W9-CBZ-840

CONCISE BIOGRAPHICAL COMPANION TO INDEX ISLAMICUS

HANDBOOK OF ORIENTAL STUDIES

HANDBUCH DER ORIENTALISTIK

SECTION ONE

THE NEAR AND MIDDLE EAST

EDITED BY

H. ALTENMÜLLER · B. HROUDA · B.A. LEVINE · R.S. O'FAHEY

K.R. VEENHOF · C.H.M. VERSTEEGH

VOLUME SEVENTY-SIX/ONE

CONCISE BIOGRAPHICAL COMPANION TO INDEX ISLAMICU

CONCISE BIOGRAPHICAL COMPANION TO INDEX ISLAMICUS

An International Who's Who in Islamic Studies from its Beginnings down to the Twentieth Century

Bio-bibliographical Supplement to Index Islamicus, 1665-1980, Volume One

A-G

BY

WOLFGANG BEHN

BRILL
LEIDEN • BOSTON
2004

This book is printed on acid-free paper.

Library of Congress Cataloging-in-Publication Data

The Library of Congress Cataloging-in-Publication Data is available on
http://catalog.loc.gov

ISSN 0169-9423
ISBN 90 04 14117 0

PRINTED IN THE NETHERLANDS

Preface

This completes the *Bio-bibliographical supplement to Index Islamicus, 1665-1980*, volume two of which was published first, in two parts, 1995 and 1996 respectively, entitled *Index Islamicus; supplement, 1665-1980*. The firm Adıyok in Millersville, Pa., is now defunct. The letters A-G and N-Z are being published now. The letters H-M have been left to the end in order to make the utmost use of the slow-moving *Dictionnaire de biographie française* which during the last ten years has merely proceeded from Lacombe to Leblois. The final volume is expected to be published in 2006.

Biographical dictionaries are the work of generations. No single person, even the greatest, would be found to contain in his memory all the biographical details included in the present dictionary. All compilers depend on the effort of generations of researchers to produce new profiles viewed under contemporary aspects. Few biographers will be found to devote so much of their time on extensive original research as Arthur Goldschmidt, Jr., State College, Pa., has done. His *Historical dictionary of modern Egypt* (2000) will stand as the biographical pharos by which the work of others will be measured for a long time to come. This, however, is not to say that others are mere copyists or plagiarists. Any intelligent person will make full use of whatever is known wherever it is to be found, supplying the sources, and adding bits and pieces that have escaped the net of others.

The history of this dictionary is quickly told; it goes back to the 1970s when Professor Goldschmidt solicited support from colleagues for a grandiose plan of a comprehensive biographical encyclopaedia of all the writers on Islam. In the end he had to limit himself to Egypt. Professor Derek Hopwood, Oxford, raised the same question at the third international conference of the Middle East Libraries Committee, held in 1981 at Berlin. He suggested a reference work along the lines of *Geographers; bio-graphical studies*, a work which has been published at London since 1977. Due to lack of organisation, or institutional backing, nothing ever came of his project either. All we ever had was the author index of the various issues of *Index Islamicus*.

It has been a long-felt shortcoming of *Index Islamicus* that little information is available about many of the authors whose articles are listed. Yet the proper appreciation of an article depends much on the credentials and the background of its writer. For example, it is worth knowing whether the translation of an Arabic text is by a casual traveller or by an official military interpreter, or to give another example, it does make a difference whether the account of an event in Kurdistan comes from the pen of a diplomat in far-away Constantinople or from a missionary at the scene of an event. A great many of the biographees listed here do not belong to the narrow circle of Orientalists. They are the men and women from all walks of life who did - or did not - succumb to the lure of the Orient and who contributed in their own way to our appreciation of that world. The majority of the twenty-one thousand odd profiles appear here for the first time in English.

No doubt some of the writers of the articles in *Index Islamicus* have been well-known over the years, but there remains a significant number about whom little is known. This biographical dictionary purports to give sufficient information so as to place each author in proper perspective and to supply select references to sources, irrespective of language. The object here has been, not so much to give all available details, as to place intelligent and resourceful researchers in a position to continue the research themselves by referring to printed genealogical works, biographies, contemporary literature, and indexes. In cases where a memoir appears in the *Dictionary of national biography* or any other easily-accessible English standard work, a minimum of detail has been given here. In every case, however, all the authorities cited should be consulted when further information is desired.

Index Islamicus, 1665-1980, lists articles of some forty thousand authors. The unfortunate editorial policy of the early compilers - and, regrettably, it was followed by this writer in his first volume - was convenient but less than useful. Reducing an author's first names to initials, leaves the poor user wondering with whom he is dealing. The stated reason why this was done is the pretentious respect for an author's personal choice of entry. There is no point dwelling on the obvious that, except in the case of monographs, authors' preference is frequently subject to a periodical's editorial policy. But even in cases when an author's first name was indeed spelled out in full in an article, Pearson and collaborators did, and still do, reduce this to initials. This constituted enormous extra work for this writer.

Apart from authors whose articles have been listed in the various volumes of *Index Islamicus, 1665-1980*, profiles have been included also of some authors whose articles ought to have been listed but

have somehow escaped the net - so far. Yet it has not been possible to supply biographical information about all the writers identified. Omitted are most pseudonyms, and authors without initial. In th
case of common surnames, like Martin, Scott and Vasil'ev, even one initial usually did not suffice f
unequivocal identification. Even with these exceptions, there remained a potential of thirty-five thou
sand odd authors to be treated. At an early stage, it was realized that such a volume of work tran
scends the ability of a retired free-lance researcher. Consequently most Oriental writers, modern a
well as ancient, have been excluded.

Consonant with the spectrum of the writers, the sources, too, reflect their international origin, but the
are obviously not comprehensive. All the entries completed after February 1998 contain sources whic
have actually been sighted, however, cited are only those of substance. It is now regretted that at th
early stages of the work, liberal use had been made of the various biographical indexes and maste
cumulations. Their accuracy leaves something to be desired. After the first eighteen months of re
search the amount of inaccuracy, irrelevance, and lacunae passed the compiler's level of toleratio
Obituary quatrains as they frequently appear in the *New York Times*, as well as their perpetuations
many indexes, have not been repeated. The same applies to most of the Islamic references in *Th
Oxford companion to Canadian history and literature*, which say nothing about the person. In case
that no published sources could be established, a library or union catalogue reference has bee
supplied whenever possible. If reference is made to the Library of Congress in addition to other refe
ences, this invariably indicates a supplementary information not found elsewhere.

The entries have been compiled in alphabetical sequence. Late additions, up-dating, and correction
have been made, although sparingly. Only the letters "A" and "B" have been completely up-dated
2003 before insurmountable computer problems put an end to the advantages of the computer. Th
length of the articles is purely accidental and is determined by the daily quota of twenty author cards a
well as personal whims and preference.

Abbreviations as found in *Vem och vad* and similar works were a source of constant annoyance.
the present work only such abbreviations are used as are listed in *the Concise Oxford dictionar*
Others occurring in the text are such as found in the sources themselves, but not identified by th
writer. This applies in particular to the Russian habit of shortening book titles. For the abbreviation
periodicals in general, reference is made also to the list of abbreviations in the various volumes
Index Islamicus, 1665-1980. The orthography of place names reflects the local official usage of th
time. The transliteration throughout is that of the Library of Congress. Diacritical signs have large
been omitted, a practice also adopted in the *Great Soviet encyclopedia*. However, there is no cor
sistency in this matter. As more sophisticated software became available diacritics were used mo
widely.

During the work on this dictionary it became obvious that the large libraries have reached the limit
meaningful collection development. For example, during ten weeks of work at the Library of Congres
at least twenty percent of the Western periodical requests turned out to be negative. The situation i
Berlin is even worse. Here, the ridiculous withdrawal of previous editions months before the new on
is put on the shelf is but a reflection on the unqualified reading room personnel. Unduly delays in boo
repairs and processing added to the frustration of the compiler, not to mention ignored requests for th
acquisition of important reference works, inconvenient annex locations for material considered of n
importance by incompetent library authorities, and insensibility to scholars' needs in general.

This writer has never been very original in the presentation of his material and is not ashamed to giv
full credit for the inclusion of titles to the suggestion of his teacher Prof. E. Birnbaum, Toronto, and fo
supplying references to the biographical sources to the advice of his friend Prof. F. Sezgin, Frankfu
am Main, who both will look with disapproval upon the decision to exclude Orientals. On a mor
general vein, a great debt is due to the benevolent influence of many members of the Middle Eas
Libraries Committee over a twenty-year period. Special thanks are due to my colleagues, Dr. Raine
Berg, Dr. Zvonko Plepelić, Erich Roth, Dr. Gennadi Wasilewitsch, and Vaclav Zeman, who wer
always ready to help out with Polish, Serbo-Croatian, Hungarian, Russian, and Czech, when the write
reached the limits of his linguistic ability.

It is with fondness that I appreciate the lifelong support of a good wife. She put me through colleg
and respected the choice of an ivory-tower subject without the least guarantee for the future. Sh
worked full-time while I spent years pursuing a strange interest at university. But more than this, at th
end of our days she sacrificed more than a decade of social life while a mute hermit in her own home
bent over the lives of people who cannot have been of the least interest to her. If her name does no
appear on the title page, this is only because the writer alone is responsible for the mistakes which
have inevitably crept into this work.

Last not least, the writer acknowledges with gratitude that this dictionary might have never bee
completed if E. J. Brill had not expressed a sustained interest to publish almost from its inception.

Key to title codes for use in locating sources

The number in parentheses after an abbreviation refers to the number of references. The sign | at the end of sources indicates the biographee's last entry in a serial publication.

Aa   van der Aa, Abraham Jacob. *Biografisch woordenboek der Nederlanden.* Haarlem, 1852-1878.

AALA   *Asien, Afrika, Lateinamerika,* Berlin.

Aalto   Aalto, Pentti. *Oriental studies in Finland, 1828-1918.* Helsinki, 1971.

ACAB   *Appleton's cyclopaedia of American biography.* New York, 1888-1901.

Adamec   Adamec, Ludwig W. *A biographical dictionary of contemporary Afghanistan.* Graz, 1987.

ADtB   *Allgemeine deutsche Biographie.* Leipzig, 1875-1912.

AfrA   Herdeck, Donald E. *African authors; a companion to Black African writing,* vol. 1. Washington, D.C., 1973.

AfrBioInd   *African biographical index,* compiled by Victor Herrero Mediavilla. München, 1999.

AfricanExp   *Directory of African experts,* 1982.

Afrikanistik   *Lexikon der Afrikanistik,* ed. H. Jungraithmayr and W. J. G. Möhlig. Berlin, 1983.

AkKisL   *Akadémiai kislexikon.* Budapest, 1989-90.

Altpreuß   *Altpreußische Biographie,* ed. Christian Krollmann. Königsberg, 1941-1967.

AmAu&B   Burke, William Jeremiah & Will D. Howe. *American authors and books, 1640 to the present,* revised by I. and A. Weiss. New York, 1962.

AmIndex   *American biographical index.* 2nd ed., comp. by Laureen Baillie. München, 1998.

AmM&WSc P   *American men and women of science:* physical and biological sciences.

AmM&WSc S   *American men and women of science:* social and behavioral sciences.

AmPeW   Roberts, Nancy L. *American peace writers, editors and periodicals.* New York, 1991.

AMS   *American men of science,* New York.

AmWomM   Leavitt, Judith A. *American women managers and administrators.* Westport, Conn., 1985.

AnaBrit   *Ana Britannica.* İstanbul, 1987-1993.

ANB   *American national biography.* New York, London, 1999.

Andrieu   Andrieu, Jules. *Bibliographie générale de l'Agenais et des parties du Condomois et du Bazadais.* Paris, Agen, 1886-91.

AnElFr   *Annuaire des études iraniennes en France.* 1ère éd., Paris, 1989- .

AnnDipl&C   *Annuaire diplomatique et consulaire de la République française.*

AnObit   *The Annual obituary.* 1- . New York, 1980- .

Arabismo   *Boletín informativo* (Agencia Española de Cooperación Internacional): Arabismo; estudios árabes en España. Madrid, Ed. Mundo Árabe e Islam, 1992- .

Artefici   *Artefici del lavoro italiano.* Roma, 1956-59. 2 vol.

ASTENE   Association for the Study of Travel in Egypt and the Near East.

AUB   American University of Beirut.

AUC   American University in Cairo.

AusBioInd	*Australasian biographical index*, ed. Victor Herrero Mediavilla. München, 1996.
Au&Wr	*Author's and writer's who's who.*
Awwad	'Awwad, Kurkis. معجم المألفين العراقيين . Baghdad, 1969.
Azan	Azan, Paul. *Les Grands soldats de l'Algérie.* Alger, 1930.
AzarbSE	*Азәрбаjчан совет енсиклопедиjасы.* Baku, 1976-1987.
Bacqué	*Représentants permanents de la France en Turquie, 1536-1991, et de la Turquie en France*, par Jean Louis Bacqué-Grammont, Sinan Kuneralp et Frédéric Hitzel. Istanbul et Paris, 1991.
BAEO	*Boletin de la Asociación Española de Orientalistas.*
Baker 78	Baker, Theodore. *Biographical dictionary of musicians*; completely revised by Nicolas Slonimsky. New York, 1978.
Baker 84	Baker, Theodore. *Biographical dictionary of musicians.* 7th ed., revised by Nicolas Slonimsky. New York, 1984.
Baldinetti	Baldinetti, Anna. *Orientalismo e colonialismo; la ricerca di consenso in Egitto per l'impreso di Libia.* Roma, 1997.
Ballesteros	Ballesteros Robles, Luis. *Diccionario biográfico matritense.* Madrid, 1912.
Baltisch	*Baltischer biographischer Index*, edited by Axel Frey. München, 1999.
BashkKE	*Башкортостан краткая энциклопедия*, general editor R. Z. Shakurov. Ufa, 1996.
BbD	*The Bibliophile dictionary.* Detroit, c1904, 1966.
BBHS	*Bio-bibliographisches Handbuch zur Sprachwissenschaft des 18. Jahrhunderts.* Tübingen, 1992- .
Behrmann	Behrmann, Georg. *Hamburgs Orientalisten.* Hamburg, 1902.
Bellier	Bellier de la Chavignerie, Émile, and Louis Auvray. *Dictionnaire général des artistes de l'école française.* Paris, 1882-85.
Bezemer	*Beknopte encyclopedie van Nederlandsch-Indië*, naar den 2. druk der *Encyclopedie van Nederlandsch-Indië*, bewerkt door Tammo Jacob Bezemer. s'Gravenhage, 1921.
BiBenelux	*Biografische index van de Benelux.* München, 1997.
BiBenelux²	*Biografische index van de Benelux.* München, 2003.
BiDAmL	*Biographical dictionary of American labor*, ed. by Gary M. Fink. Westport, Conn., 1984.
BiDAmS	Elliott, Clark A. *Biographical dictionary of American science, the seventeenth through nineteenth centuries.* Westport, Conn., 1979.
BiDInt	Kuehl, Warren F. *Biographical dictionary of internationalists.* Westport, Conn., 1983.
BiDLA	*A Biographical dictionary of the living authors of Great Britain and Ireland.* London, 1816; Detroit, 1966.
BiDMoPL	*Biographical dictionary of modern peace leaders*, ed. by Harold Josephson. Westport, Conn., 1985.
BiDMoER	*Biographical dictionary of modern European radicals and socialists*, ed. by D. Nicholls and Peter March. Vol. 1: 1780-1815. Brighton and New York, 1988.
BiDNeoM	*Biographical dictionary of neo-Marxism*, edited by Robert E. Gorman. Westport, 1985.
BiDrLUS	*Biographical dictionary of librarians in the United States and Canada.*
BiD&SB	*Biographical dictionary and synopsis of books.* Detroit, c1902, 1965.
BiDSovU	Vronskaya, Jeanne, with Vl. Chuguev. *A Biographical dictionary of the Soviet Union, 1917-1988.* London, 1989.
Bidwell	Bidwell, Robin L. *Travellers in Arabia.* Reading, 1994.
Bidwell²	Bidwell, Robin L. *Dictionary of modern Arab history.* London, 1998.

BiEncPak	*Biographical encyclopedia of Pakistan*, 1969-70. Lahore.
BiGAW	Ward, Robert E. *A Bio-bibliography of German-American writers*. White Plains, 1985.
BiLexDR	*Biographisches Lexikon zum Dritten Reich*, ed. Hermann Weiß. Frankfurt a. M., 1998.
BioB134	*Bio-bibliographies de 134 savants*. Leiden, 1979. (Acta iranica; 4e sér.; Répertoires 1)
BiobibSOT	*Биобиблиографический словарь отечественных тюркологов*. Moskva, 1974.
Biograf	*Biográf ki kicsoda*. Budapest, 2001- .
BiogrLexOö	Khil, Martha. *Biographisches Lexikon von Oberösterreich*. Linz, 1955- .
BioHbDtE	*Biographisches Handbuch der deutschsprachigen Emigration, 1933-1945*. München, 1980-1983.
BioIn	*Biography index*, 1- . New York, 1949- .
BioJahr	*Biographisches Jahrbuch und deutscher Nekrolog*. 1-18. Berlin, 1897-1917.
BioNBelg	*Biographie nationale*; publiée par l'Académie royale des sciences, des lettres et des beaux-arts de Belgique. Bruxelles, 1866- .
Bitard	Bitard, Adolphe. *Dictionnaire général de biographie contemporaine française et étrangère*. Paris, 1878.
Bitard²	Bitard, Adolphe. *Dictionnaire de biographie contemporaine française et étrangère*. 3e éd. Paris, 1887.
BJMES	*British journal of Middle Eastern studies*.
BLC	*British Library catalogue*.
BlkwERR	*The Blackwell encyclopedia of the Russian revolution*, edited by Harold Shukman. New York, 1988.
BlueB	*The Blue book; leaders of the English-speaking world*. London, New York.
BN	*Catalogue général des livres imprimés de la Bibliothèque nationale de Paris*.
Boase	Boase, Frederic. *Modern English biography*. Truro, c1892-1921; London, 1965.
Boisdeffre²	Boisdeffre, Pierre de. *Histoire de la littérature et de la langue française des années 1930 aux années 1980*. Paris, 1985.
Bonner	*Bonner Gelehrte; Beiträge zur Geschichte der Wissenschaften in Bonn*. 1- . Bonn, 1968- .
Brinkman's	*Brinkman's catalogus van boeken en tijdschriften*.
BRISMES	British Society for Middle Eastern Studies.
BritInd	*British biographical index*, 2nd cumulated and enlarged edition. München, 1998.
Brümmer	Brümmer, Franz. *Lexikon der deutschen Dichter*, 6. Aufl. Leipzig, 1913.
Brümmer²	Brümmer, Franz. *Deutsches-Dichter Lexikon*. Eichstädt, 1876-77.
BSMES	British Society for Middle Eastern Studies.
BSOAS	*Bulletin of the School of Oriental and African studies*.
Buckland	Buckland, Charles E. *Dictionary of Indian biography*. London, 1906.
Burkert	Burkert, Martin. *Die Ostwissenschaften im Dritten Reich*. 1. Teil. Wiesbaden, 2000.
Bursian	*Biographisches Jahrbuch für Alterthumskunde*, von Conr. Bursian. Berlin, 1879-1898.
BWN	*Biografisch woordenboek van Nederland*. 's-Gravenhage, 1979- .
Canadian	*Canadian who's who*.
Capeille	Capeille, Jean. *Dictionnaire de biographies roussillonaises*. Paris, 1914; reprint, Marseille, 1978.
Cappellini 1	Cappellini, Antonio. *Dizionario biografico di genovesi illustri e notabili*. Genova, 1941.

Carnoy 10²	Carnoy, Émile *dit* Henry. *Dictionnaire biographique international des écrivains.* Paris, 1903. 262 p.
Carnoy 11	Carnoy, Émile *dit* Henry. *Dictionnaire biographique international des artistes, peintres, sculptures etc.* Paris, n.d. 99 p.
Carnoy 11²	Carnoy, Émile *dit* Henry. *Dictionnaire biographique international des collectionneurs, ex-libris, livres, manuscrits etc.* Paris, 1895. 81 p.
Casanova	Casanova, Paul. *L'Enseignement de l'arabe au Collège de France.* Prais, 1910.
Casati	Casati, Giovanni. *Dizionario degli scrittori d'Italia.* A-K. Milano, 1925-1934-
Casati 2	Casati, Giovanni. *Scrittori cattolici italiani viventi.* Milano, 1928.
CasWL	*Cassell's encyclopaedia of world literature.* London, 1953, 1973.
CathWW	*The Catholic who's who and yearbook.*
ČBS	*Československý biografický slovník.* Praha, 1992.
CelCen	Sanders, Lloyd C. *Celebrities of the century.* 1881.
CentBbritOr	*A Century of British Orientalists, 1902-2001*; ed. C. Edmond Bosworth. Oxford, 2001.
Cesky	*Česky biografický slovnik XX. stoleti.* Paseka, 1999. 3 v.
ChambrBrBi	*Chambers British biographies - the 20th century*, ed. Min Lee. Edinburgh, 1993.
Chi è	*Chi è?* Roma, 1928- .
ChineseBiInd	*Chinese biographical index*, compiled by Stephan von Minden. München, 2000.
Chi scrive	*Chi scrive? Repertorio bio-bibliografico degli scrittori italiani.* Milano, 1962.
Churan	Churaň, Milan. *Kdo byl kdo v našich dějinách ve 20. století.* Praha, 1994.
Clausen	Clausen, Ursel. *Tunisie; notes biographiques.* Hamburg, 1976.
CIDMEL	*Columbia dictionary of modern European literature*, ed. Horatio Smith. New York, 1967.
CnDiAmJBi	*The Concise dictionary of American Jewish biography*, edited by Jacob Rader Marcus. Brooklyn, N.Y., 1994. 2v.
CNRS	Centre National de la Recherche Scientifique, Paris.
ConAu	*Contemporary authors.*
Cordier	Cordier, Henri. *Bibliotheca Indosinica.* Paris, 1912-1932.
Coston²	Coston, Henry. *Dictionnaire de la politique française.* Paris, 1967-82.
Couceiro	Couceiro Freijomil, Antonio. *Diccionario bio-bibliográfico de escritores.* Santiago de Compostela, 1951-1953.
Cragg	Cragg, Kenneth. *Troubled by truth; life studies in interfaith concern.* Edinburgh, 1992.
C.S.I.C.	Consejo Superior de Investigaciones Científicas.
Cuenca	Cuenca, Francisco. *Biblioteca de autores andaluces.* La Habana, 1921-1925.
CUNY	City University of New York.
CurBio	*Current biography yearbook.*
Curinier	*Dictionnaire national des contemporains*, ed. C. E. Curinier. Paris, 1901-1906.
Czy wiesz	*Czy wiesz kto to jest?* Warszawa, 1938.
DAB	*Dictionary of American biography.*
DanskBL	*Dansk biografisk leksikon*, tredje udgave. København, 1979-1984.
DanskBL²	*Dansk biografisk leksikon.* København, 1933-1944.
Dantès 1	Dantès, Alfred Langue. *Dictionnaire biographique et bibliographique.* Paris, 1875.

Dawson	Dawson, Warren R. & Eric P. Uphill. *Who was who in Egyptology,* 2d ed. London, 1972.
DBEC	*Diccionario biografico español contemporáneo.* Madrid, 1970.
DBF	*Dictionnaire de biographie française.* Paris, 1933- .
DBFC	*Dictionnaire biographique français contemporain,* 2ème éd. Paris, 1954-55.
DcAfHiB	*Dictionary of African historical biography,* 2nd ed. by Mark R. Lipschutz and R. Kent Rasmussen. Berkeley and Los Angeles, 1986.
DcAmBC	Dickinson, Donald C. *Dictionary of American book collectors.* New York, 1986.
DcAmDH	Findling, John. *Dictionary of American diplomatic history.* Westport, 1980.
DcBiPP	Vincent, Benjamin. *Dictionary of biography, past and present.* 1877.
DcBMOuvF	*Dictionnaire biographique du mouvement ouvrier français.* Paris, 1964- .
DcBrA	Waters, Grant M. *Dictionary of British artists working 1900-1950.* Eastbourne, 1975-1976.
DcCanB	*Dictionary of Canadian biography.* Toronto, 1966- .
DcCathB	Delaney, John J. & J. E. Tobin. *Dictionary of Catholic biography.* Garden City, N.Y., 1961.
DcEnc	*Dicţionar enciclopedic.* Bucureşti, 1993- .
DcEnL	Adams, William Davenport. *Dictionary of English literature.* London, ca. 1885.
DcERomân	*Dicţionar enciclopedic Român.* Bucureşti, 1962-1966.
DcEuL	Magnus, Laurie. *A Dictionary of European literature.* London, 1926.
DcIrB	Boylan, Henry. *A Dictionary of Irish biography.* New York, c1978, 1998.
DcNAA	Wallace, William Stewart. *Dictionary of North American authors.* Detroit, c1951, 1968.
DcOrL	*Dictionary of Oriental literatures.* London, New York, 1974. 3v.
DcScandB	*Dictionary of Scandinavian biography,* 2nd ed. Cambridge, 1976.
DcSandL	*Dictionary of Scandinavian literature,* edited by Virpi Zuck. New York, 1990.
DcScB	*Dictionary of scientific biography.* New York, 1970-76, 1978.
DcSpL	Newmark, Maxim. *Dictionary of Spanish literature.* New York, 1956.
De Rolandis	De Rolandis, Giuseppe M. *Notize sugli escrittori Astigiani.* Asti, 1859.
Dezobry	Dezobry, Louis Charles & Jean Louis Théodore Bachelet. *Dictionnaire général de biographie et d'histoire* etc., 5e éd. rev. Paris, 1869.
Diaz	Díaz Díaz, Gonzales. *Hombres y documentos de la filosofia española.* Madrid, 1980.
Dicc bio	*Diccionari biogràfic.* 1-3. Barcelona, 1966-1970.
DiccHist	*Diccionario historia de España.* Madrid, 1952.
Dickinson	Dickinson, Robert E. *Makers of modern geography.* London, 1969.
Dicţionar	*Dicţionar enciclopedic ilustrat.* Bucureşti, 1999.
DizBI	*Dizionario biografico degli italiani,* Roma, 1960- .
DizRN	*Dizionario del Risorgimento nazionale.* Milano, 1930-37.
DLB	*Dictionary of literary biraphhy.* 1- . Detroit, Mich., 1978- .
DNB	*Dictionary of national biography.* London, Oxford University Press
DNZB	*Dictionary of New Zealand biography.* Wellington, 1940. 2v.
DrAS	*Directory of American scholars.*
DrASCan	*Directory of Asia studies in Canada.* 1- . Ottawa, Ont., 1978- .

DrBSMES	*Directory of BRISMES members.*
DSAB	*Dictionary of South African biography.* v. 1- . Pretoria, etc., c1968, 1976- .
DtBE	*Deutsche biographische Enzyklopädie.* München, 1995-2000.
DtBiInd	*Deutscher biographischer Index.* 2. kumulierte und erw. Ausgabe. München, 1998.
DtBiJ	*Deutsches biographisches Jahrbuch.* Berlin, 1925-1929.
Dziekan	Dziekan, Marek M. *Polacy a świat arabski; słownik biograficzny.* Gdańsk, 1998.
Édouard-J.	Édouard-Joseph, René. *Dictionnaire biographique des artistes contemporains, 1910-1930.* Paris, 1910-1930.
EEE	*Εκπαιδευτική ελληνική ενκυκλοπαίδεια.* Athens, 1990-1991.
Egyptology	*Who was who in Egyptology,* 3d ed. by M. L. Bierbrier. London, 1995.
EI²	*Encyclopaedia of Islam,* 2d ed.
EIranica	*Encyclopédia Iranica.* London, 1985- .
EIS	Necatigil, Behçet. *Edebiyatımızda isimler sözlüğü,* 7th ed. Istanbul, 1972.
Elias	Elías de Molins, Antonio. *Diccionario biográfico y bibliográfico de escritores y artistas catalanes del siglo XIX.* Barcelona, 1889-95.
Embacher	Embacher, Friedrich. *Lexikon der Reisen und Entdeckungen.* Leipzig, 1882.
Eminent	*Eminent Indians who was who, 1900-1980.* New Delhi, 1985.
EmOr	*Eminent Orientalists, Indian, European, American.* Madras, 1922.
EnBulg	*Енциклоредия България.* Sofia, 1978-1996.
EncAJ	Paneth, Donald. *The Encyclopedia of American journalism.* New York, 1983.
EncAm	*Encyclopedia Americana;* international edition. New York, 1966.
EncBrit	*Encycloćdia Britannica,* 11th ed. Cambridge, 1910.
EncHung	*Enciclopedia Hungarica.* Budapest, 1992-1996.
EncicUni	*Enciclopedia universal ilustrada.* Barcelona, 1910-1930.
EncIran	*Encyclopaedia Iranica.* London, 1985- .
EncItaliana	*Enciclopedia italiana di scienze, lettere ed arti.* Roma, 1929-1949.
EncJud	*Encyclopaedia Judaica.* Jerusalem, 1971
EncJud²	*Encyclopaedia Judaica.* A-L. Berlin, 1928-1934.
EncJug	*Enciklopedija Jugoslavije.* A- . Zagreb, 1980- .
EncJug²	*Enciklopedija Jugoslavije.* Zagreb, 1955-1971.
EncLZ	*Enciklopedija leksikografskog zavoda.* Zagreb, 1966-69.
EncNI	*Encyclopedie van Nederlandsch-Indië.* 2de druk. s'Gravenhage, 1917-1939.
EncO&P	*Encyclopedia of occultism and parapsychology.* Detroit, 1984.
EncPWN	*Encyklopedia PWN w trzech tomach.* Warszawa, 1999- .
EncSlov	*Encyklopédia slovenska.* Bratislava, 1977-1979.
EncTR	Snyder, Louis L. *Encyclopedia of the Third Reich.* New York, 1976.
EncTwCJ	Taft, William H. *Encyclopedia of twentieth-century journalists.* New York, 1986.
EncWL	*Encyclopedia of world literature in the 20th century,* edited by Wolfgang B. Fleischmann. New York, 1967-1975.
EncWM	*Encyclopedia of world Methodism.* Nashville, Tenn., 1974.
EnSlovar	*Энциклопедический словарь.* S.-Peterburg, 1890-1904. 82 vols.
Erdélyi	*Erdélyi Magyar ki kicsoda.* Budapest, 2000.

Espasa	*Diccionario enciclopédico Espasa.* 1-12; apéndice 1 & 2. Madrid, 1978-1990.
EST	*Энциклопедияи совеетии точик.* 1-7. Dushanbe, 1978-1987.
EuAu	Kunitz, Stanley J. & V. Colby. *European authors, 1000-1900; a biographical dictionary of European literature.* New York, 1967.
EURAMES	*European expertise on the Middle East & North Africa, a directory of specialists and institutions*; eds. Emma Murphy, Gerd Nonneman, Neil Quilliam for EURAMES, 1993.
EVL	*Επίτομο βιογραφικό λεξικό,* Athens.
EvLB	Browning, David Clayton. *Everyman's dictionary of literary biography, English and A-merican,* compiled after John W. Cousin. 3rd ed. London, 1962.
Facey Grant	Facey, William & Gillian Grant. *Kuwait by the first photographers.* London, 1998.
FarE&A	*The Far East and Australasia.* 1 (1969)- .
Faucon	Faucon, Narcisse A. *Le Livre d'or de l'Algérie de 1830 à 1889.* Paris, 1889.
Fekete	Fekete, Márton. *Prominent Hungarians, home and abroad.* 4th ed. London, 1985.
Ferahian	Ferahian, Salwa. *Handlist of M.A. and Ph.D. theses submitted to the Institute of Islamic Studies,* (McGill University,) *1954-1995.* Montreal, McGill University, 1996.
Féraud ·	Féraud, Laurent Charles. *Les interprètes de l'armée d'Afrique.* Alger, 1876.
Fernandez	Fernández y Sánchez, Ildefonso. *Año biográfico español.* Barcelona, 1899.
Figuras	*Figuras de hoy; enciclopedia biográfica nacional.* Madrid, 1951- .
Filipsky	*Čeští a slovenští orientalisté, afrikanisté a iberoamerikanisté,* by Jan Filipský a kol. Praha, 1999.
FilmgC	Halliwell, Leslie. *Filmgoer's companion,* 8th ed. New York, 1984.
Firenze	*Catalogo cumulativo 1886-1957 del bollettino delle pubblicazioni italiane ricevute per diritto di stampa dalla Biblioteca Nazionale Centrale di Firenze.* Nendeln, 1968-1969.
Frederiks	Frederiks, Johannes G. & F. Jos. van den Branden. *Biographisch woordenboek der Noord- en Zuidnederlandsche letterkunde.* 2e dr. Amsterdam, 1888-1892.
Freeth	Freeth, Zahra D. & H. V. F. Winstone. *Explorers of Arabia.* New York, 1978.
Fuad	Fuad, Kamal. *Kurdische Handschriften.* Wiesbaden, 1970.
Fück	Fück, Johannes. *Die arabischen Studien in Europa.* Leipzig, 1955.
Fusco	Fusco, Enrico Maria. *Scrittori e idee.* Torino, 1956.
Gabriel	Gabriel, Alfons. *Vergessene Persienreisende.* Wien, 1969.
GAL	Brockelmann, Carl. *Geschichte der arabischen Litteratur,* 1898-1942.
GAS	Sezgin, Fuat. *Geschichte des arabischen Schrifttums.* 1-12. Leiden and Frankfurt am Main, 1967-2000.
Gastaldi	Gastaldi, Mario. *Dizionario delle scrittrici italiane contemporanee.* Milano, 1957.
GdeEnc	*La Grande encyclopédie.* Paris, 1885-1901.
GdLaEnc	*Grand Larousse encyclopédique.* Paris, 1960-1964.
GDU	Larousse, Pierre. *Grand dictionnaire universel.* Paris, 1865-90.
GeistigeUng	Jásznigi, Alexander. *Das geistige Ungarn; biographisches Lexikon,* herausgegeben von Oskar von Krücken [pseud.] und Imre Parlagi. Wien & Leipzig, 1918.
GeistigeWien	Eisenberg, Ludwig Julius. *Das geistige Wien.* 1- . Wien, 1893- .
Geog	*Geographers; biobibliographical studies.* 1- . London, 1977- .
GER	*Gran enciclopedia RIALP.* 1-25. Madrid, 1984-1989.
Glaeser	Glaeser, Ernest. *Biographie nationale des contemporains.* Paris, 1878.
Goldschmidt	Goldschmidt, Arthur. *Historical dictionary of modern Egypt.* Boulder, Colo., 2000.

Građa	*Građa za hrvatsku retrospektivnu bibliografiju knjiga, 1835-1940.* Zagreb, 1982- .
GrBioInd	*Griechischer biographischer Index* = *Greek biographical index,* compiled by Hilmar Schmuck. München, 2003. 3 v.
GrBr	Oxbury, Harold. *Great Britons; twentieth-century lives.* Oxford, 1985.
GSE	*Great Soviet encyclopedia.* New York and London, 1973-1983.
Gubernatis 1	Gubernatis, Angelo de. *Dizionario biografico degli scrittori contemporanei.* Firenze, 1879-1880.
Gubernatis 3	Gubernatis, Angelo de. *Piccolo dizionario del contemporanei italiani.* Roma, 1895.
GV	*Gesamtverzeichnis des deutschsprachigen Schrifttums, 1700-1910.* München, 1979-1987. 160 v.; *Gesamtverzeichnis des deutschsprachigen Schrifttums, 1911-1965.* München, 1976-1981. 150 vols.
Haan	Haan, Wilhelm. *Sächsisches Schriftsteller-Lexicon.* Leipzig, 1875.
HanRL	*Handbook of Russian literature,* edited by Victor Terras. New Haven, 1985.
HbDtWiss	*Handbuch der deutschen Wissenschaft.* Berlin, 1949. 2 vols.
HBL	*Hrvatski biografski leksikon.* Zagreb, 1983- .
HE	*Hrvatska enciklopedija.* Zagreb, 1999- .
Hellenikon	*Ελληνικον who's who,* Athens.
Henze	Henze, Dietmar. *Enzyklopädie der Entdecker.* Graz, 1978- .
Hill	Hill, Richard. *A Biographical dictionary of the Sudan.* 2nd ed. London, 1967.
Hinrichsen	Hinrichsen, Adolf. *Das literarische Deutschland.* 2. Auflage. Berlin 1891.
HisBioLexCH	*Historisch-biographisches Lexikon der Schweiz.* Neuenburg, 1921-1934.
HisDcDP	Cortada, James W. *Historical dictionary of data processing; biographies.* New York, 1987.
HL	*Hrvatski leksikon.* Zagreb, 1996-1997.
HnRL	*see* HanRL
Hoefer	*Nouvelle biographie générale,* edited by Johann C. F. Hoefer. Paris, 1852-1866.
Hvem	*Hvem er hvem,* Oslo.
IES	*Ilustrovaný encyklopedický slovník.* Praha, 1980-1982.
IJMES	*International journal of Middle East studies.*
Imperatori	Imperatori, Ugo E. *Dizionario di italiani all'estero.* Genova, 1956.
IndAu 1977	Thompson, Donald E. *Indiana authors and their books, 1917-1966.* Crawfordsville, Ind., 1974.
IndBI	*Indice biografico italiano,* 2a edizione, 1-7. München, 1997.
IndBiItal	*Indice biografico italiano,* 3a ed., T. Nappo. München, 2002.
IndexBFr	*Index biographique français.* London, 1993.
IndexBFr²	*Index biographique français,* 2ème édition cumulée et augmentée. München, 1998.
IndiaWW	*India who's who.*
IndianBiInd	*Indian biographical index,* compiled by Loureen Baillie. München, 2001.
IndiceE²	*Indice biográfico de España, Portugal e Iberoamérica.* 2a ed. München, 1995.
IndiceE³	*Indice biográfico de España, Portugal e Iberoamérica.* 3a edición corregida y amplicada, editado por Victor Herrero Mediavilla. München, 2000.
IntAu&W	*International authors and writers (who's who).*

IntDcAn	*International dictionary of anthropologists*, ed. Christopher Winters. New York, 1991.
IntMed	*International medical who's who.*
IntWW	*International who's who.*
IntWWM	*International who's who in music and musicians' directory.*
IntWWP	*International who's who in poetry.* London, 1958- .
IntYB	*The International year book and statesmen's who's who.*
IranWW	*Iran who's who.* Teheran, 1972- .
IWWAS	*International who's who in Asian studies*, Hong Kong.
JA	*Journal asiatique.*
JahrDtB	*Jahrbuch der deutschen Bibliotheken.* 1- . Leipzig, Wiesbaden, 1902- .
Jain	Jain, Naresh K. *Muslims in India.* New Delhi, 1979-83. 2v.
Jaksch	Jaksch, Friedrich. *Lexikon sudetendeutscher Schriftsteller für die Jahre 1900-1929.* Reichenberg, 1929.
JapAuFile	Kokuritsu Kokkai Toshokan (Japan). [Engl. alternative title:] *National Diet Library authority file for Japanese authors.* Tokyo, 1991.
JewEnc	*The Jewish encyclopedia.* New York & London, 1901-1906.
JNES	*Journal of Near Eastern studies.*
JRAS	*Journal of the Royal Asiatic Society.*
JRCAS	*Journal of the Royal Central Asian Society.*
JSS	*Journal of Semitic studies .*
JüdLex	*Jüdisches Lexikon.* A-R. Berlin, 1927-1930. v. 1-4.
JugoslSa	*Jugoslovenski savremenici; ko je ko u Jugoslaviji.* Beograd, 1970.
Juynboll	Juynboll, W.M.C. *Zeventiende-eeuwsche beoefenaars van het Arabisch in Nederland.* Utrecht, 1931.
Kazakhskaia	*Казахская ССР краткая энциклопедия*, vol. 1-4. Alma-Ata, 1985-1991.
KazakSE	*Казак Совет энцыклоредиясы.* Almaty, 1972-1982.
Kdo je kdo	*Kdo je kdo.* Praha, 1991- .
KDtLK	*Kürschners Deutscher Literatur-Kalender.*
Ki-kicsoda	*Ki-kicsooda? Kortársak lexikona.* Budapest, 1937.
Kim kimdir	*Günümü Türkiyesinde kim kimdir.* Istanbul.
Kirk	Kirk, John Foster. *A supplement to Allibone's critical dictionary of English literature.* Philadelphia, 1891.
Koi	*Кой кой е б България*, 1998. Sofia, 1998- .
Ko je ko	*Ko je ko u Jugoslaviji.* Beograd, 1957.
Kosch	Kosch, Wilhelm. *Das katholische Deutschland.* Augsburg, 1933-38.
Krachkovskii	Krachkovskii, Ignatii. *Die russische Arabistik*, von I. J. Kratschkowski. Leipzig, 1957.
Kraks	*Kraks blå bog.* København, 1910- .
KtoPolsce	*Kto jest kim w Polsce.*
Kuhn	Kuhn, Heinrich & Otto Boss. *Biographisches Handbuch der Tschechoslowakei.* München, 1961.
Kürschner	*Kürschners Deutscher Gelehrten-Kalender.*
KyrgyzSE	*Кыргыз Совет энциклопедиясы.* Ashgabat, 1974-1989.

Lamathière	Lamathière, Théophile de. *Panthéon de la Légion d'honneur.* Paris, 1875-1911.
LC	*Library of Congress catalog* and/or *Library of Congress name authority file.*
LEduc	*Leaders in education.* Lancaster, Pa., New York, 1932.
LexFrau	*Lexikon der Frau.* Zürich, 1953-54.
LingH	*Linguisten-Handbuch;* herausgegeben von Wilfried Kürschner. Tübingen, 1994.
LitWho	*Literary who's who.* London, 1920.
LitYbk	*Literary yearbook (and who's who),* vol. 1-22. London, 1897-1921.
LivesRem	*Lives remembered; The Times obituaries.* Pangbourne, 1991- .
Lodwick	Lodwick, Kathleen. *The Chinese Recorder index, 1867-1941.* Wilmington, Del., 1986.
LSE	London School of Economics.
LThK	Buchberger, Michael, ed. *Lexikon für Theologie und Kirche.* 2. Aufl. Freiburg, 1930-1938.
LuthC 75	*Lutheran cyclopedia;* edited by E. L. Lueker. St. Louis & London, 1975.
MacDCB 78	*The Macmillan dictionary of Canadian biography,* edited by William Stewart Wallace, 4th ed., by W. A. McKay. Toronto, 1978.
Magyar	*Magyar Nagylexikon.* Budapest, 1993- .
MagyarNKK	*Magyar ès nemzetközi ki kicsoda.* Budapest, 1992-2000.
MagyarZL	*Magyar zsidó lexikon.* Budapest, 1929.
Makers	*Makers of modern Africa.* 1- . London, 1981- .
MaláČEnc	*Malá československá encyklopedie.* Praha, 1984-1987.
Manzanares	Manzanares de Cirre, Manuela. *Arabistas españoles del siglo XIX.* Madrid, 1972.
Masarykův	*Masarykův slovník naučný.* Praze, 1925-1933.
Mason	Mason, Philip. *The Men who ruled India.* London, 1985. (An abridged version of the first edition in two volumes, 1953-1954).
Master	*Biography and genealogy master index,* 2d ed., vol. 1-8. Detroit, Mich., 1980- .
Matthieu	Matthieu, Ernest A. J. G. *Biographie du Hainaut.* Enghien, 1902-1905. 2 v.
Mayeur	Mayeur, Jean Marie & Yves Marie Hilaire. *Dictionnaire du monde religieux dans la France contemporaine.* Paris, 1985-1990.
MedWW	*The Medical who's who.* London, 1914.
Megali	*Μεγαλη ελληνικη εγκυκλοπαιδεια.* Athens, 1927-34. 24 vols.
MEJ	*The Middle East journal.*
MEL	*Magyar életrejzi lexikon.* Budapest, 1967-1969; 1978-1991.
MembriiAR	*Membrii Academiei Române, 1866-1999; dicţionar,* ed. Eugen Simion. Bucureşti,1999.
Men10	*Men of the time,* 10th edition. London, 1879.
Mendez	Méndez Bejarano, Mario. *Diccionario de escritores, maestros y oradores naturales de Sevilla y su actual provincia.* Tomo 1-3. Sevilla, 1922-1925.
Mennell	Mennell, Philip. *Dictionary of Australasian biography.* London, 1892- .
MESA	Middle East Studies Association of North America.
MEW	*Moderne encyclopedie van de wereldliteraturen.* Haarlem, 1980-1984.
Meydan	*Büyük lûgat ve ansiklopedisi.* Istanbul, Meydan-Larousse, 1969-1976.
Meyers	*Meyers Großes Konversations=Lexikon,* 6. Aufl. Leipzig, 1907-1920.
MicDcEnc	*Mic dicţionar enciclopedic.* Bucureşti, 1986.

Michaud *Biographie universelle (Michaud) ancienne et moderne.* c1854, 1967.

MidE *The Middle East and North Africa.* 1- . London, 1948- .

MIDEO *Mélanges /* Institut Dominicain d'Études Orientales du Caire.

Mifsud Mifsud Bonnici, Robert. *Dizzjunarju bijo-bibljografiku nazzjonali.* Malta, 1960.

Miliband Miliband, Sofiia D. *Биобиблиографический словарь советских востоковедо.* Moskva, 1975.

Miliband² Miliband, Sofiia D. *Биобиблиографический словарь отечественных востоковедов с 1917 г.* Moskva, 1995.

MIT Massachusetts Institute of Technology, Cambridge, Mass.

Morgan Morgan, Henry J., *ed. The Canadian men and women of the time.* Toronto, 1898; 2nd ed., Toronto, 1912.

MW *Moslem/Muslim world,* Hartford, Conn.

Nat Nat, Jan, *De studie van de Oostersche talen in Nederland in de 18e en de 19e eeuw.* Purmerend, 1929.

NatCAB *The National cyclopaedia of American biography,* vol. 1-63. New York, 1892-1984.

NatFacDr *National Faculty directory.* Detroit, 1970- .

NBN *Nouvelle biographie nationale.* 1- . Bruxelles, 1988- .

NBW *Nationaal biografisch woordenboek.* 1- . Brussel, 1964- .

NCCN *New century cyclopedia of names.* New York, 1954.

NDB *Neue deutsche Biographie.* Berlin, 1953- .

NDBA *Nouvelle dictionnaire de biographie alsacienne.* Strasbourg, 1982- .

NDNC *Nouveau dictionnaire national des contemporains,* 1-5. Paris, 1962-68.

NearMEWho *The Near and Middle East who's who.*

NEP *Nowa encyklopedia powszechna PWN.* Warszawa, 1995- .

NewC *New century handbook of English literature.* New York, 1956.

NewCathEnc *New Catholic encyclopedia.* Washington, D.C., c1967, 1981.

NewCEN *see* NCCN

NewGrDM *The new Grove dictionary of music and musicians.* London, c1980, 1995.

NieuwNBW *Nieuw Nederlandsch biografisch woordenboek.* Leiden, 1911-1937.

NÖB *Neue österreichische Biographie ab 1815.* 1- . Wien, 1923- .

NorskBL *Norsk biografisk leksikon.* 1-19. Oslo, 1923-1983.

Note Note about the author in a periodical or book.

NSMES Nordic Society for Middle Eastern Studies.

NUC *National union catalog.*

NYC New York City.

NYPL New York Public Library, New York City.

NYT *New York Times.*

ObitOF *Obituaries on file,* compiled by Felice Levy. New York, 1979.

ObitT *Obituaries from the Times.*

ÖBL *Österreichisches biographisches Lexikon, 1815-1950.* Wien, 1957- .

Opać *Opać enciklopedija.* Zagreb, 1980- .

OSK Osteuropa Sammelkatalog, edited at the Staatsbibliothek zu Berlin. Not published.

Ossorio	Ossorio y Bernard, Manuel. *Ensayo de un catálogo de periodistas españoles del siglo XIX.* Madrid, 1903-4.
OttůvSN	*Ottův slovník naučný.* Praze, 1888-1909.
Oursel	Oursel, Noémie N. *Nouvelle biographie normande.* Paris, 1886-1888.
OxCan	Story, Norah. *Oxford companion to Canadian history and literature.* Toronto, 1967.
OxCLiW	*The Oxford companion to the literature of Wales.* Oxford, 1986.
OxEng	*Oxford companion to English literature*; 4th ed. by P. Harvey. Oxford 1969.
OxFr	*Oxford companion to French literature*; ed. P. Harvey, J. E. Hesseltine. Oxford, 1966.
OxGer	Garland, Henry and Mary. *The Oxford companion to German literature.* Oxford, 1976.
OxLaw	Walker, David M. *The Oxford companion to law.* Oxford, 1980.
OxMus	Scholes, Percy A. *The Oxford companion to music*, 10th ed. London, 1974.
OxSpan	*Oxford companion to Spanish literature*; ed. by Philip Ward. Oxford, 1978.
OxThe	*Oxford companion to the theatre*, 4th ed. by Phyllis Hartnoll. Oxford, 1983.
Özege	Özege, M. Seyfettin. *Eski harflerle basılmış Türkçe eserler kataloğu.* İstanbul, 1971-82
Pallas	*A Pallas nagy lexikona.* Budapest, 1893-1897.
PeoHis	*People in history*, edited by Susan K. Kinnell. Santa Barbara, Calif, 1988.
Peyronnet	Peyronnet, Raymond. *Livre d'or des officiers des Affaires indigènes, 1830-1930.* Alger, Commissariat général du centennaire, 1930. Tome 2: Notices et biographies.
Pinto	Pinto, Juan. *Diccionario de la República Argentina.* Buenos Aires, 1950.
Poggendorff	Poggendorff, Johann C. *Biographisch-literarisches Handwörterbuch.* Leipzig & Berlin, 1863-1962.
Polre	O'Donoghue, David James. *The Poets of Ireland.* c1912, 1968.
Polski	*Polski indeks biograficzny*, compiled by Gabriele Baumgartner. München, 1998.
PorLing	*Portraits of linguists; a biographical source book for the history of Western linguistics, 1746-1963*, edited by Thomas A. Sebeok. Bloomington, Ind., 1966. 2 v. [Reprint of obituaries, most of which in the original language]
Private	Private information or questionnaire.
Prominent	*Prominent Hungarians*, ed. Márton Fekete. London, 1985.
PSB	*Polski słownik biograficzny.* 1- . Kraków, etc., 1935- .
PSN	*Příruční slovník naučný.* Praha, 1962-1967. 4 vol.
PTF	*Philologiae turcicae fundamenta.* 2v. Wiesbaden, 1959-1965.
Quem	*Quem é quem no Brasil.*
QuemPort	*Quem é alguém* (Who's who in Portugal). Lisboa, 1947.
Qui	*Qui est qui en Belgique francophone.*
Qui êtes-vous	*Qui êtes-vous*, 1908, 1924.
Quien	*Quien es quien en España.*
RCAJ	*Royal Central Asian journal.*
Rafols	Ráfols, José Francisco. *Diccionario biográfico de artistas de Cataluña.* 1-3. Barcelona, 1951-1954.
Ray	*Dictionary of national biography. Supplement*, edited by N. R. Ray. Calcutta, 1986- .
Reich	*Political leaders of the contemporary Middle East and North Africa*, edited by Bernard Reich. New York, 1990.

REJ	*Revue des études juives.*
REnAL	*The Reader's encyclopeadia of American literature.* New York, 1963.
RHbDtG	*Reichshandbuch der deutschen Gesellschaft.* Berlin, 1931.
Richter	Richter, Julius. *A History of Protestant missions in the Near East.* New York, 1910.
Riddick	Riddick, John F. *Who was who in British India.* Westport, Conn., 1998.
RNL	*Révai nagy lexikona.* 1-21. Budapest, 1911-1935.
Robinson	Robinson, Jane. *Wayward women; a guide to women travellers.* Oxford, 1990.
Romaniai	*Romániai magyar ki kicsoda.* Kolozsvár, 1997.
ROMM	*Revue de l'Occident musulman et de la Méditerranée.*
Rosenthal	Rosenthal, Eric. *Southern African dictionary of national biography.* London, 1966.
Rovito	Rovito, Teodore. *Letterati e giornalisti italiani contemporanei.* Napoli, 1922.
Ruiz C	Ruiz Cabriada, Agustín. *Bio-bibliografía del cuerpo facultativo de archiveros, bibliotecarios y arqueólogos, 1858-1958.* Madrid, 1958.
Sabater	*Diccionario biográfico español e hispanoamericano,* publicado bajo la dirección de Gaspar Sabater. Palma de Mallorca, 1959- .
Sainz	Sainz de Robles, Federico Carlos. *Ensayo de un diccionario de la literatura,* 2d ed., 1-3. Madrid, 1953-1956.
Salomone	Salomone, Sebastiano. *La Sicilia intellettuale contemporanea.* Catania, 1913.
Salses	Salses, Edmond de. *Livre d'or de valeurs humaines.* Paris, 1970.
Sampaio	Andrade, Arsénio Sampaio de. *Dicionário histórico e biográfico de artistas e técnicos portugueses.* Lisboa, 1959.
SBL	*Svenskt biografiskt lexikon.* Stockholm, 1918- .
ScBInd	*Scandinavian biographical index.* London, etc., 1994.
Schäfer	Schäfer, Richard. *Geschichte der Deutschen Orient=Mission.* Potsdam, 1932.
SchBiAr	Keller, Willy. *Schweizer biographisches Archiv.* 1-6. Zürich, 1952-1958.
Schoeberlein	Schoeberlein-Engel, John S. *Guide to scholars of the history and culture of Central Asia.* Cambridge, Mass., 1995.
Schwarz	Schwarz, Klaus. *Der Vordere Orient in den Hochschulschriften Deutschlands, Österreichs und der Schweiz.* Freiburg im Breisgau, 1980.
SchZLex	*Schweizerisches Zeitgenossen-Lexikon.* Bern, 1921.
Selim	Selim, George Dimitri. *American doctoral dissertations on the Arab world, 1883-1974.* Washington, D.C., 1976.
Selim²	Selim, George Dimitri. *American doctoral dissertations on the Arab world, 1981-1987.* Washington, D.C., 1989.
Selim³	Selim, George D. *American doctoral dissertations on the Arab world. Supplement, 1975-1981.* Washington, D.C., 1983.
Sen	*Dictionary of national biography,* edited by S. P. Sen. Calcutta, 1972-1974.
Sezgin	*Bibliographie der deutschsprachigen Arabistik und Islamkunde;* herausgegeben von Fuat Sezgin, I. Balçik, G. Degener, E. Neubauer. v. 1-21. Frankfurt a. M, 1990-1995.
Shavit	Shavit, David. *The United States in the Middle East.* New York, 1988.
Shavit, Africa	Shavit, David. *The United States in Africa.* New York, 1989.
Shavit, Asia	Shavit, David. *The United States in Asia.* New York, 1990.
SibirSE	*Сибирская советская энциклопедия.* 1-3. Moscow, 1929-1932.

Sigilla   *Sigilla veri; Lexikon der Juden, -Genossen und -Gegner.* Erfurt, 1929-1931.

SlovBioL   *Slovenski biografski leksikon.* Ljubljana, 1971-1991.

Sluglett   Sluglett, Peter. *Theses on Islam, the Middle East and North-West Africa.* London, 1983.

Smith   *The Admission register of the Manchester school;* ed. Jeremiah F. Smith. Manchester, 1866-1874.

SMK   *Svenska män och kvinnor.* Stockholm, 1942-1955.

SOAS   School of Oriental and African Studies, University of London.

Srodka   Śródka, Andrzej. *Uczeni polscy XIX-XX stulecia.* Warszawa, 1994-98.

Stache-Rosen   Stache-Rosen, Valentina. *German Indologists;* 2d ed. New Delhi, 1990.

Stenij   Stenij, S. Edv. "Die orientalischen Studien in Finnland, 1828-1875" in: *Studia orientalia* 1 (1925), pp. 271-311.

Suárez   Suárez, Constantino. *Escritores y artistas Asturianos; indice bio-bibliográfico.* 7 vols. Madrid, 1936-1959.

SUNY   State University of New York.

TatarES   *Татарский энциклопедический словарь,* ed. M. Kh. Khasanov. Kazan, 1999.

TB   *Türkiye bibliyografyası.*

Teichl   *Österreicher der Gegenwart,* hrsg. von Robert Teichl. Wien, 1951.

Temerson   *Biographie des principales personnalités françaises décédés au cours de l'année,* ed. Henri Temerson. Paris, 1956.

THESAM 1   *Le monde arabe et musulman au miroir de l'université française;* répertoire des thèses soutenues dans les universités françaises, en sciences de l'homme et de la société, sur le monde arabe et musulman, 1973-1987. THESAM 1: Maghreb, Mauritanie, Maroc, par Marie Burgat, Danièle Bruchet. Aix-en-Provence, 1989.

THESAM 2   *Le monde arabe et musulman au miroir de l'université française;* répertoire des thèses soutenues dans les universités françaises, en sciences de l'homme et de la société, sur le monde arabe et musulman, 1973-1987. THESAM 2: Algérie, Tunisie, Libye, par Jacqueline Quilès. Aix-en-Provence, 1990.

THESAM 3   *Le monde arabe et musulman au miroir de l'université française;* répertoire des thèses soutenues dans les universités françaises, en sciences de l'homme et de la société, sur le monde arabe et musulman, 1973-1987. THESAM 3: Machrek, par Jacqueline Quilès. Aix-en-Provence, 1991.

THESAM 4   *Le monde arabe et musulman au miroir de l'université française;* répertoire des thèses soutenues dans les universités françaises, en sciences de l'homme et de la société, sur le monde arabe et musulman, 1973-1987. THESAM 4: Monde arabe et musulman, Afghanistan, Empire ottoman, Iran, Pakistan, Turquie, par Marie-José Bianquis et Danièle Bruchet. Aix-en-Provence, 1992.

Thesis   Curriculum vitae in a doctoral dissertation.

ThTwC   *Thinkers of the twentieth century,* ed. E. Devine et al. London, c1983, 1987.

TurkmenSE   *Туркмен совет энциклопедиясы,* 1-10. Ashgabat, 1974-1989.

TwCAu   *Twentieth century authors.* New York, 1942, 1955.

TwCBDA   *The Twentieth century biographical dictionary of notable Americans;* edited by Rossiter Johnson. Detroit, c1904, 1968.

UCLA   University of California, Los Angeles.

UjMagyar   *Új magyar lexikon.* Budapest, 1959-1972.

UjLex   *Uj idők lexikona.* Budapest, 1936-1942.

Uj lexikon   *Uj lexikon.* Budapest, 1936. 8v.

Unesco	UNESCO. *Social scientists specializing in African studies; directory = Africanistes spécialistes de sciences sociales; répertoire.* Prepared by the Secretariat of Unesco. Paris, 1963.
UzbekSE	*Узбек Совет энциклопедиясию.* 1-14. Toshkent, 1971-1980.
Vaccaro	Vaccaro, Gennaro, ed. *Panorama biografico degli italiani d'oggi.* Roma, 1956.
Van Ess	Van Ess, Dorothy. *Who's who in the Arabian mission,* by Mrs. John Van Ess. New York, ca. 1937.
Vapereau	Vapereau, Gustave. *Dictionnaire universel des contemporains,* 6e éd. Paris, 1893.
Vem är det	*Vem är det,* Stockholm.
Vem och vad	*Vem och vad,* Helsingfors.
VIA	*Voyageurs italien en Afrique.* Roma, Ministerio delle Colonie, Ufficio Studi e Propaganda, 1931.
Vogel	Vogel, Lester I. *To see a promised land.* University Park, Pa., 1993.
Wer	*Wer ist wer; Lexikon österreichischer Zeitgenossen.* Wien, 1937.
WhAm	*Who was who in America.*
WhAmArt	*Who was who in American art.*
WhE&EA	*Who was who among English and European authors.*
WhNAA	*Who was who among North American authors.*
Who	*Who's who.*
WhoAm	*Who's who in America.*
WhoAmArt	*Who's who in American art.*
WhoAmJ	*Who's who in American Jewry.*
WhoAmL	*Who's who in American law.*
WhoAmM	*Who's who in American music.*
WhoAmP	*Who's who in American politics.*
WhoAmW	*Who's who of American women.*
WhoArab	*Who's who in the Arab world.*
WhoArt	*Who's who in art.*
WhoAtom	*Who's who in atoms.*
WhoAus	*Who's who in Australia.*
WhoAustria	*Who's who in Austria*
WhoBelgium	*Who's who in Belgium.*
WhoBlA	*Who's who among Black Americans.*
WhoCon	*Who's who in consulting.*
WhoCroatia	*Who's who in Croatia.*
WhoE	*Who's who in the East.*
WhoEc	*Who's who in economics; a biographical dictionary of major economists, 1700-1986.*
WhoEcon	*Who's who in economics; a biographical dictionary of major economists, 1700-1981.*
WhoEduc	*Who's who in education.*
WhoEgypt	*Who's who in Egypt and the Near East.*
WhoEIO	*Who's who in European institutions and organizations.*
WhoEmL	*Who's who of emerging leaders in America.*

WhoFI	*Who's who in finance and industry.*
WhoFr	*Who's who in France.*
WhoFrS	*Who's who in frontiers of science and technology.*
WhoGov	*Who's who in government.*
WhoIndia	*Who's who in India.*
WhoIsrael	*Who's who in Israel.*
WhoItaly	*Who's who in Italy.*
WhoLeb	*Who's who in Lebanon.*
WhoLib	*Who's who in librarianship.*
WhoLibI	*Who's who in library and information science.*
WhoLibS	*Who's who in library science.*
WhoLit	*Who's who in literature.*
WhoMilH	Keegan, John & A. Wheatcroft. *Who's who in military history.* 2nd ed. London, 1987.
WhoMus	*Who's who in music.*
WhoMW	*Who's who in the Midwest.*
WhoNL	*Who's who in the Netherlands.*
WhoNZ	*Who's who in New Zealand.*
WhoÖster	*Who is who in Österreich.*
WhoRel	*Who's who in religion.*
WhoRom	*Who was who in twentieth century Romania,* by Ş. N. Ionescu. Boulder, Colo., 1994.
WhoSAfrica	*Who's who in Southern Africa.*
WhoScand	*Who's who in Scandinavia.*
WhoScEu	*Who's who in science in Europe.*
WhoSocC	*Who's who in the Socialist countries.*
WhoSoCE	*Who's who in the Socialist countries of Europe.*
WhoScot	*Who's who in Scotland.*
WhoSpain	*Who's who in Spain.*
WhoS&SW	*Who's who in the South and Southwest.*
WhoSwi	*Who's who in Switzerland.*
WhoUN	*Who's who in the United Nations and related agencies.*
WhoUSWr	*Who's who in U.S. writers, editors & poets.*
WhoWest	*Who's who in the West.*
WhoWor	*Who's who in the world.*
WhoWorJ	*Who's who in world Jewry.*
WhWE	*Who was who in world exploration,* by Carl Waltman and A. Wexler. New York, 1992.
Widmann	Widmann, Horst. *Exil und Bildungshilfe.* Bern, 1973.
Wie is dat	*Wie is dat,* s'Gravenhage.
Wie is wie	*Wie is wie in Nederland,* s'Gravenhage.
Wieczynski	*Modern encyclopedia of Russian and Soviet history,* edited by J. L. Wieczynski. Vol. 1-60. Gulf Breeze, Fla., 1976-2000.
WielkoSB	*Wielkopolski słownik biograficzny,* Warszawa.

WieVlaand	*Wie is wie in Vlaanderen*, Brussel.
Wininger	Wininger, Samuel. *Große jüdische National-Biographie.* Cernăuți, 1925-1932.
WomNov	Robinson, Doris. *Women novelists, 1891-1920.* New York, 1984.
WomWWA	*Woman's who's who of America*, 1914-1915.
WorAl	*The World Almanac Book of who*, edited by Hana U. Lane. New York, 1980.
WorAu	Wakeman, John. *World authors; a companion volume to Twentieth-century authors.* New York, 1975, 1980.
WrDr	*The Writers directory*
Wrede	Wrede, Richard. *Das geistige Berlin.* Berlin, 1897-1898.
Wright	Wright, Denis. *The English amongst the Persians.* London, 1977.
WRMEA	*Washington report on Midle East affairs*, vol. 1- . Washington, D.C., 1982- .
Wurzbach	Wurzbach, Constant von. *Biographisches Lexikon des Kaiserthums Oesterreich.* Wien,
WW	*Who was who*
WWASS	*Who's who in Asian studies in Switzerland.* Geneva, 1989.
WWScand	*Who's who in Scandinavia.* A-K, L-Z. Zürich, 1981.
WWWA	*Who was who in America*
WZKM	*Wiener Zeitschrift für die Kunde des Morgenlandes*
Zach	Zach, Michael. *Österreicher im Sudan, 1820 bis 1914.* Wien, 1985.
Zananiri	Zananiri, Gaston. *Figures missionnaires modernes.* Paris, 1963.
ZDMG	*Zeitschrift der Deutschen Morgenländischen Gesellschaft*
ZKO	Zentralkatalog der Orientalia; Islamic publications down to 1993, edited by W. H. Behn at the Staatsbibliothek zu Berlin. Not published.
Zürcher	Zürcher, Erik J. *Turkey; a modern history.* London, 1993.

Aaboe, Asger Hartvig, born 26 August 1922 at København, he was educated in Denmark and received a Ph.D. in 1957 for a thesis on the history of mathematics. Since 1957 he taught his subject at various American universities. His writings include *Episodes from the early history of mathematics* (1963), and *Contributions to the study of Babylonian lunar theory* (1979). AMS, 1965, 1968, 1976 P, 1973 S, 1978 S

Aalto, Pentti, born 22 July 1917 at Pori, Finland, he was an Orientalist whose writings include *Oriental studies in Finland, 1828-1918* (1971), *Classical studies in Finland, 1828-1918* (1980). *Modern language studies in Finland, 1828-1918* (1987), and *Studies in Altaic and comparative philology* (1987). He died on 30 November 1998. WWScand, 1981

Aanavi, Don, born 17 September 1939 at N.Y.C., he was educated at City University of New York, University of Hawaii, and Columbia University, where he received Ph.D. in 1969 for *Islamic pseudo inscriptions*. From 1967 to 1969 he was an assistant curator at the Metropolitan Museum of Art, NYC, and from 1969 to 1974, professor of history of art at Lehman-Hunter College. Since 1974 he was a professor of history of art in the University of Hawaii. His writings include *Islamic arts: an exhibition of Islamic art* (1974). DrAS, 1982 H

Aaronsohn, Alexander, born in 1888 at Zikhron Ya'akov, Palestine. Before and during the first World War, he was active in anti-Turkish propaganda, and in the pro-British Nili organization. After the war, he was a founding member of the Zionist farmers' organization Benei Binyamin. During World War two, he was attached to the British Intelligence Service. His writings include *With the Turks in Palestine* (1916), *Mit der türkischen Armee in Palästina* (Bern, 1917), *Šarah: shalhevet Nili* (1942), and *Be-gan ha-mahashavot* (1943). He died in 1948. EncJud

Aarts, Paul, born in 1949 in the Netherlands, where he studied political science and international relations. He was a member of the Dutch Palestine Committee, and a founding member, as well as the secretary of the Middle East Research Associates in 1984. In 1983, he began teaching at the University of Amsterdam. His writings include *De arabische uitdaging* (1982), and *Islamisch fundamentalisme* (1986). He edited *Geld, goed en godsdienst in het Midden-Oosten* (1991). Brinkman's, 1991-95

Aartun, Kjell, a writer on Semitic linguistics who published *Zur Frage altarabischer Tempora* (Oslo, 1963), *Die Partikeln des Ugaritischen* (1974), and *Studien zur ugaritischen Lexikographie* (1991).

Abadan, Yavuz, born about 1910 in Turkey, he was in 1960 a member of the Faculty of Political Science and Law in Ankara Üniversitesi. His writings include *Harp sonu muahedelerine nazaran Lozanin hususiyetleri* (1938), *Âmme hukuk ve devlet nazariyeleri* (1952), and *Devlet felsefesi* (1959). He was honoured by the jubilee volume, *Prof. Dr. Yavuz Abadan'a armağan* (1969).

Abadan-Unat, Emine *Nermin*, born 18 September 1921 in Turkey, she studied law and political science at universities in Turkey and the U.S.A., obtaining a doctorate in 1959 from Ankara Üniversitesi for her thesis,*Bürokrasi*. Since 1966, she was a professor of political science at Ankara Üniversitesi as well as a visiting professor at universities in Germany and the United States. She was a sometime president of the Turkish Association of Social Sciences. Her writings include *Social change and Turkish women* (1963); she was joint author of *Turkish workers in Europe, 1960-1975* (1976). Kim kimdir, 1985/86, 1997/98

Abdy-Williams, Ellen Mary, born 19th cent. *see* Whishaw, Ellem Mary née Abdy, Mrs. Williams

Abaev, Vasilii Ivanovich (Василий Иванович Абаев), born 15 December 1900 at Kobi, Georgia. After secondary education at Tbilisi, 1910 to 1918, he studied Iranian linguistics at the University of Petrograd from 1920 to 1925. Thereafter he taught at Leningrad University until 1951, when he was appointed professor of Iranian studies in the Philological Institute of the Soviet Academy of Science, Moscow. He was a member of the Royal Asiatic Society, and the Société Finno-ougrienne, Helsinki. His writings include *Русско-осетинский словарь* (1950), *Историко-этимологческий словарь осетинского языка* (1958-1979), *A grammatical sketch of Ossetic* (1964), *Основ иранского языкознания* (1982), and *Нарты* (1990). BioB134, pp. 1-17; Miliband; Miliband²; Schoeberlein

Abaeva, Tamara Grigor'evna (Тамара Григорьевна Абаева), born 17 July 1927 at Khiva, Uzbekistan, she graduated from the Oriental Faculty, Central Asian State University, Tashkent, in 1951. Ten years later, she obtained a doctorate for her thesis *Очерки истории Бадахшана* (published in 1964). From 1956 until her retirement she was a member of the Oriental Institute, Uzbekistan Academy of Science. Her writings include *Памиро-Гиндустанский регион Афганистана в конче XIX-начале XX века* (1987). Miliband; Miliband²

Abawi, Mohammed Yahya, born 29 August 1929 at Kabul, where he received a law degree in 1951. He was a civil servant from 1951 until 1978; concurrently he studied at the Universität Münster from 1960 to 1964, obtaining a Dr.phil. in 1964 with a thesis entitled *Die Wirtschaftsstruktur, insbesondere die Agrarstruktur in Afghanistan*. Thereafter he taught at Kabul University until 1978. In 1981 he was in Germany as a refugee. Adamec

2

Abba, Yusufu, 20th cent., he received a B.Sc. from the Ahmadu Bello University, Zaria, Nigeria, and a M.Sc. from a university in Philadelphia, Pa. In 1979 he was lecturer at the Department of Sociology in the Ahmadu Bello University. Note about the author

d'Abbadie, Antoine Thompson, born 3 January 1810 at Dublin, he was educated at the Collège de France, Paris. From 1837 to 1848, he travelled and explored Ethiopia from north to south. He returned to France with an important collection from all branches of science, in particular Ethiopian manuscripts. It took him nearly twenty years until all the results of his exploration had been published. His writings include *Géodésie d'une partie de la Haute Ethiopie* (1860), *Douze ans dans la Haute-Ethiopie* (1868), *Géographie de l'Ethiopie* (1890). He died at his châteaux Abbadia in the Basses-Pyrénées on 19 March 1897. ACAB; DBF; Henze; Vapereau, 6e éd., 1893

Abbady, Isaac Abraham, born in 1898 at Jerusalem, he was from 1920 to 1944 chief Hebrew interpreter to the British Mandatory Administration of Palestine, and an authority on Middle Eastern affairs. Apart from many translations into Hebrew, he wrote *Benenu le-ven ha-Anglim* (1947), and *Jerusalem economy* (1950). He died in 1969. WhoIsrael, 1966/67

Abbas, Ferhat, born 24 October 1899 near Taher, Algeria, he was the first president of the Provisional Government of the Algerian Republic. He wrote *Guerre et révolution* (1962), and *L'indépendance confisquée* (1984). He died 24 December 1985. AnObit, 1985, pp. 631-633; CurBio, 1961, 1986; Master (4); MidE, 1982/83; Reich; WhoArab, 1967/68-1978/79|

'Abbas, Ihsan, born 2 December 1920 at 'Ayn Ghazzal, Palestine, he was educated at Cairo University, where he obtained a Ph.D. in Arabic literature in 1954. After teaching for ten years at the University of Khartoum, he joined the AUB, where he became chairman of the Department of Arabic and later, director of the Centre of Middle Eastern Arab Studies. Concurrently he was the editor of الأبحاث. His many writings include تاريخ النقد الأدبي عند العرب (1993). WhoArab, 1971/72-1978/79|

Abbas, Khwaja Ahmad, fl. 1939-1955. In 1939, he was on the staff of the *Bombay chronicle*, and one of the Indian delegates to the Youth Conference held at Vassar College, Poughkeepsie, N.Y. He was also a freelance writer whose writings include *Let India fight for freedom* (1943), انقلاب (1955), and *The Gun and other stories* (1985). ZKO

Abbasi, Muhammad Yusuf, born 4 September 1921 at Gujranwala, India. After obtaining a Ph.D. at Punjab University, Lahore, he was on the staff of the Pakistan Military Academy, Kakul, since 1949; and from 1962 to 1968, he taught at Government College in Nigeria. In 1974. he retired as lt.-colonel and head of the Modern Subjects Department in the Army Education Corps to become, first, professor and chairman of the Dept. of History in the Quaid-i-Azam University, Islamabad, and later, professor of history at the Dept. of History and Pakistan Studies in the Islamia University, Bahawalpur. He wrote *Muslim politics and leadership in South Asia, 1876-1892* (1981), and *London Muslim League, 1908-1928* (1988).

Abbasi, Nasreen, fl. 1976-1987. In 1979, she was staff demographer at the Pakistan Institute of Development Economics, Islamabad. She wrote *Socio-economic effects of international migration* (1980), and *Urbanization in Pakistan, 1951-1981* (1987).

Abbasov, Ali Mamed ogly, fl. 1966-1986, an Azeri writer who wrote Низами Ганчавинин "Искандарнама" поэмасы (Baku, 1966), and Азербаjчан-Афган адаби алагалари тарихиндан (Baku, 1986).

Abbasov Enver Magomed ogly, fl. 1972, an Azeri writer whose writings include Азербаjчанча-русча лугат (Baku, 1985).

Abbasov, Israfil Ismail ogly, fl. 1972, an Azeri writer whose writings include Азербаjчан фолклору XIX. аср ермани манбаларинда (Baku, 1977).

Abbate, Onofrio, born 29 February 1824 at Palermo; after completing his medical studies at the Università di Palermo, he emigrated to Egypt in 1845 and subsequently entered the Khedivial medical service. In this position he participated in the Crimean War, and accompanied the viceroy, Muhammad Said Pasha, to the Sudan (1856-1857). He was a founding member and a president of the Société khédiviale de géographie *du Caire*. His writings include *De l'Afrique centrale* (1858), *Le Soudan sous le règne du khédive Ismail* (1895), *L'Eunuchisme* (1903), *Encore le Canal Abbas II* (1912). He died 11 October 1915 in Cairo, (or, according to Hill, in Como, Italy.) DizBI; Hill

Abbate, Washington, born 12 August 1849 in Egypt, he was sent in 1861 to Paris, where he became an *élève* at the Pension Chevallier, and took courses at the Lycée Bonaparte. Concurrently with his legal studies he took classes at l'École des Hautes Études, Collège de France. Upon his return to Egypt in 1877, the Khedive Isma'il appointed him to the Auditory general. He left after two years to enter the Ministry of Justice, where he remained until his death after a long illness on 25 July 1897. Bulletin de l'Institut égyptien, 3e série, 8 (1897), pp. 177-182

Abbott, Freeland Knight, born 31 May 1919 at Hartford, Conn., he graduated from Tufts College and received a Ph. D. from Fletcher School of Law and Diplomacy. He taught at Miami University, Oxford, Ohio, and Tufts University. In 1953-1955, he was a Ford Foundation Fellow in Pakistan and went there again in 1959-1960 as a Fulbright Research Fellow. His chief interest was Middle Eastern and South Asian history on which he wrote a number of articles and the monograph *Islam and Pakistan* (1968). He was a member of several learned societies, and was interested in curriculum reform. He died suddenly at Pusan, Korea, while on sabbatic leave, 24 February 1971. WhAm 5

Abbott, George Frederick, born 19th cent., he wrote *The tale of a tour in Macedonia* (1903), *Through India with the Prince* (1906), *Israel in Europe* (1907), *Turkey in transition* (1909), *The holy war in Tripoli* (1912), *Turkey, Greece, and the great powers* (1917), *Under the Turk in Constantinople* (1920), and *Greece and the Allies, 1914-1922* (1922). LC; LitYbk, 1922; Master (4)

Abbott, Sir James, born 12 March 1807; he passed through the military college of the East India Company, Blackheath, and received a commission as second lieutenant in the Bengal Artillery on 6 June 1823. In 1839 he was sent to Khiva to negotiate the release of Russian prisoners, and concluded the terms in 1840 in St. Petersburg. From 1845 to 1853 he was commissioner of Hazara. He was also a poet and antiquarian. His writings include *The T'hakoorine, a tale of Maandoo* (1841), *A Narrative of a journey from Herat to Khiva, Moscow and St. Petersburg* (1843), *Legends, ballades, &c.* (1854). He died 6 October 1896 in Ellerslie, Isle of Wight. Boase; Buckland; DNB; Henze; IndianBilnd (4); Riddick

Abbott, Keith Edward, born about 1800; he had a Turkish background and was associated in business with James Brant, a Smyrna merchant. He was served as a British consul at Erzerum, Tehran, Tabriz and Odessa. From October 1849 to June 1850, he travelled from Tehran to Qum, Isfahan, Yazd, Kirman, Shiraz, Bushire, and from there by boat to Baghdad, returning by way of Kirmanshah and Hamadan. From Tehran he made periodic visits to the Caspian province of Gilan in order to report on and encourage the cultivation of silk which was exported to England. He made valuable reconnaissance of parts of Persia which had not been trodden before by Westerners. He died in Odessa, 28 April 1873. DNB; Gabriel; Henze; Wright

Abbott, Nabia, born 31 January 1897 at Mardin, Turkey; she was educated at the University of Allahabad, Boston University, and the University of Chicago. For some years she taught English at girls' schools in India; subsequently she was head of a girls' school in Iraq until 1923 when she went to the United States. After some ten years at Asbury College, Wilmore, Ky., she went to the Oriental Institute of the University of Chicago, where she remained until her retirement in 1963. Her writings include *The Monasteries of Fayyum* (1937), *The Kurrah papyri from Aphrodito in the Oriental Institute*, a revision of her Ph.D. thesis, Chicago, 1933 (1938), *The Rise of the North Arabic script and the Kur'anic development* (1939), *Aisha, the beloved of Mohammad* (1942), *Two Queens of Baghdad* (1946), *Studies in Arabic literary papyri* (1957-1972). DrAS, 1969 H, 1974 H, 1978 H; WhoAmW, 1961/62

Abboud, Peter Fouad, born 30 June 1931 at Jaffa, he studied at the Universsity of London, AUC, and Univ. of Texas at Austin, where he obtained a Ph.D. in 1964 for *The Syntax of Nadji Arabic*. From 1968 until his retirement he was professor of Arabic at the University of Texas. He was joint author of *Elementary modern standard Arabic* (1975-76). DrAS, 1974 F, 1978 F, 1982 F

'Abd al-Jalil, Jean Mohammed, 1904-1979 see Abd-el-Jalil, Jean Mohammed

'Abd al-Jawad, Dorothea née Schumacher, born in the last quarter of the nineteenth centry, her writings include *Eine türkische Ehe in Briefen* (1913), and *Frauenkleid und Entartung eines Jahrtausends* (1929). She died after 1932.

'Abd al-Nasir, Jamal, 1918-1970 see Nasser, Gamal Abdel

'Abd al-Rahim, Muhammad Kamil, born in 1897 in Egypt, he was educated at Fuad I University, Cairo, and Cambridge University. He was an Egyptian diplomat and sometime ambassador to the United States. His writings include *Shifā' lil-qulūb* (1967). Who's who in the Arab world, 1978/79|

Abd-el-Jalil, le père Jean Mohammed, born in 1904 in Morocco, he studied at Paris, and entered the Franciscan Order in 1928. He was ordained in 1935 and shortly thereafter appointed professor of Arabic and Islamic studies at l'Institut catholique de Paris. His writings include *Histoire de la littérature arabe* (1943). MIDEO 15 (1982), pp. 311-312; NUC, 1968-1972

Abdalla, Ahmed, born in 1950 at Cairo, he studied at the universities of Cairo and Cambridge, and in 1984, he was a special fellow of the U.N. University. He was a member of the Egyptian Organisation for Human Rights, and MESA, a free-lance researcher and author who wrote *The student movement and national politics in Egypt, 1923-1973* (1985).

Abdel Gawad Schumacher, Dorothea *see* 'Abd al-Jawad, Dorothea née Schumacher

Abdesselem, Taleb, born 19th cent. in Algeria, he studied at the Université de Paris and received a doctorate in 1911 for *L'Organisation financière de l'Empire marocain*. Subsequently he was barrister and town councillor in Tlemcen. He was an example of an emancipated multicultural Muslim. For his outstanding service to French Algeria he was awarded the *Grande médaille Gallia tutrix* by the *Revue indigène*. In 1920 he survived the abortive attempt on his life for political and personal reasons. His trace is lost after a publication in 1929. *Revue indigène* 15 (1920), p. 191

Abdoh ('Abduh), Jalal, born in 1909, he received a doctorate in 1937 from the Université de Paris. He entered the Iranian Government Service, where he served as minister, ambassador as well as permanent representative to the UN. *Iran who's who,* 1976

Abdolov, Nazarbek, born 23 February 1947 in Tajikistan, he graduated in 1969 from the State Pedagogical Institute, Dushanbe, and received his first degree in 1978 for *Особенности формирования арабо-язычной тунисской литературы XI-XX вв.* After spending five years in Algeria, he was since 1984 affiliated with the Tajikistan Pedagogical Institute. Miliband[2]

Abdugafurov (Абдугафуров), Abdurashid Khodzhaevich, born 1 May 1931 at Tashkent, he obtained a doctorate in 1970 for *Сатира в творчестве Алишера Навои*. Since 1968, he was senior researcher at the Institute for Language and Literature, Uzbek Academy of Science. His writings include *Навоий ижҳодида сатира* (1972), and *Сатира в творчестве Навои* (1972), and *Сатира Мукими* (1976). Miliband; Miliband[2]

Abdul, Musa Oladipupo Ajilogba, born 20th cent., he obtained an M.A. in 1967 from McGill University, Montreal, for *Islam in Ijebu Ode*, and in 1970, a Ph.D. for *The Qur'an; Tabarsi's commentary, his approach to theological issues*. Certainly from 1970 to 1977, he was a senior lecturer at the Department of Arabic and Islamic Studies in the University of Ibadan. His writings include *The historical origin of Islam* (1973). LC

Abdul Aziz, Mohammed *see* Aziz, Mohammed Abdul

Abdul Huq, A. M., fl. 1961-1977. His writings include *Librarianship and the Third World* (1977).

Abdul Qadir, Khan Bahadur Sheikh, 1874-1951 *see* Qadir, Abdul, Sir, Khan Bahadur

Abdullaev, Aliovsut Zakir ogly, fl. 1975-1981, an Azeri writer who published *Адабиёт форсу точик дар нимаи аввали асри XI* (1979), and *Азарбаичан дилчилийи масалалари* (1981).

Abdullaev, Ismatulla, born 10 March 1927 at Namangan, Uzbekistan, he graduated in 1944 from the local teachers' college, and in 1951 from the Oriental Faculty in the Central Asian State University. He received his first degree in 1963 for *Поэзия на арабском языке в Бухаре при Саманидах* and his doctorate in 1977 for *«Йатимат-ад-дахр» - источник по истории арабоязычной литературы народов Мавараннахра и Хорасана*. Nearly all of his other writings are in Uzbek and Dari. Miliband[2]

Abdullaev, Turgun Abdullaevich, fl. 1972-1978, an Azeri writer who published *Каталог медных и медночеканных изделий Узбекистана XVIII-XX вв* (1974); he is the joint author of *Одежда узбеков, XIX - начало XX в* (1978).

Abdullaev, Zakir Zul'fugar, born 20 December 1924 in Azerbaijan, he graduated in 1949 from the Moscow Oriental Institute and received his first degree in 1952 for *Экспансия США в Тране после первой мировой* and his doctorate in 1965 for *Формирование рабочего класса Ирана*, a work which was published in 1968. He was affiliated with the Oriental Institute, Azerbaijan Academy of Science, before he joined the Azerbaijan State University in 1966. He was appointed a professor in 1967. His writings include *Промышленность и зарождение рабочего класса Ирана в конче XIX - нахале XX вв* (1963), *Начало экспансии США в Иране* (1963) as well as works in Azeri. Miliband[2]

Abdullah, Achmed, born in 1881, a writer of English fiction who originated from the borderland of Afghanistan and India, and who attended universities in Oxford, Paris, and Berlin. His writings include *The veiled woman, a novel of West and East* (1931). He died in 1945. Master (12)

Abdur Rahman, 1934- *see* Rahman, Abdur

Abdurrahman, Prince de Condé, born in 1913 in California into a family who had fled from Europe during the revolutionary period and settled in the firmer Spanish Bourbon colony of California prior to the American conquest of that state. After service in the second World War, he left the U.S. Air Force in the rank of major, took up Arab studies at the AUB from 1950 to 1955, interrupted only by a seven-week trip to Yemen in 1953, and settled permanently in Yemen in 1956, embracing Islam and becoming a Yemeni citizen in 1958. Exiled in 1960, he was accorded citizenship in the Emirate of Sharjah until he was able to return to Yemen, in 1962, to serve the new Imam al-Badr. Brevetted lt-colonel at the battle of Maswar-Khawlan in 1963, and promoted to colonel in the honours list after the victory of Jabal Razih in the winter of 1964-65, he reached general officer's rank in 1965 on being named *aide de camp* to H.M. the Imam at the Royal GHQ in Shida with the personal rank of amir, or prince, a restoration of his ancestral title in pre-revolutionary France and Navarre. He has served also as public relations officer for GHQ and as adviser of the Ministry of Communications, in charge of postage stamp production and use, himself designing the "war stamps" of the Kingdom between 1964 and 1967. *Orient* (Opladen), vol. 10 (1969), p. 10

Abdus Subhan, born 2 December 1936 at Calcutta, he received a doctorate in 1965 at Calcutta with a thesis entitled *History of Nawab Alivardi Khan of Bengal*. He was since 1961 a professor and head of the Department of Persian, Maulana Azad College, Calcutta. His writings include *Khvudnavisht savanih hayat-i Nassakh* (1986), and he edited *Tarikh-i-Bangala-i-mahabatjangi* (Calcutta, 1963). IWWAS, 1976/77; LC

Abdus Subhan, Syed, born in 1893 in Chittagong District, he was educated at Calcutta, Aligarh, and Allahabad where he received an M.A. He participated in the non-cooperative movement of 1920-21. In the summer of 1922 he joined the teaching staff of the Department of Arabic and Islamic Studies in Dacca University, a post which held until his death on 1 June 1959. In 1945 he had gained a B.Litt. at Oxford with a thesis entitled *An enquiry into the causes of the failure of the Mu'tazilite Movement*. *Journal of the Asiatic Society of Pakistan* 4 (1959), pp. 197-199

Abedin, Syed Zainul, born 2 April 1928 at New Delhi, he received a Ph.D. in 1974 from the University of Pennsylvania with a thesis entitled *In defense of freedom; America's first foreign war, a new look at U.S.-Barbary relations, 1776-1816*. He became a director and editor-in-chief of the *Journal* of the Institute of Muslim Minority Affairs. He died in Jedda on 5 June 1993. Schoeberlein

van den **Abeele**, Marcel, born 11 July 1898 at Bruges, Belgium, he started his lifelong career in colonial agronomy in the former Belgian Congo, where he spent the years from 1922 to 1932 as a provincial agronomist and, ultimately, as inspector general of lands and forests. From 1933 until his retirement he was in government service in Bruxelles. His writings include *L'Erosion, problème africain* (1941), *Les Principales cultures du Congo belge* (2e éd., 1951). Highly decorated, he died on 18 January 1980 in Auderghem. *Hommes et destins*, vol. 5, pp. 532-533

Abeghian, Artasches, born 20 December 1877 at Astapat, Armenia, he was educated at Shusha, Tiflis, and Echmiadzin, where he graduated in 1899 from Georg Academy. After teaching at Shusha during the school year 1899/1900, he pursued his studies at Leipzig, Berlin, and Marburg, where he received a Dr. phil. for his thesis, *Vorfragen zur Entstehungsgeschichte der altarmenischen Bibelübersetzungen* (1906). He settled in Berlin, where he became in 1936 the founding editor of the *Mitteilungsblatt der Deutsch-Armenischen Gesellschaft*. Apart fom three monographs written in Armenian, his writings include *Neuarmenische Grammatik* (1936), and *Geschichte Armeniens; ein Abriß* (1948). Thesis

Abel, Armand, born 11 June 1903 at Uccle, Belgium, he was educated at l'Athénée communal de Schaerbeek, and studied at the Université libre de Bruxelles, 1920-1924. He spent the following three years teaching classics at Cairo, and at the same time learning Arabic and completing a research on Islamic ceramics, *Gaibi et les grands faïenciers égyptiens d'époque mamelouke* (1930). Since 1929 he taught Arabic as well as Islamic studies, first at the Institut des hautes études de Belgique and later, at the Université de Bruxelles and the Institut de sociologie. In the post-war era he was the incontested master of Islamics in Belgium. His writings include *Aristote; la légende et l'histoire* (1944), *Le Coran* (1951), *Le Roman d'Alexandre* (1955), *Les Musulmans noirs du Maniéma* (1960), *Introduction aux études islamiques* (1968), *Le Monde arabe et musulman* (1968). He died unexpectedly at his cottage in Awan, 31 May 1973. As a tribute his colleagues and friends published the commemoration volume *Mélanges d'islamologie; volume dédié à la mémoire de Armand Abel* (1974). *Mélanges d'islamologie*, pp. 1-5

Abel, Deryck Robert Endsleigh, born in 1918 at Salisbury, Wiltshire, he studied at the L.S.E. and specialized in economic and financial problems. He contributed extensively on history, politics, economics, and literature to a wide range of journals. His most important work was the biography, *Ernest Benn, counsel for liberty* (1960). He served as chairman of the Liberal Party Executive in 1957-1959, and had the courage to stand for election to Parliament three times, though well aware that he had little chance of success. He reached the summit of his brief career when he succeeded to the editorship of the *Contemporary review* in the summer of 1960. His writings include *A History of British tariffs, 1923-1942* (1945), *Free trade challenge* (1953), *Channel underground* (1961). He died in July or August 1965. Au&Wr, 1963

Abel, Martin, born 13 January 1912 at Hamburg, he received a Dr.phil. in 1938 from the Universität Hamburg for *Die arabische Vorlage des Suaheli-Epos "Chuo cha Herkal."* In the early 1950s he wrote articles on the contemporary Middle East, the majority of which appeared in *Zeitschrift für Geopolitik.*

Abercrombie, Thomas J., born 20th cent., he was for many years on the editorial staff of the *National geographic magazine.* He was joint author of *Ancient Egypt; discovery of its splendors* (1978).

Abercromby, John, 5th baron of Abercromby, born 15 January 1841, he entered the army in 1858 and retired as lieutenant in 1870. He was a member of the Finno-Ugrian Society, as well as other learned societies. His writings include *A Trip through the eastern Caucasus* (1889), an account of his travel from 2 July to 23 August 1888, during which he crossed the main chain of the Caucasus twice by passes little used, expect by natives. The purpose was to pass through the country of the Avars and Chechens, as he had a faint knowledge of both their languages. He died 7 October 1924. Who was who, 2

Abicht, Rudolf, born in 1850, he received a Dr.phil. in 1891 from the Universität Breslau for *Donum Wardianum carmen didacticum de linguae arabicae grammatica a Zain-ud-Din-ibn Al-Wardi compositum* and also his Dr.habil. in 1907 for *Die russische Heldensage.* He was a sometime lecturer in Polish and Russian at Breslau. His writings include *Aš'âru-l-hudalijjîna; die Lieder der Dichter vom Stamme Hudail aus dem Arabischen übersetzt* (1879). He died in 1921. Note; NUC, pre-1956; Schwarz

Abougit, Louis Xavier, fl. 1862-1873, he was a Catholic missionary in Syria who wrote *Principes de la grammaire arabe à l'usage des écoles de français en Orient* (1862).

Abourezk, James George, born 24 February 1931 at Wood, South Dakota, he was a civil engineer and United States senator. IntWW, 1990/91-1996/97; Master index (9); Who's who in America, 1976/77

About, Edmond François Valentin, born 14 February 1828 at Dieuze (Meurthe), he was a brilliant graduate of the Lycée Charlemagne, and the École normale supérieure in Paris. From 1851 to 1853 he was at the École d'Athène in Greece. Upon his return to France, he published his recollections of *Île d'Egine*, and *La Grèce contemporaine*, both in 1854. In later life he devoted himself increasingly to journalism and the editorship of *La XIXe siècle.* His writings include *Le Roi des montagnes* (1857), and *The Roman question* (1859). He was nominated to the Académie Française in 1884, but died in Paris, 16 January 1885, before having delivered his acceptance. DBF

Abraham, Alexander, fl. 1923-1936, he was a high school coach who, in 1936, was athletics consultant to the Turkish Government at the German School in Istanbul. His writings include *Sportliche Gymnastik* (1923), and *Weg zur sportlichen Höchstleistung* (1923).

Abraham, Antoine J., born 17 May 1942 at Brooklyn, N.Y., he was educated at Hunter College, CUNY, and New York University, where he obtained a Ph.D. in 1975. His main field of research was conflict studies. His writings include *Lebanon at mid-century* (1981), *Lebanon, a state of siege, 1975-1984* (1984), *Islam and Christianity* (1987), and *Khoumani* (!) *and Islamic fundamentalism* (1989). In 1993, he was professor of Middle Eastern history at New York Institute of Technology.

Abraham, Salomon Otto, born 31 May 1872 at Berlin, he studied medicine and life sciences at the Humboldt Universität, Berlin, where he received a Dr.med. for his thesis *Über den Erfolg der künstlichen Frühgeburt* (1894). Since 1896 he was at Psychologisches Institut der Universität Berlin, carrying on musicological studies on Turkish and Far Eastern music; he was the contributing editor of two musicological works. He died in Berlin, 24 January 1926. NDB

Abrahamian, Ervand, born 7 December 1940 in Iran, he studied at Oxford and Columbia Univiersity, NYC, where he obtained a Ph.D. in 1969 for his thesis *Social bases of Iranian politics.* For many years, he was a professor at Baruch College, CUNY, a post which he still held in 2003. His writings include *Iran between two revolutions* (1982), and *The Iranian Mojahedin* (1989). NatFacDr, 2003; Private

Abrahamowicz, Zygmunt, born 20 February 1923 in Galicia as a descendant of an old Karaite family. The events of the second World War postponed his Turcological studies, begun at Warszawa and completed in 1951 at Kraków. He spent nearly twenty-five years at the Wojewódzkie Archivum Panstwowe, Kraków, before moving to the Instytut Historii (Polska Akademia Nauk), in 1976, where he remained until his retirement in 1988. He belonged to a generation of archivists who were scholars at the same time. His writings include *Katalog dokumentów tureckich* (1959), *Ksiega podrózy Ewliji Czelebiego* (1969),

Historia chana Islam Gerejall (1971), *Kara Mustafa pod Wiedniem* (1973). He died in Cracow, 13 December 1990. Acta orientalia Academiae Scientiarum Hungaricae 46 (1992/93), pp. 369-372

Abrahams, Israel, born 26 November 1858 at London, he studied at Jews College, and the University of London. He was a sometime teacher at Jews College as well as reader in Rabbinic and Talmudic literature at Cambridge; but he was more important as a writer of nearly twenty books and a regular contributor to numerous periodicals as well as a founding editor of the *Jewish quarterly review* in 1889. He was one of the founders of the Jewish Historical Society of England, and a member of the Anglo-Jewish Association. His writings include *By-paths in Hebraic bookland* (1920). He died in 1925. EncJud; Who was who, 2; Wininger

Abrahams, Sir Sidney Solomon, born 11 February 1885 at Birmingham, he was a graduate of Emmanuel College, Cambridge, who represented Cambridge against Oxford in track athletics. He became a barrister-at-law and rose in the colonial courts to the position of vice-president, H.M. Court of Appeal for Eastern Africa in 1934. His writings include *Law reports containing cases determined by the High Court for Zanzibar* (1919). He died 14 May 1957. Who was who, 5

Abramov, Monashe Mishailovich, born 20 December 1926 at Samarkand, he graduated in 1946 from the Faculty of History, Samarkand State University, and received his first degree in 1959. His writings include *О письменныых источниках по истории народов Узбекистана* (1985), *Гузары Самарканда* (1989), and he edited *Вопросы истории Узбекистана* (1975). Miliband²

Abramov, Shene'ur *Zalman*, born 6 May 1908 at Minsk, he studied at Case Western Reserve University, Cleveland, Ohio, 1927-1934. Since 1939 he was in legal practice in Israel. His writings include *Perpetual dilemma; Jewish religion in the Jewish State* (1976), *ha-Yahas el ha-medinah be-kerev ha-zeramin ha-datiyim* (1982). Who's who in Israel, 1992/93; WhoWorJ, 1987

Abramowich (Abramowitz/Abramovitz), Ze'ev, born 16 July 1891 at Marinpol, Ukraine, he was educated at the universities of Odessa and Bruxelles. He settled in Israel and published on the economic history of the Middle East and the Arabs in Palestine as well as in Israel. He died in 1970. WhoWorJ, 1972

Abrams, Charles, born 16 February 1902 at Vilna, Poland, he came as an infant with his parents to the United States. He obtained a LL.B. in 1922 from St. Lawrence University, Canton, N.Y., and was admitted to the New York Bar in 1923. Afterwards he practised law in N.Y.C., specializing in city planning and housing problems. He was the recipient of numerous honours and awards. His writings include *Revolution in land* (1939), *The future of housing* (1946), *Man's struggle for shelter in an urbanizing world* (1964), *The language of cities* (1971). He died 22 February 1970. CnDiAmJBi; CurBio, 1969, 1970; Master (6)

Abramzon (Абрамзон), Saul Matveevich, born 22 June (5 July) 1905 at Dmitrovvsk-Orlovski, Russia, he was an ethnographer and specialist on Central Asia and Kazakhstan. Since 1931 he was affiliated with the Leningrad Branch of the Institute of Ethnography in the Soviet Academy of Science. His writings include *Очерк культуры киргизского народа* (1946), *Этнографические аспекты изучения современности* (1980), *Киргизы и их этногенетические и историко-культурные эвязи* (1990), a work which was originally presented in 1968 as a thesis at Leningrad. Miliband; Miliband²

Abreu, Guilherme de Vasconcellos, born 20 May 1842 at Coimbra, he wrote *Investigaçoes sobre o caracter da civiliçao árya-hindu* (Lisboa, 1878), and *Sobre a séde originaria o caracter de gente árica* (1878). He died in 1907. J. M. Etseves Pereira & G. Rodrigues, Portugal; diccionario historica, vol. 1 (1904); NUC, pre-1956

Abribat, Jules, fl. 1895-1931. His writings include the two pamphlets, *Essai sur les contrats de quasi-aliénation et de location perpétuelle auxquelles l'institution du hobous a donné naissance* (1902), and *Notice sur les officiers interprètes* [*du Service des Affaires indigènes de la Tunisie*] (1931).

Abu Ganimah, Muhammed Subhi, born 21 March 1902 at Irbid, Palestine, he received his secondary education in Damascus and Aleppo before taking up medical studies at the Universität Berlin, where he obtained a Dr. med. in 1929 for his thesis *Abul-Kasim, ein Forscher der arabischen Medizin*. Thesis

Abu Hakima, Ahmad Mustafa, born 28 August 1923 at 'Abbasiyah, Palestine, he completed high school at the British Arab College in Jerusalem in 1944 and graduated four years later from AUC. His teaching career began in Kuwait where he resided from 1953 to 1958. In 1960 he received his Ph.D. from SOAS for his thesis, *The history of Eastern Arabia, 1750-1800*. From 1960 he spent two years as a lecturer at Khartoum and then served as an Unesco at the Department of History, Zaria College in Northern Nigeria. Thereafter he taught seven years at the University of Jordan and concurrently served as a guest professor at Columbia University, N.Y.C. From 1972 until his retirement in 1983 he held the chair of Gulf history at McGill University, Montreal. His writings include *Ta'rikh al-Kuwayt* (1970), *The modern history of Kuwait* (1983),

Eastern Arabia; historic photographs (1984-86), and he was joint author of *Descriptive catalogue of Arabic manuscripts in Nigeria* (1965). He died in Ottawa, 9 April 1998. *MESA bulletin* 32 (1998), pp. 286-287

Abu Jaber, Kamel S., born 1932 at Amman, he studied political science at Syracuse University and afterwards taught successively at the University of Tennessee and Smith College from 1965 to 1969. From 1969 until 1989 he was a professor in the University of Jordan, after which time he transferred to the Government of Jordan. His writings include *The Arab Ba'th Socialist Party* (1966), a work which was presented in 1965 as his doctoral thesis at Syracuse, N.Y. WhoArab, 1997-98-2001/2002

Abu-Laban, Baha Rashid, born 23 February 1931 at Jaffa, he was educated at AUB and the University of Washington, where he obtained a Ph.D. in 1960 for his thesis *Visibility of community leaders*. Since 1960 he was a professor at various universities in the United States, Lebanon, and Canada. His writings include *An Olive branch on the family tree* (1980). AmM&WSc, 1973 S-1978 S; IWWAS, 1976-1977

Abu-Lughod, Ibrahim Ali, born 15 February 1929 at Jaffa, he studied at Universiy of Illinois, and Princeton, where he obtained a Ph.D. in 1957 for his thesis, *Arab rediscovery of Europe, 1800-1870*. Ten years later, he became professor of political science at Northwestern Univ., Evanston, Illinois. He is the editor of several collective works. AmM&WSc P, 1982; IWWAS, 1976/77; Master (3)

Abu-Lughod, Janet Lippman, born 3 August 1928 at Newark, N.J., she studied at University of Chicago, and University of Massachusetts, where she obtained a Ph.D. in 1966 for *The ecology of Cairo*. She was a consulting sociologist until 1974, when she became professor of sociological and urban affairs at Northwestern University, Evanston, Illinois. She was still active as a teacher in NYC in 1997. Her writings include *Cairo; 1001 years of the "City victorious,"* (1971), *Rabat; urban apartheid in Morocco* (1980), *Before European hegemony* (1989). AmM&WSc, 1973 S, 1978 S; ConAu, 65-68; IWWAS, 1976/77

Abu Talib Khan ibn Muhammad Tabrizi Isfahani, born in 1752., he wrote *Lubb al-siyar-u-jahan-numa*, a Calcutta Hafiz edition, and *Masir-i Talibi fi balad al-Afranji*, a narrative of his journey to Europe, 1799-1803, of which there is a translation into English (1810), which has been translated into French (1811). The French translation was translated into German in 1813, and reprinted as recently as 1987. He died probably in 1806. *Encyclopædia Iranica*; LC; Storey, 878-79

Abu-Zahra, Nadia, born about 1935 at Gizeh, Egypt, she graduated from Cairo University and subsequently worked at the National Centre for Social and Criminological Research, before studying at Oxford University. She conducted field-work in Tunisia, Kuwait, and Egypt. From 1969 to 1983, she was in Canada, including twelve years as professor of anthropology at the University of British Columbia, Victoria, B.C. Her writings include *Sidi Ameur, a Tunisian village* (1982). In 1994 she was preparing an anthropological study on the performance of Islamic rituals. AmM&WSc, 1973 S, 1976 P

Abubakar, Sa'ad, born in 1939 at Jalingo, Nigeria. After graduating from Ahmadu Bello University, Zaria, he was a lecturer at its Dept. of History for a brief period, until he became Commissioner of Education, Gongola State, in the late 1970s. His writings include *The Lamibe of Fombina* (1977, a revision of his thesis), and *Pre-colonial government and administration among the Junkun*, his inaugural lecture delivered on 26 March 1986 at the University of Maiduguri, Nigeria.

Abubakar, Saleh, fl. 1979. He received a B.A. from the Ahmadu Bello University, Zaria, and became a lecturer in the same university in 1979.

Achard, Ed. C., fl. 1923-1930. After obtaining a diploma in agronomics, he was counsellor on agriculture at the Fédération des états de Syrie in 1924. His writings include *Le coton en Cilicie et en Syrie* (1922). Note

Acharhian, Hrach'eay H. *see* Adjarian, Herachyah H.

Achenbach, Hermann, born 11 July 1937 at Weidenau/Sieg, Germany, he studied at Marburg and Würzburg, where he obtained a Dr.phil. in 1963 for *Die Halbinsel Cap Bon in Tunesien*. He was for many years a professor of geography in the Universität Kiel. His writings include *Agrarpolitische Entwicklungsprobleme Tunesiens* (1971), and *Agrargeographie Nordafrika* (1985). Kürschner, 2001

Achundoff (Achundov/Achundow), Abdul-Chalig, born about 1860 at Baku, he received his first medical doctorate from the Universität Erlangen in 1888 for his thesis *Klinische Beiträge zur Lehre vom Coloboma oculi* , and his second doctorate from the Universität Dorpat (Tartu) for his thesis *Commentar zum sogenannten Liber fundamentorum pharmacologiae des Abu Mansur Muwaffak Ben Ali el-Hirowi* in 1892.

van **Ackere**, V. Constant, born 19th cent., he was in 1916 a judge at the Mixed Tribunal, Alexandria, Egypt. He rose from vice-president of the Mixed Court of Appeal, Alexandria, in 1934, to its president in 1941.

For the same period he was a member of the Société sultanieh d'économie politique, de statistique et de législation. He was joint author of *Le statut contemporaine des étrangers en Égypte vers une réforme du régime capitulaire* (1933). Note; NUC, pre-1956

Ackerman, Phyllis, born 26 September 1893 at Oakland, Cal., she was educated at the University of California, Berkeley, where she obtained her Ph.D. in 1917 for *Essays on Hegel's Phaenomenologie*. After museum work in California, she was from 1942 to 1952 a professor at the School of Asiatic Studies in the Asia Institute, N.Y.C.,. Her writings include *Tapestry, the mirror of civilization* (1933), *Guide to the Exhibition of Persian art* (New York, 1940). She is best remembered for *A survey of Persian art* in seventeen volumes which she published jointly with her husband Arthur Upham Pope. She died in 1977. WhoAmW, 1961/62

Acland, Peter Bevil Edward, brigadier, O.B.E., born 9 July 1902, and educated at Eton and Oxford, he was with the Sudan Political Service from 1924 to 1940. In 1962 he was appointed Justice of the Peace. He died on 9 January 1993. *Who's who*, 1979-1993

Acoluthus (Akolut), Andreas, born 6 March 1654 at Bernstadt, he was a student of August Pfeiffer and studied Semitic languages at Wittenberg and Leipzig, where he gained the *gradum magisterii* and subsequently taught philosophy and theology. He later served as *diaconus* and professor of Hebrew at the Gymnasio Elisabethano in Breslau and was elected member of the Königlich-Preußische Akademie der Wissenschaften. He wrote *De aqvis amaris maledictionem inferentibus, vulgo dictis zelotypiæ* (Leipzig, 1682), and *Alcoranica sive specimen Alcorani quadrilinguis, arabici, persici, turcici, latini* (1701). He died in 1704. Dziekan; *Grosses vollständiges Universal-Lexicon* (1732, reprinted, 1961); *Przegląd orientalistyczny* 56 (1965), pp. 325-333

Acquaviva, Antoine, fl. 1936-1960, he wrote *La condition civile des étrangers au Maroc* (1937), a work which was originally presented in 1936 as a thesis at Montpellier, and *Droit d'asile à Fès* (1960).

Acquaviva, Savino, born 19th cent., his writings include *L'ora presente nella legislazione civile italiana* (1905), and *L'avvenire coloniale d'Italia e la guerra* (1917).

Ådahl, F. D. Karin, born 12 December 1942 at Leksand, Sweden, she studied at Uppsala, where she received a doctorate in 1981 for *A Khamsa of Nizami of 1439; origin of the miniatures*. She became affiliated with the Museum of Far Eastern Antiquities, Stockholm. In 1993 she was a professor of fine art in Uppsala Universitet. She was joint author of *Arabiska handskrifter* (1989). EURAMES, 1993; IWWAS, 1975/76

Adair, A. R., he served in 1938 as an assistant magistrate and collector in Bihar and was one of four Indian Civil Service officers who, on the completion of their probationary period in Great Britain, travelled from London to India in an open automobile. Note

Adalet, the pseudonym of a writer of English fiction who flourished between 1890 and 1896 and who published *Hadjira, a Turkish love story* (London and New York, 1896).

Adam, André, born 30 July 1911 at Saint-Lô (Manche), he was a graduate of the Lycée Louis-le-Grand and École Normale Supérieure, Paris, and subsequently taught at French and Franco-Muslim schools in Morocco (1937-1949), before becoming a director of various academic institutes in Morocco (1950-1960). Afterwards he was a professor of sociology at Aix-en-Provence (1962-1970) and at the Université de Paris V from 1970 until his retirement in 1980. His writings include *La maison et le village dans quelques tribus de l'Anti-Atlas* (1951), *Une enquête auprès de la jeunesse musulmane du Maroc* (1963), *Histoire de Casablanca* (1968), *Bibliographie critique de la sociologie, d'ethnologie et de géographie humaine du Maroc* (1972). He died in Paris, 29 June 1991. Unesco; WhoFr, 1966/67-1990/91

Adam, Paul August Marie, born 7 December 1862 at Paris, he was a widely travelled symbolist writer who won considerable reputation for his historical and sociological novels. His writings include *Les impérialismes et la morale des peuples* (1908). He died in Paris, 1 January 1920. DBF

Adam, Quirin François *Lucien*, born 31 May 1833 at Nancy, he was from 1859 to 1883 a magistrate in various cities of eastern France; afterwards he was transferred to Rennes. He was also an accomplished linguist of the languages of eastern South America as well as the dialects of the Lorraine. In recognition of his work, he was made a member of the Académie Stanislas at Nancy, and delegated by the Ministry of Public Education as its representative to various international congresses. His writings include *De l'harmonie des voyelles dans les langues ouralo-altaïques* (1874), *Les classifications, l'objet, la méthode, les conclusions de la linguistique* (1882). He died in 1918. Vapereau, 6e éd., 1893

Adam, Thomas Ritchie, born 7 May 1900 at Brechin, Scotland, he was educated at Merchiston Castle School and the University of Edinburgh. After four years of professional work in Melbourne, Australia, he went to the United States in 1930 as a professor of political science, first at Occidental College, Cal.

(1930-1937), and from 1949 to 1990 at New York University. His writings include *The Civic value of museums* (1937), *The Museum and popular culture* (1939), *Education for international understanding* (1948), and *Modern colonialism* (1955). He died in New York on 13 October 1990. Master (3); Unesco; *Who was who in America*, 10

Adam, Werner, born in 1935 in Germany, he was a journalist who studied at Würzburg and Heidelberg. From 1968 to 1978 he was correspondent of the *Neue Zürcher Zeitung* and *Tagesspiegel*, Berlin, in India and Pakistan. Afterwards he was correspondent of the *Frankfurter Allgemeine Zeitung* in Scandinavia. His writings include *Indien* (1977) and *Das Scheitern am Hindukusch: Afghanistan ist nicht zu unterjochen* (1989). *Wer ist wer* 29 (1990/91)

Adamec, Ludwig Warren, born 10 March 1924 at Wien, he studied political science and journalism at UCLA, where he received a Ph.D. in 1966 with a thesis entitled *Trends in Afghan foreign policy*. From 1966 until his retirement, he was a professor at various American universities as well as visiting professor at the University of Baluchistan, Quetta, 1981-1982. Since 1950, he travelled extensively in the Middle East, where he spent altogether seven years for the purpose of language study and research. He was the leading authority on Afghanistan. His writings include *Afghanistan, 1900-1923; a diplomatic history* (1967), *Historical and political gazetteer of Afghanistan* (1972-1979), *Historical gazetteer of Iran* (1976-1988), *Biographical dictionary of contemporary Afghanistan* (1987), *Historical dictionary of Afghanistan* (1991), and *Afghan wars, revolutions, and insurgencies* (1996). DrAS, 1974 H, 1978 H, 1982 H; Master (4)

Adamoli, Giulio, born 29 February 1840 at Besozzo, Italy, he was educated at the Università di Pavia. From June 1869 to October 1870, he travelled in Kirgizia and Turkestan in order to study silk cultivation. Under the auspices of the Società geografica italiana he studied the economic situation in Morocco in 1876. His writings include *Da San Martino a Mentana* (1892). He died in Cairo on 25 December 1926. *Dizionario biografico degli Italiani*

Adamov, Evgenii Aleksandrovich (Евгений Александрович Адамов), born in 1881, he wrote *Европейские державы и Греция* (1922), *Европейские державы и Туртсия* (1924-26), *Constantinople et les détroits* (1930-32), *Дипломатия Ватикана в начальную эпоху империализма* (1931), *Die Aufteilung der asiatischen Türkei* (1932), *Die Diplomatie des Vatikans zur Zeit des Imperialismus* (1932).

Adamova, Adel' Tigranovna, fl. 1971-1985, she was joint author of *Миниатюы кашмирских рукописуй* (1976), and *Миниатюры рукописи, розмы "Шахнаме" 1333 года* (1985). LC

Adamović, Milan, born 7 September 1939 at Bobota, Hungary, he was from 1985 to 1994 a director of the Seminar für Turkologie und Zentralasienkunde in the Universität Göttingen. His writings include *Das osmanisch-türkische Sprachgut bei R. Lubenau* (1977), *Konjugationsgeschichte der türkischen Sprache* (1985). Kürschner, 1996, 2001, 2003

Adams, Charles Clarence, born 15 January 1883 at West Sunbury, Pa., he received a Ph.D. in 1928 from the University of Chicago for his thesis, *The modern reform movement in Egypt and the caliphate*, a work which was published in 1933 entitled *Islam and modernism in Egypt*. He studied also at the Kennedy School of Missions, Hartford Seminary Foundation, and was ordained in 1908. He went out to Egypt in 1909, and died in Cairo, 9 March 1948. During the last ten years of his life he was dean of the School of Oriental Studies at the American University at Cairo. Shavit; Master (2)

Adams, Charles Joseph, born 24 April 1924 at Houston, Texas, he was a graduate of Baylor University, Waco, Texas, and did graduate work at the University of Chicago. In 1952 he began his long association with the newly-founded Institute of Islamic Studies at McGill University, Montreal. In 1953, however, he was appointed to a teaching position at Princeton. The following year, he was awarded a three-year Ford Foundation Foreign Training and Research Scholarship. He returned to McGill for one year before leaving North America for a twenty-month research residency in Pakistan. It was during this period, in 1955, that he was awarded a Ph.D. by the University of Chicago for *Nathan Söderblom as an historian of religions*. Upon his return to North America, he took up a new appointment as fellow of McGill's Institute of Islamic Studies, whose director he was from 1964 to 1980. His writings include *A Reader's guide to the great religions* (1965). In 1991, he was honoured by *Islamic studies presented to Charles J. Adams*. Canadian who's who, 1970-1979; ConAu, 17-18

Adams, Doris Goodrich, 1925- *see* Phillips, Doris Goodrich née Adams

Adams, Harriet Chalmers, born in 1875 at Stockton, Cal., and educated by private tutors, she travelled through Mexico and became a student of Latin American affairs, but she travelled also widely in the Middle East. Her writings include *Adventurous sons of Cadiz*. She died on 17 July 1937. Master (5); WhAm, 1

Adams, Mark Edward, born 1 May 1946 at Jacksonville, Fla., he studied at the University of Oklahoma, and University of Toronto, where he received a Ph.D. Since 1992 he was a professor of medicine at the University of Calgary. He wrote *Agricultural extension in developing countries* (1982). Canadian,1992-2000

Adams, Michael (Evelyn), born 31 May 1920 at Addis Abeba, he was educated in England. Since 1968 he was a director of the Council for the Advancement of Arab-British Understanding. His writings include *Suez and after* (1958), *Voluntary Service Overseas* (1968), *The Middle East: a handbook* (1971), *Publish it not* (1975), *Nahostkonflikt und Menschenrechte* (1981). ConAu 33-36; MidE, 1982/83

Adams, Robert McCormick, born 23 July 1926 at Chicago, he graduated from the University of Chicago after war-time service. Over a fifteen-year period, he repeatedly conducted archaeological field work in Iraq, Saudi Arabia, Iran, and Syria. He became a member of the University of Chicago in 1956, and was provost of the University from 1982 to 1984. He wrote *Level and trend in early Sumerian civilization* (1956), *Land behind Bagdad* (1965), *Behavioral and social science research* (1982). Master (8); MidE, 1982/83; Shavit; WhoAm, 1994-2002|

Adams, Thomas W., fl. 1964-1972. His writings include *Cyprus between East and West* (1968), and *Chipre entre o leste e o oeste* (1970).

Adamson, Donald A., Dr., fl, 1973-1982, he was a sometime member of the School of Biological Sciences in Mcquarie University. His writings include *A Land between two Niles* (1982). He was joint author of *The origin of the soils between the Blue and the White Nile Rivers* (1976).

Adamu, Mahdi, born in 1939 at Ngaski, Sokoto State, Nigeria., he was educated at Ahmadu Bello University, Zaria, and the University of Birmingham, where he obtained a Ph.D. From 1974 to 1982 he was at the Centre for Nigerian Cultural Studies, Zaria. In 1982 he was appointed vice-chancellor of the University of Sokoto. His writings include *The Hausa factor in West African history* (1978); he was joint editor of *Pastoralists of the West African savanna* (1986). Africa who' who, 1991, 1996

Adanson, Jean Baptiste, born in 1732 at Aix-en-Provence, he was from 1754 to his death in 1804 a dragoman at Aleppo. He is best remembered for his aquarelles of Middle Eastern subjects. DBF

Adas, Michael P., born 4 February 1943, he received a Ph.D. in 1971 from the University of Wisconsin for *Agrarian development and the plural society in Lower Burma, 1852-1941*. His writings include *Prophets of rebellion* (1979). In 1974, he was appointed professor of history at Rutgers University, New Brunswick, N.J., where he was still active in 1997. Note

Addison, Frank, fl. 1926-1951, his writings include *Jebel Moya* (1949), and *The Wellcome excavations in the Sudan* (1949-1951).

Addison, James Thayer, born 21 March 1887 at Fitchbury, Mass., he was educated at Harvard and Episcopal Theological School, Cambridge, Mass.; he was ordained in 1913. From 1915 to 1940 he was a lecturer, and later professor, at the Episcopal Theological School, Cambridge, Mass.; from 1940 to 1946 he was administrative vice-president of the National Council of the Protestant Episcopal Church in the U.S.A. and in executive charge of the foreign missionary work of the Church. He was a sometime staff member of St. John's University, Shanghai. He wrote *Life beyond death in the beliefs of mankind* (1932), *The Christian approach to the Moslem* (1942), *Our expanding Church* (1951). He died on 13 February 1953. WhAm, 3

Adekson, J. Bayo, fl. 1976-1981 he received a Ph.D. in 1976 from Brandeis University, Waltham, Mass., for *Military organization in multi-ethnically segmented societies*. He wrote *Nigeria in search of a stable civil-military system* (1981). LC

von **Adelburg**, Ed., fl. 1829-1855, he translated from the Turkish, *Auswahl türkischer Erzählungen aus dem "Humajun-namé"* (1855).

Adelkhah, Fariba, born 25 April 1959 at Tehran, she gained a doctorate in anthropology in 1990 and afterwards was a researcher with l'équipe "Sciences sociales du monde iranien contemporain" at the C.N.R.S., Paris. Her writings include *La révolution sous le voile; femmes islamiques d'Iran* (1991); she was joint author of *Termidor en Iran* (1993), and *Un péril islamiste?* (1994). Private

Aderholdt, Hans Hermann, he was in 1938 the Tehran-based correspondent of the German news agency *Deutsches Nachrichtenbüro*. Note about the author

Adger, John Bailey, born in 1810, he was an American Presbyterian minister who, starting in 1840, assisted Dr. Elias Riggs with the translation of the Old Testament into modern Armenian. He wrote *Christian missions and African colonization* (Columbia, S.C., 1857), and *My life and times, 1810-1899* (1899). LC

Adilov, Musa I., fl. 1968-1982, he was an Azeri author whose writings include *Система повторов в азербайджанском языке* (1968), *Синтаксические повторы в азербайджанском языке* (1974), *Азербаичан дилинин лексик-семантик гурулушу масалалари* (1982).

Adıvar, Abdülhak *Adnan*, born in 1882 at Gallipoli, Turkey, he graduated from the Mekteb-i Idadi and the Tibbiye in 1905. He spent the following four years in emigration in Berlin, returning to Turkey in 1909 to serve as a medical administrator in Constantinople until 1920. In the following five years he was engaged politically in the founding of the Turkish Republic. In 1925, he went once more to western Europe for political reasons. His *La science chez les turcs ottomans* (1939) is the result of his research and lectureship at the École des Langues Orientales in Paris during the years 1929 to 1939. He returned to Istanbul, and in the following year became responsible for the publication of the *Islâm ansiklopedisi*. His writings include *Bilgi Cumhuriyeti haberleri* (1945). He died in Istanbul in 1955. AnaBrit; *Türkiye Diyanet Vakfı Islâm ansiklopedisi*

Adıvar, Halide Edib, born in 1884 at Constantinople, she graduated in 1901 from the American High School in Üsküdar. She was a professor of English, a writer, and a deputy of the Turkish National Assembly. In 1917 she married Abdülhak Adnan Adivar, with whom she spent the years from 1925 to 1939 in self-imposed exile, first in England, and from 1929 to 1939 in Paris. She died in Istanbul on 9 January 1964. AnaBrit; DcOrL; EIS; EncWL

Adjarian, Herachyah H., born in 1876., he wrote *Catalog der armenischen Handschriften in der Bibliothek des Sanassarian-Institutes zu Erzerum* (1900), *L'influence de la langue turque sur l'arménien* (1902), *Classification des dialectes arméniens* (1909), *Katalog der armenischen Handschriften in Täbris* (1910), *Katalog der armenischen Handschriften in Novo-Bayazet* (1924), *Armenisches etymologisches Wurzelwörterbuch* (Erevan, 1926-1932). He died in 1953.

Adle, Chahryar, born 3 February 1944 at Tehran, he received a doctorate from the Université de Paris in 1977 for *Siyaqi Nezam, Fotouhat-e homayuni*. His main field of research was art and urban development in greater Iran, where he participated in excavations. For his work he was awarded the *Médaille de bronze* by the C.N.R.S., where he was a sometime director of research. He was the editor of *Art et société dans le monde iranien* (1982), and joint editor of *Téhéran, capitale bicentenaire* (1992). With J. L. Bacqué-Grammont he published *Les Ottomans, les Safavides et la Géorgie* (1991). LC; Private; THESAM, 4

Adler, Bruno Wilhelm Karl Adolph, born 26 October 1874 at Voronezh, Russia, he studied natural sciences at the universities of Moscow and Leipzig, where he obtained a Dr.phil. in 1901 for *Der nordasiatische Pfeil*. He was professor of ethnology and related subjects at Kazan (1922) and Moscow (1934) universities. His writings include *Возникновение одежды* (1903). Thesis; TatarES

Adler, Cyrus Hirz, born 13 September 1863 at Van Buren, Ark., he graduated in 1883 from the University of Pennsylvania, Philadelphia, Pa., and then studied Assyriology at Johns Hopkins University, gaining his Ph.D. in 1887. He remained at the University and taught Semitics, becoming assistant profesor in 1890. In later life, he was active in American-Jewish affairs. From 1916 to 1940, he was sole editor of the *Jewish quarterly review*. He died in Philadelphia, Pa., 7 April 1940. CnDiAmJBi; CurBio, 1940; EncJud.; Master (15); Wininger

Adler, Elkan Nathan, born 24 July 1861 at London, he was a lawyer who had unusual opportunities to visit all the major Muslim countries of the time, and built up a remarkable private library, of which he published a summary *Catalogue of Hebrew manuscripts in the collection of E. N. Adler* (1921). The majority of his collection went to the Jewish Theological Seminary of America, N.Y.C. He died on 15 September 1946. EncJud; *Who was who*, 4; Wininger

Adler, Felix, born 13 August 1851 at Alzey, Germany, he came to the United States as a child and was educated at Columbia University, N.Y.C., where he obtained a Ph.D. in 1870. Thereafter he studied theology, philosophy and linguistics at the Hochschule für die Wissenschaft des Judentums as well as the Universität Berlin. After his return to America, he was lecturer in Hebrew and Oriental literature at Cornell University, 1874-1876. In 1876 he founded the Society for Ethical Culture, N.Y.C. He was a founding editor of the *International journal of ethics*. His writings include *Creed and deed* (1877), *An ethical philosophy of life* (1918). He died in N.Y.C., 24 April 1933. CnDiAmJBi; EncJud.; Master (18); Wininger; WhAm, 1

Adler, Jacob Georg Christian, born 6 Dezember 1756 at Arnis, Germany, he was a clergyman who had also studied Oriental languages. In his *Descriptio codicum quorundem cuficorum* (1780) he descibed some of the Kufic Korans in the Copenhagen Library, and in *Museum cuficum Borgianum velitris* (1782-1792), some Arabic coins. From 1789 to 1794 he edited Johann J. Reiske's unpublished text and translation, *Abulfedae Annales muslemici arabice et latine* (1789-1794). But he was primarily interested in the text of the Bible:

Kurze Übersicht einer biblischkritischen Reise nach Rom (1783). In *Nonnulla Matthaei et Marci enunciata* (1784) he commented on the linguistic peculiarities of these two Gospels with reference to Syriac. He died on a journey in Gikau, 22 August 1834. ADtB; DtBE

Adler, Richard, fl. 1942-1943, he was a sometime consultant to the Banque Misr. Note about the author

Ado Bayero, Alhaji, 1930- *see* Bayero, Alhaji Ado

Adomeit, Hannes, born in 1942, he received a doctorate in political science. His writings include *Soviet risk-taking and crisis behaviour* (1973), *Die Sowjetmacht in internationalen Krisen und Konflikten* (1983), and *Die Sowjetunion als Militärmacht* (1987).

Adonts (Adonz/Адонц), Nikolai Georgevich, born 10 (22) January 1871, he graduated in 1899 from St. Petersburg University and subsequently served as a professor from 1916 to 1920. In 1930 he became professor at the Université de Bruxelles. His writings include *Towards the solution of the Armenian question* (1920), *Samuel l'arménien, roi des Bulgares* (1938), *Histoire de l'Arménie* (1946), *Études arméno-byzantines* (1965), and the English translation of his thesis, originally presented at St. Petersburg in 1908, *Armenia in the period of Justinian* (1970). He died on 27 January 1942. GSE

Adossidès (Adosides), Anastasios, born in 1873 at Constantinople, he was a Greek journalist who went to Paris and became a founding editor of the periodical *l'Hellénisme* (1904-1912). While in Paris, he published his *Arméniens et Jeunes-turcs: les massacres de Cilicie* (1910). Upon his return to Greece in 1912, he entered provincial politics in the Greek Islands. He died in Athens in 1942. EEE

Adossides, Nicholas C., fl. 1909, he was the son of a high Ottoman official who had served for forty-six years under four sultans. After a brief service with the Turkish Foreign Office, he had to flee from the country on account of his liberal tendencies. He studied in Paris and London; thereafter he lectured in Britain and the United States on Eastern affairs, and took an important part in the propaganda which succeeded in deposing Abdülhamid II. *Cosmopolitan*, 1909

Adzhiev (Аджиев), Abdulakim Magomedovich, Dr., fl. 1971-1990, he was a Soviet linguist whose writings include *Героико-исторические песни кумыков* (1971), *Жанр фольклора народов Дагестана* (1979), *Жанр сказки в фольклоре народов Дагестани* (1987), and *Проблемы межжанровых взаимосвязей в фольклоре народов Дагестана* (1990). OSK

Äfändiiev, Ogtai Äbdullkärim oghlu, 1926- *see* Efendiev, Oktai Abdulkerim ogly

Äfändiiev (Äfändi), Rasim *see* Efendiev, Rasim Samed ogly

Afentakis, D. N. *see* Aphentakes, D. N.

'Afifi, Hafiz, born in 1886 at Cairo, he was a physician and politician whose writings include الانجليز في بلادهم (1935), and على هامش السياسة بعد مسائلنا القومية (1938). He died in Cairo, 1 June 1961. Goldschmidt

Aflaq, Michel, born in 1910 at Damascus, he was educated at the Greek-Orthodox Lyceum, Damascus, and Université de Paris (*licencié en droit*). He was a sometime secondary school teacher in Damascus and a founding member of the Ba'th Party and their first leader. He was in Syrian politics until 1966 when he moved to Lebanon. His writings include في سبيل البعث (1959), and numerous reprints, *Choice of texts* (1977), *Der Anknüpfungspunkt* (1978). He died in 1989. *Who's who in the Arab world*, 1978/9

Afshar, Haleh, born 21 May 1944, she received a Ph.D. in 1975 from Cambridge University for *Land reform in Iran and Ireland*. She was a sometime lecturer at the Department of Politics and Women's Studies in the University of York. Her writings include *Islam and feminism; an Iranian case study* (1998), and she was editor of *Iran; revolution in turmoil* (1985), *Women, work, and ideology in the Third World* (1985), and *Women, state, and ideology; studies from Africa and Asia* (1987). *Directory of BRISMES members*, 1993; EURAMES, 1993; LC; Sluglett

Afshar, Iraj, born 1304/1926 at Tehran, he graduated from the Faculty of Law in the University of Tehran, where he became law librarian. From 1962 to 1979 he was director of the Central Library and, concurrently from 1969-1979, professor of history at the University. He was the founder of فارسی مقالات فهرست, the Index Iranicus, and the foremost Iranian bibliographer. His publications are so numerous that he seems to have had a way of getting his name on every title page he ever touched. On his seventieth birthday he was presented with a felicitation volume. *Iran who's who*, 1976

Afzal, Mohammad (Muhammad), born 20th cent., he was in 1971 a research demographer at the Pakistan Institute of Development Economics. His writings include *Population of Pakistan* (1974). Note; ZKO

Aga Khan, Sultan Sir Mahomed Shah, 1877-1957 see Agha Khan, Sultan Muhammad Shah, 1877-1957

Agadzhanov (Агаджанов), Sergei Grigor'evich, born 30 August 1928 at Merv., he graduated in 1950 from the Faculty of History in the State Pedagogical Institute, Ashkhabad. His writings include *Очерки истории огузов и туркмен Средней Азии IX-XIII вв* (1966), *Сельджукиду и Туркмения в XI-XII вв* (1973), *Проблемы этногенеза туркемского народа* (1977), *Библиографический указатеь историографических работ по истории народв СССР* (1987), *Государство СелЬджукидов и Средняя Азия в XI-XII вв* (1991). Miliband; Miliband²

Agaev (Агаев), Semen L'vovich, born 22 February 1935 at Kusary, Azerbaijan, he graduated in 1960 from the Faculty of History in the Azerbaijan State University, Baku, and obtained a doctorate in 1970 for *Внешняя политика Ирана в 1920-1941*. Since 1965 he was a researcher at the Institute of the People of the Near and Middle East in the Azerbaijan Academy of Sciences. His writings include *Германский империализм в Иране* (1969), *Советское ирановедение 20-х годов* (1977), *Иранская революция* (1984), *Политические и социально-экономические проблемы России и СНГ* (1994). Miliband; Milibandl

Aganin (Аганин), Rashid Abdullovich, born 10 January 1924 at Surgodi, he graduated in 1950 from the Moscow Oriental Institute and obtained a doctorate in 1959 for *Повторы и однородные парные сочетания в современном турецком языке*. Since 1968, he was a researcher at the Academy of Pedagogical Science, SSSR. His writings include *Карманный турецко-русский словарь* (1968), *Бекташи и другие* (1972). Miliband; Miliband²

Agarwala, Manmohan Lal, fl. 1895-1921. His writings include *The principles of equity, with special reference to mortgages, special reliefs and trusts* (1901), *Elements of Hindu and Mohammedan laws* (1905), *A commentary on the N.W.P. tenancy act* (1910), and *Arbitration in British India* (1921).

van **Aggelen**, Johannes G. C., born 20th cent., he was a Dutch lawyer who was at the Faculty of Law, Ain Shams University in 1976 and, ten years later, at the Centre pour les droits de l'homme des Nations Unies. His writings include *Le rôle des organisations internationales dans la protection du droit à la vie* (1986).

Agha Khan, Sir Sultan Muhammad Shah, born in 1877, he was the religious head of the Ismailis, the founder of the Aligarh Muslim University, and a politician. His writings include *Glimpses of Islam* (1944). He died in 1957. CurBio, 1957; DNB; EI²; EncAm; IntWW, 1954; Jain, pp. 54-56; Who, 1952-1956; WhAm, 3; *Who was who*, 5

Aghajanian, Akbar, born 23 August 1949 in Iran, he received a Ph.D. in 1979 from Duke University, Durham, N.C., and subsequently served as a visiting professor at Cornell University, Ithaca, N.Y. In 1989 he was a professor of sociology and demography at Shiraz University, Iran, and in 1993 he was professor at Fayetteville State University, Fayetteville, N.C., a position he still held in 1997. His writings include *The value of children and fertility in Iran* (1986), *Women and population dynamics* (1989).

Aghito, Lorenzo, fl. 1940; his writings include *Combattimenti; romanzo* (1935).

Agius, Dionisius A., born in 1945, he gained a doctorate. In 1996, he was a lecturer in Arabic at the Department of Modern Arabic Studies, Leeds. His writings include *Arabic literary works as a source of documentation for technical terms of the material culture* (1984), *Diglossic tension; teaching Arabic for communication* (1990), and *The study of Arabic in Malta, 1632 to 1915* (1990). DrBSMES, 1993; EURAMES, 1993

Aglietti, Bruno, fl. 1939-1965, his writings include *Il canale di Suez ed i rapporti anglo-egiziani* (1939), *Il governo di alcuni condomini Sudan anglo-egiziano* (1939), *L'Egitto dagli avvenimenti del 1882 ai giorni nostri* (1965).

Ago, Pietro, born 30 October 1872 at Agrigento, Italy, he graduated from a military academy. He was a general and sometime senator. Chi è, 1961; *Who's who in Italy*, 1957-58

Agostini, Enrico de, 1878- see De Agostini, Enrico

Agostino Orsini di Camerota, Paolo d', 1897- see D'Agostino Orsini di Camerota, Paolo

Agoub, Joseph (Ya'qub) Elie, born in 1795 at Cairo. His family came to France in the wake of the French retreat from Egypt in 1801, and settled in Marseille, where he started his education, including lessons in Arabic. By 1820, he had moved to Paris and published his first poetry. At the same time he began his free-lance collaboration with the Commission d'Égypte on their monumental *Description d'Égypte*, a task which, shortly thereafter, became full-time. For a few years he was also a teacher of Arabic at the École royale des jeunes langues, which was connected to the Collège Louis-le-Grand. He was an accomplished poet. His French translation of Bidpai, though completed, was never published. His writings include *La lyre brisée*,

Agrawala, Vasudeva Sharana, born 7 August 1904 at Pilkhuwa, Meerut, India, he was educated at Banares Hindu University. From 1939 to 1951, he was curator and director of various Indian museums, and from 1951 until his death in 1966, principal of the College of Indology. His writings include *A short guide-book to the Archaeological Section of the Provincial Museum, Lucknow* (1940), *Gupta art* (1948), *The heritage of Indian art* (1964), *Ancient Indian folk cults* (1970). Eminent Indians who was who, 1900-1980

de **Agreda Burillo**, Fernando, born 17 November 1945 at Madrid, he was educated at the Universidad Autonoma de Madrid, where he obtained a doctorate in 1971 in Semitic linguistics. His main fields of research were contemporary Arab studies in Spain as well as contemporary Arabic literature. He was a sometime head of the Sección de Publicaciones del Instituto de Cooperación con el Mundo Arabe, Madrid, and a member of the Asociación Española de Orientalistas. He wrote *Encuesta sobre la literatura marroquí actual* (1975), and edited *La traducción y la critica literaria; actas de las Journadas de Hispanimo Arabe, 1988* (1990).

Agrel, Henriette, fl. 1926-1928. She was joint author of *Géographie physique et géographie humaine* (Bibliographie géographique de l'Égypte, t. 1), published in 1928.

Agron (Agronsky), Gershon, born 27 December 1893 at Mena, Ukraine, he was brought to the United States in 1906, and was educated at Temple University, Philadelphia, Pa. During the first World War he served with the Jewish Legion in Palestine and remained there after demobilization. He was a journalist, and the founder of the daily *Palestine Post* in 1932. He went on special missions to Aden and Iraq to investigate relations with Palestine. From 1949 to 1951, he was director of the Israel Information Services, and from 1955 until his death on 1 November 1959, mayor of Jerusalem. He wrote *Jewish reclamation of Palestine* (1927), and *Asir ha-ne'emanut* (1964). CnDiAmJBi; EncJud; Shavit; WhoIsrael, 1958

Aguadé Bofill, Jorge, born in 1949 in la Asunción, he received a doctorate in Semitic linguistics and successively served as a professor at the Departamento de Estudios Árabes e Islámicos in the Universidad Complutense de Madrid and the Facultad de Filosofía y Letras, Universidad de Cádiz, a post which he still held in 1997. He translated *Kitab al-ta'rij* of 'Abd al-Malik ibn Habib (1991). Arabismo, 1994, 1997

Agüero Doná, Celma, fl. 1971-1992. He was a sometime professor of African history at Centro de Estudios de Asia y Africa, El Colegio de México. He is the joint author of *Campesinado e integración nacional: Asia, Africa y América Latina* (1982), *La diversidad prohibida: resistencia étnica y poder de estado* (1989), and *Peasantry and national integration* (1981).

Aguiar Aguilar, María de la Maravillas, born 20th cent., she received a diploma in Spanish philology and a doctorate in Arabic philology. She was a professor at the Departamento de Estudios Árabes, Universidad de La Laguna, Santa Cruz de Tenerife. Arabismo, 1992, 1994, 1997

Aguilar Sebastián, Victoria, born 20th cent., she received a doctorate in Semitic philology, with special reference to medieval history of Morocco. She was affiliated with the Instituto de Filología, C.S.I.C. before she be came a professor of Arabic at the Universidad de Murcia in 1994. She was joint author of *Repertorio bibliográfico de las relaciones entre la Peninsula Ibérica y el Norte de África* (1989). Arabismo, 1992, 1994, 1997

Aguilera, Cesáreo see Rodrígez Aguilera, Cesáreo

Aguilera Pleguezuelo, José, fl. 1953-1994, he received a doctorate in law and subsequently practised law in Madrid. His field of research was Muslim jurisprudence in Islamic Spain. Arabismo, 1994, 1997

Aguirre Sádaba, Francisco Javier, born 20th cent., he received a doctorate in Semitic philology and successively became a professor of Arabic and Islamic studies, particular law, institutions and material culture in al-Andalus and the Maghreb at Almería and Jaén. He was joint author of *Introducción al Jaén islámico* (1979). Arabismo, 1992, 1994, 1997

Agwani, Mohammed Shafi, born 2 March 1928 at Udaipur, India, he received a doctorate in 1954 from the Rijksuniversiteit te Utrecht for *The United States and the Arab world, 1945-1952* (1955). Afterwards he taught at the Institute of Islamic Studies, Muslim University, Aligarh, and the School of International Studies in the Jawaharlal Nehru University, New Delhi. His writings include *The Lebanese crisis, 1958* (1965), *Communism in the Arab East* (1969), *Politics in the Gulf* (1978), *Islamic fundamentalism in India* (1986), and *Religion and politics in West Asia* (New Delhi, 1992). India who's who, 1993/1994

Ahamed, Emajuddin see Ahmed, Emajuddin

al-**Ahdab**, Ibrahim Husayn, born 21 March 1921 at Beirut, he was educated at École supérieure des Travaux publics de Paris. From 1928 to 1944, he was a civil engineer in Beirut; afterwards he held various diplomatic posts. *Who's who in Lebanon*, 1970/71

Ahi, Laylá Ayman, born 1308/1929, she was an author of textbooks for elementary schools as well as a translator. Her writings include *Hadiyah-i Shah-i Pariyan* (1345/1966). *Kitab'ha-yi Iran*; NUC

Ahlgreen, Hermann Schelenz, 1848-1922 *see* Schelenz Ahlgreen, Hermann

Ahlmann, Hans Jakob Konrad Wilhelmsson, born 14 November 1889 at Karlsborg, Sweden, he was successively a professor of geography at Uppsala and Stockholm. His writings include *La Libia settentrionale* (1930), *Glaciological research on the North Atlantic coasts* (1948). He died in 1974. SMK; *Vem är det*, 1949-73

Ahlqvist, Carl *August* Engelbrekt, born 7 August 1826 at Kuopio, Finland, he studied philosophy and linguistics at Helsingfors University, where he received a doctorate in 1863 for *Suomalainen runous-oppi kielelliseltä kanna nalta.* Afterwards he did much to promote Finnish as a national language. In order to foster Finnish literature, he founded the periodical *Suometar*, to which he contributed numerous articles under the pseudonym Oksanen. Three times he conducted linguistic field work in northern Russia and Siberia. His writings include *Forskninger på de ural-altaiska språkens område* (1871), *Über die Sprachen der Nord-Ostjaken* (1880), and *Wogulische Sprachtexte* (1894). He died in Helsingfors, 20 November 1889. Aalto; *Finsk biografisk handbok*; Meyers; ScBInd (7)

Ahluwalia, Manjeet Singh, born in 1941, he received a Ph.D. in 1978 from Aligarh Muslim University for his thesis, *Muslim expansion in Rajasthan.* Since 1973 he taught at the Department of History in the Punjabi University, Patiala. In 1988, he was professor of history at Himachal Pradesh University. His writings include *History of Himachal Pradesh* (1988).

Ahlwardt, Theodor *Wilhelm*, born 4 July 1828 at Greifswald, Germany, he studied at the universities of Greifswald and Göttingen, where he received a Dr.phil. in 1851. After study of Islamic manuscripts in Gotha and Paris, he became a librarian at Greifswald from 1856 to 1865. Concurrently he taught Oriental philology. He is remembered best for his monumental *Verzeichniss der arabischen Handschriften der königlichen Bibliothek zu Berlin*, a task to which he dedicated the twenty best years of his life, and which enabled Carl Brockelmann half a century later to write his *Geschichte der arabischen Litteratur.* His writings include *Über Poesie und Poetik der Araber* (1856), *Chaled elahmar's Qasside* (1859), and *Bemerkungen über die Echtheit der alten arabischen Gedichte mit besonderer Berücksichtigung der sechs Dichter* (1872). He died in Greifswald on 2 November 1909. DtBE.; Fück, 191; Hinrichsen; Vapereau

Ahmad, Abdulhamid Muhammad, born 31 July 1931 at Cairo., he studied at Fouad I University, Cairo, SOAS and, from 1957 to1963, the Universität Hamburg, where he received a Dr.phil. in 1963 for *Die Auseinandersetzung zwischen Al-Azhar und der modernistischen Bewegung in Ägypten.* His writings include *Die wirtschaftliche Bedeutung Kuwaits und der Scheichtümer des Arabischen Golfes* (1965).

Ahmad, Anis, Dr., born 20th cent., his writings include *Muslim women and higher education* (1982), *Prayers of the Holy Prophet* (1992). LC

Ahmad, Aziz, born 11 November 1913 at Barabanki, India, he graduated from Osmania University, Hyderabad, India, and received a B.A. (Hons) from the University of London. From 1938 until partition, he taught English at Osmania University. In 1949 he went to Pakistan, where he rose to the position of director of the Department of Films and Publications for the Government of Pakistan. He returned to London in 1957 as a lecturer in Urdu and Indian Islam at SOAS, and in 1962 emigrated to Canada at the invitation of the University of Toronto. He remained a professor at the Department of Islamic Studies until he died from cancer, 16 December 1978. He had two careers: one as a novelist who achieved international recognition when in 1971 Unesco published his *The shore and the wave*; his other career began with the publication of *Islamic modernism in India and Pakistan* (1967), followed by *An Intellectual history of Islam in India* (1969), *Studies in Islamic culture in the Indian environment* (1969), and *History of Islamic Sicily* (1975). In 1983 a commemoration volume was published: *Islamic society and culture; essays in honour of Professor Aziz Ahmad.* Au&Wr, 1963; Private

Ahmad, Bahauddin, he was in 1966 a deputy director-general of the Pakistan Export Promotion Bureau. Note

Ahmad, Feroz U., born 26 January 1938 at Delhi, India, he was educated at St. Stephens College, Delhi, and SOAS, where he obtained a Ph.D. in 1966 for *The Committee of Union and Progress in Turkish policies, 1908-1913.* In 1993, he was professor of history in the University of Massachusetts at Boston. He was on the editorial board of the *International journal of Middle East studies* His writings include *The Young Turks*

Turks (1969), *The Turkish experiment in democracy* (1977), *Ittihatçılıktan Kemalizme* (1985), and *The making of modern Turkey* (1993).

Ahmad, Ilyas, 1891-1960 *see* Ilyas Ahmad

Ahmad, Imtiaz, born 1940, he wrote *Modernization and social change among Muslims in India* (1983), *Ritual and religion among Muslims of the Sub-continent* (1985), and he edited *Caste and social stratification among the Muslims* (1973), and *Family, kinship, and marriage among Muslims in India* (1976). LC

Ahmad, Ishtiaq, born in 1937, he wrote *Anglo-Iranian relations, 1905-1919* (1974).

Ahmad, Jamil-ud-Din, born in 1911, he resided in Karachi in 1958. His writings include *The Indian constitutional tangle* (1941), *Quaid-e-Azam as seen by his contemporaries* (1966), *Glimpses of Quaid-i-Azam* (1990). LC; Note

Ahmad, Kazi Saiduddin, born in 1904, he wrote *Major natural regions* (1950), and *A Geography of Pakistan* (1964). He died in Lahore, 28 November 1970. *Geographical journal*, 137 (1971), p. 272

Ahmad, Khurshid, born 23 March 1934 at Delhi, India, he was educated at Karachi University, where he was a sometime lecturer and professor. Since 1973 he was director-general of the Islamic Foundation at Leicester, UK. His writings include *Islam and the West* (1970), *Family life in Islam* (1974), and *Pakistan's economic challenge and the budget* (1979). IWWAS, 1976/77; Who's who, 1993-2002

Ahmad, Muhammad Khalaf Allah, born in 1904 in Sohag Governorate, Egypt, he was educated at al-Azhar and University of London. In 1942, he was head of the Department of Arabic, University of Alexandria, in 1952, dean of its Faculty of Arts, and in 1972, director of the Institute of Arab Research and Studies. He edited *Colloquium on Islamic culture in its relation to the contemporary world*, Princeton, N.J. (1953). Who's who in the Arab world, 1971/72, 1978/79

Ahmad, Muhammad Tawfiq, he was in 1962 the editor of البريد الاسلامي, Cairo.

Ahmad, Muneer, born 1 January 1936 at Lyallpur, India, he studied at the University of the Panjab, Lahore, and Universität Münster, where he received a Dr.phil. in 1965 for *Demokratische Entwicklung in der pakistanischen Beamtenschaft*. His writings include *Legislatures in Pakistan* (1960), and *The civil servant in Pakistan* (1964). Thesis

Ahmad, Mushtaq, born in 1919, he was educated at LSE and Columbia University, N.Y.C. He was in 1950 and 1951 a researcher at the Pakistan Institute of International Affairs, Karachi, and in 1959, assistant editor of the *Morning news*, Karachi. His writings include *The economy of Pakistan* (1950), *The United Nations and Pakistan* (1955), *Government and politics in Pakistan* (1959), *Pakistan's foreign policy* (1968), *Pakistan at the crossroads* (1985), *Politics in crisis* (1987), and *Business ethics in Islam* (1993). His last book is a revision of his doctoral thesis, submitted to Temple University, Philadelphia, Pa., in 1984, and entitled *Business ethics in the Qur'an: a synthetic exposition of the Qur'anic teachings pertaining to business*. He died before its publication. LC

Ahmad, Nafis, born in 1912 at Gulaothi, India, he was educated at Aligarh University, and the University of London, where he obtained a Ph.D. in 1953. Afterwards he was lecturer and professor of geography at various universities in India as well as in West Pakistan. His writings include *The basis of Pakistan* (1947), *Muslim contribution to geography* (1947), *An economic geography of East Pakistan* (1976), *A new economic geography of Bangladesh* (1976), and *Muslims and the science of geography* (1980). IWWAS, 1975/76

Ahmad, Naveed, born 20th cent., she was in 1976 a researcher at the Pakistan Institute of International Affairs, Karachi. She wrote *Europe and the Third World* (1985), and she was the joint author of *Productivity and cost control for the small and medium-size firm* (1980).

Ahmad, Qadeeruddin, born in 1909, he was a sometime chief justice of the High Court of Sind and Baluchistan. In 1972 he was a member of the Pakistan delegation to the U.N. General Assembly. His writings include *The constitution of the Islamic Republic of Pakistan* (1974), and *Maqasid o masa'il-i Pakistan* (1984).

Ahmad, Qazi Kholiquzzam, born in 1943, he wrote *Development communication and grassroots participation: Bangladesh case* (1988), *Upgrading of technology for rural industries in Bangladesh* (1988); in 1980, he edited *Development planning in Bangladesh*. LC

Ahmad, Qeyamuddin, born in 1930, he was in 1956 a research fellow at K.P. Jayaswal Research Institute, Patna. He received a Ph.D. in 1961 from Patna University for a thesis which, in a revised form, was published in 1966 entitled *The Wahhabi movement in India*. In 1988 he was still active as a professor of history at Patna University. His writings include *Corpus of Arabic and Persian inscriptions of Bihar* (1973), *Mazharul Haque* (1976), *Patna through the ages* (1988). LC

Ahmad, Riaz, born 16 April 1942 at Sharaqpur, India, he was educated at Punjab University, and received a M.Litt.in 1969 from Cambridge University. He was a sometime lecturer at International Peoples College, Elsinore, Denmark, and in 1973 a cataloguer and Middle East specialist at Cleveland Public Library. His writings include *Constitutional and political development in Pakistan, 1951-1954* (1981), *Quaid-i-Azam's role in South Asian political crisis, 1921-1924* (1989). IWWAS, 1976/77

Ahmad, Sayyid Maqbul, F.R.A.S., born in 1919, he received a B.Litt. in 1947 at Oxford University, and three years later, a D.Phil. for *The geography of India in the works of al-Idrisi*. His writings include *Indo-Arab relations* (1969); and he was joint author of *Historical geography of Kashmir* (1984). LC; Sluglett

Ahmad, Shabbir, fl. 1958, he was in 1970 affiliated with the Institute of Education in the University of Sind, Hyderabad, Pakistan. He wrote *Researches in the history of education* (1970).

Ahmad, Shaikh *Mahmud*, born in 1927, he wrote *Economics of Islam* (1947), and *Social justice in Islam* (2d ed., 1975). He died in 1962. LC

Ahmad, Viqar, born 20th cent., he was in 1967 a lecturer in general history at Karachi University. Note

Ahmad, Ziauddin, born in 1930, he received a Ph.D. in 1963 at Harvard for *Deficit financing, supply response and inflation in less developed economies*. He was deputy governor of the State Bank of Pakistan from 1978 to 1983, and director general of the International Institute of Islamic Economics, Islamabad, from 1983 to 1988. His writings include *The present state of Islamic finance movement* (1985), *Al-Quran, divine book of eternal value* (1989), *Shaheed-e-Millat, Liaquat Ali Khan, builder of Pakistan* (1990), and *Islam, poverty, and income distribution* (1991). LC; Note

Ahmad Amin, 1886-1954 *see* Amin, Ahmad

Ahmad 'Isá (Ahmed Issa Bey), Dr., he was an Egyptian historian of medicine and botany. His writings include *Histoire des bimaristans (hôpitaux) à l'époque islamique* (Cairo, 1928), and *Dictionnaire des noms des plantes en latin, français, anglais et arabe* (1930). He died in July 1946. Isis 37 i/ii (1947), p. 81

Ahmad Kamal, born in 1267/1851 at Cairo, he was a sometime professor of ancient history at Cairo University, and director of the Egyptian Museum in Cairo. His writings include *Livre des perles enfouies et du mystère au sujet des indications des cachettes, des trouvailles et des trésors* (1907). He died in Cairo on 5 October 1923. Egyptology; GAL S II, p. 735; Goldschmidt

Ahmad Khan, Muin-ud-Din, born 20th cent., he was in 1972 with the Islamic Research Institute, Tariqabad (Rawalpindi). His writings include *A bibliographical introduction to modern Islamic development in India and Pakistan, 1700-1951* (1959), *Muslim struggle for freedom in Bengal* (1960), *Selections from Bengal government records on Wahhabi trials* (1961), *History of Fara'idi movement in Bengal* (1965), *Titu Mir and his followers in British Indian records* (1977), *Muslim communities of South-East Asia* (1980); and he edited *Labor administration: profile on Bangladesh* (1987). LC

Ahmad Shafiq, born in 1860 at Cairo, he was a civil servant and a politician whose writings include *L'esclavage au point de vue musulman* (1891), *L'Égypte moderne et les influences étrangères* (1931), *Hawliyat Misr al-siyasiyah* (1926-1931), and *Mudhakkirati fi nisf qarn* (1934-1937). He died in 1940. Goldschmidt; LC

Ahmad Zaki, born in Muharram 1284/1867 at Alexandria, he graduated from the École d'administration, Cairo, and obtained a *licence en droit* in 1888. He entered the Ministry of the Interieur as translator in October 1888, and within one year, was appointed translator at the Council of Ministers, becoming general secretary of the Council in 1911, a position he held until his retirement in 1921. During his term of office he was the driving force behind the reform of Arabic typography at the Bulak government press in the widest sense. He died in Gizeh, 5 July 1934. Al-Andalus 2 (1934), pp. 461-462; BIE 17 (1935), pp. vii-xix; Goldschmidt; REI 8 (1834), pp. 383-392

Ahmadi, 'Abd al-Rahim, born in 1304/1925 at Kirman, Iran, he was educated at Paris, Tehran, and George Washington University, Washington, D.C. He was a chancellor of Iran Free University. Iran who's who, 1976

Ahmed, Abbasuddin, born 27 October 1901 at Cooch Behar, West Bengal, he was a musician who made his début in the musical world as a singer of Bengali modern music. Early in the 1930s he became almost the sole exponent of Bengali folk music on records, on radio and in films. He died on 30 December 1959.

19

Ahmed, Akbar Salahudin, born 15 January 1943 at Allahabad, India, he studied at the universities of Birmingham, Cambridge, and London, where he obtained a Ph.D. in 1978 in anthropology from SOAS for his thesis, *The economic and social organisation of selected Mohman Pukhtun settlements*. He was a sometime Commissioner of Quetta. In 1988 he taught at Selwyn College, Cambridge. His writings include *Discovering Islam* (1988), *Toward Islamic anthropology* (1987), *Postmodernism and Islam* (1992), and *Living Islam: from Samarkand to Stornoway* (1993). IntAu&W, 1982; LC; Sluglett

Ahmed, Bashir, fl. 1979, he was a writer on international affairs and was the joint author of *Expansion of employment and income through local resource mobilisation: a study of three villages in Pakistan* (1984). LC

Ahmed, Emajuddin, born 20th cent., he received a Ph.D. in political science from Queen's University, Kingston, Ontario, and became an associate professor at Dacca University in 1980. His writings include *Bureaucratic elites in segmented economic growth* (1980), and *Bureaucratic elites in Pakistan and Bangladesh* (1985). LC

Ahmed, Jamal Mohammed, born in 1917 in the Sudan, he received a B.Litt. in 1956 from Oxford University for his thesis, *Social and political thought in Egypt, 1900-1914*. Thereafter he was a critic and historian who taught for twenty years, first in Sudan Government schools, and then as professor of English at Khartoum University. Afterwards he was Sudan's ambassador to Arab countries and Turkey, 1957-1959, and to Ethiopia, 1959-1964, and his country's permanent delegate to the United Nations, 1964-1966. Later he was ambassador to the United Kingdom. His writings include *The intellectual origins of Egyptian nationalism* (1960), *Wijdan Afriqiya* (1974), as well as translations into Arabic. Sluglett

Ahmed, Manzoor, born in 1940, he wrote *Attacking rural poverty* (1974), *The economics of nonformal education* (1975) and, together with Philip H. Coombs, *New paths to learning for rural children and youth* (1973). LC

Ahmed, Munir-ud-Din, born 22 November 1934 at Rawalpindi, India; he was an Ahmadiyya Pakistani, educated at Panjab University, Lahore, and the Universität Hamburg, where he received a Dr. phil. in 1968 for *Muslim education and the scholars' social status up to the fifth century Muslim era in the light of Ta'rikh Baghdad*. From 1967 until his retirement he was a research fellow at the Deutsches Orient-Institut, Hamburg. IWWAS, 1975/76

Ahmed, Nafis, 1912- see Ahmad, Nafis

Ahmed, Nasim, fl. 1960-1968, he was in 1960 the London correspondent of the Karachi *Dawn*.

Ahmed, Nazir, born in 1915, he was in 1960 a director-general of the Central Statistical Office, Karachi. His writings include *Socio-economic survey, Rawalpindi, 1960* (1960). Note

Ahmed, Nisar, M.A., Ph.D., fl. 1965, he was a sometime editor and secretary of the Numismatic Society of India, Banaras Hindu University, Varanasi.

Ahmed, Qadeeruddin, 1909- see Ahmad, Qadeeruddin

Ahmed, Samina, born 20th cent., she was in 1977 a researcher at the Pakistan Institute of International Relations, Karachi. Note

Ahmed, Sayed Giasuddin, born 20th cent., he was in 1975 assistant professor of public administration at Dacca University. Note

Ahmed, Tauheed, born 20th cent., he was a staff demographer at the Pakistan Institute of Development Economics, before he entered the civil service. Note

Ahmed Abdullah, 1881- see Abdullah, Achmed

Ahmed Ali, 1910-1994 see Ali, Ahmed

Ahmed Reşid, born 19th cent., he was in 1931 a professor of international law at İstanbul Üniversitesi, in 1935, a professor at the Académie de droit international de La Haye; he was a sometime legal counsellor to the Turkish foreign ministry. He was the translator of *La quintessence de la philosophie de Ibn 'Arabi*, by Mehmed 'Ali 'Ayni (1926). BN; LC; Note

Ahmed Resmi Efendi, Giridi, 1700-1783. He was an Ottoman statesman and historian. His writings include *Wesentliche Betrachtungen, oder Geschichte des Krieges zwischen den Osmanen und Russen in den Jahren 1768 bis 1774*, übersetzt von Heinrich F. Diez (1813). Virginia H. Aksan wrote *An Ottoman statesman in war and peace; Ahmed Resmi Efendi* (Leiden, 1995). EI²; NUC, pre-1956

Ahmed Rıza, born in 1859 at Constantinople, he went in 1883 to Paris to study at the Institut agronomique. He became a journalist and politician who was in French exile from 1889 to 1908 working for the liberalization of Turkey through his journal *Meşveret*. In 1908 he returned to Turkey where he became deputy of Constantinople and, later, president of the Chamber of Deputies. He wrote *Tolérance musulmane* (1897), and *La faillite morale de la politique occidentale en Orient* (1922). He died in Istanbul in 1930. AnaBrit; *Correspondance d'Orient* 22 (1930), 137-138; Meydan; Zürcher

Ahmed Rüstem Bey (Alfred), 1862-1934 *see* Bilinski, Ahmed Rustem de

Ahrari, Mohammed E., born 20th cent., he received a Ph.D. in 1976 from Southern Illinois University for his thesis *The dynamics of oil diplomacy*. He was a sometime professor at East Carolina University in the 1980s, and later, professor of Middle Eastern and Southwest Asian affairs at Air War College, Montgomery, Ala. His writings include *OPEC, the failing giant* (1986). *MESA roster of members*, 1990

Ahrens, Heinz, born 13 July 1943 at Potsdam, Germany, he obtained a Dr.phil. in 1977 from the Universität Heidelberg for his thesis, *Bestimmungsgründe und Alternativen divergierender regionaler Wachstums- verläufe in Entwicklungsländern*. In 1976, he was a research fellow at the Südasien Institut der Universität Heidelberg. His writings include *Aspekte sozialer Ungleichheit in Südasien* (1975). IWWAS, 1976/77

Ahrens, Peter Georg, born 27 April 1920 at Berlin, he was there educated. After military service during the second World War, from which he returned wounded, he studied architecture at Braunschweig. In 1953, he was a consulting architect at the Ministry of Public Works in Ankara. In the following year, he was a successful participant in the international town planning contest of the City of Ankara. In 1960, he acted as town planning consultant in Tehran. From 1962 until his retirement, he was a professor at the Technische Universität Berlin. His writings include *Entwicklung der Stadt Tehran* (1966), originally presented as his Dr.ing. thesis at Technische Universität Berlin. Kürschner, 1976-1992|; Note

Ahrens, Wilhelm Ernst Martin Georg, born 3 March 1872 at Lübz, Germany, he obtained a Dr.phil. in 1895 from the Universität Rostock for his thesis, *Über eine Gattung n-fach periodischer Functionen von n-reellen Veränderlichen*. His writngs include *Mathematische Spiele* (1907), *Latein oder Deutsch? Die "Sprachen- frage" bei der Herausgabe der Werke Leonhard Eulers* (1910), *Altes und Neues aus der Unterhaltungs- mathematik* (1918). He died in Rostock, 25 May 1927. DtBE

Ahrweiler, Hélène née Glykatzi (Αρβελέρ-Γλύκαζη), born 29 August 1926 at Athens, she was educated at Athens and received doctorates from the Sorbonne, Paris. Since 1967 she was a professor at the Sorbonne and later served as president and chancellor of universities in France. In 1998 she was honoured by *Eupsychia; mélanges offerts à Hélène Ahrweiler*. Her writings include *Recherches sur l'administration de l'Empire byzantin aux IX-XIe siècle* (1960), *Idéologie politique de l'Empire byzantin* (1975), *Μοντερνισμοσ και Βυζαντιν* (1992), she was joint author of *The Great libraries; from antiquity to the Renaissance* (2000), and she edited *Géographie historique du monde méditerranéen* (1988). EVL, 1993/94-2001; WhoFr, 1984/85-2003/2004

Ahsan, Abdush-Shakoor, Dr., fl. 1969 at University Oriental College, Lahore. His writings include *Modern trends in the Persian language* (1976), and *An Appreciation of Iqbal's thought and art* (1985). LC

al-Ahwani, 'Abd al-'Aziz, born in Egypt, he studied at Cairo, where he later taught Arabo-Spanish studies. His writings include الشعر في والابتكار العقم ومشكلة الملك سناء ابن (1962), and العربية الوحدة ازمة (1972). LC; MIDEO 15 (1982), pp. 313-314

Aichele, Walther, born 27 January 1889 at Höhefeld, Germany, he studied at Heidelberg, Halle, and Freiburg in Sachsen, obtaining a Dr.phil. in 1915 from the Universität Heidelberg for *Biblische Legenden der Schi'iten aus dem Prophetenbuch des Hoseini*. He was a joint author of *Zigeunermärchen* (1926). Thesis

Aidarov (Айдаров), Gubaidulla, born 18 June 1921, he was since 1959 associated with the Institute of Language and Literature, Kazakhstan Academy of Sciences. He wrote Язык орхонского памятника Бильге-кагана (1966), Эпиграфиеа Казахстана (1971), Язык орхонских памятников древнетюрк- ской пись-менности VIII века (1971), and Орхон ескерткиштеринин текси (1990). Kazakhskaia, v. 3, p. 62

Aidin, E. Nouhie, fl. 1931, she was for eighteen years a headmistress of the Church Missionary Society School in Isfahan, and wrote the pamphlet, *Iran - then and now* (1949). Note about the author

Aigle, Denise, born 2 August 1953 at Neuilly-sur-Seine, she was a researcher at the Institut Français de Recherche en Iran, and taught at the Institut National des Langues et Civilisations Orientales, Paris. Her field of study was medieval history and hagiography. She was a member of the Société Asiatique and the Association des Historiens médiévistes de l'Enseignement. AnEIFr, 1989, 1997; *Livres disponibles*, 2004; Note

Aimé-Giron, Noël, born 22 August 1884 at Paris, he was educated at École des Hautes Études and the Sorbonne. He joined the consular service in the Middle East, where he studied Arabic, Persian, Turkish, and Hebrew. He wrote *Textes araméens d'Égypte* (1931). He died suddenly in 1941.

Aimel, Georges, fl. 1918-1923, he wrote *Travaillons donc à bien penser* (1919), and *La politique et le réel* (1923).

Aimilianides (Aimilios/Emilianides), Achilleas K., born in 1903 at Nicosia, he studied law at Athens, Genève, den Haag, and Heidelberg, and obtained a doctorate. His writings include *Παλαιά Κύπρος* (1933), *Χρύσιλλα* (1938), *Hellenic Cyprus* (1946), *Histoire de Cypre* (1962), *Nouvelles cypriotes* (1965), and *Symphonie de la rédemption* (1966). He died in 1978. EEE; WhE&EA

Ainsworth, William Francis, born 9 November 1807 at Exeter, he became in 1827 a licentiate of the Royal College of Surgeons, Edinburgh. He later studied in London, Paris, and Bruxelles, gaining practical experience of geology in France. In 1835, he was appointed surgeon and geologist to the expedition to the Euphrates under Francis R. Chesney. Shortly afterwards he was placed in charge of an expedition to the Christians of Chaldaea, a journey which he described in *Travels and researches in Asia Minor, Mesopotamia, Chaldea, and Armenia* (1842). His other writings include *A Personal narrative of the Euphrates Expedition* (1888). He died in Wolverton Gardens, Hammersmith on 27 November 1896. DNB, S i

Ainsztein, Reuben, born in 1917 at Vilnius, Russian Poland, he studied at the Université libre de Bruxelles. After war-time service in the RAF, he became a journalist for the BBC and Reuters, specializing in East European affairs. In his later years he worked as a researcher for the *Sunday Times* of London. He was a historian of the Holocaust. His writings include *The Warsaw Ghetto revolt* (1979). He died in Little Hadham, Herfordshire, England, on 6 December 1981. *Annual obituary*, 1981, pp. 731-732

Airas, Pentti, born 20th cent., he received a Ph.D. in 1956 at Helsinki University for *Yksilö ja suhteensa yhteisöön J. V. Snellmanin historianfilosofiassa*. His writings include *Die geschichtlichen Wertungen Krieg und Frieden von Friedrich dem Großen bis Engels* (1978), and *Sodan ja rauhan motiivit* (1981).

Ait Ahmed, Hocine, born 24 August 1926 at Ain el-Hamam, Algeria, he was educated in Algeria and at the universities of Lausanne and Nancy, and obtained a doctorate in law. He became a journalist and was first a member of the Algerian FLN and, later, of the Provisional Algerian Government. His writings include *La guerre et l'après-guerre* (1964), *L'Afro-fascisme* (1980), *Mémoires d'un combattant* (1983), and *L'affaire Mécili* (1989). *Africa who's who*, 1991, 1996

Aitmambetoy, Diuishe Osmanovich (Дюйше Османович Айтмамбетоы), born in 1921, his writings include *Дореволюционные школы в Киргизии* (1961), *Школьное дедо в Туркестане* (1963), and *Культура киргизского народа* (1967). KyrgyzSE

Aizenshtein (Айзенштейн), Natal'ia (Natta) Avrumovna, born 14 March 1923 at Odessa, she graduated in 1944 from the Moscow Oriental Institute. Since 1957, she was at the Oriental Institute of the Academy of Sciences of the USSR. Her writings include *Из истории туретского реализма* (1968), *Саид Фаик и его новеллы* (1971), and *Избранные произведения писателей Среднего Востока* (1979); she is the joint editor of *Наша улица* (1962). Miliband; Miliband²

Aizetmüller Sadnik, Linda, 1910- *see* Sadnik Aizetmüller, Linda

Ajami, Fouad, born 18 September 1945 in Lebanon, he was a sometime professor of Islamic studies at Johns Hopkins University, Baltimore, Md. His writings include *The Global populists* (1974), *The Arab predicament* (1981), and *The vanished Imam* (1986). ConAu, 167

Ajdari, Ahmad, born early 20th cent., he was an Iranian economist who in 1962 taught at the Université de Paris. His writings include *Asie du sud-ouest, Proche et Moyen-Orient; statistiques économiques et sociales* (Paris, 1961), and he was a joint author of the exhibition catalogue *Prestige du tapis persan* (1960). BN; Note

Akaad, M. Kamal *see* 'Aqqad, Muhammad Kamal al-

Akabirov, Said Fazyl, fl. 1971, he was a joint author of *Узбекского-русский словарь* (Moscow, 1959). LC

Akbaba, Iskender, fl. 1980, he was a retired Turkish colonel.

Akbaev (Акбаев), Shakman Khuseinovich, fl. 1971, he wrote *Фонетика диалектов карачаево-балкарского языка* (Cherkessk, 1963). LC

Akbar, Syed Ali, 1891-1984 *see* Ali Akbar, Syed

Akçura, Yusuf, born in 1876 or 1879 at Simsar, he was a Volga Tatar by birth and active in Young Turk activities while studying at the Harbiyye, Constantinople. He graduated in political science at Paris and became a politician. He was a sometime president of the Türk Tarih Kurumu. He is the subject of David S. Thomas' Ph.D. thesis, *The life and thought of Yusuf Akçura*. He died in Istanbul in 1935. Meydan; TatarES; Zürcher

Akhavi, Shahrough, born 10 June 1940., he received a Ph.D. in 1969 from the University of South Carolina for *The Egyptian image of the Soviet Union, 1954-1968*. He subsequently became a professor and taught for nearly twenty years at his alma mater. His writings include *Religion and politics in contemporary Iran* (1980). LC

Akhmar, Q., 1900-1969 see Akhmerov, Kasim Zakirovich

Akhmedov (Ахмедов), Bori Akhmedovich, born 12 August 1924 at Karasu, Uzbekistan, he graduated in 1953 from the Oriental Faculty, Central Asian State University, Tashkent; and in 1960 he joined the Oriental Institute of the Uzbekistan Academy of Sciences. He received a doctorate in 1974 for *Балхское ханство в XVI - первой половине XVIII вв.* His writings include *Государство кочевых узбеков* (1965), *История Балха* (1982), *Историко-географическая литература Срелней Азии XVI-XVIII вв.* (1985), and *Из истории Средней Азии и Восточного Туркестана XV-XIX вв.* (1987). Miliband; Miliband²; Schoeberlein

Akhmerov (Ахмеров), Kasim Zakirovich, born in 1900, near Ufa, he received a doctorate in philology in 1963 and was appointed a professor in 1965. His writings include *Ортографический словарь башкирского литера-турного языка для начальной и средней школу* (1952), *Башкирско-русский словарь* (1958), *Русско-башкирский словарь* (1964). He died in 1969. BashkKE

Akhmerov (Ахмеров), Rid Biktimirovich, fl. 1952; he was joint author of *Безвышечная эксплуатация нефтяных скважин* (1963).

Akhmetgaleeva, IAlkyn Safovna (Ялкын Сафовна Ахметгалеева), fl. 1970; her writings include *Исследование тюркоязычного памятника "Кисекбаш китабы"* (1979). LC

Akhmet'ianov, Rifkat Gazizianovich (Рифкат Газизянович Ахметьянов), born in 1933, he received a doctorate in philology in 1994. His writings include *Сравнительное исследование татарского и чувашского языков* (1978), *Общая лексика духовной культуры народов Среднего Поволжья* (1981), and *Проблемы лексикологии и терминологии татарского языка* (1993). LC; TatarES

Akhmetov (Ахметов), Zaki Akhmetovich, born 4 May 1928 in Kazakhstan, his writings include *Казахское стихосложение* (1964), *Современное развитие и традиции казахской литературы* (1978), *Очерки истории русской советской литературы Казахстана* (1985), and *Батырлар жыры* (1989). KazakSE

Akhramovich (Ахрамович), Roman Timofeevich, born 13 November 1923 at Minsk, he graduated in 1949 from the Moscow Oriental Institute and receiveded a doctorate in 1968 for *Общественные движения и государственная политика Афганистана после второй мировой войны*. Since 1962 he was director of the Oriental Institute of the Soviet Academy of Sciences. His writings include *Афганистан после второй мировой войны* (1961), *Афганистан в 1961-1966 гг.* (1967), *История и филология* (1987). He died 10 February 1989. Miliband; Miliband²

Akhtar, Jamila, fl. 1963, she was joint author of *Village life in Lahore District* (1960). LC

Akhtar, M. A., he was in 1974 an assistant professor of economics at Guilford College, and in 1975 an associate professor of economics at Jacksonville State University. Note

Akhtar, Sardar Mohammad, born in 1904, his writings include *Emigrant labour for Assam tea gardens* (1939), *Pakistan, a developing economy* (1966), and *Economic development of Pakistan* (1983). LC

Akhtar, Shameem, born 20th cent., he was a sometime professor and director, Institute of European Studies at Karachi University. He wrote *British Guiana: a study of Marxism and radicalism in the Carribean* (1962). LC

Akhund, Hameeda, she was in 1958 a researcher at the Pakistan Institute of International Affairs, Karachi.

Akhunzianov, Galimzian Khalimzianovich (Галимзян Халимзянович Ахунзянов), born in 1925, he received a doctorate in 1974 from the University of Kazan for *Идиомы: исследование на материале татарского языка*. His writings include *Татарская лексика в семантико-грамматиче-ском аспекте* (1988). LC; TatarES

Akimushkin, Oleg Fedorovich, born 17 February 1929 at Penza, Russia, he graduated in 1953 from the Oriental Faculty of the Leningrad State University. Since 1954 he was affiliated with the Leningrad Section of the Oriental Institute, Academy of Science. His writings include *Очерки истории культуры средневекового Ирана* (1984); he was joint author of *Персидские и таджикские рукописи Института народов Азии АН СССР* (1964), *Рукописная книга в культуре народов Востока* (1987), and *Суфизм в контексте мусульманской культуры* (1989). Miliband; Miliband²; Schoeberlein

Akins, James Elmer, born 15 October 1926 at Akron, Ohio, he there graduated from its University. After teaching in Lebanon from 1951 to 1952, he entered the Foreign Service and successively served in Damascus, Beirut, Kuwait, and Baghdad. He was ambassador to Saudi Arabia until his dismissal in 1975. Thereafter he became a consultant on foreign policy and energy in Washington, D.C. He was a contributing author to *Oil and security in the Arab world; the proceedings of an international symposium* (1980). IntWW, 1991-1998/99]; Shavit

Akinsanya, Adeoye A., born 5 June 1944 at Lagos, Nigeria, he was educated in Nigeria and the United States, where he obtained a Ph.D. in 1973 from the University of Chicago for *The Nigerianisation of the western Nigeria higher public service*. Afterwards he was professor of political science at the University of Lagos until he joined the University of Ilorin, where he delivered his inauguration lecture on 6 December 1984 entitled *Transnational corporations and economic nationalism in the Third World*. His writings include *The Expropriation of multinational property in the Third World* (1980), *Multinationals in a changing environment* (1984), and *Strategies for dismantling apartheid* (1990). Africa who's who, 1991, 1996

Akkad, Salah el- *see* 'Aqqad, Salah al-

Akmut, A. A., born in 1921, he was in 1973 a secretary of the Pakistan Institute of International Affairs, Karachi. His writings include *Challenge to poverty* (1970). LC

Aknouni, E., *pseud. see* Maloumian, Khatchadour

Akolut, Andrzej, 1654-1704 *see* Acoluthus, Andreas

Aksel, H. Avni, born in the 1890s, he graduated in 1918 at Constantinople, and in 1944 he was chief surgeon at the Haseki Hastahanesi in Istanbul. He was a member of the Turkish Medical Mission which visited the UK in the 1940s. Note about the author

Aksel'rod, Moisei Markovich (Моисей Маркович Аксельрод), born 24 December 1897 at Smolensk, he graduated in 1923 from the Faculty of Law in the State Lomonosov University, and in 1924 from its Department of Arabic. The following three years he was posted to the Soviet Embassy in Jiddah. He published also under the pseudonym M. A. Rafik. He died 18 April 1940. Miliband; Miliband²

Aksentijević, Mirko, born on 13 September 1922; he was in 1971 an editor of the Tanjug news agency. His writings include *Kurdi: borba za autonomiju* (1966), *Palestinski dosije* (1979), *Nemoguce* (1982). LC

Aktan, Reşat, Dr.; in the 1960s and 1970s, he was for over ten years a professor of economics at the Faculty of Political Science in Ankara Üniversitesi. His writings include *Türkiye'de ziraat mahsulleri fiyatları* (1955), *Türkiye ziraatinde prodüktivite* (1966), *Türkiye iktisadi* (1968); and he edited *Analysis and assessment of the economic effects [of] Public law 480 Title I program [in] Turkey*. LC

Aktan, Tahir, M.A., LL.D., born 20th cent., he was in 1967 a professor of public administration at the Middle East Technical University, Ankara. He was joint author of *The Public service in Turkey* (1955)

Akyüz, Kenan, born in 1911 at Yanya, Turkey, he obtained a doctorate in 1947 for *Tevfik Fikret*. After teaching at Turkish high schools for a number of years, he joined Ankara Üniversitesi Dil ve Tarih-Cografya Fakültesi in 1944. His writings include *Yabancılar için Türkçe dersleri* (1965), *Encümen-i Dâniş* (1975), *Modern Türk edebiyatının ana çizgileri* (1979), and he edited Fuzûlî's *Türkçe divan* (1958). EIS

Akzin, Benjamin, born 6 May 1904 at Riga, he was educated at the universities of Wien, Paris and Harvard. From November 1936 to September 1938, he served as a member of the World Excecutive of the New Zionist Organization, and successively represented that organization before the Palestine Partition Commission in Jerusalem, the Evian Refugee Conference, and various bodies of the League of Nations, which dealt with Palestine. He stayed in the United States until 1949, when he settled permanently in Israel. His writings include *Procedures of peace-making* (1943), *New states and international organizations* (1955), *Israel; high-pressure planning* (1966), and numerous works in Hebrew. He died in Jerusalem in 1985. EncJud; WhoIsrael, 1966-1978; WhoUN, 1975; WhoWorJ, 1965

Al Samman, Tarif *see* Samman, Tarif Al

'Alā', Husayn, born in 1882 in Iran, and educated at Westminster School and the University of London, he was admitted to the English Bar. He was a close confidant of both the Pahlavis, a sometime director of the

National Bank of Iran, ambassador to the U.S.A., minister in various governments, and prime minister. He established the Iranian Society for the Preservation of National Monuments. He died on 13 July 1964. In 1965, a Persian commemoration volume was published, *Yādnāmah-i shād-ravān-i Husayn 'Alā'.* CurBio, 1951, 1964; *Dā'irat al-ma'ārif-i mawzū'ī-i dānish-i bashar* (Tehran, 1349/1970); NYT, 14 July 1964, p. 33, cols. 4-5; WhAm, 4

Alaev, Leonid Borisovich, born 20 October 1932 at Moscow, he graduated in 1954 from the Faculty of History in the State Lomonosov University. Since 1956 he was a research fellow at the Oriental Institute of the Soviet Academy of Science. He wrote Южная Индия: социально-экономическая истории XIV-XVIII вв. (1964), Сельская община в Северной Индии (1981), Типы общественных отношений на Востоке в средние века (1982). Miliband; Miliband²

Alagöz, Cemal Arif, fl. 1967 in Ankara. His writings include *Türkiye karst olaylari hakkinda bir araştirma* (1944), and *Sivas çevresi ve doğusundan jips karstı olayları* (1967) LC

Äläkbärov, Aidyn Gulam oglu see Alekperov, A. K.

Alam, Iqbal, born 20th cent., he was from 1974 to 1983 a research demographer at the Pakistan Institute of Development Economics, Islamabad. He was joint author of *Fertility levels, trends and differentials in Pakistan* (1983), and joint-editor of *The revolution of Asian fertility* (1993). LC

Alamgir, Mohiuddin, born in 1943, he wrote *An analysis of national accounts of Bangladesh* (1972), *Bangladesh; a case of below poverty level equilibrium trap* (1978), *Famine in South Asia* (1980), and *The state of world rural poverty* (1992). LC

al-'Alami, Musá, B.A., LL.B., O.B.E., born 8 May 1897 in Palestine, he was admitted to the English Bar in 1923 and two years later he was appointed to the Palestine Government as junior legal adviser, rising to the position of government advocate in 1933. He relinquished his government service in 1942 to take up active Arab political work, and was one of the principal negotiators with neighbouring Arab states on Arab League problems, on behalf of the Palestinian Arabs. When no agreement could be arrived at on the constitution of a unified Palestinian Arab committee, he was chosen as sole representative of all Arab Palestinian parties as the delegate to Arab unity conferences. After the establishment of Israel he sought and discovered adequate water in the Jordan valley near Jericho and founded there his Arab Development Society, the well-known agricultural training school for refugees and their children. He wrote *'Ibrat Filastin*, 2d ed. (1949). He died in Amman, 8 June 1984. Sir Geoffrey Furlonge wrote *Palestine is my country; the story of Musa Alami* (1969). AnObit, 1984, pp. 295-296; *Near and Middle East who's who; Palestine, Trans-Jordan,* 1945-46; NYT, 8 June 1984, p. 28, col. 1

Alani, Salman H. see 'Ani, Salman Hasan al-

Alarcón y Santón, Maximiliano Augustin, born 21 December 1880 at La Roda (Albacete), Spain, he wrote *Textos árabes en dialecto vulgar de Larache* (1913), *Archivo gneral de la Corona de Aragón* (1940), and *Los documentos árabes diplomáticos del Archivo de la Corona de Aragón* (1940). He died in Madrid in 1933. *Al-Andalus* 1 (1933), pp. 193-199

Äläsgärzadä, Ä. see Alesker-Zade, Azhdar Ali ogly

Alauddin, Miss Talat K., born 20th cent., she was in 1977 a research assistant at the Pakistan Institute of Development Economics, Islamabad, later becoming a staff economist. She compiled the bibliography *Status of women and socio-economic development* (1977). LC; Note about the author

d'Alaux, Gustave, born in 1816, he wrote *L'Empereur Soulouque et son empire* (1856), and its translation, *Aragón visto por un francés durante la primera guerra carlista* (1985). He died in 1885. LC

Alavi, Buzurg, born 12 February 1904 at Tehran, he was educated in Iran and in Germany. In the early 1930s he taught at Tehran and became politically affiliated with Taqi Erani. In 1937 he was arrested for violation of a 1933 anti-communist law. He and fifty-two others remained in prison until the Allied occupation of Iran in the autumn of 1941. He became a founder of the Tudeh Party and editor of its party organ, *Mardum.* He was in East Germany when, in mid-August 1953 Musaddiq's nationalist government was overthrown. He remained in East Berlin, teaching Persian literature at Humboldt-Universität, and writing. He visited Iran briefly in 1979 and 1980, but returned to East Berlin, where he died on 17 February 1997. His writings include *Geschichte und Entwicklung der modernen persischen Literatur* (Berlin, 1964.) Grair O. Movsesian wrote Творчество Бозорга Аляви (1980). Jan Rypka, *History of Iranian literature* (1968)

Alavi, Hamza, born in 1921, he was in 1966 a Pakistani resident in Britain and vice-chairman of the Campaign against Racial Discrimination. Together with Fred Halliday he edited *State and ideology in the Middle East and Pakistan* (1988). LC

Alazard, Jean, born in 1887. His writings include *L'Orient et la peinture française au XIXe siècle* (1930); he was joint-author of *Initiation à l'Algérie* (1957). After his death in 1960, a commemorative volume was published in 1963 entitled *Jean Alazard; souvenirs et mélanges*. LC

Alban, Karl, born 20th cent., he studied at the Universität Marburg, where he obtained a Dr.phil. in 1951 for *Der Einfluß Rainer Maria Rilkes auf das englische Schrifttum*. In 1974, he was director of the Deutsche Evangelische Oberschule, Cairo. Note

Albarracín Navarro, Joaquina, fl. 1953. After obtaining a doctorate in Semitic philology, she taught Islamic ethnology and women's clothing and jewellery at the Universidad de Granada. Her writings include *El Marquesado del Cenete* (1986). Arabismo, 1992, 1994, 1997

Albaum, Melvin, born 13 July 1936 at NYC, he was educated at Hunter College, NYC, University of Wisconsin, and Ohio State University, where he obtained a Ph.D. in 1969. His writings include *Geography and contemporary issues* (1973). ConAu vol. 53-56

Alber, Oskar, fl. 1967, he was joint author of *Isolieröle; theoretische und praktische Fragen*, published by the Rhenania-Ossag Mineralölwerke, Hamburg, in 1938. LC

Albergoni, Geneviève, born 20th cent., her writings include *L'eau du puisant; une communauté oasienne du Sud-tunisien* (1987), a work which was originally presented as her thesis in 1981. LC

Alberoni, Giulio, born 21 May 1664 at Fiorenzuola, Italy, he was an Italian-Spanish prelate and statesman who died in Rome, 16 June 1752. His writings include *Cardinal Alberoni's scheme for reducing the Turkish Empire to the obedience of Christian princes* (1736). DizBI; Encyclopedia Americana

Albert, André, fl. 1922, he was a Jesuit whose writings include *Cameroun français* (1937), and *Au Cameroun français* (1943). LC

Albert, Gottfried, born 19th cent., he was from 1888 to 1903 editor of the *Mitteilungen des Deutschen Exkursions-Klubs in Constantinopel*. Note

Albert, Pierre, born 19th cent., he was from 1906 to 1907 *officier-interprète* at the Cercle de Colomb, Algeria.

Albertini, Eugène François, born 2 October 1880 at Compiègne (Oise), he was educated at the Lycée Henri IV, and École Normale Supérieure, Paris. He was a professor at the Collège de France and inspecteur général des antiquités et des musées de l'Algérie. In 1920 he went to Algeria, where he was active in the Société historique and a regular contributor to the *Revue africaine*. His writings include his *thèse complémentaire, Les Divisions administratives de l'Espagne romaine* (1923), and *Roman Africa* (1927); he was a joint-author of *L'Afrique du nord française dans l'histoire* (1937). He died in Paris in 1941. Revue africaine 85 (1941), 139-140

Alberts, Elizabeth, born about 1925 at Medina, N.Y., she was from 1943 to 1947 an undergraduate with a four-year State scholarship at the University of Buffalo, N.Y.; after a one-year teaching fellowship from Washington State College, she received her M.Sc. in experimental psychology. From October 1952 to 1954, she accompanied her husband, Robert Charles Alberts, to Iran where she also joined the Point four Social Development Staff in 1953, but was later assigned to the Public Administration Division and assumed responsibility as the American Technician for the Project 78 USOM/I "Project for Improving Selection and Placement of Personnel." It was in this capacity that she was engaged in the Testing and Vocational Guidance Unit which later became affiliated with the Institute for Administrative Affairs under the name of Personnel Management & Research Center, Faculty of Law, University of Tehran. Monthly report of the PMCR, September 1957

Alberts, Otto Friedrich, born 18 November 1851 at Stargard, Germany, he studied mathematics, natural sciences, and medicine at Halle, Berlin, Greifswald, and Jena, where he obtained a Dr.med. in 1875 for *Zur Casuistik der Behandlung von Varieen Schwangerer*. His writings include *Linguistisch-medizinischer Beitrag zur Culturgeschichte der Türken* (1890), *Aristotelische Philosophie in der türkischen Literatur des 11. Jahrhunderts* (1899), and *Der türkische Text der bilingualen Inschriften der Mongolei* (1900). NYPL; Thesis

Alberts, Robert Charles, born 22 January 1925 at Buffalo, N.Y., he studied at Washington State University, and the University of Chicago and received a Ph.D. in 1963 from the University of Wisconsin for *Social structure and cultural change in an Iranian village*. Throughout his career, he conducted research in practical problems of social, political, economic, and environmental change. From October 1952 to 1954, he was chief community analyst, U.S. Operations Mission, Iran; afterwards he held a one-year teaching appointment at Beliol College; since 1959 he was with the U.S. Government, the Human Science Research, Inc., and the Research Analysis Corporation. His writings include *A comprehensive evaluation of OEO community* *action programs on six selected American Indian reservations* (1966), *The Golden voyage* (1969), *The Good provider: H. J. Heinz* (1973), *George Rogers Clark and the winning of the old Northwest* (1975), *The Shaping of the point: Pittsburgh's Renaissance Park* (1980), and *The Pitt: the story of the University of Pittsburgh* (1986). AmM&WSc, 1973 P

Albin, Michael W., born 10 November 1942 at Gary, Ind., he was educated at Notre Dame University, and the University of Chicago. He was a sometime president of the Middle East Librarians Association and for over fifteen years chief of acquisition at the Library of Congress. IWWAS, 1976/77; Private

Albiruni, A. H., pseud. *see* Ikram, Sheikh Mohammad, 1908-1973

Albitreccia, Antoine, born in 1892, he received a doctorate in 1942 from the Université de Paris for *La Corse, son évolution au XIXe siècle et au début du XXe siècle*. His writings include *La Corse* (1935), *Le plan terrier de la Corse au XVII siècle* (1942). Together with Paul Wohl he published *Road and rail in forty countries* (1935). He died in 1945. LC

Albrecht, Edelgard née Weihmann, born in 1937, she obtained a Dr.phil. in 1964 from the Universität München for her thesis *Das Türkenbild in der ragusanisch-dalmatinischen Literatur des 16. Jahrhunderts*. She wrote *Ortsnamen Serbiens in türkischen geographischen Werken des XVI.-XVIII Jahrhunderts* (1975).

Albrecht, Max, born 19th cent., he received a doctorate in 1871 from the Universität Halle for his thesis *Über einige vom Grubengas sich ableitende Sulffonsäuren*. He also wrote *Das Erdöl und seine Produkte* (1896). His trace is lost after a publication in 1906. LC

Albrecht-Carrié, René, born in 1904, he obtained a Ph.D. in 1938 from Columbia University for *Italy at the Paris Peace Conference*. He was a sometime professor of history at Barnard College, New York. His writings include *Europe after 1815* (1952), *A Diplomatic history of Europe since the Congress of Vienna* (1958), and *Adolph Theirs, or, the triumph of the bourgeoisie* (1977). LC

Albright, Charlotte F., born 16 March 1945 at Spartenburg, she was educated at the University of Washington, where she received a Ph.D. in 1976. She specialized in the music of the Middle East; she was a sometime outreach director for the Middle East Center, University of Washington, Seattle. Together with E.-F. Bodman, she was the author of *A Middle East film sampler* (1983), she was also joint editor of *A Resource guide for Middle Eastern studies* (1983). MESA Roster of members, 1982-1990

Albright, Frank P., fl. 1955. His writings include *Johann Ludwig Eberhardt* (1978), and *The American archaeological expedition in Dhofar, Oman, 1952-1953* (1982). LC

Albright, William Foxwell, born 24 May 1891 at Coquimbo, Chile, to American parents, he was a graduate of Upper Iowa and Johns Hopkins universities. He was a professor of Semitic languages at Johns Hopkins, and for over ten years served as director of the American Schools of Oriental Research. His writings include *The Archaeology of Palestine and the Bible* (1932). He died in Baltimore, Md., on 19 September 1971. CurBio, 1955; Master (8); Shavit; WhAm, 5

Album, Stephen, born 20th cent., he was a numismatist who had studied at the University of California, Berkeley, and obtained a M.A. in 1969. He wrote *Catalogue of California merchants tokens* (1971). MESA Roster of members, 1990

de **Alciati de Grihon**, Vicomte, fl. 1845. Supported by the French Ministère de la Guerre, he, together with Sainte-Croix Pajot, travelled in the Yemen, 1844-1845. Henze

Alcock, Sir Rutherford, born in 1809 at London, he was British consul in China and Japan from 1844 to 1865, when he returned to England. From 1876 to 1878 he was president of the Royal Geographical Society of London. He died in London, 2 November 1897. DNB, Suppl., v. 22; Henze; Who was who, 1897-1915

Alcouffe, A., he was in 1957 an *ingénieur sub-divisionnaire des mines*. Note about the author

Alcover i Sureda, Antonio Maria, born 2 February 1862 in Mallorca, he wrote *Estudios sobre la historia de Mallorca antes del siglo XIII* (1894), and *Aplec de rondaies mallorquines* (1913-1930). He died in Palma de Mallorca, 8 January 1932. Dicc. bio; Sainz, 1953

de **Aldécoa**, Marcel, born 19th cent., he wrote *Cours d'arabe marocain* (Paris, 1914), and *Précis de grammaire arabe; arabe littéraire* (Paris, 1926).

Alder, Garry J., born 20th cent., he wrote *Beyond Bokhara; the life of William Moorcroft* (1985).

Aldrich, Thomas Bailey, born on 11 November 1836 at Portsmouth, N.H., he was educated at Harvard

University. He was a writer, and editor of the *Atlantic monthly* from 1881 to 1890. His writings include the autobiographical novel *Story of a bad boy* (1870). He died 19 March 1907. DAB; WhAm, 1

de **Aledo**, Marqués, fl. 1952 *see* Herrero (y) de Collantes, Ignacio

Alekperov, A. K. (Aidyn Gulam oglu Ălăkbărov), born 20th cent., his writings include *Фонематическая система современного азербайджанского языка* (1971), and *Лексическая семантика простых глаголов в современном азербайджанском языке* (1983). LC

Aleksandrov, Vasilii Aleksandrovich, born 19th cent., his writings include *Туркмения и ее курортные богатства* (1930), *Киргизия и ее курортные богатства* (1931). LC

Alekseev, Mikhail Egorovich, born 20th cent., his writings include *Сравнительно-историческая морфология аваро-андийских языков* (1988), he was joint author of *Задачи по лингвистике* (1991).

Alekseev, Valerii Pavlovich, born 20th cent., his writings include *Краниометрия* (1964), *География человеческих рас* (1974); he was joint author of *Туркмены в Среднеазиатском междуречье* (1989). LC

Alekseev, Vasilii Mikhailovich, born 2 (14) January 1881 at St. Petersburg, he was a Sinologist who graduated in 1902 from the Faculty of Oriental History at St. Petersburg University. He died on 12 May 1951. Miliband; Miliband²

Alekseev, Vladimir Mikhailovich, born 15 August 1923 at Novo Frolovskom, he graduated in 1950 from the Moscow Oriental Institute and received his first degree in 1954 for *Государственный бюджет Турции*. In 1966 he conducted field-work in Turkey. His writings include *Внешняя политика Турции* (1961). Miliband; Miliband²

Alekseeva, Tat'iana Ivanovna, fl. 1955, she was joint author of *Антро-экологические исследования в Туве* (1984), and she edited *Антропология - медицине* (1989). LC

Aleksić-Pejković, Ljiljana, fl. 1953, her writings include *Stav Francuske prema Srbiji za vreme druge vlade Kneza Miloša i Mihaila* (1957), and *Naučni skup Srbija u završnoj fazi velike istočne krize, 1877-1878* (1980).

Aleksieva, Afrodita, fl. 1972, her writings include *Българо-балкански културни взаимоотношения, 1878-1944* (1986), and *Преводната проза от груцки през Вузраждането* (1987). LC

Alemany y Bolúfer, José, born in 1866 at Culler (Valencia), he obtained a doctorate in philosophy and letters in 1889; and was a sometime professor of Hebrew at the universities of Granada and Madrid. His writings include *La antigua versión castellana del Calila y Dimna* (1915), and *La geografía de la Península ibéra en los escritos árabes* (1919-1921). Sabater; Sainz, t. 2

Alès, Adhémard d', born in 1861, he was a Jesuit and a sometime professor of theology at the Institut Catholique, Paris. His writings include *La théologie de Saint Cyprien* (1922), and *Providence et libre arbitre* (1927). He died in 1938. LC

Alesker-Zade, Azhdar Ali ogly, born in 1895 at Baku, he graduated in 1928 from the Oriental Faculty, Azerbaijan State University. He retired from the Oriental Institute, Azerbaijan Academy of Science in 1962. In 1965, he edited Nizami Ganjavi's *Laylá va Majnun*. He died on 18 September 1964. Miliband; Miliband²

Alexander, Erich, born 2 December 1880 at Berlin, he studieded at the Universität Rostock, where he received a Dr. jur. in 1902 for *Die rechtliche Natur der Erfüllung*. In 1929 he was director general of the Deutsche Orientbank. Wer ist's, 1928

Alexander, George Glover, LL.M., fl. 1925, he wrote *The administration of justice in criminal matters* (1911).

Alexander, Sir James Edward, born 16 October 1803 in Scotland, he was educated at Edinburgh, Glasgow, and the Royal Military College, Sandhurst. He was present with the Persian army during the war of 1826 with Russia, and went to the Balkans during the Russo-Turkish war of 1829. His writings include *Travels from India to England, comprehending a visit to the Burma Empire, and a journey through Persia , Asia Minor, European Turkey, etc., 1825-1826* (1827), and the autobiography *Passages in the life of a soldier, or, military service in the East and West* (1857). He died in Ryde, Isle of Wight, 2 April 1885. Buckland; DNB, Suppl.; Henze

Alexander, Lewis McElwain, born 15 June 1921 at Summit, N.J., he was a professor of geography at Harpur College, SUNY, from 1949 to 1960, and afterwards until 1981 at the University of Rhode Island. Since 1982 he was with the U.S. Department of State. His writings include *Offshore geography of north-western Europe* (1963), *Marine regionalism in the southeast Asian seas* (1982). AmM&WSc, 1973 S; WhoAm, 1974-76

Alexander, Mark, fl. 1950-1953, he was a journalist of the *Twentieth century*, stationed in the Middle East. Note

Alexander, Sidney Stuart, born 3 May 1916 at Forest City, Pa., he was educated at King's College, London, and Harvard University, where he received a Ph.D. in 1945 for *Financial structure of American corporations since 1900*. Since 1956 he was professor of economics at M.I.T. His writings include *La cienca de la economica* (1962); he was joint author of *Economics and the policy makers* (1959); and he was joint editor of *Economic development and population growth in the Middle East and Pakistan* (1972), and *Political dynamics in the Middle East* (1972). AmM&WSc, 1973 S

Alexander, Yonah, born 25 December 1931 at Grodno, Poland, he was educated at Roosevelt University (B.A.), University of Chicago, College of Jewish Studies, and Columbia University, where he received a Ph.D. in 1965. He was professor at various NYC colleges and universities since 1961. His writings include *The role of communications in the Middle East conflict* (1973), *Crescent and star* (1973), *Perspectives on terrorism* (1983); he is joint editor of *The United States and Iran; a documentary history* (1980). ConAu 61-64

Alexander à Sigismundo, fl. 1724, he was a Flemish Roman Catholic monk in Cochin, Malabar.

Alexandre, Pierre Hippolyte Henri Charles, born 3 December 1922 at Alger, he received a diploma in anthropology from the University of London. He was secretary general of the Centre de hautes études administratives sur l'Afrique et sur l'Asie moderne de l'Université de Paris, 1954-58. His writings include *Le groupe dit pahouin* (1958), *Langue et langage en Afrique noire* (1967), and its translation, *An introduction to languages and language in Africa* (1972). LC; Unesco

Alexandrescu-Dersca, Maria Matilda, fl. 1942, her writings include *La campagne de Timur en Anatolie* (1942), and *Nicolae Iorga, a Roumanian historian* (1972).

Alexieva, Afrodita *see* Aleksieva, Afrodita

Alfassa, Maurice, fl. 1938, he wrote *La crise ouvrière récente des chemins de fer anglais* (1908).

Alfaya González, José Maria, born 20th cent., he was in 1992 a director of the Centro Cultural "Antonio Machado" in Madrid. Note

Alföldi, András (Andrew), born 27 August 1895 at Pomáz, Hungary, he received a doctorate from Budapest University in 1919, and was also granted several honorary degrees by European universities. From 1919 to 1923 he was a member of the Hungarian National Museum; and from 1923 to 1947, he taught at universities in Hungary. In 1955 he went to the Institute for Advanced Studies, Princeton, N.J., where he remained until his death on 12 February 1981. He was an archaeologist and historian who wrote predominantly on Roman history in German. His writings include *Early Rome and the Latins* (1965). Int'IWW, 1981-82; Magyar; WhAm, 8

Alfonso de Macerata, born 19th cent., he was a Capucin Father from Italy who wrote *Mission catholique d'Aden en Arabie* (1869).

Alger, John Goldworth, born in 1836, he was a journalist and author whose writings include *The new Paris sketchbook* (1887), *Englishmen in the French revolution* (1889), *Glimpses of the French revolution* (1889), and *Napoleon' British visitors and captives, 1801-1815* (1904). He died in 1907.

Algosaibi, Ghazi A., 1940- *see* al-Qusaybi, Ghazi 'Abd al-Rahman

Alhegelan, Sheikh Faisal *see* Hejailan, Sheikh Faisal Abdul Aziz al-

Ali, Abdullah Yusuf, C.B.E., born 4 April 1872. After education at Bombay University and St. John's College, Cambridge, he joined the Indian Civil Service in 1895. He was a member of several Royal institutions and barrister-at-law of Lincoln's Inn. His writings include *The message of Islam* (1940). He died on 10 December 1953. M. A. Sherif wrote *Searching for solace; a biography of Abdullah Yusuf Ali* (Kuala Lumpur, 1994). Who was who, 5

Ali, Ahmed, born 1 July 1910 at Delhi, he was educated at the Muslim University, Aligarh, and Lucknow University. He was an Urdu writer whose writings include *Twilight in Delhi* (London, 1940), *Muslim China* (Karachi, 1949), and *The golden tradition; an anthology of Urdu poetry* (1973). He died in Karachi, 14 January 1994. Annual of Urdu studies 9 (1994), pp. 6-56

Ali, Hamid, fl. 1950, he was deputy trade director for Pakistan in London. Note

Ali, Karamat, born 20th cent., he received a Ph.D. in 1978 from Vanderbilt University, Nashville, Tenn., for his thesis *Agricultural modernization and human fertility in developing countries*. In 1982, he was assistant professor of economics at Bahauddin Zakriya University, Multan. He was editor of, and contributor to, *Pakistan; the political economy of rural develpoment* (1982). LC; Note

Ali, Mehrunnisa, born 20th cent., she obtained an M.A. from a Canadian university. In 1972 she was a research officer in the Pakistan Institute of International Affairs, and in 1991, associate professor of political science at the University of Karachi. She edited *Pak-Afghan discord: a historical per-spective; documents, 1855-1979* (1990). LC

Ali, Muhammad, M.A., LL.B., born in December 1875, he was an Indian Muslim nationalist leader whose writings include *Islam, or the natural religion of man* (1912), *Early caliphate* (1932), *A manual of hadith* (1944). He died in London, 4 January 1931. EI²

Ali, Nasr El Hag, he was in 1965 a director of the joint Unesco-I[international] A[ssociation of] U[niversities] Research Programme in Higher Education. Note

Ali, Radja, viceroy of Riau, Sumatra; he died in 1805. *Ensiklopedia Indonesia* (Bandung, 1954-56)

Ali, Sheikh Rustum, born 1 February 1932 in Bangladesh, he was educated at Dacca University, New York University, and American University, where he received a Ph.D. in 1975 for his thesis, *The use of oil as a weapon of diplomacy; a case study of Saudi Arabia*. His writings include *Saudi Arabia and its oil diplomacy* (1976), *The trilemma of world oil policies* (1984), *Oil, turmoil, and Islam in the Middle East* (1986), *Oil and power* (1987), *The international organizations and world order dictionary* (1992). International who's who in Asian studies,I 1976/77; LC

Ali, Syed Ameer, born 6 April 1849 at Cuttack, Orissa, he was educated in India as well as in England, where he was called to the bar in 1873. Upon his return to India, he was a professor of law, a politician, magistrate, and judge. In his later years, he returned to England and was chairman of the Woking Mosque Committee. His writings include *A critical examination of the life and teachings of Mohammed* (1873), *The personal law of the Mahommedans* (1880), *The law relating to gifts, trusts, and testamentary dispositions among the Mahommedans* (1885), *The spirit of Islam* (1896), *A short history of the Saracens* (1898). He died in England in August 1928. Shan Muhammad wrote a biography, *The Right Honorable Syed Ameer Ali; personality and achievement* (New Delhi, 1991). Buckland; DNB; Eminent; Jain

Ali, Syed Amjad, born 5 July 1907 at Delhi, India, he was educated at Government College, Lahore, and subsequently entered the Pakistan Government Service. After serving as Pakistan's ambassador to the United States from 1953 to 1955, he became Pakistan's minister of finance, making economic planning a priority, then served as his country's ambassador to the United Nations until 1994. His writings include *The record and responsibilities of the Economic and Social Council* (1952), and *The Muslim world today* (1985). In 1992, he published his autobiography entitled *Glimpses*. He died in Lahore, 5 March, 1997. Jain, p. 90; LC; WhoUN, 1975; WRMEA 16 i (June/July 1997), p. 121

Ali, Syed Waris Ameer, born 12 October 1886, he was educated at Wellington College and Balliol, Oxford. After taking his degree, he entered the Indian Civil Service to join the judicial branch, where he had a distinguished career until 1929. On his retirement to England during the second World War he was from 1939 to 1945 War Services Adviser to the High Commissioner for India. He died 2 April 1975. Who was who, 7

Ali, Zaki, fl. 1934-1960 *see* Zaki Ali

Ali Akbar, Syed, born in October 1891 at Hyderabad, India, he graduated from Wilson College, Bombay. He received an M.A. in economics at Cambridge. From 1916 until his retirement, he was in government service. His writings include *The German school system* (1932), *Education under Asaf Jah VII* (1935), and *Education and democracy* (1954). He was a sometime vice-president of *Islamic culture*. He died on 18 April 1984. Islamic culture 58, no. 2 (April 1984)

Ali Kemal Bey, born in 1869 at Constantinople, he was educated at the Mülkiye school. After graduating in 1899 from l'École libre des sciences politiques, Paris, he became a journalist and politician. After the Turkish revolution of 1909, he had to flee the country and spent much of his exile in France, Egypt, Britain, and Austria. On 19 March 1899 he became a member of the Société asiatique. He was kidnapped and murdered by followers of Mustafa Kemal Atatürk in Izmir, 18 November 1922. His writings include *Iki hemşire* (1315/1897), and *Fetret* (1913). He was the editor of the journal *Ikdam*. There is a poor and brief biography by Zeki Kuneralp, entitled *Ali Kemal; a portrait* (1993), and also *Gazetecinin infazi* (1997), by Osman Öztürk. AnaBrit; EI²; Meydan

Ali Nouri, born 19th cent., his writings include *Nasreddin Khodjas Schwänke und Streiche* (1904), *Unter dem Scepter des Sultans* (1905), *Abdul-Hamid in Karikatur* (1910). NUC, pre-1956

Ali Paşa, Mehmed Emin, born in 1815 at Constantinople, he was an Ottoman grand vizier and died in Bebek, on 7 September 1871. EI²; Meydan

Ali Zade, Abdulkerim Ali ogly, born 11 (24) January 1901 at Bil'gya, Azerbaijan, he graduated in 1930 from the Leningrad Oriental Institute and received a doctorate in 1954 for his thesis *История Азербайджана XIII-XIV вв.* He published works by Nizami Ganjavi (1947), Rashid al-Din Tabib (1957), and Muhammad ibn Hindushah Nakhjavani (1964). GSE; Miliband

Alía Medina, Manuel, fl. 1954, his writings include *Caracteristica morfograficas y geologicas de la zona septentrional del Sáhara español* (1945), *Contribución al conocimiento geomorfológico de las zonas centrales del Sáhara español* (1949), *Datos geomorfológicos de la Guinea continental española* (1951). LC

Aliabadi, Ahmad Ali, born in 1911 in Persia, he went to the United States in 1933 to study at Columbia University and New York University, where he received a Ph.D. in education in 1937. Two years later, he was awarded a doctorate in law at Washington University. Upon his return to Iran, he became a senior civil servant. Iran who's who, 1974

Alibert, Léon Henri Lucien, born 19th cent., he was a lieutenant with the Service des renseignements at Mogador, Morocco. Note

Aliboni, Roberto, born in 1940, he studied law and economics at the Università di Roma and subsequently taught at the universities of Napoli and Perugia. In 1990, he was director of studies at the Istituto Affari Internazionali, Roma. His writings include *Integrazione in Africa orientale* (1970), *The Red Sea region* (1985); and he edited *Arab industrialisation and economic integration* (1979), and *Southern European security in the 1990s* (1992). LC

Aličić, S. Ahmed, born 20th cent., his writings include *Uredenje bosanskog ejaleta od 1789 do 1878 godine* (1983), *Muhime defteri* (1985), *Turski katastarski popisi nekih područja zapadne Srbije XV i XVI vek* (1985); and he was joint author of *Hercegovina* (1981). LC

Aliev, Fuad Mamed Bagir ogly, born 20th cent., his writings include *Антииранские выступления и борьба против турецкой оккупации в Азербайджане в первой половине XVIII в* (1975), *Миссия посланника русского государства А. П. Волныского в Азербайджане* (1979), *Азербайджано-русские отношения* (1985); he is the editor of *Дружба* (1985). LC

Aliev, Gamid Zeinal Abidin ogly, born 15 May 1921 at Amirkheir, Armenia, he graduated in 1946 from the Faculty of History in Erevan State Teachers Institute and received a doctorate in 1967 for *Младотурецкая революция и внутренняя политика турецкого правительства в 1908-1918 гг.* Since 1957 he was affiliated with the Azerbaijan Academy of Science, Baku. His writings include *Бојук октјабр ва хариуи шарг* (1987). LC; Miliband; Miliband²

Aliev, Gazanfar IUsif-ogly (Газанфар Юсиф оглы), born 15 May 1930 at Gandja (Kirovabad), he graduated in 1953 from the Oriental Faculty in the Azerbaijan State University, Baku. Since 1956 he was affiliated with the Oriental Institute, Soviet Academy of Science. His writings include *Легенда о Хосрове и Ширин в литературах народов Востока* (1960). He died 23 April 1984. Miliband²; Narody Azii i Afriki, 1984, no. 6, pp. 208-9

Aliev, Rustam Musa ogly, born 13 January 1929 in Azerbaijan, he graduated in 1951 from the Oriental Faculty, Leningrad, received his first degree in 1954 for *Критический текст Гулистана Саади*, and his doctorate in 1968 for *Проблемы восстановления поэтического наследия Саади Ширази*. He was appointed a professor in 1970, and since 1985 he was affiliated with the Oriental Institute of the Azerbaijan Academy of Science. His writings include *Песни и думы народов* (1955), *Каталог арабски рукописи [Академия Наук Азербайджанской ССР]* (1984), and the translations, *Гулистан* (1957), and Nizami Ganjavi's *Стихотворения и поэмы* (1981), *Собрание сочинений* (1985-1991). Miliband²

Aliev, Salekh Mamed ogly, born 12 December 1929 at Gandja (Kirovabad), Azerbaijan, he graduated in 1952 from the Oriental Faculty in the Azerbaijan State University, Baku. Since 1959 he was affiliated with the Oriental Institute in the Soviet Academy of Science. He travelled to Turkey (1967), Bulgaria (1967), and Iran (1968). His writings include *Нефть общественно-политическое развитие Ирана в XX в.* (1985); he edited *Современный Ирани: справочник* (1993). Miliband; Miliband²; OSK

Aliiarov, Suleiman Sardar ogly (Сулейман Сардар оглы Алияров), fl. 1956, he was a professor of history. His writings include *Нефтяные монополии в Азербайджане в период первой мировой войны* (1974), and *XIX асрда Азербайјанын аграр гурулушу* (1988). LC

Alikhanov-Avarskii, Maksud, born in 1846, he was a Russian lieutenant whose writings include *В гостях у шаха: очерки Персии* (1898), *Поход в Хивы - кавказских отрядов, 1873* (1899). He died in 1907. LC

Alimov, Abid Akhmed, born 25 March (7 April) 1900 at Allagulovo, he graduated in 1930 from the Institute of Red Professorship, Moscow. From 1930 until his death, he was affiliated with the Oriental Institute in the Soviet Academy of Science. He was joint editor of *Очерки по истории Востока в эпоху империализма* (1934). He died 30 January 1935. Miliband; Miliband²

Alis, Harry, pseud., 1857-1895 *see* Percher, Jules Hippolyte

Alishan, Ghewond (Leumond) Margar, born 6 (18) July at Constantinople, he was an Armenian poet, linguistic, and historian. His writings include *Sissouan, ou l'Arméno-Cilicie* (1899). He died in Venice, 9 (22) November 1901. GSE; LC

Alishan, Leonardo P., born in 1951 at Tehran, his writings include *Dancing barefoot on broken glass* (1991). LC; Note

Alizade, Abdulkerim Ali ogly *see* Ali Zade, Abdulkerim Ali ogly

Alkan, M. Türker, fl. 1980. His writings include *12 Eylül ve demokrasi* (1986), and *Siyasal bilinç ve toplumsal değişim* (1989). LC

Alkazaz, Aziz, born in 1942 in Iraq, he studied economics and sociology at the universities of Berlin and Kiel. Since 1967, he was a researcher at Deutsches Orient-Institut, Hamburg. His writings include *Die Entwicklung der irakischen Wirtschaft* (1981). Private

Alkim, U. Bahadir, fl. 1949, he was a Turkish archaeologist whose writings include *Anatolie* (1969), English and German translations in the same year, and *Ikiztepe* (1988). He died in 1981. LC

Alkin, Erdogan, born 20th cent., he was educated in Turkey and the United States; in 1979 he was professor of economics at Istanbul Üniversitesi. His writings include *Turkey's international economic relations* (1982); with Süleyman Barda he wrote *Diş ticaret teoresi* (1967). LC

Alkin, Mecdet, Dr.; he was in 1941 a trade attaché at the Turkish Embassy in Berlin. Note

Allain, Jean Claude, fl. 1971. His writings include *Agadir 1911, une crise impérialiste en Europe pour la conquête du Maroc* (1976), *Joseph Caillaux* (1978), a work which was originally submitted in 1974 as a thesis at the Université de Paris I; he also wrote *L'Europa nell'orizzonte del mondo* (1984-1985). LC

Allais, Yvonne, born 4 September 1891 at Clermont-Ferrand, she was educated at Rennes and Paris. After teaching at various *lycées*, she succeeded Mme de Crésolles in 1942 and resumed responsibility of the excavations at Djemila (Cuicul), Algeria, until her retirement in 1956. Her writings include *Djemila*(1938). She died in 1981. Hommes et destins, vol. 7, pp. 20-21

Allan, James Wilson, born 5 May 1945, he was in 1996 a keeper of Eastern Art at the Ashmolean Museum in Oxford. His writings include *Persian metal technology* (1979), *Nishapur* (1981), *Metalwork of the Islamic world* (1986), and *Islamic ceramics* (1991). Who's who, 1993-2004

Allan, John, born in 1884, he was as a sometime lecturer in Sanskrit at the University of Edinburgh, and a keeper of Coins and Medals in the British Museum, London. His writings include *Catalogue of the coins in the Indian Museum*, vol. 4 (1906), *Catalogue of the coins of the Gupta dynasties* (1914), *Catalogue of the coins of ancient India* (1936). He died 26 August 1955. Who was who, 5

Allan, John Anthony, born 29 January 1937 in England, he was educated at Durham University, and SOAS, London, where he obtained a Ph.D. in 1971 for his thesis, *Changes in the economic use of land in the vicinity of Tripoli, Libya*. In 1990 he was a professor of geography at SOAS. His writings include *A select and airphoto bibliography of Libya* (1970), *Libya; the experience of oil* (1981), *Japan in the contemporary Middle East* (1993). IWWAS, 1975/76; LC

Allana, Ghulam Ali, born in 1906 and educated at D. J. Sind College, Karachi, and Fergusson College, Poona, he became a poet and a prose writer. His writings include *Presenting Pakistani poetry* (1961), *Quaid-e-Azam Jinnah* (1967), *Survey of libraries in the Province of Sind* (1978), *Folk music of Sind* (1982). He was a sometime mayor of Karachi, president of the Federation of Chamber of Commerce and Industry, Pakistan, vice-chairman of the Economic Committee at the U.N., member of the West Pakistan Legislative Assembly, member of the Governing body of the International Labour Organization, Geneva, and president of the International Organization of Employers, Bruxelles.

Allard, J., fl. 1958, he was a general in the Corps d'Armée d'Alger. Note

Allard, Michel Adrien, born 27 January 1924 at Brest, France, he entered the Compagnie de Jésus in 1942 and was stationed in the Lebanon. He was a sometime director of the Institut des Lettres Orientales. From

1975 until his death he was professor of Islamic studies at the Université de Lyon II. His writings include *Le problème des attributs divins dans la doctrine d'al-Aš'ari* (1965), and *Textes apologétiques de Juwaini* (1968). He was killed shortly before leaving the Lebanon when a mortar shell hit his room in the night of 15 to 16 January 1976. *Hommes et destins*, vol. 4, 17-21; IWWAS, 1975/76

d'Allemagne, Henry René, born in 1863, his writings include *Histoire du luminaire depuis l'époque romain jusqu'au XIXe siècle* (1891), *Du Khorassan au pays des Bakhtiaris; trois mois de voyage en Perse* (1911), *Les Accessoires du costume et du mobilier depuis le XIIIe jusqu'au milieu du XIXe siècle* (1982), *La Maison d'un vieux collectionneur* (1948). LC

Allen, Bernard Meredith, M.A., LL.D., born in 1864 at Stoke Newington, he was educated at Highgate and Oxford University. His writings include *The story behind the Gospels* (1926), *Gordon and the Sudan* (1931), and his reminiscences *Down the stream of life* (1948). WhE&EA

Allen, E. T., Rev., fl. 1921, he was a sometime missionary of the Presbyterian Church (U.S.A) in Persia. Note

Allen, George Venable, born 3 November 1903 at Durham, N.C., and educated at the local Duke Uni-versity and at Harvard, he entered the foreign service in 1930, and was ambassador to Iran from 1946 to 1948. He wrote *Report on India* (1954). He died in Washington, D.C., on 11 July 1970. Master (5); Shavit; WhAm, 5

Allen, Harold Boughton, born 4 August 1891 at Carlton, N.Y., he was a graduate of Rutgers University. Between the two world wars he was an officer in the Near East Relief in the Middle East and North Africa. His writings include *Come over into Macedonia; the story of a ten-year adventure in uplifting a war-torn people* (1943), *Studies in rural education; rural welfare in Iran* (1943), *Rural education and welfare in the Middle East* (1946), *Rural reconstruction in action; experience in the Near and Middle East* (1953). He died after a traffic accident, 10 July 1970. LC; Shavit

Allen, Henry Elisha, born 13 June 1902 at Orange, N.J., he was educated at Yale and the University of Chicago, where he obtained a Ph.D. in 1930 for his thesis, *The Turkish transformation; a study in social and religious development*. Thereafter he was a university professor and community administrator in the United States. He died 27 June 1985. WhAm, 8

Allen, James de Vere, born in 1936, he wrote *Swahili regalias* (1976), *Lamu* (1971), *Swahili origins* (1992). He died in 1990. LC

Allen, James Garland, born in 1900, he was in 1935 affiliated with the University of Colorado. His writings include *Naval history and strategy; a syllabus and guide to reading for Naval history 3, University of Colorado* (1944), and *A guide to the study of the history of the British Empire* (1949). LC

Allen, M. J. S., fl. 1975, he was a sometime member of H.M.'s Diplomatic Service who travelled extensively in Jordan and the Arabian Peninsula where he gained practical experience of falconry. Note

Allen, Orson P., born 6 November 1827 at Smyrna, N.Y. After graduation from Amherst College, and Andower Theological Seminary he sailed from Boston with his wife, Caroline R. Wheeler, and arrived in Smyrna, Turkey, in December 1853. Stationed for a one-year term as missionary at Trebizond, the couple was then sent to Harput, where they stayed until 1896, when Mrs. Allen's failing health compelled their return to the United States. After his wife's death, Rev. Allen spent many years in the U.S. before returning to Turkey with his daughter, Annie T. Allen, a Woman's Board Mission for the Pacific missionary, and made his home with her in Bursa station until the pressure of the first World War compelled them to withdraw to Constantinople, where he died on 21 June 1918. *Missionary herald*, 114 (1918), p. 438

Allen, Roger Michael Ashley, born 24 January 1942 in Devon, England, he received a D.Phil. in 1967 from Oxford University for *An annotated translation and study of the third edition of "Hadith Isa ibn Hisham" by Muhammad al-Muwailihi*. He was for over twenty years a professor of Arabic literature in the University of Pennsylvania, Philadelphia, Pa. His writings include *A study of Hadith 'Isa ibn Hisham*, a work which is based on his thesis, *The Arabic novel* (1982), and he was a joint editor of *Modern Arabic drama* (1995). DrAS, 74 F; IntAu&W, 1989; *MESA Roster of members*, 1977-1990; Sluglett

Allen, Roland, born 29 December 1869 at the Friary, Derby, England, and a graduate of St. John's College, Oxford, he was ordained in 1892 at the Clergy Training School, Leeds. In the same year he was accepted as a missionary by the Society for the Propagation of the Gospel and sent out to North China in 1895. With interruptions, he served there until 1903, when he returned to England, where he became an advocate of the ideas of the independent native Churches as well as the World Dominion Movement. In 1931, he went to Kenia, where he remained until his death in June 1947. His writings include *Missionary methods* (1912), and *The ministry of the spirit* (1960). He is the subject of two biographies: *Reform of the ministry; a study in the* *work of Roland Allen*, by David M. Paton (1968), and *Roland Allen; sein Leben und Werk*, by Hans W. Metzner (1970). Lodwick

Allen, Thomas Gaskell, Jr., he wrote *Across Asia on a bicycle; the journey of two American students from Constantinople to Peking* (1894). LC

Allen, William, born in 1793 at Weymouth, Dorset, he entered the Royal Navy in 1805 and accompanied the expedition to Niger under R. Landers, 1832-1834. In 1849 he travelled through Syria and Palestine and afterwards advocated the construction of a canal between the Mediterranean Sea and the Gulf of Aqaba. His writings include *Picturesque views on the River Niger* (1840), *A narrative of the expedition sent by H.M.'s Government to the River Niger in 1841* (1848), and *The Dead Sea, a new route to India* (1855). He died in 1864. DNB; Henze

Allen, William Edward David, born 6 January 1901 at London, and educated at Eton, he was a sometime Information Officer and special correspondent in the Near and Middle East. His writings include *The Turks in Europe* (1919), *A history of the Georgian people* (1932), *Guerilla war in Abyssinia* (1943), *Caucasian battlefields* (1953), *Problems of Turkish power in the sixteenth century* (1963). He died 18 September 1973. LC; WhE&EA; *Who was who*, 7

Allgrove, Joan, born 18 December 1928 in England and educated at Reading University, she became in 1960 a keeper of Textiles at the Whitworth Art Gallery, and subsequently attached to the University of Manchester. Her interest in the Islamic world was stimulated by a period of study in Isfahan. She was joint author of *The Qashqa'i of Iran* (1976). Ill-health forced her to retire prematurely in 1982. She was married in second marriage to her colleague D. M. McDowell. She died 15 February 1991. *Iran* 29 (1991), p. vi

Alling, Joseph Tilden, born 19 January 1855 at Rochester, N.Y., and educated at the University of Rochester, he became a businessman, community officer, and president of Alling & Cory Co., Rochester, N.Y., from 1908 to 1935. He died in Rochester, N.Y., 20 September 1937. WhAm, 1

Alling, Paul Humiston, born 15 July 1896 at Hamden, Conn., he was educated at the University of Pennsylvania, Philadelphia, Pa., and in 1921 he entered the U.S. Foreign Service. He was a consul in the Middle East and North Africa. He died 18 January 1949. WhAm, 2

von Allioli, Joseph Franz, born 10 August 1793 at Sulzbach, Germany, he received a doctorate in 1816, and was ordained a Catholic priest in the same year. Thereafter he studied Oriental languages at Wien, Roma, and Paris. He taught at the universities of Landshut and München from 1821 to 1834. Since 1838 he was at Augusburg, where he died on 22 May 1873. DtBE

Allison, Anthony Clifford, he was a member of the Oxford University Mount Kenya Expedition of 1949. In 1951 he was affiliated with the Anthropological Laboratory, Department of Human Anatomy, Oxford. He was joint editor of *Immunosuppressive and antiinflammatory drugs* (1993). Note

Allison, Oliver Claude, C.B.E., born 28 May 1908 at Stafford, and educated at Cambridge, he was from 1938 to 1948 a missionary in Juba, Somalia, and afterwards bishop in the Sudan until 1974. He wrote *A pilgrim church's progress* (1966). He died on 7 June 1989. *Who was who*, 8

Allix, André François Emile, born 3 September 1889 at Gap (Hautes-Alpes), and educated at Grenoble and Paris. After obtaining his teaching diploma at Lyon, he taught there from 1914 until 1918, when he moved to the Lycée Champollion in Grenoble. It was here that he researched his study of the *Massif de l'Oisans* , for which he was awarded a doctorate by the Université de Grenoble in 1929. Already in 1928, he had moved back to Lyon, where he had been appointed to the Chair of Regional Geography at the Faculté des Lettres, a post he held until his retirement. Almost concurrently, from 1928 to 1959, he was the editor of the *Revue de géographie de Lyon*. Academically, his most important appointment was that of *recteur* of the Académie de Lyon since 1944. His writings include *Géographie pour l'enseignement secondaire* (1934), and *Géographie des textiles* (1957). He died 27 May 1966. *Revue de géographie de Lyon* 41 (1966), 95-98; WhoFr, 1965/66

Allix, Jean Pierre, fl. 1958, he was a joint author of several geography textbooks, including *Travaux pratiques de géographie* (1969). BN

Allman, Timothy D., born 16 October 1944 in Florida, he was from 1970 to 1978 a student at St. Antony's College, Oxford, concentrating on Indo-China. Private

Allmen-Joray, France von, fl. 1971 he was a joint author of *Le Mariage; lieu d'un rapport entre famille et société*, a study of the Secrétariat d'État au plan, Association algérienne pour la recherche démographique, économique et sociale, Alger, published in the late 1970s. LC

34

Allmen-Joray, Malik von, fl. 1971, he was a joint author of *Le Mariage; lieu d'un rapport entre famille et société*, published in the late 1970s.

Allon, Yigal, born 10 October 1918 at Kefar Tavor, Palestine; he was an Israeli politician and military officer who studied at the Hebrew University, Jerusalem, and at Oxford. His writings include *Shield of David* (1970), and *My father's house* (1976). He died in Afulah, Israel, in 1980. AnObit, 1980; CurBio, 1980; EncJud; Master (8)

Allotte de la Fuÿe, François Maurice, born in 1844, he wrote *Documents présargoniques* (1912).

Allouni, Abdel Aziz, Dr., he was born in Syria and graduated from AUB. He did graduate work at Cornell University, Ithaca, N.Y., and the Graduate Faculty of Political and Social Science, New York. In 1957, he was counsellor at the Embassy of the United Arab Republic in Washington, D.C., and in 1971, ambassador of Syria in Pakistan. *Who's who in the Arab world, 1967/68, p. 769*

Allum, Percy, Dr., he was in 1979 a reader in politics in the University of Reading, and sponsored by the Inter-University Council for Higher Education to teach in the University of Khartoum. His writings include *The Italian Communist Party since 1945* (1970), and *State and society in Western Europe* (1995). LC

'Allūsh, Nājī, born in 1935 at Bir Zeit, Palestine. His writings include الحركة القومية العربية (Beirut, 1975), and الثورة الفلسطنية (1970), and فكر حركة المقاومة الفلسطنية (1993). LC

Allworth, Edward Alfred, born 1 December 1920 at Columbia, S.C., he received a Ph.D. in 1959 from Columbia University, New York, for his thesis, *The Soviet Russian impact on Uzbek literary activity*. In 1961 he was appointed professor of Turco-Soviet studies at Columbia. His writings include *Uzbek literary politics* (1965), *Central Asian publishing and the rise of nationalism* (1965), *The nationality question in Soviet Central Asia* (1973), and *Soviet Asia, bibliographies; a compilation of social science and humanities sources on the Iranian, Mongolian, and Turkic nationalities* (1975). ConAu, 101; Schoeberlein; WhoAm, 1980/81-1984/85

Almagià, Roberto, born 17 June 1884 at Firenze, he was a sometime professor of geography at the universities of Padua and Roma. His writings include *Studi geografici sopra le frane in Italia* (1907-1910), *La questione de la Palestina* (1918), and *Palestine* (1932). He died in 1962. LC; *Who's who in Italy, 1958*

Almagor, Ella, fl. 1979, born 20th cent., she wrote *Kitve-ha-yad shel Midreshe R. David ha-Nagid; mehkar bibliyografi* (1995), and she edited ذم الدنا, of Ibn Abī Dunyā (1984). LC

Almagro Bosch, Martin, born 17 April 1911 at Tramacastilla, Spain, he was educated at the universities of Valencia and Madrid, where he obtained a doctorate in 1935; afterwards he studied at Wien and Marburg. From 1968 to 1981 he was director of the Museo Nacional Arqueológico, Madrid. He excavated widely in the Middle East. His writings include *Prehistoria del norte de Africa y del Sáhara español* (1946), *Ampurias, history of the city and guide to the excavations* (1956). He died in Madrid, 28 August 1984. Egyptology

Almagro y Cárdenas, Antonio, born in 1856 at Granada, he was a sometime professor of Arabic and Hebrew at the universities of Salamanca and Granada. He contributed to *La Ilustración española* and *La Alhambra* (Granada), as well as to other literary periodicals. His writings include *Museo granadino de antigüedades árabes* (1886), and *Estudios sobre las inscripciones árabes de Granada* (1877). LC; Mazanares, pp. 197-199; Ossario; Sabater

Almagro Gorbea, Antonio, born 20th cent., he received a doctorate and was in 1981 a professor at the Escuela de Arquitectura de Madrid, specializing in the restauration of Islamic architecture. His writings include *Tres monumentos islámicos restaurados por España en el mundo árabe* (1981), *El palacio omeya de Amman* (1983), and he edited *Fotogrametria y reprentación de la arquitectura* (1988). Arabismo, 1992-1997

Almásy, György (Georg), Dr., born 15 October 1864 at Kétegyháza, Hungary, his writings include *Utazásom orosz Turkesztánba* (1901), and *Vándorutam Ázsia szívébe Írta* (1903). He died in Graz, Austria, 22 September 1933. Magyar; *Magyar életrejzi lexikon*, Budapest, 1967-69

Almásy, Lászlo Ede de, born 22 August 1895 at Borostyankő, Hungary, he travelled widely in northeastern Africa and wrote *Récentes explorations dans le Désert libyque, 1932-1936* (Le Caire, 1936), and *Unbekannte Sahara; mit Flugzeug und Auto in der Libyschen Wüste*, a translation of his *Az ismeretlen Sahara* (Leipzig, 1939). He died in Salzburg, 22 March 1951. Magyar; MEL, 1967-69

Almkvist, Herman Napoleon, born 28 April 1839 at Stockholm, he was a sometime professor of Semitic languages at Uppsala Universitet. He travelled in Turkey and Egypt in 1877-78. His writings include *Die Bischari-Sprache in Nordost-Afrika* (1881-85), *Nubische Studien aus dem Sudan, 1877-78* (1911). He died in Uppsala, 30 September 1904. Aalto, p. 43; Hill; *Svensk biografiskt lexikon*

Alnasrawi, Abbas Abdel-Karim, born 20th cent., he received a Ph.D. from Harvard in 1965 for *Financing economic development in Iraq*. Afterwards he was a professor of economics at the University of Vermont. His writings include *Arab oil and United States energy requirements* (1982), *OPEC in a changing world economy* (1985), *Arab nationalism, oil, and the political economy of dependency* (1991), *The Economy of Iraq; oil, wars, destruction of development and prospects, 1950-2010* (1994). AmM&WSc, 1978 S; *MESA Roster of members*, 1977-1990; NatFacDr, 1995-2003

Alon, Ilai, born 20th cent., his writings include a Hebrew translation of Averroes (1985), and *Socrates in medieval Arabic literature* (1991). LC

Alonso, Carlos, O.S.A., born 20th cent., he wrote *Los mandeos y las misiones católicas en la primera mitad del s. XVII* (1967), *Una gloria del Levante español* (1971), and *Augustinian law and charism* (1988). LC

Alonso, Dámaso, LL.L., M.A., Ph.D., Litt.D., born 22 October 1898 at Madrid, he was a writer and poet, and a professor of Romance languages at the Universdad de Madrid. He was a visiting professor at many universities throughout the world. His writings include *La lengua poética de Góngora* (1938). GER; MEW; *Who's who in Spain*, 1963

Alonso Alonso, Manuel, S.J., born in 1893, he wrote *Teologia de Averroës* (1947), *Temas filosoficos medievales; Ibn Dawud y Gundisalvo* (1959), and the translation of al-Farabi, *La ciudad ideal* (1985). LC

Alonso y Sanjurjo, Eugenio, born 19th cent., his writings include *Apuntes sobre los proyectos de abolición de la esclavitud en las islas de Cuba y Puerto Rico* (1874). His trace is lost after a publication in 1881. LC

Alp, Tekin *see* Tekinalp, Munis

Alpat, Sabahaddin, fl. 1971, he was a sometime president of the State Institute of Statistics, Turkey.

Alpatov, Mikhail Vladimirovich, born 27 November (10 December), 1902 at Moscow, he studied fine art at Moscow University and became professor of history of art. His writings include *Geschichte der altrussischen Kunst* (1932), *Russian impact on art* (1950). GSE; Int WW, 41th (1977/78)

Alpers, Edward Alter, born 23 April 1941 at Phiiadelphia, Pa., he studied at Harvard and London, where he obtained a Ph.D. in 1966. Afterwards he was a professor of history at UCLA., he wrote *The East African slave trade* (1967), *Ivory and slaves* (1975), *Walter Rodney, revolutionary and scholar* (1982). *Directory of American scholars*, 1982

Alphandéry, Paul, born in 1875. His writings include *Les idées morales chez les hétérodoxes latins au début du XIIIe siècle* (c1903, 1983), *La chrétienté et l'idée de croisade* (1954). He died in 1932. LC

Alpher, Joseph, born 20th cent., he was atttached to the Jaffee Center for Strategic Studies, Tel-Aviv University in 1992. His writings include *Israel's Lebanon policy* (1984), *The Decade of the 1990s* (1990), and he edited *War in the Gulf; implications for Israel* (1992). LC

Alport, Cuthbert James McCall, Baron of Colchester, born 22 March 1912, he was educated at Pembroke College, Cambridge. He was a Conservative politician. His writings include *Kingdoms in partnership* (1937), *Hope in Africa* (1952), and *The sudden assignment* (1965). He died 28 October 1998. Who, 1980-1999

Alport, E. A., fl. 1963, he was a sociologist whose special area of study was the Maghrib.

Alquier, Jeanne, wife of Prosper Alquier (1890-1958), she was an archaeologist in her own right and excavated at Zana, Algeria. In 1931 she was awarded the Médaille Paul Blanchet and in 1941 she was keeper at the Musée Stéphane Gsell, Algiers. With her husband, she published *La Chettaba et les grottes à inscriptions latines du Chettaba et du Taya* (Constantine, 1929). *Revue africaine* 72 (1931), 365-369

Alric, Arthur, born 19th cent., he wrote *Un diplomate ottoman en 1836 (affaire Churchill), traduction... de l'«Éclairissement» (Tebstreh) d'Akif-Pacha, ministre des affaires étrangères de Turquie* (Paris, 1892), and *Le paradis de Mahomet, suivi de l'Enfer, d'après le Coran et le Prophète*, traduit de l'arabe (Paris, 1892). BN

AlRoy, Gil Carl, born 7 November 1924 at Cernauti, Romania, he studied at City College of New York, and Princeton University, where he obtained a Ph.D. in political science for his thesis *Radicalism and modernization; the French problem* (1962). He was a sometime professor of political science at Hunter College. His writings include *The involvement of peasants in internal wars* (1966), *Behind the Middle East conflict* (1975), *The Kissinger experience* (1975), *The Middle East uncovered* (1979). AM&WSc, 1968; CnDiAmJBi; *Who's who in the East*, 1977

Alsayyad, M. M., 1916- *see* Sayyad, Muhammad Mahmud al-

Alsdorf, Ludwig, born 8 August 1904 at Laufersweiler, Germany, he studied Oriental languages, including Arabic and Persian at Heidelberg, Hamburg and Berlin, and received a Dr.phil. in 1928 at Hamburg with a thesis on Indian literature. Thereafter he was professor of Indology at various German universities. From 1930 to 1932 he was a reader in German language at Allahabad University. In all, he made a dozen visits to India. He wrote *Indien* (1940). He died in Buchholz, 25 March 1978. DtBE; Stache-Rosen, pp. 239-40

Alt, Albrecht, born 20 September 1883 at Stübach, Germany, he received a doctorate in 1909 from the Universität Greifswald for his thesis, *Israel und Ägypten; die politischen Beziehungen der Könige von Israel und Juda zu den Pharaonen.* Thereafter he was professor of Biblical studies at the universities of Basel, Halle, and Leipzig. He died in Leipzig, 24 April 1956. Dawson; DtBE; Egyptology

Altamira y Crevea, Rafael, born 10 February 1866 at Alicante, he was educated at Valencia, and became a professor at Oviedo and Madrid, and a sometime member of the International Court of Justice, den Haag. In 1944 he emigrated to Mexico. His writings include *La enseñanza de la historia* (1891), and *Cuenteos de Levante* (1895). He died in Mexico City, 1 June 1951. IndiceE³ (9); *Isis*, 43 (1952), p. 117; MEW; Sabater; Sainz

Altaner, Berthold, born 10 September 1885 at St. Annaberg, Germany, he studied Catholic theology at the Universität Breslau, where he obtained a doctorate in 1910. His writings include *Patrologie* (1938). He died in Bad Kissingen, 30 January 1964. DtBE

Altekar, Ananta Sadashiv. His writings include *A history of village communities in western India* (1927), and *Catalogue of the Gupta gold coins in the Bayana hoard* (1954). LC

von **Alten**, Georg Karl Friedrich Viktor, born 24 April 1846 at Potsdam, Germany, he was a Prussian officer and a lecturer at the military college (Kriegsakademie), Potsdam, he wrote *Studies in applied tactics* (1908), and *Die Kriege, vom Altertum bis zur Gegenwart* (1912). He died in Berlin, 28 April 1912. DtBE

Alter, S. Neale, Rev.; he was a missionary and director of the Jibrail Rural Fellowship Centre, Lebanon, in 1955. He wrote *Studies in Bahaism* (Beirut, 1923). LC

Altheim, Franz, born 6 October 1898 at Frankfurt am Main, he was for many years a professor of history at the universities of Frankfurt, Halle, and Berlin, where he taught classical history as well as history of religion. His writings include *Attila und die Hunnen* (1951), its translation, *Attila et les Huns* (1952), and with his wife, Ruth Stiehl, *Die Araber in der alten Welt* (1964-68). He died in Münster, 17 October 1976. DtBE; HbDtWiss; Kürschner, 1931-1976; *Wer ist wer*, 1950-1971/73

Altheim née **Stiehl**, Ruth, born 13 March 1926 at Forst, Lausitz, Germany, she studied at Halle, Erlangen and Freie Universität, Berlin, where she received a Dr.phil. in 1951 for *Fünf Gedichte aus dem Diwan des Ka'b Ibn Zuhair* and also a Dr.habil. in 1956 for *Die Datierung der kapitolinischen Fasten.* She was a professor at Freie Universität Berlin until 1976, when she became a professor of ancient history, and director, Institut für Epigraphie, Universität Münster. She was joint author, with her husband, Franz Altheim, of *Die Araber in der alten Welt* (1964-68). Kürschner, 1961-1996|; Thesis; *Wer ist wer*, 1976/77-1995/96|

Altmann, Alexander, born 16 April 1906 at Kassa, Austro-Hungary, he studied at Humboldt Universität, Berlin, where he received a Dr.phil. in 1931 for his thesis, *Die Grundlagen der Wertethik.* In the same year, he started serving as rabbi in Berlin, and concurrently lectured in philosophy at the Rabbinerseminar zu Berlin. In 1938 he was appointed rabbi of Manchester. Afterwards he settled in the United States. His writings include *Studies in religious philosophy and mysticism* (1969), *The meaning of Jewish existence* (1991). With S. M. Stern he published *Isaac Israeli* (1958). In 1982 he was presented with the felicitation volume *Mystics, philosophers, and politicians; essays in Jewish intellectual history in honor of Alexander Altmann.* He died in 1987. CnDiAmJBi; DrAS, 1982 P; EncJud.; WhoAm, 1978; WhoWorJ, 1987; Wininger

Altoma, Salih Jawad, born 23 September 1929 at Kerbala, Iraq, he was educated at the universities of Baghdad and Harvard, where he obtained a Ph.D. in 1957 for *The teaching of classical Arabic to speakers of colloquial in Iraq.* He was a professor of Near Eastern languages and cultures and comparative literature at Indiana University from 1964 until his retirement. His writings include *Palestinian themes in modern Arabic literature* (1969), *Modern Arabic poetry in English translation; a bibliography* (1993), as well as works in Arabic. DrAS, 1982

Altrincham, Edward William Macleay Grigg, Baron of Tormarton, born 8 September 1879, he was educated at Oxford. He was a sometime editor of *The Times*, a politician, and Minister Resident in the Middle East, 1944 to 1945. His writings include *The British Commonwealth* (1944), and *British foreign policy* (1944). He died on 1 December 1955. *Who was who*, 5

Altstadt-Mirhadi, Audrey L., born 16 November 1953, she graduated in 1975 from the University of Illinois and received her Ph.D. in 1983 from the University of Chicago for *The Azerbaijani Turkish community of Baku before World War I*. She received post-doctoral fellowships from the Russian Research Center at Harvard University and the George F. Kennan Institute of Advanced Russian Studies. She conducted research in Baku during 1980-81 and 1984-85 and was the first American to gain access to the Azerbaijan State Historical Archives. She was a member of the History Department in the University of Massachusetts at Amherst. Her writings include *The Azerbaijani Turks* (1992). LC; Note; WhoE, 1993/94

Alvarado Socastro, Salustio, born 20th cent., he received a doctorate in Semitic philology, with special refrence to apocryphal literature. He was a professor at the Departamento de Filología Eslava in the Universidad Complutense de Madrid. Arabismo, 1992, 1994, 1997

Alvarez, David J., fl. 1974. His writings include *Bureaucracy and cold war diplomacy; the United States and Turkey, 1943-1946* (1980); he was joint editor of *Religion and society in the American West* (1987). LC

Álvarez de Morales y Ruiz-Matas, Camilo, born 20th cent., he obtained a doctorate in 1992 in philosophy and letters and became affiliated with the Escuela de Estudios Arabes, C.S.I.C., Granada. His writings include *"El libro de la almohada" de Ibn Wafid de Toledo* (1980), and he edited and translated *Mujtasar fi l-tibb; compendio de medicina* (1992). Arabismo, 1994, 1997

Álvarez Millán, Cristina, born 20th cent., she received a diploma and a doctorate in Semitic philology, with special reference to Arabic and Islamic studies. She was successively affiliated with the Universidad Complutense de Madrid and the Wellcome Institute for the History of Medicine, London. Arabismo, 1992, 1994, 1997

Álvarez-Perez, José, fl. 1877, he was a contributor to *La Ilustración española y americana*. His writings include *La cacerias en Marruecos; aventuras autenticas de un español* (1870). Ossorio

Álvarez-Rubiano, Pablo, born 7 June 1910 at Almadén, Spain. After studies at Valencia and Madrid, he was professor at various Spanish universities. His writings include *Pedrarias Dávila; contribución al estudios de la figura del "Gran justador"* (1944), a work which was originally presented as his doctoral dissertation, Madrid, 1939. LC; Who's who in Spain, 1963

Álvaro Zamora, María Isabel, born 20th cent., she received a doctorate in history of art, with special refrence to Aragon ceramics. She was a lecturer in fine art at the Universidad de Zaragoza. Her writings include *Saber ver el arte* (1974), *Cerámica y alfarería de Zaragoza* (1981), and *La cerámica de Teruel* (1987). Arabismo, 1992, 1994, 1997

d'Alverny, André, born around the end of the nineteenth century, he studied from 1929 to 1933 at the Jesuit Convent in Bikfaya, Lebanon, where he suffered the traditional Arabic teaching methods. In 1933 he returned to France to start studies in philosophy. In June 1937 he registered two theses titles at the Sorbonne, *Un savant syrien du IXe siècle, Qusta ibn Luqa*, and *L'épître de Qusta ibn Luqa sur la différence entre l'esprit et l'âme*, but his preoccupation with theological studies prevented the completion of his work. The outbreak of the second World War changed all his plans. In 1942 he departed for Lebanon by way of an intended brief stop-over in Tunis. Events turned this visit into a three-year residence. In 1945 he could finally continue his journey to Bikfaya, where he remained nineteen years until he died in 1966. His writings include *Petite introduction au parler libanais* (1964), *Manuel de langue arabe* (1965), *Cours de langue arabe* (1967). Arabica 14 (1967), pp. 1-4

d'Alverny, Marie-Thérèse, born 25 January 1903 at Boën (Loire), she was a medievalist who had studied at Strasbourg and Paris. From 1928 until her retirement in 1962 she was at the Bibliothèque Nationale de Paris as librarian and *conservateur*. Her writings include *Avicenne en Occident* (1993), *Pensée médiévale en Occident*, ed. by Charles Burnett (1995). She died 26 April 1991. WhoFr, 1977/78-1990/91

Alvi, Sajida Sultana née Malik, born 28 February 1941 at Amritsar, India, she received a Ph.D. in 1967 from the University of the Punjab, Pakistan. In 1993 she was teaching at the Institute of Islamic Studies, McGill University, Montreal. Her research focused on Indo-Islamic intellectual history. She was a gold medalist of the University of the Punjab, and was awarded research fellowships in 1981, 1985, and 1987. She was a member of MESA and wrote *Advice on the art of governance: an Indo-Islamic mirror for princes* (1989). LC

Alvie, Zahira, fl. 1975; she was a sometime researcher at the Pakistan Institute of Development Economics.

Alwan, Abdul Sahib H., born in 1926 at Kazimiyah, Iraq, he received a Ph.D. in 1957 from the University of Wisconsin for his thesis, *The process of economic development in Iraq*. He was Minister of Agrarian Reform in Iraq from 1963 to 1965, and in 1968, project manager of the UNDP pre-investment survey of the north-western zone of the United Arab Republic. His writings include *Dirāsat fī al-islāh al-zirā'i* (1961), and *The role of agrarian reform in the reconstruction and development of Iraqi agriculture* (1977). LC

'**Alwan**, Muhammad Yusuf, Ph.D., he was in 1975 a professor of comparative law at the Faculty of Law in the University of Jordan. His writings include القانون الدولي العام (1978). Note

Alyami, Ali Hassan, fl. 1979, he received a Ph.D. in 1977 from Claremont Graduate School for his thesis, *The impact of modernization on the stability of the Saudi monarchy.*

Am Zehnhoff, Albert J., Dr., born in 1941, he was resident in Trogen, Switzerland, in 1973. He was a sometime professor of geography and wrote *Portugal; Kunst, Kultur und Landschaft* (1979), as well as other European travel guides. LC

Amad, Adnan, born 13 June 1936 at Jerusalem, he was educated at St. George's School, Jerusalem, 1942-1954, and afterwards studied at AUB, and the universities of Wien, and Köln, where he receivned a Dr.phil. in 1969 for his thesis *Die politische-soziale Problematik der arabischen Einheitsbestrebungen.* His writings include *Israeli League for Human and Civil Rights* (1973), and *Documents and reports on Israeli violations of human and civil rights* (1975). LC

d'Amade, Albert Gérard Léo, Comte, born 24 December 1856 at Toulouse, he graduated in 1876 from the École spéciale militaire and was posted to Constantine and Sétif, Algeria. He was a member of the Tunis expeditionary force, 1881-1882. With the rank of general, he participated in the pacification of Morocco, about which he wrote *Campagne de 1908-1909 en Chaouïa* (1911). He died in Fronsac (Gironde) on 11 November 1941. *Hommes et destins*, vol. 7, pp. 26-29

Amador, Mariano, born 19th cent., he contributed to the *Rivista contemporánea* from 1897 to 1899.

Amador de los Rios y Serrano, José, born in 1818 at Baena, Spain, he was a historian, but also a writer. His writings include *Études historiques, politiques et littéraires sur les juifs d'Espagne* (1861), *Monumentos mahometanos* (1877). He died in Sevilla in 1878. IndiceE³ (1)

Amador de los Rios y Villata, Rodrigo, born in 1843 at Madrid, he received a doctorate of law and was since 1911 a director of the Museo Arqueológico Nacional, Madrid. His writings include *Inscripciones árabes de Sevilla* (1875), *Inscripciones árabes de Córdoba* (1878), and *Estudio acerca de las enseñas musulmanas del Real monasterio de las Huelgas* (1893). He died in Madrid in 1917. LC; Sainz

Amady, Gabriel, born 20th cent., he was in 1972 *substitut général* at the Court of Appeal, Fort-Lamy, Chad.

Amady, Nathé, born 20th cent., he was in 1980 attorney general at the Court of Appeal, N'Djaména, Chad.

Amaldi, Daniela, fl. 1975. Her writings include *Pagino di un codice copto-arabo nel Museo nazionale di S. Matteo a Pisa* (1982). LC

Amalfi, Gaetano, born 14 July 1855 at Piano di Sorrento, he qualified in 1880 for law and became a magistrate and writer whose writings include *Canti del popolo di piano di Sorrento* (1883), and *Segregazione indeterminata* (1907). Chi è, 1908; IndBiltal (2)

Amalric, fl. 1926; he was an *ingénieur agronome*, an agricultural inspector in Casablanca, and joint author of *Esquisse agronomique et agrologique de la région de Sétif* (1922). BN

Aman, Muhammad Muhammad, born 3 January 1940 at Alexandria, Egypt., he obtained a Ph.D. in 1968 from the University of Pittsburgh for his thesis, *Analysis of terminolgy, form and structure of subject headings in Arabic literature and formulation of rules for Arabic subject headings.* In 1969 he was a library science librarian and lecturer in the School of Library and Information Science, Pratt Institute, Brooklyn, N.Y. His writings include *Arab states author headings* (1973), and *Arab periodicals and serials; a subject bibliography* (1979). ConAu, 49-52; Master (4)

Aman Allah, Amir of Afghanistan, born in 1892, ruler of Afghanistan from 1919 to 1929, at first with the title of amir, and from 1926 on with that of shah. In 1929 he went into exile in Italy, where he died on 21 September 1961. EncIran

Amani, Mahdi, born in 1308/1929, he was an Iranian sociologist whose writings include *Ravish'ha-yi tahlili-i jam'iyat'shinasi* (1964), and *Quelques aspects démographiques de la population d'Iran* (1968). LC

Amantos, Konstantinos Ioannou, born 2 August 1874 at Chios, Greek Aegaen Island, he was an elementary school teacher in his home town before studying from 1899 to 1903 at the Universität München, where he obtained a Dr.phil. for his thesis *Die Suffixe der neugriechischen Ortsnamen.* Afterwards he was professor of Greek history at Athens University. His writings include Σχέσεις Ελλήνων και Τούρκων (1955). He died in Athens in 1960. EEE

Amanzholov, Altai Sarsenovich, born 2 June 1934 at Alma-Ata, he received a doctorate in 1975 from the University of Alma-Ata for *Материалы и исследования по истории дренетюркской письменности.* He was a professor of Kazakh philology in the Kazakh Pedagogical Institute. His writings include *Глагольное управление в языке древненетюркских памятников* (1969). *Казахская ССР краткая энциклопедия,* vol. 3

Amanzholov, Sarsen Amanzhol, born 27 December 1903, he wrote *Казак тили грамматикасы* (1955), and *Вопросы диалектологии и истории казахского языка* (1959). He died 28 January 1958. *Казахская ССР краткая энциклопедия,* vol. 3; KazakSE

Amar, Émile, born 19th cent., he obtained a doctorate of law in 1913 at Paris for *L'organisation de la propriété foncière au Maroc.* He was the editor and translator of *Al-Fakhri; histoire des dynasties musulmanes depuis la mort de Mohamet jusqu'à la chute du khalifat abbaside de Bagdad* (1910.) NUC

Amar Nat'h, born in 1822, he was in Indian government service until 1845, and spent the rest of his life in intellectual pursuits. He wrote *Zafar'namah-i Ranjit Singh,* of which a Panjabi edition was published in 1983. He died from cholera on 1 August 1867. LC; Storey, 668-669

Amari, Michele Benedetto Gaetano, he was born 6 July 1806 at Palermo. The political views expressed in *La guerra del vespro siciliano* (1843) compelled him to live in exile until the establishment of the Risorgimento. He studied Arabic under Reinaud and de Slane in Paris, and published the first part of *Storia die musulmani di Sicilia* (1854). From 1860 to 1873 he was professor of Arabic language and literature at Palermo. His writings include *Biblioteca arabo-sicula* (1857), *I diplomi arabi del Reale archivio fiorentino* (1863), and *Le epigrafi arabiche de Sicilia* (1875-1879). He died in Firenze, 16 July 1889. *Deutsche Rundschau* 60 (1889), 438-447; DizBI; EEE; Fück

Amat, Charles, born 1852, he was a medical doctor who published in *Gazette médicale de Paris.* He wrote *Le M'zab et les M'zabites* (Paris, 1888). BN

Amato, Angelo, born 21 December 1909 at Paterno (Catania), he was a professor of *scienza delle finanze,* and a sometime director, Istituto di Scienze economiche dell'Università di Messina. His writings include *Finanza di guerra* (1940), *Lineamenti di scienza delle finanze* (1954), *Lineamenti del bilancio dello Stato e del sistema tributario italiano* (1957), *Finanza pubblica* (1965), and *Il nostro sistema tributario dopo la riforma* (1973). IndBiltal (1)

Ambashthya, Brahmadeva Prasad, born 20th cent., he was in 1962 affiliated with the K. P. Jayaswal Research Institute, Patna. His writings include *Decisive battles of Sher Shah* (1977), and *Non-Persian sources on Indian medieval history* (1984). LC; Note

Ambros, Arne Amadeus, born 2 May 1942 at Wien, he received a Dr.phil. in 1972 from the Universität Wien for *Die morphologische Funktion des Systems der Vokalqualitäten im Althocharabischen.* He was an assistant at the Oriental Institute, Universität Wien, a lecturer at the Orient-Akademie der Hammer-Purgstall-Gesellschaft, and concurrently a court interpreter. From 1972 to 1974 he was visiting professor at UCLA. His writings include *Einführung in die moderne arabische Schriftsprache* (1969), and *Damascus Arabic* (1977). Kürschner, 1992-2003

Ambrose, Gwilyn Prichard, fl. 1931. He wrote *A history of Wales* (1947).

Ambrosini, Gaspare, born 24 October 1886 at Favara, Italy, he was professor of constitutional law in the Università di Roma, and a sometime president of the Assemblea constituente. His writings include *L'Italia nel Mediterraneo* (1927), *Paesi sotto mandato* (1927), *I problemi del Mediterraneo* (1937), *The Regime of the Straits* (1941). Chi è, 1928-1961; Who's who in Italy, 1980

Amedroz, Henry Frederick, a descendant of a Huguenot family, he was born in 1854, and educated at Winchester, where he gained a scholarship in 1866. He passed the examination for Turkish dragomans in 1877, but was rejected on medical grounds. He was called to the bar in 1882, and for several years was one of the bar reporters in the Chancery Courts. During this time he took up the study of Arabic, and afterwards spent much of his life in private research at libraries, both English and foreign, containing Arabic MSS. His writings include *The historical remains of Hilâl al-Sâbi* (1904), and *History of Damascus, 263-555 A.H., by Ibn al-Qalânisi* (1908). He died in March 1917. JRAS, 1917, pp. 632-633

Ameer Ali, Syed, 1849-1928 *see* Ali, Syed Ameer

Ameer Ali, Syed Waris *see* Ali, Syed Waris Ameer

Amélineau, Émile Clément, born 28 August 1850 at La Chaize-Giraud (Vendée), he wrote *La géographie de*

l'Egypte à l'époque copte (1893), and other works on the pre-Islamic period of Egypt. He died in Châteaudun on 12 January 1915. Dawson; DBF; Egyptology

Amer, Moustafa, born 16 June 1896 at Cairo, he studied at Cairo and Liverpool; he became professor of geography at the University of Cairo, and later, rector of the University of Alexandria, and director-general of the Egyptian Antiquities Service. He died in 1873. Egyptology

Ames, David Wason, born 30 May 1922 at Crawfordsville, Ind., he received a Ph.D. in 1953 from Northwestern University for his thesis, *Plural marriage among the Wolof in the Gambia*. With Anthony V. King he published *Glossary of Hausa music and its social context*. AM&WSc, 1973 S; Unesco

Ames, Joseph, 1689-1759, he was a bibliographer and antiquary whose writings include *Typographical antiquities, being an historical accout of printing in England* (1749). DNB

Amicis, Edmondo de, 1846-1908 see De Amicis, Edmondo

Amin, Ahmad, born in 1886 at Cairo, he was an educator, a lecturer in Arabic, an author, and a member of the Arabic Language Academy. Two of his works have been translated into English, *My life; the auto-biography of an Egyptian scholar, writer, and cultural leader* (1978), and *Orient and Occident; an Egyptian's quest for national identity* (1984). He died in Cairo, 30 May 1954. William Eugene Shepard completed a Ph.D. thesis in 1973 entitled *The faith of a modern Muslim intellectual; the religious aspects and implications of the writings of Ahmad Amin*. BioIn, 12; Goldschmidt; Selim

Amin, Hafizullah, born in 1929 at Kabul, he studied in the United States from 1962 to 1965 but without taking a degree. In 1979, he was prime minister, foreign minister, and president of Afghanistan. He was killed on 27 December 1979. Adamec

Amin, Muharram Muhammad, born in 1921 in Sulaymaniyah, Iraq, he was a Kurdish author whose writings include *Mam Homar*, (1954), and *Gird-i shahidan* (1958).

Amin, Osman, Dr., born in 1905, he completed post-graduate studies at Paris and was a sometime professor of philosophy, as well as a dean, at Cairo University. He died after a long illness on 17 May 1978. MIDEO 14 (1980), pp. 398-404

Amin, Samir (ibn) Farid, born 4 September 1931 at Cairo, he was educated at the Université de Paris. Afterwards he was professor of economics at various French universities. His writings include *L'économie du Maghreb* (1966), ازمة المجتمع العربي (1985), and *Future of socialism* (1990). Africa who's who, 1991-1996; AnaBrit; IntWW, 1990/91-2001|; LC; Master (5); MidE, 1982/83

Amin, Sayed Hassan, born in 1948, he was an international lawyer and arbitrator, specializing in developing countries and the Middle East. His writings include *International and legal problems of the Gulf* (1981), *Commercial law of Iran* (1986), *Law and justice in contemporary Yemen* (1987), *Commercial arbitration in Islamic and Iranian law* (1988), and *Law, reform, and revolution in Afghanistan* (1991). LC

Amin, Tahir, born 20th cent., he studied international relations at Quaid-i-Azam University, Pakistan, and Carleton University, Ottawa. In 1984 he started a teaching career at Quaid-i-Azam University. He wrote *Afghanistan crisis* (1982). LC

Amin, 'Uthman, 1905-1978 see Amin, Osman

'Amir, Ahmad, fl. 1965, he wrote مالية دولة اتحاد الجمهورية العربية (1973). LC

'Amir, Ibrahim, fl. 1973, he was foreign affairs editor of the Cairo المصور, and wrote الارض و الفلاح (1956).

Amir Moezzi, Mohammad Ali, born 26 January 1956 at Tehran, he was educated at the Sorbonne, where he received a doctorate for his thesis, *Le guide divin dans le shî'isme originel*, in 1990. His main fields of research were Shi'ism, Sufism, and Islamic philosophy. He was a contributor to *Abstracta iranica*. In 1993, he was professor of Islamic studies at École pratique des Hautes études, Paris. AnEIFr, 1995, 1997; Private; THESAM, 4

Amiranashvili, Shalva IAsonovich, born in 1899 at Oni, Georgia, he was a historian of Georgian and Iranian art. His writings include the translations, *Georgian art* (1968), *Georgian metalwork* (1971), and *Kunstschätze Georgiens* (1971). GSE

Amirchanjanz (Amirkhanianz), Abraham, born 30 November 1838 at Shusha, Azerbaijan, he was educated by his father who taught him Persian, Azeri, and Arabic. In 1857, at the death of his father, who had worked

41

for the Evangelische Missionsgesellschaft in Basel, he was compelled by the Russian government to retire from Russia. Dr. F. M. von Zaremba of the Missionsgesellschaft arranged for him to study at Tartu (Dorpat), from where he was sent to the Basel Mission Institute from 1859-1865. He had to be ordained Lutheran pastor, since only Lutheran activities were tolerated in Russia. After he had completed his studies, the situation in Transcaucasia was such as to oblige him to work for thirteen years in the Armenian evangelical movement in Constantinople, before being stationed at the Tiflis Mission, soon to be exiled to Orenburg and, shortly thereafter, to Finland. Largely unsupported by any organization, he spent the last twenty years of his life among the Muslims of Varna, Bulgaria. His writings include *Die ökonomische Lage der Armenier in der Türkei*, a translation from the Armenian (1879), *Der Koran; eine Apologie des Evangeliums* (1905), as well as translations of the Koran into Armenian and Ottoman Turkish. Fifteen years before Atatürk, he published a project of the Turkish alphabet in Latin script. He died in Varna, 16 February 1913. *Muslim world*, vol. 29 (1939), pp. 394-400

Amirsadeghi, Hossein, fl. 1971, he wrote *The imperial Iranian family* (1977), and he edited *Twentieth century Iran* (1977), and *The security of the Persian Gulf* (1981). LC

Amitai (Amitay), Yossi, he obtained an M.A. in 1986 from the University of Tel-Aviv for *Mapam, 1948-1954*. His writings include *'Iltonut tahat kibush, 1968-1977* (1987), and *Ahavat-'amim be-mivhan* (1988). LC

Amjad, Rashid, born 30 July 1947, he was a sometime student at Queen's College, Cambridge, and in 1982, an assistant professor of economics, Punjab University, Lahore. His writings include *Private industrial investment in Pakistan, 1960-1970* (1982); he was joint author of *Industrial relations and the political process in Pakistan, 1947-1977* (1982), and *Quantitative techniques in employment planning* (Geneva, I.L.O., 1990); and he edited *Human resource planning; the Asian experience* (1987), and *To the Gulf and back; studies on the economic impact of Asian labour migration* (1989). LC

Ammar, Abbas Mustafa, born 10 December 1907 at Shammah, Egypt, and educated at the universities of Cairo, Manchester, and Cambridge, he received a Ph.D. in 1940 from the University of Manchester for *The people of Sharqiya*. Afterwards he was university teacher in England and Egypt. In later life, he held several political appointments in Egypt. His writings include *A demographic study of an Egyptian province* (LSE, 1942), *al-Madkhal al-Sharqi li-Misr* (1946). *Africa who's who*, 1991; LC; Unesco; WhoArab, 1978/79-1984/85|

'Ammar, Hamed Mustafa, born 25 February 1921 at Aswan, Egypt, he received a Ph.D. in 1951 from the London Institute of Education for his thesis *A study of growing up in an Egyptian village community*. Afterwards he was a sometime Egyptian regional advisor for human resource development with U.N.E.S.O.B. In 1986 he was regional consultant to the United Nations. His writings include *Growing up in Egypt* (1954), في اقتصاديات التعليم (1964), and في بناء البشر (1985). Unesco; WhoArab, 1978/79, 1984/85|

Ammor, M'Hamed, fl. 1980, he was a sometime president of the Court of Appeal in Rabat.

Amos, Sir Maurice Sheldon, born 15 June 1872 he was educated privately as well as at Cambridge and Paris. He was a barrister-at-law since 1897, a sometime judge in Cairo, judicial adviser to the Egyptian Government, and director of the Khedivial Law School. His writings include *The English constitution* (1930), *British justice* (1940) and, with Pierre Armijon, *A collection of problems and excercises in the civil and commercial law of Egypt* (1904). He died on 10 June 1940. *Who was who*, 3

Amos, Sheldon, born in 1835, he was a sometime reader in jurisprudence, University of London, who for health reasons settled in Egypt, where he practised law. His writings include *The science of law* (1874), and *Fifty years of the English constitution* (1880). He died in Egypt, 3 January 1886. DNB, vol. 22

Amouzegar, Jamshid, 1923- see Amuzgar, Jamshid

Ampère, Jean Jacques Antoine, born 12 August 1800 at Lyon, he was a man of letters and an historian. In the winter of 1844-5 he visited Abu Simbel and the Second Cataract in pursuit of antique remains, a journey described in his *Voyage en Égypte et en Nubie* (1868). His other writings include *La Grèce, Rome et Dante* (1848), and *La science et les lettres en Orient* (1865). He died in Paris, 26 or 27 March 1860. DBF; Hill

Amps, L. W., O.B.E. He was a civil engineer who served at the War Office with the Pioneer Corps which he left in the rank of lieuenant-colonel. In 1953, he was a director of the Gulf Engineering Company. Note

Amrouche, Jean, born 7 February 1906 at Ighil Ali, at Little Kabylia, Algeria, he was a descendant of a Catholic family and educated in Tunis and l'École normale, St-Cloud. Afterwards he was a teacher in

Tunis, a radio commentator, and an essayist in Algeria and Paris, where he died on 16 April 1962. His writings include *Un algérien s'adresse aux Français* (1994). A friend of his, Armand Guibert, wrote his biography *Jean Amrouche, 1906-1962* (1985). Hommes et destins, vol. 2, pp. 10-11; MEW

Amrouche, Marie-Louise Taos, born around the beginning of the twentieth century in North Africa into a Catholic Berber family. She was the daughter of Fadhma Aït Mansour Amrouche, born in 1882, and the sister of Jean Amrouche, 1906-1962. Under the title of *Le grain magique* (1966), she published a French version of the Berber poems and proverbs which her mother had collected. She also wrote *Jacinthe noire* (1972), and *L'amant imaginaire* (1975). LC; Note

Amuzgar, Jamshid, born 25 June 1923 in Persia, he was a graduate of the University of Tehran, and afterwards studied in the United States, where he obtained a Ph.D. from Cornell University in 1951 for his thesis *The passage of oscillatory waves over a reef.* He was a sometime prime minister of Iran. Iran who's who, 1976; Master (3); MidE, 1982/83

Amuzgar, Parviz, born in 1938 at Meshed, Iran, he taught English language and literature at the universities of Istanbul and Tehran. Iran who's who, 1976

Anabtawi, Samir N., born 4 December 1933 at Jaffa, Palestine, he graduated from Oberlin College and obtained a doctorate from Yale in 1960. He served on the faculties of Dartmouth College and the University of California, and was a member of the Center for International Studies at Princeton before joining the Department of Political Science at Vanderbilt University, Nashville, Tenn. In 1987 he was advisor to the College of Graduate Studies, King Saud University, Riyadh. He wrote *Palestinian higher education in the West Bank and Gaza* (1986). LC; AM&WSc, 1978 S

Anand, Balwant Singh, born in 1909, he wrote the autobiographical story *Cruel interlude* (1962), *Guru Namak; religion and ethics* (1968), *Baba Farid* (1975), and *The Sikhs and Sikhism* (1982).

Anand, Mulk Raj, born in 1905 at Peshawar, India, he was educated at the universities of the Punjab, London, and Cambridge, and was a founding member of the Progressive Writers' Movement in India, 1938. His writings include *Persian painting* (1931), *Album of Indian paintings* (1973), *Folk tales of Punjab* (1974), and a number of historical stories. Au&Wr, 1963; ChambrBrBi; LC; Master (15); MEW

Ananikian, Mardiros Harootioon, born in 1875. His writings include *Armenian mythology* (1925). He died in 1924, probably in Hartford, Conn. LC

Anasian, Akop Sedrakovich, 1904- *see* Anasyan, Hakob Sedrak'i

Anastas Mari, al-Karmili, born 5 August 1866 at Baghdad, he was educated at the Jesuit College of Beirut, in Chèvremont, Belgium, and Montpellier, France. In 1880 he entered the order of the Carmelites and became headmaster of the Carmelite school in Baghdad, to which he bequeathed his rich collection of books and manuscripts. Apart from theological works, he composed works on the history of Baghdad, and a history of Iraq, *Khulasat ta'rikh al-'Iraq* (1919). In later life he wrote almost exclusively articles on lexicography, which he published in 1933 entitled *Aghlat al-lughawiyin al-aqdamin.* His writings include *Nushu' al-lughah al-'Arabiyah* (1938). He died in Baghdad at the beginning of 1947. Kurkis 'Awwad published his biography, *al-Ab Anastas Mari al-Karmili* (1966). GAL S III, 493-494; Isis 38 (1848), p. 246; LC

Anastasiadou, Iphigenia, born in 1943, her writings include Ο Βενιζέλος και το Ελληνοτουρκικο συμφωνο φιλιας του 1930 (Athens, 1982). She died in 1980. LC

Anastasijević, Dragutin N., born 18 (30) July 1877 at Kragujevac, he studied at the universities of Beograd and München, where he received a Dr.phil. in 1905 for his thesis, *Die paränetischen Alphabete in der griechischen Literatur.* Since 1906 he taught at the University of Beograd, where he later held the chair of Byzantine studies until his retirement. His writings include *Otac Nemanin* (1914). He died 20 August 1950. Byzantion 22 (1952), pp. 532-537; Građa

Anasyan, Hakob Sedrak'i (Акоп Седракович Анасян), born 15 (28) May 1904 at Eskişehir, Turkey, he was a graduate of the Armenian Academy, Venezia. In 1947 he became a member of the Institute of History in the Armenian Academy of Sciences, Erevan. He obtained a doctorate in 1961 for his thesis Освободительные движения в Западной Армении в XVII в. His writings include Армянские источники о падении Византии (1957), and *Manr erker* (La Verne, Calif., 1988). LC; Miliband

Anawati (Qanawati), Georges Chehata, born 6 June 1905 at Alexandria, Egypt, he studied pharmacy at the Université St-Joseph de Beirut (1922-1926), and also chemistry at the École de chimie industrielle de Lyon (1926-1928). He subsequently operated a pharmacy and chemical laboratory with his two brothers in Alexandria. During this time he became increasingly exposed to the religious vocation. Particularly Yusuf

Karam encouraged him to enter the priesthood. In 1934 he became a Dominican novitiate in Amiens, France, and was ordained four years later in Kain, Belgium. After four years of study at Algiers, he returned to Egypt in 1944. Through the good offices of Youssef Eche, he was able to spend three months in the libraries of Istanbul (1949), researching his مؤلفات بن سينا (1950) for the Avicenna celebrations. In 1953 he became director of the newly founded Institut Dominicain d'Études orientales du Caire. During all his life he had been in close contact with the leading Islamicists, and was a visiting professor at numerous universities in Europe and North America. His writings include تأريخ الصيدلة والعقاقير (1959), *Études de philosophie musulmane* (1974), *La métaphysique du Shifa'* (1978-1985). With M. Borrmans he published *Tendances et courants de l'islam arabe contemporain* (1982-83). He and his longtime collaborator, Louis Gardet, were honoured by the felicitation volume *Recherches d'islamologie* (1977). He died in Cairo, 28 January 1994. *Journal asiatique* 282 (1994), pp. v-x

Anawati, Marie-Marcel, 1905-1994 *see* Anawati, Georges Chehata

Ancel, Jacques, born 22 July 1906 near Paris, he was educated at Paris. From 1905 to 1907 he was a school teacher in Vannes and Péronne. After obtaining diplomas in history and geography he taught in Paris until 1914. During his military service in the first World War, he discovered the Balkans, to which most of his publications relate. In 1926 he left secondary school teaching to spend the rest of his life at the Institut des Hautes Études Internationales, Paris. His main achievement was his thesis, *Macédonie, son évolution contemporaine* (Paris, 1930). His writings include *Manuel historique de la question dO'rient* (1923), *Peuples et nations des Balkans* (1926). His last years were clouded by the war. He was arrested by German troops in 1941, but released after three months, early in 1942. He died in the following year. *Geographers* 3 (1979), pp. 1-6

Ancelle, J., capitaine, fl. 1888. His writings include *Les explorations au Sénégal et dans les contrées voisines depuis l'antiquté jusqu'à nos jours* (1886), and jointly with général Faidherbe and capitaine H. Brosselard-Faidherbe, *Le Soudan français* (1881-1888). BN

Anchieri, Ettore, born 4 July 1896 at Crevoladossa, Italy, he was educated at the universities of Genève and Pavia, and obtained a doctorate in 1921. Since 1954 he taught at the Università di Padova. His writings include *Il canale di Suez* (1937), *Storia della politica inglese nel Soudan* (1939), *La questione palestinese, 1915-1939* (1940), *Constantinopoli e gli Stretti nella politica russa* (1948), *La diplomatica contemporanea* (1959), and *Histoire des origines de la 2e guerre mondiale* (1965). Chi è, 1961; Wholtaly, 1958; WhoWor, 1974/75

Ancona, Alesandro d', 1835-1914 *see* D'Ancona, Alessandro

Andel, Horst J., born in 1933. His writings include *Kommen morgen die Araber?* (Zürich, 1976), and *Nahost-Report* (1976). LC

Anderlind, Ottomar Viktor, born O. V. Leo, on 9 March 1845 at Greiz, Germany, he received a Dr.phil. from the Universität Jena in 1868 for *Plan für die Einrichtung der Forststatistik im Deutschen Reiche*. From 1870 to April 1881 he was a lecturer at the Forstakademie Tharand, and from 1882 to 1886, he travelled in the Mediterranean countries. His writings include *Die Landwirtschaft in Egypten* (1889), and *'Avodat ha-adamah* (1891). He wrote the autobiography *Leben, Wirken und Schaffen Ottomar Viktor Anderlinds* (1905). Thesis

Anderson, Bernard, born in the first half of the twentieth century, he received a Ph.D. in history. From 1947 until his retirement in 1978, he was librarian of the University of Bombay as well as head of its Department of Library Science. Note

Anderson, Elizabeth, born 19th cent., she was an American Red Cross nurse who spent the last two years of the first World War in France. After the armistice she was one of the first Americans to serve in Kars, Turkey, from June to December 1920. Note

Anderson, J. Lowrie, fl. 1937-1938, he was a sometime United Presbyterian missionary in the Egyptian Sudan. Note

Anderson, Sir James Norman Dalrymple, born 29 September 1908, he was educated at St. Lawrence, Ramsay. After a brilliant student career reading law at Trinity College, Cambridge, he forsook the prospect of a lucrative career at the Bar, and entered the mission field in 1932 to work with the Egyptian Mission. In 1939 his knowledge of Arabic led him into Intelligence where he was employed on Arab affairs. He returned to Cambridge in 1946 and subsequently joined SOAS as a lecturer (1947), soon to occupy the chair of Oriental laws. His research work concentrated on the movements for legal reform in various Muslim countries. He, more than any other scholar, embodied the teaching of Islamic law in England. Academically, his most important appointment was that of director of the Institute of Advanced Legal Studies, London, a post which he held from 1959 to 1976. A leading Evangelical, his constant interest in missionary work was

44

crowned by the presidency of the Bible Churchmen's Missionary Society. He was granted an honorary doctorate in divinity in 1974. The knighthood, which came to him in 1975, was particularly a tribute to this work for the Church. He left an autobiography entitled *An adopted son* (1958). His other writings include *Islamic law in Africa* (1954), and *Law reform in the Muslim world* (1976). He died 2 December 1994. Au&Wr, 1963; ChambrBrBi; MES 32 (1996), pp. 218-219; MidE, 1982/83; *The Times* 7 December 1994; Unesco; Who, 1980-1995

Anderson, John, born 4 October 1833 at Edinburgh, he was a natural scientist and medical doctor who went to India in 1864. In the following year, he was put in charge of the Indian Museum, Calcutta. His writings include *A report of the expedition to western Yunan* (1871), *Zoology of Egypt* (1892-1902), and *A contribution to the herpetology of Arabia* (1896). He died in Matlock, 15 August 1900. DNB

Anderson, Jon Wilson, born 25 February 1946, he was an American-born anthropologist who obtained a Ph.D. in 1979 from the University of North Carolina for *Doing Pakhtu; social organization of Ghilzai Pakhtun in Afghanistan*. In 1978 he started teaching anthropology at his alma mater; and from 1993 to 1997 he was attached to the Catholic University of America, Washington, D.C. He was a member of MESA. Private

Anderson, Lisa S., born 16 October 1950. She obtained a Ph.D. in 1981 from Columbia University for *States, peasants and tribes; colonialism and rural politics in Tunisia and Libya*. In 1985 she was professor at Harvard, and in 1991, a professor of political science, and director of the Middle East Institute, Columbia University. Her writings include *The State and social transformation in Tunisia and Libya* (1987). Note

Anderson, Margaret E., born about 1941, she was educated at Queen's University, Kingston, Ontario, McGill University, Montreal, where she received an M.A. in 1965 for *The Relationship of the Amir al-Hakam I with the Maliki fuqaha' in al-Andalus*. In 1973, she started teaching library science at the University of Toronto. Her writings include *Arabic materials in English translation; a bibliography* (1980). Ferahian; LC

Anderson, Matthew Smith, born 23 May 1922 at Perth, Scotland, he was educated at the University of Edinburgh. After obtaining a doctorate and a lectureship at Edinburgh from 1947 to 1949, he became a lecturer, and since 1961 reader, in history at the LSE. His writings include *Britain's discovery of Russia* (1958), *The Eastern question, 1774-1923* (1966), and *The Great powers in the Near East, 1774-1923* (1970). Au&Wr, 1963; ConAu, 13; WhoWor, 1978

Anderson, Nikolai Karl Adolf, born 24 September 1845 at Kullina-Mühle, Estonia, he received a Dr.phil. in 1891 from the Universität Dorpat for his thesis, printed in 1879, *Studien zur Vergleichung der ugrofinnischen und indogermanischen Sprachen*. He was from 1894 to 1905 a professor of Finno-Ugric languages at Kazan. He died in Narva on 9 March 1905. Baltisch (3)

Anderson, Samuel, he was a missionary who was teaching at Robert College, Bebek, Istanbul in 1922. In the following year, he was in Los Angeles. MW 12 (1922), p. 61

Anderson, Samuel Edwin, born in 1866, he wrote *Where God and science meet; a story of the energy that is matter, life and mind* (Boston, 1938). LC

Anderson, Totton James, born 26 May 1909 at Beirut, he was educated at the University of California, Berkeley, and University of Southern California, where he obtained a Ph.D. in 1947 for *The presidential speech as an instrument of foreign policy, 1937-1940*. Afterwards he started a life-long association with his alma mater. He was joint author of *Introduction to political science* (1967). He died in California, 28 January 1992. ConAu R1; WhAm, 10

Anderson, Sir Warren Hastings, K.C.B., C.B., born 9 January 1872 at Aldershot, he was educated at Marlborough and the Royal Military College, Sandhurst. He was major-general at the General Staff, Allied Forces in Turkey, 1922-1923, commanded Baluchistan District, Quetta, 1924-1927, and was afterwards Quartermaster-General to the Forces. His writings include *Outline of the development of the British Army...up to 1914; notes for four lectures delivered at the Staff College, Camberley* (1920). He died in London on 10 December 1930. DNB; *Who was who, 3*

Anderssen, Walter, born 31 December 1882 at Breslau, Germany, he received a Dr.jur. in 1908 from the Universität Heidelberg for *Die Haussuchung*. His writings include *Der Wert der Rechtsgeschichte und seine Grenzen* (1911), and *Vergleichendes Verfassungsrecht der Gegenwart* (1914). He died after 1937. LC

Andersson, Johan Gunnar, born 3 July 1874 at Knista, Sweden, he was an archaeologist and explorer who had studied at Uppsala and later taught geography at his alma mater. His writings include *Preliminary report on archaeological research in Kansu* (1925), and *Strövtåg i tid och rum* (1958). He died in 1960. SBL

Andhyarujina, Rustom Bhicaji, B.A., LL.B., fl. 1930 in Bombay. His writings include *Our Hindu-Muslim problem; a solution* (1947), and *Principles of rent control; Indian, Pakistani, and English rent acts* (1952). ZKO

Andouard, Ambroise, born in 1839 at Pontivy (Morbihan), he was educated at Nantes, where he became a pharmacist and professor at the Université. His writings include *Nouveaux éléments de pharmacie* (1847), and *Les progrès de l'agriculture dans la Loire-inférieure depuis un siècle* (1889). He died in 1914. DBF

Andrae, Tor Julius Efraim, bishop, born 9 July 1885 at Vena, Sweden, he studied Semitic languages and history of religion at Uppsala Universitet, where he received a doctorate in 1947 for his thesis, *Die Person Muhammeds in Lehre und Glauben seiner Gemeinde*. His writings include *Mohammed, the man and his faith* (1936; German ed., 1932; Spanish ed., 1933; French ed., 1945; Swedish ed., 1967), *Islamische Mystiker* (1960), and *In the garden of myrtels* (1987). He died in Vena, Sweden, 9 July 1947. In the same year was published *Tor Andrae in memoriam*. Geo Widengren wrote *Tor Andræ* (1947). SBL; SMK; *Vem är det*, 1925-1941

Andraos, Adly, born 1905 or 1907 at Luxor, Egypt, and educated at the Jesuit College in Cairo; he studied law at Aix-en-Provence and at the Sorbonne as well as at the Ecole Libre des Sciences Politique, Paris. Upon his return to Cairo, he became barrister at the Mixed Court and subsequently deputy public prosecutor (1937-1942), director of the Mixed Courts Administration (1943), and judge at the Mixed Court of Alexandria. Afterwards he was appointed to the Royal Cabinet and later to the Foreign Office, where he was much involved in establishing diplomatic relations between Egypt and the Vatican. In 1949 he became Egyptian ambassador at Athens, and in 1952, at Paris. He was obliged to take early retirement on account of political intrigues common in Egypt at the time. Although his publications reflect his legal background, he was deeply interested in Egypt's Coptic heritage so that he became a member of the Association des Amis et des Eglises et de l'Art coptes when it was founded in 1934. He died in 1974. *International who's who*, 1954; *Bulletin de la Société d'archéologie copte* 21 (1974), pp. 213-216; WhoFr, 1953/54

André, A., fl. 1960, he was in 1975 affiliated with the Laboratoire de géomorphologie et de cartographie, Institut scientifique chérifien, Rabat. He wrote *Contribution à l'étude scientifique de la province de Tarfaya* (1975). LC

André, Pierre J., *capitaine de l'infanterie coloniale*, fl. 1921. In 1957 he had retired from the military with the rank of general. His writings include *La Cilicie et le problème ottoman* (1921), *Islam et les races*, under the pseudonym Pierre Redan (1922), *L'islam noire; contribution à l'étude des confréries religieuses islamiques en Afrique occidentale* (1924), *L'Asie menace, l'Afrique attend* (1953), and with J. Bührer, *Ce que devient l'islam devant le monde moderne* (1952). LC

Andrea, Alfred John, born in 1941, he was educated at Boston College and Cornell University, where he obtained a Ph.D. in 1969 for his thesis, *Pope Innocent III as crusader and canonist; his relations with the Greeks of Constantinople*. Since 1967 he was a professor of history in the University of Vermont. He was joint author of *The living past* (1975). DrAS, 1982 H

Andréadès, Andreas Michael, born in 1876 in Corfu, he completed his formal education at the Université de Paris in 1901 with his thesis, *Essai sur la fondation et l'histoire de la Banque d'Angleterre, 1694-1844* . The following year, he started a lifelong career with the University of Athens, which ended when he resigned from the chair of economics only weeks before his death on 29 May 1935. He wrote widely on Greek and Byzantine economic history, both in French and Greek; for many years he was the editor of the *Bulletin d'Orient*. He represented his country at the Peace Conference of 1918, and the Danube Conference, Paris, 1920-1921. His writings include the English translation of his *History of the Bank of England* (1907), Περι της οικονομικής διοικήσεως της Επτανήςου επι Βενετοκρατιας (1914),*The Near East and the European war* (1916), *La destruction de Smyrna et les dernières atrocités turques en Asie mineure* (1923), *A history of Greek public finance* (1923), and Μαθήματα Δημοσιας Οικονομιας (1923-1927). *Byzantion* 10 (1935), pp. 803-807; EEE; WhE&EA

Andreas, Friedrich Carl, born 14 April 1846 at Batavia (Dutch East Indies), he studied Oriental languages at German universities and received a Dr.phil. in 1868 from the Universität Erlangen. Afterwards he went to Copenhagen to study Pahlavi MSS. In his capacity as epigrapher and archaeologist, he participated in the 1875-76 expedition to Persia. He stayed on in Persia for private research until 1882, when he became postmaster-general of Persia. After his return to Germany, he taught Persian and Turkish at Berlin from 1883 until 1903, when he was invited to become professor of Iranian studies at Göttingen. He wrote *Die Babi's in Persien* (1896), *Bruchstücke einer Pehlevi-Übersetzung der Psalmen* (1910), and with Franz Stolze, *Die Handelsverhältnisse Persiens* (1885). Colleagues and friends published *Festschrift Friedrich Carl Andreas zur Vollendung des siebzigsten Lebensjahres* (1916). He died in Göttingen in 1930. DtBE; NDB

Andreasian (Andreasyan), Dikran (Tigran), born in 1888, he became associated with the Deutsche Orient-Mission in Potsdam. His writings include two works in Armenian and the two pamphlets *Comment un*

drapeau sauva quatre mille arméniens (Paris, 1916), and *A Red Cross flag that saved four thousand* (1916). LC

Andreasian, Ruben Napoleonovich, born 31 August 1929 at Moscow, he was since 1956 a researcher at the Institute of World Economy and International Relations. He was authorized to attend international meetings in the Third World as well as in the West. His writings include *Арабские страны, нефть и дифференциация* (1984), *Арабске страны* (1986), *Нефть и арабские страны в 1973-1983 гг* (1990). He died 22 May 1986. Miliband; Miliband²

Andree, Richard, born 26 February 1835 at Braunschweig, Germany, he studied natural sciences at the Universität Leipzig, and was one of the founders of the cartographic firm Velhagen & Klasing in Leipzig. His writings include *Ethnographische Parallelen und Vergleiche* (1878-89). He died in München in 1912. DtBE

Andreescu, Ştefan, he wrote *Vlad Ţepeş* (1976), and *Restitutio Daciae* (Bukureşti, 1980-1989). LC

Andreev, A. P., born 19th cent., his writings include *Отъ Владикавказа до Тифлиса* (1891), and *Революця языкознаия: яфетическа акдемика И. Я. Марра* (1929). LC

Andreev, Aleksandr Ignat'evich, born 12 March 1887, he was a historian and a specialist in the history of Siberia. His writings include *Петр Великий* (1947), and *Russian discoveries in the Pacific and in North America in the eighteenth and nineteenth centuries* (1952). He died on 12 June 1959. GSE; LC

Andreev, Grigorii Andreevich, born 11 February 1922 at Paniskoe, he graduated in 1951 from the Moscow Oriental Institute. Since 1962 he was a research fellow at the Oriental Institute of the Soviet Academy of Sciences. His writings include *Индонезийское государство* (1974). Miliband; Miliband²

Andreev, Mikhail Stepanovich, born 11 September 1873 at Tashkent, he was an ethnographer and linguist. His writings include *По этнологии Афганистан: долина Панджишир* (1927), *Таджикт долины Хуф* (1953-1958), and he was joint author of *Ягнобские тексты* (1957). He died 10 November 1948. BiobibSOT, pp. 103-105; GSE

Andrejević, Andrej, born 20th cent., his writings include *Aladža džamija u Foči* (1972), and *Исламска монументална уметност XVI века у Југославији* (1984). LC

Andréjevich, Vladimir, pseud. *see* Osman Bey

de **Andrés Martinez**, Gregorio, O.S.A., born 20th cent., he wrote *Catalógo de los códices griegos desaparecidos de la Real Biblioteca de El Escorial* (1968), *El helenismo en España en el siglo XVII* (1976), and he was the editor of *Recordanzas en tiempo del Papa Luna* (1987). LC

Andrevich, Vladimir, born circa 1830 *see* Osman Bey

Andrew, George Findlay, Rev., O.B.E., F.R.G.S., born 19th cent., he was a missionary under the China Inland Mission and went to China in 1908. He spent a year (1931-1932) in the United States and Great Britain. He wrote *The Crescent in north-west China* (1921). Chinese recorder, 1932

Andrews, Charles Freer, born 12 February 1871 at Newcastle-on-Tyne, he was educated at Pembroke College, Cambridge, and ordained in 1896-1897. He went to India in March 1904 to serve in the Cambridge Mission to Delhi. His writings include *North India* (1908), *The renaissance in India; its missionary aspect* (1912), *Mahatma Gandhi's ideas* (1929), *The true India* (1939). He died a bachelor in India, 5 April 1940. ChambrBrBi; Kenneth Cragg, *Troubled by truth* (1992), pp. 32-51; *Who was who*, 3

Andrews, Clarence Edward, born 25 November 1883 at N.Y.C., he was educated at Yale University, where he obtained a Ph.D. in 1908 for *Richard Brome; a study of his life and works*. Afterwards he was a professor of English at various American universities. During an adventurous trip across the Moroccan Atlas he collected Berber songs. As an incident of this journey he was held prisoner for some time in the castle of a said in the Valley of the Souss. He published his experiences in *Old Morocco and the forbidden Atlas* (1923). He died in 1932. LC; WhAm, 1

Andrews, Frederick Henry, born 19th cent., he wrote *Catalogue of wall-paintings from ancient shrines in Central Asia and Sistan* (1933), *Descriptive catalogue of antiquities discovered by Sir A. Stein...during his explorations in Central Asia, Kansu, and eastern Iran* (1935), and *Wall paintings from ancient shrines in Central Asia* (1948). LC

Andrews, Peter Alford, born 31 October 1936 at Lyme Regis, Dorset/Devon, he received a doctorate in 1980 from the University of London for *Felt tent in Middle Asia*. He was a sometime member of the Institut für Völkerkunde in Köln. His writings include *Ethnic groups in the Republic of Turkey* (1989); and with S.

Azadi, *Mafrash, gewebte Transporttaschen als textile Bilder des Orients* (1985), and with Mügel Andrews, *Türkmen needlework* (1976). LC; Schoeberlein

Andrews, Walter Guilford, Jr., born 20th cent., he was in 1984 a professor of Turkish at the Department of Near Eastern Languages and Civilizations in the University of Washington. His writings include *The Tezkere-i şu'ara of Latifi* (1970), *An introduction to Ottoman poetry* (1976), and *Poetry's voice, society's song* (1984). LC

Andrianov, Boris Vasil'evich, he was in 1966 a senior researcher at the Ethnographic Institute in the Soviet Academy of Science. He wrote *Население Африки* (1964), and he was joint author of *Этническая экология: теория и практика* (1991), and joint editor of *Страны Африкии: политико-экономический справочник* (1988). He died in 1992. LC; Schoeberlein

Andrić, Ivo, born 10 October 1892 at Dolac near Travnik, Bosnia, he received a Dr.phil. in 1924 from the Universität Graz for *Die Entwicklung des geistigen Lebens in Bosnien unter der Einwirkung der türkischen Herrschaft*. An English translation of this work was published in 1990, entitled *The development of spiritual life in Bosnia under the influence of Turkish rule*. In later life he became a writer whose stories have been translated into many languages. He was awarded the Nobel Prize for Literature, 1961. He died in Belgrade, on 13 March 1975. Au&Wr, 1963; ConAu, 1981; CurBio, 1962, 1975; HBL; LC; Master (16); MEW

Andrus, Alpheus Newell, born 17 July 1843 at N.Y.C., he graduated in 1864 from Williams College and in 1867 from Union Theological Seminary; he was ordained in 1868. In 1869 he went as a missionary of the American Board in Turkey to Mardin, where he spent fifty years. The crowning work of his life was the translation of the New Testament into Kurdish. He had proceeded with this work as far as the fifth chapter of the Book of Revelation, when he died in Poughkeepsie, N.Y., on 11 January 1919. Missionary herald 115 (1919), pp. 107-108; Shavit

Andrzejewski, Bogumil Witalis, he was born 1 February 1922 at Poznan, Poland. At the outset of the second World War he fled to Turkey and later served in the Free Polish Forces in North Africa. After studies in England he was a lecturer at SOAS from 1952 until his retirement. His writings include *The declension of Somali nouns* (1964), *Próba ognia i próba czasu* (1972), *Indicator particles in Somali* (1975), *Literatures in African languages* (1985), and *Prodroż do krajów legendarnych* (1985); he edited *Hikmad Soomaali*, by Muuse Haaji Isma'iil Galaal (1956). He died in England, 2 December 1994. Africa (Roma) 50 (1995), pp. 117-118; Index Islamicus (4); NEP; Przegląd orientalistyczny, 1995, p. 113; Unesco

Anees, Munawar Ahmad, born in 1948 at Karachi, he studied at the University of the Punjab and Indiana University, where he received a doctorate in 1980. His main field of research was Islamic studies, biology, and information science. He was a member of MESA, editor-in-chief of *Periodica Islamica*, a founding editor of the *International journal of Islamic and Arabic studies*, and editor of the *Journal of Islamic science*. His writings include *Islam and biological futures* (1989), and *The Kiss of Juda; affairs of a brown sahib, Salman Rushdi* (1989).

Aneizi (Anesi), Ali Noureddine *see* Anisi, 'Ali Nur al-Din

Anet, Claude, pseud., 1868-1931 *see* Schopfer, Jean

d'Anfreville de la Salle, L., Dr., he wrote *Notre vieux Sénégal* (1909), *Sur la côte d'Afrique* (1912); and, with A. Thiroux, *La maladie du sommeil et les trypanosomiases animales au Sénégal* (1911). BN; LC

Angeli, Fedor Afanas'evich, fl. 1961. he wrote *Молдовиэ* (1984); he was joint author of *Исследования по истории стран Юго-Восточной Европы в новое и новейшее время* (1983); and he was joint editor of *Сионистские сеятели лжи* (1986). LC

Angelini, Gennaro, born 19th cent., he wrote *Lettere inedite d'illustri scrittori del secolo XVI* (Roma, 1882), and *Le tombe dei re latini a Gerusalemme* (Perugia, 1902). BLC

Angell, James Burrill, born 7 January 1829 at Scituate, R.I., he graduated from Brown University and also studied in Europe. He was professor of modern languages and literatures at Brown University, and afterwards, president of various American universities. He published his memoirs, *Reminiscences* (1912). He died in Ann Arbor, Mich., 1 April 1916. DAB; Master (19); Shavit; WhAm, 1

Angelov, Dimitur Simeonov, born 2 February 1917 in Bulgaria, he graduated from Sofia University and subsequently became a professor of history from 1949 until his retirement. He wrote *Богомилствого в България* (1947), *На живот смьрт* (1955), *Le Bogomilisme en Bulgarie* (1972), *Les Balkans au moyen âge* (1978), *Formation of the Bulgarian nation* (1978), *Bulgaria's contribution to the development of spiritual culture in the middle ages* (1980), and *Булгарска военна история* (1983). GSE; LC; Master (2)

Anger, Helmut, born about 1900, he received a Dr.phil. in 1925 from the Universität München for *Der Kontinentalbundsgedanke in den Jahren 1895 bis 1906*. His writings include *Die wichtigste geographische Literatur über das Russische Reich seit dem Jahre 1914* (1926), and *Die Deutschen in Sibirien; eine Reise durch die deutschen Dörfer Westsibiriens* (1930).

Anghelescu, Mircea, born in 1941 at Bucureşti, he wrote *Literatura română şi Orientul* (Bucureşti, 1975); he was joint author of *Dicţionar de termeni literari* (1995), and joint editor of *Romano-Arabica* (1974-76). DcEnc

Anghelescu, Nadia, Dr., born 20th cent., she wrote *Curs de sintaxă a limbii arabe moderne* (Bucureşti, 1972), *Tratat de lingvistică generală* (Bucureşti, 1972), *Introducere in Islam* (1993), and *Langage et culture dans la civilisation arabe* (Paris, 1995). LC

Anginieur, Claude Marie Charles Fernand, born 19th cent., he was a French captain who travelled extensively in Asia before the first World War. He wrote *En Asie centrale: Turkestan, Thibet, Cachemir, 1903* (Paris, 1904.) He was killed in the War in 1914. DBF

Anguélov, Dimitre, 1917- *see* Angelov, Dimitur Simeonov

Angulo Iñiguez, Diego, born 18 July 1901 at Valverde del Camino (Huelva), Spain, he studied history and history of art at the universities of Sevilla, Madrid, and Berlin, and became a professor at the Universidad de Madrid. His writings include *Arquetectura mudéjar sevillano de los siglos XIII, XIV y XV* (1932), and *Historia del arte* (1954). *Who's who in Spain*, 1963

Anhegger, Robert, born 14 October 1911 at Wien, where he spent the first eight years of his life, followed by four years in Rotterdam, and, since 1923, in Zürich, where he received a Dr.phil. in 1945 for *Beiträge zur Geschichte des Bergbaus im Osmanischen Reich*. He was an internationalist but also a firm believer in the cultural unity of Greater Germany without its political connotation of the 20th century. In 1940 he settled permanently in Istanbul, where he became a kind of private cultural ambassador, first at the University and, in the post-war era, at the Goethe-Institut. In the early 1950s he was married to Muallâ Eyüboglu. On the occasion of his seventy-fifth birthday he was honoured by the felicitation volume *Türkische Miscellen* (1987). He died about 2002. Widmann, pp. 108, 290

Anhoury, Jean, fl. 1925. His writings include *Aperçu sur l'agriculture égyptienne* (1929).

al-'Ani, 'Awni, fl. 1967, he wrote *Praxis der Projektplanung mit der Netzplantechnik* (1971), and *Die Zukunft in den Griff bekommen* (1973). LC

al-Ani, Salman Hasan, born 10 June 1935 at 'Anah, Iraq, he received a Ph.D. in 1963 from the University of Indiana for *Phonology of contemporary standard Arabic*. Afterwards he became a professor of Arabic linguistics at his alma mater. He was a member of MESA. His writings include *Arabic phonology; an accoustical and physiological investigation* (1970). LC; Private

Anikeev, Nikolai Petrovich, born 16 July 1925 at Krutoe, Tula Oblast, Russia, he graduated in 1953 from the Moscow Oriental Institute and received a doctorate in 1971 at Moscow for *О материалистических традициях в индийской философии*. His writings include *Выдающийся мыслитель и поэт Мухаммад Икбал* (1959). Miliband; Miliband²

Anisi, 'Ali Nur al-Din, Dr., born in 1904 at Benghazi, he was a Libyan politician, diplomat, and businessman, a sometime chairman of the Sahara Bank, and president of the Intellectual Society of Libya. WhoArab, 1978/79

Anisimov, Leonid Nikolaevich, born 20th cent., he wrote *Европа, проблемы безопасности и сотрудничества* (1982), *Проблема Кипра* (1986), and *Трудовой договор* (1989). LC

Anisimov, Vasilii Mikhailovich, born 20th cent., he wrote *Слагаемые экономии* (1984). LC

Anisuzzaman (Anisujjamana), Muhammad, he was attached to the National Institute of Public Administration, Dacca, in 1967. His writings include *Bangladesh public administration and society* (1979), *Family planning workers and service delivery in rural Bangladesh* (1980), and he was joint author of *Planning for local development* (1989). LC; Note

Anistas Mari, al-Karmili, 1866-1947 *see* Anastas Mari, al-Karmili

Anjum, Muhammad S., born 20th cent., he was a research economist at the Pakistan Institute of Development Economics, Islamabad, in 1978, and a staff economist, Pakistan Economic Analysis Network Project, Chemonics International Consulting Division, Islamabad, in 1989. He was joint author, with Kamil

Lodhi and **Agha Abbas Raza**, of *Pakistan's dairy industry; issues and policy alternatives* (1989). LC; Note about the author; ZKO

Anklesaria, Bahramgore Tehmurasp, born in 1873 at Bombay, he received an M.A. at Bombay. Afterwards he was appointed a lecturer in Pahlavi and Avestan at Sir J. J. Zarthoshti Madressa, later becoming its principal. He was for many years honorary secretary of the K. R. Cama Oriental Institute and editor of its *Journal.*. His writings include *Ethics of old Iran* (1937); he edited *Zand-Akasih, Iranian or greater Bundahišn* (1956), and *The Pahlavi Rivayat of Aturfarnbag and Farnbag-Sroš* (1956). He died in 1944. EncIran

Ankori, Zvi, born in 1920, he received an M.A. in 1950 from the Hebrew University, Jerusalem, for *ha-Baladah ha-'Ivrit*. His writings include *Karaites in Byzantium* (1957), *The continuing Zionist revolution* (1971), and *Yahadut ve Yavnut Notsrit* (1984). LC; Note

Annaklychev, Sh., fl. 1974, he was the editor of *Традиционные туркменские прадники, развлечения и игры*, of Ata Dzhikiev (Ashkhabad, 1983). LC

Annandale, Thomas *Nelson,* born in 1876; he was a sometime director of the Zoological Survey of India. His writings include *Fasciculi malayenses* (1903-1904), and *The Faroes and Iceland* (1905). He died on 10 April 1924. LC; Who was who, 2

Annanurov, Ata, born 20th cent., his writings include *Туркмен дилинин язув ядыгерликлеринде ишлигин аналитик формалары* (1977); he edited *Диалект лексикасы* (1980), and *Геокленский диалект туркменского языка* (1991). LC

Annenkov, Mikhail Nikolaevich, born 1835 in Russia, he was a surveyor, engineer, and army officer who saw action at the siege of Geok-Tepe, during which he was seriously wounded. As general of the Russian military transport he was an expert on Central Asian affairs and instrumental in the construction of the Trans-Caspian Railway, 1880-1887. He was fraudulously involved in a number of other railway projects and dismissed in 1895. He wrote *La guerre de 1870 et le siège de Paris* (1872), *Ахалъ-Текинский оазисъ и пути въ Индию* (1881). He died in St. Petersburg, 22 January 1899. Geographische Zeitschrift, 1899, p. 535

Annet, Armand Léon, born 5 June 1888 at Paris, he entered the French civil service in Equatorial Africa in 1911, and became a governor. His writings include *Aux heures troublées de l'Afrique française, 1939-1943* (1952), *Je suis gouverneur d'outre-mer* (1957), and *Le poste à bois* (1972). He died in Paris, 25 April 1973. Hommes et destins, vol. 1, pp. 23-30

Annoni, Antonio Marco, fl. 1922-1932, an Italian geographer who wrote *Breve corso di geografia economica diviso in sei parti. parte V: Asia; parte VI: Africa* (Milano, 1927).

Anokhin, A. V., he wrote *Материалы по шаманству у алтайцев, собранные во время Путешествий по Алтаю в 1910-1912 гг. по поручению Русского комитета по изкчению Средней и Восточной Азии* (Leningrad, 1924). BLC

Anrich, Ernst, born 9 August 1906 at Straßburg, he was from a family who left the city before the return of the French in November 1918 and relocated in Bonn. During his study there he became a militant national socialist. He received a Dr.phil. in 1931 from the Universität Bonn for *Die jugoslavische Frage, 1870-1914*. From 1932 to 1940 he taught modern history at Bonn. During the German occupation of Alsace, he returned to Straßburg, where he had considerable influence within the university on account of his political affiliation. After the war he returned to Germany, where he was a founder of the Wissenschaftliche Buchgesellschaft in Tübingen, 1949-1953, and later in Darmstadt. His writings include *Die englische Politik im Juli 1914* (1934), *Deutsche Geschichte, 1918-1939* (1942), *Der Sozialismus der Linken* (1973), and *Das ist erforderlich* (1990). Kürschner, 1935; LC; NDBA

Ansari, A. S. Bazmee, d. 1989 see Bazmee Ansari, A. S.

al-**Ansari**, 'Adnan Mahmud, born in 1930 in Iraq, he received a Dr.phil. in 1959 from the Universität Hamburg for *Die rechtliche Natur der Arabischen Liga*. His writings include *Die Verfassung des Libanon, der Vereinigten Arabischen Republik und des Irak* (1960), and المشكلة المائية في بحث فقهي (1962). Awwad

Ansari, 'Ali Quli Khan, born in 1247/1868 in Persia, he was a Persian career diplomat who had learned Russian and French in Trebizond and Astrakhan during his father's tenure of foreign service in these cities. In 1928 he was Persian foreign minister. He died in 1940. EncIran

Ansari, Asloob Ahmad, born in 1925, he wrote *Tanqīd o takhlīq* (1963), *Arrows of intellect; a study of William Blake's gospel of the imagination* (1965), and *Naqsh-i Ghālib* (1970). Between 1973 and 1976 he edited a number of studies on English writers for the Department of English, Aligarh Muslim University. LC

Ansari, M. Z. A., M.A., fl. 1936, he was gold medalist, honoursman, and a sometime research scholar of Allahabad Univerity. Note about the author

Ansari, Muhammad Abdul Haq, he wrote *The Ethical philosophy of Miskawaih* (1964), and *Maqsad-i zindagī ka Islāmī tasavvur* (1970). LC

Ansari, Zafar Ishaq, born 20th cent., he received his M.A. in 1959 from McGill University for *An inquiry into the interrelationship between Islam and nationalism in the writings of Egyptians, 1945-56*, and his Ph.D. in 1966 for *The early development of Islamic fiqh in Kufah*. In 1960 he was a lecturer in Islamic history at the University of Karachi, and in 1990, professor at the International University, Islamabad. He translated *Qadianism* from the Urdu of Abulhasan A Nadvi (1967). Ferahian; NUC, 1973-77

Ansay, Tugrul, born 20th cent., he was in 1981 a professor of law at Ankara Üniversitesi. His writings include *American-Turkish private international law* (1966), *Anonim şirketler hukuku dersleri* (1970); with Don Wallace he edited *Introduction to Turkish law* (1978). ZKO

Anschütz, Helga, born in 1928 in Germany, she received a Dr.phil. in 1955 from the Universität Hamburg for *Die NSDAP in Hamburg*. She travelled to the Assyrian Christians in Kurdistan and wrote *Die syrischen Christen von Tur Abdin* (1984). LC; Private

Anstock, Heinz, born in 1909. After being dismissed from the Universität Bonn he went to Turkey by way of Switzerland. At Istanbul he became a literary adviser to publishing houses and a lecturer. In 1942, he accidentally became a founding member of the German Department at İstanbul Üniversitesi. In 1961, he was appointed director of the Deutsche Schule (Alman Lisesi) in Istanbul, a post which he still held in the mid-1970s. His writings include *Deutsche Syntax* (Istanbul, 1954); *90 Jahre Deutsche Schule in Istanbul* (1958); and he was a joint author of *Türkler için Almanca* (Istanbul, 1938-1939). Widmann, p. 106

Antes, Peter, born 29 October 1942 at Mannheim, Germany, he received a Dr.phil. in 1971 from the Universität Freiburg i. Br. for *Zur Theologie der Schi'a*. Since 1973 he was a professor of comparative religion in the Universität Hannover. His main fields of interest were Islam, modern Hinduism, and problems of the systematic science of religion. His writings include *Prophetenwunder in der Aš'ariya bis al-Gazali.* (1972), *Der Islam als politischer Faktor* (1980), *Ethik und Politik im Islam* (1982), and with Bernhard Uhde, *Das Jenseits der Anderen* (1972), and *Islam, Hinduismus, Buddhismus; eine Herausforderung des Christentums* (1973). IWWAS, 1975/76; Kürschner, 1980-2003

Anthony, John Duke, born about 1940 at Richmond, Va., he was educated at Richmond and held degrees from the Virginia Military Institute and the Graduate School of the Foreign Service of Georgetown University. He received a Ph.D. from Johns Hopkins University in 1973 for *The governments and political dynamics of the Lower Gulf area*. Since the early 1970s he was professor of political science at the School of Advanced International Studies in Johns Hopkins University. He was a sometime president of the National Council on US-Arab Relations, and a fellow of MESA. His writings include *Arab states of the Lower Gulf* (1975), and *Historical and cultural dictionary of the Sultanate of Oman and the emirates of Eastern Arabia* (1976). MESA Roster of members, 1990; Note

d'Anthouard de Wasservas, Albert François Ildefonse, born 12 October 1861 at Versailles, he was a colonial administrator who served in Indochina and Madagascar, before becoming deputy of the resident-general M. Pichon in Tunisia from 1902 to 1906. From 1911 to 1913 he was *commissaire-directeur de la Dette Publique d'Égypte*. His writings include *L'Expédition de Madagascar en 1895* (1930), and *Réflections sur notre politique coloniale en Tunisie* (1914). He died at the Chateaux de Saint-Maurice, 10 October 1945. Hommes et destins, vol. 8, pp. 1-2; Qui êtes-vous, 1924

Antia, Edulji Kersaspji, born in 1842 at Navsari, Gujarat, he there received his early education and became priest (*ervad*). From 1876 until his death in 1913, he was a lecturer in Avestan at the Sir Jamshetjee Jeejeebhoy Madressa, Bombay. EncIran

Antoine, Maurice, born 26 February 1886 at Caen (Calvados), he studied at Caen and became a professor of natural sciences at the Lycée Lyautey in Casablanca. He remained there until his retirement in 1949, when he became for three years an inspector of Antiquités préhistoriques du Maroc. His writings include *Les grandes lignes de la préhistoire marocaine* (1952), and *Coléoptères carabiques du Maroc* (1955). He died in Casablanca, 10 November 1962. Hommes et destins, vol. 7, pp. 30-32

Antoine, Robert, M.A. (Sanskrit), Ph.Lic., S.J., born in 1914, he wrote *Religious Hinduism* (1964), and *Rama and the bards* (1975). LC

Antonenko, B. A., born 20th cent., he wrote *Аграрные преобразования в доколхозном таджикском кишлаке* (Dushanbe, 1987), and he was a joint contributor to *Таджикистан в братской семье народов СССР* (Dushanbe, 1972).   LC

Antonius, George, born in 1892, he was educated at Victoria College, Alexandria, Egypt, and graduated in 1914 from King's College, Cambridge.   During the first World War he found employment in the censorship office in Egypt.   In 1921 a chance encounter brought him to Palestine, where he entered the Department of Education as chief inspector.   But his tastes lay more in the political than in the educational sphere, and it was not long before special use was made of his services.   In 1927 he accompanied Sir Gilbert Clayton to conduct the negotiations with Ibn Sa'ud that led to the Treaty of Jeddah.   For these services he was made C.B.E.   He resigned from Government service in 1930 and entered the employment of Mr. C. R. Crane as senior associate for the Near East in the New York Institute for Current World Affairs.   It was during this time that he began to collect material for his book *The Arab awakening* (1938).   In later life he was gradually drawn more into the forefront of Arab politics.   When in 1939 the Arab Delegation went to London for the Palestine Peace Conference, he accepted their offer of the post of general secretary.   He died in Jerusalem at the age of fifty on 21 May 1942.   JRCAS, 1942

Antonov (Antonoff), Nikola A., born 9 January 1888 at Sofia, he was a sometime Bulgarian minister in Ankara and Moscow.   For the National Committee for a Free Europe, Washington, D.C., he wrote *The Bulgarian crisis, The confiscations, The constitutional evolution of Bulgaria,* and *The establishment of the communist regime in Bulgaria,* and *Trends toward union on the Balkans,* all of which were microfilmed by the Library of Congress in 1953.   He died 18 April 1973.   EnBulg

Antonov, Nikolai Klimovich, born 20th cent., he wrote *Материалы по исторической лексике якутского языка* (1971), *Лекции по тюркологии* (1976), and *Якутский язык* (1987).   LC

Antonova, Koka Aleksandrovna, born 10 (23) March 1910 at St. Petersburg, she graduated in 1931 from the Moscow State University and received a doctorate in 1950 for *Религиозная поли-тика Акбара*.   She was joint author of *История Индии* (1973), and its translation *A history of India* (1979).   LC; Miliband; Miliband²

Antoun, Richard Taft, born 31 March 1932 at Worcester, Mass., he was educated at Williams College, Johns Hopkins University, and Harvard, where he received a Ph.D. in 1963 for *Kufr al-Ma, a village in Jordan*.   Afterwards he was professor of anthropology at various American universities until his retirement.   In 1955-56, he was a Fulbright scholar in Egypt.   He was president of MESA, 1981-1982, and a member of the American Schools of Oriental Research and the Society for Iranian Studies.   His writings include *Arab village; a social structure study of a Jordanian peasant community* (1972), *Low-key politics* (1979), *Muslim preacher in the modern world; a Jordanian case* (1989), and he was joint author of *Syria; society, culture, and polity* (1991).   LC; Private

Antraygues, E. R., fl. 1939, he was in 1923 an administrator with the Inscription maritime, and a lecturer at the École de Navigation maritime, Bordeaux.   His writings include *Notions de droit maritime international* (Paris, 1923), and *Pour développer notre marine marchande* (1927).   BN

Antropova, Valentina Vasil'evna, fl. 1947, she was in 1971 affiliated with the Ethnographic Institute N. N. Miklukho-Maklaia in the Soviet Academy of Science.   Her writings include *Культура и быт коряков* (1971).

Antuña, Melchor Martinez, O.S.A., fl. 1921, he wrote *Abenhayán de Córdoba y su obra histórica* (1925), *El polígrafo granadino Abenaljatib en la Real Biblioteca del Escorial* (1926), *Sevilla y sus monumentos árabes* (1930), and *Ibn Hayyan de Córdoba y su historia de la España musulmana* (1946).   BLC; LC

Antweiler, Anton, born 12 October 1900 at Köln, he was ordained in 1925 and received a Dr.phil. in 1933 from the Universität Bonn for *Unendlich; eine Untersuchung zur metaphysischen Wesenheit Gottes*.   Afterwards he was a professor of theology at various German universities.   He wrote *Der Begriff der Wissenschaft bei Aristoteles* (1936), *Die Anfangslosigkeit der Welt nach Thomas von Aquin und Kant* (1961), and *Gott als Geheimnis des Lebens* (1983).   He died in Andernach, 4 October 1981.   DtBE; Kürschner

Anus, François, fl. 1932, he contributed the illustrations to *Les châteaux des croisés en Terre Sainte*, tome 1, by Paul Deschamps (1934).   BLC

Anvaripour, Mark, fl. 1966, he was a sometime acting director, American Friends of the Middle East, Iran.

Anwar, Mumtaz A., born in 1937, he wrote *Doctoral research on Pakistan; a bibliography* (1976), *Urban public libraries in Pakistan* (1983), *Information services in Muslim countries; an annotated bibliography* (1985), and he was joint author of *Pakistan; a bibliography of books and articles published in the United Kingdom, 1947-1964* (1969).   LC

Anzhiganova, Ol'ga Petrovna, fl. 1973, she received her first degree in 1974 for *Именные словосочетания в хакасском языке* (1974). Her writings include *Khakas tíll* (1987). LC; OSK

Ap-Thomas, Dafydd Rhys, fl. 1940, he wrote *A primer of Old Testament text criticism* (1947), and the pamphlet *The Society for Old Testament Study; a short history, 1917-1967* (Manchester, 1967). BLC; LC

Apcar, Mrs. Diana, born 19th cent., she was in 1922 attached to the Near East Relief. Her writings, which centre on the Armenian massacres at the beginning of the twentieth century, include *Peace and no peace* (1912), *The great evil* (1914), and *On the cross of Europe's imperialism; Armenia crucified* (1918). LC

Aphentakes, D. N., fl. 1939-1947, he wrote about agricultural credit in the Balkans and Turkey, and published *Ἡ ἀγροτική πιστίς ἐν Τουρχία, Βουλγαρία, Γιουγχοσλαβία, χαι Ἑλλάδι ὀργάνωσις χαι ἐξέλιξισ* (Athens, 1947). NUC, pre-1956

Apor, Éva, born 26 September 1937 in Budapest. After Iranian studies at the universities of Budapest and Tehran, and field work in Gileki dialectology, she received a doctorate at Budapest in 1968. From 1976 until her retirement she was head of the Oriental Collection of the Library of the Hungarian Academy of Sciences. Her writings include *Hungarian publications on Asia and Africa, 1950-1962; a selected bibliography* (1963), *The Persian manuscripts of the Vambery bequest* (1971), and she edited *Jubilee volume of the Oriental Collection of the Library of the Hungarian Academy of Sciences, 1951-1976* (1978), *A Scheiber-könyvtár katalogúsa = Catalogue of the Scheiber Library* (Budapest, 1992), and *Old routes of western Iran*, by Sir Aurel Stein (1994). Biograf, 2002; LC; MagyarNKK, 1994, 1996, 1998; 2000; Private

Apostolides, Dr. B., born about 1850, he wrote *Essai d'interpretation de l'inscription pré-hellénique de l'île de Lemnos* (Alexandria, 1887), *Essai sur l'hellénisme égyptien et ses rapports avec l'hellénisme classique et l'hellénisme moderne* (Paris, 1898-1899), and *Γλωςςικαῖ μελέται ἐξ αφορμέ των ακαδημαϊκών αναγνωςματων τυκ. Ν. Γ. Χατζεδακι* (Cairo, 1904-1906). BN; OSK

Appelt, Heinrich, born 25 June 1910 at Wien, he received a Dr.phil. from the Universität Breslau and became a professor of medieval history first at Graz and from 1963 until his retirement at Wien. His writings include *Die Urkundenfälschungen des Klosters Trebnitz* (Breslau, 1940), and *Privilegium minus* (1973). He died in 1998. DtBIlnd (2);; Kürschner, 1996; Teichl; *Who's who in Austria*, 1953-1996

Applegate, Joseph Roye, born 4 December 1925 at Wildwood, N.J., he received a Ph.D. in 1955 from the University of Pennsylvania for his thesis *Shilha; a descriptive grammar with vocabulary and texts*. From 1969 until his retirement he was a professor of linguistics and African studies at Howard University, Washington, D.C. His writings include *An outline of the structure of Shilha* (1958), *An outline of the structure of Kabyle* (196-?), and *The structure of Riff* (1963). DrAS, 1969, 1974 F, 1978 F, 1982 F

Aptowitzer (Aptovitzer), Avigdor (Victor/Vigdor), born 16 July 1871 at Tarnopol, Galicia, he studied at the Universität Wien and the Israelitische Theologische Lehranstalt (1900-1907), where he subsequently taught Biblical exegesis and philosophy from 1909 to 1938, when he emigrated to Jerusalem. In his later years his work was considerably impaired by his loss of sight. His writings include *Kain und Abel in der Agada, den Apokryphen, der hellenistischen, christlichen und mohammedanischen Literatur* (1922), and *Ma'amarim lezikhron Rabi Tsevi Perets Hayut* (1933). He died in Jerusalem on 5 December 1942. DtBE; EncJud; LC

al-'Aqqad, Muhammad Kamal, fl. 1963, he was joint author of several English-language monographs on the geology of Egypt. His writings include علم الصخور النارية (Asyut, 1961). LC

al-'Aqqad, Salah al-Din, Dr., born 7 November 1929, he was in 1968 a professor of modern history at Ain Shams University. His writings include الطيرات السياسية في الخليج (1983), المغرب العربي (1958), *The Legendary claims of Iraqi historical rights in the State of Kuwait* (1990). LC; Unesco

Aquilina, Joseph (Gużè), LL.D., born 7 April 1911, he studied Semitic languages at SOAS, where he received a Ph.D. in 1940. From 1937 to his retirement in 1976 he held the chair of Maltese and Oriental languages in the University of Malta. In 1972 he became president of the International Association of Studies on Mediterranean Civilizations. His writings include *The structure of Maltese* (1959), *Maltese meteorological and agricultural proverbs* (1961), *Papers in Maltese linguistics* (1961), *Teach yourself Maltese* (1966), *Maltese-English dictionary* (1987). The *Journal of Maltese studies* honoured him with *Across cultures; Festschrift edition in honour of Prof. Gużè Aquilina* (1977). He died 8 August 1997. Aljamía 10 (1998), p. 27; LC

Arab, Émile, fl. 1921, he received a medical doctorate from the Faculté de médecine de Beyrouth. Note

Arabadzhian (Арабаджян), Artem Zavenovich, born 15 December 1922 at Tbilisi, Georgia, he graduated in 1949 from the Moscow Oriental Institute, and received a doctorate in 1952 for *Социально-экономические корни монархии Реза-шаха и реакционая сущность ее экономической политики.* Since 1994 he was a trade commissioner of Russia in Iran. His writings include *Иран: сборник статей* (1973), *Иран – изменения в отраслевой структуре экономини в 60-70 годах* (1983), *Иран и Пакистан* (1987), *Иранская революция, 1978-1979* (1989), and *Истори духовности; религия и атеизм* (1993). LC; Miliband; Miliband[2]

al-'Arabi, Mahmud Isma'il, Dr., he was in 1969 head of the Technical Office of the Productivity and Vocational Training Department, Cairo. His writngs include *A modern apprenticeship scheme in the U.A.R.* (1960). LC; Note

el-Araby, Kadri Mohamed Gharib, born 1931, he received a Ph.D. in 1967 from New York University for his thesis,*Planning in the U.A.R; problems and prospects.*

Arafat, Walid (ibn) Najib, born in 1921 at Nablus, Palestine, he graduated from the University of London, where he also received a Ph.D. in 1953 for *A critical introduction to the study of the poems ascribed to Hassān ibn Thābit.* From 1973 to his retirement, he was a professor of Arabic and director, Institute of Arabic and Islamic Studies, University of Lancaster. In 1971 he edited *Diwan Hassan ibn Thabit.* Sluglett; WhoArab, 1999/2000-2003/4

Arafat, Yasir, the pseudonym of Muhammad 'Abd al-Ra'uf 'Arafat al-Qudwah al-Husayni, born 24 August 1929 in Jerusalem, he studied engineering at the University of Cairo, 1952-1956. From 1957 to 1965 he was an engineer in Kuwait. Since 1968 he was president of al-Fath. There are biographies by Thomas Kiernan, *Arafat, the man and the myth* (1976), and by Peter Jacobs, *Yassir Arafat; Versuch einer Lebensbeschreibung* (1985). AnaBrit; CurBio, 1971, pp.9-11, 1991; EEE; IntWW, 1974/5-2002; Master (29); MidE, 1978-1982/83; WhoArab, 1978/79-2003/4

Aragonnès d'Orcet, Gaspar Marie *Stanislas* Xavier, born 12 March 1835 at the Château de Paulhac near Brioude (Haute-Loire), he was a student at the Jesuit Séminaire d'Isuere near Moulins from 1850 to 1852 when he was sent to Paris to prepare for entrance to Saint-Cyr. After two years at l'École spéciale militaire de Saint-Cyr he received a commission in 1857 to the 1er Carabiniers as *sous-lieutenant.* After the battle of Sedan he was imprisoned in Germany from September 1870 to April 1871. His repeated requests for overseas' service did not materialize until 1880 when he was posted to the 4th Régiment de chasseurs d'Afrique at Mascara with the rank of lieutenant-colonel. He later served in Tunisia until 1884 when he returned to metropolitan France. He resigned in 1897 with the rank of brigadier general to his estate in Retz near Dornes (Nièvre). His writings include *Frœschwiller; Sedan et la commune; lettres et souvenirs publiés avec une notice biographique par L. Le Peletier* (1910). He died on a religious pilgrimage to Roma on 18 May 1900. DBF; *Frœschwiller; Sedan et la commune,* pp. 1-18; Lamathière

Arakélian, Hambartzoum, born in 1855, his writings include *La question arménienne au point de vue de la paix universelle* (1901), and *Contes et nouvelles* (Paris, 1916). LC

Arakin, Vladimir Dmitrievich, born 6 (19) July 1904 at Moscow, he graduated in 1926 from the Leningrad Institute of Modern Oriental Languages. After obtaining a doctorate for *История преподавания иностранных языков в России,* he became a lecturer, and later professor, at various institutions of higher learning in the Soviet Union. He was the compiler of a number of Russian dictionaries. He died on 1 November 1983. Miliband; Miliband[2]

Aralov, Semen Ivanovich, born 18 (30) December 1880 at Moscow, he was a Soviet military officer, politician, and diplomat, who served also in Turkey. His writings include *Воспоминания советского дипломата, 1922-1923* (1960), and its Turkish translation *Bir Sovyet diplomatının Türkiye hatırları* (1967). GSE; LC

Arambourg, Camille, born in February 1885 at Paris, he was a sometime professor of geology at the Institut National Agronomique, and the Musée National d'Histoire Naturelle, Paris, where he spent the last forty years of his life. His writings include *Les poissons crétacés du Jebel Tselfat, Maroc* (Rabat, 1954). He died in Paris in November 1969. *Hommes et destins,* vol. 1, pp. 30-39

Arandarenko, Georgii Alekseevich, born in 1846. His writings include *Досуги в Туркестане, 1874-1889* (1889), and *Бухара и Афганистан в начале 80-х годов XIX века* (1974). LC

Arapov, Dmitrii IUr'evich, born 16 May 1943 at Erevan, he graduated in 1966 from the Faculty of History, Moscow State University and received his first degree in 1978 for *История изучения Бухарск. ханства в*

русской востоковедческ. дореволюцирн. историонпафии. He was since 1972 affiliated with his alma mater. His writings include *Бухарское ханство в русской востоковедческой историографии* (1981). Miliband²

Arapova, Tat'iana Borisovna, born 17 November 1938 at Leningrad, she graduated in 1961 from the Faculty of History, Leningrad State University and received her first degree in fine art in 1973 for *Китайский фарфов конца XIV - пераой трети XVIII в.* She was since 1965 attached to the Hermitage Museum, Leningrad. Her writings include *Китайский фарфор в собрании Эрмитажа* (1977), *Hermitage* (1980), and *Китайские расписные эмали* (1988). Miliband²

Arar, Abdullah, Dr. fl. 1969. In 1988 he was a senior regional officer, Land and Water Division, Food and Agricultural Organization, Roma. He wrote *Treatment and re-use of waste-water* (1988). LC

Arasly, Gamid Mamed Tagi ogly, born in 1909 at Gandzha, Azerbaijan, he graduated in 1932 from the Faculty of Philology, Azerbaijan State Pedagogical Institute, and received his first degree in 1943 for *Азербайджанская литература XIII-XVI вв.*, and his doctorate in 1954 for *Азербайджанская литература XVII-XVIII вв.* He was a lecturer since 1944 and appointed a professor in 1956. He died 20 November 1983. His writings include *Имаддин Несими; жизнь и творчество* (1972), its translation, *Imaddin Nesimi; life and creative activity* (1973), and he was join editor of *Низами и Фузули* (1962). Most of his writings are in Azeri. AzarbSE, vol. 1, p. 383; GSE; Miliband; Miliband²

Arasteh, Abdel Reza, born 27 September 1927 at Shiraz, he received a Ph.D. in 1953 from Louisiana State University with a thesis entitled *Foundation of modern educational methods.* He was successively a professor of analytical psychology at Tehran, a faculty member of the Department of Psychology, George Washington University Medical School, and also director of interdisciplinary research at the Psychiatric Institute of Washington. His writings include *Education and social awakening in Iran* (1962), *Man and society in Iran* (1964), *Rumi, the Persian; rebirth in creativity and love* (Lahore, 1965), *Faces of Persian youth* (1970), and *Growth to selfhood; the Sufi contribution* (1980) . AmM&WSc, 1973 S, 1978 S; ConAu 105; Iran WW, 1976; WhoAm, 1984-92; WhoE, 1989/90

Arat, Gabdul Reşit Rahmeti (Rachmati/Rachmatullin), born 15 April 1900 at Kazan. The chaos following the Russian revolution brought him to Berlin in the early 1920s in order to act on behalf of his Tatar countrymen. Concurrently he studied comparative Turkic linguistics at the Humboldt Universität, Berlin, where he received a Dr.phil in 1928 for his thesis, *Die Hilfsverben und Verbaladverbien im Altaischen.* In 1933 he was invited to join the Philosophical Faculty in Istanbul Üniversitesi, where he remained until his death on 29 November 1964. His writings include *Kutadgu biliğ* (1947), *Eski Türk şiiri* (1965). Meydan; TatarES; *Ural-altaische Jahrbücher* 38 (1966), pp. 133-134

Arat, Zehra F., born 20th cent., he was a professor of political science in the State University of New York, College at Purchase, certainly from 1991 to 2003. He wrote *Democracy and human rights in developing countries* (1991). LC; NatFacDr, 2003

Arató, Endre, born 8 November 1921 at Komárom, Hungary, he was a historian who was for many years attached to the Hungarian Academy of Science. His writings include *Sociálne motívy slovenského národného hnutia v. r. 1845-48* (1952), *A memzetiségi kérdés története Magyarországon, 1790-1848* (1960), and *Kelet-Európa története a 19. század elsó két harmadábar* (1969). He died in Budapest, 30 August 1977. Magyar

Araújo Oliveira, Hermes de see Oliveira, Hermes de Araújo

al-'Arawi, 'Abd Allah Muhammad see Laroui, Abdallah Muhammad

Arazi, Albert, born 20th cent., he received a doctorate in 1974 from the Université de Paris IV for *Recherches sur la poésie satirique au IIème siècle de l'hégire.* In 1989 he was professor of Arabic literature at the Hebrew University, Jerusalem. His writings include *La réalité et la fiction dans la poésie arabe ancienne* (1989), and *Amour divin et amour profane dans l'islam médiéval à travers le divan de Khalid al-Katib* (1990). LC; THESAM, 4

d'Arbaud-Jouques, Joseph Charles André, marquis, born 11 May 1769 at Aix-en-Provence, he was a politician and administrator, and a founding member of the Académie d'Aix as well as the Académie de Marseille. His writings include *Troubles et agitations du Département du Gard en 1815* (1818). He died in Aix-en-Provence, 5 June 1849. DBF

Arberry, Arthur John, born 12 May 1905 at Portsmouth, he studied at Pembroke College, Cambridge, followed by two years in Cairo as head of the Department of Classics from 1932 to 1934. He returned to

Britain as assistant librarian at the India Office, London. He briefly was professor of Persian at SOAS, from which he transferred to the chair of Arabic in 1946. In the following year, he was elected Sir Thomas Adam's Professor of Arabic at Cambridge. He was fully aware of the necessity to introduce the study of the contemporary Middle East into Cambridge, and he took the initiative in setting up the Middle East Centre there. He had a truly amazing output of published work. In latter years he was beset by ailments which caused him distress of heart and physical disability hard for a man of his intellectual energy to bear. Still, he carried out his literary research, and, even if with mechanical difficulty, to write. Almost to his last moment he was collating the printed text of a work of al-Sha'rani with a MS from the Chester Beatty Arabic collection which he knew so well. He died 20 October 1969. Au&Wr, 1963; BSOAS 33 (1970), 364-367; *Index Islamicus (3); Iran 8* (1970), pp. vii-viii; JRAS, 1970, 96-98; *Proceedings of the British Academy* 58 (1972), 355-366; *Who was who*, 6

Arbman, Erik *Holger*, born 8 September 1904 at Bettna, Sweden, he studied at Nyköping, Stockholm, and Uppsala, where he received a doctorate in 1937 for *Schweden und das karolinische Reich*. He became a historian and archaeologist at Swedish universities. His writings include *Birka, Sveriges äldesta handelsstad* (1939), *Äldre kulturer i Rajputana* (1954), and *The Vikings* (1961). He died on 25 January 1968. *Svenska män och kvinner; Vem är det*, 1967

Arbos, Philippe Joseph, born 30 July 1882 at Mosset (Pyrénée-orientales), and educated at the Lycée Louis-le-Grand and École Normale Supérieure, Paris, he received a doctorate in 1922 for *La vie pastorale dans les Alpes françaises*. In 1919 he was appointed professor of geography at the Université de Clermont-Ferrand, where he remained until his retirement. His writings include *L'Auvergne* (1932). He died in Andancette (Dôme) on 16 November 1956. *Geographers 3* (1979), 7-12; WhoFr, 1955/56

Arbos Ayuso, Federico, born 20th cent., he received a doctorate in Semitic languages and became a professor of Arabic language and literature at the Departamento de Estudios Arabes e Islámicos in the Universidad Complutense de Madrid. He specialized in contemporary Arabic literature. Arabismo, 1994, 1997

Arbuthnot, Foster Fitzgerald, born 21 May 1833 at Belgaum, Bombay presidency, he was an author and Orientalist whose writings include *Early ideas* (1881), *Persian portraits* (1887), and *Arabian authors* (1890). He died in London, 25 May 1901. DNB

Arbuthnot, Sir Robert Keith, born 9 September 1801 at Edinburgh, he was with the Bombay civil service from 1819 to 1847. On 20 March 1828 he was married to Ann Fitzgerald, the daughter of Field Marshall Sir John Fitzgerald. He died in Firenze, 4 March 1873. Boase; Egyptology; IndianBilnd (2)

Arcas Campoy, Maria del Dulce Nombre, born 20th cent., she received a doctorate in Semitic studies, and became a professor in the Universidad de La Languna, Santa Cruz de Tenerife Tíno, where she was professor from 1992 to 1994. Arabismo, 1992, 1994, 1997

Arce, Agustin, he was a Franciscan Father, fl. 1952. His writings include *Itinerario a Jerusalén, 1703-1704, de fray Eugenio de San Francisco* (1940), *Expediciones de España a Jerusalén, 1673-1842, y la Real Cédula de Carlos III sobre los Santos Lugares en su ambiente internacional* (1958), *Catalogus descriptivus illustratus operum in Typographia Ierosoymorum Franciscati impressorum* (Jerusalem, 1969), and *Getsemani* (1971). LC

Archer, Charles, born 18 August 1861 at Perth, Scotland, he joined the Indian Staff Corps in 1885 and advanced to the rank of lieutenant-colonel. He served mainly in Baluchistan and retired in 1916. His publications include translations from the Norwegian. He died 20 November 1941. IndianBilnd (2); *Who was who*, 4

Archer, John Clark, born 23 December 1881 at Wilna, Md., he received a Ph.D. in 1922 from Yale University for his thesis *The mystical element in the life of Mohammed*. He was an educational missionary in India from 1907 to 1911. Afterwards he was a lecturer and later professor of missions and comparative religion at various American universities. His writings include *Faiths men live by* (1934), and *The Sikhs in relation to Hindus, Moslems, Christians, and Ahmadiyyas* (1946). He died on 7 July 1957. *Who was who in America*, v. 3

Archer, Raymond Leroy, born 31 October 1887 at Adonis, W.Va., he studied at universities in America and Germany and received a Ph.D. in 1935 from Hartford Theological Seminary for *Muhammadan mysticism in Sumatra*. He was ordained in 1911, and afterwards served as a missionary in Southeast Asia. WhAm 8

Archer, William George, born 11 February 1907, he was educated at Emmanuel College, Cambridge. In 1930 he entered the Indian Civil Service, where he remained until his retirement in 1948. Afterwards he was from 1949 to 1959 a keeper at the Indian Section in the Victoria and Albert Museum, London. His writings include *Kalighat paintings* (1971), *Indian paintings from the Punjab Hills* (1973), and *Visions of courtly India* (1976). He died 6 March 1979. *Who was who*, 7

Archibald, Raymond Clare, born 7 October 1875 in Colchester County, N.S., he was educated at Mt. Allison College, N.B., and universities in Cambridge, Mass., Berlin, Paris, and Straßburg, where he obtained a doctorate in 1900 for his thesis *The cardioide and some of its related curves.* He was a mathematician, librarian, and violonist. He died 26 July 1955. Canadian who's who; WhA,m 3

Archinard, Louis, born 11 February 1850 at Le Havre, he graduated in 1870 from the Polytechnique, Paris. He served as an officer in Africa south of the Sahara, and retired with the rank of general. In his report to his authorities, *Le Soudan français* (1891), he tells the story of the conquest of French Equatorial Africa. He died in Villiers-le-Bel (Seine-et-Oise), on 8 May 1932. BLC; Curinier, v. 3, p. 193; DBF

del **Arco y Garay**, Ricardo, born in 1888 at Granada, he was a historian who was educated at the Universidad de Valencia. His writings include *Huesca en el siglo XII* (1921), *Zaragoza histórica* (1928), *Repertorio de manuscritos referentes a la historia de Aragón* (1942), and *Notas de folklore altoaragonés* (1943). He died in Huesca on 8 July 1955. DBEC; Who's who in Spain, 1963

Ardagh, Sir John Charles, major-general, C.B., C.I.E., K.C.M.G., born 9 August 1840 at Comragh House, he was educated at Trinity College, Dublin, and graduated from the Royal Military Academy, Woolwich. He served fifteen years in various capacities in the Ottoman Empire and the Anglo-Egyptian Sudan. He was granted an honorary LL.D. by Trinity College, Dublin. He died 30 September 1907. DNB; Hill; Who was who, 1

Ardaillon, Édouard-Muller, born 4 May 1867 at Mazères (Ariège), he was a graduate of the École Normale Supérieure and was from 1892 to 1896 with the École française d'Athènes. In 1897 he received a doctorate for his two theses, *Les mines du Laurion dans l'antiquité* and *Quomodo Græci collocaverint portus et ædificaverint.* In the same year he became a professor of geography at the Université de Lille. In 1908 he was invited to be president of the Université d'Alger, an office which he held until his death, 21 September 1926. DBF

Ardant, Philippe Marie Joseph Maurice, born 21 July 1929 at Saint-Priest-sous-Aixe (Haute-Vienne), he received a doctorate in 1956 from the Université de Paris for *La responsabilité de l'État du fait de la fonction juridictionnelle.* He spent two years each as a professor at the universities of Rabat and Beirut before becoming professor at various French universities. From 1965 to 1967 he was cultural attaché at the French Embassy in China. His writings include *L'administration chinoise* (1968), and *Institutions politiques et droit constitutionnel* (1991). WhoFr, 1993/4-2002/3

Ardaschir, K. K., born 19th cent., he was educated in France and England. During the Balkan War he served in the Ottoman Army, and later went to Egypt and India, as a writer and lecturer. Asia, August 1921

Ardel, Ahmet, fl. 1964. His writings include *Umumi coğrafya dersleri* (1960).

d'**Ardenne de Tizac**, Jeab Raymond Marie Henri, born 17 May 1877 at Lacapelle-Marival (Lot), he was for many years a director of the Musée Cernuschi, Paris, which specializes in Oriental art. His writings, partly under his pseudonym Jean Viollis include *Déclices de Fez* (1923), and *L'art chinois classique* (1926). He died in Paris, 17 December 1932. DBF

Ardouin-Dumazet, Victor Eugène, born 12 January 1852 at Vizille (Isère), he obtained a modest education in evening courses while working as a clerk in Lyon. After service in the Franco-Prussian War of 1870-71, he requested to be stationed in Algeria, where he entered the *Service des officiers indigènes* and advanced to *archiviste de 1ère classe.* During his brief stay at Tlemcen, he became engaged in the foundation of a geographical society, and, under the pseudonym of Dumazet, produced his first publication, *La question de l'Ouest*, a study of the Moroccan question. After his return to metropolitan France, he was a correspondent to the *Courrier de Tlemcen, Courrier de Lyon*, and *La Gironde*. During the 1881 insurrection of the Bou-Amana, he was despatched to the Sud-Oranais by the *Indépendance belge.* He was a member of the Société de géographie de Paris, and vice-president of the Association des Écrivains militaires maritimes et coloniaux, and, since 16 September 1896, Chevalier de la Légion d'honneur. His writings include *L'armée et la flotte de 1891 à 1892* (1892), and *Voyage en France* (1893-1899). Curinier, v. 3 (1901), p. 204

Areán González, Carlos Antonio, born in 1921, he studied philosophy and literature at the Universidad de Santiago de Compostela, where he received a doctorate for his thesis, *Ramón de Bastera, su obra histórica y literaria* (1950). He was an art critic and historian. His writings include *Hacia el imperio* (1939), and *Cultura autóctona hispana* (1973). DBEC; Couceiro

Aref al-Aref, born in 1892 *see* al-'Arif, 'Arif

Arendonk, Cornelis van, born in the last quarter of the 19th century, he received a doctorate in 1919 from the Rijksuniversiteit te Leiden for his thesis *De opkomst van het Zaidietische imamaat in Yemen.* LC

Arends, Al'fred Karlovich, born 4 (16) October 1893 at St. Peterburg, he graduated in 1926 from the Leningrad Oriental Institute. His writings include *Персидско-русский словарь физических терминов* (1928), *Краткий синтаксис современного персидского литературного языка* (1941); he was joint editor of *Бухарский вакф XIII в: факсимили* (1979). He died 20 June 1977. Miliband; Miliband²

Arène, Paul Auguste, born 26 June 1843 at Sisteron (Alpes-de-Haute-Provence), he abandoned his university career in favour of writing at the age of twenty-three. He wrote *Vingt jours en Tunisie, août 1882* (1883); he was joint author of *La France colonisatrice* (1983). He died in Antibès on 17 December 1896. DBF; LC

Arens, Hans Jürgen, born 20th cent., he received a doctorate in 1974 from the Universität Bochum for *Die Stellung der Energiewirtschaft im Entwicklungsprozess Afghanistans*. His other writings include *Zur Theorie und Technik räumlicher Verteilung von Energieversorgungsanlagen* (1975). LC

Arens, Werner, born 20 December 1924 at Wenden, Germany, he received a Dr.theol. in 1965 from the Universität München for his thesis *Die kirchliche Mannesjugend der Gegenwart und das Problem ihrer Führerbildung*. From 1969 until his retirement he was a professor of theology in the Universität Osnabrück. His writings include *Kirche im Jahr 2000* (1992). Kürschner, 1996-2003

Areshian (Areshyan/Арешян), S. G., fl. 1945, his writings include *Русские писатели об Армении; сборник* (Erevan, 1946), and *Армянская печать и царская цензура* (Erevan, 1957). LC; OSK

Argente y del Castillo, Balmodero, born in 1877, he was a lawyer and a sometime chancellor of the Instituto de España, Madrid. His writings include *Legislación escolar vigente en España* (1904), *El derecho vingente en España* (1906), *Tierras sombrías* (1909), *Henry George, su vida, sus doctrinas* (1912), *La esclavitud proletaria* (1913), *Al margen de la vida* (1916), and *La reforma agraria* (1932). He died in 1965. Ossorio; Who's who in Spain, 1963

Argo, Abram M., he was born Abram Markovich Gol'denberg. His writings include *Сатирические очерки из истории русской литературы* (1939), *Из зарубежных поэтов* (1958), *Десятая муза* (1964), *Своимиглазами* (1965), *За много лет* (1969); and he is joint author of *Против тьмы* (1958). LC; OSK

Argynbaev, Khalel Argynbaevich, born 21 September 1924 in Pavlodar Oblast, he received a doctorate in 1975 at Alma-Ata for *Семья и брак у казахов* and was appointed a professor in 1982. He was joint author of *Казахи: историко-этнографического исследования* (1995, and he edited *Новые материалы по археологии и этнографии Казахстана* (1961). Казахская ССР краткая энциклопедия, vol. 3

Argyriou, Astérios, born 22 November 1935, his writings include *Les exégères grecques de l'Apocalypse à l'époque turque, 1453-1821* (Thessaloniki, 1982), and *Macaire Makrès et la polémique contre l'islam* (Citta del Vaticano, 1986). EVL, 1993/94, 1996/97

Argyropoulos, Perikles Alexandrou, born in 1881 at Athens, he wrote Ὁ Μακεδονικὸς Ἀγονάς, αρομνεμο-νεύματα (1984). He died in Athens in 1964. EEE

'Aridah, Antun, born 18th cent., he was a Maronite Christian from Tripolis, Lebanon, and professor of Oriental languages, who contributed to *Fundgruben des Orients*. Under the name A. Aryda he wrote *Institutiones grammaticae arabicae* (Wien, 1813-1815). LC

Arié, Rachel, fl. 1954. She was awarded an honorary doctorate by the Universidad de Granada. Her writings include *L'Espagne musulmane au temps des Naṣrides* (1973), *Études sur la civilisation de l'Espagne musulmane* (1990), *L'occident musulman au bas moyen âge* (1992), and *El reino Nasri de Granada, 1232-1492* (1992). LC

Arieli (Loebl), Yehoshua, born 26 July 1916 at Karlsbad (Karlovy Vary), Bohemia, he received a Ph.D. in 1955 from the Hebrew University, Jerusalem, for his thesis, written in Hebrew, on the "history of the concept of individualism in the United States, 1840-1912." Afterwards he was professor of history at the Hebrew University, Jerusalem. His writings include *Individualism and nationalism in American ideology* (1964). Who's who in Israel, 1980/81

Ariëns Kappers, Cornelius Ubbo, born in 1877 at Groningen, he was educated at Leeuwarden and the Universiteit van Amsterdam. He was associated with the Neurologisches Institut, Frankfurt am Main, from 1906 to 1908, when he was appointed a professor, and later director, at the Central Institute for Brain Study at Amsterdam. He left this post in 1929 to join the Amsterdam Municipal University as a professor of comparative anatomy of the central nervous system. He was a visiting professor at Peking, A.U.B., and

American universities. He was granted honorary doctorates by Yale University and the universities of Chicago, Dublin, and Glasgow. His writings include *The Anthropology of the Near East* (1932), and he was joint author of *An Introduction to the anthropology of the Near East in ancient and recent times* (1934). He died on 29 July 1946. NUC, pre-1956; NYT, 30 July 1946, p. 23, col. 4

al-'Arif, 'Arif, born in 1892 at Jerusalem and educated in Constantinople, he wrote *Die Beduinen von Beerseba* (1938), *Bedouin love, law and legend* (1944), *Nakbat Bayt al-Muqaddas* (1947-1955). WhoArab, 1978/79

Arin, Félix, born in the last quarter of the nineteenth century, he received a doctorate in 1909 from the Université de Paris for his thesis *Recherches historiques sur les opérations usuraires et aléatoires en droit musulman*. His writings include *Le régime légal des mines dans l'Afrique du nord* (1913). In 1920 he published a French translation of I. Goldziher's *Vorlesungen über den Islam*.

'Aris, Thabit, born in Syria; he was a politician and sometime ambassador to East European countries. Who's who in the Arab world, 1978/79

Aristarches, Demetrios, born 19th cent., he was a sometime Turkish chargé d'affaires in Firenze, and a member of several international learned societies. He published his *Mémoires d'Aristarchi-Bey* (1888); he was the editor of two fascicles of *Le Mémorial diplomatique d'Orient* (Athens, 1876). BN

Aristova, Tat'iana Federovna, born 16 August 1926 at Moscow, she graduated in 1929 from the Moscow Oriental Institute, and in 1953 she obtained a doctorate in ethnography for her thesis *Курды Ирана*. Her writings include *Материальная культура курдов XIX-перевой половины XX в.* (1990). Milibanb; Miliband²

Arjomand, Said Amir, born 26 December 1946 at Tehran, he received a Ph.D. in 1980 from the University of Chicago. Afterwards he was professor of sociology at S.U.N.Y., Stony Brook. He had visiting appoint-ments in England and Germany, and was a member of MESA. His writings include *The turban for the crown* (1988), and *The political dimensions of religion* (1993). Private

Arjona Castro, Antonio, born in 1938, he received a doctorate in 1979 for *La problación de Córdoba en el siglo XIX; sanidad y crisis demográfica en la Córdoba decimonónica*. In 1992 he was affiliated with the Real Academia de Córdoba, and in 1997 he was a director of the Instituto de Estudios Califales, Córdoba. He was an authority in medical history and geography of Moorish Spain. His writings include *Andalusia musulmana; estructura politico-administrativa* (1980), *Anales de Córdoba musulmana, 711-1108* (1982), *"El libro de la generación del feto, el tratamiento de las mujeres embarazadas y de los recien nacidos" de 'Arib Ibn Sa'id* (1983), *La sexualidad en la España musulmana*, 2. ed. (1990), and he was joint author of *Abdarrahmán III y su época* (1991). Arabismo, 1992, 1994, 1997; LC

Arkelian, H. see Arakélian, Hambartzoum

Arkell, Anthony John, born 29 July 1898 at Hinxhill, Kent, he was educated at Bradfield College and Queen's College, Oxford. He was ordained in the Anglican Church. In 1920 he joined the Sudan Political Service in which he held various political posts culminating in Acting Deputy-Governor of Darfur, 1932-37. In later life he became an archaeologist and a sometime lecturer in Egyptology at the University of London. His writings include *Early Khartoum* (1949), and *History of the Sudan from the earliest times to 1921* (1955). He died in Chelmsford, 26 February 1980. Au&Wr, 1963; Egyptology; Who was who, 7

Arkhangel'skii, Nikolai Porfir'evich, born in the last quarter of the nineteenth century. His writings include *Сборник матерьялов по преподаванию русского языка в нерусской школе* (Tashkent, 1926), and *Среднеазиатские вопросы географической терминологии и транскрипции* (Tashkent, 1935).

Arkhangel'skii, Sergei Ivanovich, born 10 (22) January 1882 at Semenov, Russia, he was a graduate of Moscow University and a sometime professor of medieval history in the University of Gorki. His writings include *Аграрное законодательство английской революций, 1649-1660 гг.* (1940), and *Крестянские движения в Англии в 40-50 х годах 17 века* (1960). He died in Gorki, 7 October 1958. GSE

Arkoun, Mohammed, born 1 February 1928 in Algeria, he studied at the Université de Paris and received a doctorate in 1969. His writings include *Contribution à l'étude de l'humanisme arabe en 4e/10e siècle*; *Miskawayh* (1970), *Essai sur la pensée islamique* (1973), *Ouvertures sur l'islam* (1989), and *Rethinking Islam* (1994). IWWAS, 1976/77; Unesco

Arlès, Jean Paul, born 20th cent., he received a doctorate of law in 1962 from the Université de Toulouse for his thesis, *Structures économiques et programme de développement pour le Rif*. In 1966 he was attached to the International Labour Office.

Arlotto, Anthony Thomas, born 1 September 1939 at Jersey City, N.J., he was a graduate of Boston College, who also studied at the Rijksuniversiteit te Leiden, the University of Washington, Seattle, and

Harvard, where he obtained a Ph.D. in 1966 for his thesis *The Uighur text of Hsüan Tsang's biography.* Afterwards he was for some years a professor of linguistics at Harvard. His writings include *Introduction to historical linguistics* (1971). ConAu, 33-36; DrAS, 1969, 1974 F

Armajani, Yahya, born 3 November 1908 at Rasht, Iran, he was a graduate of Princeton Theological Seminary, and received a Ph.D. in 1939 from Princeton University for his thesis, *A critical study and translation of the Arabic and Persian sources concerning the Saffarid period.* He was a sometime dean of Alborz College, Iran, and professor at Macalester College, St. Paul, Minn. He wrote *Iran* (1972), and, with Thomas M. Ricks, *Middle East; past and present* (1970). DrAS, 1982

Armand, Paul, born 14 March 1840 at Cahors (Lot), he taught history and geography at the Lycée de Marseille and was a founder of the Société de géographie de Marseille. He died in Marseille, 26 July 1894. DBF

Armbruster, Adolf, born in 1941 at Tălmaci, Sibiu, Romania, he was a sometime member of the Institutul de Istorie "N. Iorga," Bucharest. In 1981 he emigrated to Germany. His writings include *Romanitatea românilor; istoria unei idei* (Bucureşti, 1972). WhoRom

Arminjon, Pierre, born 23 July 1869, he received a doctorate in law in 1895 from the Université de Paris for *Droit romain - droit français.* He was a sometime professor at l'École khédiviale de droit du Caire, as well as a member of the Tribunal mixte du Caire, and a professor of law at Genève, Lausanne and the Académie de droit international de La Haye. Columbia University, New York, conferred on him an honoray doctorate. Together with Sir Maurice S. Amos, he published *A collection of problems and exercises in the civil and commercial law of Egypt* (1904). His own writings include *Étrangers et protégés dans l'Empire ottoman* (1903), and *L'enseignement; la doctrine et la vie dans les universités musulmanes d'Egypte* (1907). SchBiAr 4 (1954), pp. 12-13; WhoSwi, 1950/51

Armistead, Samuel Gordon, born 21 August 1927 at Philadelphia, Pa., he was educated at Princeton University where he received a Ph.D. in 1955. Afterwards he was a professor of Spanish at various American universities. His writings include *Seis romancerillos de cordel sefardies* (1981); he was joint editor of *Judeo-Spanish ballads from New York* (1981). In 1995 he was honoured by *Oral tradition and Hispanic literature; essays in honor of Samuel G. Armistead.* DrAS, 1969, 1974 F, 1978 F, 1982 F; IntAu&W, 1977; WhoAm, 1974/75-1980/81|

Armstrong, Hamilton Fish, born 7 April 1893 at N.Y.C., he graduated in 1916 from Princeton University. In 1917 he was appointed military attaché to Serbian War Mission in the United States. Afterwards he was managing editor of *Foreign affairs* from 1922 to 1928. His writings include *The new Balkans* (1926), and *Where the East begins* (1929). He died in May 1973. CurBio,1948, 1973; WhAm, 5

Armstrong, Harold Countenay, C.B.E., born 20 October 1892, he was educated at Worcester and Oxford. As captain in the British Army he travelled widely in the Middle East. In the post-World War one period he was assistant and acting military attaché to the High Commissioner in Constantinople, special service officer in the War Office, and on Headquarters Staff of the Allied Army of Occupation. In February 1927, he went to Cyprus as the British delegate on the Commission for the Assessment of Damages suffered in Turkey. His writings include *Turkey in travail* (1925), *Grey wolf, Mustafa Kemal* (1933), *Lord of Arabia, Ibn Saud* (1934), and its German translation *Ibn Saud, König im Morgenland* (1936). He died on 25 August 1943. Who was who, 4

Arnakis (Αρνάκης), George Georgiades, born 2 July 1912 at Constantinople, he was a graduate of Robert College, and also studied at Athens University. He taught at various American universities before he became a professor of history in the University of Texas, Austin, in 1961. His writings include *Οι πρώτοι Οθωμανοί* (Athens, 1947), and he was joint author of *The Near East in modern times*, 3 vols. (1969-73). He died in 1976. DrAS, 1974, 1978; EEE; Hellenikon, 1965

Arnaldez, Roger Antoine, born 13 September 1911 at Paris, he was professor of philosophy at universities in Egypt and France until his retirement in 1978. His writings include *Mahomet* (1970), *Le Coran* (1983), *Trois messengers pour un seul Dieu* (1983), *L'islam* (1985), *Aspects de la pensée musulmane* (1987), and *Jésus dans la pensée arabe* (1988). Who's who in France, 1996/97-2003/2004

Arnaud, Édouard Joseph, born 19th cent., he was a French army captain and joint leader of the *Mission Arnaud-Cortier*, which is the subject of their joint publication, *Nos confins sahariens; étude d'organisation militaire* (1908). His trace is lost after a publication in 1916. LC

Arnaud, F. Eugène, born in 1826 at Crest (Drôme), where his father served as a Calvinst pastor. After also training for the ministry, he successively became a pastor at Crupies and Vans until 1865, when he returned to Crest and remained there until his death in 1905. He wrote predominantly about Protestantism in France. His writings include *Palestine ancienne et moderne* (1868). DBF

Arnaud, Jacqueline, born 1933, she was a recognized authority on African Francophone and comparative literature. From 1958 to 1963 she taught in Morocco and subsequently in Tunisia. She was an admirer of Kateb Yacine and contributed in no small way to his literary success. Until her death on 14 January 1987, she taught at the Université de Villetaneuse (Paris-XVIII), where a commemorative colloquium was held from 2-4 December 1987. Her writings include *Anthologie des écrivains français du Maghreb* (1969); *Recherches sur la littérature maghrébine de langue français;: le cas de Kateb Yacine* (1982), a work which was originally presented in 1978 as her thesis at Paris, and *La littérature maghrébine de langue française* (1986). *Annuaire de l'Afrique du nord* 25 (1986), p. 603; THESAM, 1

d'Arnaud Bey, Joseph-Pons, born 1812, he was a French engineer who, in the service of Muhammad Ali of Egypt, participated in expeditions to the sources of the White Nile. He died in Chatou (Seine-et-Oise) on 8 June 1884. DBF; Henze; Hill

Arnaud, L., born 19th cent., he was a French *interprète militaire* who published a history of the Oulad Nail in several installments in the *Revue africaine* between 1862 and 1873. Note

Arnaud, Marc Antoine, born 18 August 1835 at Alger, he served in the Corps des interprètes militaires in Algeria and rose from the rank of *interprète auxiliaire de 2e classe* (28 February 1860) to *interprète titulaire de 1ère classe* (28 February 1873). In 1866 he became editor-in-chief of *al-Mubashshir*, the Arabic edition of the official gazette. He was a member of the Société historique algérienne. His writings include *Les roueries de Dalila, conte traduit des Milles et une nuits* (1879). Féraud, p. 343

Arnaud, Robert, born 16 February 1873 at Moustapha, Algeria, he was educated at the Lycée and the Faculté de droit, Alger, as well as the École coloniale, Paris. He was an administrator in French West Africa until his retirement in 1936. Under the pseudonym of Robert Randau he wrote fiction set in Algeria and West Africa. His writings include *Les algérianistes* (1911), *Afrique occidentale française* (1912), *Le chef des portes-plumé* (1922), *Les explorateurs* (1929), *Des blancs dans la cité des noirs* (1935), *Isabelle Eberhardt* (1945). He died in 1950. Hommes et destins, vol. 1, pp. 39-43

Arnaud, Thomas Joseph, born at Lurs (Basses-Alpes), he had been a pharmacist with an Egyptian regiment before serving the Imam of Yemen in the same capacity. In 1843 he set out from Sanaa in search of inscriptions at Marib; he attached himself to one of the regular camel trains and reached the area. After only a few days among the ruins, he considered it prudent to catch the return caravan. He arrived back in Sanaa without mishap. His trace is lost in 1850. Bidwell, p. 171; Henze

Arnberger, Erik, born 22 April 1917 at Wien, received a Dr.phil. in 1961 from the Hochschule für Welthandel, Wien, for *Erdöl im Mittleren Osten*. In his later years he was director of the Institut für Kartographie der Österreichischen Akademie der Wissenschaften, Wien. His writings include *Beiträge zur Landwirtschaftsgeographie von Niederösterreich* (1948), and he edited *Kartographie der Gegenwart in Österreich* (1984). For many years he was a joint editor of *Mitteilungen der Österreichischen Geographischen Gesellschaft*. Who's who in Austria, 1982/83

Arne, Ture Algot Johnson, born 7 May 1879, he studied at Uppsala, where he received a doctorate in 1914 for his thesis *La Suède en Orient; études archéologiques*. His writings include *Excavations at Shah Tepé, Iran* (1945), and *Svenskarna och Österlandet* (1952). He died in Stockholm, 2 August 1965. Svenska män och kvinnor; Vem är det, 1965

von **Arneth**, Joseph Calasanza, Ritter, born 12 August 1791 at Leopoldschlag, Austria, he studied at the universities of Linz and Wien. In later life he became director of the k.k. Münz- und Antiken-Kabinet, Wien. He contributed extensively to learned journals, and wrote *Geschichte des Kaiserthumes Oesterreich* (1827). He died in Karlsbad, 21 October 1863. DtBE; Egyptology; Wurzbach

Arnett, Edward John, C.M.G., born 19th cent., he was educated at St. Catherine's College, Cambridge, and was a sometime Senior Resident in the Southern Provinces of Nigeria. His writings include *Gazetteer of Sokoto Province* (1920), and *Gazetteer of Zaria Province* (1920). He died on 10 May 1940. Who was who, 3

Arnett, Mary Flounders, she obtained a Ph.D. in 1966 from Dropsie University, Philadelphia, Pa., for her thesis, *Qasim Amin and the beginning of the feminist movement in Egypt.*

Arnold, Adolf, born 20 March 1935 at Lehrte, Germany, he received a Dr..phil. in 1979 for *Untersuchungen zur Wirtschaftsgeographie Tunesiens und Ostalgeriens*. He was a professor of geography at Hannover and wrote *Agrargeographie* (1985). Kürschner, 1992-2003

Arnold, Sir Arthur, born in 1833 at Gravesend, Kent, he was a journalist and philo-Hellenic, and from 1880 to 1885 a radical Liberal M.P. Cambridge University awarded him an honorary LL.D. His writings include *Through Persia by caravan* (1877), and *Social politics* (1878). He died in 1902. DNB; Who was who, 1

Arnold, Friedrich August, born 16 November 1812 at Halle, Germany, he studied Oriental languages at Halle and received a Dr.phil. in 1841 for *Libri Aethiopici Fetha Negest*. He was a senior schoolmaster at the Latina in the Franckeschen Stiftungen, Halle, and a part-time professor at the Universität. His writings include *Imrilkaisi carmen* (1836), *Palästina* (1845), *Septem mo'allakat* (1850), *Chrestomathia arabica* (1853), and *Abriss der hebräischen Formenlehre* (1867). He died in Halle in 1869. ADtB; Fück, 173

Arnold, Matthew, born 24 December 1822 at Laleham, England, he was educated at Rugby, Winchester and Balliol College, Oxford. He was a critic, poet, and essayist whose writings include *Literature and dogma* (1883). He died in Liverpool, 15 April 1888. DNB; Master (32)

Arnold, Sir Robert *Arthur*, born 28 May 1833, he was a Liberal politician, a sometime Justice of the Peace and a member of the Greek Committee, London, as well as the Eastern Question Association, London. His writings include *From the Levant, the Black Sea, and the Danube* (1868), and *Through Persia by caravan* (1877). He died on 20 May 1902. DLB, vol. 32 (1984), pp. 3-27, vol. 57 (1987), pp. 3-28; DNB; Who was who, 1

Arnold, Sir Thomas Walker, born 19 April 1864; he was educated at Magdalen College, Cambridge. His work on Islam began in 1888 when he joined what is now the Muslim University of Aligarh. After ten years' work there he became professor of philosophy at Government College, Lahore, and afterwards dean of the Oriental Faculty, Punjab University. In 1904 he was appointed assistant librarian at the India Office, London. From 1921 until his death on 9 June 1930, he held the Chair of Arabic at SOAS. His writings include *The preaching of Islam* (1896), *The caliphate* (1924), and *Painting in Islam* (1928). As joint-editor he took part in a work that stands as his most enduring monument, the *Encyclopædia of Islam*. Al-Andalus 1 (1933), pp. 201-204; Buckland; DNB; Fück; IndianBilnd (1); Who was who, 3

Arnold, Wolfgang, Dr., fl. 1963 in Wuppertal, Germany, he wrote *Personelle Einkommensverteilung in Entwicklungsländern*. LC

Arnold-Forster, Hugh Oakeley, born in 1855, and educated at Rugby and University College, Oxford, he was a sometime Secretary of State for War, and a Member of Parliament. His writings include *History of England* (1897), and *English socialism of to-day* (1908). He died on 12 March 1909. DNB; Who was who, 1

Arnot, Robert, born in 1860, he wrote *Armenian literature* (London, 1902), and *Turkish literature, comprising fables, belles-lettres and sacred traditions* (London, 1902). LC

Arnot, Sandford, fl. 1827 at the London Oriental Institution. His writings include *A sketch of the Indian press during the last ten years* (1829), *Indian cookery as practised and described by the natives of the East* (London, 1831), and with Duncan Forbes, *A grammar of the Hindustani tongue in the Oriental and Roman characters* (1844). BLC

Arnoulet, François, he was joint author of *Études d'histoire contemporaine tunisienne, 1846-1871* (Aix-en-Provence, Institut d'histoire des pays d'outre-mer, 1973.) LC

Arntz, Égide Rodolphe Nicolas, born 1 September 1812 at Kleve, Germany, he studied at the universities of München, Jena, Bonn, and Heidelberg. Visiting home in April 1834, he was suspected of subversive activities in the student movement (*Burschenschaft*) and decided to evade to Belgium, where he made a brilliant career. In 1835 he received a doctorate from the Université de Liège, and from 1838 until his death he was a professor of law at the Université de Bruxelles, and a permanent member of the Conseil d'administration. He was a founder of *La Belgique judiciaire* (1842-1883). His writings include *Précis méthodique des règlements consulaires* (1876). He died in Ixelles, 23 August 1884. ADtB; *Biographie nationale* (Bruxelles), t. 30, pp. 84-95

Aro, Jussi Taneli, born 5 June 1928 at Lapua, Finland, he came from a pietist home and majored in Assyriology and comparative Semitics, with a bent for religions and folklore. He received a doctorate from the University of Helsinki for his thesis, *Glossar zu den mittelbabylonischen Briefen* (1957). In the same year, he, together with Armas Salonen, brought to completion the Finnish translation of *Koraani* started by Knut Tallqvist. From 1965 until his death on 11 May 1983, he held the chair of Oriental literature at his alma mater. He was a humble and deeply religous man, with a compassion for the weak and oppressed, and as such a contributor to the collective work *Assyrier – vilka är de* (1978). He always felt like a stranger among his academic colleagues. His writings include *Abrahamin perillisel* (1970), *Juutalaisuuden ja Islamin peruspiirteitä* (1978). Temenos 19 (1983), pp. 139-141; Vem och vad, 1975, 1980

Arpad, Marcel, born 19th cent., he wrote *Zigeunererzählungen und Volksdichtungen in Versen* (Halle, 1909).

Arri, Giovanni Antonio, from Asti, Italy, he was a theologian, author of works on archaeology, a sometime assistant at the Biblioteca della Regia Università, and a member of the Accademia delle Scienze di Torino. His writings include *Novas observationes in quodam numos Abbasidarum aliosque Cuficos* (Torino, 1835), *Nouvelles observations sur l'inscription latino-punique de Leptis* (1837), and *Storia degli arabi e di alcuni celebri popoli contemporanei* (Paris, 1840). De Rolandis; IndBiltal (1)

Arribas Paláu, Mariano, fl. 1953-1992., he receivd a doctorate in Semitic languages. In 1953 he was deputy director of the Instituto Muley el-Hasan at Tetuán. He was a sometime professor in the Universidad Complutense de Madrid. His writings include *Catálogo de autores de la biblioteca, sección europea* (Tetuán, 1953), *Una embajada marroquí enviada a España en 1792* (Tetuán, 1953), *Musulmanes de Valencia apresados cerca de Ibiza en 1413* (Tetuán, 1955), and *Cartes árabes de Marruecos en tiempo de Mawlay al-Yazid* (1961). LC

Arrighi, Gino, born 16 July 1906 at Lucca, Italy, he received a doctorate in mathematics and became a naval and mechanical engineer. He was a sometime professor in the Università di Pisa and wrote *Contributo ad una teoria generale degli operatori* (Roma, 1947); he also edited a number of early works on mathematics. Lui chi è, 1969; WhoWor, 1978; Who*s who in Italy, 1957/58

Arsanis, G. V., fl. 1961. His writings include *Вводный курс современного ассирийского языка* (Moscow, 1973). LC

Arsenev, Nikolai Sergeevich, born in 1888, he was a Russian Orthodox theologian who taught in Russia (1914-1920), Germany, Poland, France, and finally at St. Vladimir's Orthodox Theological Seminary in New York. His writings include *Ostkirche und Mystik* (München, 1925), *Mysticism and the Eastern Church* (1926), *Православная церков и западное христианство* (Warszawa, 1929), *Православие, католичество, протестантизм* (Paris, 1930), and *We beheld His glory* (New York, 1936.) LC

Arsenian, Seth, born 2 April 1902 at Van, Turkey, he was educated at Robert College, Constantinople, and Columbia University, N.Y.C., where he received a Ph.D. in 1937 for *Bilingualism and mental development*. Afterwards he became a professor of psychology at American universities. During the second World War he served with the Bureau of Overseas Intelligence of the Office of War Information. He was joint author of *Councelling in the YMCA* (1954). AM&WS, 1978 S

Arsh, Grigorii L'vovich, born abou 1900, he wrote *Албания и Эпир в конц XVIII - начале XIX в.* (1963), he was joint author of *Краткая история Албании* (1965), *Русско-турецкая война 1877-1878 гг. и Балканы* (1978), and he edited *Общественные и культурные связи народов СССР и Балкан XVIII-XX вв.* (1987). LC

Arsharuni, Arshaluis Mikhailovich, born 17 (29), November 1896 in the Vilayet Kars, Turkey, he graduated in 1920 from the Faculty of History and Philology, Warsaw Uniwersity in Rostov-on-Don. His writings include *СССР и народы Востока* (1925), *Бехаизм* (1930), *Бабизм* (1931); he was joint author of *Эпос советского Востока* (1930), *Ислам* (1931), and *Очерки панисламизма и пантюркизма в России* (1931). He also published in Armenian. He died 20 October 1985. Miliband; Miliband²

Arshi, Imtiyaz Ali Khan, born 8 December 1904 in India, he was a sometime director of the Rampur Raza Library. He died in 1981. Hamdard Islamicus 4 ii (1981), pp. 101-103; Jain

Arslan, 'Adil, Amir, born in 1883, he was in 1938 resident in Saffron Walden, Cambridgeshire, and a member of the Royal Central Asian Society. His writings include his reminiscences, *Dhikrayāt*, published in 1962. He died in 1954. LC

Arslan, Emin, born 1 July 1868 (or, according to Pinto, in 1873) at al-Shuwayfat, Ottoman Lebanon, he was educated at the Université des pères Jésuites de Beyrouth. In 1894 he was in Paris where he founded the journal *Kashf al-niqāb* and, in the following year, *Jeune Turquie*. In 1909 he was a witness to the counter-revolution in Constantinople. He was a sometime Ottoman consul in Belgium and France as well as vice-governor of Lebanon. In his later years he emigrated to Argentina. His writings include works in Arabic and the publications in Buenos Aires, *Final de un idilio* (1917), *La revolución Siria contra el mandate francés* (1926), *Verdadera historia de Las desencantades* (1935), and *Los árabes, reseña historico-literaria y leyendas* (1941). He died in 1942. Curinier, v. 3 (1901), p. 202; Pinto

Arslan, Shakib (Chékib), born 5 December 1869, of Druze parents at al-Shuwayfat, Lebanon, he studied in Beirut, partly under Muhammad 'Abduh. He was a politician, a sometime member of the Turkish Parliament for Hawran, and editor of *La Nation arabe* (Genève, 1930-1938). His writings include *Our decline and its causes* (1944), and his Arabic autobiography in 1969. He died in 1946. *Hommes et destins,* vol. 7, pp. 32-36; ZKO

Arslanian, Artin Hagop, born in 1942, he received a Ph.D. in 1974 from UCLA for *The British military involvement in Transcaucasia, 1917-1919*. He was a sometime member of the staff of Belmont Abbey College, Belmont, N.C. *MESA Roster of members,* 1990; NUC, 1979

Arslanlı, Halil, born 26 October 1904, he received a doctorate in 1942 from Istanbul Üniversitesi for his thesis *Türk hukukunda devletçiliğin anonim şirketlerin ehliyeti üzerine tesiri*. Afterwards he was professor of commercial law at İstanbul Üniversitesi. His writings include *Fikrî hukuk dersleri* (1954), and *Anonim şirketler* (1959-1961). He died on 29 April 1964. A commemorative volume was published in 1978 entitled, *Ord. Prof. Dr. Halil Arslanlı'nın anısına armağan.*

Arsunar, Ferruh, fl. 1943, he wrote *Türk çocuk oyunlasindan örnekler* (1955), *Gaziantep folkloru* (1962), and *Türk Anadolu halk türküleri* (1965). LC

Artamonov, Leonid Konstantinovich, born in 1859, he was a Russian army officer, engineer, and geographer. His writings include Северный Азербайджан (Tiflis, 1890), and Через Эфиопию к берегам Белого Нила (Moscow, 1979). Henze; LC

Artamonov, Mikhail Illarionovich, born in 1898 at Vygolevo, Russia, he was an archaeologist and a sometime director of the Ermitage, Leningrad. His writings include Очерки древнейшей истории хазар (1936), История хазар (1962), *Goldschatz der Skythen in der Ermitage* (1970), *The dawn of art* (1974), and Киммерийцы и Скифы (1974). He died 29 July 1972. AzarbSE; GSE; TatarES; *Who's who in the USSR,* 1965/66

Artaud, Adrien Jean Marie, born 26 September 1859 at Marseille, he was a sometime president of the Marseille Chamber of Commerce, and the director of *La Méditerranée,* 1929-1934. His writings include *Bericht über die dringende Notwendigkeit, in den deutschen und österreich-ungarischen Absatzgebieten Fuß zu fassen* (Jena, 1915), and *Finance et bon sens* (1922). *Qui êtes-vous,* 1924

Artbauer, Otto Cesar, born in 1879, he wrote *Afrikanische Sittenbilder; die Welt des Halbmonds wie sie weint und lacht* (1911), *Kreuz und quer durch Marokko; Kultur- und Sittenbilder* (1911), *Die Riffpiraten und ihre Heimat* (1911), and *Kreuz und quer durch Marokko; das Ende des letzten Sultanats* (1925).

Arthy, Elliott, born in 1765, he was a surgeon in the African and West Indian Merchants' service and wrote *The seaman's medical advocate* (London, 1798). He died after 1800. BritInd (1); Master (2)

Artin, Ya'qub Pasha, born 15 April 1842 at Cairo, he was an Armenian who was educated in Constantinople and France before he learned Turkish, Persian, and Arabic. From 1878 to 1879 he was in the service of Khedive Ismail, and, in 1881, he joined the Institut d'Egypte. He was an administrator until 1906. In 1908 he accompanied the Khedive Tawfiq on his travels to the Sudan. The University of St. Andrews in Scotland awarded him an honorary doctorate. His writings include *Contes populaires inédites de la vallée du Nil* (1895), and *Contribution à l'étude du blason en Orient* (1902). He died in 1919. Goldschmidt; *Hommes et destins,* vol. 4, pp. 33-35

de Artiñano y Galdácano, Pedro Miguel, born in 1879, he wrote *Exposición de hierros antiguos españoles* (1919), and *Catálogo de la Exposición de orfebrería civil española* (1925). He died in 1934. LC

Artonne, Pierre André, born 20 August 1882 at Clermont-Ferrand, he was educated at Paris, where he became an honorary librarian of the Ministère des Affaires Étrangères, member of the Commission des Archives diplomatiques, and editor-in-chief of *Archivum*. His writings include *Le mouvement de 1314 et les chartes provinciales de 1315* (1912). He died in Paris, 3 June 1957. *Who's who in France,* 1953/54-1957/58

Arunova, Marianna Rubenovna, born 24 June 1929 at Leningrad, she graduated in 1952 from the Oriental Faculty, Leningrad, and received a doctorate in 1956 for Рост феодальной эксплуатации и борьба народных масс Ирана в 30-40 гг. XVIII в. She was joint author of Государство Надир-шаха Афшара (1958), Афганистан; экономика, политика, история (1984), and Очерки истории формирования государственных границ между Россией, СССР и Афганистаном (1994). LC; Miliband; Miliband[2]

Aruri, Naseer Hasan, born 7 July 1934 at Jerusalem, he received a Ph.D. in 1967 from the University of Massachusetts for his thesis, *Jordan; a study in political development, 1921-1965*. He later became a professor of political science first at Southeastern Massachusetts University and then at the University of Massachusetts, Darmouth. He was affiliated with Amnesty International, Middle East Watch, and the *Third world quarterly*. He was joint author of *Reagan and the Middle East* (1983). LC; Private

Arvanitakes, Georgios L., born in 1872 at Jerusalem, his writings include the two pamphlets, *On the answer*

of the Bulgarian socialists (London, 1918), and *Sur la réponse des socialistes bulgares* (Genève, 1918). He died in Athens in 1946. EEE; LC

Arveiller, Raymond, fl. 1963-1987. His writings include *Contribution à l'étude des termes de voyage en français* (1963), and *L'œuvre poétique de Falquet de Romans* (1987). LC

Aryda, A. fl. 1809 *see* 'Aridah, Antun

Arzruni, Krikor (Grigor), Dr., fl. 1879 at Tiflis, he was an Armenian writer who had two of his papers translated into German: *Die ökonomische Lage der Armenier in der Türkei*, translated by A. Amirchanjanz (St. Petersburg, 1879), and *Die Hungersnoth in Türkisch-Armenien* (Tiflis, 1880). LC

Arzumanian, Ol'ga Agazhanovna, born 5 July 1928 in Armenia, she graduated in 1953 from Erevan State University and received her first degree in 1965 for *Вопросительое предложение в современном персидском языке*. Miliband²

Arzumetov, IUldash Safarovich (Юлдаш Сафарович Арзуметов), fl. 1973, his writings include *Медицинские взгляды Ибн Сины* (Tashkent, 1983). LC

al-Asad, Hafiz, born 6 October 1928 at Lattakia, he came from a poor Alawite peasant family named Wahsh (wild beast) and changed his family name to Asad (lion) and made an unprecedented rise to the supreme position of Syria's president in 1970. His writings include *Ka-dhalika qala al-Asad* (1984), and *Sani' ta`rikh al-ummah wa-bani majd al-watan* (1986). Patrick Seale wrote a biography, *Asad of Syria; the struggle for the Middle East* (1988). He died on 10 June 2000. CurBio, 1975, 1992; IntWW, 2002; Master (8); MidE, 1982/83; Reich

Asad, Muhammad, born Leopold Weiss, on 2 July 1900 at Lemberg, Austria-Hungary, the son of a Jewish barrister, he studied history of art, and philosophy at the universities of Wien, Praha, and Berlin, where he was influenced by the intelllectual coterie of the 1920s. During this time he made a living as a newspaper correspondent for the *Frankfurter Zeitung*. When his uncle invited him to Jerusalem, he became exposed to Zionism about which he sent critical dispatches back to Germany. These were published as a book entitled *Unromantisches Morgenland* (1924). He continued to travel extensively in the Middle East, and inasmuch as he became personally and religiously involved in the region, he became increasingly alienated from the West. He took up studying Arabic at Cairo. In 1926, he and his wife broke with the past, embraced Islam, and settled in Saudi Arabia. His life up to this point is the subject of his *The road to Mecca* (1954, German translation, 1992). In the 1940s he was engaged in the Pakistan movement, culminating in his service as Pakistan's minister plenipotentiary to the U.N. But his disapproval of many aspects of political Islam made him withdraw to Morocco where he worked on a translation of the Koran and al-Bukhari's *Sahih* (1978). He considered the Islamic revolution in Iran a disaster for the Muslim world, and died in self-imposed exile on 20 February 1992 in Mijas, Spain. *IRCICA* newsletter, no. 28 (April 1992), p. 16; *Periodica Islamica* 2, no. i (1992), p. 4.

Asadullaeva, S. Kh., fl. 1971, she edited *Художественный и металл Азербайджана* (Baku, 1984).

Asanaliev, Usengazy A., fl. 1971, his writings include *Литология и рудоносность девонских и нижне-каменноугольных отложений среднинго Тянь-Шаня* (Frunze, 1974).

Asanov, Aleksei Alekseevich, fl. 1972, he wrote *Памятники архитектуры средневекового Хорезма* (Tashkent, 1971). LC

Asboeck, Anton, born 20 July 1882 at Steinhöring, Germany. After extramural matriculation he studied at the Universität München, where he received a Dr.phil. in 1913 for *Das Staatswesen von Priene in hellenistischer Zeit*. His writings include *Die Bürgerrechtsbücher der Stadt Burghausen* (1939).

Aschenbrenner, Joyce Cathryn, born 24 March 1931 at Salem, Oregon, she received a Ph.D. in 1967 anthropology from the University of Minnesota for *Endogamy and social status in a West Punjab village*. Under a Fulbright-Hays Grant she did field work in West Pakistan (1964-1965) and sponsored by the American Philosophical Society, in India (1967). She subsequently served as a professor at various American universities. Her writings include *Lifelines; Black families in Chicago* (1975). AmM&WSc, 1973 S, 1976 P

Ascherson, Paul Friedrich August, born 4 July 1834 at Berlin, he studied medicine and botany at the Universität Berlin, where he received a doctorate in 1855 for *Studiorum phytographicorum de Marchia Brandenburgensi specimen*. In 1873 he became a professor of botany at his alma mater. He accompanied G. Rohlfs on his expedition to the Libyan Desert, and G. Schweinfurth to the Bahariyah Oasis. He died in Berlin on 6 March 1913. Henze

Aschmann, Gottfried, born in 1884, he was a career diplomat who was a junior diplomat (*Botschaftsrat*) in Ankara from 1932 to 1933. Afterwards he was head of the Press Section in the German Foreign Office. DtBilnd (1); Wer ist's, 1935

Ascoli, Graziadio Isaia, born 16 July 1829 at Gorizia, Italy, he was a student of comparative linguistics, and a member of the Deutsche Morgenländische Gesellschaft. His writings include *Studi orientali e linguistici* (Milano, 1854), *Studi critici* (1861), *Zigeunerisches* (Halle, 1865), and *Lezioni di fonologia comparata del sanscrito, del greco e del latino* (Torino, 1870). He died in Milano, 21 January 1907. DizBI; IndBiltal (20)

Asdrachas, Spyros Ioanni, born 7 May 1933 at Argostoli, Ionian Islands, he studied at Athens. His writings include Μηχανισμοί της αγροτικής οικονομίας στην Τουρκοκρατία (1978), Ζητήματα ιστορίας (1983), and Ιστορικά απεικάσματα (1995). EEE; EVL, 1993/94-2001; LC

el-Asfahany, Nabya *see* al-Isfahani, Nabiyah

Asfandyari, Hasan, 1245 H. Sh.-1323/1944 *see* Isfandiyari, Hasan

Asfour, John, born 15 January 1902 at Shefa Amr, near Haifa, he was an Anglican and educated at Bishop Gobat School, Jerusalem. He served his apprenticeship to the law as chief clerk of the District Court in Haifa; he then was called to the bar and became an advocate defending Arabs in the troubles of 1929 and 1936-1939 in Palestine. He was long engaged in developing labour organizations in Palestine, and also turned his attention to anti-Zionist activities. While attending the World Trade Unions' Conference in London, 1945, he studied labour organization in the United Kingdom. Who's who in Palestine and Jordan, 1945/46

Ashbee, Charles Robert, born 17 May 1863 at Isleworth, Kent. His father's people were Kentish yeomen who traced their descent among the hop gardens for hundreds of years; and his mother's people were Hamburg merchants who had intermarried for generations with England, whose forebears had once been cosmopolitan Jews. He was educated at King's College, Cambridge, and became an architect, designer, and townplanner. From 1918 to 1922 he was Civic Adviser to the Palestine Administration first in a military and then a civil capacity. During his time in Jerusalem, he prepared plans for the reconstruction of the city and the preservation of its historic shrines as well as for the revival of the arts and crafts of Palestine. His writings include *A Palestine note book, 1918-1923* (1923), and *Lyrics from the Nile* (1938). He died on 23 May 1942. ChambrBrBi; Who was who, 4

Ashbel, Dov, born in December, 1895, at Jerusalem, he was educated at the Teachers' Seminary, Jerusalem, and Universität Berlin. After service with the Turkish Army during the first World War, he taught for a number of years in labour settlements in Palestine before becoming a meteorologist. His writings include *Temperature and relative humidity in Palestine and surrounding countries* (1945), and *Meteorological data for Palestine* (1939-1955), as well as numerous works in Hebrew. Who was who in Palestine and Jordan, 1945

Ashcom, Benjamin Bowles, born 22 December 1903 at Everett, Pa., he was educated at Pennsylvania State College, and the University of Michigan, where he received a Ph.D. in 1938; afterwards he was professor of Spanish at Wayne State University, Detroit. His writings include *Functional Spanish review grammar and composition* (1945), and *A descriptive catalogue of the Spanish comedias sueltas in the Wayne State University Library and the private library of Prof. B. B. Ashcom* (1965). DrAS, 1969, 1974 F

Asher, Catherine Ella Blanshard, born 20th cent., she received a Ph.D. in 1984 from the University of Minnesota for her *The patronage of the Sher Shah Sur*. In 1997 she was a professor of fine art in the University of Minnesota, Minneapolis, a post which she still held in 2003. Her writings include *Architecture of Mughal India* (1992), and she was joint editor of *Perceptions of South Asia's visual past* (1994). NatFacDr, 2003

Ashford, Douglas Elliott, born 8 August 1928 at Lockport, N.Y., he spent fourteen months of study in Morocco for his Ph.D. thesis, *Political change in Morocco* (Princeton, 1960). He was a Rhodes scholar and an intelligence officer in the U.S. Air Force. In 1961 he was a professor of government at the University of Indiana, and since 1964, professor at Cornell University. His writings include *Perspectives of a Moroccan nationalist* (1964), *Morocco-Tunisia; politics and planning* (1965), *National development and local form; political participation in Morocco, Tunisia and Pakistan* (1967), and *Policy and politics in Britain* (1980). AM&WSc, 13th ed., 1978; ConAu, 73; Unesco

Ashkenazi, Tovia, he was born in the Ukraine and spent some years in Palestine before settling in the United States in 1945. He received a doctorate from the Sorbonne. His writings include *Tribus semi-nomades de la Palestine du nord* (1938), *Colloquial Arabic course* (Pittsburgh, 1947), *A Bibliographical list of writings, 1922-1924, with published biographical notes* (Washington, D.C., 1954), and he was joint author of *Treaties, agreements and pronouncements: Palestine* (Pittsburgh, 1947).

al-'Ashmawi, Salih, fl. 1948. He was a sometime vice-president of the Muslim Brotherhood in Cairo, and personal envoy of Amin al-Husayni, the Grand Mufti of Jerusalem. Note

Ashraf, Ahmad, born 21 September 1934 at Tehran, he studied at the University of Tehran and the New School for Social Research, N.Y.C. He taught at several universities in the United States. From 1971 to 1981 he was director of the Social Research Bureau in Tehran. He was an editor of the *Encyclopædia Iranica*, and he wrote موانع تاریخی رشد سرمایه‌داری در ایران دوره قاجریه (1359/1980). Private

Ashraf, Kunwar Mohammad, born in 1903, he wrote *Life and conditions of the people of Hindustan* (Karachi, 1978). In 1966 he was honoured by *Kunwar Mohammad Ashraf, an Indian scholar and revolutionary*. He died in Berlin in 1962. Jain, p. 102

Ashraf, Muhammad, born in 1907, he wrote *A catalogue of the Persian manuscripts in the Salar Jung Museum and Library* (Hyderabad, 1965-66), *The postmarks of Hyderabad* (1967), and *A concise descriptive catalogue of the Arabic MSS in the Salar Jung Museum and Library* (Hyderabad, 1978). LC

Ashraf, Syed (Abu Nasr) *Ali*, born in 1924, he was educated at the universities of Dacca and Cambridge, where he received a Ph.D. for *English poetry and its audience from 1910 to 1945*. He served at Dacca University as a lecturer and reader (1947-1954) and Rajshahi University as a reader and head of the English Department (1955-1956), before joining Karachi University. His writings include *Muslim traditions in Bengali literature* (1985). LC; Note

Ashrafi, Mukaddima Mukhtarovna, born 5 July 1936, she was in 1990 a senior research fellow at the Institute of History in the Tajik Academy of Sciences. Her writings include Персидско-таджикская поэзия в миниатюрах XIV-XVI вв. (1974), and Из истории развития миниатюры Ирана XVI в. (1978). Schoeberlein

Ashrafian (Ашрафян), Klara Zarmairovna, born 15 September 1924 at Erevan, she was a graduate of Moscow State University, where she also received a doctorate in 1966 for a monograph. Her writings include Аграрный строй Северной Индии (1965), Феодализм и Индии (1977); she was joint author of История народов Восточной и Центральной Азии с древнейших времен до наших дней (1986), and joint editor of Узловые проблемы истории докапиталистических обществ Востока (1990). Miliband²

Ashton, Sir Arthur *Leigh* Bolland, born 20 October 1897 at London, he was a graduate of Balliol College, Oxford, who in his later years was director and secretary, Victoria and Albert Museum, London. His writings include *Introduction to the study of Chinese sculpture* (1924), and he edited *The art of India and Pakistan; a commemorative catalogue of the exhibition held at the Royal Academy of Arts, London, 1947-1948* (1950). He died in London, 12 March 1983. BritInd (1); Who's who in art, 1934; Who was who, 8

Ashton, Horace D., born in the last quarter of the 19th century, he devoted twenty-four years of his life to travelling in remore parts of the world. He accompanied Theodore Roosevelt on several expeditions and did exploring and mapping in Columbia and Haiti. In 1920 he visited French North Africa, filming in the Sahara, and climbing in southern Tunisia. He was a fellow of the Royal Geographical Society, and a member of the Explorers' Club of New York and of the New York Academy of Sciences. Asia, December 1923 and 1924

Ashtor, Eliyahu, born Eduard Strauss on17 September 1914 at Wien, he concurrently studied at the Universität Wien and the Israelitisch-Theologische Lehranstalt, and received a Dr.phil. in 1936 for *Baibars al-Mansuri und Ibn al-Furat als Geschichtsquellen*. In 1938 he emigrated to Jerusalem where he submitted a second doctoral dissertation in 1944. Five years later he began an tortuous career as a professor of Islamic civilization at the Hebrew University, Jerusalem. His writings include *Mavo le-mishpat ha-Islam* (1958), *Les métaux précieux et balance des payments du Proche-Orient à basse l'époque* (1971), *The Jews of Moslem Spain* (1973), and *A social and economic history of the Middle East in the middle ages* (1976). He died in Jerusalem on 2 November 1984. Asian and African studies (Haifa) 19 (1985), pp. 119-121; WhoIsrael, 1966/67-1980/81

Ashurbeili (Ашурбейли), Sara Balabekova, born 14 (27) January 1906 at Baku, she graduated in 1941 from the Azerbayjan State University, Baku, where she also received a doctorate in 1965. Her writings include Очерк истории средневекового Баку (1964), Государство Ширваншахов VI-XVI вв. (1983), and Экономические и культурные связи Азербайджана с Индией в средние века (1990). AzarbSE, vol. 1, p. 516; LC; Miliband; Miliband²

al-Asil, Naji, born in 1897 in Baghdad, he studied at Constantinople and AUB, where he graduated in 1917. Thereafter he was in private practice as a physician for two years in Baghdad, but his interest in history and diplomacy diverted him from pursuing a medical career and in 1921 he was posted to London by King Husayn of the Hijaz as Plenipotentiary. In 1923 as spokesman for Arab interests, he represented Iraq at the Lausanne Conference. Upon his return to Baghdad in 1925, he became a founding member of the University al-Bayt where he taught ancient history and Islamic philosophy. In 1932 he was transferred to the Ministry of Foreign Affairs, of which he became director-general in 1934. As Foreign Minister he signed the Treaty of Sa'dabad. He was obliged to retired in 1937. From 1944 to 1958 he was director-general of the Iraq Antiquities Department. His writings include في مواطن الآثار (1945), and *Recent archaeological activity in Iraq* (1956). He died in Baghdad on 16 February 1963. Awwad; *Iraq* 25, no. 2 (1963), pp. ii-iv

Asimov, Mukhammad Saifiddinovich, 1920-1996 *see* Osimi, Mukhammad Saifiddinovich

Asín y Palacios, Miguel, born 5 July 1871 at Zaragoza, he lost his father as a child so that the modest means of the family restricted his education to the local university. This, however, did not stop him from registering as extra-mural student at the Conciliar Seminary of Zaragoza and reciting his first Mass in 1895. As suddenly as he had embraced the ecclesiastical life, he abandoned it. His decision to study Arabic and Islamics was due to the influence of J. Ribera y Tarrago, who held the chair of Arabic at Zaragoza. They became befriended and collaborated with many scholarly projects and Asín was sponsored by him at his reception into the Real Academia Española in 1919. But unlike his teacher, Asín was mainly interested in the history of religious ideas in Islam, in particular Sufism, a subject he had chosen for his thesis in 1901, *Algazel, dogmática, moral, ascética*. In 1903 he was appointed to the chair of Arabic at Madrid. His was a life of scholarship interrupted only by the years of enforced idleness during the Spanish civil war. He wrote *La psicologia segun Mohidin Abenarabi* (1906), *La espiritualidad de Algazel y su sentido cristiano* (1934-41), *Contribución a la toponimia arabe de España* (1940), and *Crestomatia de árabe literal* (1942). He died in San Sebastian, 14 August 1944. Diaz; Fück; GER; I.I. (8); MW 35 (1945), 273-280; *Speculum* 21 (1946), pp. 376-77

Asinari di San Marzano, Roberto, born in 1894, he wrote *Dalla piana somala all'altipiano etiopico* (1935). His trace is lost after a publication in 1941. LC

Askari, Hasan, born 20th cent., he was joint author, with Muhammad S. Abdullah, of *Islam in a plural world; Christian-Muslim encounter in a German perspective* (Bimingham, 1982) and, with Jon Avery, *Towards a spiritual humanism; a Muslim-humanist dialogue* (Leeds, 1991). LC

Askari, Hossein, Dr., born 20th cent., he was a sometime advisor on international economic and financial matters to the Ministry of Finance and National Economy of Saudi Arabia, advisor to the executive director of the International Monetary Fund, and a visiting professor at George Washington University. His writings include *Middle East economics in the 1970s* (1976), *Saudi Arabia's economy* (1990); he was joint author, with George Kozmetsky, of *Evaluation of the conversion of U.S. industry and the national energy plan* (Austin, Tex., Graduate School of Business, U. of Texas, 1978), and, with John Thomas Cummings, of *Taxation and tax policies in the Middle East* (1982). LC; Note

al-'Askari, Ja'far Pasha, 1885-1936 *see* Ja'far Pasha al-'Askari

Askari, Syed Hasan, born in 1901, he was in 1956 a professor of history at Patna College, Patna. His writings include *Reflections of the awakened* (London, 1983), *Aspects of the cultural history of medieval Bihar* (Patna, 1984), *Collected works* (1985), *Iqbal namah* (1985), *Amir Khusrau as a historian* (Patna, 1988), and *Islam and Muslims in Bihar* (Patna, 1989). In 1968 he was honoured by the *Prof. Syed Hasan Askari felicitation volume.* LC; Note

Aslam, Mian Muhammad, Dr., born 20th cent., he was in 1983 an agricultural economist at the University of Agriculture, Faisalabad. His writings include *Some dimensions of rural food* (Faisalabad, Bonn 1983); and he edited *Report of the delegation of Pakistan's agricultural experts to India, 1986* (Islamabad, 1986). LC

Aslam, Mohammad, born 20th cent., he was an agronomist and joint author of *Wheat in the rice-wheat cropping system of the Punjab* (Islamabad, 1989). LC

Aslanapa, Oktay, born 17 December 1914 at Kütahya, Turkey, he was educated at Bursa, Istanbul Üniversitesi, and Wien, where he received a Dr.phil. in 1943 for *Die osmanischen Beiträge zur islamischen Baukunst.* From 1963 until his retirement he was a professor of Turkish and Islamic art at Istanbul Üniversitesi. His writings include *Osmanlılar devrinde Kütahya çinileri* (1949), *Türkische Fliesen und Keramik in Anatolien* (1965), *Turkish art and architecture* (1971), *Kıbrıs'da Türk eserleri* (1975), *Kirim ve kuzey Azerbaycan'da Türk eserleri* (1979), *Osmanlı devri mimarisi* (1986), and *Türk halı sanati'nin bin yılı* (1987). ConAu, 37-40; Meydan

Aslanov, Martiros Grigor'evich, born 2 (14) November 1897, he wrote Афганско-русский словарь (1966), 2nd ed. entitled Пушту-русский словарь (1985); and he was joint author of Бенгальский язык (1962). He died 21 February 1977. Miliband[2]

al-**Asmar**, Fawzi, born in 1937 at Haifa, he attended Central Connecticut State University, and the University of Exeter, where he received a Ph.D. He taught at St. Antony's College, Oxford, Bradford University, and the American University, Washington, D.C. His writings include *Ard al-mi'ad* (1969), *To be an Arab in Israel* (1975), *Dreams on a mattress of thorns* (1976), *The wind-driven reed* (1979), and *Through the Hebrew looking-glass* (1986); he was joint author, with Uri Davis, of *Towards a socialist republic of Palestine* (1978).

Asmus, Valentin Ferdinanovich, born 18 (30) December 1894 at Kiev, where he received a doctorate from the University. Since 1939 he was a professor of philosophy at Moscow University. His writings include *История античной философии* (1965), *Платон* (1969), *Историко-философские этюды* (1984); he was joint author of *Единство научного знания* (1988). He died in 1975. GSE; LC

Asmussen, Jes Peter, born 2 November 1928 at Aabenraa, Denmark, he studied at the Theological Faculty, Københavns Universitet, where he received a Dr.phil. in 1966. Since 1960 he was professor of Iranian studies at Copenhagen. In 1973 he was elected member of the Royal Danish Academy of Sciences. His writings include *Tekster til Islam* (1972), *Manichaean literature* (1975), and, with Jørgen Læssøe, *Illustreret religionshistorie* (1968). Kraks, 1990-2002/3; WWScand, 1981

Asopa, Sheel K., born 20th cent., she was in 1967 a research scholar, and in 1986, associate professor of political science in the University of Rajasthan, Jaipur. Her writings include *Military alliance and regional cooperation in West Asia* (1971), a work which was originally presented as her thesis at the University of Rajasthan, *The foreign policy of modern Turkey* (1971), *Oil, arms, and Islam in the Gulf* (1986), and *Soviet Union and the Third World; from dogmatic Marxism to Glanost* (1990). LC

Aspe-Fleurimont, Lucien Auguste, born in 1862, he wrote *La Guinée française* (1900), and *L'organisation économique de l'Afrique occidentale française* (1901). LC

Aspinion, Robert, fl. 1954, he was in 1937 an *interprète-lieutenant* and in 1946 a *commandant*. His writings include *Contribution à l'étude du droit coutumier berbère* (1937), *Contribution à l'étude du droit berbère marocain* (Casablanca, 1946), and *Apprenons le berbère* (1953). BN; LC; Note

Assabghy, Alexandre (Iskander), born 19th cent., he was in 1926 a lawyer in the claims section of the Ministry of Foreign Affairs in Cairo. His writings include *Les questions de nationalité en Égypte* (Cairo, 1926), *Les accords de Montreux pour la suppression des capitulations et les tribunaux mixtes en Égypte* (Alexandria, 1937), *Apprenons le berbère* (Rabat, 1953), and *Les passions humaines; chroniques judiciaires* (Cairo, 1954). LC

Assad, Hafez, born 1928 see al-Asad, Hafiz

Assad, Mohammad Naim, born 15 October 1939 at Kabul, he studied at Kabul University and until 1964 also worked at the office of university affairs, partly for, and with, his future thesis supervisor. In 1969 he went to study in Germany on an Afghan grant. He received a Dr.rer.pol. in 1972 from the Universität Erlangen for *Das zentralbankpolitische Instrumentarium in ausgewählten orientalischen Ländern*. His writings include *Probleme der Mitarbeiterführung in Afghanistan* (1981), and he was joint author of *Betriebswirtschaftliche Probleme in afghanischen Industrieunternehmen* (1977). LC; Thesis

Assadullah, Mohammed, 1900-1992 see Asad, Muhammad

Assaf, Michael, born 3 May 1896 at Lodz, Russia, he pursued Oriental studies at Berlin before emigrating to Palestine in 1920, where he became a founding member of the Histadrut. In 1963 he was the Middle East specialist at the Hebrew daily *Davar*. His writings include *Die arabisch-nationale Bewegung in Palästina* (Prague, 1936), and *The Arab movement in Palestine* (New York, 1937). Near and Middle East who's who, 1945/46; WhoIsrael, 1949-1969/70; WhoWorJ, 1978

Assas y de Ereño, Manuel, born in 1813 at Santander, Spain, he was a barrister, antiquary, and professor of Sanskrit. He died in Madrid, 18 June 1880. Ossorio

Asseff, Alberto Emilio, Dr., fl. 1980 in Argentina. His writings include *Proyección continental de la Argentina; de la geohistorica a la geopolítica nacional* (Buenos Aires, 1980). NUC, 1981

Asselain, Jean Charles, he was a sometime member of the Faculté de droit et des sciences économiques de Paris. His writings include *Le budget de l'éducation nationale, 1952-1967* (Paris, 1969). BN

Asser, Tobias Michaël Carel, born 28 August 1838 at Amsterdam, he studied at the Universiteit and, at the age of twenty-four, became a professor of commercial and private international law at Amsterdams Athenaeum. He was instrumental in founding the Institut de droit international, and was repeatedly arbitrator in peace settlements, for which he was awarded the Nobel prize in 1911. His writings include *La*

Convention de la Haye du 14 novembre 1896 relative à la procédure civile (1901). He died in 's-Gravenhage, 29 July 1913. BWN, II, 15-17; EncJud; Wininger

Assfalg, Julius, born 6 November 1919 at Hohenaschau, Germany, he studied at the Universität München, where he received a Dr.phil. in 1957 for *Die Ordnung des Priestertums, tartib al-kahanut; ein altes liturgisches Handbuch der Koptischen Kirche.* Afterwards he was professor at München. His writings include *Georgische Handschriften* (1963), *Syrische Handschriften* (1963), and he edited *Geschichte der kirchlichen georgischen Literatur* (1955). Kürschner, 1996-2001|

Assouline, Albert, fl. 1963, he was a sometime head of the Division du Plan, Rabat, Morocco.

Astakhov, Georgii Aleksandrovich, born 29 December 1896 (10 January 1897), he graduated from Moscow State University. His writings include *От султаната к демократической Турции; очерки из истории кемализма* (1926). He died on 14 February 1942. Miliband; Miliband²

Astakhov, S., he wrote *Империалистическая сущность сионизма* (1975). LC

Astley, Hugh John Dukinfield, born 29 September 1856, he was educated privately and at Trinity College, Dublin, and ordained in 1881. He was a fellow of the Royal Anthropological Institute and a sometime vice-president of the British Archæological Association. His writings include *Prehistoric archæology and the Old Testament* (Edinburgh, 1908), and *Biblical anthropology compared with the folklore of Europe* (London, 1929). He died on 2 March 1930. Who was who, 3

Astor, William Waldorf, 3rd Viscount Astor, born 13 August 1907, he was educated at Eton and New College, Oxford. He was a sometime secretary to the Earl of Lytton, and parliamentary private secretary to Sir Samuel Hoare. His writings include *Our imperial future* (1943). He died on 8 March 1966. ChambrBrBi; Who was who, 6

Aswad, Barbara Carlene née Black, born 5 January 1937 at Kalamazoo, Mich., she studied at the universities of Edinburgh and Michigan, where she received a Ph.D. in 1968 for *Land, marriage and lineage organization among sedendarized pastoralists in the Hatay.* In 1974 she started a teaching career at Wayne State University, Detroit, where she was still active in 2003. Her writings include *Property control and social strategies in settlers in a Middle East plain* (1971), and she edited *Arabic speaking communities in American cities* (1974), and joint editor of *Family and gender among American Muslims* (1996). NatFacDr, 2003; Private

Asylgaraev, Sh. N., born 20th cent., he wrote *К вопросы этнической истории татарского народа* (1987), and he was joint author of *К формированию языка татар Поволжья и Приуралья* (Kazan, 1985), and *Исследования по лексике и грамматике татарского языка* (Kazan, 1986). LC

'Aṭa', Galib, 1880-1947 see Ataç, Galip

Atabaki, Turaj, born 23 February 1950 at Tehran, he studied in Iran, the Netherlands and England and received a doctorate in 1990. He was a member of several learned societies, and a professor of Iranian and Central Asian studies at the Rijksuniversiteit te Utrecht. His writings include *Kurdistan in search of ethnic identity* (1991), *Azerbaijan; ethnicity and autonomy in twentieth-century Iran* (1993), he was joint author of *Centraal-Azië* ('s-Gravenhage, 1994), and *Baku documents; union catalogue of Persian, Azerbaijani, Ottoman Turkish and Arabic serials and newspapers in the libraries of Azerbaijan* (1995). LC; Schoeberlein

Ataç, Galip, born in 1880 at Constantinople, he took his medical training at the Faculté de médecine in the Université de Montpellier. During the first World War he worked in hospitals in Medina, Amman and Syria, and in his later life, in Istanbul and Ankara, where he died in 1947. His writings include *Tibbî müsahabeler* (1328/1912), *Tib Fakültesi Istanbul Darülfununu* (1341/1925), and *Tib tarihi* (1341/1925). Meydan

Atagarryev, Egen, born 15 June 1934, he was educated at Ashkhabad Pedagocial Institute and received a doctorate. His writings include *Материальная культура Шехр-Ислама* (1973), *Ачык мейдандакы музей* (1977), *Средневековый Дехистан* (1986) *Тарихда гален ызлар; публицистик очерк-лер = Отголоски древности* (1989), and he was editor of *Первобытный Турк-менистан* (1976). LC; Schoeberlein

Atamirzaeva, Sarakhon Atamirzaevna, fl. 1974, she wrote *Акустико-артикуляционный анализ усбек-ской речи применительно к речевой аудиометрии* (Tashkent, 1972), and *Экспериментально-фоне-тическое исследование наманганского говора усбекского языка* (Tashkent, 1974). LC

Ataöv, Türkkaya, born 24 June 1932 at Gelibolu, Turkey, he was educated at Robert College, Istanbul, as well as Syracuse University. He was a professor of international relations at Ankara Üniversitesi and travelled extensively in the Islamic world. His writings include *Sovyet Rusya'da işçilerin bugünkü durumu* (1960), *Turkish foreign policy, 1939-1945* (1965), *Amerika, NATO ve Türkiye* (1969), *NATO and Turkey*

(1970), *Ermeni sorunu; bibliografya* (1981), *Documents on the Armenian question* (1985), and *The Ottoman archives and the Armenian question* (1986). Kim kimdir, 1985/86-2000; LC

al-Atasi, Hashim, born in 1876 at Homs, he was a Syrian politician and a sometime president of the Syrian Constituent Assembly. He died in 1960. David Commis, *Historical dictionary of Syria* (1996); Note

Atasi, Nadir, fl. 1968, he was a sometime head of the Job Evaluation Deptartment, Iraq Petroleum Company, Syria. Note

Atasoy, Nurhan, born 12 February 1934 at Reşadiye, Turkey, she studied at Istanbul Üniversitesi, where she received a doctorate in Islamic art in 1959, and afterwards became a professor of history of art. Her writings include *Ibrahim Paşa Sarayi* (1972), *Türk minyatür sanati bibliyografyası* (1972); and she was joint author of *Turkish miniature painting* (1974), *L'art de l'islam* (1990), and *Iznik; la poterie en Turquie ottomane* (1990). Schoeberlein

Atatürk, Mustafa Kemal, born in 1881 in Saloniki, he was educated at the military colleges of Monastir and Constantinople. He was an army officer and the first President of the Turkish Republic. He died in Istanbul, 10 November 1938. A. L. Macfie wrote a recent biography, *Atatürk* (1994). AnaBrit; EI²; Master (24); Zürcher

Atay, Falih Rifki, born in 1893 at Constantinople, he was a member of the Turkish Parliament and editor-in-chief of *Usul*, Ankara. His writings include *Ateş ve güneş* (1335/1919), *Bizim akdeniz* (1934), *Hind* (1944), *Mustafa Kemal'in mütareke defteri* (1955), *Atatürkçülük nedir* (1969), and *The Atatürk I knew* (1981). He died in Istanbul, 20 March 1971. EIS; Meydan

Athar, Alia Nasreen, born 20th cent., she was joint author, with M. A. Anees, of *Hadith and sira literature in Western languages* (1980), and *Guide to sira and hadith literature in Western languages* (1986). LC

Atherton, Alfred Leroy, born 22 November 1921 at Pittsburgh, Pa., he graduated from Harvard University. He entered the foreign service in 1947 and became a career diplomat, being posted throughout the Middle East until his retirement in 1984. He wrote *Egypt and United States interests* (1988). Master (6); MidE, 1982/83; Shavit; *Who's who in America*, 1996-2003

Atherton, James S., fl. 1954, he wrote *The books at the wake; a study of literary allusions in James Joyce's Finnegans wake* (c1959, 1974). LC

Atil, Esin, born 11 June 1937 at Istanbul she was educated at the American College for Girls, Istanbul, Western College for Women, Oxford, Ohio, and University of Michigan, where she received a Ph.D. in 1969, for *Surname-i Vehbi; an eighteenth century Ottoman book of festivals.* She was a curator at various U.S. universities and art galleries. Her writings include *Ceramics in the world of Islam* (1973), *The brush and the masters* (1978), *Renaissance of Islam; art of the Mamluks* (1981), *The art of Süleyman the Magnificent* (1987), and several exhibition catalogues. *Who's who in America*, 1996|

Atiya, Aziz Suryal, born 5 July 1898 in Egypt, he received a Ph.D. in 1933 at SOAS for *Nicopolis; a study based on Eastern and Western sources, and an examination of the battlefield and its approaches,* and a Litt.D. in 1939 at Liverpool for *The crusade in the late middle ages.* He became a professor at the University of Utah ,where he established in 1962 its Middle East Center. In the mid-1930s he collaborated with Paul Kahle at the Universität Bonn. He later was instrumental in establishing the Marriott Library at Utah. He died on 24 September 1988. DrAS, 1969-1982 H; *Index Islamicus* (4); IntWW, 1974-1993/94; Master (8); WhoWor, 1971/72

Atiyah, Edward Selim, born in 1903, he was in 1945 instrumental in founding the Arab Office, London, in order to inform the British public about the Arab point of view on the Palestine question. A free-lance writer since 1949, he fought for recognition of the Arab problems by Western countries through contributions to periodicals, notably the *Quarterly review* and the *Spectator.* His writings include *An Arab tells his story* (1946), *al-'Arab* (1961), *L'âne du Liban* (1963), and he was joint author of *Palästina; Versprechen und Enttäuschungen* (1970). He died in 1964. IntWW, 1957-1964/65; WhE&EA; WhoWor, 1974/5

'Atiyah, Yusuf Dib, born in 1832 in northern Lebanon. His Maronite parents turned him out of doors in February 1865, because of his leaning towards the teaching of Protestant missionaries. He found refuge with the American missionary Dr. Jessup. Having studied Arabic under the direction of an uncle, he continued a student throughout his life, attaining an unusual knowledge of both the Bible and the Koran. Equipped with some formal theological training, though not ordained, he became a persuasive preacher in Greater Syria. His best known publication is *Bakurah*, first published in Leipzig. Sir William Muir considered the work so valuable that he produced an English translation, *Sweet first-fruits*, (London, 1893), for use in Islamic countries where Arabic was not well understood. He published also *Minar al-haqq*, and a good many other writings, all of which anonymously on account of his modesty. He died in Tripoli al-Sharq, on 25 May 1926, at the age of ninety-four. *Missionary review of the world* 49 (1926), pp. 798-800

Atiyeh, George Nicholas, born 21 May 1923 at Amyun, Lebanon, he was educated at AUB and the University of Michigan, where he received a Ph.D. in 1954 for *Avicenna's conception of miracles*. From 1967 until his retirement, he was head of the Near East Section at the Library of Congress, Washington, D.C. His writings include *Al-Kindi, the philosopher of the Arabs* (1966), *The contemporary Middle East, 1948-1973; an annotated bibliography* (1975), and he edited *The book in the Islamic world* (1995). ConAu, 57-60; DrAS, 1969-1982 H; IWWAS, 1976/77; Master (2)

Atkin, Muriel Ann, born 17 December 1946 at N.Y.C., she received a Ph.D. in history from Yale University in 1976. In 1980 she was appointed a professor of history at George Washington University, Washington, D.C., a position which she still held in 1999. Her writings include *Russia and Iran, 1780-1828* (1980), and *The subtlest battle; Islam in Soviet Tajikistan* (1989). DrAS, 1982; LC; NatFacDr, 1999; Schoeberlein

Atkins, Richard Alexander, fl. 1973, he received a Ph.D. in 1968 in history from the University of California, Berkeley, for his thesis *British policy towards Egypt, 1876 to 1882*. He was a sometime professor of history at the University of California, Riverside. Note

Atkins, Miss Eunice M., born in January 1882 at Elk River, Minn., she was educated at the local high school and also at Hamline University, St. Paul. She was appointed on 25 February 1908 a missionary under the Woman's Board of Missions of the Interior and sailed in August for Turkey, where she joined the Erzurum station. Although she carried the burden of the girls' school, she was drawn to the women and children in the villages around the city. She was hoping to have the opportunity of doing village work. She died in Erzurum about 18 March 1914 from smallpox. *Missionary herald* 110 (1914), pp. 225-226

Atkinson, James, born 9 March 1780 in the county of Durham, he studied medicine at Edinburgh and London, and subsequently accepted the post of medical officer on board an East Indiaman. In 1805 he was appointed an assistant surgeon in the Bengal service near Dacca. In the leisure afforded by his not very arduous duties he devoted himself to the study of Persian. He was a sometime professor of Persian at Fort William College, and founding editor of the *Calcutta annual register*. From 1838 to 1841, he went to Afghanistan with the Army of the Indus. His writings include *Customs and manners of the women of Persia, translated from the original Persian manuscript* (1832), *The Sháh Námeh of the Persian poet Firdausi, translated and abridged in prose and verse* (1832), and *Sketches in Afghaunistan* (1842). He died 7 August 1852. Boase; BritInd (3); Buckland; DNB; IndianBiInd (2)

Atkinson, Thomas Witlam, born of humble parentage at Cawthorne, Yorkshire, 6 March 1799, he had to earn his own living at the age of eight as a bricklayer's labourer. In 1819 he was a stone-carver, and from 1835 to 1840 he worked as an architect in Manchester. In 1842 he travelled to Germany, and later to St. Petersburg, from where he set out in 1848 on a forty thousand miles journey to Siberia and Central Asia. He wrote *Oriental and western Siberia; a narrative of seven years' explorations and adventures in Siberia, Mongolia, the Kirghis steppes, Chinese Tartary and part of Central China* (1858). He died on 13 August 1861. Boase; BritInd (8); DNB; Henze; Master (4)

Atsarkina, Estir Nikolaevna, fl. 1954, she wrote Сильвестр Щедрин (1978), and other biographies of Russian artists. In 1962 and 1965 she edited Очерки по русскому и советскому искусству. LC

Attalides, Michalis (Michael) Antone, born 15 November 1941 at Leonarisso, Cyprus, he was educated at LSE and Princeton University, where he received a Ph.D. for *Social change and urbanization; a study of Nicosia*, in 1974. Afterwards he taught at universities in the UK, Cyprus, and Germany. In 1991 he was an ambassador in France. His writings include *Cyprus, nationalism and international politics* (1979), *Social change and urbanization in Cyprus* (1981), and he edited *Cyprus reviewed; the result of a Seminar on the Cyprus Problem, held in 1976 by the Jus Cypri Association* (Nicosia, 1977). EVL; WhoFr, 1992/93-1995/96|

d'**Attanoux**, Joseph Bernard, 1853-1921 *see* Bernard d'Attanoux, Antoine Casimir *Joseph*

al-**Attas**, Syed Muhammad Naquib, born 5 September 1931 at Bogor, Java, he studied at McGill University, Montreal, where he received an M.A. in 1962 for *Raniri and the Wujudiyyah of 17th century Acheh*. He received a Ph.D. in 1966 from the University of London for *The mysticism of Hamsah Fansuri*. He was Dean of the Faculty of Arts in the University of Malaya, Kuala Lumpur, and visiting professor at American universities. Since 1990, he was founding-director of the International Institute of Islamic Thought and Civilization. His writings include *Raniri and the wujudiyyah of the 17th century Acheh* (1966), and *Islam dalam sejarah dan kebudayaan Melayu* (1972). Ferahian; WhoWor, 1974/75

Attia, Mahmoud Ibrahim, fl. 1953, he was a sometime director of the Geological Survey of Egypt, and wrote *Topography, geology and iron-ore deposits of the District of East Aswân* (Cairo, 1955). LC

Aubert, Louis, born in 1876, he received a doctorate in 1911 from the Université de Paris for *L'assimilation douanière dans les rapports de la France et de ses colonies*. His writings include *Paix japonaise* (1906), *Américains et Japonais* (1908), and *The reconstruction of Europe* (1925). LC

Aubert, Pierre, born 8 March 1888 at Arras (Pas-de-Calais), he was an administrator in French West Africa between the two world wars and died in Paris, 27 December 1972. *Hommes et destins*, vol. 7, p. 11

Aubert-Roche, Louis Rémy, born 25 November 1810 at Vitry-le-François (Marne), he studied at Paris, where he received a doctorate in medicine in 1833. He travelled in Abyssinia and Egypt, and practised at Alexandria before becoming a medical officer at the construction of the Suez Canal. He returned to France in 1869, where he died on 22 December 1874. His writings include *De la peste ou typhus en Orient* (1840), and *Rapport sur l'état sanitaire et médical des travailleurs et des établissements du canal maritime de l'isthme de Suez* (1865). DBF; Hill

d'**Aubignosc**, L. P. Brun, born 18th cent., he took part in the French expedition to Egypt and remained in the Near East until 1806. In April 1830 he was sent to Tunis to find out the Bey's views towards possible French incursions into North Africa. He submitted important reports concerning the Algerian situation in general to General de Bourmont. At the time of the French conquest of Alger, he was *interprète de 1ére classe*. Afterwards he was head of the colonial police in North Africa. His writings include *La Turquie nouvelle jugée au point de vue où l'on amenée des réformes du sultan Mahmoud*. He died after 1843. DBF; Féraud, p. 185; Peyronnet, p. 14

Aubin, Eugène, born in 1863, his full name was Léon Eugène Aubin Coullard Desclos or Descos. He wrote *Le Maroc d'aujourd'hui* (1904), *Morocco of to-day* (1906), *Marruecos en nuestros días* (1908), and *La Perse d'aujourd'hui* (1908). BN; LC; Oursel

Aubin, Françoise, born 17 February 1932 at Paris, she received a doctorate in East Asian studies in 1965 from the Université de Paris. Her main fields of research were Islam in China, and Mongolia, where she conducted field work. She was *directeur de recherche* at the CNRS, and at the Centre d'Études et de Recherches Internationales de la Fondation Nationale des Sciences Politiques, Paris. She was a member of the Société asiatique and was awarded a *médaille de bronze* by the CNRS. Her writings include *Études Song in memoriam Étienne Balazs* (1973-76), and *Écrits récents sur le Tibet et les Tibétains; bibliographie commentée* (1993). Private; Schoeberlein

Aubin, Jean, born 191927, he was a French Iranist who, between 1971 and 1988, acted as thesis supervisor of a good many young Iranists at the Université de Paris. His writings include *Matériaux pour la biographie de Shâh Ni'matullah Walî Kermânî* (1956), *Deux sayyids de Bam au XVe siècle* (1956), *L'ambassade de Gegorio Pereira Fidalgo à la cour de Châh Soltân-Hosseyn, 1696-1697* (1971). In subsequent years his interest took a different direction so that he no longer wanted to be identified with the field of Islamic studies. AnEIFr, 1989; Private

Auboyer, Jeannine, born 6 September 1912 at Paris, she received diplomas from the École du Louvre and the École pratique des Hautes-Études. She was a sometime keeper at the Musée Guimet, and from 1965 until her retirement, keeper-in-chief of the French National Museums. Her writings include *Le trône et son symbolisme dans l'Inde ancienne* (1949), *Arts et styles de l'Inde* (1951), *L'Afghanistan et son art* (1968), and *The art of Afghanistan* (1968). She died on 6 February 1990. WhoFr, 1963/64-1989/90

Aubry, Paul, Dr., born in 1858 at Saint-Brieuc (Côtes-du-Nord), he was an anthropologist whose writings include *La contagion du meurtre; étude d'anthropologie criminelle* (Paris, 1887). After a tour of Europe he wrote *Autour de l'Europe* (1888). He died in St.-Brieuc in 1899. DBF

Aucagne, Jean, fl. 1974, he was a contributor to *L'unique Israël de Dieu; approches chrétiennes du mystère d'Israël* (1987). LC

Aucapitaine, baron Henri, born 5 November 1832 at Saint-Maurice near La Rochelle, France, he enlisted in the *Tirailleurs algériens*, but saw action also in Syria. He soon became an officier and was able to use his military promotion in the *Bureaux arabes* (1865) to pursue ethnographic and linguistic studies. In 1867 he was *chef d'annexe* at Beni-Mansour and Chevalier de la Légion d'honneur; a promising career was ahead of him when he died from cholera, 25 September 1867. DBF; Henze; Peyronnet, p. 311

Aucher-Éloy, Pierre Martin Remi, born 2 October 1793 at Blois, he studied pharmacy and botany at Orléans and Paris. He was attached to the military hospital service until he returned to Blois after Waterloo. He acquired a book collection and made a futile attempt at operating a printing press in Blois and later also in

Paris between 1826 and 1829. As an avid botanist, he explored the Loir-et-Cher region, and applied to be sent on a scientific mission to Russia. Although this attempt failed, he became secretary to a Russian prince at St. Petersburg, where he made the acquaintance of the Turkish ambassador Halil Paşa whom he then followed to Constantinople in order to establish a Turko-French periodical. In spite of limited financial resources he decided to set out on travels in the Near and Middle East in order to bring together a botanical and zoological collection with the intention of serving scholarship. He sent thousands of specimens to private individuals and institutions, but remained a private scholar without private means. In the end he lost his library and thousands of insects in a fire. Physically weakened, he died in Julfa near Isfahan, 6 October 1838. His writings include *Relations de voyages de 1830 à 1838* (1843). DBF; Gabriel, pp. 102-117

Auchterlonie, James Paul Crawford, born in 1948, of British parents in Germany. After Arabic studies at Oxford and Tunis, he was librarian for Arabic and Islamic studies at the University of Lancaster until 1981, when its courses were discontinued. Since that time he was at Exeter University in the same capacity. He was the outstanding British Arabic librarian of his day and dominated the UK Middle Eastern library scene. He was an officer of the SCONUL Advisory Committee on Orientalist Materials as well as the Middle East Library Committee, of which he was repeatedly chairman or secretary. He was a regular and conscientious reviewer for the *British journal of Middle Eastern studies* almost from its inception in 1973. His writings include *Union catalogue of Arabic periodicals in British libraries* (1977), *Arabic biographical dictionaries; a summary guide and bibliography* (1987), *Yemen*, published in the *World bibliographical series* in 1998; and he was editor of *Middle East and Islam; a bibliographical introduction, supplement, 1977-1983* (1986); and *Introductory guide to Middle Eastern and Islamic bibliography* (1990). Private

Audebeau Bey, Charles, born 28 September 1861 at Saint-Maximin (Var), he graduated in 1879 from the École d'arts et métiers d'Aix-en-Provence. Afterwards he spent a year of practice work at various workshops of the P.L.M. Railway in Arles. He had a first taste of Egypt during the spring of 1882 as a technician with the Société agricole industrielle du delta du Nil, however, the events of that year obliged him to leave Egypt for a year and a half. On his return trip to Alexandria, he made a profitable visit to the Société du percement de l'isthme de Corinthe. In October 1883 he became municipal topographer in Alexandria, and shortly thereafter entered the Administration des Domaines de l'État égyptien as engineer. When he retired after thirty-seven years of service, he had become *ingénieur-en-chef*. Under the modest title *Rapport présenté à la Commission des Domaines de l'État égyptien au sujet des expériences relatives à l'influence de la nappe souterraine sur les cultures de coton* (1909), he published four technical monographs of his prolonged observations concerning the subterranean water-level of the state lands in the Nile Delta. He also served in missions to Morocco, and Palestine. In 1920 he was awarded C.B.E., and in 1925, Chevalier de la Légion d'honneur. He died in Garches near Paris, 18 August 1939. *Bulletin de l'Institut égyptien* 22 (1940), pp. 5-14

Audebert, Claude France, born 20th cent., he received a doctorate in 1973 from the Université d'Aix-Marseille I for his thesis, *Un aspects de l'i'gaz au IV (Xème) siècle, d'après al-Hattabi.* His writings include *Al-Hattabi et l'inimitabilité du Coran* (1982). LC; THESAM, 4

Audinet, Eugène Louis André, born in 1859, he received a doctorate from the Faculté de droit de Poitiers in 1883 for his thesis, *Des actions qui naissent des délits.* Afterwards he was a professor of law. He wrote *Notions élémentaires d'instruction civique* (Poitiers, 1912). LC

Audisio, Gabriel, born 27 July 1900 at Marseille, he was a writer and civil servant in Algeria from 1920 to 1959. He spent the last years of his life in Issy-les-Moulineaux, where he died on 25 January 1978. He wrote essays, stories, poetry, and contributed to radio and television. His writings include *Hommes au soleil* (1923), *Trois hommes et un minaret* (1926), *La vie de Haroun-al-Rachid* (1930), *Harun al-Rashid, caliph of Baghdad* (1931), *Algérie méditerranée* (1957), and *Hannibal* (1961). *Hommes et destins*, vol. 4, pp. 39-43; MEW

Audoin, born 19th cent., he wrote *Afrique équatoriale française; mission d'études du bassin du Tchad, octobre 1913-juillet 1914* (Paris, 1922). NUC, pre-1956

Audouin-Dubreuil, Louis, born 4 August 1887 at St. Jean-d'Angély (Charente-inférieure), he was an army officer, and an explorer who, in the service of André Citroën, pioneered motor vehicle transportation in the Sahara and in Central Asia. His writings include *Sur la route de soie; mon carnet de route de la Méditerranée à la mer de Chine* (1935), *La guerre de Tunisie* (1945), *Aventures de guerre en Tunisie* (1946), and, with G. M. Haardt, *Across the Sahara by motor car* (1924), *La croisière noire; expédition Citroën* (1927). He died in Zarzis, Tunisia, in January 1960. *Hommes et destins*, vol. 1, pp. 44-47; Peyronnet, p. 925

Audroing, Jean François, fl. 1975, his writings include *Mathématiques linéaires* (1977), and *Démographie* (1978). LC

Auezov, Mukhtar Omarkhanovich, born in 1897 in Chingistan, he studied at the universities of Leningrad and Tashkent, and was a writer, a professor of literature and a member of the Kazakh Academy. He died on 27 June 1961. DcOrL, vol. 3, pp. 22-23; GSE; *Казахская ССР краткая энциклопедия*, vol. 4, pp. 134-136; TatarES

Aufhauser, Johann Baptist, born 7 September 1881 at Moosham near Regensburg, Germany, he received a Dr.phil. in 1910 from the Universität München for *Die Heilslehre des hlg Gregor von Nyssa*. Afterwards he was a professor of history of religions at München. His writings include *Asien am Scheideweg* (1933). He died in Ölberg, 8 August 1963. DtBE; Kürschner, 1935-1961

Aufrère, Léon. He was joint author of *La vie dans la région désertique nord-tropicale de l'ancien monde* (Paris, 1938). LC

Augagneur, Jean Victor, born 16 May 1855 at Lyon, he received a medical doctorate in 1886 from the Université de Paris. Afterwards he was a professor of medicine at Lyon until 1890, when he entered politics. For a number of years after the first World War he was governor of French Equatorial Africa. His writings include *Erreurs et brutalités coloniales* (1927). He died in Paris, 24 April 1931. AfrBioInd; DBF; *Hommes et destins*, vol. 3, pp. 35-39; IndexBFr² (7)

Augapfel, Julius, born 19th cent., he received a Dr.phil. in 1914 from the Universität Wien for *Babylonische Rechtsurkunden aus der Regierungszeit Darius II,*. His writings include *Babylonische Rechtsurkunden aus der Regierungszeit Artaxerxes I und Darius II* (Wien, 1917). NUC, pre-1956

Augias, L., fl. 1904-1911, he was a sometime French *officier interprète de troisième classe*.

Augier, Pierre, fl. 1968-1973, he was a sometime member of the Centre de recherches anthropologiques, préhistoriques et ethnographiques, Algiers.

Augiéras, Ernest Marcel, born in 1882, he joined the French army in 1902. His lifelong association with the Sahara began in 1913 when he was stationed with the Bureau des Affaires indigènes d'Algérie in Touat Gourara. Twice he crossed the Erg Chech. In 1927 he was asked by the American W. P. Draper to explore the route from Algeria to Senegal, an enterprise which became to be known as the Mission Augiéras-Draper. His explorations contributed greatly to the geographical, geological, and ethnographical knowledge of a region that had been largely ignored until then. He retired from active service in 1932, but retained close relations with the Institut de recherches sahariennes until his death in 1958. His writings include *Le Sahara occidental* (1919), *Chronique de l'Ouest saharien, 1900-1930* (1930), *D'Algérie au Sénégal: Mission Augiéras-Draper, 1927-1928* (1930-1931), and *La grande chasse en Afrique* (1935). Peyronnet, 923; *Travaux de l'Institut de recherches saharinnes* 17 (1958), pp. 11-12

Aujard, Robert, he was an architect and town-planner who, in 1958, was head of the Service de l'urbanisme du Maroc. Note

Aul, Joseph, born 4 March 1894 at Jedomělice. His writings include *V zemi Tamerlanově a Zarathustrově* (1923-24), *Čingischán, bič boží* (1936), *Derviš na Pousti, bucharská rapsodie* (1937), and *Karavanou do Indie* (1947). He died in Praha, 15 July 1956. Filipsky

Aulas, Marie Christine, born 20th cent., she received a doctorate in 1978 from the Université de Paris I for *L'évolution de l'Égypte, 1970-1973*. She was joint author of *L'Égypte d'aujourd'hui; permanence et changements, 1805-1976* (1977), and *La campagne de contrôle des naissances en Égypte, 1980-1981* (1982). LC; THESAM, 3

Auldjo, John, F.R.G.S. He made the 14th ascent of Mont Blanc, and wrote *Narrative of an ascent to the summit of Mont Blanc, on the 8th and 9th of August, 1827* (London, 1828), and *Journal of a visit to Constantinople, and some of the Greek Islands in the spring and summer of 1833* (London, 1835). He died in 1857. Boase

Aulneau, Joseph, born in 1879, he received a doctorate in 1902 from the Université de Poitiers for his thesis, *La circonstription électorale*. His writings include *La Turquie et la guerre* (Paris, 1915), *Le drame de l'Allemagne* (1924), and *Histoire de l'Europe centrale* (1926). LC

Duc d'Aumale, Henri Eugène Philippe Louis d'Orléans, son of King Louis Philippe, born 16 January 1822 at Paris. He distinguished himself in the early conquest of Algeria, and, in 1847, became governor-general of France's African possessions. After the 1848 revolution, he went into exile in England until allowed to return to France in 1889, having willed his Chantilly estates to the Institut de France. His writings include *Les zouaves et les chasseurs à pied* (1855), *The military institutions of France* (1869), *History of the princes of Condé in the XVIth and XVIIth centuries* (1872), and, under the pseudonym V. de Mars, articles in *Revue* *des deux mondes.* He died at Zucco, Sicily, 7 May 1897. Azan, pp. 30-36; DBF; *Séances et travaux de l'Académie des sciences morales et politiques*, n. s., 49 (1898), pp. 31-78

Aumassip, Ginette, fl. 1972, her writings include *Néolithique sans poterie de la région de l'oued Mya, Bas-Sahara* (1972), and she was joint author of *Le Shati; lac pléistocène du Fezzan* (1982). LC

Aumerat, Joseph François, born 11 December 1818 at Marseille, he went in 1842 to Algeria as a journalist. His writings, published partly under the pseudonym Marteau, include *L'antisémitisme à l'Alger* (Alger, 1885), and *Souvenirs algériens* (Blida, 1898). DBF

Aumeunier, Viviane, fl. 1966, she was a sometime member of the Centre de recherches sur l'Afrique méditerranéenne d'Aix-en-Provence. Note

Aurigemma, Salvatore, born 10 February 1885 at Monteforte Irpino (Avellino), Italy, he received a doctorate in lettres and became a keeper of antiquities at various Italian institutions. His writings include *L'area cementriale cristiana di Ain Zára presso Tripoli di Barberia* (1932), and *L'arco quadrifronte di Marco Aurelio e di Lucio Vero in Tripoli* (1970). Wholtaly, 1957/58

Aurivillius, Carolus, born 2 August 1717 at Stockholm, he was a professor of Greek and Oriental languages at Uppsala Universitet. His writings include *Disputatio philologica de usu dialecti arabicæ in indaganda vocum ebraicarum significatione* (1747), and *Dissertationes ad sacras literas et philologiam orientalem pertinentes* (1790). He died in Uppsala, 19 January 1786. *Svenska män och kvinnor*

Ausiello, Alessandro, fl. 1941, his writings include *La Francia e l'indipendenza della Siria e del Libanon* (1938), *Storia dell'espansione coloniale spanola* (1938), *La politica italiana in Libia* (1939), and *Tunisi, Gibuti e l'Oriente Mediterraneo* (1939). LC

Aussel, Jean Marie, he received a doctorate in 1953 from the Université de Montpellier for his thesis, *Essai sur la notion de tiers en droit civil français.* In 1958 he held a cross-appointment as *professeur agrégé* at the Faculté de droit de Strasbourg and the Institut des Hautes Études de Tunis. Note

Ausserer, Carl/Karl, born 28 May 1883 at Schloß Lichtenwald, Austria, he was educated at Seitenstetten and Trent before studying at the Institut für Österreichische Geschichte, and Österreichisches Historisches Institut in Roma. He was attached to the Österreichische Nationalbibliothek from 1911 until retirement in 1946, with the exception of military service during both world wars. He published several monographs dealing with the geography of the Austrian Alps. He died of a cardiac arrest on 16 May 1950. *Mitteilungen des Österreichischen Staatsarchiv* 4 (1951), pp. 391-392

Austin, Herbert Henry, British brigadier-general, born 1 June 1868. In the course of two surveys on the western frontiers of Abyssinia in 1899-1901, he travelled from Omdurman overland to Mombasa, 1900-1901. In 1909 and 1910 he was in charge of operations in the Persian Gulf for the suppression of gun-running, and from 1915 to 1919, he was in Mesopotamia, where he was a charge of the Assyrian refugee camp at Baquba at the edge of the desert. He wrote several autobiographical works including *Among swamps and giants in Equatorial Africa* (1902), and *The Baquba refugee camp* (1920). He died on 27 April 1937. Hill; *Who was who*, 3

Austin, R. W. J. He was translator of *Sufis of Andalusia; the 'Ruh al-quds' and 'al-Durrat al-fakhirah' of Ibn Arabi* (1971), and joint author of *Le monde arabe; tradition et renouveau* (1977), *The Arab world; yesterday, today and tomorrow* (1979). LC

Austruy, Jacques Jean Paul, born 24 July 1930 at Paris, he was educated at the Lycée Louis-le-Grand and the Université de Paris. Afterwards he was a professor at various French universities. He wrote *Structure économique et civilisation* (1960), a work which was originally presented in 1958 as his thesis at the Université de Paris, entitled *La notion de structure et l'analyse économique, approche structurelle de l'économie de l'Égypte contemporaine.* He also wrote *L'islam face au développement économique* (1961), *Le scandale du développement* (1965), and he was joint author of *Le droit et le future* (1985). WhoFr, 1971/72-2000|

Autard de Bragard, fl. 1869-1874, he contributed articles on Egyptian subjects to the *Revue maritime et coloniale* and the *Bulletin de la Société d'acclimatation.* BN

Autin, Jean Louis, born 20th cent., he received a doctorate in 1976 from the Université de Montpellier for *Le droit économique algérien; l'examen des institutions juridiques au service de l'analyse de la formation sociale.* He was a sometime assistant lecturer at the Institut des sciences juridiques d'Alger. Note; THESAM, 2

Avalov, Zurab Davidovich, born 19th century, he was a member of a well-known Georgian family, a member of the Russian State Duma, and one of the representatives of Georgian interests during the negotiations with the Turks at Batum, and with the Germans at Poti, during the spring and summer of 1918. He subsequently represented the *de facto* Georgian Government in Berlin, and, after the armistice, in London. During the Paris Peace Conference, he was a member of the Georgian Delegation in Paris, and later at San Remo. He was the author of several works on Georgian history and jurisprudence including *Децентрализация и замоуправление во Франции* (1905), and *The independence of Georgia in international politics, 1918-1921* (1940). Note

Lord **Avebury**, Sir John Lubbock, born 30 April 1834 at London, he was educated at Eton. Although a banker, he pursued an active interest in pre-history and archaeology. He died 28 May 1913. BritInd (20); DNB; Egyptology; Who, 1903-1912; *Who was who*, 1

Avellan, Mikael (Michael), born 1736, he took a degree in Oriental philology at Turku and was appointed a lecturer in Hebrew, Arabic, and Greek philology. His writings include *Dissertation historico-philologica de causis puritatis ac floris perennis linguae Arabicae* (1761). He died in 1806 or 1807. Aalto; ScBInd (1)

Averroes, the pseudonym of an active organizer and publicist for the socialist Palestinians, and one of the founders of *al-Fath*, who flourished from 1969 to 1970 and came to believe in a peace settlement. Note

Avery, Bennett Franklin, born 21 September 1901 at Vassar, Mich., he was a graduate of the University of Michigan, and was from 1926 to 1941 a professor of anatomy at UAB; from 1944 to 1949, he served as a director general of public health in Iran, and as adviser to the Iranian Ministry of Health. AMS, 1965

Avery, Myrtilla, fl. 1900-1941, her writings include *The Exultet rolls of south Italy* (1927), a work which was simultaniously presented as a thesis at Radcliffe College, Harvard University. NUC, pre-1956

Avery, Peter William, born in 1930 in Britain, he was a lecturer of Persian, and a fellow of King's College, Cambridge. On his retirement he was presented with the felicitation volume *Persian and Islamic studies in honour of Peter W. Avery* (1990), but his reputation was based more on King's College than on his own achievements. His writings include *Thirty poems*, of Hafiz (1952), and *Modern Iran* (1965). Private

Avetaranian, Johannes, 1861-1919 see Awetaranian, Johannes

d'**Avezac de Castera Macaya**, Marie Armand Pascal, born 18 April 1800 at Tarbes (Hautes-Pyrénées), he studied at Paris and spent nearly all his active life until retirement in 1862 with the Ministère de la Marine, where he was for many years keeper at the archives. His writings include *Études de géographie critique sur une partie de l'Afrique septentrionale* (1836). He died on 14 January 1875. DBF

Avi-Yonah, Michael, born 26 September 1904 at Lemberg, Galicia, he was educated at the University of London. Thereafter he was professor of archaeology and history of art at the Hebrew University, Jerusalem. His writings include *A history of classical art* (1969), *The Holy Land from the Persian to the Arab conquests* (1977), and *Art in ancient Palestine* (1981). He died in 1974. EncJud; WhoIsrael, 1973/74

Avierinos, Christo D., born 13 September 1893 in Palestine, he completed his secondary education in Cairo and studied medicine at Athens. Afterwards he practised at the Greek Hospital in Cairo, before continuing his studies at Wien and Berlin, where he received a Dr.med. in 1924 for *Über Chalikosis*. His writings include *Le problème de l'insuffisance coronarienne* (1941), and, with Paul Sbath, the edition and translation of *Deux traités médicaux, par Sahlan ibn Kaysan* (1953). NUC, pre-1956

Avigdor, S. His writings include *Agriculture égyptienne; renseignements généraux à l'usage de l'Afrique du nord* (Le Caire, 1937). NUC, pre-1956

Avila Navarro, Maria Luisa, born 20th cent., she received a doctorate in Semitic philology and was throughout the 1990s affiliated with the Escuela de Estudios Árabes, C.S.I.C., Granada. Her writings include the condensed version of her doctoral thesis, *La sociedad hispanomusulmano al final del califato; approximación a un estudio demografico* (1985). Arabismo, 1992, 1994, 1997; LC

Avineri, Shlomo, born 20 August 1933 at Bieldko, Silesia, he was educated at the Hebrew University, Jerusalem, LSE, and the University of London. His writings include *Israel and the Palestinians* (1971), *Marx's socialism* (1973), *The making of modern Zionism* (1981), *Moses, Hess, prophet of communism and Zionism* (1985), and he was joint editor of *Communitarianism and individualism* (1972). ConAu, 25-28; MidE, 1982/83

Aviram, Alexander, fl. 1957-1970, he was a senior Tel Aviv municipal official who served as civilian administrator for the Military Government in Gaza. Note

Avnery, Uri, born 10 September 1923 at Beckum, Germany, he was a sometime member of the Israeli Parliament, and editor-in-chief of the weekly *Ha'olam Hazeh*. His writings include *Israel without Zionists*

(1968), *My friend, the enemy* (1986), and *Wir tragen das Nessos-Gewand* (1991). ConAu 105, new rev., 25; Wholsrael, 1972-2001; WhoWor, 1974/5, 1976/77; WhoWorJ, 1965, 1972, 1978

d'Avril, Louis Marie *Adolphe* baron, born 17 August 1822 at Paris, he studied law at Paris, and in 1847 entered the Ministère des Affaires étrangères, where he remained until his retirement in 1883. His writings include *L'Arabie contemporaine* (1868), *Voyage sentimental dans les pays slaves* (1876), and *Négociations relatives au traité de Berlin* (1878). He died at Château de Coppières on 27 October 1904. DBF

'Awad, Ahmad Hafiz, born in 1874 or 1877 at Damanhur, Egypt, he was a journalist and for twenty years the editor of كوكب الشرق . His writings include خيال الظل (1924), and فتح مصر الحديث (1925). He died in 1950. Goldschmidt

'Awad, Fu'ad Hashim, B.Sc., M.Sc., Ph.D., born 11 August 1928 at Suez, he was educated at the universities of Cairo, Manchester, and Leeds, where he received a Ph.D. in 1956. He was a professor of economics at Cairo and also served with the United Nations Organisation and the Egyptian Government. *Africa who's who, 1991-1996; Who's who in the Arab world, 1987/87-2003/4*

'Awad, Hassan Muhammad, fl. 1959, he was in 1964 a professor of geography at the Kulliyat al-Adab in the Université de Rabat. His writings include جغرافية المدن المغربية على ضوء تطورها الديموغرافي الحالي (1964). LC

'Awad, Luwis, born 1914 or 1915 in Egypt, he was educated at the universities of Cairo, Princeton, and Oxford. Until 1954 he was professor at the Faculty of Arts in the University of Cairo. Irmgard Schrand submitted a dissertation in 1992 at the Universität Hamburg *Louis Awad, ein ägyptischer Kritiker und Denker*. His writings include دراسات في النقد و الادب (1963), الثورة و الادب (1967), and دراسات ادبية (1989). He died in 1990. Goldschmidt; WhoArab, 1978/79-1999/2000|

Awad, Mohamed *see* Muhammad, Muhammad 'Awad

'Awad, Muhammad Hashim, born 15 April 1935 at Khartoum, he studied economics at the University of Khartoum and LSE, where he received an M.Sc. in 1963 for *The export marketing of Sudan cotton since the war*, and a Ph.D. in 1966 for *The economics of internatl marketing in the Sudan*. He was for ten years at the Faculty of Economics in the University of Khartoum, which he left in 1973 to enter politics, culminating in Minister of Cooperatives in 1977. He was a member of the American Economic Association. His writings include استغلال و فساد الحكم في السودان (1965), *Economic Islamisation in the Sudan* (1984); and he was editor of *Socio-economic change in the Sudan* (1983). Sluglett; *Who's who in the Arab world, 1988/89-2003/4*

al-'Awadi, Badriyah 'Abd Allah, born in 1944 in Kuwait, she was educated at Cairo University and University College, London. She was a professor and dean, Department of International Law in Kuwait University. Her writings include *al-Qanun al-dawli lil-bihar fi al-Khalij al-'Arabi* (1976), and *Huquq al-tifl fi Kuwayt* (1979). *Who's who in the Arab world, 1995/96-2003/4*

'Awdah, Mahmud, he was a sometime professor and chairman of the Qism al-Ijtima', Kulliyat al-Adab in 'Ayn Shams University. His writings include القرية المصرية بين التأنيخ وعلم الاجتماع (1972), and الفلاحون و الدولة (1979). LC; Note

Awetaranian, Helene Caroline Martha née von Osterroht, born 9 May 1857 at Strellentin und Küssow, Kreis Lauenburg, Pommeria, she was the wife of Johannes Awetaranian. She died in Sommerfeld, Niederlausitz, 20 July 1942. *Genealogisches Handbuch des Adels, Adlige Häuser, B v (1961), p. 274*

Awetaranian, Johannes, born Mehmed Şükrü Efendi Emirzade on 30 June 1861 at Erzerum, Turkey, he was baptized on 28 February 1885 at the Tiflis Svenska Missionsförbundet. Through their good offices he trained as a missionary in Sweden and subsequently served with them for ten years in the Caucasus, Persia and Kashgar, where he concurrently produced an Uighur translation of the New Testament. Printing and publishing matters brought him to Berlin, where he met Helene von Osterroht, his future wife. They were married in Berlin on 20 June 1900. From November 1900 until 1918, he was a missionary of the Deutsche Orient-Mission first in Varna and Shumla, and then in Plovdiv, Bulgaria. He produced numerous tracts in Turkish, Persian, Uighur, and Mukri Kurdish. In 1905 he published his biography *Geschichte eines Muhammedaners, der Christ wurde*. In the summer of 1918 he went for medical treatment to Wiesbaden, but never recovered and died on 11 December 1919. *Der christliche Orient 21 (1920), pp. 34-38*

Axon, William Edward Armytage, born 13 January 1846 at Manchester, he was a journalist and author who took an active interest in education, temperance, and food reform. His writings include *Lancashire gleanings* (1883). He died on 27 December 1913. *Who was who, 1*

Ayache, Albert, fl. 1958, his writings include *Le Maroc; bilan d'une colonisation* (1956), *Marokko* (1959), and *Le mouvement syndical au Maroc* (1982). LC

Ayad, Boulos Ayad, born 3 May 1928 in Egypt, he was educated at Cairo and Ain Shams universities, and the Higher Institute of Coptic Studies. In 1963 he received a Ph.D. from Cairo University for his thesis *al-Aramiyun fi Misr.* Thereafter he was a professor at the University of Utah, and later, professor of archaeology and ancient languages of the Middle East in the University of Colorado, Boulder. His writings include *The topography of Elephantine* (1967), *The Jewish-Aramaean communities in ancient Egypt* (1975), and *The Jewish-Aramaean civilization and its relationship to the ancient Egyptian civilization* (1982). WhoWest, 1989/90, 1992/93|

El **Ayadi**, Habib, fl. 1968, he was a professor at the Faculté des sciences juridiques, politiques et sociales de Tunis. His writings include *Droit fiscal* (1989). LC

Ayalon, David, born in 1914 at Haifa, he studied Islamic civilization, Arabic and Jewish history at the Hebrew University, Jerusalem, to which AUB was added later. After his release from service in the British Army, he received his doctorate in 1946 from H.U.J. In 1949 he was invited to establish its Department of History of the Modern Middle East, a post which he held until his retirement in 1983. His writings include *L'esclavage du mamelouk* (1951), *Gunpower and firearms in the Mamluk Kingdom* (1956), and *Outsiders in the lands of Islam* (1988). A bibliography of his works can be found in *Studies in Islamic history and civilization in honour of Professor David Ayalon* (Jerusalem, 1986), pp. 13-18. He died in Jerusalem, 25 June 1998. MESA bulletin 32 ii (1998), p. 286; WhoWorJ, 1972

Ayandele, Emmanuel Ayankanni, born 12 October 1936 at Ogbomosho, Nigeria, he was educated at Baptist Boys High School, Oyo, University College Ibadan, and King's College, London. Afterwards he was a university professor and chancellor in Nigeria. He wrote *The missionary impact on modern Nigeria, 1842-1914* (1966), and *The educated elite in the Nigerian society* (1974). Africa who's who 1991-1996; African biographical index, 1999 (2)

Ayape Amigot, Fernando, born 20th cent., he received a diploma in Arabic language and literature from the Université de Paris. He was in 1992 a director of Medios, Comunicación e Imagen, Idea 10, Madrid. His writings include *La crisis económica mondial y el petroléo* (1977), and *España-Israel; un reencuentro en falso* (1987). Arabismo, 1992|; LC

Ayari, Chedli, born 24 August 1933 at Tunis, he studied law and economics at Paris, where he re-ceived a doctorate. He served with the United Nations, the International Bank for Reconstruction and Development, the Faculté de Droit de Tunis, and the Tunisian diplomatic service as well as the Government. Africa WW, 1991-1996; Master (3); MidE, 1982/83; Orient (Opladen) 18 (März 1977), pp. 5-6

Aybar, Celâl, fl. 1948, his writings include *Belçika nüfusu* (1935), *Bulgaristan nüfusu* (1935), and *Teorik ve teknik istatistik dersleri* (1941). LC

Aybay, Rona, born 10 May 1935 at Istanbul, she was in 1977 an associate professor of public law and human rights at the Middle East Technical University, Ankara. Her writings include *Amerikan, Ingiliz ve Türk hukuk sistemlerinde yurt dışını çıkma ve yurta girme özgürlüğü* (1975), *Kadının uyrukluğu üzerinde evlenmenin etkisi* (1980), and *Yurttaşlık (vatandaşlık) hukuku* (1982); she was joint editor of *Murat Sarıca armağanı* (1988). Kim kimdir, 1997/98-2000; LC

Aygen, Reşat Enis, born 1 June 1909 at Constantinople, where he graduated from the Faculty of Arts in 1930. He was a journalist and writer who wrote *Gece konuştu* (1935), *Toprak kokusu* (1944), and *Despot* (1957). EIS; Meydan

Ayiter, Mehmet Kudret, born 31 August 1919 at Göttingen, Germany, he taught since 1946 in various capacities at the Faculty of Law in Ankara Üniversitesi. His writings include *Medeni hukukta tasarruf muameleleri* (1953), *Roma hukuku dersleri* (1960), and *Das Staatsangehörigkeitsgesetz der Türkei* (1970). Kim kimdir, 1985/86-2000

Ayman, Laylá, 1929- see Ahi, Laylá Ayman

Aymard, Léopold Louis, *capitaine*, born 19th, he wrote *Les Touareg* (Paris, 1911). NUC, pre-1956

Aymé, Victor, fl. 1904, he wrote *L'Afrique française et le transsaharien* (Paris, 1891). NYPL

Aymo, Joseph, *capitaine*, born 20 November 1912 at Bastia, he was attached to the Ministère du Sahara, and a sometime member of the Centre de Hautes Études d'Administration Musulmane, Paris. Unesco

Ayoub, Mahmoud Mustafa, born 1 June 1935, he received a Ph.D. from Harvard University in 1975 for his thesis, *Redemptive suffering in Islam.* He was in 1982 affiliated with the University of Toronto, and in 1990 he was a professor of religion at Temple University, Philadelphia, Pa. His writings include *The Qur'an and its*

its interpreters (1983), *Islam and the Third Universal Theory* (1987), and *Islam; faith and practice* (1989). MESA Roster of members, 1982-1990

Ayoub, Victor Ferris, born in 1923 at Detroit, Mich., he graduated in 1949 from Antioch College, Yellow Springs, and received a Ph.D. in 1955 from Harvard for *Political structure of a Middle East community; a Druze village in Mount Lebanon.* From 1956 to his retirement in 1986 he was a professor of anthropoogy at Antioch College. AmM&WSc, 1973 S; MESA Roster of members, 1977; WhoWor, 1991/92

El-Ayouti, Yassin, born 14 April 1928 at Kanayat, Egypt, he was educated at Cairo, New Jersey universities, and New York University, where he received a Ph.D. in 1966 for his thesis *The Afro-Asian interpretation of the U.N. Charter's concept of dealing with non-self-governing territories, 1945-1963.* Since 1962 he was an Egyptian U.N. officer for political affairs as well as a visiting professor at universities in New York State. His writings include *The United Nations and decolonization* (1971), and *The Organization of African Unity after ten years* (1975). ConAu, 29-32, new rev., 14; WhoArab, 1995/96

Ayres, Henry F, born 7 December 1889 at London, he was an engineer who reveived a B.Sc. from the University of London and subsequently spent nearly forty years in Egypt and the Sudan in the Government's service but also in private enterprise. He was a sometime president of the Chamber of Commerce in Cairo. Who's who in Egypt and the Near East, 1951

Ayrout, Henry Habib, S.J., born 20 May 1907 at Cairo, he was educated at the Université de Lyon, where he received a doctorate in 1938. From 1962 until his death, he was in charge of the Collège de la Sainte-Famille, Cairo. His writings include *Moeurs et coutumes des fellahs* (1938), *Fellahs* (1942), The *fellaheen* (1945), and *Liaisons africaines* (1975). He died from a cardiac arrest in New York during an official visit to the United States on 10 April 1969. Hommes et destins, vol. 4, pp. 43-44

Ayub Khan, Mohammad, born in 1907 at Rehana, India, he was educated at Aligarh Moslem University and the Royal Military College, Sandhurst. He advanced through the grades to become general of the Pakistan Army and was president of Pakistan from 1958 to 1969. His writings include *Ayub, soldier and statesman; speeches* (1966). He died on 20 April 1974. CurBio, 1959, 1974; Jain, p. 107-108; Who was who, 7; WhAm, 6

Ayubi, Nazih Nasif Mikhail, born 22 December 1944 at Cairo, he there received his first degree and took a D.Phil. in 1975 at Oxford for *Bureaucratic evolution and political development; Egypt, 1952-1970.* After a brief professorship at Cairo University, he was for four years at UCLA. In 1983 he moved to the University of Exeter as key appointment in the development of Middle East studies. In 1990 he received the unusual compliment of a double promotion to a readership, which was followed by fellowships, held at the University of Manchester and at the European University Institute, Firenze. At the time of his death on 4 December 1995, in Exeter, he was under consideration for a personal chair. His writings include *Bureaucracy and politics in contemporary Egypt* (1980), *Political Islam* (1991), *Over-stating the Arab state* (1995), and *Distant neighbours* (1995). BRISMES newsletter 10, no. 2 (March 1996), p. 1; MESA bulletin 30 i (1996), pp.137-141; Sluglett

Ayverdi, Ekrem Hakki, born 22 December 1899 at Constantinople. His writings include *XVIII asirda lâle* (1950), *Fâtih devri mi'mârîsi* (1953-1961), and *Makaleler* (1985). He died on 24 April 1984. AnaBrit; Meydan

Azadi, Siawosch, born in 1935 in Berlin, he graduated in economics and was since 1963 in the Oriental rug and textile business in Germany. He was the author of exhibition and sales catalogues, and wrote *Mafrash, gewebte Transporttaschen* (1985), and *Teppiche in der Belutschen-Tradition* (1986). LC

Azadian, A., Dr.Sc., he was in 1925 a chemist at the Laboratoire de l'Administration de l'hygiène publique and a member of the Institut d'Égypte. His writings include *Les eaux d'Égypte* (1930). BN; Note

Azadovskii, Mark Konstantinovich, born in 1888 at Irkutsk, Russia, he was an ethnographer who graduated in 1913 from St. Petersburg University. He became a professor at Russian universities. His writings include *Литератур и фольклор* (1938), *Горький и Сибирь* (1969), and *Sibirian tale teller* (1974). He died in Leningrad on 24 November 1954. GSE

Azam, Kousar Jabeen, born in 1943, he received a Ph.D. in 1974 in political science from Osmania University. He wrote *Political aspects of national integration* (1981). LC

Azam, P., commandant, fl. 1946-1960. He was a sometime member of the Centre de Hautes Études d'Administration musulmane, Paris. Note

Azan, Paul Jean Louis, born 22 January 1874 at Besançon (France), he graduated from the military college of Saint-Cyr, and received a commission as *sous-lieutenant* (1897) with the 2e Zouaves, stationed first in Oran and then at various posts on the Moroccan frontier: Nemours, Tlemcen, Lalla-Maghnia, and Sebdou. Through his extensive duties in the frontier region, he came to be interested in the life and customs of the local inhabitants. His experiences during that time provided him with the material for his *Recherches d'une solution de la question indigène en Algérie* (1903). Concurrent to his military duties, he pursued literary studies which culminated in a doctorate from the Université de Paris for *Annibal dans les Alpes*. This achievement made such furor that the *ministre de la Guerre* appointed him to the *état-major de l'armée*, where he became one of the chief collaborators of its *Revue de l'histoire*. He completed his military career in 1936 as chief of the French forces in Tunisia. He was highly honoured, became president of the Académie des sciences coloniales, and remained an active historian until his death in Lons-le-Saunier in 1951. His writings include *Sidi-Brahim* (1905), *Souvenirs de Casablanca* (1911), *L'expédition de Fez* (1924), *Conquête et pacification de l'Algérie* (1931), and *L'Empire français* (1943). Curinier, v. 5, p. 87; *Hommes et destins*, 2, pp. 33-35

Azar, Antoine, Dr., fl. 1969, he taught at the Faculté de Droit et des Sciences économiques de Beyrouth, and was a member of the Comité directeur et du Centre de recherches de l'Association libanaise des sciences politiques. His writings include *Le Liban face à demain* (1978), *Liban à l'épreuve* (1982), and *Plaidoyer pour un sénat* (1985). LC; Note

Azar, Edward Elias, born 2 March 1938 in Lebanon, he graduated in 1960 from AUB. He worked for ARAMCO for four years before pursuing his graduate studies in political science at Stanford University, where he received a Ph.D. in 1969 for *International political integration : the case of the U.A.R.* (1969). He taught at Michigan State University from 1968 to 1971, and the University of North Carolina, 1971-1981, before joining the University of Maryland. He was an editor of *International interactions* from 1972 to 1987, and associate editor of *Peace science journal* from 1980 until 1991. He helped pioneer the application of quantitative analysis of international conflict issues, globally and in the Middle East. His writings include *International events interaction analysis* (1972), *Probe for peace* (1973), *Dimensions of interaction* (1975). He died on 18 June 1991 after a long struggle with AIDS. *MESA bulletin* 25 (1991), pp. 310-311

Azarakhsh, Hasan 'Ali, born in 1917 at Tehran, he received a medical doctorate in 1941 from the University of Tehran. He was a sometime director of the Iranian Narcotics Administration, and U.N. consultant in narcotic control. *Iran who's who*, 1976

Azarpay, Guitty, born 28 October 1939, she began to study in Iran, continued in England, and finished at the University of California at Berkeley, where she received a Ph.D. in 1968 for her *Urartian art and artifacts; a chronological study*. She also wrote *Sogdian painting* (1981). LC; Schoeberlein

Azcárraga y Bustamante, José Lois de, born 26 October 1918 at Vitoria, Spain, he studied law at the universities of Valladolid, Santiago de Compostela, and Madrid, where he received a doctorate in 1950. Thereafter he was for many years a professor of civil as well as maritime law at various Spanish universities. His writings include *El corso marítimo* (1950), *La Carta de las Naciones Unidas y su posible reforma* (1955), *Derecho internacional marítimio* (1970), and *Derecho del mar* (1983). DBEC

El **Azem**, Sadik, 1936- see 'Azm, Sadiq Jalal al-

Azfar, Jawaid, born in 1939, he received a Ph.D. in 1972 from Harvard for *The income distribution in Pakistan before and after taxes, 1966-1967*. After his death in 1983, a commemorative volume was published, *Employment distribution and basic needs in Pakistan; essays in honour of Jawaid Azfar* (1986).

Azhar, Barkat Ali, born in 1927, he received a Ph.D. in 1954 from the University of Illinois for *A consideration of the factors conditioning the economic development of Pakistan*. In 1972, he was an honorary advisor to the Pakistan Institute of Development Economics, and a joint economic advisor, Ministry of Finance, Government of Pakistan, Islamabad. LC; Note

Azhar, Mohammad, born 20th cent., he was in 1975 a staff demographer at the Pakistan Institute of Development Economics, Islamabad. He was joint author of *Change and differentials in men's knowledge of attitude towards, and practice of, family planning in Pakistan during the 1960s* (1977). LC; Note

Azimdzhanova (Azimzhonova), Sabakhat (Sabokhat) Azimdzhanovna, born 31 December 1922 at Tashkent, she graduated in 1942 from the Faculty of History in the Tashkent Pedagogical Institute. Twenty years later, she received a doctorate at Tashkent for Государство Бабура в Кабуле и Индии. She attended international meetings in the Eastern bloc as well as in the Third World. Since 1950, she was director of the Oriental Institute of the Uzbekistan Academy of Science. Her writings include Женщины зарубежного Востока и современность (1988). Miliband; Miliband²; UzbekSE, vol. 1, p. 180

Aziz, Mohammed Abdul, he was in 1955 a professor of international relations at the Department of International Relations in Dacca University. His writings include *The Union Parishad in Bangladesh*. LC

Aziz, Sartaj, born 7 February 1929 in Mardan, India, he was educated at Punjab University, and Harvard. Since 1950, he was an official in the Pakistani Government and, since 1971, active in international organizations. His writings include *Industrial location policy in Pakistan* (1969), *Rural development; learning from China* (1978), and *Agricultural policies for the 1990's* (Paris, 1990). ConAu, 111; WhoUN, 1975

Aziz Ahmad, 1913-1978 *see* Ahmad, Aziz

Azizi, Ali Asghar, born in 1914 at Qazvin, Persia, he received a doctorate in pharmacology at Tehran, and later studied in western Europe. He was a sometime teacher of Persian in the Universität Wien. He was attached to the consular service in Austria and Germany, where he organized friendship associations and was responsible for the surveillance of Iranians studying in these two countries. *Iran who's who,* 1976

al-'Azm, Sādiq Jalāl, born in 1936 at Damascus, he received a doctorate and taught at A.U.B., Hunter College of the City University of New York, and Damascus University. His writings include *Kant's theory of time* (1967), نقد الذكر الديني (1969), *The origins of Kant's arguments in the Antimonies* (1972), دراسات في الفلسفة الغربية الحديثة (1974), ذهنية التحريم؛ سلمان رشدى (London, 1992), and *Unbehagen in der Moderne; Aufklärung im Islam* (1993). *Who's who in the Arab world, 1978/79|*

al-'Azmah (Azmeh), 'Azīz Malak, born 23 or 24 July 1947 Damascus, he studied at the universities in Alexandria, Beirut, Tübingen, and Oxford, where he received a D.Phil. in 1977 for *Ibn Khaldun in modern scholarship*. He was a fellow of the British Society for Middle Eastern Studies, a member of the Arab Writers' Union, and the Arab Philosophical Society. His writings include *al-Yasar al-Sihyuni* (1969), *Arabic thought and Islamic societies* (1991), *Ibn Khaldun* (1993), and *Muslim kingship; power and the sacred in Muslim, Christian and Pagan politics* (2000). Publisher's catalogue; Sluglett; WhoArab, 2001/2002, 2003/2004

Azmayish, 'Ali, born in 1322/1942 in Iran, he was in 1978 vice-chancellor of the Faculty of Law as well as director of the Institute of Penal Law and Criminology in the University of Tehran. Note

Azmeh, Aziz, 1947- *see* al-'Azmah, 'Aziz

Azmi, M. Raziullah, born 20th cent., he was in 1980 a research fellow at the Area Study Centre for Africa, North and South America in the Quaid-i-Azam University, Islamabad. His writings include *Pakistan-Canada relations, 1947-1982* (1982). Note

Aznabaev, Akhmer Mukhametdinovich, fl. 1971, his writings include Политическое сознание и само-сознание личности (Ufa, 1985), and Историческая морфология Башкрпского языка (Ufa, 1976). LC

Azoo, Rizkallah F., born 19th cent., he was associated with the Asiatic Society of Bengal and wrote *Annotated glossary to the ar-Rawzatu' z-Zakiyyah* (Calcutta, 1908); and, with Henry E. Stapleton, *Alchemical equipment in the eleventh century, A.D.* (Calcutta, 1905); and he jointly compiled *Gems of Arabic literature, being the English translation of Ar-Rauzat-uz-Zakiah* (Ahmedabad, 1916). He died in 1911. BLC; LC

Azoulay, Élie Edmond, born 19th cent., he received a doctorate in 1921 from the Université d'Alger for *De la condition politique des indigènes musulmans d'Algérie; essai critique sur la loi du 4 février 1919*. His trace is lost after a publication in 1933. NUC, pre-1956

Azuar Ruiz, Rafael, born in 1921, he received a diploma in geography and history, with special reference to medieval Moorish archaeology. He was in 1992 a curator at the Museo Arqueológico Provincial de Alicante. His writings include *Alicante y lo alicantino* (1980), *Castellología medieval alicantina, area meridional* (1981), *La Rabíta Califal de la Dunas de Guardama* (1989); he edited *Fortificaciones castillos de Alicante* (1991); and he was joint editor of *Urbanismo medieval del pais valenciano* (1993). Arabismo, 1992|; LC

'Azzam, 'Abd al-Rahman, born 8 March 1893 at al-Shawbak, Egypt, he studied medicine at the University of London from 1910 to 1913. For the following ten years he was engaged militarily in Egypt and Libya. In 1923, he was elected member of the first Egyptian Parliament; he held several posts in successive governments before he became seceretary-general of the Arab League, 1945-1952 His writings include. يطل الابطال او ابرز صفات النبي محمد (1938), and *The eternal message of Muhammad* (1964). His memoirs in Arabic were published in 1977. He died in 1976. CurBio, 1947; Goldschmidt; WhoArab, 1986/87

'Azzam, Samīrah, born in 1927 at Akka, Palestine, she was a writer whose writings include العيد من النافذة (1971), and ظل الكبير (1986). *Who's who in the Arab world, 1981/82*

Azzi, Robert, fl. 1973, he was a photographer who published coffee-table books. These include *An Arabian portfolio* (1976), *Damascus, ash-Sham* (1982), and *Tufts University* (1988). LC

Baade, Fritz, born 23 January 1893 at Neuruppin, Germany, he received a Dr.rer.pol. in 1924 from the Universität Göttingen for his thesis, *Die Wirtschaftsreform des Großbetriebes in vorkapitalistischer Zeit*. From 1926 to 1930 he was director of the Forschungsstelle für Wirtschaftspolitik, Berlin; from 1934 to 1946, an agricultural consultant in Turkey; and from 1948 until his retirement in 1961, a director of the Institut für Weltwirtschaft, Kiel. His writings include *Exports and invisible receipts in Turkey* (1961), *The race to the year 2000* (1962), and *Dynamische Weltwirtschaft* (1969). He died ca. 1973. Wer ist wer, 1971/73; Widmann

Baali, Fuad G., born 12 February 1930 at Baghdad, he received a Ph.D. in 1960 from Louisana State University for his thesis, *Land tenure and rural social organization; a study in southern Iraq*. From 1968 until his retirement he was professor of sociology at Western Kentucky University. His writings include *Falsafat Ikhwan al-Safa' al-ijtima'iyah wa-al-akhlaqiyah* (1958), *Introductory sociology* (1970), *Urban sociology* (1970), and *Society, state, and urbanism* (1987). AM&WS, 1973 S

Baarda, Tjitze, born 8 July 1932 at Vogelenzang, Netherlands, he received a doctorate in 1975 from the Vrije Universiteit te Amsterdam for his thesis, *The Gospel quotations of Aphrahat, the Persian sage*. Since 1954 he taught in various capacities at the Vrije Universiteit. His writings include *De betrouwbaarheid van de envangeliën* (1967). Wie is wie, 1984/88

Baarmann, Johannes Georg Karl Friedrich, born 19 August 1858 at Eisleben, Germany, he studied at the universities of Berlin and Halle, where he received a Dr.phil. in 1882 for his thesis *Ibn al-Haitam's Abhandlung über das Licht*.

Baas, Johann Hermann, born 24 October 1838 at Bechtheim, Germany, he received a Dr.med. in 1860 from the Universität Gießen for his thesis, *Die Resektion im Ellenbogen*. Thereafter he practised medicine. His writings include *Grundriß der Geschichte der Medicin* (1876), *Outlines of the history of medicine and the medical profession* (1889), and *Die geschichtliche Entwicklung des ärztlichen Standes* (1896). He died in Worms, 10 November 1909. DtBE

Baazova, Lili Khaimovna, fl. 1960. She wrote *Avganet'is bibliograp'ia* (1979). LC

Baba, Bay Nüzhet, fl. 1944, he was a leading member of the Turkish Press Association. Note

Babaa, Khalid I., fl. 1965, his writings include his letters to the editors of Canadian newspapers under the title *Facts vs. misstatements*, published by the Arab Information Centre, Ottawa, in 1960. NUC, pre-1956

Babaev, F., fl. 1945, he edited Икбал-намэ (1947), and Лайли и Маджнун (1965). LC

Babaev, Koin Rakhimovich, born 20th cent., he received a doctorate in 1974 for his thesis, Тыркизмы в лексико-семантической системе современного русского литературного языка. His writings include Туркмен дилинин стилистикасы (1989). LC

Babakhanov, Sh. Z. *see* Bobokhonov, Shamsuddin Z.

Babakhodzhaev, Marat Abdusamatovich, born 31 October 1929 at Termez, Uzbekistan, he graduated in 1951 from Tashkent University, and four years later he received a doctorate for his thesis, Освободительная война народов Афганистана против английских захватчиков в 1838-1942 гг. His writings include Борьба Афганистана за независимость, 1838-1942 (1960), Герат эпохи Алишера Навои (1968), Усьекисеон ва Афганистон (1970), and Очерки социально-экономической и политической истории Афганистана (1975). LC; Miliband

Baban, Ismail Hakki, born in 1876 at Baghdad, he was a writer and politician who died in 1913 in Constantinople. Meydan

Babelon, Ernest Charles François, born 7 November 1854 at Sarrey (Haute-Marne), he was keeper at the Cabinet des médailles and wrote *Manuel d'archéologie orientale* (1888), and *Manual of Oriental antiquities* (1889). He died 3 January 1924. DBF

Babikian, Norma Salem *see* Salem-Babikian, Norma

Babinger, Franz Karl Heinrich, born 15 January 1891 at Weiden, Germany, he pursued Indological studies and received a Dr.phil. in 1915 from the Universität München for *Gottlieb Siegfried Bayer; ein Beitrag zur Geschichte der morgenländischen Studien im 18. Jahrhundert*. His military service in Turkey during the first World War changed the direction of his research towards Turkish studies Since 1921 professor in Berlin, his career came to a sudden halt in 1934, when the National Socialists dismissed him from office. He found refuge in Rumania where he taught until 1948, when he became the first holder of the chair of history and culture of the Near East and Turkish studies in the Universität München. He retired in 1958. His writings include *Geschichtsschreiber der Osmanen und ihre Werke*

(1927), and *Mehmed der Eroberer und seine Zeit* (1953). He died from cardiac arrest while swimming at Durrës, Albania, 23 June 1967. *Anali Gazi Husrev-begove Biblioteke* 1 (1972), pp. 143-145; DtBE; I.I. (3); Thesis; *Welt des Islams* 38 (1998), pp. 1-8

Babled, Henry, born 5 June 1862 at Nîmes, he received a doctorate in 1892 from the Faculté de droit de Paris for his thesis, *Droit romain: La cura annonae chez les romains - Droit français: Les syndicats de producteurs et détenteurs de marchandises au double point de vue économique et pénal*. From 1893 to 1899 he was a professor of law at the École française de droit du Caire. Thereafter he taught at the Université d'Aix-Marseille. He died 19 May 1909. DBF

Babouskos, Konstantinos Anastasiou, 1921- *see* Vavouskos, Konstantinos Anastasiou

Bacaicoa Arnaiz, Dora, fl. 1953, her writings include *Notas hispano-marroquies en dos comedias del siglo de oro* (Tetuán, 1955), *Zóhora la Negra y otros cuentos* (Tetuán, 1955), and *Inventario provisional de la Hemeroteca del Protectorado*, redactado por Dora Bacaico Arnaiz, jefe de dicho establecimiento, con la colaboración de Manuel Requena Córdoba (Tetuán, 1953). NUC, pre-1956

Baccanti, Alberto, born 25 November 1718 at Casalmaggiore (Cremona), he was a clergyman who attended the theological seminaries in Lodi and Milano. His writings include *Maometto, legislatore degli arabi e fondatore dell'Impero musulmano* (1791). He died in Casalmaggiore, 30 April 1805. DizBI

Baccar, Taoufik, born 20th cent., he was in 1980 atttached to the Faculté des lettres de Tunis. His writings include *Mahmoud Sehlili* (1986), *Ma'a Tawfiq Bakkar* (1990); he was joint author of *Écrivains de Tunisie; anthologie* (1981). LC

Bach, Emilie, born 2 July 1840 at Neuschluß, Bohemia, she founded in 1873 the Fachschule für Kunststrickerei, Wien. Her writings include *Muster stilvoller Handarbeiten* (1879), *Neue Muster im alten Stil* (1887-1894), and its English and French translations, *New patterns in old style*; and *Ouvrage nouveaux de style ancien*. She died in Wien, 30 April 1890. ÖBL

Bach Hamba, Mohammed *see* Bash Hanbah, Muhammad

Bacharach, Jere Lehman, born 18 November 1938 at New York City, he was educated at Trinity College, Conn., Harvard, and University of Michigan, where he obtained a Ph.D. in 1967 for his thesis, *A study of the correlation between textual sources and numismatic evidence for Mamluk Egypt*. Since 1982 he was a professor of history at the University of Washington, Seattle, Wash., and for many years editor of the *MESA bulletin*. His writings include *A Near East studies handbook* (1974); and he was editor of *Monetary change and economic history in the medieval Muslim world*, by A. S. Ehren-kreutz (1992), and *Restoration and conservation of Islamic monuments in Egypt* (1995). DrAS, 1982

Bachatly, Charles, born in 1909 in Egypt. His formal study was concerned with the pre-history of Egypt, but the course of his research changed when he became secretary of the newly founded Société d'archéologie copte. The success of its *Bulletin* was largely due to his efforts. His writings include *Bibliographie de la préhistoire égyptienne* (1942), *Le monastère de Phoebammon dans la Thébaïde* (1961). He died 16 June 1957. *Bulletin de la Société d'archéologie copte* 14 (1950-57), 249-250

Bache, Paul Eugène, born 26 November 1812 at Paris, he was a writer and a civil servant in Algeria from 1839 until his death at the end of 1863. His writings include *Ali, ou cent sonnets* (1846), and *Les Oranais; poésies* (1850). DBF

Bacher, Wilhelm (Benjamin Swew), born 12 January 1850 at Liptó-Szent-Miklós, Hungary, he studied Semitic and Oriental languages, with special emphasis on Arabic and Persian, at the universities of Budapest, Breslau, and Leipzig, where he obtained a doctorate in 1871 for his thesis, *Nizâmî's Leben und Werke und der zweite Theil des Alexanderbuches*. He pursued his studies at the Rabbiner Seminar in Breslau where he was ordained rabbi in 1876. In 1877, after having served in the previous year as rabbi of the Szeged community, he was invited to Budapest to join the faculty of the newly founded Rabbinical Seminary. He was appointed to teach Biblical studies and Hebrew language and literature, and in all these fields he kept lecturing until his death on 25 December 1913. During the last six years of his life he served also as Rector of the Seminary. He was the only scholar of his generation who studied Judeo-Persian literature. His writings include *Ein hebräisch-persisches Wörterbuch aus dem 14. Jahrhundert* (1900). EncJud; Filipsky; GeistigeUng; Magyar; MagyarZL; RNL; UjLex; Wininger; *The Rabbinical Seminary of Budapest, 1877-1977, a centennial volume*, ed. by M. Carmilly-Weinberger (1986), pp. 194-202

Bachhofer, Ludwig, born 30 June 1894, he was a lecturer at the Universität München from 1928 to 1935. His writings include *Die frühindische Plastik* (1929), *Early Indian sculpture* (1929), and *A short history of Chinese art* (1946). Kürschner, 1928/29-1935|

Bachinskii, N. M., fl. 1950. His writings include *Резное дерево в архитектуре Средней Азии* (1947), and *Антисейстика в архитектурных памятниках Средней Азии* (Moscow, 1949).

Bachmann, Peter, born 27 February 1936 at Leipzig, Germany. After study at the Freie Universität Berlin he was a professor of Islamic studies at Göttingen. His writings include *Galens Abhandlung darüber, daß der vorzügliche Arzt Philosoph sein muß* (1965). Kürschner, 1996-2003

Bachmann, Walter, born 8 May 1883 at Plauen, Germany, he studied architecture at the Technische Hochschule, Dresden, where he received a Dr.phil. in 1913 for his thesis, *Kirchen und Moscheen in Armenien und Kurdistan*. His writings include *Felsreliefs in Assyrien* (1927). LC

Bachrouch, Taoufik, born 20th cent., he was in 1972 a professor at the Université de Tunis. His writings include *Formation sociale barbaresque et pouvoir à Tunis au XVIIe siècle* (1977), *Les élites tunisiennes du pouvoir et de la dévotion* (1989), and *Le saint et le prince en Tunisie* (1989). LC

Bachur, Yona, born in 1928, he received a degree in literature from the Hebrew University, Jerusalem, and became a literary critic and lecturer in modern Hebrew literature. He died in 1991. LC

Backvis, Claude Joseph Elie, born 24 April 1910 at Schaerbeck, Belgium, he studied philosophy and Slavonic languages and received a doctorate in 1931 from the Université libre de Bruxelles. Thereafter he was a professor at Bruxelles. His writings include *Le dramaturge Stanislas Wyspiański* (1952), and *Renesans i barok w Polsce* (1993). LC; Who's who in Belgium and Luxembourg, 1962

Bacon, Elizabeth Emaline (Mrs. A. E. Hudson), born 29 July 1904 at Whittier, California, she was educated in Switzerland, France, and the United States. In 1951 she received a Ph.D. from the University of California at Berkeley for *The Hazara Mongols of Afghanistan; a study in social organization*. She edited two handbooks for the Human Relations Area Files, *India* (1955), and *Uttar Pradesh* (1955), and wrote *Obok; a study of social structure in Eurasia* (1958). ConAu, 1; WhoAmW, 1968/9

Bacon, John M., fl. 1900. "The Rev. had a plan to use the prevailing westerly winds to launch a balloon in the Sudan in the hope of reaching the Persian Gulf. He had already crossed the Irish Sea in that way and on another occasion just missed a collision with St.Paul's Cahtedral." Bidwell, p. 210

Bacqué-Grammont, Jean Louis, born 12 June 1941, he received a doctorate in 1980 from the Université de Paris I for his thesis, *Ottomans et Safavides au temps de Shah Isma'il*. He was a sometime *directeur de recherche* at the CNRS, Paris. His writings include *Mustafa Kemal Atatürk et la Turquie nouvelle* (1982), *Les Ottomans, les Safavides et leurs voisins* (1987), and he was joint author with Anne Kroell of *Mamlouks, Ottomans et Portugais en Mer Rouge* (1988), and with Chahyar Adle of *Les Ottomans, les Safavides et la Géorgie* (1991). AnEIFr, 1989; LC; Schoeberlein; THESAM, 4

Badal, Raphael Koba, born 20th cent., he received a Ph.D. in 1977 from SOAS for his thesis, *British administration in Southern Sudan*. Thereafter he taught political science at the Faculty of Economic and Social Studies in the University of Khartoum. His writings include *The 1971 Local Government Act; the case of the Southern Region* (1979), *Oil and regional sentiment in the southern Sudan* (1983), and *Origins of the underdevelopment of the southern Sudan* (1983). LC; Sluglett

Badaoui, Abd el Hamid, 1887-1965 *see* Badawi, 'Abd al-Hamid

Badaoui, H. Bahgat *see* Badawi, Hilmi Bahjat

Badawi, 'Abd al-Hamid, born 13 March 1887 at al-Mansurah, Egypt, he was educated at the Faculty of Law, Cairo, and the Université de Toulouse, where he received a doctorate in law. He became an Egyptian foreign minister and judge at the International Court of Justice. His writings include *Le développement de la notion de privilège* (Grenoble, 1912). He died in August, 1965. Revue égyptienne de droit international 21 (1965), pp. 1-4; WhAm, 4

Badawi, 'Abd al-Rahman, fl. 1958 at Cairo University, he wrote *Le problème de la mort dans la philosophie existentielle* (1964), *Histoire de la philosophie en islam* (1972), *La transmission de la philosophie grecque au monde arabe* (1987), and *Défense du Coran contre ses critiques* (1989). LC

Badawi, 'Ali Muhammad, fl. 1932, he was joint author of *Nouveau code pénal égyptien annoté* (1939). LC

Badawi, Ahmad Zaki, born in 1910, he was an adviser on labour affairs to the League of Arab States. His writings include *Législation du travail en Egypte* (1946), *A dictionary of the social sciences; English-French-Arabic* (1978), *Dictionary of education* (1980), and *Mu'jam al-sikritariyah wa-al-idarat al-makatib* (1991); he was joint author of *Dictionnaire juridique; français-arabe* (1983). LC

Badawi, Gamal, A., born in 1939 in Egypt. During his student days he was active in the Muslim Students' Association of the United States and Canada. After he obtained a Ph.D. in 1970 from Indiana University, Bloomington, for *Some analytical and operational aspects of job vacancy data*. He became a professor in the School of Management, Halifax, N.S., where he was still active in 1997. His writings include a number of Islamic pamphlets between 1972 and 1979, and *al-Fitnah al-ta'ifiyah fi Misr* (1980). LC; NatFacDr, 1995-97

Badawi, Hilmi Bahjat, Dr. fl. 1932, he was a professor of civil law at the Faculty of Law, Cairo. He wrote *Usul al-iltizamat* (1943). LC

Badawi, Jamal A., b. 1939 *see* Badawi, Gamal A.

Badawi, Muhammad *Mustafá*, born 10 June 1925 at Alexandria, Egypt, he was educated at the universities of Alexandria, London, and Oxford. From 1961 to 1980 he was Unesco expert on modern Arabic culture, and from 1967 until his retirement in 1992, a university lecturer in modern Arabic studies at St Antony's College, Oxford. He was awarded the King Faisal International Prize for Arabic Literature in Riyadh in March 1992. His writings include *A critical introduction to modern Arabic poetry* (1975), *Modern Arabic literature and the West* (1985), *Modern Arabic drama in Egypt* (1987), *Early Arabic drama* (1988), and *Short history of modern Arabic literature* (1993). AfricaWW, 1991; ConAu, 49-52

Baddeley, John Frederick, born in 1854, he was a special correspondent of the *Standard* in Russia, where he resided for thirty-five years. He was the author of *The Russian conquest of the Caucasus* (1908), *The rugged flanks of the Caucasus* (1940), and other writings. He died in 1940. LC

Baddeley, Welbore St. Clair, born in 1856 at St. Leonard's-on-Sea, Sussex, he was educated at Wellington College, Wokingham. His writings include *Legend of the death of Antar* (1881), and *Bedoueen legends and other poems* (1883).

Badeau, John Stothoff, born 24 February 1903 at Pittsburgh, Pa., he graduated from Union College, Schenectady, N.Y., and New New Brunswick Theological Seminary. From 1928 to 1930 he served as a missionary in Mosul, and from 1930 to 1935 in Baghdad. Thereafter he was variously, professor, dean, and president at the American University in Cairo from 1936 to 1953. He was a sometime ambassador to Egypt, and, from 1964 to 1971, professor of Middle Eastern studies at Columbia University. His writings include *The emergence of modern Egypt* (1953), and his autobiography, *The Middle East remembered* (1983). He died 25 August 1995. Master (3); MESA bulletin 29 (1995), pp. 287-288; Shavit

Baden-Powell, Baden Henry, born in 1841. After education at Oxford he was in the Bengal Civil Service from 1861 to 1889. His writings include *Creation and its records* (1886), *The land-systems of British India* (1892), *A short account of the land revenue and its administration in British India* (1894), and *The Indian village community* (1895). He died in Oxford, 2 January 1901. Riddick; Who was who, 1

Bader, Otto Nikolaevich, born 29 June 1903 at Aleksandrovskoe, Ukraine, he was an archaeologist who gained a doctorate in 1963 and was appointed a professor in 1965. His writings include *Археологические памятники их охрана и методы первичного изучения* (1938). He died in 1979. GSE; LC; TatarES

Badger, George Percy, born in 1815 at Chelmsford, he grew up in Malta, in some poverty, and without much formal education. He never went to a university, nor took any academic post - his doctorate was awarded by the Archbishop of Canterbury in 1873. After studying at the Church Missionary Society, Islington, he was sent as a delegate to Eastern Churches. His writings include *The Nestorians and their rituals* (1852), a translation of Salil ibn Ruzayq, *History of the imams and sayyids of Oman* (1871), and *English-Arabic lexicon* (1881). He died on 8 December 1888. British Society for Middle Eastern Studies bulletin 11 (1984), pp. 140-145; Buckland; DNB

Badi, Shamsadin Mamedovich, fl. 1971. His writings include *Аграрные отношения в современном Иране* (1959), *Рабочий класс Ирана* (1965), and *Городские средние слои Ирана* (1977). LC

Badia i Margarit, Antoni Maria, born in 1920 at Barcelona, he was since 1948 a professor of linguistics at the Universidad de Barcelona. His writings include *Los complementos pronominalo-adverbiales derivados e inde en la Península Ibérica* (1947), and *Gramàtica de la llengua catalana* (1994). Dicc. bio

Badiny, Francisco Jos *see* Jos Badiny, Francisco

Badr, Jamal Mursi (Gamal Moursi), Dr., fl. 1955, he was an adjunct professor of law at New York University, and a former justice of the Supreme Court of Algeria. His writings include *al-Niyabah fi al-tasarrufat al-qanuniyah* (1968), and *State immunity; an analytical and prognostic view* (1984). LC

Badrah'i, Faridun, born in 1315/1936 in Iran, he received a Ph.D. In 1350/1961 from Tehran University. His writings include *Ravish-i nivishtan-i panivis* (1970), and *Guzarishi dar barah-i Farhangistan-i Iran* (1976). LC

Badre (Badr), Albert Y., born in 1912, he was joint author, with Simon G. Siksek, of *Manpower and oil in Arab countries* (Beirut, AUB, 1960). NUC, 1968-1972

Badri, Hajjah Kashif, fl. 1979, she took a M.Sc. in history, was a founding member of the Sudan Women's Union, a member of its Executive Committee, and its chairman, 1956-1957. Since 1983 she was chief representative of the League of Arab States Mission for India. Her writings include *al-Harakah al-nisa'iyah fi al-Sudan* (1984), and *Women's movement in the Sudan* (1986). LC

Badri, Malik B., fl. 1967. His writings include *Saykulujiyat rusum al-atfal* (1966), *Islam and alcoholism* (1976), and *The dilemma of Muslim psychologists* (1979). LC

el **Badry**, Mohamed Abdel-Rahman, born 16 November 1920 at Cairo, he studied at Cairo and London, where he received a doctorate in statistics from the Imperial College of Science and Technology. For seventeen years he was a professor of statistics at Cairo University before he became UN population expert. In 1986 he was back in Cairo at the Demographic Centre. His writings include *Demographic projections in historical perspective* (1981), and *Aging in developing countries* (1986). LC; Unesco; *Who's who in the Arab world*, 1978/9

Badt, Hermann, born 13 July 1887 at Breslau, Germany, he received a Dr.jur. in law in 1909 from the Universität Breslau for *Die rechtliche Natur der Grundsätze über die materielle Rechtskraft der Zivilurteile*. In 1919 he studied the colonization in Syria and Palestine during a brief journey. Afterwards he was a politician in high office in the German Government, the first Jew to do so. After the national socialists' rise to power in 1933, he was dismissed and emigrated to Palestine, where he died in Jerusalem in September 1946. DtBE; Wininger

Baer, Eva née Apt, born 20 February 1920 at Berlin, she studied at the Hebrew University, Jerusalem, and SOAS, where she received a Ph.D. in 1963 for *The sphinx and the harpy in medieval Islamic art*. Thereafter she was a professor of Islamic art and archaeology at Tel Aviv University until her retirement. Her main fields of research were metalwork, iconography, and ornament. She was a member of the Israel Oriental Society, Israel Exploration Society, and MESA. Her writings include *Sphinxes and harpies in medieval Islamic art* (1965), and *Metalwork in medieval Islamic art* (1983). LC; Private; Sluglett

Baer, Gabriel, born 13 January 1919 at Berlin, he was educated at AUB and the Hebrew University, Jerusalem, where he received a Ph.D. in 1957. For thirty years he was a professor of modern history of Islamic countries at the Hebrew University. His writings include *History of landownership in modern Egypt* (1962), *Egyptian guilds in modern times* (1964), *Studies in the social history of modern Egypt* (1969), and *Fellah and townsman in the Middle East* (1982). He died shortly after his sabbatical year spent in the United States on 22 September 1982 in Jerusalem. ConAu, 5; *der Islam* 61 (1984), pp. 8-9

Baesjou, René, fl. 1972. His writings include *An Asante embassy on the Gold Coast* (Leiden, Afrika-Studiecentrum, 1979). LC

Baethgen, Friedrich Wilhelm Adolf, born 10 January 1849 at Lachem, Germany, he studied at Göttingen and Kiel, where he received a Dr.phil. in 1878 for *Untersuchungen über die Psalmen nach der Peschita*. He subsequently taught Biblical subjects at Halle, Greifswald, and Berlin. His writings include *Fragmente syrischer und arabischer Historiker* (1884), *Beiträge zur semitischen Religionsgeschichte* (1888), and *Die Psalmen* (1897). He died in Rohrbach, 5 September 1905. DtBE

Baeva, Sonia, fl. 1966, she was a literary historian at the Bulgarian Academy of Science. Her writings include *Петко Славейков; живот и творчество* (1968), and *Петко Р. Славейков* (1980). LC

Baevskii, Solomon Isaakovich, born 24 July 1923 at Mogilev, Ukraine, he took his first degree at Leningrad in 1946, he received a doctorate in 1953 for *Модальные значения глагольных форм современного персидского языка*. His writings include *Описание персидских и таджикских рукописей Института народов Азии* (1962); he edited *Фарханг-и зафангуйа ва джаханпуйа* (1974). LC; Miliband; Miliband²

Bag, Amulya Kumar, born in 1937, he received a Ph.D. in 1969 from the University of Calcutta for his thesis, *History of the development of mathematics in ancient and medieval India*. Under the title, *Mathematics in ancient and medieval India*, he published a revised version of his thesis in 1979. In 1975 he was a member of the Indian National Science Academy, New Delhi. LC

Bagatti, Bellarmino, born 11 November 1905 at Lari, Italy. When he was seventeen years old he took the habit of Saint Francis at Mount La Verna in Toscana; he was ordained priest six years later. In 1931 he was sent to the Pontifico Istituto di archeologia cristiana, Roma, where in 1934, he was awarded a doctorate in Christian archaeology for his thesis, *Il cimitero di Commodilla o dei martiri Felice ed Adautto sulla via delle sette chiese*. Since 1935 he held a chair at the Studium Biblicum Franciscanum in Jerusalem, teaching Christian archaeology and topography of Jerusalem. In 1941 he collaborated with Father Sylvester Saller, OFM, in beginning the series *SBF Collectio maior*. In 1951, together with Father Donato Baldi, he founded the review *SBF Liber annuus*. From 1968 to 1978 he was the director of the Studium. For many years he taught also at the Franciscans' Studium Theologicum Hierosolymitanum of the Custody of the Holy Land. In recognition of his work he received a number of honours and distinctions between 1955 and 1982. His writings include *L'archeologia cristiana in Palestina* (1962), and *Excavations in Nazareth* (1969). He died at the Franciscan Friary of Saint Saviour in Jerusalem, 7 October 1990. Annual of the Department of Antiquities of Jordan 34 (1990), pp. 9-11

Bagchi, Prabodh Chandra, born in 1898. His writings include *Le canon bouddhique en Chine* (1927-38), *India and China* (1950), and *India and Central Asia* (1955). He died in 1956. LC

Baggally, John Wortley, fl. 1936, he was a graduate of Herford College, Oxford, and a barrister-at-law, Inner Temple. His writings include *Ali Pasha and Great Britain* (1938), and *Greek historical folksongs* (1968). LC

Bagirov, Mir Dzhafar Abbasovich, born in 1896, he wrote Пути развития местного хозяйства в Азербайджане (1925). LC

Bagley, Frank Ronald Charles, born in 1915, he showed early promise at school and won a scholarship to Eton but his life was soon thereafter dogged by family misfortune and tragedy. He read Modern Greats at Balliol College, Oxford, and joined the Foreign Office in 1938. He was a keen linguist, acquiring French, Italian, German, Dutch, Arabic and Persian. Between 1942 and 1952 he was variously stationed as British consul in Baghdad, Djakarta, and Isfahan. For a few years he taught Arabic at the Institute of Islamic Studies in McGill University, Montreal. From 1959 until his retirement in 1981 he taught Persian studies at the School of Oriental Studies, Durham University. His writings include *Ghazali's book of councel for kings* (1964), and *From darkness into light; women's emancipation in Iran*, a translation from the Persian (1977). His numerous articles reflected the breadth of his understanding of Islamic and Middle Eastern studies. His final years were marked by deteriorating health and eventual blindness; he died in 1997. BRISMES newsletter 12 i (1997), p. 4; Private

Bagley, William Chandler, born 15 March 1874 at Detroit, Mich., he was educated at Michigan State College, University of Wisconsin, and Cornell, where he received a Ph.D. in 1900 for his thesis, *The apperception of the sentence; a study in the psychology of language*. For over twenty years he was a professor at Teachers College, Columbia University. His writings include *The educative process* (1905), and *The standard practices of teaching* (1932). He died on 1 July 1946. WhAm, 2

Bagnani, Gilbert, born 26 April 1900 at Roma, he was educated at the Università di Roma, where he received a doctorate in 1921. Afterwards he completed post-doctoral work at the Scuola archeologica di Atene. In his later years, he was professor of classics at Trent University, Peterborough, Ontario. His writings include *The Roman Campagna and its treasures* (1926), and *Rome and the papacy* (1929). He was presented with the felicitation volume, *The Mediterranean world; papers presented in honour of G. Bagnani, D.Litt., F.R.S.C., LL.D., on his 75th birthday*. He died in the late 1970s. LC; Canadian who's who, 1973/75

Bagnold, Ralph Alger, born 3 April 1896, at Davenport, England, he was educated at the Royal Military Academy, Woolwich, and Cambridge University. He spent much of his military service in the Middle East where he organized and led numerous explorations in the Libyan Desert and elsewhere. His writings include *Libyan sands; travel in a dead world* (1935), and *The physics of blown sand and desert dunes* (1941). He died 28 May 1990. Master (3); Who was who, 8

Baha' al-Din, Ahmad, born in 1927, he was an Egyptian journalist and writer whose writings include *Ayyam laha ta'rikh* (1967), *Shari'at al-sultah fi al-'alam al-'Arabi* (1984), and *Yawmiyat hadha al-zaman* (1991). He died in 1996. Goldschmidt; LC

Bahadori, Mehdi N., born 20th cent., he was in 1979 affiliated with the Department of Mechanical Engineering, Pahlavi University, Shiraz. He was joint author of *Solar energy application in buildings* (1979). LC

Bahadur, Kalim, born in 1936, he received a doctorate in 1976 from Jawaharlal Nehru University for his thesis, *The Jama'at-i-Islami of Pakistan*. Thereafter he was for well over ten years professor of

Pakistan studies at the Centre for South, South East, and Central Asian Studies, School of International Studies, New Delhi. His writings include *South Asia in transition* (1986). LC

El **Bahay**, Mohammed, 1905- *see* Bahi, Muhammad al-

Bahcheli, Tozun, born 20th cent., he received a Ph.D. in 1972 from the LSE for his thesis, *Communal discord and the stake of interested governments in Cyprus, 1955-1970*. Thereafter he was a professor of political science at King's College, University of Western Ontario, London. His writings include *Greek-Turkish relations since 1955* (1990). LC

von **Bahder**, Egon, born 11 May 1896 at Berghof in Kurland, Germany, his writings include *Herden, Hirten und Herren; durch Steppen und Städte in Turkestan* (1926), *Russische Sprachlehre* (1942), *Enver Pascha; Kampf und Tod in Turkestan* (1943), and *Kleine Geschichte aus Rußland* (1949). KDtLK, 1928-1937/38

Bahgat, Aly, born in 1858 in the province of Beni Suef, Upper Egypt, he was educated in Cairo, where he becamer a teacher of Arabic at the Institut français d'archéologie orientale. He was a fellow researcher of van Berchem as well as Max Herz, whom he succeeded as director of the Egyptian Museum in 1915. He was joint author of *Fouilles d'al-Foustât* (1921), and *La céramique musulmane de l'Égypte* (1930). He died on 27 March 1924. Islam 14 (1925), p. 378

al-**Bahi**, Muhammad, born 23 August 1905 at Asmaniyah, Egypt, he studied Arabic literature, psychology, and education at al-Azhar. In 1932 he was sent on government grant to Hamburg, where he finished his formal education in 1936 with a doctorate for his thesis, *Muhammad 'Abduh; eine Untersuchung seiner Erziehungsmethoden zum Nationalbewußtsein und zur nationalen Erhebung in Ägypten.* In 1961 he had advanced to director-general of the Islamic Culture Administration in Egypt. His writings include *al-Fikr al-Islami fi tatawwurih* (1971), *Islam fitrat Allah* (1976); and he was joint author of *Islam communautaire* (1984). LC

Bahnini, Ahmad, born in 1909, he had been an interpreter for ten years, before he was called to the bar at Fez in 1942. He was a president of the Supreme Court of Morocco, president of the Social Democratic Party, and from 1963 to 1965, prime minister. WhoWor, 1974; WhoArab, 1978/79-1988/89|

Bahrami, Mehdi, born in 1905 in Iran, he studied art and archaeology at Paris and Berlin and received a doctorate in 1937 for *Recherches sur les carreaux de revêtement lustré dans la céramique persane.* Thereafter he taught at Tehran University and became a director of the Tehran Museum. He wrote *Gurgan faïences* (1949). He died in Hamburg following an emergency operation on 29 October 1951. Artibus Asiae 14 (1951), p. 251

Bahroun, Sadok, fl. 1971, he wrote *La planification tunisienne* (1968). LC

Bahur, Yonah, 1928-1991 *see* Bachur, Yona

Baião, António, born 10 October 1878 at Ferreira do Zêzere, Portugal, his writings include *Estudos sombre a inquisição portuguesa* (1919-1920), and he was joint author of *História da expansão portuguesa no mundo* (1937). Quem é alguém, 1947

Baiburdi, Chingiz Gulam-Ali, fl. 1964, he wrote Жизни и творчество Низари, персидского поэта XIII-XIV вв. (1966). LC

Baichura, Uzbek Sh., born 6 January 1923, his writings include Звуковой строй татарского языка (1959). LC

Baid, Samuel, born in 1938, he was in 1976 on the staff of the *Samachar* (News Agency), New Delhi. He was joint author of *Pakistan; an end without a beginning* (1985). LC

Baiev, Georg Gappo, born 9 September 1869 at Vladikavkaz (Ordzhonikidze), Caucasus. For a number of years he was educated privately in the Baltic provinces near the German border. He studied law at Odessa and in 1894 started to practise law in his home town. As one of the first Ossetes, he entered municipal politics in 1905. Five years later he became mayor. In the wake of the Russian revolution he fled the Caucasus in 1921 and went to Berlin via Constantinople. For five years he made a scanty livelihood as a joint editor of Russian and Ossetic publications. Not until 1926 did he obtain a lectureship at the Seminar für Orientalische Sprachen, Berlin, where he died on 24 April 1939. Wolfgang Lentz in Mitteilungen der Ausland-Hochschule an der Universität Berlin 41 (1938), 179-186

Baig, Sir Abbas Ali, born in 1859, he was educated in Bombay and served in high office in the Imperial Indian Government. Sir Afsar ul-Mulk wrote a short biographical sketch, *Sir and Lady Abbas Ali Baig* (London & Woking, 1926). He died on 1 June 1932. Eminent; Jain, p. 118; Who was who, 3

Baig, Mirza Qadeer, born 27 April 1931 at Ajmer, India, and educated at Sind University, Karachi, and SOAS, London, where he received a Ph.D. in 1964 for his thesis, *The role of Shaikh Ahmad of Sarhind in Islam in India*. After a brief lectureship in Islamic history at Government College, Nawabshah, West Pakistan, he joined the Department of Islamic Studies in the University of Toronto in 1964 and remained there until his death on 5 June 1988. During his term of office as president of the Moslem Society of Toronto, the Jami Mosque was established.   Private; Sluglett

Baikie, William Balfour, born 27 August 1825 at Kirkwall, Orkney, he took a degree in medicine at Edinburgh and entered the Royal Navy as an assistant surgeon.   He participated in two Niger expeditions and spent the last seven years of his life at the confluence of the Quorra and Benue where he explored the country, opened up the navigation of the Niger, and translated part of the Bible into Hausa.   His writings include *Narrative of an exploring voyage up the rivers Kwóra and Binue* (1856), and *Translations from Genesis in Fulde* (1876).   He died in Sierra Leone on his way home on 12 December 1864.   DNB; Embacher; Henze

Baikova, Nataliia Borisovna, born in 1894 at Tiflis, she graduated in 1949 from the Tashkent State Teachers' Institute and received her first degree in 1950 in history and archaeology at Tashkent for her thesis, *К вопросу о русско-индийских торговых отношениях в XVI-XVII вв*. From 1942 to 1964 she was a research fellow at the Uzbekistan Academy of Science.   Her writings include *Роль Средней Азии в русско-индийских торговых связях, первая половина XVI-вторая половина XVIII в*. (1964). She died in Tiflis on 11 March 1964.   Miliband; Miliband²

Bailey, Clinton, born about 1935, he was educated at Dartmouth, Hebrew University, and Columbia, where he obtained a Ph.D. in 1966 for his thesis, *The participation of the Palestinians in the politics of Jordan*.   He had a first-hand knowledge of the Bedouin of the Sinai and Negev with whom he periodically lived and studied from 1968 to 1988.   Since 1973 he taught in the Department of Middle Eastern and African History, Tel Aviv University.   His writings include *Jordan's Palestinian challenge, 1948-1983* (1984), and *Bedouin poetry from Sinai and the Negev; mirror of a culture* (1991).   LC

Bailey, Frederick George, born 24 February 1924 at Liverpool, he studied at Oxford and Manchester, where he obtained a doctorate in 1954.   Since 1964 he was a professor of anthropology at the University of Sussex, Brighton.   His writings include *Caste and the economic frontier* (1957), *Tribe, caste, and nation* (1960), *Politics and social change; Orissa in 1959* (1970), *Debate and compromise* (1973), *Morality and expediency* (1977), and *The tactical uses of passion* (1983).   AmM&WS, 1976 P; ConAu, 13-16, new rev., 9; WrDr, 1990/92-1994/96

Bailey, Frederick Marshman, born 3 February 1882, he was educated at Edinburgh Academy, Wellington College, and Sandhurst. In 1905 he entered the Indian Political Department, from which he retired with the rank of colonel. His writings include *Mission to Tashkent* (1946). Arthur H. Swinson wrote *Beyond the frontiers; the biography of colonel F. M. Bailey, explorer and special agent* (1971). He died on 17 April 1967.   Who was who, 6; Who's who in India, Burma & Ceylon, 1937

Bailey, Sir Harold Walter, born 16 December 1899 at Devizes, Wiltshire, he was from 1936 to 1967 a professor of Sanskrit in Cambridge University. In 1993 he was awarded the Denis Sinor Medal for Inner Asian Studies. His writings include *Zoroastrian problems in the ninth-century books* (1943), and *Khotanese Buddhist texts* (1951). He died on 11 January 1996.   BSOAS 60 (1997), p. 109; Who, 1979-1996; CentBritOr, pp. 11-48

Bailey, Moses, he was in 1933 an associate professor of Old Testament at Hartford Theological Seminary. He wrote *The prophetic word, ancient and modern* (Philadelphia, Pa., 1968).   NUC, 1968-1972

Bailey, Thomas Grahame, born in 1872, his writings include *The languages of the northern Himalayas* (1908), *An English-Panjabi vocabulary* (1919), and *A history of Urdu literature* (1932). He died in 1942. BLC; LC

Baillaud, Émile, born 24 September 1874 at Leyssac (Aveyron), he received a degree in 1897 from École des sciences politiques for his thesis, *Royal Niger Company*. He accompanied the Mission Trentinian to Niger in the winter of 1898/99, and visited Guinea in 1901-1903. In 1906 he retired from his position as colonial administrator and settled first in Toulouse and later in Marseille, where he served as a director of the Institut Colonial de Marseille until his death in March of 1945. His writings include *Sur les routes du Soudan* (1902), and *La politique indigène de l'Angleterre en Afrique occidentale* (1912).   Hommes et destins, vol. 1, pp. 50-52

Baillet, Pierre, born 20th cent., he wrote *Les rapatriés d'Algérie en France* (1976), a study based on his unpublished doctoral dissertation.   LC

Baillie, Neil Benjamin Edmonstone, born in 1799, his writings include *The Moohummudan law of inheritance* (1832), *The land tax of India* (1853), and *A digest of Mohummudan law* (1865). He died on 14 April 1883. Boase; LC

Bailward, A. C., born about the middle of the nineteenth century, he entered the Royal Artillery in 1874 and retired in 1905 with the rank of brigadier-general. In 1906 he joined the Central Asian Society and for several years served on the Council. He was a quiet man, one for whom "I" was, if not dead, at least a very dormant letter. He talked little and wrote less about his travels which took him to Asia Minor, Mesopotamia, and Persia. He died in London, on 9 November 1923. *Journal of the Central Asian Society* 11 (1924), pp. 114-115

Bain, Robert Nisbet, born 18 November 1854 at London. Although he was out of England for only four brief periods, he acquired, unaided, a high degree of proficiency in no less than twenty foreign languages. In 1883 he entered the Department of Printed Books at the British Museum, London. His writings include translations from many languages. He died in Battersea Park, 5 May 1909. DNB

Bainier, Pierre Frédéric, born 4 September 1834 at S.-Julien-lès-Montbéliard (Doubs), he held varied teaching positions in Montbéliard, Mulhouse, and Strasbourg until the Franco-Prussia war, after which he had to leave Alsace. He settled in Marseille, where he organized the École supérieure de commerce, and became a founding member of the Société de géographie de Marseille. His writings include *Géographie commerciale de l'Algérie* (1874), and *La géographie appliquée à la marine, au commerce, à l'agriculture, à l'industrie et à la statistique: Afrique* (1878). He died in S.-Mande, 23 April 1903. DBF; NDBA

Bains, Joginder Singh, born 20th cent., he was in 1981 a professor of political science in the University of Delhi. His writings include *Studies in political science* (1961), *India's international disputes* (1962), *Political science in transition* (1981); he was joint editor of *Perspectives in political theory* (1980). LC

Baipakov, Karl Moldakhmetovich, born 17 November 1940, he was joint author of *Древние города Казахстана* (1971), *Древний Отрар* (1972), and *Позднесредневекоый Отрар* (1981). Schoeberlein

Bairacli Levy, Juliette de, born in 1912, her writings include *The yew wreath* (1947), *As Gypsies wander* (1953), *Summer in Galilee* (1960), *A Gypsy in New York* (1962), and *Herbal handbook for farm and stable* (1976). LC

Bairamova, Luiza Karimovna, born in 1935, she received a doctorate in 1984 and was appointed a professor in 1987. Her writings include *Русско-татарский фразеологический словарь* (1980), and she was joint author of *Сопоставительный синтаксис русского и татар-ского языков* (1989). TatarES

Baird, Andrew Cumming, born in 1883, he was educated at Airdie Academy, Glasgow and Berlin universities. From 1919 to 1938 he was Regius Professor of Divinity and Biblical Criticism, King's College, University of Aberdeen. His writings include *Christian fundamentals* (1926). He died on 12 January 1940. Who was who, 3

Baishev, Saktagan Baishevich, fl. 1978, his writings include *Победа социализма в Казахстане* (1961), *Вопросы казахской филологии* (1964), he was joint author of *Население и трудовые ресурсы Казахстана* (1979). LC

Baissette, Gaston, born in 1901, his writings include *Hippocrate* (1931), and *Aux confins de la médecine* (1977). In 1984 was published *Exposition "Gaston Baisette et la civilisation de la vigne."* He died in 1977. LC

Baistrocchi, Alfredo, born 20 September 1875 at Rimini, Italy, he was an admiral who wrote *Un programma di pacificazione e di valorizzazione della Libia* (1920), and *Elementi di arte navale* (1948). He died in Roma, 19 November 1954. Chi è, 1948; DizBI

Bajolle, Léon Céline Marius, born 9 July 1856 at Marseille. After passing through the military college of S.-Cyr, which he had entered in 1874, he received and commission as *sous-lieutenant*. He spent most of his military career in Algeria and retired after the first World War with the rank of general. He wrote *Le Sahara de Ouargla de l'oued Mia à l'oued Igharghar* (1887). He died in Nancy, 24 February 1945. DBF

Bajpai, Krishna Datta, born in 1917, his writings include *Sagar through the ages* (1964), and *Indian numismatic studies* (1976). In 1989 a felicitation volume was dedicated to him, *History and art; essays on history, art, culture, and archaeology presented to Prof. K. D. Bajpai in honour of his fifty years of Indological studies.* LC

Bajpai, Shiva Chandra, born in 1931, he was in 1962 affiliated with Saugar University, Sagar. His writings include *The northern frontier of India* (1970), and *Kinnaur in the Himalayas* (1981). LC

Bajraktarević, Fehim, born 14 November 1889, he was educated at the universities of Sarajevo and Wien, where he obtained a doctorate in 1917 for his thesis, *Die Lamiya des Abu Kabir al-Hudali*. Since 1924 he taught at Belgrade University first at the Faculty of Philosophy and since 1926 at the Department of Oriental Philology. His writings include a translation of Firdawsi, *Рустем и Сухраб* (1928). He died in February 1970. JugoslSa, 1970

Bajraktarević, Sulejman, born 3 September 1896 at Gornji Vakuf, he was educated in his home town and studied in Istanbul, Sarajevo, and Wien, where he took a degree in 1922 in international economics. His interest in Oriental studies developed gradually. It was not until 1948 that he started to work in the Oriental Collection of the Yugoslav Academy of Science, Zagreb, where he remained until his retirement in 1969. He died in Zagreb on 20 March 1977. HBL; *Prilozi za orijentalnu filologiju* 27 (1977), pp. 287-292

Bakaev, Cherkes Khudoevich, born 10 December 1912 at Sinâk, Turkey, he was educated at Erevan, where he received a doctorate in 1971 for *Язык курдов СССР*. His writings include *Курдско-русский словарь* (1957), *Говор курдов Туркмении* (1962), and *Осногы курдской орфографии* (1983). LC; Miliband

Bakali, Mahmud, born 19 January 1936 at Đakovica, Serbia, he was a party official and politician and, in 1970, a member of the presidium of the Yugoslav Peace League. JugoslSa, 1970; Note

Bakalopoulos (Vakalopoulos), Apostolos Euangelou, born in 1909 at Volos, Greece, he was a historian who taught at the University of Thessalonika. His writings include *Thesor, son histoire, son administration de 1453 à 1912* (1953), *A history of Thessaloniki* (1963), Ιστορια της Μακεδονιας (1969), *Origins of the Greek nation* (1970), *Histoire de la Grèce moderne* (1975). EEE; LC

Baker, George Percival, fl. 1978, he wrote *Mountaineering memories of the past* (privately printed in 1951). BLC

Baker, John Norman Leonard, fl. 1944, his writings include *A history of geographical discovery and exploration* (1931), and *Jesus College, Oxford, 1571-1971* (1971). NUC

Baker, Julian Alleyne, born in 1845, he was a nephew of Sir Samuel White Baker, and entered the Royal Navy in 1868. He was a participant of various expeditions and campaigns in the Sudan and promoted to rear-admiral in 1903. He died in Malvern, England, in 1922. Hill

Baker, Robert Lee, born in 1901, his writings include *Oil, blood and sand* (1942), and he was the editor of *Business leadership in a changing world* (1962). LC

Baker, Sir Samuel White, born 8 June 1821 at London. After a desultory education - he studied also at Frankfurt am Main - he embarked on a career of exploration and travel, particularly in Northeast and East Africa. He was the first Englishman to serve in high office under the Egyptian Government, a task in which he was in no way supported by the British Foreign Office. In 1870 he was sent by the Khedive Ismail to the Sudan in command of a military expedition to annex the Upper Nile to Egypt and to suppress the slave-trade there. His writings include *The Nile tributaries of Abyssinia, and the Sword Hunters of the Hamran Arabs* (1867), *Ismailia; a narrative of the expedition to Central Africa for the suppression of the slave trade* (1874), and *The Egyptian question* (1884). He died at his estate in Sandford Orleigh, Devonshire, on 30 December 1893. Richard Hall wrote a biography, *Lovers on the Nile* (1980). BLC; DLB 166 (1996), pp. 3-21; Henze; Hill

Bakhash, A. Shaul, fl. 1971, he received a D.Phil. in 1972 from Oxford University for his thesis *Reform and the Qajar bureaucracy, 1870-1900*. His writings include *Iran, monarchy, bureaucracy and reform under the Qajars* (1978), *The politics of oil and revolution in Iran* (1982), and *The reign of the ayatollahs* (1985). LC; Sluglett

Bakhrushin, Sergei Vladimirovich, born in 1882 at Moscow, he was educated in his native city and later became a professor of history at Moscow University. His writings include *Очерки по истории колонизации Сибири в 16. и 17. вв.* (1927). He died in Moscow on 8 March 1950. GSE; TatarES

Bakhshi, Goverdham Lal, born 20 September 1917 at Dehriala Segana (Rawalpindi), India, he taught mathematics for nearly twenty years in Patiala before embarking on a career in Public Instruction, Punjab. He wrote *Towards better education* (1971). India who's who, 1977/78; LC

Bakhtiar, Ali Asghar, born in 1917 at Isfahan, he took degrees in architecture at Tehran universities and became a head of the Architectural Department in the National Insurance Company of Iran. IWWAS, 1976/77

Bakhtiar, Chapour (Shapour), born in 1916 in Persia, and educated in Paris and Beirut, he was a deputy minister in the Government of Muhammad Musaddiq and imprisoned several times during the reign of the last shah. He was prime minister from January to February 1979, when he resigned after the return of Ayatollah Khomeini. His writings include *Ma fidélité* (1982), and *Si va haft ruz pas az si va haft sal* (1982). He was assassinated in his Paris exile on 8 August 1991. Jean-Yves Chaperon wrote *Enquête sur l'assassinat de Chapour Bakhtiar* (1992). IntWW, 1991/92; LC; MidE, 1982/83

Bakhtiar, Laleh Mehree, born 29 July 1938 at Tehran. From 1960 to 1976 she was married to Nader Ardalan with whom she published *The sense of unity* (1973). Since 1979 she wrote several pamphlets for the Islamic Propagation Organization, Tehran. Her writings include *Sufi; expressions of the mystic quest* (1976), *Traditional psychoethics and personality paradigm* (1993), and *Moral healer's handbook* (1994). ConAu, 69; LC

Bakhtiyar, Shapur *see* Bakhtiar, Chapour

Bakkar, Tawfiq *see* Baccar, Taoufik

Bakker, D., Dr., he was in 1972 affiliated with the Theological School "Duta Watjana," Jogjakarta, Indonesia. Note

Baklanov, Nikolai Borisovich, fl. 1947, his writings include *Тульские и кашмирские заводы* (1934), and *Архитектурные памятники Дагестана* (1935). LC

Bakoš, Ján, born 2 March 1890 at Modra, Slovakia, he studied at Göttingen but, on account of the first World War, it was not until 1928 that he received his Dr.phil. for his thesis, *Die Bezeichnung der Vokale durch Konsonantenzeichen in den nordsemitischen Sprachen*. From 1931 until his retirement in 1964 he taught North Semitic languages and cultures at the Comenius University, Bratislava. His writings include *Psychologie de Grégoire Aboulfaradj dit Barhebraeus* (1948), and *La psychologie d'Ibn Sina d'après son oeuvre* (1956). He died on 22 March 1967. *Archiv orientalni* 35 (1967), 181-182; *Asian and African studies* (Bratislava) 26 (1990), pp. 7-8; Filipsky; Schwarz

al-Bakr, Hasan Ahmad, born in 1914 at Baghdad, he was from 1968 to 1979 president of Iraq. His writings include *Masirat al-thawrah* (1971), *al-Thawrah 'alá tariq al-taqaddum* (1977), and *Ausgewählte Reden* (1978). GSE; LC; MidE, 1982/83

Bakradze, Dimitrii Zakhar'evich, born in 1826, he was a Georgian historian, ethnographer, and archaeologist who wrote *Археологическое путешествие по Гурии и Адчаре* (1878). He died in 1890. GSE; LC

Bakri (Bakry), Bashir, born in 1918, he studied at Cairo, Oxford, and Paris and subsequently entered the Sudanese Foreign Service. WhoArab, 1978/79

Baktay, Ervin, born 24 January 1890 at Dunaharaszti, Hungary, he was an Orientalist whose writings include *India müveszeti* (1958), *Körösi Csoma Sándor* (1962), and *Die Kunst Indiens* (1963). He died in Budapest, 7 May 1963. Magyar

Balaban Bey Ince, fl. 1386-1389, he was a Turkish army commander who was present at the battle of Kosova in 1389. Meydan

Balafreij (Balafreige), Ahmed, born in 1908 in Morocco and educated at the universities of Paris and Cairo, he was exiled by the French and returned to Morocco in 1955 to become Minister of Foreign Affairs and later Prime Minister. MidE, 1982/83; WhoArab, 1978/79

Balagna Coustou, Josée, born about 1940, she belonged to the higher library echelon at the Bibliothèque Nationale, Paris, before she accepted a position at the Institut du Monde Arabe, Paris, in 1989. Her writings include *L'imprimerie arabe en Occident* (1984), *Arabe et humanisme dans la France des derniers Valois* (1989), and *Ouda, princesse marocaine* (1991). Private

Balaguer Prunes, Anna M., his writings include *Las emisiones transicionales árabe-musulmanes de Hispania* (1976).

Balakaev, Maulen Balakaevich, born 7 November 1907, he was a Kazakh scholar who received a doctorate in 1951 and was appointed a professor in 1952. His writings include *Казак тили* (1955), *Основные типы словосочетаний в казахском языке* (1957), *Современный казахский язык* (1959); and he was joint author of *Казахский литепатурния язык* (1987). Казахская ССР краткая энциклопедия, vol. 3

Balans, Jean Louis, fl. 1977, he was joint author, with Christian Coulon and Jean-Marcel Gastellu, of *Autonomie locale et integration nationale au Sénégal* (1975). LC

Balansa, Benjamin, born 19th cent., he was a French botanist who during his travels explored the Algerian Sahara in 1852, Lydia, Cilicia, and Phrygia from 1854 to 1856, Lazistan in 1866, and Morocco in 1867. He died on a Far Eastern journey in Tonkin in 1892. DBF; Henze

Balard, Michel, born 20th cent., he received a doctorate in 1976 from the Université de Paris I for his *thèse d'état, La Romanie génoise; études sur les relations politiques et économiques de Gênes avec l'Orient byzantin.* His writings include *La Romanie génoise, XIIe-début du XVe siècle* (1978). He was joint author of *Des barbares à la Renaissance; moyen âge occidental* (1973). LC; THESAM, 4

Balaÿ, Christophe Louis Marie, born 12 August 1949 at Veauche (Loire), he studied at Paris and took doctorates in 1979 and 1988. He taught modern Persian literature at the Institut national des langues et civilisations orientales, Paris. From 1979 to 1983 he was *pensionnaire scientifique* at the Institut Français d'Iranologie de Téhéran. His writings include *Genèse du roman persan modern* (1989), and he was joint author, with Michel Cuypers, of *Aux sources de la nouvelle persane* (1983). AnEIFr, 1989, 1997; LC; Private; THESAM, 4

Balázs, Judit, born about 1945, she received a doctorate in 1977 from the Hochschule für Ökonomie, Berlin, for her thesis, *Einige Grundzüge und Entwicklungstendenzen in den erwerbswirtschaftlich geführten staatlichen Industrieunternehmungen der Türkei.* Her writings include *Die Türkei, das Phänomen des abhängigen Kapitalismus* (1984), and *Lessons of an attempt at stabilization; Turkey in the 1980s* (Budapest, Hungarian Scientific Council for World Economy, 1990). LC

Balba', 'Abd al-Mun'im, born in 1919, he received a Ph.D. in 1956 from the University of Illinois for his thesis, *The Mitscherlich equation as applied to express the relationships between plant composition and the soil nutrients.* His writings include *al-Ard wa-insan fi al-watan al-'Arabi* (1973), and *Adwa' 'alá al-zira'ah al-'Arabiyah* (1975). LC

Balbi, Adriano, born in 1782 at Venezia, he was a geographer and statistician. His writings include *Atlas éthnographique du globe* (1826), *Abrégée de géographie* (1833), *An abridgement of universal geography* (1835), *Allgemeine Erdbeschreibung* (1857), and *Statistical essay on the libraries of Vienna and the world* (1985). He died in 1848. LC

Balcet, Giovanni, born in 1950, he taught international economy at Università di Perugia. His writings include *Industrializzazione, multinazionali e dipendenza tecnologica* (1981). LC

Balck, Konrad Friedrich August Henry *William*, born 19 October 1858 at Osnabrück, Germany, he was an army officer whose writings include *Taktik* (1904-1910, 6 vols.), *Entwicklung der Taktik im Weltkriege* (1920), and *Development of tactics* (1922). He died in Aurich on 15 June 1924. DtBE

Baldacci, Antonio, born 3 October 1867 at Bologna, he was a geographer and natural scientist whose lifework was the exploration of the Balkans. His writings include *Itinerari albanesi, 1892-1902* (1917), and *L'Albania* (1929). Chi è, 1931-1948

Baldensperger, Louise, fl. 1931, she was joint author of *From cedar to hyssop; a study in the folklore of plants in Palestine* (1932). LC

Baldensperger, Philip James, born in 1856, his writings include *The immovable East; studies of the people and customs of Palestine* (1913), and *Les maladies des abeilles* (1928). NUC

Baldi, Bernardino, born 5 June 1553 at Urbino, he studied medicine and philosophy at Padova. He was a mathematician and miscellaneous writer and, perhaps, the most universal genius of his age. He composed an Arabic grammar and produced a translation of the Targum of Onkelos, an Aramaic paraphrase of the Pentateuch. His writings include *Cronica di matematici* (1707). He died in Urbino on 10 October 1617. DizBI; *Encyclopædia Britannica*, 11th ed.

Baldick, Julian, born 20th cent., his writings include *Mystical Islam* (1989), *Imaginary Muslims* (1993), and he was joint author, with George Morrison, of *History of Persian literature* (1981). LC

Baldissera, Eros, born 17 March 1944 at Venezia, he received a doctorate in 1971 from the Università di Cafoscari (Venezia). He became a teacher of Arabic language and literature at the Università di Venezia, specializing in epigraphy and modern Arabic literature. He conducted field work in Syria and Oman. He was a member of the Istituto per l'Oriente, Roma, the Union européenne des arabisants et islamisants, and the Istituto italiano per il Medio e Estremo Oriente. Private

Baldry, John, fl. 1975, he wrote *Textiles in Yemen; historical references to trade and commerce* (London, The British Museum, 1982). LC

Baldus, Rolf D., born 20th cent., he received a doctorate in 1976 from the Universität Marburg for his thesis, *Zur operationellen Effizienz der Ujamaa Kooperative Tansanias*. In the 1980s he was attached to the German Foundation for International Development. Note

Baldwin, C. Stephen, he was joint author, with M. Badrud Duza, of *Nuptiality and population policy* (1977).

Baldwin, E. F., fl. 1884-1890. "He served as a Baptist minister in North Carolina, and in 1884 he conducted an exploratory investigation of Algeria for the Foreign Missions Board of the Southern Baptist Convention. When the convention decided not to enter this mission field, he became a missionary in the English Kabyle Mission in 1884 and was the first superintendent of the Southern Morocco Mission. He severed his relations with the Kabyle Mission in 1888 and launched into independent missionary work in Morocco until 1890 when he moved to Syria." David Shavit, *The United States in the Middle East* (1988), p. 21

Baldwin, George Benedict, born 25 April 1920 at Cambridge, Mass, he was educated at Princeton and M.I.T., where he took a Ph.D. in economics in 1952. Afterwards he taught at a number of American universities before working for the International Bank for Reconstruction and Development where, in 1971, he was deputy director of the Population and Nutrion Projects Department. His writings include *Beyond nationalization; the labour problems of British coal* (1955), *Industrial growth in South India* (1959), and *Planning and development in Iran* (1967). AM&WS, 1973 S; WhoUN, 1975

Baldwin, Hanson Weightman, born 22 March 1903 at Baltimore, Md., he graduated from the United States Naval Academy, 1924, was a sometime *New York Times* military editor, and an author who was the recipient of the Pulitzer Prize, 1942. His writings include *Strategy for victory* (1942), *The price of power* (1948), and *Middle East in turmoil* (1957). He died 13 November 1991. CurBio, 1942, 1992; WhAm

Baldwin, Roger Nash, born 21 January 1884 at Wellesley, Mass., he was a graduate of Harvard, and was awarded honorary doctorates from the universities of Washington, Yale, and Brandeis. He was a conscientious objector and was sentenced in the Federal Court, New York, for violation of the selective service law. He was for thirty years director of the American Civil Liberties Union. His writings include *Human rights, world declaration and American practice* (1950); he was joint author of *Civil liberties and industrial conflict* (1938). He died on 26 August 1981. AmM&WS, 1978 S; ConBio, 1940, 1981; WhAm, 8

Balén García, Fernando, fl. 1948, he was a sometime director of the Hydrographic Institute of the Navy. *Who's who in Spain*, 1963

Balfet, Hélène, fl. 1955, she received two doctorates from the Université de Paris for her theses, *Céramique ancienne en Proche-Orient, Israel et Liban* and *Poterie féminine et poterie masciline au Maghreb*, in 1962 and 1977 respectively. Her writings include *Les poteries modélées d'Algérie dans les collections du Musée du Bardo* (1957), and *Pour la normalisation de la description des poteries* (1972). LC; THESAM, 1

Balfour, Francis, born in the 1740s, he received a doctorate on 12 June 1781 from Edinburgh University for his thesis, *De gonorrhoea virulenta*. He entered the East India Company's medical service in Bengal as assistant surgeon in 1769, and retired in 1807 to Edinburgh. He wrote *The forms of Herkern, a Persian letter-writer* (1781), and he contributed papers on Oriental subjects to the Asiatic Society of Bengal. He died after 1816. DNB

Balfour-Paul, Hugh *Glen*cairn, born 23 September 1917, he was educated at Magdalen College, Oxford. He served in the Middle East during World War two and in the Sudan Political Service for the next nine years until 1977. He was then a diplomat in various Middle East countries, in three of them as Britain's ambassador. He was an honorary fellow at the Centre for Arab Gulf Studies at Exeter University. His writings include *History and antiquities of Darfur* (1955), *Iraq, the contemporary state* (1982), and *The end of Empire in the Middle East* (1991). Who, 1979-2003

Balić, Smail, born 26 August 1920 at Mostar, Bosnia, he went to school in Mostar, followed by a one-year course at an Islamic institution at Sarajevo. He studied Oriental and Slavic linguistics at the universities of Leipzig, Breslau, and Wien, where he received a Dr.phil. in 1944 for *Die geistigen Triebkräfte im bosnisch-herzegowinischen Islam*. Since 1963 he was orientalist librarian at the Österreichische Nationalbibliothek, Wien. His writings include *Ruf vom Minaret* (1963), *Kultura Bošnjaka* (1973), *Die Kultur der Bosniaken* (1978), and *Der Islam im Spannungsfeld von Tradition und heutiger Zeit* (1993). *Who's who in Österrreich*, 1983

Baligot de Beyne, Arthur, born probably in 1820, he was a French journalist who lived in France, Romania, and Turkey. He wrote *Corespondenţă cu Alexandru Ioan Cuza şi Costache Negre* (1986). He died 7 January 1884. LC

Baljon, Johannes Marinus Simon, born 18 July 1919 at Modjowarno, he studied theology and Oriental languages at the universities of Leiden and Utrecht, where he received a doctorate in 1949 for his thesis, *The reforms and religious ideas of Sir Sayyid Ahmad Khan*. His writings include *Modern Muslim Koran interpretation* (1961), and *Religion and thought of Shah Wali Allah Dihlawi* (1986). Wie is wie, 1984/88, 1994/96

Balkan, Gündüz, born 3 August 1933 at Izmir, he received a doctorate in 1963 from the Universität Würzburg for his thesis *Ermittlung der Selbstkosten und Preiskalkulation in den VEB*. Afterwards he was professor at various Turkish universities. His writings include *İş degerlendirmesi* (1980). Kim kimdir, 1985/86-2000

Ball, John, O.B.E., D.Sc., born in 1872, he was educated at the Royal College of Science and Mines, London, Bergakademie Freiberg, and Universität Zürich. In 1897 he joined the Survey of Egypt where he was engaged in the geographical and geological explorations in Egypt, Sinai, and the Sudan. His writings include *Bahia Oasis; its topography and geology* (1903), *The geography and geology of west-central Sinai* (1916), *Contributions to the geography of Egypt* (1939), and *Egypt in the classical geographers* (1942). He died on 12 July 1941. Egyptology; Hill; Who was who, 4

Ball, Nicole, fl. 1979, she wrote *Regional conflicts and the international system* (1974), and she was joint editor of *The structure of the defense industry* (1983). LC

Ball, Warwick, born 24 August 1931 in Australia, he was an archaeologist whose writings include *Persian landscape; a photographic essay* (1978), and *Archaeological gazetteer of Afghanistan* (1982). LC; Schoeberlein

Ballaloud, Jacques, born 20th cent., his writings include *Droits de l'homme et organisations internationales; vers un nouvel ordre humanitaire mondial* (1984). LC

Balland, Daniel, born 29 October 1943 at Rambouillet (Yvelines), he took a degree at the Université de Paris after his study, 1962-1967, and conducted field work in Afghanistan. Afterwards he became *maître de conférences* at the Université de Paris. He was a member of the Société asiatique, the Société de géographie de Paris, and the Association pour l'avancement des études iranienne. AnEIFr, 1989, 1997; Private; Schoeberlein

Ballantrae, Bernard Edward Fergusson Baron, 1911-1980 *see* Fergusson, Bernard Edward

Ballardini, Gaetano, born 1 October 1878 at Faenza, Italy, he was the founder and first director of the Museo internazionale delle ceramiche, Faenza. His writings include *Coppe d'amore nel secolo XV* (1928), and *Ceramiche di Faenza* (1938). He died in Faenza, 26 May 1953. Chi è, 1948; DizBI

Ballas, Shimon, born 6 March 1930 at Baghdad, he received a doctorate in 1974 from the Sorbonne, Paris, for *La "naksa" dans le roman, le théâtre et la nouvelle arabe, 1967-1973*. Afterwards he worked as a journalist in Israel. His writings include *Ash'ab mi-Bagdad* (1970), *Sipurim Palestiniyim* (1970), *ha-Sifrut ha-'Arvit betsel ha-milhamah* (1978), and *La littérature arabe et le conflit au Proche-Orient* (1980). THESAM, 4; Who's who in Israel, 1992/93

de **Ballesteros**, Mercedes née Gaibrois y Riaño, born in 1891 or 2, she was the daughter of a sometime Colombian diplomat in Paris. She was married to a Spaniard and died in Madrid in 1960. She was a novelist and historian whose writings include *Historia del reinado de Sancho IV de Castillo* (1922-28). IndiceE³ (2); LC

Ballesteros y Beretta, Antonio, born in 1880 at Roma, he received a doctorate in 1906 in philosophy and letters from the Universidad de Madrid. Afterwards he was professor of history at the universities of Sevilla and Madrid. His writings include *Historia de España y su influencia en la historia universal* (1818-1941), *Síntesis de historia de España* (1920), and *Geschichte Spaniens* (1943). He died in Madrid in 1949. DBEC

Balletto, Laura, born 20th cent., she was a medievalist whose writings include *Statuta antiquissima Saone, 1345* (1971), *Genova, Mediterraneo, Mar nero, secc. XII-XV* (1976), and *Genova nel duecento* (1983). LC

Balley, Paul, born 19th cent., he took a law degree, and a diploma at the École spéciale des langues orientales vivantes, Paris. In 1917 he was *administrateur-adjoint de commune-mixte* of Belezma, Algeria. Note

Ballif, L., born 19th cent., he was in 1921 a captain in the French armed forces who was joint author of *Le combat aérien* (1917). BN; LC; Note

Ballini, Ambrogio, born 19 July 1879 at Asola (Mantova), he studied at the Università di Bologna and successively was a professor of Sanskrit at the universities of Padova, Milano, and Roma. He died in Roma, 20 March 1950. DizBI

Ballod, Francis, 1882-1947 *see* Balodis, Francis Aleksandrs

Ballu, Albert, born 1 June 1849 at Paris, where he was also educated. He was the architect of the Hôtel de Ville de Paris and other municipal buildings in France. Since 1884 he was *architecte diocésain* at Algiers. In 1886 he became *chevalier de la Légion d'honneur*. His writings include *Les ruines de Timgad* (1897), and *Théâtre et forum de Timgad; état actuel et restauration* (1902). He died after 1923. DBF

Baloch, Inayatullah, born 28 December 1946, he received a Dr.phil. in 1987 from the Universität Heidelberg for his thesis, *The problem of "Greater Baluchistan"* (1987).

Baloch, Nabi Bakhshanshah Alimuhammad Khan, born 16 December 1917 in Sind, he was educated at Bombay University, Muslim University of Aligarh, and Columbia University, where he received an Ed.D. in 1949. Afterwards he held teaching positions at Karachi University and the University of Sind, Hyderabad. In 1980 he was a director of the Institute of Historical and Cultural Research, Quaid-i-Azam University, Islamabad. His writings include *Musical instruments of the lower Indus Valley of Sind* (1966), and *Pakistan; a comprehensive bibliography of books and government publications with annotations, 1947-1980* (1981).

Balodis, Francis Aleksandrs, born in 1882 at Valmiera (Wolmar), Lithuania, he studied in Dorpat (Tartu), Moscow, and München, where he received a Dr.phil. in 1912 for *Prolegomena zur Geschichte der zwerghaften Götter in Ägypten*. Afterwards he taught ancient Near Eastern subjects at various universities. In 1926 he received a doctorate in historical sciences fo his thesis on the capitals of the Golden Horde, where he had excavated from 1919 to 1921. His writings include *Некоторые материалы по истории лаеьшскаго племени с IX по XIII столетне* (1910), and *Våld och frihet* (1941). He emigrated to Sweden in 1940 and died in Stockholm 8 August 1947. Egyptology; LC

Balog, Paul, born 15 August 1900 at Budapest, he studied at Budapest and Pécs and received a doctorate in medicine in 1924. The economic conditions in Hungary obliged him to emigrate in 1926 to Cairo, where he soon became director of the Italian Hospital, a position which he held until 1961, when he retired to Roma. His interest in Islamic numismatics and metrology developed particularly through his acquaintance with Marcel Jungfleisch. His writings include *Umayyad, 'Abbasid and Tulunid glass weights and vessel stamps* (1976), and *The coinage of the Ayyubis* (1980). He died in Roma, on 6 November 1982. I.I.(4)

Balogun, Ismail Ayinia Babatunde, born 24 January 1930 at Lagos, he was educated in Nigeria and studied at Kano and SOAS, London, where he received a doctorate, in 1967, for *A critical edition of Ihya' al-sunna wa-Ikhmad al-bid'a of 'Uthman b. Fudi popularly known as Usumanu dan Fodio*. Afterwards he was professor of religion as well as dean at Nigerian universities. His writings include *Islam versus Ahmadiyya in Nigeria* (1976), and *Utilizing religions for peaceful unity and progress in Nigeria* (1981). Africa who's who, 1991-1996; Sluglett

Balogun, Saka Adegbite, born 26 May 1938 at Ogbomosho, Nigeria. After obtaining a doctorate from the University of Ibadan, he taught history at various Nigerian universities. Africa who's who, 1991-1996

Balout, Lionel, born 18 April 1907 at Nantes. He received a doctorat from the Université de Paris in 1956. He was a sometime dean of the Faculté des lettres d'Alger, a director of the Musée du Bardo, and editor-in-chief of *Libyca*. His writings include *Les hommes préhistoriques du Maghreb et du Sahara* (1955), *Préhistoire de l'Afrique du nord* (1955), and *Algérie préhistorique* (1958). LC; Unesco

Balsan, Franç‫ ois, born 25 June 1902 at Chateauroux (Indre). After his formal education and training he worked for over ten years in the family's factory without taking a day off in order to pursue his travel ambitions in later life. His writings include *Dans le désert du Béloutchistan* (1946), *L'étreinte du Kalahari* (1950), *À travers l'Arabie inconnue* (1954), *Inquiétant Yémen* (1961), *Aventures au Yémen* (1970), and *Au Registan inexploré* (1973). He died 26 November 1972. Hommes et destins, IV, pp. 51-52

Balta, Paul, born 1929. He was for many years *le Monde* correspondent in Algeria. His writings include *La politique arabe de la France* (1973), *Iran-Iraq; une guerre de 5000 ans* (1987), and *Le grand Maghreb; des indépendances à l'an 2000* (1990); he published also several works with Caudine Rulleau, among them *L'Iran insurgé* (1979). LC

Balta, Tahsin Bekir, born in 1902, he was a professor of law at Ankara Üniversitesi and wrote *Idare hukuku* (1972). In 1974 a commemorative volume was published, *Prof. Dr. Tahsin Bekir Balta'ya armağan*. He died in 1972. LC

Bamieh (Ba Miyah), 'Aydah Adib, she received a Ph.D. in 1970 from SOAS for her thesis, *The development of the novel and short story in modern Algerian literature*. In the 1980s she taught at the University of Florida, Gainesville, where she was still active in 1997. Her writings include the Arabic translation of her thesis, *Tatawwur al-adab al-qisasi al-Jaza'iri* (1982). NatFacDr, 1995-1997; Note Sluglett

Bańczerowski, Jerzy, fl. 1975, his writings include *Konsonantenalternation im Ostlappichen* (Poznań, 1969), and *Wstęp do językoznawstwa* (1982). LC

Banerjee, Anil Chandra, fl. 1931, his writings include *The eastern frontier of British India* (1946), *The Rajput states and British paramountcy* (1980), and *Two nations* (1981). LC

Banerjee, Brajendra Nath, fl. 1924, his writings include *Begam Samru* (1925), *Dawn of India* (1927), and *Begams of Bengal, mainly based on state records* (1942). LC

Banerjee, Debendra Nath, born in 1895. His writings include *Early land revenue system in Bengal and Bihar* (1936), and *Early administrative system of the East India Company in Bengal* (1943). LC

Banerjee, Rakhal Das, 1885-1930 see Banerji, Rakhal Das

Banerjee, Romesh Chandra, fl. 1939, his writings include *The story of Khilafat* (1919). LC

Banerjee, S. K. see Banerji, Sukumer

Banerji, Adris, born in 1909, his writings include *Origins of the early Buddhist church art* (1967), and *Archaeological history of south-eastern Rajasthan* (1970). LC

Banerji, Arun Kumar, born in 1944, his writings include the revision of his thesis submitted at the University of London, in 1972, entitled *India and Britain, 1947-1968* (1977), and *Aspects of Indo-British economic relations, 1858-1898* (1982). LC

Banerji, Brajendra Nath see Banerjee, Brajendra Nath

Banerji, Nripendra Chandra; born in 1885, he received a Dr.phil. in 1935 from the Universität Köln for his thesis, *Völkerrecht und Kriegsrecht im alten Indien*. He also published his autobiography, *At the cross-roads, 1885-1949*. (1950). He died in 1949. NUC, pre-1956

Banerji, Rakhal Das, born in 1885 or 6 at Berhampore, India, he graduated in 1909 from Presidency College, Calcutta. From 1910 to 1926 he was at the Archaeological Survey of India, and from 1928 until his death he was professor of Indian history at Benares Hindu University. His writings include *The origin of the Bengali script* (1919), *History of Orissa* (1930-1931), *The age of the imperial Guptas* (1933), and *Eastern Indian school of medieval sculpture* (1933). He died in 1930. Eminent

Banerji, Sukumer, fl. 1943, he was a sometime reader in Indian history at Lucknow University. His writings include *Humayun Badshah* (1938-1941), based on his thesis, University of London, 1925. LC

Banerji-Sastri, Ananta Prasad, born in 1894, his writings include *Evolution of Magadhi* (1922), "an introduction to a dissertation accepted by Oxford University for the degree of doctor of philosophy;" and *Early inscriptions of Bihar and Orissa* (1927). LC

Bănescu, Nicolae, born 16 December 1878 at Călăraşi, Rumania, he received a Dr.phil. in 1915 from the Universität München for his thesis, *Die Entwicklung des griechischen Futurums von der früh-byzantinischen Zeit bis zur Gegenwart*. His writings include *Chipuri şi scene din Bizanţ* (1927), *Le déclin de Famagouste* (1946), *Les duchés byzantines de Paristrion* (1946), and *L'ancien état bulgare et les pays roumaines* (1947). He died in Bucureşt, 11 September 1971. LC; MembriiAR

Baneth, David Hartwig (Zvi), born in 1893 at Krotoszyn, Poland, he received a Dr.phil. from the Universität Berlin for his thesis *Beiträge zur Kritik und zum sprachlichen Verständnis der Schreiben Muhammeds*. He was professor of Arabic language and literature at the Hebrew University, Jeru-salem, from 1936 to 1959, but taught there also during most of the time while serving as assistant librarian at the Jewish National and University Library, 1924 to 1937. "Those who knew him intimately were aware of the tragedy which pervaded his life. Demanding from himself perfection, he was averse to any writing on his side. He wrote, so to say, only when forced by circumstances. An unususllay high percentage of his writings is found in jubilee and memorial volumes, in book reviews, or reactions to articles published by others." (S. D. Goitein). He died in 1973. *Studia orientalia memoriae D. H. Baneth dedicta*, Jerusalem, 1979

Bang-Kaup, Willy, born 9 August 1869 at Wesel, Germany, he studied Turkish, and English language and literature, and from 1895 to 1914 held the chair of English and German philology in the Université de Louvain. From 1920 until his death he was at the Ungarisches Institut, Berlin. He died in Darmstadt, 8 October 1934. DtBE; *Index Islamicus* (5); Kürschner, 1928/29, 1931

Bani Sadr, Abol Hassan, born 21 March 1934 at Hamadan, Iran, he was a politician who was president of the Islamic Republic of Iran from 1980 until 1981 when he had to go into exile in France. He wrote *Bayaniyah-'i Jumhuri-i Islami* (1979), *Quelle révolution pour l'Iran?* (1980), *Fundamental principles and precepts of Islamic government* (1981), *L'espérance trahie* (1982), *Le complot des ayatollahs* (1989), and *Le Coran et les droits de l'homme* (1989). CurBio, 1981; IntWW, 1996/97; MidE, 1982/83

Bank, Alisa Vladimirovna, born in 1896 at St. Petersburg, she graduated in 1928 from Leningrad University and received her doctorate in 1975 for *Прикладное искусство Византии IX-XII вв.* Her writings include *Byzantine art in the collections of Soviet museums* (1977), and *Искусство Византии в собраниях СССР* (1977). Miliband; Miliband²

Banks, Mary Macleod, Mrs., born 19th cent. at Edinburgh, her writings include *An alphabet of tales* (1904-1905), *Memories of pioneer days in Queensland* (1931), and *British calendar customs* (1946). LC; Master (2)

Banks, David Jonathan, born in 1945, he received a Ph.D. in 1969 from the University of Chicago for his thesis, *Malay kinship.* In 1995 he was professor of anthropology at New York State University, Buffalo, a post which he still held in 2003. His writings include *Trance and dance in Malaya* (1976), *From class to culture; social conscience in Malay novels since independence* (1987); he edited *Changing identities in modern Southeast Asia* (1976). LC; NatFacDr, 1995-2003

Banks, Edgar James, born 23 May 1866 at Sunderland, Mass., he was a graduate of Amherst College, and Harvard University. He studied also at the Universität Breslau, where he took a Dr.phil. in 1896 for *Sumerisch-babylonische Hymnen.* He spent a good many years in the Near East between 1897 and the first World War, as a teacher, archaeologist, mountaineer, and in the US foreign service, before teaching Oriental languages and archaeology at the universities of Toledo and Pennsylvania. His writings include *Bismya, or, The lost city of Adab* (1912), and *An Armenian princess; a tale of Anatolian peasant life* (1914). He died in Eustis, Fla., 4 or 5 May 1945. Master (5); Shavit; WhAm, 3

Banks, Miriam Amy, fl. 1928-1938, she contributed articles to the *Bulletin* of the Rhode Island School of Design, Providence, R.I. NUC, pre-1956

al-**Banna'**, 'Ali, fl. 1967, his writings include *al-Intaj al-zira'i fi Lubnan* (1970). NUC, 1968-1972

Bannerth, Ernst, born in 1895, he received a Dr.phil. in 1941 from the Universität Wien for *Ein altosmanisches Destan.* His writings include *Hindustani-Briefe* (1943), *Islam heute, morgen* (1958), *Der Pfad der Gottesdiener* (1964), *Islamische Wallfahrtsstätten Kairos* (1973), and translations of classical Arab authors. LC

Banning, Hubert, born 24 October 1882 at N.Y.C., he was a graduate of Columbia College, N.Y.C., and studied at the universities of Berlin and Erlangen, where he received a Dr.phil. in 1909 for *Muhammad ibn al-Hanafija; ein Beitrag zur Geschichte des Islams des ersten Jahrhunderts.* Thesis

Banninga, John J., Rev., D.D., Dr., fl. 1923, he was a missionary and sometime principal of the Union Theological College, India. His writings include *With the read triangle in Mesopotamia.* This is the typewritten account of the travels and work with John X. Miller in 1918. Lodwick; NUC, pre-1956

Banse, Ewald Hermann August, born 23 May 1883 at Braunschweig, Germany, he studied geography at the universities of Berlin and Halle. He became an editor and free-lance writer. In 1912 he founded the periodical *die Erde.* In 1933 he was appointed a professor of geography at the Technische Hochschule Hannover. His writings include *Tripolis* (1912), *Das Orientbuch* (1914), *Die Türkei* (1915), *Die Länder und Völker der Türkei* (1916), *Die Türken und wir* (1917), *Wüsten, Palmen und Basare* (1921), and *Kleine Geschichten aus Asien; Erlebtes und Erlesenes* (1940). He died in 1953. Kürschner, 1931-1950: Master (3); Wer ist's, 1935

Banzarov, Dorzhi, born 1823 in Siberia, he was a graduate of Kazan University. After working at the Asiatic Museum, St. Petersburg, 1847-1848, he explored Siberia from 1850 to 1855. He wrote *Черная вера или шаманство монголов* (1891). He died in Irkutsk in 1855. GSE; TatarES

Baqai, I. H., fl. 1948, he was a sometime staff member of the Indian Records Office, New Delhi, and during the war of independence he was at the Far Eastern Bureau of the British Ministry of Information. He later served as a research assistant in the Pakistan Institute of International Affairs. He wrote *Books on Asia* (1947). LC; Note

Baqai, Moin(uddin), fl. 1969-1979, his writings include *Pakistan's economic progress* (1969), *Developing planning and policy in Pakistan, 1950-1970* (1973). In 1986 he edited the commemorative volume, *Employment, distribution, and basic needs in Pakistan; essays in honour of Jawaid Azfar.* LC

Baquet, René Léopold Marcel, born in 1909, he received a doctorate in 1932 from the Université de Bordeaux for his thesis, *L'hygiène publique aux États-Unis.* In 1957 he was president of the Société de médecine du Maroc. Note

Baraban, Léopold, born 19th cent. In the service of the French Department of Agriculture he went on a mission to Tunisia. His writings include *À travers la Tunisie; études sur les oasis, les dunes, les forêts, la flore et la géologie* (Paris, 1887). His trace is lost after a publication in 1890. BN

Barabanov, A. M., fl. 1945, he wrote *Хроника Мухаммеда Тахира ал-Карахи о дагестанских войнах в период Шамиля* (1941).

Barag, Dan Pinhas, born 13 September 1935 at London, he studied at the Hebrew University of Jerusalem and taught there since 1969. His writings include *Catalogue of Western Asiatic glass at the British Museum* (1985). LC; WhoWorJ, 1972

Barak, Michael *see* Bar-Zohar, Michel

Barakaeva, Gul'sum B., fl. 1971, she wrote *Краткий таджикского-английский словарь* (1968), and joint author of *Лугати англиси-точики* (1970). LC

Barakat, Halim Isber, born 4 December 1936, he received a Ph.D. in 1966 in social psychology from the University of Michigan for *Alienation from the school system.* Afterwards he taught sociology for six years at the AUB. In 1979 he was affiliated with the Center for Contemporary Arab Studies at Georgetown University. He was both a novelist and a sociologist. His writings include *Days of dust* (1974), *Social reality in the contemporary Arab novel*, and *Contemporary North Africa* (1984). LC

Barakat, Salim Mohammed, born in 1930, he was for over thirty years affiliated with the Institut français d'études arabes de Damas. He died of cardiac arrest on 5 June 1999.

Barakatullah, Mohammed, born about 1870, he was a Bengal revolutionary who at one time set up a Azad India Government in Afghanistan. He wrote *The Khilafat* (London, 1924), and *Le khalifat* (Paris, 1924). He died 1927 or 1928 in Germany. Eminent; Jain, p. 121-122; NUC, pre-1956

Baram, Phillip Jason, born 29 July 1938 at Woonsocket, R.I., he was educated at Brown University, Hebrew Universitty, Jerusalem, and Boston University, he received a Ph.D. in 1976 for *The Department of State's view of the Middle East through 1945.* From 1967 to 1975 he taught history at various American colleges. His writings include *The Department of State in the Middle East, 1919-1945* (1978). ConAu, 85-88

Baramki, Dimitri Constantine, born 8 November 1909 at Jerusalem, he received a doctorate in 1952 from the University of London for his thesis, *Arab culture and architecture of the Umayyad period.* Under the Palestine Mandate he was an archaeological officer. Since the 1950s he taught at the AUB. His writings include *The Archaeological Museum of the American University of Beirut* (1967), *The coins exhibited at the Archaeological Museum, AUB* (1968), and *The art and architecture in ancient Palestine* (1969). MidE, 1982/83; WhoWor, 1974; Who's who in Lebanon, 1986/87

Barani, Syed Hasan, fl. 1938, he wrote in Urdu *al-Bīrūnī* (Aligarh, 1927). SOAS

Barannikov, Aleksei Petrovich, born in 1890 at Zolotonosha, Ukraine, he graduated in 1914 from Kiev University. Since 1922 he was professor of Indological studies at Leningrad State University. His writings include *Краткая грамматика хиндустани* (1926), *Словарь (урду-русско-английский) к образцам современной прозы хиндустани* (1930), *Українські цигани* (1931), and *Хиндустани* (1956). He died on 4 September 1952. GSE; LC

Barannikov, Petr Alekseevich, fl. 1965 in Moscow, his writings include *Бхарат-Индия* (1977), and *Языковая ситуация в ареале языка хинди* (1984). LC

Baranov, Pavel Aleksandrovich, born in 1892 at Moscow, he graduated in 1917 from the University. Afterwards he was professor of botany at Tashkent University. From 1933 to 1938 he headed a Pamir expedition. He died in 1962. GSE

Baranowski, Bohdan, born in 1915, he was since 1950 a professor of history at Uniwersytet Lodzki. His writings include *Polska a Tatarszczyzna w latach, 1624-1629* (1948), *O dawnej Lodzi* (1976), and *Polskie zainteresowania z XVIII i XIX wieku kulturą Gruzji* (1982); he was joint author of *Historia Gruzji* (1987). LC; NEP

Baransi, Salah, fl. 1963, he was a sometime school teacher and leader of the Israeli-Arab nationalists. Note

Bárány-Oberschall, Magda, born in 1905, she studied at Budapest University where she received a doctorate in 1929 under her maiden name, Oberschall, for her thesis, *A holland és flamand festészet nemzeti sajátsági.* Her writings include *Konstantinos Monomachos császár korónája = The crown of the Emperor Constantine Monomachos* (1937), *Magyarországi miseruhák* (1937), its translation, *Ungarländische Messegewänder* (1938), *Magyar bútorok* (1939), its translation, *Hungarian furniture* (1939), and the translation, *Die eiserne Krone der Lombardei und der lombardische Königsschatz* (1966). NUC, pre-1956

Bárányné Oberschall, M., 1905 *see* Bárány-Oberschall, Magda

Barashkov, Petr Petrovich, fl. 1951, he wrote *Краткий терминологический словарь Якутского языка* (1955); he was joint author of *Взаимовлияние эвенкийского и якутского языков* (1975), and he edited *Словарь географических названий Якутской АССР* (1987). LC

Barate, Claude, born 20th cent., he was in 1978 a director of the Centre d'études d'administration locale, Université de Perpignan. Note

Barathon, Jean Jacques, born 20th cent., he was in 1980 a *maître-assistant* at the Université de Poitiers, where he received a *doctorat d'état* in 1987 for his thesis, *Bassins et littoraux du Rif oriental.* He was joint author of *Études méditerranéennes* (1978). LC; THESAM, 1

Baratier, Édouard, he was a sometime keeper of the Archives des Bouches-du-Rhône. His writings include *Documents de l'histoire de la Provence* (1971), *Histoire de Marseille* (1973), and *Histoire de la Provence* (1978). He died before 1987. LC

Baratta, Antonio, he wrote *Constantinopoli nel 1831* (Genova, 1831), and *Constantinopoli effigiata e descritta con una notizia su le celebri sette chiese dell'Asia Minore ed altri siti osservabili del Levante* (Torino, 1840). NUC, pre-1956

Barault-Roullon, Charles Hippolyte, he wrote *Dangers pour l'Europe; origine, progrès et état actuel de la puissance russe; question d'Orient au point de vue politique, religieux et militaire* (1854).

Barb, Heinrich Alfred, Dr., fl. 1857-1878, he was a sometime professor of Persian at Polytechnisches Institut in Wien as well as Orientalische Akademie, Wien. His writings include *Persische Chrestomathie* (1857), *Über die Conjugation des persischen Verbums* (1861), *Proverbes ottomans* (1885), and *Transkriptions-Grammatik der persischen Sprache* (1886). GV

Barbar, Leo, Dr., fl. 1930, he wrote *Zur wirtschaftlichen Grundlage des Feldzuges der Türken gegen Wien im Jahre 1683* (Wiener staatswissenschaftliche Studien; 13, Heft 1, 1916). GV

Barbaroux, Charles Ogé, born 16 August 1792 at Marseille, he took a law degree at Aix-en-Provence and subsequently practised law, journalism, and writing until the revolution of 1848, when he became prosecutor-general at Alger. For a number of years he was also a member of the *Comité consultatif de l'Algérie,* as well as vice-president of the *Conseil supérieur de l'Algérie.* His writings include *Resumé de l'histoire des États-Unis* (1824), *Mémoires de Robert Guillemard, sergent en retraite, 1805-1823* (1826), and its translation, *Adventures of a French sergeant* (1826). He died in Vaux, 5 July 1867. DBF

Barbedette, Frédéric, he was in 1913 a *conseiller général* and mayor of Djidjelli, Algeria, *délégué financier,* and secretary of the central bureau of the Société de Géographie d'Alger. Note

Barber, M. C., fl. 1984, he received a Ph.D. in 1968 from the University of Nottingham for his thesis, *The Grand Masters of the Order of the Temple.* Sluglett

Barbet, Charles born in 1864, he published in Alger: *Au pays des burnous* (1898), *La perle du Maghreb (Tlemcen); visions et croquis d'Algérie* (1907), *Dans le Nord dévasté* (1921), and *Questions sociales et ethnographiques; France - Algérie - Maroc* (1921). NUC, pre-1956

Barbet de Vaux, Marie (Mme. Amédée Phalipau) *see* Vaux Phalipau, Marie

Barbiano di Belgioioso, Cristina (Trivulzio), 1808-1871 *see* Belgioioso, Principessa Cristina di

Barbié du Bocage, Amédée Victor, born in 1832 at Paris, he was a secretary and archivist of the Société de Géographie de Paris. His writings include *De l'introduction des Arméniens catholiques en Algérie* (1855), *Madagascar, possession française depuis 1642* (1859), and *Le Maroc; notice géographique* (1861). He died in 1890. DBF

Barbié du Bocage, Jean Guillaume, born in 1795 at Paris, he was a geographer and wrote *Traité de géographie élémentaire pour les études classiques suivant l'atlas* (1846). DBF, p. 314, bottom

Barbié du Bocage, Victor Amédée, 1832-1890 *see* Barbié du Bocage, Amédée Victor

Barbiellini-Amidei, Bernardo, born 24 January 1896 at Roma, he wrote *Le relazioni fra le civiltà dell'Oriente mediterraneo* (1937), *La base di Singapore* (1938), and *Elementi per uno studio linguistico e politico del Caucaso* (1938). Franci Molinari wrote his biography, *Bernardo Barbiellini Amidei, il fascista del dissenso, 1896-1940* (1982). He died in 1940. Chi è, 1940

Barbier, Joseph Victor, born 3 March 1840 at Nancy, he was a geographer and cartographer, and the founder of the Société de Géographie de l'Est in Nancy. His writings include *Le livre d'or de la géographie dans l'est de la France* (1881), and *Essai d'un lexique géographique* (1886). He died in Nancy, 7 September 1898. DBF

Barbier, Maurice, born in 1937, he wrote *Le conflit du Sahara occidental* (1982), and *Voyages et explorations au Sahara occidental au XIXe siècle* (1985); he edited *Enjeux sahariens; Table ronde du CRESM, 1981* (1984). LC

Barbier de Meynard, Charles *Adrien* Casimir, born at sea on a voyage from Constantinople to Marseille, 6 February 1826, he was educated at the École des jeunes langues, Paris, where he also taught for a few years after graduation. In 1850 he was sent as a dragoman to Jerusalem but had to return to Paris the following year on account of ill health. The only other direct contact he had with the Orient was from 1854 to 1855, when he participated in the French mission to Persia under Comte de Gobineau. From 1863 until his death in 1908 he was a professor of Turkish at the École des langues orientales vivantes and, concurrently, professor of Persian at the Collège de France.. Since 1884 he was *officier de la Légion d'honneur*. For many years he served as a *président* of the Société asiatique. His writings include *Dictionnaire turc-français* (1881). Curinier; DBF; Elranica; Fück; JA, 10e série, 12 (1908), 338-351

Barbir, Karl K., born in 1948, he received a Ph.D. in 1977 from Princeton University. In 1991 he taught history at Siena College, Loudonville, N.Y., and in 2003 at SUNY, Albany, N.Y. His writings include *Ottoman rule in Damascus, 1707-1758* (1980). MESA Roster of members, 1982-1990; NatFacDr, 2003; ZKO

Barbot, Michel, born 20th cent., he received a doctorate in 1977 from the Université de Paris IV for his thesis, *Évolution de l'arabe contemporain; les sons du parler de Damas*. His writings include *Évolution de l'arabe moderne* (1981). LC; THESAM, 3

Barbot de Marni, Nikolai Pavlovich, born in 1829 in Russia, he was a professor of geology at the St. Petersburg Mining Institute and headed an expedition to the Kalmyk Steppe in 1860 and 1862. He wrote Геологическій очеркъ Херсонской губерніи (1869). He died in 1877. GSE

Barbour, Kenneth Michael, born 8 October 1921 at Naini Tal, India, he was educated at New College, Oxford, where he received a B.Litt. in 1953 for *A geographical study of representative communities in the summer rainfall belt of the Anglo-Egyptian Sudan* and a D.Phil. in 1972 for *The growth, location, and structure of Egyptian industry*. He taught geography at universities in Khartoum, London, and Ibadan. His writings include *The Republic of the Sudan* (1961). He was joint editor of *Nigeria in maps* (1982). AfrBioInd (1); ConAu, 5-8; Sluglett; Unesco

Barbour, Nevill, born 17 February 1895 at Eastbourne, Sussex, he studied at St. John's College, Oxford, after serving as an officer in the first World War. He spent some time in Tangier and Spain before settling in Palestine in the 1930s to become for some time a local correspondent of *the Times*. During the second World War he joined the BBC as Arabic public relations officer, a post from which he retired in 1956. His writings include *Palestine - star or crescent?* (1947), and *Morocco* (1965). He died in December 1972. ConAu, 5-8

Barbudo Duarte, Enrique, born 6 July 1906 at Cadiz, he was a naval officer and diplomat whose writings include *Cultura naval* (1945), and *Diccionario marítimo* (1965). DBEC

Barbut, Marcel, he was in 1955 an *inspecteur-général de l'Agriculture*. His writings include *L'évolution de l'agriculture et de l'élevage traditionels en Afrique du nord* (Alger, 1952). NUC, pre-1956

Barceló, Carmen, born 20th cent., she received a doctorate in Semitic philology and was a sometime professor of Arabic and Islamic studies in the Facultad Filología, Universidad de Valencia. She translated from the Arabic, *Un tratado catalán medieval de derecho islámico* (1989), and she was joint author of *Numeros y cifras en los documentos arábigohispanos* (1988), and *La ceramica calital de Benetússer; la decoracio calligráfica* (1990). Arabismo, 1992, 1994, 1997; LC

Barcelo, José Mohedano *see* Mohedano Barcelo, José

Barceló i Perelló, Miquel, born 20th cent., he received a doctorate in history, particularly medieval Andalusian history and numismatics. Throughout the 1990s he was a professor of medieval history in the Universidad Autónoma de Barcelona. Arabismo, 1994, 1997; EURAMES, 1993

Barceló Torres, Maria del Carmen, born 20th cent., she wrote *Otros poetas también valencianos* (1977), and *Minórias islámicas en el país valenciano* (1984), a work which was originally submitted at Madrid as her doctoral dissertation. She was joint author, with Antonio Gil Albarracin, of *La mezquita almohade de Fiñana, Almeria* (1994). In 1992 she was area coordinator for Arab and Islamic studies in the Universidad de Córdoba. EURAMES, 1993; LC

Barchard, David, born 9 June 1947, his writings include *Turkey and the West* (1985). LC

Barchín Isper, Michel, born 20th cent., he received a medical doctorate, specializing in history of Arabic medicine. He was a sometime director del Banco de Sangre, Osuna (Sevilla). Arabismo, 1992-97

Barchudarian, Johannes, born 1 March 1864 at Akulis, a Russo-Persian border town, he was educated in Tiflis and Erevan, and studied at the universities in Leipzig, Chur, and Jena, where he obtained a Dr.phil. in 1889 for *Inwiefern ist Leibniz in der Psychologie ein Vorgänger Herbarts.*

Barcía Trelles, Camilo, born 15 July 1888 in Spain, he studied at Oviedo, Madrid, and Berlin, and taught international private law at the universities of Murcia, Valladolid, and Santiago de Compostela. His writings include *La política exterior norteamericana de la postguerra* (1924), *El imperialismo del petróleo y la paz mundial* (1925), and *Derecho internacional privado* (1936). He died in Santiago de Compostela, 4 December 1977. Revista de política internacional 154 (1977), pp. 5-6; Suárez

Barclay, Harold Barton, born 3 January 1924 at Newton, Mass., he received a Ph.D. in 1961 from Cornell University for *An ethnographic study of an Arab Sudanese village in suburban Khartoum*, a revised version of which he published in 1964 entitled *Buurri al Lamaab, a suburban village in the Sudan*. He taught at AUC, Knox College, Illinois, University of Oregon, and, since 1966, the University of Alberta. His writings include *People without government* (1982), and *Culture; the human way* (1986). American men and women of science, 1973 S; Shavit

Barclay, Sir Thomas, born 20 February 1853 at Dunfermline, Scotland, he studied classics and law at Oxford, Paris, and Jena. He was a barrister-at-law who generally lived in France. From 1876 to 1882 he was a correspondent of *the Times* in Paris. Thereafter he practised law in Paris. He contributed to the major British periodicals. His writings include *Les effets de commerce dans le droit anglais* (1884), *Problems of international practice and diplomacy* (1907), and *The Turco-Italian war and its problems* (1912). He died on 20 January 1941. Curinier, vol. 5 (1906), p. 120; Who was who, 4

Bárczi, Géza, born 9 January 1894 at Zombor, Hungary, he was from 1952 to 1969 a professor of linguistics at Budapest University. His writings include *Magyar szófejtő szótár* (1941), and *Néprajzi tanulmányok* (1949). He died in Budapest, 7 November 1975. Magyar

Bardey, Alfred Xavier, born 23 September 1854 at Besançon, he was a merchant in Aden and organized regular caravans to Somalia and Abyssinia. He was particularly interested in the coffee trade from Harar, where he established the first European trading factory in 1880. He spent many years on the coast of south-western Arabia and collect information for the French Government. His writings include *Barr-Adjam; souvenirs d'Afrique orientale* (1981). He died in Vaux-les-Prés on 16 January 1934. Henze; Hommes et destins, vol. 4, pp. 53-55

Bardin, Pierre, fl. 1952, his writings include *La vie d'un douar* (1965), and *Algériens et Tunisiens dans l'Empire ottoman* (1979). LC

Bardon, Jean Baptiste Xavier, fl. 1870, his writings include *Épisode de l'insurrection des Kabyles en Algérie, 1870-1871* (Limoges, 1884), and *Histoire nationale de l'Algérie* (Paris, 1886). BN

Bardoux, Achille Octave Marie *Jacques*, born 27 May 1874 at Versailles, he received a doctorate in English literature in 1900 from the Sorbonne for *Le mouvement idéaliste et social dans la littérature anglaise au XIX siècle; John Ruskin*. He was a politician and a sometime lecturer at the École libre des sciences politiques. His writings include *Souvenir d'Oxford* (1898), *J. Ramsay Macdonald* (1924), and *Les origines du malheur européen* (1948). He died 15 August 1959. DBFC, 1954-55; Who was who, 5

Bardy, Gustave, fl. 1853, his writings include *L'Algérie et son organisation en royaume* (Paris, 1853), and *Solutions pratiques algériennes*, 2e éd. (Alger, 1881). BN

Bareilles, Bertrand, born in 1859, his writings include *Les Turcs, ce que fut leur empire* (1917), *Constantinople, ses cités franques et levantines* (1918), *Un Turc à Paris, 1806-1811; relation de*

voyage et de mission de Mouhib Effendi (1920), and *Le drame oriental; d'Athènes à Angora* (1923). He died in 1933. BN; LC

Baréty, Léon Jean Jacques, born 18 October 1883 at Nice, he studied at the École des sciences politiques, where he received a doctorate in law. In 1919 he entered politics. At the Chambre des députés he formed the Groupe parlementaire du Maroc in order to pursue his country's colonial interests. In 1925 he became vice-president and later president of the Comité de l'Afrique française. He wrote *L'évolution des banques locales en France et en Allemagne* (1908); and he edited *La politique coloniale de la France* (1924). He died in Nice, 10 February 1971. *Hommes et destins*, I, pp. 53-54

Barfield, Thomas Jefferson, born 21 April 1950 at Atlanta, Ga., he studied at the University of Pennsylvania and at Harvard, where he received a Ph.D. in 1978 for *The Central Asian Arabs of Afghanistan*. He repeatedly conducted field work in Afghanistan, Sinkiang, and Pakistan. He taught anthropology at Wellesley College and Harvard University, and in 1989 became professor and chairman of the Department of Anthropology in Boston University. His writings include *The perilous frontier; nomadic empires and China* (1989), and *The nomadic alternative* (1993); with Albert Szabo he published *Afghanistan; an atlas of indigenous domestic architecture* (1991). Private; Schoeberlein

Bar-Gal, Yoram, Dr., he was an Israeli geographer whose writings include *Nahal Kaziv* (Haifa, 1969), and he was joint author, with A. Soffer, of *Geographical changes in the traditional Arab villages in northern Israel* (1981). LC

Bargebuhr, Frederick Perez, born Fritz Paul on 24 May 1904 at Hamburg, he emigrated in the mid-1930s and received a Dr.phil. in 1947 from the Universität München with a thesis entitled *Ibn-Mammati; über das Beamtentum unter Saladin*. Since 1947 he was a sometime teacher of Latin and modern languages as well as a professor of religion in the United States. His writings include *Salomo Ibn Gabriol, ostwestliches Dichtertum* (1976). He died in Hamburg in 1978. *Biographisches Handbuch der deutschsprachigen Emigration nach 1933* (1980-83); *der Islam* 56 1979), p. 11

Barger, Thomas C., fl. 1972, he wrote *Arab states of the Persian Gulf* (1975). LC

Bargès, Jean Joseph Léandre, born 27 February 1810 at Auriol (Bouches-du-Rhône), he completed his studies at the Grand Séminaire de Marseille, and was professor at the Petit Séminaire from 1831 to 1833. After his ordination in 1834, he was appointed vicar of Notre-Dame du Mont in Marseille and again professor at the Petit Séminaire. Still in the same year he resigned his functions and devoted himself to private tutoring. He spent a number of years in Algeria until he was appointed a professor of Hebrew at the Sorbonne in 1842. His writings include *Tlemcen, ancienne capitale du royaume de ce nom, sa topographie, son histoire; souvenirs d'un voyage* (1859), *Complément de l'histoire des Beni-Zeiyan, rois de Tlemcen* (1887), and *Inscriptions arabes qui se voyaient autrefois dans la ville de Marseille* (1889). He died in Auriol, 2 April 1896. DBF; Wininger

Bargigli, Rita, fl. 1979, he writings include *Il roseto* (1979), and *"Riccioli" in 'Unsuri e Farruhi* (1983).

Bargrave, Robert, fl. ca. 1650, he was a British traveller who made an overland journey from Constantinople to Dunkerque.

B'ari, Shmuel, fl. 1959 *see* Be'eri, Shemuel

Bariand, Pierre, fl. 1972, he was a sometime keeper of the Collection of Minerals at the Faculté des sciences, Sorbonne, Paris. His writings include *Preliminary metallogenic map of Iran* (1965), *Marvellous world of minerals* (1977), and *Larousse des pierres précieuses* (1985). LC

Barine, Louise *Cécile* Bouffée, Mme Charles Vincens, called Arvède, born 17 November 1840 at Paris, she was a historian and art critic. She died in Paris. 14 November 1908.. DBF

Baring, Evelyn, Earl of Cromer, 1841-1917 *see* Cromer, Evelyn Baring, Earl of

Barišić, Franjo, fl. 1954, he was a medievalist at Belgrade University whose writings include Чуда Димитрија Солунског као историки извори (1953); and he edited Споменица Милана Будимира (1967). NUC

Barjot, Pierre Émile Marie Joannès, born 13 October 1899 at Blanc (Indre), he was a vice admiral in the French navy and during the 1956 Suez war he was commander-in-chief of the French contingent of the allied forces. His writings include *Le Débarquement du 8 novembre 1942 en Afrique du nord* (1946), and *Vers la marine de l'âge atomique* (1955). He died 1 February 1960. DBFC, 1954/55; IndexBFr² (1); WhoFr, 1955/56-1959/60

Barkan, Ömer Lûtfi, born in 1903, he was educated at Edirne. With short interruptions, he taught at Istanbul Üniversitesi until his retirement. His writings include *Türk toprak hukuku tarihinde Tanzimat ve 1274 tarihli arazı kanunnamesi* (1940), and *Süleymaniye Cami ve imareti inşaatı* (1972). He died in Istanbul, 23 August 1979. *Turcica* 13 (1981), 7-9

Barkechli, Mehdi, born 1921 *see* Barkishli, Mahdi

Barker, Benjamin, fl. 1826, he was an agent of the Church Missionary Society, London, who visited Syria. *Missionary register,* 1826

Barker, J. Ellis, born Otto Julius Eltzbacher on 9 May 1870 at Köln, Germany, he was a prolific writer who warned Britain of the danger of a war with Germany. He was also a founder of the New Health Society. His writings include *The great problems of British statesmanship* (1917). He died 16 July 1948. *Who was who,* 4

Barker, John, born 9 March 1771 at Smyrna, he was educated in England and entered the British diplomatic service in 1797. In 1833 he retired to Suediah, near Antioch. His writings include *Syria and Egypt under the last five sultans of Turkey* (1876). He died in Betias, Syria, 5 October 1849. DNB; Egyptology

Barker, John Walton, born 7 October 1933 at N.Y.C., he received a Ph.D. in 1961 from Rutgers University for *Manuel II Palaeologus; a study in late Byzantine statesmanship.* Afterwards he taught at the University of Wisconsin, Madison, where he was still active in 1997. His writings include *Justinian and the later Roman Empire* (1966), and *The use of music and recordings for teaching about the middle ages* (1988). Master (2); NatFacDr, 1995; Who's who in America, 1986/87, 1988/89|

Barker, Muhammad Abd-al-Rahman, born 2 November 1929 at Spokane, Wash., he graduated from the University of Washington and received a Ph.D. in 1959 from the University of California, Berkeley, for *A Klamath grammar.* Afterwards he taught at universities in Canada, Pakistan, and the United States. He was joint author of several Baluchi and Urdu readers. AmM&WS, 1973 S; DrAS, 1974-1982 F; IntAu&W, 1989; IWWAS, 1976/77; WhoAm, 1988/89

Barker, William Burckhardt, born about 1810 in Syria, he was educated in England. He was a sometime professor of Oriental languages at Eton College. In August 1835 he undertook a journey to the scarcely known sources of the Orontes. His writings include *Lares and penates, or, Cilicia and its governors* (1853), *A practical grammar of the Turkish language* (1854), and *A short historical account of the Crimea* (1855). He died in Sinop, 28 January 1856. DNB; Henze

Barker, William C., captain, I.N., fl. 1842. He was "attached to the Mission to Schwá." His account of the attempt to reach Harar can be found in Sir Richard F. Burton, *First footsteps in East Africa* (1856), pp. 595-622. BLC

Barkeshli, Mehdi, born 1921 *see* Barkishli, Mahdi

Barkhowdaryan, J. *see* Barchudarian, Johannes

Barkishli, Mahdi, born in 1291/1921 at Tehran. After studies at universities in Tehran and Paris, he taught music in Iran. His writings include *L'art sassanide, base de la musique arabe* (1947), *La musique traditionnelle de l'Iran* (1963), and *Musiqi-i Farabi* (1975). Iran who's who, 1974 and 1976

Barkley, D. G., fl. 1899. He wrote *Directions for revenue officers in the Punjab* (Lahore, 1875). LC

Barkow, Jerome H., born 18 January 1944 at N.Y.C. In 1970 he obtained a Ph.D. degree at the University of Chicago with his thesis, *Hausa and Maguzawa; process of group differentiation in a rural area in North Central State, Nigeria.* In 1980 he started teaching at the Department of Anthropology in Dalhousie University, Halifax, N.S., where he was still active in 1997. His writings include *The adapted mind* (1991). Canadian, 1996

Barlette, Henri. In 1912 he was a military veterinarian and head of the Service de la Jumentière de Tiaret, Oran.

Barlette, Léonard, fl. 1912-1913. He was a sometime deputy administrator in Draa-el-Mizan, Algeria.

Barlow, Thomas Lambert, fl. 1898. In 1908 he published with John F. A. MacNair, *Oral tradition from the Indus, comprised in tales.* BLC

Barnard, Leslie William, Rev., born 22 January 1924 at Bromley, Kent, he was educated at Oxford and Southampton University. Afterwards he was lecturer in theology at the University of Leeds. His writings include *Studies in the Apostolic Fathers and their background* (1967), *The Graeco-Roman and*

Oriental background of the iconoclastic controversy (1974), and *Studies in Church history and patristics* (1978). IntAu&W, 1977

Barnds, William J., born 20th cent., he was in 1971 a senior research fellow, Council of Foreign Relations, New York. His writings include *India,Pakistan, and the great powers* (1972), and *Foreign affairs kaleidoscope* (1974). He was still active in 1977. LC

Barnes, Ernest, captain, he was in 1903-1904 affiliated with the Archaeological Survey of India. NUC

Barnes, Sir Hugh Shakespear, born in 1853, he joined the Indian Civil Service in the 1870s, but transferred to the Foreign Department of the Government of India in 1879, in time to be sent in 1880 to act as Political Officer at Kandahar. Afterwards he served many years in Baluchistan. In 1905 his long services in India came to end and he pursued a business life in the City of London, where he died on 15 February 1940. JRCAS 27 (April 1940), pp. 248-150; *Who was who*, 3

Barnes, James Strackey, major, born in 1890, his writings include *The universal aspects of fascism* (1922), and *Fascism* (1931). LC

Barnes, John Robert, born 20th cent., he was in 1974 affiliated with the Department of History, U.C.L.A. His writings include *An introduction to the religious foundations in the Ottoman Empire* (1986). LC

Barnes, Lemuel Call, born 6 November 1854 at Kirtland, Ohio, he was educated at Kalamazoo College, and Newton Theological Institution, and ordained a Baptist minister. His writings include *Two thousand years of mission before Carey* (1900), and *Elemental forces in home missions* (1912). He died 18 July 1938. WhAm, 1

Barnes, W. J., fl. 1968, he was a London journalist with many years' experience as an editorial executive on the staffs of British newspapers. He worked and travelled extensively in the Middle East and in Africa, where he studied underdeveloped countries, their problems and their needs. He published a pamphlet, *The United Nations and the press* (1967). LC

Barnett, Richard David, born 23 January 1909 at Acton, England, he was educated at Cambridge and the British School of Archaeology at Athens. He was Keeper of the Department of Western Asiatic Antiquities in the British Museum, which he had joined in 1955. His writings include *A catalogue of the Nimrud ivories* (1957), and *Ancient ivories in the Middle East* (1982). He died 29 July 1986. *Who was who*, 8

Barnett, Tony, born 16 June 1945, he taught at the School of Development Studies, University of East Anglia, Norwich. His writings include *The Gezira scheme* (1977), *Sudan; state, capital, and transformation* (1988), and *Sudan; the Gezira scheme and agricultural transition* (1991). LC

von **Barnim**, Adalberg Johann Baptist, Baron, born 22 April 1841, he and the German naturalist Robert Hartmann set out in 1859 on a scientific expedition to the Blue Nile. He fell ill with fever in the Sudan and died on 12 July 1860. In 1863 his travel journal was published under the title, *Reise des Freiherrn Adalbert von Barnim durch Nord-Ost-Afrika in den Jahren 1859 und 1860, beschrieben von seinem Begleiter Dr. Robert Hartmann.* ADtB, vol. 2, p. 82; DtBE

Barns, J. W., F.R.G.S., he was a civil engineer and a sometime member of H.M. Bombay Public Works Department. He died before 1867.

Barnum, Henry Samuel, Dr., born in 1837 at Stratford, Conn., he graduated from Yale University in 1862, and Auburn Theological Seminary in 1867. In the same year he joined the Eastern Turkey Mission and served in Harput and Van from 1868 to 1884, when he was called to Constantinople. For nearly twenty-five years he was in charge of the periodicals published at Constantinople for the Board's Turkish Mission. After his wife, Helen Randle, had died on 31 January 1914, he returned to the U.S.A., where he died in Verona, N.J., 10 December 1915. *Missionary herald* 112 (1916), p. 65; Shavit; WhAm, 1

Barnum, Herman Norton, born 5 December 1826 at Auburn, N.Y., he went In 1860 as a missionary of the American Board in Turkey to Harput, where he remained until his death on 19 May 1910. Shavit; WhAm, 1

Barnum, Mary née Goodell, born in 1835 in the United States. she was married to Rev. Herman Norton Barnum of the American Board in Turkey in 1860, and went with him to Harput. Except for furloughs, she remained in Turkey even after her husband's death, and died in Harput, 9 May 1915. *Missionary herald* 111 (1915), p. 358

Barny, Frederick Jacob, born in 1873 at Basel, Switzerland, he was educated at the Theological Seminary, Rutgers University, New Brunswick, N.J. He went out to the Arabian Mission and served in nearly every station (Basrah, 1902; Muscat, 1919; Kuwait, 1933) as well as having been loanded on one occasion to a sister mission in South India, to help in an emergency. From pioneer days he was almost continuously on the Language Committee, and also rendered conspicious service in translation. He was still active, in 1941, in Queens Village, N.Y. He was joint author of *History of the Arabian Mission* (1926). Van Ess

Barois, Julien Hippolyte Eugène, born in 1849, he was involved in the planning of the *transsaharien* and subsequently spent nearly thirty years in Egypt, where he became engineer-in-chief of Ponts et Chaussées, and principal secretary to the Ministry of Public Works in Egypt. His writings include *Les irrigations en Égypte* (1887), and its translation, *Irrigation in Egypt* (1889). He died in Paris, 27 December 1937. DBF; IndexBFr² (1)

Baron, David, born ca. 1833. He was the founder of the Christian Testimony to Israel and born in Russia as a Jew. His writings include *The ancient scriptures and the modern Jew* (1900). He died in London in 1904. BLC

Baron, Salo (Shalom) Wittmayer, born 26 May 1895 at Tarnow, Austria, he studied at the Universität Wien, where he received a Dr.phil. in 1917, and at the Jüdisches Pädagogium, Wien, where he was ordained. From 1926 to 1929 he was a lecturer and librarian at the Jewish Institute of Religion, N.Y.C., and from 1930 until his retirement in 1963, he held the Miller Chair of Jewish History at Columbia University. His writings include *Die Judenfrage auf dem Wiener Kongress* (1920), and *Modern nationalism and religion* (1947). In 1975 he was honoured with the *Salo Wittmayer Baron jubilee volume on the occasion of his eightieth birthday*. He died 25 November 1989. CnDiAmJBi; EncJud.; Kürschner, 1931; WhAm, 10; WhoWorJ, 1987; Wininger

Baroni, Adolph, born 19th cent., he was in Palestine during most of the British campaign of the first World War. He had an authoritative and special knowledge of Palestine on account of his research in Palestine and the Near East. Note in *Asia* 18 (1918)

Baroody, George M., fl. 1980, he was a sometime member of the Law Department of the Arabian American Oil Company, representing ARAMCO and its employees before the Shariah Courts and assisting in negotiations with various ministries of the Saudi Arabian Government. In 1975 he became executive vice-president of Texas Eastern Arabian Ltd. in London. Note

Baroody, Jamil Murad, born 8 August 1905 at Suq al-Gharb, Lebanon, he was a graduate of AUB, and lived in the United States since he went there in 1939 as a member of the Lebanese Commission to the New York World's Fair. In 1943 he taught Arabic and lectured on Arab culture at Princeton University. Since 1959 he was deputy Permanent Representative of Saudi Arabia at the United Nations. He died in New York, 4 March 1979. ConAu, 85; Master (3); WhoUN, 1975

Barou, Jacques, born in 1949, he received a doctorate in ethnology and a diploma in urbanism. His writings include *Travailleurs africains en France* (1972), and *La place du pauvre; histoire et géographie sociales de l'habitat HLM* (1992); he was joint editor of *L'immigration entre loi et vie quotidienne* (1993). LC

Baroudi, Mohamed Firzat, born 25 March 1937 at Damascus, he received his first education in his home town and from 1959 to 1969 studied sociology and economics at the Universität Köln, where he received a Dr.phil. for *Die Bedeutung städtischer Agglomerationen im Modernisierungsprozeß ... des arabischen Mittleren Ostens*. In 1974 he was still active in Hamburg. NUC, 1973-1977; Thesis

Barral de Montferrat, marquis Horace Dominique, born in 1854 at Bahia, Brazil, he was a sometime secretary of the Société d'histoire diplomatique. His writings include *Etude sur l'histoire diplomatique de l'Europe* (1880), *Dix ans de paix armée entre la Fance et l'Angleterre, 1783-1793* (1893), and *De Monroë à Roosevelt* (1905). IndexBFr² (1); BN; Note

Barrantes y Moreno, Vicente, born 24. March 1829 at Badajoz, Spain, he studied at the local Seminary. Since 1848 he was in various capacities atttached to the Ministerio de Ultramar. His writings include *Apuntes interesantes sobre las Islas Filipinas* (1869). He died in Madrid, 16 October 1898. Diaz

de las **Barras y de Aragon**, Francisco, born 26 or 28 October 1869 at Sevilla, he studied natural sciences and became first a professor at the Universidad de Oviedo from 1898 to 1919 and then at Sevilla and Madrid. In 1912 he conducted field work in northern Morocco. Cuenca; Mendez

Barrat, Jacques, born 20th cent., he received a doctorate in 1971 from the Université de Paris for his thesis, *Kabul, capitale de l'Afghanistan.*

Barrau-Dihigo, Lucien, born in 1876, he received a doctorate in 1921 from the Université de Tours for his thesis, *Recherches sur l'histoire politique du royaume Austurien, 718-910*. His writings include *Historia politica del Reino Asturino* (1989). He died in 1931. LC; NUC, pre-1956

Barrault, Alexis, born 9 September 1812 near Sarrelouis, France, he was a metallurgist and railroad engineer who was committed to the colonization of Algeria and the construction of the Suez Canal. With his brother, Émile Barrault, he wrote *Politique du canal de Suez* (1956). He died in 1867. DBF

Barrault, Pierre Ange Casimir Émile, born 17 March 1799 at Paris, he was a sometime *professeur des lettres* at the Collège de Sorèze. He was a Saint-Simonist and wote *Religion saint-simonienne* (1832), *Orient et Occident; études politiques, morales, religieuses pendant 1833-1834* (1835), and with Edmond de Cadalvène, *Histoire de la guerre de Méhémed-Ali contre la Porte ottomane en Syrie et en Asie mineure* (1837). He died in Paris in1869. DBF

Barré, Paul, fl. 1896, he was a sometime secretary of the Société de propagande coloniale. His writings include *Fachoda et le Bahr-el-Ghazal* (1898). BN

Barre, Raymond Octave Joseph, born 12 April 1924 at Saint-Denis de la Réunion, he studied at the Université de Paris and l'Institut d'Études politiques, where he received a doctorate for his thesis, *La période dans l'analyse économique* (1950). From 1951 to 1954 he was in Tunisia as a professor at l'Institut des Hautes études de la Université de Tunis. Since the late 1950s he was involved in government. CurBio,1977; Master (4); *Who's who in France*, 1975/76-1997/98

Barresi, Concetta Ferial, fl. 1978-1984, an Italian Arabist and translator of modern Egyptian literature.

Barret, Philippe, born in 1945, his writings include *D'un deuxième monde à l'autre; essai prospectif sur l'Europe du sud et le monde arabe* (1977).

Barrett, Charles Raymond Booth, born in 1850, his writings include *Battles and battlefields in England* (1896), *History of the XIII. Hussars* (1911), and *The 7th, (Queen's own) Hussars* (1914). LC

Barrett, Douglas Eric, he was Keeper of Oriental Antiquities, British Museum, London. His writings include *Islamic metalwork in the British Museum* (1949), *Early Cola architecture and sculpture* (1974), and with Basil Gray, *Painting of India* (1963), and its translation, *La peinture indienne* (1978). BLC

Barrier, Norman Gerald, born 22 August 1940 at Statesville, N.Y., he studied at Duke University, Durham, N.C., where he received a Ph.D. in 1966 for *Punjab politics and the disturbances of 1907*. In 1967 he was apponted a professor of South Asian history and director of the South Asia Center, University of Missouri at Columbia, a post which he still held in 1995. His writings include *The Punjab in nineteenth-century tracts* (1969), *Banned; controversial literature and political control in British India, 1907-1947* (1974), and *India and America; American publishing on India, 1930-1985* (1986). ConAu, 53-56; NatFacDr, 1995

Barrion, Georges, born 19th cent., he was an *ingénieur-agronom* who was sent by the Ministry of Agriculture on a mission, about which he reported in *Le développement de l'élevage du bétail dans la République Argentine, l'Algérie et la Tunisie* (1890). BN

Barron, John Bernard, lieut.-colonel, O.B.E., M.C., he was in the 1920s a director of Revenue and Customs, Government of Palestine; in 1923 he was superintendent of the Census. His writings include *Mohammedan wakfs in Palestine* (1922). BLC; LC; Note

Barrouquère-Claret, C., born 19th cent., his writings include *Setat, centre historique de la Chaouïa* (1919).

Barrow, Sir Edmund George, major-general, born 28 January 1852, he joined the army in 1871 and was with the Indian Contingent in Egypt, 1882; and in the Intelligence Branch, Bengal, 1885-1887, when he served on the Lockhart Boundary Commission to Chitral, Kafiristan, Hunza, and Wakhan. His writings include *The Sepoy officer's manual* (1880). He died 3 January 1934. Buckland; Riddick; *Who was who*, 3

Barry, Michael (Mike), born in 1948 in New York, he spent many years in Afghanistan and then settled in France. His writings include *Afghanistan* (1974), and *Le royaume de l'insolence; la résistance afghane du Grand Moghul à l'invasion soviétique* (1984). LC

Barry, William Francis, Very Rev. Canon, D.D., born 21 April 1849 at London, he was canon of Birmingham and professor of philosophy and theology at various British colleges. His writings include *The Papal monarchy from St. George the Great to Boniface III* (1901), and *The Papacy and modern times* (1911). He died 15 December 1930. *Who was who*, 3

Bärschneider, Edeltraud, born 20th cent., she received a doctorate in 1976 from the Institut für Tropische Landwirtschaft und Veterinärmedizin, Leipzig, for her thesis, *Die Entwicklung der landwirtschaftlichen Selbstverwaltungsbetriebe in der Demokratischen Volksrepublik Algerien*.

Barse, Jules, born in 1812, he was a Paris toxicologist whose writings include *Manuel de la Cour d'assises dans les questions d'empoisonnement* (1845). DBF

Barsoumian, Hagop Levon, born 20th cent., received a Ph.D. in 1980 from Columbia University for his thesis, *The Armenian 'amira' class of Istanbul.* LC

Barstow, Robbin Wolcott, born 18 February 1890 at Glastenburg, Conn., he was from 1910 to 1912 a tutor in the American Board of Commissioners for Foreign Missions Boys' School in Mardin, Turkey. Afterwards he was a high ranking Church official and active in the United States ecumenical movement. He wrote *Getting acquainted with God* (1928). He died 17 September 1962. WhAm, 4

Bartal, Moshe, he was in 1963 head of the Arab Department of the Histadrut. Note

Bartalini, Ezio, born 24 June 1884 at Monte San Savino (Arezzo), he received doctorates in law and letters. From 1903 to 1915 he was the founding publisher of *La Pace*, Genova. From 1933 to 1945 he taught Latin and Italian at Istanbul Üniversitesi. His writings include *Pietro Nenni* (1946). Chi è, 1961; *Who's who in Italy, 1957/58*

Bartels, Herwig, born 10 June 1934 at Bremen, Germany, he received a Dr.jur. in 1965 from the Universität Köln for his thesis, *Das Waqfrecht und seine Entwicklung in der Libanesischen Republik*. He entered the German foreign service and was an ambassador to Jordan. Wer ist wer, 1990/91-1995/96|

Bartelt, Ernst, born in 1938, he trained as a bookbinder, but entered the service of the Staatsbibliothek, Berlin. He was entrusted with the mounting and restoring of manuscripts, in which task he displayed a quite remarkable ability and skill. He was permitted to undertake work elsewhere. From 1980 to 1981, he spent half a year in San'a', Yemen, setting up facilities for, and teaching, the restoration of library materials. He retired in the late 1990s. Private; Sezgin

Bartet, Albéric Joseph Alfred Louis, born 7 August 1871 at Saint-Denis de la Réunion, he was educated first at Rochefort (Charente-Maritime) and then the École du service de santé de la Marine, Bordeaux, where he received a doctorate in 1893. Afterwards he spent ten years as a medical officer in French West Africa. He wrote *Colonne expéditionnaire dans le Haut-Dahomy* (1898). He died in Reims, 27 February 1968. *Hommes et destins*, vol. 1, pp. 58-61

Barth, Hans Karl, born 10 April 1938 at Jarek, Yugoslavia, he was since 1977 a professor of geography at the Universität Tübingen. His writings include *Der Geokomplex Sahel* (1977), *Mali; eine geografische Landeskunde* (1986); he was joint author of *Natural resources and problems of land reclamation in Egypt* (1987). In 1985 he edited *Beiträge zur Geomorphologie des Vorderen Orients*. Kürschner, 1996-2003

Barth, Heinrich, born 16 February 1821 at Hamburg, he studied at the Universität Berlin, where he received a doctorate in 1844 for his thesis, *Corinthiorum commercii et mercaturae historiae particula*. He was a geographer and explorer, particularly of the Sahara and the central Sudan. His writings include *Travels and discoveries in North Africa and Central Africa* (1857), *Reisen und Entdeckungen in Nord- und Central-Afrika* (1867-58), and *Reise durch das Innere der Europäischen Türkei* (1864). He died in Berlin, 25 November 1865. ADtB; DtBE; Behrmann; Egyptology; Embacher; Henze; Master (3); NDB

Barth, Jacob, born 3 March 1851 at Flehingen, Germany, he studied at the Rabbinerseminar zu Berlin and afterwards Oriental languages at Leipzig and Strasbourg. In 1875 he received a Dr.phil. from the Universität Leipzig for his thesis *Ta'lab's Kitâb al-Fasih nach den Handschriften von Leiden und Berlin*. At the age of twenty-three, he became lecturer at the Rabbinerseminar zu Berlin. Since 1860 he was concurrently a professor at the Universität Berlin. His writings include *Die Nominalbildung in den semitischen Sprachen* (1889-91), and *Etymologische Studien zum semitischen, insbesondere hebräischen Lexikon* (1893). He died in Berlin, 24 October 1914. DtBE; EncJud; Fück, 242; NDB; Wininger

Barth, Thomas Fredrik Weybye, born 22 December 1928 at Leipzig, he studied at the University of Chicago and Cambridge University, where he received a Ph.D. in 1957 for *The Political organisation of Swat Pathans*. Afterwards he was a professor of social anthropology at universities in Norway as well as visiting professor in the United States and the Sudan. His writings include *Principles of social organization in southern Kurdistan* (1953), *Nomads of South Persia* (1961), *Social-antropologiska problem* (1971), and *Features of person and society in Swat* (1981). ConAu, 65-68; *Hvem er hvem, 1973-94*

Barthas-Landrieu, Thérèse, she wrote *L'oasis d'Arbaïn* (1941). LC

Barthel, Günter, born 17 March 1941 at Erfurt, Germany, he received a doctorate in 1966 from the Universität Leipzig for his thesis, *Zur Industrialisierung der Türkei*. Since 1970 he was a professor of Islamic studies at Leipzig. His writings include the translation, *Industrialization in the Arab countries of the Middle East* (1972); a Russian translation was published in 1975. Kürschner, 1996-2003

Barthélemy, Adrien, born 24 August 1859 at Paris, he studied Sanskrit and Avesta at the École pratiques des Hautes études, where he received a diploma in 1884. Concurrently he obtained diplomas in Arabic, Turkish, and Persian at the École des languages orientales. Afterwards he entered l'Affaires étrangères, where he was employed in varied positions at consulates in Syria, North Africa and Zanzibar. From 1909 until his retirement in 1929 he was professor at l'École pratique des Hautes études des langues orientales, Paris. His writings include *Dictionnaire arabe-français* (1935-36). He died in Emancé near Rambouillet, 18 December 1949. JA 239 (1951), pp. 239-241

Barthélemy Saint-Hilaire, Jules, born 19 August 1805 at Paris, he is best known as a Greek scholar. From 1838 to 1852 he was professor of Greek and Latin philosophy at the Collège de France. In 1855 he accompanied F. de Lesseps on his journey to Egypt to explore the Isthmus of Suez. His writings include *Egypt and the great Suez Canal* (1857), *Mahomet et le Coran* (1865), and *L'Inde anglaise; son état actuel, son avenir* (1865). He died 24 November 1895. Buckland; DBF

Barthelet, L., he was in 1927 *secrétaire-général* of the Ligue des Familles nombreuses françaises d'Algérie.

Barthelot, Jean, he was in 1977 a colonel and *secrétaire-général* at the Défense National. He contributed to *Golfe persique et océan indien; bilan et perspectives* (Téhéran, 1977). LC

Barthold, Wilhelm, 1869-1930 see Bartol'd, Vasilii Vladimirovich

Bartholdy, Jacob Ludwig Salomo, born 13 May 1779 at Berlin, he studied at the Universität Königsberg. In 1806 he became a Lutheran. He travelled in Italy, Asia Minor, and Greece; he attended the Congress of Vienna and was afterwards Prussian chargé d'affaires in Italy. His writings include *Bruchstücke zur näheren Kenntniss des heutigen Griechenlands* (1805), *Voyage en Grèce, 1803 et 1804* (1807), and *Der Krieg der Tiroler Landleute im Jahr 1809* (1814). He died in Roma, 27 July 1825. ADtB; DtBE; Egyptology; NDB; Wininger

Bartholomae, Christian, born 21 January 1855 at Forst, Germany, he studied classics and comparative philology at the universities of München, Erlangen and Leipzig, and received a Dr.phil. in 1878 from the Universität Leipzig for *Das Verbum im Avesta* (1878), and a Dr.habil. in 1879 at Halle.. He taught successively in Halle, Münster, Straßburg, and Heidel-berg. His writings include *Altiranisches Wörterbuch* (1904). He died in Langeoog, 9 August 1925. DtBE; Elranica; NDB

Bartholomaei, I. A., 1813-1870 see Bartolomei, Ivan Alekseevich

Bartholomew, Geoffrey Wilson, born in 1927, he was a barrister-at-law of Gray's Inn, and New South Wales, a sometime professor of law at the University of Singapore, and dean, Faculty of Law at the New South Wales Institute of Technology. His writings include *The commercial law of Malaysia; a study in the reception of English law* (1965). In 1975 he edited *Malaya law review legal essays in memoriam Bashir Ahmad Mallal*. LC

Barthou, Louis Jean Firmin, born 25 August 1862 at Oloron-Ste-Marie (Basses-Pyrénées), he studied at Bordeaux and Paris, where he received a doctorate in 1886. He was a politician who was at the Chambre des députés from 1888 to 1922 and afterwards at the Sénat. He was assassinated together with King Alexander of Yugoslavia, whom he was accompanying during the state visit in Marseille, on 9 October 1934. He wrote *La bataille du Maroc* (1919). Curinier, II, pp. 313-314; DBF; NDBA

Bartina y Gassiot, Sebastián, S.J., born 11 June 1917 at Gerona, he studied classics, philosophy, and theology in Italy and Spain, and ordained in 1948. He was since 1952 a professor at the Facultad de Teología de Barcelona. His writings include *Verso y versificación; tratado de métrica castellana* (1955), *Hacia los orígenes del hombre* (1956), and *Cifras coptas y cultura árabe* (1968). DBEC

Bartl, Peter, born 26 November 1938 at Cottbus, Germany, he received a Dr.phil. in 1967 from the Universität München for his thesis, *Die albanischen Muslime zur Zeit der nationalen Unabhangigkeitsbewegung*. Since 1973, he was a member of the Seminar für Geschichte Osteuropas at the Universität München. His writings include *Der Westbalkan zwischen spanischer Monarchie und Osmanischem Reich* (1974), and *Grundzüge der jugoslawischen Geschichte* (1985). Kürschner, 1996-2003

Bartlett, William Henry, born 26 March 1809 at Kentish Town, London, he was a topographical artist who, in the course of his employment, travelled in Greece and the Near East, including Greater Syria and Arabia. His writings include *The Nile boat* (1849), *Footsteps of our Lord and his apostles in Syria,*

Greece and Italy (1851), *Jerusalem revisited* (1854), and *Gleanings on the overland route* (1864). He died homeward bound at sea, 13 September 1854. His correspondence is in the Archive of the Griffith Institute, Ashmolean Museum, Oxford. DNB; Egyptology; WhAm, 1

Bartoccini, Renato, born 25 August 1893 at Roma, he went in 1920 on an archaeological mission to Egypt. He was a sometime superintendent of antiquities in Tripolitania. His writings include *Guida del Museo di Tripoli* (1922), and *Le antichità della Tripolitania* (1926). Chi è, 1931, 1940; IndBiltal (1)

Bartol'd (Barthold), Vasilii Vladimirovich, born 3 (15) November 1869 at St. Petersburg, he was an outstanding historian of Central Asia untouched by the straight-jacket of Marxist interpretation of history. He studied at St. Petersburg, where he received a doctorate for *Туркистан в эпоху монгольского нашествия.* He died 19 August 1930. BiobibSOT, pp. 117-119; *Index Islamicus* (10); Krachkovskii; Miliband; Miliband²; TatarES

Bartolomei, Ivan Alekseevich, born 28 November 1813 in Russia, he served as a general in the Crimea and the Caucasus. He was also a collector of Sassanid coins. He died on 5 October 1870. EnSlovar; Henze; Wieczynski

Barton, George Aaron, born 12 November 1859 at Farnham, P.Q., he was a graduate of Haverford College and Harvard Univeristy. Until his retirement in 1932 he taught Semitic languages and history of religion at American universities. His writings include *Archæology and the Bible* (1916), and *The religions of the world* (1917). He died in Weston, Mass., 28 June 1942. *Canadian who's who*, 1910-12; DAB; Shavit; WhAm, 2

Barton, James Levi, born 23 September 1855 at Charlotte, Vt., he responded to the missionary call while a student at Hartford Theological Seminary and in 1885 went to Turkey as a missionary. He was stationed in Harput until 1892. In the following year he became president of Euphrates College but returned to the United States in 1894, when his wife's health made it necessary for them to stay in America. Subsequently he served until 1927 as a secretary of the American Board of Commissioners for Foreign Missions. His writings include *The missionary and his critics* (1906), *Daybreak in Turkey* (1908), *The Christian approach to Islam* (1918). He died in Brookline, Mass., 21 July 1936. *Missionary review of the world* 59 (1936), 422-423; Shavit; WhAm, 1

Barton, Sir William Pell (Peel), K.C.I.E., born in 1871, he was educated at Worcester College, Oxford, and University College, London. In 1893 he entered the Indian Civil Service, where he served in the North West Frontier Province, Kohat, Swat and Chitral. His writings include *India's North-West Frontier* (1939). He died 28 November 1956. IndianBiInd (2); Riddick; WhoIndia, 1927; *Who was who*, 5

Bartoš, Milan F., Dr., born 10 November 1901 at Beograd, he received a doctorate from the Sorbonne in 1927 for *Exposé de droit international privé notamment du droit international commercial selon la législation et la jurisprudence yougoslave en Serbie* (1927). He was a professor at Belgrade University. His writings include *Savremeni međunarodni problemi* (1955). Ko je ko, 1957; JugoslSa, 1970

Bartsch, Gerhart, born 1 September 1902 at Rawitsch, Germany, received a doctorate in 1925 from the Universität Breslau for his thesis, *Der Solling*. From 1942 until his retirement he was professor of geography at the Universität Gießen. He died between 1991 and 1996. Kürschner, 1950-1992

Bartsch, Hans Werner, born 24 April 1915 at Kiel, Germany, he received a Dr.theol. in 1939 from the Universität Heidelberg for his thesis, *Gnostisches Gut und Gemeindetradition bei Ignatius von Antiochien*, and later taught theology at the Universität Frankfurt am Main. His writings include *Entmythologisierende Auslegung* (1962). He died in Gießen, 27 December 1983. Kürschner, 1980, 1983

Bartsch, Reinhart, born 5 April 1948 at Hamburg, he received a doctorate in 1976 from the Universität Hohenheim for his thesis *Die Ökonomik der chemischen Schädlingsbekämpfung im bewässerten Baumwollanbau in der Gezira, Sudan.* For eight months he conducted field work at the Gezira Agricultural Research Corporation, Wad Medani, 1974-1975. His writings include *Economic problems of pest control* (1991). LC

Bartsch, William Henry, born 18 January 1933 at Washington, D.C., he studied at Washington and Lee University, Lexington, Va., the University of Virginia, and SOAS, where he received a Ph.D. in 1970 for his thesis, *Labour supply and employment-creation in the urban areas of Iran, 1956-1966.* Afterwards he was a U.S. Foreign Service officer, 1958-1961, and research economist at the International Labour Office, Genève, 1969-1973. His writings include *Employment and technology choice in Asian agriculture* (1977), and *Doomed at the start; American pursuit pilots in the Philippines* (1992). He was joint author of *The economy of Iran; a bibliography* (1971). Sluglett; WhoWor, 1984/85

Barua, Beni Madhab, born in 1888 in Bengal, he was educated in India and at the University of London, where he obtained a doctorate. His writings include *A history of pre-Buddhistic Indian philosophy* (1921). The *B. M. Barua commemoration volume* was published in 1949. He died in 1948.

Barua, Benu Prasad, born in 1936, he was in 1984 a professor of political science at the University of Chittagong. His writings include *Politics and constitution - making India and Pakistan* (1984), a revision of his Ph.D. thesis submitted in 1967 at the University of London, and *Eminent thinkers in India and Pakistan* (1991). LC

Baruch (Barruch), Jacob *Jules*, born 17 February 1853 at Nice, he was a military interpreter in Algeria and rose from the rank of *interprète auxiliaire de 2e classe* (27 May 1872) to *interprète auxiliaire de 1re classe* (18 March 1876). His writings include *Cours d'arabe parlé* (1898). His trace is öost after an article in 1903. Féraud, 363

Barudel, Joseph, fl. 1957-1984, he was a medical doctor whose writings include *Des gravelles et de leur traitement par les eaux de Vichy* (Lyon, 1971). BN

Baruk, Gaston David, born 18 January 1908 at Sousse, Tunisia, he was educated at l'École supérieure de commerce, Paris. In 1948 he was vice-president of the Association professionnelle de la minoterie marocaine. WhoWor, 1974/75

Barwani, Ali Muhsin, fl. 1976, he was minister of foreign affairs in the former freely elected Government of Zanzibar, and leader of the Zanzibar Nationalist Party. He wrote *I was Nyerere's prisoner* (1975). AfrBioInd (1); LC

von **Bary**, Erwin, born 22 February 1846 at München, he studied medicine at the universities of Leipzig and Zürich. On the encouragement of Gerhard Rohlfs, he settled at Malta to prepare for explorations of the Sahara. Between 1876 and 1877 he made repeated excursions deep into Tuareg country, where he met death on 3 October 1877 under circumstances which have never been determined. "Il fut un des derniers adeptes de cette école d'explorateurs du milieu du siècle qui ont eu pour seule ambition le développement des connaissances humaines" (Henri Schimer). His writings, *Sahara-Tagebuch, 1876-1877*, were edited by Erica von Bary in 1977. DtBE; Embacher; Henze; *Hommes et destins*, vol. 7, pp. 49-51

Barzani, Mustafa, born 1904 in Kurdistan, he came to prominence in the wake of the second World War, when he became the leader of the Kurds in their struggle for self-determination. His success was due to the military capabilities of his tribe. From his tribal seat in Barzan he pressed the Iraqi government to promise improvement of cultural and social services. When these promises were not honoured, serious fighting ensued. Outnumbered, he had to retreat and make his way to Iran. After having failed to reach an agreement with the Iranian government concerning political asylum, he and his followers rallied to the emerging army of the Mahabad Republic, where he was nominated one of four generals. The collapse of the Kurdish Republic in December, 1946, marked the beginning of his twelve-year uneventful asylum in the Soviet Union. The overthrow of the Iraqi monarchy in 1958 offered him the chance to return triumphantly to Baghdad. But the Qasim regime soon began to assert its authority over Kurdistan and he retreated to Barzan. By 1961 the political situation led to open war with the disgruntled Kurds. The following nine-year war ended in 1970 with an agreement on Kurdish autonomy. Barzani emerged as a charismatic leader. But this reprieve was to last only four years. In his old age he was reduced to a pawn in the Iran-Iraq border dispute over the Shatt al-'Arab. When the two countries settled their differences at the expense of the Kurds in 1975, Mullah Mustafa had to seek refuge in Iran, never to return to the political scene. He died in 1979 while on visit in the United States. EncIranica

Basagana, Ramon, fl. 1971, he was joint author of *Habitat traditionnel et structures familiales en Kabylie* (Alger, Centre de recherches anthropologiques, préhistoriques et ethnographiques, 1974).

Baschmakoff, A., 1858-1943 see Bashmakov, Aleksandr Alesandrovich

Basdevant, Pierre, born 22 March 1914 at Grenoble, he was graduated from the Faculté de droit de Paris and the École libre des sciences politiques. Afterwards he entered the French foreign service. He died on 29 November 1980. *Who's who in France*, 1879/80

Basetti-Sani, Giulio, O.F.M., born 6 January 1912 at Firenze, his writings include *Louis Massignon* (1971), *L'islam e Francesco d'Assisi* (1975), *Il Corano nella luce di Cristo* (1977), and its English translation, *The Koran in the light of Christ* (1977). LC

Başgil, Ali Fuad, born in 1892/93, he received a doctorate and became a professor of law at Instanbul Üniversitesi. His writings include *La question des détroits* (1928), *Ricali mühemmei siyasiye* (1928),

Demokrasi yolunda (1961), *Din ve lâiklik* (1962), and *La révolution militaire de 1960 en Turquie* (1963).
LC

Başgöz, Ilhan, born in 1923, his writings include *Biografik Türk halk hikâyeleri* (1948), *Educational problems in Turkey* (1968), *Turkish folklore reader* (1971), and he edited *Studies in Turkish folklore, in honor of Pertev N. Boratav* (1978). LC

Bash Hanbah, Muhammad, born in 1881 in Tunis, he was a sometime interpreter and deputy judge. In 1913 he went to Turkey and, later, to Genève where he published *La revue du Maghreb*. He died in Berlin in 1920. He wrote *Le peuple algéro-tunisien et la France*, edited by Mahmoud Abdel-Moula (1991). LC

Basharin, Georgii Prokop'evich, fl. 1955, he was a sometime member of the Institut Istorii, Akademiia Nauk SSSR. His writings include *История аграрных отношений в Якутии* (1956), *Обозрение историографии дореволюционной Якутии* (1965), and *Социально-экономические отношения в Якутии* (1974). LC

Basheer, Tahseen Mohamad, born 5 April 1925 at Alexandria, Egypt, he graduated from Alexandria University and went for graduate studies to Princeton and Harvard universities. In 1955 he joined the Egyptian foreign service. His publications include *A conversation with Ambassador Tahseen Basheer; reflections on the Middle East peace process* (1981). WhoArab, 1981/82-2003/2004

Bashir, Ahmad, he received a Ph.D. in 1952 from SOAS for his thesis, *The religious policy of Akbar*. His writings include *Akbar, the great Mughul* (1967). Sluglett

Bashir, Iskandar E., born 20th cent., he was in 1974 a senior lecturer at the Department of Political Studies and Public Administration, AUB. His writings include *Planned administrative change in Lebanon* (1965), *Civil service reforms in Lebanon* (1977), and *Dawlat al-Imarat al-'Arabiyah al-Muttahidah* (1982). LC

Bashiri, Iraj, born 31 July 1940 at Bihbahan, Iran, he was a sometime professor of Iranian studies and Turkish at the University of Minnesota, Minneapolis. His writings include a revised version of his University of Michigan thesis,'*To be' as the origin of syntax* (1973), *Hedayat's ivory tower* (1974), *Persian; 70 units* (1975) and *The black tulip* (1984). DrAS, 1974, 1978, 1982; LC; Schoeberlein

Bashkirov, Andrei Vasil'evich, born 12 (24) October 1899 at Telezhniki Lipetskogo, Russia, he graduated in 1930 from the Leningrad Oriental Institute and received a doctorate in 1938 for his thesis, *Развитие промышленности в Иране*. His writings include *Рабочее и профсоюзное движение в Иране* (1948), and *Экспансия английских и американских империалитов в Иране, 1941-1953* (1954). He died 10 November 1976. Miliband; Miliband²

Bashmakov, Aleksandr Aleksandrovich, born in 1858 in Russia, he was an ethnographer who settled in France after the Russian revolution. His writings, partly under the pseudonyms Philharmonius and Vieschii Oleg, include *Cinquante siècles d'évolution ethnique autour de la mer Noire* (1937), and *Le matérialisme juif* (193-?). His papers are at Columbia University Library. He died in 1943. LC

Basile, Antoine, born 20th cent., his writings include *Commerce extérieur et développement de la petite nation* (Bey-routh, 1972), *Investing in free export processing zones* (1984), and *Debt equity conversions* (1990). LC

Basilov, Vladimir Nikolaevich, born 18 January 1937, his writings include *Культ святых в исламе* (1970), and *Древние обряды верования и культы народов Средней Азии* (1986); he was joint author of *Домусульманские веровaния и обряды в Средней Азии* (1975). LC; Schoeberlein

Basiner, Theodor Friedrich Julius, born 3 January 1816 at Dorpat, he received a Dr.phil. in 1848 from the Universität Königsberg. He accompanied the Russian mission to Khiva under G. Danilevski, 1842-1843, as a botanist. His writings include *Naturwissenschaftliche Reise durch die Kirgisensteppe nach Chiwa* (1848). He died in Wien in 1862. Baltisch (2); Henze; LC

Baskakov, Nikolai Aleksandrovich, born 9 (22) March 1905 at Sol'vychegodsk, Russia, he graduated in 1929 from Moscow State University and received a doctorate in 1950 *Каракалпакский язык*. He was an outstanding Turkologist with a profound knowledge of Turkic peoples and tribes of the Soviet Union. The list of his publications brings to light a gold mine of linguistic erudition ranging from Karakalpak to Altai Turkic, including investigations into philological problems within the Turkic world. His writings include *Русско-уйгурский словарь* (1940), *Каракал-пакский язык* (1951), and *Тюркская лексика в "Слове о полку Игореве"* (1985). He died in Moscow, 26 August 1996 Miliband; Miliband²; Przegląd orientalistyczny 1996, p. 223; TatarES; Turkic languages 2 (1998), pp. 161-170; UAJ 38 (1966), pp. 149-159

Baskerville, Beatrice Catherine, b. 1878, d. 1955 *see* Guichard, Beatrice Catherine née Baskerville

Basmadjian, Krikor Jagob, born 19th cent., his writings include *Essai sur l'histoire de la littérature ottomane* (1910), *Histoire moderne des Arméniens, 1375-1916* (1917), and *Numismatique générale de l'Arménie* (1936). LC

Başman, Avni, born in 1887 at Constantinople, he graduated in 1908 from the Faculty of Law and subsequnetly joined the Department of Education, where he became inspector-general of the Turkish students abroad. From 1950 to 1954 he was secretary-general of the Democratic Party. He died in 1965. Meydan

Basri, Meer (Mir) S., born 19 September 1911 (or, according to Kurkis Awwad, in 1912), at Baghdad, he was an economist and civil servant whose writings include *A'lam al-Yahud fi al-'Iraq al-hadith* (1983). LC; WhoWor, 1974/75

Bass, George Fletcher, born 9 December 1932 at Columbia, N.C., he graduated from Johns Hopkins University, Baltimore, Md., and the Universitiy of Pennsylvania. He was taught classical archaeology at University of Pennsylvania, and, since 1980, anthropology at Texas A & M University, a post which he still held in 1995. His writings include *Archaeology under water* (1966), *A history of seafaring based on underwater archaeology* (1972), and he edited *Ships and shipwrecks of the Americas* (1988). DrAS, 1974-1982 H; Master (3); NatFacDr, 1995; WhoAm, 1988/89-2003

Bassermann, Alfred, born 9 February 1856 at Mannheim, Germany, he studied law at the universities of Heidelberg, Berlin, and Kiel and became a civil servant. In 1886 he resigned and began to travel extensively in Italy, where he began his Dante research. From 1892 to 1921 he translated the *Divina commedia* into German. In 1897 he published *Dantes Spuren in Italien.* He died in Königsfeld, 3 May 1935. DtBE; NDB

Basset, André, born 4 August 1895 at Lunéville (Meurthe-et-Moselle), he received a doctorate in 1929from the Université de Paris for his thesis, *Le verbe berbère.* He was foremost a linguist and a Berber scholar. He taught at colleges in Morocco, and at the Institut des hautes études marocaines, before he was invited in 1930 to the chair of Berber at the Faculté des Lettres d'Alger. In 1940 he succeeded Edmond Destaing at the École des Langues Orientales, Paris, a position which he held until his death on 24 January 1956. His writings include *Atlas linguistiques des parlers berbères* (1936-1939), *Cours berbère* (1937), and *Textes berbères de l'Aurès* (1961). Hommes et destins, II, pp. 41-42

Basset, Henri, born 7 November 1892 at Lunéville (Meurthe-et-Moselle), he grew up in Algiers. During the first World War he was seriously wounded and sent to Morocco in 1916 to teach at the École supérieure de la langue arabe. In 1920 he became the schoool's deputy director. He received two doctorates from the Faculté des lettres d'Alger in 1920, *Essai sur la littérature des Berbères* and *Le culte des grottes au Maroc.* He died from his war-time injuries, 12 April 1926, in Rabat. DBF; *Hommes et destins*, vol. 2, p. 43

Basset, René Marie Joseph, born 24 July 1855 at Lunéville (Meurthe-et-Moselle), he studied at l'École des Langues Orientales and l'École Pratique des Hautes Études, Paris. Since 1880 he was a lecturer in Arabic, and later director, at the École Supérieure des Lettres d'Alger. He was an authority on Berber languages and knew North Africa and its inhabitants from extensive travels. His writings include *Contes populaires berbères* (1887), and *Études sur les dialectes berbères* (1894). He died on 4 January 1924. A commemoration volume was published in 1928: *Mémorial Henri Basset.* DBF; Fück; *Hommes et destins*, vol. 2, pp. 43-44; *Index Islamicus* (3)

Bassett, James, born 31 January 1834 at Mundos, Ontario, he graduated from Wabash College and Lane Theological Seminary. In 1871 he went as missionary of the Presbyterian Board to Urmia and one year later he had his own printing press; after 1882 he was in charge of the Eastern Persia Mission. He also collaborated with the translation of the Bible into Persian. His writings include *The land of the imams; a narrative of travels and residence* (1886), and *A narrative of the founding and fortunes of the Eastern Persia Mission* (1890). He translated *Jaghatái Tartar, or Takah Turkoman St. Matthew* (London, 1880). He died in Los Angeles, 10 March 1906. BLC; DAB; Shavit

von **Bassewitz**, Hans Joachim Th., born 11 November 1898 at Schwerin, Germany, he studied law, history and Oriental languages at the universities of Rostock and Berlin. He received diplomas in Turkish and Persian. In the early 1920s he was in the German foreign service and posted to Kabul, Rome, Moscow, and Constantinople. Wer ist's, 1935

Bassim, Tamara Omar, fl. 1963, he wrote *La femme dans l'œuvre de Baudelaire* (1974). LC

Bassiouni, M. Cherif, born in 1937 at Cairo, he studied law at the universities of Dijon, Genève, Cairo, and Indiana. Since 1964 he was teaching law at DePaul University, Chicago. His writings include *The law of dissident and riots* (1971), and *International criminal law* (1980). ConAu, 29-32; LC

Basso, Jacques A., fl. 1975, his writings include *Les groupes de pression* (1983). LC

Baştav, Şerif, Prof. Dr., born 20th cent., his writings include *Bizans imparatorlugu tarihi* (1989), and *Osmanlı Türk-Macar tarihi münasebetlerinde ilk devir* (1991), and he edited *Ordo portae; decription grecque de la Porte* (1947). LC

Baster, Albert Stephen *James*, born in 1904, he was a sometime economic adviser on the staff of UNRWA, and chief of the U.N. African and Middle East Studies Section as well as visiting professor at Princeton University. His writings include *The imperial banks* (1929), *The twilight of American capitalism* (1937), and its translation, *Le crépuscule du capitalisme américain* (1939). He died in N.Y.C., 24 August 1957. LC; NUC, pre-1956; ObitOF, 1979

Bastiaensen, Michel, born 5 April 1944 at Antwerp, he studied Romance philology at Siena and Bruxelles, where he took also a degree in Persian in 1966. His writings include *L'Orient de l'incroyant* (1984), and *Ange de Saint-Joseph* (1985). IntAu&W, 1982

Bastian, Adolph, born 26 June 1826 at Bremen, Germany, reveived a Dr.med. in 1850 from the Universität Würzburg. From 1851 to 1865 he travelled the world, including Syria, Palestine and Egypt. From Qusayr he crossed to Arabia and continued by caravan to Aden. Since 1866 he was a director of the Museum für Völkerkunde, Berlin, as well as a professor at the Universität. His writings include *Ethnologische Forschungen* (1871-73). He died on an expedition in Port-of-Spain, Trinidad, on 2 February 1905. DtBE; Embacher; Henze

Bastico, Ettore, born 9 April 1876 at Bologna, Italy, he was a field marshall and military writer whose writings include *Il ferro Terzo corpo in A.O.* (1937). He died 1 December 1972. Chi è, 1936-1961; IndBiltal (2); Wholtaly, 1958

Bastide, Henri de la, 1916-1986 *see* La Bastide d'Hust, comte Henri Martin de

Bastide, Roger Marius César, born 1 April 1898 at Nîmes, he studied at the universities of Bordeaux and Paris. For many years he was a director of l'École Pratique des Hautes Études and a professor at the Faculté des Lettres de Paris. His writings include *Les problèmes de la vie mystique* (1931), *The mystical life* (1934), *Éléments de sociologie religieuse* (1935), and *Estudios afro-brasileiros* (1951-52). He died in 1974. LC; Unesco; WhoFr, 1971/72

Bastuni, Rustum, of Haifa, born about 1922, he studied architecture at the Haifa School of Architecture. In 1957 he was an Arab labour leader; he was also a sometime Mapam member of the second Knesset. Note

Basu, Basanta Kumar *see* Bose, Basanta Coomar

Bataillard, Paul Théodore, born 23 March 1816 at Paris. After legal studies and graduation from l'École des chartes in 1841, he became an archivist at the Faculté de médecine de Paris. He was sympathetic to Romanian revolutionary ideas and interested in the European Gypsies. He died in Paris on 1 March 1894. DBF; Vapereau

Bataillon, Louis Jacques, fl. 1977, he was joint editor of *La production du livre universitaire au moyen âge; exemplar et pecia* (Paris, C.N.R.S., 1988). LC

Bataillon, Marcel Édouard, born 20 May 1895 at Dijon (Côte-d'Or), he graduated from Lycée Louis-le-Grand, Paris, l'École normale supérieure, and l'École des hautes études hispaniques. He became a professor in Lisbon, Bordeaux, and Algiers. From 1945 to 1965 he was attached to the Collège de France. His writings include *Le roman picaresque* (1931), *Érasme et l'Espagne* (1937), and *Le docteur Laguna, auteur du Voyage en Turquie* (1958). He died in Paris, 4 June 1977. WhoFr, 1965/66-1977/78

Batal, James, born in 1901, his writings include *Assignment Near East* (New York, 1950). LC

Batcheller, George Sherman, born 25 July 1837 at Batchellerville, N.Y., he was a graduate of Harvard Law School and became a prominent New York lawyer and politician. He served for fifteen years at the Mixed Courts of Egypt and the Court of Appeals respectivly. He died in Paris, 2 July 1908. DAB; Shavit

Bate, John Drew, born in 1836, his writings include *A dictionary of the Hindee language* (1875), and *An examination of the claims of Ishmael as viewed by Muhammadans* (1884). He died in 1924. LC

115

Bateman-Champain, Sir John Underwood, born 22 July 1835 at London, he was educated at Cheltenham College. After passing through the military college of the East India Company at Addiscombe, he obtained a commission as second lieutenant in the Bengal engineers in 1853 and went to India in the following year to become principal of the Thomason College at Rurki until the outbreak of the Mutiny. From 1862 to 1872 he was engaged in the construction of the Indo-European telegraph line. He was a member of the Society of Telegraph Engineers. He died in San Remo, 1 February 1887. Boase; BritInd (1); Buckland; DNB, v. 22; Riddick

Bateni, M. R. see Batini, Muhammad Riza

Bates, Daniel Guild, born 12 March 1941 at Long Beach, Calif., he studied at the University of Michigan and Universität Freiburg, and was a National Defense Foreign Language fellow. Since 1971 he was a professor of anthropology at Hunter College, New York, a post which he still held in 1995. His writings include *Nomads and farmers; a study of the Yörük* (1973); he was joint author of *Peoples and cultures of the Middle East* (1983), and *Human adaptive strategies* (1991). AmM&WS 12 (1973); LC

Bates, Michael Lawrence, born 14 October 1941 at Louisville, Ky., he studied at the University of Chicago, where he received a Ph.D. in 1975 for *Yemen and its conquest by the Ayyubids of Egypt*. Since 1977 he was a curator of Islamic Coins at the American Numismatic Society in New York. In the winter term 1996, he taught a seminary at the History Department, UCLA, entitled "Money before machinery." His writings include *Islamic coins* (1982). DrAS, 1982

Bates, Miner Searle, born in 1897, he was affiliated with the United Christian Missionary Society and the International Red Cross Society. His writings include *Half of humanity* (1942), *Religious liberty; an inquiry* (1945), and *China in change* (1969). He died in 1978. Lodwick; LC; *Ohio authors and their books*, edited by William Coyle, 1962

Bates, Ülkü Ülküsal, born 3 December 1938 at Constanţa, Romania, he studied at Istanbul Üniversitesi and the University of Michigan, where he received a Ph.D. in 1970 for *The Anatolian mausoleum of the twelfth, thirteenth and fourteenth centuries*. In 1971 he started teaching at Hunter College, C.U.N.Y., a post which he still held in 2003. IWWAS, 1976/77; NatFacDr, 1995-2003

Bateson, Mary Catherine, born 8 December 1939 at N.Y.C., she studied at Radcliffe College and Harvard University, where she received a Ph.D. in 1963 for *A study of linguistic pattern in pre-Islamic Arabic poetry*. Afterwards she was a professor of anthropology, visiting professor, and dean at universities in the United States and Iran. Her writings include *Approaches to semiotics* (1964), *Arabic language handbook* (1967), *Structual continuity in poetry* (1970), *With a daughter's eye; a memoir of Margaret Mead and Gregory Bateson* (1984), and *Our own metaphor* (1991). LC; WhoAm, 1982-84; WhoAmW, 1981-82, 1991/92

Bathily, Abdoulaye, born 20th cent., he studied at the Centre of West African Studies, University of Birmingham, where he received a Ph.D. in 1976 for *Imperialism and colonial expansion in Senegal in the nineteenth century*. Afterwards he was a lecturer in history at Dakar University. His writings include *Les portes de l'or; le royaume de Galam de l'ère musulmane au temps des négriers* (1989). Africa who's who, 1991, 1996; LC

Batiffol, Pierre Henri, born 27 January 1861 at Toulouse, he was educated at the Séminaire de Saint-Sulpice, Paris, and l'École des Hautes Études. He received doctorates in letters and divinity, and an honorary D.Lit. (Oxford). He was a director of the Institut catholique de Toulouse. His writings include *Saint Grégoire le grand* (1928), and its translation, *Saint Gregory the Great* (1929). He died in Paris, 13 January 1929. DBF; WhE&EA

Bātinī, Muhammad Rizá, born 1313/1935, he was a professor of linguistics at Tehran University. His writings include *Masā'il-i zabānshināsī-i navīn* (1354/1975), *Zaban va tafakkur* (1354/1975), and *Chahār guftār dar bārah-i zabān* (1976). LC

Batissier, Louis, born 29 June 1813 at Bourbon-l'Archambault (Allier), he was sent in 1846 on a mission to Greece, Syria, and Asia Minor, primarily in quest of crusader monuments. Two years later he was appointed French consul at Aleppo, a post which he held until 30 March 1861, when he resigned on account of poor health. His writings include *Éléments d'archéologie nationale* (1843), and *Histoire de l'art monumental dans l'antiquité et au moyen âge* (1845). He died in Enghien, 8 June 1882. Dawson; Egyptology; Vapereau

Batllori i Munne, Miquel, born 1 October 1909 at Barcelona, he studied in Spain and Italy and received a doctorate in history in 1941 from the Universidad de Madrid. A Jesuit since 1928, he was ordained in 1940. His writings include *Cultura e finanze* (1983). Dicc. bio; WhoSpain, 1963; WhoWor, 1978/9

Batmanov, Igor Alekseevich, his writings include *Северные диалекты киргизского языка* (1938), *Язык енисейских памятников древнетюрской письменностн* (1959), and *Таласские памятники древнетюрской письменности* (1971). LC

Bator, Angelika, born 20th cent., she received a Dr.phil. in 1972 from the Universität Leipzig for her thesis, *Die Haupttendenzen der amerikanischen Nahostpolitik seit dem Ende des zweiten Weltkrieges*. Her writings include *Dokumente zur Asienpolitik des amerikanischen Imperialismus, 1945-1980* (1983), and she was joint author, with Wolfgang Bator, of *Unterwegs nach Damaskus* (1964), and *Die DDR und die arabischen Staaten; Dokumente, 1956-1982* (1984). LC

Batowski, Henryk, born in 1907, he was from 1955 to 1977 a professor of history at Universytet Warszawski. In 1986 he edited *Studia Polono-Danubiana et Balcanica*. NEP

al-Batrawi, Ahmad Mahmud, born 12 July 1902 at Kesna, Egypt. After his studies at Cairo University he joined its Anatomical Institute. In 1940 he received a doctorate in anthropology from the University of London for *The racial history of Egypt and Nubia from pre-dynastic to present times*. In 1929-1934 he participated in the Mission archéologique de Nubie, and afterwards published the *Report on the human remains* (1935). He died in Cairo in November 1964. Egyptology; Sluglett

Batsieva (Бациева), Svetlana Mikhailovna, born 30 January 1930 at Leningrad, she graduated in 1951 from Leningrad University, where she also received eight years later a doctorate for *Историко-философский трактат Ибн-Халдун "О природе общественной жизни людейю."* Her writings include *Историко социологический трактат Ибн Халдуна Мукаддима* (1965). In 1984 she was a contributing author to *Арабские рукописи Института Востоковедения; краткий ката-лог*. She died 19 January 1982. LC; Miliband; Miliband²

Battal-Taymas, Abdullah, born in 1882, his writings include *Ibnü-Mühennâ lûgati* (1934), and *Kazan Türkçesinde atasözleri ve deyimler* (1968). He died in 1969. LC; TatarES

Battandier, Jules Aimé, born 8 January 1848 at Annonay (Ardèche), he received a doctorate in natural sciences from the Université de Paris and in 1929 became a professor at the Faculté de médecine et de la pharmacie d'Alger. His writings include *L'Algérie; le sol et les habitants, flore, faune, géologie, anthropologie, resources agricoles et économiques* (1898). He died at Alger, 18 September 1922. DBF

Battersby, Harold Ronald Eric, born 16 November 1922 at Guildford, Surrey, he graduated from the University of Toronto and pursued post-graduate studies at the University of Pittsburgh and Indiana University, Bloomington, where he received a Ph.D. in 1969 for *The Uzbek novel as a source of information concerning material culture, Uzbek town planning, urban development and structures based on information given in Asqad Mukhtor's novel "Sisters."* Since 1970 he was a professor of anthropology, College of Arts and Science, SUNY at Geneseo. AmM&WS 12 (1973); Schoeberlein

Battesti, Térésa Pascale, born 2 June 1934 at Paris, she was an anthropologist and a sometime curator at the Musée de l'homme, Paris. She was joint author of *La pierre et l'homme* (1987). Schoeberlein

Battine, Cecil William, captain, born in 1867, his writings include *The crisis of the Confederacy* (London, 1905), and *A military history of the War* (London, 1916). BLC; LC

Battle, Lucius Durham, born 1 June 1918 at Dawson, Ga., he was an administrator of educational institutions and a diplomat. IntWW, 1990/91-2002; Master (5); Who's who in America, 1996-2003

Batunskii, Mark Abramovich, born 10 December 1933 at Voroshilovgrad, Ukraine, his family was evacuated to Central Asia in 1941 and he graduated in 1956 from Tashkent University. Thereafter he was a research fellow in the Institute of Philosophy and Law of the Uzbek Academy of Sciences. In 1962 he received a doctorate at Tashkent for his thesis, *К критике теоретических основ западно-европейского буржуазного исламоведения*. Since 1968 he was attached to the Institute of Sociology, Akademiia Nauk SSSR. Nevertheless, he was not allowed to pursue a career in the framework of the Soviet academic world, partly because of his support of the Muslim case at home and in neighbouring countries, and partly on account of his sympathies with Jewish culture. He had to publish under a pseudonym and after 1985 abroad. In the period of *perestroika* he was allowed to attend international conferences in Western countries. In 1990/91 he was a visiting professor at the Seminar für Osteuropäische Geschichte in the Universität Köln. Two years later, he emigrated to Germany. Ill health kept him from realizing his academic plans. He died in Köln, 12 April 1997. Central Asian survey 16 iii (1997), pp. 439-440; Miliband

Batur, Selçuk, born 13 December 1939 at Istanbul, he studied architecture at İstanbul Teknik Üniversitesi, 1962-1969. Afterwards he was a lecturer at its Faculty of Architecture. Kim kimdir, 1985/86

117

Baty, Thomas, D.C.L., LL.D., born in 1869 at Stanwix, Cumberland, he was educated at Queen's College, Oxford, and Trinity College, Cambridge. He was a barrister and legal adviser whose writings include *Britain and sea law* (1911), *Canons of international law* (1930), and *Polarized law with an English translation* (1986). He died 9 February 1954. LC; WhE&EA; Who was who, 5

Batzell, Elmer E., he was in 1957 a petroleum consultant to the Republic of Turkey. Together with Walton Hale Hamilton he published *Patents and free enterprise* (Washington, U.S. Goverment Printing Office, 1941.) LC

Bau, Milli, born in 1911, her writings include *Iran wie er wirklich ist* (1971), and *Der fruchtbare Halbmond* (1975). LC

Baud-Bovy, Samuel, born in 1906, he received a doctorate in 1936 from the Université de Genève for his thesis, *La chanson populaire grecque du Dodécanèse*. He wrote *Poésie de la Grèce moderne* (1946), and he translated Christo Zalocosta, *La Grèce, sanctuaire de la Méditerranée* (1948). BN; LC

Baude, Jean Jacques, baron, born 19 February 1792 at Valence (Drôme), he was a politician, a *député*, and a sometime editor of the Paris *Temps*. He was a partisan of surrendering Algeria, an opinion he explained in a brochure published in 1835, *Alger, du système à suivre*. He went to North Africa as a member of the Commission set up to determine the indemnities due to the expropriated indigenous inhabitants. He died in Paris, 7 February 1862. DBF

Baudet, Roger, he was in 1954 head of the *Travaux pratiques* at the School of Dentistry, Kabul. He was the founder and first president of the Groupement philatélique de Kaboul. Note

de **Baudicour**, Louis, born in 1815 at Paris, he was a French settler who founded a small Catholic colony near Blidah, Algeria, where he hoped to have a constructive influence upon his Arab neighbours. He was also a strong supporter of the Maronites who he wanted to see settled in Algeria. His writings include *Des indigènes de l'Algérie* (1852), *La guerre et le gouvernement de l'Algérie* (1853), *La colonisation de l'Algérie* (1856), *La France au Liban* (1879), and *Dawr Faransa fi Lubnan* (1982). He died in Paris, 15 May 1883. DBF; NYPL

Graf von **Baudissin**, Wolf Wilhelm Friedrich, born 26 September 1847 at Sophienhof near Kiel, Germany, he studied theology and Oriental languages at a number of German universities. In 1870 he received a Dr.phil. from the Universität Leipzig for his thesis, *Translationis antiquae arabicae libri Iobi quae supersunt nunc primum edita*. Afterwards he taught Biblical subjects at the universities of Straßburg, Marburg, and Berlin, where he died 6 February 1926. His writings include *Studien zur semitischen Religionsgeschichte* (1876-1878). DtBE; LC; NDB

Bauer, Gérard François, born 8 June 1907 at Neuchâtel, he studied at l'École libre des sciences politiques de Paris. He was a trade counsellor and diplomat. On his eightieth birthday he was honoured by *Un homme et son empreinte; hommage à Gérard Bauer* (1987). LC; Who's who in Switzerland, 1950/51

Bauer, Hans, born 16 January 1878 at Grasmannsdorf near Bamberg, Germany, he started his studies at the Pontifica Università Gregoriana, Roma, but it was not until 1906 that he began his Oriental studies at the universities of Berlin and Leipzig, where he received a Dr.phil. in 1910 for *Die Tempora des Semitischen*. In 1922 he became a Protestant. From 1923 until his death on 6 March 1937 he was a professor at the Universität Halle. He wrote *Die Dogmatik al-Gazali's* (1912). DtBE; EncJud; NDB

Bauer, Ignacio, 1891- *see* Bauer y Landauer, Ignacio

Bauer, Leonhard, born in 1872, he was a school teacher and member of the Deutsche Palästina-Verein. His writings include *Volksleben im Lande der Bibel* (1903), *Das palästinensische Arabisch; die Dialekte des Städters und des Fellachen* (1910), and *Wörterbuch des palästinensischen Arabisch* (1933). Note

Bauer, Victor, of Stettin, Germany, born 19th cent., he received a doctorate in 1904 from the Universität Freiburg i. Br. for *Zur inneren Metamorphose des Centralnerven-Systems der Insecten*. He was a sometime director of fisheries in Turkey and, in 1919, a director of the Institut für Seeforschung and Seenbewirtschaftung, Langenargen am Bodensee. In 1918 he was joint author of *Die Heuschreckenplage und ihre Bekämpfung auf Grund der in Anatolien und Syrien während der Jahre 1916 und 1917 gesammelten Erfahrungen*. In 1936 he published *Zentraleuropa, ein lebendiger Organismus*. Note; NUC, pre-1956

Bauer, Yehuda M., born 6 April 1926 at Praha, he studied at the University of Wales and the Hebrew University, Jerusalem, where he received a Ph.D. in 1960 and subsequently taught history and became head of the Institute of Contemporary Jewry. His writings include *From diplomacy to resistance; a history of Jewish Palestine, 1939-1945* (1970), and *The Jewish emergence from powerlessness* (1979). ConAu, 29-32; IntAu&W, 1977; WhoWorJ, 1972-1987; *Writers directory,* 1976/78-2003

Bauer y Landauer, Ignacio, born in 1891, he received a doctorate in 1912 from the Universidad Central de Madrid for *Joaquin Murat y los últimos tiempos de su reinado en Nápoles.* His writings include *Tánger ha de ser español* (192-), and *Apuntes para una bibliografía de Marruecos* (1922). NUC, pre-1956

Bauermeister, Karl, born 24 September 1888 at Straßburg, he studied at the universities of Straßburg and Marburg. In 1911 he received a Dr.phil. from the Universität Straßburg for *Der Mainzer Erzbischof Berthold von Henneberg als Landesfürst, 1484-1504.* NUC pre-1956

Baumann, Eberhard, born 27 May 1871 at Lübenow, Germany, he studied theology at Tübingen, Leipzig, and Berlin. He travelled in Palestine at the end of the nineteenth century. From 1905 to 1906 he was a member of the Deutsches Institut für Altertumswissenschaft, Jerusalem. From 1907 until his retirement he was a pastor in Halle and later in Stettin. He died in Plön on 1 February 1956. DtBE

Baumann, Heinz, of Frankenthal, Germany, fl. 1962. Together with Manfred Röder he published *Plastoponik: Schaumkunststoffe in der Agrarwirtschaft* (1967). LC

Baumann, Herbert, born 2 June 1938 at Bollstedt, Germany, he received a Dr.phil. in 1965 from the Universität Leipzig for *Die Wiederherstellung des unabhängigen algerischen Staates.* Afterwards he was a member of the Institut für Theorie des Staates und des Rechts, Berlin. His writings include *Staatsmacht, Demokratie und Revolution in der DVR Algerien* (1980), and *Revolutionäre Demokratie in Asien und Afrika* (1989). Kürschner, 1996|

Baumann, Jürgen, born 13 February 1931 at Hamburg, Germany, he received a Dr.jur. in 1967 from the Universität Hamburg for *Die Absicht der Zueignung.* Afterwards he joined the judiciary in Bremen. Thesis

Baumer, Franklin Le Van, born 10 May 1913 at Johnstown, Pa., he studied at Yale University, where he received a Ph.D. in 1938 for *The early Tudor theory of kingship.* Afterwards he taught at New York University, 1937 to 1963, and from 1963 until retirement in 1983, he was Randolph W. Tonsend Professor of History at Yale. His writings include *Main currents of Western thought* (1952). He died on 14 September 1990. DrAS, 1982; WhAm, 10

Bäumer, Gertrud, born 12 September 1873 at Hohenlimburg, Germany, she studied political science and philosophy at Berlin, where she received a Dr.phil. in 1905 for *Goethes Satyros.* She was a leader of the women's liberation movement, the editor of *Die Hilfe,* and *Die Frau,* and, from 1910 to 1919, the president of Bund deutscher Frauenvereine. Her many writings include *Frau und Sport* (1980). She died in Bethel near Bielefeld, 25 March 1954. DtBE

Baumer, Michel C., born 13 May 1928 at Boulogne-Billancourt, (Hauts-de-Seine), he studied at several French universities. Since 1974 he was adviser, Special Sahalian Office, United Nations, N.Y.C. His writings include *Towards a strategy for development in the Sahelian and Sudano-Sahelian zones* (1973), and *Noms vernaculaires soudanais utiles à l'écologiste* (1975). LC; WhoUN, 1975

Baumgart, Winfried, born 29 September 1938 at Streckenbach, Germany, he received a Dr.phil. in 1966 from the Universität Saarbrücken for *Deutsche Ostpolitik im Sommer 1918.* Since 1973 he was a professor of history at Mainz, and a visiting professor in Washington, D.C., Paris, Glasgow, and Riga. His writings include *Deutschland im Zeitalter des Imperialismus* (1972), and *Der Imperialismus* (1975). Kürschner, 1996-2003

Baumgarten, Helga, born in 1947 at Stuttgart, Germany, she studied political science, history, and journalism at Tübingen, SUNY at Stony Brook, L.S.E., and Göttingen. From 1977 to 1979 she was a lecturer at A.U.B., and in 1980 she was a member of the Arbeitsstelle Moderner Vorderer Orient, Berlin. Her writings include *Palästina, Befreiung in den Staat* (1991). LC

Baumgarten, Jörg Holger, Dr. phil., he studied history of art and Turkish, and was a sometime member of the Schnütgen-Museum, Köln. He wrote *Kölner Reliquienschreine* (1985). LC

Baumstark, Anton Joseph Maria Dominikus, born 4 August 1872 at Konstanz, Germany, he studied classics and Oriental languages at the Universität Heidelberg and received a Dr.phil. in 1894 from the Universität Leipzig for *Lucubrationes syro-Graecae.* In 1901 he went to Roma, where he was a founder of *Oriens christianus.* After research in Palestine and Egypt, 1904-1905, he taught Semitic studies and comparative liturgies at Katholieke Universiteit Nijmegen, and Arabic and Islamic studies at the Rijksuniversiteit te Utrecht. From 1930 until his retirement he was a professor at the Universität

Münster. His writings include *Syrisch-arabische Biographien des Aristoteles* (1898). He died in 1948. Bonner, vol. 8, pp. 347-349; DtBE

Baur, Gustav Adolf Ludwig, born 14 July 1816 at Hammelbach, Germany, he studied theology and Oriental languages at Gießen, where he received a Dr.phil. in 1841 for *De Anicio Manlio Severino Boëthio*. Afterwards he was a professor of theology at his alma mater from 1847 to 1861. His writings include *Geschichte der alttestamentlichen Weissagung* (1861). He died in Leipzig in 1889. DtBE

Bauron, Pierre, abbé, his writings include *Les rives illyriennes; Istrie, Dalmatie, Montenegro* (Paris, 1888), and *De Carthage au Sahara* (Tours, 1893). BN

Bausani, Alessandro, born 29 May 1921 at Roma, he studied at the Università di Roma, where he received a doctorate in 1943 for his thesis, *Sviluppi storici della sintassi neopersiana*. From 1944 to 1956 he taught Persian language and literature at Roma. From 1957 to 1971 he was at Napoli, and from 1971 until his retirement again at Roma. His writings include *Il Corano* (1965), *Le letterature del Pakistan e dell'Afghanistan* (1968), *The Persians from the earliest days to the twentieth century* (1971), and *L'islam* (1980). He died in 1988. A commemoration volume was published in 1991, *Yad-nama in memoria di Alessandro Bausani*. Chi è, 1961; IWWAS, 1976/77; Wholtaly, 1980

Bautier, Robert Henri, born 19 April 1922 at Paris, he studied at l'École nationale des chartes, Faculté des lettres de Paris, and l'École des hautes études. From 1961 unitl his retirement in 1990 he was a professor of diplomatics and archival studies at the École nationale des chartes. His writings include *Recherches sur l'histoire de la France médiévale* (1991). LC; WhoFr, 1996/97-2002/2003

Bauzil, Vincent, fl. 1946, he was a sometime *ingénieur en chef des Ponts et Chaussées* and *directeur général adjoint de l'Office du Niger* who wrote *Traité d'irrigation* (1952). LC; Note

Baviera, Giovanni, born 19 July 1875 at Modica, Italy, he was in 1948 a professor of history of Roman law at the Università di Napoli. His writings include *Il diritto internazionale dei romani* (1898). Chi è, 1948, 1961; LC

Baxter, Craig, born 16 February 1929 at Elizabeth, N.J., he was a graduate of the University of Pennsylvania, where he received a Ph.D. in 1967. He became a Foreign Service officer with assignments in India and Pakistan. His writings include *District voting trends in India* (1969), *The Jana Sangh; a biography of an Indian political party* (1969), *Bangladesh, a new nation in an old setting* (1984); and he edited *Zia's Pakistan* (1985). ConAu 25-28, new rev., 11, 26, 52; Master (2); WrDr, 1974/76-1998/2000

Baxter, Edna May, born 30 June 1890 at Nichols, N.Y., she studied at a number of American universities and became a writer on religious education. From 1926 to 1960 she was a professor of education at Hartford Seminary Foundation. She travelled for five months around the Mediterranean. Her writings include *The beginnings of our religion* (1968), and *Ventures in serving mankind* (1984). ConAu, 1; WhoAmW, 1961/62; Writers directory, 1986/88

Baxter, James, C.M.G., born 1 October 1886, he was educated at St Andrew's University. He was a sometime professor of economics at the Cairo Law School. From 1919 to 1928 he was financial secretary to the Egyptian Ministry of Finance. He later served as a financial adviser to the Governor of Burma. He wrote the *Report of Indian immigration* (1941). He died 18 September 1964. BLC; Who was who, 6

Baÿ, Dr., born 19th cent., he was in 1907 secretary-general of the Institut égyptien au Caire.

Bayart, Jean François, born 20th cent., he received a doctorate in political science. He wrote *L'état au Cameroun* (1979), and he was joint author of *La politique par le bas en Afrique noire* (1992). LC

Bayat, Mangol, (Mrs.) Philipp, born in 1937, she received a Ph.D. in 1971 from U.C.L.A. for her thesis, *Mirza Aqa Khan Kirmani, nineteenth century Persian revolutionary thinker*. Her writings include *Mysticism and dissent* (1982), and *Iran's first revolution; Shi'ism and the constitutional revolution of 1905-1909* (1992). LC; NUC, 1973-77

al-Baydani, 'Abd al-Rahman, born 9 August 1926 at Cairo, his writings include *Asrar al-Yaman* (1962). He was still active in 1975. LC

de **Baye**, Amour Auguste Louis *Joseph* Berthelot, baron, born 31 January 1853 at Paris, he was the first historian of barbaric art and devoted all his life to the study of Merovingian jewellery, in the quest of which he travelled all over Europe and to the south of Russia. His writings include *L'archéologie préhistorique* (1888), *A travers quelques villes historiques de la Russie* (1901), and *Chez les Tatars de Crimée; souvenirs d'une mission* (1906). He died in Paris, 3 June 1931. DBF

Bayer, Edmund Alfred, born 12 February 1848 at Erfurt, Germany, he studied philology and history at the universities of Jena, Halle, and Leipzig, where he received a Dr.phil. in 1875 for his thesis, *Gobelinus Persona*. Since 1890 he published Friedrich Rückert's private papers. He died in November 1908. Brümmer; Wrede

Bayer, Franz, Prof. Dr., born 19th cent., he was joint author, with James Connor, of *Deutsch-türki-sches Konversationsbuch zum Gebrauche für Schulen und Reisen* (Heidelberg, 1907). NUC, pre-1956

Bayer, Theodor (also Theophile or Gottlieb) Siegfried, born 6 January 1694 at Königsberg, Prussia, he studied theology, philisophy and Oriental languages at Königsberg from 1710 to 1715. A travel grant from the city enabled him to travel in Germany. During his visit to Halle, he made the aquaintance of August Hermann Francke and also studied Arabic under J. H. Callenberg and, briefly, Solomon Negri. On his visit to Leipzig in 1717 he received a bachelor and master's degree in 1716 and 1717 respectively, and also compiled a hand-list of the Oriental MSS of the Leipzig Municipal Library. After his return to Königsberg, he was first a librarian and then a deputy head of the Kathedralschule until 1725, when he accepted an invitation from the newly-established St. Petersburg Academy. He taught there until 1737, when he decided to return with his family to Königsberg, but he died in St. Petersburg, on 10 February 1738, before leaving. He wrote several works on the history of the Caucasus. He is the subject of Franz Babinger's doctoral dissertation entitled *Gottlieb Siegfried Bayer; ein Beitrag zur Geschichte der morgenländischen Studien im 18. Jahrhundert.* BiobibSOT, pp. 114-115; DtAB; Krachkovskii

Bayerle, Gustav, born 19 May 1931 at Budapest, he studied at the University of Rochester and Columbia University, where he received a Ph.D. in Turkish history for his thesis, *The detailed register of the district of Novigrad of 1570*. Since 1966 he was professor and chairman of the Department of Uralic and Altaic Studies, Indiana University, Bloomington. His writings include *Ottoman diplomacy in Hungary* (1972), and *Ottoman tributes in Hungary* (1973), *Alo Raun bibliography* (1980), and *The Hungarian letters of Ali Pasha of Buda, 1604-1616* (1991). DrAS, 1982; LC

Bayero, Alhaji Ado, born 25 July 1930 at Kano, Nigeria, he was educated at Kano Arabic schools from 1934 to 1939. He studied at the School for Arabic, Kano, and the Clerical Training College, Zaria. He was ambassador to Senegal, Emir of Kano, chancellor of the University of Nigeria and, since 1975, chancellor of the University of Ibadan. Africa who's who, 1991, 1996

Bayet, Charles Marie Adolphe Louis, born in 1849 at Liège, Belgium, he graduated from l'École normale and spent some years at the Écoles françaises d'Athènes et de Rome. Upon his return home, he received a doctorate in 1879. He subsequently held cross-appointments at the Faculté des Lettres and École nationale des beaux-arts de Lyon. In 1891 he became *recteur* of the Academy de Lille. His writings include *Recherches pour servir à l'histoire de la peinture et de la sculpture chrétiennes en Orient avant la querelle des iconoclastes* (1879), and *L'art byzantin* (1883). He died in 1918. Curinier, vol. 5 (1906), p. 396

Bayhum, Muhammad Jamil, 1889- see Beyhum, Mohamed Jamil

Bayle-Ottenheim, Jacques, he was in 1972 a *conseiller technique* at the Centre de Recherche de l'École Supérieure des Sciences Économiques et Commerciales, Paris. He was joint author of *La sous-traitance* (1973). LC; Note

Bayley, Sir Edward Clive, born in 1821, he entered the Indian Civil Service in 1842 and served in the North-West Province and the Punjab. From 1869 to 1874 he was vice-chancellor of Calcutta University. His writings include *The history of India as told by its own historians* (1886). Buckland; DNB

Bayly, Christopher Alan, born 20th cent., he received a Ph.D. in 1970 from Oxford University for his thesis, *The local roots of Indian politics*. He was a sometime member of St. Catherine's College, Cambridge. His writings include *Rulers, townsmen and bazars* (1983), and *Indian society and the making of the British Empire* (1988). LC

Bayne, Edward Ashley, fl. 1950-1971, he wrote *Persian kingship in transition* (1968). LC

Baynes, Herbert M., born 19th cent., he wrote *Dante and his ideal* (London, 1891), *The idea of God and the moral sense in the light of language* (London, 1895), *Ideals of the East* (London, 1895), and *The way of the Buddha* (London, 1906). LC

Bayol, Jean-Marie, born 24 December 1849 at Eyguières (Bouches-du-Rhône), he was educated at Lycée de Nîmes, l'École de médecine navale de Toulon, and received a medical doctorate from the Université de Montpellier in 1874. In the same year he became a medical officer in the French Navy. In the course of his duties, he explored French Equatorial and West Africa up to Bamako. His writings include *Voyage en Sénégambie, Haut-Niger, Bambouck, Fouta-Djallon et Grand-Bélédougou, 1880-1885* (1888). He died 3 October 1905. Henze; *Hommes et destins*, vol. 2, pp. 59-66

Bayon, Peter Georg Heinrich (according to the c.v. in his doctoral dissertation) or Enrico Pietro, and *Henry* Peter, born of Swiss-British lineage on 29 February 1876 at Genova, Italy, he studied at the Polytechnikum in Zürich, and the universities of Zürich, Genève, and Würzburg, where he received a Dr. med. in 1902 for *Erneute Versuche über den Einfluß des Schilddrüsenverlustes*. After a course at the London School of Tropical Medicine, he made a series of voyages as ship surgeon. During the last twenty years of his life as pathologist at Cambridge he took much interest in medical history. He was a founding member of the British Society for the History of Science. In 1938 Cambridge University conferred on him an honorary doctorate. He died at Little Shelford, Cambridge, on 20 October 1952. *British medical journal*, nos. 4796 & 4799 (6 and 27 December 1952), pp. 1260-61, 1424; WhE&EA

Baz, Faruq al- (El), born in 1938 at Zagazig, Egypt, he was educated in Egypt and the United States where he received a Ph.D. in 1964 from the School of Mines and Metallurgy, University of Missouri. He was affiliated with the National Air and Space Museum, Washington, D.C., from 1973 to 1982. His writings include *Say it in Arabic, Egyptian dialect* (1968), and *al-Fada' wa-mustaqbal al-insan* (1977); and he was editor of *Deserts and arid lands* (1984), and joint editor of *Desert land forms of southwest Egypt* (1982), and *Physics of desertification* (1986). ConAu, 25-28, new rev., 10, 26, 51; LC; Master (4)

Baz, Jean Georges, born in 1908 at Dayr al-Qamar, Lebanon, he studied law at the Université Saint-Joseph de Beyrouth, the Faculté française de droit de Beyrouth, and the Faculté de droit de Lyon. Afterwards he was a magistrate, judge, and president of the Court of Appeal. WhoLeb, 1970/71

Bazamah, Muhammad Mustafa, he was a writer on the history of Tripolitania, whose works were published in Benghazi and Tripolis and include *Bidayat al-ma'sah* (1961), *Madinat Binghazi 'abra al-ta'rikh* (1968), and *Qarinah wa-Barqah* (1973). LC

Bazán, Bernardo Carlos, born 26 October 1939 at Mendoza, Argentina, he studied at the Universidad nacional de Cuyo, Mendoza, and the Université catholique de Louvain, where he received a doctorate in philosophy in 1967 and a doctorate in medieval studies in 1971. Since 1979 he was a professor of philosophy at the University of Ottawa. DrAS, 1978 & 1982

Bazargan, Fereydoun, born 20th cent., he received a doctorate in 1963 from the Université de Lausanne for *Étude comparée de la politique éducative et des problèmes scolaires dans six pays d'Orient: Iran, Égypte, Irak, Liban, Pakistan, Turquie.* LC

Bazarian, Carl J., born 20th cent., he was a partner in East-West Group, Ltd., an investment banking and consulting firm specializing in the Middle East. During the 1970s, he worked on Middle East financial and economic developments at the Board of Governors of the Federal Reserve System, on the Treasury Department's U.S.-Saudi Arabia Joint Economic Commission, and at the Overseas Private Investment Corporation. He wrote *The Gulf states* (1980). LC

Bazarova, Dolores Kh., born 20th cent., she was joint author, with Sh. Shukurov, of *Усбекское советское языкознание; библиографические очерки по 1982* (1986). LC

Baziiants (Базиянц), Ashot Padvakanovich, born 12 November 1919 at Astrakhan, he graduated in 1941 from the Azerbaijan State Teachers' Institute, Baku. Since 1953 he was a research fellow at the Oriental Institute of the Academy of Sciences, SSSR. His writings include *Правда интереснее легенд* (1975), and *Над архивом Лазаревых* (1982). In 1963 he edited *Труды Сесси по вопросам истории и экономики Афганистана, Ирана, Турции.* LC; Miliband; Miliband[2]

Bazin, Louis René Pierre, born 29 December 1920 at Caen (Calvados), he studied at the Faculté des lettres de Paris and the École nationale des langues orientales vivantes. In 1972 he received a doctorate for his thesis, *Les calendriers turcs anciens et médiévaux*. From 1978 until his retirement in 1990 he was a professor at the Université de Paris III. His writings include *Introduction à l'étude pratique de la langue turque* (1968), *Les systèmes chronologiques dans le monde turc ancien* (1991) and *Les Turcs, des mots, des hommes* (1994). LC; THESAM, 4; *Who's who in France*, 1996/97-2002/2003

Bazin, Marcel, born 7 April 1944 at Paris, he studied at the École nationale des langues orientales vivantes, where he obtained diplomas in Turkish and Persian. He received doctorates in 1970 and 1980. In 1995 he was a professor at the Université de Reims and joint director of *Studia Iranica*. His writings include *Le Tâlech* (1980), and, with Christian Bromberger, *Gilân et Âzarbâyjân oriental* (1982). AnEIF, 1989, 1997; LC; Schoeberlein; THESAM, 4

Bazmee Ansari, A. S. He was an associated member of the Executive Committee and a contributor to the *Encyclopaedia of Islam*, 2nd edition. He died on 25 March 1989.

al-**Bazzaz**, 'Abd al-Rahman, born 20 February 1913 at Baghdad, he studied at the University of Baghdad and King's College, London. He was an Iraqi government official until he lost favour and was arrested in 1968. His many writings include *On Arab nationalism* (1965), and *al-'Iraq min al-ihtilal hattá al-istiqlal* (1967). Awwad; LC; WhoWor, 1974/75

Beach, Milo Cleveland, born 12 July 1939 at Rochester, N.Y., he received a Ph.D. in 1969 from Harvard University for *Painting at Bundi and Kota*. Since 1988 he was a director of Arthur M. Sackler Gallery in the Freer Gallery of Art, Washington, D.C. His writings include *Gods, thrones, and peacocks* (1965), *The Grand Moghul* (1978), *Early Mughal painting* (1987), and *Mughal and Rajput painting* (1992). *Who's who in America*, 1996-2003; *Who's who in the East*, 1993 & 1995/96

Beadnell, Hugh John Llewellyn, born 14 October 1874, he was educated at King's College, London, and the Royal School of Mines. He spent ten years with the Geological Survey of Egypt and mapped large areas of the Nile Valley and the Libyan Desert. He received numerous awards from geographical and geological societies. His writings include *Dakhla Oasis* (1901), *Baharia Oasis* (1903), *An Egyptian oasis; an account of the Oasis of Kharga in the Libyan Desert* (1909), and *The wilderness of Sinai* (1927). He died in London, 2 January 1944. Egyptology; *Who was who*, 4

Beale, Truxton, born 6 March 1856 at San Francisco, he was a graduate of Pennsylvania Military College, Chester, and Columbia University Law School. From 1891 to 1892 he was appointed Minister to Persia, where he obtained permission for American missionaries to hold land. Between 1894 and 1896 he travelled in Central Asia. In 1916 he edited *The man versus the state; a collection of essays by Herbert Spencer*. He died near Annapolis, Md., 3 June 1936. Shavit; WhAm, 1

Beals, Carleton, born 13 November 1893 at Medicine Lodge, Kansas, he graduated from the University of California in 1916 and became a free lance journalist and author of more than forty-five books. He died 26 June 1979. CurBio, 1941 & 1979; LC

Beaman, Ardern George Hulme, born in 1857, he was an accomplished linguistic, skilled in Turkish, Arabic, and Russian. He originally entered the consular service as student-interpreter and was assigned to Beirut, Damascus, and Cairo. He was an expert on all matters touching Egypt during the last fifty years of his life. He defended the leaders of the revolt of Ahmad Urabi Pasha in the courts at Alexandria in 1882. In 1896 he was a war correspondent of the London *Standard* in the Dongola campaign. His writings include *Twenty years in the Near East* (1898), and *The dethronement of the Khedive* (1929), a work which contains a posthumous introduction. He died 23 July 1929. BritInd (1); Hill; *Who was who*, 3

Beames, John, born 21 June 1837, he entered the Indian Civil Service in 1858 and served until retirement in 1893, mainly in Bengal. His writings include *A comparative grammar of the Aryan languages* (1872-79), *Grammar of the Bengali language* (1894), *Beames' contributions to the political geography of the subahs of Awadh, Bihar, Bengal, and Orissa in the age of Akbar* (1976), and *Memoirs of a Bengal civilian* (1984). Buckland; LC; Mason, pp. 193-200

Bean, Lee Lawrence, born 22 August 1933 at Salt Lake City, Utah, he received a Ph.D. in 1969 in sociology from Yale University. He was a sometime demographic adviser to the Pakistan Institute of Development Economics until he became associate director, Demographic Division, at the Population Council in New York. In 1997 he was still active at the University of Utah. He was joint author of *Family planning in Pakistan* (1968). AmM&WS, 1973

Beard, Michael Crowell, born 28 March 1944, he received a Ph.D. in 1974 from Indiana University, Bloomington, for his thesis, *Sadeq Hedayat's "Blind Owl" and the West; a study in the transmission of genre*. He was a staff member of the English Department, University of North Dakota, Grand Forks, from 1990 to 2003. His writings include *Hedayat's "Blind Owl" as a Western novel* (1990). He was joint editor of *Naguib Mahfouz; from regional fame to global recognition* (1993). NatFacDr, 1995-2003

Beaton, A. C., he was in 1939 an Assistant District Commissioner, Mongalla Province, Anglo-Egyptian Sudan. In 1936 he published, with G. O. Whitehead, *Likikirilen, Bari fables* (London, 1932). Note; WhoEgypt, 1951

Beaton, Donald *Leonard*, born 20 June 1929, he was a Canadian-born British journalist and defence authority. He was correspondent of *the Guardian*, director of studies, the Institute of Strategic Studies, and editor of the *Round table*. His writings include *Must the bomb spread?* (1966), and *Struggle for peace* (1966). He died 9 June 1971. ConAu 29-32

Beatty, Bessie, born 27 January 1886 at Los Angeles, she was a radio commentator, journalist, and author. Her writings include *A political primer for the new voter* (1912), and *The red heart of Russia* (1919). She died 6 April 1947. CurBio, 1944 & 1947

de **Beauchamp**, Joseph, born 29 June 1752 at Vesoul (Haute-Saône), he was an astronomer who, in 1767, entered the *ordre des Bernardins*. When his uncle was appointed Bishop of Babyion in 1776, he accompanied him on the journey. Setting out from Bagdad, he travelled independently to Persia. In the last decade of the eighteenth century he accomplished missions in Egypt and Turkey. He died in Nice, 19 November 1801. DBF; Henze

Beauclerk, George Robert, he was a British captain who wrote *A jouney to Morocco in 1826* (London, 1828), and its German translation in *Ethnographisches Archiv*, 39 (1829), pp. 1-216. Henze; Sezgin

Beaufort, Emily Anne, 1826-1887 *see* Strangford, Emily Anne née Beaufort, viscountess

Beaufort, Sir Francis, born in 1774 at Collon, he was a hydrographer and rear-admiral who, under the orders of the Lords Commissioners of the Admiralty, surveyed the south shore of Turkey. The results he published in *Karamania, or a brief description of the south coast of Asia Minor and of the remains of antiquity* (1817), and its German translation, *Karamanien* (1821). Boase; BritInd (8); Henze

Beaufre, André, born 29 January 1902 at Neuilly-sur-Seine (Seine), he was a French general of the army. His writings include *An introduction to strategy* (1965), *L'expédition de Suez* (1966), and *Die Suez-Expedition* (1968). He died 13 February 1975. ConAu, 65-68; *Who's who in France*, 1959/60-1975/76

Beaugé, Charles, born 19th cent., he was an *ingénieur-divisionnaire* of the Egyptian State Railways at Asyut and wrote *A travers la Haute-Égypte; vingt ans de souvenirs* (1923). NUC, pre-1956

Beaujot, Roderic P., born 22 April 1946 at Whitewood, Sask., he studied at the University of Alberta, where he received a Ph.D. in 1975. In 1976 he began a teaching career as a sociologist and demographer with the University of Western Ontario, London, Ont., a post which he still held in 2003. In 1973 he was joint author of a brief discussion paper entitled *Direct observation as a mode of census evaluation; the Moroccan census of 1971*. His other writings include *Growth and dualism* (1982), and *Population change in Canada* (1991). Canadian, 1996-2002; NatFacDr, 1995-2003

Beaumier, Jean Baptiste Marie Augustin, called *Auguste*, born 22 February 1823 at Marseille, he studied Arabic and spent some time in Morocco before joining the Corps du dragomanat. He was assigned to consulates in Mogador, Tanger, Tunis, and Rabat, later to become a vice-consul. He was the translator of *Roudh el-katas; histoire des souverains du Maghreb*, ascribed to Abu Muhammad Salih ibn Abd al-Halim al-Gharnati (1860). He died in Bordeaux, 30 January 1876. DBF; Embacher; Henze

de **Beaumont**, Adalbert, vicomte, fl. 1865. His writings include *Recherches sur l'origine du blason et en particulier sur la fleur de lis* (Paris, 1853). With E. Collinot he published 1883 in Paris *Ornements arabes, Ornaments de la Perse*, and *Ornaments turcs*. BN; NUC, pre-1956

de **Beaumont**, Gaston du Boscq, b. 1857 *see* Du Boscq de Beaumont, Gaston

Beaumont, Joan, born 25 October 1948 at Adelaide, she received a Ph.D. from King's College, London, and became a lecturer in social science at Deakin University, Victoria, Australia. Her writings include *Comrades in arms; British aid to Russia, 1941-1945* (London, 1980), and the pamphlet *The evolution of Australian foreign policy, 1901-1945* (East Melbourne, Vic., Australian Institute of International Affairs, Victorian Branch, 1989). In 1995 she edited *Australia's war, 1914-1918* (Leonards, NSW, Australia, 1995). *Who's who in Australia*, 2000-2003

Beaumont, Peter, born 21 June 1940, he was a sometime lecturer in geography in the University of Durham. In 1993 he was head of the Department of Geography, Saint David's University College, University of Wales at Dyfed. His writings include *River regimes in Iran* (1973), and *Environmental management and development in drylands* (1989); he was joint author, with Gerald H. Blake and J. M. Wagstaff, of *The Middle East; a geographical study* (1976); and he was joint editor of *Agricultural development in the Middle East* (1985). LC

Beaumont, Roger Alban, born 2 October 1935 at Milwaukee, Wisc., he studied at the University of Wisconsin and Kansas State University, where he received a Ph.D. in 1973. From 1965 to 1973 he taught at the University of Wisconsin. Since 1974 he was a professor of history at Texas A & M University, where he was still active in 1997. His writings include *Military elites* (1974), and *Sword of the Raj; the British Army in India* (1977). DrAS, 1982; NatFacDr, 1995

de **Beaurepaire**, Charles, fl. 1957, he held a law degree and a diploma *d'études juridiques supérieures*. Note

Beauvois, Daniel, born 20th cent., he published translations from the Polish and edited *Pologne, l'insurrection de 1830-1831* (Université de Lille III, 1982), and *Les confins de l'ancienne Pologne, Ukraine, Lituanie, Biélorussie* (Lille, 1988). LC

Beavan, R., fl. 1880, captain, F.R.G.S., C.M.Z.S., Bengal Staff Corps, assistant-superintendent, Survey of India. *Proceedings of the Royal Geographical Society*, 1880

Beawes, William, fl. 1745, he wrote a *Narrative of a journey from Aleppo to Basra in 1745,* which was edited and published by Alexander D. M. Carruthers in his *The desert route to India* (London, 1929). BLC

Beazeley, George Adam, lieut.-colonel, born 7 July 1870, he was educated at the Royal Military Academy, Woolwich, and the School of Military Engineering. From 1897 to 1925 he was attached to the Survey of India. During World War one he served in Mesopotamia, where he was shot down while flying. His writings include *Reconnaissance survey from aircraft* (1927). He died 8 May 1961. LC; *Who was who*, 6

Beazley, Sir Charles *Raymond*, born 3 April 1868 at Blackheath, England, he was educated at King's College, London, and Balliol College, Oxford. From 1906 to 1933 he was a professor of history at the University of Birmingham. He was a visiting professor in the United States and in Germany, and awarded honorary doctorates at Breslau and Oxford. His writings include *Dawn of modern geography* (1897-1906), and *Carpini and Rubruquis, Friar travellers, 1245-1255* (1903). He died 1 February 1955. *Who was who*, 5

Beazley, Elisabeth, fl. 1971, she wrote *Design and detail of the space between buildings* (London, 1960) and, with Michael Harverson, *Living with the desert; working buildings of the Iranian Plateau* (Warminster, 1982).

Becerra Fernandez, Manuel, born 19th cent., he was a Spanish engineer who published the brochure *Notas referentes a la tribu de Kelaia (Rif) y el ferrocarril de Melilla a las minas de Beni-Buifrur* (1909). NUC, pre-1956

Béchade, Henri, fl. 1858, he wrote *La chasse en Algérie* (Paris, 1860). BN

Bechhoefer, William B., he wrote *Serai Lahori; traditional housing in the old city of Kabul* (College Park, Md., School of Architecture, University of Maryland, 1975.) NUC, 1978

Bechtold, Peter Klaus, born 5 December 1937 at Wertheim, Germany, he studied at Portland State University and Princeton, where he received a Ph.D. in 1967 for *Parliamentary elections in the Sudan*. Between 1964 and 1982, he visited the Sudan on nine different occasions for field research. In 1968 he became a professor of government and political science at the University of Maryland, College Park, Md. In 1983 he was chairman for Near Eastern and North African Studies at the Foreign Service Institute, U.S. Department of State. His writings include *Politics in the Sudan* (1976). AmM&WS, 1973, 1978

Bechtoldt, Heinrich, born 28 January 1911 at Frankfurt am Main, he was a sometime professor of political science at the universities Tübingen and Stuttgart-Hohenheim. He wrote *Staaten ohne Nation* (1980). He died 23 March 1990. Kürschner, 1980-1987

Beck, Alexander, born 5 August 1900 at Basel, he received a Dr.jur. in 1927 from the Universität Heidelberg for his thesis, *Das Unrechtsbewußtsein in den deutschen Strafgesetzentwürfen*. He was a professor emeritus of the Universität Bern. His writings include *Römisches Recht bei Tertullian und Cyprian* (1930). He was honoured by *Itinera iuris; Arbeiten zum römischen Recht und seinem Fortleben* (1980). He died in Bern, 9 December 1981. Kürschner, 1976-1983

Beck, Edmund *Michael*, Pater, born 6 November 1902 at Huldessen, Germany, he received a Dr.phil. in 1959 from the Universität München for his thesis, *Die Koranzitate bei Sibawaih*. In 1961 he was affiliated with the Collegio S. Anselmo, Roma. His writings include *Ephräms Polemik gegen Mani und die Manichäer* (Louvain, Scriptorum Christianorum Orientalium,1978). Kürschner, 1961|; LC

Beck, Lois Conchita Grant, born 5 November 1944 at Bogota, Columbia, she studied anthropology at Portland State University and the University of Chicago, where she received a Ph.D. in 1977 for her thesis, *Local organization among Qashqa'i nomadic pastoralists in southwest Iran*. For a year, in 1970-71, she lived with members of the Qermezi, a sub-tribe of the Qashqa'i Confederation in Iran. In 1980 she became a professor at Washington University, St. Louis, Mo., a post which she still held in 2003. Her writings include *The Qasqa'i of Iran* (1986), and *Nomad; a year in the live of a Qashqa'i tribesman in Iran* (1991), and she edited *Women in the Muslim world* (1978). NatFacDr, 1995-2003; WhoAm, 1996, 2003

Beck, Michael, born 1902 *see* Beck, Edmund Michael

Beck, Peter J., born 20th cent., he wrote *The international politics of Antarctica* (New York, 1986). ZKO

Beck, Sebastian, Prof., born in 1878, his writings include *Neupersische Konversations-Grammatik* (1914) and, with Alexander Tehrani, *Iran* (Berlin, 1943); and he was joint editor of *Der islamische Orient; eine Sammlung gemeinnütziger orientalischer Schriften zur Föderung des Studiums islamischer Sprachen* (Heidelberg, 1917-1920). NUC, pre-1956

Beck, Theodore, born in 1859, he was educated at the University of London and Trinity College, Cambridge. In 1883 he was appointed Principal of the Muhammadan Anglo-Oriental College in Aligarh. He died in Simla, 2 September 1899. Buckland; IndianBilnd (1); *Muhammadan Anglo-Oriental College magazin*, n.s., 7 (October 1899), pp. 1-21; Riddick

Bečka, Jiří, born 16 October 1915 at Praha, he studied Oriental languages and Middle Eastern history at Universita Karlova, Praha, where he received a doctorate in 1954. Since 1952 he was a member of the Oriental Institute of the Czechoslovak Academy of Sciences. His writings include *A study of Pashto stress* (1969), *Úvod do paštského jazyka* (1979), and *Sadriddin Ayni, father of modern Tajik culture* (1980), and as joint author, *Islám a česke země* (1998). Kdo je kdo, 1991/92; Schoeberlein

Becker, Abraham Samuel, born 7 February 1927 at N.Y.C., he studied at Harvard and Columbia University, where he received a Ph.D. in 1959 for his thesis, *Economics of the cotton textile industry of the USSR, 1928-1955*. Since 1957 he was affiliated with the Rand Corporation, Santa Monica, Cal., for who he wrote a number of research memoranda. He was joint author of *The economics and politics of the Middle East* (1975). AmM&WS, 1973 S, 1978 S; ConAu, 33-36

Becker, Beatrix, 1941- see Pfleiderer-Becker, Beatrix

Becker, Carl Heinrich, born 12 April 1876 at Amsterdam, he studied at the universities of Lausanne, Heidelberg and Berlin. From 1900 to 1902 he travelled to Spain, Egypt, the Sudan and Turkey. He became a teacher of Semitic philology, a professor of Oriental history, and director of the Oriental Institute at Hamburg. He was editor of *der Islam*, a Prussian Minister of Education, and a pioneer of Islamic studies who contributed two chapters on early Islamic history to the *Cambridge medieval history*. He did interesting and encouraging research but lost contact and did not find his way back from public life. His writings include *Das Erbe der Antike in Orient und Okzident* (1931). But he is best remembered for his *Islamstudien* (1924-1932). He died in Berlin, 10 February 1933. Bonner, vol. 8, pp. 330-337; DtBE; Fück

Becker, Fridolin, Prof., born in 1854, he wrote *Die schweizerische Kartographie* (1900), *Über den Klausen auf neuer Gebirgsstrasse* (1900), and *Karte von Jerusalem und Mittel-Judäa für Palästina-Reisende* (1914). He died in 1922. LC; NUC, pre-1956

Becker, Friedrich, he was joint author of *Yabanci işçiler için bilgiler Federal Almanya'daki hak ve görevleriniz* (Wiesbaden, 1973.)

Becker, Seymour, born 15 September 1934 at Rochester, N.Y., he received a Ph.D. in 1963 from Harvard University for his thesis, *Russia's Central Asian protectorates; Bukhara and Khiva, 1865-1917*. He was a sometime professor of history at Rutgers University, New Brunswick, N.J. His writings include *Russia's protectorates in Central Asia; Bukhara and Khiva, 1865-1924* (1968), and *Nobility and privilege in late Imperial Russia* (1985). ConAu, 25-28 rev.; DrAS, 1974, 1978, 1982; LC; Schoeberlein

Becker y Gonzáles, Jerónimo, born in 1857, he was a political writer and editor of the Madrid periodicals *La Regencia* (1889), *El Clamor* (1891), *El Nacional* (1894), and collaborated with *La España moderna* and *Ilustración española*. He was a member of the Real Academia de la Historia. His writings include *España y Marruecos* (1903), *Historia de Marruecos* (1915), and *Tratados, convenios y acuerdos referentes á Marruecos y la Guinea española* (1918). He died in 1925. LC; Ossorio

Beckingham, Charles Fraser, born 18 February 1914 at Houghton, Huntingdonshire, he studied at Queen's College, Cambridge. After graduation he joined the Department of Printed Books of the British Museum, where Arabic began to occupy an increasingly important place in his private study. In the 1940s, he saw service with the military intelligence in the Middle East. It was not until 1951 that he entered academic life at Manchester University as a lecturer in Islamic history, becoming professor of Islamic studies in 1958. From 1969 until his retirement in 1981 he was a professor at SOAS. During his latter period he was also president both of the Hakluyt Society and the Royal Asiatic Society. He pursued a lifelong interest in travel and exploration in the Indian Ocean and adjoining countries both prior and during the arrival of Europeans in the area in the 16th century. His writings include *Some records of Ethiopia, 1593-1646* (1954), and a volume of his collected articles. He died 30 September 1998. *Asian affairs* n.s., 30 (1999, p. 127; Bulletin of the Association for the Study of Travel in Egypt and the Near East, no. 7 (1999), p. 14; Who's who, 1973-1999

Beckwith, John Gordon, born 2 December 1918 at Southend, England, he was a graduate of Exeter College, Oxford. He rose from assistant keeper at the Victoria and Albert Museum, London, in 1948 to keeper at his retirement. Concurrently he was a visiting professor at universities in the United States, and Slade Professor of Fine Art, Oxford University, 1978-79. He wrote *Caskets from Cordoba* (1960), and *The art of Constantinople* (1961). He died 20 February 1991. ConAu, 9-12; Who, 1977-1991

Beddie, James Stuart, born in 1902, his writings include *A family history* (1986). LC

Beddis, Rex Anthony, fl. 1963-1971, he was a British geographer whose writings include *Africa, Latin America and the lands of the south-west Pacific* (1968), and *Asia and North America* (1969). BLC; LC

Beddoe, John, born 21 September 1826 at Bewdley, England, he studied at University College, London, and the Universität Wien. Afterwards he was a professor of anthropology at Bristol University, assistant physician, Civil Hospital Staff in the Crimean War, and president of a number of learned societies. His writings include *Memoires of eighty years* (1910). He died 19 July 1911. Master (3); Who was who, 1

Bedeau, Marie *Alphonse*, born 19 August 1804 at Vertou (Loire-Inf.). After a military career in metropolitan France he participated in the conquest of Algeria since 1838. With the rank of general he became commander of Tlemcen in 1841, and was in charge of the operations in Oranie. As commanding officer of the Division de Constantine he distinguished himself in the administration and pacification of the region. At the end of 1847 he was recalled to France, where he died in Nantes, on 30 August 1863. Azan, pp. 102-106; Peyronnet, p. 96

Bédier, Charles Marie *Joseph*, born 28 January 1864 at Paris, he was a medievalist and educated at the Lycée Louis-le-Grand. After graduation from l'École Normale Supérieure in 1886, he taught at the universities of Halle and Fribourg. In 1893 he received a doctorate from the Université de Paris for his thesis, *De Nicolao Museto*. Afterwards he was a professor at the École Normale Supérieure and the Collège de France. His writings include *Les Fabliaux; études de littérature populaire et d'histoire du moyen âge* (1893). He died in August 1938. BN; *Hommes et destins*, vol. 4, pp. 62-64

Bedir-Khan, Kamuran (Qamiran) Ali, born in 1894 in Syria, he studied in the Ottoman Empire and from 1922 to 1926 at the Universität Leipzig, where he received a Dr.jur. for his thesis, *Das türkische Eherecht nach den Grundsätzen der hanafitischen Lehre*. Afterwards he practised law in Beirut and Damascus, where he published Kurdish periodicals and was active in the Kurdish movement. In 1947 he moved to Paris, where he subsequently became a professor of Kurdish at the Sorbonne. He published in Kurdish and French on politics and Kudish language and literature. He died in 1978. EncIran

Bedjaoui, Mohammed Benali, born 21 September 1929 at Sidi-bel-Abbès, Algeria, he studied law at the Université de Grenoble, where he received a doctorate in 1958 for *Fonction publique internationale et influences nationales*. Since 1958 he was engaged in the Algerian freedom movement. He was Algerian Minister of Justice, ambassador to France, and permanent representative to the UN. His writings include *La révolution algérienne et le droit* (1961), and *Succession d*états* (1971). Africa who's who, 1991-1996; IntWW, 1974-2002; WhoFr, 1979/1980-1983/84; WhoUN, 1975; WhoWor, 1974/75-1978/79

Bedore, James M., born 20th cent., he was in 1977 a research assistant at the Royal Institute of International Affairs, London. He was joint author, with Louis M. Turner, of *Middle East industrialization* (1979). LC

Bedoucha-Albergoni, Geneviève *see* Albergoni, Geneviève

Bedr-Chan, Kamuran Ali, 1894-1978 *see* Bedir-Khan, Kamuran Ali

Bedrosian, Robert, born 20th cent., he received a Ph.D. in 1979 from Columbia University for his thesis, *The Turco-Mongol invasions and the lords of Armenia in the 13th-14th centuries*. He published translations from the Armenian as well as *Armenia in ancient and medieval times* (New York, Armenian National Education Committee, 1985). LC

Bedwell, William, 1563-1632, he was the first modern English Arabist, but during most of his life an isolated figure. The principal result of his studies was an Arabic lexicon which was never printed, although he bequeathed the manuscript to Cambridge University with a fount of Arabic type for that purpose. Alastair Hamilton wrote a biography, *William Bedwell, the Arabist* (1985). DNB

Beebe, B. T. born 20th cent., he received a Ph.D. in 1970 from the University of St. Andrews for his thesis, *Edward I and the crusades*. Sluglett

Beech, Harlan P., fl. 1912, he wrote *A geography and atlas of the Protestant missions* (1906). NUC

Beech, Mervyn Worcester Howard, born 19th cent., he wrote *The Suk; their language and folklore* (Oxford, 1911), and *Aids to the study of ki-Swahili* (1918). BLC; LC

Beek, Wiero Jan, born 6 July 1932 at den Haag, he studied engineering at the Technical University Delft and received a doctorate in 1962. Afterwards he was a professor; from 1970 to 1987 he was director, Unilever. His writings include *Stofoverdracht door beweeglijke grensvlakken* (1963), *Transport phenomena* (1975), and *De toekomst van onze voedingsmiddelenindustrie* (1984). LC; Wie is wie in Nederland, 1994/96

Beeley, Brian William, born about 1936. In 1959 he received a Ph.D. in 1959 from the University of Durham for his thesis, *The individual and changing rural society in Malta*. During his later career, he taught at the Open University at Brighton. His writings include *The farmer and rural society in Malta* (1959), *Köysel Türkiye bibliyografyası* (1969), and *Rural Turkey; a bibliographic introduction* (1969). In 1997 he was still affiliated with the Open University. LC; Sluglett

Beeley, Sir Harold, born 15 February 1909, he was a graduate of Queen's College, Oxford, and from 1930 to 1939 lectured in history at various English universities. In 1946 he entered the Foreign Service and was successively British Ambassador to Saudi Arabia (1955), Assistant Under-Secretary at the Foreign Office (1956-58), and Ambassador to the United Arab Republic (1967-69). He wrote *Disraeli* (1936). He died 27 July 2001. IntWW, 1974/2002; Master (4); Who, 1956-2001

Beeman, William Orman, born 1 April 1947 at Manhattan, Kan., he studied at Wesleyan University and the University of Chicago, where he received a Ph.D. in 1976 for *The meaning of stylistic variation in Iranian verbal interaction*. Afterwards he was a professor at various American universities. In 1995 he was a professor of anthropology at Brown University, Providence, R.I., a post which he still held in 2003. His writings include *Culture, performance and communication in Iran* (1982), and *Language, status, and power in Iran* (1986). LC; NatFacDr, 1995-2003; Who's who in the East, 1979/80

Beer, Bernhard, born in 1801 at Dresden, Germany, he was privately educated in the Talmud, Hebrew as well as in modern languages and literatures, and studied at the Universität Leipzig. He was active in Jewish community life in Saxony and through his writings and personal conduct achieved considerable success towards Jewish civil equality. His writings include *Das Leben Abraham's nach der Auffassung der jüdischen Sage* (1859). He died in Dresden, 1 July 1861. DtBE; EncJud; Wininger

Beeri, Eliezer, born in 1914 at Mannheim, Germany, he studied at the Universität Berlin and was a sometime director of the Arab Workers' Department at the Israeli Ministry of Labour. His writings include *Army officers in Arab politics and society* (1970), *ha-Palestinim tahat snilton Yarden* (1978), and *Reshit ha-sikhsukh Yiśra'el-'Arab, 1882-1911* (1985). LC; Who's who in Israel, 1972, 1973/74|

Be'eri, Shemu'el, fl. 1959, he was a sometime editor of the *New outlook* but left journalism in 1970 to become a kibbutz school teacher. Note

Bees, Nikos Athanasiou, born in 1882, he was a Greek writer on palaeography, manuscripts and history of art. His writings include *Die Inschriftenaufzeichnung des Kodex sinaiticus graecus 508 und die Maria-Spiläotissa-Klosterkirche bei Sille (Lykaonien); mit Exkursen zur Geschichte der Seldschukiden-Türken* (Berlin, 1922). He died in 1958. NUC, pre-1956

Beeson, Irene, born 20th cent., she was a free lance writer for Beirut newspapers and lived in Cairo in 1970. She was joint author, with D. Hirst, of *Sadat* (1981). LC

Beeston, Alfred Felix Landon, born 23 February 1911, he was educated at Westminster School and Christ Church College, Oxford. From 1935 to 1955 he was affiliated with the Department of Oriental Books at the Bodleian Library and subsequently served until his retirement in 1979 as Laudian Professor of Arabic at Oxford. Despite his considerable shyness, he was a convivial soul, at his best with small groups of students and colleagues. The esteem in which he was held resulted in two felicitation volumes, *Sayhadica* (1987), and *Arabicus Felix Luminosus Britannicus* (1991). He was greatly touched by these, but what gave him most pleasure was his Emeritus Fellowship at St. John's. The college and its chapel were the focal points of his life for almost forty years, and there can have been no place more fitting for him to collapse and die than at the college gates on 29 September 1995. He never married. BSOAS 60 (1997) p. 117; CentBritOr, pp. 50-71; JSS 41 (1996), pp. 199-201; Private; The Times, 6 October 1995; Who, 1984-1996

Beffa, Marie Lise, born 1 February 1942 at Nice, she received a doctorate from the Université de Paris, where she became a *maître de conférences*. Her writings include *Éléments de grammaire mongole* (1975). She was joint author of *Manuel de langue mongole* (1975), and joint editor of *Figures du corps* (1989). LC; Schoeberlein

Beg, Abdulla Anwar. His writings include *The poet of the East; the life and work of Sir Muhammad Iqbal* (Lahore, 1939), *The life and odes of Ghalib* (Lahore, 1941), and *Hayat-i Iqbal* (Delhi, 1974). LC

Beg, M. Afzal, born 20th cent., he was a research economist at the Pakistan Institute of Development Economics, before he became in 1972 a professor at the Institute of Statistics, University of the Punjab, Lahore. Note

Beg, Mirza Arshad Ali, born 20th cent., he studied chemistry at the universities of Karachi and British Columbia, where he received a Ph. D. He was a senior research officer at the Pakistan Council of Scientific and Industrial Research, before he became the director of its facilities in Karachi in 1985. His writings include *New dimensions in sociology* (1987). LC; Note

Begdeli, Gulamhusein, fl. 1962, his writings include *Shărg ădăbijjatynda "Khosrov va Shirin" movzusu* (Baku, 1970), and *Ustad Shariyar la görüsh* (Tehran, 1979). LC

Begley, Wayne Edison, born 29 December 1937 at Kenvir, Ky., he studied at several American universities and received a Ph.D. in 1966 in Oriental studies from the University of Pennsylvania for his thesis, *The chronology of Mahayana Buddhist architecture and painting at Ajanta*. Since 1966 he was a professor of Indian and Islamic studies at the University of Iowa. His writings include *Monu-mental Islamic calligraphy from India* (1985). WhoAmArt, 1995/96

Begmatov, Ernst Azimovich, fl. 1975, his writings include *Hozirgi uzbek adabii tilining leksik qatlamlari* (1985); he was a contributor to *Ономастика Узбекистана* (1989). LC

Begović, Mehmed Dž, born 8 April 1904, he was a sometime lecturer at Belgrade University. His writings include *Шеријатско брачно право* (1936), and *Вакуфи у Југославији* (1963). EncJug; JugoslSa, 1970; Ko je ko, 1957

Béguin, Hubert, born 23 July 1932 at Gand, Belgium, he received a doctorate in geography from the Université de Liège, He was from 1956 to 1961 a research fellow at the Institut national d'Étude agronomique du Congo, and a United Nations expert from 1963 to 1968. Afterwards he was *maître de conférences* at the Université de Liège. His writings include *Modèles géographiques pour l'espace rural africain* (Bruxelles, 1964). LC; Qui est qui en Belgique francophone, 1981/85

Béguinot, Augusto, born 17 October 1875 at Paliano (Frosinone), Italy, he studied at the Università di Roma. Since 1900 he was a research fellow at the Istituto botanico di Padova, where he pursued an interest in Mediterranean botany. His writings include *Contributo alla flora dell'Armenia* (1912), and *La botanica* (1920). He died in Genova, 3 January 1940. DizBI; LC

Béguinot, Francesco, born 1 August 1879 at Paliano (Frosinone), Italy, he studied Oriental languages at the Scuola orientale and the Università di Roma. He was a sometime professor of Berber languages at the Istituto Universario Orientale di Napoli and a director of the Sezione di africanistica. His writings include *Cronaca abbrevieta d'Abissinia* (1901), *Il berbero Nefûsi di Fassâto* (1931), and *Istituzioni musulmane* (1938). He died in Napoli, 2 March 1953. DizBI; I.I. (3)

de **Behagle**, Ferdinand, born in 1857 at Ruffec (Charente), he started life as a captain in the merchant marine and subsequently served from 1885 to 1891 as an administrator of mixed communities in Algeria. During the last years of his life he was involved in the establishment of French commercial routes from the Congo to the Mediterranean by way of the Chad. His last mission ended on the gallows in Dikoa in mid-September 1899. Hommes et destins, vol. 9, pp. 23-26

El-**Behairy**, Mohammed, born in 1931, In 1961 he received a Ph.D. in 1961 from Ohio State University, Columbus, for his thesis, *The Suez Canal in world politics, 1941-1961*. NUC, 1968-1972

Behari, Bankey, B.Sc., LL.B., born in 1905, he originally trained as a lawyerand was the author of two standard legal texts. He later pursued an interest in mysticism and in 1940 became a Hindu monk. He later lived as a hermit at Vrindaban, India. His writings include *Mysticism in the Upanishads* (Gorakhpur, 1940), *The story of Mira Bai* (Gorakhpur, 1941), *Selections from Fariduddin Attar's Tadhkaratul-auliya* (Lahore, 1961), and *Sufis, mystics and yogis of India* (Bombay, 1962). Note

Beheschti, Mohammed, born 30 September 1926 at Shiraz, where he attended primary and secondary schools from 1935 to 1950. From 1952 to 1959 he studied agriculture at the Landwirtschaftliche Hochschule Stuttgart-Hohenheim, where he obtained a Dr.phil. in 1959 for *Die Agrarverfassung und die sich daraus ergebenden Perspektiven für die Entwicklung . . . im Iran.* LC

Behm, Ernst, born 4 January 1830 at Gotha, Germany, he studied medicine at the universities of Jena, Berlin, and Würzburg, where he received a Dr.med. in 1853 for his thesis, *Über die Physiologie der Milz*. Through travel literature he discovered his passion for geography. In 1856 he became editor of the *Geographische Mitteilungen des Geographischen Instituts von Gotha*. Together with Hermann Wagner he published since 1872 *Die Bevölkerung der Erde*. He died in Gotha, 15 March 1884. DtBE

Behm, Jonny, *pseud.*, born 1898 *see* Joost, Elisabeth

Behn, Wolfgang Hermann Lewin, born 14 September 1931 at Dessau, Germany, he was educated in Breslau, Franckeschen Stiftungen, Halle, and Rostock. By the time he left high school with undistinguished marks in 1948, he had attended seven different schools in ten years, of which one year was spent in a war-time evacuation camp, and half a year lost during the aftermath of the war. The political climate prevented his completing an apprenticeship as photographer. In 1953 the family emigrated to the United States, where he soon had to register with the local draft board and start serving in the 10th Infantry Division at Fort Riley, Kansas, on 2 January 1955. He deserted in August of the same year and emigrated to Toronto, Canada. During the winter of 1957-58 he travelled in Europe and took the Cours de civilisation française at the Sorbonne. From 1958 to 1959 he was a full-time student at Harbord Collegiate Institute in Toronto. Afterwards he travelled with his wife overland by scooter from Paris to Damascus and back. After passing the Ontario grade thirteen high school examinations in 1962, he pursued Islamic studies at University College, Toronto, from 1962, gaining a B.A. (Hons.) with the class of 1966. After a winter semester at Hamburg, he returned to Toronto to take an M.A. in Islamic studies, followed by a B.L.Sc. in 1969. The following three years, he was Islamic book selector at the University of Toronto Library, adding some five thousand vernacular publications annually to its research collection. In 1972 he accepted an offer from the Staatsbibliothek, Berlin, to become editor of the Union catalogue of Islamic publications as well as Persian subject specialist, a position which he held until his retirement in 1996. His professional development was greatly influenced by J. D. Pearson's Middle East Libraries Committee in the UK, and the British Society for Middle Eastern Studies, of which he was a founding member. He translated from the German, *The Zahiris*, by I. Goldziher (1971); from the Dutch, *Muhammad and the Jews of Medina*, by A. J. Wensinck (1975); from the Arabic, *Orient and Occident*, by Ahmad Amin (1984). Between 1979 and 1984 he collected, compiled and published four bibliographies of non-commercial literature on the Islamic revolution in Iran. Concurrently he launched the *Islamic book review index*, published annually from 1982 to 1992, when his time was taken up increasingly by *Index Islamicus, 1665-1905* (1989), and its *Supplement, 1665-1980*, in two parts (1995-1996). Independence was a quality of his character; a solitary worker, he found joy in his labours. He had a life-style to the point of austerity. His regular and early hours enabled him to produce the maximum of work every day. He wasted nothing, least of all, time. His was a disciplined life of a bio-bibliographer, to which he freely committed himself from day to day, year to year. Apart from this, he also had his diversion, particular sports, which he practised to his old age. AnEIF, 1987, 1997; DrBSMEs, 1993; EURAMES, 1993; IWWAS, 1975-77; JahrDtB, 1973-1993

Behnstedt, Peter, born in 1944, he received a Dr.phil. in 1973 from the Universität Tübingen for his thesis, *Viens-tu, est-ce que tu viens, tu viens? Formen und Strukturen des direkten Fragesatzes im Französischen*. His writings include *Die Dialekte der Gegend von Sa'dah, Nord-Jemen* (1987), and *Glossar der jemenitischen Dialektwörter in Eduard Glasers Tagebüchern* (1993). LC

Behrends, Frederick Otten, born 10 August 1934 at Wilmington, N.C., he received a Ph.D. in 1962 from the University of North Carolina for his thesis, *Bishop Fulbert and the diocese of Chartres, 1026-1028*. In 1977 he became a professor of history at the University of North Carolina, Chapel Hill, a post which he still held in 1995. His writings include *The letters and poems of Fulbert of Chartres* (1976). DrAS, 1982; NatFacDr, 1995

Behrens, Gerhard Leonidas, born 5 January 1938 at Piraeus, Greece, he received a Dr.jur. in 1970 from the Universität Hamburg. for his thesis, *Internationales und interpersonales Privat- und Prozeßrecht in Jordanien*. In 1997 he was president of the Deutsch-Arabische Handelskammer, Cairo. His writings include *Das Kollisionsrecht Jordaniens* (1970). Wer ist wer, 1996/97-2002/2003

Behrens, Helmut, born 22 February 1947 at Hannover, he studied at the Technische Universität Berlin, where he received a Dr.phil. in 1978 for *Die Profanbauten von Christoph Hehl; eine Studie zur Architektur der Hannoveranischen Schule*. In 1977 he became a civil servant in Kiel. Thesis

Behrens-Abouseif, Doris, born ca. 1940, she studied at the Universität Hamburg. where she received a Dr.phil. in 1972 for her thesis, *Die Kopten in der ägyptischen Gesellschaft von der Mitte des 19. Jahrhunderts bis 1923*. She was a visiting professor at AUC, München, Harvard, and Freiburg im Breisgau. Her writings include *The minarets of Cairo* (1985), *Fath-Allah and Abu Zakariyya, physicians under the Mamluks* (1987), *Islamic architecture in Cairo* (1992), and *Egypt's adjustment to Ottoman rule* (1994). Kürschner, 1996-2003

Behrman, Lucy C., born 1940 *see* Creevey, Lucy E.llsworth

Behrmann, Walter, born 22 May 1882 at Oldenburg, Germany, he received Dr.phil. in 1906 from the Universität Göttingen for his thesis, *Über die niederdeutschen Seebücher des 15. und 16. Jahrhunderts*. He taught geography at several German universities; when he retired he was a professor at the Freie Universität Berlin. He died there in 1955. DtBE; Kürschner, 1925-1954

Behrnauer, Walter Friedrich Adolph, born 8 March 1827 at Bautzen, Saxony, he was from 1852 to 1857 affiliated with the k.k. Hofbibliothek Wien, and since 1857 with the Königliche Öffentliche Bibliothek zu Dresden. He was a sometime lecturer in Turkish language and literature. In October 1868 he approached the Library of Congress, Washington, D.C., with the purpose of obtaining a publication grant for his *Risala djahsarijja*, by Ibn Zaidun, and *Kirk wizir*, by Scheichzade. His writings include *Die vierzig Veziere oder weisen Männer* (Leipzig, 1851), *Quellen zur serbischen Geschichte* (Wien, 1857), and *Sulaiman's Tagebuch* (Wien, 1858). Haan

Behzadi, Ismail Pasha ogly, his writings include Произведение Раванди *"Рахет-ус-судур ве аjет-ус-сурур"* как исторический источник (Baku, 1963).

Beigel, Georg Wilhelm Sigismund, born 25 September 1753 at Ippesheim, Bavaria, he studied law at the Universität Leipzig, where he received a doctorate. In 1786 he entered the foreign service of the Elector of Saxony. In 1813 he was appointed librarian at the Dresden public library, a post he held until 1826 when he retired for reasons of poor health. He died in Dresden, 25 January 1837. DtBE

Beijan, Dr. A. see Bizhan, Asad Allah

Beilis, Vol'f Mendelevich, born 24 March 1923 at Vasil'kov, Ukraine, he was educated in Kiev and received a doctorate in 1975 for his thesis, Сочинения Масуда ибн Намдар как источник по истории Аррана и Ширвана нахала XII вю и памятник средневековой арабской литературы. He edited Mas'ud ibn Namdar, Спорник рассказов, писем и стихов (1970), andТрактат о хирургии и инструментах; факсимиле рукописи (1983). LC; Miliband; Miliband²

Beinin, Joel, born 21 November 1948 at Philadelphia, Pa., he studied at Princeton and the University of Michigan, where he received a Ph.D. in 1982 for his thesis, *Class conflict and national struggle; labor and politics in Egypt, 1936-1954*. Afterwards he was a professor of history at Stanford University. He was a member of the American History Association, the Middle East Studies Association of North America, and review editor of *Middle East report*. His writings include *Was the red flag flying there; Marxist politics and the Arab-Israeli conflict in Egypt and Israel, 1948-1965* (1990). With Zachary Lockman he published *Workers on the Nile* (1987). LC; NatFacDr, 2003; Private

Beisembiev, Kasym Beisembievich, born 5 September 1919, he received a doctorate in philosophy in 1960. His writings include Очерки истории общественнодолитической и философсдлой мысли Казахстана (1976), and he was joint editor of Великие ученые Средней Азии и Казахстана (1965). Kazak SE

Beishenaliev, Shukurbek, born in 1928 at Ak-Talaa, Kirgizia, his writings include *The horned lamb* (1969), Стальное перо (1987), and Сын Сарбая (1987). Kyrgyz SE

Beit-Hallahmi, Benjamin, born 12 June 1943 at Tel Aviv, he studied at the Hebrew University of Jerusalem and Michigan State University, where he received a Ph.D. in 1970. In 1973 he became a lecturer in psychology at the University of Haifa. His writings include *Psychoanalysis and religion; a bibliography* (1978), *The Israeli connection* (1987), and its translation, *Schmutzige Allianzen* (1988). ConAu, 105; WhoIsrael, 1990/92-2001

Beitullov (Бейтуллов), Mekhmed, born 20th cent., he wrote Животът на населението от турски произход в НРБ (Sofia, 1975). LC

Bejarano Robles, Francisco, born in 1900, he was since 1924 an archivist and librarian at the Ayuntamiento de Málaga. His writings include *Documentos para el estudio del abastecimiento y auxilio de la plazas portuguesas en Marruecos, desde el sur de España* (Tanger, 1941), *Fiestas de moros y cristianos en la Provincia de Málaga* (Tetuán, 1949), *Repartimiento de Comares, 1487-1496* (1974), and *Las calles de Málaga* (1984). LC; Note

Bejtić, Alija, born 1 May 1920 at Kukavicama near Rogatice, Bosnia, his writings include *Bibliografija štampanik radova o Sarajevu do kraja 1954 godine* (1964), and *Ulice i trgovi Sarajeva* (1973). He died on 7 July 1981. LC; Prilozi za orientalnu filologiju 31 (1981), pp. 7-9

Beke, Charles Tilstone, born 10 October 1800 at Stepney, Middlesex. After a brief business career, he studied law at Lincoln's Inn. The Universität Tübingen awarded him a doctorate for his contributions to Oriental subjects. From 1840 to 1843 he explored Abyssinia. His writings include *The British captives* *in Abyssinia* (1865), and *The late Dr. Charles Beke's discoveries of Sinai in Arabia and of Midian* (1878). He died in London, 31 July 1874. DNB; Embacher; Henze; Hill

Beke, Ödön, bon 20 May 1883 at Komáron, Hungary, he was a school teacher from 1920 to 1947, before he became a professor at Budapest University. His writings include *Finnugor határozós szerkezetek* (1914), *Tscheremissische Märchen, Sagen und Erzählungen* (Helsinki, 1938), and *Mari szövegek* (1957-1961). He died in Budapest, 10 April 1964. Magyar

Bekimov, Moldaniiaz, born in 1882, a Kazak ethnographer. Kazak SE

Bekmakhanova, Nailia Ermurkhanovna, fl. 1972. Her writings include *Легенда о Невидимке* (1968), *Формирование многонационального населения Казахстана и Северной Киргизии* (1980), *Многонациональное население Казахстана и Киргизии в эпоху капитализма, 60-е годы XIX в. – 1917 г.* (1986), and *Qazaq SSR tarikhi* (1987). LC

Bekhzadi, I. P. *see* Behzadi, Ismail Pasha ogly

Bekir Sami Bey, born in 1865 in the Caucasus, he was a Turkish politician who was delegated to the London Conference of 1921. He died in Istanbul in 1933. AnaBrit; Meydan

Bekker, August *Immanuel*, born 21 May 1785 at Berlin, he studied philology at the Universität Halle, where he also obtained a doctorate. Afterwards he was invited to lecture at the newly established Universität Berlin. In 1815 he was elected to the Berlin Academy. Between 1815 and 1839 he visited the major libraries in Italy, Paris, and England. He published more than one hundred editions of classical writers. He died in Berlin, 7 June 1871. ADtB

Bektaev, Kaldybai Bektaevich, born 27 November 1920, his writings include *Статистико-информационная типология тюркского текста* (1978), and *Oryssh-qazaqsha matematikalyq sozdik = Русского-казахский математический словарь* (1986). *Казахская ССР краткая энциклопедия,* vol. 3, p. 107; LC

Bel, Alfred Marie Octave, born 14 May 1873 at Salins (Jura), to a family of humble circumstances. After completing his secondary education at Besançon in 1890 he had to take a post as *répétiteur* at the Collège d'Auxerre. In 1891 he followed his brother to Algeria, where for two years he was *répétiteur* at the Collège de Blida, followed by two years at the Lycée d'Oran. After a year of military service, he resumed his teaching at Oran for yet another two years. By that time he had taught himself Arabic in order to understand the country and the people to which he was attracted. In 1897 he received a certificate in Arabic, followed by a position at the Lycée d'Alger. He advanced rapidly in the École des lettres d'Alger and in 1899 became a *professeur des lettres* at the Médersa de Tlemcen, a position he held until 1904, when he was appointed its director. For thirty years he held this position which gave him the opportunity to educate young Muslims and, at the same time, pursue his researches on Islam. Concurrently he was a director of the Musée archéologique de Tlemcen. At his retirement in 1935 he had all intention of spending the rest of his life in Tlemcen but the political climate compelled him to leave the country and settle in Meknès where he died 18 February 1945. His writings include *Les Benou Ghanya* (1903), *Les industries de la céramique de Fès* (1918), *Zahrat el-âs (La fleur du myrte), par el-Djaznâi* (1923), and posthumously *L'islam mystique* (1988). Émile Janier in an unidentified publication, pp. 66-75

Bel, Marguerite A., fl. 1936. Under the auspices of the Gouvernement général de l'Algérie, she published the pamphlet, *Les arts indigènes féminins en Algérie* (Alger, 1939). NUC, pre-1956

Beládiez Navarro, Emilio, born 28 December 1916 at Zaragoza, he studied at the Universidad de Madrid, and subsequently entered the Foreign Service. In 1951 he was ambassador in Tehran. His writings include *Almanzor, un césar andaluz* (1959), *Diplomacia y diplomáticos* (1975), and *Españolas reinas de Francia* (1979). DBEC; WhoSpain, 1963

Belal, Abdel Aziz, born 23 October 1932 at Taza, Morocco. he studied economics at Rabat and Toulouse. Afterwards he devoted his energy to the Moroccan Party of Progress and Socialism and to teaching at the universities of Rabat and Casablanca. His writings include *Développement et facteurs non-économiques* (1980), and *Aziz Belal tel qu'il fut* (1982). He died in a mysterious fire accident at the Chicago Hilton Hotel while on an official visit to the United States. Hommes et destins, vol. 7, pp. 57-60

Belan, Vasilii Georgievich, fl. 1972-1991. His writings include *Таджикская советская литература в социалистических странах* (1971), *Восток : книги на иностранных языках Отдела иностранной литературя : каталог, 1966-1975 гг.* (1976-1981), and *Таджикистан в литературе на иностранных языках, 1976-1980* (1983). LC

Bélanger, Charles Paul, born 29 May 1805 at Paris, he was a botanist who was for many years in the service of the Ministère de la Marine et des Colonies and travelled throughout the world, including the Caucasus and Persia. From 1853 until his death, 18 November 1881, he organized the Botanical Gardens at St-Pierre de la Martinique. Henze; *Hommes et destins*, vol. 4, pp. 67-70

Belck, Carl Eugen *Waldemar*, born 5 March 1862 at Danzig, Germany, he received in 1888 a Dr.phil. from the Universität Halle for his thesis, *Über die Passivität des Eisens*. His writings include *Beiträge zur alten Geographie und Geschichte Vorderasiens* (1901). NUC, pre-1956

Beldiceanu, Nicoară Nădejde, born 25 February 1920 at Bucureşti, he was educated in his hometown. In 1948, he emigrated to Germany to study at München, where he received a Dr.phil. in 1955 for his thesis, *Der Feldzug Bajezids II. gegen die Moldau und die Schlachten bis zum Frieden von 1486*. He finally settled in the Paris region and received his second doctorate in 1973 from the Université de Paris IV for his *thèse d'état, Institutions et économie de l'Empire ottoman*. From 1965 to his retirement in 1986 he was affiliated with the C.N.R.S. His writings include *Recherche sur la ville ottomane au 15e siècle* (1973), and *Le timar dans l'État ottoman* (1980). He died in Grigny (Essonne), 19 December 1994. LC; Schwarz; THESAM, 4; *Turcica* 27 (1995), pp. 311-323; WhoRom

Beldiceanu-Steinherr, Irène, born 20th cent., she obtained a Dr.phil. in 1956 from the Universität München for her thesis, *Scheich Üftade, der Begründer des Celvetijje-Ordens*, and in 1983, her second doctorate from the Université de Paris III for her *thèse d'état, Le monde préottoman et ottoman à la lumière des archives de Turquie*. Her writings include *Recherches sur les actes des règnes des sultans Osman, Orkhan et Murad I* (1967). LC; Schwarz; THESAM, 4

Belenitskii (Беленицкий), Aleksandr Markovich, born in 1904 in Smolensk Oblast, Russia, he graduated In 1930 from Tashkent University. In recognition of his published works he received a doctorate in 1967. His writings include a translation of al-Biruni, *Собрание сведении для познания драгоценностей: минералогия* (1963), and *Средневековый город Срндней Азии* (1973). He died 15 June 1993. LC; Miliband; Miliband[2]

Belfiglio, Valentine John, born 8 May 1934 at Troy, N.Y., he studied at Union University, Albany, N.Y., and the University of Oklahoma, where he received a Ph.D. in 1970 for his thesis, *The foreign relations of India with Bhutan, Sikkim and Nepal between 1947-1967*. From 1967 to 1970 he taught at the University of Oklahoma, Norman, and in 1970 he a became professor of history and government at Texas Woman's University, Denton, a post which he still held in 2003. His writings include *The United States and world peace* (1971). ConAu, 49-52; NatFacDr, 1995-2003

Belfour, Francis Cunningham. In 1830 he published a translation from the Persian, *The life of Sheikh Mohammed Ali Hazin*, and in 1836, a translation from the Arabic, *The travels of Macarius*, patriarch of Antioch. NUC, pre-1956

Belge, Burhan, born in 1899, he was in 1939 a chief counsellor at the Press Department, Ministry of the Interior, Ankara. In 1936 he edited the collective work, *Die neue Türkei*. Note; NUC

Belgesay, Mustafa Reşit, born in 1889, he was a professor at the Faculty of Law, İstanbul Üniversitesi, and a prolific writer on Turkish law. His writings include *Kur'an hükümleri ve modern hukuk* (1963). LC; NUC

Belgioioso, Principessa Cristina di Trivulzio, born 28 June 1808 at Milano, she was a patriotic writer who enthusiastically supported the Italian freedom movement. After the suppression of the uprising in Romagna, she emigrated to Paris, where she published several periodicals, and where her home became a meeting place for celebrities. She returned to Italy in 1848 and worked for the national renaissance and financed volunteers. After the confiscation of her property was annulled in 1857, she founded the newspaper *Italia*. Her writings include *L'Italia e la rivoluzione nel 1848* (1849), *Souvenirs d'exil* (1850), *Emina; récits turco-asiatiques* (1856), *Asie mineure et Syrie; souvenirs de voyages* (1858), and *Scènes de la vie turque* (1858). She died in Milano, 15 July 1871. DizBI; Meyers; OxFr

Belgorodskii (Belgorodsky), N. A., fl. 1935, he wrote *Современная персидская лексика* (Moscow, 1936). NUC

Belgrave, Sir Charles Dalrymple, born 9 December 1894 at Montreux, Switzerland , he was educated at Belford School and Lincoln College, Oxford. During the first World War he served in several Camel Corps in the Middle East. He was a sometime United Kingdom Adviser to the Ruler of Bahrain. His writings include *Siwa, the Oasis of Jupiter Ammon* (1923), *Personal column* (1960), and *The Pirate Coast* (1966). He died 28 February 1969. *Who was who*, 6; WhoArab, 1971/72-1978/79|

Belgrave, James *Hamed* Dacre, born 22 April 1929 at Bahrain. he studied at AUB and SOAS. From 1947 to 1948 he was with the Palestine Police, and since 1956, United Kingdom Public Relations Officer, Bahrain Government. His book, *Welcome to Bahrain; a complete illustrated guide for tourists and travellers* has gone through nine editions and was translated into Arabic. WhoArab, 1971/72-1986/87|

Lord **Belhaven and Stenton**, Robert Alexander Benjamin Hamilton, lieutenant colonel, born on 16 September 1903, at Mount Abu, India, he was educated at Eton and the Royal Military College, Sandhurst, and served as political officer among the independent tribes of the Aden Protectorate from 1934 to 1939. During this time he did much walking, often with a single companion, throughout the western Aden Protectorate of which he may be regarded as the last of the explorers. He marched from the coast up through the wild Arqub Pass. His writings include *The Kingdom of Melchior; adventure in south-west Arabia* (1949), and his autobiography, *The Uneven road* (1945). He died 10 July 1961. Bidwell, pp. 177-178; *Scottish biographie* (1938); *Who was who*, 6

Belhedi, Amor, born 20th cent., he received a doctorate in 1977 from the Université de Tunis for his thesis, *Le chemin de fer et espace tunisien*, which was published, in 1980, entitled *Le chemin de fer et l'espace en Tunisie; transport et organisation de l'espace.* LC

Beliaev (Беляев), Evgenii Aleksandrovich, born in 1895 at Rzhev, Russia, he graduated in 1922 from the Moscow Oriental Institute, where he taught in subsequent years. He wrote *Арабы, ислам и арабский халифат в раннее средневековье* (1966), and *Arabs, Islam and the Arab caliphate in the early middle ages* (1969). He died in Moscow, 5 September 1964. GSE; Miliband; Miliband²

Beliaev (Беляев), Igor' Petrovich, born 18 November 1923 at Baku, he graduated in 1951 from the Oriental Institute, Moscow. In 1969 he received a doctorate in economics. From 1954 to 1956 he was a representative of Sovinform-Bureau in Syria and Lebanon. Afterwards he was for over thirteen years *Pravda* correspondent in the Middle East and Africa. His writings include *Американский империализм в Саудовской Аравии* (1957), *День седьмой, как день первый ...* (1979), and *Тоько два года* (1985). He died 10 April 1993. LC; Miliband; Miliband²

Beliaev (Беляев), Viktor Ivanovich, born 11 May 1902 at Tashkent, he graduated in 1925 from Leningrad University. From 1936 to 1959 he was a palaeographer and Arabist at the Oriental Institute, Leningrad. His writings include *Арабские рукориси Бухарской коллекции Азиатского музея Института востоковедения АН СССР* (1932), and *Арабская проза* (1956). He died in Leningrad, 7 May 1976. LC; Miliband; Miliband²

Beliavskii, IU. *see* Biellawski, Józef, 1909-

Belik, Mahmut R., fl. 1949, a writer on Turkish law who wrote *Milletlerarası harp selâhiyetinin tahdidi ve milletlerarası ihtilâfların sulh yolu ile halli usulleri* (1956), and *Milletlerarası tahkim ve adli tesviye* (1965). LC

Belik, Mübeccel, 1928- *see* Kiray, Mübeccel Belik

Belilos, Léon, fl. 1943, he published three works privately in Alexandria, Egypt, *Aux citoyens du monde nouveau* (1943), *From global war to global peace* (1944), and *La santé libératrice* (1952); in Paris he published *Unir les hommes* (1956). NUC

Bélime, Émile A., born 28 July 1883 at Lyon-Villeurbanne, he studied at l'École technique de La Martinière and became an *ingénieur des Travaux Publics de l'État.* He served in Morocco before the first World War, and in French West Africa thereafter. In 1932 he established l'Office du Niger of which he was a director until 1944. In 1951 he became founding director of the Comité du Sahara français. His writings include *Les irrigations du Niger* (1923), *La production du coton en Afrique occidentale française* (1925), *Les travaux du Niger* (1940), and *Gardons l'Afrique* (1950). He died in July 1969. *Hommes et destins* vol. 1, pp. 72-73

Belin, François Alphonse, born 31 July 1817 at Paris, he graduated from the École des langues orientales, Paris. In 1845 he became an interpreter at the French Consulate in Erzurum, from where he was moved to the Consulate in Cairo in 1852. From 1868 until his retirement in 1877 he was *secrétaire interprète* with the rank of consul-general at the French Embassy in Constantinople. His writings include *Extrait d'un mémoire sur l'origine et la constitution des biens main morte en pays musulmans* (1854), *Étude sur la propriété foncière en pays musulmans* (1862), *Essais sur l'histoire économique de la Turquie* (1865), *De l'instruction publique et du mouvement intellectuel en Orient* (1866), *Caractères, maximes et pensées de Mir Ali Chir Nevâû* (1866), *Histoire de l'Église latine à Constantinople* (1872). He died in Constantinople in 1878. Vapereau

Belin, Jean Paul, fl. 1920, he wrote *Le commerce des livres prohibés à Paris de 1750 à 1789* (1913), *Le mouvement philosophique de 1748 à 1789* (1913), and *Les relations entre la France et la Grande-Bretagne* (1916). NUC, pre-1956

Belin de Monterzi, or Montrezy, fl. 1760, he was an Orientalist who wrote *Histoire de Mehmet II* (Paris, 1764), and *Lettres turques, historiques et politiques* (Paris, 1764). Hoefer

de **Bélinay**, Frédéric, fl. 1938, he wrote *Sur le sentier de la guerre* (Paris, 1920). NUC, pre-1956

Beling, Willard Adolph, born 16 March 1919 at Grand Bend, N.D., he was educated at U.C.L.A. and Princeton University, where he received a Ph.D. in 1947 for his thesis, *The Hebrew variant of the first Book of Samuel compared with the Old Greek and recensions*. Afterwards he was for ten years a director of socio-economic research and planning with the Arabian American Oil Company. Thereafter he held academic posts in universities throughout the United States. He was a sometime editor of the *Maghreb digest*. His writings include *Pan-Arabism and labor* (1960), and *King Faisal and the modernisation of Saudi Arabia* (1980). AmM&WS, 1973 S, 1978 S; ConAu, 53-56; WhoWest, 1976

Belkherroubi, Abdelmadjid, he received a doctorate of law in 1971 from the Université de Lausanne for his thesis, *La naissance et la recon-naissance de la République algérienne*. Schwarz

Belkhodja, Abdelkader, fl. 1953, he was a sometime honorary minister of agriculture in Tunisia. With Jeanne Belkhodja he published *Les africains du nord à Gennevilliers* (1963). LC; Note

Bell, Alured Gray, born 19th cent., he wrote *The beautiful Rio de Janeiro* (1914). LC

Bell, Arthur *Clive* Howard, born 16 September 1881 at East Shefford, England, he was a critic of politics, art and literature. His writings include *Landmarks in nineteenth century painting* (1927), *An account of French painting* (1931), and *Enjoying pictures* (1934). He died 18 September 1964. ChambrBrBi; ConAu, 89-92; Master (11); OxfordEng

Bell, Coral, professor, his writings include *Negotiation from strenght* (1962), a work which was first conceived as a Ph.D. thesis for the University of London. He wrote also *The debatable alliance* (1964), and *The diplomacy of detente* (1977). LC; Note

Bell, Fitzroy, b. 19th cent. see Bell, Robert Fitzroy

Bell, Sir Gawain Westray, born 21 January 1909, he was educated at Hertford College, Oxford. He was attached to the Sudan Political Service in 1931, and seconded to the Government of Palestine in 1938. Afterwards, until his retirement, he held various military and political offices throughout the Middle East. In 1983 he published *Shadows on the sand; the memoirs of Sir Gawain Bell*. He died 26 July 1995. IntWW, 1974-1977; Who's who, 1974-1995

Bell, Gertrude Margaret Lowthian, born 14 July 1868 at the family estate, Washington Hall, Durham, she studied at Queen's College, London, and at Oxford, where she was the first girl to take first class honours in history. Since the late 1880s, she was a traveller in the Middle East, and a scholar of private means, working temporarily as assistant political officer to promote British interests in the Middle East. He writings include *Safar nameh; Persian pictures*, (published anonymously in 1894), *The desert and the sown* (1907), and *The letters of Gertrude Bell* (1927). Her archive of photographs and papers is in the University of Newcastle upon Tyne. Harry V. F. Winstone published her biography in 1978, Marie-José Simpson published *La Dame de Bagdad, Gertrude Bell* in 1992, and Caroline T. Marshall received a Ph.D. in 1968 from the University of Virginia for her thesis, *Gertrude Bell; her work and influence in the Near East, 1914-1926.*. She died in Baghdad in the night of 11 to 12 July 1926. Bidwell; Index Islamicus (7); ChambrBrBi; Robinson, p. 4-6; Selim; Who was who, 2

Bell, Sir Harold *Idris*, born 2 October 1879 at Epworth, Lincolnshire, he was a classics scholar and a graduate of Oxford, who did post-graduate studies at Berlin and Halle. He was at the British Museum since 1903 and retired in 1944 as keeper of manuscripts, and Edgerton Librarian. His writings include *Jews and Christians in Egypt* (1924), *Egypt, from Alexander the Great to the Arab conquest* (1948), and *Cults and creeds in Græco-Roman Egypt* (1953). He died in 1967. Egyptology; Who was who, 6

Bell, J., fl. 1945, he was a broadcaster and sometime member of the British Council staff in Ankara.

Bell, J. Bowyer, born 15 November 1931 at New York City, he graduated from Washington and Lee University, Lexington, Va., and received his Ph.D. in 1958 at Duke University, Durham, N.C. Afterwards he taught at various American institutes of higher learning. His writings include *The long war; Israel and the Arabs since 1946* (1969), *The myth of the guerrilla* (1971), and *Terror out of Zion* (1977). ConAu, 17-20

Bell, John, born in 1691 at Antermony, a small estate in Scotland, he attended Glasgow University from 1707 to 1711 and qualified as a medical doctor in 1713. The following year he set out for St. Petersburg where he enlisted in the service of Peter the Great and was sent to Persia as a member of a trade and diplomatic mission, spending a year and a half in the country. He had no claim to Oriental scholarship. On the business of his mission he was discretly silent, probably for reasons of state. But he was a shrewd observer, with an eye for telling detail, and his sober factual style contrasted notably with that of his more florid English predecessors. He wrote *Travels from St. Petersburg in Russia to diverse parts of Asia* (1763). He died in Antermony in 1780. Roger Stevens in: *Iran* 16 (1978), 178-182; DNB

Bell, Joseph Norment, born 20th cent., he received a Ph.D. in 1971 from Princeton University for his thesis, *The Hanbalite teaching on love*. His writings include *Love theory in later Hanbalite Islam* (1979), and the translation of 'Abd al-Hakim Qasim, *The seven days of man* (1996). LC

Bell, Mark Sever, V.C., C.B., born 15 May 1843 at Sydney, N. S. Wales, he was educated at King's College, London, and entered the Royal Engineers in 1862. He participated in military campaigns throughout Asia, rising to the rank of colonel, and was aide-de-camp to Queen Victoria, 1887-1900. He travelled widely over generally unknown parts of China, Central Asia, Persia, Kurdistan, and Asia Minor. He died 26 June 1906. *Who was who, 1*

Bell, Richard, born in 1876 in Scotland, he took courses in arts and divinity at Edinburgh, where he obtained an M.A., in 1897, and a D.D. He studied for a time in Germany. On his return he became assistant to the Profesor of Hebrew at Edinburgh, where part of his duty was to teach Arabic; he also acted as examiner in divinity. He then became a minister of a country parish in Wamphray, remaining there until he went back to Edinburgh in 1921, first as lecturer and then reader in Arabic. He retired at the age limit in 1947. His life was uneventful and it was not until the end of his life that he visited Arabic-speaking lands. It was once said that if anyone was to complete Lane's lexicon, Bell was the man. His first idea was to devote himself to Arabic mathematics, working on the manuscripts in the university library, but he gave that up and spent his life in the study of the Koran. The first-fruits of this were his Gunning lectures, *The origins of Islam in its Christian environment* (1925). The principles learned in the study of the Old Testament were applied to the Koran and in the lay-out of his translation he made it clear that it was a much-edited book and that its composition was more complicated than the Muslim authorities allowed. He is now best remembered for his *Introduction to the Qur'an* (1953), and its revised edition by W. Montgomery Watt (Edinburgh, 1970). He died in 1952. A.S. Tritton in JRAS, 1952-53, p. 180

Bell, Robert *Fitzroy*, born 19th cent., he studied at Edinburgh. In 1937 the University of Edinburgh Students' Representative Council published *Fitzroy Bell commemoration*. BLC

Bell, Thomas *Evans*, born in 1825, he was a political writer and a major who published also under the pseudonym Indicus. His writings include *The Mysore reversion* (1865), *Our great vassal empire* (1870), *The Bengal reversion* (1872), and *The Annexation of the Punjaub* (1882). He died in 1887. BLC; LC

Bellamy, James Andrew, born 12 August 1925 at Evansville, Ind., he was a graduate of Centre College, Ky., and received a Ph.D. in 1956 from the University of Pennsylvania in 1956 for *Social contrasts in Islam as seen in Muslim literature*. In 1968 he became a professor of Arabic at the Uni-versity of Michigan, Ann Arbor. His writings include the translation of 'A. b. M. Ibn Sa'id, *The Banners of the champions* (1989) as well as being joint editor of contemporary Arabic readers. DrAS, 1974 F, 1978 F, 1982 F; WhoAm, 1974/5-1980/81|

Bellanger, Eugène *Stanislas*, born 7 June 1814 at Tours, he was educated in his home town and in Paris. He was a merchant and discoverd his literary interests after a journey to Romania. In 1846 he was sent on an official mission to Turkey in quest of documents relating to Turkish history as well as seeking information as to the state of public education in the Ottoman Empire. He died of an unknown disease, which he had contracted in Damascus, without having realized his proposed history of the Ottoman Empire. His writings include *Trois ans de promenade en Europe et en Asie* (1842), and *Le Kéroutza, voyage en Moldo-Valachie* (1846). He died on 18 April 1859. His biography by Georges Cioranesco appeared 1981 in Thessaloniki under the title *La mission de Stanislas Bellanger dans l'Émpire ottoman*.

Bellemare, Alexandre, he wrote *Grammaire arabe* (Paris, 1850), *Abrégé de géographie à l'usage des écoles arabes-françaises* (Paris, 1853), and *Abd el-Kader* (Paris, 1863). In 1867, his Arabic grammar had gone through seven editions. LC; NUC, pre-1956

Bellet, Daniel, born in 1864 at Saint-Julien-de-l'Escap (Charente-Inférieure), a pupil of, and successor to, Jules Fleury, he was brought up in the classical tradition of French political economy, and devoted his whole life to the organization and popularization of the ideas of his masters. A voluminous writer and frequent contributor to the *Journal des économistes*, his principal role was to be found in the organizations with which he was associated rather than in original contributions to economic science. Since 1906 he was the permanent secretary of the Société d'économie politique, secretary-general of the Ligue du libre-échange, of which he was one of the principal founders, and professor at the École libre des sciences politiques. His latest publications, *La mentalité teutonne* (1916), and *Le commerce allemand* (1916), were the vehicle for his feeling of profound repugnance against the spirit and genius of the German Empire. He died on 11 October 1917. Personal and smpathetic notices of his career from the pen of his colleagues, Yves Guyot, Eugène d'Eichthal, and Raphaël-Georges Lévy, are to be found in the *Journal des économistes* for November 1917, pp. 289-294.

Bellew, Henry Walter, born 30 August 1834 at Nusserabad, India, he took a M.D. at St. George's Hospital, London. In 1856 he went to India in the Bengal Medical Service. In the following two years he accompanied Sir H. B. Lumsden's mission to Kandahar; thereafter he was Civil Surgeon in Peshawar. He was on several other missions and, during the second Afghan War, actes as Political Officer at Kabul. His writings include *A general report on the Yusufzais* (1864), *A dictionary of the Pukhtu language* (1867), *From the Indus to the Tigris* (1874), *Kashmir and Kashghar* (1875), and *Afghanistan and the Afghans* (1879). He died in Farnham Royal, Bucks., 26 July 1892. Buckland; Embacher; Henze; IndianBilnd (2); Riddick

Belli, Themata, fl. 1881, he was a writer on Afghanistan who published in *Rivista militare italiana*.

Bellingeri, Giampiero, born 20th cent., he wrote *Molla Penah Vaqif; vita e Qošma* (Venezia, 1983). LC

Bellinghausen, Rudolf, born 10 February 1939 at Bad Honeff, Germany, he studied economics at the Universität Bonn, where he received a Dr.rer.pol. in 1966 for *Entwicklungspolitik in einer gemischten Wirtschaftsordnung; das Beispiel Indiens*. Afterwards he was for three years a lecturer at Kabul University before becoming a civil servant at the Ministry for Economic Cooperation, Bonn.

Bellman, Dieter, born 4 November 1934 at Freital, Germany, he studied at the Universität Halle, where he received a Dr.phil. in 1966 for *Das Anstandsbuch des Ibn al-Wašša'*. From 1966 to 1970 he was director of the Kultur- und Informationszentrum der DDR, Damascus, before becoming director of Orientalisches Institut in the Universität Leipzig, a post which he held until his retirement. His writings include *Grundzüge der geistig-kulturellen Entwicklung der arabischen Staaten* (1977), and *Arabische Kultur der Gegenwart* (1984). Kürschner, 1996|; Wer ist wer, 1996/97-2002/2003

Bellot, fl. 1945-46, he was a sometime lieutenant in the *Service des affaires indigènes d'Algérie*.

Beloshapkin, Denis Kipriianovich, born in 1902 in the Ukraine, he graduated in 1930 from the Leningrad Oriental Institute and received his first degree in 1955 for *Экономическя политика праящих кругов Ирана в военные и послевоенные годв (1941-1953)*. He was a trade commissioner with the Soviet Legation in Iran before he became a lecturer in 1960. He died 19 June 1977. Miliband; Miliband²

Belot, Jean Baptiste, born 1 March 1822 at Lux, Bourgogne, he studied at the Université de Dijon and entered the Société de Jésus in 1842. Afterwards he spent three years in Algeria teaching and studying Arabic. He was ordained in Bordeaux in 1852 and sent to Rome, 1855-58. In 1865 he was posted to Lebanon, where he remained until his death on 14 August 1904. His writings include *Dictionnaire arabe-français* (1890). Arabica 25 (1978), 1-9; Fück

Belova, Anna Grigor'evna, born 1 May 1933 at Sevastopol, she graduated in 1955 from the Leningrad Oriental Faculty and received her first degree in 1964 for *Формообразование имен в арабском языке*. Since 1965 she was affiliated with the Oriental Institute in the Soviet Academy of Science. Miliband; Miliband²

Belova, Kaleriia Antoninovna, born 18 December 1938 in the Mari Autonomous Soviet Socialist Republic, she obtained a doctorate In 1969 for her thesis, *Основные политические и идеологические теченя в Турции после 1960 года*. Miliband; Miliband²

Belova, Ninel' Koz'minichna, born 4 February 1927 at Moscow, she obtained a doctorate in 1956 for her thesis, *Революционное движение в Иранском Азербайджане в период революции 1905-1911 гг.* Afterwards she taught at the Institute of the People of the Orient, Moscow University. In 1988 she contributed to the collective work *Новая история Ирана*. Miliband; Miliband²

Beltrame, Giovanni, born 11 November 1824 at Valeggio, Italy, he went in 1853 as a missionary to the Sudan, where he was one of the founders of the Roman Catholic mission station of Holy Cross on the Upper White Nile. He made important contributions on the Dinka language, which he was one of the first to study. His writings include *Grammatica della lingua denka* (1870), and *Il Sennaar e lo Sciangàllah; memorie* (1879). He died in Verona, 8 April 1906. DizBI; Henze; Hill; VIA, pp. 63-64

Beltrán, Luis, born 6 September 1932 at Salamanca, Spain, he studied at the Universidad de Salamanca and the University of Michigan, where he received a Ph.D. in comparative literature in 1972. Since 1977, for over twenty years, he taught Spanish and comparative literature at Indiana University, Bloomington. His writings include *La cultura hispanica en Africa negra* (1970), *Razones de buen amor* (1977). and *La arquetectura del humo* (1986). DrAS, 1974-1982; LC

Beltz, Walter, born in 1935, he taught religion at the Universität Halle and at Beirut since 1970. His writings include *Das Tor der Götter* (1978), *Die Mythen des Koran* (1980), *God and gods* (1983), *Sehnsucht nach dem Paradies* (1989), and *Wieviel Religion braucht der deutsche Staat* (1992). Kürschner, 1996-2003; LC

Belyaev, Igor, 1923- *see* Beliaev, Igor' Petrovich

Belzoni, Giovanni Battista, born 5 November 1778 at Padova, he trained for the priesthood but, abandoning his intention, married and went to England in 1803. He went to Egypt in 1815 where he was engaged in the excavation of antiquities. He died from dysentery in Benin while on a journey of discovery to Timbuctu on 3 December 1823. Stanley Mayes wrote *The Great Belzoni* (c1959, 2004). DizBI; DNB; Egyptology; Henze; Hill; Hoefer; VIA, pp. 29-31

Bémont, Frédy. His writings include *L'Iran devant le progrès* (1964), *Les villes de l'Iran* (1969-73), and *L'Iran depuis 1962* (1971). LC

Benaboud, Muhammad M., born 20th cent., he received a Ph.D. in 1978 from the University of Edinburgh for his thesis, *A political and social histoty of Seville under Banu 'Abbad*. Sluglett

Benachenhou, Abdellatif, born 31 March 1943 in Algeria, he wrote *Formation du sous-développement en Afrique* (1976), *Le tiers-monde en jeu* (1981), and *Développement et coopération internationale* (1982). AfrBioInd (1); LC

Ben Achour, Yadh, born 20th cent., he was a sometime professor at the Faculté de droit et de sciences politiques et économiques de Tunis. His writings include *L'état nouveau et la philosophie politique et juridique occidentale* (1980), *Droit administratif* (1982), and *Politique, religion et droit dans le monde arabe* (1992). LC

BenAicha, Hedi, born 27 April 1952 in Tunisia, he studied at the Sorbonne, where he received a doctorate under Claude Cahen in 1979. He subsequently went to the United States, where he took an M.L.Sc. at the University of Maryland, College Park, in 1985. In 1991 he was an Arabic bibliographer and head of the Arabic Preservation Project at Princeton University Library. Private

Ben Ali, Mohamed Ridha, born 20 November 1920 at Gafsa, Tunisia, he studied at the Université de Tunis and became a lawyer and politician. He was a sometime attorney general, Supreme Court of Appeal, and Minister of Justice. Africa who's who, 1991-1996

Benard, Cheryl, born in 1953, she received a Dr.phil. and became attached to the Universität Wien and was also affiliated with Forschungsstelle für Politik und Zwischenmenschlichen Beziehungen, Wien. Her writings include *Die ganz gewöhnliche Gewalt in der Ehe* (1978), *Das Gewissen der Männer: Geschlecht und Moral; Reportagen aus der orientalischen Despotie* (1992). With Zalmay Khalilzad she published *The government of God, Iran's Islamic Republic* (1984). Kürschner, 1996-2001|

Benardout, Raymond, his writings include *Turkish rugs* (1975), *Nomadic Persian and Turkoman weaving* (1977), *Caucasian rugs* (1979), and *Exhibition catalogue* of an exhibition held at Raymond Benardout (Gallery), London, from 23 October to 4 November 1978. LC

Ben Arieh, Yehoshua, born in 1928, he retired in 1998 as Rector of the Hebrew University, Jerusalem. His writings include *The changing landscape of the Central Jordan Valley* (1968), and *The rediscovery of the Holy Land in the nineteenth century* (1979). In 1997 he attended the Oxford conference on *Travellers in Egypt*. LC

Benattar, Raoul, fl. 1963, he was in 1968 a barrister at the Tunisian *Cour de cassasion*.

Benavides Moro, Nicolás, born 7 November 1883 at La Bañeza, Spain, he received a doctorate in 1926 for his thesis, *La colonización y el acta Torrens en el norte de Africa*. He became a professor of military science and military history at the Spanish Staff College. WhoSpain, 1963

Ben Barka, Mehdi, 1920- *see* Bin Barakah, Mahdi

Ben Cheneb, Mohammed, born in 1869 in Algeria, he graduated in 1898 from l'École des lettres d'Alger and subsequently taught at various *medersas* in Constantine and Algiers before becoming professor of modern Arabic at the Faculté des lettres d'Alger in 1927. His writings include *Catalogue des manuscrits arabes conservés dans les principales bibliothèques algériennes; tome 2: Grande Mosquée d'Alger* (1909), and *Abû Dolâma, poète bouffon de la cour des premiers califes abbasides* (1922). He died in Alger, 5 February 1929. AfrBioInd (2); *Hommes et destins*, vol. 7, pp. 64-65; JA 214 (1929), pp. 359-365

Ben Cheneb, Saâdeddine, born 26 February 1907 at Alger, the son of Mohammed Ben Cheneb. After studies at Alger and Paris he was a school, college, and university teacher in Algeria and Tunisia. From 1947 to 1949 he was French Minister to Saudi Arabia. His writings include *La poésie arabe moderne* (1946), and *Contes d'Alger* (1946). He died in 1968. AfrBioInd (2); *Hommes et destins*, vol. 7, pp. 66-67

Benchétrit, Maurice, fl. 1966, his writings include *L'érosion actuelle et ses conséquences sur l'aménagement en Algérie* (1972). LC

Ben Choaib, Abou Bekr Abdessalam, born 19th cent., he was in 1906 a teacher at the Shaykh Sanusi Mosque at Tlemcen, and in 1908, a municipal councillor. His writings include the pamphlet *Une délégation de notables musulmans algériens à la foire de Rabat* (Oran, 1918). Note; NUC, pre-1956

Benda, Harry Jindrich, born in 1919, he received a Ph.D. in 1955 from Cornell University, Ithaca, N.Y., for *The crescent and the rising sun; Indonesian Islam under the Japanese occupation of Java, 1942-45*. Afterwards he was an assistant professor of history at the University of Manchester. His publications include *The crescent and the rising sun* (1958). He died in 1971. BioIn, 9 (3) & 10 (1)

Ben-Dak, Joseph D., born 2 Januray 1943 at Haifa, he studied at the Hebrew University, Jerusalem, and the University of Michigan. He was on the board of directors of the Israeli Peace Research Society and a research fellow of the Israeli Institute for the Study of International Affairs. His writings include *Political unification and regional integration; a working bibliography* (1978). WhoIsrael, 1992/93

Ben Dhia, Abdelaziz, he was in 1973 a *maître assistant* at the Faculté de droit de Tunis, and in 1991 a Tunisian Minister of Defense. Note

Ben-Dor, Gabriel, born 16 April 1944 in Hungary, he studied political science at Hamline University, St. Paul, Minn, and Princeton, where he received a Ph.D. in 1972 for his thesis, *The politics of innovation and integration; a political study of the Druze community in Israel*. His alma mater conferred on him an honorary doctorate in 1986. His writings include *The Druzes in Israel* (1979). In 1987 he was joint editor of *Conflict management in the Middle East*. He was Rector of the University of Haifa in 1993. WhoIsrael, 199/93

Benedetti, Achille, born 15 April 1881 at Marsala, Sicily, he was a journalist, covering the Moroccan campaign against Abd El Krim from 1925 to 1926. His writings include *Dal Sahara al Ciad* (1935), and *La guerra equatoriale* (1936). Chi è, 1936, 1948

Benedetti, Vincent, comte, born 29 April 1817 at Bastia. After studying law at Paris, he was an *élève consul* in Alexandria (1840), consul in Cairo (1845), consul-general in Palermo (1848), deputy secretary at the Constantinople Embassy (1852), and appointed minister to Persia in 1855, a post which he declined. Until his retirement in 1871, he accomplished various diplomatic missions at home and abroad. In 1877, he was elected to the *Conseil général* of Corsica, and re-elected in 1883. He wrote *Ma mission en Prusse* (1871), *Essais diplomatiques* (1895). He died in Paris, 28 March 1900. BDF; Index BFr (2); Vapereau

Benedetto, Luigi Foscolo, born 24 February 1886 at Torino, he was a linguist, critic, editor, and professor of French literature at the Università di Firenze. His writings include *The travels of Marco Polo* (1931), and *Il libro di messer Marco Polo* (1932). He died in 1966. Chi è, 1936

Benedick, Richard Elliot, born 10 May 1935 at N.Y.C., he was a graduate of Columbia University, and a diplomat who was Program Economist in Tehran, 1959-1961, and in Karachi, 1963-1964. In 1979 he was coordinator of Population Affairs at the U.S. Department of State. Based on his Harvard thesis, he published *Industrial finance in Iran* in 1964. His writings also include *Ozon diplomacy* (1991). WhoAm, 1980-2003

Benedict, Peter, born in 1938, he was an anthropologist whose writings include *Türkiye: coğrafi* (1971), and *Ula, an Anatolian town* (1974). He contributed to the collective work *Sudan, the Rahad Irrigation Project* (1982). LC

Benedikt, Heinrich, born 30 December 1886 at Wien, he was professor of modern history at the Universität Wien from 1947 until his retirement in 1958, when he became chairman of

Zeitungswissenschaftliche Institut der Universität Wien. His writings include *Das Königreich Neapel unter Kaiser Karl VI.* (1927), and *Damals im alten Österreich; Erinnerungen* (1979). In 1957 he was honoured by *Festschrift für Heinrich Benedikt.* WhoAustria, 1969/70

Beneitez Cantero, Valentín, fl. 1955, his writings include *Vocabulario español-arabe marroquí* (Tetuán, 1949), *La problación de la zona españa del Mogreb* (1950), *La alimentación en Marruecos* (Tetuán, 1951), and *Sociología marroquí* (Tetuán, 1952). LC

Beneva, A. R., 1913-1984 *see* Binava, 'Abd al-Ra'uf

Benfey, Theodor, born 28 January 1809 at Nörten, Germany, he received a Dr.phil. in 1828 from the Universität Göttingen for *Observationes ad Anacreontis fragmenta genuina.* After converting to Christianity in 1848, he was appointed professor of Sanskrit at Göttingen, a position he held until his retirement. His writings include *Über das Verhältnis der ägyptischen Sprache zum semitischen Sprachstamm* (1844), and *Geschichte der Sprachwissenschaft und orientalischen Philologie in Deutschland* (1869). He died in Göttingen, 26 June 1881. Buckland; DtAB; JudEnc; Stache-Rosen, pp. 32-33; Wininger

Benhazera, Maurice. born 19th cent., he was from May to November 1905 an *officier-interprète de 2e classe* on reconnaissance in Touareg territory. In 1914 he was a legal interpreter at Aïn-Beïda (Constantine). His writings include *Six mois chez les Touareg du Ahaggar* (1908). Note; NUC, pre-1956

Benhima, Mohamed, born 25 June 1924 at Safi, Morocco. After matriculation in Marrakesh, he studied medicine at the Université de Nancy, where he received a doctorate. He was a rural medical practioner in Morocco until independence in 1956, when he was attached to the Ministry of Health. In 1961 he was Minister of Public Works, and in the following year, Minister of Commerce and Industry. AfrBioInd (5); AfricaWW, 1996; IntWW, 1996-1997; MidE, 1982/83; *Orient* (Opladen) 14 (1974), p. 102

Bénier, Charles, fl. 1956-57, he was an *ingénieur agronome.* Note

Benigni, Rudolf, fl. 1973, his writings include *Österreichische Botschaftsberichte über arabische Länder; Register zu den im Haus- und Staatsarchiv in Wien befindlichen Akten der Kaiserlichen Internuntiatur.* LC

Benin, Stephen David, born in 1947 in New York, he graduated from the University of Rochester, N.Y., and did graduate studies at Indiana University and the University of California at Berkeley, where he received a Ph.D. in 1970. Since 1981, he was a professor of comparative religion and Jewish studies at the University of Washington, Seattle. His writings include *The footprints of God; divine accommadation in Jewish and Christian thought* (1993). DrAS, 1982 H; LC

Benis, Adam Jerzy, born in 1898, he studied at Genève, Paris, Wien and Warszawa, and became a historian and diplomat. He edited *Une mission militaire polonaise en Égypte* (1938). He died in 1935. Dziekan

Benítez, Cristóbal, fl. 1886, he wrote *Mi viaje por el interior del Africa* (Tanger, 1889). NUC, pre-'56

Benítez de Lugo, Antonio, born in 1841 at Sevilla, he received a doctorate and was a sometime lecturer at the Facultad de Derecho, Universidad de Sevilla. He wrote *Filosofía del derecho* (1872). Mendez; NUC, pre-1956

Benitez Sánchez-Blanco, Rafael, born in 1949, he received a doctorate and was in 1979 a professor of modern history at the Universidad de Valencia, and in 1993, at the Universidad de Valladolid. His writings include *Moriscos y cristianos en el Condado de Casares* (1982); he was joint author of *Poder, familia y consanguinidad en la España del antiguo régimen* (1992). EURAMES, 1993; LC; Note

Benito del Caño, Ciro, fl. 1926, he was joint author with Rafael Roldán y Guerro, of *Cerámica farmaceutica; apuntes para su estudio* (1928).

Benito Ruano, Eloy, born 1 December 1921 at Madrid, he was a professor of history at the Universidad de Madrid. His writings include *Toledo en el siglo XV; vida política* (1961). WhoSpain, 1963

Benjamin, Samuel Greene Wheeler, born to American missionaries, 13 February 1837, at Argos, Greece. After graduating in 1859 from Williams College, he studied law and art. For some years he worked at the Albany State Library. From 1883 to 1885, he was the first U.S. Minister to Persia. He was also an accomplished painter of marine subjects. His writings include *Persia and the Persians* (1886), *Persia* (1888), and *The life and adventured of a free lance* (1914). He died 19 July 1914. NewCEN; Shavit; WhAm, 1

Benjamin Shimun, Mar Shi'mun XX, born 19th century., he was a Patriarch of the Nestorians and was killed in 1918 through the treachery of Simco Agha of the Shekak Kurds. Major A. D. W. Bentinck

Benjelloun, Abdelkrim, fl. 1959, he was a sometime Moroccan Minister of National Education. Note about the author

Benjelloun, Abdelmajid, 1919- see Bin Jallun, 'Abd al-Majid

Benjenk, Munir P., born 24 June 1924 in Turkey, he was educated at Robert College, Instanbul, and LSE, 1945-1949. He was an international finance officer. From 1972 to 1980 he was regional vice-president of the International Bank for Reconstruction and Development. In 1994 he lived in London. IntWW, 1990/91-1994/95|; WhoUN, 1975

Ben Khedda, Ben Yousef, born in 1920 at Blida, Algeria, he was a trained chemist and a politician in the Front de libération nationale, and detained from 1954 to 1955. From 1960 to 1961 he was prime minister of the Algerian Provisional Goverment, but arrested in 1964. Africa who's who, 1991-1996; Makers of modern Africa, 1996; Middle East and North Africa, 1978-1981

Ben-Meir, Gad, fl. 1961, he was a sometime editor of al-Ta'awun, an Arabic quarterly published by the Arab Workers' Department of the Histadrut, Tel-Aviv. Note

Ben-Moshe, Eliezer, fl. 1959, he was a veteran Israeli observer of the Middle East scene and, in 1960, a commentator for the Israeli daily Lamerhav, and the New outlook. New outlook

Bennathan, Esra, born 4 February 1923, his writings include The economics of ocean freight rates (1969). In the 1990s he produced a number of discussion papers on industrialization and haulage for the World Bank. LC

Benndorf, Werner, pseud., born Werner Treydtke, 24 June 1912 at Leipzig, Germany, he studied Oriental languages and philosophy of religion at the Universität Leipzig, travelled throughout the Mediterranean countries, and lived for a year in Morocco. After his return he was literary adviser to various publishing houses in Leipzig. His writings include Arabische Glut (1936), Menwer; Geschichte eines arabischen Knaben (1939), Eine andalusische Nacht (1940), and Das Mittelmeerbuch (1940). He died in a car accident in Leipzig after his release as prisoner of war, 18 July 1945. DtBE

Bennett, Arthur King, born 27 March 1881 at Watkins Glen, N.Y., he was a graduate of the University of Michigan and studied medicine at the universities of Liverpool and Paris. From 1904 to 1914 he was a medical missionary in the Dutch Reformed Church in America, serving in its Arabian Mission at Basrah and Matrah, Oman. He returned to the United States in 1916 and practised in Marquette, Mich., where he died 13 September 1966. Facey Grant, pp. 56-58; NatCAB; Shavit

Bennett, Crystal M., Mrs., OBE, FSA, born in 1918. Biographical details can presumably be found in Alastair Northedge's Studies on Roman and Islamic 'Amman; the excavations of Mrs. C.-M. Bennett and other investigations (1992). She died in 1987. LC

Bennett, Sir Ernest Nathaniel, born in 1865 or 1868, he was a war correspondent for the Westminster gazette in the Nile campaign of 1897-98, and in 1911 to 1912 served a captain in the Ottoman Army in Tripoli and Thrace. He was a member of Parliament, 1906 to 1910, and 1929 to 1945. His writings include The downfall of the dervishes (1898), and With the Turks in Tripoli (1912). He died in Chart Sutton, Maidstone, 2 February 1947. Hill; Who was who, 4

Bennett, Frederic Mackarness, born 2 December 1918 at Torquay, Devonshire, he was educated at Westminster School, served in the 1939-1945 war, and was called to the English bar, Lincoln's Inn, 1946. He was a British government official and was knighted in 1964. He died 14 September 2002. Who, 1997-2002; WhoWor, 1976

Bennett, Ian, his writings include Book of American antiques (1973), History of American painting (1973), and Complete illustrated rugs & carpets of the world (1977). LC

Bennett, John Godolphin, born in 1897 at London, he was educated at the Royal Military Academy, Woolwich, the School of Military Engineering, Chatham, and SOAS, London. He was a sometime principal of the International Academy for Continuous Education. His writings include The crisis in human affairs (1948), Christian mysticism and Subud (1961), Spiritual psychology (1964), and Journeys in Islamic countries (1974). IntAu&W, 1972; LC

Bennett, Margaret N., she was in 1975 a research assistant at SOAS, London. Note

Bennigsen, Alexandre A., born 20 March 1913 at St. Petersburg, he went to Paris in 1924 and studied at the Université de Paris, where he received a doctorate in 1935. In the mid-1950s he was elected to a personal chair of history of non-Arabic Islam at l'École des hautes études en sciences social, Paris, a position he held until his retirement in 1983. His writings include Russes et Chinois avant 1917 (1974); he was joint author of a number of monographs on Islam in the USSR. He died 2 June 1988. ConAu, 125; DrAS, 1978 H; Index Islamicus (5); Schoeberlein; TatarES

Bennouna, Mohamed, born 1943 at Marrakesh, he was a sometime professor of law at the universities of Nice and Rabat. His writings include *Le consentement à l'ingérence militaire dans les conflits internes* (1974), and *Traité du nouveau droit de la mer* (1985). AfrBioInd (1); LC

Benoist, Charles, born 31 January 1861 at Courseulles-sur-Mer (Calvados), he was a politician, diplomat, and sociologist. In 1895 he was appointed to the chair of constitutional history of continental Europe at the École des sciences politiques. His writings include *L'Organisation du travail* (1905), *La Question méditerranéenne* (1928), and *Les Maladies de la démocratie* (1929). He died at his birthplace, 11 August 1936. DBF

Benoist, Edmond, fl. 1899. He studied at l'École des langues orientales, Paris, and was joint editor of *Documents arabes relatifs à l'histoire du Soudan: Tarikh es-Soudan, par Abderrahman ben Abdallah es-Sa'di* (1898-1900). BN

Benoist-Méchin, Jacques Michel Gabriel Paul, baron, born 1 July 1901 at Paris, he was a graduate of Lycée Louis-le-Grand and the Faculté des lettres de Paris. He was a journalist, and later, editor and director of the Paris agency of the International News Service. During the 1940s he was a diplomat, politician, and briefly, professor at l'École libre des sciences politiques. Since 1950 he was a private historian. His writings include *Fayçal, roi d'Arabie* (1975), and *Ibn-Séoud ou la naissance d'un royaume* (1991). Fr. Maxence wrote *Jacques Benoist-Méchin, historien et témoin du Proche-Orient* (1994). He died in Paris, 24 February 1983. IndexBFr² (2), NDNC, 1961/62; WhoFr, 1971-1983/84

Benoit, Fernand Marie Louis Alphonse, born 9 September 1892 at Avignon, he studied at the Collège Stanislas, École des chartes, Faculté des lettres de Paris, and École française de Rome. From 1928 to 1931 he was head of the Service de presse in the Cabinet du résident général at Tunis and Rabat. Thereafter he was in various capacities attached to museums in the south of France. His writings include *L'Afrique méditerranéenne* (1931), and *L'Émpire de Fez; le Maroc du nord* (1931). He died on 2 April 1969. NDNC, 1963; WhoFr, 1969/70

Benoit, François, born in 1870, he received a doctorat in 1897 and became affiliated with the development of the Institut d'art in the Université de Lille from 1899 to 1939. His writings include *L'archi-tecture: antiquité; l'Orient médiéval et moderne; l'Occident médiéval du romain au roman; l'Occident médiéval romano-gothique et gothique* (1911-1934). He died in Argenteuil, 31 May 1947. *Revue archéologique* 6e série, vol. 39 (1952), pp. 100-101

Ben-Or, Juda Leib, born in 1897 at Cairo, he was educated at universities in Cairo and London. Before and after the creation of Israel he was an officer in the Department of Education, responsible for Jewish and Arab education respectively. WhoIsrael, 1968

Bénot, Yves, fl. 1967, his writings include *Idéologies des indépendances africaines* (1969), *Qu'est-ce que le développement?* (1973), *Les indépendances africaines* (1975), and *Les parlementaires africains à Paris, 1914-1958* (1989). LC

Ben-Porath, Yoram, born in 1937 at Ramat-Gan, Palestine, he studied at the Hebrew University, Jerusalem, and Harvard, where he received a Ph.D. in 1967 for his thesis, *Some aspects of the life cycle of earnings*. He taught at Chicago, Harvard, and UCLA, before his appointment as professor at the Hebrew University, Jerusalem. Under a grant from the Ford Foundation, he and Emanuel Marx published the report, *Some sociological and economic aspects of the refugee camps in the West Bank* (1971). His writings include *The Arab labor force in Israel* (1966). WhoEcon

Ben-Shammai, Haggai, born 20th cent., his writings include *Hikre 'Ever va-'Arav* (1993), and he was joint author of *Sefer Yerushalayim* (1987-1991).

Bensidoun, Sylvain, born 20th cent., her writings include *L'agitation paysanne en Russie de 1881 à 1902* (1975), *Le dynamisme de la vallée du Zeravšan* (1979); originally presented as her thesis at the Université de Clermont, 1972, *Samarcande et la vallée du Zerafchan* (1979), and *Alexandre III, 1881-1894* (1990). LC

Bensimon-Donath, Doris, born 9 January 1924 at Wien, she studied at the univrsities of Lyon, Lille, and Aix-en-Provence and received a doctorate in sociology from the Sorbonne, Paris, in 1969. Her writings include *Évolution du judaïsme marocain sous le Protectorat français* (1968), *L'Intégration des juifs nord-africains en France* (1971); in 1989 she edited the collective work *Judaïsme, sciences et technologies*. LC; WhoWorJ, 1972, 1978

Ben Slama, Hamadi, fl. 1969, he was a sometime président de Chambre à la Cour de cassation, Tunis. Note

Benson, Edward Frederic, born 24 July 1867 at Wellington College, Berkshire, England, he was educated at King's College, Cambridge, and worked at Athens for the British Archaeological School, 1892 to 1895, and in Egypt for the Hellenic Society in 1895. Thereafter he travelled in Algeria, Egypt, Greece, and Italy and became a novelist whose writings include *The outbreak of war, 1914* (1933). He died 29 February 1940. ChambrBrBi; New century encyclopedia of names; Who was who, 3

Bensusan, Samuel Levey, born 29 September 1872 at Dulwich, England, he was educated at City of London School and Great Ealing School. He was an editor, author, literary adviser to Theosophical Publishing House, and special correspondent in Morocco, Spain, Portugal, Italy, Germany, and Canada. His writings include *Morocco* (1904). He died 11 December 1958. Master (4); Who was who, 5

Bent, James Theodore, born 30 March 1852 at Baildon, England, he graduated in 1875 from Oxford University. He was an explorer who, together with his wife Mabel, conducted archaeological research in the Eastern Mediterranean, Arabia, and East Africa. His writings include *The Ruined cities of Machonaland* (1892), and *The Sacred city of the Æthiopians* (1893). He died in London from malaria, 5 May 1897. Bidwell; DNB, 1st suppl.; Henze

Bent, Mabel Virginia Anna, born 19th cent., she was educated privately and was married to James Theodore Bent whom she accocompmanied on many of his journeys, including to Bahrain and Hadhramaut in 1893. Her writings include *Anglo-Saxons from Palestine* (1908), and, with her husband, *Southern Arabia* (1900). She died on 3 July 1929. Bidwell; Who was who, 3

Bentham, Sir Samuel, born 11 January 1757, he was a gifted shipwright who travelled in Russia, where he participated in the war against Turkey in 1787. He died 31 May 1831. DNB

Bentinck, A. D. W., major, born 19th cent., he served with his regiment, the 3rd Coldstream Guards, from 1909 to 1911 in Egypt. From 1913 to 1914 he was seconded to the King's African Rifles, and served in Somaliland, where he was wounded. In 1916 and 1917 he served with the Egyptian army, and between 1917 and 1920 was under the orders of the Foreign Office in Abyssinia. From 1922 to 1923 he commanded a battalion of Assyrians Levies in Mesopotamia. JCAS 12 (1925), 122-135

Bentley, G. W., fl. 1933, he was an R.A.F squadron leader and was awarded the Distinguished Flying Cross. Note

Bentov, Mordecai, born in 1900 at Grodzisk, Poland, he was a member of Kibbutz Mishmar Haemek, a sometime Minister of Housing and Development, a member of the Executive Committee of MAPAM, and the author of books on the Jewish-Arab world. His writings include *Yisrael, ha-Palestina'im veha semol* (1971). He died in 1985. EncJud; LC

Ben-Tsur, Avraham, 1924- see Ben-Tzur, Avraham

Bentwich, Joseph Solomon, born 3 February 1902 at London, he was educated at Trinity College, Cambridge. He went to Palestine in 1924 and was successively attached to the Department of Education under the Mandate Government and Israel. His writings include *Education in Israel* (1965). He died in 1982. EncJud; Who's who in Israel, 1980/81; WhoWorJ, 1972

Bentwich, Norman De Mattos, born 28 February 1883 at London, he was a scholar of Trinity College, Cambridge, 1901-1903, and was admitted to Lincoln's Inn in 1908. The universities of Aberdeen, Melbourne, and Jerusalem conferred on him honorary doctorates. Under the Mandatory Government of Palestine he served as attorney-general, 1918-1931. Afterwards he was a professor of international relations at the Hebrew University. His writings include *England in Palestine* (1932). He died 8 April 1971. Asian affairs 58 (1971), p. 200; EncJud; Who was who, 7; WhoWorJ, 1965; Wininger, vol. 1 & 6

Ben-Tzur (Ben-Zur), Avraham, born 1 August 1924 at Dortmund, Germany, he was a founding member of the Kibbutz Lehavot Habashan, a Middle East correspondent for the daily *al-Hamishmar*, and a free-lance writer who wrote *The Syrian Baath Party and Israel* (1968). LC; WhoWorJ, 1972

Benveniste, Émile, born 27 April 1902, he received a doctorate in 1935 from the Université de Paris for his thesis, *Origines de la formation des noms en indo-européen*. In 1927 he was appointed department head at l'École Pratique des Hautes Études, and in 1937 he accepted the chair of comparative grammar at the Collège de France, two positions he held concurrently until poor health compelled him to resign in 1969. His writings include *Problems in general linguistics* (1971), and *Études sogdiennes* (1979). In 1975 he was honoured by *Mélanges linguistiques offerts à Émile Benveniste*. He died 3 October 1976. JA 265 (1977), 1-7; WhoFr, 1975/76

Benveniste (Benvenisti), Meron Shmuel, born 21 April 1934 at Jerusalem, he studied at the Hebrew University. From 1960 to 1965 he was attached to the Ministry of Tourism. Afterwards he was a municipal official and, in 1974, deputy mayor of Jerusalem. His writings include *The Crusaders in the*

Holy Land (1970), *Conflict and contradictions* (1986), *Intimate enemies* (1995); and, with Shlomo Khayat, *The West Bank and Gaza atlas* (1988). ConAu, 65-68; LC; WhoWorJ, 1972

Benyoussef, Amor, he received a docatorate in economics and was in 1967 a demographic expert in the International Labour Organization, Genève. His writings include *Populations du Maghreb et communauté économique à quatre* (1967). LC

Ben Youssef, Salah, born in 1907 or 1908 on Djerba, Tunisia, he was a militant nationalist and from 1948 to 1955 secretary general of the Tunisian Neo-Destour Party, but a partisan of Tunisian Pan-Arab and Islamic politics, and the main rival to President Habib Bourguiba. He was exiled twice and assassinated, 12 August 1961, in Frankfurt, Germany, in circumstances which have never been determined officially. He is the subject of *Le Nouvel état aux prises avec le complot youssefiste, 1956-1958*, edited by Mohamed Sayah (1982-83). AfrBioInd (2); LC; Makers, 1981, 1996

Benzing, Johannes, born 13 January 1913, he received a Dr.phil. in 1939 from the Auslands-Hochschule, Berlin, for his thesis, *Über die Verbformen im Türkmenischen*. Thereafter he was a professor of Turkology at various German universities and, in 1958, visiting professor at Istanbul Universitesi. His writings include *Einführung in das Studium der altaischen Philologie und der Turkologie* (1953). Kürschner, 1996-2001|

Benzinger, Immanuel Gustav Adolf, born 21 February 1865 at Stuttgart, Germany, he studied at the Universität Tübingen, where he received doctorates in divinity and philosophy. Afterwards he was for nearly ten years a pastor of a country parish. From 1897 to 1902 he was editor of the *Zeitschrift des Deutschen Palästina-Vereins*. In 1902 he went for ten years to Palestine as a school teacher of the Hilfsverein der Deutschen Juden. From 1912 until his retirement he was successively professor at the University of Toronto, University of Meadvielle, Pa., and Riga University, where he died on 12 March 1935. His writings include *Hebräische Archäologie* (1894). DtBE

Benzmann, Hans, born 27 September 1869 at Kolberg, Prussia, he studied law at the Universität Berlin and then entered the Bureau of Statistics. He was a sometime archivist of Paliament. Through extramural literary studies he received a Dr.phil. in 1912 from the Universität Greifswald for his thesis, *Die soziale Ballade in Deutschland*. In 1922 he retired as civil servant and became a free-lance writer. His writings include *Die deutsche Ballade* (1925). He died in Berlin, 7 January 1926. DtBE

Benzoni, Alberto, born in 1935, his writings include *Documenti del socialismo italiano* (1968), and *Il movimento socialista nel dopoguerra* (1968). LC

Ben-Zur, Avraham, 1924- *see* Ben-Tzur, Avraham

Ben-Zvi, Itzhak, born 6 December 1884 at Poltava, Ukraine, he was the second president of Israel. He died in office, 23 April 1963. EncJud.; Wininger, vol. 6

Be'or, Haim, fl. 1976, he was a sometime *al-Hamishmar* correspondent on Histadrut affairs.

Beradze, Grigorii Grigor'evich, fl. 1971, his writings include Материалы по историй Ираногрузин-ских ваимоотношений в начале XVII века (1988). LC

Bérard, Maurice Robert Georges, born 17 March 1891 at Paris, he studied at l'École des sciences politiques and Faculté de droit, Paris. He was attached to the Banque de Syrie et du Grand-Liban since its foundation in 1919 and became its *directeur-général* in 1934, when he succeeded Félix Vernes. In 1936 he became the Bank's president. He was *officier de la Légion d'honneur*. *Correspondance d'Orient* 26 (septembre 1934), pp. 108-109; WhoFr, 1955/56-1977/78

Bérard, Victor, born 10 August 1864 at Morez-du-Jura, he was a graduate of l'École Normale Supérieure, *docteur ès-lettres*, member of l'École française d'Athènes, and director of Greek studies at l'École les Hautes Études. In 1920 he was elected senator from Jura and re-elected in 1924. His writings include *La Révolution turque* (1909), *Révolutions de la Perse* (1910), and *Le Problème turc* (1917). He died in Paris, 13 or 14 November 1931. *Correspondance d'Orient* 23 (1931), p. 207; DBF

Béraud, Roger Charles Jean, born 27 July 1915 at Billom, France, he studied law at the universities of Toulouse and Aix-en-Provence, and received a doctorate. From 1943 to 1969, he was presiding judge of the Tribunal de grande instance at Aix-en-Provence. His writings include *Les Mesures de sûreté en droit allemand* (1937). WhoWor, 1978

Berberian, Manuel, he was in 1976 attached to the Tectonic and Seismotectonic Research Section, Geological Survey of Iran. He wrote *Contribution to the seismotectonics of Iran* (1976). LC; Note

Berbrugger, Louis Adrien, born 11 May 1801 at Paris, he studied at the Collège Charlemagne and l'École des chartes. He was an lexicographer, scholar, editor, indefatigable archaeologist, commander of the Légion d'honneur, corresponding member of l'Institut de France, and author of two dozen books and nearly two hundred and fifty scholarly articles. In 1835 he founded a library in Alger, which ultimately became the National Library of Algeria of today. He died in Alger, 2 July 1869. DBF; *Hommes et destins*, vol. 7, pp. 72-73

van **Berchem**, Max, born 16 March 1863 at Genève, he studied natural sciences, Oriental languages, and history of art at the universities of Leipzig, Straßburg, and Berlin. In 1886 he received a Dr.phil. from the Universität Leipzig for his thesis, *La propriété territoriale et l'impôt foncier sous les premiers califes*. After extensive travels in the Middle East he settled as a private scholar in his home town and pursued epigraphic researches. His writings include *Inscriptions arabes de Syrie* (1897), and *Matériaux pour un Corpus inscripionum Arabicarum* (1894-1903). He died in Genève, 7 March 1921. DtBE; Fück; *Index Islamicus* (5)

Bercher, Léon, born in 1889, he studied Arabic at Alger and afterwards enlisted for four years in the 1st Régiment de Spahis as an interpreter. In 1916 he accompanied the French military mission to the Hejaz. In the 1920s he began his career as a jurist and professor. He received a doctorate in 1926 from the Faculté de droit de Paris for his thesis, *Les délits et les peines de droit commun prévus par le Coran*. He was attached to l'École Supérieure de Langue et de Littérature Arabes, Tunis, and was head of the Service de l'interprétariat du Gouvernement tunisien. He translated several of I. Goldziher's works into French, as well as C. Brockelmann's *Geschichte der arabischen Literature*. His writings include *Lexique français-arabe* (1938), and editions with translations of 'Abd Allah b. Abi Zayd, al-Ghazzali, and A. b. M. al-Quduri. He died in the night of 23 to 24 January 1955. *Index Islamicus* (5)

Berchet, Federico, fl. 1899, his writings include *Relazione degli scavi in Piazza S. Marco* (Venezia, 1892); and with Agostino Sagredo he published *Il Fondaco dei Turchi in Venezia; studi storici et artistici con documenti inediti e tavole illustrative* (Milano, 1860). NUC, pre-1956

Bercovitch, Jacob, born in 1947, he was in 1991 a senior lecturer in international relations, University of Canterbury in New Zealand. His writings include *Social conflict and third parties; strategies of conflict resolution* (1984), a work which he originally presented as his doctoral thesis at LSE. LC

Berdimuratov, Esenmurat, fl. 1971, he received a doctorate and was appointed a professor; his writings include Лексикология совремеииого каракалпаского языка (Nukus, 1968), *Hāzirgi qaraqalpaq tili* (Nokis, 1979); and he edited Некоторые вопросы филологий (1981).

Berdyev, Ovliakuli, fl. 1970, his writings include Древней земледельцы Южного Туркменистана (Ashkhabad, 1969), and Докуз айлап Овганыстана (Ashgabat, 1977). LC

Berecz, Antal, born 16 August 1836 at Boldog, Hungary, he was an educator, geographer, and a founder of the Hungarian Geographical Society. He died in Budapest, 14 September 1908. Magyar

Berengian, Sakina, born 28 April 1919 at Tabriz, she graduated from the University Tehran, and studied at Berkeley, Calif., and Columbia, NYC, where she received a Ph.D. in 1956 for her thesis, *Poets and writers from Iranian Azerbaijan in the twentieth century*. She was an assistant professor of Persian at the Department of Islamic Studies in the University of Toronto from 1966 until her death from cancer in Toronto, 10 July 1971. Private

Beres, Louis René, born in 1945, he received a Ph.D. in politics from Princeton University and became a professor of political science at Purdue University, West Lafayette, Ind., a position which he still held in 2003. His writings include *The management of world power* (1973), and *America outside the world; the collapse of U.S. foreign policy* (1987). LC; NatFacDr, 1995-2003

Berezin (Béresine), Il'ia Nikolaevich, born in 1818 in Perm Oblast, he was one of the most important Russian Orientalists of the nineteenth century, and a professor at Kazan University from 1846 to 1855, and afterwards until his retirement at Saint Petersburg. From July 1842 to August 1845 he travelled throughout the Middle East and the Balkans. His writings include Грамматика персидскаго языка (1853), and *Recherches sur les dialects persans* (1853). He died in St. Petersburg in 1896. BiobibSOT, pp. 123-126; Embacher; EncIran; GSE; Henze; Krachkovskii; TatarES

Berg, Cornelius Christiaan, born 18 December 1900 at Rotterdam, he studied at the Rijksuniversiteit te Leiden, where he became a professor of Javanese from 1928 to 1949. His writings include *Maya's hemelvaart in het Javaanse Buddhisme* (1969-1980). Who's who in the Netherlands, 1962/63; Wie is dat, 1948

Berg, Hans Walter Magnus, born 20 October 1916 at Varel, Germany, he studied at the University of Michigan and Universität München, where he received a Dr.phil. in 1943 for *Studien zum Problem der amerikanischen Neutralitätspolitik*. He was for nearly twenty years chief correspondent for Asian affairs at the German radio and televison network. His writings include *Gesichter Asiens* (1983), and *Das Erbe der Großmoguln* (1988). IntAu&W, 1982; LC; Wer ist wer, 1996/97-2002/2003; WhoWor, 1982

Berg, Lev Semenovich, born in 1876 at Bendery, Bessarabia, he was a geographer and biologist who graduated from Moscow University and taught at Leningrad University for most of his life. His writings include *Рыбы пресныхъ водъ Росейской империи* (1916), and *Бессарабія* (1918). His major works have been translated into English, French, and German. He died in Leningrad, 24 December 1950. GSE

van den **Berg**, Lodewijk Willem Christiaan, born 19 October 1845 at Haarlem, Netherlands, he studied at the Universiteit te Leiden and received a doctorate in 1868 for *De contractu "do ut des" jure Moham-medano*. From 1870 to 1877 he held a number of legal and administrative positions in the Neder-landsch-Indië. In 1887 he succeeded A. W. T. Juynboll at the Universiteit te Delft. He wrote *Diritto musulmano de' contratti* (1877), *Le Hadhramout et les colonies arabes dans l'archipel indien* (1886), and *Principes du droit musulman selon les rites d'Abou Hanifah et de Châfi'é* (1986). He died in 1927. EncNI; LC

Berg, Viktoria, 1941- see Meinecke-Berg, Viktoria

Bergan, Asbjörn, fl. 1976, he wrote *Personal income distribution and personal savings in Pakistan* (1966). LC

Bergdolt, Ernst Friedrich, born 31 July 1902 at München, he received a doctorate in botany in 1926 from the Universität München for his thesis, *Untersuchungen über Marchantiaceen*. Thereafter he was a lecturer at the University and attached to the Munich botanical gardens. Kürschner, 1940/41

Berge, Adol'f Petrovich, born in 1828, his writings include *Dichtungen transkaukasischer Sänger des XVIII und XIX. Jahrhunderts in adserbeidshanischer Mundart* (Leipzig, 1868), and *Dictionnaire persan-français* (Paris, 1868). He died in 1886. NUC, pre-1956

Bergé, Marc, born 20th cent., he received a doctorate in 1974 from the Université de Lille III for his *thèse d'état*, *Essai sur la personalité morale et intellectuelle d'Abu Hayyan al-Tawhidi*. In 1978 he was attached to the Université de Bordeaux III. His writings include *Les Arabes* (1978), and *Pour un humanisme vecu* (1979), and he edited and translated *Épître sur les sciences* of 'Ali b. M. al-Tawhidi (1964). LC; THESAM, 4

Bergeon, Benoit Charles, born 11 February 1870 at Caluire-et-Cuire (Rhône), he studied law at Paris and settled in Marseille where he was a municipal politician until 1938. He later moved to Paris where his trace is lost in 1946. He wrote *La Liberté des mers et le désarmement naval* (Paris, 1932). DBF

Berger, Earl, fl. 1965, he was born and educated in Toronto, Ontario, and took a Ph.D. in economics at LSE. He was a sometime lecturer in politics at the University of Ghana, Legon, and the Institute of Public Administration, Achimota. He then became a journalist for the Toronto *Globe and mail*. During the time of the Sinai War he lived in Jerusalem. He wrote *The Covenant and the sword* (1965). LC

Berger, Elmer, born 27 May 1908 at Cleveland, Ohio, he was a graduate of the Hebrew Union College, Cincinnati, and the University of Cincinnati, Ohio; he was ordained in 1932. His legacy comprises two major themes, one, Judaism as a universal religion which does not assume a nationality, and two, equality of Jews, Muslims and Christians in Palestine/Israel. He was successively founder, executive director and executive vice-president of the American Council for Judaism, 1943-1967, and after 1968, a founder and president of the American Jewish Alternatives to Zionism. His writings include *Who knows better must say so* (1955), *Letters of an-anti-Zionist Jew* (1978). He died at his home in Long Boat Key, Fla., 6 October 1996. WhoWorJ, 1965; WRMEA 15, no. 6 (January/February 1997), pp. 24 & 84

Berger, François, fl. 1922, he was a writer on Morocco and wrote *Moha ou Hammou le Zaïani, un royaume berbère contemporain au Maroc, 1877-1921* (Paris, 1929). LC

Berger, Morroe, born 25 June 1917 at N.Y.C., he studied at City College of New York and Columbia University, where he received a Ph.D. in 1950 for his thesis, *Equality by statute*. From 1952 until his death on 7 April 1981, he was a professor of sociology at Princeton University. His writings include *The Arab world today* (1962), and *Islam in Egypt today* (1970). CnDiAmJBI; ConAu, 1 rev.; Master (4); MidE, 1982/83; WhoWorJ, 1972, 1978; WhAm, 7

Berger, Peter Ludwig, born 17 March 1929 at Wien, he received a Ph.D. in 1954 in sociology from the New School for Social Research, New York. He was a sociologist, theologian, and writer who taught at a number of American universities. From 1981 until his retirement he taught at Boston University. His writings include *Facing up to modernity* (1977), and *Modernisation and religion* (1981). BioIn, 14; ConAu, 1 revised; Master, 1981-85 (3); WhoAm, 1988/89; *Who's who in the East*, 1974

Berger, Philippe, born 15 September 1846 at Beaucourt, Alsace, he studied theology at Strasbourg and received a doctorate at Montauban in 1873, but renounced his ministry and became a Semitic scholar. From 1892 to 1910 he held the chair of Hebrew at the Collège de France. His writings include *Histoire de l'écriture dans l'antiquité* (1891). He died in Paris, 24 March 1912. Curinier, II, 117; DBF; NDBA; Vapereau

Berger de Xivrey, Jules, born in 1801 at Versailles, he was a deputy keeper at the Bibliothèque nationale, Paris, and elected in 1839 to the Académie des inscriptions et belles-lettres. He died in Saint Sauveur-lès-Bray (Seine-et-Marne), 29 July 1863. DBF

Bergeret, Jean, born 20th cent., he received a doctorate in 1977 from the Université de Paris IV for *L'art seldjoukide de Konya de la fin du XIIe siècle à la fin du XIIIe siècle*. NUC, 1981; THESAM, 4

Berggren, Jacob, born 11 March 1790 at Sörbo, Sweden, he studied at Uppsala University and received a doctorate of divinity in 1844. In the 1810s he was a clergyman at the Swedish Legation in Constantinople from where he travelled to the Near and Middle East. He was twice invited to teach Arabic at the University of Kharkov, but declined on both occasions. After his return to Sweden, he was a pastor of a country parish at Skällwik and Linköping. His writings include *Resor i Europa och Osterländere* (1826), *Reisen in Europa und im Morgenlande* (1826-1834), *Guide français-arabe vulgaire des voyageurs et des Francs en Syrie et en Égypte* (1844), and *Proverbs arabes* (1948). He died on 2 September 1868. Henze; Krachkovskii, pp. 70-71; SMK

van den **Bergh**, Simon, born 16 November 1882 at Osch, Germany, he received a Dr.phil. in 1912 from the Universität Freiburg im Breisgau for his thesis, *Umriss der muhammedanischen Wissenschaften nach Ibn Haldun*. He devoted all his working life to Islamic philosophy. He went as a refugee from Paris to England, where he settled in Oxford. His writings include *Die Epitome der Metaphysik des Averroes* (1924), and, in the Unesco collection of great works, *The incoherence of the incoherence*, by Averroes (1954). LC

Berghaus, Peter, born 20 November 1919 at Hamburg, Germany, he received a Dr.phil. in 1949 and became a director of the Landesmuseum Münster. Kürschner, 1976-2003

van den **Berghe**, Louis Camiel Silvere, 1923- see Vanden Berghe, Louis Camiel Silvere

Berghoff, Carl, born 19th cent., he was a German official in the service of the Egyptian Government. He was a photographer in Khartoum, when the governor-general of the Sudan appointed him an inspector for the repression of the slave trade. He accompanied the governor of Fashoda on his march against the Mahdis and was killed in the battle of Jabal Qadir in 1881. Hill

Bergman, Samuel (Shmuel) Hugo, born 25 December 1883 at Praha, he studied there and received a doctorate. From 1916 to 1919 he was a librarian at Prague University Library. In 1920 he was appointed chief librarian of the National Library, Jerusalem, a position which he held until 1935. Concurrently, he was a lecturer at the Hebrew University; later becoming its first dean. In 1924 he founded the Hebrew bibliographical journal *Kiryat sefer*. His writings include *Untersuchungen zum Problem der Evidenz der inneren Wahrnehmung* (1908). He died 18 June 1975. DtBE; *Near and Middle East who's who*, 1945-1946; WhoIsrael, 1972; Wininger

Bergmann, Alexander, born in 1878, he received a Dr.jur. in 1902 from the Universität Freiburg im Breisgau for *Das Verhältnis der Gesellschaftsschulden zu den Privatschulden eines Gesellschafters nach BGB*. He was a sometime high official in the Prussian Ministry of Justice. His writings include *Der Ausländer vor dem Standesamt* (1926), and *Internationales Ehe- und Kindschafts-recht* (1926). Note; NUC, pre-1956

Bergmann, Arthur Aharon, born about 1900 at Berlin, he received a Dr.jur. in 1929 from the Universität Berlin for his thesis, *Die Einflußnahme öffentlicher Körperschaften auf den Aufsichtsrat*. From 1948 to 1953 he was Director of Inland Revenue and Finance, the Government of Israel. His writings include *Developing countries and international fiscal law* (1969). WhoWorJ, 1972

von **Bergmann**, Benjamin Fürchtegott Balthasar, born 17 November 1772 at Arrasch, he studied at the universities of Leipzig and Jena in the early 1780s. For a number of years he was a private tutor and teacher in Riga and Moscow. In 1802 and 1803 he explored the Kalmyk settlements of Central Asia. Since 1804 he was a pastor in Rujiena, Livonia. He was an honorary member of the Societas Latina, Jena. His writings include *Nomadische Streifzüge unter den Kalmüken* (Riga, 1804), *Die Kalenderunruhen in Riga in den Jahren 1585 bis 1590* (Leipzig, 1806), *De Kalmukken* (Amsterdam, 1820). *Peter der Grosse als Mensch und Regent* (Königsberg, 1823), and *Voyage chez les Kalmuks* (1825), and Исторія Петра Великаго (Sanktpeterburg, 1840-41). He died at his family estate, Gut Blussen near Wenden, 16 August 1856. Baltisch (1); DtBE

von **Bergmann**, Eduard, born 19th cent. at Rujiena, Livonia, where he became a pastor. Towards the end of the nineteenth century he was a missionary of the Deutsche Orient-Mission, Potsdam. He served in Diyarbakir and later founded orphanages in Urmiya and Khoi. He died of typhoid fever, 26 September 1900.

Ritter von **Bergmann**, Ernst, born 4 February 1844 at Wien, he studied Egyptology at Wien and Göttingen and became a keeper at the Ägyptische Sammlung as well as the Orientalische Münzen in the Kunsthistorisches Museum, Wien. He died in Wien, 26 April 1892. Egyptology; ÖBL

Bergmann, Herbert, fl. 1973, his writings include *The impact of large-scale farms on development in Iran* (1975).

Bergmann, Hugo, 1883-1975 *see* Bergman, Samuel Hugo

Bergmann, Theodor, born 7 March 1916 at Berlin, he received a doctorate in 1955 in agrarian economics from the Landwirtschaftliche Hochschule Stuttgart-Hohenheim for his thesis, *Wandlungen der landwirtschaftlichen Betriebsstruktur in Schweden*. In the service of the U.N. Development Fund, he spent twelve months on a development plan in Antalya, Turkey. His writings include *Soziale Sicherung und landwirtschaftliche Bevölkerung* (1956), *Agrarpolitik und Agrarwirtschaft sozialistischer Länder* (1979), and *Mechanisation and agricultural development* (1981). Kürschner, 1980-1992|

Bergna, Costanzo, born 4 November 1884 at Cantù (Como), Italy, he was ordained in 1908 and became a Franciscan missionary in Libya and Abyssinia. His writings include *La mission francescana in Libia* (Tripoli, 1924), and *Tripoli dal 1510 al 1850* (Tripoli, 1925). He died in Addis Abeba, 12 December 1941. DizBI

Bergsträsser, Gotthelf, born 5 April 1886 at Oberlosa, Germany, he studied philosophy and linguistics at the Universität Leipzig, where he received a Dr.phil. in 1911 for his thesis, *Die Negationen im Kor'an*. In 1914 he travelled to Constantinople, Syria, and Egypt. Since 1915 he was sucessively a professor at Constantinople, Berlin, Königsberg, Heidelberg, and München. He did valuable work on translations from the Greek. His writings include *Einführung in die semitischen Sprachen* (1928), *Grundzüge des islamischen Rechts*, edited by Joseph Schacht (1935), and *Introduction to the Semitic languages* (1983). He died in consequence of a mountaineering accident on Mount Watzmann, 16 August 1933. DtBE; Fück; NDB; Kürschner, 1926

Bérillon, Lucie, fl. 1901, her writings include *La Préparation au bonheur* (1933), and *Le Bonheur et l'adaption à la vie*; préface du docteur Edgar Bérillon, [1859-1948,] (Paris, 1944) LC

Berindei, Dan, born in 1923 at Bucureşti, he was a writer on modern history and diplomatic relations. During the late 1980s he lived in exile. His writings include *Din începuturile diplomaţiei româneşti moderne* (1965), *L'année révolutionnaire 1821 dans les pays romains* (1973), and *Cucerirea independenţei, 1877-1878* (1977). LC; WhoRom

Berindei, Mihnea, fl. 1972, he was joint author, with Gilles Veinstein, of *L'Empire ottoman et les pays roumains, 1544-1545* (1987). LC

Berindranath, Dewan, born in 1932, he was in 1972 a political commentator on current affairs in New Delhi. His writings include *Nasser, the man and the miracle* (1966), *The War with Pakistan* (1966), *War and peace in West Asia* (1968), and *Private life of Yahya Khan* (1974). LC; Note

Beringer, Christoph, born 10 June 1929 at Passau, Germany, he received a Ph. D. in 1955 from Michigan State University for his thesis, *The method of estimating marginal value productivities of input and investment categories on multiple enterprise farms*. From 1955 to 1968 he was a professor of agricultural economy in the University of Idaho. His writings include *Land fragmentation ... in the N.W.F.P. of West Pakistan* (Peshawar, 1962), and *The use of agricultural surplus commodities for economic development in Pakistan*. (1964). WhoUN, 1975

Berkes, Niyazi, born 21 September 1908 in Cyprus, he studied at Istanbul and Chicago and became a professor at Ankara Üniversitesi and the Institute of Islamic Studies, McGill University, Montreal. His writings include *The development of secularism in Turkey* (1964), *Atatürk ve devrimler* (1982), and *Teokrasi ve laiklik* (1984). In 1976 he was honoured by the felicitation volume *Essays on Islamic civilisation*. Canadian, 1964-1970

Berkhan, Oswald, born 19 March 1834 at Blankenburg, Germany, he received a Dr.med. in 1856 from the Universität Würzburg. He established the first school for the mentally retarded as well as special classes for pupils with speech impediments at elementary schools in Braunschweig. His writings include *Über Störungen der Sprache und Schriftsprache* (1889). He died in Braunschweig, 15 February 1917. DtBE

148

Berki, Osman Fazil, fl. 1954, he received a doctorate in law in 1941 from the Université de Genève for his thesis, *La succession ab intestat dans le droit international privé de la Turquie*. Afterwards he was a professor of law at Ankara Üniversitesi. His writings include *Kanun ihtilâfları* (1954), and *Devlet hususî hukuku* (1956). LC; Schwarz

Berki, Şakir, fl. 1954, he wrote *Medeni hukuk* (1969), and he was joint author of *Islâm hususi hukukunu ana prensipleri, "Kuranda hukuk"* (1956). LC

Berkin, Necmettin M., born in 1918, he received a Dr.jur. in 1949 from the Universität Freiburg im Breisgau for *Das Zwangsausgleichverfahren im türkischen Recht und die kritischen Ansichten über die Verbesserung dieses Verfahrens*. He later became a professor at Hukuk Fakültesi Istanbul Üniversitesi. His writings include *Icra hukuku dersleri* (1969), and *Iflâs hukuku* (1970). LC; Schwarz

Berkman, Ali Ümit, born 14 November 1946 at Ankara, he received a doctorate in 1975 and subsequently taught at the Middle East Technical University, Ankara. Together with Metin Heper, he published *Development administration in Turkey* (1980). Kim kimdir, 1985/86-2000

Berl, Alfred, fl. 1899-1938, he was an eminent French publicist and a member of the Ligue française pour la Défense des droits de l'hellénisme. He was joint author of *La Grèce devant le Congrès* (1919).

Edle von **Berks**, Maria, pseud., Mara Cop Marlet, born in 1859 at Livorno, she was a writer and playwright, who wrote *Südslavische Frauen* (1888). She died in 1910. DtInd (2); KDtLK, 1907, 1908; ÖBL

Berlin, Charles, born 17 March 1936 at Boston, Mass., he studied at Harvard University, where he submitted an honors thesis in 1958 entitled *The Jewish press in Palestine, 1863-1914*. In 1962 he was appointed Lee M.Friedman Bibliographer in Judaica at Harvard College Library. His writings include *Index to festschriften in Jewish studies* (1971). DrAS, 1972-1982; Master (3); NUC, 1956-'57; WhoWorJ, 1972

Berliner, Abraham, born 1 May 1833 at Obersitzko, Germany, he was a self-taught scholar who was awarded an honorary doctorate in 1866 by the Universität Leipzig for his edition of Rashi's commentary on the Pentateuch. He was subsequently invited to teach at the Universität Berlin. When the Rabbiner-Seminar zu Berlin was founded, he lectured in Jewish history and literature. He visited most of the Jewish library collections in Europe and collected an important private library, parts of which he bequeathed during his lifetime to H. Brody, Prague, A. Marx, New York, and A. Freiman, Frankfurt. The rest was donated to the Stadtbibliothek Frankfurt a. M. His writings include *Geschichte der Juden in Rom* (1983). He died in Berlin, 22 April 1915. EncJud; Wininger

Berliner, Rudolf, born 14 April 1886 at Ohlau, Germany, he studied history of art at the universities of Berlin, Heidelberg, and Wien. In 1910 he received a doctorate. After two years' overseas travel, which included the Middle East, he became a curator at the Bayerische Nationalmuseum. Between 1933 and 1939 he spent some years in a concentration camp. He subsequently emigrated to the United States. His writings include *Weihnachtskrippen* (1955). He was joint author of the pamphlet *Silberschmiedekunst aus Kurdistan* (1922). He died in Forest Grove, Oregon, 16 October 1961. DtBE

Berman, Ariel, fl. 1975 at Haifa, he wrote *Islamic coins* (1976). LC

Berman, Mildred, born 26 November 1926 at Boston, Mass., she received a Ph.D. in 1963 from Clark University for her thesis, *The role of Beersheba as a regional center*. In 1966 she became a professor at the Department of Geography in Boston University. WhoAmW, 1972/73|

Bermúdez Pareja, Jesús, fl. 1965, he wrote the pamphlet *El Partal y la Alhambra alta* (1977). LC

Bernadotte af Wisborg, greve Folke, born in 1895 at Stockholm, he was a diplomat, and president of the Swedish Red Cross, who was chosen as mediator to seek peace in the Arab-Jewish conflict in Palestine. He was assassinated in Jerusalem by members of the Stern Group in 1948. CurBio; EncJud

Bernand, Étienne, born 11 July 1923 at Bruxelles, he was from 1950 to 1956 a professor at Ain Shams University, Cairo, and since 1965, professor of Greek language and literature at Université de Besançon. His writings include *Recueil des inscriptions grecques du Fayoum* (1975-81). WhoFr, 1981-2002/2003

Bernand, Marie née Baladi, born in 1923, she was the wife of the French Islamicist Étienne Bernand and attached to the Institut français d'archéologie orientale du Caire. She received a doctorate in 1977 from the Université de Paris IV for her thèse d'état, *L'épistémologie mutazilite, d'après le "Mugni XII."* Her writings include *L'Accord unanime de la communauté comme fondement des status légaux de l'islam, d'après Abu al-Husayn al-Basri* (1970), and *Le Problème de la connaissance d'après le Mugni du cadi 'Abd al-Gabbar* (1982). She died 16 June 1993. Annales islamologiques 27 (1993), p. vii; Index Islamicus, 1995 (2); THESAM, 4

Bernard, Augustin, born in 1865 at Chaumont-sur-Tharonne (Loir-et-Cher), he taught geography of North Africa at the École supérieure des lettres d'Alger from 1894 until 1902, when he accepted the chair of geography and colonization at the Sorbonne, a position which he held until his retirement in 1935. From Paris he made annual visits to one part or the other of North Africa and was one of the most active members of the Comité de l'Afrique française. For many years he was general secretary as well as counsellor of the Commission interministrielle des Affaires musulmanes. He left an enormous literary legacy. His writings include *La Pénétration saharienne, 1830-1906* (1906), *Les Confins algéro-marocains* (1911), *Enquête sur l'habitation rurale des indigènes de la Tunisie* (1924). He died 29 December 1947. DBF; *Hommes ed destins*, vol. 2, pp. 71-81; *Index Islamicus* (2)

Bernard, Frédéric Charles Émile, general, born 21 December 1851 at Arras (Pas-de-Calais), he graduated in 1871 from the École Polytechnique, and subsequently participated in military operations in Algeria. In 1880 he accompanied the Missions Flatters which explored the feasibility of a Trans-Saharan railway. His writings include *Carnet d'itinéraires de la division d'Alger* (1880), *Quatre mois dans le Sahara* (1881), *Carte des régions parcourues par les deux missions Flatters* (1882), *Note au sujet de quelques monuments de pierres brutes relevées chez les Touareg Azgar* (1885), and *Deux missions françaises chez les Touareg en 1881-1882* (1896). He died near Nice in 1927. DBF; LC

Bernard, Maurice, fl. 1928-1936, he was a lt.-colonel in the French Army. Together with J. Ladreit de Lacharrière and Henri J. Simon, he published *La pacification du Maroc, 1907-1934* (Paris, 1936). BN

Bernard, P. (Madame), born 19th cent., she wrote *Ali et Aicha; livre de lecture courante en arabe parlé* (Oran, 1906). NUC, pre-1956

Bernard, P., fl. 1954, he was an *ingénieur des Ponts et chaussées*. Note

Bernard, Yvelise, born about 1950, she studied at the Université de Lyon and was a sometime librarian in Lyon and active in the International Middle East Libraries Committee. She subsequently became a professor at the Faculté des lettres et des sciences humaines at the Université nationale d'Abidjan. Her writings include *L'Orient du XVIe siècle à travers les récits des voyageurs français* (1988), a work which was originally submitted in 1982 to the Université de Lyon as a doctoral thesis. She edited *D'Alexandrie à Istanbul; pérégrinations dans l'Empire ottoman, 1581-1583* (1991). LC; Private

Bernard d'Attanoux, Antoine Casimir *Joseph*, born 18 March 1853 at Aix-en-Provence, he was a graduate of the military college of Saint-Cyr, which he had entered in 1872. In September of 1880 he resigned from the military in order to conduct explorations in North Africa. Later, he was sent on a mission to the Touareg Azdjer to negotiate their acceptance of French domination. He wrote *La Marche du tourisme à pied* (Alger, 1908). He died in November 1921. Curinier I, p. 59; DBF; Henze

Bernard de Jandin, R. fl. 1908-1913, he received a doctorate in 1899 from the Faculté de droit de Paris for his thesis, *Des professions que les étrangers peuvent excercer en France.* NUC, pre-1956

Bernasconi, Piero, born 17 October 1889 at Varese, Italy, he was a publisher who, in 1924, became the director of *Rivista delle colonie e dell'Oriente.* Chi è, 1928, 1931, 1936

Bernath, Mathias W., born 11 October 1920 at Sagul-Segenthau, Germany, he received a doctorate in 1951. He was a professor at the Freie Universität Berlin and, concurrently, director at the Südost-Institut, München. His writings include *Habsburg und die Anfänge der rumänischen Nationalbildung* (1972). Kürschner, 1992-2003; LC

Bernatzik, Emmy née Winckler, fl. 1974, she was the wife of the Austrian ethnographer Hugo Adolf Bernatzik, 1897-1953. She wrote *Afrikafahrt; eine Frau bei den Negern Westafrikas* (1936), and she was also joint author of *Südostasien* (1979). LC; Wer ist wer (Wien), 1937

Bernaudeau, A., fl. 1918, he wrote *L'Arabe parlé tunisien; nouveau procédé de figuartion en caractères latins* (Tunis, 1918). NUC, pre-1956

Berne de Chavannes, Pierre, fl. 1928, he wrote *Introduction au capitalisme intégral* (Clermont-Ferrand, 1940); he was joint translator of *L'état musolinien*, par Tomaso Sillani (Paris, 1931). NUC, pre-1956

von **Berneck**, Karl Gustav, born in 1803, he was a historical novelist who published some of his works under the pseudonym Bernd von Guseck. His writings include *Das Buch der Schlachten* (1856), *Deutschlands Ehre* (1864), and *König Murats Erbe* (1865). He died in 1871. LC

Berner, Alfred, born 10 April 1910 at Heinrichswalde, Germany, he received a Dr.phil. in 1937 from the Universität Berlin for his thesis, *Studien zur arabischen Musik auf Grund der gegenwärtigen Theorie und Praxis in Ägypten.* He later became affiliated with the Museum für Völkerkunde, Berlin, and the

Staatsbibliothek, Berlin, before he became director of the Institut für Musikforschung, Berlin. His writings include *Die Berliner Musikinstrumenten-Sammlung* (1952). Kürschner, 1934-1996|

Berner, Wolfgang, born 1 February 1923 at Wallerfangen, Germany, he was for many years a director of the Bundesinstitut für Osteuropäische und Internationale Studien, Köln. He wrote *Die iranisch-sowjetische Zusammenarbeit im wirtschaftlich-technischen Bereich* (1974), and many other brief reports on international communist parties. Kürschner, 1992-2003

Bernhard, Ludwig, born 4 July 1875 at Berlin, he studied at the universities of Berlin and München and received a doctorate in 1902 at Berlin. He was a sometime professor at the universities of Posen, Greifswald, Kiel, and Berlin, where he was the director of the Staatswissenschaftliche Seminar. His writings include *Undesirable results of German social legislation* (1914), and *Die Polenfrage* (1920). He died in Berlin, 16 January 1935. Kürschner, 1926, 1931; NDB

Bernhard, Manfred, fl. 1980, he wrote *Experimentelle Untersuchungen über die Zerkleinerung von Gersten- und Maissilage mit Walzenmühlen* (1967). LC

Bernheimer, Richard, born in 1907, he was an authority on renaissance and baroque art and author of *Romantische Tierplastik und die Ursprünge ihrer Motive* (1931), *Wild men in the middle ages* (1952), and *The nature of representation* (1962). He died in Lisbon, 7 June 1958. Master (4)

Bernier, Tudy, born 18 April 1913 at Quiberon (Morbihan), he began to study law but soon opted for a military career. In 1939 he graduated from the military college in Saint-Maixent. After the second World War he spent some years in Indochina before he was posted to Djibouti. In 1953 he was attached to the Centre de Hautes Études d'Administration Musulmane, Paris. His expertise in Arab affairs and competence in Arabic effected his employment in North Africa. He was struck by illness on 25 August 1963. *L'Afrique et l'Asie* 64 (1963), 88-89

Bernis, Carmen, fl. 1954, she wrote *Trajes y modas en la España de los Reyes Católicos* (1978). LC

de **Bernis**, Gérard, 1928- see Destanne de Bernis, Gérard René Camille

Bernleithner, Ernst, born 4 January 1903 at Wien, he was a geographer whose writings include *Kirchenhistorischer Atlas von Österreich* (1967). He died in Wien, 4 March 1978. Kürschner, 1970, 1976

Bernshtam (Bernstam), Aleksandr Natanovich, born in 1910 at Kerch, Ukraine, he graduated In 1931 from Leningrad University and received a doctorate in 1942 for his thesis, История Кыргыз и Киргизстанас древнейших времен до монгольского завоевания. From 1946 to 1952 he was a professor of archaeology at his alma mater. His writings include Историко-археологические очерки Центрального Тян-Шаня и Памиро-Алая (1952). He died in Leningrad, 10 December 1956. GSE; KyrgyzSE, vol. 1, p. 475; Miliband; Miliband²

Bernstein, Fritz Leon, born 1 January 1888 at Breslau, Germany, he studied at the universities of Breslau and Berlin and received a Dr.phil. in 1913 from the Universität Straßburg for his thesis, *Des Ibn Kaisan Kommentar zur Mu'allaka des Imru'ulkais.* Schwarz; Thesis

Bernstein, George Heinrich, born in 1787 at Cospeda, Thuringia, he studied at the Universität Jena and became a Syriac scholar and professor successively at Berlin and Breslau. His writings include *Carmen arabicum* (1816), *De initiis et originibus religionum in Oriente* (1817), and the unfinished *Lexicon linguae syriacae* (1857). He died in Lauban, 5 April 1860. ADtB; DtBE

Bernstein, Marver Hillel, born 7 February 1919 at Mankato, Minn., he received a Ph.D. in 1948 from Princeton University for *Enforcing government regulations.* He there subsequently served as a professor from 1947 to 1972, when he became a president of Brandeis University, Waltham, Mass. His writings include *Regulating business by independent commission* (1955), and *The politics of Israel* (1957). He died on 1 March 1990. ConAu 1 revised; DrAS, 1982; WhoWorJ, 1972; WhAm, 10

Bernus, Edmond, born 3 June 1929, he studied geography at Paris and received a *docteur ès-lettres.* He was in 1963 affiliated with the Institut français d'Afrique noire, Abidjan, where he specialized in agrarian and social problems. His writings include *Les Illabakan, une tribu touarègue saharienne et son aire de nomadisation* (1974), *Touaregs nigériens* (1981), and *Touaregs; chronique de l'Azawak* (1991). Together with Suzanne Bernus he published *Touaregs* (1983). LC; Unesco

Bernus, Marthe see Bernus-Taylor, Marthe

Bernus, Suzanne, born 20th cent., she was an ethnographer who, in 1972, was affiliated with the C.N.R.S. Her writings include *Henri Barth chez les Touaregs de l'Air; extraits du journal de Barth, 1850* (1972); together with Edmond Bernus she published *Touaregs* (1983). In 1986 she edited the collective work *Le fils et le neveu; jeux et enjeux de la parenté touarègue.* LC

Bernus-Taylor, Marthe, fl. 1972, her writings include *L'Art en terre d'islam* (1988). and *Arabesques et jardins de paradis* (1989). Together with Annie Caubet she published *Le Louvre; Near Eastern antiquities* (1991). LC

Berouti, L., fl. 1980, he was affiliated with the International Labour Office, Geneva, and responsible for the organisation of its Afghanistan Mission. His writings include *Employment and manpower problems and policy isues in the Arab countries* (1984). LC; Note

Berov, Liuben Borisov, born 6 October 1925, he was since 1971 a professor at Sofia University. His writings include *Bulgaria's economic development through the ages* (1980), and *An Outline of Bulgaria's geography and economy* (Sofia, 1984). Koi, 1998; LC

Berque, Augustin, born 11 March 1884 at Nay (Pyrénée-Atlantiques), he was educated in Algeria and taught himself Arabic. For over ten years he was a deputy administrator in Algeria. From 1919 until his death he was affiliated with the Direction des Affaires indigènes du gouvernement général, a position in which he experienced administrative and political isolation. His writings include *Art antique et art musulman en Algérie* (1930), and *L'Algérie, terre d'art et d'histoire* (1937). He died 11 September 1947. Hommes et destins, vol. 7, pp. 26-27; RA, 91 (1947), 152-157

Berque, Jacques Augustin, born 4 June 1910 at Molière, Algeria, he received a classical French education in the humanities and obtained the *agrégation des lettres* from the Sorbonne in 1932. Afterwards he spent two years with a tribe in the Hodna region of Algeria in order to perfect his Arabic. In 1934 he entered the colonial service in Morocco as an official in the Service des Affaires Indigènes and remained there until his resignation in 1953, when he became a Unesco expert in Egypt. He was subsequently appointed a professor at the Sorbonne, where he remained until his retirement in 1981. He held a year-long appoinment at the University of Texas, and spent shorter stays elsewhere. His writings include *Les Structures sociales du Haut-Atlas* (1955), *Histoire sociale d'un village égyptien au XXème siècle* (1957), and a translation of the Koran. His main works were translated into English. He died at his family's estate in Saint Julien-en-Born, 22 June 1995. ConAu, 85-88; Index Islamicus, 1995 (7); MESA bulletin 29 (December 1995), 149-150; Unesco; WRMEA, July/August 1995

Berrady, Lachmi, fl. 1966, he was joint author of *La formation des élites politiques maghrébines* (1973). LC

Berré, François Marie Dominique, born 15 September 1857 at Saint-Méen-le-Grand (Ille-et-Vilaine), he received a religious education and in 1877 entered the Order of St. Dominique. He was ordained in 1882. He became a missionary at Van, and later Mosul, where he exerted considerable influence on account of his relations with the authorities in the Vilayet, so that he was able to promote apostolic interests in the region. He died of angina pectoris, 4 April 1929.

Berreby, Jean Jacques, born 23 October 1927 at Alger, he was a journalist who had studied at l'École nationale des langues orientales vivantes, Paris. His writings include *La Péninsule arabique* (1958), and *Le Golfe persique* (1959). WhoFr, 1971/72-2002/2003

Berriau, Henri Marie Martin, born at Erbray (Loire-inférieure). After passing through the military college of Saint-Cyr, he received a commission as *sous-lieutenant* in 1894. Four years later he was appointed to the Service des Affaires indigènes de l'Algérie, and successively posted to El-Goléa, Ghardaïa, and Aïn-Sefra. On account of the good impression he made on general Lyautey at a meeting at Beni Ounif in 1903, he advanced rapidly, becoming head of the Bureau subdivisionnaire d'Aïn-Sefra in 1904, recipient of the Croix de la Légion d'honneur in 1907, and head of the Compagnie saharienne de la Saoura in 1908. In 1915 he was lieutenant-colonel and head of the Services des renseignments in Morocco. The basis of his political success seems to have been his understanding and respect of the native population. He was promoted to colonel in 1917. He died on 17 December 1918. His writings include *L'Officier de renseignements au Maroc* (1918). Peyronnet, p. 538

Berry, Burton Yost, born 31 August 1901 at Fowler, Ind., he was a graduate of Indiana University and a foreign service officer at the U.S. Department of State until 1954, when he resigned. But he continued to live in the Middle East as a writer and researcher. His writings include *The Burton Y. Berry* [coin] *Collection* (1961-1962), and *Out of the past; the Istanbul Grand Bazaar* (1977). ConAu, 85-88

Berry, John A., fl. 1972., he was a U.S. Army officer and, from 1969 to 1971, an assistant professor of Middle Eastern studies at the U.S. Military Academy.

Bersot, Henri, fl. 1938, his writings include *Die Fürsorge für die Gemüts- und Geisteskranken in der Schweiz* (Bern, 1936), simultaneously published in French entitled *Que fait-on en Suisse pour les malades nerveux et mentaux?* He also wrote *Destins de la psychiatrie suisse* (Berne, 1946). LC

Bertacchi, Cosimo, born 29 January 1854 at Pinerolo, Italy, he was a professor of geography successively at the universities of Messina (1895-1899), Palermo (1900-1910), Bologna (1910-1912), and Torino (1912-1929). His writings include *L'Afganistan nel conflitto eventuale fra l'Inghilterra e la Russia* (1880), and *Dante geometra* (1887). Chi è, 1928-1940; IndBI (4)

Bertagaev, Trofim Alekseevich, born 6 October 1905 at Bulusa, he graduated in 1930 from Irkutsk State University and received a doctorate in 1948 for his thesis Лексика монгольских языков. He was from 1953 to 1976 affiliated with the Institute of Philology in the Soviet Academy of Science. His writings include Грамматика бурятского языка (1962), and Лексика современных монгольских литературных языков (1974). He died 12 April 1976. LC; Miliband; Miliband²

Berteaut, Sébastien, born 10 April 1807 at Marseiile, he was a writer on maritime communication and, since 1848, a secretary of the Marseille Chamber of Commerce. His writings include *Marseille et les intérêts nationaux qui se rattachent à son part* (1845), and *Ferdinand de Lesseps et son œuvre* (1874). He died in Marseille, 14 December 1874. BN; DBF

Berteil, Louis, born in 1904, he was a French general whose writings include *L'Armée de Weygand* (1975), and *La France dans un monde dangereux* (1977). LC

Bertel's, Andrei Evgen'evich, born 8 February 1926 at Leningrad, he graduated in 1949 from the Moscow Oriental Institute and received a doctorate in 1972 in Iranian studies. He was from 1953 to 1979 affiliated with the Oriental Institute, Soviet Academy of Science. His writings include Насир-и Хосров и исмаилизм (1959), and Персидский юмор (1962), and he was joint editor of Антология таджикской поэзии (1957). He died 23 February 1993. LC; Miliband; Miliband²

Bertel's, Evgenii Eduardovich, born in 1890 at St. Petersburg, he graduated in 1920 from the Department of Oriental Languages, Petrograd University. He then joined the Asiatic Museum of the Academy of Sciences of the USSR, where he remained until his death, 7 October 1957. He wrote Очерк истории персидской литературы (1928). EST; GSE; I.I. (4); Miliband; Miliband²; TurkmenSE

Berthault, Pierre, fl. 1923-1936, he was an agronomist and received a doctorate in natural sciences. With François Berthault he published *Le Blé* (1923). LC

Berthelot, André Marcel, born 20 May 1862 at Paris, he studied history and geography. At the age of twenty-six, he was appointed a *maître de conférences* in history of Roman and Grecian religions at l'École des hautes études, Paris. In 1894 he entered politics and business, without abandoning entirely his scholarly endeavours. His writings include *L'Afrique saharienne et soudanaise, ce qu'en ont connu les anciens* (1927). He died 6 June 1938. Curinier, v. 2, p. 277; DBF

Berthelot, Marcellin Pierre Eugène, 1827-1907 see Berthelot, Pierre Eugène Marcellin

Berthelot, Philippe Joseph Louis, born 9 October 1866 at Sèvres (Hauts-de-Seine), he entered the diplomatic service in 1889 in Lisbon. In 1902 he was sent on a mission to the Far East, and upon his return in 1904, he was put in charge of the newly created *service d'Asie*. For twenty-five years he played a leading role in the political life of France. He died in Paris, 22 November 1934. DBF

Berthelot, Pierre Eugène *Marcellin*, born 25 October 1827 at Paris, he was one of the great French scientists and educators of the nineteenth century without ever having obtained a formal degree. All the contemporary learned societies considered it an honour to have him as a member. His writings include *Les Origines de l'alchimie* (1885), and *Thermochimie* (1897). He died in Paris, 18 March 1907, and was buried in a state funeral at the Panthéon. DBF; Curinier, v. 2, p. 276; Ind BFr (9); Vapereau

Berthelot, Sabin, born 4 April 1794 at Marseille. Through his service in the merchant marine, he came to the Canary Islands in 1820, where he entered the service of a rich land owner of Tenerife and managed his botanical garden. There he met the British botanist Philip B. Webb and became his collaborator. Together they explored the Islands and published their *Histoire naturelle des Canaries* between 1836 and 1850. Alone, he published in 1840 *De la pêche sur la côte occidentale de l'Afrique*. He was a founder of the Société d'ethnographie and an honorary citizen of Santa Cruz de Tenerife, where he died 10 November 1880. DBF

Bertherand, Émile Louis, born 21 August 1821 at Valenciennes, France, he received a medical doctorate from the Université de Strasbourg in 1845, and in 1847 joined the Bureaux arabes d'Algérie. He was a military surgeon in the Armée de l'Afrique until his resignation around 1874. At sometime he practised medicine in Lille as well as at the Hospice musulmane d'Alger. He wrote *Médicine et hygiène des Arabes* (1855). His *Hygiène musulmane* was published in a Portuguese translation in 1876, entitled *Hygiene mahometana*. He died in Cheliff, Algeria, 2 June 1890. DBF; Vapereau

Bertherand, François *Alphonse*, born in 1815 at Bazeilles (Ardennes), he joined the Corps de santé militaire in 1834 and received a doctorate in 1837 from the Faculté de médecine de Paris. In 1852 he became chief medical officier in the division d'Alger, and participated in the campaigns in Kabylia. He died in Alger in December 1887. DBF

Berthier, Pierre, born 20th cent., he received a doctorate in 1982 from the Université d'Aix-Marseille for his thesis, *La Bataiile de l'oued el Makhazen dite "bataille des trois rois,"* a work which was published in 1985. In the same year he became affiliated with the C.N.R.S. LC; THESAM, 1

Bertholon, Lucien Joseph, born 30 September 1854 at Metz, he studied medicine at Lyon, where he received a doctorate in 1877. He was a medical officer in Tunisia until 1890, when he resigned in order to practise at the French colony of Tunis. He later taught at the Sadiqi and Alawi colleges. In 1894 he founded the *Revue tunisienne*. In 1894, 1902, and 1912 he was elected president of l'Institut de Carthage. He died 4 August 1915 in Lyon, where he had gone for medical treatment. His writings include *Recherches anthropologiques dans la Berbérie orientale* (1913). *Revue tunisienne*, 1915, pp. 3-22

Berthon, Louis, born 19th cent., he wrote *Supplément à l'ouvrage "L'industrie minéral en Tunisie"* (1931). LC

Berthoud, Adolphe, fl. 1880, his writings include *L'autonomie de l'Algérie* (Alger, 1862). BN

Bertin, George, born in 1848, he was a Assyriologist and a member of the Royal Asiatic Society. His writings include *Abridged grammar of the languages of the cuneiform insciptions* (London, 1888), and *The population of the fatherland of Abraham* (London, 1893). He died in 1891. BLC; LC

Bertman, Martin A., born 20th cent., he was in 1981 a professor of philosophy at S.U.N.Y., Potsdam. His writings include *Research guide to philosophy* (1974), and *Body and cause in Hobbes* (1991). LC

Bertocci, Peter J., born in 1938, he received a Ph.D.in 1970 in anthropology from Michigan State University for his thesis, *Elusive villages; social structure and community organization in rural East Pakistan*. His writings include *Bangladesh history, society and culture* (1973).

Bertola, Arnaldo, born 15 August 1889 at Sostegno, Italy, he received a doctorate in law and was from 1920 to 1928 a president of the Aegean Islands' Court of Justice, Rhodes. Since 1931 he pursued a teaching career at the universities of Urbino, Pavia, and Torino. His writings include *Il regime dei culti in Turchia* (1925), and *Il regime dei culti nell'Africa* (1939). Chi è, 1936-1961; Who's who in Italy, 1958

Bertola, Ermenegildo, born 12 July 1909 at Vercelli, Piedmont, he was affiliated with the Università cattolica as a professor. His writings include *La filosofia ebraica* (1947), *Saggi e studi di filosofia medioevale* (1951), and *Salomon ibn Gabirol, Avicebon* (1953). In 1987 he contributed to the collective work, *Etica e pragmatica*. Chi è, 1948

Bertoldi, Vittorio, born 2 April 1888 at Trient (Trento), Austria, he studied at the Universität Wien, where he received a Dr.phil. for his thesis, *Die trientischen Pflanzennamen; eine onomasiologische Unter-suchung*. He was successively professor of comparative linguistics at the universities of Napoli and Cagliari. His writings include *Colonizzazioni nell'antico Mediterraneo occidentale alla luce degli aspetti linguistici* (1950), *La storicità dei fatti di lingua* (1951), and *La linguistica* (1953). He died in Rome, 8 June 1953. Chi è, 1948; DizBI

Bertolotti, Davide, born 2 September 1784 at Torino, Italy, he was a prolific writer whose publications include *Storia delle crociate* (1833), and *Gli Arabi in Italia* (1838). He died in Torino in 1860. DizBI

Berton, Peter Alexander Menquez, born 11 June 1922 at Bialystock, Poland, he studied at Wasada University, Japan, and Columbia University, where he received a Ph.D. in 1956 for his thesis, *The secret Russo-Japanese alliance of 1916*. From 1945 to 1947 he was a deputy assistant censor, Supreme Command Allied Powers. Since 1969 he was a professor of international relations at the University of Southern California. His writings include *Soviet works on China* (1959), and *Soviet works on Southeast Asia; a bibliography* (1967). AmM&WS, 1973 S, 1978 S; WhoWest, 1974-1976

de **Bertou**, Jules, comte, fl. 1838, he was a French explorer who travelled in Palestine. His writings include *Essai sur l'état politique des provinces de l'Empire ottoman* (1839), *Essai sur la topographie de Tyr* (1843), and *Le mont Hor, le tombeau d'Aaron, Cadès; étude sur l'itinéraire des Israélites dans le désert* (1860). BN; Henze

Bertram, Sir Thomas *Anton*, born 8 February 1869, he was educated at London and Cambridge, and called to the bar in 1893. He later joined the Colonial Service. His writings include *The Colonial Service* (1930). With J. W. A. Young he wrote *The Orthodox Patriarchate of Jerusalem; report of the Commission appointed by the Government of Palestine to inquire and report upon certain* controversies between the Orthodox Patriarchate of Jerusalem and the Arab Orthodox community (1926). He died 16 September 1937. Who was who, 3

Bertrand, François Marie, l'abbé, born 26 October 1807 at Fontainebleau (Seine-et-Marne), he studied at the Seminary of Saint-Sulpice and served for many years at the parish of Herblay before he became canon of Versailles. His writings include *Chrestomathie hindoustani* (1847), and *Dictionnaire universel historique et comparatif de toutes les religions du monde* (1848-51). He died in 1881. BN; IndexBFr (3); LC; Vapereau

Bertrand, Gustave, born 19th cent., he gained a medical doctorate and was in 1916 a *médecine-major* and head of the Service médical indigène of the Arbaoua District in Morocco. Note

Bertrand, Henri Casimir, born 15 July 1829 at Nîmes, he graduated from the military college of Saint-Cyr and participated in the 1855 Crimean campaign. From 1871 to 1875, he was attached to the Bureaux des Affaires indigènes d'Algérie and a *commandant supérieur* at Tiaret. Afterwards he served until 1887 as commanding officer at Sousse. He died in Nîmes, 21 March 1904. DBF; Peyronnet, p. 896

Bertrand, Jean Jacques Achille, born in 1884, he received a doctorate in 1914 from the Université de Paris for his thesis, *Cervantes et le romantisme allemand*. His writings include *Sur les vieilles routes d'Espagne* (1931). LC

Bertrand, Olivier, fl. 1972, he was at one time attached to the Centre d'études et de recherches sur les qualifications. His writings include *Le livre français sur les marchés mondiaux* (1957), and with Pierre Maréchal he published *Les ouvriers qualifiés à travers les différents régimes de qualification dans les pays de la CEE* (issued also in English and German in 1981). LC; Note

Bertrand, Pierre, fl. 1955, he was an *ingénieur des travaux publics*. Certainly until 1959, he was an *administrateur* at the Institut national de la statistique et des études économiques. His writings include *Dix ans d'économie marocaines, 1945-1955* (Paris, 1955), and *Manuel pratique de la voirie urbaine* (Paris, 1961). LC

Bertrandon de la Brocquière, fl. 1432, he wrote *Le voyage d'outremer et retour de Jérusalem en France par la voie de terre, pendant des années 1432 et 1433* (1804), and its English translation, *The travels of Bertrandon de la Brocquière to Palestine* (1807). NUC, pre-1956

Berza, Mihai, born 23 August 1907 at Tecuci, Romania, he studied history at Iaşi University, where he also received his doctorate. From 1931 to 1935 he studied at the Şcoala română in Rome. He spent the following academic year at l'École Pratique des Hautes Études. He had a long academic career and was a director of the Institutul de studii sud-est europene din Bucureşti and president of the Comitetul naţional român de studii sud-est europene. In 1965 he published a biography of Nicolae Iorga. He died 5 October 1978. WhoRom; Südost-Forschungen 38 (1979), pp. 266-268

Besançon, Jacques, born 20th cent., he received a doctorate in 1975 from the Université de Paris VII for his thesis, *Recherches géomorphologiques en Beqaa et dans le Liban intérieur*. His writings include *L'homme et le Nil* (1957), and *Géographie de la pêche* (1965). LC; THESAM, 3

Besant, Sir Walter, born in 1836 at Portsea, England, he was a novelist whose many writings include *The life and achievements of Edward Henry Palmer* (1883); together with him he published *Jerusalem, the city of Herod and Saladin* (1871). He died in Hampstead, 9 June 1901. DLB, vol 135 (1994), pp. 38-46, vol. 190 (1998), pp. 32-42; DNB; Who was who, 1

Bese, Lajos (Louis), born 1 October 1926 at Ligeti, Hungary, he was a curator of the Oriental collection at the Library of the Hungarian Academy of Science, Budapest. He died in Budapest, 18 June 1988. MEL, 1978-1991

Beshevliev (Beševliev), Veselin Ivanov, born 25 March 1900 at Sofia, he studied at Halle, Jena, and Würzburg and became affiliated with Sofia University as a professor, specializing in Balkan philology, epigraphy, and history. His writings include Епиграфски приноси (1952), and *Bulgarisch-byzantinische Aufsätze* (1978). EnBulg; LC

Beshir, Mohamed Omer, born 3 December 1926 at Karima, Sudan, he graduated from Gordon Memorial College, Khartoum, and joined the Sudan Government's Department of Education as a primary school teacher. Despite his active role in the left-wing politics of post-war Sudan, the Department nominated him for further study at Queen's College, Belfast, where he took a B.Sc.Econ. in 1956. He completed his post-graduate study at Linacre College, Oxford, where he received his B.Litt. in 1966 for his thesis *Educational development in the Sudan, 1899-1956*. After service in the Sudan Government, he returned to St. Antony's College, Oxford, for research and lecturing. He was granted honorary doctorates from the University of Hull and the University of Juba. His greatest work was the establishment of a private university, Ahlia University College. His writings include *The Southern Sudan* (1968), *Revolution and nationalism in the Sudan* (1977), and *Terramedia, themes in Afro-Arab relations* (1982). He died 29 January 1992. *Africa* (London) 62 (1992), pp. 435-438; Unesco

Besnard, Auguste Edmond Jean, born in 1866, he was awarded in 1938 the *Mérite libanais de première classe* for his contribution to Lebanon's culture and education as secretary-general of the Mission Laïque Française. In addition, a street in Aleppo was named after him. In 1951, Gustave Goujon and Pierre Deschamps published a brief biography, *Edmond Besnard, 1866-1949.* BN

Besnier, Maurice, born in 1873 at Paris, he studied at l'École normale supérieure and l'École française de Rome. Throughout his life he pursued an interest in Roman antiquities. He lectured in classical antiquities and history at the Université de Caen, and offered a weekly class at l'École des Hautes-Études, Paris. His writings include *L'Île tiberine dans l'antiquité* (1902), *Géographie ancienne du Maroc* (1904), and *La Tunisie punique* (1904). He died 4 March 1933. DBF

Bessel-Hagen, Erich, born 12 September 1898 at Berlin, he studied at the Universität Berlin, where he received a Dr.phil. in 1920 for his thesis, *Über eine Art singulärer Punkte der einfachen Variationsprobleme in der Ebene.* His trace is lost after a publication in 1932. Thesis

Besset, G., lieutenant, born 19th cent., he wrote *Réconnaissances au Sahara; d'In Salah à Anguid et à Tikhammar* (1904). NUC, pre-1956

Bessière, Lucien, he was in 1939 a *professeur agrégé* in history and geography at the Lycée d'Alger. Concurrently he served as an archivist at the Société de Géographie d'Alger et de l'Afrique du Nord and in charge of its *Bulletin.* Note

Besson, Ferny, born in 1913, she was a novelist whose writings include *Sahara, terre de vérité* (1965).

Besson, Maurice, born in 1885, his writings include *Les Colonies allemandes et leurs valeur* (1917), *Le Général comte B. Boigne, 1751-1830* (1930), *Histoires des colonies françaises* (1931), and *Les Aventuriers français aux Indes, 1775-1820* (1932). NUC, pre-1956

Best, Kershaw Thorpe, born 19th cent., he wrote *An etymological manual* (1887), and *Shakesperiana* (1889). BLC

Besterman, Theodore Deodatus Nathaniel, born 18 November 1904 in England, he was privately educated and from 1931 to 1938 served as a special lecturer in the School of Librarianship, the University of London. His writings include *The beginnings of systematic bibliography* (1935), *A world bibliography of bibliographies* (1939-1940), and *UNESCO; peace in the minds of men* (1951). He died 4 June 1980. DNB; Master (10); Who was who, 7

Besthorn, Rasmus Olsen, born 29 October 1847 at Hillerød, Denmark, he studied Arabic at Københavns Universitet. A university grant enabled him to study Arabic manuscripts at the Bibliothèque nationale de Paris in the spring of 1885 for his 1889 doctoral thesis entitled *Ibn Zaiduni vitam scripcit epistolamque ejus ad Ibn-Dschahbarum scriptam nunc primum edidit.* When his thesis supervisor, August F. von Mehren, retired in 1898, he had hoped to succeed him as professor of Semitic and Oriental languages at the university, but he was disappointed and had to settle for a career as journalist. He was joint editor of *Euclides Elementa ... arabice et latine ediderunt* (1893-1910), and *Die astronomischen Tafeln des Muhammad ibn Musa al-Khwarizmi* (1914). He died in Charlottenlund on 20 August 1921. DanskBL; DanskBL²

Betger, Evgenii Karlovich, born in 1887 at Tashkent, he studied from 1906 to 1909 at Heidelberg, and graduated in 1914 from Kiev University. His writings include *Указатель к газете "Туркестанские веломости" за 1870-1892* (Tashkent, 1926), and *Краткий справочник* (1958). He died in 1956. Miliband; Miliband²

Bethmann, Erich Waldemar, born 4 September 1904 at Berlin, he was educated in Germany, the United States, England, and at the AUB, and served as an Adventist missionary in Asyut (1929-1933), al-Husn and Irbid, Jordan (1933-1936), Mosul and Baghdad (1936-1939). During World War two he was interned in India. Since 1946, he resided in the United States, where he was one of the founders of the American Friends of the Middle East. He was married in second marriage to the American journalist Dorothy Thompson. His writings include *Bridge to Islam* (1950), *Decisive years in Palestine* (1957), *Yemen on the treshold* (1960), and *Steps toward understanding Islam* (1966). ConAu, 2; Master (3); WrDr, 1982-1992/94|; WRMEA 10 (May/June 1991), pp. 41 & 60

Bettoli, Parmenio, born 13 January 1835 at Parma, Italy, he was a prolific author and playwright whose writings include *Tripoli artistica e commerciale* (1912). He died in Bergamo, 16 March 1907. DizBI

Bettrán y Róspide, Ricardo, born in 1852, he wrote *La Guinea española* (Barcelona, 1901). He died in 1928. NUC, pre-1956

Betts, Richard Kevin, born 15 August 1947 at Easton, Pa., he studied politics at Harvard University, where he received a Ph. D. in 1975 for *Soldiers, statesmen, and the resort to force*. He successively served as a professor of government at Harvard and Brookings Institution, Washington, D.C. His writings include *Soldiers, statesmen and cold war crises* (1977). ConAu, 85-88

Betz, Anton, born 23 February 1893 at St. Ingbert, Germany, he studied law at Würzburg, Freiburg im Breisgau, and Bonn, where he received at Dr.rer.pol. in 1924 for his thesis *Beiträge zur Ideengeschichte der Staats- und Finanzpolitik der deutschen Zentrumspartei*. Afterwards he was a journalist and later, owner of a publishing empire. In 1963, he was honoured by *Festschrift für Anton Betz*. His writings include *Zeit und Zeitung; Notizen aus acht Jahrzehnten, 1893-1973* (1973). He died in Düsseldorf, 11 December 1984. DtBE; Wer ist wer, 1984

Beuchelt, Eno, born 6 March 1929 at Leipzig, he received a Dr.phil. in 1961 from the Universität Köln for his thesis, *Kulturwandel bei den Bambara von Ségou*. Until 1992 he was a professor of ethnology at Köln. His writings include *Mali* (1966) *Niger* (1968), *Ideengeschichte der Völkerpsychologie* (1974), and *Die Afrikaner und ihre Kulturen* (1981). Kürschner, 1992|

van der **Beugel**, Ernst Hans, born 2 February 1918 he studied at Amsterdam and was in government service from 1945 to 1960. From 1966 until his retirement in 1984, he was a professor of international relations at the Rijksuniversiteit te Leiden. His writings include *From Marshall aid to Atlantic partnership* (1966), and *Nederland in de westelijke samenwerking* (1966). IntWW, 1974-1992/93|; WhoNL, 1962/63; WhoWor, 1974/75; Wie is dat, 1956

Beulé, Charles Ernest, born 29 June 1826 at Saumur, he was a graduate of l'École normale supérieure, and a student at l'École française d'Athènes. In 1857, he succeeded to the chair of archaeology at the Bibliothèque impériale. He was a member of the Académie des inscriptions since 1860, and, since 1862, permanent a secretary of the Académie des beaux-arts. His writings include *L'Acropole d'Athènes* (1854). He died in Paris, 4 April 1874. DBF

Beumelburg, Walther, born 4 October 1894 at Traben-Trarbach, Germany, he served during the first World War as an army officer in the Ottoman Empire. After the war, he became a writer for press and radio. Since 1934 he was served as head of the radio station Reichssender Berlin. Wer ist's, 1935

Beurdeley, Georges Ernest, born 17 May 1863 at Tonnerre (Yvonne)., he entered the French civil service in 1883 at the Préfecture de la Seine. In 1897 he was tranferred to Dahomy, later to Abomey. He became a *directeur des affaires politiques* and Justice of the Peace of the territory extending to Porto Novo, 1898-1899. He died on the eve of his retirement in Pondichery, 24 August 1921. Hommes et destins, vol. 7, p. 31

Beurmann, Karl Moritz von, born 28 July 1835 at Potsdam, Germany, he studied the Ingenieurschule in Berlin and served as an army officer in Erfurt before studying Oriental languages at the Universität Breslau. In 1860, he explored East Africa from Egypt to Nubia and northern Abyssinia. In the following year he went to Wadai in search of the astronomer Eduard Vogel. He reached Mao, in what is now Chad, and lost his life in February 1863, probably not without the approval of the Sultan of Waddai. He wrote *Vocabulary of the Tigré language* (Halle, 1868), and *Voyages et explorations, 1860-1863; Nubie, Soudan, Libye, Fezzan, Lac Tchad* (1973). ADtB; AfrBiolnd (1); DtBE; Embacher; Henze; Hill; Hommes et destins, vol. 9, pp. 36-38

Beuscher, François, born in 1869 at Paris, he was a prominent political journalist in Alger as well as an editor of the *Indépendant de Constantine* and the *Dépêche algérienne*, Alger. From 1928 until his retirement in 1941, he was affiliated with *l'Echo d'Alger*. He died in Alger in September 1952. Hommes et destins, vol. 7, pp. 82-84

Bevan, Anthony Ashley, born 19 May 1859 at Trent Park, Barnet, England, he was educated at Cheam, Surrey, Lausanne, and Straßburg. He became a Fellow of Trinity College and Lord Almoner's Professor of Arabic, Cambridge. His writings include *A short commentary on the Book of Daniel for the use of students* (1892), and *The Naka'id of Jarir and al-Farazdak* (1905-1912). He died in 1933. Who was who, 3

Bevan, Bernard, fl. 1930, he wrote *History of Spanish architecture* (London, 1938). NUC, pre-1956

Beveridge, Annette Susannah Akroyd, born in 1842, she translated *The history of Humayun* (1902), and edited and translated the *Bábar-Náma* in 1905 and 1922 respectively. She died in 1929. BLC; LC

Beveridge, Henry, born in 1837, he was educated at Queen's College, Belfast, and joined the Bengal Civil Service, serving in India from 1858 to his retirement in 1893. His writings include *A comprehensive history of India* (1862), *The district of Bákarganj* (1876), and *The trial of Maharaja Nanda Kumar* (1886). He died in 1929. BLC; IndianBiInd (2); LC

Beville, lieutenant-colonel Francis Granville, born 24 March 1867, he was in 1896 acting consul at Muscat, and from 1896 to 1897 a consul. From 1900 to1904, he was Political Agent, Bundelkhand. He died 21 April 1923. IndianBiInd (3); *Who was who*, 2

Bevis, John, born in 1693 at Tenby, England, he graduated from Christ Church, Oxford and subsequently studied medicine, astronomy, and optics. He was a member of the Royal Academy of Berlin, and a corresponding member of the Paris Academy. He died in 1771. DNB

Bevis, Richard Wade, born 4 June 1937 at NYC., he studied at Duke University and the University of California at Berkeley, where he received a Ph.D. in 1965 for *The comic tradition on the London stage, 1737-1777*. He later taught English for ten years at AUB, before joining the Department of English in the University of British Columbia, a post which he still held in 1995. His writings include *Bibliotheca orientalia; an annotated checklist of early English travel books on the Near and Middle East* (1973). DrAS, 1974, 1978; NatFacDr, 1995

Bewer, Julius August, born 28 August 1877 at Ratingen, Germany, he studied at the Union Theological Seminary of New York, and Columbia University, where he received a Ph.D. in 1920 for his thesis, *The history of the New Testament canon in the Syrian Church*. In 1922 the Universität Göttingen conferred on him an honorary doctorate of divinity. For many years, until his retirement in 1945, he was a professor of Hebrew and cognate languages at the Union Theological Seminary. He died 31 August 1953. WhAm, 3

Bey, Frauke, 1941- *see* Heard-Bey, Frauke

Beyer, Franz, born 27 May 1892 at Bautzen, Germany, he graduated from the Fürstenschule St. Alfa, Meißen and served from 1911 to 1918 as a lieutenant in the Imperial Navy, where he was an eyewitness to the German intervention in Finland. After the war, he was a police officer and an extramural student at the universities of Düsseldorf, Köln, and Münster, where he received a Dr.jur. in 1927 for his thesis, *Das deutsche Einschreiten in Finnland 1918*. His writings include *Das Leitbild des deutschen Offiziers* (1964). Thesis

Beyhum, Mohamed Jamil, born in 1889 at Beirut, he was in 1914 a member of the Syrian national congress charged with nominating Faysal, King of Syria. He was president of the Muslim Youth Association in 1932, and a sometime president of te Lebanese Academy. His many writings include *Falsafat al-ta'rikh al-'Uthmani* (1925), and *Urubat Lubnan* (1969). *Who's who in Lebanon*, 1970/71

Beylerian, Arthur, he wrote *Les Grandes puissances, l'Empire ottoman et les Arméniens dans les archives françaises, 1914-1918* (1983). LC

Beylié, général Léon Marie Eugène, born 26 November 1849 at Strasbourg, he graduated from the military college Saint-Cyr, and spent the greater part of his military service in the Far East. It was only during the last three years of his life that he excavated in North Africa. His writings include *L'Inde sera-t-elle russe ou anglaise?* (1884), *Mon journal de voyage de Lorient à Samarcande* (1889), *Prome et Samara; voyage archéologique en Birmanie et en Mésopotamie* (1907), and *La Kalaa des Beni-Hammad; une capitale berbère* (1909). He died on the Mekong River, 15 July 1910. DBF; NDBA

Beylis, V. M., 1923- *see* Beilis, Vol'f Mendelevich

Beyran, Joseph Melcon, born in 1825, he was a medical doctor who was affiliated with the Académie impériale de médecine. His writings include *La Turquie médicale au point de vue des armées expéditionnaires et des voyageurs* (Paris, 1854), and *Notice sur la Turquie; aperçu topographique, industrie, propriété, instruction publique, armée française, Koran, capitulations, hommes d'état, réformes* (Paris, 1855). He died in 1865. BN; LC

Beyries, J., fl. 1930-1935, he wrote *Proverbes et dictions mauritaniens* (Paris, 1930). NUC, pre-'56

Beyssade, Jacques, born 21 March 1911, he received a doctorate in law, and specialized in Algerian legal problems. He was a member of the Centre de Hautes Études d'Administration musulmane. In 1946 he participated in preparing the Statut de l'Algérie. In the same year, he produced the memoir, *De l'accession des musulmans de l'Algérie à la citoyenneté française*. His writings also include *Le Régime législative de l'Algérie* (1955). He died overworked at his office in Alger, 2 January 1960. *L'Afrique et l'Asie moderne* 49, 1er trimestre (1960), pp. 85-86; LC

Beyssade, Pierre, born in 1906, he was a member of the Centre de Hautes Études Administration musulmane. He wrote *La Guerre d'Algérie* (1968), *La Ligue arabe* (1968), and *L'agonie d'un monde* (1973). *L'Afrique et l'Asie moderne* 49, 1er trimestre (1960), pp. 85-86; LC

Beytullov, Mekhmed *see* Beitullov, Mekhmed

Bezault, Bernard, born 19th cent., his writings include *Épuration des eaux d'égout* (Paris, 1901), and *Assaissement des villes* (Paris, 1912). BN; NUC, pre-1956

Bhalla, Ajit S., fl. 1967, he was a sometime resident associate, Economic Growth Center, Yale University. Subsequently he was chief of the Technology and Employment Branch at the International Labour Office, Genève, and Hallsworth Professorial Fellow in Economics, University of Manchester, England. With Dilmus D. James he published *New technologies and development* (1988). He edited *Small and medium enterprises* (1991), and *Environment, employment, and development* (1992). LC

Bhambhri, Chandra Prakash, born 28 March 1933 in India, he studied at Agra University, where he received a Ph.D. in 1959. In 1968 he was a reader at the Department of Political Science in the University of Rajasthan, Jaipur. His writings include *Substance of Hindi policy* (1959), *Bureaucracy and politics in India* (1971), and *World Bank and India* (1981). IntAu&W, 1977

Bhandarkar, Devadatta Ramkrishna, born 19 November 1875, he was Carmichel Professor of Ancient Indian History and Culture, Calcutta University. His writings include *Lectures on the ancient history of India* (1919), and *Lectures on ancient Indian numismatics* (1921). He died 30 May 1950. Eminent; Ray

Bhandarkar, Sir Ramkrishna Gopal, born 6 July 1837, he was an Orientalist and social reformer, educated at Ratnagiri and Elphinstone College, Bombay. Until his retirement in 1893, he taught Sanskrit and Oriental languages at Indian schools and colleges. He was awarded an honoray Dr.phil. by the Universität Göttingen. His writings include *Early history of the Dekkan down to the Mahomedan conquest* (1884). He died in August 1925. Buckland; EmOr; IndianBiInd (7); Who was who, 2

Bhanu, Dharma, fl. 1955 *see* Dharma Bhanu

Bhargav, Abhay, born 20th cent., he was in 1976 a research fellow at the South Asia Studies Centre, Department of Political Science, University of Rajasthan. Note

Bhargava, Ganti Suryanarayana, born 20th cent., he was in 1977 an assistant editor at the *Hindustan times*, New Delhi. His writings include *The battle of NEFA* (1964), *India and West Asia* (1967), *Pakistan in crisis* (1969), *India's Watergate* (1974), *Morarji Desai* (1977), *South Asian security after Afghanistan* (1983), and *Benazir, Pakistan's new hope* (1989). LC

Bhargava, Krishna Dayal, born in 1912, his writings include *Descriptive list of Mutiny papers in the National Archives of India* (New Delhi, 1960-1979). LC

Bharier, Julian, born 20th cent., he received a Ph.D. in 1968 from SOAS for *Capital formation in Iran, 1900-1965*. His writings include *Economic development in Iran, 1900-1970* (1971). LC; Sluglett

Bhatnagar, G. D., born 20th cent., he received a Ph.D. in 1965 from the University of Lucknow for *Awadh under Wajid Ali Shah*, a work which was published in 1968. LC

Bhatt, Shashikant K., fl. 1974. Together with Pradeepchand Kailashchandra Sethi he published *Ratlam state coinage* (1980). ZKO

Bhattacharjee (Bhattacherjee), Binoy, born in 1929, he wrote *Cultural oscillation; a study of Patua culture* (Clacutta, 1980). LC

Bhattacharya, Aparna, fl. 1970, he wrote *Religious movements of Bengal and their socio-economic ideas* (1981), a work which was originally submitted as the author's thesis at Patna University. ZKO

Bhattacharya, Bhabani, born in 1906 at Bhagalpur, India, he studied at Patna University and the University of London, where he received a Ph.D. in 1934. He was an author and a journalist. BioIn, 10; ConAu, 5 rev.; IntWW, 1978/79-1985/86; Master; WhoWor, 1974; WrDr, 1988-90

Bhattacharya, D. K., fl. 1973, his writings include *Prehistoric archaeology; a comparative study of human succession* (Delhi, 1972), *Anthropologists in India* (1978), and *Old stone age tools* (1979). LC

Bhattacharya, Dinesh Chandra, fl. 1953, he wrote *History of Navya Nyaya in Mithila* (Darbhanga, Mithila Institute of Post-Graduate Studies and Research in Sanskrit Learning, 1958). LC

Bhattacharya, Sukumar, born in 1923, he received a Ph.D. in 1953 from the University of London for his thesis, *The East India Company and the economy of Bengal from 1704 to 1740*, a work which was published in 1954. In 1956 he served on the University Grants Commission, New Delhi. His other writings include *The Rajput states and the East India Company* (1972). He died in 1969. LC

Bhattacharyya, Asoke Kumar, born 1 February 1919 at Calcutta, he was a curator, and later director, at the Archaeological Section, the National Museum, New Delhi, and a sometime lecturer at Calcutta University. His writings include *Indian coins in the Musée Guimet* (1971). WhoWor, 1974-1976

Bhattacharyya, Narendra Nath, Dr., born in 1934, his writings include *India's puberty rites* (1968), *History of Indian cosmogonical ideas* (1971), *Ancient Indian rituals and their social contents* (1975), and *The geographical dictionary; ancient and early medieval India* (1991). LC

Bhattacharyya, Paresh Nath, fl. 1930, he was in 1940 an assistant curator, Archaeological Section, Indian Museum. He wrote *A hoard of silver punch-marked coins from Purnea* (Delhi, Archaeological Survey of India, 1940). BLC; NUC, pre-1956

Bhattacharyya, Sudhindra Nath, fl. 1929-1934, he wrote *A history of Mughal north-east frontier policy* (Calcutta, 1929). BLC; NUC, pre-1956

Bhattasali, Nalini Kanta, 1888-1947, he was a sometime curator at the Dacca Museum, and wrote *Coins and chronology of the early independent sultans of Bengal* (Cambridge, 1922). LC; Note

Bhatti, Allah Ditta, fl. 1969, he published *A bibliography of Pakistan demography* (Karachi, 1965). BLC; LC

Bhatty, I. Z., fl. 1980, he was a director-general of the National Council of Applied Economic Research, India, and chief of the Afghanistan Employment Policy Mission. His writings include *The impact of the price rise in petroleum* (1976), and *Technological change and employment* (1978). LC

Bhim Singh see Singh, Bhim

Bhola, Pritam Lal, fl. 1977, he was in 1986 an assistant professor at the South Asia Studies Centre, University of Rajasthan, Jaipur. His writings include *Pakistan-China relations* (1986), a work which was partly submitted as a requirement for the Ph.D. degree at the University of Rajasthan in 1982. He also wrote *Benazir Bhutto; opportunities and challenges* (Jaipur, 1989). LC

Bhutani, Surendra, born in 1943, his writings include *Israeli-Soviet cold war* (Delhi, 1975), and *The United Nations and the Arab-Israeli conflict* (1977). LC

Bhutto, Zulfikar Ali, born 5 January 1928 at Larkana, India, he studied at the University of California, Berkeley, and Christ Church, Oxford, and was called to the bar, Lincoln's Inn, London, in 1953. From 1971 to 1977, he was prime minister and foreign minister of Pakistan. He was arrested after a coup d'état, condemned to death, and executed at Rawalpindi, 4 April 1979. His writings include *Politics of the people* (1973), *Thoughts on some aspects of Islam* (1976), and *From my death cell* (1980). Sayid Ghulam Mustafa published the biography, *Bhutto, the man and the martyr* (1993). ConAu, 53; Master (10); *Who was who*, 7

Bhuyan, Suryya Kumar, 1894-1964, he received a Ph.D. in 1949 from the University of London for his thesis, *Anglo-Assamese relations, 1771-1826*. His writings also include *Early British relations with Assam* (1928), and *Atan Buragohain and his times* (1957). BLC; LC

Bianca, Stefano, born about 1945, he received a doctorate in 1973 from the Eidgenösische Technische Hochschule, Zürich, for his thesis, *Baugestalt und Lebensordnung im islamischen Stadtwesen*. He was an architect and town planner who had a first-hand knowledge of Middle Eastern urban problems from extended field work. His writings include *Architektur und Lebensform im islamischen Stadtwesen* (1975), *Städtebau in islamischen Ländern* (1980), *La città degli altri* (1989), and *Hofhaus und Paradiesgarten* (1991). LC; Schwarz

Bianchi, Thomas Xavier, born 25 June 1783 at Paris, he studied at l'École des jeunes de langues at Constantinople and became a dragoman at the Smyrna consulate. In 1815 he accompanied two Persian ambassadors to Paris, where he then stayed on to became a professor of Turkish at l'École des jeunes de langues, and subsequently holder of the chair of Turkish. His writings include *Vocabulaire français-arabe* (1831). He died in Paris, 14 April 1864. DBF; Vapereau

Bianchi, Ugo, born in 1922, he was a professor of history of religion at the Università di Roma. His writings include *Zaman i Ohrmazd; lo Zoroastrismo nelle sue origini e nella sua essenza* (Torino, 1958). LC; Wholtaly, 1980

Bianconi, François, born in 1840, his writings include *La Question d'Orient dévoilée* (1876), and *Ethnographie et statistique de la Turquie d'Europe et de la Grèce* (1877). LC

Bianquis, Anne-Marie née Torquebiau, born about 1935, and since 1963 married to Thierry Jean Joseph Bianquis, she was an Arabist and a professor of history. Her writings include La réforme agraire dans la Ghouta de Damas (1989), a work which was submitted partially as a thesis for a doctorat de 3e cycle at the Université de Lyon in 1980. She was joint author of La Syrie d'aujourd'hui (1980), a work which was prepared by the Centre d'études et de recherches sur l'Orient arabe contemporain. Private; THESAM, 3

Bianquis, Thierry Jean Joseph, born 3 August 1935 to French educator parents at Broummana, Lebanon, he received his primary and secondary education in Lebanon and in France, where he later studied history at the Université de Lyon. Since 1960 he taught at institutions of higher learning successively in Algeria, France, and Lebanon. He participated in excavations at Fustat and Rahbah-Mayadin. From 1975 to 1981, he was director of the Institut Français d'Études Arabes de Damas. In 1984, he received a doctorat d'état from the Université de Paris I for his thesis Damas et la Syrie sous la domination fatimide; essai d'interprétation de chroniques arabes médiévales, a work which was published in two parts, 1986 and 1989. In 1990, he was appointed professor of Islamic history and civilization at the Université Lumière-Lyon. Private; THESAM, 3

Biard d'Aunet, Georges, 1844- see Z. Marcas, pseud.

Biarnay, S., born in 1879 at Saint-Laurent-du-Pont (Hautes-Alpes), he grew up in Algeria but later went to Morocco, where he entered the Télégraphes chérifiens. Shortly before the first World War he was appointed a director of the Service de contrôle des Habous. His writings include Étude sur le dialecte de Ouargla (1908), Étude sur les dialectes berbères du Rif (1917), and Notes d'ethnographie et de linguistique nord-africaines (1924). He died in 1918. RA 59 (1918), pp. 494-498

Biarnès, Pierre Marie Esprit, born 17 January 1932 at Tulette (Drôme), he studied at the Faculté de droit de Paris. From 1959 to 1960, he was attached to the Chamber of Commerce, Dakar and from 1962 to 1985, he was a correspondent to le Monde, Paris, for West Africa. His writings include L'Afrique aux africains (1980), and Les Français en Afrique noire, de Richelieu à Mitterand (1987). Who's who in France, 1996/97-2002/2003

Biasutti, Renato, born 22 March 1878 at San Daniele del Friuli, he studied at the Università di Firenze, where he became an assistant at the Museum and the Istituto de antropologia until 1912. He then became successively a professor of geography at the universities of Napoli and Firenze until his retirement in 1953. His writings include Studi di antropogeografia generale (1912), I tipi umani (1925), and La casa rurale nella Toscana (1938). He died in Firenze, 3 March 1965. Chi è, 1961; DizBI; Wholtaly, 1958

Bibby, Thomas Geoffrey, born 14 October 1917 at Heversham, England, he studied at Caius College, Cambridge. Since 1956, he was an archaeologist and a keeper at the Forhistorik Museum, Århus. His writings include The Testimony of the spade (1956), and Preliminary survey in East Arabia, 1968 (1973). He died 6 February 2001. ASTENE 11 (2001), p. 15; Au&Wr, 1971; ConAu 1 rev.; IntAu&W, 1977; LC; WhoWor, 1976

Biberstein-Kazimirski, Adalbert (Albert, Wojciech), 1808-1887 see Kazimirski-Biberstein, Adalbert

Bicknell, Herman, born in 1830 in England, he received a medical doctorate in 1854 from the College of Surgeons and became an assistant army surgeon, first in Hong Kong, and later in Lahore, where he also studied Oriental languages. Soon after his return to England in 1860, he resigned his commission, and devoted himself entirely to travel and languages. In the early 1860s, he made the hajj, posing as a British convert and made the greater part of the journey in European dress. He duly performed all the rites, but excused himself from going on to Medina because of the heat. He died on 14 March 1875, following an accident in an attempt to ascent the Matterhorn. Bidwell; Buckland; DNB

Bidarmaghz, Sohrab, born 11 April 1933 at Tehran, he studied medicine at the Universität Wien from 1957 to 1960, and agriculture from 1960 to 1964. He received a doctorate in 1970 at Gießen for Steigerung und Rationalisierung der Agrarproduktion im Iran mit Hilfe kooperativer Maßnahmen. From 1964 to 1966 he was a lecturer at the Faculty of Agriculture, Pahlavi University, Shiraz. Thesis

Bidault, Georges Augustin, born 5 October 1899 at Moulins (Allier), he studied at the Collège des Jésuites de Bollange, and at the Faculté des lettres de Paris. He was successively a professor of history at Valencienne, Reims, and Paris, a député, and a minister in government. In 1943, he succeeded to Jean Moulin at the head of the Conseil National de la Résistance. His writings include Algérie, l'oiseau aux ailes coupées (1958), and D'une résistance à l'autre (1965). He died in Paris, 27 January 1983. Hommes et destins, vol. 5, pp. 64-65; WhoFr, 1983/84

Biddulph, Charles Hubert, 1898-1966, his writings include Coins of the Pandyas (1966), and Coins of the Cholas (1968). LC

Biddulph, Cuthbert Edward, born in 1850, he was a British civil servant whose writings include *Afghan poetry of the seventeenth century* (1890), and *Four months in Persia, and a visit to Trans-Caspia* (1892). He died in 1899. BLC; Henze; IndianBilnd (1)

Biddulph, Harry, born in 1872, he was a brigadier-general in the Royal Engineers and served in the Tirah Expedition of 1897, and the Waziristan Expedition of 1902. He died 21 April 1952. Who was who, 5

Biddulph, Sir Michael Anthony Shrapnel, born in 1823, he was a general who served throughout the Crimean campaign, in the Afghan war of 1878-80, and was present at the occupation of Kandahar. He died 23 July 1904. Buckland; Henze; *Who was who*, 1

Biddulph, Robert, General Sir, born 26 August 1835 at London, he served in the Crimean War, the Indian Mutiny campaign, and was High Commissioner for Cyprus from 1879 to 1886. His writings include *Lord Cardwell at the War Office* (1904). He died 18 November 1918. Who was who, 2

Bidwell, Robin Leonard, born 25 August 1927 in the UK, he was educated at Downside and Pembroke College, Cambridge. His first taste of the Middle East came when he was posted to the Suez Canal Zone as an Intelligence Corps sergeant. He became a political officer in the Western Aden Protectorate in 1955, where he remained until 1959. His real Middle Eastern travels began thereafter when he was appointed Oxford University Press travelling editor. In 1965 he returned to Cambridge on a Hayter Scholarship to work under Professor Robert Serjeant. He earned his Ph.D. in 1968 for his thesis, *The French administration of tribal areas of Morocco*. This is were his regular career ended. He became a private scholar without private means. In the seventies and eighties he was an underpaid, under-appreciated, under-used, part-time secretary of the Middle East Centre in Cambridge, but he was a man of tremendous fun and puckish humour; nothing was sacred and beyond his ubiquitous wit. His pranks have to be seen as part of his nowadays outmoded eccentricity, which probably contributed to his talents being less appreciated than they might have been. His writings include *Travellers in Arabia* (1976), *The two Yemens* (1983), and *Dictionary of modern Arab history* (1998). He died in his sleep in Coney Weston, 10 June 1994. BJMES 21 (1994), pp. 152-153; LC; Private

Bieber, Friedrich Julius, born 24 February 1873 at Wien and deprived of formal education at an early age, he eventually taught himself African languages and ethnography. His expertise was recognized by the Austrian authorities who sent him on several missions to Abyssinia. His collection is now in the Völkerkunde-Museum in Wien. His writings include *Kaffa, ein altkuschitisches Volkstum in Innerafrika* (1922-1923). Otto Stradal published his biography, *Der Weg zum letzten Pharao; Leben und Werk des österreichischen Afrikaforschers Friedrich Julius Bieber.* He died in Wien, 3 March 1924. *Mitteilungen der Geographischen Gesellschaft, Wien,* 77 (1934), pp. 302-303; ÖBL

von **Bieberstein**, Rogalla, 19th cent. *see* Rogalla von Bieberstein

Biegman, Nicolas H., born 20th cent., his writings include *The Turco-Ragusan relationship* (1967), and *Egypt's side-shows* (1992). ZKO

Biehl, Max, born about 1900, he received a Dr.phil. in 1928 from the Universität Hamburg for his thesis, *Die Wirtschaft des Fernen Westens*. His writings include *England als Wucherbankier* (1940), and *Das Entwicklungspotential der Bewässerungswirtschaft in Pakistan und Hinterindien* (1970). LC

Bielawski, Józef, born 12 August 1909 or 1910 at Stara Wieś, Poland, he studied law at Kraków before embarking on Oriental studies, which he completed in 1947. He taught Islamic studies at Uniwersytet Warszawski from 1948 until his retirement. His writings include a translation of the Koran into Polish, and *Historia literatury arabskiej* (1968). In 1984, he was honoured by a jubilee volume *Księga dla uczczenia 75 rocznicy urodzin Józefa Bielawskiego.* He died 19 September 1997. Dziekan; NEP; *Rocznik orientalistyczny* 43 (1984), 7-10; *Studia arabistyczne i islamistyczne* 5 (1997), pp. 3-4 [in English]; WhoSocC,1978

Bieling, Alexander, born 1 May 1847 at Berlin, he was a professor at a secondary school in Berlin, and a literary critic. He died in Berlin, 9 September 1897. BioJahr, 4 (1900), p. 63*; LC

Bierman, Irene A., born about 1945, she studied at Harvard and the University of Chicago, and was a professor of history of art at UCLA. In 1994, she became the fifth director of the Center for Near Eastern Studies at UCLA. She was joint editor of the exhibition catalogue *The warp and weft of Islam; oriental carpets* (1978). WhoAmArt, 1991-1996

Biermann, Frédéric *Charles*, born 9 March 1875 at Lausanne, he was a sometime professor of geography at Lausanne and later Neuchâtel. His writings include *La Maison paysanne vaudoise* (1946). LC; WhoSwi, 1950/51

Bietti, Giambattista, born 29 April 1907 at Padua, he was a sometime professor of ophthalmology at the universities of Sassari, Pavia, and Parma. His writings include *La vitamine in oftalmologia* (1940). Chi è, 1961; Who's *who in Italy*, 1957/58

Bigelow, Poultney, born 10 September 1855 at New York City, he was a graduate of Yale (1874), and Columbia Law School (1882). From 1875 to 1876 he made a trip around the world in a sailing ship, and later took a canoe through the Iron Gates of the Danube. He was a founder of *Outing*. He lectured at principal universities on modern history and administration. His writings include *White man's Africa* (1898). He died 28 May 1954. Who was who, 5; *Who was who in America*, 3

Biggio-Cao, Giuseppe, 1861-1934. In 1977, E. Acquaro published *La collezione Biggio; antichità puniche a Sant' Antioco.* LC

Biggs-Davidson, Sir John Alec, M.P., born 7 June 1918, he was a graduate of Magdalen College, Oxford, and served with the Royal Marines during the war, stationed in India. He joined the Indian Civil Service. A short spell at headquarters in New Delhi was followed by other postings leading up to that of Commissioner of Deri Ghazi Khan, a remote district in tribal Baluchistan. In later life, he showed strong leanings towards imperialism. He was a member of the Punjab Boundary Commission, and, back in England, the Conservative Research Department, as well as the Suez Group as soon as he entered the House of Parliament. His writings include *The Uncertain Ally* (1957). He died 17 September 1988. *Asian affairs* 20 (1989), p. 124; *Who was who*, 8

Bigiavi, Edoardo D., fl. 1911, his writings include *Dell'opera degli italiani in Egitto* (1906), *Noi e l'Egitto* (1911), and *Dell'evoluzione del regime fondiario musulmano in Egitto* (Livorno, 19--). Firenze

Bigley, Loretta Imeldia, born about 1900 at Emmetsburg, Iowa, she served as a public health nurse with the Near East Relief Organization in Aintab, Turkey, 1919-1921, before studying at Chicago and Columbia. Since 1931, she was a public health administrator in the USA. She wrote *Community clinics; the hospital outpatient department and nonhospital clinics* (1947). WhoAmW, 1964/65

Bigot, Henri, fl. 1916, his writings include *Des traces laissées en Provence par les Sarrasins* (Paris, 1908). NUC, pre-1956

Bih'azin (pseud.), Mahmud (or Muhammad) I'timadzadah, born in 1915 at Rasht, Persia, he completed high school and went to France on a government scholarship to study engineering. Upon his return to Iran, he worked for the Navy and the Ministry of Education. Around 1940 he became involved in the Tudeh Party, and subsequently pursued a career as translator and writer; his first collection of short stories appeared in 1944. His political opposition to the Pahlavis led to several periods of incarceration. During the revolution of 1978 to 1979, he was a leading voice for Marxist Tudeh views. In the mid-1980s the Islamic Republic put him in jail. His writings include *Mihmān-i īn āqāyān* (1975), and *Naqsh-i parand* (1365/1986). Jan Rypka, *History of Iranian literature* (1968), p. 413

Bihishti, Muhammad, born 1926 see Beheschti, Mohammed

Bihzadi, Hamid, born in 1312/1934, he took a doctorate and became a professor of law and political science at Tehran University. His writings include *Qudrat'hā-i buzurg va sulh-i bayn al-milalī* (1976).

Biishev, Akriam G/Gheibatovich., born 16 April 1926, he graduated in 1956 in Oriental languages from Moscow State University. From 1956 to 1986 he was a research fellow, and head of the Section of Bashkir language, literature, and history in the Bashkir Academy of Science. His writings include *"Первичные" долгие гласные в тюркских языках* (Ufa, 1963), and *Bashqort khalqynyng tarikhy hăm azatlyq korăshe* (Ufa, 1993). BashkKE; LC

Bijlefeld, Willem Abraham, born 8 May 1925 at Tobelo, Indonesia, he studied at Groningen and Utrecht, where he received a doctorate of divinity in 1959 for his thesis, *De islam als na-christelijke religie.* From 1964 to 1966, he was a professor of Arabic at Ibadan. Since 1966, he was a professor at Hartford Theological Seminary and, concurrently, editor of the *Muslim world.* DrAS, 1974 & 1982

Bil, Hikmet, born in 1918, his writings include *Atatürk'ün sofrasi* (1955), and *Kıbrıs olayi ve içyüzü* (1976). LC

Bilainkin, George, born 12 February 1903, he was a diplomatic correspondent, writer, and lecturer. His writings include *Diary of a diplomatic correspondent* (1942), and *Cairo to Riyadh diary* (1950). He died 16 March 1981. Who was who, 8

Bilge, Ali Suat, born 4 November 1921 at Istanbul, he received a doctorate of law from the Université de Genève for his thesis, *La responsabilité internationale des états et son application en matière d'actes législatifs.* He was a sometime professor of law at Ankara Üniversitesi, an ambassador, and

Minister of Justice. His writings include *Milletlerarası politika* (1966), and *Güç komşuluk* (1992). IntWW, 1974/75-1998/99|; WhoUn, 1975

Bilge, Necip, fl. 1961, he received a doctorate in 1941 from the Université de Genève for his thesis, *La captivité civile des personnes morales en droit civil suisse*. He was a sometime professor of private law at Ankara Üniversitesi Hukuk Fakültesi. His writings include *Borçlar hukuku özel borç münasebetleri* (1962), and *Hukuk başlangıcı dersleri* (1975). LC

Bilgrami, Hamid Hasan, Dr., fl. 1952, his writings include *Glimpses of Iqbal's mind and throught; brief lectures delivered at London, Cambridge and Oxford* (Lahore, 1954); he was joint author of *The concept of an Islamic university* (1985). LC

Bilgrami, Syed Ali, born 10 November 1851 or 1853 in India, he was educated at Patna and Lucknow, as well as Thomason Civil Engineering College, Rurki. In 1879, he joined the service of the Nizam of Hyderabad. He retired in 1901 to settle in England, where he was a sometime lecturer in Mahratti at Cambridge. He died on 22 May 1911. Buckland; IndianBiInd (2); Jain, p. 133-134; *Who was who*, 1

Bilgrami, Syed Hossain, born 18 October 1842 or 1844 at Sahibganj, Gaya, India, he was educated at Patna, Bhagalpur, and Calcutta. From 1866 to 1872, he was a professor of Arabic at Canning College, Lucknow, and a sometime editor of the *Lucknow times*. From 1873 to 1883, he was private secretary to Sir Salar Jung, and from 1887 until his resignation in 1909, in Government service. His writings include *Life of Sir Salar Jung*. He died on 3 June 1926. Eminent; Jain; *Who was who*, 2

von **Bilguer**, A., Dr., born 19th cent., he was in 1912 a correpondent for *Nord und Süd* in Tripolitania. His trace is lost after a publication in 1914. Note

Bilharz, Theodor Maximilian, born 23 March 1825 at Sigmaringen, Germany, he took a Dr.med. at Tübingen and became an anatomist. In 1850, he followed his former professor to his appointment at Cairo University. In 1855, he himself was appointed professor of internal medicine at the Cairo Medical Academy. Ernst Senn wrote a biography, *Theodor Bilharz; ein deutsches Forscherleben in Ägypten, 1825-1862* (1931). He died in Cairo, 9 May 1862. ADtB; DtBE; Hill; *Orient* (Opladen), 3 (1962), 116

de **Bilinski**, Ahmed Rustem (Rüstem Bey), born in 1862, he was a sometime Turkish chargé d'affaires in Washington. His writings include *The world war and the Turco-Armenian question* (Berne, 1916), *La guerre mondiale et la question turco-arménienne* (Berne, 1918), and *La crise proche orientale et la question des détroits de Constantinople* (Roma, 1921). He died in 1934. AnaBrit; Meydan

Bilinsky, Yaroslav, born 26 February 1932 at Lutsk, Ukraine, he attended school in Germany, 1945-1951, and graduated from Harvard in 1954. In 1958, he received a Ph.D. from Princeton for *Ukrainian nationalism and the Soviet nationality policy after World War two*. Thereafter he was a professor of political science at various American universities. His writings include *French economic aid and the socio-economic development of Tunisia* (1970). AmW&WS, 1973; ConAu, 13-16; LC; WhoE, 1977-79

Biliotti, Adrien, born in the last quarter of the 19th century, he received a doctorate of law in 1909 from the Université de Paris for his thesis, *La Banque impériale ottomane*. His writings include *Législation ottomane depuis le rétablissement de la constitution 1324/1908* (1912). LC

Bilkert, Henry Arjen, born 24 January 1892 at Kalamazoo, Mich., he was a graduate of New Brunswick Theological Seminary, and served in the Arabian Mission from 1917 until killed by a Bedouin raiding party, 21 January 1929. Shavit

Bilkur, Şefik, fl. 1951, he wrote *National income of Turkey* (Ankara, 1949). NUC, pre-1956

Bill, James Alban, born 2 March 1939 at La Crosse, Wisc., he graduated in 1961 from Assumption College, Worcester, Mass., as class valedictorian, and received a Ph.D. in 1968 from Princeton University for his thesis, *The Iranian intelligentsia*. In May 1989, he was awarded an honorary doctorate by his alma mater. He did extensive field work in the Middle East and Central Asia, beginning with a two-year residence in Iran between 1965-1967. He successively was a professor of government, and a director, at the University of Texas, and the College of William and Mary, Williamsburg, Va. His writings include *The politics of Iran* (1972), and *The Eagle and the Lion* (1988). AmM&WS, 1973 S, 1978 S; ConAu, 114; LC; Private

Billeh, Victor Yacoub Issa, born in 1942., he received a Ph.D. in 1969 from the University of Wisconsin for *Cultural bias in the attainment of concepts of the biological cell by elementary school children*. NUC, 1968-72

Bilquees, Faiz, fl. 1976-1993, he was a sometime staff economist at the Pakistan Institute of Development Economics, Islamabad. Note

Bilsel, Cemil, born in 1880, his writings include *Lozan* (1933), *Devletler hukuku* (1934-41), and *Birleş-miş milletler* (1946). LC

Bin 'Abd Allah, 'Abd al-'Aziz, professor, born 28 November 1923 at Rabat, his writings include *Clartés sur l'islam* (1969), and *al-Falsafah wa-al-akhlāq 'inda Ibn al-Khaṭīb* (1953). LC; MidE, 1978-1982; WhoArab, 1981/82-1984/85|

Bin Barakah (Ben Barka), al-Mahdi, born in 1920, he was a professor of mathematics at the Université de Rabat, a president of the former Moroccan Consultative Assembly, one of the leaders of the Moroccan National Union of Popular Forces, as well as chairman of the Afro-Asian Solidarity Committee. His writings include *Option révolutionnaire au Maroc* (1966). He died in 1965. AfrBioInd (3); LC; Makers, 1981, 1991, 1996

Bin Jallun, 'Abd al-Majid, born in 1919 at Casablanca, he was a Moroccan writer whose writings include *Hadhihi Marrakush* (1949), *Êtres et choses, le même silence* (1976), and *Approches du colonialisme espagnol et du mouvement nationaliste marocain dans l'ex-Maroc khalifien* (1988). LC

Binark, Mehmet Ismet, born 28 February 1941 at Istanbul, he was a bibliographer whose writings include *Türk sefer ve zaferleri bibliyografyası* (1969), he edited *Türk-Avrupa Topluluğu bibliyografyası* (1990), and he was joined editor of *World bibliography of translations the meanings of the Holy Qur'an* (1980). Kimkimdir, 1997/98-2000; LC

Binava, 'Abd al-Ra'uf, born in 1913 at Kandahar, Afghanistan, he was a Pashto writer and politician. He went for medical treatment to the United States and died in 1984. Adamec

Binder, Friedrich, fl. 1941-1948, he received a Dr.phil. in 1938 from the Universität Wien for his thesis, *Die materiellen Grundlagen der Beduinenkultur*. Schwarz

Binder, Henry, born in 1855, his writings include *Au Kurdistan, en Mésopotamie et en Perse; mission scientifique du Ministère de l'instruction publique* (Paris, 1887). BN; LC

Binder, Leonard, born 20 August 1927 at Boston, he was a graduate of Harvard University, where he also received a Ph.D. in 1956 for *Islamic constitutional theory and politics in Pakistan*. In 1955, he was a Ford Foundation Fellow in Pakistan. He taught at UCLA and Chicago. His writings include *Religion and politics in Pakistan* (1961), *On a moment of enthusiasm* (1978), and *Islamic liberalism* (1988). AmM&WS, 1973; ConAu, 61; MidE, 1982/83; WhoAm,1974-78

Bindloss, Harold, born in 1866, he was a writer who spent several years at sea and in various colonies. His writings include *In the Niger country* (1898). He died 30 December 1945. Who was who, 4

Binet, Jacques Émile Eugène, born 1 June 1916 at Gretz, (Seine-et-Marne), he received a doctorate of law in 1945 from the Université de Paris, and in 1963 another doctorate from Dakar University for his thesis, *Sociétés de danse chez les Fang du Gabon*. He was from 1955 to 1975 affiliated with the Office de la recherche scientific et technique d'outre-mer. Since 1977 he was a professor of African sociology at Paris. His writings include *Afrique en question* (1965), *Psychologie économique africaine* (1970), and *Migrations et appauvrissement culturel en Afrique* (1980). Unesco; WhoWor, 1987

Binger, Louis Gustave, born 14 October 1856 at Strasbourg, he was a French army officer sent on a two-year exploration of the Niger and the Ivory Coast. He was a sometime administrator of the Ivory Coast. His writings include *Essai sur la langue bombara* (1886), and *Du Niger au Golfe du Guinée par le pays de Kong et la Mossi* (1890-92). He died in l'Isle-Adam, 10 November 1936. AfrBioInd (9); Hommes et destins, vol. 8, pp. 32-35; NDBA

Binkevich, Evgeniia Reingol'dovna, fl. 1949, she wrote Устное творчество народов СССР; библиографический указатель (1940). LC

Binney, Edwin, born in 1925, he was an art collector whose writings include *Indian miniature painting* (1973). BioIn, 15; LC

Binnie, Geoffrey Morse, born 13 November 1908, he was a civil engineer who specialized in the design and buildings of dams in the more remote parts of the world. During the 1950s he developed his innovative engineering technique which he used to such good effect during his construction of the Dokan Dam in northern Iraq. In 1956, he faced his greatest task, the design and construction of the Mangla Dam on the River Jhelum in West Pakistan. He died 5 April 1989. Asian affairs 20 (1889), pp. 385-86; Who was who, 8

Binswanger, Karl, born in 1947, he studied at the Universität München where he received a Dr.phil. in 1977 for his thesis, *Untersuchungen zum Status der Nichtmuslime im Osmanischen Reich des 16. Jahrhunderts*. From 1978 to 1980, he was a research fellow at the Institut für Geschichte und Kultur des Nahen Ostens, München. Since 1981, he was a free lance jornalist. He was joint author of *Türkisch-islamische Vereine als Faktor deutsch-türkischer Koexistenz* (1988). LC; Schwarz

Binyon, Robert *Laurence*, born 10 August 1869 at Lancaster, England, he was a graduate of Trinity College, Oxford, and a sometime keeper of Prints and Drawings, British Museum, London. His writings include *The court paintings of the Grand Moguls* (1921), and *The spirit of man in Asian art* (1935). He died 10 March 1943. *Ars* Islamica 11-12 (1946), pp. 207-209; Who *was who*, 4; WhAm, 2

Biollay, Émile, fl. 1976, his writings include *Le Valais en 1813-1814 et sa politique d'indépendance* (Martigny, 1970). LC

Bion Smyrniadis *see* Smyrniadis, Bion

Biot, Jean-Baptiste, born 21 April 1774 at Paris, he was a mathematician, physicist, and astronomer. He died in Paris, 3 February 1862. DBF; Egyptology

Biran, Yaïr, fl. 1975, he was joint author, with G. Sella, of *El mul Golan* (1976). LC

Birand, Mehmet Ali, born in 1941 at Istanbul, he was a sometime head of the Bruxelles Office of the Turkish daily newspaper *Milliyet*. His writings include *Bir pazar hikayesi* (1977), *12 Eylül, saat 04.00* (1984), *The general's coup in Turkey* (1987), *Shirts of steel* (1991), and *APO ve PKK* (1992). Kim kimdir, 1985/86-2000; LC

Birch, B. P, he was in 1963 affiliated with Padgate Training College, University of Southampton. Note

Birch-Reynardson, Henry Thomas, 1892-1972 *see* Reynardson, Henry Thomas Birch

Birchenough, Sir Henry, born in 1853, he was a sometime Justice of the Peace, a business executive, and a government official. He died 12 May 1937. Who *was who*, 3

Bircher, André (Andreas), born in 1838 in Switzerland, he was a merchant in Cairo, a founder of the Khedivial Geographical Society, and a judge on the Commercial Tribunal. He died in 1926. Egyptology

Bird, F. L., born 19th cent., he lived in Persia from the time of the financial reorganization of the country in 1911 until the close of the war. As an instructor in history in the large American School in Tehran, he had ample opportunity for studying the political situation of the country. His trace is lost after a publication in 1921. Asia, 1919

Bird, Isabella Lucy, 1831-1904 *see* Bishop, Isabella Lucy née Bird

Bird, James, born in 1797 and educated at King's College, Aberdeen, he was an army surgeon in India, and a member of the Royal Asiatic Society. His writings include *The political and statistical history of Gujarat, translated from the Persian* (1835). He died in 1864. BLC; Boase; Henze; IndianBilnd (3)

Bird, Kai, fl. 1977, he was a sometime assistant editor of *The Nation*. He was joint author, with L. Lifschultz, of *Bangladesh, the unfinished revolution* (1979). LC

Bird, Mary Rebecca Stewart, born in 1859, she joined the Church Missionary Society in 1891 and shortly thereafter openend a dispensary for Muslim women deep in the Isfahan bazaar where Christians rarely pernetrated. She had no medical training yet, once the ice was broken, women flocked to her for treatment. The *mullahs* preached against her in the mosques and encouraged their followers to insult her as she rode unveiled through the bazaar's crowded alleyways; they tried to shut and bolt her doors, but with the help of her patients she reopened them. Despite all opposition she persisted in her good works and won the devotion of her many patients. She wrote *Persian women and their creed* (1899). She died in Kerman in 1914. Four biographies were published: Clara C. Rice, *Mary Bird in Persia* (1916), and *Mary Bird, the friend of the Persians* (1920), Constance Savary, *She went alone; Mary Bird* (1942), and Jessie Powell, *Riding to danger; the story of Mary Bird of Persia* (1949). BLC; NUC, pre-1956; Wright, p. 120

Bird, Sir Wilkinson Dent, born 4 May 1869, he was educated at the Royal Military College, Sandhurst, and from 1897 and 1898 served in the Niger Expedition as well as on the N.W. Frontier of India. His writings include *A chapter of misfortunes; the battles of Ctesiphon and of the Dujailah in Mesopotamia* (1923). He died 6 January 1943. Who *was who*, 4

Birdwood, Christopher Bromhead Birdwood, 2nd Baron, born 22 May 1899, he was a graduate of the Royal Military College at Sandhurst. He served in India until 1945 when he retired with the rank of lieutenant-colonel from the Indian Army. His writings include *A continent decides* (1953), *Two nations and Kashmir* (1956), and *Nuri as-Said* (1959). He died 5 January 1962. BLC; LC; Who *was who*, 6

Birdwood, Sir George Christopher Molesworth, born 8 December 1832 at Belgaum in the Southern Mahratta country, he took a medical doctorate at Edinburgh and joined the Bombay Medical Staff in 1854. He was a sometime professor at Grant Medical College, Bombay, a J.P. as well as a Sheriff of Bombay, and affiliated with the India Office from 1871 to 1902. His writings include *The industrial arts of India* (1880). He died 28 June 1917. *Asiatic review* 12 (1917), pp. 229-30; DNB; *Who was who*, 2

Birge, John Kingsley, born 4 March 1888 at Bristol., Conn., he was educated at Yale and Hartford Seminary Foundation. He first was in Turkey from 1914 to 1922 as a professor at the International College in Smyrna (Izmir). After the Graeco-Turkish war he helped in relief work and served on a commission for the exchange of prisoners. He returned in 1927 to engage in publication work under the American Board of Commissioners for Foreign Missions in Istanbul. He was an authority on Turkish language, literature and history, and headed the revision of the *Redhouse English-Turkish dictionary* (1950). From 1943 to 1944 he was chairman of the Turkish Area and Language Studies at Princeton. His writings include *The Bektashi order of dervishes* (1938), which was first begun in partial fulfilment of the requirements for a Ph. D. at the Kennedy School of Missions at Hartford in 1935, and *Turkey between two world wars* (1944), and *Guide to Turkish area study* (1949). He died in Istanbul, 14 August 1952. *Isis*, 43 (1952), p. 367; Shavit

Biriukov (Бирюков), Pavel Ivanovich, born in 1860 in Russia. He was a writer and public figure who was acquainted with L. Tolstoi and began to publicize the latter's religious teaching. His writings include *Л. Н. Толстои* (1911-13). The work has been translated into English, French, and German. He died in Genève, 10 October 1931. GSE

Biriukovich (Бирюкович), Rimma Makhmudovna, fl. 1975, she was a linguist whose writings include *Морфология чулымско-тыркского языка* (1979-81) and contributed to *Актуальные проблемы языковой номинации* (1988). LC

Birkbeck, Major-General Sir William Henry, born 8 April 1863, he joined the army and served in Afghanistan. He died 16 April 1929. *Who*, 1905-1929; *Who was who*, 3

Birkeland, Harris, born 30 July 1904 at Vikebygd, Norway, he studied theology, and received a doctorate in philosophy in 1933. From 1946 until his death in 1961 he taught Semitic studies at Oslo. His writings include *Akzent und Vokalismus im Althebräischen* (1940), *Altarabische Pausalformen* (1940), and *Lærebok i hebraisk grammatik* (1967). *Hvem er hvem*, 1948, 1955, 1959

Birkenmajer, Aleksander Ludwik, born in 1890, he was a historian and a sometime librarian successively at Poznan, Kraków, and Warszawa. His writings include *Studja nad Witelonem* (1921), and *Rocznik woyskowy Królestva polskiego, 1817-1830* (1929). He died in 1967. NEP

Birks, John Stace, born in 1947, he studied geography, economics and geology at Leeds, Liverpool and Durham and received a doctorate. Sincen 1979 he was successively a research fellow at the Department of Economics, University of Durham, and the Institute for the Study of Sparsely Populated Areas, University of Aberdeen. His writings include *Across the savannahs to Mecca* (1978), *Arab Republic of Egypt; country case study* (1978), and *Arab manpower* (1980). LC; Note

Birnbaum, Eleazar, born 23 November 1929 at Hamburg, he was educated at Liverpool and London after the family's emigration in 1933. His diploma in Hebrew palaeography and epigraphy (1949) was followed by a B.A. in Arabic (1950), and Turkish (1953) from SOAS. For the next seven years he was at Durham University, building up large collections of Arabic, Persian, Turkish and Hebrew books. His hand-written catalogue cards remain a lasting personal memorial to this day. From 1960 to 1964 he served as Near Eastern bibliographer at the University of Michigan, Ann Arbor. In 1964 he was invited to teach Islamic studies and Middle Eastern bibliography at the University of Toronto, where he was the kindest and most considerate of teachers, even with his less gifted students. Upon his retirement in 1995 he became professor emeritus. He was the recipient of numerous fellowships and research awards, did extensive research travel in the Middle East and Central Asia, and acted as consultant on Middle Eastern manuscripts and artifacts to museums and dealers in North America. His writings include a transliteration scheme for Ottoman Turkish, *Books on Asia* (1971), and *The book of advice, the Kabus-name* (1981). At the time of writing a *Festschrift* for his forthcoming seventy-fifth birthday was being prepared. *Canadian who's who*, 1995-2003; Private; Schoeberlein; WhoWorJ, 1987

Birnbaum, Salomon Asher, born 24 December 1891 at Wien, he was educated at the universities of Wien, Zürich, Berlin, and Würzburg, where he gained a Dr. phil. in 1922 with a thesis entitled *Das hebräische und aramäische Element in der jiddischen Sprache*. He was lecturer in Yiddish at the Universität Hamburg until 1933, when he emigrated to the United Kingdom to become an authority on Hebrew paleography. Although he retired in 1958 from the University of London, his curiosity had not abated in his late nineties, and one of his last birthdays was affectionately remembered by echoes of *hear, hear!* from the participants of a London meeting of Middle East librarians. His writings include

Grammatik der jiddischen Sprache (1918), and *The Hebrew scripts* (1954-1971). He spent the last twenty years of his life in Toronto, Ontario, where he died in 1989. BioHbDtE; EncJud; Kürschner, 1925-1935; Private; *Wer ist's*, 1928; WhoWorJ, 1965, 1987; Wininger

Birnja, P. B. *see* Byrnia, Pavel Petrovich

Birot, Pierre, born 16 June 1909 at Meudon (Hauts-de-Seine), he received a doctorate in 1937 from the Université de Paris for his thesis, *Recherches sur la morphologie des Pyrénées orientales franco-espagnoles*. Since 1932 he was a professor at various French universities. His writings include *General physical geography* (1966). With Jean Dresch he published *La Méditerranée et le Proche-Orient* (1953-56). *Who's who in France*, 1955/56-1979/80|

Birsen, Kemaleddin, born in 1899, he received a doctorate and was in 1961 a professor of private law at Istanbul Üniversitesi. His writings include *Borçlar hukuku dersleri* (1944), and *Medeni hukuk dersleri* (1954). LC

Bisbee, Eleanor, born about 1892, she was a professor of philosophy at Robert College and the American College for Girls in Istanbul from 1936 to 1942. After her return to the United States, she lectured extensively on Middle Eastern, in particular Turkish, affairs. Her writings include *The people of Turkey* (1946), and *The new Turks* (1951). She died in 1956. *Asia and the Americas* 43 (March 1943), p. 139; MEJ 4 (1950), p. 170; *New York times* 20 April 1956, p. 25

Bischoff, Theodor, fl. 1871-1882, he wrote *Tuhaf al-anbā' fi ta'rīkh Halab al-Shahbah* (Beirut, 1880). LC

Bishai, Wilson Basta, born 18 May 1923 at Minia, Egypt, he was a graduate of Harvard, and received a Ph.D. in 1959 from Johns Hopkins University, Baltimore, Md., for his thesis, *The Coptic influence on Egyptian Arabic*. He taught at his alma mater, Foreign Service Institute, Washington, D.C., Harvard, and Defense Language Institute, Monterey, Cal. His writings include *Concise grammar of literary Arabic* (1971), and *Humanities in the Arabic-Islamic world* (1973). WhoE, 1975

Bishop, Eric Francis Fox, Rev., born in 1891, he served in Palestine under the Church Missionary Society, and was principal of the Newman School of Missions, Jerusalem, from 1927 to 1948. From 1949 until his retirement in 1956, he was a lecturer in Arabic in the University of Glasgow. His writings include *The light of inspiration and secret of interpretation* (1957), and *The prophets of Palestine* (1962). He died 20 November 1976. A very personal obituary by K. S. S. Kamal appeared in *Muslim world* 67 (1977), pp. 223-225. IntAu&W, 1976/77; WrDr, 1971/73-1976/78

Bishop, Harry Coghill Watson, born in the 19th cent., he wrote *A Kut prisoner* (London, 1920).

Bishop, Isabella Lucy née Bird, born in 1831, she was a world traveller and a travel writer. In 1854 she travelled in North America, Australia, and Oceania. She later visited Persia, and in 1901, she crossed Morocco and the Atlas Mountains on a two thousand-mile journey. Her writings include *Journeys in Persia and Kurdistan* (1891). She died in Edingburgh, 7 October 1904. DLB 166 (1996), pp. 29-49; Henze; Master (4); Robinson, pp. 81-83; *Who was who*, 1

Bishop, William Warner, Jr., born 10 June 1906 at Princeton, N.J., he was a graduate of the University of Michigan, and from 1931 to 1976, a professor of law at the Law School in the University of Michigan. His writings include *International law* (1953), and *Background to revolution in Africa* (1976). He died 26 July 1987. WhAm, 9

al-Bishri, Salim, born in 1248/1832 at al-Bishr, Egypt, he was in 1909 a rector of al-Azhar, Cairo. He died in 1335/1916. Goldschmidt; LC

Bisisu (Bseisu), Mu'in Tawfiq, born in 1926, he was a poet, politician, member of the Palestine National Council, held several high ranking positions in the Palestinian Liberation Organization, and was the cultural adviser to the PLO Executive Committee Chairman, Yasir Arafat. In 1981 he was awarded the Lotus Prize, the highest award of the Afro-Asian Writers' Association. He later was the editor of the Arabic edition of *Lotus*. His writings include *Filastin fi al-qalb* (1965), its translations, *Palästina im Herzen* (1982), *С Палестино в серце* (1983), and *Descent into the water; Palestinian notes from Arab exile* (1980). He died of a heart attack in a London hotel, 24 January 1984. *Afkar international* 1 i (June 1984, pp. 68-69; LC

Biskupski, Ludwik, he attended in 1955 the 80th Congrès des sociétés savants at Lille. His writings include *L'origine et l'historique de la représentation officielle du Saint-Siège en Turquie* (1968), and *L'Institut français et son activité scientifique et littéraire 1895-1970* (1970), both of which were published in Istanbul. LC; Note

168

Bisnek, A. G., fl. 1935, he was joint author of *Библиография библиографии Седней Азии* (1936). LC

von Bissing, Friedrich Wilhelm, Freiherr, born 22 April 1873 at Potsdam, he studied classics and later excavated at Abu Gurob. He was a professor of Egyptology at the Universität München. His writings include *Der Bericht des Dior über die Pyramiden* (1901), and *Geschichte Ägyptens im Umriß* (1904). He died in Oberaudorf, 12 January 1956. DtBE; Egyptology; Kürschner, 1925-1954; LC

Bisson, Jean, born 28 November 1930 at Constantine, Algeria, he received a doctorate in 1954 from the Université de Paris for his thesis, *Le statut international du Sud-Ouest africain*. He was a sometime professor at the Université de Tours. His writings include *Le Gourara; étude de géographie humaine* (1957), and *Le Maghreb* (1985). LC; Unesco

Bisson de la Roque, Fernand, born 30 June 1885 at Bourseville (Somme), he studied at the École des langues orientales, and École du Louvre, Paris, and excavated in Palestine as well as in Egypt. His writings include *Rapport sur les fouilles d'Abou-Roasch* (1924-25), and *Rapport sur les fouilles de Médamoud* (1926). He died in Paris, 1 May 1958. Egyptology

Bistany, Butrus, 1819-1883 *see* al-Bustani, Butrus ibn Bulus

Bittel, Kurt, born 5 July 1907 at Heidenheim, he was affiliated with Deutsches Archäologisches Institut from 1930 until his retirement. His writings include *Die Felsbilder von Yazilikaya* (1934), and *Hattuscha, Haupstadt der Hettiter* (1983). A commemorative volume, *Kurt Bittel zum Gedächtnis*, was published in 1992. He died at his birth-place, 30 January 1991. DtBE; Kürschner, 1966-1987; LC; WhoWor, 1974

Bittner, Maximilian, born 12 April 1869 at Lobositz, Bohemia, he studied at Wien and later was a professor of Oriental languages at the Universität Wien as well as professor of Arabic and Persian at the Konsularakademie. He was a sometime editor of the *Wiener Zeitschrift für die Kunde des Morgenlandes*. His writings include *Der Einfluss des Arabischen und Persischen auf das Türkische* (1900), and *Die heiligen Bücher der Jeziden* (1913). He died in Mödling, 7 April 1918. DtBE; NDB; LC; ÖBL

Bivar, Adrian David Hugh, he gained a first class degree in Classical studies at Oxford, and studied Arabic and Persian at Beirut and Shiraz. After military service in India before partition he was appointed a research lecturer in ancient history at Christ Church, Oxford, and presented his doctoral thesis on the history and archaeology of the Kushan and Kushano-Sasanian periods. In 1956 he was appointed Museum Curator in the Nigerian Antiquities Service, being mainly concerned with Arabic manuscripts and Islamic armour, weapons, and buildings. Since 1960 he was a lecturer in Central Asian archaeology at SOAS. He was director of the Royal Asiatic Society from 1971 to 1974, and secretary of the Corpus Inscriptionum Iranicarum since 1971. His writings include *Catalogue of the western Asiatic seals in the British Museum.* BioB134; BLC; LC

Bixby, James Thompson, born 30 July 1843 at Barre, Mass., he was a 1870 graduate of Harvard School of Divinity, and received a Dr.phil. in 1885 from the Universität Leipzig. He was a Unitarian clergyman whose writings include *The new world and the new thought* (1902). He died in Yonkers, N.Y., 26 December 1921. DAB; WhAm, 1

Bjerrum, H., fl. 1925, his writings include *St.John's Gospel in Musulman Tamil* (1919). BLC

Björck (Böjrk), Gudmund, fl. 1936, he wrote on Greek veterinary medicine in Arabic translation, and contributed to *le Monde oriental* (Uppsala). GAS III, p. 349

Björkman, Walther, born 19 June 1896 at Lübeck, he was a Turkologist and a professor at universities in Germany, Sweden, and Turkey. His writings include *Ofen zur Türkenzeit* (1920), and *Beiträge zur Geschichte der Staatskanzlei im islamischen Ägypten* (1928). Kürschner, 1940/41-1996

Bjørnbo, Axel Anthon, born 20 April 1874 at København, he studied at København and München, where he received a doctorate in 1901 for his thesis, *Studien über Menelaos' Sphärik*. He became a historian of mathematics and a librarian. His writings include *Die mathematischen S. Marco-Handschriften in Florenz* (1976). With Seb. Vogel he edited *Alkindi, Tieus und Pseudo-Euklid, drei optische Werke* (1912). He died in Hellerup, 6 October 1911. DanskBL; Dansk²

Blache, Jules Adolphe Lucien, born 28 January 1893, he received a doctorate in 1931 from the Université de Grenoble for his thesis, *Les massifs de la Grande Chartrouse et du Vorcors*. From 1944 to 1946, he was Préfet de Meurthe-et-Moselle. He retired as rector of the Université d'Aix-Marseille. His writings include *L'homme et la montagne* (1933), and *Le grand refus* (1945). He died 6 April 1970. WhoFr, 1957/58-1969/70|; *Who was who*, 6

Blachère, Régis, born 30 June 1900 at Montrouge (Hauts-de-Seine), he followed a career as an Arabist in Morocco until 1935, when he established himself at Paris. His writings include *Introduction au Coran* (1947), *Le problème de Mahomet* (1952), *Analecta* (1975) as well as a French translation of the Koran (1957); he was joint author of *Dictionnaire arabe-français-anglais* (1967). He died in Paris, on 7 August 1973. *Hommes et destins*, vol. 7, pp. 87-88; *Index Islamicus* (5); WhoFr, 1971/72

Blachier, fl. 1955, he was a sometime *conseiller* at the Court of Appeal at Algiers. Note

Black, Charles Edward Drummond, fl. 1905-1909, his writings include *A Memoir on the Indian surveys, 1875-1890* (1891), and *The Marquess of Dufferin and Ava* (1903). LC

Black, Claud Hamilton Griffith, Lt.-Colonel, born 19th century, he was a graduate of the Royal Military College, Sandhurst, and joined the Indian Cavalry in 1901. He died 25 June 1946. Who was who, 4

Black, Cyril Edwin, born 10 September 1915 at Bryson City, N.C., he was a graduate of Duke University, Durham, N.C., and received a Ph.D. in 1941 from Harvard for *The beginnings of constitutional government in Bulgaria, 1878-1885*. From 1939 to 1986 he taught at Princeton. He was a sometime adviser to the American delegation on the Security Council Balkan Commission. His writings include *The establishment of constitutional government in Bulgaria* (1943), and *The dynamics of modernization* (1966). He died in Princeton, 18 July 1989. NUC, pre, 1956; WhAm, 10

Black-Michaud, Jacob, born 24 October 1938 at London, he was a graduate of Oxford and received a Ph.D. from SOAS in 1976 for his thesis, *The economics of oppression; ecology and stratification in an Iranian tribal society*. He spent eighteen months doing sociological fieldwork among nomadic tribesmen in the Middle East. His writings include *Cohesive force; feud in the Mediterranean and the Middle East* (1975), and *Sheep and land; the economics of power in a tribal society* (1986). He died 6 March 1985. ConAu, 61-64; LC; Sluglett

Blackburn, John *Richard*, born 14 November 1939 at Sault St. Marie, Ontario, Canada. he graduated in 1962 from the University of Toronto where he received a Ph.D. in 1971 for *Turkish-Yemenite political relations, 1538-1568*. He was a member of the Department of Islamic Studies at Toronto from 1964 until his retirement. His research in Ottoman and Yemeni history is based on fieldwork in Ottoman collections in Istanbul. He was a member of MESA and the American Research Institute in Turkey. *MESA Roster of members*, 1977-1990; Private

Blacker, Latham Valentine *Stewart*, born in 1887, he was a graduate of the Royal Military College Sandhurst, and served in Waziristan, Turkistan, Afghanistan, and Kurdistan, he wrote *On secret patrol in High Asia* (1922), and *Tales from Turkestan* (1924). He died 19 April 1964. Who was who, 6

Blackman, Aylward Manley, born 30 January 1883 at Dawlish, Devon, he was privately educated and studied at Queen's College, Oxford. He was an Egyptologist whose specialty was Egyptian religion. His list of works is a long one and includes *Egyptian myth and ritual* (1932). His drawings are in the Archive of the Griffith Institute, Ashmolean Museum, Oxford. He died in Abergele, 9 March 1956. Dawson; Egyptology; *Who was who*, 5

Blackman, Winifred Susan, born 14 August 1872 at Preston Richards, Westmoreland, she was a graduate of Oxford and participated in the Percy Sladen Expedition to Egypt from 1922 to 1925. Her writings include *The Fellahin of Upper Egypt* (1968). She died 12 December 1950. Egyptology; *Who was who*, 4

Blackmore, Rev. Josiah T. C., fl. 1930, he was a sometime missionary of the Methodist Episcopal Church in Algeria, and superintendent of the Kabylie district. Note

Blagden, Charles Otto, born 30 September 1864, he was a graduate of Corpus Christi College, Oxford. He held various administrative and judicial posts in Malacca and Singapore until his retirement on ground of ill-health in 1897. From 1917 to 1935 he was a lecturer at SOAS. His writings include *Catalogue of manuscripts in European languages belonging to the Library of the India Office* (1916). He died 25 August 1949. Who was who, 4

Blagova, Galina Fedorovna, born 31 August 1927 at Moscow, she graduated in 1950 from the Moscow State University, where she also received a doctorate in 1954 for her thesis, *Характеристика грамматического сторя (морфологии) староузбекского литературного языка конца XV века по "Бабур-наме"*. Since 1954 she was editor-in-chief of *Вопросы языкознания*. Her writings include *Тюркское склонение в ареально-историческом освещении* (1982), and *Бабур-наме: язык, прагматика текста, стиль* (1994). LC; Miliband; Miliband²

Blaikie, Piers M., born 29 January 1942, his writings include *Family planning in India* (1975), and *The political economy of civil erosion in developing countries* (1985). LC

Blaise, A., born 19th cent., he was a professor at l'École de médecine d'Alger and died while giving his first general pathology class in 1900. He had been a member of long-standing of the Société de géographie d'Alger, and was an active participant at the Congrès de géographie, held in Alger. He advocated the creation of a chair of subtropical medicine at Alger, as well as a widening of naturalization. His writings include *Lathyrisme médullaire spasmodique*. *Bulletin de la Société de géographie d'Alger* 6 (1901), pp. 613-614

Blaise, Jacques, fl. 1972, he was affiliated with the Institut géologique Albert Lapparent, Paris. His writings include *Le Précambrien du Tazat, sa place dans les structures du Hoggar oriental* (Paris, 1967). LC

Blake, Anthony George Edward, born in 1939, his writngs include *A seminar on time* (1980), and *The intelligent enneagram* (1996). LC

Blake, Frank Ringgold, born 9 February 1875 at Baltimore, Md., he received a Ph.D. in 1902 from Johns Hopkins University, Baltimore, Md., for his thesis, *The so-called intransitiv verbal forms in the Semitic languages*. He was a sometime professor at Johns Hopkins, and a member of the American Oriental Society. His writings include *A resurvey of Hebrew tenses*. LC; WhNNA

Blake, Gerald Henry, born 1 February 1936, he received a Ph.D. in 1963 from SOAS for his thesis, *A study of the meaning of rural planning from the Lachish region in Israel*. In 1992 he was a reader in geography, and director, International Boundaries Research Unit, University of Durham, UK. His writings include *Misurata, a market town in Tripolitania* (1968); and he was joint author of the *Cambridge atlas of the Middle East and Africa* (1987). LC; Sluglett

Blake, Isabel M., fl. 1917, her writings include *Fez and turban tales* (1920). LC

Blake, Robert Pierpont, born 1 November 1886 at San Francisco, he took undergraduate honours in Greek at California, and at Harvard passed general examination for the Ph.D. in both classics and history. Moving on to Berlin, he pursued his developing interest in Oriental languages. In 1911 he visited St. Petersburg and was inspired to take up Armenian and Georgian. From 1918 to 1920 he was lecturer in the Russian University at Tiflis, and later a professor at the State University of Georgia, where he lectured in Georgian. From 1920 until his death on 9 May 1950, he was at Harvard teaching Georgian and Armenian, as well as courses on the economic development of the Mediterranean world, and on the Byzantine and Ottoman empires. *Armenian affairs* 1 (1950), pp. 312-314; *Harvard University gazette* 46 vi (28 October 1950), pp. 34-35; Shavit; WhAm, 3

Blaker, William Frederick, Colonel, born 9 April 1877 at Tynemouth, Northumberland. During the first World War he served with General Headquarters Staff of the Mesopotamian Expeditionary Force. He died 20 August 1933. *Who was who, 3*

Blanár, Vincent, Dr., fl. 1970, his writings include *Príspevok ku štúdiu slovenských osobných a pomiestnych mien v Mad'arsku* (1950), and *Lexikalno-sémantická rekonštrukcia* (1984). LC

Blanc, Edouard, born 15 April 1858 at Paris, he joined the Administration des Eaux-et-Forêts in 1876 and later transferred to Ponts-et-Chaussées as an engineer for southern Tunisia, where he performed preliminary explorations for the Trans-Saharan railway project. From 1890 to 1900, he was involved in scientific as well as diplomatic missions in Central Asia and North Africa. His writings include *Chasses à l'impossible* (1889). He died in 1923. Curinier, vol. 3 (1901), pp. 82-83

Blanc, Haim, Dr., born in 1926 in Romania, he was a sometime member of the Department of Linguistics at the Hebrew University, Jerusalem. He wrote *Studies in North Palestinian Arabic* (1953), and *Communal dialects in Baghdad* (1964). He died in 1984. *Jerusalem studies of Arabic* 12 (1989), pp. iii-vii; LC

Blanc, Jean-Charles, born 20th cent., he was in 1978 affiliated with *le Monde*, Paris. His writings include *Afghan trucks* (1976), and *L'Afghanistan et ses populations* (1976). LC

Blanc, Paul, fl. 1875, his writings include *Manuel algérien* (1871), and *La vie du colon en Algérie* (1874). BN

Blanc, Robert, born 25 May 1921 at Vincennes, he was a sometime member of the Service de statistique du Maroc, chief of the Service de statistique de l'Afrique occidentale française, Dakar, and an *administrateur* at the Institut national de la statistique et des études économiques. Unesco

Blancard, Louis, born in 1831, he was a sometime archivist of the Département des Bouches-du-Rhône. His writings include *Le besant d'or sarrazines pendant les croisades* (1880), and *Documents inédits sur le commerce de Marseille au moyen-âge* (1884-85). He died in 1902. LC; NUC, pre-1956

Blanchard, Francis, born 21 July 1916 at Paris, he studied from 1934 to 1937 at l'École des sciences politiques, Paris. From 1940 to 1941 he was Résident général de France in Tunisia, and from 1974 to 1984, director-general of the International Labour Organization. IntWW, 1974-2002; WhoFr, 1983-2002/2003; WhoUN, 1975; WhoWor, 1974-78

Blanchard, Georges, born in 1873, he received a doctorate in 1898 from the Université de Grenoble for his thesis, *Étude sur la formation et la constitution politique de l'État indépendant du Congo*. Certainly from 1903 to 1913 he was a professor at l'École français de droit du Caire. His writings include *Histoire du droit publique français* (1908). LC; Note

Blanchard, Raoul, born in 1877, his writings include *Cours de géographie; la France et ses colonies* (1923), and *Asie occidentale* (1929). NUC, pre-1956

Blanchard, William Oscar, born in 1886, he was an American geographer and joint author of *Economic geography of Europe* (1931). He died in 1952. Bioln, 3; LC

Blanché, Ferdinand, born 19th cent., he was a sometime director of l'École d'Aïn-el-Turck, Algeria. His trace is lost after a publication in 1915. Note

Blanchet, Paul, born 3 August 1870 at Paris, he studied at l'École normale and was later a professor at the Collège de Constantine. He was an Arabist who carried on explorations in northeastern Africa as well as southern Tunisia. For the Trans-Saharan railway project he explored western Adrar. On his return from the mission he contracted yellow fever and died in Dakar, 6 October 1900. DBF; *Bulletin de la Société de géographie d'Alger* 3 (1900), pp. 351-353; *Revue de la Société de géographie de Tours* 17 (1900), pp. 13-15

von Blanckenburg, Peter, born 2 July 1921 at Kardemin, Germany, he received a Dr.agr. in 1952 from the Universität Göttingen for his thesis, *Die heimatvertriebenen Landwirte*. From 1964 until his retirement he was a professor of agronomy at the Technische Universität Berlin. His writings include *Agricultural extension systems in some African and Asian countries* (1984). Kürschner, 1992-2003

Blanckenhorn, Max Ludwig Paul, born 15 (or 16) April 1861 at Siegen, Germany, he studied geology at Göttingen, Bonn, Straßburg and Berlin, and received a doctorate in 1855 from the Universität Bonn for his thesis, *Die Trias am Nordrande der Eifel*. From 1879 to 1899 he was a member of the Geological Survey of Egypt in Cairo. He travelled extensively in the Middle East. His writings include *Geologie Ägyptens* (1901), *Naturwissenschaftliche Studien arn Toten Meer und im Jordantal* (1912), *Syrien, Arabien und Mesopotamien* (1914), and *Ägypten* (1921). He died in Marburg, 13 January 1947. DtBE; NDB; Thesis

Bland, Nathaniel, born 3 February 1803, he was educated at Eton and Christ Church College, Oxford, and became a distinguished Persian scholar. His writings include *Persian chess, illustrated from Oriental sources* (1850), and *On the Muhammedan science of tâbír, or interpretation of dreams* (1866). In later life he took to gambling, had to sell his estate, and committed suicide, 10 August 1865. Buckland

Blandy, Richard John, born 8 December 1938 at Vila, Vanuatu, New Hebrides, he studied at St. Peter's College, Adelaide, and Columbia University, NYC. From 1963 to 1972 he was affiliated with the International Labour Office, Genève. He was a sometime professor at the University of Melbourne. His writings include *How labour markets work* (1982). WhoAus, 1983-1998|

Blanqui, Jérôme Adolphe, born 21 November 1798 at Nice, he was the founding editor of *Journal des économistes*, and from 1830 until his death, 29 January 1854, a director of l'École spéciale du commerce, Paris. His writings include *L'Histoire de l'économie politique en Europe* (1837), its translations into Danish, English and German, and *Algérie; rapport sur la situation économique des nos possessions dans le nord de l'Afrique* (1840). DBF

Blaramberg, Johann (Ivan Fedorovich) von, born 8 April 1800 at Frankfurt am Main, he studied law at the Universität Gießen. Since 1823 in Russian service, he explored the Caucasus and Central Asia. From 1837 to 1840, he accompanied a Russian embassy to Persia, during which time he travelled on to Meshed, Herat and Isfahan. For several years, he was a director of the Topographical Department of the Russian Ministry of War. Between 1872 and 1875, Emil von Sydow published his *Erinnerungen aus dem Leben des kaiserlich-russischen General-Lieutenant Johann von Blaramberg*. He died in Simferopol, 22 December 1878. DtBE; Henze; Wieczynski

Blasdell, R. A., Rev., fl. 1945, he spent some time in Malaya with the Methodist Church of Southern Asia. In 1945 he was on the staff of Leonard Theological College, Jubbulpore, and also served for a period at the Henry Martyn School of Islamic Studies, Aligarh. He wrote *Sa-biji bĕneh, tĕrkarang oleh, R. A. Blasdell* (Singapore, 1954). LC

Blaškovič (Blaskovics), József, born 12 June 1910 at Imel, formerly Hungary, he attended Teachers College in Bratislava, and pursued Oriental studies at the universities of Budapest and Praha, where he received a doctorate in 1950 for his thesis, *Listiny Vysokej Porty vo veci obsadenia Košíc*. Since 1952 he was a professor at Universita Karlova. His writings include *Dějiny nové turecké literatury* (1953), and *Arabische, türkische und persische Handschriften der Universitäts-Bibliothek in Bratislava* (1961). He died in Praha, 6 July 1990. Asian and African studies (Bratislava), 16 (1980), pp. 9-18; Filipsky: LC

Blatter, Ethelbert (Edelbert), S.J., born 15 December 1877 at Appenzell, Switzerland, he was educated in Switzerland and England. In 1904 he was appointed a professor of botany at St. Xavier's College, Bombay. His writings include *Flora of Aden* (1914-16), and *Flora Arabica* (1919-36). He died in 1934. Kosch; WhE&EA

Blau (de Wangen), Joyce, born in 1932 at Cairo, she was from 1962 to 1966 affiliated with the Centre pour l'Étude des problèmes du monde musulman contemporain, Université libre de Bruxelles. From 1970 until her retirement she was a professor of Kurdish at the Institut national des langues et civilisations orientales, Paris. Her writings include *Dictionnaire kurde-français-anglais* (1965), and *Les Kurdes et le Kurdistan; bibliographie critique* (1989). In 1973 she received a doctorate from the Sorbonne nouvelle for her thesis, *Le kurde de 'Amadiya et de Djebel Sindjar*. THESAM, 3

Blau, Ludwig (Lajos), born 29 April 1861 at Putnok, Hungary, he received a doctorate in 1887 from the University of Budapest, and in the following year he was ordained at the Landes-Rabbinerschule, Budapest. In 1889 he became a professor of Hebrew and Aramaic at the Landes-Rabbinerschule, where he became the first professor of the Seminary chosen from amongst its graduates. Concurrently he was also its librarian from 1899 to 1922; since 1913 he was its director. His writings include *Massoretische Untersuchungen* (1898). *Zur Einleitung in die Heilige Schrift* (1894), *Das altjüdische Zauberwesen* (1898). For forty years he was also editor of *Magyar Zsidó szemle*. He died in 1936. EncJud; Magyar; The Rabbinical Seminary of Budapest, 1877-1977, a centennial volume, ed. by M. Carmilly-Weinberger (1986), pp. 194-202; Wininger

Blau, Otto Hermann, born 21 April 1828 at Nordhausen, Germany, he was graduate of Schulpforta, and studied theology, philosophy and Oriental languages at Halle and Leipzig. He entered the Prussian diplomatic service in 1852, and served at the Legation in Constantinople, from where he travelled throughout Asia Minor. After the conclusion of the German-Persian trade agreement of 1857, he travelled overland to Persia. In 1858 he was consul at Trapezunt; in 1861 he went on a mission to Herzegovina and Montenegro, followed by an appointment as consul at Sarajevo in 1870. Since 1873 he was consul-general at Odessa, where he committed suicide, 27 February 1879. His writings include *Commerzielle Zustände Persiens* (1858). Embacher; Henze; Pallas

Blau, Yehoshua (Joshua), born 22 September 1919 at Cluj, Romania, she was a sometime professor of Hebrew and Semitic languages at Tel Aviv and later Jerusalem. Her writings include *The emergence and linguistic background of Judeo-Arabic* (1965), *The renaissance of modern Hebrew and modern Arabic* (1981), and *Studies in Middle Arabic and its Judaeo-Arabic variety* (1988). WhoIsrael, 1966/67-1992/93

Blaudin de Thé, Bernard Marie Samuel, born in 1920, he was a sometime *commandant* of the Compagnie méhariste de l'Erg oriental. His writings include *Historique des compagnies méharistes, 1902-1952* (1955), and *Essai de bibliographie du Sahara français* (1959). LC

Blauensteiner, Kurt, born in 1907 in Austria, his writings include *Georg Raphael Donner* (Wien, 1944). He was killed in action on the Eastern Front, 18 February 1943.

Blaustein, Albert Paul, born 12 October 1921 at New York City, he studied law at the University of Michigan and Columbia University. He was a civil and human rights lawyer as well as a special studies consultant. His writings include *The American lawyer* (1954), and *Manual of foreign legal periodicals and their index* (1962). He was joint author of *The Arab oil weapon* (1977). He died in 1994. ConAu, 1-4; Master (6); WrDr, 1976/78-1996/98|

Blayac, Joseph, fl. 1899-1922, his writings include *Esquisse géologique du Bassin de la Seybouse et de quelques régions voisines* (1912). NUC, pre-1956

Blayney, Thomas Lindsey, born 3 December 1873 (or 1874) at Lebanon, Ky., he was a graduate of Center College of Kentucky, Danville, Ky., studied at several European universities and received a Dr.phil. in 1906 from the Universität Heidelberg for his thesis, *Thomas Moore, ein irischer Dichter*. He was a professor of modern languages as well as history of European art at United States universities. He also served as a university and museum administrator. He died 13 March 1971. Thesis; WhAm, 5

Blazquez y Delgado Aguilera, Antonio, born in 1859 at Almadén del Azogue, Spain, he was a sometime professor at the Academia de Administración Militar and *bibliotecario perpetuo* of the Real Sociedad Geográfica. His writings include *Via romana de Tanger á Cartago* (1902), and *Estudios geográfico-históricos de Marruecos* (1913). He died in Madrid, 14 February 1950. DBEC

Bleaney, Carol *Heather*, born about 1946 in Great Britain, she was from 1976 to 1990 an Islamic bibliographer at the Centre for Middle Eastern and Islamic Studies in the University of Durham. Since 1990 she was joint editor of *Index Islamicus* at the Islamic Bibliography Unit at the Cambridge University Library. Her writings include *Lebanon* (World bibliographical series; 1991). Private

Blechman, Barry M., born 7 April 1943 at N.Y.C., he was educated at Queens College, CUNY, and received a Ph.D. in 1971 from Georgetown University for *The consequences of Israeli reprisals*. In the 1970s he was attached to the Brookings Institution, and the U.S. Arms Control and Disarmament Agency, Washington, D.C. His writings include *A quantitative description of the Arab-Israeli interactions, 1949-1969* (1971). He was joint author of *Force without war* (1978). ConAu, 97; WhoAm, 1980-83

Bleiber, Fritz, born 19 February 1898 at Wien, he received a Dr.phil. in 1921 from the Universität Wien for his thesis, *Der Sprachschlüssel des Scheich Mahmud.*. Thereafter he was successively a librarian at Wien and Kiel. He was a sometime professor of international law at Wien and Kabul. His writings include *Die Entdeckung im Völkerrecht* (1933), *Der Völkerbund* (1939), and *Handwörterbuch der Diplomatie und Außenpolitik* (1959). He died in Wien, 13 May 1959. Kürschner, 1940/41, 1954, 1961; Teichl; WhoAustria, 1954-1957/58

Bleichsteiner, Robert, born 6 January 1891 at Wien, he received a Dr.phil.in 1913 from the Universität Wien for *Die Götter und Dämonen der Zoroastrier in Firdusis Heldenbuch von Eran*. He was a librarian at the Forschungsinstitut für Osten und Orient and subsequently a keeper at the Asian Section in the Museum für Völkerkunde, Wien. He wrote *Kaukasische Gesänge* (1919), and edited *Wörterbuch der heutigen mongolischen Sprache* (1941). Brill, Leiden, posthumously published *The library of the late Robert Bleichsteiner* (1955). He died in Wien, 10 April 1954. DtBE; Schwarz; WhoAus, 1954

Blennerhassett, Rowland Ponsonby, born 22 July 1850, at Kells, Ireland, he was educated at Christ Church College, Oxford, and became a justice of the peace who practised at the Parliamentary Bar. He died 7 April 1913. Who was who, 1

Blerzy, J. *Henri*, born 30 July 1830 at Rozoy (S.-et-M.), he graduated from l'École polytechnique and in 1852 joined the French telegraph service, where he remained until his retirement. His writings include *Les Colonies anglaises* (1879). He died in Paris about 1904. DBF

Blessich, Aldo, born 19th cent., he was a professor of geography at the Università di Napoli and later at the Istituto superiore di scienze economiche e commerciali di Roma. He was a sometime secretary of the Società africana d'Italia. His writings include *La geografia alla corte aragonese in Napoli* (1897), and *Un geografo italiano del secolo XVIII, Giovanni A. R. Zannono* (1898). Chi è, 1931, 1936, 1940, 1948; Rovito

Bleuchot, M. *Hervé*, born 20th cent., he received a doctorate in 1970 from the Université d'Aix-Marseille for his thesis, *Les Libéraux français au Maroc, 1947-1956*. In 1993 he was attached to l'Institut de recherches et d'études sur le monde arabe et musulman, Aix-en-Provence. His writings include *Les Libéraux français au Maroc, 1947-1955* (1973), *Chroniques et documents libyens, 1969-1980* (1983), and *Les Cultures contre l'homme? Essai d'anthropologie historique du droit pénal soudanais* (1944). In 1991 he was a joint editor of *Sudan; history, identity, ideology.* EURAMES; LC; THESAM, 1

Blieske, Dorothea, born 11 May 1934 at Poblotz, Germany, she studied at the universities of Berlin and Tübingen, where she received a Dr.phil. in 1966 for her thesis *Šahin-e Širazis "Ardašir-Buch."* She was a Persian subject specialist at the Tübingen Universitätsbibliothek from 1961 to 10 April 1978, when she committed suicide. Jahrbuch der Deutschen Bibliotheken 47 (1977), p. 382

Blind, Karl, born 4 September 1826 at Mannheim, Germany. he studied at Heidelberg and Bonn and was a leader of the German revolution 1848 in Baden. He was court-martialled; saved from death through flaw in Grand Ducal proclamation; refuge in France, banished, refuge in England. He died in Hampstead, near London, 31 May 1907. DtBE; DtBlnd² (4); Who was who, 1

Blinkhorn, Thomas A., fl. 1969, he wrote *People of the land* (1972). NUC, 1973-1977

Blishchenko, Igor' Pavlovich, fl. 1960, he received a doctorate in law. His writings include Агрессия Израиля и международное право (1970), Дипломатическое право (1972), and the translation *Terrorism and international law* (1984). LC

Bliss, Daniel, born 17 August 1823 at Georgia, Vt., he was a missionary under the American Board of Commissioners for Foreign Missions for seven years, before serving for fifty years as founding president, and president emeritus, at the Syrian Protestant College in Beirut. He wrote an autobiography, *The reminiscences of Daniel Bliss* (1920). He died in Beirut, 27 July 1916. DAB; NCCN; Shavit; WhAm, 1

Bliss, Edwin Elisha, born 12 April 1817 at Putney, Vt., he was a Protestant missionary at Trabzon, 1843-1851, and Merzifon, 1851-1856, before transferring to Constantinople, where he edited (1865-1892) the *Avedaper*, printed in Turkish and Armenian. He wrote *Condensed sketch of the missions of the American Board in Asiatic Turkey* (1877), and a Bible handbook in Armenian. He died in Constantinople, 20 December 1892. DAB; NCCN; Shavit; WhAm, H

Bliss, Edwin Munsell, born 12 September 1848 at Erzerum, he grew up in Constantinople, attended Robert College, Amherst College, and Yale Divinity School. He was intermittently an agent for the Bible Society and and editor of the *Encyclopedia of missions*. He travelled extensively in the Middle East. His writings incude *The Turk in Armenia, Crete, and Greece* (1896), *Turkey and the Armenian atrocities* (1896), and *The missionary enterprise* (1908). He died in Washington, D.C., 6 August 1919. DAB; NCCN; Shavit; WhAm, 1

Bliss, Frederick Jones, born 23 January 1859 at Suq al-Gharb, Syria, he was an archaeologist under the Palestine Exploration Fund from 1891 to 1900. He excavated in Palestine and directed archaeological work at Jerusalem and other localities. His writings include *Excavations at Jerusalem, 1894-97* (1898), *The development of Palestine exploration* (1906), and *The religions of modern Syria and Palestine* (1912). He died in White Plains, N.Y., 4 June 1937. DAB; NCCN; Shavit; WhAm, 4

Bliss, Howard Sweetser, born 6 December 1860 at Suq al-Gharb, Syria, he was a graduate of Amherst College, and studied at Oxford, Berlin, and Göttingen. He served as a pastor in the United States, before succeeding his father as president of the Syrian Protestant College, Beirut. In 1919 he attended the Paris Peace Conference as an expert on Syrian and Near Eastern affairs. He died in Saranac Lake, N.Y., 2 May 1920. DAB; NatCAB; NCCN; Shavit; Who was who 2; WhAm, 1

Bliss, Isaac Grout, born 5 July 1822 at Springfield, Mass., he graduated from Amherst College and Andover Theological Seminary. On 4 May 1847, he was ordained at West Springfield, on 8 May he married Eunice Day, and on 23 June together they sailed for Turkey to serve as missionaries of the American Board at Erzerum. His zeal soon exhausted his strength so that in 1851 he was obliged to return to America with broken health. For five years he performed pastoral duties in Massachusetts, but in 1856 he accepted an appointment from the American Bible Society as its agent for the Levant, with Constantinople as his residence. His lasting contribution was the organization of the agency, and particularly the distribution of the Bible. At the request of the Mission, he also undertook the distribution of all other missionary books published at Constantinople. This task brought him into direct contact with missionaries and colporters in Turkey, Syria, Egypt, and Persia. The Bible House at Constantinople originated in his mind, and was built by funds largely raised by him. His writings include *Twenty-five years in the Levant; Bible work in the Turkish Empire* (1893). He died in Asyut, Egypt, on 16 February 1889. *Missionary herald* 85 (1889), pp. 141-142; Shavit

Bliss, Joseph, J.P., born in 1853, he was educated at Edinburgh University, he was a sometime Liberal M.P. who died 12 December 1939. Who was who, 3

Bliss, Richard Mitchell, born 16 December 1929 at Washington, he studied at Yale and New York University. He was a banker and business executive, specializing in Middle East affairs. WhoAm, 1974-1978; WhoWor, 1978/79

Bliss, William Dwight Porter, born 20 August 1856 at Constantinople, he was educated at Robert College, Amherst College, and Hartford Theological Seminary. He was a Christian socialist and preached his gospel of social salvation with a sheer disregard of personal consequences. He died a poor man on 8 October 1926. His writings include *Handbook of socialism* (1895); he was joint editor of *The new encyclopedia of social reform* (1908). DAB; WhAm, 1

Blitzer, Charles Robert, born 8 November 1944 at Pasedena, Cal., he was a graduate of Stanford University, where he also received his Ph.D. in 1971 for *A perspective planning model for Turkey, 1969-1984*. He became affiliated with the World Bank and was a visiting professor at American universities. In 1975 he was joint editor of *Economic-wide models and development planning*. He was author or joint author of a number of working papers for the National Bureau of Economic Research, e.g. *Project appraisal and foreign exchange constraints* (1987). WhoE, 1991/92

Bloch, Adolphe, Dr., fl. 1903-1914, he was a French anthropologist. Note

175

Bloch, Alfred, born 18 April 1915 at Basel, where he studied comparative linguistics and Islamics. From 1949 until retirement he was a professor at the Universität Basel where he also taught Hebrew at its Faculty of Divinity. He left an unfinished work, *Die Bedeutung der altarabischen Dichtung für die vergleichende Literaturwissenschaft.* He died in Basel, 11 July 1983. DtBE

Bloch, Ariel Alfred Karl, born 14 May 1933 at Heidelberg, he studied at the Hebrew University, Jerusalem, and Universität Münster, where he received a Dr.phil. in 1962 for *Die Hypotaxe im Damaszenisch-Arabischen mit Vergleichung zur Hypotaxe im Klassisch-Arabischen.* He taught in Germany until 1965, when he was appointed professor of Semitic languages and linguistics at the University of California, Berkeley. His writings include *Studies in Arabic syntax and semantics* (1986), and, as joint author, *The Song of songs, a new translation* (1955). ConAu 41-44; DrAS, 1974 F, 1978 F; Schwarz

Bloch, Ernst *Theodor*, born 19th cent., he received a Dr.phil. in 1893 from the Universität Leipzig for *Vararuci und Hemacandra.* He was an Indologist whose writings include *Supplementary catalogue of the archaeological collection of the Indian Museum* (1911). LC

Bloch, Isaac, born 17 July 1848 at Soultz, Alsace, he studied at Strasbourg and the Rabbinical Seminary, Paris. In 1873 he entered the service of the Alliance israélite universelle. From 1878 to 1889 he was chief rabbi of Algeria; he returned to France in 1890 to succeed to the same office in Nancy. His writings include *Inscriptions tumulaires des anciens cimitières israélites d'Alger* (1888). He died in Nancy, 22 February 1925. DBF; NDBA; Wininger

Bloch, Stella, born in 1901, she was a New York writer and translator who published *Dancing and drama East and West* (1922). WhoLit, 1929-1931

Blochet, Gabriel Joseph *Edgar*, born 12 December 1870 at Bourges (Cher), he studied Arabic, Persian, Turkish and Urdu at l'École des langues orientales, and history and philology at l'École pratique des hautes études, Paris. He received a doctorate for a thesis on Zend-Pahlevi lexicography. From 1895 until his retirement in 1930 he was a keeper at the Bibliothèque nationale. His writings include *Les sources orientales de la Divine comédie* (1901), *Études de grammaire pehlevie* (1905), *Introduction à l'histoire des Mongols de Fadl Allah Rashid ed-Din* (1910), *Muslim painting* (1929), and several catalogues of Arabic, Persian, and Turkish manuscripts. He died in 1937. NUC, pre-1956; *Revue de turcologie = Türk bilik rewüsü* 8 (1938), 320-324

Blochmann, Heinrich (*Henry*) Ferdinand, born 8 January 1838 at Dresden, he graduated from Kreuzschule and studied at Leipzig and Paris. He served in the British Army in India, as an interpreter to the Pacific and Orient Company, and in 1860 was made assistant professor of Urdu and Persian at the Calcutta Madrasa. After graduation from Calcutta University in 1861 he was a president of the Cacutta Madrasa from 1865 until his death on 13 July 1878. He was philological secretary to the Asiatic Society of Bengal and wrote *The prosody of the Persians* (1872). Buckland; DNB S 1; *Index Islamicus* (2); IndianBiInd (1); Riddick

de **Blociszewski**, Joseph, born 14 July 1867 at Paris, he graduated from the Lycée Louis-le-Grand and in 1889 completed his law and also received a diploma from l'École des sciences politiques, Paris. Three years later, he accepted a professorial appointment at the Konsularakademie, Wien, where he taught diplomatic history until the outbreak of the first World War, the years of which he spent under strict surveillance in an internment camp. In late 1918, he returned to Paris to take up a position as an editor with *le Temps,* soon to become head of its foreign service, a position which he held until his death. Concurrently he was lecturing at l'Institut des hautes études internationales. During the last years of his life he was a member of l'Institut de droit international, and served as a legal adviser to the Polish embassy in Paris. He died in 1928. *Revue générale de droit international public* 36 = 3e série, no. 3 (1929), pp. 121-124

Block, Sir Adam Samuel James, born 25 June 1856 at Lucknow, he was educated at Clifton College and entered the consular service at Constantinople as a student interpreter. In 1903 he was appointed by the Council of Foreign Bondholders to represent British and Dutch interests on the Council of Administration of the Ottoman Public Debt. For his service he was decorated by the Sultan of Turkey. He died 16 April 1941. Who was who, 4

de **Blocqueville**, Henri de Coulibœuf, fl. 1860-61, he left a description of his *Quatorze mois de captivité chez les Turcomans,* a work which has been translated into German, *Gefangener bei den Turkomanen* (1980), and into Turkish, *Türkmenler arasinda* (1986). LC

Blohm, Dieter, born 27 May 1942 at Merseburg, Germany, he studied general and Oriental philology, particularly Indian languages, and received a Dr.phil. in 1969 from the Universität Leipzig for *Der Relativsatz im modernen Hocharabischen.* After some time with a Leipzig publisher, he was since 1966 a researcher in Orientalistisches Institut, Universität Leipzig. He edited *Studien zur arabischen*

Linguistik (1989). He was in 2003 affiliated with the Seminar für Arabistik, Freie Universität Berlin. Kürschner, 2003; Thesis

Blöhm, Julius, born 19th cent., he made a journey to Mesopotamia in 1884. Note

Blomdus, Jean, fl. 1885. His writings include the pamphlet, *Réponse à l'enquête ministérielle au sujet du bon emploi militaire des cadres d'instruction dans l'infanterie et des sous-officiers rengagés en particulier* (Paris, 1896). BN

Blomeyer, Arwed, born 16 December 1906 at Wilhelmshaven, Germany, he received a Dr.jur. in 1929 from the Universität Jena for his thesis, *Die außerpositiven Grundlagen des Privat-eigentums*. He was a professor of law at various German universities. His writings include *Zivilprozeßrecht* (1985). He died in Berlin, 8 May 1995. Kürschner, 1940/41-1992

Blomfield, Rosamund Seline née Graves, born in the 19th centuy at Dublin, she was married in 1877 to Rear-Admiral Sir Richard M. Blomfield, 1835-1921, with whom she spent more than twenty-five years of residency in Alexandria, where her husband had been Comptroller of the Port since 1879. *Who was who*, 2

Blondel, André, born in 1878, he received a doctorate in 1927 from the Université Aix-Marseille for his thesis, *Le contrôle juridictionnel de la constitutionnalité des lois*. In 1932 he was a professor of law at the Faculté de droit de Dijon. His writings include *Essai sur les institutions municiplaes de Chartres* (1903), and *La Conférence de Montreux et le nouveau régime des Détroits* (1938). LC

Blondel, Georges, born 8 March 1856 at Dijon, he was a sociologist who received a doctorate in 1881 in law. Thereafter he taught at Lyon, Lille, and the Collège de France, Paris. His research centered on the German and Austrian questions. His writings include *La France et le marché du monde* (1901), *Tempête sur l'Europe* (1937), and many works on Germany. He died in Paris, 31 July 1948. LC

Bloom, Clark C., born in the first half of the 20th century, he was in 1974 a member of the American Economic Asociation. He wrote *State and local tax differentials and the location of manufacturing* (1956), and *How the American economy is organized*, both of which were published by the Bureau of Business and Economic Research, College of Commerce, University of Iowa. LC; NUC, 1956-1967

Bloomfield, Barry Cambray, born 1 June 1931 at London. He was successively librarian of SOAS, director of the India Office Library and Records, and director of Collection Development at the British Library, London. His writings include *W. H. Auden; a bibliography* (1964), and *Theses on Asia accepted in the United Kingdom* (1967). He died 26 February 2002. ConAu 9-12; Who, 1984-2002; WrDr, 1980/82-1998/2000

Bloomfield, Valerie Jean née Philpot, born ca. 1935, she was married in 1958 to Barry Cambray Bloomfield. She was a librarian at the Institute of Commenwealth Studies, London. Her writings include *Coomonwealth elections, 1945-1970; a bibliography* (1976), and she was joint author of *Theses on Africa accepted by universities in the United Kingdom and Ireland* (1964). Private

Bloss, John F. R., Dr. he was from 1933 to 1955 with the Sudan Medical Service, and from 1953 to 1955, deputy director, Ministry of Health. In 1982 he was a participant at the Sudan Historical Records Conference, Durham, UK.

Blount, Sir Henry, born 15 December 1602 at Tittenhanger, Herfordshire, he graduated in 1618 from Trinity College, Oxford, and studied law at Gray's Inn. In May 1634 he set out on an eleven-month journey through the Balkans to Egypt. The publication of his *Voyage to the Levant* (1638), at once established his fame as an author and a traveller. The work was translated into German in 1687. He died 9 October 1682. DNB; Sezgin

von Blücher, Wipert Carl Wilhelm, born 14 July 1883 at Schwerin, Germany, he studied at Heidelberg, München, Berlin, and Rostock, where he received a Dr.jur. in 1911 for *Der Kontokorrentverkehr nach §355 des Handelsgesetzbuches*. In 1911 he entered the diplomatic service. His writings include *Zeitwende in Iran; Erlebnisse und Beobachtungen* (1949), its translation, *Safarnamah-i Blushir* (1984), *Deutschlands Weg nach Rapallo* (1951), *Gesandter zwischen Diktatur und Demokratie* (1951), and *Wege und Irrwege der Diplomatie* (1953). LC; Wer ist wer, 1955-1962; Wer ist's, 1935

Blue, Lionel, born 6 February 1930, he was educated at Balliol College, Oxford, University College, London, and the Leo Blaeck College, London. Since 1967 he was a lecturer at the Leo Blaeck College. His writings include *To Heaven, with Scribes and Pharisees* (1975), and *A Backdoor to heaven* (1979). LC; Who, 1987-2003

Bluhm, Julius, fl. 1864, his writings include *Kurzgefaßte Darstellung des gegenwärtigen Standpunktes des Kriegsmarinewesens in Europa und Amerika* (1848), and *Die Politik der Zukunft vom preußischen Standpunkte* (1858). LC

Blum, André S., born in 1881, he studied at the Sorbonne and received a *doctorat ès lettres* and also a diploma from l'École du Louvre, Paris. His writings include *Histoire générale de l'art* (1921), *Les origines du papier* (1935), and its translation, *On the origin of paper* (1934), and *La route du papier* (1946). NUC, pre-1956

Blum, Robert *Stephen*, born 4 March 1942 at Cleveland, Ohio, he was a graduate of Oberlin College, and received a Ph.D. in 1972 from the University of Michigan. He taught in the United States until 1977 when he was appointed director of the Graduate Programme in Music at York University, Toronto, Ont. His writings include *Ethnomusicology and modern music history* (1991). IntWWM, 1984

Blum, Yehuda Zvi, born 2 October 1931 at Bratislava, he studied at the Hebrew University, Jerusalem, and the University of London, where he received his Ph.D. He was a professor of law at Jerusalem and a sometime Irsaeli representative to the U.N.O. His writings include *Secure boundaries and Middle East peace in the light of international law* (1971), and *For Zion's sake* (1987). IntWW, 1979-2002; LC; MidE, 1979-1982/83; WhoWor, 1978-1997/98

Blumberg, Harry, born 27 August 1902 or 1903 at N.Y.C., he studied at universities in N.Y.C. and received a Ph.D. in 1929 from Harvard for his thesis, *Averroës' Epitome of Aristotle's Parva naturalia*. From 1956 until retirement he was a professor of Hebrew at Hunter College of the City University of New York. His writings include *Modern Hebrew* (1946-52). He died in Ann Arbor, Mich., 28 April 1983. CnDiAmJBi; ConAu, 73-76; WhoWorJ, 1965, 1972

Blumenthal, David Reuben, born 28 December 1938 at Houston, Texas, he received a Ph.D. in 1972 from Columbia for *The commentary of R. Hoter Ben Shelomo to the thirteen principles of Maimonides*. Since 1976 he was a professor of religion at Emory University, Atlanta, Ga. He edited *Understanding Jewish mysticism* (1978-82), and *Approaches to Judaism in medieval times* (1984-85). DrAS, 1978 P, 1982 P; LC

Blumentritt, Ferdinand (Fernando), born 10 September 1853 at Prag, he was a geologist, philologist and high school teacher whose writings include *Die Philippinen* (1900), and its translation, *The Philippines* (1980). He died in September 1913. DtBiInd (3); Jaksch; LC

Blundell, A. S. Moss, fl. 1924-1926, he translated from the French of André Servier, *Islam and the psychology of the Musulman* (1924), and *Spain and the Riff*, by Jean and Jérôme Tharaud (1926). BLC

Blunt, Anne Isabella née Noel Baroness Wentworth, born 22 September 1837 at London, she was the wife of Wilfrid Scawen Blunt and accompanied him on his travels. She was an intrepid horse-woman, an accomplished musician, and an observant traveller. Her Arabic was so perfect and so classical that hardly any Arab could understand a word that she said. Her writings include *Bedouin tribes of the Euphrates* (1879), and *Pilgrimage to Nejd* (1881). She died in Cairo, 15 December 1917. Bidwell; DLB 174 (1997), pp. 41-53; DNB; Freeth, pp. 269-289; Henze; Robinson

Blunt, Sir Edward Arthur Henry, born 14 March 1877, he graduated from Corpus Christi College, Oxford, entered the Indian Civil Service in 1901 and served until 1935. His writings include *The Caste system of Northern India* (1932), and *The I.C.S., the Indian Civil Service* (1937). He died 29 May 1941. Who was who, 4

Blunt, James T., fl. 1799, he was a British army officer who accomplished a reconnaissance mission to North-eastern Deccan, January to May, 1795. Henze

Blunt, Wilfrid Scawen, born in 1840, he entered the Diplomatic Service in 1858, but left in 1869. In 1872 he inherited sufficient wealth to be as eccentric as he wished. He explored Algeria, Egypt, Palestine, and penetrated Najd to Hail. Under safe conduct from its amir, he reached Bushire whence he sailed for India. He spoke fluent but ungrammatical Arabic and had an enthusiasm for Arabic literature of which he produced translations which can still be read with pleasure. He was strongly sympathetic with weak nations and attributed their underdevelopment to the influence of imperialism. He was such a noisy critic of British policy everywhere abroad that he went to jail. His writings include *The future of Islam* (1882), *Ideas about India* (1885), *Atrocities of justice under British rule in Egypt* (1906), and *The secret history of the English occupation of Egypt* (1907). Elizabeth Longford wrote a biography, *A pilgrimage of passion, the life of Wilfred Scawen Blunt* (1979); he is also the subject of an Oxford B.Litt. thesis in 1961 by G. Scott entitled *W. S. Blunt, anti-imperialist*. He died in 1922. Bidwell, pp. 146-49; DNB; DLB 174 (1997), pp. 41-53; Freeth, pp. 269-289; Goldschmidt; Who was who, 2

Bluzet, René, fl. 1894-97, he was a lieutenant in the French Marine Corps and the topographer in the *colonne J.-C. Joffres*, who surveyed the Timbuctu region in 1894. Henze, vol. 3, p. 714

Blyden, Edward William, born 3 August 1832 at Charlotte-Amalie, Virgin Islands. His parents originally descenced from Eastern Nigeria. His mother, a school teacher, supplemented his primary school education with private studies at home. The family were members of the Dutch Reformed Church. Failing to be admitted to U.S. colleges on account of his colour, he went to Monrovia. There he made a living as a correspondent for the *Liberia herald* and lay preacher since 1853. He rose to the rank of Secretary of State of Liberia, 1864, and Ambassador Extraordinary in London, 1905. He was a controversial figure who spent his life attempting to disprove myths of racial superiority and advancing interest in an understanding of African customs and institutions. His writings include *Christianity, Islam, and the Negro race* (1889). He died in Sierra Leone, 7 Februray 1912. Makers, 1981-1996

Blyth, Estelle, born in the 19th century, the daughter of George F.P. Blyth, Bishop of Jerusalem, 1887-1914. Her writings include *Jerusalem and the crusades* (1913), *Warrior saints* (1916), and *When we lived in Jerusalem* (1927). Who was who, 1

Boak, Arthur Edward Romilly, born 29 April 1888 at Halifax, N.S., he was a graduate of Queen's University, Kingston, Ont., and received his Ph.D. in 1911 from Harvard for *The Roman magistri*. From 1914 until retirement he was a professor of history at the University of Michigan. His writings include *A history of Rome to 565 A.D.* (1921). He died 16 December 1962. Canadian, 1936-37; WhAm, 4

Boase, Thomas Sherrer Ross, born 31 August 1898, he was educated at Rugby School and Magdalen College, Oxford. He was a professor of history of art, University of London, 1937-1947, and chairman, British School at Rome, 1965-72. He was a fellow of the British Academy and was awarded an honory doctorate by St. Andrews. His writings include *Castles and churches of the crusading kingdom* (1967), *Kingdoms and strongholds of the crusaders* (1971), and *Death in the midle ages* (1972). He died 14 August 1974. BritInd (1), Who was who, 7

Bobek, Hans, born 17 Juni 1903, he received a doctorate in 1926 for his thesis, *Innsbruck, eine Gebirgsstadt*. He was a lecturer at Berlin and Freiburg before becoming a professor of geography at the Institut für Geographie der Universität Wien. His writings include *Iran; Probleme eines unterentwickelten Landes* (1962). He died in Wien, 15 February 1990. Dickinson, pp. 167-168; DtBE; Kürschner, 1961-1987; WhoAus, 1957/58-1982/83

Bobichon, François *Henri*, born 2 May 1866 at Saint-Étienne (Loire), he served as an officer in French Equatorial Africa and accompanied missions in quest of the route from Gabon to Tchad and the Nile. He was a sometime Minister of Colonies, and a *gouverneur honoraire des colonies*. His writings include *Le vieux Congo français et l'A.E.F.* (1938). He died in Paris, 16 September 1939. AfrBioInd (1), Hommes et destins, vol. 7, pp. 36-44

de **Boblaye**, Émile Le Puillon, born 16 November 1792 at Pontivy (Morbihan), he graduated from l'École polytechnique and served with the Corps des ingénieurs géographes until he retired in 1840 with the rank of *chef d'escadron au corps d'état-major*. Shortly thereafter he was elected *député* for Pontivy. His writings include *Géologie et minéralogie* (1833), and *Description d'Égine* (1835). He died in Paris, 4 December 1843. DBF

Bobokhonov, Shamsuddin Z., fl. 1971, his writings include al-Bukhari's *Адаб дурдоналари = al-Adab al-mufrad* (1990), and *Хадис илминин пешволари* (1992). LC

Bobzin, Hartmut, born 16 August 1946 at Bremen, he studied theology and Oriental languages at Marburg, where he received a Dr.phil. in 1974 for *Die 'Tempora' im Hiobdialog*, and also a Dr.habil. in 1986 for *Der Koran im Zeitalter der Reformation*. He was subsequently appointed a professor of Oriental languages and Islamic studies at Erlangen. His writings include *Der Koran; eine Einführung* (1999). Kürschner, 1992-2003; Thesis

Bocandé, Bertrand, born about 1800 at Nantes, he was a natural scientist and an explorer who spent more than ten years in Portuguese Guinea. Henze

Boccara, Bruno, born 20th cent., he was a sometime lawyer at the Cour de Paris. He wrote *L'Impôt truqué* (1985), and *La Grande peur de 1992; réalités et mirages du barreau français* (1988). LC

Bocco, Riccardo, born in 1957 in Italy, he received diplomas in cultural anthropology from the Università di Torino, and in development studies from the Université de Genève. In 1984 he joined the Institut de recherche sur le monde arabe contemporain, Lyon, as a research fellow. Since 1985 he was a faculty member at the Institut universitaire d'études du développement, Genève. In 1993 he was joint editor of *Steppes d'Arabies; états, pasteurs, agriculteurs et commerçants*. WWASS

Bochard, Arthur, born in 1858, he wrote *L'Évolution de la fortune de l'état* (1910), and *Les Lois de la sociologie économique* (1913). LC

Bocheński, Feliks, fl. 1971, he was a sometime member of the Economic Department of the International Bank for Reconstruction and Development. In 1948 and 1949 he visited Egypt and Lebanon as a member of the Bank's missions to study general economic conditions in those countries. His writings include *The economic structure of Poland* (1944). Note

Bocher, Charles Philippe, born 27 November 1816 at Paris. After passing through the military college of Saint-Cyr in 1838 he took part in the Algerian campaign of La Moricière. After also participating in the Crimean War he resigned from the army. His writings include *Lettres de Crimée, souvenirs de guerre* (1877), *Lettres et écrits militaires; Afrique et armée de l'Orient* (1897), and *Mémoires* (1907-09). He died in Paris, 14 April 1908. DBF

Bock, Franz, born 3 May 1823 at Bartscheid, Germany, he was ordained in 1850, and thereafter served as a clergyman in Krefeld, Aachen, and Köln. During his extensive travels in Europe, Asia, and North Africa he collected medieval art and artifacts which form the stock of the Museum Bock in Aachen. His writings include *Geschichte der liturgischen Gewänder des Mittelalters* (1856-71). He died in Aachen, 1 May 1899. DtBE

Bockel, Alain. In 1967 he was a professor of law at the Faculté de droit de Tunis. His writings include *La participation des syndicats ouvriers aux fonctions économiques et sociales de l'état* (1965), *L'administration camerounaise* (1971), *Droit administratif* (1978), and *De l'apartheid à la conquête du pouvoir* (1986). LC

Bockwitz, Hans Heinrich, born 4 September 1884 at Waldheim, Germany, he studied at Berlin, Grenoble, and Erlangen, where he received a Dr.phil. in 1910 for his thesis, *J.-J. Gourd und seine Trois dialectiques*. He was a director of the Buch- und Schriftmuseum, Leipzig, and after the second World War, a director of the Deutsche Bücherei. He wrote *Zur Kulturgeschichte des Papiers* (1935). He died in Leipzig, 2 December 1954. DtBE

Bocti, Guiseppe *see* Bokti, Guiseppe

von **Bode**, Arnold *Wilhelm*, born 10 December 1845 at Calvörde, Germany, he was a lawyer who later studied history of art and received a doctorate in 1870. Since 1872 he was affiliated with the Königliche Museen in Berlin. His writings include *Vorderasiatische Knüpfteppiche aus alter Zeit* (1902), its translation, *Antique rugs from the Near East* (1970), and *Die Kunst der Frührenaissance in Italien* (1923). He wrote an autobiography, *Mein Leben*. (1930). He died in Berlin, 1 March 1929. DtBE

de **Bode**, Clement Augustus Gregory Peter Louis, Baron, son of a French-Russian couple, he was born in the beginning of the 19th century. From his father he inherited claims of indemnity for property in Alsace confiscated at the commencement of the French revolution in 1789, which he prosecuted with unremitting energy. His writings include *Travels in Luristan and Arabistan* (1845), and the translation from the Russian of N.V. Khanykov, *Bokhara, its amir and its people* (1845). BN; Men10

Bodenheimer, Friedrich Simon, born 6 June 1897 at Köln, Germany, he studied biology and received a doctorate at Bonn in 1922 for his thesis, *Beiträge zur Kenntnis der Kohlschnake*. He was affiliated with the Hebrew University, Jerusalem, until 1938, when he became a visiting professor at Ankara Üniversitesi and consultant to the Turkish Ministry of Agriculture. In 1943 he was an entomological adviser on locust control in Iraq. His writings include *Die Schädlingsfauna Palästinas* (1930), *Problems of animal ecology* (1938), *Studies on the honey bee and beekeeping in Turkey* (1941), and *Türkiye'nin coccidea'si* (1949). He was joint editor of *Ergebnisse der Sinai Expedition 1927 der Hebräischen Universität Jerusalem* (1929). He wrote an autobiography, *A biologist in Israel* (1959). He died in 1959. EncJud; Kürschner, 1931; NearMEWho, 1945/46; WhoIsrael, 1949-1958; Wininger, v. 6

Bodenheimer, Levi, born 13 December 1807 at Karsruhe, Germany, he was a sometime rabbi at Hildesheim and Krefeld. His writings include *Das Testament unter der Benennung einer Erbschaft* (1847). He died in Krefeld, 25 August 1867. Wininger

Bodenheimer, Simon, 1897-1959 *see* Bodenheimer, Friedrich Simon

Bodichon, Eugène, born in 1810 at Mauves, near Mantes (Yvelines). Shortly after he received a medical doctorate at Paris in 1835, he settled in Algeria, where he was engaged in the social, geographical, and economic development of the colony. He was married to Barbara Leigh Smith, an English feminist. His writings include *Considérations sur l'Algérie* (1845), *Études sur l'Algérie en Afrique* (1847), and *De l'humanité* (1866). He died in Alger at the beginning of 1885. DBF

Bodley, Ronald Victor Courtenay, Major, born 3 March 1892 at Paris. After passing through the Royal Military College, Sandhurst, he was a military attaché at the British Embassy in Paris. While attending the Paris Peace Conference, 1919, he made the acquaintance of Thomas E. Lawrence and left the Army. For eight years he lived in the Sahara with a Bedouin tribe. Thereafter he was an author and a film script writer. His writings include *Algeria from within* (1927), *The gay deserters* (1945), *The*

Messenger; the life of Muhammed (1946), and *The soundless Sahara* (1968). With Lorna Hearst he wrote *Gertrude Bell* (1940). His trace is lost after his last publication. WhAm, 9

Bodman, Herbert Luther, Jr., born 29 August 1924 at NYC. As a graduate student in Arab history at Princeton, he conducted field research in Arab history and political institutions with a grant from the Ford Foundation. He received a Ph.D. in 1955 from Princeton for *Political factions in Aleppo, 1760-1826*. After a brief career at the U.S. Information Agency, he was a professor of history at Indiana University. DrAS, 1974 H, 1978 H, 1982 H

Bodroligeti, András J. E., born 5 August 1925 at Tiszaigar, Hungary, he studied at Budapest, and was appointed in 1972 professor of Turkish and Persian at UCLA. His writings include *A fourteenth century Turkish translation of Sa'di's Gulistan* (1969), *The Persian vocabulary of the Codex Cumanicus* (1971), and *Halis's story of Ibrahim* (1975). DrAS, 1974 F, 1978 F, 1982 F; Schoeberlein

Boehm, Georg, born 21 December 1854 at Frankfurt/Oder, Germany, he studied geology and palae-ontology at Straßburg, Göttingen and München, and conducted field research in Italy, Greece, Russia, and the Far East. Since 1888 he was a professor at the Universität Freiburg, Germany, where he died 18 March 1913. DtBE

Boehmer, Julius, born 6 September 1866 at Barmen, Germany, he studied theology at Halle, Basel, and Bonn, and received doctorates at Tübingen, 1898, and Göttingen, 1920. He was a pastor to various congregations. His writings include *Eupen-Malmedi bleibt deutsch* (1941). His trace is lost after his last publication. Kürschner, 1926-1935; Wer ist's, 1912, 1922, 1935; WhE&EA

Boehmer, Rainer Michael, born 2 December 1930 at Königsberg, East Prussia, he received a Dr.phil. in 1961 from the Freie Universität Berlin for *Die Entwicklung der akkadischen Glyptik*. He was an archaeologist at Heidelberg. His writings include *Kleinfunde aus der Unterstadt von Bogazköy* (1979). Kürschner, 1980-2003; Thesis

Boelcke, Willi Alfred, born 20 September 1929 at Berlin, he received a Dr.phil. in 1955 from Humboldt Universität, Berlin, for his thesis, *Die feudale Gutsherrschaft in der Oberlausitz*. He was a professor of social and economic history at the Universität Hohenheim since 1962. His writings include *Krupp und die Hohenzollern* (1956), and *Die Macht des Radios* (1977). Kürschner, 1976-2003; Wer ist wer, 1986-1997/98; WhoWor, 1978

Boele van Hensbroek, Pieter Andreas Martin, 1853-1912. He was a bookseller, publisher, editor, bibliographer, and author whose writings include *De beoefening der Oostersche talen in Nederland en zijne overzeesche bezittingen 1800-1874* (1875). He was joint author of *Het Museum Mesdag en zijne stichters* (ca. 1910). BiBenelux (3)

de **Boer**, Tjitze J., born 28 May 1866 at Wirdum, Netherlands, he studied at Bonn and Straßburg, where he received a Dr.phil. in 1894 for *Die Ewigkeit der Welt in Algazzali und Ibn Rošd*. His writings include *Die Widersprüche der Philosophie nach Al-Gazzali und ihr Ausgleich durch Ibn Rošd* (1894), *Geschichte der Philosophie im Islam* (1901), and its translation, *The history of philosophy in Islam* (1903). He died in 1942. Thesis

Boéresco, Mihai (Michel) B., born 19th cent., he received a doctorate in 1899 from l'Université de Paris for his thesis, *Étude sur la condition des étrangers d'après la législation roumaine, rapprochée de la législation française*. NUC, pre-1956

Boesch, Hans Heinrich, born 24 March 1911 at Zürich, he was an expert in the field of physical, regional, and economic geography. He joined the Universität Zürich in 1941 and was appointed direc-tor of the Geographisches Institut in the following year. His writings include *A geography of world economy* (1964), and its translation, *Weltwirtschaftsgeographie* (1966). He died 16 August 1978. ConAu, 116; Kürschner, 1976; WhoSwi, 1968/69-1978/79; WhoWor, 1974-1978

Boev, IUrii Alekseevich, fl. 1965, his writings include Ближний Восток во внешней политике Франций (1964), and Критика буржуазных концепций политики империалистических госу-дарств на Ближнем Востоке (1979). LC

Boev, Radi, fl. 1975, his writings include Военният флот на България 1879-1900 (Sofia, 1969), and Варненци в Отечествената война 1944-45 (Sofia, 1972). LC

Bogdanov, D. P., fl. 1913, his writings include Материалы для геологической карты Алтая (1910), and Материалы для геологие Алтая (1914). OSK

Bogdanov, Leonid Stanislas, 1881-1945 *see* Dugin, Leonidas Stanislas

Bogdanova, Medine Iskanderovna, born in 1908, her writings include *Токтогул Сатылганов* (1959), *Киргизский героический эпос Манас* (1960); and she edited *История литератур народов Средней Азии и Казахстана* (1960). She died in 1962. Kyrgyz SE

Bogdanović, Dejan, born in 1933, he received a doctorate in 1964 from Tehran University. In 1995 he was keeper of the Persian collection at the Bibliothèque de l'Institut national des langues et civilisations orientales, Paris. His writings include the translation from the Persian, *Le livre des sept vizirs* (1976). AnEIFr; LC

Boggs, Samuel Whitemore, born 3 March 1889 at Coolidge, Kan., he was a graduate of Berea College which awarded him an honorary doctorate in 1949. He also studied at Yale and Columbia universities. He was a geographer, and fellow of the Royal Geographical Society, who had a career in geographical and related societies. His writings include *International boundaries* (1940). He died on 14 September 1954. NatCAB, v. 45, p. 493; WhAm, 3

Boghdadi, Hassan, fl. 1955, he received a doctorate in law, and was a sometime professor of civil law as well as international private law at Alexandria University, where he was later dean of the Faculty of Law. He wrote *Origine et technique de la distinction des statuts personnel et réel en Égypte* (1937). *Who's who in the Arab world*, 1968

Bogoliubov, Mikhail Nikolaevich, born in 1918 at Kiev, he graduated in 1941 from Leningrad University, and he also received a doctorate in 1956 for his thesis, *Ягнобский (ново-согдийский) язык*. Since 1959 he was dean of the Oriental Department at Leningrad. His writings include *Согдийские документы с горы Муг* (1960). IntWW, 1975/6-1978/9; Miliband; Miliband²

Bogoutdinov, Alautdin Makhmudovich, born 22 November (5 December) 1911, he receceived his doctorate in 1951. He wrote *Избранные произведения* (1980), and he edited *Матери-алы по истории Компартии Таджикистана* (1963). He died 23 February 1970. Kyrgyz SE; Turkmen SE

Bogti, Guiseppe *see* Bokti, Guiseppe

Bohas, Georges, born in 1946, he received two doctorates from the Université de Paris for his theses, *Métrique arabe classique et modernes* (1975), and *Contribution à l'étude de la méthode des grammairiens arabes en morphologie* (1979). In 1990, he was a professor at the Université de Paris VIII. He was joint author of *Étude des théories des grammairiens arabes* (1984), and *The Arabic linguistic tradition* (1990); and he edited *Développements récents en linguistique arabe et sémitique; séminaire* (1993). LC; THESAM, 4

Bohdanowicz, Leon, fl. 1941, his writings include *Les Musulmans en Pologne* (Jerusalem, Section du bien-être du soldat du Quartier général des forces armées polonaises en Moyen Orient, 1947).

Böhlau, Helene, born 22 November 1856 at Weimar, Germany, she was a privately educated author. On a journey to the Orient, she met a Russian Jew who, in order to marry her in second marriage, converted to Islam and adopted the name Omar al-Raschid Bey. They lived for a number of years in Constantinople before she returned to Germany, in 1910, where she died in Widdersberg, 22 March 1940. Josef Becker wrote a biography, *Helene Böhlau* (1988). DtBE; OxGer

von **Bohlen**, Peter, born 13 March 1796 at Wüppels near Jever, Oldenburg, he started life as a taylor's apprentice, was a buttler, cook, and waiter before he entered the Johanneum in Hamburg. He studied Oriental languages at Halle, Bonn, Berlin, and Königsberg. In 1826 he was appointed professor at Berlin. His writings include *Das alte Indien mit besonderer Rücksicht auf Aegypten* (1830). He edited Sanskrit as well as Arabic texts, *Commentatio do Motenabbio* (1824), and *Carmen arabicum Amâli dictum*, by 'Ali ibn 'Uthman al-Ushi (1849). He also wrote his *Autobiographie* (1841). He died in Halle, 6 February 1840. DtBE; Stache-Rosen, pp. 15-16

Böhm, Julius, fl. 1893, he wrote *Mineralien-comptoir … Collectionen* (Brünn, n.d.) LC

Bohn, Helmut, born 18 November 1914 at Recklinghausen, Germany, his writings include *Vor den Toren des Lebens; in russischer Kriegsgefangenschaft, 1944-47* (1949), *Die Sozialisten und die Verteidigung* (1957), and *Siegen ohne Krieg* (1959). KDtLK, 1952, 1958

Bohndorff, Friedrich, born 16 August 1840 at Plau, Saxony, he started life as a goldsmith's apprentice but soon took to wandering. His stations were France, Italy, and Africa. In 1874 he entered the service of C. G. Gordon Pasha, and penniless in 1879, that of Wilhelm Junker. Afterwards he took service under the Congo Free State and subsequently with the Deutsche Ostafrikagesellschaft. His trace is lost in 1887. Henze; Hill

Böhtlingk (Бётлингк), Otto von, born 30 May 1815 at St. Petersburg, he studied there and at Dorpat, Berlin, and Bonn. At first his scholarship was directed to the study of Arabic and Persian, but he became celebrated as a worker in Sanskrit. His writings include *Kritische Bemerkungen zur zweiten Ausgabe von Kasem-Bek's türkisch-tatarischer Grammatik* (1848), and *Über die Sprache der Jakuten* (1851). He died in Leipzig, 1 April 1904. BiobibSOT, pp. 127-128; Buckland; *Indogermanische Forschungen* 17 (1904/5), pp. 131-136, reprinted in PorLing, vol. 1, pp. 261-268; Stache-Rosen, pp. 48-49

Boigey, Maurice Auguste Joseph, born in 1877, he received a doctorate in 1912 from l'Université de Paris for his thesis, *Le massif des Beni Snassen; géographie physique, climatologie, ethnographie*. His writings include *Manuel scientifique d'éducation physique* (1923), *La science des couleurs et l'art du peintre* (1923), and *Manuel de massage* (1950). LC

Boiko, Konstantin Alekseevich, born 11 April 1930 at Leningrad, he received his first degree in 1977 from the Oriental Institute, Moscow, for his thesis, *Арабская историческая литература в Испании*. He was since 1975 affiliated with the Leningrad Section of the Oriental Institute in the Soviet Academy of Science. His writings include *Араб-ская историческая литература в Египте, VII-IX вв.* (1983), and *Арабская историческая литература в Египте, IX-X вв.* (1991). LC; Miliband²

Boinet, A. fl. 1882, he edited *Qāmūs jughrāfī lil-qutr al-Misrī* (Cairo, 1899). ZKO

Boinet, Édouard Louis Désiré, born 13 February 1859 at Marly-la-Ville (Seine-et-Oise), he was a medical army officer in the Far East, and since 1891 at Aix-Marseille, where he died in 1938 or 1939. He was a member of l'Académie de médecine. DBF; Index BFr² (2)

Bois, Alexis, commandant, fl. 1886, he wrote *Sénégal et Soudan; travaux publics et chemins de fer* (1886), and *Sénégal et Soudan; de Dakar au Niger* (1887). BN; NUC, pre-1956

Bois, Jules, born in 1871, he was a French author and dramatist whose writings include *Le Satanisme et la magie* (1895), and *Le Mystère et la volupté* (1901). He died in 1943. BioIn, 1; LC

Bois, Thomas, born 6 May 1900 at Dunkerque, France, he wrote *L'âme des Kurdes à la lumière de leur folklore* (1946), its translation, *Kurdische Volksdichtung* (1985), *Connaissance des Kurdes* (1965), and its translation, *The Kurds* (1966). WhoLeb, 1963/64

Boisboissel, Yves Marie Jacques Guillaume de, born 7 May 1886 at Paris, he passed through the military college of Saint-Cyr, and was posted to French West Africa as a *méhariste*. He was a sometime *aide-de-camp* to Général Lyautey. He resigned from the army with the rank of *général de corps d'Armée*, and commander-in-chief, l'Afrique occidentale française. His writings include *Peaux noires, cœurs blancs* (1931), and *Dans l'ombre de Lyautey* (1953). He died in Paris, 17 February 1960. *Hommes et destins*, vol. 1, pp. 91-93

Boisnard, Magali, born in 1882 at Orange (Vaucluse), she came at an early age with her parents to Algeria, where she studied history, Arabic, and the sociology of its inhabitants. At eighteen, she published her first poetry, followed by *Rimes du ble* (1905). She was married to a French physician with whom she spent many years on the fringes of the Sahara. Her writings include *L'Alert au désert; la vie saharienne pendant la guerre* (1916), *Le Roman de la Kahena d'après les anciens textes arabes* (1925), and *Le Roman de Khaldoun* (1930). She died in 1945. *Hommes et destins*, vol. 4, pp. 478-80

Boissel, Jean, fl. 1975, his writings include *Gobineau; l'Orient et l'islam* (1973), and *L'Iran moderne* (1975); he edited *Œuvres* of Comte de Gobineau (1983-1987). LC

Boissonade, Prosper Marie, born 23 January 1862 at Requista (Aveyron), he was a professor of history and economics at Poitiers. His writings include *Travail dans l'Europe chrétienne au moyen âge* (1921), and its translation, *Life and work in medieval Europe* (1927). He died 9 March 1935. DBF

Boital, Fabius, fl. 1856-1882, he was a poet whose writings include *Nasser-ed-Din Schah et la Perse; la légende et l'histoire* (Paris, 1875). BN

Bojanić-Lukać, Dušanka, fl. 1952, her writings include *Turski zakoni i zakonski propisi* (1974), *Видин и Видинският санджак през 15-16 век* (1975), and *Turske vojne zastave u Cetinskim muzejima* (1981). LC

Boker, George Henry, born 6 October 1823, he was a poet, playwright, and diplomat. As Minister to Turkey he negotiated a treaty recognizing the status of naturalized American citizens. He recommended the purchase of Bab al-Mandab by the United States. He died in 1890. DAB; Shavit; WhAm, H

Bokti (Bogti), Guiseppe, fl. 1809, he was a sometime Austrian vice-consul in Rosetta, Egypt.

Boktor, Amir, born in 1896, he received a Ph.D. in 1936 from Columbia University for his thesis, *School and society in the Valley of the Nile.* He was a sometime dean of AUB. His writings include *The development and expansion of education in the United Arab Republic* (1963). LC

Boland, Bernard Johan, fl. 1968, his writings include *The struggle in modern Indonesia* (1982), and he was joint author, with I. Farjon, of *Islam in Indonesia; a bibliographical survey* (1983). LC

Boldyrev, Aleksandr Nikolaevich, born in 1909 at St. Petersburg, he graduated in 1931 from the Leningrad Institute of History, Philology, and Linguistics. In 1954 he received a doctorate at Leningrad for *Таджикский писатеь XVI в. Зайнаддин Васифи и его произведение "Удивительные собы-тия."* His writings include *Каталог восточных рукописей Академии наук Таджикской ССР* (1960). He died 4 June 1993. Miliband; Miliband²

Bolens, Lucie, born in 1933, she received a doctorate in 1972 from the Université de Paris for her thesis, *Les Méthodes culturales au moyen âge d'après les traités d'agronomie andalous; traditions et techniques.* Since 1975 she was a professor of history at l'Université de Genève. Her writings include *Agronomes andalous du moyen âge* (1981), *La Cuisine andalouse, un art de vivre* (1990), and *L'Andalousie du quotidien au sacré* (1991). LC; THESAM, 4

Bolgiani, Valeska Voigtel, died 1876 see Voigtel-Bolgiani, Madame Valeska Müller

Bolitho, Henry Hector, born 28 May 1898 in New Zealand, he was a prolific author and lecturer, especially in the United States. His writings include *Beside Galilee; a diary in Palestine* (1933), and *A Biographer's notebook* (1950). He died 12 September 1974. ConAu, 9-10 & 53-56; Who was who, 7

Boll, Michael Mitchell, born 3 March 1938 at Antigo, Wisc., he received a Ph.D. in 1970 from the University of Wisconsin, Madison, for his thesis, *The social and political philosophy of Semen L. Frank.* He was affiliated with Radio Free Europe and the U.S. Information Agency, Washington, D.C., before he was appointed in 1970 a professor of Soviet history at San Jose State University, where he was still active in 1998. His writings include *Cold war in the Balkans* (1984). DrAS, 1974, 1978, 1982 H; LC

Bolla-Kotek, Sybille, born 8 June 1913 at Preßburg, Austria-Hungary, she studied at the Deutsche Universität Prag, where, under her maiden name, Bolla, she received a Dr.jur. in 1938 for her thesis, *Die Entwicklung des Fiskus zum Privatrechtssubjekt.* Since 1949 she was a professor of law at the Universität Wien, concurrently pursuing an interest in Orientalism. Her writings include *Untersuchungen zur Tiermiete und Viehpacht im Altertum* (1940). WhoAustria, 1969/70

Bolland, Wilhelm (Willi, Wely Bey), born in the 19th century, he was a sometime teacher of German and Turkish in Constantinople and Berlin. His writings include *Deutsches Lehrbuch für Türken* (1910), *Erstes türkisches Lesebuch für Deutsche* (1915), and *Türkisch für Offiziere und Mannschaften* (1917). His trace his lost after his contribution to *Mitteilungen des Seminars für orientalische Sprachen* in 1928.

Bolle, Johann, Dr., born in 1850, he was sometime member of the k.k. Versuchsanstalt für Seidenzucht und Weinbau in Görz (Gorizia), Austria-Hungary. His writings include *Der Seidenbau in Japan* (1898), *Anleitung zur Kultur des Maulbeerbaumes* (Görz, 1908), and *La Bachicoltura al Giappone* (1915). GV; NUC, pre-1956

Bollecker-Stern, Brigitte see Stern, Brigitte

Boller, Anton, born 2 January 1811 at Krems, Austria, he studied medicine but dropped it in order to pursue private studies in linguistics. In 1845 he became the first lecturer in Sanskrit at the Universität Wien. Since 1850 he was also a professor of comparative linguistics. He was a member of the Akademie der Wissenschaften, Wien. He died in Wien, 19 January 1869. ADtB; DtBE; ÖBL; Wurzbach

Bolling, George Melville, born 13 April 1871 at Baltimore, Md., he received a Ph.D. in 1896 from Johns Hopkins University for his thesis, *The participle in Hesiod.* He was a professor of Sanskrit, Greek, and comparative literature at various American universities. WhNAA; WhAm, 5

Bologa, Valeriu Lucian, born in 1892 at Braşov, Rumania, he received a doctorate and was a professor of the history of medicine at the Universitatea din Cluj. His writings include *Contribuţiuni la istoria medicinei din Ardeal* (1927). He died in 1971. LC; WhoRom

Bolotnikov (Bolotnikoff), Aleksei Aleksandrovich, born in 1894, he was joint author of *Восток* (1935), and joint editor of *Литература Ирана X-XV в.* (1935), and *Рубайят*, by 'Umar Khayyam (1935). NYPL

Bol'shakov, Oleg Georgievich, born 3 June 1929 at Kalinin, Russia, he graduated in 1951 from the Oriental Faculty at Leningrad. He was an archaeologist who wrote *Путешествие Абу Хамида ал-*

Гарнати в Восточную и Центральную Европу (1971), *Средневековый город Ближ-него Востока 7- середина 13 в.* (1984), and *История халифата* (1989). LC; Miliband; Miliband²; Schoeberlein

Bolsover, George Henry, born 18 November 1910, he studied at Liverpool and London, where he received a Ph.D. in 1933 for *Great Britain, Russia and the Eastern Question, 1832-1841*. He had a brief teaching career, and was for five years an attaché and first secretary at the British Embassy, Moscow, before becoming an academic administrator. He died 15 April 1990. Sluglett; Who, 1970-1990

Bolton, Henry Carrington, born 28 January 1843 at N.Y.C., he was a graduate of Columbia University, and pursued studies in chemistry at Paris, Heidelberg, Berlin, and Göttingen, where he received a Dr.phil. in 1866 for his thesis, *On the fluorine compounds of uranium*. He was a professor of chemistry at various American colleges. He died 19 November 1903. DAB; WhAm, 1

Bölükbaşı, Rıza Tevfik, 1869-1949 *see* Rıza Tevfik Bölükbaşı

Bombaci, Alessio, born 27 August 1914 at Castroreale, Sicily, he started studying law, but later changed to Oriental languages at Napoli. After two years' teaching at the Università di Roma, he was appointed a professor at Istituto orientale di Napoli. His writings include *Storia della letteratura turca* (1956), and, with S. J. Shaw, *L'imperio ottomano* (1981). *Studia Turcologica memoriae Alexii Bombaci* was published in 1982. He died 29 January 1979. Chi è, 1948-1961; Index Islamicus (4)

Bomford, Trevor, fl. 1895-1924, he wrote the pamphlet, *The Afghan wars and modern research* (London, 1921). BLC

Bompard, Louis *Maurice*, born 17 May 1854 at Metz, he studied law and afterwards entered provincial politics. Through the good offices of his predecessor at the *préfecture du département du Nord*, Paul Campon, he, too, entered the foreign service in Tunisia (1884). It was not until 1909 that he was posted once more to the Muslim world - for five years in Constantinople. He retired from the diplomatic service in 1919 and died in Grasse (Alpes-Maritime), 7 April 1935. His writings include *Législation de la Tunisie* (1888), *La Politique marocaine de l'Allemagne* (1916), and *L'Entrée de la Turquie dans la guerre* (1919). Bacqué, p. 77; DBF

Bon, Michel Marie, born 5 July 1943 at Grenoble (Isère), he graduated from l'École nationale d'administration, and became an *inspecteur des finances*. His writings include *Le Dialogue des dialogues* (1967), and *Accompagner les personnes en fin de vie* (1994). WhoFr, 1985/86-2002/2003

Bonacci, Giuliano, born 19th cent., he was a journalist and correspondent to *Corriere della sera* and travelled extensively in Italy and abroad. He wrote *Gli ultimi giorni de Bengasi turca* (1912). Rovito

Bonamy, André Paul Henri, born in 1880, his writings include *Les Deux rives du Sahara* (Paris, 1924), and *Territoires africaines sous mandat de la France* (Paris, 1930). NUC, pre-1956

Bonan, Joseph, fl. 1951, he was a former *bâtonnier* and director of the *Gazette des tribunaux du Maroc*. He wrote *Code de commerce maritime et textes annexes* (Casablanca, 1953). LC

Bond, Harriet L., fl. 1933, she was the wife of an American Consul who served in Pakistan, India, and Denmark, before returning to Wyoming. Note

Bond, William Ralph Garneys, born 12 December 1880, he was educated at Eton, and New College, Oxford, and became an officer in the Sudan Political Service. He died in 1952. Who was who, 5

Bondarevskii, Grigorii L'vovich, born 25 January 1920 at Odessa, he graduated in 1948 from Moscow University, where he also received a doctorate in 1965 for his thesis, *Борьба за Персидский залив, Аравийский полуостров и Красное море на рубеже XIX-XX вв.* From 1951 to 1956 he was a dean of the Central Asian University at Tashkent. His writings include *Багдадская дорога и проникновение германского империализма на Ближний Восток, 1888-1903* (1955), *Hegemonists and imperialists in the Persian Gulf* (1981), *Muslims and the West* (1985); and, with Leonid V. Mitrokhin, *Failure of three missions; British diplomacy and intelligence ... in Central Asia* (1987). Miliband; Miliband²

Bondoux, Georges, born 22 February 1870 at Villeneuve-sur-Yonne, he received a doctorate in law in 1895 from the Université de Paris for his thesis, *Les Règles du flagrant délit dans le Code d'instruction criminelle et dans les lois postérieures*. He was a sometime *substitut, procureur, président*, and *juge* in the French legal administration. BN; Qui êtes-vous, 1924

Bonebakker, Seeger Adrianus, born 21 September 1923 at Wisch, Netherlands, he studied at the Rijksuniversiteit te Leiden, where he received a doctorate in 1956 for his thesis, *The Kitab naqd al-ši'r of Qudama b. Ga'far al-Katib al-Bagdadi*. He was a professor at Leiden and Columbia University, before being appointed in 1969 a professor at UCLA. His writings include *Materials for the history of Arabic rhetoric* (1975), and *Hatimi and his encounter with Mutanabbi* (1984). DrAS, 1974-1982 F; LC

Bonelli Hermande, Emilio, born in 1854 at Zaragoza, he studied in France and Italy. He was a Spanish officer posted to the west coast of Africa, from where he explored the Sahara and negotiated a Spanish "protectorate" over the territory of Río de Oro. He was also an editor of several periodicals in Madrid. His writings include *El imperio de Marruecos y su constitución* (1882), *Sahara* (1887), and, with Manuel Scheidnagel, *Colonización española* (1893). AfrBioInd (2); LC; Ossorio

Bonelli, Luigi, born 20 September 1865 at Brescia, Italy, he was a student of modern languages at the Accademia Scientifico Letteraria di Milano, and concurrently taught himself Arabic. In 1887 he catalogued the Islamic manuscripts of the Biblioteca Casanatense, Roma. He went on missions to Constantinople, 1890, and Malta, 1894. On the invitation of the King of Egypt, he compiled abstracts of Ottoman *firmans*. He taught at the Istituto orientale di Napoli, whose director he was from 1914 to 1916. His writings include *Elementi di grammatica turca osmanli* (1899), *Detti proverbiali persiani* (1941), and a translation of the Koran. He died in Napoli, 26 January 1947. Chi è, 1928-1940; DizBI; Index Islamicus (2)

Bonelli Rubio, Juan María, born 6 May 1904 at Madrid. After passing through the Escuela Naval Militar, he joined the Cuerpo Nacional de Ingenieros Geógrafos in 1930. He was a member of the Academia de Doctores, and received numerous awards. His writings include *Notas sobre la geografía humana de los territorios españoles del Golfo de Guinea* (1944). DBEC; Figuras

Boneschi, Paul, fl. 1925-55, he contributed to French, Italian and American periodicals. NUC, pre-1956

Bonet Correa, Antonio, born 20 October 1925 at La Coruña, Spain, he studied at the Universidad de Compostela and l'École du Louvre, and became a professor of history of art at the Universidad de Murcia. His writings include *Manuel Colmeiro* (1954), *El barroco en España y Mexico* (1966), and *Andalucía barroca* (1978). DBEC; LC

Bonét-Maury, Amy *Gaston* Charles Auguste, born 2 January 1842 at Paris, he studied theology at Genève and Strasbourg, where he received a doctorate in 1867 for his thesis, *J. Bunsen, un prophète des temps modernes*. Thereafter he was a pastor and a professor at the Faculté protestante de Paris. His writings include *L'islamisme et le christianisme en Afrique* (1906), and *L'unité morale des religions* (1913). He died in Paris, 23 June 1919. DBF; LC

Bonét-Maury, Claude Marie Gaston, born 6 December 1897, he studied at l'École alsacienne de Paris, and graduated from the Faculté de droit de Paris. From 1923 to 1932 he was a barrister at the Cour de Paris. He was an expert on river communication and was a member of several international river commissions. He died in Paris, 8 March 1981. NDBA

Bonfante, Pietro, born 29 June 1864 at Poggio Mirteto, Italy, he graduated in law from the Università di Roma. His writings include *Storia del diritto romano* (1903), and its translations into French (1928), and Spanish (1944). He died in Roma, 21 November 1932. DizBI; LC

Bonfanti, Adriano, le Père, born in 1931 in Piemonte, he successively taught history and was an editor of *Nigrizia*, an Italian missionary periodical, before he left for Central Sudan in 1959. He was expelled by the Khartoum authorities in 1963. His writings include *Espulsi dal Sudan* (1964). LC

Bonghi, Ruggiero, born 21 March 1826 at Napoli, he was a prolific writer, professor, scholar, politician, and the founder of two major newspapers, *La Stampa*, and *Il Nazionale*, as well as the periodical *La Cultura*, in 1882. His writings include *Il Congresso di Berlino e la crisi d'Oriente* (1878). He died in Torre del Greco, 22 October 1895. BiDMoPL; BiD&SB; DizRN; EncBrit; IndBI (16); Meyers

Bonhoure, Eugène, born in the first half of the 19th century, his writings include *L'Indo-Chine* (1900). His trace is lost after a publication in 1908. NUC, pre-1956

Boniface, Philippe, he was in 1935 a *contrôleur civil* in Morocco.

Bonilla y San Martín, Adolfo, born in 1875 at Madrid, he received doctorates in law and liberal arts, and became a literary scholar, philosopher, and editor. His writings include *Historia de filosofía española* (1908-1911), and *El derecho aragonés en el siglo XII* (1920). After his death in 1926, the University of Madrid published *Estudios eruditos in memoriam Adolfo Bonilla y San Martín* (1827-30). CIDMEL; DcSpL; Sabater; Sainz

Bonin, Charles Eudes, born 26 June 1865 at Poissy (Yvelines), he was a graduate of l'École des chartes. After a diplomatic career in the Far East, he went on a mission to Urumchi, Kuldja, and

Samarkand, from where he continued by rail to the Caspian Sea. He died in Barcelona, 30 September 1929. *Hommes et destins*, vol. 6, pp. 44-46

Bonine, Michael Edward, born in 1942, he received a Ph.D. in 1975 from the University of Texas for *Yazd and its hinterland*. In 1977 he was appointed professor of Middle Eastern geography in the Department of Near Eastern Studies, University of Arizona, Tucson, a position he still held in 2003. He was joint editor of *The Middle Eastern city and Islamic urbanism; a bibliography* (1994), and editor of *Population, poverty, and politics in Middle Eastern cities* (1997). LC; NatFacDr, 1995-2003

Boniteau, Maurice, born 19th cent., he published the pamphlet, *Rapport sur l'invasion du criquet pèlerin en Egypte* (Le Caire, 1904). NUC, pre-1956

Bonjean, François Joseph, born 26 December 1884 at Lyon, he was a writer and teacher of French language and literature successively in Egypt, Syria, and Morocco. He spent his later years in Rabat, where he married a local Muslim. His writings include *Au Maroc en roulotte* (1950). He died in Rabat, 12 May 1963. *Hommes et destins*, vol. 2, pp. 96-97

Bonjean, Jacques, fl. 1954, he was a doctor of law whose writings include *L'unité de l'Empire chérifien* (1955), and *Tanger* (1967). LC

Bonn, Charles, born in 1942, he received two doctorates from the Université de Bordeaux III for his theses, *Besoins culturels et expression artistique francophone en Algérie* and *Le Roman algérien contemporain de langue française*, in 1972 and 1982 respectively. His writings include *Littérature maghrébine* (1976), *Le Roman algérien de langue française* (1985), *Lecture présente de Mohammed Dib* (1988), *Kateb Yacine, Nedjma* (1990), and *Bibliographie de la littérature maghrébine, 1980-1990* (1992). LC; THESAM, 2

Bonn, Gisela, born in 1909, she was a writer of travel literature and travel guides. Her writings include *Marokko; Blick hinter den Schleier* (1950), *Neue Welt am Nil; Tagebuchblätter* (1953), *Neue Welt am Atlas* (1955), *Das Doppelgesicht des Sudan* (1961), *Unter Hippies* (1968), and *India and the Subcontinent* (1974). KDtLK, 1963-1988; LC; Wer ist wer, 1990/91-1995/96

Bonnafont, Jean Pierre, born in 1805 at Plaisance (Gers), he joined the Garde royale in 1827 and took part in the Algerian conquest as a medic. In 1834 he received his medical doctorate from the Université de Montpellier. He retired to Antony, where he lived until 1890. His writings include *Réflexions sur l'Algérie, particulièrement sur la province de Constantine* (1837), and *Douze ans en Algérie, 1830 à 1842* (1880). DBF

Bonnaud, Robert, he wrote *Itinéraire* (1962), a work on Algerian history. LC

Bonné, Abraham *Alfred*, born 16 November 1899 at Nürnberg, he studied at Erlangen, München, and Frankfurt a.M. Until 1930 he was a leading statistician of the Keren Hayesod in Palestine. From 1931 to 1948 he was affiliated with the Economic Archives for the Near East. Thereafter he was a professor of regional economics and sociology at the Hebrew University, Jerusalem. He died in 1959. EncJud; NearMEWho, 1945/46; New outlook 3 (April 1960), pp. 15-26; WhoIsrael, 1958

Bonneau, Alexandre, born 24 April 1820 at Exoudun (Deux-Sèvres), he graduated in 1842 in law from the Université de Paris. From 1845 to 1847 he was an administrator in Algeria. In 1854 he joined *la Presse* as a journalist and editor. He was one of the first to appreciate the value of physical fitness. His writings include two pamphlets published in 1860, *Les Turcs et la civilisation*, and *Les Turcs et les nationalités*. He died in November 1890. DBF; Vapereau

Bonnefous, Marc Elie Jean, born 5 January 1924 at Bordeaux, he graduated in 1947 from l'Ecole nationale d'administration and received a doctorate in law in 1948 from the Université de Bordeaux. He was a career diplomat. His writings include *Perspectives de l'agriculture marocaine* (1949), *Les Palmeraie de Figuig* (1952), *Europe et tiers monde* (1961), and *Le Maghreb; repères et rappels* (1990). WhoFr, 1990-2002/2003; WhoWor, 1974/75

Bonnel de Mézières, Albert Louis Marie Joseph, born 9 February 1870 at Cambrai (Nord), he was a military officer posted to the French Sudan. In 1901 he transferred to the French Colonial Administration, retiring in 1907. He died in Oualata on a mission in 1942. DBF; Hill; *Hommes et destins*, vol. 8, pp. 49-51

Bonnemain, François Louis, born 18 October 1817 at Bastia, he was the adopted son of Cheikh El-Bechir of the Haljoutes. In 1836 he joined the Corps des gendarmes maures, and in 1851, he was a captain of the spahi. In 1956 he was sent on a mission to Ghadamès. He died at the hospital of La Calle, 13 January 1867. DBF; Féraud, pp. 267-79; Henze

Bonnenfant, Paul, born 20th cent., he was affiliated with l'Institut de recherches et d'études sur le monde arabe et musulman, Aix-en-Provence, specializing in the domestic architecture and anthropology of the Arabian Peninsula. His writings include *Bibliographie de la peninsule Arabique* (1980), *Les Maisons tours de Sanaa* (1989), and, as joint author, *Les Vitreaux de Sanaa* (1981), and *L'Art du bois à Sanaa* (1987). EURAMES; LC

Bonner, Arthur, born 4 October 1922 at N.Y.C., his writings include *Among the Afghans* (1987), *Averting the apocalypse; social movements in India today* (1990), and *Alas! What brought you here? The Chinese in New York, 1800-1950* (1997). Schoeberlein

Bonnet, Edmond, born 8 April 1848 at Beaune (Côte-d'Or), he started studying law but later changed to medicine. He received a medical doctorate in 1876 but never practised, instead, he accepted a chair of botany. In 1883 he explored Tunisia and Sud-Oranais. He bequeathed a large portion of his estate to the Académie de Dijon. He died in Paris, 3 October 1922. DBF

Bonnet, Jean Charles, born in 1936, his writings include *Les Pouvoirs publics français et l'immigration dans l'entre-deux-guerres* (1976). LC

de **Bonneuil**, Marie Édith, fl., 1934, he wrote *Bivouacs aux étoiles* (1938), a work on the Italo-Ethiopian war of 1935-36. LC

de **Bonneval**, Léon Paul Marie Deshayes, 1860-1931 see Deshayes de Bonneval, Léon Paul Marie

Bonniard, F., he received a doctorate in 1934 from l'Université de Paris for his thesis, *Le Tell septentrional en Tunisie*. In the same year he wrote the supplementary thesis, *Les lacs de Bizerte*, and also published *La Tunisie du nord*. LC

Bono, Francesco, fl. 1942, his writings include *Attualita' dell'urbanistica italiana* (1953). Firenze; NUC, pre-1956

Bono, Salvatore, born 11 December 1932 at Tripoli, Libya, he received a doctorate in 1955, and subsequently taught history and institutions of Afro-Asian countries at the Faculty of Political Science, Perugia, specializing in the modern and contemporary history of the Mediterranean, particularly the relations between Europe and the Arab and Ottoman countries. His writings include *I corsari barbareschi* (1964), *Le relazioni commerciali fra i paesi del Maghreb e l'Italia nel medioevo* (1967), *Storiografia e fonti occidentali sulla Libia, 1510-1911* (1982), *Siciliani nel Maghreb* (1989), and *Corsari nel Mediterraneo* (1993). Since 1982 he was the editor of *Islàm; storia e civiltà*. EURAMES; LC; Private

Bonola, Federico, born in 1839 at Milano, he spent most of his life in Cairo, where he was for many years secretary general of the Société khédiviale de géographie. His writings include *I patrioti italiani; storie e biografie* (1869-70), and *L'Egypte et la géographie* (1889). He died in Cairo, 17 December 1912. DizRN; *Index Islamicus*, 1995 (1)

Bonsal, Stephen, born 29 March 1865 at Baltimore, Md., he was a man of private means and took post-graduate diplomas in German and Italian literatures at Heidelberg and Wien. After losing his fortune at the races, he entered journalism with the *New York herald*. He was a special correspondent in the Bulgarian-Serbian conflict of 1885, and in the Macedonian insurrection of 1890. His writings include *Morocco as it is* (1892), and *Unfinished business* (1944), a work for which he was awarded the Pulitzer prize in 1945. He died in Washington, D.C., 8 June 1951. DAB; NewCEN; *Who was who*, 5; WhAm, 3

Bonte, Pierre, born 20th cent., he received a *doctorat du 3e cycle* in 1970 from the Université de Paris for his thesis, *Production et échanges chez les Touareg Kel Gress du Niger*. LC

Bontems, Claude, born about 1940, his writings include *Manuel des institutions algériennes de la colonisation turque à l'indépendance* (1976), and *La guerre du Sahara occidental* (1984). LC

Bontinck, François, born in 1920, he took a doctorate in ecclesiastic history. His writings include *Aux origines de l'État indépendant du Congo* (1966), *L'autobiographie de Hamed ben Mohammed el-Murjebi Tippo Tip, traduite et annoté* avec Koen Janssen (1974), and *Les missionnaires de Scheut au Zaire, 1888-1988* (1988). LC

Bonvalot, Pierre Gabriel Édouard, born in 1853 at Epagne (Aube), he travelled in Europe, 1873-1880, before he was sent by the Ministère d'éducation on a mission to Central Asia. He made several more journeys which included visits to Afghanistan and, notably with the Prince Henri d'Orléans, to Chinese Turkestan. His writings include *En Asie centrale; de Moscou en Bactriane* (1884), *En Asie centrale; du Kohistan à la Caspienne* (1885), *Du Caucase aux Indes à travers le Pamir* (1889), *De Paris au Tonkin à travers le Tibet inconnu* (1892), and its translation, *Across Tibet* (1892), and *Les Chercheurs de routes* (1924). He died in Paris, 9 December 1933. DBF; Henze; Meyers; *Who was who*, 3

188

Bonzom, E., fl. 1897-1898, his writings, all published in Alger, include *De la production et de l'amélioration de la race chevaline en Algérie* (1874), *La production ovine en Algérie* (1886), *Algérie devant le Parlement* (1891), and *La France algérienne; ressources et puissance que l'Algérie apporte à la France* (1898). NUC, pre-1956

Bonzon, Jacques, born in 1871, he was a lawyer whose writings include *Cent ans de lutte sociale* (1894), *Le Crime et l'école* (1896), *La Debâcle des placements russes* (1919), and *Les Emprunts russes et les Rothschild* (1924). NUC, pre-1956

Boodberg, Peter Alexis, born 8 April 1903 at Vladivostok, he was a cadet at a military school in St. Petersburg when the first World War erupted. In 1915 he was sent to Harbin for safety. In Manchuria he turned to the study of philology. In the summer of 1920, he went to San Francisco. Four years later he graduated in Oriental languages from the University of California, Berkeley, where he also received his Ph.D. in 1930 for *The art of war in ancient China*. In 1934 he joined Berkeley as an instructor in Oriental languages and became professor emeritus in 1970. He was recalled to active service as irreplacable in 1973. His health began to fail rapidly and he died of a heart attack on 29 June of that year. His writings include *Notes for collectors of Chinese antiques* (1943). JAOS 94 (1974), pp. 1-13

Boorman, James A., B.B.A., 1964; LL.B., 1966, University of Texas; LL.M., 1974, George Washington University; lt-commander, U.S. Navy, the Judge Advocate General's Corps, Office of the Staff Judge Advocate, Commander in Chief, Pacific. *Journal of international law and economics*, 1974

Booth, Sir George *Arthur* Warrington, born 28 October 1879, he studied at New College, Oxford, and was called to the bar in 1905. He practised law in London and Alexandria, Egypt, and was a sometime judge in the Mixed Tribunal, Cairo. He died 22 March 1972. Who was who, 7

Booth, John Nicholls, born 12 August 1912 at Meadville, Pa., he was a graduate of McMaster University, a clergyman, magician, writer, and photographer. His writings include *The quest for preaching power* (1943), *Fabulous destinations* (1950), and *The story of the Second Church in Boston* (1959). WhoAm, 1974/75-1998

Booth, Newell Snow, Jr., born 18 November 1927 at Boston, Mass., he received a Ph.D. in 1956 from Boston University. He was a professor of religion at Miami University, a post which he still held in 1998. He edited *African religions; a symposium* (1977). DrAS, 1974-1982 P; NatFacDr, 1995-98; WhoRel, 1975

Bor-Ramenskii, Evgenii Georgievich, fl. 1940. His writings include *1 Мая* (1938), *Кто такие гитлеровцы* (1942), and *Первая маевка в Москве* (1969). LC; NUC, pre-1956

Borah (Borrah), Moayyidul Islam, fl. 1939-41, he received a Ph.D. in 1931 from SOAS for his thesis, *The life and works of Amir Hasan Dihlavi*. He was the translator of *Baharistan-i-Ghaybi*, by Mirza Nathan (Gauhati, 1936). BLC; LC; Sluglett

Boratyni, Tytus Liwiusz, 1617-1681 *see* Burattini, Tito-Livio

Boratav, Pertev Naili, born 2 September 1907 at Daridere, Bulgaria, at the time, the Ottoman province of Edirne, he was a Turkish folklorist who studied at Istanbul and at l'École des langues orientales, Paris. He taught in Turkey until 1947. Thereafter he collaborated in the founding of the Turkish collection at Stanford University, Calif., before he went to France, in 1952, where he was attached successively to the CNRS and l'École pratique des hautes études. His writings include *Folklor ve edebiyat* (1939), *Zaman zaman içinde* (1958), *100 soruda Türk folkloru* (1973), and *Türkische Volkserzählerkunst* (1975). Two commemorative volumes were published in 1978, *Quand le crible était dans la paille*, and *Studies in Turkish folklore, in honor of Pertev N. Boratav,* LC; Meydan

Borch-Jensen, M., fl. 1953, he was affiliated with the Danske Missionsselskab, and wrote *Ved milepælen; 50 aars dansk mission i Arabien* (1954). NUC, pre-1956

Borchardt, Paul, fl. 1929, he was joint author of *Silberschmiedearbeiten aus Kurdistan* (Berlin, 1922). NUC, pre-1956

von Borcke, Astrid, fl. 1973. She was affiliated with the Bundesministerium für Ostwissenschaftliche und Internationale Studien, Köln. She wrote innumerable brief studies and reports on the communist world including *Die Ursprünge des Bolschewismus* (1977), *Die Intervention in Afghanistan* (1980), and *Gorbachev's perestroika; can the Soviet system be reformed?* (1987). LC

Bordat, Gaston, born 19th cent., he was in 1906 the founding editor of the *Revue des Français.* NUC

Bordeaux, Joseph *Paul Émile*, général, born 3 August 1866 at Thonon (Haute-Savoie), he graduated in 1885 from the military college of Saint-Cyr and was posted to Algeria. From 1908 to 1909 he was a member of the French military mission to Greece. His writings include *L'Orient hellénique contemporain; missions, observations, souvenirs* (1948). He died in Thonon, 15 January 1951. DBF

Bordet, Pierre, born in 1914 at Dijon, he was a geologist and clergyman, and a sometime member of the Institut géologique Albert de Lapparent, Paris. His writings include *Les volcans récents du sud du Dacht-e Nawar, Afghanistan central* (1976). In 1986 he was honoured by the felicitation volume, *Évolution des domains orogéniques d'Asie méridionale.* LC; Note

Boré, Eugène, born 15 August 1809 at Angers, he studied the main languages of the Middle East, and in 1833 was appointed a professor at the Collège de France. In the service of the Académie des inscriptions he went on a scientifique mission to Persia. In 1850 he was ordained at Constantinople and appointed Father Superior at the Collège de Bebek, Constantinople. For fifteen years he promoted French Catholic interests in the Near East, until he became *supérieur général des Lazaristes.* His writings include *Correspondance et mémoires d'un voyageur en Orient* (1840), and *La Question des Lieux saints* (1850). He died 3 May 1878. DBF

Borecký, Miloš, born 28 December 1903 at Prag (Praha), he was a Czech Iranist who wrote *O jmenných větách v památkách staro-iránských* (1932). He died in Washington, D.C., 18 March 1954. Filipsky; NUC, pre-1956

Borel, Pierre Joseph, called Pétrus, born 26 June 1809 at Lyon. After training as an architect in Paris, he turned to literature. The last years of his life were spent in Algeria in the Colonial Service, but he was dismissed for inefficiency some time before he died in Mostaganem, 14 July 1859. BiD&SB; DBF; OxFr

Borella, François Charles, born 16 February 1932 at Nancy, he studied at Nancy and Paris. Excepting a four-year term spent as *assesseur du doyen* at the Faculté de droit d'Alger from 1962 to 1966, he was a professor at the Faculté de droit et des sciences économiques, Université de Nancy from 1955 until retirement. His writings include *L'Evolution politique et juridique de l'Union française depuis 1946* (1958). In 1984 he edited *Corpus électoral de la Lorraine.* WhoFr, 1989/90-2001/2002|

Borelli, Octave, born 28 March 1849 at Marseille, he received the education of the time, but earned his law degree at the age of nineteen. In 1874 he was a councillor at the Prefecture Tarn et Garonne. His subsequent municipal activities are somewhat shrouded. He felt compelled to leave France and emerged in Egypt at the time when a dual control by England and France was established over the land. In July 1879 he was appointed *avocat conseil* at the Ministry of Finance under the Khedive Tawfiq. In November 1879 he became a member of the Club khédivial, and from then on rose quickly to prominence in the local French community. In the 1882 Urabi trial he represented the Egyptian Government. From 1884 to 1896 he was the sole owner and editor of the *Le Bosphore égyptien.* In 1900 he returned to France. He spent the last years of his life between Le Cap near St. Tropez and Paris. His book *Choses politiques d'Égypte* (1895) is the collection of the articles which he had contributed anonymously to his journal. He is best remembered for his *La Législation égyptienne annotée* (1892). He died in Paris, 25 July 1911. ROMM 30 (1980), pp. 71-99

Borenius, Carl *Tancred*, born 14 July 1885 at Viipuri (Viborg), Finland, he was educated at his home town and at Helsingfors University. He taught history of art at University College, London, from 1914 to 1947. Concurrently he served as a temporary diplomatic representative of Finland. He died 2 September 1948. Aikalaiskirja, 1934; Vem och vad, 1931, 1936, 1941; WhE&EA; WhoLit, 1925-1931; Who was who, 4

Boretzky, Norbert, born 10 January 1935 at Breslau, Germany, he received a Dr.phil. in 1962 from the Universität Bonn for *Der Tempusgebrauch in Kurbskijs "Istorija velikago knjazja moskovskago."* Thereafter he was a professor at the Universität Bochum. His writings include *Der türkische Einfluß auf das Albanische* (1970). Kürschner, 1983-2003

Borg, Alexander, his writings include *Cypriot Arabic* (1985). LC

Borgnis-Desbordes, Gustave, général, born 22 October 1839 at Provins (Seine-et-Marne). After passing through l'École polytechnique and l'École d'application de Metz, he served in Indochina, before being posted to the French Sudan, from 1876 to 1884. He died from dysentery in Hanoi, 18 July 1900. DBF; *Hommes et destins*, vol 4, pp. 95-106; IndexBFr² (1)

Borgoiakov, Mikhail Ivanovich, born 5 May 1930, he received a doctorate in 1978 in philology at Alma-Ata for his thesis, *Проблема формирования и развития хасского язьикаю.* His writings include *Развитие падежных форм и их значений в хасском яхыке* (1976), and *Источники и история изучения хасского языка* (1981). He died 15 October 1983. LC

Boris, Gilbert, born 30 June 1905, he was a brillant student of Latin, Greek, philosophy, and law, but it was the Arab world, the life of the desert, that appealed to him. In 1926 he joined the Spahis at Sfax,

Tunisia, and soon thereafter, the Compagnie saharienne at Touat-Gourara as a non-commissioned officer. From 1926 to 1930 he patrolled the Central Sahara with his *méharistes Chaamba*. The next few years he was employed by the Haut-Commisaire de France en Syrie, Services des renseignemnts, successively at Beirut, Damascus, and Deir ez-Zor. When he returned to France in 1934, he completed his formal studies at l'École des langues orientales, Paris, the Sorbonne, and the Musée de l'homme. From 1935 to 1938 he carried on field work in the Douz Oasis, Tunisia, interrupted only by a six-month term at the Institut français du Caire. After he war he was affiliated with the C.N.R.S., completing his researches on Douz, when he died suddenly 17 April 1950. He wrote *Lexique du parler des Marazig* (1958). IBLA 14 (1951), 57-59; *Journal asiatique*, n° 239 (1951), pp. 355-57

Borisov, Andreii IAkovlevich, born in 1903 at Volgovitsy, he graduated in 1929 from Leningrad University. He was a Semitic scholar and Iranist, and exceptionally well trained in Arabic. He discovered the Arabic original of the Latin "Theology" of the Pseudo-Aristotle. He died following the Leningrad ordeal of 1942 in Orekhovo-Zuevo, 10 July 1942. Krachkovskii; Miliband; Miliband[2]

Born, Wolfgang, born 21 October 1893 at Breslau, Germany, he was a professor of history of art at various American colleges, from 1937 until his death in New York City, 15 June 1949. BioIn, 2; DcNAA; Kürschner, 1950

Bornecque, Jules Charles Constant, born 17 October 1838 at Massevaux (Haut-Rhin), he was a graduate of l'École polytechnique. After serving in the army from 1868 to 1889, he returned to his alma mater as an assistant treasurer. He was a writer on military affairs. His writings include *Rôle des fortifications dans la dernière guerre d'Orient* (1881). He died in Paris, 18 July 1911. DBF; NDBA

Börner, Armin, born 20th cent., he received a Dr.phil. in 1980 from the Universität Leipzig for his thesis, *Genesis und Evolution der antikolonialen Bewegung im Sudan*. Sezgin

Boroianu, C., fl. 1972, he edited *Texte vechi românești; album de paleografie româno-chirilică* (București, 1971).

Borolina, Irina Vasil'evna, born 27 March 1927 at Moscow, she graduated in 1948 from the Faculty of Philology, Moscow State University. Her writings include *Абдулла Каххар: очерк творчества* (1957), and she edited *Прач лани: турецкая народная в переводах Наум И. Гребнева* (1966). Miliband; Miliband[2]; NUC, 1968-72

Borovkov, Aleksandr Konstantinovich, born in 1904 at Tashkent, he graduated in 1928 from the Oriental Faculty, Central Asian University. His writings include *Учебник уйгурского языка* (1935), *Вопросы грамматики и истории восточных языков* (1958), and *Лексика среднеазиат-ского тефсира XII-XIII вв.* (1963). He died in Leningrad on 12 or 15 November 1962. GSE; Kazak SE; *Казахская ССР краткая энциклопедия*, vol. 3, p. 119; Miliband; Miliband[2]

Borozdin, Il'ia Nikolaevich, born in 1883 at Yaroslavl, Russia, he graduated in 1907 from Moscow University. His writings include *Новейшие археологические открытия в Крыму* (1925). He died on 13 October 1959. LC; Miliband; Miliband[2]

Borrah, Moayyidul Islam *see* Borah, Moayyidul Islam

Borrás Gualis, Gonzalo M., born 15 September 1940 at Valdealgorfa, Spain. After taking a doctorate he was appointed in 1987 a professor of history of art at the Universidad de Zaragoza. Concurrently he was director of the Instituto de Estudios Turolenses. His writings include *Arte mudéjar aragonés* (1985), and *El arte mudéjar en Teruel y su provincia* (1987). Arabismo, 1994, 1997; LC

Borrel, Eugène Marie Valentin, born 22 August 1876 at Lisboa, he was a French violinist and musicologist who wrote also on Turkish music. He died in Paris, 19 February 1962. LC

Borrey, Francis Maurice, born 8 April 1904 at Besançon, he was a student at Louis-le-Grand, Paris, and received a medical doctorate at Paris. In 1931 he entered the French Colonial Medical Service as a surgeon. After the war, he specialized in aeronautic medicine. He repeatedly was a member of French Cabinets, where he served as Minister of Agriculture as well as Education. His writings include *Coopération technique entre la France et les pays en voie de développement dans le domaine de l'aviation civil* (1967). He died 6 May 1976. *Hommes et destins*, vol. 9, p. 48; Unesco; WhoFr, 1965/66-1975/76

Borrmans, Maurice, born in 1925 at Lille, he was affiliated with the Pontifici Istituto di studi arabi e d'islamica. His writings include *Statut personnel et famille au Maghreb de 1940 à nos jours* (1977), *Orientations pour un dialogue entre chrétiens et musulmans* (1981), and its translation, *Guidelines for dialogue between Christians and Muslims* (1990). With G. C. Anawati he published *Tendances et courants de l'islam arabe contemporain* (1982-83). LC

Borschak (Borshchak), Elie (Il'ko), born 19 July 1892 at Kherson, Ukraine, he was an historian who spent most of his adult life in France, writing extensively in both French and Ukrainian, primarily on eighteenth century Ukraine and Franco-Ukrainian relations. His writings include *Huit mois à la Santé, journal, 1940-41* (1946), and *La Légende historique de l'Ukraine* (1949). He died in Paris, 11 October 1959. LC

Borshchevskii, IUri Efimovich, born 20 January 1924 at Petrograd, he was an Iranist by training but with interests far beyond that, or any, discipline. His entire career was spent in the Institute of Oriental Studies of the Academy of Sciences. He was joint author of *Книга о простаках Дахо-наме* (1968), and *Персидские миниатюры XIV-XVII вв.* (1968). In 1960 he edited *Джахан-наме*, by Bakran. He died in Leningrad, 31 March 1983 or 2 April 1984. Miliband²; *Narody Azii i Afriki* 1984 v, 206-207; *Russian review* 43 (1984), pp. 111-129

Borthwick, Bruce Maynard, born 2 May 1938 at Port Jefferson, N.Y., he was a graduate of Syracuse University and received a Ph.D. in 1965 from the University of Michigan for his thesis, *The Islamic sermons as a channel of political communication in Syria, Jordan and Egypt*. In 1964 he started a teaching and administrative career in the Department of Political Science, Albion (Mich.) College, a post which he still held in 1998. He wrote *Comparative politics of the Middle East* (1980). AmM&WS 13 (1978); LC; NatFacDr, 1995-1998

Bosc, Robert, fl. 1974, he was affiliated with the Institut catholique de Paris. His writings include *La Société internationale et l'Église* (1961-68), *Sociologie de la paix* (1965), *Le Tiers monde dans la politique internationale* (1967), and *Guerres froides et affrontements de 1950 à 1980* (1973). LC

Bosch, Gulnar H. née Kheirallah, born 31 October 1909 at Lake Preston, S.D., she graduated in 1929 from the Art Institute, Chicago, and received a Ph.D. in 1952 in Oriental languages from the University of Chicago for her thesis, *Islamic book-bindings; twelfth to seventeenth centuries*. In 1941 she began a teaching career in history of art at a variety of American colleges. With Guy Petherbridge she wrote *Islamic bindings and bookmaking; a catalogue of an exhibition* (1981). DrAS, 1978 H; WhoAm, 1986; WhoAmW, 1970/71-1975/76

Bosch Vilá, Jacinta, born 14 April 1922 at Figueras, Spain, he studied at Barcelona and Madrid and took doctorates in philosophy and law. He was a professor of Arabic and Islamic institutions at various Spanish universities. His writings include *El Oriente arabe en el desarrollo de la cultura Marca Superior* (1954), and *Historia de Sevilla; la Seville islamica* (1984). He died 18 November 1985. A commemorative volume appeared in 1991: *Homenaje al Prof. Jacinto Bosch Vilá*. DBEC; I.I. (4); *Who's who in Spain*, 1963

Boscheinen, Hans, fl. 1959, he was affiliated with Dresdner Bank, Hamburg. Note

Bose, Basanta Coomar, born 19th cent., his writings include *Conquest of Bengal* (1926), and *Mahomedanism* (1931) LC

Bose, Fritz, born 26 July 1906 at Stettin, Germany, he received a Dr.phil. in 1935 from the Universität Berlin for his thesis, *Die Musik der Uitoto*. Thereafter he was a department head at the Institut für Lautforschung and its successor, the Institut für Musikforschung, Berlin. His writings include *Lied der Völker; die Musikplatten des Instituts für Lautforschung an der Universität Berlin; Katalog* (1936), and *Musikalische Völkerkunde* (1953). Since 1963 he was an editor of *Jahrbuch für musikalische Volks- und Völkerkunde*. He died in Berlin, 16 August 1975. DtBE; Kürschner, 1940/41-1970; *Wer ist wer*, 1969/70

Bose, Swadesh R., Dr., fl. 1963, he was in 1971 an economist at the Pakistan Institute of Development Economics, Karachi, and in 1973 an acting director of the Bangladesh Institute of Development Economics. He was joint author of *The Pakistan export bonus scheme* (1963), and *Some basic considerations on agricultural mechanization in West Pakistan* (1969). In 1970 he edited *Studies on fiscal and monetary problems*. LC

Bosis, Adolfo de, born in 1863 at Ancona, Italy, he was a poet who settled in Roma in his youth and lived there until his death in 1924. CIDMEL, 1947; LC; Master (1)

Boškov, Vančo, born 8 January 1934 at Negotino, Macedonia, he studied Arabic and Turkish at Sarajevo University, and thereafter was affiliated with the National Archives, Skopje. He was a some-time assistant in Turkish literature at Sarajevo, before being appointed in 1980 professor at Skopje University. He died in 1984. The commemoration volume, *Osmanistische Studien zur Wirtschafts- und Sozialgeschichte in memoriam Vančo Boškov* (1986), contains an obituary by H. G.Majer. LC

Bošković, Đurđe, born 11 April 1904 at Beograd, he was affiliated with the Archaeological Institute, Beograd. His writings in-clude *L'Art médiéval en Serbie et en Macédoine* (1948), *Arhitektura sredñeg veka* (1957), and *Stari Bar* (1962). He was joint author of *Ulcinj* (1981). JugoslSa, 1970; Ko je ko, 1957

Bošković, Mirko, born 14 March 1918 at Zdenci, Orahovica, his writings include *Društveno-politički sistem Jugoslavije* (1963). JugoslSa, 1970; LC

Boson, Giovanni *Giustino*, born 15 December 1883 at Valgrisanche, Italy, he was educated at Aosta, and the Pontificia Università Gregoriana, Roma. After he gained a doctorate in divinity and a *licenza biblica*. From 1910 to 1914 he studied at München, where he received a Dr.phil. in 1914 for his thesis, *Les métaux et les pierres dans les inscriptions assyro-babyloniennes*. He was a sometime professor of Semitic philosophy at the Università cattolici del S. Cuore di Milano and R. Università di Torino. His writings include *Le quattro prime parabole del romanzo "Barlaam o Giosafatte"* (1914), and *Assiriologia* (1918). Casati 2; Dantès I; LC; Schwarz

Bossard, Raymond, born 20th cent., he received two doctorates in 1978 from the Université de Montpellier for his theses, *Mouvements migratoires dans le Rif oriental*, and *Un espace de migration; les travailleurs du Rif oriental et l'Europe*. LC; THESAM, 1

Bossavy, fl. 1939 in Morocco, where he was a *garde général* of the Service des Eaux et Forêts. Note

Bossavy, Georges, colonel, born 20 October 1906 at Toulon, he contributed to *Revue de défense nationale* in 1957 and 1958.

Bosshard, Walter E., born 8 November 1892 at Richterswil, Switzerland, he was a graduate of the Teachers' College, Zürich, and studied history of art at Firenze and Zürich. He worked in Southeast Asia, and accompanied the German Central Asian Expedition, 1927-1928, before he became a correspondent to international news agencies, and, since 1939, to the *Neue Zürcher Zeitung*. He spent four years in the Middle East. His writings include *Durch Tibet und Turkestan* (1930), *Indien kämpft* (1931), *Erlebte Weltgeschichte; Reisen und Begegnungen eines neutralen Berichterstatters im Weltkrieg 1939-1945* (1947), *Gefahrenherd der Welt, der Mittlere Osten* (1954), and *Im goldenen Sand von Aswan* (1962). He died in Torremolinos, Spain, 18 November 1975. DtBE; WhE&EA; WhoSwi, 1966/67-1972/73

Boswell, Alexander Bruce, born in 1884 at Ashbourne, Derbyshire, he was a graduate of Lincoln College, Oxford, who spent five years as an assistant librarian in Warszawa, followed by six years as a research fellow in Polish at Liverpool. He was a professor emeritus of the University of Liverpool. His writings include *Poland and the Poles* (1919), and *The Eastern boundaries of Poland* (1943). He died 9 January 1962. Who was who, 6

Bosworth, Clifford *Edmund*, born 29 December 1928 at Sheffield, he studied at Oxford and Edinburgh, where he received a Ph.D. in 1960 for his thesis, *The transition from Ghaznavid to Seljuq rule in the Islamic East*. He was a professor of Islamic studies at home and abroad, and emeritus professor of Arabic studies, Manchester University. He was an editor of EI², and a member of the Royal Asiatic Society and the British Institute of Persian Studies. His writings include *The Islamic dynasties* (1967), *Sistan under the Arabs* (1968), *The later Ghaznavids* (1977), and *History of the Saffarids of Sistan and the maliks of Nimruz* (1994). A felicitation volume, *Studies in honour of Clifford Edmund Bosworth*, was published in 2000. ConAu, 13-16, new rev., 7; Sluglett; Who, 1993-2003

Botham, Mark Edwin, born 17 April 1892 at Fengsiang, NW China, where his parents had been missionaries, he was brought to England when still a child, shortly after his father's death from typhoid fever. He entered Bedford Grammar Preparatory School, from which he passed after two years to the School for the Sons of Missionaries at Blackheath. In 1919 he entered upon a business career in a London bank. In the autumn of 1913, he applied to, and was accepted by, the China Inland Mission on the recommendation of his pastor. With a Certificate in Religious Studies from the University of London, he sailed for China in company with his widowed mother in September 1915. After a period of study at the Mission's language school at Anking, he was designated for work among the Muslims in Lanchow. In addition to the study of Chinese he devoted himself to Arabic. For some five years he engaged in widespread itinerant work throughout Northwest China. Early in the summer of 1917 he ventured to visit even Hochow. His arduous travels necessitated a short period of rest at the coast in 1921, but soon he travelled again for the Committee on work for Moslems throughout east and central China. He was also instrumental in the formation of the Moslem Evangelization League. In the spring of 1922 he returned briefly to the Kansu Mission's School, soon to assume again his travels. In his early years in China, he contracted rheumatic fever, and during his last journeys he was again afflicted by illness. In March 1923, little realizing how brief a span of life yet remained, he was married to Miss E. Olive Trench, and it was hoped that by residence in a lower altitude than that of NW China his health would improve. This expectation was not realized. On the 29th of August, 1923, he died from septic endocarditis. MW 14 (1924), pp. 269-274; E. O. Trench, *Two pioneers, life sketches of Thomas and Mark Botham* (1924)

Botham, Olive M. *née* Barclay, born about 1865, she served with the China Inland Mission, and on 14 June 1889, she married, in Paoning, the Rev. Thomas E. S. Botham., also of the C.I.M. After he had died from typhoid fever at Fengsiang, she returned to England in the mid-1890s for the education of her children. When it was her son Mark E. Botham's turn to serve under the C.I.M., she sailed with him for China in September 1915. She was still active in 1938. Lodwick; MW 14 (1924), pp. 269-274

Bothmer, Heinz, born 14 August 1865 at Hannover, he studied modern languages at Genève, was in the service of the Ottoman Empire since 1892, and an honorary Imperial Ottoman Consul. His writings include *Kreta in Vergangenheit und Zukunft* (1899), *Serbien unter König Peter I.* (1905), and *Das deutsche Dorf* (1909). He died before 1928. Wer ist's, 1909, 1912, 1922

Bot'ianov (Ботьянов), Ivan Vasilii, born ca. 1800, he studied at the Oriental Institute of the Foreign Ministery and the University of St. Petersburg, where graduated in 1824. He published translations, particulary the *Mu'allaqat Labid* in 1827. Later he was an interpreter of some rank at the Black Sea Fleet, but continued to produce translations from Arabic and Persian literatures, the last of which were published in 1867. Krachkovskii, p. 106

Botoran, Constantin, fl. 1974, his writings include *Relaţiile româno-egiptene in epoca şi contemporană* (Bucureşti, 1974), and *Solidaritate militantă* (1974). LC

Botta, Paul Émile (Paolo Emilio), born 6 December 1802 at Torino, he studied medicine and natural sciences at Paris, and then made a tour of the world as a ship's surgeon. In 1822, he entered the service of Muhammad Ali as a military physician in the Arabian campaigns. In 1842, he was appointed consul in Mosul and concurrenly sent on a mission under the Société asiatique to find Nineveh. He resigned from the consular service in 1869, and died in Achères-sous-Bois, 29 March 1870. His writings include *Relation d'un voyage dans l'Yémen, entrepris en 1837 pour le Musée d'histoire naturelle de Paris* (1841), and *The buried city of the East, Niveveh* (1851). DBF; Egyptology; Embacher; Henze; Hill; Imperatori; Vapereau

Botte, Louis Alexandre, born in 1883 at Paris, he was an engraver and sculptor who was awarded several prizes. He was made an officer of the Légion d'honneur in 1914. His writings include *Au cœur du Maroc* (1913). Édouard-J.

Botti, Giuseppe, born 3 November 1889 at Vanzone di S. Carlo (Novara), he studied classical philology and Christian literature at Torino. It was during his time as teacher at various schools in Torino that he took up Egyptology. He later became professor of Egyptology at Firenze and Roma. He died in Firenze, 27 December 1968. In 1984 appeared a commemoration volume, *Omaggio a Giuseppe Botti.* Chi è, 1961; Dawson; DizBI; Egyptology; Wholtaly, 1957/58

Bottomley, John *Anthony*, born 3 March 1927 at Port Elizabeh, South Africa, he was a graduate of the University of British Columbia, and received a Ph.D. in 1961 from the University of Virginia for his thesis, *Agricultural credit in Tripolitania.* He taught in the U.S., Singapore, and Australia, before he was appointed in 1966 a professor of economics, and chairman, the School of Social Sciences, University of Bradford (UK). His writings include *Factor pricing and economic growth in underdeveloped rural areas* (1971). WhoWor, 1978/79

Bottomley, Sir Norman Howard, Air Chief Marshall, born 18 September 1891, he was educated at Halifax, and the Université de Rennes. He served in the military until retirement in 1948, when he became Director of Administration, B.B.C. until 1954. He died 13 August 1970. Who was who, 6

Botzaris, Alejandro, fl. 1953, his writings include *Africa e o communismo* (1859-61), *Africa, continente negro o rojo?* (1960), *Communist dogma and the African nationalisms* (1961), and *Communist penetration in Africa* (1961). LC

Bou el-Moghdad, Si, 19th cent. see Bu el Moghdad, Si

Bouabid, Abdarrahim, born 21 March 1920 at Salé, Morocco, he was educated in Rabat and studied in Paris, where he received a diploma in law. He was a member of the Istiqlal Party, and Minister of State in the first Moroccan Government, 1956. Although still listed in *Who's who in the Arab world*, 1993/94, according to Robin Bidwell, he died in the late 1980s. AfrBioInd (2); AfricaWW, 1991

de **Boüard**, Michel, born 5 August 1909 at Lourdes, he was a sometime dean of the Société de l'École des chartes, Paris. His writings include *Manuel d'archéologie médiévale* (1975). In 1982, he was presented with the felicitation volume, *Mélanges d'archéologie et l'histoire médiévales.* He died 28 January 1989. Who's who in France, 1981/82-1987/88

Boubakeur, al-Sayyid al-Hajj Abu Bakr *Hamzah* al-Siddiqi, born 15 June 1912 at Géryville, Algeria, he was educated at Alger and Paris. He was a politician and clergyman, and an honorary rector of the

Paris Mosque. His writings include a French translation of the Koran, and *Trois poètes algérien de langue arabe populaire* (1990). He died 4 February 1995. NDNC, 1961/62; WhoFr, 1993/94-1994/95; *Who's who in the Arab world*, 1978/79; *Who's who in the world*, 1974/75

Boucau, Eugène *Henri*, born 22 July 1887 at Pau (Basse-Pyrénées), he studied geography at Bordeaux and Paris, fought in the first World War, and spent a few months in North Africa. He then taught geography at various *lycées*, notably Condorcet (1923-30), and Louis-le-Grand (1930-40), where he prepared students for the geography courses at l'École nationale de la France d'outre-mer. He died in 1956. *Hommes et destins*, vol. 7 , p. 53

Bouchardat, Apollinaire, born 23 July 1806 at l'Isle-sur-Serein (Yonne), he was a pharmacist and a medical doctor who taught at the Faculté de médecine de Paris. He resigned in 1855 exclusively to pursue his scientific researches. His writings fill ten columns in the *Catalogue général des livres imprimés de la Bibliothèque nationale*. He died in Paris, 7 April 1886. DBF; LC

Boucharlat, Rémy, born 22 November 1948 at Lyon, he received a doctorate in 1974 from the Université de Paris for his thesis, *Le sud-ouest de l'Iran à l'époque sassanide; essai d'inventaire archéologique*. Thereafter he carried on field work in Iran, the Persian Gulf, and Kazakhstan. He was a *directeur de recherches*, CNRS, Lyon, and joint author of *Arabie orientale, Mésopotamie et Iran méridional* (1984), and *Fouilles de Tureng Tepe* (1987). EURAMES, 1993; Private; Schoeberlein; THESAM, 4

Bouche, Denise, born in the first half of the 20th century, she received a doctorate in 1974 from the Université de Paris I for *L'Enseignement dans les territoires français de l'Afrique occidentale de 1817 à 1920*. He was since 1968 a professor of contemporary history at the Université de Nancy II. LC

de **Boucheman**, Albert, capitaine de l'armée de terre, 1906-1941, his writings include *Matériel de la vie bédouine* (Damas, 1935), and *Une petite cité caravanière, Suhné* (1937). Index BFr² (1)

Boucher, André, born in 1879 at Dun-sur-Auron (Cher), he was an *abbé* and *directeur* of the Oeuvres du diocèse de Bourges until 1920, when he was put in charge of the Oeuvre apostolique pour les missions étrangères in Paris. He was an editor of *Revue d'histoire des missions*, and *Études missionaires*, and successively president of the Conseil parisien de la Propagation de la Foi, 1926, l'Oeuvre de St-Pierre Apôtre pour le clergé indigène, 1929, and head of the Union missionnaire du Clergé, 1936. His writings include *Petit atlas des missions catholiques* (1931), and *L'Action missionnaire* (1931). He died in Paris, 17 August 1937. *Hommes et destins*, vol. 5, pp. 79-80

Boucher, Louis, born in 1857 at Sancergues (Cher), he took a medical doctorate in 1883 at Paris. He was a physician and head at the Rouen General Hospital. He was a president of the Société normande de géographie, a municipal politician, and attached to the Académie des sciences, belles-lettres et arts de Rouen. His writings include *La Salpêtrière; son histoire de 1656 à 1790* (1883), and *Conférence antialcoolique* (1917). He died in Rouen, 1 March 1940. DBF

Boucher, Richard, born in 1843, he studied Arabic at l'École des langues orientales, Paris, and, in 1863, set out on a long journey to Algeria and Tunisia to study North African Arabic. Thereafter he went to Constantinople, where he copied the *diwan* of al-Farazdaq, which he edited and translated in 1870. In the 1880s he departed once more for the Orient, where, exhausted, he died in Tehran in October 1886. *Journal asiatique*, 8e série, 12 (1888), pp. 41-42

Bouchon-Brandely, Germain, born at Bort (Corrèze), he was a student of natural sciences, particularly pisciculture. In 1873 he entered the civil service as an inspector of ocean fishery, advancing to inspector general of fisheries in 1887. He submitted several reports on the state of pisciculture in France and the neighbouring countries to the Minister of the Marine and Colonies, most of which were published in the *Journal officiel*. He was joint author of *Les pêches maritimes en Algérie et en Tunisie* (1891). He died in Paris, 24 June 1893. DBF

Bouda, Karl, born 10 February 1901 at Hamburg, he received a Dr.phil. in 1933 from the Universität Berlin for his thesis, *Der Dual des Obugrischen mit einem Exkurs über die Suffixlockerheit*. In 1942 he was appointed a professor at the Universität Erlangen. His writings include *Baskisch-kaukasische Etymologien* (1949), and *Die Verwandtschaftsverhältnisse der tschutschischen Sprachgruppe* (1952). He died in Nürnberg, 30 July 1979. Kürschner, 1950-1980; *Wer ist wer*, 1958

Boudahrain, Abdallah, he was in 1979 a barrister in Casablanca, and in 1984, *enseignant-chercheur* at the Faculté de droit, Rabat. His writings include *Droit social marocain* (1984), *Nouvel ordre social international et migrations dans le cadre du monde arabe et de l'espace euro-arabe* (1985), and *La Sécurité sociale au Maroc* (1989). LC

195

Boudard, René, born 20th cent., his writings include *Gêne et la France dans la deuxième moitié du XVIIIe siècle* (1962), *La "Nation corse" et sa lutte pour la liberté entre 1744 et 1769* (1979), and *Figures et moments de l'histoire creusoise au temps de la Révolution et de l'Empire* (1989). LC

Boudera, Ismail, born in 1823 at Marseille, he was a military interpreter in Algeria, who rose from the rank of *interprète temporaire* (28 February 1853) to *interprète principal* in 1872. For most of his military life he was posted to the Bureau arabe in Lagouat. He accomplished a mission to Ghat, and accompanied Mircher and Polignac to Ghadamès. He was a member of the Société historique algérienne, and the Société de géographie de Paris. He died in Alger, 16 November 1878. Henze; Peyronnet, p. 375

Boudet de Puymaigre, Théodore Joseph, 1816-1901 *see* Puymaigre, Théodore Joseph Boudet de

Boudin, Jean Christian Marc François Joseph, born 27 April 1806 at Metz. He was a student at the Hôpital d'instruction de Metz. In 1832 he was attached to the military hospital in Marseille, where he founded the ephemeral *Gazette médical*. In 1837 he was in charge of the medical service during the second expedition to Constantine, where he remained for three years. On his return to France, he had a successful medical career. He was also an outstanding member of the Société d'anthropologie. His writings include *Essai de géographie médicale* (1843), *Histoire statistique de la colonisation de la population an Algérie* (1853), and *Études anthropologiques* (1864). He died 9 March 1867. DBF

Boudot-Lamotte, Antoine, born 20th cent., he received a doctorate in 1974 from the Université de Paris IV for his thesis, *Ahmad Šawqi, l'homme et l'œuvre*. He was affiliated with the Institut français de Damas. His writings include *Contribution à l'étude de l'archerie musulmane* (1968). LC; THESAM, 3

Boudy, P., fl. 1935, he was a sometime director at the Service des Eaux et Forêts au Maroc. His writings include *Économie forestière nord-africaine* (1948-1955). LC

Boué, Ami, born 16 March 1794 at Hamburg, he studied medicine at Edinburgh and geology from 1817 to 1826 at Berlin, Wien, and Paris. Since 1835 he lived at his estate in Bad Vöslau, Austria. He was a member of the London Geological Society, the Akademie der Wissenschaften in Wien, and a founding member of the Société géologique de France. He knew Turkey from travels in 1836-38. His writings include *La Turquie d'Europe* (1840), its translation, *Die europäische Türkei* (1889), *Der ganze Zweck und der hohe Nutzen der Geologie* (1851), and *Recueil d'itinéraires dans la Turquie d'Europe* (1854). He died in Bad Vöslau, 21 November 1881. DtBE; ÖBL

Bouhdiba, Abdelwahab, born in 1932 at Kairouan, he lived in 1970 at Tunis. His writings include *Criminalité et changement sociaux en Tunisie* (1965), *Sociologie du développement africain* (1971), *La sexualité en islam* (1975), its translation, *Sexuality in Islam* (1985), and *Raisons d'être* (1980). AfriBioInd (2); Clausen, pp. 138-139; LC; Note

Bouhouche, Ammar, fl. 1965, he received a Ph.D. in 1971 from the University of Missouri for his thesis, *Conditions and attitudes of migrant Algerian workers in France*. His writings include the translation of his thesis, *Conditions et attitudes des travailleurs algériens émigrés en France* (1979), and an Arabic work on bureaucracy in contemporary society. LC

de Bouillane de Lacoste, Émile Antoine Henri, born about 1865, he was a French officer who was a *sous-lieutenant* in 1888, and advanced through the grades to become *commandant* in 1904. He was sent on a mission to study the feasibility of extending the Trans-Siberian railway across Manchuria, the results of which are the subject of his report *A travers la Mandchourie; le chemin de fer de l'Est-chinois* (1903). Thereafter he travelled for several years across Persia, Baluchistan, Mongolia, and Afghanistan. His writings include *Autour de l'Afghanistan* (1908), and *Au pays sacré des anciens Turcs et des Mongols* (1911). He died in Montélimar, 25 September 1937. DBF

Bouillier, François (*Francisque*) Cyrille, born 12 July 1813 at Lyon, he was an orphan who studied philosophy, took a doctorate in 1839, and was designatated for the chair of philosophy at the Faculté de Lyon. In 1846 he made an incursion into liberal politics, but the 1848 revolution, for which he had struggled, came for him as such a surprise that he turned conservative for the rest of his life. Under the *Empire* he became president of the Université de Clermont, and inspector general of secondary education. He was compelled to retired in 1879. He published his memoirs, *Souvenirs d'un veil universitaire* (1897). He died in Simandre (Isère), 27 September 1899. DBF

Bouin, fl. 1917, he was a veterinarian *aide-major* with the Service de l'Élevage, Groupe vétérinaire mobile in Marrakesh. Note

Bouinot, Jean, born 20th cent., he received a doctorate in 1982 from the Université de Paris I for his thesis, *Temps et espace en gestion communale*. His writings include *La Nouvelle gestion municipale* (Paris, 1977). He was joint author of *L'influence des finances municipales sur les processus de* *croissance urbaine* (1977), and joint editor of *Contributions pour la gestion des études dans les collectivités locales* (1982), and *Projet de ville et projets d'entreprise* (1993). LC; THESAM, 2

Boulad, Émile, born 19th cent., his writings include *Propositions de réformes législatives en Egypte* (Le Caire, 1913). LC

Boulad d'Humières, Jean, he was joint author of *The Private ship letter stamps of the world* (1985).

Boulaine, Jean Louis, born in 1922, he received a doctorate in 1957 at Alger for his thesis, *Étude des sols des plaines du Chélif*. In 1987 he was a professor of pedology at the Institut national agronomique de Paris. His writings include *L'Agrologie* (1971), *Géographie des sols* (1975), and *Histoire des pédologues et de la science des sols* (1989). LC

Boulanger, Robert, born in 1926, he was a writer of travel guides for the *Guides bleues*, Paris, which include *Liban* (1955), *Moyen-Orient; Liban, Syrie, Jordanie, Irak, Iran* (1956), the English and German translations in 1966, *Tunisie* (1971), and *Iran, Afghanistan* (1974). LC

Boulangier, Edgar, born in 1850, he was an engineer with the Service des ponts et chaussée. His writings include *Un Hiver au Cambodge* (1888), *Voyage à Merv* (1888), and *Notes de voyages en Sibérie* (1891). LC

Boularès, Habib, born 29 July 1933 at Tunis, he was educated in Tunis and received a diploma in economics at Paris, and in journalism at Strasbourg. He started life as an editorial manager for local Tunisian newspapers. Thereafter he was a member of parliament, ambassador, and minister of various porfolios until 1974, when he was excluded from the Destour Party and went into exile in Paris. His writings include *Tunisie d'aujourd'hui* (1965), *Murad al-Thalith* (1973), *L'Islam; la peur et l'éspérance* (1983), and its translation, *Islam; the fear and the hope* (1990). Clausen, pp. 139-142; LC

Boulay de la Meurthe, Alfred, comte, born 3 November 1843 at Paris, he entered the Conseil d'État, Section de l'Intérieure et des Cultes, in 1868, but had to resign in the wake of the 1870 revolution. Thereafter he wrote for *le Commerce*, and was a founding member of the Société d'histoire diplomatique, Société d'histoire contemporaine, and Société de l'histoire de Paris. He wrote *Le Directoire et l'expédition d'Egypte* (1885). He died in Paris, 3 September 1926. DBF

Boulger, Demetrius Charles de Kavanagh, born 14 July 1853, he was educated at Kensington Grammar School and privately. He contributed to all the leading periodicals on questions relating to India, China, Egypt, and Turkey since 1876. He was in 1885 a founding editor of the *Asiatic quarterly review*. His writings include *The Life of Yakoob Beg* (1878), *Central Asian portraits* (1880), *Central Asian questions* (1885), *The Life of General Gordon* (1896), *The Story of India* (1897), *India in the nineteenth century* (1901), and *Belgium of the Belgians* (1911). He died in 1928. Buckland; Who was who, 2

Boulhol, P., he was in 1941 an inspector with the Service des Eaux et Forêts, Morocco. Note

Boulifa, 'Ammar ben Sa'id, born in 1870, he was a sometime lecturer in Berber language at the Faculté des lettres and the École normale d'Alger. His writings include *Une Première année de langue kabyle* (1897), *Recueil de poésies kabyles* (1904), *Textes berbères en dialects de l'Atlas marocain* (1908), *Lexique kabyle-français* (1913), *Le Djurdjura à travers l'histoire* (1925). He died in 1931. LC

Boulin, Jean, fl. 1972, he was a sometime member of the Laboratoire de géologie historique, Paris. He wrote *Méthodes de la stratigraphie et géologie historique* (1977). LC; Note

Boullata, Issa J., born 25 February 1929 at Jerusalem, he was educated at De La Salle College, Jerusalem, and the University of London, where he received a Ph.D. in 1969 for his *Badr Shakir al-Sayyab, the man and his poetry*. He was Academic Deputy Headmaster at St. George's School, and lecturer in Islamic studies at St. Goerge's College, Jerusalem, before he emigrated to the U.S.A. in 1968. He was a sometime professor of Arabic and Islamic studies at the Hartford Seminary Foundation, and the Institute of Islamic Studies, McGill University. For more than ten years he was an editor of the *Muslim world*. In 1972 he was a recipient of the Arberry Memorial Prize. In 2000 he was honoured by *Professor Issa J. Boullata; a profile of an intellectual exile*. DrASCan, 1983; Private; Sluglett

Boullata, Kamal, born 28 May 1942 in Palestine, he was an artist and writer who lived in Washington, D.C. He was the editor of *Women of the Fertile Crescent; an anthology of modern poetry by Arab women* (1978), and *The world of Rashid Hussein* (1979). LC; Note

Boullier. In 1920 he served as a captain with the Service géographique du Maroc. Note

Boulos, Afif *see* Bulos, Afif Alvarez

Boulouis, Jean, born 20th cent., he received the "Prix Paul Deschanel" for his 1951 Paris doctoral thesis. He was a professor at the Université de Paris, whose writings include *Essai sur la politique des subventions administratives* (1951), and *Cours de droit administratif* (1968). BN; LC; Note

Boulton, Laura Theresa Craytor, born at Conneaut, Ohio, her year of birth being given variously as 1889 and 1899. She was a graduate of Denison University, Granville, Ohio, and the University of Chicago. After studying music at Chicago and abroad, she held a variety of university posts which included the teaching of primitive and liturgical music. Between 1929 and 1968 she made several trips to Africa, either as music collector or as a member of academic expeditions. Her writings include *The Music hunter, the autobiography of a career* (1969). She died in Bethesda, Md., 16 October 1980. Shavit-Africa; WhoAmW, 1970-71; WhAm, 7

Bouman, Johan, born 1 March 1918 at Amsterdam, he received a doctorate in 1959 from the Rijksuniversiteit te Utrecht for his thesis, *Le Conflit autour du Coran et la solution d'al-Baqillani*. Thereafter he was a professor at Bruxelles, AUB, Bochum, and, from 1973 until retirement, at Marburg. His writings include *Gott und Mensch im Koran* (1977), *Das Wort vom Kreuz und das Bekenntnis zu Allah* (1980), *Christentum und Islam im Vergleich* (1982), and *Der Koran und die Juden* (1990). Kürschner, 1980-1996; Wer ist wer, 1997/98

Boumédienne, Houari, born 23 August 1927, he received an Islamic secondary education and studied at Tunis and Cairo. He was a soldier, politician, and for fourteen years president of Algeria. His *Discours du président Boumédienne* were published in 1970, 1972, 1975, 1976, 1978, and 1979. He died 27 December 1978. Makers, 1981, 1991, 1996; Master (10); WhAm, 7

Bounoure, Gabriel, his writings include *Souvenirs littéraires et problèmes actuels; allocution et conférence prononcées à Beyrouth en avril 1946* (Beyrouth, 1946), and *Edmond Jabès; la demeure et le livre* (1984). He died in 1969. LC

Bouquet de la Grye, Jean Jacques *Anatole*, born in 1827, he graduated in 1847 from l'École polytechnique and became a hydrographer and cartographer. In 1861 he made a study of the Port of Alexandria, Egypt. His writings include *Paris, port de mer* (1892). He died in Paris, 22 December 1909. DBF

Bourcart, Jacques Paul, born 5 July 1891 at Hueberwiller (Haut-Rhin), he took a doctorate in science and became a geologist, explorer of the Sahara, and an oceanographer. He was the author of several maps of Morocco, and joint author of *La Faune des calcaires cambriens de Sidi Mouça d'Aglou* (1931). He died 24 June 1965. WhoFr, 1963/64-1965/66

Bourdarie, Paul, born 18 July 1864 at Montfaucon (Lot), he started life in a Paris *droguerie*, in 1884. In 1893 he was sent on a mission to the Congo to study various agricultural problems. On his return to France in the following year, he was appointed secretary general of the Société africaine de France, in which position he was involved in the organization of explorations to Egypt and other parts of Africa. Since 1906 he was the editor of the *Revue indigène*, and since 1908, professor of history and African sociology at the Collège des sciences sociales. He died in Nice, 13 July 1950. DBF; Hommes et destins, vol. 1, pp. 101-102

Bourde, Paul Anthelme, born 21 May 1851 at Voissant (Isère), he started life on a farm, followed by two years in an office of the Service des Ponts et chaussée de Lyon. After the Franco-Prussian war he went to Paris, where he joined the staff of *le Temps* and proved to be a talented journalist. He spent several years in Algeria and Tunisia. Since 1890 he was an administrator in Tunisia. His writings include *Russes et Turcs, la guerre d'Orient* (1878), *À travers l'Algérie; souvenirs de l'excursion parlementaire* (1879), and *De Paris à Tonkin* (1885). He died in Paris, 27 October 1914. DBF; Hommes et destins, vol. 1, pp. 103-104

Bourdet, Claude, born 28 October 1909 at Paris, he studied mathematics and philosophy, and taught at Versailles and Zürich before entering French politics as *ministre de l'Économie nationale*, 1936-39, Concurrently he pursued a journalistic career. He was a member of the Counseil national de la Résistance. His writings include *L'Europe truquée; supranationalité* (1977). He died 20 March 1996. DBFC, 1954/55; WhoFr, 1963/64-1995/96

Bourdieu, Pierre Félix, born 1 August 1930 at Denguin (Basses-Pyrénées), he was educated at the Lycée de Pau and Louis.le-Grand, Paris, and graduated from the École normale supérieure. From 1958 to 1960 he taught sociology at the Faculté des lettres d'Alger; and in 1982 he was appointed to the chair of sociology at the Collège de France. His writings include *Sociologie de l'Algérie* (1958), its translation, *The Algerians* (1962), *Règles de l'art* (1992), its translation, *The rules of art* (1996), *Question de sociologie* (1980), its translation, *Sociology in question* (1993). He was joint author of *Le Déracinement; la crise de l'agriculture traditionnelle en Algérie* (1964). He died in Paris from cancer, 23 January 2002. Unesco; WhoFr, 1989/90-2000/2001

198

Bourdillon, Sir Bernard Henry, born 3 December 1883 at Emu Bay, Tasmania, he was a graduate of St. John's College, Oxford, and in 1908 entered the Indian Civil Service. During the first World War he was posted to Mesopotamia where, after the war, he was secretary to the High-Commissioner, and successively Acting High-Commissioner, 1925-1926. His writings include *The Future of the Colonial Empire* (1945). He died 6 February 1948. *Who was who*, 4

Bourdillon, Sir James Austin, born in 1848 at Madras, he entered the Indian Civil Service in 1870 and went out to India. He was a colonial administrator, member of the Bengal Legislative Council, acting Lieutenant-Governor of Bengal, and Resident in Mysore. He died in 1909. Buckland; IndianBilnd (2); Riddick; *Who's who*, 1903-1909; *Who was who*, 1

Bourdon, Claude, fl. 1934, his writings include *Anciens canaux, anciens sites et ports de Suez* (1925).

Bourdon, Joseph *Gaston*, born 4 October 1830 at Nîmes, he graduated from the military college of Saint-Cyr and rose to the rank of general in 1888. He spent the years 1862 to 1870, and 1871 to 1875 in Algeria. He died 27 October 1896. DBF

Bourdon, Léon Marie Antoine, born 10 May 1900 at Mâçon (Saône-et-Loire), he studied at l'École normale supérieure, and took a doctorate in history. He was a member of l'École française de Rome, 1924-1926, director of l'Institut français au Portugal, 1928-1935, and thereafter taught successively at Toulouse and Paris. WhoFr, 1965/66-1971/72

Bourély, Michel, fl. 1962, his writings include *Droit public marocain* (1966), and he was a contributing author to *Droit et l'espace* (1988). LC

Bourgeois, Émile, born 24 July 1857 at Paris, he was a graduate of l'École normale supérieure, and received a doctorate in 1885 from the Faculté des lettres de Paris for *Quodomo provinciarum romanorum*. He held a brief appointment as professor of history at the Lycée d'Alger. Since 1882 he was a professor of modern political and diplomatic history successively at Caen, Lyon, and Paris. His many writings include *Le Capitulaire de Kiersy-sur-Oise* (1885). He was an illustrious historian who died almost unnoticed during the vacation doldrums of the summer of 1934. DBF; *Who was who*, 3

Bourgeot, André, fl. 1972, his writings include *Le Désert des Kel Ahaggar* (1982). LC

de **Bourges**, Jacques, born about 1630 at Paris, he was a missionary under the Société des Missions étrangères, and left for the Far East in 1660. Shortly after arriving in Siam, he returned to Rome to report on his mission. The report was published under the title, *Relation du voyage de monseigneur l'évêque de Beryte par la Turquie, la Perse, les Indes &c. jusqu'au royaume de Siam* (1666), and its German translation, *Wahrhaffte und eigendliche erzehlung von der reise auss Frankreich zu wasser und zu lande nach China* (1671). He went out again to Siam in 1666, and later went to China until expelled in 1712. He died as a refugee in Siam, 9 August 1714. DBF

Bourgey, André Georges Laurent, born 9 September 1936 at Saint-Étienne (Loire), he was educated at *lycées* in Lyon and Alger, and studied geography at l'Université de Lyon. He was successively affiliated with the Faculté des lettres de Lyon, the Institut de géographie du Proche-et Moyen-Orient, Beirut, and the Centre d'études et de recherches sur le Moyen-Orient contemporain, Beirut, before being appointed a professor, and subsequently director, at the Institut nationale des langues et civilisations orientales, Paris. Since 1993 he was administrator of the Institut du monde arabe, Paris. He was joint author of *Industrialisation et changements sociaux dans l'Orient arabe* (1982), and *Migrations et changements sociaux dans l'Orient arabe* (1985). WhoFr, 1990/91-2002/2003

Bourgin, Georges, born in 1879 at Nevers (Nièvre), he studied law at l'École des chartes, Paris, and in 1904 entered the service of the Archives nationales. He was a keeper of the Section ancienne when he died in September 1958. For fifteen years he was a professor at l'École pratique des hautes études, where he gave a course on economic and social history, and especially on the history of labour. He was a member of the Comité des travaux historiques, as well as other learned societies. He was joint author of *Inventaire du fonds de l'Algérie aux Archives nationales* (Alger, 1929). BioIn, 5; Index BFr² (3)

Bourguet, Pierre Marie d'Audibert Caille du, 1910-1988 *see* Du Borguet, Pierre Marie d'Audibert C.

Bourguiba, Habib, born 3 August 1903 at Monastir, Tunisia, he was the first president after the abolition of the Tunisian monarchy, but deposed as president-for-life on 7 November 1987. He wrote *La Tunisie et la France; vingt-cinq ans de lutte pour une co-opération libre* (1954). Derek Hopwood wrote the biography, *Habib Bourguiba of Tunisia, the tragedy of longvity* (1992). He died in Monastir, 6 April 2000. AfricaWW, 1991; Clausen, 146-156; IntWW, 1978/79-1997/98; MidE, 1982/83; Reich, 119-126

Bourham, Abdul-Aziz *see* Burham, 'Abd al-'Aziz

Bouriant, Urbaine, born 11 April 1849 at Nevers (Nièvre), he studied law at Paris, and later, Egyptology under Maspero. In 1881 he became a member of the French archaeological mission to Cairo. Two years later he was appointed deputy director of the Bulaq Museum, and, in 1886, head of the Mission française. Since 1898 he was inflicted by hemiplegia and compelled to return to France, where he died in Vannes, 19 June 1903. His writings include *Chansons populaires arabes en dialecte du Caire, d'après les manuscrits d'un chanteur des rues* (1893). Dawson; DBF; Egyptology

Bourjade, Gaston, fl. 1888, his writings include *Notes chronologiques pour servir à l'histoire de l'occupation française dans la région d'Aumale, 1846-1887* (Alger, 1891). BN

Bourke-Burrowes, D. fl. 1931, he was a correspondent of *the Times* in Persia. Note

Bourlon, Abel, fl. 1947-1960, he was a sometime member of the Centre de hautes études d'administration musulmane, Paris, and in 1958, *commandant de Cercle*, Tera, République du Niger. Note

Bourmont, Louis Auguste Victor de Ghaisne, comte, born 2 September 1773 at the Château de Bourmont (Anjou), he was a graduate of l'École militaire de Sorèze. Throughout his life he switched his alliance many times from Napoleon to the Bourbons and back again. His greatest victory was the conquest of Alger in 1830, which procured him the rank of *maréchal de France*. Even thereafter he had a checkered career in Portugal and Spain. When he at last returned to France, he had almost entirely lost his popularity and accordingly retired for the rest of his life to his estate in Anjou, where he died 27 October 1846. Gustave Gautherot published *La Conquête d'Alger, 1830, d'après les papiers inédits du maréchal de Bourmont, commandant en chef de l'expédition* (1929). DBF; EncAm; EncBrit; Meyers

Bourne, Kenneth, born 17 March 1930 at Wickford, Essex, he was a graduate of the University of Exeter, and received his Ph.D. in 1955 at LSE. He was a research fellow in history at the University of Reading, before he was appointed in 1957a lecturer in international history at LSE. He wrote *The Foreign policy of Victorian England, 1830-1902* (1970). ConAu, 25-28 & 11 new rev.; WrDr, 1982/84-1994/96|

Bournoutian, George A., born 25 September 1943 at Isfahan, he was educated at the University of California, awarded several fellowships, and in 1993 became a professor of history at Iona College, New Rochelle, N.Y., a post which he still held in 2003. His writings include *Eastern Armenia in the last decades of Persian rule, 1807-1828* (1982) - a work which was originally presented in 1976 as Ph.D. thesis at U.C.L.A. entitled - *Eastern Armenia on the eve of the Russian conquest: the Khanate of Erevan* and *The Khanate of Erevan under Qajar rule, 1795-1828* (1992). NatFacDr, 1995-2003; Private

Bouron, Narcisse Firmin Léon Henri, *capitaine*, he wrote *Les Druzes* (Paris, 1930), *Kalaat Allah, "la forteresse de Dieu;" roman* (Paris, 1937), *Le second drame de Maubeuge; histoire de la 101e division de forteresse* (1947), and *Druze history* (1952). LC

Bourquelot, Émile, fl. 1863, he was a keeper at the Bibliothèque de Provins (Seine-et-Marne). His writings include *Souvenirs de voyage d'un Provinois dans le sud de l'Italie, 1865* (1867), *En Algérie; souvenirs du Provinois* (1881), and *Promenades en Egypte et à Constantinople* (1886). BN

Bourrel, fl. 1860, he was a French warrant-officer. In the service of the Governor of Senegal, he explored the territory of the Brakna, north of the River Senegal, June to October 1860. Henze

Bourrilly, Joseph, born 21 March 1878 at Toulon, he studied law at Aix-en-Province. During the first years of the first World War he served in eastern Morocco, in Taza, Bou Ladjeraf, and Safsafat. During the final years, he was relieved of his military duties to serve as a professor at Oudja and Rabat. He stayed on in Morocco after the war and was a magistrate, archaeologist, and ethnographer. His writings include *Éléments d'ethnographie marocaine* (1932). He died in Casablanca, 15 January 1929. *Hommes et destins*, vol. 7, pp. 93-95

Bourrilly, Victor Louis, 1872-1945, he was a sometime professor at the Faculté des lettres d'Aix-en-Provence. He was joint author of *Histoire de la Provence* (1966). LC; Note

Bouscaren, Anthony Trawick, born 7 July 1920 at Winchest, Mass., he was a Yale graduate who received his Ph.D. in 1951 from the University of California at Berkeley for *Christian democracy in European government and politics*. He taught political science at various military and civilian institutions in the United States. His writings include *Soviet expansion and the West* (1949), *International migrations since 1945* (1963), and *Enduring the Soviets* (1987). AmM&WS, 1973 & 1978; ConAu, 1

Bouslama, Abdelmajid, born 2 March 1924 at Hammamat, Tunisia, he studied law at Tunis, where he received a *licence en droit*. Thereafter he was a magistrate in Tunis, rising to the position of Deputy Attorney General in 1975. Clausen, pp. 160-161

Bousquet, Georges, born in 1846, his writings include *Agents diplomatiques et consulaires* (1883), and *La Banque de France et les institutions de crédit* (1885). IndexBFr² (1); LC

Bousquet, Georges Henri, born in 1900, he was a specialist on Islamic law, a subject on which he published widely. From 1932 to 1956 he read North African sociology at the Faculté de droit d'Alger. His writings include *Précis élémentaire de droit musulman* (1936-40), *Du droit musulman et de son application effective dans le monde* (1949), *Justice français et coutumes kabiles* (1950), *Les Berbères* (1967), and *L'Ethique sexuelle de l'islam* (1990). He died in 1978. LC

Bousquet-Deschamps, Jacques *Lucien*, born 16 June 1798 at Marmande (Lot-et-Garonne). As a young man he went to Paris, where he published *Application de l'enseignement mutuel à l'étude de la langue latine* (1819). Thereafter he was editor-in-chief of *l'Aristarque* until suppressed by censorship. He was harassed, imprisoned, escaped, spent years in Spanish exile, returned, and died after a checkered journalistic career around 1850 in Paris. DBF

Boussac, P. O. G. Hyppolyte, born at Narbonne (Aude), he was an architect who contributed articles on ancient Egyptian subjects to *la Nouvelle revue* and the *Journal of the Royal Institute of British architects* between 1895 and 1897. Bellier, suppl., p. 96

Bousser, Marcel, he received a doctorate in 1934 from the Université de Bordeaux for his thesis, *Les Transports intérieurs au Maroc français, leur concurrence*. He was joint author of *Bibliographie marocaine, 1923-1933* (1937). LC

Boustani, Habib S., he was in 1927 a leader of the Parti national libanais. His writings include *Pour l'agriculture égyptienne* (1920). LC; Note

Boustany, Fouad Ephrem, born 15 August 1906 at Deir el-Kamar, Lebanon, he was a Maronite Christian, and studied at the Université de Saint-Joseph, Beirut. From 1953 to 1970 he was the first dean of the Lebanese University. He was an authority on Lebanese history, pre-Islamic history, and Arabic poetry. He won awards for his work in education from his own government, the Vatican, France, Morocco, Tunisia, and Iran. He died in Beirut of a heart attack, 1 February 1994. WhoLeb, 1970/71, 1982/83; IntWW, 1973/74-1978/79; WRMEA 12 ii (1994), p. 113

Boustany, Salah el-Din (Salaheddine) Youssef, born 7 April 1927 at Cairo, he was a journalist and owner of Maktabat al-'Arab in Cairo. His writings include *Bonaparte's Egypt in picture & word* (Cairo, 1986), as well as works in Arabic. IntAu&W, 1989; IWWAS, 1975/76; Master; WhoWor, 1984/85

Boustead, John Edmund *Hugh*, Colonel Sir, born 14 April 1895 in Ceylon, he was educated at the Royal Naval College, Osborne, and, interrupted by his desertion, served in many parts of Africa and Asia until retirement in 1935, when he transferred to the Sudan Political Service. In 1966 he was awarded the Lawrence of Arabia Memorial Medal by the Royal Central Asian Society. He wrote *The Wind of morning, the autobiography of Hugh Boustead* (1971). He died in Dubai, 3 April 1980. ConAu, 97; Master; Who was who, 7

Boutakoff, A., 1816-1869 *see* Butakov, Aleksei Ivanovich

Bouteflika, Abdelaziz, born 2 March 1937 at Oudja, Algeria, he was an officer in the Armée de libération nationale. After Algerian independence, he was a member of parliament, minister, president of the UN General Asssembly. AfrBioInd (6); AfricaWW, 1991; IntWW, 1997/98-2002/2003; MidE, 1982/83

de **Bouteiller**, Georges, born 13 January 1913 at Boulogne-sur-Mer (Pas-de-Calais), he studied at the Faculté de droit d'Alger, and the Faculté des lettres de Paris. After passing through the military college of Saint-Cyr, he was an officer in Algeria, and subsequently served with Affaires indigènes du Maroc. From 1967 to 1975 he was ambassador to Saudi Arabia. His writings include *L'Arabie Saoudite* (1981), and *Tiers-monde islamique tiers du monde* (1987). WhoFr, 1975/76-1981/82|

Boutillier, Jean Louis, born 23 October 1926 at Paris, he received a *doctorat ès siences économiques* from the Université de Paris and was a sometime member of the Office de la recherche scientifique et technique d'outre-mer, Paris. His writings include *Bongouanou, Côte d'Ivoire; étude socio-économique d'une subdivision* (1960), and *La moyenne vallée du Sénégal* (1962). African biographical index, 1999 (1); LC; Unesco

Boutros-Ghali, Boutros, born 14 November 1922 at Cairo, the son of a wealthy Coptic family, he studied law and political science at Cairo and Paris, where he received a doctorate in 1949 in international law. He was brought into political life by Egyptian president Anwar al-Sadat in 1974 and served as Secretary General of the U.N., 1992 to 1996. He wrote *L'Organistaion de l'unité africaine* (1969), *Les Conflits des frontières en Afrique* (1972), and *al-Siyasah al-kharijiyah al-Misriyah* (1991).

Africa, 1991-1996; Goldschmidt; IntWW, 1997/98-2002; Makers, 1996; MidE, 1982/83; *Time*, 2 Dec. 1991, p. 28; Unesco; Who, 1998-2003; WhoAm, 1999; WhoArab, 1986/87-2003/2004; WhoFr, 2002

Boutros-Ghali, Mirrit, 1908- *see* Ghali, Mirrit Boutros

Boutruche, Robert, born 21 October 1904 at Chailland (Mayenne), he studied at the Faculté des lettres de Rennes, and received a *doctorat ès lettres*. He was a medievalist at Strasbourg, 1947-58, and at Paris, 1958-73. His writings include *Seigneurie et féodalité* (1959). In 1976 appeared *La Noblesse au Moyen Âge, XIe-XVe siècles; essais à la mémoire de Robert Boutruche*. He died 15 November 1975. WhoFr, 1965/66-1975/76

Bouty, J., fl. 1878-1901, he was an engineer affiliated with the Département d'Oran, Algeria, and an adviser to the Commission du transsaharien. BN; Note

Bouvat, Lucien, born in 1872, he was a graduate of l'École nationale des langues orientales as well as l'École pratique des hautes études, Paris. He started life at the editorial offices of *Archives maro-caines* and *Revue du monde musulman*, where he produced excerpts from the Muslim press, which often appeared anonymously. Since 1926 he worked in a similar capacity for the *Bulletin périodique de la presse turque*, issued by the Ministère des Affaires étrangère. On the recommendation of Barbier de Meynard and Octave Houdas, he was accepted as a member of the Société asiatique in 1899. He later became the librarian of the Société. Apart from his innumerous anonymous writings, he wrote *L'Empire mongol* (1927), and *Les Barmékides d'après les historiens arabes et persans* (1828), a work which was translated into Persian in the early 1970s. He died in Paris in 1942. *Journal asiatique* 242 (1954), pp. 267-269

Bouvé, Clement Lincoln, born 27 May 1878 at Hingham, Mass., he was a graduate of Harvard and Harvard Law School, and a lawyer at the Register of Copyrights, Library of Congress, Washington, D.C. He died 14 January 1944. WhAm, 2

Bouverot, fl. 1920, he was a sometime battailon commander, and *commandant* of the Cercle de la Haute Moulouya, Morocco. *Bulletin de la Société de géographie du Maroc*, 1920/22

Bouvier, Jean, born 27 June 1914 at Paris, he received a diploma from l'École supérieure de commerce de Paris. Thereafter he was a business executive, and from 1936 to 1956, *administrateur directeur général* of the Établissements Bouvier in Casablanca. WhoFr, 1975/76-1981/82|

Bouvier, René, born 2 January 1883 at Grenoble, he received a *doctorat ès sciences*, and was a sometime president of the Société des Papeteries de l'Indochine. His writings include *Le Denier des grands Mogols; la vie d'Aureng Zeb* (1947). WhoFr, 1953/54

de **Bouville**, Carlos, fl. 1845, his writings include *France et Algérie* (Pithiviers, 1850). BN

Bouy, Ernest, born 23 April 1904 at Saint-Marcellin (Dauphiné). After he received a doctorate in law from the Université de Lyon, he was appointed *maître de conférences* at l'École des hautes études juridiques de Rabat. Concurrently he participated in the elaboration of the industrial legislation of the Moroccan Protectorate. Since 1941 he was an insurance executive. His writings include *Le Problème de la main-œuvre et la législation du travail au Maroc* (1930). WhoFr, 1953/54-1977/78|

Bouyges, Maurice, le père, S.J., born in 1878, he was a specialist in Islamic philosophy and its connection with medieval European scholasticism, in particular studies in al-Ghazzali, Averroes, and al-Farabi. In his grandios project, the *Bibliotheca Arabica scholasticorum*, he published seven works. He edited al-Ghazzali's *Tahâfut al-falasifa* (1927), and wrote *Essai de chronologie des œuvres de al-Ghazali* (1959). He died 22 January 1951. *Isis* 43 (1952), p. 117; *Proche Orient chrétien* 1 (1951), p. 142

Bouyx, Emmanuel, fl. 1972, he was a sometime member of the Laboratoire de géologie historique, Paris. His writings include *Contribution à l'étude des fonctions anté-ordoviciennes de la Meseta méridi-onale* (1970). LC; Note

Bovier-Lapierre, Paul Henri Hippolyte, born 18 November 1873 at Grenoble, he was a natural scientist who entered the Société de Jésus in 1895. He taught science intermittently in Egypt, Lebanon, and Paris, until an accident prevented his using a microscope. From then on he concentrated on the study of ancient Egyptian history. He died in Beirut, 26 May 1950. Egyptology; *Hommes et destins*, v. 2, pp. 123-124

Bovill, Edward William, born 25 December 1892, he was a graduate of Trinity College, Cambridge, and a sometime vice-president of the Hakluyt Society. His writings include *Caravans of the old Sahara* (1933), *The Battle of Alcazar* (1952), *The Golden trade of the Moors*, 2nd ed. (1968), and *The Niger explored* (1968). He died 19 December 1966. *Who was who*, 6

Bowden, Bertram Vivian, Baron Bowden, born 18 January 1910, he was a graduate of Emmanuel College, Cambridge. He was a Physics Master, and carried on radar research in England and the

United States. He was a sometime principal of the University of Manchester Institute of Science and Technology. His writings include *Faster than thought* (1953). He died 28 July 1989. Who was who, 8

Bowder, Geoffrey, he was in 1978 a lecturer in Arab studies at the University of Durham. Note

Bowdon, Walter Syden, Rev., born in 1873 at London, he was a graduate of St. John's College, Cambridge, and a sometime vicar of Walsgrave. He travelled extensively throughout the world. His writings include *Re-interpretations; old beliefs re-represented from the point of view of modern thought* (1930). WhE&EA

Bowen, Harold, fl. 1929, his writings include *The life and times of Ali Ibn 'Isa, the Good Vizier* (1928), *British contributions to Turkish studies* (1945), and he was joint author of *Islamic society and the West* (1950). LC

Bowen, John Charles Edward, born 8 October 1909, he was a graduate of Oxford, and served in the Indian Army and the Indian Political Service, 1932-1947. He was successively District Commissioner in India and Nigeria, 1950-1963. His writings include *Poems from the Persian* (1948), *The Golden pomegranate; a selection from the poetry of the Mogul Empire in India* (1957), *Translation or travesty* (1973), and *Plain tales of the Afghan border* (1982). IndianBilnd (1); IntWWP, 1977

Bowen, John Eliot, born in 1858 at Brooklyn, N.Y., he was a journalist who received a Ph.D. in 1886 from Columbia University for his thesis, *The Conflict of the east and the west in Egypt*. He died in Brooklyn, N.Y., 3 January 1890. DcNAA

Bowen, Richard LeBaron, born 2 April 1919 at Providence, R.I., he was a graduate of Princeton University and took a Ph.D. degree at MIT in 1949. He was a professional chemical engineer with an intense interest in the Arabian Peninsula. He worked for the Arabian American Oil Company from 1945 to 1947 in Saudi Arabia. In the winter of 1950 he was technical and engineering adviser to the American Foundation for the Study of Man, Arabian Expedition, which conducted archaeological excavations in South Arabia. He was joint author of *Archaeological discoveries in South Arabia* (1958). AMS, 1965 P; AmMWSc, 1971 P - 1979 P; Shavit; WhAm, 6

Bowen-Jones, Howard, born 25 May 1921 at Ammanford, Wales, he was and graduate of Cambridge, a sometime professor of geography at the University of Durham (UK). His writings include *Change in development in the Middle East* (1981). DrBSMES, 1993; Unesco

Bower, Sir Graham John, born 15 June 1848 at Dingle, Ireland. After passing through the Naval Academy, Gosport, Hamshire, he served as a naval man and controversial diplomat in the Mediterranean, on the coast of Africa, in the East Indies, Britain, and Australia. He died in London, 2 August 1933. DSAB, 5; Who was who, 3

Bower, Hamilton, Maj.-Gen. Sir, born 1 September 1858, he was educated at Edinburgh Collegiate School, and passed through the Royal Naval School, New Cross. He entered the Army in 1880, and as officer of the 17th Bengal Cavalry, he travelled in 1889 with Henri Dauvergne in Turkestan and the Pamir Mountains, and in 1891, with W. G. Thorold, in Tibet, the results of which he published in *Diary of a journey across Tibet* (1894). In 1896 he participated in the expedition to Dongola, Sudan. He died 5 March 1940. Henze; Who was who, 3

Böwering, Gerhard Heinrich, born 20 October 1939 at Mönchen-Gladbach, Germany, he studied at Würzburg, Panjab University, and McGill University, Montreal, where he received a Ph.D. in 1974 for his thesis, *A textual and analytical study of the Tafsir of Sahl al-Tustari*. Since 1980 he was a professor of Islamic studies at the University of Pennsylvania, Philadelphia. He wrote *The mystical vision of existence in classical Islam* (1980). DrAS, 1978 F, 1982 F; Ferahian

Bowers, John Zimmerman, born 27 August 1913 at Catonsville, Md., he was a graduate of Gettysburg College, and received his M.D. in 1938 from the University of Maryland. He was awarded an honorary doctorate by the Université d'Aix-en-Pronvence. He was a physician and educator whose writings include *Medical education in Japan* (1965). Master; WhoAm, 1974/75-1978/79

Bowett, Derek William, born 20 April 1927 at Manchester, he was educated at Downing College, Cambridge, and Manchester, where he received his Ph.D. in 1951. He was a lecturer in law at Manchester, 1951-1960, and since 1960 at Cambridge. His writings include *Self-defense in international law* (1958), *The Law of international institutions* (1963), and *The Legal regime of islands in international law* (1979). ConAu, 9-12; Who, 1989-2003

Bowie, Leland Louis, born 20th cent., he received a Ph.D. in 1970 from the University of Michigan for *The protégé system in Morocco, 1880-1904*. After conducting field work in Egypt, 1973 to 1974, he became a professor of Middle Eastern history at Temple University, Philadelphia, Pa.

Bowker, John Westerdale, born in 1935, he taught religious studies successively at Oxford, Cambridge, and Lancaster universities. Since 1984 he was Fellow and Dean, Trinity College, Cambridge. His writings include *The Targums and Rabbinic literature* (1969), *The Problems of suffering in religions of the world* (1970), and *The Meaning of death* (1991). WrDr, 1976/78-1996/98|

Bowles, Thomas Gibson, born 15 January 1842, he was educated at King's College, London. After a brief service in the Inland Revenue, he left for journalism. In 1892 he turned active politician. His writings include *Maritime warfare* (1878), and *Gibraltar; a national danger* (1901). L. E. Naylor wrote a biography, *The irrepressible Victorian, the story of T. G. Bowles, journalist, parliamentarian and founder editor of the original "Vanity fair"* (1965). He died in Algeciras, 12 January 1922. DNB; Who was who, 2

Bowman, Humphrey Ernest, born 26 July 1879, he was a graduate of Oxford, and served in the Egyptian Civil Service (1903-1923), in the Sudan, and later in Mesopotamia, and for many years in Palestine. He wrote *Middle East window* (1942). He died 23 March 1965. Who was who, 6

Bowman, Isaiah, born 26 December 1878 at Waterloo Township, Ont., he was educated in the United States and received his Ph.D. in 1909 from Yale University. He was a professor of geography at various American universities, and from 1935 until retirement in 1948, president of Johns Hopkins University, Baltimore, Md. Throughout his life he was awarded several honorary doctorates. He died 6 January 1950. Canadian, 1936/37-1948; DAB, 4; Who was who, 4; WhAm, 2

Bowman, James Edward, born 5 February 1923, he was a physician and educator who took his medical doctorate at the University of Chicago, where he later was a professor of pathology, and served on the Committee on Genetics. From 1955 to 1961 he was at the Shiraz Medical Center. WhoAm, 1976/77-1984/85

Bowman, John, born 13 May 1916 at Ayr, Scotland, he was a graduate of Glasgow University, and received a D.Phil. in 1951 from Oxford for his thesis, *The Pharisees and Rabbinic studies*. He taught Hebrew and Semitic studies at Glasgow and Leeds, before accepting an appointment as professor and chairman of the Department of Middle Eastern Studies in Melbourne University in 1959. On his retirement in 1978, he became professor emeritus. He was a founder and editor of *Abr-Nahrain*. His writings include *Samaritan documents relating to their history, religion and life* (1977). IWWAS, 1976/77; WhoAus, 1980-1997|; WhoWor, 1978-1990/91

Bowman, Thomas Sutton, he received a Ph.D. in 1925 from the University of London for his thesis, *A survey of the results of boring for oil in Egypt*. His writings include *Report on boring for oil in Egypt* (Cairo, 1925-1931). NUC, pre-1956; Sluglett

Bowman, Waldo Gleason, born 26 September 1900 at Lawrence, Kan., he was a graduate in civil engineering of the University of Kansas, and for many years an editor of *Engineering news record*, and from 1942 to 1944, a war correspondent in North Africa and the Middle East. His writings include *American military engineering in Europe* (1945). WhoAm, 1976/77

Bowra, Sir Cecil *Maurice*, born 8 April 1898 at Kiukiang (Chiu-chiang), China, he was a graduate of New College, Oxford, and an authority on classical Greek literature. His writings include *Tradition and design in the Iliad* (1939), and *Inspiration and poetry* (1955). He died 4 July 1971. Charles Drage wrote a biography, *Servants of the Dragon Throne, being the lives of Edward and Cecil Bowra* (1966). ConAu, 29-32; Iran 10 (1972), pp. iii-iv; Master (12); Who was who, 7; WhAm, 5

Bowra, Edward Charles Macintosh, born in 1841, he attended schools in Rugby, Dartford, and Swaffham. He later went to the City of London College. In 1860 he secured a place in the London Customs House, but a few months later, he abandoned his stool to volunteer to actively aid the cause of Garibaldi in Italy. In 1861 he was back in England, where he found employment with the Chinese Maritime Customs, spending the rest of his tragically short life in China. He arrived during the closing stages of the Taiping rebellion, helped General C. G. Gordon to storm Soochow; rising rapidly in the Service, he was chosen to conduct a senile and mutinous mandarin round Europe. He later organized the Chinese section of the Vienna Exhibition of 1873 and drove his frail and over-worked body to death two nights before his thirty-third birthday, 1874. BioIn 8

Boxhall, Peter, Major, fl. 1966-1974. When in the Army, he led expeditions to Socotra Islands, and Murzuk in South Libya, and later served in Muscat and Oman. After he left the Army, he was a director of Save the Children Fund in the Yemen Arab Republic. Arabian studies 1 (1974)

Boyce, Annie née Stocking, born 19th cent., she lived with her husband, the missionary Arthur Clifton Boyce, for over twenty-five years in Tehran. She was fluent in Persian and thus able to have access to Persian women of all classes. Asia, 1933

Boyce, Arthur Clifton, born 24 November 1884 at Tuscola, Illinois, he was a graduate of Lafayette College, and received a Ph.D. in 1933 from the University of Chicago for his thesis, *The comparison of two forms of Persian writing.* He was a teacher in Persia, before becoming principal of the American Boys' School in Tehran, and later vice-president of Alborz College, Tehran. He died in Duarte, California, 30 August 1959. BioIn, 5; Selim; Shavit

Boyce, Mary, born 2 August 1920 at Darjeeling, she was a graduate of Cambridge, where she took a doctorate in Oriental studies in 1952. She was a lecturer in Anglo-Saxon literature and archaeology at the Royal Holloway College, London, before she started her long and distiguished career in Iranian studies at SOAS. In 1972 she was awarded the Burton Gold Medal for work among the Zoroastrians of Iran, 1963-64. Her writings include *Catalogue of the Iranian manuscripts in Manichaean script in the German Turfan collection* (1960), *A History of Zoroastrianism* (1975), and *Zoroastrianism; its antiquity and constant vigour* (1992). BioB134; Schoeberlein

Boyd, Derek, lieutenant-colonel, born in 1913, he wrote *Royal Engineers* (London, 1975). LC

Boyd, Elizabeth Isabella Macnaghten, born 19th cent., she was an editor of the *Women's international quarterly*, of the World's Young Women's Christian Association, and she also edited *Women workers of the Orient*, by Margaret E. Burton (1920). BLC

Boyd, Harper White, born 14 September 1917 at Tampa, Fla., he was a graduate of Beliol College, and received a Ph.D. in 1952 from Northwestern University, Evanston, Illinois. Thereafter he was a professor of marketing and related subjects at various American universities. From 1960 to 1964, he was successively project director, Executive Management Program, Egypt, and consultant, Management Development Institute, Egypt. In 1995 he was Donaghey Distinguished Professor of Marketing, University of Arkansas, Little Rock. AmM&WS, 1973 S, 1978 S; ConAu 13-16; LC

Boyd, James Oscar, born 17 October 1874 at Ranway, N.J., he was a graduate of New York University, Princeton Theological Seminary, and Princeton University, where he received a Ph.D. He taught at Princeton Theological Seminary, was a pastor of a Presbytarian congregation, secretary of the American Bible Society for the Levant, and affiliated with the Young Men's Christian Association. He died 13 August 1947. WhNAA; WhAm, 2

Boyd-Orr, John, Baron, 1880-1971 *see* Orr, John Boyd, Baron Boyd Orr

Boyé, A. J., fl. 1931, he wrote *La "denuntiatio," introductive d'instance sous le principat* (Bordeaux, 1922). LC

Boyer, le Père Auguste M., S.J., fl. 1897-1906, he was a Sanskrit scholar who contributed to the *Journal asiatique* and *Muséon.* He was joint editor of *Kharosthi inscriptions discovered by Sir Aurel Stein in Chinese Turkestan* (1929). BN

Boyer, Noël, fl. 1949, he was a sometime member of the Palestine Peace Commission. Note

Boyer, Pierre Marie, born 22 November 1918 at Camarès (Aveyron), he was educated at the Faculté des lettres, and École nationale des chartes, Paris. He was *conservateur en chef* at the Archives nationale, Paris, and from 1968 until retirement, head of the Archives d'outre-mer, Aix-en-Provence. His writings include *L'Evolution de l'Algérie médiane* (1960), and *La Vie quotidienne à l'Alger* (1964). WhoFr, 1979/80-1995/96|

Boyer-Banse, L., born 19th cent., he received a doctorate in law in 1902 from the Université de Paris for his thesis, *La propriété indigène dans l'arrondissement d'Orléansville.* He was a sometime barrister in the Cour d'Appel d'Alger, and secretary of the central office of the Société de géographie d'Alger. His trace is lost after a publication in 1912. Note; NUC, pre-1956

Boyko, Konstantin Alekseevich, born 20th cent., he received a doctorate in 1978 from the Oriental Institute, Moscow, for his thesis, Арабская историческая литература в Испании.

Boylan, Patrick John, born in 1939, he was a local historian whose writings include *The Falconer papers* (1971), and he contributed to *Leicester Guildhall; a short history and guide* (1981). LC

Boyle, Frederick, born in 1841, his writings include *Camp notes; stories of sport and adventure in Asia, Africa, and America* (1874), and *The Narrative of an expelled correspondent* (1877). LC

Boyle, John Andrew, born in 1916 at Worcester Park, Sussex. After taking his first degree at the University of Birmingham, he studied Oriental languages at Berlin and London, where he received a Ph.D. in 1947 for his thesis, *Studies on the "Tarikh-i-jahan-gusha" of Juvayni.* He was head of the Department of Persian Studies in the University of Manchester, a member of the Governing Council of the British Institute of Persian Studies, and sat on the Editorial Board of the *Cambridge history of Iran* and the Advisory Board of *Iran-shenâsi*. His writings include *A Practical dictionary of the Persian language* (1949), and the translations from the Persian, *The history of the World-Conqueror* (1958), and *The Ilahi-nama; or, Book of God* (1976). He died 19 November 1978. BioB134; *Index Islamicus* (5); Private; Sluglett; WrDr, 1976/78; *Who was who*, 7

Boyle, John Edward Whiteford, born 8 March 1935 at Milwaukee, Wis., he studied in the United States, the Institut Franco-Iranien, and Tehran University. He was a journalist and a CIA executive. From 1958 to 1962 he was successively director, American Friends of the Middle East, Tehran, Tunis, and Alger, and from 1959 to 1962, member of the board of directors, Pahlavi Foundation, Tehran. His writings include *Beyond the present prospect* (1977). Master (1); WhoAm, 1992-1996; WhoWor, 1982

Bozeman, Adda Bruemmer, born 17 December 1908 at Geistershof, Latvia, she was educated at l'École libre des sciences politiques, Paris, and was a barrister-at-law in Berlin, den Haag, and London. She was a profesor of history and international relations at various American universities from 1943 until retirement in 1978, when she became professor emerita. Her writings include *Regional conflicts around Geneva* (1949), and *Strategic intelligence & statecraft* (1992). ConAu, new rev. 3; DrAS, 1974 H, 1978 H, 1982 H; IntAu&W, 1977-1991/92; Unesco; WhoAm, 1974/75-1988/89; WhoAmW, 1968/69-1974/75; WrDr, 1982/84-1998/2000

Bozer, Ali, born in 1925 at Ankara, he received a doctorate in law from the Université de Neuchâtel. He was a member of Parlaiment, and, in 1986, vice-chairman of Milliyetçi Demokrasi Partisi. His writings include *Sigorta hukuku* (1981). Kim kimdir, 1985/86-1999|

Božović, Rade, born 20th cent., he received a doctorate in 1971 from the Univerzitet u Beogradu for his thesis, *Kultura slobodnog vremena*. His writings include *Arapi u usmenoj narodnoj pesmi na srpskohrvatskom jezičkom području* (1977), and he edited *U krilu zlatna jabuka* (1988). LC

Bozzo, Anna, born 2 May 1946 at Genova, Italy, she studied at the universities of Genova and Bonn, and received a diploma in Arabic from the Pontificio Istituto di Studi Arabi e di Islamistica di Roma. She conducted field work in Algeria, and was a professor of history and institutions of the Near East and North Africa at the Facoltà di Scienze Politiche, Istituto Universitario Orientale di Napoli. Her writings include *L'Algeria nei documenti dell'Archivio di Stato di Napoli* (1992), and she contributed to *Storia dell'Africa e del Vicino Oriente* (1979). LC; Private

Braat, Wouter Cornelius, fl. 1966, he was joint author of *De Holdeurn bij Berg en Dal, centrum van pannenbakkerij* (Leiden, 1946). LC

Braatz, Werner Ernst, born in 1929, he received a Ph.D. in 1969 from the University of Wisconsin for his thesis, *Neo-conservatism in crisis at the end of the Weimar Republic*. He was a professor of history at the University of Wisconsin, Oshkosh. LC; NatFcDr, 1995-1998

Brabazon, Reginald, 12th Earl of Meath, born in 1841 at London, he was educated at Eton and subsequently went for some years to Germany. After his return, he successively served with the Foreign Office and the diplomatic service, where he remained until his retirement. Since 1873 he and his wife devoted themselves to social and philanthropic work. His writings include a collection of his articles, *Social arrows* (1886), *Memories of the nineteenth century* (1923), and *Memories of the twentieth century* (1924). He died in London in 1929. DNB; Who, 1899-1924; *Who was who* 3

Braches, Ernst, born 8 October 1930, he studied at the Universiteit van Amsterdam, where he received a doctorate in 1973. He was an *assistent* at Amsterdam from 1957 to 1965, and successively a keeper at the Leidse Universiteitsbibliotheek, the Rijksmuseum Meermanno Westraenianum Museum van het Boek, and the Universiteit van Amsterdam. His writings include *Het boek als nieuwe kunst, 1892-1903* (1973), *Engel en afgrond* (1983), and *De tijd van het boek* (1988). *Wie is wie in Nederland*, 1984/88, 1994/96

Brackenbury, Sir Henry, born 1 September 1837, he passed through the Royal Military Academy, Woolwich, and subsequently joined the Indian Civil Service, serving in India, Ashanti, Cyprus, and Zululand. He commanded the River Column, Egypt, 1884-85 and was promoted major-general for distinguished service in the field. He died in Nice, 20 April 1920. Buckland; DNB; Hill; IndianBilnd (1); Riddick

Braden, Charles Samuel, born 19 September 1887 at Chanute, Kansas, he received a Ph.D. in 1926 from Northwestern University for *Religious aspects of the conquest of Mexico*. He was a missionary from 1914 to 1925, when he was appointed professor of history and literature of religions at Northwestern University, Evanston, Illinois. On retirement he became professor emeritus. His writings include *Modern tendencies in world religions* (1933), *The world's religions* (1939), *The Scriptures of mankind* (1952), and *Christian science today* (1958). *Who was who in America*, 9

Bradley, Amos Day, born 9 October 1905 at Wakefield, Pa., he was a graduate of Pennsylvania State College, and received a Ph.D. in 1929 from Columbia University for his thesis, *The geometry of repeating design and geometry of design for high schools*. He subsequently served as a professor of mathematics at Hunter College. His writings include *Mathematics for air and marine navigation* (1942). AMS,1965; AmMWSc, 1973 P

Bradley, John Francis Nejez, born in 1930, his writings include *Civil war in Russia, 1917-1920* (1975), and *War and peace since 1945* (1989). LC

Bradley, Julia, born 27 March 1911 at Upper Hutt, New Zealand, she was a journalist, editor of weekly suburban newspapers, copywriter in advertising agency, feature writer for dailies and radio. IntAu&W, 1982

Bradley-Birt, Francis Bradley, F.R.G.S., born 25 June 1874, he was an Oxford graduate who entered the Indian Civil Service in 1898. He was assistant magistrate in Bengal, assistant director, Local Resources, Mesopotamia, and attached to the British Legation in Tehran. His writings include *The Romance of an Eastern capital* (1906), *Through Persia from the Gulf to the Caspian* (1909), *Twelve men of Bengal in the nineteenth century* (1910), and *Bengal fairy tales* (1920). He died 11 June 1963. Who was who, 6

Brady, David, born about 1945 in the UK., he was for over twenty years a librarian with special responsibility for Oriental books of the main collection in John Rylands University Library of Manchester, and a member of the Middle East Libraries Committee, U.K. His writings include *Middle Eastern and Judaic studies; a guide to research resources*, 4th ed. (1997). Private

Bragin, N. I., fl. 1966, his writings include Борьба греческого народа за свободы и независимость (Moscow, 1948). LC

Braginskii, Iosif Samuilovich, born in 1905 at Baku, he graduated in 1931 from the Moscow Oriental Institute and received a doctorate in 1954 for his thesis, Опыт исследования элементов народного поэтического творчества в памятниках древней и средневековой таджикской письменности. He was a Tajik scholar and since 1957 editor-in-chief of Народы Азии и Африки. In 1958 he was appointed professor at the Akademiia nauk Tadzhikskoi SSR. His writings include Поэты Таджикистана (1947), Иранское литературное наследие (1984), Куллият-и диван-и Рудаки (1984). In 1987 he was joint editor of Гуругли; таджикский народный эпос. His "Автобиография" was published in Восток, 1995 iv, pp. 148-156. He died 23 July 1989. EST; GSE; *Index Islamicus*, 1995, p. 7 (2); Miliband; Miliband[2]

Braginskii, Vladimir Iosifovich, born 11 January 1945 at Moscow, he graduated in 1969 from the Institute of Oriental Languages, Moscow and received his first degree in 1972 for a dissertation entitled «Основные вопросы развития повествовательных форм малайского стиха» and his doctorate in 1984 for Генезис и развитие средневековой малайсеой литературры. Since 1969 he was affilaited with an Oriental Institute. He was joint editor of Художественные традициилитерату Востока и современность (1986), and Повесть о Бах-тиаре (1989). Miliband; Miliband[2]

Brahaspati, K. C. D., born 15 January 1915 at Rampur, India, he was a musicologist, writer, and Orientalist who received a doctorate in music. He was a fellow of Sangeet Natak Academy, and from 1950 to 1965, a professor of Hindi and Dharmashastras. WhoIndia, 1970-1974/75

Brahim Seid, Joseph, 1927-1981 see Seid, Joseph Brahim

Brahmanchari, Sir Upendranath, born 7 June 1875 at Jamalpur, Bihar, he studied medicine and chemistry and received a medical doctorate in 1904. After medical research with Sir Neil Campbell in Dacca, he pursued independent kala-azar research. He died in 1946. Eminent

Braibant, Charles Maurice, born 31 March 1889 at Villemonble (Seine), he studied in Paris, where he received diplomas from the Faculté de droit, École des chartes, and École de hautes études. He was an archivist and palaeographer who was head of the Service des archives et bibliothèques de la Marine from 1919 to 1944, when he was appointed director of Archives de France. His writings include essays, historical studies, and belles-lettres. He died 23 April 1976. WhoFr, 1963/64-1975/76

Braibant, Guy Maurice, born 5 September 1927 at Paris, he was a graduate of l'École nationale d'administration and l'Institut d'études politiques, Paris. He served as *auditeur* at the Conseil d'État, and since 1977 as a professor at the Institut d'études politiques. His writings include *La Planification en Tchécoslovaquie* (1948). WhoFr, 1975/76-2002/2003; WhoWor, 1990/91

Braibanti, Ralph John D., born 29 June 1920 at Danbury, Conn., he was a graduate of Western Connecticut State College, and received a Ph.D. in 1949 from Syracuse University. He taught political science at Kenyon College until 1953, when he was appointed a professor, and, since 1977, director of Islamic and Arabian development studies in Duke University, Durham, N.C. Concurrently, he was from 1960 to 1962 chief adviser to the Civil Service Academy, Lahore. His writings include *Research on the bureaucracy of Pakistan* (1966). WhoAm, 1982-1988/89; WhoWor, 1984/85

Braig, Carl (Karl), born 19 February 1853 at Kanzbach, Germany, he studied at the Universität Tübingen and became first a pastor in Wildbach and then successively a professor of philosophy and theology at the Universität Freiurg im Breisgau, where he died 24 March 1923. DtBE

Brailsford, Henry Noel, born in 1873 at Mirfield, Yorkshire, he was educated at Glasgow, where he was a sometime professor of logic, before becoming lead-writer for a number of British newspapers. From 1897 to 1918 he was variously engaged in political and humanitarian affairs in the Balkans. His writings include *Macedonia* (1906), and *Rebel India* (1931). He died 23 March 1958. Master (10); Who was who, 5

Brain, Belle Marvel, born 4 August 1859 at Springfield, Ohio, she was an educator, missionary, and associate editor of the *Missionary review of the world*, 1914-1917. Her writings include *Fifty missionary programmes* (1901), and *From every tribe and nation* (1927). She died in Schenectady, N.Y., 25 May 1933. DcNAA; Master (5); WhAm, 1

Brain, Robert John, born in 1933 at Hobart, Tasmania, he was a graduate of the University of Tasmania, and received a Ph.D. from University College, London, where he was appointed lecturer in anthropology in 1965. His writings include *Bangwa kinship and marriage* (1972), *Into the primitive environment* (1972), *Friends and lovers* (1976), *The Tribal impulse* (1976), and *The Decorated body* (1979). ConAu 73-76; WhoWor, 1980/81

Brakel, Lode Frank, born about 1940, he was a sometime professor at the Universität Hamburg. His writings include *The Hikayat Muhammad Hanafiyyah, a medieval Muslim-Malay romance* (1975), and *The poems of Hamzah Fansuri* (1986). He died at age forty, 4 June 1981. LC

Bräker, Hans Gerhard, born 25 April 1921 at Seehausen, Germany, he received a Dr.phil. in 1950 from der Universität Göttingen for his thesis, *A. L. v. Schlözers Rußland- und Slavenbild*. Since 1961 he was a director, Bundesinstitut für Ostwissenschaftliche und Internationale Studien, Köln. He wrote *Es wird kein Frieden sein; der islamische Orient …* (1992). His numerous brief studies include *Islam - Sozialismus - Kommunismus* (1968). He died 11 August 1997. Kürschner, 1980-1996|

Brambach, Wilhelm, born 17 December 1841 at Bonn, Germany, he studied philology and music at Bonn, where he received a Dr.phil. in 1864 for his thesis, *De consulatus romani mutata inde a Caesaris temporibus ratione prolusio*. Thereafter he was an assistant at the university library. In 1866 he was appointed a lecturer in classical philology at the Universität Freiburg im Breisgau. Since 1872 he was a director, Badische Hof- und Landesbibliothek, Karlsruhe. In his later years he was head of the Münz-Kabinett in Karlsruhe, where he died 26 February 1932. DtBE; Master

Brambeus, Baron, pseud., 1800-1858 *see* Senkovskii, Osip Ivanovich

Brame, Michael Keith, born in 1944, he received a Ph.D. in 1970 from M.I.T. for *Arabic phonology*. In 1998 he was teaching linguistics at the University of Washington at Seattle, a post which he still held in 2003. His writings include *Conjectures and refutations in syntax and semantics* (1976). He contributed to *Semantics and grammatical theory* (1978), and jointly edited *A Festschrift for Sol Saporta* (1986). LC; NatFacDr, 1998-2003

Brammer, Lawrence Martin, born 20 August 1922 at Crookston, Minn., he was a graduate of St. Cloud State University, and received a Ph.D. in 1950 from Stanford University. Since 1964 he was an educational psychologist at the University of Washington. His writings include *Therapeutic psychology* (1960), and *The Helping relationship* (1973). AmM&WS, 1973 S, 1978 S; WhoAm, 1984-1988/89

Bramsen, John, born 18th cent., he wrote *Letters of a Prussian traveller; description of a tour through Sweden, Prussia, Austria, Hungary, Istria, the Ionian Islands, Egypt, Syria, Cyprus, Rhodes, the Morea, Greece, Calabria, Italy, the Tyrol, the banks of the Rhine, Hannover, Holstein, Denmark, Westphalia, and Holland* (1818), and its partial translation, *Reise durch die Ionischen Inseln, Aegypten, Syrien und Palästina* (1819). LC

Brand, Charles Macy, born 7 April 1932 at Stanford, Cal., he was a graduate of Stanford, and received a Ph.D. in 1961 from Harvard University for *Byzantium and the West*. After teaching history for two years at San Francisco State College, he successively was a professor and chairman, Department of History, Bryn Mawr College. His writings include *Byzantium confronts the West, 1180-1204* (1968), and *Icon and minaret* (1969). ConAu 21-24; DrAS, 1974 H - 1982 H; WhoAm, 1984-1988/89; WhoE, 1986-1991/92

Brandel-Syrier, Mia (Miya), fl. 1947, her writings include *Black woman in search of God* (London, 1962), and she translated *The Religious duties of Islam as taught and explained by Abu Bakr Effendi* (Leiden, 1960). LC

van den **Branden**, Albertus, he was affiliated with the Institut orientaliste in the Université de Louvain, Belgium. His writings include *Les Inscriptions thamoudéennes de Philby* (1950), *Histoire de Thamoud* (1960), and *Les Inscriptions dédaniets* (1962). LC

Brandenburg, Dietrich, born in 1928, he was an ophthalmologist and Orientalist whose writings include *Islamische Baukunst in Ägypten* (1966), *Priesterärzte und Heilkunst im alten Persien* (1969), *Der Tâj Mahâl* (1969), *Die Baumeister des Propheten* (1971), *Medizinisches bei Herodot* (1976), *Islamic miniature painting in medieval manuscripts* (1982), and *Die Ärzte des Propheten* (1992). He died at the age of sixty-six in Berlin, 28 December 1994. LC

Brandenburg, Erich, born 10 September 1877 at Danzig, Germany, he studied at Berlin, München, Genève, and Marburg, where he received a Dr.phil. in 1906 for *Über praehistorische Grotten in Phrygien*. He was a professor at Leipzig, and an editor of the *Historische Vierteljahrschrift*. He travelled in Greater Syria before the first Wold War. His writings include *Über Felsarchitektur im Mittelmeergebiet* (1915), and *Die Felsarchitektur bei Jerusalem* (1926). He died in 1936. Kürschner, 1925-1935; LC

Brandes, Georg Morris Cohen, born 4 February 1842 at København, he studied law and philosophy and received a gold medal of the University in 1862 for his treatise, *Die Schicksalsidee der Alten*, as well as a considerable travel grant. Since 1870 he was a literary critic and a professor in Denmark, Norway, and Germany. His writings include *Main currents in nineteenth century literature* (1901-1905), *Reminiscences of my childhood and youth* (1906), and *The World at war* (1917). He died in København, 19 February 1927. DanskBK; DanskBL²; EncAm; EncJud; Wininger

Brandes, Jan Laurens Andries, born 13 January 1857 at Rotterdam, he studied theology at Amsterdam and Oriental languages at the Rijksuniversiteit te Leiden, where he received a doctorate in 1884 for his thesis, *Bijdrage tot de vergljkende klankleer westersche afdeeling van de Maleisch-Polynesische taalfamilie*. The same year he left for Java. His writings on Malayan and comparative literatures include studies on *Kalilah wa-Dimnah*, the *Ten Viziers*, and the *Tuti-namah*. He died in Batavia, 26 June 1905. Bezemer; EncNI

Brandl, Ludwig, fl. 1975, he was a clergyman who wrote *Ärzte und Medizin in Afrika* (1966), its translation, *A Short history of medicine in Africa* (197-?), and he was joint editor of *Kirche in der Gesellschaft; Dimensionen der Seelsorge* (1992). LC

Brandl, Rudolf Maria, born 1 July 1943 at Stockerau, Austria, he received a Dr.phil. in 1970 and was since 1982 a professor of musicology at the Universität Göttingen. Kürschner, 1987-2003

Brandon Oscar Henry, born 9 March 1916 at Reichenberg (Liberec), Austria, he was a journalist and lecturer, and awarded an honorary doctorate. From 1939 to 1982, he was an associate editor for the *Sunday Times* of London. His writings include *As we are* (1961), *Anatomy of error* (1969), *The Retreat of American power* (1973), and *Special relationships* (1988). He died 20 April 1993. BlueB, 1976; ConAu 49-52; IntAu&W, 1989-1993; IntWW, 1975-1991/92; Who, 1985-1993; WrDr, 1980/82-1990/92

Brands, Horst Wilfrid, born 22 May 1922 at Bad Oeynhausen, Germany, he received a Dr.phil. in 1952 from the Universität Marburg for *Azerbaidschanisches Volksleben und modernistische Tendenz in den Schauspielen Mirza Feth-'Ali Ahundzadehs*. He was head of the Oriental Department at the Frankfurt University Library, before he was successively professor of Turkish studies at Gießen, Mainz, and Frankfurt am Main. His writings include *Studien zum Wort-bestand der Türksprachen* (1973). Kürschner, 1976-2003; Schwarz

Brandt, Jürgen, born 4 November 1935 at Berlin, he studied at the Universität Leipzig, to which one year was added at the Institute of Oriental languages at the Moscow State Lomonosov University, 1961-62. He received doctorates from the Universität Leipzig for his theses, *Die Politik des französischen Imperialismus in Syrien und Libanon* (1966), and *Syrien/Libanon - Renaissance einer nationalen Identität* (1980). Since 1963 he was attached to Orientalisches Institut in der Universität Leipzig. He probably lost his tenure after German re-unification in 1992. Kürschner, 1992|; Sezgin; Thesis

von **Brandt**, Max August Scipio, born 8 August 1835 at Berlin, he served in the Prussian Army and entered the diplomatic service and serving as consul and ambassador in Japan and China. His writings include *Die englische Kolonialpolitik und Kolonialverwaltung* (1906), and his autobiography, *Dreiunddreißig Jahre in Ost-Asien* (1901). He died in Weimar, 24 March 1920. DtBE; DtBIlnd (6)

Branellec, René, fl. 1953, he travelled extensively in the Near and Middle East as well as in India. Note

Brann, Markus, born 9 July 1849 at Rawicz (Posen), Prussia, he was a rabbi in Breslau and Pless, before being appointed a professor of exegesis and history at the Jüdisch-theologische Seminar, Breslau. He was for many years the editor of the *Monatsschrift für Geschichte und Wissenschaft des Judentums*. His writings include *Geschichte der Juden in Schlesien* (1896-1917). He died in Breslau, 28 September 1920. DtBE; EncJud; Wininger

Brant, James, born about 1800, he was a British vice-consul in Trabzon, 1830, consul in Erzerum, 1836, and in Damascus from 1856 until retirement in 1860. Twice, in 1835 and 1838, he explored Armenia and eastern Turkey from Batum to the confluence of the Euphrates and Murat rivers, as far west as Kayseri. He died in Cliftonville, Brighton, 24 November 1861. Boase; Henze

Braquehaye, Charles, born 19th cent., he was affiliated with the Ministère de l'instruction publique, and a corresponding member of the Comité des sociétés des beaux-arts, Bordeaux. His trace is lost after a publication in 1907. Note

Brásio, António Duarte, born in 1905 at Penela, he studied at Coimbra, and was ordained in 1932. Thereafter he was a professor at the Colégio Missionário de Godim (Régua) and Viana. His writings include *A Missão e Seminário da Huíla* (1940), *Os prêtos em Portugal* (1944), and *História e missiologia* (1973), and he edited *Monumenta missionaria africana* (1952-71). In 1989 appeared the commemorative volume, *Elogio do Padre António Brásio*. He died in 1985. LC; *Quem é alguém (Who's who in Portugal)*, 1947

Braslavski, Joseph, born in 1896 in the Ukraine, he came to Palestine as a young boy. In 1927 he went to Berlin to study Semitics. On his return he became a lecturer in geography at the Teachers' Seminary in Tel Aviv. He wrote on topography, archaeology, and the physical geography of Palestine. He died in 1972. EncJud; LC; WhoIsrael, 1952

Brass, Adolf, born 13 June 1888 at Eindhoven, the Netherlands, he studied at München and Bonn, where he received a Dr.phil. in 1919 for *Eine neue Quelle zur Geschichte des Fulreiches Sokoto*. Sezgin; Thesis

Brass, Paul Richard, born 8 November 1936 at Boston, Mass., he was a Harvard graduate who received his Ph.D. in 1964 from the University of Chicago for his thesis, *The Congress Party organization in Uttar Pradesh*. Since 1965 he was a professor of political science and Asian studies at the University of Washington, Seattle, a post he still held in 1998. His writings include *Factional politics in an Indian state* (1965), and *Language, religion and politics in North India* (1974). American men and women of science, 1973 S, 1978 S; ConAu 17-20; NatFacDr, 1995-1998

Braswell, George Wilbur, born 30 May 1936 at Emporia, Va., he was a professor of Church history at Southeastern Baptist Theological Seminary, Wake Forest, N.C., a post he still held in 1998. His writings include *To ride a magic carpet* (1977), and *Understanding world religions* (1983). ConAu, 112; DrAS, 1982; NatFacDr, 1995-1998

Brătianu, Gheorghe Ioan, born in 1898 at Ruginoasa, Romania, he was a historian and politician whose writings include *Énigme et un miracle historique; le peuple romain* (1937), *Études byzantines d'histoire économique et sociale* (1938), *Die geschichtliche Missions Ungarns* (1941), and *La Mer Noire* (1969). He died 1953 in Iaşi. DcEnc; MicDcEn; WhoRom

Braude, Benjamin, born 18 October 1945 at Providence, R.I., he was a graduate of Harvard, where he also received his Ph.D. in 1978. Since 1978 he was a professor of history at Boston College, Chestnut Hill, Mass., a post which he still held in 2003. He was joint editor of *Christians and Jews in the Ottoman Empire* (1982). ConAu 111; LC; NatFacDr, 1995-2003

Braudel, Fernand Paul, born 24 August 1902 at Luméville (Meuse), he studied at the Faculté des lettres de Paris, where he received his doctorate in history. He was a professor at Alger, 1924 to 1932, and then taught at various Parisian institutions. He was a historian of international reputation, whose works have been translated into many languages. He was awarded more than ten honorary doctorates and was a member of many prestigious academies and learned societies. His writings include *Civilisation matérielle, économie et capitalisme* (1967). He died 28 November 1985. WhoFr, 1975/76-1985/86

Brault, Julien, born 16 November 1862 at Rennes (Ille-et-Vilaine), he studied medicine at l'Université de Paris, served for a short period as a military physician, and since 1897 taught tropical medicine at Alger. His writings include *Hygiène et prophylaxie des maladies dans les pays chauds* (1900), and *Pathologie et hygiène des indigènes musulmans d'Algérie* (1905). He died in 1916. DBF

Braum, Harald Erich, born 1 June 1893 at Wien, he studied law and Oriental languages at the Universität Wien, where he took a Dr.jur. and thereafter was affiliated with the Handelsmuseum, before being appointed a professor at the Wirtschaftsuniversität, Wien. Wer ist's, 1922, 1935; WhoAustria, 1954

Braun, Dieter, he wrote *Deutsche Kulturpolitik im Ausland* (1966). LC

Braun, Edmund Wilhelm, born 23 January 1870 at Epfenbach, Germany, he studied at Freiburg, Leipzig, and Heidelberg, where he received a Dr.phil. in 1895 for *Ein Trierer Sacramentar vom Ende des X. Jahrhunderts*. He was a sometime director of the Schlesisches Landesmuseum, and the Kaiser Franz Josef Museum, Troppau, and editor of its *Mitteilungen*. He was joint author of *Kunst und Kultur in Böhmen, Mähren und Schlesien; Ausstellung im Germanischen National-Museum zu Nürnberg* (1955). Jacksch; Wer ist's, 1922, 1935

Braun, Fernand, born 13 May 1882 at Alexandria, Egypt, he studied at l'École française de droit, Cairo, and the Faculté de droit, Paris, where he received a doctorate. He was a barrister in the Mixed Court of Appeal, Alexandria, editor-in-chief of the *Journal du Caire*, founding director of the *Revue d'Egypt et d'Orient*, 1900-1914, and secretary general of the Association France-Égypte. His writings include *Le Régime des sociétés par action aux États-Unis* (1924). WhoFr, 1953/54-1959/60|

Braun, Frank Hans, born in 1940, he received a Ph.D. in 1971 from the University of Texas at Austin for his thesis, *The role of the intelligentsia in modernization; the case study of Morocco*. LC

Braun, Fritz, born 27 November 1873 at Danzig, Germany, he started life as a school teacher in Constantinople, 1900-1905. After his return home, he continued to teach in various towns, and distinguished himself as a local historian. His writings include *Orientalische Landschaften* (1906), *Landeskunde der Provinz Westpreußen* (1912), *Der neue Balkan* (1913), and *Ostmärkische Städte und Landschaften* (1914). He died in Danzig, 22 January 1931. Altpreuß

Braun, Hellmut, born 27 July 1913 at Saronno, Italy, he studied Oriental languages, religion, and history at the Auslandshochschule Berlin, and received a Dr.phil. in 1946 from the Universität Göttingen for his thesis, *Ahval-e Šah Isma'il*. He was a librarian, head of department, and professor at Hamburg. He was responsible for the German romanization schedules for the Islamic languages, including Kurdish, Pashto, and Urdu. JahrDtB, 1959-1997/98; Kürschner, 1996-2003; Schwarz

von **Braun**, Joachim, born 10 July 1950, his writings include *Ernährungssicherungspolitik in Entwicklungsländern; ökonomische Analyse am Beispiel Ägyptens* (1984), and he was joint authour of *The effects of food price and subsidy policies on Egyptian agriculture* (1983). LC

Braun, Julius, born 16 July 1825 at Karlsruhe, Germany, he studied theology, philology, and history of art from 1850 to 1853. He subsequently travelled in Egypt, Syria, and Greece, before being appointed professor successively at Heidelberg, Tübingen, and München. His writings include *Naturgeschichte der Sage* (1864), *Gemälde der mohammedanischen Welt* (1870), and *Geschichte der Kunst in ihrem Entwicklungsgang durch alle Völker der Alten Welt* (1873). He died in 1869. DtBE

Braun, Karl *Ferdinand*, born 6 June 1850 at Fulda, Germany, he was a physicist who, together with Marconi, was awarded the 1909 Nobel Prize for Physics. Friedrich Kurylo wrote a biography, *Ferdinand Braun, Leben und Wirken des Erfinders der Braunschen Röhre* (1965). He died in Brooklyn, N.Y., 20 April 1918. EncAm; DtBE

Braun, Maximilian, born 6 November 1903 at St. Petersburg, Russia, he received a Dr.phil. in 1934 from the Universität Leipzig for his thesis, *Die Anfänge der Europäisierung im Kunstschrifttum der moslimischen Slaven in Bosnien und Herzegovina*. He was a professor of Slavic studies and chairman of the Seminar für Slavische Philologie, Göttingen. His writings include *Der Aufstieg Rußlands vom Wikingerstaat zur europäischen Großmacht* (1940), and *Russische Dichtung im neunzehnten Jahrhundert* (1947). He died in Göttingen, 17 July 1984. Kürschner, 1940/41-1983

Braun, Ursula, born in 1937, she studied law and political science at Hamburg, Cambridge, and den Haag. Between 1961 and 1972 she repeatedly visited the Arab countries, delivering guest lectures at Rabat. She was a free lance consultant to the Stiftung Wissenschaft und Politik, Ebenhausen, and a trustee of the Deutsche Orient-Stiftung. Her writings include *Nord- und Südjemen im Spannungsfeld interner und globaler Gegensätze* (1981), and *Der Kooperationsrat Arabischer Staaten am Golf* (1986). In 1993 she was a member of the British Society for Middle Eastern Studies. EURAMES; LC

Braune, Walther, born 20 October 1900 at Brandenburg, Germany, he received a Dr.phil. in 1928 from the Universität Königsberg for his thesis, *Die Futuh al-gaib des 'Abd al-Qadir*. He was for many years a professor of divinity at Berlin. His writings include *Der islamische Orient zwischen Gegenwart und Zukunft* (1960). He died in 1988. Kürschner, 1950-1992; Private

Brauner, Siegmund, born 23 March 1934 at Burkartshain, Germany, he studied at Leipzig where he received a Dr.phil. in 1960. He was successively a professor, and director, Institut für Afrikanistik, Leipzig. His writings include *Lehrbuch des modernen Swahili* (1979), and he was joint author of *Lehrbuch der Hausa-Sprache* (1966). Kürschner, 1996-2003

Braunholtz, Hermann Justus, born 12 October 1888 at Cambridge, where he attended the University. He was a keeper at the Department of Ethnography in the British Museum, London, a sometime president of the Royal Anthropological Institute, and editor of its *Journal*. He died 4 June 1963. Unesco; WhE&EA; *Who was who*, 6

Bräunlich, Erich, born 15 September 1892 at Hamburg, he received a Dr.phil. from the Universität Leipzig in 1921 for his thesis, *The well in ancient Arabia*. He was a professor at Leipzig, Greifswald, Königsberg, and Leipzig, where he was successively acting chairman of the Oriental Institute, and dean of the Faculty of Philosophy. For a number of years he was an editor of *Islamica*. His writings include *Bistam ibn Qais, ein vorislamischer Beduinenfürst und Held* (1923). It is said that he died of a malignant disease in a Yugoslav prisoner of war camp only days before his fifty-third birthday in 1945. Fück, p. 310; Kürschner, 1940/41; WhE&EA; ZDMG 100 (1950), pp. 37-41

Braunthal, Julius, born 5 May 1891 at Wien, he started life as a bookbinder in Austria. After the first Wold War he entered the public service, and from 1920 to 1934 he was a political editor. In his British exile he was a foreign editor and later affiliated with the Socialist International. His writings include *History of the International* (1966). He died in 1972. ConAu, P 2; EncJud; LC

Brausch, Georges E. J.-B., born 31 October 1915 at Nottingham, UK., he received a doctorate in 1953 from the Université libre de Bruxelles. He was a sometime reader in social anthropolgohy and sociology at the University of Khartoum, and a *directeur d'études* at the Université libre de Bruxelles. His writings include *Bashqara area settlements, 1963; a case study in village development in the Gezira scheme* (1964); he was joint author of *Belgian administration in the Congo* (1961). LC; Unesco

Brauw-Hay, Elizabeth A. de *see* De Brauw-Hay, Elizabeth A.

Bravmann, Meier Max, born 3 July 1909 at Eppingen, Germany, he studied Semitic philology, Assyriology, Persian, and philosophy and received a Dr.phil. in 1934 from the Universität Breslau for his thesis, *Materialien und Untersuchungen zu den phonetischen Lehren der Araber.* His writings include *Studies in Arabic and general syntax* (1953), *The Arabic elative* (1968), *The spiritual background of early Islam* ((1972), and *Studies in Semitic philology* (1977). Thesis

Bravo Villasante, Carmen Ruiz, *see* Ruiz Bravo Villasante, Carmen

Brawer, Moshe, born 3 November 1919 at Wien, he was educated at Jerusalem and received his Ph.D. in 1959 from the University of London for his thesis, *The frontiers of Israel.* Since 1969 he was a professor of geography at Tel Aviv University. His writings include *Gevul ha-tsafon shel Erets-Israel* (1970). Sluglett; WhoWorJ, 1972, 1987

Bray, Sir Denys de Saumarez, born 29 November 1875, he was a graduate of Balliol College, Oxford, who entered the Indian Civil Service in 1898 and served in the Punjab, the North-West Frontier, and Baluchistan, where he conducted the first complete census. His writings include *The Brahui language* (1909-34), *Statistical analysis of the tribes of Baluchistan* (1911), and *The Life story of a Brahui* (1913). He died 19 November 1951. IndianBilnd (3); WhE&EA; *Who was who*, 5

Brayer, A., born about 1775 in France, he was a physician who wrote *Neuf ans à Constantinople; observations sur la topographie de cette capitale, l'hygiène et les mœrs de ses habitants, l'islamisme et son influence* (Paris, 1836), and *Médecine simplifié* (1841). He died in 1848. BN; Dezobry; Oursel

Bréal, Michel Jules Alfred, born 26 March 1832 at Landau, Germany, he studied at Weißenburg, Metz, Paris, and Berlin, and was successively affiliated with the Lycée Louis-le-Grand, Département des manuscrits à la Bibliothèque royale, Collège de France, and École pratique des hautes études, Paris. His writings include *Mélanges de mythologie et de linguistique* (1877). He died 28 November 1915. Curinier, vol. 3 (1901), p. 244; DBF; PorLing, vol. 1, pp. 440-453 (2); Vapereau; Wininger

Breasted, James Henry, born 27 August 1865 at Rockford, Illinois, he started life as a clerk in local drugstores, before studying at Yale and Berlin. He later became an outstanding Egyptologist and held several academic posts of distinction, notably in the University of Chicago, where he was a director of the Oriental Institute. His writings include *The Dawn of conscience* (1933), and *Ancient times; a history of the early world* (1935). He died in N.Y.C., 2 December 1935. Dawson; Egyptology; Hill; Master (20); Shavit; *Who was who*, 3; WhAm, 1

Breccia, Alessandro, Dr. He wrote *Il porto d'Alessandria d'Egitto* (Le Caire, Société royale de géographie d'Egypte, 1927). LC

Breccia, Annibale *Evaristo*, born 18 July 1876 at Offagna (Ancona), he studied ancient history at Roma and then became a director of the Graeco-Roman Museum in Alexandria, Egypt until 1931, when he accepted the chair of classical antiquity in the Università di Pisa. He was a president of the University when he retired in 1941. His writings include *Municipalité d'Alexandrie* (1914), and *Con sua Maestà il Re Fuad all'oasi di Ammone* (1929). He died in Roma, 28 July 1967. Chi è, 1928-1961; DizBI; Egyptology; Wholtaly, 1957/58

Brecher, Irving, born 1 February 1923 at Montreal, P.Q., he was a graduate of McGill University, Montreal, and received his Ph.D. in 1951 from Harvard. He was a professor of economics at various American universities, and since 1985, professor emeritus, McGill University. From 1960 to 1961 he was joint director of the Pakistan Institute for Development Economics, Karachi. He was joint author of *Foreign aid and industrial development in Pakistan* (1972). Canadian, 1997-2002; WhoAm, 1984-2003

Brecher, Kenneth, born 7 December 1943 at NYC., he was a graduate of M.I.T., and became a research physicist and professor of astronomy and physics at various American universities. WhoAm, 1986/87

Brecher, Michael, born 14 March 1925 at Montreal, he was a graduate of McGill University, Montreal, and received a Ph.D. in 1953 from Yale University for his thesis, *The struggle for Kashmir*. Thereafter he was for over ten years a professor of international relations in the Department of Political Science, McGill University. His writings include *Decisions in Israel's foreign policy* (1974), and, with Benjamin Geist, *Decisions in crisis* (1980). Canadian, 1958-2002; DrASCan, 1983; IWWAS, 1975/76

Breck, Allen duPont, born 21 May 1914 at Denver, Colo., he received a Ph.D. in 1950 from the University of Colorado. Since 1946 he was a professor in the Department of History, the University of Colorado, Denver. His writings include *The Centennial history of the Jews of Colorado* (1960). ConAu, 13-16; DrAS, 1969 H, 1974 H, 1978 H; WhoAm, 1974-2003; WhoWest, 1974-1989/90

Breck, Joseph, born 3 February 1885 at Allston, Mass., he was a Harvard graduate who also studied art in Europe, 1907-1908. He became a curator and director of museums in Minneapolis and N.Y.C. He published museum guides and catalogues, and was a joint author of *The James F. Ballard Collection of Oriental rugs* (1923). He died 2 August 1933. Who was who in America, 1

Breckenridge, James Douglas, born 8 August 1926 at N.Y.C., he was a graduate of Cornell University, Ithaca, N.Y., and received his Ph.D. from Princeton University. He was a professor of history of art at Johns Hopkins University, Baltimore, Md., and later at Northwestern University. He died in 1982. DrAS, 1982; LC; WhoAmArt, 15th ed., 1982

Breckle, Siegmar Walter, born 27 February 1938, he was a scholar of bionomics, in particular of the Muslim world. He was joint author of *Tropical and subtropical zonobiomes* (1986). In 1983 he edited the collective work, *Forschungen in und über Afghanistan*. Kürschner, 1987-2003; LC

Bredero, Adriaan Hendrik, born in 1921, he was a professor of medieval history at the Vrije Universiteit te Amsterdam until his retirement in 1986. His writings include *Bernhard von Clairvaux im Widerstreit der Historie* (1966), and *Clung et Cîtaux au douxième siècle; l'histoire d'une controverse monastique* (Amsterdam, 1985). Brinkman's, 1986-1990

Bredi, Daniela, fl. 1976, her writings include *Il trattato libico-marocchino del 13 agosto 1984* (Pisa, 1984). ZKO

Bredin, George Richard Frederick, born in 1899, he was an Oxford graduate who entered the Sudan Political Service in 1921. From 1941 to 1948 he was Governor of Blue Nile Province, and served on the Governor-general's Council, 1943-1948. He was also chairman, Gordon Memorial College Trust Fund. Upon his return to England, he was a university administrator. He died 30 September 1983. Who was who, 8

Breebaart, Deodaat Anne, born in 1927, she received a Ph.D. in 1961 from Princeton University for *The develop-ment and structure of the Turkish futuwah guilds*. NUC, 1956-67

Breese, Gerald William, born 4 June 1912 at Horseheads, N.Y., he was a Yale graduate who received his Ph.D. in 1947 from the University of Chicago. He was a professor of sociology at Princeton from 1959 to 1977, when he became professor emeritus. His writings include *Urbanization in newly developing countries* (1966), and *Urban Southeast Asia; a selected bibliography* (1973). He died in 1995. BlueB, 1973/74, 1975, 1976; Master (2); WhoAm, 1974-1988; WrDr, 1982-1998/2000

Bregel', IUrii Enokhovich, born 13 November 1925 at Moscow, where he was educated and also received his doctorate in 1961. From 1956 to 1973 he was affiliated with the Oriental Institute, Soviet Academy of Science. His writings include Хорезмикие туркмены в XIX веке (1961), Пословицы и поговорки народов Востока (1961), Документы архива хивинских ханов по истории и *этнографии Каракалпаков* (1967), and *The role of Central Asia in the history of the Muslim East* (1980). In 1988 he edited *Firdaws al-iqbal; history of Khorezmi*. He was also the translator of C.A. Storey's *Persian literature* into Russian. LC; Miliband²; Schoeberlein

Bréhier, Louis, born 5 August 1868 at Brest, he taught a various *lycées* before he accepted in 1900 the chair of history of antiquity and the middle ages at the Faculté des lettres de Clermont-Ferrand. Since 1925 he was a member of the Académie des inscriptions. His writings include *L'Église et l'Orient au moyen âge* (1907), and *Grégoire le grand, les états barbares et la conquête arabe* (1938). He died in Reims, 13 October 1951. BioIn, 3; DBF; *Isis* 43 (1952), p. 55

Brehm, Alfred Edmund, born 2 February 1829 at Renthendorf, Germany, he was a naturalist who, from 1847 to 1854, travelled extensively in Egypt, Nubia, the Sudan, Spain, and Siberia. He became successively director of the Zoologischer Garten, Hamburg, and the Aquarium, Berlin. His writings include *Reise-Skizzen aus Nord-Ost-Afrika* (1855-63). He died in his home town, 11 November 1884. Embacher; EncAm; GSE; Henze; Hill

Breil, Jacques, born 25 March 1918 at Brie (Ariège), he studied at Toulouse and Paris, and became an administrator at the Service national des statistiques, a sometime director of the Service statistique de l'Algérie, and a professor at the Faculté de droit d'Alger. Since the 1960s he was a business executive. He wrote *La Population des départements algériens* (1955). Unesco; WhoFr, 1973/74-1981/82|

von **Breitenbach**, Bernhard, ca. 1440-1497 *see* Breydenbach, Bernhard von

Brémard, Frédéric, fl. 1951, he received a doctorate in law and wrote *L'Organisation régionale du Maroc* (1949), and *Les Droits publics et politiques des Français au Maroc* (1950). LC

Brémond, Edouard, born in 1868, he was an Arabist. As a lieutenant-colonel he was *sous-chef d'état-major* with the 35th Army Corps, in the capacity of which he became acquainted with the Islamic world in North Africa. In 1916 he was head of the French military mission to Jiddah, and from 1919 to 1920 he was chief administrator in Cilicia. After his return to France he advanced to the rank of general and became affiliated with the Centre des Hautes Études Militaires. His writings include *Le Hedjaz dans la guerre mondiale* (1931), and *Berbères et Arabes* (1942). *Bulletin de la Société de géographie d'Oran* 76 (1953), pp. 41-42

Brend, Barbara, born 16 February 1940 at London, she was a graduate of Newnham College, Cambridge. For her 1987 Ph.D. from SOAS, she received the Frederick Richter Memorial Prize. She was a free lance researcher and lecturer at the British Museum and the British Library, specializing in Persian, Mughal, and Ottoman painting. Her writings include *Islamic art* (1991). LC; Private

Brendemoen, Bernt, born in 1949, his writings include *Tyrkisk-norsk ordbok* (1980), and he was joint editor of *Riepmočála, essays in honour of Knut Bergsland* (1984). LC

Brendl, Oskar, born in 1910, he wrote *Die Bundes-Republik Kamerun; eine historisch-wirtschafts-geographische Studie* (Hagen, 1965). LC

Brenez, J., fl. 1971, he was a sometime professor at the Société pour le développement économique et sociale. He wrote the report, *Enquête démographique en Mauritanie, 1964-1965* (1966). LC

Brenner, Henricus, fl. 1724, he was the editor of *Epitome commentariorum Moysis Armeni* (1723). BLC

Brenner, Louis, born 19 June 1937 at Memphis, Tenn., he was a graduate of the University of Wisconsin, and received a Ph.D. in 1968 from Columbia University for his thesis, *The Shehus of Kukawa; a history of the al-Kanemi dynasty of Bornu*. From 1967 to 1980 he was a professor at the African Studies Center, Boston University. His writings include *Originality of thought and method in West African Islamic teaching* (1980), *The West African Sufi* (1984), *Réflexions sur le savoir islamique en Afrique de l'ouest* (1985); and he was joint author of *Inventaire de la Bibliothèque 'umarienne de Ségou conservée à la Bibliothèque Nationale, Paris* (1985). DrAS, 1974 H, 1978 H, 1982 H; LC

Brenner, Richard, born 20 June 1833 at Merseburg, Germany, he was a forest ranger who took part in the East African expedition under C. C. von der Decken, 1864-1865. From 1870 to 1871 he carried on commercial reconnaissance along the coast of East Africa, South Arabia, and the Persian Gulf. In 1871 he was appointed Austrian consul at Aden. He died in Zanzibar, 22 March 1874. ADtB; Embacher; Henze

Brenner, Yehojachin Simon, born 24 December 1926 at Berlin, he studied at the universities of Basel, Jerusalem, and London. He was a professor of economics, and a university administrator in various capacities in Ghana, Turkey, and the Netherlands. Since 1972 he was a professor at the Rijksuniversiteit te Utrecht. His writings include *Theories of economic development and growth* (1966), *Capitalism, competition and economic crisis* (1984), *Maatschappelijk klimaat en economisch elan* (1990), *The*

Rise and fall of capitalism (1991); and he was joint editor of *Visies op verdeling* (1986). ConÄu, 21-24, new rev., 11; IntAU&W, 1989; Wie is wie, 1994/96; WrDr, 1976-1998/2000

Brentjes, Burchard, born 20 February 1929 at Halle, he attended a local middle school, including grades six to ten. At the age of sixteen he joined the Communist Party, and became secretary of the Party's youth wing. After a make-up semester at the Universität, he was from 1946 to 1952 a regular student in archaeology, receiving a Dr.phil. in 1953 for *Untersuchungen zur Geschichte des Pfluges*. From 1960 until retirement in 1994, he was a professor of Middle Eastern archaeology at Halle. His writings include *Die Söhne Ismaels* (1971), *Die Araber* (1971-1975), *Drei Jahrtausende Armenien* (1974), *Das alte Persien* (1978), *Volksschicksale am Hindukusch* (1983), *Die Ahnen Dschingis-Chans* (1988), and *Die Kunst der Mauren* (1992). Au&Wr, 1971; Günther Buch, *Namen und Daten wichtiger Personen der DDR*, 4th ed. (Berlin, Bonn, 1987); Kürschner, 1992-2003; Schoeberlein

Brentjes, Helga née Wilke, born about 1930, she received a Dr.phil. in 1961 from the Universität Halle for *Die Imamatslehre der Muslims nach Asch'ari*. She was a researcher and the wife of Burchard Brentjes. Au&Wr, 1971; Schwarz

Brentjes, Sonja, born 21 August 1951 at Halle, she studied at the universites of Dresden, Leipzig, and Halle, where she received a Dr.phil. in 1977. She specialized in the socio-cultural context of science in Islam, particularly regarding mathematics. She was a member of Deutscher Mathematikerverein, and Middle East Medievalists. She was a recipient of grants from C.N.R.S., and the Rockefeler Foundation. She was joint editor of *Geschichte der Naturwissenschaften* (1983). LC; Private; Schoeberlein

Brepohl, Friedrich Wilhelm, born 3 April 1879 at Caternberg, Germany, he was a clergyman who was a foreign editor in Firenze, 1899 to 1902, and in Locarno, 1902 to 1906. Thereafter he was a preacher in Serbia and Hungary, 1906-1908. During the first World War he was a director of the Deutsche Evangelische Kriegsgefangenen-Fürsorge, and editor of the journal *Christlicher Botschafter für Kriegsgefangene*. As an exile German in the post-war period, he was much concerned with the German settlements abroad. His writings include *Die Wolgadeutschen im brasilianischen Paraná* (1927). His trace is lost after his address at a German-Brasilian teachers' conference, *Volkstum, Muttersprache und Schule; ein Gruß aus dem fernen Brasilien an die Nassauer im lieben alten Heimatland* (1931). LC; Wer ist's, 1922, 1928, 1935

Bresciani-Turroni, Costantino, born 26 February 1882 at Verona, he was a professor of political economy at various Italian universities, and a sometime executive director, International Bank for Reconstruction and Development, Washington, D.C. His writings include *The Economics of inflation* (1937), *Introduzione alla politica economica* (1942), its translation, *Einführung in die Wirtschaftspolitik* (1948), and *Lezione di teoria economica* (1946). He died in Milano, 7 December 1963. Chi è, 1948; DizBI; WhAm, 7

Bresnier, Louis Jacques, born 11 April 1814 at Montargis (Loiret), he was a printer who had acquired a classical education in his spare time and was encouraged to take courses at the École des langues orientales, Paris, where he became a student of Sylvestre de Sacy. It was on his recommendation that Bresnier was charged with applying the School's teaching tradition to Algiers, where he started Arabic courses on 17 October 1836. Some years later, he became also examiner of prospective military interpreters without ever having been formally admitted to the Corps des interprètes de l'armée d'Afrique. Still, he was in a position to re-organize and rejuvenate the Corps. In 1853 he was awarded the *Croix de la Légion d'honneur*. His writings include *Anthologie arabe élémentaire* (1852), *Cours pratique et théorique de langue arabe* (1855), *Éléments de calligraphie orientale* (1855), *Chrestomathie arabe* (1857). He died suddenly when entering the library in Algiers in the morning of June 21st, 1869. DBF; Féraud, 372-381; Fück, p. 154

Bresnitz von Sydačoff, Philipp Franz, born 2 November 1868 at Wien, he studied philosophy at the Universität Wien and later became a journalist. He travelled in the Near East, Russia and the Orient where he had contact to the King of Serbia and the Prince of Bulgaria. Suspected of high treason by the Sultan of Turkey, he was incarcerated in Belgrade, 1893, but able to flee to Semlin (Zemun), where he founded the *Semliner Tageblatt*. After his return to Wien, he published his memoirs, *Fünf Jahre am Hofe des Königs von Serbien* (1895). He also wrote *Im roten Hermelin; vom alten zum neuen Rußland* (1922). His trace is lost after his last publication. DtBE; Wer ist's, 1909

Bresse, Louis, born in 1868, he wrote *Le Montenegro inconnu* (1920). His trace is lost after an article published in 1925. LC

Bresson, Gilbert, fl. 1955, he wrote *Histoire d'un centre rural algérien: Fort-de-l'Eau* (Alger, 1957).

Bressonnet, Maurice Jean August, born in 1872, he received a doctorate in 1902 from the Université de Paris for his thesis, *De la qualité de bellingérant dans la guerre continentale*. Thereafter he entered the diplomatic service. IndexBFr²

Bretanitskii (Bretanicky), Leonid Semenovich, born in 1914 at Odessa, he graduated in 1938 from the Faculty of Architecture, Azerbaijan Pedagogical Institute, Baku, and in 1961 he received a doctorate at Baku for his thesis, *Зодчество Азербайджана XII-XV вв. и его местои в архитектуре народов Переднего Востока*. His writings include *Кировабад* (1960), *Баку* (1965), *Архитектура Советского Азербайджана* (1972), *Искусство Азербайджана IV-XVIII веком* (1976), its translation, *Die Kunst Aserbaidschans vom 4. bis zum 18. Jahrhundert* (1988), and *Художественное насладие Переднего Востока эпохи феодализма* (1988). He died in 1979. LC; Miliband

Bretholz, Wolfgang, born 28 August 1904 at Brünn, Austria-Hungary, he received a Dr.jur. in 1926 from the Universität Leipzig for his thesis, *Das System der presserechtlichen Verantwortlichkeit*. He edited *Das sowjetrussische Presserecht* (Berlin, 1931), and wrote *Ich sah sie stürzen* (1955), and *Aufstand der Araber* (1960). He lived for many years in Lausanne, where he died 31 August 1969. KDtLK, 1958-1967

Breton, André Lucien Eugène, born 13 July 1902 at Mâcon (Saône-et-Loire), he studied law and successively served as a professor of law, and dean, at the Faculté de droit et des science économiques d'Alger, 1933-1962. WhoFr, 1953/54-1973/74|

Breton, Ernest François Pierre Hippolyte, born 21 October 1812 at Paris, he took courses at l'École de droit as well as at painters' studios. He visited Italy in 1829, and collaborated in the production of various illustrated publications. In 1823 he published *Les Monuments de tous les peuples*. For his *Histoire de la peinture à fresque en Italie au XVIe siècle* he was awarded a gold medal by the Académie des inscriptions. In the 1850s he travelled to excavations in Italy and Greece. Since 1838 he was a member of the Antiquaires de France. He died 29 May 1875. DBF

Bretschneider (Bretshneider), Emilii Vasil'evich (Эмилий Васильевич Бретшнейдерь), born on 3 or 4 July 1833 at St. Petersburg or Riga. Having obtained his medical doctorate from the University of Dorpat (Tartu) he entered the service of the Ministry of Foreign Affairs in 1862 and was appointed to the Russian Legation in Tehran. In 1866 he was appointed physician to the Russian Legation at Peking. Except for two furloughs, in 1871 and 1878, he remained in Peking until retirement in February 1884. During his residence there he had the good fortune to be associated with the Archimandrite Palladius, and with him took full advantage of the opportunity afforded in the splendid library of Chinese works attached to the Mission. His writings include *On the knowledge possessed by the ancient Chinese of the Arabs and the Arabian colonies* (1871). He died in St. Petersburg, 29 April (12 May) 1901. *Journal* of the China Branch of the Royal Asiatic Society 33 iii (1899/1900), 69-72; *T'oung pao*, 2e série, 2 (1901), pp. 192-197

Brett, M. K., fl. 1972, he was a sometime keeper of Textiles at the Royal Ontario Museum, Toronto.

Brett, Michael, fl. 1974, he received a Ph.D. in 1969 from SOAS for *Fitnat al-Qayrawan; a study of traditional Arabic historiography*. Thereafter he was a lecturer in history of North Africa at SOAS. He was joint author of *The Moors; Islam in the West* (1980), and its translation, *Die Mauren* (1986). Sluglett

Breulier, Louis Adolphe, born 29 May 1815, his writings include *Du droit de perpétuité de la propriété intellectuelle* (1855), *Éléments de linguistique et de philosophie* (1857), *Du régime de l'invention* (1862), and contributions to periodicals. Index BFR²; Oursel

Brewer, Josiah, born 1 June 1796 at Monterey, Mass., he was a graduate of Yale College and Andover Theological Seminary and served as a missionary in Greece and Turkey. His writings include *A Residence at Constantinople in the year 1827* (1830), and *Patmos and the seven churches of Asia* (1851). He died in Stockbridge, Mass., 19 November 1872. Master (5); Shavit

Brewer, William Dodd, born 4 April 1922 at Middletown, Conn., he was a graduate of Williams College, and Fletcher School of Law and Diplomacy. For a number of years he was an instructor at American colleges, before entering the U.S. Foreign Service in 1947. He served in various capacities throughout the Muslim world until 1978. BlueB, 1973/74, 1975, 1976; WhoAm, 1974-1988/89; WhoAmP, 1973/74-1977/78

Brewster, Beverly J., née Kline, born 19 October 1938 at Chicago, she was a garduate of Indiana University, a librarian, instructor at library schools, and an indexer. In 1978, she was associated with the Graduate Department of Library and Information Science, The Catholic University of America, Washington, D.C. She wrote *American overseas technical assistance, 1940-1970* (1976). BiDrLUS, 1970; WhoLibS, 1966

216

Brewster, David Pearson, Rev., born in 1930, he spent the year 1962/63 studying Arabic at Tunis. In 1975 he received a D.Phil. from Oxford for his thesis, *Philosophical discussions of prophecy in medieval Islam*. His writings include *Al-Hallaj, Muslim mystic and martyr* (1976). LC; Sluglett

Brewster, Paul G., born 5 November 1898 at Stendal, Ind., he received a B.S. in 1920 from Oakland City College (Ind.), and an A.M. in 1925 from the University of Oklahoma. He held a variety of positions at American colleges and universities. His writings include *Ballads and songs of Indiana* (1940), and *American nonsinging games* (1953). IndAu, 1917

Breycha-Vauthier, Arthus Carl von, born 1 July 1903 at Wien, he studied at Wien, London, and in Belgium. In 1928 he became a librarian at the League of Nations, and in 1945, he was appointed United Nations' chief librarian, and concurrently served as a professor of library science in Genève. From 1964 to 1968 he was Austrian ambassador to Lebanon, Syria, Jordan and Kuwait. Thereafter he was director of the Diplomatische Akademie, Wien. His writings include *Österreich in der Levante* (1972), and *Österreich und der arabische Nahe Osten* (1976). Master (3); WhoAustria, 1954-1982/83

von **Breydenbach**, Bernhard, born ca. 1440 in Germany, he was a canon in Mainz who went on a pilgrimage to the Holy Land from April to November 1483. His travel account, *Peregrinatio in terram sanctam* (Mainz, 1486), was published initially in Latin but soon reached a wider audience through its translations into French, German, Italian, and Spanish. He died in Mainz, 5 May 1497. Henze

Breydy, Michael, born in 1928 in Lebanon, he studied at Salamanca, Roma, and Heidelberg. In 1984 he was appointed to the chair of Nahöstliche Orientalistik and chairman of the Institut für Christlich-Arabische Literatur in the Universität Witten/Herdecke. His writings include *Études sur Sa'id ibn Batiq et ses sources* (1983), *Das Annalenwerk des Eutychius von Alexandrien* (1985), *Maroniten vom VII. bis XVI. Jahrhundert* (1985), and *Études maronites* (1991). He died in 1994. LC; Note

Brezianu, Andrei, fl. 1980, his writings include *Odiseu în Atlantic* (Cluj-Napoca, 1997). LC

Brian, Doris, (Mrs. Hepner), born about 1910 at Philadelphia, Pa., she graduated in 1934 from Barnard College, N.Y., and received an A.M. from the Institute of Fine Arts, New York University. She was successively an editior, manager, and director of a number of art journals in New York as well as a contributor to scholarly periodicals. WhoAmW, 1958; Master (1)

Brice, William Charles, M.A., fl. 1951. His writings include *South-west Asia* (1967). In 1978 he edited *The environmental history of the Near East and Middle East since the last ice age*. Under the patronage of the EI² he published *An historical Atlas of Islam* (1981). LC

Bricteux, Auguste, 1873-1937, he was affiliated with the Université de Liège, and wrote *Au pays du lion et du soleil* (1908); and translated *Contes persans*, traduits sur un manuscrit inédit de la Bibliothèque de Berlin (1910), and *Les Comédies de Malkom Khan* (1933).

Bridge, F. Roy, born 20th cent., he received a Ph.D. in 1966 from the University of London for *The diplomatic relations between Great Britain and Austria-Hungary, 1906-1912*. His writings include *The Habsburg monarchy, 1804-1918* (1967), and *The Habsburg monarchy among the great powers, 1815-1918* (1990). He edited *Austro-Hungarian documents relating to the Macedonian struggle, 1896-1912* (1976). LC

Bridge, John N., born 20th cent., he received a Ph.D. in 1975 from the University of Durham for his thesis, *Financial growth and economic development; a case study of Lebanon*. He was a member of the American Economic Association. Sluglett

Bridgman, Herbert Lawrence, born 30 May 1844 at Amherst, Mass., and a 1866 graduate of Amherst College. He had been in the newspaper work since 1864, becoming business manager of *The Standard Union* in 1889, a position he held until his death. He was a prominent figure in U.S. national journalism, and an enthusiast of polar exploration. In 1905 he went up the Nile as far as Gondokoro, stopping on the return voyage at Khartoum and meeting with Sir Reginald Wingate. In 1913 he made a tour of Bulgaria and the Near East and wrote of his experiences there. His alma mater awarded him an honorary doctorate in 1920. He died in mid-Atlantic aboard the state schoolship *Newport*, 24 September 1924. DAB, 2; Shavit-Africa

Bridier, Manuel, fl. 1980, he was a French socialist whose writings include *Évolution des structures de l'État* (1963). LC

Brieger-Wasservogel, Lothar, born 6 September 1879 at Zwickau, Germany, he was an art critic who wrote for the *Vossische Zeitung* in Berlin until 1933, when he had to emigrate to Shanghai. He traded in antiquities until he was able to return to Berlin after the war, where he died 23 March 1949. His writings include *Ein Jahrhundert deutscher Erstausgaben* (1925), and *Die großen Kunstsammler* (1931). DtBE; Kürschner, 1931; Wininger

de **Brière**, he was a member of the Société asiatique, Paris, and wrote *Essai sur le symbolisme antique d'Orient* (Paris, 1847), and *Histoire du prix fondé par le comte de Volney ... pour la transcription universlelle des langues en lettres européennes* (Paris, s.d.) BN

Brieux, Alain, fl. 1975, his writings include *La publicité du seizième au vingtième siècle* (196-), and *Histoire des sciences* (Paris, 1971). LC

Briffault, Robert Stephen, born in 1876 at London, he was educated privately in Firenze and London. He practised as a surgeon and served in the first World War. His writings include *The Decline and fall of the British Empire* (1938), and *L'Angleterre et l'Egypte* (194-). He died 11 December 1948. Who was who, 4

Briggs, Frank Shrewsbury, Rev., fl. 1930, he contributed to the *Journal of the Bombay Natural History Society*, and the *Moslem world*. He was affiliated with the Methodist Mission, Ghazipur, U.P., India. WhE&EA

Briggs, Herbert Whittaker, born 14 May 1900 at Wilmington, Del., he received a Ph.D. in 1925 from Johns Hopkins University, for *The doctrine of continuous voyage*. He was an international lawyer, and a professor at Oberlin College from 1928 to 1969, when he became emeritus professor of international law at Cornell University, Ithaca, N.Y. He was editor of *The law of nations* (1952). He died 6 January 1990. AmM&WS, 1973 S, 1978 S; DrAS, 1974 P, 1978 P, 1982 P; Master (1); WhAm, 10

Briggs, John, born in 1785, he joined the East India Company's Madras Army in 1801, served in the Mahratta wars, and accompanied Sir J. Malcolm on his mission to Persia in 1810. He was successively Resident at Satara and Nagpur. In 1838 he retired with the rank of major-general. He translated Farishtah's *Muhammadan power in India*, and the *Siyar-ul-muta'akhkhirin* from Persian into English. He died 27 April 1875. DNB; Buckland; IndianBilnd (2); Riddick

Briggs, Lloyd Cabot, born 27 June 1909 at Boston, Mass., he received a Ph.D. in 1952 from Harvard for his thesis, *The pre-neolithic inhabitants of Northwest Africa*. He was a sometime research associate at Harvard. His writings include *The Living races of the Sahara Desert* (1958), and he was joint author of *No more for ever; a Saharian Jewish town* (1964). He died in 1975. Bioln 10; AmM&WS, 1973 S, 1976 P; Master (1); Unesco

Briggs, Martin Shaw, born in 1882 at Otley, Yorkhire, he was a graduate of Leeds University, who practised as an architect in London. He was a Fellow of the Royal Institute of British Architects. His writings include *Muhammadan architecture in Egypt and Palestine* (1924), and *Everyman's concise encyclopaedia of architecture* (1959). He died 13 October 1977. Who was who, 7

Brignon, Jean, born 16 August 1931, he was a sometime professor of history at the Faculté des lettres de Rabat, and joint author of *Histoire du Maroc* (Paris, 1967), and *Découverte de Fès* (1972). WhoArab, 1981/82, 1984/85

Brigol, Madeleine, born about 1935 *see* Rouvillois-Brigol, Madeleine

Brill, Robert Howard, born 7 May 1929 at Irvington, N.J., he received a Ph.D. in 1955 in physical chemistry from Rutgers University, New Brunswick, N.J. He specialized in archaeological chemistry and art conservation. He edited *Science and archaeology; papers* (1971), and he was joint author of *Studies in early Egyptian glass* (1993). AmM&WS, 1973 P -2003 P; Bioln 7

Brincat, Giuseppe, fl. 1971, he edited *Rime*, by Giovan Matteo di Meglio (1977). LC

Brincat, Joseph M., born 20th cent., his writings include *Malta, 870-1054; al-Himayari's account* (Valetta, 1991). ZKO

van den **Brincken**, Anna Dorothee, born 23 December 1932 at Essen, Germany, she received a Dr.phil. in 1957 from the Universität Münster for her thesis, *Studien zur lateinischen Weltchronik bis in das Zeitalter Ottos von Freising*. She was a professor of medieval history at various German universities. Her writings include *Das Stift St. Mariengraden zu Köln* (1969), *Die "nationes christianorum orientalium" im Verständnis der lateinischen Historiographie* (1973), and *Kartographische Quellen; Welt-, See- und Regionalkarten* (1988). Kürschner, 1980-2003

Bringau, born 19th cent., he was an electrical engineer in Fez when he and his family were assassinated during the 1911 turmoil. Note

Brinner, William Michael, born 6 October 1924 at Alameda, Calif., he was a graduate of the University of California at Berkeley, where he also received a Ph.D. in 1956 for *Damascus during the reign of*

Sultan Barquq, according to Ibn Sasra. He was since 1964 a professor of Near Eastern languages at the University of California, Berkeley. He edited and translated from Ibn Sasra *A chronicle of Damascus, 1389-1397* (1963), he translated al-Tabari's *Prophets and patriarchs* (1984), and edited *Like all the nations; a symposium* (1987). In 2000 he was honoured by *Judaism and Islam; boundaries, communication and interaction.* DrAS, 1969 H, 1974 H, 1978 H, 1982 H; Master (3)

Brinsley, John Harrington, born 29 December 1933 at N.Y.C., he was a graduate of Cornell University, Ithaca, N.Y., who, after bar admission, practised law and was a visiting lecturer at various American universities. WhoAm, 1982-1988/89

Brinton, Jasper Yeates, born 5 October 1878 at Philadelphia, Pa., where he grew up and studied. He was a sometime assistant U.S. attorney and, in 1919, a member of the American Military Mission to Armenia. In 1921 he was appointed to the Mixed Courts of Egypt. He stayed there until his death in August, 1973. He was a founding member of the Egyptian Society of International Law. His writings include *The Mixed Courts of Egypt* (1930), *The American effort in Egypt* (1972), and *A contribution to the history of the Alexandria Archaeological Society, 1935-1939, a recollection by one of its past presidents* (1973). Shavit; *Who was who in America*, 6

Brintzinger, Ottobert Ludwig, born 6 December 1929 at Tübingen, he received a Dr.jur. in 1957 from the Universität Basel, and in 1959 entered public service. His writings include *Rückwirkung des Art. 12 der Genfer Flüchtlingskonvention von 1951?* (1966). *Wer ist wer*, 1997/98-2002/2003

Brion, Émile François Marie, born in 1852, he translated *Vocabulaire des poudres et explosifs*, by Ferdinando Salvati (Paris, 1895). LC

Brisch, Klaus, born 7 February 1923 at Oppeln, Germany, he was an archaeologist, and from 1966 to retirement in 1988, a director of the Museum für Islamische Kunst, Berlin. His writings include *Fenstergitter und verwandte Ornamente der Hauptmoschee von Córdoba* (1966), as well as two museum catalogues. He died in Berlin, 9 February 2001. Kürschner, 1992-1996; *Wer ist wer*, 1991/92

Briscoe, John, born 30 July 1948 at Brakpan, South Africa, he studied at the University of Cape Town, and received a Ph.D. in environmental engineering in 1976 from Harvard University. From 1976 to 1978 he was affiliated with the Cholera Research Laboratories, Bangladesh. In 1996 he was a senior economist and division chief, World Bank, Washington, D.C. His writings include *The role of water supply in improving health in poor countries, with special reference to Bangladesh* (1977). He was joint author of *Water for rural communities* (1988). AmM&WS P, 1982-2003; LC

Briscoe, William Richard Brunskill, born 14 January 1855, he was a graduate of Trinity College, Cambridge, and a barrister-at-law who practised in Egypt from 1897 to 1906. He was a sometime Crown Prosecutor for Egypt, and from 1924 to 1925 a judge in the Mixed Tribunal of Tangier. He died 23 August 1930. *Who was who*, 3

de **Brissac**, Pierre Simon Charles Timoléon de Cossé, Duc, born 13 March 1900 at Paris, he served four years in the armed forces, before he became an engineer and subsequently a business executive. His writings include *Histoire des ducs de Brissac* (1952), its translation, *The Dukes of Brissac* (1954), and *En autres temps, 1900-1939* (1972). He died 4 April 1993. WhoFr, 1981/82-1992/93

Brissaud- Desmaillet, Georges Henri, born in 1869 at Carcassonne (Aude), he was a graduate of the military college of Saint-Cyr, and l'École de guerre. He resigned from the army in 1931 with the rank of general. He died in Paris, 14 November 1948. DBF

Brito, Eduino, fl. 1956, he was a sometime Portuguese *chef de porto do quadro administrativo.* Note

Britsch, Jacques Paul Léon Jules, born 10 September 1906 at Broye (Saône-et-Loire), he studied at the facultés de droit at Alger, Paris, and Beirut, and received a diploma in advanced Islamic studies from the Université de Paris. After passing through the military college of Saint-Cyr, he was successively posted to North Africa and Syria, 1928-1936. He retired in 1963 with the rank of colonel. His writings include *Perspectives sahariennes* (1956). WhoFr, 1973/74-1981/82|

Britt, George William Hughes, born 5 October 1895 at Millerburg, Ky., he was a journalist who worked for a variety of American newspapers, and taught news writing at Columbia University, N.Y.C. During the second World War, he worked for the U.S. Office of War Information in the Middle East. In the early 1950s he spent eighteen months in Lebanon. His writings include *Christians only; a study in prejudice* (1931), *Forty yeears - forty millions; the career of Frank A. Munsey* (1935), and *The fifth column is here* (1940). He died in Hightstown, N.J., 4 February 1988. AmAu&B; ConAu, 124

Brittain, Mary Zwemer, she published the tract, *Arab lands* in the series, *Land and peoples*, (New York, Holiday House, 1947). LC

Britton, Nancy née Pence, she was born at Madison, Wisc., and graduated from Northwestern University. For a number of years she was affiliated with the Museum of Fine Arts, Boston. Her writings include *A study of some early Islamic textiles* (1938), *East of the sun* (1956), and *The inspired folly* (1971). Au&Wr, 1971; LC

Briullova-Shashkol'skaia, N. V., fl. 1927, her writings include the booklet *Как жит между собою народам России?* (1917), and *Народности России и их требования* (n.d.) OSK

Brives, Abel, born 1868, he received a *doctorat ès sciences* in 1897 for *Les terrains tertiaires du bassin du Chélif et du Dahra*. From 1901 to 1907 he accompanied Capt. Larras on his hydrographic explorations in Morocco. Thereafter he was affiliated with the Service des territoires du Sud-algérien. At the end of his career he was appointed in 1929 a professor of applied mineralogy at the Université d'Alger. His writings include *Voyages au Maroc, 1901-1907* (1909), *Contributions à l'étude des gîtes metallifères de l'Algérie* (1918), and *Considérations hydrologiques sur l'Algérie* (1925). DBF

Brix, Joseph, born 27 June 1859 at Rosenheim, Germany, he was a town planner and ecologist with an interest in the Islamic world. He was granted an honorary doctorate by the Universität München. His writings include *Aus der Geschichte des Städtebaues in den letzten 100 Jahren* (1912), and *Die Stadtentwässerung in Deutschland* (1934). He died in Berlin, 10 January 1943. NDB; Kürschner, 1925-1940/41; Wer ist's, 1928, 1935

Broadley, Alexander Meyrick, born 19 July 1847. After his bar admission, he practised law in Tunis, and represented the Bey of Tunis in his differences with the French Republic, events which are the subject of his book, *The last Punic war; Tunis, past and present* (1882). He was later a senior counsel of Arabi Pasha and the other state-prisoners. For many years he held the appointment of Standing Counsel to the Khedive Ismail Pasha. His writings include *How we defended Arabi and his friends; a story of Egypt and the Egyptians* (1884), and *Collectana Napoleonica* (1905). He died 16 April 1916. BritInd (1); Who was who, 2

Broadribb, Donald, born in 1933 at Rochester, N.Y., he lived in Perth, Western Australia, where he was in private practice as an analytical psychologist since 1975. He edited the *Bibliography of the Samaritans*, by L. A. Mayer (1964), and wrote *The dream story* (1987). LC; Note

Brocherel, Giulio (Jules), born 19th cent., his writings include *Alpinismo* (Milano, 1898), and *En Asie centrale - les Kirghizes - les Mont Célestes* (Paris, 1902). BN

Brock, Henry Le Marchant, born 5 May 1889 at Guernsey, where he was also educated. He served in the British Armed Forces and retired with the rank of Air Commodore. In 1930 he served in the North West Frontier Province of India. He died 11 March 1946. Who was who, 6

Brock, Peter de Beauvoir, born 30 January 1920 at Guernsey, he studied at Oxford where he received a doctorate in 1948, and a second doctorate from Universytet Jagielloński, Kraków, in 1950. He was a professor of history at London and N.Y.C., before he was appointed in 1966 a professor at the University of Toronto. His writings include the revision of his Oxford thesis, *The political and social doctrines of the Unity of Czech Brethren in the fifteenth and early sixteenth centuries* (1957), *Slovak national awakening* (1976), *Polish revolutionary populism* (1977), and *The Mahatma and Mother India* (1983). Canadian, 1996-2002; ConAu, 9-12, new rev. 5; DrAS, 1974, 1978 H; IntAu&W, 1982-1989; WrDr, 1976/78-2003

Brock, Robert, born in 1889 at Penzance, Cornwall, he was a journalist and newspaper executive in British India. His writings include *The Simon report on India* (1930). WhE&EA

Brockelmann, Carl, born 17 September 1868 at Rostock, Germany, he received a Dr.phil. in 1890 from the Universität Straßburg for his thesis, *Das Verhältnis von Ibn-El-Atirs "Kamil" zu Tabaris "Ahbar."* He was successively a professor at Breslau, Königsberg, Halle, and Berlin. Since 1945 he lived in Halle. His writings include *Grundriß der vergleichenden Grammatik der semitischen Sprachen* (1908-1913), and *Geschichte der islamischen Völker und Staaten* (1939), a work which has been translated into many languages. But he is best remembered for his monumental *Geschichte der arabischen Litteratur* (1898-1949), which has been translated even into Arabic. He died in Halle, 6 May 1956. DtBE; Index Islamicus (9); Kürschner, 1925-1954; Wer ist wer, 1955; Wer ist's, 1935

Brockhaus, Hermann, born 28 January 1806 at Amsterdam, he studied Oriental languages at Leipzig, Göttingen, and Bonn, and received a Dr.phil. in 1838 from the Universität Leipzig. He was a professor of Oriental languages successively at Jena and Leipzig, and was practicularly interested in Indian literature. His writings include the edition and translation of *Die Lieder des Hafis, Persisch mit dem Commentare des Sudi* (1854-1860). He died in Leipzig, 5 January 1877. DtBE; EncAM; EncBrit; GdeEnc; GDU; Meyers; NDB; Stache-Rosen, pp. 28-29

Brocki, Zygmunt, fl. 1975, he was a Polish writer on lexicography and geography. His writings in-clude *Polskie wybrzeże* (1954), *Die polnische Küste* (1954), and *Michałki z kambuza* (1979). LC

Brocklebank, Richard *Hugh* Royds, born in 1889, he wrote *A turn or two I'll walk to still my beating mind; commentary on a private collection* (London, 1955). LC

Brockway, Archibald *Fenner*, Baron Brockway, born 1 November 1888 at Calcutta, the son of missionaries. His anti-colonial views turned him into a life-long socialist. One of his oldest dreams was to contribute to an Israeli-Arab peace settlement. He was a member of numerous peace, disar-mament, and liberation campaigns, on which he published widely. His writings include *The Colonial revolution* (1973), and *Towards tomorrow; the autobiography of Fenner Brockway* (1977). He died 28 April 1988. Who was who, 8

Brockway, Duncan, born 23 July 1932 at Manchester, N.H., he was a graduate of St. John's College, Annapolis, and Princeton. He was ordained in 1956, and received an M.A. in library science in 1960 from Rutgers University. He had a career as a clergyman and librarian. Master (3); WhoAm, 1974-1988/89

Brockway, Thomas Parmelee, born 21 November 1898 at Clinton, N.Y., he was a graduate of Reed College, and received a Ph.D. in 1937 from Yale University. He was a professor of history and political science at various American universities. His writings include *Battles without bullets* (1939), *A peace that pays* (1944), *Dollars, goods and peace* (1948), and *Basic documents in United States foreign policy* (1957). ConAu, P 2

Brode, Johann Wilhelm *Heinrich*, born 9 July 1874 at Schwerz, Germany, he was educated at Tübingen, Halle and Berlin, where he studied Suaheli and Arabic for three years. In 1898 he received a Dr.jur from the Universität Greifswald for *Über das Verhältnis der reinen Schenkung zur Schenkung von Todeswegen*. In the same year he entered the foreign service as a dragoman, posted variously to Zanzibar, Mombasa, Jaffa and Jerusalem. His writings include *Tippoo Tib, the story of his career in Central Africa* (1907), *British and German East Africa* (1911), and several joint publications in German. Wer ist's, 1912, 1922, 1928, 1935

Brodin, Eric, fl. 1968, his writings include *Sweden's paradise lost; the decline of the Swedish welfare state* (1984). LC

Brodkin, Edward Irwin, born 26 February 1936 at Montreal, P.Q., he was a graduate of McGill University, Montreal, and took a Ph.D. in history at Cambridge. In 1978 he was appointed professor of history at Connecticut College, New London, a post which he still held in 2003. DrAS, 1974, H 1978 H, 1982 H; NatFacDr, 1995-2003

Brodney, Spencer, born 29 August 1883 at Melbourne, he studied at Melbourne and London and became a staff member of a variety of Australian, English, and American newspapers and periodicals, in particular, *Events*, and *Current history*. He died in May 1973. WhAm, 6

Brodskaia, D. F., fl. 1963, he was joint author of *Докторские и кандидатские диссертации защищенные в Институте Востоковедения Академия Наук СССР с 1950 по 1970 гг* (1972). LC

Brogan, Olwen, fl. 1960, he was affiliated with the British School at Rome, and a joint author of *Ghirza, a Libyan settlement in the Roman period* (1984). LC

de **Broglie**, Jean, Prince, born 21 June 1921 at Paris, he was in the public service and a politician. He was assassinated 24 December 1976. IndexBFr² (1); NDNC, 1962/63; WhoFr, 1966/67-1975/76

Brohi, Allahbukhsh Karimbukhsh, born in 1915, he was a scholar, lawyer, statesman, and a sometime minister of justice in Pakistan. His writings include *An adventure in self-expression* (1955), *Fundamental law of Pakistan* (1958), *Islam and the modern world* (1968), and *Testament of faith* (1975).

Broido, Grigorii Isaakovich, born in 1885, he wrote *Национальный и колониальный вопрос* (1924), and *Восстание киргиз в 1916 г.* (1925). LC

Broke, Sir Arthur de Capell, 1791-1858 *see* Brooke, Sir Arthur de Capell

Bromage, T. N., M.B.E., he was a major in the Grenadier Guards and served for a number of years with Sir John Glubb in the Arab Legion. He later was assistant military attaché in Amman. Note

Bromberger, Christian, born 25 October 1946 at Paris, he studied at the Sorbonne, and the Musée de l'Homme, Paris, and took his doctorate in 1990. He was a professor of ethnology in the Université de Provence, Aix-en-Provence, and director of the Laboratoire d'ethnologie méditerranéenne compa-rative. He conducted field work in Iran and was a member of the European Association of Social Anthropology as well as an editorial member of several scholarly journals. His writings include *Habitat,* *architecture and rural society in the Gilan Plain* (1989), and he was joint author of *Gilân et Âzarbâyjân oriental* (1982). AnElFr, 1995; EURAMES; Private

Bromberger, Edgar, born in 1889 at N.Y.C., he was a 1910 graduate of New York University Law School, and an honorary member of the class of 1930 of the United States Military Academy. He practised law in N.Y.C. until 1934, when he started a civic service career. From 1945 until retirement because of ill health in 1950, he served as Chief New York City Magistrate. During his time, his courts made progress with dealing with sociological problems. He died 17 March 1956. Bioln, 4; Master (2); NYT 18 March 1956, p. 18

Bromhead, Sir Benjamin Denis Gonville, born 7 May 1900, he passed through the Royal Military College, Sandhurst, and in 1919 joined the Indian Army. He served in Mesopotamia, Waziristan, and the North West Frontier of India. He died 18 March 1981. Who was who, 8

Brömmer, Wolfgang, fl. 1980, he was a German leftist political activist who contributed to ephemeral periodicals.

Broms, Henri, born in 1927, his writings include *Two studies in the relations of Hafiz and the West* (1868), *How does the Middle Eastern literary taste differ from the Europeans* (1972), and *The Middle Eastern thinking as expressed in language and style* (1982). LC

Bron, Michał, fl. 1975, his writings include *Wojna hiszpańska, 1936-1939* (1961), and *Bitwa nad Ebro i udział w niej Polaków* (1976). LC

Brondel, Georges, born 25 May 1920 at Lyon, he was a graduate of the École nationale des mines, and a mining engineer in the public service. WhoEIO, 1982, 1985

Brönner, Wolfram, fl. 1979, he wrote *Der Nahostkonflikt und die Palästina-Frage* (1979), *Afghanistan - Revolution und Konterrevolution* (1980), and *Ölkrise und arabische Ölländer* (1980), all of which were published in Verlag Marxistische Blätter, Frankfurt am Main.

Brönnle, Paul, F.R.G.S., F.R.Hist.S., member of the R.A.S., born 16 September 1867 at Markgrönin-gen, Germany, he received a Dr.phil. in 1895 from the Universität Halle-Wittenberg for his thesis, *Die Commentatoren des Ibn-Ishak und ihre Scholien*. He was a sometime associate editor at the *Encyclopædia Britannica*. He edited classical Arabic texts and *Vor 45 Jahren; Worte aus großer Vergangenheit* (Leipzig, 1915). Literary yearbook, 1904, 1910; Master (1)

Bronstein, Leo, born in 1902 or 1903 in Poland, but he spent his later years as an art historian in the United States where he died, 1 June 1976. His writings include *Altichiero, l'artiste et son œuvre* (1932), *Fragments of life, metaphysics, and art* (1953), and *Kabbalah and art* (1980). ConAu 65; Bioln 10

Brooke (Broke), Sir Arthur de Capell, born 22 October 1791, he graduated from Magdalen College, Oxford, and entered the army. He retired with the rank of major. Much of his early life was spent in foreign travel. His writings include *Sketches in Spain and Morocco* (1831). He died 6 December 1858. Boase; Britlnd (1); DNB; Master (1)

Brooke, Christopher Nugent Lawrence, born 23 June 1927, he was a graduate of Cambridge University and served as a professor of history at Liverpool and London, before he was appointed Dixie Professor of Ecclesiastic History and Fellow of Gonville and Cains College, Cambridge. His writings include *Europe in the central middle ages* (1964), *Medieval Church and society* (1971), and *The monastic world* (1974). ConAu 5-8, new rev., 2,18; IntAu&W, 1976-1989; Who, 1982-2003; WhoWor, 1982-1990/91; WrDr, 1976-2003

Brooke, Sir James, born 29 April 1803 near Benares, he was educated at Norwich, ran away from school and was made a cadet of infantry in Bengal. He was invalided in the Burma war and resigned from the East India Company's service in 1830. In 1838 he privately went to Borneo, where he made a political career. When he finally left Sarawak in 1863, he had been British commissioner and consul-general of Borneo. He died 11 June 1868. Emily Hahn wrote *James Brooke of Sarawak, a biography* (1953). DNB; Embacher; Henze; IndianBilnd (2) LC

Brooke-Popham, Sir Henry *Robert* Moore, born 18 September 1878, he was educated at Haileybury, Sandhurst, and Staff College, and then entered the Army. He was commandant of the newly created R.A.F. Staff College from 1921 to 1925, and promoted to air marshal in 1935. With the outbreak of the Italo-Abyssinian crisis, he was sent to Cairo as air commander-in-chief Middle East. From 1940 to 1942 he had a luckless spell of duty in the Far East and left active service. He died 17 August 1953. His private papers are in Rhodes House Library, Oxford. JRCAS 41 (1954), pp. 61-62; DNB; Master (5); Who was who, 5

Brooks, Ernest Walter, born 30 August 1863 at Hambledon, Hants., he was educated at Eton and Cambridge, and awarded an honorary doctorate in 1927 by the Université de Louvain. He was a student of late Roman, Byzantine, and early medieval history, a Syriac scholar, and a Fellow of the British Academy. He died 26 March 1955. *Who was who*, 5

Broome, Michael R., fl. 1976, he wrote *A handbook of Islamic coins* (London, 1985). LC

Broomfield, Gerald Webb, born 26 May 1895 at London, he was an Anglican priest and church administrator for education in East Africa, and a canon chancellor of Zanzibar Cathedral. His writings include *Colour conflict* (1943), *The chosen people* (1954), *Towards freedom* (1957), and *Sarufi ya Kiswahili* (1975). He died in September 1976. ConAu 5-8, 103, 5; Master (2); WhE&EA

Broomfield, John Hindle, born 16 July 1935 at Whangarei, New Zealand, he was a graduate of the University of Canterbury, and received his Ph.D. from the Australian National University. He taught history at the University of Michigan, Ann Arbor, before he was appointed in 1969 a professor of history and director of its Center for South and Southeast Asian Studies. His writings include *Elite conflict in a plural society; twentieth-century Bengal* (1968). ConAu, 25-28; DrAS, 1974 H, 1978 H, 1982 H

Broomhall, Marshall, born in 1866 at London, he was for twenty-seven years an editorial secretary of the China Inland Mission. His writings include *Islam in China* (1910), and *The Bible in China* (1934). He died in 1937. Lodwick; WhE&EA

Brosche, Karl Ulrich, born 8 November 1939 at Helmstedt, Germany, he received a Dr.rer.nat. in 1967 from the Universität Göttingen for *Struktur- und Skulpturformen im nördlichen und nordwestlichen Harzvorland.* He was for over twenty years a professor of geography in the Freie Universität Berlin. Kürschner, 1980-2003

Broselow, Ellen I., born in 1949, she received a Ph.D. in 1976 from the University of Massachusetts at Amherst for her thesis, *The phonology of Egyptian Arabic.* NUC, 1980

Brosnahan, Tom, born 27 April 1945 at Bethlehem, Pa., he was a graduate of Tufts University, and from 1967 to 1970 a Peace Corps worker in Turkey. Since 1968 he worked as a teacher of English, as a writer and translator. He wrote *Turkey on 5 dollars a day* (1971), *Turkey, a travel survival kit* (1985), and numerous Berlitz travel guides, some of which were published also in translation. ConAu, 119

Brosse, Marii Ivanovich, 1802-1880 *see* Brosset, Marie Felicité

Brosselard, Charles, born in 1816, he spent most of his life in Algeria, starting as *secrétaire des commissariats* of Blidah and Bougie, where learned the local languages. He later was an army interpreter, prefect, and director of Algerian Affairs at the Ministry of Interior. His writings include *Dictionnaire français-berbère* (1844), and *Les khouan; de la constitution des ordres religieux musulmans en Algérie* (1859). He died in Paris, 29 March 1889. DBF

Brosselard-Faidherbe, Henri François, born 3 June 1855 at Paris, he was a cartographer who served as a captain at Headquarters, Ministry of War. In connection with the projected Trans-Saharan railway, he explored the Sahara as far south as Timbuctu. His writings include *Voyage de la mission Flatters au pays des Touareg Azdjers* (1883), *Rapport sur la situation dans la vallée du Sénégal en 1886; insurrection de Mahmadou-Lamine* (1888), and *Casamance et Meliacorée; pénétration au Soudan* (1892). He died in Coutances, 19 August 1893. DBF; Henze

Brosses, Charles de, born 7 February 1709 at Dijon, he was one of the first to interest himself in the study of man. His writings include *Histoire des navigations aux terres australes* (1756), *Le Culte des dieux fétiches* (1760), *Terra australis cognita* (1766-68), and *Traité de la formation méchanique des langues et des principes physiques de l'etymologie* (1801). He died in Paris, 7 May 1777. DBF; Master (4); OxFr

Brosset, Diego, born in 1898, he joined the French army in 1915, and after the war passed through the military college, Saint-Maixent. During the second World War he served with the Free French Forces in the Middle East. He was killed in a vehicle accident, 20 November 1944. His writings, published under the pseudonym Charles Diego, include *Sahara; roman* (1935), and *Un Homme sans l'Occident* (1946). Hommes et destins, vol. 1, pp. 135-137

Brosset, Marie Félicité, in his Russian form, Marii Ivanovich Brosse, born 5 February 1802 at Paris, he originally pursued ecclesiastic studies and taught for a few years at Jesuit colleges, but soon moved to Paris to study Oriental languages, however, in the most modest circumstances. After a few years as a printer, he found a position as a teacher of Caucasian languages in St. Petersburg, 1837. He became a member of the Russian Academy, a librarian, and keeper at the Ermitage before he returned to

France, where he died in Châtellerault, 3 September 1880. G. S. Buachidze wrote a biography, *Mapu Броссе, страницы жизни* (1983). DBF; IndexBFr² (2); LC; Vapereau

Brou, Alexandre, born 26 April 1862 at Chartres, he was a Jesuit priest who taught at Jesuit colleges from 1894 to 1924. Thereafter he was for twenty years the editor of the periodical *Études*. His writings include *Cent ans de missions, 1815-1934; les jésuites missionnaires* (1935), *Sur les frontières de l'Église* (1942), and *Au pays des dieux* (1946). He died in Laval, 12 March 1947. Mayeur I, p. 58-59

Brouard, Maurice, he was a *médecin-major de 2e classe*, and from April 1922 to July 1925, chief medical officer at Beni Ounif, Algeria. Peyronnet, p. 824

Brough, Owen Lavar, born 29 March 1916 at Tremonton, Utah, he was a graduate of Utah State University, and received a doctorate in agricultural economy in 1950 from Iowa State University. He was a professor at various American universities. In 1973 he was affiliated with the Arid Lands Agricultural Development Program, Ford Foundation, Beirut. He was joint author of the booklet, *Crop and livestock production possibilities* (1958). AmM&WS, 1973 S

Brouk, S. I., 1920- see Bruk, Solomon Il'ich

Broussais, Émile Octave, born 20 June 1855 at Paris, he studied law and Oriental languages and later was successively a barrister-at-law, and president of the Conseil général d'Alger. He was elected to the Chambre des députées in 1910. He proved to be an ardent patriot and political realist who favoured colonial politics and opposed pan-Islamic trends. When he was defeated at the 1919 elections, he returned to his legal profession in Algiers where he died around 1945. His writings include *De Paris au Soudan; Marseille-Alger-Transsaharien* (1891), and *Conférence sur la pénétration saharienne par les voies ferrées et les lignes télégraphiques* (1900). DBF; Peyronnet, p. 925

Brouwers, Paul Henri, S.J., born 27 August 1932 at Sydney, he studied at the Berchnamianum in the Netherlands, and l'Université Saint-Joseph, Beirut. Since 1970 he was general manager, Imprimerie catholique, Beirut. WhoWor, 1984

Brown, Arthur Judson, Rev., D.D., Dr., born 3 December 1856 at Holliston, Mass., he was a graduate of Wabash College, and from 1895 to 1929 secretary of the Presbyterian Board of Foreign Missions. His writings include *The foreign missionary* (1907), *The Chinese revolution* (1912), *Japan in the world of to-day* (1928), and *Memoirs of a centenarian* (1957). He died in N.Y.C., 11 January 1963. BiDInt, 1983; Lodwick; Master (6)

Brown, Cecil Hooper, born 3 December 1943 or 44 at Jackson, Tenn., he was a graduate of Tulane University, where he also received a Ph.D. in 1971 for *An ordinary language approach to transformational grammar and to formal semantic analysis of Huastee terminologiacal systems*. He was successively a professor of anthropology, and chairman of department, Northern Illinois University, DeKalb, where he was still active in 1998. His writings include *Language and living things* (1984). ConAu 109; LC; NatFacDr, 1995-1998

Brown, Cecil Jerem(a)yne, born in 1886, he was educated at Ipswich, and Trinity College, Oxford. Thereafter he was successively a reader in English at Lucknow and Allahabad. His writings include *Catalogue of coins in the Provincial Museum, Lucknow* (1920), and *The coins of India* (1921). He died 25 October 1945. Who was who, 4

Brown, Clement Henson, born in 1900, he was from 1921 to 1951 affiliated with the Egyptian Ministry of Agriculture. His writings include *Egyptian cotton* (1953). LC; Note

Brown, Constantine, born about 1889 in Rumania, he emigrated to the United States and became a foreign news analyst, and foreign correspondent for the *Chicago daily news*, stationed for nearly five years in Istanbul. His writings include *The American diplomatic game* (1935), and *International communism* (1957). He died in Washington, D.C., 23 February 1966. BioIn 2, 7; ObitOF, 1979

Brown, Demetra (Vaka), born in 1877 on Büyükada (Prinkipo), Sea of Marmara, she was educated at schools in Constantinople, France, and New York. She was on the editorial staff of *Atlantis*, a Greek newspaper in N.Y.C., and a teacher of French at Comstock School until 1904, when she married Kenneth Brown. She travelled throughout the Balkans and Asia Minor, was in Greece during the first World War, and travelled to Constantinople in 1921 to write for *Asia magazine*. Her writings, many under the pen-name Demetra Vaka, include *Haremlik* (1909), *In the shadow of Islam* (1911), *A child of the Orient* (1914), and *The unveiled ladies of Stamboi* (1923). She died in Chicago, 17 December 1946. Master (6); Shavit; Who was who in America, 2

Brown, Elizabeth Atkinson Rash, born 16 February 1932 at Louisville, Ky., she was a graduate of Swathmore College, and received a Ph.D. in 1961 from Radcliffe College for *Charters and leagues in*

early fourteenth century France. After teaching history for a few years at Harvard, she was appointed in 1974 a professor of history at Brooklyn College, specializing in medieval history. DrAS, 1978, H 1982 H

Brown, Ernest Faulkner, born 7 March 1854, he was a graduate of Trinity College, Oxford. From 1899 to 1920 he was a superior, Oxford Mission to Calcutta, and canon of St. Paul's Cathedral, Calcutta. His writngs include *Pastoral epistles with introduction* (1917). He died 31 January 1933. Who was who 3

Brown, Harold *Vivian* Bigley, born 20 August 1945, he was a graduate of Oxford, who was resident in Jeddah from 1975 to 1979. Since 1996 he was a director, Business Link, Department of Trade and Industry. He was joint editor of *Islamic philosophy and the classical tradition* (1972). Who, 1988-2003

Brown, Helen Mitchell, fl. 1974, she was a writer on numismatics.

Brown, Helen White. born 20th cent., she was in 1994 a senior assistant keeper, Heberden Coin Room, Ashmolean Museum, Oxford. Her writings include *Index to register of Queen Anne Parish* (1960), and *Some descendants of John Sheldon of Rhode Island* (1964). DrBSMES, 1993

Brown, Horatio Robert Forbes, born 16 February 1854 at Nice, he studied at Oxford, and in 1879 went to settle in Venice, where he became a historian of Venice. His writings include *Studies in the history of Venice* (1907). He died in Italy, 19 August 1926. DNB; Who was who, 2

Brown, Ian, born 20th cent., he was a graduate of St. Andrew's University, and later taught English in Cairo and travelled extensively in Syria, Jordan and the Occupied Territories of Israel before being sent to Iraq by Terre des hommes. He was the Swiss charity's last educational representative in Iraq, working two and one-half years with the boy prisoners at Ramadi before being expelled. In early 1990, he took up another assignment for Terre des hommes, managing a programme for orphans in Ethiopia. His writings include *Khomeini's forgotten sons; the story of Iran's boy soldiers* (1990).

Brown, Irving Joseph, born 20 November 1911 at N.Y.C., he was from 1945 to 1955 the European representative of the American Federation of Labor, and later became a sometime AFL-CIO director of international affairs. He died 10 February 1989. Who was wo in America, 9

Brown, John Porter, born 17 August 1814 at Chillicote, Ohio., he studied Arabic and Turkish in Turkey, where he was a U.S. foreign service officer until his death in Constantinople on 28 April 1872. His writings include *The dervishes; or, Oriental spiritualism* (1868), and *Turkish evening entertainment*, translated from the Turkish of Ahmed ibn Hemdem, the ketkhoda, called Sohaibe (1850). DAB, 3; Shavit; Who was who in America, 3

Brown, Judith A., born 20th cent., she received a Ph.D. in 1964 from Durham University for her thesis, *A geographical study of the evolution of the cities of Teheran and Isfahan.* Sluglett

Brown, Kenneth, *Mrs.*, 1877-1946 *see* Brown, Demetra (Vaka)

Brown, Kenneth Lewis, born in 1905, he received a Ph.D. in 1969 from UCLA for *The social history of a Moroccan town; Salé, 1830-1930.* In 1990 he was a senior lecturer in sociology in the University of Manchester. His writings include *People of Salé; tradition and change in a Moroccan city* (Manchester, 1976). MESA *Roster of members*, 1977-1990; NUC, 1973-1977

Brown, L. Dean, born in 1920 at N.Y.C., he was educated at Wesleyan College, and the Imperial Defence College, London. He joined the U.S. Foreign Service in 1946 and served until retirement in 1975. From 1975 to 1987 he was a president of the Middle East Institute, Washington, D.C. His writings include *The land of Palestine* (1982). IntWW, 1974-1990/91|; Master (1)

Brown, Leon Carl, born 22 April 1928 at Mayfield, Ky., he received a Ph.D. in 1962 from Harvard for *Tunisia under the French protectorate.* He was appointed in 1966 a professor of Near Eastern history and civilization at Princeton, became its director of the Near Eastern studies program in 1970, and Garrett Professor of foreign affairs in 1976. Concurrently he was a U.S. Foreign Service officer in Lebanon and the Sudan, as well as a Fulbright fellow. His writings include *State and society in independent North Africa* (1966), *The Tunisia of Ahmed Bey* (1974), and *International politics and the Middle East* (1984). ConAu, 117; DrAS, 1974, 1978, 1982; WhoAm, 1974-1988/89

Brown, Michel E., born 20th cent., he was in 1974 affiliated with Cornell University, Ithaca, N.Y., and a joint author of *A model of cartel formation* (1976).

Brown, Neville George, born 8 April 1932 at Watlington, Oxfordshire, he was a graduate of New College, Oxford, and University College, London. He successively served as a lecturer, Royal Military Academy, Sandhurst, the Institute for Strategic Studies, London, became a defence correspondent of the *New statesman*, and a lecturer in political science and international affairs, Birmingham University.

His writings include *Strategic mobility* (1963), *Arms without Empire* (1967), *The future global challenge* (1977), *Limited world war* (1984), and *The strategic revolution* (1992). ConAu, 9-12; Master (1)

Brown, Peter Robert Lamont, born 26 July 1935 at Dublin, he was a graduate of Oxford, and later taught medieval history at U.K. universities and, since 1978, at the University of California, Berkeley. His writings include *The world of late antiquity, from Marcus Aurelius to Muhammad* (1971), and *Power and persuasion in late antiquity* (1992). ConAu, new rev., 13; Master (1); Who, 1985-2003

Brown, Percy, born in 1872, he studied at the School of Art, Birmingham, and later excavated in Upper Egypt for the Egypt Exploration Fund. In 1899 he entered the Indian Educational Service and was successively principal, Mayo School of Art, and curator, Museum, Lahore, and principal, Government School of Art, Calcutta. His writings include *Picturesque Nepal* (1912), *Indian paintings under the Moghuls* (1924), and *Indian architecture* (1942-43). He died 22 March 1955. IndianBiInd (3); WhoIndia, 1927; Who was who, 5

Brown, Philip Marshall, born 31 July 1875 at Hampden, Me., he was a graduate of Williams College, and Harvard. He entered the Foreign Service in 1900 and was posted to Constantinople and later in Egypt and Palestine. From 1913 until retirement in 1935, he was a professor of international law at Princeton University. His writings include *Foreigners in Turkey* (1914). He died in Williamstown, Mass., 10 May 1966. Shavit; Who was who in America, 4

Brown, R. Weir, LL.B., fl. 1925, he was a writer on international law.

Brown, Richard Jay, born 22 January 1922 at Council Bluffs, Iowa, he was a graduate of State University of Iowa, where he also received a Ph.D. in 1955 for *Public criticism of secondary school history teaching*. From 1965 to 1967 he served as a cultural exchange officer in Tehran. Thereafter he was a professor of history and education at Wisconsin State University until 1968 when he was appointed a director, Nicolet College and Technical Institute. DrAS 1969 H; LEduc, 1974

Brown, Stuart E., born 20 July 1942, he received an M.A. in 1969 from the Institute of Islamic Studies, McGill University, Montreal, and also his Ph.D in 1976 for *The "Young Tunisia" Movement*. In the 1990s he was affiliated with the Sub-Unit on Dialogue, World Council of Churches, Geneva. His writings include *The Nearest in affection* (1995). Ferahian; LC

Brown, Theo, born in 1914, he was a folk-lorist whose writings include *The fate of the dead; a study in folk-eschatology in the West Country after the Reformation* (1975). LC

Brown, Theodore Burton, fl. 1946-1983 *see* Burton-Brown, Theodore

Brown, Theodore Nigel Leslie, M.A., fl. 1947, he wrote *The History of the Manchester Geographical Society, 1884-1950* (Manchester, Manchester University Press, 1971). LC

Brown, Vivian, 1945- *see* Brown, Harold Vivian Bigley

Brown, William Norman, born 24 June 1892 at Baltimore, Md., he was a graduate of Johns Hopkins University, who spent some of his boyhood years with his missionary parents in India. From 1922 to 1924, he was again in India as a professor of English; and from 1926 until his retirement in 1966, he was professor of Sanskrit in the University of Pennsylvania. His writings include *India, Pakistan, Ceylon* (1951), *The United States and India and Pakistan* (1953), and selected articles entitled *India and Indology* (1978). he was honoured by *Indological studies in honor of W. Norman Brown* (1962). He died in West Chester, Pa., on 22 June 1975. Master (6); Shavit - Asia

Brown, William R., he was from 1960 to 1962 a deputy principal officer at the U.S. Legation in Ta'iz, Yemen, and in 1963 became a Foreign Service officer assigned to the Agency for International Development. He wrote *The Last crusade; a negotiator's Middle East handbook* (1980). Note

Browne, Donald Roger, born 13 March 1934 at Detroit, he was a graduate of the University of Michigan, where he also received a Ph.D. in 1958 for *The history and programming policies of RIAS, Berlin*. He was a sometime professor of speech-communication at the University of Minnesota. His principal scholarly activity was in the field of comparative and international broadcasting. His writings include *The Voice of America* (1976), and *Comparing broadcasting systems* (1989). DrAS, 1974 E, 1978 E, 1982 E; WhoAm, 1988-2003

Browne, Edward Granville, born on the family estate in Gloucestershire, 7 February 1862. Initially he studied medicine at Cambridge, but soon turned to Oriental studies. His year in Persia, 1887-1888, he described in *A Year amongst the Persians* (1893). In spite of a life-long love for the country, he never again set foot on Persian soil. At Cambridge he was Adams Professor of Arabic, but he is best known for his achievements in the field of Persian studies. Since he was bred to wealth and status, and a rich man in his own right, he could please himself in virtually everything he did and said. His main legacy is the *Literary history of Persia* (1902-1924), in four volumes. He died near Cambridge, 5 January 1926. CentBritOr, pp. 74-86; DNB; EncIran; Flück; Krachkovskii; Wright

Browne, Laurence Edward, born 17 April 1887 at Northampton. After obtaining his degree at Sydney Sussex College, Cambridge, followed by ordination and a curacy, he was a lecturer at St. Augustine's College, Canterbury (1913-1920), and Bishop's College, Calcutta (1921-1925). It was in India that his interest in Islam was awakened. He taught from 1930 to 1934 at the Henry Martyn School of Islamic Studies in Lahore. It was during this period that he completed the work for which he is best known, *The Eclipse of Christianity in Asia* (1933). For this work the Cambridge University awarded him an honorary doctorate in divinity. After a furlough in 1935, circumstances forced him to stay in England for the rest of his life. He did full-time university teaching only after the second World War at Manchester and Leeds, where he resigned from the chair of theology on reaching the age of sixty-five. He died at a nursing home in Sussex, 29 May 1986. MW 56 (1966), 328-329; *Who was who,* 8

Browne, W. H., born 19th cent., he was an English missionary to the Assyrian Christians who served in Qudschani (Hakkari), from 1886 until his death in 1910.

Browne, William George, born 25 July 1768 at London. After disappointing studies at Oxford, he pursued private legal studies, which he relinquished on becoming independent upon his father's death. In 1792 he travelled to Alexandria and on to the Sudan, returning via Constantinople in 1798. From 1800 to 1802 he travelled again in Turkey and the Levant. On his last journey to Persia he was murdered near Tabriz in the summer of 1813. His *Travels in Africa, Egypt, and Syria, from the year 1792 to 1798* (1799) were published soon in French and German translations. Dawson; DNB; Egyptology; Hill

Brownfeld, Allan Charles, born 26 November 1939 at N.Y.C., he received a J.D. degree in 1964 from Marshall-Whyte School of Law, College of William and Mary. He was a journalist and speech writer for U.S. politicians. In 1986 he was an associate editor of *AIM report*, and associate editor of the *Lincoln review*. His writings include *The New left* (1968), *Dossier on Douglas* (1970), and *The Revolution lobby* (1985). WhoE, 1991

Browning, Robert, born 15 January 1914 at Glasgow, he was educated at the University of Glasgow, and Balliol College, Oxford. He was a professor of classics and ancient history in the University of London from 1947 to 1981, when he became a professor emeritus. His writings include *Byzantium and Bulgaria* (1975), *The Byzantine Empire* (1980), and *The Greek world* (1985). He died 11 March 1997. ConAu, 33-36, new rev., 13; IntAu&W, 1982-1989; Who, 1982-1995; WrDr, 1982-1998/2000

Brownlee, William Hugh, born 17 February 1917 at Sylvia, Kansas. After he received his Ph.D. in 1947 from Duke University, he was for two years a fellow at the American Schools of Oriental Research. Thereafter he was a professor of Old Testament, Claremont Graduate School and University Center, Claremont, Calif. His writings include *The meaning of the Dead Sea scolls for the Bible* (1964). ConAu, 9-12; Master (2); WrDr, 1976-1984/86|

Bruce, Charles Edward, born 23 March 1876, he was a graduate of Wellington College, and the Royal Military College, Sandhurst. He joined the Indian Political Department in 1901, and served in the North West Frontier Province and Afghanistan. He died 24 January 1950. IndianBInd (3); *Who was who,*4

Bruce, Frederick Fyvie, born 12 October 1912, he was a distinguished student of Greek and Latin at Aberdeen, Cambridge, and Wien, and became a professor of Biblical history and literature at various universities in the U.K. and abroad. His many writings include *The Teacher of Righteousness in the Qumran texts* (1957). He died 11 September 1990. *Who was who,* 8

Bruce, J. F., M.A., fl. 1944-1947, he was a sometime professor of history, Panjab University, Lahore.

Bruce, James, born 14 December 1730 at Kinnaird, Scotland, he spent part of his early life studying Arabic and Ethiopic. As a British consul at Alger, he made an archaeological tour of the Barbary Coast. He reached Egypt in 1768, and set out to explore the sources of the Nile. His writings include *Travels to discover the source of the Nile* (1790). He died in 1794. James M. Reid wrote *Traveller extraordinary; the life of James Bruce of Kinnaird* (1968). Dawson; DNB; Egyptology; Hill; Henze; Wright

Bruce, Robert, Dr., born about 1825 in Ireland, he had been a missionary of the Church Missionary Society in India for well over ten years, when, in 1869, he was granted permission to visit Persia on the way back to his work in the Punjab, with the purpose of revising in Julfa (Isfahan) Henry Martyn's Persian translation of the Bible, a translation not unimportant for the mission in India. His leave of absence from India became permanent in 1875. When he retired in 1893, he was able to supervise the printing of his revision in 1895 in Leipzig at the cost of the British Bible Society. Richter, 329-330; Wright, 118-119

Bruch, Henri Frédéric *Edouard*, born 11 July 1835 at Strasbourg, he received a medical doctorate in 1860 from the Université de Strasbourg for *De la fécondation*. Thereafter he was an ophthalmologist at l'École de médecine d'Alger. In 1900 he attended the French Medical Congress. NDBA; Note

Brücher, Wolfgang, born 30 May 1941 at Mühlheim, Germany, he received a Dr.phil. in 1969 from the Universität Tübingen for his thesis, *Die Erschließung des tropischen Regenwalds ... der Anden*. He was appointed in 1976 a professor of geography at the Universität Saarbrücken. He was joint author of *Industriegeographie der Bundesrepublik Deutschland and Frankreichs* (1991). Kürschner, 1980-2003

Bruchhausen, Karl H. N. von, born in 1851, he was an army officer who retired with the rank of major. His writings include *Der Werdegang des italienischen Heeres* (Berlin, 1906), and *Der kommende Krieg; eine Studie über die militärische Lage Deutschlands* (Berlin, 1906). NUC, pre-1956

von Brück, Max Karl Franz, born 27 February 1904 at Kempten, Germany, he studied law at München and Erlangen, where he received a Dr.jur. in 1933 for *Der Begriff des Jagens unter besonderer Berücksichtigung des bayerischen Rechts*. He was a journalist and editor, and a joint author of *Ein Jahrhundert Frankfurter Zeitung, 1956-1956* (1956). Wer ist wer, 1955-1987/88|

von Brücke, Ernst Wilhelm, Ritter, born 6 June 1819 at Berlin, he studied at Heidelberg and Berlin, where he received a doctorate in 1842 for *De diffusione humorum per septa mortua et viva*. He was successively a professor of physiology at Königsberg, and director, Physiologisches Institut in Wien. From 1882 to 1885 he was vice-president of the Akademie der Wissenschaften in Wien. His researches include optics and chromatology; he developed a phonetic alphabet. His writings include *Grundzüge der Physiologie und Systematik der Sprachlaute* (1856). ÖBL

Brückmann, Werner C. Ph., born 28 September 1907 at Mannheim, Germany, he studied at Genève, München, Frankfurt, and Berlin, to which Kansas State University, Lawrence, was added a year or two later. In 1942 he received a Dr.jur from the Universität Hamburg for his thesis, *Eine Untersuchung über die Verbeamtung des deutschen Richters nebst Vorschlägen zur Wiederherstellung echten Richtertums*. Since 1938 he was employed in the German judiciary, and later in the foreign service. In 1955 he was a German consul at Atlanta, Ga. Thesis; Wer ist's, 1955

Bruel, Gilbert *Georges*, born 23 May 1871 at Moulins (Allier), he graduated in 1895 from l'École coloniale, Paris, and thereafter served as a colonial administrator in French Equatorial Africa until 1910, when he returned to Paris. His writings include *Bibliographie de l'Afrique équatoriale française* (1914), and *L'Afrique équatoriale française* (1918), a work for which he was awarded the Prix Lucien de Reinach by the Académie des sciences morales et politiques, and the Prix Delalande-Guérineau by the Académie des sciences. He died at his estate des Vayots in Neuilly-le-Réal, 31 October 1944. Hommes et destins, vol. 4, pp. 135-145

Brügel, Johann Wolfgang, born 3 July 1905 at Auspitz, Austria-Hungary, he studied law at Karls Universität, Praha, 1923-28. He went into exile in France and subsequently in the U.K., returning to Czechoslovakia after the war, but went back to London in November 1946, where his trace is lost in 1978. His writings include *Tschechen und Deutsche, 1918-1938* (1967). BioHbDtE

Brüggemann, Werner, fl. 1979, he was a joint author of *Teppiche der Bauern und Nomaden in Anatolien* (1982), its English translation, *Rugs of the peasants and nomads of Anatolia* (1983), and *Pflanzliche Bauelemente der Seldschuken in Kleinasien* (1989). LC

Bruggey, Jürgen, born 20th cent., he received a doctorate in 1970 from the Technische Hochschule München for his thesis, *Mesozoikum und Alttertiär in Nord-Paktia*. Schwarz

Brugman, Jan (Johan), born 9 May 1923 at Zaandam, Netherlands, he was from 1948 to 1960 in the Dutch foreign service, posted mainly to Cairo. In 1960 he received a doctorate from the Rijksuniversiteit te Leiden for his thesis, *De betekenis van het Mohammedaanse recht in het hedendaagse Egypte*. Since 1961 he taught Arabic at Leiden. His writings include *An introduction to the history of modern Arabic literature in Egypt* (1984), and *De zuilen van de islam* (1985); he was joint author of *Arabic studies in the Netherlands* (1979). LC; Wie is wie, 1984/88

Brugmann (Brugman), Karl Friedrich Christian, born 29 June 1919 at Wiesbaden, Germany, he studied at Halle and Leipzig, where he received a Dr.phil. in 1871 for his thesis, *De graecae linguae productione suppletoria*,. He was a professor of comparative philology successively at the universities of Freiburg and Leipzig. His writings include *Problem der homerischen Textkritik und der vergleichenden Sprachwissenschaft* (1876), and *Elements of the comparative grammar of the Indo-Germanic languages* (1888-95). He died in Leipzig, 29 June 1919. DtBiJ 2 (1917/20); GSE; Indogermanisches Jahrbuch 7 (1919), pp. 143-148, reprinted in PorLing, vol. 1, pp. 575-580; NDB; Wer ist's, 1912

Brugsch, Ernst Mohammed, born 12 January 1860 at Berlin, the son of Heinrich Karl B., he was a translator and Arabist whose writings include *Arabisch-deutsches Handwörterbuch* (1924), and *Die Erzählung von der Sklavin Tawaddud aus Tausend und eine Nacht* (1924). He died 21 August 1929. DtBiJ 11 (1929)

Brugsch, Heinrich Ferdinand Karl, born 18 February 1827 at Berlin, he was one of the greatest German Egyptologist of his day, and one of the profoundest and most original scholars in Europe in an age that produced veritable giants in this field. In 1853 he was sent to Egypt by the Prussian government, and led a Prussian embassy to Persia, 1860-61. His writings include *Reise der k. preuss. Gesandtschaft nach Persien* (1862-63), its Persian translation in 1988, *Reise nach der großen Oase El Khargeh* (1878), *Egypt under the Pharaohs; a history derived entirely from the documents* (1891), and the autobiography, *Mein Leben und Wandern* (1894). He died in Berlin, 9 September 1894. Dawson; DtBE; DtBiInd (5); Egyptology; Embacher; EncBrit; GSE; Henze; Hill; NDB

Bruhns, Fred C., fl. 1955. He spent the years 1948 to 1950 with the International Refugee Organization, working on the European displaced persons' problem as a Resettlement, Repatriation, and Placement Officer. In 1952-53 he held a Ford Foundation grant to study the Arab refugee problem. *Middle East Journal* 9 (1955), p. 130

de **Bruijn**, Johannes Thomas Pieter, born in 1931, he was a sometime professor of Persian in the Department of Middle Eastern and Islamic Studies, Rijksuniversiteit te Leiden. His writings include *Of piety and poetry* (1983), and *Islam, norm, ideaal en werkelijkheid* (1984). He was a joint author of *Dichter en hof; verkenningen in veertien culturen* (1986). EURAMES, 1993; LC

van **Bruinessen**, Maarten Martinus, born in 1946 at Schoonhoven, Netherlands, he studied physics and ethnology at the Rijksuniversiteit te Utrecht. Since 1966 he travelled extensively in the Middle East. From 1974 to 1976 he carried on ethnographic field reseach in Kurdistan, which became the subject of his doctoral thesis, *Agha, shaikh, and state*, submitted in 1978 to the Rijksuniversiteit te Utrecht. Since 1979 he taught Turkish, Kurdish, and Indonesian Islam successively at Utrecht and Leiden. His writings include *Turkije in crisis* (1982), and the translation, *Agha Scheich und Staat* (1989); he was a joint translator of *Evliya Çelebi in Diyarbekir* (1988). Private

Bruins, Evert M., fl. 1969, his writings include *Nouvelles découvertes sur les mathématiques babyloniennes* (1952); he was joint author of *Textes mathématiques de Suse* (1961). LC

Bruk, Solomon Il'ich, born 1 July 1920 at Rogachev, Belorussia, he graduated in 1947 from the School of Geography, Moscow State University, and received a doctorate in 1964 for his thesis, Основные проблемы этнической географии. He was a sometime deputy director of the Miklukho-Maklai Institute of Ethnography, USSR Academy of Sciences. His writings include Население мира; этнодемографический обзор (1965), its translation, *La population du monde; aperçu ethnodémographique* (1983), *L'Ethnographie des pays du Moyen-Orient* (1966), and *Ethnographic processes; the world population at the threshold of the 21st century* (1985). LC; Miliband; Miliband²

Brulé, Jean Claude, born 20th cent., he was in 1987 a professor of geography at the Université de Tours. LC

Brulez, Wilfrid, born in 1927 at Blankenberge, he was a sometime professor of modern economic and social history in Gent University. His writings include *Correspondance de Richard Pauli-Stravius* (1955), *De firma della Faille en de internationale handel van Vlaamse firma's in de 16e eeuw* (1959), *Marchands flamands à Venise* (1965), and *Der Kolonialhandel und die Handelsblüte der Niederlande in der Mitte des 16. Jahrhunderts* (1969). LC

Brummer, Rudolf Max, born 23 April 1907 at Radebeul, Germany, he studied at Leipzig and the Sorbonne, and was successively a professor of Romance philology at Breslau, Rostock, Berlin and Mainz. His writings include *Bibliographia Lulliana* (1976). He died in München, 1 October 1989. Kürschner, 1950-1987; WhoWor, 1974-1978

Brun, Conrad Malte, 1775-1826 *see* Malte Brun, Conrad

Brun, Filip, 1804-1880 *see* Bruun, Filip Jacob

Brun, Thierry André, born about 1940, he was a French agronomist who received a Ph.D. in 1974 from the University of California at Berkeley for his thesis, *Hormonal disturbances and liver dysfunction in infantile malnutrition*. In 1990 he was affiliated with the Center for Analysis of World Food Issues, College of Agriculture and Life sciences, Cornell University, Ithaca, N.Y. LC; Note

Brun-Rollet, Antoine, born 25 July 1807 at Saint-Jean-de-Maurienne (Savoie), he was educated at a theological seminary until 1827, when he accepted employment with a Marseille commercial enterprise. He was sent to Egypt, where worked as an subordinate until 1830 when he entered the service of J. M. F. Vaissière, a French merchant. He rapidly made a fortune by trading on his own account and went to the Sudan in the following year and established a trading post, living the life of a native. He accompanied the governor-general of the Sudan, Ahmad Pasha, on the latter's expedition to Taka in 1840. His own activities necessitated trips up the Nile between 1843 and 1845, which he described in *Le Nil blanc et le Soudan; études sur l'Afrique centrale, mœurs et coutumes des sauvages* (1855). After he was appointed in 1855 Sardinian vice-consul at Khartoum, he made one more journey to the Bahr al-Ghazal region in 1856. He died in Khartoum, 25 September 1858. DBF; Hill; Henze

Brundage, James Arthur, born 5 February 1929 at Lincoln, Nebr., he was a graduate of the University of Nebraska, and received his Ph.D. in 1955 from Fordham University, N.Y. After teaching for a few years at Fordham, he was appointed in 1964 a professor of history in the University of Wisconsin, Milwaukee. His writings include *The Crusades; a documentary survey* (1962), *Medieval canon law and the crusader* (1969), and *Law, sex, and Christian society in medieval Europe* (1987), and he edited *The Crusades; motives and achievements* (1964). ConAu 5-8, new rev., 7; DrAS 1969 H, 1974 H, 1978, 1982 H; IntAu&W, 1976-1991/92; WhoAm, 1974-1988/89; WhoMW, 1992/93

Brundage, William H., fl. 1977, he was a sometime instructor at the United States Air Force Academy, Colorado. Note

Brunel, Camille, born 19th cent., he was a sometime *commissaire délimitateur*. In 1906 he had retired from a position as chief topographer. Note

Brunel, Clovis Félix, born 19 February 1884 at Amiens, he was educated at the Lycée Henri IV, l'École des chartes, la Sorbonne, and l'École pratique des Hautes Études, Paris. He was an archivist and palaeographer until he was appointed in 1919 a professor at l'École des chartes, becoming its director in 1930. In 1937 he was elected a member of the Académie des insciptions et belles-lettres. His writings include *Les plus anciens chartes en langue provençale* (1926), *Bibliographie des manuscrits littéraires en ancien provençal* (1935), and numerous editions of medieval texts. He died, 8 December 1971. Pierre Marot wrote *Notice sur la vie et les travaux de M. Clovis Brunel, lue dans la séance du 8 mars 1974* (Paris, Académie des Inscriptions, 1974). DBFC; IndexBFr² (2); WhoFr, 1953/54-1971/72

Brunet, Louis Pierre Joseph Emmanuel, his date of birth is variously given as 23, 24 and 29 July 1846 and 1847 at Saint-Denis, Ile de la Réunion. He was a lawyer, *député*, senator, a sometime vice-president of the Commission des affaires extérieure et des protectorats, and a partisan of French colonialism and justice in the Indian Ocean and adjacent areas. His writings include *La France à la Madagascar, 1815-1895* (1895), and *L'Œuvre de la France à Madagascar* (1903). He died suddenly 26 December 1905. Curinier, vol. 4 (1903), p. 252; DBF; *Hommes et destins*, vol. 4, pp. 148-150

Brunet, Roger, fl. 1956, he was a contributor to the Marxist journal *La pensée*.

Brunet-Millon, Charles, fl. 1912, he wrote *Les Boutriers de la mer des Indes; affaires de Zanzibar et de Mascate* (Paris, 1910). NUC, pre-1956

Bruneton, Ariane, born in 1944, she studied sociology, ethnology, and ethnographic cinematography, as well as Berber language at l'École nationale des langues orientales vivantes, and Musée de l'Homme, Paris. From 1967 to 1971 she carried on field work in Morocco, especially on diet and food habits. Concurrently she was an associate expert in the Nutrition Division of the Food and Agricultural Organization, Roma, from 1970 to 1971. Since 1972 she did research in rural France on both the food habits and the women of that area. Note

Brunhes, Léon Victor *Jean* Baptiste, born 25 October 1869 at Toulouse. After graduating in 1889 from l'École normale supérieure, he pursued studies under a scholarship of the Thiers Foundation. In 1902 he received a doctorate for his thesis, *L'irrigation, ses conditions géographiques dans la péninsule Ibérique et l'Afrique du nord.* Thereafter he was a professor of geography at the universities of Fribourg and Lausanne. His writings include *Étude de géographie humaine* (1902), *Human geography* (1920), and *Races* (1930). He died in Boulogne-sur-Seine, 25 August 1930. DBF; DcScB

Bruni, Giraldo (Gerardo), born 30 June 1896 at Cascia (Perugia), he received a doctorate in 1922 for his thesis, *La metafisica di F. Suarez.* Under the Carnegie Endowment for International Peace he went to the United States where he studied library science at Ann Arbor, Mich., and Columbia, N.Y.C. From 1929 to 1946 he was a librarian at the Vatican. His writings include *Riflessioni sulla scolastica* (1927), its translation, *Progressive scholasticism* (1929), and *La biblioteca moderna, la sua fisionomia i suoi problemi.* He died in Roma, 10 December 1975. DizBI

Brunialti, Attilo, born 2 April 1849 at Vicenza, he studied law at Padova, and thereafter was appointed a professor successivlely at various Italian universities. His writings include *Cli eredi della Turchia*

(1880), *Algeria, Tunisia e Tripolitania; studii di geografia politica sugli ultimi avvenimenti africani* (1881), *L'Italia e la questione coloniale* (1885), and *Le colonie degli Italiani, con appendice*(1897). He died in Roma, 2 December 1920. DizBI

Brunner, Christopher J., fl. 1977, he edited *A man of enterprise; the short writings of Josiah Harlan* (New York, Afghanistan Forum, 1987). LC

Brunner, Otto, born 21 April 1898 at Mödling, Austria, he received a Dr.phil. in 1922 from the Universität Wien for *Österreich und die Walachei während des Türkenkrieges von 1683 bis 1699*. He was for over ten years affiliated with the Staatsarchiv, Wien, before he was appointed a professor of Austrian history in the Universität Wien. On his sixty-fifth birthday he was honoured by *Alteuropa und die moderne Gesellschaft, Festschrift für Otto Brunner* (1963). He died in Hamburg, 12 June 1982. DtBE; Kürschner, 1931-1980; WhoAustria, 1955-1964

Brunner-Traut, Emma, born 25 December 1911 at Frankfurt am Main, she received a Dr. phil., became a private scholar, a sometime lecturer at Cairo University, and an associate of the Ägyptische Abteilung, Staatliche Museen Berlin. Her writings include *Der Tanz im alten Ägypten* (1938), *Kleine Ägyptenkunde* (1982), and *Die Kopten* (1982). She was joint author of *Die ägyptische Sammlung der Universität Tübingen* (1981), *Osiris, Kreuz und Halbmond* (1984), and joint editor of *Die fünf großen Weltreligionen* (1974), and *Ägypten; Kunst- und Reiseführer* (1988). Kürschner, 1961-2003

Brünnow, Rudolf Ernst, born 7 February 1858 at Ann Arbor, Mich., he was a graduate of Trinity College, Dublin, and studied at Basel, Tübingen, and Straßburg, where he received a Dr.phil. in 1884 for *Die Charidschiten unter den ersten Omayyaden*. In 1910 he was appointed professor of Semitic studies at Princeton. His writings include *Chrestomathy of Arabic prose-pieces* (1895), *Die Provincia Arabica auf Grund zweier in den Jahren 1897 und 1898 unternommenen Reisen* (1904-1909), and *Arabische Chrestomathie aus Prosaschriftstellern* (1913). He died 14 April 1917. Fück; WhAm, I

Bruno, Andrea, born in 1931, she was a professor of architecture and affiliated with the Politecnico di Torino. In 1989 she edited *Corsi di perfezionamento*. LC; Note

Bruno, Henri, born 29 April 1888 at Cherchell, Algeria, he received all his education in Alger, and his doctorate in 1913 from the Sorbonne for *Contribution à l'étude du régime des eaux en droit musulman*. He pursued a legal career in France and Morocco, 1909-1932, and concurrently a university teaching career at Rabat, where he was affiliated with the Institut des Hautes Études Marocaines since 1913. He was joint author of *Répertoire alphabétique de la jurisprudence de la Cour d'appel de Rabat* (1947-1955). He died in an automobile accident, 15 February 1948. Hespéris 36 (1949), pp. 3-5

Brunot, Louis, born in 1904, his writings include *Yailah; ou, l'arabe sans mystère* (1921), *Glossaire judéo-arabe de Fès* (1940), *Au seuil de la vie marocaine* (1950), and *Introduction à l'arabe marocain* (1950). LC

Brunov, Nikolai Ivanovich, born in 1898 at Moscow, he was a graduate of Moscow University, and was apointed professor of history of art at its School of Architecture in 1934. His writings include Храм Василия Блаженного в Москве (1988). GSE; LC

Bruns, Paul Jacob, born 18 July 1743 at Preetz, Germany, he studied theology at the universities of Lübeck and Jena. He was appointed in 1781 a professor of history at the Universität Helmstedt, and in 1796 a professor of Oriental languages. After the closing of the university, he went to Halle as professor of philosophy. His writings include *Allgemeine Literärgeschichte zum Behuf akademischer Vorlesungen* (1804). He died in Halle, 17 November 1814. ADtB; DtBE; DtBilnd (6)

Brunschvig, Robert, born 6 October 1901 at Bordeaux, he studied classical philology at l'École normale supérieure, Paris. Thereafter he taught with a brief interruption in Tunis, from 1922 to 1946. During the Vichy regime, he worked tirelessly on behalf of the persecuted Jews of Algeria. From 1947 to 1968 he was successively a professor of Islamic history at Bordeaux, professor of Islamic studies at the Sorbonne, and director of l'Institut d'études islamqiues, Paris. Concurrently he was for many years a joint editor of *Studia islamica*. His writings include *La Berbérie orientale sous les Hafsides* (1940-47). He died 16 February 1990. EncJud; Index Islamicus (3); WhoWor, 1974-76; WhoWorJ, 1965

Brunschwig, Henri, born 2 June 1904 at Mulhouse (Haut-Rhin), he was educated at Mulhouse and Strasbourg, and thereafter successively affiliated with the Lycée Henri IV, l'École nationale de la France d'outre-mer, l'École pratique des hautes études, and l'Institut des sciences politiques, Paris. His writings include *La Colonisation française du Pacte colonial à l'Union française* (1949), *Mythes et réalités de l'impérialisme colonial français, 1871-1914* (1960), its translation, *French colonialism, 1871-1914; myths and realities* (1966), and *Noirs et Blancs dans l'Afrique noire française; ou, comment le colonisé devient colonisateur, 1870-1914* (1983). NDBA; Unesco; WhoFr, 1965/66-1987/88

Brunyate, Sir William Edward, born 12 September 1867, he was a graduate of Trinity College, Cambridge, and called to the bar, Lincoln's Inn, 1894. He entered the Khedivial service in 1898. In 1899 he was sent to the Sudan to assist Lord Kitchener in drafting fundamental laws for the newly occupied country. During the first World War he was a counsel to the Sultan of Egypt, and legal adviser to H.B.M.'s Residency, Cairo. From 1921 to 1924 he was vice-chancellor of Hong-Kong University. He edited the *Report of Committee with reference to the sale of government lands in the Sudan* (1904). He died 29 August 1943. Goldschmidt; Hill; *Who was who, 4*

Brusa, A. fl. 1940, he wrote *Le Rhodesie nell'Eurafrica di domani* (Milano, 1941).

Brush, John Edwin, born 2 September 1919 at Jefferson, Pa., he spent most of his early years in India where his parents were Baptist missionaries. He was a conscientious objector and assigned alternative service, 1943-47. He graduated from Bucknell University and received a Ph.D. in 1952 from the University of Wisconsin for *Trade centers of southwestern Wisconsin*. Since 1951 he taught geography at Rutgers University, New Brunswick, N.J. AmM&WS, 1973 S, 1978 S; ConAu 33-36; IWWAS, 1976/77; WrDr, 1976/78-1984/86|

Brush, Stanley Elwood, born 8 November 1925 at Khargpur, Bengal, India, he graduated in 1948 from Bucknell University and received a Ph.D. in 1971 from the University of California for *Protestants in the Punjab; religion and social change in an Indian province in the nineteenth century*. He taught at Forman Christian College, Lahore, from 1958 to 1963, before being appointed in 1967 a professor of history at the University of Bridgeport, Conn. DrAS 1969 H, 1974 H, 1978 H, 1982 H; IWWAS, 1976/77

Brussilowsky, Jean, born 20h cent., he was in 1969 a *conservateur* at the library of the Institut international d'administration publique [Paris.] Note

Bruton, Henry Jackson, born 30 August 1921 at Dallas, Texas, he graduated from the University of Texas and received a Ph.D. in 1952 from Harvard. From 1958 to 1960 he was a financial adviser to the International Cooperation Administration, Tehran. He taught successively at Yale, Bombay, and Karachi, before being appointed in 1962 a professor of economics at Williams College, Williamstown, Mass. His writings include *A survey of recent contributions to the theory of economic growth* (1956), and *Principles of development economics* (1965). In 1992 he published a World Bank comparative study on *Sri Lanka and Malaysia*. He was joint author of *The Pakistan export bonus scheme* (1963). AmM&WS, 1973 S; ConAu 21-24; WhoAm, 1974/75-1988/89

Brutskus (Brutzkus), IU. (Julius) D., born 25 December 1870 at Palanga, Courland, he studied medicine at Moscow and later settled in St. Petersburg where he was a historian, communal worker, and active in the Zionist movement until obliged to emigrate to Palestine via France. His writings include Письмо хазарского еврея от X века (Berlin 1924). He was joint editor of Сборник памяти А. Д. Идельсрна (Berlin, 1925). He died in Israel in 1951. EncJud; Wininger

Bruun (Brun), Filip Jacob, born 18 August 1804 at Frederikshavn, Denmark, he went in 1832 to Odessa where he taught at first at the Lycée Richelieu and, since 1866, at the University. His writings include *Notices historiques et topographiques concernant les colonies italiennes de Gazarie* (1866), and Черноморскне (1874). He died 15 June 1880. Meyers

Bruun, Malthe Conrad, 1775-1826 *see* Malte Brun, Conrad

Bruun, Peter *Daniel*, born 27 January 1856 at Asmild Kloster, Viborg, Denmark, he was an army officer and a traveller. His writings include *Algier och Sahara* (1893), *Huleboerne i syd Tunis* (1895), its translation, *The Cave dwellers of southern Tunisia* (1898), *Afrika* (1901), *Plevna - Schipka* (1915), and *Paa de tyrkiske Fronter, 1914-1915* (1922). He died in Hellerup, 22 September 1931. DanskBL; DanskBL²

Bruun, Philippe, 1804-1880 *see* Bruun, Filip Jacob

de **Bruyn**, Cornelis, born in 1652 at s'Gravenhage, Netherlands, he was a traveller whose travel accounts have been translated into many languages. These include *Reizen door de vermaardste deelen van Klein Asia* (1698), its translation, *Voyage au Levant* (1700), *Reizen over Moskovie, door Persie en Indië* (1711), and its translation, *Voyage par la Moscovie en Perse* (1718). He died near Utrecht in 1726 or 27. EncIran; GdeEnc; NieuwNBW

van **Bruyssel**, Ernest Jean, born 1 July 1827 at Bruxelles, he was an archivist and historian who travelled extensively since his early days. Since 1868 he was variously posted as a Belgian consul - in 1899 to Tunis. He retired in 1906. His writings include *La Vie sociale et ses évolutions* (1907). He died in Roma, 2 May 1914. BioNBelg

Bruzon, Paul, born 11 June 1877 at Moustiers-sur-le-Lay (Vendée), he received a medical doctorate in 1904 for *La Médecine et les religions*. He was sent on missions to the Orient in 1907, 1909, 1911, 1912, and 1913. IndexBFr² (1); *Qui est-ce*, 1934

Bruzonsky, Mark A., fl. 1975, he was the editor of the 1977 edition of *The Middle East; U.S. policy, Israel, oil, and the Arabs* and in 1987, a joint editor of *Security in the Middle East; regional change and great power strategies*. MESA *Roster of members*, 1990

Bryan, Rev. John Thomas Ingram, M.A., M.Litt., B.D., Ph.D., born 12 May 1868 in Canada, he studied at Toronto, Ont., Halifax, N.S., the University of California, and University of Pennsylvania, where he received his doctorate for *The feeling for nature in English pastoral poetry*. He was successively rector of various parishes in Canada and America, professor of English in Japan, and professor of Japanese history and civilization at Cambridge University. He died 31 August 1953. WhLit, 1930, 1931; *Who was who*

Bryan, William Jennings, born 19 May 1860 at Salem, Illinois, he studied law and afterwards practised in Illinois and Nebraska. He was the Democratic presidential candidate in 1896, 1900, and 1908. He was opposed to trusts and imperialism. He made a tour around the world, 1905-1906. His "British rule in India" from *India* of 20 July 1906 was repeatedly re-issued, as well as in Turkish and Urdu translations. His writings include *The Old world and its ways* (1907). He died 26 July 1925. DAB; Master (6); WhoLit, 1924, 1925, 1926; *Who was who*, 2; WhAm 1; ZKO

Bryce, James Bryce, Viscount, born 10 May 1838 at Belfast, he studied both at Glasgow and Oxford, to which Heidelberg was added a year or two later. His *The Holy Roman Empire* (1863) won him the Arnold Prize. He was called to the bar in 1867 and practised until 1882, as well as being Regius Professor of civil law at Oxford. He was a liberal member of Parliament, and a founder of the League of Nations. His writings include *Transcaucasia and Ararat* (1877), where he had travelled the previous year. He died in Sidmouth, 22 January 1922. DLB 166 (1996), pp. 79-90; DNB; NCCN; *Who was who*, 2

Bryde, Brun-Otto, born 12 January 1943, he received his Dr.jur. in 1971 from the Universität Hamburg for his thesis, *Zentrale wirtschaftspolitische Beratungsgremien in der parlamentarischen Verfassungsordnung*. He was a professor of law at the Universität Gießen, and a sometime visiting lecturer at the University of Addis Abeba. His writings include *The Politics and sociology of African legal development* (1976). Kürschner, 1983-2003

Bryer, Anthony Applemore Mornington, born 31 October 1937, he was a Scholar of Balliol College, Oxford, to which the Sorbonne, and Athens University were added a year or two later. He had a long association with the University of Birmingham, where he was director of the Centre for Byzantine, Ottoman, and Modern Greek Studies. His writings include *Byzantium and the ancient East* (1970), as well as two collections of his articles, *The Empire of Trebizond and the Pontos* (1980), and *Peoples and settlement in Anatolia and the Caucasus, 800-1900* (1988). Who, 1993-2003

Bryer, D. R. W., fl. 1976, he received a D.Phil. in 1971 from the University of Oxford for his thesis, *The origins of the Druze religion*. Sluglett

Brykina, Galina Anatol'evna, born 16 January 1929, her writings include *Карабулак* (1974), and *Юого-западная Фергана в первой половине I тысячелетия насей эры* (1982). LC; Schoeberlein

Bryson, Thomas Archer, born 16 March 1931 at Savannah, Ga., he was a graduate of Yale, and received a Ph.D. in 1963 from the University of Georgia for *Woodrow Wilson, the Senate, public opinion and the Armenian mandate question, 1919-20*. He taught at DeKalb College from 1965 to 1967, when he was appointed a professor of history at West Georgia College, Carrellton, Ga. His writings include *American diplomatic relations with the Middle East, 1784-1975* (1977), *Tars, Turks, and tankers* (1980), and *Seeds of Mideast crisis* (1981). DrAS, 1969 F

Brzozowski, Karol, born 29 November 1821 at Warszawa, he was a poet who spent some time as an emigrant in Turkey and Mesopotamia. He died in Lwow, Galicia, 5 November 1904. Dziekan; PSB

Brzozowski, Marian (Marie), born in 1803 in Poland, he was an emigrant whose writings include *La guerre de Pologne en 1831* (Leipzig, 1833). He died in 1876. PSB

Brzuski, Witbold Kazimierz, fl. 1974, his writings include *Zapożyczenia arabskie w dawnym i wsółczesnym języku amharskim* (1983). LC

Bseisu, Mu'in Tawfiq, born 1926 *see* Bisisu, Mu'in Tawfiq

Bu el-Moghdad, Si, 19th cent., he was a *qadi* at St.-Louis, Senegal, whence he started the *hajj* on the first leg overland to Mogador (Es-Saouira), Morocco, December 1860 to March 1861. Henze

Bubenik, Vit Moric, born 31 March 1942 at Nove Mesto, Czechoslovakia, he received doctorates in 1967 and 1969 from the University Brno, Czechoslovakia. In 1983 he was a professor of linguistics at Memorial University of Newfoundland, St. John's, Nfld. His writings include *The Phonological interpretation of ancient Greek* (1983). DrAS, 1978 F, 1982 F; DrASCan, 1983

Bubnova, Liudmila Sigizmundovna, fl. 1957, she was the author of a number of biographies, and the editor of *Дечко Узунов* (1981), and *Александр Бубнов* (1981). LC

Bubnova, Mira Alekseevna, born 4 November 1929, she studied at Tajik State University. Her writings include *Добыча полезных ископаемых в Средней Азии в XVI-XIX вв.* (1975). She contributed to *Шедевры древнего искусства и культуры Таджикистана* (1983), and she was joint author of *История Таджикистана; указатель советской литературы, 1917-1983* (1986). LC; Schoeberlein

Bucaille, Maurice Henri Julien, born 19 July 1920 at Pont-l'Evèque (Calvados), he studied law at Lyon, Paris, and Yale, to which Arabic was added a few years later. He was a physician in Paris and an avid student of comparative religion. His works were awarded a prize by the Académie française. His writings include *La Bible, le Coran et la science* (1976), its translation, *The Bible, the Qur'an, and science* (1992), *Les Momies des pharaons et la médecine* (1987), and its translation,*Mummies of the pharaohs* (1990). Two of his works have been translated into Arabic. WhoFr, 1953/4-1987/88|; ZKO

Bučan, Daniel, born 31 March 1943 at Split, Yugoslavia., he graduated in 1965 from Beograd University. His writings include *Realistički racionalizan Ibn-Haldun iz Mukaddime* (1976), and *Al-Gazali i Ibn Rušd* (1991). IWWAS, 1976/77

Bucci, Onorato, born 20th cent., his writings include *Introduzione allo studio storico e giuridico dell'Oriente Mediterraneo* (Romae Institutum Utriusque Iuris Pontificia Universitas Lateranensis, 1976). LC

Buchanan, Angus, born in 1886 at Kirkwall, Orkney Islands, he trained as an architect in Scotland and was for more than ten years engaged in his profession, chiefly in Canada. Then, owing to medical advice, he gave up architecture for an outdoor life. His last year in Canada, 1914, he spent on a zoological expedition to Barren Grounds, N.W.T. He went home from the arctic regions to enter the World War and, after three years' service in East Africa, was invalided home with the rank of captain. In 1919-1920 he made his first journey to Aïr, Sahara, on behalf of Lord Rothschild. At this time he conceived the idea of crossing the Sahara from south to north. This he did, in 1922-1923, taking some sixteen months in all for the task. The collection of birds and animals that he brought back have established for the first time the wild life of the Sahara. The journey was carried out entriely by camels, from railhead in the south to railhead in the north, some thirty-five thousand miles. His writings include *Three years of war in East Africa* (1919), *Exploration of Aïr* (1921), and *Sahara* (1926). Asia, May 1926; OxCan; WhE&EA

Buchanan, Claudius, Rev., born 12 March 1766, he received doctorates in divinity from the universities of Glasgow and Cambridge, and was ordained in 1795. He went in 1797 to India, where he was from 1799 to 1807 a professor and vice-provost, College of Fort William. When the latter appointment was abolished he devoted himself to the promotion of Christianity and to native education. He made two prolonged tours in southern and western India before returning to England in 1808. His writings include *Christian researches in Asia* (1810), and *Colonial ecclesiastical establishment* (1813). He died 9 February 1815. Buckland; Master (4); Riddick

Buchanan, Sir George Cunningham, born 20 April 1865 at Islington, he was a civil engineer who went to Basrah at the end of 1915 as adviser to Sir John Nixon, the commander-in-chief of the Mesopotamian campaign, on all matters connected with the port, its administration, engineering works, and river conservancy. He described his work at Basrah in his book *The Tragedy of Mesopotamia* (1938). He died 14 April 1940. DNB; Who was who, 3

Buchanan, James Robertson, he received a Ph.D. in 1927 from the University of Edinburgh for his thesis, *Muhammad's idea of the last judgment and its sources*. NUC, pre-1956; Sluglett

Buchanan, Milton Alexander, born 17 July 1878 at Zurich, Ont., he graduated in modern languages from the University of Toronto and was a fellowship student at Chicago, to which Paris and Madrid was added a year or two later. He returned to Chicago in 1906 to take a Ph.D. for *El Esclavo del demonio*. He was immediately invited to teach Romance languages at his alma mater, a post which he held until his retirement in 1946. He was elected a member of the Royal Society of Canada in 1935. His writings include *Spanish in the golden age* (1942). He died 7 March 1952. Master (3); Minutes of proceedings of the Royal Society of Canada, 1955, pp. 69-73

Buchère, Edouard, born in 1884, he was a colonial administrator. IndexBFr² (1)

Bucherer-Dietschi, Paul A., born 29 September 1942 at Diepoldsau, Switzerland. After studying architecture at Luzern, and ethnology at Basel, he carried on field-work in Iran, Afghanistan, and Pakistan in 1971 and 1972. Upon his return home, he founded the Afghanistan-Archiv in Liestal, and became the director of the Foundation Bibliotheca Afghanica. He edited *Schmuck und Silberschmiedearbeiten in Afghanistan und Zentralasien* (1981), and *Textilhandwerk in Afghanistan* (1983); with Chr. Jentsch he edited *Afghanistan; Ländermonographie* (1986). Private; Schoeberlein; WWASS, 1989

Buchet, Gaston, fl. 1892-1906. In 1903 he published a "Rapport sur une mission scientifique dans le nord du Maroc." BN

Büchler, Sándor (Alexander), born 27 September 1870, he was a professor of Hungarian Jewish history at Budapest University. His writings include *A zsidók története Budapesten a legrégibb időktől 1867-ig* (1901). He was deported in 1944 to Auschwitz, where he died. EncJud; UjLex

Buchroither, Manfred F., Dr., fl. 1980, he was affiliated with the Institut für Kartographie at the Austrian Academy of Science. His writings include *Erläuterung zur Karte der Landsat-Bildlineamente von Österreich* (1984). LC

Buchta, Richard, born 19 January 1845 at Radlow, Galicia, he was a painter and photographer who went to Egypt in 1870. From 1878 to 1880 he was variously enlisted as photographer and explorer and returned with the very first photographs from the Anglo-Egyptian Sudan, published in 1881 under the title *Die oberen Niltäler; Volkstypen und Landschaften dargestellt in 160 Photographien*. He visited Egypt again in 1885. His historical works include *Der Sudan und der Mahdi* (1884), and *Der Sudan unter ägyptischer Herrschaft* (1884). He died in Wien, 29 July 1894. DtBE; DtBiInd (3); Henze; Hill; ÖBL; Pallas; Zach, pp. 165-167

Buchthal, Hugo, born 11 August 1901 at Berlin, he studied at Berlin, Heidelberg, and Hamburg, where he received a Dr.phil. in 1933 for *Codex Parisinus Graecus 139*. Since 1934 he was resident in London. He was successively affiliated with the Hebrew University, Jerusalem, the Warburg Institute and the University of London, teaching history of art and history of Byzantine art. His writings include *A handlist of illuminated Oriental Christian manuscripts* (London, Warburg Institute, 1942), and *Miniature painting in the Latin kingdom of Jerusalem* (1957). He died in 1996. BioHbDtE; Who, 1974-1997

Buchvarov (Бъчваров), Mikhail Dimitrov, born 22 April 1929 at Eski Dzhumaya, Bulgaria, he was a writer on philosophy and historiography, and since 1973 a secretary of the Bulgarian Academy of Science. His writings include *Методологически проблеми на историята на философията* (1970), and the translation, *Eleven centruries of Bulgarian philosophical thought* (1973). EnBulg

Buck, Dorothy Louisa Marian, Madame Chavanne, born in 1897, she was the wife of a French officer at the Affaires indigènes de Tunisie. Her writings include *The new lotus-eaters* (1928), *The last oasis* (1932), and *The harem window* (1938). Who was who in literature, 1930, 1931

Buck, Oscar MacMillan, born 9 February 1885 at Cawnpore, India, and a graduate of Ohio Wesleyan University and Drew Theological Seminary, he was a missionary in India from 1909 to 1913, and afterwards a pastor and professor of missions and comparative religion in the United States. His writings include *India looks at her future* (1930). Master (3); Shavit - Asia; WhAm, 1

Buckingham, James Silk, born 25 August 1786 at Flushing, Cornwall, he was sent to sea in 1796. In 1815 he travelled overland from Egypt to India as a merchant. In 1818, at Calcutta, he bought out the *Calcutta journal*, attacked the Government so vigorously that his licence was revoked and he was deported from the country in 1823. Back in England, he conducted the *Oriental herald and colonial review*, the *Colonial review*, and was connected with other journals. From 1832 to 1837 he was M.P. for Sheffield. His writings include *Travels in Palestine* (1821), *Travels in Mesopotamia* (1827), *Travels in Assyria, Media, and Persia* (1829), *The Buried city of the East, Niniveh* (1851), and *Autobiography of James Silk Buckingham* (1855). He died in Stanhope Lodge on 30 June 1855. Boase; BritInd (12) Buckland; Henze; IndianBiInd (4); Riddick

Buckland, Charles Edward, born 19 September 1847, he was educated at Laleham, Eton, and Ballio College, Oxford, and in 1870 joined the Civil Service in Bengal. He retired in 1904. His writings include *Bengal under the lieutenant-governors* (1902), and *Dictionary of Indian biography* (1906). He died 10 October 1941. IndianBiInd (4); Riddick; Who was who, 4

Buckler, Francis William, M.A., born in 1891, he was a sometime Allen scholar at the University of Cambridge and a lecturer in history, University College, Leicester. His writings include *Harunu'l-Rashic and Charles the Great* (1931), *Firdausi's Shahnamah and the Genealogie Regni Dei* (1935), and *Legitimacy and symbols; the South Asian writings* (1985). He died in 1960. LC

Buckley, James Lane, born 9 March 1923 at N.Y.C., he was a graduate of Yale University and admitted to the bar in 1949. From 1953 to 1970 he was vice-president and a member of the board of directors of the family's Catawba Corporation. In 1971 he became a Republican senator from New York. His writings include *If men were angels* (1975). BlueB, 1973/74, 1975, 1976; ConAu 61-64; Master (5)

Buckley, Wilfred, born 13 June 1873, he was educated at Giggleswick School. He was the founder and chairman of the National Clean Milk Society, 1915-1928. He pursued an interest in glass and wrote *The art of glass, illustrated from the Wilfred Buckley Collection in the Victoria and Albert Museum* (1939), and a number of pamphlets on glass. He died 26 October 1933. Who was who, 3

Buda, Aleks, born in 1911 at Elbasan, Ottoman Albania, he studied in Austria before the war and was a sometime director of the National Library, Tirana, as well as a professor of history at Tirana University. His writings include *Shkrime historike* (1986). In 1985 he edited *Fjalor enciklopedik shqiptar*. WhoSocC, 1978

Budagov, Lazar' Zakharovich, born 12 April 1812 at Astrakhan, he studied at Moscow and Kazan universities and later became a professor at St. Petersburg. His writings include *Практическое руководство турецко-татарского адербиджанскаго наречия* (1857), and *Стравнительный словарь турецко-татарских напечий со включением употребительнейших слов арабских и персидских и с переводом на русский язык* (St. Petersburg, c1869-1871, 1960). He died on 30 December 1878. AzarbSE, vol. 2, p. 338; BiobibSOT, pp. 130-131; TatarES

Budagova, Zärifä Ismaiyl gyzy, born 28 April 1929 at Erevan, she received a doctorate in 1963 from Baku University for her thesis, *Простое предложе-ние в современном азербайджанском литера-турном языке*. In 1968 she was appointed professor of Azeri. Her writings include *Азербайджан-ский язык* (1982), and *Основы грамматики современного азербайджанского языка* (1987). AzarbSE; LC

von **Budberg**, Peter A., 1903-1973 see Boodberg, Peter Alexis

Budde, Hans Jürgen, born 29 August 1935, he received a Dr.rer.pol. in 1969 from the Universität Köln for his thesis, *Der Temperatur- und Feuchtigkeitsbegriff; eine Untersuchung im Rahmen der wirtschaftlichen Warenlehre*. In 1997 he was a director of Verband der Industriellen Energie- und Kraftwirtschaft, Essen. Wer ist wer, 1994/95-2000/2001|

Budde, Karl Ferdinand Reinhard, born 13 April 1850 at Bensberg, Germany, he studied theology at Berlin, Utrecht, and Bonn where he received a doctorate in divinity in 1873. He was a professor of theology at the Universität Straßburg from 1889 to 1900, and at the Universität Marburg from 1900 until retirement in 1921. His writings include *Die Religion des Vokes Israel bis zur Verbannung* (1900), its translation, *Religion of Israel to the exile* (1899), and *Geschichte der althebräischen Literatur* (1906). He died in Marburg, 29 January 1935. DtBE; Kürschner, 1925-1928/29; Master (1)

Buddruss, Georg Artur Andreas, born 30 November 1929 at Lappienen, Germany, he received a Dr.phil. degree in 1954 from the Universität Frankfurt am Main. He was a professor of Indology successively at Tübingen and Mainz. His writings include *Die Sprache von Sau in Ostafghanistan* (1967), and *Khowar-Texte in arabischer Schrift* (1982). IWWAS, 1976/77; Kürschner, 1966-2003; Schoeberlein; WhoWor, 1978

Büdel, Julius, born 8 August 1903 at Molsheim, Alsace, he was successively a professor of geography at the universities of Berlin, Göttingen, and Würzburg. His writings include *Die morpho-logische Entwicklung des südlichen Wiener Beckens* (1933), and *Klima-Geomorphologie* (1981). He died in Würzburg, 28 August 1983. Kürschner, 1961-1983

Budenz, József, born 13 June 1836 at Rasdorf, Germany, he studied at the Universität Göttingen where he received a Dr.phil. in 1858 for his thesis, *Das Suffix χός (ιχός, αχός, υχός) im Griechischen*. He then went to Hungary, where in 1872 he became a professor in the Department of Altaic Studies, Budapest University. He pursued an interest in the relation of Hungarian to Turkic and Finno-Ugrian languages. His writings include *Ugrische Sprachstudien* (1869-70), and *Magyar-ugor összehasonlító szótár* (1873-81). He died in Budapest, 15 April 1892. GSE; Magyar; RNL; UjLex

Budhraj, Vijay Sen, born in 1923, his writings include *Hindi* (1957), and *Soviet Russia and the Hindustan Subcontinent* (1973). LC

Buechler, Sándor (Alexander), 1870-1944 see Büchler, Sándor

Buechner, Thomas Scharman, born 25 September 1926 at N.Y.C., he was a graduate of Princeton and continued his studies abroad. He had a long museum career at various American institutions, starting at the Metropolitan Museum of Art, N.Y.C. His writings include *Norman Rockwell, artist and*

236

illustrator (1970). He was the founder of the *Journal of glass studies*, in 1959. ConAu 49-52; Master (3); WhoAmA, 1973-2001/2002

Buehrig, Edward Henry, born 4 October 1910 at Minier, Illinois, he was a graduate of the University of Chicago, where he also received his Ph.D. in 1942 for *American intervention in Europe, 1917*. In 1934 he began a lifelong teaching career at Indiana University, Bloomington. His writings include *Woodrow Wilson and the balance of power* (1955), and *The U.N. and the Palestinian refugees* (1971). He died 31 August 1986. AmM&WS, 1973 S, 1978 S; ConAu 37-40; IndAu, 1917; WhAm, 9

Buell, Paul David, born 24 August 1941 at Glendale, Calif., he received a Ph.D. in 1977 from the University of Washington for *Tribe, qan and ulus in early Mongol China*. He became a free lance writer and photographer, resident in Seattle. He contributed to *Chinese medicine on the Golden Mountain* (1984). LC; NUC, 1980; Schoeberlein

Buell, Raymond Leslie, born 13 July 1896 at Chicago, he graduated from Occidental College, Los Angeles, received his doctorate in 1923 from Princeton. After teaching for five years at Harvard, he was affiliated with the Foreign Policy Association of NYC from 1927 to 1939, when he joined the staff of Time, Inc. His writings include *The Washington conference* (1922), *International relations* (1925), *The native problem in Africa* (1928), *Liberia, a century of survival* (1947). He died in Montreal, 20 February 1946. Shavit-Africa; WhAm, 2

Buesco, Victor, born in 1911 at Craiova, Romania, he was a professor of classical philology and Romanian, and taught at the University of Bucharest until 1940, and from 1945 at Universidade de Lisboa. His writings include *Problèmes de critique et d'histoire textuelle* (1942), *A fost odată* (1951), and *Introdução à cultura clássica* (1970). He died in 1971. WhoRom

Buffault, Pierre Hippolyte Marie Joseph, born 5 November 1866 at Yzeurre (Allier), he was a lifelong forester as *garde général des Eaux et Forêts* in various parts of France, and successively a secretary, vice-president, and president of the Société commerciale de Bordeaux; *officier de la Légion d'honneur,* and *commandeur du Mérite agricole.* His writings include *Histoire des dunes maritimes de la Gascogne* (1942). He died in Bordeaux, 12 February 1942. Index BFr² (1); *Revue trimestrielle* de la Société de géographie commerciale de Bordeaux, 1941-47, fasc. 1, pp. 3-6

Bugeaud, Thomas Robert, Marquis de la Piconnerie, Duc d'Isly, Maréchal de France, born 15 October 1784. His military career followed the political changes in France, as well as the military fortunes in Algeria of the time. When he handed over Algeria to his successor, Duc d'Aumale, in 1847, he could claim to have transformed a country of three million enemies into a French Algeria, submitted, colonized, and pacified. His writings include *L'Algérie; des moyens de conserver et d'utiliser cette conquête* (1842), *De la colonisation d'Algérie* (1847), and *Histoire de l'Algérie française* (1850). He died of cholera, during active service, in Paris, 10 June 1849, and was buried in Invalides. Azan, pp. 61-78; DBF; *Hommes et destins,* vol. 1, pp. 108-114

Bugéja, Manuel, born 19th cent., he was in 1939 an honorary *administrateur principal* of *Communes mixtes* and *commissiare général* of the central bureau of the Société de géographie d'Alger et de l'Afrique du nord. His writings include *Souvenirs d'un fonctionnaire colonial; 34 ans d'administration algérienne* (1939). Note

Bugéja, Marie, born in the 19th century at Moisan, Algeria, she had an intimate and personal knowledge of Algerian social conditions from her travels in rural Algeria. She was a lifelong activist for Algerian women's rights, for which she struggled in her numerous works and lectures. Her engagement won her many honours, *officier de l'Académie* (1925), *officier de l'Instruction publique* (1929), and *officier Nichan iftikhar* (1935). The City of Paris awarded her the *Grand Prix du Centenaire de l'Algérie,* 1930, for her *Nos sœurs musulmanes* (1921). Her writings include *Visions d'Algérie* (1929), *Enigme musulmane* (1938), and *Cœur de Kabyle* (1939). *Hommes et destins,* vol. 4, pp. 153-155

Buheiry, Marwan Rafat, originally Mirvin Ogden-Smith, born in 1934, the son of a Lebanese Muslim father and an Armenian mother. He was raised mainly by an English stepfather, attended an English private school in Lebanon before becoming an undergraduate at AUB. He received a Ph.D. in 1974 from Princeton for *Anti-colonial sentiment in France during the July Monarchy; the Algerian case.* For the following ten years he was a professor at AUB and concurrently a part-time director of the International Section of the Institute for Palestine Studies. In 1985 he was appointed the first director of the Centre for Lebanese Studies, Oxford, but died only months after taking up his position in 1986. His writings include *U.S.threats of intervention against Arab oil, 1973-79* (1980). Vatikiotis *in* BSOAS 54 (1991), pp. 634-635

Buhl, Frants Peder William, born 5 September 1850 at København, he studied theology and Oriental languages at Københavns Universitet, and Universität Leipzig. He was a professor at København from

1881 to his retirement, interrupted by eight years at Leipzig. His writings include *Kanon und Text des Alten Testaments* (1891), *Muhammeds liv* (1903), its translation, *Das Leben Muhammeds* (1930), and *Muhammeds religiøse forkyndelse efter Qurânen* (1924). He died in Hillerød. 29 September 1932. DanskBL; DanskBL²; Fück, 305-6; KDtLK, 1895-98; Meyers; WhE&EA; *Who was who*, 3

Buhl, Marie Louise, born 2 March 1918 at Randers, Denmark, she studied at Københavns Universitet where she received a doctorate in 1959. She was a keeper at the Nationalmuseet, København, and concurrently a lecturer in Near Eastern archaeology at Københavns Universitet. Her writings include *Skatte fra det gamle Persien* (1968), and *The Near Eastern pottery* (1983); she was joint author of *Shilch; the Danish excavations at Tall Sailun* (1969). Kraks, 1990-2002/2003

Buhle, Johann Gottlieb Gerhard, born 29 September 1863 at Braunschweig, Germany, he studied philology and philosophy at Göttingen and Helmstedt. In 1794 he was awarded a medal of distinction for his book *Calendarium Palaestinae oeconomicum*. In 1785 he was appointed professor of a philosophy at Göttingen. From 1811 to 1813 he taught at Moscow University. He returned in 1814 to teaching in Braunschweig, where he died 11 August 1821. ADtB, v. 3, pp. 509-510; DtBE; DtBilnd² (9)

Bühler, Johann *Georg*, born 19 July 1837 at Borstel, Germany, he studied classical philology and Oriental languages, including Zend, Persian, Armenian, and Arabic at Göttingen where he later taught briefly until 1863 when he was appointed a professor of Sankrit and Oriental languages at Elphinstone College, Bombay. From 1880 until his death he was a professor at the Universität Wien where he founded Orientalisches Institut and Indogermanische Gesellschaft. The University of Edinburgh conferred on him an honorary doctorate. His writings include *Indische Palaeographie* (1896). He drowned in Lake Constance, 8 April 1898. ADtB; Buckland; DtBE; NDB; ÖBL; Stache-Rosen, pp. 83-85

Buijtenhuis, Robert, fl. 1976. He was a sometime sociologist at the Afrika-Centrum, Leiden. His writings include *Mau Mau - twenty years after* (1973), *Revolutie in zwart Afrika?* (1975), *Le Frolinat et les révoltes populaires du Tchad, 1965-1976* (1978), *Essays on Mau Mau* (1982), and *Democratization in sub-Saharan Africa. 1989-1992* (1994). Brinkman's; LC

Buis, Georges Paul, general, born 24 February 1912 at Saigon, he was educated at Toulon, Marseille, La Flèche, and Saint-Cyr. During the second World War he served with the Free French Forces in Palestine and Syria, and after the War, in Morocco (1947-1950), Iran and Afghanistan (1951-1955), and Algeria (1958-1961). Until his retirement in 1972, he was attached to various military institutions in France. His writings include *La Grotte; roman* (1961), *La Barque* (1968), and *Les Fanfares perdues* (1975). He died 12 June 1998. WhoFr, 1965/66-1997/98|

Buisson, B., fl. 1916-1923, he was a sometime honorary director of l'Enseignement primaire, Tunis.

Buisson d'Armandy, Aimé Prosper Édouard Chérubin Nicéphore, born 5 November 1793 at Pernes (Vaucluse). After passing through the military College, Saint-Cyr in 1813, he participated in the final campaigns of *l'Empire* in Spain. Thereafter he entered the Garde Royal, but was dismissed in 1816. For a number of years he travelled in Egypt, Persia and India, was appointed consul at Mokha in 1824, and Damietta in 1830. Under Louis Philippe, he was reintegrated in the army and sent to North Africa where he rose to the rank of general. He retired in 1859, and died in Carpentras (Vaucluse), 3 July 1873. DBF; Index BFr² (2)

Buist, David Simson, Major-General, born 29 September 1829, he entered the Army in 1848 and served in the Indian Army throughout the Mutiny. He died 16 January 1908. *Who was who*, 1

Al Bukhari, Alhaji Junaidu b. Muhammad, Wazir of Sokoto, fl. 1979, he received a D.Litt. from Ahmadu Bello University. Note

Bukinich, D. D., fl. 1938, he was joint author of *Земледельческий Афганистан* (1929). LC

Bulatov, Mitkhat Sagadatdinovich, born 18 April 1907, he took a doctorate in architecture. His writings include *Мавзолей Саманидов-жемчужина архитектуры Средней Азии* (1976), and *Геометрическая гармонизация в архитектуре Средней Азии IX-XV вв.* (1978). He was joint editor of *Архитектура Узбекистана; алманах* (1989). Kazak SE; LC

Bülbül, Mehmet, born 8 February 1939 at Samsun, he received a doctorate in 1963 from the Universität Kiel for *Staatliche Förderung der Landwirtschaft in der Türkei*. Since 1979 he taught at Ankara Üniversitesi Ziraat Fakültesi. Kim kimdir, 1985/86-2000|

Bulcke, Camille, Father, 1909-1982, he was affiliated with the India Catholic Literature Committee. His writings include *A technical English-Hindi glossary of general terms* (1955). BLC; LC

Bulgakov, Pavel Georgievich, born 6 July 1926 or 1927 at Tashkent, he graduated in 1951 from the Oriental Faculty of Leningrad State University and received a doctorate in 1967. He was since 1964 affiliated with the Oriental Institute of the Uzbek Academ<y of Science. He was joint editor of *Абу Али ибн Сина; к 1000-летию со дня рождения* (1980), and joint author of *Мухаммад ал-Хорезми* (1983). He died in 1994. LC; Miliband; Miliband²; Schoeberlein

Bullard, Arthur, born 8 December 1879 at St. Joseph, Mo., he was in 1905 a foreign correspondent in North Africa, and later in the Balkans and the European war. After the war he was associated for many years with the League of Nations. His writings, partly under the pseudonym Albert Edwards, include *The Barbary Coast* (1913), and *Diplomacy of the Great War* (1916). He died in Genève, 10 September 1929. Master (4); Shavit; Who was who in America, 1

Bullard, Sir Reader William, born 5 December 1885, he was a London dock labourer's son without any university education, and one of that now forgotten band of specialist diplomats of the Levant Consular Service. He rose from student interpreter in pre-1914 Constantinople to become ambassador in Tehran during the second World War. In between, he was military governor of Baghdad at the end of the first World War, and had two spells of duty in Arabia, first as consul in Jeddah, 1923-25, and then as minister there, 1936-39. He never succumbed to the fascinations of the Middle East and showed considerable reservations in his dealings with the Persians. He ended his career as director of the Institute of Colonial Studies, Oxford. His writings include *Britain and the Middle East* (1951), his -autobiography, *The camels must go on* (1961), *Letters from Tehran; a British ambassador in World War II Persia* (1991), and *Two kings in Arabia; Sir Reader Bullard's letters from Jeddah* (1993). He died in 1976. Britlnd (1); DNB; Who was who, 7

Bulliet, Richard Williams, born 30 October 1940 at Rockford, Illinois, he graduated from Harvard, where he also received his Ph.D. in 1962 for *An interpretation of early Islamic history; Muhammad's mission and the evolution of the state*. He taught successively at Harvard, the University of California, Berkeley, and Columbia, where he was still active in 2003. His writings, partly under the pseudonym Clarence J.-L. Jackson, include *The patricians of Nishapur* (1972), *The camel and the wheel* (1975), *Conversion to Islam in the medieval period* (1979), *The Gulf scenario* (1984), *The Sufi fiddle* (1991), and *Islam, the view from the edge* (1994). ConAu 57-60, new rev., 7; NatFacDr, 1995-2003

Bullock, Humphrey, Brigadier, born 9 January 1899, he was educated at Dover College and the Royal Military College, Sandhurst. During the first World War he served with the Indian Army in Mesopotamia and Salonika, and thereafter in India until partition. His writings include *Indian cavalry standards* (1930), and *Indian infantry colours* (1931). He died 19 November 1959. Who was who, 5

Bullock, Walter Frederick, born about 1873, he was for thirty years a New York correspondent for the London *Times* and *Daily mirror*. He retired in 1936. He died at the age of sixty-nine in New York City, 1 May 1942. ObitOF, 1979

Bulmer-Thomas, Ivor, born in 1905 at Cwmbran, Monmouthshire, he was an outstanding scholar at Oxford and variously represented Oxford against Cambridge at athletics. In 1926 he became Welsh International Cross-country Runner. He became a chief leader write as well as Parliamentary Under-Secretary of State for the Colonies. His writings include *Coal in the new era* (1934), and *Gladstone of Hawarden* (1936). He died 7 October 1993. BioIn 1; WhE&EA; Who, 1951-1994; WrDr, 1976-1996/98

von **Bulmerincq**, Alexander Michael Karl, born 24 May (5 June) 1868 at St. Petersburg, he studied at Dorpat and four years at Leipzig; and received his Dr.phil. in 1894 from Dorpat University for *Das Zukunftsbild des Propheten Jeremia aus 'Anathoth*. He was the last Arabist and Semitic scholar at Dorpat. His writings, which centre on Biblical archaeology and exegesis, include *Der Prophet Maleachi* (1926-32), and related works. The University of Aberdeen conferred on him in 1906 an honorary doctorate in divinity. He died in 1938. Baltisch (7); Krachkovskii, p. 148; Kürschner, 1931, 1935; Wer ist's 1912

Bulos, Afif Alvarez, born about 1930, he received a Ph.D. in 1961 from Harvard for his thesis, *The structure of the triliteral verb in Arabic*. His writings include *Arabic music* (1955), and the revision of his thesis, *The Arabic triliteral verb* (1965). LC

Buluç, Sadettin, born 25 September 1913 at Van, Turkey, he was educated at Sivas Erkek Lisesi, studied German language at Schulpforta in 1931, and pursued Turkish studies, from 1932 to 1937, at the Universität Breslau, where he received a Dr.phil. in 1938 for *Untersuchungen über die alt-osmanische anonyme Chronik der Bibliothèque nationale zu Paris, Suppl. turc, 1047*. His trace is lost after a publication in 1941. Thesis

Bulus, 'Afif *see* Bulos, Afif Alvarez

Bulwer, Sir William *Henry* Lytton Earle, Baron Dalling and Bulwer, born 13 February 1813 at London, he was educated at Cambridge. After diplomatic service in Europe, he served at the Ottoman Porte in Constantinople from August 1858 to August 1865, when he returned home and retired from the diplomatic service. His writings include *An autumn in Greece* (1826), and a number of biographies. He died suddenly in Napoli on 23 May 1872. DNB; Richter, p. 175

Bumke, Peter Joachim, born about 1940, he studied at the Südasien Institut, Heidelberg, and received a Dr.phil. in 1970 from the Universität Heidelberg for *Die Miao; Sozialgeschichte und politische Organisation.* He was a sometime director of the German Max Mueller Bhavan, Hyderabad, and joint editor of *Images of rural India in the 20th century* (1992). LC

Bumpus, Bernard, fl. 1979, he was joint author of *Seventy years of international broadcasting* (Paris, Unesco, 1984). LC

Bunakov, E. V., fl. 1960, he wrote Ненецкий национальный округ (1936).

Bunce, Valerie, born 16 February 1949 at Pontiac, Mich., she received a Ph.D. in 1976 from the University of Michigan for *Elite succession and political change in communist and democratic systems.* She was successively a professor of political science at Northwestern University, Evanston, Illinois, and professor of government at Cornell University, Ithaca, N.Y., where she was still active in 1998. Her writings include *Do new leaders make a difference?* (1981). LC; NatFacDr, 1995-1998

Bunche, Ralph Johnson, born 7 August 1904 at Detroit, Mich., he was a graduate of U.C.L.A., and Harvard, and became a professor of political science at Howard University, Washington, D.C. As acting mediator on Palestine in 1948-49 he succeeded in reaching cease-fire arrangements in the Arab-Israeli war, for which he received the Nobel Peace Prize of 1950. His writings include *A World view of race* (1936), and *The Political status of the Negro in the age of FDR* (1973). He died in N.Y.C., 9 December 1971. Master (9); Shavit; Who was who in America, 5

von **Bunge**, Alexander Andreevich, born 24 September 1803 at Kiev, he was educated at Dorpat, where he received a medical doctorate in 1825. The following year, he accompanied his teacher, K. Fr. von Ledebour, on a scientific expedition to the Altai Mountains. In the service of the Russian Academy of Science he again visited the region in the summer of 1832. He was a professor at Kazan, 1833-36, and at Dorpat, 1836-67. From 1858 to 1859 he accompanied N.V. Khanykov on the expedition of the Russian Geographical Society to Khurasan. His writings include *Beiträge zur Kenntniss der Flor Russlands und der Steppen Central-Asiens* (1851). He died 18 July 1890. Baltisch (7); Embacher; EnSlovar; Henze; TatarES

Buniiatov, Ziia Musaevich, born 24 December 1921 at Astara, Azerbaijan, he graduated in 1950 from the Oriental Institute, Moscow, and received a doctorate in 1963 at Baku for his thesis, Азербайджан в VII-IX вв., a work which was published in 1965. He was affiliated with the Oriental Institute, Azerbaijan Academy of Science since 1964 and appointed a professor in 1965. His writings include Государство атабеков Азербайджана, 1136-1225 годы (1978). He published a critical edition with Russian translation entitled Китаб талхис ал-асар ва аджа'иб ал-малик ал-кассар, by 'Abd al-Rashid al-Bakuwi (1971). Miliband; Miliband²

von **Bunsen**, Ernst, born 11 August 1811 at Roma, where his father was the Prussian representative at the Vatican. He himself became a Prussian officer and served until 1849, having intermittently spent some time with his father in London, while the latter had a spell of duty in England. In the early 1850s, he returned to London, where his main interests lay in literary study. His writings include *Die Einheit der Religionen im Zusammenhange mit den Völkerwanderungen der Urzeit und der Geheimlehre* (1870), *Biblical chronology* (1874), *The Angel-messiah of Buddhists, Essenes, and Christians* (1880), and *Essays on Church history; Islam or true Christianity* (1889). He died in London, 13 May 1903. DNB, Suppl., 1901-1911

Bunsen, Georg Friedrich, born 7 November 1824 in Roma, he received a doctorate in 1852 from the Universität Bonn for *De Azania Africae littore oriental.* After travels in France, Italy, and England, he made a living on his agricultural estate. He later entered liberal politics and was successively a member of the Prussian Parliament and the German Reichstag. He died 22 December 1896. BioIn 6; DtBE

Bunsen, Sir Maurice William Ernest De, 1852-1932 *see* De Bunsen, Sir Maurice William Ernest

Buonazia, Lupo, born 18 July 1844 at Prato, Italy, he studied law at the Università di Pisa, to which Leipzig and Beirut was added a year or two later. From 1885 until his death on 12 January 1914 he was a professor of Arabic at the Università di Napoli. His writings include *Regole della grammatica arabe* (1900). *Rivista degli studi orientali* 6 (1914/15), pp. 1410-13

Buonfanti, Maurizio (Maurice), died in 1885, he was an Italian traveller who claims to have crossed from Tripolitania via Murzuq and Timbuctu to Lagos. The credibility of his account is disputed. He died in West Africa. Henze

Bur-Markovska, Marta, fl. 1972, her writings include *Балканите и унгарският пазар през XVIII век* (1977), and *Българският народ под османско владичество, от XV до началото на XVIII в.* (1983). LC

Burattini (Boratyni), Tito-Livio, 1617-1681, he was a physicist whose writings include *Misura universale di Tito Livio Burattini*, ed. L. A. Birkenmajer (Kraków, 1897). Dziekan; PSB

Burbiel, Gustav, fl. 1969, he received a Dr.phil. in 1950 from the Universität Hamburg for his thesis, *Die Sprache Isma'il Gaspyralys.*

Burchardt, Hermann, born 18 November 1857 at Berlin. His parents' wealth afforded him extensive travels throughout the world, but particularly in the Middle East. In 1892 he received a formal diploma in Arabic from the Orientalisches Seminar zu Berlin. After a prolonged stay in Damascus, he conducted ethnological expeditions in Arabia, Persia, and East Africa. In the course of his journeys he amassed a valuable collection of thousands of photographes of places never previously visited by Westerners, which was later presented to the library of the Orientalisches Seminar. After spending almost a year in the Yemen, partly in the company of the Italian vice-consul Benzoni, he fell victim to marauders on his way from Mokka (Mocha, al-Mukha) to San'a', 18 December 1909. In 1926 Eugen Mittwoch edited *Aus dem Jemen; Hermann Burchardts letzte Reise durch Südarabien*, with the Arabic of Ahmad ibn Muhammad al-Jaradi (al-Garadi). EncJud; Facey Grant; Meyers; Wininger

Burchuladze, Ermolai Evseevich see Burčulaže, Ermolai Evseevich

Burckhardt, Johann Ludwig, born 25 November 1784 at Lausanne. After studies at Leipzig and Göttingen, he went to London, in 1806, with introductions to Sir Joseph Banks, a member of the African Assocation. Burckhardt offered his paid, professional services to attempt to reach Timbuktu with the pilgrim caravans which returned from Mecca. In 1809 he sailed for Malta, from where he went to Mecca via Aleppo. When he eventually reached Cairo, in poor health, he had to linger in the city because no caravan that would take him to Timbuktu was expected in the foreseeable future. He died in Cairo on 15 October 1817, and was buried in a Muslim cemetery near Bab al-Nasr Cairo, where Roger O. De Keersmaecker discovered his grave in 1984 (*ASTENE bulletin*, no. 11 (April 2001), pp. 18-19). Two months later, the first caravan for four years left for Tmbuktu. He had died with the main purpose of his life unfulfilled, the exploration of the sources of the Niger. All his works were published posthumously; they include *Travels in Egypt and Nubia* (1819-20), *Reisen in Syrien, Palästina und der Gegend des Berges Sinai* (1823), *Description de l'Arabie* (1841), and *Viaggi in Arabia* (1844). In 1969 Katherine Sim published his biography entitled *Desert traveller; the life of Jean Louis Burckhardt*. Bidwell; EncJud; *Encyclopædia Britannica*, 11th ed.; Henze; Hill

Burckhardt, Titus, born in 1908. Although he first saw the light of day in Firenze, he was the scion of a patrician family of Basel and a schoolmate of Frithjof Schuon. This was the beginning of an intimate friendship and a deeply harmonious intellectual and spiritual association that was to last a lifetime. He devoted all his life to the study and exposition of the different aspects of wisdom and tradition. In the 1930s he spent a few years in Morocco and immersed himself in the Arabic language. In the 1950s and 1960s he was the artistic director of the Urs Graf Publishing House in Olten near Basel. His writings include *Introduction aux doctrines ésotériques de l'islam* (1955), its translation, *An introduction to Sufi doctrine* (1959), *Alchemie, Sinn und Weltbiild* (1960), its translations, *L'alchimie science et sagesse* (1967), *Alchemy, science of the cosmos, science of the soul* (1967), *Fes, Stadt des Islam* (1960), *Sacred art in East and West* (1967), *Die maurische Kultur in Spanien* (1970), its translation, *Moorish culture in Spain* (1972), *Art of Islam* (1976), its translation, *L'art de l'islam* (1985), and the translations from the Arabic, *De l'homme universel* (1953), and *La sagesse des prophètes* (1955). He died in Lausanne in 1984. Freeth, pp. 91-120; I.I. (10)

Burčulaže (Burchuladze), Ermolai Evseevich, fl. 1952. His writings include *Soc'ialsturi erebi ganvit'arebis axal etapze* (T'bilisi, 1965). LC

Burdon, Sir John Alder, M.A., F.R.G.S., born 23 August 1866, he was a Hausa scholar of Christ's College, Cambridge, and commanded the Royal Niger Constabulary during the operations in Niger territory, 1898-99. He was repeatedly Resident of the Sokoto Province. He died 9 January 1933. Who was who, 3

Burdukov, Aleksei Vasil'evich, born in 1883, he was a Mongolian scholar whose writings include *Разговорник монгольского языка с подробным оглавлением каждого урока, подстрочным и алфавитным спрварями* (1935). He died 15 March 1943. Miliband; Miliband[2]

Büren, Rainer, born in 1941, he studied law, political science, and Islamics at Bonn, Cairo, Paris, and Kiel, where he received a Dr.phil. in 1972 for *Nasser's Ägypten als arabisches Ver-fassungsmodell*. From 15 February 1972 until Dezember 1975 he was director of Deutsches Orient-Institut, Hamburg. Thereafter he was head of the Middle East and Africa Section at the Stiftung Wissenschaft und Politik, Ebenhausen. His writings include *Gegenwartsbezogene Orientwissenschaft in Deutschland* (1974), and *Ein palästinensischer Teilstaat* (1982). Note; Schwarz

Buret, M. T., fl. 1928, he was a sometime professor at the Institut des hautes études marocaines. His *Cours gradué d'arabe marocain* was reprinted several times in the 1940s and 1950s. LC

van **Burg**, Pieter Frederick Jan, born in 1925, he received a doctorate in 1962 from Landbouwhogeschool Wageningen for his thesis, *Interne stickstofbalans, produktie van droge stof en veroudering bij gra*. In 1963, he taught at the Lycée Moulay Ismaïl, Meknès. He was affiliated with the European Grassland Federation, and a joint author of *Sugar beet* (1983). Brinkman's, LC, Note

Burg, Steven L., born 28 March 1950, he received a Ph.D. in 1980 from the University of Chicago for his thesis, *Conflict and regulation, decision-making, and institutional adaption in a multinational state; the case of Yugoslavia since 1966*. He was a professor of political science at Brandeis University, Waltham, Mass., in 1995, a post which he still held in 2003. His writings include *Conflict and cohesion in socialist Yugoslavia* (1983), and *The political integration of Yugoslavia's Muslims* (1983). LC; NatFacDr, 1995-2003

Burgard, Raymond, fl. 1931, his writings include *L'Expédition d'Alexandre de la conquête de l'Asie* (1937), and *La Découverte de la terre* (1942). LC

Burgat, François, born 20th cent., he received a doctorate in 1980 from the Université de Grenoble II for *Les villages socialistes dans la révolution agraire algérienne*. In 1988 he was affiliated with the Institut de recherches et d'études sur le monde arabe et musulman, Aix-en-Provence. His writngs include *Islamisme au Maghreb* (1988), *The Islamic movement in North Africa* (1993), and he was joint author of *Les villages socialistes de la révolution agraire algérienne, 1972-1982* (1984). LC; THESAM, 2

Burgel, Guy, fl. 1967, he was a French geographer whose writings include *Pobia; étude géographique d'un village crétois* (Athènes, 1965), *La Condition industrielle à Athènes* (1972), *Athènes* (1975), *Croissance urbaine et développement capitaliste* (1981), and he was a contributing author to *La C.E.E. méditera-néenne* (1990). LC

Bürgel, Johann Christoph, born 16 September 1931 at Gottesberg, Silesia, Germany, he studied at Frankfurt a.Main, was an exchange student at Ankara in 1956/57, followed by Arabic studies in Jordan, Bonn, and Göttingen, where he received a Dr.phil. in 1960 for *Bahtiyar und 'Adud ad-Daula; ein Beitrag zur Geschichte der frühen Buyiden*. From 1970 until his retirement he was head of Islamwissen-schaftliche Abteilung, Universität Bern. In 1983 he was the recipient of the Friedrich Rückert prize of the City of Schweinfurt. His writings include *Drei Hafis-Studien* (1975), *The feather of Simurgh* (1988), *Allmacht und Mächtigkeit; Religion und Welt im Islam* (1991), and the translation *Licht und Reigen* (1974). IWWAS, 1975/76; Kürschner, 1970-2003; WhoWor, 1982/83, 1987; WWASS, 1989

Burgelin, Henri, fl. 1974, he was a sometime professor at the Institut d'études politiques, Paris. His writings include *La Société allemande, 1871-1968* (1969). LC

Burgemeister, Burghard, born about 1930, he received a Dr.phil. in 1958 from Humboldt Universität, Berlin, for his thesis, *Emil Adolf Roßmäßler, ein demokratischer Pädagoge*. He was a director of Säch-sische Landesbibliothek, Dresden. His writings include *Regionalkundliche Bibliotheksarbeit* (1968). LC

Burger, André, born in 1896, he was a classicist and medievalist whose writings include *Les Mots de la famille φvω en grec ancien* (1925), *Lexique de la langue de Villon* (1957), and *Turold, poète de la fidélité* (1977). LC

Burger, Jean Jacques, fl. 1969, he was a sometime *directeur général* of the Société Pétrolière Française en Algérie. Note

Burgess, Charles Henry, born 1808 or 9, son of a London banker. His interest in Oriental trade had been aroused by a plausible Armenian whom he had met in London and who had persuaded him to accompany a valuable consignment of British merchandise, which the Armenian was shipping to Tabriz. He reached Tabriz in July 1828 and for the next eight years was busy himself, albeit unsuccessfully, in seeking his fortune by trading with England. In 1836 the Persian Crown Prince entrusted him with the task of buying some £30,000 worth of muskets and other military equipment in London. Instead he absconded with the money advanced to him for this purpose and never returned to Persia, leaving behind not only debts but two illegitimate children by an Armenian mistress and, most tragic of all, his brother Edward, whom the Persians held hostage on Charles' account for the rest of his life. His wayward brother Charles, who had been living for some years at Aix-la-Chapelle, died around 1855, suffering dreadfully from the advanced stages of syphillis. His letters were edited by Benjamin Schwartz and published in 1942 entitled *Letters from Persia by Charles and Edward Burgess, 1828-1855.* NUC, pre-1956; Wright, pp.96-99

Burgess, James, born 14 August 1832 at Kirkmahoe, Scotland, he was a sometime director-general of the Archæological Surveys of India, and an honorary member of several international learned societies. His writings include *On the Muhammadan architecture of Bharoch, Cambay, Dholka, Champanir, and Mahmudabad in Gujarat* (1896), *The Ancient monuments, temples and sculptures of India* (1897), and *The Chronology of modern India, 1494-1894* (1913). He died 5 October 1916. Who was who, 2

Burgess, Julian, fl. 1970, he wrote *Interdependence in southern Africa; trade and transport links in south, central and east Africa* (London, Economist Intelligence Unit,1976).

Burgess, Oliver, born about 1860, he was a missionary under the China Inland Mission and arrived in Shanghai on 21 December 1890. On 7 December 1897 he was married to the co-missionary, Miss A. C. Thomson, at Paoning. He later served at Chefoo. His trace is lost after his last arrival in China from Australia on 21 March 1926. Lodwick

Burggraff, Pierre, 1803-1881, he wrote *Principes de grammaires général* (Liège, 1863).

Burgoyne, Michael Hamilton, born 20th cent., he received a Dr.phil. in 1979 from Oxford for *The architectural development of the Haram in Jerusalem under the Bahri Mamluks.* In the late 1980s and early 1990s he was a lecturer at Mackintosh School of Architecture in Glasgow. His writings include *Mamluks Jerusalem; an architectural study* (1987). Directory of BSMES members, 1993; LC; Sluglett

Burguière, Paul Maurice Jean, born 19 August 1918 at Bordeaux, he studied at Bordeaux and Paris, and taught at Istanbul Üniversitesi Edebiyat Fakültesi from 1945 to 1951. In 1960 he received a doctorate for his thesis, *Histoire de l'infinitif grec.* Thereafter he was a professor of *grammaire des langues classiques* at l'Université de Bordeaux III. In 1985 he published a critical edition and translation of Saint Cyril of Alexandria entitled *Contre Julien.* WhoFr, 1975/76-1988/89|

Burham (Bourham), 'Abd al-'Aziz, fl. 1948, he he received a *docteur ès lettres* and was a sometime professor at the Faculté des lettres, Alexandria, Egypt. His writings include *De la condition de la femme dans l'antiquité hébraïque* (Alexandrie, 1959). NUC, pre-1956

Buri-Gütermann, Johanna, born 20th cent., she received a Dr.phil. in 1970 from the Universität Wien for *Der Satzbau in der Sprache der osmanischen Urkunden aus der Zeit von Mehmed Fatih bis Süleyman-i Qanuni,* a work which was published in 1972. LC; Schwarz

Burian, Orhan, born about 1913, he was a leading specialist in English studies in Turkey, and died at the age of thirty-nine in 1952 or 53. His writings include *Kıraliçe Elizabeth'den üçüncü Sultan Murata gelen hediyenin hikâyesi* (1951), *Canın yongası* (1954), *Denemeler, eleştiriler* (1993). JRCAS 40 (1953), pp. 301-2

Buringh, Pieter, born 20th cent., he received a doctorate in 1951 from Landbouwhogeschool, Wageningen, Netherlands, for his thesis, *Over de bodemgesteldheid rondom Wageningen.* He was a professor of soil science and affiliated with the Centre for World Food Market Research, Wageningen. His writings include *Soils and soil conditions in Iraq* (1960), and *Introduction to the study of soils in tropical and subtropical regions* (1968). LC

Burkart, James Ellsworth, fl. 1962-67, he was a sometime director, American Friends of the Middle East, Jordan. Note

Burke, Edmond, born 30 July 1940 at Washington, D.C., he was a graduate of the University of Notre Dame and received his Ph.D. in 1970 from Princeton for *Moroccan political responses to French penetration, 1900-1912.* He was in 1968 a professor of history at the University of California, Santa Cruz, a post which he still held in 2003. His writings include the revised version of his thesis, *Prelude to protectorate in Morocco* (1976). In 1988 he edited *Global crises and social movements.* DrAS, 1974, H 1978 H, 1982 H; NatFacDr, 1995-2003; Selim

Burke, Samuel Martin, born 3 July 1906 at Martinpur, India, he took an M.A. in 1928 at Government College, Lahore. He entered the Indian Civil Service in 1931, and, after partition, the Pakistani Foreign Service, where he remained until 1961 when he was appointed a professor and consultant in South Asian studies at the University of Minnesota. His writings include *Pakistan's foreign policy* (1973),

Mainsprings of Indian and Pakistani foreign policies (1974), and *Akbar, the greatest Mogul* (1989). AmM&WS, 1973 S, 1978 S; ConAu 49-52; IntWW, 1974-1983/84; IWWAS, 1976/77; WhoWor, 1974/75-1978/79

Burkett, Mary Elizabeth, O.B.E., born in Northumberland, England, she was a graduate of the University of Durham, a sometime teacher of art and crafts, and from 1963 until her retirement in 1986, a director of Abbott Hall Art Gallery. In 1962 she spent seven months in Turkey and Iran. Her writings include *Old photographs of the Lake District* (1974). Who, 1979-2003; WhoWor, 1978/79

Burkhard, Karl Friedrich, born 2 September 1824 at Leipheim, Bavaria, he studied theology, philosophy, and Oriental philology at the universities of Erlangen, Halle, and Leipzig, where he received a Dr.phil. in 1846 for his Latin thesis on the Turkish dialects of Central Asia, with special reference to the Kazan area. In 1847 he pursued post-doctoral studies at St. Petersburg, where he also served as a private tutor at the home of Lieutenant-general von Mühlen. In 1848 he declined a professorship in German at the Imperial Armenian Institute, Moscow, and returned to München. Since 1851 he taught classical philology, Hebrew, and French at high schools in Austria, advancing to the position of professor in 1868. From 1870 to his retirement in 1890 he was a professor, and later director, at the k.k. Franz Joseph Gymnasium in Wien. He died 19 February 1893. Bursian, v. 17 (1894), pp. 87-92

Burki, Riffat Jahan, born ca. 1938 in India, she was educated at Punjab University and the University of Durham where she received a Ph.D. in 1868 for her thesis, *The main philosophical ideas in the writings of Muhammad Iqbal*. She was a somtime deputy director in the Bureau of National Research and Reference, Ministry of Information and National Affairs, Government of Pakistan. Note

Burki, Shahid Javed, born 20th cent., he was in 1964 a Public Service Fellow of the Kennedy School of Government, Harvard University, and a sometime director of the Rural Works Programme of West Pakistan. In 1992 he was affiliated with the World Bank. His writings include *Pakistan under Bhutto* (1980), *Pakistan, a nation in making* (1986), and *Historical dictionary of Pakistan* (1991). LC; NUC

Burman, Dalim Chandra, he was in 1980 a research fellow at Dacca University. Note

Burmester, Oswald Hugh Ewart, Dr., fl. 1939, his writings include *The Egyptian, or Coptic Church* (1967). He was joint author of the *Catalogue of the Coptic and Christian Arab MSS preserved in the Cloister of Saint Menas, Cairo* (1967), and *Catalogue of the Coptic and Christian Arabic MSS preserved in the Library of the Church of Saints Sergius and Bacchus, Cairo* (1977). He died before 1985. LC

Burn, Henry Pelham, Brig.-Gen., born 1 May 1882, he entered the Army in 1901 and served in South Africa, 1901-1902. He died 10 July 1958. Who was who, 5

Burn, Richard, fl. 1895, he was a British traveller who crossed the Bakhtiyari territory from Isfahan to Shushtar in the autumn of 1894. Henze

Burn, Sir Richard, born 1 February 1871 at Liverpool, he was a graduate of Oxford, and served in the Indian Civil Service from 1891 until retirement in 1927. He was a contributor to the *Cambridge history of India*, and joint editor of the *Imperial gazetteer of India*. He died 26 July 1947. IndianBiInd (5); Who was who, 4

Burn, William Laurence, born 15 October 1904 at Wolsingham, England, he was a graduate of Oxford, a barrister-at-law, and since 1944 a professor of modern history at the University of Newcastle upon Tyne. His writings include *The British West Indies* (1951). He died 11 July 1966. Who was who, 6

Burnes, Sir Alexander, born 2 November 1805 at Montrose, Scotland. While serving in the army of the East India Company, he made himself acquainted with Urdu and Persian, and thus obtained an appointment as interpreter at Surat in 1822. Transferred to Cutch in 1826 as assistant to the Political Agent, he turned his attention to the history and geography of north-western India. In subsequent years, his travels were extended through Afghanistan across the Hinukush to Bukhara and Persia. In 1836 he undertook a political mission to Dost Mohammad at Kabul. He returned to Kabul as political officer in 1841, where he was killed during the Afghan insurrection, 2 November 1841. His writings include *Travels into Bokhara* (1834), its translations into French and German (1835), Italian (1842), Russian (1848), and *Cabool, being a personal narrative of a journey to, and residence in that city, in 1836, 7, and 8* (1842). Buckland; DNB; Embacher; EncBrit; GdeEnc; Henze; I.I. (2); IndianBiInd (6); Riddick

Burnes, James, born 12 February 1801 at Montrose, Scotland, he was a trained physician and arrived in Bombay in company with his brother Alexander in 1821. He accompanied the field force which, in 1825, captured Cutch in Sind. In 1837 he was appointed garrison surgeon of Bombay. Impaired health compelled him to resign in 1849 and return to England, where he died 19 September 1862. His writings include *A Narrative of a visit to the court of Sinde; a sketch of the history of Cutch* (1829). Buckland; DNB; Henze; IndianBiInd (5)

Burnet, Etienne, born 11 October 1873, he wrote *Lucrète, notre contemporain* (Tunis, 1984). He died in Tunis, 20 December 1960. LC

Burnett, Charles S. F., Dr., fl. 1980, he was a sometime lecturer at the Warburg Institute, London. His writings include the critical editions and translations, *De essentiis*, of Hermann of Carinthia (1982), and *De mundi celestis terrestisque constitutione* (1988).   *Directory of BSMES members*, 1993

Burnouf, Denis, fl. 1961-1974, he wrote *Turcorama* (Paris, Hachette, 1967). LC

Burnouf, Émile Louis, born 25 August 1821 at Valognes (Manche), he studied at Paris and was appointed in 1854 a professor of Oriental studies at Nancy. In 1867 he was a director of l'École française d'Athènes. After his return to France, he settled in Paris as a Sanskritist. His writings include *Méthode pour étudier la langue sanscrite* (1859), *Histoire de la littérature grecque* (1869), and *La Légende athénienne* (1872). Buckland; DBF; Vapereau

Burns, Eedson Louis Millard, born 17 June 1897 at Westmount, P.Q., and educated at the Royal Military College, Kingston, Ont., he became a chief of staff, UN Truce Supervision Organisation, Palestine, 1954-55, and commander, UN Emergency Force, 1956-59. His writings include *Between Arab and Israeli* (1962), *General mud; memoirs of two world wars* (1970), and *A Seat at the table* (1972). He died 13 September 1985. Canadian, 1936, 1948-1985; Who 1968-1985; *Who was who*, 8

Burns, James David, born 13 December 1932 at Seattle, Wash., he was a graduate of Whitman College, Wala Wala, Wash., a practising trial attorney in Seattle, and a collector of art, particularly rugs. His writings include *The Caucasus* (1987). LC; WhoAmL, 1979

Burns, John, born 20 October 1858 at London, he was a Labour MP, 1882-1918, who was convinced of the injustice of the first World War. A number of biographical studies can be found under his main entry in the BLC to 1975. He died 24 January 1943. *Who was who*, 4

Burns, Norman, born 14 November 1905 at Versailles, Ohio, he graduated from Wittenberg University, where he also earned a law degree; he received a master's degree in economics from Yale. From 1929 to 1932 he was an assistant professor of economics at AUB. Thereafter he held U.S. State Department assigments as deputy director of the International Administration Office for the Near East, South Asia and Africa, director of the U.S. Operations Mission to Jordan, and director of the Foreign Service Institute. He also served as chief economic adviser to the U.N. Relief and Works Agency in Beirut from 1953 to 1956. After his retirement he lectured on Middle East economic problems at Johns Hopkins School of Advanced International Studies and served on the Middle East Institute's board of governors. His writings include *The Tariff of Syria, 1919-1932* (1933). He was the editor of *The Administration of higher institutions under changing conditions* (1947). He died of renal failure at his home in Falls Church, Va., 25 December 1994. MidE, 1982/83; Shavit; WhoAm, 1974-1978/79; WRMEA, March 1995

Burns, Robert Ignatius, S.J., born 16 August 1921 at San Francisco, he entered the Society of Jesus in 1940, and received a Ph.D. in 1958 from Johns Hopkins University, Baltimore, Md. He was a professor of history at the University of California from 1947 until retirement, and a visiting professor at American, Canadian, and European universities. His writings include *Islam under the Crusaders* (1973), *Medieval colonialism* (1975), *Muslims, Christians, and Jews in the Crusader Kingdom of Valencia* (1984), and *Foundations of Crusader Valencia* (1991). ConAu, 17-20, new rev. 7, 26; DrAS, 1969 H, 1974 H, 1978 H, 1982 H; IntAu&W, 1977-1989; WhoAm, 1976, 1989/90-2003

Burns, William Haywood, his writings include *The Voices of Negro protest in America* (1963), and its translation, *Voces de protesta de los negros en Estados Unidos* (Buenos Aires, 1964). LC

Buron, Robert Gaston Albert, born 27 February 1910 at Paris, he was educated at Paris and received a doctorate in 1938 from the Faculté de droit de Paris for his thesis, *Les obligation du trustee au droit anglais*. He was a sometime municipal magistrate, and a minister. From 1963 to 1967, he was president of the Centre de développement of the Organization for Economic Cooperation and Development, Paris. His writings include *Carnets politiques de la guerre d'Algérie, par un signataire des accords d'Évian* (1965), *Decision-making in the development field* (1966), and *Les Dernières années de la IVe République; carnets politiques* (1968). He died 28 April 1973. WhoFr, 1959/60-1973/74

Burov, Nikolai Appolonovich, born in 1885, he published in 1923 in a Russian journal the article, "Точные науки в Туркестане в 1917-1922 г.г.", an off-print of which is to be found in the N.P.Y.L. LC

Burr, Angela Margaret Rose, born 20th cent., she received a Ph.D. in 1974 from SOAS for her thesis, *Buddhism, Islam, and spirit beliefs and practices and their social correlates in two southern Thai coastal fishing villages*. Sluglett

Burr, Charles Barton, fl. 1805-1819, he was a sometime member of the Bombay establishment of the East India Company. BLC; NUC, pre-1956

Burr, Malcolm, D.Sc., born in 1878 at Blackheath, UK., he was educated at New College, Oxford, and the Royal School of Mines. He was a corresponding member of the American Entomological Society. In April 1946, he was resident in Istanbul as acting correspondent of the Government of India. His writings include *In Soviet Siberia* (1931), *Dersu, the trapper* (1996), and translations from the Russian. He died in 1954. BioIn 3; LC; WhE&EA

Burrell, Robert Michael, fl. 1972, he studied at St. Andrews and SOAS, where he received a Ph.D. in 1979 for his thesis, *Aspects of the reign of Muzaffar al-Din, Shah of Persia, 1896-1907*. Thereafter he was a lecturer in contemporary history of the Near and Middle East at SOAS. His writings include *The Persian Gulf* (1972). In 1989 he edited *Islamic fundamentalism; papers of a seminar*. Sluglett

Burrill, Kathleen Ruth Frances, née Griffin, born 8 March 1924 at Canterbury, Kent, she was a graduate of Columbia University and received a Ph.D. in 1964. From 1947 to 1955, she was an officer of the British Council, Ankara, and thereafter successively lecturer, professor and chairman, Center of Turkish Studies, Columbia University, N.Y.C. , where she was still active in 1998. Her writings include *The quatrains of Nesimi* (1972); she was joint editor of *Archivum Ottomanicum*. NatFacDr, 1998; *Who's who in America*, 1988/89-2003; *Who's who in the East*, 1985-1991/92

Burroughs, Franklin Troy, born 12 November 1936 at Wilmington, Calif., he received a Ed.D. in 1964 from U.Ç.L.A. for his thesis, *Foreign students at U.C.L.A.; a case sudy in cross-cultural education*. For over fifteen years he was a professor of English as secondary language in Iran, interrupted only by a one year spell of teaching in Saudi Arabia. LEduc, 1974

Burrowes, Robert Dennis, born 21 July 1935 at Orange, N. J., he received a Ph.D. in 1967 from Princeton for his thesis, *Adolf Augustus Berle, Brandeis of the future*. Since 1961 he was a professor of political science at New York University. His writings include *The Yemen Arab Republic; the politics of development* (1987), and *Historical dictionary of Yemen* (1995).

Burrows, Sir Bernard Alexander Brocas, born 3 July 1910, he was educated at Eton, and Trinity College, Oxford. He entered HM Foreign Service in 1934. He was the first Foreign Service officer to be Political Resident in the Persian Gulf from 1953 to 1958. Thereafter he served as ambassador to Turkey until 1962. After his retirement he was a consultant to the Federal Trust for Education and Research. His writings include *Footnotes in the sand* (1990). He died 7 May 2002. BlueB, 1973/74, 1975, 1976; IntWW, 1974-1992/1993; IntYB, 1978-1998; Who, 1974-2002

Burrows, Eric Norman Bromley, S.J., born in 1882, he was an English poet and Assyriologist. His writings include *Archaic texts* (1935), and *The Gospel of the infancy and other Biblical essays* (1940). He died in 1938. BioIn 3; Master (2)

Burrows, Millar, born 26 October 1889 at Wyoming, Ohio, he was a graduate of Cornell, and Yale universities, served as a Presbyterian minister, and was a professor of Biblical history and literature. While he was director of the American Schools of Oriental Research, Jerusalem, the Dead Sea scrolls were discovered, on the subject of which he wrote two best-selling books. From 1954 to 1957, he was president of Middle East Relief. His writings include *Founders of great religions* (1931), *Palestine is our business* (1949), and *The Dead Sea scrolls* (1955). He died in Ann Arbor, Mich., 29 April 1980. BioIn 4, 12; ConAu 81, 97; CurBio 56, 80 new; Master (5); Shavit; Who, 1974-1980; WWWA, 7; WrDr, 1976-1980/82

Burt, Richard B., he was in 1975 an assistant director of the International Institute of Strategic Studies, London. His writings include *Congressional hearings on American defense policy; an annotated bibliog-raphy* (1974), and *New weapons technologies* (1976). LC

Burthe d'Annelet, Jules Louis Charles de, lt.-colonel, born 11 February 1870 at Paris, he served with the Spahis sahariens, and later took part in the Chari campaign, 1903-1906. After the first World War he served in Tunisia, the Corps d'occupation de Constantinople, and Syria. After his retirement from the army, he pursued colonial explorations in French Africa. From 1928 to 1931 he made a 25,000 km tour of the Sahara. DBF; Peyronnet, p. 925

Burton, Harry McGuire, Major, born in 1898, he went in 1927 to Turkey as a language student, one of the first Englishmen to be accorded the privilege of living with a Turkish family for several years. After a seven-year absence, he returned to Turkey on a visit. Note

Burton, John, born in 1929, his writings include *The Collection of the Qur'an* (1977), and *The Sources of Islamic law* (1990). LC

Burton, John Wear, born in 1915 in Australia, he was a graduate of the University of Sydney, and received his Ph.D. from the University of London. He was a reader in international relations at University College, London, and since 1978, at the University of Kent. His writings include *The Alternative; a dynamic approach to our relations with Asia* (1954), *Systems, states, diplomacy and rules* (1968), *Conflict & communication* (1969), and *World society* (1972). BlueB, 1973/74, 1975, 1976; ConAu 103; IntYB, 1980-1998; WrDr, 1980-1998/2000|

Burton, Reginald George, General, born 8 July 1864 at Daventry, Northamptonshire. After passing through the Royal Military College, Sandhurst, he served in India until his retirement in 1920. His writings include *History of the Hyderabad Contingent* (1905), and *The Mahratta and Pindari war* (1910). He died 2 February 1951. Master (1); WhE&EA; Who was who, 5

Burton, Sir Richard Francis, 1821-1890, he was an amazing explorer, orientalist, linguist, and man of letters. His discovery of Lake Tanganyika and his pilgrimage to Mecca in Muslim disguise are mighty achievements. No traveller in Arabia - apart from T. E. Lawrence - has attracted more biographies and the first was published ten years before his death. A bibliography of his own works runs to more than three hundred pages and includes sixty full-length volumes. James A. Casada published *Sir Richard F. Burton; a biobibliographical study* (1990). Bidwell; Buckland; DLB 166 (1996), pp. 98-119; Embacher; EncAm; EncBrit; EncicUni; Freeth, pp. 121-152; Fück; GdeEnc; *Index Islamicus* (6); Henze; Magyar; Meyers; RNL

Burton-Brown, Theodore, B.A., fl. 1946-1983, he was a British archaeologist whose writings include *Studies in third millenium history* (1946), *Excavations in Azarbaijan, 1948* (1951), *The Coming of iron to Greece* (1955), *Early Mediterranean migration* (1959), *Second millenium archaeology* (1978), *Kara Tepe* (1979), and *Westward migration* (1983). BLC; LC

Burton-Page, John, fl. 1980, he wrote *Ahmadabad* (Bombay, 1988).

Burtt, Joseph, fl. 1929. Under the auspices of the Armenian Committee of the Society of Friends, he wrote *The people of Ararat* (London, 1926). LC; Note

Bury, George *Wyman*, born in 1874, he was an army officer who had fought with Moroccan rebels in 1895. At the beginning of the twentieth century he made the first serious attempt to explore the interior of southern Arabia. His writings, party under his South Arabian pseudonym Abdullah Mansur, include *The Land of Uz* (1911), *Arabia infelix; or, the Turks in Yemen* (1915), and *Pan-Islam* (1919). Bidwell; LC

Bury, John Bagnell, born 16 October 1861 at Monaghan, Ulster, he was a graduate of Trinity College, Dublin, a classical scholar and historian. He received honorary doctorates of Aberdeen, Dublin, Durham, Edinburgh, Glasgow, and Oxford. His writings include *The Ancient Greek historians* (1909). He died in 1927. DNB; Master (16)

Bury, John Patrick Tuer, born 30 July 1908 at Cambridge, he was a graduate of Corpus Christi College, Cambridge, who spent his entire teaching career at Cambridge. His writings include *Gambetta and the national defence* (1936), and *The College of Corpus Christi, 1822 to 1952* (1952). ConAu 17-20; IntAu&W, 1976-1991/92; WrDr, 1976-1988/90|

Busard, Hubert Lambertus Ludovicus, born in 1923, his writings include *Quelques sujets de l'histoire des mathématiques au moyen âge* (1968), *The Translation of the Elements of Euclid from the Arabic into Latin by Hermann of Carinthia* (1977), and *The First Latin translation of Euclid's Elements commonly ascribed to Adelard of Bath* (1983). LC

Busbecq (Busbeck/Bousbecq/Bousebecque), Augier (Ogier) Ghislain de, born at Comines, Flanders. In the service of Emperor Ferdinand I he was sent to Constantinople, in 1555, as ambassador to Sultan Süleyman the Magnificent. While there, he suffered imprisonment for a time, but succeeded in concluding a treaty of peace which was ratified in 1562. His writings include *Legationis Turcicae epistolae quatuor* (1589), and its translations into several languages. He died in Rouen, 28 October 1592. BioNBelg; EncAm; EncBrit; GdeEnc; Henze; *Index Islamicus* (2); Magyar; Meyers; Meydan; RNL

Busch, Briton Cooper, born 5 September 1936 at Los Angeles, he was a graduate of Stanford University and received a Ph.D. in 1965 from the University of California, Berkeley, for his thesis, *British policy in the Persian Gulf, 1894-1914*. In 1963 he was appointed professor of history at Colgate University, Hamilton, N.Y., where he was still teaching in 1998. His writings include *Britain and the Persian Gulf, 1894-1914* (1967), *Britain, India, and the Arabs, 1914-1921* (1971), *Mudros to Lausanne; Britain's frontier in West Asia, 1918-1923* (1976), and *Whaling will never do for me* (1993). ConAu, 21-24, new rev., 8; NatFacDr, 1995-1998; Master (5); Selim

Busch, Charles David, born in 1929, he received a Ph.D. in 1960 from Cornell University, Ithaca, N.Y. for his thesis, *An Investigation of mole drain deterioration and of a method of extending drain life*. In

1979, he was an associate professor of agriculture engineering at Auburn University, Auburn, Alabama. NUC

Busch, Clemens (Klemens) August, born 20 May 1834 at Köln, he studied law and Oriental languages at Berlin, where he received a Dr.phil. in 1859 for *Specimen doctrinae de copticae linguae praepositionibus ac particulis*. In 1861 he entered the Prussian diplomatic service as a student interpreter in Constantinople. He served as a foreign service officer and counsellor to the German chancellor at the Congress of Berlin in 1878. He died in Bern, 25 November 1895. DtBE; Meyers; NDB

Busch, Julius Hermann *Moritz*, born 13 February 1821 at Dresden, he studied theology and philosophy at Leipzig from 1842 to 1846. Disheartened by the revolution of 1848, he went in 1851 to the United States, but returned the following year. From 1856 to 1859 he was in the service of Österreichischer Lloyd in the Levant, as a result of which he published the travel guides, *Aegypten* (1858), *Griechenland* (1859), and *Türkei* (1860), From 1859 to 1864 he was a full-time editor of the *Grenzboten*. He was appointed to the press bureau of the Prussian foreign service in 1870. Until his resignation in 1873, he was in charge of consular affairs in St. Petersburg and, later, of operations in the Levant. His writings include *Eine Wallfahrt nach Jerusalem* (1861), *Abriss der Urgeschichte des Orients bis zu den medischen Kriegen* (1868), and *Wunderliche Heilige* (1879). He died in Leipzig, 16 November 1899. DtBE; Embacher; EncAm; Meyers; *Sigilla veri*

Busch, Klemens August, 1834-1895 *see* Busch, Clemens August

Busch, Moritz, 1821-1899 *see* Busch, Julius Hermann Moritz

Busch, Ruth Chipman, born 25 September 1931 at Ann Arbor, Mich., she was a graduate of Cornell University, and received a Ph.D. in 1970 from the University of Arizona. Thereafter she was a professor of sociology and anthropology at Auburn University, Auburn, Ala. AmM&WS, 1973S, 1978S

Busch-Zantner, Richard, born 4 January 1911, he received a Dr.phil. in 1938 from the Universität Erlangen for his thesis, *Agrarverfassung, Gesellschaft und Siedlung in Südosteuropa*. Thereafter he was with the Bavarian civic service. His writings include *Albanien, neues Land im Imperium* (1939), and *Bulgarien* (1941). He died on duty at the eastern front, 25 August 1942.

Buschendorf-Otto, Gisela, fl. 1961, she was joint author, with Karl-Heinz Otto, of *Felsbilder aus dem sudanesischen Nubien* (1993).

Büscher, Horst, born 20th cent., he received a Dr.phil. in 1967 from the Universität Köln for *Sozial schwache Bevölkerungsschichten und Gesellschaftspolitik in Entwicklungsländern ... Afghanistan, a work* which was published under the title *Die Industriearbeiter in Afghanistan* (1969). He was joint author of *Betriebswirtschaftliche Probleme in afghanischen Industrieunternehmen* (1977). LC; Schwarz

Bushell, Stephen Wootton, born 28 July 1844, he was a surgeon in England until 1868 when he went out to Peking to fill the post of physician to the British legation there. On returning to England he devoted himself to the study of Chinese art and archaeology. His writings include *Oriental ceramic art* (1896), and *Description of Chinese pottery and porcelain; being a translation* (1910). He died 19 September 1908. DNB

Bushev, Petr Pavlovich, born in 1899 at St. Petersburg, he graduated in 1929 from the Oriental Institute, Leningrad, and was from 1951 to his death in 1981 affiliated with the Oriental Institute, Soviet Academy of Science. His writings include *Герат и англо-иранская война 1856-1857 гг.* (1959), *История посольсв и дипломатических отношений русского и иранского государсв в 1586-1612 гг.* (1976), and *Посольство Артемия Волыиского в Иран в 1715-1718 гг.* (1978). LC; Miliband; Miliband²

el-**Bushra**, Mahammad el-*Sayed*, he received an M.A. in 1964 from LSE for his thesis, *The Urban geography of north and central Sudan*, and a Ph.D. in 1970 from Bedford College, London, for *The Khartoum conurbation; an economic and social analysis*. He was in 1976 a senior lecturer in geography at the University of Khartoum. His writings include *An Atlas of Khartoum* (1976). LC; Sluglett

Bushuev, Semen Kuz'mich, fl. 1937, his writings include *Борьба горцев за независимость под руководством Шамиля* (1939), *Крымская война, 1853-1856 гг.* (1940), and *Из истории внешне-политических отношений в период присоединения Кавказа к России* (1955). OSK

Buskirk, Dale, born 12 December 1943 at Anacortes, Wash., a graduate of the University of Washington, who received a Ph.D. in 1976 from Ohio State University for *Islam and modernization; the Indonesian case*. IWWAS, 1976/77

Busquet, Raoul, 1881-1955, he was a sometime chief archivist at the Département Bouches-du-Rhône. His writings include *L'Œuvre du Conseil général des Bouches-du-Rhône* (1932), and *Histoire de Marseille*, of which no less than eight editions were published until 1945. LC

Busquets Mulet, Jaime (Juan), born 26 November 1898 at Palma de Mallorca, he was since 1931 a professor of colloquial Arabic at the Escuela de Comercio de Palma de Mallorca. His writings include the critical edition and translation, *El hijo del sultán y la hija del carpintero; cuento popular en dialecto de Tetuán* (1953), and *Gramática elemental de la lengua árabe* (1954). He died 14 January 1971. *Boletin de la Asociation Española de Orientalistas* 7 (1971), pp. 6-7

Buss, Georg, born 9 September 1850 at Köln, he was a trained architect, and editor of *Moderne Kunst* (Berlin, 1887-1914.) His writings on arts and crafts include *Der Fächer* (1904), *Das Kostüm in Vergangenheit und Gegenwart* (1906), and *Aus der Blütezeit der Silhouette* (1913). Wrede, v. 3, p. 28

Bussagli, Mario, born 23 September 1917 at Siena, he was since 1958 a professor of Indian and Central Asian art at the Università di Roma. His writings include *Profili dell'India antica e moderna* (1959), *Il Tâj Mahal* (1965), *Culture e civiltà dell'Asia centrale* (1970), and the translations, *Painting of Central Asia* (1963), *Oriental architecture* (1974), *Architektur des Orients* (1975), *Indian miniatures* (1976), *La Peinture de l'Asie centrale* (1978). He was joint author of *Arte de vetro* (1991). Chi è, 1961; LC; Wholtaly, 1980

Busse, Heribert, born 26 April 1926 at Duderstadt, Germany, he studied at Mainz and SOAS, and became a lecturer at Hamburg, a visiting professor at Bordeaux, 1970-71, and a professor at Bochum, and from 1973 to 1991 a professor, and later director, Seminar für Orientalistik, Kiel. His writings include *Untersuchungen zum islamischen Kanzleiwesen und zur Verwaltungsgeschichte an Hand turkmenischer und safawidischer Urkunden* (1959) - a work which was orginally presented in 1956 at Mainz as his doctoral thesis - *Chalif und Großkönig; die Buyiden im Iraq, 945-1055* (1969), *Jerusalemer Heiligtumstraditionen in altkirchlicher und frühislamischer Zeit* (1987), *Die theologischen Beziehungen des Islams zu Judentum und Christentum* (1988), and its translation, *Islam, Judaism, and Christianity; theological and historical afflictions* (1998). Kürschner, 1970-2003; Schwarz

Bussert, Rudolf, fl. 1967, he wrote *Prozess- und Zwangsvollstreckungsrecht für Betriebswirte* (Wiesbaden, 1972). LC

Bussi, Emilio, born 13 April 1904 at Rovigo, Italy, he received a doctorate in law in 1935 and was appointed a professor of law successively at Cagliari and Modena. His writings include *Ricerche intorno alle relazione fra retratto bizantino e musulmano* (1933), *Principi di diritto musulmano* (1943), *Evoluzione storica dei tipi di stato* (1948), and *Esperienze e prospettive; saggi di storia politica e giuridica* (1976). Chi è, 1948, 1957, 1961; Wholtaly, 1957/58

Bussink, Willem C. F., born 12 June 1929, he was joint author of *Malaysia, growth and equity in a multiracial society* (1980), and a contributing author to *Poverty and the development of human resources* (Washington, D.C., The World Bank, 1980), and *Poverty reduction in India* (1991). LC

Busson, Henri, born in 1870, he was in 1900 a teacher at the Lycée de Clermont-Ferrand. His writings include *Géographie générale* (1913); he was joint author of *Notre empire coloniale* (1910), and *La France d'aujourd'hui et ses colonies* (1920). LC; Note

Busson de Janssens, Gérard, *docteur en droit*, fl. 1953-1960, he was a sometime member of the Centre de hautes études d'administration musulmane, Paris, and chief of the Division des investissements privés, Délégation générale du Gouvernement, Alger. Note

Bussy, Albert Charles, born 6 April 1864. After passing through a French school of infantry, he received a commission as *sous-lieutenant* on 17 March 1887, and on ministerial orders was assigned to the Service des Affaires indigènes de l'Algérie on 1 February 1893. He remained there until 1910 when he was posted to the Service des renseignements du Maroc. During the first World War he saw action as a commander of a regiment. He retired from active service with the rank of colonel of the 57th Regiment at Rochefort. Peyronnet, pp. 519-520

al-**Bustani**, Butrus ibn Bulus, born in 1819 at Dibbiyah, Lebanon, he studied at the Maronite Seminary, 'Ayn Warqah. From his early years he was influenced by the American Mission in Beirut, and later became a Protestant and dragoman at the American Consulate. He founded a high school in Beirut and, in 1870, the newspaper *al-Jannah* and subsequently the ephemeral *al-Junaynah*, and lastly the fornightly *al-Jinan*. He is best remembered for his dictionary, *Muhit al-muhit*. He died 1 May 1883. GAL II, p. 495

al-**Bustani**, Fu'ad Afram, 1906- *see* Boustany, Fouad Ephrem

Bustany, Basil K. I., he received a Ph.D. in 1969 from the American University for his thesis, *Monetary policy and economic development in Iraq, 1950-1964*. In 1980 he was an economic adviser to the executive director of the Middle East Group at the World Bank in Washington, D.C. His writings include *The currency board system in Iraq, 1932-1949* (Baghdad, 1984). LC; Selim

Busuladžić, Mustafa S., fl. 1942, he wrote *Jedna sjajna stranica islamske historije* (Sarajevo, 1935). Grada

Busygin, Evgenii Prokof'evich, born in 1914, he was an ethnographer, geographer and historian; who received a doctorate in 1963 and was appointed a professor in 1965. His writings include *Русское сельское население Среднего Поволжья* (1966); he was joint author of *Пусское население чувашской АССР* (1960), and *Этнографиянародов Средного Поволжья* (1985). LC; OSK; TatarES

Butaev, Inal, fl. 1922, he wrote *Национальная революция на востоке; проблема Турции* (Leningrad, 1925). OSK

Butakov, Aleksei Ivanovich, born 7 (19) February 1816, he was an officer in the Imperial Russian Navy, who explored and surveyed the Sea of Aral and the Syr Darya, 1848-1859. He died in Bad Schwalbach, Germany, 11 July 1869. Embacher; EnSlovar; GSE; Henze

Butani, Dayo Hasomal, fl. 1975, his writings include *Baba Hariram, saint of Sind* (1981), *The future of Pakistan* (1984), and *The melody and philosophy of Shah Latif* (1991). He died in 1989. LC

Buthaud, Étienne François Robert, born 21 April 1909 at Poitiers, he was a graduate of the Faculté de droit de Poitiers, and from 1936 to 1954 served successively as a justice of the peace, judge, and tribunal president in Tunisia. He was joint author of *Les Corporations tunisiennes: Le souk des barbouches; Le gardiennage des souks* (194-). WhoFr, 1969/70-1977/78|

Butler, Alfred Joshua, Dr., born in 1850, he was a sometime fellow of Brasenose College, Oxford, and Eton College. He was in 1880 a tutor to the Khedive of Egypt. His writings include *Court life in Egypt* (1887), *The Arab conquest of Egypt and the last thirty years of the Roman domination* (1902), *Babylon of Egypt* (1914), *Islamic pottery* (1926), and *Sport in classic times* (1930). He was joint editor of *The Churches and monasteries of Egypt and some neighbouring countries* (1985). He died 4 October 1936. Who was who, 3

Butler, Howard Crosby, born 7 March 1872 at Croton Falls, N.Y., he was a graduate of Princeton and Columbia, to which study at the American School of Classical Studies in Rome and Athens was added a year or two later. He was from 1895 to 1922 a lecturer in architecture, art and archaeology at Princeton. He repeatedly conducted archaeological expeditions in Syria. His writings include *Architecture and other arts* (1903), and *Early churches in Syria* (1929). He died on his way home from his last expedition, in Neuilly, France, 13, 14 or 15 August 1922. DAB; Shavit; WhAm, 1

Butler, Pierce, born 19 December 1886 at Claredon Hills, Illinois, he was educated at Columbia University and theological seminaries in the United States. He was a sometime lecturer in history of printing and bibliographic methods, and a professor of library history at the University of Chicago. His writings include *The Origin of printing in Europe* (1940). He died 28 March 1953. Master (3); WhAm, 3

Butler, Richard Austen, afterwards Baron Butler of Saffron Walden, born 9 December 1902 in the Punjab. He was a conservative politician, and deeply impressed by M. K. Gandhi. He published his autobiography, *The Art of the possible* (1971). He died 8 March 1982. DNB; Who was who, 8

Butler, Stephen Seymour, born in 1880, he joined the 3rd Northumberland Fusilliers in 1897, and advanced through the grades to become major-general. He served predominantly in the Middle East and Africa. He died 16 July 1964. Who, 1943-1964

Butler, William Elliott, born 20 October 1939 at Minneapolis, Minn., he received a Ph.D. in 1963 from Johns Hopkins University, Baltimore, Md. After teaching in the United States until 1970, he was appointed a professor of comparative law at the University of London. His writings include *Legislation of the Chinese Soviet Republic, 1931-1934* (1981), and he edited *The legal system of the Chinese Soviet Republic, 1931-1934* (1983), and *Perestroika and the rule of law; Anglo-American and Soviet perspectives* (1991). ConAu 25-28, new rev., 11; Who, 1986-2003

Butorac, Franjo, fl. 1980, he was joint author of *Povijest Rijeke* (Rijeka, 1988). LC

Butros, Albert Jamil, born 25 March 1934 at Jerusalem, he received a Ph.D. in 1963 from Columbia for his thesis, *English loanwords in the colloquial Arabic of Palestine, 1917-1948*. In the same year he was appointed a professor of English at the University of Jordan. Selim; WhoWor, 1982/83

Butros-Ghali, Butros, 1922- see Boutros Ghali, Boutros

Butterfield, Sir Herbert, born 6 October 1900 at Oxenhope, Yorkshire. After Cambridge, he was Regius professor of modern history at Cambridge, 1963-68. His writings include *International conflict in the twentieth century* (1960). He died 20 July 1979. ConAu 1; Master (10); *Who's who*, 1965-1979; *Writers directory*, 1974/76-1980/82

Butterworth, Charles E., born 9 July 1938 at Detroit, Mich., he was a graduate of Michigan State University, and received a Ph.D. in 1967 from the University of Chicago for his thesis, *Rhetoric and reason; a study of Averroës' Commentary on Aristotle's Rhetoric*. Since 1969 he was a professor of government and politics at the University of Maryland, where he was still teaching in 2003. His writings include *Philosophy, ethics and virtuous rule* (1986). *National Faculty directory*, 1995-2003; Selim; *Who's who in the East*, 1991/92

Buttigieg, Joseph A., born 20 May 1947 at Hamrun, Malta, he was educated in Malta, England, and the United States, where he received a Ph.D. in English in 1976 from SUNY, Binghampton. He was a professor of English in Malta and America, ultimately at the University of Notre Dame, where he was still teaching in 2003. DrAS, 1978 E, 1982 E; NatFacDr, 1995-2003

Buttiker, Wilhelm, born in 1921 in Switzerland, he received a doctorate in natural science in 1948 at Zürich. Thereafter he carried on field-work in Saudi Arabia. He was a counsellor to the Saudi Arabian Commission on the Protection of the Environment. WWASS, 1989

Buttin, Charles, born in 1856, his writings include *Catalogue de la collection d'armes anciens européennes et orientales de Charles Buttin* (1933). NUC, pre-1956

Buttin, François, born 10 April 1897 at Rumilly (Hte-Savoie), he was an *agent général pour le Maroc* with the Compagnie d'assurance l'Abille, and an expert in the Tribunaux du Maroc. He was editor of *Catalogue de la collection d'armes anciens*, by Charles Buttin. WhoFr, 1965/66|

Buttin, Paul, fl. 1960-64, his writings include *Positions d'un chrétien en terres d'Afrique de 1944 à 1950* (Meknès, 1950), and *Le Drame du Maroc* (1955); he was a contributing author to *Contacts en terres d'Afriques* (Meknès, 1946). NUC, pre-1956

Büttner, Friedemann, born 18 May 1938 at Göttingen, he studied German literature and performing arts, and later political science and philosophy as well as Islamics at München, London, and Oxford. He received a Dr.phil. in 1979 from the Universität München for his thesis, *Die Krise der islamischen Ordnung; Studien zur Zerstörung des Ordnungsverständnisses im Osmanischen Reich*. Since 1979 he was a professor of Islamic studies at the Freie Universität Berlin. He was joint author of *Ägypten* (1991), and joint editor of *Reform und Revolution in der islamischen Welt* (1971), and *Les Migrations dans le monde arabe* (1991). Kürschner, 1983-2003; LC

Butzer, Karl Wilhelm, born 19 August 1934 at Mülheim, Germany, he was a graduate of McGill University, Montreal, where he received a B.Sc. (Hons). He received a Dr.rer.nat. in 1957 from the Universität Bonn for his thesis, *Stratigraphy and climate in the Near East*. Since 1959 he was successively professor of geography and/or anthropology at the University of Wisconsin, Madison, the University of Chicago, and the University of Texas at Austin, where he was still teaching in 1995. In 1982 he received the Fryxell Award of Interdisciplinary Research. His writings include *Early hydraulic civilization in Egypt* (1976), and *Archaeology as human ecology* (1982). AmM&WSc, 1973 S, AmM&WSc,1989-2003 P; Bioln 13; *Contemporary authors*, 21-24, 8 new rev.; IntAu&W, 1976-1989; *Who's who in America*, 1976-1986/87; WrDr, 1976-1996/98

Buvry, Louis Leopold, born in 1822, he received a Dr.phil. from the Universität Jena for his thesis, *De Algeriae incolis eorumque situ, origine et moribus*. In the mid-1850s he explored Algeria, particularly the eastern parts. He was a sometime editor of the *Zeitschrift für Akklimatisation*. His writings include *Algerien und seine Zukunft unter französischer Herrschaft* (Berlin, 1855). Henze

Buxton, Edward North, born 1 September 1840. After study at Trinity College, Cambridge, he was engaged in public service, and for forty-two years verderer of Epping Forest. His writings include *On either side of the Red Sea* (1895), and *Two African trips* (1902). He died 9 January 1924. *Who was who*, 2

Buxton, Harold Jocelyn, Rt. Rev., born in 1880, he served in the Caucasus and Cyprus. His writings include *Substitution of law for war* (1925), *Transcaucasus* (1926), and *A Mediterranean window* (1954). He was joint author of *Travel and politics in Armenia* (1914). He died 12 March 1976. ConAu, 104; Who, 1961-1976; *Who was who*, 7

Buxton, Leland William Wilberforce, born in 1884, he was educated at Cambridge, and a close friend of Aubrey Herbert with whom he travelled in the Yemen. Later they were shipwrecked off Bahrain. He had also been active in the Balkans, fighting with guerilla bands against the Turks. The first World War found him at the Arab Bureau in Cairo, where he wrote for the *Arab bulletin*, specializing in Abyssinian affairs. After the war he was a successful stock-broker. His writings include *The Black sheep of the Balkans* (1920), *The Devil's river* (1924), and *Count Blitzki's daughter* (1925). He died in 1967. Arab bulletin 1 (1986 reprint), p. xxv; Bidwell, 174; BLC

Buxton, Leonard Halford Dudley, born 18 April 1889, he was educated at Exeter College, Oxford, and since 1928 a University reader in physical anthropology. His writings include *Primitive labour* (1924), and *Peoples of Asia* (1925). He died 5 March 1939. Who was who, 3

Buxton, Noel, 1869-1948 *see* Noel-Buxton, Noel Edward

Buxton, Patrick Alfred, born 24 March 1892, he was a graduate of Trinity College, Cambridge. After qualification in medicine, he took up a commission in the Royal Medical Corps and was posted to Mesopotamia and north-western Persia. In 1921 he was appointed entomologist to the Medical Department in Palestine. After his return to England, he was appointed head of the Department of Entomology in the London School of Hygiene and Tropical Medicine, where he remained until his death on 13 December 1955. His writings include *Animal life in deserts* (1923). DNB; WhE&EA; Who was who, 5

Buy, Jacques, fl. 1966, his writings include *Towards the geo-economic recognition of a second Europe* (Strasbourg, Council of Europe, 1979). LC

Buzeskul, Vladislav Petrovich, born in 1858 at Popovka, Ukraine, he was a professor of history at the University of Kharkov, specializing in history of ancient Greece. His writings include *История афьинской демократии* (1909), and *Открытия XIX и начала XX века в ооласт истории древнего мира* (1923-24). He died in Kharkov, 1 June 1931. GSE; OSK

Buzzard, Rear-Admiral Sir Anthony Wass, born 28 April 1902, he was a graduate of the Royal Navy colleges at Osborne and Dartmouth, a founding member of the Institute of Strategic Studies, and a director of Naval Intelligence, London, from 1951 to 1954. After his retirement, he was associated with the International Department of the British Council of Churches. He died in Guildford, 10 March 1972. ObitT, 1971; Who was who, 7

Byam, Wiliam, born 19 August 1882, he was a trained physician who entered the Royal Army Medical Corps in 1904. He was attached to the Egyptian Army, 1908 to 1916. From 1951 to 1953 he was director of the Princess Tsehai Memorial Hospital, Addis Abeba. He was a philatelist. He wrote the autobiography *Dr. Byam in Harley Street* (1962), and the reminiscences *The Road to Harley Street* (1963). He died 25 October 1963. WhE&EA; Who was who, 6

Bychvarov, Mikhail Dimitrov, 1929- *see* Buchvarov, Mikhail Dimitrov

Byé, Maurice, born 30 November 1905 at Marseille, he was a graduate of the Faculté de droit de Lyon, and thereafter a professor of law at Toulouse, 1931-46, and from 1946 until his death on 6 May 1968, a professor of political economy at the Faculté de droit et des Sciences économiques de Paris. In 1945 he taught at l'École française de droit, Cairo. His writings include *Relations économiques internationales* (2nd ed., 1965). He died 6 May 1968. WhoFr, 1957/58-1967/68

Bykov, Aleksei Andreevich, born in 1896 at St. Petersburg, he graduated in 1923 from the Leningrad State University. He was a numismatist, specializing in Oriental, particularly Arabic, numismatics. In 1938 he succeeded R. R. Fasmer as keeper at the Numismatic Collection at the Ermitage, Leningrad. Much of his work was published in *Труды Отдела нумисматики государственного Эрмитаж*. His writings include *Монеты Турции XIV-XVII вв.* (1939), and *Монеты Китая* (1969). He died on 27 January 1977. Krachkovskii; Miliband; Miliband²

Byng, Edward John, born 21 January 1894 at Budapest, he served with the Ottoman army, boxed in the 1912 Olympics, and held a doctorate from Oxford. From 1922 to 1934, he worked as a journalist for United Press. Thereafter he was a radio commentator and free-lance writer. His books include *A Five-year peace plan* (1943), *The World of the Arabs* (1944), and its translation, *Die Welt der Araber* (Berlin, 1953). He wrote an autobiography, *Of the meek and mighty* (1939). He died in New York City, 15 February 1962. NYT, 16 Feb. 1962, p. 29, col. 3

Bynon, James F. G., fl. 1975, he edited the proceedings *Hamito-Semitica* (1975), and the papers *Current progress in Afro-Asiatic linguistics* (1984). LC

Bynon, Theodora, fl. 1975. Her writings include *Historical linguistics* (1977), its translation, *Lingüística histórica* (1981); she was joint editor of *Hamito-Semitica* (1975), and *Studies in the history of Western linguistics in honour of R. H. Robins* (1986). LC

Byrne, Eugene Hugh, born 16 November 1882 at Baraboo, Wisc., he was a graduate of the University of Wisconsin, where he also received his Ph.D. in 1915 for his thesis, *Commercial contracts of the Genoese in the Syriac trade of the twelfth century.* He was a professor of history at American universities from 1911 until his retirement in 1949. His writings include *Genoese shipping in the twelfth and thirteenth centuries* (1930). He died 23 September 1952. BioIn 3, 4; WhAm, 7

Byrnia, Pavel Petrovich, fl. 1955-74, his writings include *Сельские поселения Молдавии XV-XVIII вв.* (1969), *Молдавский средневековый город в Днестровско-Прутском междуречье* (1984); and he edited *Археологические исследования средневековых памятников в Днестровско-Прутском междуречье* (1985). LC

Byroade, Henry Alfred, born 24 July 1913, he was a 1937 graduate of West Point. After his resignation from the U.S. Army in 1952, he was appointed an assistant Secretary of State for Near Eastern, South Asian and African affairs. He served as ambassador to Egypt in the years in which the U.S. withdrew its offer to finance the Aswan High Dam, and during the Suez crisis of 1956. He later served as ambassador to Afghanistan and Pakistan, retiring from the Foreign Service in 1977. He died of cardiopulmonary arrest in Washington, D.C., 31 December 1993. Master (7); WRMEA 12, no. 6 (February/March 1994), p. 112

Byron, Robert, born in 1905 in England, and a trained archaeologist from Oxford. His interest in architecture, painting, and history kept him travelling through Greece, Turkey, India, Tibet, as well as Afghanistan, Persia, and Central Asia until the second World War. His writings, partly under the pseudonym Richard Waughburton, include *Europe in the looking glass* (1926) *The Byzantine achievement* (1929), *First Russia, then Tibet* (1933), and *The road to Oxiana* (1937). He was a dauntless, erudite man, who won distinction in more than one field. He is believed to have been killed by enemy action at sea in 1941. DLB 195 (1998), pp. 8-19; *Journal of the Royal Asiatic Society* 28 (1941), pp. 474-76

Bystrzonowski (Bystrzanowski), Ludwik Tadeusz Szafraniec, born 24 August 1797 at Krakau (Kraków), Austria, he wrote *Sur la Serbie dans ses rapports européens avec la question d'Orient* (Paris, 1845). He died 27 August 1878. Dziekan; PSB

Bz'oza, Hanoch, fl. 1958. He was a sometime editor of the communist Hebrew organ "New paths."

Cabanelas Rodríguez, Darío, O. F. M., born 20 December 1916 at Trasalba (Orense), Spain, he graduated in 1946 from the Universidad Central de Madrid where he also received a doctorate in 1948 with a thesis entitled *Juan de Segovia y el problema islámico.* He was a professor of Arabic in the Universidad de Granada and also served as a secretary of the journal *Miscelánea de estudios árabes y hebraicos*, and as executive secretary, Patronato de la Alhambra y del Generalife. His writings include *El morisco granadino Alonso del Castillo* (1965), *Ibn Sina de Murcia, el mayor lexicógrafo de al-Andalus* (1966), *Poesía arábigo andaluza* (1984), and *El techo del salon de Comares en la Alhambra* (1988). In 1987 he was honoured by *Homenaje al prof. Darío Cabanelas Rodríguez.* He died 18 September 1992. *Cuadernos de la Alhambra* 29/30 (1993/94), pp. 13-19; Who's who in Spain, 1963

Cabaton, Antoine, born 11 December 1863 at Nérondes (Cher), he came from a family of modest substance, went to school in Orléans, and studied at l'École du Louvre and l'École des Hautes Études, Paris. For many years he held a subordinate position at the Bibliothèque nationale, Paris. From 1920 to 1933, he held the Chair of Malay at l'École des langues orientales de Paris. His writings include *Java, Sumatra, and the other islands of the Dutch East Indies* (1911), and *L'Indochine* (1932). He died 25 November 1942. *Archipel* 26 (1983), pp. 17-24

Cabello y Lapieda, Luis Maria, fl. 1863, he was a contributor to *Resumen de arquitectura* (1897), *Correspondencia de España* (1903), and *Arquitectura, bellas artes y decoración* (1903). Ossorio

Cabezudo Astráin, José, born in 1901, he wrote *Tafalla ... * (Pamplona, 1971). NUC, 1968-72

Cable, Alice Mildred, born in 1878, she for some time studied science before joining the China Inland Mission, first arriving on 12 February 1902 at Shanghai. She was sent to work in a school in Shansi under Miss Eva French. They later persuaded their authority that there was work to do for them in the Gobi Desert. They went to the edge of the Gobi Desert and during their fifteen years' work there they crossed the desert five times. Whenever they heard of an oasis in the desert they made their way there, a Bible in hand, wearing Chinese clothes and speaking also Turki, which they had studied. When she visited China in 1921, she had retired. Together with Francesca France, she published *Dispatches from north-west China* (1925), *The Gobi Desert* (1942), *The Bible in mission lands* (1947), and *George Hunter, apostle of Turkestan* (1948). She died in 1952. Phyllis Thompson wrote *Desert* *pilgrim; the story of Mildred Cable's venture for God in Central Asia* (London, 1957). JRCAS 39 (1952), pp. 207-208; DLB 195 (1998), pp. 20-27; Lodwick; Robinson

Cabrera, Carmelo García, he wrote *Tenerfe* (Barcelona, 1962), *Informe sobre la situación actual de las pesquerías en el banco sahariano* (Madrid, 1975), and he was joint author of *Escómbridos de las Islas Canarias* (Madrid, 1974). LC

Cabrillana Ciezar, Nicolás, he was director of the Archivo Histórico Provincial de Almería and subsequently the Archivo de la Delegación de Hacienda de Málaga. His writings include *Documentos nationales refenrentes a los moriscos* (1978), and *Almería morísca* (1982). LC

Caby, Gaston, he received a doctorate in 1924 from the Université de Paris for his thesis, *Le principe de l'indissolubilité du mariage et la séparation de corps en droit italien*. He was a sometime professor at the Faculté de droit de l'Université Fouad 1er, Cairo. His writings include *Cours de droit commerial* (Cairo, 1948), and *Introduction à l'étude du droit civil* (Cairo, 1948). Note; NUC, pre-1956

Cáceres Plá, Francisco de Paula, fl. 1899, he collaborated with the publication of *La Alhambra* (1902), *La Ilustración española y americana*, as well as other periodicals. Ossorio

Cachia, Pierre Jacques Elie, born 30 April 1921 at Fayum, Egypt, he studied at AUC and the University of Edinburgh, where he received a Ph.D. degree in 1951 for his thesis, *Taha Husayn; his place in the Egyptian literary renaissance*. Thereafter he taught modern Arabic literature successively at AUC, Edinburgh, and Columbia University, NYC, until his retirement from the Chair of Arabic Language and Literature in June 1991. From 1991 to 1992 he was a fellow at Woodrow Wilson International Center, Washington, D.C. He was co-founder and joint editor of the *Journal of Arabic lit-erature*. His writings include *An overview of modern Arabic literature* (1990). ConAu, 25-28; IntAu&W, 1977; Private; Sluglett; WhoAm, 1976-80; WrDr, 1976-80

Caclamanos, Demetrius, 1872-1949 *see* Kaklamanos, Demetrios

Cadell, Sir Patrick Robert, born 6 May 1871, he was a graduate of Balliol College, Oxford, and was in the Indian Civil Service from 1891 to 1926. His writings include *History of the Bombay Army* (1938). He retired with the rank of colonel. He died 22 November 1961. Who was who, 6

Cadell of Grange, Henry Moubray, born 27 January 1892, he passed through the Royal Military College, Woolwich, and subsequently joined the Royal Engineers. During the first World War he served in Saloniki and Palestine. He died 6 November 1967. Who was who, 6

Cadenat, Pierre, he was a member of the Société de géographie et d'archéologie d'Oran and, in 1938, *receveur de l'enregistrement* in Tiaret, Algeria. His writings include *Nouvelles recherches dans la nécropole gallo-romaine d'Ussubium* (1982). LC; Note

Cader, Abdul-Cader, born 25 June 1925 at Erbil, Iraq, he took a German Dipl.Ing. degree and received a doctorate from the Technische Universität Berlin for his thesis, *Räumliche Disparitäten der Lebensgrundlagen im irakischen Kurdistan* (1977). LC; Schwarz

Cadiot, J. In 1952 he was head of the Services agricoles régionaux de Rabat.

Cadman, Sir John, born 7 September 1877 at Silverdale, Staffordshire, he was an emeritus professor of Birmingham University, and chairman of the Anglo-Iranian Oil Company. He died 31 May 1941. Who was who, 4

Cadora, Frederic Joseph, born 21 February 1937 at Jerusalem, he was a graduate of Emory University, and received his Ph.D. in 1966 from the University of Michigan for *An analytical study of inter-dialectal lexical compatibility in Arabic*. Since 1967 he was a professor at the Department of Judaic and Near East Languages and Literatures, Ohio State University. His writings include *Interdialectal lexical compatibility in Arabic* (1979), and *Bedouin, village, and urban Arabic* (1992). DrAS, 1974-1982

Cadoux, Gaston, born in 1857, he wrote *Tunisie, Algérie; six semaines en Afrique du nord* (1923). LC

Cady, Putnam, clergyman, born 13 May 1863, he was a graduate of Princeton University as well as Princeton Theological Seminary. Since 1898 he was a lecturer in archaeology at Union College, N.Y., and since 1907, a fellow of the Royal Geographical Society. Who was who in America, 4

Caetani, Leone, born 12 September 1869 at Roma, where he also studied Oriental languages and literatures, and obtained a doctorate in 1891. After travels in North Africa and the Near East, he decided to write *Annali dell'Islam*, a comprehensive history of the Muslim peoples to the time of the Ottoman conquest of Egypt in 1517. But the material gathered in twenty years was such as to fill ten volumes for the period down to the caliphate of Ali (661 A.D.) alone. At that point the project was

254

abandoned and the accumulated research material handed over to the Fondazione Caetani per gli studi musulmani at the Accademia nazionale dei Lincei in 1924. His other notable works are *Studi di storia orientale* (1911), and *Onomasticon Arabicum* (1915). He died at Vancouver, B.C., 25 December 1935. DizBI; Fück, pp. 297-299; MW 26 (1936), pp. 299-300

Cafer Seydahmet (Seydamet), Kirimli, born in 1889 in the Crimea. After the Russian October Revolution he was Minister of Foreign Affairs of the short-lived Crimean Republic until 1921. He went into exile, where he published *Gaspirali Ismail Bey* (1934). Wschod 6 iii (listopad 1935), pp. 19-24

Caferoğlu, Ahmet, born 17 April 1899 at Ganja, Azerbaijan, he was educated at Samarkand and Ganja, and began his study at Kiev and Baku (1920). In the wake of the political turmoil in Azerbaijan, he continued his study at Istanbul and later at Breslau, where he received a Dr.phil. degree in 1930 for his thesis, *75 Azärbajganische Lieder "Bajaty" in der Mundart von Gängä*. After his return to Istanbul he was professor of Turkish linguistics. His writings include *Uygur sözlüğü* (1934-38). Meydan; Ural-altaische Jahrbücher 32 (1960), pp. 88-89

Caferzade, Azize, 1921- see Jäfärzadä, Äzizä Mämmäd gyzy

Çağa, Tahir, born 25 February 1913 at Beykoz, Turkey, he studied at the Istanbul Teachers College and subsequently became a school teacher in Istanbul from October 1929 to December 1934. From 1934 to 1939 he studied law at Zürich and received a doctorate in 1939 for his thesis, *Konkurrenz deliktischer und vertraglicher Ersatzansprüche nach deutschem und schweizerischem Recht*. His writings include *Deniz ticareti hukuku* (1979). LC

Cagigas, Isidro de las. His writings include *Los mozárabes* (1947-48), *Andalucía musulmana* (1950), *Sevilla almohade* (1951), and *Tratados y convenios referentes a Marruecos* (1952). LC

Cagnat, René Louis Victor, born 10 October 1852 at Paris, he graduated from l'École normale supérieure and subsequently taught at the Collège Stanislas. Shortly after obtaining his doctorate in 1880, he went on an archaeological mission to Tunisia on behalf of the Ministère de l'Instruction publique, the results of which were published under the title *Explorations épigraphiques et archéologiques en Tunisie* (1883-1886). After a teaching interlude at Douai, he was appointed to the Chair of Epigraphy and Roman Antiquities at the Collège de France. His writings include *Les monuments historiques de Tunisie* (1898). He died in Paris, 27 March 1937. DBF

Cagne, Jacques, fl. 1968, born in Morocco, he took a *doctorat d'état* in Arabic and Islamic studies. His writings include *Nation et nationalisme au Maroc* (1988). LC

Cahen, Claude Louis Alfred, born 26 February 1909 at Paris, he graduated from l'École normale supérieure, and received his *agrégation d'histoire*. After the second World War he was appointed professor at the Université de Strasbourg and later at the Sorbonne. For over twenty years he was editor-in-chief of the *Journal of the economic and social history of the Orient*. The topical range of his academic interest went far beyond the strictly sociological and economic phenomina. There is hardly a major Orientalist journal in the West, or even a fascicule in the new edition of the *Encyclopædia of Islam* that does not contain a contribution of Cahen. His writings include *Pre-Ottoman Turkey* (1968), *Les peuples musul-mans dans l'histoire médiévale* (1977), and *Orient and Occident au temps des croisades* (1983). Impaired vision during his last years put an end to his work in the late 1980s. He died in Paris, 18 November 1991. JA 28 (1993), pp. 1-17; JESHO 35 ii (1992), 105-109; MESA bulletin 26 (1992), 154-6; MidE 1982/83

Cahnman, Werner Jacob, born 30 September 1902 at München, he studied at the universities of Berlin and München, where he received a doctorate in 1927 [1929] for his thesis, *Der ökonomische Pessimismus und das Ricardosche System*. After his imprisonment at the Dachau concentration camp he went to the United States. Until his retirement in 1966, he was a sociologist at various American universities. His writings include *Völker und Rassen im Urteil der Jugend* (1965). A commemoration volume was published in 1983, *Ethnicity, identity, and history, essays in memory of Werner J. Cahnman*. He died 27 in Queens, N.Y., September 1980. AmW&WS, 1973-1982; CnDiAmJBI; Contemporary authors, 49; IntAu&W, 1977; LC

Cahours de Virgile, fl. 1896, he contributed to the periodical *À travers le monde* (Paris).

Cahu, Jules Nicolas Théodore, born 5 December 1854 at Beaugency (Loiret). After passing through the military College of Saint-Cyr, he was *chef du secrétariat* of General Boulanger. In 1883 he resigned from the army to pursue a literary interest. His writings include *Au pays des Mauresques* (1882), and *Des Batignolles au Bosphore* (1890). Under the pseudonym Théo Critt, he published popular literature. He died in Beaugency, 28 October 1928. DBF

255

Cahun, David *Léon*, born 23 June 1841 at Haguenau, Alsace, he was a deputy keeper at the Bibliothèque Mazarine in Paris, and concurrently taught at the Faculté des Lettres. His writings include *La vie juive en Alsace* (1886), and *Introduction à l'histoire de l'Asie; Turcs et Mongols des origines à 1405* (1896). He died in Paris, 30 March 1900.   DBF; NDBA; Wininger

Caillard, Sir Vincent Henry Penalver, born 23 October 1856, he was educated at Eton, and after passing through the Royal Military College at Woolwich, he joined the Royal Engineers. He served in various capacities in the Middle East. His writings include *Imperial fiscal reform* (1903). He died on 18 March 1930.   Who was who, 3

Caillé, Jacques. He took doctorates in arts and law, and was a sometime *directeur d'études* at the Institut des Hautes Études marocaines, as well as a corresponding member of the Institut de France. His writings include *Organisation judiciaire et procédure marocaines* (1948), *Petite histoire de Rabat* (1950), *La mosquée de Hassan à Rabat* (1954), *La procédure judiciaire de l'immatriculation foncière au Maroc* (1956), and *Le consulat de Tanger des origines à 1830* (1967).   LC

Cailliaud, Frédéric, born 9 June 1787 at Nantes, he was since 1809 resident in Paris, where he pursued an interest in mineralogy and archaeology. From 1815 to 1818 he was in the service of the Viceroy of Egypt prospecting for minerals. He returned to Egypt in 1820 to accompany the military expedition of Isma'il Pasha to the Sudan. His monumental account of the journey was published under the title *Voyage à Méroé, au Fleuve Blanc au-delà de Fâzogl, dans le midi du royaume de Sennâr, à Syouah et dans cinq autres oasis, fait dans les années 1819, 1820, 1821 et 1822.* (Paris, 1826-1827). He died in Nantes, 1 May 1869.   DBF; Embacher; Henze; Hill; Vapereau

Caillié, René, born 17 November 1799 at Mauzé (Deux-Sevres), he grew up in a family of modest substance. After a two-year preparation among the Brakna Moors, he set out to become the first of the Saharan travellers to reach Timbuctu on 4 May 1828. He left his *Journal d'un voyage à Tombouctou et à Djenné* (1830), and its English translation, *Travels through Central Africa to Timbuctoo* (1992). He died impoverished, 25 May 1828.   Embacher; *Géographie* 49 (1928), pp. 173-204; Henze; *Hommes et destins* I, pp. 115-118

Cain, Mead T., born 11 October 1946, he wrote *Class, patriarchy, and the structure of women's work in rural Bangladesh* (1979), *Women's status and fertility in developing countries* (1984), and *The world on paper* (1994). In 1990 he was joint editor of *Rural development and population; institutions and policy.*   LC

Cairns, John Campbell, born 27 April 1924 at Windsor, Ontario, he was a graduate of the University of Toronto, and received a Ph.D. in 1952 from Cornell University for his thesis, *France in the international crisis, 1911-1914.* From 1952 until his retirement he was professor at Toronto. In 1978 he edited *Contemporary France.*   Canadian, 1970-1996; ConAu 13-14; DrAS, 1974-1982

de Caix (de Saint-Aymour), Robert, born 5 February 1869 at Paris, he studied at the Faculté de droit de Paris and l'École des sciences politiques. From 1893 until 1918, he was attached to the *Journal des débats* as a diplomatic commentator. Since 1919 he was in active diplomatic service in Greater Syria. His writings include *Fachoda, la France et l'Angleterre* (1899). He died 12 March 1970.   DBF; *Hommes et destins* I, pp. 118-120

Calassanti-Motylinski, Adolphe de (Gustaw Adolf Kalasanty Motyliński), born 15 February 1854 at Mascara, Algeria, he was a *répétiteur* at the Lycée d'Alger before he joined the Corps des interprètes in 1875. From 1882 to 1887 he was posted to the M'Zab, where he pursued an interest in Berber studies. Thereafter he was lecturer at the Medersa de Constantine. In 1906 he undertook an arduous exploration of the Sahara, as a con-sequence of which he died of overwork, 2 March 1907. His writings include *Le dialecte berbère de R'édamès* (1904), and *Textes touaregs en prose* (1984).   *Bulletin de la Société de géographie d'Alger et de l'Afrique du nord* 12 (1907), pp. 119-122; DBF; Dziekan; Peyronnet, p. 401

Calasso, Giovanna, fl. 1970, she wrote *Un'epopea musulmana di epoca timuride* (1979).   LC

Calcat, A., fl. 1958, he was in 1961 *inspecteur* and *chef* of the Service de l'agriculture et du paysanat du Sahara.

Calchi Novati, Giampolo, born 20 June 1935 in Italy, he was a professor at the Università di Pisa, his writings include *L'Africa nera non è indipendante* (1964), *Le rivoluzioni nell'Africa nera* (1967), *De-colonizzazione e Terzo mondo* (1979), and *Le lezione del Libano* (1985).   Wholtaly, 1980

Calder, Norman, born in 1950 at Buckie, Scotland, he went to Wadham College, Oxford, in 1979 to read Oriental studies. During 1976-1979 he completed his thesis, *The structure of authority in Imami Shi'i jurisprudence*, at SOAS. From 1980 to 1997 he was a lecturer in Arabic and Islamic studies in the

256

University of Manchester. His writings include *Studies in early Muslim jurisprudence* (1993). He died 13 February 1998. *MESA bulletin* 32 ii (1998), p. 288

Calderini, Aristide, born 18 October 1883 at Taranto, Italy, he was a professor of classical antiquities in the Università cattolica del Sacro Cuore, Milano. He died in 1968. *Chi è*, 1957; DizBI; LC; Wholtaly, 1958

Caldéron, Serafín Estébanez, 1799-1867 *see* Estébanez Caldéron, Serafín

Calero Secall, Maria Isabel, fl. 1975. She took a doctorate in Semitic linguistics. Certainly from 1992 to 1994 she was attached to the Facultad de Filosofía y Letras, Universidad de Málaga.

Caley, Earle Radcliffe, born 14 May 1900, he took a Ph.D. in 1928 at Ohio State University. From 1928 to 1942 he was a professor of chemistry at Princeton and afterwards joined his alma mater until retirement in 1960. WhAm, 8

Freiherr von **Call zu Rosenburg und Kulmbach**, Guido, born 6 September 1849 at Triest, he entered the Levant consular service at Tehran. From 1875 to 1894 he filled a variety of diplomatic posts in the Ottoman Empire. He was attached to development schemes of the Tauern railway as well as the port of Triest. He retired from public service in 1911 and moved in 1916 to Graz, where he died 12 May 1927. DtBE; ÖBL

Callahan, Raymond Aloysius, born 30 November 1938 at Trenton, N.J., he received a Ph.D. in 1967 from Harvard University for his thesis, *The reorganization of the East India Company's armies, 1784-1798*. Since 1967 he was a professor of history at the University of Delaware. His writings include *The East India Company and army reforms, 1783-1798* (1972). ConAu 69-72; DrAS, 1974-82

Callan, Hugh, born 19th cent., he wrote *Wanderings on wheel and on foot through Europe* (1887), *The story of Jerusalem* (1891), *From the Clyde to the Jordan; narrative of a bicycle journey* (1895), and *Heart cures* (1912). BLC

Callard, Keith Brendon, born in 1924, he wrote *The political forces in Pakistan, 1947-1959* (1959). Until his death in 1961 he had appointments at the Department of Political Science and the Institute of Islamic Studies in McGill University, Montreal. LC; *Macmillan dictionary of Canadian biography*

Callari, Roberto, born 20 August 1928 at el-Kef, Tunisia. After study in Tunisia, France, and Italy, he received a doctorate in 1954 at Paris. He taught briefly at the Università di Roma, before being appointed deputy secretary for the Middle East at the Italian embassy in Libya. He died at sea off Tripoli, 17 July 1966. *Oriente moderno* 46 (1966), p. 549

Callier, Camille Antoine, General, born 7 March 1804 at Saint-Omer (Pas-de-Calais), he was a graduate of the Polythechnique and l'École des ingénieurs géographes, Paris. In the service of the French government he roamed over Asia Minor and Greater Syria and subjected them to a critical topographical study. The French Foreign Ministry sent him to Egypt in 1839. He died in Paris on 12 January 1889. DBF; Henze

Calmard, Jean Marcel, born in 1931, he received a doctorate from the Université de Paris for his thesis, *Le culte de l'imam Hussein; étude sur la commémoration du drame de Kerbala dans l'Iran pré-safavide*, in 1975. He was a specialist of Islamic history of Iran, and attached to the CNRS, Paris. He was the editor of *Études safavides* (1993). AnNEIFr, 1995; THESAM, 4

Caloyanni, Mégalos A., born in 1869, he was a judge whose writings include *La Protection de l'enfance en Égypte* (Cairo, 1913), and *L'Organisation de la Cour permanente de justice et son avenir* (1932). LC

Calverley, Edwin Elliott, born 26 October 1882 at Philadelphia, Pa., he graduated from Princeton University in 1906 and took his M.A. in 1908. In 1909 he graduated from Princeton Theological Seminary, having been ordained the previous year in the Presbyterian Church in the United States. He was married to Eleanor Jane Taylor, M.D. From 1909 to 1930 they served as missionaries under the Reformed Church in America in Arabia and the Persian Gulf. During several furlough periods he pursued studies at the Kennedy School of Missions at the Hartford Seminary Foundation. In 1923 he receiced a Ph.D., *magna cum laude*, in Arabic and Islamic studies. After an illness in 1930 he became an instructor at the School of Missions and retired as professor of Arabic and Islamics in 1952. Throughout this period numerous honours, privileges and special opportunities came his way because of his recognized scholarship. His writings include *Worship in Islam; a translation with commentary and introduction, of al-Ghazzâli's Book of the Ihyá on the worship* (1925); originally presented as his thesis, Hartford, 1923. He also published *An Arabian primer* (1920), *An Arabian reader* (1925), *Islam; an introduction* (1958). For many years he was the editor of *The Moslem world*. He died in Hartford, Conn., on 21 April 1971. MW 57 (1967), 176-185; Shavit; WhAm, 7

Calverley, Eleanor Jane *née* Taylor, born 24 March 1886 at Woodstown, N.J., she received her M. D. from the Woman's Medical College of Pennsylvania at Philadelphia in 1908. In September 1905 she married Edwin E. Calverley with whom she served as medical missionary under the Reformed Church in America at Bahrain, the Persian Gulf, Basrah, and Amarah from 1909 to 1930. She returned with her husband to the U.S. and settled in Hartford, Conn. Her writings include *How to be healthy in hot climates* (1949), *My Arabian days and nights* (1958). She died in Hartford, Conn., 21 or 22 December 1968. MW 57 (1967), 178-185; Shavit

Calvez, Jean Yves, born 3 February 1927 at Saint-Brieux (Côtes-du Nord), he entered in 1943 the Compagnie de Jésus, and was since 1953 a professor of social philosophie at the Faculté de philosophie de Chantilly. His writings include *La Pensée de Karl Marx* (1956), *Aspects politiques et sociaux des pays en voie de développement* (1971), *Foi et justice* (1985), and *Tiers monde - un monde dans le monde* (1989). WhoFr, 1994/95-2002/2003

Calvo Moralejo, Gaspar, O.F.M. His writings include *Emigrante ... hay camino* (1973), and *Un cordobés en Damasco* (1975). LC

Calvocoressi, Peter John Ambrose, born 17 November 1912 at Karachi, he studied at Eton College and Balliol College, Oxford, and was called to the bar in 1935. He assisted at the Nuremberg war tribunal, 1945 to 1946, and became a publisher and lecturer. He wrote *Nuremberg, the facts, the law, and the consequences* (1947) and *Resilient Europe* (1991). With Guy Wint he published *The Middle East crisis* (1957). ConAu 65-68; IntAu&W, 1976-77; IntWW, 1974-1997/98; Who's who, 1974; WrDr, 1980

Calzaroni, J. A., fl. 1923, he was a sometime director of l'École d'Hennaya, Algeria.

Camaj, Martin, born in 1925 at Dukagjin, Albania, he pursued Slavic studies at Beograd and Roma, where he received a doctorate in 1960 for *"Il Messale" di Gjon Buzuku*. After a few years at Roma, he accepted a lectureship in Albanian at the Universität München, where he was able to pursue also his interest in Albanian literature. His writings include *Lehrbuch der albanischen Sprache* (1969), *Albanian grammar* (1984), and *Selected poetry* (1990). He in 1992. Südost-Forschungen 51 (1992), pp. 283-286

Câmara Cascudo, Luis da, 1899- *see* Cascudo, Luis de Câmara

Camariano-Cioran, Ariadna, born in 1906 at Peristeri, Greece, she was a historian whose writings include *Academiile domneşti şi Iaşi* (1971), and *Les académies princières de Bucarest et de Jassy et leurs professeurs* (Thessaloniki, 1974). She died in 1993. LC; WhoRom

Camau, Michel, Dr., political scientist. His writings include *La notion de démocratie dans la pensée des dirigeant maghrébins* (1971), *Pouvoirs et institutions au Maghreb* (1978), *La Tunisie* (1989), and with Hédi Zaïem and Hajer Bahri, *État de santé; besoin médical et enjeux politiques en Tunisie* (1990).

Cambier, Guy, a medievalist who was editor of *La vie de Mahomet par Embricon de Mayence* (1962), *Le monde grec* (1975), and *Christianisme d'hier et d'aujuord'hui; hommage à Jean Préaux* (1979). LC

Cambon, Jules Martin, born 5 April 1845 at Paris, he was a French government official in Algeria from 1874 to 1878, and governor-general of Algeria from 1891 to 1897. He wrote *Le diplomate* (1926). He died in Vevey, Switzerland, 19 September 1935. DBF; Hommes et destins, II, pp. 161-167

Cambon, Pierre Paul, born 20 January 1843 at Paris, he was in French provincial politics until he was appointed, on 25 February 1882, minister plenipotentiary charged with the functions of French Resident Minister in Tunis, followed by appointments as ambassador in Madrid (1886), Constantinople, and London. He was awarded *commandeur de la Légion d'honneur*, 6 January 1886. Five years later, he became member of the Académie des sciences morales et politiques. His writings include *Correspondance, 1870-1924* (1940-46). He died in Paris, 29 May 1924. Bacqué, 75; DBF; Hommes et destins II, pp. 161-167

Cambuzat, Paul Louis. His writings include *L'évolution des cités du Tell en Ifrîkiya du VIIe au XI siècle* (1986). LC

Cameron, Donald Andreas, born 19 June 1856, he was educated at a private school, and from 1885 to 1888 a British consul in the Sudan. He later filled a variety of consular and judicial positions in Egypt and Tangier until his retirement in 1911. His writings include *Arabic-English vocabulary* (1892), and *Egypt in the nineteenth century* (1898). He died 21 January 1936. Hill; Who was who, 3

Cameron, George Glenn, born 30 July 1905 at Washington, Pa., he was a graduate of Washington and Jefferson College, and received a Ph.D. from the University of Chicago in 1932. He was a scholar of pre-Islamic history of Iran, teaching the first part of his career at Chicago and the latter part at the University of Michigan. His writings include *History of early Iran* (1936). In 1976 he was presented with *Michigan Oriental studies in honor of George G. Cameron.* BioB134; BioIn 12; ConAu 89-92; DrAS, 1974-78; WhoAm, 1974-78; WhoWor, 1974; WhAm, 7; Shavit

Cameron, Verney Lovett, born 1 July 1844 at Radipole (Dorset), he was primarily an African explorer before he travelled in the Middle East in search of an overland route to India, 1878 to 1879. He died after falling off a horse in Soulsbury, 27 March 1894. Henze; Men10

Cameron Watt, Donald, born 17 May 1928 at Rugby, he changed his name about 1964 from Watt to Cameron-Watt. After Oriol College, Oxford, he joined the British Foreign Office. From 1946 to 1948 he served in the British Army, Intelligence Corps. Since 1954 he was affiliated with LSE, teaching international history. His writings include *Britiain and the Suez Canal* (1956), *Documents on the Suez crisis* (1957), and *Personalities and policies* (1965). In 1992 he was honoured by *Power, personalities, and policies; essays in honour of Donald Cameron Watt.* Au&Wr, 1971; IntAu&W, 1976, 1977; ConAu 77-80, new rev. 14; Who, 1974-2002; WhoWor, 1980/81

Camerota, Paolo d'Agostino Orsini di, 1897- *see* D'Agostino Orsini di Camerota, Paolo

Camilleri, Carmel, born 19 November 1922 at Porto-Farina, Tunisia., he was in 1965 attached to the Faculté des lettres et des sciences humaines de Tunis, and in the 1980s, a sometime professor at the Université de René Descartes, Paris. Publications include *Applications du test positif de Louisa Düss à des groupes d'enfants tunisiens et européens de Tunis* (1964), *Les "nouveaux jeunes"* (1983), and *Cultural anthropology and education* (1986). LC; Unesco

Camilleri, J. J., fl. 1977. He was joint author of *Kwartett; gabra ta' poeziji minn J. J. Camilleri [et al.]* (Malta, 1965). ZKO

Cammann, Schuyler Van Rensselaer, born 2 February 1912 at NYC., he was a graduate of Yale University and received a Ph.D. from Johns Hopkins University, Baltimore, Md., in 1949. He was a sometime professor of East Asian studies at the University of Pennsylvania, and a member of archaeological expeditions to Afghanistan and Turkey. His writngs include the extensively revised edition of his Ph.D. thesis, *Trade through the Himalayas* (1951), and *The land of the camel* (1951). ConAu 9-10; DrAS, 1974-1982

Camón y Aznar, José, born in October of 1898 at Zaragoza, Spain. The exact day and year of his birth vary in the reference souces. He was a sometime university professor and dean, as well as a director of the Museo Lázaro Galdiano of the Consejo Cientificas Superior de Investigaciones. His writings include *Joyas de la pintura religiosa* (1929-30), and *Filosofía del arte* (1974). Lomba Fuentes published in 1984 *El pensamiento de Camón Aznar.* He died in 1979. DBEC; Figuras; LC; Sabater; WhoSpain, 1963

Camós Cabruja, Lluís, born in 1892 at Palamós, he wrote *Retablo de la Barcelona pretéria* (1943). Rafols

Camp, Glen D., Jr. He wrote *Berlin in the East-West struggle, 1958-61* (1971). LC

Campani, Romeo, fl. 1910. His writings include *Calendario arabo* (1914), and the translation of Ibn Kathir al-Faghani, *Il "libro dell aggregazione delle stelle"* (1913). LC

Campbell, Charles Grimshaw, born in 1912, he was a major in the British Army, as well as a student of Arabic folklore and dialects. He was last posted near Benghazi, Libya, before he died on 31 March 1953. His writings include *Tales from the Arabic tribes* (1949), *Race and religion* (1953), *Told in the market place; a collection of the stories told by the Arab tribes of the lower Euphrates* (1954), and a German translation, *Arabische Geschichten von Gaunern und Schelmen* (1964). BLC; LC

Campbell, Clifton P., Dr. born 20th cent., he was a sometime consultant on vocational education training in Saudi Arabia. In 1998, he was a professor at the University of Tennessee, Knoxville. He was the editor of *Education and training for work* (Lancaster, Pa., 1996). NatFacDr, 1998

Campbell, Cyril. He wrote *The Balkan war drama* (1913). LC

Campbell, Donald Ralph, born 19 November 1918 at Foxboro, Ontario. After graduating from the University of Toronto (1949), and Oxford University, he held a variety of academic posts in Canada. From 1962 to 1964 he was economic advisor and director of planning, Government of Jordan. From 1970 to 1972 he held a similar post in Kenya. He was joint author of *Canadian agriculture in the seventies* (1970). Canadian, 1967/69-1984

Campbell, Dugald, born in 1871. In the service of the National Bible Society of Scotland he undertook an expedition to sell the Scriptures, mainly in Arabic and French, throughout the Sahara. For the same purpose he made another tour from Senegal to the Anglo-Egyptian Sudan. When he retired as a missionary in 1937 it was his intention to spend the rest of his days in Johannesburg, South Africa. His writings include *On the trial of the veiled Tuareg* (1928), *Wanderings in the widest Africa* (1931), *Camels through Libya; a desert adventure from the fringes of the Sahara to the oases of Upper Egypt* (1935), and *With the Bible in North Africa* (1944).

Campbell, George, K.C.S.I., Sir, born in 1824, he entered the Indian Civil Service in 1842, and was called to the bar from Inner Temple in 1854. In 1858 he was appointed Judicial and Financial Commissioner in Oude. His writings include *Modern India* (1852), *The ethnology of India* (1872), *The Afghan frontier* (1879), and *Memoirs of my Indian career* (1893). He died in Cairo, 18 February 1892. BiD&SB; Mason; Men 10

Campbell, James, born about 1787, he was an assistant surgeon in the Honorable East India Company's Service and went to Persia with Sir John Malcolm. From 1810 to 1814 he was surgeon to Prince Abbas Mirza. In 1814 he accompanied Sir Gore Ouseley to Russia but later became the Legation doctor in Tehran, where he died in 1818, aged thirty-one. Wright, p. 55; *Journal of the Central Asian Society* 18 (1931), p. 223

Campbell, John Coert, born 8 October 1911 at NYC., he was a graduate of Harvard University and received his Ph.D. for his thesis, *French influence and the rise of Roumanian nationalism, 1830-1857*, in 1940. He was a member of the Policy Planning Staff at the U.S. Department of State, and later a senior fellow and director of studies at the Council on Foreign Relations. His writings include *Defense of the Middle East* (1958). ConAu 1 rev.; DrAS, 1974-1982; WhoAm, 1974-1978

Campbell, Robert Bell, born in 1926 at Boston, he became a Jesuit in 1944. After basic religious studies, he obtained an M.A. from Harvard, and a doctorate, in 1972, from the University of Michigan for his thesis, *The Arabic journal al-Mashriq; its beginning and first twenty-five years.* He taught at Baghdad College, and al-Hikmah University, Baghdad. He later was a specialist in Arabic literature at the Centre d'études pour le monde arabe moderne in the Université Saint-Jospeph, Beirut. His writings include *A'lam al-adab al-'Arabi al-mu'asir* (1996). LC; Selim

Campbell, Sir Ronald Hugh, born 27 September 1883, he entered the British Foreign Service in 1907 and was a sometime ambassador to France and Portugal. He died 15 November 1953. Quem é alguém, 1947; Who was who, 5

Campbell, Sheila D., born in 1938, her writings include *The Malcove Collection* (1985), *The mosaics of Antioch* (Toronto, 1988), and *The mosaics of Aphrodisias in Caria* (Toronto, 1991). LC

Camperio, Manfredo, born 30 October 1826 at Milano, he was a captain in the Italian army and pursued an interest in African trade. For this purpose he founded *l'Esploratore* in 1877. In the service of the Società d'esplorazione commerciale in Africa he explored Tripolitania in 1880. His writings include *Da Assah a Dogali; guerre abissine* (1887), *Manuale tigrè-italiano* (1894), and *Autobiografia* (1917). He died in Napoli, 29 December 1899. DizBI; Henze; Hill; Sezgin; VIA

Campion-Vincent, Véronique, fl. 1970, she was joint author of *Légendes urbaines; rumeurs d'aujourd'hui* (1992); in the same year she edited *Des fauvres dans nos campagnes.* LC

de **Campos**, José Augusto Correira, born 5 December 1890 in Portugal, he studied at the Universidade de Coimbra and the Escola de Guerra. His writings include *Arqueologia árabe em Portugal* (1965), and *Monumentos da antiguidade árabe em Portugal* (1970). Quem é alguém, 1947

de **Campou**, Ludovic, his writings include *Un empire qui croute, le Maroc contemporain* (1896), *La Tunisie française* (1887), and *Causeries géographiques* (1889). BN; LC

Campredon, Jean Pierre, born 20th cent., he was in 1986 joint editor of *France, océan Indien, mer Rouge.* LC

Camps, Arnulf, O.F.M., he received a doctorate in 1957 from the Université de Fribourg for his thesis, *Jerôme Xavier and the Muslims of the Mogul Empire.* In 1988 he edited *Oecumenische inleiding in de missologie.* LC; NUC, pre-1956

Camps, Gabriel, born in 1927, he was a archaeologist whose writings include *Monuments et rites funéraires protohistoriques* (1961), *Amekni, neolithique ancien du Hoggar* (1969), *Berbères* (1980), and *L'Afrique du nord au féminin* (1992). LC

Camps Cazorla, Emilio, born 31 October 1903 at Fuensanta de Martos, Spain, he was an archaeologist and a specialist in medieval history of art, a keeper at the Museo Lázaro and director of the Arqueológico Nacional. His writings include *Arquitectura califal y mozarabe* (1929). He died 28 January 1952. *Archivo español de arqueología* 25 (1952), p. 209; Figuras

Camps-Faber, Henriette, born 1928, her writings include *L'Olivier et l'huile dans l'Afrique romaine* (1953), *Les Bijoux de grande Kabylie* (1970), and *Bijoux berbères d'Algérie* (1990). LC

Camussi, H., fl. 1908, he wrote *La rage, son traitement et les insectes vésicants chez les arabes* (1888). BN; NUC, pre-1956

Cana, Frank Richardson, born in 1865 at Brampton, England, he was a journalist and a departmental editor with the *Encyclopædia Britannica*. His writings include *The great war in Europe* (1920). He died 9 January 1935. Who was who, 3

Canac, André, fl. 1955, he received a doctorate in law. In 1958 he was a deputy judge at the Tribunal civil d'Alger, and in 1959 a judge at the Tribunal de grande instance de Tizi-Ouzou. His writings include *La justice musulmane et le juge de paix en Algérie* (1958). LC

Cañada Juste, Alberto, born 20th cent. After he received a doctorate in philosophy and letters, he specialized in medieval history. In 1992 he was a professor of medieval history in the Universidad de Pamplona, a post which he still held in 1997. His writings include *La campaña musulmana de Pamplona año 924* (1976). Arabismo, 1992, 1994, 1997

Canal, Joseph, born in 1852, his writings include *Géographie générale du Maroc* (1902), and *Tabarca et la Kroumirie* (1932). LC

Cañamaque y Jiménez, Francisco de Paula, born 22 December 1851 at Gaucín, Spain, he was a historian and politician whose writings include *Las islas Filipinas* (1880). He was also editor of a number of periodicals. He died in Madrid, 23 December 1891. Ossorio

Canamas, Christine, born 20th cent., she was joint author of *Cours d'arabe maghrébin* (1979), and *Le tour de la gram-maire arabe en 80 pages* (1986). LC

Canard, Marius, born 26 December 1888 at Dracy-Saint-Loup (Saône-et-Loire), he studied before and after the first World War at the Université de Lyon as well as l'École des langues orientales, Paris, where he received a diploma in 1924. In 1927 he was appointed professor at the Faculté des lettres d'Alger, where he spent the remainder of his career. He was a leading Islamist and an accomplished Byzantinist whose writings include *Receuil de textes relatifs au califat abbaside al-Mu'tacim à al-Mu'tamid* (1951), and *Byzance et les musulmans du Proche Orient* (1973). He died in September 1982. Arabica 33 (1986), pp. 251-262

Canazzi, Auguste, fl. 1961, he was in 1953 a deputy attorney general in the Cour d'appel de Tunis.

Cancel, Jean, born 4 February 1876 at Loubens (Ariège), he was a graduate of the military college of Saint-Cyr and admitted to the Bureau des Affaires indigènes in 1903, posted as *adjoint stagiaire* at Ghardaïa, Laghouat and El-Aricha. In 1909 he was in charge of the Compagnie saharienne at Touat, and in 1913 he was *chef du Bureau* and administrator at Géryville. After serving in Morocco and the World War, he returned to the Bureau des Affaires indigènes in 1925. Since 1927 he was head of the Service des Affaires indigènes. Peyronnet, p. 821

Cândea, Virgil, born in 1927 at Focşania, Rumania, he was a professor of history of diplomatic relations in the University of Bucharest. His writings include *Les études sud-est européennes en Roumanie* (1966), *Outline of Romanian history* (1977), and *Romanian culture abroad* (1982). LC; WhoRom

Candler, Edmund, born in 1874, he was a *Daily mail* and *Times* correspondent. His writings include *Unveiling of Lhasa* (1905), *The long way to Baghdad* (1919), and *Youth and the East, an unconventional autobiography* (1924). He died in 1924. LitYbk, 1921; LitWho, 1920

Canestrini, Giuseppe, born 17 July 1807 at Trento, Italy, he studied statistics and political economy. His writings include *La scienza e l'arte di stato* (1862). He died in Firenze, 28 November 1870. LC; DizBI

Canfield, Robert Leroy, born 5 July 1930 at Yale, Okla., he was an anthropologist whose writings include *Faction and conversion in a plural society; religious alignments in the Hindu Kush* (1973); he was joint editor of *Revolutions & rebellions in Afghanistan* (1984), *Afghanistan and the Soviet Union; collision and transformation* (1989), and in 1991 he edited *Turko-Persia in historical perspective*. LC; Schoeberlein

Canivet, R. G., fl. 1906. Together with M. Fort he wrote *L'Égypte; pages de littérature et d'histoire* (Paris, 1923). NYPL

Cankova-Petkova, Genoveva *see* TSankova-Petkova, Genoveva

Canney, Maurice Arthur, born 18 March 1872 at London, he was educated at Oxford and called to the bar in 1908. He was emeritus professor of Semitic languages and literatures in the University of Manchester. His writings include *Materials for Hebrew composition* (1913). He died 16 May 1942. WhE&EA; *Who was who*, 4

Canning, R. Gordon, fl. 1924-1929, he contributed articles to the *Contemporary review*.

Canning, Stratford, first Viscount Stratford de Redcliffe, born in 1786, he was educated at Eton and King's College, Cambridge, and entered the diplomatic service in 1807 as a clerk in the foreign office. Later, as ambassador, he negotiated several treaties to protect British interests the Balkans and the Levant from the time of the treaty of Bucharest in 1812 to the middle of the nineteenth century. His writings include *The Eastern question* (1881). Stanley Lane-Poole wrote the *Life of the Right Honorable Stratford Canning* (1888). He died in 1880. Boase; CelCen; DNB; EncAm; EncBrit; EncicUni; EncItaliana; GdeEnc; GDU; Pallas; Meyers

Cannon, Byron David, born 24 September 1940, he received a Ph.D. in 1970 from Columbia University for his thesis, *The politics of judicial reform; Egypt, 1876-1891*. In 1988 he was attached to the University of Utah. His writings include *Politics of law and the courts in nineteenth-century Egypt* (1988). In 1987 he edited *Teritoires et sociétés au Maghreb et au Moyen Orient* (1987). LC

Cannon, Garland Hampton, born 5 December 1924 at Fort Worth, Texas, he was a graduate of the University of Texas, where he also received a Ph.D. in 1954 for *Oriental Jones, a biography*. Afterwards he held a variety of positions at American universities. Since 1966 he was professor of English and linguistics at Texas A & M University. He spent several years in Afghanistan, India and Thailand. His writings include *The life and mind of Oriental Jones* (1990). ConAu 33-36; DrAS, 1974-1978; Master (4)

Cannon, William Austin, born in 1870, he received a Ph.D. in 1903 from Columbia University for his thesis, *Studies in plant hybrids*. In 1913 he was attached to the Desert Laboratory, Tucson, Arizona. His writings include *Botanical features of the Algerian Sahara* (1913). NUC, pre-1956

Canova, Giovanni, born 10 October 1944 at Feltre, Italy, he received a doctorate in 1971 from the Università di Venezia. He was a specialist in popular Islam, legends and folk epics. He conducted field work in Egypt and the Yemen. He was professor of Islamic studies at Venezia and a member of the Istituto per l'Oriente, Roma. He was joint translator of *Poesie*, by Nizar Qabbani (1976). Private

Cansacchi di Amelia, Giorgio, born 24 June 1905 at Pinerolo, Italy, he was a sometime dean and vice-president of the Facoltà di Economia e Commercio in the Università di Torino. His writings include *L'occupazione dei mare costieri* (1936), and *Elementi di legislazione bancaria* (1951). Chi è, 1957, 1961; Wholtaly, 1957/58

Cantacuzino, Sherban, born 6 September 1928, he was educated at Magdalene College, Cam-bridge. He was a private architect and editor of the *Architectual review*. His writings include *Modern houses of the world* (1964), and *Great modern architecture* (1966). Who's who, 1982-1997

Cantarellas Camps, Catalina, fl. 1971, her writings include *La arquitectura mallorquina desde la Ilustración a la Restauración* (1981), and *Pedro de Alcántara Peña* (1984). LC

Cantarino, Vicente, born 12 May 1925 at Larida, Spain, he was educated at the Valencia Arch-bishopric Seminary, 1942 to 1945. He studied at the Pontificia Università di Roma before completing his formal education in 1962 with a Dr.phil. from the Universiät München for *Der neuaramäische Dialekt von Gubb 'Abdin; Texte und Übersetzung*. Since 1965 he was a professor of Hispano-Arabic studies, Indiana University, Bloomington. His writings include *Syntax of modern Arabic prose* (1974-75), *Arabic poetics in the golden age* (1975), and *Entre monjes y musulmanes* (1978). DrAS, 1974; LC

Canteins, Jean. His writings include *Phonèmes et archétypes* (1972), *Sauver le mythe* (1986), and *Miroir de la shahada* (1990). LC

Cantera Burgos, Francisco, born 22 November 1901 at Miranda de Ebro, Spain. After his study at the universities of Madrid and Valladolid, he was a professor of Hebrew at the Universidad de Madrid. His writings include *El judío Salamantino Abraham Zacut* (1931), *Abraham Zacut, siglo XV* (1935), and *Sinagogas españolas* (1955). WhoSpain, 1963

Cantine, James, born 3 March 1861 on an old farm in Ulster County, he entered New Brunswick Seminary in 1886, and soon after graduation he became a missionary of the Reformed Church of America and sailed for Beirut where he began to study Arabic. Being first in the field, he led in the planning and reconnaissance of the land, which resulted in the selection of Basrah as the first station of the Arabian Mission, which he founded with his friend S. M. Zwemer. In 1924 he was instrumental in founding also the United Mission in Mesopotamia. On account of ill health he returned to the United

States in 1929, and shortly thereafter he resigned from active service. He wrote *The golden milestone; reminiscences of pioneer days fifty years ago in Arabia with S. M. Zwemer* (1938.) He died in Kingston, N.Y., after a long illness, 1 July 1940. Facey Grant, p. 56; MW 30 (1940), p. 331; Shavit

Cantineau, Jean, born 9 June 1899 at Epinal (Vosges), he was from 1928 to 1933 a research scholar in the Institut français de Damas. He received a doctorate from the Université de Paris for his thesis, *Le dialecte arabe de Palmyre*, in 1934. Since 1947 he held the chair of Arabic at l'École nationale des langues orientales vivantes, Paris. His writings include *Inscriptions palmyréniennes* (1930), and *Manuel élémentaire d'arabe oriental* (1953). A commemoration volume was published in 1960: *Études de linguistique arabe; mémorial Jean Cantineau*. He died in Sainte-Geneviève-des-Bois, 8 April 1956. WhoFr, 1955/56; *Word* 12 (1956), p. 115; ZDMG 108 (n.f. 33, 1958), pp. 14-20

Cantor, Milton, born 11 June 1925 at NYC., he graduated in 1947 from Brooklyn College and received a Ph.D. in 1954 from Columbia University for *The life of Joel Barlow*. He held a variety of positions at American universities before he was appointed professor of history at the University of Massachusetts in 1963. He was joint editor of *Main problems of American history* (1987). DrAS, 1974, 1978, 1982

Cantor, Moritz Benedikt, born 23 August 1829 at Mannheim, Germany, he studied mathematics at Heidelberg, Göttingen and Berlin, where he received a doctorate in 1851. From 1860 until his retirement he was a pofessor of mathematics at Heidelberg. His writings include *Mathematische Beiträge zum Kulturleben der Völker* (1863). He died in Heidelberg, 10 April 1920. DtBE; LC; Sezgin

Cantori, Louis Joseph, born 29 June 1934, he received a Ph.D. in 1966 from the University of Chicago for his thesis, *Organizational basis of an elite political body; the Egyptian Wafd*. In 1984 he was chairman of the Dept. of Political Science in the University of Maryland. His writings include *Comparative political systems* (1974). Together with Iliya Harik he edited *Local politics and development in the Middle East* (1984). AmM&WS, 1973 S,1978 S; ConAu 29-32 rev.

Cao, Giuseppe Biggio, 1861-1934 *see* Biggio-Cao, Giuseppe

Capenny, S. H. F., fl. 1899. He wrote *The arts and crafts of the nations* (London, 1910). BLC

Capitaine, Hippolyte Félix, born 16 November 1837 at Paris. After the completion of his medical study he joined the French navy as a surgeon. He visited Cyprus, Egypt, the Indian Ocean and repeatedly Algeria. Since 1876 he was attached to *L'Exploration*. He died in Paris in 1880. DBF; Embacher

Capitan, Joseph *Louis*, born 19 April 1854 at Paris, he was a physician and anthropologist. Since 1892 he lectured at l'École d'anthropologie and was the founder of l'Institut international d'anthropologie. His writings include *La Préhistoire* (1922), and *L'Humanité primitive dans la région des Eyzies* (1924). He died in Paris, 1 September 1929. DBF

Capitant, Maurice, fl. 1936, he received a doctorate from the Université de Paris for his thesis, *De la détermination des individus dont le statut juridique est influencé par les traités de droit privé*, in 1927, and a second one from Harvard Law School in 1930 for his thesis, *Fundamental principles of the Anglo-American rules of conflict of laws*. NUC, pre-1956

Capot-Rey, Robert E., born 16 December 1897 at Agen (Lot-et-Garonne), he was educated at Bordeaux and Paris. Despite having lost his right leg in the first World War, he devoted the best years of his life to geographical exploration of the Sahara. In 1935 he was invited to the Faculté des lettres d'Alger. He was first secretary and later director of the Institut de recherches sahariennes. His writings include *Borkou et Ounianga* (1961). He died in Nîmes, 4 May 1977. *Geographers* 5 (1981), pp. 13-19; *Hommes et destins*, vol. 4, pp. 162-164; Unesco; WhoFr, 1967/68-1971/72

Cappe, Heinrich Philipp, fl. 1842, he wrote several books on German numismatics which include *Die Münzen der deutschen Kaiser und Könige des Mittelalters* (1848-57), and *Beschreibung der Münzen von Goslar* (1860). NUC, pre-1956; Sezgin

Capra, Giuseppe, born 3 October 1873 at Ponte S. Martino, Italy, he was a professor of geography at Roma and Perugia. His writings include *L'italiano in Australia e Nuova Zelanda* (1914), and *L'Africa centro-australe e l'emigrazione italiana* (1924). Chi è, 1948; NUC, pre-1956

Capus, Jean *Guillaume*, born 25 August 1857 at Esch-sur-Alzette, Luxembourg, he received a doctorate in 1879 in natural sciences and thereafter accompanied several French missions to Central Asia, Afghanistan, and Indochina. He was a sometime professor of agriculture at l'École coloniale and l'Institut agronomique de Nogent-sur-Marne. His writings include *A travers le royaume de Tamerlan* (1892) and *A travers la Bosnie et l'Herzégovine* (1896). He died in Boulogne-sur-Seine, 27 April 1931. DBF; *Hommes et destins*, vol. 1, pp. 126-127; NUC, pre-1956

Caputo, Eugenio, colonel. He wrote *Il Lazio* (1926). NUC, pre-1956

de **Caqueray de Valoline**, Gaston Marie Joseph, comte, born in 1869, he was joint author of *La marine et le progrès* (1901). LC; NUC, pre-1956

Caquot, André Marcel, born 24 April 1923 at Epinal (Vosges), he was educated at the *lycées* de Vesoul and Louis-le-Grand, Paris, as well as the École Normale Supérieure, Paris. Since 1955 he was a *directeur d'études* at l'École pratique des hautes études, Paris, and since 1972, a professor of Hebrew and Aramaic at the Collège de France. He was joint author of *Ugaritic religion* (1980). LC; *Who's who in France*, 1979-1997

Carabaza Bravo, Julia María, born 20th cent., she received a doctorate in Semitic philology and became a professor of Arabic and Islamic studies at the Departamento de Filologias Integradas in the Universidad de Sevilla. She is said to have published *Kitab al-Filahah al-Nabatiyah* (1991). Arabismo, 1992, 1994, 1997

Caraci, Giuseppe, born 23 December 1893 at Firenze, he was a professor of geography who held a variety of positions at Italian universities from 1925 to 1946. His writings include *Disegno geografico della Bulgaria* (1933), *Le materie prime* (1954), and *Il petrolio* (1955). He died in Roma, 28 September 1970. DizBI

Caradon, Hugh Mackintosh Foot, Baron, born 8 October 1907, he was educated at St. John's College, Cambridge. From 1929 to 1937 he was Administrative Officer, Government of Palestine, and afterwards held a variety of positions in the Middle East. From 1964 to 1970 he was UK representative to the UNO and is known as "the father" of Security Council Resolution 242. His writings include *The future of Jerusalem* (1980). He died 5 September 1990. Who was who, 8

Carali, Paolo/Paul, died 1952 see Qar'ali, Bulus

Caralp, Raymonde, fl. 1951, he was joint author of *Études de géographie des transports* (1978). LC

de **Caraman**, Adolphe de Riquet, comte, fl. 1841, his writings include *Anet, son passé, son état actuel, notice historique* (1860). NUC, pre-1956

Carandell, Luis, born 24 February 1929 at Barcelona, where he was also educated. He was a sometime correspondent in the Middle and the Far East. His writings include *Vivir en Madrid* (1967), and *Los españoles* (1968). DBEC

Caravaglios, Cesare, born 6 April 1893 at Alcamo, Sicily, he was a musician and ethnographer whose writings include *L'anima religiosa della guerra* (1935), *Il folklore musicale in Italia* (1936), and *Saggi folklore* (1938). He died in Roma, 15 January 1937. DizBI

Caravita, Giovanni, born 25 November 1933 at Milano, he taught at the Università di Milano and was elected to parliament in 1979. His writings include *Vita religiose dei Dinka* (1989). Who's who in Italy, 1980

Carayol, Angel Paul, born 19th cent., he received a doctorate in 1906 from the Université de Paris for his thesis, *La législation forestière de l'Algérie*.

de **Carcaradec**, Marie, fl. 1977, her writings include the English translation from the French, *Mural ceramics in Turkey* (1981).

Carcopino, Jérôme Ernest Joseph, born in 1881 in France, he was an educator and classicist whose writings include the translation, *Daily life in ancient Rome* (1940), *Aspects mystiques de la Rome païenne* (1941), and *Le Maroc antique* (14th edition, 1948). He died in 1970. LC

Cardahi, Choucr, born in 1890, he was a sometime Lebanese minister, president of the Cour de Cassation au Liban, professor at l'École française de droit de Beyrouth, and l'Académie de droit international de La Haye. His writings include *Les hommes de loi* (1937), *Droit et morale; le droit modern et la législation de l'islam au regard de la morale* (1950), and *La vente en droit comparé occidental et oriental* (1968). WhoWor, 1974

Cardaillac, Denise, born 20th cent., she received a doctorate in 1972 from the Université de Montpellier for her thesis, *La polémique anti-chrétien du manuscrit aljamiado n° 4944 de la Bibliothèque nationale de Madrid*. zKO

Cardaillac, Louis, born first half 20th cent. After he had received a doctorate in 1973 from the Université de Montpellier III for his *thèse d'état*, *La polémique anti-chrétienne des Morisques ou l'opposition de deux communautés*, he became a professor at his alma mater. His writings include *Morisques et chrétiens; un affrontement polémique, 1492-1640* (1977), its translation, *Moriscos y* *cristianos* (1979), and he was editor of *Les morisques et l'inquisition* (1990), and *Tolède, XII.-XIII.; musulmans , chrétiens et juifs* (1991). LC; THESAM, 4

Cardaire, Marcel Philippe, born 24 August 1916, he received his secondary education in Beirut and served as a French army officer in the campaigns in Europe and Indochina. He was attached to the Centre de hautes études d'administration musulmane à Paris, and spent ten years in French Equatorial Africa. His writings include *Contribution à l'étude de l'islam noir* (1949-50), and *L'islam et le terroir africain* (1954). He died 18 June 1959. *L'Afrique et l'Asie* 48 (4e trimestre 1959), pp. 75-76

Carden, Guy, born 31 July 1944 at Chicago, he graduated from Harvard, where he also received his Ph.D. in 1970 for *Logical predicates and ideolect variation in English*. In 1980 he became a professor of linguistics at the University of British Columbia, Vancouver, a post which he still held in 2002. His writings include a revised version of his thesis entitled *English quantities* (1976). DrAS, 1974, 1978, 1982 F; NatFacDr, 2002; Private; WhoWor, 1987/88

Cárdenas, Antonio Almagro, 1856- *see* Almagro y Cárdenas, Antonio

Cárdenas y Espejo, Francisco de, born in 1816 at Sevilla, he was an academic and a politician who, in his early career, was the editor of the Sevilla *El Conservador* (1839) and *Revista de Andalucía*. His writings include *Ensayo sobre la historia de la propiedad en España* (1873-75). He died in Madrid, 2 July 1898. NUC, pre-1956; Ossorio

Cardi, Beatrice de *see* De Cardi, Beatrice

Cardin de Cardonne, A., fl. 1834, he was the translator of *Journal d'Abdurrahman Gabarti pendant l'occupation fran☐ aise en Egypte* (1838).

Cardini, Franco, born in 1940 at Firenze, he was a historian specializing in the middle ages. He taught at the Università di Bari until 1989, when he was appointed to the chair of medieval history at the Università di Firenze. His writings include *Il movimento crociato* (1972), *Il Barbarossa* (1985), and *Noi e l'islam; un incontro possibile?* (1994). Wholtaly, 1995

Cardon, Émile, born 24 June 1824 at Paris, he was a journalist who travelled for many years in Europe, the Middle East, and North Africa. His writings include *Étude sur l'agriculture et la colonisation de l'Algérie* (1860). He died in 1899. DBF

Cardona, Giorgio Raimondo, born in 1943, his writings include *Linguistica generale* (1969), and *Introduzione all'etnolinguistica* (1976). In 1988 he was joint editor of *Bilinguismo e biculturalismo nel mondo*. LC

Carette, Antoine Ernest Hippolyte, born 23 May 1808, he was admitted in 1828 to l'École polytechnique. He participated in the conquest of Algeria; as *capitaine du génie* he was a member and secretary of the Commission Scientifique that explored Algeria from 1840 to 1842. He later was a *directeur des fortifications* at Arras, a position from which he retired in 1868. His writings include *Étude des routes suivies par les Arabes dans la partie méridionale de l'Algérie et de la régence de Tunis* (1844), and *Recherches sur l'origine et les migrations des principales tribus de l'Afrique septentrionale* (1853). He died in France in 1890. DBF; Henze

Carey, A. D., born in the 19th century, he was a member of the India Civil Service and travelled in Chinese Turkestan and along the northern frontier of Tibet from 1885 to 1887, visiting Khotan, Korla, Turfan, and Yarkand. Henze

Carey, Andrew Galbraith, born about 1889, he was a vice-president and director of Carey Machinery Company of Baltimore from 1930 to 1946. He was called to Washington in 1941 as a consultant on machine tools to the Secretary of War. In 1945 he was a member of the Secretariat at the San Francisco Conference to organize the United Nations, and from 1953 to 1954 he was chief of the industry division of the Mutual Security Agency at Rome. Together with his wife, Jane Perry Clark, he wrote *The web of modern Greek politics* (1968). He died 2 September 1974. NYT, 4 September 1974, p. 32

Carey, Jane Perry née Clark, born in 1898 at Washington, D.C., she was a graduate of Vassar College, Poughkeepsie, N.Y., and received a Ph.D. from Columbia University for *Deportation of aliens from the United States to Europe*, in 1931. She was a member of various state, federal, international and academic boards. From 1938 to 1953 she was a professor of government at Columbia. Her writings include *The role of uprooted people in European recovery* (1948). She died 24 October 1981. ConAu 73-76; Master (3); WhAm, 8

Carile, Antonio, he was a sometime professor of medieval history at the Università di Bologna. His writings include *La cronachistica veneziana di fronte alla spartizione della Romania nel 1204* (1969), and *Per una storia dell'imperio latino di Constantinopoli* (1972). Wholtaly, 1980

Carl, Louis, born 11 November 1924 at Paris, he was joint head of the Missions Hoggar-Tibesti, and joint author, with Joseph Petit, of *Tefedest; méharée au Sahara central* (1953), and its English translation, *Mountains in the desert* (1954), as well as *La Ville de sel; du Hoggar au Tebesti* (1954). LC; Unesco

Carlberg, Bertold, fl. 1936, he received a doctorate in 1924 in geography from the Universität Greifswald for his thesis, *Die Städte des westlichen Hinterpommerns*. NUC, pre-1956

Carle, Georges, fl. 1933-1945, he was an *ingénieur* whose writings include *Hydraulique agricole et industrielle en Syrie* (1923), and *Rapport sur la culture du coton au Maroc en 1924* (1925). NUC, pre-1956

Carless, Hugh Michael, born 22 April 1925, he was educated at SOAS, London, and Cambridge. He entered the Foreign Service in 1950 and served in a variety of positions, among them Kabul and Tehran. Who's who, 1974-1997

Carless, Rosia Maria née Frontini, she was married in 1956 to Hugh Michael Carless. She was a writer on pottery.

Carless, Thomas G., born in 1807, he was a British naval officer who served in the Indian Navy. From 1830 to 1833 he accompanied reconnaissance expeditions along the coasts of Arabia, East Africa, and the Indian Subcontinent. In 1837 and 1838 he plied the waters of Somaliland and the Persian Gulf. He died from small pox at Bushire, Persia, 16 December 1848. Henze; *Journal of the Royal Geographical Society* 19 (1849), pp. xli-xlii

Carleton, Alford, born 26 March 1903 at Albany, N.Y., he was a graduate of Oberlin College and Hartford Theological Seminary, where he received a doctorate in 1937 for his thesis, *Millet system for the government of minorities in the Ottoman Empire*. He served as a missionary under the American Board of Commissions for Foreign Missions in Turkey and Syria from 1924 to 1953. He retired in 1970, and died in Columbus, Ohio, 22 August 1983. IntWW, 1974/75; Shavit

Carlier, Émilie (Thévenin), born in the 19th century, she was the wife of a French consul in Armenia and wrote *Au milieu des massacres; journal de la femme d'un consul de France en Arménie* (1903). NUC, pre-1956

Carlone, Pierre François *Augustin* Théophile, born 11 October 1812 at Nice, his writings include *Un Charivari à Nice; chronique historique de l'an 1600* (1853), and *Vestiges épigraphiques de la domination gréco-massaliote et de la domination romaine dans les Alpes-Maritimes* (1868). He died in Nice, 11 March 1872. BN; DBF

Carlsen, Bodil Hjerrild, born 25 October 1942 at Ribe, Denmark, he studied classics and Iranian linguistics at Københavns Universitet, where he was a professor of Iranian philology in 1977. BioB134

Carlson, Sevinç Diblan, born in the first half of the twentieth century at Istanbul, she was a graduate of the American College for Girls, Istanbul, and received a doctorate of law from Istanbul Üniversitesi. She was a member of the Institut of Administrative Law and Administration at Istanbul before she became a senior staff member and Asia expert at the Center for Strategic and International Studies, Georgetown University, Washington, D.C. Her writings include *Malaysia, search for international unity and economic growth* (1975), and *Indonesia's oil* (1977). IWWAS, 1976/77; LC

Carlyle, Joseph Dacre, born in 1759, he was an Arabist whose writings include *Maured al-Latafet Jemaleddini filii Togri-Bardii* (1792), *Specimens of Arabian poetry* (1796), and *Poems, suggested chiefly by scenes in Asia-Minor, Syria, and Greece* (1805). He died in 1804. BLC; LC

Carman, Harry James, born 22 January 1884 at Greenfield, N.Y., he received a Ph.D. in 1919 from Columbia University for his thesis *The street surface railway franchises of New York City*. Afterwards he held a variety of positions at American universities. He wrote *Social and economic history of the United States* (1930-1934). He died 26 December 1964. Who was who in America, vol. 4

Carmel, Alex, born 17 June 1931 at Berlin, he was a senior lecturer in history at Haifa since 1969. His writings include *Toldot Hefah bi-yeme ha-Turkim* (1969), its German translation, *Geschichte Haifas in der türkischen Zeit* (1975), *Palästina-Chronik, 1853-1882* (1978), and *Christen als Pioniere im Heiligen Land* (1981). WhoWorJ, 1978

Carmichael, Joel, born 31 December 1915 at NYC., he studied Oriental languages at Oxford and Paris and became a free-lance journalist specializing in Europe and the Middle East. His writings include *The shaping of the Arabs* (1967), *Arabs today* (1971), and *The satanizing of the Jews* (1992). ConAu 1 rev.

Carmody, Francis James, born 4 December 1907 at San Francisco, he received a Ph.D. in 1932 from Harvard University for his thesis, *The "Opera-comique en vaudevilles"* at Paris. After-wards he was a professor of French in the University of California at Berkeley. His writings include *Differentie scientie astrorum* (1943), and *Innovations in Averroes' De caleo* (1982). DrAS, 1974; LC; WhoAm, 1974

Carmoly, Eliakim David, originally Goschel David Baer/Behr, born 5 August 1802 at Sulz, Alsace, he studied Hebrew and Talmud at Colmar, French and German at Paris, where he was also attached to the Bibliothèque nationale for a number of years. In 1833 he was appointed rabbi of Belgium at Bruxelles, a position he held until 1839, when criticism caused him to resign and pursue his interests in Paris. His writings include *Histoire de médecins juifs anciens et modernes* (1844), and *Biographie des israélites de France* (1868). He died in Frankfurt a.M., 15 Februry 1875. EncJud; NDBA; Wininger

de **Carné**, Louis Joseph Marie, comte, born in 1844, his writings include *Voyage en Indo-Chine et dans l'empire chinois* (1872), and its English translation *Travels in Indo-China and the Chinese Empire* (1872). He died in 1870. BN; NUC, pre-1956

Carnock, Frederick Archibald Nicolson, 2d Baron, born 9 January 1883, he joined the 15th, the King's, Hussars in 1903 and served in India, where he was aide-de-camp to the Viceroy of India, 1911-13. His writings include *History of the 15th, the King's, Hussars, 1914-1922* (1932). He died 31 May 1951 or 1952. Who was who, 5

Carnoy, Albert Joseph, born 7 November 1878 at Louvain, Belgium, he held a variety of positions at universities in Europe and the United States. His writings include *The religion of ancient Persia* (1934), and *Dictionnaire étymologique de la mythologie gréco-romaine* (1957). He died in Louvain, 12 January 1961. NBW, vol. 1; WhoBelgium

Caro Baroja, Julio, born 13 November 1914 at Madrid, he received a doctorate in philosophy and letters from the Universidad de Madrid. He was a historian and anthropologist, specializing in the history of the Moriscos of Granada and the sociology of the Muslims of the Sahara. He held a variety of academic positions in Spain and elsewhere. His writings include *La casa en Navarra* (1982), and *Estudios saharianos* (1990). In 1978 he was presented with *Homenaje a Julio Caro Baroja*. DBEC; OxSpan; Unesco

Caroe, Sir Olaf Kirkpatrick Krunse, born 15 November 1892 at London, he was educated at Winchester and Magdalen College, Oxford. He was an army officer who entered the Indian Civil Service in 1919 and served in a variety of posts in the North West Frontier Province, Baluchistan and the Persian Gulf. His writings include *Wells of power* (1951), and *The Soviet empire; the Turks of Central Asia and Stalinism* (1953). He died 23 November 1981. DNB; IntAu&W, 1976-77; Who was who, 8; Who's who, 1974-1982

Caron, Nelly Renée, born 15 May 1912 at Dieppe (Seine-Inférieure), she studied at the Paris Conservatoire and was a music journalist as well as a professional musician. She was a founding member of the Centre d'études de musique orientale, Paris. Her writings include *Iran* (Les traditions musicales, 1966). WhoFr, 1975/76-1987/88

Carp, L. W., fl. 1978, he was a chairman of the International Rumi Society. Note

Carpenter, Frank George, born 8 May 1855 at Mansfield, Ohio, he was a journalist whose travels, which extended over thirty-six years, took him to nearly every part of the world. As late as 1921, he started on fresh journeys. Attacks of illness failed to discourage him; his last one overtook him in Nanking, China, 18 June 1924. His writings include *Cairo to Kisumu* (1923), and *From Tangier to Tripolis* (1923). DAB, vol. 3; Who was who in America, 1

Carpov, Paul Theodor, he was from 1741 to 1747 affiliated with the Universität Rostock, Germany. He died in 1761. NUC, pre-1956

Carr, David William, born in 1936, he was in 1980 a program economist at the USAID Mission in Nouakchott, Mauritania. He was previously posted at Damascus, Beirut, Amman, Aden and Jiddah. His writings include *Foreign investment and development in Egypt* (1979). LC

Carr, James A., born in 1920, he published in 1994 the bibliography, *American foreign policy during the French revolution; Napoleonic period, 1789-1815.* LC

Carra de Vaux, Bernard, baron, le père, born 3 February 1867 at Bar-sur-Aube, he was educated at the Collège Stanislas and Polythechnique. He was a sometime professor of Oriental languages at l'Institut catholique de Paris, and a founder of the *Revue de l'orient chrétien.* His writings include *Le* *livre de l'avertissement et de la revision* (1896), *Avicenne* (1900), *Gazali* (1902), and *La doctrine de l'islam* (1921-1926). He died in 1953. Carnoy 10²; DBF; Fück; *Islamic studies* 10 (1971), pp. 201-207

de **Carranza**, Fernanza, fl. 1950, his writings include *La guerra santa por mar de los corsarios berberinos* (1932), *Estudios sobre las provincias de Yebala y el Rif* (1933), and *Ensayos históricos muslimes* (1945). NUC, pre-1956

Carré, Jean Marie, born 1 March 1887 at Maubert-Fontaine (Ardenne), he was a professor of comparative literature at universities in France, Cairo and NYC until his retirement in 1956. His writings include *Voyageurs et écrivains français en Égypte* (1932). He died 6 January 1958. Who's who in France, 1957/58

Carré, Jean Olivier, he studied philosophy and theology at Paris; Arabic at l'Université St.-Joseph, Beirut, and l'Institut français d'études arabes, Damascus; and sociology at l'École des hautes études, obtaining doctorates in 1969 and 1977. His writings include *Enseignement islamique et idéal socialiste* (1974), parts of which were submitted at the Sorbonne for his doctorat d'état in 1969, *Mystique et politique* (1982), *L'Orient arabe aujourd'hui* (1991), and *L'utopie islamique dans l'Orient arabe* (1991). THESAM, 3

Carreira, Antonio, born 28 October 1905 at Ilha do Fogo, Cape Verde Islands. After studies at the University of Lisbon, he became a colonial administrator. His writings include *O tráfico de escravos nos rios de Guiné e ilhas de Cabo Verde, 1810-1850* (1981), and the translation, *The people of the Cape Verde Islands* (1982). Unesco

Carrer, Franz, born about 1920, he graduated in 1948 in agriculture from the Hochschule für Bodenkultur, and then entered public service on the provincial level in Tirol, and later at the federal level in Wien. From 1951 to 1953 he was in charge of the European Recovery Program, and later dealt with export affairs, and personally visited many of Austria's trade partners. Note about the author

Carreras y Artau, Joaquin, born in 1894 at Girona, Spain, he received a doctorate in 1923 from the Universidad de Barcelona for his thesis, *Ensayo sobre el voluntarismo de J. D. Duns Scot.* He was a member of l'Institut d'Etudis Catalans, Barcelona, and the Consje Superior de Investigaciones Cientifico de Madrid. His writings include *Introduccion a la filosofía* (6th ed., 1946). Dicc bio

Carreras y Candi, Francesch, born in 1862, his writings include *Argentona histórica* (1891), and *L'aljama de jehéus de Tortosa* (1928). He died in 1937. Dicc bio

Carrère, Claude, born in 1929, he wrote *Barcelone; centre économique à l'époque des difficultés, 1380-1462* (1967), and its translation into Catalan in 1977-78. LC

Carrère d'Encausse, Hélène, born 6 July 1929 at Paris, she was a professor of history at l'Université de Paris, and a member of l'Académie française since 1990. In 1994, she was elected to the European Parliament, and in 1999, she became the first woman to be elected permanent secretary to the Académie française. Her writings include *Réforme et révolution chez les Musulmans de l'Empire russe* (1966), *L'émpire éclaté* (1978), and *Islam and the Russian Empire* (1988). Schoeberlein; WhoFr, 1993/94-1999

Carret, Jacques, capitaine, fl. 1957, his writings include *Régime des cultes en pays musulmans* (1955), *Le maraboutisme et les confréries religieuses musulmanes en Algérie* (1959), and *Le reformisme en islam* (1959). BN; LC

Carretto, Giacomo E., born in 1939 at Roma, he was a member of the Turkish Studies Association whose writings include *Hars-Kültür; nascita di una cultura nazionale* (1979), *Saggi su Meş'ale* (1979), and *Un sultano prigioniero del Papa* (1989). In 1983 he was joint author of *Maometto in Europa; arabi e turchi in Occidente, 622-1922*, a work which was published a year later in French and German. LC

Carriazo Arroquia, Juan de Mata, born in 1899 at Jódar, Spain, he was a sometime professor of history at the universities of Granada and Madrid, as well as an archaeologist. His writings include *El Carambolo* (1978), *Protohistoria de Sevilla* (2d ed., 1980), and *Crónica de Juan II de Castilla* (1982). He was presented with *Homenaje al professor Carriazo* (1972-73). DBEC

Carrier, J. M., fl. 1980, he wrote *Viet Cong motivation and moral* (Santa Monica, Cal., Rand Corporation, 1966, i.e. 1977). LC

Carrière, Pierre, fl. 1972, he was affiliated with l'Université Paul Valéry de Montpellier. His writings include *L'Albanie* (1978), and *Les problèmes de l'agriculture soviètique* (1979). LC

Carro Martínez, Antonio, born 3 May 1923 in Lugo, Spain, he wa a sometime professor of law and political science at the Universidad de Madrid. His writings include *Introducción a la ciencia política* (1957), and *Derecho político* (1959). IntWW, 1974-81; Quien, 1993; WhoSpain, 1963, 1994; WhoWor, 1978

Carroll, Michael, born in 1935, he spent his childhood in India. After leaving Cambridge, he did an extensive tour by Land Rover, donkey, and other forms of conveyance through Turkey, Perisa, Afghanistan, India and Nepal. He wrote *From a Persian tea-house* (1960), and *Gates of the wind* (1965). NUC, 1956-1967

Carrubba, Robert William, born 1 August 1934 at NYC., he was a graduate of Fordham University and received a Ph.D. in 1964 from Princeton for his thesis, *The arrangement and structure of Horace's Epodes*. After teaching in New York State from 1964 to 1969, he was appointed professor at Pennsylvania State University in 1974. DrAS, 1974, 1978, 1982

Carruthers, Alexander *Douglas* Mitchell, born 4 October 1882 at London, he was educated at Haileybury and Trinity College, Cambridge. He started in quite a humble way at the Royal Geographical Society but eventually took part in expeditions which advanced his career. He travelled in Turkestan and the countries south-east of Syria. His writings include *Arabian adventure to the Great Nafud Desert in quest of the Oryx* (1935), and *Beyond the Caspian; a naturalist in Central Asia* (1949). He died 23 May 1961 or 1962. Bidwell, pp. 134-135; DNB; *Who was who*, 6

Carruthers, Ian Douglas, born 20th cent., his writings include *Economic aspects and policy issues in groundwater development* (1981). In 1983 he edited *Aid for the development of irrigation*. LC; *Who's who in science in Europe*, 7th ed. (1991)

Carsalade du Pont, Jules Marie Louis de, born 16 February 1847 at Simorre (Gers) and ordained in 1871, he was a professor at the Séminaire d'Auch, where he pursued an interest in local history and archaeology. He was the founder of the Société archéologique d'Auch, as well as the Musée archéologique d'Auch. In 1900 he was invested as Bishop of Elne. His writings include *Documents inédits sur la Fronde en Gascogne* (1883). He died 29 December 1932. DBF

Carson, Beryl, fl. 1926. As a participant in the Congress of Orientalists, he spent some weeks in Turkey travelling to Ankara. Note

Carson, George Barr, Jr., born 16 October 1915 at Ancon, Canal Zone, he received a Ph.D. in 1942 from the University of Chicago for *The Chevalier de Castellux, soldier and philosopher*. After a variety of positions in American universities, he was a professor of history at Oregon State University from 1961 until his retirement. His writings include *Electoral practices in the U.S.S.R.* (1955). DrAS, 1974, 1978, 1982

Carson, William Morris, born 7 November 1924. Under grants from the Ford Foundation, he spent the years from 1951 to 1953 in Egypt doing graduate research which resulted in *The Mehalla report* (1953). Thereafter he held a variety of academic and managerial positions in the United States and the Third World. AmM&WS, 1973 S, 1978 S; WhoUN, 1975

Carswell, John William, born 16 November 1931 at London, he was a sometime professor of fine art at Beirut, London and Chicago. His writings include *New Julfa; the Armenian churches and other buildings* (1968). In 1972 he published, with C. J. F. Dowsett, *Kütahya tiles and pottery from the Armenian Cathedral of St. James, Jerusalem*. WhoAm, 1982-1988/89

Cart, Léon, 1869-1916. He wrote *Au Sinai et dans l'Arabie pétrée* (1915). LC

Cartellieri, Alexander Georg Maximilian, born 19 June 1867 at Odessa, he studied history at Tübingen, Leipzig and Berlin, where he received a Dr.phil. in 1891 for his thesis, *Philipp II August von Frankreich bis zum Tode seines Vaters*. From 1902 until his retirement in 1935 he was a professor of history at Jena. His writings include *Der Vorrang des Papsttums zur Zeit der ersten Kreuzzüge* (1941). He died in Jena, 16 January 1955. DtBE; Kürschner, 1931-1954

Carter, April, born in 1937, her writings include *Direct action* (1962), *Non-violent action* (1966), and *Authority and democracy* (1979). LC

Carter, Francis William, born 4 July 1938 at Wednesfield, Staffordshire. He was educated at Sheffield, Cambridge, and London. In 1975 he received a Dr.nat.sc. from the Universita Karlova, Praha. Since 1967 he taught geography at University College, London, specializing in Eastern Europe. His writings include *Dubrovnik (Ragusa), a classic city-state* (1972), and *Trade and urban development in Poland* (1994). In 1993 he was joint editor of *Environmental problems in Eastern Europe*. IntAu&W, 1967, 1977; LC; WhoWor, 1976/77

Carter, George Edward Lovelace, fl. 1917-1924, he was affiliated with the Archaeological Survey of Kashmir. BLC

Carter, Henry John, born in 1813, he was a naval surgeon who participated in coastal reconnaissance along the shores of north-eastern Arabia in 1844 to 1845. He wrote *Geological papers on western India, including Cutch, Sinde, and the south-east coast of Arabia* (1857). He died in 1895. BLC; Henze

Carter, John R. L., born in 1934, his writings include *Leading merchant families of Saudi Arabia* (1979), *Tribes in Oman* (1982), and *Merchant families of Kuwait* (1984). LC

Carter, Martha Limbach, born 12 July 1935 at Cleveland, Ohio, she was a graduate of Skidmore College and received a Ph.D. in 1970 from Case Western Reserve University. BioB134; Schoeberlein

Carter, Michael G., born 20th cent., he received a D.Phil. in 1967 from Oxford University for his thesis, *A study of Sibawaihi's principles of grammatical analysis.* Afterwards he was affiliated with the University of Sydney (1981) and New York University (1990). He edited *Arabic linguistics* (1981), and *Studies in the history of Arabic grammar* (1990). LC; Sluglett

Carter, Theresa Howard, born 15 May 1929 at Millbrook, N.Y., she was educated at Syracuse, the University of Pennsylvania, and Bryn Mawr (Pa.) College. Since 1960 she was affiliated with the University Museum of the U. of Pennsylvania, Philadelphia, and participated in excavations in North Africa and the Middle East. DrAS, 1974; Shavit; WhoAm, 1974-1982; WhoAmW, 1974/75, 1975/76

Carter, Thomas Francis, born 26 October 1882, he received a Ph.D. in 1925 from Columbia University for his thesis, *The invention of printing in China and its spread westward.* He wrote *Periods of Chinese history and parallelism* (1925). He died 6 August 1925. NUC, pre-1956

Carteret, Hubert, fl. 1949, his writings include *Code de droit pénal et de procédure criminelle* (Casablanca, 1952). BLC; LC

Carton, Louis Benjamin Charles, born 16 June 1861 at S.-Omer (Pas-de-Calais). After completing his medical studies with a doctorate from the Université de Lille, he entered the *Corps de santé militaire* and was posted to Gabès, Tunisia, while pursuing an interest in the history of Carthage. He was a founding member of the Société archéologique de Sousse, and a sometime vice-president of the Institut de Carthage. His writings include *Ruines de Dougga* (1910). He died in Paris in December 1924. Carnoy 11²; DBF

Caruel, Teodoro, born 27 June 1830 at Chandernagor, India, he studied at the Università di Firenze, where he spent most of his career as a botanist. His writings include *Epitome florae Europae terrarumque affinium; sistens plantas Europae, Barbariae, Asiae occidentalis et centralis et Sibiriae* (1892-1897). He died in Firenze, 4 December 1898. In 1899 was published *In memoria di Teodoro Caruel, ricordo.* DizBI

Carus, W. Seth, born 20th cent., he was throughout the 1990s affiliated with the Center for Strategic and International Studies, Washington, D.C. His writings include *The genie unleashed: Iraq's chemical and biological weapons program* (1989), *Ballistic missiles in the Third World* (1990), and *Ballistic missiles in modern conflict* (1991). LC

Carvajal Ferrer, Francisco *Javier*, born in 1926 at Barcelona, he was an architect and is the subject of *Javier Carvajal* (1991). Espasa, ap. 1

de **Carvalho**, Henrique Martins, fl. 1969, he was a sometime professor at the Universidade Técnica de Lisboa. His writings include *Aspectos da crise do pensamento contemporâneo* (1952), *Portugal e o Pacto do Atlantico* (1953), and *O Pacto do Atlantico e a política mundial* (1955). LC

Carvely, Andrew, fl. 1969. He worked and travelled extensively in the Middle East and North Africa, including four years in Libya. His writings include *U.S.-U.A.R. diplomatic relations and Zionist pressures* (1969). LC

Casamar Perez, Manuel. After he received a diploma in philosophy and lettres, majoring in history, he specialized in Islamic art, particularly ceramics. In 1992 he was a deputy director of the Museo Romántico de Madrid. He was joint author of *La España árabe; legado de un paraiso* (1990). LC

Casanova, Eugenio, born 17 January 1867 at Torino, he began his long career as an archivist at the Archivio di Stato di Firenze in 1886. His writings include *Gli archivi provinciali del mezzogiorno d'Italia e della Sicilia* (1914). He died in Roma, 22 December 1951. Chi è, 1931-1940; DizBI

Casanova, Jean Joseph, born 11 June 1934 at Ajaccio, he was educated at the Lycée Carnot, Tunis, and the Facultés de droit et des lettres, Paris, and at Harvard University. He held a variety of French university posts and was a sometime government consultant. His writings include *Principes d'analyse économique* (1970). WhoFr, 1969/70-1997

Casanova, Paul, born in 1861 at Orléansville, Algeria, he was a graduate of l'École normale, and received a diploma from l'École des langues orientales vivantes, Paris. He was a librarian at the Département des médailles of the Bibliothèque nationale, a professor of Arabic at the Collège de France, and since 1900, a deputy director of the Institut français d'archéologie orientale at Cairo, where he died 23 March 1926. His writings include *Histoire et description de la citadelle du Caire* (1894-97), and *Mohammed et la fin du monde* (1911-14). He was the translator of Ibn Khaldun's *Histoire des berbères et des dynasties musulmanes de l'Afrique septentrionale* (1925-26). DBF

Casartelli, Louis Charles, Rt. Rev., born 14 November 1852 at Manchester, he received a doctorate in 1884 from the Université de Louvain for his thesis, *La philosophie religieuse du mazdéisme sous les Sassanides*. From 1900 to 1903, he was professor of Zend and Pahlavi at Louvain, and afterwards until 1920, lecturer on Iranian languages at the University of Manchester. Since 1906 he was president of the Manchester Dante Society. His writings include *The popes in the Divina commedia of Dante* (1921). He died 18 January 1925. *Who was who,* 2

Casati, Gaetano, born 4 September 1838 at Ponte d'Albiate, Italy, he joined the Bersaglieri in 1839 and served in the Topographical Section until he retired from the army with the rank of captain in 1879 to join the staff of *l'Esploratore*, Milano. In 1880 he travelled in the service of the Società d'esplorazione commerciale to East and Equatorial Africa. His writings include *Dieci anni in Equatoria e ritorno con Emin Pascia* (1891), an work which was translated into several languages. He died in Como, 7 March 1902. DizBI; *le Globe* 41 (1902), pp. 168-170; Henze; Hill; VIA

Casciaro Ramírez, José Maria, born 20th cent., he received doctorates of divinity and Semitic philology, specializing in the Islamic influence upon scholastic theology. In 1992 he was a professor of New Testament studies at the Universidad de Navarra. His writings include *El diálogo teológico de Santo Tomás con musulmanes y juíos* (1969). LC

Cascudo, Luis da Câmara, born 30 December 1899 at Natal, Brazil, he was a professor of *historia da civilização* and history of music. His writings include *Dante Alighieri e a tradição popular no Brasil* (1963), and *Folclore do Brasil* (1967). LC; Quem, 1951

Case, Paul Edward, fl. 1947, he was an assistant to Dr. Luther M. Winsor, an American adviser on irrigation to the Iranian Government, and given a war-time assignment to meet the head of the Bakhtiyaris and obtain their cooperation for the construction of a road and a dam in their territory. Note

Casemajor, Roger, born 25 September 1912 at Gafsa, Tunisia, he received his secondary education at the Lycée Carnot, Tunis, and his diploma in law from the Université de Dijon in 1937. He was attached to the Centre de hautes études d'adminstration musulmane, Paris, and made his career in Tunisia, where he served successively at the Résidence générale, the Haut-Commisariat, and the Ambassade de France. He died 19 September 1959. *L'Afrique et l'Asie* 49 (1er trimestre 1960), pp. 84-85

Casey, Elizabeth Temple, born 24 September 1901 at Providence, R.I. From 1956 until her retirement, she was a curator of Oriental art at the Museum of Art, Rhode Island School of Design. She wrote *The Lucy Truman Aldrich Collection of European porcelain figures of the eighteenth century* (1965). WhoAmW, 1970-1978

Casey, James Gerard, born in 1944, he was a sometime lecturer in history at the University of East Anglia. His writings include *The Kingdom of Valencia in the seventeenth century* (1979). LC

Cash, William Wilson, D.S.O., born 12 June 1880, he was a missionary in Egypt, served as an army chaplain in the Middle East, and became a Church Missionary Society administrator in his later years. His writings include *The Moslem world in revolution* (1925), *The expansion of Islam* (1928), *Persia old and new* (1929), *The changing Sudan* (1930), and *Christendom and Islam* (1937). He died 18 July 1955. *Who was who,* 5

Casie Chitty, Simon, 1807-1860 see Chitty, Simon Casie

Casimir, Michael J., born 20th cent., he wrote *Flocks and food; a biocultural approach to the study of pastoral foodways* (1991). In 1992 he was joint editor of *Mobility and territoriality; social and spatial boundaries among foragers, fishers, pastoralists, and peripatetics.* LC

Casiño, Eric Salcedo, born in 1936, his writings include two brief monographs, *Muslim folk art in the Philippines* (Manila, 1967), and *Ethnographic art of the Philippines* (Manila, 1973). LC

Caskel, Werner, born 5 March 1896 at Danzig, he studied at Tübingen and Berlin, saw war-time service in the Ottoman Empire, and received a doctorate in 1925 from the Universität Mannheim for his thesis, *Das Schicksal in der altarabischen Poesie*. He was attached to the Oppenheim-Stiftung for many years, particularly from 1933 to 1945, when he was barred from teaching for political reasons. From 1946 to 1964 he was a professor at Berlin and subsequently at Köln. In 1968 he was honoured by *Festschrift Werner Caskel*. His writings include *Gamharat an-nasab, das genealogische Werk des Hišam ibn Muhammed al-Kalbi* (1966). He died 28 January 1970. DtBE; Kürschner, 1966; Schwarz

Casoni, Giovanni, born 15 January 1783 at Venezia, he was a naval engineer and in charge of the Venetian dockyards in 1852. A year before his death, he was appointed director of the Museo di marina at Venezia. He died 30 or 31 January 1857. DizBI

Caspani, Egidio, a clergyman, fl. 1946. He was joint author of *Afghanistan, crocevia dell'Asia* (Milano, 1951). NUC, pre-1956

Caspar, Robert, born 20th cent., he was a professor of theology and Islamic mysticism; in 1994 he was a consultant editor of *Islam and Christian-Muslim relations*. His writings include *Traité de théologie musulmane* (1987), and *Pour un regard chrétien sur l'islam* (1990).

Caspari, Carl Paul, born 8 February 1814 at Dessau, Germany, he studied Semitic languages at Leipzig, and after his baptism in 1838, he continued with theology at Berlin. In 1857 he was invited to teach Biblical exegesis at Christiania (Oslo). His writings include translations from the Arabic as well as *Bibleske afhandlinger* (1884), and *Grammatica arabica in usum scholarum academicarum* (1848), a work which was repeatedly reprinted and appeared in its first English edition by W. Wright in 1859. He died at Christiania, 11 April 1892. ADtB; Fück, pp. 199-200; NorskBL; Wininger

Cassar Pullicino, Guze/Joseph, born in 1921, his writings include *Il-folklore Malti* (1960), *Studies in Maltese folklore* (1976), and *Femmes de Malte dans les chants traditionels* (1981). LC

Cassavetes, Nicholas J., born 19th cent., he was in 1919 a director of the Pan-Epirotic Union in America, and vice-president of the League of the Friends of Greece. His writings include *Epirus and Albania* (1919), *The question of northern Epirus at the Peace Conference* (1919), and *Near East problems* (1944). LC; Note

Casserly, Gordon, born in the 19th century at Dublin, he was educated at Dublin University. In 1900 he went with the Indian Expeditionary Force to China for the Boxer War. After the first World War he resigned from the Army for ill-health contracted on service. He continued to travel extensively. His writings include *The land of the Boxers* (1903), *Life in an Indian outpost* (1914), *Algeria to-day* (1923), and *Tripolitania* (1943). He died 4 April 1947. Who was who, 4

Casson, Lionel, born 22 July 1914 at N.Y.C., he was a graduate of New York University, where he received a Ph.D. in 1939 for his thesis, *Nine papyrus texts in the New York University collec-tion*. From 1936 until his retirement he was a professor of classics at N.Y.U. His writings incude *Ancient trade and society* (1984). ConAu 9-10; DrAS, 1974-1982

Casson, Ronald William, born 3 July 1942 at Chicago, he was a graduate of the University of Illinois, and received a Ph.D. in 1972 from Stanford University for his thesis, *Kinship terminilogy and kinship organization in a Turkish village*. Since 1978 he was a professor of anthropology at Oberlin College. His writings include *Language, culture and cognition* (1981). DrAS, 1974, 1978, 1982

Casson, Stanley, born 7 May 1889. After Oxford, and the British School at Athens, he served with the Salonika Force from 1916 to 1918, and in Constantinople and Turkestan in 1919. Thereafter he was a reader in classical archaeology at Oxford. His writings include *Hellenic studies* (1920). He died 17 April 1944. Who was who, 4

Castagné, Joseph A., fl. 1935, he was a keeper at the Museum of Orenburg. His writings in Russian and French include Надгробныя сооруженія киргизских степей = *Les monuments funéraires de la steppe des Kirghizes* (1911), *Les Basmalchis* (1925), and *Les musulmans et la politique des soviets en Asie centrale* (1925). LC

Castaing, Alphonse, born in 1822, he was a sometime editor of *Annuaire de la Société d'ethnographie*, Paris. His writings include *Ethnographie de la France à l'usage des écoles* (1885). He died in 1888. BN

Castañeda, Jorge, born 1 October 1921 at Mexico City., he was a career diplomat, a representative to international organizations, and a professor of international public law. His writings include *México y el*

orden internacional (1956), *Valor jurídico de las resoluciones de las Naciones Unidas* (1967), and *Legal effects of United Nations resolutions* (1969). IntWW, 1985/86; WhoUN, 1975; WhoWor, 1976-1978

Castañeda y Alcover, Vicente, born 7 March 1884 at Madrid, he received a doctorate of law, and was a sometime president of the Sociedad de bibliófilos españoles. Since 1920 he was permanent secretary of the Real Academia de la Historia. He died in 1958. Espasa; Ruiz C

Castejón Calderón, Rafael, fl. 1962, he wrote *Los juristas hispano-musulmanes* (1948). LC

Castejón y Martínez de Arizala, Rafael, fl. 1945, his writings include *Guía de Córdoba* (1930), *La busca de la felicidad* (1975), and *Medina Azhara, la ciudad palatina de los califas de Córdoba* (1976?).

Castel, Georges, born 20th cent., he received a doctarate in 1979 from the Université de Lyon II for his thesis, *Matériaux pour une étude de l'architecture rurale et désertique en Egypte*. He was affiliated with the Institut français d'archéologie orientale du Caire. His writings include *Deir el-Médineh, 1970; fouilles* (1980), and *Gebel el-Zeit* (1989). LC; THESAM, 3

Castel, Jorge. He wrote *La actividad de España en Marruecos desde principios del siglo XIX hasta la paz de Tetuán de 1860* (Madrid, 1960).

Castelar Ripoli, Emilio, born in 1832 at Cadiz, he was a professor of history and philosophy, and a politician whose writings include *La cuestion de Oriente* (1876), *La guerras de America y Egypto* (1883), and *Crónica internacional* (1897-98). He died in 1899. EncAm; EncBrit; Espasa; GER; Meyers

Castell, Edmund, born in 1606 at Tadlow, Cambridgshire, he studied first at Emmanuel College, Cambridge, but afterwards changed to St. John's. His great work was the compiling of his *Lexicon heptaglotton, Hebraicum, Chaldaicum, Syriacum, Samaritanum, Æthiopicum, Arabicum, conjunctim* (1669). Over this book he spent eighteen years, employing fourteen assistants, one of whom was J. M. Wansleben. By an expenditure of £12,000 he brought himself to poverty, for his lexicon, though full of the most unusual learning, did not find purchasers. He was later made prebendary of Canterbury and professor of Arabic at Cambridge. He died in 1685 at Higham Gobion, Bedfordshire, where he was rector. EncBrit; EncicUni; GdeEnc; GDU; Μεγαλι ελλινικβ εγκυκλοπαιδεια, vol 13 (1930), p. 959; Pallas; RNL

Castellan, Antoine Laurent, born 1 February 1772 at Montpellier, he was a painter, engraver, and traveller. His writings include *Lettres sur la Grèce, l'Hellespont et Constantinople* (1811), and *Mœurs, usages, costumes des Othomanes* (1812), and its translations into English and German. He died in Paris, 2 April 1838. DBF; Hoefer

Castellan, Georges Gabriel, born 26 September 1920 at Cannes. Until his retirement in 1979, he was a professor of history at various French universities. His writings include *Histoire de l'armée* (1948), *Histoire de la Roumanie* (1984), and the translation, *History of the Balkans* (1990). WhoFr, 1997/98

Castellane, Louis Charles *Pierre* de, born 25 October 1824 at Paris, he was an army officer in Algeria and later served in the Crimean war. After his retirement in 1855 he was a consul in Ancône and Budapest. His writings include *Souvenirs de la vie militaire en Afrique* (1852), *Military life in Algeria* (1853), and *Madgy; souvenirs de l'armée anglaise en Crimée* (1878). He died in Paris, 16 April 1883. DBF

Castellani, Vittorio M., fl. 1925, he was a sometime consul-general of Italy in Zürich, and wrote *La questione di Tangeri* (1926). Vaccaro

Castelli, Giulio, born 13 August 1882 at Genova, he was a political scientist and journalist. His writings include *L'estraterritorialità fittizia degli stranieri al Marocco* (1911), *Il XXIII anno santo* (1925), *Gli anni santi* (1949), and *La Chiesa e il fascismo* (19519. Chi è, 1928-1948; Firenze

Castelli, Mosé, born in 1816 at Firenze, he went in 1832 to Egypt, where he operated the printing house *Matba'at Kastilli*, or *al-Kastilliyah*. He died in 1884. A Francesco Gabrieli (1964), pp. 217-223

Castellino, Giorgio Raffaele, born in 1903, he wrote *Grammatica accadica introduttiva* (1970). LC

Castells, Francis de Paula, Rev., fl. 1916, his writings include *Origin of the Masonic degrees* (1928), and *Prehistoric man in Genesis; a study in Biblical anthropology* (1929). BLC

Castiau, Marcel, born 19th cent., he wrote *La Chine actuelle* (Bruxelles, 1926). NUC, pre-1956

Castiglioni, Arturo, born 10 April 1874 at Trieste, he was a professor of medicine and history of medicine at universities in Europe and America, and a member, or honorary member, of the major medical academies. His writings include *Storia della medicina* (1927). He died in Milano, 21 January 1953. DizBI de **Castiglioni**, Carlo Ottavio, conte, born 23 October 1785 at Milano, he was a linguist and attached to the Brera and Milano museums. His writings include *Mémoire géographique et numismatique sur la partie orientale de la Barbarie* (1826), and *Del'uso cui erano destinati i vetri con epigrafi cufiche e della origine, estensione e durata di esso* (1847). He died in Cornigliano near Genova, 10 April 1849. DizBI

Castiglioni, Giovanni Battista, born 3 January 1931 at Padua, he was since 1966 a professor of geography at the Università di Padua. Wholtaly, 1995

Castle, Edgar Bradshaw, born 23 December 1897, he studied at Oxford, and was a professor of education at the University of Hull until his retirement. From 1961 to 1965 he was a visiting professor at Makerere, Uganda. His writings include *Ancient education and today* (1961), *Principles of education for teachers in Africa* (1965), and *Growing up in East Africa* (1966). He died 10 September 1973. Who was who, 7

Casto, Earle Ray, born in 1884, his writings include *Building Bible names* (1939). He died in 1940. LC

Castonnet des Fosses, Henri, born 8 June 1846 at Angers, he was a president of the Société de géographie commerciale de Paris and travelled extensively. His writings include *Le Maroc* (1885), and *L'Inde française au XVII siècle* (1900). He died in Paris, 2 May 1898. DBF

Castrén (Кастрен), Matthias Alexander, born 2 December 1813 at Tervola, he received two doctorates at Helsinki with theses entitled *De affinitate declinatione in lingua Fennica* and *De nominum declinatione in lingua syraena* in 1839 and 1844 respectively. In the service of the St. Petersburg Academy of Science he travelled in northern Russia and Central Asia from 1838 to 1849. His writings include *Elementa grammatices syrjaenae* (1844), *Elementa grammatices tscheremisse conscripsit* (1845), and *Ethnologische Vorlesungen über die altaischen Völker* (1857). He died in Helsinki, 7 May 1852. BiobibSOT; GSE; ScBInd (3)

de **Castries**, Henri Marie de la Croix, comte, born 28 December 1850 at Paris, he graduated from the military college, Saint-Cyr, and was posted to Blida, Algeria, in 1874. Until 1880 he served with the Service des Affaires Indigènes. His writings include *Islam; impressions et études* (1896), and *Moulay Ismail et Jacques II* (1903); and he edited *Les Sources inédites de l'histoire du Maroc de 1530 à 1845* (1905). He died 10 May 1927. DBF; Hommes et destins II, 181-186; Peyronnet, p. 368

Castrillo Márquez, Rafaela, born 20th cent., she completed her study with a doctorate in Semitic philology. Certainly from 1992 to 1997 she was a professor of Arabic at the Universidad Complutense de Madrid. Her writings include the translation, *El Africa del Norte en el "A'mal al-A'mal" de Ibn al-Jatib* (1958), *58 incunables de medicina en la Universidad de Madrid* (1971), *Rhazes y Avicena en la Bibliotheca de Madrid* (1984), and *Catalogo de obras impresas en el siglo XVI* (1985). Arabismo, 1994, 1997

Castro, Antonio Paes de Sande e, fl. 1887, his writings include *Égypte* (Paris, 1901). LC

Castro, Francesco, fl. 1964, his writings include *Materiali e richerche sul nikah al-mut'a* (1974); and he edited *Scritti di diritto islamico* (1976). LC

de **Castro García**, Lázaro, his writings include *Historia de la muy noble y leal villa de Palenzuela* (1969), *La necrópolis de Pallentia* (1971), and *El Coro del Templo de Santoya, Palencia* (1974). LC

Castro-Rial y Canosa, Juan Manuel, born 9 February 1913, he completed his study with a doctorate in law and became a career diplomat. DBEC

Cat, Édouard Charles, born in 1856 at Arras (Pas-de-Calais), he was a professor of history and geography at the Faculté d'Alger. His writings include *Petite histoire de l'Algérie, Tunisie, Maroc* (1888-91), *Essai sur la province romaine de Mauritanie césarienne* (1891), and *À travers le désert* (1892). He died in 1903. Bulletin de la Société de géographie d'Alger 8 (1903), pp. 197-198; DBF

Catafago, Joseph, fl. 1848-1873. He wrote *An Arabic and English literary dictionary* (London, 1858).

Catalán Menéndez-Pidal, Diego, born in 1928, he was educated at Salamanca and Madrid and taught at various European universities before his appointment as professor of literature at the University of California at San Diego. His writings include *La escuela lingüística española y su concepción del lengaje* (1955), *Por campos del romancero* (1970), and the translation, *Crónica del moro Rasis* (1974). DrAS, 1974-1982; LC

Cataluccio, Francesco. His writings include *Il conflitto italo-etiopico* (1936), *Storia del nazionalismo arabo* (1939), *Balcani e Stretti nella politica russa* (1950), and *La questione coloniale nel'età moderna* (1950). LC

Catarivas, Daniel. He was joint author of *Histoire de Jérusalem d'Abraham à nos jours* (1965). LC

Cate, Curtis Wilson, born 22 May 1924 at Paris, he was a graduate of Harvard University and also studied at Paris and Oxford. He was a foreign correspondent and European editor of the *Atlantic monthly*. His writings include *Antoine de Saint-Exupéry* (1970), *George Sand* (1975), and *The ideas of August* (1978). ConAu, 53-56; LC; WhoE, 1979/80

Catellani, Enrico Levi, born 12 June 1856 at Padova, he was a professor of law at the Università di Padova and became a senator in 1920. His writings include *Il dirirro internazionale privato e i suoi recenti progressi* (1883-1888), and *Le colonie e la Conferenza di Berlino* (1885). He died in 1940. Chi è, 1928; IndBI (5)

Catford, Sir John Robin, born 11 January 1923, he was educated at the University of St Andrews and St John's College, Cambridge. From 1946 to 1955 he was in the Sudan Civil Service, and from 1982 to 1993, Secretary for Appointments to the Prime Minister and Ecclesiastical Secretary to the Lord Chancellor. *Who's who*, 1997

Cathy, Armand, born 19th cent., he was in 1907 a member of the Société de géographie de Marseille.

Caton, Margaret Louise, born 20th cent., she received a Ph.D. in 1983 from the University of California, Los Angeles, for *The classical "tasnif"; a genre of Persian vocal music.* LC

Caton-Thompson, Gertrude, born 1 February 1888 at London, she was educated privately and was a specialist in pre-dynastic Egypt. She carried on field work at Abydos, the Northern Faiyum Oasis, and in the Hadhramawt. She was highly honoured and awarded an honorary doctorate by Cambridge University in 1954. Her writings include *The Desert Fayum* (1935), and her reminiscences *Mixed memoirs* (1983). Her notes, papers, correspondence, etc., on pre-historic Faiyum are in the Archive of the Griffith Institute, Ashmolean Museum, Oxford. She died 18 April 1985. Egyptology; Who was who, 8

Catrice, Paul, born in 1905, he was affiliated with the Centre des hautes études d'administration musul-mane, Paris. His writings include *Paul Drach, ancien rabbin et orientaliste chrétien* (1978). LC

Catroux, Georges Albert Julien, born 29 January 1877 at Limoges, he was a graduate of the military college of Saint-Cyr, and the Centre des Hautes Études Militaires. He had a military, administrative, and diplomatic career in Algeria, Morocco, Europe, and the Near and the Far East. He served as Governor-General of Algeria, Commissioner for the Coordination of Muslim Affairs and as French ambassador to the Soviet Union. His writings include *Deux missions en Moyen-Orient, 1919-1922* (1958). He died 21 December 1969. WhoFr, 1953; Who was who, 6

Catsiapis, Jean, fl. 1977, he was an assistant at the Université de Paris and wrote *La Grèce, dixième membre des communautés européennes* (1980).

Catta, Emmanuel, fl. 1966, he was head of the Service des Études et de Documentation Générale at the Compagnie française des Pétroles, and attached to the Centre des Hautes Études Administratives pour l'Afrique et l'Asie Modernes.

Cattan, Henry, born 26 February 1906 at Jerusalem, he studied journalism at London, and law at Paris. He was a member of the Palestine and Syrian bars since 1932, and a sometime tutor at the Jerusalem Law School. His writings include *Palestine and international law* (1973), *Jerusalem; politics and government* (1981), and *The Palestine question* (1988). He died in Paris, 17 April 1992. ConAu, 29-32; WrDr, 1976/78-1990/92; WRMEA 11 ii (July 1992), p. 100

Cattaui, Joseph Aslan Pasha, born in 1861, he was an Egyptian senator, and vice-president of the Jewish Community in Cairo. Since 1 December 1924 he was Minister of Finance. He was a sometime director of the National Bank of Egypt. His writings include *Coup d'œil sur la chronologie de la nation égyptienne* (1931), and *Le Khédive Isma'il et la dette de l'Égypte* (1935). He died in 1942. EncJud; Wininger

Catteloup, Bon Auguste, fl. 1839-1863, his writings include *Recherches sur la dyssenterie du nord de l'Afrique* (1851), *De la cachexie paludénne en Algérie* (1852), and *Essai d'une topographie médicale du bassin de Tlemcen* (1854). BN; NUC, pre-1956

Caucig, Franz von, fl. 1959-1969, he spent nearly thirty years in the Middle East, where he was a correspondent for the Vereinigte Wirtschaftsdienste, Frankfurt, and the Bundesstelle für Auslands-information, Köln. His writings include two travel guides, *Türkei* (1956), and *Jordanien und Libanon* (1962). Sezgin

Caudel, Maurice, fl. 1899. His writings include *Supplément à la "Législation de Tunisie" de Maurice Bompard* (1896), and *Les premières invasions arabes dans l'Afrique du nord* (1900). BN

Caudhuri, E. Ema. Phayeja Ahamada *see* Choudhury, A. M. Faiz Ahmad

Caulk, Richard Alan, born in 1937, he was a student of Ethiopian history and completed his Ph.D. work in 1966 at the University of London with the presentation of his thesis, *The origins and development of the foreign policy of Menelik II, 1865-1896*. Thereafter he taught history at Addis Abeba from 1966 to 1977, when he returned to the United States. He taught briefly at UCLA and Columbia, before he obtained a position at Camden College of Rutgers University, and held it until his death in September 1983. *International journal of African historical studies* 17 (1984), p. 200

Cauneille, August François, born 20 September 1911 at Caudiès-de-Fenouillères (Pyrénées-Orientales), he graduated in 1931 from the military college, Saint-Cyr. In 1938 he took a preparatory course at the Service des Affaires Indigènes d'Algérie et de Tunisie and was then posted to the Compagnies sahariennes de l'Ouest. In April of 1939 he began his Saharan sojourn in western Algeria which was to last, nearly uninterrupted, for fourteen years. From 1951 to 1953 he served as batttalion com-mander in the Fezzan until ill-health obliged him to resign from the military. He was brevetted at the Centre de hautes études d'administration musulmane, Paris, 12 July 1954. After his retirement he was much involved in the local history and community affairs of his native town. His writings include *Les Chaanba (leur nomadisme); évolution de la tribu durant l'administration française* (1968). He died 8 September 1965. *L'Afrique et l'Asie* 72 (1965), pp. 72-73; Unesco

Causeret, Charles, born 19th cent., he received a doctorate in 1886 from the Faculté des lettres de Paris for his thesis, *De Phædri sermone grammaticae observationes*. His writings include *Béranger* (1895), and *Ce qu'il faut connaître de Rabelais* (1927). BN

Caussin de Perceval, Armand Pierre, born 11 January 1795 at Paris, he was a graduate of the Collège des jeunes de langue, and since 1814, *élève interprète* in Constantinople. He visited Syria and Lebanon, and, for a year, was a dragoman in Aleppo before returning to Paris in 1821. In 1822 he was appointed to the chair of colloquial Arabic at Paris, and in 1849, admitted to the Académie des inscriptions. His writings include *Grammaire arabe vulgaire* (1824), and *Essai sur l'histoire des arabes* (1847-48). He died in January of 1871. DBF; Fück

Caussin de Perceval, Jean Baptiste Jacques Antoine, born in 1759, he was since 1778 affiliated with the Département des manuscrits at the Cabinet des antiques, Paris. He was a sometime professor of Arabic at the Collège de France. He translated and/or edited works of Ibn Yunus, al-Hariri, al-Nuwayri, and al-Zawzani as well as *Alf laylah wa-laylah*, and *al-Mu'allaqāt*. BN; DBF; Fück

Cauvain, Henri Alexis, born in 1815, he studied law at Paris and he beame a barrister in the Cour de Paris, and an editor at *le Constitutionnel*. His writings include *Code de faillites* (1841), and *De la colonisation de l'Algérie* (1857). He died 13 October 1858. DBF; Vapereau

Cauvet, Gaston Edouard Jules, born 23 May 1860 at Douai (Nord). On 6 October 1881, one year after his graduation from the military college of Saint-Cyr, he joined the Service des Affaires indigènes de l'Algérie. He was the last of a breed of scholarly military administrators who spent his entire career at the former *Bureaux arabes*. During his term at El-Goléa he experimented successfully with artesian irrigation (1888-1890). In 1902 he was posted to In-Salah to organize the Compagnie des Oasis sahariennes du Tidikelt. His writings include *Le chameau* (1925-26), and *Les berbères en Amérique* (1930). He died in Alger, 24 March 1950. Peyronnet, pp. 478-80; *Travaux de l'Institut de Recherches Sahariennes* 7 (1951), pp. 7-14

Cauvin, Charles, born in 1868 at Toulouse, he was a captain in the *Infanterie coloniale*, and an explorer of the Sahara and the French Sudan. He organized the Senegal *méharistes* in Timbuctu (1905) in order to provide support for the French forces coming from southern Algeria. He defeated the Senoussis in 1911 and was *chef du territoire de Tombouctou* until 1914. He served in the European war until he was wounded in 1917. His writings include *Une reconnaissance en Afrique centrale; combat de Fouka, Tchad* (1912). He died 6 September 1929. BN; DBF

Cavaignac, Godefroy Éléonore Louis, born in 1801 at Paris, he was a politician who spent a number of years in Algeria. He died in Paris, 5 May 1845. DBF

Cavallaro, Evaldo. In 1976 he published *Infrastrutture e decollo economico; il caso dello Zaire*. LC

Cavallo, Adolph Salvatore, born 20th cent., he was successively affiliated with the Museum of Fine Arts, Boston, and the Metropolitan Museum of Art, New York. His writings include *Needlework* (1979), and *Medieval tapestries in the Metropolitan Museum of Art* (1993). LC

Cavanagh, John Henry, born 20 August 1955 at Boston, Mass., he studied at Dartmouth College and Princeton University. After being affiliated with the World Health Organization, Genève, he became in 1983 a fellow of the Institute for Policy Studies, Washington, D.C. He was joint author of *The world in their web; dynamics of textile multinationals* (1981), *Plundering paradise* (1993), and *Global dreams*

(1994). In 1985 he edited *Meeting the corporate challenge; a handbook on corporate campaigns.* LC; WhoAm, 1988-1998

Cave, Sir Basil Shillito, born 14 November 1865, he was in the British consular service posted predominantly to East Africa until his retirement in 1924. He died 9 October 1931. Who was who, 3

Cavendish, Lady Lucy Caroline (Lyttelton), 1841-1925. Her writings include *Lyrical poems* (1912), and *Diary of Lady Frederick Cavendish;* edited by John Bailey (1927). LC

Cavero, Maria Luisa, fl. 1971, she wrote *Granada; poemas traducidos y presentados* (1969). ZKO

Cavid Bey, Mehmed, born in 1875 at Salonika (Selânik), he was a graduate of the Yüksek Mülkiye Okulu, Constantinople, and a Young Turk economist, financier, and a politician. Under Atatürk, he was tried on charges of high treason and, although nothing was proved against him, he was hanged in Ankara, 26 August 1926. His writings include *'Ilm-i iktisad* (1905-1912). EI²; Meydan; Zürcher

Cayré, Fulbert, born 19th cent., he wrote *Précis de patrologie* (1927), and its translation, *Manual of patrology and history of theology* (1927-30). LC

Cazacu, Matei, born 20th cent., his writings include *L'histoire du Prince Dracula en Europe centrale et orientale* (1988), originally presented as his thesis, (*élève diplômé* at the École pratique des hautes études). In 1987 he was a contributing author to *Sprachen und Nationen im Balkanraum.* LC

de **Cazalès**, Edmond, born 31 August 1804 at Grenade (Haute-Garonne), he studied law and was a *juge auditeur,* before turning to theology. He was ordained in 1843, and in 1845, he was appointed director of the Séminaire de Nîmes. His writings include *Études historiques et politiques sur l'Allemagne contemporaine* (1853), and *Nos maux et leurs remèdes* (1876). He died 23 January 1876. BDF

Cazalet, Victor Alexander, lieutenant-colonel, born 27 December 1896, he was educated at Eton and Christ Church College, Oxford. He had a military, political and diplomatic career, and travelled extensively in the Middle East. He died 4 July 1943. Who was who, 4

Cazel, Fred Augustus, born 25 February 1921 at Asheville, N.C., he received a doctorate in 1948 from Johns Hopkins University, Baltimore, Md. From 1947 until his retirement he held a variety of positions at American universities. His writings include *Roll of divers accounts for the early years of the reign of Henry III* (1982). ConAu 9-10; DrAS 1974, 1978, 1982

Cazemajou, Gabriel Marius, born 10 December 1864 at Marseille, he was a captain in the Corps of Engineers and explored the direct route from Nefta, southern Tunisia, to Ghadamès, Fezzan. He was killed on a subsequent exploration in Zinder country, Niger, 5 May 1898. DBF; Henze

Cazenave, Jean, born 19th cent., he was in 1923 a *professeur agrégé* at the Lycée d'Alger. His writings include *La Colonisation en Algérie* (1900). NUC, pre-1956

Cazès, David, born in 1851 at Tetuan, he was a Moroccan historian and educator who was affiliated with the Alliance israélite universelle almost from its inception. His writings include *Essai sur l'histoire des Israélites de Tunisie* (1888), and *Notes bibliographiques sur la littérature juive-tunisienne* (1893). He died in 1913. BN; EncJud

Céard, Louis Joseph, born 24 July 1878 at Chaumont (Haute-Marne), he was a medical doctor who spent the years from 1923 to 1929 at Colombe-Béchar, Algeria. *Médecin commandant* since 25 September 1928, he was of real influence in the region. Together with the doctors H. J. E. Foley and Lucien Raynaud he published a large number of medical, social as well as economic studies. He wrote *Heures vecues* (1911). BN; Peyronnet, p. 824

Ceccaldi, Colonna, 1865- *see* Colonna Ceccaldi, Georges

Cecchi, Antonio, born 28 January 1849 at Pesaro, Italy, he was a naval officer and an explorer of the sources of the Nile. In 1894 he was consul in Zanzibar. He was killed in the Lafole massacres, 26 November 1896. In 1982, Francisco Bonasera published *L'opera geografico-economico di Antonio Cecchi.* DizBI; Embacher; Henze; LC; Rivista delle colonie 9 (1935), pp. 111-121; VIA, 71-73

Cecconi, Osiris, born 20th cent., he received a doctorate in 1975 from the Université de Paris I for his thesis, *Croissance et typologie culturelle.* His writings include *La société industrielle* (1972), *Croissance économique et sous-développement culturel* (1975), and *Désir et pouvoir* (1983). LC

Cecil, Cecil O. He was a lieutenant in the U.S. Air Force, and received his M.A. in 1964 from the School of Advanced International Studies, Johns Hopkins University, Baltimore, Md.

Cederquist (Cederqvist), Karl, born 28 October 1854 at Fellingbro, Sweden, he studied at the Johannelunds Missionsinstitut and thereafter served as a missionary in Addis Abeba, whence he made evangelistic tours among the Abyssinians and Galla between 1898 and his death 11 November 1919. SMK

Cedillo, Conde de, 1862-1934 *see* López de Ayala, Jerónimo Conde de Cedillo, visconde de Palazuelos

Ćehajić, Džemal, fl. 1969, his writings include *Derviški redovi u jugoslovenskim zemljama sa posebnim osvrtom na Bosnu i Hercegovinu* (1986), and he translated *Bulbulistan* from the Persian of Shaykh Fawzi (1973). LC; ZKO

Cejpek, Jiří, born 20 February 1921 at Wien, but educated in Praha, where he also received a Dr.phil. for *Iranica; einige Bemerkungen über manche Ausdrucksweisen der durativen Aktionsart im Iranischen.* Thereafter he was attached to a variety of institutes of the Czechoslovak Academy of Sciences. His writings include contributions to Jan Rypka's *History of Iranian literature.* He died 18 April 1986. *Archiv orientální* 56 (1988), 62-63

Celal Nuri, 1877-1939 *see* Ileri, Celal Nuri

Celâsun, Merih, he was in 1971 an instructor at the Department of Mathematics in the Middle East Technical University, Ankara. His writings include *Perspectives of economic growth in Turkey* (1974), and *Sources of industrial growth and structural development; the case of Turkey* (1983). LC

Celentano, Giuseppe, fl. 1974, his writings include *Due scritti medici di Al-Kindi* (1979), and *L'epistola di Al-Kindi sulla sfera armillare* (1982). LC

Célérier, Jean, born 30 November 1887 at Château-Ponsac (Haute-Vienne), he was a graduate of l'École normale supérieure and served, and was wounded, in the first World War. Since 1917 he first taught in Morocco and then in Casanblanca and Rabat, where he became a professor at l'Institut des hautes études marocaines. His writings include *Le Maroc* (1931). He died at his retirement retreat in Pau, 12 August 1962. *Revue de géographie du Maroc* n° 3/4 (1963), pp. 7-8

Čelić, Džemal, fl. 1953. His writings include *Sarajevo i okolica* (1979), and *Sarajevo and its surroundings* (1980); in 1969 he was joint author of *Stari mostovi u Bosni i Hercegovini.* LC

Celil, Celile, 1936- *see* Dzalil, Dzahlile

Cella, Pado della, born in 1792 at Stefano d'Aveto, Italy, he was a physician and accompanied Ahmad, the son of the Pasha of Tarabulus, on a punitive expedition during which he collected plants for Dr. Domenico Viviani (1772-1840), who described them in his *Florae libycae specimen* (1824). His writings include *Viaggio da Tripoli di Barberia alle frontiere occidentali dell'Egitto* (1819), and the translations, *Reise von Tripoli an die Grenzen von Aegypten* (1821), and *Narrative of an expedition from Tripoli in Barbary to the western frontier of Egypt* (1822). He died in Genova, 22 May 1854. LC; VIA, pp. 33-34

Celnarová, Xénia, born 18 April 1944 in Slovakia, she was a contributing author to *Premeny sveta v literatúrach* (1990). LC; Schoeberlein

Celsius, Olof, born 19 July 1670 at Uppsala, he was a student of Oriental languages and botany, and successively appointed to the chairs of Greek, Oriental languages, and theology, and filled the office of provost of the cathedral at Uppsala. He died in Uppsala, 24 June 1756 EncAm; GDU; Meyers; SBL

Cemal Paşa, Ahmed, born in 1872 at Mytilene, Ottoman Turkey, he was successively *mutasarrif* of Üsküdar, *vali* of Adana, and later of Baghdad, military governor of Constantinople, commander of the first Army Corps, and Minister of the Navy. During the first World War he was governor-general of Syria and chief-of-staff of the Ottoman forces operating on the Egyptian front. His writings include *Memoirs of a Turkish statesman, 1913-1919* (1973). He was assassinated in Tiflis, 21 July 1922. AnaBrit; EI²; Meydan; *Orient & Occident* 2 (1922), pp. 536-37; *Orient-Rundschau*, 15 September 1922, pp. 1-3; Zürcher

Cemil, Mesud, fl. 1942, his writings include *Tanburî Cemil'in hayatı* (1947). NUC, pre-1956

Cénival, Pierre Hellouin de, born 20 November 1888 at Château de la Marre (Bretagne), he studied law, and graduated in 1912 from l'École des chartes. From 1919 to 1927 he was a keeper at the Archives et Bibliothèque du Protectorat à Rabat. He was a sometime director of l'Institut des hautes études marocaines. He edited the *Chronique de Santa-Cruz du Cap de Gué* (1934). He died in 1937. DBF; *Hommes et destins*, vol. 7, pp. 112-113; *Index Islamicus* (2)

Censoni, Domenico, fl. 1947, his writings include *L'Italia nel Sudan orientale* (1941), and *La politica francese nel Vicino Oriente* (1948). Firenze; NUC, pre-1956

Centlivres-Demont, Micheline, born 16 June 1930 at Rotterdam, she received a doctorate in 1971 from the Université de Neuchâtel for her thesis, *Une communauté de poitiers en Iran*. Her writings include *Faïences des XIXe et XXe siècles* (1975). In 1983 she edited *Migrations en Asie*, and in 1988 she jointly published with her husband *Et si on parlait de l'Afghanistan?* LC; Schoeberlein; WWASS, 1989

Centlivres-Demont, Pierre, born 7 August 1933 at Mont-la-Ville, Switzerland, he received a doctorate in 1972 for his thesis, *Un bazar d'Asie centrale*. From 1974 until his retirement he was a professor of anthropology and director of the Institut d'ethnologie de l'Université de Neuchâtel. His writings include *L'ethnologie dans le dialogue interculturel* (1983), and *Paysannerie et pouvoir en Afghanistan* (1985). In 1988 he was joint author, with his wife, of *Et si on parlait de l'Afghanistan?*. IWWAS, 1975/76; LC; Schoeberlein; *Who's who in Switzerland*, 1996/97; WWASS, 1989

Çepel, Necmettin, Dr., born in 1928 at Bursa, he was since 1963 a professor at Toprak Ilmi ve Ekoloji Enstitüsü Istanbul Üniversitesi. His writings include *Orman ekoloji* (1978), and *Ekoloji terimleri sözlüğü* (1982). Kim kimdir, 1985

Cepollaro, Armando, fl. 1941, his writings include *I Swahili e la loro lingua* (1962), and he was joint editor of *I paesi africani; profili storico-geografici* (1967). LC

Cerbella, Gino, fl. 1953, his writings include *Nuhab; letture scelte ad uso delle scuole medie coloniali* (1936), and *Le caratteristiche dei Tuàregh del Sud Libico* (1943), and he was joint author, with Mustafa Ageli, of *Le feste musulmane in Tripoli; appunti etnografici* (1949). LC

Cereceda, J. D., 1881-1943 *see* Dantín Cereceda, Juan

Çernis, Volf, he was a sometime member of the Istanbul bar. His writings include *Tatbikattan çizgiler* (1962). He died 8 February 1977. LC

Cernovodeanu, Paul, born 18th cent., he received a Dr.habil. in 1811 in classical philology at Jena, and later studied Persian under Hammer-Purgstall at Wien. Through the good offices of his teacher he was in 1826 appointed a professor of Oriental languages at Erlangen, a post which he held until 1840.

Cernovodeanu, Paul I., fl. 1967, his writings include *Societatea feudală românească văzută de călători străini* (1973), *Revista istorică română, 1931-1974* (1977), and the translation *England's trade policy in the Levant* (1972). Together with Dimitrie Cantemir he published *Extracts from the "History of the Ottoman Empire"* (1973). LC

Cerović, Vasilije, born 20th cent., he was in 1973 a colonel in the Yugoslav Army. His writings include *Karakter i zadaci Jugoslovenske narodne armije* (1966). LC

Cerqua, Clelia Sarnelli *see* Sarnelli Cerqua, Clelia

Cerulli, Enrico, born 15 February 1898 at Napoli. After pursuing Ethiopic and Islamic studies at university, he carried on field work in Somaliland and Abyssinia for well over ten years, and four years in Iran from 1950 to 1954. He was a member of the major academies, and received honorary doctorates from Bruxelles, Roma, and Manchester. His writings include *The folkliterature of the Galla of southern Abyssinia* (1922), *Documenti arabi per la storia dell'Etiopia* (1931), and *Islam di ieri e di oggi* (1971). BioB134; Chi è, 1948; IntWW, 1974-1981/82; Unesco; WhoWor, 1974

Cervera, Francesc Maria, born in 1858 at Valencia, he entered the Franciscan Order and served in Morocco. In 1908 he was appointed Apostolic vicar of Morocco and bishop of Fessea. In 1923 he was titular archbishop of Pompeiòpolis. He died in Tanger, 1926. Dicc bio

Cervin, Vladimir Bohdan, born 12 March 1914 at St. Petersburg, he was educated at Wien, AUB, Bruxelles, and Praha, where he received a doctorate in social psychology in 1948. He spent almost six years in Afghanistan studying social conditions. Following research and teaching at Montreal universities, he was a professor of psychology at the University of Windsor, Ontario. AmM&WSc, 1973 S, 1978 S

César, Vitoriano José, 1860-1939. His writings include *Invasões francesas em Portugal* (1904-1910), and *A fundação de monarquía portugesa* (1927). LC

Cesari, Cesare, born 28 March 1870 at Modena, Italy, he was a general and affiliated with the Istituto Coloniale Italiano; he was a sometime professor of colonial studies at Università di Roma. His writings include *L'Asia turca; la futura questione d'Oriente* (1914), *Questione del vicino Oriente* (1914), *Colonie e possedimenti coloniali* (1923), *Problemi d'Oriente e imperialismo americano* (1939), and *L'imperio coloniale francese; origini e sviluppo* (1941). Chi è, 1928-1940

Cesàro, Antonio, born 25 April 1901 at Napoli. After Arabic studies at the Istituto Orientale di Napoli, he was for some time affiliated with the Ministerio dell'Africa Italiana in Tripolitania, before becoming director of the Ufficio Studi del Governo della Libia in 1934. In the 1940s and 1950s he taught Arabic and Berber languages at Napoli. His writings include the translation from the Arabic of 'Abd al-Salam ibn 'Uthman, *Santuari islamici nel secolo XVII in Tripolitania* (Tripoli, 1933). He died in Napoli, 3 June 1968. *Annali* (di) *Istituto Orientale di Napoli*, n.s. 18 (1968), pp. 469-470

Ceulemans, Pierre Maurice, born 2 December 1934 at Bruxelles, he was a banker who wrote *La Question arabe et le Congo, 1883-1892* (1959). WhoWor, 1976/77

Ceyp, A. J., fl. 1888-1892, he was for many years a teacher at the Tehran Military Academy. Note

Chabanier, Eugène, fl. 1931-1954, he wrote *L'Expression verbale des valeurs numériques et des fonctions des anciens grecs aux occidentaux du debuts de la Renaissance éclairée par un théorème d'Aristote* (1954). NUC, pre-1956

Chabas, Jean, fl. 1959, his writings include *Le Mariage et le divorce dans les coutumes des Ouolofs habitant les grands centres du Sénégal* (1952). LC

Chabas y Llorens, Roque, born 9 May 1844 at Dénia, Spain, he was a clergyman and historian whose writings include *Historia de la ciudad de Dénia* (1874), *Los mozárabes valencianos* (1891), and *Génesis del derecho foral de Valencia* (1902). He died in Valencia, 20 April 1912. Dicc bio; Ossorio

Chabassière, Jules Antoine, born 18 April 1836 at Châteauneuf-sur-Loire, he originated from a family of modest substance. After some time spent in the Service hydrologique, he enlisted in the 3e régiment de zouaves. Since 1860 he was attached to the Algerian Service topographique and served as a *triangulateur* and *calculateur de trigonométrie*. Thereafter he held civic offices and pursued an interest in archaeology. His writings include *La sécurité en mer; étude d'un bateau genre bi-coque* (1883), *Question des eaux, assainissement et irrigation de la plaine, desséchement de 2500 hectares de marais; requête à M. le gouverneur général de l'Algérie au nom de tous les habitants* [du] *Département de Constantine, commun d'Aïn-M'Lila* (1884), and *Une année de mairie dans le fief des Ouled-Rahmoun, 17 septembre 1893* (1893). At the Congrès des Sociétés savantes, held 1899 in Toulouse, he was awarded the *Palmes d'Officier d'Académie*. BN; Carnoy 10²

Chabaud-Arnault (Arnauld), born in 1839, he was the author of *Histoire des flottes militaires* (1889), and is also said to be called Adolphe and Charles. BN; DBF

Chabert, Alexandre Vladimir, born 7 April 1915 at Toutrakan, Bulgaria, he received a doctorate in 1940 for his thesis, *La coopération en Roumanie*. From 1958 to 1960 he was a professor at the Faculté de droit d'Alger. Since 1961 he was a professor at Strasbourg. His writings include *Essai sur les mouvements des prix et des revenues en France de 1798 à 1820* (1945-49). Unesco; WhoFr, 1975-1982

Chabert, Thomas, 1766-1841, professor of Oriental languages. His writings include *Hadji Bektache, ou la création des Janissaires, drame en langue turque* (Vienne, 1810), and the translation, *Latifi, oder biographische Nachrichten von vorzüglichen Dichtern* (Zürich, 1810). BN; Neuer Nekrolog der Deutschen

Chabot, Jean Baptiste, born 16 February 1860, he was a Syriac scholar whose writings include *Les Langues et les littératures araméennes* (1910), and *La Littérature syriaque* (1935), as well as catalogues of Syriac manuscripts in various library collections. He died 7 January 1948. NUC, pre-1956

Chabouillet, Pierre Marie Anatole, born 18 July 1814, he was a numismatist who in 1832 joined the Cabinet des médailles in the Bibliothèque royale, Paris. His writings include *Catalogue des poinçons, coins et médailles du musée monétaire de la Commission des monnaies et médailles* (1833), and *Catalogue général et raisonné des camées et pierres gravées de la Bibliothèque impériale* (1858). He died 5 January 1899. BN; DBF

Chabrier, Jean-Claude, fl. 1974, he received doctorates in medicine, and musicology in 1976 from the Université de Paris IV for his thesis, *Un mouvement de réhabilitation de la musique et du luth, 1907 à 1975*, and a diploma in Oriental languages. In 1993 he was a research fellow at the Séminaire pratique d'analyse des musiques traditionnelles, CNRS, Paris. EURAMES; LC; THESAM, 3

Chabrov, Georgii Nikolaevich, born 19 January 1904 at St. Petersburg, he there graduated in 1927 from the Faculty of Philology and Material Culture. In 1936 he joined the Republic Museum of Arts in Tashkent. From 1948 to 1966 he was affiliated with the Central Asian State University, Tashkent, and subsequently headed the bibliographical division of the USSR Nizami State Pedagogical Institute, Tashkent. He received a doctorate in historical sciences in 1966 and in 1968 became a professor. He edited Некоторые вопросы международных отношений на Востоке (1960), and he was joint editor of История Средней Азии и Узбекистана (1956). He died on 22 January 1986. Manuscripta orientalia 6, no. 4 (2000), pp. 58-59; UzbekSE, vol. 12, p. 462

Chachanof, Alexander, 1866- *see* Khakhanov, Aleksandr Solomonovich

Chackerian, Richard, born 20th cent., his writings include *Federal aids to Washington State and local governments* (1966). He was joint author of *Political development and bureacracy in Libya* (1977), and *Power in society* (1984). LC

Chad, Carlos, S.J., born 20th cent., his writings include *Les Dynastes d'Emèse* (1972), a work which the author presented originally in 1967 as his thesis at the Université de Paris. LC

Chadbourn, Philip Hemenway, fl. 1919. He was a lieutenant in aviation and from 1916 to 1917, special assistant to the American Ambassador to Russia at Petrograd. *Asia*, 1919

Chadwick, Nora née Kershaw, born 28 January 1891 in England, and educated at Newnham College, Cambridge, she was a lecturer in English language and literature at British universities, an honorary life fellow of Newnham College, Commander of the Order of the British Empire, as well as recipient of honorary doctorates. Her writings include *Russian heroic poetry* (1932), *The beginnings of Rusian history* (1946), and, with V. Zhirmunsky, *Oral epics of Central Asia* (1969). She died 24 April 1972. ConAu 1; WhE&EA

Chaffetz, David, born 20th cent., his writings include *Afghanistan, Russia's Vietnam?* (1979), and *A Journey through Afghanistan* (1981). LC

Chafik, Ahmad, 1860-1940 *see* Ahmad Shafiq

Chaghatai (Chaghtai), Muhammad Abdulla, born 23 November 1896 at Lahore, he was educated at Government Technical School, and Mayo School of Arts, both Lahore, and the Thomason Engineering College, Rurki. From 1914 to 1933 he pursued a teaching career in India. In 1936 he travelled to Europe, followed by art study at Paris from 1936 to 1938, and received a doctorate in letters for his thesis, *Le Tadj Mahal d'Agra*. Thereafter he taught again in India until partition, when he moved back to Lahore to pursue his interest in research and teaching, but predominantly occupied by his publishing enterprise in order to make a living. His writings include *The Badshahi Masjid* (1972), and *Pak o Hind men Islami khattati* (1976). *Ancient Pakistan* 2 (1965/66), pp. 215-219; LC

Chaikin, Konstantin Ivanovich, born in 1889 at Moscow, he graduated in 1916 from Lazarev Institute of Oriental Languages, Moscow. Thereafter he was an interpreter at the Soviet legation in Iran. He wrote *Краткий очерк новейшей персидской литературы* (1928). He died in 1939. Miliband

Chaikovskaia (Чайковская), Angelina Ivanovna, fl. 1975, her writings include *Тюркская грамматика в арабоязычных филологических трактатах XIII-XIV вв.* (1981).

Chaillé-Longue, Charles, born 2 July 1842 at Princes Anne, Md., he joined the Egyptian Army in 1869, and in 1874, was chief of staff to General C. Gordon in the Sudan. In the service of the Khedive Ismail he went on a secret mission to Uganda, and on his return journey he explored the sources of the Nile and its adjacent territory. On account of poor health he returned to the United States in 1877 to study law at Columbia University. He returned to Egypt in 1882 to practice international law in Alexan-dria. His writings include *Central Africa* (1876), *L'Afrique centrale* (1888), *The three prophets* (1884), *L'Egypte et ses provinces perdues* (1892), *My life in four continents* (1912). "He wrote bombastically of his own exploits and was a reckless detractor of Gordon; he rendered some service to the American subjects of Alexandria during the bombardment and troubles of 1882" (Hill). He died in Virginia Beach, Va., 24 March 1917. DAB; Henze; Hill; Shavit-Africa; WhAm, 1

Chaillet, L. His writings include *Concordance inédite des calendriers grégorien et musulman* (Alger, 1857). BN

Chailley (Chailley-Bert), Joseph, born 4 March 1857 at St.-Florentin (Yonne), he received a doctorate in 1882 from the Faculté de droit de Paris for his thesis, *L'adultère à Rome avant et sous la loi Julia*. He was a sometime professor at l'École des sciences politiques, founder of l'Institut colonial international, and a politician. His writings include *L'émigration des femmes aux colonies* (1897), *La colonisation de l'Indo-chine* (1892), and *L'Inde britannique* (1910). He died in 1928. DBF

Chailley, Marcel, born 16 September 1910 at Douai (Nord), he was a graduate of the military college, Saint-Cyr, and was predominantly posted to French Africa. His writings include *Notes sur les 'Afar de la région de Tadjoura* (1966). He died in Vanves, 4 October 1962. *Hommes et destins*, I, pp. 135-136

Chailley-Bert, Joseph, 1857-1928 *see* Chailley, Joseph

Chaillou, Lucien, fl. 1979, he was a sometime mayor, and delegate to the Assemblée algérienne. He wrote *Textes pour servir à l'histoire de l'Algérie au XVIIIe siècle* (1979), and edited *L'Algérie en 1781; mémoire du consul Césaire Philippe Vallière* (1974). LC

Chaine, M., born in 1873, his writings include *Grammaire éthiopienne* (1907), and *La chronologie des temps chrétiens de l'Égypte et de l'Éthiopie* (1925). NUC, pre-1956

Chaitanya, Krishna. His writings include *Manuscript, Moghul and Deccani traditions* (1979). ZKO

Chaix, Paul Georges Gabriel, born 1 October 1808 at Crest (Drôme), he studied at the Université de Genève, and was a professor of geography and history at Genève from 1836 until his retirement in 1883. In the 1840s he travelled to Greece and Egypt. He was a president of the Société physique de Genève. His *Précis de géographie élémentaire* went through six editions until 1864. He died in 1901. DBF

Chaix-Ruy, Jules, born 7 November 1896 at Avignon. After obtaining a doctorate in letters, he held a variety of teaching positions at colleges and universities throughout France. From 1948 to 1960 he was a professor of philosophy at the Faculté des lettres d'Alger. His writings include *Les Dimensions de l'être et du temps* (1953), *Ernest Renan* (1956), and *Kafka* (1968). WhoFr, 1967/68-1975/76

Chakhtoura, Maria, fl. 1972, she wrote *La guerre des graffiti; Liban, 1975-1978* (1978). LC

Chakravarti, Sukha Ranjan, born 20th cent., he received a doctorate from Nagpur University and served as a faculty member at the South Asia Studies Centre, University of Rajasthan, Jaipur, from 1972 to 1992. In 1994 he was affiliated with the South Asian Studies Division of the School of International Studies, Jawarharlal Nehru University, New Delhi. His writings include *Bangladesh* (1986), and *Foreign policy of Bangladesh* (1994). LC

Chakravarty, Amiya Chandra, born 10 April 1901 at Serampore, Bengal, he was educated in India and at Oxford, where he received a doctorate in 1936. He was for many years associated with Rabindranath Tagore, partly as his private secretary. Thereafter he was a professor of English literature and lectured in the United States and throughout the world. His writings include *The dynasts and the post-war age in poetry* (1938), *The Indian testimony* (1953), and *Modern humanism* (1968). ConAu 1 rev.; DrAS, 1974; IntAu&W, 1977; LC

Chakravarty, Sukha Ranjan *see* Chakravarti, Sukha Ranjan

Chakraverti, Ashish K., fl. 1968, he was joint author of *Structural interdependence of the Turkish economy* (Ankara, 1970), and *Flow-structure of imports, Turkish economy, 1967 and 1968* (Ankara, 1973). LC

Chalandon, Fernand, born 10 February 1875 at Lyon, he graduated in 1899 from l'École des chartes. He became an archivist and palaeographer whose writings include *Essai sur le règne d'Alexis Ier Comnène* (1900), a work for which he was awarded the prix Bordin of the Académie des inscriptions. He died in Lausanne, 31 October 1921. DBF

Chalatianz, Bagrat *see* Khalat'iants', Bagrat

Chaliand, Gérard, born in 1934, he was a sometime chairman of the Association France Kurdistan. His writings include *La question kurde* (1961), *Le malheur kurde* (1992), *Les bâtisseurs d'histoire* (1995), *Les empires nomades de la Mongolie au Danube* (1995), and the translation *The Kurdish tragedy* (1994); and he was joint author of *L'Algérie indépendante* (1972), and *Le génocide des arméniens, 1915-1917* (1980). LC

Chalilov, Džabar Asadulla ogly *see* Khalilov, Dzhabbar Asadulla ogly

Challemel-Lacour, Paul Armand, born 19 May 1827 at Avranches (Manche), he was a graduate of l'École normale supérieure, and thereafter taught at *lycées* in Pau and Limoges. From 1851 to 1859 he was in political exile. After his return, he was one of the foremost orators on the French political scene. His writings include *Études et réflexions d'un pessimiste* (1901). He died in Paris, 26 October 1896. BiD&SB; DBF; EncAm; EncBrit; GdeEnc; Meyers

Challet, J., fl. 1954-1962 in Rabat, he was a *paysagiste* and attached to the Service de l'urbanisme.

Challita, Mansour, fl. 1962-1978, his writings, all of which were published in Rio de Janeiro, include *A literatura árabe* (196-), *A vida e a obra de Gibran* (1962), *As mais belas páginas da literatura árabe* (1967), *Do Oriente Médio* (1973), and *Arábia Saudita* (1978). LC; NUC, 1956-1967

Challot, Jean Paul, born 25 May 1903, he was a trained agronomist who spent thirty-four years in the Administration des Eaux et Forêts in Morocco. As chief of the Service de la Défense et de la Restauration des Sols he was particularly concerned with the human aspect of this problem. Since 1942 he was attached to the Centre de Hautes Études d'Administration Musulmane à Paris. He died 6 September 1964. *L'Afrique et l'Asie* 68 (1964), pp. 69-70

Chalmers, Sir Robert, Baron Chalmers, born 18 August 1858 at London. After study at Oriel College, Oxford, he entered the Home Civil Service in 1882. In 1913 he accepted the Governorship of Ceylon. He was a member of the Pali Text Society, and received honorary doctorates from Glasgow, Oxford, Cambridge, and St. Andrews. His writings include *History of currency in the British colonies* (1893), and the translations *The Jataka* (1895), and *Buddha's teachings* (1932). He died in Oxford, 17 November 1938. *Proceedings of the British Academy* 25 (1939), pp. 321-332

Chalmeta Gendrón, Pedro, he received a doctorate in Semitic linguistics, specializing in Islamic history and institutions. He was a sometime professor at the Departamento de Estudios Árabes e Islámicos, Universidad Complutense de Madrid. His writings include *El "señor del zoco" en España; edades media y moderna* (1973), and an edition of Ibn al-'AttA8r, *al-Wathā'iq wa-al-sijillat* (1983).

Chalmin, Pierre, commandant, fl. 1953. His writings include *L'officier français de 1815 à 1870* (1957).

Chaloian, V. K. *see* Ch'aloyan, Vazgen Karapeti

Chalon, Louis, fl. 1969. His writings include *L'histoire et l'épopée castillane du moyen âge* (Paris, 1976). LC

Chalon, Renier Hubert Ghislain, born 4 December 1802 at Mons, Belgium, he obtained a doctorate in law in 1824 from the Université de Louvain for his Latin thesis on the prerequisites for the civil marriage. Afterwards he was a tax-collector in Cuesmes (Hainaut) for a number of years until he obtained a high position in the administration in Bruxelles. He resigned from the civil service on 11 December 1867. He published well in excess of one hundred articles on Belgian numismatics. It was he who introduced Oriental numismatics to the *Revue belge de numismatique et de sigillographie* whose editor he was for a number of years. He even learned Arabic and had an impressive collection of this *curieuse numismatique*. His writings include *Recherches sur les monnaies des comtes de Hainaut* (2 vol., 1848-1854). *Revue belge de numismatique* 45 (1889), pp. 452-464

Ch'aloyan, Vazgen Karapeti, his writings include Армянский ренессанс, (1963), Восток - Запад (1968), and Развитие философской мысли в Армении (1974). LC

Chalus, Paul, fl. 1959, he wrote *L'homme et la religion* (1963). LC

de **Chalvet de Rochemonteix**, Frédéric Josephe *Maxence* René, marquis, born 5 February 1849 at Clermont-Ferrand, he was educated at colleges in Paris and Alger, and then studied African languages, including Berber, at Paris where he also had his first encounter with Egyptology. In November 1875, he was sent by the Ministère de l'Instruction publique on a mission to Egypt. From 1879 until 1887 he served as deputy administrator with the Commission des Domaines de l'État égyptien. Poor health obliged him to return in 1887 to Paris where he lectured in Egyptology at the Sorbonne. His writings include *Le Temple d'Edfou* (1897-1918). He died in Paris, 30 December 1891. Dawson; DBF; Egyptology

Chamas, Sami, fl. 1949, his writings include *La loi du 27 novembre 1947 sur le régime municipal et la gestion des intérêts locaux au Liban* (1949), and *L'état et les systèmes bancaires contemporains* (1965).

de **Chamberet**, Charles *Gabriel* Tyrbas, *général*, born 27 September 1816 at Besançon, he was a graduate of the Polytechnique and École d'état-major. In 1847 he was sent on a mission to Africa. His writings include *Manuel du légionnaire* (1852). He died in 1880. DBF

de **Chamberet**, Raoul, fl 1910, he wrote *Enquête sur la condition du fellah égyptien, au point de vue de la vie agricole, de l'éducation, de l'hygiène et de l'assistance publique* (Dijon, 1909).

Chamberlain, Muriel Evelyn, born in 1932 at Syston, England, she was a graduate of St. Hilda's College, Oxford, where she also received a Ph.D. in 1961. Afterwards she taught at London and Swansea. Her writings include *The new imperialism* (1970), *Britain and India* (1974), *British foreign policy in the age of Palmerston* (1980), and *Decolonization; the fall of the European empires* (1985). In 1994 she was joint author of *L'Europe et l'Afrique de 1914 à 1970*. ConAu 93-96

Chamberlin, William Henry, born 17 February 1897 at Brooklyn, N.Y., he was educated at Penn Charter School, Philadelphia, Pa., and Haverford (Pa.) College. He was a journalist, a Moscow and Far Eastern correspondent, and a lecturer at American colleges. His writings include *The Russian revolution, 1917-1921* (1935), *Japan over Asia* (1937), and *Japan in China* (1940). He died 12 September 1969. WhAm, 5

Chambers, Richard Leon, born 27 September 1929 at Brundidge, Ala., he received a Ph.D. in 1968 from Princeton for *Ahmed Cevdet Paşa; the formative years of an Ottoman transitional*. Afterwards he taught at AUB and Princeton, before accepting a professorship of Turkish language and civilization at the University of Chicago in 1962. He was joint editor of *Contemporary Turkish short stories* (1977). DrAS, 1978, 1982

Chambers, Robert, born 1 May 1849 at Norwich, Ontario, he was graduate of Queen's University, Kingston, Ontario, and Princeton Theological Seminary. He joined the American Board's Turkish Mission in 1879, serving first in the Erzurum field. In 1891 he took charge of the Bithynia High School at Bardizag, where he accomplished remarkable results. Owing to war conditions, he returned to the United States in 1915 and devoted himself to raising relief funds to be sent to Turkey. He died in Newton, Mass., 2 April 1917. *Missionaty herald* 113 (1917), pp. 221-222

Chambers, Sir William, born in 1726. As a youth he went to sea and made a voyage to China. Later he devoted himself to architecture, which he studied in Italy. Upon his return to England he became a famous and prosperous architect. His writings include *A dissertation on Oriental gardening* (1772), and the translation, *Abhandlung über die orientalische Gartenkunst* (1775). He died in 1796. DNB; Sezgin

Chambers, William Nesbet, born 22 February 1853 at Norwich, Ontario, he was a graduate of Queen's University, Kingston, Ont., and received doctorates in divinity from Queen's as well as Princeton. Since 1879 he was a missionary under the American Board of Commissioners for Foreign Missions and served in Turkey. His writings include *Yoljuluk; random thoughts on a life in imperial Turkey* (1928). He died 7 August 1934. WhAm, 2

Chambre, Henri Joseph, born 13 January 1908 at Chambéry (Savoie), he was a mining engineer who joined the Société de Jésus in 1933. His writings include *Le Marxisme en Union soviétique* (1955), *Christianisme et communisme* (1959), and *L'Union soviétique et le développement économique* (1967). He died 8 October 1994. WhoFr, 1977/78-1994/95

de **Chambrun**, Aldebert Pineton, he was a French military officer. He died 22 April 1962. LC

Chamla, Marie Claude, fl. 1965, he was a sometime *directeur de recherche* at the C.N.R.S. His writings include *Les populations anciennes du Sahara et des régions limitrophes* (1968), and *L'anthropologie biologique* (1971). In 1976 he was joint author of *Croissance des algériens de l'enfance à l'âge adulte.* LC

Chamonard, Joseph, born in 1866, he was affiliated with l'École française d'Athènes, and a translator of Flavius Josephus works into French. LC

Champ, Maxime, born in 1900, he received a doctorate in 1928 at Alger for his thesis, *La commune mixte d'Algérie.* In 1951 he was a *sous-directeur du commerce* of the Gouvernement général de l'Algérie. His writings include *Les communes en Algérie* (1933). LC

Champagne, David C., fl. 1975, he wrote *Afghanistan, background and status of global crisis* (1980).

Champain, John Underwood Bateman, 1835-1887 *see* Bateman-Champain, John Underwood

Champault, Francine *Dominique*, fl. 1956, her writings include *Une Oasis du Sahara nord-occidental; Tabelbala* (1969), she edited *Vie juive au Maroc* (1986), and she was joint author of *La Main; ses figurations au Maghreb et au Levant* (1965), *Lunes d'Arabie* (1987), and its translation, *Arabian moons.*

de **Champeaux**, Gérard, fl. 1980, he was joint author of *Introduction au monde des symboles* (1966).

Champion, Jacques, born in the late 1910s, he was affiliated with the Centre d'études et de documentation sur les problèmes africains et leur rapport avec l'immigration, la rencontre des cultures et les échanges culturels at the Université de Grenoble. His writings include *Les Langues africaines et la francophonie* (1974), and *Langage et pédagogie en France et en Afrique* (1986). LC

Champlouis, A. V. Nau de *see* Nau de Champlouis, A. V.

Chamrajev, Murat *see* Khamraev, Maratbek Karimovich

Chamussy, René, fl. 1971, he wrote *Chronique d'une guerre; Liban, 1975-1977* (1978). LC

Chamy, Georgio (Georges), fl. 1958, he was an Egyptian-born orientalist and journalist, a graduate of the Jesuit College of Beirut as well as the French College of Alexandria. Note

Chancel, Ausone de, born in 1808, he was an administrator whose writings include *Anges et diables* (1835), *D'une immigration de noirs libres en Algérie* (1858), and *Cham et Japhet* (1859). In 1848 he published jointly with E. Daumas *Le Grand Désert.*

Chand, Bool, fl. 1933, his writings include *The German government* (1942), *The Japanese government* (1944), and *Lord Mahavia* (1948). LC

Chanderli, Abdel-Kader, born in 1915, he was an Algerian diplomat and business executive, who was educated at the Université de Paris. From 1956 to 1962 he was a representative of the Front de libération nationale in the United States of America. WhoWor, 1974/75

Chandler, George, born 2 July 1915 at Birmingham, he was educated at the University of London, where he received a Ph.D. in 1951. He was a sometime city librarian in Liverpool. His writings include *Dudley as it was and as it is to-day* (1949), and *Libraries in the East; an international and comparative study* (1971). He died 9 October 1992. ConAu 9-10; Master (5); Who, 1979-1993

Chandler, Richard, born in 1738, he was educated at Winchester and was a fellow of Magdalen College, Oxford. He was a classical antiquary who made a tour of exploration in Asia Minor and Greece at the expense of the Society of Dilletanti from 1764 to 1766. His writings include *Travels in Asia Minor* (1775), and its translation, *Reisen in Klein Asien* (1776). He died 9 February 1810. DNB

Chandra, Moti, born 26 August 1909 in India, he received a doctorate in 1933 from the University of London. He was a curator of the Art Section, Prince of Wales Museum, Bombay. His writings include *Jain miniature paintings from western India* (1949), and *The technique of Mughal painting* (1949). He died 17 December 1974. Eminent; LC

Chandra, Satish, M.A., D.Phil., born in 1922, he was in 1967 a professor of history at the University of Rajasthan, Jaipur. His writings include *Parties and politics at the Mughal Court* (1959), *The 18th century in India* (1986), and *The Indian Ocean; explorations in history, commerce and politics* (1987). He translated from the Persian, *Letters of a king-maker of the eighteenth century* (1972). LC

Chandrasekhara Rao, P., LL.D., fl. 1965, he wrote *The new law of maritime zones* (1983). LC

Chankov, Dimitrii Ivanovich, fl. 1957, his writings include Согласные хакасского языка (1957), Русско-хакасский словарь (1961), and *Pos tilining chooghy* (1989). LC

Channebôt, A. fl. 1869-1891, his writings include *L'Empire ottoman, esquisse d'un projet de colonisation de la Cyrénaïque* (1869), *Politique méditerranéenne* (1880), and *L'Empire ottoman, l'Italie et la France* (1891). BN

Chanoine, Charles Paul *Jules* or *Julien*, born 18 December 1870 at Paris. After passing through l'École spéciale militaire de Saint-Cyr he was posted to French West Africa, where he was killed in the course of a military insubordination in Niger, 16 July 1899. DBF; *Hommes et destins*, vol. 2, pp. 194-197

Chantre, B., Madame, fl. 1893, her writings include *A travers l'Arménie russe* (1892), and *En Asie mineure; souvenirs de voyages en Cappadoce et en Cilicie* (1896-98). BN

Chantre, Ernest, born 13 January 1843, he was attached to the Muséum de Lyon from 1871 to 1910, during which period he repeatedly undertook ethnographic and anthropological explorations in Asia Minor, Egypt, and Tripolitania. In 1901 he received a doctorate from the Université de Lyon for his thesis, *Paléontologie humaine; l'homme quartenaire dans le bassin du Rhône.* His writings include *Les arméniens; esquisse historique et ethnographique* (1896). He died in Ecully (Rhône), 24 November 1924. DBF; Vapereau

Chantréaux, Germaine *see* Laoust-Chantréaux, Germaine

Chanzy, Antoine Eugène *Alfred*, born 18 March 1823 at Nouart (Ardennes), he enlisted in the army at Metz in 1840; after passing through the military college of Saint-Cyr, he received a commission as *sous-lieutenant* in 1843 to serve with the 1er Zouaves. He spent the next sixteen years in Algeria, most of the time with the Bureaux arabes. On 28 July 1848 he was appointed to the *Cabinet du gouverneur général* in charge of Arab affairs. In 1851 he became captain in the Foreign Legion, and in the following year, *Chevalier de la Légion d'honneur.* Recalled to metropolitan France in 1859, he participated in the operations in Italy and Syria before returning to Algeria in 1870 to join the expedition against the Ouled Sidi Cheikh. He was a successful general in the Franco-German war of 1870-1871. He returned to Algeria in 1873 as governor. His writings include *Campagne de 1870-1871: la deuxième armée de la Loire* (1871). He died suddenly in Châlons-sur-Marne, 4 January 1883. DBF; Peyronnet, 277-284

Chapal, Philippe, fl. 1971, he received a doctorate in 1967 from the Université de Grenoble for his thesis, *L'arbitrabilité des différends internationaux.* LC

Chapira, Bernard, born in 1880, he was an Old Testament scholar whose writings include *Sifre 'Ezra u-Nehemyah* (1955), and *ha-Nusah ha-mekori shel sefer Tehilim* (1956). LC

Chapman, Alex H., he was In 1956 an assistant to the vice-president of the Arabian American Oil Company. Note

Chapman, Duane, born in 1940. He was a sometime professor of resource economics at Cornell University, Ithaca, N.Y., and a member of the American Economic Association. His writings include *Energy resources and energy corporations* (1983). LC

Chapman, Richard A., Dr. From 1974 to 1988 he rose from reader to professor at the Department of Politics in the University of Durham, England. His writings include *Decision making* (1968), *The higher Civil Service in Britain* (1970), *Teaching public administration* (1973), and *The art of darkness* (1988).

Chapman, [T.] He was a British Army captain who was in 1873 Sir Douglas Forsyth's secretary on the mission to Yakub Beg, the Emir of East Turkestan. Note

Chapman-Andrews, Sir Edwin Arthur, born 9 September 1903, he was educated at University College, London, the Sorbonne, and St. John's College, Cambridge, where he studied Oriental languages. In 1926 he entered the Levant Consular Service, from which he retired as British Ambassador at Khartoum in 1961. He was a vice-president of the Royal Central Asian Society, and a member of the Council of the Anglo-Arab Association. He died 10 February 1980. Note; *Who was who*, 7

Chapot, Marc Joseph *Victor*, born 20 November 1873 at Grenoble, he was a professor at l'École des Beaux-arts de Paris, and an honorary *conservateur* at the Bibliothèque de l'Université de Paris. His writings include *La frontière de l'Euphrate de Pompée à la conquête arabe* (1907), *L'organisation des bibliothèques* (1910), *Le monde romain* (1927), and its translation, *The Roman world* (1928). He died in 1954. WhoFr, 1953/54

Chapoutot-Remadi, Mounira, fl. 1972, she was a professor at the Université de Tunis and wrote *Itinéraire du savoir en Tunisie* (1995). LC

Chapra, Mohammed Umer, born about 1930., he received a Ph.D. in 1961 from the University of Minnesota for his thesis, *Inflation and monetary policy in Pakistan, 1951/51-1959/60*. He was a sometime economic adviser to the Saudi Monetary Agency, an economist at the Pakistan Institute of Developing Economics, and a professor at the Institute of Islamic Research, Pakistan. His writings include *The economic system of Islam* (1971), *Towards a just monetary system* (1985), and *Islam and economic development* (1993). LC; NUC, 1956-67

Chaput, Ernest, born in 1880, he was a professor of geography at l'Université de Dijon, and from 1928 to 1939, at Istanbul Üniversitesi. His writings include *Voyages d'études géologiques et géomorphogéniques en Turquie* (1936). He died in 1943. *Hommes et destins*, vol. 7, p. 114

Chaquéri (Shakeri/Shakiri), Cosroe (Khosrow), born in 1938 in Iran, he received a doctorate in 1980 from the Université de Paris III with a thesis entitled *Le Parti communiste iranien; genèse, développement et fin, 1916-1932*. He was a political activist in the anti-Shah movements in France and Germany. In the late 1980s he went to the United States, where he was attached to the *Encyclopaedia Iranica*. His writings include *La social-démocratie en Iran* (1979), *Le mouvement communiste en Iran; documents* (1979), *L'Union soviétique et les tentatives de soviets en Iran* (Tehran, 1983), and *The Soviet Socialist Republic of Iran, 1920-1921* (1995). ConAu 154; LC; Private; THESAM, 4

Charak, Sukhdev Singh, born in 1923, his writings include *Maharaja Ranjitdev and the rise and fall of the Jammu Kingdom* (1971), *Himachal Pradesh* (1978-79), and *Life and times of Maharaja Ranbir Singh* (1985). LC

Charanis, Peter, born 15 August 1908 at Lemnos, Aegean Islands, he received a Ph.D. in 1935 from the University of Wisconsin, and in 1980, an honorary doctorate from the University of Thessaloniki. From 1938 until his retirement in 1976 he was a professor of history at Rutgers University. His writings include *Church and state in the late Roman Empire* (1939), and *The Armenians in the Byzantine Empire* (1963). He died 23 March 1985. ConAu 37-40; DrAS, 1974-1982; *Who's who in America*, 1974-1978; Whm 8

Charbonneau, Jean Eugène Marie, born 2 May 1883 at Segré (Marne-et-Loire), he was a graduate of École spéciale militaire de Saint-Cyr, and was a *général de division* when he retired. He spent many years in French Equatorial, West, and North Africa. He was a member of the Académie des Sciences d'Outre-Mer, and the recipient of literary awards. His writings include *Sur les traces du pacha de Tombouctou* (1936), and *Maroc; vingt-troisième heure* (1938). He died 1 October 1973. WhoFr, 1959/60-973/74

Charbonneau, Pierre, Dr., fl. 1951-1955, he was successively *médecin-chef* at the Nouvel hôpital musulman de Casablanca, and l'Hôpital Maurice Gaud de la région de Fès. Note

Charbonneau, René Jean Marie, born 2 April 1911 at Rochefort (Charente-Maritime). After passing through the military college of Saint-Cyr, he was a colonial army officer in Africa and the Far East. After his resignation in 1947, he was an *inspecteur commercial* of the Société Paris-Outre Mer and made more than twenty trips on their behalf to Black Africa. His writings include *Essais sahariens; au Tibesti* (1937), and he was joint author of *Marchés et marchands d'Afrique noire* (1961). WhoFr, 1983/84-1989/90

Chard, Frederic de la Court. His writings include *Power system engineering* (1962), and *Electricity supply* (1970). LC

Chardin, Sir John (Jean), born in 1643 at Paris. In 1665 he set out on his first mercantile journey to the East Indies and spent six years in Isfahan, from where he returned with the most authentic information of the political and military state of Persia. He was later appointed minister plenipotentiary of the King of England. His writings include *Journal de voyage en Perse* (1686), and its translation *Travels into Persia* (1686). He is the subject of the doctoral thesis, *Une approche de l'Orient; Jean Chardin*, by Olivier Bonnerot, Strasbourg, 1971. He died in 1713 DBF; DNB; Embacher; EncBrit; EncAm; GDU; Henze; Meydan; Meyers; OxFr; THESAM, 4

Chardonnet, Jean Charles Albert, born 9 September 1913 at La Rochelle, he was educated at the Lycée Louis-le-Grand and l'École normale supérieure, Paris, and reveived a doctorate in geography in 1947 from the Université de Paris for his thesis, *Le relief des Alpes du sud*. He was a professor at various French universities. His writings include *Géographie industrielle* (1962-65), and *Les grandes puissances* (1967-69). WhoFr, 1969/70-1981/82

de **Charency**, Charles Félix Hyacinthe, Comte Gouhier, born 8 November 1832 at Paris. After the completion of his legal studies, he became a politician and educator with particular interest in the improvement of public instruction. He was also a lifelong ethnographer and linguist. He contributed innumerable articles to a wide range of periodicals, and wrote *La langue basque et les idioms de l'Oural* (1862-1866). He died 12 March 1916. Carnoy 10²; DBF

Charfi, Mohamed, born 20th cent., he was since 1969 variously *chargé d'enseignement, maître de conférences,* and *professeur* at the Faculté de droit et des Sciences politiques et économiques de Tunis. His writings include *Introduction à l'étude de droit* (1983). LC

Chargelègue, Jack, fl. 1960, his writings include *L'Espagne, 25 francs par jour* (1965), and *L'Italie, 25 francs par jour* (1966). BN; NUC, 1968-1972

Chariev (Чариев), Azam, he received a doctorate in 1976 at Moscow for his thesis, *Притяжательная конструкция с родительным радежом в узбекском языке.* His writings include *Процессформирования идейно-нравственного облика советской молодежи* (1981). LC

Charignon, Antoine Joseph Henri, born in 1872, his writings include *Les chemins de fer chinois* (Pékin, Imprimerie des Lazaristes, 1914), and *La grande Java de Marco Polo en Cochinchine* (Saigon, 1930). NUC, pre-1956

Charles, Eunice A., born 20th cent., she received a doctorate in 1972 from Boston University for her thesis, *A history of the kingdom of Jolof (Senegal), 1800-1890.* Thereafter she was a faculty member at the Southern Illinois University at Carbondale. Her writings include *Precolonial Senegal* (1977), and *Pan-Africanism in French-speaking West Africa* (1982). LC

Charles, Henri, S.J., born in 1900, his writings include *Jésuites missionnaires; Syrie, Proche-Orient* (1929), *Le christianisme des arabes nomades sur le limes et dans le désert syro-mésopotamien aux alentours de l'hégire* (1936), and *Tribus moutonnières du Moyen-Euphrate* (1939). LC; NUC, pre-'56

Charles, Raymond, born 25 July 1901 at Sidi-Bel-Abbès, Algeria, he studied at the Faculté des lettres et de droit d'Alger and received a doctorate in law as well as a diploma in Islamic law. Thereafter he practised law and taught at universities. His writings include *Le statut de Tanger, son passé, son avenir* (1927), *Histoire du droit pénal* (1955), *L'âme musulmane* (1958), *L'évolution de l'islam* (1960), and *L'étoile rouge contre le croissant* (1962). *Who's who in France*, 1965/66-1993/94

Charles, Robert P., fl. 1967, his writings include *Étude anthropologique des nécropoles d'Argos* (1963), and *Anthropologie archéologique de la Crète* (1965). LC

Charles-Dominique, Paule, fl. 1952, he produced together with G. H. Bousquet a partial translation of Ibn Hanbal's *K. al-Wara' wa-al-iman* in 1952. GAS I, 507

Charles-Roux, François, born 19 November 1879 at Marseille, he entered the Foreign Service in 1902 at St.Petersburg and subsequently served at Constantinople, Cairo and elsewhere. He was a president of the Suez Canal Company. His writings include *La production du coton en Égypte* (1908), *L'Angleterre et l'expédition française en Égypte* (1925), *France et chrétiens d'Orient* (1939), *Missions diplomatiques françaises à Fès* (1955), and *Souvenirs diplomatiques d'un âge révolu, 1902-1914* (1956). He died 17 August 1961.   DBFC, 1954/55; WhoFr, 1953/54-1959/60; *Who was who*, v. 6

Charles-Roux, Jules, 1841-1918 see Roux, Jules Charles

Charleston, Robert Jesse, born 3 April 1916, he was educated at New College, Oxford. From 1963 to 1976 he was a keeper at the Department of Ceramics, Victoria and Albert Museum, London. His writings include *Roman pottery* (1955). He died 4 December 1994.   Au&Wr, 1971; Who, 1974-1995; WrDr, 1976-1980

Charlesworth, Dorothy, fl. 1958, she was an archaeologist and published brief guides to monuments and historic buildings in Britain; these include *Aldborough Roman town and museum* (1979).   LC

Charlet, Charles Marie Louis Édouard, born about 1872. After passing through the military college of Saint-Cyr, he received in 1895 a commission as *sous-lieutenant* and spent the following two years with an infantry regiment in France before being assigned to the Zouaves. He entered the Service des Affaires indigènes de l'Algérie in February 1899 at the Bureau arabe in Boghar. In 1901 he participated in the conquest of the Saharan oases in the Algerian extreme South. Being the adventurous type, he went on furlough in Morocco and secretly collected intelligence information and took photographs at Aïn Mellouk. This escapade, though admired by his authorities, resulted in his transfer to Mzab. There he started to study the culture of the local population and perfected his Arabic, even obtaining a diploma. From 1904 to 1907 he was posted successfully to El Abiodh Sidi Cheikh. In the winter of 1907 to 1908 he participated in the large military operations in Morocco. In October 1908 he was once more with the Service des Affaires indigènes at the Central Government in Algiers, where he also received the *croix de chevalier de la Légion d'honneur*. Until the outbreak of the first World War, his duties necessitated inspections and assignments as far south as Timbuctu. His writings include *Au Sahara avec le commandant Charlet*, published posthumously in 1932. In 1914 he went with a regiment of the Zouaves to the trenches of the Campagne where he died in action on 25 September 1915.   Peyronnet, pp. 509-513

Charlier, Robert Edouard, born in 1906, his writings include *L'état et son droit* (1984). In 1981 he was honoured by the publication of *Service public et libertés; mélanges offerts au professeur Robert-Edouard Charlier*.   LC

Charmes, Gabriel, born 7 November 1850 at Aurillac (Cantal). After classical studies he joined his brother in Paris and became a journalist, specializing in foreign affairs. Inflicted by tuberculosis, he sought relief in southern Mediterranean countries. His writings include *Cinq mois au Caire et dans la Basse-Égypte* (1880), *L'avenir de la Turquie, le panislamisme* (1883), *La Tunisie et la Tripolitaine* (1883), *Politique extérieure et coloniale* (1885), and *Les stations d'hiver de la Méditerranée* (1885). He died 19 April 1886.   DBF

Charmes, Jacques, born 20th cent., he was in 1980 an economist affiliated with the Institut national de la statistique de Tunisie. His writings include *Études sur l'emploi aux Antilles et en Tunisie* (1982). In 1985 he was joint author of *In-service training in Tunisia*.   Note

Charmetant, le père Jacques Joseph Félix, born 20 June 1888 at Saint-Maurice-l'Exil (Isère), he graduated from the Grand séminaire de Lyon, and was ordained in Alger in 1868. He was a missionary of the Pères Blancs and travelled extensively in the Sahara, Kabylie, and French Equatorial Africa. He prepared the arrival of the Pères Blancs in Zanzibar. His writings include *Études et souvenirs d'Afrique; d'Alger à Zanzibar* (1882), *Martyrologe arménien* (1896), and *L'Arménie argonisante et l'Europe chrétienne* (1897). He died in Aix-les-Bains, 22 July 1921.   Curinier, vol. 5 (1906), p. 344; DBF

Charmoy (Шармуа), François Bernard, born 14 May 1793 at Soultz (Haut-Rhin), he studied Hebrew and Arabic at school before he went to Paris in 1810 to take courses at the Faculté de droit, the École spéciale des langues orientales vivantes, and the Collège de France. Upon the recommendation of his teacher Sylvestre de Sacy, he went to St. Petersburg in 1817 to accept the chair of Persian language and literature at the Pedagogical Institute. In 1821 he changed to the chair of Persian and Turkish at the Oriental Institute of the Ministry of Foreign Affairs. He spent eighteen years in Russia until his health compelled him to move to the mild climate of the Provence. He was the translator of *Relation de Mas'oudy et d'autres auteurs musulmans sur les anciens slaves* (1832-33), and *Chèref-nameh; ou, Fastes de la nation kourde* (1868-75). He died in Aouste in 1869.   BiobibSOT, pp. 289-290; DBF; EnSlovar; Fück, 156; Krachkovskii, 116, 117; NDBA; *l'Orient, l'Algérie et les colonies françaises* 1 (1866/67), pp. 143-144; Wieczynski

Charnay, Claude Joseph *Désiré*, born 2 May 1828 at Fleurieux-sur-l'Arbresle (Rhône), he was a traveller and archaeologist who was mainly an explorer of Latin America, but he also visited the Yemen in 1898. He died in Paris, 24 October 1915. DBF; Embacher; Henze

Charnay, Jean *Paul*, born 20th cent., he received a doctorate in 1977 from the Université de Paris X for his *thèse d'état, Sociologie religieuse de l'islam*. In 1980 he was a director of the Centre d'études et de recherches sur les stratégies et les conflicts at the Sorbonne, Paris. His writings include *L'ambivalence dans la culture arabe* (1967), *Islamic culture and socio-economic change* (1971), *Les contreorients* (1980), *L'islam et la guerre* (1986), and *La vie musulmane en Algérie d'après la jurisprudence de la première moitié du XXe siècle* (1991). LC; THESAM, 4

Charnock, Richard Stephen, born 11 August 1820, he was educated at King's College, London, and admitted an attorney in 1841. He travelled through the whole of Europe, and also visited North Africa and Asia Minor. His major interest was anthropology, archaeology, and philology, including Oriental languages. In 1871 he was elected president of the Anthropological Society of London. His writings include *Local etymology* (1859). He died in 1904. Men10; Vapereau

Charon, Cyrille, fl. 1920, he wrote *Histoire des patriarcats melkites (Alexandrie, Antioche, Jérusalem) depuis le schisme monophysite du sixième siècle jusqu'à nos jours* (1909-10). NUC, pre-1956

Charpentier, Carl Johan, born 30 April 1948 in Sweden, he was educated at Uppsala Universitet, where he received a doctorate in 1972 for his thesis, *Bazaar-e tashqurghan; ethnographical studies in an Afghan traditional bazaar*. With a special visa, he spent the years from 1969 to 1973 as a social anthropologist in Kabul, where he had contacts with King Zahir Shah as well as the communist opposition leaders. Thereafter he was attached to the Etnografiska Institutionen, Uppsala. His writings include *Kommer aldrig revolutionen?* (1977), *Afghanistan, landet på Världens tak* (1992), and the translation, *Afghanistan mellem Mekka & Moskva* (København, 1980). IWWAS, 1975/76

Charpentier, Jarl Hellen Robert Toussaint, born 17 December 1884 at Göteborg, he received a doctorate of Sanskrit and Indo-European languages and taught these subjects at Uppsala. His writings include *Kleine Beiträge zur indoiranischen Mythologie* (1911), *De indoeuropeiska spr͞ ken* (1915), and *The Indian travels of Apollonius of Tyrana* (1934). He died in Uppsala, 5 July 1935. SMK

Charters, David A., born 12 September 1949, he received a Ph.D. in 1980 from King's College, London, for his thesis, *Insurgency and counter-insurgency in Palestine, 1945-1947*. He was a sometime director of the Centre for Conflict Studies in the University of New Brunswick. His writings include *The British Army and Jewish insurgency in Palestine* (1989). LC

Charton, Albert. In 1923 he had received his *agrégation* and was attached to the Université de Casablanca.

Charvet, Claude, fl. 1892-1896, he wrote *Notes sur l'Algérie, par un algérien* (1892). BN

Charvet, Jean Paul, born about 1945, he obtained a *doctorat d'état* and was since 1970 affiliated with the Université de Paris X - Nanterre. His writings include *Les Greniers du monde* (1985), *La Guerre du blé* (1988), and *La France agricole en choc* (1994). LC

Charvin, Robert, born 20th cent., he obtained a *doctorat en droit* and became a professor at the Université de Nice, and dean of its Faculté de droit et des sciences économiques. His writings include *Justice et politique* (1968), and *Les relations internationales des états socialistes* (1981). In 1988 he was joint author of *Le syndrôme Kadhafi*. LC

Charyiarov (Чарыяров), Biashim, fl. 1973-1985, he was a Turkologist from Ashkhabad, whose writings include *Turkmen dilining grammatikasy = Грамматика туркменского языка* (1977), and *Большои русского-туркменский словарь* (1986). LC

Charykov (Tcharykow), Nikolai Valerievich, born in 1855, his writings include *Посольство в Рим и служба в Москве* (1906), and *Glimpses of high politics through war and peace, 1855-1929; the autobiography of N. V. Tcharykow, serf-owner, ambassador, exile* (1931). He died in 1930. LC

de **Chassey**, Francis born 20th cent., he received a doctorate in 1972 from the Université de Paris for his thesis, *Contribution à une sociologie du sous-développement*. His writings include *L'étrier, la houe et le livre* (1977), and *Mauritanie, 1900-1975* (1978). LC

Chassignet, Louis Maximilian Modeste, born 11 July 1817 at La Malgrange near Nancy, he graduated in 1849 from the *Polytechnique*, and also passed through l'École d'application de Metz. From 1853 to 1857 he was posted to North Africa, where he participated in several expeditions to the Grande

Kabylie. He was also a member of the Syrian campaign. His writings include *Essai historique sur les institutions militaires depuis les temps les plus reculés jusqu'en 1789* (1869). He died in 1893. DBF

Chassinat, Émile Gaston, born 5 May 1868 at Paris, he was originally a printer working at the Imprimerie nationale. In 1888 he began to study Egyptology at l'École des hautes études. He went to Cairo in 1895 as a member of l'Institut français d'archéologie orientale, whose director he became three years later. He died in Saint-Germain-en-Laye, 26 May 1948. Egyptology

Chastel, Étienne Louis, born in 1801 at Genève, he was a pastor and professor of theology at Genève. His writings include *Histoire de la destruction du paganisme dans l'empire d'Orient* (1847), and the translations, *The charity of the primitive Churches* (1857), and *Christianity in the nineteenth century* (1874). He died in 1886. BN; Dantès 1

Chasteland, Jean Claude, fl. 1969, his writings include *Demographie; bibliographie et analyse* (1961), and *Les Politiques de population dans le tiers monde huit ans après Bucarest* (1984). LC

Chatel, François D., he was in 1962 an *assistant administratif* and economic expert at the Moroccan Ministry of the Interior. Note

Chatelain, René Julien, baron, lieutenant-colonel, born 17 March 1771 at Versailles, he served in the Egyptian, Italian, and Spanish campaigns. His writings include *Le Guide des officiers de cavalerie* (1817), and *Mémoire sur les moyens à employer pour punir Alger et détruire la piraterie des puissances barbaresques* (1828). He died in Paris, 4 March 1836. DBF

Chatelain, Yves, born in 1902, his writings include *Duc Durtain et son œuvre* (1933), and *La vie littéraire et intellectuelle en Tunisie de 1900 à 1937* (1937), a work for which he received the Prix de Carthage. LC

Chatelet, Aristide, fl. 1933, his writings include *Jean-Gabriel Perboyre de la Congrégation de la mission (Lazaristes) martyr* (1943). LC

Chatelus, Michel, fl. 1969, his writings include *Stratégies pour le Moyen-Orient* (1974).

Chater, Melville, born in 1878 in the United States, he was a writer of fiction before he became a contributor to the *National geographic magazine*, Washington, D.C. He travelled extensively in Europe and Asia Minor, and was associated with the Near East Relief. WhNAA

Chatterjee, Ashok Kumar, he was in 1973 affiliated with the Degree College, Ghazipur. He wrote *The Yogacara idealism* (1962), and other Buddhist works. LC

Chatterton-Hill, Georges, Dr., born in 1883, his writings include *Heredity and selection in sociology* (1907), *The sociological value of Christianity* (1912), *Individuum und Staat* (1913), and *The philosophy of Nietzsche* (1914). On behalf of the Deutsch-Irische Gesellschaft he edited the *Irische Blätter*, v. 1-2 (1917-1918). LC

Chattopadhyaya, Mrs. Kamaladevi, born 3 April 1903 at Mangalore, India, she was educated at Mangalore, Bedford College, London, and LSE. Her writings include *Handicrafts of India* (1975), *Tribalism in India* (1978), and *Indian women's battle for freedom* (1983). J. Brij Bhushan wrote *Kamaladevi Chattopadhyaya; portrait of a rebel* (1976). IntAu&W, 1989; IntWW, 1980-1983

Chauchar, Marie L. Ach., *capitaine*, his writings include *Examen critique des Mémoires sur l'Algérie rédigés par le brigadier Don Crispin de Sandoval et Don Antonio Madera y Vivero* (Paris, 1854), and *Espagne et Maroc, campagne de 1859-1860* (Paris, 1862). BN

Chaudhary, Abdul Ghafour, born in 1934, he received LL.B. and LL.M. degrees from the University of Leeds. He was a barrister-at-law and advocate in Lahore High Court and the Supreme Court of Pakistan, and a sometime chief editor of the *All Pakistan reporter* as well as a professor at the Hamayat-i-Islam Law College, Lahore, and a consultant editor of the *Law notes*, Lahore. His writings include *Company law in Pakistan* (1964), and *The law Latin lexicon* (1979). LC

Chaudhary, Muhammad Ali, born 20th cent., he was in 1978 a senior research economist at the Pakistan Institute of Development Economics, Islamabad. His writings include *An economic analysis of level and structure of irrigation water changes* (1981). LC

Chaudhri, A. T., he was in 1954 a researcher at the Pakistan Institute of International Affairs, Karachi. He was joint editor of *In Sind today* (1951). Note

Chaudhri, Mohammed Ahsen, Dr., he was in the 1950s a researcher at the Pakistan Institute of International Affairs, Karachi. He was joint author of *Pakistan and regional pacts* (1958), *Pakistan and*

290

the great powers (1970), and *International law and the United Nations* (1988). In 1984 he edited *Pakistan and regional security*. LC

Chaudhry, M. Anwar, born 20th cent., he was In 1974 a research economist at the Pakistan Institute of Development Economics. Note

Chaudhry, Muhammad Ghaffar, born in 1942, he was in 1972 a research economist at the Pakistan Institute of Development Economics. He received a Ph.D. in 1980 from the University of Wisconsin at Madison for his thesis, *The green revolution and income equality*. He was joint author of *Structural change in Pakistan's agriculture* (1989). LC

Chaudhry, Naseer A., born 20th cent., he was in 1976 a director, Pakistan Family Welfare Council, Lahore. Note

Chaudhry, Shahid Amjad, born 15 August 1945, he was in 1994 a joint editor of the World Bank technical paper, *Civil service reform in Latin America and the Carribean*. LC

Chaudhuri, Muzaffer Ahmed, he received a Ph.D. in 1960 from the University of London for his thesis, *The civil service in Pakistan*. Thereafter he was a lecturer in political science at the University of Dacca. His writings include *Government and politics in Pakistan* (1968), and *Rural government in East Pakistan* (1969). LC

Chaudhury, Rafiqul Huda *see* Chowdhury, Rafiqul Huda

Chaudri, Nazir Ahmad Khan. His writings include *Commonwealth of Muslim states* (1972), *The making of a lawyer* (1976), and *Thoughts on Pakistan and Pan-Islamism* (1977). LC

Chaudruc de Crazannes, Jean César Marie Alexandre, baron, born 21 July 1782 at Crazannes (Charente-Maritime), he was a civil servant and an archaeologist, and a sometime keeper of historic monuments at the Département du Gers, and later, *inspecteur conservateur* of Antiquities at the Département de Charente-Inférieure. His writings include *Antiquités de la ville de Saintes* (1820). He died at Castelsarrasin, 15 August 1862. DBF

Chaulet, Claudine, born 21 April 1931 at Longeau (Haute-Marne), she studied at the Université d'Alger and the Musée de l'Homme, Paris. Her writings include *La Mitidja autogérée; enquête sur les exploitations autogérées agricoles d'une région d'Algérie* (1971), and *La terre, les frères et l'argent; stratégie familiale et production agricole en Algérie depuis 1962* (1987), a work which was originally presented in 1984 as her thesis for a *doctorat d'état* at the Université René Décartes, Paris. Unesco

Chaulet, Pierre, born 20th cent., he was a sometime professor at the Matiben Pneumo-Phthisiology Unit, Beni-Messous Hospital, West Algiers UHC. He wrote *Childhood tuberculosis still with us* (1992).

Chaurand de Saint-Eustache, Felice de, born in 1857, he was in 1908 a major general. His writings include *Come l'esercito italiano entrò in guerra* (1929). LC

Chautard, Jean, born in the 19th century, he received a doctorate in 1905 from the Université de Paris for his thesis, *Étude sur la géographie physique et la géologie du Fouta-Djallon*. His writings include *Les gisements de pétrole* (1922). NUC, pre-1956

Chauvet, Adolphe, fl. 1861-1891, he was joint author, together with Dr. Émile Isambert, of *Itinéraire déscriptif, historique et archéologique de l'Orient* (1861), and *Syrie, Palestine, comprenant le Sinai, l'Arabie pétrée et la Cilicie* (1892)

Chauvin, Victor Charles, born 26 December 1844 at Liège, he studied at l'École normale des humanités de Liège, where he also took courses in Hebrew, Arabic, and law. In 1863 he changed exclusively to law and received a doctorate in 1869. Thereafter he practised law until 1872, when he succeeded his teacher Pierre Burggraf as professor of Oriental languages and Islamic law. He was a demanding and elitist teacher who admitted only above-average students when they were ready for explanations of difficult texts. The few students he had, all became distinguished Orientalists. His writings include *Bibliographie des ouvrages arabes ou relatifs aux Arabes* (1892-1909). He died at Liége on 19 November 1913. BioNBelg, v. 29 (1956/7), cols. 445-8; Fück; Vapereau

Chauvin-Beillard, Auguste, fl. 1851, his writings include *De l'Empire ottoman, de ses nations et de sa dynastie, 1841-1845* (1845). NUC, pre-1956

de **Chavagnac**, Maurice Gabriele, fl. 1886. he travelled in 1881 throughout Morocco. BN

Chavanne, Dorothy Louisa Marian née Buck, 1897- *see* Buck, Dorothy Louisa Marian

Chavanne, Joseph, born 7 August 1846 at Graz, Austria. After study at Prague, he travelled in the new world as well as in central and northern Africa. From 1874 to 1885 he was attached to the Meteorologische Zentralanstalt, Wien, and concurrently he was an editor of the *Mitteilungen der Geographischen Gesellschaft in Wien*. His writings include *Die Sahara; oder, Von Oase zu Oase; Bilder aus dem Natur- und Volksleben in der großen afrikanischen Wüste* (1879). He died in Buenos Aires, 7 December 1902, where he had been living since 1885. Embacher; Henze; ÖBL

Chavannes, Emmanuel Édouard (or Edmond), born 5 October 1865, he was educated at Lyon and Lausanne, and studied Chinese at l'École des langues orientales. He was a professor of Chinese at le Collège de France. His writings include *Documents sur les Tou-Kiue (Turcs) occidentaux* (1903). He died in Paris, 20 January 1913. DBF

Chavchavadze, Tinatin Aleksandrovna, born 29 April 1928 at Tbilissi, she graduated at Tbilissi in 1949, and received a doctorate in 1961 from the Akademiia Nauk SSSR, Institut Narodov Azii for her thesis *Научное наследие П. А. Чихачева*. Her writings include *Именное словосложение в ново-персидском языке* (1981). LC; Miliband

Chaventré, André, fl. 1972, his writings include *Évolution anthropo-biologique d'une population touarègue* (1983). LC

Chavush'ian, Arkadii Nikolaevich, fl. 1965, he was joint author of *Сырьевые ресурсы Азии, Австралии, Океании* (1987). LC

Chavy, Paul, born 19 July 1914 at Saint-Florent, France, he was from 1948 until his retirement a professor of French at Dalhousie University, Halifax, N.S. His writings include *Traducteurs d'autrefois, moyen âge et Renaissance; dictionnaire* (1988). In 1992 he edited *Littérature générale, littérature comparée; actes du XIème Congrès de l'Association internationale de L.C.* DrAS, 1974, 1978, 1982

Chawla, R. L., Dr., born 20th cent., he was in 1994 affiliated with the Indian Council for Research on International Economic Relations. He was editor of the symposia papers *Development cooperation or strengthening international economic relations* (1992), and joint editor of *Cooperation for growth* (1994). LC

Chawla, Vijay, he was in 1972 a research fellow at the South Asia Studies Centre, Jaipur. He wrote *India and the super powers* (1973). LC

Chazan, Robert, born about 1940, he received a Ph.D. in 1967 from Columbia University, N.Y.C., for his thesis, *Thirteenth-century Jewry in northern France*. In 1997 he was a professor of Hebrew and Judaic studies at New York University. His writings include *Daggers of time* (1989), *European Jewry and the first crudade* (1987), *Barcelona and beyond* (1992), and *In the year 1097; the first crusade and the Jews* (1992). LC

Cheboksarov, Nikolai Nikolaevich, born in 1907 at Simbirsk, Russia, he graduated in 1930 from the Moscow State University, and in 1949 he received a doctorate from the Akademiia Nauk SSSR, Institut Etnografii, for his thesis, *Северные китайцы и их соседи*. He was from 1943 to 1980 affiliated with the Institute of Ethnography, Soviet Academy of Science. In 1968 he was joint editor of *Очерки общей этнографии* (1968). He died 1 February 1980. LC; Miliband; Miliband[2]

Chedeville, Édouard, fl. 1969, he was in 1980 joint editor of *Notes sur les 'Afar de la région de Tadjoura*, by Marcel Chailley. LC

Chédiac, Charles, fl. 1911-1916, he lectured from 1910 to 1912 in agrarian economics, in French as well as in Arabic, at the Egyptian University, Cairo,. Baldinetti, pp. 79-80

Cheema, Aftab Ahmad, born 20th cent., he was in 1978 a research economist at the Pakistan Institute of Development Studies in Islamabad. Note

Cheesman, Robert Ernest, colonel, born 18 October 1878 at Westwell, Kent, he was an ornithologist who served with the British Army in India and Mesopotamia. He mapped parts of the Arabian coast, and spent eleven weeks at Hufuf from where he travelled to Jabrin. His writings include *Summary notes on vegetable growing in Mesopotamia in 1917* (1918), *In unknown Arabia* (1926), and *Lake Tana and the Blue Nile* (1936). He died 13 February 1962. DNB; Who was who, 6

Chéhab, Maurice, born in 1904 at Homs, he was a student at the Jesuit college in Beirut where he received a French *baccalauréat* in 1924. The following four years, he studied at the Sorbonne, École pratique des hautes études, Institut catholique and the Louvre. When he returned to Beirut, he was appointed keeper at the Musée national. From 1942 to 1982 he was head of the Service des

Antiquités, the last twenty years of which with the title *directeur général*. He died on Christmas Eve, 1994. Syria 73 (1996), pp. 205-206

Chehabi, Houchang Esfandiar, born 22 February 1954 at Tehran, he received a Ph.D. in 1986 from Yale University for his thesis, *Modernist Shi'ism and politics*. Thereafter he was an associate professor of government and social studies at Harvard University. His writings include *Iranian politics and religious modernism* (1990), and in 1995 he was joint author of *Politics, society, and democracy*. LC; Private; Schoeberlein

Chehata, Chafic (Shafiq T. Shehata), he was a sometime professor of law, economics and social sciences at l'Université de Paris II. His writings include *Essai d'une théorie générale de l'obligation en droit musulman* (1936), *Théorie générale de l'obligation en droit musulman hanéfite* (1969), and *Études en droit musulman* (1971). LC

Cheikh, Yédali Ould, he was in 1980 Minister of Justice and Islamic Affairs, Mauritania.

Cheikho (Shaykhu), Louis, born 5 February 1859 at Mardin. After passing through the Séminaire oriental de Ghazir, Lebanon, he entered the Compagnie de Jésus in 1874. He was an Arabist and researcher, the founder of, and for twenty-five years an indefatigable contributor to, *al-Machriq*. His writings include *al-Majānī al-adab* (1885-88), and *Les manuscrits des auteurs arabes chrétiens depuis l'islam* (1924). He died in Beirut, 2 or 7 December 1927. l'Asie française, 28 (1928), pp. 79-81; Fück

Chejne, Anwar George, born 15 August 1923 at Rahbah, Lebanon, he studied at Bogota, Columbia, the Asia Institute, N.Y.C., and the University of Pennsylvania, where he received a doctorate in 1954 for his thesis, *Succession to the rule in Islam*. He was a professor at Wayne State University, Michigan, before he became a professor of Middle Eastern languages at the University of Minnesota from 1966 until his retirement. His writings include *The Arabic language; its role in history* (1969), *Muslim Spain* (1974), and *Islam and the West; the Moriscos* (1983). ConAu 25-28; ConAu 18 new rev.; DrAS, 1974; IntAu&W, 1977; LC; WrDr, 1976/78-1988/90

Chekhovich, Ol'ga Dmitrievna, born in 1912 at St. Petersburg, she graduated in 1932 from Leningrad and received a doctorate in 1968. Her writings include *Самаркандские документы XV-XVI вв.* (1974). In 1979 she was joint editor of *Бухарский вакф XIII в.* She died in Moscow, 27 January 1982. LC; Miliband; Народы Азии и Африки, 1982, no. 3, pp. 218-219

Chelhod, Joseph, born 6 December 1919 at Aleppo, he was educated at French institutions, including the Lycée français, at Aleppo. From 1939 to 1946 he worked as a school teacher and concurrently pursued an interest in research. He contributed several articles to local journals and translated Durkheim's *Education et sociologie* into Arabic. In 1946 he enrolled at the Faculté des lettres de Paris where he received a *docteur ès lettres* degree in 1952 with a thesis entitled *Sacrifice chez les Arabes*, and a complementary thesis entitled *Les faits sociaux sont-ils des choses?* He was a French national since 1955, and he became a *maître de recherche* in October 1963. Since 1972 he was affiliated with the C.N.R.S., and concurrently lectured in cultural anthropology of the Arab East at the Université de Paris. In 1984 he was promoted to *directeur de recherche*. His writings include *Fi al-lughah wa-al-ijtima'* (1931), *Introduction à la sociologie de l'islam* (1958), *Les structures du sacré chez les Arabes* (1965), *Le droit dans la société bédouine* (1971), and *L'Arabie du sud* (1984-85). He died at the end of 1994. Chroniques yéménites, 1995, pp. 4-9; WhoWor, 1976/77-1982/83

Chelhot, Victor, fl. 1959, he wrote *al-Naz'ah al-kalamiyah fi uslub al-Jahiz* (1964). NUC, 1956-1967

Chelkowski, Peter Jan, born 10 July 1933 at Lubliniec, Poland, he studied at the Uniwersytet Jagielloński, Kraków, and Tehran University, where he received a Ph.D.. Since 1978 he was a professor of Near Eastern studies at New York University. He wrote *Mirror of the invisible world* (1975), and edited *The scholar and the saint* (1975), *Ta'ziyeh, ritual and drama in Iran* (1979), and *Ideology and power in the Middle East* (1988). DrAS, 1974-1982

Chelmsford, Frederic John Napier Thesiger, Lord and Viscount, born 12 August 1868 at London, he was educated at Winchester and Magdalen College, Oxford. From 1916 to 1921 he was Viceroy of India. His writings include *Montagu-Chelmsford report* (1918), and *Constitutional and national development in India* (1981). He died 1 April 1933. DNB; Riddick; Who was who, 3

Chemillier-Gendreau, Monique, born about 1935, she was since 1958 married to professor Pierre Chemillier. She was a professor at the Université de Paris VII. Her writings include *Culture et santé* (1985), and *Humanité et souverainités* (1995); she was joint author of *Introduction à la sociologie politique* (1971), and *Quelques questions de pouvoir et de responsabilité dans le domaine médical* (1985).

Chemoul, Maurice, he was in 1936 a *professeur agrégé* at the Lycée d'Oujda, Morocco. Note

Chen, John Hsüeh-Ming, born 24 June 1931 in China, he studied at Columbia, New York University, Virginia Polytechnic Institute and Virgina State University, University of Wisconsin, University of Denver, and the University of Pennsylvania, where he received a Ph.D. in 1968. He held the posts of professor of education and of international Asian studies in various universities in the United States, and was a noted Orientalist. His writings include *Bibliotherapy* (1963), and *Vietnam; a comprehensive bibliography* (1973). Master (2); Note about the author; WhoLibS, 1966

Chen, Lincoln Chih-ho, born 12 February 1942 in China, he studied at Princeton and Harvard, where he received an M.D. in 1968. He was affiliated with the Population Council, N.Y.C., and a sometime program officer in Bangladesh. His writings include *Disaster in Bangladesh* (1973), *Recent fertility trends in Bangladesh* (1976), and he was joint editor of *Diarrhea and malnutrition* (1982). ConAu 49-52

Chen, Zalman, he was in 1968 a senior official in one of Israel's government ministries. Note

Chenavard, Marie Antoine, born 4 March 1787 at Lyon, he studied at the École des beaux-arts de Paris, and travelled in the Balkans, the Near and the Middle East. He was an architect of the Département du Rhône, a profesor at l'École des beaux-arts, a corresponding member of l'Institut de France, a member of l'Académie de Lyon, honorary president of the Société académique d'architecture, chevalier de la Légion d'honneur and l'ordre du Sauveur de Grèce. He was joint author of *Relation du voyage fait en 1843-44, en Grèce et dans le Levant* (1846). He died in Lyon, 29 December 1883. Dantès 1; DBF; I.I. (1); Vapereau

Chénebaux, A., fl. 1946-1961, he was a sometime member of the Centre de Hautes Études d'Administration Musulmane, Paris. Note

Chenery, Hollis Burnley, born 6 January 1918 at Richmond, Va., he received a Ph.D. in 1950 from Harvard University for his thesis, *Engineering bases of economic analysis*. He was a sometime lecturer in economics at Harvard, and a vice-president of the International Bank of Reconstruction and Development. He was joint author of *Arabian oil, America's stake in the Middle East* (1949), *Turkish investment and economic development* (1953), and *Industrialization and growth* (1986). He was joint editor of the *Handbook of development economics* (1988-1989), but died during the preparation of the 3rd volume (1995). AmW&WS, 1973-1978; IntWW, 1974-1978; LC; WhoAm, 1976-1978; WhoUN, 1975; WrDr, 1980

Cheng, Bin, born 21 January 1921 in China, he received a Ph.D. in 1950 from the University of London and an LL.D. in 1966. Since 1950 he was a professor of air and space law, and dean of the Faculty of Law at London. His writings include *General principles of law as applied by international courts and tribunals* (1953), and *The law of international air transport* (1962). Au&Wr, 1971; IntAu&W, 1976-1977; WhoWor, 1974/75-1976/77

de **Chénier**, Louis, born 3 June 1722 at Montfort-sur-Boulzane (Aude), and educated at the Collège des Doctrinaires de Limoges, he was a merchant and a sometime French consul. His writings include *Recherches historiques sur les Maures* (1787), and *Un chargé d'affaires au Maroc; la correspondance, 1767-1782*, edited by Pierre Grillon (1970). He died in Paris, 26 May 1795. Hommes et destins, 1, 141-143

Chenu, Marie Dominique, born in 1895, he was a clergyman whose writings include *Les études de philo-sophie médiévale* (1939), *Pour une théologie du travail* (1955), *La doctrine sociale de l'Église comme idéologie* (1979), and the translation *Nature, man, and society in the twelfth century* (1968). He was honoured by the jubilee volume, *L'hommage différé au Père Chenu* (1990). He died on 2 November 1990. LC

Chepelev, Vladimir Nikolaevich, fl. 1936, his writings include Искусство советского Узбекистана (1935), Об античной стадии в истории искусства народов СССР (1941); and he was joint author of Искусство советской Туркмении (1934). LC

Chepelevtskaia (Чепелевецкая), Gertruda L'vovna, her writings include Сузани Узбекистана (1961), and she was joint author of Музей восточных культур (1957). LC

Chepurina, P. IA., fl. 1935. Author of Каримские брачные договоры (1927), and Орнаментное шитье Крыма (1938). LC

Chéradame, André Marie Joseph, born in 1871, he received in 1905 a doctorate from the Université de Paris for his thesis, *De la condition juridique des colonies allemandes*. His writings include *La question d'Orient* (1903), *La colonistaion et les colonies allemandes* (1905), *Le chemin de Bagdad* (1915), and *Douze ans de propagande en faveur des peuples balkaniques* (1913). LC

Ch'eraz, Minas, 1852-1929 *see* Tchéraz, Minas

Cherbonneau, Jacques *Auguste*, born in 1813 at La Chapelle-Blanche (Indre-et-Loire), he was a graduate of the Lycée Charlemagne and l'École des langues orientales, Paris. He was the first professor of Arabic when the Chair was established at Constantine in 1846. In 1863 he was appointed director of the Collège arabe français d'Alger, and in 1879, professor of colloquial Arabic at l'École des langues orientales vivantes, Paris. His writings include *Anecdotes musulmanes, texte arabe; ou, Cours d'arabe élémentaire* (1847), *Dictionnaire arabe-français* (1876), and the translations, *Histoire de Chems-Eddine et de Nour-Eddine; extraite des Mille et une nuits* (1853), and *Fables de Lokman* (1883). He died 11 December 1882. DBF; Fück, 203; *Revue de géographie* 12 (1883), pp. 42-45; Vapereau

Cherbuliez, Charles *Victor*, born 18 July 1829 at Genève, of a family of clergymen and professors, in all likelihood of French origin. At school he acquired a taste for literature and philosophy. In 1849 he went to Paris where he was greatly influenced by Taine, Renan and Sainte-Beuve. In the following year, he went to Germany and stayed in Bonn and Berlin. Upon his return to Genève in 1852 he married, started to give private lessons, and began to write for the *Revue critique des lvres nouveaux*. In 1859 he went to the East, visiting Constantinople, Smyrna and Athens. After his return he published *À propos d'un cheval; causeries athéniennes* (1860), a work which was republished entitled *Un cheval de Phidas* (1864). Following the success of his first books, he was invited to become a contributor to the *Revue des deux mondes*. He moved to Paris where, since 1875, he published under the pseudonym Gustave Valbert foreign policy reports which were unanimously appreciated. He died in Combs-la-Ville (Seine-et-Marne), 2 July 1899. André Célières received a doctorate at Paris for *Victor Cherbuliez, romancier, publiciste, philosophe*, a work which was published in 1936. DBF; IndexBFr² (4)

Cherdantsev, Gleb Nikanorovich, born in 1885, his writings include *Средне-азиатские республнки* (1928), and he edited *Экономическая география* (1954). He died in 1958. LC

Chérel, Jacques, fl. 1960-1964, his writings include the translation, *The traditional sector and rural development in Mauritania*. NUC, 1968-1972

Cherel, Jean, fl. 1971, he was an agronomist and in 1964 an expert for technical cooperation affiliated with the Secrétariat à l'agriculture of the Tunisian Government.

Cherfils, Christian, born in 1858, his writings include *Un Essai de religion scientifique* (1898), *Canon de Turner* (1906), *L'Esthétique positiviste* (1909), and *Bonaparte et l'islam, d'après les documents français et arabes* (1914). He died in 1926. LC

Cherif Chergui, Abderrahman, fl. 1972, his writings include *La Ideología islámica* (1977), a work which was originally submitted as his doctoral thesis at the Universidad de Madrid. LC

Chériff Vanly, Ismet, born 21 November 1924 at Damascus, he studied at AUB, and the universities of Lausanne and Genève. In 1956 he was a founding member of the Kurdish Students Society in Europe, Wiesbaden, and from 1959 to 1961, their president in Paris, where he was concurrently attached to the Institut national des langues et civilisations orientales as a lecturer in Kurdish studies. From 1962 to 1964, and from 1974 to 1975, he was a spokesman for General Mustafa Barzani. In 1965 a Syrian courtmartial sentenced him to death. He survived an assassination attempt despite two shots in the head in Lausanne on 7 October 1976. In 1979 he was a founding member and the first secretary-general of Yekbun, the Kurdish Liberation and Progress Party, which operated clandestinely since 1986. He was a president of the Institut kurde de Paris, member of the Kurdish Academy, and president of the planning committee of l'Union pour la décolonisation et la libération du Kurdistan since 1990. His writings include *Le Kurdistan irakien, entité nationale* (1970), and *Survey of the national question of Turkish Kurdistan* (1971), as well as its German translation. LC; Private

Cherkasov, B., he was in 1963 a correspondent for the Soviet News Press Agency.

Cheraskov, Petr Petrovich, his writings include *Франция и Индокитай, 1945-1975* (1976), *Агония империи* (1979), and *Распад колониальной империи Франции* (1985). LC

Cherkasova, Natal'ia Valentinova, fl. 1949, she was joint author of *Искусство советского Узбекистана* (1960), and *Folk art in the Soviet Union* (1990); and joint editor of *Художники советской Киргизии* (1951), and *Традиционное искусство и современные промыслы народов Севера и Сибири* ... (1981). LC

Cherkasskii, Leonid IAkovlevich, his writings include *Стратегия мира* (1972), *СССР никомы не угрожает* (1977), *Азия; проблемы безопасности* (1981), and he was joint author of *Борьба СССР за обеспечение прочного и справедливого мира на Ближнем Востоке, 1967-1980* (1981). LC

Cherkasskii, Mark Abramovich, fl. 1959, his writings include *Тюркский вокализм и сингармонизм* (1965). LC

Cherniakhovskaia (Черняховская), Neonila Ivanova, born 22 May 1929 at Kiev, she graduated in 1953 from the Moscow State University and was awarded a doctorate in 1966. Thereafter she was affilliated with the Akademiia Nauk SSSR. Her writings include *Развитие промышленности и положение рабочего класса Афганистана* (1965), and *Проблемы экономической помощи развивающимся странам Азии и Африки* (1987), and she was joint author of *Афганистан* (1973). In 1990 she edited *Структурные реформы и экономисеское развитие; опыт Африки в 80-е годы*. LC; Miliband

Cherniavsky, Michael, born about 1923, he was a graduate of the University of California, where he also received his Ph.D., and a sometime research assistant to Ernst Kantorowicz at the Institute for Advanced Study at Princeton. He taught at Wesleyan, Chicago, Rochester, and S.U.N.Y., Albany, before being appointed Andrew Mellon Professor of History at the University of Pittsburgh. His writings include *Tsar and people* (1961); in 1967 he edited *Prologue to revolution; notes on A. N. Iakhontov on the secret meetings of the Council of Ministers, 1915.* He died 12 July 1973. LC; *New York times*, 18 July 1973, p. 40, col. 4

Chernikov, Sergei Sergeevich, born 24 July 1909 at Belgorod, he was an archaeologist whose writings include *Восточный Касахстан в эпоху бронзы* (1960), and *Загадка золотого кургана* (1965). He died in Moscow, 7 October 1976. KazakSE; LC

Chernovskaia, Valentina Veniaminovna, fl. 1975, her writings include *Формирование египетской интеллигенции в XIX - первой половине XX в.* (1979). LC

Chéron, Albert, he was a professor whose writings include *Précis de procédure locale appicable en matière civile et commerciale dans les départments du Rhin et de la Moselle* (1930); and he was joint author of *Nouveau code pénal égyptien annoté* (1939). LC

Chérot, Auguste, born about 1812 at Nantes, and educated at the Polytechnique and l'École des mines, he was an industrialist, economist, municipal politician as well as secretary-general of the Société académique de Nantes. He was the author of a great number of periodical articles and pamphlets which include *Les grandes compagnies de chemin de fer en 1877* (1877). BN; DBF

Cherry, William Thomas, born 11 October 1872 at Bowmanville, Ontario; he was a missionary in the Straits Settlements. and wrote *Geography of British Malaya* (1923). He died in Ridley Park, Pa., on 12 October 1941. Shavit - Asia

Cherry, William Thomas, Jr., fl. 1916-1930s, the son of Rev. William Thomas Cherry, 1872-1941.

Chertan, Evgenii Evgen'evich, fl. 1969, he wrote *Русско-румынские отношения в 1859-1863 годах* (1968), and he was the editor of *Балканскии историческии сборник* (1968). LC

Cherville, Asselin de, fl. 1809-1814, he was a French dragoman, who knew the German traveller Ulrich J. Seetzen from Cairo. Fück, 163

Cherzoï (Shirzoi), Wali, born in 1936 at Kabul, he was educated in Afghanistabn and Switzerland. In 1969 he was an honorary dean of the Faculty of Law and Political Science, Kabul. Adamec

Cheshire, Harold Theodore, born in 1890, he edited the *Czech-English dictionary* (1935).

Chesnais, Jean Claude Louis, born 27 October 1948 at Plessix-Balisson (Côtes-du-Nord). After he received doctorates in demography as well as economy, he became attached to the CNRS, l'École nationale d'administration, and l'École polytechnique. In 1989 he was head of the Social Economics Department, l'Institut national d'études démographiques. His writings include *Les mortes violentes en France depuis 1826* (1976), *Le revanche du Tiers-monde* (1987), and *Le crépuscule de l'Occident* (1995). LC; WhoFr, 1997/98

Chesneaux, Jean Marie Auguste, born 22 October 1922 at Paris, he was a graduate of the Lycée Henri-IV and the Faculté des lettres, Paris. In 1955 he was appointed director of l'École pratique des hautes études. His writings include *L'Extrême-Orient de 1840-1914, Chine et Japon* (1955), *Du passé faisons table rase?* (1976), and its translation, *Pasts and futures* (1978). WhoFr, 1973/74-1977/78

Chesney, Francis Rawdon, born in 1789, he was a general, the explorer of the Euphrates, and founder of the overland route to India. His writings include *The expedition for the survey of the rivers Euphrates and Tigris* (1850), *The Russo-Turkish campaigns of 1828 and 1829* (1854), and *Narrative of the Euphrates Expedition* (1868). He died in 1872 or 1876. Boase; DNB; Embacher; Henze

Chesney, George M., he was a general whose writings include *India under experiment* (London, 1918). Master (7); OxEngl

Chesney, Sir George Tomkyns, General, born 30 April 1830 at Tiverton, Devonshire. After passing through the military college of the East India Company at Addiscombe, he obtained a commission as second lieutenant in the Bengal Engineers in 1848. He was posted to India from 1850 to 1891. His writings include *Indian polity* (1868), and *The battle of Dorking; reminiscences of a volunteer* (1871). He died 31 March 1895. Boase; DNB

Chester, Colby Mitchell, born 29 February 1844 at New London, Conn., he was a graduate of the U.S. Naval Academy, and in command of the cruiser *Kentucky* in 1900 at Constantinople to support American damage claims. After his retirement in 1906 he returned to Turkey where he obtained concessions for a railway and for mining. He was a sometime professor of naval science at American universities. He died 4 May 1932. DAB, suppl. I; Shavit; WhAm, 1

Chester, Frank Dyer, born 2 December 1869 at Newton Lower Falls, Mass., he received a Ph.D. in 1894 from Harvard for his thesis, *The "Book of songs", by Ali al-Isbahani.* Thereafter he was a Roger Fellow of Harvard in Damascus, 1895-96, and in Budapest, 1896-97. From 1897 to 1908 he was a consul in Budapest. He died 14 June 1938. WhAm, 1

Chester, Greville John, 25 October 1830 at Denton, Norfolk, he was privately educated, took his degree at Balliol College, Oxford, and after being ordained, served at different parishes throughout England until ill-health forced him to retire. He wintered abroad for many years and frequently visited Egypt, Syria and Palestine. It is as collector and supplier of antiquities that he is best remembered today. He obtained a large series of Arabic glass weights for the British Museum. He died in London, 23 May 1892. Boase, suppl.; Egyptology

Chevaldonné, François Claude Robert, born 15 November 1929 at Epieds, he studied at the Université de Clermont-Ferrand and received a doctorate from the Université de Paris VIII for his thesis, *La communication intégrale*, in 1979. The work was published commercially in 1981. He was a sometime section head at the Bureau de la Formation Professionnell, Ministère des Travaux Publics, Rabat. In 1962 he was attached to the Équipe inter-disciplinaire de recherches en sciences humaines, Rabat. THESAM, 2 Unesco

Chevalier, Auguste Jean Baptiste, born 23 June 1873 at Dromfront (Orne). Although he originated from a family of modest substance, he was able to study natural sciences and obtain a doctorate in 1901 from the Université de Paris for his thesis, *Monographie des myricacées.* In 1898 he accompanied the mission to the Soudan français under General de Trentinian as a botanist. His writings include *L'Afrique centrale française* (1907), *Études sur la flore de l'Afrique centrale française* (1913), and *L'Agriculture coloniale* (1942). He died in Paris, 4 June 1956. Hommes et destins IX, pp. 83-87

Chevalier, Célestin Marie Bernard, l'abbé, born in 1867, he was a sometime professor of philosophy and flourished in Alexandria, Egypt, in 1906. In 1934 he was awarded the Prix de concours internationale de l'Institut catholique de Paris for his work, *La Mariologie de Saint Damascène.* He also wrote *Le Frère de Dolorès, au Paraguay en 1729* (1946). LC

Chevalier, Jean Marie, born 4 June 1941 at Paris, he studied at Paris and Michigan State University. Thereafter he taught at Alger, Rabat, Grenoble and Paris. He was a sometime *administrateur* of the Banque nationale de Paris, and since 1984, a consultant on energy to the World Bank. His writings include *La pauvreté aux États-Unis* (1971), *Le nouvel enjeu pétrolier* (1973), and its translation, *The new oil stakes* (1975), *L'économie en question* (1977), and *Économie de l'energie* (1986). WhoFr, 1997/98

Chevalier, Louis, born 29 May 1911 at l'Aiguillon-sur-Mer (Vendée), he was a graduate of the Lycée Henri-IV as well as l'École normale supérieure, Paris. In 1950 he received a doctorate from the Université de Paris for his thesis, *Les fondements économiques et sociaux de l'histoire politique de la région parisienne, 1848-1870.* Thereafter he was affiliated with the Institut d'études politiques and the Collège de France, Paris. His writings include *Les paysans* (1947), *Le problème démographique nord-africain* (1947), *Démographie générale* (1951), and *Les parisiens*; postface de Jean-Pierre Garnier (1985). ConAu, 85-88; IntWW, 1974-1978; WhoFr, 1967/8-1987/88; WhoWor, 1974-1978

Chevalier, Michel Pierre Aurèle, born 13 September 1921 at Bar-le-Duc (Meuse), he was a professor at a number of lycées before he joined the Faculté des lettres de Toulouse in 1946. He later became a professor of geography at the Faculté des lettres de Besançon, and its *doyen* from 1960 to 1964. From 1964 to 1975 he was *recteur* de l'Académie de Rouen, and from 1981 to 1987 he was affiliated with the Sorbone. His writings include *La vie humaine dans les Pyrénées ariégeoises* (1956), and *Les montagnards chrétiens du Hakkâri et du Kurdistan septentrional* (1985). WhoFr, 1979/80-2000

hevalley, Abel, born 4 July 1868 at Mouilleron-en-Pareds (Vendée), he was sent from 1893 to 1898 a *mission pédagogique* to Egypt. Thereafter he was a contributor to *le Temps*, specializing in reign, particularly British, affairs. From 1905 to 1921 he was in the diplomatic service. He was a iter of poetry and prose, whose *La reine Victoria* (1902), won him the recognition of the Académie ançaise. He died 30 December 1933. DBF; WhE&EA

hevallier, Dominique, fl. 1960, his writings include *La société du Mont Liban à l'époque de la ré-lution industrielle en Europe* (1971), and *Ville et travail en Syrie du XIXe au XXe siècle* (1982); in 987 he was editor of *Renouvellements du monde arabe, 1952-1982*. LC

hevallier, Jean, fl. 1942, he received a doctorate in law in 1932 from the Université de Rennes for his esis, *De l'effet déclaratif des conventions et des contrats*. He was joint author of *Droit civil, 1ère née* (1974). LC; NUC, pre-1956

hevallier, Jean Jacques, born in 1900, he received a doctorate in law in 1925 from the Université de ancy for his thesis, *La competence juridictionnelle en matière de contraventions de voirie*. In 1937 he as a professor of international public law at the Faculté de droit in the Université de Grenoble. His ritings include *Histoire de la pensée politique* (1979-1984). He died in 1983. LC

hevance, J. P., he was in 1956 an *élève-administrateur* at France d'Outre-Mer.

hevrillon, André Louis, born 3 May 1864 at Ruelle (Charente), he was educated in France and ngland, and received a doctorate in 1894 for his thesis, *Sydney Smith et la renaissance des idées érales en Angleterre*. He taught English until ill-health compelled him to resign in 1896 and pursue a erary career. He made several journeys to the Middle East and North Africa. His writings include erres mortes (1897), *Un Crépuscule d'islam; Maroc* (1906), *Les Puritains du désert* (1927), and 'sions du Maroc* (1933). He died in Paris, 10 July 1957. DBF

hew, Samuel Claggett, born 31 August 1888 at Baltimore, Md., he was from 1920 to 1954 a pro-ssor of English at Bryn Mawr (Pa.) College. His writings include *The Crescent and the rose; Islam d England during the Renaissance* (1937). He died 15 January 1960. WhAm, 3

heyne, Thomas Kelly, born 18 September 1841 at London, he was an Old Testament scholar, a ellow of the British Academy, and from 1868 to 1882, a Fellow of Balliol College, Oxford. He died 16 ebruary 1915. DNB; EncAm; Who was who, 1

heynet, Jean Claude, born 20th cent., he received a doctorate in 1987 from the Université de Paris I r his *thèse d'état, Milieux et foyers de perturbation dans l'Empire byzantin de 963 à 1204*. His ritings in-clude *Études prosopographiques* (1986). LC; THESAM, 4

hézy, Antoine Léonard, born 15 January 1775 at Neuilly, he was educated at the Collège de Na-arre, and was the favorite student of Silvestre de Sacy. He was designated to take part in the xpédition d'Égypte but had to return home when he fell ill in Toulon. Through the good offices of his acher, he was the first appointee to the chair of Sanskrit at the Collège de France in 1814. He was e of the founders of the Société asiatique. He died from cholera in Paris, 3 September 1832. Dantès DBF; EncAm; Fück, 154; Hoefer; Index BFr (3)

hézy, Wilhelmine (Helmina) Christiane (Christina) née von Klencke, born 26 January 1783 at Berlin, e wrote poetry and prose from the age of fourteen. In 1805 she married A. L. Chézy. After her ook, *Leben und Kunst in Paris seit Napoleon* (1805-1807), was confiscated by the French authorities, e returned to Germany, where she joined the anti-Napoleonic movement. She lived successively in eidelberg, Berlin, Dresden, Wien and Genève. Her writings include the autobiography, *Unvergesse-es; Denkwürdigkeiten aus dem Leben von Helmina von Chézy* (1858). She died 28 February 1856. 3F; DtBE

hhatari, R. S., colonel, he was in 1953 a delegate of Pakistan to the United Nations. Note

hiauzzi, Gioia, born 20th cent., she was in 1988 affiliated with the Instituto universitario orientale di apoli. Her writings include *Africa settentrionale* (1982), and *Cicli calendariali nel Magreb ...; materiali metodologia per lo studio di un ordinamento* (1988). LC

hichele-Plowden, Sir Trevor John Chichele, born in 1846, he was educated at Winchester. He ntered the India Civil Service, and went out to Bengal in 1868, and served in the Government of India. e was at the Home Department in 1872, the Foreign Department in 1877. He later was Resident in urkish Arabia, and Consul-general in Baghdad. Thereafter he again served in India until 1890. He ied 5 November 1905. Buckland; Riddick; Who was who, 1

Chicherov, Vladimir Ivanovich, born in 1907 at Viazniki, Russia, he graduated in 1928 from the Moscow State University, where he later received his doctorate and was appointed a professor. He was a folklorist whose writings include the translation *Russische Volksdichtung* (1968), and *Школы сказителей Заонежья* (1982); in 1955 he edited *Сусско народно-поэтическое творчество в Татарской АССР.* He died in 1957 in Moscow. GSE; LC

Chidiac, Robert, he received a doctorate in law and was in 1966 a judge in the Court of Appeals and a lecturer at the Université libanaise. Note

Chidiak (Shidyaq), Jean (Phaïm), born 24 December 1821 in Lebanon, he was an interpreter with the Corps des interprètes de l'armée d'Afrique and rose from the rank of *interprète temporaire* (30 December 1846) to *interprète titulaire de 3e classe* (25 December 1861). After having been stationed to various posts in Algeria, he participated in the French campaign in Syria in 1860. He became *chevalier de la Légion d'honneur* in 1864; he retired from the military on 15 May 1867. Féraud, p. 300

Chierici, Luigi, born 14 July 1823 at Bologna, he was a medical doctor who practised in Corfu and Constantinople from 1850 to 1860. In 1861 he returned to Torino and later moved to Bologna and Firenze, from where he moved to Roma, where his trace is lost in 1875. DizBI

Chiha, Michel, his writings include *Liban d'aujourd'hui* (1942), *Palestine* (1957), its English translation in 1969, *Visage et présence du Liban* (1964), and *Propos d'économie libanaise* (1964).

van der **Chijs**, Jacobus Anne, born in 1831, his writings include *De Nederlanders te Jakatra* (1860) and *Mijne reis naar Java in 1869 en terugkeer over Engelsch Indië, Palestina ... en 1870* (1874). He died in 1905. LC

Chikhachev (Tchihatchef/Tschichatscheff), Petr Aleksandrovich (Петр Александрович Чихачев), he was born in 1808 in Gachina near St. Petersburg. He was a geographer and geologist who spent most of his life outside Russia, travelling extensively in Asia Minor between 1847 and 1863. In 1877 and 1878 he visited Spain, Algeria, and Tunisia. His writings include *Voyage scientifique dans l'Altaï oriental et les parties adjacentes de la frontière de la Chine* (1845), *Lettres sur la Turquie* (1859), *Asie mineure* (1853-68). The Académie des sciences de Paris awards the Prix Tchihatchef in his honour. He died in Firenze in 1890. Embacher; EnSlovar; GSE; *Nouvelle revue* 67 (1890), 159-161

Chikhani, Roger, born 25 November 1923 at Bikfaya, Lebanon, he studied at the Faculté droit de l'Université de Saint-Joseph, Beirut, and practised law since 1945. From 1974 to 1978 he was a president of the Lebanese Bar. In 1982 he was appointed Minister of Justice and Information. WhoLeb 1980/81, 1982/3, 1986/7, 1988/9, 1990/1

Child, Theodore, born in 1846 or 1855 at Liverpool, he was a miscellaneous author who spent twenty years in Paris and travelled throughout Europe. His writings include *Summer holidays, travelling notes in Europe* (1889), and *The praise of Paris* (1893). He died from cholera near Tehran, 2 November 1892. Boase, suppl.; LC

Childe, Blanche Lee de Triqueti, born 19th cent., her writings include *Le Général Lee* (1874), and *Un hiver au Caire; journal de voyage en Egypte* (1883). She died in 1886. NUC, pre-1956

Childers, Erskine B., born in 1929, he was a lifelong partisan of Arab self-determination, and Palestinians' rights in particular. In *The road to Suez* (1962) he "exposed the perfidity of the British French, and Israelis over Suez in 1956." His other writings include *Common sense about the Arab world* (1960), and *Arab nationalism* (1964). From 1966 until 1989, he was a senior adviser to the UN director-general for Development and International Economic Co-operation in N.Y.C. He "fulminated against what he saw as the abuse of the United Nations during the Gulf War." When he retired from the UN in 1989, he was soon in the limelight again. Jointly with Sir Brian Urquhart, he issued a series of proposals for making the UN work, culminating in his last, *A world in need of leadership; tomorrow's United Nations* (1990). He died on 25 August 1996. WRMEA 15 (October 1996), p. 24

Childs, James Rives, born 6 February 1893, a graduate of Randolph-Macon College and Harvard, he was a correspondent for the Associated Press, attached to the American Relief Administration in Russia, and was in the Diplomatic Service from 1923 to his retirement in 1953. He was for eighteen years in the Near and Middle East, and in 1934 and 1935 travelled some ten thousand miles by motor vehicle throughout Iran. Under the pseudonym Henry Filmer he wrote *The pageant of Persia; a record of travel by motor in Persia* (1936), and *Escape to Cairo* (1938). He wrote an autobiography, *Foreign Service farewell; my years in the Near East* (1969), and *Vignettes; or, autobiographical fragments* (1977). Shavit; WhoAm, 1948/49-1970/71

299

Childs, W. J., fl. 1916-1924, he wrote *Across Asia Minor on foot* (1917). Together with Mr. Headlam-Morley, historical adviser to the Foreign Office, he prepared a "Memorandum respecting Cyprus," 28 December 1924. BLC

Chimenti, Elisa, fl. 1967, her writings include *Chants de femmes arabes* (1942), *Légendes marocaines* (1959), and its translation, *Tales and legends of Morocco* (1965). LC

Chipp, Sylvia A., born 21 May 1942 at Albany, N.Y., she studied at Rochester and Syracuse, N.Y., where she received a Ph.D. in 1970 for her thesis, *The role of women elites in a modernizing country; the All Pakistan women's Association.* In 1970 she was appointed a professor of political science at Northeastern Oklahoma State University. AmM&WS, 1973 S, 1978 S; IWWAS, 1976/77

Chipp, Thomas Ford, born in 1886, he received a doctorate in science in 1927 from the University of London for his thesis, *The Gold Coast forest.* His writings include *The Forest officers' hand-book of the Gold Coast* (1922). He died in 1931. LC

Chirgwin, Arthur Mitchell, Rev., born 5 April 1885, he was educated at University College, London, and trained for the ministry at Richmond Theological College. He was attached to the London Missionary Society, and was a sometime research secretary of the United Bible Society. The University of Aberdeen conferred on him an honorary doctorate in divinity. His writings include *An African pilgrimage* (1932), *The Bible in world evangelism* (1954), and *These I have known* (1964). He died 29 June 1966. LC; *Who was who*, 6

Chirikov, Egor Ivanovich, fl. 1849-1860, he was a Russian commissar charged with mediating in the Turco-Persian boundary settlement, 1849-1852, about which he reported in his travel diary, *Путеной журнал Е. И. Чирикова, русскаго комиссара-посредника по турецко-персидском разграниче-нию, 1849-1852* (1875). OSK

Chirkuh, Bletch, fl. 1930 *see* Shirkuh, Blih'ch

Chirol, Sir Ignatius *Valentine*, born 23 May 1852. After early training in the Foreign Office, he travelled extensively, mostly in the Near and Middle East, and became a director of the Foreign Department of *The Times.* In 1912 he was appointed to the Royal Commission to enquire into the Indian Public Service. His writings include *The Egyptian problem* (1920), and *India, old and new* (1921). He died 22 October 1929. DNB; *Who was who*, 3

Chisholm, Archibald Hugh Tennent, born 17 August 1902 at London, he was from 1928 to 1972 affiliated with the Anglo-Iranian Oil Compahy in Iran, Kuwait and London. He died 22 November 1992. WhE&EA; *Who's who*, 1974-1993

Chishti, Sumitra, born 15 March 1932 at Arasikere, India, she was in 1988 appointed a professor at the Centre for International Politics, Jawaharlal Nehru University, New Delhi. Her writings include *India's trade with East Europe* (1973), *India's terms of trade, 1930-1968* (1974), a work which is based on her doctoral thesis submitted to the Indian School of International Studies, New Delhi, and *Reconstructing of international economic relations* (1991). IndiaWW, 1995/96; LC

Chittick, Hubert *Neville*, born 18 September 1923 at Hove, Sussex, he went to East Africa from the Sudan in 1957 to be the first keeper of antiquities in Tanganyika. In 1961 he was appointed director of the British Institute of History and Archaeology in Eastern Africa one year after it had been established in Dar es Salam. He supervised the move of its headquarters to Chiromo Mansion in Nairobi three years later, and continued in this post until his retirement in 1983. He had further fieldwork plans in mind but, just after his achievements had been recognized by the award of the OBE, he died suddenly and unexpectedly in Cambridge, 27 July 1984. His writings include *Kilwa, an Islamic trading city on the East African coast* (1974). *Azania* 19 (1984), pp. 1-3; IWWAS, 1975/76

Chittick, William C., born 29 June 1943, he was for over twenty years a professor of comparative literature at SUNY, Stony Brook, specializing in Persian literature, a position he still held in 1997/98. His writings include *The Sufi doctrine of Rumi* (1974), *The Sufi path of knowledge* (1989), *Faith and practice of Islam; three thirteenth-century Sufi thinkers translated* (1992), *Imaginal wolds; Ibn al-'Arabi* (1994), and the translations from the Persian, *The spiritual life* (Tehran, 1982), and *The Sufi path of love* (1983). LC

Chitty, Simon Casie, 1807-1860, his writings include *The Ceylon gazetteer* (1834), *The castes, customs, manners and literature of the Tamils* (1934), and *The Tamil plutarch* (1982). LC

Chklaver, Georges, fl. 1937, he received a doctorate in 1929 from the Université de Paris for his thesis, *Le droit international dans ses rapports avec la philosophie du droit.* He edited *Constantinople et les détroits,* by E. A. Adamov (1930-32), and *Au service de la Russie,* by A. P. Izvol'skii (1937). LC

Chlala (Shallalah), Joseph, fl. 1947. After the completion of legal studies, he became a librarian to the Cour d'appel mixte du Caire. His writings include *Répertoire du droit de travail* (1955), and the Arabic *Dictionnaire pratique français-arabe; droit, commerce, finance* (1973). LC

Chlenova, Nataliia L'vovna, fl. 1956, her writings include *Хронология памятников карасукской эпохи* (1972), *Карасуские кинжжалы* (1976), *Оленные камни как исторический источник* (1984), and *Памятники конца эпохи бронзы в Западной Сибири* (1994). LC

Chmielowska, Danuta, fl. 1975, her writings include *La Femme turque dans l'œuvre de Nabi, Vehbi et Vasif* (Varsovie, 1986). LC

Chobanian (Tchobanian), Arshag, born in 1872, his writings include *Chants populaires arméniennes* (1903), *La femme arménienne* (1918), and *La roseraie d'Arménie* (1918-1929), as well as the translation *The people of Armenia* (1914). He died in 1954. LC

Chochiev, Vitalii Georgievich, born 6 October 1925 at TSkhinvali, Georgian SSSR, he graduated in 1950 from the Oriental Faculty, Tbilissi State University. His writings include *Ирано-турецкнй мирный договор 1639 г. и Грузия* (1954). Miliband

Chodzidlo, Theophil, fl. 1946, his writings include *Die Familie bei den Jakuten* (1951). LC

Chodźko, Aleksandr Borejko, born 30 August 1804 at Krzywicze, Poland, he studied Oriental languages at Wilno/Vilna and St. Petersburg, 1824-1830. He entered the Russian diplomatic service and served as a translator and interpreter at the Missions in Tabriz and Tehran, and as a consul in Rasht. From 1852 to 1855 he worked for the French foreign ministry. He later was a professor of Persian and Slavic studies at Paris until his retirement in 1883. His writings include *Specimens of the popular poetry of Persia* (1842), *Le Ghilan, les marais caspiens* (1850), *Grammaire persane* (1852), and *Le théâtre persan* (1878). He died in Noisy-le-See, near Paris, 19 Decmber 1891. Dantès I; Elranica; Henze; PSB

Chokai-ogly (Çokay/Czokai-ogly/Tchokaï Ogly), Mustafa, born in 1890, he was a prominent Turkestani nationalist and president of the Provisional Government of Autonomous Turkestan, which was elected by the Extraordinary Congress of Turkestan Muslims in November, 1917, and which was suppressed as a result of the bombardment of Kokand by troops of the Tashkent Sovnarkom on 31 January 1917. He fled the USSR in 1919 and settled in France, but kept numerous connections in Turkey, Persia, and Afghanistan. His writings include *Chez les soviets en Asie centrale* (1928), *Туркестан под властью Советов* (1935), and *1917 yılı hatıra parçaları* (1988). He died in 1941. In 1953, his private papers and his library were sold by his widow to what is now the Bibliothèque de l'Institut national des langues et civilisations orientales, Paris. BN; LC; ZKO

Cholnoky, Jenő, born 23 July 1870 at Veszprém, Hungary, he was a geographer whose writings include *A Balaton színtüneményei* (1906), and an autobiography, *Utazágaim, élményeim, kalandjaim* (1942). He died in 1950. LC; RNL

Chombart de Lauwe, Jean, born 17 July 1909 at Compiègne (Oise), he was an agronomist and a *docteur ès sciences économiques*. His writings include *Pour une agriculture organisée* (1949), and *Gestion des exploitations agricoles* (1957). LC; WhoFr, 1965/66-1995/96

Chombart de Lauwe, Paul Henry, born in 1912, he was a sociologist and affiliated with the CNRS. His writings include *Des hommes et des villes* (1963), *Aspirations et transformations sociales* (1970), *La fin des villes* (1982), and *Culture - action des groupes dominés* (1988). LC

Chomsky, Noam Avram, born 27 December 1928 at Philadelphia, Pa., he received a Ph.D. in 1955 from the University of Pennsylvania for his thesis, *Transformational analysis*. Since 1957 he was a professor of linguistics at M.I.T., prominent not only in his own field but also in the American radical movement. His writings include *Syntactic structures* (1965), *Peace in the Middle East?* (1974), and *The fateful trial* (1983). CnDiAmJBi; ConAu 17-18; EncJud; Master (12); WhoAm, 1974-1997

Ch'opomyan, Arshak, 1872-1954 *see* Chobanian, Arshag

Chopra, M. S., he was in 1951 a major-general in the Indian Army.

Chopra, Surendra, fl. 1965, author of *UN mediation in Kashmir* (1971), *Post-Simla Indo-Pak relations* (1988), and *Pakistan's thrust in the Muslim world* (1992). LC

Chossat, Marcel, S.J., born in 1863, his writings include *Les Jésuites et leurs œuvres à Avignon, 1553-1768* (1896), *La guerre d'après le droit naturel chrétien* (1918), and *La somme des sentences* (1923). LC

Chottin, Alexis, fl. 1924, he was attached to the Service des arts indigène du Protectorat de la République française au Maroc. His writings include *Chants d'arabes d'Andalousie* (193-?), *Corpus de musique marocaine* (1931), and *Tableau de la musique marocaine* (1939), a work for which he was awarded the Prix du Maroc in 1938. LC

Chou, Yi-liang, fl. 1946, he received a Ph.D. in 1944 from Harvard University for his thesis, *Tantrism in China*. LC

Choubert, Georges, he was in 1941 a geological engineer and head of the Brigade de Draa et Souss of the Mission hydrogéologique, Morocco, and in 1960, he received a doctorate from the Université de Paris for his thesis, *Histoire géologique du précambrien de l'Anti-Atlas*. He was joint author of *La géologie marocaine* (1948), and joint coordinator of *Atlas géologique du monde* (1976-1987). LC

Choublier, Max, born 30 March 1873. After obtaining a doctorate of law, he lectured at l'École française de droit du Caire, from 1897 to 1900, when he entered the French consular service, spending ten years in Macedonia. He resigned in 1912 to pursue an interest in commercial affairs. His writings include *La question d'Orient depuis le traité de Berlin* (1897). He died in Palamos, Spain, on 29 August 1933. DBF; LC

Choucair, Néjib, fl. 1926, he was a secretary-general of the Comité syro-palestinien.

Choudhury, A. K. M. Alauddin, fl. 1974, he was in 1972 attached to the Pakistan-SEATO Cholera Research Laboratory.

Choudhury (Caudhuri/Chowdhury), A. M. Faiz Ahmad, born in 1917. After the completion of his religious education, he took the B.A. subsidiary examination in Arabic and English in 1942 and his B.A. (Hons.) in Persian at the University of Dacca in 1943. He passed the M.A. (Final) examination in Urdu as a private candidate in 1955. He did post-graduate work at Tehran University, 1952-1953. Thereafter he joined the University of Dacca as a lecturer in Persian and Urdu, a position which he still held in 1968. His writings include *Bengali to Urdu dictionary* (1966). LC

Choudhury, Golam Wahed, born 1 January 1926 at Habigunj, India (East Pakistan), he was educated at Calcutta and Columbia University, where he received a Ph.D. in 1956 for his thesis, *The first Constitutional Assembly of Pakistan, 1947-1954*. In 1957, he joined Dacca University, and in 1963, he was head of the Department of Political Science. He was a sometime assistant secretary of the Pakistan Institute of International Affairs as well as a visiting professor at the Southeast Asian Institute of Columbia University. His writings include *China in world affairs* (1982), and *Islam and the contemporary world* (1990). ConAu, 25-28; IntAu&W, 1977

Chouémi, Moustafa, fl. 1959, his writings include *Le verbe dans le Coran* (1966), and, with Régis Blachère, *Dictionnaire arabe-français-anglais* (1967). LC

Choupaut, Yves Marie, fl. 1969, he was a journalist for *Paris-Normandie* and *Radio France*. His writings include *Les Amants du pont du Gard* (1993). LC

Chowdhury, A. H. M. Nuruddin, fl. 1962-1971, he was an economist and affiliated with the Economic Office of the Asian Development Bank. His writings include *Regional Cooperation for Development* (1965), *Inflation in developing member countries* (1982), and he was joint author, with Marcelia C. Garcia, of *Rural institutional finance in Bangladesh and Nepal* (1993). LC

Chowdhury, A. M. Faiz Ahmad *see* Choudhury, A. M. Faiz Ahmad

Chowdhury, Rev. D. A., B.D., fl. 1934, he was a convert from Islam and in charge of the work of the work of the Church of Scotland Mission at Budge-Budge, near Calcutta.

Chowdhury, Malik K., he was in 1968 a senior lecturer in economics at Karachi University. His writings include *The first five-year plan; economic development ... in Bangladesh* (New Haven, Conn., Yale University, Economic Growth Center, 1975). ZKO

Chowdhury (Chaudhury), Rafiqul Huda, fl. 1975, a writer on demography and population studies whose work includes *Married women in urban occupations of Bangladesh* (1976). LC

Ch'owgaszyan, Babken L, born 1923 *see* Chugaszian, Babken Levonovich

Chrétien, Maxime, he received a doctorate in law in 1936 from the Université de Lille for his thesis, *Les règles de droit d'origine juridictionnelle*. He was a sometime professor at the Faculté royale de droit du Caire. His writings include *Réforme fiscale* (1949), and *Histoire de l'Égypte moderne* (1951).

Christ, Hermann, born 19th cent., in Switzerland, he received a Dr.med. in 1894 from the Universität Basel for his thesis, *Über den Einfluß der Muskulatur auf die Herztätigkeit*. He was a medical missionary at Urfa, Turkey, from December 1898 to April 1903, when he had to return on account of his wife's ill-health. *Der Orient* (Potsdam), 1923, p. 31

Christelow, Allan, born 8 July 1947, he received a Ph.D. and was a professor at the Department of History, Idaho State University, Pocatello, certainly until 1998. His writings include *Muslim law courts and the French colonial state in Algeria* (1985). In 1994 he edited *Thus ruled the Emir Abbas; selected cases from the records of the Emir of Kano's Judicial Council.* LC

Christensen, Arthur Emanuel, born 9 January 1875 at København, he was appointed in 1919 to the chair of Iranian Philology in Københavns Universitet. His writings include *Romanen om Bahram Tschôbîn* (1907), *Études sur le Zoroastrisme de la Perse antique* (1928), and *Études sur le persan contemporain*, a work though completed during the war in 1944, it was not published until 1970. In 1945, he was honoured by the jubilee volume *Øst og West; afhandlinger tilegnede Professor Dr. phil. Arthur Christensen*. He died in Charlottenlund, 31 March 1945. L.P. Elwell-Sutton, *British Society for Middle Eastern Studies bulletin* 10 (1983), pp. 59-68; DanskBL

Christensen, Dieter, born 17 April 1932 at Berlin, he received a Dr.phil. in 1957 from the Freie Universität Berlin for his thesis, *Musik der Kate und Sialum; Beiträge zur Etnographie Neuguineas* and became a curator at the Museum für Völkerkunde, Berlin, from 1958 to 1972. Thereafter he was a professor of musicology and director of the Center for Ethnomusicology at Columbia University. He frequently carried on field-work in eastern Turkey and Oman. WhoAmM, 1983

Christian, Viktor, born 30 March 1885 at Wien, he studied philology and archaeology at the Universität Wien, where he also received a doctorate in 1910. Until 1924 he was attached to the Naturhistorisches Museum, Wien. Thereafter he was a professor of Semitic linguistics, and later, Dean of the University. His writings include *Die sprachliche Stellung des Sumerischen* (1932), *Altertumskunde des Zweistromlandes* (1940), and *Untersuchungen zur Land- und Formenlehre des Hebräischen* (1953). In 1956, he was honoured by the *Festschrift für Professor Dr. Viktor Christian*. He died in Walchsee, 28 May 1963. DtBE; WhE&EA; WhoAustria, 1954-1959/60

Christiansen-Weniger, Friedrich Johann Georg, born 17 April 1897 at Hamburg, he received a doctorate in 1922 at Breslau with a thesis entitled *Der Energiebedarf der Stickstoffbindung durch die Knöllchenbakterien*. From 1928 to 1929 and 1930 to 1940, he was successively a lecturer at the Yüksek Ziraat Okulu, Ankara, and Ankara Üniversitesi and concurrently a consultant to the Turkish Ministry of Agriculture. His writings include *Die Grundlagen des türkischen Ackerbaus* (1934), and *Ackerbauformen im Mittelmeerraum ... dargestellt am Beispiel der Türkei* (1970). He died in Eckernförde, 22 March 1989. Kürschner, 1961-1987; Wer ist wer, 1971/73; Widmann

Christides, Vassilios/Vasileios, born ca. 1940, he received a Ph.D. in 1970 from Princeton with a thesis entitled *The image of pre-Islamic Arab in the Byzantine sources*. Thereafter he was a professor of Byzantine history at the University of Thessaloniki. His writings include *The conquest of Crete by the Arabs* (1984). EVL; LC

Christie, Anthony, born first half 20th cent., his writings include *Chinese mythology* (1968).

Christie, Archibald H., fl. 1922-1942, his writings include *Traditional methods of pattern designing* (1910), 2nd edition published in 1929. NUC, pre-1956

Christie, Ella R., fl. 1920, she wrote *Through Khiva to Golden Samarkand; the remarkable story of a woman's adventurous journey alone through the deserts of Central Asia to the heart of Turkestan* (London, 1925).

Christie, Thomas Davidson, born 21 January 1843 at Sion Mills, Ireland, he was an engineer who later studied at Beloit College, followed by three years at Andower Theological Seminary. He then joined the Commission of the American Board as a missionary to Central Turkey, in 1877. Fluent in Turkish after one year's immersion, he served first at Maraş and later at Tarsus. Following the 1909 Armenian massacres, he was engaged in relief work. In 1915 he was expelled by the Turkish authorities, returning only for a short time after the war. He died in Pasadena, Cal., 25 May 1921. *Missionary review of the world*, n.s., 35 (1922), pp. 788-796; Shavit

Christie, William Melville, fl. 1901, he wrote *Palestine calling* (London, 1940). BLC; NUC, pre-1956

Christodoulou, Demetrios, born 1 January 1919 at Nicosia, he received a Ph.D. in 1954 from LSE for his thesis, *The evolution of the rural land use in Cyprus*. After public service in Cyprus, he joined the Food and Agriculture Organization of the United Nations, in 1973. From 1982 to 1985 he was Minister of Agriculture in Cyprus. His writings include *The Unpromised land; agrarian reform and conflict worldwide* (1990). LC; Sluglett; WhoUN, 1975

Christophe, Louis A., fl. 1962-1966, his writings include *Abou-Simbel et l'épopée de sa découverte* (Bruxelles, 1965), and *Campagne internationale de l'Unesco pour la sauvagarde des sites et monuments de Nubie* (1977). LC; NUC, 1956-1967

Christopher, W., lieutenant, born in 1814. "After entering the Navy, he was employed for five years in the surveys of the coasts and islands of the Red Sea, and for the next five years in the surveys of the Maldive Islands, the Gulf of Manaat and Chagos Archipelago, under Capt. Moresby. He subsequently surveyed the east coast of Africa, in command of the *Tigris* brig of war. It was then, that, having made a journey into the interior he discovered a large stream, which he named Haines river ... After this he was employed in the Indus flotilla under Capt. Powell, chiefly in Seinde, and afterwards in ascertaining by surveys how far up the rivers Indus, Sutlej, Chenab, and Ravee were navigable by steam. In July, 1848, he joined the force under Lieut. Edwardes operating before Mooltan, and received his death-wound while pointing out the way to a detachment of troops advancing to support the force already in the trenches." *Journal of the Royal Geographical Society* 19 (1849), p. lxi

Christy, Cuthbert, born in 1863. After taking a medical doctorate at Edinburgh, he was a surgeon and explorer who served in many parts of Africa and India. His writings include *Mosquitos and malaria* (1900), and *Big game and Pygmies* (1924). He died 29 March 1932. Hill; *Who was who*, 3

Chromov, A. L. see Khromov, Al'bert Leonidovich

Chroust, Anton (Toni) Hermann, born 28 January 1907 at Würzburg, Germany, he studied at universities in Germany, Italy, France and Britain. In 1929 he received a Dr.jur. from the Universität Erlangen for his thesis, *Die Einführung des Code Mapoleon im Großherzogtum Würzburg*. Thereafter he was a professor of law at American universities. His writings include *Socrates, men and myth* (1957), *The rise of the legal profession in America* (1965), and *Aristotle; new light on his life* (1973). ConAu, 1; WhoAm, 1974-1978

Chubin, Shahram, Dr., born in 1940, he was in 1979 a co-ordinator of the Regional Security Programme at the Institute for Strategic Studies, London. His writings include *Foreign relations of Iran* (1974), *Soviet policy towards Iran and the Gulf* (1980), *Iran and Iraq at war* (1988), and he edited *Germany and the Middle East* (1992). LC

Chubinashvili, Georgii Nikolaevich, born 21 November 1885, he was a writer on Georgian art and architecture whose writings include *Архитекура Кахетии* (1956-59), *Вопросы истории искусства* (1970), and *Хандиси* (1972). In 1977, M. I. Barkava and E. Dolize published the bio-bibliography, *Гиоргий Чубинашвили; биобиблиографья*. He died 14 January 1973. LC; NUC, 1982

Chufrin, Gennadii Illarionovich, born 20th cent., his writings include *Сингапур* (1970), *Экономическая интеграция в Азии* (1975), and *Экономическая интеграция развивающихся стран Азии* (1983); he was joint author of *Наука и техника в странах АСЕАН* (1990).

Ch'ugaszian (Chukaszian), Babken Levonovich, born 18 March 1923 at Tabriz, he graduated in 1951 at Erevan, and received his first degree in 1962 for *Армяно-иранске литературные связи в V-XVIII веках*. From 1963 to 1965 he was deputy director of the Institute for Literatures, Armenian Academy of Science. Miliband; Miliband²

Chukov, Boris V. he edited *Писатели Египта, XX век*, by N. K. Kotsarev (1975), and *Писатели Сирии и Ливана, 1946-1975*, by A. S Roitenburd (1979). LC

Chuloshnikov, A. P., fl. 1932-1936, his writings include *Очерки по истории казак-киргизского народа в связи с общими судьбами других тюркских племен* (1924), and *Восстание 1755 в Башкирии* (1940). LC

Chumachenko, Erika Georgievna, fl. 1966, she wrote *В. О. Ключевский, источниковед* (1970).

Chumakaeva, M. Ch., born 20th cent., she received a doctorate in 1972 for her thesis, *Консонантизм алтайского языка*. She was joint editor of *Как это сказать по-алтайски* (1990). LC

Chumovski, Teodor A., born 1913 see Shumovsii, Teodor Adamovich

Churakov, Mikhail Vasil'evich, fl. 1955, his writings include *Народное движение в Магрибе род знаменем хариджизма* (1990). LC

Churchill, Charles Wesley, born in 1911, he received a Ph.D. in 1942 from New York University for his thesis, *The Italians in Newark, a community study*. He was attached to the Economic Research

304

Institute, American University of Beirut. He was joint author of *The city of Beirut* (1954), and joint editor of *Readings in Arab Middle Eastern societies and cultures* (1970). Note

Churchill, Edward, fl. 1975, he was a graduate of Harvard, and a doctoral candidate in history at the University of Pennsylvania. He taught at Kent State and Rutgers University, and had been repeatedly to India as well as Pakistan on research in social history and the Muslim community. Note

Churchill, Sidney John Alexander, born 1 March 1862, he was privately educated in Britain and entered the Persian Telegraph Department of the Government of India in 1880. In 1886, he was attached to the Legation of Tehran. He later was in the consular service. He was a collector of Oriental manuscripts. His writings include *Oriental carpets* (1892-96). He died 11 January 1921. *Who was who, 2*

Churchill, Sir Winston Leonard Spencer, 1874-1965, British wartime prime minister whose writings include *A history of the English-speaking peoples* (1956-58). DNB; *Who was who, 6*

Chvyr', Liudmila Anatol'evna, born 13 November 1944, her writings include *Таджикские ювелирные украшения* (1977), and *Уйгуры Восточного Туркестана и соседние народы в конце XIX-начале XX в.; очерки* (1990). LC; Schoeberlein

Chwolson, Daniel A., 1819-1911 *see* Khvol'son, Daniel Avraamovich

Ciachir, Nicolae/Nikolae, born in 1928 at Vaisal, Bessarabia, he was a historian of the Balkans whose writings include *100 ani de la Unirea Principatelor* (1958), *România în sud-estul Europei* (1968), *Soliman Magnificul* (1972), and *Diplomația europeană în epoca modernă* (1984). LC; WhoRom

Ciasca, Raffaele, born 24 May 1888 at Rionero in Vulture (Potenza), he received a doctorate in 1913 for his thesis, *L'origine del "programma per l'opinione nazionale italiana" del 1847-1848*, which was published in 1916. Thereafter he was a professor at the Università di Cagliari. His writings include *Storia delle bonifiche del Regno di Napoli* (1928), and *Storia coloniale dell'Italia contemporanea da Assab all'Impero* (1938). He died in Roma, 18 July 1975. DizBI; Unesco

Ciecierska-Chłapowa, Teresa, fl. 1964, she was affiliated with the Uniwersytet Jagielloński, Kraków. Her writings include *Krytyka społeczno-polityczna w dramatach Orhana Aseny* (1982). LC

Cieślak, Edmund, born 7 July 1922 at Toruń, Poland, he studied at the universities of Lille and Toruń, where he received a doctorate in 1950. Thereafter he was a professor of history, specializing in the local history of Gdańsk. His writings include *Dzieje Gdańska* (1969), and its translation, *History of Gdańsk* (1988). Kto Polsce 3 (1993); LC

Cigar, Norman L., born 2 May 1948, he received a D.Phil. in 1976 from Oxford University for his thesis, *An edition and translation of the chronicles from Muhammad al-Qadiri's "Nashr al-Marhani."* In 1978, he was attached to the Department of History in the University of Wisconsin at Madison, and in 1994, to the U.S. Marine Corps School of Advanced Warfighting. He published numerous brief bibliographies on the greater Middle East in the *Vance bibliographies* series. His writings include *Agriculture and rural development in the Fertile Crescent* (1981), and *Genocide in Bosnia; the policy of ethnic cleansing* (1995). LC; Sluglett

Cigielman, Victor, fl. 1962 *see* Cygielman, Victor

Cilardo, Agostino, fl. 1976, he was affiliated with the Istituto universitare orientale di Napoli. His writings include *Studies on the Islamic law of inheritance* (1991). LC

Çiller Tansu U., born 24 May 1946 (some sources say 1945) at İstanbul, she graduated from Robert College, Bebek, İstanbul, and also studied economics at American New England universities. She was a member of Doğru Yol Partisi and became Turkey's first woman prime minister in 1993. She persuaded the West that she was Turkey's only answer to Islamic fundamentalism and the European Union rewarded her with a long-coveted customs union agreement. Çiller, who made her husband, Özer Ucuran, take her maiden name, was nicknamed Turkey's "iron lady with a smile." But while she was tough on Kurds, she had less success battling 150 per cent inflation. She spent her four years of premiership fighting to retain power rather than wielding it. Her writings include *Türk sanayiinin büyümesindeki kaynaklar* (1981), *II düzeyinde milli gelir dağılımı* (1982), and *Kritik politika* (1987). IntWW, 1996-1998|; IntYB, 1996-2001; Kim kimdir, 1985/86, 1997/98, 1999; *The Times* magazine, 23 March 1996, p. 18

Cillov, Halûk, born 20 May 1920 at Izmir, he received a doctorate in economics in 1949. Thereafter he was a professor of statistics and economics at Istanbul Üniversitesi. His writings include *Türkiye ekonomisi* (1962), and its Russian translation, *Экономика Турции* (1971). Kim kimdir, 1985/86; LC

Cimino, Massimo, born 6 August 1908 at Nicastro, Italy, he received a doctorate in mathematics in 1933. Thereafter he was a professor of astronomy at various Italian universities before he became attached to the Museo astronomico e copernicano di Roma. His writings include *Lezioni di astronomia* (1966). Chi è, 1961; Wholtaly, 1980; WhoWor, 1974/75, 1976/77

Cimmino, Francesco, born in 1864 at Napoli, he was a sometime professor of Sanskrit at the Università di Napoli. His writings include *Dal poema persiano Jusuf e Zuleicha di Mewlana A. Giami* (1899). He died in 1939. IndBI (6); Rovito

Ciobanu, Veniamin, fl. 1975, his writings include *Jurnal ieşcan la sfirşit de veac* (1980), *Relaţiile politici romăno-polone între 1699 şi 1848* (1980), *Les pays roumains au seuil du 18e siècle* (1984), *Ţările romăne şi Polonia, secolele XIV-XVI* (1985), *La cumpănă de veacuri* (1991), and *Politice şi diplomaţie în secolul al XVII-lea* (1994). LC

Cioeta, Donald James, born in 1945, he received a Ph.D. in 1979 from the University of Chicago for his thesis, *"Thamarat al-funun," Syria's first Islamic newspaper, 1875-1908.* In 1990 he was affiliated with the University of Washington and a member of MESA. MESA roster of members, 1982-1990

Ciopiński, Jan, fl. 1964, his writings include *Elementy retoryczne w "Kanuni mersiyesi" Bakiego* (1982). LC

Ciorănesco, Georges, born in 1918 or 1919 in Romania, he graduated in law from the Universitatea din Bucureşti. After the communist take-over he fled to the West, where he was a collaborator with Radio Free Europe. He later settled in France. His writings include *La mission de Stanislas Bellanger dans l'Empire ottoman* (1981), and *Bessarabia, disputed land between East and West* (1985). He died in 1993. LC; WhoRom

Cipolla, Carlo, conte, born 26 September 1854 at Verona. After his study of history and philosophy at Verona and Padova, he was appointed professor of modern history at the Università di Torino. His writings include *Compendio della storia politica di Verona* (1899). and *Scritti di Carlo Copolla, 1854-1916.* He died in 1916. DizBI; LC

Cipolla, Carlo Manlio, born 15 August 1922 at Pavia, Italy, he studied at Pavia, Paris and LSE. Afterwards he was a professor at various Italian universities. In 1959 he taught at the University of California at Berkeley. His writings include *Studi di storia della moneta* (1948), *Le avventure della lira* (1975), *The monetary policy of fourteenth-century Florence* (1982), and *Miasmas and disease* (1992). Chi è, 1957, 1961; ConAu, new rev. 2; LC; IntAu&W, 1976; WrDr, 1976-1988

Cipriani, Lidio, born 17 March 1894 at Firenze, he was an anthropologist at Firenze and carried on extensive field-work in Africa and India. His writings include *Arabi dello Yemen e dell'Higiaz* (1939), *Abitazioni indigene dell'Africa orientale italiana* (1940), and *The Andaman Islanders* (1966). He died in Firenze, 18 October 1962. Chi è, 1928-1961; DizBI; Wholtaly, 1957/58

de Circourt, Anne Marie Joseph *Albert*, comte, born 25 June 1809 at Bouxières-aux-Chênes (Meurthe). After passing through l'École de marine, he went to the Middle East in 1826, and took part in the siege of Alger in 1828. For political reasons he had to resign from the Navy in 1830. Thereafter he was a writer and editor. His writings include *Histoires des Mores Mudejares et des Morisques* (1846). He died 15 June 1895. DBF

Cirilli, Gustave, born 19th cent., he was a diplomat whose writings include *Album de Smyrne* (1883), *Droit international; le régime des capitulations, son histoire, son application, ses modifications,* and *Journal du siège d'Adrianople* (1913). BN; NUC, pre-1956

Čirkovič (Tchirkovitch), Stevan, born in 1898, he received a doctorate in law in 1926 from the Université de Paris for his thesis, *L'Institut américain de droit international.* In 1952 he was a professor at l'Institut des hautes études internationales de l'Université de Paris. His writings include *Le droit international nouveaux* (1926). NUC, pre-1956

Cirot, Georges, born 25 February 1870 at Neuilly-sur-Seine, he was a graduate of l'École normale supérieure de Paris, and was appointed in 1896 a professor at the Faculté de droit de Bordeaux and in 1933 a director of l'École des hautes études hispaniques. His writings include *Études sur l'historiographie espagnole* (1904), and *Histoire générale de l'Espagne* (1905). He died in Bordeaux on 27 November 1946. DBF

de Cirre, Manuela Manzanares, 1910- *see* Manzanares de Cirre, Manuela

Cirtautas, Ilse D. *see* Laude-Cirtautas, Ilse D.

Císcar Pallarés, Eugenio, his writings include *Las cortes valencianas de Felipe III* (1973); and he was joint author of *Moriscos i agermanats* (1974). LC

Cissoko, Sékéné Mody, fl. 1969, he was a *professeur secondaire* in Mali and originated from Dinguira in the Kayes region, south-west of Mali. His writings include *Tombouctou et l'Empire Songhay* (1975), *Contribution à l'histoire politique du Khasso dans le Haut-Sénégal* (1986), *Le Khasso face à l'Empire toucouleur et à la France dans le Haut-Sénégal* (1988); he was joint author of *Recueil des traditions orales des Mandingue de Gambie et de Casamance* (1974). LC

Ciszewski, Stanislaw Bronisław, born 18 December 1865 at Krążku, he was a Polish ethnologist folklorist and a professor who received a Dr.phil in 1897 from the Universität Leipzig for his thesis, *Künstliche Verwandtschaft bei den Südslaven*. His writings include *Prace etnologiczne* (1925-1926). He died in Warszawa, 27 May 1930. LC; PSB

Citarella, Armand O., born 12 March 1921 at Napoli, he received a doctorate in 1949 from the Università di Napoli. Thereafter he was a professor of classics at St. Michael's College, Winooski, Vt. He was joint author of *Ninth-century treasure of Monte Cassino in the context of political and economic developments in Italy* (1983). DrAS, 1982

Ciurea, Doina, fl. 1970, author of *Descifrări* (Bucureşti, 1977), and *Ion Ion; roman* (1991). LC

Civera Simón, Gregorio, born in 1909. His writings include *Algelia, punto clave de una encrucijada histórica* (1957). NYPL

Clagett, Brice McAdoo, born 6 July 1933 at Washington, D.C., he studied law at Princeton, Allahabad and Harvard, where he received a Ph.D. in 1954. He was successively attached to the U.S. Supreme Court, the International Court of Justice, and the U.S.-Iran Claimants Commission. WhoAm, 1988; WhoAmL, 1978-1996/97

Clagett, Marshall, born 23 January 1916 at Washington, D.C., he received a Ph.D. in 1941 from Columbia University for *Giovanni Marliani and late medieval physics*. He taught at variety of American universities before he joined the Institute for Advanded Study, Princeton, in 1964. His writings include *Greek science in antiquity* (1955), and *The science of mechanics in the middle ages* (1959). ConAu 1, new rev. 5; DrAS, 1974, 1978, 1982; WhoAm, 1974-1988/89

Clairmont, Christoph Walter, born 13 February 1924 at Zürich, he studied at Oxford and Zürich, where he received a Dr.phil. in 1950 for *Das Parisurteil in der klassischen Kunst*. Since 1966 he was a professor of classics and archaeology at Rutgers University, New Brunswick, N.J. His writings include *Die Bildnisse des Antinous* (1966), *Gravestone and epigram; Greek memorials* (1970), *Excavations at Salona, Yugoslavia, 1969-1972* (1975), and *Catalog of ancient and Islamic glass* (1977). DrAS, 1974

Clairmonte, Frédéric, fl. 1970, he received a doctorate in 1958 from the Université de Genève for *Le libéralisme économique et les pays sous-développés*. His writings include *Economic liberalism and underdevelopment* (1958), and its translation, *Liberalismo económico y subdesarrollo* (1963), and he was joint author, with John Cavanagh, of *The world in their web; dynamics of textile multinationals* (1981). In 1988 he wrote for the World Council of Churches' Commission on the Churches Participation in Development the pamphlet, *Mechanics of financial capital; merger mania and insider trading.*

de **Claparède**, Arthur, 1852-1911, his writings include *Annuaire universel des sociétés de géographie* (1892), *A travers le monde* (1894), *En Algérie* (Genève, 1896), *Catalogue des livres de la Société de géographie de Genève* (1897), and *Corfou et les Corfiotes* (Genève, 1900). BN; NUC, pre-1956

Clapier-Valladon, Simone, fl. 1960, she received diplomas in philosophy, psychology and ethnology. In 1983 she was a professor at the Université de Nice. She wrote *Panorama du culturalisme* (1976); she was joint author of *L'approche biographique; réflexions épistémologiques sur une méthode de recherche* (1983), and she was joint editor of *Les femmes et la vie* (1989). LC

Clapp, Frederick Gardner, born 20 July 1879 at Boston, he graduated from M.I.T. From 1902 to 1908, he was attached to the U.S. Geological Survey, and afterwards he became a consulting and petroleum geologist. He conducted explorations also in Iran and Afghanistan. His writings include *Geology of eastern Iran* (1940). He died in Chickasha, Okla., 18 February 1944. Shavit; Shavit - Asia; Master (3)

Clapp, Gordon Rufus, born 28 October 1905 at Ellsworth, Wisc., he was a university administrator before he became chairman of the board of directors of the Tennessee Valley Authority from 1946 to 1954. He headed the 1949 U.N. Economic Survey Mission to the Middle East. In 1955 he and David E. Lilienthal formed the Development and Resources Corporation to provide planning and administrative services to foreign countries in resource development work. Following a visit to Iran in February 1956, their company agreed to work for the Iranian Plan Organization in developing the Khuzistan region. He died 28 April 1963. *Who was who in America*, 4

Clapperton, Hugh, born in 1788 at Annan, Dumfries, Scotland, he served in the merchant marine and the Royal Navy before he joined the Bornu Mission to Central Sudan in 1821. He travelled from Tripoli to Sokota in 1822. He died at the end of the unsuccessful second mission near Sokota, 13 April 1827. His wrote *Journal of a second expedition into the interior of Africa* (1829), a work which was immediately translated into Dutch and German. He was joint author of *Narratives of travels and discoveries in Northern and Central Africa* (1926). DNB; Embacher; Henze

Clark, Alden Hyde, born 26 June 1878 at Minneapolis, Minn., and a graduate of Amherst College, Columbia University, and Union Theological Seminary, he served as a missionary in India from 1904 until his retirement in 1947. He wrote *India on the march* (1930). Shavit - Asia; WhAm, 4

Clark, Brian Drummond, fl. 1973, he was joint author of *Kermanshah, an Iranian provincial city* (1969), and *Environmental impact assessment; a bibliography with abstracts* (1980). LC

Clark, Edward C., born 20th cent., he was in 1974 a professor at the University of Texas at El Paso.

Clark, Edwin H., fl. 1969, he published, with Mohammed Ghaffar, *Installation of private tubewells in West Pakistan, 1964-1967* (1968), *Purchase of water from private tubewells* (1968), *An analysis of private tubewells costs* (1969), and, with Swadesh R. Bose, *Some basic considerations on agricultural mechanization in West Pakistan* (1969). NUC, 1968-1972

Clark, Francis Edward, born 12 September 1851 at Aylmer, P.Q., he was a graduate of Dartmouth College and Andover Theological Seminary. In 1881 he founded the Society for Christian Endeavor. His writings include *Training the Church of the future* (1902), and *Memories of many men in many lands; an autobiography* (1922). He died 25 May 1927. Master (11), Who was who in America, 1

Clark, Sir George Norman, born 27 February 1890 at Halifax, West Yorkshire, he was a professor of history at both Oxford and Cambridge and, in 1943, became Regius Professor of Modern History at Cambridge. He was knighted in 1953. His writings include *The Dutch alliance and the war against French trade, 1688-1697* (1923). He died 16 April 1979. ConAu 85-88; IntWW, 1974-1978; Master (6); Who was who, 7

Clark, Harlan Bendell, born 5 January 1913 at Brookfield, Ohio. After graduating from Fletcher School of Law and Diplomacy, he entered the foreign service in 1937. During his career, he served many years in the Muslim world. He retired in 1970. Shavit

Clark, Henry Martyn, Dr., born 19th cent., he edited on behalf of the Panjab Text Book Committee *The Panjábí dictionary*, prepared by Munshi Gulab Singh (1895). He wrote *Robert Clark of the Panjab* (1907). NUC, pre-1956

Clark, John, born 26 July 1909 at Chicago, he received a Ph.D. in 1935 from Princeton for *The stratigraphy of the Chadron formation in the Big Badlands of South Dakota*. He was a sometime vice-president and field director of the Central Asiatic Research Foundation, Pittsburgh, and a curator at the Chicago Natural History Museum. He wrote *Hunza, lost kingdom of the Himalayas* (1957). AmM&WS, 1973 S, 1976 P

Clark, John Rosslyn, born 20th cent., he joined in 1990 the Turkish Studies Association. His writings include *Turkish Cologne; the mental maps of migrant workers in a German city* (1977). LC

Clark, Larry Vernon, born 19 July 1943 at Lodi, Calif., he was a graduate of Indiana University, where he received a Ph.D. in 1975 for his thesis, *Introduction to the Uyghur civil documents of East Turkestan, 13th-14th centuries*. Thereafter he was a professor of Altaistic linguistics at his alma mater. DrAS, 1978; Schoeberlein

Clark, Peter John Alleguen, OBE, born 17 May 1939 at Sheffield, he graduated in 1962 from the University of Keele and received a Ph.D. in 1971 from the University of Leicester for a thesis entitled *Henry Hallam, historian*, and a diploma in higher Arabic in 1974 from the Civil Service Commission. He taught mathematics at Ankara College and English at the British Council, 1962-63. He successively taught at Leicester and Dunde from 1964 to 1967, when he began a thirty-two year affiliation with the British Council. After his resignation he became a director of the Middle East Cultural Advisory Services, a post which he stillheld in 2001. His writings include *Marmaduke Pickthall, British Muslim* (1986). He was a fellow of the Royal Geographical Society (1982), the Institute of Linguistics (1993), and a member of the British Society for Middle East Studies (1995), and the Society of Authors (1999). Private

Clark, Philip Jason, born in 1920, he received a Ph.D. in 1953 from the University of Michigan for his thesis, *Relative viability of albino and normal paradise fish*. In 1955 he was affiliated with the Institute of Human Biology in the University of Michigan. LC

Clark, Richard Charles, born 9 December 1935 at Yonkers, N.Y., he received a Ph.D. in 1971 from Columbia University for his thesis, *St. Ambrose's theory of church-state relations*. In 1972 he was appointed professor of government and politics at St. John's University, Jamaica, N.Y. Concurrently he was a book review editor of the *Review of national literatures*. AmM&WS, 1973 S

Clark, Robert, born in 1825, he was a graduate of Trinity College, Cambridge, and ordained in 1850. Thereafter he served as a missionary under the Church Missionary Society and was posted to the Punjab. Henry Martyn Clark wrote a biography, *Robert Clark of the Panjab, pioneer and missionary statesman* (1907). He died in 1900. Boase

Clark, Walter Eugene, born 8 September 1881 at Digby, N.S., he was a Harvard graduate and received a Ph.D. in 1906 for his thesis, *Quid de rebus Indiois scirent Graeci prisci quaeritur*. Thereafter he pursued studies at Berlin and Bonn. He was successively professor of Sanskrit at Chicago and Harvard. He died 30 September 1960. Canadian, 36-67; *Who was who in America*, 4

Clark, W(illiam) A(lexander) *Graham*, born 14 August 1879 at Raleigh, N.C., he was a business executive and later a commercial agent with the Department of Commerce and Labor, investigating markets abroad for American cotton mill products, visiting most of the countries of the world between 1906 and 1910. He died 24 January 1953. *Who was who in America*, 3

Clarke, Sir Andrew, born 27 July 1824 at Southsea, he was a colonel commandant, Royal Engineers, and a colonial official. He served in India from 1875 to 1880. He was joint author of the *Report on the Maritime Canal, connecting the Mediterranean at Port Said, with the Red Sea at Suez* (1879). He died 29 March 1902. BLC; DNB; *Who was who*, 1

Clarke, Sir Caspar Purdon, born 21 December 1846 at London, he was an architect, archaeologist, and museum director. He edited the translation, *Oriental carpets* of the k.k. Österreichisches Handels-Museum, Wien (1892-96). He died in London, 29 March 1911. DAB; DNB; WhoAm 1; *Who was who*, 1

Clarke, Dorothy Clotelle, born 16 July 1908 at Los Angeles. After she received a Ph.D. from UCLA, she taught Spanish at a variety of American universities and retired in 1976 from UCLA. Her writings include *Romance literature* (1948). IntAu&W, 1977; WhoAmW, 1958, 1961, 1964; WrDr, 1976-1996/98

Clarke, Edward Daniel, born 5 June 1769 at Willington, Sussex, he was an antiquary and a mineralogist who travelled throughout the old world from 1799 to 1802. His writings include *Travels in various countries of Europe, Asia, and Africa* (1810-1823), and the translation, *Reise durch Russland und die Tartarei* (1817). William Otter wrote a biography, *The life and remains of the Rev. E. D. Clarke*. He died 9 March 1822. DNB; Egyptology; Embacher; Henze; Master (8)

Clarke, George Sydenham, Baron Sydenham of Combe, born in 1848, he was educated at the East India Company's college, Haileybury. After passing first into and first out of the Royal Military Academy, Woolwich, he joined in 1868 the Royal Engineers. He soon made his name as an instructor on the Woolwich staff; then had a spell of active service in the Egyptian and Sudan campaigns. Thereafter he was among the most prominent and able exponents and creators of the great schemes of naval and military reorganization and inmperial defence. As a civil administrator he won equal distinction as governor of Bombay from 1907 to 1913. His writings include *Imperial defence* (1897), and *My working life* (1927). He died in 1933. DNB; JRCAS 20 (1933), pp. 308-309; *Who*, 1903-1932; *Who was who*, 3

Clarke, Henry Wilberforce, born in 1840, he was a captain and Iranist. He wrote a *Persian manual* (1877), and he translated, *The Sikandar name e bara*, of Nizami Ganjavi (1881), *The Divan*, of Hafiz (1891), and *A dervish text book from the 'Awarifu-l-ma'arif*, of 'Umar b. Muhammad al-Suhrawardi (1980). He died in 1905. LC

Clarke, Hyde, born in 1815 at London, he was a miscellanous writer who published *Colonization, defence, and railways in our Indian Empire* (1857), and *The early history of the Mediterranean populations* (1882). He died in London in 1895. BiD&SB

Clarke, James Franklin, born 5 June 1906 at Monastir, Ottoman Empire, he received a Ph.D. in 1938 from Harvard University for his thesis, *Bible societies, American missionaries, and the national revival of Bulgaria*. Thereafter he taught at various American universities and was later attached to U.S. Government agencies. His writings include *The pen and the sword; studies in Bulgarian history* (1988). DrAS, 1974, 1978, 1982

Clarke, James Freeman, born 4 April 1810 at Hanover, N.H., he was a graduate of Harvard College (1829), and Harvard Divinity School (1833), and ordained in the same year. He was a minister, library trustee, non-resident professor, member of the Board of Overseers of Harvard College, and a prolific writer. His writings include *The great religions* (1870), and *Steps of belief* (1876). He died 8 June 1888. DAB; WhAm, H

Clarke, John Innes, born 7 January 1929 at Bournemouth, Dorset, he received a Ph.D. in 1955 for his thesis, *A geographical study of nomadic migrations in Tunisia, 1881-1890*. He taught geography successively at the universities of Aberdeen and Durham. His writings include *The Iranian city of Shiraz* (1963). He was joint author of *Kermanshah, an Iranian provincial city* (1969), and editor of *Populations of the Middle East and North Africa* (1972). Sluglett; Unesco; Who, 1990-2003

Clarke, Peter Bernard, born in 1940, he received an M.Phil. in 1974 from the University of London for his thesis, *The Ismaili Khojas; a sociological study of an Islamic sect in London*. Thereafter he was attached to the Department of History and Philosophy of Religion at King's College, London. His writings include *West Africa and Islam* (1982), and *West Africa and Christianity* (1986). He was joint author of *Islam in modern Nigeria* (1984). LC; Sluglett

Clarke, Somers, born 22 July 1841 at Brighton, Sussex, he was educated privately and became an architect and archaeologist. From 1902 until his death on 31 August 1926 he lived in Egypt, where he was involved in excavations and the restoration of historic buildings. His writings include *The Unrest in Egypt* (1919). His notebooks, notes, plans, tracings, photographs, and correspondence, including el-Kâb material, are in the Griffith Institute, Ashmolean Museum, Oxford. Egyptology; Who was who, 2

Class, Heinrich, born 29 February 1868 at Alzey, Germany, he studied law at Freiburg im Breisgau and Gießen and practised his profession at Mainz. He was a conservative politician and affiliated with Alldeutscher Verband. His writings include *West-Marokko deutsch!* (1911). Under the pseudonym Einhart he published several editions of *Deutsche Geschichte*, and under Daniel Fryman, *Wenn ich der Kaiser wär* (1913). He wrote the autobiography, *Wider den Strom* (1932). He died in Jena, 16 April 1953. DtBE; Wer ist's, 1928, 1935

Claudot, Hélène, born 20th cent., she received a doctorate in 1979 from the Université d'Aix-Marseille for her thesis, *La sémantique au service de l'anthropologie; recherche méthodologique et application à l'étude de la parenté chez les Touaregs*, a work which was published in 1982. She was a contributing author to *Textes touaregs en prose* (1984). LC; THESAM, 2

Claudot, J., he was in 1959 a senior official with the Service des Eaux et Forêts and a director of the Station de recherches et d'expérimentation forestières de Rabat. Note

Clausen-Engelbracht, Ursel, born in 1938, she studied Arabic at the universities of Mainz and Bonn and received a diploma in translation and interpretation. In 1965 she joined the Deutsches Orient-Institut, Hamburg. Her writings include *Tunisie; notes biographiques* (1976), *Der Konflikt um die West-sahara* (1978), and *Demokratisierung in Mauritanien* (1993).

Clauson, Sir Gerard Leslie Makins, K.C.M.G., O.B.E., F.S.A., born in 1891, he was a soldier, public servant, high-level business man, outstanding Orientalist, in particular, a Turkologist, and a private scholar not intimately connected with the university and academic world. He was educated at Eton and became a scholar of Corpus Christi Coellege, Oxford. His writings include *Sanglax, a Persian guide to the Turkish language* (1960), *Turkish and Mongolian studies* (1963), and *An etymological dictionary of pre-thirteenth century Turkish* (1972). He died 1 May 1973 or 1974. CentBritOr, pp. 88-100; Index Islamicus (5); Who was who, 7; WhoWor, 1974

Clauß, Ludwig Ferdinand, born 8 February 1892 at Offenburg, Germany, he received a Dr.phil. in 1921 from the Universität Freiburg im Breisgau for his thesis, *Die Totenklagen der deutschen Minnesänger*. He was an anthropologist and an assistant to Edmund Husserl. On three occasions he spent years carrying on field-work in the Arab world, where he lived among the Bedouin. His writings include *Rasse und Seele* (1926), *Als Beduine unter Beduinen* (1933), *Umgang mit Arabern des Ostens* (1949), and *Weltstunde des Islams* (1963). He died 13 January 1974. Kürschner, 1961-1966; Kürschners Deutscher Literatur-Kalender, 1961-1966; Wer ist wer, 1971/73; Wer ist's, 1928, 1935

Clauss, Max Weber, Dr. phil., fl. 1970, his writings include *Treffpunkt der Zukunft; die wirtschaftliche Entwicklung der Hannover-Messe* (1984). LC

Clauzel, Jean, he was a colonial administrator affiliated with France Outre-Mer, and posted to the Soudan français from 1946 to 1958, and to the Sahara français from 1960 to 1961. Thereafter he was a professor at l'Institut E.D.E.S. His writings include *L'exploitation des salines de Taoudenni* (Alger, 1960). NUC, 1956-1967

Clavé, Jules, born in 1826, he wrote *Études sur l'économie forestière* (Paris, 1862). LC

Clavel, Jean Pierre, born 4 August 1922 at Lausanne, he was educated at the universities of Lausanne and Basel; he received an honorary doctorate. He was a chief librarian of the Bibliothèque cantorale et universitaire de Lausanne, and president of the Ligue des bibliothèques européennes de recherche. His writings include *L'évaluation des bibliothèques universitaires* (1984). WhoSwi, 1973/74-1992/93; WhoWor, 1974/75, 1976/77

Clavel, Leothiny S. (Leopoldo Leothiny), born in 1945, his writings include *They are also Filipinos* (1969), and *Agrarian reform in the Philippines* (1980). LC

Clavier, Henri, fl. 1954, he was a Protestant clergyman whose writings include *Études sur le calvinisme* (1936), *En Grèce* (1952), and *Algérie d'hier et d'aujourd'hui* (Strasbourg, 1955). LC

Clayton, Sir Gilbert Falkingham, Brig.-Gen., K.C.M.G., K.B.E., born 6 July 1875 at Ryde, Isle of Wight, he was educated at the Royal Military Academy, Woolwich, and joined the Egyptian Army in 1900. Six years later he transferred to the Sudan Civil Service. In 1914 he was a director of military intelligence in Cairo, and in 1927 he negotiated the Treaty of Jiddah with Saudi Arabia. He died in Baghdad, while British High Commissioner for Iraq, 11 September 1929. DNB; Hill; *Times* 12 Sept. 1929; *Who was who,* 3

Cleaves, Francis Woodman, he received a Ph.D. In 1942 from Harvard for his thesis, *A Sino-Mongolian inscription of 1362.* In 1969 he edited a *Manual of Mongolian astrology and divination.* LC

Clédat, Jean, born 7 May 1871 at Périgueux, he began to study at l'École des arts, Paris, but soon transferred to l'École du Louvre and the Collège de France to take up Egyptology. He was a sometime lecturer at l'École d'anthropologie, Paris, and since 1900, affiliated with a variety of archaeological missions in Egypt. He died 29 July 1943. Egyptology

Clegg, Ian, born in 1943, his writings include *Industrial democracy* (1969), and *Workers' self-management in Algeria* (1971).

Cleinow, Georg, born 27 April 1873 at Dolhobyczów, Russian Poland. From 1883 to 1893 he trained as a military, followed by travels in Russia. Upon his return, he had to abandon his military ambitions due to an accident. He started to study political economy and Slavic history at the Universität Königsberg. From 1909 to 1920 he was an editor of *Die Grenzboten.* He later was a lecturer at the Hochschule für Politik, Berlin, and head of the Eurasiatisches Seminar. His writings include *Das Recht der Ausländer in der Union der S.S.R.* (1925), *Roter Imperialismus* (1931), and *Verlust der Ostmark* (1934). He was joint author of *Turkestan, die politisch-historischen und wirtschaftlichen Probleme Zentralasiens* (1942). He died in Berlin, 20 October 1936. DtBE; *Wer ist's,* 1928, 1935

Cleland, William *Wendell*, born 14 December 1888 at Aledo, Illinois, he studied at Princeton and Harvard, where he received a Ph.D. in 1936 for *The population problem in Egypt.* He was a Church and municipal administrator in the U.S. before he began his lifelong association with Egypt, and the American University at Cairo in particular. From 1954 to 1958 he was a professor of Middle East studies at the American University, Washington, D.C. He died in Highland Park, Ill., 4 December 1972.

Clem, Ralph S., born 9 October 1943, he was joint author of *Nationality and population change in Russia and the USSR* (1976), and editor of the *Research guide to the Russian and Soviet censuses* (1986). LC

Clemen, Carl Christian, born 30 March 1865 at Sommerfeld, Germany, he received a Dr.phil. in 1890 from the Universität Leipzig for *Die religionsphilosophische Bedeutung des stoisch-christlichen Eudämonismus in Justins Apologie.* He was a professor of divinity successively at Halle and Bonn. His writings include *Die nichtchristlichen Kulturreligionen in ihrem gegenwärtigen Zustand* (1921), and *Der Einfluß des Christentums auf andere Religionen* (1931). He died in 1940. DtBE; *Wer ist's,* 1928, 1935

Clemens, Ekkehard, Dr., fl. 1968. he was affiliated with a German agency for technical cooperation. He contributed to *Agricultural development in West Sumatra* (1976). LC

Clément, A., fl. 1853, supported by the Société de géographie de Genève, he travelled in the company of the last ruling Pasha of Sulaymaniyah from Constantinople to Samsun, and then overland to the Persian Gulf, visiting also Kurdistan, 1853-56. Note

Clement, Edward Henry, born 19 April 1843 at Chelsea, Mass., he was a graduate of Tufts College. As a journalist in New York, Newark, and Boston he followed sedulously the fortunes of several oppressed races. He died in Concord, Mass., 7 February 1920. DAB; WhAm, 1

Clément, Jean-François A., born 20th cent., he was in 1971 affiliated with the Faculté des lettres et sciences humaines, Rabat. Note

Clément-Mullet, Jean Jacques, born 17 January 1796 at Lusigny-sur-Barse (Aube), he was an industrialist but also a student of Oriental languages. He contributed translations of Arabic natural science works to the *Journal asiatique*, and translated *Le livre de l'agriculture*, of Ibn al-'Awwam (1864-67). His writings also include *Essai sur la minéralogie arabe* (1868). He died in Paris, about 1865. DBF; Fück, 204; IndexBFr³ (1)

Clément-Simon, Frédéric, fl. 1907-1908, he contributed to *Revue de Paris* and *Revue d'histoire diplomatique*.

Clémentel, Étienne, born 29 March 1864 at moulin de Mézard, near Clermont-Ferrand, where he also studied law and liberal arts. He had a brief career in municipal politics before he was elected to the Chambre des députés in 1900. In 1905 he joined the cabinet Rouvier as minister for the colonies, in the capacity of which he pursued a policy of cooperation with the local population. He died 25 December 1936. DBF

Clements, Frank Alexander, born 10 January 1942 at Edinburgh, he was a graduate of Loughborough School of Librarianship and a fellow of the Library Association. In 1985 he was a librarian and co-ordinator of research at the College of St. Mark and St. John, Plymouth, and in 1993, he had become head of Learning Services. His writings include *T.E. Lawrence; a reader's guide* (1973), *The emergence of Arab nationalism* (1976), *Oman, the reborn land* (1980), and *Arab regional organizations* (1992). IntAu&W, 1982

Clemons, James T., born 17 October 1929, he was affiliated with Wesley Theological Seminary, Washington, D.C. His writings include *An index of Syriac manuscripts containing the Epistles and the Apoc-alypse* (1968), and *What does the Bible say about suicide* (1990). In 1990 he was also editor of *Perspectives on suicide*. LC

Clemow, Frank Gerard, born 19th cent. A graduate of Edinburgh and Cambridge, he was a physician and public health officer for a number of years attached to the British Embassy, Constantinople. His writings include *The cholera epidemic of 1892 in the Russian Empire* (1893), *The Indian Plague Commission* (1902), *The geography of disease* (1903), *Report on sanitary matters in Mesopotamia, the Shiah holy cities and on the Turco-Persian frontier* (1916). He died 25 February 1939. LitYbk, 1922; WhE&EA; WhoLit, 1926; Who was who, 3

Cleray, Edmond, born 19th cent., he received a doctorate in 1900 from the Université de Paris for his thesis, *De la mise en valeur des biens communaux*. His writings include *L'affaire Favras, 1789-90* (Paris, 1932). NUC, pre-1956

Clerc, Alfred Joseph, born 19 August 1829 at Paris, he went in 1833 with his orientalist uncle, Dr. Nicolas Perron, to Egypt, where he was educated by his uncle and by eminent Arab writers. He returned to Paris in 1846 to complete his studies at the École spéciale des langues orientales, and the Collège de France. In 1852 he was appointed a director of the École arabe-française in Constantine, Algeria. Afterwards he entered the Corps des interprètes militaires, where he rose from the rank of *interprète titulaire de 3e classe* (21 December 1853) to *interprète principal* (28 February 1873). He was a founding member of the Société historique algérienne, member of the Société asiatique, Chevalier de la Légion d'honneur (11 January 1876), and for many years editor-in-chief of *al-Mubashshir*, the Algerian official gazette. He published numerous articles in the *Encyclopédie du XIXe siècle* and the *Encyclopédie Firmin-Didot*. In 1877, he edited his uncle's *L'islamisme, son institution, son influence et son avenir*. Féraud, pp. 336-337

Clerc, F., he was in 1959 a head of the Bureau des programmes à la C.A.T., Rabat. Note

de Clercq, Frederik Sigismund Alexander, born 7 April 1842 at Zutphen, Netherlands, he was a sometime Dutch Resident at Riouw, and carried on geographic as well as ethnographic explorations in the Dutch East Indies. His writings include *Het Maleisch der Molukken* (1876), and *Ethnographische beschrijving van het west- en noord-kust van Nederlandsch Nieuw-Guinea* (1893). He died in 1906. Henze; EncNI

Clerget, Marcel, fl. 1932, his writings include *Le Caire; étude de géographie urbaine et d'histoire économique* (1934), and *La Turquie, passé et présent* (1938). NUC, pre-1956

Clerget, Pierre, born in 1874, he was in 1923 a director of l'École supérieure de commerce de Lyon, and a member of the Mission d'études économiques dans le Levant. His writings include *Manuel d'économie commerciale* (1909), and *Géographie économique* (1912). NUC, pre-1956

Clerget de St-Léger, Henri Marie Louis François, born 1 June 1875 at Roulans (Doubs), he enlisted in the army on 24 October 1894, and after passing through the military college of St-Maixent, which he had entered in 1898, he received a commission as *sous-lieutenant* on 1 April 1899. From 1903 to

1910 he served a first turn with the Bureau des Affaires indigènes d'Algérie, attached to the Command of the Oases Territories. From 1913 to 1915 he was with the Bureau for a second turn, during which time he was first in charge of the Compagnie saharienne at Tidikelt, later at Touat-Gourara, and, finally, at Saoura. He was a captain (1910), and Chevalier de la Légion d'honneur (1916). He died in action during the first World War. Peyronnet, p. 616

Clerin-Lison, Rose M., born in 1945, she wrote *Taxation planning for Middle East operations* (1978), a work which was originally submitted at Bruxelles as a requirement of the final degree of l'École supérieure des sciences fiscales. LC

Clérissse, Henry, fl. 1931, his writings include *La Guerre du Rif et la Tache de Taza* (1927), *30000 kilomètres à travers l'Afrique française* (1934), and *Espagne, 36-37* (1937). NUC, pre-1956

Clerk, Claude, fl. 1851, he was a British officer who travelled in 1857 from Tehran to Herat, and returned the following year by way of Shahrud. Henze

Clermont-Ganneau, Charles Simon, born 19 February 1846 at Paris, he was a student at l'École des langues orientales vivantes, Paris. From 1867 to 1871 he served as *drogman-chancelier* to the Consulat de France in Jerusalem. Concurrently he pursued an interest in Semitic archaeology and paleography, partly in the service of the Palestine Exploration Fund. He held the chair of archaeology and Oriental epigraphy at the Collège de France, Paris, and was instrumental in exposing a number of archaeological forgeries. His writings include *Études d'archéologie orientale* (1880-97), and *Les fraudes archéologiques en Palestine* (1885). He died 15 February 1923. DBF; Who was who, 2

Clermont-Tonnerre, François Amédée Marie, born 19 September 1906 at Paris, he was educated at the Lycée Henri IV, the Sorbonne, and the École nationale des chartes. He was an agriculturist, journalist and administrator. In 1936 he was a *député de la Somme*. He was joint author of *Le Manifeste paysan; essai d'une doctrine humaniste appliquée à l'agriculture française* (1937). He died 2 December 1979. WhoFr, 1953/54-1979/80

Cleveland, Ray Leroy, born 29 April 1929 at Scotbluff, Nebr., he received a Ph.D. from Johns Hopkins University, Baltimore, Md., where he was attached as an archaeologist until 1966, when he joined the University of Saskatchewan, Regina, as a professor of history. His writings include *An ancient South Arabian necropolis* (1965), and *The Middle East and South Asia, 1967* (1967). ConAu 21-22; DrAS, 1974, 1978, 1982; Shavit; WrDr, 1976/78-1998/2000

Cleveland, William Lee, born 23 April 1941, he was for many years affiliated with the Department of History in Simon Fraser University, Burnaby, B.C., a post which he still held in 1998. His writings include *The making of an Arab nationalist* (1971), *Atatürk viewed by his Arab contemporaries* (1982), and *Islam against the West* (1985). LC

Clevenger, W. M., born 20th cent., he received a B.Litt. in 1971 from Oxford for his thesis, *British reactions to the Young Turks, 1908-12; a study in the formation of attitudes.* Sluglett

Clevenger, William Murrie, fl. 1968, he served in the 1960s as an American consul in Meshed. Note

Clifford, Robert Laning, born 19 February 1912 at Evanston, Illinois, he was a graduate of Princeton, Harvard, and the Army and Navy Staff College. He served in South East Asia Command from 1943 to 1945 and was an Economic Officer of the American Embassy in Rangoon from 1948 to 1949. While serving in the American Legation, Beirut, from 1950 to 1951, he made contact with the Arabian-American Oil Company. Subsequently he followed petroleum matters in other developing countries as a Foreign Service Officer and as a United Nations Economic Adviser. He was joint author of *Naval gunfire support of the landings in Sicily* (1984). WhoAmP, 1977/78

Cline, Walter Buchanan, born in 1904, he received a Ph.D. in 1936 from Harvard for his thesis, *The sources of metals and techniques of metal working in Negro Africa.* His writings include *Notes on the people of Siwah and El Garah in the Libyan Desert* (1936), *Mining and metallurgy in Negro Africa* (1937), and *The Teda of Tibesti, Borku, and Kawar in the Eastern Sudan* (1950). LC

Clinton, Jerome Wright, born 14 July 1937 at San Jose, Cal., he was a graduate of Stanford University, and received a Ph.D. in Persian and Arabic literature in 1972 from the University of Michigan. He was from 1962 to 1964 with the Peace Corps in Iran as a teacher of English, from 1972 to 1974 a director of the Tehran Center of the American Institute of Iranian Studies, and thereafter a professor at the Department of Near Eastern Studies in Princeton University, a post he still held in 1998. He was a sometime council member of the Society for Iranian Studies, a member of the editorial board of *Edebiyat*, a founding member of the Middle East Literary Seminars, and a trustee and frequent member of the executive committee of the American Institute of Iranian Studies for over twenty years.

His writings include *The divan of Manuchihri Damghani; a critical study* (1972). DrAS, 1974, 1978, 1982; Private

Clive, Robert Henry, Baron, born 29 September 1725 in England, he joined the East India Company's service and reached Madras penniless in 1744. He had a brilliant career in India, where he became the chief founder of the empire of British India. He returned to England in shattered health in 1766 and became a victim to opium. He committed suicide in 1774. Buckland; DNB; EncAm; EncBrit; GDU; Mason; Meyers

Clive, Robert Henry, Sir, born 27 December 1877, he was educated at Magdelen College, Oxford, and entered the Foreign Service in 1902. He served in the Muslim world at Cairo, Tangier, and Tehran. He died 13 May 1948. DNB; ObitOF 79; Who was who, 4

Cloarec, Paul Jean Armand Marie, born 11 October 1860 at Morlaix (Finistère), he served with the French Navy until his resignation in 1901, when he started lecturing in naval tactics at l'École de guere. Concurrently he was affiliated with l'École des sciences politiques and the Collège libre des sciences sociales. He was a director of the review *La Ligue maritime*. His writings include *La renaissance de notre marine marchante* (1919), and *La politique et la méthode* (1920). Under the pseudonym J. Hunier he published *Du navire de combat* (1890). He died in Cannes in May 1951. Curinier 5, 325; DBF

Clogg, Richard, born in 1939, in 1986 he had been for over fifteen years a lecturer in modern Greek history at the School of Slavonic and East European Studies, King's College, London. His writings include *A short history of modern Greece* (1979), and *Parties and elections in Greece* (1987). He was joint editor of *Greece under military rule* (1972). LC

Cloquet, Louis André Ernest, born 11 October 1818 at Paris, he studied medicine, was an intern in surgery in 1840, and received a doctorate in 1846 from l'Université de Paris for his thesis, *De l'hématocèle vaginale*. A few months later, he left for Tehran to accept an appointment as counsellor and physician to the Shah of Persia. He died in 1855 from having inadvertently taken a strong dose of cantharidin. DBF; *Revue de l'Orient* 4 (1856), 507-16

Clos, Paul Jean, born 7 September 1915 at Morlaas (Basses-Pyrénées), he was a graduate of l'École polytechnique and an *ingénieur en chef des ponts et chaussées* who served in Morocco from 1947 to 1961. WhoFr, 1965/66-1979/80

Close, Sir Barry, born about 1750, he was appointed a cadet of infantry at Madras in 1771 and promoted major-general in 1810. In 1784 and 1787 he conducted political negotiations with the commissioners from Tippoo Sultan for the adjustment of disputed territory. In both cases, the force of talents alone arrested the encroachments of the Sultan, without the necessity of an appeal to arms. His distinguished services in the war of 1790-92, were fairly appreciated by Earl Cornwallis. He died in England, 20 April 1813. *Asiatic annual register* 11 (1809), pp. 457-458; DNB

Close, Harold Wilberforce, born in 1888, he received a Ph.D. In 1922 from Princeton for his thesis, *Acid catalysis in lactone formation*. In 1927 he was a professor of chemistry at AUB. LC

Clot, André, born 20th cent., he was a historian and journalist who spent a number of years in Turkey and the coun-tries of the former Ottoman Empire. His writings include *Soliman le magnifique* (1983), *Haroun al-Rachid et le temps des Milles et une nuit* (1986), and its translation, *Harun al-Raschid, Kalif von Bagdad* (1988), *Mehmed II, le conquérant de Byzance* (1990), and *L'Égypte des Mamelouks, l'empire des esclaves, 1250-1517* (1996). LC

Clot Bey, Antoine Barthélemy, born 5 November 1793 at Grenoble, he studied medicine at Marseille and Montpellier, then practised as a surgeon in Marseille until appointed a surgeon-in-chief in Egypt by Muhammad 'Ali. With interruptions, he stayed in Egypt from 1825 until his retirement in 1860. During this time he created a public health service and a centre of medical education. He was a collector of antiquities and wrote *Aperçu général sur l'Égypte* (1840). He died in Marseille, 28 August 1868. DBF; Egyptology; Goldschmidt; Hill; Vapereau

Cloudsley-Thompson, John Leonard, born 23 March 1921 at Murree, India, he was educated at Pembroke College, Cambridge, where he received a Ph.D. in 1950. Since 1972 he was a professor of zoology in the University of London. He was lecturer and/or visiting professor in Khartoum, Kuwait, and Nigeria. ConAu 17-18, new rev., 8; IntAu&W, 1982; WrDr, 1982/84-1998/2000

Clough, W. Lynndon, fl.1938, he was a teacher at the Doon School at Dehra Dun, India, and travelled in Iran in the summer of 1938. Note

Cloulas, Ivan Émile Jean Martial, born 26 December 1932 at St.-Junien (Hts-Vienne), he was a graduate of l'École des chartes and received a doctorate in history in 1968 from the Sorbonne. Since

1957 he was a keeper at the Archives nationales, Paris. His writings include *La vie quotidienne dans les châteaux de la Loire* (1983), *Charles VIII et le mirage italien* (1986), *Les Borgia* (1987), and its translation, *The Borgias* (1989). WhoFr, 1981/82-1997/98; WhoWor, 1989

Cloupet, 18th cent., he originated from Île de France and travelled to Arabia and the Yemen in 1788.

Clouston, William Alexander, 1843-1896, his writings include *Literary curiosities and eccentricities* (1875), *Popular tales and fictions, their migrations and transformations* (1877), *Arabian poetry for English readers* (printed privately in Glasgow, 1881), *Flowers from a Persian garden* (1890), and *Some Persian tales, from various sources* (1892). LC

Clouzot, Henri, born 17 September 1865 at Niort (Deux-Sèvres), he was a regional newspaper man and a journalist. In 1895 he was briefly attached to the Archives des Deux-Sèvres. His writings include *L'Ancien théâtre en Poitou* (1901). He died 24 September 1941. DBF

Clozel, Marie *François* Joseph, born 29 March 1860 at Annonay (Ardèche). During his military service he made his first contact with Africa and the Muslim world in Algeria, 1881 to 1882. From 1885 to 1886 he studied Arabic at Alger and then entered the Service de la propriété indigène as a deputy interpreter. Soon afterwards he was transferred to French Equatorial Africa, where he was attached to several missions or posted as an administrator. He spent his entire career from 1892 to 1918 in black Africa. His writings include *Haute Sangha, Bassin du Tchad, les Bayas; notes ethnographiques et linguistiques* (1896), and *Les Coutumes indigènes de la Côte-d'Ivoire* (1902). He died 11 March 1918. *Hommes et destins*, vol. 8, pp. 84-88

Clubb, Oliver Edmund, born 16 February 1901 at South Park, Minn., he was a graduate of the University of Minnesota, and California College in China. He was in the U.S foreign service from 1928 until his retirement in 1952, when he became a lecturer at the East Asia Institute in Columbia University. His writings include *China and Russia* (1971), and his autobiographical *The witness and I* (1974). He died in N.Y.C., 9 May 1989. Master (4); Shavit - Asia

Cluzel, Augustin Pierre, born 6 March 1815 at Montclar (Aveyron), he was a Lazarist priest and a missionary in Urmia from 1852 until his death, 12 August 1882. In 1874 he was ordained apostolic deputy in Persia. Among the pamphlets he wrote is *Sur l'état de la mission de Perse et la necessité d'établir une imprimerie chaldéenne et de construire une église à Ourmiah* (1876). DBF

Clyne, Anthony, born in 1890, he was a journalist. WhE&EA; WhoLit, 1928-1931

Coale, Ansley Johnson, born 14 November 1917 at Baltimore, Md., he was a graduate of Princeton University, where he also received his Ph.D. in economics in 1947. Since 1976 he was an associate director, Office of Population Research at Princeton. He wrote *The problem of reducing vulnerability of atomic bombs* (1947) and he was joint author of *Population growth and economic development in low-income countries* (1958). AmW&WS, 1973 S, 1978 S; WhoAm, 1974-1978

Coan, Frederick Gaylord, D.D., born 23 May 1859 at Urmia, Persia, he was a graduate of Western and Princeton theological seminaries and served as a missionary under the Prebyterian Board of Foreign Missions in Persia from 1885 to 1923. He wrote an autobiography, *Yesterdays in Persia and Kurdistan* (1939). He died in Shreve, Ohio, 23 March 1943. Shavit

Coatalen, Paul, Dr., fl. 1969, he received a doctorate from the Université de Paris V for his thesis, *Les Chleuhs de Tafraout*, in 1972. He was attached to the Département d'études arabes, Paris III, and in 1993, a professor and research fellow at the Centre de documentation d'études juridiques, économiques et sociales du Caire. EURAMES; THESAM, 1

Coate, Miss Winifred A., fl. 1951-1953, she was a member of the Church of England and attached to the Church Missionary Society Refugee Relief Centre at Zarqa, Jordan.

de **Coatgoureden**, René Joseph Marie, born 13 January 1880 at Quimper (Finistère). After passing through the military college of Saint-Cyr, which he had entered in 1899, he received a commission as *sous-lieutenant* on 1 October 1901. Except for four years which he spent in Morocco, he was attached to the Bureau des Affaires indigènes de l'Algérie from 1905 to 1914, stationed variously in El-Aricha, Toüggourt, Géryville, Colomb, Ghardaïa, and Laghouat. During the first World War he served in France where he was killed in action in 1918. Peyronnet, p. 617

Coatman, John, born 5 November 1889, he was educated at Manchester University and Pembroke College, Oxford. He joined the Indian Police Service in 1911 and was a sometime director of Public Information, Government of India, member of the Indian Legislative Assembly, honorary professor of political science in Delhi University, professor of Imperial economic relations in the University of London, editor and controller of B.B.C., and director of research in the social sciences in St. Andrews

University. His writings include *Years of destiny, India, 1926-1932* (1932), and *India, the road to self-government* (1941). He died 1 November 1963. Who was who, 6

Cobb, Standwood, born 6 November 1881 at Newton Highlands, Mass., he was a graduate of Dartmouth College and of Harvard Divinity School. He was a Bahai and taught at Robert College, Constantinople, until 1910, when he returned to the U.S. to teach. His writings include *The real Turk* (1914), and *Security for a failing world* (1934). He died in Chevy Case, Md., 28 December 1982. Shavit

Cobban, Helena, born 31 October 1952, she was a sometime reporter on the London *Sunday Times*. In 1991 she was a scholar-in-residence at the Foundation for Middle East Peace in Washington, D.C. Her writings include *The Palestinian Liberation Organization* (1984), *The making of modern Lebanon* (1985), and *The superpowers and the Syrian-Israeli conflict* (1991). LC

Cobbold, Evelyn, Lady, 1867-1963, she claims to have been the first European woman to have performed the *hajj* as a Muslim. She seems to have had a splendid time and was able to find many upper class ladies with whom she could take tea and engage in polite conversation. Her writings include *Pilgrimage to Mecca* (1934). Bidwell, p. 137; Robinson, p. 41

Cobbold, Ralph Patteson, fl. 1900., he wrote *Innermost Asia travel and sport in the Pamirs* (London, 1899). NUC, pre-1956

Cobham, Catherine, fl. 1975 she was an Arabist, who specialized in modern Arabic literature, and a member of the British Society for Middle Eastern Studies. In 1993 she was a teaching fellow at the Department of Arabic Studies in the University of St. Andrews. She published the translations *The harafish*, of Najib Mahfuz (1994), and *Beirut blues*, of Hanan al-Shaykh (1995). DrBSME, 1993; LC

Cobham, Claude Delaval, born 30 June 1842, he was a graduate of Oxford University, who was from 1878 to 1907 Commissioner of Lacarna, Cyprus. He published in 1886 a bibliography of Cyprus, which was repeatedly up-dated until 1929. He translated from the Turkish *The laws and regulations affecting waqf property* (1899), and wrote *The patriarchs of Constantinople* (1911). He died 29 April 1915. Who was who, 1

Cocâtre-Zilgien, André, born 10 May 1924 at Paris, he received a doctorate in law in 1950 from the Univer-sité de Paris. He was a professor of law at Alexandria, Egypt, 1951-1952, and the Institut des hautes études françaises du Caire, 1952-1954. Thereafter he taught in French West Africa and at various French universities. His writings include *Remarques impertinents sur la question juive* (1972). He died 1 June 1996. Unesco; WhoFr, 1965/66-1995/96; WhoWor, 1976-1978/79

Coccioli, Carlo, born 15 May 1920 at Livorno, Italy, he was educated at the universities of Napolli and Roma, and received a doctorate in colonial affairs. He was primarily an author of *belles-lettres*, whose writings include *11 agosto; scritti di partigiani* (Firenze, 1945). Bioln 2; ConAu, new rev. 9; Master (2); MEW

Coche, Raymond, general, born 26 January 1904 at Valence (Drôme), he was a graduate of the École spéciale militaire de Saint-Cyr, and was posted to North Africa, 1925-1933, where he was in charge of the special mobile detachments of Ouargla and Béni-Abbès, and policed and explored large parts of the eastern and western Sahara. Peyronnet, p. 926; WhoFr, 1959/60-1967/68

Cochelet, Charles, born in 1786 at Charleville, (Ardennes), he was a sometime paymaster-general in Catalonia and, after a shipwreck, captured, sold and resold as a slave in Morocco before he was liber-ated. After his return to France, he wrote *Naufrage du brick français La Sophie, perdu, le 30 mai 1819, sur la côte occidentale d'Afrique, et captivité d'une partie des naufragés dans le désert de Sahara* (Paris, 1821), and its translation, *Narrative of the shipwreck of the Sophia, on the 30th of May, 1819, on the western coast of Africa and of the captivity of a part of the crew in the desert of Sahara* (London, 1822). DBF

Cocheris, Jules, 1866-1935, he received a doctorate in law in 1903 from the Université de Paris for his thesis, *Situation internationale de l'Égypte et du Soudan*. His writings include *Mademoiselle de La Chesnaye* (1928). BN; LC

Cochin, Denys Marie Pierre Augustin, born 1 September 1851, he was educated at the Lycée Louis-le-Grand and the Université de Paris. From 1893 to 1914 he was a member of the Chambre des députés. In 1915 he was appointed under-secretary of state, but resigned in 1917 over religious issues. His *L'évolution et la vie* (1886), won him an award from the Académie française. His writings include *Affaires marocaines; discours prononcés à la Chambre des députés* (1912). He died 24 March 1922. DBF

Cochran, Joseph Plumb, Dr., born in 1855 to missionary parents in Persia. As a youngster he went to America to carry on his studies at Yale University and Buffalo Medical College. He returned to Persia in 1878 to serve as a medical missionary. In 1880, through the generosity of friends in the West-minster Presbyterian Church, Buffalo, N.Y., he laid the foundations of the Westminster Hospital in Urmia. He was twice decorated for his professional services among the subjects of the Shah, and presented to the Shah in 1888. He died of typhoid fever, 18 August 1905. R. E. Speer wrote his biography, *The Hakim Sahib* (1911). Missionary review of the world, n.s., 19 (February 1906), pp. 99-104; Shavit

Cochran, Katharine née Hale, of Minneapolis, born 19th cent., she was a graduate of Vassar College, Poughkeepsie, N.Y. She was married to Joseph Plumb Cochran on 21 August 1878, and went with him to Persia in the same year. Her trace is lost in 1927.

Cochrane, Sir Ralph Alexander, Air Chief Marshall, born 24 February 1895 in Scotland, he was posted to the Middle East from 1921 to 1928, with an absence of three years. He died 17 December 1977. DNB; Who, 1974-1977; Who was who, 7

Cochut, Pierre *André*, born in 1812 at Paris, he was an economist and one of the first contributors to the *Revue des deux mondes*. His writings include *Les Associations ouvrières* (1851). He died in Paris in 1890. DBF; Hoefer; IndexBFr² (1); NUC, pre-1956; Vapereau

de **Cock**, André, fl. 1947, his writings include *Le Congo belge et ses marques postales* (Forest-Bruxelles, 1931). NUC, pre-1956

Codazzi, Angela, fl. 1915-1956, born at Milano, she was a professor of geography and a director of the Istituto di geografia e Istituto di lingua e letteratura arabe in the Università di Milano. Her writings include *Le edizioni quattrocentesche e cinquecentesche della "Geografia" di Tolemeo* (1950), and *I paesi del petrolio del Medio Oriente* (1955). Gastaldi

Codera y Zaydin, Francisco, born in 1836 at Fonz (Aragón), he studied Arabic at Madrid and after-wards taught at Granada and Zaragoza until 1874 when he accepted the chair of Arabic at Madrid. He was the founder of the academic study of the history of Moorish Spain. Since 1868 he published clas-sical Arabic sources on Islamic Spain. He was the first writer of a *Tratado de numismática arábigo-española* (1879). A collection of his articles, *Estudios crítico de historia árabe española* was published in 1917. His writings include *Misión histórica en la Argelia y Túnez* (1892), and *Decadencia y des-aparición de los Almoravides en España* (1899). In 1904 he was honoured by the jubilee volume *Homenaje à D. Francisco Codera*. He died in 1917. Fück; I.I. (2); IndiceE (7)

Codman, Charles Russell, born about 1896, he was a 1915 graduate of Harvard College and a veteran of both world wars. He visited Morocco at the time of the 1925 Riff uprising. He was president of the Boston real estate concern Codman & Codman, Inc. His writings include *Contact* (1937), and *Drive* (1957). He died 26 August 1956. LC; NYT, 26 August 1956, p. 84

Codrington, Humphrey William, fl. 1913-28, his writings include *Catalogue of the coins in the Colombo Museum* (1914), and *The liturgy of Saint Peter* (1936). He was joint author of *Commentaries on the Jacobite Liturgy, by George, Bishop of the Arab tribes, and Moses Bar Kepha* (1913).

Codrington, Kenneth de Burgh, born 5 June 1899, he was a professor emeritus of Indian archae-ology in the University of London, where he had taught at SOAS. He was joint author of *The art of India and Pakistan* (1956). He died 1 January 1986. Who was who, 8

Codrington, Oliver, died in 1921, he was a sometime editor of the *Numismatical chronicle* and author of *Some rare and unedited Arabic and Persian coins* (1889), and *A manual of Musulman numismatics* (1904). NUC, pre-1956

Codrington, William Melville, born 16 December 1892 and educated at Oxford, he was a soldier, foreign service officer, and business executive. He died 29 April 1963. Who was who, 6

Coedès, George, born in 1886, he started life as a teacher of German, 1908-1909, before he pursued East Asian studies at l'École pratique des hautes études, Paris, leading to a career in the same field. In 1958 he was elected to the Académie des inscriptions et belles-lettres. He died in Paris, 2 October 1969. Hommes et destins, vol. 1, pp. 151-153

Coelho, Vincent Herbert, born 20 July 1917. After Madras University he entered the Indian Civil Service. After the partition of India, he was a Foreign Service officer and ambassador. His writings include *Sikhim and Bhutan* (1970), and *Across the Palk Straits* (1976). IntWW, 1974/75-1977/78; Master (2)

Coello de Portugal y Quesada, Francisco, born in 1822 in Jaén, Spain, he was a military officer who, after his retirement from the army, pursued an interest in geography. He died in 1894. Cuenca, vol. 2, 96

Cogniart, Paul Jean, fl. 1956, he was associated with the Cour d'appel de Douai. His writings include *La prostitution; étude de science criminelle* (1939), originally presented as his thesis at the Université de Lille, and *Les jurisdictions françaises au Maroc, 1913-1957* (1966). He was joint author of *Procédure pénale* (1971). LC

Cohen, Abner, born 11 November 1921, he was an anthropologist who received a Ph.D. in 1961 from the University of Manchester for *The social organization of Arab villages in Israel*. His writings include *Arab border-villages in Israel* (Manchester, 1965), *Two-dimensional man* (1974), *Politics of elite culture* (1981), and *Masquerade politics* (1993). In 1974 he edited *Uran ethnicity*. LC; Sluglett

Cohen, Aharon, born 3 October 1910 at Britshani, Bessarabia, he was the founding director of the Arab department of ha-Shomer ha-tsa'ir, 1940-1950, an authority on the Arab world, and a sometime member of the editorial board of the *New outlook*. His writings include *Yisrael veha-'olam ha-'aravi* (1964), its translation, *Israel and the Arab world* (1970), and *The reminiscences of Aharon Cohen* (1975). ConAu 69--72; WhoIsrael, 1966/67-1978

Cohen, Amnon, born 1 August 1936 at Tel Aviv, he was educated at the Hebrew University, Jerusalem, where he later became a professor of Arabic and Middle Eastern history. His writings include *Palestine in the 18th century* (1973), *Political parties in the West Bank under the Jordanian regime* (1982), *Yehudim be-shilton ha-Islam* (1982), its translation, *Jewish life under Islam* (1984), and *Economic life in Ottoman Jerusalem* (1989). ConAu 77-80; Master (1)

Cohen, Boaz, born 26 February 1899 at Bbridgeport, Ct., he was a graduate of City College, New York, N.Y., was ordained at the Jewish Theological Seminary, in 1924, and received a Ph.D. in 1936 from Columbia University for his thesis, *Mishnah and Tosefta*. He was an authority on Jewish and Roman law at the Jewish Theological Seminary. His writings include *An annotated bibliography of the Rabbinic responsa of the middle ages* (1930), *Law and tradition in Judaism* (1959), and *Jewish and Roman law; a comparative study* (1966). He died in N.Y.C., 11 December 1968. CnDiAmJBi; EncJud; NYT, 12 December 1968, p. 47

Cohen, David, born 24 July 1922 at Tunis, he received diplomas from l'École des langes orientales, Paris, and a doctorate in 1977 from the Université de Paris III for his *thèse d'état, La phrase nominale et l'évolution du système verbal en sémitique*. In the 1990s, he was a *directeur d'études* at l'École pratique des hautes études in the Université de Paris III. His writings include *Le Parler arabe des Juifs de Tunis* (1964-75), *Études de linguistique sémitique et arabe* (1970), and *L'Aspect verbal* (1989). THESAM, 3; Unesco

Cohen, Erik, born in 1932, he was an anthropologist who was affiliated with the Department of Sociology and Anthropology in the Hebrew University, Jerusalem. His writings include *Bibliography of the kibbutz* (1964), *The city in the Zionist ideology* (1970), and *Bibliography of Arabs and other minorities in Israel* (1974). LC

Cohen, Gustave David, born 24 December 1879 at Saint-Josse-Ten-Noode-Les-Bruxelles, he was a medievalist, theatre scholar and author of a standard work on liturgical drama, *Histoire de la mise en scène dans le théâtre religieux français du moyen-âge* (1906). He was a professor of French literature successively at Leipzig, Amsterdam, Strasbourg, and Paris, and the founder and dean of the Free School of Higher Studies, the Free French University, that functioned in the United States during World War two. His writings include *Histoire de la chevalerie en France au moyen-âge* (1943), and *Anthologie de la littérature française du moyen-âge* (1946). He died in Paris, 11 June 1958. BioIn 4, 5; OxThe, 1983; NYT, 12 June 1958, p. 31; WhoFr, 1953/54-1957/58

Cohen, Hayyim J., born 1930, he received a Ph.D. in 1962 from the Hebrew University, Jerusalem. His writings include *ha-Yehudim ha-Tsiyonit be-'Irak* (1969), *ha-Yehudim be-artsot ha-Mizrah ha-tikhon be-yamenu* (1972), and its translation, *The Jews of the Middle East* (1973). LC

Cohen, Israel, born 24 April 1879 at Manchester, he studied at Jews' College and University College, London. He was a journalist and Zionist leader. On behalf of the Zionist Organization he visited many Jewish communities throughout the world. His writings include *The Zionist movement* (1945), and his autobiography, *Jewish pilgrimage* (1956). He died 26 November 1961. EncJud; Master (2); Who was who, 6

Cohen, Joseph, born 1 November 1817 at Marseille, he was a lawyer and an active journalist in Aix-en-Provence, where he was the founder of *Le Mémorial d'Aix*. He was particularly interested in the Jewish community in Alger. In 1842 he was sent on an official mission to the city to study the condition of the Jews and recommend means to their improvement. He remained until 1848, when he returned to Paris to pursue his journalist career. He was the editor of *La vérité israélite; receuil d'instruction religieuse* (1860-62), and wrote *Les déicides; examen de la divinité de Jésus-Christ ...* (1861), and *Les Pharisiens* (1877). He died in Paris, in December 1899. EncJud; GdeEnc; Vapereau; Wininger

318

Cohen, Joseph Louis (Lewis), 1891-1940, he was an economist and a sometime member of the Labour Zionist Organization. CnDiAmJBi; WhE&EA; *Who was who*, 3

Cohen, M. *see* Tekinalp, Munis

Cohen, Marcel Samuel Raphaël, born 6 February 1884 at Paris, he obtained his *baccalauréat* at the Lycée Condorcet and graduated in 1905 from l'École des langues orientales. He then studied Indo-European linguistics and Semitic languages at the Collège de France, l'École des hautes études, and the Sorbonne. His thesis, *Le parler arabe des Juifs d'Alger* won him the Prix Volnay for 1912. He struggled all his life for the recognition of the Hamito-Semitic family and for an intensive study of it. In 1931 he organized in Paris the Groupe linguistique d'études chamito-sémitique devoted to that subject. His writings include *Documents sudarabiques* (1934), *Traité de langue amharic* (1936), *Le langage, structure et évolution* (1950), and its translations into Chinese, English, Japanese, and Polish. His career did not develop entirely according to his abilities and to his expectations. He was never appointed to the Collège de France, nor did he occupy the chair of Semitic languages at the Sorbonne, but he was granted honorary degrees by several universities, among them the University of Manchester. His wife was his main help in all the work he did, and his main support for more than sixty years. He died 5 November 1974. BSOAS 38 (1975), pp. 615-22; Unesco; WhoFr, 1955/56-1973/74; *Who was who*, 7

Cohen, Mark R., born 11 March 1943, he was In 1990 a professor of Near Eastern studies at Princeton University. His writings include *Jewish self-government in medieval Egypt* (1980), originally presented in 1976 as his thesis at the Jewish Theological Seminary of America, New York. He was joint editor of *Jews among Arabs* (1989). LC; *MESA roster of members, 1982-1990*

Cohen, Michael Joseph, born 29 April 1940 at London, he was a graduate of the University of London and received a Ph.D. in 1971 from LSE. He was a sometime professor of history at Bar Ilan University, Ramat Gan, Israel. His writings include *Palestine, retreat from the Mandate* (1978), *Palestine and the great powers, 1945-1948* (1982), *The origins and evolution of the Arab-Zionist conflict* (1987), and *Palestine to Israel; from mandate to independence* (1988). ConAu 129; LC

Cohen, Ronald, born 22 January 1930 at Toronto, Ont., he was a graduate of the University of Toronto, and received his Ph.D. in 1960 from the University of Wisconsin for his thesis, *The structure of Kanuri society*. He was successively a professor of anthropology at Toronto, McGill University, Montreal, Northwestern University, Evanston, Ill., and University of Florida, Gainesville. His writings include *Dominance and defiance; a study of marital instability in an Islamic African society* (1971). ConAu, new rev. 13; Unesco; WhoAm, 1980-1988/89

Cohen, Saul Bernard, born 28 July 1925 at Malden, Mass., he was a graduate of Harvard University, where he also received his Ph.D. in 1955 for his thesis, *Haifa, Israel's link to the world*. He became a professor of geography at Boston College and, in 1965, director of the Graduate School of Geography, Clark University, Worcester, Mass. His writings include *Geography and politics in a divided world* (1963), *Jerusalem bridging the four walls* (1977), *Jerusalem undivided* (1980), and *The geopolitics of Israel's border question* (1987). AmM&WS, 1974-1988/89 P; CnDiAmJBi; Master (3); WhoAm, 1974/75-1988/89; WhoWorJ, 1972-1987

Cohen, Shalom, born 12 February 1926 at Baghdad, he was for over twenty years on the staff of *ha-'Olam ha-zeh*. His writings include *ha-'Olam ha-zeh* (1972), and *Mitsrayim* (1978); he was editor of *Jewish liturgy* (1975). WhoWorJ, 1972, 1978

Cohen, Stuart A., born in 1946, he was a professor of history at Bar-Ilan University, Ramat Gan, Israel. His writings include *British policy in Mesopotamia, 1903-1914* (1976), and *English Zionists and British Jews* (1982). He was joint author of *A gazetteer of Jewish political organization* (1981), and joint editor of *Conflict and consensus in Jewish political life* (1986). LC

Cohen, William Benjamin, born 2 May 1941 at Jacobstad, Finland, he received a Ph.D. in 1968 from Stanford University for his thesis, *Rulers of empire; the French colonial service in Africa, 1860-1960*. He was successively a professor of history at Nothwestern University, Evanston, Illinois, and Indiana University at Bloomington. His writings include *The French encounter with Africans; white response to Blacks, 1530-1880* (1980). CoAu 37-40; DrAS 1974, 1978, 1982; WhoAm, 1984-1994; WrDr, 1976-1998/2000

Cohen, Yohanan, born 31 December 1917 at Lodz, Russia, he was a sometime leading Liberal member of the Ramat Gan Municipal Council, an Israeli diplomat and, from 1971 to 1982, director of the Department of Historical Research in the Israeli Ministry of Forreign Affairs. WhoWorJ, 1978, 1987

Cohen-Hadria, Elie, Dr., born in 1898, he wrote *Du protectorat français à l'indépendance tunisienne, souvenir d'un témoin socialiste* (1976). LC

Cohen-Sidon, Shlomo, fl. 1963, he was a sometime attorney prominent in local Israeli affairs.

Cohen-Stuart, Abraham Benjamin, born 17 March 1825 at 'sGravenhage, Netherlands. After study at Leiden and Delft, he spent over twenty years in the Dutch East Indies. His writings include *Kawi oorkonden in facsimile* (1875). He was joint author of the *Catalogus der Bibliotheek van het Bataviaasch Genootschap van Kunsten en Wetenschappen* (1864). He died in Batavia, 6 February 1876. EncNI; Nieuw NBW], v. 3, pp. 246-47

Cohen-Stuart, J. W. Th., he was joint author of *Oost-Indonesië* (1948). NUC, pre-1956

Cohn, David Lewis, born in 1896, he was a graduate of Yale University, and a free lance author whose writings include *God shakes creation* (1935), *This is the story* (1947), and *Where I was born and raised* (1948). He died 12 December 1960. AmAu&B

Cohn, Haim Hermann, born 11 March 1911 at Lübeck, Germany, he settled in Palestine in 1930, but returned to Germany to take his doctorate in 1933. He was an attorney-general of Israel, 1953-1960. His writings include *Human rights in Jewish law* (1984). In 1971 he was presented with the felicitation volume, *Of law and man; essays in honor of Haim H. Cohn.* EncJud; MidE, 1982/83; WhoIsrael, 1956-1992/93

Cohn, Robert Allen, born 4 September 1939, he was a graduate of Washington University, St. Louis, 1961. He was a sometime editor-in-chief of the *St. Louis Jewish light,* and president of the American Jewish Press Association. WhoRel, 1975, 1977, 1985

Cohn-Wiener, Ernst, born 25 December 1882 at Tilsit, East Prussia, he received a Dr.phil. in 1907 from the Universität Heidelberg for his thesis, *Über den Codex Bruchsal I der Karlsruher Hof- und Landesbibliothek.* He was a lecturer in history of art at the Humboldt-Akademie. In 1924-25 he travelled in Russia and Central Asia, studying art and architecture. Forced to leave Germany in the 1930s, Robert Byron helped to procure him a librarianship in India. His writings include *Turan; islamische Baukunst in Mittelasien* (1920), *Kunstgewerbe des Ostens* (1923), *Asia; Einführung in die Kunstwelt des Ostens: Indien, China, Japan, Islam* (1929), and *Die jüdische Kunst* (1929). He died in New York City, 13 April 1941. CnDiAmJBi; LC; Wininger

Coindreau, Roger, born 7 March 1891 at la Roche-sur-Yon (Vendée). After passing through l'École navale, 1909-1911, he served in the navy and l'Armée d'Orient in Syria and Cilicia, 1919. From 1929 to 1944 he was *directeur des ports marocains* Port-Lyautrey-Kénitra and Rabat-Salé. After his retirement he was a director of Editions africaines Perceval. His writings include *La Casbah de Mehdia* (1946), *Les corsairs de Salé* (1948), and *Le Maroc* (1953). He died 17 December 1964. *Hommes et destins* I, pp. 153-154

Çokay, Mustafa, 1890-1941 *see* Chokai-ogly, Mustafa

Coke, Richard, born in 1891 at Nottingham, he was a sometime Baghdad correspondent for the *Daily Mail* and also correspondent for the *Egyptian gazette* and the *Times of India.* His writings include *The heart of the Middle East* (1925), *Baghdad, city of peace* (1927), and *The Arab's place in the sun* (1929). WhE&EA

Cola Alberich, Julio, born 22 June 1918 at Beniparrell (Valencia), he started his university career as a professor of experimental biology and later added anthropology to his teaching. He was associated with the Universidad Central. His writings include *Los naturalistas hispano-musulmanes de al-Andalus* (1947), *Amuletos y tatuajes marroquíes* (1949), *Escenas y costrumbres marroquíes* (1950), and *Anatomia del terror mundo* (1973). DBEC; LC; Unesco

Colacrai de Trevisán, Miryam, fl. 1978, her writings include *El mundo desarrollado en la Antártica* (1986), and *Enfoques teóricos y doctrinarios que dominaron las relaciones entre los paises del Cono Sur durante los setenta* (1988). LC

Cold, Edith, born about 1885, she was a missionary worker in Hadjin, Turkey, until the beginning of 1926. Since September 1926 she was affiliated with the Chicago Office of the Woman's Board of Missions of the Interior. Note

Coldstream, William, born about 1840. After High School in Edinburgh from 1851 to 1856, he went to the University, where he gained the Stratton Prize. He entered the Indian Civil Service in 1860 and went to India, where he was posted to the Punjab. He was assistent secretary of the Punjab Exhibition of 1864, and rose early to the grade of deputy commissioner. He made a close study of the Indian vernaculars and read many of the classics in their original texts. After retirement he helped substantially to obtain recognition of Persian and Urdu in the London University matriculation. In 1914 he was awarded the Kaiser-i-Hind Gold Medal. His writings include *Records of the Intelligence*

Department of the Government of the North-West Provinces of India during the Mutiny of 1857 (1902). He died in London, 24 April 1929. Asiatic review, n.s., 25 (1929), pp. 476-78; *Times* 26 April 1929

Cole, Donald Powell, born 21 March 1941 at Byran, Texas, he was a graduate of the University of Texas and received a Ph.D. in 1972 from the University of California at Berkeley for his thesis, *The social and economic structure of the Al Murrah, a Saudi Arabian Bedouin tribe*. Since 1971 he was a professor of anthropology at AUC. His writings include *Nomads of the nomads, the Al Murrah Bedouin of the Empty Quarter* (1975), and *Saudi Arabian Bedouin* (1978). He was joint author of *Arabian oasis city; the transformation of 'Unayzah* (1989). LC; Master (2); Selim; WhoWor, 1989/90

Cole, Juan Ricardo Irfan, born 23 October 1952 at Albuquerque, N. Mex., he was a graduate of Northwestern University. Between 1982 and 1990 he carried on field work in India, Egypt, and Pakistan. In 1990 he was appointed a professor of Middle Eastern history at the University of Michigan and later director of its Center for Middle Eastern and North African Studies. He was a sometime member of the editorial board of *Iranian studies* and review editor of the *International journal of Middle East studies*. His writings include *Roots of Indian Shi'ism in Iran and Iraq* (1988), originally presented as his Ph.D. thesis, in 1984, at UCLA entitled *Imami Shi'ism from Iran to North India, 1722-1856; state, society and clerical ideology in Awadh*. He also wrote *Colonialism and revolution in the Middle East* (1993), and *Sacred space and holy war* (2002). Publisher's catalogue; Private; LC; Selim²

Colebrooke, Henry Thomas, born 15 June 1765 at London, he was privately educated and entered the East India Company in 1782, where he served until his return to England in 1814. His writings include *A grammar of the Sanscrit language* (1805). He was the first great Sanskrit scholar of Europe, and died in total blindness, 10 March 1837. His son, Sir Th. E. Colebrooke, wrote *The life of H. T. Colebrooke* (1873). Buckland; DNB

Colebrooke, Sir Thomas Edward, born 19 August 1813 at Calcutta, he was educated at Eton, an M.P., and served three terms as president of the Royal Asiatic Society. His writings include *Two visits to the Crimea in the autumns of 1854 and 1855* (1856), and *Life of the Honourable Mountstuart Elphinstone* (1884). He died in London, 11 January 1890. Boase; Buckland

Coles, Anne, fl. 1975, she was joint author of the pamphlet *A windtower house in Dubai* (1975). LC

Coletti, Alessandro, fl. 1971-1985, his writings include *Grammatica della lingua persiana* (1977), *Grammatica e dizionario della lingua curda* (1979), *Grammatica della lingua pashtu afgana e pakistana* (1980), *Quaderno turco* (1980), and *Baluchi of Mirjave; Likû couplets* (1981). ZKO

Colie, Stuart Edgar, born 21 February 1922 at Brooklyn, N.Y., he was a graduate of Yale and received a Ph.D. in 1962 from Princeton for his thesis, *MacCarthyism and some European images of America*. He was associated with the U.S. State Department in Germany, before he became a professor of political science at various American universities. AmM&WS, 1973, 1978

Colin, fl. 1880-88, he was a French navy surgeon who accompanied the mission under Isidore A. M. Derrien to the Upper Senegal, 1880-81. In the service of the French colonial administration he explored the Upper Falémé River, Senegal, in April and May of 1888. Henze

Colin, Auguste, fl. 1826-1847, he was a traveller and author of a number of pamphlets under twenty pages each, all published in Paris: *Le cri du peuple* (1831), *Percement de l'Isthme de Suez* (1847), and *L'Angleterre et l'Égypte* (1851). BLC; BN

Colin, Eugène, fl. 1890-93, he was a *pharmacien-major* at the military hospital in Vichy, and a writer on the bacteriology of mineral water. BN

Colin, Georges Séraphin, born 4 January 1893 at Champagnole (Jura), he was a graduate of l'École des langues orientales vivantes, Paris. Towards the end of the first World War he was posted to Morocco, where he was soon appointed an *interprète auxiliaire* at the Service des Renseignements. For thirty-three and thirty-six years respectively, until his retirement in 1963, he held concurrently academic and consular positions in Morocco, and the chair of Moroccan Arabic at l'École des langues orientales vivantes, Paris. His writings include *Pour lire la presse arabe* (1937), *Chrestomathie marocaine* (1939), and *La vie marocaine* (1953). He died 24 January 1977. AnnDipl&C, 1927; *Hommes et destins*, vol. 7, pp. 128-29; *Index Islamicus* (2)

Colin, Jean Pierre, fl. 1980-1985, he was a profesor at, and chairman of, the Centre d'études des relations internationales in the Université de Reims. His writings include *Le Gouvernement des juges dans les communautés européénnes* (1966). LC

Colish, Marcia Lillian, born 27 July 1937 at Brooklyn, N.Y., she was a graduate of Smith College and received a Ph.D. in 1965 from Yale University for her thesis, *The mirror of language*. For over twenty years she was associated with Oberlin College. Her writings include *The Stoic tradition from antiquity to the early middle ages* (1985). ConAu, new rev. 10; DrAS, 1974, 1978, 1982; IntAu&W, 1989; WhoAm, 1986/87-1995; WrDr, 1974/76-1998/2000

Collaer, Paul-Henri, born in 1891 at Boom, Belgium, he was an ethno-musicologist whose writings include *Atlas historique de la musique* (1960), its translation, *Historical atlas of music* (1968), and *Musique traditonnelle sicilienne* (1980). He was joint editor of *Nordafrika* (Leipzig, 1983). WhoMus, 1972

Collante, José R., fl. 1936 at Jolo, Sulu, Philippines, he was joint author of *Local taxing power* (1966).

Collantes de Terán Sánchez, Antonio, he received a doctorate in 1977 from the Universidad de Sevilla for his thesis, *Sevilla en la Baja Edad Media*. His writings include *Archivo Municipal de Sevilla; catálogo* (1977), and *Guía del Archivo Municipal* (Sevilla, 1977). LC

Collet, Collet Dobson, born 31 December 1812, he was affiliated with the Society of Arts, London, and was a member of several committees for obtaining the repeal of certain duties and taxes. His writings include *History of the taxes on knowledge; their origin and repeal* (London, 1899). He died in 1898. Boase

Collet, Léon William, born 23 September 1880 at Fiez, Switzerland, he was a geologist and a professor of geology at the Université de Genève from 1918 to 1944. His writings include *Les Lacs, leur mode de formation - leurs eaux - leur destin* (1925), and *The Structure of the Alps* (1927). He died in 1957. WhoSwi, 1950/51

Colliard, Claude Albert, born 14 July 1913 at Marseille, he received a doctorate in 1938 from the Université d'Aix-Marseille for his thesis, *Le prejustice en droit administratif français*. His writings include *Droit international et histoire diplomatique* (1948), *Institutions internationales* (1956), *The Law and practice relating to pollution control in France* (1976), and *Les Régimes parlementaires contemporains* (1978). LC

Collignon, Léon *Maxime*, born 9 November 1849 at Verdun, he graduated in 1868 from l'École normale, Paris. For a number of years he taught rhetoric at the Lycée de Chambéry. After travels and study in Italy, Greece and the Near East, he held the chair of antiquities at Bordeaux and later, the chair of archaeology at the Sorbonne. His writings include *Mythologie figurée de la Grèce* (1883), and its translation *Manual of mythology in relation to Greek art* (1890). He was a highly honoured scholar, and a member of the Académie des inscriptions. He successively lost his two wives and his only daughter; he died in Paris, 15 October 1917. DBF

Collignon, René, born 16 February 1856 at Metz, Lorraine. After taking a degree in medicine, he was a medical officer before setting up a practice in Cherbourg, in 1909. He was also an accomplished anthropologist and ethnologist. His writings include *Les âges de la pierre en Tunisie* (1887), and *Anthropologie du sud-ouest de la France* (1895). He died in Jaulny, 27 March 1932. DBF

Collin, Bernadin René, Evêque, born 9 May 1905 at La Mure (Isère), he studied law at Dijon, and at the Facultés catholiques de Lyon. He was ordained Franciscan priest in 1929. His writings include *Les lieux saints* (1948), *Pour une solution au problème des lieux saints* (1974), and *Rome, Jérusalem et les lieux saints* (1981). He died 27 April 1985. WhoFr, 1965/66-1984/85

Collin, Edouard, he received a doctorate in 1951 from the Faculté de droit de l'Université de Nancy for his thesis, *L'expansion économique du Maroc moderne*.

Collin, Matthäus Kasimir, born 3 March 1779 at Wien, he took a doctorate in law in 1804 at the Universität Wien. He was a sometime professor of aesthetics and history of philosophy at the Universität Kraukau, and since 1812, at the Universität Wien. From 1818 to 1821 he was an editor of the *Jahrbücher der Litteratur*. He died in Wien, 23 November 1824. DtBE; ÖBL

Collin-Delavaud, Claude, fl. 1960, his writings include *Les Régions côtières du Pérou septentrional* (1968), *Pérou* (1976), and *Territoires à prendre; le marché face aux idéologies* (1988). LC

Collinder, Erik Alfred Torbjörn (*Björn*), born 22 July 1894 in Sweden, he was from 1933 to 1961 a professor of Finno-Ugrian languages at Uppsala. His writings include *The Lapps* (1949), *Språket* (1959), *Sprachverwandtschaft und Wahrscheinlichkeit* (1964), and *Survey of the Uralic languages*, 2nd edition (1969). He died 20 May 1984. A commemorative volume was published in 1984 entitled *Linguistica et philologica; Gedenkschrift für Björn Collinder*. LC; Vem är det, 1941-1983

Collins, J. Walter, born about 1895 at London, he was for many years the Istanbul correspondent of the London *Times*, and, since 1932, he was Middle East manager of United Press. From his headquarters in Cairo he directed and covered every major news story from the Mediterranean to the Indian Ocean. He died 19 August 1956. NYT, 19 August 1956, p. 92, col. 3

Collins, L. J. D., fl. 1975, he received a Ph.D. in 1969 from the University of London for his thesis, *The fall of Shaikh Ahmed Khan and the fate of the people of the Great Horde, 1500-1504.* Sluglett

Collins, Robert Oakley, born 1 April 1933 at Waukegan, Illinois, he was a graduate of Dartmouth College, to which study at Oxford was added a few years later. He received a Ph.D. in 1959 from Yale University for his thesis, *The Mahdist invasions of the southern Sudan, 1883-1898.* He was a professor at Williams College before being appointed professor of history at the University of California, Santa Barbara, where he taught until his retirement. His writings include *The Southern Sudan* (1967), *Europeans in Africa* (1971), and *The waters of the Nile; hydropolitics* (1990). He was joint author of *Egypt and the Sudan* (1967), and *Requiem for the Sudan* (1994). ConAu 1, 9-10, new rev., 4, 22; DrAS, 1974, 1978, 1982; IntAu&W, 1977-1989; Selim; Unesco; WhoAm, 1984-1998; WhoWest, 1987-1989/90; WrDr, 1986-1998/2000

Collot, Claude. He was a sometime professor of history at Alger and Nancy. His writings include *Les Institutions de l'Algérie durant la période coloniale* (1987). He was joint author of *Le mouvement national algérien; textes, 1912-1954* (1978). He died in 1977. Revue de l'Occident musulman et de la Méditerranée 25 (1978), pp. 141-145

Collotti-Pischel, Enrica, born in 1930 at Rovereto (Trento), she was an expert on East Asian affairs and successively associated with the Istituto per gli Studi di Politica Internazionale, Torino, Bologna and, in 1998, with the Università di Milano. Her writings include *Le origini ideologiche della rivoluzione cinese* (1958), *La révolution ininterrompue* (1964). In 1991 she edited *Cina oggi.* Wholtaly, 1998

Cöln, Franz Joseph Maria, born 14 May 1873 at Linz am Rhein, Germany, he began his study with one semester of philosophy and Oriental languages at Bonn in 1893, but in the autumn of the same year, he changed to theology at the Bischöfliche Priesterseminar, Trier. After ordination, he spent three years in pastoral service. In 1900 he obtained a three-year leave of absence to complete his Oriental studies at the Universität Berlin, where he received a Dr.phil. in 1903 for his thesis, *Die anonyme Schrift "Abhandlung über den Glauben der Syrer."* Schwarz; Thesis

Colomb, Louis Joseph Jean François Isidore de, born 6 January 1823 at Figeac (Lot). After passing through the military college of Saint-Cyr, he received a commission as *sous-lieutenant* in 1840 and posted to North Africa. On 20 April 1844 he entered the Service des bureaux arabes. After four years of duty at Mascara, followed by two years at Oran, he was transferred to Géryville in 1854; there he stayed six years as *chef d'annexe.* His rise to the rank of general was due mainly to his successful operations in the Algerian extreme south, where he established French authority. From then on, he could pursue also his scientific interests. His writings include *Exploration des ksours et du Sahara de la province d'Oran* (1858), *Notice sur les oasis du Sahara et des routes qui y conduisent* (1860). He produced several valuable maps of Gourara, Touat, Tidikelt, and Tafilalet which were used when the project of the Trans-Saharan railway came under discussion.. When he retired from active service, the locality Béchar was re-named Béchar-Colomb in his memory. He died in Autoire (Lot), 19 November 1902. DBF; Henze; Peyronnet, 291-294

Colombain, Maurice Émile François, born in 1887, he was in 1937 head of the Co-operative Section at the International Labour Office, Geneva. His writings include *L'Organisation internationale du travail et le mouvement coopératif* (1944), and *Les coopératives et l'éducation de base* (Paris, Unesco, 1950), a work which was published simultaneously in French and Spanish. LC

Colombe, Marcel, fl. 1943, he was in 1951 a secretary of the Centre de l'Orient contemporain at the Institut d'études islamiques, and in 1955, a professor at l'École nationale des langues orientales vivantes, Paris. He received a doctorate in 1972 from the Université de Paris I for his *thèse d'état, L'Orient arabe et les Grandes Puissances, de la fin de la second guerre mondiale à la première conférence des Etats non-engagés.* His writings include *L'évolution de l'Égypte, 1924-1950* (1951), and *Orient-arabe et non-engagement* (1973). LC; THESAM, 3

Colomer, André, born 5 April 1927 in Algeria, he studied law at Alger and Paris, where he received his *agrégation* in 1955. He was a professor of law at Alger until independence, when he moved to the Université de Montpellier. His writings include *Droit musulman* (1963). WhoWor, 1980/81

Colonieu, Victor Marie, born 19 January 1826 at Orange (Vaucluse), he attended the École polytechnique in Paris from 1845 to 1847, and became *capitaine du génie* in 1853. During his Algerian service he began to associate with the local population in order to understand them. His authorities permitted him to spend some time in an isolated Arab environment in the attempt of pacification and civilization. This experience benefited his military career. At the age of thirty-four he became *commandant supérieur* at Géryville; he was able to play his role as mediator, judge, physician, and diplomat. Later, during the insurrection of Bou Amara, he played once more an important role. In 1889 he was made *grand officier de la Légion d'honneur*, in January 1891 he retired from active service and settled in Mostaganem where he died 16 September 1902. His writings include *Le Tracé central du chemin de fer trans-saharien* (1880). DBF; Peyronnet, pp. 303-307

Colonna, Fanny, fl. 1972, she received a doctorate in 1987 from the Université de Paris III for her thesis, *Les paysans et le savoir*. She was a political scientist whose writings include *Instituteurs algériens, 1883-1939* (1975). In 1983 she edited the reprint of *Formation des cités chez les populations sédentaires de l'Algérie*, by Émile Masqueray. LC; THESAM, 2

Colonna Ceccaldi, Georges, born in 1865, he was a archaeologist who published in the *Revue archéologique*. His writings include *Monuments antiques de Chypre, de Syrie et d'Égypte* (Paris, 1882). BN; NUC, pre-1956

Colósio, Stefano, born 19th cent., his writings include *Les lois de la guerre dans l'ancien droit musulman* (Tunis, 1911). NUC, pre-1956

Colpe, Carsten Ludwig, born 19 July 1929 at Dresden, Germany, he received a Dr.phil. in 1955 from the Universität Göttingen for his thesis, *Der Manichäismus in der arabischen Über-lieferung*. He was a professor of religious studies, first at Göttingen, and from 1973 until his retirement at the Freie Universität Berlin. His writings include *Problem Islam* (1989). IWWAS, 1975-1976; Kürschner, 1966-2001

Colquhoun, Archibald Ross, born in March 1848 of Cape of Good Hope, he was educated at Edinburgh University and abroad. In 1871 he entered the Indian Public Works Department. After he retired from public service in 1894, he travelled extensively in Asia. His writings include *Amongst the Shans* (1885), and *Russia against India* (1900). He died 18 Decmeber 1914. Buckland; Who was who, 1

Colson, Achille, born about 1815. In 1844, he came as a captain to Perpignan, and in 1855, he had been promoted *commandant*. He pursued a private interest in numismatics and wrote *Notice sur les monnaies qui ont en cours en Roussillon* (Perpignan, 1853). BN; Capeille

Colson, Alexander, Dr., fl. 1845-1882, he was a numismatist who published in the *Numismatic chronicle* and the *Revue de la numismatique belge*. BN

Colson, Jean Philippe, fl. 1975, his writings include *L'Office du juge et la preuve dans le contentieux administratif* (1970), a work which was originally presented as a doctoral thesis at Montpellier. NUC

Colston, Raleigh Edward, born of American parents 31 October 1825 at Paris, he went to the United States in 1842. He was a graduate of, and professor at, the Virginia Military Institute. After service in the Confederate Army, he conducted a private military school. In 1874 he was appointed to the Egyptian General Staff with the rank of brigadier-general. He conducted expeditions in the Nubian Desert and in Kordofan. A serious injury by a fall from a camel put an end to his military career. His reports were published in the *Bulletin de la Société khédiviale de géographie*. In 1878 he returned to America where he died totally disabled from the effects of his African injuries after two years at a Confederate soldiers' home in Richmond, Va., 29 July 1896. Henze; Hill; Shavit

Colucci, Guido, fl. 1930-1948, he was an engraver and a member of the Société nationale des Beaux-Arts. Édouard-J.

Colucci (Bey), J., fl. 1862-1887 in Alexandria, Egypt, he wrote *Réponses à douze questions sur le choléra de 1865 en Égypte* (Alexandrie, 1866). BN

Colucci, Massimo, fl. 1927, his writings include *Principe di diretto consuetudinario della Somalia italiana meridionale* (1924), *Il controllo sulle giurisdizioni indigene nell'ordinamento giudizaro eritreo* (1938), and *Il regime della proprietà fondiaria nell'Africa italiana* (1942). NUC, pre-1956

Colucci, Tullio, born 7 April 1885 in Italy, he was a sometime secetary-general for the colonies. His writings include *Dal vecchio al nuovo socialismo* (Milano, Società editrice socialista "Avanti," 1912). Chi è, 1936; NUC, 1956

Columbeanu, Sergiu, fl. 1967-1978, his writings include *Cruciadele* (1971), *Cnezate şi voievodate româneşti* (1973), and the translation *Grandes exploitations domaniales en Valachie au XVIII siècle* (1974). He was joint author of *Vlad Dracul* (1978). LC

Colvill, W. H., born 19th cent., he was an English assistant surgeon who travelled around 1867 overland from Bushire to Lingah, along the shores of the Persian Gulf. Henze

Colvin, Sir Auckland, born 8 March 1838 at Calcutta. After education at Eton and Haileybury, he entered the Indian Civil Service, where he served chiefly in the North West Province until his retirement in 1892, interrupted by a three-year spell of duty as financial adviser to the Khedive, 1880-1883. He wrote *John Russell Colvin* (1895), and *The making of modern Egypt* (1906). Buckland; DNB; Goldschmidt; Mason; Who was who, 1

Colvin, Ian Goodhope, born 23 November 1912, he was a British journalist and author of works on contemporary world affairs. His writings include *Chief of Intelligence* (1951), *The rise and fall of Moise Tshombe* (1968), and *The Chamberlain Cabinet* (1971). He died 20 April 1975. ConAu 57-60; LC

Colvin, Lucie Gallistel, born in 1943, she received a Ph.D. in 1972 from Columbia University, N.Y.C., for her thesis, *Kajor and its diplomatic relations with Saint-Louis de Sénégal, 1763-1861*. Thereafter she was a professor of African American studies in the University of Maryland, Baltimore. Her writings include the *Historical dictionary of Senegal* (1981). LC

Colvin, Peter J. B., M.A., B.A., Dip. Lib., A.L.A., born about 1950, he was for over twenty years, principal assistant librarian for the Islamic Near East and Middle East at SOAS, and a sometime secretary of the Middle East Libraries Committee. Private

Comay, Michael S., born 17 October 1908 at Cape Town, he was educated in South Africa and served with the South African Army during the second World War. Since 1945 he resided in Israel, where he pursued a diplomatic and ambassadorial career since 1948. In the 1960s he was Israel's chief delegate to the United Nations. His writings include *U.N. peace-keeping in the Israel-Arab con-flict, 1948-1975* (1976), and *Zionism, Israel, and the Palestinian Arabs* (1983). He died in Israel, 6 November 1987. Who, 1980-1988; WhoIsrael, 1978; WhoWorJ, 1965

Combe, Étienne, born 29 January 1881, he was joint editor of *Répertoire chronologique d'épigraphie arabe* (1931), and *al-Ilmam bi-al-i'lam*, by al-Nuwayri (1968). He died 9 July 1962. LC

Combes, Edmond, born 18 June 1812 at Castelnaudary (Aude), he was a Saint Simonian and was educated at the École de droit de Toulouse. In 1833 he travelled from Cairo to Suakin by way of Dongola, Khartoum and Berber, leaving a "purple-tinted account of his journey," *Voyage en Égypte, en Nubie, dans les déserts de Beyouda, des Bicharys et sur les côtes de la Mer Rouge* (1846). He was employed as the local agent of the Compagnie nanto-bordelaise which attempted to open up trade with Abyssinia through the Red Sea in 1840 to 1841. He died in Damascus, 22 April 1848. Hill; Henze

Combès, Jean Louis, fl. 1945, he was a sometime director of the Centre des arts et traditions populaires de Djerba. His writings include *Les femmes et la laine à Djerba* (1946), and, with André Louis, *Les poitiers de Djerba* (1967). LC

Combes, Pierre Paul, born 13 June 1856 at Paris, he entered the Seminaire d'Issy and was ordained, but left the diaconate in 1879 to pursue his literary interests. In 1886 he founded the Librairie uni-verselle in Paris; in 1891 he went on an archaeological excursion to Spain and the Balearic Islands, and in the following year he journeyed to the Sahara in the service of the *Dépêche coloniale* and the *Journal des débats*. Upon his return to Paris in 1897, he founded the Institut encyclopédique, and engaged in public education, contributing widely to periodicals, often with a moral and religious purpose. His writings include *L'Abyssinie en 1896; le pays, les habitants, la lutte italo-abyssine* (1896), and *L'île de Crète* (1897). He died in Paris, 6 March 1909. DBF

Comhaire, Jean Louis Léopold, born 29 June 1913 at Seraing, Belgium, he held doctorates in law and philosophy, and resided in South Orange, N.J., in 1956. His writings include *Urban conditions in Africa* (1952), *Aspects of urban administration in tropical and southern Africa* (1953), and he was joint author of *Le nouveau dossier Afrique* (1975). Unesco

Commeaux, Charles, fl. 1972-85, he was a sometime resident in Saint-Genis-Laval (Rhône), near Lyon, and taught literature and history of art. His writings include *La vie quotidienne chez les Mongols de la conquête* (1972), *La vie quotidienne en Bourgogne au temps des ducs de Valois* (1979), and *Les conclaves contemporains, ou, les aléas de l'inspiration* (1985). LC

Commines de Marsilly, C. R. Adolphe de, born 25 June 1824, he was a writer on the socio-economic conditions and the industry of northern France. He entered the École polytechnique in 1843, and was later an *ingénieur au corps de mines*. In 1866 he became a director of the mines in Anzin (Nord). He died 10 May 1889. DBF

Commissariat, Menekshah Sorabshah, born in 1881, he was a sometime professor of history and principal, Gujarat College, Ahmedabad. He delivered the Thakkar Vassonji Madhavji lectures of the University of Bombay for the year 1930-1931. His writings include *Studies in the history of Gujarat* (1935), and *A history of Gujarat* (1938). LC

Compagni, Vittoria Perrone, fl. 1975, she edited *De occulta philosophia libri tres*, of Cornelius Agrippa (1992). LC

Comparetti, Domenico Pietro Antonio, born 7 July 1835 at Roma, he was a classicist, medievalist, literary historian, and a critic. His writings include *Researches respecting the Book of Sindibâd* (1882). He died in Firenze, 20 January 1927. DizBI; EncicUni; GdeEnc; Meyers; *Who was who*, 2

Compiègne, Louis Alphonse Henri *Victor* du Pont, marquis, born 22 July 1846 at Fuligny (Aube). From his early life he was a traveller and explorer of the Tropics. From 1875 to 1876 he was a secretary of the Société khédiviale de géographie du Caire, and later their president. His writings include *L'Afrique équatoriale* (1875), and *Voyages, chasses et guerre* (1876). He died in a duel, 28 February 1877. DBF; *Hommes et destins*, IX, p.98

Comstock, Alzada Peckham, born 23 November 1888 at Waterford, Conn., she studied at Mount Holyoke College, to which LSE and Sorbonne was added a year or two later. In 1921 she received a Ph.D. from Columbia University for her thesis, *State taxation of personal incomes*. She later taught economics at Mount Holyoke and Barnard colleges. Her writings include *Taxation in the mod-ern state* (1929). She died 15 January 1960. LC; *Who was who in America*, 3

Comyn, David Charles Edward Ffrench, born in 1877, he entered the Black Watch in 1898, and advanced to the rank of major. He wrote *Service and sport in the Sudan; a record of administration in the Anglo-Egyptian Sudan* (1911). BLC; CathWW, 1926, 1930, 1931, 1934, 1936

Comyn-Platt, Sir Thomas, born in 1875, and educated privately, he served as honorary attaché at the British Embassy in Constantinople, and thereafter at the Foreign Office until invalided in the first Wold War. His writings include *The Turks in the Balkans* (1906), *By mail and messenger; private letters mainly from Constantinople and the Near East, covering a period of twelve years before the war* (1925), and *The Abyssinian storm* (1935). He died 18 March 1961. LC; *Who was who*, 6

Conacher, James Blennerhasset, born 31 October 1916 at Kingston, Ont., he was a graduate of Queen's University, Kingston, Ont., and received a Ph.D. in 1949 from Harvard for his thesis, *Canadian participation in the Sicilian campaign, 1943*. He was a professor of history at the University of Toronto from 1946 until 1983, when he became professor emeritus. His writings include *Britain and the Crimea, 1855-56; problems of war and peace* (1987). Canadian, 1981-1993; DrAS, 1974, 1978, 1982

Concas, Víctor María, born 12 November 1845 at Barcelona, he was a captain in the navy who participated in the Spanish colonial campaigns. He published monographs and contributed to several periodicals. He died in 1916. DiccBio; EncicUni; LC; Ossorio

Concasty, Marie Louise, fl. 1954, her writings include *Les manuscripts grecs* [du] *Département des manuscrits* (Paris, 1958), and the editions of several works by A. Gobineau. LC

Concolato, Jean Claude, he received a doctorate in 1976 from the Université de Grenoble II for his thesis, *Le Soudan; politique et accumulation primitive*. LC; THESAM, 3

Conde, José Antonio, born 28 October 1766 at Peraleja (Cuenca), he was educated at the university of Alcalá. In 1795 he obtained a post in the royal library and in 1799 he published a "mediocre edition of the Arabic text of al-Idrisi's *Descripcion de España de Xerif Aledris*" (EncBrit), with notes and a translation. He was a member of the Real Academia Española and the Real Academia de la Historia. His *Historia de la dominación de los árabes en España* (1820-25), was translated into German (1824-25), French (1825), and English (1854). His "prententions to scholarship have been severely criticized by Dozy, and his history is now discredited" (EncBrit). He also wrote *Memoria sobre la moneda arabiga y en especial la acuñada en España por los principes musulmanes* (1982). He died in poverty in Madrid, 12 June (or 20 October) 1820. EncBrit; Espasa; Fück; Manzanares; Meyers; Sainz

Conder, Claude Reignier, born 29 December 1848 at Cheltenham, Gloucestershire, he was a Royal Navy officer and led the Palestine Exploration Fund sponsored mapping party to Palestine from the spring of 1881 to 1882. The results were published under the title *Survey of western Palestine* (1881), and *Survey of eastern Palestine* (1889). His other writings include *Palestine* (1889), and *The Latin kingdom of Jerusalem* (1897). He died in Cheltenham, 16 February 1910. DNB; Henze; *Who was who*, 1

Condorelli, Luigi, fl. 1978, his writings include *La funzione del riconoscimento di sentenza straniere* (1967), and *Il giudice italiano e i trattati internazionali* (1974). LC

Condurachi, Emil, born 3 January 1912 at Scîenteia-Iaşi, Rumania, he was an archaeologist and a professor of history at Bucharest University. His writings include *Histria* (1959), its translations into

326

English and German, *L'archéologie roumaine au XXe siècle* (1963), and *Daco-Romania antiqua; études d'archéologie et d'histoire ancienne* (1988). He died in Bucureşti, 16 August 1987. LC; WhoRom

Conestabile della Staffa, Giovanni Carlo (Giancarlo), conte, born 2 January 1824 at Perugia, he was a professor of archaeology at the Università di Perugia, specializing in antiquities, art, and in his later years, also in Etruscan research. He died near Perugia, 21 July 1877. DizBI; EncBrit; EncicUni; Meyers; NUC, pre-1956

Confer, Carl Vincent, born 12 June 1913 at Greencastle, Ind., he was a graduate of De Pauw University in 1934, and received a Ph.D. in 1939 from the University of Pennsylvania with a thesis entitled *Lyautey and the Moroccan problem, 1903 to 1907*. He was a professor of history at various American universities, specializing in the colonial question in France since 1870. Since 1978, he was professor emeritus, Syracuse University. His writings include *France and Algeria* (1966). ConAu, 21-22; DrAS, 1974, 1978; IndAu; Selim; Unesco

Congreve, Richard, born 4 September 1818 at Leamington Hastings, England, he was educated at Rugby and Oxford, where he taught for the better part of ten years. In 1848 he visited Paris, where he came under the spell of positivism, including the religious cult. In the early days of the movement in London, he took the chief part in the establishment of the propaganda. He died 5 July 1899. DNB, v. 22, Suppl.; Master (4)

Conker, Orhan, fl. 1937, his writings include *Les Chemins de fer en Turquie et la politique ferroviaire turque* (1935), *Türk-Rus savaşları* (1942), and *Milli ideal* (1943). LC

Conn, Harvie Maitland, born 7 April 1933 at Regina, Sask., he was a graduate of Calvin College (1954) and Westminster Theological Seminary, Chestnut Hill, Pa. (1957). He was a pastor in New Jersey and a missionary in Korea before he was appointed a professor of missions and apologetics in Chestnut Hill, Philadelphia, Pa., in 1972. His writings include *Contemporary world theology* (1973). WhoRel, 1975, 1977

Connelly, Bridget Ann, born 20 April 1941 in Minnesota, she studied at the University of Minnesota, to which the universities of Besançon and Tunis were added a few years later. In 1974 she received a Ph.D. from the University of California at Berkeley for her thesis, *The oral-formulaic tradition of Sirat Bani Hilal*. She taught Arabic at Cornell University, before she was appointed a professor of rhetoric at the University of California, Berkeley, where she was still active in 1998. Her writings include *Arabic folk epic and identity* (1986). In the following year, she was awarded the Chicago Folklore Prize. ConAu, 127; NatFacDr, 1998

Connor, James, born in the 18th century, he was a missionary and went to the Middle East in furtherance of the objects of the Church Missionary Society. His journal, chiefly in Syria and Palestine, is contained as an appendix in *Christian researches in the Mediterranean from 1815 to 1820*, by William Jowett, and published in 1828. His writings include *Visit of the Rev. James Connor in 1819 and 1820 to Candia, Rhodes, Cyprus, and various parts of Syria and Palestine* (1822). BLC

Conolly, Arthur, born 2 July 1807, he was educated at Rugby and Addiscombe, entered the East India Company in 1822, and joined the Bengal Cavalry in 1823. From a sick leave in England, he returned to India by way of St. Petersburg, Tabriz, Qazwin, Tehran, Astrabad, Sabzavar, Meshed, Herat, Kandahar and Sind. His abortive excursion from Astrabad to Khiva nearly cost him his life when he fell into the hands of marauding Turcomans. His report, *Journey to the north of India, overland from England through Russia, Persia and Afghanistan* (1830), threw the first light on the lower courses of the Atrak and Gurgan rivers. From 1834 to 1838 he was attached to the Political Department in Rajputana. He made another journey via Wien, Constantinople, Baghdad and Herat. He joined Sir W. Macnaghten's staff at Kabul in 1840. In September of the same year, he was sent as envoy to Khiva via Merv, and to Khokand, and, on the invitation of the Amir Nasir Allah of Bukhara, sent through Colonel Charles Stoddart, went there, but was treacherously imprisoned in late 1841. By the Amir's order both were publicly beheaded, 17 June 1842. His few letters described their sufferings in their dungeon. His prayer-book, full with his writing, was delivered to his sister in London in 1862. Buckland; Henze

Conolly, Edward Barry, a brother of Arthur and born in 1808, he was the first explorer of the Sistan depression in eastern Persia which he penetrated from Herat in 1839. He was a captain in the Bengal Cavalry and commandant of Sir W. Macnaghten's escort at Kabul, when he was killed fighting in the Kohistan under Sir R. Sale, 20 September 1840. Buckland; Henze; NUC, pre-1956

Conolly, Violet, born in 1899 at Glasnevin, Ireland, she was a specialist in Soviet studies, and received a doctorate, and a diploma from the Graduate Institute of International Studies, Geneva, in 1933. She served for many years at the Foreign Office and Chatham House. Her writings include

Soviet economic policy in the East; Turkey, Persia, Afghanistan, Mongolia and Tana Tuva, Sin-kiang (1933), *Soviet trade from the Pacific to the Levant* (1935), *Soviet tempo; a journal of travel in Russia* (1937), and *Siberia today and tomorrow* (1975). She died in 1988. ConAu 124; *Times* 13 January 1988, p. 14

Conrad, Dieter, born in 1932, he studied at Freiburg, Heidelberg, Tübingen, and Ann Arbor, Michigan, where he received an M.A. in comparative law. For many years he was a member of the Südasien-Institut, Heidelberg. Repeatedly he carried on field-work in India, Pakistan, and Bangladesh. His writings include *Freiheitsrechte und Arbeitserfassung* (1965), the revision of his 1963 Heidelberg doctoral thesis. In 1994 he was joint editor of *Bangladesh; dritte Heidelberger Südasiengespräche.*

Conrotte, Manuel, born in 1862 at Madrid, he was educated at the Academia de Administración Militar. He was a lawywer and military officer who contributed to several periodicals. His writings include *España y los paises musulmanes durante el ministerio de Floridablanca* (1909). His trace is lost in 1913. EncicUni; Ossorio

Consiglio, Carlo, fl. 1944, his writings include *"Italia fuente de poesia" e altri studi di letteratura spagnola* (Bari, 1955). Firenze

Constable, Archibald George, major, born in 1822, his writings include *Afghanistan* (1879), a lecture delivered before the American Geographical Society, 14 January, 1879. He died in 1882. LC

Constable, Charles Golding, born in 1821, he was a British naval officer who entered the service of the East India Company in 1839. Together with lieutenant Arthur W. Stiffe he surveyed the Kathiawar Coast of India, 1852-53, and the Persian Gulf, 1857-60. He was joint editor of *The Persian Gulf pilot, including the Gulf of Oman* (London, Hydrographic Office, 1864). He died in London, 18 March 1879. BLC; Embacher; Henze

Constable, Giles, born 1 June 1929 at London, he received his undergraduate and graduate degrees from Harvard. He then taught at the State University of Iowa, before he was appointed professor of history at Harvard. He was a sometime director of Dumbarton Oaks Research Library. His writings include *Monastic tithes* (1964), and *Medieval monasticism; a select bibliography* (1976). He was joint editor of *Petrus Venerabilis, 1156-1956; studies and texts* (1956). His collected articles were also published. DrAS, 1974, 1978, 1982; WhoAm, 1974-1986/87

Constable, William George, born 27 October 1887 at Derby, he was educated at Cambridge, and then went to London and, joining the Inner Temple, read for the bar, to which he was called in 1914. But the direction of his career changed after a horrific experience in 1916. Thereafter he gave up law and looked to the arts for a living, first in England and, since 1938, at "the other Cambridge," Mass. He was the author of several catalogues of art exhibitions. He died in the United States, 3 February 1976. DNB; WhoAmA, 1973, 1976; *Who was who, 7*; *Who was who in America, 6*

Constantelos, Demetrios John (Dimitris Stachys), born 27 July 1927 at Spilia, Greece, he was educated at Holy Cross Greek Orthodox Theological School, Princeton Theological Seminary, at Rutgers University, where he received a Ph.D. in 1965 for his thesis, *Philanthropia and philanthropic institutions in the Byzantine Empire, 330-1204.* He was a pastor in Perth Amboy, N.J., 1955-64, and from 1971 to 1986, a professor of history and religious studies at Stockton State College. His writings include *Orthodox theology and diakonia* (1981), *Byzantine society and church philanthropy from the fourth crusade through the fall of Constantinople* (1985), and *Βυζαντινή κλερονομία; θεολογία, ιστορία, παίδεία* (1990). ConAu 21-22, new rev. 8, 24, 49; DrAS 1974, 1978; Master (1); WrDr 1976-1998/2000

Constantin, François, born 20th cent., he was a lecturer and a deputy director at the Faculté de droit et des sciences économiques de l'Université de Pau. His writings include *Les Voies de l'islam en Afrique orientale* (1987); he was joint author of *Les Communautés musulmanes d'Afrique orientale* (1983), and joint editor of *Arusha (Tanzanie), vingt ans après; journées d'études* (1988). LC

Constantin, Julien Noël, 1857-1936, he wrote *La Nature tropicale* (1899). NUC, pre-1956

Constantinescu, Nicolae A., born in 1885 at Scorţeni, Romania, he was a teacher in France, before he was appointed professor of history at Bucharest University. His writings include *Noua istorie a Românilor de N. Iorga* (1940), *Proverbe turceşti* (1972), *Dicţionar onomastic Român* (1963), and *Lectura textului folcloric* (1986). He died in Prahova in 1961. WhoRom

Constantinescu, Radu, fl. 1978, his writings include *Moldova şi Transilvania în vremea lui Petru Rateş* (1978), and *Dionisie din Pietrari miniaturist şi caligraf* (1982). LC

Constantini, Otto, born in 1904 in Austria, he received a Dr.phil. in 1927 from the Universität Innsbruck for his thesis, *Die Entwicklung der Tiroler Landesverteidigung, 1511-1631.* He was a secondary school teacher, historian and geographer whose writings include *Leben und Wirken eines öster-*

reichischen Geographieprofessors und Erwachsenenbildners (1969), and *Linzer Erinnerungen aus dem 19. Jahrhundert* (1983). BiogrLexOö

Constantinian, F. Pierre, fl. 1903-1914, he was an Armenian of Maraş, Turkey. After study at the Séminaire oriental Saint François Xavier in the Université Saint-Joseph, Beirut, he served as a missionary at Zeytun (Süleymanli) in 1909, and in 1914, as a *curé* at Maraş. Note

Constantinides, Pamela M., fl. 1980, she received a Ph.D. in 1971 from LSE for her thesis, *Sickness and the spirits; a study of the zaar spirit possession cult in the northern Sudan.* Her writings include *Symbols and sentiments* (1977). LC; Sluglett

Contenau, Georges, born 9 April 1877 at Laon (Aisne), he obtained doctorates in medicine and arts, as well as a diploma from l'École nationale des langues orientales vivantes, Paris. He was a keeper of Oriental antiquities at the Musée du Louvre, and subsequently a lecturer, professor, and university administrator at Paris and Bruxelles. His writings include *Manuel d'archéologie orientale*, 4 vol. (1927-1947), and *Les civilisations anciennes du Proche-Orient* (1945). He died 22 March 1964. BioIn, 7; WhoFr, 1963/64

de **Contenson**, Ludovic Guy Marie du Bessey, baron, born 28 February 1861 at Lyon, he was a graduate of the military college, Saint-Cyr, and resigned from the military with the rank of captain in 1903. He travelled to Syria in 1892, and to Armenia in 1897. His writings include *Chrétien et musulmans; voyages et études* (1901), and *Les réformes en Turquie d'Asie* (1911). He died in 1936. Curinier, vol. 4 (1903), p. 35; DBF; LC

Conti, Giovanni, born in 1937, his writings include *Rapporti tra egiziano e semitico nel lessico egiziano dell'agricoltura* (1978), and *Studi sul bilitterismo in semitico e in egiziano* (1980). LC

Conti Rossini, Carlo, born 25 April 1872 at Salerno, he received a doctorate in law from the Università di Roma in 1894. From 1899 to 1903 he was director of the Affari Civili in Eritrea. He pursued a career as a high official in the Ministero del Tesoro and as a brilliant scholar of Ethiopic studies. His writings include *L'Abissinia* (1929), *Chrestomathica arabica meridionalis epigraphica* (1931), and *Grammatica elementare della lingua etiopica* (1941). He died 21 August 1949. Chi è, 1936, 1940, 1948; Hommes et destins, vol. I, pp. 157-158; I.I. (2); IntWW, 1947-1950; Isis 41 ii (1950), p. 201

Continente Ferrer, José Manuel, born early 20th cent., he obtained a doctorate in Semitic linguistics, and was a sometime professor at the Departamento de Estudios Árabes e Islámicos in the Universidad Autónoma de Madrid. His writings include Ibn al-Khatib's *Poesia árabe clasica; antología* (1981). He died on 2 September 1999. Arabismo, 1994, 1997

Contini, Fulvio, fl. 1953. In 1931 he prepared several school texts for the Italian Ministero delle Colonie. Firenze

Contini, Gianfranco, born 4 January 1912 at Domodossala, Italy, he was a sometime professor of Romance philology at the Università di Firenze, and editor of *Teatro religioso del medioevo fuori d'Italia* (1949). Chi è, 1957, 1961; Wholtaly, 1980, 1983; WhoWor, 1980/81

de **Contreras**, Juan, born 19th cent., he was director of *El Hispano Americano* (Madrid, 1903). Ossorio

Contreras y Muños, Rafael, born 28 September 1826 at Granada, he was a writer, artist, architect, and a sometime editor of the Granada *La Constancia*, and in charge of the conservation works at the Alhambra. His writings include *Del arte árabe en España* (1875), and *Recuerdos de la dominación de los árabes en España* (1882). He died 29 March 1890. Cuenta; LC; Ossorio

Contu, Giuseppe, fl. 1975, he was affiliated with the Istituto universitario orientale, Napoli. His writings include *Gli aspetti positivi e i limiti del laicismo in Salâmah Mûsâ* (1980). LC

Cöntürk, Hüseyin, born in 1918 at Izmir, he was educated at Istanbul Teknik Üniversitesi. His writings include *Behçet Necatigil ve Edip Cansever üstüne* (1964). EIS, 1975

Conway, Agnes Ethel, afterwards Horsfield, fl. 1909-1935, she was an archaeologist whose writings include *A Ride through the Balkans, on classic ground with a camera* (1917), *Henry VII's relations with Scotland and Ireland, 1485-1498* (1932), and she was joint author, with Sir William Martin Conway, of *The children's book of art* (1909). BLC; BritInd

Conway, William Egbert, born 5 April 1918 at Red Bluff, Calif., he retired, in 1978 as librarian of the William Andrews Clark Memorial Library at UCLA. He was joint editor of *William Andrews Clark, Jr., his cultural legacy* (1985). BiDrLUS, 1970; LC

Conway, Sir Wiliam Martin, Baron Conway of Allington, born 12 April 1856 at Rochester (Kent), he was educated at Trinity College, Cambridge, and was a sometime Roscoe professor of art at University College, Liverpool, Slade professor of fine art at Cambridge, and director-general of the Imperial War Museum. He was a passionate mountaineer who, from 1872 to 1901, missed very few Alpine seasons. His writings include *Dawn of art in the ancient world* (1891), *The Alps* (1904), *The sport of collecting* (1914), *Palestine and Morocco, lands of the overlap* (1923), and *Episodes in a varied life* (1932). He died 19 April 1937. DNB; Henze; Who was who, 3

Conybeare, Frederick Cornwallis, born in 1856, he was a graduate of Oxford, a fellow of the British Academy, and received honorary doctorates from Gießen and St. Andrews. His writings include *The Dreyfus case* (1898), *Myth, magic, and morals* (1909), and *The story of Ahikar from the Aramaic, Syriac, Arabic, Armenian, Ethiopic, Old Turkish, Greek and Slavonic versions* (1913). He died 9 January 1924. Who, 1924; Who was who, 2

Conze, Egbert, born 6 April 1945 at Meisdorf, Germany, he started life as an agriculturist, before he received a B.Sc. from the University of Minnesota, and an M.A. from Cornell. He completed his formal education with a doctorate in agronomy from the Universität Göttingen for his thesis, *Ökonomische Beurteilung von Maßnahmen zur Begrenzung der Umweltbelastung in der tierischen Produktion*. Since 1975 he was an executive of the Deutsche Landwirtschafts-Gesellschaft, Frankurt am Main. Thesis

Cook, Sir Edward Mitchener, born in 1881, and educated at Clare College, Cambridge, he joined the Indian Civil Service in 1904. From 1931 to 1940 he was governor of the Bank of Egypt. He wrote the tract, *Britain and Turkey; the causes of the rupture* (1914). He died 6 August 1955. Who was who, 5

Cook, Gordon Charles, born 17 February 1932 at Wimbledon, he was a physician with special interest in tropical and infectious diseases. He was a lecturer at the London School of Hygiene and Tropical Medicine, as well as a visiting lecturer in Third World countries. Who, 1994-1998

Cook, John Manuel, born 11 December 1910, the son of Sir Edward Mitchener Cook. After being wounded and invalided out, he went to the Middle East Centre for Arab studies. From 1958 to 1976, he was a professor of ancient history and classical archaeology at Bristol University. His writings include *The Greeks in Ionia and the East* (1963), and *The Persian Empire* (1983). He died 2 January 1994. Who, 1974-1994

Cook, Joseph W., Dr. born in 1883, he served as a medical missionary in Persia from 1912 to 1917 when he resigned for health reasons. He returned to Hamadan in 1929 for a final spell of duty, but died of typhoid fever, 7 January 1932.

Cook, Nilla Cram, born in 1908, she was an expert in Western and Oriental languages, and joined Ghandi's movement for independence in 1931. She was the first American admitted to his model colony. In 1941 she went to Iran to continue research into Oriental art and literature begun in India. In 1942-43 she travelled and studied in Afghanistan, returning to Iran in the autumn of 1943. She was then engaged by the Iranian Ministry of the Interior to found a department of theatre, and organize the national opera and ballet, being concurrently employed in cultural relations for the American Embassy in Tehran. In 1946 she resigned both posts to found the "Studio for the Revival of the Classical Arts of Iran." Her writings include *My road to India* (1939), and *The way of the swan; poems of Kashmir* (1958). She died in Neunkirchen, Austria, 11 October 1982. ConAu 108

Cooke, Brian Kennedy, 1894-1963 see Kennedy-Cooke, Brian

Cooke, Francis T., fl. 1925-1938, he received a Ph.D. in 1934 from Hartford for his thesis, *Ibn al-Qaiyim's Kitab al-ruh, a translation with introduction and annotation*. Selim

Cooke, James Jerome, born 2 August 1939 at Baltimore, Md., he received a Ph.D. in 1969 from the University of Georgia for his thesis, *Eugène Étienne and new French imperialism, 1880-1910*. Since 1979 he was a professor of history at the University of Mississippi, where he was still active in 1998. His writings include *New French imperialism, 1880-1910* (1973), and *France, 1789-1962* (1975). DrAS, 1974, 1978, 1982; NatFacDr, 1998; Selim

Cookey, Sylvanus John Sodienye, born in 1934, his writings include *Britain and the Congo question, 1885-1913* (1968), and *King Jaja of the Niger Delta* (1974). LC

Cooksey, Joseph James, born in 1872, he joined the North African Mission in 1896, at first stationed in Sousse, Tunisia, but soon afterwards as first resident missionary in Kairouan. He was highly esteemed on account of his personality as well as his fluency in Arabic, particularly during his latter years in Tunis. His wife's health compelled him to return to England in 1926. His writings include *The* *land of the vanished Church; a survey of North Africa* (1926), and *Religion and civilization in West Africa* (1931). He died in Blackheath, 23 November 1940. MW 31 (1941), p. 320

Cooley, John Kent, born 25 November 1927 at New York City., he was educated at Zürich, Wien, Dartmouth College, and Columbia University. He was a free lance writer, and a civilian employee and interpreter with U.S. military groups. Later he was a special North African and Middle East correspondent of *The Christian science monitor*, 1965-1978, and Pentagon correspondent, 1978-1980, stationed in Lebanon. He was a senior associate of the Carnegie Endowment for International Peace in 1980-81. His writings include *Baal, Christ, and Mohammed* (1965), *Green march, black September; the story of the Palestinian Arabs* (1973), *Libyan sandstorm* (1982), its translation, *Kadhafi; vent de sable sur la Libye* (1982), and *Payback* (1991). ConAu 13-14; LC; WhoAm 1976/77; WhoWor, 1974-1978; WrDr, 1976-1990/92

Cooley, William Desborough, born 16 March 1795 in Ireland. After education by a private tutor he entered Trinity College, Dublin, in 1811, and graduated in the spring of 1816. By the end of the 1820s he was "well known in [London] literary, scientific and especially geographical circles. His greatest fame and influence came in a period which coincided with the first three or four decades of the existence of the Royal Geographical Society; in fact, his career was closely involved with that institution. It can hardly be said that the relationship was an untroubled one for Cooley was a pricky character who long bore a grudge against the Society's officials. But it was the great explorers of inner Africa who resented him most and their views conditioned subsequent verdicts on him. ...Nevertheless, Cooley's work is worthy of note in the story of the development of the subject in Britain, more particularly where that story invloves the Royal Geographical Society and its offspring, the Hakluyt Society, which he founded [in 1846.] Through the R.G.S. Cooley did have some influence on the course of African exploration. In recent years, too, historians of Africa have come to realize that some of the evidence for his 'theorectical discoveries' in the continent is unobtainable elsewhere and throws useful light on developments in tropical Africa however incorrect the topographical conclusions Cooley drew from it may have been." His writings include *History of maritime and inland discovery* (1830-31), its translations into Dutch (1835-37) and French (1840), *The Negroland of the Arabs examined and explained* (1841), *Inner Africa laid open* (1852), and *Dr. Livingstone and the Royal Geographical Society* (1874). He died 1 March 1883. DNB; Roy C. Bridges, *Geographical journal* 142 (1976), pp. 27-47, 274-286

Coolidge, Archibald Cary, born 6 March 1866 at Boston, Mass., he studied at Berlin, Paris, and six years at Freiburg, leading to a Dr.phil. in 1892 for *Theoretical and foreign elements in the formation of the American constitution*. Since 1893 he was a professor of history and director of library at Harvard. For three months he was attached to the 1919 Peace Conference. His writings include *Origins of the Triple Alliance* (1917), and *Ten years of war and peace* (1927). He died 14 January 1928. DAB; WhAm 1

Coolidge, William Augustus Brevoort, born 28 August 1850 near New York, he was educated in the United States, Guernsey, and Exeter College, Oxford. He was a priest, professor of English history, and a mountaineer. Since 1875 he was a life fellow of Magdalen College, Oxford. The Universität Bern conferred on him an honoary doctorate in 1908. His writings include *The Alps in nature and history* (1908), and *Alpine studies* (1912). He died in 1926. Who, 1924; Who was who, 2

Coomaraswamy, Ananda Kentish, born 22 August 1877 at Colombo, Ceylon, he was a trained chemist and geologist and later pursued an interest in Oriental art. He was a sometime research fellow in Indian, Persian and Muhammadan art at the Museum of Fine Arts in Boston. His writings include *Rajput painting* (1916), *Introduction to Indian art* (1923), and *History of Indian and Indonesian art* (1927). He died in Needham, Mass., 9 September 1947. DAB, suppl. 4; Eminent; I.I. (3); WhNAA; *Who was who, 2; Who was who in America, 2*

Coombs, Philip Hall, born 15 August 1915 at Holyoke, Mass., he was a graduate of Amherst College, Mass., and afterwards continued studies at Chicago and Hoover Institution, Stanford University. He briefly taught economics at American universities before becoming a national and international executive for educational and cultural affairs. His writings include *The technical frontiers of education* (1960), *What is educational planning?* (1970), and *Future critical world issues in education* (1981). BlueB, 1976; ConAu 17-18, new rev. 8; IntWW, 1979-1983/84; WhoAm, 1974-1982/83; WhoWor, 1974-1982/83; WrDr, 1980/82-1990/92

Coon, Carleton Stevens, born 23 June 1904 at Wakefield, Mass., he received a Ph.D. in 1928 from Harvard for his thesis, *A study of the fundamental racial and cultural characteristics of the Berbers of North Africa, as exemplified by the Riffians*. He was a university lecturer, a curator of ethnology at the Philadelphia University Museum, and a professor of anthropology at the University of Pennsylvania until his retirement in 1963. During the early years of his career, he conducted anthropological and archaeological field-work throughout the Muslim world. His writings include *Measuring Ethiopia and flight into Arabia; an account of an anthropological expedition in Ethiopia and Arabia, 1933-1934*

(1935), *Caravan; the story of the Middle East* (1951), *Cave explorations in Iran, 1949* (1951), and an autobiography, *Adventures and discoveries* (1981). He died 3 June 1981. BlueB, 1976; ConAu 5-6, new rev. 2; Master (9); Selim; *Who's who in America*, 1980

Cooney, John Ducey, born 3 August 1905 at Boston, Mass., he was a graduate of Harvard College and successively a curator at the Brooklyn Museum and the Cleveland Museum of Art. He served one term as director of the American Research Center in Cairo. His writings include *Late Egyptian and Coptic art* (1943). He died in 1982. BioIn, 10, 13; Egyptology; WhoAmA, 1973, 1976

Cooper, A. R. C., fl. 1926, he was a squadron-leader in the Royal Air Force and served for three years in Mesopotamia. *Journal of the Central Asian Society* 13 (1926), p. 148

Cooper, Alfred Duff, Viscount Norwich, born 22 February 1890 at London, he was a graduate of New College Oxford, who joined the Foreign Service in 1913, and later entered Parliament. His writings include *Talleyrand* (1932), *The second World War* (1939), *Old men forget; the autobiography of Duff Cooper* (1953), and *A durable fire; the letters* (1983). He died 1 January 1954. DNB; Master (7)

Cooper, Elizabeth (Mrs. Clayton Sedgwick Cooper), born 10 May 1877 at Homer, Iowa, she was a widely known writer who spent a great part of her life in travelling for the purpose of investigating the condition of women in various countries. Her writings include *The women of Egypt* (1914), and *The harim and the purdah; studies of Oriental women* (1915). She died in 1945. AmAu&B; LC; Master (3); WhNAA; *Who was who in America*, 5

Cooper, Frederick Henry, 1826 or 7-1869, he was a Punjab employee. He wrote *The crisis in the Punjab, from the 10th of May until the fall of Delhi* (1858), and he was joint author of *The handbook of Delhi* (1863). BLC; LC; Mason, pp. 169-171

Cooper, John, born 24 August 1947, he was a sometime lecturer in Persian at Cambridge University. He pursued an interest in Islamic legal philosophy as well as the application of new technology to the editing and publishing of Islamic manuscripts. His writings include the annotated translation of al-Tabari's *Commentary on the Qur'an*, vol. 1 (1987). He died 9 January 1998. Private

Cooper, Mark Neal, born about 1950, he received a Ph.D. in 1979 from Yale University for his thesis, *The transformation of Egypt*. His other writings include *Trends in liability awards* (1986). LC

Cooper, Merian C., born 24 October 1894 at Jacksonville, Fla., and educated at the U.S. Naval Academy, he was a trained newspaperman with the spirit of the explorer. He sailed in the South Seas, visited Abyssinia and, in 1925-1926, made the annual Zardah Kuh migration with the Baba Ahmadi Bakhtiyaris in the Zagros Mountains. He spent six months with them producing the documentary film *Grass*. He also wrote the book *Grass* (1925). He died 21 April 1973. Master (5); Shavit; WhAm 5

Cooper, Richard Stefan, born 23 August 1935 at Elmira, N.Y., he was a graduate of Princeton, and received a Ph.D. in 1973 from the University of California at Berkeley for his *Ibn Mammati's rules for the ministries; translation with commentary of the Qawanin al-dawanin*. Since 1970 he was attached to the Collection Development Office, General Library, University of California. From 1973 to 1975 he was vice-president of the Middle East Librarians Association. IWWAS, 1975/76; Selim; WhoLibl, 1982

Cooper, Robert Leon, born in 1931, he received a Ph.D. in 1965 from Columbia University for his thesis, *The ability of deaf and hearing children to apply morphological rules*. He was joint author of *The languages of Jerusalem* (1991); he edited *Language spread* (1982), and *Sociolinguistic perspective on Israeli Hebrew* (1983). LC

Coordes, Gerd (Gerhard), 1839-ca.1890, he was a geographer and educator whose writings include *Pädagogische Blüten; allgemeine Erziehungslehre in Aussprüchen bedeutender Pädagogen aller Zeiten und Völker* (Frankfurt, 1882). NUC, pre-1956

Copeland, Paul W., M.A., fl. 1955, he wrote *The land and people of Syria* (*Portraits of the nation series*, 1964), and *The land and people of Libya* (1967). LC

Coppola, Carlo, born 1 October 1938 at Wooster, Ohio, he was a graduate of John Carroll University, Cleveland, Ohio, and received a Ph.D. in 1975 from the University of Chicago for his thesis, *Urdu poetry, 1935-1970; the progressive episode*. He was a professor of Hindi and Urdu linguistics, and chairman of the Area Studies Program at Oakland University, Rochester, Mich. He was joint translator of *Eleven poems, and introduction, translation from the Urdu of Faiz Ahmad Faiz* (1971), and he edited *Marxist influence and South Asian literature* (1974). DrAS, 1978, 1982; WhoUSWr, 1986/87-1988

Coque, Roger, born 1 March 1923 at Bonneuil, France, he received a doctorate in 1962 from the Sorbonne. From 1951 to 1957 he served as instructor in the Tunisian higher educational system.

After his return to France, he was attached successively to the CNRS and the universities of Poitiers, Lille and Paris. His writings include *La Tunisie présaharienne* (1962), *Nabeul et ses environs* (1964), and *Géomorphologie* (1977). WhoWor, 1971/72, 1974/75

Coquebert de Montbret, Eugène, born 8 February 1785 at Hamburg, Germany. On account of an accident, he lost his speech at the age of five. In spite of this handicap, his intelligence and tremendous memory enabled him to master Latin, Greek, and several modern langauges, including Arabic. Since 1806 he was attached to the Bureau de statistique of the Ministry of the Interior, and later transferred to the Ministry of Agriculture. In 1816 he was appointed translator at the Ministry of Foreign Affairs. He produced an extract of Ibn Khaldun's *Prolegomena*. He bequeathed his important library to the Rouen municipal library. He died in Rouen in 1849. DBF

Coquelle, P., born in 1858, he was a writer on history and published *Le royaume de Serbie* (1894), and *Histoire du Monténégro et de la Bosnie* (1895). LC

Coquery, Michel Louis, born 10 June 1931 at Le Mans, he was a professor of geography at the Sorbonne from 1961 until his retirement. He was joint author of *Atlas classique Larousse* (1969). WhoFr 1993/94-1997/98

Coquery-Vidrovitch, Catherine Marion, born 25 November 1935 at Paris, she was a professor of contemporary history at the Université de Paris VII - Denis Diderot. Her writings include *La découverte de l'Afrique* (1965), *Le Congo au temps des grandes compagnies concessionnaires, 1898-1930* (1972), originally presented as her thesis, Paris, 1970. She also wrote *Société paysannes du Tiers-monde* (1980), and *Les Africaines* (1994). WhoFr, 1977/78-1997/98

Coquin, François Xavier, fl. 1957, his writings include *La révolution russe* (1962), *La révolutionm de 1917* (1974), and *Des pères du peuple au père des peuples; la Russie de 1825 à 1929* (1991). LC

Coquin, René Georges, fl. 1978, he received a doctorate in 1975 from the Université de Paris for his thesis, *Livre de la consécration du sanctuaire de Benjamin*. His writings include *Les Canons d'Hippolyte* (1966). LC

Cora, Guido, born 20 December 1851 at Torino, he was educated at Torino and Leipzig and became a professor of geography. He founded the periodical *Cosmos*, in 1873. In 1874 and 1876 he undertook scientific travels to Greece and North Africa. He died in 1917. Embacher; IndBI

Čorbe, Klime, fl. 1971, he was joint author of *Makedonija; razvoj i perspektive* (1960). LC

Corbet (Corbett), Eustace Kynaston, born 22 June 1854, he was a graduate of Balliol College, Oxford, English secretary to the Khedive Tawfiq, 1895-91, in various capacities at the Native Court of Appeal, Cairo, 1891-1908, and director of the Egyptian Educational Mission to England, 1908-1913. His writings include *Lessing's Nathan the wise, translated into English* (1883). He died 21 March 1920. BLC; *Who was who*, 2

Corbett, Percy Ellwood, born 20 December 1892 at Tyne Valley, P.E.I., he was a graduate of Huntingdon Academy, and completed graduate studies in Montreal and Oxford. He was awarded a honorary LL.D. form the University of Melbourne in 1938. He served as dean of the Faculty of Law in McGill University, Montreal, as well as assistant legal advisor at the International Labour Office in Genève. In 1956 he was a member of the Center of International Studies, Princeton University. His writings include *Canada and world politics* (1928), *Britain, partner for peace* (1946), and *The growth of world law* (1971). Canadian, 1936-1952

Corbetta, Carlo, fl. 1883, he was an Italian traveller who wrote *Sardegna e Corsica* (1877). LC

Corbin, Henry, born 14 April 1903 at Paris, he was educated at Paris and started his career as a librarian, and later keeper, at the Bibliothèque nationale de Paris. In the service of the Institut français d'archéologie d'Istanbul, he went on a mission to Turkey in 1939. In 1946 he was appointed director of the Département d'iranologie de l'Institut franco-iranien de Téhéran. In 1954 he succeeded Louis Massignon to the *chaire d'islamisme* at l'École pratique des hautes études, Paris. He was an Iranist and Arabist who contributed greatly to a fundamental re-orientation of Islamic studies. His writings, many of which have been translated into English, include *Avicenne et le récit visionnaire* (1952-56), *L'imagination créative dans le soufisme d'Ibn Arabi* (1958), *L'École shaykhi en théologie shi'ite* (1967), *Histoire de la philosophie islamique* (1964), and *L'homme de lumière dans le soufisme iranien* (1971). In 1977 he was honoured by *Mélanges offerts à Henry Corbin*. He died in Paris, 7 October 1978. BioB 134; *Hommes et destins* VII, pp. 133-34; I.I. (13); WhoFr, 1971/72-1977/78

333

Corbon, Jean, born in 1924, he was in 1961 a lecturer at the Institut de lettres orientales in the Université de Beyrouth. His writings include *L'église des Arabes* (1977), and *Liturgie de source* (1980), and its translation, *The wellspring of worship* (1988). He was joint author of *La parole de Dieu* (1966).

Corbyn, Ernest Nugent, born 2 April 1881, he was a Cambridge graduate who, in 1904, joined the Sudan Political Service, where he then spent his entire career. He was a secretary of the Royal African Society as well as editor of its *Journal*. He died 26 May 1961. Who was who, 6

Corcelle, Joseph, born 20 January 1858 at Ceyzerien (Ain). After studies of law and arts, he became a professor of history and geography successively at Épinal, Le Puy, Lyon and Chambéry. He was a contributor to the *Revue de géographie* as well as regional periodicals. His writings include *Les pays de l'Ain* (1904). He died in Ceyzerien, 25 March 1921. DBF

Corcos, David, born in 1917 at Mogador, Morocco, he was a sometime staff member at the *Encyclopaedia Judaica*. His writings include *Studies in the history of the Jews of Morocco* (1976). He died in 1975. LC

Cordell, Dennis Dale, born 1 January 1947 at St. Louis, Mo., he was a Yale graduate, and a Peace Corps worker in Chad from 1968 to 1970. He received a Ph.D. in 1977 from the University of Wisconsin at Madison for his thesis, *Dar al-Kuti*. Since 1977 he was a professor of history at Southern Methodist University, Dallas, Texas, where he was still active in 1998. His writings include *Dar al-Kuti and the last years of the trans-Saharan slave trade* (1985). He was joint editor of *African population and cap-italism* (1987). DrAS, 1978, 1982; LC; NatFacDr, 1998

Cordero Torres, José María, born 14 December 1909 at Almeria, Spain, he was a sometime lecturer in international and colonial law and policy at the Universidad de Madrid. Since 1955 he was a Supreme Court magistrate. His writings include *El africanismo en la cultura hispánica contemporanea* (1949), *La missión africana de España* (1956), and *La decolonización* (1965). WhoSpain, 1963

Cordes, Rainer, fl. 1985, he received a doctorate in 1981 from the Universität Göttingen for his thesis, *Die Binnenkolonisation auf den Heidegemeinheiten zwischen Hunte und Mittelweser*. He was joint author of *Bedouins, wealth, and change* (1980). LC

Cordier, Henri, born 18 October 1849 at Nouvelle-Orléans. A seven-year stay in the nineteenth century in China determined his lifelong orientation toward the Far East. He was for forty years a professor at the École nationale des langues orientales vivantes, Paris. In 1890 he founded the journal *T'oung Pao*. His writings include *Les études chinoises, 1891-1902* (1898-1903). He died in Paris, 16 March 1925. Revue du monde musulman 62 (1925), pp. 139-140

Cordun, Valéry, born 26 July 1918 at Alehki, Ukraine, he was educated in Sofia and, from 1949 to 1972, worked as a literary translator in Bucureşti, concurrently pursuing an interest in folklore research. In 1974 he went to Germany, where he taught at an evening school. WhoWor, 1982/83

Coret, Alain, born 27 July 1930 at Anglet (Pyrénées-Atlantiques), he received a doctorate in economics from the Sorbonne, and a diploma from the Institut d'études politiques de Paris.. He was a civil servant, and a sometime head of the credit division, General Secretariat of the Council of Europe. His writings include *Le condominium* (1960). He contributed to *Qu'est-ce qu'un groupement fédératif d'entreprise?* (1976). LC; WhoEIO, 1982, 1985

Corfus, Ilie, a writer who published *Agricultura ţării româneşti în prima jumătate a secolului al XIX-lea* (1969), its translation, *L'agriculture en Valachie durant la première moitié du XIX siècle* (1969), *Agricultura în ţarile române, 1848-1864* (1982), and *Documente privitoare la istoria României culese* (1983). LC; OSK

Corivan, Nicolae, born in 1904 at Galaţi, Romania, he was a sometime professor of history successivetly at Iaşi and Suceava. His writings include *Lupta diplomatică pentru cucerirea in-dependenţiei României* (1977), and *Relaţiile diplomatice ale Româneie de la 1859 la 1877* (1984). LC; WhoRom

Corkill, Norman Lace, born 11 June 1898, he was educated at Liverpool, where he received a M.D. in 1936. From 1927 to 1963, he served as a health officer, and professor of zoology and tropical medicine, in many Arab countries and Iran, as well as in Liverpool. His writings include *Snake and snake bite in Iraq* (1932). He died 26 September 1966. BLC; Who was who, 6

Corm, Georges Antoine Georges, born in 1940 at Alexandria, he received a doctorate in law from the Faculté de droit et sciences économiques, and a diploma from the Institut des sciences politiques, Paris. He was a sometime representative of financial institutions in Beirut, as well as a lecturer in political science at the Université de Saint-Joseph, Beirut. His writings include *Politique économique et* *planification au Liban* (1964), *Les Finances d'Israël* (1968), *Contribution à l'étude des sociétés multi-confessionnelles* (1971), *Le Proche-Orient éclaté* (1983), *Fragmentation of the Middle East* (1988), *L'Europe et l'Orient* (1990), and *Conflits et identités au Moyen-Orient, 1919-1991* (1992). LC; WhoLeb, 1970/71-1997/98

Cornelius, A. R., born in 1903, he was a sometime chairman of the Pakistan Pay and Services Commission. His writings include the tracts *Scheme for establishment of zakat* (1970), and *The ethical basis for democracy in Pakistan* (1971). Note

Cornelius, Paul Frederick Sinel, he contributed articles on marine biology to the *Bulletin of the British Museum* (natural history) in 1975 and 1979. LC

Cornet, Roger, he was in 1968 a research fellow at the Centre africain des sciences humaines appliquées, Aix-en-Provence. He was joint author of *Comune et société rurale en Algérie* (1968). BN

Cornetz, born 19th cent., he was in 1912 a civil engineer and a secretary of the Section technique of the Société de géographie d'Alger. Note

Cornevin, Robert, born 26 August 1919 at Malesherbes (Loiret), he was educated at l'École nationale de la France d'outre-mer and received a doctorate from the Sorbonne in 1960. He was an anthropologist and a sometime secretary of the Académie des sciences d'outre-mer and, at the end of his career, *administrateur en chef de la France d'outre-mer.* His writings include *Histoire de l'Afrique* (1956), *Le Togo* (1967), and *Histoire du Zaire* (1989). With Marianne Cornevin he published *Histoire de l'Afrique des origines à nos jours* (1964), and its translation, *Geschichte Afrikas von den Anfängen bis zur Gegenwart* (1980). He died 14 December 1988. IntAu&W, 1977, 1982; Unesco; WhoFr, 1975/76-1988/89; WhoWor, 1984-1989

Cornish, Vaughan, born 22 December 1862 at Debenham, Suffolk, he was a geographer and a lecturer. His writings include *Ocean waves and kindred geophysical phenomena* (1934). He died in Camberley, 1 May 1948. DNB; WhE&EA; *Who was who*, 4

Cornwall, Sir James Handyside Marshall, 1887-1985 see Marshall Cornwall, Sir James Handyside

Cornwall, Peter Bruce, born in the first half of the 20th century, he studied Arabian history and archaeology at Oxford and Harvard. He carried on anthropological research in Bahrain and Saudi Arabia in 1941-42. he received a Ph.D. in 1944 from Harvard for his thesis, *Dilmun, the history of Bahrein Island before Cyrus.* NUC, pre-1956

Cornwallis, Sir Kinahan, born 19 February 1883. At Oxford University he read Arabic and held records as an athlete. In 1906, he joined the Sudan Civil Service and also worked in the Egyptian Ministry of Finance. He was associated with Intelligence from the start of the first World War and was one of the first members of the Arab Bureau, Cairo. He specialized in Asir, editing the *Handbook* on the area. As director of the Bureau, he edited most numbers of the *Arab bulletin*. After his retirement in 1935, he was ambassador in Baghdad from 1941 to 1945. Gertrude Bell regarded him as "a tower of strength and wisdom." After the war, King Faisal, chosen as King of Iraq, refused to go there unless Cornwallis accompanied him as adviser. He died 3 June 1959. R. L. Bidwell, *Arab bulletin* 1 (1986 reprint), p. xxv; *Who was who*

Corò, Francesco, born 3 October 1882 at Venezia, he was a journalist, a writer on history, archaeology and ethnography, and a periodical editor. His writings include *Vestigia di colonie agricole romane; Gebel Nafusa* (Roma,1929), *La via del sud* (Tripoli, 1930), and *Settantasei anni di dominazione turca in Libia, 1835-1911* (Tripoli, 1937). Chi è, 1940, 1948; Firenze; IndBI

Corominas, Joan (John), born in 1905 at Barcelona, he received a doctorate in 1931 from the Universidad de Madrid for his thesis, *Vocabulario aranés*. He was successively professor of linguistics at Barcelona, the Universidad Nacional de Cuyo, Argentina, and the University of Chicago. His writings include *Mots catalans d'origens aràbic* (1936), *Estudios de etimología hispánica* (1942), and *Diccionario crítico-etimológico de la lengua castellana* (1954). DcSpL; OxSpan; Master (2)

Ćorović, Vladimir, born 15 October 1885, a writer on Balkan history, his writings include Босна и Херцеговина (1925), Историја Југославије (1933), Борба за независност Балкана (1937), and Историја Босне (1940). He died 16 October 1941. LC

Corradini, Piero, he was a Sinologist and Japanologist whose writings include *La Cina* (1969), *La Mongolia moderna* (1978), and *Introduzione alla storia del Giappone* (1992). LC

Corré, Alan David, born 2 May 1931 at London, he studied at London and Manchester, and received a Ph.D. in 1962 from the University of Pennsylvania for his thesis, *The structure of Tamil.* From 1963

until his retirement he was a professor of Hebrew studies at the University of Wisconsin, Milwaukee. His writings include *The daughter of my people; Arabic and Hebrew paraphrases of Jeremiah 8.13-9.23* (1971), *Understanding the Talmud* (1975), *A diskionary and chrestomathy of modern Judeo-Arabic* (1989), and *Icon programming for humanists* (1990). In 1992 he edited *The quest for social justice, II.* ConAu, 37-40; DrAS, 1974, 1978, 1982; WhoWorJ, 1972

Corréard, Joseph, born in 1792, he was an engineer, a bookseller and editor in Paris, and a writer on military affairs. His writings include *Recueil de documents sur l'expédition et de la prise de Constantine par les Français en 1837* (1838), and *Guide maritime et stratégique dans la mer Noire, la mer d'Azof, et sur le théâtre de la guerre en Orient* (1854). He was also an editor of the *Journal des sciences militaires.* He died 21 April 1870. DBF; Vapereau

Correia Afonso, John, born 15 July 1924 at Benaulim, Goa, he was a graduate of St. Xavier's College, Bombay, and in 1953 received a doctorate from the University of Bombay. He entered the Society of Jesus in 1946, and was variously a professor of history at, or a president of, St. Xavier's College. From 1965 to 1970 he was successively a provincial superior of the Society of Jesus, Bombay, and assistant to the superior general, Roma. His writings include *Jesuit letters and Indian history* (1955), *The soul of modern India* (1960), and *The Ignation vision of India* (1991); he was the editor of *Letters from the Mughal court* (1980), and *Indo-Portuguese history* (1981). ConAu, 33-36, new rev. 13; LC; WhoWor, 1989

Correia de Campos, José Augusto, born 1890 *see* Campos, José Augusto Correia de

Correll, Christoph, born 19 August 1940 at Berlin, he studied at Wien and München, where he received a Dr.phil. in 1969 for his thesis, *Materialien zur Kenntnis des neuaramäischen Dialekts von Bah'a.* He was a sometime professor of linguistics at the Universität Konstanz. His writings include *Untersuchungen zur Syntax der neuwestaramäischen Dialekte des Antilibanon* (1978). Kürschner, 1992, 1996; Schwarz; Thesis

Corriente Cordoba, Federico, born in 1940, he obtained a doctorate in Semitic linguistics, and was a sometime lecturer in Arabic literature at the Universidad de Zaragoza, where he was still active in 1997. His writings include *Diccionario español-árabe* (1970), *Problemática de la pluralidad en semítico* (1971), *Las mu'allaqat; antologia y panorama de Arabia preislamica* (1974), *A grammatical sketch of the Spanish Arabic dialect bundle* (1977), *Gramática árabe* (1980), and *Nuevo diccionario español-árabe* (1988). Arabismo, 1992, 1994, 1997; LC

Corrigan, H. S. W., fl. 1967, he received a Ph.D. in 1953 from the University of London for his thesis, *British, French and German interests in Asiatic Turkey, 1881-1914.* Sluglett

Corry, Cyril Eugene, captain, born about 1894. In 1915 he was posted to the 14th Hussars and served with his regiment until 1917, when he joined the Iraq Police. After a few months' experience as Station House Officer at Amara and Basra, he was promoted to police commissioned rank as Assistant Commandant at Baghdad, where he witnessed the troubles of 1920. This was followed by two years in the Southern Desert with the Camel Corps, and six years as Inspecting Officer of Police in southern Iraq, where he took an active part in the operations for establishing Government authority in the marshes. After spells of duty in Diyalá, Kut, and Diwaniyah in 1933, he was transferred to the north as inspecting officer for the *liwa's* of Mosul and Arbil, a post which he held until he retired from the service of the Iraqi Government in 1947. He was about to take up a new appointment under the British military administration in North Africa, when he died at his home in Darlington after a short illness, aged fifty-three, 18 November 1947. He wrote *The blood feud* (1937). JRCAS, vol. 35 (1948), p. 103

Corsepius, Hans Günther, fl. 1939, he was a pastor and affiliated with the Deutsche Orient-Mission, Potsdam. He wrote *Der Islam im Angriff* (1938).

Corsi, Mario Carlo, born 19 June 1882 at Pistoia, Italy, he was a writer of historical biographies, whose works include *A traverso il Gebel* (1914). He died in Roma, 3 April 1954. DizBI

Corsi Prosperi, Anna, fl. 1977, she was joint editor of Ceseri Frullani's *Gl'avvenimenti del lago di Fucecchio e modo del suo governo* (1988). LC

Corso, Raffaele, born 8 February 1885 at Nicotera (Catanzaro), he studied law and received a doctorate in 1906 for his thesis *Proverbi giuridici italiani.* From 1914 to 1921 he was the first professor in Italy to give lectures in ethnography at the Istituto di antropologia dell'Università di Roma. Since 1922 he taught ethnography at the Istituto orientale di Napoli. In 1946 he was the founding editor of *Folklore*, Napoli. His writings include *Africa italiana, genti e costumi* (1940), *Africa; cenni razziali* (1941), and *Studi africani* (1950). He died in Napoli, 29 July 1965. DizBI

Cortabarría Beitia, Ángel, fl. 1950, he was a Dominican priest who received a doctorate in Arabic philosophy, specializing in Muslim Spain. Arabismo, 1992, 1994, 1997

Cortambert, Louis Richard, born in 1809 in France, he was an abolitionist, a writer, journalist, and traveller. He emigrated to the United States as a youth. His writings include *États-Unis d'Amerique* (1867), and *Religion du progrès* (1884). He died in Hyères, 26 January 1884. AmAu&B; DAB, DBF; DcNAA; WhAm, H

Cortambert, Pierre François *Eugène*, born 12 October 1805 at Toulouse. At the age of twenty he was a teacher in Paris and collaborated in the production of the *Dictionnaire géographique universelle* by Picquet. Throughout his life he was a teacher and popularizer of geography. He was a member of the Société de géographie de Paris from 1836 and its general secretary, 1853-1854, when he joined the geographical section of the Bibliothèque nationale, Paris, and became a keeper in 1863. He died in Passy, 5 March 1881. DBF; Geog, 2

de **Cortanze**, H., he was in 1903 a French vice-consul in Samsun, Turkey. Note

Cortelazzo, Manlio, born 19 December 1918 at Padua, he was a dialectician and a sometime professor at the Università di Padova. He was a prolific writer on his specialty. His writings include *L'influsso linguistico greco a Venezia* (1970). In 1989 he was honoured by the felicitation volume *La dialettologie italiana oggi; studi offerti à Manlio Cortelazza*. In 1990 he edited *L'ambiente e il paesaggio*. IndBI (1); LC; Wholtaly, 1988, 1990, 1992, 1994

Cortese, Emilio, born 25 September 1856 at Alexandria, he was a geologist attached to the R. Ufficio geologico. From 1910 to 1911 he explored Arabia from Chena (Shannah?) to Qusayr. His writings include *Metallurdia dell'oro* (1904), *Traversata del deserto arabico da Chena à Cosseir* (1912), and *Geologia pratica* (1932). He died in Firenze, 4 October 1936. DizBI

Cortesi, Fabrizio, born 8 June 1879 at Roma, he was a botanist who obtained a doctorate in botany in 1902 from the Università di Roma for a thesis on orchids. His writings include *Manuale di botanica agraria* (1908), *Botanica farmaceutica* (1910), and *Piante medicinali coltivate* (1942). He died in Roma, 29 June 1949. DizBI

Corti, Roberto, born 26 July 1909 at Firenze, he was a professor of botany at the Facoltà di agraria dell'Università di Firenze. His writings include *Flora e vegetazione del Fezzán e della regione di Gat* (1942). Chi è, 1961

Cortiana, Rino, born in 1944, he was a writer whose works include *I poeti della Comune* (1971), and *L'azzurro di Giotto* (1982). He was a contributing author to *7 poeti del Premio Montale: Roma 1988* (1989). LC

Cortier, Maurice Adrien, born 9 August 1879. After passing through the military college of Saint-Cyr in 1899, he joined the French Marines. Since 1901 he was posted to French West Africa. After accompanying the Mission Cauvin to the Saharan salt-pits, he and captain Arnaud organized the *méharistes*, as a consequence of which he crossed the Sahara from Alger to Gao to Saint-Louis de Sénégal in 1907. In the service of the Ministère des colonies, he explored the *Sahara soudanais*, an enterprise which became known as the Mission Cortier, 1908-1910. Two years later he was part of a group that made a study of a possible trans-African railway. His writings include *Mission Arnaud-Cortier: nos confins sahariens* (1908). He died in the opening campaign of the first World War in Ville-sur-Tourbe, 25 September 1914. DBF

Coryate, Thomas, born about 1577, he was a sometime student at Oxford and travelled extensively in Europe in 1608. From 1612 to 1617 he travelled to Greece and continued overland to India, but most of his important travel journal has been lost. He wrote *Coryate's crudities; reprinted from the edition of 1611, to which are now added his letters from India* (1776). Michel Strachan wrote a biography *The life and adventures of Thomas Coryate* (1962). He died in Surat in 1617. CasWL; DNB; EncAm; Master (11); MEW; OxEng

Corzo Sánchez, Ramón, fl. 1978, his writings include *Osuna de Pompeyo e César; excavaciones en la muralla republicana* (1977). In 1982 he edited the *Historia de los pueblos de la Provincia de Cádiz*. He was a contributing author to *Algeciras* (1983). LC

Cosentino, Giuseppe, born 11 or 12 February 1852 at Palermo, he was a sometime lecturer in palaeography and Latin diplomatics at Regia Università di Palermo, and the editor of *Nuovi documenti sulla Inquisizione in Sicilia* (1885-86). His last known article was published in 1910. Casati[2]; Gubernatis[3]; Salomone

Coseriu, Eugenio, born in 1921 at Mihăileni, Romania, he studied in Italy. In the late 1940s, he taught Romanian at the Università di Milano, followed by twelve years at the Universidad de Montevideo, Uruguay. Since 1966 he was a professor of linguistics at the Universität Tübingen, Germany. In 1971 the University of Bucharest conferred on him an honorary doctorate. His writings include *Textlinguistik* (1980), *Sprachkompetenz* (1988), and *Limba română în față occidentului* (1994). Kürschner, 1966-1996; LC; WhoRom

Cosim, S., pseud. *see* Phocas Cosmetatos, Spuridon Pan

Coşkun, Gülay, fl. 1969-86, she received a doctorate in 1969 from Ankara Üniversitesi for her thesis, *Türk ve Amerikan hukukunda grup sigortasi ve çeşitleri*. She was a sometime assistant director at the Budget Department, Finance Ministry, Ankara, as well as a university lecturer. Her writings include *Bütçe reformu (nedenleri) ve program bütçe sistemi* (1976), and *Devlet bütçesi; Türk bütçe sistemi* (1986). LC

Coslovi, Franco, 1949-1993, he studied Indian Islam, particularly the Naqshbandi order, at the Facoltà di lettere dell'Università di Roma, to which Lahore and SOAS, London, was added in 1973 and 1975 respectively. Under a scholarship he continued his studies at the Seminario di Iranistica dell'Università di Venezia since 1981, and in 1991/92 he taught Urdu language and literature. His obituary in *Rivista degli studi orientali* 67 i-ii (1993/94), pp. 197-199, contains a list of his articles. To this should be added his contribution to the collective work, *India tra Oriente e Occidente* (1991). LC

Cosquin, Emmanuel Georges, born in 1841 at Vitry-le-François (Marne), he was a follower of La Tour du Pin whom he assisted in the founding of workers' circles. He contributed to *le Français* and *le Moniteur*, upholding conservative and royalist ideas, and attended the international congresses of Catholics as well as congresses of popular traditions. His writings include *Les contes indiens et l'Occident* (1922), and *Études folkloriques* (1922). He died in 1919. DBF

de **Cossé Brissac**, Philippe, born in 1905. Even before he obtained his formal diploma in archival palaeography from the École française des Chartes in 1928, he was invited to collaborate in the research project *Les sources inédites de l'histoire du Maroc*. He remained a lifelong collaborator despite the project's faltering fortunes between 1937 and 1947, when he advanced to the position of director of the Section historique du Maroc. He died in Genève, 20 May 1963. Andalus 28 (1963), pp. 237-238

de **Cossé-Brissac**, Pierre, duc, 1900-1993 *see* Brisaac, Pierre Simon Charles Timoléon de Cossé

de **Cossio y Martinez Fortún**, José Maria, born in 1893 at Valladolid or Santander, Spain. he was educated at the Instituto de Santander and at the universities of Valladolid and Madrid. He was a literary critic who contributed numerous articles to magazines, reviews, and papers. His writings include *Fábulas mitologicas de España* (1952). CIDMEL; DBEC; Figuras; OxSpan; Sabater; Sainz; WhoSpain, 1963

de **Cosson**, Charles Alexander, baron, fl. 1881-1920, his writings include *Catalogue of the exhibition of ancient helmets and examples of mail at the Archaeological Institute, from June 3rd to June 16th, 1881* (1985). He wrote the introduction to Sir Guy F. Laking's *A record of European armour and arms* (1920-1922). LC

Cosson, Ernest St.-Charles, born 22 July 1819 at Paris, he studied medicine and botany and received a medical doctorate in 1847 from the Université de Paris. In 1852 he accompanied the Commission scientifique de l'Algérie as a botanist and, during the following six years, explored North Africa. The results, entitled *Itinéraire d'un voyage botanique en Algérie*, he published in the *Bulletin de la Société botanique* in 1857. His monographs include *Compendium florae atlanticae* (1882-88). He died in Paris, 31 December 1889. DBF; Henze; NUC, pre-1956

Costa, Émile Jacques, born 15 February 1927, he studied law at Alger and Paris. For over twenty years he was a member of the Human Resources Department at the International Labour Office, Genève. His writings include *Youth training and employment schemes in developing countries* (1972). WhoUN, 1975

Costa, Horacio Luís de la, 1916-1977 *see* De la Costa, Horacio Luís

Costa, Julio Salom *see* Salom Costa, Julio

Costa, Paolo M., born in 1932, he was associated with the Bureau of Antiquities, Sanaa. His writings include *The pre-Islamic antiquities at the Yemen National Museum* (1978), *The hinterland of Sohar* (1987), and *L'uomo e l'ambiente nella Peninsula Araba* (1991). He was joint author of *Yemen, paesi di costruttori* (1977). LC

Costard, George, born in 1710 at Shrewsbury, he was a fellow of Wadham College, Oxford, and chosen proctor of the University in 1742. He was a writer on astronomy and his works are still worth consulting for the frequent references to, and citations from, Hebrew and Arabic texts. He died in Twickenham, in 1782. DNB

Coste-Floret, Paul, born 9 April 1911 at Montpellier, he received a doctorate in law in 1935 from the Université de Montpellier for his thesis, *La nature juridique du droit de propriété d'après le code civil et depuis le code civil*. His ten-year teaching career at Alger and Montpellier was interrupted in 1945 when he served as assistant attorney general at the International Tribunal in Nürnberg. He later was a government official. He died 28 August 1979. IntWW, 1972/73-1979/80; IntYB, 1978-1985; WhoFr, 1953/54-1979/80; WhoWor, 1971/2-1978/79

Costello, Desmond Patrick, born 31 August 1912 at Auckland, New Zealand. He was educated at Auckland University College, and Trinity College, Cambridge. During the second World War he served in Greece and North Africa. After the war he was for six years a secretary at the New Zealand Legation in Moscow. In 1955 he was appointed professor of Russian at Manchester University. He translated *The blind owl*, of Sadiq Hidayat (1958), and edited *Russian folk literature* (1967). He died 23 February 1964. Who was who, 6

Costello, Edmund W., brig.-general, born 7 August 1873, he served in the Punjab Infantry since 1894, and was awarded V.C. in 1897. During the first World War he was posted to Mesopotamia. He died 7 June 1949. Who was who, 4

Costello, Vincent Francis, he received a Ph.D. in 1970 from the University of Durham for his thesis, *Settlement relations in the city and region of Kashan, Iran*. His writings also include *Urbanization in the Middle East* (1977). Sluglett

Costescu, Eleanora, she was a writer of historical biographies which include *Gheorge Petraşcu* (1975), and *Meštrović* (1978). LC

Cotard, Charles, fl. 1875-1892, he was a civil engineer who was affiliated with the Société des ingénieurs civils. He contributed to *le Génie civil*, and *l'Explorateur*, and wrote *Note sur l'aménagement des eaux* (1877). BN

Côte, Marc, born about 1940, he received a doctorate in 1977 from the Université d'Aix-Marseille for his thesis, *Mutations rurales dans les hautes plaines de l'Est algérien*. From 1966 to 1986 he was a lecturer in geography successively at Dijon and Constantine. In 1989 he was lecturing at Aix-en-Provence. His writings include *Mutations rurales en Algérie* (1980), *L'espace algérien* (1983), and *L'Algérie, ou, L'espace retourné* (1988). LC; THESAM, 2

Cotelle, Henri, born about 1821. he was an employee at the Trésor à Alger, where he learned Arabic and successively advanced to the position of dragoman at the French consulates in Tunis, and Tanger. His *Le langage arabe ordinaire, ou, Dialogues arabes élémentaires destinés aux Français qui habitent l'Afrique* went through three editions between 1850 and 1858. He collected more than two hundred manuscripts on Arabic grammar as well as other works on the history of Africa which became part of the Bibliothèque d'Alger when he died at the age of thirty-six in Quiers (Loiret), 19 June 1857. DBF

Cotran, Eugene, born 6 August 1938 at Jerusalem, he was educated at Alexandria, Egypt, Leeds, Cambridge, and London, and was called to the bar from Lincoln's Inn in 1959. He was a sometime High Court Judge in Kenya, and a Circuit Judge in England. In 1994 he was a visiting professor of law with reference to Africa and the Midle East, and chairman of the Centre for Islamic and Middle Eastern Law at SOAS, London. His writings include *The law of marriage and divorce* (1968), and *Casebook on Kenya customary law* (1987). He was joint author of *Readings in African law* (1970). Unesco; Who, 1993-98

Cotsonis, H. I., 1905- *see* Kotsones, Hieronymos

Cott, Perry Blythe, born 27 March 1939 at Columbus, Ohio, he was a graduate of Princeton, where he also received a Ph.D. in 1937 for *Siculo-Arabic painted ivories of the twelfth and thirteenth centuries*. He was a sometime chief curator, National Gallery, Washington, D.C. Selim; WhoAmA, 1959, 1966, 1970

Cotta, Carl *Bernhard* von, born 24 October 1804 or 8 at Klein-Zillbach, Germany, he was educated privately as well as at the Bergakademie Freiberg, where he was appointed a professor of geology in 1842. He was an important scholar and a philosopher of geology in a time of increasingly detailed research. In the service of the Russian Government, he travelled to the Altai Mountains in 1868. He died in Freiberg, 14 September 1879. DcScB; DtBE; DtBilnd; Embacher; EnSlovar

Cottam, Richard Walter, born 1 October 1924 at Provo, Utah. As is customary for Mormons, he engaged in a brief period of missionary activity for the Church. In 1954 he received a Ph.D.from Harvard University for his thesis, *Iran; a case study of nationalism*. Thereafter he studied at Tehran under a Fulbright scholarship, from 1951 to 1952. He served in the division of covert opera-tions in the CIA between 1953 and 1958, serving the early part of that time in Washington and then seconded as a political officer to the Embassy in Tehran during 1956-1958. From 1970 until retire-ment, he was a professor at the University of Pittsburgh. For many years a critic of the U.S. support for the Shah of Iran, he played an active part in the early negotiations for the release of the American Embassy hostages, serving as a go-between for the State Department with Iranian officials, most notably Foreign Minister Sadiq Qutbzadah, his friend of many years. His writings include *Nationalism in Iran* (1964), and *Iran and the United States* (1988). He died of cancer, 29 August 1997, at the University of Pittsburgh Medical Center. MESA *bulletin* 31 (1997), pp. 203-205; WRMEA 16 v (Jan./Feb. 1998), p. 152

Cotte, Narcisse, born in the first half of the nineteenth century, he was a sometime professor at the Collège de Tunis and, from 1855 to 1858, successively attached to the consulate-general of France, Tanger, and the *vice-consulat* of France, Rabat. He wrote *Le Maroc contemporain* (1860). LC

Cottenest, commandant, born about 1870, he joined the army on 20 May 1889, and after passing through the military college of Saint-Maixent, he received a commission as *sous-lieutenant*. Upon his request, he was posted to the Service des Affaires indigènes de l'Algérie on 20 October 1898. He was *adjoint de 1ère classe* in the Bureau arabe, Malla-Marnia (Oran), in 1914, and captain in the 2nd Light Infantery Battailon in Africa, detached to the Service des renseignements, Casablanca, in 1914. He is remembered mainly for his raid one thousand miles into Touareg country to revenge the assassination of P. F. Flatters, and to establish permanently French supremacy in the Sahara. He was killed in action in the Bois des Marquises, 25 September 1914. Peyronnet, p. 484

Cottevieille-Giraudet, Rémy, fl. 1938, he was joint author of *Rapport sur les fouilles de Médamond* (1926). LC

Cotton, Harry *Evan* Auguste, born 27 May 1868 at Midnapore, Bengal, he was educated at Oxford and called to the bar from Lincoln's Inn in 1893. He practised law at Calcutta until retirement from India in 1906. Thereafter he was a journal editor in London, a Member of Parliament, and a founding member of the governing body of SOAS. His writings include *Calcutta, old and new; a historical and descriptive handbook to the city* (1907). He died 7 March 1939. Who, 1921; *Who was who*, 3

Cotton, Julian James, 1869-1927, he was a colonial judge and and antiquary. His writings include *List of inscriptions on tombs or monuments in Madras possessing historical or archaeological interest* (1905), and *A book of Corpus verses* (1909). BritInd (2); LC

Cottrell, Alvin J., born in 1924 at Bordentown, N.J., he received a Ph.D. In 1960 from the University of Pennsylvania for his thesis, *Western and communist attitudes towards conflict*. After teaching at Wharton School in the University of Pennsylvania in the 1950s, he worked at the Instiue for Defense Analyses and directed an arms control project for the Kennedy Administration's military staff. He later taught at the National War College, Georgetown University, before joining the Defense Department's Office of International Security Affairs. His writings include *Arms transfer and U.S. foreign and military policy* (1980), and *The United States and the Persian Gulf* (1984). He died in Alexandria, Va., 24 February 1984. ConAu, 112; LC

Cottu, Charles, born 13 March 1778 at Paris. After graduation from the Polytechnique, and a brief service with the Artillerie de la Marine, he completed his law training at Paris and became a magistrate and a judge in the Tribunal d'appel de Paris. He was sent to Britain to prepare a documentation for a possible reform of the French judiciary. He was a fervent legitimist, though anticlerical. His writings in-clude *De l'administration de la justice criminelle en Angleterre* (1830), *Théorie générale des droits des peuples et des gouvernements appliquée à la Révolution de juillet* (1832), and *Guide politique de la jeunesse* (1838). His trace is lost after his last publication. BN; DBF

Coudreau, Henri Anatole, born 6 May 1859 at Sonnac, (Charente-Maritime), he started life as a notary's clerk, but later studied at l'École de Cluny and, in 1880, obtained a post as geography teacher at the trade school in Reims. At first he toyed with the idea of North African exploration. He made short contributions on ethnography and applied for participation in the Flatters Mission to the Sahara. After being turned down, but set on exploration at all cost, he accepted a post in Cayenne. South America became his speciality until he died there in 1899. His writings include *Le Pays de Wargla; les peuples de l'Afrique et Hartmann*. BN; DBF; Henze

Coufoudakis, Van, fl. 1974, he was a sometime vice-chancellor of Academic Affairs and a professor of political science, Indiana University - Purdue University, Fort Wayne. He was editor of *Essays on the Cyprus conflict* (1976). LC

Coufourier, Édouard Auguste, born 11 November 1882, he was a graduate of l'École des langues orientales vivantes, Paris, successively an interpreter in Mazagan, Tanger, and Casablanca, *gérant* at the consulates in Mogador, and Marrakesh, and vice-consul in Marrakesh. He was still in active consular service in 1921. AnnDipl&C, 1927, 1929/30

Couland, Jacques, fl. 1964-1974, his writings include *L'éveil du monde arabe* (1964), *Israël et les états arabes* (1968), *Israël et le Proche-Orient* (1969), and *Le mouvement syndical au Liban* (1970). LC

Couleau, Julien, fl. 1945, his writings include *Le Paysannerie marocaine* (1968), and he was joint author of *Le Maroc* (1977). LC

Coulon, Alfred, fl. 1913-1930, he was a sometime *instituteur* at Alger, and from 1928 to 1930 a director of l'École d'application, El-Biar, Alger. Note

Coulon, Christian, fl. 1975, his writings include *Le marabout et le prince; islam et le pouvoir en Afrique noire* (1981), and *Les musulmans et le pouvoir en Afrique noire* (1983). He was joint author of *Autonomie locale et intégration nationale au Sénégal* (1975), and *L'islam au féminin* (1990); he was joint editor of *Charisma and brotherhood in African Islam* (1988). LC

Coulond, Lucien, 1883-1966 *see* Helsey, Lucien Edmond Marie Coulond *called Édouard*

Coulson, Noel James, born 18 August 1928 at Blackrod, Lancashire, he was a graduate of Keble College, Oxford, and called to the bar from Gray's Inn in 1961. He spent much of his academic career at SOAS. In 1965/66 he was a dean of law at Ahmadu Bello University, Zaria, Nigeria. He was a frequent visiting professor at American law schools. His writings include *History of Islamic law* (1964), *Conflicts and tensions in Islamic jurisprudence* (1969), *Succession in the Muslim family* (1971), and *Commercial law in the Gulf states* (1984). He died 30 August 1986. ConAu, 120, 124; I.I. (2); LC

Coult, Allan D., fl. 1968-1977, he was a member of the International Society of Psychedelic Anthropology, and the editor of *Pschedelic anthropology* (1977). LC

Coulter, John Wesley, born 8 May 1893 at Pettigo, Ireland, he received a Ph.D. in 1926 from the University of Chicago for his thesis, *The geography of the Santa Lucia Mountain region*. He was a sometime professor of geography at the University of Cincinnati. After his retirement he lived in Middlebury, Vt. Most of his more than one hundred publications center on the Pacific. He received two awards for articles that appeared in the *Journal of geography*. His writings include *Fiji, little India in the Pacific* (1942), and *The drama of Fiji* (1967). AmAu&B; LC; NatCAB, 55, p. 281-82

Couput, Gustave, fl. 1900, his writings include *Les Laines et l'industrie lainière de l'Algérie à l'exposition de 1889* (1889), and *L'olivier* (1904). BN

Cour, Auguste, born in 1866, he received a doctorate in 1920 from the Université d'Alger for his complementary thesis, *La dynastie marocaine des Beni Wattâs, 1420-1554*. He was a sometime professor at the Médersa in Tlemcen, Algeria. His writings include *L'établissement des dynasties des chérifs au Maroc et leur rivalité avec les Turcs de la Régence d'Alger, 1509-1830* (1904), *Catalogue des manuscrits arabes conservés dans les principales bibliothèques algérienne; Médersa de Tlemcen* (1907). He died 10 January 1945. Andalus 10 (1945), pp. 459-460

Courau, Jean, born in 1866, he was a civil engineer who contributed to *le Genie civil* and the *Journal des économistes*. He wrote *Les Chemins de fer de l'Algérie-Tunisie* (Paris, 1891). NUC, pre-1956

Courbage, Youssef, born 20th cent., he wrote *La situation démographique au Liban* (1973-74); he was joint author of *Chrétiens et Juifs dans l'islam arabe et turc* (1992), and its translation, *Christians and Jews under Islam* (1997). LC

Courbin, Paul, born in 1922, he was a graduate of l'École normale supérieure, and joined l'École française d'Athènes in 1949, becoming its secretary-general from 1954 to 1959. A trained Hellenist, he held the chair of Archéologie historique et de civilisation matérielle at l'École des hautes études en sciences sociales for over thirty years. His writings include *Qu'est-ce que l'archéologie?* (1982), and its translation, *What is archaeology* (1988). He died in 1994. Syria 74 (1997), p. 221

Couret, René, fl. 1967, his writings include *Guide bibliographique sommaire d'histoire militaire et coloniale française* (1969). LC

Courtade, Antoine, born in 1857, he was a medical doctor whose writings include *Anatomie, psysiologie et séméiologie de l'oreille* (1893), and *Manuel pratique du traitement des maladies de l'oreille* (1895). His trace is lost after an article published in 1913. BN; LC

Courtade-Cabessanis, Pierre, born 3 January 1915 at Bagnères-de-Bigorre (Hautes-Pyrénées), he was a member of the Central Committee of the French Communist Party, a prominent journalist, writer, a staff member of *l'Humanité*, and the newspaper's Moscow correspondent in his later years. His writings include *Essai sur l'antisociétisme* (1946), and *Albania; travel notebook* (1956). He died in Paris, 14 May 1963. WhoFr. 1963/64

Courteille, Abel Pavet de, 1821-1889 *see* Pavet de Courteille, Abel Jean Baptiste Marie Michel

Courtellemont, Gervais, 1863-1931 *see* Gervais-Courtellemont, Jules

Courtenay, William James, born 5 November 1935 at Neenah, Wisc., he was a graduate of Vanderbilt University, Nashville, Tenn., and received his Ph.D. in 1967 from Harvard Divinity School for his thesis, *The Eucharistic thought of Gabriel Biel.* From 1966 until retirement he was a professor of history in the University of Wisconsin at Madison. His writings include *Schools and scholars in fourteenth-century England* (1987), and *Capacity and volition; a history of the distinction of absolute and ordained power* (1990). A collection of his articles was published under the title *Covenant and causality in medieval thought* (1984). ConAu, 9-10; DrAS, 1974, 1978, 1982; WhoAm, 1988/89-1995

Courtet, Jules Jean Joseph Laurent Édouard, born 9 July 1807 at Isle-sur-Sorgue (Vaucluse), he was a sometime *sous-préfet* and *chevalier de la Légion d'honneur.* His writings include *Dictionnaire géographique, historique, archéologique et biographique ... de Vaucluse* (1857). He died in Val-les-Bains, 4 August 1881. LC; Vapereau

Courtney, David, born about 1920, he went to the Middle East in the service of the British Government in 1943. Before and after the second World War he was a newspaper corresopndent in Turkey and Israel respectively. He wrote *Column one* (Tel Aviv, 1953). His trace is lost after his last publication in 1957. LC

Courtney, Leonard Henry, Lord of Penwith, born 6 July 1832 at Penzance, Cornwall, he was a graduate of St. John's College, Oxford in 1851, and became a fellow of his college in 1856. He joined the staff of *The Times*, and sat for over twenty-five years in the House of Commons. He was in turn Under-Secretary for the Home Department, for the Colonies, Financial Secretary to the Treasury, and Deputy Speaker of the House of Commons, and was created a peer in 1913. He was one of the vice-presidents of the Royal Economic Society. His writings include *The working constitution of the United Kingdom* (1901). He died 11 May 1918. DNB

Courtois, Christian, born 20 July 1912 at Cognac (Charente), he started studying modern languages, but soon changed to ancient languages. On his request he was appointed professor at the Lycée d'Alger, 1935, and remained there until his appointment to the Faculté des lettre d'Alger. Upon the completion of his two theses, *Les Vandales et l'Afrique* and *Victor de Vita et son œuvre*, in 1955, he became *maître de conférences.* His writings include *Timgad, antique Thamvgadi* (1951), and *Bibliographie de l'histoire de l'Afrique du nord* (1953). He died after a car accident in Lyon, 8 August 1956. Index Islamicus (2); Revue africaine, 101 (1957), pp. 433-434

Courtois, Henry, born 6 October 1839 at Toulouse, he was the son of a Toulouse banker and, after his father's death, pursued an interest in geography at his estate, the Château de Mudes (Lot-et-Garonne). His writings include the multi-volume *Géographie de la France par voies de communications; chemins de fer ...* (1872-76). His trace is lost after an article published in 1887. Andrieu

Courtois, Jacques Claude, fl. 1961, he was attached to the Mission archéologique d'Alasia. His writings include *Les habitats protohistoriques de Sainte-Colombe près d'Orpierre (Hautes-Alpes) dans le cadre des civilisations* (1975). LC

Courtois, Victor, S.J., fl. 1938-47, he was the editor of the *Avicenna commemoration volume* of the Iran Society, Calcutta (1956). LC

Courtot, lieutenant-colonel, fl. 1926, he was head of the Cabinet militaire du Résident général de Tunisie and pursued a long interest in the problems of native politics and the questions of the southern parts of Tunisia which he explored in 1925. Peyronnet, p. 925

Coury, Ralph M., born 20th cent., he received a Ph.D. in 1984 from Princeton for his thesis, *Abd al-Rahman Azzam and the development of Egyptian Arab nationalism.* Selim[2]

Cousens, Henry, 1854-1934, he was a member of the Royal Asiatic Society and a sometime super-intendent, Archaeological Survey of India. His writings include *Lists of antiquarian remains in His High-ness the Nizam's territories* (1900), *Bijapur and its architectural remains* (1916), and *The antiquities of Sind, with historical outline* (1929). LC

Cousin, Jean Philippe, born 4 September 1902 at Cognac (Charente), he studied at Bordeaux and Paris, where he received a doctorate for his thesis, *Études sur Quintilien*, in 1935. His writings include *Bibliographie de la langue latine, 1880-1948* (1951). He died in 1981; a commemoration volume, *Hommage à Jean Cousin*, was published in 1983. LC

Coutelle, Jean Marie Joseph, born in 1748 at Le Mans, he was a physicist and an army colonel who made the first French excavations at Alexandria in 1798 and picked up the fist of a colossus of Ramses II in Memphis in 1799, now in the British Museum. He produced much meteorological material, and an account of his travel in Sinai with a Bedouin caravan, a paper on the construction of the pyramids and a proposal for bringing one of the Luxor obelisks to Paris (1800). He died in Auteil in 1835. DBF; Hoefer

Coutière, Suzanne, fl. 1937. she was chief of pharmacy at the Hôpital d'Oran and, since 1936, a member of the Société de géographie et d'archéologie d'Oran. Note

Coutsinas, Georges, fl. 1975, he was a research fellow in the Institut d'étude du développement économique et social in the Université de Paris, and joint author of *La croissance des quantités globales en L'Afrique de l'ouest de 1947 à 1964* (1967). LC

Couve de Murville, Jacques *Maurice*, born 24 January 1907 at Reims, he was a politician and diplomat, and mediator in the Lebanese civil war, 1975. His writings include *Une politique étrangère, 1958-1969* (1971), and its translation, *Außenpolitik* (1973). IntWW, 1974-1990/91; Master (4); Who, 1974-1998; WhoFr, 1953/54-1997/98

Couvreur, Gérard, fl. 1964, he received a doctorate in 1978 from the Université de Strasbourg for his thesis, *Éssai sur l'évolution morphologique du Haut Atlas centrale calcaire*. THESAM, 1

Couyat, Jules, fl. 1911, he was an archaeologist whose writings include *La Route de Myos-Hormos et les carrières de porphyre rouge* (1909), and *Les Inscriptions hiéroglyphiques et hiératiques du Ouâdi Hammâmât* (1912), both of which were published by the Institut français d'archéologie orientale, Cairo.

Couzinet, Paul, born 27 September 1900 at Toulouse, he was educated at Toulouse and Paris, where he received a doctorate in 1928 for his thesis, *La réparation des atteintes portées à la propriété im-mobilière par les groupements administratifs*. He spent most of his academic career at Toulouse, where he held the chair of international public law until 1943, when he accepted the chair of administrative law, a post he held until his retirement. He was a sometime editor of the *Revue de droit constitutionnel français*. A felicitation volume, *Mélanges offerts à Paul Couzinet*, was published in 1974.

Covernton, James Gargrave, born in 1868. He was a graduate of St. John's College, Oxford, and a member of the Indian Education Service. His writings include *Vernacular reading books in the Bombay Presidency* (1906). He died 20 July 1957. Who was who, 5

Cowan, David, born in 1929, he was a linguist whose writings include *Modern literary Arabic* (1958), and its translation, *Langue arabe, langage quotidien en Égypte* (1980). Private

Cowan, Hendrik Karel Jan, born 18 June 1907 at Batavia, he was educated at s'Gravenhage and studied at the Rijksuniversiteit te Leiden, where he received a doctorate in 1937 for his thesis, *De "Hikajat Malém Dagang," Atjèhsch heldendicht*. He was an anthropologist, a sometime director of Domestic Affairs, and a deputy chairman of the Raad van Diensthoofden of the Government of Dutch New Guinea. His writings include *Grammar of the Sentani language* (1966). Wie is dat, 6 (1956)

Cowan, J. Ronayne, fl. 1978 at the University of Illinois, he was joint author of *Spoken Hausa* (1976).

Cowan, Laing Gray, born 31 May 1922 at Galt, Ont., he was a graduate of the University of Toronto and received a Ph.D. in 1950 from Columbia University. He taught at Columbia, from 1947 to 1971, and at SUNY, Albany, thereafter. His writings include *The economic development of Morocco* (1958), *Local government in West Africa* (1958), *The dilemmas of African independence* (1964), and *Privatization in the developing world* (1990). AmM&WS, 1973 S, 1978 S; LEduc, 1974; Unesco

Cowan, William George. born 17 November 1929 at St. Petersburg, Fla. After he received a Ph.D. in 1960 from Cornell University, Ithaca, N.Y. for his thesis, *A reconstruction of proto-colloquial Arabic*, he worked for the U.S. Department of State in Beirut from 1960 to 1964. From 1971 until his retirement he was a professor of linguistics at Carleton University, Ottawa, Ont., and concurrently a visiting professor at many universities. Canadian, 1987-1994; DrAS, 1974, 1978, 1982; Selim

Cowdrey, Herbert Edward John, born 29 November 1926 at Basingstoke, Hants, he was educated at Trinity College, Oxford. He was a sometime chaplain and, since 1956, a fellow and tutor at St. Edmund Hall, Oxford. His writings include *The Cluniacs and the Gregorain reform* (1970), *The age of Abbot Desiderius* (1983), *Popes, monks, and crusaders* (1984), and the collection of his articles, *The crusades and Latin monasticism, 11th-12th centuries* (1999). WhoWor, 1984/85

Cowell, Edward Blythe, born 23 January 1826 at Ipswich, Suffolk, he started life as a merchant's clerk and studied Persian before he graduated from Magdalen Hall, Oxford, in 1854. He taught in India until 1867, when he was appointed the first professor of Sanskrit at Cambridge, a post he held until his death, 9 February 1903. His writings include *The Maitri Upanishad* (1870). Buckland; DNB

Cowper, Henry Swainson, born 17 June 1865 at Harrow near London, he was an antiquary who made an archaeological excursion in the area east and southeast of Tripolis in Libya. His writings include *Through Turkish Arabia; a journey from the Mediterranean to Bombay* (1894), and *The Hill of the Graces* (1897). His collection of Egyptian antiquties was presented to the British Museum in 1943. He died in Bowness-on-Windermere, 7 April 1941. Egyptology; Henze; WhE&EA; *Who was who*, 4

Cox, Albertine née Jwaideh, born about 1930 in Iraq, she was educated in Iraq and at Oxford, where she became the first Arab woman to obtain the B.Litt. *and* D.Phil. for her respective theses, *Municipal government in Bagdad from 1869 to 1914* (1953), and *Land and tribal administration of Lower Iraq under the Ottomans from 1869-1914* (1957). In 1966, she joined the Department of Islamic Studies in the University of Toronto, where she remained until her retirement. Private; Sluglett

Cox, Cyril, fl. 1919, he was a paymaster lt.-commander, R.N.R. Note

Cox, Frederick John, born 27 January 1914 at Tacoma, Wash., he was a graduate of the University of California at Berkeley, where he also received his Ph.D. in 1947. He was a professor of Middle Eastern history at the universities of Alabama and Cairo, and a professor emeritus of history, Portland State University, since 1979. He was joint author of *The Soviet Union and the Middle East; a documentary record* (1987). DrAS, 1974, 1978, 1982; LC

Cox, Sir George William, Rev., born 10 January 1827 at Benares, he was a graduate of Trinity College, Oxford. His writings include *The Crusades* (1874), *The Greeks and the Persians* (1876), and *History of the establishment of British rule in India* (1881). He died 9 February 1902. DNB; Master (4); *Who was who*, 1

Cox, Hiram, born about 1760 in Britain, he was a captain of the Bengal Army and a British colonial agent who was sent on a mission to Burma, 1796-1797. After his return to India, Lord Wellesley entrusted him with resettling thousands of Arakanese who had fled to Chittagong from Arakan. His writings include *Journal of a residence in the Burmhan Empire, and more particularly at the Court of Amara-poorah* (1823), and its translation, *Voyage du capitaine Hiram Cox dans l'émpire des Birmans* (1825). He died of fever in the unhealthy Chittagong district in 1799. G. P. Ramachandra, *Journal of Southeast Asian studies* 12 (September 1981), pp. 433-451; Henze

Cox, Sir Percy Zachariah, major-general, born 20 November 1864. After passing through the Royal Military College, Sandhurst, he joined the Indian Staff Corps and served in the Indian Political Department. In 1899 he began his long and distinguished connection with the Persian Gulf as consul at Muscat. He skilfully defeated the schemes of Germany for securing a terminus for the Baghdad Railway in the Persian Gulf, or for securing a monopoly of the pearl fisheries through the shadowy claims of the Sultan. He died 20 February 1937. Philip P. Graves wrote a biography, *The life of Sir Percy Cox* (1941). Buckland; DNB; Who, 1921, 1932; *Who was who*, 3

Cox, Raymond, born in 1856, he was a director of the Musée de Lyon. His writings include *L'art de décorer les tissus, d'après les collections du Musée historique de la Cambre de commerce de Lyon* (1900), *Catalogue sommaire des collections du Musée historique des tissus* (Lyon, 1902), and *Les soieries d'art depuis les origines jusqu'à nos jours* (1914). BN; LC

Coxe, Antony Hippisley, 1912-1988 *see* Hippisley Coxe, Anthony Dacres

Coyajee, Sir Jahangir Cooverjee, born 11 September 1875, he was educated at Cains College, Cambridge, and a sometime professor of political economy, Presidence College, Calcutta, and from 1930 to 1931 its president. His writings include *India and the League of Nations* (1932), *Iranian and Indian analogues of the legend of the holy grail* (1939), and *Studies in the Shahnameh* (1939). He died in July 1943. Who, 1932; *Who was who*, 5

Coÿne, Abel André, born 11 October 1835 at Laroche-Chalais (Dordogne), he enlisted in 1855 in the army. After passing through the military college of Saint-Cyr, which he had entered in 1858, he received a commission as *sous-lieutenant* at the 58e de Ligne on 1 Ocober 1860. He entered the Service des affaires indigènes de l'Algérie on 23 December 1861, and was stationed to a variety of Saharan posts until assigned to the headquarters of the Tunisian expeditionary corps on 20 January 1882. He retired from active service with the rank of battailon commander. His writings include *Une ghazzia dans le Grand Sahara* (1881). Peyronnet, pp. 451-452

Cozens-Hardy, William Hepburn, born 22 November 1868, he was a graduate of University College, London, followed by a career in the British judiciary, 1899-1907. Jointly with Walter Burton Harris, he published *Modern Morocco; a report on trade prospects, with some geographical and historical notes* (1919). He died 18 June 1920. LC; *Who was who, 2*

Crabbs, Jack Austin, born 16 May 1938, he received a Ph.D. in 1972 from the University of Chicago for his thesis, *The historians of Egypt, 1798-1922*. For over ten years he was a professor of history in the California State University, Fullerton, where he was still active in 1998. His writings include *The writing of history in nineteenth-century Egypt* (1984). NatFacDr, 1998; Selim

Crabites, Pierre, born 17 February 1877 at New Orleans, he studied at Tulane University and the Université de Paris, and was admitted to the bar in 1900. He practised in New Orleans until 1911, when he was appointed a presiding judge in the Cairo Mixed Tribunal, a post which he held for fourteen years. He had resigned from the Bench, and was about to take up a professorship in the University of Louisana, when, on the entry of the U.S. into the second World War, he joined the diplomatic service. At the time of his death on 11 October 1943, was in Baghdad as legal assistant to the American Minister to Iraq. His writings include *Gordon, the Sudan and slavery* (1933), *The winning of the Sudan* (1934), *Americans in the Egyptian Army* (1938), and *The spoiliation of Suez* (1940). Hill; Shavit; *Who was who in America, 2*

Cragg, Albert *Kenneth*, born 8 March 1913, he received a D.Phil. in 1950 from Oxford for his thesis, *Islam in the twentieth century*. He was an Anglican with a conservative evangelical background who had learned his Arabic when he was a chaplain in Beirut from 1939 to 1947. During this time he also lectured in philosophy at AUB. In 1953 he became a professor of Arabic and Islamics at the Kennedy School of Missions of the Hartford Seminary Foundation, and also assumed the editorship of the *Muslim world*. He was a sometime assistant bishop of Jerusalem, and Oxford. His writings include *Call of the minaret* (1956), *Counsels in contemporary Islam* (1965), *Jesus and the Muslim* (1985), *The Arab Christian* (1992), and *Troubled by truth* (1992). Con Au, 17-18, new rev. 7; Sluglett; Who, 1970-1998; WrDr, 1976/78-1998/2000

Craies, William Feilden, born 31 October 1854 at Brisbane, Queensland, he was educated at Winchester College, New College, Oxford, and called to the bar in 1882. He practised law. His writings include *A treatise on statute law* (1906). He died 23 October 1911. *Who was who, 1*

Craig, Albert *James* Macqueen, born 13 July 1924, and educated at Liverpool and Oxford, he was ambassador to Syria, 1976-79, to Saudi Arabia, 1979-84, visiting professor of Arabic, Oxford, 1985-91. His writings include *Shemlan; a history of the Middle East Centre for Arab Studies* (1998). *Directory of BRISMES members*, 1993; MidE, 1982/83; Who, 1974-2002

Craig, Daniel, born 20th cent., he was in 1978 a Ph.D. candidate in anthropology under a National Science Foundation graduate fellowship at the University of California at Berkeley. Note

Craig, James Ireland, born 24 February 1868 at Buckhaven, Scotland, he was educated at Edinburgh and Cambridge, and from 1896 to 1918 in the service of the Egyptian Government. His writings include *Anthropometry of modern Egyptians* (1911), *Egyptian irrigation* (1913), and *Egypt in the post-war economy* (1945). He died 26 January 1952. Master (1); WhE&EA; *Who was who, 5*

Craig, Richard Blythe, born 28 January 1935 at Blytheville, Ark., he was a graduate of the University of Missouri at Columbia, where he also received his Ph.D. for his thesis, *Interest groups and the foreign policy*, in 1970. In 1969 he was appointed a professor of political science in Kent State University, where he was still active in 1998, specializing in international narcotics diplomacy. His writings include *The bracero program; interest groups and foreign policy* (1971). AmM&WS, 1973 S; ConAu, 53-56; NatFacDr, 1998

Craig-Martin, Paul F., fl. 1952. Before the second World War he was on the staff of the Commonwealth Economic Committee and later went to Washington as a member of the British Food Mission to North America. He subsequently was an agricultural economics adviser in the International Bank, and was the Bank's representative at several Food and Agriculture Organization conferences and at meetings of the International Cotton Advisory Committee. His writings include *Oils and fats* (1949), and *Hides and skins* (1952). *Middle East journal*

Cramer, Frederick H., born at Berlin in 1906, he was trained in history and law at Humboldt Universität, Berlin, Columbia Law School, N.Y.C., and received a doctorate from the Universität Zürich. In 1937 he settled in the United States, where he taught, from 1945 to his tragic accident in 1954, ancient and modern European history at Mount Holyoke, serving also as chairman of the department. His writings include *Astrology in Roman law and politics* (1954). He died near Toulouse, 4 September 1954. *American historical review* 60 (1955), p. 493

Cramer, Johannes, born 8 November 1950 at Heidelberg, he studied at Darmstadt, where he received a Dr.Ing. in 1980 for his thesis, *Gerberhaus und Gerberviertel in der mittlealterlichen Stadt*. After a year or two as a research fellow at the Deutsches Archäologisches Institut, Istanbul, he was appointed professor at the Universität Bamberg, specializing in architectural problems of urban renewal. He was joint author of *Istanbul-Zeyrek* (1982). *Kürschner; Thesis*

Crampon, Louis Ernest, born 7 June 1829 at Laon (Aisne), he was educated in Reims and in Paris at the Faculté de droit, l'École des chartes, and l'École d'administration. His publications *De la neutralité de l'Autriche dans la guerre d'Orient* (1854), but particularly *La politique médiatrice de l'Allemagne* (1855), opened him the door to the Direction politique at the Ministry of Foreign Affairs. He was a member of the international commission set up to re-organize the Lebanon in 1860. From 1863 to his retirement, 26 March 1889, he served as consul in many parts of the Near and Middle East. His writings include *Rapport sur le commerce français aux îles Philippines* (1884). *DBF*

Crampton, Richard J., born 23 November 1940, he received a Ph.D. from the University of London for his thesis, *The diplomatic relations between Great Britain and Germany in the Balkans and eastern Mediterranean from the Agadir crisis to the murder at Sarajevo*, in 1970. His writings include *The hollow detente* (1979), *Bulgaria, 1878-1918* (1983), *A short history of modern Bulgaria* (1987), and *Eastern Europe in the twentieth century* (1994). *LC; Sluglett*

Crane, Charles Richard, born 7 August 1858 at Chicago. As a young man he lived for nearly a year in Bukhara and Samarkand, eating the native food and making friends with everyone, while Asia cast his spell upon him. Very wealthy, he used his money more especially to foster education, and was a trustee of Robert College in Constantinople and president of the Women's College. After the first World War he was commissioned by President Wilson to examine the question of the United States accepting a mandate for Syria. He later visited the Yemen and, at the invitation of King 'Abd al-'Aziz, Saudi Arabia in 1930. He died in Palm Springs, Cal., 15 February 1939. His papers, 1873-1934, are at Oberlin College Archives. *JRCAS, 26 (1939), pp. 361-362; LC; Shavit; Who was who in America, 1*

Crane, Howard Grant, born 20th cent., he received a Ph.D. in 1975 from Harvard University for his thesis, *Materials for the study of Muslim patronage in Saljuq Anatolia; the life and works of Jalal al-Din Qaratai*. Certainly from 1982 to 1998, he was a professor of art history and chairman in Ohio State University, Columbus. His writings include *Ca'fer Efendi: Risale-i mi'mariyye* (1987). *MESA roster of members, 1982-1990; NatFacDr, 1998; NUC, 1982*

Crangle, John V., born 25 June 1940 at Sioux Falls, S Dak., he was a graduate of the University of South Dakota, and received a Ph.D. in 1968 from the University of South Carolina. He was a professor of history at variety of American universities. *DrAS, 1974*

Cranz, Ferdinand Edward, born 5 August 1914 at Barmen, Germany, he was a graduate of Syracuse University and received his Ph.D. in 1938 from Harvard for *Aristotelianism in medieval political theory*. He was a professor at the Department of History, Connecticut College, New London, Conn., from 1942 to retirement. He edited *A bibliography of Aristotle editions, 1501-1600* (1984). *DrAS, 1974, 1978, 1982*

Crapanzano, Vincent, born 15 April 1939 at Glen Ridge, N.J., he was a Harvard graduate and received his Ph.D. in 1970 from Columbia University for his thesis, *The Hamadsha*. In the same year he was appointed a professor of anthropology at Princeton. His writings include *The Hamadsha, a study in Moroccan ethnopsychiatry* (1973), its translation, *Die Hamadša, eine psychiatrische Untersuchung in Marokko* (1981), *Tuhami, portrait of a Moroccan* (1980), its translation, *Tuhami, Portrait eines Marokkaners* (1983), *Waiting, the Whites of South Africa* (1985), and *Hermes' dilemma and Hamlet's desire* (1992). *AmM&WS, 1973 S, 1976 P; ConAu, 53-56, new rev. 5; Selim*

Crapuchet, Simone, fl. 1971, her writings include *Sciences de l'homme et professions sociales* (1974), and *Bagatelle, 1930-1958; la Maison de santé protestante de Bordeaux* (1992). *LC*

Crary, Douglas Dunham, born 10 September 1910 at Warren, Pa., he was a graduate of the University of Michigan at Ann Arbor, where he also received his Ph.D. in geography in 1947, and taught since

1963. In March 1948 he drove a pick-up truck the length of the Nile Valley from Alexandria to Khartoum, shipping by river steamer from Aswan to Wadi Halfa. AmM&WS, 1973 S, 1976 P; Unesco

Craufurd, Charles William Frederick, born 28 March 1847, he was a lieutenant-commander in the Royal Navy. He died 24 September 1939. Who, 1932; Who was who, 3

Crawford, J. Forrest, bon in 1901, he received a Ph.D. in 1931 from the University of California at Berkeley for *Some chemical and histological changes occurring during the growth of pear shoots.* NUC, pre-1956

Crawford, Lyndon S., born 24 March 1852 at North Adams, Mass., he graduated in 1876 from Williams College and in 1879 from Hartford Theological Seminary. In the autumn of the same year he sailed for Turkey, where he served as a missionary in Trebizond under the American Board of Commissioners for Foreign Missions. He died after surgery in Trebizond, 26 September 1918. *Missionary herald*, 115 (1919), p. 11

Crawford, Osbert Guy Stanhope, born 28 October 1886 at Bombay, he was educated at Oxford University. Subsequently he became interested in archaeology and carried on excavations in the Sudan and in Britain. His writings include *The Fung Kingdom of Sennar* (1951), and his autobiography, *Said and done* (1955). His maps, plans, and drawings are in the Griffith Institute, Ashmolean Museum, Oxford. He died in Southampton, 28 November 1957. DNB; Egyptology; Who was who, 5

Crawford, Robert Webb, born 25 March 1924, he received a Ph.D. in 1955 from Princeton for *A history of Aleppo, 478-579.* He was a sometime consultant to performing and visual arts institutions. He was the editor of *In art we trust; the board of trustees in the performing arts* (1981). Selim

Crawford, Walter Ferguson, Sir, born 11 April 1894, he studied at Sidney University, and New College, Oxford, and was a Rhodes scholar in 1915. He was a British Political Service officer in Iraq, the Sudan, and Palestine. He died 28 March 1978. Who was who, 7

Crawfurd, John, born 13 August 1783 on Islay island, Inner Hebrides, he successively studied and practised medicine in Edinburgh until 1803, when he received a medical appointment in India, where he served for five years with the army in the North-West Provinces. He later served in south-eastern Asia before returning to Britain, where he died in London, 11 May 1868. His writings include *A history of the Indian Archipelago* (1820), *Journal of an embassy from the Government of India to the Court of Ava* (1829), and *A descriptive dictionary of the Indian islands & adjacent countries* (1856). DNB; Embacher; Henze

Crawley, Charles William, born 1 April 1899 at London, he spent all his academic career at Cambridge, where he was successively tutor, lecturer, fellow and honorary fellow, Trinity College. His writings include *The question of Greek independence; a study of British policy in the Near East, 1821-1833* (1930). He died 6 October 1992. BlueB, 1976; ConAu, 109; Who, 1974-1993

Crawshaw, Nancy, born in 1914 at Vevey, Switzerland, she was a privately educated journalist and photographer. She contributed numerous articles to magazines, reviews, and papers, and wrote *The Cyprus revolt* (1978). Au&Wr, 1971; IntAu&W, 1982

Crawshay-Williams, Eliot, lt.-colonel, born 4 September 1879, he was educated at Eton and Trinity College, Oxford. He joined the army in 1900 and served in England and India, from where he returned overland through Persia and Russia, 1903-1904. He later served with the Colonial Office in Egypt and Sinai. His writings include *Across Persia* (1907). He died 11 May 1962. Master (6); Who was who, 6

Crecelius, Anahid Tashjian, born in 1937, she was the wife of Daniel Neil Crecelius, and a member of the American Public Health Association. In 1998 she was a professor of home economics at California State Polytechnic University, Ponoma. ConAu, 139; NatFacDr, 1998

Crecelius, Daniel Neil, born 15 January 1937 at St. Louis, Mo., he was a graduate of Colorado College, and received a Ph.D. in 1967 from Princeton University for *The ulema and the state in modern Egypt.* He was since 1964 a professor of history at California State University, Los Angeles. His writings include *The roots of modern Egypt* (1981); and he edited *Eighteenth-cetury Egypt; the Arabic manuscript sources* (1990). ConAu, 139; DrAS, 1978, 1982; IWWAS, 1976/77; Selim

Credland, Arthur G., fl. 1975, his twenty-eight page monograph, *The Diana of Hull* was published by The Kingston-upon-Hull Museums and Art Galleries(1979). LC

Creevey, Lucy Ellsworth, born 2 July 1940 at Cambridge, N.Y., she was a graduate of Smith College and, under the name Lucy Creevey Behrman, received her Ph.D. in 1967 from Boston University for *The political influence of Muslim brotherhoods in Senegal.* Her *Muslim brotherhoods and politics in Senegal* she also published under this name in 1970. She was appointed in 1967 a professor of political science at the University of Pennsylvania, Philadelphia; since 1997 she was teaching political science at the University of Connecticut. She was joint author of *The heritage of Islam; women, religion and politics in West Africa* (1994), and she edited *Women farmers in Africa; rural development in Mali and the Sahel* (1986).. ConAu, 29-32; NatFacDr, 1997, 1998; WhoE, 1989-1991/92

Crema, C. F. born 19th cent., he was in 1882 a *capitano* of the Stato Maggiore and accompanied an Italian embassy from Tanger to Morocco and Mogador. Henze

Crémazy, François *Laurent*, born 11 August 1837 at Saint-Paul de la Réunion, he was a barrister and judge in various French overseas territories. His writings include *L'Ile de la Réunion et Madagascar* (1861). He died after 1904. DBF

Cremer, Jacob Theodoor, born 30 June 1847 at Zwolle, the Netherlands, he was a business executive of the Deli Tobacco Plantations in the Dutch East Indies, and a sometime member of the Board of Administrators of the Suez Canal Company. His writings include *De toekomst van Deli* (1881), and *Koloniale politiek* (1891). He died in Amsterdam, 14 August 1923. BWN; WhAm, 1

Cremona, Antonio, fl. 1892-1968, his writings include *Delle origini di Caltagirone* (1892), *The development of Maltese as a written language and its affinities with other Semitic tongues* (1928), *A manual of Maltese orthography and grammar* (1929), *Il-fidwa tal-bdiewa* (1936), *Taghlim fug il-kitba maltija* (1938), *Il-knisja ta' Sarria* (1968), and he edited *Antologija ta' proża maltija* (1970). NUC, pre-1956

Crépy, Auguste Paul Omer, born 19 January 1865 at Lille, he was a president of the Société de géographie de Lille from 1908 to 1936 and, since 1918, Chevalier de la Légion d'honneur. His writings include *A travers les États-Unis* (1890). He died 3 March 1936. DBF

Crespi, Gabriele, born 20th cent., he was a professor of Arab studies and Middle Eastern history, and affiliated the Maghreb Project of the Ministry of Foreign Affairs at Gallazate (Varese), Italy. His writings include *Gli Arabi in Europa*, its translation, *Die Araber in Europa* (1983), and *Maometto il profeto* (1988). Directory of BRISMES members, 1993; EURAMES, 1993; Sezgin

Crespin, Joseph C., fl. 1897-1905, he was a medical doctor whose writings include *La fièvre typhoïde dans les pays chaudes, régions prétropicales; Algérie* (1901), a work which won him the Académie des sciences' Prix Bellion for 1899. LC

Cressaty, S. M., le comte, fl. 1904, his writings include *L'Égypte d'aujourd'hui* (1912), and *La Syrie française* (1915). LC

Cressey, George Babcock, born 15 December 1896 at Tiffin, Ohio, he studied at a variety of American universities. After a professorship at the University of Shanghai from 1923 to 1929, he was a professor of geology and geography at Syracuse University from 1929 until his death on 21 October 1963. His writings include *Asia's lands and peoples* (1944), *Crossroads; land and life in southwest Asia* (1960). Master (3); Shavit - Asia; WhAm, 4

Cresson, Rebecca Shannon, fl. 1953, she was the wife of a sometime American Quaker educator in the Middle East. Note

Cresson, William Pen, born 17 September 1872 at Claymont, Del., he studied at the University of Pennsylvania and at Paris, before he received his Ph.D. in 1922 from Columbia University for his thesis, *The Holy alliance; the European backgound of the Monroe doctrine*. From 1909 to 1917 he was a member of the Foreign Service, and from 1920 to 1928, a professor of international law and diplomatic history at various American universities. His writings include *Persia; the awakening East* (1908). He died in Stockbridge, Mass., 12 May 1932. DcNAA; Who was who in America, 1

Cresswell, E., Dr., fl. 1972, he was an adviser to the Food and Agriculture Organization, United Nations Development Programme, Riyadh. Note

Cresswell, Robert, born in 1922, he was an anthropologist whose writings include *Éléments d'ethnologie* (1975); and he was joint author of *Memorandum on traditional rural housing* (1976). LC

Cresti, Federico, born 19 January 1948 at Roma, he was a *maître-assistant* at the Université d'Alger, 1977-1986, and a lecturer from 1989 to 1992. In the same year, he received a doctorate from the Università di Siena. He was a member of the Società degli Africanisti Italiani. His writings include *Documenti sul Maghreb dal XVII al XIX secolo: archivio storico della Congregazione "De Propaganda Fide"* (1988), *Conservazione e islam* (1990), and *Oasi di italianità: la Libia della colonizzazione agraria tra fascismo, guerra e indipendenza, 1935-1956* (1996). He was joint author of *Occupational profiles in the restoration and rehabilitation of the architectural heritage* (1992). LC; Private

Creswell, Sir Keppel *Archibald* Cameron, born 13 September 1879 at London, where he was educated at Westminster School and the City and Guilds Technical College. He found himself in Palestine at the end of World War one. Through fortuitous circumstances he became responsible for the registration and preservation of medieval monuments. His travels in the Middle East led to the publication of his *Early Muslim architecture* (1932-40). Under the Royal Egyptian patronage he concentrated his research on the Muslim monuments of Egypt. He was professor of Muslim Art and Archaeology at the University of Cairo, and subsequently AUC, of which he was distinguished emeritus professor at his death in Cairo, 8 or 9 April 1974. His writings include *A bibliography of the architecture, arms and crafts of Islam* (1961). ConAu, P1; Index Islamicus (4); Master (2); Times 13 April 1974, p. 14; Who was who, 7

Cretella, Luigi, born in 1868, he received a doctorate in 1891 from the Università di Roma. His writings include *L'ideale di Salvator Rosa e le "Satire"* (1899). IndBl (1); Rovito

Crewe-Milnes, Robert Offley Ashburton, Marquess of Crewe, born 12 January 1858 at London, he was a graduate of Trinity College, Cambridge, and became a politician. From 1910 to 1915, he was secretary of state for India. He received honorary degrees from several English universities. He died 20 June 1945. DNB; Master (2); Who was who, 4

Crews, Clyde F., born 20 November 1944 at Louisville, Ky., he was a graduate of Bellarmine College, Louisville, received a Ph.D. in 1972 from Fordham University, and was ordained Roman Catholic priest in 1973. He was a professor of theology and, later, also chairman of the Department of Theology at Bellarmine College. Concurrently he was a curator of the Cathedral Museum of Louisville. His writings include *Presence and possibility; Louisville Catholicism and its Cathedral* (1973), and *Fundamental things apply* (1983). ConAu, 116

Crinò, Sebastiano, born 29 November 1877 at Barcellona Pozzo di Gotto, Sicilia, he studied Latin, Greek, geography, and history at Messina. In the 1930s he was a professor of geography at the Università di Cagliari. His writings include *Imago mundi* (1928-34), *La scoperta della carta originale di Paolo dal Pozzo Toscanelli che servì di guida a Cristoforo Colombo per il viaggio verso il nuovo mondo* (Firenze, 1941), and *Testo-atlante di storia antica* (1946). Chi è 2 (1931), 3 (1936)|; Firenze; Salomone

Crispi, Francesco, born 4 October 1818 in Sicilia, he was educated at the Seminario greco-albanese de' Siciliani, and the Facoltà di giurisprudenza, Palermo, where he recieved a doctorate in 1843. He practised law in Napoli until 1848, when he became a politician and statesman. He died in Napoli, 11 August 1901. DizBI, v. 30, pp. 779-799; EncAm; EncBrit; EncicUni; GdeEnc; Meyers

Crispo-Moncada, Carlo, fl. 1889, he was affiliated with the Scuola di lingua e letteratura araba nella Reale Università di Palermo. His writings include *Sul taglio della vite di Ibn al-Awwam* (1891), and *I codici arabi nuovo fondo della Biblioteca Vaticana* (1900). Note

Crist, Raymond E., born 11 October 1904 at Seven Mile, Ohio, he graduated from the University of Cincinnati in 1925, to which graduate studies at Cornell, Zürich, Bonn, and Grenoble were added later. In 1937 he received a *dr. ès lettres* degree from the Université de Grenoble for his thesis, *Étude géographique des llanos du Venezuela occidental.* He was a field geologist in Latin America before he turned to teaching geography at American universities. ConAu, 73-76

Critchlow, James, born 9 July 1926 at Springfield, Mass., he was a graduate of M.I.T., and a sometime senior U.S. Government analyst of Soviet affairs specializing in Central Asian politics and, later, a fellow at the Russian Research Center, Harvard University. He wrote *Nationalism in Uzbekistan* (1991). LC; Schoeberlein

Critchlow, Keith, born 16 March 1933, he was educated at Summerhill School, Battersea Polytechnic, St Mountnis School of Art, London, and the Royal College of Art, London. He was an architect and concurrently a college professor. His writings include *Islamic patterns; an analytical and cosmological approach* (1976). Zodiac 22 (1973), pp. 212-213

Critt, Théo, pseud., 1854-1928 *see* Cahu, Jules Nicolas *Théodore*

Crocetti, Camillo Guerrieri, 1891- *see* Guerrieri-Crocetti, Camillo

Crocker, Herbert Edmund, born 10 September 1877, he was a lieutenant-colonel who served during the first World War in Turkey and Mesopotamia. He died 13 May 1962. Who was who, 6

Crocker, Richard Lincoln, born 17 February 1927 at Roxbury, Mass., he was a graduate of Yale University, where he received a Ph.D. in 1957 for his thesis, *The repertoire of proses at Saint Martial de Limoges.* After teaching for a few years at Yale, he was in 1971 appointed a professor of music at the University of California, Berkeley. His writings include *History of musical style* (1966), and *The early medieval sequence* (1977). DrAS, 1974, 1978, 1982; Master (2)

Crocquevieille, Jean, born 3 May 1925. Following his graduation from l'École nationale de la France d'outre-mer, he served in French Equatorial Africa, particularly Chad. After six years of service he was admitted to the Centre de hautes études d'administration musulmane, Paris. From 1959, until his death after a long illness on 6 August 1963, he was *contrôleur financier* in Oran, Secrétariat général pour les Affaires Algériennes. *L'Afrique et l'Asie* 64 (1963), p. 89

de Croizier, Edme Casimir Baudier, marquis, born 16 November 1848 at Neuilly, he studied law at Paris. From 1865 to 1870, he made a tour of the world, visiting also Egypt, Turkey, and Greece. After serving as consul of Greece in Paris, 1871-72, he pursued a very active interest in international orientalism. His writings include *Les Intérêts européens en Asie; la Perse et les Persans* (1873), and *L'Art khmer* (1875). He died between 1911 and 1929. DBF

Crolla, Guido, born in 1897, he was an Italian diplomat. Note

Crombet, Paul, born in 1786 at Namur, Belgium, he served as an officer in the Royal Dutch Navy and, since 1828, he was a professor at l'École royale de marine. His writings include *Les souvenirs d'Italie de Paul Crombet, officier belge de la Marine royale des Pays-Bas, 1817-1826* (1941). LC

Crombie, Alistair Cameron, born 4 November 1915, he was educated at Melbourne and Cambridge, and taught history of philosophy and science at London, 1946-53, and at Oxford, 1953-83. He was a visiting professor at universities throughout the world, and received an honorary doctorate from the Université de Paris, 1993. His writings include *Augustin to Galileo* (1952), and *Science in the later middle ages and early modern times* (1969). He died 9 February 1996. BlueB, 1976; Master (2); Who, 1974-1996; WrDr, 1976-1998/2000

Cromer, Sir Evelyn Baring, Earl of, born 26 February 1841 at Norfolk, he was educated at Ordnance School, Carshalton, and the Royal Military Academy, Woolwich. He entered the Royal Artillery in 1858. From 1872 to 1876, he was private secretary to the Viceroy of India and, since 1877, in the Diplomatic Service in Egypt. He died in London, 29 January 1917. Buckland; DNB; Egyptology; EncAm; EncBrit; EncicUni; Goldschmidt; Hill; Master (5); Meyers; *Who was who, 2*

Crommelin, Claude August, born 22 December 1878 at Nieuw-Amstel, the Netherlands, he was educated at Amsterdam and studied at Leiden, where he received a doctorate in 1910 for *Metingen betreffende de toestandsvergelijking van argon*. Throughout his career he was in varied capacities attached to the Kamerlingh Onnes Laboratorium, Leiden. His writings inculde *Het Natuurkundige Laboratorium der Rijksuniversiteit te Leiden in de jaaren 1904-1922* (1922). He died in Leiden, 1 July 1965. BWN, vol. 1, pp. 125-126

Crone, Desmond Roe, colonel, born 24 September 1900 at Willesden, Middlesex, he joined the Survey of India in 1924 and served in the North-West Frontier from 1930 to 1933, particularly with the Indo-Afghan Boundary Commission. He died 23 November 1974. WhE&EA; *Who was who, 7*

Crone, Gerald Roe, born 16 September 1899 at Willesden, Middlesex, he was a graduate of St. John's College, Cambridge. He was a librarian and map curator at the Royal Geographical Society from 1934 to 1966, and had a long association with the Hakluyt Society. His writings include *The Voyages of Cadamosto and other documents on western Africa in the second half of the fifteenth century* (1937). He died 6 October 1982. *Geographical journal* 149 (1983), pp. 270-273; WhoWor, 1971/72 & 1974/75

Crook, Henry Tipping, born in 1854, he was a civil engineer, a voluntary captain, and associated with the Manchester Tactical Society. His writings include *War-game maps* (1888), *Maps of the Ordnance Survey* (1892), and *Studies in practical topography* (1909). BLC; BritInd (2)

Crooke, William, born 6 August 1848, he was educated at the Grammar School, Tipperary, and at Trinity College, Dublin, and was a member of the Indian Civil Service in the North Western Province and Oudh from 1871 until retirement in 1896. He was a magistrate and a collector, and wrote *The Tribes and castes of the North Western Province and Oudh* (1896), and *The North-western provinces of India; their history, ethnology and administration* (1897). He died 25 October 1923. Buckland; *Who was who, 2*

Croon, Hans. In 1960 he was a German consul general.

Crose, Kenneth LaVerne, born 26 December 1915 at San Diego, Calif., he was a graduate of Anderson (Ind.) College, and received a Ph.D. in 1955 from the Hartford Seminary Foundation. He was a missionary teacher in Syria, Egypt, and Iran, from 1940 to 1948. After his return to the United States, he taught at Warner Pacific College, 1955-1966, and Anderson (Ind.) College, from 1966 until his retirement in 1981, when he became professor emeritus. DrAS, 1974, 1978; IWWAS, 1976/77

Crosnier de Varigny, Charles Auguste Hippolyte *Henry*, born 13 November 1855 at Honolulu, Hawai, he received doctorates in 1884 from the Faculté de médecine de Paris, and in 1886 from the Faculté des sciences de Paris. He was a sometime municipal councillor at Montmorency (Val d'Oise), and in 1891 and 1893 sent by the Ministry of public instructiuon to Britain, Russia, and the United States. His writings include *En Amérique; souvenirs de voyages* (1894), and *La mort et la biologie* (1926). Curinier; *Qui êtes-vous*, 1924

Crosnier de Varigny, Charles Victor, born 25 November 1829 at Versailles, he early in life went to Honolulu to pursue commercial interests. In return for his services in the negotiations for a trade agreement, the French Government appointed him chancellor of the Consulate of France. On the death of the consul in 1862, he acceded to that position. On the accession to the throne of Hawai, King Kamehameha V offered him the post of minister of finance. Authorized by the French Government to accept, he became a member of the Hawaian Privy Council, foreign minister, and president of the Council. In 1868 he was sent to Europe to negotiate trade agreements with France, Italy, and Russia. He resigned his functions after the 1870 war and retired to Montmorency (Val d'Oise), where he died in 1899. His writings include *Nouvelle géographie moderne des cinq parties du monde* (1890-92), and *Fourteen years in the Sandwich Islands, 1855-1868* (1981). *Bulletin de la Société de géographie d'Alger* 4 (1899), pp. 223-228; DBF; Lamathière; LC

Crossland, Cyril, born in 1878 at Sheffield, he received a D.Sc. in 1917 from the University of London for *Desert and water gardens of the Red Sea*. The Sudan Government engaged him to report on the possibilities of establishing a pearl-fishing industry on the Red Sea coast, and in 1906 he was appointed director of a specially created pearl fisheries department. After it was abolished in 1923, he retired from the Sudan and lived for some years in Copenhagen where he died in 1943. Hill; Sluglett

Crossley, John, Rev., he was in 1972 a general adviser for the Islam in Africa Project, Ibadan.

Crosson-Duplessix, born 1 January 1865 at Melecey (Haute-Saône). After the Polytechnique he passed through l'École d'application de Fontainebleau and was commissioned into the corps of engineers. He served in the French Sudan, 1892-1894, and a few years later he was posted to the Ivory Coast to report on the possibilities of building a railway. After the first World War he served in Algeria and Morocco, retiring with the rank of general. He died on 5 December 1931. DBF

Crouch, Philip Andrew, born 6 December 1916 at Perry, Iowa, he graduated in 1937 from Central Bible College, Springfield, Mo. From 1939 to 1941 he was a student at AUC. In 1946 he received his M.A. from Hartford Seminary Foundation, followed by postgraduate studies at UCLA. He spent twenty years as a missionary in Egypt. From 1957 until his retirement, he was successively a teacher and administrator at the Central Bible College. WhoRel, 1975

Crouchley, Arthur Edwin, born in 1903, his writings include *Investment of foreign capital in Egyptian companies and public debt* (1936), and *The economic development of modern Egypt* (1938). LC

Crow, Francis Edward, born 31 May 1863. After education at Honiton Grammar School, he started life as a student interpreter in the Levant in 1885. From 1890 until his retirement in 1927 he served as British consul posted throughout the Middle East. He wrote *Arabic manual; a colloquial handbook in the Syrian dialect* (1901). He died 9 December 1939. BritInd (3); *Who was who*, 3

Crow, Ralph Earl, born 20th cent., he received a Ph.D. in 1964 from the University of Michigan for his thesis, *The civil service of independent Syria, 1945-58*. He was a sometime member of the Department of Political Studies and Public Administration, AUB, and taught public administration for more than twenty years at various universities in Egypt, Jordan, and Lebanon. He was joint author of *Fihris al-mu'allafat al-'Arabiyah fi al-idarah al-'ammah* (1967). LC; Selim

Crowe, Sybil Eyre, fl. 1943, she wrote *The Berlin West African Conference, 1884-1885* (1942).

Crowe, Yolande, born 20th cent., she received a Ph.D. in 1973 from SOAS for her thesis, *Divrigi; Ulu cami and hospital*. She was joint author of *Les Arts de l'islam* (1976). Sluglett

Crowfoot, Grace Mary née Hood, born 3 November 1878 at Nettleham, Lincolnshire. After her marriage she played a considerable part in starting the Government maternity service in the Sudan. Concurrently she studied primitive weaving techniques of the Sudanese Bedouins. Her writings include *Some desert flowers collected near Cairo and the Sudan* (1914), *Methods of hand spinning in Egypt and the Sudan* (1931), *From cedar to hyssop; a study in the folklore of plants in Palestine* (1932), and, with her husband, *Early ivories from Samaria* (1938). She died in Geldeston, Norfolk, 20 March 1957. Egyptology

Crowfoot, John Winter, born 28 July 1873 at Wigginton, Staffordshire. After Oxford he travelled in Greece, Asia Minor, and Cyprus. He was a lecturer in classics for two years, before he worked for the

Eygptian Ministry of Education from 1901 to 1914, when he entered the service of the Sudan Government. From 1927 to 1935 he was director, British School of Archaeology at Jerusalem. His writings include *Early churches in Palestine* (1941), and, with his wife, *Early ivories from Samaria* (1938). He died in Geldeston, Norfolk, 6 December 1959. BritInd (1); Egyptology; *Who was who*, 5

de Crozals, Jacques Marie Ferdinand Joseph, 1848-1915, he was a professor of history and geography whose writings include *Les Grandes époques de l'histoire depuis l'antiquité jusqu'à la fin des croisades* (1887), *Les Peulhs; études d'ethnologie africaine* (1882), and *L'unité italienne* (1898). BN; NUC, pre-1956

Croze, Henri, fl. 1926, his writings include *Souvenirs du vieux Maroc* (1952). LC

Crozier, Andrew Joseph, born 20 September 1944 at Peebles, Scotland, he was since 1969 a lecturer in modern history at University College North Wales, Bangor. In 1983 he received a doctorate from LSE. His writings include *Appeasement and Germany's last bid for colonies* (1988). WhoWor, 1987/78

Crozier, Brian Rossiter, born 4 August 1918 at Kuridala, Queensland, he attended Peterborough College, 1930-35, and Trinity College of Music, London, 1935-36. He was a newspaperman, sub-editor, features editor, correspondent, free-lance art and music critic, and radio commentator. He was the founding director of the Institute for the Study of Conflict, London, 1970-1979. His writings include *The Morning after; a study of independence* (1963), *Neo-colonialism* (1964), *Soviet objectives in the Middle East* (1974), and *Strategy of survival* (1978). ConAu, 9-10, new rev. 3; Au&Wr, 1971, IntAu&W, 1976-1991/92; IntWW, 1978/79-1984/85; Who, 1974-1998; WhoWor, 1980/81-1984/85; WrDr, 1976/78-1998/2000

Crudgington, James W., fl. 1952, he served with the British forces in the Middle East, including Libya, in 1941-42, and with the Civil Affairs section of the U.S.Army in Cairo during 1942-43. For the remainder of the war he was with the Allied Military Government in Italy and returend to Firenze in 1950-51 for research at the Centro di studi coloniali on Italo-Arab relations from 1908 to 1923. MEJ

Cruickshank, A. A., born 20th cent., he received a D.Phil. in 1963 from the University of Oxford for his thesis, *The growth of the opposition in Turkish politics, 1919-1946*. In 1968 he was a member of the Department of Political Science, University of Otago, Dunedin, New Zealand. Sluglett

Cruise O'Brien, Donal, born 20th cent., he received a Ph.D. in 1968 from LSE for his thesis, *The Mourides of Senegal; the socio-economic structure of an Islamic order*. He was a sometime lecturer in African politics at SOAS. His writings include *Charisma and brotherhood in African Islam* (1988). Sluglett

Cruttenden, Charles J., fl. 1834-1848, he was a lieutenant in the Indian Navy and took part in the coastal reconnaissance of the South Arabian coast under Stafford B. Haines. Early in 1834 he spent two months on Socotra, and in July 1836 he travelled from Mocha via Bayt al-Faqih to San'a where he remained nearly a month. He visited the coast of Somalia in 1848. Bidwell; Henze

Cruz Hernández, Miguel, born 15 January 1920 at Málaga, he studied at Madrid and was appointed professor of philosophy at Salamanca in 1961. In 1992 he was professor emeritus of the Universidad Autónoma de Madrid Cantoblanco. His writings include *La metafísica de Avicenna* (1949), *Filosofía hispano-musulmana* (1957), and *Historia del pensamiento en al-Andalus* (1985). Arabismo, 1992, 1994, 1997; Master (1); Quien, 1993; WhoSpain, 1963

Cruz Herrera, José, born in 1890 at Cadiz, he was a painter. José Riquelme Sánchez wrote a biography, *Vida y obra del pintor José Cruz Herrera* (1987). He died in 1972. LC

Cryan, Robert W. W., born about 1866 at Dublin, where he was educated at Belvedere College. After graduation, he made extensive travels in Europe, which are the subject of his *Glimpses of sunny lands* (1896). He wrote many articles which he intended to collect in book form. He died in Bordighera, 4 April 1907. Polre

Csányi, Károly, born 3 or 7 September 1873 at Györ, Hungary, he studied fine art and received a doctorate in architecture in 1896. He was a keper at the Budapest Museum of Aplied Arts. His writings include *A középhori épitőmüvészet formái* (1910), and the translation *Geschichte der ungarischen Keramik* (1954). He died in Budapest, 30 December 1955. GeistigeUng.; MEL, 1967-69

Csillaghy, Andrea, fl. 1974, she was affiliated with the Istituto di iranistica, uralo-altaistica e caucasologia dell'Università degli studi di Venezia. She edited the conference papers, *La lingua e la cultura ungherese come fenomeno areale* (1977), and *Studi miscellanei uralici e altaici dedicati ad Alessandro Kőrösi-Csoma* (1985). LC

Csillik, Bertalan, Dr., born 28 December 1889 at Tiszanána, Hungary, he edited *Omar Khajjám Rubáijatjának kisebb kéziratai a Párisi Bibliothèqie nationale-ban* (1933). He died in Szeged, 2 January 1978. MEL, 1978-1991

Csoma, Sándor, 1784-1842 *see* Kőrösi Csoma, Sándor

Csongor, Barnabás, he received a doctorate in 1947 from Budapest University for his thesis, *Ujgúr írásos kínai szórványok.* He was joint author of *A kinai nevek és szavak magyar átirása* (1993). LC; NUC, pre-1956

Cszewski, Stanislaw, 1865-1930 *see* Ciszewski, Stanislaw Bronisław

Cubertafond, Bernand, born 20th cent., he received a doctorate in 1979 from the Université de Limoges for his thesis, *La République algérienne démocratique et populaire.* Thereafter he was a lecturer at l'Université de Limoges. His writings include *Algérie contemporaine* (1981), and *Province, capital Limoges* (1987). LC

Cubrilović, Vasa, born 13 January 1897, his writings include Политичка прошлост Хрвата (1930), and Србија од 1858 до 1903 (1938). LC

Cucheval-Clarigny, Philippe Athanase, born 1 February 1821 at Calais, he was a graduate of l'École normale supérieure. Prevented from accepting a professorship at Angers, he served as librarian of l'École normale, concurrently taking courses at l'École des chartes leading to a diploma in archival palaeography in 1846. He wrote for *le Constitutionnel* until political events prompted him to enter politics. His writings include *L'équilibre européen après la guerre de 1870* (1871). He died 3 November 1895. DBF

Cucinotta, Ernesto, born 20 February 1887 at Pace del Mela, Messina, he received a doctorate in law from the Università di Messina, and later taught at the Università di Roma. He was a sometime judge in the Mixed Court of Egypt, and a legal adviser at the Italian Ministry of Foreign Affairs. His writings include *Diritto coloniale italiano* (1933), *Il diritto commerciale fluviale dell'Egitto* (1937), and *Il conflitti di leggi nell'Africa italiana* (1943). Chi è, 1957, 1961; IndBI (1); Unesco

Cuda, Alfred, born 26 December 1908 at Potsdam, where he trained as a construction worker before he enrolled in the Technische Universität Berlin and in 1939 took a doctorate for his thesis, *Stadtaufbau in der Türkei.* He was called to the eastern front in 1939, and posted to the western front in October of the same year. Thereafter his traced is lost. Thesis

Cuinet, Vital, d. 1896. His writings include several editions of *La Turquie d'Asie* (1890-95), and *Syrie, Liban et Palestine; géographie administrative, statistique* (1896). NUC, pre-1956

Cuisenier, Jean Henri Eugène, born 9 February 1927 at Paris, he taught geography at the secondary school in Carthage, Tunisia, and was a professor of sociology at l'Institut des hautes études de Tunis, from 1956 to 1959. Since 1968 he was chief curator at the Musée national des arts et traditions populaires, Paris, and, since 1971, *directeur de recherche* at the C.N.R.S., Paris. His writings include *Économie et parenté; leurs affinités de structure dans le domaine turc et dans le domaine arabe* (1975), a work which was originally presented in 1971 as his thesis at Paris. He also published the translation, *French folk art* (1977). ConAu, 73-76, new rev. 20; Unesco; WhoFr, 1989/90-1997/98

Cuisinier, Jeanne Adèle Lucie, Dr., born in 1890, she was a French anthropologist affiliated with the C.N.R.S., Paris. Her writings include *La Danse sacrée en Indochine et en Indonésie* (1951). EncO&P; Master

Čulić, Branko, he was joint author of *Narodno Biloteka Bosne i Hercegovina, 1945-1965* (1965), and editor of *Bibliografija članaka iz bosanskohercegovačkih godinsjaka i periodičnih zbornika, 1945-1970* (1979). LC

Culin, Robert *Stewart*, born 13 July 1858 at Philadelphia, he was a director and curator of museums in Philadelphia and N.Y.C., from 1892 until his death in Amityville, Long Island, N.Y., 8 April 1929. Master (2); Shavit - Asia

Cullum, Leo A., S.J., born about 1902 at Jersey City, he graduated from Weston College, earned a M.A. from Boston College, and received a doctorate from the Pontificia Università Gregoriana, Roma. He was a professor of theology and rector at San Jose Seminary in the Philippines. He died aged 86 in Manila, 24 April 1988. NYT, 30 April 1988, p. 11

Cultrera, Guiseppe, born 14 July 1877 at Chiaramonte Gulfi, Ragusa, he obtained a doctorate in letters and a diploma from the Scuola archeologica di Atene. Thereafter he held a variety of museum posts. His writings include *Estetica dell'edilizia e dell'urbanistica* (1952). Chi è? 1928-1961; Wholtaly, 1958

Culwick, Mrs. G. M., fl. 1954, her writings include *A Dietary survey among the Zande of the southwestern Sudan* (1950), and *Diet in the Gezira irrigated area, Sudan* (1951). With her husband, Arthur Theodore Culwick, she published *Ubena of the Rivers* (1935).

Cumberland, Roger Craig, born in 1895 at Verne, Calif., he was a Presbytarian missionary who began his service with the United Mesopotamian Mission in 1923, at first in eastern Persia, going soon afterwards to Mosul, and then to Dohuk, northern Iraq. He made long trips to the villages of tribesmen, living with the people and establishing Christian centres among them. He had mastered their language and knew their customs. On Sunday, 12 June 1938, he was murdered in his home by two Kurds, who called ostensibly for obtaining books, and who shot him when his back was turned. Note

Cumming, Constance Frederica Gordon, 1837-1924 *see* Gordon-Cumming, Constance Frederica

Cummings, Sir Duncan Cameron, born 10 August 1903. After Caius College, Cambridge, he joined the Sudan Political Service in 1925. He was Chief Administrator, Cyrenaica, in 1942, Chief Secretary to the British Administration in Eritrea in 1941, served with distinction in several posts in the area during the war, and was Chief Administrator of Eritrea from 1951 until Eritrea was handed over to Ethiopia in September, 1952. He died 10 December 1979. BlueB, 1976; *Geographical journal* 146 (1980), pp. 158-159; *Who was who, 7*

Cummings, John Thomas, born 20th cent., he received a Ph.D. in economics in 1974 from Tufts University, Medford, Mass., where he afterwards taught economics. He was joint author of *Middle East economics in the 1970s* (1976), *Oil, OECD and Third World* (1978), and *Taxation and tax policies in the Middle East* (1982). In 1990 he served as a senior economist in Riyadh. LC

Cummins, Ian, fl. 1978, his writings include *Marx, Engels, and national movements* (1980). He was a contributing author to *The Expats guide to Kuwait* (1982). LC

Cumont, Franz Valéry Marie, born 3 January 1868 at Alost, Belgium, he was a sometime professor of history at the Université de Gand, and a curator at the Musée du cinquantenaire, Bruxelles, and awarded honorary doctorates by the universities of Oxford, Cambridge, and Dublin. He was honoured by *Mélanges Franz Cumont*. (1936). He died 19 or 20 August 1947. Bioln, 1 & 4; WhE&EA; *Who was who, 4*

Cumston, Charles Green, born in 1868, he wrote *An Introduction to the history of medicine* (1926).

Cuneo, Paolo, fl. 1977, his writings include *L'architettura della scuola regionale di Ani nell'Armenia medievale* (1977), and *Storia dell'urbanistica; il mondo islamico* (1986). LC

Cunliffe-Owen, Frederick, born in the 19th century, he had a lengthy association with the Near and Middle East in various capacities since 1912. In 1918, he completed a mission to Central Arabia, involving many months spent with Ibn Sa'ud, the ruler of Najd; in June 1919, he was put in charge of the Assyrian refugee camp, Baqubah, twenty-seven miles east of Baghdad. He later was Director of Repatriation in the Civil Government of Mesopotamia, and from 1923 to 1926, attached to the Settlement Commission, Greece. He died 10 January 1946. JCAS, 9 (1922), pp. 86-94; *Who was who, 4*

Cunningham, Alexander, born 23 January 1814 at Westminister, he went to India in 1833 to join the Bengal Engineers. After participating in several military operations, he explored and surveyed Ladakh. He was posted to the North-West Frontier of India from 1958 to 1861, when the British Government appointed him the first director of the Archaeological Survey of India. His writings include *Ladakh, physical, statistical, and historical* (1854). He died in South Kensington, 28 November 1893. DNB, vol. 22; Henze

Cunningham, Francis A., S.J., born 16 October 1908, his writings include *Essence and existence in Thomism* (1988). LC

Cunningham, Robert Baily, born in 1937, he received a Ph.D. in 1967 from Indiana University for his thesis, *An approach to the problem of development, achievement, alienation, and dogmatism among Jordanian teachers.* He was a sometime professor in McMaster University, Hamiltion, Ont; for over fifteen years he was a professor at the Department of Political Science, University of Tennessee, Knoxville, a post which he still held in 1998. His writings include *The bank and the bureau; organizational development in the Middle East* (1988). He was joint author of *Management turnover in Tennessee* (1985). LC; NatFacDr, 1998

Cunningham, William Alfred, born 31 August 1877 at Brixton, England. After studies at the Royal College of Science, London, he obtained a diploma as associate in 1898. In 1899 he was appointed demonstrator in zoology at the Royal College of Science in Dublin. In February 1901 he went to study at the Universität Jena where he received a Dr.phil. in 1902 for his thesis, *Studien an einer Daphnide,*

Simocephalus sima. He left England in March, 1903, on a biological expedition to the Birket el-Qurun Lake in the Fayoum Province of Egypt. Thesis

Cunnison, Ian George, born 13 February 1923 at Milngavie, Scotland, he was a graduate of Cambridge and received a D.Phil. in 1952 from Oxfod. Thereafter he was for three years in the service of the Sudan Government, followed by a lectureship in anthropology at the University of Manchester. He taught Middle Eastern sociology in the University of Hull from 1967 until his retirement. His writings include *The Luapula peoples of northern Rhodesia* (1959), and *Baggara Arabs; power and the lineage in a Sudanese nomad tribe* (1966). Unesco

Cuno, Kenneth M., born 4 January 1950 at Syracuse, N.Y., he received a Ph.D. in 1985 from UCLA for his thesis, *Landholding, society and economy in rural Egypt, 1740-1850.* He was a visiting professor at the Center for Arabic Studies, AUC, for five years before he was appointed a professor of history in the University of Illinois, Urbana-Champaign. His writings include *Landholding, society, and economy* (1985), and *The pasha's peasants* (1992). ConAu, 147; Selim²

Cunsolo, Ronald Salvatore, born 3 May 1923 at N.Y.C., he was a graduate of New York University, where he also received a Ph.D. in 1961 for *Enrico Corradini and Italian nationalism.* He spent most of his academic career as a professor of history at Nassau Community College, Garden City, N.Y. His writings include *Italian nationalism* (1990). WhoE, 1981/82-1983/84

Cuny, Charles, born 30 June 1811 at Goin (Moselle), he started his education at the Séminaire de Montigny but later trained as a military pharmacist at Metz and served in Algeria from 1833 to 1837, when he joined the Egyptian service as a military surgeon. He married the daughter of Louis M. A. Linant de Bellefonds Bey. In 1853 he qualified as a civilian physician with the medical authorities in Paris. In 1857 he set out on a journey of exploration to Darfur, travelling by way of Dongola and al-Ubaiyad. His writings include *Journal de voyage de Siout `El-Obéid du 22 novembre 1857 au 5 avril 1858* (1863). His biography by Hippolyte Roy, *La vie heroïque et romantique du docteur Charles Cuny*, was published in 1930. He died in 1858. The sources vary in the details of his life. DBF; Egyptology; Embacher; Henze; Hill

Cuny, Léon, born 24 April 1838 at Morhange (Moselle), he graduated from the military college, St-Cyr, and served in Algeria since 1878. He was from 1898 until his retirement in 1900 an *inspecteur technique de la gendarmerie* in Algeria and Tunisia with the rank of general. He died 18 April 1912. DBF

Cunynghame, Henry Hardinge, born 8 July 1848, he joined the Royal Engineers before he decided to go to Cambridge with a view to the bar. In 1870 he entered St. John's College and, reading for the Moral Science Tripos, came under the influence of Alfred Marshall. After leaving Cambridge, his avocations were incredibly various, but he slowly found his way from the bar into the Civil Service by way of a remarkable succession of secretaryships of committees and Royal Commissions. One of his outstanding achievements was the foundation of the London Polytechnics. He died 3 May 1935. *Economic journal* 45 (1935), pp. 398-406; *Who was who*, 3

Cuoq, Joseph, le Père, born 23 March 1917 at Saint-Didier-en-Velay, he spent two years at the Séminaire gréco-catholique, Rayaq (Riyaq), Lebanon, where he learned his classical Arabic. He was an active advocate of the Muslim-Christian dialogue and an historian, having obtained his doctorate in 1975 from the Université de Paris for his thesis, *Recueil de sources arabes concernant l'Afrique occidentale du VIIIe au XVe siècle.* At Alger he founded *la Revue de presse,* and at Paris, the *Cahiers nord-africains.* His writings include *Les Musulmans en Afrique* (1975), *Histoire de l'islamisation de l'Afrique de l'ouest* (1984), and *Islamisation de la Nubie chrétienne* (1986). He died 26 July 1986. *Hommes et destins*, vol. 9, pp, 106-108; *IBLA*, 49 (1986), pp. 387-88; MIDEO 18 (1988), p. 406

Cuperly, Pierre, born 20th cent., he received a doctorate in 1982 from the Université de Paris IV for his *thèse d'état, Professions de fois ibadites.* His writings include *Introduction à l'étude de l'ibadisme et de sa théologie* (1984), and *Prières des fils d'Abraham* (1992). LC; THESAM, 4

Cupşa, Ion, his writings include *Arta militară a Moldovenilor în a doua jumătate a secolului al XV. lea* (1959), *Bătălia de la Vaslui* (1975), and *Participarea României la înfrîngerea Germaniei naziste* (1985).

Curatola, Giovanni, born in 1953 at Firenze, his writings include *Soltaniye II* (1979), *The Simon and Schuster book of oriental carpets* (1982), *Kalat-i Nadiri; note sul 'Barocco' indo-persiano* (1983), *Oriental carpets* (1983), and *Le arti nell'islam* (1990). LC

Cureton, William, born in 1808 at Westbury, Shropshire, he was a graduate of Oxford and ordained priest in 1832. He was employed at the Bodleian Library, where he had ample opportunities of pursuing his interest in Oriental languages. He was later transferred to the British Museum, where he made valuable contributions to Syriac studies. His writings include the *Catalogus codicum orientalium qui in Britannico asservantur, pars II* (1846-52). He died 17 June 1864. DcBiPP; DNB; Fück, 190; LuthC 75

Curiel, Raoul, born at the beginning of the 20th century, he studied at the Institut de civilisation indienne de la Sorbonne. From 1954 to 1958 he was a director of the Department of Archaeology and Museums, Pakistan. In 1960, he was attached to the Direction des musées de France. He was an unassuming, withdrawn, but extremely helpful scholar who was joint author of *Le Trésor monétaire de Qunduz* (1965), and *Une Collection de monnaies de cuivre arabe-sasanides* (1984). Studia iranica 11 (1982), pp. 7-13

Curmi, Giovanni, born about 1900, he wrote *Tre nomi maltesi* (1930), *Colloqui e cronache* (1956), *Quante cose di te* (1962), and *Epistolarju romantiku* (1965). LC

Currie, Sir James, born 31 May 1868 at Edinburgh, he was educated at Edinburgh and Oxford, and then joined the Sudan Civil Service, where he served as director of education and, during the last ten years or so, concurrently as a principal of Gordon College, Khartoum. Thereafter he was in the British Civil Service. He died in Cambridge, 17 March 1937. DNB; Hill; *Who was who*, 3

Currie, Lady Mary Montgomerie, née Lamb, Singleton, born in 1843 at Beauport, Sussex, she was a writer of poetry and prose under the pseudonym Violet Fane. Her writings include *Under cross and crescent; poems* (1896). She died in 1905. DNB; *Who was who*, 1

Curtin, Philip DeArmond, born 22 May 1922 at Philadelphia, Pa., he was a graduate of Swarthmore (Pa.) College and received a Ph.D. from Harvard in 1953 for his thesis, *Revolution and decline in Jamaica, 1830-1865*. After teaching history at his alma mater for three years, he was appointed a professor of history at the University of Wisconsin. His writings include *Economic change in pre-colonial Africa* (1975), and *Cross-cultural trade in world history* (1984). He was the editor of *Africa and the West* (1972). Paul E. Lovejoy edited the felicitation volume, *Africans in bondage; studies in slavery and slave trade; esssays in honor of Philip D. Curtin on the occasion of his twenty-fifth anniversary of African Studies at the University of Wisconsin* (1986). ConAu, 13-16; DrAS 1974, 1978, 1982; WhoAm, 1974-1989/90; WhoWor, 1974/75

Curtis, William Eleroy, born 5 November 1850 at Akron, Ohio, he was a graduate of Western Reserve College, Hudson, Ohio, and a sometime journalist who travelled in the Middle East for the *Chicago herald*. His writings include *To-day in Syria and Palestine* (1903), *Egypt, Burma and British Malaysia* (1905), *Around the Black Sea* (1911), and *Turkestan, the heart of Asia* (1911). He died in 1911. DAB; Shavit; *Who was who in America*, 1

Curtiss, Richard Holden, born 13 June 1927 at Grand Rapids, Mich., he was a graduate of the University of Southern California and joined the Department of State in 1951, and was transferred in 1953 to the U.S. Information Agency. His foreign service assignments included Indonesia, Turkey, Iraq, Syria, Greece, and Lebanon. In 1976 he became the U.S.I.A.'s deputy director for the Near East and South Asia, and received the Agency's highest professional recognition by the Edward R. Murrow Award for Excellence in Public Diplomacy. He was chief inspector of the Agency when he retired in 1980. He wrote *A changing image; American perceptions of the Arab-Israeli dispute* (1986). WhoAm, 1974-1976

Curtiss, Samuel Ives, born 5 February 1844 at Union, Conn., he was a graduate of Amherst and Union Theological Seminary of New York, to which were added a year at Bonn and four years at Leipzig, where he received a Dr.phil. for his thesis, *De Aaronitici sacerdotie atque Thorae elohistoricae origine*, in 1876. He spent most of his academic career with the Chicago Theological Seminary. His writings include *Primitive Semitic religion today* (1902), and its translation, *Ursemitische Religion im Volksleben des heutigen Orients* (1903). He died in London, 22 September 1904. DAB; Master (6); NatCAB 13, p. 395-96; WhAm, 1

Curtze, Ernst Ludwig Wilhelm *Maximilian*, born 8 April 1837 at Ballenstedt, Germany. After study at the Universität Greifswald, he taught mathematics at the Gymnasium in Thorn. His writings include *Urkunden zur Geschichte der Mathematik im Mittelalter und der Renaissance* (1902). He died in Thorn in 1903. Altpreuß; DcScB

Curwen, Eliot, born in 1865, he was educated at Mill Hill School and studied at St. John's College, Cambridge, and at the London Hospital, qualifying in 1889. In 1894 he went to China as a medical missionary under the London Missionary Society, but had to return to England in 1900 for reasons of health. He settled at Hove in 1901 and soon began to take an active interest in local archaeology. He was for thirty-five years a member of the Council of the Sussex Archaeological Society and for seven years its chairman. He died 15 March 1950. *Antiquaries journal* 30 (1950), p. 237; BritInd (3)

Curwen, Eliot Cecil, born in 1895 at Peking, he was an English physician who pursued an interest in antiquities. His writings include *The archaeology of Sussex* (1937). LC; WhE&EA

Curzon of Kedleston, George Nathaniel, born 11 January 1859 at Kedleston, Derbyshire, he was educated at Eton, and Balliol College, Oxford. He was a statesman, and Viceroy and Governor-General of India, 1899-1904. He travelled in Central Asia, Persia, Afghanistan, and the Pamirs. His writings include *Russia in Central Asia* (1889), *Persia and the Persian question* (1892), and *The Pamirs and the source of the Oxus* (1896). He died in London, 20 March 1925. Kenneth V. Rose wrote *Curzon, a most superior person* (1985). Buckland; DNB; Henze; Mason; *Who was who*, 2; Wright

Cushing, Caleb, born 17 January 1800 at Salisbury, Mass., he was a graduate of Harvard University and Harvard Law School. After practicing law, he became a state and federal politician. From 1855 to 1857, he was attorney general of the United States. He died in Newburyport, Mass., 2 January 1879. Master (19); Shavit - Asia; WhAm, H

Cust, Sir Edward, born in 1794 at London, he was a general and a military historian. He died in 1878. DNB

Cust, Lionel George *Archer*, born 6 June 1896, he was educated at Eton College and was with the Palestine Civil Service from 1920 to 1939. During the time he was there, he served in every district of Palestine, was *aide-de-camp* to Sir Herbert Samuel, private secretary to Sir John Chancellor, and acting District Commissioner in Jerusalem during some of the most difficult times right up to the riots of 1939. He died 22 May 1962. *Who was who*, 6

Cust, Sir Lionel Henry, born in 1859 at London, he was educated at Eton and Cambridge. He was an art historian at the Department of Prints and Drawings, the British Museum, London, from 1884 to 1895, when he became the director of the National Portrait Gallery. He died 12 October 1929. *Contemporary review* 171 (1947), pp. 110-115; DNB; LitYbk, 1907-1922; WhoLit, 1924-26; *Who was who*, 3

Cust, Robert Needham, born 24 February 1821. After education at Eton and Haileybury, he entered the Bengal Civil Service in 1843, and retired in 1867. He served in the North West Province and the Punjab. He was called to the bar from Lincoln's Inn in 1855, took part in the settlement of the Punjab after the Mutiny in 1858, and was Home Secretary to the Government of India from 1864 to 1865. He was a sometime honorary secretary of the Royal Asiatic Society. The University of Edinburgh awarded him a LL.D. in 1885. His writings include *Essay on the prevailing methods of the evangelization of the non-Christian world* (1894), and *Memoirs of the past of a septuagenarian* (1899). He died 28 October 1909. Buckland; *Who was who*, 1

Cutler, Allan Harris, born 16 October 1936 at Chicago, he was a graduate of the University of Southern California where he received a Ph.D. in 1963 for his thesis, *Catholic missions to the Moslems to the end of the first crusade*. He taught medieval history and Western comparative religions successively at California State College, San Diego, and Temple University, Philadelphia, Pa. He was joint author of *The Jew as ally of the Muslim; medieval roots of anti-Semitism* (1986). DrAS, 1974, 1978; Master (1); Selim

Cutler, Anthony, born 18 February 1934 at London, he was a graduate of Cambridge, and received a Ph.D. in 1963 from Emory University. After teaching at Emory University until 1967, he was appointed professor of art history at Pennsylvania State University, University Park, Pa., a post he held until his retirement. His writings include *Transfiguration* (1975), and *The aristocratic psalters in Byzantium* (1984). DrAS 1974, 1978, 1982; NatFacDr, 1998

Cutrera, Antonino, born in 1863, his writings include *I ricottari, la mala vita di Palermo; contributo di sociologia criminale* (Palermo, 1896), and *L'archivio del senato di Trapani del secolo XIV al XVIII* (Trapani, 1917). His trace is lost after an article published in 1931. IndBI (1); NUC, pre-1956

Cutts, Elmer Henry, born 15 May 1908 at Silvercliff, Colo., he was a graduate of the University of Washington and received a Ph.D. in 1940 from Harvard for his thesis, *British educational policy in India under the East India Company*. He was a professor of history at various American universities. He died 4 August 1960. *Who was who in America*, 4

Cuvelier, Gaston, he was in 1966 a *commissaire principal honoraire de la Sûreté nationale*. Note

Cuvillier, Jean, born 16 February 1899 at Ambleteuse (Pas-de-Calais), he was a professor at the Lycée français du Caire, 1922-30, a lecturer at Cairo University, 1930-38, and a professor of geology at the Sorbonne, 1938-57. He received a doctorate in 1930 from the Sorbonne for his thesis, *Révision du nummulitique égptien*. He died 25 September 1969. DBFC; WhoFr, 1959/60-1969/70

Cvetkova, Bistra Andreeva, 1926-1982 *see* TSvetkova, Bistra Andreeva

vetler, Jiři, fl. 1969. He was affiliated with Brno University. He was joint author of *Bibliografie česko-ovenské balkanistiky za léta, 1978-1982* (1984). LC

viić, Krsto (Christopher) F., born 3 October 1930 at Nova Gradiška, Croatia, he was resident in ngland from 1954. In 1980 he was a staff member of the *Economist*. His writings include *Remaking ·e Balkans* (1991), and *Pogled izvana* (Zagreb, 1994). LC

ygielman, Victor, fl. 1962, he was an Israeli journalist writing for the Paris *Nouvel observateur*, a ·ember of the *New outlook* editorial board and, in 1994, a founding member of the *Palestine-Israel ·urnal of politics, economics, and culture.*

zapkiewicz, Andrzej, born in 1924, he was affiliated with Kraków University. His writings include *prachproben aus Madaba* (Krakau, 1960), *The verb in modern Arabic dialects* (1975), and *Arabic ·ioms* (1983). He was joint editor of *Studia Indo-Iranica* (1983), and joint author of *Nata'allamu al-·gata al-'Arabijja* (1990). He died in 1990. Dziekan; LC

zapkiewicz, Maria (Opozda), fl. 1969, she was attached to the Instytut Historii Kultury Materialnej, ·olska Akademia Nauk. She was joint author of *Skarb monet arabiskich z okolic Drohiczyna nad ·ugiem* (1960), and contributing author to *Skarb monet arabskich z Klukowicz powiat Siemiatycze ·964)*. NUC, 1956-1967

zaplicka, Marie Antonina, born in 1886 near Warszawa, she studied at London and Oxford, where ·he obtained a diploma in anthropology in 1912. She took part in the Oxford Anthropological ·xpedition to the Yenesei Valley, 1914/15. From 1916 to 1919 she was a lecturer in ethnology to the ·xford School of Anthropology. Her writings include *My Siberian year* (1916), and *The Turks of ·entral Asia in history and at the present day* (1918). She died 2 June, 1921. PSB; Who was who, 2

zaykowski, Fouad Bey Muzaffer, fl. 1898, he was a military inspector of the *haras* in the Ottoman ·mpire. Le Tour du monde, 1901

zebe, Gyula, born 17 February 1887 at Mezőtúr, Hungary, he was a philologist whose writings include · *veszprémvölgyi oklevél görög szövegel* (Budapest, 1916). He drowned in Balatonszentgyörgy, 13 ·uly 1930. MEL, 1967

zeglédy, Károly, born 21 December 1914 at Pápa, Hungary, he first studied Protestant theology ·ince 1932 at Debrecen University, and then pursued Oriental studies at Belfast and Utrecht from 1936 · 1939. He taught Arabic and Semitics at Budapest from 1942 to his retirement in 1984, and was ·ead of the Department of Semitic philology and Arabic studies since 1963. His writings include *A ·önges veláris spiráns az ugariti semi feliratokban nemet kovonattal = Die stimmhafte Velare spirans in ·en ugaritisch-semitischen Inschriften mit deutschem Auszug* (1940), and *Magyar őstörténeti ·anulmányok* (1985). Arabist 8 (1994), pp. xi-xv; Magyar ki kicsoda, 1990; MagyarNKK, 1992, 1994, 1996

zekalski, Józef Stanisław, born 28 March 1895 at Piotrków Trybunalski, Poland, he was a professor ·f geography and geology. He died in Poznan, 29 February 1976. Dziekan; WielkoSB

zekanowski, Jan, born 6 October 1882 at Głuchów, he studied at Berlin and Zürich, where he ·eceived a Dr.phil. in 1907 for his thesis, *Verhältnis der Kopfmasse zu den Schädelmassen*. He was ·uccessively professor at Lwów, 1913-41, and Poznań, 1946-60. His writings include *Forschungen im ·il-Kongo-Zwischengebiet* (1917), *Czlowiek w czasie i przestrzeni* (1934), *W głąb lasów Aruwimi* ·1958), and *Teoria i empiria w Polskiej Szole Antro-pologiczneij* (1985). He died 20 July 1965. Czy ·iesz; NEP; Unesco

zermak, Wilhelm, born 10 September 1889 at Wien, he studied Semitics, Egyptology and African ·nguistics at the Universität Wien where he received a Dr.phil. in 1911 for his thesis, *Proben und ·tudien über die Nominalform fu'lul im Altarabischen*. He took part in excavations at the Pyramids, ·912-1914. In the first World War he served as an officer in Syria, where he also pursued linguistic ·tudies. In 1925 he was appointed professor of African studies at Wien; Egyptology was added to his ·eaching duties in 1931. His writings include *Kordufannubische Studien* (1917), *Die Laute der ·gyptischen Sprache* (1931-34), and *Der Rhythmus der koptischen Sprache* (1931). DtBE; Egyptology; ·ürschner; NYT, 14 March 1953, p. 15, col. 3; Schwarz

on Czetsch-Lindenwald, Hermann, born in 1901, he was a pharmacist whose writings include ·alben, Puder, Externa (1944). He was joint author of *Hilfsstoffe für Pharmazie und angewandte Ge-·iete* (1963).

zirbusz, Géza, Dr., born 17 September 1853 at Kassa, Hungary, he was a priest and a professor of ·eography. His writings include *A délmagyarországi bolgárok ethnographiai magánrajzai* (1880), and · *kárpátok hegyeinek ès folyóinak nevei* (1908). He died in Budapest, 10 July 1920. MEL, 1967 von

von **Czoernig von Czernhausen**, Karl, born 5 May 1804 at Tschernhausen, Bohemia, he studied law and he entered the Austrian civil sevice in 1828. In 1841 he was appointed head of the Austrian statistical office in Wien. He re-organized the Austrian merchant marine. His writings include *Ethnographie der österreichischen Monarchie* (1857). He died in Görz, 5 October 1889. ÖBL; Wurzbach

Czokai-ogly, Mustafa *see* Chokai-ogly, Mustafa

Czołowski-Sas, Aleksandr, born 27 February 1865 at Bakończyce, Poland, he received a doctorate and became an archivist and historian at Lwów. His writings include *Wysoki Zamek* (1910), and *Historja Lwowa* (1925-27). He died in Lwów, 17 July 1944. NEP

Dąb-Kalinowska, Barbara, fl. 1977 at Warszawa, she received two doctorates and wrote *Ziemia piekło, raj* (1994). LC

Dabbāgh, Muhammad 'Abd al-Hayy, born in 1935, his writings include *Nazrah tahlīlīyah fī al-masādi al-mālīyah al-Lubnānīyah wa-dawr al-masraf al-markazī* (1978). LC

Dabbs, Jack Autrey, born 31 January 1914 at Mercury, Texas, he was a graduate of the University of Texas at Austin, where he also received his Ph.D. in 1950 for *The political and military administration of Marshall François-Achille Bazaine in Mexico*. He was a professor of linguistics at Texas A&M University until 1980, when he became a professor emeritus. Concurrently he was a director of the American Language Institute, Baghdad, from 1953 to 1957. His writings include *Spoken Bengali* (1965), and *Word frequency in newspaper Bengali* (1966). ConAu, 17-20; DrAS, 1978, 1982; Master (1) WhoAm, 1974/75-1978/79

Dąbrowski, Jan Konstanty, born 21 December 1890 at Krosna, Poland, he studied at the Uniwersytet Jagielloński, Kraków. His writings include *L'Année 1444* (1952), and *Dawne dziejopisarstwo polskie* (1964). He died in 1965. LC; Czy wiesz

Dąbrowski, Krzysztof, born 25 May 1931 at Lublin, he studied archaeology at the Uniwersytet Warszawski where he also received two doctorates. He was an archaeologist at the Polish Academy of Sciences and a lecturer. His writings include *Kalisz w starożytności i w Średniowieczu* (1956), *Śladami Etrusków* (1970), *Z przeszłości Kalisza* (1970), and *Polacy nad Lemanem* (1995). WhoWor 1978/79

Dachraoui (al-Dashrawi), Farhat, he wrote *Le Califat fatimide en Maghreb* (1981), a work which was originally presented in 1970 as a doctoral thesis at the Université de Paris IV. LC

Dacier, Bon Joseph, Baron, born in 1742 at Valognes (Manche), he was a member of the Académie française and a permanent secretary of the Académie des inscriptions. He died in Paris, 4 February 1833. DBF; Egyptology; Index BFr (12)

Dacier, Édouard *Émile* Gabriel, born 4 April 1876 at Orléans, he studied at l'École des chartes and concurrently at l'École du Louvre, and completed his formal education with a thesis submitted at the Université de Toulouse in 1898 entitled *Florimond Robertet, secrétaire du roi et trésorier de France*. He was an archivist palaeographer and for twenty-six years a collaborator in the production of the *Catalogue des imprimés* of the Bibliothèque Nationale de Paris, as well as an editor of a number of exhibition catalogues. His writings also include *En canoë sur la Meuse de Charleville à Liège* (1906). He died 30 June 1952. BN; DBF

Dadabhoy, Sadequa, born 20th cent., he was in 1979 a graduate student at the University of California at Davis. His writings include *Determinants of the length of life in Asian, African, and Latin American countries* (1976). He was joint author of *Do schools care about equality?* (1977). LC

Dadant, P. M., fl. 1973, he wrote the pamphlet, *Shrinking international airspace as a problem for future air movements briefing* (1978), and he prepared a project report for the U.S. Air Force. LC

Dadashev, Tofik Pasha-ogly, born 2 May 1929 at Baku, he was a graduate of Leningrad University and for many years attached to the Azerbayjan Museum of History. He received a doctorate in 1967 for his thesis, *Реформы в области образования и пробема подготовки кадров в Турции,1923-1939*. His writings include *Просвещение в Турции в нрвейшее время, 1923-1960* (1972). Miliband

Daddah, Moktar Ould, born 25 December 1924 at Boutilimit, Mauritania, he was educated at a Koranic school, studied law in Senegal and France, and thereafter practised law in Dakar before turning to politics. He was the first president of the République de Mauritanie. AfricaWW, 1 (1981); IntWW, 1974-1990/91; Master (4); WhoArab, 1981/82-1984/85; WhoWor, 1974/75

Dadiani (Дадяни), Lionel' IAkovlevich, fl. 1975, his writings include *Критика идеологии и политики социалсионизма* (1986); and he was a contributing author to *Сионизм в системе империализма; очерки истории и современность* (1988). LC

Daes, Erica Irene A., born 18 September 1925 at Chania, Crete, she studied at Athens, den Haag, Cambridge, and London. She was an expert on human rights and minorities and since 1974 attached to United Nations' institutions. In 1991 she was the representative of Greece to the U.N. General Assembly. Her writings include *The individual's duties to the community and the limitation of human rights and freedoms under article 29 of the Universal Declaration of Human Rights* (1983). LC; WhoUN, 1975, 1992

Daftari, Ali Akbar, born 8 July 1889 at Tehran, he was educated in Tehran at the Deutsch-Persische Höhere Lehranstalt, and the College of Law, where he received a *licencié en droit*. Afterwards he was *conseiller légiste* to the Afghan Ministry of Foreign Affairs, Kabul, and lawyer in Tehran courts. In 1933, he was attached to the Iranian Legation in Berlin, where he received a Dr.jur. from Humboldt Universität in 1935 for his thesis, *Geschichte und System des iranischen Strafrechts*. Thesis

Dağlarca, Fazıl Hüsnü, born 26 August 1914 at Constantinople. For fifteen years he served as an officer in the army. After his resignation in 1950, he held a government position for a number of years. In 1959 he set up a bookshop and a small publishing business in Istanbul, and pursued a interest in poetry. His writings include *Daha* (1943), *Haydi* (1968); and *Brot und Taube*; Nachdichtungen aus dem Türkischen von Gisela Kraft (1984). DcOrL, 3; EIS, 1972, 1978; IntA&W, 1976; LC; Meydan

Dagorn, René, he received a doctorate in 1972 from the Université de Paris III for his thesis, *La geste d'Ismaël dans l'onomastique et la tradition arabes*. It was published in 1981. LC; THESAM 4

Dagorne, A., fl. 1969, he was joint editor of *Géographes d'auhourd'hui; mélanges offerts en hommage au doyen F. Gay* (1984). LC

D'Agostino Orsini di Camerota, Paolo, born 24 December 1894 or 1897 at Napoli, he was attached to the Istituto superiore di studi corporativi di Roma. His writings include *Che cosa e' l'Africa* (1936), *Francia contro Italia in Africa* (1939), and *La colonizzazione africana nel sistema fascista i problemi della colonizzazione nell Africa italiana* (1941). Chi è? 1948

Dagradi, Piero, born 20 September 1926, he was a sometime professor of geography at the Università di Bologna. His writings include *Elementi di geografia umana* (1975), *Introduzione alla geografica umana* (1979), and *Geografica del mondo arabo e islamico* (1994). LC; Wholtaly, 1980

Dahan, Constant, fl. 1918, he was a lawyer resident in Tanta, Egypt, in 1916, and a member of the Société sultanieh d'économie politique, de statistique et de législation. His writings include *De la dernière maladie en droit musulman, rite hanafite* (Le Caire, 1912). NUC, pre-1956

Dahan, Sami, he was born in Syria, and since 1966 a professor at the University of Amman. Who's who in tne Arab world, 1971/72; Who's who in the world, 1974/75

Dahinten, Gisela, fl. 1961, she was associated with the Goethe-Institut, Tehran. Her writings include *Die Geisterszenen in der Tragödie vor Shakespeare* (1958), originally presented as her doctoral thesis at the Universität Göttingen in 1956. NUC, 1956-67

Dahiya, Mahinder Singh, born in 1947, he received a Ph.D. from Aligarh Muslim University in 1975. His writings include *Office of the governor in India* (1979). LC

Dahl, Valdemar Ferdinand, 1801-1872 *see* Dal', Vladimir Ivanovich

Dahm, Horst, born 7 July 1940 at Mannheim, Germany, he studied political economy at the universites of Heidelberg and Bonn. He received a Dr.jur. in 1967 from the Universität Kiel for *Die Patinkin-Kontroverse*. In the same year he obtained a position as assistant at the Universität Regensburg. Thesis

Dahncke, Monika, 1943- *see* Rochan Zamir-Dahncke, Monika

Dahoodi (Dahudi), Zuhdi Kurshid al-, born in 1940 at Tuz Khurmatu, Iraq, he was a primary school teacher, 1961-63, and active in the Kurdish rebellion. After five years in prison, he went to former East Germany, where he studied philosophy and history at the Universität Leipzig, obtaining a Dr.phil. in 1976 for his thesis, *Geschichtslehrbücher und -pläne im Irak*. After teaching positions at Mosul and Benghazi, he returned to Leipzig to teach modern history. His writings include *Die Kurden; Geschichte, Kultur und Überlebenskampf* (1987), *Tollwut; kurdische Erzählungen* (1991), and *Das längste Jahr* (1993). LC; Schwarz

Daiber, Hans, born 1 April 1942 at Stuttgart, he studied at Tübingen and Saarbrücken, where he received a Dr.phil. in 1967 for his thesis, *Die arabische Übersetzung der Placita philosophorum*. In 1977 he was appointed a professor of Arabic and Islam at the Vrije Universiteit te Amsterdam. His writings include *Das theologisch-philosophische System des Mu'ammar Ibn-'Abbas as-Sulami* (1973), *Ein Kompendium der aristotelischen Meteorologie* (1975), *Aetibus Arabus* (1980), *Catalogue of the Arabic manuscripts of the Daiber Collection* (1988), and *Bibliography of Islamic philosophy* (1999). Kürschner, 1996; Schwarz; WhoWor, 1980/81, 1982/83

Daillier, Pierre Louis Lucien, born 13 September 1905 at Norroy-le-Sec (Meurthe-et-Moselle). After passing through the military college, Saint-Cyr, he was posted to Tunisia and Morocco from 1926 to 1942, interrupted only by his attending l'École supérieure de guerre from 1936 to 1938.. He resigned from the military with the rank of general in 1965. His writings include *Terre d'affrontements, le Sud tunisien* (1985), and *Le 4e R.T.M.* (1991). He died 24 April 1992. WhoFr, 1979/80-1991/92

Dajani, Majed, fl. 1958, he obtained a Ph.D. and became a president of the Arab Bankers Association, London. His writings include *Oil, money, and politics* (1984). LC

Dajani-Shakeel, Hadia Ragheb, born in the 1930s, she received a Ph.D. in 1972 from the University of Michigan for her thesis, *al-Qadi al-Fadil, his life and political career*. She was a professor at the Department of Islamic Studies in the University of Toronto from the 1960s until her retirement. She was joint editor of *The jihad and its time* (1991). LC; Selim

Dakhshleiger, Grigorii Fedorovich, born 2 September 1919 at Odessa, he was a writer on Kazakhstan, whose writings include *Турксиб* (1953), *Социально-экономические преобразования в ауле и деревне Казахстана, 1921-1929 гг.* (1965), and *Историография Советского Казахстана* (1969). He died 1 August 1983. Kazak SE; LC

Dal' (Даль), S. K., fl. 20th cent., he was a writer on Armenia whose works include *Hayastani manr mowshtakavor kendaninerĕ* (1947), and *Животный мир Армятской ССР* (Erevan, 1954). LC

Dal', Vladimir Ivanovich, born in 1801 at Lugansk, he was also called Valdemar Ferdinand Dahl, and used the pseudonym Kazak Luganskii. He studied medicine at Dorpat University. As a military physician he participated in the campaigns against the Ottoman Empire and Poland. In the early 1830s he resigned from the navy and entered civilian government service in Orenburg Province where he pursued an interest in folklore and linguistics. He died in Moscow in 1872. Joachim T. Baer wrote the biography, *Vladimir Ivanovič Dal' as a belletrist* (1972). BiD&SB; CasWL; DanskBL; DcBiPP; DLB 198 (1999), pp. 110-118; EnSlovar; GSE; HnRL; Wieczynski

von **Dalberg**, Johann *Friedrich* Hugo, Freiherr, born in 1752 at Herrnsheim, Germany, he studied law at Erfurt and Göttingen, and had a brief ecclesiastic career in Trier, Worms, and Speyer. Thereafter he pursued an interest in natural science and musicology. His writings include *Über die Musik der Inder* (1802), *Geschichte einer Drusen-Familie* (1808), and *Über Meteor-Cultus der Alten* (1811). He died in Aschaffenburg in 1812. ADtB; Master (17); LC; NDB

Dale, Godfrey, born 19th cent., he was a sometime canon, chancellor, and archdeacon of Zanzibar and was attached to the Universities' Mission to Central Africa. His writings include *Bondei exercises* (1894), *The contrast between Christianity and Mohammadanism*; four lectures delivered in Christ Church Cathedral, Zanzibar (1904), *Islam and Africa* (1925), and *The peoples of Zanzibar* (1929). In 1931 he also published a Swahili translation of the Koran, *Tafsiri ya Kurani ya Kiarabu, kwa lugha ya Kisawahili*. WhE&EA

Dale, Mary Wood née Bliss, born in January 1857 at 'Abeih ('Abayh), Lebanon, she was the daughter of Daniel Bliss, the first president of the American University of Beirut. In 1905, she organized the Woman's Hospital of the American University of Beirut, which, under her administration, grew until it had 102 beds and a school of nursing with fifty-six students of many nationalities. She died in Beirut, 8 March 1930. From a note in an unidentified missionary periodical

Dale, Stephen Frederic, he received a Ph.D. in 1972 from the University of California at Berkeley for his thesis, *Islam and social conflict; the Mappilas of Malabar, 1498-1922*. In 1980 he was a professor of Islamic and South Asian history at Ohio State University, Columbus, a position he still held in 1998. His writings include *Islamic society of the South Asian frontier* (1980), and *Indian merchants and Eurasian trade, 1600-1750* (1994). NatFacDr, 1998; Selim

Dalenberg, Cornelia, born at the end of the 19th century at South Holland, Illinois, she was educated at Hope College, Mich., and West Side Hospital Training School for Nurses, Chicago. After joining the Arabian Mission she served first in the hospital in Bahrain (1921) where her duties led her up to the marshes of southern Iraq. In 1930 she was transferred to Amarah, Iraq, to take charge of the women's clinics, where she was still active in 1946. Note

Dalgleish, Walter Scott, born in 1834 at Edinburgh, he was a correspondent of the *Times* since 1878, and a text-book writer. He died 15 February 1897. *Who was who*, 1

Dalin, S., pseud., 1889-1962 *see* Dallin, David Julievich

Dall'Armi, Giuseppe, fl. 1941, he was a sometime director-general at the Ministero dell'Africa Italiana.

Dallas, William Liscombe, fl. 1879-1908, he was attached to the Meteorological Department, India, and wrote *Investigation into the mean temperature, humidity and vapour tension conditions of the Arabian Sea and Persian Gulf* (Calcutta, 1894). NUC, pre-1956

Dallaway, James, 1763-1834, he was educated at Trinity College, Oxford. After taking orders he served a curacy in the neighbourhood of Stroud. Through his connection as a fellow of the Society of Antiquaries he was appointed chaplain and physician to the British embassy in Constantinople in the 1790s. His writings include *Constantinople, ancient and modern* (1797), and its translations, *Constantinople ancienne et moderne* (1799), and *James Dallaway's Reise nach Constantinopel, der Ebene von Troja, und in die Levante* (1801). BiDLA; DcBiPP; DNB

Dalleggio d'Alessio, Eugenio (Eugène), born 7 October 1888 at Constantinople, he was a member of the Institut français d'études byzantines and the Centre d'études d'Asie mineure. His writings include *Relatione dello stato della cristianita di Pera e Constantinopoli* (1925), and *Le pietre sepolcrali di Arab Giami* (1942). Hellenikon, 1965; LC

Dallet, Jean Marie, le père, fl. 1939, his writings include *Le verbe kabyle* (1953), *Contes kabyles inédits* (1967), and *Dictionnaire kabyle-français* (1982-85). He died in 1972. LC

Dallin, David Julievich, born David Lewin on 24 May 1889 at Rogachev, Russia, he also used the pseudonym S. Dalin. He was educated at St. Petersburg, Berlin, and Heidelberg, where he received a Dr.phil. in 1913 for his thesis, *Theorie des Existenzminimums*. He was expelled from Germany in 1935, and since 1940 resident in the United States, where he became a Soviet affairs specialist. His writings include *Soviet Russia and the Far East* (1948), *The rise of Russia in Asia* (1949), and *Soviet espionage* (1955). He died 22 February 1962. AmAu&B; Au&Wr, 1971; CnDiAmJBi; NYT, 22 February 1962, p. 25, col. 1; TwCA, 1st suppl.; WhAm, 4

Dalling and Bulwer, Henry Lytton Bulwer, Baron, 1801-1872 *see* Bulwer, William *Henry* Lytton Earle

Dall'Oglio, Marino, Dr., he was joint author of *Turkish rugs in Transylvania* (1977), a French translation and revision of *Tapis turcs*, by G. Végh and K. Layer, published in 1925. LC

Dalman, Gustaf Hermann, born G. A. Marx, on 8 June 1855 at Niesky, Silesia, he began to study In 1874 at the Theologisches Seminar der Brüdergemeinde in Gnadenfeld and returned in 1881 as a teacher. In 1886 he joined the Institutum Judaicum, Leipzig, and in 1895 he was appointed professor at Leipzig. He visited Palestine in 1899, became director of the Palästina-Institut, and in 1917, a professor at Greifswald. "He had a profound knowledge of Jewish sources ... and although always writing from a Christian angle, he evinced a sincere sympathy with traditional Judaism." His writings include *Palästinischer Diwan; als Beitrag zur Volkskunde Palästinas* (1901). He died in Herrnhut, 19 August 1941. DtBE; EncJud; LuthC, 1975; WhE&EA

Dalrymple, William, lieutenant-colonel, fl. 18th cent. As an army major he travelled in Spain and Portugal. His writings include *Travels through Spain and Portugal in 1774, with a short account of the Spanish expedition against Algiers, in 1775* (1777), and its translation, *Voyage en Espagne et en Portugal dans l'année 1774* (1783). BN

Dalton, Edward Tuite, born in 1815, he entered the army in 1835 and rose to the rank of major-general. He served in the tribal area on the Tibetan frontier. His writings include *The descriptive ethnology of Bengal* (1872), and *The tribal history of eastern India* (1872). He died 30 December 1880. Buckland

Dalton, James Cecil, born 31 August 1848 at Halifax, N.S., he was educated at military colleges in England and served in the Afghan campaign of 1880. He retired from the military with the rank of major-general in 1910. He was the author of a military handbook. He died 12 May 1931. Master (2); WhE&EA; *Who was who*, 3

Dalton, Ormonde Maddock, 1866-1945, he was a Welsh archaeologist and classicist who was educated at New College, Oxford. He entered in 1895 the Department of British and Mediæval Antiquities and Ethnography, British Museum. He was its keeper when he retired in 1928. He wrote

Treasure of the Oxus (1905), *Byzantine art and archaeology* (1911), and he was the author of several museum catalogues and guide-books. DNB; *Who was who*, 4

Dalton, William G., born about 1940, he received a Ph.D. in 1970 from the University of Manchester for his thesis, *The social structure of an oasis community in Libya*. Thereafter he was a teacher at Columbia University in 1973, and throughout most of the 1990s, a professor of anthropology at the University of New Bunswick, Fredericton, N.B. NatFacDr, 1993-1998; Sluglett

Daly, Amor, fl. 1969, he wrote the pamphlet *Le Programme de planning familial en Tunisie* (1969). ZKO

Daly, El Sayed A. el-., he was in 1966 attached to Rutgers University, New Brunswick, N.J., where he received a Ph.D. in 1967 for *An econometric model of growth with reference to the U. A. R.* Selim

Daly, Martin W., born about 1940, he received his M.A. in 1974 from the Institute of Islamic Studies, McGill University, Montreal, P.Q., and his Ph.D. in 1977 from SOAS for his thesis, *The governor-generalship of Sir Lee Stack in the Sudan, 1917-1924*. In 1980 he became a research fellow at the University of Durham. In the 1990s he was a professor of history successively at Memphis State University, and University of Tennessee, Chattanooga, where he was still active in 1998. His writings include *Empire on the Nile* (1986), *Imperial Sudan* (1991), and *Sudan* (World bibliographical series, 1992). *Directory of BRISMES members*, 1993; NatFacDr, 1998; Sluglett

Daly, William Michael, born 27 December 1920 at Great Barrington, Mass. He was a graduate of Boston College, and received a Ph.D. from Boston University in 1955 for his thesis, *The concept of Christendom in the Western crusade chronicles of the twelfth and thirteenth centuries*. Since 1971 he was a professor of history at Boston College. DrAS, 1974, 1978, 1982; LC

Dalyell of the Binns, Gordon, born 16 January 1887, he was educated at the Royal Military College, Sandhurst, and served in India and the Persian Gulf until his retirement in 1938. He died in 1953. *Who was who*, 5

van **Dam**, Nikolaos, born 1 April 1945 at Amsterdam, he studied political science Arabic at Amsterdam where he received a doctorate in 1977 with a thesis entitled *De rol van sektarianisme, regio-nalisme en tribalisme bij de strijd om de politieke macht in Syrië*. In 1971 he joined the Dokumentatie-centrum voor Nieuwst Geschiedenis at Amsterdam University, and from 1975 to 1980 he was attached to the Middle East Seciton at the Ministerie van Buitenlandse Zaken. He was subsequently served as ambassador in the Middle East. His writings include *The struggle for power in Syria* (1979), and *Nederland en de Arabische wereld* (1987). *Directory of BRISMES members*, 1993; EURAMES, 1993; Wie is wie, 1984-88, 1994-96

Damad Ferid Paşa, born 1853 at Constantinople, he was one of the last grand vezirs of the Ottoman Empire and died in exile in Nice in 1923. EI²; Meydan

Damais, Louis Charles, 1911-1966, he was a South East Asian scholar whose writings include *Cent deux poèmes indonésiens, 1925-1950, mis en français* (1965), and *Répertoire onomastique de l'épigraphie javanaise* (1970). LC

Damant, Guybon Henri, born 9 May 1846 and educated at St Paul's School, London, and Christ's College, Cambridge, he entered the Indian Civil Service and went out to Bengal in 1869. He was Political Agent in the Naga Hills, Assam, where he was killed on duty on 14 October 1879. He took a keen interest in literature and philology. Some of his articles were published in 1976 entitled *Tales from Bangladesh*. Buckland

Damaschino (Δαμασκηνου), Nicholaos (Nicolas), fl. 1858-1882, his writings include *Traité des magasins généraux (docks) et des vents publiques de marchandises en gros* (1860), *Λόγος περι των ἀρχαίων ανωτάτων συνεδρίων της Γαλλιας* (1882), and *Discours sur les anciens parlements français* (1882). BN; LC

Dame, Mrs. L. P., born about 1900, she was the wife of the medical missionary Louis Paul Dame and accompanied him to the Governor of Hasa, Arabia, in the summer of 1933. Note

Dame, Louis Paul, born 16 December 1886 at Groningen, the Netherlands, he was a graduate of Lewis Institute, Chicago, and Illinois Medical College. He served in the Medical Corps in the first World War, and under the Arabian Mission of the Reformed Church in America in Bahrain from 1919 to 1936. During this period he made a series of journeys through Arabia. In recognition of his notable explorations, the Royal Geographical Society of Great Britain appointed him a fellow. He was later a medical adviser to the Arabian American Oil Company, before returning to the United States in 1941, where he died in Rockford, Illinois, 3 July 1953. *Missionary review of the world*; Shavit

Dames, Mansel Longworth, born in 1850 at Bath, he spent his childhood and youth in Ireland and Devonshire, and without any special education passed for the Indian Civil Service in 1868. He went to India in 1870. His service was spent in the Panjab and the North West Frontier. He became Deputy Commissioner of the Jhang, Dera Ismail Khan, and Dera Ghazi Khan districts, and finally Commissioner of Rawalpindi Division. He retired in 1897. His was the story of an uneventful career, but he was anything but a mere official. He was a fine Oriental linguist and a master of the languages he studied. His writings include *A sketch of the northern Baluchi language* (1881), *The Baloch race* (1904), *Popular poetry of the Baloches* (1907), and *A textbook of the Balochi language* (1922). He died in 1922. *Journal of the Royal Asiatic Society,* 1922, pp. 301-304

Damianov, Simeon Angelov, born in 1926, his writings include *Франция и българската национална революция* (1968), *Великата френска революция* (1987). He was honoured with *България, Балканите и Европа: доклати от конференция, посветена на 65-годишнината от рождението на проф. д-р Симеон Дамянов, 1991* (1992). LC

Damis, John James, born 16 June 1940 at Portland, Ore., he was a graduate of Harvard, and received his Ph.D. in 1970 from Fletcher School of Law and Diplomacy for his thesis, *The free-school movement in Morocco, 1919-1970.* Since 1972 he was teaching at Portland State University, where he was still active in 1998. His writings include *Conflict in Northwest Africa* (1983). ConAu, 118; NatFacDr, 1998; Selim

Dammann, Ernst, born 6 May 1904 at Pinneberg, Germany, he received a Dr.phil. from the Universität Kiel in 1929 for his thesis, *Beiträge aus arabischen Quellen zur Kenntnis des negerischen Afrika.* He taught history of religion and African studies successively at the universities of Hamburg, Berlin, and Marburg. His writings include *Die Religionen Afrikas* (1963). Kürschner, 1950-1996; Schwarz; Unesco

Damme, Mark van, fl. 1964, he was a Turkologist who contributed the article "Rabghuzi" to EI², and was a joint editor of *Evliya Çelebi's book of travels* (1988).

Damodaran, Ambady Krishnan, born 29 June 1921, he was the son of Krishna Menon, and educated in India as well as in the United States. He was a diplomat and in 1977/78, a honorary professor of diplomatic studies at Jawaharlal Nehru University, New Delhi. In 1980 he was a senior fellow at the Centre for Studies in Diplomacy, International Law, and Economics, School of International Studies, New Delhi. He edited *Krishna Menon at the United Nations; India and the world* (1990). IndiaWW, 1978/79, p. 166, 1979/80, p. 174

Damon, Theron Johnson, born 25 February 1883 at Concord, Mass. After graduation from Harvard he spent a year travelling in Europe and then spent a year working on the Kansas City *Star.* Following that stint he went to Constantinople to teach at Robert College. For the better part of the period from 1906 to 1929, he made a living in Turkey teaching, and helping out at the American Embassy as courier to Berlin. He served at Washington, D.C., as captain during the war, and was assigned to the peace-making council at Versailles. During the depression he started a shop in N.Y.C. for old Near Eastern art and craft work. In the late 1930s he became associated with the American Antiquarian Society and the Worcester Art Museum. During the second World War he accepted an appointment in the Office of War Information, specializing in Near Eastern matters. He retired soon after the war. He died in a convalescent home in Weston, Mass., 25 April 1973. *Proceedings of the American Antiquarian Society* 83 (1974), pp. 189-192

Damsté, Henri Titus, born 28 January 1874 at Huisduinen, the Netherlands, he was educated at Leiden and Delft, and entered the Dutch colonial service, posted to Batavia, in 1894. He served throughout the Dutch East Indies, and became an expert on the history, language and literature of Atjeh. His strained relations with his superiors lead to his early retirement in 1923. After his return to Leiden, he pursued academic interests. He was a member of learned Dutch societies and an editor of the *Koloniaal tijdschrift.* He died in Leiden, 6 January 1955. BWN

Dan, Mihail S., fl. 20th cent., his writings include *Cehi, Slovici şi Români in Veacurile* (Bucureşti, 1944), *Sub flamura Táborului* (Bucureşti, 1959), *Un stegar al luptei antiotomane, Iancu de Hunedoara* (1974); he was joint editor of *Corespondenţa lui Vincenţiu Babeş* (1973-1983). LC

Dan, Pierre, born about 1580 in France. At an early age he entered the order of the Trinitarians. As a superior he was sent on a mission to Alger in 1631 to ransom Christian captives. He returned in 1635 with forty-two liberated Christians. During his mission he had a chance to study the country. This mission is the subject of his *Histoire de Barbarie et de ses corsaires* (1649). He is said to have died in the same year. DBF

D'Ancona, Alessandro, born 20 February 1835 at Pisa, Italy, he studied at the universities of Firenze and Torino. He was a literary critic and Dante scholar. From 1860 until his retirement he held the chair of Italian literature at Pisa, where he died 8 November 1914. His writings include *La poesia popolari italiani* (1878), *Le opere minori di Dante Alighieri* (1906), *Scritti danteschi* (1912). DizBl; EncJud; Wininger

Danby, Miles William, born 23 May 1925 at Eastbourne, Sussex, he was educated at London, where he also studied architecture. He was a pracising architect before teaching in Ghana and the Sudan. Since 1970 he was a professor of architecture and head of department at Newcastle University. His writings include *Grammar of architectural design, with special reference to the tropics* (1963), and *Moorish style* (1995). ConAu 13; LC

Dandamaev, Mukhammed Abdul Kadyrovich, born 2 September 1928 in Daghestan, he graduated in 1952 at Leningrad, where he also received a doctorate in history in 1958 for his thesis, *Бехистунская надпись как источник по истории начала царствования Дария I*. His writings on ancient history include *Persien unter den ersten Achämeniden* (1976), *Slavery in Babylonia* (1984); he was joint author of *Культура и экономика Древнего Ипана* (1980), and *The culture and social institutions of ancient Iran* (1989). LC; Miliband

Dane, Sir Louis William, born 21 March 1856 at Chichester, he was a British colonial administrator who served as settlement officer, Gurdaspur, 1887, and foreign secretary to the Government of India, 1903. He had a fluent command of Persian and headed the Mission to Kabul, 1904 to 1905, to negotiated a treaty with the amir of Afghanistan. His writings include *Final report of the revised settlement of the Gurdaspur district in the Punjab* (1892). He died in London, 22 February 1946. Buckland; DNB; *Who was who*, 4

Danecki, Janusz, fl. 1973-1991, he received a doctorate from the Uniwersytet Warszawski in 1982 for his thesis, *Literatura i kultura w imperium kalifów*. LC

Danesch, Mostafa, 1944- see Danish Shari'atpanahi, Mustafá

Daneu Lattanzi, Angela, born in 1901 at Alexandria, Egypt, her writings include *I manoscritti ed incunaboli miniati della Sicilia* (1965), and *La miniatures italienne du Xe au XVIe siècle* (1969) as well as editions of medieval texts. Gastaldi

Danforth, Loring Mandell, born 15 September 1949 at Newton, Mass., he was a graduate of Amherst College and received a Ph.D. in 1978 from Princeton University for his thesis, *The Anastenaria; a study in Greek ritual therapy*. He carried on field work in Greece and on two occasions he was a teaching fellow at Athens. Since 1978 he was a professor of anthropology at Bates College, Lewiston, Me., a position he still held in 1998. His writings include *The death rituals of rural Greece* (1982), and *Firewalking and religious healing* (1989). ConAu, 111; LC; NatFacDr, 1998

Dani, Ahmad Hasan, born 20 June 1920 in India, he was a gold medal graduate of the Banaras Hindu University, and received a Ph.D. from the University of London in 1955. He was a sometime superintendent of archaeology in India, West and East Pakistan. From 1963 to 1971 he was a professor and chairman of the Department of Archaeology in the University of Peshawar. Since 1981 he was a professor emeritus, Quaid-i-Azam University, Islamabad. His writings include *Bibliog-raphy of the Muslim inscriptions of Bengal* (1957), *Muslim architecture in Bengal* (1961), *Indian palaeography* (1963), *Alberuni's Indica* (1973), *Quaid-i-Azam and Pakistan* (1981), and *Recent archaeological discoveries in Pakistan* (1988). BioB134; ConAu, 13; Schoeberlein

Daniel, Abraham H., born 22 April 1925 in Bulgaria, and resident in Israel since 1946, he received a doctorate in 1963 from the Université de Paris for his thesis, *La coopération de production et de services en Israel*. His writings include *Labor enterprises in Israel* (1976), and *Ko'operrativim be-mivhan* (1989). He died 21 August 1988. LC; WhoWorJ, 1978

Daniel, Elton Lee, born 7 May 1948 in North Carolina, he was educated at the University of North Carolina, New York University, and the University of Texas, where he received a Ph.D. in 1978 for his thesis, *Iran's awakening; a study of local rebellions*. In 1998 he had been a professor of history at the University of Hawai, Honolulu, for over ten years. He was a graduate chairman and director of World Civilization Program. His writings include *The political and social history of Khurasan under Abbasid rule* (1979), its Persian translation in 1988, and the translation, *A Shi'ite pilgrimage to Mecca, 1885-1886; the Safarnâmeh of Mirza M. Hosayn Farâhâni* (1990). NatFacDr, 1998; Private

Daniel, Francisco Salvador, ca. 1830- ca. 1871, he was a musician who played a particular role in the dreadful insurrection that ravaged Paris at the end of the 1870-71 war. His writings include *La musique arabe, ses rapports avec la musique grecque et le chant grégorien* (Alger, 1863), *La musique arabe* (1879), and *Musique et instruments de musique du Maghreb* (1986). IndexBFr² [incorrect reference]

365

Daniel, Jean, born 21 July 1920 at Blida, Algeria, he was educated in Alger as well as in Paris. He was a journalist, editor and a sometime correspondent for *l'Express*, Paris. He was a sympathetic observer of North African affairs and close to the leaders of the F.L.N. His writings include *De Gaulle et l'Algérie* (1986). WhoFr, 1965/66-1998/99

Daniel, Norman Alexander, born 8 May 1919 at Manchester, he was educated at Queen's College, Oxford, and Edinburgh University, where he obtained a Ph.D. in 1956 for *The concept of Islam in Latin writers of the middle ages*. He served for many years as British Council representative in various countries and held the appointment of cultural attaché in Cairo. He was an eminent consultant and historian of intercultural relations. His writings include *Islam and the West* (1960), *Islam, Europe, Empire* (1966), and *The Arabs and medieval Europe* (1975). He died in Toronto, Ont., on 11 August 1992. ConAu 57; MIDEO 21 (1993), pp. 579-81; Sluglett

Daniel, Odile, fl. 1975-77, her writings include *Albanie; une bibliographie historique* (Paris, 1985).

Daniel, Robert Leslie, born 1 May 1923 at Detroit, Mich., he was a graduate of Miami University and received a Ph.D. in 1954 from the University of Wisconsin for his thesis, *From relief to technical assistance in the Near East, a case study; Near East Relief and Near East Foundation*. He taught at a number of American universities until 1957, when he was appointed professor of history at Ohio University, Athens, ending his career as chairman of department. His writings include *American philanthropy in the Near East* (1970). ConAu, 33; DrAS, 1982; Selim

Danielcik, Hans Peter, born about 1900, he received a Dr.jur. in 1925 from the Universität Heidelberg for his thesis, *Die Rechte nationaler Minderheiten nach dem Versailler Vertrag*. His writings include *Deutsch-lands Selbstversorgung* (1932), *Aktiengesetz* (1937), and *Verwaltungsvereinfachung* (1941). His trace is lost after a publication in 1944. NUC, pre-1956

Danielli, Iacopo, born 11 November 1859 at Buti near Pisa, he studied natural sciences at Pisa but transferred for graduate studies in anthropology to l'Istituto di studi superiori, Firenze, in 1888. He was a sometime teaching assistant in anthropology at the Institute, before he engaged in philosophical studies in Berlin from 1890 to 1895. He was a member of the anthropological societies of Paris and Bruxelles. During the last years of his life he was active in socialist politics. He wrote a number of pamphlets which include *Tecnica antropologia* (Pisa, 1888). He died 19 April 1901. DizBI

Daniëls, Carel Eduard, 1839-1909, he was a Dutch medical doctor. LC

Daniels, Charles M., fl. 1975, he was a sometime lecturer in archaeology at the Department of Archaeology, University of Newcastle upon Tyne. His writings include *The Garamantes of southern Libya* (1970); he was joint author of *Soba; archaeological research at a medieval capital on the Blue Nile* (1991). LC

Danielsen, Niels Skovgaard, born 20 May 1933 at Hellerup, Denmark, he was a graduate of Københavns Universitet and received a doctorate from Aarhus Universitet in 1968. He was a professor of Germanic philology successively at København and Odense since 1968, as well as a visiting professor at Firenze, Wien, Toronto, and Galaway. His writings include *Zum Wesen des Konditionalsatzes* (1968). He died 1 October 1987. Kraks, 1987; Kraks, register, 1910-1993; WhoWor, 1980/81

Danielsson, Arne, born 20th cent., he was in 1967 a curator at the Armémuseum, Stockholm.

Danilov, Viktor Petrovich, fl. 1957, he was a writer on land tenure and social conditions in Russia. His writings include Очерки истории коллективизации Сельзкого хозяйста (1963), Советская доколхозная деревня (1979), and *Rural Russia under the new regime* (1988). LC

Danilov, Vladimir Ivanovich, born 20th cent., he was a Russian Turkologist whose writings include Средние слои в политической жизни современной Турции (1968), 7000 километров по Турции (1975), Политическая борьба в Турции (1985), Турция 80-х (1991); and he was an editor of Турция, история, экономика, политика (1984), and Османская империя (1986). LC

Daninos, Guy, born in 1929, he received a doctorate in 1976 from the Université de Nancy II for his thesis, *Les romanciers algériens de langue française depuis 1965*. His writings include the trade edition of his thesis, *Les nouvelles tendances du roman algérien de langue française* (1979), *Aspects de la nouvelle poésie algérienne de langue française* (Sherbrooke, P.Q., 1982), and *Comprendre Tribaliques d'Henri Lopes* (1987). LC; THESAM 2

Danish Shariʻatpanahi, Mustafá, born 2 May 1944 at Semnan, Iran, he studied at the universities of München, Bonn, and Köln, where he received a Dr.phil in 1976 for his thesis, *Die Politik Groß-britanniens und Rußlands in der iranischen bürgerlichen Revolution, 1905-1911*. LC

Dankoff, Robert Martin, born 24 September 1943 at Rochester, N.Y., he received a Ph.D. in 1971 from Harvard University for his thesis, *Ethnographic studies in the Diwan lughat al-Turk*. He was a member of MESA, and certainly from 1990 to 1999 a professor of Near Eastern languages and civilizations at the University of Chicago. His writings include *The Turkic vocabulary in the Farhang-i Zafân-gûyâ* (1987), *An Evliya Çelebi glossary* (1991); and the translations *Wisdom of royal glory; a Turko-Islamic mirror for princes* (1983), and *The intimate life of an Ottoman statesman, Melek Ahmed Pasha, as portayed in Evliya Çelebi* (1991). MESA *Roster of members*, 1990; NatFacDr, 1998-1999; Schoeberlein; Selim

Dann, Uriel, born 6 May 1922 at Berlin, he went to Palestine in 1933. In the second World War he served in the British Army and subsequently joined the Israeli Army, where he served as an officer in its intelligence branch, intently watching, listening to and monitoring Israel's eastern neighbours. His true passion was history and while in the Israeli Army he pursued his education by correspondence, acquiring a B.A. in history from the University of London. He subsequently earned two doctorates, the first from the Hebrew University, Jerusalem, and the second from Oxford. He was a professor at the Moshe Dayan Center for Middle Eastern and African Studies, Tel Aviv University. His writings include *Studies in the history of the Transjordan, 1920-1949* (1984), and *King Hussein and the challenge of Arab nationalism* (1989). He died in Tel Aviv, 19 October 1991, from injuries suffered when he was hit by an automobile. A memorial volume was published in 1995 entitled *The Hashemites in the modern Arab world; essays in honour of the late professor Uriel Dann*. ConAu, 25; *Index Islamicus* (2); MESA *bulletin* 26 i (1992), p. 153; WhoIsrael, 1972

Danner, Mary Ann Koury, 1948- see Danner-Fadae, Mary Ann née Koury

Danner, Victor, born in 1926, he received a Ph.D. in 1970 from Harvard University for *Ibn 'Ata' Allah, a Sufi of Mamluk Egypt*. In 1990 he was a professor of Near Eastern languages and culture at Indiana University, Bloomington. His writings include the translation *The book of wisdom of Ibn Ata Allah* (1978). LC; MESA *Roster of members*, 1990; Selim

Danner-Fadae, Mary Ann née Koury, born 13 March 1948 at Louisville, Ky., she was a graduate of AUB and received a Ph.D. in 1988 from Indiana University for a translation with introduction of Ahmad ibn 'Ata' Allah's *Miftah al-falah wa-misbah al-arwah*. She was a sometime manager of the Middle Eastern Studies Collection, Indiana University Library, and a part-time teacher, specializing in Sufism and Arabic literature. She received two Arabic translation awards, the first from the American Association of Teachers of Arabic in 1985, and the second from the Translation Center, Columbia University in 1990. Her writings include *The remembrance of God in Sufism* (1986). Private

Danon, Abraham Josef, born in 1857 at Edirne, Ottoman Empire. After his education in Edirne, he was attached to the Alliance Israelite Universelle and founded a Jewish seminary in Constantinople, and he was the founding editor of *Yosef ha-da'at*, or, *El Progresso*, a journal in Ladino, Hebrew, and Turkish in Hebrew characters. During the first World War he taught Hebrew in Paris. He died in 1925. EncJud; Wininger

Danon, Vitalis, fl. 1955, his writings include *Aron le colporteur; nouvelle juive nord afrcaine* (Tunis, 1933), and *Ninette de la rue du Péché; nouvelle populiste* (Tunis, 1939). LC

Danova, Nadja Khristova, fl. 1972, her writings include Националният въпрос в гръцките политически програми през XIX век (Sofia, 1980); and she was joint editor of Изследвания в чест на академик Николай Тодоров (1983), Книга за българските хаджии (1985), and Културнопросветуи центрове и институции на балканските народи XV-XIX в. (1989). LC

Dansette, Béatrice née Mouton, born about 1950, she was married on 12 October 1968 to Hubert Dansette, a deputy director of the Citibank, Paris. She received a doctorate from the Université de Paris IV for her thesis, *Les Pélerinages occidentaux en Terre Sainte aux XIVème et XVème siècles*, in 1977. THESAM 3; WhoFr., 1997/98

Dansker, Ol'ga L'vovna, fl. 1960, she was a writer on Tajikistan and edited *С. А. Самосуд; статьи, воспоминания, письма* (Moscow, 1984). LC

Dantan, J. L., fl. 1908, he received a doctorate in 1921 from the Université de Paris for his thesis, *Recherches sur les antipathaires*. His writings include *L'ostréiculture en Tunisie* (1932). NUC, pre-1956

Dantín Cereceda, Juan, born in 1881 at Madrid, he was a geographer whose writings include *Resumen fisiográfico de la Peninsula Ibérica* (1912), *Ensayo acerca de las regiones naturales de España* (1922), and *Historia de la tierra* (1922). He died in 1943. Espasa; LC

Dantsig, Boris Moiseevich, born in 1896 at Nezhin, Ukraine, he graduated in 1919 from the Faculty of Law at Kiev, and received a doctorate in 1965. He was the author of country studies on Turkey, 1937,

1938, 1940, 1949; Iraq, 1940, 1955; and Syria, 1940. He also wrote *Ближний Восток в русской науке и литературе* (1973). He died 16 August 1973. LC; Miliband

Danvers, Frederick Charles, born 1 July 1833 at Hornsey, he was a civil and mechanical engineer who spent forty years in various departments of the India Office, London. His writings include *India* (1877), and *The Portuguese in India* (1894). He died 17 May 1906. Buckland; DNB; *Who was who,* 1

Danvila y Collado, Manuel, born 3 December 1830 at Valencia, he was an historian, politician, eloquent lawyer, and a member of the Comisión de codificación in 1876. His writings include *La expulsión de los Moriscos españoles* (1889). He died in Málaga, 21 February 1906. DiccHist; EncicUni; Indice E (2)

Danziger, Raphael, born about 1940, he received a Ph.D. in 1977 from Princeton University for his thesis, *Abd-al-Qadir and the Algerians; resistance to the French and international consolidation.* For the Commission on International Affairs, American Jewish Congress, he wrote the pamphlet, *The decline of Egyptian-Israeli relations.* (1984). LC

Dar, Saeeduddin Ahmad, he was in 1976 a chairman of the Department of International Relations in the University of Islamabad. He edited *Selected documents on Pakistan's relations with Af-ghanistan* (1988). LC

Daras, Charles, he was a French local historian and, in 1981, an honory president of the Société archéo-logique et historique de la Charente. His writings include *Angoumois roman* (1961), *Église de Charente* (1972), and *Les Templiers en Charente* (1981). LC

Darasz, Zdzisław, fl. 1974, his writings include *Od moderny do ekspresjonizmu* (Wrocław, 1982). LC

Daraz, Sa'id *Muhammad 'Abd Allah*, born in 1894, he received a doctorate from the Sorbonne, Paris, for his thesis, *La morale du Koran.* He was a sometime professor at al-Azhar, Cairo. His writings include the translation of his thesis, *Dustur al-akhlaq fi al-Qur'an* (1973), and *Wa-thiyabaka fa tahhir* (1978). He died in 1958. LC

Darbinian-Melikian, M. O., fl. 1964, he was an editor and translator of Armenian historical works which include *Путевые заметки*, by Simeon Lekhetsi (1965), and *История анонимного повество-вателя Псевдо-Шапух Багратуни* (1971). LC

Darby, George O. S., fl. 1936, he received a Ph.D. in 1932 from Harvard for his thesis, *An astrological manuscript of Alfonso X.* LC

Darcel, Alfred, 1818-1895, he was joint author of *L'Art architectural en France* (1866-67). LC

d'Arcy Todd, Elliott, 1808-1845 *see* Todd, Elliott d'Arcy

Dard, A. R., fl. 1925, he was a sometime imam of the London Mosque. His writings include *The hadith* (1934), and *Life of Ahmad, the founder of the Ahmadiyya movement* (1948). NUC, pre-1956

Dardaud, Gabriel, fl. 1940, his writings include *Trente ans au bord du Nil; un journaliste dans l'Égypte des derniers rois* (1987). He was joint author of *Les émirats mirages; voyage chez les pétrocrates* (1975). LC

al-**Dardiri**, Yahyá Ahmad, fl. 1973, he obtained a doctorate in law and wrote *Makanat al-'ilm fi al-Qur'an* (1944), and *Arkan al-Islam al-khamsah* (1951). LC

Daressy, Georges Émile Jules, born 19 March 1864 at Sourdon (Somme). After study at l'École des hautes études he went to Egypt as a member of the Mission archéologique française in 1886 and was made assistant keeper at the Bulaq Museum the following year. He was a prolific contributor to jour-nals. He retired in 1923 in Sourdon where he died 28 February 1938. Curinier, 4, p. 136; DBF; Egyptology

Dareste de la Chavanne, Antoine Elisabeth *Cléophas*, 1820-1882, he was educated at l'École des chartes and taught history successively at the Collège de Rennes, Collège de Stanislas, Paris, facultés des lettres at Grenoble as well as Lyon, where he was appointed dean in 1865. His *Histoire de France depuis les origines jusqu'à nos jours* won him the Grand Prix Gobert. DBF; EncBrit; IndexBFr² (5); EncicUni; EncItaliana; GdeEnc; Meyers; Vapereau

Darin-Drabkin, Haim, born 13 October 1908 at Warszawa, he studied at Warszawa, Paris, and Lyon and emigrated to Palestine in 1934. In the late 1950s and early 1960s he was an economic advisor to the Ministry of Labour, and in 1967, head of the Economic, Sociological, and Statistical Research Division of the Israel Housing Ministry. For many years he was the chairman of the editorial board of the *New outlook.* His writings include *ha-Hevrah ha-aheret* (1961), its translations, *The other society*

(1963), and *Der Kibbuz* (1967), *Land policy and urban growth* (1977), and he was joint author of *The economic case for Palestine* (1978). He died in 1979. LC; WhoIsrael, 1966/67, 1969/70, 1972; WhoWorJ, 1965

Darity, William Alexander, born 15 January 1924 at Flat Rock, N.C., he was a graduate of Shaw University, and received a Ph.D. in 1964 from the University of North Carolina for his thesis, *Contraceptive education; the relative cultural and social factors related to applied education.* From 1953 to 1961 he served with the World Health Organization as consultant in health education with the U.N. Relief and Works Agency for Palestine Refugees; he was a W.H.O. visiting professor of health education at AUB, and a Regional Health Adviser for seventeen countries of the region. Since 1965 he served as a professor, head of department and dean at Amherst University. He was joint author of *Labor economics* (1984). AmM&WS, 1973-1989; NatFacDr, 1998; WhoAm, 1974/75-1978/79; WhoBIA, 1980/81, 1985, 1988; WhoWor, 1976/77

Darkó, Jenö (Eugen), 1880-1940, he was a Byzantine scholar whose writings include *Byzantinisch-ungarische Beziehungen in der zweiten Hälfte des XII. Jahrhunderts* (1933), and *Az ösmagyar hadmüvészetfejlödése és hatasa nyngateurópára* (1934). UjMagyar

Darkot, Besim, born in 1903 at Constantinople, he was a geographer who studied at Istanbul Üniversitesi and Université de Strasbourg. His writings include *Kartografya dersleri* (1939), *Türkiye iktisadi coğrafyası* (1955), and *Modern büyük atlas* (1975). Meydan

Darlow, John J., fl. 1914-1937, he was affiliated with the Permanent Philatelic Congress, London, and joint compiler of *A history of the Philatelic Congress of Great Britain* (1914). BLC; LC

Darmesteter, James, born 28 March 1849 at Château-Salins (Moselle), he was from a Jewish family of modest substance, delicate, puny, and almost deformed, but the greatest authority of his time on Zoroastrian literature. In honour of this illustrious French Iranist and philologist the Association James Darmesteter was founded in Paris in 1922. His writings include *Lettres sur l'Inde; à la frontière afghane* (1888). He died 19 October 1894. Buckland; *Contemporary review* 67 (1895), pp. 81-104; DBF; EncAm; EncBrit; EncicUni; EncIran; EncItaliana; EncJud; GdeEnc; Meyers; Sigilla; Wininger

Darmon, Amran, born in July 1815 at Oran, Algeria, he was an interpreter in the Corps des interprètes de l'armée d'Afrique and rose from the rank of interprète temporaire (19 June 1836) to interprète 1re classe (16 January 1852); he was awarded chevalier de la Légion d'honneur (22 December 1852). He retired from military service on 8 January 1870, and settled in Mascara, where he died on 17 October 1878. Féraud, 263; *Revue africaine* 22 (1878), p. 475

Darmon, Raoul, fl. 1965, his writings include *La situation des cultes en Tunisie* (Paris, 1930), and *La Goulettes et les Goulettois* (Tunis, 1969). LC

Darmstaedter, Ernst, born 13 January 1877 at Mannheim, Germany, he was a chemist and historian of natural sciences. His writings include *Die Alchemie des Geber, übersetzt und erklärt* (1922), *Arznei und Alchemie; Paracelsus-Studien* (1931); and he was joint editor of *Acta Paracelsica.* Kürschner, 1925, 1926, 1928/29, 1931, 1935; Sigilla; Wer ist's, 1935

Darricau, Raymond, fl. 1960, he was a *professeur* whose writings include *À cœur de l'histoire de Quercy; Alain de Solminihac* (1980), *Vie et œuvres de sainte Marguerite-Marie Alacoque* (1990); and he was joint author of *Le diocèse de Bordeaux* (1974). LC

Darrouy, Henri, fl. 1953, he was a sometime administrative secretary-general of the Commission d'aide aux Nord-africaines dans la métropole. Note

Darrouy, Lucienne Jean, fl. 1945 *see* Jean-Darrouy, Lucienne

Darrouzès, Jean, born in the early 20th century, his writings include *Epistoliers byzantins du Xe siècle* (1960), *Documents inédits d'ecclesiologie byzantine* (1966), *Recherches sur les οφφίχια de l'église byzantine* (1970), and the collection of his articles, *Littérature et histoire des textes byzantins* (1972). He edited *Notitiae episcopatum Ecclesiae Constantinopolitanae* (1981). LC

Darskii, Erikh Nikolaevich, he was a writer on fine art, whose writings include *Искусство Оъединенной Арабсеой Республики, Ливана, Туниса, Судана, Индии, Цейлона, Индонезии, Камбоджи, Австралии* (1959); he was editor of *Вдадимир Стельмашонок* (1983). LC

Dart, Raymond Arthur, born in 1893 at Toowong, Queensland, he took his medical training in Australia, and became a surgeon in Sydney, as well as a captain in the Australian Army Medical Corps in the first World War. He was a lecturer in histology at London, and a professor of anatomy at Johannesburg. He also gave a series of lectures on the origin of man on the South African Broadcasting network, including *Beyond antiquity, Africa's place in the human story* (1954); and *The missing link* (1959). He died 22 November 1988. BioIn, 14, 15; ConAu, P-1; IntWW, 1974/75-1978; Master (12), NUC, pre-1956; Who, 1973-1988; WhoSAfrica, 1986/87, 1987/88, 1988/89; Who was who, 8

Darvai, Moricz, born 14 December 1849 at Aszód, Hungary, he was a secondary school teacher, and from 1872 until his retirement in 1911, a director. Thereafter he was an art critic and translator. His writings include *Üstökösök és meteorok* (1888), and *Benvenuto Cellini* (1907). GeistigeUng; RNL

Darwin, John, born 29 June 1948, he was a graduate of St. John's College, Oxford, and received a D.Phil. in 1976 for his thesis, *The Lloyd George coalition government and Britain's imperial policy in Egypt and the Middle East, 1918-22*. His writings include *Britain, Egypt, and the Middle East* (1981), *Britain and decolonisation* (1988), and *The end of the British Empire* (1991). LC; Sluglett

Das, Harihar, F.R.Hist.S., born in 1895 in Bengal, he was a journalist educated at Calcutta, London, and Oxford where he received a B.Litt. in 1923 for his thesis, *Sir William Norris, Bart., and his embassy to Aurangzeb, 1657-1702*. His writings include *The life and letters of Toru Dutt* (1921), and *The Norris embassy to Aurangzib* (1959). Master (1); Sluglett; WhE&EA

Das, Sarat Chandra, born 18 July 1849, he was educated at Chittagong and the Calcutta Presidency College, where he later joined its Engineering Department. In 1874 he was appointed head master of the Bhutia Boarding School, Darjeeling, where he began to study Tibetan. He visited Lhasa twice. From 1896 to 1904 he served the Government of Bengal as Tibetan interpreter. His writings include *Indian pandits in the land of snow* (1893), and *An introduction to the grammar of the Tibetan language with texts* (1915). He died in 1917. Buckland

Das, Taraknath, born 15 June 1884 near Calcutta, he was a Bengali college student, fled India in 1906, and founded *Free Hindustan* while a U.S. immigration interpreter in Vancouver, 1908. Forced out by British pressure, he spent a year at Norwich University, Northfield, Vt., urging, wherever he could, Indian freedom from British rule. Again the British persuaded the Administration to dismiss him. He nevertheles stayed in the United States, where he obtained a Ph.D. in 1924 from Georgetown University, and became a lecturer in history and international relations at several universities from 1934 to 1947. His writings include *India in world politics* (1923), its translation, *Indien in der Weltpolitik* (1932), and *British expansion in Tibet* (1928). He died in New York City, 22 December 1958. *American historical review*, 64 (1959), p. 831; Eminent; PeoHis

Dascalakis, A., 1903- see Daskalakes, Apostolos Basileiou

Da Schio, Almerico, born 25 November 1836 at Costozza di Longare (Vicenza), he studied law at Padova from 1855 to 1860. After practising law for a number of years, he began in 1865 to pursue an interest in the Padova observatory and started to study mathematics. He subsequently became director of the meteorological observatory of the Accademia Olimpica di Vicenza, a post which he held until 1918. He was a member of numerous learned societies. His writings include *Di due astrobali in caratteri cufici* (Venezia, 1880). He died in Vicenza on 28 November 1930. DizBI; Gubernatis 1; Gubernatis 3

Dasgupta, Kalpana, born in 1941, she held her B.A. and M.A. from Patna University, and her M.S. from Syracuse University, N.Y. In 1975 she was an assistant librarian at the National Council of Applied Economic Research in India, specializing in social science documentaion, as well as language problems and urbanization in India. She edited *Women on the Indian scene* (1976), and wrote *Mass communication in India* (1982). LC

Dashevskii, G., fl. 1924, and author of *Фашистская пятя колонна в Испании* (1938). LC

Dashkevich, IAroslav Romanovich, his writings include *Армянские колонии на Украине* (1962), and *Каменные бабы Причерноморскнх степей* (1982); he edited *Украинско-армянскне связи в XVIII веке* (1969). LC

Dashrawi, Farhat al- see Dachraoui, Farhat

Daskalakes, Apostolos Basileou, born 24 September 1903, he was educated at Athens University and the Sorbonne. For several years he was a journalist and foreign correspondent of various Athens newspapers before he was appointed professor of medieval and modern history at Athens. He later served as vice-chancellor of the University, and cultural counsellor, Ministry of Foreign Affairs. He was an honorary professor of a number of European universities. His writings include *Κοραῆς και Κόδρικας η μεγάλη φιλολογικη διαμάχη των Ελλήνων, 1815-1821* (1966), *Κείμενα; πηγές της ιςτορίας τῆς Ελληνικής Επαναςτάςεως* (1968), and *Ιστορία της Ελληνικής Χωροφυλακής, χρονικης περιόδου, 1936-1950* (1973). Hellenikon, 1965; IntWW, 1974/75-1983; LC

Daskawie, Mohammed Abdul Qayyum, fl. 1931-1978, he was a Christian convert and since 1928 a professor at Gordon College, Rawalpindi. Note

Dastugue, Elisabeth Jean *Hyacinthe* Dominique, born 8 June (or July) 1827 at Maubourguet (Hautes-Pyrénées), he joined the Chasseurs à pied in 1848 and soon thereafter was transferred to the Spahis where he became sous-lieutenant in 1851. In the Service des Bureaux arabes he quickly advanced through the grades to become lieutenant-colonel, particularly after his successful operations at Garet-Sidi-Cheikh in 1865. With the exception of the 1870-71 war, he remained in Algeria until invalided home in 1876. In 1878 he was recalled for service in Corsica, where he died in Bastia, 15 January 1880. DBF; Henze; Peyronnet, p. 345

Daszkiewicz, Jarosław R. *see* Dashkevich, IAroslav Romanovich

Datta, Kalikinkar, born in 1905 in Bihar, he was educated at Calcutta, where he received a Ph.D. and later lectured in history. He was a sometime vice-chancellor of Magadh and Patna universities. His writings include *Alivardi and his times* (1939), *The Dutch in Bengal and Bihar* (1948), *Anti-British plots and movements before 1857* (1970), and *Economic condition of Bengal Subah in the years of transition, 1740-1772* (1984). LC; WhoIndia, 1970, p. 412; 1972, p. 493; 1973, p. 439

Dattari, Giovanni, born 19th cent., he was an Italian coin collector and antiquary in British service, and residing in Cairo. His writings incude *Monete imperiali greche* (Cairo, 1901), and *I medaglioni di Tarso e qualli d'Aboukir* Milano, 1907). He died in 1923. Egyptology; NUC, pre-1956

Dauer, Alfons Michael, born 16 April 1921 at Bamberg, Germany, he was in 1977-78 a professor at the Academy of Music and Dramatic Arts, Graz, Austria. His writings include *Zur Syntagmatik des ethnographischen Dokumentationsfilms* (Wien, 1980). Kürschner, 1980-1996; WhoAustria, 1977/78

Daugan, Albert Joseph Marie, born 31 December 1866 at Rennes. After graduation from the military college Saint-Cyr and l'École de guerre, he was posted to Algeria in 1903 and served there and in Morocco until the war. In 1922 he was attached to the Résident général du Maroc and employed in Marrakesh and southern Morocco. During the Riff war he commanded the northern front. He retired with the rank of general and died 16 June 1952. DBF

Daula, A. M., fl. 1936, he received a Ph.D. from the University of London and became a lecturer at Government College, Ludhiana, Punjab. Note

Daumas, Jacques, born 24 February 1906 at Toulouse, he was an employee of the Compagnie universelle du Canal maritime de Suez since 1936. He was an excellent sportsman and a mountaineer who spent much of his time climbing in the Sinai. He was a founder of the Société d'études historiques et géographiques de l'Isthme de Suez. His writings include *Sur les traces de Moïse* (1942), and *La Péninsule du Sinaï* (1951), a first-class guide-book for which the Académie des sciences awarded him the Prix Tchihatcef for 1953. He died in Auxerre, 13 December 1982. Hommes et destins, v. 7, pp. 142-143

Daumas, Melchior Joseph *Eugène*, born 4 September 1803 at Delémont, Switzerland, he participated in the French conquest of Algeria as a French officer and later was appointed director of the Bureaux des affaires arabes in Alger. He took a keen and sympathetic interest in the Algerian people, particularly the Bedouins. His writings include *Le Sahara algérien* (1847), *Le grand désert* (1848), *Les chevaux du Sahara* (1857), its translation, *The horses of the Sahara* (1863) and *La femme arabe* (1912), and its translation, *Women of North Africa* (1943). He died 29 April 1871. DBF; Embacher; EncicUni; GdeEnc; Henze; Index BFr²; Meyers; Vapereau

Daumont, Alexandre, fl. 1837, his writings include *Voyage en Suède* (Paris, 1834). BN

Dauney, William, born in 1800 at Aberdeen, he was a trained lawyer. In the Advocates' Library in Edinburgh he discovered what is now known as the "Skene MS," a collection of English and Scottish dances from the 17th century, which he transcribed and published in 1837 as *Ancient Scottish melodies*. He died in Georgetown, British Guiana, where he was a colonial solicitor-general, 28 July 1843. Baker 84

Daunou, Pierre Claude François, born 18 August 1861 at Boulogne-sur-Mer, he had a brilliant career at the local Collège des Oratoriens, and joined the order at Paris in 1777. He served as professor at various seminaries from 1780 to 1787, when he was ordained priest. In 1792 he was elected a deputy and became an active and influencial politician and statesman as well as a historian. He edited the *Journal des savants* after 1816. He died in Paris, 20 June 1840. CelCen; DBF; DcBiPP EncAm; EncBrit; EncicUni; GdeEnc; Index BFr² (12); Master (3); Meyers

Dauphin, Jacques Marie Alexandre, born 30 April 1915 at Paris, he was educated at Rouen. After completing his studies at the facultés de droit et des lettres de Paris, he obtained a diploma in Chinese and Japanese from l'École nationale des langues orientales vivantes. He was a journalist who spent the years from 1948 to 1962 in the Middle East. His writings include *Incertain Irak; tableau d'un royaume avant le tempête, 1914-1953* (1991). WhoFr, 1975/76-1981/82

Daura, Bello, his writings include *Introduction to classical Hausa* (1970); and he was joint author of *Hausa customs* (1968).

Daussy, Pierre, born 8 October 1792 at Paris, he was a member of the Corps des ingénieurs hydrographes. After a career at French ports and in Paris, he became a sometime keeper of the Dépôt des cartes et plans at the Ministère de la Marine. He was a member of the Académie des sciences and died in Paris, 5 September 1860. DBF

Dautry, Jean, born 27 July 1910 at Désertines (Allier), he was a professor of social history. During the 1920s and 1930s he was a militant member of various extreme leftists; in 1941 he joined the French communist party. His writings include *Le percement de l'isthme de Suez* (1947), and *Histoire de la révolution de 1848 en France* (1948). He was a contributor to the Marxist periodical *La Pensée*. He died in Paris, 6 March 1968. DcBMOuvF, v. 24 (1985), pp. 105-106

Dauvergne, Henri, fl. 1892, he was a French traveller who set out from Srinagar in June of 1889 to explore the Pamirs, eastern Turkestan, and Kashmir. Henze

Dauvillier, Jean Georges Henri, born 19 August 1908 at Epinay-sur-Orge, he studied at the Faculté de droit de Paris and École des languages orientales anciennes de l'Institut catholique de Paris. He was successively professor of history of canon law at the universities of Paris and Toulouse. His writings include *Le mariage dans le droit classique de l'Église* (1933), *Le mariage en droit canonique oriental* (1936), and a collection of his periodical articles entitled *Histoire et institutions des églises orientales au moyen âge* (1983). He died 5 February 1983. WhoFr, 1981/82-1983/84

Daux, A., he wrote *Voyages et recherches en Tunisie, 1868* (Paris, Microéd. Hachette, 1971).

Dauzat, Albert, born 4 July 1877 at Guéret (Creuse), he was educated in Paris, where he took four degrees and later was attached to l'École des hautes études from 1910 until his retirement in 1947. During the period 1947-48, he gave a course on linguistics at the Université d'Alger. However, his best known work, *Dictionnaire étymologique des noms de famille et prénoms de France* (1951), was severely criticized by some contemporary specialists. He died in Paris, 31 October 1955. Biol, 4; DBF; NYT, 2 November 1955, p. 35, col. 4; *French review* 29 (April 1956), pp. 418-419; WhoFr, 1955/56

Davar, Firoze Cowasji, fl. 20th cent., his writings include *Art and morality, and other essays* (Bombay, 1935), *Iran and its culture* (Bombay, 1953), *Iran and India through the ages* (Bombay, 1963), and *Socrates and Christ* (Ahmedabad, 1972). BLC; LC

Davary, Gholam Djelani, born 15 January 1943 at Kabul, he studied Afghan history and geography at Kabul from 1963 to 1968, but subsequently changed to Iranian studies in Germany, first at Hamburg, and later at Kiel. His writings include *Baktrish; ein Wörterbuch auf Grund der Inschriften* (1982). BioB134; LC

Daveau, Suzanne, born 20th cent., she was in 1959 a lecturer at the Faculté des lettres et sciences humaines de Dakar. Her writings include *Recherches morphologiques sur la région de Bandiagara* (1959); she was joint author of *Bibliográfica de Portugal* (1982); and editor of *Geografia de Portugal, por O. Ribeiro e H. Lautensach* (1987-91). LC

Davenport, William Arthur, born in 1883. After passing through the Royal Military College at Sandhurst, he was commissioned into the West Yorkshire Regiment but in 1912 attached to the Egyptian Army. He was in action in the Sudan and Gallipoli. In October 1916, he was posted to the Hejaz in command of Egyptian troops and stayed there during the rest of the war. He sent many reports upon their activities to the *Arab bulletin*. R.L. Bidwell, Arab bulletin 1 (1986 reprint), p. xxv

Daver, A. M., 1921- see Dauer, Alfons Michael

Daver, Abidin, born 8 February 1885 at Constantinople, he was a sometime editor of the Istanbul dailies, *Cumhuriyet* and *la République*, and an authority on naval and military matters. In 1939 he was elected a deputy from Istanbul at the Millet Meclisi. He later served as chief statistical and publications officer in Istanbul and taught at Galatasary Lisesi. His writings include *Dünkü buyünkü yarinki Istanbul* (1944), *Türk denizciliği* (1947), and *Barabros Hayrettin Paşa* (1953). He died in Istanbul, 8 February 1954. NYT, 10 February 1954, p. 29, col. 4

Davesiès de Pontès, Charles Jules Lucien, born 9 Septembre 1806 at Orléans, he was educated in Paris and in 1824 entered l'École navale d'Angoulême. In 1826 he came as a midshipman to the shores of Egypt without seeing much action there. He stayed on in the Near East, succumbing to the history, archaeology, and civilization of Greece and its islands, but disgusted by the idleness to which he was condemned, he resigned from the navy in 1834. He returned to Paris, where he contributed articles about his travels to various periodicals. In later life he was a municipal administrator. His writings, most of which were published posthumously, include *Études sur l'Orient* (1864), *Notes sur la Grèce* (1864), *Études sur l'Angleterre* (1865), and *Études morales et religieuses* (1869). He died in Passy, 28 December 1859. BN; DBF

Davey, Richard Patrick Boyle, born 12 July 1848, he was educated in Italy. In 1870 he left Europe for America, where he soon distinguished himself as a journalist. He returned to England in 1880 and joined the staff of the *Morning Post*. In 1893-94 he visited Constantinople, a journey which he described in *The sultan and his subjects* (1897). In the early years of the twentieth century he was resident in London. He contributed to periodicals and also wrote *The Tower of London* (1910). BritInd (5); LitYbk, 1904, 1907, 1910, 1911, 1912, 1913; *Men and women of the time*, 15th ed., 1899

Davico, Rosalba, fl. 1973, her writings include *Dalla rivoluzione dei consumi del XVIa secolo alla rivolizione francesco* (1977), and *'Peuple' et notables (1750-1816); essais sur l'Ancien Régime* (1981).

David, Clément *Joseph*, Mgr., 1829-1890, he was a Dominican priest from Mosul. His writings include *Éléments de grammaire française exposés en arabe* (Mossoul, 1865), *Antiqua Ecclesiae Syro-Chaldaicae traditio circa Petri Aposteli* (Roma, 1870), *Grammaire de la langue araméenne* (Mossoul, 1879), and *Grammatica aramaica seu Syriaca* (Mausil, 1896). Bahman Fadil 'Affas is said to have published an Arabic biography in 1985 entitled *Iqlimis Yusuf Dawud*. Khayr al-Din al-Zirikli, *al-A'lam*, 3rd ed., Beirut, 1970, v. 1, p. 343

David, Cyrille, fl. 1973, she was a professor at the Faculté de droit d'Alger and wrote *L'Impôt sur le revenue des ménages; assiette imposable* (1987). LC

Dávid, Géza, born 22 August 1949 at Budapest, he was a professor of Turkish, whose writings include *A Simontornyai szandzsák a 16 században* (1982), and *Útiszótár magyar-török* (1987). MagyarNKK, 1990, 1992, 1994, 1996, 1998

David, Jean Claude, he received a doctorate from the Université de Lyon II for his thesis, *Le Paysage urbain d'Alep*, in 1972. His writings include *Le waqf d'Ipšir Paša à Alep* (1982). LC; THESAM 3

David, Joseph, 1829-1890 *see* David, Clement Joseph

David, Jules Antoine, fl. 1882, his writings include *Le Péché originel* (1842), *Analogie et divergence entre les légendes religieuses de la Bible et du Koran* (1884), *Orient; traductions et imitations de poésies arabes et persanes* (1884), and he was joint author of *Syrie ancienne et moderne* (1848). BN; NUC, pre-1956

David, Madeleine V., born in 1902, her writings include *Les Dieux et le destin en Babylonie* (1949); she was editor of *Du culte des dieux fétiches*, by Charles de Brosses (Paris, 1989). LC

David, Philippe, born in 1932 at Paris, he was a sometime magistrate, and resident in Maradi, Niger, 1962-64, and in Dakar in 1969. His writings include *Les Navétanes* (1980), and *La Côte d'Ivoire* (1986). LC

David, René, born 12 January 1906 at Paris. After studies at the universities of Paris and Cambridge he received a doctorate in 1928 from the Université de Paris for his thesis, *La protection des minorités dans les sociétés par action*. He was successively professor of law at Grenoble, Paris, Aix-en-Provence, and Firenze. He was an honorable bencher of the Inner Temple, and received several honorary doctorates. His writings include *Cour de droit civil comparé* (1953), *Preliminary draft of the Ethiopian civil code* (1954), *Arbitrage dans le commerce international* (1982), its translation, *Arbitration in international trade* (1985); and he was joint author of *Major legal systems in the world today* (1978). WhoFr, 1975/76-1979/80

David, Robert, fl. 1897, his writings include *La pêche maritime au point de vue international* (Paris, 1897). BN

David-Bey, Melik S., fl. 1922, his writings include *La Langue arabe en 30 leçons* (Paris, 19--), *Manuel de la langue arménienne* (Paris, 1919); and he edited *Documents officiels concernant les massacres arméniens* (1920). LC

David-Neel, Alexandra Eugénie Marie Louise, born 24 October 1868 at Saint-Mandé (Seine), she was educated at Belgian schools and studied at the Faculté des lettres de Paris. She was an Orientalist, an explorer of the Far East, a practising Buddhist, and the first white woman to enter Lhasa in 1924. In December 1943 she was resident in Chinese Turkestan. Her writings include *Mystiques et magiciens du Thibet* (1929), *La lampe de sagesse* (1969), *Sons des nuées d'orage* (1980), and *Le sortilège du mystère* (1983). She died 8 September 1969. BioIn, 8, 9, 11; ConAu 25; EncO&P, 1978; Master (2); NYT 9 September 1969, p. 47, col. 1; Robinson, pp. 9-10; WhoFr, 1969/70

David-Weill, Jean Alexandre, born 27 February 1898 at Paris, he was educated at the Lycée Carnot, Paris, and obtained a doctorate in law as well as diplomas in Arabic and Persian from l'École nationale des langues orientales. In 1927-28 he was an *attaché libre* at l'Institut d'archéologie orientale du Caire, where he returned during the period from 1933 to 1936 as a research fellow. Between 1931 and 1936 he published the *Catalogue général du Musée arabe du Caire*. In 1938 he was appointed assistant keeper at the Louvre and, at the end of the same year, also lecturer in history of Islamic art at l'École du Louvre. He retired in 1968 and died 30 May 1972. *Journal asiatique* 260 (1972), pp. 215-216; WhoFr, 1969/70

Davidian, Harutun, Dr. born in 1924 at Tehran, he received a M.D. in 1948 from Tehran University, and a diploma in psychology in 1958 from the University of London. He was head of the Department of Psychiatry, Ruzbeh Hospital, and a member of the Faculty of Medicine at Tehran University, as well as a member of the World Health Organization's Advisory Panel on Mental Health. His writings include the Persian translation of work on psychopathology by an unidentified Western writer, in 1345/1966. IranWW, 1974, 1976; *Fihrist-i kitab'ha-yi chapi-i Farsi*, vol. 1, col. 611 (1352/1973)

Davidian, Marie Louise, she was in 1960 attached to the American University, Beirut. Note

Davidovich, Elena Abramovna, born 24 December 1922 at Krasnoiarsk, Russia, she graduated from Tashkent University in 1945, and received a doctorate in 1964 from Dushanbe University for her thesis, *Нумизматичекие данные по социально-экономической и политической истории Средней Азии.* She was a research fellow in Tajikistan from 1951 to 1971, and thereafter attached to the Oriental Institute of the Academy of Science of the USSSR. Her writings include *История монетного дела Средней Азии* (1964), *Денежное хозяйство Средней Азии после монгольского завоевания* (1972), *Клады древних и средневековых монет Таджикистана* (1979), *История денежного обращения средневековой Средней Азии; медные монеты ... в Мавераннахре* (1983), and *Корпус золотых и серебряных монет шейбанидов:XVI век* (1992). LC; Miliband; Schoeberlein

Davids, Jules, born 10 December 1920 at Brooklyn, N.Y., he was a graduate of Brooklyn College and received a Ph.D. in 1947 from Georgetown University, Washington, D.C. He was a professor of history at Georgetown, as well as a research associate at its Center for Strategic Studies since 1965. His writings include *America and the world of our time* (1960). DrAS, 1974, 1978, 1982

Davids, Thomas William *Rhys*, born 12 May 1843 at Colchester, Essex. After education at Brighton and the Universität Breslau, he entered the Indian Civil Service in Ceylon, where he was first led to acquire a first-hand knowledge of Pali and to make the acquaintance of Buddhist civilization. After his return home he was instrumental in the formation of the Pali Text Society. In 1882 he was appointed professor of Pali at London University, where he served until 1904, when he accepted the chair of comparative religion at Manchester University. He died in Chipstead, Surrey, 27 December 1922. *Asiatic review*, n.s., 19 (1923), pp. 359-362; Buckland; Who, 1903-1921; *Who was who*, 2

Davidson, Alexander Elliott, colonel, born in 1880, he was educated at the Royal Military Academy, Woolwich, and afterwards served in the Royal Engineers. He died 29 January 1966. *Who was who*, 6

Davidson, Flora Marion, born in 1879, she was resident in Peshawar in 1920 and in 1945. Her writings include *Hidden highway; experiences on the northwest frontier of India* (1948), and *Wild frontier* (1957). LC

Davidson, Herbert Alan, born 25 May 1932 at Boston, he was for ten years a professor of Hebrew, Islamic and Jewish philosophy at Harvard, before he was appointed professor of Hebrew at UCLA in 1972. His writings include *The philosophy of Abraham Shalom* (1964), a work which was originally written as a doctoral dissertation for Harvard in 1959. He also wrote *Proofs of eternity, creation and the existence of God in medieval Islamic and Jewish philosophy* (1987), and *Alfarabi, Avicenna and Averroes on intellect* (1992). ConAu, 17 DrAS, 1974, 1978, 1982

Davidson, John, born in 1797, he was educated at a private academy in London and trained as a chemist and drugist before studying medicine at Edinburgh. For health reasons he gave up medicine and travelled to southern Italy. In January 1836 he went to Morocco with the intention of reaching Timbuctu by way of the Sahara. He set out in November of the same year but fell victim to marauders. His diary and some of his letters were published by his brother entitled *Notes taken during travels in Africa* (1839). DNB; Egyptology; Embacher; Henze

Davidson, John, born in 1845, he was educated at Winchester. In 1863 he entered the Army and in 1866 joined the Panjab Cavalry; he was assistant adjutant-general of the Panjab Frontier Force in 1875. He served in the Jowaki-Afridi expedition, 1877-78; the Afghan campaign, 1878-79; the Waziri expedition, 1880. He was military secretary, Panjab Government, 1885-86, and colonel on Staff,

374

Chitral, 1896-98. His writings include *Notes on the Bashgali (Kafir) language* (Calcutta, 1902). He died in 1917. Buckland; NUC, pre-1956

Davidson, J(oseph) Leroy, born 16 March 1908 at Cambridge, Mass., he was a Harvard graduate and took a Ph.D. at Yale University. Thereafter he was a professor of Asian art at various American universities. In 1963-64 he participated in an archaeological expedition to India. His writings include *The Lotus Sutra in Chinese art* (1954), and *Art of the Indian subcontinent* (1968); he was editor of *Harper's encyclopedia of art* (1937), and *New standard encyclopedia of art* (1939). He died 18 March 1980. WhoAm, 1980; WhoAmA, 1973, 1978, 1984; Who was who in America, 8

Davidson, Lawrence, born about 1950, he received a Ph.D. in 1976 from the University of Alberta. In 1990, he was a professor of history at West Chester (Pa.) University, a post which he still held in 2003. He was a contributor to *Tributaries of history* (1991). MESA Roster of members, 1990; NatFacDr, 1998-2003

Davidson, Sir Nigel George, C.B.E., born in 1873. After Oxford he was called to the bar from Inner Temple, London, in 1899. He served as counsellor to the High Commissioner for Iraq from 1923 to 1924, and was a legal secretary, Sudan Government, from 1926 to 1930. He died in 1961. Who was who, 6

Davidson, Roderic Hollett, 1916-1996 *see* Davison, Roderic Hollett

Davidson, Thomas, born 25 October 1840 in Scotland. After graduation with honours from the University of Aberdeen in 1860, he taught at various British schools until 1866, when he emigrated first to London, Ontario, Canada, and a year later to the United States. He eventually settled at the East Coast. He was a radical individualist. For several years he took extensive walking tours through Greece during his half-year vacations. He spent most of the period from 1878 to 1884 in Italy. His writings include *The education of the Greek people* (1894), and *History of education* (1900). He died in N.Y.C., 14 September 1900. EncAm; DAB

Davidson-Houston, James Vivian, captain, born 20 November 1901 at Dublin, he was a career officer from the Royal Military Academy, Woolwich, and a military attaché. His writings include *Armed diplomat; a military attaché in Russia* (1959). He died 25 October 1965. ConAu 5

Davies, Christopher Shane, born 8 December 1939 at Bargoed, Wales, he was a graduate of Indiana University where he also received a Ph.D. in 1970 for his thesis, *The reverse commuter transit problem in Indianapolis*. Since 1969 he was a professor of geography at the University of Texas, a position which he still held in 1998. AmM&WS, 1973 S, 1976 P; NatFacDr, 1998

Davies, Cuthbert Collin, born 16 April 1896, he was educated at Aberystwyth and Cambridge, served in the Third Afghan War, 1919, and participated in the operations in Waziristan, 1921-22. He was a lecturer in Indian history at SOAS, and since 1965 reader emeritus in Indian history in the University of Oxford. His writings include *The problem of the North-West Frontier, 1890-1908* (1932), *Warren Hastings and Oudh* (1939), and *An historical atlas of the Indian peninsula* (1949). He died 5 November 1974. Au&Wr, 1971; WhE&EA; Who, 1964-1975; Who was who, 7

Davies, David Hywel, born 30 April 1924 at Ruthin, Wales, he was a lecturer in geography at the University of Baghdad from 1951 to 1954, and later a professor and dean at the University of Rhodesia. His writings include *Land use in central Cape Town* (1965), and *Lousak, Zambia; some town planning problems* (1969). WhoSAfrica, 1986/87, 1987/88, 1988/89, 1989/90

Davies, Harold Richard John, born 4 January 1931 at Liverpool, he received a B.Litt. in 1961 from the University of Oxford for his thesis, *Certain aspects of the economic and social geography of the part of the Sudan between the White and Blue Nile north of the Machar Marshes*. He was a lecturer in geography at the University of Khartoum, 1955 to 1960, as well as University College of Swansea. He specialized in human and historical geography with reference to Africa, especially the problems of development in the arid areas of the continent. His writings include *Tropical Africa; an atlas for rural development* (1973). Sluglett; Unesco

Davies, Philip E., fl. 1979, he was an associate regional director of Safe the Children. Note

Davies, Raymond Arthur, born 15 March 1908 at Montreal, P.Q., he was a correspondent for Canadian journals and the Canadian Broadcasting Corporation. He covered the major events throughout the world, including Iran, Egypt, and North Africa during 1944 and 1945. His writings include the personal recollection, *Odyssey through hell* (1946), as well as *Printed Jewish Canadians, 1685-1900* (1955). Canadian, 1948, 1949

Davies, Reginald, C.M.G., born 17 November 1887. After Cambridge he entered the Sudan Political Service in 1911, and was Resident, Dar Masalit, Anglo-Egytian Sudan, since 1920. He later served in

Egypt until his retirement in 1953. His writings include *The camel's back; service in the rural Sudan* (1957). He died 18 December 1971. Who was who, 7

Davies, Roger Paul, born 7 May 1921 at Berkeley, Calif., he was a graduate of the University of California at Berkeley, and the U.S. Army War College. He joined the U.S. diplomatic service in 1946 and served throughout the Middle East. From 1965 to 1974 he was Deputy Assistant Secretary of State for Near Eastern and South Asian Affairs. He was assassinated in Cyprus and died 19 August 1974. NYT 20 August 1974, p. 1, col. 6-p. 4, col. 5; Who was who in America, 6

Davies, Thomas Witton, born 28 February 1851 at Nantyglo, Montmouthshire, he studied mathematics, classical languages, philosophy, and theology at the Baptist College, Pontypool, from 1872 to 1877. Two years later he received a B.A. degree from the University of London. He served as a pastor in Merthyr Tydfil until the end of 1880, when he was appointed professor of classical languages and Hebrew at the Baptist College, Haverfordwest. Since 1892 he concurrently was a professor of divinity and dean, Midland Baptist College, professor of Old Testament studies, Congregational Institute, and lecturer in Arabic and Syriac, University College, Nottingham. In 1898 he received a Dr.phil degree from the Universität Leipzig for his thesis, *Magic, divination, and demonology among the Hebrews and their neighbours*, a trade edition of which was published in 1910 entitled *"Magic," black and white; charms and counter charms*. He also wrote *Heinrich Ewald, orientalist and theologian, 1803-1903; a centenary appreciation* (1903). LitYbk, 1904-1922; Thesis

Davis, Albert Richard, born 3 February 1924, he was a Sinologist who taught Oriental languages, classical Chinese, and Oriental studies successively at Canberra University and the University of Sydney since 1948. WhoAus, 1971, 1974, 1977, 1980, 1983

Davis, Asa J., fl. 1964, she was attached to the exhibition *"Blueprint for change"* (1995) at the Queens Borough Public Library, Jamaica, N.Y. LC, Name authorities, 1987-96

Davis, Eric M., born 31 March 1946, he was in 1998 a professor of political science at Rutgers University, New Brunswick, N.J. His writings include *Bank Misr and the political economy of industrialization in Egypt, 1920-1941* (1977), and *Challenging colonialism* (1983); he was joint editor of *Statecraft in the Middle East; oil, historical memory and popular culture* (1991). LC; NatFacDr, 1998

Davis, Floyd James, born in 1920, he was in 1960 head of the Department of Sociology, Hamlin University; and in 1980 he was attached to the Department of Anthropology and Social Work, Illinois State University. His writings include *Society and the law* (1962); he was joint editor of *The collective definition of deviance* (1974). LC

Davis, George Washington, born 7 December 1902 at Pittsburgh, Pa., he received a Ph.D. in 1932 from Yale University. He was a clergyman; and from 1938 until his retirement he was a professor of Christian theology at Crozer Theological Seminary, Chester, Pa. His writings include *Existentialism and theology* (1957). He died 13 February 1962. Who was who in America, 4

Davis, James Lindsay Reeve, born 16 June 1936 at Hull, U.K., he settled in Australia in 1968. He was educated at King's College, Auckland, New Zealand, and Cambridge. After five years of lectureship in law at the University of Canterbury, New Zealand, he was appointed reader in law at the Australian National University in 1971, a position which he still held in 1989. WhoAus, 1994-1998

Davis, Sir John Francis, born in 1795, he was an officer of the East India Company and a diplomat who accompanied the embassy of Lord Amherst to China and remained there until 1848. His writings include *Sketches of China* (1841), and *Vizier Ali Khan* (1844). He died in England in 1890. CelCen; DcBiPP; DNB, v. 22; Henze

Davis, John Herbert, born 9 October 1904 at Wellsville, Mo., he was a graduate of Iowa State University and received a Ph.D. in 1950 from the University of Minnesota for his thesis, *An economic analysis of the tax status of farmer cooperatives*. He was an agricultural economist in U.S. government service until 1954, when he was appointed a director at Harvard Graduate School. He was president of the American Middle East Refugee Aid, Inc., from 1968 to 1976. His writings include *The evasive peace; a study of the Zionist-Arab problem* (1968). BioIn 3, 5, 15; IntYB, 1978, 1979, 1980, 1982; Shavit

Davis, Leslie A., born in 1876 at Port Jefferson N.Y., he graduated in 1898 from Cornell University, and also received a degree from George Washington University Law School. After a brief period as a Manhattan lawyer, he began a career in the foreign service of the U.S. State Department in 1912. He was appointed consul at Harput, Turkey, in 1914, where he served until April 1917. He later served at a variety of foreign service posts at Archangel, Helsinki, Oporto, Zagreb, Patras, Lisbon, and Glasgow. His writings include two pamphlets written in 1922 for the U.S. Dept. of Commerce on Finnish economics, and *The Slaughterhouse province* (1989). LC

Davis, Peter Hadland, born 18 June 1918, he was a reader in botany in the University of Edinburgh. His writings include *Flora of Turkey and the Aegean Islands* (1965-67). Who's who of British scientists, 1971/72

Davis, Ralph Henry Carless, born 7 October 1918 at Oxford, he was a medievalist who taught for fourteen years each at Merton College, Oxfod, and the University of Birmingham. His writings include *A history of medieval Europe* (1957), *The medieval warhorse* (1989), and *From Alfred the Great to Stephen* (1991). He was honoured by *Studies in medieval history presented to R. H. C. Davis* (1985). He died 12 March 1991. ConAu 5 rev.; Master (3); Who, 1974-1991; WrDr, 1976-1994/96

Davis, Ronald Wayne, born 23 August 1943 at Cleveland, Ohio, he was a graduate of Bowling Green University, 1964, and received a Ph.D. in 1968 from Indiana University at Bloomington for his thesis, *Historical outline of the Kru Coast, 1500 to the present.* Since 1971 he was a professor of history at Western Michigan University, Kalamazoo, Mich., a position which he still held in 1998. His writings include *Ethnohistorical studies on the Kru Coast* (1976). DrAS, 1974, 1978, 1982; NatFacDr, 1998

Davis, Susan Schaefer, born in 1943, she received a Ph.D. in 1978 from the University of Michigan for her thesis, *Formal and nonformal roles of Moroccan village women.* She was a private scholar and a consultant whose writings include *Patience and power; women's lives in a Moroccan village* (1983). Together with Douglas A. Davis she wrote *Adolescence in a Moroccan town; making social sense* (1987). LC; MESA *Roster of members*, 1990

Davis, Uri, Dr., fl. 1977-1994. He was a vice-chairman of the Israeli League for Human and Civil Rights, and a senior fellow, Centre for Near Eastern and Islamic Studies, University of Durham. His writings include *Utopia incorporated* (1977), *Israel, an apartheid state* (1987), *The state of Palestine* (1991), and with Fawzi al-Asmar, *Towards a socialist republic of Palestine* (1978). Directory of BRISMES members, 1993

Davis, William Morris, born 12 February 1850 at Philadelphia, Pa., he was a professor of geography at Harvard. He had been to Turkestan. His writings include *Physical geography* (1898). He died 5 February 1934. BioIn, 2, 4; Master (14); Who was who in America, 1; Wininger

Davis, William Stearns, born 30 April 1877 at Amherst, Mass. After receiving a Ph.D. from Harvard in 1905, he became a professor of medieval and modern European history at a variety of American universities. His wrings include *A short history of the Near East* (1922). He died 15 February 1930. Master (12); Who was who in America, 1

Davison, Roderic Hollett, born 27 April 1916 at Buffalo, N.Y., he grew up at Robert College, Istanbul, where his father was a teacher. After three years of study in Turkey, he continued in the United States where he received a Ph.D., under the name of R. H. Davidson, from Harvard University in 1942. Since 1954 he held the chair of modern European history with reference to the Middle East at George Washington University. Concurrently he was a visiting professor at Princeton, Johns Hopkins, and Harvard. He had researched in the archives of Istanbul, London, Paris, and Wien. His writings include *Reform in the Ottoman Empire, 1856-1876* (1963), a revised version of his doctoral thesis, *Turkey* (1968), *Turkey, a short history* (1981), and *Essays in Ottoman and Turkish history, 1774-1923* (1990). He died 23 March 1996. DrAS, 1974, 1978, 1982; Master (1); MESA bulletin 30 i (1996), p. 137-141; Private; Turcica 29 (1997), pp. 9-11; WhoAm, 1974-1995

Davletshin, Tamurbek Mukhammedovich, born in 1917, he was a Tatar who remained in Germany after the second World War. His memoirs from 1952 to 1978 are in the Bakhmeteff Archive, Columbia University, N.Y.C. His writings, partly under the pseudonym I. Idelev, include *Cultural life in Tatar Autonomous Republic* (1953), *Советский Татарстан* (1974), and *Tatarisch-deutsches Wörterbuch* (1989). He died before 1992. LC

Davran, Bülent, born 12 September 1912 at Constantinople, he was educated at the İstanbul Alman Lisesi and received a Dr.jur. in 1940 from the Universität Göttingen for his thesis, *Vom islamischen zum türkischen Recht.* He was a professor of law at İstanbul Üniversitesi Hukuk Fakültesi since 1945. His writings include *Mukayseli medeni hukuk dersleri* (1968); he was joint author of *Almanca-Türkiye büyük lûgat = Grosses deutsch-türkisches Wörterbuch* (1944). Schwarz; Türkiye'de kim kimdir, 1977

Davray, Henry D., born 4 or 14 August 1873 at Paris, he was educated at the Sorbonne and the University of London. He was an editor and correspondent, a writer and translator, as well as a lecturer at the universities of Paris and Bruxelles. He was awarded Officier de la Légion d'honneure and C.B.E. He died 21 January 1944. Qui êtes-vous, 1924; WhE&EA; Who was who, 4

Davydov, Aleksandre Davydovich, born 27 July 1928 at Rostov, he was a graduate of the Oriental Institute, Moscow, 1951, and since 1956 attached to the Academy of Science, SSSR. His writings include *Аграрный строй Афганистана* (1967), *Афганистан* (1973), *Сельская община и патронимия в странах Ближнего и Среднего Востока* (1979), *Афганистан; экономика, политика, история* (1984), *Аграрное законодательство Демократической Республики Афганистан* (1984), *Мелкотоварное крестьянское хозяйство в странах Ближнегр и Среднего Востока* (1989), and *Афганистан; войны могло не быть* (1993); and he was ediitor of *Ирригация в странах Ближнего и Среднего Востока* (1985), and *Афганистан; проблемы войны и мира* (1996). LC; Miliband

Dawe, Morley Thomas, O.B.E., born in 1880, he was an agriculturist, and in 1906 an officer in charge of the Botanical, Forestry, and Scientific Department, Uganda, and in 1938 director of Agriculture and Fisheries in Palestine. His writings include *Report on a botanical mission through the forest districts of Buddu and the Western and Nile provinces of the Uganda protectorate* (1906). BritIn (1); Master (1)

Dawisha, Adeed (ibn) Isam, born 2 November 1944 at Baghdad, he was a graduate of Lancaster Universiy and received a Ph.D. in 1975 from LSE for his thesis, *The U.A.R. and the Arab East, 1958-1963*. He was a member of the Department of Politics, Lancaster University, Bailriggs, and a senior research associate at the International Institute for Strategic Studies before being appointed professor at George Mason University, Fairfax, Va. His writings include *Egypt and the Arab world* (1976), *Saudi Arabia's search for security* (1980), its translation, *Saudi-Arabien und seine Sicherheitspolitik* (1980), *Syria and the Lebanese crisis* (1980), *The Arab radicals* (1986); and he was joint editor of *Beyond coercion; the durability of the Arab state* (1988). ConAu, 102, new rev. 18; Sluglett; WrDr, 1982-1990/92

Dawisha, Karen Lea née Hurst, born 2 December 1949 at Colorado Springs, Col., she was a graduate of Lancaster University, Bailriggs, and received a Ph.D. in 1975 from LSE, London for her thesis, *The foundations, structure and dynamics of Soviet policy toward the Arab radical regimes, 1955-1961*. She was a sometime lecturer in politics at the University of Southampton before being appointed in 1985 a professor of government and politics at the University of Maryland, College Park, Md., a post which she still held in 1998. Her writings include *Soviet policy towards Egypt* (1979), and *Eastern Europe, Gorbachev, and reform* (1988). ConAu, 120; NatFacDr. 1998; Sluglett

Dawkins, Clinton Edward, Sir, born in 1859, he was educated at Cheltenham and Balliol College, Oxford, and entered the India Office in 1884. He was Under Secretary of State for Finance in Egypt, 1895, and financial member of the Supreme Council in India, 1899-1900. His writings include the appendix to A. M. Milner, *England in Egypt*, 11th ed. (1904). He was awarded C.B. in 1901 and K.C.B. in 1902. He died 2 December 1905. Buckland; *Who was who*, 1

Dawkins, John McGillivray, fl. 1934-1944, his writings include *Zinc and spelter; notes on the early history of zinc from Babylon to the 18th century* (Oxford, Zinc Development Association, 1950). BLC

Dawkins, Richard McGillivray, born in 1871 at Surbiton, he had entered classics rather later than many of his contemporaries, but won a fellowship at Emmanuel College, Cambridge, and in 1906 he was appointed director of the British School at Athens, a post which he resigned in 1914 when an inheritance gave him financial freedom to pursue his first love, philosophy. He was for many years professor of Byzantine and modern Greek at Oxford. His writings include *Modern Greek in Asia Minor; a study of the dialects* (1916), and *Modern Greek folktales* (1953). He died in Oxford, 4 May 1955. BioIn, 3, 4; ObitT, 1951-60; WhE&EA; *Who was who*, 5

Dawlatābādī, Sadīqah (Dolatabadi, Sadighé), born 1264/1885, she was a director of the Persian journal زنان زبان, and in 1924 visited Paris as a delegate of the Persian committee for the rights of women. He writings include آداب معاشرت زنان (Tihran, 1333/53). She died in 1341/1962. Note; Persian name authority file in Farsi (1367/1997)

Dawlaty, Khairullah, he was in 1971 affiliated with the Faculty of Agriculture, Kabul University, and in 1977 with the Department of Agricultural Economy and Rural Sociology, University of Tennessee. He was joint author of the pamphlet, *Wheat farming in Afghanistan* (1970), and *Underdevelopment in Tennessee* (1977). LC

Dawletschin, Tamurbek, 1917- see Davletshin, Tamurbek Mukhammedovich

Dawn, Clarence *Ernest*, born 6 December 1918 at Chattanooga, Tenn., he received a Ph.D. from Princeton in 1948 for his thesis, *The project of Greater Syria*. He was a professor of history at the University of Illinois since 1949 and concurrently from 1971 to 1975 director of the Tehran Research Unit. From 1981 to 1982 he was a fellow at the Institute of Advanced Studies, Hebrew University, Jerusalem. His writings include *From Ottomanism to Arabism* (1973). DrAS, 1974, 1978, 1982; Selim; WhoAm, 1974-1996; WhoWor, 1974/75

Dawood, Hassan Aly, born in 1917, he received a Ph.D. in 1950 from Michigan State College of Agriculture and Applied Sciences for his thesis, *Economic aspects of land tenure in Egypt.* Selim

Dawson, Alec John, born in 1872 in London. After an apprenticeship in the merchant marine, he travelled extensively throughout the world. He spent much time in Morocco when not in England. He wrote on imperial and colonial interests, particularly Canadian interests. His writings, partly under the pseudonym Howard Kerr, include *Bismillah; a story* (1898), *African nights' entertainment* (1900), its translation, *Marokkanische Geschichten* (1904), and *Things seen in Morocco* (1904). He died in 1951 or 1952. Morgan, 1912; WhE&EA

Day, Florence Ely, fl. 1956, she received a Ph.D. in 1940 from the University of Michiganfor her thesis, *Mesopotamian pottery; Parthian, Sassanian, early Islamic.* Selim

Day, Gerald Wayne, born 6 August 1945 at Springfield, Illinois, he was a 1967 graduate of Illinois State University, and received a Ph.D. in 1978 from the University of Illinois for *Genoese involvement with Byzantium, 1155-1204.* He was appointed professor of history at the University of Miami, Coral Gables, in 1981. His writings include *Genoa's responde to Byzantium, 1155-1204* (1988). DrAS, 1982

Dayton, John E., fl. 1968, his writings include *Minerals, metals, glazing and man* (1978), and *The discovery of glass* (Cambridge, Mass, Peabody Museum of Archaeology and Ethnology, 1993).

D'Costa, A., S.J., fl. 1960 in India, he wrote *The Christianisation of the Goa Islands, 1510-1567* (1965), a work which was originally presented as a doctoral thesis in the Faculty of Church History, Pontificia Università Gregoriana Roma. LC

De, Amalendu. born in 1930, he was in 1978 a professor at the Department of History, Jadavpur University. His writings, mostly in Sankrit, also include *Roots of separatism in nineteenth century Bengal* (1974), and *Islam in modern India* (1982). LC

De Agostini, Enrico, colonel, born in 1878, his writings include *La populazioni della Cirenaica* (Tripoli, 1922), *Notize sulla regione di Cufra* (Bengasi, 1927), *Le prime avanguardie nelle conquista dell'impero* (1937); and the translation from the Arabic, *Santuari islamici nel secolo XVII in Tripolitania* (Tripoli, 1933). NUC, pre-1956

Deambrosis, Delfino, born 8 December 1871 at Firenze, he was a general and a sometime lecturer in geography at the Università di Pisa. His writings include *Geografia militare razionale* (1920-34), *Fondamenti di geografia umana* (1924), and *L'Italia jonico-libica* (1935). Chi è, 1936, 1940, 1948

De Amicis, Edmondo, born 21 October 1846 at Oneglia (Imperia), Italy, he was a writer and editor whose extensive travels supplied him with much material for his stories. He is best known for his *Cuore* (1886), translated as *A boy's life at school* (1901), and also *The heart of a boy* (1912); his other writings include *Marocco* (1876), *Constantinople* (1878), *Morocco; its people and places* (1879). He died in Bordighera on 11 March 1908. DizBl; IndBiltal (6)

Dean, Bashford, born 28 October 1867 at N.Y.C., he received a Ph.D. in 1890 from Columbia University. He was a zoologist who was a sometime curator of arms and armour at the Metropolitan Museum of Art, N.Y.C, where he was instrumental in gathering an assemblage of arms and armour that ranked fourth in importance among such collections. He later became a professor of fines arts at New York University. He wrote several exhibition catalogues. In 1927 appeared *A miscellany of arms and armor, presented to B. Dean.* He died 6 December 1928. DAB; DcNAA; Master (3); NatCAB, vol. 21, p. 29; WhAm, 1

De Andrés Martinez, Gregorio, O.S.A. *see* Andrés Martinez, Gregorio de

Dearden, Ann, fl. 1950. She was resident in Tripolitania from 1947 to 1950, during which time she travelled extensively throughout the Middle East as correspondent for the *Manchester guardian.* Previously she was a diplomatic correspondent on its London staff. Her writings include *Jordan* (1958); she was editor of *Arab women* (1983). Middle East journal, 1950

Dearden, Seton, born in 1905, he spent twenty years in the Middle East, during the war in the army, and afterwards in the foreign service. He was a writer of historical biographies which include *The Arabian knight; a study of Sir Richard Burton* (1936), *and A Nest of corsiars, the fighting Karamanlis of Tripoli* (1973). LC

Deasy, George F., born 20 February 1912 at Cincinnati, Ohio, he received a Ph.D. in geography in 1948, and then served with the U.S. Department of State and the U.S. War Department until 1950 when he was appointed a professor of geography at Penn State University. His writings include *A Geographic study of Manchurian agriculture* (1936); and he was joint author of *Atlas of world affairs* (1946). AmM&WS, 1973, 1976

Deasy, Henry Hugh Peter born in 1866 at Dublin, he was educated at Bournemouth and Dublin. After eleven years' service in the British Army, he retired with the rank of major to explore Central Asia. He received the Founders' Gold Medal from the Royal Geographical Society for exploring and survey work in Central Asia for nearly three years. He also set a record in motoring by driving 450 miles in twenty-one hours. He wrote *In Tibet and Chinese Turkestan* (1901). Buckland; Henze; WhE&EA

De Baer, Oliver Rudston. He was educated at Harrow, where he was later head of the School. After his National Service he obtained an open scholarship at Trinity College, Cambridge, where he afterwards taught. With the moral support of the Royal Central Asian Society he and some friends of his at the University of Cambridge set out on an Afghanistan expedition in 1955, which he descibed in *Afghan interlude* (London, 1957). Journal of the Royal Central Asian Society, 1956

Debanne, Odilon, born 19th cent., he received a diploma in Arabic and was a sometime inspector of education in Algeria, a post from which he had retired in 1938. He was a member of the Commission administrative of the Société de géographie et d'études coloniales, Marseille. Note

Debarnot, Marie Thérèse, born 20th cent., she received a doctorate in 1980 from the Université de Paris IV, for her thesis, *Les clefs d'astronomie d'Abou al-Rayhan M. b. A. al-Biruni*. Her writings include *La trigono-métrie sphérique chez les arabes de l'est à la fin du Xe siècle*; texte établi et traduit d'al-Biruni (1985). LC; THESAM 4

Debatin, Helmut Felix, born 26 September 1926 at Konstanz, Germany, he studied law at the Universität Freiburg im Freisgau, where he received a Dr.jur. in 1951 for his thesis, *Die dogmatische Auslegung des §145 des Strafgesetzbuches*. He served for many years at the German Internal Revenue Service, Bonn. In 1974 he became assistant secretary-general, Controller, Office of Financial Service at the United Nations in NYC. He was joint author of *Handbook on the United States-German tax convention* (1966). Wer ist wer 21 (1981); WhoUN, 1975

Debbasch, Charles, born 22 October 1937 at Tunis, he received a doctorate in 1961 from the Université d'Aix-Marseille for his thesis, *Procédure administrative contentieuse et procédure civile*. Except for the academic year 1962/63 spent at Grenoble, he was a professor of law, and later dean, Faculté de droit, at the Université d'Aix-Marseille. In 1989 he was honorary president of the university. His writings include *La République tunisienne* (1962); he was joint author of *La Tunisie* (1973), and *La société française* (1989). IntWW, 1982-1998/99; WhoFr, 1975/76-1997/98

Debets (Дебец), Georgii Frantsevich, born in 1905 at Tomsk, Russia, he was an anthropologist whose writings include Антропологические исследования в Афганистане (1965), and its translation, *Physical anthropology of Afghanistan* (1970). He died in Moscow, 19 January 1969. GSE; Kazak SE

De Bode, Clement Augustus Gregory Peter Louis, Baron, fl. 1845 see Bode, Clement A. G. P. L..

Debon, Alfred Adrien, fl. 1912, his writings include *Faut-il transformer l'armée française* (1911), and *Notre parlementarisme et la défense nationale en 1914* (1915). NUC, pre-1956

De Borchgrave, Arnaud, born 26 October 1926 at Bruxelles, he was an editor, author, and lecturer. Since 1951 he was senior editor and chief foreign correspondent of *Newsweek*, New York. He was joint author of *The spike* (1980). ConAu, 13; IntAu&Wr, 1989; Master (1); WhoAm, 1974-1998; WhoE, 1986-1997/98; WhoWor, 1976-1998

Déborde de Montcorin, Emmanuel, born 1 July 1858 at Paris. After he took a law degree at Paris, he entered the Ministère D'Instruction publique, a post which he resigned in 1918. Thereafter he was a keeper at the Musée Maisons-Laffitte. His writings include *Premier écho; recueil de poésies, 1884-1888* (1888). He died in Moret-sur-Loing (Seine-et-Marne), 11 December 1941. DBF

De Bosset, Charles Philip, his writings include *Proceedings in Parga and the Ionian Islands* (1819), and *Parga and the Ionian Islands* (1821). NUC, pre-1956

De Brauw-Hay, Elizabeth A., she received a law degree from the University of Glasgow and was a member of a research team of the International Bureau of Fiscal Documentation, Amsterdam. She was joint editor of *Income taxation in eastern Africa* (1980). LC

Debré, François, fl. 1969, his writings include *Biafra, au II* (1968), *Cambodge; la révolution de la forêt* (1976), *Les Chinois de la diaspora* (1976), *Le livre des égarés* (1979), and *Les fêtes d'automne* (1981). LC

Debré, Michel Jean Pierre, born 15 January 1912 at Paris, he was educated at the Lycée Louis-le-Grand and the Faculté de droit de Paris. He was prime minister of France from 1959 to 1962. His writings include *L'Artisanat, classe sociale* (1934), and *La République et ses problèmes* (1952). He died 2 August 1996. IntWW, 1974-1994/95; Master (7); Who, 1974-1997; WhoEIO, 1982; WhoFr, 1953/54-1995/96; WhoWor, 1974-78

De Bruijn, J. T. P., 1931- *see* Bruijn, Johannes Thomas Pieter de

Dębski, Bronisław Anton, born 26 June 1874 at his family's estate Przybojewo near Zakroczym, Russian Poland, he was educated privately and at Warszawa. He studied botany, zoology, physics and chemistry at Universytet Jagielloński, Kraków, from 1892 to 1893 when he changed to the Universität Bonn where he received a Dr.phil. in 1899 with a thesis entitled *Weitere Beobachtungen an Chara fragilis Desv.* Unable to accept a post at his alma mater, he spent some time in Egypt. He died in 1927. Dziekan; PSB; Thesis

De Bunsen, Sir Maurice William Ernest, born 8 January 1832 at London, he was educated at Rugby and Christ Church, Oxford, and entered the diplomatic service in 1877. He was the unofficial mediator in the Franco-Spanish dispute, 1911-1912. He died 21 February 1932. DNB; *Who was who*, 3

De Bunsen, Victoria Alexandrina née Buxton, born in 1874, her writings include *The Soul of a Turk* (1910), *Old and new in the countryside* (1920), and *Charles Roden Buxton* (1948). LC

Deburaux, Édouard Léopold Joseph, born in 1864, his writings, partly under the pseudonym Léo Dex, include *Voyages aériens au long cours* (1894), *Au Pays des Touaregs* (1901), and *Du Tchad au Dahomey en ballon* (1903). He died in 1904. LC

Debus, Allen George, born 16 August 1926 at Chicago, he was a professor of history of sciences and medicine at the University of Chicago. His writings include *The English Paracelsians* (1966), and *Science and education in the seventeenth century* (1970). AmM&WS, 1986-1998/99 P; ConAu, 37, new rev. 14; DrAS, 1974, 1978, 1982; IntAu&Wr, 1977-1989; Master (2); WhoAm, 1974-1998; WrDr, 1980-1998/2000

De Candole, Eric Armar Vully, born 14 September 1901. After Oxford he joined the Sudan Political Service in 1923 and served the first four years at Gordon College, Khartoum; he remained in the Sudan until 1946, when he was seconded to Cyrenaica. In the mid-fifties he was with the Kuwait Oil Company in charge of external affairs. His writings include *The Life and times of King Idris of Libya* (1990); an Arabic translation was published the year previously. He died 7 July 1989. Who, 1982-1988; *Who was who*, 8

De Cardi, Beatrice Eileen, she was born 5 June 1914. After working for the British Government, she was active in archaeological research in the area between Pakistan and the Persian Gulf since 1948. Upon retirement in 1973 she was awarded OBE. She was also a recipient of the Richard Burton Medal of the Royal Asiatic Society in 1993. She continued her archaeological research well into retirement. Her writings include *Excavations at Bampur, 1966* (1970), *Qatar archaeological report; excavations, 1973* (1978), and *Archaeological surveys in Baluchistan, 1948 and 1957* (1983). Who, 1979-1998

Decei, Aurel, born in 1905 at Gura Râului, Romania, he was an orientalist and a senior research fellow at the N. Iorga Institute for History, Bucureşti. His writings include *Istoria Imperialui otoman pînă la 1656* (1978), and *Relaţii româno-orientale* (1978). He died 24 April 1976. I.I. (2); WhoRom

Déchaud, Ed., born 19th cent., he was a secretary of the Chambre de commerce d'Oran, Algeria, 1905-1908. His writings include *Le commerce algéro-marocain* (Alger, 1906), *Oran, son port, son commerce* (Oran, Chambre de Commerce, 1914), and *Lyautey* (Rabat, 1942). BN; NUC, pre-1956

Decheix, Pierre Jean, born 29 March 1927 at Paris, he received a doctorate in law, and was a some-time secretary-general of l'Institut international de droit des pays d'expression française. He served as a magistrate in Cameroon, 1957-61, and in Mali, 1961-62. WhoFr, 1993/94-1997/98

Déchy, Mór (Moritz von), born 4 November 1851 at Budapest. Although he explored the Himalayas, he is best remembered for his seven expeditions to the Caucasus from 1884 to 1902, which he described in his three-volume work, *Kaukasus; Reisen und Forschungen* (1905-1907). He also wrote *Kaukázus; kutatásaim és élményeim a Kaukazusi havasokban* (1907). He died in Budapest, 8 February 1917. Embacher; Henze; Meyers; Pallas; RNL; UjMagyar

De Cillis, Ugo, fl. 1928-1942, his writings include *Relazione sull'attivita'[della] stazione sperimentale di granicoltura Benito Mussolini per la Sicilia* (1931-32). Firenze; IndBI (1)

von der **Decken**, Klaus, born in 1934 at Berlin, he studied geography, political science, and geology at the universities of Hamburg, Innsbruck, and Freiburg im Breisgau, where he received a doctorate in 1969 for his thesis, *Thailands Seefischerei.* In the same year he became a member of the Südasien-Institut, Heidelberg, as a researcher. LC

Decle, Lionel, 1859-1907, his writings include *Three years in savage Africa* (1898), *Trooper 3809, a private soldier of the third republic* (1899), and *The new Russia* (1906). LC

Decleva, Enrico, born 18 April 1941, he was in 1980 a professor of history at the Università di Milano. His writings include *Da Adua a Sarajevo* (1971), *L'Italia e la politica internazionale dal 1870 al 1914* (1974), and *Etica del lavoro, socialismo, cultura populare; Augusto Osimo* (1985). WhoItaly, 1980

Décobert, Christian, born 20th cent., he received a doctorate in 1977 from the Université de Paris III for his thesis, *Phonologie comparée de trois parlers arabes du Tchad*. In 1987 he was attached to the C.N.R.S., Paris. His writings include *Phonologies arabes du Tchad* (1985); and he was joint author of *Linteaux à épigraphes de l'oasis de Dakhla* (1981). LC; THESAM 4

Decorse, Gaston *Jules*, born 10 October 1873 at Saint-Maurice (Seine). After completing his medical studies at Paris in 1898, he went with the French army to Madagascar as a military physician. In 1902 he participated in the Mission Chari - Lac Tchad, in the course of which he travelled over seven thousand miles in largely unexplored territory, a journey which he described in *Géographie médicale; Chari et lac Tchad* (1905), and *Du Congo au lac Tchad* (1906). He was later involved in a feasibility study of ostrich farming in southern Tunisia. He was joint author of *Rabah et les Arabes du Chari* (1905). He died in Paris, 26 August 1907. DBF

De Cosson, Emilius Albert, 1850-1889, he was a British officer who, in 1873, travelled from Masawa by way of Aduwa to Gondar and on via Gallabat and Gedaref to Khartoum, Berber, and Suakin, a journey which he described in *The Cradle of the Blue Nile* (1877). He was on the commissariat and transport staff of the British Army at Suakin in 1885. He wrote of his war experiences in *Days and nights of service with Sir Gerald Graham's Field Force at Suakin* (1886). Hill

Decottignies, Roger Edmond Eugène, born 11 April 1923 at Fourmies (Nord), he received a doctorate in law in 1949 from l'Université de Lille. He was a professor of law at Paris, and a dean, Faculté de droit et des sciences économiques, Université de Dakar. His writings include *Les Présomptions en droit privé* (1950); and he was joint author of *Les Nationalités africaines* (1963). Unesco; *Who's who in France*, 1961/62-1993/94

Decour, Humbert, born 1882, he received a medical doctorate in 1907 from l'Université de Lille. In 1931 he was a *médecin commandant* and attached to the Service des affaires indigènes, Résidence général de France à Tunis. He was author of the pamphlet *Notice sur le service médical dans les territoires militaires du sud* (Bourg, 1931). He was still active in 1953. NUC, pre-1956

Decourdemanche, Jean Adolphe (*see also* Osman Bey), born in 1844 at Paris, he was a member of the Société asiatique and the Société philologique. He was a sometime financial director of the journal *le Globe*. He bequeathed his interesting collection of Islamic coins to the Cabinet des Médailles. His writings include *Fables turques* (1882). He died in Paris in 1914, 1915 or 1916. BN, DBF; *Grande Larousse encyclopédique* (1960-69); LC; *Revue numismatique*, 4e série, t. 20 (1916), pp. 123-124

Decraene, Philippe Michel René, born 5 October 1930, he was an editorial writer in charge of Black African affairs, *le Monde*, since 1958. His writings include *Tableau des parties politiques de l'Afrique au sud du Sahara* (1963), *Le panafricanisme* (1970), *Lettres de l'Afrique atlantique* (1975), and *L'expérience socialiste somalienne* (1977). WhoWor, 1971/72, 1974/75

Decroux, Paul, born 9 June 1904 at Reignier (Hautes-Savoie), he received a doctorate in law in 1931 from the Université de Lyon with a thesis entitled *La vie municipale au Maroc*. He was successively attached to the Institut des hautes études d'administration musulmane, Paris, Institut des hautes études marocaines, Rabat, and the Faculté de droit, Dakar. His writings include *Les Sociétés au Maroc* (1950), *L'Autonomie de la volonté et l'ordre public en droit conventionnel marocain* (1952), *De l'application des lois nationales au Maroc* (1955), and *Le Droit des sociétés dans le Maroc moderne* (1961). He died 18 October 1989. Unesco; WhoFr, 1969-1989/90; WhoWor, 1978/79

Décsy, Gyula Jozsef, born 19 March 1925 at Negyed, Hungary, he received a doctorate in letters from Budapest University. He was a lecturer in Hungarian in Germany until 1977, when he was appointed a professor of Uralic and Altaic studies in Indiana University at Bloomington. His writings include *Einführung in die finnisch-ugrische Spachwissenschaft* (1965), *Yurak chrestomathy* (1966), and *Die linguistische Struktur Europas* (1973); all of them are listed in *Gyula Décsy Bibliographie, 1947-1975* (Wiesbaden, 1975). DrAS, 1978, 1982; Kürschner, 1966, 1970, 1976; MagyarNKK, 1990, 1992

Dedering, Sven Emanuel, born 10 December 1897 at Nyköping, Sweden, he received a doctorate in 1927 with a thesis entitled *Aus dem Kitab Fath al-bab fi-l-kuna wa-l-alkab*. He was a professor of Arabic at Uppsala Universitet. His writings include *Ein Dialog über die Seele und die Affekte des*

Menschen (1936), and *Die Widerlegung der Irrgläubigen und Neuerer*, von M. b. A. al-Malati (1936). He died 23 September 1986. Vem är det, 1941-1987

Deeb, Marius K., born 15 December 1941 at Jaffa, he received a Ph.D. in 1971 from Oxford with a thesis entitled *The Wafd and its rivals*. Thereafter he was for a number of years a professor of political science at Kent State University, Ohio. In 1979 he was a visiting professor at Princeton. His writings include *Party politics in Egypt* (1979), *The Lebanese civil war* (1980); and he was joint author of *Libya since the revolution* (1982). IWWAS, 1976/77; Sluglett

Deedes, Sir Wyndham Henry, born 10 March 1883. After Eton he joined the British Army. On account of his acquaintance with Turkish, which he had learned in Malta, he was seconded for employment with the Turkish gendarmerie. He later was responsible for relief and settlement of refugees at Smyrna, and served as military attaché at Constantinople, 1918-19. As a supporter of Zionism, he was appointed first Chief Secretary to the Palestine Government in 1920. His writings include *A Few facts about Turkey* (1945). John Presland wrote a biography, *Deedes Bey* (1942). The Anglo-Israel Association published *Memories of Sir Wyndham Deedes* in 1958. Bioln, 4, 5, 10; DNB; Who, 1929-1956; Who was who, 5

Deér, József, born 4 March 1905 at Budapest, he was a professor of medieval history and taught successively at the universities of Szeged, Budapest, Bern, and Wien. His writings include *Heidnisches und Christliches in der altungarischen Monarchie* (1934), *L'evoluzione dell'idea dello stato ungherese* (1941), *Papsttum und Normannen* (1972), and he edited *Magyarok és románok* (1943-1944). He died in 1972. AkKisL; Kürschner, 1954, 1961, 1966; LC

Dees, Joseph L., fl. 1959, he served as an instructor at the Collège de garçons in Sétif, Algeria, from 1936 to 1937. In the summer of 1956 he was a student at AUB. Note

Deeva, Evgeniia Aleksandrovna, fl. 1962, she was joint author of Памятники революционной славы Ташкента (1969), and a contributing author to Революция 1905-1907 гг. в Узбекистане (1984). LC

Deflers, Albert, born 16 October 1841 at Doullens (Somme), he was a botanist with relations in Egypt, where he spent many a winter making an inventory of the plants along the Nile in the early 1880s. In the service of the French Ministère de l'Instruction publique he went on a botanical mission to Arabia in 1887, visiting Aden, Hadhramaut, and southern Arabia, travels which he described in *Voyage au Yémen, journal d'une excursion botanique faite en 1887 dans les montagnes de l'Arabie heureuse* (1889). He also wrote *L'exploration scientifique de lÉgypte sous le règne de Mohammed Ali* (1896). He died 4 October 1921. DBF

De Forest, Henry Albert, 1814-1858, he was a medical missionary in Syria, 1842-1854. Shavit

Defrance, Ph., fl. 1957, he was a sometime head of the Service de la Défence des végétaux, Maroc.

Defrates, John Francis, born 19 April 1923 at London, he was educated at Oxford and since 1953 attached to a variety of United Nations' organizations. In 1971 he was appointed director of Public Information and Contributions Office of the U.N. Relief and Works Agency for Palestine Refugees in Beirut. WhoUN, 1975

Defrémery, Charles François, born 8 December 1822 at Cambrai (Nord), he was educated at the Lycée Louis-le-Grand, l'École des langues orientales, and Collège de France, Paris, and was a student of Caussin de Perceval and É. Quatremère. He became a specialist in Islamic history and geography, and succeeded St. Guyard at the Collège de France. His writings, most of which appeared in *Journal asiatique*, include *Recherches sur le règne de Barkiarok, sultan seldjoukide* (1853). He was joint editor and translator of Ibn Batutatah's *Voyages* (1848-1858). He died 19 August 1883. CelCen; DBF; Egyptology; Enclran; Fück, p. 202; Journal asiatique 8e série, 4 (1884), pp. 27-29

De Gaury, Gerald Simpson Hillairet Rutland Vere, born of Huguenot extraction on 1 April 1897 at London, he joined the Hampshire Regiment from the Oxford University Officers' Training Corps in August 1914. He fought on the Somme and at Gallipoli, where he was wounded. While convalescing he took up the study of Arabic. This led to his secondment from the regular army for employment with the Iraq Levies in 1923. Thereafter, his career as a soldier-diplomat was in the Middle East, where he travelled extensively. He was on friendly terms with the royal Iraqi family as well as with King Ibn Saud. He served as a diplomat in Jeddah, Tehran, Baghdad, Damascus, and Cairo. In retirement after a period at the Foreign Office, he became a writer whose works include *Arabian journey and other desert travels* (1950), *Rulers of Mecca* (1951), *The new state of Israel* (1952), and *Faisal, King of Saudi Arabia* (1966). He died on 12 January 1984 at his home in Brighton, where he had lived for the last twenty years of his life. Asian affairs 15 (1984), pp. 227-228; ConAu, 13 rev.; ConAu 112, 73 new rev.; Facey Grant; Master (2); WrDr, 1976/78-1984/86

Degen, Kurt H., born 16 July 1904 at Berlin, he received a Dr.phil. in 1931 from the Universität Würzburg for his thesis, *Die Bamberger Malerei des 15. Jahrhunderts*. He was a keeper at museums successively in Dresden, Bautzen, Breslau, and Gera. His writings include *Die Bau- und Kunstdenkmäler des Landkreises Breslau* (1965). Kürschner, 1940/41, 1950

Degen, Rainer, fl. 1974, he was a professor of Semitic philology at München. His writings include the revision of his 1967 Marburg thesis, *Altaramäische Grammatik der Inschriften des 10.-8. Jh. v. Chr.* (1969); and he was joint author of *Neue Ephemeris für semitische Epigraphik* (1972). Kürschner, 1987-2003; Schwarz

Degener, Albert, born 29 March 1899 at Bernburg, Germany, he studied economics at Halle, Greifswald, and Praha, and received a Dr.jur. in 1923 from the Universität Greifswald for his thesis, *Die Siedlungsbestrebungen der Anhaltinischen Staatsregierung*. He served with the German Chamber of Commerce in Wien, 1925-27, New York, 1928-41, Athens, 1942-44, and Amsterdam, 1944-45. From 1952 to his retirement in 1969, he was a secretary-general of the German-Arab Chamber of Commerce in Egypt. His writings include *American firms dealing with Germany* (1933); and he was editor of the *German-American commerce bulletin* (1961-). He died in München, 30 October 1969. LC; *Der Orient* 10 (1969), p. 38

Degener, Volker W., born 12 June 1941 at Berlin, he was a writer whose works include *Kehrseiten und andere Ansichten* (1973), and *Heimsuchungen; Roman* (1975). KDtLK, 1984; Wer ist wer, 1985, 1986

Degert, Antoine, born 9 December 1859 at Téthien (Landes), he was ordained priest in 1885. After obtaining a degree from l'Institut catholique de Toulouse, he taught at the Collège libre de Dax since 1887. In 1894 he received two doctorates from the Faculté des lettres de Bordeaux for his theses, *Le cardinal d'Ossat, evêque de Rennes et de Bayeux*, and *Quid ad mores ingeniaque Afrorum cognoscenda conferant sancti Augustini sermones*. In 1899 he was appointed professor at l'Institut catholique de Toulouse; he became dean of the Faculté des lettres de Toulouse in 1902. His writings on Church history include *Histoire des séminaires français jusqu'à la révolution* (1912). After his retirement in 1926 he lived at his native village, where he died 7 March 1931. DBF

Dégez, Albert, fl. 1961, he was a town planner and conservationist whose writings include *Restaurer en Bretagne* (1978). LC

De Giorgi, Luigi, fl. 1965, his writings include *Culto gemelli nel Sudan meridionale* (Bologna, 1964). LC

De Golyer, Everette Lee, born 9 October 1886 at Greensburg, Kan., he was a 1911 graduate of the University of Texas, a petroleum geologist, and a collector of books on the history of science and technology. His library, although originally promised to the University of Oklahoma, was deposited at Southern Methodist University. His writings include *Bibliography on the petroleum industry* (1953). The University of Oklahoma published a handlist of the *E. De Golyer Collection in the history of science and technology* (1953). He died in Dallas, Texas, 14 December 1956. BioIn, 2, 4, 5, 6, 9; DcAmBC; Master (5); NatCAB, vol. 43, pp. 12-14

Degouy, Jean Baptiste Charles *Robert* Mathieu, rear-admiral, born 16 May 1852 at Toulouse, he was a graduate of l'École navale. In 1881 he participated in the campaigns against Tunisia, particularly in the conquests of Sfax and Gabès. He later was a distinguished writer on naval matters. His writings include *La Guerre navale et l'offensive* (1917). He died in Étretat, 9 August 1942. DBF

Degré, Gerard L, born 21 January 1915 at Havanna, he received a Ph.D. in 1943 from Columbia University for his thesis, *Society and ideology*. In 1968 he was appointed a professor of sociology at the University of Waterloo, Ontario. His writings include the pamphlets, *Science as a social institution* (1955), and *Realignments of class consciousness in the military and bourgeoisie in developing countries: Egypt, Peru and Cuba* (1970). AmM&WS, 1973 S, 1978 S; LC

De Gregorio, Giacomo, 1856-1936 *see improper entry under* Gregorio, Giacomo de

De Groot, Joanna, born 13 September 1947, she was in 1993 a lecturer in history in the University of York. Her writings include *Women's studies in the 1990s* (1993). LC

Degurov, Anton Antonovich, 1766-1849 *see* Du Gour, Antoine Jeudy

Dehaussy, Jacques, born 7 April 1924 at Aigurande (Indre), he received a doctorate in law from the Université de Paris, and became a professor of public as well and international public law successively at Paris, and Dijon, where he was also *doyen* of the Faculté de droit et des sciences économiques. WhoFr, 1963/64-1995/96

Dehée, René, born in 1898 at Raismes (Nord), he studied literature, history, and geography at the Université de Lille, and later served with the French army in North Africa. He died on military service in 1928 in Togo. Note

Dehérain, Henri, born 31 March 1867 at Paris, he received a doctorate in 1897 from the Université de Paris for his thesis, *Le Soudan égyptien sous Mehmet Ali*. He was a geographer and historian, but basically a library man. Although he visited Egypt in quest of material for his thesis, he became a deputy librarian at the Bibliothèque de l'Institut de France in 1899, and remained there until he retired in 1934 with the position of keeper. From 1903 until his death in 1941, he was attached in various capacities to the *Journal des savants*. His writings include *Figures colonials françaises et étrangères* (1931). Hommes et destins, vol. 2, pp. 253-254; Qui êtes-vous, 1924

Dehn, Paul, born 9 August 1848 at Berlin, he was a bookseller and a writer on political and social matters. His writings include *Deutschland und die Orientbahnen* (1883), *Deutschland und Orient in ihren wirtschaftlichen Beziehungen* (1884), and *Die Völker Südosteuropas und ihre politischen Probleme* (1909). He died in 1938. DtBilnd (2); KDtLK, 1910-1939; Wer ist's, 1912, 1922, 1928, 1935

Dehqani-Taft, Hassan Barnaba, born 14 May 1920 at Yazd, Persia, he was ordained Anglican priest in 1950. He served in Iran until 1976, and thereafter in Jerusalem; since 1982 he was an assistant bishop of Winchester. His writings include and *Design of my world* (1959), and *The Hard awakening* (1981), as well as works in Persian. ConAu, 106; Who, 1983-1998

Dei Gaslini, Mario, born 31 October 1893 at Paderno Dugnano, Italy, he was a journalist, writer, and lecturer whose writings include *Piccolo amore Beduino* (1926), *Paradiso nell'inferno; usi e costumi abissini* (1937), *L'Italia sul Mar rosso* (1938), *Morgane nel deserto* (1938), and *L'ora X degli arabi* (1956). Casati; Chi è, 1931, 1936, 1940

Deighton, Herbert Stanley, fl. 1942-1968, he was a sometime professor of history at Cairo University. He delivered the British Council winter lecture series, 1942/43 and 1943/44 at the Jerusalem Y.M.C.A. He was the general editor of *The Oxford introduction to British history* (1951). BLC; LC

Deimler, Rev. J. G., fl. 1872, he was joint translator of Rudolf Fr. Gau, *The Goal of the human race, or the Development of civilisation* (London, 1892). BLC

Deinhardstein, Johann Ludwig, 1794-1859, he was a playwright, a deputy-director of the Wiener Burgtheater, a professor of aesthetics at the Universität Wien, official censor of books, and from 1818 to 1849 an editior of *Jahrbücher der Literatur*. DtBE; DtBilnd (10); ÖBL; OxGer

Dei Sabelli, Luca, fl. 1929-1966, his writings include *Nazioni e minoranze etniche* (1929), *Storia di Abissinia* (1936-38), and *Il controllo sui traffici marittimi e l'Italia* (1940). Firenze; NUC, pre-1956

Déjeux, Jean, born in 1921 at Albi (Tarn), he entered the Grand séminaire tunisien des Pères blancs in 1942, was mobilized the following year, and ordained priest at Carthage in 1952. He spent more than twenty years in Algeria, followed by some years in Tunisia. He did not settle for good in Paris until 1981. He was a specialist on Francophone writing of North Africa; French universities from Yaoundé to Sherbrooke, Québec, considered it an honour to have him lecture. His writings include *Littérature maghrébine de langue française* (1973), *La Littérature algérienne contemporaine* (1975), *Djoh'a; héros de la tradition orale arabo-berbère* (1978), and *Le Sentiment religieux dans la littérature maghrébine de langue française* (1986). He died of a heart attack on the métro station Saint-Germain-des-Près, 17 October 1993. Cahiers d'études maghrébines 6/7 (1994), p. 284

Dekmejian, Richard Hrair, born 3 August 1933 at Aleppo, he was a graduate of the University of Connecticut, and received his Ph.D. in 1966 from Columbia University for his thesis, *The dynamics of the Egyptian political system*. Thereafter he was a professor of political science at SUNY, Binghampton, from 1964 until his retirement. His writings include *Egypt under Nasir* (1971), *Patterns of political leadership* (1975), and *Islam in revolution; fundamentalism in the Arab world* (1995). IWWAS, 1975/76

De La Bère, Rupert, captain, born in 1887, he was in 1924 a professor at the Royal Air Force Cadel College, Cranwell, Lincs. His writings include *A history of the Royal Air Force College, Cranwell* (1954). LC

Delaborde, Léon Emmanuel Simon Joseph, 1807-1869 *see* Laborde, *Léon Emmanuel Simon J. de*

Delaby, Laurence, fl. 1975. His writings include *Chamanes toungouses* (1977). LC

De la Costa, Horacio Luís, born 9 May 1916 at Mauban, Philippines, he graduated in 1935 from Ateneo de Manila. In the same year, he entered the Society of Jesus and later, as a professor, taught at his alma mater, where he specialized in history of the Roman Catholic Church in the Philippines. He was ordained at Woodstock College, Md., in 1946 and received a doctorate in 1951 from Harvard for his thesis, *Jurisdictional conflicts in the Philippines during the XVI and XVII centuries*. His writings include *The Jesuits in the Philippines* (1961), *Asia and the Philippines* (1967), and *Challenges for the Filipino* (1971). He died in Manila in 1977. Catholic historical review 63 (July 1977), pp. 497-498; Master (2)

Deladrière, Roger, he received a doctorate in 1974 from the Université de Paris IV for *La profession de fois d'Ibn Arabi*, and became a professor of Islamic philosophy and civilization. His writings include the translations from the Arabic, *Le Tabernacle des lumières* (1981), *Traité de soufisme; les maîtres et lea étapes* (1981), and *Enseignement spirituel; traités, oraisons et sentences* (1983). LC; THESAM 4

Delafosse, Ernest François *Maurice*, born 20 December 1870 at Sancergues (Cher) he enrolled in 1890 at l'École des langues orientales vivantes, Paris, where he studied not only Arabic, but also pursued studies in African languages. In 1894 he published a *Manuel dahoméen*. In the same year, he entered the Corps des affaires indigènes in the Ivory Coast. He remained an administrator in French West Africa until his retirement in 1919, interrupted by teaching spells in Paris and explorations in the French Sudan. Back in Paris, he taught at his alma mater and l'École coloniale. In 1920 he was the founding editor of *Revue d'ethnographie et des traditions populaires*. His writings include *Les Noirs de l'Afrique* (1922); with his father-in-law, Octave Houdas, he edited and translated from the Arabic *Tarikh el fettach, ou Chronique du chercheur* (1913). He died 23 November 1926. DBF #9; Hommes et destins, vol. 1, pp. 181-187

Delafosse, Jules Victor, born 2 March 1843 at Pontfarcy (Calvados). After completing his studies at Paris, he made several journeys in Europe. Since 1870 he was an editor, a founder of journals, and active in politics. His writings include *Vingt ans au parlement* (1899), *Théorie de l'ordre* (1901), *France au dehors* (1908), and *Contre l'Allemagne; France et Maroc* (1911). He died 1 February 1916. DBF, #7; Curinier, vol. 5 (1906), p. 3-4; IndexBFr² (9)

Delage, Pierre Alexis *Émile*, born 16 March 1855 at Angoulême. Early in life he had to work for a living at a variety of trades. In the mid-1820s he began to write for French journals. This gave him the chance to travel to Algeria and Spain, where he established commercial connections which he pursued with changing fortune since 1885. He died about 1910 DBF #3; Curinier, vol. 3 (1901), p. 15

Delaissé, Léon M. J. His writings on medieval illuminated manuscripts include *De gouden eeuw der Vlaamse miniatuur* (1959), *La miniature flamande* (1959), *A century of Dutch manuscript illumination* (1968), and he was joint author of *Illuminated manuscripts* (1977). He died in January 1972. LC

De Lancey Forth, Nowell Barnard, born in 1879, he joined the British Army and advanced through the grades to become lieutenant-colonel. He served in the Egyptian Army from 1907 to 1916 in Kordofan, Palestine, and on the Egyptian-Cyrenaican border. He died in 1933. Who was who, 3

Delanoue, Gilbert, born 20th cent., he received a doctorate in 1977 from the Université de Paris IV for his thesis, *Moralistes et politiques musulmans dans l'Egypte du XIXème siècle*. He was editor of *Les Intellectuels et la pouvoir; Syrie, Égypte, Tunisie, Algérie* (1986). LC; THESAM 3

Delaporte, J. Honorat, fl. 1816-1846, his writings include *Abrégé chronologique de l'histoire des Mamlouks d'Égypte* (1816), *Fables de Loqmân, adaptées à l'idiom arabe en usage dans la régence d'Alger* (1835), *Principes de l'idiom arabe en usage à l'Alger* (1836), and *Guide de la conversation français-arabe*, 2e éd. (1841). BN; NUC, pre-1956

De Laporte, Jacques Denis, born 14 April 1777 at Paris, he was educated at the École des langues orientales, Paris. He was attached to the Napoleonic expedition as interpreter. Afterwards he was employed in the Ministry of Foreign Affairs and successively consul in Tripoli en Barbarie, Algiers, Mogador and Meknès. He returned to France in 1841 and died in Paris, 28 January 1861. His writings include *Dictionnaire français-berbère* (1844), *Spécimen de la langue berbère* (1844). DBF; Féraud, pp. 195-199

Delaporte, René Edgard, born 7 January 1876 at Blidah, Algeria, he received a classical education in Algeria and then went to Paris. In 1894, he enrolled at l'École des hautes études commerciales. After graduation, he pursued a literary interest and published collections of poetry, *Fleurs fanées*, in 1895, and *Étoiles filantes*, in 1897. During those years he also travelled to Ceylon and Singapore where he studied the economic conditions and gathered information for the advancement of French economic interests. On his return voyage he made a six-month stop over in Egypt and brought back with him material for the book *Dans la Haute-Égypte* (1898), a work in which he described both the monuments from the past as well as the contemporary economic resources. Shortly thereafter he visited Palestine, Syria, Greece, the European parts of Turkey, and Central Europe. Upon his return to Paris in 1899, he was appointed a professor of business administration at l'École commerciale of the Paris Chamber of Commerce, and at the Institut commercial. He later was an examiner at l'École des hautes études commerciales. In 1907, he was director of the Section commerciale annexée au Gymnase de Nicosie, and a member of the Société de géographie de Marseille. His book *Les Levantines* (1902), won him an award from the Académie de Bordeaux. His other writings include *L'île de Chypre* (1913). Curinier, tome 3 (1901), p. 104

Delapraz, Micheline, fl. 1965, she was joint author of *Afghanistan* (Neuchâtel, 1964). NUC, 1968-1972

Delarozière, Marie Françoise, she was a writer on Mauritania; her works include *Désert, ma citadelle* (1969), *Formes et couleurs en Mauritanie* (1976), *Les Perles de Mauritanie* (1985); and she was joint author of *Il était une fois ...en Mauritanie* (1968). LC

De la Serna y Gutierrez Repide, Alfonso, 1922- *see* Serna y Gutierrez Repide, Alfonso de la

Delatre, Louis Michel James Lacour, born 9 May 1815 at Paris, he lived in Italy until 1831, and later studied in France. He seems to have attended public lectures on Greek, Arabic, and Turkish at the Bibliothèque nationale de Paris in 1851, and, perhaps, became attached to consulates in the Near East. He later was resident in Firenze, possibly as a professor. His writings include *Chants d'exil* (1843), *La Langue française dans ses rapports avec le sanscrit et avec les autres langues indo-européennes* (1854), and *Saggi linguistici* (Firenze, 1873). He died probably after 1893. BN; DBF; NUC, pre-1956

Delattre, Pierre, born in 1903, he was an accomplished pianist, and even a composer, but he followed the advice of his father, a clergyman, and turned to literature. His musical training and his extraordinary ear explain his brilliant success as a phonetician. He had received a diploma in phonetics from the Sorbonne, and a Ph.D. from Ann Arbor - but above all, he taught himself. He was not an academic climber. His studies, his teaching, his very presence enhanced many institutions: Wayne University from 1925 to 1940, Oklahoma from 1941 to 1947, Pennsylvania from 1948 to 1954, Colorado from 1955 to 1964, Santa Barbara from 1964 until his sudden death of a heart attack on 1 July 1969. His writings include *Les Difficultés phonétiques du français* (1948), and *Les Exercises structuraux, pour faire?* (1971). He was also an athlete and a sportsman. French review 43 (1969), p. 4-5

Delau, Louis, fl. 1940, he wrote *Morocco, a country of Islam* (Casablanca, 194-). NUC, pre-1956

De La Valette, John, born in 1883 in Java, he was educated at Batavia and Amsterdam. His writings in- clude *An Atlas of the progress in Nawanagar* (1932), *British trade with Holland* (1934), *The Conquest of ugliness* (1935); and he edited *Papers on Indian states development* (1930). WhE&EA

Delavaud, Claude Collin *see* Collin Delavaud, Claude

De Laveleye, Emile Louis Victor, 1822-1892 *see* Laveleye, Emile Louis Victor de

Delavignette, Robert Louis, born 29 March 1897 at Sainte-Colombe-sur-Seine, he served as a sympathetic colonial administrator in rural French Sudan from 1922 to 1930. He later served as a director of l'École nationale de la France d'outre-mer and governer-general of France d'outre-mer. His writings include *Les Paysans noirs; récits soudanais en douze mois* (1931), for which he was awarded the Grand prix de la littérature coloniale, 1932, *Petite histoire des colonies françaises* (1941), *La Paix nazaréenne* (1942), for which he was awarded the Prix de l'Académie Française, 1943, and *Robert Delavignette on the French Empire; selected writings* (1977). He died in Paris, 4 February 1976. DBFC, 1954/55; IntWW, 1974/75, 1975/76; Hommes et destins, v. 4, pp. 228-237; NDNC, 1961/62

Delaville le Roulx, Joseph Marie Antoine, born 15 August 1855 at Paris, he completed his studies at l'École des chartes in 1878, and received a doctorate in 1886 for his thesis, *La France en Orient au XIVe siècle; expéditions du maréchal Boucicant*. In the late 1870s he was a member of l'École française de Rome, and spent the years 1878/79 and 1879/80 in Malta doing research at the archives of the Ordre de S.-Jean de Jérusalem. He was a private scholar of considerable means and could well do as he pleased and visit the archives of France and elsewhere. His writings include *Les Archives, la bibliothèque et le trésor de l'ordre de Saint-Jean de Jérusalem à Malte* (1883), *Cartulaire de l'ordre des Hospitaliers de St-Jean de Jérusalem*, 4 vol. (1894-1906), *Les Hospitaliers en Terre Sainte et à Chypre, 1100-1310* (1904), and *Les Hospitaliers à Rhodes* (1913). He died at his château in Touraine, 4 November 1911. DBF

Delawarde, Jean Baptiste, born in 1900, he received a doctorate in 1937 from the Université de Clermont for his thesis, *La vie paysanne à la Martinique; essai de géographie humaine*. LC

Delaye, Théophile Jean, fl. 1934-1959, he was a sometime head of the photographic section of the Service géographique du Maroc, editor of *Revue de géographie du Maroc*, corresponding member of l'Académie des sciences d'outre-mer, and an illustrator of books on North Africa. LC

Delbrel, Gabriel, born about 1872, he left France for Algeria in the autumn of 1890 to fit himself by the study of Arabic for a three-year journey into Morocco. At Tlemcen he made the acquaintance of a prominent trader who gave him letters of recommendation to the chiefs of the Angad tribes on the frontier of Morocco. Wearing Arab dress. but not concealing his nationality, he was well received at Oujda. After falling under suspicion once, he assumed the character of a Turk, and was careful thereafter to observe Muslim practices. Detained for several months among the Angad by intertribal quarrels, he set out in November 1891, with the *qa'id* Hamada al-Buzegawi, for Fès. There he found his way, in the train of the *qa'id*, into the presence of the Sultan. On his way back to Algeria he fell sick and was arrested by one of the sons of the Sultan. He succeeded in escaping to the Beni-M'ter, Berbers dwelling between Fès and the chain of the Middle Atlas. When these Berbers were ordered to join the Sultan's force moving against Tafilalet, he accompanied them. He was denounced and brought before the Sultan, but was spared at the intercession of Muley Abdul-Aziz, the future ruler of Morocco. Delbrel acquired the friendship of the prince, and was allowed to move about the country without being greatly annoyed. His stay in Tafilalet lasted from 10 to 19 November, 1893. As a captive under surveillance, he followed the Sultan's army to Marrakesh, and there determined to make his escape. After a forced march of two days and a half, he reached Mazagan (El-Jadida), where he took refuge with the French consul. The Sultan sent out horsemen in pursuit of the fugitive, but he had changed his Arab costume for a European dress and embarked in safety on 8 of January 1894. Eight days later he reached Marseille. He wrote *España en Marruecos* (1909), and *Geografia general de la provincia del Rif y Kabilas* (1911). Journal of the American Geographical Society of N.Y. 26 (1894), pp. 551-555

Delbrück, Berthold, born 26 July 1842 at Putbus, Germany, he studied philosophy and comparative linguistics at Halle and Berlin, and received two doctorates from the Universität Halle for his theses, *De inifinitivo graeco* in 1863, and *De usu dativi in carminibus Rigvedae* in 1867. Since 1870 he was a professor of philosophy at Jena, and since 1873 he also taught Sankrit and comparative linguistics. He died in Jena, 3 January 1922. DtBE; DtBilnd (6); *Indogermanisches Jahrbuch* 8 (1920/21), pp. 259-266, reprinted in PorLing, vol. 1, pp. 489-496; Stache-Rosen, pp. 99-100; *Wer ist's*, 1909, 1912

Delcroix, M., fl. 1922, he was a director of the Service des municipalités in Egypt. Note

Deleau, Jacques, fl. 1973, he received a doctorate from the Université de Paris in 1941 for his thesis, *La nature du droit du banquier sur l'effet contrepassé en comte courant*. He was joint author of *Traité formulaire des tribunaux de commerce* (1955). LC

Deleau, Paul, fl. 1957. His writings include *Étude géologique des régions de Jemmapes, d'Hammam-Meskoutine et du col des Oliviers* (Alger, 1938). LC

Delebecque, Jacques, born in 1876, he was a journalist and writer who had travelled in North Africa and Greece. He contributed to *Revue universelle* and *l'Action française*. For his collaboration with the latter one he was condemned in 1946 to ten years in prison. His writings include *Gordon et le drame de Khartoum* (1935), and *Vie du Général Marchand* (1936). He died 23 April 1957. DBF

Delécluze, Etienne Jean, born 26 February 1781 at Paris, he was a renown painter who also pursued literary ambitions. His writings include *Antar, roman bedouin*; imité de l'anglais par Terrick Hamilton (1819), and *Dante Alighieri; ou, La poésie amoureuse* (1848). He died in Versailles, 12 July 1863. Bioln, 2, 4, 5; DBF; IndexBFr² (6); Meyers; Vapereau

Deledalle, Gérard, he was a professor of philosophy at the Université de Perpignan. His writings include *L'existentiel, philosophies et littératures de l'existence* (1949), *La pédagogie de John Dewey* (1965); and he was joint editor of *Semiotics and pragmatics; proceedings* (1989), and editor of *Signs of humanity; proceedings* (1992). LC

De Lens, Mme A.-R., fl. 1915-1925 see Lens, A.-R. de

De Leon, Edwin, born in 1818 at Charleston, S.C., he graduated in 1837 from Carolina College and was admitted to the South Carolina bar in 1840. He became a journalist and served as editor of several newspapers. He later served for eight years as American consul in Egypt. His writings include *The Khedive's Egypt* (1877), *Under the stars and under the crescent* (1887), and *Thirty years of my life on three continents* (1890). He died in NYC, 1 December 1891. BiD&SB; Bioln, 4, 14; CnDiAmJBi; DcNAA; EncJud; Master (8); NatCAB, vol. 4, p. 94; Shavit; WhAm, H

De Leone, Enrico, born 9 May 1906 at Roma, he received a doctorate of law from the Università di Roma, and a doctorate in political science in 1929 from the Università di Padua. He was a sometime professor of Islamic law and Berber common law at the Université d'Alger, and later taught at the Institut des hautes-études de Rabat. From 1932 to 1953 he was an official at the Ministero dell'Africa Italiana. Since 1963 he was a professor of law at Cagliari. His writings include *Studi di diritto coloniale* (1935), *L'Italia in Africa* (1955), *La colonizzazione dell'Africa del nord* (1957-60), *L'Impero ottomano nel primo periodo delle riforme* (1967), *Reminiscenze maghrebine* (1973), and *Riformatori musulmani del XIX secolo nell'Africa e nell'Asia mediterranee* (1973). Unesco

Delheure, Jean, his writings include *Le mariage à Ouargla; texte berbère* (1971), *L'hydraulique traditionnelle à Ouargla et au Mzab* (1975), *Dictionnaire mozabite-français* (1984), *Faits et dires du Mzab* (1986), and *Aggeraw n iwalen teggargrent-tarumit = Dictionnaire ouargli-français* (1987). LC

Delhomme, Etienne Charles Ferdinand, born 12 July 1884 at Paris. After passing through the military college Saint-Cyr, he participated in the campaign on the Algero-Moroccan border. He later served as an intelligence officer in Morocco until the outbreak of the first World War, during which he served in metropolitan France. Wounded, he returned to Morocco in 1915 as head of the Bureau d'enseignements d'Agadir. He subsequently had a career in Syria in the 1920s and again in the 1940s. He died in Paris, 5 September 1944. DBF

De L'Hoste, Edward Paterson, lieutenant-colonel, fl. 1840, his writings include *Sinde, a field for commercial and Christian enterprise* (1861), *Sinde and its capabiblities with reference to the projected canal* (1863), and *Delhoste's observations on Sind*, edited by Mubarak Ali (1987). BLC; LC

Delibanes (Delivanis), Demetrios Ioannou, born 3 April 1909 at Wien, he grew up and was educated in Greece, where he completed legal studies. He received a doctorate in 1934 from the Université de Paris for his thesis, *La politique des banques allemandes en matière de crédit à court terme*. He was successively professor at the universities of Athens and Thessaloniki. His writings include *Greek monetary developments, 1939-1948* (1949), *Παραδόσεις εφηρμοσμένης πολιτικής οικονομίας* (1960), *Économie sous-développée* (1963), *Die internationale Liquidität* (1965), and *L'Influence de l'inflation sévissant depuis 1939* (1970). EVL, 1993/94; Hellenikon, 1965; IntWW, 1974/75; WhoWor, 1974-1989/90

Delilez, Jean Pierre, born 24 October 1928 at Grasse (Alpes-Maritime), he completed his studies in sociology and economics at Paris in 1952. His writings include *La Planification dans les pays d'économie capitaliste* (1968), *Les Monopoles* (1970), *Türklere karşı Ermeni komitecileri* (1973), and *L'Etat du changement* (1977). LC; Unesco

Delingette Alfred *Charles*, born 14 November 1878 at Vannes (Seine), he was an army captain, topographer, and explorer who accompanied the Mission (Henry) Moll to Chad, 1909-1910. He and his wife, Louise, were they first to cross the African continent from Oran to the Cape of Good Hope by car, an achievement for which both of them were highly decorated and honoured. Qui est-ce?, 1934

Deliorman, Altan, fl. 1965, his writings include *Mustafa Kemal* (1959), *Atatürkün hayatındaki kadınlar* (1961), *Yugoslavya'da Müslüman-Türk'e büyük darbe* (1975), and *Tanıdığım Atsız* (1978). LC

Delitzsch, Franz Julius, born 23 February 1813 at Leipzig, he was an orientalist and Lutheran theologian of Jewish descent. He maintained a genuine understanding of, and affection for, Judaism and worked for the conversion of the Jews to Christianity. With a view to this end he edited the periodical *Saat auf Hoffnung* (seed of hope), and founded a Jewish missionary college for the training of theologians. He translated the New Testament into Hebrew. He was successively professor of Semitics at Erlangen and Leipzig, where he died 4 March 1890. DtBE; DtBilnd; EncBbrit; EncJud; LuthC 1975; Master; Sigilla

Delitzsch, Friedrich Conrad Gerhard, born 3 September 1850 at Erlangen, he was a professor of Assyriology successively at Leipzig, Breslau, and Berlin, and the author of many books on Oriental philology. He also wrote *Wo lag das Paradies* (1881), and *Babel und Bibel* (1902), and its translation, *Babel and Bible* (1902). He died 19 December 1922. DtBE; DtBilnd; EncJud; LuthC 1975

Delivanis, Dimitrios J., 1909- see Delibanes, Demetrios Ioannou

Delk, Robert Carlton, born 5 July 1920 at Hamilton, Ontario, he received a Ph.D. in 1953 from the University of Wisconsin, and thereafter taught history at various American universities until 1980, when he was appointed chairman of the Division of Social Sciences at Pikeville College, Kentucky. He contributed articles and reviews to history and education periodicals. ConAu, 45; DrAS 1974, 1978, 1982

Dell, Anthony, fl. 1925, his writings include *The Church in Wales* (1912), *Isles of Greece* (1926), and *Llama land* (1927). LC

Della Valle, Carlo, fl. 1933-35, his writings include *Lecco e il suo territorio* (Roma, 1954), *Le bonifiche di Maccarese e di Albanese* (Napoli, 1956), and *La popolaziane industriale nella provincia di Como* (1961). Firenze; NUC, pre-1956

Della Valle, Pietro, born in 1586, he came from a noble Roman family. His early life was divided between the pursuits of literature and arms. He visited the Holy Land by way of Constantinople, and acquired a good knowldege of Turkish and a little Arabic. From 1615 to 1626 he made a journey to India. There are numerous editions and translations of his *Viaggii di Pétro della Valle il Pellegrino*. He died in 1652. AnaBrit; *Cambridge history of Iran*, vol. 6 (1986); DcBiPP; EncBrit; EncItaliana; GdeEnc

Dellinger, David T., born 22 August 1915 at Wakefield, Mass., he completed his studies at Yale University, to which Oxford and the Union Theological Seminary of New York was added later. Thereafter he served as a minister in New Jersey. He was a pacifist and moral dissenter who served two prison terms as a draft resister in World War two because he opposed the war as evil and useless; he also questioned the allies' motives because they supported some fascist regimes, restricted immigration, had business deals with the Axis powers. His writings include *Revolutionary violence* (1970), *Vietnam revisited* (1986), and *From Yale to jail* (1993). BioIn, 10, 11, 13, 14; ConAu, 65; Master (5)

Dell'Omodarme, Marcello, fl. 1980, his writings include *Europa, mito e realtà del processo d'integrazione* (Milano, 1981). LC

Del Mar, Alexander, born 9 August 1836 at N.Y.C., he was educated in England and Spain, and became a political economist and a mining engineer, partly in U.S. government service. His writings include *A history of money in ancient countries* (1885), *A history of monetary systems* (1895), and *Barbara Villiers; or, A history of monetary crimes* (1899). He died in Little Falls, N.J., 1 July 1926. CnDiAmJBi; DAB; DcNAA; EncAm; Master (10); NatCAB, vol. 4, p. 189; WhAm, 1

Delmas, Claude, born in 1920, his writings include *Quel avenir pour la France* (1956), *La Guerre révolutionnaire* (1959), *L'Alliance atlantique* (1962), *Armements nucléaires et guerre froide* (1971), and *L'Europe et le Tier monde* (1976). LC

Delmas, Joseph, born about 1832, he was a geographer and historian who taught for over forty years at the Lycée de Marseille. He was a contributor to the *Bulletin de la Société de géographie et d'études coloniales de Marseille*. He died at the age of eighty-seven, 13 July 1919.

Del Medico, Henri E., born in 1896 at Constantinople, he left Turkey in 1922 to study Semitics in France and Italy. He was a translator of Ugaritic texts and the Dead Sea scrolls. His writings include *Le Mythe des Esséniens des origines à la fin du moyen âge* (1958), *L'Enigme des manuscrits de la mer Morte* (1957), and its translation, *The Riddle of the Scrolls* (1959). EncJud; LC

Delmet, Christian, Dr., fl. 1973. He received a doctorate in 1980 from the Université de Paris X for his thesis, *Histoire, peuplement et culture du Djabal Guli, Soudan*. In 1993 he was attached to CNRS. He was joint editor of *Sudan; history, identity, ideology* (1991). EURAMES; THESAM 3

Deloncle, Antoine Benoît *François*, born 14 August 1856 at Cahors (Lot), he studied at the Sorbonne and graduated in 1877 from l'École des langues orientales vivantes. For a short time thereafter, he was a lecturer in Hindu studies, and a correspondent to several Parisian newspapers for the Orient, Russia, and greater Germany. In the early 1880s he was attached to the Foreign Ministry; from 1889 to 1914 he was a *député*. He died in 1922. DBF

Deloncle, J. L., fl. 1898-1906, he was attached to the Exposition universelle internationale de 1900, Paris, and the Ministère du Commerce, de l'industrie, des postes et des télégraphes. BN; Note

Delor, Jean, fl. 1946, he was joint author of the pamphlet *L'Enseignement musical à l'école enfantine* (Genève, Département de l'instruction publique, 1967). LC

Delorme, Achille Félix, born 13 April 1831 at Bellème (Orne). After the completion of legal studies at Paris, he became secretary to the Conférences des avocats. As the first recipient of the Prix Paillet, he took his place at the bar in the Cour d'appel, and became known for his opposition to the Empire through his articles in *l'Électeur libre*. He sat at the centre left in the Assemblée nationale. He did not seek re-election in 1876 and retired. His writings include *L'Église unie à l'État, revue d'antiques* (1865). He died 10 August 1888. Curinier, vol. 5 (1906), p. 328; DBF

Delorme, Paul, born in 1866, he was a senior official at the Bureau du commerce et de l'industrie of the Gouvernement général de l'Algérie. His writings include *Le Commerce algérien* (1906). BN; NUC

Delpech, Adrien Pierre, born 31 December 1848 at Boufarik, Algeria, he was from 25 September 1867 to 16 April 1872 an *interprète auxiliaire* in the Corps des interprètes de l'armée d'Afrique; in 1876 he became *interprète judiciaire*. He was a member of the Société historique algérienne, and still active in 1913. Féraud, p. 316

Delpey, Geneviève, she received a doctorate in 1939 from the Université de Paris for her thesis, *Les Gastéropodes mésozoïques de la région libanaise*. Her writings include include *Gastéropodes mésozoïques de l'ouest de Madagascar* (1948). LC

Delphin, Gaëtan, born 27 May 1857 at Lyon. After Arabic studies at l'École des langues orientales vivantes, Paris, he went to Algeria as an interpreter at various courts of justice. He later became a teacher of Arabic at primary schools in Alger until 1881, when he was offered the chair of Arabic at the

Collège de Blida. In 1883 he accepted the chair of Arabic at Alger, a position he still held in 1904. He wrote *Complainte arabe sur la rupture du barrage de Saint-Denis-du-Sig* (1886), *Notes sur la poésie et la musique arabes dans le Maghreb algérien* (1886), *Fas, son université et l'enseignement supérieur musulman* (1889), and *Recueil de textes pour l'étude de l'arabe parlé* (1891). DBF; Index BFr² (2)

Delprat, Raymond, fl. 1960, he was joint author of *Développement, révolution solidaire* (1967). LC

Del Prete, Pasquale, born 16 January 1911 at Bari, Italy, he was a sometime professor of administrative law at the Università di Catania, and since 1960 president of the Università di Bari. His writings include *La responsabilità dello schiavo nel diritto penale romano* (1937). *Chi è?* 1957, 1961; IndBI (2)

DeLuca, Anthony R., fl. 1977, he was for over fifteen years a professor at the Department of Humanities, Emerson College, Boston, a post which he still held in 1997. His writings include *Great power rivalry at the Turkish Straits* (1981). LC; NatFacDr, 1985-1999

De Luca, Maria Amelia, fl. 1976, she was a joint translator of Nizar Qabbani, *Poesia* (Roma, Istituto per l'Oriente, 1976).

De' Luigi, Giuseppe, born 27 June 1881 at Carpi di Villabartolomea, Italy, he was a professor of history of colonization at the Istituto orientale di Napoli. He visited North Africa in 1933. His writings include *Il Mediterraneo nella politica europea* (1925), *La Francia nord-africana* (1936), and *Corso di storia dell'Africa* (1949). *Chi è?* 1931, 1936, 1940, 1948

Delumeau, Jean, born 18 June 1923 at Nantes, he was a graduate of l'École normale supérieure. In 1975 he accepted the chair of Histoire des mentalités religieuses dans l'Occident moderne in the Collège de France. He received three honorary doctorates and was highly honoured and decorated. His writings include *Vie économique et sociale de Rome* (1957-59). ConAu, 97-100; WhoFr, 1971/72-1997/98; WhoWor, 1989/90

Deluz, Jean Jacques, fl. 1964, his writings include *Le Propriétaire du bâtiment ou de l'ouvrage* (Lausanne, 1979), and *L'Urbanisme et l'architecture d'Alger* (1988). LC

Delval, Raymond, fl. 1972, his writings include *Les Musulmans au Togo* (1980), *Les Musulmans d'Abidjan* (1980), *Musulmans français d'origine indienne* (1987), and *Les Musulmans en Amérique latine et aux Caraïbes* (1992). LC

Delvert, Jean Laurent, born 19 May 1921 at Vincennes (Seine), he was a professor of geography successively in Vietnam, Cambodia, Algeria (1960-62), and from 1962 until his retirement in 1990 at the Sorbone. His writings include *Le Paysan combadien* (1961), *L'Asie méridionale* (1981), and *L'Asie tropicale* (1983). WhoFr, 1984/85-1997/98

Del Vita, Alessandro, born 15 January 1885 at Arezzo, Italy, he was an archaeologist, art critic, and a director of museum at his home town. His writings include *La ceramica nazionale romana ai tempi di Augusto* (1938), and *Guida di Arezzo* (1953). *Chi è*, 1928, 1931, 1936, 1940, 1948

Delvolvé, Pierre Charles Marie, born 16 September 1940 at Malause (Tarn-et-Garonne), he received a doctorate in law, economy and social sciences from the Université de Paris. From 1967 to 1971 he was a professor at the Université Saint-Joseph de Beyrouth, and thereafter successively at Toulouse and Paris. His writings include *L'Administration libanaise* (1971), and *L'Acte administratif* (1983). WhoFr, 1984/85-1997/98

Delye, Gérard, born in 1932, he was a zoologist. LC

Demaëght, Laurent *Louis* Philippe, born 13 January 1831 at Petite Synthe (Nord), he joined the army at he age of seventeen and became *sous-lieutenant* three years later. He entered the Bureaux arabes in Algeria on 25 June 1858. From October 1870 to September 1871 he was *commandant supérieur* at Biskra. He took early retirement to be free to pursue his academic interests. He was a founding member of the Société de géographie et d'archéologie de la province d'Oran in 1878, where, except for a few months as president in 1881, he served as vice-president from 24 May 1880 until his death on 26 April 1898. His writings include the *Catalogue raisonné des objets archéologiques contenus dans le Musée d'Oran* (1895). DBF; Peyronnet, pp. 335-336

Demanche, Georges, born in 1855, he was from 1885 to 1904 an editor of the *Revue française de l'étrangère et des colonies*, et *Exploration*. His writings include *Cinquante années de peuplement: Canada* (1928), and *Évasions militaires de 1870-71* (1931). LC

Demandt, Karl Ernst, born 6 April 1909 at Apia, Samoa, he received a doctorate in 1934, and became a medievalist, and a lecturer at the Institut für Archivwissenschaften, Marburg. His writings include *Regesten der Grafen von Katzenelnbogen* (1953-57). He died 30 June 1990. Kürschner, 1961-1987

Demangeon, Albert, born 13 June 1872 at Gallion (Eure), he was a graduate of l'École normale supérieure. After completing his geographical studies with two doctorates, he was successively a professor at the universities of Lille and Paris. His writings include *L'Empire britannique* (1923), its translations into English and German, and *Problèmes de géographie humaines* (1942). He died in Paris, 25 June 1940. BioIn, 8; DBF; WhE&EA

Demanget, P., born 19th cent., he was an *expert-syndic*, resident in Cairo, and in 1928 a member of the Société Fouad 1er d'économie politique, de statistique et de législation. His trace is lost after a publication in 1943. Note

De Marchesetti, Carlo, 1850-1926 *see* Marchesetti, Carlo von

De' Marignolli (Marignola), Giovanni, 1297-1359 *see* Marignolli, Giovanni

De Martino, Carlo, born in 1931, his writings include *Se la tua poesia e' qualcosa che esiste* (1976).

De Mayer, Jenny E., born 19th cent. in Russia, she was a self-supporting missionary in Russia, the Ukraine, and among the Sarts in the Caucasus. In the 1910s she tried to establish a dispensary and Bible shop in Jiddah. She travelled extensively in Central Asia and visited Meshed. She wrote *Adventures with God*; introduction by Samuel M. Zwemer (1942). LC; Note

Dembiński, Henryk, born 16 January 1791 at Strzałków, Galicia, he studied from 1807 to 1809 at the Ingenieurakademie Wien. He served in the Polish army and advanced through the grades to become general. In 1833 he went to Egypt to reorganize the Syrian troops for Muhammad Ali. From 1851 to his death on 13 June 1864, he was resident in Paris. His writings include *Mein Feldzug nach und in Litthauen und mein Rückzug von Kurszany nach Warschau* (Leipzig, 1832), its translation, *Mémoires sur la campagne de Lithuanie* (1832), *Rzut oka na ostatnie wypadki rewolucyi polskiéj* (Paryż, 1837), and *Deminsk Magyarországon* (Budapest, 1874). Dziekan; ÖBL; PSB; RNL; Wurzbach

Demchenko, Pavel Epifanovich, fl. 1957, his writings include *Иракский Курдистан в огне* (1963), and *Иовый день Йемена* (1963). LC

Demeerseman, André, born 20 August 1901 at Hazebrouck (Nord), he began his studies in 1926 at the Centre d'étude de la langue et de la culture arabe, Tunis, founded by the Pères Blancs in the same year. Since 1928, he was a staff member of the Centre, and from 1931 to 1954, its director under the current name, l'Institut des Belles Lettres Arabes. In 1937, he founded its journal, *IBLA*, and remained its director until 1975. From 1957 to 1963, he was *supérieur régional* of the Pères Blancs de Tunisie, and concurrently *vicaire général* of the Evêque de Carthage from 1948 to 1965. His writings include *Tunisie, terre d'amitié* (1955), *La Famille tunisienne et les temps nouveaux* (1967), and *Lumière et ombre au Maghreb* (1970). He died 31 August 1993. IBLA 56 ii (1993), pp. i-ii; Unesco

Demel von Elswehr, Hans, born 14 April 1886 at Teschen (Silesia), he received doctorates in law and Egyptology. He later was a director of the Egyptological and Oriental collections at Kunsthistorisches Museum, Wien. He died in Wien, 28 December 1951. DtBE; DtBIlnd (1); Egyptology; Teichl

Demény, Lajos (Ludovic), born 6 October 1926 at Kisfülpös, Rumania, he obtained a doctorate in history. His writings include *Bethlen Gábor és kora* (1982), *Carte, tipar şi societate la români în secolul al XVI-lea* (1986); and he was joint editor of *Székely oklevéltár* (1983). MagyarNKK; Romaniai

Demeny, Paul George, born 24 December 1932 in Hungary, he was educated in Budapest and received a Ph.D. in 1961 from Princeton University for his thesis, *Investment allocation and population growth*. He was a professor of economy at the universities of Michigan and Hawaii, and since 1971 a director at the Population Council, New York. His writings include *International aspects of population policies* (1982), and *World population growth and prospects* (1989). AmM&WS, 1973 S

Demesinova, Nazipa Khabievna, born 28 December 1929, she was since 1963 affiliated with the Institute of Philology, Kazakhstan Academy of Science; she received a doctorate in 1982. She wrote *Сопоставительная грамматика русского языков* (1966), *Развите синтаксиса современного казахского языка* (1974), *Синтаксическая стилистика современного казахского языка;* and she edited *Казахское слово в русском художественном тексте* (1990). Kazakhskaia, vol. 3; OSK

Demetriades, Evros I., he received a Ph.D. in 1976 from LSE for his thesis, *An economic evaluation of industrialization policies in Cyprus, 1962-1971*. His writings include *The process of industrialization in Cyprus* (1984), and he was joint editor of *Population and human resources development in Cyprus* (1992). Sluglett

Demidchik, Vladimir Pavlovich, fl. 1971, his writings include *Суданская поэзия XX в.* (1972); he was editor of *Проблемы восточного источниковедения* (1980), and he was joint editor of *Восток и взаимодействне литератур* (1987). LC

Demidov (Demidoff), Pavel Grigor'evich, born in 1738, he was a great traveller and at the same time a benefactor of Russian scientific education. He founded an annual prize for Russian literature, awarded by the Academy of Sciences. His writings include *Catalogue systematique des livres de la bibliothèque de Paul de Demidoff* (Moscou, 1806). He died in 1821. EncBrit; EnSlovar

Demidova, Margarita Ivanovna, fl. 1963, she was a writer on library matters, and edited *Система методического раководста организацией депозитарного хранения библиотечных фондов* (1985). LC

Demiéville, Paul, born 13 September 1894 at Lausanne, he was educated at Paris, where he received a diploma from l'École des langues orientales vivantes. From 1946 to 1965 he was professor of Chinese at the Collège de France. He received honorary doctorates of Louvain and Roma. His writings include *Philosophes taoïstes* (1980), and *Buddhism and healing* (1985). He died 23 March 1979. BioIn, 12; IntWW, 1969/70-1979/80; JAOS 99 (1979), pp. 553-555; WhoFr, 1957/58-1979/80; WhoWor, 1974/75-1978/79

D'Emilia, Antonio. For many years he was affiliated with the Facoltà di giurisprudenza di Roma. His writings include *La compravendita nel capitolo XXXIII del Nomocanone di Ibn al-'Assal* (1938), *Il waqf ahli secondo la dottrina di Abu Yusuf* (1938), *Appunti di diritto bizantino* (1940-41), and *Diritto musulmano* (1941). Firenze

Dëmin, Aleksandr Ivanovich, born 13 December 1926 at Moscow, he graduated in 1955 from the Institute of History, Moscow State University, and received his first degree in 1968 in economics for a monograph. His writings include *Вопросы лиманного орошения лугов на местном стоке в условиях Центральной Якутии* (1963), *Сельское хозяйство современного Ирана* (1967), and *Современная иранская деревня* (1977). He died 7 July 1991. LC; Miliband[2]

Demirgil, Demir, born 2 February 1927 at Istanbul, he was a staff member of the Faculty of economics, İstanbul Üniversitesi, since 1959. Thereafter he was a professor of economics at Boğaziçi Üniversitesi, Istanbul. His writings include *Türkiye'de sermaye-emek münasebetleri* (1969), and *The Turkish economy* (1980). A jubilee volume, *Demirgil memorium = Demirgil'e armağan*, was published in 1990. Kimdir, 1985/86; Türkiye bibliyografyasi

Demko, George Joseph, born 10 April 1933 at Catasauqa, Pa., he received a Ph.D. in geography in 1964 from Penn State University and subsequently taught geography at a variety of universities before he became affiliated with the National Science Foundation, Washington, D.C. His writings include *The Russian colonization of Kazakhstan, 1896-1916* (1969), *Population geography; a reader* (1970); and he was joint editor of *The Art and science of geography; U.S. and Soviet perspectives* (1992). AmM&WS, 1973 S, 1976 P

Demogeot, Jacques August, his second first name is erroneously given as Claude. He was born in 1808 at Paris and became a literary historian, and a professor of rhetoric and literature at a variety of French universities. His writings include *Histoire de la littérature française* (1852), and *Histoire des littératures étrangères* (1880). He died in Paris in 1894. BiD&SB; DBF; IndexBFr² (4)

Demontès, Victor, born 19th cent., he received a doctorate in 1918 from the Université de Paris for his thesis, *La colonisation sous Bugeaud*. He was a professor at the Lycée d'Alger and a secrétaire-général of the Société de géographie d'Alger. His writings include *L'Algérie économique* (1922-30), *L'Algérie agricole* (1930), and *L'Algérie industrielle* (1930). LC

De Montmorency, James Edward Geoffrey, born 6 December 1866 at Greenwich, he was educated at Cambridge and called to the bar from Middle Temple in 1892. From 1920 until his retirement in 1932 he held the chair of Quain Professor at University College, London. He died 9 March 1934. DNB; Who, 1921-1932; Who was who, 3

De Moor, Eduardus Cornelius Maria, 1936- *see* Moor, Eduardus Cornelius Maria de

De Morgan, Jacques Jean Marie, 1857-1924 *see* Morgan, Jacques Jean Marie de

Demorgny, Gustave, born in 1869, he studied law at the Faculté de droit de Paris, where he received a doctorate in 1899 for his thesis, *Les principales réformes financières en Indo-Chine de 1897 à 1899*. From 1912 to 1923 he was a lawyer in the service of the Persian government and concurrently taught at the Classe impériale and l'École des sciences politiques, Tehran. His writings include *La question du Danube* (1911), *Essai sur l'administration de la Perse* (1913), *Les institutions financière de la Perse* (1915), and *La question persane et la guerre* (1916). L'Asie française 13 (1913), pp. 328-330; LC

Demoulin, Françoise, fl. 1926, she was joint auhor of *Croissance des algériens de l'enfance à l'âge adulte* (1976). LC

Demoulin, Robert Léon Hubert, born 8 May 1911 at Huy, Belgium, he was from 1939 to 1981 a professor of history at the Université de Liège. His writings include *L'Université de Liège de 1936 à 1966; notices historiques et biographiques* (1967), and *Cent cahiers = Honderd bijdragen* (1987). Qui, 1981-1985; WhoBelgium, 1962

Demoz, Abraham, born 8 December 1935 at Asmara, Ethiopia, he was educated in Ethiopia and received a Ph.D. in 1964 from U.C.L.A. He taught ten years in Addis Ababa until 1974, when he was appointed professor of linguistics at Northwestern University, Evanston, Illinois. WhoAm, 1982/83

Denais, Joseph Remy, born 21 October 1851 at Beaufort-en-Vallée (Maine-et-Loire), he was a journalist whose writings, partly under pseudonyms, include *La Turquie nouvelle et l'ancien régime* (1909). He died 20 October 1920. DBF

Denaro, Victor F., born in 1896, his writings include *The Houses of Valetta* (Malta, 1967), and *The Goldsmiths of Malta and their marks* (Firenze, 1972). LC

Dendias, Michael, born 8 November 1902 (or 1899) on Paxos, Greece, he received a doctorate in 1932 from the Université de Paris for his supplementary thesis, *La question cypriote aux points de vue historique et du droit international*. He was a professor in the Faculty of Law of Athens University. His writings include *L'Organisation du Proche-Orient et le mouvement de rapprochement balkanique* (1935), *The Cypriote question* (1937), and *Διοικητικον δίκαιον* (1942). Hellenikon, 1965; LC

Déneux, Gabriel Charles, born in 1856 at Paris, he was a painter. In 1907 he held a special exhibition of his paintings, most of which of African themes, representing the product of a journey to Morocco and the Sahara. He published a few pamphlets including *La Peinture à l'encaustique avec les couleurs inaltérables* (1892). BN; DBF

Deney, Nicole, fl. 1962, she was a political scientist and a research fellow in the Centre d'étude des relations internationales de la Fondation nationale des sciences politiques. In the academic year 1960/61 she was the recipient of a scholarship of the American Association of University Women. Her writings include *Bombe atomique française et opinion publique internationale* (1962). LC

von **Denffer**, Dietrich Ahmad, born in 1949 in Germany, he was attached to the Islamic Foundation, Leicester, UK. His writings include *The Fulani evangelisation scheme in West Africa* (1980), *Christian presence in the Gulf region* (1981), *Literature on hadith in European languages; a bibliography* (1981), *Research in Islam* (1983), *'Ulum al-Qur'an; an introduction* (1984), and *Kleines Wörterbuch des Islam* (1986). LC

Deng, Francis Mading, born 1 January 1938 at Abyei, Sudan, he was educated at Khartoum University, Yale Law School, and SOAS. He was variously Sudanese ambassador and foreign minister, as well as visiting lecturer. His writings include *Tradition and modernization; a challenge for law among the Dinka of the Sudan* (1971), a revision of his 1968 thesis, Yale University, *Africans of two worlds, the Dinka in the Afro-Arab Sudan* (1978); and he was joint editor of *The British in the Sudan, 1898-1956* (1984). ConAu, 157; WhoArab, 1981-1997/98

Denham, Dixon, born 1 January 1786 at London, he entered the army in 1811. In 1822 he joined Dr. Oudney and Hugh Clapperton at Murzuk, Fezzan, where they had been sent by the British Government via Tripoli on their way to the central Sudan. The expedition made its way across the Sahara to Bornu, where they arrived in February 1823. Here he accompanied a slave-raiding party into the country south of Bornu. When Oudney and Clapperton set out for Hausa country in 1823, he remained behind and explored the shores and rivers of Lake Chari, principally with a view to tracing the course of the Niger and ascertaining its estuary. After his return to England by way of Tripoli, he was promoted lieutenant-colonel in 1826 and sent to Sierra Leone as superintendent of liberated Africans. He died only weeks after he was appointed governor of Sierra Leone, 8 May 1828. His writings include *Narrative of travels and discoveries in northern and central Africa in the years 1822, 1823, and 1824* (1826), and its translations, *Voyages et découvertes dans le nord et dans les parties centrales de l'Afrique* (1926), and *Beschreibung der Reisen und Entdeckungen im nördlichen und mittleren Afrika* (1927). DcBiPP; DNB; Embacher; EncBrit; EncicUni; GdeEnc; Henze; Meyers

Denhardt, Edith Tilton, 1914-1996 *see* Penrose, Edith Tilton

Deniel, Raymond, S.J., born in 1929, his writings include *De la savane à la ville* (1968), *Croyances religieuses et vie quotidienne; islam et christianisme à Ouagadougou* (1970), *Religions dans la ville;*

croyances et changements sociaux à Abidjan (1975), *Femmes des villes africaines* (1985), and *Oui, patron; boys cuisiniers en Abidjan* (1991). LC

Denike, Boris Petrovich, born in 1885 at Kazan, he graduated from Kazan University, and taught literature and history at Moscow University since 1920. In 1925 he was appointed a professor. His writings include *Искусство Средней Азии* (1927), *Живорись Ирана* (1938), and *Архитектурный орнамент Средней Азии* (1939). He died 14 October 1941. GSE; Miliband; Miliband²; TatarES

Deniker, Joseph, born of French parents at Astrakhan on 6 March 1852, he was educated in Russia, and trained in engineering. In this capacity he travelled extensively in the petroleum districts of the Caucasus and Europe. In 1876 he settled in Paris and studied at the Sorbonne. He became a naturalist and anthropologist. In 1888 he was appointed chief librarian of the Musée d'histoire naturelle de Paris. His writings include *Les races de l'Europe* (1899-1908), and *Les races et les peuples de la terre* (1900). He died in 1918 in Paris. Curinier, v. 3, p. 139; DBF; EncBrit; EncicUni; GdeEnc; GSE; Wininger, v. 6

Denis, Ferdinand Jean, born 13 August 1798 at Paris. Although his parents expected him to follow a diplomatic career, he preferred to study languages, and travel. In his thirties, he settled in Paris, where he was appointed in 1838 keeper at the Bibliothèque Ste.-Geneviève. He was joint author of *Fondation de la régence d'Alger; histoire des Barberousse, chronique arabe du XVIe siècle* (1837). He died 2 August 1890. DBF

Denis, Pierre, général de brigade, born in 1923, he was a graduate of the military college, Saint-Cyr, and obtained a diploma from the Centre de hautes études sur l'Afrique et l'Asie modernes. He served seven years in the Sahara successively as head of the dromedary platoon of the Compagnie de la Saoura with headquarters in Tindouf, and the support platoon of the Compagnie de la Zousfana with headquarters in Colomb-Béchar. From 1958 to 1960, he was commanding officer of the Compagnie méhariste du Tidikelt-Hoggar with headquarters in Tamanrasset. In 1976 he received one of his four doctorates for his thesis, *Les Reguibats l'Gouacem*. His writings include *Les Derniers nomades* (1989), and *L'Armée française au Sahara* (1991). LC; THESAM, 1

Denis de Rivoyre, Barthélemy Louis, 1837- *see* Rivoyre, Barthélemy Louis Denis de

Denisov, Petr Vladimirovich, fl. 1962, his writings include *Религиозные верования чуваш* (1959), *Этнокультурные параллели дунайских бодгар и чувашей* (1969), and *Религия и атеизм чувашского народа* (1972). LC

Denizeau, Claude, fl. 1954, he received a doctorate in 1982 from the Université de Paris III for his thesis, *Recherches sur le lexique de Gahiz*. His writings include *Dictionnaire des parlers arabes de Syrie, Liban et Palestine*; supplément au *Dictionnaire arabe-français* d'Adrien Barhélemy (1960), and he was joint author of the *Dictionnaire arabe-français-anglais* (1967). LC; THESAM 4

Denker, Bedriye, 1931- *see* Tolun-Denker, Bedriye

Dennett, Daniel Clement, born in 1910, he received a Ph.D. in 1939 from Harvard for his thesis, *Marwan ibn Muhammad; the passing of the Umayad caliphate*. His writings include *Conversion of poll tax in early Islam* (1950). He died in 1947. Selim

Dennis, Alfred Pearce, born in 1869, he was a graduate of Princeton University, where he also received a Ph.D. in 1894. Thereafter he taught history and politics at various colleges and universities until 1907, when he accepted a position in the U.S. government service as economist. His writings include *The romance of world trade* (1926). He died in 1931. WhAm, 1

Dennis, George Thomas, born 17 November 1923 at Somerville, Mass, he was educated at American universities, the Pontifical Institute for Oriental Studies, Rome, and ordained Roman Catholic priest in 1954. He taught history and theology at Loyola University, Los Angeles, and the Catholic University of America, Washington, D.C. His writings include *The reign of Manuel II Palaeologus in Thessalonica, 1382-1387* (1960), *Three Byzantine military treatises* (1985), and his collected articles entitled *Byzantium and the Franks* (1982). DrAS, 1974, 1978, 1982; WhoE, 1983/84, 1985/86; WhoRel, 1985

Dennis, James Shephard, born 15 December 1842 at Newark, N.J, he was a graduate of Princeton University and Princeton Theological Seminary. He served as a missionary posted to Sidon and Zahlah from 1868 to 1891. From 1873 to 1891 he was also a professor at the Theological Seminary in Beirut. After his return to the States he was historian and statistician of missions for the Presbyterian Board of Foreign Missions. His writings include *A sketch of the Syrian mission* (1872), *Christian missions and social progress* (1897-1906), and *The modern call of missions* (1913). He died in Montclair, N.J., 21 March 1914. DAB; DcNAA; NatCAB, v. 22, pp. 320-21; Shavit; WhAm, 1; Who, 1908, 1909; *Who was who*, 1

Denny, Frederick Matheson, born 2 March 1939 at Burlington, Vt., he was a graduate of the College of William and Mary, and received a Ph.D. from the University of Chicago in 1974 for his thesis, *Community and salvation; the meaning of the ummah in the Qur'an*. He taught at various universities until 1978, when he was appointed a professor of religious studies at the University of Colorado, Boulder, where he was still active in 1999. His writings include *An introduction to Islam* (1985), and *Islam and the Muslim community* (1987). NatFacDr, 1997-99; WhoRel, 1992

Denny, Walter Bell, born 20th cent., he received a Ph.D. in 1971 from Harvard for his thesis, *The ceramics of the Mosque of Rustem Pasha and the environment of change*. He was a professor of fine arts successive-ly at Harvard and the University of Massachusetts, Amherst. His writings include *Oriental and Islamic art* (1974), and the exhibition catalogue, *The image and the world* (1976). MESA *Roster of members*, 1990; NatFacDr, 1997-99; Selim

Denomy, Alexander Joseph, born 21 June 1904 at Chatham, Ontario, he was a graduate of the University of Western Ontario, and received a Ph.D. in 1934 from Harvard. Since 1935 he taught history of comparative literature in various capacities at the Pontifical Institute of Medieval Studies in the University of Toronto. His writings include *The heresy of courtly love* (1947). He died 19 July 1957 while visiting friends in Massachusetts. Canadian, 1948-1955; *Speculum* 33 (1958), pp. 461-62; WhE&EA

Denoyer, Pierre, born 24 October 1901 at Paris, he received diplomas from the Faculté des lettres, the Faculté de droit, and l'École libre des sciences politiques, Paris. He was a foreign correspondent and a newspaper editor. He spent three months in Egypt in 1921, and in the spring of 1924 he was sent by *La liberté* to make a study of the situation in Tunisia. For most of the 1930s he was New York and Washington correspondent for *le Petit Parisien*. From 1938 he worked for his newspaper in Paris until 1940, when he became active in the *Résistance*. He was one of the founders of *Défense de la France*. He had a brief career at *France soir* and *le Figaro* before becoming editor-in-chief of the French edition of *The Reader's digest*. His writings include *La presse contemporaine* (1948), and *La presse dans le monde* (1950). He died 19 August 1965. BioIn, 2, 7; NYT, 20 August 1965, p. 29, col. 3; WhoFr, 1959/60-1965/66

Densuşianu (Densusianu), Ovidiu, born in 1873 at Făgăraş, Romania, he studied philology at Paris and Roma, and thereafter taught at Bucharest University, where he specialized in Romanian language and literature. His writings include *Histoire de la langue roumaine* (1901), *Vieaţa păstorească în poesia noastră populară* (1922-23), and its translation, *La vita pastorale nella poesia popolare romena* (1936). He died in 1938. DcEnc; WhoRom

Dent, Clinton Thomas, born in 1850, he was educated at Eton and Trinity College, Cambridge. He was a surgeon with the police force and a mountaineer who repeatedly explored in the Caucasus. His writings include *Above the snow line; mountaineering sketches* (1885), and *Mountaineering* (1892). He died in 1912. BritInd (3); *Who was who*, 1

Dentice di Frasso, Luigi, born 19 August 1861 at Brühl, Austria, Italian senator. He died in Roma, 28 July 1947. Artefici

Deny, Jean Joseph Thadée, born 12 July 1879 at Kiev, where his father was a secondary school teacher. He was educated at the Lycée Richelieu in Odessa, and the Lycée Louis-le-Grand in Paris. He studied concurrently at l'École des langues orientales vivantes and the Faculté de droit de Paris. Fom 1904 to 1908 he was successively dragoman and vice-consul in Beirut, Jerusalem, Tripolis, and Maraş. Interrupted only by war-time service and a mission to Egypt, 1926-1930, he held the chair of Turkish at l'École des langues orientales vivantes from 1920 until his retirement in 1949. He was one of the great Turkologist of the century. His writings include *Grammaire de la langue turque, dialecte osmanli* (1921), *Sommaire des archives turques du Caire* (1930), and *Principes de grammaire turque* (1955). In 1958 he was honoured by the jubilee volume, *Jean Deny armağanı*. He died in Gérardmer, 5 November 1963. AnaBrit; *Index Islamicus* (7); Meydan; *Qui êtes-vous*, 1924

Denz, Adolf, born 12 February 1935 at Dortmund, Germany, he studied classical philology and Semitics and received a Dr.phil. in 1963 from the Universität München for his thesis, *Struktur-analyse der pronominalen Objektsuffixe im Altsyrischen und klassischen Arabisch*. Since 1975 he was professor of Semitics at München. His writings include *Die Verbalsyntax des neuarabischen Dialektes von Kwayriš* (1969). Kürschner, 1976-1996; Schwarz

Déonna, Waldemar, born 24 September 1880 at Cannes. For his *Statues de terre cuites dans l'antiquité* he was awarded a *docteur ès lettres* in 1907 from the Université de Genève. He taught there from 1920 to 1956, and held the chair of archaeology and history of art. Concurrently he was a director of the Musées d'art et d'histoire de Genève. His recognition came rather late; it was not until 1946 that he became *correspondant étranger* of the Académie des inscriptions et belles-lettres. He was a scholar who worked to the limit of his power for nearly half a century. His many writings include

Les Arts à Genève des origines à la fin du XVIIIe siècle (1942), and *Der Orient-Teppich* (1947). He died 3 May 1959. Revue archéologique 2 (1959), pp. 103-6; WhoSwiss, 1951/52

Depont, Octave Emmanuel, born 17 September 1862 at La Champenoise (Indre), he entered the French administration at Constantine, Algeria, in 1880 and was an *administrateur de communes mixtes* from 1883 to 1893, when he entered the Service des Affaires indigènes et du personnel militaire du Gouvernement général de l'Agérie. He returned to metropolitan France in 1901, where he was an administrator in various *départements*. After his retirement he was active in social and cultural work among the Muslims of Paris. In 1932 he was a member of the Commission d'Études de l'Hôpital Franco-Musulman, and a lecturer in Arabic and Kabyle at the École des Infirmières de la Seine. His writings include *L'Algérie du centenaire* (1928), *Vocabulaire français-kabyle* (1933), and *Les Berbères en France* (1937); he was joint author of *Les Confréries religieuses musulmanes* (1897). DBF

Deprez, Jean Paul Germain, born 13 January 1928 at Vesoul (Haute-Saône), he received a doctorate in 1953 from the Université de Rennes for his thesis, *La Lésion dans les contrats aléatoires*. He was a professor of law at Rennes and Paris, and also taught at Dakar University. Unesco

Dequin, Horst Friedrich Ernst, born 9 April 1927 at Neeberg auf Usedom, Germany. After war-time service during the last six months of the war, and six-year training in an agricultural establishment, he studied agronomy at the Technische Universität Berlin from 1952 to 1956. In 1962 he received a Dr.phil. at Berlin for his thesis, *Die Landwirtchaft Saudisch-Arabiens*. In 1973 he joined the Food and Agriculture Organization of the United Nations. His writings include *Agricultural development in Malawi* (1970), *Arabische Republik Jemen* (1976), and *Indonesien* (1978). Schwarz; Thesis; WhoUn, 1975

Deramey, Jules, fl. 1893-1899, he contributed a number of articles on early Christianity in Arabia and Ethiopia to the *Revue de l'histoire des religions*. BN

Derbil, Süheyp Nizami, fl. 1956, he was a professor of law whose writings include *Idare hukuku* (1940-49), and *Kooperatifler* (1945). LC

Derbisaliev, Abdsattar Bagisbaevich, born 15 September 1947 in Kazakhstan Oblast, he graduated in 1969 from a teachers' college and received his first degree in 1977 for "*Основные этары развития арабоязычной литературы Марокко,*" and a doctorate in 1987 for *Эволюция марокканской арабоязыцной словесности.* Since 1977 he taught Oriental philology at Kazan State University. His writings include *Эстетика аль-Фараби* (1980), and *В стране "1001 ночи: очерки* (1986). Miliband²

Dercle, Charles Ursmar, born 23 August 1866 at Teteghem (Nord). After medical studies at Lyon, he was a physician in the Territoires du Sud of Algeria from 1895 to 1906. In 1906 he was sent to Settat, Morocco, to establish a hospital which became widely acclaimed. He was an accomplished Arabist and published *De la pratique de notre médecine chez les arabes; vocabulaire arabe français d'expressions médicales* (1904). Peyronnet, p. 825

Đerđa, Josip, born 18 February 1911 at Zadar, Croatia, he was a diplomat and politician, and a sometime ambassador to India and the United Arab Republic. In 1974 he was vice-president of the Federal Government, Beograd. His writings include *Svet u 1965* (1966). He died in Beograd, 18 February 1990. HBL; JugoslSa, 1957; Ko je ko, 1970; LC; WhoWor, 1971/72, 1974/75 (no substance)

Derenbourg, Hartwig, born 17 June 1844 at Paris, he was educated at Göttingen and Leipzig, to which l'École des langues orientales, Paris, was added a year or two later. He received a Dr. phil. in 1867 from the Universität Göttingen for *De pluralium linguae arabicae et aethiopicae formarum omnis generis origine et indole scripsit et Sibavaihi capita de plurali ed...* . In 1879 he was appointed professor of Arabic, and in 1866 professor of Islam at l'École des hautes études. He collaborated with his father in the great edition of Saadia and the edition of Abu al-Walid, and also produced a number of important editions of other Arabic writers, including *'Oumâra du Yémen, sa vie et son œuvre* (1897-1904). He also published *Les Manuscrits arabes de l'Escurial* (1884), and *Opuscules d'un arabisant, 1868-1905* (1905). A memorial volume, *Mélanges Hartwig Derenbourg*, was published in 1909. He died in Paris, 12 April 1908. Curinier, v. 5 (1906), pp. 265-66; DBF; EncBrit; EncJud; Fück; Wininger

Derenbourg (Derenburg), Joseph, born 21 August 1811 at Mainz, he studied Semitics under Georg W. Freytag at Bonn before he settled in Paris, where he was a considerable force in the educational revival of Jewish education. He made great contributions to the knowledge of Saadia, and planned a complete edition of Saadia's works in Arabic and French. He also wrote *Les Fables de Loqman le sage* (1850), *Essai sur l'histoire et la géographie de la Palestine* (1867), and *Deux versions hébraïques du livre de Kalîlâh et Dimnâh, la première accompagnie d'une traduction française* (1881). He was awarded the Légion d'honneur in 1869. He died in Bad Ems, 29 July 1895. DBF; DtBE; EncBrit; EncJud; Fück; Wininger

Derendinger, Jean *Robert*, fl. 1912, he wrote *Vocabulaire pratique du dialecte arabe centre-africain; dialect arabe des rives du Tchad au Ouadaï* (1923). NUC, pre-1956

Der-Hagopian, Nishan, fl. 1918, he wrote *Out of inferno* (Philadelphia, 1949). NUC, pre-1956

Déribéré, Maurice, born 7 July 1907 at Auneau (Eure-et-Loire), he was a trained engineer who became a production manager, head of a research laboratory, and head of the Centre d'éclairagisme of the Compagnie des lampes Mazda. His many writings, partly with Paulette Déribéré, include *La Couleur dans la publicité et la vente* (1969), *L'Éthiopie, berceau de l'humanité* (1972), *Au Pays de la reine Saba* (1977), and *Histoire mondiale du déluge* (1978). He died 10 June 1997. NDNC 3 (1964); WhoFr, 1967/68-1996/97

D'Erme, Giovanni M., born 12 February 1935 at Cori (Latina), he was educated at the universities of Bari, Roma, and Tehran. From 1969 to 1973 he was a professor of Persian at the Università di Venezia, and thereafter successively attached to the Istituto universitario orientale di Napoli and Istituto per l'Oriente di Roma. Since 1995 he was dean of the Faculty of Arts, Istituto universitario orientale di Napoli. His writings include *Grammatica del neopersiano* (1979). WhoItaly, 1997

Dermenghem, Émile, born 3 January 1872 or 1892 at Paris, he studied archival palaeography at the Université de Paris, and became head of the Archives de la Délégation générale du Gouvernement en Algérie. His writings include *Joseph de Maistre, mystique* (1923), *Contes kabyles* (1945), *Archives du Gouvernement général de l'Algérie, série X, dons et acquisitions; répertoire par G. Esquer et É. Dermengham, archiviste-bibliothécaire du Gouvernement général de l'Algérie* (Alger, 1954), *Mahomet et la tradition islamique* (1957), and its translations, *Muhammad and the Islamic tradition* (1958), and *Muhammed in Selbstzeugnissen und Bilddokumenten* (1960). LC; NUC, pre-1956; Unesco

Dermigny, Louis, fl. 1954, his writings include *Cargaisons indiennes; Solier et Cie, 1781-1793* (Paris, 1950-60), *Sète de 1666 à 1880; esquisse de l'histoire d'un port* (Montpellier, 1955), and *La Chine et l'Occident; le commerce à Canton au XVIIIe siècle, 1719-1833* (Paris, 1964). LC

Dernova, Varvara Pavlovna, born 22 October 1906 in Tatar ASSR, she received a doctorate in 1974 in musicology. Her writings include *Народная мызыка в Хазахстане* (1967), and *Гармония Скрябина* (1968). Казахская ССР краткая энциклопедия, vol. 3, pp. 179-180; KazakSE

Dernschwam von Hradiczim, Hans (Johannes), born 23 March 1494 in Brüx, Bohemia, he studied at the universities of Leipzig, Wien, and Roma, and belonged to the Vienese humanist school. He later was a private tutor to royalty of Budapest and Preßburg. In 1553 he went with an imperial embassy to the Ottoman Porte, a journey which is described in *Hans Dernschwam's tagebuch einer reise nach Konstantinopel und Kleinasien*, edited by Franz Babinger (1923). DtBE; DtBilnd; Henze

Derouet, Michel, fl. 1957, he received a doctorate in law in 1940 from the Université de Paris for his thesis, *Le Jury en matière civile dans le droit anglais et dans le droit anglo-américain*. LC

Déroulède, L., he received a doctorate in 1895 from the Faculté de droit de Bordeaux for his thesis, *De la prise à partie, législation ancienne, moderne et étrangère*. BN; LC

Derrécagaix, Victor Bernard, born 14 December at Bayonne, he was a graduate of the Lycée Saint-Louis, Paris, and the military college, Saint-Cyr, He was posted to the 3e Zouaves in Algeria, 1856, and participated in the campaigns against the Berber. In June 1861 he was *aide de camp* of general Yusuf. In the following year he was employed in topographical works in Algeria, particularly in a survey of the territory of the Oulad Sidi Cheikh in the southern part of Oran Province. In 1890 he accomplished another geodetic and topographical mission in Algeria and Tunisia. His writings include *Recits d'Afrique; Yusuf* (1907). He died 11 April 1915. DBF; Henze

Derrett, John *Duncan Martin*, born 30 August 1922 at London, he was a graduate of Jesus College, Oxford, and received a Ph.D. from SOAS. After war-time service in India, he began his career at SOAS in 1949, culminating in emeritus professor of Oriental laws in 1982. His writings include *Hindi law, past and present* (1957), *Introduction to legal systems* (1968), and *The death of a marriage law* (1978). He was presented with *Indology and the law; studies in honour of Professor J.. Duncan M. Derrett* (1982). ConAu, 13-16, new rev. 6, 21, 44; Master (2); Who, 1985-2003; WrDr, 1976-1998

Derrida, Fernand, born 14 August 1920 at El-Biar, Algeria, he was a professor of law at l'Université d'Alger. His writings include *L'Obligation d'entretien; obligation des parents d'élever leurs enfants* (1952), a work which was originally presented in 1947 as his doctoral thesis at l'Université d'Alger, *La Réforme du règlement judiciaire et de la faillite* (1969); and he was joint author of *Redressement de liquidation judiciaire des entreprises* (1986). LC; Unesco

Derrien, Isidore Antoine Michel, born 7 February 1839, he was a graduate of the military college, Saint-Cyr, and l'École d'état-major. He was employed in topographic works in Algeria, accomplished a geodetic mission in Palestine, as well as the first topographic survey of Upper Senegal. His writings include *Le Chemin de fer transsahrien d'Oran au Touat* (1879), and *Les Français à Oran depuis 1830 jusqu'à nos jours* (1886). He died in August of 1904. DBF; Henze; *Index Islamicus*, 1665-1905, p. 6

Derrouch, André Marie Émile Armand, born 7 October 1912 at Toulouse, he studied at Toulouse and Paris, and received a doctorate in law from the Université de Toulouse for his thesis, *L'Institut de France; son statut juridique*. After three years' service in the Cour d'appel de Toulouse, he started an administrative career in Morocco from 1939 to 1944. After the war, he held various civil administrative positions in Morocco until 1956. Concurrently he was a lecturer at the Institut des hautes études marocaines, and a professor at the École marocaine d'administration. From 1957 to 1961 he was posted to Algeria. His writings include *Le Droit du travail au Maroc* (1948), *L'Economie marocaine* (1953), and *Études relatives aux clauses économiques des traités concernant le Maroc* (1955). NDNC, vol. 5 (1968); WhoFr, 1969/70-1981/82|

Dershowitz, Alan Morton, born 1 September 1938 at Brooklyn, N.Y., he graduated (magna cum laude) from Brooklyn College and Yale University. He was the recipient of honorary doctorates of the universities of Yeshiva and Haifa, and a lawyer of the last resort. In 1967 he was appointed professor of law at Harvard Law School, a position he still held in 1997. His writings include *The Best defense* (1982); and he was joint author of *Psychoanalysis, psychiatry, and law* (1967). BioIn, 11, 12, 15; ConAu, 25-28 rev., 11 new rev., 44 new rev.; DrAS, 1974, 1978, 1982 P; Master (3); NatFacDr, 1997; WhoAm, 1979-1998; WhoAmL, 1979-1998/99; WhoWorJ, 1972-1987

Dervaux, Adolphe, born in 1871 at Paris, he was an architect who made himself a name with reinforced concrete railway stations. He was a president of the Société française des urbanistes. His writings include *L'Edifice et le milieu* (1919). He died in Paris in 1948. DBF; IndexBFr²

Dervichyan, Yervanth A., fl. 1895-1919, he wrote the pamphlet *Réflections sur les origines des races en Turquie et leurs incompatibilités* (Lausanne, 1919). NYPL

Derville, Henry, fl. 1923, he wrote *L'âme africaine* (1941). NUC, pre-1956

Derzhavin, Nikolai Sevast'ianovich, born in 1877, he was a Slavic scholar, president of Leningrad University, 1922-1925, director of the Institute of Slavic Studies, Leningrad, 1931-1934, its head from 1947 to 1953, and a member of the Presidium of the Academy of Sciences. His writings include *Prof. N. S. Derschawin über Makedonien* (1918), *Les rapports bulgaro-serbes et la question macédonienne* (1918), *Сборник статей и исследований в области славянской филологии* (1941), *Die Slaven im Altertum* (1948), and *Slavii în vechime* (Bucuresti, 1949). He died in Leningrad, 26 February 1953. GSE; NYT, 28 February 1953, p. 17, col. 4

Derzhavin, Vladimir Vasil'evich, born in 1908 at Kologriv, Russia, he came to poetry from painting, which he had studied at the art studio Vkhutemas in Moscow. He edited *Избранные четверо-стишия персидско-таджикских поэтов-классиков* (1965), and he translated *Из "Шах-наме"* (1969), and *Стена Искандела* (1970). He died in 1975. EST; LC; *Soviet literature*, 1981 vii, 131-136

Desai, Ziyaud-Din Ahmed, born 17 May 1925 at Dhandhuka, Gujarat, he received a doctorate in Persian literature from Tehran University. He was a lecturer in Persian at government colleges in Ahmedabad, Bombay, and Rajkot until 1953, when he joined the Archaeological Survey of India. His writings include *Mosques of India* (1966), *Indo-Islamic architecture* (1970), *Muslim inscriptions from Rajasthan* (1971), *Centres of Islamic learning in India* (1978), *A topographical list of Arabic, Persian and Urdu inscriptions of South India* (1989), and *Malfuz literature* (1991). LC; WhoIndia, 1973, p. 439, 1974/75, p. 449, 1977/78, p. 362

Desalle, Eusèbe François de *see* Salles, Eusèbe François comte de

Desanti, Dominique, born at the end of the first World War, he interrupted his studies in 1940 to join the *résistance*. In 1944 he was a war-correspondent. He became a journalist who travelled extensively and published in French communist periodicals as well as in the UK and communist countries. His writings include *L'année ou la terre a tremblé* (1947), *Nous avons choisi la paix* (1949), *Bombe ou paix atomique* (1950), *Côte-d'Ivoire* (1962), and *Les socialistes de l'utopie* (1971). In 1985 he was awarded the *prix de l'essai* of the Société des gens de lettres. Boisdeffre²; LC

Deschamps, C., French officer, born 19th cent., he was n 1906 a lieutenant with the 4e Spahis, and in 1914, a captain with the 2e Dragons, posted to Casablanca. Note

Deschamps, Émile Félix, born in 1857, he was a sometime editor of *Revue de l'Extrême-Orient.* His writings include *Au pays d'Aphrodite, Chypre* (1898), *En Palestine* (1903), *Les femmes d'Oncle Sam* (1913), and *Le Krak des Chevaliers* (1929). BN; NUC, pre-1956

Deschamps, Gaston, born 5 January 1861 at Melle (Deux-Sèvres). After graduation from l'École normale supérieure, and *agrégation* in 1885, he was appointed a member of l'École française d'Athènes. He travelled in Asia Minor. After his return to Paris he published *La Grèce d'aujourd'hui* (1892), a work which was awarded by the Académie française. He later was appointed a professor at the Collège de France. His writings include *Sur les routes d'Asie* (1894), *À Constantinople* (1913), and *La Somme dévastée* (1921). He died in Paris, 15 May 1931. BN; DBF

Deschamps, Hilaire, général de la cavalerie, born 19 August 1857 at Mauzac (Dordogne). After graduation from the military college of Saint-Cyr he was posted to Algéria from 1882 to 1889. He served in metropolitan France until his retirement in 1919. He was awarded Commandeur de la Légion d'honneur in 1914. He died in Brantôme (Dordogne), 4 January 1936. DBF

Deschamps, Léon, born 6 July 1849 at Campeaux (Calvados). After studies at the Sorbonne, he was a professor of history at the Lycée du Mans until his retirement in 1909. In 1898 he received a doctorate from the Université de Paris for his thesis, *La Constituante et les réformes; la réforme sociale coloniale.* He devoted his retirement to the defence of the interests of employees and the Ministère de l'Éducation Nationale in the journal *la Solidarité*, which he had founded in 1904. His writings include *Études élémentaires sur le coton* (1885), *Histoire de la question coloniale en France* (1891), and *Les colonies pendant la révolution* (1898). DBF

Deschamps, Paul, born 19 September 1888, he was a graduate of the Lycée Louis-le-Grand and l'École nationale des chartes, where he later served until 1927, when he became *conservateur* at the Musée des Monuments français. He was elected to the Académie des inscriptions et belles lettres in 1942, and awarded the Légion d'honneur. His writings include *French sculpture of the Romanesque period* (1930), *Le Crac des Chevaliers; études historiques et archéologique* (1934), *Les châteaux des croisées en Terre Sainte* (1934-39), and *La défense du royaume de Jérusalem* (1939). DBFC, 2e éd., 1954/55; WhoFr, 1953/54|

Deschanel, Paul Eugène Louis, born 13 February 1856 at Bruxelles, he was educated at the Collège Saint-Barbe and the Lycée Concordet, Paris. In 1878 he became sub-prefect of Dreux. He entered the Chambre des députés in 1885 as member for Eure-et-Loire, became vice-president of the Chambre des députés in 1896, and its president from 1898 to 1902, and again from 1912 to 1920. In 1898 he was elected to the Académie française. He died 28 April 1922. Curinier, v. 3 (1901), p. 313-14; DBF; EncAm; EncItaliana

Des Chesnais, René, le père, fl. 1881, his writings include *En felouque sur le Nil; souvenirs de Basse-Nubie et de Haute-Égypte* (Tours, 1897), and *Vie de Notre Seigneur Jésus-Christ* (1907). BN

Des Cilleuls, Jean, médecin-général, born in 1885, his writings include *Au corps du cavalerie avec le Service de santé, septembre 1939 - juin 1940* (1948). LC

Descloitres, Claudine, born 20 August 1928 at Jaulgonne (Aisne), she was educated at l'École de haut enseignement commmercial pour les jeunes filles, Paris, and the Faculté de droit d'Alger. She was the founding director of the Centre universitaire de documentation économique et sociale, Institut de recherche économique et sociale d'Alger from 1955 to 1957. Her writings include *La Psychologie appliquée en Afrique; bibliographie* (1968), and she was joint author of *L'Algérie des bidonvilles* (1961). Unesco

Descloitres, Robert Jean Denis, born 27 September 1928 at Paris, he was educated at Paris and Alger, and became an anthropologist specializing in Third World sociology. His writings include *Les Travailleurs étrangers, leur adaption au travail industriel et à la vie urbaine* (1967), its translation, *The Foreign worker* (1967); and he was joint author of *L'Algérie des bidonvilles* (1961), and *Commune et société rurale en Algérie* (1968). Unesco

Desclos (Descos), Léon Eugène Aubin Coullard, 1863- see Aubin, Eugène

Desdevises du Dézert, Théophile Alphonse, born in 1822, he was a college professor of geography at Blois and Bordeaux, and, after his *agrégation*, at Brest, Limoges, Angers, and Douai. After the completion of two theses, he was successively professor of geography at the Faculté des lettres de Clermont, and Caen. His writings include *Géographie ancienne de la Macédoine* (1863), and *La France dans l'Extrême-Orient* (1884). DBF

Desfeuilles, Paul, born in 1866, he was a professor at secondary schools. His writings include *Les Colonies françaises: l'Algérie* (1931), and *Les Colonies françaises: le Maroc* (1932). LC

Desfontaines, René Louiche, born 13 February 1750 at Tremblay (Ille-et-Vilaine), he was educated at the Collège de Reims, and studied medicine at Paris, but soon turned to botany. In the service of the Académie française he explored Tunisia and Algeria as a botanist from 1783 to 1786. His writings include *Voyages dans les régences de Tunis et d'Alger* (1838). He died in Paris, in 1833. DBF; Henze

Desfossés, Edmond, born in 1815, his writings include *Affaires d'Orient; la disgrâce de Sidi Moustapha Khasnadar* (1875), *Affaires d'Orient; la Tunisie, histoire, finances, politique* (1877), *Affaires d'Orient; la question tunisienne et l'Afrique septentrionale* (1881), and *Tunisie sous le protectorat et son annexion à l'Algérie* (1886). BN; LC

Des Godins de Souhesme, Gaston, born 11 May 1841 at Vouziers (Ardennes), he studied at Strasbourg, and was an administrator with the Trésorerie d'Afrique from 1865 to 1878, when he became editor-in-chief of *Nouvelliste de l'Algérie*. In 1884 he founded in Turkey the ephemeral *Revue française*, of which he published ten issues. His writings include *Tunis; histoire, mœurs, gouvernement* (1875), *Tunis* (1880), and *Au pays des Osmanlis* (1894). BN; DBF

Desgrand, Louis, born in 1809 at Annonay (Ardèche), he was the founder of the Société de géographie de Lyon in 1873, and its president until his retirement in 1892. He regularly spent his the winter months in Egypt. His writings include *De l'influence des religions sur le développement économique des peuples; simple étude* (1884). He died 22 June 1893. DBF

Des Hautesrayes, Michel Ange André Le Roux, 1724-1795, he was an Oriental interpreter who since 1751 held the chair of Arabic at the Collège de France. Casanova; DBF; Fück; IndexBFr² (5)

Deshayes, Jean Fernand, born 11 February 1924 at Paris. After studies at l'École normale supérieure, he continued at l'École française d'Athènes from 1949 to 1952. After his *agrégation* he pursued an interest in pre-historic excavations around the eastern Mediterranean. A long affiliation with the C.N.R.S. at Beirut broadened his interest to include the area of greater Iran to the borders of China. Successively a professor at Lyon and Paris, he assured the training of young French archaeologists. His writings include *La Nécropole de Ktima* (1963), and *Les Civilisations de l'Orient ancien* (1969). He died in Tunisia, 15 April 1979. A commemoration volume was published in 1985: *De l'Indus aux Balkans; recueil à la mémoire de Jean Deshayes*. Hommes et destins, t. 7, pp. 148-149; WhoFr, 1967/68-1977/78; WhoWor, 1974/75, 1976/77

Deshayes de Bonneval, Léon Paul Marie, born 6 May 1860 at La Flèche (Sarthe). After passing through the military college of St-Cyr, which he had entered in 1878, he received a commission as *sous-lieutenant* on 1 October 1880, and advanced to the rank of *général de division* in 1918. During his thirty-five years of service in Algeria and Tunisia he became an authority on North African topography. His writings include *Toute l'Algérie en circuit* (1923), *Circuits sahariens* (1929). He died in Algiers, 23 March 1931. DBF; Peyronnet, 725

Deshen, Shlomo A., born 13 June 1935, he was a graduate of the Hebrew University of Jerusalem, and received a Ph.D. in 1967 from the University of Manchester for his thesis, *Religion and ethnicity in an Israeli local election*. Since 1968 he was a lecturer in social anthropology at Tel-Aviv University. His writings include *A Case of breakdown of modernization in an Israeli immigrant community* (1964), *The Mellah society; Jewish community life in Sherifian Morocco* (1989), *Blind people; the private and public life of sightless Israelis* (1992); and he was joint author of *The Predicament of homecoming* (1974). ConAu, 57-60; Sluglett; Wholsrael, 1976; WhoWorJ, 1978

Desheriev, IUnus Desherievich, fl. 1957, he wrote Бацбийский язык (1953), *Development of non-Russian languages in the USSR; principles and practice* (1957), Социальная лингвистика (1977); and he was joint editor of Русский язык в национальных республиках Советского Союза (1980).

Desika Chari, Sir Tirumalai, born in 1868. After education at Presidency College, Madras, he was a lawyer active in municipal and local civic institutions, 1909-1925. He was knighted in 1922. His writings include *South Indian coins* (1933). He died 9 July 1940. Eminent; Who, 1921-1936; *Who was who*, 4

Desimoni, Cornelio, born 16 September 1813 at Gavi (Alessandria), he was a historian and geographer who received his *aggregazione* from the Facoltà di filosofia e di lettere, Università di Genova, in 1881. His writings include *Saggio storico sulla musica in Liguria*, a cura di M. Tarrini (1987), and numerous contributions to periodicals. He died in Gavi, 29 June 1899. DizBI; IndBI (2); LC

Desio, Ardito, born 18 April 1897 at Palmanova (Udine), he received a Dr.rer.nat., was a fellow of the Royal Geographical Society, a geologist and past director of the Istituto di geologia in the Università di Milano. During the war he served with the Alpine troops. In 1938 he discovered the first deposits of natural oil and gas in Libya. He later led several expeditions in the Himalaya and Karakorum. He was highly decorated for his achievements. His writings include *Le isole italiane dell'Egeo* (1931), *Geology of the Upper Shaksgam Valley, Xinjiang* (1980); and he edited *Geology of Central Badakhshan and* *surrounding countries* (1975).   *Chi è*, 1936-1961;   IntWW;   IndBI (3);   Who, 1974-1999;   Wholtaly, 1980-1998; WhoWor, 1974/75-1978/79

Désiré-Vuillemin, Geneviève M., fl. 1958, she received a doctorate in 1961 for her thesis, *Essai sur le gommier et le commerce dans les escales du Sénégal.* She was affiliated with the Institut pédagogique national. Her writings include *Les rapports de la Mauritanie et du Maroc* (1960), *Contributions à l'histoire de la Mauritanie de 1900 à 1934* (1962), *Kango Moussa, empereur du Mali* (1963), *Histoire de la Mauritanie* (1964), and *Le monde libyco-berbère dans l'antiquité* (1964).   LC

Desjardins, Albert Michel, born 28 April 1838 at Beauvais, he was educated at Sainte-Barbe and l'École de droit de Paris. He received two doctorates in law in 1862 for his theses, *De jure apud Franciscum Baconum*, and *Les plaidoyers de Démosthène.* He was professor of Roman law at Nancy and later held the chair of criminal law at Paris. His writings include *Le ouvoir civil au Concile de Trente* (1870), and *Les Cahiers des États généraux en 1789 et la législation criminelle* (1883). He died in Beauvais, 21 January 1897.   DBF;   IndexBFr² (4)

Desjobert, Amédée, born 15 January 1796 at Orsay (Seine-et-Oise), he was a trained agriculturist, and a *député* for Seine-Inférieure from 1833 to 1848. He was an opponent to French colonization in North Africa. His writings include *L'Algérie en 1846* (1846), and *État sanitaire de l'armée* (1848). He died in Paris, 28 April 1853.   DBF;   IndexBFr² (3)

Desmaisons, Baron Jean Jacques Pierre, born in 1807, he gained a medical doctorate at Chambéry and went to Russia in 1831. His writings include the edition and translation, *Histoire des Mongols et des Tatares*, by Ebülgâzi Bahadır Han (St. Petersburg, 1871-1874), and *Dictionnaire persan-français* (Roma, 1908-1914). He died in 1873.   BiobibSOT, pp. 155-156

Desnottes, L. In 1921, he was a *contrôleur civil suppléant*, assigned as assistant to the *Chef du Contrôle* of Safi, Morocco.

De Solliers, Felix, 1845-1910 *see* Dessoliers, Louis *Félix*

De Somogyi, Joseph, 1889-1976 *see* Somogyi, József

De Souza, Alfred, born 11 January 1930 at Zanzibar, he was educated at Melbourne, Columbia University, and Delhi. His writings include *Indian public schools; a sociological study* (1974), a revised version of his 1971 University of Delhi thesis; *Children in creches; day care for the urban poor* (1979); and *The social organisation of aging among urban poor* (1982).   IntAu&W, 1977;   LC

Desparmet, Joseph, born 6 February 1863 at Béguey (Gironde), he received an arts degree in 1884 from the Université de Lyon and successively taught at the colleges of Cluny and Villefranche-sur-Saône unti 1891. Since nothing kept him in France at the time, he took the opportunity to start teaching French and Latin at the Collège de Tlemcen in the same year. Concurrently he studied colloquial Arabic and made contact with the local population. After he received his first diploma in Arabic in 1897, he took a leave of absence from teaching to take Arabic at l'École supérieure des lettres d'Alger. From then on he advanced rapidly in his career as Arabist, culminating in his *agégation d'arabe* in 1906. He kept teaching at the Grand Lycée d'Alger until 1921 when he requested a transfer to the Lycée Moustapha, where he remained until his retirement in July of 1928. From then on he was resident alternatively in Alger and Les Vans (Ardèche), his wife's place of origin. There he died on 13 March 1942. His writings include *Enseignement de l'arabe dialectal d'après la méthode directe* (1903-1905), and *Coutumes, institutions, croyances des indigènes de l'Algérie* (1913).   *Revue africaine* 87 (1943), pp. 251-268

Despax, Michel, fl. 1961, he received a doctorate in 1957 from the Université de Toulouse for his thesis, *L'entreprise et le droit.* In 1982 he was president of the Université [des sciences sociales] de Toulouse-Le Mirail. His writings include, *Le Droit du travail* (1967), *Le Droit de l'environnement* (1980), *The Law and practice of pollution control in France* (1982), and its translation, *Lois et pratique concernant le contrôle de la pollution en France* (1983).   LC

Despois, Jean Jacques, born 19 January 1901 at Paris. After he received his *agrégation* in history and geography in 1924, he secured a position at the Collège Sadiki in Tunis and began to study the country. However, the two theses which he submitted to the University of Paris in 1935 deal with Libya, *La colonisation italienne en Libye*, as well as *Djebel Nefousa; étude géographique.* He was later appointed a professor at the Faculté des lettres d'Alger. His writings include *La Tunisie* (1930), *La Tunisie orientale; Sahal et basse steppe* (1940), *La Géographie humaine [du Fezzan]* (1946), *L'Afrique du nord* (1949), *L'Afrique blanche française* (1949-53), *Le Hodna, Algérie* (1953), and *Le Djebel Amour, Algérie* (1957). He died 6 July 1978.   *Hommes et destins*, v. 7, pp. 150-51;   Unesco;   WhoFr, 1961/62-1979/80;   WhoWor, 1974/75, 1976/77

Des Portes, A., born 19th cent., he was a navy officer who accompanied a French minister from Tanger by way of Larache to Fès and back via Meknès in 1877, resulting in a reliable surveyance of the return jouney. Henze

Desportes, Edmond, his writings include *Procédure et voies d'exécution en matière musulmane algérienne* (1949), and *La Chambre de révision musulmane et le pourvoi en annulation* (1952). LC

Desprairies, Pierre Charles, born 10 June 1921 at Bayeux (Calvados), he was educated at the Lycée Louis-le-Grand, la Faculté des lettres de Paris, and l'École nationale d'administration. He was a *président-directeur général* of the Société des pétroles d'Afrique équatoriale, 1959-1966, and the Société française des pétroles d'Iran, 1967-1974. He was awarded the Légion d'honneur. His writings include *La Crise d'energie* (1982); and he was editor of *Les Ressources de pétrole; rapport complet* (1978). LC; WhoFr, 1953/54-1997/98

Despréaux, Élise, born in 1870, she was a teacher and founder of a school. She edited a number of short collective works on the history of Latvia, and wrote *Trois ans chez les tsars rouges* (Paris, 1930). IndexBFr² (1); NUC, pre-1956

Desprez, Félix *Hippolyte*, born 7 September 1819 at Breteuil (Eure), he studied law and became a politician and diplomat. He had a first-hand knowledge of the Balkans and Turkey, and was a delegate to several European conferences, among them the Congress of Berlin, 1878. In 1880 he became French ambassador to the Vatican, his last post before retirement in 1884. He had been *grand officier de la Légion d'honneur* since 1870. His writings include *Les Peuples de l'Autriche et de la Turquie* (1850). He died in Paris, 24 September 1898. DBF

Dessigny, Charles Martial René, born 28 October 1861 at Oulch-le-Château (Aisne), he enlisted in the army in 1882, and after passing through the military college of St.-Maixent, which he had entered in 1887, he received a commission as *sous-lieutenant* on 12 March 1888. He entered the Bureau des Affaires indigènes de l'Algérie in 1893 and held a variety of posts at Ghardaïa, Lalla-Marnia, Oran, Touggourt, and Aïn-Sefra, an area which he came to know well, and about whose population and and customs he made valuable reports. Battalion commander since 1910, *officier de la Légion d'honneur*, he was promoted to lieutenant-colonel during the first World War. He remained associated with the military even after his retirement. Peyronnet, p. 880

Dessoliers, Louis *Félix*, born 2 February 1845 at Alger, he received a doctorate in 1873 from the Faculté de droit de Paris for his thesis, *Des Argentarii, en droit romain, et du Crédit foncier, en droit français*. He was a regular contributor to *La Dépêche d'Alger*, and a *député* from 1882 to 1885, when he returned to private life. He published a number of reports submitted to the Chambre des députés or to the Syndicat commercial algérien in the interest of trade and industry. His writings include *Organisation politique de l'Algérie* (1894), *L'Algérie libre; étude économique sur l'Algérie* (1895), and *La Question des chemins de fer d'intérêt général dans la nouvelle organisation administrative et financière de l'Algérie* (1901). He died 5 January 1910. BN; DBF; IndexBFr² (1)

Dessouki, Ali E. Hilal, born 20th cent., he received a Ph.D. in 1972 from McGill University, Montreal, for his thesis, *The origins of socialist thought in Egypt, 1882-1922*. In 1980, he was a visiting professor at the universities of California and Princeton. In 1990, he was a professor of political science at Cairo University. His writings include *Democracy in Egypt* (1978); he was editor of *The Iran-Iraq war; issues of conflict...; proceedings* (1981), and joint editor of *The foreign policy of Arab states* (1984). LC; MESA Roster of members, 1982-1990; Selim

Dessoulavy, Charles Louis, born 19th cent., he received a doctorate in 1901 for his thesis, *St Anselme et son action sur la philosophie du moyen-âge*. His writings, partly under the pseudonym Luigi Cappadelta, include *A Maltese-Arabic word-list, showing which of the corresponding Arabic roots are shared by other Semitic tongues or used in the Quran* (1938), *Index Breviarii romani* (1939), and *Gate of the East and garden of Semitic roots* (1939-41). BLC; LC

Destaing, Léon *Edmond*, born 19 January 1872 at Rozet-Fluans (Doubs). After training as a primary school teacher, he was granted a position in Algeria, where he taught at Alger from 1894 to 1902, concurrently taking lessons in Arabic and Berber at l'École supérieure des lettres d'Alger. From 1902 to 1914 he was professor at medersas in Tlemcen, St. Louis du Sénégal and Alger. For personal reasons he returned to Paris in 1915 and became the first holder of the chair of Berber studies at l'École des langues orientales vivantes; concurrently he lectured at l'École coloniale. His writings include *Étude sur le dialecte berbère des Beni Snoûs* (1907-11), *Dictionnaire français-berbère* (1914), *Étude sur la Tachelhit du Soûs* (1920), *Textes arabes en parler des Chleuhs du Sous* (1937), and *Textes berbères en parler des Chleuhs du Sous* (1940). He died in L'Hay-les-Roses near Paris, 27 December 1940. DBF; *Hommes et destins*, vol. 4, p. 249; *Index Islamicus* (3)

Destains, Eugène, born in 1793 at Paris, he studied Oriental languages in order to qualify for the diplomatic service, but in 1812 he was drafted into the army. Discharged after being seriously wounded, he completed his studies and published translations from the Arabic and Turkish in the *Mercure étranger*. He founded the *Annales de la littérature et des arts* in 1818. As a staunch royalist, he was concurrently director of the *Gazette de France*. In 1829 he was appointed *secrétaire-interprète* at Headquarters of the Armée d'Alger. The evening before he was to sail for Algeria he committed suicide, 17 May 1830. DBF; Hoefer; IndexBFr² (1)

Destanne de Bernis, Gérard René Camille, born 10 November 1928 at Bordeaux, he studied at the Facultés de droit et des lettres de Paris and became a professor of social sciences at the universities of Lille and Grenoble. From 1954 to 1959, he taught at l'Institut des hautes études de Tunis. He was a contributor to the collective work, *L'Afrique de l'indépendance politique à l'indépendance économique* (1975), and joint editor of *Les Multinationales* (1980). Unesco; WhoFr, 1965/66-1984/85

De Stefani, Carlo, born 9 May 1851 at Padova, he studied law and political economy, but later pursued an interest in geology. He died in Firenze, 12 November 1924. DizBI; IndBI (1)

Destenave, George Mathieu, general, born 17 May 1854 at Saint-Cricq (Landes). After graduation from the military college, Saint-Cyr, he was posted to the 2d Régiment Zouaves in 1893, and participated in the campaigns against the French Soudan. He served in French Equatorial Africa and on the Chari from 1900 to 1902. He was awarded the Légion d'honneur. He wrote the pamphlet *La Région du Tchad d'après les travaux du lieut.-col. Destenave et du capt. Truffert*. He died in Toulon, 23 December 1928. DBF; NUC, pre-1956

Destombes, Marcel, Dr. h.c., born in 1905, he was attached to the Département des cartes et plans at the Bibliothèque nationale, Paris, and the Commission on Ancient Maps, International Geographical Union. His writings include *Catalogue des cartes gravées au XVe siècle* (1952). He died in Paris on 26 November 1983. LC; NUC, pre-1956

Destrée-Donckier de Donceel, Annette, born 22 March 1934 at Bruxelles, she received a diploma in history in 1955, and a doctorate in Oriental philology and history in 1973, both from the Université libre de Bruxelles. She there taught Persian language and history, as well as Muslim art and history. Her writings include *Les Fonctionnaires belges au service de la Perse 1898-1915* (1976), and *L'Afrique méditerranéenne* (1977). BioB134; LC

Destro, Adriana, born 18 June 1937 at Verona, she was in 1977 a researcher in the Istituto di Glottologia, Università di Bologna. Thereafter she lectured in anthropology at Trieste until she was appointed a professor at Bologna in 1986. Her writings include*Villaggio palestinese* (1977), *L'ultima generazione* (1984), *In caso di gelosia* (1989), its translation, *The law of jealousy; anthropology of Sotah* (1989); and she edited *Le politiche del corpo* (1994). Wholtaly, 1997, 1998

Desvaux, Nicolas Gilles Toussaint, general, born 1 November 1810 at Paris, he prepared for l'École polytechnique but when the time came, the 1830 revolution broke out. He graduated from l'École de cavalerie de Saumur in 1831. With the support of his authorities, he was able to study in museums and libraries. In 1837 he even obtained a six-month leave of absence to travel to Italy and the Orient. From 1840 to 1859 he was stationed in Algeria; in 1853 he was awarded the Légion d'honneur. In 1864 he was appointed *sous-gouverneur* of Algeria, a post which he held until recalled to Paris in 1866. He kept a regulary diary since 1831. On 29 June 1884 he recorded his activities during the morning; in the afternoon he was found dead. DBF; Vapereau

Desvergers, Marie (Marin) Joseph *Adolphe Noël*, born 2 June 1805 at Paris, he studied law and physical and natural sciences, and subsequently entered l'École des langues orientales in Paris. In 1837 he published *Vie de Mahomet*, by Abu al-Fida, with text, translation and notes, followed in 1840 by *Histoire de l'Afrique*, Ibn Khaldun's text, accompanied by the notes of Ibn al-Athir and Nuwayri, with translation and notes. His other writings include *Abyssinie* (1847), *Arabie* (1847), and *L'Étrurie et les Étrusques* (1862-1864). He died in Nice, 2 January 1867. Fück; Hoefer; Index BFr² (2); *L'Orient, l'Algérie et les colonies françaises* 1 (1866/67), pp. 174-76, 191-92; Vapereau

Des Villettes, Jacqueline, born 20th cent., she wrote *La Vie des femmes dans un village maronite libanais Aïn el Kharoubé* (Tunis, 1964). NUC, 1956-67

Dethan, Georges, born 8 May 1923 at Paris, he was educated at the Lycée Henri IV and l'Ecole nationale des chartes. He was a trained archivist and palaeographer who also obtained a degree in law. From 1947 to 1988 he was a keeper at the Archives du Ministère des Affaires Étrangères. His writings include *Mazarin, un homme de paix à l'âge baroque* (1981), and *Guerre et pouvoir en Europe au XVIIe siècle* (1991). LC; WhoFr, 1971/72-1997/98

Dethier, Jean Jacques. In 1985 he received a Ph.D. from the University of California at Berkeley for his thesis, *The political economy of food prices in Egypt*. He was affiliated with the World Bank. His writings include *Trade, exchange rate, and agricultural pricing policies in Egypt* (1989); he was joint author of *Technological innovation in agriculture; the political economy of its rate and bias* (1985). LC

De Tray, Dennis N., born 8 January 1944, he was in 1977 an adviser at the Pakistan Institute for Development Economics, Islamabad. His writings include *Fiscal restraints and the burden of local and state taxes* (1981), and *Schooling policy in Malaysia* (1985). He also published several short monographs. LC

Dettmann, Klaus, born 20th cent., he received a Dr.phil. in 1967 from the Universität Erlangen-Nürnberg for his thesis, *Damaskus, eine orientalische Stadt zwischen Tradition und Moderne*. He was a professor of cultural geography at the Universität Bayreuth for at least ten years. His writings include the translation from his German original, *Urban development in the north of the Indus Valley* (1982). Kürschner, 2003; Schwarz; *Wer ist wer*, 1990/91-1996/97

De Unger, Edmund, fl. 1986, he was joint author of *Islamic metal work* (1976), and *Islamic carpets and textiles in the Keir Collection* (1978). LC

Deutsch, Robert, born 19th cent., he was an engineer who spent nearly a year in the service of the Syndicat d'entreprises de chemins de fer en Turquie, investigating the feasibility of a railway from al-Hudaydah to San'a'. He returned to Wien in 1912, where he still flourished in 1918.

Deutscher, Isaac, born 3 April 1907 near Kraków, Austria-Hungary, he received an orthodox Jewish education and upbringing. He was a member of the communist party since 1926, but expelled in 1932. He emigrated to England before the second World War and acquired a reputation as expert on Soviet Russia and communism. His writings include *Stalin* (1947), *Ironies of history* (1966), and *Russia after Stalin* (1969). He died a lifelong Marxist in Roma, 19 August 1967. BioIn, 2, 6, 8, 9, 10, 11; ConAu, 5-8 rev.; EncJud; ObitOF, 1979; WhAm, 5; WhE&EA; *Who was who*, 6

Devalle, Susana Beatriz Cristina, born 31 May 1945 at Buenos Aires, she studied at Buenos Aires and Mexico, and received a D.Phil degree from SOAS in 1989. She was a professor of social anthropology at El Colegio de México since 1973. Her writings include *Multi-ethnicity in India* (1980), and *Discourses on ethnicity* (1992); she edited *La diversidad prohibida* (1989). ConAu, 147; LC

Devédeix, born 19th cent. In 1911 he had retired as *capitaine commandant* of the French Spahis in Chari Tchad. Note

De Vega, Guillermo C., he attended Philippine schols and in 1962 earned a Ph.D. in political history in Pakistan. He was a presidential assistant of Philippine President Ferdinand E. Marcos since 1966 and was shot to death in Manila, 27 October 1975. NYT, 28 October 1975, p. 14, col. 5

Develay, Albert, born 19th cent., he travelled in Armenia and Kurdistan around 1890, and published an Armenian work in 1892 in Wien. NYPL

Deverdun, Gaston, fl. 1970, his writings include *Inscriptions arabes de Marrakech* (1956), *Marrakech des origines à 1912* (1959-66), and he was joint author of *La Mosquée al-Qaraouiyn à Fès, avec une étude sur les inscriptions de la mosquée* (1968). LC

Devereux, Robert Essex, born 9 December 1922 at Beaver Dam, Wisc., he graduated from Indiana University in 1944 and received a Ph.D. in 1961 from Johns Hopkins University, Baltimore, Md.. He was with the Department of the Army from 1946 to 1963, when he joined the U.S. Department of State. In 1990 he was a member of the School of International Studies at Johns Hopkins. His writings include *The first Ottoman constitutional period* (1963), and he edited *Muhakamat al-lughatain*, by Ali Shir Navai, with translation and notes in 1966. ConAu, 5-8; MESA Roster of members, 1977-1990

Devéria, Jean *Gabriel*, born 7 February 1844 at Paris, he took an interpreter course for Chinese at l'École des langues orientales, Paris, and then advanced from consular officer to first interpreter at the French Legation in Peking. He was elected member of the Académie des inscriptions in 1897, and professor of Chinese at l'École des langues orientales in 1899. He was joint author of *Inscriptions de l'Orkhon par l'Expédition finnoise 1890* (1892). He died 12 July 1899. DBF

Devernois, Guy, fl. 1960-1963, he was a *directeur d'études* at the Société d'édition d'enseignement supérieur in the 1970s. His writings include *Élaboration du plan national 1970-74; enseignement*. LC

De Verteuil, Charles Robert Joseph, fl. 1953, his writings include *Yellow dust* (1953), *Last train to Shanghai* (1978); and he was joint author of *The teenage marketplace* (1975). LC

Deviatkina, Tamara Filippovna, born 29 September 1918, she was a 1940 graduate of the Moscow State University and received a doctorate in 1953 for her thesis, *Борьба рабочего класса и массовое антиимпериалистическое движение в Индии в 1919-1922 гг.* She was since 1953 a researcher in the Oriental Institute, Soviet Academy of Science. Her writings include *Индийский национальный конгресс 1947-1964* (1970), and *Зарождение коммунистического движеня в Индии* (1978). LC; Miliband; Miliband²

Devic, L. Marcel, born in 1832 at Peyrusse (Aveyron), he was educated at the Collège de Cahors, where he pursued an interest in pure science, but not in order to teach. Still, in his younger years, he was a physics professor at l'École normale d'Auteuil. But he was soon attracted to the study of Oriental languages under A. P. Caussin de Perceval in Paris. Thanks to a remarkable aptitude, he learned one after another, Arabic, Hebrew, Persian, Turkish, and Malay. During the last years of teaching he turned towards comparative philology and lectured in comparative grammar of Indo-European languages at the Faculté des lettres de Montpellier as *maître de conférences*. His writings include *Les aventures d'Antar, fils de Cheddad* (1864), *Dictionnaire étymologique des mots français d'origine orientale* (1876), *Les merveilles de l'Inde, al-'Aja'ib al-Hind, de Buzurg ibn Shahriyar al-Ramhurmuzi* (1883-86), *Pays des Zendjs; ou, La côte orientale d'Afrique au moyen âge* (1883), and *Une traduction inédite du Coran* (1883). He died in 1888. *Bulletin de la Société de linguistique de Paris* v. 6, n° 32 (1888), pp. ccxxvi-ccxxvii

Dévigne, Roger, born 11 September 1886 at Angoulême, he was educated in Angoulême and Paris, where he received a diploma in letters. He was awarded the Légion d'honneur. His *Maison sur la mer* won him the Prix Moréas for 1937, and his *Le légendaire de France à travers notre folklore oral* was awarded by the Académie française in 1942. He died 28 October 1965. DBFC, 1954/55; *Qui est-ce*, 1934; WhoFr, 1955/56

Devillars, Pierre, fl. 1950, his writings include *L'immigration marocaine en France* (Paris, 1954). LC

de Villers, Gauthier, born in 1940 at Bruxelles, he received a doctorate in sociologie from the Université de Louvain and became affiliated with the Centre d'étude et de documentation africaine de Bruxelles; in 1993 he was its director. His writings include *L'État démiurge; le cas algérien* (1987), *Zaïre, 1990-1991; faits et dits de la société* (1992), and *De Mobutu à Mobutu* (1995). EURAMES, 1993

de Visscher, Fernand Marie Émile, born 14 October 1885 at Gent, Belgium, he studied Roman law at the University and subsequently taught at his alma mater from 1919 to 1932, when it became an integral part of Flanders, a decision which he disapproved of. He at once accepted a chair in the Facultés catholiques de Lille and stayed on until 1936. He spent his last twenty academic years teaching Roman law at the Université catholique de Louvain. His writings include *Études de droit romain* (1931). He died in Herent, 15 December 1964. NBN, vol. 2, pp. 133-34; *Revue belge d'archéologie* 35 (1966), pp. 115-118 = vol. 36 (1967), pp. 186-189

Devisse, Jean Joseph, born 14 November 1923 at Amiens (Somme), he studied at the Faculté des lettres de Paris, and received a doctorate in 1973 for his thesis, *Hincmar de Reims*. He was a historian of the middle ages at various French universities. From 1958 to 1963 he taught at the Université de Dakar. In 1969 he began his affiliation with the Comité scientifique international pour la rédaction d'une histoire générale de l'Afrique à l'Unesco, and since 1973 he was a *maître de conférences* at Paris VIII (Vincennes). WhoFr, 1977/78-1981/82|

Devlin, John F., born in 1926, he was a specialist in modern history of the Fertile Crescent, and a fellow of MESA from 1982 to 1990. His writings include *The Ba'th Party* (1976), *Syria, modern state in an ancient land* (1983); and he was joint author of *Iraq, paramount power of the Gulf?* (1989). LC

de Vocht, Henri Alphonse (Hendrik Alfons), born 15 July 1878 at Turnhout, Belgium, he studied at the Université Catholique de Louvain where he subsequently served as a professor until his retirement in 1950. His writings include *De invloed van Erasmus op de engelsche tooneelliteratur der XVI° en XVII° eeuwen* (1908), *Inventaire des archives de l'Université de Louvain, 1426-1797* (1927), and *Monvmenta hvmanistica lovaniensia* (1934). He died 17 July 1962. WhoBelgium, 1957/58; *Who's who in Belgium and Luxemburg*, 1962

Devonshire, Henriette Caroline, born in 1864 at Le Havre, she was a writer on, and lecturer in, Islamic art. Her writings include *Rambles in Cairo* (1920), *Quatre-vingts mosquées et autres monu-ments musulmans du Caire* (1925), and *L'Égypte musulmane et les fondateurs de ses monuments* (1926). LC; NUC, pre-1956; WhE&EA

DeVore, Ronald M., born 20th cent., he received a Ph.D. in 1973 from Indiana University for his thesis, *British military consuls in Asia Minor, 1878-1882*. He was a fellow of MESA, and an executive director of the American Association of Attorney-Chartered Public Accountants in 1990. His writings include *The Arab-Israeli conflict* (1976). LC; MESA Roster of members, 1977-1990

Devoulx, Albert, born in 1826 at Marseille, he grew up in Algeria where he acquired a perfect command of Arabic. He entered the Bureaux du Gouvernement général and later was *sous-chef du bureau* at the Préfecture d'Alger. He was for many years a keeper at the Archives arabes, Service de l'enseignement et domaines à Alger, and an honorary treasurer-archivist of the Société historique algérienne. His writings include *Le Raïs Hamidou* (1858), and *Les archives du consulat général de France à Alger* (1963). He died 17 November 1876. DBF; *Revue africaine* 20 (1876), pp. 514-517

Devoulx, Alphonse, born about 1800. During forty years of his life, he diligently followed all phases of life in Alger, laying the groundwork for his son Albert's researches. He died shortly before his son. *Revue africaine* 20 (1876), pp. 415-416

Devreesse, Robert, born 20 May 1894 at Cisai-Saint-Aubin (Orne), he was a graduate of l'Institut catholique de Paris, an apostolic proto-notary, and for many years attached to the Vatican Library. He received a doctorate in 1945 from the Université de Paris with a thesis entitled *Le patriarcat d'Antioch depuis la paix de l'église jusqu'à la conquête arabe*. His writings include *Introduction à l'étude des manuscrits grecs* (1954). WhoFr, 1954/55-1957/58|

De Vries, Bert, born 4 March 1939 in the Netherlands, he was educated at Calvin College, and received a Ph.D. in 1967 from Brandeis University for his thesis, *The style of Hittite epic and mythology*. Since 1967 he was a professor of history, and since 1980 also chairman of department, Calvin College, positions which he still held in 1997. He was joint editor of *Perspectives of global change* (1997). DrAS, 1974, 1978, 1982; *MESA Roster of members*, 1977; NatFacDr, 1997

Devrim, İzzet Melih, born 6 June 1887 at Jerusalem. After he graduated from Galatasaray Sultanîsini, he studied law at Istanbul and Paris, where he received a doctorate in 1938. He was a writer, playwright, and lecturer. From 1940 to 1942 he taught French at the Turkish Harb Akademisi. His writings include *Tezadd* (1917), its translation, *Gegensätze* (1917), and *Her güzelliğe âşık* (1938). He died in Istanbul, 15 June 1966 EIS; Meydan

De Waal Malefijt, Annemarie, born 23 May 1914 at Amsterdam, she was a graduate of Columbia University, where she also received a Ph.D. in 1960 with a thesis entitled *The Javanese population of Surinam*. In 1960 she began her affiliation with Hunter College, City University of New York. At the time of her death of cancer on 15 December 1982, she was professor emerita of anthropology. Her writings include *Religion and culture* (1968). ConAu, 61-64, 109; NYT 18 December 1982, p. 34, col. 6

Dewachter, Michel, fl. 1971, he was joint editor of *Monuments of Egypt; the Napoleonic edition* (1987), and *L'égyptologie et les Champollion; recueil d'études* (1994). LC

von **Dewall**, Adolf Friedrich, born 28 April 1834 at Cheribon, Java, the son of Hermann von de Wall (1807-1873), he grew up like a native child, a fact which made it natural to become an authority on the Malay language in later life. From 1852 to his retirement in 1877 he was a colonial official who also profitted from his linguistic competence in Sudanese and Javanese. He died in Batavia, 6 July 1909. EncNI, vol. 1 (1917), p. 596; NieuwNBW, vol. 8 (1930), cols. 386-387

Dewall, Hermann T. von, 1807-1873 *see* Wall, Hermann Theodor Friedrich Karl E. W. A.. C. von de

Dewdney, John Christopher, born 8 June 1928 at Woodford, Essex, he was a professor of geography at the University of Durham. From 1965 to 1967 he taught at Fourah Bay College, U.C., Sierra Leone. His writings include *A geography of the Soviet Union* (1965), *Turkey* (1971); and he was joint author of *Cambridge atlas of the Middle East and North Africa* (1987). ConAu, 103; IntAu&W 1976, 1977; WhoWor, 1976/77; WrDr, 1974/76-1998/2000

Dewulf, Eugène Édouard Désirél, born 30 March 1831 at Hoymille (Nord). After his graduation from l'École polytechnique and l'École d'application de Metz, he joined the army engineers. He retired with the rank of general. He was an accomplished mathematician who was fluent in Arabic. He served in Algeria, with interruptions, until 1870. He died in Aix-en-Provence, 14 April 1896. DBF; Peyronnet, p. 806

de **Wulf**, Maurice Marie Charles Joseph, born in 1867, he was a Belgian historian of medieval philosophy, whose writings include *Histoire de la philosophie médiévale* (1900), its translation into English, 1909, German, 1913, Italian, 1913, and Dutch, 1947, and *Scholasticism old and new* (1903). He died 23 December 1947. Isis 39 (1948), p. 69; Master (1)

Dex, Léo, *pseud.*, 1864-1904 *see* Deburaux, Édouard Léopold Joseph

Deyell, John S. fl. 1974, he was a scholar of economic history and its interface with numismatics. He was a sometime first secretary at the Canadian High Commission, New Delhi. His writings include *Living without silver; the monetary history of early medieval North India* (1990). LC

Deyrolle, Théophile, 19th cent., he was a natural scientist who visited the Caucasus in 1868, and Lazistan and Armenia in 1869. Henze

Dezos de la Roquette, Jean Bernard Marie Alexandre, born 31 October 1784 at Castelsarrasin (Tarn-et-Garonne). Early in life he went to Paris, where he started as *chef du bureau* at the Caisse d'amortissement. He also served for some time in the Garde nationale, and was later admitted as *avocat* in the royal court, Paris. When his relative, General Dessolle, was appointed minister of foreign affairs, he became a member of his cabinet, and was later made a *rédacteur*, a position which he held until 1825. He was a prolific writer on geographical matters. He died in 1868. DBF; NUC, pre-1956

Dezsó, László, born in 1927, his writings include *Очерки по истории эакарпатских говоров* (1967), *Studies in syntactic typology and contrastive grammar* (1982), and *A XVI-XIX. szádasi kar-pátukrán nyelvemlékek magyar jövevényszavai* (1989). LC

Dhaher, Ahmad J. *see* Zahir, Ahmad Jamal

Dharma Bhanu, M.A., Ph.D., professor, fl. 1956, his writings include *History and administration of the North-Western Provinces, subsequently called the Agra Province, 1803-1858* (1957), a revision of his 1955 Agra University thesis, and *The province of Agra, its history and administration*, (2nd ed., 1979).

Dhoquois, Guy, he was in 1983 a *maître assistant* in historical sociology at the Université de Paris VII. His writings include *Critique du politique* (1983), and *Histoire de la pensée historique* (1991). LC

Diachenko, Vasyl' Dmytrovych, fl. 1956, he was an anthropologist whose writings include *Антропологічний склад українского народы* (1965). NUC, pre-1956; OSK

Diakonoff, I. M., 1915- *see* D'iakonov, Igor' Mikhailovich

D'iakonov, Igor' Mikhailovich, born 30 December 1914 (12 January 1915) at Petrograd, he graduated in 1938 from the Faculty of History and Philology, Leningrad State University, and received a doctorate in 1960. From 1936 to 1959 he was affiliated with the Ėrmitazh, Leningrad. His writings include *Развитие земельных отношений в Ассирии* (1949), *Языки древней Передней Азии* (1967), *Geographical names according to Urartian texts* (1981); and he edited *Ancient Mesopotamia* (1966), and *Лирическая поэзия древнего Востока* (1984). LC; Miliband; Miliband²

D'iakonov, Mikhail Mikhailovich, born 13 (26) June 1907, he studied at Oslo, specializing in Iranian subjects, and graduated in 1930 from the Faculty of Linguistics and Material Culture, Leningrad State University. He received a doctorate in 1946 for his thesis, *Очерки по истории древнего Ирана*. He advanced from lecturer in 1938 to professor in 1949. During the last years of his life he was a professor of history at Moscow University. His writings include *Фердоуси; жизнь и творчество* (1940), *У истоков древней культуры Таджикистана* (1956), *Очерк истории древнего Ирана* (1961), as well as translations of Persian classical texts. He died in Moscow, 8 June 1954. EncIran; EST; LC; Miliband; Miliband²

D'iakonova, Natal'ia Vasil'evna, born 28 November (11 December) 1907 at St. Petersburg, she graduated from the Oriental Faculty of the Leningrad State University in 1930, and was successively attached to the Museum of History, Samarkand, the Ukrainian Oriental Institute, Kharkov, and the Ermitage, Leningrad. Her writings include *Два дидактических отрывка Шахнаме Фирдоуси* (1946), *Хотанске древиости* (1960), and *Искусство народов зарубежного Востока в Эрмитаже* (1962). LC; Miliband; Miliband²

D'iakonova, Vera Pavlovna, fl. 1958. She was a Russian archaeologist who excavated in southern Siberia. LC

D'iakov, F. V., fl. 1930. His writings include *Проблема наследования в колхосах* (Baku, 1930). LC

D'iakov, Nikolai Nikolaevich, born 18 June 1953 at Leningrad, he graduated in 1976 from the Leningrad Oriental Faculty, where he also received his first degree in 1980 for a thesis on the political history of Algeria from 1892 to 1918. His writings include *Младоалжирцы и антиколониальная борьба в Алжире* (1985). LC; Miliband²

Diamantara, Achilleos Z., fl. 1905, his writings include *Η Νήσος Μεγίνη, ουνοπτική περιγραφή αναγνωσθείσα εν τη αδελφότητι των κασζελλοριζίων κατά δεκέμβριου του 1893 υπό Αχιλλέωσ Ζ. Διαμανταρά* (1894). BN

Diamanti, Octave, born 19 September 1864 at Cairo, where his father was physician to the viceroys 'Abbas Pasha and Sa'id Pasha. He studied at Paris, where he received a law degree in 1885; thereafter he was a student at l'École des sciences politiques; he took the oath before the Cour d'appel in 1889. A few months later, he left for Persia, where he stayed two years as secretary to the president to the Council of State. Concurrently he was a representative of the Chambre de commerce française de Constantinople, and an interim *chargé d'affaires* of the Belgian Legation at Tehran. In 1892 he went on a mission to the government of Russian Turkestan to discuss a possible extension of the Trans-caspian railway. He made two journeys during which he visited Central Asia and the Pamirs, including Bukhara. He returned by way of St. Petersburg, where he reported to the ministers of defence and finances, and, under the auspices of the French ambassador de Montebello, put the finishing touch to the negociations. Upon his return to Paris in 1893, he accomplished a mission for the Ministry of Trade and Commerce to Egypt, Syria, and Palestine. After his return, he lectured at several French geographical societies, trying to popularize those far-away regions in the interest of the French economy. His travel reports were published in *Revue bleue, Revue scientifique*, and *Nouvelle revue*. On 28 September 1898 he was appointed director of the Compagnie Coloniale et des Mines d'or de la côte Ouest de Madagascar. He was president of the Section d'explorations of the Société de géographie commerciale, a member of the Société de géographie de Paris, the Union coloniale, the Comité de propagande of the Alliance française, and a corresponding member of several learned sociéties. Curinier, v. 2, pp. 221-222

Diamond, William, born 20 December 1917 at Baltimore, Md., he was a graduate of Johns Hopkins University, Baltimore, where he also received a Ph.D. in 1942 for his thesis, *The economic thought of Woodrow Wilson*. He was a banker who was affiliated with the International Bank for Reconstruction and Development, as well as the World Bank. His writings include *Development banks* (1957), and *Bancos de fomento* (1957). AmM&WS, 1978 S; BlueB, 1976; ConAu, 65-68; Master (3); WhoE, 1991/92

de **Dianous** (Dianoux), Hugues Jean, fl. 1954, his writings include *L'Afrique "portugaise" dans l'oeuvre de René Pélissier* (Paris, Institut National des Langues et civilisations orientales, 1989). LC

Diarra, Mamadou, born 15 September 1925 at Dakar, he studied law at the Université de Paris, where he received a *doctorat d'état* in 1972. He was a financial adviser to the president of the Conseil du Sénégal and a head of the Bureau d'études at the Ministère de la fonction publique et du travail. His writings include *Les états africaines et la garantie monétaire de la France* (Dakar, 1972), *Justice et développement au Sénégal* (1973), and *Le Sénégal, concession royale; histoire de la colonie* (1973). The latter two publications represent portions of his Paris thesis. He also wrote *Memento de la fonction publique* (1982). AfricaWW, 1996; LC

Diarra, Tiémoko Diatigui, born 20th cent., he was in 1969 an attorney-general and president in the Cour d'appel du Mali. Note

Dias Farinha, António see Fariiha, António Dias

Diatlov, Viktor Innokent'evich, born 20 January 1949 in Irkutsk Oblast, he graduated in 1972 in history fro Irkutsk State University and received his first degree in 1977 with a thesis on modern Egypt. Affiliated with his alma mater since 1976, he became a lecturer in 1984. His writings include Крупная буржуазия в Египте накануне революции 1952 года (1983), and he was joint editor of Страны и народы Востока; пути развития. Тезисы докладов к региональной конференции (1988). LC; Miliband²

Díaz Esteban, Fernando, fl. 1985, he received a doctorate in 1975 from the Universidad de Madrid for his thesis, *Sefer 'Oklah wĕ-'Oklah; colección de listas de palabras destinades a conservar la integridad del texto hebreo de la Biblia entre los judios de la edad media.* LC

Díaz Garcia, Amador, born 20th cent., he received a doctorate in 1973 from the Universidad de Granada for his thesis, *El dialecto árabe-hispánico y el "Kitab fī lahn al-âmma" de Ibn Hišam al-Lajmi.* Thereafter he was appointed a professor of Arabic at Granada, a position which he still held in 1997. His writings include *Devocionario mosrisco en árabe dialectal hispánico* (1981). Arabismo, 1992, 1994, 1997; EURAMES; LC

Díaz de Villegas, José, his writings, partly under the pseudonym Hispanicus, include *El estrecho de Gibraltar* (1953), *Oriente frente a Occidente entre la paz y la guerra* (1956), *Africa septentrional; Marruecos, el nexo del Estrecho* (1961), and he was joint author of *Plazas y provincias africanas españolas* (1962). NUC, 1956-67

Dib, Pedro, his writings include *Essai sur une théorie des mobiles en droit civil hanefite* (Beyrouth, Imprimerie catholique, 1952). LC

Diba, Farhad, born 29 April 1937 in Iran, he studied history and politics at M.I.T. and Oxford, where he received an M.A. in 1960. For many years, he was a researcher at Oxford University and a member of the British Society for Middle Eastern Studies. His writings include *Mohammad Mossadegh; a political biography* (1986). DrBSMES 1993; EURAMES; *MESA Roster of members*, 1982-1990; Private

Diblan Carlson, Sevinç *see* Carlson, Sevinç Diblan

Dicca, J., Dr., born 19th cent. In 1893, he had resigned his position as *professeur de matière médicale* at l'École impériale de médecine et de pharmacie militaire, Val de Grace. Note

Dicey, Edward James Stephen, born in 1832 at Claybrook, Leicestershire, he was called to the bar from Gray's Inn, but he did not practise. He became a journalist whose writings include *The Morning Land* (1870), *England and Egypt* (1881), *The story of the khedivate* (1902), and *Egypt and the future* (1907). He died in 1911. BiD&SB; BioIn, 6; *Concise DNB*, Index and epitome to the 1901-1911 supplement, p. 32 (the reference to 2 Suppl. i. 497 has not been confirmed); DcBiPP; DcEnL; NewC; *Who was who*, 1

Dichy, Joseph, born 20th cent., he was in 1993 a professor of Arabic and Islamic studies at the Faculté des langues in the Université Lumière-Lyon 2. EURAMES, 1993

Dick, Ignace, born in 1926 at Aleppo, he was educated at the Seminary of St. Ann, Jerusalem, and the Université de Louvain, where he obtained a doctorate. He later became a priest of the Roman Melkite Catholic Church in Aleppo. His writings include *Qu'est-ce que l'Orient chrétien?* (1965), and its translation, *What is the Christian Orient?* (1967); he edited *Maymar fi wujud al-khaliq wa-al-din al-qawim*, by T. Abu Qurrah (1982). ConAu, 25-28, new rev. 12; LC

Dicken, Mrs. Alice Mary, born in 1885, she was a novelist who wrote under the pseudonym Thora Stowell. Her writings include *The seller of perfumes* (1923), *The black camel* (1927), *The desert flower* (1928), *Ways of birds* (1937), and *The scarlet flute* (1951). BLC; NUC, pre-1956

Dickerhof, Harald, born 6 November 1941 at Edenkoben, Germany, he was a professor of medieval history at the Katholische Universität Eichstädt. His writings include *Land, Reich, Kirche im historischen Lehrbetrieb an der Universität Ingolstadt* (1971), a revison of his thesis, München, 1971. Kürschner, 1996

Dickerson, George, fl. 1974, he was a public information officer of the United Nations Relief and Work Agency. Note

Dickie, Archibald Campbell, born in 1868 at Dundee, he was architect to the Palestine Exploration Fund, 1894-97, and a member of the executive committee from 1906 until his death in 1941. He was joint author of *Excavations at Jerusalem, 1894-1897; plans and illustrations by A. C. Dickie* (1898). BLC; BioIn, 15

Dickie, James, 1934- *see* Zaki, Yaqub

Dickinson, Eric Charles, born in 1892, he was a graduate of Exeter College, Oxford, and a sometime professor of English literature, Government College, Lahore, principal, Sadiq Egerton College, Bahawalpur. He held the chair of English at Muslim University, Aligarh, from 1921 to 1927. His writings include *Laolus and other poems* (Aligarh, 1924); he was joint author of *Kishangarh painting* (1959). He died in 1951. NUC, pre-1956; WhE&EA

Dickson, Bertram, captain, born 19th cent., he was in 1910 a British military consul at Van, Turkey, and travelled in the surrounding country, particularly in Kurdistan east of the Tigris. Note

Dickson, Charles H., fl. 1860, he was a British vice-consul and a traveller who explored five different routes of the Sahara between Tripoli and Ghadamès from 1849 to 1854. Henze

Dickson, Gladys, born 19th cent., she was affiliated with the Palestine Exploration Fund, and translated from the Arabic *A Jerusalem Christian treatise on astrology* (London, 1909). NUC, pre-1956

Dickson, Harold Richard Patrick, born in 1881, he was educated at Oxford and in 1903 joined the 1st Connaught Ranger. Having joined the Indian Army in 1908, his knowledge of Arabic led to his appointment to Mesopotamia in 1914. At the end of the war he was appointed Political Agent, Bahrain, and in 1920 returned as Political Officer to Iraq. He was present at the 'Uqayr Conference of 1922. After a spell in India he returned to the Gulf as secretary to the Political Resident. In 1929 he took the post of Political Agent, Kuwait. He and his wife (d. 1990), author of *Forty years in Kuwait*, were to devote the rest of their lives to Kuwait. His writings include *The Arab of the desert* (1949), and *Kuwait and her neighbours* (1956). He died in 1959. BritInd (1); Facey Grant, pp. 80-82; *Who was who*, 5

Dickson, Martin Bernard, born 22 March 1924 at Brooklyn, N.Y., he joined the U.S. Army, where he was inducted into the OSS [Office of Strategic Studies] and learned Persian in Michigan, Greek in Egypt and Greece, and Chinese and Russian in China. After the end of the war he pursued more formal studies at the University of Washington and Princeton University, where he received a Ph.D. in 1958 for his thesis, *Shah Tahmasb and the Uzbeks*, in the course of which he added Arabic and Turkish to his expertise. His studies in sixteenth-century Central Asian and Iranian history took him to the Sorbonne, to Istanbul, Tehran and Tabriz, where he spent four years. He spent his entire professional career at Princeton, where he was professor of Near Eastern studies until his death from heart and kidney disease on 14 May 1991. His writings include *The Houghton Shahnameh* (1981). A jubilee volume was published in 1990: *Intellectual studies in Islam*. MESA *bulletin* 25 ii (1991), pp. 307-308

Dickson, Violet Penelope Lucas-Calcraft, Dame, born 3 September 1896 at Gautby, Lincolnshire, she was educated in Britain and Switzerland. She entered the Arab world by accident when, in 1920, she was married to Major Harold Dickson, an officer in the Indian Army. She spent most of her life in Kuwait, where her husband was political agent. She was a member of the Royal Society of Asian Affairs, received the Lawrence of Arabia Medal in 1961, and was awarded M.B.E., C.B.E. and D.B.E. Her writings include *The wild flowers of Kuwait and Bahrain* (1955), and the autobiography, *Forty years in Kuwait* (1921). She died in London, 4 January 1991. *Asian affairs* 22 (1991), pp. 240-41; Au&Wr, 1971; Facey Grant; IntAu&W, 1976, 1977, 1982; Who, 1977-1991

Diculescu, Vladimir Gh., fl. 1970-1977, his writings include *O manufactură de ceramică la Tirgu-Jiu, 1832-1863* (1956), *Viaţa cotidiană a Ţării Româneşti în documente, 1800-1848* (1970), and *Bresle, negustori şi în Ţara Românească* (1973). OSK

Didden, Horst, fl. 1968-1969, his writings include *Irak; eine sozio-ökonomosche Betrachtung* (1969).

Didier, Charles Emmanuel, born in 15 September 1805 at Genève, where he studied law and sciences. After mediocre success in journalism and fiction writing, he travelled in Europe and the Middle East. His writings include *Promenade au Maroc* (1844), *Cinquante jours au désert* (1857), *Séjour chez le Grand-chérif de la Mekke* (1857), its translation, *Soujourn with the Grand Sharif of Makkah* (1985), *500 lieues sur le Nil* (1858), and *Les nuits du Caire* (1860). He also wrote two un-informative and sensational books on his journey through the Sudan, published in Paris in 1857 and 1858. During his last travels he lost his eyesight nearly completely. He committed suicide in Paris on 8 March 1864. J. A. Sellards wrote a biography, *Dans le sillage du romantisme; Charles Didier* (1933). BiD&SB; Henze; Hill; IndexBiF² (3); Vapereau

Dieck, Alfred, born 4 April 1906 at Großsalze, Germany, he received a Dr.phil. and became an archaeologist. His writings include *Die europäischen Moorleichenfunde* (1965), *Schwarz liegt das Moor* (1971), *Sagen, Märchen und Geschichten um Karlstein im Landkreis Berchtesgadener Land* (1977). Kürschner, 1980, 1983, 1987, 1992|

Diehl, Katherine née Smith, born 16 May 1906 at Manheim, Pa, she was educated at Millersville Normal School, Boston University, Emory University, and the University of Michigan. She taught mathematics in Delta, Pa., before becoming a librarian in 1938. She was in East Pakistan and West Bengal as a librarian from 1959 to 1962, when she was appointed a professor at the Graduate School of Library Science in Rutgers University. Her writings include *Early Indian imprints* (1964), *Primary sources for 16th-19th century studies in Bengal, Orissa, and Bihar libraries* (1971), *Printers and printing in the East Indies to 1850* (1990); and she edited Lewis Ferdinand Smith's English translation of Mir Amman Dihlavi, *The tale of the four durwesh* (1970). ConAu, P-1; WhoLibl, 1982; WhoLibS, 1955, 1966

Diehl, Michel Charles, born 4 July 1859 at Strasbourg, he was an archaeologist and historian of art, who became a professor of archaeology at the Université de Nancy in 1888. From 1899 until his retirement he was professor of Byzantine archaeology at the Université de Paris. He was an indefatigable worker despite being inflicted by blindness in his old age. His writings include *Histoire de l'Empire byzantin* (1919), and *History of the Byzantine Empire* (1925). He died in Paris, 2 November 1944. *Byzantion* 17 (1944/5), pp. 414-416; DBF; NDBA

Diels, Friedrich Ludwig Emil, born 24 September 1874 at Hamburg, he studied botany at the Universität Berlin, where he received a doctorate in 1896 for his thesis, *Vegetations-Biologie von Neu-Seeland*. Since 1906 he was a professor at Marburg, and was later successively appointed director of the Botanical gardens and professor of botany in Berlin. He was a president of the Gesellschaft für Erdkunde, Berlin. He died in Berlin, 7 March 1945. DtBE

Diem, Werner, born in 1944, he received a doctorate in 1968 from the Universität München for his thesis, *Das Kitab al-ǧim des aš-Šaibani*. He held the chair of Oriental philology in the Universität Köln since 1976. His writings include *Hochsprache und Dialekt im Arabischen* (1974), *Arabische Briefe auf*

Papyrus und Papier aus der Heidelberger Papyrus-Sammlung (1991), and *al-Ism wa-al-sifah fi al-nahw* (1994). Kürschner, 1976, 1980, 1983, 1987, 1992, 1996

Dien, Albert E., born 13 July 1927 at St. Louis, Mo., he was a graduate of the University of California at Berkeley, where he also received his Ph.D. in 1962. After teaching Chinese at the University of Hawaii from 1960 to 1962, he was appointed professor of Chinese studies at Stanford University, a position which he still held in 1997. DrAS, 1974, 1978, 1982; NatFacDr, 1997

Diener, Carl, born 11 December 1862 at Wien, where he studied geography and also received a doctorate in 1883 for his thesis, *Das Zemmtal und seine Umrandung*. Thereafter he visited Syria and Lebanon. Since 1897 he was a professor of geology at the Universität Wien. He died 6 January 1928. DtBE; DtBilnd; Henze; *Mitteilungen* der Geographischen Gesellschaft in Wien, 1928, pp. 93-95; NDB; ÖBL

Diener, Paul, born in 1939, he was educated at the University of Wisconsin, Milwaukee, and Stanford University, where he received a Ph.D. in 1979 for his thesis, *To the making of man; new evolutionism in anthropological theory*. He held teaching positions at Island School, San Juan, Puerto Rico, the University of South Dakota, Yale University, the University of California at Riverside, and Stanford University. In 1978 he was a data analyst at the Southern Wisconsin Health Systems Agency in Milwaukee. LC

Dienes, Leslie Dennis, born 2 January 1938 at Nábrád, Hungary, he was a graduate of McGill University, Montreal, P.Q., and received a Ph. D. in geography in 1968 from the University of Chicago. In 1972 he was appointed a professor of geography at the University of Kansas, Lawrence, a position which he still held in 1999. His writings include *Soviet energy policy and the hydrocarbons* (1978), *The regional dimensions of Soviet energy policy* (1979), and *Soviet Asia; economic development and national policy choices* (1987). AmM&WS, 1976 P; NatFacDr, 1997-1999

Diercks, Gustav, born 13 January 1852 at Königsberg, Germany, he studied classical and oriental philology at Berlin and Paris and received a Dr.phil. In 1871 he became a professor of Sanskrit, Persian, and Arabic at the Università di Napoli. He later went to Cairo as a librarian. In 1875 he visited North Africa, Spain, India, and North America. Since 1891 he was a foreign correspondent to leading newspapers, and also taught at the Humboldt Akademie, Berlin. His writings include *Die Araber im Mittelalter und ihr Einfluss auf die Kultur Europa's* (1875), *Geschichte Spaniens von den frühesten Zeiten bis auf die Gegenwart* (1895-96), *Die Marokkofrage und die Konferenz von Algericas* (1906), *Kreuz und Halbmond* (1910), and *Hie Allah; das Erwachen des Islam* (1914). He died in Berlin, 13 January 1934. DtBE; DtBilnd (5); *Wer ist's*, 1928

Diergart, Paul, born 16 January 1875 at Duisburg, Germany, he was a chemist who worked for some time at the Königliche Porzellan Manufaktur, Berlin. He later lectured in, and contributed articles on, the history of science. He was a member of the Gesellschaft für Geschichte der Medizin, der Naturwissenschaften und der Technik. DtBilnd (1); *Wer ist's*, 1922, 1928, 1935

von **Diest**, Walther, born in 1851, he was a Prussian colonel. In the service of the Königliche Akademie der Wissenschaften he conducted a survey of the region around Pergamon in 1886. From there he continued by way of Kütaya and Eskişehir to Amasra and then followed the coast to Constantinople, a journey which he described in *Von Pergamon über den Dindymos zum Pontus* (1889). He later travelled again in central Asia Minor in 1892 and 1896. His writings include *Von Tilsit nach Angora im Frühjahr 1896* (1898); and he was joint author of *Neue Forschungen im nordwestlichen Kleinasien* (1895). He died after 1913. Henze

Dieterici, Carl Friedrich Wilhelm, born 23 August 1790 at Berlin. After he studied political economy at the universities of Köinigsberg and Berlin, he entered the Ministry of Cultural Affairs in 1820. Since 1835 he was head of the Bureau of Statistics, and since 1847, a member of the Preußische Akademie der Wissenschaften. He died in Berlin, 29 July 1859. DtBE; DiBilnd (2); NDB

Dieterici, Friedrich Heinrich, born 6 July 1821 at Berlin, he studied theology and Oriental languages at Berlin, Halle, and Leipzig, and received a Dr.phil. in 1846 from the Universität Berlin for *De antologia arabica Tsaalebii unio actatis appellata*. After his Dr.habil. in 1846, he travelled in the Orient from 1847 to 1850, when he was appointed professor of Arabic language and literature at Berlin. His writings include *Chrestomathie ottomane* (1854), and *Arabisch-deutsches Handwörterbuch zum Koran und Thier und Mensch* (1881). He also edited and translated works of al-Farabi, al-Mutanabbi, al-Tha'alibi, and Ikhwan al-Safa'. He died in Berlin, 18 August 1903. DtBE; DtBilnd (4); Embacher; Fück, 173; NDB

Dieterlen, Germaine, born 15 May 1905 at Paris, she received a *doctorat d'état* in ethnology in 1949 from the Université de Paris, a second doctorate in 1951 for her thesis, *Essai sur la religion bambara*, and diplomas from l'École pratique des hautes études, and l'École pratique des langues orientales.

412

She held the chair of Black African religions at l'École pratique des hautes études. Her writings include *Les âmes des Dogons* (1941), and *Le titre d'honneur des Arou, Dogon, Mali* (1982). A jubilee volume was published in 1978: *Systèmes de signes; texctes réunis en hommage à Germaine Dieterlen*. LC; Unesco

Dietrich, Albert, born 2 November 1912 at Hamburg, he received a Dr.phil. in 1937 from the Universität Leipzig for his thesis, *Arabische Papyri aus der Hamburger Staats- und Universitäts-bibliothek*. He taught at the Universität Heidelberg since 1949. His writings include *Arabische Briefe aus der Papyrussammlung der Hamburger Staats- und Universitätsbibliothek* (1955). Kürschner, 1983-96

Dietrich, Ernst Ludwig, born 28 January 1897 at Groß-Umstadt, Germany, he studied theology and Islamic subjects at the Universität Gießen, where he received a Dr.phil. in 1925 for *Der Mahdi Mohammed Ahmed nach arabischen Quellen*. Thereafter he attended the Priester- seminar in Friedberg. From 1934 to 1945 he was *Landesbischof* of the Evangelische Landeskirche Hessen-Nassau. Since 1949 he taught at the Orient-Institut Frankfurt am Main, and since 1956 at the Universität Frankfurt. He died in Wiesbaden, 20 January 1974. DtBE; DtBilnd; Kürschner, 1970; Schwarz; Wer ist's, 1935

Dietze, Joachim, born 16 Oktober 1931 at Dresden, Germany, he completed German and Slavic studies with two doctorates. Thereafter he held various positions as a professor and librarian at Dresden, Leipzig, Berlin, Weimar, and Halle. His writings include *August Schleicher als Slavist* (1966), *Die Sprache der ersten Novgoroder Christen*; and he edited *275 Jahre Universitäts- und Landes-bibliothek in Halle/Saale* (1971). JahrDtB, 1993, 1995/96; Kürschner, 1992, 1996

Dieulafoy, Jane Paule Rachel née Magre, born into a wealthy family on 29 June 1851 at Toulouse. In 1870 she married Marcel Dieulafoy and joined him in l'Armée de la Loire during the Franco-Prussian war. From that time, she adopted masculine costume and a short haircut in her extensive travels and her mundane Parisian life. She studied drawing and sculpture, knew several European languages, and acquired some knowledge of Moroccan Arabic. She accompanied her husband on an unpaid assignment in Persia, as a *collaborateur* - she used the masculine form purposely - covering on horseback all the itinerary of the voyage from Marseille to Athens, Istanbul, Erevan, Tehran, and by way of Bushire and Mesopotamia to Susa, 1881-1882. She was fascinated by Persia, and wrote profusely on the country, and photographed and processed on the spot men and women with the camera obscura she carried along with a cumbersome photographic material. She managed to penetrate into the private women's quarters, *andaruns*, and left vivid descriptions of the lives of secluded women of all ranks. Her writings include *La Perse, la Chaldée et la Susiane* (1887), *A Suse; journal des fouilles, 1884-1886* (1888), and *At Susa, the ancient capital of the kings of Persia* (1890). She died at the Château de Langlade, 25 May 1916. Eve and Jean Gran-Aymeric wrote a biography, *Jane Dieulafoy; une vie d'homme* (1991). Curinier I, pp. 118-119; DBF; EncIran; Master (3); LexFrau; Wer ist's, 1909

Dieulafoy, Marcel Auguste, born 3 August 1844 at Toulouse, he was a graduate of l'École poly-technique and l'École des ponts et chaussées. He took up his first position as an engineer in Algeria in 1868, at the same time pursuing an interest in archaeology. From 1871 to 1879 he held an appoint-ment at Toulouse as the architect in charge of historical monuments and came to travel extensively in England, Italy, Spain, Egypt, and Morocco. Together with his wife Jane, he repeatedly excavated in Persia from 1880 to 1887, work which is the basis of his *L'art antique de la Perse* (1884-85). His writ-ings include *Espagne et Portugal* (1913), its translations, *Art in Spain and Portugal* (1913), *L'arte in Spagna e Portogalla* (1913), *Geschichte der Kunst in Spanien und Portugal* (1913), and *El arte en España y Portugal* (1920). He died in Paris, 25 February 1920. DBF; EncIran; Pallas; RNL; Wer ist's, 1909

Diez, Erna, born 8 April 1913 at Kassa (Kaschau/Kosice), Hungary, she grew up in Hungary and retained a command of Hungarian throughout her life. She studied at the Universität Graz, where she received a Dr.phil. degree in 1937 for her thesis, *Quomodo Valerius Maximus res in factorum et dictorum memorabilium libris IX narratas exonaverit*. She remained at Graz and retired as a professor of classical archaeology. Her writings include *Flavia solva; die römischen Steindenkmäler auf Schloss Seggau bei Leibnitz* (1949). *Classica et provincialia; Festschrift Erna Diez* was presented to her in 1978. Kürschner, 1950-1996; LexFrau; WhoAustria, 9th ed., 1977/78

Diez, Ernst, born 27 January 1878 at Lölling, Austria, he studied history of art and archaeology at the Universität Graz, where he received a doctorate in 1902. Thereafter he found employment with various historical institutions in Wien before he went on an unpaid assignment to the Berliner Museen in 1908. He returned to Wien in 1911 and had the chance to accompany O. von Niedermayer on his expedition to Persia, returning by way of India, Mesopotamia, and Asia Minor. In 1926 he was appointed associate professor of history of art at Bryn Mawr, Pa., where he remained with interruptions until 1933. In 1943 he was invited to teach Islamic and Turkish art at Istanbul. He returned to Wien in 1950 and died there, 8 July 1961. His writings include *Die Kunst der islamischen Völker* (1915),

Churasanische Baudenkmäler (1918), *Einführung in die Kunst des Ostens* (1922), *Entschleiertes Asien* (1940), *Glaube und Welt des Islam* (1941), and *Iranische Kunst* (1944). DtBE; EncIran; *Kunst des Orients* 4 (1963), pp. 110-112; Kürschner, 1925-35; Teichl; *Wer ist's*, 1935

von **Diez**, Heinrich Friedrich, born 2 September 1751 at Bernburg/Saale, Germany. After legal studies at the Universität Halle, he was appointed director of the chancellery in Magdeburg and, in 1784, Prussian *chargé d'affaires* in Constantinople. On account of exceeding his powers in the negociations with the Sublime Porte, he was recalled in 1790 and forcibly retired. Since 1807 he was resident in Berlin, where he pursued an interest in oriental studies. His two contributions to Hammer-Purgstall's *Fundgruben des Orients*, seem to have left something to be desired. Hammer-Purgstall's emendations to the articles resulted in Diez's 600-page polemics entitled *Unfug und Betrug in der morgenländischen Litteratur, nebst vielen Hundert Proben von der groben Unwissenheit des Herrn von Hammer zu Wien in Sprachen und Wissenschaften* (1815), to which the accused countered with "Fug und Wahrheit in der morgenländischen Literatur, nebst einigen wenigen Proben von der feinen Gelehrsamkeit des Herrn von Diez zu Berlin in Sprachen und Wissenschaften," published in *Archiv für Geographie …und Kriegskunst* 7 (1816), pp. 137-143, 145-147. His writings include *Denkwürdigkeit von Asien* (1811-15), *Der neuentdeckte oghuzische Cyklop verglichen mit dem Homerischen* (1815), and the translation of the *Qabusnamah* in 1811, *Das Buch des Kabus*. He died in Berlin, 7 April 1817. DtBE; DtBiInd (2); Fück, p. 161; NDB

Diez Macho, Alejandro, born 13 May 1916 at Villafria de la Peña (Palencia), he was ordained priest in 1939, and studied Semitics at Barcelona, where he received a doctorate in 1953 for his thesis, *Moše ibn Ezra como poeta y preceptista*. In 1944 he became a member of the Universidad de Barcelona, where he was appointed to the chair of Hebrew in 1949. His writings include *La novelistica hebraica medieval* (1951). DBEC; EncJud; LC

Digard, Jean Pierre, born 8 May 1942 at Paris, he studied at the Sorbonne where he received a doctorate in 1973 for his thesis, *Techniques et culture des nomades baxtiâri*, published commercially in 1976. He was a *directeur de recherche* at the C.N.R.S., Paris. His writings include *L'homme et les animaux domestiques* (1990); and he edited *Le cuisinier et le philosophe* (1982), and *Le fait ethnique en Iran et Afghanistan; colloque* (1988). EURAMES; IWWAS, 1976/77; LC; Private; Schoeberlein; THESAM, 4

Digby, George Frederick Wingfield, born in 1911, he was educated at various schools in England, at the Sorbonne, and in Wien. He joined the Victoria and Albert Museum, London, and remained there for nearly forty years as keeper of textiles. His writings include *French tapestry* (1951), *Elizabethan embroidery* (1863), and *The Tapestry collection, Victoria and Albert Museum* (1980). He died 8 or 9 January 1989. ConAu, P-1; 127; *Who was who*, 8

Digby, Simon, fl. 1965, his writings include *War-horse and elephant in the Delhi Sultanate* (1871); he edited *The Royal Asiatic Society, its history and treasures* (1979), and he was joint editor of *Paintings from Mughal India* (1979). LC

Dighe, Vishvanath Govind, fl. 1937-1950, his writings include *Peshwa Bajirao I & Maratha expansion* (1944), and he was joint author of *Bombay, story of the Island City* (1949); he edited *Maratha-Nizam relations, 1792-1795* (1937). LC

Di Giura, Giovanni, born 6 January 1893 at Roma, where he studied law and received a doctorate. He then entered the diplomatic service. He wrote on diplomatic, legal, historical, and artistic matters. He was a sometime president of the Società Dante Alighieri. *Chi è?* 1940, 1948, 1957, 1961; Wholtaly, 1980

Dihqani-Taft, Hassan B., 1920- see Dehqani-Taft, Hassan Barnaba

Dijkema, Fokke Theodoor, born in 1938 in the Netherlands, he studied at the Rijksuniversiteit te Leiden, where he received a doctorate in 1977 for his thesis, *The Ottoman historical monumental inscriptions in Edirne*. He was the Oriental editor at E.J. Brill, Leiden, until his retirement in the early 1990s. Private

Dikmen, M. Orhan, born in 1915, he was a professor of economics at İstanbul Üniversitesi, and a director of the Institute of Public Finances. His writings include *Vasıtalı vergiler* (1950), *Asgarî geçim indirimi* (1956), and *Türkiyede tasarruf bonoları* (1965). LC; *Türkiye bibliyografyası*, 1964

Dildine, William G., fl. 1951, he was an American journalist who had a first-hand knowledge of Iran.

Dilger, Bernhard, born 1 March 1931 at Dresden, Germany, he studied at Bonn, Wien, and the Freie Universität Berlin, where he received a Dr.phil. in 1968 for his thesis, *Die politischen Anschauungen A. D. Gradovskijs*. He was an exchange student at Leningrad University, 1960/61, and affiliated with the

Ruhr-Universität Bochum since 1964, and in 1986, a professor of comparative education. He edited *Vergleichende Bildungsforschung* (1986). Kürschner, 1987, 1992, 1996

Dilger, Konrad, born 27 July 1935 at Dresden, Germany, he studied law and Islamic subject and received a Dr.phil. in 1967 from the Universität München for *Untersuchungen zur Geschichte des osmanischen Hofzeremoniells im 15. und 16. Jahrhundert.* He was affiliated with the Max-Planck-Institut für ausländisches und internationales Privatrecht, Hamburg, from 1969 to 1982, and then successively profesor at the universities of Hildesheim and Oldenburg. Kürschner, 1983-1996; Schwarz

Dilik, Sait, born 18 April 1932 at Kula, Turkey. After completing his economic studies at Istanbul, he studied at the Universität Freiburg im Breisgau from 1957 to 1961, where he received a Dr.phil. in 1961 for *Die Geldverfassung und die Währungspolitik in der Türkei bis 1958.* He later was a professor at, and dean of, Ankara Üniversitesi. His writings include *Türkiye'de sosyal sigortlar* (1972). Kim kimdir, 1985/86; Schwarz

Dilke, Ashton Wentworth, 1850-1883, he was a scholar of Trinity College, Cambridge, and visited Russia and Central Asia. Upon his return he read a paper on Kuldja, Sinkiang, before the Geographical Society. DNB

Dilke, Sir Charles Wentworth, 1843-1911, he studied law at Trinity College, Cambridge, and was called to the bar in 1866. Thereafter he travelled. In 1868 he was elected M.P. for Chelsea, and in 1880 appointed under-secretary of state for foreign affairs. His writings include *Greater Britain; a record of travels in English-speaking countries during 1866 and 1867* (1868), *Problems of Greater Britain* (1890), and *Imperial defence* (1892). Bioln, 14; CelCen; DcBiPP; DNB; Master (7); NewC

Dillaye, Madeleine, fl. 1931, she was a keeper at the French Archives nationales, and joint author of *Les Archives du Bureau des saisies rélles* (Paris, 1982). LC

Dillemann, Louis, fl. 1977, his writings include *Haute Mésopotamie orientale et pays adjacents; contribution à la géographie historique* (1962). LC

Dillon, Emil Joseph, born in 1854 at Dublin, he trained for the priesthood in obedience to his father's wishes, but theology attracted him much less than oriental languages to which he devoted himself under Ernest Renan at the Collège de France. He continued his studies in Austria, Germany, Belgium, and Russia, and obtained doctorates in oriental languages, comparative philology, and philos-ophy. But his true bent was towards journalism. For nearly thirty years he was a correspondent in Russia of the *Daily Telegraph.* He was a member of the Armenian Academy in Venice. His writings include *A scrap of paper; the inner history of German diplomacy* (1914), *From the Triple to the Quadruple alliance; why Italy went to war* (1915), and *The inside story of the Peace Conference* (1920). Bioln, 11; DNB

Dillon, Frank, 1823-1909, he was a landscape painter and visited Egypt first in 1854; many of his works were the outcome of this and subsequent visits to that country. DNB; Master (5)

Di Lorenzo, Michele, born in 1905 at Magliano Nuovo (Salerno), he was a journalist who specialized in arts, history, and tourism. His writings include *Guida gastronomica e dei vini d'Italia* (1973). Chi scrive; LC; Vaccaro

Dimakis, Jean (John), born 9 November 1929 at Gargaliani, Greece, he studied at the universities of Athens and Paris, where he received a doctorate. He taught at colleges in Greece, and the Université de Sherbrooke before his appointment as professor of medieval history at the Université de Montréal. He was an Alexander-von-Humboldt fellow, 1963-64. His writings include *La presse française face à la chute de Missolonghi et à la bataille navale de Navarin* (1976), and *P. Codrika et la question d'Orient sous l'Empire français et la Restauration* (1986). DrAS, 1974, 1978, 1982H; WhoAm, 1986/87, 1988/89|

Dimand, Maurice Sven, born 2 August 1892 in Austria, he received a Dr.phil. in 1916 from the Universität Wien for his thesis, *Die Ornamentik der ägyptischen Wollwirkereien.* From 1923 to 1959 he was affiliated with the Museum of Modern Art, New York. His writings include *A handbook of Mohammadan decorative arts* (1930), *A handbook of Muhammadan art* (1944), *Oriental rugs in the Metropolitan Museum* (1973), and several exhibitions catalogues. WhoAmArt, 1966

Dimanshtein, Semen Markovich, he was a Russian revolutionary and communist leader with a rabbinical diploma. He edited the Yiddish paper *Der Emess*, which was an instrument of communist propaganda. After the Russian revolution he was a commissar for education in Turkestan. His writings include Борьба ленинизма с люксембургианством (1933). He was excecuted during the Stalin purges of 1937. EncJud; LC

Dimant-Kaas, Ilana, fl. 1974, her writings include *Pravda and Trud; divergent attitudes towards the Middle East* (1974), and she was joint author of *The Soviet military involvement in Egypt, January 1970- July 1972* (1974). LC

Di Matteo, Ignazio, born in 1872 at Trabia, Sicily, he was a professor of Hebrew and Greek at the Seminario di Monreale, and later a professor of Arabic language and literature at the Università di Palermo. His writings include *La predicazione religiosa di Maometto e i suoi oppositori* (1934), and *La divinità di Cristo e la dottrina della Trinità in Maometto e nei polemisti musulmani* (1938). He died in 1948. *Chi è?* 1948|; *Rivista degli studi orientali* 26 (1951), pp. 203-204

Dimitrijević, Vojin, born 9 July 1932 at Rijeka, he was a professor of international relations at the Universitet u Beogradu, and affiliated with United Nations organizations. His writings include *Utočište na teritoriji strane države* (1969), *Međunarodne organizacije* (1971), and *Osnovi teorije međunarodnik odnosa* (1977). WhoUN, 1975

Dimitroff, Iwan, born in 1883 at Stara-Sagora, Bulgaria, he was educated at Sofia, where he started studying law. He later changed to Oriental languages at the Lazarevski Institute, Moscow, and subsequently at Berlin in 1903. He received a Dr.phil. from the Universität Berlin in 1908 for his thesis, *Asch-Schaibani und sein corpus juris "al-ǧami' as-sagir."* Schwarz; Thesis

Dimitrov, Strashimir At., prof., fl. 1960, his writings include *Бьстанието от 1850 година в България* (1972) and *История на балканските народи, 1879-1918* (1975); he edited *Георги Кастриоти Скандербег, 1468-1968* (1972), and he translated from the Turkish of Evliya Çelebi *Пьтепис* (1972). LC

Dinaux, Jean Marie Benjamin, general, born 21 October 1868 at Taninges (Haute-Savoie), he was a graduate of the military college, Saint-Cyr. During his forty-one years with the French army he had six spells of duty in Algeria totalling twenty-four years, of which he spent fifteen years in the Sahara. He was one of the most prominent members of the Service des affaires indigénes and the Compagnie des oasis sahariennes at the beginning of the twentieth century. He died in Saint-Germain-en-Laye, 22 February 1947. DBF; Peyronnet, p. 576-578

Đinđić, Slavolub, born 24 April 1935 at Krnjigrad, he was an Orientalist affiliated with the Philological Faculty, Univerzitet u Beogradu. His writings include *Ratna i revolucionarna tematika u delima Jakuba Kadrija Karaosmanoglua* (1967), a work which was originally presented as his thesis in 1965, and *Панорама савремене турске поезије* (1968), and he was joint author of *Primeri Turske proze* (1969). JugoslSa, 1970; LC

Dinerstein, Herbert Samuel, born 3 March 1919 at N.Y.C., he studied at the City College of New York, and received a Ph.D. in 1943 from Harvard for his thesis, *Soviet policy in the Near and Middle East, 1917-1923*. He was a regional analyst at the Office of War Information from 1943 to 1945, and a senior staff member for Soviet studies for the Rand Corporation from 1955 to 1966, when he was appointed professor of Soviet studies at the School of Advanced International Studies, Johns Hopkins University, Baltimore, Md. His writings include a great many pamphlets on the Soviet Union. AmM&WS, 1973 S, 1978S; ConAu, 108; LC; Selim

Dinescu-Székely, Viorica, fl. 1959, her writings include *Teatrul de umbre turc* (1982), a work which was originally presented as her thesis at Bucureşti in 1976. LC

Dinet, Alphonse *Étienne*, born 28 March 1861 at Paris, he was educated at the Lycée Henri IV, but left before graduation to attend l'École des beaux-arts. He was a landscape painter who first visited Algeria in 1884, and again in the following year, financed by a travel grant. There he made the acquaintance of the Algerian Sliman ben Ibrahim, with whom he travelled from then on. They visited the Mzab, Souf, and Egypt. Since 1910 he resided in Algeria with his friend's family and acquired a perfect command of Arabic. He converted to Islam, and with his friend performed the *hajj*. Together with his friend he wrote *Mirages; scènes de la vie arabe* (1906), *La vie de Mohammad*, its translation, *The life of Mohammad* (1918), and *Le pèlerinage à la maison sacrée d'Allah* (1930). There are two biographies: *Étienne Dinet et el Hadj Sliman ben Ibrahim*, by F. Arnaudiés (1933), and *La vie d'Étienne Dinet*, by J. Dinet-Rollince (1938). He died on a visit to Paris, 24 December 1929, and was buried in Bou Saâda. His home became the Musée Dinet. DBF; Edouard; *Hommes et destins* IV, p. 257; *Qui êtes-vous*, 1924

Dingelstedt, Victor, fl. 1891-1893, he was a corresponding member of the Société impériale russe and the Royal Geographical Society of Scotland. LC

Dinguizli, Dr. born in 1869, he received a doctorate in medicine from the Université de Bordeaux in 1897 for his thesis, *La Variole en Tunisie*. NUC, pre-1956

Dino, Güzin, his writings include *Tanzimattan sonra edebiyatta gerçekçiliğe doğru* (1954), *La genèse du roman turc au XIXe siècle* (Paris, 1973), *Türk romanının doğuşu* (1978), and *Gel zaman, git zaman* (1991). LC

Dinshaw, Viccaji, Dr. fl. 1915 at Mahaboobnagar, India, his writings include *The date and country of Zarathustra* (Hyderabad, Deccan, 1912). NUC, pre-1956

Dinsmore, John Edward, born 19th cent., he was the joint author of the second edition of *Flora of Syria, Palestine and Sinai* (1932-33), and the translation, *Die Pflanzen Palästinas* (1911). LC; Sezgin

Dinstein, Yoram, born 2 January 1936 at Tel-Aviv, he was a graduate of the Hebrew University, Jerusalem and, since 1970, a professor of international law at Tel-Aviv University. His writings include *The defence of "obedience to superior orders" in international law* (1965), and *Consular immunity from judicial process* (1966). IntAu&W, 1977; WhoIsrael, 1972-1992/93; WhoWorJ, 1978

Dintses, Lev Adol'fovich, born in 1895, his writings include *Русская глиняная игрушка* (1936-1947), and *Неопубликованные каррикатуры "Искры" и "Гудка," 1861-1862* (Moscow, 1939). NUC, pre-1956

Dionisotti-Casalone, Carlo, born 9 June 1908 at Torino, he was educated at Torino, where he received a doctorate in 1929. He taught at Torino until 1949; from 1949 to 1970 he was a professor of Italian at Bedford College, University of London. His writings include *Geografia e storia della letteratura italiana* (1967), and *Gli umanisti e il volgare fra Quattro e Cinquecento* (1968). In 1973 he was presented with *Studi di filologia e di letteratura italiana offerti a Carlo Dionisotti*. Au&Wr, 1971; Who, 1969-1998; Wholtaly, 1980, 1990, 1994, 1998

Diószegi, István, born 20 September 1930 at Szeged, Hungary, he was a professor and head, Department of Modern and World History, Budapest Eötvös Loránd University. His writings include *Ausztria-Magyarország és a francia-porosz háború, 1870-1871* (1965), *Hazánk és Európa* (1970), *Hungarians in the Ballhausplatz; studies on the Austro-Hungarian common foreign policy* (1983), and *A magyar külpolitika útjai* (1984). Fekete, 1985; LC; MagyarNKK, 1992, 1994, 1996, 1998

Diószegi, Vilmos, born 2 May 1923 at Budapest, his writings include *Samanizmus* (1962), *A pogány magyarok hitvilága* (1967), and *Tracing Shamans in Siberia* (1968). He died in Budapest, 22 July 1972. MEL, 3 (1981); LC

Diringer, David, born in 1900 at Tłumacz, Galicia, he taught at the Institute of Colonial Studies in the University of Florence from 1931 to 1938 when he moved to Britain to teach Semitic epigraphy until he became professor emeritus. During the war he was affiliated with the British Foreign Office. He was, in 1959, the founder of the Alphabet Museum, Cambridge. His writings include *Le iserizione antico-ebraiche palestinesi* (1934), *The alphabet; a key to the history of mankind* (1948), and *The hand-produced book* (1953). He died in Cambridge, 13 February 1975. ConAu, 1-4, 57-60, new rev. 6; EncJud; IntWW, 1969/70-1974/75; WhoWorJ, 1965

Diriöz, Haydar Ali, born in 1923 in Turkey, he studied Turkish language and literature at the Teachers College and the Faculty of Letters, İstanbul Üniversitesi. After 1946 he taught literature at various military, public, and private schools. For some eight years he was a director of the Ayasofya Kütüp-hanesi, İstanbul. In 1960 he was appointed lecturer at the Gazi Eğitim Enstitüsü, Ankara, and from 1966 to 1969 he served as cultural attaché at the Turkish Embassy, Tehran. Thereafter he resumed his Turkish teaching at the Gazi Eğitim Enstitüsü. His writings include *Ali Nihad Bey Tarlan* (1965); and he edited A. R. Altınay's *Lâle devri* (1973).

Dirks, Jacob, born 19 June 1811 at Leeuwarden, the Netherlands, he was educated at Leiden where he received a doctorate in 1835 for his thesis, *De judiciis vemicis*. He practised law at his home town for the next fifty years or so. He was instrumental in making the Friesch Genootschap an academic centre of Friesland. He was a prolific writer on history and auxiliary sciences. His writings include *Noord-Nederland en de kruistogten* (1851), and *Geschiedkundige onderzoekingen aangaande het verblijf der heiden of Egyptiërs in de noordelijke Nederlanden* (1850). He died in Leeuwarden, 25 November 1892. NieuwNBW, v. 4, col. 505-6

Dirks, Sabine *see* Karasan-Dirks, Sabine

Dirr, Adolf, born 17 December 1867 at Augsburg, Germany, he studied at the Sorbonne and Tiflis, and then became a teacher in the Caucasus, where he pursued an interest in Caucasian languages. Since 1913 he was a keeper, and later professor, at the Museum für Völkerkunde, München. His writings include *Grammatik der vulgär arabischen Sprache* (1893), *Dirr's colloquial Egyptian Arabic grammar* (1904), *Рутульский язык* (1911), *Praktisches Lehrbuch der ostarmenischen Sprache* (1912),

Kaukasische Märchen (1920), its translation, *Contes barbares* (1944), and *Einführung in das Studium der kaukasischen Sprachen* (1928). He died in 1928. DtBE; Kürschner, 1926; Wer ist's, 1928

Dishon, Daniel, born 20th cent., his writings include *Ma'arekhet ha-yehasim ha-ben'arviyim* (1974), and *Politics and society in Ottoman Palestine; the Arab struggle for survival and power* (1994). LC

van **Dissel**, J., fl. 1893, his writings include *Maleische chrestomathie* (Leiden, 1896). NUC, pre-1956

Di Stefano, Carmela Angela, born 20th cent., her writings include *Bronzetti figurati del Museo nazionale di Palermo* (1975), *Federico e la Sicilia; dalla terra alla corona* (1995); and she was joint author of *Palermo, Museo archeologico* (1991). LC

Distel, Ludwig, born 6 May 1874 at Nürnberg, he started to study law at München, but soon changed to geography. He was an accomplished and active mountaineer in the Austrian Alps and this kept him until 1911 from completing his thesis, *Die Formen alpiner Hochtäler im Gebiet der Hohen Tauern*. He taught at the Universität München all his life, and was an active member of the Geographische Gesellschaft in München as editor of its journal as well as its librarian. He was joint author of *Ergebnisse einer Studienreise in den zentralen Kaukasus* (1914). He died 6 August 1958. Kürschner, 1928/29; Wer ist's 1928

Disuqi, 'Ali al-Din Hilal see Dessouki, Ali E. Hillal

Ditiakin, V. fl. 1928, he was a writer on economics whose writings include *Мировая торговля в эпоху вели-кого экономического кризиса* (1921). LC

Dittberner, Helga, born 20th cent., she received a doctorate in natural sciences in 1971 from the Universität Frankfurt am Main for *Zur Geschichte der Kenntnis und Ordnung der Salze*. Schwarz

Dittel (Диттель), Vil'gel'm (Vil'iam, Villiam), born 14 May 1816 at Kazan, he visited most countries in the Caucasus and the Near and Middle East from 1842 to 1845. He died 22 July 1848. BiobibSOT, 158

Dittes, James Edward, born 26 December 1926 at Cleveland, Ohio, he was a graduate of Oberlin College, and received a Ph.D. in psychology in 1958 from Yale University. He was an instructor in science at the American School in Talas, Turkey, from 1950 to 1952, and ordained minister in 1954. In the following year, he began teaching psychology of religion at Yale University. His writings include *The Church in the way* (1967), *Minister on the spot* (1970), and *The male predicament* (1984). AmM&WS, 1973 S, 1978 S; ConAu, 61-64; DrAS, 1974, 1978, 1982P; Master (1); WhoAm, 1974-1998

Dittmer, Kerrin, fl. 1973, her writings include *Die indischen Muslims und die Hindi-Urdu-Kontroverse in den United Provinces* (1972), a work which was originally presented in 1971 as a doctoral dissertation at the Südasien Institut, Universität Heidelberg. LC

Dittmer, Kunz, born 19 September 1907 at Leipzig, he studied ethnology and history of art at München, Leipzig, and Wien, where he received a Dr.phil. in 1933 for his thesis, *Die Herkunft der Spiralornamentik in Ozeanien*. He joined the Museum für Völkerkunde, Berlin, in 1934 and remained there until called to arms in 1941. After the war he was a keeper at the Museum für Völkerkunde und Vorgeschichte, Hamburg. His writings include *Vom Grabstock zum Pflug; ein Gang durch die Wirtschaftsgeschichte* (1949), and *Die sakralen Häuptlinge der Gurunsi im Obervolta-Gebiet, Westafrika* (1961). He died on vacation in Leiden, 3 June 1969. Hommes et destins, vol. 9, pp. 148-150; Unesco

Di Tucci, Raffaele, born 25 August 1884 at Graeta, Italy, he was successively affiliated with the Archivio di Stato di Cagliari and the Archivio di Stato di Genova. His writings include *Manuale di storia della Sardegna* (1918), and *Le corporazioni artigiani della Sardegna* (1926). Casati; Chi è, 1928, 1931, 1936, 1940; Firenze

Divaev, Ăbubăkir Akhmedzhanovich, born 19 December 1856 at Orynbor, he was a folklorist, ethnographer, and linguist whose writings include *Киргизская былина о Бикете, записанная и переведенная* (1897), *О свадебном ритуале Киргизов Сыъ-Дарьинской области* (1900), *Казахская народная поэзия* (1964), and *Тарту* (1992). He died in Tashkent, 5 February 1933. KazakSE; LC

Divaris, Panaghi N., born 19th cent., he received a medical doctorate in 1912 from the Université de Paris for his thesis, *Recherches sur l'appendicite*. His writings include a number of pamphlets: *L'Exile des étudiants étrangers* (Paris, 1896), *Appel à la France; la question crétoise* (Paris, 1897), and *La Guerre gréco-bulgare et la politique russo-anglaise* (Macon, 1913). BN; NYPL

Divine, Donna Robinson, born 30 March 1941, she received a Ph.D. in 1970 from Columbia University for her thesis, *Patrons and saints; a study of the career patterns of higher civil servants in Israel*. She was a professor of government at Smith College, Northampton, Mass, 1990-1997. She was joint editor of *Women living change* (1985). MESA roster of members, 1977-1990; NatFacDr, 1997-99

Divitçioğlu, Ediz *Sencer*, born 14 February 1927 at İstanbul, he was educated at Istanbul and Paris, where he received a doctorate in 1955. He was a professor of economics at Istanbul universities until his retirement. From 1982 to 1984 he was a visiting professor at the Université de Paris, Nanterre. His writings include *Mikroiktisat* (1965), *Asya üretim tarzı ve osmanlı toplumu* (1967), *Marksist "üretim tarzı" kavramı* (1971), and *Kök Türkler* (1987). Kim kimdir, 1985/86

Diwald, Hellmut, born 13 August 1924, or, according to LC, in 1929, at Schattau, Moravia, he received a Dr.phil. in 1955 from the Universität Erlangen for his thesis, *Das historische Erkennen*. He held the chair of medieval and modern history at the Universität Erlangen from 1965 to 1985. His writings include *Die Anerkennung; Bericht zur Lage der Nation* (1970), and *Geschichte der Deutschen* (1978). He died in Würzburg, 26 May 1993. DtBE; Kürschner, 1983, 1987, 1996

Diwald, Susanne Margarete Wilzer née Hopf, born 12 September 1922 at Gleichamberg near Hildburghausen, Germany, she received a Dr.phil. in 1952 from the Universität Erlangen for her thesis, *Untersuchungen zu al-Ghazzali's K. at-Tauba*. She was a lecturer in Islamic studies at the Universität Würzburg. Her writings include *Arabische Philosophie und Wissenschaft in der Enzyklopädie* (1975). Kürschner, 1980, 1992|

Dix, Arthur, born 30 November 1875 at Haus Kölln, Germany, he studied law and political science at the universities of Königsberg, Leipzig, and Berlin, 1895-1899, and received a Dr.phil. in 1923 from the Universität Köln for *Politische Geographie*. He was an editor-in-chief of various conservative newspapers. From 1916 to 1918 he was head of the news bureau at the military representative in Sofia. His writings include *Deutscher Imperialismus* (1912), *Zwischen Beresina und Wardar; Landsturmbriefe und Balkanbilder* (1916), *Zwischen zwei Welten* (1917), *Wirtschaftskrieg und Kriegswirtschaft* (1920), and *Was geht uns Afrika an* (1931). He died in Berlin, 25 March 1935. DtBE; DtBilnd (3); KDtLK, 1912-1934; Kürschner, 1931; Wer ist's, 1912-1928

Dixey, Duncan, fl. 1906, he was a missionary under the Church Missionary Society, London. Note

Dixit, R. K., Dr., M.Com., M.Phil., Ph.D., fl. 1969, he was a sometime assistant legal adviser, Ministry of Foreign Affairs, India, and an associate professor, Department of Economic Administration and Financial Management, University of Rajasthan, Jaipur. His writings include *Role of agro-industries corporations* (1991). LC

Dixon, Abd al-Ameer Abd, he received a Ph.D. in 1969 from SOAS for his thesis, *The Umayyad caliphate, 684-705; a political study*, a work which was published in 1971. An Arabic translation was published in 1973. BLC; Sluglett

Dixon, Walter Herbert, he received a Ph.D. in 1970 from Johns Hopkins University, Baltimore, Md., for his thesis, *The Gulf of Aqaba; history, geography, and law*. Selim

Dixon, William Hepworth, born 30 June 1821 at Newton Heath, he was called to the bar from Inner Temple, London, in 1854, but he never practised. From early years he had been contributing articles to magazines, and from 1853 to 1869 he was editor of *Athenaeum*. He visited the Iberian Peninsula and North Africa in 1861 and the next year he went to the Middle East. Upon his return, he pursued an active interest in the founding of the Palestine Exploration Fund. His writings include *The Holy Land* (1865), and *British Cyprus* (1879). He died 27 December 1879. BiD&SB; CasWL; CelCen; DcBiPP; DNB; Embacher; EncAm; EncBrit; GdeEnc; Master (11); NewC

Diyarbekirli, Erol *Nejat*, born 17 June 1928 at Adapazarı, Turkey, he was appointed in 1956 an assistant at the Devlet Güzel Sanatlar Akademisi; and in 1985 he was a professor of history of art at Mimar Sinan Üniversitesi, İstanbul. His writings include *Hun sanatı* (1972). Kim kimdir, 1985/86

Dizdarević, Faik, born 25 May 1929 at Fojnica, Bosnia, he studied political science at Paris, and journalism at Beograd. He was an editor at the Yugoslav press agency Tanjug, and a sometime correspondent in Cairo. JugosSA, 1970

Dizer, Muammer, Dr., born in 1924 at İstanbul. After graduation from İstanbul Üniversitesi, he began his career as an assistant at Kandilli Observatory, Istanbul, of which he became the director in 1970. Under his directorship seismic studies in Turkey expanded. Concurrently he was a university professor. His writings include *Les Observations des taches solaires faites à l'Observatoire de Kandille, 1949-1951* (1953), *A Calculation method for the visibility curve* ... (1984), *Takiyüddin* (1990); and he was joint author of *Türkiye'de astronomi çalışmaları* (1983), a bibliography of astronomical works in Turkey, 1923-1982. He died in İstanbul, 25 November 1993. LC; Meydan; *Studies in the history of medicine and science*, n.s., 13 i (1994), p. 132

Djabri (Djabry/Jabri), Ihsan Bey El, fl. 1927-1930, he was a delegate to the Syro-Palestinian Congress on the independence of Syria in Genève. Sezgin

Djait (Ju'ayyit), Hichem, born 6 December 1935, he was educated at the Collège Sadiki, Tunis, l'École normale supérieure, and Sorbonne, Paris, where he received a *doctorat d'état* in 1981. He was for many years a professor at the Université de Tunis, and concurrently a visiting professor at the Sorbonne. His writings include *La personnalité et le devenir arabo-islamiques* (1974), *L'Europe et l'islam* (1978), its translation, *Europe and Islam* (1985), and *La grande discorde* (1989). AfricaWW, 1991; LC; WhoArab, 1981, 1995/96, 1997/98

Djalili, Mohammad-Reza, born in 1940 at Tehran, he was a sometime professor at the universities of Tehran and Paris before joining the Institut universitaire de hautes études internationales, Genève, in 1979. His writings include *L'Océan indien* (1978), *Religion et révolution* (1981), and *Diplomatie islamique* (1981). EURAMES, 1993; LC; Schoeberlein; WWASS, 1989

Djedidi, Tahar Labib, fl. 1973, he received a doctorate in 1972 from the Université d'Alger for *La Poésie amoureuse des Arabes*, a work which was published in its Arabic translation *Susiyulujiyat al-ghazal al-'Arabi* in 1981. In 1987 he was a professor of sociology at the Université de Tunis. LC

Djelani Davary, Gholam, 1943- see Davary, Gholam Djelani

Djemal Pasha, Ahmed, 1872-1922 see Cemal Paşa, Ahmed

Djerdja, Josip, 1911-1990 see Đerđa, Josip

Djian, Georges, born 19th cent., he was in 1915 a French military interpreter in Chad. Note

Djindjić, Slavolub, 1935- see Đinđić, Slavolub

Djordjevic, Dimitrije see Đorđević, Dimitrije

Djurdjev, Branislav see Đurđev, Branislav

Dlala, Habib, born 20th cent., he received a doctorate in 1986 from the Université de Strasbourg for his thesis, *La structuration et le fonctionnement de l'espace industriel tunisien*. In 1980 he was an assistant at the Department of Geography in the Université de Tunis. His writings include *L'économie industrielle dans les villes-postes du Nord-est tunisien* (19819. THESAM 2

Długosz, Jan, born in 1415, he graduated from the university of Kraków and became a statesman and historian. His *Historica Polonica* is the first, and still one of the best, historical works on Poland, first published in 1614. He died in Piatek in 1480. Dziekan; EncBrit; EncicUni; EncItaliana; GdeEnc; PSB

Dluhosh, Eric Jan, born 28 October 1927 in Czechoslovakia, he graduated from McGill University, Montréal, P.Q., and studied at Cornell and the University of California at Berkeley, where he received a Ph.D. in 1973 for his thesis, *Flexibility/variability in prefabricated housing*. He was a practising architect and a visiting lecturer in architecture. In 1997 he was affiliated with M.I.T. ConAu, 25-28; LC

Dmitriev, Evgenii, fl. 1970, his writings on Middle East affairs include Палестинский узел (1978), *The Tragedy of the Palestinian people* (1984), and Палестинская трагедия (1986); and he was joint author of Путь к миру на Ближнем Востоке (1974). LC

Dmitriev, Nikolai Konstantinovich, born 28 August 1898 at Moscow, he studied Slavic and Semitic philology at Moscow University and the Lazarev Oriental Institute, and later taught at Leningrad State University and the Oriental Institute from 1926 to 1941. After the war, he was a head of the Institute for Oriental Research, Moscow, where he remained until his death on 22 December 1954. He was in charge of several linguistic expeditions to the Turkic-speaking Soviet republics. V. D. Arakin wrote a biography, Николай Константинович Дмитриев, 1898-1954 (1972). GSE; *Index Islamicus* (6); LC; Kazak SE; Miliband; TatarES; Turkmen SE

Dmitrieva, Liudmila Vasil'evna, born 7 November 1924 at El'tse Orlovskoi, she was a 1948 graduate of the Oriental Faculty, Leningrad State University, and received a doctorate in 1951 for her thesis Язык татар Западной Сибири. Since 1966 she was affiliated with the Leningrad Section of the Philological Institute of the Soviet Academy of Science. Her writings include Описание тюркских рукописей Института народов Азии (1965-1975), and Язык барабинских татар (1981). LC; Miliband; Miliband²

Dmitrievsky, Igor, fl. 1939-1941, he was a journalist who accompanied a variety of Russian scientific expeditions to Central Asia as a writer and correspondent. Note

Dmitriyev, E. see Dmitriev, Evgenii

Dobbin, Christine E., born in 1941, she was in 1983 a visiting fellow at the Department of Pacific and Southeast Asian History, Research School of Pacific Studies, Australian National University, Canberra.

Her writings include *Basic documents in the development of modern India and Pakistan, 1835-1947* (1970), *Urban leadership in western India* (1972), *Islamic revivalism in a changing peasant economy; central Sumatra, 1784-1847* (1983), and its translation into Indonesian in 1992. LC

Dobbing, A. Herbert, fl. 1968, his writings include *Cause for concern; a Quaker's view of the Palestine problem* (Beirut, Palestine Liberation Organization, 1970). LC

Dobbs, Sir Henry Robert Conway, G.B.E., K.C.S.I., K.C.M.G., K.C.I.E., born in 1871, he was educated at Brasenose College, Oxford. He entered the Indian Civil Service in 1892, and was posted to the United Provinces of Agra and Oudh. He held a long succession of posts on the North-West Frontier, in Seistan, Afghanistan, Baluchistan, Turkish Arabia, and was consul-general for Iraq from 1923 to his retirement in 1929. He died in 1934. DNB; JRCAS, 21 (1934), pp. 708-716; *Who was who*, 3

Dobkin, Marlene, she was in 1967 affiliated with the University of Massachusetts at Boston. Note

Dobrača, Kasim, born 15 April 1910 at Vragolovima (Rogatica), Bosnia, he studied at Cairo where he received a diploma in 1935. Thereafter he was affiliated with the Gazi Husrevbegova Biblioteka, Sarajevo. His writings include the *Katalog arapskih, turskih i perzijskih rukopisa, Gazi Husrev-Begove Biblioteke u Sarajevu* (1963-1979). He died 3 November 1979. Anali Gazi Husrev-Begove Biblioteke 7/8 (1982), pp. 281-285

Dobrée, Bonamy, born 2 February 1891 at London, he was educated at Haileybury and the Royal Military Academy, Woolwich. During the war he served in France, Egypt, and Palestine, and thereafter went to Christ's College, Cambridge. From 1926 to 1929 he was a professor of English at Cairo University. In 1936 he accepted the chair of English at the University of Leeds, a post which he held until his retirement in 1955. He was awarded O.B.E. in 1929, and honorary doctorates from the Université de Dijon and the University of Kent at Canterbury. His writings include *Restauration comedy* (1924). The jubilee volume, *Of books and humankind*, was presented to him in 1964. He died 3 September 1974. Au&Wr, 1971; ConAu 5, 53-56, new rev. 4; DNB; Master (4); *Who was who*, 7

Dobretsberger, Josef, born 28 February 1903 at Linz, Austria, he studied law at Wien, and was since 1934 a professor of political economy in the Universität Graz. He was a cabinet minister from 1935 to 1936, but emigrated to Turkey in 1938, where he taught until 1941, when he went to Jerusalem. In 1942 he settled as a professor in Cairo, and also headed the Austrian section of the British Intelligence. He returned to the Universität Graz in 1946. His writings include *Das Geld im Wandel der Wirtschaft* (1946), *Katholische Sozialpolitik am Scheideweg* (1947), and its translation, *La politica sociale cattolica al bivio* (1949). He died in Wien, 23 May 1970. DtBE; Kürschner, 1931, 1935; Teichl; *Wer ist's*, 1935; *Wer ist wer* (Österreich), 1937; Widmann, pp. 126, 259

Dobriansky, Lev Eugene, born in 1918 at N.Y.C., he was a graduate of Fordham University and received a Ph. D. in 1951 from New York University for his thesis, *The social philosophical system of Thorstein Veblen*. He was successively a professor of economics at his alma mater, Georgetown University, Washington, D.C., and the National War College, as well as a visiting professor in the United States and abroad. Since 1944 he was an expert on communism and the Soviet Union, and a consultant to government and industry. His writings include *The vulnerable Russians* (1967), and *U.S.A. and the Soviet myth* (1971). ConAu 1-4, new rev. 2; LC; WhoAm, 1980-1998; WhoWor, 1987-1993/94

Dobrişan, Nicolae, fl. 1976, he was the editor of Arabic short stories translated into Romanian entitled *Cele mai ieftine, nopti; nuvele arabe* (1971). LC

Dobrodomov, Igor' Georgievich, Prof. Dr., fl. 1975 in Moscow, he was a contributor and/or editor of the following collective works: *История структурных элементов русского языка; сборник научных трудов* (1982), *Взаимодействие финно-угорских и русского языков* (1984), and *Эволюция семантических и функциональных свойств русской лексики* (1987). LC

Dobrovský, Joseph, born 17 August 1753 at Gyarmat, Hungary, he was educated at Deutsch-Brod (Nĕmecký-Brod) and Klattau, Bohemia. Since 1758 he was educated at Prag and since 1771 he studied at the university, supporting himself by private lessons. He left in the following year to begin his noviciate as a Jesuit in Brünn (Brno). When the order was dissolved in 1773, he returned to the university, where he took hermeneutics. In his academic development he gradually drifted towards Slavonic studies. His writings include *Literární a prozodická bohemika* (1779), *De antiquis hebraeorum characteribus dissertatio* (Pragae, 1783), and *Geschichte der böhmischen Sprache und Litteratur* (Prag, 1792). He died in Brünn, Moravia, 6 January 1829. BiD&SB; CasWL; EncSlov; IES; *Jahrbücher für Kultur und Geschichte der Slaven*, neue Folge, 6 (1930), pp. 209-222; MaláČEnc; Master (2); OttůvSN; Pallas; PSN; UjLex

von **Dobschütz**, Ernst Adolf Alfred Oskar Adalbert, born 9 October 1870 at Halle, Germany, he was a patristic scholar who taught successively at the universities of Jena, Straßburg, Breslau, and Halle.

Concurrently he was a visiting professor at Harvard. His writings include *Die urchristlichen Gemeinden* (1902), *Christian life in the primitive Church* (1904), *The Influence of the Bible on civilisation* (1914), and *Die Bibel im Leben der Völker* (1934). He died in Halle, 20 May 1934. DtBE; Kürschner, 1925-1931; LuthC 75; NDB; *Wer ist's*, 1928

Döcker, Richard, born 13 June 1894 at Weilheim/Teck, Germany, he graduated in architecture and biology from the Technische Hochschule Stuttgart, and afterwards found employment with the local department of town planning as an architect. He later was head of the Württemberg clearing-house of the construction industry. Since 1921 he was a practising architect in Stuttgart. After the war he became director-general of reconstruction in Stuttgart, and in 1947 he was appointed professor of architecture at his alma mater. His writings include *Typenpläne für Kleinwohnungen* (1925). He died in Stuttgart, 9 November 1968. DtBE; DtBilnd (3); Kürschner, 1950-1966; Master (3); *Wer ist wer*, 1958-1967/68

Dodd, Clement Henry, born 6 April 1926 at Chester, England, he received degrees from the universities of London, Wales, and Edinburgh, and thereafter was a professor of politics and government at Manchester, Durham, and Hull, where he remained until his retirement in 1987. He then joined the staff of the Centre for Near and Middle East Studies at SOAS as a research associate, where a modern Turkish studies program was launched under his chairmanship, a position which he relinquished in 1993. He also taught in the Middle East Technical University, Ankara, where he acted as dean of faculty, 1961-62, and Boğaziçi Üniversitesi, Istanbul, 1986. He conducted field work in northern Cyprus, and was the founder of Eothen Press, where he published many of his writings which include *Politics and government of Turkey* (1969), *Israel and the Arab world* (1970), *Democracy and government in Turkey* (1979), and *The crisis of Turkish democracy* (1983). Private; WhoWor, 1987/88

Dodd, Edward Mills, born in 1887 at Kayseri, Turkey, he was a graduate of Princeton University and Cornell Medical School. He served as a medical missionary in Persia from 1916 to 1925. During the war he did relief work among mountain peoples of Persia. After his return to the United States he acted as medical secretary to the Board of Foreign Missions of the United Presbyterian Church of North America until 1957. His writings include *The Beloved physician; an intimate life of William Schauffler* (1931), *How far to the nearest doctor?* (1933), *The Gift of the healer; the story of men and medicine in the overseas mission of the Church* (1964), and with Rose Wilson Dodd he published *Mecca and beyond* (1937). He died in Upper Montclair, N.J., 28 or 30 June 1967. LuthC 75; Master (3); NYT, 3 July 1967, p. 17, col. 5; Shavit

Dodd, Erica Cruikshank, born about 1930 at Beirut, she was a graduate of Wellesley College, and received a Ph.D. in Byzantine art in 1958 from the University of London. In 1981 she was a professor at AUB, and in 1990, at the United States Educational Foundation in Pakistan, Islamabad. Her writings include *Byzantine silver stamps* (1961), and *Byzantine silver treasures* (1974); she was joint author of *The Image of the word; a study of Quranic verses in Islamic architecture* (1981), and joint editor of *Architecture theory; student papers* (1985). LC; *MESA Roster of members*, 1990

Dodd, Peter Carter, born 20th cent., he received a Ph.D. in 1962 from Harvard for his thesis, *Role conflicts in the school principalship*. He was a recipient of a Canada Council grant and affiliated with the Depart-ment of Sociology and Anthropology, AUB. In 1990 he was a professor at the United States Educa-tional Foundation in Pakistan, Islamabad. He was joint author of *River without bridges* (1968). LC; *MESA Roster of members*, 1977 & 1990

Dodd, Stuart Carter, born in 1900 at Talas, Turkey, the son and grandson of medical missionaries, he studied psychology at Princeton, where he received a Ph.D. in 1926 for his thesis, *International group mental tests*. He became a pioneer in scientific polling techniques and a professor emeritus of sociology at the University of Washington even though he had never taken a course in sociology. He founded the Department of Sociology at AUB and served as its chairman until 1947. His writings include *Social relations in the Near East* (1931), *A controlled experiment on rural hygiene in Syria* (1934), *Dimensions of society* (1942), and *A pioneer radio poll in Lebanon, Syria, and Palestine* (1943). He died suddenly while visiting a son in Berkeley during the Christmas holidays in 1975. AmM&WS, 1973 S; Bioln, 11; ConAu, 41-44 rev.; LC; Shavit

Dodds, Dennis R., fl. 1979, his writings include *Oriental rugs; the collection of Dr. and Mrs. Robert A. Fisher in the Virginia Museum of Fine Arts* (1985). LC

Dodds, Jerrilyn Denise, born 20th cent., she received a Ph.D. in 1979 from Harvard University for her thesis, *Mozarabic architecture of the resettlement and the spiritual reconquista*. Her writings include *Architecture and ideology in early medieval Spain* (1990); and she edited *The Art of Islamic Spain; catalog of an exhibition at the Alhambra* (1992). LC

Döderlein, Johann Christoph, born 20 January 1746 at Windsheim, Germany. After the completion of his Lutheran training at the Universität Altdorf, near Nürnberg, he was a deacon in Windsheim until

1772, when he was appointed professor of theology and deacon at Altdorf. From 1782 until his death on 2 December 1792 he was a professor at Jena. He was the editor of the *Theologische Bibliothek*, 1780-1792, and joint editor of the *Biblia Hebraica* (1793). ADtB; DtBE; DtBilnd (12); LuthC, 1975

Dodge, Bayard, born 5 February 1888 at N.Y.C. After receiving degrees from Princeton, Union Theological Seminary, Occidental College and Yale University, and having been on the faculty of A.U.B from 1913 to 1919, he served as the director of Near East Relief for Syria and Palestine, 1920-1921. Above all, he was associated with the private American educational effort in the Arab world. He was appointed president of A.U.B. in 1923 and served as president of International College until his retirement in 1948. His wrings include *The American University of Beirut* (1952), *Al-Azhar* (1961), and *Muslim education in medieval times* (1962). He died 30 May 1972. ConAu, 111; Master (3); Shavit; WhAm, 5

Dodge, David Stuart, born in 1836 at N.Y.C., he was a graduate of Yale University and a clergyman. In his later years he was a president of the board of trustees of the Syrian Protestant College, Beirut. His writings include *Systematic benevolence* (1900). He died in N.Y.C., in 1921. LC; WhAm, 1

Dodge, Henry Percifal, born 18 January 1870 at Boston. After graduation from Harvard and its Law School, he studied in France, Germany, and Italy. He was admitted to the bar in 1895 and joined the U.S. Legation, Berlin, in 1899, remaining with the diplomatic service until his retirement in 1930. From 1908 to 1909 he was American minister to Morocco. He died in Zürich, 16 October 1936. Master (3); WhAm, 1

Dodson, George Everard, born 31 January 1872 at Cheetham Hill, Manchester,. he was a medical missionary under the Church Missionary Society, London, and went out to Kerman, Persia, in 1903, where he was active until the late 1920s. A "friend of Iran" wrote a biography entitled *"Dawdson,"* the *dcctor; G. E. Dodson of Iran* (London, Highway Press, 1940). BLC; MedWW

Dodykhudoev, Rakhim Khalilovich, born 15 June 1928 in Soviet Badakhshan, he studied linguistics at the Tajik State Institute, and received a doctorate in 1963 at Leningrad for his thesis, *Историческая фонетика шугнанского языка*. He taught at the Tajik State Institute since 1961. His writings include *Памирская микротопономия* (1975), and he edited *Исследования по восточным ызыкам* (1988). LC; Miliband; Miliband²

Doe, D. *Brian*, Dr., born in 1920, he was an architect and archaeologist whose writings include *Aden in history* (1965), *Socotra; an archaeological reconnaissance in 1967* (1970), *Südarabien* (1970), and *Monuments of South Arabia* (1983). LC

Doenecke, Justus Drew, born 5 March 1938 at Brooklyn, N.Y., he was a graduate of Colgate University, and received a Ph.D. from Princeton in 1966 for his thesis, *American public opinion and the Manchurian crisis, 1931-33*. He taught history successively at Colgate and Ohio universities until 1969 when he was appointed professor of social science at New College, University of Southern Florida, a position which he still held in 1997. His writings include *The literature of isolationism* (1972), and *When the wicked rise; American opinion-makers and the Manchurian crisis of 1931-1933* (1984). ConAu, 104, 43 new rev.; DrAS, 1974, 1978, 1982H; NatFacDr, 1997; WhoSSW, 1991/92, 1993/94

Doerfer, Gerhard, born 8 March 1920 at Königsberg, Germany, he came from a family of modest substance, and remained grateful to his parents for spending ten percent of the family budget on his school fees; he considered high school education a privilege and not a prerogative. As a politically unreliable person, he was inducted to paramilitary service in 1938, followed by conscription and the fate as prisoner of war until 1946. After his release, he was a simple worker in the post-war Berlin of 1946, an experience which instilled in him a lifelong reverence for manual labour. During this time he earned his matriculation as an extension school student. He studied and concurrently worked until he was granted a bursary which he accepted with humiliation and obligation. He received a Dr.phil. summa cum laude in 1954 from the Freie Universität Berlin for his thesis, *Zur Syntax der Geheimen Geschichte der Mongolen*. His writings include *Türkische und mongolische Elemente im Neupersischen* (1960-1975). He shared the fate of many Germans of his generation, the generation of sceptics, who believed in values, but not in those uttered by politicians and proclaimed in formal addresses. He considered anti-German and anti-Semitic libel equally repulsive. He was never the clever academic manager, rather he accepted the role of the ivory tower professor at the Institut für Turkologie in the Universität Göttingen which appointed him professor emeritus on his retirement. On his seventy-fifth birthday he was honoured by the jubilee volume, *Beläk Bitig; Sprachstudien für Gerhard Doerfer* (1995). His autobiography appeared in *Journal of Turkish studies* 13 (1989), pp. i-iv. EURAMES, 1993; Kürschner, 1966-2003; Schoeberlein; WhoWor, 1989/90

Doergens, Richard, born in 1839, he was a geographer who accompanied the Prussian consul Johann G. Wetzstein on topographical surveys in eastern Syria, from Damascus by way of Hauran to the ruins in

Amman. His writings include *Theorie und Praxis der geographischen Kartennetze* (Berlin, 1870). He died in 1901. DtBilnd (2); Henze; NUC, pre-1956

Doerr, Arthur Harry, born 28 August 1924 at Johnston City, Illinois, he was a graduate of Southern Illinois University, and received a Ph.D. He taught geography for twenty-three years successively at Indiana University, Northwestern University, and the University of Oklahoma until 1970, when he was appointed a professor and vice-president, Academic Affairs at the University of West Florida. In 1965 he was a summer fellow in Israel of the American Association for Middle Eastern Affairs; he spent the following eighteen months at the Pahlavi University and elsewhere in Iran. His writings include *Fundamentals of physical geography* (1990). AmM&WS, 1973 S; ConAu, 41; LEduc, 1974; Master (1); WhoAm, 1974-1988/89

Dognée, Eugène Marie Octave, fl. 1892, he contributed to archaeological periodicals and wrote *Histoire du pont des arches de Liège* (1860), *Liège; origines, histoire, monuments, promenades* (1880), and *Un officier de l'armée de Varus* (1902). BN

Dogra, Ramesh Chander, born in 1936, he received a M.Phil. from the University of London and was a principal assistant librarian for South Asia at the School of Oriental and African Studies, London. His writings include *Jammu and Kashmir* (1986), *Catalogue of early printed books on South Asia from 1586 to 1864 held in the Library of SOAS* (1988), and, in the World biographical series, *Bhutan* (1990). He was a joint author of *A handlist of the manuscripts ...at SOAS* (1978). LC

Doğramacı, Emel, born 21 December 1934 at Erbil, she studied at Baghdad, Oxford and Edinburgh, where she received a Ph.D. in 1956 for her thesis, *George Eliot and emancipation; a Turkish view*. She taught English language and literature at various Turkish academic institutes since 1965. Her writings include *Rights of women in Turkey* (1982), *Türkiye'de kadın hakları* (1982), and *Status of women in Turkey* (1984). Kim kimdir, 1985/86; Sluglett; TB, 1982

Doğrul (Dogrol), Ömer Rıza, 1893-1952, he was a Turkish journalist and a member of the Turkish Parliament. His writings include *Ekber; bir Türk dâhîsi* (1944), *Kanlı gömlek* (1944), *İslâmiyetin geliştirdiği tasavvuf* (1948), and *İlâhi bir müjde* (1952). LC; NUC, pre-1956

Doherty, Kathryn B., fl. 1968, her writings include *Jordan waters conflict* (1965).

Dohm, Robert, born about 1919, he studied political economy at the Universität München from 1951 to 1955 and then joined the Commerzbank. He became a member of its board of directors, responsible for international transactions in 1960. In 1976 he was a federal director of the Bundesverband des privaten Bankgewerbes.

d'Ohsson, Ignatius Mouradgea, 1740-1807 *see* Mouradgea d'Ohsson, Ignatius

Doi, Abdur Rahman I., born 16 July 1933 at Himmatnagar, Gujarat, India, he was educated at Bombay, and received a Ph.D. in 1964 from Cambridge for his thesis, *Muhibb Allah Ilahabadi; a study of the life and personality of Shaikh Muhibb Allah b. Mubariz b. Pir, together with a survey of his mystical theology and philosophy*. After serving successively at the University of Gujarat, University of Nigeria, Nsukka, and University of Ife, he was appointed professor and chairman of the Centre for Islamic Legal Studies, Ahmadu Bello University, Zaria, Nigeria, in 1977. His writings include *Non-Muslims under Shari'ah* (1981), and *Women in the Qur'an and the sunnah* (1988). LC; Sluglett; WhoWor, 1980/81

Doig, James Conroy, born 22 June 1929 at Washington, D.C., he was a graduate of the University of Notre Dame and pursued post-graduate studies at the Pontificia Università Gregoriana, Roma, and the Université de Louvain, where he received a doctorate in philosophy. He taught in his field at Notre Dame until 1969, when he was appointed a professor of philosophy at Clayton Junior College in the University System of Georgia at Morrow. His writings include *Aquinas on metaphysics* (1972), and *In defense of cognitive realism* (1987). DrAS, 1978, 1982; LC

Dokali, Rachid, fl. 1968, his writings include *Les mosquées en Algérie* (1970), and *Les mosquées de la période turque à Alger* (1974). LC

Dolan, John Patrick, born 7 December 1923 at Kankakee, Illinois, he was a graduate of Loyola University, and spent five years as a Roman Catholic chaplain with the U.S. High Commission in Germany. After teaching sociology and philosophy at St. Ambrose College, he was appointed in 1968 a professor of sociology at Mount St. Claire College. He was author and editor of a critically acclaimed history of the Christian Church. His writings include *History of the Reformation* (1965), and *Cathol-icism; an historical survey* (1968). He died 25 December 1981. AmM&WS, 1973 S; ConAu, 5-8, 106, new rev. 2; NYT 27 December 1981, p. 36, col. 5

Dolatabadi, Sadighé, 1885-1962 *see* Dawlatābādī, Sadīqah

Dold-Samplonius, Yvonne, fl. 1963-1975, she was joint translator of the Arabic of Archimedes' *Über einander berührende Kreise* (1975). LC

Dole, Charles Fletcher, born in 1845 at Brewer, Me. After graduation from Havard and Andover Theological Seminary, he was for over forty years a pastor in Massachusetts. He was a pacifist, but not fanatically. His writings include *The Citizen and the neighbour* (1884), *The Theology of civilization* (1899), and *My eighty years* (1927). He died in 1927. BiD&SB; BioIn, 3; DAB; DcNAA; LC; Master (3); WhAm, 1; WhNAA

Dole, Nathan Haskell, born 31 August 1852 at Chelsea, Mass., he had a varied career as a college and high school teacher, newspaper correspondent, writer with a great literary versatility, and the ability to work rapidly. He was also affiliated in an editorial capacity with the headquarters of the American Board of Commissioners for Foreign Missions at Boston. He was joint editor of *Flowers from Persian poets* (1901), and anthologies from Greek and Latin literatures. He died in 1935. BiD&SB; DcNAA; Master (17); WhAm, 1; WhNAA

Dölger, Franz, born 4 October 1891 at Kleinwallstadt, Germany, he received a Dr.phil. in 1919 from the Universität München. He was a librarian in München, and concurrently a lecturer in Greek at the Universität from 1926 to 1959. He was a member of the major academies of science on the continent, and receiced honorary doctorates from Athens, Sofia, and Thessalonike. His writings include *Byyanz und die europäische Staatenwelt* (1953). He died in München, 5 November 1968. DtBE; GSE; Kürschner, 1950-1966; *Südost-Forschungen* 28 (1969), pp. 287-288

Dolgikh, Boris Osipovich, born 18 April 1904, he was an ethnographer, specializing in Siberian minorities. His writings include *Кеты* (1934); and he was the editor of *Мифологические сказки и исторические предания нганасан* (1976). He died in 1971. GSE; LC

Dolgopol'skii, Aron Borisovich, born 18 November 1930 at Moscow. After graduation from the Moscow State Pedagogical Institute in 1954, he received a doctorate in 1958 for his thesis, *Из истории развития типов отглагольних имен деятеля от латыни к романским языкам*. His writings include *Сравнительно-историческая фонетика кушитских языков* (1973), and he was joint author of *Практическая грамматика языка иврит* (1985). LC; Miliband

Dolinina, Anna Arkad'evna, born 12 March 1923 at Petrograd, she graduated in 1949 from the Oriental Institute, Leningrad State University, where she also received a doctorate in 1953 for her thesis, *Русская литература XIX века в арабских странах*. Since 1961 she was a lecturer. Her writings include *Очерки истории арабсой литературы нового времени* (1968), and *Египет и Сирия* (1973). LC; Miliband

Dolinskaia, V. G., fl. 1964, a joint author of *Искусство Советского Узбекистана, 1917-1972* (1976). LC

Dolley, Reginald Hugh Michael, fl. 1953, he was joint author of *A bibliography of coin hoards of Great Britain and Ireland, 1500-1967* (1971), and *Early medieval coins from Lincoln and its shire* (1983). LC

Dollfus, Julesb orn 19th cent., he studied Oriental languages at Leipzig and Tübingen and was a friend of L. Krehl. He died in 1848 without having completed the edition of al-Bukhari's *Sahîh*, of which he had exerpted more than one third of the Dresden manuscript. Note

Dollfus, Lucien, fl. 1893, his writings include *Études sur le moyen âge espagnol* (Paris, 1894), and he translated the *Chanson de Roland* into Spanish, *Romancero de Roncevaux* (1897). BN; LC

Dollin du Fresnel, E., fl. 1900-1901, he was a contributor to the *Bulletin* de la Société de géographie commerciale de Paris. BN

von **Döllinger**, Johann Joseph Ignaz, born 28 February 1799 at Bamberg, Germany, he studied law and theology at the Universität Würzburg and was ordained priest in 1822 at Bamberg. In the 1840s he briefly acted as a spokesman of political Catholicism. He was a strong opponent of the dogma of papal infallibility, even after its proclamation, and was put under a ban. His writings, several of which have been translated into English, French, Portuguese, and Russian, include *Muhammad's Religion* (1838), *Die Reformation* (1846-48), and *Die Papstfabeln des Mittelalters* (1863). He died in isolation in München, 10 January 1890. ADtB, v. 48; DtBE; DtBIlnd (15); LC

Dollot, Louis Marie Auguste, born 26 November 1915 at Paris, he received a doctorate from the Sorbonne in 1941 for his thesis, *La question des privilèges dans la seconde moitié du XVIIe siècle*. He entered his diplomatic career as a French consul in Melilla in 1945. His writings include *Les Grandes migrations humaines* (1946), *Histoire diplomatique* (1948), *Mélilla, pointe africaine de l'Espagne* (1952), and *La Turquie vivante* (1957). He died 30 January 1997. *Who's who in France*, 1971/72-1996/97

Pollot, René, born 25 February 1875 at Nancy, he was a graduate of l'École libre des sciences politiques, Paris, and received a doctorate in law in 1902 for his thesis, *Les origines de la neutralité de la Belgique et le système de la barrière*. He was in the French diplomatic service from 1902 until his retirement in 1937. In 1934 he was a special envoy to Afghanistan. He later was a lecturer at the Académie de droit international, den Haag. He was a prolific writer whose works include *'Afghanistan; histoire, description, mœurs et coutumes, folklore, fouilles* (1937), and *De Tanger au Quai d'Orsay* (1956). He died 25 February 1962. DBF; WhoFr, 1953/54

Dolmetsch, Mabel, 1874-1963, she was the third wife of Eugène Arnold Dolmetsch, and a musician in her own right as well as an expert on Renaissance and Baroque dancing. Her writings include *Dances of England and France* (1949). OxMus

Dolot, Conrad Étienne *Gabriel*, born 28 May 1847 at Prémery (Nièvre), he was a graduate of the Polytechnique and l'École d'application de Metz. He served with the engineers and rose to the rank of brigadier-general in 1904. He had two spells of duty in Tunisia, and contributed a number of articles on Tunisia to the *Revue du génie militaire*. He died in 1924. DBF

Dols, Michael Walter, born 6 July 1942 at Baltimore, Md., he was a graduate of Trinity College, Hartford, Conn., and received a Ph.D. in 1971 from Princeton for his thesis, *The black death in the Middle East*. He pursued a teaching career at California State University, Hayward, from 1971 until his death on 1 December 1989. From 1985 to 1989 he was a visiting fellow at the Wellcome Unit for the History of Medicine, Oxford. His writings include *Medieval Islamic medicine; Ibn Ridwan's treatise "On the prevention of bodily ills in Egypt"* (1984), and *Majnun; the madman in medieval Islamic society*, edited by Diana E. Immisch (1992). ConAu, 69; DrAS, 1974, 1978, 1982; IWWAS, 1976/77; LC; *MESA bulletin* 24 (July 1990), pp. 152-153

von **Dombay**, Franz Lorenz, born 10 August 1758 at Wien. After graduating from the Orientalische Akademie, Wien, he accompanied an imperial embassy to Morocco. He later served at the Austrian Embassy in Madrid until 1802, when he was appointed court interpreter in Wien. His *Grammatica linguae mauro-arabiae juxta vernaculi idiomatis usum* (1800), represents the first academic contribution to the study of Arabic dialects. His other writings include *Popular-Philosophie der Araber, Perser und Türken* (Agram, 1795), *Geschichte der Scherifen oder Könige des jetzt regierenden Hauses zu Marokko* (1801), and *Grammatica linguae persicae* (1804). He died in Wien, 12 December 1810. BHS, vol. 1, p. 434; DcBiPP; Fück, pp. 151-152; Wurzbach

Dombrowski, Bruno W., born 28 November 1929 at Hannover, Germany, he received a Dr.phil. from the Universität Basel and thereafter taught classics and history for a number of years at the University of Manitoba until he was appointed a professor of classics and ancient history at Dalhousie University, Halifax, N.S., in 1966. His writings include *Der Name Europa auf seinem giechischen und altsyrischen Hintergrund* (1984). DrAS, 1974; LC

Dombrowski, Gisela, born 14 June 1937 at Berlin, she trained as a translator and interpreter, 1956-1959, worked as a foreign language secretary in Berlin, 1959-1961, and as a translator for the Deutsche Stiftung für Entwicklungshilfe, from 1962 to 1966, when she enrolled in ethnology at the Freie Universität Berlin. She received a Dr.phil. in 1975 for her thesis, *Die Auffassungen von "Sozialwissenschaft" und "Gesellschaft" bei Dürckheim und Radcliffe-Brown*. For many years she was head of the Abteilung Islamischer Orient, at the Museum für Völkerkunde, Berlin. She was a contributing author to *Boote aus aller Welt; Katalog zur Sonderausstellung* (1984). EURAMES; Thesis

Domenech Lafuente, Angel, born in 1894, his writings include *Apuntes sobre geografía de la Zona Norte del Protectorado de España en Marruecos* (3d ed., 1942), *Del territorio de Ifni* (1946), *Un oficial entre moros* (1948), and *Del islam* (1950). LC

Domet, Asis, born in 1890, his writings include *Ben Sina; dramisches Gedicht* (Wien, 1924). NUC, pre-1956; Sezgin

Domingues, José D. Garcia, fl. 20th cent., his writings include *História luso-árabe* (1945), *Egipto* (1952), *Património cultural arábico-algarvio* (1956), *Guia turístico de Silves* (1958), and he was joint editor of *Livro do almoxarifado de Silves; século XV* (1984). LC

Domínguez Bordona, Jesús, fl. 1929, his writings include *Exposición de códices miniados españoles; catálogo* (1929), *La miniatura española* (1930), its translations, *Die spanische Buchmalerei* (1930), *Spanish illumination* (1930), *Catálogo de los manuscritos catalanes de la Biblioteca nacional* (1931), and *La miniatura* (1950). LC

Domínguez Ortiz, Antonio, born 18 October 1909 at Sevilla. After receiving a doctorate from the Universidad de Madrid, he was a professor at Sevilla. His writings include *Orto y ocaso de Sevilla*

426

(1946), *La clase social de los conversos en Castilia en la edad moderna* (1955), *Alteraciones anda-luzas* (1973), *Sociedad y estado en el siglo XVIII español* (1976), and *Historia de los moriscos* (1978) DBEC; LC

Dominian, Leon, born 13 April 1880 at Constantinople, he graduated from Robert College, Constantinople, and took courses in geography at the Université de Louvain from 1898 to 1900. After travelling in Turkey, he was successively a member of the U.S. Geological Survey, taught at American universities, and served as a consul. His writings include *The frontiers of language and nationalty in Europe* (1917). He died 25 July 1935. NatCAB, vol. 25, p. 94; WhAm, 1

Dominicus, Germanus, 1588-1670 *see* Germanus (de Silesia), Dominicus

Dominique, Paule Charles *see* Charles-Dominique, Paule

Dömötör, Sándor, born 24 February 1908 at Budapest, he received a doctorate in 1930 from Szeged University for his thesis, *Betyárromantika*. His writings include *Kedvet virágoztató magyar népmesék* (1944), *Őrség* (1960), and *Hervestől Baranyáig* (1983). He died in Budapest, 15 January 1986. MEL, 1978-1991

Donald, Leland Holmes, born in 1942, he was in 1995 a member of the Department of Anthropology in the University of Victoria, B.C., a position which he still held in 1999. His writings include *Aboriginal slavery on the northwest coast of North America* (1997); he edited *Themes in ethnology and culture history; essays in honor of David F. Aberle* (1987). LC; NatFacDr, 1995-1999

Donaldson, Bess Allen, born 5 December 1879 at Galesbury, Illinois, he was a graduate of the local Knox College and taught a number of years in the state before going in 1910 to Tehran as a missionary. There she married D. Dwight M. Donaldson in 1916. They both served in Meshed until 1940 and afterwards in Lucknow, India, until their retirement in 1951. Her writings include *The wild rue, a study of Muhammedan magic and folklore in Iran and India* (1938), and her memoirs *Prairie girl* (1971), *Prairie girl in Iran and India* (1972). She died in Lakeland, Fla., 20 December 1974. MW 66 (1976), pp. 312-313; Shavit

Donaldson, Dwight Martin, born 16 December 1884 at a Presbyterian manse in Ohio. After graduating from Washington and Jefferson College in 1907, he went to the Punjab and taught at the Forman Christian College for three years. He returned to the United States for his theological education in Pittsbrugh, Pa., and at Harvard Divinity School. In 1927 he received a D.D. from Washington and Jefferson, and in the following year he was awarded a Ph.D. by the Hartford Theological Seminary. He was an evangelistic missionary of the Presbyterian Church in the United States in Meshed from 1914 until 1940, when he was invited to become the principal of the Henry Martyn School of Islamics in Lucknow, India. He served there with his wife, Bess Allen, whom he had married 1916 in Tehran, until their retirement in 1951. After returning to the United States he served for several years as pastor of a church in Alabama. His writings include *The Shi'ite religion* (1933), which was originally presented as his thesis, Hartford, Conn., 1928, and *Studies in Muslim ethics* (1953). He died in Lakeland, Fla., 11 May 1976. MW 66 (1976), 312-313

Donaldson, William J., born 20th cent., he received a Ph.D. in 1979 from the University of Durham for his thesis, *Fishing and fish marketing in northern Oman; a case study in artisanal fisheries development*. He was part of a field team of Durham University Oman Research and Development Project, 1974-1976, and thereafter a member of the Centre for Middle Eastern and Islamic Studies in the University of Durham. Note; Sluglett

Donati, Lamberto, born in 1890 at Roma, he was affiliated with the Biblioteca Vaticana, where he specialized in the history of the book. His writings include *Stampe del XV secolo della Città del Vaticano, biblioteca* (1936). IndBI (2); LC

Donau, Raymond Victor Joseph, born about 1863. After passing through the military college, Saint-Cyr, he requested service in the Bureau des Affaires indigènes. Around 1893 he was transferred to the Service de renseignements, Tunis. He remained in the Régence until his retirement as commander at a variety of posts in southern Tunisia. In 1915 he was a colonel and awarded officer of the Légion d'honneur. His trace is lost in 1929, when he was resident in Givet (Ardennes). DBF

Donazzolo, Pietro, Dr., born 19th cent., his writings include *Storia della geografia* (1902), and *I viaggiatori veneti minori, studio bio-bibliografico dell dott. Pietro Donazzolo* (1928). Firenze; NUC, pre-1956

Doncoeur, Paul, born 6 September 1880 at Nantes. After the completion of his education at Reims, he entered the Société de Jésus in 1898. He lived in self-imposed exile in Belgium until the outbreak of the war, when he volunteered for service in France. After his release from prisoner of war camp, he became a contributor to *Études*, the journal founded by the Compagnie de Jésus, and since 1920 he was its editor-in-chief. He travelled in Central Europe, the Orient, and the Americas. He died in Troussures (Oise), 21 April 1961. DBF; DBFC; Bioln, 1; Index BFr² (2)

Donia, Robert Jay, born 30 May 1945 at Akron, Ohio, he was a graduate of Hope College, and received a Ph.D. in 1976 from the University of Michigan for his thesis, *The politics of factionalism; the Bosnian Moslems in transition, 1878-1906.* He was a professor of history at Ohio State University since 1978. His writings include *Islam under the double eagle; the Muslims of Bosnia and Hercegovina, 1878-1914* (1981); and he was joint author of *Bosnia and Hercegovina; a tradition betrayed* (1994). ConAu, 155; DrAS, 1978; LC

Donidze, Gaioz Il'ich, fl. 1964, his writings include *Безличные предложения в хакасском языке* (1959); he edited *Инструкция по русской передаче географических названий* (1959), and *Словарь географических названий Антарктики* (1987). LC

Donini, Pier Giovanni, born in 1936 at Trento, Italy, he taught Near and Middle Eastern history at the Istituto universitario orientale di Napoli. His writings include *Profilo di geografia economica dell'Africa* (1975), *Israele* (1981), *Le minoranze nel Vicino Oriente e nel Maghreb* (1985), *I paesi arabi* (1987), and *Il mondo arabo-islamico* (1995). LC

Donkin, Robin Arthur, born 28 October 1928 at Morpeth, Northumberland, he was educated at the University of Durham where he received a doctorate in 1953. From 1972 to 1996 he was a reader in historical geography and a fellow of Jesus College in the University of Cambridge. His writings include *Beyond price; pearls and pearl-fishing; origins to the age of discoveries* (1998). LC; Who, 1986-1998

Donkin, William A. He was a casual traveller who made a camel journey from Touggourt in northeastern Algeria to Kano in northern Nigeria in 1933. Note

Donkin, William Fishburn, born in 1814 at Bishop Burton, Yorkshire, he studied classics and mathematics at Oxford, and became a lecturer in the subject at St. Edmund Hall, Oxford. In 1842 he was elected Savilian Professor of astronomy at Oxford. His writings include *Acoustics, theoretical* (1870). He died in 1869. DNB; BritInd (5)

Dönmez, Yusuf, born 24 April 1933 at Erzincan, Turkey, he received a doctorate in 1966, and was appointed a professor of geography at İstanbul Üniversitesi in 1970. His writings include *Trakya'nın bitki coğrafyası* (1968), and *Kütahya ovasının ve çevresinin fizikî coğrafyası* (1972). Kim kimdir, 1985/86, 1997/98

Donnelly, Alton Stewart, born 30 November 1920 at Springville, Utah, he was a graduate of the University of California at Berkeley where he also received a Ph.D. In 1960 for his thesis, *The Orenburg expedition; Russian colonial politics on the southern frontier, 1734-1740.* In 1966 he was appointed a professor of history at SUNY, Binghamton. His writings include *The Russian conquest of Bashkiria, 1552-1740* (1968). ConAu, 21-24; DrAS, 1974 H, 1978 H, 1982 H

Donnelly, Anne, she was a traveller residing in Texas in 1933. Since 1922 she had been several times to the Near East, the Far East, and the islands of the Pacific. Asia, December 1933

Donner, Fred McGraw, born 30 September 1945 at Washington, D.C., he was a graduate of Princeton, where he also received a Ph.D. in 1975 for his thesis, *The Arab tribes in the Muslim conquest of Iraq.* He pursued post-graduate studies at Shemlan, Lebanon, and the Universität Erlangen. He taught at the Department of History at Yale, 1975-1982, and thereafter was a professor of Islamic history at the Oriental Institute and Department of Near Eastern Languages and Civilizations, Chicago. From 1992 to 1994 he was president of the Middle East medievalists. He received numerous awards, grants and fellowships. His writings include *The early Islamic conquests* (1981). ConAu, 106; NatFacDr, 1995-1999; Private; WhoMW, 1988/89

Donner, Kai, 1888-1935, he undertook two travels to Siberia, 1911-1913, and 1914, and received a Dr.phil. in 1920 from Helsingfors University for *Über die anlautenden labialen spiranten und verschlußlaute im samojedischen und uralischen.* He also wrote *Siperian samojedien keskuudessa* (1923), *Ethnological notes about the Yenisey-Ostyak* (1953), and *Among the Samoyed in Siberia* (1954). LC

Donner, Otto, born 15 December 1835 at Kokkola, Finland, he received a Dr.phil. in 1863 from Helsingfors University for his thesis, *Indernas föreställingar om verldsskapelsen jemförda med Finnarnes.* He was a professor of Sanskrit at Helsinki University, and a founder of the Finno-Ugric Society. His writings include *Das Personalpronomen in den altaischen Sprachen* (1865), *Lieder der Lappen* (1876), *A brief sketch of the Scottish families in Finland and Sweden* (1884), and *Sur l'origine de l'alphabet turc du Nord de l'Asie* (1896). He died in 1909. GSE; LC; Pallas; RNL; ScBInd (4); UjLex

Donner, Wolf, born in 1923, he received a Dr.phil. in 1960 at Köln for *Die sozial- und staatspolitische Tätigkeit der Kriegsopferverbände.* He was affiliated with the Institut für Asienkunde, Hamburg. His writings *Nepal; Raum, Mensch und Wirtschaft* (1972), and *Thailand ohne Tempel* (1984). LC

Donnet, Gaston Henri Pierre, born 21 August 1867 at Le Havre, he was a journalist for the *Petit Dauphinois* in Genève, and later for *le Soir* in Paris. In the service of the Ministère des Colonies, he went in 1894 to French West Africa to study the access to the Sahara, a project which was realized only partially, and which he described in *En Sahara à travers le pays des Maures nomades* (1901). In 1905 he acted as secretary of the European Commission for the Control of the Navigation on the Danube in Galatz. He died in Soissy-sous-Étoilles (Seine-et-Oise), in September 1908. DBF; Henze

Donohue, John Joseph, born 12 January 1926, he was a graduate of the College of the Holy Cross, Worcester, Mass., and received a Ph.D. from Harvard in 1966 for his thesis, *The development of political and social institutions in Iraq under the Buwayhids, 334-403 H.; the fall and rise of the caliphate.* After teaching for a number of years in Baghdad, he was appointed director of the Center for the Study of the Modern Arab World, St. Joseph's University, Beirut. He was the editor of *Islam in transition; Muslim perspectives* (1982). ConAu 122, new rev. 48; LC; Selim

Donon, Jean, fl. 1922, his writings include *Le Régime douanier du Maroc et le développement du commerce marocain jusqu'à nos jours* (1920). NUC, pre-1956

Dontas, Domna N., M.A., Ph.D. (London), fl. 1969, the author's writings include *Greece and the Great Powers, 1863-1875* (1966), *Greece and Turkey; the regime of the Straits, Lemnos and Samo-thrace* (1987), and *The last phase of the war of independence in Western Greece* (1990). LC

Doolittle, George Curtis, Rev., 1867-1922, he was since 1893 a missionary under the American Presbyterian Church in Zahlah, Lebanon. His writings include *Forbidden paths in the land of Og; record of travels of three wise & otherwise men to the east of the Jordan River* (1900), and *Druzes of Syria; their relation to Christianity and Islam* (n.d.). LC

van **Dooren**, Petrus Johannes, born in 1926, he received a doctorate from the Rijksuniversiteit te Leiden in 1954 for his thesis, *De sociaal-economische ontwikkeling van de inheemse samenleving in Uganda.* He was a director, Department of Social Research, Koninklijk Instituut voor de Tropen, Amsterdam. His writings include *Coöperaties voor ontwikkelingslanden* (1978), and its translation, *Co-operatives for developing countries* (1982). LC

Doorenbos, Harvey, he was a member of the Division of Endocrinology at the University Hospital, Groningen, the Netherlands. He edited *Non-surgical management of malignant diseases* (1981). LC

Dopffel, Helmut *Peter*, born 2 April 1926 at Heilbronn, Germany, he studied at Tübingen, Freiburg im Breisgau, and Göttingen, to which Duke University, Durham, N.C., and Cambridge were added later. He received a Dr.jur. from the Universität Hamburg in 1967 for his thesis, *Die Wurzel der Regel locus regit actum im Römischen Altertum.* Since 1954 he was a member of the Max Planck Institut für ausländisches und internationales Privatrecht, Hamburg. Since 1961 he was a joint editor of *Rabels Zeitschrift für ausländisches und internationales Privatrecht.* Thesis

Dopp, Pierre Herman, born in 1898, his writings include *Le Contrefaçon des livres français en Belgique, 1815-1852* (Louvain, 1932), and he edited *L'Égypte au commencement du quinzième siècle, d'après le traité d'Emmanuel Piloti de Crète* (Le Caire, 1950). LC

Dor, Rémy, born 31 October 1946 at Paris, he received two doctorates from the Université de Paris for his theses, *Introduction à l'études des Kirghiz du Pamir afghan,* in 1975, and *"Si tu me dit: chant, chant!" Documents pour servir à la connaissance de la tradition orale des Kirghiz du Pamir afghan,* in 1980. His writings include *Contribution à l'étude des Kirghiz du Pamir afghan* (1975), *Die Kirghisen des afghanischen Pamir* (1978), *Chants du toit du monde* (1982), and *Le chardon déchiqueté* (1982); he edited *Quand le crible était dans la paille* (1978). LC; Schoeberlein; THESAM 4

Dor, Victor *Édouard*, born in 1840 at Vevey, Switzerland, he was educated at Lausanne and Bonn, where he received a Dr.phil. in 1863 for his thesis, *Ronsardus quam habuerit vim ad linguam Francogallicam excolendam.* His writings include *L'instruction publique en Égypte* (1872). BN; Thesis

Dora d'Istria, pseud., see Kol'tsova-Masal'skaia, Elena Mikhailovna

Doran, Charles Francis, born 31 January 1943 at Mankato, Minn, he was a graduate of Harvard and received a Ph.D. in 1969 from Johns Hopkins University, Baltimore, Md. He was a professor of political science at Texas universities and in 1991 a professor of international relations at Johns Hopkins School of Advanced International Studies, Washington, D.C. He was a member of the

Council on Foreign Relations, a regular adviser to business and government officials, provided congressional briefings and testimony on trade, security, and energy policy. His writings include *The politics of assimilation* (1971), *Domestic conflict in state relations* (1976), *Myth, oil, and politics* (1977), and *Forgotten partnership; U.S.-Canada relations today* (1985). ConAu, 73-76; Private

Dorato, Mario, born 23 July 1910 at Roma, he received a double diploma in law and letters from the Università di Roma. He was a director of the Istituto coloniale italiano (Istituto italiano per l'Africa), and the founder, and for many years the editor, of *Africa italiana*, *Continenti*, and *Voce dell'Africa*. His writings include *Libia, bastione dell'impero* (1937), and *Grandi romani in Africa e nel mondo* (1946). He died 6 September 1970. Chi è, 1948, 1957, 1961; *Hommes et destins*, v. 1, pp. 196-197; IndBI (2)

Đorđević (Djordjevic), Dimitrije, born 27 February 1922 at Beograd, his writings include *Излазак Србије на Јадранско море и Конференција амбасалора у Лондону, 1912* (1956), and *Цариски рат Аустро-Угарске и Србије, 1906-1911* (1962); and he was joint editor of *East Central European society and the Balkan wars* (1987). JugoslSA, 1970; LC

Doresse, Jean, born in 1917 at Champagne-Moyton (Charente), he was an archaeologist educated at the Lycée Henri IV, the Sorbonnne, and l'École des hautes études, Paris. His writings include *Alchimie byzantine* (1951), *Livres secrets des gnostiques d'Égypte* (1958), and its translation, *The secret books of the Egyptian Gnostics; an introduction to the Gnostic Coptic manuscripts discovered at Chenoboskion* (1986). Au&Wr, 1971

Dorez, Marie Louis *Léon*, born 17 July 1864 at Villemaur-sur-Vanne (Aube), he was educated at the Lycée de Troyes, l'École des hautes études and l'École des chartes, Paris. He was a palaeographer who spent some time in Britain and the Vatican. In 1893 he joined the Département des manuscrits in the Bibliothèque nationale de Paris. He was an editor of medieval texts, and the author of numerous articles on classical antiquity, French and Italian history, Italian literature, and miniatures, most of which were published in the *Revue des bibliothèques*. He died 25 January 1922. DBF

Dorfman, Robert, born 27 October 1916 at N.Y.C., he was a graduate of Columbia University and received a Ph.D. in 1951 from the University of California at Berkeley for his thesis, *Applications of linear programming to the theory of the firm*. In 1963 he was a professor of economics at Harvard. His writings include *The price system* (1964). AmM&WS, 1973S, 1978S; ConAu, 17-20; IntAu&Wr, 1977; Master (3); WhoAm, 1974-1999

Dori, Latif, born 7 December 1934 at Baghdad, he resided in Israel since 1951 and was a columnist for *al-Hamishmar*. Years later, he joined the editorial board of *al-Mirsad*. He was active in social, trade, and political affairs. Master (1); WhoIsrael, 1973/74, 1976, 1978|; WhoWor, 1974/75, 1976, 1978

Dorigo, Rosella, born 1 August 1945 at Venezia, she studied at the Università di Venizia, where she received a doctorate in 1970. In 1994 she was a professor of modern Arabic literature at her alma mater, specializing in nineteenth century popular Arabic drama as well as contemporary drama. She conducted field work in Syria, and was a member of the Istituto per l'Oriente, and the Union européenne des arabisants et islamisants. Private

Dorman, Harry Gaylord, Jr., born in 1906, he received a Ph.D. from Columbia University in 1948 for his thesis, *Toward understanding Islam; contemporary apologetic of Islam and missionary policy*. In 1962 he was affiliated with the Presbyterian Church in the U.S.A., and executive secretary of the Near East Christian Council. LC; Selim

Dorman, William A., born 20th cent., he was joint author of *The U.S. press and Iran* (1987).

Dorn, Boris Andreevich, born Johann Albert *Bernhard* Dorn, 11 May 1805 at Schönefeld, Germany. After studies at Halle and Leipzig, where he obtained a Dr. phil. for his thesis *De Psalterio aethiopico commentatio* (1825), he went to Kharkov in 1829 to take up a teaching position. In 1835 he followed an invitation to the Institute of Oriental Languages, St. Petersburg, where, in 1842, he became also director of the Asiatic Museum. Concurrently he worked at the Public Library as well as the Academy of Sciences where, however, he did not have the least bit of influence. He was an energetic and productive scholar who published numerous works on Central Asia, some of which were reprinted in the middle of the twentieth century. His writings include *History of the Afghans, translated from the Persian of Neamet Ullah* (1829-1836), *A chrestomathy of the Pushtu or Afghan language* (1847), *Catalogue des MSS et xylographes orientaux de la Bibliothèque impériale publique de St. Petersbourg* (1852), *Bericht über eine wissenschaftliche Reise in dem Kaukasus und den südlichen Küstenländern des Kaspischen Meres* (1861), *Caspia; über die Einfälle der alten Russen in Tabaristan* (1875). He died in St. Petersburg, 31 May 1881. Behrmann, p. 89; BiobibSOT, p. 159; EnSlovar; Fück, 157; GSE; Krachkovskii; *L'Orient, l'Algérie et les colonies françaises* 1 (1866/67), 272, 286-88; TatarES; Wieczynski

Dornier, Pierre, fl. 1949-1954, his writings include *La politesse dans les campagnes du nord de la Tunisie* (Tunis, Institut des belles lettres arabes, 1964). LC

Dornin, Pierre, fl. 1903, his writings include contributions to *Revue de géographie* as well as *Ames soudanaises* (Paris, 1906). BN

Dorofeeva, Lidiia Nikolaevna, 1922-1990 *see* Kiseleva, Lidiia Nikolaevna Dorofeeva

Dorogi, Márton, born 11 September 1911 at Szeged, Hungary, he was an ethnographer whose writings include *Adatok a szarvasi szűcsmesterséghez* (1960). He died in Püspökladány, 10 November 1980. MEL, 1978-1991

Doroshenko, Dmytro, born 8 April 1882 at Vilnius, he was an eminent historian and historiographer, who worked in Kiev and Katerynoslav and became editor of the Ukrainian Shevchenko Society in Kiev. After the 1917 revolution he became the Russian Provisional Government Commissar of Galicia and Bukovyna, then Commissar of Chernihiv Gubernia. He emigrated in 1919 and remained an important figure in the *emigré* Hetmanite Movement. As an *emigré* he held several academic posts in Europe and Canada. In 1945-51 he was the first president of the Ukrainian Academy of Arts and Sciences. His many writings include *Chevtchenko, le poète national de l'Ukraine* (1931), *History of the Ukraine* (1939), and *Die Ukraine und das Reich* (1941). He died in München, 19 March 1951. *American historical review* 56 (1950/51), p. 1040; Master (2)

Doroshenko, Elena Aleksandrevna, born 4 August 1920 at Moscow, she graduated from the Faculty of History, Moscow Univerity in 1945, and received a doctorate in 1952 for her thesis, *Антинародная политика учебников периода правления Реза-шаха Пехлеви*. She was a researcher at the Oriental Institute of the Soviet Academy of Sciences. Her writings include *Система просвещения в Иране* (1959), *Шиитское духовенство в современном Иране* (1975), and *Зороастрийцы в Иране* (1982). LC; Miliband; Miliband²

Dorr, Goldwaithe Higginson, born 21 October 1876 at Newark, N.J., he was a New York lawyer and at various times a special assistant to the U.S. Department of Justice. He was an American delegate to the International Refugee Council, 1948, and a past chairman of the American School of Prehistorical Research, and chairman of the board of Robert College, Istanbul. He wrote *A report on the cost of crime* (1931) for the U.S. National Commission on Law Observance and Enforcement. He died in Carmel, N.Y., 7 December 1977. Master (3); Shavit; WhAm, 7

Dorr, Steven R., born 18 May 1959, he graduated in computer science from the University of Minnesota. He was director of Programs at the Middle East Institute, Washington, D.C., and editor of the *Middle East journal*, before he became Director of Conferences and Programs at the Defense Intelligence College in Washington, D.C., a post which he still held in 1991. He was a specialist in Persian Gulf affairs, with particular research interests in Qatar. His writings include *Scholars' guide to Washington, D.C., for Middle East studies* (1981). LC; MESA roster of members, 1982-1990

Dorra, Albert J., fl. 1938, he was an engineer and, in 1941, attached to the Egyptian Salt and Soda Company in Cairo; in 1952, he was a technical advisor to the Egyptian Federation of Industries, and a member of the Société Fouad Ier d'économie politique, de statistique et de législation. Note

Dorraj, Manochehr, born 20th cent., he received a Ph.D. in 1984 from the University of Texas at Austin. In 1990s he was a professor of political science at the Texas Christian University, Fort Worth. His writings include *From Zarathustra to Khomeini* (1990); and he was the editor of *The changing political economy of the Third World* (1995). LC; NatFacDr, 1995

Dorri, Dzhekhangir Khabibulovich, born 21 February 1932 at Moscow, he was a graduate of the Faculty of Philology, Moscow State University in 1955, and received a doctorate in 1962 for his thesis, *Рекоторые сведения о Низари*. He was successively a researcher at the Tajik and Soviet academies of science since 1955. His writings include a number of catalogues of Oriental manuscripts of the Tajik Academy of Science and *Персидская сатирическая поэзия* (1965), *Персидская сатирическая проза* (1977), and *Мохаммед Али Джамальзаде* (1983); and he translated from the Persian of Muhammad Ali Jamalzadah, *Всякая всясина* (1967). LC; Miliband; Schoeberlein

Dorsey, James, he was in 1976 a foreign editor of *Trouw*, a group of Dutch newspapers. Note

Dorsey, William H., fl. 1972, he was a writer on Arab affairs and a past staff member of the *Arab report and record*. Note

Dortet de l'Espigarié de Tessan, Louis Urbain, born 25 August 1804 at Vigan (Gard), he trained as a hydrographer at l'École polytechnique. He accompanied hydrographical missions to the Gironde, the port of Bayonne, and the Normandie coast. From 1831 to 1833 he was on coastal reconnaisssance in

Algeria. His Algerian experiences are embodied in Auguste Bérard's *Description nautique des côtes de l'Algérie* (1837). In later years he was sent on similar hydrographical missions to Gibraltar and the Moroccan coast. He died in Paris on 30 September 1879. DBF

Doskaraev, Zhumat Doskaraevich, 1887-1972 *see* Dosqaraev, Zhumat Doskaraevich

Dospanov, Urakbai (Orakbey) Dospanovich, born 8 March 1938, he was joint author of *Qaraqalpag isimleri* (1994). LC; Schoeberlein

Dos Passos, John Roderigo, born 14 January 1896 at Chicago. After graduating from Harvard, he became a novelist who in later years aligned himself with conservative forces in the United States and repudiated his early socialist leanings. He visited the Caucasus, Persia, and Syria, a journey which he described in *Orient express* (1927). He died in Baltimore, Md., 28 September 1970. ConAu 3, 29-32 new rev.3; EncAm; Master (40); Shavit; WhAm, 1

Dosqaraev (Доскараев), Zhumat Doskaraevich, born in 1887, he was joint author of *Казак диалектологиясы* (1965), and *Диалектологический словарь казахского языка* (1969). He died 6 July 1972. KazakSE; LC

Doss, Mediha, born 20th cent., she received a doctorate in 1981 from the Université de Paris III for her thesis entitled *Le dialecte sa'idi de la région de Menya*. THESAM 3

Dos Santos Simões, João Miguel, 1907-1972 *see* Simões, João Miguel dos Santos

Dossat, Yves, *docteur ès lettres, agrégé d'histoire*. His writings include *Les Crises de l'Inquisition toulousaine au XIIIe siècle, 1233-1273* (1959), a work which is based on his 1951 Toulouse thesis; a collection of his articles, *Église et hérésie en France au XIIIe siècle* (1982); and he edited *Saisimentum comitatus Tholosani* (1966). LC

Dossie, Robert, d. 1777, he was an English chemist of whom few particulars have survived the passage of time. Before he could be duly elected to the Society of Arts on 2 April 1760, his two-year arrear of his subscription had to be paid by another member. In 1761 he received a grant of one hundred pounds for a method of purifying oil, and five years later was awarded a gold medal for "aiding to establish the manufacture of potash in North America." He was the author of several works on medical subjects including a volume of formulas entitled *The elaboration laid open; or, The secrets of modern chemistry and pharmacy revealed* (1758). "The handmaid to the arts" in *Apollo* 63 (February 1956), p. 54

Dossin, Georges, born in 1896, he was an Ugaritic scholar, a joint author of *Arslan-Tash* (1931), jointed editor of *Xe et XIe campagnes de fouilles à Ras-Shamra-Ugarit* (1941), and *Archives royales de Mari* (1950). LC

Dostal, Walter, born 15 May 1928 at Grulich, Moravia, he received a Dr.phil. in 1952 from the Universität Wien for his thesis, *Ethnologisch-linguistische Studie über das Problem der semitisch-sprechenden Völker*. He was a keeper of the Near Eastern collection, Museum für Völkerkunde, Wien, professor of ethnology and director of the Institut für Ethnologie, Universität Bern, and professor of ethnology at the Universität Wien. His writings include *Die Beduinen in Südarabien* (1967), *Handwerker und Handwerkstechniken in Tarim* (1972), *The traditional architecture of Ras al-Khaimah* (1983), *Egalität und Klassengesellschaft in Südarabien* (1985), and *Eduard Glaser Forschungen in Yemen* (1990). A jubilee volume, *Studies in Oriental culture and history*, was published in 1993. Schwarz; WhoAustria, 1996

Dostian, Irina Stepanovna, born in 1920, her writings include *Борьба сербского народа против турецкого ига XV- начало XIX в* (1958), *Россия и балканский вопрос* (1972); and she edited *Формирование национальных независимых государств на Балканах* (1986). LC

Dotson, Oscar W., fl. 1938, he was a student assistant in the Department of Geography, Emory and Henry College, Appalachian State University. Note

Dottain, Ernest, fl. 1878, his writings include *Précis d'histoire ancienne* (1857), *Précis d'histoire grecque* (1857), and *Précis d'histoire romaine* (1857). BN; NUC, pre-1956

Doublet, Jacques François, born 5 May 1823 at Coutances (Manche), he was still young when he entered primary school teaching. He served successively as *maître d'études* in his home town (1847), at Saint-Hilaire de Harcouët (1848-49), and at the Lycée de Brest (1849-50). With his *bachelier ès-lettres* diploma (1850), he went to Alger to become a sometime *répétiteur particulier*. He was a *professeur* at the Pensionat Maffre from 1851 to 1853 when he went to Bône to teach at the community college until his retirement in 1880. Since 1860 he was concurrently occupied with the founding of the Académie d'Hippone, and later was one of its prominent officers, serving as its secretary and librarian. He also served as keeper at the Musée de Bône, librarian at the Bibliothèque militaire de Bône, and vice-president of the Ligue de l'enseignement. He died in Bône, 3 December 1895. *Bulletin de l'Académie d'Hippone* 28 (1896), pp. 128-138

Doublier, Roger, fl. 1957, he received a doctorate in law, and was a sometime magistrate as well as a lecturer at the Faculté de droit d'Alger. His writings include *La Propriété foncière en A.O.E.* (1957), *Manuel de droit du travail du Cameroun* (1973), and *Le Nu et la loi* (1976). LC

Doucet, Robert, born in 1877, he received a doctorate in 1903 from the Université de Paris for his thesis, *Conversions de fonds d'état en France au XIXe siècle*. Ever since leaving l'École de droit, he remained a student of colonial affairs. He was a secretary of the Comité Dupleix, and, under the auspices of *France de demain*, he published an inquiry into colonisation, which established his reputation. He was a contributor to *Revue indigènes* and *Mois colonial et maritime*. His writings include *Notre domaine colonial* (1921), and *Commentaires sur la colonisation* (1926). He died at the age of fifty-one. *Revue indigène* 24 (jan./février 1929), p. 19

Douchy, François Médard, général, born 19 May 1867 at Dampmar (Aisne), he was educated at the Polytechnique, l'École d'application de Fontainebleau and received a commission in the corps of engineers. After completing courses at l'École supérieure de guerre in 1893, he was attached to the general staff. He was posted to Algeria for two years and thereafter lectured at l'École de guerre. During the first World War he served with the Armée d'Orient. His writings include *La Guerre turco-grecque de 1897* (1898). He died in Vannes, 19 April 1952. DBF

Doucouré, Amadou, born to a princely family of the Soninké in 1909 at Goumbou, French Soudan, he served for twenty years with the Compagnie du Niger français until 1946, when he was elected *conseiller de la République du Soudan*. He resigned from political life in 1964, and died in Bamako, on 5 September 1969. *Hommes et destins*, t. 2, pp. 275-276

Doudou, Boulaid, fl. 1970, he received a doctorate in 1961 from the Universität Wien for his thesis, *Der Tarih al-Mansuri des Ibn Nazif al-Hamawi*. Sezgin

Douel, Martial, born 10 September 1874 at Laigle (Orne), he studied law and entered the Ministère des Finances in 1893. In 1908 he was appointed *contrôleur des dépenses* with the Gouvernement général of Algeria and the Territoires du Sud, and, in 1913, *contrôleur* with the Algerian state railway. His writings include *Au pays de Salammbô* (1911), *Sept villes mortes* (1917), *L'Algérie romaine* (1930), and *Un Siècle de finances coloniales* (1930). He died in Paris, 3 October 1952. DBF

Douence, Jean Claude, born in 1940, he was affiliated with the Centre d'étude des collectivités locales, and was a professor of public law in the Université de Pau et des Pays de l'Adour. His writings include *La Mise en place des institutions algériennes* (1964), and *L'action économique locale* (1988).

Dougherty, James Edward, born 4 May 1923 at Philadelphia, Pa, he was a graduate of St. Joseph's College, Philadelphia, and received a Ph.D. in 1960 from the University of Pennsylvania. In 1951 he began a lifelong career as a teacher of political science at his alma mater. His writings include *The Politics of the Atlantic Alliance* (1964), *The Politics of war-time aid* (1978), and *The Horn of Africa* (1982). AmM&WS, 1973 S; ConAu, 111, 134; LC; Master (1)

Dougherty, James Joseph, born 14 May 1939 at Mauch Chunk, Pa, he was a graduate of the University of Notre Dame, South Bend, Ind., and received a Ph.D. in 1973 from the University of Maryland for his thesis, *American economic assistance to France and French Northwest Africa, 1941-1945*. In 1971 he was appointed a professor of history at University College, the University of Maryland. His writings include *The politics of wartime aid; American economic assistance to France and French Northwest Africa, 1940-1946* (1978). DrAS, 1978, 1982H; NUC

Dougherty, Raymond Philip, born 5 August 1877 at Lebanon, Pa., he was an archaeologist and Assyriologist who was a principal of Albert Academy, Freetown, Sierra Leone, from 1904 to 1914, and served concurrently two terms as vice-consul in Freetown. From 1918 to his death in New Haven, Conn., on 13 July 1933, he was successively a professor of ancient Near Eastern literature at Goucher College, and Yale University. His writings include *Mohammedanism* (1912), *Records from Erech* (1920), *Archives from Erech* (1923-1933), and *The Sealand of ancient Arabia* (1932). DAB, S I; DcNAA; LC; Shavit; WhAm, 1

Doughty, Charles Montagu, born in Suffolk in 1843 into a landed family traditionally connected with the Navy and the Church, he studied geology at Cambridge, but still in his early twenties decided that the vocation of his life should be to serve his native language. He took some years preparing for this task studying other languages. He spent a year in Oxford reading medieval poets. Then he wandered forth in quest of a theme. He passed through Europe and to Cairo from where early in 1875 he rode across Sinai to Petra and on to Madain Salih, where he joined a caravan setting out for Mecca. He travelled openly, without disguise, proclaiming himself a Christian. In consequence, he was entirely at the mercy of the Bedouin with whom he travelled. He made no important discoveries and was not interested in politics. He was a brave but remote man, and his assessment of life provides a testimony to many who travelled like him. In his *Travels in Arabia deserta* he set himself a lasting memorial as a writer of Victorian prose. He died in 1926. Walt Taylor wrote *Doughty's English* (1939), and Andrew Taylor, *God's fugitive; the life of C. M. Doughty* (1999). Bidwell, pp. 84-95; ConAu, 115; DLB 174 (1997), pp. 103-115; DNB; EncAm; EncicUni; Freeth;, pp. 225-267; Fück; GrBr; Henze; Master (17); Meyers; Pallas

Doughty, William Ellison, born 2 February 1873 at Jeffersonville, N.Y., he was a graduate of Syracuse University and ordained a Methodist minister in 1903. He held pastorates until 1910, when he began his eight-year service as secretary of the Laymen's Missionary Movement of the U.S. and Canada. He was associate general secretary of Near East Relief from 1924 to 1929 and national field administrator of the Near East Foundation from 1930 to 1936. He retired in 1955 as national counselor of the Near East Foundation and died 18 June 1959. His writings include *The Call of the world* (1912), *Efficiency points; studies in missionary fundamentals* (1915), and *Christ and the world today* (1937). NYT 20 June 1959, p. 21, col. 6; WhAm, 5; WhNAA

Douglas, Elmer Hewitt, born 12 January 1903 at Kingston, N.Y., he was educated at Ohio Wesleyan University, Drew University, Madison, N.J., and Hartford Seminary Foundation, where he received a Ph.D. in 1945 for his thesis, *Book of the pearl of mysteries and the treasure of the righteous, being a partial translation of Ibn al-Sabbagh al-Himyari*. In 1960 he was appointed professor of Arabic and Islamic studies at the Kennedy School of Missions of the Hartford Theological Foundation, and also assumed the editorship of the *Muslim world*. He died 5 October 1990. DrAS, 1974F

Douglas, Ian Henderson, born 12 May 1920 at Edinburgh, he received a Ph.D. in 1969 from Oxford University for his thesis, *The life and religious thought of Abul Kalam Azad*. He was successively a missionary and a director of the Henry Martyn Institute of Islamic Studies, Lucknow, India. His writings include *Abul Kalam Azad; an intellectual and religious biography* (1988), a revision of his doctoral thesis. He died in 1975. LC; Sluglett

Douglas, Fedwa Malti, 1946- see Malti-Douglas, Fedwa

Douglas, J. Leigh, 1952-1986, his writings include *The Free Yemeni Movement, 1935-1962* (1987). LC

Douglas, James Archibald, major-general, C.M.G., C.I.E., born 21 October 1862, he was a graduate of the Royal Military College, Sandhurst, and served in the Muslim world from Mesopotamia to India until his retirement in 1920. He died 2 May 1932. Who, 1929; Who was who, 3

Douglas, Roy Ian, born 28 December 1924 at London, he was educated at the University of London, and received a Ph.D. in 1952 from Edinburgh. He was called to the bar from Gray's Inn in 1956. Since 1955 he was a faculty member of the University of Surrey. He was repeatedly a Liberal candidate for Parliament. His writings include *From war to cold war, 1942-48* (1981), *World crisis and British decline, 1929-1956* (1986), *Between the wars, 1919-1939* (1992); and he edited *1939, a retrospect forty years after* (1983). ConAu, 73-76; 13, 30, 56 new rev.; LC; Who, 1998; WhoWor, 1980/81

Douglas, William Orville, born 16 October 1898 at Maine, Minn., he was a New York lawyer, a member of the law faculties at Columbia and Yale universities, and an associate justice of the U.S.Supreme Court from 1939 to 1975. His writings include *Strange lands and friendly people* (1951), its translation, *Gärender Orient* (1954), *Beyond the high Himalayas* (1953), and *The right of the people* (1958), a work which in substantial part represents the North Lectures, delivered at Franklin and Marshall College, Lancaster, Pa. in the spring of 1957. He died 19 January 1980. ConAu 9-12, 93-96, new rev. 21; Master (27); WhAm, 7; Who was who, 7

Douglas-Home, Charles Cospatrick, born 1 September 1937, he joined the staff of the London *Times* in 1965, and was its editor during his last years. His writings include *The Arabs and Israel* (1968), *Britain's reserve forces* (1969), and *Rommel* (1973). He died of cancer, 29 October 1985. ConAu, 117; IntAu&Wr, 1976; Who was who, 8; WhoWor, 1982/83

Douin, Georges, born in 1884. After graduation from l'École navale, he went as a sailor on the *vaisseau-école-d'application* first to Patagonia and Chile and on to China, where he was permitted to stay on to learn Chinese and obtain the *brevet d'interprète*. From this period originate his first publications on China. During his service with the French navy in the first World War, he made his first contact with the Near East, resulting in *La Méditerranée de 1803 à 1805; pirates et corsaires aux îles Ioniennes* (1917). With the rank of *capitaine de corvette* he joined the Compagnie du Canal de Suez as *contrôleur de navigation* in 1919. He quickly advanced to become *agent principal* of the transit at Port Said, 1927, and head of the same service at Ismailia in 1938. At the same time he pursued his interest in the history of the Canal. His researches were appreciated by King Fuad I who commissioned him for the publication of the unpublishing documents on the reign of Muhammad Ali. His writings include *La Flotte de Bonaparte sur les côtes d'Égypte* (1922), *L'Égypte indépendante, projet de 1801; documents inédits* (1924), *Mohamed Aly, pacha du Caire, 1805-1807; correspondance des consuls de France en Égypte* (1926), and *Histoire du Soudan égyptien* (1944). He died in the midst of his researches, 5 December 1944. *Bulletin de l'Institut d'Égypte* 27 (1946), pp. 89-95

Doukakes (Doukakis), Vasiles A., born in 1926 at Mytilene, Lesbos, his writings include *Accumulation du capital et calcul économique* (Alger, 1984), *Εθνικό εισόδημα και αναπαραγωγή* (1989), and *Το χρήμα στην ελληνική αρχαιότητα* (1996). EVL, 1993/94, 1996/97; LC

Douls, Camille, born 22 January 1864 at Rodez (disputed), he was educated first at Aveyron, where he lived until 1881, and thereafter at Paris. Under the impression of a voyage to the Antilles as well as an encounter with Paul Soleillet, he became a Saharan adventurer, the second European to explore its western part. He was one of the few men not driven by the dream of the Trans-Saharan railway, but rather by the profound interest in the country. A student of Arabic and the Koran, he travelled disguised as a Muslim merchant. Twice he fell into the hands of nomads, the second time, he was assassinated by his guides in Touareg country on his way to Timbuctu, 6 February 1889. Albert Roussanne published his biography, *L'Homme, suiveur de nuages, Camille Douls, saharien* (1991). DBF; Henze; Peyronnet, p. 857

Doumergue, François, born 11 May 1858 at Carcassonne, he was a school teacher in metropoitan France until 1886, when for unknown reasons he became interested in the flora of Oranie and requested a position at the Collège d'Oran in 1886. There he completed courses at l'École supérieure and qualified as a professor at the Lycée d'Oran. Together with colleagues he accomplished scientific excursions throughout the départment d'Oran, the results of which he reported in periodicals and at various meetings of the l'Association Française pour l'Avancement des Sciences. He contributed to no small degree to the completion of the geological map of Algeria. As a member of the Société de géographie de la province d'Oran, he organized the Society's library and served twice as its president. In 1926 he was appointed keeper at the Musée Demaeght. At the centennial celebrations of the foundation of Algeria, he was awarded the Légion d'honneur. His writings include *Essai sur la faune erpétologique de l'Oranie* (1901). He died 23 December 1938. DBF; *Bulletin trimestrielle* de la Société de géographie et d'archéologie d'Oran 60 (mars 1939), pp. 35-42

Doumergue, Gaston, born of modest Protestant land-owner stock on 1 August 1863 at Aigues-vives (Gard). After completing his legal training at Nîmes and Paris, he obtained his first appointment as substitute magistrat in Hanoi from 1890 to 1892; this was followed by a similar post in Alger. He later entered the Chambre des députés, was a colonial minister, premier, and served as president of the Third French Republic from 1924 to 1931. He died 18 June 1937. DBF; EncAm; *Hommes et destins*, 8, pp. 125-127; Index BFr² (7)

Doumet-Adanson, Napoléon, born in 1834 at Sète (Hérault), he was a lifelong student of natural sciences, a founding member of the Société d'horticulture et de botanique de l'Hérault and a contributor to its *Annales*. He led scientific missions to Tunisia in 1874 and 1878, to Algeria and Tunisia in 1884, and to Corsica in 1896. He was one of the first French to study the southern Tunisian *chotts* and to consider the creation of a *mer intérieure* in the Sahara. His writings include the *Rapport sur une mission botanique exécutée en 1884 dans la région saharienne, au nord des grandes chotts et dans les îles de la côte orientale de la Tunisie* (1888). He died at his family's Château de Baleine, 31 May 1897. DBF

Dournaux-Dupéré, Norbert, born 2 June 1845 at Guadaloupe. After a checkered youth, he discovered his passion for the Sahara. Driven by geographical as well as commercial interests, and encouraged by the Chambre de Commerce d'Alger and the Ministre du Commerce, he, together with E. Joubert, set out in a small party to reach Timbuctu. They were assassinated by Touareg marauders south-west of Idelès in eastern Hoggar near the Tripolitanian frontier, 17 April 1874. Henze; Peyronnet, p. 856

Dournon, A., fl. 1913-1929, he was affiliated with the Société archéologique et géographique du Département de Constantine, Algeria. He translated from the Arabic of Ibn al-'Attar *Ta'rikh balad Qusantinah* in 1913, and *Constantine sous les Turcs*, d'après [Muhammad] Salah [ibn] el 'Ant[a]ri in 1929. BLC; GAL S II, p. 688

Doury, Paul Constantin, born 18 November 1867 at St-Masmes (Marne). After passing through the military college, St-Cyr, he was admitted to the Service des Affaires indigènes de l'Algérie in January 1895 and successively stationed at Djelfa and El-Aricha. He was a highly esteemed officier on the Algero-Moroccan frontier during the crucial years when the French were trying to pacify North Africa.

At the height of his success he resigned from military service in 1919 at Algiers. He was actively involved in the preparations for the centennial celebrations of French Algeria in 1930. Peyronnet, 547-550

Doutrepont, Georges, 1868-1941, his writngs include *La Littérature et la société* (1942). LC

Doutté, Edmond, born 14 January 1867 at Évreux (Eure), he was a local administrator in the Département de la Marne until 1899, when he was granted a position in Algeria for reasons of health. He was posted to l'Aurès, but later was appointed a professor at the Medersa de Tlemcen, where he also pursued Berber studies. He was a lecturer at l'École supérieure des lettres d'Alger, but at the same time, also one of the great explorers of Morocco before 1907, when the country was still closed and hostile. Since 1907 he held the chair of Arab history and civilization at the Faculté des lettres d'Alger, and shortly thereafter also the chair of Berber linguistics. After the first World War he taught in Paris. His writings include *L'Islam algérien en l'an 1900* (1900), *La Société musulmane du Maghrib; magie et religion dans l'Afrique du nord* (1909), *Enquête sur la dispersion de la langue berbère en Algérie* (1913), and *Missions au Maroc; en tribu* (1914). He died in Alger, 7 August 1926. DBF; *Hommes et destins* vol. 4, pp. 265-267; LC

Dow, Alexander, born in Perthshire, he came as a sailor to Bengal, where he became a secretary to the governor. He entered the East India Company's military service in 1760 and advanced through the grades to become lieutenant-colonel in 1769. He published translations from the Persian and also wrote historical works on India. He died in Bhaglapur, 31 July 1779. Buckland; DcBiPP; DNB; Master (1)

Dow, Thomas Edison, born 25 May 1936 at N.Y.C., he was a graduate of Hunter College, New York, and received a Ph.D. in 1962 from the University of Pennsylvania for his thesis, *A sociological analysis of family reaction to disability and institutionalization.* He taught at various American colleges until 1971 when he was appointed a professor of sociology at SUNY at Purchase. AmM&WS, 1973S

Dowidar (Dawidar/Diwidar/Duwaydar), Mohamed, fl. 1964, he obtained a M.Sc. in economics from the University of London and was a professor of law at the Faculty of Law, University of Alexandria, Egypt. His writings include *Les Schémas de reproduction et la méthodologie de la planification socialiste* (1964), *L'économie politique, une science sociale* (1974), and *al-Iqtisad al-Misri bayna al-takhalluf wa-al-tatwir* (1978). LC

Downey, Fairfax Davis, born 28 November 1893 at Salt Lake City, he was a graduate of Yale University and became an editor, journalist, and free lance writer since 1929. His writings include *The Grande Turke, Suleyman the Magnificent* (1929), its translation, *Soliman le Magnifique* (1930), and *Burton, Arabian nights adventurer* (1931). He died in 1990. ConAu 1-4, 131; Master (9); WhE&EA; WhNAA; WrDr, 1976-1990/92

Downs, James Francis, born 20 December 1926 at Pasadena, Calif., he was a graduate of the University of California at Berkeley, where he also received a Ph.D. in 1961 for his thesis, *The effect of animal husbandry on two North American Indian tribes.* He taught at various American universities until 1970 when he was appointed a professor of anthropology at Hilo College, University of Hawaii. His writings include *Washo religion* (1961), *Two worlds of the Washo* (1966), *Cultures in crisis* (1971), *The Navajo* (1972), and *Human nature* (1973). AmM&WS, 1973 S; ConAu, 81-84; LC

Downs, Norton, born 11 February 1918, he was a graduate of theUniversity of Pennsylvania where he also received a Ph.D. in 1950 for his thesis, *Thomas Smith, scholar.* He was a professor of history at Trinity College, Hartford, Conn. He edited *Basic documents in medieval history* (1959), and *Medieval pageant; readings* (1964). He died in Hartford, Conn., 11 January 1985. ConAu 1-4, 114; DrAS, 1974, 1978, 1982H; NYT 14 January 1985, p. A-16, col. 2

Dowsett, Charles James Franck, F.B.A., born 2 January 1924, he was from 1965 to 1991 a professor of Armenian studies at Oxford. His writings include the translation *The penitential of David of Ganjak* (1961). In 1972 he published together with J. W. Carswell, *Kütahya tiles and pottery from the Armenian Cathedral of St. James, Jerusalem.* He died 8 January 1998. LC; Who, 1974-1998; WhoWor, 1978

Dowson, Ernest MacLeod, C.B.E., born 19 November 1876 in India, he was affiliated with the Survey of Egypt from 1900 to 1909, and was successively an adviser to the governments of Egypt, Palestine, Transjordan, Iraq, Zanzibar, and Kenya from 1920 to 1940. He died 26 June 1950. Who, 1921-1949; *Who was who, 4*

Dowson, John, born in 1820 at Uxbridge, he was an assistant to his uncle at the Royal Asiatic Society, a tutor at Haileybury, professor of Hindustani at University College, London, and Staff College, Sandhurst, 1855-1877. His writings include *A grammar of the Urdu or Hindustani language* (1872); his *Classical dictionary of Hindu mythology and religion, geography, history and literature* went through eight editions between 1879 and 1953. He also edited Sir H. M. Elliot's *History of India as told by its own historians*, 8 vols. (1867-1877). He died 23 August 1881. Buckland; DNB; LC

Dowson, Valentine Hugh Wilfred, colonel, born 19th cent., he lived for more than thirty years in Basrah, and was affiliated with date plantations, having gone there in 1915. During the second World War he was an intelligence officer attached to the British Embassy in Iraq, where he was responsible for the southern part of the country. His writings include *Dates and date cultivation of Iraq*, 3 vols. (1921-23), and *Dates; handling, processing and packing* (1962). LC

Doxiades, Konstantinos Apostolou, born 14 May 1913 at Stenimakhos near Romilias, he was from 1939 to 1975 a professor of town planning at the Technical University, Athens, and concurrently a visiting professor at universities throughout the world. His writings include *Ecumenopolis* (1967), *Ekistics; an introduction to the science of human settlements* (1968), *Architecture in transition (1968), The two-headed eagle; from the past to the future of human settlements* (1972), *Architectural space in ancient Greece* (1972), a translation of his 1937 Berlin thesis entitled *Raumordnung im griechischen Städtebau*, and *Building Entopia* (1975). He died in Athens, 28 June 1975. EEE; Hellenikon, 1965; Int WW, 1974; Master index (6); WhAm, 6

Doyle, Sir Arthur Conan, born 22 May 1859 at Edinburgh, he was a trained physician who took to writing. In 1895-96, during a visit to Egypt for the sake of his health, the Dongola campaign began and he was appointed honorary correspondent of the *Westminster gazette* of London. He followed the expedition in early 1896 and then returned to England. A previous trip in a Cook's steamer to Wadi Halfa and a donkey tour in the winter of 1895-96 inspired some of his writings. He died in 1930. ConAu, 122; DNB; Hill; Master (43); Who was who, 3

Doyon, Pierre Alphonse Célestre, born 30 August 1870 at Saint-Hilaire-du-Rosier (Isère), he was educated at the Jesuit Collège de Montgré, and received degrees in law and letters from the Sorbonne. He entered the diplomatic service and later practised law. He died at the Château de Montchalin (Isère), 24 December 1939. DBF

Dozon, Auguste, born 2 February 1822 at Châlons-sur-Marne. After completing his law course, he entered the foreign service in 1855 and spent his entire career in the Balkans. His writings include *Manuel de la langue chkipe ou albanais* (1878), *Contes albanais* (1881), *L'épopée serbe* (1888), and the translation from the Russian of V. P. Nalivkin, *Histoire du khanat de Khokand* (1889). He died in Versailles, in 1891. DBF; LC

Dozy, Reinhart Pieter Anne, born 21 February 1820 at Leiden, he was an eminent Orientalist, versed in Arabic as well as Spanish language and literature. His great work is the *Histoire des Musselmans d'Espagne*, 4 vols. (1861); his writings include *De Israëliten te Mekka* (1864), and a number of Arabic text editions. He died in Leiden, 29 April 1883. CelCen; EncBrit; EncicUni; EncItaliana; EncJud; Fück, p. 182; GdeEnc; NieuwNBW; OxSpan; Pallas; RNL; Wininger

Draganović, Krunoslav Stjepan, born 30 October 1903 at Brčko, he received a doctorate and became a professor of theology at Zagreb University. His writings include *Poviest Crkve u Hrvatskoj* (Zagreb, 1944); and he edited *Opći šematizam Katoličke Crkve u Jugoslaviji* (Sarajevo, 1939), and *Croazia sacra* (Roma, 1943). He died in Sarajevo, 14 June 1983. HBL; LC

Dragendorff, Johann Georg Noël, born 8 April 1836 at Rostock, Germany, he trained as a professional pharmaceutical chemist and thereafter studied at the Universität Rostock, where he received a doctorate in 1861 for his thesis, *Über Einwirkung des Phosphors auf einige Kohlensäure und borsaure Salze*. In 1862 he went to St. Petersburg as editor of the *Pharmazeutische Zeitschrift für Russland* and as legal expert on chemistry. Two years later, he was appointed a professor of pharmacology in the Kaiserliche Universität Dorpat, where he founded the bacteriological laboratory. He resigned when the Czar began to replace the German teaching staff with native Russian scholars. His writings include *Die Heilpflanzen der verschiedenen Völker und Zeiten* (1989). He died in Rostock, 7 April 1898. DtBE

Drago, Roland Louis, born 22 June 1923 at Alger, he completed his legal studies at Alger and Paris with a doctorate in 1950 from the Sorbonne for his thesis, *Les crises de la notion d'établissement public*. Thereafter he held various positions at French universities. In 1998 he was a president of the Tribunal suprême de Monaco. His writings include *Cours de science administrative* (1967). Who's who in France, 1979/80-1998/99; WhoUN, 1975

Drague, Georges, pseud., 1899-1980 *see* Spillmann, Georges Joseph Roger André

Dragunov, Aleksandr Aleksandrovich, born 8 (21) February 1900 at St. Petersburg, where he spent all his life as a Sinologist. From 1930 to 1936 he was a member of the committee on the romanization of Chinese. He died 2 February 1955. Miliband

Drakakis-Smith, David W., born 18 November 1942 or 1944, he was in 1976 a research fellow in the Department of Human Geography of the School of Pacific Studies, Australian National University, and in 1981 a lecturer at the Department of Geography, University of Keele. His writings include *Urbanization, housing, and the developing process* (1980), *The Third World city* (1987); he was joint author of *Housing problems in Ankara* (1987), and editor of *Economic growth and urbanization in developing areas* (1990). LC

Drake, Charles Francis Tyrwhitt, born in 1846 at Amersham, he visited Morocco in 1866-67, Egypt and the Sinai in 1868-69, and together with E. H. Palmer he made a topographical and archaeological survey of the desert of al-Tih as well as Edom and Moab in 1869-70; he investigated northern Syria from Hama to Aleppo in 1870. In the service of the Palestine Exploration Fund he surveyed the Holy Land in 1872. His writings include *Modern Jerusalem* (1875), and he was joint author of *Unexplored Syria* (1972). Overwork, devotion to his task, unhealthy climate, and neglect of preliminary warnings struck him down with fever, and he died in Jerusalem, 23 June 1874. DNB; Embacher; Henze

Drambiants (Drambyantz), Gagik Gurgenovich, fl. 1970, his writings include *Персидский Залив без романтики* (1968). LC

Drampian, Ruben Grigor'evich, fl. 1939, he wrote a number of biographies and *Un évangile cilicien du cercle de Thoros Roslin* (1978), *Фрески Кобайра* (1979), and *Государственная картинная Галерея Армении* (1982). LC

Draper, John William, born 23 July 1893 at Hastings-on-Hudson, N.Y., he was a professor of English literature at various American universities. His writings include *Orientalia and Shakespeareana* (1978). He died in Morgantown, W.Va., 30 November or 1 December 1976. ConAu, 9-10, 69-72; NatCAB 60, 162-63

Drapeyron, Ludovic, born 26 February 1839 at Limoge, he was a 1862 graduate of l'École normale supérieure, Paris, and received two doctorates in 1869 from the Sorbonne for his theses, *L'empereur Héraclius et l'Empire byzantin au VIIe siècle*, and *De Burgundiae historia et ratione politica, Merovingorum aetate*. He was a strong advocate of French geography teaching, for the purpose of which he founded the *Revue de géographie* in 1876. His historical writings deal with the middle ages. He died in Paris, 9 January 1901. DBF

Drašković, Radovan M., born 24 February 1889, his writings include *Ваљево у прошлости; прилози за завичајну историју* (1987). He died 25 April 1974. LC

Drayton, Geoffrey, fl. 1963, he was an editor of *Petroleum times* and affiliated with the Economist Intelligence Unit, Ltd., London. His writings include *The Market for LPG in the 1980s* (1981), and he was joint editor of *Soviet oil and gas to 1990* (1982). LC

Draz, M. Abdallah, 1894-1958 see Daraz, Sa'id *Muhammad 'Abd Allah*

Dréolle, Jean André, born 7 October 1797 at Libourne (Gironde), he was an editor of *le Constitutionnel* before he was appointed a professor of history at l'Athènes royal de Paris in 1837. He spent some years at his home town where he founded the journal *le Peuple* in 1848. He later returned to Paris to join the staff of the *Journal des débats*. His writings include *De l'influence du principe religieux sur l'homme et sur la société; cours professé à l'Athènes royal de Paris, 1837-38* (1838), and *Expédition anglaise sur le Niger pendant les années 1841 et 1842* (1845). He died 6 February 1878. DBF

Dresch, Jean, born 30 November 1905 at Paris, he was educated at Lycée Louis-le-Grand, and École Normale Supérieure, Paris. From 1931 to 1941 he was professor at the Collège musulman, and later at the Lycée in Rabat. In 1941 he received a doctorate from the Université de Paris for his thesis, *Recherches sur l'évolution du relief dans le massif central de Grand Atlas, le Haouz et le Sous*. Thereafter he taught at a variety of universities in France. Together with Pierre Birot he published *La Méditérranée et le Proche-Orient* (1953-55). He died 4 March 1994. WhoFr, 1969/70-1993/94

Dresden, Mark J., born 26 April 1911 at Amsterdam, where he completed his Indo-Iranian and classical studies, and received a doctorate in 1941 from the Rijksuniversiteit te Utrecht. He was a professor of classics at Amsterdam until 1949, when he was appointed a professor of Iranian studies at the University of Pennsylvania. He was a frequent visiting professor at American universities, and a member of learned societies and academic committees. He edited a *Modern Persian reader* in 1964. BioB134; DrAS, 1974, 1978, 1982

Dressaire, Léopold, fl. 1913, his writings include *Jérusalem à travers les siècles* (Paris, 1931). NUC, pre-1956

Dressendörfer, Peter, fl. 1978, his writings include *Islam unter der Inquisition; die Morisco-Prozesse in Toledo, 1575-1610* (1971), a work which was originally presented as doctoral thesis at the Universität Gießen in 1970. Schwarz

Dressler, Jürgen, born about 1950 at Waakhausen, Germany, he received a doctorate in agronomy from the Universität Hohenheim for his thesis, *Standortgerechter Landbau im tropischen Bergbau; Situation und Entwicklungsmöglichkeiten landwirtschaftlicher Kleinbetriebe in Rwanda*, in 1984.

Dreux, André Auguste Albert, born 5 June 1871 at Blois. After completing his arts degree, he enrolled in 1895 at l'École des chartes, Paris. It was not until 1900 that he fulfilled the requirements and received a diploma in archival palaeography for his thesis, *Le premier divorce de Henri VIII et les relations de la France et de l'Angleterre de 1527 à 1534*, a work which has never been published. He briefly served as an archivist in the Département de Lozère before becoming first the secretary to the historian Spoelberch de Lovenjoul, and later, the research associate of Henri de Castries for the history of Morocco. After the first World War he was successively professor of French language and literature at Tulane University, New Orleans, and Winona University, Minn., where he died 3 July 1931. DBF

Drew, Elizabeth, born 16 November 1935 at Cincinnati, Ohio, she was a graduate of Wellesley College, and a free lance writer, editor, and televison commentator on American politics. Most of the material in her books appeared originally as syndicated articles. Her books include *Washington journal* (1975). ConAu, 104; Master (3); WhoAm, 1974-1999; WhoAmW, 1983/84-1995/96

Drew, Frederic(k), born 11 August 1836 at Southampton, he was educated at the Royal School of Mines and entered the Geographical Survey. Since 1862, he was employed by the Maharaja of Kashmir to search for minerals and supervise his forest administration. He later was a governor of Ladakh. He travelled to Baltistan in 1863 and 1870, and Gilgit in 1870. He was a science master at Eton, where he died 28 October 1891. His writings include *The Jummoo and Kashmir territories* (1875), and the partial French translation, *Cachemir et Petit Thibet* (1877). Buckland; DNB; Henze

Drew, Jane Beverly, Dame, D.B.E., born 24 March 1911, she was a British architect and a sometime town planning adviser in West Africa and India as well as a visiting professor of architecture at various American universities. She received several honorary doctorates. Her writings include *Village housing in the tropics* (1947), and she was joint author of *Architecture and environment* (1976). She died 27 July 1996. BlueB, 1975, 1976; IntWW, 1975-1994/95; Master (6); WhE&EA; Who, 1974-1996; WhoWor, 1984-1995

Drew, Ronald Farinton, born 5 October 1922 at Toronto, he was a graduate of the University of Toronto and received a Ph.D. in 1958 from Stanford University for his thesis, *Siberia; an experiment in colonialism, a study of economic growth under Peter I*. He was a professor of history in the University of Houston, Texas, from 1954 until his retirement. DrAS, 1974, 1978, 1982

Drewes, Gerardus Willebrodus Joannes, born 28 November 1899 at Amsterdam, he studied oriental languages at the Rijksuniversiteit te Leiden, where he also received a doctorate. In 1925 he was appointed a staff adviser, Native Affairs, Jakarta, and in 1936, successively professor of Islamic law and Indonesian languages at the Faculty of Law, and dean, at Jakarta. After the war, he served at Leiden as professor of Indonesian, 1947-54, and professor of Islamic studies, 1954-1959. His writings include *Drie Javaansche Goeroe's* (1925), *Die mirakelen van Abdoelkadir Djaelani* (1938), *The romance of King Anlin Darma in Javanes literature* (1975), *Directions for travellers on the mystic path* (1977); he edited and translated *Two Achehnese poems, Hikajat Ranto and Hikajat Teungku di Menke* (1980), and he edited *Adat Atjèh* (1958). WhoNL, 1962/63; Wie is dat, 1948, 1956

Drexel, Albert, born 18 June 1889 at Hohenems, Austria, he was ordained a Catholic priest and was a sometime director of the Afrikanisches Institut zu Innsbruck. He was the editor of *Bibliotheca ethnologica linguistica africana* and the ephemeral *Innsbrucker Jahrbuch für Völkerkunde und Sprachwissenschaft*, 1925-1926. His writings include *Die Judenfrage in wissenschaftlicher Bedeutung* (1936), *Grundriss der Rassenkunde* (1941), *Albert Drexel; Schicksal und Werk eines österreichischen Gelehrten*, edited by K. Ernst Girsberg (Zürich, 1947), *Ursprung und Wesen der Sprache* (1951-52), *Sprachen der Erde* (1954), *Atlas der Völkerkunde* (1955), and *Ein neuer Prophet? Teilhard de Chardin* (2nd rev. ed., 1971). DtBilnd (1); LC

Drexl, Franz, born 25 November 1885 at Gammelsdorf, Germany, he was a secondary school teacher who had studied classical philology and received a Dr.phil. in 1909 from the Universität München for his thesis, *Achmets Traumbuch; Einleitung und Probe eines kritischen Textes*. He died in 1951. DtBilnd (2); KDtLK, 1926, 1928, 1930, 1932, 1934; Wer ist's, 1928, 1935

Dreyer, June Teufel, born 5 October 1939 at Brooklyn, N.Y., she was a graduate of Wellesley College and received a Ph.D. in 1973 from Harvard for her thesis, *Chinese communist policy toward indige-*

nous minority nationalities. After teaching at Harvard and the University of British Columbia, she was appointed a professor of political science at Miami University in 1975. In 1996 she was affiliated with with the School of Law, University of Maryland. Her writings include *China's forty million; minority nationalities and international integration* (1976), *China's political system* (1993), and she edited *Chinese defense and foreign policy* (1989), and *Asian Pacific regional security* (1990). AmM&WS, 1978; LC; Schoeberlein

Dreyfus, Hippolyte, born 19th cent., his writings include *Le Béhaïsme* (1908), *Essai sur le Béhaïsme* (1909), *The universal religion, Bahaism* (1909), and several translations of 'Abd al-Baha ibn Baha Allah into French. NUC, pre-1956

Dreyfus, Maurice René, born in 1901, he received a medical doctorate in 1928 from the Université de Paris for his thesis, *Physiologie des diverticules vésicaux*. In 1936 he was *médecin-commandant* at the Hôpital de Laghouat, Algeria. NUC, pre-1956

Driault, J.-Édouard, born in 1864 at La Neuville-sur-Essone (Loiret), he was educated at the *lycées* in Orléans and Saint-Cloud. He was a professor of history at various *lycées* from 1892 to 1920, when he accomplished a scientific mission to Greece. Upon his return in 1925, he retired from teaching. He was a prolific writer on contemporary history, particularly on the Balkans and the Near East. In 1912 he founded the *Revue des études napoléoniennes*. His writings include *La question d'Orient* (1898), *La politique orientale de Napoléon* (1904), *La formation de l'empire de Mohamed Aly de l'Arabie au Soudan, 1814-1823* (1927), and *L'éxpédition de Crète et de la Morée, 1823-1828* (1930). He was politically isolated after his appeal to Hitler to have the remains of the King of Rome returned to Paris. He died in 1947. He had converted to Greek Orthodoxy. DBF

Drijvers, Hendrik Jan Willem, born 25 September 1934 at Winschoten, the Netherlands, he studied theology and Semitic languages at the Rijksuniversiteit te Groningen, where he received a doctorate in 1965. Thereafter he was a professor of Semitic languages at his alma mater. His writings include *Bardaison of Edessa* (1966), and a collection of his articles entitled *East of Antioch; studies in early Syriac Christianity* (1984). LC; Wie is wie, 1984/88

Drikker, Khanna Natanovna, fl. 1960, her writings include *К истории коллективизации сельского хозяйства в Таджикистане в период первой и второй пятилеток* (1959), *О некоторых вопросах коренняx социально-экономических преобразований в Таджикистане в период построения социализма* (1979), and *Формировнание классов социалистического общества в Таджикистане* (1983). LC

Drimba, Vladimir, his writings include *Syntaxe comane* (Leiden, 1973), and he edited the works of Ion Heliade-Rădulescu between 1961 and 1975. LC

Driver, Sir Godfrey Rolles, born 20 August 1892 at Oxford, he was a fellow of Magdalen College, a professor of Semitic languages and a sometime librarian and vice-president at Oxford. His collection of 19th-century photographs of Jerusalem, Lebanon, etc., are now in the Griffith Institute, Ashmolean Museum, Oxford. He died 22 April 1975. BlueB, 1973/74, 1975, 1976; CentBritOr, pp. 102-138; ConAu, 21-22, 57-60; DNB; Master (4); WhAm, 6; Who, 1958-1974

Drobizheva, Leokadiia Mikhailovna, her writings include *Ленин и использование местного опыта хозяйственного строительства* (1965), *История и социология* (1971), its translation, *Soziologie und Geschichte* (1974), *Духовная общность народов* (1981); and she edited *Ethic conflict in the post-Soviet world* (1996). LC

Droin, Jean Claude, fl. 1964, he was an engineer *des ponts et chaussées* and head of the Divison départementale de la Saoura de l'Organisation saharien, Algeria. Note

Drojat, François, born 19 October 1795 at Die (Drôme), he was a trained lawyer who practised successively in Die and Paris, but his interest in archaeology gradually led him to abandon his legal profession. He was a member of the Société des antiquaires de France since 1824, and its secretary since 1826. In 1827 he started his research on Hannibal, retracing the course of his expedition in Africa and Spain; but he never published the results. His trace is lost after he stood for election in 1831. His writings include *Aperçus philosophiques* (1821), and *La Maîtresse-clef de la tour de Babel; alphabet primordial, phonétique, graphique, idéal de toutes les langues du globe* (1857). DBF; Index BFR² (2)

Droop, Adolf, born 6 September 1882 at Hannover, Germany, he studied at the universities of Göttingen, Berlin, Lausanne, Oxford, and Jena, where he received a Dr.phil. degree in 1906 for his thesis, *Die Belesenheit P. B. Shelley's nach den direkten Zeugnissen*. His writings include *Karl May;*

eine Analyse seiner Reiseerzählungen (1909). In 1917 he was resident in Berlin, where he contributed to *Islamische Welt*, a periodical of German Muslims. NUC, pre-1956

Drost, Dietrich, born 6 January 1928 at Brunshaupten, Germany, he completed his anthropological studies with two doctorates from the Universität Jena for his theses, *Der Feuerbock; Monographie eines Handgerätes* (1952), and *Töpfereitechnik in Afrika* (1959). He was successively a professor of anthropology at Jena, and a keeper at the Museum für Völkerkunde, Leipzig. Unesco

Drouet, Francis Alexandre, born in 1863, his writings include *De Marseille à Moscou par le Caucase; notes de voyage* (Rouen, 1893), and *Au nord de l'Afrique* (Nice, 1896). BN; LC

Drouiliat, René, he was in 1938 a lecturer at the Faculté de droit d'Alger. Note

Drouin, Edme Alphonse called Edmond, born in 1838 in France, he studied law at Paris, where he was called to the bar around 1860 and subsequently rose to prominence. A few years later, he abandoned his legal profession and turned to purely academic work. After 1882 he was almost exclusively occupied with Oriental numismatics so much as to dominate the field from Persia to the gates of Mongolia for a quarter of a century. His other writings include *Dictionnaire comparé des langues française, italienne, espagnole, latine, allemande, anglaise, grecque, hebraïque et arabe* (1866), *Grammaire théorique et raisonnée de la langue allemande* (1876). He died in Paris, 28 January 1904. DBF

Drouville, Gaspard, born 18th cent., he was a French cavalry colonel who travelled to Persia in the service of the czar, a journey which he described in *Voyage en Perse pendant les années 1812 et 1813* (St.-Pétersbourg, 1819-20). A Persian translation was published in 1985, even though the author's descriptions of Persian customs were by far not as new as they seemed to him. Henze; LC

Drouyn de Lhuys, Édouard, born 19 November 1805 at Paris. After completing his legal studies, he entered the diplomatic service as an attaché at the French Embassy in Madrid in 1831. In 1840 he was appointed a director of commercial affairs at the Ministère des Affaires étrangères, a post which he held until 1842, when he entered politics. After the 1848 revolution he was foreign minister until his retirement in 1870. His writings include *Les neutres pendants la guerre d'Orient* (1868). He died on 1 March 1881. CelCen; DBF; DcBiPP; GdeEnc; IndBI (2); Index BFr² (5); Glaeser; Hoefer; Vapereau

Drovetti, Bernardino Michele Maria, born 4 (not 7) January 1776 at Barbania, Piedmont, he was a trained lawyer but he early abandoned his profession. In 1863 he joined the French consular service and from that year until 1815 was consul in Cairo. During the next six years he was privately in Egypt, visiting Upper Egypt in 1816 and the Oasies in 1819 and 1820, and acquiring antiquities. Some years later, he became consul-general of France in Egypt, a post which he held until his retirement in 1830, when he returned to his native Piedmont, where he died in Torino, 9 May 1852. He played an important part in politics, exploration and the collection of antiquities. Ronald T. Ridley published *Napoleon's proconsul in Egypt; the life and times of Bernarino Drovetti* (1998). DBF; DizBI; Egyptology; Goldschmidt;Henze; Hill; Hoefer; *Hommes et destins*, v. 7, pp. 155-157

Drower, Lady Ethel Mary Stefana née Stevens, born 1 December 1879 at London, she was the wife of the British adviser to the Ministry of Justice in Baghdad, and lived in Iraq for well over ten years. Her travels in the Middle East supplied her with material for her books, part of which were published under her maiden name. Her writings include *My Sudan year* (1912), *By Tigris and Euphrates* (1923), *Cedars, saints and sinners in Syria* (1926), *Folk-tales of Iraq* (1931), and *Peacock angel* (1941). She died 27 January 1972. ConAu, 11-12; Master (2); WhE&EA; Who, 1943-1972; *Who was who*, 7

Droz, Georges André Léoplod, born 4 May 1931 at Alger. After completing his studies with a doctorate in law, he was a professor of law at the Sorbonne, and a lecturer at the Academy of International Law, den Haag. His writings include *Compétence judiciaire et effets des jugements dans le Marché commun* (1972), and *Pratique de la convention de Bruxelles du 27 septembre 1968* (1973). IntWW, 1983-1998/99; LC; WhoEIO, 1982, 1985

Drozdík, Ladislav, fl. 1964, he was joint author of *Jazyky sveta* (Bratislava, 1983). LC

Druart, Therese Anne, born 20th cent., she received a B.Phil. in 1975 from Oxford for her thesis, *The metaphysics of al-Farabi's al-Siyasa al-madaniyya*. In the 1990s she was a professor at the Department of Philosophy, Catholic University, Washington, D.C. She edited *Arabic philosophy and the West* (1988). LC; NatFacDr, 1995-1999; Sluglett

Drucker, Peter Ferdinand, born 19 November 1909 at Wien, he received a Dr.jur. from the Universität Frankfurt am Main in 1931 for his thesis, *Die Rechtfertigung des Völkerrechts aus dem Staatswillen*. He was successively an economist in England, an America correspondent for several British newspapers, and a professor of economics at various American universities. His writings include *The end of economic man* (1939), *The practice of management* (1954), and *Post-capitalist society* (1993). AmM&WS, 1973, 1978; BlueB, 1973/74, 1975, 1976; ConAu, 61-64, 46 new rev.; Master (6); Who, 1974-1998; WhoAm, 1974-1999; WhoWest, 1987-1994/95; WhoWor, 1974/5-1998; WrDr, 1980-1998/2000

Drude, Carl Georg *Oscar*, born 5 June 1852 at Braunschweig, Germany, where he also studied and received a doctorate in botany. He was successively a professor of botany and a director of the botanical gardens, Dresden. His writings include *Die Ökologie der Pflanzen* (1913). He died in Dresden, 1 February 1933. DtBE; DtBilnd (6); *Wer ist's*, 1912, 1922, 1928

Drummond, Richard Henry, born 14 December 1916 at San Francisco, he was a graduate of UCLA, received a Ph.D. in 1941 from the University of Wisconsin, and was ordained in 1947 after passing through the Gettysburg Theological Seminary. He served as a missionary in Japan from 1949 to 1962, when he was appointed a professor of ecumenical mission and history of religions at the University of Dubuque, Iowa. His writings include *Toward a new age in Christian theology* (1985). DrAS, 1974, 1978, 1982; Master (1); WhoRel, 1975, 1977, 1985, 1992/93

Drummond de Melfort, Marie Caroline Durand de Fontmagne *see* Durand de Fontmagne, Marie C.

Drummond-Hay, Grace Marguerite née Lethbridge, 1895 or 6-1946 *see* Hay, Grace Marguerite

Drummond-Hay, Robert, 1846-1926 *see* Hay, Sir Robert

Druon, Henri Valéry Marc, born 12 May 1819 at Cateau (Nord), he was educated at Cambrai and graduated in 1839 from l'École normale. He taught at a variety of French colleges. In 1859 he received a doctorate in letters from the Université de Paris for his thesis, *Études sur la vie et les mœurs de Synésius, évêque de Ptolémaïs*. He was resident in Nancy since 1885, where he was a member of l'Académie de Stanislav, and its president since 1889. He died in 1907. DBF

Druzhinin, Nikolai Mikhailovich, born 1 (13) January 1886 at Kursk, Russia, he graduated in law as well as in history and philology from Moscow University in 1918. He held various positions at the Museum of the Revolution of the USSR, Moscow University, and at several academic institutions. Before his retirement in 1964, he worked ten years in the Academy's Institute of History, where he headed a department concerned with the history of nineteenth-century Russia. He died 8 August 1986. GSE; Master (2); NYT 13 August 1986, p. D-20, col. 1; WhoWor, 1971/72, 1974/75

Druzhinina, Elena Ioasafovna née Chistiakova, born 11 April 1916, and in 1949 married to Nikolai M. Druzhinin, she was a senior researcher at the Institute of History, Soviet Academy of Sciences. Her writings include Кючук-Кайнарджийский мир 1774 года (1955), Северное Причерноморье в 1775-1800 гг (1959), and Южная Украина в период кризиса феодализма, 1825-1860 (1981). LC

von **Drygalski**, Erich, born 9 February 1965 at Königsberg, Germany, he received a doctorate in geography in 1887 from the Universität Berlin for his thesis, *Die Geoiddeformation der Eiszeit*. He qualified as lecturer in geography and geophysics at his alma mater in 1898, and became a professor in 1899. In 1906 he was invited to the newly established chair of geography at the Universität München. When he retired in 1935, he left a highly regarded department. In 1925 he was presented with the jubilee volume, *Freie Wege vergleichender Erdkunde*. He died in München on 10 January 1949. DcScB; DtBE; DtBilnd (11); Henze; Master (3)

Drysdale, Alasdair Duncan, born 20th cent., he received a Ph.D. in 1977 from the University of Michigan for *Center and periphery in Syria; a political geography study*. Throughout the 1990s, he was a professor at the Department of Geography in the University of New Hampshire at Durham. He was joint author of *The Middle East and North Africa; a political geography* (1985), and *Syria and the Middle East peace process* (1991). LC; *MESA roster of members*, 1977-1990; NatFacDr, 1995, 1999

D'Souza, Stanislaus Michael, born 29 September 1934, his writings include *Closed birth intervals; a data analytic study* (New Delhi, 1974), a work which was originally presented as a doctoral thesis, Princeton, 1971. He also wrote *A population laboratory for studying disease processes and mortality; Matlab, Comilla* (1981), and *Mortality case study, Matlab, Bangladesh* (1985). LC

D'Souza, Victor Salvatore, born 23 December 1923 at Mangalore (Karnataka), India, he was a professor of sociology, and later a dean, at Panjab University. His writings include *Social structure of a planned city, Chandigarh* (1968), *Economic development, social structure, and population growth* (1985), and *Development planning and structural inequalities* (1990). LC; WhoIndia, 1979/80-1993/94

Duarte, Adrian, 1896-1967, his writings include *Les premières relations entre les Français et les princes indigènes dans l'Inde au XVIIe siècle, 1666-1706* (Paris, 1932), *The beggar saint of Schwan*

and other sketches of Sind (Karachi, 1974), *A history of British relations with Sind, 1613-1843* (Karachi, 1976), and *The crafts and textiles of Sind and Baluchistan* (1982). LC

Dubar, Claude, fl. 1972, his writings include *Besoins de formation continue et crise économique* (1981), *La formation professionnelle continue* (1985), *La socialisation* (1991); and he was joint author of *Les classes sociales au Liban* (1976). LC

Dubash (Dubaśa), Dhunjibhai Framji, his writings include *Puratana Irana* (1934).

Dubberstein, Waldo Herman, born 21 October 1907 at Bellefont, Kansas, he was a graduate of the University of Chicago, where he also received a Ph.D. in 1934 for his thesis, *Comparative prices in later Babylonia*. He was a professor of international affairs at the National War College, and concurrently a research specialist in the U.S. Department of Defense and the Department of Justice until his retirement in 1982. He had allegedly travelled to Tripoli, Libya, under an assumed name in the spring of 1978 to discuss deployment of troops in the Middle East with Libya's military intelligence officers. The day after he was indicted on seven counts of peddling classified secrets about the Middle East to a renegade ex-CIA agent, he was found shot through the head, an apparent suicide, on Friday, 6 May 1983. He was joint author of *The glories of ancient history* (1938). BioIn, 13; DrAS, 1974, 1978, 1982; *Newsweek* 101 (9 May 1983), p. 121

Dubertret, Louis, born in 1902, he received a doctorate in 1953 from the Sorbonne for his thesis, *Géologie des roches vertes du nord-est de la Syrie et du Hatay*. He was joint author of *Manuel de géographie; Syrie, Liban et Proche-Orient* (1940), and joint editor of *Hydrogeology of karstic terrains* (1984). LC

Dubetsky, Alan R., born in 1943, he received a Ph.D. in 1973 from the University of Chicago for his thesis, *A new community in Istanbul; a study of primordial ties, work organization, and Turkish culture*.

Dubeux, Louis, born 2 November 1798 at Lisboa, where his father was chancellor at the French consulate. After the evacuation of Portugal, the family settled in Paris, and in 1816 he entered the De Bure bookshop, a family enterprise, and in 1820 the Bibliothèque royale. During his spare time he learned an enormous number of foreign languages. In 1847 he succeeded Amédée Jaubert in the chair of Turkish at l'École des langues orientales vivantes, Paris, and in 1857, Étienne Quatremère as professor of Hebrew at the Collège de France, a position he held until 1862, when it passed to Ernest Renan. His writings include *La Perse* (1841), and *Éléments de la grammaire turque* (1856). He died 4 October 1863. DBF

Dubey, Swaroop Rani, Mrs., born 20th cent., she advanced from a junior research fellow in 1973 to assistant professor at the South Asia Studies Centre, University of Rajasthan, Jaipur, in 1988. Her writings in-clude *One-day revolution in Sri Lanka* (1988). LC

Dubié, Paul, born 3 July 1908 at Estampures (Hautes Pyrénées), he completed his law studies at Toulouse and Paris and received diplomas from several schools of higher learning, including the Centre des hautes études pour l'Afrique et l'Asie moderne. He was a French colonial administrator in Mauritania and Senegal from 1933 to 1945. His writings include *La vie matérielle des Maures; les nomades, l'agriculture, le commerce, la sédentarisation des Maures et leurs activités hors de Mauritanie* (1953). WhoFr, 1963/64-1969/70

Dubief, Jean, born 28 October 1903 at Rennes, he graduated in 1920 from l'École nationale supérieure agronomique, Alger. He was from 1931 to 1942 a climatologist and head of the Observatoire de Tamanrasset, French Sahara, and a physicist at the Institut de météorologie et de physique du globe at the Université d'Alger from 1962 to 1968. His writings include *Essai sur l'hydrologie superficielle au Sahara* (1953), and *Le climat du Sahara* (1959). WhoFr, 1965/66-1998/99; WhoWor, 1974/75-1997

Dubiński, Aleksander, born 22 May 1924 in Lithuania, he received a doctorate from Uniwersytet Warszawski. He was joint author of *Słownik turecko-polski, polski-turecki* (1983). LC; Schoeberlein

Dubler, César Emil, born 14 November 1915 in Switzerland. After he received a doctorate in chemistry in 1940, he obtained a second doctorate in 1943 from the Universität Zürich for his thesis, *Über das Wirtschaftsleben auf der Iberischen Halbinsel vom XI. zum XIII. Jahrhundert; ein Beitrag zu den christlich-islamischen Beziehungen*. After completing his Orientalist training at SOAS in 1956, he became a professor of Islamic languages and culture at the Universität Zürich, a position which he held until his death, 20 July 1966. Under his chairmanship, and with personal financial sacrifice, the Orientalistisches Seminar in Zürich became a first-class research institute. His writings include *Abu Hamid el Granadino y su relación de viaje por tierras eurasiáticas* (1953), *La materia médica de Dióscorides* (1953). *Asiatische Studien* 22 (1968), pp. 146-154; *Index Islamicus* (2); Schwarz

Duboc, Émile Charles Eutrope, born 8 July 1852 at Barentin (Seine-maritime). After graduation from l'École navale, he plied the waters of West Africa from 1873 to 1875. During this time he was dispatched to the Ogowe River for hydrographical reconnaissance. He later saw naval action in China. He died in Saint-Germain-en-Laye, 31 January 1935. DBF; *Hommes et destins*, vol. 4, pp. 267-269

Dubois, Albert *Félix*, born 16 September 1862 at Dresden, Germany, where his father was in the service of the King of Prussia. He was educated at the Collège de Melun, to which l'École supérieure de commerce de Paris was added. His father's connections were conducive to his career as a correspondent to several newspapers in Berlin and Wien. In 1890 the editors of *l'Illustration* asked him to accompany, and report on, the Mission Brosselard-Faidherbe, which set out to explore Guinea and the sources of the Niger River. Four years later, he was sent out to Timbuctu to report on the arrival of the *colonne* Joffre on 12 February 1894, a journey which he described in *Tombouctou la mystérieuse* (1897), and its translation, *Timbuctu the mysterious* (1896). He was one of the founding members who financed the Société générale d'études pour le transport par automobile Dubois et Cie, intended to accomplish the *mission civilisatrice de la France* by introducing automobile transport to the French Sudan; but it was an enterprise that cost him his fortune. His writings also include *La vie au continent noir; une expédition au Soudan français* (1893). He died 1 June 1945 and was burried at Père Lachaise cemetery in Paris. DBF; *Hommes et destins*, vol. 5, pp. 178-184

Dubois, Edmond *Marcel*, born 25 July 1856 at Paris. After graduation from l'École normale supérieure in 1876, and *agrégation d'histoire et de géographie* in 1878, he was named a member of l'École d'Athènes. He travelled extensively in Greece and the Greek Islands. After submitting his doctoral theses, *De Co insula* (1884), and *Les ligues étolienne et achéenne* (1885), he was successively a lecturer at Nancy and a professor of geography at the Sorbonne. On account of the introduction of new teaching methods, he was invited to join the Masson publishing house, and a few years later, Hachette in Paris. His writings, predominantly for teaching purposes, include *Géographie économique de l'Afrique, l'Asie, l'Océanie et l'Amérique* (1889), and *La crise maritime* (1910). He died in Sèvres, 23 October 1916. DBF

Dubois, Jean Michel, fl. 1978, he was an assistant at the Institut de droit, Ben-Aknoun, Alger. Note

Dubois, Paul Jean Marie, born 19 March 1932 at Paris, he graduated in 1954 from l'École polytechnique. He was successively an administrator at the Institut national de la statistique et des études économiques du Maroc, and head of the Service central des statistiques at the Ministère de l'économie nationale, Rabat. Unesco

Dubois, R., born 19th cent., he was in 1913 a *capitaine d'Artillerie coloniale* at Tchekna (Baguirmi).

Du Bois, William Ewing, born 15 December at Doylestown, Pa, he studied the classics and became a lawyer. An affection of the voice made it increasingly difficult for him to talk so that he accepted a position as director's clerk in the Mint of the United States. He later transferred to the assay department, with whose director he jointly published. Their writings include *A manual of gold and silver coins of all nations* (1851). He died in Philadelphia, Pa., 14 July 1881. DAB

Dubois-Aymé, Jean Marie Joseph Aimé Dubois, born 1779 at Pont-de-Beauvoisin (Isère). After graduation from the École polytechnique, he served as an engineers' officer in the French campaign in Egypt as well as later collaborating in the great edition of the *Description de l'Égypte*. He served with the rank of colonel in Italy, and later turned toward politics. His writings include *Mémoire sur la ville et la vallée de Qoçeir et sur les peuples nomades ...* (1812), *Mémoire sur quelques parties de l'Égypte* (1814), and *Mémoire sur quelques tribus arabes des déserts d'Égypte* (1814). He died in Meylan, 15 March 1846. DBF; *Hommes et destins*, v. 7, p. 159-162

Dubois de Jancigy, Adolphe Philibert, born in 1795 at Paris. After participating in the final campaigns of *l'Empire*, he received a pension which enabled him to visit the East Indies, where he served as *aide de camp* to the ruler of Oudh. In 1841 he was sent on a political mission to the Far East to report on the Opium War; and in 1849, he was appointed *agent vice-consul* in Baghdad. During the last years of his political life he was attached to the Ministère d'État. His writings include *Histoire de l'Inde ancienne et moderne* (1858). He died in 1860. DBF

Dubois-Richard, Paul, born 15 January 1886 at Poitiers. After completing his legal studies at Paris, he was successively a professor of constitutional law at Montpellier and Poitiers. He founded the École de droit and the Institut international de Tours. From 1928 to 1941 he was a professor at the Faculté de droit du Caire, and a member of the Société Fouad 1er d'économie politique, de statistique et de législation. His writings include *Éléments de droit public* (Le Caire, 1937), and *Essai sur le gouvernement de l'Égypte* (Le Caire, 1941). NUC, pre-1956; WhoFr, 1955/56

Duboscq, André, born 23 February 1876 to a family from Gascogne, he was educated at the Collège de Stanislas, took courses at the Faculté de droit de Paris, and studied diplomatic sunjects. He was a correspondent to several newspapers for the Balkans, and accomplished missions for the French government in Tripolitania and the Balkans. He also spent some time in the Far East. He was diplomatic editor of *le Temps* and, since 1944, of *le Monde*. His writings include *L'Orient méditerranéen* (1917), *Le Pacifique et la rencontre des races* (1929), *Extrême-Orient, 1931-1938* (1938), and *Unité de l'Asie* (1940). He died at his office desk, 17 December 1949. DBF; DBFC, 1954/55

Du Boscq de Beaumont, Gaston, born in 1857 at Airel (Manche), he belonged to the *Conseil héraldique de France*. He travelled to North Africa, a journey which resulted in his *Une fille de France, la Tunisie* (1905), and *L'étendard vert; du Maroc à l'Égypte* (1907). DBF; NUC, pre-1956

Du Boulery, P., fl. 1852, he visited Egypt, where he collected Arabic folktales in Cairo. NUC, pre-1956

Dubouloz-Laffin, Marie-Louise, fl. 1941, her writings include *Le Bou-mergoud, folklore tunisien; croyances et coutumes populaires de Sfax et de sa région* (Paris, 1946). LC

Du Bourguet, Pierre Marie d'Audibert Caille, le Père, S.J., born 21 January 1910 at Ajaccio, he was a Coptologist and Egyptologist whose writings include *L'Art copte* (1968), and its translations, *Die Kopten* (1967), *Coptic art* (1971), *Histoire et légendes de l'Égypte mystérieuse* (1968), *Grammaire égyptienne* (1971), and *L'Art égyptien* (1973). He died in Paris, 30 December 1988. Egyptology; LC

Dubova, Nadezha Anatol'evna, born 20th cent., she edited Межэтнический мир Прикамья (1996), Новые методы, новые подходы в современной антропологии (1997); and she was joint editor of Туркмены в Среднеазиатском междуречье (1989), Русские старожилы Азербайджана; материалы по этнической экологии (1990), and Этническая экология (1991). LC

Dubuission, Patricia R., she received an M.A. in 1975 from the Institute of Islamic Studies, McGill University, Montreal, for her thesis, *Qasimi piracy and the general treaty of peace, 1820*, and also a Ph.D. in 1982 for her thesis, *A history of 'Uman and Masqat, 1750-1800*. Ferahian; Selim²

Du Camp, Maxime, born 8 February 1822 at Paris, he was a man of letters and a photographer, who travelled with Gustave Flaubert to Egypt and ascended the Nile as far as Wadi Halfa in 1850, a journey which extended also to Palestine and Syria. His photographs are of considerable historical interest. He published an album with exploratory text entitled *Égypte, Nubie, Palestine et Syrie; dessins photographiques recueillis les années 1849, 1850 et 1851, accompagnés d'un texte explicatif* (1852). His writings include *Souvenirs littéraires* (1892), its translation, *Recollections of a literary life* (1893), *Voyage en Orient, 1849-1851*, edited by Giovanni Bonaccorso (1972), and *Un voyageur en Égypte vers 1850* (1987). He died in 1894. BiD&SB; BioIn, 3, 7, 13; DBF; Egyptology; Hill; IndexBFr² (8); Master (1)

Du Cane, Sir Edmund Frederick, born in 1830 at Colchester, Essex, he served in the Royal Engineers and rose to the rank of major-general. From 1848 until his retirement in 1887 he was employed in organizing convict labour on public works in western Australia, where he proved to be a successful administrator who reorganized the mismanaged prison system. He was recalled for service in the Crimean War but when he arrived home, the war was at an end. He was a man of wide interests. He died in London in 1903. Lady Alexandra Hasluck wrote a biography, *Royal Engineer; a life of Sir Edmund Du Cane* (1973). CelCen; DNB; Master (2); OxLaw; Who was who, 1

Ducati, Bruno, born 19th cent., his writings include *Compendio di diritto musulmano, secondo i quattro di riti fondamentali* (Bolgna, 1909), *L'islam* (1929), *Maometto* (1931), *Grammatica pratica elementare della lingua araba letteraria moderna* (Roma, Istituto coloniale fascista, 1932), *Il diritto musulmano* (1934), *Corso di lingua amharia in venti lezioni* (1936), and *I 2000 verbi amharici piu´ usati* (1939). Firenze; LC; NUC, pre-1956

DuCaurroy, Antoine Joseph, born about 1775 at Eu (Seine-Inférieure), he studied Oriental languages and became successively *instituteur*, and deputy director at l'École des jeunes de langues in Paris, and a director of the École pratique des élèves interprètes, maintained by the French in Constantinople from 1802 to 1814. He was appointed second and first dragoman in 1810 and 1811 respectively, and finally royal *secrétaire interprète* at the French Embassy in Constantinople. He retired about 1831. He was the author of "Législation musulmane sunnite, rite hanèfite", an article which appeared in several installments in the *Journal asiatique*, 1848-1853. In addition, he supplied the Commission algérienne de législation with a memoir of great usefulness for the service of the colony. DBF; Journal asiatique, 5e série, 2 (1853), 543-544

Ducci, Gino, admiral, born 18 September 1872 at Firenze, his writings include *Il Pacifico* (1939), and *Panorama politico-militare nel Medio e Estremo Oriente all'iniyio del 1941* (1941). He died in Roma, 5 January 1962. Chi è, 1936, 1940, 1948; DizBI

Ducellier, Alain, born 20th cent., he was in 1981 a professor at the Université de Toulouse-Le Mirail. His writings include *Les Bzyantines* (1963), *Miroir de l'islam; musulmans et chrétiens d'Orient au moyen-âge* (1971), *Le façade maritime de l'Albanie au moyen-âge* (1981), his collected articles entitled *L'Albanie entre Bycance et Venise, Xe-XVe siècles* (1987); and he was joint author of *Le Proche-Orient médiéval; des Barbares aux Ottomans* (1978), and *Le moyen-âge en Orient* (1990). LC

Duchac, René, he was a professor at the Department of Sociology, Université de Provence. His writings include *Sociologie et psychologie* (1963), and he was a contributing author to the collective work, *Villes et sociétés au Maghreb* (1974). LC

Du Chalieu, Robert, born 19th cent., he was a captain who spent a number of years in the French African territories in the performance of combined military and civil duties. During the first World War, he served in the intelligence department of the French army. His trace is lost after a publication in 1932. Note

Duchateau, Jean *Julien* René, born in 1833, he was an ethnographer who attended the International Congress of Orientalists, Paris, 1873. BN; NUC, pre-1956

Duchateau, Pierre, born at Marseille, he was a director of the European Economic Community, and later a head of the E.E.C Legation at the Organization for Economic Co-operation and Development. WhoEIO, 1982, 1985

Du Chaume, P.-L., fl. 1828, he was the author of a letter to the editor of the *Nouvelles annales des voyages*.

Duchemin, André, he was the author of *À l'ombre des merveilles* (Paris, 1972). LC

Duchemin, G. J., fl. 1950, his writings include *Saint-Louis de Sénégal; guide historique* (Saint-Louis du Sénégal, 1955). NUC, pre-1956

Duchêne, Achille, 1866-1947, he was joint author of *Des divers styles des jardins; modèles de grandes et petites résidences; sur l'art décoratif des jardins - jardins européens et jardins orientaux* (Paris, 1914). LC

Duchêne Ferdinand, born 30 January 1868 at Bassière-Poitevine (Haute-Vienne), he trained for law at Paris, and practised at Poitiers, before being appointed a magistrate in Algeria, where he spent his entire career, rising to the rank of *conseiller* to the Cour d'appel d'Alger. He was an honorary president of the Société de géographie d'Alger et de l'Afrique du nord. He had a solid command of Arabic, and was well acquainted with the customs of the Algerian Muslims, all of which is reflected in his writings which include *Les Barbaresques; au pas lent des caravanes* (1922), a work for which he received the Grand prix littéraire de l'Algérie in 1931. He contributed to *Mercure de France, Annales africaines*, and *l'Illustration*. He died in 1956. DBF; *Hommes et destins*, vol. 7, pp. 162-164

Duchêne, François, fl. 1973, his writings include *Beyond alliance* (1965). LC

Duchesne-Guillemin, Jacques, born in 1910 at Jupille near Liège, he received a doctorate in philosophy and letters in 1931 from the Université de Louvain for a thesis on comparative grammar, and a certificate in Indian studies from the Sorbonne in 1933. He joined the staff of the Université de Liège in 1938, where he later held the chair of Indo-Iranian studies. His writings include *Études de morphologie iranienne* (1936), and *Ormazd et Ahriman* (1953). He received an honorary doctorate of Tehran University. BioB134; LC; Qui, 1981-1985

Duchesne-Guillemin, Marcelle, fl. 1969, she was the author of the short monographs *Déchiffrement de la musique babylonienne* (Roma, 1977), and *A Hurrian musical score from Ugarit* (1984). LC

Duckerts, Jules, fl. 1899-1910, he was a sometime Belgian consul-general in Smyrna. His writings include *La Chine en 1899; rapport de la mission commerciale* (1900), *Turquie d'Asie* (1904), and *Chili; voyage d'exploration et rapport sur la situation économique* (1910). LC

Duckworth, Henry Thomas Forbes, born in 1868 at Liverpool. After Oxford he was ordained a priest of the Church of England in 1894, and in 1896 appointed to duty in Nicosia regarding the liturgy of the Eastern Church. In 1900 he was a chaplain in Cairo, and in 1901 appointed professor of Greek at Trinity College in the University of Toronto. His writings include *Pages of Levantine history* (1906), and *The Church of the Holy Sepulchre* (1922). He died in hospital, Rouen, France, 7 September 1927. BritInd (6); *Canadian men and women of the time*, 1910-1912; LC; MacDCB 78

Duclos, Louis-Jean, fl. 1977, he was in 1972 an *attaché de recherches* in the Centre d'études des relations internationales, Fondation nationale des sciences politiques, Paris. He was joint author of *Les nationalismes maghrébins* (1966). LC

Duclot, Paul, born 11 May 1880 at Toulouse. After passing through the military college, St-Cyr, he received a commission as *sous-lieutenant* in 1901. In 1908 he was posted to the Service des Affaires indigènes de l'Algérie, where, two years later, his request for transfer to the Compagnie saharienne at Tidikelt was granted. He carried out many missions in Touareg country, and against the Senoussis on the Tripolitanian frontier. A highly esteemed and decorated commander, he died in a traffic accident, 19 July 1928. Peyronnet, pp. 554-559

Du Couret, Louis Laurent, born 23 April 1812 at Huningue (Alsace), he wrote *L'Arabie heureuse; souvenirs de voyages en Afrique et en Asie*, par Hadji-Abd-el-Hamid Bey, publiés par A. Dumas (1860). These are the only facts concerning this "French traveller and perhaps charlatan. His travels to the East and indeed his identity are in doubt. There is a suspicion that Alexandre Dumas the Elder, who had a hand in the composition of at least two of his books, may have invented or coloured the story of this ambiguous person" (Hill). DBF

Ducrocq, Georges, born in 1874 near Lille, he travelled to Russia and Central Asia, a journey which he described in *Du Kremlin au Pacifique* (1905). After the armistice, 1918, he was a military attaché at Tehran, and later served with general Weygand in Syria, the impressions of which are echoed in *La belle Libanaise; Journal de Soleiman* (1930). He later was a newspaper editor and finally editor-in-chief of *la Nation*. He died 30 September 1927. DBF

Ducroquet, Paul, fl. 1908-1917, his writings include *Une Nouvelle institution sociale, la Société de prévoyance des fonctionnaires et employés tunisiens* (1899), and he was joint author of *Dictionnaire du timbre* (1873). BN

Ducros, Bernard, fl. 1963, his writings include *L'Action des grands marché financières sur l'équilibre monétaire* (1952), a work which was originally presented as a doctoral thesis at the Faculté de droit de Poitiers in 1950 entitled *Équilibre monétaire et structure financière.* LC

Ducruet, Jean, born in 1922 at Bourg-en-Bresse, he was in 1975 appointed a president of the Université Saint-Joseph, Beirut. His writings include *Les Capitaux européens au Proche-Orient* (1964). LC

Ducuing, François, born in 1817 in the Hautes-Pyrénées, he was an editor at the *Revue des deux mondes*, and elected to the French Assemblée nationale in 1871. His writings include *Les villages départementaux en Algérie* (1853), and *La guerre de montagne; Navarre, 1834-35 et Kabylie, 1841-47. Les dominations françaises; Syrie, Canada, Inde, Morée, Égypte, Plata* (1868). He died in Asnières, 20 October 1875. DBF

Duda, Dorothea, born 20th cent., she received a Dr.phil. in 1964 from the Universität Wien for her thesis, *Die Buchmalerei der Ġala'iriden.* Her writings include *Innenarchitektur syrischer Stadthäuser des 16. bis 18. Jahrhunderts* (1971). From 1983 to 1992, she published a number of catalogues of Islamic manuscripts of the Österreichische Nationalbibliothek Wien. LC; Schwarz

Duda, Herbert Wilhelm, born 18 Januar 1900 at Linz, Austria. After completing Islamic and Semitic studies at Leipzig, Prag, Wien, and Paris, he received a Dr.phil. in 1925 from the Universität Leipzig for his thesis, *Eine Übergangsperiode des Osmanischen, untersucht an den Qırk-Vezir-Erzählungen.* He conducted field-work in Turkey from 1927 to 1932. In 1936 he was appointed a professor of Islamic studies with special reference to Turkey at the Universität Breslau. In 1941/42 he was a visiting professor at Sofia. Since 1943 he taught at Wien, where he became director of the Orientalisches Institut in 1946. His writings include *Ferhad und Schirin* (1933), and *Vom Kalifat zur Republik* (1948). He died 16 February 1975. DtBE; DtBilnd (5); I.I. (2); Master (1); Schwarz; WhAm, 6

Dudgeon, Gerald Cecil, born in 1867, he was an agriculturalist and a government adviser who was educated in England, and who had studied tropical agriculture in India. He also spent some time in Persia. After his return to England, he joined the Colonial Office as superintendent of agriculture for British West African colonies and protectorates. He produced a number of brief studies on farming for the technical and scientific service of the Egyptian Ministry of Agriculture. His other writings include *The agricultural and forest products of British West Africa* (1911), and *Gossypium Spp., cotton-qotn in Egypt; history, development, and botanical relationship of Egyptian cottons* (Cairo, 1917). He died in 1930. Who was who, 3

Dudin, Samuil Martynovich, born in 1863, his writings include a translation of his Ковровые изделия Средней Азии, entitled *Teppiche Mittelasiens* (1984). LC

Dudžus, Wolfgang M. P. W., fl. 1956, he received a doctorate in 1939 from the Universität Basel for his thesis, *Paulus von Watt, Kanzler des Hochmeisters Friedrich von Sachsen.* NUC, pre-1956

Duerden, Dennis, fl. 1972, he was a sometime curator at the Museum in Jos, Northern Nigeria. His writings include *The invisible present; African art and literature* (1975). LC

Dufeil, Michel Marie, born 16 November 1922 at Jonzac, France, he was in 1991 affiliated with the Centre universitaire d'études et de recherches médiévales d'Aix-en-Provence. His writings include *Guillaume de Saint Amour et la polémique universitaire parisienne, 1250-1259* (1972), and *Saint Thomas et l'histoire* (1991). LC

Duff, Douglas Valder, born in 1901 at Rosario de Sta, Fe, Argentina. After the 1918 armistice, he spent twelve years in Palestine. In 1935 he was a special correspondent to Haile Selassie. His writings include *The Hammer of Allah* (1936), *Palestine picture* (1936), *Palestine unveiled* (1938), and *May the winds blow; autobiography* (1948). BioIn, 1, 3; LC; Master (2); WhE&EA

Duff, Sir Mountstuart Elphinstone Grant, 1829-1906 *see* Grant Duff, Mountstuart Elphinstone, Sir

Duffart, Charles, born 19th cent., his writings include *Géographie commerciale* (1892), and *Mémoire sur le choix d'un tracé du chemin de fer de Thiès au Soudan* (1909). BN

Dufour, Dany, fl. 1978, he received a doctorate in 1976 from the Université de Paris VIII for his thesis, *Étude socio-pédagogique dans un centre de formation professionnelle en Algérie.*

Dufour, Jean, Dr., born 20th cent., he was in 1971 a research assistant at the Institute of Sociology in the Université libre de Bruxelles. Note

Dufour de la Thuillerie, René Marie Frédéric, born in 1874, he was in 1929 a *commissaire général de la marine*. His writings include *De Salonica à Constantinople; souvenirs de la Division navale d'Orient, 1916-1919* (1921). NUC, pre-1956

Dufourcq, Charles Emmanuel, born 15 October 1914 at Alger, he was educated at Alger and completed his formal education with the *agrégation d'histoire et géographie* at the Sorbonne. In 1937 he started his university career at the Lycée Carnot de Tunis. He was mobilized in 1939, and after the armistice in 1940 consciously served the Vichy government as cultural counsellor in Barcelona. The repeal of his teaching licence and a ten-year exile he accepted without false shame. He lived in Barcelona until 1954 when his licence was returned, and he started teaching at the Lycée de Bugeaud d'Alger. He was a *français d'Algérie* and could not imagine that at the end of the Algerian insurrection he would be summoned to metropolitan France. From 1962 to 1967 he was actively involved in establishing the new Faculté des Lettres d'Alger. He never severed his good relations with the Université d'Alger. Upon his repatriation, he became a professor of history, first at the Université d'Amiens, and two years later at Paris-Nanterre, where he remained until his death. His writings include *L'Espagne catalane et les Maghribaux* (1966), a work which was originally his doctoral thesis in 1965, and *La vie quotidienne dans l'Europe médiévale sous domination arabe* (1978). He died in Paris, 3 March 1982. Index Islamicus (4); Moyen âge 37 (1982), pp. 509-514

Dufrenne, Suzy, she received a doctorate in 1972 from the Université de Paris IV for her thesis, *Les illustrations du Psaltier d'Utrecht*. Her writings include *L'illustration des psaltiers grecs du moyen-âge* (1966), *Les programmes iconographiques des églises byzantines de Mistra* (1970); and she was joint editor of *Der serbische Psalter; Faksimile-Ausgabe* (1978). LC

Dugas, Joseph, born 30 September 1843 at Lyon, he became a priest, and then entered the Société de Jésus, 11 November 1871. His writings include *La Kabylie et le peuple kabyle* (1877), and contributions to *Études*. He died in Alger, 24 November 1877. DBF

Dugat, Gustave, born in 1824 at Orange (Vaucluse), he studied Oriental languages under Joseph T. Reinaud and Caussin de Perceval. In 1845 he went to Algeria to establish an agricultural penitentiary. Upon his return to Paris in 1846, he worked on Arabic, Turkish, and Persian manuscripts. In 1873, he was appointed professor of Islamic history and geography at l'École des langues orientales vivantes, Paris. His writings include *Grammaire française à l'usage des Arabes de l'Algérie ... et de la Syrie* (1854), *Histoire des orientalistes de l'Europe* (1868-70) and *Histoire des philosophes et des théologiens musulmans* (1878). He died in Barjols (Var), in 1894. DBF; Index BFr² (2); Vapereau

Dugdale, Blanche Elizabeth Campbell (Balfour), born 19th cent., she was a champion of the Zionist cause and an authority on Palestine. She was employed in the Bbritish Naval Intelligence Department during the first World War. For eight years she was head of the intelligence department of the League of Nations, of which she was an executive member. She was the niece and biographer of the Earl of Balfour. Her writings include *Arthur James Balfour* (1937), and *The Balfour declaration* (1940). She died 16 May 1948. NYT, 17 May 1948, p. 19, col. 5; ObitOF, 1979

Dugdale, John, 1905-1963, he was educated at Oxford and became a Labour member of Parliament; from 1950 to 1951 he was a Minister of State for Colonial Affairs. BioIn, 6; *Who was who*, 6

Duggan, Stephen Pierce Hayden, born 20 December 1870 at N.Y.C., he was a graduate of the City College of New York, and received a Ph.D. in 1902 from Columbia University for his thesis, *The Eastern question; a study in diplomacy*. He was a professor of political science at his alma mater, and a director of the Institute of International Education, New York, from 1919 to 1946. His writings include *The League of Nations* (1919), and he was joint author of *Rescue of science and learning* (1948). He died in Stamford, Conn., 18 August 1950. BiDInt; BioIn, 3; WhAm, 3

Dugin, Leonidas Stanislas, born Leonid Stanislas Bogdanov in 1881, he was naturalized a French citizen in 1932, when he changed his name to Dugin. He studied at St. Petersburg under the brilliant faculty gathered there at the end of the nineteenth century. A lecturer in Persian before the first World War, he was in Enzeli, Persia, at the time of the Russian revolution, and a short time later he became a consul at the Russian Legation in Tehran. He then went to India, and several years was professor of Persian at Santiniketan. He was one of the first Europeans to reside in Afghanistan after its entry into the family of nations. He was an interpreter at the French Legation in Kabul from 1923 to 1927, after which time he returned to Santiniketan. He was a lecturer in Persian in Calcutta University, 1932-1941. From 1941 until his death in 1945 he was acting consular attaché at the French Legation in Kabul. He wrote *Персия в географическом, религиозном, бытовом, торгово-промышленном и администра-тивном отношении* (1909). MW 36 (1946), 278

Du Gour, Antoine Jeudy, 1766-1849, he was a Russian writer of French origin, naturalized in Russia, 1812, under the name de Gouroff. His writings include *De la civilisation des Tatars-Nogais dans le midi de la Russie europénne*. DBF

Duguid, Stephen, fl. 1970-1973, he published *Radical scholar-ship* in the *Reference bibliography* series, (Burnaby, B.C., Simon Fraser University Library, 1972). NUC, 1973-77

Duhousset, Louis *Émile*, born 18 April 1823 at Paris. After passing through the military college, Saint-Cyr, he participated in the campaigns against Roma. Thereafter he was an instructor at Saint-Cyr until 1858, when he was sent on a military mission to reorganize the army of the Shah of Persia. In the course of his mission, his studies on oriental horses brought him to the Caucasus, Georgia, Greece, and Egypt. Upon his return to France, he presented his voluminous researches and notes with his accompanying drawings to the Académie des Sciences. Two years after his return, he was sent to Algeria, where he participated in quelling the insurrection in Mascara. His report on the Djurjura populations of Tunisia, which was accompanied by 160 of his drawings, won him the *Palmes d'officier de l'Instruction publique*. His writings include *Le Cheval dans la nature et dans l'art* (1902), and *The Voyage to Persia, 1858-1860* (Tehran, ca. 1969). DBF; ZKO

Duichev (Dujčev), Ivan Simeonov, born 18 April 1907 at Sofia, his writings include *Medioevo bizantino-slavo* (1965-70), *La crise idéologique de 1203-1204 et ses répercussions sur la civilisation byzantine* (1976), and *The uprising of 1185 and the restoration of the Bulgarian State* (1985). His collected articles, entitled *Slavia orthodoxa*, were published in 1970. EnBul; LC

Duinsenbaev, Yskak Täkim oly, born 15 October 1910, he received a doctorate in 1967, and was appointed professor of Kazakh in 1971. His writings include *Казахскии лирическии эпос* (1973), and he was joint editor of *Люди вечной юности* (1971). KazakSE; OSK

von **Duisburg**, Adolf David Wilhelm, major, born 15 July 1883 on a plantation in Deli Province, Sumatra, he grew up and was educated in Germany, and was a graduate of the war college (Kriegs-akademie). He began to study Oriental languages in 1908 at the Universität Berlin, but had to interrupt his course in May of 1909, when he was posted to the Schutztruppe Kamerun in the Cameroons as an officer. From 1913 to 1914 he was Resident of the Deutsche Tschadsee Länder. During the war he had to surrender, and was interned first on Fernando Póo, and later in Spain. He resigned from the army in 1920 to become a teacher and archivist at the Deutsche Kolonialschule, Witzenhausen. In 1923 he received a Dr.phil. from the Humboldt Universität, Berlin, for his thesis, *Untersuchungen über die Mbum- und Père-Sprache*. His writings include *Grundriss der Kanuri-Sprache in Bornu* (1913), its translation, *Primer of Kanuri grammar* (1917), *Wer will in die Kolonien? Ein Wegweiser* (1938), and *Im Lande des Cheghu von Bornu* (1942). NUC, pre-1956; Thesis

Du Jonchay, Ivan, born in 1899, his writings include *L'Industrialisation de l'Afrique* (1953), *Les Grands transports mondiaux* (1978), and its translation, *Handbook of world transport* (1980). LC

Duka, Theodore (Tivadar), born 22 June 1825 at Dukafalva, Hungary. After the Hungarian war of in-dependence, he went to London, where he studied medicine and thereafter entered the East India

Company as a military surgeon, a post which he retired in 1877. He returned to London and became a regular contributor to English and Hungarian periodicals. His writings include *Life and works of Alexander Csoma de Koros*, a work which was simulaniously published in Hungarian in 1885. He died in Bornemouth, 5 May 1908. GeistigeUng; Pallas; RNL; UjLex

Ðukanović, Marija, born 7 January 1923 at Mostar, she received a doctorate in 1956 from Belgrad University for her thesis, *Rimovana autobiografija Varvari Ali-Paša*. Her writings include *Kroz tursku narodnu poeziju* (1969); she was joint author of *Primeri turske proze* (1969), and *Оријентални руко-писи* (1973); and she was joint translator of *Турске загонетке* = *Türk bilmeceleri* (1980). She died in Belgrad, 22 January 1983. JugoslSa, 1970; LC; *Priloyi ya Orijentalnu filologiju* 32/33 (1982-83), pp. v-vi

Dukas, Martha Lesley P. *see* Wilkins, Lesley

Dulaeva, Z. A. The author's writings include *Сумгаит, индустриальный гигант Азербайджана* (Baku, 1962). NUC, 1968-1972

Dulaurier, Jean Paul Louis François Édouard, born 29 January 1807 at Toulouse, he came to Paris as a young man, studied Arabic and Turkish under Silvestre de Sacy, and became interested in ancient Egyptian studies. He went to London in 1838 to study hieroplyphic and Coptic texts. He later studied Javanese and related languages which, however, he knew only from texts written in Arabic. After he added Armenian to his expertise, he was appointed professor of Armenian at the École des langues orientales vivantes, Paris, where he held the chair of Armenian since 1862. His writings include the one-volume off-print, *Les Mongols d'après les historiens arméniens* (1858-1861). His most useful work is his two-volume compilation of Armenian texts relating to the crusades, which was published as part of the *Receuil des historiens des croisades* (1869). He died in Meudon (Hauts-de-Seine), 21 December 1881. DBF; DcBiPP; Egyptology; Hoefer; Index FR² (3); Vapereau

Dulieu, Louis Ferdinand Alfred, born in 1917 in France, he received doctorates in medicine and letters. His writings include *Essai historique sur l'Hôpital Saint-Éloi de Montpellier, 1183-1950* (1953), *La pharmacie à Montpellier* (1973), *La Chirugie à Montpellier* (1975), *La Médecine à Montpellier* (1975-1979), and *La Faculté des sciences de Montpellier de ses origines à nos jours* (1981). IntMed 80; LC

Dulina, Ninel' Aleksandrovna, fl. 1972, her writings include *Османская империя в международных отношениях* (1980), and *Танзимат и Мустафа Решид-Паша* (1984). LC

Duller, Eduard, Dr., born 9 November 1809 at Wien, he studied at the Universität Wien, and was resident in Germany since 1830, where he became a poet, journalist, and a popular radical historian, particularly on account of his *Geschichte des deutschen Volkes* (1840); he also wrote *Mohammed der Prophet, Don Juan von Oesterreich; historische Novellen* (1855). He died in Wiesbaden, 24 July 1853. BiD&SB; DtBE; Hoefer; Master (19; ÖBL; OxGer

Du Loir, fl. 1639-1654, was a French traveller who set out from Marseille in Novemver 1639 on a journey to the Near East. After a stop over in Malta and Smyrna, he visited the coast of Asia Minor, arriving in Constantinople on 28 January 1640, where he remained to 10 March 1641. During that time he witnessed the ceremonies of Sultan Ibrahim's accession. He returned by way of the Peloponnese and disembarked at Venezia, 19 June 1641. He described his journey in *Voyages du sieur Du Loir* (1654). The Italian translation, *Viaggio di Levante*, was published in 1670. Hoefer

Dulout, Fernand, fl. 1933-1941, he wrote *La Terre arch ou sabga en Algérie; enquêtes partielles* (Alger, 1923), and *Des droits et actions sur la terre arch ou sabga en Algérie* (Paris, 1929). LC

Dulov, Vsevolod Ivanovich, born in 1913, he was from 1952 until his death a professor at the Irkutsk Pedagogical Institute. His writings include *Крестьянство Восточной Сибири в годы первой русской революции* (1956), and *Социально-экономическая история Тувы* (1956). He died in 1964.

Dul'zon, Andreii Petrovich, born 9 February 1900 at the German colony named Preis, on the Lower Volga. According to family legend, their roots (Doulson or Dulson) are somewhere both in southern France and near Köln. He studied philology at Saratov, gaining his doctorate in 1939 and a professor-ship in the following year. After the outbreak of the second World War his family shared the fate of other Germans and was deported to Tomsk in Siberia. Since 1941 he headed the German department of the Tomsk State Pedagogical Institute, concurrently pursuing his interest in Siberian history, archaeology, ethnography and linguistics, particularly the Turkic languages. His writings include *Кетские сказки* (1966), *Кетский язык* (1968), and *Сказки народов Сибирского Севера* (1972). He died in 1972. *Rocznik orientalistyczny* 52 ii (2000), pp. 93-102

Dumaine, Jacques Chilhaud, born in 1897, he was a French diplomat. Under the Vichy Government he was ambassador at Rio de Janeiro. In 1943 he resigned and joined the liberation movement, which he represented first in Brazil, then in Algeria. After the liberation in 1944, he became French chief of protocol. He died 12 May 1953. NYT, 13 May 1953, p. 29, col. 4

Dumanowski, Bolesław, a Polish geographer whose writings include *Zależność rozwoju stoku od budowy geologicznej* (1967); he edited *Miscellanea geographica* (1984). LC

Du Mans, Raphaël, 1612-1696 *see* Raphaël du Mans

Dumas, A., fl. 1895, he was a lieutenant with the *4e spahis* and travelled together with Gabriel M. Cazemajou in March and April 1893 from Nefta on a direct route by way of the northern Great Eastern Erg to Ghadames, from where they returned on 3 April. Note

Dumast, Prosper Guerrier de, 1796-1883 *see* Guerrier de Dumast, Auguste Prosper François

Dumazet, pseud. *see* Ardouin-Dumazet, Victor Eugène, 1852-

Dumézil, Georges Edmond Raoul, born 4 March 1899 at Paris, he was an archaeologist, linguist, and historian who taught at Warszawa, 1920-21, and Istanbul, 1925-31. From 1935 to 1968 he was *directeur d'études* at the École pratique des hautes études, Paris, and concurrently held the chair of Indo-European civilisation at the Collège de France from 1949 to 1968. His writings include *Études comparatives sur les langues caucasiennes du nord-ouest* (1932), *Notes sur le parler d'un Arménien musulman de Hemşin* (1964), and he edited *Documents anatoliens sur les langues et les traditions du Caucase* (1960-69). He died 11 October 1986. ConAu, 120, 165; Master (1); *Studia iranica* 17 (1988), pp. 95-99; WhoFr, 1975/76-1985/86

Dumke, Glenn Schroeder, born 5 May 1917 at Green Bay, Wisc., he was a graduate of Occidental College, Los Angeles, and received a Ph.D. from U.C.L.A. in 1942. He was a professor of history, president, and chancellor at California universities. His writings include *The boom of the eighties in southern California* (1944); he also published four novels under the pseudonym Glenn Pierce and Jordan Allen. He died 30 June 1989. ConAu 112, 129, new rev., 31; DrAS, 1974, 1978, 1982; LEd, 1974; WhAm, 10; WhoAm, 1974-1988/89; WhoWest, 1976-1987

Dummer, Egon, born about 1935 in Germany, he received a Dr.phil. in 1966 from Humboldt Universität, Berlin, for *Die Strategie und Taktik der Convention People's Party im Kampf für die nichtkapitalistische Entwicklung in Ghana.* Thereafter he was affiliated with the Institut für Internationale Arbeiterbewegung at the Akademie für Gesellschaftswissenschaften des Zentralkomites der SED, Berlin. He wrote *Äthiopien im Aufbruch* (1984), and he edited *Entwicklungsländer heute* (1989). LC

Dummett, Michael Anthony Eardley, born 27 June 1925 at London, he was a graduate of Christ Church, Oxford, and thereafter a professor of philosophy at Oxford until his retirement. He pursued an interest in tarot cards, an aspect of culture which is now at risk from the over grown cultural uniformity which obliterates local customs that have survived for centuries. He was a fellow of the British Academy. ConAu, 102; IntWW, 1990/91-1998/99; Who, 1974-1998; WhoWor, 1982-1998

Dumont, Arsène Jean Louis, born 21 March 1849 at La Cambe (Calvados), he studied law at Paris, but changed to demography at l'École d'anthropologie, where he became enthusiastic about Louis A. Bertillon's courses. A modest inheritance from his parents enabled him to finance his researches for ten years. He pursued researches for ten years on a moderate inheritance from his parents, hoping for an appointment to his professor's chair at l'École d'anthropologie thereafter. He was determined to commit suicide if this were not the case. But this is exactly what happened. He made valuable contributions to French demography and he had the ability to become famous. His writings include *Dépopulation et civilisation; étude démographique* (1890). He died in Paris, 31 May 1902. DBF; Oursel

Dumont, Fernand, he received a doctorate in Islamic studies, and was a high-ranking officer of the Corps des affaires musulmanes. His writings include *L'Anti sultan, ou, Al-Hajj Omar Tal du Fouta combattant de la foi* (1974). DBF

Dumont, François Marcellin *Aristide*, born 2 June 1819 at Crest (Drôme), he was a graduate of l'École polytechnique and l'École des ponts et chaussées, Paris. He was an engineer with particular interest in fresh water supply and agricultural irrigation. In 1847 he was *chef de cabinet* of the Ministre des Travaux publics, and in 1863 *ingénieur en chef*. His writings include *Des travaux publics dans leurs rapports avec l'agriculture* (1847), and *Les chemins de fer en Orient* (1868). He died 25 July 1902. Dantès 1; DBF; Glaeser; Vapereau

Dumont, Paul, born in 1945, he received doctorates from the Université de Paris IV for his thesis, *Le Village anatolien dans la littérature turque*, in 1971, and from the Université de Strasbourg II, for his thesis, *De l'Empire ottoman à la Turquie actuelle; études d'histoire politique, sociale et culturelle*, in 1987. His writings include *Mustafa Kemal invente la Turquie moderne, 1919-1924* (1983); and he was joint editor of *La Turquie et la France à l'époque d'Atatürk* (1981), *Économie et sociétés dans l'Empire ottoman; actes du colloque de Strasbourg* (1983), and *Radicalismes islamiques* (1985-1986). AnEIFr, 1997; THESAM 4

Dumont, René Fernand, born 13 March 1904 at Cambrai, he was a professor of agriculture at the Institut national agronomique from 1933 to 1974, and concurrently a professor at the Institut d'études politiques de Paris from 1946 to 1966, as well as an adviser in agronomy and agricultural planning to numerous governments and international agencies throughout the world. His writings include *L'Afrique noire est mal partie* (1962), its translation, *False start in Africa* (1966), *Paysanneries abois, Ceylan, Tunisie, Sénégal* (1972), and *Afrique étranglée* (1982), and its translation, *Stranglehold on Africa* (1983). BioIn, 8; IntWW, 1974-1996/97; WhoFr, 1967/68-1998/99

Dumont, Xavier, born 24 March 1813 at Avignon, he enlisted in the army in 1831, and received a commission as *sous-lieutenant* with the *Spahis irréguliers* in 1835; in 1836 he was a lieutenant. In 1838 he resigned from active service to become *chancelier du consulat* at Alexandria, Egypt. On 31 December 1840, he became *interprète militaire de 3e classe*, and on 21 January 1842, *interprète militaire de 2e classe*. Afterwards he became French consul at Zanzibar, where he died before 1876. His writings include *Guide pour la lecture des manuscrits arabes* (1842). Féraud, p. 229

Dumoulin, Michel, born 20th cent., he received a doctorate in 1981 from the Université catholique de Louvain for his thesis, *Italie-Belgique, 1861-1915; relations diplomatiques, culturelles et économiques.* He edited *La Correspondance entre Émile de Laveleye et Marco Minghetti* (Bruxelles, 1979). LC

von **Dumreicher**, Friedrich, born 19th cent., he received a Dr.jur. and was a lawyer, resident in Cairo. For the multi-volume collection of *Handelsgesetze des Erdballs* he wrote the sixth volume entitled *Das Handelsrecht, Wechselrecht, Konkursrecht und Seerecht Ägyptens* (1909), a work which was simultaneously published in French entitled *Le droit commercial, le droit de change ... et le droit maritime de l'Égypte*. His trace is lost after a publication in 1917. NUC, pre-1956

Du Nador, Jean, born 19th cent., he wrote the pamphlet, *À travers l'Algérie; vue d'ensemble, colons, indigènes, le vignoble* (Alger, 1903). BN

Dunan, Maurice, born 19th cent., his writings include *Histoire ancienne de peuples d'Orient* (1885), *Histoire de la Grèce ancienne* (1886), and *Histoire de l'ancien Orient et de la Grèce ancienne* (1891).

Dunbar, Archibald Ranulph, fl. 1960, his writings include *A history of Bunyoro-Kitara* (Nairobi, 1966), and *The annual crops of Uganda* (Nairobi, 1969). LC

Dunbar, David, pseud., 1929- see Baxter, Craig

Dunbar, John Greenwell, born 1 March 1930, he was educated at London and Oxford, and joined the staff of the Royal Commission on Ancient and Historical Monuments of Scotland in 1953. He was a contributor to archaeological journals. ConAu, 21-24; Who, 1985-1999

Duncalf, Frederic, born 23 March 1882 at Lancaster, Wisc., he was a graduate of Beloit College, 1904, and received his Ph.D. from the University of Wisconsin in 1909. He joined the University of Texas history department in 1909 and then taught briefly at Bowdoin College and the University of Illinois before returning to the University of Texas in 1914 as professor of medieval history. In this capacity he continued to serve until his retirement in 1951. His scholarly work in medieval history was mainly in the field of the crusades. As one of those who inspired the multiple *History of the Crusades*, he contributed several articles to the first volume published in 1956. He died 29 March 1963. *American historical review* 68 (1963), pp. 1212-1213; Master (3)

Duncan, Alistair Charteris, born 10 October 1927 at Shillong, India, and educated at Marlborough College, 1941-1945, he was successively an army officer and insurance broker before he founded the Middle East Archive, London, in 1961. He was an administrator of the World of Islam Festival in 1975-1976, and director of the World of Islam Festival Trust in 1993. His writings include *The Noble sanctuary; portrait of a holy place in Arab Jerusalem* (1972), and *Towards Islam; four essays* (1977). ConAu, 61-64; EURAMES, 1993

Duncan, Francis, born in 1836 at Aberdeen, where he graduated from Marischal College in 1855. He became an army officer who served in British North America from 1856 to 1862, and later in Egypt, rising to the rank of colonel. His writings include *Canada in 1871; or, our empire in the west* (1872), *History of the Royal Regiment of Artillery* (1872-73), and *The English in Spain* (1877). He died in Woolwich, 16 November 1888. DNB, Suppl. 1; Master (2)

Duncan, Jonathan, born 15 May 1756, he arrived at Calcutta in the East India Company's service in 1772. He was made Resident and Superintendent at Benares in 1788. During his term as Governor of

Bombay from 1795 to 1811, he suppressed scandals in the administration and infanticide. He also recognized a very large number of petty chiefs as sovereign princes. He died in Bombay, 11 August 1811. Buckland; DNB; Morgan, 41, 72, 104-105

Duncanson, Dennis J., fl. 1948. Under the auspices of the Royal Institute of International Affairs, he published his *Government and revolution in Vietnam* (London, 1968). Asian affairs 85 (1998), p. 383

Dunckley, Henry, born in 1823 at Warwick, he trained for the ministry in Scotland. In 1855 he relinquished his ministerial position to become a journalist. His writings include *The Glory and shame of Britain* (1851), *The Charter of the nations; or, free trade and its results* (1854), *The Crown and the Cabinet* (1878), and *The Crown and the constitution* (1878). He died in 1896. DNB

Dundas, Sir Charles Cecil Farquharson, O.B.E., born 6 June 1884, he spent the greater part of his colonial service in Africa. During the second World War he served as political officer in East Africa. In 1920 he was named Senior Commissioner of Tanganyika. He was Chief Secretary of Northern Rhodesia from 1934 to 1937, and Governor of Uganda from 1940 to 1944. From 1950 to 1952 he was the editor of *British Africa review*. His writings include *Kilimanjaro and its people* (1924), and the autobiography, *African cross-road* (1955). He retired in 1945 and died in London, 10 February 1956. NYT, 11 February 1956, p. 17, col. 5; *Who was who*, 5

Dundas, Lawrence John Lumley, Marquess of Zetland, Earl of Ronaldshay, born 11 June 1876, he was educated at Harrow and Trinity College, Cambridge. He joined the staff of Lord Curzon in India as an aid-de-camp, and returned home by way of Baluchistan, Persia, and Russia. His writings include *On the outskirts of empire in Asia* (1904), *An Eastern miscellany* (1911), and *India, a bird's-eye view* (1924), and its translation, *Indien aus der Vogelschau* (1925). He died in 1961. BritInd (4); DNB; *Who was who*, 6

Dundes, Alan, born 8 September 1934 at N.Y.C., he was a graduate of Yale University, and received a Ph.D. in 1962 from Indiana University for his thesis, *The morphology of North American Indian folktales*. From 1963 until his retirement he was a professor at the Department of Anthropology, University of California at Berkeley. His writings include *The study of folklore* (1965), *Life is like a chicken coop ladder; a portrait of German culture through folklore* (1984), and *Cracking jokes* (1987). AmM&WS, 1973 S; ConAu, 21-24 & new rev., 9, 26, 52; Master (2); NatFacDr, 1995-1999

von **Dungern**, Friedrich, Freiherr, born 23 July 1884 at Neuwied am Rhein, Germany. After secondary education in Wiesbaden, he studied at Freiburg i. Br., Kiel, Marburg and Leipzig, where he received a Dr.jur. in 1907 for his thesis, *Die völkerrechtlichen Grundlagen der neueren Kolonial-gründungen*. Thereafter he entered the judiciary in Wiesbaden. He wrote *Die Staatswirtschaft* (1940).

Dunham, Henry Warren, born 24 January 1906 at Ohama, Nebr., he was a graduate of the University of Chicago, where he also received his Ph.D. in 1941. He was a sometime professor of sociology at Wayne State University, Detroit. At his death he was a professor of sociology and psychiatry at State University at Stoney Brook, L.I. His writings include *Social systems and schizophrenia* (1980). He died in Port Jefferson, L.I., 16 December 1985. AmM&WS, 1973 S- 1978 S; ConAu, 13-16, 118, new rev., 8; NYT 31 December 1985, p. B-10, col. 5; WrDr, 1982/84-1986/88

Dunkel, Franz, born 30 March 1870 or 1872 at Küllstedt, Germany, he studied Oriental languages and civilization, and also received a doctorate in theology at Roma. He entered the Lazarists in 1899, and went to Palestine in 1894. From 1922 until his death on 31 October 1930, he was head of the Jerusalem branch of Deutsche Verein vom Heiligen Land. Kosch; LThK

Dunlop, Douglas Morton, born 25 February 1909, he received a D.Litt. in 1954 from Glasgow University for his thesis, *The history of the Jewish Khazars*. He was a specialist in Middle East history, and successively taught at the universities of Glasgow, St. Andrews, and Cambridge. He was a visiting professor at Columbia University, New York, 1962/63. His writings include *Arabic science in the West* (1958), *Arabic civilization to A.D. 1500* (1971), and he was the editor and translator of al-Farabi's *Fusul al-madani; aphorisms of the statesman* (1961), and *The Muntakhab Siwan al-hikmah of Abu Sulaiman as-Sijistani* (1979). He died in Cambridge, 3 June 1987. ConAu, 123; DrAS, 1974 H; Master (2); Sluglett; Who, 1974-1987

Dunmore, Charles Adolphus Murray, Earl of, 1841-1907 see Murray, Charles Adolphus

Dunn, Ethel née Deikman, born 30 March 1932 at Pueblo, Cal., and married to Stephen Porter Dunn, she was a graduate of Rollins College, and received a M.A. from Columbia University. She was a research anthropologist in California since 1964, specializing in Eastern Europe. She was joint author of *The peasants of Central Russia* (1967), *Introduction to Soviet anthropology* (1974), and *Ländliche Zuwanderer in sowjetische Städte* (1977). ConAu, 21-24; LC

Dunn, Read Patten, Jr., born in 1914., he was a graduate of Millsaps College, Miss., and founder of the International Institute for Cotton. He was a sometime member of the National Cotton Council, and the Commodity futures trading commission. His writings include *Remembering* (1992). BioIn, 12; LC

Dunn, Robert Steed, born 16 August 1877, he was a Harvard graduate and a news correspondent of many years' experience, who represented American newspapers and magazines in both the Far East and the Middle East. He served as a war correspondent throughout the Russo-Japanese War. He wrote of the Near East from a broad personal experience as aide to Rear-admiral Bristol, the American high commissioner at Constantinople. He saw behind the scenes in the Near East, where at one time he was engaged in intelligence work. He died 24 December 1955. WhAm, 3

Dunn, Ross Edmunds, born 20th cent., he received a Ph.D. from the University of Wisconsin in 1969 for his thesis, *The colonial offensive in south-eastern Morocco, 1881-1912*. Throughout the 1990s he was a professor of history at the Department of History, San Diego State University. His writings include *Resistance in the desert; Moroccan responses to French imperialism, 1881-1912* (1977), and *The adventures of Ibn Battuta* (1986). MESA Roster of members, 1977 & 1990; NatFacDr, 1995-1999; Selim

Dunn, Stanely Charles, born 19th cent., he was affiliated with the Geological Survey of the Anglo-Egyptian Sudan. His writings include *Notes on the mineral deposits of the Anglo-Egyptian Sudan* (Khartoum, 1911), and *Desert snow; on alleged novel of European Egypt* (London, 1930). BLC

Dunn, Stephen Porter, born 24 March 1928 in Massachusetts, and married to Ethel Deikman, he was a graduate of Columbia University, N.Y.C., where he also received a Ph.D. in 1959 for his thesis, *The influence of ideology upon cultural change*. He was a professor of social and cultural anthropology, specializing in Eastern Europe. His writings include *Kulturwandel im sowjetischen Dorf* (1977), *The fall and rise of the Asiatic mode of production* (1982), and he was joint author of *The peasants of Central Russia* (1967), *Introduction to Soviet anthropology* (1974), and *Ländliche Zuwanderer in sowjetische Städte* (1977). AmM&WS, 1973 S, 1978 S; ConAu, 124; Master (1)

Dunnell, Mark Boothby, born in 1864, he was a graduate of the University of Rochester, N.Y., and admitted to the bar in 1888. From 1889 to 1892 he was a deputy consul-general in Shanghai. He was the author of books on Minnesota law. He died in 1940. Master (1); WhAm, 1

Dunning, Gerald Clough, fl. 1961, he was a fellow of the Society of Antiquaries, and honoured by the jubilee volume, *Medieval pottery from excavations; studies presented to Gerald Clough Dunning*, (1974). LC

Dunsany, Edward Plunkett, 16th baron, born 29 November 1808 at Ramsgate, Kent, he entered the British Navy in 1823 and rose to the rank of admiral in 1877. His writings include *The past and future of the British Navy* (1846), *Our naval position and policy* (1859), and *Gaul or Teuton?* (1873). He died in Hastings, 22 February 1889. Boase; BritInd (4)

Dunsterville, Lionel Charles, major-general, born in 1865, he served in Waziristan and the North-West Frontier in the 1890s. In 1917 he was sent for two years on a military mission to Persia. He was the original of the Dunsterforce, and of the Kipling character "Stalky." His writings include *The Adventures of Dunsterforce* (1920), and *Stalky's reminiscences* (1928). He died in 1946. BioIn, 1, 12; ObitOF 1979; Who was who, 4; WhE&EA; Wright, pp. 177-178

Dupaigne, Bernard, born 8 February 1943 in France, he was a professor of ethnology and a director of the Musée de l'homme, Laboratoire d'ethnologie, Paris, in the 1990s. He was joint author of *Afghan embroiderie* (1993). AnEIFr, 1995, 1997; LC; Schoeberlein

Dupas, P., captain, fl. 1929-1938, he was chief of the Bureau régionale des Confins algéro-marocains.

Du Pasquier, Roger, born in 1917, he was a journalist whose writings include *Découverte de l'islam* (1979), *Le Réveil de l'islam* (1988); and he was joint author of *Le Monde arabe; tradition et renouveau* (1977), and *The Arab world; yesterday, today and tomorrow* (1979). LC

Du Paty de Clam, Antoine Amédée Mercier, born 18 February 1813 at Paris. After passing through the military colleges of Saint-Cyr and l'École de Saumur, he served in Algeria from 1851 to 1865. He died in Toulouse, 3 May 1887. DBF

Du Paty de Clam, August Charles Ferdinand Marie Mercier, born 21 February 1853 at Paris, he was a graduate of the military college of Saint-Cyr, and l'École d'état-major. After he was promoted captain in 1877, he was posted to the Carte topographique de l'Algérie. In 1881 he participated in the campaign against Tunisia. While serving with the chief of staff as an intelligence officer, he became implicated in the affair Dreyfus. His writings include *Fastes chronologiques de la ville de Sfaks* (1890). He died 6 September 1916. BN; DBF

Dupin, François Pierre *Charles*, baron, born 6 October 1784 at Varzy (Nièvre), he was a graduate of l'École polytechnique and an outstanding engineer in the French navy until 1827, when he was elected Liberal deputy for Castres. He retired from public life in 1870. His writings include *Défense des intérêts coloniaux* (1838), *La Morale, l'enseignement et l'industrie* (1838), and *Canal maritime de Suez*; deux rapports à l'Académie des sciences (1857, 1858). He died in Paris, 18 January 1873. CelCen; DBF; DcBiPP

Dupin de Saint-André, Armand, born 10 September 1840 at Saint-Antonin to a Calvinist noble family from Albi, where he studied theology at Montauban, where he received a doctorate in 1863 for his thesis, *De la méthode apologétique de Justin*. After ordination he was successively pastor at Albi, Sauveterre-de-Béarn, and Tours until his retirement in 1911. He died in Tourraine in 1921. His writings include *Livingstone* (1874), and *L'Afrique centrale, région des grands lacs* (1880). DBF

Dupin de Saint-André, Blaise Victor *Ernest*, born 29 December 1816 at Toulouse, he entered the navy through the École navale in 1833. During his long service he also participated in the Crimean campaign, 1854-1856, and was navy commander in Algeria, 1877-1878. When he resigned from active service in 1878, he had risen to the rank of rear-admiral. His writings include *Affaires d'Orient en 1839-1841* (1898). He died in 1893. DBF

Dupla, Jean, born 19th cent., he received a doctorate in 1901 from the Université de Toulouse for his thesis, *De l'interposition frauduleuse de l'article 911 C.e*, ... His writings incude *Précis de procédure pénale en droit tunisien* (1922). In 1924 he was director of the Services judiciaires tunisiennes. LC

Duplessis, Johannes, born 25 July 1868 at Cradock. After graduation from the South African College, Cape Town, he went to Edinburgh for further study in Hebrew. He subsequently studied Arabic at Halle, Germany, and then visited the Holy Land. At the end of 1893 he returned to South Africa, where he became a minister, traveller in Africa, missionary expert, author, and professor of theology. His writings include *A thousand miles in the heart of Africa; a record of a visit to the mission-field of the Boer Church in Central Africa* (1905), *History of Christian missions in South Africa* (1911), *Thrice through the Dark continent, 1913-1916* (1917), *Een toer door Afrika* (1917), and *The evangelisation of pagan Africa* (1930). He died in Stellenbosch, 16 February 1935. DSAB, v. 1, pp. 262-266; LC

Duplessis-Hergomard, fl. 1937, he was an *administrateur-adjoint de commune mixte* in Algeria. Note

Duplessy, Jean, fl. 1956, his writings include *Les trésors monétaires médiévaux et modernes découverts en France* (1985), and *Les monnaies françaises royales* (1988-1989). LC

Dupon, Jean François, he received a doctorate in 1977 from the Université d'Aix-en-Provence-Marseille for his thesis, *Contraintes insulaires et fait colonial aux Mascareignes et aux Seychelles*. Since 1969 he was a *maître-assistant de géographie* at the Centre d'enseignement supérieur littéraire de Saint-Denis de la Réunion. LC

Duponchel, Adolphe, born 18 May 1821 at Florac (Lozère). After passing through l'École poly-thechnique, he was admitted to the corps des Ponts et chaussées. He spent some time in les Landes, le Gard and Algeria before he found employment with the Département d'Hérault, where he remained until his death in 1903. After his visit to Algeria he began to popularize the Trans-Saharan railway project. His book, *Le chemin de fer transsaharien, jonction coloniale entre l'Algérie et le Soudan* (1879), did much to promote the great campagne in favour of the project in the early 1880s. His enthusiasm inspired many of the subsequent scientific missions to the Sahara. He was a president of the Société languedocienne de géographie. DBF

Dupond, Octave, fl. 1934, he received a doctorate in law in 1917 from the Université de Paris for his thesis, *Le Sénat français et le vote des lois de finance*. He was a sometime lecturer at the Faculté de droit d'Alger. His writings include *Les Délégations financières algériennes* (1930). NUC, pre-1956

Dupont-Ferrier, Joseph Marie *Gustave*, born 23 May 1865 at Vinay (Isère), he received a diploma in archival palaeography in 1888 from l'École des chartes, Paris, and a doctorate in 1902 from the Université de Paris for his thesis, *Quae fuerint tam a regibus tam a comitibus in Engolismensi "apanato" comitatu instituta*. He taught at French lycées until 1914, when he was appointed a professor of French political, administrative and judicial institutions at l'École des chartes. In 1934 he was elected to the Académie des inscriptions et belles-lettres. His writings include *Du moyen âge aux temps modernes* (1926), and *De la fin de l'Empire romain d'occident au début des temps modernes* (1938). He died in 1956. DBF; IndexBFr² (2); NUC, pre-1956; Qui êtes-vous, 1924; Temerson

Dupouy, Alain, he received a doctorate in 1976 from the Université de Paris I for his thesis, *Une nouvelle étape des relations entre la CEE et l'Algérie*. THESAM 2

Duprat, Pierre *Pascal*, born 24 March 1816 at Hagetmau (Landes), he was educated at the Séminaire l'Aire-sur-l'Adour, followed by study at the Universität Heidelberg. He was appointed a professor of history at Alger in 1840. After his return to Paris in 1844, he became a contributor to periodicals until 1847, when he became director of the *Revue indépendante*. In 1848 he was elected a representative for the Landes. Three years later, he was banned and had to go into exil in Bruxelles, where he published the philosophical and literary journal *Libre recherche*, 1855-1860. Thereafter he was resident in Lausanne, Napoli, and Torino until 1871, when he returned to France to take a seat in the Assemblée nationale. In 1881 he was appointed minister plenipotentiary to Chile. He died at sea on a return voyage to Chili after a holiday in France, 17 August 1885. His writings include *Essai historique sur les races anciennes et modernes de l'Afrique septentrionale* (1879). DBF

Dupré, Pierre, born 18th cent., he served at the French consulate in Arta, Greece, in 1794. In 1797 he was posted to Preveza, Greece, until the town was taken by the Turcs in 1798. He was attached to the French legation at Constantinople in 1803, when General Gentilly, ambassador at the time, sent him on a commercial mission to the shores of the Black Sea. On board the *Jeune Tropez* he visited Amasra, Sinop, and the port of Trebizond. At the end of the same year, he was appointed French vice-consul at Trebizond, but had considerable difficulties settling down as the Turkish authorities refused to let him enter the town. He later accompanied General Gardanne to Erzerum. He died in Trebizond, on 5 September 1820. DBF; Henze

Dupré, Pierre Louis Athanase, fl. 1881, his writings include *Dictionnaire des marines étrangères (cuirasses, croiseurs, avisos rapides); Angleterre, Allemagne, Russie, Turquie ...* (Paris, 1882). BN

Dupré, Raoul, fl. 1922, he was a professor at the Lycée in Casablanca. Note

Dupré la Tour, François, born 18 September 1900 at Ecully (Rhône), he received doctorates in physical sciences and medicine, and belonged to the Société de Jésus. From 1942 to 1959 he was professor of *physique biologique*, and dean, Faculté française de médecine de Beyrouth. WhoFr, 1961/62

Dupree, Louis Benjamin, born 23 August 1925 at Greenville, N.C., he was a graduate of Harvard and became the leading expert on the history and culture of Afghanistan. From 1959 to 1978 he was director of the American Universities Field Staff in Afghanistan and Pakistan. In later years he was a consultant of Afghan affairs to the U.S. State Department, the National Security Council, and the United Nations. He published innumerable American Universities Field Staff reports and *Afghanistan* (1973), and with his wife Nancy, *Afghanistan in the 1970s* (1974). He died 21 March 1989. AmM&WS, 1973 S, 1976 S; *Asian affairs* 20 (1989), p. 245; ConAu, 41-44 rev., 28 new rev.; EncIran; *Index Islamicus* (3); Master (2); Schoeberlein; Shavit; WhAm, 10; WhoAm, 1974-1988/89

Dupree, Nancy Marie Shakuntula Hatch, born 20th cent., she took her M.A. in Chinese at Columbia University in 1951, and was the wife of Louis Benjamin Dupree since 1966. In 1990 she was a program associate of Islamic/Arab Development Studies at Duke University, Durham, N.C. Her writings include *Historical guide to Afghanistan* (1965), *Herat, a pictorial guide* (1966), *The road to Balkh* (1967), and *The Valley of Bamiyan* (1967); she edited *The KES collection of vintage photographs; summary catalogue* (1979). LC; MESA *Roster of members*, 1990

Du Puigaudeau, Odette, 1894-1991, her writings include *Pieds nus à travers la Mauritanie, 1933-1934* (1936), its translation, *Barefoot through Mauritania* (1937), *La grande foire des dattes, Adrar mauritanien* (1937) *Tagant, Mauritanie* (1949), *La route de l'ouest; Maroc-Mauritanie* (1945), and *La piste Maroc-Sénégal* (1954). Monique Vérité wrote a biography, *Odette du Puigaudeau, une Bretonne au désert* (1992). LC

Dupuis, Jacques, born in 1912, he was an Indologist whose writings include *L'Asie médionale* (1969), *Singapour et Malaysie* (1972), and *L'Inde et ses populations* (1982). LC

Dupuy, André Roger, born in 1935, he was a biologist affiliated with the World Wildlife Fund. His writings include *Les parcs nationaux de la République de Sénégal* (1972), and *Les gardiens de la vie sauvage* (1984). LC

Dupuy, Pierre Henry, fl. 1957, he received a doctorate in 1962 from the Université de Bordeaux for his thesis, *Le trésor et la monnaie au Maroc*. In 1962 he was a member of the Faculté de droit de Rabat. His writings include *Le trésor, la croissance et la monnaie au Maroc* (Rabat, 1965). LC; ;NUC, 1973-1977

Duquesne, Abraham, born 17th cent., he was a French royal naval officer who went to Persia in 1670. He had adventures in the Far East, where he spent three years in prison. He participated in campaigns against Tripoli, Zante, Tunis, Alger, Chio, and Genova between 1681 and 1684. After 1687, he accomplished diplomatic and military missions in the Far East and Europe. He was the author of *Journal d'un voyage fait aux Indes orientales* (1692), and its translation, *A New voyage to the East-Indies in the years 1690 and 1691* (1696). He died in 1724. DBF; Index BFr² (13)

Duquesne, Jacques, born 18 March 1930 at Dunkerque, he obtained diplomas in law and political science, and became a journalist engaged in press and television. His writings include *L'Algérie; ou, la guerre des mythes* (1958), *Sujet ou citoyen* (1965), *Dieu pour l'homme d'aujourd'hui* (1970), and *Théo et Marie* (1996). LC; WhoFr, 1981/82-1998/99

Duraffourg, Valère, captain, fl. 1882-1886, he was affiliated with the Société de géographie de Lille. His writings include *Béja et ses environs* (Lille, 1886), and *Notice de géographie historique et descriptive sur la Tunisie; Sfax et ses environs* (Lille, 1890). BN

Duran, Khalid, pseud., 1939- *see* Khalid, Detlev H.

Duran, Lûtfi, born in 1921 at Antakya, Hatay, he received a doctorate in law from the Faculté de droit de Toulouse in 1949. Since 1961 he was a professor at the İstanbul Üniversite Hukuk Fakültesi. His writings include *Idare hukuku* (1982), and *Türkiye yönetiminde karmaşa* (1988). Kim kimdir, 1985/86; LC

Durand, Alfred, born in 1858 at Chantemerle (Drôme), he entered the Société de Jésus in 1876, and studied at the universities in Roma and Paris. From 1896 to 1923 he was a professor of *Écriture sainte* at the Université de Lyon. He was a regular contributor to *Études*. His writings include *L'Enfance de Jésus-Christ* (1908); and he was joint author of *Elementa grammaticæ arabicæ cum chrestomathia, lexico variisque notis* (1896-1897). He died in 1928 in Lyon. DBF; NUC, pre-1956

Durand, Alfred Joseph, born 24 April 1862 at Paris, he was a graduate of the military college, Saint-Maixent, and posted to Madagascar as a colonial administrator from 1889 to 1894. In 1898 he organized the Hova course at l'École des langues orientales vivantes, Paris, and was a professor of Hova there from 1901 until his retirement in 1922. His writings include *Essais sur la prononciation de la langue hova* (1900), *Jeune Turquie, vieille France* (1909), and *Les derniers jours de la cour hova; l'exile de la reine Ranavalo* (1933). His trace is lost after his last publication. Curinier, 3, pp. 187-188; DBF

Durand, Sir Edward (Law), born in 1845, he was from 1884 to 1886 an assistant with the Afghan Boundary Commission. His writings include *Cyrus, the Great King* (1906), and *Rifle, rod, and spear in the East* (1911). He died in 1920. BLC; Who was who, 2

Durand, Emmanuel, born 7 August 1889 at Saint-André, Réunion, he completed his doctoral thesis, *L'Ile de la Réunion et le Crédit foncier colonial*, for the Université de Paris at the outbreak of the first World War. In 1917, Lyautey called him to Morocco, where he served until independence. He was an administrator and concurrently a lecturer at the Institut des hautes études marocaines de Rabat. Based on his lectures, he published *Traité de droit public marocain* (1955). He died in le Havre, 15 December 1975. Hommes et destin, vol. 2, pp. 288-290

Durand, Guy, born 30 May 1933 at Dunham, P.Q., he was educated at the Université de Montréal, and received a doctorate in 1967 from the Faculté catholique de Lyon. Since 1968 he was a professor of *théologie morale* at the Faculté de théologie in the Université de Montréal. His writings include *Éthique de la rencontre sexuelle* (1971), *Sexualité et foi* (1983), and he was joint author of *Quel avenir* (1978), and *Quelle vie* (1978). LC; WhoRel, 1985

Durand, Huguette Marie Claude, born 17 June 1926 at Saint-Michel (Savoie), she received a doctorate in law in 1953 from the Université de Grenoble, and thereafter taught at the Faculté de droit. Her writings include *Essai sur la conjoncture de l'Afrique noire* (1957), *La monnaie et les institutions financières* (1969); and she edited *Les systèmes monétaires et bancaires étrangers* (1986). LC; Unesco

Durand, Jacques Henry, he was an agronomist and in 1955 chief of the Section pédologie of the Service des études scientifique in Algeria. His writings include *Les Sols d'Algérie* (1954), *Les sols irrigables* (1958), and *Les sols rouges et les croûtes en Algérie* (1959). LC

Durand, Jean Pierre, born in 1948, he received a doctorate in 1978 from the Université de Paris V for his thesis, *La tentative de rupture de la reproduction des rapports de production capitalistes en Algérie*. He was joint author of *L'île Maurice et ses populations* (1978), *L'Algérie et ses populations* (1982), *L'après-fordisme* (1993); and editor of *Vers un nouveau modèle productif?* (1993). In 1982 he was maître-assistant en sociologie at the Université de Rouen, and in 1993, he held a cross-appointment in sociology at the universities of Paris-Evry and Rouen. LC; THESAM 2

Durand de Fontmagne, Marie Caroline Drummond de Melfort, baronne, born about 1840, she travelled extensively in her youth. She married in 1869 but lost her husband in 1877. Thereafter she pursued an interest in music. Her writings include *Un Séjour à l'ambassade de France à*

Constantinople sous le second Empire (1902), and the translation, *Kırım harbi sonrasında İstanbul* (1977). She died after 1898. Curinier, vol. 3 (1901), p. 154; DBF

Durand-Gasselin, Jean Pierre, born 3 August 1910 at Bavilliers. After passing through the military college, Saint-Cyr, he served predominantly among the nomades of the French Soudan, modern Mali, Mauritania, and Senegal, rising to the rank of lieutenant-colonel. From 1959 to 1961 he successively served with the Cabinet of the Secetary-general for Algerian Affairs, and the Organisation Commune des Régions Sahariennes. In 1963 he became secretary-general of the Association Internationale pour le Développement et l'Aide Technique. He was a member of the editorial staff of *Afrique contemporaine*. He died 16 May 1976. *Hommes et destins*, vol. 9, p. 159; WhoFr, 1971/72-1975/76

Durand-Lapie, Paul, born in 1845 at Toulouse, he studied law and practised it until he went into teaching. He was a *professeur de lettres* at the Lycée de Montauban until his retirement in 1902. His writings include *Le Comte d'Escayrac de Lauture* (1900). He was a member of the Académie de Montauban. DBF

Durand-Viel, Georges Edmond Just, born 11 March 1875 at Le Havre, he was a graduate of l'École navale, and retired in 1937 with the rank of admiral. He was a director of the École de guerre navale and the Centre des hautes études navales from 1927 to 1928. After his retirement he was a vice-president of the Suez Canal Company. His writings include *Les campagnes navales de Mohammed Aly et d'Ibrahim* (1935). He died 8 October 1959. DBF; DBFC, 1954/55; WhoFr, 1953/54-1957/58

Durandin, Catherine, fl. 1979, her writings include *Révolution à la française ou à la russe* (1989); she was joint author of *Brésil, l'idéologie de la sécurité nationale* (1977), and *La Roumanie de Ceausecscu* (1988). LC

Durant, William James, born 5 November 1885 at North Adams, Mass, he was a graduate of St. Peter's College, Jersey City, N.J., and received a Ph.D. in 1917 from Columbia University for his thesis, *Philosophy and the social problem*. He was a prize-winning historian and philosopher whose chronicles of world history and civilization reached a mass audience. His enduring work is the eleven-volume *Story of history* (1935-1975), on which he collaborated in part with his wife. He died in Los Angeles, 7 November 1981. ConAu, 9-12, 105, new rev., 4, 61; Master (17); WhAm, 7; Who was who, 8

Durassier, Henry, fl. 1875-1890, he was a writer on naval affairs, and a contributor to *l'Armée maritime*. NUC, pre-1956

Durch, William J., he was in 1977 affiliated with the Center for Naval Analyses. His writings include *The Cuban military in Africa and the Middle East, from Algeria to Angola* (1977), *The ABM Treaty and Western security* (1988); he was joint author of *Regaining the high ground* (1990). LC

Durdağ, Mete, he received a Ph.D. in 1972 from Birmingham University for his thesis, *Some problems of development financing; a study of the Turkish development plan, 1963-67*. His writings include *Planlama açısından kamu kesiminin dengesi, ilkeler ve uygulama* (1973). Sluglett

Durdenevskii (Durdenevsky), Vsevold Nikolaevich, born in 1889, he served as an expert consultant to the Soviet Foreign Ministry after 1944. His writings include *Равноправие языкре в советском строе* (1927). He died in Moscow, 13 November 1963. NYT 16 November 1963, p. 27, col. 5

Đurđev (Djurdjev), Branislav, Prof. Dr., born 4 August 1908, he studied history and Oriental philology at the Univerzitet u Beogradu, and was later dean of the Filozofskog fakulteta u Sarajevu. His writings include *Турска власт у Црној Гори у XVI и XVII веку* (Sarajevo, 1953), originally presented as his doctoral thesis; *Dva deftera Crne Gora iz vremena Skender-bega Crnojevića* (1968-73), and *Die historisch-ethnischen Veränderungen bei den südslawischen Völkern nach der türkischen Eroberung* (1974). He died in 1993. *Prilozi za orijentalnu filologiju*, Sarajevo, 42/43 (1992-93), pp. 7-8; LC

Dureau de la Malle, Adolphe Jules César Auguste, born 2 March 1777 at Paris, he was educated privately, and collaborated in scholarly pursuits with his father. He later became interested in geography and, without ever having travelled, published *Géographie physique de la Mer Noire, de l'intérieur de l'Afrique et de la Méditerranée* (1807). After the French conquest of Algeria, he pursued an interest in the history of Roman Africa. He died in 1857. BN; DBF; Hoefer; Index BFr² (3); Vapereau

Duret-Robert, François, born 29 January 1932 at Paris, he was educated at Paris, and obtained a diploma from the Institut d'études politiques de Paris. He was a journalist from 1963 to 1995. In 1997, he became a lecturer at the École du Louvre and concurrently at the Université de Paris IX-Dauphine. His writings include *Les quatre cents coups du marteau d'ivoire* (1964); and he edited *La valeur des objets* (1977). WhoFr, 1990/91-1998/99

Durham, Mary Edith, born in 1863 at London, where she was also educated. She was a painter who travelled extensively. Her writings include *Through the lands of the Serb* (1904), *The burden of the Balkans* (1905), *High Albania* (1909), *The struggle for Scutari* (1914), *Twenty years of Balkan tangle* (1920), its translation, *Die slavische Gefahr* (1922), and *The Sarajevo crime* (1925). She died 15 November 1944. DcBrA; DNB; Master (4); Robinson, pp. 260-261; WhE&EA; *Who was who*, 4

al- Duri, 'Abd al-'Aziz K., born in 1917 at Baghdad, he was educated in Iraq, and graduated from the University of London, where he also received a Ph.D. in 1942 from SOAS for his thesis, *Studies on the economic life of Mesopotamia in the tenth century*. After his return to Iraq, he became a professor of history, and later dean of the Faculty of Arts and Science, Baghdad University. His writings include works in Arabic and the translations, *Arabische Wirtschaftsgeschichte* (1979), *The Rise of historical writing among the Arabs* (1983), and *Historical formation of the Arab nation* (1987). Awwad; LC; Sluglett

Đurić-Zambo, Divna, fl. 1965, her writings include *Beograd sa starih fotografija* (1966), its translation, *Belgrade in old photographs* (1968), *Beograd kao orijentalna varoš pod Turcima, 1521-1867* (1977), *Beograd, 1898-1914* (1980), and *Хотели и кафане XIX века у Београду* (1988). LC

Durieu de Leyritz, fl. 1895, author of *La sécurité de la justice répressive en Algérie; discours* (Alger, 1897). BN

Durieu de Maisonneuve, Michel Charles, born 7 December 1796 at Saint-Eutrope (Lot-et-Garonne). After passing through the military college, Saint-Cyr, he was posted to Algeria in the 1840s, when he participated as a biologist in the exploration of the natural resources. He travelled extensively throughout the colony to the northern borders of the Sahara. In 1853, he became director of the Bordeaux botanical gardens. His writings include *Atlas de la flore d'Algérie* (1846-49). He died in Bordeaux, 20 February 1878. BN; DBF

Düring, Ernst Carl Eduard Camille, born 6 May 1858 at Hamburg. After completing his medical studies at Tübingen, Leipzig, and Erlangen, he became successively an assistant at the Institute of Pathology, and the Hospital in Erlangen and Hamburg. In 1889, he was appointed professor of medicine at the Imperial Ottoman School of Medicine, Constantinople. After his return to Germany in 1902, he was director of a variety of medical institutions. He died in Heidelberg, 23 December 1944. DtBE; DtBiInd (4); *Wer ist's*, 1912-1935.

During, Jean, born 3 June 1947 at Mulhouse (Haut-Rhin), he received two doctorates from the Université de Strasbourg II for his theses, *L'évolution récente de la musique traditionnelle iranienne*, in 1975, and *Musique et mystique en Iran*, in 1986. He was a sometime fellow of the Iranian Academy of Philosophy as well as the Institut français de recherche en Iran. His interpretation of traditional music won him the Iran TV Prix Bârbad for 1979. His writings include *Musique et extase; l'audition mystique dans la tradition soufie* (1988), *Musique et mystique dans la tradition de l'Iran* (1989); and he was joint author of *The art of Persian music* (1991), and *Introduction au muqam ouïgour* (1991). AnEIFr, 1997; LC; Private; Schoeberlein; THESAM 4

Duroselle, Jean Baptiste Marie Lucien Charles, born 17 November 1917 at Paris, he was a university professor who had a fifty-year career in modern history and international relations teaching. His writings include *Histoire diplomatique de 1919 à nos jours*, a work which went through eleven editions between 1953 and 1993. His *L'Europe; histoire de ses peuples* (1990) won him the Prix Adolphe Bentinck for 1991. He died 12 September 1994. ConAu 9-12, new rev., 3, 18, 45; Master (1); NDNC 3 (1964); Salses; WhoWor 1989/90; WhoFr 1967/68-1994/95

Durosoy, Maurice Armand, born 20 May 1898 at Paris. After graduating from the military college, Saint-Cyr, he participated in the campaign to pacify the Central Atlas as an officer at the Bureau des affaires indigènes from 1921 to 1924. From 1924 to 1934, he was successively *aide de camp* and *chef de cabinet* to maréchal Lyautey. He was a sometime *commandant* of the École de Saumur. He retired in 1957 with the rank of *général de corps d'armée*. He died 26 September 1988. WhoFr 1969/70-1988/89

Durrani, Ashiq Muhammad Khan, fl. 1980, he was a sometime chairman of the Department of History and Pakistan Studies, his alma mater. His writings include *Multan under the Afghans, 1752-1818* (1981), a work which is based on his doctoral thesis, Bahauddin Zakariya University, Multan, Pakistan.

Durrani, Fazal Karim Khan, his writings include *The Ahmadiyya movement* (1927), *The meaning of Pakistan* (1944), *The message of Islam* (1944), and *The future of Islam in India* (1946). LC

Durrieu, Jean Marie Paul Simon, comte, born 2 October 1855 at Strasbourg, he was a medievalist and a writer on illuminated French manuscripts. He was a graduate of l'École des chartes, 1878, a research fellow at l'École de Rome, 1879, and a keeper at the Musée du Louvre from 1885 until his retirement in 1902, when he became a private scholar. He died in Paris in 1925. Curinier, v. 6; DBF

Durrieu, Joseph Emmanuel Xavier, born 22 December 1814 at Castillon (Ariège), he was a journalist, editor, and a politician who was exiled in 1851. His writings include *Le coup d'état de Louis Bonaparte* (Bruxelles, 1852), and *The present state of Morocco; a chapter of Mussulman civilisation* (London, 1854). He died in Barcelona, 6 February 1868. DBF; Vapereau

Durrieux, Alcée, born in 1869, he received a doctorate in medicine in 1901 from the Université de Paris for his thesis, *Les diverticules de la vessie*. His writings include *Samarkand, la bien gardée* (1901). DBF; NUC, pre-1956

Duru, Raymond, fl. 1960, he was joint author of *Oumm el-Amed, une ville de l'époque hellénistique aux échelles de Tyr* (1962). LC

Durupty, Michel, fl. 1968, his writings include *Institutions administratives et droit administratif tunisien* (1973), *Les entreprises publiques* (1986), and *Les privatisations en France* (1988). LC

Duruy, Jean Victor, born 11 September at Paris, he was a teacher, historian, a minister of public education, and a prolific writer. His writings include *Histoire ancienne des peuples de l'Orient* (1888), and the translation, *A general history of the world* (1898). He died in Paris, 15 November 1894. DBF; Hoefer; Index BFr² (10); Master (6); Vapereau

Dusseau, Elie Pierre *René*, born 24 December 1868 at Neuilly-sur-Seine, he studied ancient history archaeology, Semitic languages, and epigraphy at l'École des hautes études, l'École des langues orientales vivantes, and the Collège de France in Paris, to which lifelong field-work in Greater Syria was added since 1895. He was a professor at the Collège de France from 1905 to 1910, when he was appointed deputy keeper of oriental antiquities at the Musée du Louvre and concurrently a professor at l'École du Louvre. In 1923, he was elected to the Académie des inscriptions et belles-lettres. His writings include *Histoire et religion des Nosairis* (1900), *Les Arabes en Syrie avant l'islam* (1907), *Les découvertes de Ras Shamra (Ugarit) et l'Ancien Testament* (1937), and *La pénétration des Arabes en Syrie avant l'islam* (1955); he was joint author of *Voyage archéologique au Safâ et dans le Djebel ed-Drûz* (1901). He died 17 March 1958. Egyptology; Index Islamicus (2)

Düster, Joachim, born 25 August 1954 at Pforzheim, Germany, he studied from 1973 to 1980 law and Arabic at Heidelberg, Genève and Tübingen. He was the founder and director of the Oman Studies Centre, Tübingen and Pforzheim. In 1984, he entered the foreign service, and from 1987 to 1989, he was head of the consular section in Damascus, and from 1993 to 1996, consul-general in Dubai. He was a founding member of the German Omani Society. DrBSMES, 1993; Wer ist wer, 1996/97-2001/2002

Du Taillis, Jean, born in 1873 at Alençon (Orne), he was an editor at *le Figaro* and specialized in economic and colonial matters. After extensive travelling he became the newspaper's North African correspondent. He wrote on his travels and on Morocco, including *Le Maroc pittoresque* (1905), *Le nouveau Maroc; suivi d'un voyage au Riff* (1923), and *Motoring in Morocco* (1925). DBF

Duteil, Mireille, fl. 1975, she was a journalist whose writings include *Les martyrs de Tibhirine* (1996); she was joint author of *L'Algérie des Algériens; vingt ans après* (1981), and *La poudrière algérienne* (1994). LC

Dutertre, Jacques, 1612-1696 see Raphaël du Mans

Duthie, John Lowe, born 20th cent., he took his M.A. at Aberdeen University in 1971, and received a Ph.D. in 1976 from Glasgow University for his thesis, *The Role of pressure groups in the formulation of British Central Asian policy, 1856-1881*. From 1971 to 1973, he lectured at Abdullahi Bayero College, Kano, Nigeria, and from 1976 to 1979, at the University of the West Indies (Mona), Kingston, Jamaica.

Duthoit, Edmond Marie, born in 1837 at Amiens, he was an architect who died in Amiens in 1889. Bellier; DBF; Master (1)

Dutkiewicz, Józef Edward, 1903-1968, he was a professor of history and an art historian at Kraków. His writings include *Małopolska rzeźba średniowieczna* (1949), *Tarnów* (1954), and *Angelia a sprawa polska w latach 1830-1831* (1967). NEP; NUC, 1956-1972

Dutoit, Bernard, born 18 January 1933 or 1935 at Lausanne, he obtained a doctorate in law at Lausanne, and a diploma in Russian at Paris. Since 1967 he was a professor of law, and director, Centre universitaire de droit comparé, Université de Lausanne, positions which he still held in 1982. He was a contributing author to the collective work, *Répertoire de droit international privé suisse* (1982). LC; WhoWor, 1980-1982/83

Dutreuil de Rhins, Jules Léon, born in 1846 in France, he served in the French navy and later in the merchant marine. After a careful study of Central Asian geography and the publication of his *l'Asie*

centrale (1889), he applied for, and received the support of, the Ministère de l'Instruction publique and the Académie des inscriptions for a mission to Lhasa in 1891. He made an extraordinary three-thousand mile journey overland from Constantinople, visiting also Russian and Chinese Turkestan. He was drowned after being wounded in a Chinese ambush, 5 June 1894. BDF; Henze; Vapereau

Dutrieux-Rey, Pierre Joseph, born 19 July 1848 at Tournai, Belgium, he was a trained medical doctor who was invited by the Khedive Ismail to establish a school of medicine, where he later became a professor of ophthalmology. He was credited with outstanding service during the cholera epidemic of 1883 in Egypt. He also accomplished missions to Central Africa under the auspices of King Leopold II of Belgium. His writings include *Réflexions sur l'épizootie chevaline au Caire en 1876* (1877), *La question africaine au point de vue commerciale* (1880), *Vocabulaire français-kisouahili* (1880), *Le choléra dans la Basse-Égypte en 1883; relation d'une exploration médicale dans le delta du Nil pendant l'épidemie cholérique* (1884), *Aperçu de la pathologie des Européens dans l'Afrique intertropicale* (1885), and *Souvenirs d'une exploration médicale dans l'Afrique intertropicale* (1885). He died in Paris, 30 January 1889. BN; Matthieu; NUC, pre-1956

Dutt, Chinmay (Cinmoy), fl. 1954, his writings include *Catalogue of Arabic and Persian inscriptions in the Indian Museum, Calcutta* (1967), and *Selections from Avesta and Old Persian* (1973).

Dutt, Gargi, Mrs., born in 1929, she was in 1980 a professor of Chinese studies at the Centre for East Asian Studies, School of International Studies, New Delhi. Her writings include *Rural communes in China* (1967), and she was joint author of *China after Mao* (1991). LC

Dutton, Brian, born 14 July 1935 at Milton, Staffs, he was a graduate of the University of London, and obtained a doctorate in Spanish in 1965. In 1968, he was appointed a professor of Spanish at the University of Georgia, and in 1995, he was a professor of Spanish in the University of Wisconsin at Madison. He was joint author of *Cassell's new compact Spanish-English dictionary* (1969). NatFacDr, 1995

Dutton, Samuel Train, born 16 October 1849 at Hillsboro, N.H., he was a graduate of Yale University. He was a professor of school administration, and superintendent of the college schools, Teachers' College, Columbia University, a sometime trustee of the American College for Girls, Constantinople, a prominent religious layman, and as a peace worker, he assumed a key role as an organizer, coordinator, and conciliator among American peace workers and internationalists. He was joint author of *School management* (1903). He died in Atlantic City, N.J., 28 March 1919. BiDInt; DAB; Master (2); WhAm, 1

Duval, Jules, born 30 April 1813 at Rodez (Aveyron), he was a trained lawyer at the age of twenty-three and soon thereafter became a deputy magistrate, a post which he held for eight years. Influenced by the ideas of Saint-Simon, he went to Algeria in 1846. In 1847, he was a founding member of the Union agricole d'Afrique, and in 1852, he became editor-in-chief of *l'Echo d'Oran*. After his return to France, he founded *l'Économie français*, and later was a vice-president of the Société de géographie de Paris. His writings include *Histoire de l'émigration européennne, asiatique et africaine au XIXe siècle*, a work which won him an award from the Académie des sciences morales et politiques in 1861. He also wrote *Gheel; ou, Une colonie d'aliénés vivant en famille et en liberté* (1860), *Les puits artésiens du Sahara* (1867), *Un programme de politique algérienne* (1868), and *Bureaux arabes et colons* (1869). He died in a railway accident, 20 September 1870. Bulletin de la Société de géographie, 6e série, 11 (1876), pp. 353-367; DBF; Hommes et destins, vol. 2, pp. 295-298; Vapereau

Duval, Paul *Rubens*, born 25 October 1839 at Morsange-sur-Seine, he was a student of Semitic languages, particularly Aramaic, and influenced by Heinrich Ewald of Göttingen. In 1881, he published *Traité de grammaire syriaque*; under the auspices of the Académie des inscriptions et belles-lettres, he edited the Aramaic part of the *Corpus inscriptionum semiticarum* between 1886 and 1893. He was member of the Société asiatique since 1879, and, at one time or another, he was also council member, librarian, and editor of their journal. On account of his failing health, he relinquished all official functions in 1908. He died in Morsange, 10 May 1911. DBF, n° 81; Fück, p. 251

Duval, Paulette M., fl. 1974, her writings include *La pensée alchimique et le Conte du Graal* (1979), a work which she originally presented in 1975 as her thesis at the Université de Paris I under the title, *Recherches sur les structures de la pensée alchimique (Gestalten) et leurs correspondances dans le "Conte du Graal."* She was joint author of *Alchimie mystique et traditions populaires* (1983). LC

Duval, Pierre Gonzalès Charles, born 25 April 1832 at Tulle (Corrèze), he entered the Dominican Order in 1851 and was ordained in 1857. In the autumn of the same year, he was sent to Mosul where he served for thirty-eight years, the last twenty-three of which as Supérieur de la Mission dominicaine. From 1895 until his death, he was Délégue apostolique de Syrie. He wrote *La Mission des dominicains*

461

à *Mossoul* (1889). He died in Beirut, 31 July 1904.   *Actes du 80e Congrès des sociétés savantes*, Lille, 1955, pp. 503-507; DBF, n° 72

Duverger, Maurice, born 5 June 1917 at Angoulême, he was from 1942 to his retirement in 1985 a professor of law, and/or political science at a variety of French universities.   His writings include *Les Finances publiques* (1950), its translation, *Âmme maliyesi* (1955), and *Sociologie politique* (1965).   ConAu 65-68, new rev. 27;   DBFC, 1955;   IntWW 1974-1995/96;   NDNC 3 (1964), 5 (1968);   WhoFr 1965/66-1998/99;   WhoWor 1974-1994/95

Duvernois, Clément Aimé Jean Baptiste, born 6 April 1836 at Paris, he was educated at the Lycée d'Alger.   He had a checkered career as a journalist in Algeria and metropolitain France on account of his polemic writings.   He was repeatedly censored.   He later was elected to the Assemblée nationale.   He died in Paris, 9 July 1879.   Bitard; Dantès 1; DBF; Glaeser; Vapereau

Duveyrier, Henri, born 28 February 1840 at Paris, he was educated at religious colleges in Paris, the Handelshochschule and the Universität, Leipzig, where he was a student of H. L. Fleischer in Arabic.   His visit to Algeria in 1857 was the subject of his first German publication in 1858.   After his return to Paris, he made careful preparations for a scientific exploration of the Algerian Sahara.   Between 1859 and 1861 he visited Algeria as well as Touareg country.   His writings include *Exploration du Sahara* (1864), and *Les Touaregs du nord* (1864).   He committed suicide on 25 April 1892.   Bitard²; DBF; Embacher; Henze; *Hommes et destins*, vol. 7, pp. 169-172; *Revue économique française* 72 (1959), pp. 19-26

Duvignaud, Jean Octave Auguste, born 22 February 1921 at La Rochelle., he changed from his original name, Auger, in 1977.   He was educated at the Lycée Henri-IV and the Faculté de lettres de Paris, where he obtained a doctorate.   He held varied positions at French universities.   In the 1960s he was for five years chairman of the Département de sociologie at Tunis.   His writings include *Tunisie* (1965), *Chebika, mutations dans un village du Maghreb* (1968), *Change at Shibeika; report from a North African village* (1977), and *Chebika; changement dans un village du Sud-tunisien* (1991).   BiDNeoM, pp. 128-129; WhoFr, 1981/82-1998/99

Duwaydar, Muhammad, fl. 1964 *see* Dowidar, Mohamed

van **Duyl**, Anton Gillis Cornelis, born 8 December 1829 at Brielle, the Netherlands, he studied theology at the Universiteit te Utrecht.   He was affiliated with the Maatschappig tot Nut van 't Algemeen until 1862, when he became an editor of the *Rotterdamsche Courant*.   In 1865, he became editor-in-chief of the *Algemeen Handelsblad*, a position which he held for twenty years.   He was instrumental in the founding of the Nederlandsche Journalistenkring.   Frederiks; *Wie is dat*, 1902

Duyvendak, Jan Julius Lodewijk, born 28 June 1889 at Harlingen, the Netherlands, he studied Dutch literature and subsequently Chinese and Japanese at Leiden, Paris, and Berlin.   He gained his expert knowledge of modern China through his years in the diplomatic service of the Netherlands, beginning as student interpreter at he Lagation in Peking.   Since 1919 he was a professor of Chinese at Leiden, and a frequent visiting professor at Columbia University, N.Y.C.   He died in Leiden, 9 July 1954.   BioIn, 3; *Far Eastern quarterly* 14 (1955), pp. 297-298; *T'oung Pao* 43 (1954), pp. 1-33; *Wie is dat*, 1948

Duzinchevici, Gheorghe, fl. 1935, his writings include *Cuza-Vodă și revoluția polonă din 1863* (1935), *Documente din arhivele polone relative la istoria Românilor* (1935), *Ștefan cel Mare și epoca sa* (1973), and he edited *Inventarul protocoalelor primăriei Sibiu, 1521-1700* (1958).   LC

Dvoichenck-Markov, Demetrius, born 10 July 1921 at Saloniki, he was a graduate of UCLA.   After obtaining an M.A. in 1951 from Columbia University, he became a research analyst at the U.S. War Department and the Department of Defense.   In 1981, he was appointed a professor of history, geography, and Russian at Monmouth College, West Long Branch, N.J.   DrAS, 1974, 1978, 1982; WhoE, 1977/78-1988/89

Dvořák, Rudolf, born 12 November 1860 at Dřítni, he was a student of Jaromir Košut, and received a Dr.phil. in 1883 from the Universität Leipzig for his thesis, *Ein Beitrag zur Frage über die Fremdwörter im Koran*.   He was the founder of Czech orientalism.   His writings include *Abû Firâs, ein arabischer Dichter und Held* (1895), the edition of *Bâkî's Dîwân* (1911), and *Slavný básník a myslitel arabský XI. stol. Abul 'Alá* (1916). He died 1 February 1920.   Ottův slovník naučný; Masarykův slovník naučný

Dvoriankov, Nikolai Aleksandrovich, born 3 January 1923 at Moscow, he received a doctorate in 1967 for his thesis, Проблема народности современной афганской (паштунской) поэзии.   In 1970 he was appointed a professor.   His writings include Язык пушту (1960), and he edited Афганско-русский словарь (1966), and Пушту-русский словарь (1985). He died 17 December 1979.   LC; Miliband; Miliband²

Dvorniakova, Valentina Nikolaevna, born 13 November 1944 at Moscow, she graduated in 1967 from the Institute of Asian and African Studies, Moscow State University, and received her first degree in 1973 for *Жизнь и творчество Парвин Этесами, 1907-1941.* Miliband²

Dvornik, Francis (František), born 14 August 1893 at Chomyz, he was ordained Roman Catholic priest in 1916, received a diploma from l'École des sciences politiques, and a *docteur ès lettres* in 1926 from the Sorbonnne. He became a professor of church history, and later dean, at the Faculty of Theology, Universita Karlova, Praha. From 1949 to his retirement in 1964 he was a professor of Byzantine history at United States universities, and a visiting professor at the Collège de France as well as Trinity College, Cambridge. His writings include *Les Slaves, Byzance et Rome au IXième siècle* (1926), a work which won him the prix de l'Académie française for 1927, *The life of Saint Wenceslas* (1929), *Byzance et la primauté romaine* (1964), and its translation, *Byzantium and the Roman primacy* (1966). He died in Kromeriz, 4 November 1975. ConAu 1-4, 61-64, new rev. 6; DrAS 1974; IntWW 1974/75, 1975/76; WhAm, 6 & 7; WhoAm 1974/75, 1976/77

Dvoskin, Beniamin IAkovlevich, born 20 October 1923, he received a doctorate in 1968 in geography and specialized in Kazakhstan regional problems. He was joint author of *Казахская ССР* (1971), *Производительные силы Восточного Казахстана* (1976), *Проблемы расселения населения Казахстана* (1989), and *Инфраструктурно-территориальный комплекс* (1990). Казахская ССР краткая энциклопедия, vol. 3, p. 176; LC

Dwight, Harrison Gray Otis, born 22 November 1803 at Conway, Mass. After graduating from Hamilton College and Andower Theological Seminary, he became in 1831 a missionary to the Armenians in Constantinople under the American Board of Commissioners for Foreign Missions. He worked well-nigh uninterruptedly in the city. His chief power lay in the proclamation of the Gospel in Constantinople and its neighbourhood. In addition to learned treatises and periodical articles, he wrote *Researches of the Rev. E. Smith and Rev. H. G. O. Dwight in Armenia, including a journey through Asia Minor, and into Georgia and Persia, with a visit to the Nestorian and Chaldean Christians at Oormiah and Salmas* (1833), and *Christianity revived in the East* (1850). He met with his death in an unfortunate railway accident while at home on furlough, 25 January 1862. DAB; NatCAB, 10, p. 490; Richter, p. 108; Shavit; WhAm, 3

Dwight, Harrison Griswold, born 6 August 1875 at Constantinople, where he attended Robert College. After graduation from Amherst College in 1898, he was a correspondent for the *Chicago record-herald* until 1902. From 1906 to 1914 he did news work in Europe and the Middle East. After the war he attended peace conferences in Versailles and Paris. In 1920 he became a special assistant to the U.S. State Department. He was attached to the Near East and Protocol divisons until 1920. He later was for ten years an assistant director of the Frick Collection in NYC. He wrote *Constantinople, old and new* (1913), *Stamboul nights* (1916), and *Persian miniatures* (1917). He died in N.Y.C., 24 March 1959. NYT, 26 March 1959, p. 34; Shavit; WhAm, 3

Dwight, Henry Otis, born 3 June 1843 at Constantinople, he was a son of one of the founders of the Turkey missions, a graduate of Ohio Wesleyan University, and an officer in the Union Army from 1861 to 1865. From 1867 to 1872 he was the business agent of the American Board of Commissioners for Foreign Missions. His missionary language, of which he was facile master, was Turkish so that he edited the publications of the Mission in Turkish from 1872 to 1899. His books in English give abundant evidence of his exceptional fitness for the literary work of the foreign missionary. Since 1907 he was in the service of the American Bible Society in N.Y.C and its historian. His writings include *Turkish life in war* time (1881), *Treaty rights of American missionaries in Turkey* (1893), and *Constantinople and its problems* (1901). He died in Roselle, N.J., 20 June 1917. DAB; Missionary herald, 113 (1917), p. 361; Shavit; WhAm, 1

Dwyer, Daisy Hilse, born 20th cent., she received a Ph.D. from Yale in 1973 for her thesis, *Women's conflict behavior in a traditional Moroccan setting; an international analysis.* Her writings include *Images and self-images; male and female in Morocco* (1978), *Women and income in the Third World* (1983); she edited *A Home divided* (1988), and *Law and Islam in the Middle East* (1990). LC; Selim

Dwyer, Kevin, born 20th cent., he received a Ph.D. in 1974 from Yale University for his thesis, *The cultural bases of entrepreneurial activity.* He was an anthropologist who spent more than two decades studying Arab society in North Africa, and served as director of Middle East research for Amnesty International in London between 1978 and 1984. His writings include *Moroccan dialogues; anthropology in question* (1982), and *Arab voices; the human rights debate in the Middle East* (1991). LC; Private

Dybowski, Jean, born in 1857 at Paris, he graduated from l'École nationale de Grignon and became a lecturer at l'École nationale d'horticulture. In 1889 he was sent on a scientifique mission to Southern Algeria, and in 1890 to the Sahara. In the service of the Comité de l'Afrique française he also visited

Chad. After his return he was a professor of colonial agriculture at the Institut agronomique from 1893 to 1927, and concurrently taught at l'École supérieure coloniale and was an acting general director of agriculture and trade in Tunisia. His writings include *La route du Tchad* (1893), and *Traité pratique des cultures tropicales* (1902). He died 18 December 1928. DBF; Henze; *Hommes et destins*, v. 1, p. 211, v. 5, 199

Dyé, Alfred Henri, born 25 September 1874 at L'Isle-S.-Denis, he was a graduate of l'École navale. He accompanied the Mission Marchand which, setting out from the sources of the Ubangi River, tried to reach the Nile in 1897. In 1900 he participated with the French contingent against the Boxer Rebellion; in 1906-7 he led a hydrographic mission to the coast of Morocco; and in 1908 he was second in command of the Mission Mazeran, which made a feasibility study of the navigation on the Senegal River. He was appointed *commandant de la marine* at Beirut, but died in an automobile accident, shortly after he rejoined his post. His writings include *Les portes du Maroc; leur commerce avec la France* (1909). DBF

Dyer, M. G, he received a doctorate in 1972 from King's College, London, for his thesis, *The end of World War I in Turkey, 1918-1919*. Sluglett

Dyker, David A., born 6 September 1944, he was a lecturer in economics at the School of European Studies, University of Sussex. His writings include *The Soviet economy* (1976),*The future of the Soviet economic planning system* (1985), and *Yugoslavia; socialism, development, debt* (1990). LC

Dykstra, Dirk, born 1879 at Welsryp, the Netherlands, he was educated at Hope College, and Western Theological Seminary, both Holland, Mich., and ordained in 1914. He went out in 1906 to serve in the Arabian Mission until 1952. Though he had long experience in evangelistic work in all the stations and on tours, he was pre-eminent in the Mission as an architect and builder. Hospitals, particularly in Muscat, schools and residences all over the Arabian Mission bear witness to his vision and the hard painstaking work. He died in Holland, Mich., 1 November 1956. Shavit; Van Ess

Dymock, William, born 10 August 1832 or 1834, he was educated at Rugby and Oxford, and entered the Bombay Army as a medical officer in 1859 and rose to the rank of surgeon major in 1873. He was principal medical storekeeper in Bombay from 1871 to 1890. His writings include *A Catalogue (revised) of Indian drugs* (1883), *The Vegetable materia medica of western India* (1884), and *Pharmacographia indica; a history of the principal drugs of vegetable origin, met with in British India* (1890). He died in Bombay, 29 April 1892. Boase, v. 5, col., 184

Dynes, Russell Rowe, born 2 October 1923 at Dundalk, Ontario, he was a graduate of the University of Tennessee and received a Ph.D. in 1954 from Ohio State University for his thesis, *Church - sect typology*. He was a professor of sociology, and a sometime chairman of department, Ohio State University, from 1951 to 1977. From 1964 to 1965 he was a Fulbright lecturer at Ain Shams University, Cairo, and concurrently a member of staff at the Arab State Centre for Education in Community Development, Cairo. His writings include *Social problems* (1964), and he was joint author of *Acceptance of change* (1967). AmM&WS 1973 S; ConAu 9-12, new rev. 6, 23; Master (1); WhoAm, 1978-1986

Dynnik, Valentina Aleksandrovna, born in 1898, she translated from the Ossetic *Сказания о нартах; эпоса осетинского народа* (1944), *Сказания о нартх; перевод с осетинского* (1948), and *Нартские сказания; осетинский народный эпос* (1949). NUC, pre-1956

Dyrenkova, Nadezhda Petrovna, fl. 1930, her writings include *Грамматика ойротского языка* (1940), and *Грамматика шорского языка* (1941), *Грамматика хакасского языка* (1948), and *Шорский фольклор* (1948). LC; NUC, pre-1956

Dyroff, Karl, born 12 November 1862 at Aschaffenburg, Germany, he studied classical philology and Oriental languages at the universities of München, Würzburg and Berlin, and received a Dr.phil. in 1892 from the Universität München for his thesis, *Zur Geschichte der Überlieferung des Zuhair-diwans*. In 1906 he became an honorary professor of Egyptology and Arabic at München where he died 12 November 1938. DtBE; Egyptology; Kürschner, 1925-1935; Schwarz

Džambo, Jozo, born in 1949 in Yugoslavia, he was in 1985 affiliated with Bayerisches National-museum, München. His writings include *Buchwesen in Bosnien und der Herzegowina, 1800-1878* (1985); and he edited *Itinerarium der Gesandtschaft König Ferdinand I von Ungarn nach Konstantinopel, 1530* (1983). LC; Note

Dzeniskevich, Galina Ivanovna, fl. 1972, she was joint editor of *Открытие Америки продолжаеця* (1993). LC

Dzerunian, S. K., 1860-1931 *see* TSerunian, Semen Grigor'evich (Kirkovich)

Dzhabbarov, Isa Murodovich, 1929- *see* Zhabborov, Isa Murodovich

Dzhafarov (Dzhafar, Jăfăr), Akrem Saftarovich, born 5 (18) May 1905 in Azerbaijan, he received a doctorate in 1971 at Baku for his thesis, *Теоретические основы аруза и азербайджанский аруз.* He published almost exclusively in Azeri. Miliband; Miliband²

Dzhafarov, S. A., 1907-1978 *see* Jăfărov, Sălim Äbdullătif oghlu

Dzhafarzade, Aziza, 1921- *see* Jăfărzadă, Äziză Mămmăd gyzy

Dzhafarzade, Iskhak M., 1895-1982 *see* Jăfărzadă, Ishag Mămmădriza ogly

Dzhalaganiia, Irina Levanovna, fl. 1958, her writings include *Истории монетного дела в Грузии* (1958), *Монетные клады Грузии* (1975), *Иноземная монета в денешном обращении Грузии V-XIII вв.* (1979), and *Клад сасанидских и византийских монет из Цители Цкаро* (1980). LC

Dzhalil (Celil, Jalil), Dzhalile Dzhasimovich, born 26 November 1936 at Erevan, he received a doctorate in 1963 from Moscow University for his thesis, *Освободительная борьба курдского народа в 50-80.х годах XIX в.* He later became a teacher at Erevan University, specializing in folklore and history. His writings include *Восстание курдов 1880 года* (1966), *Курды Османской Империи в первой половине XIX века* (1973), *Курдская книга в Армении 1930-1980* (1981), and *Курды Советской Армении; би-блиография 1920.1980* (1987); and with O. Dzhalil he was joint author of *Курдский фольклор* (1978), and *Курдские сказы, легенды и предания* (1989). LC; Miliband; Miliband²

Dzhalil (Dzhalilov), Ordikhan Dzhasimovich, born 24 August 1932 at Erevan, he received a doctorate in 1961 from Leningrad University for his thesis, *Курдский героический эпос «Златорукий хан».* His writings include *Гражданская поэзия Джагархуна* (1966), and *Курдские пословицы и поговорки* (1972); and with Dzhalile Dzhalil he was joint author of *Курдский фольклор* (1978), and *Курдские сказы, легенды и предания* (1989). LC; Miliband; Miliband²

Dzhalilov, Ordikhane Dzhasimovich, 1932- *see* Dzhalil, Ordikhan Dzhasimovich

Dzhalilov, Shukhrat Il'khamovich *see* Zhalilov, Shukhrat Il'khamovich

Dzhamalov, Oner Baimbetovich, fl. 1958, he was the editor of the collective works *Экономические закономерности и преимущества некапиталистического пути развития* (1973), *Законо-мерности роста уровня жини населения в условиях некапиталистического развития* (1976), and *Закономерности создания и развития социалистической экономики в Узбекистане; избранные труда* (1979). LC

Dzhanashiia, Nodar Nikolaevich, born 25 May 1925 at Tiflis, he graduated in 1951 from the Oriental Faculty, Tiflis, where he also received a doctorate in 1969 for his thesis, *Исследование по морфологии турецкого глагола*, a work which was published in 1981. Since 1951 he was affiliated with his alma mater, where he was appointed a lecturer in 1965 and a professor in 1972. LC; Miliband²

Dzhangidze (Jangiże), Verena Tarasovna, born 1 September 1928 at Tiflis,she graduated in 1949 from the State University, Tiflis, and received her first degree in 1955. She was since 1950 affiliated with the Faculty of Philology, Tiflis. Her writings include *Ингилойский диалект в Азербайджане* (1978). LC; Miliband²

Dzhanmatova, Khakima Irisofna, born 21 April 1939 at Tashkent, she graduated in 1966 from the Oriental Faculty, Tashkent, and received her first degree in 1971 for *Аль-Кинди и его философские взгляды.* She was a lecturer since 1983. Miliband²

Dzharylgasinova (Jarylgasinova), Roza Shotaevna, born 14 October 1931 at Moscow, she obtained her first degree in 1962 for her thesis, *Когурёсцы.* Her writings include *Древние когурецы* (1972), *Этниеская ономастика* (1984); and she edited *Калеидарняе обычаи и обряды народов Восточной Азии; новый год* (1985), *Калеидарняе обычаи и обряды народов Восточной Азии; годовой цикл* (1989), and *Календарно-праздничная культура народов Зарубежной Азии; традиции и инновации* (1997). LC; Miliband; Miliband²

Dzhavadov (Javadov), G. D., fl. 1977, his writings include *Народная земледельческая техника Азербайджана; историко-этнографическое исследрвание* (1988). LC

Dzhidalaev, Nurislam Sirazhutinovich, fl. 1970, he obtained a doctorate in linguistics. His writings include *Тюркизмы в дагестанских языках* (1990); and he edited *Тюркского-дагестанские языковые контакты* (1982), *Местоимение в языках Дагестана* (1983), and *Тюркско-дагестан-ские языковые взаимоотношения* (1985). LC

Dzhikiev, Ata, born 29 May 1933 in Turkmenistan, his writings include *Традиционные туркмеиские праздники* (1983), and *Очерки происхождения и формирования туркменского народа в эпоху средневековья* (1991). LC; Schoeberlein

Dzhikiia, Sergei Simonovich, born 20 October 1898 in Gruziya, he graduated in 1924 from Tbilisi State University, where he also received a doctorate in 1956 for his thesis, *Простанный реестр вилайета Гюрджистан*. He was a research fellow at the Philological Institute, Georgian Academy of Science, Tbilisi, from 1936 to 1960, when he became head of its Turkish Section. Kazak SE; Miliband; Miliband²; *Советская тюркология* 1971, № 1, pp. 115-116

Dzhindi (Jindi, Jndi), Dzhauari *Adzhie* (Hajie, Hajji), born 18 (31) March 1908 at Kars Vilayeti, Ottoman Turkey, he was a collector of Kurdish and Armenian folklore, and the author of Kurdish literary works as well as translations into Russian. His writings include *Folklora körmanshchie = Русский фольклор* (Erevan, 1957), and *Shaked eposa "R'jstăme Zală" K'ordi = Курдские сказы эпоса "Ростаме Зал"* (1977). Fuad, p. xli; LC; Miliband, p. 181

Dzhugashvili (Jugašvili), Galina IAkovlevna, born 19 February 1938 at Moscow, she was a graduate of Moscow State University, and received her first degree in 1970 for her thesis, *Художественные особенности алжирского романа 50-60-х годов*. She was since 1970 affiliated with the Soviet Academy of Science. Her writings include *Алжирский франкоязычный роман* (1976). LC; Miliband; Miliband²

Dzhumagulov, Chetin Dzhumagulovich *see* Zhumagulov, Chetin Zhumagulovich

Dzhumanazarov, Umurzak *see* Zhumanazarov, Umurzoq

Dzięgiel, Leszek, born 15 August 1931 at Myłowice, Poland, he studied at Uniwersytet Jagielloński, Kraków, where he also received his doctorate in 1972. He was affiliated with the Instytut Rolnictwa i Leśnicta Kraków Tropikalnych i Subtropikalnych, Kocmyrzów. His writings include *Rural community of contemporary Iraqi Kurdistan facing modernization* (1981), *Węzeł kurdyjski; kultura, dzieje, walka o przetrwanie* (1992); he edited *Zarys etnografii górali Assamu* (1977), and *Na egzotycznych szlakach; o polskich badaniach etnograficznych w Afryce, Ameryce i Azji* (1987). He was joint editor of *Problemy metodologiczne etnografii* (1989). KtoPolske, 2001; LC; OSK; Schoeberlein

Dzierżykray-Rogalski, Tadeusz, born 19 September 1918 at Warszawa, he received doctorates in 1949 and 1951 and became a professor of anthropology and palaeopathology at Uniwersytet Warszawski. His writings include *Zdolności przystosowawcze człowieka* (1970), *Polska antropologia w Afryce* (1981), *The bishops of Faras; an anthropological-medical study* (1985); and he was joint author of *Sudan* (1980). In 1970 he edited the proceedings, *Biology of man in Africa*. KtoPolske, 1993

Dziubiński, Andrzej, born in 1936, his writings include *Maroko w XVI wieku* (1972), *Między mieczem, głodem i dżuma; Maroko w latach 1727-1830* (1977), *Podbój Maghrebu przez Francję, 1830-1934* (1984); and he was joint author of *Przed podbojem; Afryka północna i zachodnia w relacjach z XVIII i XIX wieku* (1980). LC

Dzumanazarov, IU. *see* Zhumanazarov, Umurzoq

Eagleton, Clyde, born 13 May 1891 at Sherman, Texas; he was educated at Austin, (Texas) College, and Princeton University. In 1917 he was a Rhodes scholar at Oxford, and in 1928 he obtained a Ph.D. at Columbia University, N.Y.C. From 1923 until his retirement in 1956 he was professor of international law at New York University. His writings include *The responsibility of states in international law* (1928), *Analysis of the problem of war* (1937), *International government* (1948). He died 30 January 1958. WhAm, 3; WhNAA

Eagleton, William Lester, born 17 August 1926 at Peoria, Illinois, he was a graduate of Yale University, and did post-graduate work in the Institut d'études politiques de Paris from 1948 to 1949. Thereafter he joined the U.S. Foreign Service, where he spent most of his career in the Middle East. From 1984 to 1988 he was ambassador at Damascus. His writings include *The Kurdish Republic of 1946* (1963), and *An introduction to Kurdish rugs and other weavings* (1988). WhoAm, 1980-1996|; WhoWor, 1987-89; Master (1)

Eaker, Ira Clarence, born 13 April 1896 at Field Creek, Texas, he studied at different universities and then entered the military service, where he advanced to the rank of brigadier general. He was deputy commander of the Army Air Force and chief of the air staff in Washington in 1945, and he helped set in motion the creation of the U.S. Air Force as an independent branch of the military. He died 6 August

1987. James Parton wrote *Air Force spoken here; General Ira Eaker and the Command of the Air* (1986). ConAu, 123; Master ((2); WhAm, 10; Who 1969-1987; *Who was who*, 8

Earle, Edward Mead, born 20 May 1894 at N.Y.C., he received a Ph.D. from Columbia University in 1923 for his thesis, *Turkey, the great powers, and the Baghdad railway; a study in imperialism*, a work which won him the George Louis Beer prize for the best book of the year on European diplomacy. It was published in a Turkish translation, *Bağdat demiryolu savaşı*, in 1972. He taught history at Columbia University from 1920 until 1934, when he was appointed a professor at the Institute of Advanced Study, Princeton. He was a visiting lecturer at home and abroad. He died 24 June 1954. AmAu&B; DAB, 5; Master (2); Selim; *Who was who*, 5; *Who was who in America*, 3

Earle, Ralph Anstruther, born in 1835 at Edinburgh, and educated at Harrow, he was an attaché at Paris in 1854, a private secretary to Benjamin Disraeli, when chancellor of the exchequer, from 1858 to 1859. While a member of Parliament from 1865 to 1868, he was parliamentary secretary to the Poor Law Board, 1866-1867. He died in Soden, Nassau, 10 June 1879. Boase

Earles, Joseph, fl. 1801, his writings include the translations *Letters of the Emperor Aurung-Zebe to his sons, his ministers and principal nobles, to which is prefixed his will* (Calcutta, 1788), and *Treatise on horses* (1788), a translation from a Persian version of the Sanskrit *Salihotra* into English. BLC

Early, Evelyn A., born 20th cent., she received a Ph.D. in 1980 from the University of Chicago for her thesis, *Badawi women of Cairo*. In 1991 she was press attaché for the U.S. Embassy, Rabat. Her writings include *Baladi women of Cairo; playing with an egg and a stone* (1992); and she was joint editor of *Everyday life in the Muslim Middle East*. LC; Selim²

Earthy, E. Dora, fl. 1955, she was affiliated with the Save the Children Fund.

Eastham, Jack Kenneth, born in 1901 at Poynton, Cheshire, he was educated at Salisbury, Manchester and LSE, and became a lecturer in economics at Dundee and St. Andrews, a professor of economics at Ankara Üniversitesi, and a visiting professor at the Middle East Technical University, Ankara. His writings include *Graphical economics* (1960). Au&Wr, 1971

Eastman, Alvin Clark, 1894-1959, he was an Orientalist who was affiliated with the Boston Museum of Fine Arts. He wrote *The Nala-Damayanti drawings* (1959). LC; WhoAmA, 1980 N, 1982 N, 1986 N, 1989/90 N

Eastwick, Edward Backhouse, born in 1814, he was educated at Oxford and subsequently joined the East India Company's service as a cadet in the Bombay infantry. His proficiency in Oriental languages soon led to his employment in the civil branch of the Company. Broken health compelled him to return to Europe. In 1845 he was appointed a professor of Hindustani at the East India Company's college at Haileybury. In 1860 he left England as secretary of legation to the court of Persia, where he remained three years. His writings include *A Concise grammar of the Hindustani language* (1847), *Journal of a diplomat's three years' residence in Persia* (1864), and numerous translations from the Persian and Urdu including the *Gulistan, Anwar-i Suhayli*, and *Bagh-u-bahar*. He died in 1883. BiD&SB; Buckland; CelCen; DcBiPP; DNB

Eastwood, Bruce Stansfield, born 8 February 1938 at Worcester, Mass, he was a graduate of Emory University, and received a Ph.D. in 1964 from the University of Wisconsin for his thesis, *The Geometrical optics of Robert Grosseteste*. He held varied positions in history of higher learning until 1973, when he was appointed professor of intellectual history of science at the University of Kentucky, a position which he still held in 1999. His writings include *The elements of vision; the micro-cosmology of Galenic visual theory according to Hunayn Ibn Ishaq* (1982). DrAS, 1974, 1978, 1982; NatFacDr. 1999

Eastwood, Tristram, born 6 November 1936 at Birkenhead, Cheshire, he took a degree in Slavonic languages at the University of Nottingham and became an International Labour Organization expert on co-operative education and development, serving in Turkey from 1970 to 1972. He subsequently served with United Nations' institutions. WhoUN, 1975

Eaton, Charles Le Gai Hasan, born 12 November 1941 in Switzerland and educated at Charterhouse and King's College, Cambridge, he worked for many years as a teacher and journalist in Jamaica and Egypt before joining the British diplomatic service. His writings include *King of the castle; choice and responsibility in the modern world* (1977), *Islam and the destiny of man* (1985), and its translation, *Der Islam und die Bestimmung des Menschen* (1987). LC

Eaton, Richard Maxwell, born 8 December 1940 at Grand Rapids, Mich, he was appointed a professor of history at the University of Arizona in 1972, a post which he still held in 1999. His writings include *Sufis of Bijapur* (1977), a work based on his 1972 Ph.D. thesis, submitted at the University of Wisconsin; and he was joint author of *Firuzabad, palace city of the Deccan* (1992). DrAS, 1978, 1982; LC; NatFacDr, 1995, 1999

Ebadian, Mahmoud, born about 1940, he wrote *Die Problematik der Kunstauffassung Georg Lukacz'* (1977), a work which was presented in 1978 as a thesis for a Dr.phil. at the Universität Hamburg. LC

Eban, Abba Solomon, born 2 February 1915 at Cape Town, he was a graduate of Queen's College, Cambridge, and subsequently was a research fellow and tutor in Oriental languages at Pembroke College, Cambridge. Since 1947 he served as a vocal proponent of Israel's interests, first in the U.N. from 1947 to 1959, then as Israel's ambassador to the U.S.A. from 1950 to 1959, and then in a variety of prominent posts in Israel itself, including deputy prime minister and minister of foreign affairs. His writings include *Voice of Israel* (1957), *The Promised Land* (1978), *My people* (1978), and *Personal witness; Israel through my eyes* (1992). He died on 17 November 2002. ConAu, 57-60, new rev., 26; IntWW, 1974-1998/99; Master (4); Who, 1974-1998; WhoIsrael, 1990/91; WhoWor, 1974-1989/90; WhoWorJ, 1965-1987

Ebeling, Adolf Heinrich, born 24 October 1827 (or 1823) at Hamburg. After obtaining a doctorate at Heidelberg he travelled to Brazil. From 1851 he was resident in Paris, first as a private tutor and correspondent to German newspapers, and later as a professor. In 1873 he was appointed a professor at the Cairo Military School, a position which he held until 1878, when he returned to Germany to settle permanently in Köln. His writings include *Regenbogen im Osten; die Krone des Orients - Gaselen* (1868), *Bilder aus Kairo* (1878), and *Die Sklaverei von den ältesten Zeiten bis auf die Gegenwart* (1889). He died 23 July 1896. BiD&SB; Hinrichsen

Eberhard, Elke see Niewöhner née Eberhard, Elke

Eberhard, Otto Glaubrecht Karl Theodor, born 28 November 1875 at Ludwigslust, Germany, he studied theology and philosophy at Erlangen, Greifswald, and Rostock, and became a pastor until he was appointed director of the theological seminary at Greiz. He later was a school administrator near Berlin. He visited Palestine in 1905 and was a member of the Deutsches Komitee zur Föderung der Jüdischen Palästinasiedlung. His writings include *Palästina; Erlebtes und Erlauschtes vom Heiligen Lande* (1913), and *Bildungswesen und Schulreform in der neuen Türkei* (1916). He died 26 September 1966. DtBE; Master (1); WhE&EA

Eberhard, Wolfram, born 17 March 1909 at Potsdam, Germany, he obtained a diploma from the Seminar für Orientalische Sprachen, and a Dr.phil. from the Universität Berlin in 1933 for his thesis, *Beiträge zur kosmologischen Spekulation der Chinesen der Han-Zeit*. He was a refugee from National Socialism and a lecturer in German at Peking, and a professor of Chinese culture at Ankara, before he migrated to the United States and became a professor of sociology at the University of California at Berkeley in 1952. His writings include *Minstrel tales from southeastern Turkey* (1955), *China und seine westlichen Nachbarn* (1978), and *China's minorities* (1982). He died in 1989. ConAu, 49-52, new rev., 2; Kürschner, 1950, 1954, 1970-1987|; Master (3); Widmann, pp. 150, 259

Eberman, Vasilii Aleksandrovich, born in 1899 at St. Petersburg, he graduated from the Oriental Faculty, Petrograd, in 1921. From 1919 to 1930 he was affiliated with the Asiatic Museum, Leningrad, where he specialized in Arabic poetry and miniature painting. He died 27 June 1937. Miliband; Miliband²

Ebers, Georg Moritz (Maurice), born 1 March 1837 at Berlin. Following the wish of the family, he started to study law at Göttingen but without real commitment. He later changed to Egyptology and in 1870 became a professor of Egyptology at Leipzig. His writings include *Ägypten in Wort und Bild* (1878-79). He died in 1898. ADtB, v. 45, 469-73; BioIn, 7; CelCen; Egyptology; Who was who, 1; Wininger

Ebersolt, Jean born 22 June 1879 at Montbéliard (Doubs), and educated at universities in Paris, Nancy, Berlin, and München, he obtained a *docteur-ès-lettres* at the Sorbonne in 1910. Afterwards he conducted archaeological explorations. His writings include *Les églises de Constantinople* (1913), *Constantinople byzantine et les voyageurs du Levant* (1918), *Mission archéologique de Constantinople* (1921), and *Orient and Occident* (1928-1929). He died from a coronary, in December 1933, the very day the Université de Bruxelles offered him the chair of history of art. DBF; Byzantion 8 (1933), pp. 800-805

Ebert, Adam, born in 1653 at Frankfurt on Oder, Germany, he received a doctorate of law in 1687 from the Universität Frankfurt for his thesis, *De justicia actionum Philippi II. Hispaniae & Indiarum regis*. His travels in Europe, *Reise-Beschreibung von Villa Franca, der Chur Brandenburg durch Deutschland, Holland und Brabant, England, Frankreich ... gantz Italien*, he published under his pseudonym Aulus Apronius in 1723. He died in Frankfurt, 24 March 1735. ADtB; DtBilnd (2)

Ebert, Hans Georg, born 22 July 1953 at Aue, Germany, he studied Arabic and law at the Universität Leipzig, where he received doctorates in 1982 and 1990. Thereafter he was a research fellow at Leipzig, specializing in Islamic law. He did field research in Egypt, Libya, Tunisia, and Iran. His writings include *Die Interdependenz von Staat, Verfassung und Islam im Nahen und Mittleren Osten in der Gegenwart* (1991), and he was joint author of *Die Islamische Republik Iran* (1987). Private; Thesis

468

Ebied, Rifaat Y., born 20th cent., Dr., he was in 1976 attached to the Department of Semitic Studies in the University of Leeds, and in 1993, he was a professor of Semitic studies in the University of Sydney. His writings include *Bibliography of medical Arabic and Jewish medicine and allied sciences* (1971); and he was joint editor and translator of *Arab stories - East and West* (1977), and *Affliction's physic and the curse of sorrow* (1978).

Ebon, Martin (Eric Ward), born 27 May 1917 at Hamburg, Germany, he was an author and editor who wrote on parapsychology. During the second World War he was chief of the Foreign News Section, Overseas News and Features Bureau, U.S. Office of War Information and later served with the Department of State and the Foreign Policy Association. He was a frequent lecturer at the Faculty of the New School of Social Research in N.Y.C. His writings include *World communism today* (1948), and *Prophecy in our time* (1968). ConAu, 21-24, new rev., 10, 29; EncO&P, 1978; WrDr, 1980-2000|

Eccles, Henry Effingham, born 31 December 1898 at Bayside, N.Y., he was educated at Columbia University and the U.S. Naval Academy. He joined the Navy and retired with the rank of rear admiral in 1952. His writings include *Logistics in the national defense* (1959). He died in 1986. ConAu P-1; BioIn 14, 15; WrDr 1976-1986/88

Ecevit, Bülent, born 28 May 1925 at İstanbul, he was a graduate of Robert College, Istanbul, and also studied at Ankara and SOAS. He was a journalist, writer, politician, and prime minister of Turkey. His writings include *Bu düzen değişmelidir* (1968), *Dış politika* (1976), *Ich meißele Licht aus Stein* (1976), *Şiirler* (1976), and *Değişen dünya ve Türkiye* (1990). BioIn, 10, 11, 12; CurBio, 1975; IntAu&Wr, 1989; IntWW, 1974-1998/99; IntYB, 1998 Kim kimdir, 1985/86; MagyarNKK, 1992, 1994, 1996, 1998; Master (3); Meydan; MidE, 1982/83; WhoWor, 1974-1989/90; Zürcher

Echallier, Jean Claude, fl. 1966-67, his writings include *Villages désertées et structures agraires anciennes du Touat-Gourara* (1972). LC

Echard, Nicole, born in 1937, she was an anthropologist and a lifelong research fellow at the C.N.R.S. since 1967, specializing on Central Africa, where she spent several years. From 1989 to 1991, she was president of the Association française des anthropologues. Her writings include *Étude socio-économique dans les vallées de l'Ader Doutchi Maggia* (1964), *L'expérience du passé; histoire de la société paysanne hausa de l'Ader* (1975), *Bori, aspects d'un culte de possession hausa dans l'Ader et le Kurfey, Niger* (1989); and she edited *Métallurgies africaines; nouvelles contributions* (1983), and *Les relations hommes-femmes dans le bassin du lac Tchad; Colloque Méga-Tchad* (1991). She died 21 June 1994. Journal des africanistes 64 ii (1994), 91-95

de **Echegaray**, Bonifacio, fl. 1921-1945, his writings include *La vida civil y mercantil de los vascos a través de sus instituciones jurídicas* (1923), *Derecho foral privado* (1950), and *Los sitos funerarios en el derecho consuetudinario de Navarra* (1951). NUC, pre-1956

Echols, John Minor, born 25 March 1913 at Portland, Ore., he was a graduate of the University of Virginia, and received a Ph.D. in 1940 in German philology. He served with the U.S. Department of State from 1947 to 1952, when he was appointed a professor of linguistics, and later associate director, Modern Indonesia Project in Cornell University, Ithaca, N.Y. He was joint author of two Indonesian dictionaries, and wrote *Indonesian writing in translation* (1956). BioIn, 13; ConAu, 5-8, 107, New rev., 2; DrAS, 1974, 1978, 1982; Master (1)

Eckardt, Julius T. von, fl. 1897-1899, he contributed articles to *Deutsche Rundschau* and also wrote *Von Carthago nach Karruan* ; *Bilder aus dem orientalischen Abendlande* (Berlin, 1894). Sezgin

Eckart, Bruno, born about 1870 at Sorge, Germany, a brother of Franz Hugo, he was affiliated with the Deutsche Orient-Mission at the Urfa station in 1908. During 1917 and 1918 he was attached to the Baghdad Railway in Turkey, but obliged to return to Germany after the war. Note

Eckart, Emma née Geittner, born 19th cent., she was a widowed rug designer at the Deutsche Orient-Mission's factory in Germany, when she became engaged to Franz Hugo Eckart in 1896. The following year, she went out to Urfa, Turkey, to join her husband and become the artistic director of the carpet manufacture at the Urfa Mission. She died of typhoid fever, 28 December 1901 in Urfa.

Eckart, Franz Hugo, born 14 June 1873 at Sorge near Greiz, Germany, he was a village school teacher, trained at the teachers' seminary, Greiz. He made the acquaintance of Johannes Lepsius who won him over to the cause of the Armenische Hilfsbund and go out to Urfa, Turkey, to establish the German orphanage of the Deutsche Orient-Mission. He served for twenty-two years as head of the Urfa station until arrested by the Turkish authorities after the war, allegedly for having incited the Turkish population of Urfa to the massacre of the local Armenians in 1915. He was interned on the island of Prinkipo

(Büyükada). In order to evade his transfer to Malta, he tried to escape from custody but was shot by Turkish border control near Midia (Kıyıköy) in March of 1919. Orient 1 (1919), pp. 146-148; Schäfer

Eckaus, Richard Samuel, born 30 April 1926 at Kansas City, Mo., he was a graduate of Iowa State University, and received a Ph.D. in 1954 from M.I.T. He was a professor of economics at Brandeis University, Waltham, Mass., from 1951 to 1962, when he was appointed a professor of economics, with special reference to less developed countries, at M.I.T. His writings include *Planning for growth* (1968), *Appropriate technologies for developing countries* (1977), and *Some temporal aspects of development* (1983). ConAu, 45-48; Master (2); WhoAm, 1980-1999

Eckensberger, Lutz H., born 24 November 1938 at Berlin, he received a doctorate in 1969 for his thesis, *Methodenprobleme der kulturvergleichenden Psychologie*, and was appointed a professor of psychology at the Universität Saarbrücken in 1972. His writings include *Unterrichtsprobleme an technisch-gewerblichen Ausbildungsstätten in Entwicklungsländern* (1968). Kürschner, 1976-1996; LC

Eckert, Ekkehart Hédi, fl. 1970., he received a doctorate in 1975 from the Universität Köln for his thesis, *Struktur und Funktionen der Familie in Tunesien*. Schwarz

Eckert, Jerry Bruce, born 29 March 1939 at Columbus, Ohio, he was a graduate of the University of Arizona and received a Ph.D. in 1970 from Michigan State University for his thesis, *The impact of dwarf wheats on resource productivity in West Pakistan's Punjab*. He served for many years as an agricultural development economist in Pakistan, where he was also a member of the Pakistan Water Management Team, 1972-1976. Since 1977 he was a professor at the Colorado State University, Fort Collins, a post which he still held in 1999. His writings include *The economics of fertilizing dwarf wheats in Pakistan's Punjab* (1971) NatFacDr, 1995-1999; WhoWest, 1984/85|

Eckhardt, Alexandre, 1890-1969 *see* Eckhardt, Sándor

Eckhardt, Georg Theobald *Paul*, born 16 May 1898 at Lippoldsberg an der Weser, Germany, he studied law at Berlin, and theology and philosophy at Marburg, where he received a Dr.phil. in 1923 for his thesis, *Schloß Wilhelmsthal*. Thesis

von **Eckhardt**, Hans, born in 1890, his writings include *Rußland* (1930), *Iwan der Schreckliche* (1941), and *Russisches Christentum* (1947). LC

Eckhardt, Sándor (Alexandre), born 23 or 29 December 1890 at Arad, Hungary, his writings include *Remy Belleau, sa vie, sa Bergerie* (1917), and *Balassi Bálint* (1941). He died in Budapest, 16 May 1969. Ki-kicsoda, 1937; MEL, 1981

Eckmann, János, born 21 August 1905 at Keszthely, Hungary, he was educated at Budapest and Wien, where he obtained a doctorate in 1937. He was a lecturer at Ankara, 1945-1948, and at Istanbul, 1952-1961. From 1961 to his death on 22 November 1971 he was a professor of Turkish at U.C.L.A. His writings include *Macar edebiyatı tarihi* (1946), *Chagatay manual* (1966), its translation, *Çağatayca el kitabı* (1988), and *Middle Turkish glosses of the Rylands interlinear Koran translation* (1976). Meydan; Prominent; WhAm, 6

Écochard, Michel Marie Léon, born 11 March 1905 at Paris, he was a townplanner and architect, and from 1946 to 1953, director of the Service de l'urbanisme in Morocco. Thereafter he was active in the Ivory Coast, Syria, Senegal, and Lebanon. He was awarded the first prize in the international competition for the National Museum of Kuwait. His writings include *Les bains de Damas* (1942-43), *Casablanca; le roman d'une ville* (1956), *Le problème des plans directeurs d'urbanisme au Sénégal* (1963), and *Filiation de monuments grecs, byzantins et islamiques* (1978). He died in 1985. IntWW, 1978-1984/85; WhoFr, 1971/72, 1975/76-1979/80; Revue des études islamiques 53 (1985), pp. vii-xv

Économidès, Jean G., born in Cairo, fl. 1932-1955, he was in 1941 a *chef du bureau* and proxy for the Crédit foncier égyptien, and a member of the Société Fouad Ier d'économie politique, de statistique et de législation. He later was a cultural director of the Hellenic Center, Cairo, and a member of the French-Hellenic League, Athens, as well as the France-Greece League, Paris. Note; WhoWor, 1974/75

Ecsedy, Csaba A., born in 1942, he was an anthropologist who was affiliated with the Ethnographical Museum, Budapest; his writings include *How do people travel?* (1985). LC

Ecsedy, Hilda, fl. 1964, she was joint author of *Hungarian publications on Asia and Africa, 1950-1962; a selected bibliography* (1963). LC

Ecsedy, Ildikó Mária, born 23 March 1938 at Ungvár when it was part of Hungary (later, Ukraine). Her writings include *Nomádok és kereskedők Kína határain* (1979), and she edited *Ōstarsadalom és ázsiai termelési mód* (1976). MagyarNKK, 1990, 1992, 1994, 1996, 1998; Prominent; Schoeberlein

Edbury, Peter W., born 20th cent., he received a Ph.D. in 1975 from St. Andrews University for his thesis, *The feudal nobility of Cyprus, 1192-1400*. He was a lecturer in history at University College, Cardiff. His writings include *The kingdom of Cyprus and the crusades, 1119-1374* (1991); the collection of his articles, *Kingdoms of the crusaders, from Jerusalem to Cyprus* (1999), he was joint author of *William Tyre, historian of the Latin East* (1988); and he edited *Coinage in the Latin East*; 4th Oxford Symposium on Coinage and Monetary History (1980), and *Crusade and settlement*; papers read at the 1st Conference of the Society for the Study of the Crusades and the Latin East (1985). LC; Sluglett

Eddé, Jacques, fl. 1972, his writings include *Manuel de géographie* (2nd ed., 1964). ZKO

Eddison, John Corban, born 4 November 1919 at N.Y.C., he was a graduate of Cornell University, Ithaca, N.Y., and received a Ph.D. in 1955 from M.I.T. He was an economic consultant. From 1958 to 1963 he was economic development adviser, Harvard University Advisory Group, Pakistan, and in 1971, he became an associate director, Economic Development, Harvard University Development Advisory Service. His writings include *A case study in industrial development; the growth of Indian pulp and paper industry* (1955). AmM&WS, 1973 S; WhoAm, 1980-1988/89|; WhoE, 1989/90

Eddy, David Brewer, born 20 June 1877 at Leavenworth, Kan., he was a graduate of Yale University, ordained in 1904, and received a doctorate in divinity from Wesleyan University in 1921. He was a missionary under the American Board of Commissioners for Foreign Missions from 1909 to his retirement in 1945. His writings include *What next in Turkey; glimpses of the American Board's work in the Near East* (1913), and *The social aspects of the American Board's work* (1914). He died 1 June 1914. Master (4); WhAm, 2

Eddy, George *Sherwood*, born 19 January 1871 at Leavenworth, Kan., and educated at Yale University, Union Theological Seminary, and Princeton Theological Seminary. He became a YMCA official who worked also among students in the Middle East. His writings include *India awaking* (1911), *The abolition of war* (1924), and the autobiography *Eighty adventurous years* (1955). He died in Jacksonville, Ill., 3 March 1963. Master (3); Shavit - Asia; WhAm, 4

Eddy, Mary (Mrs. William King Eddy), born in 1864, she received a medical doctorate and was the first woman in the Ottoman Empire to obtain the requisite Turkish diploma for the practice of medicine. She was a missionary of the Presbyterian Board in Syria and was posted to Tripoli, Syria, in 1881. She died 18 May 1931. Private; Richter, p. 217; Shavit

Eddy, William Alfred, born 9 March 1896 at Sidon, Syria, he was a soldier, diplomat, intelligence agent, educator and administrator who lived in the Middle East for more than thirty years. He was a graduate of Princeton, where he received a Ph.D. in 1922. Thereafter he was for five years chairman of the Department of English, AUC. He was the first United States Minister to Saudi Arabia, 1944-46, and chief of a special diplomatic mission to the Yemen, 1946. During 1947-1960, he served as a consultant to ARAMCO-TAPLINE. His writings include *F.D.R meets Ibn Saud* (1954). He died in Beirut, 4 or 5 May 1962. NatCAB, v. 49, p. 177; NYT, 5 May 1962, p. 27, col. 2; Shavit; WhAm, 4

Eddy, William King, born in the middle of the 19th cent. in Syria of missionary parents so that Arabic was his Syrian heritage. He was an itinerating missionary for twenty-eight years and spent the greater part of the year in travel from Sidon eastward beyond Hermon, southward nearly to Acre. He had a thorough grasp of Turkish law and a pre-eminent ability to cope with official and unofficial abusers of that law. He never wrote for publication. His wife, Mary, was a medical missionary. He died at a distant outpost where he intended to hold preaching and communion services on a Sunday in 1906. *Missionary review of the world*, n.s., 20 (1907), pp. 125-127

Ede, Jeffrey Raymond, born 10 March 1918, he was educated at King's College, Cambridge. During the war he served in the Inteligence Corps and thereafter entered the Public Record Office, where he retired in 1978 as Keeper of Publics Records. Concurrently he held varied positions in archival affairs. BlueB, 1976; Who, 1971-1998

Edelberg, Johan Lorentz *Lennart* Fraas, born 19 May 1915 at København, he studied natural history and geography at Københavns Universitet. He was a high school teacher at Ribe. From 1947 to 1949 he participated in the third Danish expedition to Central Asia as a botanist. The death of the expedition's ethnographer, Henning Haslund-Christensen, obliged him to take his place. As a consequence he became an expert on the Kafirs of Afghan Luristan, and the Lurs of southwestern Iran. Supported by appreciative authorities, he was repeatedly granted study leave for expeditions and research. His writings include *Nuristan buildings* (1984); and he was joint author of *Nuristan* (1979). He died in 1981. *Afghanistan journal* 9 (1982), pp. 53-54; DanskBL

Edelby, Néophyte Abdallah, born 10 November 1920 at Aleppo, he was educated at Jerusalem and Roma, ordained priest of the Melkite Church in 1944, consecrated bishop in 1962, and archbishop in 1968. His writings include *Les églises orientales catholiques* (1970), *Sulayman al-Ghazzi, sha'ir wakatib Masihi Malaki* (1984-85); and he edited *Religious freedom, canon law* (1966). LC; WhoArab, 1971/72-1984/85; WhoWor, 1974/75, 1976/77

Edel'man, Aleksandr Solomonovich, born 10 October 1926 at Moscow, he graduated in 1952 from the Oriental Section of the Faculty of Philology at Moscow. He specialized in Persian and Tajik studies. He died 19 November 1958. Miliband; Miliband²; Проблемы востоковедения6 1959, p. 244

Edelman, Bernard, fl. 1971, his writings include *Droit saisi par la photographie; éléments pour une théorie marxiste du droit* (1973), its translation, *The ownership of the image* (1979), and *La législation de la classe ouvrière* (1978). LC

Edel'man (Эдельман), Dzhoi Iosifovna, born 29 December 1930 at Moscow, he graduated in linguistics in 1953 from Moscow State University, and received his first degree in 1964 for his thesis, Язгулямский язык. His writings include *О единой научной транскрипции для иранских языков* (1963), *Дардские языки* (1965), *Основные вопросы лингвистической географии* (1968), and *Сравнительная грамматика восточноиранских языко; фонология* (1986). LC; Miliband; Miliband²

Edens, David Gilland, born 22 March 1928 at Lumberton, N.C., he was a graduate of the University of North Carolina and received a Ph.D. in 1962 from the University of Virginia for his thesis, *Economic aspects of eminent domain*. Under a grant from the Ford Foundation he was a consultant on economic development planning in Saudi Arabia, 1965/66. Since 1952 he was a professor of economics at the University of Connecticut, Storrs. His writings include *Oil and development in the Middle East* (1979). WhoE 1974/75

Edgar, Oscar Pelham, born 17 March 1871 at Toronto, he was educated at Upper Canada College, Toronto, the University of Toronto, and Johns Hopkins University, Baltimore, Md., where he received a Ph.D. in 1899 for his thesis, *A study of Shelley*. He was successively chairman of the French and English departments at Victoria College in the University of Toronto. He died in Canton, Ontario, on 7 October 1948. Bioln, 1, 2; Canadian, 1912-1948; DcNAA; Master (3); OxCan; *Who was who*, 4

Edgeworth, Michael Pakenham, born in 1812, he was educated at Charterhouse and took Oriental languages and botany at Edingburgh. After an distinguished career at the East India Company's college of Haileybury until 1831, he went to India in the Civil Service and remained there until his death on 30 July 1881. His chief publications were on botany, including *Pollen* (1877). DNB; Master (3)

Edhem, Ismail Galip, born in 1847 or 1848 in Ottoman Turkey, he was a numismatist and museum director. His writings include *Catalogue des monnaies turcomans ... du Musée impérial ottoman* (1894). He died in 1895. Meydan; NUC

Edib, Habib, fl. 1917 *see* Habib Edib

Edington, George Henry, born 10 January 1870 at Glasgow, he was a surgeon and a fellow of the Royal College of Surgeons of England. During the first World War he was a commanding officer in Turkey, Egypt, and Palestine. He died in 1943. Bioln, 3; *Who was who*, 4

Edkins, Joseph L., born 19 December 1823 at Nailworth, England, he obtained a doctorate of divinity, and became a Sinologist, linguist, and a missionary in China from 1848 to 1880. He made remarkable excursions in China. His writings include *The religious condition of the Chinese* (1859), *The evolution of the Hebrew language* (1889), and *Chinese currency* (1901). He died 23 April 1905. Henze; *Journal of the China Branch of the Royal Asiatic Society* 36 (1905), pp. 157-159; Lodwick

Edmonds, Cecil John, born in 1889, he was educated at Bedford School and Pembroke College, Cambridge. He entered the Levant Consular Service in 1910 and was posted to Iraq from 1918 until 1945. In 1922 he was seconded for service under the Iraqi Government, and from 1935 to 1945 was adviser to the Ministry of the Interior. Although no partisan of the Kurdish cause, he produced important works on the history and culture of the Kurds. He was a sometime lecturer in Kurdish at SOAS in the 1950s. His writings include *Kurds, Turks and Arabs; politics, travel and research in northeastern Iraq, 1919-1925* (1957), *A pilgrimage to Lalish* (1967); and he was joint author of *A Kurdish-English dictionary* (1966). He died in 1979. *Asian affairs* no 10 (1979), pp. 362-363; Au&Wr, 1971; ConAu, P-1, 13-14; Facey Grant, p. 83; Who, 1958-1978; *Who was who*, 7; WrDr, 1976/78, 1980/82

Edmonstone, Sir Archibald, born in 1795 at London, he was a miscellaneous writer who was educated at Eton and Oxford. In 1819 he travelled to Egypt. His visit to the Kharga and Dakhla oases he described in *A Journey to two oases of Upper Egypt* (1822). He died in 1871. BiD&SB; DNB; Egyptology; Henze

Edmonstone, Neil Benjamin, born 6 December 1765, he reached Calcutta in the East India Company's civil service in 1783 and was soon appointed Persian translator to government. In the capacity as acting private secretary to the governor-general he participated in the campaign against Tippoo Sultan and thereafter translated and published the documents found in Tippoo's palace. He later held high office in the Indian administration; he had become a member of the supreme council at Calcutta when he left India after thirty-four years' service. From 1820 until his death in 1841 he was a director of the East India Company in London. Buckland; DNB

Edsman, Carl Martin, born 26 July 1911 at Malmberget, Sweden, he obtained a doctorate of divinity in 1940 from Uppsala Universitet for his thesis *La baptême du feu*. Except for three years spent at Lund Universitet, he was at Uppsala from 1940 until his retirement. He was connected since 1959 in various capacities and functions with the Board of the Donner Institute of Research in Religious and Cultural History, Abo, Finland, and its library, the Steiner Memorial Library. His writings include *Ignis divinus* (1949), as well as numerous articles in the fields of folklore and the history of religions. *Dictionary of Scandinavian biography*, 2d ed., 1976

Edwardes, Stephen Meredyth, born in 1873, he was educated at Eton and Christ Church, Oxford, and in 1895 entered the Indian Civil Service, where he served as collector, magistrate, and secretary to government. From 1909 to 1916 he was commissioner of Police in Bombay. He retired from the Service in 1918. His writings include *Crime in India* (1924), *Babur, diarist and despot* (1926), and *Mughal rule in India* (1930). He died in 1927. Master (1); Who was who, 2

Edwards, Albert, pseud., 1879-1929 *see* Bullard, Arthur

Edwards, Arthur Cecil, born in 1881 at Constantinople, he was a carpet merchant who spent his whole working life in a detailed study not only of the marketing of oriental carpets, but also in the technique of their manufacture. As a young man, in the employ of his two uncles, he had experience of the buying and selling of oriental carpets both in Constantinople and London. Soon after the formation of the Oriental Carpet Manufacturers Ltd. in 1908, he went to Persia with a small staff to begin operations on an ever-increasing scale, opening up manufacturing branches in all the important weaving centres. In 1924, he was appointed London manager of the Company. He was recognized in London as the leading authority on oriental carpets of all types - not only of Persian qualities but also of Indian and Turkish makes, for he paid numerous visits to India and Turkey. During the second World War, he gave his time freely in the service of the Foreign Office Research Department. After his retirement he lectured to many societies, colleges, and schools. His writings include *A Persian caravan* (1928), and *The Persian carpet* (1953). He died 11 September 1951. Journal of the Iran Society 1 (1950/51), pp. 147-148

Edwards, Bela Bates, born 4 July 1802 at Southampton, Mass., he was a graduate of Amherst College and Andover Theological Seminary. He had a long career as editor of educational and religious publications before he accepted an appointment as professor of Hebrew language and literature in Andower Theological Seminary. A born philanthropist, he was interested in missionary enterprises and social reforms, including temperance and anti-slavery. He died in 1852. DAB; DcNAA; Master (9); WhAm, H

Edwards, Clara Cary Case, died in 1955, she was the wife of Arthur Cecil Edwards, 1881-1951. Her correspondence, 1911-1923, is located in Bryn Mawr College Library. LC

Edwards, Clive Thomas, fl. 1969, his writings include *Public finances in Malaya and Singapore* (1970), and *Reconstructing Australian manufacturing industry* (1978). LC

Edwards, E. W., born about 1918, he received an M.A. in 1939 from the University of Wales for his thesis, *British policy with relation to Morocco, 1902-1906*. When he retired in 1983, he had been a senior lecturer in history at University College, Cardiff, for over twenty years His writings include *British diplomacy and finance in China, 1895-1914* (1983). LC; Sluglett

Edwards, Edward, born in 1870, he ended his career as an assistant keeper at the Department of Oriental Printed Books and Manuscripts in the British Museum, London. His writings include *A catalogue of the Persian printed books in the British Museum* (1922), *A facsimile of the manuscript (Or. 9777) of Diwan i Zu'l-Fakar*, edited with introduction (1934), and he was joint author of *A descriptive list of the Arabic manuscripts acquired by the Trustees of the British Museum since 1894* (1912). LC

Edwards, Frederick Augustus, fl. 1887-1923, he was a fellow of the Royal Geographical Society and affiliated with the Hampshire Field Club. He published a number of articles on African affairs and antiquities in the *Asiatic quarterly review*. BLC

Edwards, John Arwel, he was in 1965 affiliated with the British Council, Lahore. He was joint editor of *Llantrisant new town, the case against* (1974). LC

Edzard, Dietz Otto, born 30 March 1893, he received a Dr.phil. in 1955 from the Universität Heidelberg for his thesis, *Die zweite Zwischenzeit Babyloniens*. His writings include *Cuneiform texts* (1971), and he was a joint editor of the *Reallexikon der Assyriologie* (1928), and a contributing author to *Götter und Mythen im Vorderen Orient* (1965). He died 8 January 1963. LC; Schwarz

Eekelaar, John Michael, born 2 July 1942 at Johannesburg, he obtained degrees at London and Oxford, where he was a Rhodes scholar from 1963 to 1965, and afterwards a fellow and tutor in law at Pembroke College. In 1976 he became a research fellow in the Centre for Socio-Legal Studies, Wolfson College, Cambridge. He wrote *Family, security and family breakdown* (1971). ConAu, 116

Eeman, Albert, born in 19th cent., he was in 1916 affiliated with the Attorney General of the Mixed Tribunal, Alexandria, and a member of the Société sultanieh d'économie politique, de statistique et de législation. Note

Eerdmans, Bernardus Dirks, born in 1868 at Maasdam, he received a doctorate in divinity in 1891 from the Rijksuniversiteit te Leiden for his thesis, *Melekdienst en vereering van hemellichamen in Israël's assyrische periode*. He was a preacher at Midwoud from 1896 to 1898, when he was appointed a professor of Jewish history and literature at Leiden. His writings include *Alttestamentliche Studien* (1908-1912), *De godsdienst van Israël* (1930), its translation, *The religion of Israel* (1947), and he was a joint editor of *Theologisch tijdschrift*, Leiden, 1909-1919. Wie is dat, 1902

Efendiev (Эфендиев, Äfändiiev), Oktai Abdulkerim ogly, born 26 March 1926 at Baku, he graduated from the Moscow Oriental Institute in 1950, and he received a doctorate in 1968 at Baku for his thesis, *Азербайджанское государство сефевидов в XVI веке*. His writings include *Образование Азербайджанского государства сефевидов в начале XVI века* (1961),and *Азербайджанское государство сефевидов в XVI веке* (1981). LC; Miliband; Miliband[2]

Efendiev (Эфендиев, Äfändi, Äfändiiev), Rasim Samed ogly, fl. 1959, his writings include *Azärbaijan el sänäti* (1971), *Azärbaijan dekoratif-tatbigi sänätlari* (1976), Azärbaijan khalg sänäti = *Народное искусство Азербайджана* (1984), and *Каменная пластика Азербайджана* (1986). LC

Efendieva (Эфендиева), Nilufer Zakir kyzy, born 19 May 1925 in Azerbaijan, she graduated in 1950 from the Historical Faculty, Baku, and obtained her first degree in 1963 for her thesis, *Борьба турецкого народа против французских оккупантов, 1919-1921 гг*. She was affiliated with the Near and Middle East Institute, Azerbaijan Academy of Science, since 1960. Her writings include *Борьба турецкого народа против французских оккупантов на юге Анатолии, 1919-1921 гг.* (1966). LC; Miliband; Miliband[2]

Efimenco, Nicholas Marbury, fl. 1955, he received a Ph.D. in 1948 from the University of Minnesota for his thesis, *Imperialism and the League; experiment with the mandate system*. He was affiliated with the University of Michigan. NUC, pre-1956

Efimov, Eduard Sergeevich, born 20th cent., his writings include *Планирование и развитие экономики Египта; вторая половина XX века* (1990).

Efimov, Gerontii Valentinovich, born 21 March (3 April) 1906 at Rozhdestvenskaya Khava, Russia, he graduated in 1932 from Leningrad Faculty of History and Philology and received a doctorate in 1955 at Leningrad for his thesis, *Международные отношения Китая и внешняя политика Цинского правительства в конце XIX века*. He was a historian of modern China. His writings include *Сунь Ятсен; поиск пути, 1914-1922* (1981). He died 3 June 1980. LC; Miliband; Miliband[2]

Efimov, Valentin Aleksandrovich, born 22 March 1933 at Galich, Russia, he graduated in 1957 from the Institute of Oriental Linguistics, Moscow. His writings include *Язык афганских хазара* (1965), *Яазык ормури в синхронном и исторческом освещении* (1986), and he edited *Сравнительно-историческая грамматика западно-иранских языков* (1990). Miliband; Miliband[2]

Efimova, Larisa Mikhailovna, born 20th cent., her writings include *Религиозные традиции в политической жизни современной Индонесии; 1965-1992* (1992). LC

Efrat, Elisha, born 20 April 1929 at Danzig, he received a doctorate in 1963 from the Hebrew University, Jerusalem, for a Hebrew thesis with the English added title page, *The influence of geographic factors on the physical planning of the Jerusalem region*. In 1977 he was a professor of geography at Tel Aviv University. His writings include *Urbanization in Israel* (1984), and he was joint author of *Geography of Israel* (1964). LC; WhoWorJ, 1978

Efrat, Moshe, born in 1927, he was a sometime senior research fellow at LSE and joint editor of *Superpowers and client states in the Middle East; the imbaôance of influence* (1991).

Efremov, Filipp Sergeevich, born in 1750 at Biatka (Kirov), Russia, he was a non-commisioned officer who was captured in the Orenburg steppes and enslaved in Bukhara. After he escaped he travelled in Central Asia. His writings include *Десятилетнее странствованіе и приключеніе в Бухаріи* (1786), *Странствованіе ... в Бухаріи, Хиве,Персіи и Индіи, и возвращеніе оттуда чрез Англію в Россію* (1794), and *Девятилетнее странствование* (1952). He died after 1811. BiobibSOT; GSE

Efremov, L. P., fl. 1960, his writings include *Основы теории лексического калькирования* (1974).

Efros, Israel *Isaac*, born 28 May 1891 at Ostroy, Poland, he came to the United States as a teenager. He received a Ph.D. in 1916 from Columbia Unibersity for his thesis, *The problem of space in Jewish medieval philosophy*. He was later ordained at the Jewish Theological Seminary, NYC, and served as a professor of Hebrew and Jewish literature and philosophy at universities throughout the United States. He died in Tel Aviv, 4 January 1981. BioIn, 12; CnDiAmJBi; ConAu, 102, 21 new rev.; EncJud; Master (2); WhoAmJ, 1965; Wininger

Eganian (Eganiyan), Gamlet (Hamlet) Mnatsakanovich (Mnats'akani), born 13 August 1925 at Tabriz, he graduated at Erevan in 1951. For many years, he was affiliated with the Historical Institute, and subsequently with the Oriental Institute of the Armenian Academy of Science. Miliband

Eger, Gudrun, born 20th cent., her writings include *Die Auswirkungen der religiösen und sozial-traditionellen Verhältnisse auf die bevölkerungspolitische Situation in Pakistan* (1971), *Familienplanung in Pakistan* (1973), *Familienplanungsprogramme oder Änderung der sozio-ökonomischen Verhältnisse*, a revison of her 1974 München thesis, as well as *Das Comilla-Genossenschaftsprogramm ...* (1982).

Egerton, Granville George Algernon, born in 1859, he was a graduate of the Royal Military College, Sandhurst, and rose to the rank of major-general in 1912. He served in the Afghan War, 1879-80, the Egyptian War, 1882, and the Sudan campaign, 1898. He died in 1951. BioIn, 2; Who was who, 5

Eggeling, Willi Johannes, born in 1948, he received a Dr. rer. nat. in 1973 from the Universität Bochum for his thesis, *Beiträge zur Kulturgeographie des Küçük-Menderes-Gebietes*. His writings include *Türkei; Land, Volk, Wirtschaft in Stichworten* (1978), and he was joint author of *Entwicklung und räumliche Analyse der türkischen Binnenverkehrsnetze* (1979).

Eggers, Thies, fl. 1976, he was joint author of *Iran-Engagement; Einführung in das Gesellschafts-recht, Steuerrecht und Volksaktienprogramm* (1977).

Eghiayean (Eghiayian/Yeghiyan), Biwzand (Puzant), born in 1900, he was affiliated with the Armenian Seminary at Antilyas, Lebanon. His writings, all published at the seat of the Seminary, include *Mankavarzhakan dasakhosut'iwnner* (1965), *Zhamanakakits' patmut'iwn Kat'oghikosut'ian Hayots' Kilikioy, 1914-1972* (1975), and *Karawaně; patmuatsk'ner* (1979). LC; Note

Egiazarov, Solomon Adamovich, born in 1852, he was a professor at Kazan, 1892-93, and since 1893 affiliated with Kiev university. His writings include *О водовлденіи въ Закав-казскомъ крае* (Kiev, 1896). He died after 1917. LC; OSK; TatarES

Eglar, Zekiye Suleyman, fl. 1971, she received a Ph.D. in 1958 from Columbia University, N.Y.C., for his thesis, *Vartan bhanji; institutionalized reciprocity in a changing Punjabi village*. His writings include *A Punjabi village in Pakistan* (1960). NUC, 1956-1967

Egorov, Vadim Leonidovich, born in 1938, he was an archaeologist who received a doctorate in history in 1987. His writings include *Историческая география Золотой Орды в XIII-XIV вв.* (1985). LC; TatarES

Egorov, Vasilii Georgevich, born 11 February 1880 near Kazan, Russia, his writings include *Русско-чувашский словарь* (1960), and *Этимологический словарь чувашского языка* (1964). He died 25 January 1974. BiobibSOT, p. 160; LC; *Советская тюркология*, 1974 № 1, pp. 123-124

Eguaras Ibáñez, Joaquina, born in January 1897 in Navarra, she studied philosophy and liberal arts at the Universidad de Granada, where she graduated in 1922. Three years later, she was appointed an assistant at its Facultad de Filosofía y Letras. In 1944 she received a doctorate for a thesis on *Kitāb al-filāhah*. From 1947 untill her retirement in 1967, she was a professor of Arabic at Granada. She died 25 April 1981. Qantara 2 (1981), pp. 465-468; Ruiz C

Eguchi, Paul Kazuhisa, born in 1942, he was affiliated with the Institute for the Study of Languages and Cultures of Africa and Asia, Tokyo, and the National Museum of Ethnology, Osaka. His writings include *Miscellany of Maroua Fulfulde* (1974), *An English-Fulfulde dictionary* (1986), and he was the compiler of *Fulfulde tales of North Cameroon* (1978-1984). LC

de **Eguilaz y Yanguas**, Leopoldo, born 29 September 1829 or 1830 at Mazarrón (Murcia), he was a professor of Spanish literature, and dean of the Facultad de Filosofía y Letras in the Universidad de Granada. His writings include *Glossario etimológico de las palabras españolas de orígen oriental* (1886). He died in 1906. Cuenca; EncicUni; Manzanares

Ehgartner, Wilhelm, born 23 February 1914 at Graz, Austria, he studied anthropology at Wien, where he received a Dr.phil. in 1939, and a Dr.habil. in 1957 for his thesis, *Die Schädel aus dem frühbronzezeitlichen Gräberfeld von Hainburg.* At the time of his death, he was head of the Anthropologische Abteilung, Naturhistorisches Museum, Wien. From 1960 to 1963 he was affiliated with the Unesco preservation project in Nubia. He died 9 November 1965. Bustan 7 (1966), pp. 33-34

Ehlers, Eckart, born 1 March 1938 at Duisburg, Germany, he studied geography and geology at Marburg, Kiel, and Tübingen, where received a doctorate in 1965 for his thesis, *Das nördliche Peace River Country, Alberta.* Scholarships enabled him to study at Southampton, 1959/60, and the University of Alberta, Edmonton, 1962/63. Since 1972 he was a professor of geography at Marburg. His writings include *Südkaspisches Tiefland und Kaspisches Meer ... im Jung- und Postpleistozän* (1970), *Traditionelle und moderne Formen der Landwirtschaft in Iran* (1975), and *Iran; Grundzüge einer geographischen Landeskunde* (1980). Kürschner, 1980-1992|; Schwarz; Thesis

Ehmann, Dieter, born 20th cent., he received a doctorate in 1975 from the Universität Tübingen for his thesis *Bahtiaren; persische Bergnomaden im Wandel der Zeit* (1975), a Persian translation of which was published in 1988. Schwarz; ZKO

Ehmann, Günter, born 20th cent., his writings include *Bildungspolitik und Hochschulpolitik in der Bundesrepublik Deutschland aus der Sicht praxisorientierter ... Studiengänge* (1993). LC

von **Ehrenfels**, Omar (Umar) Rolf Leopold Werner, Baron, born 28 April 1901 at Prag, Austria-Hungary, he received a Dr.phil. in 1937 from the Universität Wien. In the 1960s he was a professor of anthropology and head of department, University of Madras, and a president of the Anthropological Society of Madras. His writings include *Mother-right in India* (1941), *Kadar of Cochin* (1952), and *The light continent* (1960). LC; Unesco

Ehrenkreutz, Andrew Stefan, born 19 December 1921 in Poland, he received a Ph.D. in 1952 from SOAS for his thesis, *Contributions to the history of the Islamic mint in the middle ages.* His writings include *Saladin* (1972), and a collection of his articles, edited by J. L. Bacharach, *Monetary change and economic history in the medieval Muslim world* (1992). LC; Sluglett

Ehrensvärd, E. M. Ulla M., born in 1927, she studied history of art at Stockholm Universitet, where she also received a doctorate in 1975. Her writings include *Böcker och bibliotek* (1983), and she was joint author of *Gunnar Jarring; en bibliografi* (1977). Vem är det, 1981-1999

Ehrig, Friedrich Reiner, born 13 January 1942 at Arnstadt, Germany, he studied geography, zoology, and botany at the Universität München, where he received a doctorate in 1971 for his thesis, *Reale Vegetation und natürlicher Wald auf Korsika.* Thesis

Ehrig-Eggert, Carl, born about 1950, he received a Dr.phil. in 1983 from Ruhr-Universität, Bochum, for his thesis, *Die Abhandlung über den Nachweis der Natur des Möglichen von Yahya Ibn 'Adi.* From the 1980s throughout the 1990s he was a senior researcher in the Institut für Geschichte der Arabisch-Islamischen Wissenschaften, Frankfurt am Main. His writings include *al-Jughrafiya* (1990), and he was joint editor of the twenty-two volume *Bibliographie der deutschsprachigen Arabistik und Islamkunde* (1990-1993). Private

Ehteshami, Anoushiravan, born 21 December 1958, he studied at Nottingham City University and the University of Exeter, Devon, where he became a lecturer in Middle East politics and research fellow in international relations and strategic studies. He was the founding editor of *Middle East strategic studies quarterly*, and administrative editor of *BRISMES newsletter*. His writings include *Nuclearisation of the Middle East* (1989), *After Khomeini* (1995), and he was joint author of *War and peace in the Gulf* (1991), and joint editor of *Iran and the international community* (1991). EURAMES, 1993; LC; Private

Eichhorn, Johann Gottfried, born in 1752, he was a theologian and Biblical scholar at the Universität Jena from 1775 to 1788, when he was appointed professor of Oriental languages at Göttingen, a post which he held until his death in 1827. He was the editor of *Repertorium für biblische und morgenländische Litteratur*, 1777-1786. ADtB; BBHS; BiD&SB; CelCen; DtBE; LuthC, 1975

Eichlehner, Nikolaus, born 6 December 1904 at Raab, Hungary, he studied electrical engineering at the Technische Hochschule, Wien, and thereafter served for twenty years as a vocational school teacher, and head of department in Austrian schools. He entered the Bundesministerium für Unterricht in 1949 and was responsible for technical and vocational education. He visited Mosul in 1957, and Tehran in 1958, with a view of organizing and establishing technical schools. WhoAustria, 1967, 1969/70, 1977/78; 1982/83|

Eichler, Gert, born 21 June 1942 at Berlin-Schmargendorf, he studied geography, history, and political science at Kiel, and the Freie Universität Berlin, where he received a doctorate in 1976 for his thesis, *Algiers Sozialökonomie, 1955-1970.* Since 1974 he held an academic position in the Universität Marburg. Thesis

Eichner, Wolfgang, born 12 March 1911 at Duisburg, Germany, he studied at Kiel, Theologische Schule Bethel, Erlangen, and Bonn, where he received a Dr. phil. in 1936 for his thesis, *Nachrichten über den Islam bei den Byzantinern.* Schwarz; Thesis

Eichthal, Gustave d', born 22 March 1804 at Nancy, he was a Saint Simonian and began studying social problems, but subsequently applied himself to ethnology. He spent some time in Greece. A refugee for some time in England on the fall of Napoleon, he was permitted to return to France in 1872. His writings include *Mélanges de critique biblique* (1886), *Les trois grands peuples méditerranéens et le christianisme* (1887), and the translation, *French sociologist looks at Britain; Gustave d'Eichthal and British society in 1828* (1977). He died in Paris, 9 April 1882. BiD&SB; Bioln, 10, 11; CelCen; BDF; DcBiPP; EncJud; Wininger

von **Eichwald** (Эйхвальд), Carl Eduard, born 4 July 1795 at Mitau, Kurland, he studied at Berlin and Wien, and received a medical doctorate in 1819 at Vilna. He was a natural scientist who held the chair of zoology at Kazan from where he made a scientific excursion to the Caspian Sea and the Caucasus, 1825-1826. His writings include *Reise auf dem Caspischen Meere und in den Caucasus* (1834-37), and *Alte Geographie des Kaspischen Meeres, des Kaukasus und des südlichen Rußlands* (1838). He died in St. Petersburg, 10 November 1876. Baltisch (7); DcBiPP; DtBE; DtBilnd (7); Embacher; GSE; Henze

Eickelman, Dale Floyd, born 15 December 1942 at Evergreen Park, Illinois, he received an M.A. from the Institute of Islamic Studies, McGill University, for *Musaylimah; an anthropological appraisal,* and a Ph.D. in 1972 from Chicago for *Secret of ancestors; a study of the secularization of a Moroccan religious lodge.* Since 1989 he was a Ralph and Richard Lazarus professor of anthropology and human relations at Dartmouth College. He was a member of learned societies and a past president of MESA. His writings include *Moroccan Islam* (1976), *The Middle East; an anthropological approach* (1981), *Knowledge and power in Morocco* (1985), and *Muslim politics* (1996); he was editor of *Russia's Muslim frontiers* (1993), and joint author of *Muslim travellers; pilgrimage, migration, and the religious imagination* (1990), and *Muslim politics* (1996). Ferahian; NatFacDr, 1995-1999; Private; Selim; WhoE, 1986/87

Eickhoff, Ekkehard, born 8 June 1927 at Berlin, he received a Dr.phil. in 1954 from the Universität des Saarlandes for his thesis, *Seekrieg und Seepolitik zwischen Islam und Abendland bis zum Aufstiege Pisas und Genuas, 650-1040,* and later entered the diplomatic service. His writings include *Venedig, Wien und die Osmanen* (1970), and *Friedrich Barbarossa im Orient* (1977). Kürschner, 1976-1996; Schwarz; Wer ist wer, 1979-1998/99; WhoWor, 1984/85-1987|

Eid, Albert, born in 1886 at Cairo, he was an Egyptian antiquities dealer and collector. He died in Cairo in 1950. Egyptology

Eid, Mehanny, fl. 1955, his writings include *Zeheri catalogue for postage stamps of Egypt, U.A.R., and the Sudan,* 9th ed. (1972). LC

Eidelberg, Shlomo, born in 1918, he received a Ph.D. from Yeshiva University for his thesis, *The responsa of Rabbi Gershom ben Judah Me'or ha-Golah as a source of the history of the Jews in France and Germany.* His writings include *Jewish life in Austria in the XVth century ...* (1962), *The Jews and the crusades* (1977), and *R. Yuzpa Shamash di-kehilat Vermaiśa* (1991). LC

Eiiubi (Эйюби), Kerim Rakhmanovich, born in 1924, his writings include *Курдский диалект Мукри* (1968), and he was joint author of *Фонетика курдского языка* (1985). LC

Eikenberg, Christian, born in 1939, he was a regional representative of Kinderdorf SOS. His writings include *Marokko; Rahmenbedingungen und Struktur der marokkanischen Wirtschaft* (1977), and *Sozioökonomische Probleme der tunesischen Wasserwirtschaft* (1982). LC

Eikhval'd, Eduard Ivanovich, 1795-1876 see Eichwald, Carl Eduard von

Eiland, Murray Lee, born 9 September 1936 at Taft, Calif., he was a medical doctor, a psychiatrist, and, since 1974, president of Oriental Rug Company. His writings include *Oriental rugs* (1973), *Chinese and exotic rugs* (1979), and he was joint author of *Weavers, merchants, and kings; the inscribed rugs of Armenia* (1984). ConAu, 85-88; LC; WhoWest, 1976/77-1984/85|

Eilers, Wilhelm Max Johannes, born 27 September 1906 at Leipzig. After completing his legal studies with a Dr.jur. in 1931 from the Universität Leipzig for *Gesellschaftsformen im altbabylonischen Recht*, he pursued Oriental studies which he completed in 1938 with his thesis, *Iranische Beamtennamen in der keilschriftlichen Überlieferung*. During the war he was interned first in Iran, and later in Australia, where he taught for five years until he returned to Germany in 1952. He worked as a Persian subject specialist at the Westdeutsche Bibliothek, Marburg, and concurrently lectured at the Universität until 1958, when he was appointed a professor at Würzburg, a position he held until his retirement. His writings include *Deutsch-persisches Wörterbuch*, A-F (1959-83), *Die Al, ein persisches Kindbettgespenst* (1979), and *Geographische Namensgebung in und um Iran* (1982). He died in Würzburg, 3 July 1989. BioB134; *Index Islamicus* (3); Kürschner; LingH; Schwarz; WhoWor, 1978/79-1982/83

Eilts, Hermann Frederick, born 23 March 1922 at Weißenfels, Germany, he was brought to the United States in 1926. He was a graduate of Ursinus College, and then studied at Johns Hopkins' School of Advanced International Studies, as well as the University of Pennsylvania. He was for over thirty years in the U.S. Foreign Service, posted to the Middle East. He later was a professor and director at the Center for International Relations, Boston University. Since 1993 he was a Middle East consultant. BlueB, 1973/74, 1975, 1976; DcAmDH; IntWW, 1979-1998/99; Master (4); MidE, 1982/83; Shavit

Eimer, Helmut, born 14 June 1936 at Stettin, Germany, he pursued Oriental studies at Hamburg, Berlin, and Bonn, where he received a Dr.phil. in 1974 for his thesis, *Berichte über das Leben des Dipamkaraśrijñana*. His writings include *Tibetica Uosaliensia* (1975), and *Some results of recent Kanjur research* (1983). Kürschner, 1987-1996; LC

Einsler, Lydia née Schick, fl. 1887-1896, her writings include *Mosaik aus dem Heiligen Lande; Schilderungen der arabischen Bevölkerung Palästinas* (Jerusalem, Druck des Syrischen Waisenhauses, 1898). NUC, pre-1956

Einstein, Lewis David, born 15 March 1877 at N.Y.C. After graduating from Cc   ·sity, he entered the diplomatic service, and was posted at Constantinople before and 477 t World War. His writings include *Inside Constantinople; a diplomat's diary during the Dardanelles expedition* (1917), *Looking at Italian pictures at the National Gallery of Art, Washington* (1951), and *A diplomat looks back* (1968). He died at the American Hospital, Paris, 1 December 1967. BioIn, 7, 8; DcAmDH; EncJud; Master (1); ObitT, 1961; Shavit; WhNAA; Wininger

Einzmann, Harald, he received a doctorate in 1976 from the Universität Heidelberg for his thesis, *Religiöses Volksbrauchtum in Afghanistan; islamische Heiligenverehrung und Wallfahrtswesen im Raum Kabul*. His writings include *Ziarat und Pir-e Muridi* (1988). LC; Schwarz

Eiselt, Josef, born 3 May 1935 at Wien, he completed his study of zoology and botany with a doctorate. He was for many years a keeper of the amphibian and reptile collection at the Naturhistorisches Museum, Wien. He first visited Istanbul in 1935, and retained an interest in the Middle East throughout his career. Kürschner, 1970, 1976, 1980, 1992|

Eisemann, Gudrun, fl. 1974, she was involved in cultural and student exchange, and in charge of the Zentrale Nachkontaktsstelle, Carl-Duisberg-Gesellschaft, Stuttgart, as well as a member of the editorial staff of its journal, *Echo aus Deutschland*. Note

Eisenbach, Zvi, born 20th cent., he received a Ph.D. in 1978 from the Hebrew University, Jerusalem, for his thesis, *Megamot ve-shinuyim be-firyon ha-ukhlusiyah ha-Muslemit be-Yiśra'el*. He was joint author of *Demographic and socio-economic aspects of population aging in Israel* (1991). LC

Eisenberg, Isaac, born in 1884 at Pinsk, Russia, he was educated at the Rabbinical Seminary, Wolożin, Gouvernement Vilna. Thereafter he studied at Prag, 1893-1894, followed by two years at Berlin. He received a Dr.phil. in 1898 from the Universität Bern for his thesis, *Die Prophetenlegenden des Muhammed ben Abdallah al-Kisâî*. Thesis

Eisenbeth, Maurice, born 4 June 1883 at Paris. After a classical education at Paris, he entered the Grand séminaire israélite in 1902, and was ordained in 1912. He became great rabbi of Constantine, in 1928, of Alger in 1932, and of Algeria in 1940. He spared no effort to support and save his co-religionists during the war, a task which he described in *Pages vécues, 1940-1943* (1945). His writings include also *Le judaïsme nord-africain* (1932), *Les Juifs de l'Afrique du nord* (1936), *Les Juifs au Maroc* (1948), and *Les Juifs en Algérie et en Tunisie à l'époque turque, 1516-1830* (1952). He died 15 January 1958. DBF; *Revue africaine* 103 (1959), pp. 166-167

Eisendle, Edwin, fl. 1974, he received a Dr.phil. in 1973 from the Universität Graz for his thesis, *Das Volk der Amir im antiken Südarabien und seine Personennamen*. Schwarz

Eisenhower, Dwight David, born 14 October 1890 at Denison, Texas, he was a General of the Army, and from 1953 to 1961 the thirty-fourth president of the United States. Of Middle East relevance is the U.S. Congress resolution of 5 January 1957, usually referred to as the Eisenhower doctrine. His writings include *Peace with justice* (1961). He died 29 March 1969. Encyclopedia America; WhAm, 5

Eisenstadt, Shmuel Noah, born 10 September 1923 at Warszawa, he was educated at the Hebrew University, Jerusalem, where he also took his doctorate. He became a professor of sociology and a dean of faculty, as well as a visiting professor abroad. His writings include *The absorption of immigrants* (1954), *The development of the ethnic problem in Israel* (1986), and he was joint editor of *Political clientilism, patronage, and development* (1981). He was honoured by the jubilee volume, *Comparative social dynamics; essays in honor of S. N. Eisenstadt* (1985). ConAu, 25-28; EncJud; IntAu&W, 1977, 1982; IntWW, 1974-1998/99; Master (2); MideE, 1982/83; WhoIsrael, 1955; WhoWor, 1982-1989/90|; WrDr, 1980-1998/2000

Eisner, Jan, born 26 April 1885, he was a Slovak historian and archaeologist, and a sometime professor of archaeology at Universita Karolava, Praha. His writings include *Rukovět' slovanské archeologie* (1966). He died 2 May 1967. MaláčEnc

Eißfeldt, Otto Hermann Wilhelm, born 1 September 1887 at Northeim, Germany, he studied at Göttingen and Berlin and became a preacher. He later was a lecturer at Berlin until 1922, when he was appointed a professor of Old Testament studies at Halle, where he died on 27 April 1973. His writings include *Quellen des Richterbuches* (1925), *Einleitung in das Alte Testament* (1934), and *Von den Anfängen der phönizischen Epigraphik* (1948). DtBE; IntWW, 1969/70, 1973/74, 1974/85; Wer ist's, 1922, 1928, 1935; Wer ist wer, 1950. 1955, 1958|

Eister, Allan Wardell, born 10 February 1915 at Upper Sandusky, Ohio, he was a graduate of DePauw University, and received a Ph.D. in 1945 from the University of Wisconsin. He was a professor of sociology and head of department at home and abroad. From 1959 to 1960 he was a senior Fulbright lecturer at the University of Karachi. He was a Quaker and did civilian public service as conscientious objector, 1940-1944. His writings include *The United States and the A.B.C. powers, 1899-1906* (1951), and *Changing perspectives in the scientific study of religions* (1974). He died on 22 March 1979. AmM&WS, 1978; ConAu, 45-48, 2 new rev.; WhoAm, 1976-1978; WhAm, 7

Eitan, Israel, born 23 April 1885 at Warszawa, he was educated at Hebrew schools, the Séminaire israélite de France, the universities of Paris and Montpellier, and received a Ph.D. in 1924 from Columbia University for his thesis, *A contribution to Biblical lexicography*. He was resident in Palestine from 1904 until 1921, when he went to the United States, where he spent his last eleven years in Pittsburgh, Pa., at the Teachers Training School of the Hebrew Institute. He died 11 October 1935. CnDiAmJBi; DcNAA; WhNAA

Eivasian, Garabed (Jean Baptiste), born 10 August 1879 at Maraş, Turkey, he was a native Turkish-speaking Armenian who, from 1895 to 1907, trained at the Séminaire oriental Saint-François-Xaxier, Beirut. He served as a missionary at Maraş until 1912, when he was sent as a temporary replacement to the dangerous Zeytun (Süleymanlı) Mission, where he died of a stomach ailment, 19 August 1912.

Ekblom, Richard, born 30 October 1874 at Ekby, Sweden, he was a professor of Slavic linguistics at Uppsala Universitet from 1921 to 1939. His writings include *Die frühe dorsale Palatalisierung im Slavischen* (1951), and he edited *Rysk grammatik*, 6th ed. (1966). He died 7 April 1959. Vem är det, 1925, 1941, 1949, 1953, 1955, 1957, 1959

Ekin, Nusret, born 17 July 1932 at İzmit, Turkey, he received a doctorate in 1957, and was successively a lecturer, professor, and dean of the Faculty of Economics at İstanbul Üniversitesi. His writings include *İşgücü ve ekonomik gelişme* (1968), *Gelişen ülkelerde ve Türkiye'de bir istihdam politikası olarak küçük ölçekli işyerlerinin teşviki* (1993), and he was a joint author of several other publications. Kim kimdir, 1985/86, 1997/98

Ekrem, Hadije Selma, born about 1900 at Constantinople, she was the daughter of Ali Ekrem Bolayır, sometime governor of Ottoman Jerusalem and later governor-general of the Aegean Islands. She grew up in the Ottoman Empire. In the 1930s she was resident in the United States, where she was engaged in lecturing and writings on Turkey. Her writings include *Unveiled; the autobiography of a Turkish girl* (1930), *Turkey, old and new* (1947), and *Turkish fairy tales* (1964). Asia, 1930

Ekwensi, Cyprian Odiatu Duaka, born 26 September 1921 at Minna, Nigeria. After his graduation from Ibadan University, he studied pharmacology in the UK and the USA. After a brief career at colleges in Lagos, 1947-1956, he entered public service at the Nigerian Broadcasting Corporation, followed by the Ministry of Education. Since 1970 he was in private business and concurrently a consultant, and a writer of African stories. His writings include *Burning grass; a story of the Fulani of*

Northern Nigeria (1962), *An African night's entertainment* (1962), and *Survive the peace* (1976). AfricaWW, 1996; IntWW, 1974-1997/98; Master (20); MEW; WorAu; WrDr, 1976-1998/2000

El Araby, Kadri M. Gharib, 1931- *see* Araby, Kadri Mohamed Gharib el-

El Baz, Farouk *see* Baz, Faruq al-

El Daly, El Sayed A. *see* Daly, El Sayed A.

El-Kammash, Magdi Mohamed, 1931- *see* Kammash, Magdi Mohamed El-

El Mallakh, Ragaei, 1925- *see* Mallakh, Ragaei El-

El Sammani, Mohammed Osman, 1939- *see* Sammani, Mohammed Osman El-

Elagin, Andrei Sergeevich, Dr., fl. 1956, his writings include *Из истории героической борьбы партизан Семиречья* (1957), *Социалистическое строительство в Казахстане в годы гражданской войны, 1918-1920 гг.* (1966), and he was joint author of *Семипалатинск* (1984). LC

Elahi, Cyrus, born in 1943, he received a Ph.D. in 1970 from the American University, Washington, D.C., for his thesis, *Society and foreign policy in Iran*. NUC, 1968-1972

Elam, Yigal, born in 1936, he was an Israeli historian who received a Ph.D. from the Hebrew University, Jerusalem. His writings include *Toldot Yiśra'el ba-dorot ha-aharonim* (1967), *Me-hazon li-medinah* (1978), *ha-Haganah* (1979), *Memal'e ha-pekudot* (1990), and *ha-Shokhnut ha-Yehudit* (1990). LC

Elath, Eliahu, born E. Epstein. 30 July 1903 at Snocsk, Russia, he went to Palestine in 1925. He was in charge of the Middle East Department of the Jewish Agency for Palestine, and in 1948 became the first Israeli ambassador to the U.S.A. He was the recipient of several honorary doctorates. His writings include *ha-Bedvim* (1933), and *Zionism at the UN* (1976). He died 24 June 1990. ConAu, 13-16, 132; EncJud; IntWW, 1974-1990/91; Master (7); MideE, 1982/83; WhAm, 10; Who, 1974-1990; WhoIsrael, 1949-1985/86|; WhoWorJ, 1965, 1972, 1978

Elaut, Louis, he was a writer on the history of medicine and received a doctorate in 1956 for his thesis, *Van smeinscen lede; een Middelnederlands geneeskundig geschrift*. He wrote *Het leven van de Gentse ziekenhuizen* (1976), and he compiled *Antieke geneeskunde, in teksten van Griekse en Latijnse auteurs* (1960). LC

Elbir, Halid Kemal, born in 1921, he obtained a doctorate and became a professor at the Faculty of Law, İstanbul Üniversitesi. His writings include *Gerekçeli - notlu - sistematik Türk ticaret kanunu ve tatbikat ile alâkalı mevzuat* (1958), and *Türk borçlar hukuku* (1958). TB

Elbogen, Ismar, born 1 September 1874 at Schildberg, Germany, he studied at Jüdisches Theologisches Seminar and the Universität, Breslau, where he received a Dr.phil. in 1898 for his thesis, *Der Tractus de intellectus emendatione und seine Stellung in der Philosophie Spinozas*. He taught Jewish history and Biblical exegesis at the Collegio Rabbinico Italiano, Firenze, from 1899 to 1902, when he returned to Germany. From 1919 to his forced emigration in 1938, he was a professor at the Hochschule für die Wissenschaft des Judentums, Berlin. During the last years of his life in America, he taught at the Hebrew Union College, N.Y.C. His writings include *Der jüdische Gottesdienst in seiner geschichtliche Entwicklung* (1913), its translation, *Jewish liturgy* (1993), and he collaborated with the production of the *Jüdisches Lexikon* and *Encyclopaedia Judaica*. He died in NYC, 1 August 1943. CnDiAmJBi; DtBE; Master (3); Wininger

El'chibekov (Эльчибеков), Kudratbek, born 23 November 1938 at Gorno-Badakhshan A.O., he was a graduate of the Tajik State University in 1964 and received a doctorate in 1975 for *Рыночные отношения и проблемы экономическогою*. Since 1968 he was affiliated with the Tajik Academy of Sciences, and delegated to Isfahan, 1977 to 1980, and to Afghanistan, 1986 to 1988. Miliband[2]

Elchouémi, Moustapha *see* Chouémi, Moustafa

Elçin, Şükrü Murat, born 10 October 1912 at Phlorina (Florina), Macedonia, he obtained a doctorate in 1949, to which two years of study at the Sorbonne, Paris, was added. Since 1964 he was a professor at Hacettepe Üniversitesi, Ankara. His writings include *Türk bilmeceleri* (1970), and *Akdeniz'de ve Cezâyir'de türk halk şâirleri* (1988). Kim kimdir, 1985/86; LC

El'darova (Эльдарова), Emina (Amina) Mehrab gyzy, fl. 1964, her writings include *Искусство ашыгов Азербайджана* (1984), and she edited *Azărbaijan khalg musigisi* (1981). OSK; ZKO

Eldblom, Lars, fl. 1966, he received a doctorate in 1968 from Lund Universitet for his thesis, *Structure foncière: organisation et structure sociale; une étude comparative sur la vie socio-économique dans*

les trois oasis libyennes de Ghat, Mourzouk et particulièrement Ghadamès. He published two brief summaries of his thesis, *Land tenure - social organization and structure; a ... study of ... Ghat, Mourzouk and Ghadamès* (1969), and *Structure foncière d'une communauté musulmane* (1971). NUC, 1968-1972

Eldem, Vedat, fl. 1946, his writings include *Osmanlı İmperatorluğunun iktisadi şartları hakkında bir tetkik* (1970). LC

Elder, Earl Edgar, born in 1887 at Albia, Iowa, he was a teacher at Assiut College, a missionary, and a teacher of Arabic at the American University, Cairo. His writings include *Egyptian colloquial Arabic reader* (1927); *A commentary on the creed of Islam, by al-Taftazani* (1950), a translation originally made as a part of the requirements for the Ph.D. at the Kennedy School of Missions of Hartford Seminary; and *Vindicating a vision; the story of the American Mission in Egypt, 1854-1954* (1958). He died in 1973. LC; Shavit

Elder, Joseph Walter, born to American parents, 25 July 1930 at Kermanshah, Iran, he was a graduate of Oberlin College, and received a Ph.D. in 1959 from Harvard for *Industrialism in Hindu society.* He was a teacher of English in India, 1951-1953, and a professor of sociology and Indian studies at Oberlin College from 1959 to 1968, when he was appointed professor of sociology and Asian studies at the University of Wisconsin, Madison. He also was a consultant to several national and international foundations and institutions. He was a joint author of *Civilization of India syllabus* (1966), and *Planned resettlement in Nepal's Terai* (1976). AmM&WS, 1973 S, 1978 S; NatFacDr, 1995; WhoAm, 1974-1988/89|

Eldridge, Robert Huyck, born 13 March 1938 at N.Y.C., he was a graduate of Harvard University and became a business and financial executive. He travelled extensively in the Middle East. Canadian, 1983-1997; Master (1); WhoAm, 1974-1988/89|

Elenov, T. E., he edited *Установление советской власти в Казахстане* (1957). OSK

Elers-Napier, 1808-1870 *see* Napier, Edward Delaval Hungerford Elers

Elezović, Gligorije Gliša, born 6 January 1879 at Vučitrn, he was a linguist and historian who studied at Universitet u Beogradu, 1901-1905. His writings include *Речник косовоско-метохискот дијалекта* (1932-35), *Како су Турци после више опсада заузели* (1956), and he was joint author of *Iz Carigradskih turskih arhiva; mühimme defteri* (1951). He died in Beograd, 17 October 1960. EncJug

Elfenbein, Josef Herblit, born 9 March 1927 in California, he studied mathematics and Indo-European languages at Princeton and London, and received a Ph.D. in 1950 from Princeton for his thesis, *The Tocharian verbal system.* He taught mathematics successively at London, Tehran, and Quetta from 1961 to 1982. Since 1987 he was professor of Iranian studies and comparative linguistics at the Universität Mainz. His writings include *The Baluchi language* (1966), *A Baluchi miscellanea of erotica and poetry* (1983), and he edited *An anthology of classical and modern Balochi literature* (1990). LC; LingH

Elgood, Cyril Lloyd, born in 1892 at London, he was a graduate of Balliol College, a doctor of medicine of Oxford, and trained at St. Bartholomew's Hospital, London. He spent the greater part of his professional career as physician to the British Legation in Tehran and later as physician to the governments of Libya and the Sudan. His writings include *A medical history of Persia and the Eastern Caliphate* (1951), and *Safavid medical practice* (1970). He was a member of the British Academy. He died in the Seychelles on 29 March 1970. LC; WhE&EA

Elgood, Percival George, born 30 July 1863 at London, he was educated at the military colleges at Marlborough and Sandhurst and in 1883 entered the British Army, retiring with the rank of major in 1903. He served for many years in the Egyptian Army, and held important posts in Egyptian ministries, including Controller-General of Food Supplies of the Egyptian Government and Inspector-General of the Suez Canal during the first World War. On his retirement from military and administrative work, he continued to live in Egypt, where he devoted himself largely to literary work, including *Egypt and the army* (1924), *The transit of Egypt* (1928), *Bonaparte's adventure in Egypt* (1931), and *Egypt* (1935). He died at Villa Beata, Heliopolis, 20 December 1941. Egyptology; Hill; *Journal of the Royal Central Asian Society* , 1942, pp. 156-157; *Who was who*, 4

Elia (Iliya), Moujid, he was in 1964 in charge of the Technical Office, Productivity and Vocational Training Department, in the Egyptian Ministry of Industry. Note

El'ianov (Эльянов), Anatolii IAkovlevich, born 30 March 1929 at Moscow, he graduated from the Oriental Institute, Moscow, in 1953, and received a doctorate in 1975 for his thesis, *Рыночню отношения и проблемы экономю роста в развивающихся странах.* His writings include *Эфиопия*

(1967), *На пути в XX век* (1969); he was joint author of *Пазвивающиеся стпаны* (1983), its translations, *Los paises en desarrollo en el umbral del tercer milenio* (1984), and *Developing nations at the turn of the millenium* (1987), editor of *Актуальные социально-экономические и политические проблемы развивающихсиа стран* (1983), and joint editor of *Развивающиеся страны; экономический рост и социальныи прогресс* (1983), and its translation, *Economic growth and the market in the developing countries* (1982). Miliband; Miliband²

Elias, Ney, born 10 February 1844, he was educated in England and the continent, followed by instruction under the Royal Geographical Society of London. He later explored the Gobi Desert, Chinese Turkestan, and Afghanistan. He died in London, 31 May 1897. Gerald Morgan wrote the biography, *Ney Elias, explorer and envoy extraordinary in high Asia* (1971). Bioln, 9; Buckland; DNB, v. 1922; Embacher; EncicUni; EncJud; GdeEnc; Henze; Meyers; Pallas; RNL; Wright, p. 82

Eliash, Joseph, born 25 October 1932 at Jerusalem, he received a Ph. D. in 1966 from SOAS for his thesis, *Ali b. Abi Talib in Ithna-'Ashari Shi'i belief.* He was resident in the United States from the 1960s until his death in Oberlin, Ohio, in 1981. CnDiAmJBi; Sluglett

Eliash, Mordechai, born in 1892 at Uman, Ukraine, he received a religious education, studied law and later Oriental languages at Berlin and Oxford, where he took a B.Litt. in 1919 for his thesis, *The Risalah of Shafi'i.* He was resident in Palestine since 1919, and became the first Israeli minister to Britain. He died 11 May 1959 in London of a heart attack. Bioln, 2; EncJud; NearMEWho, 1945/46; ObitOF, 1979; Sluglett; WhoIsrael, 1949; Who was who, 5

Eliav, Arie Lova, born 21 November 1921 at Moscow, he came to Palestine in 1924. He was a student at Reading and Cambridge (UK), and received a diploma from the Hebrew University, Jerusalem, in 1959. He was a government official, member of the Knesset, a deputy minister, visiting lecturer, and a Hebrew writer on immigration and integration in Israel. English translations of his works include *The voyage of the Ulua* (1969), *Land of the Hart* (1974), and *New heart, new spirit* (1988). Bioln, 8; ConAu, 69-72, new revision, 11 & 28; EncJud; WhoIsrael, 1968-1990/91|; WhoWor, 1878/79; WhoWorJ, 1972, 1978, 1987

Eliav, Mordechai, born 28 September 1920 in Poland, he came to Palestine in 1934 and received a Ph.D. in 1958 from the Hebrew University, Jerusalem, for his thesis, *ha-Hinukh ha-Yehudi be-Germanyah.* He was a professor and chairman, Department of Jewish History, Bar-Ilan University. His writings include *Sefer ha-'aliyah ha-rishonah* (1981), and *Inter-communal relations within the Yishuv at the end of the Ottoman period* (1983). Master (1); WhoIsrael, 1973/74, 1976, 1978, 1985/86

Elie de la Primaudaie, F., fl. 1860-1872, he contributed articles to *Annales des voyages, Revue africaine,* and *Revue algérienne et coloniale,* and wrote *Études sur le commerce au moyen âge; histoire du commerce de la mer Noire et des colonies génoises de la Krimée* (Paris, 1848). BN

Elif Khan, fl. 1936, he was a press attaché at the Afghan embassy in Berlin. Note

Eliot, Alexander, born 28 April 1919 at Cambridge, Mass., he was a student at American colleges from 1936 to 1939, and later became a free lance writer. He was a member of P.E.N, Authors Guild, and Free Lance Council. His writings include *Proud youth* (1953), and *Greece, 1983-1984* (1983). AmAu&B; ConAu, 49-52, new revision 1; IntAu&W, 1982, 1989; WhoAm, 1974-1988/89|; WhoWor, 1980/81, 1982/83

Eliot, George Fielding, born 22 June 1894, he began his career as a magazine fiction writer, but later became a military correspondent and analyst. His writings include *Hate, hope and high explosives; a report on the Middle East* (1948). He died 21 April 1971. AmAu&B; Bioln, 9, 11; ConAu, 29-32; EncAJ; EncTwCJ; Master (8); WhAm, 5; WorAu

Eliot, Theodore Lyman, born 24 January 1928 at N.Y.C. After graduating from Harvard, he was in the U.S. Foreign Service from 1949 to 1978. Thereafter he was a dean at Fletcher School of Law and Diplomacy until 1985. He was a sometime ambassador to Afghanistan, and affiliated with the Center for Asian Pacific Affairs, Asia Foundation. His writings include *The Red Army on Pakistan's border* (1986), and *Gorbachev's Afghanistan gambit* (1988). LC; Master (4); WhoAm, 1974-1996|; WhoWor, 1978/79

Eliraz, Giora (Giyora), born 20th cent., she received a doctorate in 1980 from the Hebrew University, Jerusalem, for her thesis, *Intelektu'alim Mitsrim mul masoret ve-shinui, 1919-1939.*

Elisséeff, Nikita, born in 1915 at Petrograd and brought up in France, he studied at l'École des langues orientales vivantes as well as l'École pratique des Hautes études where he received all his degrees. In 1945 he became a collaborator with Robert Mantran and Jean Sauvaget at the Institut français de Damas where he later became acting deputy directeur. He was one of the last staff members to leave Damascus in 1956. He returned well before diplomatic relations between France and Syria were re-established. In 1966 he returned to France for good. His writings include *Thèmes et motifs de Mille et une nuit* (1949), *Nur ad-Din, un grand prince musulman de Syrie* (1967), *L'Orient*

482

musulman au moyen âge (1977); he was editor and translator of *La description de Damas d'Ibn 'Asakir* (1959); and he also contributed numerous articles to EI² as well as the *Encyclopédia universalis.* He died in Lyon, 25 November 1997. Revue des mondes musulmans et de la Méditerranée 83/84 (1997), pp. 283-285

Elisséeff, Vadime, born 4 May 1918 at Petrograd, Russia, and educated in France, he was a chief keeper of the Musées d'art et d'histoire of the city of Paris, and a writer on East Asian history and art. WhoFr, 1979/80-1998/99

Elkan, Walter, born 1 March 1923 at Hamburg, Germany, he received a Ph.D. in 1956 from the University of London. He was a lecturer in economics at Makerere College, Kampala from 1958 to 1960, when he joined the Department of Economics in Durham University. He spent 1973/74 in Iran with the World Bank Commission engaged in a basic economic survey. His writings include *An African labour force* (1956), *Migrants and proletarians* (1960), and *An introduction to development economics* (1973). Unesco; Who, 1974-1998

Elkins, Ethel C., she was for several years a member of the staff of the Pennsylvania Museum of Art, Philadelphia, before she became secretary to the American Institute for Persian Art and Archaeology, New York, in 1934. Note

El'kovich, Leonid IAkovlevich, fl. 1955-1979, his writings include Лотфулла Фаттахов (1960), Николай Дмитриевич Кузнецов (1962), Художники Татарии (1965), and he edited Изобразительное искусство Турменской ССР (1957). OSK

Ellehauge, Martin Olaf Marius, born in 1892 at Falster, Denmark. He was a keeper at the Department of Uniforms and Colours, Tojhus Museum, Frederiksholms, København, and the editor of *Heraldica* (1958-61). WhE&EA

Ellenberg, Hans, born 7 April 1877 at Hamburg, Germany, he studied at Kiel, where he received a Dr.phil. in 1920 for his thesis, *Islamische Kunstgewerbe nach Qazwini und Tha'alibi.* In 1947 he was a professor of Oriental philology at the Universität Jena. His writings include *Orient* (1931), *Geh' mit mir in den Orient* (1932), and *Sultan, Seraskier und Soldaten* (1937). Schwarz

Elles, Robin Jamieson, born 4 January 1907. After graduating from Trinity College, Cambridge, in 1928, he was in the Sudan Political Service for five years. After the war, he was successively a business and academic administrator. He died in 1987. Who, 1973-1987; Who was who, 8

Ellickson, Jean E., born 7 September 1935 at Cleveland, Ohio, he was a graduate of Ohio State University, and received a Ph.D. in 1972 from Michigan State University for his thesis, *A believer among believers; the religious beliefs, practices and meanings in a village in Bangladesh.* In 1971 he was appointed a professor of anthropology at Western Illinois University, Macomb, a posiition he still held in 1995. IWWAS, 1976/77; NatFacDr, 1995

Ellinger, Ilona Elisabeth Deak-Ebner, born 12 June 1913 at Budapest, she studied in Hungary, Sweden, and the United States. From 1943 to 1978 she was a professor of fine art at Trinity College, Washington, D.C. In the early 1960s, she spent a sabbatical year as a Fulbright professor of fine art in Pakistan. DrAS, 1974, 1978; WhoAmA, 1973-1997/98; WhoAmW, 1958/59

Elliot, Gertrude, born in 1855, she was the daughter of Sir Henry George Elliot, 1817-1907, and edited his *Some revolutions and other experiences* (1922). NUC, pre-1956

Elliot, Sir Henry George, born in 1817, he was educated at Eton, and Trinity College, Cambridge. He entered the British Diplomatic Service in 1841, and served as ambassador to Turkey in 1867. He died in 1907. DNB, suppl.; Who was who, 1

Elliott, Alfred Charles, born 20 September 1870. After passing through the military college, Sandhurst, he served in the Indian Army until 1893, when he passed into the civil employment in Punjab, a position which he resigned in 1923. His writings include *The chronicles of Gujrat* (1902). He died in 1952. Who was who, 5

Ellis, Alexander George, born about 1858, he passed from Merchant Taylors' School, where he was solidly grounded in Hebrew as well as in the classics, to Queens' College, Cambridge, and there took a distinguished degree in Semitic languages. Joining the staff of the British Museum in 1883, he spent the next twenty-six years chiefly in cataloguing Islamic literature, at first printed books and later both books and manuscripts, covering in this work an unusually wide field, including Persian, Turkish, and Armenian. He left the Museum in 1909 to take up the appointment of sub-librarian at the India Office where he served until his retirement. In 1930 he returned to the British Museum to give part-time service in cataloguing the Armenian library, until declining health brought this activity as well as his work for the Royal Asiatic Society, which he had joined in 1897, to a close. His astonishing powers as a bibliographer were proverbial. His recreation was walking. In his prime he would tramp vast distances across country without turning a hair, and it was only on the verge of eighty that he bowed with an ill grace to the necessity of limiting his Saturday afternoon walk to nine or ten miles. His writings include *A catalogue of the Persian printed books in the British Museum* (1922), *A facsimile of the manuscript (Or. 9777) of Diwan i Zu'l-Fakar*, edited with introduction (1934), and he was joint author of *A descriptive list of the Arabic manuscripts acquired by the Trustees of the British Museum since 1894* (1912). On 17 March 1941 he passed unnoticed from the scene at the ripe age of eighty-four. Journal of the Royal Asiatic Society, 1942, pt. 2, pp. 153-154

Ellis, Charles Grant, born 12 October 1908 at Kingston, N.Y., he studied at Princeton, and was since 1961 a research associate, Textile Museum, Washington, D.C. His writings include *Early Caucasian rugs* (1976), and *Oriental carpets in the Philadelphia Museum of Art* (1988). WhoS&SW, 1973/74, 1975/76, 1976/77

Ellis, Charles Howard, born 13 February 1895 at Sydney, he was educated at Melbourne, Oxford, and Paris. During the first World War he saw service in the Middle East and India, and later was a member of the Malleson Mission to Meshed and Central Asia in 1818-19. From 1921 to his retirement in 1953 he was an intelligence officer in the British Foreign Service. He died 5 July 1975. ConAu, P-1, 13-14; Who, 1955-1975; Who was who, 7

Ellis, Ellen Deborah, born in 1878, she graduated in 1901 from Bryn Mawr College, where she also received a Ph.D. in 1905 for her thesis, *An introduction to the history of sugar as a commodity.* Thereafter she joined Mount Holyoke College faculty as a professor of political science, later to become chairman of department, until her retirement in 1944. She was a sometime teacher at the American Women's College in Istanbul. Her papers are in Mount Holyoke College Library. She died in Wallingford, Pa., 20 December 1974. Master (1); NYT 24 December 1974, p. 22, col. 5

Ellis, George Washington, born 4 May 1875 at Weston, Mo., he graduated LL.B. in 1893 from the University of Kansas and did postgraduate studies at Howard University, and Gunton Institute of Social Economics and Sociology, N.Y.C. He was secretary at the American Legation in Liberia from 1902 to 1910, during which time he made expeditions into the interior. He accumulated an important ethnological collection which went to the National Museum in Washington, D.C. From 1917 until his death in Chicago, 26 November 1919, he practised law in that city. His writings include *The Negro culture in West Africa* (1914), *The leopard's claw* (1917). DAB; Shavit - Africa; WhAm, 1

Ellis, Harry Bearse, born 9 December 1921 at Springfield, Mass., he was a graduate of Wesleyan University, and became a staff member of the *Christian science monitor*. He repeatedly was a correspondent in Beirut and in Europe. His writings include *Heritage in the desert; the Arabs and the Middle East* (1956), *Israel and the Middle East* (1957), *Challenge in the Middle East* (1960), and *Israel, one land - two people* (1972). BlueB, 1976; ConAu, 1-4 rev., 2 new rev.; IntAu&W, 1977-1989; Master (3); Shavit; WhoAm, 1974-1988/89|; WhoWor, 1974/75, 1976/77|; WrDr, 1976-1998/2000

Ellis, Richard Stephens, born 16 December 1934 at Detroit, Mich., he was a graduate of Wabash College, and received a Ph.D. in 1965 from the University of Chicago for his thesis, *Foundation deposits in ancient Mesopotamia; archaeological and textual data.* He taught for ten years at Yale University before he was appointed a professor of classical and Near Eastern archaeology at Bryn Mawr College, Pennsylvania, in 1974. DrAS, 1974, 1978, 1982; WhoAm, 1984-1988/89|

Ellis, William Thomas, born 25 October 1873 at Allegheny, Pa., he was an editor of religious magazines and later a special correspondent in the Near and Middle East. He interviewed King Ibn Saud, and Sultan Abdülmacid. His writings include *Men and missions* (1909), *Bible lands to-day* (1927), and *Pilgrim fare from Bible lands* (1940). He died in 1950. Bioln, 2; WhNAA; Shavit; WhAm, 8

Ellsworth, Paul Theodore, born 20 November 1897 at Rutland, Vt., he received a Ph.D. in 1932 from Harvard for his thesis, *Some aspects of investment in the United States, 1907-1930.* He was a professor of economics at the University of Cincinnati, Ohio, from 1932 to 1967. His writings include *International economics* (1938), and *International economy*, 5th ed. (1975). AmM&WS, 1973, 1978 S; ConAu, 17-20

Ellul, Jacques, born 6 January 1912 at Bordeaux. After receiving a doctorate in law, he was for much of his professional life a professor of history of law at the Université de Bordeaux. He wrote more than forty books which fused his sociological beliefs in Marxism and Christianity, including *Homme et l'argent* (1979), its translation, *Money and power* (1984), *Perspectives on our age; Jacques Ellul speaks on his life and work* (19819, *FLN propaganda in France during the Algerian War* (1982), *Anarchie et christianisme*, and its translation, *Anarchy and Christianity* (1991). He died in Bordeaux, 19 May 1994. AuWr, 1971; Bioln, 10, 12, 13, 14; ConAu, 81-84, 145; Master (2); WhoWor, 1974/75

Elmandjra, Omar S., fl. 1959-1960, he was a sometime executive director at the International Bank for Reconstruction and Development, Washington, D.C.

Elmessiri, Abdelwahab Mohammad, 1938- *see* Messiri, Abdelwahab Mohammad

Elmslie, William Jackson, 1832-1872, he was a medical missionary under the Church Missionary Society from 1864 to his death, and affiliated with the Edinburgh Missionary Society. His writings include *A Vocabulary of the Kashmiri language* (1872), and *Medical missions, as illustrated by some letters and notices of the late Dr. Elmslie* (1874). William Burns Thomson wrote *A memoir of William Jackson Elmslie* (1881). BLC; Boase

Éloffe, Gabriel, born about 1835 at Paris, he was a professor of geology at the Musée d'histoire naturelle, a member of several learned societies, and a member of the organizing committee of the Congrès scientifiques de l'Exposition universelle de 1900. Curinier, vol. 2 (1901), p. 150

Eloui, Ali, fl. 1923, he was a trained physician and wrote the pamphlet, *Die moderne Frau im Morgen- und Abendland; kulturelle Betrachtungen eines Arztes und soziale Vergleiche* (Berlin, 1921). NUC

Elphinston, William G., colonel, born in the 19th cent., he served with the Desert Mounted Corps in Palestine during the first World War. He was connected with Kurdistan since 1918-1919, when he was posted to a Kurdish area near Urfa as an Assistant Political Officer. He was subsequently a member of the British mission to the Iraqi Army from 1925 to 1928. During the second World War he was in Middle East Intelligence, dealing with Kurdish affairs, and also in touch with Kurdistan when in the Middle East Section of the Political Intelligence Centre in Cairo. After the war, he was a research secretary for the Near and Middle East at Chatham House, London. JRCAS 40 (1953), pp. 174-75

Elphinstone, Mountstuart, 1779-1859, he was appointed to the Bengal civil service in 1796. As Resident of Nagpur, he went on a political mission to the Emir of Kabul in 1808. From 1819 to 1827 he was governor of Bombay. His writings include *An Account of the Kingdom of Caubul* (1815), and *History of India* (1841). Biographies are "Short memorial of the Honorable Mountstuart Elphinstone" in *Journal of the Bombay Branch of the RAS* 6 (1862), pp. 97-111, Cyril John Baron Radcliffe's Romanes Lecture of 1962, *Mountstuart Elphinstone*, and Rustom D. Choksey, *Mountstuart Elphinstone; the Indian years* (1971). BioIn, 2,6,9,14; CelCen; DcBiPP; DNB; Embacher; EncAm; EncBrit; EncicUni; EncItaliana; GdeEnc; Henze; Mason; Master (9); Meyers; Pallas; RNL

Elphinstone, William George Keith, 1782-1842, he was a successful British army officer, and appointed to the command of the Benares division of the Bengal army in 1839. Despite his age and poor health he was selected at the close of 1841 to take command of the British army at Kabul. During the disastrous retreat of the army from Kabul in January 1842, he became a prisoner of the Afghans and died, while still a captive, on 23 April 1842. BritInd (3); Buckland; DNB

Elsammani, Mohammed Osman, 1939- *see* Sammani, Mohammed Osman El-

Elsner, Jakob, born in 1692 at Saalfeld, East Prussia. After pursuing Oriental studies at Königsberg, he spent four years in Holland. Upon his return, he was appointed a professor of theology and Oriental studies at Lingen, Westphalia. He later was a preacher at Berlin, where he died in 1750. For his *Observationes sacrae in Novi Foederis libros* (1720-1728), the University of Utrecht conferred on him a D.D. degree. His writings include *Neueste Beschreibung derer griechischen Christen in der Türckey* (1737), *Nieuwste beschryving van de Grieksche Christenen in Turkyen* (1743), and *Fortsetzung der neuesten Beschreibung der griechischen Christen inder Türckey* (1747). ADtB; DtBilnd (9); NUC, pre-1956

Elsner, Jürgen, born in 1932, he received a Dr.phil. in 1964 from Humboldt Universität, Berlin, for his thesis, *Zur vokalsolistischen Vortragsweise der Kampfmusik Hanns Eislers*, and a second doctorate for *Der Begriff des maqam in Ägypten in neuerer Zeit* (1973). He was joint author of *Nord-afrika* (1983). LC; Schwarz

Elton, John, fl. 1730-1751, he was a British sea-captain who, for some time in the early 1730s, had been in the service of the Russian government, a post which he resigned with some disgust in 1738. In the spring of 1739 he travelled from Moscow to Astrakhan, where his party took a boat to Gilan with a view of establishing trade relations with England, in particular the export of English textiles in return for raw silk from Persia. He later entered the service of the Shah. He was shot in the course of Persian political rivalries in 1751. A German translation of his diary, *Tagebuch über seine Reise von Moskau nach den nördlichen Gegenden von Persien*, was published in 1790. BLC; DNB; Henze

Eltzbacher, Otto Julius, 1870-1948 *see* Barker, J. Ellis

Elwell-Sutton, Albert Sigismund, born in 1878 at Manchester, he was educated in the Royal Navy and at the University of London. During the first World War he served in the Middle East, commanding a gun-boat on the Tigris above Baghdad in 1918. On retirement, with the rank of lieut.-commander, he became known as a lecturer on geography and current affairs, partly for the University of London Extension Board. His writings include *The Evolution of Germany* (1915), and *The Chinese people* (1934). He died at the age of eighty-three, 25 October 1961. Geographical journal 127 (1961), p. 565; WhE&EA

Elwell-Sutton, Laurence Paul, born 2 June 1912 at Ballylickey, Bantry Bay, Ireland, he studied Arabic and Persian at SOAS, graduating in 1934. Thereafter he worked for the Anglo-Iranian Oil Company until 1938, when he returned to London to work at the BBC as a Persian specialist. From 1943 to 1947 he served as press attaché at the Embassy in Tehran. He was appointed a lecturer in Persian at Edinburgh in 1952, and rose to a personal chair retiring in 1982. He had a broad interest and competence in Persian matters, on which he could draw, particularly in his last work, *Bibliographical guide to Iran* (1983), when, despite of his illness, he was able to contribute all those sections, for which no contributors could be found. His writings include *A guide to Iranian area study* (1952), *Persian oil; a study in power politics* (1955), and *The Persian metres* (1976). *Qajar Iran*, studies presented to Professor L. P.Elwell-Sutton, was published in 1983. He died 2 September 1984. ConAu, 5-8, 114; Times, 2 September 1984; WhoWor, 1976/77; WrDr, 1976/78-1986/88

Elwood, Anne Katherine, Mrs., fl. 1830-1845, she was a travel writer and a biographer whose writings include *Narrative of a journey overland from England ... to India* (1830), and *Memoirs of the literary ladies of England* (1843). BLC; BritInd; LC; Robinson, pp. 14-15

Ely, Catherine Beach, fl. 1925, her writings include *The modern tendency in American painting* (1925).

Emam, Hani Shafiq, born in 1932 at Mecca, he was a trained economist from Columbia University, and became a business and financial executive, and a sometime lecturer in economics at King Abdulaziz University. Master (1); WhoArab, 1981-1999/2000

Emanuel, William Vernon, fl. 1939, his writings include *The wild ass; a journey through Persia* (1939).

Emanuelli, Pio, born 3 November 1888 at Roma, he was an astronomer at the Vatican Observatory and died in Roma, 2 July 1946. Chi è, 1928-1940; DcScB; DizBI

Ember, Aaron, born 25 December 1878 at Tulnas, Lithuania, he was a graduate of Johns Hopkins University, Baltimore, Md., where he also received a Ph.D. in 1905 for his thesis, *The pluralis intensivus in Hebrew*. From 1907 until his death on 1 June 1926, he was active at his alma mater, partly as a professor of Egyptology. He died trying to save from his burning house a manuscript of a work on which he had been working for a number of years,. CnDiAmJBi; Egyptology; WhAm, 1

Emberger, Louis Marie, born 23 January 1897 at Thann (Haut-Rhin), he started his study of pharmacy at Straßburg but completed it after the war at Lyon. From 1923 to 1936 he was in Morocco where he was for ten years head of the Service botanique and a professor at the Institut des hautes études marocaines à Rabat. His writings include *Les arbres du Maroc et comment les reconnaître* (1938), *Aperçu général sur la végétation du Maroc* (1939), and *Travaux de botanique et d'écologie* (1971). He died in Saint Sulpice, 29 November 1969. Index BFr² (1); NDBA; WhoFr, 1965/66-1969/70

Embury, Lucy, 1883- see Hubbell, Lucy née Embury

Emel'ianov, Valerii Nikolaevich, fl. 1960, his writings include *Аграрные отношения в Ливане за 25 лет независимого развития* (1969). OSK

Emeneau, Murray Barnson, born 28 February 1904 at Lunenburg, N.S., he was a graduate of Dalhousie University, studied at Oxford, and took a doctorate in 1931 at Yale University. He was a professor of Sanskrit and general linguistics at the University of California, Berkeley, until his retirement in 1971. He wrote *A Dravidian etymological dictionary* (1961), and *India and the historical grammar* (1965). BlueB, 1975, 1976; ConAu, 1-4, 5 new rev.; DrAS, 1974, 1978, 1982; Master (2); WrDr, 1976/78-1992/94

Emerit, Marcel, born 3 August 1899 at Niort (Deux-Sèvres), he studied at the Facultés des lettres et des sciences, Bordeaux, and received a doctorate in 1937 for his thesis, *Les paysans roumains*. He had a varied teaching career at l'Institut français des hautes études en Roumani, l'Université de Bucarest, la Faculté des lettres de Lille, and la Faculté des lettres d'Alger. His writings include *Les saint-simoniens en Algérie* (1941), and *L'Algérie à l'époque d'Abd-el-Kader* (1951). Revue d'histoire maghrebine 7-8 (1977), pp. 9-15; Unesco; WhoFr, 1967/68-1979/80|

Emerson, Alfred, born 19th cent., he was a student of European history, followed by graduate work in classical philology and archaeology at the Universität München, where he received a Dr.phil. in 1881 for *De Hercule Homerico*. He later was a lecturer in these subjects at Johns Hopkins University, Baltimore, Md., and the American School of Classical Studies at Athens. At the time of his retirement he was a professor of archaeology at Cornell University, Ithaca, N.Y. His writings include *An account* *of recent progress in classical archaeology, 1875-1889* (1889). He died in N.Y.C., 19 October 1943. ObitOF, 1979

Emerson, Gertrude, 1890- *see* Sen, Gertrude née Emerson

Emerson, Ralph Waldo, born 25 May 1803 at Boston, he was an American essayist, poet, and philosopher, gifted with powers of original thought and exalted literary expression. He exerted a wide and deep influence both at home and abroad. He died in Concord, Mass., 27 April 1882. BiDMoPL; BioIn, 1-15; CelCen; DAB, 3; DcBiPP; DcNAA; EncAm; EncBrit; Master (50); WhAm, H

Emerson, Rupert, born 20 August 1899 at Rye, N.Y., he was a graduate of Harvard, and took a Ph.D. in 1927 at LSE for a thesis on modern history of Germany. He was a professor of international relations at Harvard until his retirement in 1970, and concurrently a visting professor at other American universities. His writings include *Malaysia* (1937), and *Africa and the United States policy* (1967). He died 9 February 1979. AmAu&B; AmM&WS, 1973; ConAu, 1-4, 85-88, 2 new rev.; Master (1); Unesco; WhAm, 7

Emerson, Thomas, born 2 June 1870, he was a graduate of Emmanuel College, Cambridge, and thereafter entered the Indian Civil Service, arriving in India in 1894. He served in Bengal, and was a member of the Council of State from 1925 to 1926. He retired in 1927. He died 22 July 1956. Who, 1921-1956; *Who was who*, 5

Emerson, William, born 16 October 1873 at N.Y.C., he was a Harvard graduate and studied architecture at Columbia University, N.Y.C., and l'École des beaux arts, Paris. He was a practising architect in N.Y.C., and a professor of architecture, as well as a dean of the School of Architecture at M.I.T. from 1919 to 1939. His writings include *Old bridges of France* (1925), *Pages from an architects sketch book, 1900-1930* (1930), and he was joint author of *The use of brick in French architecture* (1935). He died 4 March 1957. BioIn, 4; WhAm, 3

Emilia, Antonio d' *see* D'Emilia, Antonio

Émily, Jules Michel Antoine, born 20 March 1866 at Olmato, Corsica. After completing his medical training in 1892, he entered the French colonial service as a naval surgeon and was posted to the French Sudan where he saw active service. He participated in the Mission Marchand as a medical officer, and was with him at Fashoda in 1898. He retired in 1928, with the rank of médecin-général, and inspecteur of colonial troops. He died 16 December 1944. DBF; Hill; *Hommes et destins*, v. 2, 302-304

Emin Pasha, born Eduard Carl Oscar Theodor Schnitzer, 28 March 1840 at Oppeln, Prussia. After working as a physician in the Ottoman Empire, he went to Khartoum in 1875 and entered the Egyptian service under Gordon as a medical officer, being known as Emin. His flair for foreign languages made Muslims readily accept both him and his work. He was sent on three political missions, to Bunyoro and Buganda. After the Mahdist uprising he was isolated in Central Africa and had to be liberated by a British expedition under H. M. Stanley. He later went to East Africa in the service of Germany. He was killed by slave traders in the Congo, 23 October 1892. His career inspired an extensive literature printed mostly in English and German. DtBE; EI²; Embacher; EncAm; EncJud; Henze; Hill; *Index Islamicus*, (3); Master (3); Meyers; NCCN; Pallas; Sigilla

Emiri, Ali, born in 1857 at Diyarbakır, Turkey, and educated at Mardin, he served as private secretary to Abidin Paşa before he was sent to Diyarbakır in 1879 in the capacity of high commissioner of reforms. Thereafter he was successively a'şar müdiri in the tithe administration, special treasurer (*muhasebeci*), treasurer-general (*defterdar*), and finally inspector (*müfettiş*). Deeply attached to the dynasty, he resigned on a pension half his salary at the outbreak of the 1908 revolution. This, however, still allowed him to pursue his lifelong interest in manuscripts and books. His administrative appointments to different parts of the empire had given him a chance to collect manuscripts in places as far apart as Kırşehir, Diyarbakır, Yanina, and Scutari in Albania. He was the founding editor of *Tarih ve edebiyat mecmu'ası* in 1919. His writings include *Levami' ül-Hamidiye* (1312/1894). He was a bachelor and bequeathed his library of 18,000 volumes to the Evkaf Administration. He died in Constantinople, 23 January 1924. *Journal asiatique* 204 (1924), pp. 375-379; Meydan

Emmerick, Ronald Eric, born 9 March 1937 at Sydney, he was a graduate of the University of Sydney and took a Ph.D. at Cambridge in 1965. He served for a few years as an associate professor at the Oriental Institute, Chicago, before he was appointed professor of Iranian studies at the Universität Hamburg, where he remained until his retirement. His writings include *A Guide to the literature of Khotan* (1979). AnElFr, 1995, 1997; IWWAS, 1975/76; Kürschner, 1976-1996; LingH

Emrich, Duncan Black Macdonald, born 11 April 1908 at Mardin, Turkey, he was a graduate of Brown University and received a Ph.D. from Harvard in 1937 for his thesis, *The Avicenna legend*. He pursued post-doctoral studies abroad and then was successively professor of English literature, chief of Folklore Section at the Library of Congress, and a cultural affairs officer in the U.S. Government, as well as Fulbright professor on American civilization at European universities. He died in 1977. BioIn, 3, 4, 11; ConAu, 61, 9 new rev.; Master (4); PeoHis; Selim; WhoAm, 1974, 1976; WhAm, 7

Emrich, Gerhard, born about 1945, he received a Dr.phil. in 1973 from the Universität Bochum for his thesis, *Antike Metaphern und Vergleiche im lyrischen Werk des Kostis Palamas.*

Emsalem, René, fl. 1950, his writings include *Climatologie générale* (Alger, 1975).

Emsheimer, Ernst, born 15 January 1904, at Frankfurt am Main, he received a Dr.phil. in 1928 from the Universität Freiburg im Breisgau for his thesis, *Johann Ulrich Steigleder, sein Leben und seine Werke; ein Beitrag zur Geschichte der süddeutschen Orgelkomposition.* Thesis

Enan, Hussein, fl. 1935, he was joint author of *An analysis of the factors governing the response to manuring of cotton in Egypt* (Cairo, 1935). NUC, pre-1956

Encel, Solomon, born 3 March 1925 at Warszawa, and brought to Australia in 1929, he was a graduate of the University of Melbourne, where he also took a Ph.D. in 1960. He was a professor of political science at Australian universities until his retirement in 1990. His writings include *Cabinet government in Australia* (1962), and *Equality and authority* (1970). ConAu, 115, 37 new rev.; Master (1); WhoAus, 1968-1988; WhoWor, 1989/90|

Ende, Karl Paul *Werner*, born 22 September 1937 at Wittenberg, Germany, he was a trained book-seller before he started to pursue Islamic studies at Halle, completing it with a Dr.phil. in 1965 at Hamburg for his thesis, *Europabild und kulturelles Selbstbewußtsein bei den Muslimen am Ende des 19. Jahrhunderts.* He also studied at Cairo, 1963/64. He taught at Hamburg from 1965 until 1983, when he was appointed to the chair of Islamic studies at the Universität Freiburg im Breisgau. His writings include *Arabische Welt und islamische Geschichte* (1977). Kürschner, 1980-1996; Private; Schwarz

Enderlein, Volkmar, born 21 July 1936 at Oschersleben, Germany, he received a Dr.phil. in 1958 from the Universität Jena. In 1959 he joined the Museum für Islamische Kunst, Berlin, where he later served as its director until his retirement in 2001. His writings include *Islamische Kunst* (1970), *Die Miniaturen der Berliner Baisonqur-Handschrift* (1970), *Führer durch das Islamische Museum, Berlin* (1976), *Orientalische Kelims* (1986), and *Islamische Kunst* (1990). LC; Private

Enderlin, Jakob, Dr., born 19th cent., he was a missionary under the Basel Mission at Daraw and Aswan, Upper Egypt, working among the Nubian Muslims. He had a good command of Arabic, as well as an acquaintance with the two more common Nubian dialects. During the last years of his service he was affiliated with the School of Oriental Studies at Cairo as a teacher of Nubian and Egyptian Arabic. He retired home after severe heart strain on the eve of the war. His writings include the pamphlet, *Offene Türen in Nubien* (1908). He died 15 June 1940. Der Nahe Osten

Endres, Franz Carl (Niklaus), born 17 December 1878 at München, he was a student at the Kriegs-akademie, München, where he later taught. Shortly before the first World War, he was appointed a lecturer at the war college in Constantinople and participated in the war as a commander of a Turkish army corps. As a result of his experience in the war his military career came to a sudden end when he fell seriously ill with malaria while on an information gathering trip to Palestine in 1915. The slaughter of the Armenian people by the Turkish Government against which he spoke out at the cost of the Turkish Government's withdrawing the pension to which he was entitled, the immense misery of the Turkish soldiers, as well as his observation at the German war fronts in 1917 caused him to renounce completely his military profession and adopt a pacifist position. He became a journalist and was resident in Switzerland as a free lance writer since 1926. His writings include *Nargileh* (1916), *Die Türkei* (1916), *Türkische Frauen* (1916), *Die Ruine des Orients* (1918), *Zionismus und Weltpolitik* (1918), *Die Zahl in Mystik und Glauben der Naturvölker* (1935), and *Land der Träume; ... Orient* (1935). He died in Muttenz, 10 March 1954. BiDMoPL; DtBE; DtBIlnd (4); Wer ist's, 1928

Endreß, Gerhard, born 23 October 1939 at Friedrichsdorf (Taunus), Germany, he received a Dr.phil. in 1965 from the Universität Frankfurt a. M. for his thesis, *Die arabischen Übersetzungen von Aristoteles' Schrift De caelo.* Thereafter he was a professor of Islamic studies at Frankfurt until 1975 when he was appointed at Bochum. He wrote *Zwanzig Abschnitte aus der Institutio theologica in arabischer Über-setzung* (1973), *The works of Yahya Ibn 'Adi; an analytical inventory* (1977), *Einführung in die islami-sche Geschichte* (1982), and its translation, *An Introduction to Islam* (1988). Kürschner, 1976-96; Schwarz

Eneberg, Kaarle (Karl) Fredrik, born 19 March 1841 at Närpes, Finland, he studied Oriental languages at Helsingfors, St. Petersburg, and Leipzig, and received doctorates at Helsingfors for *De pronomini-bus arabicis dissertatio etymologica* (1872), and *De pronominiibus arabicis (2): pronomina personalia* (1874). He died on a research journey to the East at Mosul in May 1876. ScBInd (3); Stenij, pp. 310-311

Eneström, Gustaf Hjalmar, born 5 September 1852 at Nora, Sweden, he was a mathematician and a librarian who studied at Uppsala, and received a doctorate at Lund. He died in Stockholm, 10 June 1923. SBL, v. 13, pp. 538-543

Enfrey, Lucienne Marie, fl. 1937, her writings include *Le Livre des harems* (1920), *Antioch* (1930), and *Une Femme entre les femmes* (1958). BN; NUC, pre-1956

at Hamburg **Engel**, Claire Éliane, born at Oran, she studied at the Sorbonne, where she received her *doctorat ès lettres* and *agrégation d'anglais*. Her writings include *A History of mountaineering in the Alps* (1950), *L'Ordre de Malte en Méditerrané, 1530-1798* (1957), *The Knights of Malta* (1964), *Histoire de l'Ordre de Malte* (1968), and *Les Chevaliers de Malte* (1972). Au&Wr, 1971

Engelbach, Reginald, born 9 July 1888 at Moretonhampstead, Devon, he was a trained engineer whose interest in Egyptology originated from a visit to Egypt during a convalescence in 1909-1910. Subsequently he studied Egyptian, Coptic and Arabic at University College, London. From 1924 until his retirement in 1941, he was a keeper at the Egyptian Museum, Cairo. He died in Cairo, 26 February 1946. Egytology; *Who was who*, 4

Engelbracht, Ursel, 1938- *see* Clausen-Engelbracht, Ursel

Engelhardt, Édouard Philippe, born 16 May 1828 at Rothau (Vosges), he studied law at the Faculté de droit de Strasbourg, was *élève-consul* at Mainz from 1850 to 1865, when he was assigned to the international commision to regulate the navigation on the Danube, 1865-1867. He was a consul-general for Serbia until 1874. He wrote *La Turquie et le tanzimat* (1882-84), *Les Protectorats anciens et modernes* (1896), and *La Question macédonienne* (1906). He died in Nice in 1916. DBF; NDBA

Engelhart, Christian C., fl. 1970, he pursued Indo-Iranian studies at the Universität Wien, and in 1969 became a teacher of German at the Hammer-Purgstall-Gesellschaft, Wien. Note

Engelke, Irmgard, born 11 March 1897 at Hannover, she studied at Berlin, Freiburg im Breisgau, and Köln, and received a Dr.phil. in 1926 from the Universität Kiel for her thesis, *Sülejman Tschelebi's Lobgedicht auf die Geburt des Propheten*. Schwarz; Thesis

Engelkemper, Wilhelm, born 17 March 1869 at Münster, Germany, he studied at Münster, Bonn, and Berlin, received a doctorate in philosophy at Roma, and a Dr.phil. in 1897 from the Universität Münster for his thesis, *De Saadiae Gaonis vita*. In 1906 he was appointed professor of Old Testament exegesis at Münster. His writings include *Die religionsphilosophische Lehre Saadja Gaons über die Hl. Schrift* (1903). Kosch; Kürschner, 1925-1935|; *Wer ist's*, 1909-1935

Enger, Maximilianus, born 14 March 1823 at Düren, Germany, he studied theology and Oriental languages and received a Dr.phil. in 1851 from the Universität Bonn for his thesis, *De vita et scriptis Maverdii*. In 1853 he published an edition of al-Mawardi's *al-Ahkam al-sultaniyah*. Fück, p. 173; Thesis

Engeström, Tor, born in 1905, he obtained a doctorate, and he was resident in Stockholm in 1959. His writings on West Africa include *Apport à la théorie des origines du peuple et de la langue peuhle* (1954). NUC, pre-1956

Engle, Anita, fl. 1976, her writings include *Ancient glass in its context* (Jerusalem, 1978), and she was editor of *Readings in glass history* (1973). LC

Englebert, Victor, born 5 February 1933 at Bruxelles, he was a professional photographer whose works include *Camera on Africa* (1970), *Camera on Ghana* (1971), and *Camera on the Sahara* (1971). BioIn, 11; ConAu, 57-60; LC

English, George Bethune, born 7 March 1787 at Cambridge, Mass., he graduated from Harvard and much later obtained a commission as a lieutenant of marines. During a call at Alexandria, Egypt, in 1820, he resigned his commission, embraced Islam, and participated in the expedition of Ismail Pasha to Sennar, a campaign which he described in *A narrative of the expedition to Dongola and Sennar* (1822). After the conquest, he resigned the Pasha's service as the expected reward was not forthcoming, and served the U.S. Government in several minor missions to the Ottoman Porte. He died in Washington, D.C. 20 September 1828. BiD&SB; DAB 3; DcNAA; Egyptology; Henze; Hill; Master (10); Shavit; WhAm, 4

English, Patrick Thomas, fl. 1953-1973, he was resident in Baltimore, Md., in 1959. His writings include *Man's march through the ages* (1937). NUC, pre-1956

English, Paul Ward, born 20 February 1936 at Worcester, Mass., he received a Ph.D. in 1965 from the University of Wisconsin for his thesis, *Settlement and economy in the Kirman Basin, Iran*. He was a professor of geography, with interest in cultural geography, and the geography of the Middle East.

He taught at various universities until 1979 when he was appointed at the University of Texas, Austin, a position he still held in 1999. His writings include *City and village of Iran* (1966), *World regional geography*, 2d ed. (1984), and *Geography; our changing world* (1990). AmM&WS, 1973, 1976; LC; *MESA Roster of members*, 1977-1990; NatFacDr, 1995-1999; WhoAm, 1980-1989/90|

Enikolopov, Ivan Konstantinovich, fl. 1954, his writings include *Пушкин на Кавказе* (1938), *Прибоедов в Грузии* (1954), and *Л. Н. Толстой в Грузии* (1978). LC

Enlart, Désiré Louis Camille, born 22 November 1862 at Boulogne-sur-Mer, he studied at l'École des beaux-arts de Paris, followed by courses in law. Being interested in architecture and archaeology, he attended l'École des chartes from 1885 to his graduation in 1889. After travels in Italy he became a *sous-bibliothéciare* at l'École des beaux-arts. From 1903 until his death he was director of the Musée de sculpture comparée du Trocadéro. Concurrently he lectured at l'École des chartes and l'École du Louvre. In the service of the Ministère de l'Instruction publique, he went on two archaeological missions to Cyprus in 1896 and 1901. His writings include *Les monuments des croisés dans la royaume de Jérusalem* (1925-27). He died in Paris, 14 February 1927. Curinier, v. 5, 13-15; DBF; *Qui êtes-vous*, 1924

Ennès, Pierre, fl. 1979, he was in 1994 *conservateur en chef* at the Département des objets d'art of the Musée du Louvre, Paris. His writings include *Histoire de la table; les arts de la table des origines à nos jours* (1994). LC

Enoch, G. Francis, fl. 1924, he was the American editor of a monthly periodical in Poona, India, in 1926. *Asia*, 1926

Enshoff, Dominikus, O.S.B., born in 1868, he was a sometime Benedictine missionary in East Africa. He died after 1909. LC

Entelis, John Pierre, born 5 November 1941 at Marseille, he was a graduate of Wesleyan University and received a Ph.D. from New York University in 1970 for his thesis, *The Lebanese Kata'ib; party transformation and system maintenance in a multiconfessional society*. He was appointed a professor at the Department of Social Sciences in Fordham University, N.Y.C., in 1970. In 1999 he was concurrently joint director of the Middle East Studies Program. His writings include *Pluralism and party transformation in Lebanon* (1974), *Comparative politics of North Africa* (1980), and *Algeria; the revolution institutionalized* (1986). AmM&WS, 1973, 1978; *MESA roster of members*, 1982-1990; NatFacDr, 1995-1999; Selim

Entessar, Nader, born 15 September 1948, he received a Ph.D. in 1976 from Saint Louis University for his thesis, *Political development in Chile during the Allende administration*. For over ten years he was a professor of political science and international relations at Spring Hill College, Mobile, Ala. His writings include *Political development in Chile* (Calcutta, 1980), and *Kurdish ethnonationalism* (Boulder, Col., 1992). *MESA roster of members*, 1990; NatFacDr, 1995-1999; NUC, 1982

Enthoven, Reginald Edward, born 23 November 1869 at St. Leonard's-on-Sea, he was educated at New College, Oxford, and entered the Indian Civil Service in 1887, remaining there until 1920. He was a student of Hindu anthropology. His writings include *The tribes and castes of Bombay* (1920), and *The folklore of Bombay* (1924). He died in 1952. BioIn, 3; Master (1); WhE&EA; *Who was who*, 5

Entwistle, William James, born 7 December 1895 in China, he was educated at the China Inland Mission Schools at Chefoo, Robert Gordon's College, Aberdeen, and the University of Aberdeen. He was King Alphonso XIII Professor of Spanish studies at Oxford since 1932, and director of Portuguese studies since 1933. His writings include *European balladry* (1939). He died suddenly in Oxford, 13 June 1952. BioIn, 2; DNB; ObitT, 1951; WhE&EA; *Who was who*, 5

Enver Paşa, born 22 November 1881 at Constantinople, he was a controversial figure in Turkish politics of the period between the Young Turks' revolution and the collapse of the Ottoman Empire. For a little over a year, he was appointed military attaché in Berlin but left in 1911 to serve in the Italo-Turkish war, the account of which he described in his *Um Tripolis* (1918), and its translation, *Diario della guerra libica* (1986). In 1913 he recaptured Edirne from the Bulgarians and became a national hero who, with Talat Paşa and Cemal Paşa, virtually ruled the country. He had fantastic Pan-Turkic schemes, but lost against Mustafa Kemal Atatürk, his hated rival. He was killed during his participation in the *basmachis* revolt in Bukhara against the Soviet regime, 4 August 1922. His writings include *Kendi mektuplarında Enver Paşa* (1986). BioIn, 12; EEE; EI²; EncAm; EncBrit; Meydan; Meyers, 1936; Zürcher

de **Epalza Ferrer**, Míkel, born 18 February 1938 at Pau (Pyrénées-Atlantiques), he was a graduate of the Universidad de Barcelona, where he also received a doctorate in 1967 with a thesis entitled *La Tuhfa, autobiografía y polemica islamica contra el cristianismo de Anselm Turmeda*. For over ten years he was a professor of Arabic and Islamic studies at the Universidad de Alicante as well as a visiting professor at the universities of Lyon, Tunis, Alger, Oran, and Cuenca. His writings include

Islam, christianisme, incroyance à la recherche d'un langage et d'une entente (1973), *Ecrits relatifs à l'histoire de l'Espagne publiés en Algérie de 1962 à 1973* (1976), and *Moros y moriscos en el levante peninsular* (1983). Arabismo, 1994, 1997; EURAMES, 1993; IWWAS, 1976/77

Eph'al, Israel, fl. 1975, he received a Ph.D. in 1982 from the Hebrew University, Jerusalem, for his thesis, *ha-Navadim bi-sefar Erets Yiśra'el*. He was a professor of Biblical history at Tel Aviv University in 1982, and a professor at the Department of History, the University of Chicago, in 1995. His writings include *The ancient Arabs; nomads on the borders of the Fertile Crescent* (1982). LC; NatFacDr, 1995

Eppel, Dov Bora, born 25 November 1917 in Poland. Since 1957 he was resident in Israel. He was a foreign affairs journalist for the Polish non-party daily *Życie Warszawy* and a lecturer in modern Persian language and literature at the Oriental Institute, Universytet Warszawski. He lectured in Persian at the Hebrew University, Jerusalem, from 1957 to 1958, and then became a foreign affairs columnist and a member of the Israeli daily, *Lamerhav*. New outlook, 1958, 1960; WhoIsrael, 1972-1976

Eppel, Michael, born 6 June 1947, he was a staff member at Oranim College in the University of Haifa in 1994. His writings include *The Palestine conflict in the history of modern Iraq* (1994). LC

Eppenstein, Franz, fl. 1939, he received a Dr.phil. in 1924 from the Universität Gießen for his thesis, *Deutschlands Milchversorgung in Frieden und Krieg*. His writings include the pamphlet, *Das türkische Volkseinkommen* (1938).

Eppenstein, Simon, born 25 August 1864 at Krotoszin, Poland. His orthodox studies at home were complemented at the Rabbiner-Seminar zu Berlin, where he was also ordained in 1889. He served as a rabbi at Briesen, West Prussia, until 1911 when he succeeded A. Berliner as lecturer in Jewish history and literature at the Rabbiner-Seminar, Berlin. He specialized in the Geonic period on which he wrote *Beiträge zur Geschichte und Literatur im geonäischen Zeitalter* (1913), and *Abraham Maimuni* (1914). He died 19 November 1920. EncJud; Wininger

Epstein, Eliahu, 1903-1990 *see* Elath, Eliahu

Epstein, Mark Alan, born 20th cent., his writings include *The Ottoman Jewish communities and their role in the 15th and 16th centuries* (Freiburg, im Breisgau, 1980), a work which was originally submitted as a doctoral thesis at the University of Washington; he was joint compiler of *Ottoman documents on Balkan Jews, XVIth-XVIIth centuries* (Sofia, 1990). LC

Epton, Nina Consuelo, born in 1913 at London, and educated at the Sorbonne, Paris, she was a writer and from 1943 to 1956 in charge of the French-Canadian Section at the BBC, London. Her writings include *Journey under the crescent moon* (1949), *Oasis Kingdom; the Libyan story* (1952), *The islands of Indonesia* (1955), *Saints and sorcerers; a Moroccan journey* (1958), *Andalusia* (1968), and *Dora Bell's village cats* (1977). Au&Wr, 1971; ConAu, 5-8, 11 new rev.; IntAu&W, 1976, 1977

Eran-Feinberg, Oded, fl. 1991, he received a Ph.D. from Indiana University in 1971 for his thesis, *Soviet thought on the role of the Communist party in the Third World*. He was affiliated with the Center for Strategic Studies, Tel Aviv University. His writings include *A comparative analysis of foreign and defense oriented research establishments in their political function in the USA and USSR, with lessons for Israel* (1979), and *Mezhdunarodniki; an assessment of professional expertise in the making of Soviet foreign policy* (1979). LC; Selim

Erb, Richard David, born 15 April 1941 at Bellmore, N.Y., he served from 1971 to 1974 as staff assistant to the president and director for international monetary affairs, Council for International Economic Policy, at the White House. From 1974 to 1976 he was deputy assistant secretary of treasury for developing nations. Thereafter he was a resident fellow at the American Entreprise Institute for Public Policy Research, Washington, D.C. His writings include *The Arab oil-producing states of the Gulf; political and economic developments* (1980); and he was editor of *Federal Reserve policies and public disclosure* (1978). IntWW, 1982-1992/93; Master (1); WhoAm, 1982/83-1986/87; WhoWor 1984/85-1987/88

von **Erckert**, Roderich, born in 1821 at Kulm, Prussia, he joined the Russian army as a young Prussian officer and rose to the rank of lieutenant-general. When he resigned in 1884 he was commander of a Caucasian division. During his service he pursued an interest in ethnographical and linguistic studies of the Caucasus. He lived in retirement in Berlin, where he wrote *Der Kaukasus und seine Völker* (1887), and *Die Sprachen des kaukasischen Stammes* (1895). He died in Berlin, 12 December 1900. Biographisches Jahrbuch, 1900, p. 577

Erckmann, Jules, capitaine, fl. 1887, his writings include *Le Maroc moderne* (1885). BN

Erdal, Marcel, born 8 July 1945 at İstanbul, he received a Ph.D. in linguistics in 1977 from the Hebrew University, Jerusalem, and later became a professor of linguistics. His writings include *Old Turkic word formation; a functional approach to the lexicon* (1991), *Die Sprache der wolgabolgarischen Inschriften* (1993); and he was joint editor of *Beläk Bitig; Sprachstudien für Gerhard Doerfer zum 75. Geburtstag* (1995). LC; Schoeberlein

Erdélyi, Istvan F., born 28 August 1931 at Nagyvárad, Romania, he was educated at Leningrad, obtained a doctorate, and became a lecturer in archaeology at Budapest. He travelled in Central Asia. His writings include the translations, *L'art des Avars* (1966), *The art of the Avars* (1966), *A magyar honfoglalás és előzményei* (1986), and *Pannoniai husnét* (1987); he was joint editor of *Археология Венгрии* (1986). Fekete; LC; MagyarNKK, 1990, 1992, 1994, 1996, 1998

Erdener, Nihal, fl. 1959, he obtained a docorate and was a lecturer in international private law at the Faculty of Law, Istanbul. His writings include *Türk devletler hususi hukuku sisteminde locus regit actum kaidesinin tatbiki* (1958). NUC, 1956-1967

Erder, Leila, fl. 1975, she received a Ph.D. from Princeton University, and was a lecturer at the Department of City and Regional Planning in the Middle East University, Ankara. She edited *Population information for city planning and management; report of a study group* (1979). LC

Erdman (Эрдман), Fedor Ivanovich, 1795-1863 *see* Erdmann, Franz

Erdmann, Carl, born 27 November 1898 at Tartu (Dorpat), he set out to study theology at Berlin in 1916 but later changed to history at München. He was a private tutor at Lisboa, 1921-1924, and obtainreceived a Dr.phil. in 1925 from the Universität Würzburg. He subsequently spent some years at the Preußisches Historisches Institut, Roma, where he began work on his *Die Entstehung des Kreuzzuggedankens* (1935), published in an English translation in 1977 under the title *The origin of the idea of crusade*. He also wrote *Idea de cruzada em Portugal* (1940). He was a collaborator in the production of *Monumenta Germaniae Historica* from 1932 to 1936, when he was barred from university activities on account of his opposition to the National Socialists. He served in the war since 1943 and died in Yugoslavia in 1945. DtBE

Erdmann, Elisabeth H., born 24 July 1942, she received a Dr.phil. in 1971 from the Universität Konstanz for her thesis, *Die Rolle des Heeres in der Zeit von Marius bis Caesar*. Since 1994 she was a professor at the Universität Erlangen-Nürnberg. Kürschner, 1994

Erdmann (Эрдман), Franz, born in 1795, he studied at the Universität Rostock and in 1819 succeeded C. M. Frähn at Kazan as a professor of Arabic and Persian. Although he was repeatedly also dean, and once deputy president, of the University, he resigned after his twenty-five-year tenure to take up a post as school administrator in the Gouvernement Novgorod because he had failed to win sympathy, or achieve very much, at Kazan. According to N. I. Veselovskii, he was "a pompous pedant and, although he knew how to surround himself with the flair of a scholar, he was ignorant and dull." In V. V. Bartol'd's laconic verdict, "he was denied acceptance as a scholar at home as well as abroad." Krachkovskii criticized his superficial use of Oriental prime material in his publications, and the way he misled influencial people in order to attain high academic offices. That he published his own silver jubilee volume, *Muhammad's Geburt und Abraha's Untergang*, in 1843 speaks for itself. His writings include *Vollständige Übersicht der ältesten türkischen, tatarischen und mongolischen Völkerstämme nach Raschid-ud-Din's Vorgange* (1841). He died in 1863. Krachkovskii; NUC, pre-1956; TatarES

Erdmann, Hanna, fl. 1985, her writings include *Orientteppiche, 16.-19. Jahrhundert* (1966), and she edited *Iranische Kunst in deutschen Museen* (1967). Together with Kurt Erdmann she published *Das anatolische Karavansaray des 13. Jahrhunderts* (1976). LC

Erdmann, Kurt Arthur Heinz, born 9 September 1901 at Hamburg, he was a historian of Sasanian and Islamic art. His career and publications were closely connected to the Islamische Abteilung of the Staatliche Museen, Berlin, where he was its director from 1958 until his death on 30 September 1964. Concurrently he lectured at the universities of Berlin, Bonn, Cairo, and Hamburg. His writings include *Europa und der Orientteppich* (1962), and *The history of the early Turkish carpet* (1977). EncIran; Kürschner, 1950, 1954, 1961; Meydan

Eredia, Filippo, born 6 February 1877 at Catania, Italy, he was a meteorologist and a sometime professor at the Università di Roma. His writings include *Tripolitania e Cirenaica; climatologia di Tripoli e Bengazi* (1912), and *Nuovi orizzonti della meteorologia* (1941). He died in Roma, 14 February 1948. Chi è, 1928, 1931, 1938, 1940; DizBI

Ereli, Eliezer, fl. 1955, his writings include *Legal framework affecting offshore oil terminals* (1973), a work which was published by the Texas Law Institute of Coastal and Marine Resources. Note

Eremeev, Dmitrii Evgen'evich, born 21 October 1928 at Briansk, Russia, he graduated in 1952 from the Oriental Institute, Moscow, received a doctorate in 1972, and was appointed a professor in 1975. He was a researcher at the Ethnographical Institute, Soviet Academy of Sciences from 1960 to 1970 when he became a lecturer at the Institute for Afro-Asian Countries, Moscow. His writings include *Страна за Черным мореь* (1968), *Юрюки* (1969), *Этногенез турок* (1971), *Турция* (1973), *На стыке Азии и Европы; очерки о Турции и турках* (1980), and its translation, *An der Nahtstelle zwischen Asien und Europa: Skizzen über die Türkei und die Türken* (1987). Miliband; Miliband²

Eremian, Suren Tigranovich, born 28 March 1908 at Tbilisi, he graduated in 1931 at Erevan, and received a doctorate in 1953 for his thesis, *Рабовладельческое общество древней Армении*. Miliband; Miliband²; WhoSocC, 1978

Eremina, Kira Nikolaevna, born 12 January 1929 at Riazan (Ryazan), she graduated in 1961 from the Institute of Oriental Languages at Moscow. Thereafter she was a researcher at the Oriental Institute, Academy of Sciences. Her writings include *К проблеме языковых контактов; Европеизмы в современном персидском языке* (1980). Miliband²

Eren, Nuri, born about 1913, he was a trained economist and held a post in the Turkish Ministry of Commerce until he became head of the Anglo-American Section of the Press Department of the Turkish Government. He was a sometime Turkish representative to the United Nations, and was an international consultant and secretary-general of the Economic Research Foundation of Turkey in 1966. His writings include *Turkey, today and tomorrow* (1964), and *Turkey, NATO, and Europe* (1978). BioIn, 2, 8; LC

Erendil, Muzaffer, born in 1921 at Adapazarı, Turkey, he was a Turkish officer and retired with the rank of major general. His writings include *Tarihte Türk-Bulgar ilişkileri* (1976), *Tarihte Türk-Iran ilişkileri* (1976), *Topçuluk tarihi* (1988), *Çağdaş orta doğu olayları* (1992), and *Dünden bu güne mehter* (1992). LC

von **Erffa**, Helmut, born in 1900 at Lüneburg, Germany, he received an M.F.A. in 1938 from Princeton University, and was a joint author of *The paintings of Benjamin West* (1986). He died in 1979. LC

Erian, Tahany Said el-, born in 1939, he received a Ph.D. in 1972 from Columbia University for his thesis, *The Public law 480 program in American libraries*. LC

Erice, Fernando Sebastián de, 1906- *see* Sebastián de Erice y O'Shea, Fernando

de **Erice y O'Shea**, José Sebastián, 1906- *see* Sebastián de Erice y O'Shea José

Erickson, John David, born 9 January 1934 at Aitkin, Minn., he was a graduate of the University of Minnesota where he also received a Ph.D. in 1961 for his thesis, *The illusion of reality in the novels of François Mauriac*. He taught at a number of American universities, was a visiting professor at the Université de Mohammed V in Morocco before he became a professor of French, and chairman of department, at Louisiana State University, Baton Rouge, in 1980. His writings include *Nommo; African fiction in French south of the Sahara* (1979). DrAS, 1974, 1978, 1982; LC; NUC, 1956-1967

Erickson, Jon Laroy, born 20h cent., he received a Ph.D. in 1965 from the University of Texas for his thesis, *English and Arabic; a discussion of contrastive verbal morphology*. He was a sometime professor of English at the University of Wisconsin. His writings include *Phases; poems, 1974-1977* (1980), and he was joint author of *Readings for the history of the English language* (1968). Selim; LC

Erim, Ismail Nihat, born in 1912 at Kandıra, Turkey, he was educated at Galatasaray Lisesi, Istanbul, and studied law at Istanbul and Paris. He was a professor of constitutional law at Ankara Üniversitesi as well as a senator. From March 1971 to April 1972 he was prime minister of Turkey. He died in Istanbul, 19 July 1980. AnObit, 1980; BioIn, 10, 11, 12; IntWW, 1979/80, 1980/81; Master (1); Meydan; Zürcher

Erinç, Sırrı, his writings include *Doğu Anadolu coğrafyası* (1953), *Klimatoloji ve metodları* (1962), and he was joint author of *Some documents concerning the geography of Turkey* (1962). LC; TB, 1954

d'**Erlanger**, Rudolphe François, born 7 June 1872 at Boulogne-sur-Seine, he was a landscape painter with a classical education. His work and his extensive travels in North Africa provided him with the opportunity to study at first hand the various peoples of North Africa. He was also interested in music, presided the Congress of Arab music in Cairo, 1932, and edited and translated *La Musique arabe*, in five volumes, 1930-1935. He died in Sidi Bou Saïd, Tunisia, 29 October 1932. DBF; Baker 1984

Erlashova (Yerlashova), Sof'ia Mikhailovna, fl. 1964, her writings include *Тенгиз Мирзасвили* (1973), *Керамика и чеканка Грузии* (1977), *Манаба Магомедова* (1982), and she edited *Живопись советской Туркмении = Painting of Soviet Turkmenia* (1975). LC

Erlikh (Erlich), Hagai, born 29 March 1942, he was a professor whose writings include *Ethiopia and Eritrea during the scramble for Africa* (1982), *The struggle over Eritrea, 1962-1978* (1983), *Ethiopia and the challenge of independence* (1986), and *Students and university in 20th century Egyptian politics* (1989), as well as writings in Hebrew on the same subjects. LC

Erlikh (Эрлих), R. L., born around the end of the nineteenth century, she started studying at Leningrad University in 1917, and later specialized in Arabic and ancient folk literature. She died in 1930. Krachkovskii, p. 200

Erlmann, Veit, born 13 February 1951 at Essen, he received a Dr.phil. in 1978 from the Universität Köln for *Die Macht des Wortes; Preisgesang und Berufsmusiker bei den Fulbe des Diamaré, Nordkamerun.* He was a professor of music-ethnology successively at the universities of Durban, South Africa, Johannesburg, and Berlin. He wrote *Booku, eine literarisch-musikalische Gattung der Fulbe des Diamaré* (1979), and *African stars; studies in Black South African performance* (1991). ConAu, 1939; Kürschner; LC

Erman, Georg Adolf, born 12 Mai 1806 at Berlin, he studied natural sciences and accompanied a Norwegian expedition to Russia and Siberia. After his return to Berlin he became a professor of physics. From 1841 to 1867 he was an editor of the *Archiv für wissenschaftliche Kunde von Russland.* He died in Berlin, 12 July 1877. DcScB; DtBilnd; Embacher; Henze

Erman, Johann (Jean) Peter (Pierre) Adolf (Adolphe), born 30 October 1854 at Berlin, of Swiss Protestant descent, he studied Egyptology at Leipzig and Berlin, where he was appointed director of the Ägyptisches Museum in 1884 and concurrently a professor of Egyptology at the Universität in 1885. His influence on Egyptology may be termed cyclonic and the greatest since Champollion. He wrote his autobiography, *Mein Werden und mein Wirken* (1929). He died in 1937. DtBE; DtBilnd (5); Egyptology; NDB

Erman, Sahir, fl. 20th cent., he was in 1958 a lecturer in law at Istanbul Üniversitesi. His writings include *Askeri ceza hukuku* (1955), *Kaçakçılık kanunu şerhi* (1973), and *Bankacılık suçları* (1984). LC

Ermatinger, Charles Joseph, born in 1921, he received a Ph.D. in 1963 from St. Louis University for his thesis, *The coalescent soul in post-Thomistic debate.* He was the editor of *Guide to microfilms of Vatican library manuscript codices available for study in the Vatican Film Library at Saint Louis Library* (1993). LC; NUC, 1956-1967

Ernazarova, Tamara Sadridinovna, born 25 August 1939 in Uzbekistan, she was a writer on archaeology and numismatics. Schoeberlein

Ernshtedt, Petr Viktorovich, born in 1890 at Gatchina, Russia, he graduated in 1913 at St. Petersburg and was appointed a professor in 1947. His writings include *Исследования по грамматике коптского языка* (1986). He died 25 December 1966. Miliband; Miliband²

von **Ernst**, Carl, fl. 1875-1880, he was affiliated with the Numismatische Gesellschaft in Wien and wrote *Die Kunst des Münzens* (Wien, 1880). NUC, pre-1956

Ernst, Carl W., born 8 September 1950 at Los Angeles, he was a graduate of Stanford University, and received a Ph.D. from Harvard in 1981 for his thesis, *Faith and infidelity in Sufism.* He taught at the Department of Religion, Pomona College, Claremont, Cal., until 1992 when he became successively a professor of religion, and chairman of department, University of North Carolina at Chapel Hill. His writings include *Words of ecstacy in Sufism* (1985), *Eternal garden; mysticism, history, and politics in a South Asian Sufi center* (1992), *Ruzbihan Baqli; mystical experience and the rhetoric of sainthood in Persian Sufism* (1996), and *The Shambhala guide to Sufism* (1997). ConAu, 163; *National faculty directory,* 1999; Private; Selim²

Ernst, Fritz, born 30 October 1905 at Stuttgart, he received a Dr.phil. in 1929 from the Universität Tübingen for *Die wirtschaftliche Ausstattung der Universität Tübingen in ihren ersten Jahrzehnten.* He was a sometime professor of modern history successively at Tübingen and Heidelberg. He was a joint editor of *Die Welt als Geschichte,* a member of the Akademie der Wissenschaften, Heidelberg, and author of *England und Indien* (1939). He died in Heidelberg, 21 December 1963. Kürschner, 1940/41, 1950, 1954, 1961; *Wer ist wer,* 1950, 1955, 1958, 1962, 1963

Erödi-Harrach, Béla, born 19 April 1846 at Szászrégen, Hungary, he travelled extensively in the Middle East until 1880, when he started a teaching career. His writings include *Keleti gyöngyök* (1871), *Hafiz dalai* (1872), *Leila ile Medsnun* (1875), *Török mozaik* (1875), *Szádi Gulisztánja* (1889), *A Fáraók országában* (1897), and *A Szentföldön* (1899). He died in 1936. GeistigeUng; Pallas; RNL; UjLex

Erol, Oğuz, fl. 1963-1979, he received a doctorate in 1950 at Ankara for a thesis on the geology and geomorphology of the region southeast of Ankara. His writings include *Ankara şehrinin gelişmesinde doğal koşulların* (1976), and *Die naturräumliche Gliederung der Türkei* (1983). LC; TB, 1979

Erpenbeck, Doris *see* Kilias, Doris (divorced Erpenbeck)

Erpenius (van Erpe), Thomas, born in 1584 at Gorkum, Holland, he studied theology at Leiden and since 1609 at Paris. He became a professor of Arabic and Hebrew at Leiden. His writings include *Proverbiorum arabicorum centuriæ duæ* (1614), *Rudimenta linguæ arabicæ* (1620), and *Historia Saracenica* (1625). He died in Leiden in 1624. EncBrit; EncJud; Flück, pp. 59-71; Juynboll; NieuwNBW, v. 8, col. 495-96

Errera, Isabelle née Goldschmidt, born 2 April 1869 at Firenze, she had sufficient private means to be an art collector and historian, specializing in ancient embroidery and lace-work. She made donations to the Royal Museum, Bruxelles, and wrote a number of catalogues, including *Collection d'anciennes étoffes réunies et décrites* (1901), *Collection de broderies anciennes* (1905), and *Collection d'anciennes étoffes égyptiennes* (1916). She also wrote *Dictionnaire répertoire des peintres depuis l'antiquité jusqu'à nos jours* (1913). She died in Bruxelles, 23 June 1929. BioNBelg, vol. 31, col. 328-332

Errera-Hoechstetter, Irène, fl. 1978, her writings include *Le conflit israélo-arabe, 1948-1974* (1974), and *La course aux armements au Proche-Orient* (1977).

Ershov, Nikolai Nikolaevich, born 30 December 1904, his writings include *Русско-таджикский разговорник* (1968), and *Альбом одежды таджиков* (1969). He died 26 September 1980. LC

Erten, Süleyman Fikri, born 1875 or 6 at Gornji Rahić near Brčko, Bosnia, he was educated at Istanbul, where he graduated from a *medrese* and the Faculty of Arts. He was a teacher at Bolu, Lazikiya, and Antalya. Concurrently he pursued an interest in archaeology and established the Archaeological Museum, Antalya. His writings include *Antalya livası tarihi* (1922), and *Tekelioğulları* (1955). He died in 1962. Anali Gazi Husrev-Begove Biblioteke 11/12 (1985), pp. 141-164

Erzakovich, Boris Girchevich, born 30 May 1908 at Akmolinsk, Kazakstan, he was affiliated with the Institute of Literatures and Arts, Kazak Academy of Science. His writings include *Песенная культура казахского народа; музы-кально-историческое исследование* (Alma-Ata, 1966), and *Музыкальное наследие казахского народа* (Alma-Ata, 1979). Казахская ССР краткая энциклопедия, vol. 3, p. 202; LC; NUC, 1956-1967

Erzakovich, Lev Borisovich, born in 1936 he was joint author of *Древний Отрар* (1972), and *Позднесредневековый Отрар* (1981). He died in 1993. LC; Schoeberlein

Esbergenov, Khozhakhmet, born 10 May 1933 in Uzbekistan, he was joint author of *Традиции и их преобразование в городском быту каракалпаков* (1975), and *Этнографические мотивы в каракалпакском фольклоре* (1988). LC; Schoeberlein

Escallier, Robert, fl. 1974, his writings include *Citadins et espace urbain au Maroc* (1981). LC

d'**Escayrac de Lauture**, Pierre Henri *Stanislas*, comte, born in 1826 at Paris, he was educated at the Collège de Juilley. Since 1844 attached to the Ministère des Affaires étrangères, he was sent on missions to Morocco; he also resided in Algeria, where he learned Arabic. After the 1848 revolution he was a man of leisure and visited North Africa and the Near East. In 1856, the viceregent of Egypt, Muhammad Sa'id Pasha, appointed him leader of an expedition to discover the sources of the Nile, but the mission failed even before leaving Cairo. Opinions are divided as to whether he was a great explorer or a mountebank. His writings include *Le désert et le Soudan* (1853), its translation, *Die afrikanische Wüste und das Land der Schwarzen am oberen Nil* (1855), *De la Turquie et des états musulmans en général* (1858), and *Voyage dans le grand désert et au Soudan* (1858). He died in Fontainebleau, on 18 December 1868. Bulletin de géographie historique et descriptive, 1899, pp. 323-369; DBF; Embacher; Henze; Hill; Hommes et destins, v. 7, pp. 178-180

d'**Eschavannes**, E., the author of *Notice historique sur la maison de Lusignan; son illustration en Occident et en Orient* (1853), and *Histoire de Corinthe; relation des principaux événements de la Morée* (1854). BN

d'**Eschavannes**, Jouffroy, b. 1810 *see* Jouffroy d'Eschavannes, Joseph Louis Édouard

Eschelbacher, Ruth, 1930- *see* Lapidoth, Ruth née Eschelbacher

Escholier, Raymond, born 25 December 1882 at Paris, he was a sometime secretary at the Direction des beaux-arts, and successively a keeper at the Musée Victor-Hugo, and the Petit Palais. He died on 19 September 1971. WhAm, 6; WhE&EA; WhoFr, 1953/54, 1965/66, 1967/68, 1969/70, 1971/72; WhoWor, 1974/75

Escott, Bickham Aldred Cowan Sweet, fl. 1956 *see* Sweet-Escott, Bickham Aldred Cowan

Escovitz, Joseph H., fl. 20th cent., he received an M.A. in 1974 from McGill University, Montreal, for his thesis, *A study of "al-Durar al-kamina"* as a source for the history of the Mamluk Empire. His writings include *The office of qâdî al-qudât in Cairo under the Bahri Mamluks* (1984), a work which he originally presented as his doctoral thesis also at McGill in 1978. Ferahian; LC

Escribano Ucelay, Victor, born 13 February 1913 at Madrid, he held a diploma in town planning and was a sometime municipal architect of Córdoba. His writings include *La Calahorra* (Córdoba, 1961), and *Estudios sobre terrenos de bujeo* (Madrid, 1961). WhoSpain, 1963; NUC, 1956-1972

Esenberlin, Iliyas, born 10 January 1915 at Atbasar, Tselinograd Oblast, he was a Kazak writer who was well known for his novels on the pre-Soviet period of Central Asian history. His writings include *On tomdyq shygharmalar zhinaghy* (1984). He died 5 October 1983. *Central Asian survey* 2 (1983), pp. 1-3; KazakSE vol. 4, p. 180

Esenkova, Enver, fl. 1960, his writings include *Türk dilinde Fransız tesiri* (1959), *İhtilâl...* (1962), *Connaissance des Turks et de la Turquie* (1967), and *Fransız dili grameri* (1967). NUC, 1956-1967

Esenov, Khairbolat Mukanovich, born 6 May 1931, his writings include *Qazaq tilindegi kurdelengen soilemder* (1974), and *Sabaktas kurmalas söjlemnin kurylysy* (1982). *Казахская ССР краткая энциклопедия*, vol. 3, p. 204; OSK

Eshai Shimun. He was the Catholicos Patriarch of the Church of the East and the Assyrian Nation, who sent a petition on behalf of the Assyrians to the secretary general of the United Nations' Conference, San Francisco, 1945. The text was published in 1946 entitled *The Assyrian national petition presented to the world security conference at San Francisco, May 7, 1945.* LC

Esin, Emel née Tek, born in 1914 at Constantinople, she was educated at Istanbul and Paris where she obtained a doctorate in medieval Turkish cultural history. Since 1941 she was married to the Turkish diplomat Seyfullah Esin, whose post in Moscow afforded her first visit to Central Asia in 1941 resulting in her *Türkestan seyahatnamesi* (1959). She was a free lance writer until 1983 when she was nominated a member of Atatürk Kültür Merkezi, Ankara. Her writings include *Turkish miniature painting* (1960), *Mecca, the Blessed, Medinah, the Radiant* (1963), *Antecedents and development of Buddhist and Manichean Turkish art in Eastern Turkestan and Kansu* (1967), *A history of pre-Islamic and early Islamic Turkish culture* (1980), and *The culture of the Turks* (1986). She died in 1987. *Inex Islamicus* (3); IWWAS, 1976/77

Esin, Necmettin, fl. 1964, he was the editor of *Kemalettin Kamu* (1975). TB, 1975

Eslami Nodooshan, M. A. *see* Islami Nudushan, Muhammad 'Ali

d'Espérey, Franchet, 1856-1942 *see* Franchet d'Espérey, Louis Félix Marie François

Esperson, Pietro, born 2 March 1833 at Sassari, Sardinia, he was a practising lawyer and a professor of international law at the universities of Sassari and Pavia. His writings include *Diritto cambiario internazionale* (1870). He died in 1917. *Chi è*, 1908; Gubernatis; Gubernatis 3

Espitalier, Albert, born in 1874, his writings include *Napoléon et le rois Murat, 1808-1815* (1910), its translation, *Napoleon and King Murat* (1912), and *Vers brumaire; Bonaparte à Paris* (Paris, 1914). NUC, pre-1956

Esposito, Bruce John, born 9 February 1941 at N.Y.C., he was since 1976 a professor of history at the University of Hartford, Conn., a position which he still held in 1999. His writings include *Energy developing in China* (1979). AmM&WS, 1973 S; DrAS, 1974, 1978, 1982; NatFacDr, 1995-1999; Schoeberlein

Esposito, John Louis, born 19 May 1940 at Brooklyn, N.Y.C., he was a graduate of St. Anthony College and received a Ph.D. in 1974 from Temple University for his thesis, *Muslim family law in Egypt and Pakistan.* He taught at Rosemont College until 1972, when he was appointed professor of religious studies, and later chairman of department, at the College of the Holy Cross, Worcester, Mass. His writings include *Women in Muslim family law* (1982), *Islam, the straight path* (1988), *The Islamic threat; myth or reality* (1992), and he was editor of *Islam and development* (1980), and *Political Islam* (1997). ConAu, 116; DrAS, 1978, 1982; NatFacDr, 1995; Private

Esquer, Gabriel, born 12 April 1876 at Caunes-Minervois near Carcassonne, he studied at l'École des chartes and was appointed chief archivist of the Département du Cantal in 1903. In 1908, he became *archiviste-bibliothècaire* of the Gouvernement général de l'Algérie and in 1910, *administrateur* of the Bibliothèque nationale d'Alger, positions which he held until 1942 and 1948 respectively. His writings include *Les Débuts de l'administration civile à Alger; le personnel* (1912), *Iconographie historique de l'Algérie* (1929), and *Histoire de l'Algérie* (1950). He died in 1961. Hommes et destins, vol. 4, pp. 297-298

van **Ess**, Josef, born 18 April 1934 at Aachen, Germany, he received a Dr.phil. in 1959 from the Universität Bonn for his thesis, *Die Gedankenwelt des Harit ibn Asad al-Muhasibi*. Since 1968 he was a professor of Islamic studies at Tübingen. His writings include *Die Erkenntnislehre des 'Adudad-din al-Ici* (1966), *Zwischen Hadit und Theologie* (1975), and *Anfänge muslimischer Theologie* (1977). Kürschner, 1970-1996; Schwarz

Essad, Mahmoud, fl. 1926 *see* Mahmoud Essad

Essad Bey (Leo Noussimbaum), born in 1905 at Baku, where his father owned an oil field. He was educated abroad, chiefly in Germany, and he wrote usually in German. His writings include *Öl und Blut im Orient* (1930), *Zwölf Geheimnisse im Kaukasus* (1930), *Der Kaukasus* (1931), *Stalin* (1931), *Mohammed; Biographie* (1932), *Das weiße Rußland* (1932), *Flüssiges Gold; der Kampf um die Macht* (1933), *Allah ist groß* (1936), and *Reza Schah* (1936). He died in 1942. LC; NUC, pre-1956

van der **Essen**, Léon Jean, born 12 December at Antwerpen (Anvers), he studied history and was appointed in 1910 a professor at the Université catholique de Louvain. He also was a visiting professor at Chicago, Oxford, Utrecht, Nijmegen, Belfast, Montpellier and Groningen. He wrote *A Short history of Belgium* (1916), and *L'Université de Louvain, 1425-1940* (1945). WhoBelgium, 1957/58, 1962

von **Essen**, Otto Ludwig Rudolph Heinrich, born 20 May 1898 at Hamburg, he was a professor of phonetics at the Universität Hamburg. His writings include *Grungbegriffe der Phonetik* (1962). He was honoured by a jubilee volume, *Festschrift für Otto von Essen anläßlich seines 80. Geburtstages* (1979). He died in Hamburg, 6 February 1983. Kürschner, 1950-1983; Wer ist wer, 1955, 1958, 1962, 1967/68

del **Estal**, Gabriel, fl. 1959, his writings include *La dialéctica de los "dos reinos" en la filosofía augustiniana del derecho y del estado Parte sistemática* (1959), *Viento de pentecostés en el Monte Vaticano* (1962), and *Sociedad inconforme* (1973). NUC, pre-1956

del **Estal**, Juan Manuel, fl. 1960, his writings include *El voto de virginidad en la primitiva iglesia de Africa* (1959), and *Institución monástica de San Augustín desde sus orígenes hasta la muerte del Fundador* (1965). LC

Estébanez Calderón, Serafín, born 27 December 1799 at Malaga, he studied law at Granada and subsequently practised law until 1822 when he became a professor of rhetoric and poetry at Malaga. His writings include *Escenas andaluzas* (1847), *Manual del oficial en Marruecos* (1844), *De la conquista y perdida de Portugal* (1885), and *Cristianos y moriscos* (Hamburgo, 1922). He died in Madrid, 5 February 1867. IndiceE (20); Manzanares. pp. 105-118

Esterhazy, Louis Joseph Ferdinand, 1807-1857 *see* Walsin Esterhazy, Louis Joseph Ferdinand

Esteve Guerrero, Manuel, born 25 July 1905 at Jerez, Spain, his writings include *Jerez de la Frontera; guída official de arte* (1952), and *Excavaciones de Asta Regia* (1962). He died 27 November 1956.

Esteves Pereira, Francisco Maria, born 9 August 1854, his writings include *Historia dos martyres de Nagran; versão ethiopica* (1899). He died in 1924. NUC, pre-1956

Estier, Claude, born in 1925 at Paris, he was educated at the Lycée Carnot and l'École libre des sciences politiques, Paris. He was a newspaper editor and a socialist leader. His writings include *La gauche hebdomadaire, 1914-1962* (1962), *Pour l'Algérie* (1964), and *L'Égypte en révolution* (1965). WhoFr, 1973/74-1998/99

d'**Estourmel**, François Marie *Joseph* Louis, born in 1783, he had a varied administrative career until 1824. In 1832 he visited Italy, Palestine, and Egypt, a journey which he described in *Journal d'un voyage en Orient* (1844). He died in Paris, 13 December 1853. DBF; Egyptology; GdeEnc; Michaud

d'**Estournelles de Constant**, Paul Henri Benjamin Balluet d'Estournelles de Constant de Rebecques, born 22 November 1852 at La Flèche (Sarthe), he was a graduate of the Lycée Saint-Louis and l'École des langues orientales vivantes, Paris. He entered the diplomatic service in 1876, and was posted to Tunis, Montenegro, Turkey, and the Netherlands. Appointed to the Cour permanente d'arbitrage at den Haag in 1900, he founded the *Bulletin de la conciliation internationale* in 1906, was the French delegate at the Conference of the Haag the following year, and was the Nobel laureat in peace for 1907. He died in 1924. EncAm; BioIn, 9, 11, 15; Curinier, vol. 5 (1906), pp. 345-6; DBF; Qui êtes-vous?, 1924

d'**Estry des Frames**, Guillaume Henry Jean, comte, 1829- *see* Meyners d'Estry, Guillaume Henry J.

497

szer, Ambrosius K., fl. 1971, his writings include *Das abenteuerliche Leben des Johannes Laskaris Kalopherus; Forschungen zur Geschichte der ost-westlichen Beziehungen im 14. Jahrhundert* (1969).

'Eszlary, Charles, fl. 1954, his writings include *Les Français en Hongrie pendant les guerres napoléoniennes et mondiales* (Paris, 1966). NUC, 1956-1967

sztergár, Marianne, born in 1935, she received a Ph.D. in 1971 from the University of California at San Diego for her thesis, *The generative phonology of nouns and vowel harmony in Hungarian*. NUC, 973-1977

te, Muhlis, born 23 October 1904, he received a doctorate and was successively a professor at Istanbul and Ankara. In 1950 he entered politics. His writings include *Köy bölgelerimizde kurulacak küçük sınaî işletmeler* (1943), *İşletme ekonomisi dersleri* (1946), *State exploitation in Turkey* (1951), and *Probleme der Assoziierung der Türkei mit der Europäischen Wirtschaftsgemeinschaft* (1963). He also was the editor of *Türk ekonomisi* since 1943. IntWW, 1974-1985/86; LC; Meydan

thé, Carl Hermann, born 13 February 1844 at Stralsund, Germany, he studied classics at Greifswald, and Oriental languages at Leipzig, where he was a student of H. L. Fleischer. In 1868 he presented his thesis at the Universität München, where he subsequently taught Oriental languages. In 1872 he was invited to continue the work of E. Sachau at the Bodleian Library, Oxford, particularly the cataloguing of the Persian, Turkish and Afghan manuscripts. Concurrently he accepted to catalogue the Persian manuscripts of the India Office Library. In 1875 he was appointed a professor of Oriental languages at University College of Aberythwyth, a post which he held until 1914. Since return to his post was denied to him after the summer holiday on the Rhine, he continued to work on the manuscripts of the India Office Library during the war. His writings include *Morgenländische Studien* (1870), *Catalogue of Persian manuscripts in the Library of the India Office* (Oxford, 1903), and *Catalogue of Oriental manuscripts, Persian, Arabic, and Hindustani* (Aberystwyth, 1916). He died unnoticed by friend and foe in Bristol, 7 June 1917. *Acta orientalia Academiae scientiarum hungaricae* 48 (1995), pp. 37-50; Brümmer; Brümmer²; EnclIran *Wer ist's*, 1909, 1912, 1922, 1928; *Who was who*, 2

them, Muhlis, born 23 October 1904 at Constantinople, he was a graduate of the Austrian St. Georg-Schule in Constantionple and the Realgymnasium in Weimar. He studied at the Universität Leipzig rom 1925 to 1929, when he received a Dr.phil. for his thesis, *Der Hafen von Stambul und seine Organisation*. Thesis

therton, Percy Thomas, born 4 September 1879, he was educated privately in France. During the war, he served in Egypt, Palestine, and Mesopotamia. From 1918 to 1924, he was British consul-general and political resident at Kashgar in Chinese Turkestan, and served as additional assistant judge in H.B.M. Supreme Court for China. His writings include *In the heart of Asia* (1925). He died 30 March 1963. WhE&EA; *Who was who*, 6

tienne, Bruno, born 20th cent., he received a doctorate in 1965 from the Université d'Aix-Marseille for his thesis, *Les problèmes juridiques des minorités européennes au Maghreb*. He was a sometime professor of political science at Aix-Marseille III. His writings include *L'Islamisme radical* (1987), and *Abdelkader* (1994), and he was joint author of *Ils ont rasé la Mésopotamie* (1992).

tienne, Eugène Napoléon, born 15 December 1844 in Algeria, he was educated at lycées in Alger and Marseille. After he completed his training in France, he returned to Algeria in 1881 and ran as a Gambettist republican for the Chambre des députées. Elected as an announced champion of the colon minority, he dedicated his life to their cause. Among the representatives of French Algeria, he did more to fix the ideals of *Algérie française* on Algeria than any other person. He became the heart of colon supremacy. He was the founder of the Comité de l'Asie française. After his death on 13 May 1921, his friends established the Foundation Eugène Etienne in his memory. His writings include *Les compagnies de colonisation* (1897). Roland Villot wrote *Eugène Étienne, 1844-1921* (1951). *Bulletin de a Société de géographie d'Oran* 41 (1921), pp. 97-103; Curinier, vol. 1, pp. 2-3; DBF; MW 65 (1975), pp. 39-53

tienne, Gilbert, born in 1928 in Switzerland, he received a degree in law in 1951 from the Université de Neuchâtel, a diploma in 1954 from the École des langues et civilisations orientales, Paris, and a doctorate in 1955 at Neuchâtel. He was a faculty member of the Institut universitaire de hautes études internationales, Genève, since 1962, and concurrently a consultant to the World Bank. His writings include *De Caboul à Pékin; rythmes et perspectives d'expansion économique* (1959), *Bangladesh, development in perspective* (1979), *Le Pakistan, don de l'Indus* (1989), and he was joint author of *Suisse - Asie; pour un nouveau partenariat* (1992). WWASS, 1989; LC

ttinghausen, Richard, born 5 February 1905 at Frankfurt am. Main, he held a varied of positions in the American academic art world until he was appointed a professor of fine arts at New York University in 1967. He died 2 April 1979. BlueB, 1975, 1976; CnDiAmJBi; ConAu, 65-68, 85-88, new rev., 9; DrAS, 1974, 1978; I.I. (4); IntWW, 1974-1978/79; Schwarz; WhAm, 7; WhoAm, 1974-1978/79; WhoAmA, 1973-1985; WhoWor, 1974/75

Etzioni, Amitai Werner, born 4 January 1928 at Köln, he was educated at the Hebrew University, Jerusalem, and received a Ph.D. in 1959 from the University of California at Berkeley for his thesis, *The organizational structure of the kibbutz*. He was a sometime staff member of the Institute of War and Peace Studies, Columbia University, N.Y.C., and director of the Center for Policy Research. In 1980 he was appointed a professor at the Department of Sociology, George Washington University, D.C. His writings include *Bi-ferots ha-portsim* (1952), and *The Active society* (1968). AmM&WS, 1973, 1978; BioIn, 12; CnDiAmJBi; ConAu, 1-4, new rev., 5, 22; Master (2); NatFacDr., 1995; WhoAm, 1974-1999; WhoE, 1977/78; WhoWorJ, 1965, 1972, 1978; WrDr, 1980-1988/90

Etzioni-Halavy, Eva née Horowitz, born 21 March 1934 at Wien, she was educated at the Hebrew University, Jerusalem, where she also received her Ph. D. in 1971. Thereafter she was a sociologist at universities in Australia and Israel. Her writings include *The political culture in Israel* (1977), *National broadcasting under siege* (1987), and *The Elite connection; problems and potential of Western democracy* (1993). ConAu, 127, new rev., 58; WhoIsrael, 1992/93; WhoWorJ, 1978, 1987

Etzold, Thomas Herman, born 2 June 1945 in St. Clair County, Illinois, he received a Ph.D. in 1970 from Yale University for his thesis, *Fair play; American principles and practice in relations with Germany, 1933-1939*. Since 1981 he was director of Strategic Research, U.S. Naval War College, Newport, R.I. ConAu, 81-84, New rev., 14; DrAS, 1974, 1978; IntAu&W, 1982

Eubank, Weaver Keith, born 8 December 1920 at Princeton, N.J., he was since 1964 a professor of history, Queens College, CUNY. His writings include *Paul Cambon, master diplomatist* (1960), *Summit conferences, 1919-1960* (1966), *The origins of World War II* (1969), *Summit at Tehran* (1985), and *The bomb* (1991). ConAu, 5-8, 2 new rev.; DrAS, 1974, 1978, 1982; WhoE, 1981/82

Eudel, Paul Charles Théodore, born 23 October 1837 at Crotoy (Somme). After his education at Nantes, he spent two years in Réunion, where an oncle was a rich farmer. Upon returning to France, he joined a large commercial firm in Nantes. Concurrently with his mercantile activities, he contributed to local periodicals and pursued an interest in art collecting. His writings include *Constantinople, Smyrne et Athènes; journal de voyage* (1885), *L'Ofévrerie algérienne et tunisienne* (1902). He died on 18 November 1911. Carnoy 11², p. 7; DBF

Euelpides (Evelpidi), Chrysos, born in 1895 at Constantinople, his writings include *La Réforme agraire en Grèce* (1926), *Les Etats balkaniques; étude comparée politique, sociale, économique et financière* (1930), *Ουτοπίες και πραγματικότητες* (1945), *Πολιτικα* (1945), and *Οικονομιχη και κοινωνικη ιστορία της Ελλάδος* (1950). He died in Athens in 1971. EEE; NUC, pre-1956

Eulenberg, Herbert, born 25 January 1876 at Mühlheim, Germany, he was a trained lawyer who turned dramatist and novelist. His writings include *Die Inseln Wak Wak; eine Erzählung aus 1001 Nacht frei bearbeitet* (1922). He died in Düsseldorf, 4 September 1949. CIDMEL; DtBE; Master (2); OxGer

Europaeus, David Emmanuel Daniel, born 1 December 1820 at Savitaipale, Finland, he was a folklorist and linguist whose writings include *Svenskt-finskt handlexikon* (1853). He died in St. Petersburg, 15 October 1884. NUC, pre-1956; ScBInd (2)

Eustache, Daniel, fl. 1955-1978, his writings include *Corpus des dirhems idrisites et contemporains* (Rabat, 1971). LC

Eustache, Gonzague, born in 1845 at Alignan-du-Vent, France, he was a medical doctor and a sometime member of the *comité d'études* of the Société de géographie de Lille. He died in 1910. DBF

Euting, Julius, born 11 July 1839 at Stuttgart, he was educated at the Seminar, Blaubeuren, from 1857 to 1861, and thereafter studied theology at the Evangelisches Stift, Türbingen. Concurrently he pursued an interest in Oriental languages. He received a doctorate in 1862 for a thesis on the Koran and spent a year of post-doctoral studies at Paris, London, and Oxford. In 1866 he became librarian at the Evangelisches Stift, Tübingen, and two years later, a keeper at the Tübingen University Library. In 1871 he became the first German librarian at the Universitätsbibliothek Straßburg. From 1900 to his retirement in 1909 he was its director. During the years 1883 and 1884 he visited North and Central Arabia for the purpose of archaeological and epigraphical studies, travels which he desribed in *Tagebuch einer Reise in Inner-Arabien* (1896-1914). In 1880 he was appointed a professor at the Faculty of Philosophy. His writings include *Nabatäische Inschriften aus Arabien* (1885). He died a bachelor in Straßburg on 2 January 1913. DtBE;Henze; *Islam* 4 (1913), pp. 121-122; Pallas; RNL

Euzennat, Maurice, born 15 November 1926 at Mont-Saint-Aignan (Seine-Inférieure), he was an archaeologist and a member of l'École française de Rome from 1951 to 1954, a professor at l'Institut les hautes études marocaines at Rabat in 1955, and a director of Antiquités du Maroc from 1955 to 1962. His writings include *Les Découvertes archéologiques de la Bourse à Marseille* (1968). WhoFr, 1961/62-1998/99; WhoWor, 1989/90|

Evan, William Martin, born 17 December 1922 at Ostrow, Poland, he was a graduate of the University of Pennsylvania and received a Ph.D. in 1954 from Cornell University for his thesis, *Occupation and voluntary associations*. In 1975 he was a professor of sociology and management at the University of Pennsylvania. His writings include *Organizational experiments* (19719, and *Organization theory* 1976). AmM&WS, 1973 S, 1978 S; ConAu, 2 new rev.; WhoAm, 1978-1999; WhoE, 1975/76, 1977/78

Evans, Sir Arthur John, born 8 July 1851 at Nash Mills, Herts., he studied modern history at Oxford and later became a keeper at the Ashmolean Museum, Oxford. His travels in the Balkans are the subject of *Through Bosnia and Herzegovina on foot during the insurrection, August and September, 1875* (1876). He also wrote *The Palace of Minos* (1921-1935). He died 11 July 1941. BioIn, 2, 4, 5, 6, 8, 12, 14; DNB; EEE; Egyptology; GrBr; OxEng; *Who was who*, 4

Evans, Edward Payson, born in 1831 at Remsen, N.Y., he was a graduate of the University of Michigan who travelled and studied abroad from 1857 to 1862. He was a professor of modern languages and literatures at his alma mater from 1862 to 1867. He died in 1917. DAB; Master (2); TwCBDA; WhAm, 4

Evans, Hubert John Filmer, born 21 November 1904, he was educated at the City of London School and Jesus College, Oxford, where he studied Oriental languages, with particular reference to Persian. He joined the Indian Civil Service in 1928 and was a district magistrate in the United Provinces for eight years. He was appointed president of the Delhi Municipal Council in 1938 and from 1942 to 1945 was secretary of the Delhi Administration. Transferring to the Foreign Service when India became independent, he served as ambassador. After his retirement he worked for five years at the Central Asian Centre. He was honorary secretary of the Royal Central Asian Society from 1965 to 1968 and for some years chairman of the editorial board of *Asian affairs*. He died 28 June 1989. *Asian affairs* 20 (1989), p. 387; Who, 1974-1988; *Who was who*, 8

Evans, John Martin, born 2 February 1935 at Cardiff, he was educated at Oxford, and since 1975 a professor of English at Stanford University, a position which he still held in 1999. His writings include *Notes on Milton's works* (1967), and *'Paradise lost' and the Genesis tradition* (1968). ConAu, 85-88; DrAS, 1982; NatFacDr, 1995-1999; WhoAm, 1980-1988/89|

Evans, Lewis, born in 1853, he was the founder of the Lewis Evans Collection of scientific instruments in the Old Ashmolean Building at Oxford. He died 25 September 1930. *Who was who*, 3

Evans, Robert John Weston, born 7 October 1943, he was a lecturer in modern history at Brasenose College, Oxford, and since 1997 a Fellow of Oriel College, and Regius Professor of Modern History at Oxford. His writings include *Rudolf II and his world* (1973), and *The making of the Habsburg monarchy* (1979). Who, 1985-1999

Evans, Trefor Ellis, born 4 March 1913, he was a distinguished Arabist, and one who had served in various Middle Eastern countries at critical moments in their history. Through most of the war he was private secretary to Lord Killearn, British ambassador to Egypt, and he was again in Cairo, as Oriental counsellor, from the fall of King Farouk to the Suez crisis of 1956. During the Algerian war of independence he served as consul-general in Alger, and later was appointed ambassador to Syria, 1964-67, and Iraq, 1968-69. In 1969 he was appointed to the chair of international politics at the University of Wales. His writings include *Mission to Egypt (1934-1946); Lord Killearn* (1971). He died suddenly in Aberystwyth on 16 April 1974. BRISMES *bulletin* 1 (1974/75), p. 41; Obit T, 1971-75; Who, 1955-74; *Who was who*, 3

Evans-Pritchard, Sir Edward Evan, 1902-1973, he received a Ph.D. in 1928 from the University of London for his thesis, *The social organisation of the Azande of the Bahr al-Ghazal province of the Anglo-Egyptian Sudan*. He visited Egypt and Libya in 1932. During the war he served one year as political officer in the Alawite territory of Syria before being posted in November 1942 as political officer to the British Administration of Cyrenaica, where he spent two years, the greater part of them among the more nomadic sections of the Bedouin. In 1949 he was appointed professor of social anthropology and fellow of All Souls College, Oxford. His writings include *The Political system of the Anuck of the Anglo-Egyptian Sudan* (1940), and *The Sanusi of Cyrenaica* (1949). In 1972 he was honoured by the jubilee volume, *Essays in Sudan ethnography*. He died in 1973. Au&Wr, 1971; BioIn, 1, 10, 12, 13, 14; ConAu, 65-68; DNB; EEE; Sluglett; *Who was who*, 7; WhoWor, 1974/75; WorAu, 1971

Evatt, Sir George Joseph Hamilton, born in 1843, he was educated at the Royal College of Surgeons and Trinity College, Dublin. He entered the Army Medical Service in 1865, served in India,

Afghanistan, and the Middle East and retired with the rank of major-general. His writings include *Ambulance organization, equipment, and transport* (1884). He died in 1921. Who was who, 2

Eveland, Wilbur Crane, born 1 July 1918 at Spokane, Wash., he served in the U.S. Marine Corps and the Army until 1960. He was a covert associate but never an actual member of the Counter Intelligence Corps. Since 1966 he was a free lance consultant in Beirut to oil companies. His experiences during nearly thirty years in the Middle East he described in *Ropes of sand; America's failure in the Middle East* (1980), and its Arabic translation, *Hiban min ribal* (1985). ConAu, 101

Evelpidi, C., 1895-1971 see Euelpides, Chrysos

Evers, Friedrich *Wilhelm*, born 24 JUly 1906 at Söhlde, Germany, he was a professor of geography at the Technische Hochschule, Hannover. His writings include *Finland im Spannungsfeld zwischen Ost und West* (1969). He died in Isernhagen, 18 July 1983. Kürschner, 1950-1983; Wer ist wer, 1955-1974/75|

Eversley, George John Shaw-Lefevre, 1st Baron, born 12 June 1831, he was educated at Eton and Trinity College, Cambridge. He was an M.P. and a sometime Civil Lord of the Admirality as well as chairman of important committees in the House of Commons. His writings include *The Turkish Empire, its growth and decay* (1917). He died in 1928. DNB; Who was who, 2

Evert- Kappesowa, Halina, fl. 1953, her writings include *Studia nad historią wsi bizantyńskiej w VII-IX wieku* (1963). LC

Evrard, James B., fl. 1974, he received a Dr.phil. in 1974 from the Universität München for *Zur Geschichte Aleppos und Nordsyriens im letzten halben Jahrhundert der Mamluken-herrschaft.* Schwarz

Evriviades, Marios L., fl. 1976, his writings include *The U.S. and Cyprus; the politics of manipulation in the 1985 U.N. Cyprus high level meeting* (Athens, 1992). LC

Evron, Boaz, born 6 June 1927 at Jerusalem, he was a writer, journalist, and theatre critic, affiliated with *Yedi'ot aharonot* since 1964. His writings include *Midah shel herut* (1975), and *Jewish state or Israeli nation* (1995). LC; WhoIsrael, 1990/91, 1992/93

Evron, Yair, born 27 November 1931, he was a graduate of the Hebrew University, Jerusalem, and received a Ph.D. in 1971 from LSE for his thesis, *Nuclear options in a regional sub-system; the case of Israel*. He later became a lecturer at the Hebrew University. His writings include *The Middle East* (1973), *The Demilitarization of Sinai* (1975), *The Role of arms control in the Middle East* (1977), *War and intervention in Lebanon* (1987), and *Israel's nuclear dilemma* (1994). LC; Sluglett

Evtiukhova, Lidiia Alekseevna, fl. 1947, she was an archaeologist whose writings include *Археологические памятники енисейских кыргызов* (Abakan, 1948). LC

Ewald, Christian Ferdinand, born in 1802 at or near Bamberg, Germany, of Jewish parentage, he became a Lutheran in 1822 and was affiliated with the Society for Propagating the Gospel among the Jews, London, as an ordained Anglican. He was a missionary in North Africa and travelled overland from Tunis to Tripolis and back, in 1835, a journey which he described in *Reise von Tunis über Soliman, Nabal, Hammomet, Susa, Sfax, Gabis, Gerba nach Tripolis, und von da wieder zurück nach Tunis im Jahre 1835* (Nürnberg, 1837-38). He later served as chaplain to the first Anglican bishop of Jerusalem. He died in Norwood, 9 August 1874. DNB, vol. 22, p. 622; Henze; Sigilla

Ewald, George *Heinrich* August, born 16 November 1803 at Göttingen, he studied theology, classical philology, and Semitic languages at Göttingen where, except for ten years at Tübingen, he taught throughout his academic career. He was one of the outstanding orientalists of his time and the founder of Semitic philology in Germany. His writings include *Grammatik der hebräischen Sprache* (1828), its translation, *Syntax of the Hebrew language* (1879), *Grammatica critica linguae arabicae* (1831-33), and *Über die arabisch geschriebenen Werke jüdischer Sprachgelehrten* (1844). He died in Göttingen in 1875. Thomas Witton Davies wrote *Heinrich Ewald, orientalist and theologian, 1803-1903; a centenary appreciation* (1903). ADtB; BdD; BiD&SB; CelCen; DtBE; DtBInd (8); EncAm; EncBrit; EncicUni; EncItaliana; Fück, p. 167; GdeEnc; Meyers; NDB; Pallas; RNL; Stache-Rosen, pp. 22-23

Ewer, Walter, born in 1784, he was privately educated and joined the Bengal Civil Service in 1803 and served for ten years as superintendent of police in Bengal, Bihar, and Orissa. He was a judge in the *Sadr* Court, N.W.P., when he resigned in 1840. He died in London, 5 January 1863. Boase; Buckland

Ewert, Christian, born 11 April 1935 at Stuttgart, he was a professor of history of art at the Universität Bonn since 1980. His writings include *Spanisch-islamische Systeme sich kreuzender Bögen* (1968-80), *Islamische Funde in Balaguer und die Aljafería in Zaragoza*, and its translation, *Hallazgos islamicos en Balaguer y la Aljafería de Zaragoza* (1979). Kürschner, 1980-1996

Ewing, Arthur F., born in 1915, his writings include *Industry in Africa* (1968), *Planning and policies in the textile finishing industry* (1972), and *Journey towards one world* (1992). LC

Ewing, Arthur Henry, born 18 October 1864 at Saltsburg, Pa., he was a graduate of Washington and Jefferson College, Western Theological Seminary, Pittsburgh, Pa., and Johns Hopkins University, Baltimore, Md., where he received a Ph.D. in 1901 for *The Hindu conception of the functions of breath*. He was a missionary in India from 1890 until his death in Allahabad, India, 13 September 1912. Shavit - Asia; WhAm, 1

Exner-Erwarten, Felix Maria, born 23 August 1876 at Wien, he studied mathematics, physics, and chemistry at the Universität Wien. He was a sometime professor at Innsbruck and since 1917 director of the Zentralanstalt für Meteorologie und Geodynamik, Wien. His writings include *Dynamische Meteorologie* (1917). He died in Wien, 7 February 1930. DtBE

Eydoux, Henri Paul, born 16 March 1907 at Tarbes, he was educated at Paris, where he received a diploma from l'École libre des sciences politiques. He was attached to the French government in Algeria since 1933. In 1934 he was secretary general of the Exposition du Sahara, Paris. His writings include *L'Exploration du Sahara* (1938), *L'Homme et le Sahara* (1943), *L'Archéologie, résurrection du passé* (1970), *A la recherche des mondes perdus* (1967), and its translation, *In search of lost worlds* (1971). He died 7 May 1986. WhoFr, 1969/70-1985/86

Eyice, Mustafa Semavi, born 3 December 1923, or 2 January 1924, at Constantinople, he was since 1948 a professor of fine arts at İstanbul Üniversitesi and concurrently a visiting professor at Ankara, Bochum, and Paris. His writings include *Son devir Bizans mimârisi* (1963), *Galata ve kulesi = Galata and its tower* (1969), and *Ayasofya* (1984). He was honoured by the jubilee volume, *Semavi Eyice armağanı; İstanbul yazıları* (1992). Kim kimdir, 1985/86, 1997/98

Eynaud, Albert Laurent Léoplod, born 7 January 1843, he studied law and joined the French foreign service in 1843. He served at consulates in Erzerum, Smyrna, Suez, and Tunis until released from active duty for political reasons in 1878, and finally dismissed in 1881. His writings include *Scènes de la vie orientale* (1874), and *Exposé pratique de la procédure civile française dans les échelles du Levant* (1875). DBF

Eyre, Sir Vincent, born 22 January 1811, he was educated at Norwich and Addiscombe, and served in the Army in India from 1828 until his retirement in 1863. He wrote *Journal of imprisonment in Affghanistan* (1843), *The Military operations at Cabul, which ended in the retreat and destruction of the British Army, January 1842* (1843). He died in Aix-les-Bains, 22 September 1881. Boase; DcBiPP; DNB;

Eyriès, Jean Baptiste Benoît, born 25 June 1767 at Marseille, he completed his study at the Collège de Juilly. With the intention of entering mercantile shipping, he travelled in the western world. After the French revolution he was employed in several diplomatic negociations as an interpreter. After 1805 he pursued a literary career, collaborating with the production of the *Encyclopédie moderne*, the *Journal des voyages*, and the *Biographie universelle*. He was a joint founder of the *Nouvelles annales des voyages*, and a founding member of the Société de géographie. He died in Graville-Sainte-Honorine, 13 June 1846. DcBiPP; DBF

Eysenbach, Mary Locke, born 19 December 1932 at Harford, Conn., she received a Ph.D. in 1970 from Stanford University for *American manufactured exports, 1879-1914*. She was a U.S. Foreign Service officer until 1962. In 1978 she was appointed professor of economics and dean of college, Knox College, Galesburg, Illinois, a position which she still held in 1995. NatFacDr., 1995; WhoAm, 1982-1988/89|

van **Eysinga** (Eijsinga), Philippus Pieter Roorda, 1796-1856 *see* Roorda van Eysinga, Philippus P.

Eyssautier, L.-A., fl. 1897, his writings include *La Propriété indigène en Algérie* (Alger, 1898), and *Cours criminelles musulmanes et tribunaux répressifs indigènes* (Alger, 1903). BN; NUC, pre-1956

Eyssautier, Louis Charles, born 26 February 1914 at La Tronche (Isère), he was educated at l'École polytechnique and l'École nationale supérieure des mines, Paris. He was an engineer and a business executive successively in Morocco and France. His writings include *L'Industrie minière du Maroc* (1952). WhoFr, 1959/60-1981/82|

Eyth, Eduard Friedrich Maximilian, Dr., born 6 May 1836 at Kirchheim, Germany, he studied at the Polytechnikum, Stuttgart, and later travelled in France and Belgium. In 1861 he accepted a position as mechanical engineer at John Fowlers' steam plough manufacturers, Leeds. In the service of the company he spent three years at the estates of the Egyptian Prince Halim Pasha. He returned to Germany in 1882 as a prosperous man. Since 1885 he was instrumental in the foundation of the

Deutsche Landwirtschaftsgesellschaft, whose director he remained until 1896. His writings include *Der Kampf um die Cheopspyramide* (1902), and *Blut und Eisen; Erlebnisse eines deutschen Ingenieurs in Ägypten* (1914). He died in Ulm, 25 August 1906. CasWL; DtBE; LC; OxGer

Ezenkin, Valerii Stepanovich, fl. 1972, his writings include *Путь к роману* (1976), and *Теоретические основы чувашской литературной критики, 1917-1970-е гг.* (1992). LC

Ezquerra Abadia, Ramón, born 22 January 1904 at Almuniente, Huesca, Spain, his writings include *La conspiración del duque de Híjar* (1934), and *Resumen de geografía de España*, 2. ed. (1950). IntAu&W, 1976; NUC, pre-1956

Faaland, Just, fl. 1974, he was a sometime director of the Chr. Michelsens Institut for Videnskap og Åndsfrihet, Bergen. His writings include *Aid and influence* (1981); and he was joint author of *The economy of Kenya* (1967), *The economy of Tanzania* (1967), *The economy of Uganda* (1967), *Bangladesh; the test case of development* (1981), *The political economy of development* (1986); and he edited *Population and the world economy in the 21st century* (1982). LC

Faath, Sigrid, born 3 August 1952 at Offenbach, Germany, she studied at the universities of Heidelberg and Hamburg and received a Dr.phil. in 1989 for her thesis, *Herrschaft und Konflikt in Tunesien*. She specialized in the political systems of the Maghreb where she repeatedly conducted field work. She was a fellow of the Deutsches Orient-Institut, Hamburg, and concurrently a lecturer at the Universität Hamburg. She was a joint editor of *Wuqûf;* her writings include *Die Banû Mîzâb* (1985), and *Algerien; gesellschaftliche Strukturen und politische Reformen zu Beginn der neunziger Jahre* (1990). EURAMES; Private

Faber, Michael (Mike) Leslie Ogilvie, born 12 August 1929 at London, he was educated at Eton, Oxford, University of Michigan, and Cambridge. He was a foreign correspondent for British papers in the Third World, 1954-1960. Thereafter he was a lecturer in economics as well as a senior economist to various governments. From 1982 to 1987 he was director of the Institute of Development Studies, Brighton. Unesco; Who, 1984-1998

Fabert, Léon, born 13 June 1848 at Nantes, he was a journalist at Paris until 1889 when he accepted a mission of information to French West Africa, even though he had not the least competence in colonial affairs. In 1893 the governor of Senegal sent him on yet three other missions to Adrar in the Sahara. He left no written reports on his travels. He died in Marseille, 10 January 1896. DBF; Henze

Fabia, Charles, fl. 1945-1971, his writings include *Les Caractéristiques principales du droit des sociétés par action dans le nouveau Code de commerce libanais* (1946), and he was joint author of *Code de commerce libanais annoté; précis de droit commercial libanais* (1974). LC

Fabié y Escudero, Antonio Maria, born 15 June 1832 at Sevilla, he was a lawyer, politician, and philosopher. His writings include *Disertaciones jurídicas sobre el desarrollo histórico del derecho* (1885), and *Estudio filológico* (1885). He died in Madrid, 3 December 1899. Diaz; EncicUni; Espasa; IndiceE (4)

Fabó, Bertalan (Berthold), born 25 May 1868 at Taktakenéz, Hungary, he obtained a doctorate in law but never practised. Since 1900 he pursued an interest in musicology. He was also the founder of the Magyar Zsidó Múzeum in Budapest. His writings include *A magyar népdal zenei fejlödése* (1908). He died in Budapest in utter destitute, 29 October 1920. EncHung; GeistigeUng; MagyarZL; Wininger

Fabri, Charles Louis (Károly Lajos), born 18 November 1899 at Budapest, he obtained a doctorate and was affiliated with the Archaeological Survey of India. He catalogued and arranged the finds at Mohenjo-Daro, and reorganized the Central Museum, Lahore, for the Punjab Government. He assisted Sir Aurel Stein for some years on archaeological expeditions and research. Since May 1938 he was field director in charge of excavations at Bhera of the Panjab Exploration Fund, of which he was a joint founder. His writings include *A history of Indian dress* (1961), and *History of the art of Orissa* (1974). Géza Bethlenfalvy compiled and edited *Charles Louis Fabri, his life and works* (1980). He died in Delhi, 7 July 1968. MEL, 1978-91

Fabri, Felix, born Felix Schmid (also known as Faber and Felix von Ulm), in 1438 or 1441/42 at Zürich, he entered in 1452 the Dominican convent, Basel, and completed his noviciate at Basel and Pforzheim. From 1477 until his death he was principal preacher at the order's convent in Ulm. He travelled extensively in Germany, Italy, and Palestine. His two pilgrimages to the Holy Land in 1480 and 1483-84 are the subject of his *Pilgerfahrt des Bruders Felix Faber ins Heilige Land* (1965), and *Voyage en Eygpte de Félix Fabri, 1483* (1975). There are three biographies, Max Häussler, *Felix Fabri aus Ulm* *und seine Stellung zum geistigen Leben seiner Zeit* (1914), and Hilda F. M. Prescott, *Friar Felix at large* (1950), and *Once to Sinai* (1958). He died in Ulm, 14 May 1502. BioIn, 12; DtBE; EncJud; Henze

Fabricius, Adam Kristoffer, born 18 July 1822 at Bøvling, Denmark, he was a clergyman and a historian whose writings include *Los historiadores españoles en pruebas escogidas* (1858), *Forbindelserne mellem norden og den spanske halvø i ældre tider* (1882), and *Minder i Normandiet* (1897). He died in København, 24 August 1902. DanskBL; DanskBL²

Fabricius, Ernst, born 9 July 1857 at Darmstadt, Germany, he received a Dr.phil. in 1881 from the Universität Straßburg for *De architectura graeca*. A travel grant from the Deutsches Archäologisches Institut enabled him to visit the Mediterranean countries before he accepted a position at the Antikenmuseum, Berlin. After his Dr.habil. in 1886 from Berlin, he became the first holder of the chair of ancient history at the Universität Freiburg im Breisgau. His writings include *Die Besitznahme Badens durch die Römer* (1903). He died in Freiburg, 22 March 1942. DtBE; Kürschner, 1925-1940/41

Facey, William, born in 1948 in Rhodesia and brought up in England, he studied classics, philosophy and history of art at Oxford before becoming involved in the Arabian Peninsula. Since then he worked as a planning and research consultant on numerous projects to set up museums of archaeology, and history and natural history of the Arabian states. He was a director of the London Centre of Arab Studies. His writings include *Riyadh; the old city, from its origins until the 1950s* (1992), and he was joint author of *The Emirates by the first photographers* (1996), *Saudi Arabia by the first photographers* (1996), and *Kuwait by the first photographers* (1998).

Fackenheim, Emil Ludwig, born 22 June 1916 at Halle, Germany, he studied at the Hochschule für Wissenschaft des Judentums, Berlin, was ordained rabbi in 1939, and continued his study at Halle, Aberdeen, and the University of Toronto, where he received a Ph.D. in 1945 for his thesis, *"Substance" and "perseity" in medieval Arabic philosophy, with introductory chapters on Aristotle, Plotinus and Proclus*. He was a professor of philosophy at Toronto until 1983. His writings include *Paths to Jewish belief* (1960), and *Metaphysics and historicity* (1961). After his retirement he was resident in Israel. BioIn, 13; BlueB, 1973/74, 1975, 1976; Canadian, 1970-1979; DrAS, 1974, 1978, 1982; EncJud; IntAu&W, 1976-1989; Master (3); Selim; WhoAm, 1974-1988/89; WhoIsrael, 1973/74-1992/93; WhoWorJ, 1965-1987; WrDr, 1986-1990/92

Fadeev, Anatolii Vsevolodovich, fl. 1951-1955, his writings include *Россия и восточный кризис 20-х годов XIX века* (1958), *Россия и Кавказ первой тпети XIX в.* (1960), *Россия и народы Северной Азии* (1965), and *Идейные связи и культурная жизн народов дореформенной России* (1966). LC

Fadeeva, Irina Evgen'evna, fl. 1975, her writings include *Мидхат-паша; жизнь и деятельность* (1977). LC

Fadel, Mohamed, fl. 1925, he was editor of the ephemeral newspaper *Die ägyptische Flagge*, Berlin.

Faduma, Orishatukeh, born in 1860, the son of Nigerian Yoruba parents who were converted to Christianity before the birth of their son. He was educated at the Missionary High School for Boys in Sierra Leone, the University of London, and Divinity School, Yale University. From 1895 to 1914 he was principal of Peabody Institute, Troy, N.C., under the American Missionary Association. Afterwards he was for two years principal of the Missionary Collegiate School in Sierra Leone, five years in the Sierra Leone Education Department, serving as an Inspector of Schools, tutor in the Teacher Training Department, and officer in charge of the Government Model School. In 1925 he was instructor in Latin and English literature at Lincoln Academy, Kings Mountain, N.C., under the American Missionary Association. His writings include *The Defects of the Negro Church* (1904). LC

Fafunwa, Ali Babatunde, born in 1923, he obtained a doctorate and became a tutor at Ahmadiyya College, Lagos. In 1986 he was a pro-chancellor, University of Calabar. Since 1990 he was Federal honorary Minister of Education. His writings include *New perspectives in African education* (1967), *History of Nigerian higher education* (1971), *History of education in Nigeria* (1974), *Up and down; a Nigerian teacher's odyssey* (1991), and he was joint ediitor of *Education in mother tongue* (1989). AfricaWW, 1991, 1996; IntYB, 1998; WhoWor, 1978/79, 1980/81

Fagan, Christopher George Forbes, born 15 March 1856, he was educated at Harrow and joined the Army in 1875. He served in the Afghan war, 1879-80, and was political agent and consul at Basra, 1897, and Muscat, 1898. He resigned in 1907 with the rank of lieutenant-colonel and died 9 July 1943. Buckland; *Who was who*, 4

Fagan, Sir Patrick James, born 5 July 1865, he graduated from St. John's College, Cambridge, and entered the Indian Civil Service. He held executive posts until his retirement in 1923. He died 26 June 1942. *Who was who*, 4

Fagnan, Edmond, born 5 December 1846 at Liège. After the completion of his study at the Université de Liège with a doctorate in law, he obtained a diploma in Arabic, Persian, Turkish, and Hebrew from the École des langues orientales vivantes, Paris. In 1873 he joined the Département des manuscrits of the Bibliothèque nationale, where he collaborated in the production of Oriental historians in the series, *Recueil des historiens des croisades*. In 1884 he was appointed a professor of Arabic and Persian at l'École des lettres d'Alger, a post which he held until his retirement in 1919. From 1892 to 1904 he belonged to the Bureau de la Société historique algérienne. He was a loner, and his judgment of men and events was generally unequivocal without the slightest trace of compromise; he knew no differentiation. His writings include *Concordance du manuel de droit de Sidi Khalil* (1889), and *Additions aux dictionnaires arabes* (1923). He died in Alger, 28 February 1931. DBF; *Revue africaine* 72 (1931), pp. 139-42

Fagnani, Emma Everett née Goodwin, 19th cent., of Charlestown, Mass. She was the wife of Guiseppe Fagnani with whom she visited Constantinople in 1864 as guests of the American ambassador Henry Bolwer. She wrote *The Art life of a XIXth century portrait painter, Joseph Fagnani, 1819-1873*, edited by Charles Prospero Fagnani (1930). DizBI; NUC, pre-1956

Fago, Vincenzo, born in 1870, 1873 or 1875 at Taranto (Apulia), he was a poet and an art critic, and from 1910 to 1911, editor of the *Bulletin de la Bibliothèque* (Section des langues européennes) *de l'Université du Caire*. His writings include *Discordanze* (1905), and *Arte araba* (1909). He died in 1941. Baldinetti, pp. 84-90; *Chi è*, 1928; IndBI

Fahmi, Aziza, fl. 1967, she received a doctorate in 1961 from the Universität Wien for her thesis, *Internationale Flüsse und der Nil*. Schwarz

Fahmi, Isma'il, born 2 October 1922 at Cairo, he graduated in 1945 from the Faculty of Law at Cairo and subsequently joined the Ministry of Foreign Affairs. He served as foreign minister, ambassador, and U.N. representative. He was in charge of negotiations with Israel. He died in Cairo after surgery on 21 November 1997. Goldschmidt; MideE, 1982/83; WRMEA 16 v (Jan./Feb. 1998), p. 152; WhoArab, 1978/9

Fahmy-Bey, Jeanne née Puech-d'Alissac, born 17 April 1861 at Bessèges (Gard), she was married in 1879 to the Egyptian medical student Salim Fahmi at Montpellier. Later that year they settled in Cairo. She accompanied her husband when he was posted to Jedda, Alexandria, and lastly Tanta, where he became *médecin-en-chef* of the hospital. She learned Arabic and explored the Delta. Encouraged by her husband, she began to contribute articles to Cairene and French periodicals. Despite being engaged in the Egyptian feminist movement, it is believed that for convenience she adopted the male *nom de plume*, Jehan d'Ivray, at that time. She remained in Egypt until her husband's death in 1919, when she returned to Paris. Her writings include *Bonaparte et l'Égypte* (1914), *La Lombardie au temps de Bonaparte* (1919), *L'Égypte éternelle* (1921), and *Promenade à travers le Caire* (1928). She died in Vichy, 19 September 1940. *Hommes et destins*, vol. 4, pp. 381-382

Fähndrich, Hartmut Ernst, born 14 October 1944 at Tübingen, he received a Ph.D. in 1972. from UCLA for his thesis, *Man and men in Ibn Khallikan*. Since 1978 he taught Arabic and Islamic studies at the Eidgenössische Technische Hochschule, Zürich, and since 1990 he was founding chairman of the Schweizerische Gesellschaft Mittlerer Osten und Islamischer Kulturen. His writings include *Nagib Machfus* (1991), and the translations *Treatise to Salah ad-Din on the revival of the art of medicine* (1983), and *Die Söhne der Zeit* (1984). EURAMES; LC; Selim; WWASS, 1989

Fahrnschon, Helmut, born 17 March 1923 at Frankenthal, Germany, he was educated at Karlsruhe, Mainz, and Franfurt a.M., where he studied law and economics. Since 1958 he held executive posts in industry, and since 1958 he was director of the Centrale Marketinggesellschaft. On his sixtieth birthday he was honoured by the jubilee volume, *Agrarmärkte & Agrarmarketing; Strategien im grünen Markt*. Wer ist wer, 1976/77-1992/93|

Faidherbe, Louis *Léon* César, born 3 June 1818 at Lille, he was educated at the Polytechnique and l'École d'application de Metz. He had a successful career as military officer and colonial administrator in Algeria and French West Africa from 1844 until the late 1860s, when poor health obliged him to resign with the rank of general. After the Franco-Prussian war he pursued a political career in metropolitan France. His long residence in Senegal had provided him with the opportunity to study African languages as well as the pre-Roman civilization of North Africa. In recognition of his archaeological work he was elected a member of the Académie des inscriptions et belles-lettres in 1884. His writings include *Collection complète des inscriptions numidiques (libyques) avec des aperçus ethnographiques sur les Numides* (1870), *Essai sur la langue poul* (1875), *Langues sénégalaises* (1887), and *Le Sénégal* (1889). He died in 1889. BioIn, 6, 11; *Bulletin de la Société de géographie de Lille* 84 (1940), pp. 2-11; DBF; *Hommes et destins*, vol. 1, pp. 230-234, vol. 5, pp. 202-203

Faidutti-Rudolph, Anne Marie, fl. 1961, her writings include *L'Immigration italienne dans le sud-est de la France* (Gap, 1964). LC

Fairbairn, Andrew Martin, born 4 November 1838 in Scotland, he was educated at Edinburgh, Berlin, and Glasgow. He was a Congregational minister, a sometime principal of Airedale College, Bradford, and Mansfield College, Oxford, and received several honorary doctorates throughout his life. His writings include *Studies in the philosophy of religion and history* (1876), and *Religion in history and in modern life* (1884). He was honored by the jubilee volume, *Mansfield College essays, presented to the Rev. Andrew M. Fairbairn* (1909). Charles N. Foshee wrote a biography, *Andrew Martin Fairbairn, philosopher of the Christian religion* (1958). He died 9 February 1912. BioIn, 2; DNB; LuthC, 1976; Who was who, 1

Fairchild, David Grandison, born 7 April 1869 at Lansing, Mich., and a graduate of Kansas State College of Agriculture, he became an agricultural explorer and went on expeditions to many parts of the world. He was the first chief of the Plant Introduction Section, U.S. Dept. of Agriculture, 1906-1928. His writings include *Exploring for plants* (1931). He died 2 August 1954. Master (5); Shavit; Shavit - Asia; WhAm, 3

Fairfield, Roy Philip, born 17 May 1918 at Saco, Me., he was a graduate of Bates College, and received a Ph.D. in 1953 from Harvard University for *Saco, Maine, 1865-1900*. He taught at a number of American colleges and universities before he was appointed a professor of social sciences at Union Graduate School, Yellow Springs, Ohio, in 1970. His writings include *Sands, spindles, and staples; a history of Saco, Maine* (1956). AmM&WS, 1973 S; ConAu, 33-36; LEduc, 1974; WhoMW, 1876/77

Fairhurst, Harry, M.A., A.L.A., fl. 1978, he was a sometime librarian, University of York, UK., and joint author of *University of Ghana library planning report, 1970* (1970). LC

Fairman, Walter T., Dr., born 24 April 1874, he succeeded Arthur T. Upson at the Nile Mission Press and worked there for years. Later, he joined the American United Presbyterian Mission and remained in it. He was known throughout the Nile Valley for his fluency in Arabic, but he outstayed his strength, and before he retired to Clacton-on-Sea in June 1939 he was a broken man. He survived on his special diet which was a great difficulty. Finally, after only two days in bed, he succumbed on 11 October 1941. MW 32 (April 1942), p. 166

Fairservis, Walter Ashlin, born in 1921 at Brooklyn, N.Y., he received a Ph.D. in 1958 from Harvard for *The comparative stratigraphy of the Indo-Iranian borderlands*. He was an anthropologist and affiliated with the American Museum of Natural History from 1949 to 1953. In 1968 he was appointed a professor of anthropology at Vassar College, Poughkeepsie, N.Y., a post which he still held in 1995. He wrote *Archaeological studies in the Seistan Basin of southwestern Afghanistan and eastern Iran* (1961), *Before the Buddha came* (1972), and *The Harappan civilization and its writing* (1992). LC; NatFacDr, 1995; Shavit

Faivre, Charles, fl. 1956, he was joint author of the booklet, *Les Etrangers d'Auvergne; les immigrants en Suisse; la femme algérienne* (Paris, Etudes sociales Nord-africaines, 1969). LC

Fajkmajer, Karl, born 12 August 1884, he completed his history study at the Universität Wien with a Dr.phil. He was a member of the Institut für Österreichische Geschichtsforschung from 1905 to 1907, when he joined the municipal archival service in Wien. He was a collaborator with the production of a comprehensive local history of the city of Wien. His writings include *Skizzen aus Alt-Wien* (1914). He was killed in action near Monfalcone, 16 May 1916. DtBE; ÖBL

Fakhouri, Hani I., born 20th cent., he received a Ph.D. in 1969 from Michigan State University for his thesis, *Kafr el-Elow, an Egyptian village in transition*. He was a sociologist affiliated with the University of Dayton in 1968, and a professor of anthropology and chairman, University of Michigan at Flint, from 1990 to 1999. MESA *Roster of members*, 1990; NatFacDr, 1995-1999; Selim

Fakhrutdinov, Ravil' Gabdrakhmanovich, born in 1937, he was an archaeologist and historian who received a doctorate in 1990. His writings include *Археологические памятники Волжско-Камской Булгарии и ее территория* (1975), *Очерки по истории Воложской Булгарии* (1984), *Altyn Urda häm tatarlar* (1993), and he edited *Историческая демография татарского народа*, by D. M. Iskhakov (1993). LC; TatarES

Fakoussa, Hassan A., Dr.jur., fl. 1940-1961, he was a sometime head of the department of international law at the League of Arab States, and in 1961 in charge of its Bonn information office.

Falah, Salman Hamud, born 16 February 1935 at Kafr Sami'a, Palestine, he was a graduate of the Hebrew University, Jerusalem, and received a Ph.D. from Princeton. He was a sometime coordinator of Druze Affairs at the Israeli Prime Minister's Office, and chief inspector of Arab education in the

Ministry of Education. His writings include *Toldot ha-Deruzim be Yisrael* (1974), and *Fusul fi ta'rikh al-Duruz* (1979). LC; Wholsrael, 1978, 1980/81-1985/86

al-**Falaki**, Mahmud Ahmad Hamdi, 1815-1885, he was an Egyptian astronomer who was educated at the Polythechnique, Paris. EI²; Goldschmidt; Hill

Falaturi, Abdoljavad, born 19 January 1926 at Isfahan, Persia, he was a sometime director of the Islamische Wissenschaftliche Akademie, Köln, and concurrently a professor at the Universität Köln. His writings include *Katalog der Bibliothek des schiitischen Schrifttums im Orientalischen Seminar der Universität zu Köln* (1988). On his sixty-fifth birthday he was honoured by the jubilee volume, *Gottes ist der Orient - Gottes ist der Okzident* (1991). Kürschner, 1976-1996

Falck (Falk), Johan Peter, born in 1725 at Kockstorp i Broddetorps, Västergötland, Sweden, he was since 1763 residing in Russia and Central Asia, where he died in Kazan on 31 March 1774. His writings in-clude *Beyträge zur topographischen Kenntniss des Russischen Reichs* (St. Petersburg, 1785-86). BiobibSOT, pp. 275-276; SBL

Falcon, Norman Leslie, born 29 May 1904, he graduated from Cambridge and in 1927 joined the Anglo-Iranian Oil Company. He served in Persia until 1936, undertaking extensive geological surveys as well as oilfield development. Later he took part in the exploration drilling pro-gramme in Great Britain and became increasingly interested in the application of air photography to geology. He served in the Intelligence Corps during the second World War, his duties including the study of air photo-graphs, and he was awarded the United States Bronze Star. After the War, he was concerned with a wide range of geological problems in Europe and the Middle East. He was chief geologist of the British Petroleum Company, 1955-1965, and a member of the Natural Environment Research Council, 1968-1971. He was a vice-president of the Royal Geographical Society. He died 31 May 1996. Nature 173 (20 March 1954), p. 523; Who, 1969-1996

Falconer, Forbes, born 10 September 1805, he studied Hebrew, Arabic, and Persian at Aberdeen, Paris, and German universities, and became a professor of Oriental languages at University College, London. His writings include *Tuhfat ul ahrar, The gift of the noble; being one of the seven poems entitled the Haft aurang, of Mulla Jami* (1848), and *Salman u Absal, an allegorical romance; being one of the seven poems entitled the Haft aurang, of Mulla Jami* (1850). He died 7 November 1853. Buckland; DNB

Falev, Pavel Aleksandrovich, born 8 October or December 1888 at St. Petersburg, where he studied Arabic, Persian, Turkish and Tatar literature from 1908 to 1912. The following year he did post-graduate research at Gotha, Dresden, and Leipzig. He was successively an assistant at the Museum of the St. Petersburg Faculty of Oriental Languages and a lecturer in Turkish. He died 3 July or August 1922. BiobibSOT, pp. 274-275

Falina, Avrora Ivanovna, born 15 December 1923 at Irkutsk, she completed her academic training in 1951 with the unpublished dissertation, Государство Ильханов как этап развития феодализма на Ближнем и Среднем Востоке. She published the translation, Переписка, from Rashid al-Din Tabib, in 1971. She died 23 September 1986. Miliband; Miliband²

Falk, Johann Peter, 1725-1774 *see* Falck, Johan Peter

Falk, Richard Anderson, born 13 November 1930 at NYC. After graduation in the universities of Pennsylvania, Yale, and Harvard, he became a professor of law at the Woodrow Wilson School, Princeton University, and a member on the editorial board of the *Third world quarterly*. His writings include *Human rights and state sovereignty* (1981), and *Reviving the World Court* (1986). BlueB, 1973/74, 1975, 1976; CnDiAmJBi; ConAu, 5-8, 12 new rev.; NatFacDr, 1995; WhoAm, 1974-1982/83|

Falk, Stephen John, born 6 July 1942 at Warminster, England, he was educated at Rugby and Cam-bridge. He started work as a porter at Sotheby's, London, and later catalogued books. He collab-orated with Mildred Archer on the production of *Indian miniatures in the India Office Library* (1981), a work which established his reputation as an art scholar. His writings include *Qajar paintings* (1972), *Indian painting* (1978), and *Paintings from Mughal India* (1979). All but his first work have appeared under the name Toby Falk. He died of cancer, 10 January 1997. ConAu, 124, 156

Falk, Toby, 1942-1997 *see* Falk, Stephen John

Falke, Jacob, born 21 June 1825 at Ratzeburg, Germany, he studied liberal arts at Erlangen and Göttingen. He was a keeper at the Germanisches Nationalmuseum, Nürnberg, from 1855 to 1858, when he moved to Wien to become librarian and director of the Fürstlich-Liechtensteinschen Samm-lungen. From 1864 to his retirement he was successively keeper and director, Österreichisches

Museum für Kunst und Industrie. His writings include *Geschichte des modernen Geschmacks* (1866), and *Hellas und Rom* (1878). He died in Lovran near Opatija, 8 June 1897. BbD; BiD&SB; DtBE; ÖBL

von **Falke**, Otto, born 29 April 1862 at Wien, where he studied history, art, and archaeology. A travel grant enabled him to visit Roma before he entered the Kunstgewerbemuseum, Berlin. Until his retirement in 1927 he was successively museum administrator at Köln and Berlin. In 1928 he became the founder and principal contributor to *Pantheon*. His writings include *Romanische Leuchter und Gefäße* (1935). He died in Schwäbisch-Hall, 15 August 1942. DtBE; ÖBL; WhE&EA *Who was who*, 7

Fal'kovich, Svetlana Mikhailovna, born in 1932, she was a research fellow in the Institute of Slavic and Balkan Studies, Soviet Academy of Sciences. Her writings include *Идейно-политическая борьба в польском освободительном движении 50-60 годов XIX века* (1966), and *Польша на путях развития и утверждения капитализма* (1984). LC

Fall, Ould Ahmed Mohamed, fl. 1972, he was a sometime director of the Mauritanian judicial and penitentiary administration. Note

Fallers, Lloyd Ashton, born 29 August 1925 at Nebraska City, Neb., he was a graduate of the University of Chicago, and studied also at LSE. Between 1950 and 1957 he spent four years at the East African Institute of Social Research in Kampala, Uganda; from 1957 until his death he was professor of anthropology, first at the University of California at Berkeley, and finally at the University of Chicago. His writings include *Bantu bureaucracy* (1956), *Law without precedent* (1969), *Inequality* (1973), *The social anthropology of the nation-state* (1974). He died in Chicago, 4 July 1974. Unesco; WhAm, 7

Fallers, Margret Chave, born 12 July 1922 at Sioux Falls, S.Dak., she was a graduate of Oberlin College, and from 1960 to 1970, a professor of anthropology at the University of Chicago. Her writings include *The Eastern lacustrine Bantu* (1960). Unesco; WhoAmW, 1974/75

Fallmerayer, Jakob Philipp, born 10 December 1790 near Brixen, Austria, he studied theology at Salzburg, and classical philology at Landshut. After military service, he taught at high schools. His *Geschichte des Kaiserthums von Trapezunt*, published in 1827, won him the 1823 essay competion of the Danish Academy of Science. In 1831 he set out on his first tour of the Near East, which he described in *Fragmente aus dem Orient* (1845). He was counsel to the Bavarian archduke, and future king, Maximilian, on Balkan affairs, 1844-1846. After some turbulent political years and exile in Switzerland, he returned to München, in 1850, where he spent the rest of his life writing and travelling. His theory of the Albanian origin of the modern Greeks resulted in much animosity, particularly from Greeks and clerics. He received a honorary doctorate of the Universität Tübingen, and he was a member of the Bavarian, Hungarian, and Austrian academies of science. His life and works are the subject of three Austrian doctoral theses. His writings include *Geschichte der Halbinsel Morea während des Mittelalters* (1830-36), and *Das albanesische Element in Griechenland* (1857-61). He died in München, 26 April 1861. ADtB; BbD; BiD&SB; CelCen; DtBE; EEE; ÖBL; Wurzbach

Fallot, Ernest, born in 1855 at Marseille, he entered the colonial administration in Senegal in 1884 and transferred to Tunis in 1887 to become successively director of the Service des renseignements et des contrôles civils, director of agriculture and trade, head of the Service du commerce et de l'im-migration. He returned to France in 1905. He was a member of the Société de géographie de Marseille. His writings include *Par delà la Méditerranée; Kabylie, Kroumirie* (1887), *Notice géographique, administrative et économique de la Tunisie* (1888), *La solution française de la question du Maroc* (1904), and *Le peuplement français de l'Afrique du nord* (1906). He died in Colombe (Hauts-de-Seine) on 23 April 1929. DBF

Falls, J. C. Edwald, born in 1885, his writings include *Beduinen-Lieder der Libyschen Wüste* (1908), *Drei Jahre in der Libyschen Wüste* (1911), its translation, *Three years in the Libyan Desert* (1913), and *Der Zauber der Wüste* (1922). LC

Famchon, Yves Joseph Jérôme, born 16 February 1918 at Piriac-sur-Mer (Loire-inférieure), he studied at the Faculté de droit de Paris and the Institut d'études politiques, and received diplomas in *études supérieures d'économie politique* as well as *hautes études internationales*. He was a customs' inspector from 1937 to 1948, when he became a lawyer in the Court of Appeal, Paris. His writings include *L'Allemagne et le Moyen-Orient* (1957), and *Maroc; d'Algésiras à la souveraineté économique* (1960); and he was joint author of *La Jurisprudence communautaire en matière de douane* (1992). WhoFr, 1984/85-1990/91|

Fane, Violet, pseud., 1843-1905 *see* Currie, Mary Montgomerie, née Lamb, Singleton, Lady

Fănescu, Mihail, fl. 1968, he was a Romanian archivist whose writings include *Catalogul documentelor Țării Românești din Arhivele Statului* (1974-93). LC

Fanfoni, Giuseppe, fl. 1978, he was affiliated with the Istituto di Studi del Vicino Oriente, Università di Roma. His writings include *Appunti per un corso sulle techniche di restauro* (Cairo, 1976), and he edited *Sonqi Tino* (1979).

Fanjul García, Serafín, born 20th cent., he held a doctorate in Semitic philology and was a professor of Arabic language and literature at the Universidad Autónoma de Madrid, specializing in folklore and anthropology. His writings include *El Mawwal egipcio; expresión literaria popular* (1976), and *Literatura popular árabe* (1977). Arabismo, 1992, 1994, 1997

Fanon, Frantz Omar, 1925-1961, he was a West Indian physician, psychiatrist, and philosopher of social revolution, born in Martinique and educated in Martinique and France. His writings include *Les Damnés de la terre* (1961). Irene L. Gendzier wrote a biography, *Frantz Fanon; a critical study* (1973), and B. Marie Perinbam *Holy vio-lence; the revolutionary thought of Frantz Fanon* (1982). He died of leukemia. AfrBioInd (1); ConAu, 89-92, 116; IndexBFr² (1); Master (9); WorAu

Fanshawe, lieutenant-general, Sir Hew Dalrymple, born in 1860, he served in Egypt, the Sudan, India, and Mesopotamia. He died in 1957. Who was who, 5

Fántoli, Amilcare, fl. 1941, his writings include *Piccola guida della Tripolitania* (1925), *Nuova guida della Tripolitania* (1930), *Elementi preliminari del clima dell'Etiopia* (1940), and *Le pioggie della Libia* (1952). Firenze

Faqqusah, Hasan A., fl. 1940-1961 see Fakoussa, Hassan A.

Faradzhev, Alikuli Sattar ogly, his writings include *Mukhtăsăr dilchilik lughăti* (1960), and Зарождение и развитие экономической мысли в Азербайджане в эпоху феодализма (1986). LC

Farag, Sami Assaad, fl. 1980, he was a director, Anti-Narcotics General Administration, Cairo, and a sometime member of the International Narcotics Control Board.

Farag, Wadie M., fl. 1937, he received a doctorate in 1926 from the Université de Paris for his thesis, *Le Rôle des tribunaux mixtes et indigènes d'Égypte en matière de statut personnel*. His writings include *L'Intervention devant la Cour permanente de justice internationale* (1927). LC

Faragó, Ladislav (László), born 1 September 1906 at Csurgo, Hungary, he worked as journalist in Hungary, 1924-1928, Berlin, 1928-1935, and since 1935 as foreign correspondent for the Associated Press, the *New York times* and other newspapers. His writings include *Palestine on the eve* (1936), *Palestine on the crossroads* (1937), *Arabian antic* (1938), *The riddle of Arabia* (1939), *The axis grand strategy* (1942), and *Burn after reading* (1961). He died in NYC, 15 October 1980. CnDiAmJBi; ConAu, 65-68, 102, 12 new rev.; Master (1); MEL, 1978-1991; WhoAm, 1974-1978/79; WhoWor, 1974-1978/79

Farah, Bulus, fl. 1959, he was one of the founders of the Arab labour movement in Palestine and a sometime leading member of the Communist Party. His writings include *Muqaddimat fi ta'rikh al-'Arab al-ijtimā'ī* (1962), and *al-Harakah al-'ummalīyah al-'Arabīyah al-Filastinīyah* (1987). LC

Farah, Tawfic Elias, born 12 August 1946 at Nazareth, he was a graduate of California State University at Fresno, and received a Ph.D. in 1975 from the University of Nebraska for his thesis, *Aspects of consociationalism and modernization; Lebanon as an exploratory test case*. He was a sometime professor of political science at Kuwait, editor of *Arab affairs*, and since 1979 president of the California Educational Services Group. His writings include *Aspects of modernization and consociationalism; Lebanon as an exploratory test case* (1975); and he was editor of *Political behavior in the Arab states* (1983), and *Pan-Arabism and Arab nationalism* (1987). WhoEmL, 1987; WhoWest, 1980-1998/99

Fărăjov, Å. S. see Faradzhev, Alikuli Sattar ogly

Fard-Saidi, Mohammad, born in 1941, he received a Ph.D. in 1974 from the University of Pennsylvania for his thesis, *Early phases of political modernization in Iran, 1870-1925*. In 1977 he was a professor at the Faculty of law and political science, Tehran University. He was joint author of *Recent trends in Middle East politics and Iran's foreign policy options* (Tehran, 1975). LC

Fareed, Sir Razik, born in 1893 or 1895, he was a sometime Ceylonese M.P., and a Moor by race and a Muslim by religion. He died 23 August 1984. LC; Who, 1974-1984; Who was who, 8

Farès (Faris), Bishr, born in 1906 at Zagazig, Egypt, he received a doctorate in 1932 from the Sorbonne for his thesis, *L'honneur chez les Arabes avant de l'islam*. His writings include *Une miniature religieuse de l'école arabe de Bagdad* (1948), and *Vision chrétienne et signes musulmans* (1961). He died in February 1961. Arabica 10 (1963), pp. 113-120; WhoArab, 1974/75, 1978/79, 1981/82, 1984/85

Fargues, Philippe, born 17 October 1948 at Paris, he received a doctorate in 1973 from l'École pratique des hautes études, Paris, for his thesis, *Aspects idéologiques de l'enseignement de l'histoire en Égypte*. He was affiliated with the U.N.O. in Lebanon and Cameroon from 1972 to 1977. Since 1983 he was a *directeur de recherche* at the Institut national d'études démographiques, Paris, and acting director of the Centre de documentation d'études juridiques, économiques et sociales, Cairo. His writings include *Les Champs migratoires internes en Syria* (1979); he was joint author of *The Atlas of the Arab world; geopolitics and society* (1991), *Chrétiens et Juifs dans l'islam arabe et turc* (1992), its translation, *Christians and Jews under Islam* (1997); and he was joint editor of *L'Economie de la paix en Proche-Orient* (1995). LC; THESAM 4; WhoWor, 1989/90

Farhang, Mir Muhammad Siddiq, born in 1915 at Kabul, he was a graduate of Kabul University, and received degrees in the UK and USA. He was a sometime chief librarian of the Kabul public library and a staff member of the Kabul teachers' college. His writings include *Saffariyan* (1955), and *Afghanistan dar panj qarn-i akhir* (1988). He died in 1989. Adamec; LC

Farhangi, Setareh née Ghaffari, 1958- see Ghaffari-Farhangi, Setareh

Farhat, Moncef, fl. 1973, he was a sometime *assistant* at the Faculté de droit de Tunis. Note

Farhi, André, fl. 1974, he was joint author of *Le Nouveau déséquilibre mondial* (1973), and *La Crise de l'impérialisme et la troisème guerre mondiale* (1976). LC

Farias, Paulo Fernando de Moraes see Moraes Farias, Paulo Fernando de

Farineaux, M., fl. 1930, he was a sometime *inspecteur de Douanes*, and a member of the Société de géographie commerciale du Havre. Note

Farinha, António Dias, he was affiliated with the Instituto de Linguas Africanas e Orientas. His writings include *História de Mazagão durante o periódo filipino* (Lisboa, 1970). LC

Faris, Nabih Amin, born 1 October 1906 at Nazareth, he was educated at Bishop Gobat School, Jerusalem, the American University, Beirut, and at Princeton, where he received a Ph.D. in 1935 for his thesis, *The antiquities of South Arabia*. After a long academic association with Princeton, he went back to A.U.B., where he remained for the rest of his life. He served as professor of Arab history, and for a long time was chairman of the Department of History. His writings include *Arab archery* (1945), *The crescent in crisis* (1955), *The book of knowledge* (1962). He died in Beirut, 14 February 1968. MW 58 (1968), p. 193; Selim

Farjenel, Fernand, died in 1918, his writings include *La Morale chinoise, fondement des sociétés d'Extrême-Orient* (1900), *Les Peuples chinois, ses mœurs & ses institutions* (1904), *A Travers la révolution chinoise; mes séjours dans le sud et dans le nord* (1914), and its translation, *Through the Chinese revolution; my experiences in the south and north* (1915). LC

Farjoun, Emanuel, born in 1944, he was a professor of mathematics at the Hebrew University, Jerusalem. His writings include *Laws of chaos; a probability approach to political economy* (1983). LC

Farkas, Gyula (Julius) von, born 27 September 1894 at Eisenstadt (Kismarton), Austria-Hungary. After completing his studies at Budapest, he went to Ungarisches Institut, Berlin, where he remained until 1945. During the last years of his life he was a professor of Finno-Ugric philology at Göttingen, where he died, 12 September 1958. I.I. (2); MEL, 1967-69; Südost-Forschungen, 18 (1959), p. 181

Farley, J. G., fl. 1971, he was a sometime assistant district officer for the Government of Northern Nigeria, and a senior lecturer in the Department of History and International Relatios, with special reference to Africa, at the Royal Naval College, Greenwich. Note

Farley, James Lewis, born 9 September 1823 at Dublin, he was a chief accountant of the Ottoman Bank, Beirut, from 1857 to 1860, when he was appointed accountant-general of the state bank at Constantinople. After his return to England, he became an expert on Near Eastern affairs, and a frequent contributor to British newspapers. In 1870, he was appointed consul in Bristol for the Ottoman Sultan, a post which he held until 1884. His writings include *Two years in Syria* (1858), *The massacres in Syria* (1861), *Banking in Turkey* (1863), *Modern Turkey* (1872), *The decline of Turkey* (1875), *Cross or crescent* (1876), *Turks and Christians* (1876), *Egypt, Turkey and Asiatic-Turkey* (1878), and *Turkey* (1886). He died in London in 1885. BiD&SB; Boase; DcBiPP; DNB; Men, 1875, 1899; NewC

Farman-Farma'iyan (Farmayan), Hafiz, born in 1927 in Persia, he was a director of the Center for Middle Eastern Studies at Tehran, before immigrating to the United States. He was a sometime director of the Iranian Studies Program in the Center for Middle Eastern Studies at the University of Texas, Austin. His writings include *Iran; a selected and annotated bibliography* (1951). Private

Farmer, Henry George, born 1882 at Birr, Ireland, he was a musicologist and Arabist from the University of Aberdeen and received a Ph.D. in 1926 from the University of Glasgow for his thesis, *A Musical history of the Arabs, from the time of idolatry to the time of the Buwaihids*. His writings include *History of Arabian music to the XIIIth century* (1929), its Persian translation in 1987, *Historical facts for the Arabian musical influence* (1930), *The organ of the ancients, from Eastern sources* (1931), *Music, the priceless jewel; from the Kitab al-'Iqd al-farid of Ibn 'Abd Rabbihi, edited and translated* (1942), and *Oriental studies, mainly musical* (1953). He died 30 December 1965. Sluglett; WhE&EA, *Who was who*, 6

Farmer, Leslie George, fl. 1969, his writings include *We saw the Holy City* (1944), *Bethlehem today* (1947), and *Land of the Gospel* (1963). BLC

Farooq, Daniel M., fl. 1961, he was a sometime member of the Pakistan Institute of Development Economics and joint author of *A statistical history of district boundary changes in Pakistan, 1881-1961* (1964), and *Family planning in Pakistan* (1968). LC; Note

Farooq, Ghazi Mumtaz, fl. 1968, he was a sometime senior population economist at the International Labour Office. His writings include *Population and employment in developing countries* (1985), and he was joint author of *Fertility and development* (1988), and joint editor of *Fertility in developing countries* (1985). LC

Farooqui, M. *Naseem Iqbal*, fl. 1974, he was a sometime staff demographer at the Pakistan Institute of Development Economics, and joint author of *Complete life tables for Pakistan and provinces* (1969), and *The state of population in Pakistan, 1987* (1989). LC

Faroqhi, Suraiya Roshan Nadira Erica, born 2 October 1941 at Berlin, she attended elementary school in India and Indonesia (1947-1952), and high school in Bonn (1953-1959). She studied at Istanbul, Bloomington, Ind., and Hamburg, where she received a Dr.phil. in 1967 for her thesis, *Die Vorlagen (telhise) des Großwesirs Sinan Paşa an Sultan Murad III*. She was a sometime professor at the Middle East Technical University, Ankara, and the Nahost-Institut, München; a recipient of a Gibb Fellowship, Harvard, 1983-84; a Rockefeller Fellowship, Washington University, St. Louis, Mo., 1990; a joint editor of the *Cambridge history of Turkey*, 1990-1992; and a member of the editorial board of *Lexikon des Mittelalters*. In 2001/2002 she was a fellow at Wissenschaftskolleg zu Berlin. Her writings include *Towns and townsmen of Ottoman Anatolia* (1984), *Herrscher über Mekka* (1990), and *Coping with the state; political conflict and crime in the Ottoman Empire* (1995). Kürschner, 1987-2003; LC; *MESA roster of members*, 1990; Private; Thesis

Farouk, Abdullah, born in 1928, he was in 1972 a professor and chairman of the Department of Commerce in the University of Dacca. His writings include *Measuring benefits of development projects* (1966), *The vagrants of Dacca City* (1978), *Time use of rural women; a six-village survey in Bangladesh* (1979), and *Changes in the economy of Bangladesh* (1982). LC

Farouk-Sluglett, Marion, 1936- *see* Sluglett, Marion

Farquhar, David Miller, born 23 January 1927 at Washington, D.C., he received a Ph.D. in 1960 from Harvard University for his thesis, *The Ch'ing administration of Mongolia up to the nineteenth century*. He was a professor of pre-modern Chinese history at UCLA from 1964 until his death in Los Angeles after a long battle with emphysema on 9 August 1985. He was a specialist on the history of the Altaic peoples, especially the Mongols, and their relation with the Chinese. DrAS, 1974, 1978, 1982; *Journal of Asian studies* 45 (1986), pp. 1127-1128

el **Farra**, Muhammad Hussain, born 20 April 1921 at Khan Younes, Palestine, he was educated at Boston University and the University of Pennsylvania Law School. He taught at American universities from 1955 to 1959, when he joined the Jordanian foreign service. His writings include the pamphlets, *Algeria and the United Nations* (1956), and *Arab nationalism and the United Nations* (1958). IntWW, 1973/74, 1975/76; NUC, 1956-1967; WhoArab, 1978/79, 1981/82

Farran, Charles D'Olivier, born 9 September 1923 at West Denton, England, he received a Ph.D. from the University of Sheffield and was called to the bar from Lincoln's Inn. He was successively a lecturer in law at Sheffield and Liverpool from 1947 to 1958, and a sometime senior lecturer and chairman of the Department of International Comparative Law in the University of Khartoum. His writings include *Matrimonial laws of the Sudan* (1963). Unesco

Farrell, Wilfrid Jerome, 1882-1960, he was a senior scholar and a fellow of Cambridge, and a student at the British School of Archæology, 1906-1910. He served in the Intelligence Corps in the Middle East, and later in the Education Service in Iraq and Palestine. *Who was who*, 5

Farrer, Reginald John, 1880-1920, he was educated privately and at Balliol College, Oxford. He was a horticulturist who travelled extensively in the Far East. During 1914 and 1915 he explored in China's

Kansu province. His writings include *In old Ceylon* (1908), and *On the eaves of the world* (1917). Euan H. M. Cox wrote *Farrer's last journey, Upper Burma, 1919-1920* (1926). BioIn, 2, 3, 4, 9, 13; Who was who, 2

Farrère, Michel, pseud., 1949-1990 *see* Thieck, Jean Pierre

al-**Farsi** (Farsy), Fouad Abdul Salem, born in 1946, he was a sometime Saudi Arabian minister of information and professor at King Saud University. His writings include *Saudi Arabia; a case study in development* (1978), a work which was originally presented as a doctoral thesis at Duke University, Durham, N.C., and *Modernity and tradition; the Saudi equation* (1990). IntYB, 1998

Fartash, Manuchehr, born in 1924 at Tehran, he entered the ministry of foreign affairs in 1944, and later obtained a doctorate in law from the Université de Paris. IranWW, 1974

Faruki, Kemal A., born in 1923, he was a barrister-at-law and a sometime professor of law at Karachi, and editor of *Pakistan horizon*. His writings include *Islamic constitution* (1952), *Islamic jurisprudence* (1962), *The evolution of Islamic constitutional theory and practice from 610 to 1926* (1971), and *Islam today and tomorrow* (1974). LC

al-**Faruqi**, Isma'il Raji, born 1 January 1921 in the coastal region of Jaffa. His youth was clouded by the gathering tensions which beset the inter-war period of the British Mandate. His later trauma of those events needs to be understood in any reckoning with his religious thought which became increasingly involved with the vision of an "Islamicisation of all knowledge," and is manifested in his *Toward Islamic English* (1986). He was educated at AUB; the Institute of Islamic Studies, McGill University, Montreal; Indiana University; and Harvard. At the time of his death he was professor at Temple University, Philadelphia. He died at the hands of an armed intruder at his home, 27 May 1986. Cragg; MW 76 (1986), 251-252

al-**Faruqi**, Lois Lamya Ibsen, born 1926 in Montana, she studied to be a pianist at the universities of Montana and Indiana. After three years of teaching at Butler University, she turned her attention to Islamic studies, guided initially by her husband. Study at McGill University, Montreal, was followed by a Ph.D. at Syracuse University with the thesis *The nature of the musical art of Islamic culture* (1974). She was adjunct professor of religion and art at Temple University from 1977 until her assassination at her home, 27 May 1986. Her writings include *An annotated glossary of Arabic musical terms* (1981), *Islam and art* (1985), *Women, Muslim society and Islam* (1988). Ethnomusicology 32 (1988), pp. 265-268

Faruqi, Nisar Ahmed, born in 1934, his writings include *Early Muslim historiography* (Delhi, 1979), and other works in Urdu. LC

Farzad, Mas'ud, born in 1906 in Persia, he was a sometime professor at Pahlavi University, Shiraz. His writings include *The metre of the robàà'i* (1942), *Haafez and his poems* (1949), and *Persian poetic metres* (1967). IranWW, 1974; NUC, pre-1956

Fasholé-Luke, Edward William, he was editor of *Christianity in independent Africa* (1978).

al- **Fasi**, 'Allal , born in 1910 at Fès, he received an early Islamic education before reading law. He took to politics in 1930 and later became a teacher of theology at the university until 1933 when he was exiled by the French colonial authorities. After Moroccan independence, his reputation earned him an appointment as adviser to Sultan Mohammed V. In 1960 he was elected president of the Istiqlal Party, which he had founded earlier. He resigned from government service in 1963 and returned to teaching Islamic law at Rabat. His writings include *The Independence movements in Arab North Africa* (1954), and *Défense de la loi islamique* (1974). He died of a heart attack on 13 May 1974. DcOrL; Makers, 1996; Reich

Fasmer, Richard Richardovich, born in 1888 at St. Petersburg, he was a graduate of the Oriental Faculty, St. Petersburg and at the time of his death, 1 December 1936, keeper of the numismatic collection at the Ermitage, Leningrad. His writings include *Ein im Dorfe Staryi Dedin in Weissrussland gemachter Fund kufischer Münzen* (Stockholm, 1929), *Chronologie der arabischen Statthalter von Armenien* (1931), and its Armenian translation (Wien, 1933). Krachkovskii, pp. 225, 233; Miliband, p. 570

Fatás Cabeza, Guillermo, born in 1944, he was a sometime lecturer in ancient history at the Universidad de Zaragoza. His writings include *Diccionario de términos de arte y elementos de arqueología y numismática* (1973), *La Sedetania* (1973), a work which is based on his Zaragoza doctoral thesis; and he was joint author of *Zaragoza 1563* (1974), *Heráldica aragonesa* (1990), and *Blasón de Aragon; el escudo y la bandera* (1995). LC

Fatemi (Fatimi), Nasrollah Saifpour, born in 1909, 1910, or 1911 at Nain, Persia, he was a publisher and editor of an Iranian provincial newspaper for over ten years, as well as a politician. In 1946 he emigrated to the United States, where he became successively a professor of political science at Princeton, and Fairleigh Dickinson University, Teaneck, N.J. His writings include *While the United States slept* (1982), and he was joint author of *Sufism, message of brotherhood, harmony and hope* (1976), and *Love, beauty, and harmony in Sufism* (1978). He died in N.Y.C., 23 March 1990. ConAu, 77-80, 131; LC; WhAm, 10; WhoAm, 1986/87, 1988/89; WhoWor, 1984-1987/88

Fathy, Hassan, born 23 March 1900 at Alexandria, Egypt, he studied architecture and graduated in 1926 at Fouad 1st University, Cairo, where he later taught architecture, and became chairman of the Department of Architecture, College of Fine Arts. He was a proponent of building with inexpensive local resources, and he created many superb buildings and complexes using, and derived from, traditional mud-brick buildings with domes and vaults. His writings include *Le pays d'utopie* (1949), *Gourna; a tale of two villages* (1969), its translation, *Construire avec le peuple* (1970), and *The Arab house in the urban setting* (1972). He died in Cairo, 30 November 1989. BioIn, 10, 14; ConAu; Goldschmidt; LC; Makers, 1996; Master (2)

Fatimi, Sayyid Qudratullah, fl. 1968, he was a sometime professor and director, Regional Cooper-ation for Development Institute, Pakistan Branch, Islamabad. His writings include *Pakistan movement and Kemalist revolution* (1977), as well as works in Urdu. Note

Fattenborg, Hans (Hannu) Henrik, born 8 October 1769 at Pohja (Pojo), Finland, he was a professor of Greek at Åbo Akademi, Finland, and as such also responsible for Oriental languages, but in praxis this was limited to Hebrew; he only gave private lessons in elementary Syriac and Arabic. In 1811 he became the first holder of the chair of Oriental languages and remained in this post also after 1812 when the University was transferred to Helsingfors. He died in 1844. ScBInd (5); Stenij, p. 271

Faublée, Jacques, born 24 March 1912 at Saint-Quentin, he received a diploma from l'École des langues orientales vivantes, Paris, and a doctorate in 1953 from the Université de Paris for his thesis, *Les esprits de la vie à Madagascar*. He worked for twenty-five years at the Musée national d'histoire naturelle, Paris, and then taught until his retirement at l'École nationales des langues orientales vivantes. Unesco

Faublée-Urbain, Marcelle, born 20th cent., her writings include *L'Art malgache* (Paris, 1963), and she was joint author of *La Divination malgache par le Sikidy* (Paris, 1970). BN; NUC, 1956-1972

Faucher, Léon Léonard Joseph, born 8 September 1803 at Limoges, he was a journalist, a politician, who twice served as minister of the interior, and a writer on political economy. He died in Marseille on 14 December 1854. DBF; DcBiPP; EncAm; EncBrit; EncicUni; GdeEnc; Meyers; Pallas; RNL

Fauchille, Paul, born in 1858 near Lille, he studied at Douai and Paris, where he received a doctorate in 1882 for his thesis, *De la théorie des risques dans la vente en droit romain. Du blocus maritime en droit français*. He was a lawyer to the Court of Appeal, Paris, and collaborated in the production of the *Recueil de jurisprudence général* of Dalloz. In 1894, he was a joint founder of the *Revue générale de droit international public*. He was a founding director of the Institut des hautes études international de Paris, where he lectured for many years. He died 9 February 1926. DBF; OxLaw

Faucon, Narcisse Alexandre, born in 1857 at Sotteville-lès-Rouen, he started his literary career as an editor with the *Journal de Sotteville* and advanced to become chief editor. After a turbulent resignation in 1878, he went to Algeria to become chief editor of *l'Echo d'Oran*. His writings include *Le livre d'or de l'Algérie* (1890), and *La Tunisie avant et depuis l'occupation française* (1893). He died in 1926. DBF

Faulds, Andrew Matthew William, born 1 March 1923 in Tanganyika, where his father was a missionary. He was an actor for many years, and appeared in three seasons at Stratford-upon-Avon, and over thirty movies. He was M.P. since 1967 and from 1974 to 1997 affiliated with the Parliamentary Association for Euro-Arab Cooperation. He died 31 May 2000. FilmgC, 1984; IntYB, 1980-1985; Who, 1982-2000; WhoWor, 1980/81

Fauquenot, Émile, born 28 February 1897 in France. After service in the first World War, he was put at the disposition of the French mandatory power in Syria in the *Corps des Conseillers contrôleurs*, and, except one three-year interruption, remained there until 1946. In 1940, he received a diploma in *hautes études d'administration musulmane* for his *mémoire* "Les vicissitudes du traité franco-syrien de 1936." From the end of 1948 to 1956 he served in Morocco. He died 2 September 1966. L'Afrique et l'Asie 75 (1966), pp. 72-75

Faure, Adolphe, born in 1913 in Morocco, he was a professor of Arabic at l'Institut des hautes études in Rabat until 1964, when he retired and became a mayor of Carnoux-en-Provence, where he died on 27 July 1983. He edited *al-Tashawwuf ilá rijal al-tasawwuf*, by Yusuf b. Y. al-Tadili (1958). Hespéris Tamuda 22 (1984), pp. 3-4

Faure, Andre Bertrand Pierre *Fernand*, born 16 March 1853 at Ribérac (Dordogne), he was a lawyer at Bordeaux since 1873, and received his doctorate in 1878 for his thesis, *Droit romain: histoire de la préture; droit français: de l'institution contractuelle*. Since 1880 he was a professor of law at Bordeaux, where he became concurrently engaged in municipal affairs. In 1885 he was elected a *député* and soon established an reputation for financial matters. In 1892 he was concurrently appointed professor of financial legislation at the Faculté de droit de Paris, a post which he held for thirty years. He died in Paris, 6 November 1929. DBF

Faure, Claude, born 9 March 1881 at Bourges, he was educated at a Carthusian institution in Lyon and Lycée Henri IV in Paris. He entered l'École des chartes in 1901 and spent the years from 1906 to 1908 at l'École française de Rome. He was successively an archivist at French *départements*, and the Gouvernement général de l'Afrique Occidentale Française from 1909 to 1941. In the first World War he also served in the Armée de l'Orient and was seriously wounded in Macedonia. He published several repertories of archives at home and abroad. In 1932 he received two doctorates from the Université de Grenoble. He died in Ampuis (Rhône), 23 February 1942. DBF

Faure, Fernand, 1853-1929 *see* Faure, André Bertrand Pierre *Fernand*

Faure, François *Félix*, born 30 January 1841 at Paris, he was a shipowner in le Havre and an authority on matters concerning shipping, trade and the colonies. He entered the Chambre des députés in 1881 and was elected president of France in 1895, a post which he held until his death in Paris, 16 February 1899. DBF; EncAm

Faure, Henri Paul Lucien, born 18 December 1903 at Tlemcen, Algeria, he was an agromomist educated in Alger, Paris and Montpellier. He was *délégué général adjoint* of the Organisation commune des régions sahariennes from 1958 to 1963, and a member of the Conseil économique et social au titre des personnalités qualifiés pour leur connassaince des problèmes économiques et sociaux d'outre-mer from 1962 to 1969. In 1962 he went on a mission to Tehran to negotiate the technical and economic cooperation between France and Iran. WhoFr, 1965/66-1979/80|

Faure, Raoul, fl. 1954, he was a sometime chief engineer and head of the Services agricoles régionaux in Morocco. Note

Faure-Biguet, Gabriel Isidore, born 13 December 1838 at Crest (Drôme). After graduation from l'École polytechnique in 1857 he went on to l'École d'application d'état-major. He rose to the rank of general and had three spells of duty in Algeria. His writings include *Histoire de l'Afrique septentrionale sous la domination musulmane* (1905), and *Abrégé des successions en droit musulman d'après le poème de la Tlemsâniya et le commentaire d'el A'snoûni* (1912). He died in Valence, 9 July 1919. DBF; Peyronnet, p. 433

Faurot, Lionel, fl. 1877-1887, he received a doctorate in 1895 from the Université de Paris for his thesis, *Études sur l'anatomie, l'histologie et le développement des actinies*. NUC, pre-1956

Fauvel, Albert Auguste, born in 1851 at Cherbourg, he studied Manchu at l'École des langues orientales vivantes, Paris, and entered the Chinese customs administration in 1872. In 1885, he was appointed an inspector of the Messageries maritimes, and was sent on numerous missions, particularly to the Seychelles. He was a contributor to newspapers and journals. He died in Cherbourg on 3 November 1909. DBF; *Hommes et destins*, vol. 2, pp. 308-309

Favaro, Antonio Vittorio Eugenio Maria, born 21 May 1847 at Padova, he studied mathematics and engineering at Padova, Torino, and Zürich. In 1872 he was appointed professor of statics and of the history of mathematics at the Università di Padova. His writings include *Galileo Galilei; e lo studio di Padova* (1883), *Carteggio inedito di Ticone Brahe, G. Keplero e di altri celebri astronomi e matematici dei secolo XVI, e XVII.* (1886), and *Archimede* (1912). He died in Padova, 30 September 1922. EncAm; EncicUni; EncItaliana; IndBI (7); LC; Meyers; Pallas; RNL

Favé, Ildefonse, born 28 April 1812 at Dreux (Eure-et-Loire), he was educated at l'École polytechnique, and l'École d'application de Metz. He was an artillery officer and a writer on military matters, specializing in explosives and artillery. He took part in the Crimean War and later lectured in military science at the Polytechnique. He resigned with the rank of general in 1874 and died in Paris, 14 March 1894. His writings include *Cours d'art militaire* (1877), and the translation, *The Emperor Napoléon's new system of field artillery* (1854). DBF; Index BFr² (4); Vapereau

Favenc, Bernard, fl. 1922, he was in 1916 a judge in the Mixed Tribunal, Alexandria, and in 1928, a *conseiller* in the Mixed Court of Appeal, Alexandria; he was a member of the Société sultanieh d'économie politique, de statistique et de législation. Note

514

Favoreu, Louis, born 5 September 1936 at Luc-de-Béarn (Basses-Pyrénées), he studied law at Paris, where he received his doctorate and *agrégation*. He was a professor of law as well as a dean and president at various French universities. In 1996, he was appointed international judge to the Constitutional Court of Bosnia-Hercegovina. Between 1985 and 1997 he received six honorary doctorates. His writings include *Du déni de justice en droit public français* (1965), and *L'île Maurice; encyclopédie politique et constitutionnelle* (1970). WhoFr, 1981/82-1998/99

Favre, Camille, born 19th cent. In April and May 1874 he made an archaeological excursion together with B. E. de Mandrot to Cilicia. From modern Iskenderun they travelled north by way of Erzin (Yeşilkent) to the Ceyhan River, visited the Misis Mountains and went on to Adana, the Bolkar Dağı to Tarsus and Mersin whence they continued along the coast. Henze

Favreau-Lilie, Marie Louise, fl. 1974-1986, her writings include *Studien zur Frühgeschichte des Deutschen Ordens* (1974), a work which was originally presented in 1972 as her doctoral thesis at the Universität Kiel, and *Die Italiener im Heiligen Land; vom ersten Kreuzzug bis zum Tode Heinrichs von Champagne, 1098-1197* (1989), a work for which she received a second doctorate in 1983. LC

Favret, Jeanne Hélène, born 26 September 1934 at Sfax, Tunisia. After receiving a *agrégation* in 1958, she specialized in European settlers in North Africa, and pursued advanced studies successively at l'Institut de hautes études de Tunis and l'Institut d'ethnologie, Paris. She was a sometime *professeur* of philosophy at the Lycée de Quimper. Unesco

Fawcett, Frederick, born in 1853, he joined the Bengal Police in 1878 and rose to the rank of Deputy Inspector-General of Police in 1905, a post which he held until he retired in 1912. His writings include *On the Saoras (or Savaras), an aboriginal hill people of the eastern ghats of the Madras Presidency* (Bombay, 1901). *Indian biographical dictionary*, 1915

Fawcett, James Edmund Sandford, born 16 April 1913, he was a sometime legal adviser to the Foreign Office, and to the UK delegation to the United Nations, and the British Embassy, Washington, D.C. In 1977, he became chairman of the British Institute of Human Rights. He wrote *The Application of the European Convention on Human Rights* (1969), and *Lights on human rights* (1987). He died 24 June 1991. BlueB, 1975, 1976; ConAu, 97-100; IntWW, 1973/74-1985/86; IntYB, 1982, 1983; Who, 1974-1991

Fawcett, Percy Harrison, born in 1867 at Torquay, Devon, he was educated at the Royal Military College, Woolwich, then joined the Army and served in Europe and the Far East. In 1901, he went on a mission to the interior of Morocco. His writings were published in newspapers and journals. He died in 1925. *Who was who*, 3

Fawcett, William Lyman, fl. 1875, his writings include *Gold and debt; an American hand-book of finance* (1877). NUC, pre-1956

Fawdah (Foda), 'Izz al-Din, born in 1923, he was a sometime professor at Cairo University. His writings include *The projected Arab court of justice* (1957), *Israeli belligerent occupation and Palestinain armed resistance in international law* (1970), as well as works in Arabic. LC

Fawzi, Husayn, born 11 July 1900 at Cairo, he studied medicine in Egypt and later belonged to a group of young intellectuals who launched the journal *al-Fajr*. In 1925 he received a five-year government scholarship to study oceanography and marine zoology in France. Upon his return he became Egypt's first oceanographer and later was appointed director of fisheries research in Alexandria, and subsequently served as professor of zoology at Alexandria University. Between 1955 and 1960 he served as under-secretary of state at the Ministry of Culture, and for several years he was the chief editor of *al-Majallah*. He was an active member of the Institut d'Égypte, functioning as its president between 1968 and 1974. His writings include *An Egyptian Sindbad; journeys in the Indian Ocean* (1938), and *Tales of old Sindbad* (1943). He died in Cairo, 20 August 1988. *Asian and African studies*, Haifa, 23 (1989), pp. 97-99; Goldschmidt

Fawzi, Mahmud, born 1900 at Cairo, he was a career diplomat who served King Faruq, and emerged from the military revolution of 1952 as the leading diplomat of president Jamal 'Abd al-Nasir (Nasser). Under president Sadat he was successively prime-minister and vice-president of Egypt until he resigned from office in 1974. He was the author of a number of books in Arabic. He died in Cairo, 12 June 1981. AnObit, 1981, pp. 384-85; Goldschmidt; Makers, 1996; Master (5); WhoArab, 1978/79

Fawzi, Saad el Din I., born in the Sudan, he studied at St. Andrews and London, where he received a Ph.D. in 1954 for his thesis, *The origins and development of the labour movement in the Sudan*. A trade edition, *The labour movement in the Sudan, 1946-1955*, was published in 1957. Thereafter he was a professor of economics at the University of Khartoum. WhoArab, 1981/82, 1984/85

Fawzy, Didar, fl. 1978, his writings include *La République du Soudan, 1956-1966* (1975). LC; NUC; ZKO

Fay, Gérard, he received a doctorate in 1972 from the Université de Paris VII for his thesis, *Recherches sur l'organisation de la vie rurale et sur les conditions de la production dans la basse montagne rifaine.* THESAM 1

Fay, Sidney Bradshaw, born 13 April 1876 at Washington, D.C., he was a graduate of Harvard where he received a Ph.D. in 1900 for his thesis, *The Fürstenbund of 1875.* He was a professor of history at Dartmouth College, Smith College, and Harvard, as well as a lecturer at Amherst College, Columbia, and Yale. He was a president of the Near Eastern History Teachers Association and the American Historical Association as well as a member of learned societies at home and abroad. His writings include *The origins of the World War* (1928). He died in 1967. Master (5); WhAm, 4, 5; *Who was who*, 6

Fay, William, born in 1948 in Rhodesia and brought up in England, he studied classics, philosophy, and history of art at Oxford before becoming involved in the Arabian Peninsula in 1974. Since then he has worked as a planning and research consultant on numerous projects to set up museums of the archaeology, history and natural history of the Arabian states. In 1999, he was a director of the London Centre of Arab Studies. His writings include *Oman, a seafaring nation* (1979), and he was joint author of *Kuwait by the first photographers* (1998).

Fayein, Claudie, born in 1912, she received a medical doctorate in 1940 from the Université de Paris and became affiliated with the Musée de l'homme, Paris. Her writings include *Une française, médecin au Yémen* (1955), its translation, *Hakima, eineinhalb Jahre Ärztin im Jemen* (1956), *Yemen* (1975), and *Vie de femmes au Yémen; recits de Nagiba* (1990). LC

Fazlul Haq (Huq), Abul Kasem, born 26 October 1873 at Chakhar, East Bengal, he was privately educated, graduated with triple honours from Presidency College, Calcutta, in 1894, took an M.A. in mathematics two years later, and his B.L. in 1897. He was a college teacher and a journalist until 1906 when he entered the government service as a deputy magistrate for six years. From then on he was active as a lawyer, but foremost as a politician. From 1913 until partition he was associated with the Bengal Legislative Assembly. He served under the East Pakistan Government until 1958. His writings include *Memorable speeches of Sher-e-Bangla* (1978). He died in Dacca, 27 April 1962. A. S. M. Abdur Rab wrote *Fazlul Haq; life and achievements* (1967). BioIn 6, 8; Sen, vol. 2, pp. 135-138; NYT 28 April 1962, p. 25, col. 5

Fazlur Rahman, 1905-1966 *see* Rahman, Fazlur

Fazlur Rahman, 1919-1988 *see* Rahman, Fazlur

Fazy, Edmond, born in 1870, he was a teacher and journalist. His writings include *Les Turcs d'aujourd'hui, ou Le Grand Karagheuz; la Porte, le palais, certains financiers, le corps diplomatique, intermède, le sultan* (1898), and *Anthologie de l'amour turc* (1905). He died in 1910. BN; NUC, pre-1956

Fazylov, Ergash Ismailovich, born 10 March 1933 at Kaunchi, Uzbekistan, he was a graduate of the Moscow Institute of Oriental Languages and received a doctorate in 1967 from Tashkent University for his thesis, *Староузбекский язык; Хоресмийские памятники XIV века.* His writings include *Кадимги обидалар ва Алишер Навоий тили* (1969), *Фрагменты неизвестного старотюрского памятника* (1970), he was joint author of *Русские тюркологи и узбекское языкознание* (1979), joint translator of *Изысканный дар тюркскому языку; грамматический трактат XIV в. на арабском языке* (1978), and he edited *"Юсуфу Зулайхо" достони морфологияси* (1988). Miliband²

Fazylov (Fozilov), Mulladzhan F., fl. 20th cent., his writings include *Спрвъ выражении современного таджикского языка* (1963), *Истины; изречення персидского и таджикского народов, их поэтов и мудрецов* (1968), *Пословичные рассказы* (1973), and *Словарь таджикско-персидских пословиц, поговорок и афоризмов* (1975). LC; NUC, 1973-1977

Fedalto, Giorgio, fl. 1975, his writings include *Ricerche storiche sulla posizione giuridica ed ecclesiastica del greci a Venezia nei secoli XV e XVI* (1967), *Perché le crociate* (1980), *La chiesa latina in Oriente* (1981), *Le chiese d'Oriente* (1984), and he edited *Hierarchia ecclesiastica orientalis* (1988).

Fedchenko, Aleksei Fedorovich, born in 1913 at Mineral'nikh Vodakh, he graduated from the Tomsk Polytechnical Institute in 1938. Since 1953 he was a research fellow in the Oriental Institute of the Soviet Academy of Science. His writings include *Ирак в борьбе за независимость, 1917-1969* (1970), and he was joint author of *Международный сионизм; история и политика* (1977). He died 15 May 1983. Miliband; Miliband²; *Народы Азии и Африки*, 1983, № 5, p. 218

Fedchenko, Aleksei Pavlovich, born in 1874, he was a naturalist who made two remarkable excursions to the Alai Valley, the Khanate of Kokand, and the Zeravshan Valley from 1868 to 1869 and again from 1870 to 1871. He gathered enormous zoological and botanical collections in areas previously little known or explored. His writings include *Reise in Turkestan*, text and t.p. in Russian, 3 vols (1874-88), and *Путешествие в Туркестан* (1950). While on a visit to Germany and Switzerland he went on a glacial ascent of Mount Montblanc, an enterprise which ended in his death on 15 September 1873. Bioln, 15; Embacher; Geog, 8; GSE; Henze, p. 204; NUC, pre-1956

Fedchina, Vera Nikolaeva, fl. 1957, her writings include *Как создавалась карта Средней Азии* (1967). LC

Fedden, Henry Romilly, born 26 November 1908 at Burford, England, he was educated at Magdalene College, Cambridge. He was a writer, traveller, and a notable mountaineer. As secretary of the Historic Buildings Committee, he was the keeper at the National Trust for Places of Historic Interest or Natural Beauty's aesthetic standards. He was appointed deputy director general in 1968 and on his retirement received the C.B.E. His writings, partly under the pseudonym Robin Fedden, include *The land of Egypt* (1939), *Syria; an historical appreciation* (1946), *Crusader castles* (1950), its translation, *Kreuzfahrerburgen im Heiligen Land* (1959), and *The continuing purpose; a history of the National Fund, its aims and work* (1968). He died 20 March 1977. Apollo 105 (May 1977), p. 399; Bioln, 8, 11; ConAu, 9-12; Who, 1969-1977; Who was who, 7

Fedden, Robin, pseud., 1908-1977 see Fedden, Henry Romilly

Feddersen, Martin, born 26 November 1888, he studied at the Universität Hamburg where he received a Dr.phil in 1924 for his thesis, *Die Kanzeln des "Eiderstedter Typus."* For many years he was affiliated with the Museum für Kunst und Gewerbe, Hamburg. His writings include *Chinesi-sches Kunstgewerbe* (1939). He died in Hamburg, 4 February 1964. Kürschner, 1950, 1954, 1961.

Feder, Ernst, born 18 March 1881 at Berlin, he studied at Berlin and München and received a doctorate in law in 1938 from the Université de Genève for his thesis, *Le contrôle dans les sociétés anonymes anglaises (auditors)*. He was a journalist and political editor at the *Berliner Tageblatt* from 1919 to 1931. He briefly practised law in Berlin before emigrating to France in 1933, and to Brazil in 1941. In 1957 he returned to Berlin where he died in 1964. His writings include *Begegnungen* (1950), and *Heute sprach ich mit ...; Tagebücher eines Berliner Publizisten, 1926-1932* (1971). His papers are now at the Leo Baeck Institute. Bioln, 8; EncJud; LC; WhE&EA; Wininger

Federici Vescovini, Graziella, fl. 1979, she was editor of *Il "Lucidator dubitabilium astronomiae" di Pietro d'Abano* (1988). LC

Federmann, Henri, born 10 September 1823 at Göttingen, Germany, he was naturalized a French citizen and an interpreter in the Corps des interprètes de l'armée d'Afrique. He advanced from *interprète auxiliaire* (5 May 1848) to *interprète principal* (27 January 1866). He was a member of the Société historique algérienne and *chevalier de la Légion d'honneur* (11 August 1859). He died during active service, 12 October 1872. Féraud, p. 292

Federspiel, Howard Manley, born 10 March 1932 at Springville, N.Y., he was a graduate of Capital University, received an M.A. in 1961 from the Institute of Islamic Studies, McGill University, Montreal, for his thesis, *Hajj Muhammad Amin al-Husayni*, and also a Ph.D. in 1966 for *The Persatuan Islam*. He was a researcher and analyst before being appointed a professor of political science at Winthrop College, S.C. In 1995 he taught at the Department of Social Science in Ohio State University, Newark, and in 1999, at McGill University. His writings include *Muslim intellectuals and national development in Indonesia* (1992). AmM&WS, 1973 S, 1978 S; Ferahian; Selim

Fedorenko, Vsevolod Mikhailovich, born 8 January 1912 in Russia, he was in the diplomatic service from 1946 to 1948, and from 1954 to his death on 25 January 1989 he was affiliated with the Oriental Institute of the Soviet Academy of Science. Miliband²

Fedorov, Georgii Borisovich, fl. 1955, he obtained a doctorate in history. His writings include *Археология Румынии* (1973); he was joint author of *Памятники древних славян* (1974), and he edited *Население центральной части Днестровско-Прутского междуречья в X-XII вв.* (1982). LC

Fedorov, IAkov Aleksandrovich, 1902-1982, his writings include *Ранние тюркина Северном Кавказа* (1978), and *Историческая этнография Северного Кавказа* (1983). LC

Fedorov-Davydov, German Alekseevich, born in 1931, he was an archaeologist, historian and numismatist who received a doctorate in 1966 and in 1969 was appointed a professor. His writings include *Монеты рассказывают* (1963), *Курганы, идолы, монеты* (1968), *Монеты Московской Руси* (1981), and the translations *Die Goldene Horde und ihre Vorgänger* (1972), and *The Culture of the Golden Horde cities* (1984). LC; TatarES

Fedorova, Irina Evgen'evna, born 11 January 1951 at Moscow, she was a graduate in linguistics of the Moscow State University in 1973, and was a researcher at the Oriental Institute of the Soviet Academy of Science since 1979. In 1980, she received her first degree for her thesis, *Политика Англии в Иране в начале XX века (1905-1914)*. She was joint author of *Политика Велико-британни и США на Среднем Востока в английской и американской историографии* (1989). Miliband[2]

Fedotov, Mikhail Romanovich, born 20th cent., his writings include *Средства выражения модальности в чувашском языке* (1963), *Исторические связи чувашского язика угро-финнов* (1965), and *Чувашский язык в семье алтайских языков* (1980-1986). LC

Fedozzi, Prospero, born 12 July 1872 at Metelica (Macerata), he was a professor of international law at the Università di Palermo and subsequently at Genova. His writings include *Saggio sul protettorato* (1897). He died in Genova, 19 January 1934. Casati; Chi è, 1931; DizBI

Féghali, Michel, born 10 July 1877 at Kfarabida, Lebanon, he received a doctorate in 1918 from the Université d'Alger with a *thèse complémentaire* entitled *Études sur les emprunts syriaques dans les parlers arabes du Liban*. He was a Maronite clergyman, and a professor at the Faculté des lettres de Bordeaux as well as the l'École nationale des langues orientales vivantes, Paris. His writings include *Du genre grammatical en sémitique* (1924), *Contes, légendes, coutumes populaires du Liban et de Syrie* (1935), and *La famille maronite au Liban* (1935). He died 3 June 1945. Al-Andalus 10 (1945), p. 464; Qui est-ce, 1934

Fehér, Géza, born 4 August 1890 at Kunszentmiklós, Hungary, he studied at the University of Debrecen where he received a doctorate in Hungarian history. After the war he spent half a year at the Hungarian Institute, Constantinople, and later was employed at the Oriental Section of the Municipal Library, Budapest. He was a lecturer in history at Debrecen from 1924 to 1944 when he became a lecturer at Istanbul. From 1948 until his death on 10 April 1955 he was a member of the Archaeo-logical Section in the Hungarian National Museum, Budapest. His writings include *Bulgarisch-ungarische Beziehungen in den V.-XI. Jahrhunderten* (1921). EnBulg; MEL, 1967-69; Südost-Forschungen 14 (1955), pp. 454-455; UjMagyar

Fehér, Geza, fl. 1973, his writings include *Craftsmanship in Turkish-ruled Hungary* (1975), *Török miniaturák a magyarországi hódoltság koráról* (1975), its translation, *Turkish miniatures from the period of Hungary's Turkish occupation* (1978) A *magyar történelem oszmán török ábrázolásokban* (1982), and *Bulgar Türkleri tarihi* (Ankara, 1984). LC

Fehérvári, Géza, born 6 May 1926 at Eger, Hungary, he received a Ph.D. in 1960 from SOAS for his thesis, *Development of the mihrab down to the fourteenth century*. He was a lecturer in Islamic art at the University of London since 1963. His writings include *Islamic pottery* (1973), *Islamic metalwork in the eighth to the fifteenth century in the Keir Collection* (1976), *Az Iszlám művészet története* (1987), and he was joint author of *1400 years of Islamic art; a descriptive catalogue* (1981). Fekete; MagyarNKK, 1992, 1994, 1996, 1998; Sluglett

Feigl, Maria, fl. 1955, she received a Dr.phil. in 1951 from the Universität Köln for her thesis, *Quellenstudien zu Alberts des Großen Kommentar zum Liber de causis*. Sezgin

Feilberg, Carl Gunnar, born 20 October 1894 at København, he was a geographer and ethnographer who received a doctorate in 1944 from Københavns Universitet for his thesis, *La tente noire; contri-bution ethnographique à l'histoire culturelle des nomades*. His writings include *Afrika; een Verdensdel lukker sig up* (1945), and *Les Papis; tribu persane de nomades montagnards du sud-ouest de l'Iran* (1952). He died in Hellerup, 6 January 1972. DanskBL

Feinberg, Nathan, born 6 June 1895 at Kovno (Kaunas), Russia, he studied at Zürich and Genève where he received a doctorate in law. From 1924 to 1927 and 1934 to 1945 he practised law in Palestine, from 1931 to 1933 he lectured at Genève, and from 1945 to his retirement he was a professor of law, and dean, Hebrew University, Jerusalem. His writings include *The Arab-Israel conflict in international law* (1970), *On an Arab jurist's approach to Zionism and the State of Israel* (1971), and *Studies in international law, with special reference to the Arab-Israel conflict* (1979). EncJud; IntAu&W, 1977, 1982, 1986, 1989; IntWW, 1972/73-1985/86; Master (1); MideE, 1982/83; NearMEWho, 1945/46; WhoIsrael, 1956-1985/86|; WhoWor, 1974/75-1978/79; WhoWorJ, 1965, 1972

Feinerman, James Vincent, born 30 October 1950 at Chicago, he graduated from Yale University where he also received a Ph.D. in East Asian languages and literature. He studied and lectured in China, and was admitted to the New York bar in 1981. Since 1985 he was a lecturer at the School of Law, Georgetown University, Washington, D.C, a post which he still held in 1999. DrAS 1982; Master (2); NatFacDr, 1995-1999; WhoEmL, 1987

Feis, Herbert, born 7 June 1893 at NYC, he was a graduate of Harvard University where he also received an Ph.D. in 1920 for his thesis, *An investigation of wage principles underlying a policy for industrial peace*. He lectured in economics at various American universities until 1929 when he entered the government service as an economic adviser and consultant. He was a sometime member of the Institute for Advanced Study, Princeton. His writings include *The changing patterns of international economic affairs* (1940), and *Petroleum and American foreign policy* (1944). He died 2 March 1972. CnDiAmJBi; ConAu, P-1, 9-10, 33-36; Master (7); WhAm, 5; WorAu

Feiwel, Raphael Joseph, born 23 April 1907 at Köln, he spent his early years working and residing in Palestine. He later was a broadcaster and periodical editor in Britain. His writings, published partly under the pseudonym Tosco Raphael Fyvel, include *No ease in Zion* (1939), its translation, *L'Anglais, le Juif et l'Arabe en Palestine* (1939), *The insecure offenders* (1961), *The frontiers of sociology* (1964), and *Intellectuals today* (1968). He died in France in 1985. ConAu, 117, 129; LC

Fékar, Benali, born 19th cent., he received a doctorate in 1908 from the Université de Lyon for his thesis, *L'usure en droit musulman et ses conséquences pratiques*. His writings include *Leçons d'arabe dialectal marocain, algérien*, 2e éd. (Lyon, 1914). NUC, pre-1956

Fekete, Lajos, born 12 June 1891 at Tardos, Hungary, he was a trained historian and archivist and began his career at the National Archives, Budapest. From 1938 to his retirement in 1966 he was succesively a lecturer in, and professor of, Turkology. His writings include *Einführung in die osmanisch-türkische Diplomatik der türkischen Botmässigkeit in Ungarn* (1926), *Budapest a török korban* (1944), and *Die Siyaqat-Schrift in der türkischen Finanzverwaltung* (1955). He died in 1969. I.I. (4); UjMagyar

Feki, Ahmed Hassan el-, born in 1911, he was educated at the Cairo military academy as well as Staff College, and Gunnery Staff College, UK. He was a career diplomat and thereafter a high official in the Egyptian ministry of foreign affairs. IntWW, 1971/72-1975/76; WhoArab, 1971/72-1993/94

Fekrat, M. Ali, born 24 July 1937, he was a graduate of AUB and received a Ph.D. in 1969 from Indiana University for his thesis, *International monetary reserves for an expanding world economy; a theoretical inquiry*. In 1967 he was appointed professor of business economics at Georgetown University, Washington, D.C., a post which he still held in 1999. He was joint author of *Iran; economic development under dualistic conditions* (1971), and joint editor of *Impediments to U.S.-Arab economic relations* (1989). ConAu 45-48; NatFacDr 1995-1999

Feld, Otto, fl. 1968, his writings include *Studien zur spätantiken und byzantinischen Kunst* (1986). LC

Feldbæck, Ole, born 22 July 1936, he received a doctorate in 1969 from Københavns Universitet for his thesis, *India trade under the Danish flag, 1772-1808*. Since 1968 he was a professor at the Institut for Økonomisk Historie in Københavns Universitet. His writings include *Slaget på Reden* (1985), and he was joint author of *Kolonierne i Asien og Afrika* (1980). Kraks, 1990-1998

Feldman, Herbert H. S., born in 1910 at London, he was called to the bar from Gray's Inn. He went to India in 1941 as a soldier and later was successively a temporary civil servant and a contractor in Pakistan. He knew Urdu and wrote extensively on Pakistani matters. His writings include *A constitution for Pakistan* (1955), *Karachi through a hundred years* (1960), *From crisis to crisis; Pakistan, 1962-1969* (1972), and *The end and the beginning; Pakistan, 1969-1971* (1975). He died in 1976. His private papers from 1954 to 1976 are housed in Duke University Library, Durham, N.C. ConAu, 29-32; LC

Feldmann, Leopold, born 22 March 1802 at München, he was a playwright and a journalist who visited Greece from 1836 to 1840. He died in Wien, 26 March 1882. ADtB; BbD; BiD&SB; Wininger; ÖBL; Wurzbach

Feldmann, Wilhelm, born 2 February 1880 at Wilhelmshaven, Germany, he studied law and literature at the universities of Marburg, München, Berlin, and Freiburg im Breisgau, where he received a Dr.phil. in 1902 for his thesis, *Friedrich Justin Bertuch*. He was a journalist and correspondent to various German newspapers, and served as war correspondent during the Balkan War as well as the first World War. His writings include *Kriegstage in Konstantinopel* (1913), *Reise zur Suesfront* (1917) and *Felix Faller, ein Schwarzwaldmaler* (1950). Wer ist's, 1928, 1935

Felix, Günther, born 20th cent., he received a Dr.jur. in 1954 from the Universität Köln for his thesis, *Ermessensausübung im Steuerrecht*. He wrote extensively on German internal revenue legislation. Kürschner, 1992, 1996; LC

Felkin, Robert William, born in 1853 at Beeston, England, he was a medical doctor, trained at the universities of Edinburgh and Marburg. In 1878 he joined a party of missionaries of the Church Missionary Society, London, on a journey to Uganda. He was later in correspondence with Emin

Pasha when the latter was isolated in Equatorial Africa. He was joint author of *Uganda and the Egyptian Sudan* (1882). He died in 1926. Henze; Hill

Fell, Edward Nelson, born in 1857, he was an American mining engineer who spent a number of years as manager of the Spassky Mining Company, an English concern, on the Kirghiz steppes. His writings include *Russian and nomad; tales of the Kirghiz Steppes* (1916). AmIndex (1)

Fell, Winand, born 13 December 1837 at Aachen, Germany, he studied Catholic theology and Semitic languages at the universities of Münster and Bonn. He was ordained in 1861 at Köln, where he served as a priest until 1869 when he continued his Oriental studies at Berlin and Leipzig, completing his formal education with the thesis, *Canones apostolorum Aethiope*. He taught at a secondary school in Köln from 1873 to 1886 when he was appointed a professor of Old Testament exegesis at the Universität Münster. His writings include *Indices ad Beidhawii commentarium in Coranum* (1878). He died in Münster, 5 July 1908. BioJahr, 1908; DtBE; *Wer ist's*, 1908

Fellman, Jack, fl. 1976. In 1973 he was affiliated with Bar-Ilan University. His writings include *The revival of a classical tongue; Eliezer Ben Yehauda and the modern Hebrew language* (1973). LC

Fellmann, Walter, born in 1931, he received a Dr.phil. degree in 1963 from the Universität Halle for his thesis, *Die Bedeutung des Nahostöls und die anglo-amerikanischen Rivalität im Kampf um die Kontrolle der Erdölquellen im Vorderen Orient.* LC; Schwarz

Fellowes, Peregrine E. C., fl. 1971. He was a sometime consulting editor of the *New Middle East* and previously affiliated with the Foreign Office and Shell.

Fellows, Charles, Sir, born in 1799 at Nottingham, he was a mountaineer and an archaeologist. His writings include *A journal written during an excursion in Asia Minor* (1839), its translation, *Ein Ausflug nach Kleinasien und Entdeckungen in Lycien* (1853), *An account of discoveries in Lycia* (1841), and *Travels and researches in Asia Minor, more particularly in the Province of Lycia* (1852). He died in 1860. BiD&SB; DcBiPP; DNB; Embacher; Henze

Fels, Edwin, born 11 November 1888 on Corfu, he studied geography at the Universität München, and had a career as a lecturer and professor of economic geography, spending the last twenty years before his retirement in Berlin. His writings include *Das Weltmeer in seiner wirtschafts- und verkehrs-geographischen Bedeutung* (1932). He died in München, 19 May 1983. DtBE; Kürschner, 19311983

Felvinczi Takáts, Zoltán, born 7 April 1880 at Nagysomkut (Şomcuta Mare,) Austria-Hungary, he studied law at Budapest but soon changed to art subjects and left for the universities of München and aftwards Berlin. Upon his return to Budapest he continued with fine art, mainly Far Eastern art, until he received a doctorate. Just after the turn of the century he started his career as a curator, first at the National Galery, and then at the Museum of Fine Arts (Szépüvészti Múzeum), Budapest. In 1919 he became the first director of the Hopp Ferenc Keletázsiai Müvészeti Múzeum, Budapest. He was a sometime professor at the universities of Pécs, Szeged, and Kolozsvár (Cluj). He died in Budapest on 4 December 1964. Geistige Ung; Magyar; MEL, 1967-69; *Oriental art* 11 (1965), p. 125

Felze, Jacques, fl. 1935. His writings include *Au Maroc inconnu* (Grenoble, 1935). LC

Fenaux, Henri, fl. 1972. He was a sometime lecturer at the Faculté de droit et des sciences économiques d'Alger.

Fendrich, Walter, fl. 1969. He was an ornithologist and for many years a staff member of the Natur-historisches Museum, Wien, and the Österreichische Vogelwarte.

Fenech, Edward C. He received a Ph.D. in 1975 from the University of Leeds for his thesis, *An analytical and comparative study of contemporary journalistic Maltese*. His writings include *Contemporary journalistic Maltese* (1978). LC; Sluglett

Fenech, Soledad Gibert *see* Gibert Fenech, Soledad

Fenelon, Kevin Gerard, born 6 December 1898 at London, he was affiliated successively with the universities of Edinburgh and Manchester until 1951. He intermittenly served as statistical adviser to Middle Eastern countries until 1976. Form 1958 to 1961 he served as a professor at AUB. His writings include *The economics of transport* (1925), and *The United Arab Emirtaes; an economic and social survey* (1973). He died 12 March 1983. ConAu, 73-76; Master (1); WhE&EA

Fénelon, Paul, born 4 January 1903 at Trémolat (Dordogne), his writings include *La Terre, les continents, l'Union française* (1949), and *Vocabulaire de géographie agraire* (1970). LC

520

Fenn, Christopher Cyprian, fl. 1886-1888, he was a missionary and affiliated with Oxford University. BLC

Fenn, David, fl. 1867, he was a missionary and joint author of *Concordance to the Tamil New Testament* (1878). BLC

de **Fenoyl**, Maurice, S.J., fl. 1939, his writings include *Le Sanctoral copte* (Beyrouth, 1960), and he was joint author of *Coutumes religieuses coptes* (Le Caire, 1953). LC

Fenster, Erwin, born 28 October 1938 at Bad Wörishofen, Germany, he studied classical philology and Byzantinism at the Universität München and received a Dr.phil. in 1968 for *Laudes Constantinopolitanae*. In the autumn of 1968, he obtained a position as a research fellow at the Institut für Byzantinistik und neugriechische Philologie at his alma mater. In 1978, he was resident in Augsburg. Thesis

Fenton, Paul Bernard, fl. 1980, he obtained a doctorate in Oriental languages at Paris, and was a sometime professor at the Département des études hebraïques, Université de Strasbourg. His writings include *The treatise of the pool*, by Obadiah ben Abraham Maimonides (1981), and *Reshimat kitve-yad be-'Arvit-Yehudit be-Leningrad* (1991). EURAMES, 1993; LC

Fentzloff, Helmuth E., born in the 1890s in Germany, he attended school and the Technische Hochschule at Danzig. In 1925, he was awarded the Schinkel-Plakette of the Berliner Architekten- und Ingenieur-Verein and thereafter worked in various capacities as an engineer of hydrodynamics in Bavaria. He received a Dr.ing. in 1956 from the Technische Hochschule Karlsruhe for his thesis, *Systematik der Wassernutzung*. His trace is lost after a publication in 1961. Thesis

Fenwick, Charles Ghequiere, born 26 May 1880 at Baltimore, Md., he was a graduate of the local Loyola College and received a Ph.D. in 1912 from Johns Hopkins University, Baltimore, for his thesis, *The neutrality laws of the United States*. He was an expert on international law, for thirty years a professor of political science at Bryn Mawr College, and for more than sixty years associated with the American Society of International Law. His writings include *Cases on international law* (1935), and *Foreign policy and international law* (1968). He died in Baltimore, 24 April 1973. *American journal of international law* 67 (1973), pp. 501-4; BiDInt; ConAu, 41-44; OxLaw; WhAm, 5 & 6

Féral, Gabriel, fl. 1951, his writings include *Note sur l'emploi agricole dans le delta du fleuve Sénégal dans le cadre des futurs aménagements hydro-agricoles* (1975), *Esquisse sur la situation de l'emploi en Mauritanie* (1977), and *Le tambour des sables* (1983). LC

Féraud, Charles Laurent (Laurent-Charles), born 5 February 1829 at Nice. After the Lycée de Toulon, he went in 1845 to Algeria as a civil servant. From 1850 to 1878 he belonged to the Corps des interprètes militaires where he advanced to the highest rank. Attached to Maréchal Mac Mahon from 1851 to 1872, he participated in all operations in the Province of Constantine and in Kabylie. From 1878 to 1881 he was consul in Tripoli, Libya, and thereafter, diplomat in Tangiers where he died in office, 19 December 1888. His writings include *Histoire des villes de la province de Constantine* (1869), *Les interprètes de l'armée d'Afrique* (1876), *Annales tripolitaines* (1927). Mohamed A. el-Wafi published *Charles Féraud et la Libye, ou portrait d'un consul de France à Tripoli au XIXe siècle* (1977). DBF; Peyronnet, 199-203; *Revue africaine* 55 (1911), 5-15

Feraud-Giraud, Louis Joseph Delphin, born in 1819 at Marseille, he received a doctorate in law from the Université d'Aix-en-Provence and then served as lawyer in the court of Marseille. He later served in the court of appeal at Aix-en-Provence, and the foreign ministry as a member of a commission for the reorganization of justice in the Orient. His writings include *De la justice française dans les échelles du Levant et de Barbarie* (1859). He died in 1908. DBF; Glaeser; Vapereau

Ferber, Stanley H., born 11 November 1927 at Brooklyn, N.Y., he was a graduate of Brooklyn College and received a Ph.D. in 1963 from New York University for his thesis, *Crucifixion iconography in Carolinian ivory carvings of the Liuthard and Metz groups*. Since 1973 he was a professor of history of art, and later chairman, SUNY, Binghampton. He was joint editor of *Islam and the medieval West; a loan exhibition* (1975). DrAS, 1974, 1978

Ferchiou, Sophie, born in 1931, she was an anthropologist whose writings include *Les Femmes dans l'agriculture tunisienne* (1985). AfricanExp; LC

Ferdinand, Klaus Vilhelm, born 19 April 1926 at Herlufsholm, Denmark, he was affiliated with the Ethnographical Collection of the Forhistorik Museum, and Århus Universitet, from 1957 to 1993. His writings include *Bedouins of Qatar* (1993), and he was joint editor of *Islam; state and society* (1988). Kraks, 1990-1998; Schoeberlein

521

Ferembach, Denise, born 25 November 1924 at Paris, she received a doctorate in 1956 from the Université de Paris for her thesis, *Constantes crâniennes, brachycrânie et architecture crânienne*. For many years she was affiliated with the CNRS. Her writings include *La nécropole épipaléolithique de Taforalt, Maroc oriental* (1962), and *Diagrammes crâniens sagittaux et mensurations individuelles des squelettes ibéromaurusiens de Taforalt* (1965); she was joint editor of *L'homme, son évolution, sa diversité* (1986). WhoWor, 1982/83

Ferenc, Aleksander, fl. 1979, he received a doctorate in 1976 from Universytet Warszawski for his thesis, *Histoire des Oromo (Galla), d'après les sources amhariques*.

Ferguson, Charles Albert, born 6 July 1921 at Philadelphia, Pa., he was a graduate of the University of Pennsylvania where he also received his Ph.D. in 1945 for his thesis, *The phonology and morphology of standard colloquial Bengali*. He was a professor of linguistics and a visiting professor at various American universities. From 1967 until his retirement he was at the Department of Linguistics, Stanford University. His writings include *Lessons in contemporary Arabic* (1960), *Language structure and language use* (1970), and *Cognitive effects of literacy* (1981). He was honoured by the jubilee volume, *Festschrift in honor of Charles A. Ferguson* (1986). ConAu 69-72, 46 new rev.; DrAS 1974, 1978, 1982; WhoAm, 1974-1988/89|

Ferguson, Donald William, fl. 1906, his writings include the edition *Travels of Pedro Teixeira; with his "Kings of Harmuz," and extracts from his "Kings of Persia."* (London, Printed for the Hakluyt Society, 1902). BLC

Ferguson, Phyllis, born 20th cent., she lived in Nigeria from 1963 to 1966, where she taught at Ibadan and co-operated with the Department of Antiquities in a study of the Esie stone figures. From 1966 to 1968 she pursued graduate studies at Northwestern University. Thereafter she studied at Newnham College, Cambridge, where she received a Ph.D. in 1972 for her thesis, *Islamization in Dagbon; a study of the Alfanema of Yendi*. Her writings include *Aspects of Muslim architecture in the Dyula region of western Sudan* (1968), a work which she originally submitted as her M.A. thesis under the name Phyllis Ferguson Stevens at Northwestern University. NUC, pre-1956; Sluglett

Ferguson, Richard Saul, born 28 July 1837 at Carlisle, he was educated at St. John's College, Cambridge, and was called to the bar from Lincoln's Inn in 1862. He was a sometime president and editor, Cumberland and Westmoreland Antiquarian and Arachæological Society. He died 3 March 1900. DNB; *Who was who*, 1

Fergusson, Bernard Edward, Baron Ballantrae, born 6 May 1911. After Eton and the Royal Military ACollege, Sandhurst, he joined the Black Watch in 1931. He served in the Middle East, India, and Burma, and as instructor at the Royal Military College. He retired with the rank of brigadier in 1958. He held several honorary doctorates. His writings include *Beyond the Chidwin* (1945), and *The Black Watch and the King's enemies* (1950). He died 28 November 1980. Au&Wr, 1971; ConAu, 9-12, 105, new rev. 7; DNB; IntAu&Wr, 1976, 1982; Master 4); WhoNZ, 1964, 1968; *Who was who*, 7

Fernandes, Leonor E., born about 1950, she received a Ph.D. in 1980 from Princeton University for *The evolution of the Khanqah institution in Mamluk Egypt*. In 1995 she taught - possibly only temporarily - in the Department of Near Eastern Languages and Literatures, New York University. Her writings include *The evolution of a Sufi institution in Mamluk Egypt; "the Khanqah"* (1988). NatFacDr, 1995

Fernández-Cuesta y Merelo (Merello), Raimundo, born 5 October 1897 at Madrid, he was a notary, politician, and diplomat whose writings include *Discursos sobre temas jurídicos, 1945-46* (1947), and *El movimento politico español* (1952). DBEC; WhoSpain, 1963

Fernández-Duro, Cesáreo, born 25 February 1830 at Zamora, Spain, he was a naval officer and an historian whose writings include *Memorias históricas de la ciudad de Zamora, su provincia y obispado* (1882-83), *La conqista de las Azores en 1583* (1886), and *El derecho á la ocupación de territorios en la costa occidental de Africa* (1900). He died 5 June 1908. EncicUni; Espasa; IndiceE (4)

Fernández González, Etelvina, born in 1945 at Mieres (Oviedo), Spain, she gained a doctorate in letters in 1978 from the Universidad Complutense de Madrid, specializing in medieval art. She was in 1992 a professor in the Universidad de León. Her writings include *La escultura románica en la zona de Villaviciosa* (1982), a work which is an abridged version of her doctoral thesis. Arabismo, 1992; Note

Fernández y González, Francisco, born in 1833 at Albacete, Spain, he studied philosophy and liberal arts and was a sometime dean of the Facultad de Filosofía y Letras, Universidad de Madrid. A member of the Real Academia de la Historia and Real Academia de Ciencias Morales y Políticas, Madrid, he wrote *Plan de una biblioteca de autores árabes* (1861), *Estado social y político de los*

Mudéjares de Castilla (1866) and he edited and translated the *Historia de Al-Andalus*, of Ibn 'Idhārī al-Marrākushī. He died in Madrid in 1917. EncicUni; Espasa; IndiceE³ (5); Manzabares

Fernández y González, Manuel, born in 1821 at Sevilla, he was a dramatist as well as a writer of prose and poetry. His writings include *Allah-Akbar (Dios es grande); leyenda de las tradiciones del sitio y conquista de Granada* (1849), and *La Alhambra; leyenda árabes* (1856). He died in 1888 in Madrid. EncicUni; IndiceE³ (18)

Fernández Guerra y Orbe, Aureliano, born in 1816 at Granada, he was a professor of history and literature successively at Granada and Madrid, and a sometime permanent secretary of the Real Academia Española. His writings include *Historia de España desde la invasión de los pueblos germánicos hasta la ruina de la monarquía visigoda* (1890-96). He died in Madrid in 1894. BbD; BiD&SB; EncicUni; EncItaliana; Espasa; IndiceE (4); Meyers

Fernández Manzano, Reynaldo, born 20th cent., he received a degree in medieval history, specializing in Arabic and Mozarab musicology. He was in 1992 the director of the Centro de Documentación Musical de Andalucia at Granada. His writings include *De las melodías del reino nazari de Granada a las estructuras musicales cristianas; la transformación tradiciones musicales hispano-árabes en la Península Ibérica* (1985). Arabismo, 1992

Fernández Navarro, Lucas, born 3 January 1869 at Madrid, he was a mineralogist and a professor of natural sciences at various Spanish universities. His writings include *El mundo de los minerales* (1900). He died in Madrid in 1930. EncicUni; Espasa

Fernández Puertas, Antonio, born 20th cent., he gained a doctorate in letters, specializing in Islamic art. He was in 1992 a professor in the Departamento Arabe, Universidad de Granada. His writings include *Plano guía de la Alhambra* (1979), and *La fachada del Palacio de Comares = The facade of the Palace of Camares* (1983). Arabismo, 1992

Fernau, Friedrich Wilhelm, born 22 April 1913 at Görlitz, Germany, he studied political science at München, Leipzig, and Berlin, where he received a Dr.rer.pol. in 1937 from the Orientalische Seminar for his thesis, *Die wehrwirtschaftliche Bedeutung des Orients für Großbritannien und das britische Weltreich*. Until 1941 he was in charge of the Near Eastern Division at IG-Farben, Berlin, and concurrently contributed articles to newspapers. In 1942 he became affiliated with the military attaché at the German consulate general, Istanbul. After the war, he was a journalist and editor until his retirement in 1978. He regularly visited the Middle East, and was a member of the board of directors of the Nah- und Mittelostverein, Hamburg. His writings include *Flackernder Halbmond* (1953) and *Patriarchen am Goldenen Horn* (1967). He died in Bremen, 20 July 1980. DtBE; Schwarz

Fernea, Elizabeth Jane née Warnock, born 21 October 1927 at Milwaukee, Wisc., she was a graduate of Reed College, Portland, Ore. She collaborated with her husband Roger Alan on the fieldwork in Iraq and Egypt. She later was a professor of English at the University of Texas at Austin. Her writings include the autobiographical works *Guests of the sheik* (1965), *A view of the Nile* (1970), and *A street in Marrakesh* (1979); she was joint editor of *Middle Eastern women speak* (1977), and joint author with her husband of *The Arab world; personal encounters* (1985). ConAu, 13-16, New rev., 12 & 29; NatFacDr, 1995; Shavit; WhoSSW, 1986/87; WRMEA 11 ii (Aug./Sept. 1992, p. 48

Fernea, Robert Alan, born 25 January 1932 at Vancouver, Wash., he received a Ph.D. in 1959 from the University of Chicago for his thesis, *Irrigation and social organization among the El Shabana, a group of tribal cultivators in southern Iraq*, a work which is based on his field research in a small town of southern Iraq from 1956 to 1958. In 1960 he moved to Egypt to conduct an anthropological survey in Nubia behind the future Aswan Dam. He spent the years from 1971 to 1972 in Morocco. He was affiliated with AUC and Harvard before he started his lifelong association with the Center for Middle Eastern Studies, University of Texas at Austin, as a professor of anthropology. His writings include *Sheikh and effendi* (1970), and *Nubians of Egypt, peaceful people* (1973). AmM&WS, 1973, 1978; ConAu, 33-36, new rev., 29; Master (1); MideE, 1982/83; NatFacDr, 1995; Selim; Shavit; WhoAm, 1984-1988/89

Ferragne, André, his writings include *Le précambrien et le paléozoïque de la province d'Orense, nord-ouest de l'Espagne* (1972), a work which was originally presented as his thesis at Bordeaux. LC

Ferrand, Bernard, fl. 1975, he was a sometime *assistant* at the Institut de droit, Constantine, Algeria.

Ferrand, Paul *Gabriel* Joseph, born 22 January 1864 at Marseille, he studied at Paris, where he received a diploma from l'École des languages orientales vivantes, and then entered the Corps consulaire. He served throughout the world, including ten years at Madagascar and for a shorter period in Persia, at Bandar Bushir and Rasht, as vice-consul. He died 3 February 1935. DBF; Fück; *Hommes et destins*, vol. 3, pp. 199-200

Ferrand-Eynard, Pierre, fl. 1960, he was an officer of the Affaires algériennes and successively *adjoint militaire* and *chef par interim* of S.A.S. at Messad, Algeria. He spoke fluently Arabic and was sent on an administrative mission to the Oulad Naïl in the northern Sahara from February to October, 1960.

Ferrandi, Jean, born 13 July 1882 at Bergerac (Dordogne), he studied at the Collège Ste-Barbe, Paris, where he obtained a diploma in law. After passing through the military college, Saint-Cyr, in 1905, he spent nearly his entire career until the war in French Africa as *méhariste*, soldier, arbitrator, explorer, ethnographer and geographer, serving in Bahr al-Ghazal and Borku, where he also collected scientific information for the Muséum d'histoire naturelle. Gravely wounded on his arms during the European war, he returned to the French colonies to become successively chief of the general staff in French West Africa, military commander of the Sanjak Alexandrette, and chief of the 4e Bureau at the general staff of general Dufieux in Morocco. He retired with the rank of colonel in 1927 and died suddenly in Arcueil, on leaving a veterans' meeting. His writings include *Conquête du Cameroun-nord, 1914-15* (1928), *Le Centre-africain français, Tchad, Borkou, Ennedi; leur conquête* (1930), and *De la Bénoué à l'Atlantique* (1931). DBF

Ferrandis Torres, José, born in 1900 at Valencia, he was an archivist and a sometime lecturer in numismatics and epigraphy at the Universidad de Madrid. His writings include *Los vasos de la Alhambra* (1925), and *Marfiles árabes de Occidente*. He died in Madrid in 1948. Espasa; IndiceE (2)

Ferrandis Torres, Manuel, born in 1898 at Madrid, he was a lawyer and a sometime professor of history. His writings include *Historia general de la cultura* (1934), and *Interpretación política de la historia de España*. He died in Sangüesa in 1973. Espasa

Ferrar, Robert Louis, born in 1938, he received a Ph.D. in 1968 from the University of Oregon for his thesis, *Econometric models of education as applied to Central America*. He was a sometime professor of economics at the American University, Cairo. NUC, 1968-1972

Ferrara, Reno, fl. 1953, his writings include *Problemi e prospettive dei trasporti urbani in Europa* (1959), *Trasporti pubblici e sviluppo economico* (1961), and *Aspetti aziendali e sociali dell'economia dei trasporti terresti* (1966).

Ferrard, Christopher G., fl. 1971, he received a Ph.D. in 1979 from the University of Edinburgh for his thesis, *Ottoman contributions to Islamic rhetoric*. Sluglett

Ferrari, Giorgio E., fl. 1959, his writings include *Documenti marciani e principale letteratura sui codici veneti di epopea carolingia* (Venezia, 1962). NUC, 1968-1972

Ferrari, Guglielmo, born 17 February 1850 at Isola della Scala (Verona), he was for thirty years an art critic and *direttore artistico* of *Tribuna illustrata*. Chi è, 1908

Ferrari, Jean, born 20th cent., he received a doctorate in 1976 from the Université de Paris IV for his thesis, *Les sources françaises de la philosophie de Kant*. He was joint editor of *Égalité; actes du colloque franco-italien de philosophie politique, 1988* (1990). LC

Ferrari Bravo, Luigi, fl. 1980, his writings include *La prova nel processo internazionale* (1958), *Diritto internazionale e diritto interno nelle stipulazione dei trattati* (1964), *Responsabilià civile e diritto internazionale privato* (1973), and *Lezioni di diritto internazionale* (1976). NUC, 1973-1977

Ferré, André, fl. 1977, he was awarded a doctorate in 1971 from the Université de Paris for his thesis, *Ahbar al-duwal al-munqati'a de Ĝamal al-Din Ali ibn Zafir*. ZKO

Ferré, Lucien, born 20 September 1899 in Algeria, he served with a regiment of the Tirailleurs algériens during the final stages of the first World War. From 1922 to 1938 he was an administrator of various mixed communities in Algeria, particularly in the Aurès area, the cradle of insurrections; special assignment during the second World War, sous-préfet of the difficult arrondissements of Batna, Médéa, Guelma, and Tizi-Ouzou, where he maintained a calmness unknown elsewhere. He was seriously hurt during a police operation in the Grande Kabylie 1946. As sous-préfet of Briey, in 1948, he pacified the social disturbances in the industrial and mining centres of Longwy and Villerupt, creating the first community centre for North Africans in Lorraine. During the 1954 events in Algeria, he was a member of commissions inquiring into tortures, war crimes, and concentration camps. As assistant to General Bollardière, he headed the new arrondissement Alger-Est in 1956. This successful experiment of linking administration and military brought honour to the general but transfer to Palestro to the sous-préfet. Under pressure of the Comités de salut publics, he was appointed *contrôleur général* and *directeur interdépartemental* of the Protection civile at Alger in 1958, but sent into forced retirement two years later. While translating the Koran, and as a consequence of his contacts with Muslim subordinates, he converted to Islam and adopted the name Mohammed Al-

Bachir. Relieved of all restrictions, he published *Chroniques d'un sous-préfet converti à l'islam; d'une insurrection à une autre, 1939, 1945, 1954, 1960* (1990). LC

Ferreiro y Peralta, Martín, born in 1830 in Spain, he was a geographer and served as secretary to the Instituto Geográfico y Estadístico and the Sociedad Geográfica de Madrid. His writings include *Atlas geográfico de España, islas adyacentes y posesiones españolas de ultramar* (186-?). He died 5 April 1896. Ballesteros; Ossario

Ferrer, Manuel, fl. 1913, he was a lawyer and served with the Centro de Expansión Comercial of the Ministerio de Fomento asa commercial agent in Morocco.

Ferret, Pierre Victor Adolphe, born 30 May 1814 at Réalmont (Tarn). After passing through the military college, Saint-Cyr, he was admitted to l'École d'application d'état-major. In 1839 he and his classmate, J. G. Galinier, were granted a leave of absence from the military to accompany the explorer Edmond Combes to Abyssinia. He spent eight months in Cairo studying Arabic, before setting out on the pilgrim route to Mecca, surveying the Hijaz mountain range on the way, and arriving at Massawa in October 1840, one year after departing from Marseille. After a year and a half in Abyssinia, they arrived back in Toulon on the 1st of March 1843 laden with several cases of geological, cartographical and astronomical data, which they jointly prepared for publication during the following years. Ferret later was posted repeatedly to Algeria and retired with the rank of general in 1879. He was joint author of *Voyage en Abyssinie dans les provinces du Tigré, du Samen et de l'Amhara* (1847). He died a bachelor in Réalmont, 4 September 1882. DBF; Henze

Ferrette, Jules, he appears to have been born in France of Protestant parentage in the first part of the nineteenth century. In his youth he was received into the Catholic Church, and in 1851 he entered the novitiate of the newly erected French Province of the Friars Preachers at Flavigny. He was given the religious name of Raymond. After his profession in 1852 he was sent to Paris and later to Grenoble for his studies in philosophy and theology. By 1854 he was in Roma, living with the Italian Dominicans at S. Maria sopra Minerva, but their observances were not austere enough to satisfy Frère Raymond. He obtained permission to move to S. Sabina on the Aventine to a community of ultra-strict observance *à la française*. He was raised to the priesthood by Cardinal Patrizi on 2 June 1855 and ordered to join the Dominican Mission of Mesopotamia and Kurdistan. He sailed to Beirut on 6 September 1855, bound for Mosul. Within less than a year he apostatized, and on 22 June 1856 he left Mosul for Damascus, where he offered his services to the Irish Presbyterian Mission. With the name of Mar Julius, Bishop of Iona, he later went to Britain where he found a warm welcome and where his credentials were taken on their face value. In 1874 he fades out of the British picture. Eventually he made his way to North America. Finally he returned to Europe and settled first at Lausanne and later at Genève, where in 1903, he published *Les rites essentiels du christianisme* and died shortly thereafter, without having reconciled with the Roman Church. His writings include *The Romish baptism as judged by Protestant theology* (Belfast, 1859), and *The gospel of Matthew in Arabic* (London, 1863). He died in 1903. Peter F. Anson, *Bishops at large* (1965), pp. 31-47

Ferri, Ferruccio, born 19th cent., he wrote *Il Golfo persico e la ferrovia di Bagdad* (Roma, 1913). ZKO

Ferrier, Joseph Pierre, fl. 19th cent., he was a French army officer who came to Persia in 1839 as an instructor in the Persian army, however, considered it prudent to resign after a while. He decided to offer his services in India and set out on the overland journey from Baghdad on 1 April 1845. This proved to become an extremely difficult enterprise. At the end of the summer he had to admit defeat in Baluchistan and was obliged to return to Baghdad whence he reached India by boat. When he returned to France in 1847, he was unable to find a publisher for his valuable travel journal. His writings, which first appeared in an English translation nine years later, include *Caravan journeys and wanderings in Persia, Afghanistan and Belouchistan* (1856), *History of the Afghans*, translated from the unpublished manuscript by Capt. William Jesse (1858), and *Voyages en Perse, dans l'Afghanistan, le Béloutchistan et le Turkestan* (1860). Gabriel; Henze

Ferrier, Ronald W., born 20th cent., he received a Ph.D. in 1970 from Cambridge for his thesis, *British-Persian relations in the seventeenth century*. His writings include *The history of the British Petroleum Company* (1982-94); he was joint author of *Twentieth century Iran* (1977); editor of *The arts of Persia* (1989); and joint editor of *Oil in the world economy* (1989). LC; Sluglett

Ferriol, F., born 19th cent., he was awarded a medical doctorate in 1909 from the Université de Toulouse. In 1922, he was a medical officer with the Groupe sanitaire mobile de l'Atlas, Marrakech.

Ferro, Gaetano, born 2 April 1925 at Stella (Savona), he was a journalist and a professor of geography. He lectured successively at Trieste and Milano before his appointment at Genova in 1973, a post which he held until his retirement in 1987. His writings include *I navigatori portoghesi sulla via* *delle Indie* (1974), *Geografia e libertà; temi e problemi di geografia umana* (1983), *La Liguria e Genova al tempo di Colombo* (1988), and *Carte nautiche dal medioevo all'età moderna* (1992). Chi scrive; Vaccaro; Wholtaly, 1997, 1998

Ferro, Marc Roger, born 24 December 1924 at Paris, he studied at Grenoble and Paris and was awarded doctorates in history and letters. He taught for eight years at a secondary school in Oran, was for four years associated with the C.N.R.S before he became *directeur d'études* at l'École pratique des hautes études, Paris, in 1969. Thereafter he was successively a lecturer and professor at l'École polytechnique for twenty-two years. His writings include *La révolution russe de 1917* (1967), *Cinéma et histoire* (1977), *L'histoire sous surveillance; science et conscience de l'histoire* (1985), and *Suez; naissance d'un tiers monde*, 2nd ed. (1987). ConAu, 77-80; WhoFr, 1979/80-1998/99

Ferron, Jean, fl. 1954, his writings include *La Tunisie antique* (Tunis, 1968), and he was joint author of *Orants de Carthage* (1974). LC

Ferry, Edmond Victor, born 22 April 1861 at Nancy, he was a graduate of the military college, Saint-Cyr, and l'École de guerre. During his military career he was posted to the French Sudan from November 1898 to July 1900. He retired with the rank of brigadier-general in 1917. His writings include *La France en Afrique* (1905), and *De Moukden à Nancy* (1907). He died in Paris, 31 July 1936. DBF

Ferry, Robert, born 20 January 1920 at Paris, he was awarded diplomas and certificates from the Université de Paris, l'École polytechnique, l'École professionnelle des hautes études, l'École nationale de langues orientales, and the Centre des hautes études administratives sur l'Afrique et l'Asie modernes (C.H.E.A.M.) He was an ethnologist and historian, and a sometime *chef* du Bureau, État-Major, Djibouti, and deputy director of the C.H.E.A.M. Unesco

Ferté, Louis *Henri*, 1821-1903, he was a *professeur* of rhetoric. His writings include *Vie de Sultan Hossein Baikara*; traduit de Khondémir (1898), and *Rollin, sa vie, ses œuvres et l'université de son temps* (1902). BN; NUC, pre-1956

Ferwerda, Floris Livingstone, fl. 1937, he received a Ph.D. in 1940 from Princetonfor his thesis, *The Hispano-Mauresque carved ivory inscriptions of the tenth and eleventh Christian centuries*. Selim

Feser, Robert A., born 27 July 1940 at Karlsruhe, Germany, he studied ethnology and Turkology at Tübingen and München where he received a Dr.phil. in 1978 for his thesis, *Die infiniten Verbalformen des Osmanisch-Türkischen*. Thesis

Fesharaki, Fereidun, born in 1947, he received a Ph.D. in 1973 from the University of Surrey for his thesis, *The development of the Iranian oil industry, 1901-1971*. In 1976, he was affiliated with the Institute for International, Political and Economic Studies, Tehran. His writings include *Development of the Iranian oil industry* (1976), *Revolution and energy policy in Iran* (1980), and he was joint author of *OPEC, the Gulf, and the world petroleum market* (1983). LC; Sluglett

Festa, Aldo, fl. 1940, his writings include *La Spagna e il Marocco, 1844-1912* (Roma, 1943). NUC

Fetisov, Mikhail Ivanovich, fl. 1960, his writings include *Литературные связи России и Казахстана 30-50-е годы 19 века* (1956), *Народный поэт чувашии П. П. Хузангаи* (1957), *Русско-казахские литературные отношения в первой половине 19 века* (1959), and *За-рождение казахской публицистики* (1961). NUC, 1956-1968

Février, James Germain, born in 1895 at Clérac (Charente-Maritime), he was educated at Saintes and Poitiers before entering l'École Normale Supérieure in July 1914. In 1920, he started a nearly forty-year teaching career at the Section des sciences historiques et philologiques in the École Pratique des Hautes Études, Paris, many years of which also as its director. His writings include *La Religion des Palmyréniens* (1931), and *L'Histoire de l'écriture* (1948). He died 15 July 1976. Journal asiatique 265 (1977), pp. 9-13

Février, Louise, born about 1925, she was the widow of Dr. Février who had practised medicine in Tangier and who went with his wife and three children, aged thirteen, seventeen, and twenty-one, to Aden in 1947 on a two-year contract from the Ruling Family. Her trace is lost in 1976. R. L. Bidwell

Février, Paul Albert, born about 1931 at Fréjus, he studied history and archaeology at Aix-en-Provence and l'École des chartes, and received a doctorate in 1964 for his thesis, *Le développement urbain en Provence de l'époque romaine à la fin du XIVe siècle*. He was a professor and administrator whose writings include *Art de l'Algérie antique* (1971), *Approches du Maghreb romain* (1989-90); and he was joint editor of *Villes et campagnes dans l'Empire romain; colloque* (1982). He died 10 April 1991 at the age of sixty. Commemoration volumes were published in 1992 and 1995 respectively: *Paul-Albert*

Février parmi nous; textes rassemblés lors des obsèques à Fréjus et de la journée de commémoration à l'Université de Provence, and *Omaggio a Paul Albert Février*. LC

Feyzioğlu, Feyzi Necmeddin, fl. 1961, he was awarded a doctorate in law, and later was a professor of private law at İstanbul Üniversitesi for over fifteen years. His writings include *Zilyedlikte iadenin mevzuu ve şümulü* (1958), *Şuf'a hakkı* (1959), and *Aile hukuku dersleri* (1971). NUC, 1968-1972; TB

Feyzioğlu, Turhan, born 19 January 1922 at Kayseri, he studied law both at Istanbul and Ankara, to which Oxford was added later on. He was a professor of law at Ankara Üniversitesi, a sometime member of parliament and a minister. His writings include *Kanunların anayasaya uygunluğunun kazaî murakabesi* (1951), *Büyük tehlike; komünizm* (1969), *Millet yolunda* (1975), and *Atatürk ve milliyetçilik* (1986). Master (2); Meydan; MideE, 1982/83; WhoWor, 1974/75-1989/90; Zürcher

Ffoulkes, Charles John, born in 1868, he studied at Oxford without taking a degree, but was awarded an honorary D.Litt. in 1936. He was a curator at the Tower armouries and later the first curator at the Imperial War Museum. He died in Oxford, 22 April 1947. DNB; Master (4); *Who was who*, 4

Ficheur, Louis *Émile*, born 15 August 1854 at Rilly-Ste-Syre (Auber), he was awarded a doctorate in 1890 from the Faculté des sciences de Paris for his thesis, *Les terrains écocènes de la Kabylie du Djurjura*. He was a science teacher in Algeria and subsequently a professor of geology and mineralogy at l'École supérieure des sciences d'Alger. He was affiliated with the Club alpin français, section de l'Atlas. His writings include *Itinéraires de la Grande Kabylie* (1886), and *La Kabylie du Djurjura* (1891). DBF

Fichtner, Eckhardt, fl. 1972, He was awarded a Dr.sc.agr., and later lectured at the Hochschule für Landwirtschaftliche Produktionsgenossenschaften at Meißen. Kürschner, 1992

Fickeler, Paul, born 7 April 1893 at Riesa, Germany, he received a Dr.phil. in 1928 for his thesis, *Der russische Altai*. He was a private scholar, specializing in cultural geography. His writings include *Der Altai; eine Physiogeographie* (1925). He died in Siegen, 24 June 1959. Kürschner, 1950-1961

Ficker, Adolph, born 14 June 1816 at Olmütz, Austria-Hungary, he studied at the Universität Wien, where he received a Dr.phil. (1835) and Dr.jur. (1842). He was successively a professor at Laibach and Olmütz, before he was appointed head of the department of administrative statistics at the ministry of trade and commerce in 1853. From 1870 until his retirement he was posted to the ministry of cultural affairs and education. His writings include *Die Völkerstämme der österreichisch-ungarischen Monarchie* (1869). He died in Wien, 12 March 1880. DtBE; ÖBL; Wurzbach

Fidel, Camille, born in 1878, he went on missions to Libya in 1920 and 1922. His writings include *Les Intérêts économiques de la France au Maroc* (1903), *Les Premiers jours de la Turquie libre; lettres d'un témoin* (1909), *La Paix coloniale française* (1918), and *Une Mission en Tripolitaine, 1920* (1921). LC

Fidel, Kenneth, born in 1936, he received a Ph.D. in 1969 from Washington University for *Social structure and military intervention; the 1960 Turkish revolution*. He was in 1995 a professor at the Department of Sociology, De Paul University, Chicago. He wrote *Military organization and conspiracy in Turkey* (1970); and he was editor of *Militarism in developing countries* (1975). LC; NUC, 1968-1972

Fiedler, Wilfried, born 20th cent., he obtained a doctorate and became affiliated with the Zentralinstitut für Sprachwissenschaft, Akademie der Wissenschaften der DDR. He was joint author of *Albanische Volksmusik* (1965). NUC, 1956-67

Field, Claud Herbert Alwyn, 1863-1941, he worked nine years among the lower classes in London before he became a missionary under the Church Missionary Society, London, among the Afghans, mainly in the Peshawar region, from 1892 to 1903. His writings include *Heroes of missionary enterprise* (1908), *With the Afghans* (1908), *Mystics and saints of Islam* (1910), *The charm of India* (1911), *A Dictionary of Oriental quotations* (1911), *Persian literature* (1912), and the translations of al-Ghazzali, *The Confessions of al-Ghazzali* (1909), and *The Alchemy of happiness* (1910). NUC, pre-1956

Field, Gary Robert, born in 1934, he received a Ph.D. in 1964 from the University of Oregon for his thesis, *Political involvement and political orientations of Turkish law students*. In 1968, he was a professor of political science at San Fernando Valley State College, Northridge, Cal., and in 1990, a deputy director, Office of Near Eastern and South Asian Analysis, Central Intelligence Agency, Langley, Va. MESA *Roster of members*, 1977-1990

Field, Henry, born 15 December 1902 at Chicago, he was a graduate of New College, Oxford, and also studied at Heidelberg and Harvard. He was an anthropologist specializing in early Middle Eastern civilization, and a sometime curator of physical anthropology at the Field Museum of Natural History, Chicago. His writings include *The early history of man* (1927), *The Arabs of central Iraq* (1935), *The*

527

track of man; adventures of an anthropologist (1953), *Ancient and modern man in southwestern Asia* (1956-61), and *Body-marking in southwestern Asia* (1958). He died in 1986. AmM&WS, 1973 S, 1976 P, 1979 P; ConAu, 69-72, 118; Master (9); Shavit; WhAm, 9

Field, Joseph Albert, fl. 1972, he was joint author of *L'Algérie, de Gaulle et l'armée, 1954-1962* (1975), a work which was translated from the English manuscript. LC

Field, Michael, born in 1949, he was a sometime Gulf correspondent for the *Middle East economic digest* but later became a free-lance writer who travelled extensively in the Middle East. His writings include *A hundred million dollars a day* (1975), *The merchants; the big business families of Arabia* (1984), and *Inside the Arab world* (1995). LC

de **Fiennes**, Jean Baptiste Hélin, born 9 October 1669 at Saint-Germain-en-Laye, he was a student at the Collège Louis-le-Grand, Paris. In 1686 F. Pétis de La Croix, took him along to Egypt, where he was appointed in 1692 first dragoman at the consulate in Alexandria. Transferred to Cairo in 1695, where he served in the same capacity, he returned to Paris in 1706 and in 1714 succeeded to Pétis de La Croix in the chair of Arabic. In 1718 he accompanied Dussaux on his voyage to Tripoli, Tunis, and Alger. In 1729 he was sent to Tripolis to conclude a treaty with the Barbary corsairs. He died in 1744 in Paris. Casanova; DBF; Hoefer; Michaud

de **Fiennes**, Jean Baptiste, born in 1710 at Saint-Germain-en-Laye, the son of Jean Baptiste Hélin de Fiennes, he was educated at the collèges de Navarre and Beauvais, and learned Oriental languages from his father. In 1729 he was sent to the embassy at Constantinople to deepen his language skills. When he returned he had a perfect command of Arabic, Persian, and Turkish. In 1739 he was nominated a professor at the École des jeunes de langue. In 1742 he was sent to Tunis to support the French ambassador, and in the following sent to To Tripoli on a mission, of which he left an account. He was a *secrétaire interprète* to the King when his father died in 1744; he succeeded to the chair of Arabic at the Collège de France in 1748. When again dispatched in 1751 to Tripoli to protest against the excesses of the Barbary corsairs he heard nothing but platitudes. He died in 1767. Casanova; DBF; Hoefer; Michaud; *Revue tunisienne*, 1931, pp. 339-43

Fierro Bello, Maria Isabel, born 20th cent., she received a doctorate in Semitic philology, specializing in the Islamic history of al-Andalus as well as in Malikite law. In 1992 she was an academic assistant in the Departamento de Estudios Árabes, C.S.I.C., Madrid. Her writings include *La heterodoxia en al-Andalus durante el periodo omeya* (1987), and she edited and translated from the Arabic of Muhammad ibn Waddāh, *Kitāb al-Bida'* (1988). Arabismo, 1992

Fiey, Jean Maurice, born 30 March 1914 at Armentières (Nord), he was a Dominican priest sent as a missionary to Mosul in 1939 and remained there until expelled in 1973. He received two doctorates from the Université de Dijon, for his theses, *Les diocèses du Maphrianat syrien*, in 1972, and *Histoire des églises orientales de l'Irak actuel*, 1978. He held a variety of teaching positions in Iraq from 1939 to 1973 and thereafter was affiliated with the Centre des Pères Dominicains at Beirut. His writings include *Chrétiens syriaques sous les Mongols* (1975), *Nisibe, métropole syriaque orientale et ses suffragants des origines à nos jours* (1977), *Chrétiens syriaques sous les Abbasides surtout à Bagdad* (1980), and *Pour un Oriens Christianus Novus; répertoire des diocèses syriaques orientaux et occidentaux* (1993). He died at his desk in the night from 10 to 11 November 1995. BioB134; MIDEO 23 (1997), pp. 471-473; THESAM 3

Figanier, Joaquim Abreu, born 21 August 1898 in Portugal, he studied Arabic at l'Institut des hautes études marocaines de Rabat from 1936 to 1938. He successively taught Arabic at the Faculdade de Letras and Escola Colonial at Lisboa from 1938 to 1948, but he was led to pursue a career in secondary school teaching where his pedagogical qualities were unanimously appreciated. He repeatedly was a visiting lecturer at the Université de Bordeaux and l'Institut catholique de Paris. His career obviously left him little time for research. His writings include *História de Santa Cruz do Cabo de Gué (Agadir), 1505-1541* (1945), *Fr. Joãa de Souza, mestre e intérprete de língua arábica* (1949), and *Moedas arábica* (1949-1959). He died in Lisboa, 15 August 1962. al-Andalus 27 (1962), pp. 467-468

Figueroa, Manuel Ruiz *see* Ruiz Figueroa, Manuel

Fikret, Tevfik, 1867-1915 *see* Tevfik Fikret, Mehmed

Filchner, Wilhelm, born 3 September 1877 at München, he was a military officer who studied geodesy and geography at the Universität München. Although he is now primarily remembered for his Antarctic expeditions, his explorations in Asia were no less important. He went to Samarkand in 1900, riding on horseback across the huge Pamir ridge from the Russian side. This sporting venture aroused his scientific curiosity and was followed by his first expedition to Tibet in 1903-5. In 1926-28 and 1934-8 he led two further expeditions to Tibet. In 1939-40 he conducted a magnetic survey of Nepal. He spent the second World War interned in India. His writings include *Hui-Hui; Asiens Islamkämpfe* (1928), *Bismillah; vom Huang-ho zum Indus* (1938), and his autobiography, *Ein Forscherleben* (1950). He died in Zürich, 7 May 1957. Bioln, 4; DtBE; *Geographical journal* 124 (1958), pp. 114-145

Filesi, Teobaldo, born 17 January 1912, he received doctorates in law and political science, and was a sometime officer at the Ministero dell'Africa italiana. His writings include *Trasformazione e fine del colonialismo* (1955), *Il Dey d'Algeri a Napoli e a Livorno, 1824-1833* (1974), *Profilo storico-politico dell'Africa* (1974), *L'immagine dell'Africa; nelle tesi di laurea della Pontifica Università urbaniana, 1935-1981* (1981), and *Un secolo di rapporti tra Napoli e Tripoli, 1734-1835* (1983). Unesco; Vaccaro; Wholtaly, 1958

Filhol, René Marc, born 25 April 1911 at Poitiers, he was educated at the Université de Poitiers where he became successively a lecturer, professor, and dean, Faculté de droit. He was an honorary professor at the Centre d'études supérieures de civilisation médiévale, a member of the Société Jean Bodin, and other learned societies. WhoFr, 1961/62-1981/82|

Filipović, Milenko S., born 8 November 1902 at Bosanski Brod, Bosnia, he completed his school education in Visoko and Tuzla, and then went for studies in ethnography to Universitet u Beograd, where he was awarded a doctorate in 1928 for a thesis on the ethnic origin of the population near Visoko. He was a professor at Skopje from 1930 to 1941, a visiting professor at Harvard in 1952, and a professor of human geography and ethnology at Sarajevo from 1955 until his retirement in 1962. In 1964, after long efforts, he found a home in Beograd, where he finally had access to a good library collection for the last five years of his life. His writings include *Visočki cigani* (1932), and *Among the people, native Yugoslav ethnography* (1982). He died 22 April 1969. *American anthropologist* 10 (December 1969), pp. 558-560; EncJug; Ko je ko, 1957; *Südost-Forschungen* 28 (1969), pp. 289-290

Filipović, Nedim, born 7 February 1915 at Glamoč, Herzegovina, he was a professor of Oriental languages at Universitet u Beogradu, and an honorary professor of philosophy at Sarajevo. He was joint editor of *Savjetovanje o istoriografiji Bosne i Hercegovine, 1945-1982* (1983). JugoslSa, 1970

Filippani-Ronconi, Pio, born in 1920 at Madrid of an old Romanian emigrant family, he received a doctorate in 1949 for an Indological thesis. Supported by a grant, he studied Iranian history and Sufism at the University of Tehran in 1953. After a four-year assistantship at the Università di Roma, he went to the Istituto universitario orientale di Napoli, where in due course he became director of the department of Indology. His writings include *Avviamento allo studio del pensiero orientale* (1959), *Ismaeliti ed "Assassini"* (1973); he translated *Il libro dello scioglimento e della liberazione* of Nasir Khusraw (1959), and he edited *Umm al-kitab* (1966). BioB134

Filippi, Filippo de, born 20 April 1814 at Milano, he was a professor of zoology at Torino. In 1862, he accompanied an Italian embassy to Persia. His writings include *Note di un viaggiò in Persia, 1862* (1865). He died in Hongkong, 9 February 1867. Embacher; Henze

Filippi, Louis, fl. 1935. He was a *professeur honoraire* at the Lycée d'Alger, and president of "Bastion de France."

Filitti, Ioan C., born in 1879 at Bucureşti, he was a lawyer and historian whose writings include *Opere alese* (Bucureşti, 1985). He died in 1945. WhoRom

Filliozat, Jean Lucien Antoine, born 4 November 1906 at Paris. After his studies at the Université de Paris he was attached to the Bibliothèque nationale from 1936 to 1941, when he became *directeur d'études* of Indian philology at the École pratique des hautes études, Paris. From 1952 to 1978 he was a professor at the Collège de France. His writings include *État des manuscrits sanscrits, bengalis et tibétains de la collection Palmyr Cordier, Bibliothèque nationale* (1934), *Doctrine classique de la médecine indienne* (1949), and its translation, *The classical doctrine of Indian medicine, its origins and its Greek parallels* (1964). He died 27 October 1982. Bioln, 15; IntWW, 1972/73-1982/83; WhoFr, 1955/56-1983/84; WhoWor, 1974/75-1980/81

Fillitz, Hermann, born 20 April 1924 at Wien, he received a doctorate in 1947. He was a director of the Sammlung für Plastik und Kunstgewerbe, Kunsthistorisches Museum Wien, 1958; director of the Österreichisches Institut, Roma, 1965; a professor at Basel, 1967; and a professor at Wien, 1974. Kürschner, 1961-1996; WhoAustria, 1957/58-1996

Filmer, Henry, pseud., b. 1893 *see* Childs, James Rives

Filonenko, Viktor Iosifovich, born 19 November 1884 at Tula, Russia, he studied at St. Petersburg. His writings include Загадки крымских татар (1926). His trace is lost in 1958. BiobibSOT, pp. 277-278

Filonik, Aleksandr Oskarovich, born 3 May 1944 at Moscow, he was a graduate of the Moscow Institute of Oriental Languages in 1967. Since 1971 he was a research fellow in the Oriental Institute of the Soviet Academy of Sciences. His writings include *Аграрный строй Судана, 1820-1970* (1975), he was joint author of *Финансовые структуры Ближнего Востока* (1996), he edited *Арабские страны; политика и экономика* (1997), and he was joint editor of *Арабский Восток; сборник статей* (1997), and *Сирийская Арабская Республика* (1997). Miliband²

Fil'shtinskii, Isaak Moiseevich, born 7 October 1918 at Kharkov, Ukraine, he graduated at Moscow in 1945, and received a doctorate in 1993 for his thesis, *Социокультурная функция словесного искусства в средневековом арабо-мусульманском обществе*. Since 1958 he was affiliated with the Oriental Institute of the Soviet Academy of Science. His writings include *Арабская литература; краткий очерк* (1964), its translation, *Arabic literature* (1966), *Арабская классическая литература* (1965), *История арабской литературы* (1985), *История арабской литературы X-XVII века* (1991), and he was a joint translator of *Жизнеописание Сайфа, сына цария Зу Язана* (1987), and *Царевич Камар аз-Заман и царевна Будур*, from the Arabian Nights in 1988. Miliband; Miliband²

Financıoğlu, Yurdakul, fl. 1970, he was born in Turkey and worked as a journalist since 1953. He was parliamentary correspondent for two leading newspapers, *Cumhuriyet* and *Hurriyet*, as well as editor of the opposition paper *Ulus*.

Finazzo, Giancarlo, fl. 1976, his writings include *I musulmani e il cristianesimo alle origini del pensiero islamico* (Roma, 1980). LC

Finbert, Elian Judas, born 12 June 1896 or 1899 at Jaffa, he grew up and was educated in Minyat al-Qamh, Egypt. He later attended the Collège Saint-Louis, Tanta, operated by the Pères des Missions africaines de Lyon. While working as a pharmacist's apprentice, he began to write poetry which was published by the local press. Although he was later sent to Genève to forget his literary ambitions and complete his training, he gave up pharmacy and instead enrolled in literature at the University. After voluntary service in the first World War, he returned to Egypt for a few years. He left the country in 1930, never to return. His writings include *Le fou de Dieu* (1933), a work for which he was awarded the Prix Renaissance, *Le Nil, fleuve du paradis* (1933), and *Le Livre de la sagesse arabe* (1958). He died in Chartres in 1977. *Hommes et destins*, vol. 4 , pp. 312-313

Finch, George Augustus, born 22 September 1884 at Washington, D.C., he was an international lawyer and a legal scholar. He worked for the State Department until 1911. Thereafter he was closely associated with the American Society of International Law; concurrently he served in various capacities from assistant editor to honorary editor-in-chief at the *American journal of international law*. He was also affiliated with the Carnegie Endowment for International Peace. He died 17 July 1957. BiDInt; BioIn, 3, 4; WhAm, 3

Findeisen, Hans, born 28 February 1903 at Berlin, he studied at Berlin where he received a Dr.phil. in 1929 for his thesis, *Die Fischerei im Leben der sibirischen Völkerstämme*. He was an assistant at the Museum für Völkerkunde, Berlin, 1922-1934, and a sometime lecturer at the Seminar für Orientalische Sprachen, Berlin. For many years he was affiliated with the Institut für Menschen- und Menschheitskunde, Augsburg. His writings include *Reisen und Forschungen in Nordsibirien, 1927-1928* (1929), and *Das Schamanentum dargestellt am Beispiel der Bessenheitspriester nord-eurasiatischer Völker* (1957). Kürschner, 1950, 1954, 1961|

Fındıkoğlu, Ziyaeddin Fahri, born in 1901 or 2 at Erzurum, Turkey, he was educated at Kayseri and Istanbul, and received doctorates in 1935 from the Université de Strasbourg for his thesis, *Ziya Gökalp, sa vie et sa sociologie*, and his complementary thesis, *Essai sur la transformation du code familial en Turquie*. He was a sometime professor at İstanbul Üniversitesi. His writings include *Bayburtlu Zihni* (1950), *Türkiyede kooperatifçilik* (1953), and *Karl Marx ve sistemi* (1975). He died in 1974. LC; Meydan

Findley, Carter Vaughn, born 12 May 1941, he was a graduate of Yale University and received a Ph.D. in 1969 from Harvard for his thesis, *From re'is efendi to foreign minister; Ottoman bureaucratic reform and the creation of the Foreign Ministry*. He was a professor of history at Ohio State University, Columbus, since 1972. He was a member of the Turkish Studies Association. His writings include *Bureaucratic reform in the Ottoman Empire* (1980). ConAu, 102; DrAS, 1978, 1982; *MESA Roster of members*, 1990; NatFacDr, 1995-1999

Finefrock, Michael M., born 20th cent., he received a Ph.D. in 1976 from Princeton University for his thesis, *From sultanate to republic; Mustafa Kemal Atatürk and the structure of Turkish politics, 1922-1924*. He was a staff member of the Department of History, College of Charleston, S.C., throughout the 1990s. NatFacDr, 1995-1999; NUC, 1978

Finer, Herman, born 24 February 1898 at Herta, Bessarabia, he was educated at London, where he later was a lecturer at LSE. After the war he was a professor at Chicago until his retirement in 1963.

From then until his death he was a professor of political science at Northwestern University, Evanston, Illinois. His writings include *Foreign governments at work* (1921), and *Theory and practice of modern government* (1932). He died 4 March 1969. AmAu&B; CnDiAmJBi; EncJud; ObitT, 1961; WhAm, 5; *Who was who*, 6

Finger, Seymour Maxwell, born 30 April 1915 at N.Y.C, he was a graduate of Ohio University. After the war he held a variety of diplomatic posts, and from 1971 until his retirement in 1985 he was a professor of government and international organizations at N.Y.C. universities. He was editor of *The new world balance and peace in the Middle East; reality or mirage*; a colloquium (1975). BlueB 1973/74, 1975, 1976; ConAu, 104; Master (3); WhoAm, 1974-1988/89; WhoAmP, 1969/70-1983; WhoWorJ, 1965, 1972, 1978, 1987

Fink, Harold S., born 16 September 1903 at Garland, Texas, he was a graduate of the University of Minnesota and received a Ph.D. from Princeton, in 1936, for his thesis, *Anonymi Gesta Francorum Iherusalem expugnatium; a chronicle of the first crusade and the Kingdom of Jerusalem, 1095-1106*. He spent his academic career as a professor of history at the University of Tennessee, Knoxville. DrAS, 1974, 1978; Selim

Fink, Julius Thomas, born 18 April 1918 at Wien, he received a doctorate in physical geography in 1944 from the Universität Wien for his thesis, *Morphologische und lithogenetische Untersuchungen im Raum von Maria-Zell*. He was a professor at the Hochschule für Bodenkultur, Wien. He was a joint editor of the *Mitteilungen der Österreichischen Geographischen Gesellschaft*. He died in Wien, 2 April 1981. DtBE; Kürschner, 1961-1980; WhoAustria, 1959/60-1977/78

Finkel, Joshua, born 6 October 1893 at Warszawa, he came to the U.S.A. as a boy. He was a graduate of New York University, ordained at the Jewish Theological Seminary, and received a Ph.D. in 1927 from Dropsie University. From 1937 to his retirement he was a professor of Semitic languages and literature, Bernard Revel Graduate School, Yeshiva University, N.Y.C. His edition *Thalath rasa'il*, by al-Jahiz (1924), was based on his research in Egypt, 1924-1926. He died in NYC, 12 February 1983. EncJud; NYT 16 February 1983, Section B, p. 8, col. 4; WhoWorJ, 1965

Finkel'shtein, Mikhail Borisovich, fl. 1970, his writings include *Именные словосочетания в русском языке и их узбекско соответствия* (1980). LC

Finley, John Park, born 11 April 1854 at Ann Arbor, Mich., he was educated in the Ypsilanti school system and completed the course in classical education at the State Normal School, Michigan, in 1869. He received a B.Sc. in 1873 from Michigan State Agricultural and Mechanical College, and a M.Sc. in 1882 in recognition of his proficiency in meteorology. He also completed a one-year law course in 1875. In 1877, he enlisted in the U.S. Army Signal Service. He was sent to the Signal Service school at Fort Whipple, Va., and in 1877 he started training for assistant to the non-commissioned officer in charge of a weather station. After he completed his army schooling, he was detailed as assistant to the sergeant in charge of the Signal Service Station in Philadelphia, Pa., where his interest in tornados began. His forecasting and analysis activities made him the centre of controversy during most of his professional life and led to open debate in the literature, but he set precedents in meteorological forecasting. His interest continued even when he had achieved the rank of captain and was civil governor of Zamboanga District, Moro Province, Philippines. After his retirement as a colonel he again became active as a private meteorologist, first establishing a business that provided insurance underwriters with meteorological data for assessing risks, and then opening a school of theoretical and applied meteorology and climatology. His writings include *Tornados* (1887), and *The Subanu* (1943). He died in 1943. *Bulletin of the American Meteorological Society* 66 (1985), pp. 1389-95, 1506-10

Finn, Robert Patrick John, born 19 December 1945 at N.Y.C., he was a graduate of St. John's University, N.Y., and received a Ph.D. in 1978 from Princeton for his thesis, *The early Turkish novel, 1872-1900*, a work which was published commercially, together with its Turkish translation, *Türk romanı ilk dönem, 1872-1900*, in 1984. After serving briefly as an assistant professor of history at AUB, he entered the U.S. Foreign Service in 1978. DrAS, 1978

Finney, Davida M., fl. 1937, she was a missionary under the United Presbyterian Church of North America and posted to Ramleh, Egypt. Her writings include *Tomorrow's Egypt* (Pittsburgh, Pa., 1939), and *Village reborn; the transformation of the people of a village in Central Egypt after they had learned to read in an all-village literacy campaign*, as told by Adib Galdas to Davida Finney. (New York, Committee on World Literacy and Christian Literature, 1958). LC

Finney, Minnehaha, 1867-1965, she was a missionary under the United Presbyterian Church of North America to Egypt Mission and stationed to Tanta in 1917. She was an associate editor of *Women's missionary magazine* of the United Presbyterian Church until her retirement in 1937. Her papers, 1915 to 1931, are at the Historical Society of Philadelphia, Pa. LC

Finnie, David H., born in 1924, he was a lawyer whose writings include *Desert enterprise* (1958), *Pioneers east* (1967), *Shifting lines in the sand* (1992), and *The joyful world of Harry Caesar* (1993).

Finó, José Federico, born 30 July 1907 at Santa Fé, Argentina, he studied at Paris and Buenos Aires, and was a sometime professor of library science. His writings include *Castillos y armaduras de la Francia feudal* (1960), and *Forteresses de la France médiévale* (1967). IndiceE (1)

Finot, Louis, born 20 July 1864 at Bar-sur-Aube, he was a trained archivist and palaeographer at the Bibliothèque nationale, before he turned to Indian and East Asian studies. In 1898 the Académie des Inscriptions et belles-lettres sent him on a scientific mission to Hanoi, which he soon institutionalized in the form of l'École française d'Extrême-Orient, and served on four occasions as its director. He also served as professor at the Collège de France, *directeur d'études* at l'École pratique des hautes études, and was a member of the Académie des Inscriptions et belles-lettres. He died in Toulon, 16 May 1935. DBF

Finster, Barbara, born 29 August 1938 at Berlin-Grünau, she studied oriental philology and history of art at Tübingen, Istanbul and Saarbrücken, and received a Dr.phil. in 1972 from the Universität Tübingen for her thesis, *Die Mosaiken der Umayyaden-Moschee von Damaskus*. As a recipient of various grants, she conducted field research in Afghanistan, Iran, Iraq, and Yemen from 1971 to 1985. Since 1996 she was a professor of Islamic history of art and archaeology at the Universität Bamberg. Her writings include *Frühe iranische Moscheen* (1991); and she was joint author of *Sasanidische und frühislamische Ruinen im Iraq* (1977). Kürschner, 1992, 1996; Thesis

Fioletov, Nikolai Nikolaevich, 1891-1943, his writings include Очерки христианской апологетики (1992). LC

Fiorani Piacentini, Valeria, fl. 1979. Her writings include *Turchizzazione ed islamizzazione dell'Asia centrale, VI-XVI secolo d. Cr.* (1974), and *L'emperio ed il regno di Hormoz, VIII- fine XV secolo d. Cr.* (1975). LC

Fiore, Silvestro, born 12 January 1921 at Sousse, Tunisia, he was a graduate of the Collège Ste.-Marie, and Collegio Italiano, Tunis, and received a Dr.phil. in 1956 from the Universität Köln for his thesis, *Über die Beziehungen zwischen der arabischen und der frühitalienischen Lyrik*. He taught variously French, Italian, and Arabic in Tunisia, Germany and the U.S.A. His writings include *Voices from the clay* (1965). He died in 1972 or 1973. ConAu, 17-20; LC; Schwarz

Fiori, Hermann, fl. 1937-1947, his writings include *Bibliographie des ouvrages imprimés à Alger de 1830 à 1850* (Alger, 1938). NUC, pre-1956

Fiorini, Matteo, born 14 August 1827 at Felizzano (Alessandria), he studied mathematics at the Università di Torino. He was a sometime professor of geodesy at the Università di Bologna, specializing in the history of cosmography. His writings include *Le projezioni delle carte geografiche* (1881), *Le sfere cosmografiche e specialmente le sfere terresti* (1893-94) and its translation, *Erd- und Himmelsgloben, ihre Geschichte und Konstruktion* (1895). He died in Bologna, 14 January 1901. DizBI

Firkovich, Abraham ben Samuel, born 27 September 1786 at Luts'k (Łuck), Ukraine, he was a controversial Karaite leader active in Evpatoria, Crimea. In his quest for old manuscripts he travelled to Palestine, Egypt, the Caucasus, and Constantinople. He died in Chufut-Kale, Crimea, 4 (17) June 1874. The two Firkovich collections in the former Imperial Public Library, St. Petersburg, are among the largest single collections of Hebrew manuscripts in existence today. Hermann L. Strack wrote a biography, *Abraham Firkowitsch und der Werth seiner Entdeckungen* (1880). EncicUni; EncJud; GdeEnc; JüdLex; Krachkovskii; PSB; Wininger

Firminger, Walter Kelly, Rev., D.D., born in 1870 he was educated at Merton College, Oxford, he was a priest in Mombasa, a member of the Universities Mission to Central Africa, and for nine years an archdeacon of Calcutta. His writings include *Alterations in the Ordinal of 1612* (1898), and *The early history of Freemasonry in Bengal and the Punjab* (1906). He died in 1940. Who, 1909-1936; Who was who, 3

Firsov, Nikolai Nikolaevich, born 30 September 1864 at Kazan, he was a graduate of Kazan University, where he later became of professor of Russian history. His writings include Русскія торгово-промышленныя компаніи въ 1-ю половины XVIII столѣтія (1896), Чтенія по исторіи Сибири (1915), and Прошлое Татарии (1926). He died in Moscow, 7 April 1934. GSE; TatarES

First, Ruth, Dr., born in 1925 at Johannesburg, South Africa, she was educated at the University of Witwatersrand, where she joined the Communist Party. She later became a member of the African National Congress. She was an unrelenting opponent of the Afrikaner Nationalist regime. After her release from a 117-day solidary confinement in 1963, she left South Africa, never to return. From 1973 to 1979 she lectured at the University of Durham on the sociology of underdevelopment. Thereafter she was resident in Mozambique where she was killed in her office when she opened a letter bomb on 17 August 1982. Her writings include *The barrel of a gun* (1970), and *Libya, the elusive revolution* (1974). AnObit, 1982; BioIn, 13; ConAu, 53-56, 107, new rev., 10; Master (2)

Fischel, Marcel, Dr., fl. 1913, his writings include *Le thaler de Marie-Thérèse; étude de sociologie et d'histoire économique* (Paris, 1912). NUC, pre-1956

Fischel, Walter Joseph, born 12 November 1902 at Frankfurt, Germany, he received a Dr.rer.pol. in 1924 from the Universität Gießen for his thesis, *Der Historismus in der Wirtschafts-wissenschaft*, and a Dr.phil. in 1928 at Frankfurt am Main for his thesis, *Die jüdische Pädagogik in der tannaitischen Literatur*. He was a lecturer in Germany, Palestine, South Africa, and various universities in the United States. His writings include *Jews in the economic and political life of medieval Islam* (1937), *Ibn Khaldun and Tamerlane* (1952), and *Ibn Khaldun in Egypt* (1967). He died 14 July 1973. AmAu&B; BioIn, 10; CnDiAmJBi; ConAu, 23-24, 41-44; NYT, 16 July 1973, p. 32, col. 3; WhAm, 6; WhoWor, 1971/72-1974/75; WhoWorJ, 1965, 1972

Fischer, Adolf, born in 1877, his writings include *Orient* (1924), *Menschen und Tiere in Südwestafrika* (1930), and *Südwester Offiziere* (1935). NUC, pre-1956

Fischer, Alfred Joachim, born in 1909 at Altkloster, Germany, he was educated in Western Prussia. Since 1923 his family was resident in Berlin where he later worked as a journalist for liberal newspapers. In 1933 he emigrated first to Czechoslovakia and then went on to Scandinavia, the Balkans, Palestine, and Turkey, from where he escaped in 1939, at the last minute, to Britain. He was interned in Australia until 1943, when he returned to London where he wrote for several English newspapers. After the war he was a roving reporter for radio and press throughout the world. In 1959 he again took permanent residency in Berlin. His writings include *Grækenland i dag* (1948), and *In der Nähe der Ereignisse; als jüdischer Journalist in diesem Jahrhundert* (1991). LC

Fischer, Andreas, born 15 April 1865 at Brienzwyler, Switzerland, he was an elementary school teacher who, after obtaining his Dr.phil. for his thesis *Goethe und Napoleon* (Bern, 1899), taught at a secondary school in Basel. He was an experienced mountaineer and twice visited the Caucasus, the first time in 1889 on the invitation of the famous English mountaineer D. W. Freshfield in a search expedition. He perished climbing in the Swiss Alps on 21 July 1912. His travel accounts were published posthumously entitled *Hochgebirgswanderungen in den Alpen und im Kaukasus* (1913).

Fischer, August Wilhelm Hermann Gustav, born 14 February 1865 at Halle, he studied theology and Oriental languages at Halle, Berlin, and Marburg, and received a Dr.phil. in 1889 from the Universität Halle for his thesis, *Biographien von Gewährsmännern des Ibn Ishaq*. He taught Arabic at the Seminar für Orientalische Sprachen, Berlin, from 1896 to 1900, when he succeeded A. Socin in the chair of Arabic at the Universität Leipzig. He was an outstanding linguist, competent in classical as well as colloquial Arabic, which he knew from repeated visits to North Africa and the Ottoman Empire. His writings include *Das marokkanische Berggesetz und die Mannesmann'sche Konzessionsurkunde* (1910), and he was joint editor of *Arabische Chresthomatie aus Prosaschrifstellern* (1948). He was also an editor of *Islamica*. He died in Leipzig, 14 February 1949. BioIn, 2; DtBE; Fück, pp. 309-310; Schwarz

Fischer, Dietrich Max, born 22 September 1941 at Münsingen, Switzerland, he was a graduate of the Universität Bern, and received a Ph.D. in 1971 from New York University for his thesis, *A dynamic model to calculate optimal price strategies for associations of raw material exporting countries, with special reference to OPEC*. He was a professor of economics at New York University, 1976-1978, and thereafter associated with international organizations. His writings include *Major global trends and causal interactions among them* (1981), and *Preventing war in the nuclear age* (1984). ConAu, 117; WhoE, 1983/84

Fischer, Ernst W., born 17 May 1884 at Plauen, Germany, he received a Dr.phil. in 1920 from the Universität Farnkfurt for his thesis, *Boden- und Mietpreise*. His writings include *Vom deutschen Wesen und den fremden Völkern* (1918), and *Neubaupolitik und Wohnungsnot* (1927). NUC, pre-1956

Fischer, Georges, born 26 January 1917 at Satu-Mare, Transylvania, he received a doctorate in 1946 from the Université de Genève for his thesis, *Les rapports entre l'Organisation internationale du travail et la Cour permanente de justice internationale*. His writings include *Le Conseil économique et social* (1955), *Problèmes internationaux relatifs aux pays sous-développés* (1955), and he was the editor of the proceedings of the colloquium, *Armement, développement, droit de l'homme*, désarmement (1985). Unesco

Fischer, Jan Bernard, fl. 1962, he received a Ph.D. in 1961 from Dropsie for his thesis, *The Arabic transmission of the Poetics of Aristotle*. Selim

533

Fischer, Johann Jacob, fl. 1875-1877, his writings include *Reiseskizzen; durch Nordafrika; Land und Leute* (Zürich, 1904), and *Reiseskizzen; durch die Asiatische Türkei; Land und Leute* (Zürich, 1906). NUC, pre-1956

Fischer, Joseph, historian of cartography, born 19 March 1858 at Quadrath near Köln, he studied theology and philosophy at Münster and München, entered the Society of Jesus in 1881 at Exaten, the Netherlands, and studied history and geography at Innsbruck and Wien, 1892-1894. Until his retirement he taught the latter two subjects at the Gymnasium Stella Matutina, Feldkirch. He spent the last years of his life at Schloß Wolfegg, where he died 26 October 1944. It was at the library of that castle that he made some of his main discoveries in 1899. DtBE; *Isis* 37, no. 3/4 (1947), p. 183

Fischer, Karl August, fl. 1935-1960, he was a high civil servant at the Bavarian ministry of education. *Wer ist's*, 1935|

Fischer, Karl Heinz, Dr.ing., born 23 June 1919 at Würzburg, Germany, he was a sometime professor of farm management at the Universität Erlangen, and a consultant at Abu Ghraib, Iraq, and at Alexandria. His writings include *Die Technik in der Innenverwaltung bäuerlicher Beriebe* (1947), and *Die Verkehrswirtschaft im Landbau* (1952). Kürschner, 1980|

Fischer, Klaus, born 23 November 1919 at Zittau, Germany, he was from 1966 until his retirement a professor of history of Oriental art at the Universität Bonn. His writings include *Dächer, Decken und Gewölbe indischer Kultstätten und Nutzbauten* (1974), and he was joint author of *Indische Baukunst islamischer Zeit* (1976). Kürschner, 1976-1992|

Fischer, Louis, born 29 February 1896 at Philadelphia, Pa., he started life as a school teacher, but soon followed the lure of greater exitement as a foreign correspondent, specializing on Soviet affairs. From 1961 until his death he was a research associate and a lecturer at the Woodrow Wilson School of Public and International Affairs, Princeton University. He was the winner of the National Book Award for 1964 for his *The life of Lenin*. His writings also include *Oil imperialism* (1926), its translation, *Ölimperialismus* (1927), and *Men and politics; an autobiography* (1941). He died in Hackensack, N.J., 17 January 1970. Bioln, 1, 2, 3, 4, 8, 9, 13; CnDiAmJBi; ConAu, 1-P, 11-12, 25-26; DAB, 8; EncAJ; NYT, 17 January 1970, p. 31, col. 5, REnAL; TwCA; *Who was who*, 6

Fischer, Ludolph, born 27 April 1900 at Hamburg, he was a professor of tropical medicine at various German universities, and from 1938 to 1941 and 1950 to 1952, a medical counsellor in Kabul. His writings include *Afghanistan; eine geographisch-medizinische Landeskunde* (1968). *Wer ist wer*, 1955, 1958, 1962, 1963|

Fischer, Ludwig Hans, born 2 March 1848 at Salzburg. After study at the Akademie der Bildenden Künste, Wien, he was resident in Roma from 1875 to 1877, and thereafter in Wien. He travelled to North Africa and East Asia. He was a painter, archaeologist, ethnologist, and travel writer whose works include *Ragusa und Umgebung* (1897), and he edited *Historische Landschaften aus Österreich-Ungarn* (1880-84). He died in Wien, 25 April 1915. DtBE; ÖBL

Fischer, Michael Max Jonathan, born in 1946, he received a Ph.D. in 1973 from the University of Chicago for his thesis, *Zoroastrian Iran between myth and reality*. In 1995, he was a staff member of the Department of Anthropology, M.I.T. His writings include *Iran, from religious dispute to revolution* (1980), and he was joint author of *Debating Muslims; cultural dialogues in postmodernity and tradition* (1990). NatFacDr, 1995

Fischer, Paul David, Dr.jur., born in 1836 at Berlin, he was a business executive, and later a high official in the German ministry of post and communications. His writings include *Die Telegraphie und das Völkerrecht* (1876), *Post und Telegraphie im Weltverkehr* (1879), *Italien und die Italierner* (1899), and its translation, *L'Italia e gli italiani* (1904). He died in Berlin, 13 March 1920. *Wer ist's*, 1909

Fischer, Theobald, born 31 January 1846 at Kirchsteitz, Germany, he received a Dr.phil. in 1868 from the Universität Bonn for his thesis, *Qvales se praebverint principes stirpis Wettinicae Rvdolfo et Adolfo regibus*. He was a sometime professor of geography at Kiel and Marburg. He was an expert on the Mediterranean countries, particularly Morocco, which he knew from his extensive travels.. His writings include *Der Ölbaum* (1904), and *Mittelmeerbilder* (1906). He died in Marburg, 18 September 1910. DtBiInd (5); Henze

Fischer, Wolfdietrich, born 25 March 1928 at Nürnberg, he received a Dr.phil. in 1959 from the Universität Erlangen for his thesis, *Die demonstrativen Bildungen der neuarabischen Dialekte*. He was a professor of Islamic studies at Erlangen from 1964 to his retirement in 1995. His writings include *Farb- und Formbezeichnungen in der Sprache der altarabischen Dichtung* (1965), *Grammatik des klassischen Arabisch* (1972), and he was joint author of *Lehrgang für die arabische Schriftsprache der Gegenwart* (1977). Kürschner, 1976-1996

Fischer-Galati, Stephen Alexander, born 1924 at Bucureşti, he was a graduate of Harvard University, where he also received his Ph.D. in 1949. Since 1966 he was a professor of history, and later also director, Center for Slavic and European Studies, University of Colorado, Boulder. His writings include *Ottoman imperialism and German Protestantism, 1521-1555* (1959), *Rumania; a bibliographical guide* (1963) and *Twentieth century Rumania* (1970). ConAu, 127; DrAS, 1974, 1978, 1982; WhoRom

Fischl, Hanns, Dr.jur., born 8 July 1883 at Brünn, Moravia, his writings include *Das österreichische Luftfahrtsrecht* (1929). Jacksch

Fish, Radii Gennadievich, born 28 October 1924 at Leningrad, he graduated in 1949 from the Moscow Oriental Institute. Since 1959 he was a member of the Soviet Writers' Union. His writings include *Писатели Турции* (1963), *Назым Хикмет* (1968), its translation, *Nazımın çilesi* (1969), and *Назум сердца; липика Назыма Хикмета* (1977), and *Турецкие дневники* (1977). Miliband; Miliband[2]

Fisher, Alan Washburn, born 23 November 1939 at Columbus, Ohio, he was married to Carol Garrett. He was a graduate of DePauw University and received a Ph.D. in 1967 from Columbia University for his thesis, *The Russian annexation of the Crimea, 1774-1783*. In 1966 he started his lifelong teaching career at the Department of History, Michigan State University, East Lansing, specializing in Russian and Turkish history. His writings include *The Crimean Tatars* (1978). ConAu, 53-56; DrAS, 1974, 1978, 1982; NatFacDr, 1995-1999; WhoMW, 1988/89; WhoAm, 1980-1988/89|; WrDr, 1986/88-1990/92

Fisher, Allan George Bernard, born 26 October 1895 at Christchurch, New Zealand, he was a graduate of the University of Melbourne, and received a Ph.D. in 1921 from LSE. He was successively a professor of economics in New Zealand, Australia, England, and the United States. He was joint author of *Slavery and Muslim society in Africa* (1970). He died in London in January 1976. ConAu, 33-36; WhoNZ, 1956-1968; *Who was who, 7*

Fisher, Anna L., fl. 1899-1933, she was an American whose genius for organizing and directing enterprises in social service and traditional handicrafts put her in charge of various projects in Europe, the Near East, the United States, and Mexico. Her interest in the Arab world began in 1919 in Damascus where, although engaged in civilian work under the short-lived Arab Government, she was honoured with the military rank of captain in the army. Her admiration for King Faisal during that régime led her in 1928, after he was King of Iraq, to accept his invitation to make prolonged industrial and photographic surveys of Iraq. Note

Fisher, Carol née Garrett, born 26 June 1940 at Columbus, Ohio, she was married to Alan W. Fisher, 24 August 1963. She studied at New York University and Michigan State University, where she received a Ph.D. in 1981 for her thesis, *The pictorial cycle of the Siyer-i Nebi*. She was a sometime coordinator of Educational Programs, Kresge Art Museum, Michigan State University, and an adjunct professor of history of art, specializing in Islamic, particularly Ottoman Turkish, art history, at M.S.U., a position which she still held in 1999. She was editor of *Brocade of the pen; the art of Islamic writing* (1991). She was a member of the Turkish Studies Association. NatFacDr, 1995-1999; Private; Selim[2]

Fisher, Harold Henry, born 15 February 1890 at Morristown, Vt. As a member of the American Relief Administration in Russia shortly after the first World War and with the encouragement of Herbert Hoover, he initiated the collection of sources on current Russian history which was destined to become later the Hoover Institution on War, Revolution and Peace at Stanford University. From the very inception of the Institution, he served as executive chief in addition to his lecturing a weekly seminar. Although his main interest was in the field of Russian history, he demonstrated an absorbing interest in the continent of Asia. For several years he also served as news analyst for C.B.S. and N.B.C radio stations. In addition to his numerous duties he was also a professor at Stanford University, and after retirement he taught at Columbia University, San Franscisco State University, and Mills College. He died 15 November 1975. AmAu&B; Bioln, 10; ConAu, 61-64; *Russian review* 35 (1976), pp. 231-232; WhAm, 6 & 7; WhNAA

Fisher, Humphrey John, born 20 September 1933 at Dunedin, New Zealand, he was a graduate of Harvard, and received a D.Phil. degree from Oxford in 1959 for his thesis, *Ahmadiyya; a study in contemporary Islam in West Africa*. Since 1952 he taught African history at SOAS; concurrently he taught at University College, Ibadan, in 1959. He was joint author of *Slavery and Muslim society in Africa* (1970), and he was joint editor of *Rural and urban Islam in West Africa* (1987). ConAu, 33-36; Sluglett

Fisher, Sydney Nettleton, born 8 August 1906 at Warsaw, N.Y., he was a graduate of Oberlin (Ohio) College, and received a Ph.D. in 1935 from the University of Chicago for his thesis, *Sultan Bayezit II and the foreign relations of Turkey*. After two teaching spells at Robert College, Istanbul, he was a professor of history at Ohio State University until his retirement. His writings include *The Middle East;*

a history (1959). He died 10 December 1987. His private papers, 1929-1985, are at Oberlin College Archive. DrAS, 1974, 1978, 1982; LC; Master (2); WhAm, 9; WhoAm, 1974/75-1986

Fisher, T., fl. 1934, he was in Algeria in the spring of 1914, when he was witness to a spring rain dance. Note

Fisher, William Bayne, born 24 September 1916 at Darwin, Lancashire, he studied at the Université de Paris, where he took his doctorate just before the war with a thesis on the population of France. He then became a geographical editor on the staff of the *Encyclopædia Britannica*. During the war he served in the Middle East. He was then sent as a liaison officer with the French in Syria. Thereafter he successively taught geography at Manchester, Aberdeen, and Durham, specializing in the geography and population of the Middle East. His writings include *The Middle East; a physical and regional geography* (1950), a work which saw five editions until 1978, and *The oil states* (1980). He died in 1984. BlueB, 1973/74, 1975, 1976; ConAu, 65-68, 113; *Iran* 23 (1985), p. v; Master (4); MideE, 1982/83; Unesco; Who, 1957-1984; *Who was who*, 8; WrDr, 1976/78-1984/86

Fisk, Brad, fl. 1952, he was in 1950/51 a lecturer in geography at the Higher Teachers' Training College (Dar al-Mu'allimin al-'Aliyah), Baghdad. Note

Fiske, Fidelia, born in 1816, she was a graduate of Mount Holyoke Seminary and then served as a missionary schoolteacher to the Nestorians at Urmia, Persia, 1843-1857. After her return to the States, she taught at Mount Holyoke from 1859 to 1864. She died at the place of her birth, Shelburne, Mass., 26 July 1864. Her private papers are at Mount Holyoke College Library. DAB; LC; *Missionary review of the world*, n.s., 22 (1909), 341-352; Shavit; WhAm H

Fita y Colomé (Colomer), Fidel, born 31 December 1835 or 1 January 1836 at Arenis de Mar, Spain, he studied European languages as well as Hebrew, Arabic, and Sanskrit at Barcelona. He entered the Society of Jesus and served his noviciate at Nivelles, Belgium. He was a sometime director of the Real Academia de la Historia. His writings include *Epigrafía romana de la ciudad de Leon (1866), and La España hebrea* (1889-98). He died 13 January 1917. Dicc bio; EncicUni; Espasa; IndiceE (4); Ossorio

Fitger, Emil August, born 15 December 1848 at Delmenhorst, Germany, he was self-employed until he joined the staff of the *Weserzeitung* in 1878, later to become its editor-in-chief until his death in Bremen on 9 April 1917. His writings include *Die Rückwirkung des ostasiatischen Krieges auf das Völkerrecht* (1904), and *Unsere zukünftige Handelspolitik namentlich mit Österreich* (1916). DtBE; NDB; *Wer ist's*, 1909-1912

Fitt, Robert Louis, born 9 August 1905, he was a British engineer, specializing in irrigation and water supplies. He travelled extensively over a period of seven years on behalf of Sir Alexander Gibb and Partners, who were consulting engineers to various Persian authorities. He was also employed in the Sudan and Iraq. He died 24 September 1994. Who, 1976-1994

Fitter, Kaikhosrow Ardeshir, fl. 1936, his writings include *Colloquial Persian as absolutely neccessary for travellers in Iran* (Bombay, 1948).

Fitting, Johannes *(Hans)* Theodor Gustav Ernst, born 23 April 1877 at Halle, Germany, he studied natural sciences at Halle and Straßburg. After three years as an assistant at Leipzig and Tübingen, he travelled to the tropics. After his return, he was a professor of botany successively at Straßburg and Halle. From 1912 to 1946 he was a professor at Bonn. He died in Köln, 6 July 1970. DtBE; Kürschner, 1931-1966; *Wer ist's*, 1909-1922

Fitz, Angelika, fl. 1979-80, she was affiliated with the Zentralinstitut für Geschichte at the Akademie der Wissenschaften, Berlin. Note

Fitz, Peter Richard, born 17 January 1925 at Wien, he was educated at Wien and Innsbruck, where he took a Dr.jur. in 1950. He headed two economic missions to Iran in 1970 and 1971. He later was head of the Asia, Australia and Oceania Section in the Austrian Federal Ministry of Economics, Division of Trade Policy and Export. WhoAustria, 1969/70-1982/83

Fitzau, August, born in 1861, he received a doctorate in 1888 from the Universität Leipzig for his thesis, *Die Nordwestküste von Agadir bis St. Louis*. NUC, pre-1956

Fitzclarence, George Augustus Frederick, first Earl of Munster, major-general, born in 1794, he was educated at a private schoool and afterwards at the Royal Military College, Marlow. He served on the continent until transferred to India in 1814. After the campaigns against the Mahrattas, 1816-1817, he was entrusted with duplicates of documents to be taken overland to England, a journey which is the subject of his *Journal of a route across India and through Egypt to England in 1817-1818* (1819). He was a member of the Royal Asiatic Society since 1824, for many years their vice-president, and was chosen president in 1841. In 1827 he was nominated by the Society member of a committee to prepare a plan for publishing translations of oriental works, and was subsequently appointed vice-president of the Oriental Translation Fund. He was also president of the Society for the Publication of Oriental Texts. He committed suicide in 1842. DcBrBl; DNB; Egyptology

Fitzgerald, Dennis Alfred, born in 1903, he entered the U.S. Agricultural Adjustment Administration in 1933. After the war, he became secretary-general of the International Emergency Food Council in 1946. He later served as deputy director, Foreign Operations Administration, Washington, D.C. His writings include *Corn and hogs under the Agricultural Adjustment Act* (1934), *Principles of technical cooperation* (1959), and *Operational and administrative problems of food aid* (1965). Bioln 1

Fitzgerald, Edward, born 31 March 1809 in England, he was a poet whose writings are mostly modelled translations of foreign writers, including Umar Khayyam and Farid al-Din al-'Attar. He died in 1883. Alfred M. Terhune wrote *The life of Edward Fitzgerald* (1947, reprinted 1980). BiD&SB; CasWL; DNB; EncAm; EncBrit; EncicUni; EncItaliana; GdeEnc; MEW; Meyers; OxEng; RNL

Fitzgerald, Gerald Milnes, born in 1883, he was educated at Eton and Trinity College, Cambridge, he was an archaeolgist whose writings include *Beth-shan excavations, 1921-1923; the Arab and Byzantine levels* (1931). WhE&EA

Fitzgerald, Michael L., born in 1937, he was a research scholar in the Instituto Pontifico di Studi Arabi, Roma, and a temporary lecturer at Makerere University, Kampala, Uganda, in 1971. He was editor of *Mensch, Welt, Staat im Islam* (1977), and joint editor of *Moslems und Christen - Partner?* (1977).

Fitzgerald, Robert Geoffrey, fl. 1927, he was a sometime judge in the Tribunal mixte de Tanger.

Fitzgerald, Seymour Gonne Vesey, 1884-1954 *see* Vesey-Fitzgerald, Seymour Gonne

Fitz-Gerald, William George, born 19th cent. Under the pseudonym Ignatius Phayre he published *The shrine of Sebekh* (1911), *America's day* (1918), and *Can America last?* (1933). NUC, pre-1956

Fitzgerald, Sir William James, born in 1894 at Cappawhite, Ireland, he was educated at Trinity College, Dublin. He was called to the bar from King's Inn, Dublin, 1922, and thereafter served in British Africa until 1937, when he was appointed attorney general in Palestine. Since 1944 he was chief justice in Palestine. He died in 1989. NearMEWho; Who, 1943-1989; *Who was who*, 8

Fitzler, Mathilde Auguste Hedwig. She received a Dr.phil. in 1931 from the Universität Köln for her thesis, *Die Handelsgesellschaft Felix v. Oldenburg & Co., 1753-1760; Beitrag zur Geschichte des Deutschtums in Portugal im Zeitalter des Absolutismus.* In 1935 she was resident in Berlin.

Fitzmaurice, Gerald Henry, born in 1865, he was a graduate of the Royal University of Ireland, he entered the Foreign Service in 1888. On his retirement in 1921, he had served in a variety of positions in the Ottoman Empire, from vice-consul, to British commissioner, chief dragoman, first secretary, and consul. He wrote *Reports by vice-consul Fitzmaurice from Birecik, Ourfs, Adiaman, and Behesni ... 1896.* He died in 1939. BLC; *Who was who*, 3

Fitzner, Rudolf, born 3 October 1864 at Küstrin, Germany, he received a Dr.phil. in 1899 from the Universität Halle for his thesis, *Der Kagera-Nil.* His writings include *Die Regentschaft Tunesien; Streifzüge und Studien* (1895), *Niederschlag und Bevölkerung in Kleinasien* (1902), *Forschungen in der bithynischen Halbinsel* (1903), *Aus Kleinasien und Syrien* (1904), *Beiträge zur Klimakunde des Osmanischen Reiches und seiner Nachbargebiete* (1904-1907). He was a sometime editor of the *Deutsches Kolonial-Handbuch.* Wer ist's, 1935

Fixler, Leslie Donald, born in 1927, he received a Ph.D. from New York University in 1960 for his thesis, *The economics of price discrimination.* He was in 1975 a professor of economics at the American University, Beirut. NUC, 1956-1967

Flamand, Georges Barthélemy Médéric, born 9 February 1861 at Paris. After classical studies, he was a student at the Musée d'histoire naturelle. Through the good offices of the director of l'École supérieure des sciences d'Alger he came to Algeria in 1880 and became his assistant in the mineralogical laboratory. For the Service de la carte géologique d'Alger he then conducted a geological study from Cape Djenet to the Moroccan frontier. After his appoinment to the chair of geology of the Sahara at Alger, 1894, he explored the Touat region, the Great Eastern Erg, and the Oueds sud-oranais. On an official mission to the extreme south of Algeria in 1899, he established the frontier between Algeria and the Sahara in face of hostilities from the local population. He continued his exploration also after his appointment as director of the Service géographique des territoires du sud de l'Algérie in 1905. He received a doctorate in 1911 from the Faculté des sciences de Lyon for his

537

thesis, *Recherches géologiques et géographiques sur le haut pays de l'Oranie et sur le Sahara.* His writings include *Alger* (1890), and *De l'Oranie au Gourara* (1898). He died in 1919. BN; DBF; Henze

Flament, Jean Charles *Pierre*, born 3 June 1878 at Paris, he graduated from l'École des chartes in 1899 and then served for a few years at the Bibliothèque nationale de Paris as an archivist palaeographer. He held the same position successively in the Departments of Allier and Pas-de-Calais. He was also a local historian. He died in action near Verdun, 1 August 1916. DBF

Flandin, Eugène Napoléon, born 1809 at Napoli, he was designated in 1839 to accompany the French ambassador de Sercey to Persia; he stayed until 1841. Together with P. Coste he returned with a considerable number of documents which they published in their *Voyage en Perse de MM. Eugène Flandin, peintre, et Pascal Coste, architecte* (1851). At the end of 1843, he and P. É. Botta left on an official mission to Niniveh and Khorsabad to make drawings of the Assyrian ruins. His writings include *L'Orient* (1853-1867), and *Histoire des chevaliers de Rhodes depuis la création de l'ordre à Jérusalem jusqu'à sa capitulation à Rhodes* (1864). He died in Tours in 1876. DBF; Embacher; Henze; Hoefer; IndexBFr²; Master (2); Vapereau

Flapan, Simha, born 27 January 1911 at Tomaszow, Poland, he was a sometime secretary of the Jewish-Arab Association, a member of the Executive Committee of Mapam, and founding editor of *New outlook* in 1957. His writings include *5. June 1967; der arabisch-israelische Krieg* (1969), *Zionism and the Palestinians* (1979), and *The birth of Israel* (1987). WhoWorJ, 1972, 1978

Flasche, Rainer, born 17 September 1942 at Hannover, Germany, he received a Dr.phil. in 1971 from the Universität Marburg for his thesis, *Geschichte und Typologie afrikanischer Religiosität in Brasilien.* Since 1975 he was a professor of religious studies at Marburg. Kürschner, 1992, 1996

Flatow, Egon, born 13 February 1898 at Berlin, he served in the first World War and then studied medicine at the universities of Berlin and Freiburg im Br., where he received a Dr.med. in 1924. Thesis

Flattet, Guy, born 30 September 1915 at Paris, he studied at Paris and Lausanne, where he received doctorates in law. He spent his whole academic career at Lausanne. In 1985, he was honoured by a jubilee volume, *Mélanges Guy Flattet.* He died 2 March 1994. WhoFr, 1965/66-1993/94

Flavell, Geoffrey, born 23 February 1913 in New Zealand, he was educated in New Zealand and England, where he qualified in medicine, specializing in cardio-thoracic surgery. During the war he served in North Africa, and after the war he was a visiting lecturer for the British Council in the Middle to Far Eastern universities. He died 28 November 1994. Who, 1959-1995

Fleet, John Faithful, born 1847, he was educated at Merchant Taylors' School and University College, London. He joined the Indian Civil Service in 1867 and served in Bombay. In 1883 he became epigrapher to the Government of India and in the following year was awarded Companion of the Indian Empire. He later served as Commissioner in Bombay. He retired in 1897. From 1885 to 1891 he was editor of the *Indian antiquary.* The Universität Göttingen conferred on him an honorary doctorate in 1892. He died in 1917. Buckland; Who was who, 2

Fleisch, Henri, S.J., he received a doctorate in 1944 from the Université de Paris for his thesis, *Les verbes à allongement vocalique interne en sémitique.* His writings include *Introduction à l'étude des langues sémitiques* (1947) - the best recent statement on the place of Arabic in the general context of Semitic languages - *L'arabe classique* (1956), and *Études d'arabe dialectal* (1974). LC

Fleischer, Ezra, born 7 August 1928 at Timisoara, Rumania, he was a law graduate of the Universitatea din Bucureşti and received a Ph.D. from the Hebrew University, Jerusalem, for his Hebrew thesis on R. Joseph ibn Abitur's works. He was a sometime lecturer in medieval Hebrew literature at the Hebrew University. LC; WhoWorJ, 1972, 1978

Fleischer, Heinrich Leberecht, born 21 February 1801 at Bad Schandau, Germany, he studied theology in Germany, to which Arabic, Persian, and Turkish at Paris was added from 1824 to 1828. He was a professor of Oriental languages at Leipzig from 1835 until his retirement. His reputation as a teacher attracted students from all over Europe and made Leipzig the outstanding centre of Arabic studies. He was instrumental in the founding of the Deutsche Morgenländische Gesellschaft in 1845. He died in Leipzig, 10 February 1888. ADtB; CelCen; DtBE; Fück, pp. 170-173; EncBrit; EncicUni; EncItaliana; GdeEnc; Meyers; Pallas; RNL

Fleischhacker, Hans, born 10 March 1912 at Töttleben, Germany, he received a Dr.phil. in 1935 from the Universität München for his thesis, *Über die Vererbung der Augenfarbe.* He was a professor of biological sciences at the Universidad de El Salvador, 1965-1967, and from 1971 until his retirement he was a professor of anthropology at the Universität Frankfurt am Main. Kürschner, 1992|

Fleischhammer, Manfred, born 22 July 1928, he received a Dr.phil. in 1955 from the Universität Halle for his edition of *Muhammad Ibn Hibban's K. Mašahir 'ulama' al-amsar, ein Werk der islamischen Traditionskritik nach dem Leipziger Unikum.* From 1956 until his retirement he was a professor of Arabic and Islamic studies at the Universität Halle. He was joint author of *Chrestomathie der modernen arabischen Prosaliteratur* (1978). Kürschner, 1992|; Schwarz

Fleischmann, B. W. *Paul*, born 3 October 1865 at Fürstenwalde, Germany, he studied theology and Oriental languages at Berlin and Breslau, and was a pastor before he became superintendent of the Deutsche Orient-Mission, Potsdam. He became editor of its journal after the death of Johannes Lepsius. His writings include *Das Heilige Land in Wort und Bild* (1904), and *Alttestamentliche Lyrik* (1916). Wer ist's, 1909-1935

Fleming, Jackson, fl. 1919-1933, he was an American political writer who went as the special correspondent of *Asia* to study international and domestic problems of the Near and Middle East after the war. He met European officials as well as local nationalists. Note

Flemming, Barbara H., born 28 May 1930 at Hamburg, she received a Ph.D. in 1961 from UCLA for her thesis, *Landschaftsgeschichte von Pamphylien, Pisidien und Lykien im Mittelalter.* She was a professor at the Universität Hamburg from 1971 to 1977, when she was appointed a professor of Islamic studies and Turkology at the Rijksuniversiteit te Leiden, a position she held until her retirement. In 2003 she was still resident in the Netherlands. Her writings include a catalogue of *Türkische Handschriften* (1968). EURAMES, 1993; Kürschner, 1976-1992|; LC; Private; Schwarz

Flemming, Johannes Paul Gotthilf, born 12 January 1859 at Kölleda, Germany, he studied theology and Oriental languages at Leipzig, Berlin, and Göttingen, where he received a Dr.phil. in 1883 for his thesis, *Die große Steinplatteninschrift Nebukadnezars II.* He was successively a librarian at the university libraries of Göttingen, Bonn, and the Königliche Bibliothek, Berlin. In 1905 he accompanied a German embassy to Abyssinia, where he acquired eighty Ethiopian manuscripts for the latter library. He edited and translated a number of Ethiopian and Syrian texts. He died in Berlin, 4 September 1914. DtBE

Fletcher, Arnold Charles, born 17 November 1917 at Chicago, he was a graduate of Linfield College and received a Ph.D. in 1953 from the University of Southern California for his thesis, *A history of the Afghan nation.* He was employed by the Government of Afghanistan for three years, taught history in California, and was affiliated with the Los Angeles Police Commission. He made three research trips to Central Asia. His writings include *Afghanistan, highway of conquest* (1965), and he was joint author of *A history of civilization* (1969). ConAu, 17-20

Fletcher, Joseph Francis, born 14 July 1934 at Raleigh, N.C., he was a graduate of Harvard, where he also received a Ph.D. in 1965 for his thesis, *The Erdeni-yin erike as a source for the reconciliation of the Khalkha, 1681-1688.* He was a professor of East Asian languages and history at Harvard from 1966 to his death of cancer on 14 June 1984. DrAS, 1974, 1978, 1982; NYT 16 June 1984, p. 28, col. 2

Fletcher, Max Ellis, born 23 August 1921 at Preston, Idaho, he was a graduate of the University of Washington, a Fubright scholar at LSE, and received his Ph.D. in 1957 from the University of Wisconsin for his thesis, *Suez and Britain.* From 1958 to 1984 he was a professor of economics at the University of Idaho, Moscow. His writings include *Economics and social problems* (1979). AmM&WS, 1973, 1978; WhoAm, 1974-1988/89|

Fletcher-Cooke, John, Sir, born 8 August 1911 at Burnham, Buckinghamshire, he was educated at Paris and Oxford. He spent almost thirty years in HM's Overseas Civil Service, predominantly in the Middle East and Africa. He was under-secretary to the Government of Palestine, 1946-1948, and special representative for Palestine at the United Nations in 1948. He wrote on Middle Eastern, African, Commonwealth, and United Nations issues. His writings include *The emperor's guests, 1942-1945* (1971), an autobiographical account of his time as a Japanese prisoner of war. He died 19 May 1989. BlueB, 1973/74, 1975, 1976; ConAu, 102; Master (2); Who, 1958-1989; Who was who, 8; WrDr, 1976/78-1990/92

de **Fleuriot de Langle**, Alphonse Jean René, vicomte, born 16 May 1809 at the Château de Pradalan (Finistère). After passing through l'École navale d'Angoulême he took part in the capture of Alger, 1830, as a naval officer. He served several years suppressing the slave trade on the coasts of Africa, participated in the Crimean campaign of 1855, and later served in the Indian Ocean. He retired with the rank of vice-admiral in 1874 and died in Paris, 22 July 1881. DBF

Fleury, Antoine, fl. 1977, his writings include *La politique allemande au Moyen-Orient, 1919-1939; étude comparative* (1977), a work which was originally presented as a doctoral thesis in 1974 at the Université de Genève, *La pénétration allemande au Moyen-Orient, 1919-1939* (1977), and he edited Швейцария-Россия; контакты и разрывы = *Suisse-Russie; contacts and ruptures* (1994). Schwarz

Fliche, Henri Marie Thérèse André, born 8 June 1836 at Rambouillet, he was a pupil who left school with undistinguished grades, entered second last at l'École forestière de Nancy, but graduated first of the class of 1859. From 1880 to his retirement in 1902 he was a botanist at Nancy and spent his vacations travelling in Europe, and once also in Algeria. He died in Nancy, 28 November 1908. DBF

Flindt, Torben W., fl. 1979, he was a member of the Danish Arms and Armour Society and also a member of the Danish Writers' Society. He visited Uzbekistan as well as Tajikistan. His writings include *Blå skygger* (1972), and *Gamle våben; katalog* (1976). LC

Flinn, Peter, fl. 1968, he was a sometime BBC radio commentator who spent ten years in the Middle East. Note

Flohn, Hermann Gerhard, born 19 February 1912 at Frankfurt am Main, he received a Dr.rer.nat. in 1934 from the Universität Frankfurt, and a Dr.phil.nat., in 1941 from the Universität Würzburg. He was employed by the German national meteorological service from 1935 to 1945, and was a professor at the Universität Bonn from 1961 to 1977. His writings include *Vom Regenmacher zum Wettersatelliten* (1968) *Abhandlungen zur allgemeinen Klimatologie* (1971), and *Tropical circulation pattern* (1971). He was honoured by a jubilee volume, *Klimatologische Forschung; Festschrift für Hermann Flohn zur Vollendung des 60. Lebensjahres* (1974). Kürschner, 1961-1992|; WhoWor, 1980/81

Floor, Willem M., born 1942 in the Netherlands, he received a doctorate in 1971 from the Rijksuniversiteit, Leiden, for his thesis, *The guilds in Qajar Persia*. He was affiliated with the Dutch Ministerie van Buitenlandse Zaken until the late 1980s, when he accepted a position at the World Bank, Washington, D.C., where he was still active throughout the 1990s. His writings include *Commercial conflict between Persia and the Netherlands, 1712-1718* (1988); and he was joint author of *De Iraanse revolutie; achtergronden* (1980), and *Twenty years of Iranian power struggle; a bibliography of 951 political periodicals from 1962 to 1981* (1982). Brinkman's; LC; Private

Flore, Vito Dante, fl. 1972, his writings include *Trasporti marittimi e Mercato comune europeo* (Roma, 1959), *I trasporti marittimi; teoria economica, intervento dello stato* (Roma, 1960), and he was editor of *Porti e terminali industriali* (Milano, 1972). LC

Florensov, Nikolai Aleksandrovich, born in 1909 at Kiev, he graduated from the University of Irkutsk in 1936. He was a geologist of Eastern Sibiria and Central Asia. His writings include Байкальский рифт (1968). He died 21 March 1986. GSE; LC

Flores, Alexander, born 21 March 1948 at Wuppertal, Germany, he received a doctorate in 1980 from the Universität Münster with a thesis entitled *Nationalismus und Sozialismus im arabischen Osten*. He taught successively at Berlin, Essen, Birzeit, Erlangen-Nürnberg, Würzburg, and Essen. His writings include *Intifada, Aufstand der Palästinenser* (1989); and he was joint editor of *Palästinenser in Israel* (1983). Kürschner, 1996, 2003; LC; Sezgin

Florescu, Radu Radu N., born 23 October 1925 at București, he was a graduate of Christ Church College, Oxford, and received his Ph.D. in 1959 from Indiana University for his thesis, *The Roumanian problem in Anglo-Turkish diplomacy, 1821-1824*. He was a sometime professor of history at Boston College. His writings include *History of science in Rumania* (1955), and *The struggle against Russia in the Romanian principalities, 1821-1854* (1962). ConAu, 41-44; DrAS 1974, 1978, 1982; NUC, pre-1956-1967

Floriano, Luis, he was in 1972 affiliated with the Universidad de Oviedo, Spain. Note

Florinsky, Michael Timofeevich, born in 1894 at Kiev, he was educated at Kiev, Petrograd, LSE, and Columbia University, where he received a Ph.D. in 1931 for his thesis, *The end of the Russian Empire*. He was affiliated with Columbia throughout his academic career as a professor of economics. His writings include *Integrated Europe?* (1955). He died in Switzerland, 10 October 1981. AmAu&B; BioIn, 13; ConAu, 1-4, 105, new rev., 5; IntAu&W, 1977, 1982; WhAm, 10; WhE&EA; WrDr, 1976/78-1984/86

Florit y Arizcun, José Maria, born in 1866 at Madrid, he was a sometime keeper at the Armería Real. His writings include *Catalogo de las armas del Instituto de Valencia de Don Juan* [Madrid] (1927). Ossorio

Florovskii, Antonii Vasil'evich, born in 1884, he was a sometime professor of economics at Praha. His writings include *Čeští jesuité na Rusi* (1941), *Česko-ruské obchodní styky v minulosti, X-XVIII století* (1954), and *От Полтавы до Прута* (1971). He died in 1968. NUC, pre-1956; PSN

Flory, Maurice Adolphe Marie, born 19 June 1925 at Paris, he studied at the Faculté de droit and the Institut d'études politiques. For three years he served as a professor of international law at Rabat, and since 1971 he was at Aix-en-Provence, where he became director of the Centre de recherches et d'études sur les sociétés méditerranéennes. From 1967 to 1971 he was head of the Mission universitaire et culturelle française in Morocco. His writings include *Les régimes politiques des pays arabes* (1968), and *Droit international du développement* (1977). WhoFr, 1979/80-1999; WhoWor, 1974/75, 1976/77

Flory, Vera Elizabeth, fl. 1940, she was affiliated with Cumberland University, Lebanon, Tenn. Note

de **Flotte de Roquevaire**, René, born in 1875, his writings include *Cinq mois de triangulation au Maroc* (1909), and he was joint author of *Atlas d'Algérie et de Tunisie* (1923). NUC, pre-1956

Flouriot, Jean, fl. 1966, he was joint author of *Atlas de Kinshasa* (Paris, 1975). LC

Flournoy, Francis Rosebro, fl. 1932, he received a Ph.D. in 1927 from Columbia University for his thesis, *Parliament and war*. His writings include *British policy towards Morocco in the age of Palmerston* (1935). NUC, pre-1956

Flower, Richard Lancelot Gallienne, born 22 March 1937 at London, he studied at Cambridge and the Freie Universität Berlin, where he received a Dr.phil. for *Die Entwicklung von Sadeq Hedayät in seinen literarischen Werken*. He was a sometime assistant at the Seminar für Iranische Philologie, Berlin, and a research fellow at the Universität Bonn, 1978-1981. His writings include *Sadeq-e Hedayät, 1903-1951; eine literarische Analyse* (1977). IWWAS, 1975/76; Kürschner, 1976-2003; Schwarz

Floyer, Ernest Ayscoghe, born in 1852, he served as a British telegraph engineer in India, and later was inspector-general of Egyptian telegraphs from 1878 until his death in Cairo on 1 December 1903. In 1891, he was appointed by the Khedive to the command of an expedition to the desert south of Wadi Halfa, the outcome of which is the subject of his *Étude sur le Nord-Etbai entre le Nil et la mer Rouge* (1893). In his other work, *Unexplored Baluchistan* (1882), he describes his Indian experiences prior to his Egyptian engagement. He died in 1903 in Cairo. DNB; Hill; Gabriel; Henze

Flückiger, Frédéric Auguste, born 1828 at Langenthal, Switzerland, he studied at several universities and received a doctorate from the Universität Heidelberg. Thereafter he practised pharmaceutical chemistry until he was appointed professor of pharmacology successively at the universities of Bern and Straßburg. He died in Bern in 1894. DtBE; NDBA

Fluehr-Lobban, Carolyn, born 6 January 1945 at Philadelphia, Pa., she was a graduate of Temple University and received a Ph.D. in 1973 from Northwestern University for her thesis, *An anthropological analysis of homicide in an Afro-Arab state, the Sudan*. She conducted field research in the Sudan, Egypt, and Tunisia. For the better part of the 1990s, she was a professor of anthropology at Rhode Island College, Providence, R.I. She wrote *Modern Egypt and its heritage* (1990), *Islamic society in practice* (1994), and together with her husband, Richard A. Lobban, *Historical dictionary of the Sudan* (1992); she was editor of *Ethics and the profession of anthropology* (1991), and *Against Islamic extremism; the writings of Muhammad Sa'id al-Ashmawy* (1998). NatFacDr, 1995-1999; Private; Selim

Flügel, Gustav, born in 1802 at Bautzen, Germany, he studied theology and Oriental languages at Leipzig, 1821-1824. In 1829/30 he also studied Arabic, Persian, and Turkish at Paris. From 1832 until his early retirement on account of ill health in 1850, he was a professor at the Fürstenschule in Meißen. He published the Koran with a concordance, and he edited the seven-volume biographical dictionary of Hajji Khalifah (1853-58). He died in Dresden in 1870. CelCen; DcBiPP; DtBE; Fück, p. 157; NDB

von **Flügge**, Wilhelm, fl. 1948, his writings include *Deutsche Verwaltung* (Hamburg, 1948), and he was joint author of *Düngemittel im Kriege* (1917). GV, 1911-1965; NUC, pre-1956

Flury, Samuel, born 20 April 1874 at St. Isabella, Brazil, he studied theology at Basel and Berlin, and then became a teacher of music and German. An invitation in 1899 enabled him to spent three years in Egypt. After his return to Europe, he studied modern linguistics in Switzerland, to which three years of English in Britain was added. From 1907 until his retirement he taught English at the Obere Realschule in Basel. There he came under the influence of the epigraphist Max van Berchem, but the only time in which he could work properly on ornamental epigraphy were the summer holidays. His work was recognized particularly by the American Insitute for Persian Art which awarded him a stipend for work in Paris and Berlin, and small though it was, it resulted in many important studies. His writings include *Islamische Schriftbänder* (1920). He died 24 January 1935. Ars islamica 2 (1935), pp. 235-240; *Bulletin of the American Institute for Persia Art* 4 (1935/36), pp. 51-53

Flye Sainte Marie, Jean, born 22 May 1896 to a family with a long military tradition. After war-time service he passed through the military college, Saint-Cyr. In 1920, he was posted to the Syrian steppe for three years, and in 1924, he entered the camel corps of the Affaires Indigènes d'Algérie. Among his many exploits was a two thousand-mile reconnaisssance in three months as far as Taoudenni to safeguard the desert tracks and wells. From 1929 to 1939 he served at the Affaires Indigènes du Maroc. He retired from active service in 1948 to return to the Centre de Hautes Études d'Administration Musulmane, Paris, where he had been a student in 1938. He became a research assistant of Robert Montagne, and a consultant on North African affairs. He died 5 June 1964. *L'Afrique et l'Asie* 67 (1964), pp. 73-74

Flye-Sainte-Marie, Marie Pierre, born 8 March 1869 at Avallon (Yonne). After passing through the military college, Saint-Cyr, he was with the rank of captain, when he was seconded in 1902 to the Service des Affaires d'indigène in North Africa. During the twelve years he spent there he distinguished himself in reconnaissance operations at Erg Iguidi in the Sahara and, much later, in western Morocco. He served with the French army intelligence from 1913 to 1916, when he became commander of a North African native unit in the Great War. In 1920 he served at Aïn-Tab (Gaziantep). He resigned with the rank of general in 1927 and died, *grand officier de la Légion d'honneur*, in Arradon (Morbihan), 3 January 1956. DBF

Foà, Rodolfo, born 22 March 1875 at Casale Monteferrato, he was a journalist. In 1907 he founded in Roma *L'Italia all'estro*. He was a war correspondent to the *Gazetta del popolo* and the *Chicago daily news*. He later was a contributor to *Giornale d'Italia*. Chi è, 1928, 1931, 1936; Firenze

Fobes, Francis Howard, born 1 August 1881 at Somerville, Mass., he received his undergraduate and graduate education at Harvard, where he earned a Ph.D. in 1912. He also received a B.A. from Oxford University. He taught Greek and Latin at Harvard from 1908 to 1913. From 1920 until his retirement in 1948 he was professor of Greek at Amherst College. He had a broad range of interests, which varied from kite-flying to the publication of modern and ancient works on his own hand-operated press. In 1932 he completed the design of his Brenner Greek type His writings include *Philosophical Greek; an introduction* (1957). He died 16 September 1957. NatCAB 47, pp. 347-48; NYT 18 September 1957, p. 33, col. 2

Foch, René, born in 1924, he obtained a doctorate in law and an additional degree from the École nationale de la France d'outre-mer. In 1958 he was appointed director of the External Relations Division at Euratom. WhoAtom, 1969, 1977

Focillon, Henri, born in 1881 at Dijon. After l'École normale supérieure he was a professor of literature at colleges in Bourges and Chartres. Travels to North Africa were the first incentive to publish works on North African epigraphy. Since 1913 he taught history of art at Lyon and was concurrently a keeper at the Musée municipale. In 1935 he was appointed professor of history of medieval art at the Sorbonne. He left on a lecture tour to Yale University, New Haven, Conn., in 1938, but was unable to return on account of the war and died there, 3 March 1943. BioIn, 2, 6; DBF; Master (2)

Fock, A., born 19th cent., he was a civil engineer whose writings include *Algérie, Sahara, Tchad* (Paris, 1891), *Chemin de fer transsaharien* (1929), and *Examen critique du Rapport ... pour le chemin de fer transsaharien et transafricain français à deux branches* (1930). BN; NUC, pre-1956

Focke, Friedrich, born 28 February 1890 at Wengerich, Germany, he studied at Greifswald, Berlin, and Münster, where he received a Dr.phil. in 1911 for *Quaestiones Plutarcheae de Vitarum parallelarum textus historia*. He was a sometime professor of classical philology and a president of the Universität Tübingen. His writings include *Entstehung der Weisheit Salomons* (1913), *Herodot als Historiker* (1927), and *Ritte und Reigen; Volkskundliches* (1941). He died in Hechingen, 11 March 1970. Kürschner, 1935-1970; Wer ist's, 1935

Foda, Ezeldin, 1923- see Fawdah, 'Izz al-Din

Födermayer, Franz, born 13 September 1933 at Grieskirchen, Austria, he received a Dr.phil. in 1964 from the Universität Wien for *Die musikwissenschaftlichen Phonogramme Ludwig Zöhrers von den Tuareg der Sahara*. In 1973 he was appointed professor of musicology at Wien. His writings include *Zur gesanglichen Stimmgebung in der außereuropäischen Musik* (1971). Kürschner, 1976-2003; Schwarz; WhoAustria, 1982/83

Fodor, Ferenc (Francis), 1887-1962, his writings include *Conditions of production in Hungary* (1921), *Magyar föld, magyar élet* (1937), and he was editor of *Osteuropäisches Jahrbuch*. NUC, pre-1956

Fodor, István, born 16 March 1920 at Budapest, his writings include *The rate of linguistic change* (1965), *The problems in the classification of the African languages* (1966), *Miro jó a nyelvtudomány?* (1968), *Pakkas und andere afrikanische Vokabularien vor dem 19. Jahrhundert* (1975), and he was joint editor of *Language reform; history and future* (1983-84). LC; MagyarNKK, 1998

Fogg, Walter, fl. 1935-1941, he received an M.A. in 1928 from the University of Manchester for his thesis, *The influence of physical conditions upon human life in the Sebou Basin*.

Fogg, William Perry, 1826-1906, his writings include *"Round the world;"* letters from Japan, China, India, and Egypt (1872), and Arabistan, or, the land of the *"Arabian nights,"* being travels through Egypt, Arabia, and Persia, to Bagdad (1875). LC; Master (1)

Fokeev, German Vasil'evich, born 13 January 1933, he graduated in 1956 from the Moscow State Institute for International Relations. He received a first degree in 1963 for his dissertation, *Колониальная политика Англии в Африке после второй мировой войны, 1945-1963 гг.*, and a doctorate in 1978 for his thesis, *Проблемы меджунарых отношений в Африке и внешне-политической деятельности государства Африки*. Since 1981 he was a professor at his alma mater. His writings include *Они не хотят уходить* (1965), *Внешняя политика стран Африка* (1968), *Внешнеполитические про-блемы современной Африки* (1975). Miliband[2]

Fokker, A. A., fl. 1893, he receiced a doctorate in 1895 from the Rijksuniversiteit te Leiden for his thesis, *Malay phonetics*. He was a sometime teacher of Malay at the Openbare Handelsschool in Amsterdam. His writings include *Toen ik Indisch student was* (1902), and *Maleisch leesboek* (1903). NUC, pre-1956

Fokos-Fuchs, David Raphael, 1884- see Fuchs, Dávid Ráfáel

Folcker, Erik Gustaf, born in 1858, he was affiliated with the National Museum, Stockholm, and an editor of the *Medenlanden* of the Svenska Slöjdföreningen. Note

Folda, Jaroslav Thayer, born 25 July 1940 at Baltimore, Md., he was a graduate of Princeton and received a Ph.D. from Johns Hopkins University, Baltimore, in 1968. Thereafter he was appointed professor of history of art, and later chairman of department, University of North Carolina at Chapel Hill, a position which he still held in 1999. His writings include *Crusader manuscripts illustration at Saint-Jean d'Acre, 1275-1291* (1976). ConAu, 127; DrAS, 1982; NatFacDr, 1995-1999; WhoAmA, 1980-1997/98

Foley, Charles Maurice O'Connell, born 1904 at Jhelum, India, he was educated at Beaumont College, and University College, London. He was a journalist who began his career on the Chicago *Tribune*'s famed Paris *Tribune*, and later worked fifteen years as foreign editor on the *Daily Express*. In 1955, he sailed for Cyprus, where he founded and edited the independent English daily newspaper *Times of Cyprus*. His writings include *Commando extraordinary* (1954), *Island in revolt* (1962), *Legacy of strife; Cyprus from rebellion to civil war* (1964); and he was joint author of *The struggle for Cyprus* (1975). He died 30 May 1995. Au&Wr, 1971; Bioln, 5; ConAu, P-1, 13-16, 148; Time, v. 72 (15 September 1958), p. 75

Foley, Henry Joseph Edmond, born 11 April 1871 at Vignory (Haute-Marne), he was since 1896 in Algeria, at first as a medical officer at the hospitals of the Division d'Oran, and from 1906 to 1914, as head of the Infirmerie indigène at Beni Ounif-de-Figuig. Subsequently he was director of the Services de santé des Territoires du Sud algérien from 1917 to 1921, when he retired from the military to become head of the Service des Laboratoires sahariens at the Institut Pasteur d'Algérie. He was an officer of the Légion d'Honneur, and greatly honoured by learned societies and academies. In 1916 he was a recipient of the Prix Monthyon. He died in Vignory (Haute-Marne), 2 August 1956. Peyronnet, 826; Travaux de l'Institut de Recherches Sahariens 15 (1957), pp. 7-10

Foley, Rolla, she received a Ph.D. in 1956 from Columbia University for her thesis, *Work songs of the Arab*. Her writings include *Song of the Arab; the religious ceremonies, shrines, and folk music of the Holy Land Christian Arab* (New York, 1953). LC; Selim

Folkerts, Menso, born 22 June 1943 at Eschwege, Germany, he received a doctorate in 1967. After teaching at the Universität Oldenburg, he was appointed a professor at the Institut für Geschichte der Naturwissenschaften, Universität München. He wrote *Mittelalterliche mathematische Handschriften in westlichen Sprachen in der Herzog August Bibliothek, Wolfenbüttel* (1981). Kürschner, 1992-2003

Follet, René, S.J., he was joint editor of *Codex Hammurabi; transcriptio et versio Latina* (1950). His article in *Rivista degli studi orientali*, v. 31 (1956), was published posthumously. LC

Folliot de Crenneville, Victor, Graf, born 19th cent., his writings include *Die Insel Cypern in ihrer heutigen Gestalt* (Wien, 1879). NUC, pre-1956

Foltz, William Jay, born 24 January 1936 at Mount Vernon, N.Y., he was a graduate of Princeton and received a Ph.D. in 1963 from Yale University. Since 1962 he was a professor of political science at Yale. In 1985 he was director of the Africa Project, Council of Foreign Affairs. His writings include *From French West Africa to the Mali Federation* (1965), and he was joint editor of *Arms and the African* (1985). AmM&WS, 1973 S, 1978 S; ConAu, 9-12

Fonahn, Adolf Mauritz, born 15 June 1873 at Hedrum, Norway, he studied medicine and Oriental languages, and became a lecturer at the Universitetet i Oslo. He was a medical historian whose writings include *Zur Quellenkunde der persischen Medizin* (Leipzig, 1910), and *Arabic and Latin anatomical terminology* (Kristiana, 1922). He died in Oslo, 21 August 1940. *Isis* 37 i-ii (1947), p. 81; NorskBL

Foncin, Pierre François Charles, born in 1841 at Limoges, he was for many years a school-teacher before he started to lecture in economic geography at Bordeaux in 1874. After he obtained his doctorate in 1877, he held the newly created chair of geography at the Faculté des lettres de Bordeaux. In 1879 he became dean of the Académie de Douai, in the capacity of which he was instrumental in the establishement of the Union géographique du Nord de la France. He later served for thirty years as director-general of public education. He died in Paris, 16 December 1916. DBF

Fonde, Jean Julien, fl. 1943. His writings include *J'ai vu une meute de loups* (1969), *Traitez à tous prix ...* (1971), and *L'Arche de lumière* (1985). LC

Fonseca, Fernando Venâncio Peixoto da, fl. 1959-1985, he was a linguist whose writings include *Método prático de língua Romena* (1963), and *O português entre as línguas do mundo* (1985). LC

Font Rius, José (Josep) María, born in 1915 at Barcelona, he studied at Barcelona and received his doctorate at Madrid. He was a professor of history at Barcelona since 1954. The universities of Montpellier and Bordeaux conferred upon him honorary doctorates. His writings include *Orígines del régimen municipal de Cataluña* (1946), *Instituciones medievales españolas* (1949), *Cartas de problación y franquicia de Cataluña* (1969), and *Guía de la cátedra de historia del derecho español* (1971). Dicc bio

Fontaine, Alfred L., fl. 1947 his writings include *Monographie cartographique de l'Isthme de Suez, de la péninsule du Sinaï, du nord de la chaîne arabique* (1955). LC

Fontaine, Claude, born 8 October 1928 at Paris, he received a *doctorat ès lettres* in 1953 at Toulouse, followed by several post-doctoral degrees. For several years he was a psychologist at the Centre d'études des sciences humaines, Tunis, and a professor at l'École Avicenne, Tunis. Unesco

Fontaine, Jean Marie André, born 2 December 1936 at Saint André, he studied at Tunis, Paris, and Aix-en-Provence, where he received a *doctorat d'état* in 1977 for his thesis, *Mort-résurrection; une lecture de Tawfiq al-Hakim.* He was a *conservateur* at the library of the Institut des Belles Lettres Arabes, Tunis, from 1968 to 1984, and since 1975 also the director of its journal, *IBLA*. His writings include *Vingt ans de littérature tunisienne, 1956-1975* (1977), and *La Littérature tunisienne contemporaine* (1990). Private; THESAM 3

Fontana, Maria Vittoria, born 20th cent., her writings include *La leggenda di Bahram Gur e Azada* (Napoli, 1986), *Iconografia dell'Ahl al-bayt; immagini di arte persiana* (1994), and she was editor of *La ceramica medievale di San Lorenzo Maggiore in Napoli; atti del Convegno, 1980* (1984). LC

Fontane, Marius Étienne, born 4 September 1838 at Marseille. At the age of seventeen he became attached to a commercial firm trading with the Orient. On one of his travels he came in contact with Ferdinand de Lesseps who engaged him as his secretary. Despite his administrative responsibilities he early displayed literary ambitions of various genres, novels, political economy, and history. His writings include *Le canal maritime de Suez* (1869). In his fourteen-volume *Histoire universelle* (1881-1910), he published individual volumes also on the Middle East and related subjetcs. Implicated in the Panama case, he was condemned to two years in prison on 10 February 1893. He died in 1914. DBF

Fontaneau de Touchenard, Pierre Émile Ferdinand, born 8 January 1925 at Alger, he was educated at Alger and Paris, and received doctorates in law and political science. He was successively a lawyer to the court of appeal at Alger and Paris, and since 1952 a professor of law at Alger, Montpellier, and Nice. He later also served as a consultant to the government on Algerian affairs, as well as an academic ad-ministrator on a national and international level. His writings include *L'électrification de l'Algérie* (1952), *Essais sur les investissements* (1957), and *Tableaux fiscaux européens* (1971). WhoFr, 1971/72-1998/99

Fontanier, Victor, born 23 September 1796 at S.-Flour, France, he studied pharmacy before his graduation from l'École normale in 1817. In 1821 he was sent as *naturaliste* to the French Embassy at Constantinople. His official function permitted extensive travels in all parts of the Ottoman Empire. In 1838 he became French vice-consul at Basra, a post which offered him the chance to visit also Arabia. He later served in the Netherlands and the Far East. His writings include *Voyages en Orient, 1821 à 1829* (1829), *Voyage dans l'Inde et dans le golfe Persique par l'Égypte et la mer Rouge* (1844-1846), and *Narrative of a mission to India, and the countries bordering the Persian Gulf* (1844). He died in Civita Vecchia, 26 May 1857. DBF; Henze; Hoefer; Vapereau (1861)

de **Fontenelle**, Julia, 1790-1842 *see* Julia de Fontenelle, Jean Sébastian Eugène

Fontes, Juan Torres, fl. 1944-1963 *see* Torres Fontes, Juan

de **Fontgalland**, Bernard Heurard, born 24 June 1917 at Paris, he was educated at Lyon and Paris. He became an *ingénieur des ponts et chaussées* and was a former student of l'École polytechnique. He was successively a director of railways in Cameroon and Dakar-Niger, 1945-1953. From 1966 to 1971 he was head of research at the Société national des chemins de fer. His writings include *Le Système ferroviaire dans le monde* (1980), its translation, *The World railway system* (1984), and *Cheminot sans frontière* (1988). WhoFr, 1981/82-1994/95|

Fontin (Fontin-Clozel), Paul Jean, born 19 November 1859, he studied law, followed by courses at l'École des sciences politiques, section diplomatique, and became a secretary to the director of *le Soleil*. He later entered journalism as a political editor, specializing in martime affairs. He was a sometime librarian of the Ministère de la Marine. From 1915 to 1919 he was *directeur du cabinet* of the governor-general of Algeria. His writings include *Les Lois du nombre et de la vitesse dans l'art de la guerre* (1894), and *Réformes navales* (1899). His trace is lost after a publication in 1929. *Dictionnaire de biographie française*

de **Fontmagne**, Marie Caroline Drummond de Melfort Durand, born 19th cent., *see* Durand de Fontmagne, Marie Caroline Drummond de Melfort, *baronne*

de **Fontpertuis**, Adalbert Frout, 1825- *see* Frout de Fontpertuis, Adalbert

de **Fonvielle**, Wilfrid, born 21 or 24 July 1824, 1826 or 1828 at Paris, he was a political activist in his youth, known to the police as a dangerous social element. After the coup d'état of 2 December 1851, he was deported to Algeria, where he established the newspaper *l'Algérie nouvelle*. He was pardoned in 1859 and returned to France, where he continued his journalistic career and, at the same time, became interested in aeronautics. He later tried unsuccessfully to enter politics and turned exclusively to literary pursuits. His writings cover a wide range of subjects and include the pamphlets, *La Croisade en Syrie* (1860), and *L'Empereur en Algérie* (1860). He died in Paris, 24 April 1914. BiD&SB; Curinier, vol. 2 (1901), pp. 227-8; DBF; DcBiPP

Foord, Edward A., born 19th cent., his writings include *The Byzantine Empire, the rearguard of the European civilization* (1911), *Napoleon's Russian campaign of 1812* (1914), and *The Last age of Roman Britain* (1925). LC

Foot, Rosemary, born 4 June 1948, she was in 1975 a research student at LSE and thereafter a sometime lecturer in international relations at the School of English and American Studies in the University of Sussex. Her writings include *The Wrong war* (1985), *A Substitute for victory* (1990), and she was a contributing author to *South Asian security and the great powers* (1986). LC

Foote, Helen S., born in 1892, she served with the Cleveland Museum of Art for thirty-six years prior to her retirement in 1958. Her position at that time was associate curator of decorative arts. She died suddenly on 11 August 1969. *Bulletin of the Cleveland Museum of Art* 56 (December 1969), p. 365

Foradori, Ezio, fl. 1914, he was in 1953 a business executive residing in Innsbruck, Austria. *Who's who in Austria*, 1954, 1955, 1957/58|

Forand, Paul Glidden, born 30 May 1933 at New Medford, Mass., he was a graduate of Harvard and received a Ph.D. in 1962 from Princeton University for his thesis, *The Development of military slavery under the Abbasid caliphs*. He held various academic positions until he was appointed professor of Arabic at the University of Kentucky, Lexington, in 1970. *Dictionary of American scholars*, 1974, 1978, 1982; Private; Selim

Forbes, Andrew D. W., fl. 1976, his writings include *Warlords and Muslims in Chinese Central Asia; a political history of Republican Sinkiang, 1911-1949* (1986), and he was editor of *The Muslims of Thailand* (1988). LC

Forbes, Archibald, born in 1838 at Boharm, Scotland, as the son of a Prsbyterian minister, he was educated at King's College, Aberdeen and served six xears in the military before becoming editor and part proprietor of the London *Scotsman*. In 1870 he joined the staff of the *London news*. His writings include *Afghan wars* (1891), and *Czar and sultan; the adventures of a British lad in the Russo-Turkish war of 1877-1878* (1894). BbD; *Biographical dictionary and synopsis of books*; Buckland; DNB; Master (3); *Who was who*, 1

Forbes, Duncan, born in 1798 at Kinnaird of a family of modest substance. His schooling was of the scantiest, and he knew no English until his early teens. He became a village schoolmaster before studying at St. Andrew's. Thereafter he taught in Calcutta from 1823 to 1826, when he returned home to become a professor of Oriental languages at London until 1861. His writings include *A Grammar of the Persian language* (1844), *The History of chess* (1860), *A Dictionary, Hindustani and English* (1862-

1866), *Arabic reading lessons* (1864), and *A catalogue of Oriental manuscripts, chiefly Persian, collected within the last five and thirty years* (1866). He died 17 August 1868. Buckland; DNB

Forbes, Frederick, M.A., born in 1808, he was a graduate of Marischal College, Aberdeen. He joined the East India Company service as an assistant surgeon in 1832. At the time of his visit to the Somali Coast in 1833 he was attached to the Indian Navy. He later was an officer of the Bombay Medical Staff and was the first European, in 1838, to explore Jabal Sinjar, northern Mesopotamia, inhabited by the Yezidis. Three years later, he travelled from Trebizond (Trabzon) by way of Tehran to Meshed, and on southward to Turbat-i Haydariyah, Birjand, and Tabas to the lower Hari Rud River, where he was killed in the summer of 1841. His writings include *Thesis on the nature and history of the plague, as observed in the north western provinces of India* (Edinburgh, 1840). Henze; *International journal of African historical studies* 19 (1986), pp. 679-691

Forbes, Henry Ogg, born 30 January 1851 at Drumblade, Scotland, he studied medicine until the loss of one eye in an accident obliged him to give up. After travels in Portugal, 1875-77, he later carried on explorations in the Malay Archipelago. Under the auspices of British museums he was joint leader of a zoological expedition to Socotra. His writings include *A naturalist's wanderings in the Eastern Archipelago* (1885), and *The natural history of Sokotra and Abd-el-Kuri* (1903). He died 27 October 1932. BbD; BiD&SB; Henze; WhE&EA; *Who was who*, 3

Forbes, Joan *Rosita* née Torr, in second marriage Mrs. A. T. McGrath, born 16 January 1895, she was a famous travel-writer who aptly named her first book *Unconducted wanderers*. Still in her twenties, she made a name for herself by romantic exploits described in still more romantic books. In heavy disguise she visited the Libyan oasis of Kufra where only one European had preceded her. Her writings include *The secret of the Sahara; Kufara* (1921), *From Red Sea to Blue Nile* (1925), *Conflict; Angora to Afghanistan* (1931), and *Forbidden road; Kabul to Samarkand* (1937). She died in 1967. Bidwell; ConAu, 116; DLB 195 (1998), pp. 85-99; DNB; Master (2); ObitT, 1961; Robinson, pp. 91-92; *Who was who*, 6

Forbes, Lesley E., Mrs. Harding, born about 1940 in Britain, she was since the mid-1970s a keeper of Oriental books at the University of Durham Library, and for over twenty years, Islamic librarian at its Middle East Centre. She was active in the SCONUL Advisory Committee on Orientalist Materials as well as the Midlle East Libraries Committee. Her writings include *Early Western books, 1500-1599* (1987). Private

Forbes, Robert Humphrey, born 15 May 1867 at Cobden, Illinois, he was a graduate of the University of Illinois and received a Ph.D. in 1916 from the University of California. He was a pioneer agriculturalist, environmentalist, conservationist, and water specialist at home and abroad. From 1918 to 1922 he was agronomist to the Société sultanienne d'agriculture du Caire. His writings include *Le coton dans la vallée moyen du Niger* (1926). He died in 1968. Charles C. Colley wrote a biography, *Century of Robert H. Forbes* (1977). LC; Shavit; WhAm, 5

Forbes, Rosita, 1895-1967 *see* Forbes, Joan *Rosita* née Torr

Forcade, Eugène, born in 1820 at Marseille. After an early employment at a banking establishment, he turned towards journalism and published *Le Sémaphore* in Marseille from 1837 to 1840, when he went to Paris. There he worked as a journalist, notably for the *Revue des deux mondes*, and as an editor and founder of periodicals. His writings include *Histoire des causes de la guerre d'Orient* (1854), and its translation, *Storia delle cause della guerra d'Oriente* (1854). He died outside Paris, 7 November 1869. DBF; DcBiPP

Forcade La Roquette, Jean Louis Victor *Adolphe*, born 8 April 1820 at Paris, he studied law and became a lawyer in the court of appeal at Paris in 1841. His role in the coup d'état of December 1851 determined his future political role. He was a member of the Conseil d'État and after 1860 held several portefolios. In 1862 he went on a fact-finding mission to Algeria. His writings include *Enquête sur le commerce et la navigation de l'Algérie; rapport* (1863). He died in Paris, 15 August 1874. CelCen; *Dictionnaire de biographie française*

Forchheimer, Karl, Dr., born 29 July 1880 at Prag, he studied at Prag and Wien. He served at the Austrian Ministry of the Interior until 1938 and thereafter lectured in economics at Oxford from 1939 to 1948. His writings include *Gesetze und Verordnungen für die Zeit des Krieges* (1914), *Die Vorschriften über die Arbeitslosenversicherung* (1932), and *Keynes' neue Wirtschaftslehre* (1952). WhoAustria, 1954, 1955, 1957/58|

Ford, Jeremiah Denis Matthias, 1873-1958, he was Smith Professor Emeritus of French and Spanish languages at Harvard University. WhAm, 3; *Who was who*, 5

Ford, Joseph Francis, born in 1912, he was a China expert in the British diplomatic service and was posted to Shanghai, Chungking, and Peking. From 1974 to 1978 he was director of the Great Britain-China Centre. He died in 1993. Who, 1969-1993

Ford, Olga Gemes, fl. 1980, she was a graduate of the Technische Universität, Berlin, and a sometime lecturer at the City of Leicester Polytechnic and School of Architecture. WhoArt, 1980-1998

Forde, Cyril Daryll, born 16 March 1902 at Tottenham, Middlesex, he obtained a Ph.D. in 1928 from the University of London. He was a sometime professor of geography and anthropology, University of Wales, head of the Department of Anthropology, University College in the University of London, and director of the International African Institute. His writings include *Habitat; economy and society* (1934), and *The Yoruba-speaking people of south-western Nigeria* (1951). Unesco

Forder, Archibald, Rev., born in 1863, he was a sometime superintendent of the Nile Mission Press, Jerusalem Branch. His writings include *With the Arabs in tent and town* (1902), *Ventures among the Arabs in desert, tent, and town; thirteen years of pioneer missionary life with the Ishmaelites of Moab, Edom and Arabia* (1905), *Daily life in Palestine* (1912), *In and about Palestine* (1919), *In brigands' hands and Turkish prisons, 1914-1918* (1920).

Forey, Alan John, fl. 1977, he was affiliated with the University of Durham. His writings include *The Templars in the Corona de Aragon* (1973). LC

Forget, Jacques, born 6 January 1852 at Chiny, Belgium, he studied Oriental languages at Louvain, to which the universities of Roma and Beirut were added a year or two later. He received a doctorate in 1882 from the Université de Louvain for his thesis, *De vita et scriptis Apharaatis, sapientis Persae*. He was appointed professor of Arabic at Louvain in 1885, and taught this subject until his retirement in 1932. Concurrently he held the chair of Syriac from 1900 to 1932. Since 1913 he was also director of the Arabic Section of the *Corpus scriptorum christianorum orientalium*. His writings include the edition and translation of Avicenna's *Le Livre des théorèmes et des avertissements* (1892). He died in Louvain, 10 July 1933. BioNBelge vol. 33, pp. 319-322

Forgeur, Adrien, baron, born 19th cent., he was in 1916 a professor at l'École sultaniyeh de droit, and a member of the Société sultanieh d'économie politique, de statistique et de législation, Cairo. His trace is lost after a publication in 1921. Note

Forgues, Paul *Émile* Daurand, born 20 April 1813 at Paris, he received a law degree in 1833. After a brief political interlude and service as secretary of the Conférence des avocats in 1837, he returned to journalism, his first profession. For unknown reason, he became interested in English literature while continuing to contribute articles to a wide range of French publications. After 1861 he specialized in foreign affairs, particularly British politics. After his health broke down in 1870, he retired to Cannes, where he died on 22 October 1883. His writings include *La révolte des Cipayes; épisodes et récits de la vie anglo-indienne* (1861). DBF

Forichon, Robert, he was in 1937 *contrôleur civil suppléant* in Morocco, and in 1951, *chef* of the Cercle de la moyenne Moulouya. Note

Forke, Ernst Conrad *Alfred*, born 12 January 1867 at Bad Schöningen, Germany, he studied at the universities of Genève, Berlin, and Rostock, where he received a Dr.jur. in 1890. Thereafter he studied Chinese and served for a number of years as a consular interpreter in China. From 1903 to 1935 he was successively Sinologist at Berlin and Hamburg. He died in Hamburg, 9 July 1944. DtBE

Forlong, James George Roke, born in 1824, he was a trained engineer and joined the Indian Army in 1843, and served until 1857. The following two years he travelled extensively. He later was involved in special public works, became superintending engineer in Bengal, North West Province, and Rajputana from 1861 to 1871. From 1872 until his retirement in 1877, he was secretary and chief engineer in Oudh. He was well versed in Indian religions and folklore. His writings include *Short studies in the science of comparative religions* (1897), and *Faith of men; a cyclopædia of religions* (1906). He died 29 March 1904. Buckland

Formichi, Carlo, born 14 February 1871 at Napoli, he was an authority on Indian civilization and a sometime president of the Italian Royal Academy. His writings include *L'ora dell'India* (1942), and *India, pensiero e azione* (1944). He died in Roma, 13 December 1943. Chi è, 1928-1940; DizBI

Formosinho, José dos Santos Pimenta, born 22 May 1888 at Lagos (Algarve), Portugal, he studied law at Coimbra and subsequently practised at Portimao. He was also affiliated with the Museu Regional de Santo António, Lagos. Quém é alguém, 1947

Fórneas Besteiro, José Maria, fl. 1973, he received a doctorate in Semitic philology and letters and taught Arabic at Granada. In 1994 he was a *catedrático emeritus* in Arabic at the Universidad de Granada. He edited Averroes' *Kulliyat fi al-tibb* (1987). Arabismo, 1992, 1994, 1997

Forrer, Ludwig, born in 1897, he received a Dr.phil. in 1923 from the Universität Zürich for *Die osmanische Chronik des Rustem Pascha*, and Dr.habil. in 1942 from the Universität Leipzig for his edition and translation of *Südarabien nach Al-Hamdani's "Beschreibung der arabischen Halbinsel."* Schwarz

Forst, Hermann, born 8 October 1858 at Koblenz, Germany, he received a Dr.phil. in 1882 from the Universität Bonn for his thesis, *Über Buchanans Darstellung der Geschichte Maria Stuarts.* His writings include *Das Fürstentum Prüm* (Bonn, 1903). GV, 1700-1910

Forst, Robert Drane, fl. 1976, he received a Ph.D. in 1970 from the University of Texas for his thesis, *Labor and traditional politics in Morocco.* Selim

Forst-Battaglia, Jakob, born 9 May 1950 at Wien, he studied history, Slavonic languages and literature at the Universität Wien, where he received a Dr.phil. in 1974 for his thesis, *Die polnischen Konservativen Galiziens und die Slawen, 1866-1879.* He was a lecturer at the Institut für Slawistik in the Universität Wien until 1983, when he became cultural attaché at the Austrian Embassy, Moscow. His writings include *Polnisches Wien* (1983). WhoAustria, 1982/83|

Forst de Battaglia, Otto, born 21 September 1889 at Wien, the offspring of a former affluent Polish family, he studied at Wien and Bonn, and received doctorates in law as well as in history. After the war he was predominantly a critic and spent much time in Switzerland, France, and Belgium, where he made the acquaintance of prominent European politicians. From 1937 to 1945, he was for a time in the diplomatic service of the Polish Government at home and in exile. In 1948 he accepted a professorship at the European College at Bruxelles. His writings include *Jan Sobieski* (1946), and its translation, *Jan Sobieski, król Polski* (1983). He died in Wien, 3 May 1965. Czy wiesz, 1938; DtBE; NEP; WhoAustria, 1955-1964

Forster, Johann Reinhold, born of Scottish extraction on 22 October 1729 at Dirschau, Germany, he was educated at Berlin and, following his father's expressed wish, studied theology at Halle, while retaining an interest in Oriental languages and philosophy. From 1753 to 1764 he was a country pastor. But he was a restless man, at odds with himself and the world. He abandoned his cure and went on an unsuccessful mission to southern Russia in the service of the Russian Government in 1865. The following year he moved with his family to England. In 1772 he was offered to accompany J. Cook on his three-year tour around the world. He returned to Halle as professor of natural history in 1870. His writings include *Geschichte der Entdeckungen und Schiffahrten im Norden* (1784), and its translations, *History of voyages and discoveries made in the north* (1786), *Histoire des découvertes et des voyages faits dans le Nord* (1788), *The Resolution journal of Johann Reinhold Forster, 1772-1775* (1982). He died in Halle, 9 December 1798. Michael E. Hoare wrote *Tactless philosopher, Johann Reinhold Forster, 1729-1798* (1975). BiD&SB; BioIn, 2; DtBE; Embacher; Henze; OxCGer, 1986

Forstner, Martin, born 23 August 1940 at Nürnberg, he studied Islamic subjects at the Universität Mainz, where he received a Dr.phil. in 1968 for his thesis, *Das Kalifat des Abbasiden al-Musta'in.* Thereafter he started teaching at his alma mater. He was affiliated with the Gesellschaft für Österreichisch-Arabische Beziehungen. His writings include *Al-Mu'tazz billah; die Krise des abbasidischen Kalifats* (1976), *Das Wegenetz des zentralen Maghreb im islamischer Zeit* (1979), *Der allgemeine Teil des ägyptischen Strafrechts* (1986), *Materialien für den Arabischunterricht* (1988), and the pamphlet, *Algerien; Demokratie ohne Demokraten* (1994). Kürschner, 1970-1996; Schwarz

Forsyth, Sir Thomas Douglas, born in 1827 at Birkenhead, England, he was educated at Sherborne, Rugby, and the East India Company's College at Haileybury. He served in India from 1847 to his resignation in 1877. At the Company's college in India he gained competence in Persian, Urdu, and Hindi. He accomplished misions to Ladakh in 1867, and in the following year was sent to Russia on a diplomatic mission to obtain from the Russian government an acknowledgement that certain disputed territories belonged to the Amir of Afghanistan. He led other missions to Yarkand in 1870 and to Kashgar in 1877. His writings include *Report of a mission to Yarkund in 1873* (1875), *Ost-Turkestan und das Pamir-Plateau nach den Forschungen der britischen Gesandtschaft 1873 und 1874* (1877), and *Autobiography and reminiscences of Sir Douglas Forsyth* (1887). He died in Eastbourne on 17 December 1886. Buckland; CelCen; DNB; Embacher; Henze

Forté, Albert N., fl. 1952, he obtained a doctorate in law, and for over thirty-five years was a member of the Société Fouad Ier d'économie politique, de statistique et de législation. In 1952 he was *chef du Contentieux* at the National Bank of Egypt. His writings include *Les banques en Égypte* (Paris, 1938). Note; NUC, pre-1956

Forte, David Francis, born 2 November 1941 at Somerville, Mass, he was a graduate of Harvard, and received a Ph.D. in 1974 from the University of Toronto for his thesis, *The policies and principles of Dean Rusk*. He taught political science successively at the University of Toronto and Skidmore College, Saratoga Springs, N.Y., until 1974, when he became a judge. In 1980 he was appointed a professor at the College of Law in Cleveland State University, a position which he still held in 1999. ConAu, 53-56; Master (1); NatFacDr, 1980-1999; Private

Fortescue, L. S., born 19th cent., he was a captain in the British Army stationed in northern India until the spring of 1917, when he was transferred to Mesopotamia. In the following year he thrice made the three hundert-odd-mile journey from Basrah to Baghdad on horseback. Having privately studied Persian, he was sent to Persia in 1918 and attached to the Norperforce as assistant political officer at Qazvin until 1920, when he was detailed to compile a report for General Headquarters Baghdad on the region of North Persia. Note

Forth, Nowell Barnard de Lancey, 1879-1933 *see* De Lancey Forth, Nowell Barnard

Fortin, Ernest Leonard, born 17 December 1923 at Woonsocket, R.I., he studied in the United States and at Paris, where he received a *dr. ès lettres* degree. He was a sometime professor of Christianity and politics and a professor of theology at Boston College, Chestnut Hill, Mass, a position which he still held in 1995. His writings include *Christianisme et culture philosophique au cinquième siècle* (1959), and *Political idealism and Christianity in the thought of St. Augustine* (1972). DrAS, 1974, 1978; Master (2); NatFacDr, 1995

Fortnum, Charles Drury Edward, 1820-1899, he was an English art collector and benefactor of the University of Oxford. His writings include *Maiolica; a historical treatise on the glazed and enamelled earthenwares of Italy, with marks and monograms, also some notice of the Persian, Damascus, Rhodian, and Hispano-Moresques wares* (1896). BioIn, 12, 13; DNB, vol. 22; Who was who, 1

Fortunatov, P. K., fl. 1953, his writings include *Война 1877-1878 гг. и освобождение Болгарии* (1950), and its translation, *Der Krieg 1877/78 und die Befreiung Bulgariens* (1953). NUC, pre-1956

Foskett, Douglas John, born 27 June 1918 at London, he was a librarian educated at London. When he retired in 1983, he was director of Central Library Services and Goldsmiths' Librarian in the University of London. His writings include *Information service in libraries* (1958), and *Classification and indexing in the social sciences* (1963). Au&Wr, 1971; BioIn, 15; ConAu, 1-4; IntAu&W, 1976, 1977, 1982, 1989; Master (1); Who, 1978-1999; WhoWor, 1978/79-1989/90

Fosset, Robert, he received a doctorate in 1979from the Université de Montpellier III for his thesis, *Société rurale et organisation de l'espace; les bas-plateaux atlantiques du Maroc moyen.* THESAM 1

Fossier, Robert Marcel, born 4 September 1927 at Vésinet (Yvelines), he was educated at l'École des chartes and the Sorbonne, Paris. He was successively an archivist-palaeographer, a college and a university professor of medieval history until his retirement in 1993. His writings include *Paysans d'Occident, XIe-XIV siècle* (1984), and its translation, *Peasant life in the medieval West* (1988). WhoFr, 1993/94-1999

Fossum, Ludvig Olsen, born 5 June 1879 at Wallingford, Iowa, he graduated in 1902 from the Norwegian Lutheran Seminary and served as pastor at Slayton, Iowa, from 1902 to 1905 when he went as missionary to the Nestorians in Urmia for the first time. In 1911 he returned for a second time to Kurdistan and worked there until he and the remaining missionaries were forced to leave in 1916 on account of the war and food shortage. He arrived in America on 21 September 1916 and continued his Kurdish literary work. In 1919 he returned to Kurdistan for the last time to work in the Red Cross Service as the district commander of the Near East Relief in Erivan where he died from nervous exhaustion and convulsions, 10 October 1920. His writings include *Muhammedanismen; land, forholde og personlighed der frembragte den* (1911), *Kurdish prayer book* (1918), *A practical Kurdish grammar* (1919). MW 11 (1921), p. 88; Shavit

Foster, Benjamin Read, born 15 September 1945 at Bryn Mawr, Pa., he was a graduate of Princeton University. In 1981 he was appointed a professor of Assyriology at Yale University. He also was a sometime teacher of Arabic. His writings include *Umma in the Sargonic period* (1982), a work which is a revision of his 1975 Yale thesis. DrAS, 1982; NatFacDr, 1995-1999

Foster, Brian, born in 1920 at Sunderland, England, he studied at the University of Durham and obtained a doctorate from the Université de Paris. He was successively lecturer at the universities of Southampton and Durham. His writings include *The changing English language* (1968), and he edited *The local port book of Southampton for 1435-36* (1963). Au&Wr, 1971; ConAu, 112; IntAu&W, 1976, 1977; WrDr, 1976/78

Foster, Frank Hugh, born in 1851 at Springfield, Mass., he was a graduate of Harvard, and Andover Theological Seminary, and received a Dr.phil. in 1882 from the Universität Leipzig for his thesis, *The doctrine of the transcendent use of the principle of causality in Kant, Herbart and Lotze*. He became a clergyman and a professor of philosophy and Church history at various American colleges. He died in Oberlin, Ohio, in 1935. DAB, Suppl. 1; LuthC, 1975; Master (1); WhAm, 1

Foster, I. J. C. (Jack), born in 1907 at London, he began as a student of physics; this was followed by three years of school-teaching. His zeal for learning and spirit of intellectual enquiry led him to Trinity College, Cambridge, to read theology and later Oriental languages. But it is as a librarian that he is chiefly remembered. In 1945 he became reference assistant at Bristol University Library. He soon went to Durham University Library, where he remained until his retirement, becoming successively the first special cataloguer for older books, assistant librarian in charge of the separate Oriental Section, and, in 1958, keeper of Oriental books. In the twenty-three years of his service he built up the Library from a few shelves of books to a collection of national importance, numbering over 100,000 volumes and covering the entire Orient from its origins to the present day. It was his pride that there were few Oriental languages in the library with which he did not have some acquaintance, and none at all that he was not prepared to tackle, should the need arise. The same enthusiasm was displayed in his private researches. Many of his bibliographical researches found their way into J. D. Pearson's *Index Islamicus*, and into the various supplements by this writer. He was a valuable member of the Middle East Libraries Committee since its inception in 1966. He died on 16 or 17 September 1978. Diana Grimwood-Jones in *BRISMES bulletin* 6 i (1979), pp. 79-80; Private

Foster, John Webster, fl. 1952-1963, he was a technical director for water resources, Aero Service Ltd., Beirut, in 1963. His writings include *Groundwater geology of Lee and Whiteside Counties, Illinois* (1956). NUC, 1956-67

Foster, Kenelm, fl. 1952, his writings include *God's tree; essays on Dante and other matters* (1957), and *The two Dantes, and other stories* (1977), and he was joint translator of *Aristotle's De Anima ... and the commentary of St. Thomas Aquinas* (1951). LC

Foster, R., fl. 1838, he was a British naval captain and traveller in Arabia who surveyed the Aden peninsula in 1839. Henze

Foster, Sue Molleson, born at the end of the nineteenth century, she was a trained librarian and began her professional service in the New York Public Library, 1911-1922. She transferred to the Missionary Research Library, N.Y.C., in 1931 and remained there until 1935. She served in the adjacent and related Library of Union Theological Seminary from 1935 until her retirement in 1963. From 1932 to 1965 she prepared the survey of periodicals published quarterly in the *Muslim world*. She had a reading knowledge of French, German and Italian and was familiar with the library resources of N.Y.C. so that her service has been characterized by competence in stating simply and succinctly the gist of the articles. MW 55 (1965), p. 389

Foster, Sir William, born in 1863, he was educated at Cooper's Grammar School and the University of London. He joined the India Office in 1882, and was registrar and superintendent of records from 1907 to 1923. He served as honorary secretary to the Hakluyt Society, 1893-1902, and was a president of the Society from 1928 to 1945. His writings include *Early travels in India* (1921), *England's quest for eastern trade* (1933), and its translation, *England und der Orienthandel* (1939). He was the editor of several travel accounts as well as India Office lists. He died in 1951. Buckland; *Who was who*, 5

Fotheringham, John Knight, born in 1874, he was educated at London and Oxford, and was a student of the British School at Athens. He taught classics and ancient history at London. His writings include *Marco Sanudo, conqueror of the Archipelago* (1915). He died in 1936. DNB; *Who was who*, 3

Fotos, Evan, fl. 1955, he was a sometime instructor at Roberts College, Istanbul. Note

Foucart, George(s), born in 1865 or 1866 at Paris or Versailles, he was an Egyptologist, a professor at the Faculté des lettres, Aix-en-Provence, and later a director of l'Institut français du Caire from 1916 to 1927. According to the obituary presented by Étienne Drioton delivered during the session of l'Institut d'Égypte on Monday, 1 November 1943, he died "le 18 mai dernier." *Bulletin de l'Institut d'Égypte* 26 (1944), pp. 21-30; *Chronique d'Égypte* 21 (1946), pp. 81-88; DBF; Egyptology; *Revue archéologique* 36 (1950), pp. 103-106

de Foucaucourt, J. Baron, 1896-1939, his writings include *De l'Algérie au Soudan par le Sahara; 5000 kilomètres en automobile dans le désert et la brousse* (1928), and *Vingt mille lieues dans les airs; tour d'Europe, tour d'Afrique dans un petit avion de tourisme* (1938). NUC, pre-1956

Foucauld, Charles Eugène, vicomte de, Frère Marie Albéric, born 15 September 1858 at Strasbourg. After undisciplined school and army life, he explored Algeria and Morocco from June 1883 to May 1884 on his own account. He was ordained priest in 1901, and in 1905 he decided to devote himself to a solitary priesthood among the pagans and Muslims in the French Sahara, at the same time becoming an authority on Tuareg. His writings include *Reconnaissance au Maroc, 1883*-1884 (1888), *Écrits spirituels* (1923), *Meditations of a hermit* (1930), *L'Évangile présenté aux pauvres du Sahara* (1938), and *Dictionnaire touareg-français; dialecte de l'Ahaggar* (1952). He fell victim to marauders in Tamanrasset, Ahaggar Mountains, 1 December 1916. DBF; EncItaliana; GER; Henze; *Hommes et destins* II, pp. 310-321; *Index Islamicus* (4); NDBA; *Partisan review* 51 iv/52 i (1984/85), pp. 663-674; Peyronnet, p. 501

de **Fouchécour**, Charles-Henri, born 23 August 1925 at Séméac (Hautes-Pyrénées), he studied at the Sorbonne Nouvelle, where he received his doctorate in 1984. He was a sometime director of the Institut des études iraniennes, Paris. He was the driving force behind *Abstracta iranica* from its inception in 1978 until 1985. His writings include *La déscription de la nature dans la poésie lyrique persane du XIe siècle* (1969), *Éléments pour un manuel de persan* (1974), *Éléments de persan* (1981), *Moralia; les notions morales dans la littérature persane du 3e/9e au 7e/13e siècle* (1986), and he was joint editor of *Études irano-aryennes offertes à Gilbert Lazard* (1989). AnEIFr, 1997; EURAMES, 1993

Foucher, Alfred Charles Auguste, born 21 November 1865 at Lorient (Morbihan), he was educated at Paris and from 1888 to 1891 he was successively a professor at the lycées of Vendôme and Chartres. He became interested in the relations of India and ancient Greece and studied briefly at l'École des hautes études where he was awarded a three-year travel grant from the City of Paris. He went to the Orient and stayed predominantly at Kandahar and the Peshawar region from 1891 to 1894. Upon his return home in 1895, he received his diploma and became a lecturer at l'École des hautes études. Thereafter he became an archaeological traveller and administrator, partly in the service of the Ministère de l'Instruction publique. In 1922 he obtained the exclusive rights to French archaeological excavations for thirty years from the Afghan Government. In 1928 he was elected a member of the Académie des Inscriptions et belles-lettres, and in 1929 he resumed his teaching at the Sorbonne. His writings include *Sur la frontière indo-afghane* (1901). He died 21 March 1952. *Artibus Asiae* 15 iv (1952), pp. 348-351; DBF; *Hommes et destins*, vol. 4, pp. 140-141

Fougère, Louis, born 9 October 1915 at Paris, he studied at Lille, and was a technical adviser to the Moroccan Government, 1956 1959. In 1965 he was *maître des requêtes* at the Conseil d'État, Paris. He later served in missions to various African states from 1959 to 1960. His writings include *La fonction publique* (1966), its translation, *Civil service systems* (1967), and *Le Conseil d'État, son histoire ...*, *1799-1974* (1975). Unesco

Fougères, Gustave Adolphe François, born 24 April 1863 at Baume-les-Dames (Doubs), he was a classicist who studied at the École normale supérieure, Paris, followed by a research fellowship at l'École française d'Athènes in 1885. He spent the following year travelling on the coast of Asia Minor. After his return to France he became a lecturer in classical antiquities at Lille. Thereafter he taught classics at the Sorbonne in various capacities, interrupted only by his directorship of l'École d'Athènes from 1913 to 1919. In 1922, he was elected member of the Académie des inscriptions et belles-lettres. He died in Paris, 7 December 1927. DBF

Fouilloux, Gérard, fl. 1966, his writings include *La Nationalisation et le droit international public* (1962), and he was joint editor of *Recueil de textes relatifs au droit international de l'air et de l'espace* (1982-83). LC

Fouly, Mohamed M. el-, fl. 1973, he was an agronomist who edited the proceedings, *Agricultural health chemicals and their effects on ecological systems in Egypt* (1980), and *Role of potassium in crop production* (1980). LC

Fouquet, fl. 1927, he was a lieutenant in the Geographical Service of the French Army, and accompanied captain Duprez, commander of the Compagnie saharienne des Ajjers, on a reconnaissance of the Tummo Mountains region on the border of Niger, producing an invaluable map of this region. Peyronnet, 924

Fouquet, Daniel Marie, born 16 March 1850 at Doué-la-Fontaine (Maine-et-Loire). After the completion of his medical studies at Paris, he was successively an *assistant* at the Collège de France and l'École des Hautes-Études. He was resident in Cairo since 1881, where he practised medicine, and collected antiquities. His writings include *Contribution à l'étude de la céramique orientale* (1900), and *Collection du Dr. Fouquet du Caire* (1922). He died in Cairo in August 1914. Curinier, v. 5, p. 103; Egyptology

Fouquier, Achille Louis Alfred Gabriel, born 21 February 1817 at Rouen, he was a graduate of l'École des mines de Paris, and a prospector in Europe and the Middle East His writings include *Macédonie, Tunisie; anecdotes de voyages* (1879). He died about 1895. DBF; Oursel

Fourcade, Pascal Thomas, born 2 June 1768 at Pau (Pyrénées-Atlantiques), he was educated by the Jesuits and became a periodical editor with Jacobin leadings. In 1796, he applied for consular service in the Orient. He was first sent to Canea, Crete, but after Turkey declared war on France, he was interned and kept at Pera (Beyoğlu) until 1801. After his return to France, he was appointed consul-general at Sinope. He went there by way of Constantinople, where he stayed six months with the French ambassador, and arrived at his destination in the summer of 1803. He took his appointment seriously and, having learned Turkish, was in a position to further French interests owing to his good offices amongst administrative and commercial circles of the town. He had broad interests and on his extensive travels identified many ancient sites. He was serious wounded by marauders at Sinope on 11 December 1807. After a year's recuperation he left Sinope on 17 February 1809, and, travelling by way of the Crimea and central Europe, he returned to Paris in the spring of 1809. In the summer of the following year he was elected a corresponding member of the Académie des Inscriptions et belles-lettres. Six months later he was appointed consul-general at Thessaloniki, where he arrived in April of 1813. He died on 11 September 1813. DBF; Michaud

Fourchault, Alexandre Edmond Constant, born 19 August 1817 at Orléans, he attended military schools and colleges but was repeatedly expelled for reprehensible conduct, and his promotion to officer deferred. He saw his first overseas service in Algeria in 1853; in 1855, he participated in the Crimean campaign. Interrupted only by the Franco-Prussian war, he then served in Algeria from 1856 to 1877, when he resigned with the rank of colonel, disappointed not having been promoted general. In his retirement he began medical studies. He died from tetanus, 10 April 1884. DBF

Foureau, Fernand, born 17 October 1850 at Saint-Barbant (Hte-Vienne). From 1876 to 1877 he set out on his first exploration of the Algerian Sahara together with Louis Say. In the course of his travels in southern Algeria during the following two years, he, together with F. Fau and A. Foureau, founded the Compagnie de l'Oued Rirh for the cultivation of date palms, the drilling of artesian wells, and the establishment of new oases. It was in the vicinity of Biskra that he learned Arabic and the Berber dialects, and became familiar with the ways of the desert. From 1882 to 1897 he made nine explorations in the territory between Touggourt, El Goléa, and Ghadamès; however, since he did not share the illusions of Duveyrier and Flatters regarding the favourable character of the Touareg, he travelled slowly, with great caution, on camel back, and almost solidary, accompanied only by some Chambaa guides. His 1898 to 1900 mission to the Sahara became known as the Mission Foureau-Lamy. His writings include *Ma mission de 1893-1894 chez les Touareg Azdjer* (1894). He died 17 January 1914. Curinier, v. 3 (1901), pp. 298-299; DBF; EncBrit; EncicUni; EncItaliana; Henze; Meyers; RNL

Fourgous, Jean, fl. 1927, he obtained a doctorate in law and wrote *L'Arbitrage dans le droit français au XII et XIV siècle* (Paris, 1906). NUC, pre-1956

Fourmestraux, Eugène, born in 1815 at Lille. Shortly after the conquest of Alger, he went to Algeria as a military accountant, advancing to the position of deputy paymaster. He later entered the civilian administration and became secretary-general of the Préfecture d'Alger. He retired in 1880. His writings include *L'instruction publique en Algérie* (1880), and *Les budgets de l'Algérie et de la Tunisie* (1882). DBF

Fourmont, Étienne, born 23 June 1683 at the seigniorial estate Herblay (Val-d'Oise). An orphant since childhood, he grew up at his uncle's who wanted him to take orders. At the Séminaire des Trente-trois, he learned Greek, Hebrew, and Arabic, but in the end, he abandoned a clerical career and, in 1713, he was admitted to the Académie des Inscriptions et belles-lettres. Two years later he succeeded Antoine Galland in the chair of Arabic at the Collège de France, to which the chair of Hebrew became to be added, but his lasting reputation is based on his later studies in Chinese linguistics. He died 18 December 1745. Casanova; DBF; DcBiPP; Egyptology; IndexBFr² (5)

Fournel, Marc, fl. 1887, his writings include *La Tunisie; le christianisme et l'islam dans l'Afrique septentrionale* (1886), and *La Tripolitaine; les routes du Soudan* (1887). BN

Fournel, Marie Jérôme Henri, born 25 January 1799 at Paris, he started to train as a painter, but later studied at the Polytechnique, followed by l'École des mines. After extensive geological explorations on foot in France, Switzerland, and Italy, he became a mining engineer in 1822. In Paris, he became involved in the Société saint-simonienne, and when B. P. Enfantin was obliged to leave France, he accompanied him to Egypt. There he submitted plans for building a canal at the Isthmus of Suez, a project which, although approved of by Muhammad Ali, was rejected on pressure from the British. After his return to France he became estranged from the Saint Simonians. He turned to prospecting, with an interest in railways. In the service of the Ministère de la guerre he went on a mineralogical mission to Algeria in 1843. His writings include *Richesse minérale de l'Algérie* (1849), *Étude sur la conquête de l'Afrique par les Arabes, et recherches sur les tribus berbères qui ont occupé le Maghreb* *central* (1857), and *Les Berbères; étude sur la conquête de l'Afrique par les Arabes, d'après les textes arabes imprimés* (1875-81). He died in Blois, 21 July 1876. DBF; Vapereau

Fournier, Eugène Yves Antoine Marie, born 28 December 1871 at Saint-Brieuc (Nord), he studied natural sciences at Paris and Marseille, and became attached to the Carte géologique de France in 1894. After obtaining his diploma in the summer of the same year, he was awarded a travel grant to study the geology of the Caucasus. Upon his return in 1896, he submitted his thesis, *Description géologique du Caucase central.* He successively taught geology and mineralogy, held a chair, and was dean, at Besançon, interrupted only by war-time service. He died in 1941. DBF; *Qui êtes-vous,* 1924

Fournier, Joseph Xavier, born 4 July 1872 at Marseille, he studied law at Aix-en-Provence and then joined the Archives départementales des Bouches-du-Rhône as assistant archivist. Thereafter he became archivist of the Chambre de commerce de Marseille, head of its historical service, and secretary of the Société de géographie de Marseille. In 1911, he was elected member of the Académie de Marseille, in 1920, awarded *chevalier* of the Légion d'honneur, and in 1941 became permanent secretary of his Académie. His writings include *La Chambre de commerce de Marseille* (1920). He died in Marseille, 16 April 1949. DBF

Fournier de Flaix, Ernest Jacques, born 13 November 1824 at Bordeaux. After completing his studies, he had a brief career as a contributor to various journals. In 1867 he established the short-lived journal, *le Précurseur,* at Bordeaux. Thereafter he went to Paris as a contributor to *Journal des économistes* and *Nouvelle revue.* In 1882, he founded *Revue de la finance* which in the following year changed its title to *Revue des banques.* In 1891, prior to the conclusion of the Franco-Russian political-economic agreements, he was sent on an economic fact-finding mission to Russia. He returned to France by way of the Ottoman Empire and Germany. His writings include *Études économiques et financières* (1883), and *L'Indépendance de l'Égypte et le régime international du canal de Suez* (1883). He died in Sèvres (Hauts-de-Seine), 13 April 1904. DBF

Fournier-Lefort, J., fl. 1892-1907, he was an editor of the *Revue forézienne* and *Revue du Sud-est,* as well as author of the pamphlet, *Le Paix universelle* (Paris, 1911). NUC, pre-1956

Fournol, Étienne Maurice, born 16 June 1871 at Saint Affrique (Aveyron), he received a doctorate in 1896 from the Université de Paris for his thesis, *Bodin, prédécesseur de Montesquieu.* He became an administrator at the Ministère des Travaux publics, and was elected a *député* in 1909. His writings include *Les Volets du diptyque* (1920), *Le Moderne Plutarque* (1923), and *Manuel de politique française* (1933). IndexBFr² (1); NUC, pre-1956

Fourtau, René, born 19th cent., his writings include *Calatogue des invertébrés fossiles de l'Égypte, représentés dans les collections du Geological Museum au Caire* (1913). NUC, pre-1956

de **Foville**, Alfred, born 26 December 1842 at Paris. After the École polytechnique he worked for a year in Rouen as an *élève-ingénieur télégraphiste* before continuing his studies at the Faculté de droit de Paris, École des chartes, and École des beaux-arts. Thereafter he entered the civil service and advanced to become head of the Bureau de statistique at the ministry of finance. Since 1878 he was a lecturer in statistics and economic geography at l'École des sciences politiques, where he held the chair of public finance since 1880. In 1893, he became head of the Direction des monnaies et médailles, and in 1909, permanent secretary to Georges Picot. Since 1896 he was a member of the Académie des sciences morales et politiques. His writings include *La transformation des moyens de transport et ses conséquences économiques et sociales* (1880), a work which received an award from the Académie des sciences morales et politiques, and *La monnaie* (1907). He died 14 May 1913. DBF

Fowle, James Luther, born 29 December 1847 at Woburn, Mass., he was a graduate of Amherst College and Andover Seminary. Together with his wife, Caroline Farnsworth, he went to Turkey under the American Board of Commissioners for Foreign Missions in 1878, and was assigned to Cesarea in 1885. Having acquired an excellent command of both written and colloquial Turkish, he became well acquainted with the ways and thoughts of all classes of people in his field. During his service of thirty-three years he saw the organization of a good number of evangelical Armenian and Greek Churches. He returned home in June 1911 and died in Newton, Mass., 16 May 1917. *Missionary herald* 113 (1917), pp. 319-320

Fowle, Sir Trenchard Craven William, born in 1884, he devoted most of his life to the Orient. He spent over thirty years in India, Persia, Aden, and Iraq, and for the last ten years he served in the Persian Gulf, first as political agent, Muscat, and from 1932 as political resident at Bushire. He retired in 1939 with the rank of lieutenant-colonel. He was created C.B.E. in 1929 and K.C.I.E. in 1937. His writings include *Travels in the Middle East* (1916). He died 23 February 1940. *Journal of the Royal Central Asian Society* 27 (July 1940), p. 382; *Who was who,* 3

Fowler, Gary Lane, born in 1934, he received a Ph.D. in 1969 from Syracuse University for his thesis, *Italian agricultural colonization in Tripolitania*, an Arabic translation of which was published in 1988. In 1999, he was a professor of anthropology and geography at the University of Illinois, Chicago. His writings include *Appalachian migration* (1980). NatFacDr, 1999; Selim

Fowler, Sir John, born in 1817 in England, he was created K.C.M.G. for services in Egypt and the Sudan. He died in Bournemouth in 1898 or 1899. CelCen; DcBiPP; DNB; Egyptology; Hill; *Who was who*, 1

Fox, Gertrude Lillian, born 28 July 1922 at Cambridge, Mass., she was a trained librarian who started her career as a cataloguer at Brown University, Providence, R.I., in 1944. In 1964, she went to State College, Salem, Mass. WhoAmW, 1974/75

Fox, Marshall N., born 19th cent., he edited Robert J. Davidson's *Life in West China* (1905). His trace is lost after a publication in 1917. BLC

Fox, Samuel Ethan, born in 1954, he received a Ph.D. in 1982 from the University of Chicago for his thesis, *The structure of the morphology of Cairene Arabic*. His writings include *CLS book of squibs; cumulative index, 1968-1977* (1977). LC; Selim²

Foy, Karl Arthur Philipp Heinrich, born 17 November 1856 at Ludwigslust, Germany, he studied modern languages at first but soon changed to classics at the Universität Leipzig where he received a Dr.phil. in 1879 for his thesis, *Studien zur Lautlehre des Vulgärgriechischen*. He was a some-time professor of Turkology. His writings include *Lieder vom Goldenen Horn* (1888). He died in 1907. NUC, pre-1956; Thesis

Fozilov, Ergash Ismailovich, 1933- see Fazylov, Ergash Ismailovich

Fozilov, M. see Fazylov, Mulladzhan F.

Fraas, Oskar Friedrich von, born 17 January 1821 at Loch, Germany, he was a trained theologian who had concurrently studied palaeontology and geology. In 1851, he was appointed keeper of the mineralogical and palaeontological collections at Stuttgart. He made extensive scientific explorations in Egypt, Arabia, and Lebanon. His writings include *Aus dem Orient* (1867), and *Drei Monate am Libanon* (1876). He died in Stuttgart, 22 November 1897. DtBE; Embacher; Henze

Frade Merino, Ferdando, born in 1917, his writings include *Sectas y movimientos de reforma en el islam* (Tetuán, (1952), *Compendio de religion musulman* (Tetuán, 1955), and *El islam y su cuna* (1981). LC

Fradejas Lebrero, José, born 20th cent., his writings include *La calle de Toledo* (1954), *Ceuta en la literatura* (1961), and he was editor of *Sendebar; libro de los engaños de las mujeres* (1981), and *Novela corta del siglo XVI* (1985). LC

Fraehn, Christian Martin, 1782-1851 see Frähn, Christian Martin Joachim

Fraenkel, Adolf Abraham Halevy, born 17 February 1891 at München, he studied at München, Marburg, Berlin, and Breslau. He was a mathematician and taught successively at Marburg and Kiel, and from 1921 to 1959 at the Hebrew University, Jerusalem. He died in Jerusalem, 15 October 1967. BioIn, 7; ConAu, 159; DcScB; DtBE; WhoIsrael, 1956, 1958; WhoWorJ, 1965

Fraenkel, Gerd, born 25 December 1919 at Frankfurt, Germany, he was educated at Jerusalem and received a Ph.D. in 1962 from Indiana University for his thesis, *A generative grammar of Azerbaijani*. He was a professor of linguistics in the United States. His writings include *Israel* (1963), *What is language?* (1965), *Writing systems* (1965), *Language in culture* (1967), and *Languages of the world* (1967). He died in 1970. ConAu, 1-P; 11-12

Fraenkel, Leo, fl. 1964, he was a sometime director, American Friends of the Middle East, Morocco.

Fraenkel, Siegmund, born 7 April 1855 at Frankfurt/Oder, he studied Semitic languages at Leipzig, Berlin, and Straßburg, and received a Dr.phil. in 1877 from the Universität Straßburg for his thesis, *Beiträge zur Erklärung der mehrlautigen Bildungen im Arabischen*. He obtained his Dr.habil. in 1880 from the Universität Breslau for his thesis, *De vocabulis in antiquis Arabum carminibus et in Corano peregrinis*. From 1886 to his retirement he was a professor of Semitic languages at Breslau. His writings include *Aramäische Fremdwörter im Arabischen* (1886). He died in Breslau, 11 June 1909. DtBE; Fück, p. 243; JüdLex; Schwarz

Fragistas (Φραγκίστας), Charalampos Nikolaou, 1905- see Phrankistas, Charalampos Nikolaou

Fragner, Bert Georg, born 27 November 1941 at Wien. After studies at the universities of Wien and Tehran, he obtained a Dr.phil. in 1970 from the Universität Wien for his thesis, *Geschichte der Stadt*

Hamadan und ihrer Umgebung. He repeatedly carried on field-work in Iran and Central Asia. For six years each, he was professor of economic and cultural history of Iran and Central Asia at the universities of Freiburg i. Br. and Berlin, before becoming chairman of the Seminar für Iranistik in the Universität Bamberg in 1989, a post which he held until his retirement. His writings include *Persische Memoirenliteratur als Quelle zur neuesten Geschichte Irans* (1979), *Repertorium persischer Herrscherurkunden* (1980). Kürschner, 1980-2003; Schoeberlein

Fragnito, Gigliola, fl. 1979, her writings include *Memoria individuale e costruzione biografica: Becadelli, Della Casa, Vettori* (1978). LC

de **Fraguier**, Gabriel, born 15 June 1904, he was a French military officer who served seventeen years overseas, with Kurdish units in Syria and later in the Régiment étranger de Cavalerie in southern Tunisia. After completing a course at the Affairs Indigènes d'Alger in 1933, he was posted to the Companie Saharienne de la Saoura, where he participated in the operations in southern Morocco from 1933 to 1934. For his conduct in this campaign he was awarded the *Croix de Chevalier* of the Légion d'honneur. He had another spell of duty in the Sahara from 1938 to 1949, when he successively headed the post of the Affairs Indigènes at Beni-Abbès and the annexes of El Oued, Géryville, and Touat. He distinguished himself particularly in the disastrous winter of 1946 when he assured the economic survival of the nomadic population of Géryville. In 1948, he joined the Centre des Hautes Études d'Administration Musulmane, Paris, as a Saharan specialist. In the following year, he became head of the general staff of the Inspection des Territoires du Sud, and, in 1952, director of the curriculum of the Affairs Indigènes d'Alger. He soon ran into the incomprehensibility of the administrative authorities regarding his views on the social and economic transformation of the Sahara. Rather than compromising on what he considered consonant with realities and the interests of the Saharan population, he resigned from active service with profound regrets. He remained in the reserves with the rank of lieutenant-colonel, and died 23 March 1963. *L'Afrique et l'Asie* n° 63 (1963), pp. 74-75

Frähn (Френ), Christian Martin Joachim, born 4 June 1782 at Rostock, Germany, he studied Oriental languages at Rostock. After he obtained a doctorate, he was offered the chair of Arabic at the University of Kazan. He remained for ten years, teaching Arabic, Persian, and Turkish, conducting numismatic researches at the same time. In 1818, he was offered the directorship of the Asiatic Museum, St. Petersburg. He remained there until his death on 28 August 1851. During his St. Petersburg years he specialized in Russian history, based on Arabic sources. His writings include *Beiträge zur muhammedanischen Münzkunde aus St. Petersburg* (1818), *De musei Sprewitziani mosquæ numis Kuficis nonullis ante hac ineditis* (1825), *Die Münzen der Chane von Ulus Dschutschi's* (1832), and *Adnotationes in varia opera numismatica, edidit B. Dorn* (1877). BibibSOT, pp. 279-281; CelCen; DcBiPP; DtBE; EncBrit; GdeEnc; GSE; Krachkovskii, 72-74

Fraisse, André, born 31 May 1909 at Saint-Chamond (Loire), he was a colonial administrator, particularly in the Far East. After the war, he served in French Africa, where he was the last commander of the Cercle Français at Nioro-du-Sahel in the French Sudan. His writings include *Trames entrecroisées; roman* (1954), and *Marche dans les solitudes; roman* (1955). He died in 1987. Hommes et destins, vol. 8, pp. 150-151

Frajese, Attilio, born 11 November 1902 at Roma, he was a sometime professor of mathematics at the Università di Roma. His writings include *Attraverso la storia della matematica* (1949), *La matematica nel mondo antico* (1951), and *Platone e la matematica nel mondo antico* (1963). Chi è, 1961; Wholtaly, 1958

Frajzyngier, Zygmunt, born 3 April 1938 at Radom, Poland, he was educated at Uniwersytet Warszawa, where he received a doctorate, and at the University of Ghana, where he received an M.A. in 1965. He taught briefly at Ahmadu Bello University, Kano, before being appointed professor of linguistics at the University of Colorado, Boulder, in 1982, a position which he still held in 1995. His writings include *A Pero-English and English-Pero vocabulary* (1985). DrAS, 1982; NatFacDr, 1995

Frame, John Davidson, M.D., fl. 1927, he spent twenty-one years at Rasht, Persia, as a medical missionary under the Board of Foreign Missions of the Presbyterian Church in the U.S.A. His writings include *Dr. Dawood* (1951), and *Personality; development in the Christian life* (1961). LC

Franc, Julien, fl. 1934, he received a *doctorat ès lettres* in 1928 from the Université de Paris for his thesis, *L'Histoire de la colonisation de l'Algérie*. He was a sometime *professeur* at the Lycée d'Alger. His writings include *La Colonisation de la Mitidja* (1928).

France, John, born 20th cent., he was in 1994 a senior lecturer at University College, Swansea. His writings include *Victory in the East; a military history of the first crusade* (1994). LC

Franceschini, Ezio, born 25 July 1906 at Vill'Agnedo (Trento), he was a medievalist successively at the universities of Milano and Padova. His writings include *Studi e note di filologia latina medievale* (1938), and *Leggenda minore di S. Caterina da Siena* (1942). He died 21 March 1983. Chi è, 1948; LC

Franchet d'Espérey, Louis Félix Marie François, born 25 May 1856 at Mostaganem, Algeria, he was a graduate of Saint-Cyr and l'École de guerre. He served in North Africa in 1876 and 1912. After the war, he was commander of the allied occupation force at Constantinople, and later was made inspector-general in North Africa. He retired with the rank of *maréchal de France*. In 1934 he was elected member of the Académie française. A. L. Grasset and P. J. L. Azan wrote his biography in 1920 and 1949 respectively. He died in 1942. DBF; EncAm; *Hommes et destins*, v. 1, pp. 246-250

Franchini, Jean, born 19th cent., he originated from Chios, Argean Sea, and studied at the Séminaire oriental Saint François Xavier in the Université Saint-Joseph, Beirut. In 1914 he was a Roman Catholic priest at Chios. Note

de **Franciosi**, Charles Marie Xavier, born 23 December 1846 at Pérenchies (Nord), he joined the French army in 1870 and advanced through the grades to become a lieutenant. He served in Tunisia from 1881 to 1887, and in Algeria in 1889. He was generally employed in topographical works. Lamathière

Francis, Raymond Iskandar, fl. 1973, his writings include *Taha Hussein, romancier* (1945). LC

Francis, Richard M., he was in 1973 a lecturer at the Department of International Politics, Aberystwyth.

Franck, Adolphe, born 9 October 1809 at Liocourt (Moselle). After rabbinical education at Alaincourt, he studied medicine, but changed to philosophy after 1830, when universities opened their doors also to non-Catholics. He was a professor of philosophy at Douai, Nancy, and the Sorbonne, and in 1854 accepted a chair at the Collège de France. He was an indefatigable worker and did not retire until he was senventy-eight years old. His writings include *Études orientales* (1861), *Philosophie et religion* (1867), *Philosophie et droit civil* (1886), and its translation, *Felsefe-i hukuk-ı medeniye* (1917). He died in Paris, 11 April 1893. BiD&DS; DBF; EncJud; Master (1); Meyers; Özege #5468; Vapereau; Wininger

Franck, Dorothea née Seelye, married to Peter G. Franck in 1944, she received a Ph.D. in 1919 from Columbia University for her thesis, *Moslem schisms and sects, being the history of the various philosophic systems developed in Islam*. She worked until 1948 in the U.S. Department of State's cultural program, first handling the exchange of professors and specialists with the Middle East, and later serving as head of the Education Unit in the Division of Exchange of Persons. Her writings include the pamphlet, *In the minds of men* (1946), and together with her husband she published *Implementation of technical assistance* (1951), she edited *Islam in the modern world; a series of addresses* (1951). LC; *Middle East journal*, 1950; Selim, 1883-1968, #783

Franck, Peter Goswyn, born 11 December 1913 at Berlin, he studied at Berlin, Basel, and received a Ph.D. in 1954 from the University of California. He was a sometime economic adviser to the Government of Afghanistan and a professor of economics at Robert College, Istanbul, from 1956 to 1966, when he was appointed a professor at the College of Business Administration, Syracuse University, N.Y. His writings include *Obtaining financial aid for a development plan* (1954), and *Afghanistan between East and West* (1960). AmM&WS, 1973

Franck, Thomas Martin, born 14 July 1931 at Berlin, he was a graduate of the University of British Columbia. He was appointed professor of law at the School of Law, New York University in 1960, a position which he still held in 1999. Concurrently he held innumerable related academic and professional positions. His writings include *Race and nationalism* (1960), and *Fairness in international law and institutions* (1995). BlueB, 1973/74, 1975, 1976; ConAu, 33-36; DrAS, 1974, 1978, 1982; NatFacDr, 1995-1999; WhoAm, 1980-1999; WhoAmL, 1983-1988/89; Unesco; WrDr, 1982/84-1998/2000

Francke, August *Hermann*, born 5 November 1870 at Gnadenfrei, Germany, he was a teacher at a missionary school in Saxony, before went to Fairfield, England, to attend a missionary school in preparation for his assigment in the Moravian Mission. In 1896 he went out to the western Himalayas to serve for fourteen years as a missionary. After the war, he worked on manuscripts at Göttingen. In 1925 he was appointed an associate professor at Berlin, even though he had never studied and had not gained a degree. His writings include *A history of western Tibet* (1907), *Antiquities of Indian Tibet* (1914), *Durch Zentralasien in die indische Gefangenschaft* (1921), and *Geistesleben in Tibet* (1925). He died 16 February 1930. GV, NUC, pre-1956; Stache-Rosen, pp. 173-175

Francklin, William, born in 1763. After Trinity College, Cambridge, he served in the East India Company from 1782 until his retirement in 1825 with the rank of lieutenant-colonel. He also enjoyed considerable reputation as an oriental scholar. During his tour of Persia in 1786 he lived for eight months with a Persian family, and was thus enabled to communicate a fuller account of the manners of the people than had before appeared. His writings include *Observations made on a tour from Bengal to Persia in the years 1786-87* (1790), *The History of the reign of Shah Allum* (1798), and its translation, *Geschichte Shah Allums, Kaisers von Hindostan* (1800). He died in 1839. Buckland; DNB; Henze

de **Franclieu**, E., he was president of the jury set up for the Exposition agricole d'Alger in 1851.

Franco, Moïse (Moses), born in 1864 at Constantinople, he studied at the École normale orientale israélite, Paris, and became an historian and a schoolmaster in the employ of the Alliance Israélite Universelle. He was a principal of several Jewish schools in the Middle East, established the Jewish school at Safed, Palestine, and was schoolmaster of the A.I.U. schools in Shumla, Bulgaria, and Gallipoli, Turkey. His writings include *Essai sur l'histoire des Israélites de l'Empire ottoman depuis les origines à nos jours* (1897). He died in Gallipoli, in 1910. Encyclopædia Judaica, 1930; Jewish encyclopedia, 1903; JüdLex; Wininger

Franco Sanchez, Francisco, born 20th cent., he was in 1992 affiliated with the División de Estudios Árabes e Islámicos in the Universidad de Alicante. His writings are said to include *Muhammad Aš-Šafra* (1990). Arabismo, 1992

François, A., born 19th cent., he was a French naval lieutenant who in the spring of 1877 accompanied the French minister plenipotentiary de Vernouillet on his journey from Tanger by way of Larache to Fès. Henze

François, Georges Alphonse Florent Octave, born in 1874, he received a doctorate in 1900 from the Faculté de droit de Paris for his thesis, *Le budget local des colonies.* He was a sometime *sous-chef* at the Ministère des Colonies. His writings include *Finances coloniales* (1903), *Notre colonie du Dahomey, sa formation, son développement, son avenir* (1906), *L'Afrique Occidentale française* (1907), and *Le Gouvernement général de l'Afrique occidentale française* (1908). BN; NUC, pre-1956

François, Roger Marceau, born 9 March 1901 at Nancy, he was a chemical engineer who had received a doctorate. He conducted carbo-chemical as well as petrochemical research and from 1925 to 1939 accomplished innumerable scientific and industrial study missions the world over. He held executive positions in related industrial enterprises at home and abroad. WhoFr, 1965/66-1971/72

Francolini, Bruno, born 23 April 1903 at Firenze, he was a colonial administrator in Italian East Africa, 1929-1935, and concurrently from 1931 to 1933, director of *Corriere della Somalia.* He later became a professor of colonial geography successively at Napoli and Firenze. His writings include *Africa bianca; panorami fra Mediterraneo e Sahara* (1932), *Africa d'oggi* (1937), *Il lavoro italiano in Tunisia* (1939), *Bianchi e neri in Africa* (1944), *Corso di geografia; l'Africa* (1953), *Il Medio Oriente; profilo geo-politico* (1958), and *Nuovi mondi afro-asiatici* (1964). Chi è, 1948, 1957, 1961; Chi scrive; Vaccaro; Wholtaly, 1958

Françon, André, fl. 1969, his writings include *La Propriété littéraire et artistique en Grande-Bretagne et aux États-Unis* (1955), and he was editor of *Les Correspondances inédites; conference* (1984). LC

Franda, Marcus Francis, born 16 August 1937 at Nassawaupee, Wisc., he was a graduate of Beloit College, and held several prestigeous fellowships before he received his Ph.D. in 1966 for his thesis, *The federalizing process in India.* He was for many years a political scientist at Colgate University, Hamilton, N.Y., and thereafter a director, Institute of World Affairs, Salisbury, Conn. Throughout the better part of the 1990s he was a professor at the Department of Government and Politics, College Park, Md. His writings include *Political development and political decay in Bengal* (1971), and *Radical politics in West Bengal* (1971). AmM&WS, 1973, 1978; ConAu, 21-24, new rev., 9; NatFacDr, 1995-1999; WhoE, 1983-1989; WrDr, 1976/78-1984/86

Frandon, Ida Marie, fl. 1963, her writings include *L'Orient de Maurice Barrès* (1952), *"Assassins" et "Danseurs mystiques" dans Une enquête aux pays du Levant de Maurice Barrès* (1954), *Barrès précurseur* (1983), and she was editor of *Un homme libre, Maurice Barrès; presenté* (1988). LC

Frangi, Abdallah, born in 1943 at Beersheba, Palestine, he was resident in Germany from the early 1960s and studied political science and medicine at the Universität Frankfurt, but without taking a degree. After the terrorist attack on the 1972 Olympic games in München, he was exiled, but returned soon thereafter and became a public relations manager for the Palestine Liberation Organization in Bonn, a position which he held for over twenty years. His writings include *PLO und Palästina* (1982). Tagesspiegel, Berlin, no. 14716, 24 Oktober 1993

Frangipani, Agenore, his writings include *L'equivoco abissino* (Milano, 1936). NUC, pre-1956

Frank, Carl, born 7 February 1881 at Nürnberg, he received a Dr.phil. in 1906 from the Universität Leipzig for *Bilder und Symbole babylonisch-assyrischer Götter.* He was a professor of Assyriology at the Universität Straßburg until 1918, and thereafter, at Berlin. His writings include *Türkische Erzähler, übersetzt mit Einleitung* (1920). He died 2 November 1945. Kürschner, 1925-1940/41; NUC, pre-1956

Frank, Helmut, born 15 April 1912 at Berlin, he studied at the universities of Berlin and Bonn, where he received a Dr.phil. in 1936 for his thesis, *Mischna mit arabischen Glossen; Leningrader Fragment Nr. 262*. In 1937, he was ordained rabbi and served a community in Worms until 1939, when he emigrated to the U.S.A. He was an East coast rabbi until 1973. DtBilnd (1); Schwarz

Frank, Josef, born 30 June 1881 at Regensburg, Germany, he studied at München and Erlangen and thereafter was a professor of experimental physics at the Technische Hochschule München. He was joint author of *Ein Astrolab aus dem indischen Mogulreiche* (1925). He died in Freising, 27 January 1953. DtBE; Kürschner, 1931-1950

Frank, Lewis Allen, born 16 January 1938 at Silver City, N.Mex., he completed his studies at U.C.L.A. with an M.A., specializing in Soviet affairs. He was a sometime consultant on military-political decision-making. His writings include *Arms trade in international relations* (1969), and *Soviet nuclear planning* (1977). AmM&WS, 1973, 1978

Frank, Richard Martin, born 12 December 1927 at Louisville, Ky., he was a graduate of the Catholic University of America, Washington, D.C., where he received a Ph.D. in 1959 for his thesis, *The Jeremias of Pethion ibn Ayyûb al-Sahhâr*. He later served as a professor of Semitic and Egyptian languages and literatures at his alma mater. His writings include *Beings and their attributes; the teaching of the Basrian School of the Mu'tazila* (1978), *Creation and the cosmic system; al-Ghazâlî & Avicenna* (1992), and *Al-Ghazali and the Ash'arite School* (1994). DrAS, 1974, 1978, 1982; Selim

Frank-Kamentskii, Izrail' Grigor'evich, born 13 February 1880 at Vilna (Vilnius), Russia, he studied at Leipzig, Berlin, Göttingen, and Königsberg, where he received a Dr.phil. in 1911 for his thesis, *Untersuchungen über das Verhältnis der dem Umajja b. Ali 's-Salt zugeschriebenen Gedichte zum Koran*. His writings include Памятники египетской религии в фиванский период (1917). He died in Vilna, 4 April 1937. Miliband; Miliband²; NUC, pre-1956; Schwarz

Franke, Alwin Wilhelm *Otto*, born 27 September 1863 at Gernrode, Germany, he studied at several German universities and received a doctorate in 1884 for an Indological thesis. Thereafter he specialized in Chinese studies and was in the diplomatic service as an interpreter at Peking, Tientsin, and Shanghai. In 1909 he was appointed to the newly created chair of Chinese at the Kolonialinstitut, Hamburg. From 1923 to 1931 he was a professor at Berlin. His writings include *Beiträge aus chinesischen Quelle zur Kenntnis der Türkvölker und Skythen Zentralasiens* (1904), *Geschichte des Chinesischen Reiches* (1932-52), and *Erinnerungen aus zwei Welten* (1954). He died in Berlin 5 August 1946. DtBE; Kürschner, 1915-1940/41

Franke, Elisabeth, 1886-1931, her writings include *Hinter dem Schleier; ein Schrei der Not aus der mohammedanischen Frauenwelt* (Frankfurt a. M., 1908), as well as contributions to *Missionspädagogische Blätter* and *Moslem world*. N.Y.P.L.

Franke, Herbert, born 27 September 1914 at Köln, he studied at Köln, Bonn, and Berlin, and received doctorates in law and philosophy. He was a professor of East Asian studies at the Universität München from 1952 until his retirement. From 1960 to 1965 he was an editor of the *Zeitschrift der Deutschen Morgenländischen Gesellschaft*. His writings include *Geld und Wirtschaft in China unter der Mongolen-Herrschaft* (1949), and *Sinologie* (1953). IntWW, 1972/73-1996/97; Kürschner, 1954-2003

Frankel, Joseph, born 30 May 1913 at Lwów, Galicia, he was a graduate of the University of Lwów, and received a Ph.D. from the University of London in 1950. He taught at London and Aberdeen, before being appointed a professor of politics at the University of Southampton, 1962-1978. His writings include *The Making of foreign policy* (1963), and *International relations in a changing world* (1979). He died 13 January 1989. Au&Wr, 1971; ConAu, 5-8, 3 new rev.; IntAu&W, 1976, 1977, 1982; Who, 1972-1988; *Who was who*, 8; WrDr, 1976/78-1990/92

Frankel, Zacharias, born 30 September 1801 at Prag, he was a rabbi in Bohemia and Germany, editor of the *Zeitschrift für die religiösen Interessen des Judentums*, 1844-1846, and the founder of the *Monatsschrift für Geschichte und Wissenschaft des Judentums*. Since 1854 he was director of the Jüdisch-Theologisches Seminar, Breslau, where he died 13 February 1875. DtBE; EncJud; Vapereau; Wininger

Frankenberg, Hermann Julius *Wilhelm*, born 18 October 1868 at Kassel, he studied theology at the Universität Marburg, where he received a doctorate in 1895 for his thesis, *Die Composition des deuteronomischen Richterbuches*. He was a pastor, and the editor of *Abhandlung zur semitischen*

558

Religionskunde und Sprachwissenschaft (1918), and *Die syrischen Clementinen mit griechischem Paralleltext* (1937). DtBilnd (1)

von **Frankenberg und Proschlitz**, Werner E. V. E., born 19th cent., he was an officer in the German general staff and retired with the rank of major-general. *Wer ist's,* 1905-1912

Frankfurter, Felix, born 15 November 1882 at Wien, he came to the U.S.A. in 1894. After graduating at N.Y.C., he studied at Harvard and Oxford to become a professor at Harvard from 1914 to 1939, when he became an associate justice of the U.S. Supreme Court until his retirement in 1962. He died in Washington, D.C., 22 February 1965. CnDiAmJBi; ConAu, 124; DAB, 7; EncJud; NYT, 23 February 1965, p. 1, col. 6, p. 26, col. 1; WhAm, 4; WhoWorJ, 1965; Wininger, Suppl

Frankl, Pinkus (Pinkas) Friedrich (Fritz), born 28 February 1848 at Ungarisch-Brod, Moravia, he was privately educated and studied at the Jüdische-theologisches Seminar, Breslau, and the Universität Halle, where he received a Dr.phil. in 1871 for his thesis, *Beiträge zur Kunde des "Galam" und der muslimischen Secten.* In 1877 he accepted the invitation to become rabbi in Berlin. His writings include *Ein mutazilitischer Kalâm aus dem X. Jahrhundert, als Beitrag zur Geschichte der moslemischen Religionsphilosophie* (1872), and *Studien über die Septuaginta und Peschito zu Jeremia* (1873). He died in Johannisbad, 22 August 1887 (or 23 July 1885). ADtB; DtBE; EncJud; *Jewish encyclopedia*; JüdLex; ÖBL; Wininger

Frankl, Theodor, Dr. med., Dr. phil., he was in 1930 resident in Prag. His writings include *Die Anatomie der Araber* (1930), and *Die Entstehung des Menschen nach dem Koran* (1930). LC

Frankl Ritter von **Hochwart**, Ludwig August, born 3 February 1810 at Chrast, Bohemia, he studied medicine at Padova and Wien. In 1838 he became a secretary of the Jüdische Kultusgemeinde, Wien, whose directorship he assumed some years later. He was the founder of the literary journal, *Sonntags-Blätter.* He visited Palestine and Egypt. His writings include *Libanon; ein poetisches Familienbuch* (1855), and *Nach Jerusalem*: (1) Griechenland, Kleinasien, Syrien. (2) Palästina. (3) Aus Egypten (1860). He died in Wien, 12 March 1894. ADtB, vol. 48; BiD&SB; Meyers; ÖBL; Vapereau, 1863; Wininger

Frankle, Eleanor, born in 1943 at N.Y.C., she was a graduate of New York University and received a Ph.D. in 1948 from Columbia University for her thesis, *Word formation in the Turkic languages.* She was a sometime professor of linguistics at an American college in Mexico. In 1990 she was a member of the Turkish Studies Association. IWWAS, 1976/77

Franklin, James Henry, born 13 May 1872 at Pamplin, Va, he was a graduate of Richmond College, Va., and Southern Baptist Theological Seminary, and obtained two doctorates. He held pastorates in Colorado until 1912, when he became foreign secretary of the American Baptist Foreign Missionary Society, supervising work in China, Japan, the Philippines, and Europe. He also visited Africa as a special commissioner. He served as a member of the International Missionary Council for many years. From 1934 to 1944 he was president of Crozer Theological Seminary, Chester, Pa. He was awarded the *Légion d'honneur* by France. His writings include *In the track of the storm* (1919), *Ministers of mercy* (1919), *The Christian crisis in China* (1931), and *Never failing light* (1933). He died in Richmond, Va., 23 March 1961. NYT 24 March 1961, p. 27, col. 5; WhAm, 5

Franko, Ivan, born in 1856 in Galicia, he studied at Lemberg (Lwów) and Wien, where he received a Dr.phil. degree in 1893 for his thesis, *Der Roman von Barlaam und Josaphat.* He was a writer and historian whose writings include Галицько-руські рароднї Приповідкі (1901), and Панськи жарты (1928), and its translation, *The Master's jests* (1979). He is the subject of several biographies. He died in 1916. GSE; Master (6); ÖBL

Franko, Lawrence George, born 3 November 1942 at Kingston, N.Y. After graduating from Harvard University, he received an M.A. from the Fletcher School of Law and Diplomacy. In 1966/67, he was a technical assistant to the Tunisian Government. Thereafter he held a variety of positions at American universities and was a sometime professor at the European Institute of Business Administration, Fontainebleau, and a deputy assistant director, U.S. Congressional Budget Office, Washington, D.C. ConAu, 37-40; WhoE, 1989/90

Franses, Michael, fl. 1979, his writings include *An introduction to the world of rugs* (1973), and he was joint author of *Aspects of the weaving and decorative arts of Central Asia* (1980), and *Kelims, gewebte, gestickte und gewirkte Teppiche des Orients* (1980). LC

Franz, Erhard, born in 1938, he received a Dr.phil. in 1969 from the Freie Universität Berlin for his thesis, *Das Dorf Icadiye,* based on field-work in Turkey, 1966/67. Since 1972, he was a research fellow at the Deutsches Orient-Institut, Hamburg. His writings include *Kurden und Kurdentum* (1980), and a number of bibliographies and editions of newspaper clippings. Schwarz

Franz, Heinrich Gerhard, born 19 January 1916 at Dresden, Germany, he received a Dr.phil. in 1941 from the Universität Berlin for his thesis, *Die Kirchenbauten des Christoph Dietzenhofer*. He was a professor of history of art successively at the universities of Mainz and Graz. His writings include *Hinduistische und islamische Kunst Indiens* (1967), *Palast, Moschee und Wüstenschloß* (1984), and *Von Baghdad bis Córdoba; Ausbreitung der islamischen Kunst* (1984). Kürschner, 1954-2003

Franz (Pasha), Julius, fl. 1881-1912, he was a Hungarian Jewish engineer and architect whose writings include *Die Baukunst des Islam* (1887), and *Kairo* (1903). Egyptology; Sezgin, vol. 13, p. 430

Franz-Willing, Georg, born 11 March 1915 at Bad Aibling, Germany, he studied at the Universität München, 1937-1939, and received a Dr.phil. in 1942. He was successively employed with the Südostinstitut, München, Institut für Kultur- und Sozialforschung, München, Ost-Europa Institut, München, and Militärgeschichtliches Forschungsamt, Freiburg im Breisgau. His writings include *Die Hitlerbewegung* (1962), and *Die bayerische Vatikangesandtschaft, 1803-1934* (1965). Kürschner, 1961-1992; Wer ist wer, 1998/99; WhoWor, 1987/88, 1989/90

Fraser, Alexander Thomas, born 19th cent., his writings include *An Historical review of the principal Jewish and Christian sites at Jerusalem* (1881), *Darkness in the land of Egypt, and light in the dwellings of the children of Israel* (1884), *The Drift of Buddhism from India, to the Mongols, and Thibet* (1905), and *The Volcanic origin of coal and modern geological theories* (1909). BLC

Fraser, David Stewart, born 16 August 1869 at Invergordon. After education at Aberdeen, he had some experience of commercial affairs in London before accepting employment with the Bank of Bengal in Calcutta, contributing articles to a local paper at the same time. After voluntary service in the South African war, he had the good fortune to apply for employment with *The Times* at the right time and was lucky soon to come up with an account of the Battle of the Yalu River which was quoted throughout the world. He remained a Far and Middle Eastern correspondent until he retired to Vancouver, B.C., in 1940. He later moved to Washington, D.C., where he died 19 May 1953. Obit T, 1951

Fraser, James Baillie, born in 1783 at Edinburgh of well-to-do parents, he had acquired a taste for eastern travel after two months in the Himalayas in 1815. In 1821 he left India in company with the surgeon Andrew Jukes and reached Tehran, from where he set off for Mashad. Because of unsettled political conditions, he was unable to proceed to Bokhara, instead he explored the Caspian shores and Kurdistan before returning to England. His travel accounts, though covering new ground, made little contribution to systematic geography. He died in 1856. BiD&SB; Buckland; DNB; Gabriel; Henze; Wright

Fraser, Sir John Foster, born in 1868 at Edinburgh, he trained as a journalist at provincial papers in the Midlands before he went ot London in 1892. He became a roving reporter and correspondent, travelling by any means. In 1896 he journeyed around the world by bicycle. His writings include *The Land of veiled women; some wanderings in Algeria, Tunisia and Morocco* (1911). He died in 1936. WhE&EA; Who was who, 3

Fraser, T. H., he was in 1934 a professor of economics at the Egyptian University, and in 1941, resident in Cairo and a member of the Société Fouad 1er d'économie politique, de statistique et de législation. Note

Fraser-Tytler, Sir William Kerr, lieutenant-colonel, born in 1886, he was a graduate of Christ Church College, Oxford, and entered the Indian Army in 1910 and served in India until 1941. His writings include *Hunting talk* (1919), and *Afghanistan; a study of political developments in Central Asia* (1950). He died in 1963. Who was who, 6

Frashëri, Kristo, 20th cent., his writings include *Gjergj Kastrioti-Skandabeg, nacio hero de Albanio* (Tirana, 1967), *George Kastrioti-Scanderbeg, the national hero of the Albanians* (1962), *Georges Kastriote-Skanderbeg, heros national des Albanais* (1962), *Abdyl Frashëri, 1839-1892* (1984); and he edited *Historia e popullit shqiptar* (1968-69). LC

Frasso Dentice, Luigi, 1861-1947 *see* Dentice di Frasso, Luigi

Frati, Lodovico, born 13 December 1855 at Bologna, he was a keeper of manuscripts at the Univer-sity Library, Bologna, from 1883 to 1923. His writings include *Miscellanea dantesca* (1884), *La donna italiana secondo i più recenti studi* (1899), and *Il settecento a Bologna* (1923). He died in 1941. Chi è, 1928, 1931, 1936, 1940; IndBI (7)

Frauberger, Heinrich, born in 1845, his writings include *Die Geschichte des Fächers* (1878), *Zweck und Ziel der Gesellschaft zur Erforschung jüdischer Kunstdenkmäler zu Frankfurt* (1900), *Über alte*

Kultusgegenstände in Synagoge und Haus (1903), and *Verzierte hebräische Schrift und jüdische Schrift und jüdischer Buchschmuck* (1909). NUC, pre-1956

Frayssinet, Jean, fl. 1976, he was a sometime staff member of the Centre de recherches administratives de la Faculté de droit et de science politique, Aix-en-Provence. His writings include *La bureaucratique; l'administration française face à l'Informatique* (1981), and he was joint author of *Administration et justice administrative face aux administrés* (1972). LC

Frazee, Charles Aaron, born 4 July 1929 at Rushville, Indiana, he was a graduate of St. Meinrad College and received a Ph.D. in 1965 from Indiana University for his thesis, *The Orthodox Church of Greece from the revolution of 1821-1852*. He taught successively at Indianapolis and Bloomington from 1956 to 1970 when he was appointed a professor of history of art at California State University, Fullerton. He conducted research in the Balkans and Tunisia. His writings include *The Orthodox Church and independent Greece, 1821-1852* (1969), and *Catholics and sultans* (1983). ConAu, 37-40; DrAS, 1974, 1978, 1982; WrDr, 1980/82, 1984/86

Frazer, Sir James George, born 1 January 1854 at Glasgow, he was educated at Glasgow and Trinity College, Cambridge, where he was elected fellow in 1879. Although he pursued his interests in classical literature throughout his life and studied law in obedience to his father's wishes, he made his most enduring contributions in the field of anthropology and from 1907 to 1932 was professor of social anthropology at the University of Liverpool. His works have been translated into Arabic, Armenian, and Russian. He died in Cambridge, 7 May 1941. CasWL; ConAu, 118; DNB; EncAm; *Hommes et destins*, vol. 5, p. 215; Master (23); *Who was who*, 4

Frease, Edwin Field, born 28 December 1862 at Canton, Ohio, he was a graduate of Taylor University, where he also received a doctorate in divinity. He had studied law but in 1885 he became a clergyman and joined the East Ohio Conference of the Methodist Episcopal Church. In 1888 he went to India as a missionary and served in Bombay and Baroda. In 1910 he left India to become home superintendent of the North Africa Mission, supervising the work of missionaries and native Christian preachers and teachers in Algeria and Tunisia until his retirement in 1932. He died in Canton, 22 April 1938. NYT, 23 April 1938, p. 15, col. 3; Shavit

Frech, Fritz Daniel, born 17 March 1861 at Berlin, he received a doctorate in 1885 from the Universität Berlin for his thesis, *Die Korallenfauna des Oberdevons in Deutschland*. He was a mining engineer and a sometime professor whose writings include *Geologie Kleinasiens im Bereich Bagdadbahn; Ergebnisse eigener Reisen* (1916), *Die Grundlagen türkischer Wirtschaftsverjüngung* (1916) and *Der Kriegsschauplatz in Armenien und Mesopotamien* (1916). Wounded in the war, he died in 1917. *Geographische Zeitschrift* 23 (1917), p. 551; NUC, pre-1956; Sezgin

Frechtling, Louis Earl, born 19 June 1913 at Hamilton, Ohio, he was a graduate of Miami University, and a Rhodes scholar at Queen's College, Oxford, 1936-39, where received a D.Phil. for his thesis, *British policy in the Middle East, 1874-80*. He was employed with the Foreign Policy As-sociation, N.Y.C., and thereafter with the U.S. Department of State. Master (1); WhoAm, 1972/73, 1974/75, 1976/77; WhoWor, 1974/75

Frederick, Edward, 1784-1866, he entered the Bombay army in 1799 and retired in 1838 with the rank of general. His writings include *Report on the military expenditure of the East India Company* (1831), and *Remarks on the government of India* (1839). BLC; Boase

Freed, Rita, fl. 1970, her writings include the eight-page pamphlet, *The war in the Middle East* (1973). NUC, 1973-1978

Freedman, Robert Owen, born 18 April 1941 at Philadelphia, Pa., he was a graduate of the University of Pennsylvania and received a Ph.D. in 1969 from Columbia University, N.Y.C. From 1975 he was a professor of political science, and later dean of Graduate School, Baltimore Hebrew College. In 1989 he served on a Brookings Institution delegation that went to Tunis to discuss the Middle East peace process with Yasir Arafat and other PLO leaders. His writings include *Soviet policy toward the Middle East since 1970* (1970), and *Moscow and the Middle East* (1991), and he was editor of *World politics and the Arab-Israeli conflict* (1979), *The Middle East since Camp David* (1984). ConAu, 33-36, 13 new rev.

Feer, Adela M., 1857-1931 *see* Goodrich-Freer, Ada (Adela), Mrs. H. H. Spoer

Freeland, Humphrey William, born in 1814, he was a graduate of Christ Church College, Oxford, in 1836, and called to the bar from Lincoln's Inn in 1841. From 1859 to 1863 he was a M.P. for Chichester. His writings include translations from European languages, *Poems* (1848), and *Lectures and miscellanies* (1857). He died in 1892. BritInd (2); NUC, pre-1956

561

Freeman, Edward Augustus, historian, born in 1823, his writings include *History of Norman conquest of England* (1867-79), *The Ottoman power in Europe* (1877), and *The Turks in Europe* (1877). He died in Alicante, 16 March 1892. BbD; BiD&SB; BritInd; CasWL; CelCen; DcBiPP; DNB; Master (12)

Freeman, Lewis Ransome, born in 1878 at Genoa Junction, Wisc., he was a bachelor who travelled extensively throughout the world and later served as a war correspondent attached to military units. His last monograph seems to be *Brazil's deserved destiny* (1941). AmAu&B; WhAm, 4

Freeman-Grenville, Greville Stewart Parker, born 29 June 1918 at Hook Norton, England, he had a varied record of teaching and research in the Middle East and Muslim Africa, especially on pre-colonial Africa. His writings include *The medieval history of the coast of Tanganyika* (1962), *Chronology of African history* (1973), *The Beauty of Cairo; a historical guide* (1981), *The Beauty of Jerusalem and the holy places* (1983), *The New atlas of African history* (1991), and a collection of his articles entitled *The Swahili coast, 2nd to 19th centuries* (1988). ConAu, 5-8, 3 new rev.; IntAu&W 1986-1993/94; WrDr, 1976/78-1998/2000

Freiman, Aleksandr Arnol'dovich, born in 1879 at Warszawa, he received a Dr.phil. in 1906 from the Universität Wien for his thesis, *Pand-Namak i Zartušt*. He was a research fellow at the Oriental Institute of the Soviet Academy of Science from 1934 until his death, 19 January 1968. His writings include *Хорезмийский язык* (1951). Miliband; Miliband²; Schwarz

Freimann, Aron, born 5 August 1871 at Filehne (Wieleń), Prussia, he studied history and Oriental languages at Berlin and received a Dr.phil. in 1896 from the Universität Erlangen for his thesis, *Die Isagoge des Porphyrius*. From 1897 to 1933 he was head of the Judaica Section in the Stadtbibliothek Frankfurt a.M., and concurrently, from 1900 to 1922, he was editor of the *Zeitschrift für hebräische Bibliographie*. Deposed in 1933, he went to America in 1939, where he served as a consultant in bibliography to the N.Y.P.L. until 1945. He was an expert in Hebrew bibliography and early printing. His writings include *Katalog der Judaica und Hebraica* (Frankfurt am Main, 1932). He died in 1948. EncJud; Wininger

Freimark, Peter, born 25 October 1934 at Halberstadt, Germany, he received a Dr.phil. in 1967 from the Universität Münster for his thesis, *Das Vorwort als literarische Form in der arabischen Literatur*. In 1972 he was appointed professor of history of German Jewry at the Institut für die Geschichte der Deutschen Juden, Hamburg. His writings include *Judentore, Kuggel, Steuerkonten* (1983), and he edited *Große fremde Religionen* (1977). Kürschner, 1976-2003; Schwarz; WhoWor, 1978/79

Freitag, Anton, born 4 January 1882 at Altenbeck, Germany. After local primary education, he entered the Missiehuis St.-Michaël in Steyl, the Netherlands, for humanistic studies. In 1901, he transferred to the philosophic-theological Lehranstalt of the Steyler Missionsgesellschaft, St. Gabriel near Wien, where he pursued advanced studies in philosophy. After he had become a full member of the Gesellschaft des Göttlichen Wortes zu Steyl (Missionarissen van het Goddelijk Woord), he read theology for four years. In 1908 he was ordained priest at St. Gabriel. Thereafter his authority posted him to Steyl to become acquainted with missionary work. In 1910 he began with his doctoral work at the Universität Münster, where he received a D.D. in 1915 for his thesis, *Historisch-kritische Untersuchung über den Vorkämpfer der indianischen Freiheit, Don Fray Bartolomé*. His writings include *Die Missionen der Gesellschaft des Göttlichen Wortes* (1912), *Emigranten voor God* (1949), and *Mission und Missionswissenschaft* (1962). LC; NUC, pre-1956; Thesis

Freivalds, John, born 12 March 1944 in Latvia, he was a graduate of Georgetown University, Washington, D.C. After serving as a Peace Corps worker, he served as an economist for a leading U.S. consulting form. He spent two years in Iran, participating in agricultural planning. He was founder and director of *Agribusiness*, a worldwide magazine. His writings include *Grain trade* (1976), *The famine plot* (1978), and *Successful agribusiness management* (1985). ConAu, 69-72; Master (1); WhoMW, 1988-1990/91

Fremantle, John Morton, born in 1876, he was educated at Eton and Oxford, and served as a military officer in the African campaigns of the early twentieth century. After political appointments in British West Africa, he was a lecturer in Hausa at Oxford and Cambridge. He was editor of the *Gazetteer of Muri Province* (1922). He died in 1936. Who was who, 3

Frémy, Édouard, born 29 September 1843. After he received his diploma in law, he served with the Ministère des Affaires étrangères where he was employed for many years as supernumerary in the Direction politique until he finally was fully employed with pay starting in 1870. He served as archivist until 1880 when he was granted time off for his personal researches in the *archives diplomatiques*. His writings include *Essai sur les diplomates du temps de la Ligue* (1873), *Lamartine diplomate* (1885), and

Un Curé poitevin, Jean-Baptiste Chauvin, curé de Persac (1900). His trace is lost after his last publication. DBF

Fren, Kh. D., 1782-1851 *see* Frähn, Christian Martin Joachim

French, David H., he was in 1989 a member of the British Institute of Archaeology, Ankara. His writings include *Roman roads and milestones of Asia Minor* (1981-88); he edited *Studies in the history and topography of Lycia and Pisidia* (1994), and he was joint editor of *The Eastern frontier of the Roman Empire; proceedings* (1989). LC

French, H. B., fl. 1945, he was a sometime member of the British Council staff, Ankara. Note

French, Joseph Charles, born in 1883, he was an official in the Indian Civil Service who had an intimate acquaintance with the Himalayas from marches and camp fires. He spent much of his spare time to the study of Indian art. His writings include *The Art of the Pal Empire of Bengal* (1928), and *Himalayan art* (1931). LC

French, Roger Kenneth, born 12 April 1938 at Coventry, England, he was a graduate of St. Catherine's College, Oxford, where he also received his D.Phil. in 1965. He was a lecturer in history of science at Leicester and Aberdeen, and from 1975, at Cambridge, where he was con-currently director of the Welcome Unit for the History of Medicine. His writings include *Robert Whytt, the soul, and medicine* (1969), and he was joint author of *Before science; the invention of the friars' natural philosophy* (1996). ConAu, 118, 42 new rev.; WhoWor, 1978/79

Frend, William Hugh Clifford, born 11 January 1916 at Shottermill, Surrey, he was a graduate of Keble College, Oxford, where he also obtained his D.Phil. degree. He was a research fellow at the University of Nottingham, a lecturer in divinity at Cambridge, and from 1969, a professor of ecclesiatical history in the University of Glasgow. He received honorary degrees from Cambridge, Oxford and Edinburgh. He served as vice-president, and president, of the European Commission for Comparative Study of Ecclesiatical History. His writings include *The Domastic Church; a movement of protest in Roman North Africa* (1952), *The early Church* (1966), and a collection of his artices entitled *Town and country in the early Christian centuries* (1980). ConAu, 21-24, 9 new rev.; IntAu&W, 1982; Who, 1971-1999; WhoWor, 1989/90; WrDr, 1982/84-1998/2000

Frenkel, Leopoldo, born in 1947, he was resident in the Argentine in 1980. He completed his studies with a doctorate in law, and was the founder of *Pensamiento y nación*, a periodical which ceased publication with no. 6 (1982). His writings include *El justicialismo* (1984). LC

Frenzke, Dietrich, fl. 1980, he received a Dr.phil. in 1955 from Humboldt-Universität, Berlin, for his thesis *Die produktiven Verbalklassen des Altrussischen*. His writings include *Die Rechtsstruktur des Sowjetblocks* (1981), and he was joint editor of *Macht und Recht im kommunistischen Herrschaftssystem* (1965). LC

Frere, Sir Henry Bartle Edward, born 29 March 1815 at Clydach, Wales, he was a graduate of the East India Company's college of Haileybury. With special permission he journeyed to India overland through Egypt, across the Red Sea, and from Mocha in an Arab dhow to Bombay. He was for many years an assistant revenue commissioner and also employed in investigating land assessments. From 1859 to 1862, he was a member of the Governor-General's Supreme Council. In 1872, he was sent to Zanzibar to negotiate a treaty for the suppression of the slave trade. He was an eminent public servant and earnest in his religious views. His writings include *Eastern Africa as a field for missionary labour*, (1874), *On the impending Bengal famine* (1874), and *Afghanistan and South Africa* (1881). He died 29 May 1884 and was buried in St. Paul's Cathedral, London.. Buckland; DNB; Mason; Master (3)

Frescaly, Marcel, 1856-1886 *see* Palat, Justin Marcel

Fresco (Frisko), Abraham, fl. 1882-1898, he was a Jewish scholar whose writings include *Sefer Berakh et Avraham* (1861 or 62), reprinted in 1993 or 94. LC

Fresco, Jacques, he was in 1940 head of Technical Service at General Statistics, Egypt, and a member of the Société Fouad 1er d'économie politique, de statistique et de législation for over twelve years. Note

Frescobaldi, Dino, fl. 1976, he was a journalist whose writings include *Nasser* (1970), *La sfida di Sadat* (1977), and *La riscossa del profeta* (1988). LC

Freshfield, Douglas William, born 27 April 1845, he was educated at Eton and Oxford, and admitted to the bar in 1870, but never practised law. He was a man of private means and pursued his interest in travel and mountaineering beyond the beaten tracks. His writings include *Travels in the Central*

Caucasus and Bashan (1869), *The exploration of the Caucasus* (1896), and *Hannibal once more* (1914). He was for many years editor of the *Alpine journal* and member of council of the Royal Geographical Society. He died in 1934. Bioln, 2, 5; DNB; Henze; Master (2); WhE&EA; *Who was who*, 3

Freshfield, Edwin Hanson, born about 1864, he was educated at Winchester and Trinity College, Cam-bridge, and grew up to share his father's interests in the City of London and in Byzantine antiquities. He served thrice on the Council, in 1900, 1903, and 1909, and was a Trustee of the British School at Athens and a member of the Society for the Promotion of Roman Studies. He was master of the Vintners' Company in 1931 and one of his Majesty's lieutenants for the City of London. His writings include *Byzantine guilds, professional and commercial ... rendered into English* (1938). He died 15 May 1948, at the age of eighty-four. *Antiquaries journal* 29 (July 1949), p. 246

Fresnel, Fulgence, born 15 April 1795 at Mathieu (Calvados), he first studied Chinese, and that well enough to do some translations, but in the end he enrolled at l'École des langues orientales vivantes where he had Sylvestre de Sacy as a teacher in Arabic and Persan. He complemented his studies at the Maronite Congrégation de la Propagation de la foi in Roma, and then visited Egypt and Cairo in 1831. He eventually entered the diplomatic service as a consular agent at Jiddah, a post which left him sufficient time to travel to southern Arabia in quest of Himyarite inscriptions which he endeavoured to decipher. After his return to Paris, he was sent on an archaeological mission to Mesopotamia in 1851, where he died in Baghdad, 30 November 1855. His writings include *Lettres sur l'histoire des Arabes avant l'islamisme* (1836). DBF; Henze

Freudenheim, Tom Lippmann, born 3 July 1937 at Stuttgart, Germany, he was a graduate of Harvard, and was a sometime curator, or museum director, at N.Y.C., Berkeley, Calif., Baltimore, Md., and Worcester, Mass. In 1986 he was appointed assistant secretary for museums, Smithonian Institution, Washington, D.C. WhoAm, 1974-1988/89; WhoAmA, 1973-1997/98; WhoE, 1974-1989

Freudenthal, Jakob, born 20 June 1839 at Bodenfelde, Germany, he was educated at Jüdisch-Theologisches Seminar, Breslau, its Universität, and the Universität Göttingen where he received a Dr.phil. in 1863 for his thesis, *Über den Begriff des Wortes φαντασια bei Aristoteles*. Thereafter he taught at the Samsonschule, Wolfenbüttel, until he became a lecturer in classical languages and history of religion at the Jüdisch-Theologisches Seminar, Breslau. Since 1878, he was a professor of philosophy at the Universität Breslau, where he specialized in Greek philosophy. His writings include *Die durch Averroes erhaltenen Fragmente Alexanders zur Metaphysik des Aristoteles*. He died in Schreiberhau (Szklarska Poręba), Silesia, 1 July 1907. EncJud²; Wininger

Freund, Leonhard, born at Breslau, Germany, he studied law, received a doctorate, and practised law in Leipzig. His writings include *Über Recht auf Wahrheit* (1862), *Thaten und Namen; Forschungen über Staat und Gesellschaft* (1871), *Hinaus; Kulturbild aus dem Zentrum des modernen Anti-semitismus* (1889), and *Lug und Trug nach moslemischem Recht und nach moslemischer Polizei* (1894). He died in München, 2 October 1895. Wininger

Freund, Wolfgang Slim, born in 1939, he studied sociology, political science, modernen history as well as French, at Freiburg im Breisgau, Lausanne, Tunis, Cairo, and Köln, where he received a Dr.phil. in 1970 for his thesis, *Die Djerbi in Tunesien*. He was a research fellow at Köln, 1974-77, associate professor of sociology at Ain Shams University, Cairo, 1974-75, and concurrently a visiting professor at AUC, *professeur associé* at the Université de Strasbourg, 1982, and at the Université de Tunis, 1983. He was founder and editor of *die Dritte Welt* quarterly. His writings include *Das arabische Mittelmeer* (1974), and *Welche Zukunft für den Iran* (1981). Schwarz

Fréville, Ernest, fl. 1907-1913 in Reims, he was a sometime *receveur particulier des finances*, and a member of the Académie nationale de Reims. He visited Morocco and Turkey. His writings include *Conférence fait à Reims* (1908), and *Constantinople; mœurs, usages, coutumes* (1909). BN

Frey, Albert Romer, born 17 February 1858 at N.Y.C., he was a civic employee and a sometime secretary of the Shakespeare Society of New York. His writings include *Sobriquets and nicknames* (1887), and *A dictionary of numismatic names* (1917). He died in N.Y.C., 19 January 1926. Bioln, 2; DcNAA; Master (1); WhAm, 4

Frey, Frederick Ward, born 16 June 1929 at Cleveland, Ohio, he was a graduate of the local Western Reserve University, and a Rhodes scholar who received his Ph.D. in 1962 from Princeton for his thesis, *Political leadership in Turkey; the social background of the deputies to the Grand National Assembly, 1920-1957*. He taught at M.I.T. until 1974 when he was appointed a professor of political science, and later chairman of the graduate program in international relations, at the University of Pennsylvania, a post which he still held in 1995. His writings include *The Turkish political elite* (1965), and *Regional variations in rural Turkey* (1966). AmM&WS, 1973, 1978; ConAu, 53-56; NatFacDr, 1995; WhoAm, 1974-1984; WhoWor, 1974/75

Frey, Ulrich J. M., born 30 June 1872 at Breslau, Germany, he joined the Prussian Army in 1892 and resigned in 1921 with the rank of lieutenant-colonel. From 1917 to 1918 he was posted to the Turkish Army. After he received a Dr.phil. in 1922 from the Universität München for his thesis, *Das Hochland von Anatolien mit besonderer Berücksichtigung des abflußlosen Gebietes*, he was in charge of the courses for military interpreters of the Reichswehr, München. He was joint author of *Vorder- und Südasien in Natur, Kultur und Wirtschaft* (1931). Kürschner, 1926-1935|; Schwarz; Wer ist's, 1928, 1935

Frey, Wolfgang, born 14 August 1942 at Rechberghausen, Germany, he was a professor of botany successively at the universities of Tübingen, Gießen and, since 1981, Berlin. He was joint author of *Gliederung der Vegetation und ihre Darstellung im Tübinger Atlas des Vorderen Orients* (1977), *Die Vegetation des Maharlu-Beckens bei Širaz* (1977), *Vegetation und Flora des Zentralen Hindukuš* (1978), and *Die Vegetation im Vorderen Orient* (1989). Kürschner, 1992

Freyer, Barbara Regine, 1935- *see* Stowasser, Barbara Regine née Freyer

Freytag, Eva-Maria née Köhler, born 18 October 1942 at Breslau, Germany. After Iranian as well as library studies at the Humboldt Universität, Berlin, she obtained a Dr. phil. for her thesis, *Das Bibliothekswesen und die Bibliographie in Iran* (1976). From 1976 until her retirement she was Persian subject specialist at the Staatsbibliothek zu Berlin. Private

Freytag, Georg Wilhelm Friedrich, born 19 September 1788 at Lüneburg, Germany, he studied theology and philosophy at Göttingen. In 1815, he came to Paris as a Prussian chaplain. He remained in Paris and completed his Oriental studies. In 1819, he was appointed professor of Oriental languages at Bonn, where he specialized in Arabic linguistics. He published several classical Arabic texts with Latin translation as well as *Darstellung der arabischen Verskunst* (1830), and *Lexicon Arabico-Latinum* (1830-37). He died in Dottendorf, 16 November 1861. ADtB; CelCen; Bonner, vol. 8, pp. 293-295; DcBiPP; DtBE; DtBilnd (4); Fück, pp. 166-167; NDB

Freytag, Iris, born in 1951, she studied political science at Hamburg, 1972-1978. She was a free lance journalist specializing in international politics and development programs in North Africa. Private

Frézouls, Edmond, born in 1925, he was a graduate of l'École normale supérieure, a member of l'École française de Rome, 1949 to 1951, a research fellow at l'Institut français d'archéologie de Beyrouth, 1951-1954, and successively a keeper and director at the Musée du Bardo, Tunis, 1951-1959, when he was appointed a professor of Roman archaeology at the Faculté des Sciences historiques de l'Université de Strasbourg. From 1976 to 1982, he was its dean. He died in 1995. Syria, 74 (1997), pp. 221-222

Frick, Fay Arrieh, born 17 August 1923 at Milwaukee, Wisc., she was a graduate of the University of Chicago and received a Ph.D. in 1971 from the University of Michigan for her thesis, *A typology of Fustat ceramics*. She was a sometime professor of history of art at A.U.B. and San Diego State University. Selim; WhoAm, 1982/83; WhoWest, 1980

Frick, Heinrich, born 2 November 1893 at Darmstadt, Germany, he studied theology at Gießen and Tübingen, and received a Dr.phil. in 1919 for his thesis *Ghazalis Selbstbiographie; ein Vergleich mit Augustins Konfession*. He successively taught theology and history of religion at the universities of Gießen and Marburg. His writings include *Vergleichende Religionswissenschaft* (1928), and *The Gospel, Christianity and other faiths* (1938). He died in Marburg, 31 December 1952. DtBE; Kürschner, 1926-1950; Schwarz; Wer ist's, 1935

Fridman, Leonid Abramovich, born 7 July 1930 at Moscow, he was a graduate of Moscow State University and received a doctorate in 1970 for his thesis, *Аграрные отношения и развитие производительных сил в сельском хозяйстве Египта, 1882-1952*. He was a sometime professor of economics and director of the Centre for Comparative Social and Economic Studies at his alma mater. His main field of interest was the social and economic structures of underdeveloped countries. His writings include *Капиталическое развитие Египта, 1882-1939* (1963), and *Египет,1882-1952; социально-экономическя структура деревни* (1973). Miliband; Miliband²

Fridolin, Major, 1815- *see* Valbezen, Eugène Anatole de

Friedemann, Anna, born 19th cent., she was a missionary under the Deutsche Orient Mission, Potsdam, and went out to Urmia in November 1900 to take up the directorship of the German Orphanage and remained there until expelled at the end of 1914. She described her Persian experiences in the unidentified *Mutter Annenbuch* (Missionsverlag der Deutschen Orient-Mission, Potsdam). Private

Friederich, Rudolf Hermann Theodoor, born 7 January 1817 at Koblenz, he studied Semitic languages and Sanskrit at the universities at Berlin and Bonn. In the service of the East Indian Army he came to the Dutch Indies in 1844 and became a librarian at the Bataafsch Genootschap. He was joint author of *Codicum arabicorum in bibliotheca Societatis Artium et Scientiarum quae Bataviae floret asservatorum catalogum* (1873). He died 28 July 1875. EncNI; NieuwNBW

Friedgut, Theodore H., born 1 February 1931, he was a graduate of the University of Toronto and Hebrew University, Jerusalem, and an exchange student in Moscow, 1969-70. He received his Ph.D. in 1972 from Columbia University for his thesis, *Citizen participation in Soviet local government*. He was a sometime professor of Russian studies at the Hebrew University. His writings include *Soviet anti-Zionism and anti-Semitism; another cycle* (1984). ConAu, 89-92; Private

Friedl, Erika Loeffler, born 6 February 1940 at Wien, she studied at the Universität Wien and received a Dr.phil. in 1964 from the Universität Mainz for her thesis, *Träger medialer Begabung im Hindukush und Karakorum*. She was affiliated with the Oriental Institute, Chicago, and Western Michigan University, where she was a professor of anthropology since 1968. Her writings include *Women of Deh Koh; lives in an Iranian village* (1989), its translation, *Die Frauen von Deh Koh* (1991), and she was joint editor of *In the eye of the storm; women in post-revolutionary Iran* (1994). ConAu, 147

Friedländer (Friedlaender), Israel, born 8 September 1876 at Kovel (Kowel), Ukraine. He was brought up in Warszawa where he received a private education. In 1895 he enrolled at the Rabbiner-Seminar für das Orthodoxe Judentum, Berlin, and concurrently studied Semitic languages at the Universität until 1900, when he transferred to the Universität Straßburg, where he received his Dr.phil. in 1901 for *Der Sprachgebrauch des Maimonides; ein lexikalischer und grammatischer Beitrag zur Kenntnis des Mittelarabischen*. The following three years he lectured in Semitics at Straßburg. In 1904 he accepted a professorship at the Jewish Theological Seminary, N.Y.C. In 1919 he went on a humanitarian mission to Jewish communities of Eastern Europe where he fell victim to bandits in 1920. His writings include *Arabisch-deutsches Lexikon zum Sprachgebrauch des Maimonides* (1902), and *Die Chadhirlegende und der Alexanderroman* (1913). Baila R. Shargel wrote a biography, *Practical dreamer, Israel Friedlaender and the shaping of American Judaism* (1985). CnDiAmJBi; DAB, 4; DcNAA; EncJud; Schwarz; WhAm, 1

Friedländer, Paul, fl. 1964, he received a doctorate in 1963 for his thesis, *Die regionale Spezifik der neokolonialistischen Wirtschaftsexpansion Westdeutschlands im Nahen und Mittleren Osten*. He was joint author of a supplementary thesis submitted in 1976 at Potsdam, entitled *Grundprobleme der Strategie und Politik des Imperialismus gegenüber Entwicklungsländern in der internationalen Klassenauseinandersetzung der Gegenwart*. Schwarz

Friedlander, Robert A., Ph.D., fl. 1978., he was a professor of law at Ohio Northern University College of Law. He was editor of *Terrorism; documents of international and local control* (1979-81), and joint editor of *Self-determination; national, regional, and global dimensions* (1980). LC; NUC

Friedlander, Saul, born 11 October 1932 at Praha. At the outbreak of the war his family fled to France and later went into hiding. He was sent to a Catholic boys' school and embraced Catholicism. When priests told him that his parents were deported and killed, he took up the Zionist cause. He was a graduate of l'Institut d'études politiques, Paris, and received a doctorate in 1963 from the Graduate Institute of International Studies, Genève, for his thesis, *Le rôle du facteur américain dans la politique étrangère et militaire de l'Allemagne, 1939-1941*. He served at the World Zionist Organization, the Israeli Ministry of Defense, and thereafter divided his time between Israel and Californa, teaching contemporary history. His writings include *Pie et le III Reich* (1964), and he was joint author of *Arabes et Israéliens; un premier dialogue* (1974). BioIn, 12; ConAu, 130; NatFacDr, 1995; WhoIsrael, 1969/70-1992/93; WhoWorJ, 1972

Friedli, Richard, O.P., born in 1937 in Switzerland. From 1967 to 1971 he was a professor of social ethics at the National University of Rwanda., and thereafter, professor of religious studies and missions at the Université de Fribourg. In 1973 he received a doctorate in divinity for his thesis, *Fremdheit als Heimat*. His writings include *Frieden wagen* (1981), *Mission oder Demission* (1982), and *Zwischen Himmel und Hölle; die Reinkarnation* (1986). WWASS, 1989

Friedman, Andrew L., fl. 1972, he was a sometime lecturer in economics in the University of Bristol. His writings include *Industry and labour; class struggle at work and monopoly capitalism* (1977). LC

Friedman, Ellen G., born 8 March 1939 at N.Y.C., she was a graduate of New York University where she also received her Ph.D. in 1975. In 1978 she was appointed a professor of history at Boston College, Chestnut Hill, Mass., a position which she still held in 1999. Her writings include *Spanish captives in North Africa in the early modern age* (1983). DrAS, 1982; NatFacDr, 1959-1999

Friedman, Harry J., born 11 January 1926 at Trenton, N.J., he was a graduate of Rutgers University, New Brunswick, N.J., and received a Ph.D. in 1956 from the University of Pittsburgh for his thesis, *Consolidation of India since independence*. He was appointed professor of political science at the University of Hawai in 1962, a position which he still held in 1995. AmM&WS, 1973; NatFacDr, 1995

Friedman, Howard Martin, born 26 September 1941 at Springfield, Ohio, he was a graduate of Ohio State University, and received law degrees from Harvard Law School and Georgetown University. He was a member of the Ohio Bar and a sometime professor of law at the University of Toledo, Ohio. NatFacDr, 1995-1999; WhoAmL, 1977/78-1985/86; WhoEmL, 1987/88

Friedman, Isaiah, born 28 April 1921 at Łuck, Poland, he was educated at the Hebrew University, Jerusalem, where he also received his doctorate in 1964. He was a research fellow in Israel and England from 1965 to 1971, when he was appointed professor of history and political science at Dropsie University, Philadelphia, Pa. His writings include *The question of Palestine, 1914-1918* (1973), and *Germany, Turkey, and Zionism, 1897-1918* (1977). ConAu, 53-56; IntAu&W, 1977

Friedman, Reuben, born 14 December 1892, he was a graduate of Temple University School of Medicine, Philadelphia, since 1916, a professor of clinical dermatology at his alma mater, and on the staff of Temple University Hospital, where he died 4 February 1956, of acute myocardial infarction. *Journal of the American Medical Association* 16 iii (19 May 1956), p. 255

Friedman, Saul S., born 8 March 1937 at Uniontown, Pa., he was a graduate of Kent State University where he also received his Ph.D. in 1969. He was a welfare and social workers in Ohio, a college instructor in history, and appointed professor of history at Youngstown (Ohio) State University in 1969, a position which he still held in 1999. His writings include *No haven for the oppressed* (1973), a work which was originally submitted as his doctoral thesis, and *Without future; the plight of Syrian Jewry* (1989). ConAu, 57-60; DrAS, 1974, 1978, 1982

Friedman, Victor Allen, born 18 October 1949 at Chicago, he was a graduate of Reed College, and received his Ph.D. in 1971 from the University of Chicago for his thesis, *The grammatical categories of the Macedonian indicative*. In 1975 he was appointed professor of Balkan and Slavic linguistics at the University of North Carolina, Chapel Hill, a position which he still held in 1995. He was a member of the Turkish Studies Association. NatFacDr, 1995; WhoSSW, 1984/85

Friedmann, Yohanan, born 28 March 1936 at Zakamenne, Czechoslovakia, he was educated at the Hebrew University, Jerusalem, and received a Ph.D. in 1966 from the Institute of Islamic Studies, McGill University, Montreal. His writings include *Shaykh Ahmad Sirhindi* (1971), a revision of his thesis, and *Prophecy continuous; aspects of Ahmadi religious thought* (1989). ConAu, 33-36; Ferahian; WrDr, 1976/78-1998/2000

Friedrich, Johannes, born 27 August 1893 at Leipzig, where he also studied and taught ancient Near Eastern languages until 1950, when he went to the Freie Universität Berlin. His writings include *Aus dem hethitischen Schrifttum* (1925), *Entzifferung verschollener Schriften und Sprachen* (1954), its translation, *Extinct languages* (1957), as well as its translations into Chinese (1979), and Persian (1986), and *Geschichte der Schrift* (1966), as well as its translation into Persian in 1989. He died in Berlin, 12 August 1972. DtBE; Kürschner, 1926-1979; Master (3)

Friedrich, Wolfgang Uwe, born in 1952, he received a Dr.phil. in 1982 from the Universität Göttingen. In 1999, he was a professor of political science and sociology at the Universität Hildesheim. His writings include *Bulgarien und die Mächte, 1913-1915* (1985), a work which was originally submit-ted as doctoral thesis, and *DDR, Deutschland zwischen Elbe und Oder* (1989). Kürschner, 1996-2003; LC

Friedrichsen, Max H., born 21 June 1874 at Hamburg, he was a professor of geography successively at Rostock, Bern, Greifswald, Köningsberg, and Breslau. He visited the Caucasus in 1897, and Tien Shan in 1902. He died 22 August 1941. DtBE; Kürschner, 1925-1935; NDB; Sigilla; Wer ist's, 1909-1935

Friendly, Alfred, born 30 December 1911 at Salt Lake City, he was a graduate of Amherst College. He was a journalist and reporter for American and British periodicals, and the recipient of the Pulitzer Prize for international reporting, 1968, for coverage of the Arab-Israeli war. His writings include *Israel's oriental immigrants and Druzes* (1972), and *The battle of Manzikert, 1071* (1981). He died in Washington, D.C., 7 November 1983. AnObit, 1983, pp. 520-521; CnDiAmJBi; ConAu, 101, 111; BlueB, 1973/74, 1975, 1976; IntAu&W, 1977, 1982; IntWW, 1972/73-1983/84; WhoWor, 1978/79

Friendly, Alfred, Jr., born in 1938, he was a journalist and a correspondent to *Atlantic monthly, New York Times*, and *Newsweek*. ConAu, 152

Frierman, Jay David, born 17 May 1923 at Los Angeles, he was a graduate of the University of California, Berkeley. He held a variety of positions as a teacher of history, curator and director of museums, and lecturer in Near Eastern archaeology. He edited *The Natalie Wood Collection of pre-Columbian ceramics from Chupícuaro* (1969). WhoWest, 1976/77, 1978/79

Frifelt, Karen, fl. 1968, she was affiliated with Aarhus Universitet, and a member of the Association of South Asian Archaeologists in Western Europe, 1985. Her writings include *The Island of Umm-an-Nar* (1995), and she edited *South Asian archaeology, 1985; papers* (1989). LC

Friggieri, Oliver, born 27 March 1947 at Floriana, Malta, he studied at Malta and did post-doctoral research at the Università di Milano. He was a lecturer in Maltese and literary theory at Malta since 1976. His writings include *Cultura italiana a Malta nell'ottocento e nel primo novecento* (1977), *Storja tal-letteratura maltija* (1979), its translation, *Storia della letteratura maltese* (1986), *Dun Karm* (1980), and the translation of his *L-istramb*, entitled *A turn of a wheel*, in the Unesco collection of representative works, 1987. WhoWor, 1978/79-1989/90|

Friš, Oldřich, born 7 May 1903, he was professor of Indology at Universita Karlova, Praha, and dean of the Faculty of Philology. In 1954 he succeeded V. Lesný in the chair of Indology. He was also editor-in-chief of *Archiv orientální* and *Nový Orient*. He died 14 January 1955. Archiv orientální 23 (1955), pp. 2-5; IES; PSN

Frisch, Alfred, born Jewish on 7 July 1913 at Heidelberg, he was baptized a Catholic in 1937. He studied at Heidelberg, Genève, Bordeaux, Alger, and Lyon, where he received a diploma in law. He joined the *résistance* in France during the war. After 1945, he was Paris correspondent to German dailies, and a radio commentator. His writings include *Une réponse au défi de l'histoire* (1954), its translation, *Großmacht der Technokratie* (1955), and *Dictature pour les pauvres?* (1963). DtBiIndex (1)

Frison-Roche, Roger, born 10 February 1906 at Paris, he was a writer on mountaineering and explorations. His writings include *L'Appel du Hoggar* (1936), *La Piste oubliée* (1950), its translation, *The Lost trail of the Sahara* (1952), *Carnet sahariens; l'appel du Hoggar et autres méharées* (1975), and *50 ans de Sahara* (1976). WhoFr, 1969/70-1998/99

Frissard, Pierre François, born 27 July 1787 at Paris, he was a graduate of l'École polytechnique and l'École des Ponts et chaussées. He had a varied record of service in canal, harbour and rail construction throughout France. He was a sometime professor of maritime construction at l'École des Ponts et chaussées, and was sent on a mission to Algeria in 1850. His writings include *Notes prises au cours de ports de mer* (1849). He died from cholera, 2 September 1854. DBF

Friters, Gerard Martin, born 4 December 1911 at Berlin, he studied at the Université de Genève, where he received a doctorate in 1939 for his thesis, *The international position of Outer Mongolia*. He was a lecturer in political science at Bristol, London, Durham, and the University of the Punjab, Pakistan, until 1961, when he was appointed a professor at Université Laval, P.Q. His writings include *Outer Mongolia and its international position* (1949). AmM&WS, 1973 S

Fritsch, Gustav Theodor, born 5 March 1938 at Cottbus, Germany, he studied natural sciences and medicine at the universities of Berlin, Breslau and Heidelberg, and received a doctorate in 1862. Since 1867 he was in various capacities affiliated with medical institutes in Berlin. On his extensive travels to South Africa, Persia and Egypt he carried on anthropological and ethnographical studies. His writings include *Ägyptische Vokstypen der Jetztzeit* (1904). He died in Berlin, 12 June 1927. DtBE; Embacher; Henze; Master (3)

von **Fritsch**, Karl Georg Wilhelm, born 11 November 1838 at Weimar, Germany, he was a geologist who held various positions as a professor at the universities in Frankfurt and Halle. He explored Madeira and the Canary Islands in 1862 and Morocco in 1872. He died 9 January 1906. DtBE; Embacher; Henze

Fritzler, Karl, born 6 March 1880, he received a Dr.phil. in 1917 at Berlin for his thesis, *Die so-genannte Kirchenordnung Jaroslaws*. He was a sometime lecturer in Russian affairs at the universities of Darmstadt and Frankfurt am Main, as well as editor of *Südöstliche Warte*. His writings include *Zwei Abhandlungen über altrussisches Recht*. Kürschner, 1926-1940/41

Friz, Karl, fl. 1955, his writings include *Die Stimme der Ostkirche* (1959), and contributions to *Evangelische Missions-Zeitschrift*. LC

Frobenius, Leo Viktor, born 29 June 1873 at Berlin, he was a self-taught ethnographer and an extentric. It took him a long time to gain recognition from academically trained colleagues. He began his researches at museums of man and special libraries at home. His first publications on the origin of African culture as well as masks and secret societies, published in 1898, found little sympathy with academics. In 1904, he started with field-work, visiting the countries from the Maghrib to the Equator, between the Cameroons and the Red Sea. Initially, he collected folklore, but he progressively turned to pre-historic paintings and engravings, becoming an expert on primitive African art. His expeditions in the Nubian Desert and Tripolitania resulted in a unique collection of copies of rock drawings, later to be housed at the Völkermuseum, Frankfurt am Main. Under his influence the Deutsche Gesellschaft für Kulturmorphologie, as well as the periodical *Paideuma*, were founded in 1938. His writings, much of which has been translated into French, include *Probleme der Kultur* (1901), *Volksmärchen der Kabylen* (1921-22), *Erzählungen aus dem Westsudan* (1922), *Kulturgeschichte Afrikas* (1933), its translation, *La civilisation africaine* (1987), and *Die Felsbilder des Fezzans* (1937). He died at Biganzola, Lago Maggiore, 9 August 1938. DtBE; EnCAm; *Hommes et destins*, vol. 2, pp. 321-324

Frödin, John Otto Henrik, born 16 April 1879 at Uppsala, he received a doctorate in 1914 from Uppsala Universitet for his thesis, *Geografiska studier i St. Lule älvs källområde*. He was a geographer who travelled extensively in the Muslim world. His writings include *Recherches sur la végétation du Haut Atlas. Vem är det*, 1941-1953|

Froehner, Reinhard, born 16 February 1868 at Dresden, Germany, he received a doctorate in 1902 from the Universität Bern for his thesis, *Die Stellung der Kreisthierärzte in Preußen*. He was a sometime veterinarian at Fulda. His writings include *Kulturgeschichte der Tierheilkunde* (1952). LC

Froelich, Jean Claude, born 14 November 1914 at Marseille, he was a graduate of l'École polytechnique and also studied at l'École nationale de la France d'Outre-mer, and received a doctorate in law. He served in French West Africa during the war and was a sometime *directeur d'études* at the Centre des hautes études administratives sur l'Afrique et l'Asie modernes, Paris, as well as a professor of ethnology at the Institut des hautes études d'Outre-mer. His writings include *La tribu Konkomba du nord Togo* (1954), *Cameroun, Togo; territoires sous tutelle* (1956), *Les Musulmans d'Afrique noire* (1962), *La Horde de Gor* (1967), and *Les Nouvaux dieux d'Afrique* (1969). He died in Paris, 26 March 1976. *Hommes et destins*, vol. 2, pp. 326-327; Unesco

Froggatt, Sir Peter, born 12 June 1928, he was educated at Belfast and Dublin. He was a sometime medical doctor at the Institute of Clinical Science, Belfast, and affiliated with Queen's University, Belfast, from 1959 to 1976, the last five years of which as dean of the Faculty of Medicine. His inaugural lecture delivered before the Queen's University of Belfast on 6 May 1970, entitled *Modern epidemiology*, was published in the same year. He was the recipient of numerous awards and honours. Who, 1977-1999

Fröhlich, Hermann, born 18 March 1837 at Gleiwitz, Germany, he studied at the universities of Bratislava and Berlin, where and received a medical doctorate in 1860 for his thesis, *De morbis oesophagi morbis nonnulla*. Thesis

Frohß, Elfgard, fl. 1979, he was a member of the Sektion Afrika und Nahostwissenschaften in the Universität Leipzig. Note

Froidevaux, Henri, born in 1863 at Paris, he prepared for a teaching career and submitted two Latin theses at the Sorbonne in 1891. After briefly teaching at the Lycée de Vendôme, he became associated with the chair of colonial geography at the Faculté de droit de Paris and, in 1898, secretary of its Office colonial. In 1904, he was appointed to the chair of modern and contemporary history at the Institut catholique de Paris, a position which he held until his retirement in 1938. Since 1915, he had been dean of the Institut. For many years he was a director of the journal *L'Asie française*. He died in Versailles, 20 January 1954. DBF

Frolov, Dmitrii Vladimirovich, born 14 September 1946 at Moscow, he graduated from the Institute for Afro-Asian Countries, Moscow State University, in 1970. His writings include Классический арабский стих; история и теория аруза (1991), and he was editor of Арабская средневековая культура и литература (1978). Miliband²

Frolova, Ol'ga Borisovna, born 29 June 1926 at Petrozavodsk, Russia, she graduated in 1950 from the Oriental Faculty, Moscow State University, and became a lecturer there in 1970. Her writings include Мы говорим по-арабски (1972), Поэтическая лексика арабской лирики (1984), and she was joint author of Новое лицо (1974). Miliband; Miliband²

Frolow, A., fl. 1955, his writings include *Recherches sur la déviation de la IVe croisade vers Constantinople* (Paris, 1955). NUC, pre-1956

Fromentin, Eugène Samuel Auguste, born 24 October 1820 at La Rochelle, he began to study law at Paris but early turned to landscape painting. In 1842, he travelled to Algeria, and it was after this journey that he began painting Algerian desert scenes. He visited Algeria twice between 1848 and 1852. The fruit of these wanderings were not only numerous pictures but also two literary works descriptive of his travels, *Un été dans le Sahara* (1956), and *Une année dans le Sahel* (1859). He died 27 August

1876. Biographies were published by Louis Gonse (1881), Prosper Dorbec (1926), Arthur R. Evans (1964), and Marie Anne Eckstein (1970). BiD&SB; CasWL; DBF; DcBiPP; EncAm; EncBrit; Faucon; *Hommes et destins*, v. 8, pp. 198-202; Meyers

Fromkin, David Henry, born 27 August 1932 at Milwaukee, Wisc., he was a graduate of the University of Chicago, and was admitted to the Bar of Chicago, 1953, New York, 1959, and U.S. Supreme Court, 1963. His writings include *The question of government* (1975), *The independence of nations* (1981), and *A peace to end all peace* (1989). ConAu, 109; WhoAmL, 1983; WhoE, 1970/71-1973/74

Fromont, Pierre Jules Auguste, born 29 December 1896 at Rigny-le-Ferron (Aube), he was educated at Rennes, Nancy, and Paris, and was a graduate of l'École normale supérieure. He received a doctorate in 1924 from the Université de Nancy for his thesis, *Le régime juridique de l'électrification des campagnes dans la région lorraine.* He served at the Faculté de droit de Paris, l'Institut national agronomique, and l'Institut des hautes études françaises en Égypte. His writings include *Démographie économique* (1947), *Cours d'économie rurale* (1953), and *L'Agriculture égyptienne et ses problèmes* (1954). He died 19 May 1959. WhoFr, 1953/54-1959/60

Fronzaroli, Pelio, fl. 1955, he was affiliated with the Università di Firenze. His writings include *La fonetica ugaritica* (1955), *Studi yemeniti* (1985), and he was editor of *Studies on Semitic lexicography* (1973), *Studies on the language of Ebla* (1984), and *Miscellanea eblaitica* (1988-90). LC

Frothingham, Arthur Lincoln, born 21 June 1859 at Boston, he was educated at Roma and Leipzig, specializing in Oriental languages. He was a sometime lecturer in archaeology at Johns Hopkins University, Baltimore, Md., and a professor of history of art and ancient history and archaeology at Princeton. He was a founder of several academic journals. He died in 1923. AmAu&B; DAB; DcNAA; WhAm, 1

Frout de Fontpertuis, Adalbert, born 8 December 1825 at Rennes (Ille-et-Vilaine). After college he joined the army and served seven years as a quartermaster. Thereafter he entered municipal politics and contributed articles to French periodicals. He was a sometime member of the editorial staff of *Le Xxe siècle.* DBF

Frowein, Jochen Abraham, born 8 June 1934 at Berlin, he received a Dr.jur. and successively served as a professor of law at the universities of Bochum, Bielefeld, and Heidelberg, and was a director of the Max-Planck-Institut, Heidelberg. He was a joint editor of a number of collective works on international private law. InWW, 1983-1998/99; Kürschner, 1970-2003

Fruzzetti, Lina Maria, born 22 August 1942 at Keren (Cheren), Eritrea, she was a graduate of Rosary College, River Forest, Illinois, and received a Ph.D. in 1975 from the University of Minnesota for her thesis, *Conch-shells bangles, iron bangles; an analysis of women, marriage, and ritual in Bengali society.* She taught anthropology in various capacities at Brown University, Providence, R.I., for over twenty-five years. From 1977 to 1979 she taught at the University of Khartoum. Her writings include *The gift of a virgin; women, marriage, and ritual in a Bengali society* (1982), *Kinship and ritual in Bengal; anthropological essays* (1984), and *Culture and change along the Blue Nile* (1990). ConAu, 113; NatFacDr, 1995-1999

Fry, Jane Beverley, 1911-1996 *see* Drew, Jane Beverly

Fry, Maxwell John, born 12 February 1944 at Maidenhead, Berkshire, he was a graduate of LSE and received a Ph.D. in 1971 from the University of London for his thesis, *Financial aspects of Turkey's economic development.* Thereafter he had a varied record of teaching at Morley College, Middle East Technical University, Ankara, City University of London, University of Hawaii, Boğaziçi Üniversitesi, and the University of California. His writings include *Finance and development planning in Turkey* (1972), *The Afghan economy* (1974), and he was joint author of *Money and banking in Turkey* (1979). Sluglett; WhoWest, 1984

Fry, Roger Eliot, born 14 December 1866 at London, he was an artist, art critic, art historian, translator, and a writer on art, particularly Chinese art. He died of injuries sustained in a fall, 9 September 1934. ConAu, 115; DNB; Master (4); WhAmArt 85; *Who was who*, 3

Frye, Richard Nelson, born 10 January 1920 at Birmingham, Ala., he was a graduate of the University of Illinois and received a Ph.D. in 1946 from Harvard University for a translation and study of Narshakhi's *History of Bukhara.* He spent three years at the Office of Strategic Services, Washington, D.C., before he became a professor at Harvard; since 1956, he was Agha Khan Professor of Iranian Studies. His varied academic career included a year at Hamburg as successor to Wolfgang Lentz as well as some years as a director of the Asia Institute in Pahlavi University, Shiraz. He travelled extensively in Central Asia. His writings include *The heritage of Persia* (1963), *Bukhara; the medieval achievement* (1965), *Persia* (1968), *The golden age of Persia* (1975), and a collection of his articles entitled *Islamic Iran and Central Asia* (1979). Many of his works have been translated into Persian. He was honoured by the jubilee volume, *Richard Nelson Frye Festschrift ... on his 70th birthday* (1992). BioB134; BlueB, 1973/74, 1975, 1976; ConAu, 5-8, new rev., 3; DrAS, 1982; *Journal of Turkish studies* 16 (1992), pp. i-ii; MideE, 1982/83; Schoeberlein; Shavit

Fryzeł, Tadeusz, born in 1939, his writings include *Jedność arabska; idea i rzeczywistość* (1974), and *Arabska myśl socjalistyczna; doktryna socializmu arabskiego* (1985). LC

Fuad, Kamal, born in 1932 at Sulaymaniyah, Iraq. Until 1960 he was a political activist in the Communist Party of Iraq, and after its suppression, a member of the Kurdish Democratic Party of Iraq. In the early 1960s he went as a student to Communist Germany, where he found support from fellow-traveller Buzurg 'Alavi at the Humboldt Universität, Berlin. During his student days from 1963 to 1968 he was chairman of the Kurdish Students' Society in Europe, and from 1964 to 1970, member of the Central Committee of the Kurdish Democratic Party of Irak, responsible for party work abroad. In 1970 he received a Dr.phil. from the Humboldt Universität for his thesis, *Beschreibung und Interpretation der kurdischen Handschriften in den deutschen Bibliotheken*. Thereafter he returned to Iraq, where he was head of the Kurdish Section at Sulaymaniyah University until the Kurdish unrest of 1976, when he once more went to Germany, only that time to the Western part, where he enjoyed refugee status until his final return to Erbil in 1991 as a politician and lecturer. In the autumn of 2002 he was still active in Iraq. His writings include *Kurdische Handschriften* (1970). Private

Fuchs (Фукс), Aleksandra Andreevna (Apekhtina), born in 1805, her writings include *Записки Александры Фуксъ о чувашахъ и черемисахъ Казанской губернiи* (Kazan, 1840). She died in 1853. NUC, pre-1956; TatarES

Fuchs, August, born 22 June (or July) 1818 at Dessau, Germany He pursued private Spanish studies before he studied philology at Leipzig and Berlin. In 1839 he returned to Dessau as an assistant teacher and private tutor of the Prince of Anhalt-Dessau. He died in Dessau, 8 June (or July) 1847, before having obtained tenure. In his short life he displayed an exceptionally broad philological activity which encompassed also Arabic. His writings include *Über die sogenannten unregelmäßigen Zeitwörter in den romanischen Sprachen* (1840), and *Zur Geschichte und Beurtheilung der Fremdwörter im Deutschen* (1842). ADtB; DtBE; Jürgen Storost in: *Beiträge zur romanischen Philologie* 23 (1984), pp. 95-108

Fuchs, Dávid Ráfáel, born 10 December 1884 at Bisenz (Bzenec), Moravia. In early life he came to Hungary, where he graduated from university. After field-work in northern Russia from 1911 to 1913, he became a professor of philology at Budapest. His writings include *Zürjén szövegek* (1916), *Finnugor-török mondattani egyezések* (1934), *Volksdichtung der Komi* (1951), and *Syrjänisches Wörterbuch* (1959). GeistigeUng; MagyarZL; UjMagyar, vol. 2 (1960)

Fuchs, Edmond, 1837-1889 see Fuchs, Philippe Jacques *Edmond*

Fuchs, Karl Ludwig, he received a Dr.phil. in 1955 from the Universität Wien for his thesis, *Familienleben und Gesellschaftsformen nordwestafrikanischer Berberstämme*. Sezgin

Fuchs, Ludwig F., fl. 1939. His writings include *Die Glaskunst im Wandel der Jahrtausende* (Darmstadt, 1956). NUC, 1956-1967

Fuchs, Peter, born 2 December 1928 at Wien, he studied ethnology and anthropology at Wien and received a Dr.phil. He was a sometime professor of ethnology at the Universität Göttingen and conducted four expeditions to Equatorial Africa.. His writings include *Im Land der verschleierten Männer; meine Expedition zu den Tuareg* 1953), *Sudan; Landschaften, Menschen, Kulturen zwischen Niger und Nil* (1977), *Die Völker der Südost-Sahara* (1961), *Das Brot der Wüste* (1983), and *Fachi, Sahara-Stadt der Kanuri* (1989). Kürschner, 1976-1992; Unesco; WhoAustria, 1959/60, 1964, 1967, 1969/70

Fuchs, Philippe Jacques *Edmond*, born 1 April 1837 at Strasbourg, he was a graduate of l'École polytechnique in 1858, and became a professor at l'École impériale des mines in 1862. Since 1873 he had a checkered life as a prospector in France and abroad. From 1873 to 1874 he led hazardous missions in Tunisia to discover the mineral resources of the country. He died in Paris, 7 August, or September, 1889. DBF; NDBA

Fuchs, Walter, born 1 August 1902 at Berlin, he received a Dr.phil. from the Universität Berlin in 1927 for his thesis, *Die politische Geschichte des Turfangebietes bis zum Ende der T'ang-Zeit*. He lived in China from 1935 to 1950. After his return he became a professor of East Asian studies successively at Berlin and Köln. His writings include *Beiträge zur mandjurischen Bibliographie und Literatur* (1936), and *Die Bilderalben für die Südreise des Kaisers Kienlung im 18. Jahrhundert* (1976). He died in Köln, 5 March 1979. A commemorative volume, *Florilegia Mangurica; in memoriam Walter Fuchs*, was published in 1982. DtBE; LC; Schwarz

Fück, Johann Wilhelm, born 8 July 1894 at Frankfurt am Main, he studied oriental and classical philology at the universities of Halle, Berlin, and Frankfurt, where he received a Dr.phil. in 1921 for his thesis, *Muhammad Ibn Ishaq; literatur-historische Untersuchungen*. For a number of years he taught Latin and Greek as well as Hebrew at secondary schools until 1930 when he went for five years to the University of Dacca as a professor of Arabic and Islamic studies. After his return home he taught at Frankfurt until 1938 when he succeeded Hans Bauer in the chair of Semitic languages and Islamic studies at Halle. Concurrently he became director of the Oriental Faculty as well as the Library of the Deutsche Morgenländische Gesellschaft. His writings include *Arabiya; Untersuchungen zur arabischen Sprach- und Stilgeschichte* (1950), its translation, *Arabiya; recherches sur l'histoire de la langue et du style arabe* (1955), *Die arabischen Studien in Europa bis in den Anfang des 20. Jahrhunderts* (1955), and *Vorträge über den Islam* (1999). He died in Halle, 24 November 1974. *Index Islamicus* (3); Kürschner, 1970

Fuehrer (Führer), Jean Louis, born 23 April 1823 at Strasbourg, he was a freemason, a liberal, engaged in the establishment of public libraries, and a journalist of *La Bibliothèque populaire*, and *Elsässisches Volksblatt*. He was a sometime editorial secretary of the *Presse d'Alsace et Lorraine*. During the last year of his life, he was facing legal charges concerning his contributions to the *Rheinbote* when he died in Straßburg, 6 March 1883. NDBA

Fuentes Guerra, Rafael, fl. 1961, his writings include *La evolución de las ciencas exactas y aplicadas en el intercambio cultural de Oriente y Occidente* (1962), and *Maslama, de Madrid, e Ibn Hazm, de Córdoba* (1963). LC

Fuglestad, Finn, born 22 August 1942 at Stavanger, Norway, he studied at the universities of Bergen, Aix-en-Provence, and Birmingham, where he received a Ph.D. in 1976 for his thesis, *An introduction to the history of Niger in the colonial period, ca. 1897 to 1957*. Thereafter he was a research associate at the University of Birmingham, 1973-77, a visiting lecturer at University of Calforcia, Berkeley, 1977, and then held various positions at the Universitetet i Trondheim until 1981, when he was appointed a professor at Oslo. His writings include *A history of Niger, 1850-1960* (1984), and he was joint editor of *Norwegian missions in African history* (1986). Hvem, 1994

Fühner, Fritz, born 20 March 1917 at Königsberg, Germany, he was a professor of medicine at the Universität Hamburg and also served at the Faculty of Medicine, Kabul. He specialized in hygiene of underdeveloped countries. Kürschner, 1970-1992|

Führer, Jean Louis, 1823-1883 *see* Fuehrer, Jean Louis

Fuks, Aleksandra Andreevna, 1805-1853 *see* Fuchs, Aleksandra Andreevna (Apekhtina)

Fulbright, James William, born 9 April 1905 at Sumner, Mo., he gained prominence as a senator from Arkansas and is remembered for initiating the Fulbright-Hayes Act of 1946, also known as the Fulbright Scholarship. A Rhodes scholar, he taught law at the University of Arkansas, where he was appointed the university's president at the age of thirty-four. He later entered politics and served in the U.S. Senate from 1945 to 1974. His writings include *The arrogance of power* (1967). He died in Washington, D.C., 1995. BlueB, 1973/74, 1975, 1976; ConAu; IntWW, 1974-1994/95; Who, 1963-1995; WhoAm, 1986-1995; WrDr, 1976-1996/98

Fulcrand, born in 1823 at Montpellier, he graduated from l'École d'application in 1846 and served in the French army in Senegal and Algeria from 1852 to 1884, advancing through the grades to become colonel in 1877. On his retirement on 4 September 1884, he was awarded the Croix de commandeur. Peyronnet, p. 687

Fulda, Gerhard, born 17 March 1939 at Hamburg, he studied law and Arabic at the universities of Hamburg and Freiburg im Breisgau, and received a Dr.jur. in 1970 for his thesis, *Die Entwicklung des ägyptischen Sozialversicherungsrechts*. An Egyptian government grant enabled him to reside in Cairo from October 1964 to March 1966. Schwarz; Thesis

Fuleihan, Louise, fl. 1945, she was affiliated with the American Junior College for Women, Beirut.

Fuller, Abraham Richard or Richmond, major, born in 1828, he served in the Bengal Army and in the Department of Public Instruction in the Punjab. He died 20 August 1867 near Rawalpindi. An enlarged edition of his *Shah Jahan nama of Inayat Khan* was published in 1990. BLC; LC

Fuller, Americus, Rev., born about 1840, he was a graduate of Bowdoin College, Bunswick, Me., and in 1888 served as a missionary at Aintab (Gaziantep), Turkey. NUC, pre-1956

Fuller, Anne Hewlett, 1896-1983, she studied anthropology at the University of Chicago and spent the year 1937/38 in rural Lebanon as a fellow of the American Association of University Women, holding the Margaret E. Maltby Fellowship. Her writings include *Buarij, portrait of a Muslim village* (1961). LC

Fuller, Mary Lucia Bierce, fl. 1927, her writings include *The Triumph of an Indian widow; the life of Pandita Ramabai* (1928). NUC, pre-1956

Fulton, Alexander Strathern, born in 1888 at Beith, Ayrshire, he studied Semitic languages at Glasgow and briefly taught at the University of Edingburgh before entering the British Museum, London, in 1911, retiring as keeper of Oriental Printed Books and Manuscripts. At various times he also was examiner in Arabic and Hebrew at British universities. He was joint author of a number of catalogues of Arabic printed books in the British Museum. He died 25 June 1976. WhE&EA; *Who was who, 7*

Fumey, Eugène, born in 1870 at Besançon, he studied at l'École des langues orientales vivantes, Paris, where he received diplomas in Arabic, Turkish and Persan. He entered the consular service in 1893 as a student dragoman at Aleppo. After four years, he was posted to the consulate at Fez as dragoman, and in the following year, he became first dragoman at Tanger. In 1901, he led the embassy of the Sultan of Morocco to Paris, and he also took a French mission on a return visit to the Sharifian Court at Fez and Rabat. He was already a sick man when he accompanied the special envoy Saint-René Taillandier to Rabat in 1902. He died in Toulon, 27 March 1903. His writings include *Choix de correspondances marocaines pour servir à l'étude du style épistolaire administratif employé au Maroc* (1903), and the translation, *Chronique de la dynastie alaouite du Maroc, par A. b. Kh. al-Nasiri al-Salawi* (1906-7). DBF

Funck-Brentano, Christian, born 15 August 1894 at Montfermeil (Seine-et-Oise), he was a librarian and an associate of Maréchal Lyautey in Morocco. He was joint author of *Bibliographie marocaine, 1923-1933* (1937). He died in Rabat in July 1966. Coston[2]

von **Funk**, Franz Xaver, born 12 October 1840 at Abtsgemünd, Germany, he studied theology and philosophy at Ellwagen and Tübingen, where he won a prize for a political economy essay in 1862. He received a doctorate in theology in 1863, was ordained in 1864, and studied at Paris in 1865-1866. Since 1870, he was a professor of Church history, patristic studies, and Christian archaeology at the Universität Tübingen. His *Lehrbuch der Kirchengeschichte* has been translated into English and French, and published in many editions. He died in Tübingen, 24 February 1907. DcCathB; DtBE

Funk, Harald, born about 1945 in Germany, he studied Arabic language and literature at the Universität Halle and later worked in academic publishing. He was a sometime staff member of the Institut für Orientforschung, Deutsche Akademie der Wissenschaften zu Berlin. In 1999 he was a lecturer in Arabic at the Institut für Orientalistik in the Universität Halle. Private

Funston, N. John, he was a graduate of Monash University, Melbourne, and a sometime research scholar at the Australian National University. His writings include *Malay politics in Malaysia; a study of the United Malays National Organisation and Party Islam* (1980). LC

Furber, Holden, born 13 March 1903 at Boston, he was a graduate of Harvard, where he also received his Ph.D. in 1929 for his thesis, *Henry Dundas, first Viscount Melville, 1742-1811, political manager of Scotland, statesman administrator of British India*. He also received degrees from Oxford in 1925 and 1930. He held a variety of positions in the U.S. and India until 1948 when he moved to the University of Pennsylvania, where he remained until 1973. His writings include *The John Company at work* (1948), a book which the American Historical Association honoured with the Watumull Prize in 1949, *Rival empires of trade in the Orient, 1600-1800* (1976), and his collected studies entitled *Private fortunes and company profits in the India trade in the 18th century*, edited by Rosane Rocher. He died in his sleep, 19 January 1993. DrAS, 1974, 1978, 1982; *Journal of Asian studies* 52 (1993), pp. 812-813

Furedy, Christine Philippa Margaret, born 9 January 1940 at Colombo, Ceylon, she graduated from the University of Sydney in 1964, and received her Ph.D. in 1971 from the University of Sussex. Thereafter she was a professor at the Division of Social Sciences, York University, Downsview, Ont. Her writings include *The Bhadralok and municipal reform in Calcutta, 1875-1900* (1972). Canadian, 1997; DrAS, 1974-1978; DrASCan, 1978, 1983

Furlani, Guiseppe, born 10 November 1885 at Pola, Istria, he studied law at the Universität Wien, and later at Graz, where he received his doctorate in law in 1908. He received a second doctorate at Graz in 1913 for his thesis, *Beiträge zur Geschichte des Aristoteles bei den Syrern*. He later was a professor of Semitic languages. Apart from his regular duties at the Università di Roma and the Academia Nazionale dei Lincei, he was president of the Società Asiatica Italiana and a member of numerous learned societies. On his seventieth birthday he was honoured by a jubilee volume. His writings include *Religione dei yeidi* (1930). He died in Roma, 17 December 1962. Casati; Chi è, 1928-1961; DizBI; Vaccaro

Furlong, Charles Wellington, born 13 December 1874 at Cambridge, Mass., he studied art in the United States and France, and served in the U.S. Army for thirty-five years, retiring with the rank of major. Before and after the first World War, he led expeditions to Turkey and Tripolitania. After the War, he served as a military observer and intelligence officer in the Balkans and the Near and Middle East. His writings include *Tripoli in Barbary* (1911), and *Gateway to the Sahara* (1914). He died on 9 October 1967. Master (2); Shavit; WhAm, 4; WhAmArt 85

Furlonge, Sir Geoffrey Warren, born 16 October 1903, he entered the Levant Consular Service in 1926 and served more than thirty years in the Middle East and Africa, twelve years of which he spent in an almost continous period in Beirut. His writings include *The lands of Barbary* (1966), and *Palestine is my country; the story of Musa Alami* (1969). He died 15 August 1984. ConAu, 114; Who was who, 8

Furnestin, Jean, he received a doctorate in 1945 from the Université de Marseille for his thesis, *Contribution à l'étude biologique de la sardine atlantique*. In 1952, he was a director of the Institut des pêches maritime du Maroc. His writings include *Ultra-sons et pêche à la sardine au Maroc* (1953). NUC, pre-1956

Furon, Raymond Louis Charles, born 29 March 1898 at Beaumont-le-Roger (Eure), he studied geology and received a doctorate at Paris in 1926. He was for over twenty years a deputy director of the Museum national d'histoire naturelle, Paris, and thereafter a professor at the Faculté des sciences de Paris. He was a member of the Académie des sciences d'outre-mer and led missions to Afghanistan, Africa, Iran and Turkey. His writings include *L'Afghanistan* (1926), *La Perse* (1938), and *L'introduction à l'histoire de la terre* (1970). Au&Wr, 1977; WhoFr, 1961/62-1971/72|

Furrer, Konrad, Dr., 1838-1908, he was a deacon at St. Peter in Zürich. His writings include *Wanderungen durch Palästina* (1865), and *Menschheitsfragen* (1909). GV; NUC, pre-1956

Fussman, Gérard, born 17 May 1940 at Lens (Pas-de-Calais), he was a graduate of l'École nationale supérieure, and from 1972 to 1984 a professor of Sanskrit at the Université de Strasbourg. Since 1985 he held the chair of Histoire du monde indien at the Collège de France. He was joint author of *Une collection de monnaies de cuivre arabo-sasanides* (1984). WhoFr, 1988/89-1998/99

Futaky, István, born 12 May 1926 at Nyircsaholy, Hungary, he was a professor of Finno-Ugric languages at the Universität Göttingen from 1979 until his retirement in 1991. His writings include *Tungisische Lehnwörter des Ostjakischen* (1975), a work which was originally presented as a thesis at Göttingen in 1973. Kürschner, 1980-1996; Schwarz

Futrell, Michael, fl. 1979, he was a sometime professor of Russian at the University of British Columbia. His writings include *Northern underground; episodes of Russian transport and communications through Scandinavia and Finland, 1863-1917* (1963). NUC, 1956-1967

Fux, Herbert, born in 1925, he received a Dr.phil. in 1959 from the Universität Wien for his thesis, *Zur Frage des islamischen Einflusses auf das frühe chinesische Blau-Weiß*. In 1982, he was director of the Österreichisches Museum für Angewandte Kunst. His writings include *4000 Jahre ostasiatische Kunst; Ausstellung* (1978). LC; Schwarz

Fyldes, G. Burford, captain, M.C., fl. 1925-1928, he was in 1928 posted to the Sikh Regiment, Aden.

Fyvel, Tosco Raphael, pseud., 1907-1985 *see* Feiwel, Raphael Joseph

Fyzee (Faizi), Asaf Ali Asghar, born 10 April 1899 in Poona, India, he was educated at St. Xavier's College, Bombay, St. John's College, Cambridge, where he was a Foundation Scholar, and called to the bar from the Middle Temple, London, in 1924. He began practice in the Bombay High Court in 1925 and continued there until he became principal of the Government Law College and its professor of jurisprudence in 1938. After partition, he was a member of the Bombay Public Service Commission until 1949 when he was recruited for diplomatic service as ambassador in Cairo. From 1957 to 1960 he was vice-chancellor of the University of Jammu and Kashmir. After his retirement, he returned once more to Cambridge in 1962 as a Commonwealth Fellow. He died in Bombay, 23 October 1981. His writings include *The Ismaili law of wills* (1933). Cragg; IJMES 14 (1982), p. 418; *Index Islamicus* (2); WhE&EA

Gaál, Lászlo (Ladislaus), born 22 January 1891 at Karcag, Hungary, he was an Indo-Iranian scholar who died at his place of birth on 13 June 1964. MEL, 1967-69

von **Gabain**, Annemarie, born 4 July 1901 at Mörchingen, Lothringen (Lorraine), she grew up in various garrison towns where her father was stationed as a Prussian officer. She studied Chinese and Turkology at Humboldt Universität, Berlin, and did post-doctoral studies in China, 1931-1932. Through the good offices of Prof. Afetinan, she was a visiting professor at Ankara Üniversitesi, 1935-1937. In 1944 she published Özbekische Grammatik, of which only twenty advance copies were distributed. The rest was confiscated after the war on account of objectionable remarks to the Soviet Union. From 1949 until her retirement in 1966, she was professor of Turkology at the Universität Hamburg, though much in the shadow of the arrogant and domineering Spuler. She donated her private papers during her lifetime, particularly to her former student Şinasi Tekin. Friends presented her with Scholia; Beiträge zur Turkologie ... A. von Gabain zum 80. Geburtstag (1981). Her writings include Einführung in die Zentralasienkunde (1979). She died at an old age home in Berlin on 15 January 1993. Index Islamicus (5); Schoeberlein; Ural-altaische Jahrbücher 12 (1993), pp. 1-5

Gabbay, Rony E., born 20th cent. at Baghdad, he received a doctorate in 1959 at Genève for A political study of the Arab-Jewish conflict. His other writings include Communism and agrarian reform in Iraq (1978), and Economic development in a small island economy; a study of the Seychelles Marketing Board (1992). LC; Note

von der **Gabelentz**, Hans Georg Conon, born 16 March 1840 at Poschwitz, Germany, he studied law and philology at Leipzig, where he received a Dr.phil. in 1876 for his thesis, Thai-Kih-Thu, des Tscheu-Tsi Tafel des Urprinzipes mit Tschu-hi's Commentare nach dem Hoh-pih-sing-li, chinesisch mit mandschurischer und deutscher Übersetzung. He practised law from 1864 to 1878, when he was appointed a professor of East Asian languages at Leipzig. In 1899 he accepted a chair at Berlin. His re-search focused on comparative linguistics. His writings include Sprachwissenschaft, ihre Aufgaben, Methoden und bisherigen Ergebnisse (1891). He died in Berlin, 11 December 1893. DtBE; DtBIlnd (3)

Gabelli, Ottone, born 25 March 1880 at Reano del Rojale (Udine), he graduated in law in 1904 from the R. Università di Padova. He served with the Ministry of the Interior from 1905 to 1914, when he joined the Ministero delle Colonie as a secretary, advancing to the post of secretary general to the governor of Cyrenaica in 1929. He later served in similar high posts in Colonie dell'Africa Orientale. His writings include La Tripolitania della fine dalla guerra mondiale all'avvendo del fascismo (1937). He died 9 January 1939. Chi è, 1931, 1936, 1940, 1948|; Rivista delle colonie 13 (1939), pp. 13-15

Gable, Richard Walter, born 16 November 1920 at Joliet, Illinois, he graduated in 1942 from Bradley University and received his Ph.D. in 1950 from the University of Chicago for A political analysis of an employers' association. He was successively a professor of public administration and political science in Ohio State University, Stanford University, and the University of Southern California at David. From 1955 to 1957 he was a member of the University of Southern California's faculty team which assisted the University of Tehran Faculty of Law in establishing the Institute for Administrative Affairs. His writings include Changing governors; the 1982-83 transition in California (1983). AmM&WS, 1973 S, 1978 S; Note; WhoAm, 1974/75-1990

Gäbler-Kaindl, Ulrich, born 3 September 1941 at Villach, Carinthia, he received a Dr.theol. in 1969 at Zürich for Die Kinderwallfahrten aus Deutschland und der Schweiz. He was a professor of canon history, and Rektor in the Universität Basel. He served as a visiting professor at Amsterdam and Harvard. In 1996 he was awarded an honorary doctorate by Budapest University. His writings include Huldrych Zwingli im 20. Jahrhundert (1975). Kürschner, 1976-2001|; WhoSwi, 1992&93, 1996&97, 1998&99|

Gaborieau, Marc, born in 1937, he gained his agrégation de philosophie and was in 1987 an ethnologist and directeur de recherche at the Centre d'Etudes de l'Inde et de l'Asie du Sud in the Ecole des Hautes Etudes en Sciences Sociales. His writings include Minorités musulmanes dans le royaume hindou du Népal (1977), Le Népal et ses populations (1978), and he edited and translated Récit d'un voyageur musulman au Tibet (1973). AnEIFr, 1995, 1997

Gabriel, Albert Louis, born 2 August 1883 at Cerisières (Haute-Marne), he graduated in architecture from the Ecole nationale des Beaux-Arts, Paris, and came to history of art by way of his 1908 appoint-ment to the Ecole française d'Athènes, where he collaboarted with the publication of the excavations at Delos. It was there that he had a chance to prepare his licence ès lettres, which was a prelude to his private researches about Rhodes, providing him with the material for his principle doctoral thesis, La Cité de Rhodes. After the war, during which he served as interpreter with the Division navale de Syrie, he rapidly established himself as an Orientalist. The year following a first mission to Anatolia, he was nominated a lecturer in history of art at Caen and in 1925 he became a professor at the Université de Strasbourg. Concurrently, he taught archaeology at Istanbul until 1930, when he became the first director of the Institut français d'archéologie d'Istanbul, a post which he held until 1956, except the years of the war. During these years he also conducted field work in greater Syria and Persia. In 1946 he was elected to the chair of history of eastern Islamic art at the Collège de France. His other writings include *Châteaux turcs du Bosphore* (1943) and its translation, *Türk kaleleri* (1975). He died in Bar-sur-Aube, 23 December 1972. AnaBrit; Bioln 10; DBF; *Hommes edt destins*, v. 7, pp. 202-3; WhoFr, 1957/8-1971/2

Gabriel, Alfons, born 4 February 1894 at Beraun, Bohemia, he grew up in Wien. As an eighteen-year old he made a trip to North Africa, travelling by way of Kairouan to the Chott el-Djerid and the Sahara. At university he had to decide between geography, his first choice, and medicine, his second choice. He settled for medicine which, in the long run, enabled him the to pursue his main interest. He received his Dr.med. in 1920 and subsequently spent five years in the medical service on Bonaire in the Dutch West Indies. In 1926 he served as a ship's doctor to Mekka pilgrims from Indonesia to Jeddah. Supported by the modest resources of a country physician, he made three long journeys with his wife to explore the Persian deserts from 1927 to 1937, experiences which are embodied in *Weites, wildes Iran; drei Jahre Forschungsfahrten* (1939). After the war he also lectured at the Hochschule für Welthandel, Wien. In 1959 he gave up his practice in the village of Leobendorf and retired to Wien, where he died on 28 May 1976. His writings include *Marco Polo in Persien* (1963), *Vergessene Persienreisende* (1969), *Religionsgeographie von Persien* (1971), and *Die religiöse Welt des Iran* (1974). *Iranzamin* 1 i (1981), pp. 76-82; KDtLK, Nekrolog, 1971-98; Kürschner, 1961-76; *Mitteilungen der Österreichischen Geographischen Gesellschaft*, Wien, 106 (1964), pp. 71-78, and 119 (1977), p. 261; Teichl

Gabriel, Erhard F., born 27 January 1920 at Groß Stein, Silesia, he received a Dr.rer.nat. in 1952 at Hamburg for *Die wirtschaftsgeographische Karte*. He was a professor of economic geogaphy, with reference to the Middle East, at the Universität Köln since 1974. EURAMES, 1993; Kürschner, 1980-2003

Gabriel Sionita (Jibrā'īl al-Sihyūnī), born in 1577 at Ehden (Edden), Lebanon, he was educated from his early youth at the college of the Maronites. He came to Paris through the efforts of Savary de Brèves, former ambassador to Turkey, who wished to issue a polyglott Bible. He succeeded É. Hubert in the chair of Arabic at the Collège de France, a post which later included the teaching of Syriac. He received a doctorate in 1620, and was ordained in 1622. His writings include *Liber Psalmorum Davidis ... ex arabico idiomate in latinum translatus* (Roma, 1614); he was joint author of *Grammatica arabica maronitarum* (Paris, 1616); and he translated from the Arabic of al-Idrīsī, *Geographia nubiensis* (1619). He died in Paris in 1648. BN; Casanova, pp. 46-51; DcCathB; EncicUni; Fück, p. 73; GdeEnc

Gabrieli, Francesco, born 27 April 1904 at Roma, he was successively a professor of Arabic at Istituto universitario orientale di Napoli and Università di Roma. In 1984 he was honoured by *Studi in onore di Francesco Gabrieli nel suo ottantesimo compleanno*. His writings include *Al-Ma'mun e gli 'Alidi* (1929), *Il califato di Hishām* (1935), *Narratori egiziani* (1941), *Dal mondo dell'islàm* (1954), *Storia della lettera-tura araba* (1956), *Storici arabi delle crociate* (1957), its translation, *Die Kreuzzüge* (1973), *Gli Arabi* (1958), and its translation, *Geschichte der Araber* (1963). *Chi è*, 1948-1961; IndBiltal (4); Wholtaly, 1958, 1980

Gabrieli, Guiseppe, born 4 April 1872 at Calimera, nel Salento, he entered the Università di Napoli in 1891, and there studied Arabic under Lupo Buonazia. In 1895 he joined the Istituto di studi superiori di Firenze where he became a pupil of Fausto Lasinio for Arabic and of David Castelli for Hebrew. He graduated in 1895 with a thesis on the life, times and poems of the Arab poetress al-Kansa, which was published in 1899. In the same year, he completed the requirements for the diploma of Arabic in the Istituto orientale di Napoli, where his teacher was Carlo A. Nallino to whom he was runner-up in 1900 in the competition for the chair of Arabic in the Università di Palermo. In 1902 he became librarian of the Reale Academia die Lincei and later taught Arabic at the Università di Roma. During the first World War he began a long-enduring association with Prince Leone Caetani, who dedicated the fifth volume of the *Annali dell'Islam* to Gabrieli, acknowledging him as the most faithful and constant of his collaborators with this important work. Gabrieli is best remembered for his *Manuale di bibliografia musulmana* (1916). He died in Roma, 7 April 1942. *Chi è*, 1931, 1936, 1940; DizBI; IndBiltal (6)

Gabuchan, Grachiia Mikaelovich, born 24 September 1926 at Cairo, he graduated in 1953 from Erevan State University and received his first degree in 1967 for Категория артикля в арабском литературном языке. He was since 1957 affiliated with the Institute of Asian and African Studies in Moscow State University. His writings include Теория артикля и проблемы арабского синтаксиса (1972), and he was joint editor of Литературный арабский язык в текстах (1993). Miliband; Miliband²

Gacek, Adam, born 20 December 1949 at Maków, Poland, he graduated in 1973 from Uniwersytet Jagiellónski, Kraków, and the School of Library Science, Polytechnic of North London. He began his career in 1978 as a researcher at SOAS. He later became head of the Library of the Institute of Ismaili Studies, London. Since 1987 he was head of the Library of the Institute of Islamic Studies, McGill University, Montreal. He was joint editor of *Manuscripts of the Middle East*. His other writings include *Catalogue of the Arabic manuscripts in the Library of the School of Oriental and African Studies, University of London* (1981), *Catalogue of Arabic manuscripts in the Library of the Institute of Ismaili*

Studies (1981-85), *Arabic lithographed books in the Islamic Studies Library, McGill University descriptive catalogue* (1996), and *The Arabic manuscript tradition; a glossary of technical terms and bibliography* (2001). Private

Gacon, Jean, born 13 September 1904 at Neuville-sur-Saône (Rhône), he was a colonel who served in the Levant with the Services Spéciaux from 1932 to 1941, particularly at Deir ez-Zor, Antioch, Alexandrette, Baalbek, and Lattaquie. After the war he was U.N.O. observer in Palestine and served in Indochina. He was a competent local administrator with considerable experience among the Kurds, Nusayris and Armenians of northern Syria. He had been affiliated with the Centre de Hautes Etudes d'Administration Musulmane, Paris, from 1942 to 1946. His *mémoire d'entrée* as well as two reports on the *Exode des Arméniens du Moussa Dagh* and *La Bekaa* are documents of prime importance which are kept at the Centre's archives. He died 24 October 1965. *l'Afrique et l'Asie* 72 (1965), p. 74

Gadant-Benzine, Monique, born 20th cent., she received a doctorate in 1978 from the Université de Paris for her thesis, *Contribution à la lecture d'El-Moudjahid, organe centrale du FLN, 1956-1962*, a work which was published in 1988. Her other writings include *Women of the Mediterranean* (1986), *Le Nationalisme algérien et les femmes* (1995), *Parcours d'une intellectuelle en Algérie* (1995), and she was joint editor of *Femmes du Maghreb au présent; la dot, le travail, l'identité* (1990). Livres disponibles, 2003; THESAM, 2

Gaddafi, Mu'ammar Muhammad, 1942- see Qadhdhafi, Mu'ammar Muhammad al-

Gaden, Nicolas Jules *Henri*, born 24 January 1867 at Bordeaux, he graduated from the Lycée Louis-le-Grand, Paris, and passed through the military college, Saint-Cyr, in 1890. He requested service in the French Sudan, where he became successively Deputy Resident at Bandiagara, Resident at Zinder, Niger, Resident to the Sultan of Baghirmi, and acting Governor of Chad, 1905-1906. In 1908 he became commandant and administrator of the Cercle de Trazza in Mauritania. After his resignation he was nominated administrator first class of the colonies and attached to Afrique Occidentale Française. During the Great War he served in Morocco until invalided home; he subsequently entered the French civilian colonial administration in Mauritania. At the time of his retirement in 1926 he was Governor General of Mauritania. His writings include *Le poulâr dialecte peul du Fouta sénégalais* (1912), *Proverbes et maximes peuls et toucouleurs* (1931), and he edited and translated *La Vie d'el Hadj Omar, qacide en poular* (1935). He died in Saint-Louis de Sénégal, 12 December 1939. DBF; *Hommes et destins*, 8, 151-152

Gadille, J., fl. 1955, he was affiliated with the Comité de géographie du Maroc. His writings include *Exploitations rurales européennes* (Rabat, 1958).

Gadlo, Aleksandr Vil'iamovich, born 20th cent., his writings include Этническая история Северного Кавказа IV-X вв. (1979). LC

Gadzhibekov (Hajybǎǐov), Uzeir Abdul Gusein ogly (Үзеjир Әбдулһүсеjн оғлу һачыбəjов), born in 1885 at Karabagh, he originally trained for a teaching career but soon turned first to literature and then music composition. He gradually gained wide popularity also beyond his Caucasus audience. For many years he was a teacher of the Azeri musical tradition. His writings include О музыкальном искусстве Азербайджана (1966), *Āsǎrlǎrı*, ed. Kubad Kasimov (Baku, 1974), and Беш манат əнвалаты (1974). He died 23 November 1948. AzarbSE, vol. 10, pp. 147-150; BiobibSOT, p. 144; GSE

Gadzhiev (Hajyǐev), Maksud Ibragim ogly, born 10 September 1935 in Azerbaijan, he graduated in 1959 from the Oriental Faculty, Azerbaijan State University, and received his first degree in 1966 for Конахкендскии говор языка татов. He was since 1959 affiliated with the Oriental Institute in the Azerbaijan Academy of Science. He was a researcher of the State Committee for Economic Relations in Afghanistan, 1962-64 and 1979-83, and in Iran, 1966-68 and 1971-74. He was joint author of Русско-персидскии разговорник с кратким грамматическим очерком персидского языка, техническом словарем и справочинком по Ирану (Isfahan, 1973). Miliband[2]

Gadzhiev (һачыjев/Hajyǐev), Pasha Azizbala ogly, he wrote Азербайджанская советская графика 1920-1940 гг. (Baku, 1962), and Заманын боjары (Baku, 1979). OSK

Gadzhiev (Hajyǐev), Tofig I., born 20th cent., he was associated with the Azerbaijan State University. His writings include Азəрбаjчан əдəби дили тарихи (Baku, 1976), Молла Нəсрəддинин дили вə үслубу (Baku, 1983), and he was a joint editor of Азəрбаjчан дилинин таризи лексикасына даир тəдгиглəр = Исследования по исторической лексике азербайджатского языка (1988). OSK

Gadzhieva, Ninel' Zeinalovna, born 4 December 1925 at Baku, she graduated in 1948 from Moscow State University, received her first degree in 1952 for Типы придаточных предложений в современном азербайджанском литературном языке, and her doctorate in 1970 for Основные пути *развития синтаксической структуры тюркских языков.* Her writings include *Синтаксис сложно-подчиненного предложения в азербайджанском языке* (1963), *Проблемы тюркской ареальной лингвистики* (1975), *Тюркоязычные ареалы Кавказа* (1979), and *Сравнительно-историческая грамматика тюркских языков* (1986). She died 28 October 1991. Miliband; Miliband²

Gadzhieva, Sakinat Shikhamedovna, born 20th cent., her writings include *Материальная культура кумыков XIX-XX вв.* (1960), *Кумык; этнографическое исследование* (1961), *Семья и брак у народов Дагестана в XIX- начале XX в.* (1985), and she was joint author of *Женщины Советского Дагестана* (1960), and *Материальна культура даргинцев* (1967). OSK

Gadzhinskii, D. D., he wrote *В огне революционной борьбы* (Baku, 1965). NUC, 1956-67

Gaebelé, Yvonne (Robert), fl. 1948, she wrote *Créole et grande dame, Johanna Bégum* (Pondichéry, 1934), and *Une Parisienne aux Indes au XVIIe siècle* (Pondichéry, 1937). NUC, pre-1956

Gafarov, Abdullo, born 5 July 1931 in Tajikistan, he graduated in 1953 from the Faculty of History and Philology, Tajik State University, and received his first degree in 1962 for *Жизнь и творчество Мирзы Азадуллы Галиба (1797-1869).* He subsequently became affiliated with the Oriental Institute in the Tajik Academy of Science. His writings include *Мирза Асадулла Галиб* (1965), and *Индия и Пакистан* (1987). He died 25 August 1990. Miliband²

Gaffarel, Paul Louis Jacques, born 2 October 1843 at Moulins (Allier), he went to school in Paris, before studying history and geography at the Ecole normale supérieure. He taught history at second-ary schools successively in Montpellier and Marseille and in 1869 had his two theses accepted at the Sorbonne. In 1873 he started his university career at Dijon, holding the chair of history in the Faculté des lettres. In 1881 he founded the Société bourguignonne de géographie; in 1892 he was elected dean of his faculty; and in 1901 he transferred to the Faculté des lettres d'Aix-Marseille. In 1909 he became vice-president of the Société de géographie de Marseille and there he died on 27 December 1920. His prolific writings, particularly in colonial history, include *Les Colonies françaises* (1880), *L'Algérie; histoire, conquête et colonisation* (1883), *Le Sénégal et le Soudan française* (1890), *Le Conquête de l'Afrique* (1892), and *L'Expansion coloniale en Afrique de 1870 à nos jours* (1918). DBF

Gaffarov (Ghafforov), Razzak, born 15 January 1932 at Samarkand, he graduated in 1949 from the Samarkand Teachers' College and in 1953 from the Faculty of Philology in the Leninabad State Pedagogical Institute. He received his first degree in 1964 for *Язык и стиль Рахима Джалила* and his doctorate in 1981 for *Синтаксис таджикских говоров в сравнительном освещенин.* His writings include *Ленин о языке* (1966) as well as works in Tajik. Miliband²

Gafferberg, Édit Gustavovna, fl. 1936-1970, she wrote *Белуджи туркменской ССР* (Leningrad, 1969).

Gaffiot, Maurice, fl. 1928, he wrote *Les Théories sociales d'Anatole France* (Alger, 1923), and he was joint author of *L'Œuvre législative de la France en Algérie* (Paris, 1930). NUC, pre-1956

Gaffney, Patrick Daniel, born in 1947, he received a Ph.D. in 1982 from the University of Chicago. In 1982 he was associated with the Department of Sociology and Anthropology, University of Notre Dame, Ind., a post which he still held in 1990. He belonged to the Dominican Order and wrote *The Prophet's pulpit; Islamic preaching in contemporary Egypt.* (1994). MESA Roster of members, 1982-1990

Gafurdzhanova, Tamila Iusufdzhanovna, born 20 December 1935 at Tashkent, she graduated in 1959 from the Faculty of Philology, Tashkent State University and received her first degree in 1966 for *Надыр и его поэма «Хафт гулшан.»* Since 1959 she was affiliated with the Institute of Language and Literature in the Uzbek Academy of Science. Milband²

Gafurov (Ghafurov), Alimdzhan (Olim) Gafurovich, born 15 November 1931 in Tajikistan, he graduated in 1954 from the Institute of History, Moscow State University, and received his first degree in 1964 for *Лично-собственные Имена в таджикческих языке.* He was from 1963 to 1970 affiliated with the Oriental Institute, Tajik Academy of Science. His writigs include *Рассказы об именах* (1968), *Лев и кипарис; о восточных именах* (1971), *Этимология географических Имен* (1983), *Имя и история; об именах арасов, таджиков и тюрков* (1987), and works in Tajik. Miliband²

Gafurov, Bobodzhan Gafurovich, born 31 December 1908 at Ispisar, Tajikistan, he received his first degree in 1941 for *История секты исмаилитов с начала XIX в. до мировой империалистической войны* and his doctorate in 1952. He was a historian and since 1956 director of the Oriental Institute in the Soviet Academy of Science. His writings include *В. И. Ленин - великий друг народов Востока* (1960), and he was joint author of *Ал-Фараби в истории культуры* (1975) as well as works in Tajik. Russian biographies were published in 1969 and 1985. He died in Dushanbe, 12 July 1977. GSE;

578

IntWW, 1974/75-1977; *Journal of Central Asia* 3 (1980), pp. 167-172; Miliband; Miliband²; NYT,14 July 1977, p. 18, col. 5; TurkmenSE; WhoSocC, 1978

Gafurova, Kapitolina Aleksandrovna, she wrote *Борьба за интернациональое сплочение трудящихся Средней Азии и Казахстана в первые годы Советской власти* (1972). NUC, 1973-77

Gagemeister, Iulii Andreevich, 1806-1878 *see* Hagemeister, Julius von

Gagnier, Jean (John), born about 1670 at Paris. After the death of his father, his twenty-four year old mother entered a nunnery and left him in the care of the Church. He received a humanistic education, including Hebrew and Arabic, at the Collège de Navarre. After taking orders, he was made a *chanoin régulier* of the Abbey Ste-Geneviève-du-Mont, Paris, but finding life irksome, he went to England, married and became an Anglican clergyman. He taught Hebrew and Oriental languages at Oxford and was in 1777 appointed to the chair of Arabic. His writings include *De vita et rebus gestis Mohammedis*, translated from the Arabic of Abū al-Fidā', together with the text (1723). He died in 1740. BritInd (6); Dantes 1; DBF; Dezobry; DNB; Hoefer; IndexBFr² (2)

v. **Gähler**, Sigismund Wilhelm, born 20 October 1704 at Haag, he was a Danish civil servant. In the service of King Frederik V he was sent in 1752 on a trade mission to Constantinople, endeavouring to conclude a commercial treaty with the Porte. In disguise of a horse dealer, he travelled first to Wien and then by way of Hungary to Constantinople, where he was successful only after prolonged negociations. He died in Altona, 28 December 1788. DanskBL

Gaibi, Agostino, born 1 July 1891 at Bologna, he was affiliated with the Istituto Coloniale Italiano, Roma. His writings include *La guerra d'Africa, 1895-1896* (Roma, 1930), and *Storia delle colonie italiane* (Torino, 1934). Chi è, 1928, 1931, 1936, 1940|

Gaibrois de Ballesteros, Mercedes, 1891 or 2-1960 *see* Ballesteros, Mercedes née Gaibrois y Riaño de

Gaidarzhi, Gavril Arkad'evich, born 20th cent., he wrote *Гагаузский синтактис* (1973), *Гагаузско-русско-молдавский словарь* (1973), *Gagauz Türkçesinin sözlüğü* (1991); and he edited *Современная гагаузская топонимия и антронимия* (1989). LC

Gaillard, Claude, born in 1930 at Rabat, he received a *doctorat d'état* in 1956 and in 1981 was teaching at the Université d'Alger. His writings include *Economie et droit du développement* (1982), and *Le Portugal sous Philippe III d'Espagne* (1982). LC

Gaillard, Gaston, born 19th cent., he was an editor of the journal *Orient & Occident* (Paris, 1922-23). His writings include *L'Allemagne et le Baltikum* (1919), *Les Turcs et l'Europe* (Paris, 1920), and *The Turcs and Europe* (1921). His trace is lost after an article in 1957.

Gaillard, Joseph Xavier *Henri*, born 19 March 1859 at Paris, he graduated in 1883 from the Ecole des Chartes, Paris, as an archival palaeographer. Interested in teaching, he passed his *agrégation*. He was a secondary school teacher of history and geography successively in Cluny, Laval, and Poitiers until 1924, when he retired to Paris, giving up at the same time his presidency in the Société des Antiquaires de l'Ouest. His writings include *Histoire du moyen âge et des temps modernes* (1899), *Une Ville de l'islam, Fès* (1905), and *La Réorganisation du gouvernement marocain* (1916). He died in Paris on 19 January 1942. DBF; NUC, pre-1956

Gaillardon, B., born 19th cent., he wrote *Manuel du vigneron en Algérie et Tunisie* (1886). His trace is lost after a publication in 1889. NUC, pre-1956

Gaillardot, Joseph Arnaud *Charles*, born in 1814 at Lunéville (Meurthe-et-Moselle), he completed his medical studies in 1836 at Paris. Through the good offices of E. F. Jomard, he was in the same year nominated a professor of natural history at Cairo University. When war broke out between Egypt and the Porte, he became an army physician and participated in the Syrian campaign. After the treaty of London, he entered the Ottoman Army and was appointed head physician of the hospital in Saida as well as medical inspector in Syria. During the 1860 turmoil in the Lebanon, he was able to save numerous Christian families. He participated with the Mission archéologique Renan in Syria from 1861 to 1863, when he was nominated *médecin sanitaire* of France in Egypt. He later served as a director of the Ecole de médecine du Caire. He died near Beirut on 27 August 1883. DBF; Henze; IndexBFr² (1)

Gain, Edmond Eugène, born 6 September 1868 at Marle (Aisne), he was educated at the Collège de Soissons and the Sorbonne, where he received a doctorate in 1895 for *Recherches sur le rôle physiologique de l'eau de la végétation*. He was a professor of applied natural sciences at institutes and schools in Paris and Nancy. In 1893 he headed a scientifique mission on vegetal physiology to Algeria and Tunisia. He was successively affiliated with the Faculté des sciences, the Institut colonial

et agricole, and the botanical gardens in Nancy. He died in Reims on 20 March 1950. DBF; IndexBFr²
(1)

Gainullin, Mukhammad Khairullovich, born in 1903, he received a doctorate in philology in 1958, and in 1967, he was appointed a professor. He served as a director of the Kazan Branch of the Soviet Academy of Science, 1944-1953 and 1959-1961. His writings include *Татарская литература и публицистика начале XX века* (1966), and *Татарская литература XIX века* (Kazan, 1975). He died in 1985. TatarES; WhoSocC, 1978

Gairdner, William Henry Temple, born 31 July 1873 at Ardrossan, Scotland, he graduated from Trinity College, Oxford. He was an Arabist and later joined the Church Missionary Society. He became Canon of the Protestant Cathedral, Cairo, and served as associate editor of the *Moslem world*. Cairo was the centre of his life activities since 1899. A great part of his later years was given to to the training of younger missionaries. His writings include *Egyptian colloquial Arabic* (1917), *The Phonetics of Arabic* (1925), and he translated *Mishkāt al-anwār* (1924), from the Arabic of al-Ghazzālī. He died in Cairo on 22 May 1928. Constance E. Padwick wrote *Temple Gairdner of Cairo* (1929). Bioln 5; BritInd (1); LuthC, 1975; *Missionary review of the world*, 52 (1929), pp. 91-96; *Muslim world* 18 (1928), p. 226; Note; *Who was who* 2

Gaitskell, Sir Arthur, born in 1900, he was educated at Winchester, and New College, Oxford. He was for twenty years a member of the Commonwealth (formerly Colonial) Development Corporation. His writings include *Gezira; a story of development in the Sudan* (1959), *Report on land tenure and land problems in the territories of Tanganyika and Ruanda-Urundi* (1959), and *Alternative choices in development strategy and tactics; the Mekong River Project* (1973). He died in 1985. Who, 1973-1985

Gal, Allon, born in 1934 in Palestine, he was educated at a Kibbutz Teachers' College, the Hebrew University, and Brandeis University, Waltham, Mass., where he received his Ph.D. in 1975 for *Brandeis, progressivism, and Zionism*. He became an instructor and lecturer in Judaic studies. His writings include *Socialist Zionism* (1973), *Brandeis of Boston* (1980), and *David Ben Gurion and the American alignment for a Jewish state* (1988). ConAu 45-48, new rev. 1

Gǎlǎbov, Gǎlǎb D., 1882-1972 see Gülübov, Gülüb D.

Galal, Kemal Eldin, born 1 March 1903 at Ed Damer in northern Sudan, he was a graduate of a Cairene secondary school and a technical college. From 1922 to 1926 he was a student at Technische Universität, Berlin, to which journalism at Humboldt-Universität was added from 1934 to 1936. Throughout his residency in Berlin he was a free-lance writer for Egyptian periodicals. In 1938 he became *al-Ahrām* correspondent. In 1939 he gained a Dr.phil. at Berlin for his thesis, *Entstehung und Entwicklung der Tagespresse in Ägypten*. Thesis

Galand, Lionel, born 11 May 1920 at Aluze (Saône-et-Loire), he was successively a professor at l'Institut des Hautes études marocaines, Rabat, and a *directeur d'études* at Ecole pratique des Hautes études, Sorbonne, a post which he still held in 1993. His writings include *Langue et littérature berbère* (1979), and he was joint author of *Inscriptions antiques du Maroc* (1966). EURAMES, 1993; Unesco

Galand-Pernet, Paulette, born 9 December 1919 at Montchanin (Saône-et-Loire), she was successively affiliated with l'Institut des Hautes études marocaines, Rabat, and CNRS as a *maître de recherche* (honorairé). Her writings include *Une Version berbère de la Haggadah de Pesah* (1970), and *Recueil de poèmes chleuhs* (1972). EURAMES, 1993; Unesco

Galanté, Abraham, born in 1873 at Bodrum, Turkey, he was a scholar of Jewish history in Turkey and a sometime professor at Istanbul. His writings include *Türkler ve Yahudiler* (1928), *Histoire des Juifs d'Anatolie* (1937-39), and *Les Juifs sous la domination des Turcs seldjoukides* (1941). He died in 1961. AnaBrit; EncJud; JüdLex; Wininger

Galbiati, Gilberto, born 20th cent., he wrote *Il Concilio di Efeso* (Genova, 1977), *Islam e Cristianesimo, due defi a confronte* (Firenze, 1991), *Diversità dell'Islam* (Firenze, 1993), and *Testi sacri dell'Islam* (Firenze, 1999). LC; *Catalogo die libri in commercio*, 2002

Galbiati, Giovanni (Johannes), born 12 March 1881 at Carugo (Como), he studied classics and theology, including Hebrew, at Università cattolica di Milano. Since 1924 he was a *prefetto* at the Biblioteca Ambrosiana, Milano, and concurrently taught classical philology as well as Arabic and Islamic institutions at the Università cattolica. He died in Milano in 1966. Chi è, 1928-1961; DizBI; IndBiltal (5); Wholtaly, 1958

Galbraith, John Semple, born 10 November 1916 at Glasgow, he graduated in 1938 from Miami University. From 1948 to 1964 he was a professor of history at UCLA, and from 1964 to 1968 he served as chancellor of the University of California at San Diego. His writings include *The Hudson's Bay Company as an imperial factor* (1957), *Mackinnon and East Africa* (1972), and *Crown and charter*

(1974). BlueB, 1973/74, 1975, 1976; ConAu 5-8, new rev. 6; DrAS, 1974 H, 1978 H, 1982 H; WhoAm, 1974/75, 1995-2000; WhoWor, 1974/75.1987; WhoWest, 1980/81, 1982/83

Galdieri, Eugenio, born 20th cent., he was in 1974 a field director for the Istituto Italiano per il Medio ed Estremo Oriente(Roma), Centro di Restauri team in Isfahan. His writings include *Isfahan* (1972-84), *A few conservation problems concerning several Islamic monuments in Ghazni* (1978), *Esfahan; Ali Qapu* (1979), and he was joint author of *Progretto di sistemazione del Maydan-i Šah* (1969). Note; ZKO

Galdston, Iago, born in 1895 in Russia, he graduated from Fordham University, where he also received his M.D. in 1921. He was a psychiatrist who later became a professor at his alma mater. His writings include *The Meaning of social medicine* (1954), and *On the utility of medical history* (1958). He died in 1989. AmM&WS, 1973, 1976, 1979 P; Master (3); NYT, 20 December 1989, p. D23, col. 1

Galea, Guże' (Joseph), born in 1912, he studied history at Malta and Oxford. He was a member of several British learned societies as well as the Malta Society of Arts. In 1960 he was an archives assistant at the Royal Malta Library. His writings include *Żmien l-ispanjol* (1949), *Id-Dinja rota* (1968), and *Xogħol u snajja' taimgħoddi* (1969). Mifsud; ZKO

Galena, Silvan, pseud., 1855-1909 *see* Gopčević, Spiridion

Galerkina, Olimpiada Isaevna, born 24 March 1919 at Petrograd, she received her first degree in 1951 for *Материальная культура Средней Азии и Хорасана XV-XVI вв. по данным миниатюр ленинградских собраний*. In 1963 she was appointed a lecturer. Her writings include *Художник Виктор Васнецов* (1975), and *Искусство Индии древности и в средние века* (1963). She died on 5 November 1988. Miliband; Miliband²

Galgóczy, János (Johann), born 1 June 1838 at Nagykörös, Hungary, he was affiliated with an insurance company until his retirement in 1893, when he began to pursue studies in Sumerian philology which he published in German and French periodicals. His trace is lost after a publication in 1901. GeistigeUng

Galiautdinov, Ishmukhamet Gil'mutdinovich, born 1 January 1948 in Bashkiria, he received a doctorate in 1992 and, in 1994, was appointed a professor. He was joint author of *Проблемы изучения башкирских литературно-публицистических и фольклорных источников* (1982), and *Источниковедение Башкирской филологии* (1984). BashkKE

Galib (Galip), Ismail, 1847 or 8-1895 *see* Edhem, Ismail Galip

Galib 'Ata', 1880-1947 *see* Ata, Galip

Galin, Salavat Akhmadievich, born 3 March 1934 in Bashkiria, he received a doctorate in 1995 and concurrently was appointed a professor. He was joint author of *Аннотированный библиографический указатель по башкирскому устнопоэтческомы творчеству* (Ufa, 1967). BashkKE

Galindo Aguilar, Emilio, born 20th cent., he received a doctorate in philosophy, specializing in Islamic philosophy. He was a sometime director of Instituto Darek-Nyumba, Madrid. His writings include *Islam; ayer, hoy, mañana* (Madrid, 1960). Arabismo, 1992, 1994, 1997; EURAMES, 1993

Galinet, L. P., born 20th cent., his writings include the twenty-five-page booklet, *Le Monde du travail de l'Afrique française* (1904). BN

Galinier, Joseph Germain, born 27 November 1814 at Belpech (Aude), he graduated in 1835 from the military college, Saint-Cyr, and from 1837-1839 passed through the general-staff college. In 1839 he and his classmate, Adolphe Ferret, were granted a leave of absence from the military to accompany the explorer Edmond Combes on a geographical and commercial mission to Abyssinia. Galinier first spent eight months in Cairo studying Arabic, before setting out on the pilgrim route to Mecca, surveying the Hijaz mountain range on the way, and arriving at Massawa in October 1840, one year after departing from Marseille. After a year and a half he arrived back in Toulon on the 1st of March 1843 laden with several cases of geological, cartographical and astronomical data which he jointly prepared for publication during the following years. In 1851 he carried on geodesic work in Algeria. As acting commandant in 1853 at Laghouat he was in charge of operations against rebel tribesmen; in 1854 he led an expedition to the Oued Sébaou in the Algerian Sahara. After his return to metropolitan France he had a distinguished career as a general. He retired in 1878 and died in Versailles in 1887. He was joint author, with A. Ferret, of *Voyage en Abyssinie dans les provinces du Tigré, du Samen et de l'Amhara* (1847). DBF; Henze

Galitzin, E., 1804-1853 *see* Golitsyn, Emmanuil Mikhailovich

Galiullin, Tălgat Nabievich (Təлгат Галиуллин), born in 1938, he was since 1965 affiliated with the Elabuga Pedagogical Institute, and since 1971 its rector. He received a doctorate in 1981 and was appointed a professor in 1983. In 1989 he was appointed a lecturer in the University of Kazan. His writings include *Яңа урлəр яаулаганда; əдəби-тəнкыйть мəкалəлəре* (Kazan, 1972). *Дыхание времени* (Kazan, 1979), and *Безнең заман - узе жыр* (Kazan, 1982). TatarES

Galkin (Galkine), Mikhail Nikolaevich, born 19th cent., his writings include *Этнографические и исторические материалы по Средней Азии* (S. Petersburg, 1868). BN; NYPL

Galkin, Il'ia Savvich, born about 1900, he was a lecturer in contemporary history. His writings include *Германя в 1870-1914* (1940), *Дипломатия европейских держав* (1960), and *Н. М. Лубинб революионер, ученый* (1984). In 1972 he was honoured by *Проблемы новой и новойшей истории. [Проф. И. С. Галкину в связис его 70-литием посвящ]* (1972). LC; NUC, 1956-67; OSK

Freiherr von **Gall**, August Georg, born 18 September 1872 at Lemgo, Westphalia, he studied Protestant theology and Oriental languages at Halle, Berlin and Gießen, where he received a Dr.phil. in 1895 for *Die Einheitlichkeit des Buches Daniel*. He was a high school teacher at Mainz and subsequently at Gießen, where he was since 1913 a professor of Old Testament studies. His writings include *Die Herrlichkeit Gottes* (1900), and *Der hebräische Pentateuch der Samaritaner* (1914-18). He died on 4 October 1946. DtBE; Kürschner, 1931-1940/41

Gall, Lothar, born 3 December 1936 at Lötzen, East Prussia, he received a Dr.phil. in 1960 and a Dr.habil. in 1967. He was successively a professor of modern German history at Gießen, Freie Universität Berlin, and Frankfurt am Main. In 1972-73 he was a visiting professor at Oxford. His writings include *Benjamin Constant* (1963), and *1871 - Fragen an die deutsche Geschichte* (1971). ConAu 157; Kürschner, 1970-2003; WhoWor, 1989/90, 1991/92

Gallagher, Charles Frederik, born 1 May 1923, he joined the American Universities Field Service in 1956, reporting on Arab and Muslim affairs. His writings include *The United States and North Africa* (1963), and the 15-page booklet, *Turkey between two worlds; a demographic view* (1982). More than fifty of his booklets are listed in NUC, 1956-72. LC; Note; Shavit

Gallagher, John S., born 20th cent., he was a transport economist with extensive experience in transport operations, management and planning in both developed and underdeveloped countries. He worked in Nepal, Thailand and Afghanistan, as well as in Europe and the Americas. In 1979 he served as an UNTAD (United Nations Conference on Trade and Development) senior adviser within ITC's (International Teletraffic Congress) trade promotion project in Afghanistan. His work in this project was carried out with the substantive support of UNTAD's Special Programme for Least Developed, Landlocked and Island Developing Countries. His writings include *The Post Offices of Ohio* (1979). Note

Gallagher, Michael Desmond, born 20th cent., he served with the British Army. After his retirement, he was in 1980 an assistant to Government Adviser for Conservation of the Environment, Oman. He was a joint author of *The Birds of Oman* (1980). Note

Gallagher, Nancy Elizabeth, born 14 September 1942 in Alamedo County, Calif., she graduated B.S. in 1964 from the University of California at Berkeley and received her Ph.D. in 1977 from UCLA for *Epidemics in the Regency of Tunis*. She did field work in history of epidemics in Tunisia and Egypt, as well as in the international women's human rights movement. A member of MESA and the American Institute for Maghribi Studies, she was appointed a professor of history in the University of California at Santa Barbara in 1978, a post which she still held in 2003. From 1975 to 1976 she was a junior fellow of St. Antony's College, Oxford, where she wrote her dissertation. She was the recipient of a Macarthur Foundation grant in 1991. Her writings include *Arabic medical manuscripts at the U.C.L.A.* (1983), and *Egypt's other wars; epidemics and the politics of public health* (1990). Private

Galland, Antoine, born in 1646 at Rollot (Picardie), he was an Orientalist who made three journeys to the Ottoman Empire. He was the first European translator of the *Arabian nights*, which were published in twelf volumes (1704-1717), soon to be translated in turn into German and English. He also completed D'Herbelot's *Bibliothèque orientale*. Since 1709 he held the chair of Arabic at the Collège de France. His other writings include *Le Voyage à Smyrne*; un manuscrit d'Antoine Galland, ed. Frédéric Bauden (2000). He died in Paris in 1715. AnaBrit; DBF; EncBrit; EncicUni; EncItaliana; Fück, pp. 99-100; GdeEnc; GDU; IndexBFr² (12); JA 289 (2001), pp. 1-66; *Livres disponibles*, 2003; Master (2); Meyers; Pallas; RNL

de **Galland**, Charles Louis Emile, born 17 December 1851 in Algeria, he was successively a school teacher at Alger, Aix-en-Provence, Tournon, Montauban, and again Alger. His writings include *Histoire du Collège, du grand Lycée d'Alger et du petit Lycée de Bou-Aknoun 1833-1889* (1889), *Les Petits cahiers algériens* (1900), and *Alger et l'Algérie* (1924). He died in 1923. IndexBFR² (1); NUC, pre-'56

Gallego y Burín, Antonio, born 20 January 1894 or 1895 at Granada, he was a director of the Museo Arqueológico Provincial and a professor at the Universidad de Granada. His writings include *Guía de Granada* (1938), *El barocco granadino* (1956), *La Alhambra* (1963), *Los Moriscos del Reino de Granada* (1968), and *Granada; guía artística e histórica* (1982). He died in Madrid, 13 January 1961. IndiceE³ (5)

Gallenga, Antonio Carlo Napoleone, born in 1810 at Parma, where he went to school and began to study. When the French revolution of 1830 roused all Italy, the excitement of politics drew him from the study of medicine. In the following year, he left Italy for political reasons, settling abroad and earning a precarious livelihood as a journalist and by teaching and writing. His writings, partly under the pseudonym Louis or Luigi Mariotti, include *Two years of the Eastern question* (1877), *A Summer tour in Russia* (1882), and *Iberian reminiscences* (1883). He died in Wales in 1895. Toni Cerutti wrote *Antonio Gallenga, an Italian writer in Victorian England* (1974). BiD&SB; DizBI; DNB; IndBiltal (12)

Galles, René, born in 1819 at Vannes (Morbihan), he went to school in Nantes and subsequently first entered the Polytechnique in 1838 and then the Ecole d'application de l'Artillerie et du Genie de Metz, from which he graduated in 1840 as a *sous-lieutenant*. He joined the military administration and became *sous-intendant* at Vannes, Alger and Nantes. After the 1870-71 war he was appointed *intendant* of the tenth Army Corps at Rennes. In 1881 he retired to Arradou (Morbihan) to pursue an interest in archaeology and history. He died there on 12 August 1891. BN; DBF

Galletti, Mario, born in 1924, he wrote *L'ora della Spagna* (Roma, 1975). LC

Galletti, Mirella, born 20th cent., she gained a doctorate and was a member of the Gruppo di ricerca sul Medio Oriente contemporaneo, Bologna, a post which she still held in 1993. Her writings include *I Curdi nella storia* (1990). EURAMES, 1993

Galley, Micheline, born 22 November 1926, she wrote *Badr az-zîn et six contes algériens* (1971?, she was joint author of *Femmes de Malte dans les chants traditionels* (1981), and she was joint editor of *Histoire des Beni Hilal et de ce qui leur advint dans leur marche vers l'ouest* (1983). LC; ZKO

Gallez, Paul J., born in 1920 at Bruxelles, he was a historian, geographer and economist who gained a doctorate in political science, as well as a diploma in law. He lived in Argentina. His writings include *Das Geheimnis des Drachenschwanzes* (1980), and *La cola del dragon* (1990), a translation from the German translation of the author's unpublished manuscript, *Protocartographie de l'Amérique du sud du deuxième au seizième siècle*. LC

Gallico, Loris, born in 1910 at Tunis, he wrote *Storia del Partito communista francese* (1973), and *L'altro Mediterraneo tra politica e storia* (1989). LC; ZKO

Gallieni, Joseph Simon, born 24 April 1849 at Saint-Beat (Haute-Garonne), he prepared at La Flèche for admittance to the military college at Saint-Cyr. He graduated on the eve of the outbreak of the Franco-Prussian war, during which he was wounded, taken prisoner, and brought to Ingolstadt, where he spent some time at a German teacher's home. After his liberation, he served three years at Réunion. This was the beginning of a long colonial career, which can be easily followed up as he kept a meticulous day to day diary. He served in Senegal, passed through Ecole de guerre, was posted to Indo-China and to Madagascar. During the Great War he became the defender of Paris despite his poor state of health, which eventually required his resignation. He died at a Versailles hospital, 27 May 1916. His writings include *Deux campagnes au Soudan française* (1891). He is the subject of numerous biographies. AfrBioInd (4); BioIn 2, 11; DBF; Curinier 4 (1903), pp. 249-51; Embacher; Henze; *Hommes et destins*, vol. 3, pp. 212-15; IndexBFr² (4); Master (4); Vapereau; WhoMilH, 1976 & 1987

Gallissot, René, born 20th cent., he was a sometime lecturer at the Université d'Alger, before teaching at the Université de Paris. In 1969 he was affiliated with the Centre d'études et de recherches marxistes, Paris. His writings include *L'Economie de l'Afrique du nord* (1961), *Le Patronat européen au Maroc* (1964), *L'Algérie pré-coloniale* (1968), *Misère et antiracisme* (1985), *Maghreb-Algérie; classe et notions* (1987); he was joint author of *Ces migrants qui font le prolétariat* (1994); and he edited *Mouvement ouvrier, communisme et nationalismes dans le monde arabe* (1978). LC; Note

Gallman, Waldemar John, born in 1899 at Wellsville, N.Y., he graduated from Cornell University and Georgetown Law School. A year later, he entered the U.S. foreign service. His writings include *Iraq under General Nuri; my recollections of Nuri al-Said, 1954-1958* (1964). He died in 1980. BioIn 16; ConAu 11-12, 101, new rev. 76; NYT, 30 June 1980, p. D-15, cols. 4-6; WhoAm, 1974/75, 1976/77; WhAm 7

Gallo, Rodolfo, born in 1881, "he distinguished himself by his industrious research in Venetian archives and libraries and by his prolific publications on painters, architects and graphic artists of the Republic, as well as her most notable explorers, Marco Polo and Giovanni Caboto. To these labours he devoted the leisure from his regular employment in the service of the Comune di Venezia and subsequently of the Italian Government." His writings include *Il tresore di S. Marco e la sua storia* (1967). He died in 1964. Imago mundi 21 (1967), p. 115; NUC, 1968-72

Gallois, Eugène, born in 1856 at Paris, he studied music and painting, but also pursued an interest in finance and geography. In the service of the ministries of Instruction publique, and Colonies, he travelled extensively throughout the world. He was a founding member of the Société de géographie de Lille. His many writings include *La Poste et les moyens de communication des peuples à travers les siècles* (1894), *Excursion à la capitale de Tamerlan* (1898), *Aux Oasis d'Algérie et de Tunisie* (1905), and *Asie-mineure en Syrie* (1907). He died in 1916. Curinier 3 (1901), pp. 86-87; DBF; LC

Gallois, Lucien Louis Joseph, born 21 February 1857 at Metz, he went to school at Lyon and studied at Ecole normale supérieure, where he received a doctorate for *Les géographes allemands de la Renaissance*. He was an authority in ancient geography and served as a professor at the Université de Lyon from 1889 to 1893, when he was appointed a professor at the Sorbonne For fifty years he was the *cheville ouvrière* of the *Annales de géographie*, contributing numerous articles on a wide range of subjects. He died in 1941 following a road accident. Bioln 1, 2; DBF; Dickson; Qui est-ce, 1934

Gallotta, Aldo, born 20th cent., he wrote *Il turco osmanli del XVI secolo secondo il "Gasavāt-i Ḥayreddīn Paşa* (1984), and he edited *Studi preottomani e ottomani; atti* (1976), and *Studia turcologica memoriae Alexii Bombaci* (1982). LC

Gallotti, Jean, born 4 March 1881 at Irai (Orne), he must have been an architect when he left for Morocco towards the beginning of the French occupation and there lived close to General Lyautey. He subsequently returned to France and pursued an interest in literature of long standing. His writings include *Le Jardin et la maison arabe au Maroc* (1926), *Moorish houses and gardens of Morocco* (1926), and *Le Palais des papes* (1949). He died 4 February 1972. DBF; Oursel

Galloway, Christian F. J., born 19th cent., he was an English mining engineer, whose specialty was coal. While travelling in the interest of his profession in various parts of the world, he found many unusual customs. In Persia he had the opportunity of seeing the Shi'ite Muharram procession. His writings include *The Call of the West; letters from British Columbia* (1916), and *Poverty amidst plenty* (1933). Note; NUC, pre-1956

Galloway, John Herbert, born 22 January 1949 at Stranraer, Scotland, he graduated in 1960 from McGill University, Montreal, and received his Ph.D. in 1965 from the University of London. He was since 1977 a professor of geography at Victoria College in the University of Toronto. His writings include *The Sugar cane industry; an historical geography from its origins to 1914* (1989). Canadian, 1990-2002; NatFacDr, 1995-2003

Galmés de Fuentes, Álvaro, born 20th cent., he received a doctorate in 1967 in Semitic philology for *El libro de las batallas*. He was a professor of Romance philology, and a chairman of the Departamento de Árabe y Filología Románica in the Universidad di Oviedo. In 1997 he was a member of the Real Academia de la Historia and a professor emeritus, Universidad Complutense de Madrid. His writings include *Dialectología mozárabe* (1983), *Toponimia de Alicante* (1990), *Las jarchas mozárabes* (1994); he edited *Dichos de los siete sabios de Gracia* (1991); and he was honoured by *Homenaje a Álvaro Galmés de Fuentes* (Oviedo, 1985-87). Arabismo, 1992, 1994,1997; EURAMES, 1993

Galopin, Maurice Edmond Pierre, born 3 February 1921 at Guelma, Algeria, he was educated at the Lycée d'Aumale, Constantine, and the Faculté des lettres d'Alger. He received diplomas in Arabic and Berber linguistics. He was an officer of the Affaires militaires musulmanes (1944); director of the Muslim information centre at the French embassy in Tunis (1951); director of the Arabic and Kabyle service of the French radio and television in Algeria (1958); and a professor of Arabic at Ecole speciale militaire de Saint-Cyr-Coëtquidam (1961). From 1963 to his retirement in 1980 he was a liquid gas executive as well as director of the Franco-Libyan Chamber of Commerce. He died 18 June 1990. WhoFr, 1977/78-1989/90

Galster, Jørgen Georg Castonier, born 17 May 1889 at København, he studied history, Danish and Latin. In 1910 he entered the Department of coins and medals in the Nationalmuseet, København, and remained there until his retirement in 1959. His writings include *Die Münzen Dänemarks* (1939), *Coins and history; selected numismatic essays* (1959), *Næstved mønt* (1966), and *Ancient British and Anglo-Saxon coins* (1964). He died in Hässleholm, 22 May 1974. DanskBL; Kraks

Galston, Miriam S., born 8 January 1946, she received a Ph.D. in 1973 from the University of Chicago for *Opinion and knowledge in Farabi's understanding of Aristotle's philosophy*. She was in 1995 affiliated with the School of Law in George Washington University, Washington, D.C., a post which she

584

still held in 2003. Her writings include *Politics and excellence; the political philosophy of Alfarabi* (1990). LC; NatFacDr, 1995-2003; Selim³

Galt, Russell, born in 1889, he received a Ph.D. in 1936 from AUC for *The effects of centralization on education in modern Egypt.* He was successively affiliated with AUC and Susquahanna University, Selinsgrove, Pa. His writings include the booklet, *The conflict of French and British educational philosophies in Egypt* (1933). He died in 1959. NYT, 17 March 1959, p. 33, col. 3; Selim; Shavit

Galtier, Jean Mathieu *Emile*, born 23 August 1864 at Millau (Aveyron), he planned on a colonial career and started to study Arabic at l'Ecole supérieure d'Alger, but subsequently entered secondary education. He was a teacher at the Lycée in Mont-de-Marsan (Landes) in 1903, when, as an Arabist, he was nominated a member of the Institut français d'Egypte. Four years later, he obtained the position of librarian at the Musée des antiquitées égyptiennes, Cairo, however, he died there on 2 April 1908 before taking office. He was a modest scholar of ancient languages derived from, or related to Arabic, particularly Coptic. During his lifetime he edited *Foutouh al Bahnasâ* (Le Caire, 1909). After his death, his friends published some of his unpublished manuscripts entitled *Mémoirs et fragments inédits* (1912). DBF; Egyptology

Galton, Sir Francis, born in 1822 at Duderton near Birmingham, he studied medicine and subsequently graduated from King's College, Cambridge. He travelled in the Middle East from 1845 to 1846 and later also in South Africa. His writings include *Heredity genius* (1869), its translation, *Genie und Vererbung* (1910), *Essays in eugenics* (1909), and *Memories of my life* (1911). He died in 1911. AfrBioInf (5); BbD; BritInd (7); ConAu 121, 183; DcScB; DLB 166 (1996), pp. 177-83; DNB; Embacher; Henze; Hill; Master (38); Rosenthal; *Who was who* 1

Gal'tsev, V. S., fl. 1954, he wrote *Борьба за Советскую власть в Северной Осетии; спорник документов и материалов* (Ordzhonikidze, 1972). NUC, 1973-77

Galtung, Johan Vincent, born 24 October 1930 at Oslo, he gained a doctorate and became the founder of the Institut for Fredsforskning, Oslo, in 1959. He was a professor of peace research at the Universitet i Oslo from 1969 to 1977. He was awarded numerous honorary doctorates and held many visiting professorships throughout the world. His writings include *Fredsforskning* (1966), *Peace, war and defense* (1976), and *Non-violence and Israel/Palestine* (1989). Hvem er hvem, 1973-1994

Galunov, Roman Andreevich, he wrote *Русско-персидский словарь* (1936-37).

Galustian, Andranik Arutiunovich, born 20th cent., he was joint author of *Фразеологический словарь армянского языка* (1975).

Galuzo, Petr Grigor'evich, born in 1897 in Vitebsk Oblast, he gained a doctorate in history in 1965. In 1969 he was appointed a professor. His writings include *Туркестан - колония* (1929), *Аграрные отношения на юге Казахстана в 1867-1914 гг.* (1965), and he edited *Казахстан в канун Октября* (1968). He died in Alma-Ata on 9 April 1980. KazakSE, vol. 3, p. 140; *Казахская ССР краткая энциклопедия*, vol. 3 (1989), p. 146

Gálvez Vázquez, María Eugenia, born 20th cent., she gained a doctorate in Semitic philology, specializing in contemporay Arabic literature. She was a professor in the Departamento de Árabe, Facultad de Filología de Sevilla. Her writings include *El Cairo de Mahmūd Taymūr* (1974). Arabismo, 1992, 1994, 1997; EURAMES, 1993

da **Gama**, Vasco, born in 1469, he was a Portuguese navigator and discoverer of the sea-route to India. He died in 1524. AnaBrit; Henze; EncBrit; EncicUni; EncItaliana; GdeEnc; Master (33)

Gämbärov (Гәмбәров), M. G., born 20th cent., he was associated with the Azerbaijan Academy of Science. His writings on modern Arabic literature include *hафиз Ибраһимин поезијасы* (1978), and *Муасир әрәб ше'риндә сијаси лирика* (1990). LC

Gambier, James William, born 16 June 1841 at Livorno (Toscana), he was educated at Cheltenham College and became a commander in the Royal Navy. He also served as Justice of the Peace for the county of Sussex and as a *Times* special correspondent during the Russo-Turkish war. His writings include *Servia* (1878), and *Links in my life on land and sea* (1906). BritInd (1)

Gambier-Parry, Ernest, major, born in 1853, he was a graduate of Eton who entered the army and served in the Sudan where he was seriously wounded. He was a writer, painter, and musician. His writings include *Suakin, 1885; being a sketch of the campaign of the year, by an officer who was there* (1885). He died in 1936. BLC; BritInd (1); Who, 1921-1936; *Who was who*, 3

Gámir Sandoval, Alfonso, born 23 January 1899 at Granada, he was a historian whose writings include *Algunos viajeros del siglo XIX ante Malaga* (1962), and he was joint author of *Los moriscos del Reino de Granada* (1968). He died 17 November 1962. LC

Gamm, Niki, fl. 1980, he was in 1977 a member of MESA and resident in Vancouver, B.C. MESA Roster of members, 1977

Gamow (Gamov), George (Georgii Antonovich), born in 1904 at Odessa, he was a theorectical physicist and science popularizer. His writings include *Atomic energy in cosmic and human life* (1947), *One, two, three ... infinity* (1947), and its translations into Turkish, *Bir, iki, üç... sonsuz* (1964), and into Chinese in 1978. He died in 1968. AMS, 1965; ANB; ConAu 93-96, 102; CurBio, 1951, 1968; DAB; DcScB; Master (23); WhAm 5; *Who was who* 6

de **Ganay**, Solange, fl. 1924-1951, her writings include *Le Binou Yébéné* (Paris, 1942), *Les Devises des Dogons* (Paris, 1942), and she was a joint author of *La Génie des eaux chez les Dogons* (1942). BN; NUC, pre-1956

Gandilhon, René, born 22 November 1907 at Bourges (Cher), he was educated at the Lycée de Bourges and Ecole nationale des chartes, Paris. He was an archival palaeographer and received a doctorate in 1940 from the Université de Toulouse for *Politique économique de Louis XI*. He served as an archivist of the Département of Ille-et-Vilaine, 1934-41, chief curator and director of antiquities of the Département of Marne, 1941-1971, and *inspecteur général des archives*, 1971-1978. His writings include *Bibliographie générale des travaux historiques et archéologiques publiés par les sociétés savantes de la France* (1944-61). He died on 1 December 1990. WhoFr, 1963/64-1990/91

Gandin, Jean Marie, born 20th cent., he received a doctorate in 1973 from the Université de Paris for his thesis, *Luttes entre les héritiers du Sa'idien Ahmed el-Mansour et remise de Larache aux Espagnols en 1610*. THESAM, 1

Gandjei, Tourkhan, born early 20th cent., he was a writer on classical Persian literature, who edited *The Makārim al-Akhlāq; a treatise on Alishir Navaï*, by Khvandamir (1979). LC

Gandolphe, Paul Lucien *Maurice*, born 25 February 1874 at Vincennes, he studied at the Sorbonne, where he received an arts degree in 1894. On the recommendation of the Alliance française, he became for three years a lecturer at Göteborgs Universitet. He subsequently abandoned pursuit of the teaching for the career of a journalist in the Far East, the Balkans, and the Islamic world, particularly in Northwest Africa. Invalided in the first World War, he became an interpreter and section chief at the Ministry of Foreign Affairs. After the war he represented French interests at international negociations. His writings include *La Crise macédonienne; enquête dans les vilayets insurgés, september-décembre 1903* (1904), and *Système de paix et de sécurité mondiale* (1949), a work in which he propounded peace based on the collaboration of all men outside established institutions. He died in a road accident in 1947. DBF

Gandon, Francis, born 20th cent., his writings include *Sémiotique et négativité* (1986). BN; LC

Gandy, Christopher Thomas, born in 1917, he was educated at King's College, Cambridge. After serving with the Royal Air Force during the war, he entered H.M. Diplomatic Service in 1945 and retired in 1973. He spent much of his career in the Middle East. He was a senior associate member of St. Antony's College, Oxford. BlueB, 1973/74, 1975, 1976; Master (1); Who, 1966-2002

Gandz, Solomon, born 2 February 1883 at Tarnobrzeg, Austria-Hungary, he received a traditional Jewish education at home until the age of sixteen and then matriculated at the Gymnasium of Bielitz, Silesia. He received a Dr.phil. in 1911 at Wien and in 1914 completed his rabbinical training at the Israelitisch-Theologische Lehranstalt, Wien. From 1915 to 1919 he was a professor of Jewish theology in Viennese high schools. From 1923 to 1934 he was a librarian and professor of Arabic, Yeshiva University, N.Y.C. From 1942 until his death at the end of March 1954 he was research professor of history of Semitic civilization at Dropsie College for Hebrew and Cognate Learning, Philadelphia, Pa., except for the war years, 1943-45, when he was in government service. His writings include *History of science; reprints* (Berlin, 1928-36). CnDiAmJBi; Fück, p. 258; *Isis* 46 (1955), pp. 107-110; NYT, 1 April 1954, p. 31, col. 1; Wininger

Ganem (Ghānim), Chékri (Shukrī), born in 1861 in Ottoman Syria, he was a poet and politician. Condemned to death by the Turkish Government, he found refuge in France. He was a sometime editor of *Correspondance d'Orient*, and he was in 1917 one of the founders of the Comité Central Syrien in Paris and served as their president until 1921, when ill-health obliged him to retire to Antibès, (Alpes-maritimes), where he died in 1929. His writings include *Antar, pièce en cinq actes, en vers* (Paris, 1910), and *La Giaour; drame* (Paris, 1928). *Correspondance d'Orient*, vol. 12 (juillet/décembre 1919), pp. 412-417, vol. 21, n° 377 (May 1929), pp. 193-195

586

Ganiage, Jean, born 8 June 1925, he received a *doctorat ès lettres* in 1957 from the Université de Paris. From 1956 to 1961 he was a professor of contemporary history at the Université de Tunis. His writings include *La Population européenne de Tunisie au milieu du XIXe siècle* (1960), *L'Expansion coloniale et les rivalités internationales de 1871 à 1914* (1964), *Les Origines du protectorat français en Tunisie* (1968), and *Les Affaires d'Afrique du nord de 1930 à 1958* (1972). Unesco

Ganier, Germaine, born 8 October 1899 at Cherbourg, she lost her father, a colonial head of a marine battalion in Senegal, when still an infant. She went to school at Légion d'honneur establishments, first at Ecouen and then Saint-Denis, where she suffered the worst of uninspired traditional education imaginable. With the diplomas she received, she remained at these schools, becoming «*Dame*» (*professeur*), first of music and then of French history and geography. Concurrently she obtained in 1939 a *licence ès lettres* and a diploma from l'Ecole des hautes études. After having spent nearly half a century with establishments of the Education de la Légion d'honneur, she had to take early retirement in 1959. She devoted her retirement years to research in French colonial campaigns in which her father had participated, however, since 1978 her eyesight began to fail and she became nearly blind, putting an end to all of her work. Her writings include *La Politique du connétable Anne de Montmorency* (1957), and *Papiers d'Afrique* (1963). She died in 1987. AfrBioInd (1); Hommes ed destins 9, pp. 192-93

Ganiev, Abdukhafiz, born 2 November 1929 at Tashkent, he graduated in 1951 from the Central Asian State University and received his first degree in 1955 at Moscow for *Страдательный залог в современном литературном пушту*. His writings include *Очерки по глагольной фразеологии литературного пушту* (1985), and he edited *Иранская филология* (Tashkent, 1966), *Русско-татарский словаь* (1984), and he was joint editor of *Проблемы лексикологии и лексикографии татарского языка* (1992). He died on 16 January 1992. Miliband; Miliband²

Ganiev, Fuat Ashrafovich, born in 1930, he was since 1962 affiliated with the Tatar Academy of Science. His writings include *Видовая характеристика глаголов татарского языка* (1963), and *Образование сложных слов в татарском языке* (1982). TatarES

Gankovskii, IUrii Vladimirovich, born 6 April 1921 at Kharkov, he graduated in 1942 from the Faculty of History, Moscow State University, and received his first degree in 1958 for *Очерки государственного строя и военной системы державы Дуррани*, and his doctorate in 1966 for *Национальный вопрос и национальные движения в Пакимтане*. He was since 1956 affiliated with the Oriental Institute, Soviet Academy of Science. He was appointed a lecturer in 1961 and professor in 1965. His writings include *Империя Дуррани* (1958), its translation into Pashto in 1979, *Народы Пакистана* (1964), its translation, *The peoples of Pakistan* (1971), *Народная Республика Бангладеш* (1974); he was joint author of *История Пакистана* (1961), and its translation, *A history of Pakistan* (1964); *История Афганистана* (1982), and its translation, *A history of Afghanistan* (1985). Miliband; Miliband²

Gannagé, Elias A., born 20th cent., he was from 1966 to 1984 a professor at the Faculté de droit et des sciences économiques in the Université Saint-Joseph, Beirut. His writings include *La Réforme des impôts directs au Liban et en Syrie* (1947), *Economie du développement* (1962), its translation, *Economia del desarrollo* (1964), *Théories de l'investissement direct étranger* (1984), and *Economie de l'endettement internationale* (1994). Note

Gannagé, Pierre, born 18 December 1923 at Beirut, he received a doctorate in law in 1947 from the Université de Lyon. He was throughout the 1950s and 1960s affiliated with the Faculté de droit et des sciences économiques de Beyrouth as a professor of civil law and private international law. His writings include *Le Rôle de l'équité dans la solution des conflits de lois en jurisprudence française et libano-syrienne* (1949). His trace is lost after a publication in 1983. Note; WhoWor, 1974/75

Ganns, Ortwin, born about 1900, he received a Dr.habil. in 1941 at Praha for *Geologie der Zlatar Planina*. He was affiliated with Deutsche Gesellschaft der Wissenschaften und Künste, Prag. His writings include *Zur Geologie von Südost-Afghanistan* (1979), and its translation, *On the geology of SE Afghanistan* (1970). GV; Note; NUC, 1968-72

Ganshof, François Louis Arthur Marie, born 14 March 1895 at Brugge (Bruges), he studied at Gent (Gand) and Paris and served from 1923 to 1961 as a professor of medieval history and legal history at Gent. His writings include *Qu'est-ce que la féodalité* (1944), and its translation, *Feudalism* (1996). He died in Bruxelles in 1980. BioIn 12; ConAu 19-20; IntWW, 1974/75-1980; NBN, vol. 5, pp. 171-74; WhoWor, 1974/75

Ganske, Joachim, born about 1930, he received a Dr.jur. in 1960 from the Universität Köln for *Der Begriff des Nachteils bei den strafprozessualen Verschärfungsverboten*. He was the editor of *Umwandlungsrecht* (1995). LC

Ganzenmüller, Konrad, born 27 December 1841 at Zoltingen, Bavaria, he received a doctorate in 1877 from the Universität Leipzig for *Tibet nach den Resultaten geographischer Forschungen*. He was a civil servant at the statistical bureau, Dresden. He died there in 1905. BioJahr,, vol. 10 (1905), Totenliste, col. 171*

Ganzin, Eugène, fl. 1856-1859, he wrote *Léthargie de la boulangerie parisienne industriel-propriétaire à Alger* (1856), and *De la situation du credit commercial, industriel et agricole en Algérie et de son organisation par la Banque de France* (1858). BN

Garaudy, Roger, born 17 July 1913 at Marseille, he was educated at the Lycée Henri IV, and the Faculté des lettres, Paris, and completed his formal studies with the degree *docteur ès lettres*. He was a member of the Communist Party since 1933, incarcerated in a German concentration camp, served three terms at the Assemblée nationale, was its vice-president, 1956-1958, and a correspondent of *l'Humanité* in the Soviet Union. Since 1965 he was *maître de conférences* at the Faculté des lettres de Poitiers. He published his autobiography, *Parole d'homme* (1975). In 1982 he embraced Islam. His writings include *L'islam habite notre avenir* (1981), *Promesse de l'islam* (1981), its translation, *Verheißung des Islam* (1989), *L'affaire Israël* (1983), *L'islam en Occident* (1987), and *Les mythes fondateurs de la politique israélienne* (1996). WhoFr, 1965/66-2002/2003; WhoWor, 1974-1976

Garbarino, Taddeo, born 25 April 1906 at Roma, he received a doctorate in law and commerce, and became a senior tax official, a administrator of a variety of societies, journalist, and publisher. Lui, chi è

Garbell, Irene, born about 1900, she was a linguist affiliated with the Hebrew University, Jerusalem. Her writings include *The Jewish Neo-Aramaic dialect of Persian Azerbaijan* (1965) as well as a Hebrew work in 1963. Note

Garbers, Karl, born early 20th cent., he received a Dr.phil. in 1936 from the Universität Hamburg for *Ein Werk Ṯābit b. Qurra's über ebene Sonnenuhren* and a Dr.habil. in 1948 from the Universität Leipzig for *Buch über die Chemie des Parfüms und die Destillation*, translated from the Arabic of Yaʻqūb ibn Isḥāq al-Kindī. His other writings include *La matemática y la astronomía en la edad media islámica*; traducción del alemán (1954); he edited and translated *Maqāla fī-'l-mālihūliyā; vergleichende kritische arabisch-lateinische Paralleausgabe of Isḥāq ibn 'Imrān* (1977); and he was joint editor of *Quellengeschichtliches Lesebuch der Araber im Mittelalter* (1980). GV; LC; Sezgin

Garbini, Giovanni, born 8 October 1931 at Roma, he was a professor of Semitic epigraphy and philology successively at Roma, Napoli, Pisa, and again Roma. A member of the Accademia dei Lincei, Roma, he wrote *Il semitico di nord-ovest* (1960), *The ancient world* (1966), its translation, *Die Kulturen des Vorderen Orients* (1968), *Le lingue semitiche* (1972), *Storia e problemi dell'epigrafia semitica* (1979), *Il semitico nordoccidentale* (1988), and *Il Filisti* (1997). ConAu 21-24, new rev. 9, 25, 51; IndBiltal (1)

Garbuzova, Virineia Stefanovna, born in 1914 at Petrograd, she graduated in 1939 from the Faculty of Philology, Leningrad, and subsequently was affiliated with the Hermitage Museum until 1954. She received her first degree in 1956 for Сказание о Мелике Данышменде, как древнейший тюркоязычный литературный на территории Малой Азии and her doctorate in 1975 for Турецкая поэзия XIII-XX в. Her other writings include Поэты средневековой Турции (1963) and Поэты Турции (1963). Miliband; Miliband²

Garcia, Luc, born in 1937 in Benin, she wrote *Le Royaume du Dahomé face à la pénétration coloniale* (1988). LC

Garcia, Sandra Joanne Anderson, born 10 August 1939 at Buffalo, N.Y., she graduated in 1966 from Texas Western College and received her Ph.D. in 1971 from the University of Southern California for *The relationship of hypnotic suspectibility, EEG alpha, achievement, and parent's child rearing practices*. Since 1970 she taught psychology at the University of Southern Florida, Tampa. She edited *Child and families* (1991). NatFacDr, 2003; WhoAmW, 1991/92, 1993/94. 1995/96

García Alix, Antonio, born in 1852 at Murcia, he was a lawyer and politician who was appointed in 1900 a minister of public instruction. He was joint author of *Función del rey en el regimen constitucional y parlamentario* (Madrid, 1910). IndiceE³

García Antón, José, born in 1915, he gained a doctorate in history, with special reference to the Arab world and Islam. His writings include *Fortificaciones en la costa de Aguilas, siglo XVI al XIX* (1988), and *Estudios historicos sobre Aguilas y su entorno* (1992). Arabismo, 1992; LC

García-Arenal Rodriguez, Mercedes, born 20th cent., she received a doctorate in Semitic philology, with special reference to the history of the Maghreb. In 1993 she was a professor in the Departamento de Estudios Árabes, Instituto de Filologia, C.S.I.C., Madrid. Her writings include *Los Moriscos* (1975),

Los moros y judios en Navarra en la baja edad media (1984); she was joint author of *Repertorio bibliográfico de las relaciones entre la Peninsula Ibérica y el Norte de África* (1989), *Los españoles y el Norte de Africa, siglos Xv-XVIII* (1992); and she edited *Relaciones de la peninsula Ibérica con el Magreb, siglos XIII-XVI; actas* (1988). Arabismo, 1992, 1994, 1997; EURAMES, 1993

García Arias, Luis, born 24 April 1921 at Chantaga (Lugo), Spain, he was a professor of international public and private law successively at Zaragoza, Santiago de Compostela and Madrid. His writings include *La guerra moderna y la organización internacional* (1962), and *Corpus iuris gentium* (1968). He died in 1973. IndiceE³ (1); WhoSpain, 1963

García Ayuso, Francisco, born in 1835 at Valverde de Camino (Segovia), he pursued studies in the humanities at Segovia and took Arabic and Hebrew at Tánger and Tetuán. He was a sometime *profesor auxiliar* in the Universidad Central, Madrid. In 1893 he was elected a member in the Real Academia de la Lengua Española. His writings include *Los pueblos iranios y Zoroastro* (1874), *Iran, ó del Indo al Tigris; descripcion geográfica de los países iranios* (1876), and *El Afghanistan* (1878). He died in Madrid in 1897. EncicUni; IndiceE³ (1); Sainz

García Ballester, Luis, born 20th cent., at Valencia, he gained a medical doctorate, with special reference to history of medicine, and became a professor in his subject at Barcelona and Santander. His writings include *Alma y enfermedad en la obra de Galeno* (1972), *Historia social de la medicina en la España de los siglos XIII al XVI* (1976), *Medicina ciencia y minorias marginadas; los Moriscos* (1977), *Los Moriscos y la medicina* (1984), *La medicina a la Valencia medieval* (1988), *Medical licensing and learning in fourteenth-century Valencia* (1989), and he edited *Practical medicine from Salerno to the black death* (1994). Arabismo, 1992|; Note

García Banquero y Sáinz de Vicuña, Galo, born 31 May 1881 at Luanco (Asturias), he was affiliated with the Colegio provincial de médicos, La Coruña, as well as the district Academy of Physicians and Surgeons. WhoSpain, 1963

García Barriuso, Patrocinio, O.F.M., born in 1909 at Ventosa de Pisuerga (Palencia), Spain, he studied at the Colegio Franciscano de Santiago de Compostela and received a doctorate in civil and canon law. He was head of the Museo-Laboratorio de Música Marroquí de Tetuán and also affiliated with the Instituto de Estudios Africanos. His writings include *Ecos del Magrib* (1940), *La musique hispano-musulmane au Maroc* (1940), *La música hispano-musulmana en Marruecos* (1941), *Los derechos del gobierno español en la misión de Marruecos* (1968), and *San Francisco el Grande de Madrid* (1975). IndiceE³ (3)

García y Bellido Ochando, Antonio, born 10 Februray 1903 at Villanueva de los Infantes (Ciudad-Real), Spain, he studied at Madrid, Berlin, Paris, Roma, Athens, London and Oxford, gaining a doctorate in 1929. Since 1931 he was a professor of archaeology at the Universidad Central, Madrid, and a director of the Instituto Español de Arqueologia, C.S.I.C., Madrid. His writings include *Factores que contribuyeron a la helenización de la España preromana* (1934), and *Fenicios y Carthagineses en Occidente* (1942). He died in 1972. Figuras de hoy, 1950; IndiceE³ (2); WhoSpain, 1963; WhoWor, 1974/75

García Cárel, Ricardo, born in 1947 at Requena (Valencia), he gained a doctorate in history, specializing in modern history, the Inquisition, and Moriscos. He was a professor in the Universidad Autónoma de Barcelona. His writings include *Moriscos i agermanats* (1974), *Las germanías de Valencia* (1975), *Orígines de la inquisición española; el tribunal de Valencia* (1976), *Historia de Cataluña, siglo XVI-XVII* (1985), *Las culturas del siglo de oro* (1989), and *La leyenda negra* (1992). Arabismo, 1992|; LC

García Cabrera, Carmelo *see* Cabrera, Carmelo García

Garcia Domingues, José D. *see* Domingues, José D. Garcia

García Figueras, Tomás, born 18 or 19 June 1892 at Jerez de la Frontera, Spain, he was affiliated with the Spanish High Commission in Morocco. His writings, partly under the pseudonym Vial de Morla, include *Marruecos* (1939), *Notas sobre el islam en Marruecos* (1939), *Africa en la acción española* (1947), *España en Marruecos* (1947), and *Larache; datos para su historia en el siglo XVII* (1973). He died in 1981. IndiceE³ (2); Unesco; WhoSpain, 1963

García Franco, Salvador, born in 1884, he wrote *Catálogo crítica de astrolabios existentes en España* (1945), *Historia del arte y ciencia de navegar* (1947), and *Instrumentos náuticos en el Museo Naval* (1959). NUC, pre-1956

589

García de la Fuente, Arturo, fray, he wrote *Catálogo de los manuscritos franceses y provenzales de la Biblioteca de El Escorial* (1933), *Catálogo de las monetas y medallas de la Biblioteca de El Escorial* (1935), and *La miniatura española primitiva* (1936). NUC, pre-1956

García Fuentes, José Maria, born 20th cent., he wrote *La Inquisición en Granada en el siglo XVI* (1981), and he was joint author of *Cuarto viaje de Colón* (1991). LC

García Gallo de Diego, Alfonso, born in 1911 at Soria, Spain, he studied law at Barcelona and Madrid, where he gained a doctorate in 1933. He was successively a professor of history of law at Murcia, Valencia, and the Universidad Complutense de Madrid. He also served as a director of the *Anuario de historia del derecho español*. His writings include *Cedulario de Eucinas* (1990). Figuras de hoy, 1950; IndiceE³ (2); WhoSpain, 1963

García Gómez, Emilio, born 4 June 1905 at Madrid, he was one of the eminent Arabists of the twentieth century and since 1930 successively a professor of Arabic at Granada and Madrid. He served as ambassador of Spain to Iraq, Lebanon and Turkey as well as director of the Real Academia de la Historia. His writings include *Poemas arábigo-andaluces* (1930), *Cinco poetas musulmanes; biografías y estudios* (1959) as well as numerous editions and translations of classical Arab authors. He died 31 May 1995. Figuras de hoy, 1950, 1956; Index Islamicus (6); IndiceE³ (5); OxSpan; Sainz; WhoSpain, 1963

García de Herreros, Enrique, born 19th cent., he wrote *Les tribunaux mixtes d'Egypte* (Alexandrie, 1914), and *Quatre voyageurs espagnoles à Alexandrie d'Egypte* (Alexandrie, 1923). NUC, pre-1956

García-Junceda y Alvarez-Quiñones, José Antonio, bon 20th cent., he received a doctorate in medieval philosophy. In 1992 he was a professor of philosophy in the Universidad Autónoma de Madrid. His writings include *De la mistica del número al rigor de la idea; sobre la prehistoria del saber occidental* (1975), and *La cultura cristiana y San Agustin* (1986). Arabismo, 1992|

García de Linares, Ramón, born 19th cent., he was joint editor of *Los documentos árabes diplomáticos del Archio de la Corona de Aragón* (1940). NUC, pre-1956

García Maceira (Maccina), Antonio, born in 1857 at Salamanca, Spain, he served with the Cuerpo de Montes as an inspector general. His writings include *Apuntes y noticias sobre la agricultura de los arabes españoles* (1876), *Leyendas salmantinas* (1887), and *La labranza castellana y la poesía regional salmantina* (1910). EncicUni; IndiceE³ (3)

García Martín, Luis, born in 1833 at Valladolid, Spain, he collaborated for many years with the *Almanaque militar español* and the *Boletín de la Sociedad Geográfica* as well as other publications. Ossorio

García Rivera, Ventura, born 19th cent., he was since 1886 affiliated with the journal *El Liberal Coruñés*, to which *La Mañana* was added in 1896. IndiceE³ (1)

García Romo, Francisco, born in 1901, he wrote *La escultura del siglo XI* (1973). NUC, 1973-77

García Sánchez, Expiración, she received a doctorate in Semitic philology, as well as a *licencia* in geography and history. In the 1990s she was a *colaboradora científica* at Escuela de Estudios Árabes de Granada, Consejo Superior de Investigaciones Cientificas. She edited *Ciencias de la naturaleza en al-Andalus; textos* (1990). Arabismo, 1992, 1994, 1997; LC

Garcin, Jean Claude, born 10 October 1934 at Marseille, he studied at Aix-en-Provence and Lyon. In 1974 he received a doctorate from the Sorbonne for *Un centre musulman de la Haute-Egypte médiéval, Qûs*. In 1962 he was a professor at the Faculté des lettres de Tunis and in 1993 he was affiliated with the Université d'Aix-Marseille. His writings include a collection of his articles, *Espace, pouvoir et idéologies de l'Égypte médiévale* (1987). EURAMES, 1993; THESAM, 3; Unesco

Garcin de Tassy, Joseph Héliodore Sagesse Vertu, born 20 January 1794 at Marseille, he there was educated at the Petit Séminaire and the Lycée, learning at the same time the basics of colloquial Arabic by chance. In 1817 he began to study Oriental languages at Paris, where he was a student of Silvestre de Sacy, qualifying with the Arabic edition with French translation, *Les oiseaux et les fleurs; allégories morales d'Azz-Eddin Elmocaddesi*. However, he subsequently turned to Hindustani studies. Through the good offices of his teacher, he was appointed in 1828 a director of the Ecole des langues orientales, teaching Hindustani and Persian. It is not attested that he had a solid acquaintance with the languages he was teaching. He was nevertheless elected in 1838 as an Orientalist to the Académie des Inscriptions et belles-lettres. He taught until his retirement in 1877. He died in Paris on 2 September 1878. Buckland; Dantes 1; DBF; Fück, p. 155; Hoefer; Index Islamicus (2); Vapereau

Gardanov, Valentin Konstantinovich, he wrote *Общественный строй адыгкских народов* (1967), and he edited *Материалы по обычному кабардинцев* (1956), and *Кавказский этнографический сборник* (1980). LC; OSK

Gardel, Victor Marie Gabriel, born 7 January 1884 at Beziers (Hérault), he graduated from the military college, Saint-Maixent (Deux-Sèvres). In 1911 he was attached to the Service des Affaires indigènes d'Algérie at Djelfa in northern Algeria, where he perfected his command of Arabic. In 1912 he was appointed deputy military commander of Territoire des Oasis, a post which he held for two years. At the outbreak of the Great War he was on leave in metropolitan France and volunteered for combat service. He was wounded in action and subsequently died in a German prisoner of war camp in Hannoversch-Münden on 8 April 1916. Peyronnet, pp. 514-518

Garder, Michel, born in 1916, he wrote *Histoire de l'armée soviétique* (1959), its translation, *A history of the Soviet Army* (1966), and *Agonie du régime en Russie soviétique* (1965), its translations into Polish (1965) and German (1966). LC

Gardet, Louis, born in 1904 (his true identity has always been ignored), he was a brilliant student of philosophy. Under the influence of Jacques Maritain he developed from a sceptic to a firm believer. In 1933 he entered the Fraternité d'El-Abiodh Sidi Cheikh in the Sud Oranais algérien and took the name of Frère André. He was one of the most active pioneers of the contemporary Muslim-Christian dialogue. Since 1946 he resided at the Fraternité d'études des Petits Frères de Jésus near the Ecole de Théolgie des Pères Dominicains, Saint Maximin (Provence). His writings include *La Pensée religieuse d'Avicenne* (1951), *Expériences mystiques en terre nonchrétiennes* (1953), *La Cité musulmane* (1954), *Connaître l'islam* (1960), and its translation, *Der Islam* (1961). A traffic accident in 1978 had left him semi-paralysed and aphasic. He died in Toulouse on 17 July 1986. Annuaire de l'Afrique du nord 25 (1986), pp. 605-609; IBLA, 49 (1986), pp. 385-86; Islamochristiana 12 (1986), pp. 1-26; Index Islamicus (3); MIDEO 18 (1988), pp. 406-7; Zeitschrift für Missionswissenschaft 71 (1987), p. 85

Gardin, Jean Claude, born 3 April 1925 at Paris, he was an archaeologist affiliated with the CNRS. His writings include *Céramique de Bactres* (1957), *Lashkari Bazar* (1963-78); he was joint author of *Archaeological gazetteer of Afghanistan* (1982); and he was joint editor of *Representations in archaeology* (1992). AnEIFr, 1989, 1997; EURAMES, 1993; Schoeberlein

Gardiner, Arthur Zimmermann, born 31 October 1901 at Garden City, N.Y., he was in business in New York until the outbreak of the second World War, during which he served with the Foreign Economic Administration (FEA) and was a vice-president of the U.S. Commercial Company, the corporate instrument for all foreign purchasing of FEA. In 1947 he joined the U.S. Department of State, working for a year on the Turkish-Greek Aid Program. He spent 1948 with the Economic Cooperation Administration, returning to his former post in 1949 to act as a special assistant on Point Four and economic operations to Assistant Secretary McGhee, in charge of the Bureau of Near Eastern, South Asian, and African Affairs. His writings include the booklet, *Aspects of foreign aid* (1961). His papers, 1941-1975, are at the Harry S. Truman Library, Independence, Mo. He died in 1975. Note; NYT, 10 December 1975, p. 32, col. 5; WhAm 10

Gardner, Alexander Haughton Campbell, born in 1785 in North America, he was an adventurer who travelled throughout Central Asia, 1818 to 1832, from Trebizond to Lahore, where he entered the service of Maharaja Ranjit Singh as a colonel of artillery. He was the first known European to visit Kafiristan between 1826 and 1828, but the travel journal has been lost. His writings include *Soldier and traveller; memories of Alexander Gardner*, edited by Hugh Pearse (1898). He died in Jammu, 22 January 1877. Buckland; Henze; Imperial and Asiatic quarterly review, 3rd series, 6 (1898), pp. 283-299; IndianBilnd (4)

Gardner, Alice, born in 1854, she was a professor of Byzantine history in the University of Bristol since 1919. Her writings include *Julian, philosopher and emperor* (c1895, 1978), *Rome, the middle of the world* (1897), *The Lascards of Nicæa* (1912), and *A Short history of Newnham College, Cambridge* (1921). She died in 1927. Who, 1916-1921; Who was who 2

Gardner, Elinor Wight, fl. 1929, he was affiliated with the Institut d'Egypte. His writings include *Some lacustrine Mollusca from the Faiyum Depression* (Le Caire, 1932). NUC, pre-1956

Gardner, G. B., fl. 1939, he wrote *Keris and other Malay weapons*, edited by R. Lumsden Milne (Singapore, 1936). NUC, pre-1956

Gardner, George Henry, born 22 November 1909 at Denver, Colo., he graduated in 1931 from Princeton, where he also received his Ph.D. in 1961 for *Some social correlates of the transitional phase of change from the traditional to the modern way of life; an exploration among Egyptian secondary school and college youth, 1954-1955*. From 1936 to 1948 he was affiliated with American and international welfare organizations in Greece. He successively became a professor of sociology at

AUC and Alfred University, N.Y. He was a joint author of *Arab socialism* (1969). AmM&WS, 1973, 1978 S; Master (1); *MESA Roster of members*, 1977-1990; Selim; WhAm 10

Gardner, Kenneth Burslam, born 5 June 1924 at London, he went to school in Stevenage, Hertfordshire, and studied at the University of London. In 1950 he joined the SOAS Library and later became a keeper, Department of Oriental Manuscripts and Printed Books, British Museum, London. He died in 1995. BlueB, 1973/74, 1975, 1976; IntWW, 1974/75-1995/96; Private; Who, 1969-1995; WhoLib, 1954

Gardner, W. R. W., M.A., Rev., born 19th cent., he was affilated with the Christian Literature Society for India. He wrote *Christianity and Muhammedanism* (1910), *The Doctrine of man* (1913), *The Qur'anic doctrine of salvation* (1914), *The Qur'anic doctrine of sin* (1914), and *Al-Ghazali* (1919). Note

Gardos, Harald, born 20th cent., he received a Dr.phil. in 1968 from the Universität Wien for *Österreich-Ungarn und die Türkei im Kriegsjahr 1915*. He was a secretary-general of the Austrian Commission for Unesco. He writings include *Some aspects of cultural planning in Austria* (1981). LC

Garín Ortiz de **Taranco**, Felipe María, born 14 February 1908 at Valencia, he received a doctorate in history and a diploma in law. He was a professor of history of art, particularly Islamic art, in the Universidad de Valencia, and also served as a president of the Real Academia de Bellas Artes de San Carlos de Valencia. His writings include *Catálogo-guía del Museo Provincial de Bellas Artes de San Carlos* (1955), *Valencia monumental* (1959), *Vinculaciones universales del gótico valenciano* (1969), and he was joint author of *Catálogo monumental de la ciudad de Valencia* (1983). EURAMES, 1993; *Gran enciclopedia de España*, 1990; IndiceE³ (5); Quin, 1981; WhoSpain, 1963

Garipov, Talmas Magsumovich, born 31 July 1928 at Moscow, he received a doctorate in 1974 and was appointed a professor in 1979. He was a Bashkir and Turkish scholar and affiliated with the Institute of History, Language and Literature, Bashkir Section, Soviet Academy of Science. His writings include Кыпчакские языки Урало-Поволжья (1979), he was joint author of Башкирское языкознание единиц разных уровней (1987), and he was joint editor of Башкирская лексика (1966), and Русский язык в Башкирии и его взаимодействие с башкирским языком (1988). BashkKE, TatarES

Garkavets, Aleksandr Nikolaevich, born 20th cent., he wrote Конвергенция армяно-кыпчакского языка к славянским в XVI-XVII вв. (1979), Тюркские языки на Украине (1988), and he edited Османская империя в первой четверти XVII века (1984). LC; OSK

Garkavi, Avraam IAkovlevich, 1835-1919 *see* Harkavy, Abraham Elijah

Garlake, Peter Storr, born 20th cent., he wrote *The Early Islamic architecture of the East African coast* (1966), *Great Zimbabwe* (1973), *The Kingdoms of Africa* (1978), and *The Hunter's vision; the prehistoric art of Zimbabwe* (1995). LC

Garland, Herbert Gerald, born in the second half of the nineteenth century. Before the first World War, he was in the Sudan, probably as an engineer. In October 1916, he was commissioned into the Egyptian Army and sent to Rabigh, Arabia, to train Arab troops in the use of explosives. He carried out many attacks on the Hejaz Railway using a mine of his own invention. He frequently reported upon them to the *Arab bulletin*. Early in 1919, he was posted to the Arab Bureau, in the last days of which he was director and also editor of the *Bulletin*. *Arab bulletin* 1 (1986 reprint), pp. xxv-xxvi

Garle, Henry Ernest, born in 1878, he had a varied legal experience in the Near and Middle East, extending back to the Daïra Sanieh liquidation in 1905, when he represented the Khedival family in conjunction with Raymond Poincaré (1854-1934) and Lord Oxford and Asquith (1852-1928). At the close of the first World War he assisted in the reorganization of the judicature in Palestine, and, after acting for some years as Special Commissioner for Turkish Reparations at Constantinople, was the representative of the British Government on the Turkish Assessment Commission in Paris, of which he became president in 1925. His writings include *Social hygiene to-day* (1936). Note; NUC, pre-1956

Garlington, William, born 18 May 1947, he was a writer on Bahaism. His writings include *Fire and blood; a novel* (Los Angeles, Kalimat Press, 1984). LC

Garnelo y **Alvarez**, Benito, O.S.A., born 12 January 1876 at Carracedo del Monastero (Léon), he was educated at the Seminario de Astorga and the Universidad de Madrid. He pursued an ecclesiastical career at the Monasterio de El Escorial. He was an editor of *La Ciudad de Dios* and *Religión y cultura*. His writings include *Relaciones entre España e Italia durante la edad media* (1927). IndiceE³ (3)

Garnett, Miss Lucy Mary Jane, born 19th cent. at Sheffield, she was a folklorist, Orientalist and musical compiler. Her writings include *Greek-folk songs from the Ottoman northern Hellas* (1888), *Turkish life in town and country* (1904), *Home life in Turkey* (1909), *Mysticism and magic in Turkey* (1912), and *Balkan home life* (1917). She died in 1934. WhE&EA; Master (2); Who, 1908-1932; *Who was who* 3

Garnett, Richard, born in 1835 at Lichfield, England, he was a bibliophile, prolific writer and editor of the British Museum catalogue. From 1851 to 1889 he was keeper of Printed Books in the British Museum. He died in 1906. BbD; BritInd (3); DLB 184 (1997), pp. 138-51; DNB; Master (24); *Who was who* 1

Garnick, Daniel Harris, born in 1929, he received a Ph.D. in 1958 from Dropsie College, Philadelphia, for *Middle Eastern citrus industries and their markets*. He was in 1960 a lecturer in economics and Middle Eastern thought and culture in the University of Buffalo, N.Y. His writings include *Toward development of a National-Regional Impact Evaluation System and the Upper Licking Area Pilot Study* (1971). Master (2); Note; Selim

Garnier, Charles René, born 19 April 1874 at Alger, he was there educated and became a lawyer. He was a secretary of the Société de géographie de l'Afrique du nord, president of the Syndicat de la Presse algérienne, and, from 1902 to 1907, the editor of the *Revue nord-africaine*. Since in 1905 he was resident in Paris and a contributor to a variety of journals. In 1911 and 1912 he was director of *La France africaine*. His writings include the undated *Petits guides pratiques de l'Algérie*. In 1899 he published, jointly with Achille Garnier, their recollections of a journey to Morocco, *Au Pays des chérifs*. Their other writings include *Fez, la ville sainte* (1899), and *Tanger, la ville des chiens* (1899). DBF

Garnier, Louis, fl. 1947, he was a chief engineer with the *Génie rurale*, and head of the Section de l'équipement économique in Morocco. Note

Garnot, Jean Sainte Fare, 1908-1963 *see* Sainte Fare Garnot, Jean

Garratt, Geoffrey Theodore, born in 1888 at Little Tew, Oxforshire, he was educated at Rugby and Hertford College, Oxford, and subsequently entered the Civil Service of the Bombay Presidency as assistant collector and magistrate. From 1915 to 1918 he served with the Mesopotamia Expeditionary Force. After leaving the Indian Civil Service in 1922, he was for two years Berlin correspondent for the *Westminster gazette*. His writings include *The Legacy of India* (1937), *Mussolini's Roman Empire* (1938), and *Gibraltar and the Mediterranean* (1939). He died in 1942. IndianBiInd (1); CurBio, 1942; *Labour who's who*, 1927; WhE&EA; *Who was who* 4

Garrett, Herbert Leonard Offley, born 16 June 1881 at Cambridge, he graduated in 1902 from St. John's College, Oxford, and subsequently served with the Colonial Service until 1912, when he joined the Indian Educational Service. He became a professor of history and vice-principal of Government College, Lahore. He was the editor of *European adventures of northern India, 1785 to 1849* (1929), and *The Punjab a hundred years ago* (1935). He died in 1941. BritInd (3); IndianBiInd (1); *Who was who* 4

Garrett, Robert, born in 1875, he was educated by tutors while travelling with his family in Europe and the Middle East from 1889 to 1891. After graduating from Princeton and Johns Hopkins universities, he became a partner in the investment banking firm Garrett & Sons until his retirement in 1957. He was a lifelong collector of rare and exquisite books and manuscripts, part of which were published in 1937 entitled *The Descriptive catalog of the Garrett Collection of Arabic manuscripts in the Princeton University Library*. He died in Baltimore, Md., in 1961. DAB; Master (1); NatCAB, vol. 48, pp. 574-575; NYT, 26 April 1961, p. 39, col. 1; *Princeton University Library chronicle*, 10, no. 3 (April 1949), pp. 103-116; Shavit

Garrison, Fielding Hudson, born in 1870 at Washington, D.C., he was from 1903 to 1927 an editor of *Index medicus* and since 1930 a librarian at Welch Medical Library, Baltimore, Md. He died in 1935. Solomon R. Kagan wrote *Fielding H. Garrison, a biography* (1948). ANB; BioIn 5; DAB; Master (7); NatCAB, vol. 26, pp. 51-52; WhAm 1

Garrison, Jean L., born in 1945, he received a Ph.D. in 1976 from the University of Chicago for *The development of social security in Egypt*. He was in 1978 a professor in the School of Social Work, University of Oklahoma at Norman. Note; NUC, 1978

Garrity, Patrick J., born 20th cent., he was a sometime fellow, Center for Strategic and International Studies, Georgetown University, Washington, D.C. He wrote a number of study group reports on crisis management. His other writings include *Crisis control in a nuclear age* (1985), and *The future of nuclear weapons* (1990). LC

Garrod, Oliver, Dr., born early 20th cent., he trained at St. Bartholomew's Hospital and qualified in 1939. As he had joined the Territorial Army earlier that year, he went into the Royal Army Medical Corps immediately. He was posted to India in early 1941. Later, while stationed at Rawalpindi, he had ample opportunity to start his outstanding collection of Persian rugs. In the summer of 1941 he was posted to Pai force in the Persian Gulf and was stationed to Basra and then to Shaiba where he was Staff Captain Medical. He had two winter leaves in Persia in 1941 and 1942 respectively, travelling to Tehran on the trans-Iranian railway. On the second visit he went on a mission to the Caspian Sea. After working in a Malaria Field Laboratory in Baghdad he was invited to form a Medical Dispensary to work amongst the nomadic tribes of south-west Persia with a view to befriending these tribes and keeping them on the side of the Allies at a time when German infiltration in Persia was rife. He and his Persian interpreter and four other British ranks penetrated deep into the mountain ranges in Khuzistan, Luristan, Bakhtiari and the tribal districts of Fars, staying with the chieftain of several of these tribes. He collected a large amount of material about these tribes and communicated an address to the Royal Central Asian Society on his return in 1945. He was awarded the M.B.E. for his invaluable services. He subsequently worked at Barnet Hospital until his retirement in 1955. He died in September 1983. *Asian affairs*, 15 / old series 71 (1984), p. 116; Note

Garrot, Henri, born 19th cent., he wrote *La Banque de l'Algérie* (1892), *Les Juifs algériens* (1898), and *Histoire générale de l'Algérie* (1910). BN; LC

Garstang, John, born 5 May 1876 at Blackburn, Lancashire, he was educated at Jesus College, Oxford, and taught Egyptian archaeology since 1902 in various capacities. In 1904 he founded the Liverpool Institute of Archaeology. From 1947 to 1959 he served with the British Institute of Archaeology at Ankara. His writings include *The Hittite Empire* (1930), and *The Foundations of Bible history* (1931). He died in Beirut, 12 September 1956. BioIn 4 (5); BritInd (1); Dawson; DNB; Egyptology; LuthC, 1978; Master (1); NYT, 14 September 1956, p. 23, col. 4; *Revue archéologique* 2 ii (1958), pp. 102-103; WhAm 4; *Who was who* 5

Garstin, Sir William Edmund, born in 1849 in India, he was an engineer and a sometime inspector-general of irrigation and Under-Secretary of State for public works in Egypt. He died in 1925. BritInd (2); DNB; Goldschmidt; Hill; Master (1); *Who was who* 2

Garthwaite, Gene Ralph, born 15 July 1933 at Mount Hope, Wisc., he graduated in 1955 from St. Olaf College and received a Ph.D. in 1969 from U.C.L.A. for *The Bakhtiyārī khāns*. In 1975 he was appointed a professor of history in the Department of History, Dartmouth College, Hanover, N.H., a post which he still held in 1995. His writings include *Khans and shahs; a documentary analysis of the Bakhtiyari in Iran* (1983). DrAS, 1974 H, 1978 H, 1982 H; *MESA Roster of members*, 1977-1990; NatFacDr, 1995

Garton, Tessa Elizabeth H., born 29 July 1948, she was in 1995 a professor in the Department of Fine Arts, College of Charleston, S.C. Her writings include *arly Romanesque sculpture in Apulia* (1984). LC; NatFacDr, 1995

Garufi, Carlo Alberto, born 14 February 1868 at Palermo, he was a professor of palaeography and Latin diplomatics at the Università di Palermo. His writings include *Monete e conii nella storia dirotto siculo dagli arabi ai Martini* (1898). He died in Palermo, 16 September 1958. Chi è, 1931-1948; DizBI

Garulo Muñoz, María Teresa, born 20th cent., she received a doctorate in Semitic languages, with particular reference to Hispano-Arabic. She was a professor in the Departamento de Estudios Árabes e Islámicos, Universidad Complutense de Madrid. Her writings include *Los arabismos en el léxico andalúz* (1983), and *Diwan de las poetas de al-Andalus* (1986), and she translated from the Arabic of Ibrāhīm Ibn Sahl al-Isrā'īlī, *Poemas* (1984). Arabismo, 1992, 1994, 1997; LC

Garzón Pareja, Manuel, born in 1918, he wrote *La Real Casa de la Moneda de Granada* (1970), *La industria sedera en España* (1972), and *Historia de la hacienda de España* (1984). He died in 1983. LC

Garzouzi, Eva, born in 1916 at Cairo, she received a diploma from the Université de Genève and her M.A. in 1962 from New York University. She was an economist and a sometime executive of the Economic Research Department of the Central Bank of Egypt. She was a professor of economics at SUNY, Brockport, before joining Ithaca College in 1967. Her writings include *Old ills and new remedies in Egypt* (1958), and *Economic growth and development* (1972). *MESA Roster of members*, 1977-1990; WhoAmW, 1979/80

Gasanov, I. M., he wrote Частновладельческие крестьяне в Азербайджане в первой половние XIX века (1957), and Азербайджан в годы первой русской революции (1966). NUC, pre-1956

Gasanova, Ėsmiral'da IUsif-kyzy, born 30 December 1932 at Gandzh (Kirovabad), she graduated in 1955 from Moscow State University and received her first degree in 1961 for К вопросы о развитии идеологии буржуазного национазма в Турции. Since 1958 she was affiliated with the Institute of the Peoples of the Near and Middle East, Azerbaijan Academy of Science. Her writings include Идеология буржуазного национализма в Турции в период младотурок (1966), Идеи "исламского социализма" в общественно-политической мысли Турции (1994), and she edited Турция; история и современность (1988). Miliband; Miliband²

Gasbarri, Carlo, born 15 October 1907 at Roma, he was an Oratorian priest and an authority in Muslim affairs. In 1939 he started to collaborate with *l'Osservatore Romano*, becoming their editor in 1945. His writings include *La via di Allah* (1942), *Noi e l'islam* (1944), *Medioriente* (1959), and *Cattolicesimo e islam oggi* (1972). Lui chi è, 1969; Imperatori; Vaccaro

Gascoigne, Richard Frederick Thomas, born in 1851, he was a captain in the Royal Horse Guards. At the end of 1881 he went in the company of the physician H. Melladew on a hunting expedition to northern Ethiopia between the rivers Setit (Tekeze) and Barka. He died in 1937. Henze; Hill

Gashev, Boris Nikolaevich, born 28 June 1925 in Russia, he graduated in 1951 from the Institute of Foreign Trade and received his first degree in 1975 for *Государственный сектор в экономике Арабской Республики Египет за 20 лем; (1952-1972)*, a work which was published in 1978. In the service of the State Committee of Economic Relations he was in Egypt from 1966 to 1970 and subsequently became affiliated with the Oriental Institute in the Soviet Academy of Science. He was a visiting lecturer at Leipzig in 1979, Aleppo in 1984, and in Iraq in 1985. Miliband²

Gasiorowski, Mark Joseph, born 9 October 1954, he graduated from the University of Chicago and received his Ph.D. from the University of North Carolina. He subsequently became a professor of political science at Louisiana State University, Baton Rouge, a post which he still held in 2003. His writings include *U.S. foreign policy and the Shah* (1991), and he was joint editor of *Neither East nor West* (1990). LC; NatFacDr, 1995-2003

Gąsiorowski, Stanisław Jan, born 26 June 1897 at Warszawa, he studied classical archaelogy at Kraków and Wien, received two doctorates, and subsequently taught his subject at Uniwersytet Jagielloński, Kraków. His writings include *Le Problème de la classification ergologique et la relation de l'art à la culture materielle* (1936). He died in Kraków, 13 September 1962. Czy wiesz, 1938; Egyptology; *Folia orientalia* 5 (1963), pp. 227-31

Gaskin, John Calcott, born 19th cent., he was appointed a British vice-consul at Bushire, Persia, on 3 July 1893. His trace is lost after an article in 1900. BritInd (1)

Gaslini, Mario Dei, 1893- see Dei Gaslini, Mario

Gaspar y Remiro, Mariano, born in 1868 at Zaragoza, he was a professor of Arabic at Granada, where he later also served as a vice-chancellor and dean. His writings include *Los cronistas hispano judíos* (1920), *Historia de Murcia musulmana* (1925), and he edited and translated from the Arabic of Ibn al-Khaṭīb, *Correspondencia diplomática entre Granada y Fez* (1916). He died in Épila, 4 August 1925. *Aragon en la Edad Media* 14-15 (1999), pp. 499-508; EncicUni; Espasa

Gasparini, Jacopo, born 23 March 1879 at Volpago del Montello (Treviso), he was a senator and a colonial governor in Italian East Africa. In 1926 he negociated a treaty of friendship and economic relations with the Imam of Yemen. He died 16 May 1940 or 1941. Massiomo Rava wrote *Nel cuore dell'Arabia Felice; con Jacopo Gasparini nello Yemen* (1927). Chi è, 1931, 1936, 1940; *Rivista delle colonie* 15 (1941), pp. 755-68

Gasparro, Giulia Sfameni see Sfameni Gasparro, Giulia

Gasratian, Manvel Arsenovich, born 21 May 1924 at Kala Ismaillinsk, he received his first degree in 1956 for *Национальный вопрос в Турции, 1919-1939*, and his doctorate in 1977 for *Курдская проблема в Турции в новейшее время*. Since 1961 he was affiliated with the Oriental Institute in the Soviet Academy of Science. His writings include *Турция ждет перемен* (1963) *Современная Турции* (1965), *Турция в 1960-1963 годах* (1965); he was joint author of *Турции* (1965); and he edited *СССР в Турция* (1981). Miliband; Miliband²

Gasselin, Édouard, born in 1849, he wrote *Petit guide de l'étranger à Tunis* (1869), and *Dictionnaire français-arabe* (1880-86). BN; NUC, pre-1956

Gasser, Jules, pseudonym J. Romagny, born about 1865, he studied at the Faculté de médecine de Paris, where he received a doctorate. He was a sometime surgeon at l'Hôpital d'Oran, a senator and *conseiller général d'Oran*. His writings include *Le Rôle de la France au Maroc* (Oran, 1908), *Rôle sociale de la France dans l'Afrique du nord* (1924), and *La Tunisie* (1932). Qui êtes-vous, 1924

Gasser, Peter, born 12 November 1915 at Abbazia (Istria), Austria-Hungary, he received a Dr.phil. in 1940 from the Universität Wien for *Die Entwicklung des Seehandels in Triest in der Zeit Maria Theresias and Josephs II*. He was an archivist at the Austrian national archives. WhoAustria, 1954, 1955|

Gassiot, Georges, born about 1900, he wrote *Le Juge de paix et les juridictions musulmanes en Algérie* (Alger, 1950). NUC, pre-1956

Gast, Marceau, born 1 June 1927, he received a doctorate in ethnology and became a *directeur de recherche* with the CNRS. His writings include *Mils et Sorgho en Ahaggar; étude ethnologique* (1965), *Alimentation des populations de l'Ahaggar* (1968); he was joint author of *Le Lait et les produits laitiers* *en Ahaggar* (1969), and *Textes touaregs en prose* (1984); and he edited *Hériter en pays musulman* (1987). He was in 1977 a member of the Middle East Studies Association of North America. LC; Note

Gasteiger von und zu Raabenstein und Kobach, Albert Josef, born 28 March 1823 at Innsbruck, he joined in 1846 the Austrian civil service as a railway engineer. In 1860 he entered the service of Nasir al-Din Shah as head of Persian civil and military construction. With a view of road construction, he travelled in 1861 from Tehran to the Caspian provinces. From 1880 to 1881 he went on a political and military mission to the extreme southeast of the country. Through his sensational construction of the road to Mazandaran, 1863-1868, as well as the road from Meshed to Ashkhabad, 1886-1888, he became well-known and honoured throughout the region. In 1888 he returned to Austria. His writings include *Von Teheran nach Beludschistan; Reise-Skizzen* (1881). He died in Bozen on 5 July 1890. Reinhart Pohanka wrote *Der Khan aus Tirol, Albert Joseph Gasteiger* (1988). Gabriel, pp. 143-161; Henze; EncIran; ÖBL

Gaster, Moses, born 16 September 1856 at Bucureşti, the son of the Dutch consul-general, he studied at the universities of Leipzig and Breslau, was ordained rabbi at Jüdisch-Theologisches Seminar, Breslau in 1881 and then returned to Bucureşti to teach Romanian philology. On account of his outspoken propagation of Jewish emigration to Palestine as well as his protests against the treatment of the Jews in Romania, he was exiled in 1885 and went to England. He was a sometime professor of Slavic philology at Oxford. As a Zionist he was a fearless supporter of Th. Herzl when the latter came to London in 1896. His writings include *The Samaritans* (1925). He died near Reading on 5 March 1939. DNB; EncAm; EncJud; MembriiAR; WhE&EA; WhoRom; *Who was who*, 3; Wininger

Gasteyger, Curt Walter, born 20 March 1929 at Zürich, he studied law, received a Dr.jur. at Zürich and became a professor of international relations. He was a sometime director of the Programme d'études stratégiques et de sécurité internationale at Genève. He was also affiliated with various international institutions in the field. His writings include *La Sécurité de la Suisse* (1983), *Searching for world security* (1985), and he was joint author of *L'Europe et le Maghreb* (1972), and *The Missing link* (1990). Kürschner, 1980-2003; WhoSwi, 1992/93-1998/99; WhoWor, 1984-1995

Gastineau, Benjamin, born 11 July 1823 at Montreuil-Bellay (Maine-et-Loire), he started life as a compositor with *La Vraie République* and later became an editor. He was a political activist who was frequently charged with violation of press legislation - at times acquitted, at others, convicted, deported to Algeria, incarcerated or pardoned. He was a prolific writer whose writings include *Comment finissent les riches* (1849), *Comment finissent les pauvres* (1850), *Les Femmes et les mœurs de l'Algérie* (1861), and *Chasses au lion et à la panthère en Afrique* (1863). He died in Maison-Lafitte in 1904. DBF; DcBMOuvF 6 (1969), pp. 140-41; IndexBFr² (3); Vapereau

Gastinel Bey, J. B., born 19th cent., he was a pharmacist as well as a chemistry and physics teacher at al-Madrasah al-Tibbīyah, Cairo. His writings include *Mémoire sur l'arséniate de caféine et l'acide tanno-arséniate* (Paris, 1862), and *Étude topographique, chimique et médicale sur les eaux minerales de Hélouan-les-Bains* (Le Caire, 1883). BN; Note; NUC, pre-1956

Gasymov, Mamed Shamkhal ogly, born 20th cent., he received a doctorate in 1972 for Основы терминологии азербайджанского языка. His writings include Азәрбајчан дили терминоло-кијасынын әсаслары (1973), he was joint author of Терминолокијаја аид әдәбијјатын ве терминоложи луғәтлəрин библиогоафијасы (1983), and he edited Терминология мəсəлəлəри (1984). LC; OSK

Gasztowtt, Tadeusz, born 8 June 1881 at Paris, he went to school in Warszawa and in 1907 emigrated to Constantinople. His writings, partly under the pseudonym Seyfeddin, include *La Pologne et l'islam* (Paris, 1907), and *Turcya a Polska* (Paryż, 1913). He died in Istanbul in early 1936. Dziekan; PSB

Gatacre, Sir William Forbes, born in 1843 in Scotland, he was a graduate of the Royal Military College, Sandhurst, and was posted to India from 1862 to 1867. He later served also in the Sudan and South Africa and retired with the rank of major-general in 1900. After his retirement he joined the board of the Kordofan Trading Company and, while exploring rubber forests, caught fever while camping in a swamp and died there in 1906. His wife, Lady Beatrix Wickens (Davy) Gatacre wrote *General Gatacre; the story of the life and services* (London, 1910). AfrBioInd (1); BritInd (3); Buckland; DSAB, vol. 2, pp. 257-58; Hill; Riddick; Rosenthal; *Who was who* 1

Gataullin, Maliuta Fazleevna, born 7 November 1924 in Kirovsk Oblast, she graduated in 1950 from the Moscow Oriental Institute and received her first degree in 1953 for Аграрные отношения в современной Сирии. Her writings include Аграрные отношения в Сирии (1957), Экономия ОАР на новум пути (1966), and Аграрная реформа и классовая борьба в Египете (1985), a work which is a revised version of her 1981 doctoral thesis. Since 1966 she was affiliated with the African Institute in the Ыщмшуе Academy of Science. Miliband; Miliband²

Gateau, Albert, born in 1902 at Vierzon (Cher), he completed his secondary education at the Lycée d'Alger. After pursuing classical as well as Arabic studies, he qualified as a teacher, teaching at Sétif, Médéa, Mostaganem and Constantine. After his *agrégation* he was appointed a secretary of the Ecole nationale des langues orientales vivantes, Paris. When in 1941 life under occupation became intolerable, he returned to Tunisia, where he had previously taught at the Collège Sadîki. In 1944 he was invited to a professorship at l'Institut des hautes études marocaines, Rabat. He began to work on his second edition and translation of Ibn Abd al-Hakam's *Conquête de l'Afrique du nord* and, more important, on a *histoire de la Berbérie musulmane* and the foundation and rise of the Fatimid Empire. He had been seriously ill for some time when he died in 1949. *Hesperis* 37 (1950), pp. 1-3

Gatell y **Folch**, Joaquin, born 3 January 1826 at Altafulla near Tarragona, he studied law and Oriental languages. He travelled in 1860 to Morocco in search of adventure. He stayed for four years, apparently embracing Islam. Posing as a physician (*bien que je connusse rien à la médecine*), he visited the coastal regions Sus, Nun and Tekna. His writings include *Viajes por Marruecos, el Sus, Uad-Nun y Tekna* (1878). He died in Cádiz, 13 May 1879. F. Valderrama Martínez wrote a biography, *Joaquín Gatell* (1952). Embacher; EncicUni; *Gran enciclopedia de España*; Henze; IndiceE³ (1)

Gatenby, Edward Vivian, born in 1892, he was educated at Chesterfield Grammar School, Hymers College, Hull, and King's College, London, where he took a first class honours degree in English in 1920. For the next three years he taught at King's College, London, and Regent Polytechnic School. In 1923, he was appointed instructor in English at Fukushima Higher Commercial School, Japan, and there began to teach another type of English, the type which he taught for the rest of his life, English as a foreign language. After eighteen years in Japan, he started a new career in Turkey, where he was appointed in 1942 a linguistic adviser to the British Council. Concurrently he was also head of the English Department of Gazi Eğitim Enstitüsü, Ankara. From 1946 to 1954 he held the chair in English literature at Ankara Üniversitesi. He also advised governments in the Near, Middle, and Far East on their programmes of English-teaching. His writings include *The cloud-men of Yamato* (1929), *English as a foreign language* (1945), and he was joint author of *Essential English for Turkish students* (1948). He died in 1955. RCAJ 54 (1967), pp. 166-68

Gates, Caleb Frank, born in 1857, he graduated from Beloit College and the Chicago Theological Seminary. He was a missionary in Turkey from 1891 to 1902, and subsequently served until 1932 as a president of Robert College, Constantinople. He wrote an autobiography, *Not to me only* (1940). He died in 1946. ANB; DAB; Master (1); Shavit; WhAm 2, 3; *Who was who* 4

Gates, Rosalie Prince, born 20th cent., she was in 1995 a professor in the Department of History and Government, Meredith College, Raleigh, N.C. NatFacDr, 1995

Gates, Warren Everett, born 20th cent., he received a Ph.D. in 1958 from the University of Colorado for *Montesquieu and the Abbé DuBos; their literary relationship.* NUC, 1956-67

de **Gatines**, Ch., born 19th cent., he wrote *Journal d'un voyage en Orient* (Paris, 1862). BN

Gätje, Helmut, born 16 November 1927 at Bremerhaven, he came to Islamic studies through Protestant theology and Hebrew at Tübingen, where he received his Dr.phil. in 1955 for *Die parva naturalia des Aristoteles in der Bearbeitung des Averroes*, and also his Dr.habil. in 1962 for the unpublished *Fragmente des Dichters 'Adī b. ar-Riqā'.* He was affiliated with Orientalisches Seminar, Tübingen, from 1956 to 1963, when he was appointed to the newly established chair of Oriental studies in the Universität des Saarlandes, Saarbrücken, a post which he held until his death after a long illness on 8 March 1986. His lifelong researches centred on the transmission of Greek philosophy to the Arabs. *Islam* 64 (1987), pp. 1-3; Kürschner, 1974-83

Gatt, Georg, born 19th cent., he was affiliated with Deutscher Palästina-Verein as well as Palästina-Pilgerverein der Diöcese Brixen, southern Tyrol. His writings include *Die Hügel von Jerusalem* (1897), and *Sion in Jerusalem* (1900). Note; NUC, pre-1956

Gattefossé, Jean, born 26 February 1899 at Lyon, he completed his chemistry in 1918 at Lyon and became a botanist and prehistorian. From 1920 to 1945 he made botanical research expeditions and carried on agricultural and commercial missions throughout North Africa for the Institut scientifique chérifien and the Institut d'hygiène du Maroc. He was a member of several learned societies. His writings include *Bibliographie de l'Atlantide et des questions connexes* (1926). IndexBFr² (1)

Gatterer, Johann Christoph, born of humble parentage in 1727 at Lichtenau near Ansbach, he studied theology, Oriental languages, philosophy and mathematics at the Universität Altdorf. He was a school teacher at Nürnberg until 1759, when he became a professor of history at Göttingen. His writings include *Abriß der Heraldik* (1773), *Abriß der Geographie* (1775), *Abriß der Chronologie* (1777), and *Abriß der Diplomatik* (1798). He died in Göttingen in 1799. ADtB, vol. 8, pp. 410-13; DtBE; DtBiInd (13); NDB

Gatteschi, Domenico, born 19th cent., he received a doctorate in law and was in 1867 a barrister. His writings include *Manuale di diritto pubblico e privato ottomano* (1865) and its English translation *Real property, mortage and waqf, according to Ottoman law* (1884). Note; NUC, pre-1956

Gatti, Carlo, born 10 September 1875 at Predosa (Piemonte), he entered the Societas S. Francisci Salesii and spent many years in the Arab world, mainly in Palestine. An authority on the Eastern Churches, he was also an Arabist working on an Arabic-Italian dictionary modelled on the work of Jean B. Belot. He devoted nearly all of his life to this project. At the end of the war, four folio volumes had been completed, except for the last two letters of the alphabet, but due to financial difficulties of the Istituto per le Relazioni Culturali con l'Estero, under whose auspices the work was to be published, he had to cede his unpublished opus to his *Congregazione*. He was joint author of *I Riti e le chiese orientali* (Genova, 1942) He died in Roma, 19 September 1947. Oriente moderno 27 (1947), pp. 188-89

Gatto, Ludovico, born 7 May 1931 at Roma, he was a professor of medieval history successively at the Università di Catania and Università degli Studi "La Sapienza," Roma. His writings include *Medioevo voltairiano* (1972), *Per una scuola diversa* (1975), and *Viaggio intorno al concetto di medioevo* (1981). IndBiItal (1); Note; WhoItaly, 1980, 1990-2002

Gaube, Heinz, born 8 September 1940 at Böhmisch-Leipa, Bohemia, he received a Dr.phil. in 1973 from the Universität Hamburg for *Die südpersische Provinz Arragān/Kūh-Gīlūyeh von der arabischen Eroberung bis zur Safawidenzeit*. After gaining a Dr.habil. in 1977, he was since 1979 a professor of Islamic studies at Tübingen. His writings include *Arabosasanidische Numismatik* (1973), *Arabische Inschriften aus Syrien* (1978), *Iranian cities* (1979), and he was joint author of *Aleppo; historische und geographische Beiträge zur baulichen Gestaltung* (1984), and *Die Kernländer des Abbasidenreiches* (1994). Kürschner, 1983-2003

Gaucher, Gilbert, born about 1900, he was in 1948 an *ingénieur I.A.A.*, *licencié ès-sciences*. His writings include *Observations hydrogéologiques sur la plaine de Perrégaux* (1938), *Vocations culturelles et aptitudes à l'irrigation des sols des Niayes méridionales de Kayer à M'Boro* (1962), *Traité de pédologie agricole* (1968), and *Géologie, géomorphologie et hydrologie des terrains salés* (1974). Note

Gauckler, Paul, born in 1866 at Colmar, he was educated at Épinal, Nancy and Paris. He started to study mathematics but soon changed to *rhétorie supérieure*. Exhausted from his strenuous study he went in 1884 for a break to Algeria and also took courses at the Ecole des lettres d'Alger. He returned to Paris for his *agrégation* in 1889, but subsequently spent fifteen years in Algeria and Tunisia as an archaeologist. In the service of the Ministère de l'Instruction publique he studied museums and carried on archaeological missions. Since 1892 he was in Tunisia, later to become director of Antiquités et Arts de la Régence. His archaeological discoveries came to enrich the collections of the Régence, particularly those which he had founded, the Musée arabe within the Musée antique de Tunis and the Musée de Sousse. After 1906 he was affiliated with the Ecole française de Rome, when he died in 1911. He was joint author of *Les Monuments arabes* (1899), and *Musée de Sousse* (1902). DBF; NDBA

Gaud, Jean, Dr., he wrote *L'Habitat indigène au Maroc* (Rabat, 1937), and *Acarien sarcoptiformes plumicoles (Analgoïdea), parasites sur les oiseaux ralliformes et gruiformes d'Afrique* (1968). LC; Note

Gaudard, Jules Maurice, also named Goudard-Pacha, born 16 November 1828 at Azans near Dôle (Jura), he studied law at Dijon and then moved to Paris. Since the early 1860s he was in Egypt, where he was first head of the disputed claims department in the Ministry of Foreign Affairs, subsequently becoming its director general. He resigned his position and in 1883 returned to Dôle, where he died on 12 June 1888. IndexBFr² (2)

Gaudefroy-Demombynes, Jean, born 7 January 1898 at Mur-de-Selogne (Loir-et-Cher), he graduated from l'Ecole des sciences politiques and successively served as a professor of Arabic at the Sorbonne, and professor of German at the Collège d'Honfleur. His writings include *L'Œuvre linguistique de Humboldt* (1926), and *Histoire des Etats-Unis* (1947). Qui est-ce, 1934; Qui êtes-vous, 1924

Gaudefroy-Demombynes, Laurent Joseph Maurice, born 15 December 1862 at Amiens, he studied law and qualified in 1884. Ten years later he received a diploma in Arabic from l'Ecole des langues orientales vivantes, Paris, and in 1895 from l'Ecole supérieure des Lettres d'Alger. He subsequently served as a director of the Medersa de Tlemcen until 1898, when he returned to l'Ecole des langues orientales as a teacher, concurrently teaching also at l'Ecole coloniale and the Sorbonne. He later became a director of the Institut des études islamiques, Paris. Since 1935 he was a member of the Académie des Inscriptions et belles-lettres. His writings include *Les Cents et une nuits* (1911), *Les*

Institutions musulmanes (1921), its translation, *Muslim institutions* (1950), and he was joint author of *Le Monde musulman et byzantin jusqu'aux croisades* (1931). He died in Paris, 12 August 1956. DBF; DBFC, 1954/55; *Index Islamicus* (4); *Lexikon der Afrikanistik*; *Qui êtes-vous*, 1924; WhoFr, 1955/56, 1957/58

Gaudeul, Jean Marie, born 20th cent., he wrote *Appelés par le Christ; ils viennent de l'islam* (1991). LC

Gaudin, Georges *Alexandre*, born in 1838 at Talmont (Vendée), he passed through the military college at Saint-Cyr and served in two African campaigns, 1859-60 and 1869-70. In the same year he started a career as a military instructor and administrator first at l'Ecole de Saumur and then at l'Ecole d'application d'état-major. About 1880 he returned to an African unit at Tlemcen, where he participated for two years in campaigns against insurgents. He resigned from active service with the rank of brigadier-general, having served in the late 1890s in Tunisia. He died in Talmont in 1915. DBF

de **Gaudin de Lagrange**, Mlle. Emérentienne, fl. 20th cent., she received a doctorate in 1935 from the Université de Montpellier for *L'Intervention du juge dans le contrat*. In the 1960s she was a professor at the Faculté de droit et des sciences politiques et économiques de Tunis, as well as editor-in-chief of the *Revue tunisienne de droit*. Note; NUC, pre-1956

Gaudio, Attilio, born in 1930, he received a doctorate in 1983 from the Université de Paris for *Les Populations nomades de l'Ouest saharien face à la modernité*. His other writings include *Le Sahara espagnol* (1975), *Le Dossier du Sahara ocidental* (1978), *Fès; joyau de la civilisation islamique* (1982), *Maroc saharien du Tafilalet au Rio de Oro* (1985), *Sahel; sulle piste della fame* (1986), *Le Mali* (1988), *Guerres et paix au Maroc* (1991), *Les Populations du Sahara occidental* (1993), and he was joint author of *Femmes d'islam; ou, le sexe interdit* (1980), and *Etonnante Côte-d'Ivoire* (1984). LC; THESAM, 1

Gaudry, Albert Jean, born in 1827 at Saint-Germain-en-Laye, the son of a Parisian barrister, collector of minerals, and friend of geologist. At the age of twenty he became affiliated with the Muséum national d'histoire naturelle. He completed a thesis in 1852 and in the following year became an assistant at the Muséum, where his brother-in-law held the chair of palaeontology. From 1853 to 1854 he was sent on a scientific mission to Greece, Syria, Cyprus and Egypt, a journey which he described in *Recherches scientifiques en Orient entreprises par les ordres du gouvernement* (1855). He died in Paris, 27 November 1908. BioIn 14; DBF; DcScBi; Henze; MembriiAR

Gaudry, Madame Matthéa, born 19th cent., she received a docorate in law in 1928 from the Université d'Alger for *La Femme de la Chaouia de l'Aurès; étude de sociologie berbère*, a work which was published in 1929. She was in 1932 an barrister in the Cour d'appel d'Alger. Note; NUC, pre-1956

Gaulis, Madame Berthe Georges, born 19th cent., she wrote *La France au Maroc* (1919), *Le Nationalisme turc* (1921), *La Nouvelle Turquie* (1924), *La Nationalisme égyptienne* (1928), and *La Question arabe* (1930). Her trace is lost after an article in 1930. BN

Gaulis, Georges, born in 1865, he wrote *Les Questions d'Orient* (1905), and *La Ruine d'un empire; Abd-ul-Hamid* (1913). He died in 1912. BN; NUC, pre-1956

Gaulmier, Jean, born 10 March 1905 at Charenton-du-Cher, he studied at the Ecole nationale des langues orientales vivantes, Paris. He was a *professeur* in the service of the Syrian government from 1927 to 1941 at Hama, Damascus and Aleppo. After the war, he was affiliated with the Université de Beyrouth from 1945 to 1951, when he there received a *doctorate ès lettres* for his thesis, *L'idéologue Volney*. He subsequently served as a professor of history successively at Strasbourg and the Sorbonne. NDBA; WhoFr, 1965/66-1979/80|

Gaulmin, Gilbert, born in 1585 at Moulins (Bourbonnais), he was an administrator but, above all, one of the great seventeenth century scholars and linguists, particularly in Oriental languages. He wrote *Livre des Lumières; ou, la Conduite des rois*, composé par le sage Pilpay (1644), and the translations from the French, *The Instructive and entertaining fables of Pilpay* (1784), and *The Fables of Pilpay* (1886). He died in Paris in 1665. Hoefer; IndexBFr² (2); *Revue de l'histoire des religions* 177 (1970), 35-63

Gaur, Albertine née Kasser, born 9 April 1932 at Sankt Pölten, Austria, she received a Dr.phil. in 1955 from the Universität Wien for *Glaube und Brauch des deutschen Schauspielers*. Thereafter she studied Dravidian languages at SOAS. After teaching German and cultural anthropology at Rajasthan University, 1960-1963, she successively joined the India Office Library and the British Museum, London. She was councillor elected to the Royal Borough of Kingston on Thames, 1993-1997. Her writings include *Catalogue of Malayalam books in the British Library* (1971), *Second supplementary catalogue of Tamil books in the British Library* (1980), *A History of writing* (1984), the two British Library booklets, *Writing materials of the East* (1979), and *Women in India* (1980), and she was joint author of *Signs, symbols and icons; pre-history to the computer age* (1997). ConAu, 121; IntAu&W, 1989; Private

Gaury, Gerald de, 1897-1984 *see* De Gaury, Gerald Simpson Hillairet Rutland Vere

Gauss, Julia, born about 1910, she received a Dr.phil. in 1934 from the Universität Basel for *Die methodische Grundlage von Goethes Geschichtsforschung*. Her writings include *Goethe-Studien* (1961), and *Ost und West in der Kirchen- und Papstgeschichte des 11. Jahrhunderts* (1967). GV; NUC

Gautero, Francesco, born 19th cent., he was in 1928 a judge in the Mixed Tribunal, Cairo, and a member of the Société Fouad 1er d'économie politique, de statistique et de législation. His writings include *Relazione statistica dei lavori compiuti nel circondario del tribunale civile e penale di asti nel-l'anno 1902* (1903), and *Giustiziae proprieta' fondiaria in Tunisia ed Algeri* (Roma, 1912). Firenze; Note; NUC, pre-1956

Gautherot, Gustave, born in 1880 at Pierrefontaine (Doubs), he studied at Dôle, Dijon and Besançon, where he completed his doctorate in 1907 with the complementary thesis, *Sur les relations franco-helvétiques de 1789 à 1792 d'après les archives du Ministère des Affaires étrangères*. He subsequently became a professor of history of the French revolution in the Institut catholique de Paris. In 1932 he was elected a senator for Loire-Inférieure. In June 1940 he voted for full powers for Maréchal Pétain. His many writings include *La France en Syrie et en Cilicie* (1920), and *La Conquête d'Alger, 1830, d'après les papiers inédits du maréchal Bourmont* (1929). He died in Paris, 24 February 1948. DBF; IndexBFr² (1); *Qui est-ce*, 1934

Gauthier, Henri Louis Marie Alexandre, born in 1877 at Lyon, he pursued ancient Near Eastern studies at Lyon and Berlin and in 1903 became a member of the Institut français d'archéologie orientale. His writings include *Les Nomes d'Égypte depuis Hérodote jusqu'à la conquête arabe* (1935). He died in Monaco in 1950. Dawson; Egyptology

Gauthier, Léon Marie Félix, born 18 January 1862 at Sétif, Algeria, he was educated at the Lycée d'Alger. After his *agrégation* in 1884 he successively taught philosophy at the Collège de Dôle and at Blois until 1895, when he returned to Algeria. After receiving a diploma in Arabic he taught philosophy at the Ecole supérieur des lettres d'Alger. From 1910 to his retirement in 1932 he held the chair of history of Islamic philosophy at Alger. He was an authority on Averroes. His writings include *La Philosophie musulmane* (1900), *Ibn Tofaïl* (1909), *Introduction à la philosophie musulmane* (1923), and *Ibn Rochd* (1948). He died in a suburb of Alger, 11 March 1949. DBF; *Qui êtes-vous*, 1924

Gauthier, René Antonin, O.P., fl. 1947, he wrote *Magnanimité* (1951), and *La Morale d'Aristote* (1958).

Gauthiot, Charles, born 24 April 1832 at Dijon, he was a journalist who taught first at the Lycée Charlemagne and later the Ecole coloniale, Paris. Although he is remembered for his thirty-year service as a permanent secretary of the Société de géographie commerciale de Paris, he was also an active member of the Comité de l'Afrique française. From 1871 to 1887 he was an editor of the *Journal des débats*. He died 27 February 1905. DBF; Unidentified obituary in the *journal* of his Société

Gauthiot, Robert, born in 1876 at Paris, he studied at the Université de Paris, where he received a doctorate in 1913 for *Essai sur le vocalisme du sogdien*. He was a deputy *directeur d'études* at the École des hautes études, Paris. He pursued linguistic field-work in the Pamirs, and contributed to the decipherment of Central Asian languages. His writings include *De l'alphabet sogdien* (1911), and *Essai de grammaire sogdienne* (1914-1923). He died from war injuries at the Hôpital du Val-de-Grâce, Paris, 11 September 1916. DBF

Gautier, Émile Félix, born 29 October 1864 at Clermont-Ferrand, he was educated at the École Normale Supérieure, spent three years in Germany, and explored Madagascar from 1893 to 1900, before going to Alger, where he was to hold the chair of geography at the Faculté des Lettres for thirty-five years until his retirement. He accomplished various geological missions in the Algerian Sahara without neglecting its political geography. His writings include *La Conquête du Sahara* (1910), *L'Al-gérie et la métropole* (1920), *L'Islamisation de l'Afrique du nord* (1927), *Moeurs et coutumes des musulmans* (1931), *Sahara, the great desert* (1935). On his retirement in 1937 he was presented with a felicitation volume entilted *Mélanges de géographie et d'orientalisme*. He died in Pontivy (Morbihan), 16 January 1940. *Bulletin de la Société de géographie d'Oran* 64 (1943), 7-25; DBF; *Index Islamicus* (2)

Gautier, Lucien Charles (also Marie), born 17 August 1850 at Cologny, Canton de Genève, he studied theology and Semitic languages at Genève, Leipzig and Tübingen. He was a professor of Hebrew and Old Testament exegesis at the Faculté de théologie libre de Lausanne from 1877 to 1898, when he returned to Genève, where he continued to lecture sporadically. He knew the Holy Land from three study travels, 1893, 1894 and 1899. He was granted honorary degrees by the universities of Bern and Glasgow. His writings include *Souvenirs de Terre-Saint* (1898), *Autour de la Mer morte* (1901), and *Vocations de prophètes* (1901). He died in 1925. SchZLex, 1921; *Who was who* 2

Gautier, Paul, born 20th cent., he was a member of the Institut français d'études byzantines. He edited and translated from the Greek of Nicephorus Bryennius, *Histoire* (1975), and of Theophylactus, archbishop of Ochida, *Lettres* (1986). LC

Gautier-Dalché, Jean, born 31 March 1913 at Podensac (Gironde), he studied at Bordeaux and Paris and became a *professeur* at the lycées in Oujda and Rabat from 1940 to 1943. A fellow of Casa Velazquez, Madrid, from 1946 to 1949, he subsequently served seven years at the Lycée Lyautey in Casablanca, before becoming a professor at the Université de Rabat from 1949 to 1958, and at the Université de Nice from 1965 to 1981. His writings include *Historia urbana de Léon y Castilla en la edad media* (1979), and *Les Espagnes médiévales* (1984). WhoWor, 1987/88, 1989/90

Gautier van Berchem, Marguerite, born 20th cent., she was joint author, with Solange Ory, of *La Jérusalem musulmane dans l'œuvre de Max van Berchem* (Lausanne, 1978). LC

Gautsch, Charles Lionel Honoré *Arnoul*, born 20 February 1882 at Paris, he graduated from the Polytechnique and Ecole d'application de Fontainebleau. He was a general who, as a young officer before the Great War, participated in campaigns in Algeria. From 1921 to 1938 he served intermittently in North Africa. As head of the Service automobile d'Afrique du nord, he supplied indispensable support to many Saharan missions. He died in Paris in 1969. DBF; Peyronnet, p. 926

Gauvain, Marie *Auguste*, born 6 October 1861 at Vesoul (Haute-Saône), he completed his law at Paris, where he also received a diploma from the Ecole des sciences politiques. A barrister in the Cour d'appel de Paris, he specialized in international law. He was editorial secretary to the *Journal de droit international*, 1887-1891, and also editor-in-chief of *La Vie politique à l'étranger*, 1889-1890. From 1893 to 1903 he served as a secretary to the Commission européenne du Danube, and subsequently as French secretary with the Office central des Transport internationaux, 1904-1908. Until his retirement in 1926 he was director of foreign policy at the *Journal des débats*. His writings include *L'Affaire grecque* (1917), *The Greek question* (1918), and *La Question yougoslave* (1918). He died in 1931. DBF; Qui êtes-vous, 1924

Gauvin, Joseph, born 20th cent., he was in 1976 affiliated with the Faculté de philosophie du Centre-Sèvres, Paris, and joint author of *L'Aliénation dans la phénoménologie de l'esprit* (1970). Note

Gavard, Octave, born in 1874, he received a medical doctorate in 1899 from the Université de Lyon for *La Misère du corps humain*. He became a *médecin-major* and was a member of the Société de géographie d'Alger. His writings include *Heures sahariennes; voyage à travers le Djerid tunisien* (1911). BN; Note; NUC, pre-1956

Gavault, Pierre, born 19th cent., he wrote *Etude sur les ruines romaines de Tigzirt* (Paris, 1897). He died in 1895. LC

Gavazzi, Milovan, born 18 March 1895 at Gospić, he was an ethno-musicologist and served as a curator at the Ethnographic Museum, Zagreb, from 1922 to 1925, when he became a professor at Zagreb University. His writings include *Godina dana hrvatskih narodnik običaja* (1939), *Subdina stare slavenske baštine kod Južnih Slavena* (1959), and *Vrela i sudbine narodnih tradicija* (1978). He died in Zagreb, 20 January 1992. HBL

Gavillot, J.-C. Aristide, born in 1837, he wrote *L'Angleterre ruine l'Egypte* (1875), *Essai sur les droits des Européens en Turquie et en Egypte* (1875), *L'Etude sur les impôts fonciers et autres devant les droits des Européens en Egypte* (1891), and *La Juridiction et les tribunaux mixtes* (1893). BN; LC

Gavin, Carney Edward Sebastian, born 28 March 1939 at Boston, Mass., he graduated *summa cum laude* in 1959 from Boston College, did post-graduate work at Jesus College, Oxford, and received a Ph.D. in 1973 from Harvard for *The glyptic art of Syria-Palestine*. He became an archaeologist and was affiliated with the Harvard Semitic Museum. His writings include *The Image of the East; 19th-century Near Eastern photography*, edited by Ingeborg E. O'Reilly (1982). Master (2); WhoE, 1985/86; WhoRel, 1977, 1992/93

Gavin, Robert J., born 23 July 1905 at Abderdeenshire, he received his LL.B. in 1928 from the University of Aberdeen and subsequently pursued post-graduate work at LSE. He became an International Labour Office official in Switzerland as well as in the Congo. His writings include *The Scramble for Africa* (1973), and *Aden under British rule, 1839-1967* (1975). Unesco

Gavira, José, born about 1900, he received a doctorate in 1929 from the Universidad de Madrid for *Estudios sobre la iglesia española medieval*. His writings include *Catálogo de la Biblioteca de la Real Sociedad Geográfica* (1947-48), and he edited *El viajero español por Marruecos, don Joaqín Gatell, "Káid Ismail"* (1949). NUC, pre-1957-67

Gavrilov, Mikhail Filippovich, born 19th cent., he wrote *Остаки ясы и юсуна у узбеков* (Tashkent, 1929), and *Материалы к этнографии "тюрок" Ура-Тюбинского района* (Tashkent, 1929). NYPL

Gavrilović, Mladen, born 9 September 1925 at Beograd, he was a foreign politics editor of the Yugoslav press agency Tanjug as well as a correspondent of the Beograd Radio and TV in the Middle East. His writings include *Carevina na krovu Afrike* (1968), and *Ratni plamenovi roga Afrike* (1979). JugoslSa, 1970

Gavron, Daniel, born 7 December 1935 at London, he attended SOAS and successively became a kibbutz founder and leader, a public relations officer, a news editor, and a reporter. His writings include *The End of days* (1970), *Israel after Begin* (1984), and *The Kibbutz; awakening from utopia* (2000). He was the founding editor of *Palestine-Israel journal*. ConAu 29-32, new rev. 12, 99

Gay, Jules Marie Michel, born 14 January 1867 at Strasbourg, he was a graduate of the Lycée Louis-le-Grand and the École normale supérieure. He received a doctorate in 1904 from the Université de Paris for *Le Pape Clément VI et les affaires d'Orient, 1342-1352*. He was a medievalist whose writings include *L'Italie méridionale et l'Émpire byzantin* (1904), its translation, *L'Italia meridionale e l'imperio bizantino* (1980), and *Les Papes du XIe siècle et la chrétienté* (1926). He died in Lille on 1 September 1935. Byzantion 12 (1937), pp. 712-721; IndexBFr² (3)

Gay y Forner, Vicente born in 1876 or 77 at Valencia, he was a professor of political economy at the Universidad de Valladolid. His writings include *El imperialismo y la guerra europea* (1915), *Las constitutiones políticas* (1930), *Qué es el imperialismo* (1941), and *La hacienda social* (1948). He died in 1947. IndiceE³ (2); NUC, pre-1956

Gaya Nuño, Juan Antonio, born 29 January 1913 at Tardelcuende (Soria), he received a doctorate in 1934 from the Universidad de Madrid. His writings include *El románico en la provincia de Vizcaya* (1944), *El Escorial* (1947), and *Teoría del románico* (1962). He died in 1975. ConAu 81-84, new rev. 31; DBEC; IndiceE³ (2); IntAu&W, 1976

de **Gayangos y Arce**, Pascual, born 21 June 1809 at Sevilla. From 1822 onwards he was educated in France, and he is known to have attended Silvestre de Sacy's lectures. Following upon a tour of North Africa, he visited England in 1828 and, shortly afterwards, married Miss Fanny Revell, of Round Oak, Windsor, whom he had met when travelling in Algiers. On his return to Spain he entered the Treasury, and, in 1831, became interpreter to the Foreign Office. For political reasons he resigned in 1836, residing in England until 1841, when he was named professor of Oriental lamguages at the Universidad de Madrid. This post he held until 1872. He was chosen a supernumerary member of the Real Academia de la Historia on 26 January 1844, and was elected as member on 5 March 1847. He was appointed director of Public Instruction in 1881; but his tenure of office was brief, owing to the promotion to the Senate. A true student, his life is almost bare of incident, and his best monument is to be found in the catalogue of his writings which include *The history of the Mohammedan dynasties in Spain* (1840-43), *Memoria sobre la autenticidad de la Crónica denominada del moro Rasis* (1850), and *Catalogue of the Spanish manuscripts of the British Museum* (1875-93). He died in London, 4 October 1897. EncAm; EncBrit; EncicUni; Fück, p. 265; GdeEnc; *Index Islamicus* (4); IndiceE (8); Manzanares, pp. 83-101; Meyers; *Revue hispanique* 4 (1897), pp. 337-341; RNL; Sainz

Gayet, Albert Jean Marie Philippe, born 17 September 1856 at Dijon, he was an Egyptologist who went to Egypt with the Mission archéologique française of 1881. His writings include *L'Art arabe* (1893), *L'Art persan* (1895), and *L'Art copte* (1902). He died in 1916. Dawson; Egyptology

Gayet, Georges, born 2 January 1891 at Toulon, he was educated at the Faculté de droit de Paris and the Ecole coloniale, graduating in 1912. After the first World War he served for three years with the Gouvernement générale in Madagacar. When he returned to Paris in 1923, he took his doctorate in law. From 1923 to 1934 he was sent on twelve missions to various French colonies. He remained in the colonial administration until his retirement. Throughout his career he concurrently taught at the Ecole nationale d'administration, Ecole des sciences politiques, the Centre des hautes études sur l'Afrique et l'Asie moderne, the Institut des hautes études de la Défense nationale and the Ecole supérieure de guerre. He was a member of the Académie des sciences coloniales and the Comité des Travaux historiques. He was a joint author of *Madagascar, colonie française* (1931). He died in Poitiers, 15 April 1962. *l'Afrique et l'Asie* 59 (1962), pp. 75-76; *Hommes et destins*, vol. 8, pp. 156-57; Unesco

Gayot, Henri, born about 1900, he was affiliated with the Moroccan Ministère de l'Education nationale, Enseignement technique. He was joint author of *Le Décor floral dans l'art de l'islam occidental* (Rabat, 1955), *La Broderie de Meknès* (Rabat, 1956), and *La Broderie de Fès* (1959). BN

Gazeau, Théodore Paul Ambroise, called Gazeau de Vatibault, he was born in 1842 at the château de Montglonne in the community of S.-Florent-le-Vieil (Maine-et-Loire). He was a barrister-at-law and affiliated with the Gardes nationales de la Seine. Interested in French railways, he also propagated the *Trans-saharien* and the *Trans-continental africain*, but the advent of Jules Ferry put an end to his plans in 1880. He stood for elections twice but was defeated each time. His writings include *Le Trans-saharien, chemin de fer d'Alger au Soudan* (1879). He died in Nice in 1902. DBF

Gazić, Lejla, born 20th cent., she edited and translated from the Turkish, *Vakufname iz Bosne i Hercegovine XV i XVI vijek* (Sarajevo, 1985). LC

Gazit (Weinstein), Mordechai, born 5 September 1922 at Constantinople, he studied at the Hebrew University, Jerusalem, and became a politician. His writings include *The Peace progress, 1969-1973* (1983), and *President Kennedy's policy toward the Arab states and Israel* (1983). MidE, 1982/83; WhoFr, 1977/78-1979/80; WhoIsrael, 1972-2001; WhoWorJ, 1965, 1972, 1978, 1987

Gazit, Shlomo, born in 1926 in Turkey, he was educated at Tel Aviv University and subsequently entered the army. He became head of Military Intelligence. His writings include the booklet, *Israel's policy in the administered territories* (1969). IntWW, 1984/85-2002; Master (1); MidE, 1978-1982/83; WhoIsrael, 1985/86-2001; WhoWor, 1984/85

Gazizov, Riza Salakhovich, born in 1894, he wrote *Русско-татарский словарь* (1955), *Сопоставительная грамматика татарского и русского языков* (1959), and *Татарский язык* (1960). He died in 1981. TatarES

Gazov-Ginzberg, Anatolii Mikhailovich, born 17 December 1929 at Novosibirsk, he graduated in 1957 from Leningrad State University, where he also received his first degree in 1964 for *Роль звукоизобразительных истоков в образовании семитского запаса корней*. He was since 1957 affiliated with the Leningrad Oriental Institute. His writings include *Был ли язык изобразителен в своих истоках?* (1965), and *Символизм прасемитской флексии* (1974). Miliband; Miliband[2]

Gazzo, Yves, born 20th cent., he received a doctorate in 1975 from the Université de Montpellier for *Prospection et développement; le rôle et l'action du secteur rural dans les pays sahéliens*. He was in 1993 a principal administrator with the European Economic Commission in Bruxelles. His writings include *Afrique du nord d'hier à demain; essai d'analyse économique* (1979), *Pétrole et développement; le cas libyen* (1980), and *L'Endettement dans le monde* (1990). EURAMES, 1993; THESAM, 1

Geagea, Nilo, born in 1908, he was a scholar of Mariolatry whose writings include *Maria nel messaggio coranico* (ca. 1978), and its translation, *Mary of the Koran* (1984). LC

Geary, Grattan, born 19th cent., he was a journalist who went to India in 1873. He was an editor of the *Times of India* and subsequently acquired the *Bombay gazette*. He took a prominent part in Bombay municipal affairs and was at one time chairman of the Corporation of Bombay. His writings include *Through Asiatic Turkey; a narrative of a journey from Bombay to the Bosphorus* (1878), and *Burma, after the conquest* (1886). He died in 1900. Boase; Buckland; IndianBiInd (2); Riddick

Gebert, Bolesław, born in 1895, he was a labour activist whose writings include *New Poland* (1945), *Pierwsi Polacy w Stanach Ziednoczonych* (1958), and *Z Tykocina za Ocean* (1982). LC

Geddes, Charles Lynn, born 3 January 1928 at Cornvallis, Ore., he graduated in 1951 from the University of Oregon and received his Ph.D. in 1959 from SOAS for *The Yu'firid dynasty of San'a*. After five years of teaching at AUC, he became a professor of history at the University of Colerado, Denver, and concurrently a director of the American Institute of Islamic Studies. His writings include *Guide to reference books for Islamic studies* (1985) as well as a number of annotated bibliographies on Middle Eastern subjects. ConAu 49-52, new rev. 2; DrAS, 1969 H, 1974 H, 1978 H, 1982 H; Sluglett; WhoWest, 1992/93-1996/97

Geddes, Sir Patrick, born in 1854 at Ballater, Scotland, he was a biologist and sociologist. Although not trained as a geographer, he worked in areas which were or have become mainstream geography. His writings include *Town planning in Lucknow* (1916), *Town planning in Patiala State and City* (1922), and *Patrick Geddes, spokesman for man and the environment* (1972). He died in 1932. BiD&SB; BritInd (2); DNB; *Geographers*, 2 (1978), pp. 52-65; Master (23); Riddick; WhE&EA; *Who was who* 3

Gedenshtrom, Matvei Matveevich, born about 1780, he was a Russian explorer of Swedish origin (Hedenström). During his explorations of the New Siberian Islands he made many trips through Yakutia and Transbaikalia. His writings include *Отрывки о Сибири* (1830). He died in Tomsk, Russia, 20 September 1845. GSE; Henze

Gee, Ellen Margaret Thomas, born 29 January 1950 at Vancouver, B.C., she received a Ph.D. in 1978 from the University of British Columbia, Vancouver, for *Fertility and marriage patterns in Canada, 1851-1971*. Since 1992 she was a professor of sociology in Simon Frazer University, Burnaby, B.C., a post which she still held in 2003. She was joint author of *Women and aging* (1987). Canadian, 1995-2002; NatFacDr, 2003

Geertz, Clifford James, born 23 August 1926 at San Francisco, he received a Ph.D. from Harvard in 1956 for *Religion in Modjokuto*. He was a professor of anthropology and social sciences successively at the University of California, Berkeley, University of Chicago, and the Institute for Advanced Study, Princeton. His writings include *Islam observed; religious development in Morocco and Indonesia* (1968), its translation, *Religiöse Entwicklung im Islam* (1988), and he was joint author of *Meaning and order in Moroccan society* (1979). AmM&WS, 1973 S, 1978 S; ConAu 33-36, new rev. 36, 82; IntAu&W, 1991-2003; IntWW, 1989/90-2002; IWWAS, 1975-76; Master (7); Shavit - Asia; WhoAm, 1976/77-2003; WhoE, 1989/90-2003; WrDr, 1986/88-2003

Gefen, Marek, born 14 July 1917 in Czechoslovakia, he studied at Uniwersytet Jagielloński, Kraków and in 1949 emigrated to Israel, where he became an editor-in-chief of *Al Hamishmar*. WhoIsrael, 1976-1985/86

Geffcken, Friedrich Heinrich, born in 1830 at Hamburg, he studied history and law and in 1854 entered the diplomatic service. From 1872 to 1882 he was a professor of political science and pubilc law at the Universität Straßburg. His writings include *Zur Geschichte des orientalischen Krieges* (1881), *La Question du Danube* (1883), and *Frankreich, Rußland und der Dreibund* (1893). He died in München in 1896. DtBE; DtBilnd (3)

Gehman, Henry Snyder, born 1 June 1883 in Lancaster County, Pa., he graduated from Franklin and Marshall College, Lancaster, Pa., and received a Ph.D. in 1933 from the University of Pennsylvania for *The interpreters of foreign languages among the ancients; a study based on Greek and Latin sources.* After five years of service as a minister, he was from 1909 to his retirement in 1958 affiliated with the Theological Seminary, Princeton. He died in 1981. ConAu 13-16; DrAS, 1969 F, 1974 F, 1978 F, 1982 F; WrDr, 1976-1982/84; WhAm 8

Gehring, Gilbert, he wrote *Les Relations entre la Tunisie et l'Allemagne avant le Protectorat français* (Tunis, 1971). NUC, 1973-77

Gehrke, Ulrich, born about 1930, he received a Dr.phil. in 1960 from the Universität Hamburg for *Persien in der deutschen Orientpolitik während des ersten Weltkrieges*. He became affiliated with Deutsches Orient-Institut, Hamburg. He was joint author of *Die Grenzen des Irak* (1963), *Die Aden-Grenze in der Südarabienfrage, 1900-1967* (1967), and he was joint editor of *Iran* (1975). Private

Geidarov (Heidärov), Mikhail Khudair ogly, born 20th cent., he wrote Ремесленное производство в городах Азербайджана в XVIII в. (1967), Города и городское ремесло Азербайджана XIII-XVII веков (1982), and Социально-экономические отношения и ремесленные организации в городах Азербайджана в XIII-XVII вв. (1987). LC

Geiger, Abraham, born 24 May 1810 at Frankfurt am Main. After private instruction in the Talmud he studied philosophy and Oriental languages at Heidelberg and Bonn, where he completed his studies with the prize-essay, *Was hat Mohammed aus den Judentum aufgenommen?* (1833), and its translation, *Judaism and Islam* (1970). He was a leader of reformed Judaism and the founder of the *Zeitschrift für jüdische Theologie*. Since 1863 he was a rabbi at Frankfurt, and in 1870 he accepted an invitation as rabbi at Berlin, where he also taught since 1872 at the newly established Hochschule für die Wissenschaft des Judentums. He died in Berlin on 23 October 1874. DtBE; EncBrit; EncItaliana; EncJud; Fück, p. 174; GdeEnc; JüdLex; Wininger

Geiger, Bernhard, born 30 April 1881 at Bielitz-Biala, Austria-Hungary, he studied at Wien, where he also received his Dr.phil. in 1904 for *Die Mu'allaqa des Tarafa Ibn al-'Abd*. Influenced by his teacher, Leopold von Schroeder, his interest shifted to Indo-Iranian languages. In 1908 he received a Dr.habil. with a work on the *Amesha-Spentas*, and in 1919 he succeeded to von Schroeder, but concentrating in his teaching mainly on pre-Islamic Iranian philology. Dismissed after the Anschluß in 1938, he went to the Asia Institute, New York, where he remained until 1950. He was joint author of *Peoples and languages of the Caucasus* (1959). He died in N.Y.C., 5 July 1964. BioHbDtE; CnDiAmJBi; DtBE; EncJud; Fück, p. 258; NYT, 7 July 1964, p. 32, col. 6; WhoWorJ, 1965; WZKM 59/60 (1963/64), pp. 224-26

Geiger, Wilhelm Ludwig, born in 1856 at Nürnberg, he was an Indo-Iranian scholar and successively a professor at the universities of Erlangen and München. His writings include *Die Russen in Turkestan* (1885), *Die Pamirgebiete* (1887), and *Pali literature and language* (1943). He died in Neubiberg near München on 2 September 1943. DtBE; DtBilnd (3); Kürschner, 1925-1940/41: Stache-Rosen, pp. 127-29; Wer ist's, 1922-35; WhE&EA; ZDMG 98 (1944), pp. 170-188

Geijbels, M., born 20th cent., he was associated with the Christian Study Centre, Rawalpindi. His writings include *An Introduction to Islam; Muslim beliefs and practices* (Rawalpindi, 1975-77). LC; Note

Geijer, Agnes Theresa, born 26 October 1898 at Uppsala, she received a doctorate in 1938 and subsequently was a curator of textiles at Statens Historiska Museum, Stockholm. Her writings include *Oriental textiles in Sweden* (1951), *History of textile arts* (1979), and she was joint author of *Orientalische Briefumschläge in schwedischem Besitz* (1944). She was honoured by *Opera textilia variorum temporum; to honour Agnes Geijer on her ninetieth birthday* (1988). She died 17 July 1989. Vem är det, 1956-1987

Geiler, Hermann Franz, born 19th cent., he gained a Dr.oec. and was in 1919 the editor of the journal *Soziale Wirtschaft* (Berlin). His writings include *Die zentralen Kreditinstitute Deutschlands* (1935). NUC

Geilinger, Walter, born 19th cent., he received a Dr.med. in 1917 from the Universität Zürich. His writings include *Der Kilimandjaro; sein Land und seine Menschen* (1930). NUC, pre-1956

Geise, Nicolaas Johannes Cornelis, born in 1907, he was a Franciscan father who received a doctorate in 1952 from the Rijksuniversiteit te Leiden for *Badujs en Moslims in Lebak Parahiang*. LC

Geiss, Albert, born 19th cent., he wrote *De l'établissement des manuscrits destinés à l'impression; conseils pratiques* (Le Caire, Institut français d'archéologie orientale, 1906). His trace is lost after an article in 1910. NUC, pre-1956

Geissler, Friedmar, born 27 June 1920 at Dresden, he was affiliated as a lecturer with the Institut für Orientforschung, Deutsche Akademie der Wissenschaften, as well as Pädagogische Hochschule, Potsdam. His writings include *Brautwerbung in der Weltliteratur* (1955), he was joint author of *Ein Manichäisch-sogdisches Parabelbuch* (1985), and he edited and translated *Beispiele der alten Weisen des Johann von Capua*, from Bīdpā'ī (1960). He died 24 November 1984. Kürschner, 1961-1976; LC

Geist, Benjamin, Dr., born 20th cent., he was in 1976 a lecturer in foreign policy at the Hebrew University, Jerusalem. He was a joint author of *Decisions in crisis; Israel, 1967 and 1973* (1980). Note

Geitlin, Gabriel, born 3 January 1804 at Naantalissa (Nådendaal), Finland, he studied Oriental languages at St. Petersburg and received a doctorate in 1834 from Helsingfors University for *Specimen academicum Pendnameh, sive librum consiliorum Scheich Musliheddin Saadi.* He served in various capacities at his University until his retirement in 1864. Concurrently he was from 1849 to 1863 a curator of the University's collection of coins and medals. His writings include *Principia grammatices neo-persicae* (1845), and *Hebraisk grammatik* (1856). He died in 1871. Aalto; ScBInd (7); Stenij

Geiushev (Koiushov), Ziiaddin Bagatur ogly, born 20 May 1920 in Azerbaijan, he received a doctorate in 1963 and was appointed a professor in 1964. His writings include Мировоззрение Г. Б. Зардаби (1962), Этическая мысль и Азербайджане (1968), and Философская мысль в Советском Азербайджане (1980). AzarbSE, vol. 6, p. 109

Gelb, Ignace Jay, born in 1907 at Tarnów, he studied in Italy and in 1929 went to the United States, where he became affiliated until his retirement in 1976 in various capacities with the Oriental Institute, University of Chicago, as a linguistic and Assyriologist. His writings include *Inscriptions from Alishar and vicinity* (1935), and *A Study of writings* (1952). He died in 1985. ANB; CnDiAmJBi; ConAu 9-12, 118; DrAS, 1969, 1974, 1978, 1982; EncJud; IntWW, 1974/75-1983; NYT, 24 December 1985, p. B10, col. 2; Shavit; WhAm 9; WhoAm, 1974/75-1984/85

Gelb, Leslie Howard, born 4 March 1937 at New Rochelle, N.Y., she graduated *magna cum laude* in 1959 from Tufts University and received a Ph.D. in 1964 from Harvard for *Anglo-American relations, 1945-1949*, a work which was published in 1988. She was an executive assistant, or director, at a variety of government levels, mainly in the field of defence as well as national and international security. Her other writings include *The Irony of Vietnam* (1979). ConAu 103, new rev. 19; Master (2); WhoAm, 1978-2003; WhoAmP, 1979-1995/96

Gelber, Marvin Bernard, born 1 November 1912 at Toronto, Ont., he graduated in the class of 1934 from the University of Toronto. He became a member of Parliament in 1963, and subsequently an executive in cultural, philanthropic, and social institutions. WhoWorJ, 1965, 1972, 1978

Gelber, Nathan Michael, born 27 May 1891 at Lemberg (Lvov), Austria-Hungary. After a strict Jewish education he studied philosophy at Berlin and Wien, where he received a Dr.phil. for a thesis on Jewish history. He was a historian and a Zionist leader whose writings include *Die Juden und der polnische Aufstand von 1863* (1923), and *Zur Vorgeschichte des Zionismus* (1927). He died in Jerusalem in 1966. BioHbDtE; DtBE; DtBInd (1); EncJud; WhoIsrael, 1956-66/67; *Who's who in Central & East Europe*, 1933/34; WhoWorJ, 1965; Wininger

van **Gelder**, Geert Jan H., born in 1947, he received a doctorate in 1982 from the Rijksuniversiteit te Leiden for *Beyond the line; classical Arabic literary critics.* His writings include *The Bad and the ugly;*

attitudes toward invective poetry (1989), and he was joint author of *A Bibliography of Dutch publications on the Middle East and Islam* (1976), *The Arabic text of the Apocalypse of Baruch* (1986), and *De pen en het zwaard; literatuur en politiek in het Midden-Oosten* (1988). Brinkman's; LC

van **Gelder**, Hendrik Douwe, born in 1861 at Bolsward, Netherlands, he received a doctorate in 1888 at Leiden for *Mohtar de valsche profeet*. Since 1890 he was a lecturer in Persian and Turkish at his alma mater. Wie is dat, 1902

Gelfer-Jørgensen, Mirjam, born 16 December 1939 at København, she received an M.A. in 1971 from Københavns Universitet and also a Dr.phil. in 1987. In 1985 she was one of the founders of the Dansk Jødisk Museum; and in 1991 she was associated with the Library of the Museum of Art as well as her alma mater as a professor of fine art. She edited *Dansk jødisk kunst; jøder i dansk kunst* (1999). IWWAS, 1975/76; Kraks, 1999-2004; NSMES *Directory of members*, 1991

Gella, Július, born 1 June 1933 at Vrútky, Czechoslovakia, he studied Arabic at the Univerzita Komenského, Bratislava, where he also received a Ph.Dr. in 1986. He visited Egypt in 1965-66 and Libya from 1980 to 1985. Filipsky

Gellert, Johannes Fürchtegott, born 4 October 1904 at Leipzig, he studied geography at the Universität, where he received a Dr.phil. in 1929 for *Neogenbucht von Varna* and also a Dr.habil. in 1937 for *Mittelbulgarien*. He became a professor of geography at Leipzig in 1940. He was confined in South Africa from 1940 to 1944, when he returned to Germany. He was in 1949 a professor at Halle. From 1950 to his retirement in 1970 he was a professor of physical geography at Pädagogische Hochschule, Potsdam. His writings include *Politisch-geographische Entwicklung und Struktur Bulgariens* (1933), *Die Niederschlagsschwankungen im Hochland von Südwestafrika* (1955), and *Alexander von Humboldt* (1960). Kürschner, 1940/41-1976|; WhoSoC, 1978; WhoSoCE, 1989; WhoWor, 1987/88

Gellhorn, Martha Ellis, born in 1908 at St. Louis, Mo., she was a graduate of Bryn Mawr College, Pa., and became a journalist, war correspondent, and novelist. In 1940 she married Ernest Hemingway; they divorced in 1945. Her writings include *What mad pursuit* (1934), *The Heart of another* (1941), and *The Face of war* (1959). She died of cancer in London in 1998. ConAu 77-80, 164; IntAu&W, 1971-1991/92; IntWW, 1974/75-1993; Master (29); WhoAm, 1974/75-1984; WhoAmW, 1958-1974/75; WrDr, 1976/78-1998/2000

Gellner, Ernest André, born 9 December 1925 at Paris, he received a Ph.D. in 1961 from LSE for his thesis, *The Rôle and organisation of a Berber zawiya*. He taught his subject at the University of London from 1949 to 1984, when he became William Wyse Professor of social anthropology at Cambridge. His writings include *Saints of the Atlas* (1969), *The Devil in modern philosophy* (1974), *Muslim society* (1981), its translation, *Leben im Islam* (1985), *Reason and culture* (1992), and *Conditions of liberty* (1994). He died in Prague, 5 November 1995. Cesky; ConAu 5-8, 150, new rev. 4, 22; IntWW, 1974/75-1995/96; MES, 32 iv (1996), 405-6; *Morocco*, n.s., 1 (1996), pp. 1-2; Sluglett; Unesco; Who, 1973-1996; WhoWor, 1974/75-1989/90; WrDr, 1976/78-1996/98

Gelpke (-Rommel), Rudolf, born 24 December 1928 at Waldenburg, Switzerland, he studied ethnology and Islamic subjects at Swiss and German universities (1948-1951), travelled in Egypt (1949), and Tunisia (1952), and published his novel *Holger und Mirjam* (1951). He was free-lance writer until 1953 when he started on his thesis, *Sultan Mas'du I. von Gazna*, which was accepted by the Universität Basel in 1957. He lectured in Europe, the United States, and Iran until the late 1960s when he abandoned academic research and experimented with submergence in Oriental mysticism. During the last years of his life he became totally estranged from formal Western scholarship as reflected in *Vom Rausch in Orient und Okzident* (1966). During his three months' travels in central Iran he became an honorary member of an Iranian dervish order. His writings include *Die iranische Prosaliteratur im 20. Jahr-hundert* (1962), *The Story of Layla and Majnun* (1966), *Hundertundeine Geschichte aus dem Rosengarten, von Scheich Saadi* (1967). He died from a brain haemorrhage while taking a stroll in Luzern, 19 January 1972. Note; *Who's who in Switzerland*, 1972-73

Gelzer, Heinrich Carl Guido, born 1 July 1847 at Berlin, he studied classical philology and history at Basel and received a Dr.phil. in 1869 from the Universität Leipzig for *De Branchidis*. He was successively a professor of his subject at Heidelberg and Jena, where he died on 11 July 1906. His writings include *Geistliches und Weltliches aus dem türkisch-griechischen Orient* (1900), and *Vom Heiligen Berge und aus Makedonien; Reisebilder* (1904). DtBE; DtBIlnd (5); NUC, pre-1956

Gemmill, Paul Fleming, born 30 May 1889 at Muddy Creek Forks, York County, Pa., he started life as a stenographer with York Printing Co, later becoming a Y.M.C.A, assistant secretary, and from 1909 to 1917 working as an entertainer - during the last six years before graduating from Swarthmore College, also summers. He received his Ph.D. in 1925 from the University of Pennsylvania for *Collective bargaining by actors*. From 1919 to 1959 he served as a professor of economics at the University. His writings include *Britain's search for health* (1960). He died in 1976. ConAu 69-72; NYT, 5 January 1977, p. B18, cols. 1-2; WhAm 8

Gendzier, Irene Lefel (Mrs. A. J. Kfoury), born 24 March 1936 at Paris, she graduated in 1957 from Barnard College and received a Ph.D. in 1964 from Columbia University for *The politics of faith; Ya'qub Sanu'as Abu Naddara.* She subsequently joined the University of Boston, where she taught history until her retirement. Her writings include *A Middle East reader* (1969), *Frantz Fanon* (1973), and *Managing political change* (1985). ConAu 21-24; DrAS, 1969-1982 H; NatFacDr, 1995; Selim

Genevois, Henri, fl. 1955-1974, he was a Berber scholar who wrote *Ayt-Embarek; notes d'enquête linguistique* (1955), *La Famille* (1962), *L'Habitation kabyle* (1962), *Le Corps humaine* (1963), *Le Sage Bou-Amrane* (1965), *La Femme kabyle* (1969), and *Djebel Bissa* (1973). LC

Géniaux, Charles Hippolyte Jean, born 12 November 1870 at Rennes, he was a writer of novels dealing with the Bretagne or North Africa, many of which he wrote jointly with his wife Claire. His writings include *Les Musulmanes* (1909), and *La Passion d'Armelle Louanais* (1917), a work which won him the *grand prix du roman* from the Académie française. He died in Nice on 19 March 1931. DBF

Géniaux, Claire Charles, born 6 July 1879 at Rennes, she wrote *L'Âme musulmane en Tunisie* (1934) as well as other novels written jointly with her husband Charles. DBF

Genin, Izrail' Adol'fovich, born in 1897, he graduated in 1924 from the Institute of Political Economy and received his first degree in 1940 for *Экономика Турции в период мирового экономического кризика, 1929-1933 гг.* He was a lecturer since 1935. His writings include *Страны Арабского Востока* (1948), *Йемен* (1953), *Ливия* (1956), and *Империалисическая борьба за Сахару* (1962). Miliband; Miliband²

Geniusz, Mieczysław, born in 1853, his writings, partly under the pseudonym M. Negus, include the booklet, *Comment faire la société des nations* (Paris, 1917). He died in 1920. Dziekan; PSB

Genko, Anatolii Nesterovich, born in 1896 at St. Petersburg, he there studied and took his doctorate in 1935 in linguistics. From 1922 to his death on 26 December 1941, he was affiliated with the Asian Museum of the Oriental Institute, Soviet Academy of Science. His interest in the Arabic sources of Caucasian history is embodied in his 1941 treatise *«Арабский язык и кавказоведение».* Krachkovsikii; Miliband; Miliband²

Gennadios (Gennadius), James (John), born in 1844 at Athens, he entered the Greek foreign service. He was a member of the Greek Mission at the Congress of Berlin. After his retirement, he represented Greece in the Conference of the Balkan Allies in London, 1913. He was the recipient of numerous honours and decorations. His writings include works on Greek philology. He died in London in 1932. BritInd (2); EEE; Megali, vol. 8 (1928), p. 200; Who, 1921-1932; Who was who 3

Genné, Marcelle, born 20th cent., she was certainly from 1979 to 1995 a professor in the Université d'Ottawa. Her writings include *Méthodes d'investissement* (1982), and *Autosuffisance alimentaire, ou, Famine en l'an 2000; le Niger* (1991). LC; NatFacDr, 1995

Gennep, Arnold van, 1873-1957 *see* Van Gennep, Arnold

Genocchi, Giovanni, born 30 July 1860 at Ravenna, he was educated at the Pontificio Seminario Pio and received a doctorate in 1880. He was ordained in 1883. He was a missionary and professor of divinity who first visited the East in 1885, an experience which he described in *Il mio viaggio in Oriente nell'autunn dell'anno 1885* (Ravenna, 1886). He later visited the Near and Middle East with Pontifical missions. His writings include *Carteggio, 1877-1900*, ed. Francesco Turvasi (1978). He died in Roma on 6 January 1926. F. Turvasi wrote *Padre Genocchi, il Sant'uffizio e la Bibbia* (1971), and *Giovanni Genocchi e la controversia modernista* (1974). DizBI; IndBiItal (2)

Genoud, Roger, born 20th cent., he received a doctorate in 1965 from the Université de Genève for *L'Evolution de l'économie tunisienne.* NUC, 1968-72

Genov, TSonko Alipiev, he was a Bulgarian whose writings include *Памотници на бойна слава и братска прознателност* (1960), *По бойния път на освободителите, 1877-1878* (1976), and *Осваободителната война 1877-1978* (1978). LC

Gentelle, Pierre, born in 1933, he was affiliated with the Musée Guimet, Paris. His writings include *Le Blé en Afghanistan* (1972), *Etude géographique d'Ai Khanoum et de son irrigation depuis les temps anciens* (1978), *Géographie de la Chine* (1980), *Fascination desert* (1992), and he was joint author of *Afghanistan* (1985). AnEIFr, 1997; *Livres disponibles*, 2003; Schoeberlein

Gentil, Emile, born about 1800, he was a chevalier du Saint-Sépulche and wrote *Mort d'un pèlerin à Jérusalem en 1852* (Paris, 1854), and *Souvenirs d'Orient; détails nouveaux sur Malte, le Liban, la Syrie et l'Egypte* (Metz, 1855). BN

Gentil, Emile, born 4 April 1866 at Volmunster, (Moselle), he went to school in Nancy and graduated in 1885 from the École navale de Brest. After a hydrographical mission to Gabon on board the *Courbet* he requested a transfer to the colonial administration of Africa. Since 1891 an administrator in the Congo, he went between 1895 and 1897 on several missions of exploration to Lake Chad and the River Chari. Named *commissaire* of Chari in 1899, he set out to put an end to the exploits of the dreadful Rabah and his warriors. As lieutenant-governor of the Congo from 1902 to 1903, he pacified Ouaddaï, Bornu, Borku and Tibesti. His writings include *La Chute de l'empire de Rabah* (1902. He died in Bordeaux on 14 March 1914, and was buried at Père Lachaise in Paris. AfrBioInd (2); DBF

Gentil, Emmanuel, born 19th cent., he went in 1908 in the service of the Ministère de l'Instruction publique and the Ministère des Affaires étrangères on a scientific mission to Morocco. In 1909 he was a lecturer at the Université de Paris. Note

Gentil, Jean Baptiste Joseph, born 25 June 1726 at Bagnols-sur-Cèze (Gard) to a well-off family. On 13 February 1752 he left from Lorient for Pondichéry, arriving there with his regiment five months later. He participated in the Mahratta campaign until 1755 and was taken prisoner at the fall of Mazulipatum. After the capitulation of Chandernagor, he offered his services to the Nawab of Bengal. He later joined the Nawab of Oudh, Shuja'-ud-Daula, who heaped him with honours for having served as aide-de-camp in the battle of Baxter. After the English victory, he was most generous in helping less fortunate French fellow countrymen, and enrolled a body of them to serve under the Nawab. During his spare time, he studied Indian languages, history, and geography, at the same time collecting important weapons, medals, drawings as well as Oriental manuscripts in a variety of languages. After the death of the Nawab in 1775, he was compelled by the English to leave. Upon his arrival in 1778 at Paris, he offered all his collections to the king. He lived at Versailles until 1789. Having lost his pension in the French revolution, he died in poverty in Bagnols, 15 February 1799. His writings include *Mémoires sur l'Indoustan, ou Empire mongol* (1822). Buckland; DBF; Henze; Hoefer; IndexBFr² (4)

Gentil, Louis Émile, born in 1868 at Alger, he discovered his interest in the people of North Africa and Islam while still a high school student, learning Arabic at that early stage. For practical reasons, he trained in physical sciences and received his doctorate in 1902 from the Université de Paris for *Esquisse stratigraphique et pétrographique du bassin de la Tafna*. A partisan of French colonization, his scientifique exploration of Morocco can be divided into three periods. From 1904 to 1911 he accomplished six missions. First in disguise, speaking Arabic, he passed as a pious Egyptian, and later in Sharifian service; during the French conquest of Morocco from 1911 to 1913 his intimate acquaintance with the country facilitated French military operations; and from 1913 to 1924 he profitted from the pacification and explored hitherto unknown regions in the region of Oued Drac. His contribution was greatly appreciated and he was honoured by membership in several learned French academies, and a professorship at the Université de Paris. His writings include *Dans le Bled es Siba* (1906), *Le Maroc physique* (1912), and *Voyages d'exploration dans l'Atlas marocain, 1923* (1924). He died in Paris, 12 June 1925. DBF; IndexBFr² (2)

Gentile, Marino, born 9 May 1906 at Trieste, Austria, he took a doctorate in philosophy and became a professor of philosophy of history and history of philosophy in the Università di Padova. His writings include *I fondamenti metafisici della morale di Seneca* (1932), *La metafisica presofistica* (1939), *Bacone* (1945), *Come si pone il problema metafisico* (1955), and *Storia della filosofia* (1970-72). He died in Padova, 31 May 1991. Chi è, 1948-1961; DizBI; Wholtaly, 1958

Gentizon, Paul, fl. 1924-1958, he wrote *Le Drame bulgare* (1924), *Moustapha Kemal, ou, l'Orient en marche* (1929), its translation *Mustafa Kemal ve uyanan doğu* (1983), *L'Esprit d'Orient* (1930), *La Conquête de l'Ethiopie* (1936), *La Revanche d'Adoua* (1936), and *Il mito di Mussolini* (1958). LC

Genty de Bussy, Pierre, born in 1793 at Choissy-le-Roi (Val-de-Marne), he was a civil servant and from 1821 to 1822 a secretary to the governor of the Invalides. He participated in the campaign against Spain, 1823, and was sent to Greece in 1828. A *maître des requêtes* at the Conseil d'état in 1829, he was successively *sous-intendant* and *intendant* of the Régence d'Alger from 1830 to 1835. He retired from public service in 1848. His writings include *De l'Intendance militaire et de son organisation* (1834), and *De l'établissement des Français dans la Régence d'Alger* (1839). He died in Paris in 1867. DBF; Hoefer; IndexBFr² (2); Vapereau

Gentz, Jochen, born 20th cent., he received a Dr.phil. in 1959 from the Universität Bonn for *Die Bürgschaft im islamischen Recht nach al-Kāšānī.* Schwarz

Genuardi, Luigi, born 3 February 1882 at Palermo, he studied law at the Università di Palermo and received a doctorate in 1904 for *Il rito di Alfonso considerato nei suoi precedenti storici*. In 1915 he started a teaching career in the history of Italian law at the Università di Camerino. In 1932 he was invited to teach his subject at Palermo. His writings include *La presenza del giudice nel contratti privati italiano dell'alto medio evo* (1914), *Storia dal diritto italiano* (1921), and *Palermo* (1929). He died in Palermo on 28 October 1935. Chi è, 1928-1940; DizBI; IndBiltal (2)

Georgacas (Γεωργακας), Demetrius John (Ioannou), born 30 January 1908 at Sidirokastro, Peloponnesus, he studied at Athens and Berlin, where he received a Dr.phil. in 1942 for *Grundfragen des peloponnesischen Neugriechischen*. He emigrated to the United States and was from 1951 to his retirement in 1978 a professor of classics in the University of North Dakota at Grand Forks. His writings include Περι της καταγωγης των Σαρακατσαναιων και του ονόματος αύτων (1949), *Slavs in Cyprus?* (1951), and he was joint author of *Place names of southwest Peloponnesus* (1967). DrAS, 1974 F, 1978 F, 1982 F; Hellenikon, 1965

George, A. R., born 20th cent., he received a Ph.D. in 1978 from the University of Durham for *The vistometric technique of landscape evaluation; its application in a study of the Syrian tourist industry*. Sluglett

George, Hereford Brooke, born in 1838 at Bath, he was educated at Winchester College and New College, Oxford. He was called to the bar in 1864, but returned to Oxford in 1867. He was ordained in 1868 and subsequently served as a tutor of New College until 1891. His writings include *The Oberland and its glaciers* (1866), *Battles of British history* (1895), and *A Historical geography of the British Empire* (1904). He died in 1910. BritInd (1); DNB; Who, 1903-1909; Who was who 1

George, Pierre Oscar Léon, born 11 October 1909 at Paris, he studied geography at the Sorbonne, where he qualified in 1936 with his *thèse complémentaire, La Forêt de Bercé*. Since 1948 he was a professor at his alma mater. He was one of the most prolific writers and popularizers among geographers, but also a militant trade unionist. His writings include *Géographie agricole du monde* (1946), *Etude sur les migrations de population* (1952), *L'Environnement* (1971), and *Les Migrations internationales* (1976). DcBMOuvF, vol. 29, pp. 286-87; Dickinson, pp. 244-46; WhoFr, 1981/82-2002/3

Georgelin, Jean, born 20th cent., he wrote *Venise au siècle des lumières, 1669-1797* (1978), *L'Economie de Marseille - Provence; au travers de l'œuvre de Louis Pierrein* (1988), and *L'Italie à la fin du XVIII siècle* (1989). LC; Livres disponibles, 2003-2004

Georgesco (Georgescu), Vlad, born in 1937 at Bucureşti, he was a historian in Rumania until expelled in 1980. He subsequently served as director of Radio Free Europe's Rumanian Service. His writings include *Ideile politice şi iluminismul in Principatele Române 1750-1831* (1972), *Mémoires et projets de réforme dans les principautés roumaines 1831-1848* (1972), *The Romanians; a history* (1991), and he edited *Romania; 40 years, 1944-1984* (1985). He died 13 Octber 1988. DcEnc; Dictionar; LC; WhoRom

Georges-Gaulis, Berthe *see* Gaulis, Madame Berthe Georges

Georghallides, G. S., born 20th cent., he wrote *A Political and administrative history of Cyprus, 1918-1926* (1979), and *Cyprus and the governorship of Sir Ronald Storrs* (1985). LC

Georgiadès Bey, Nicolas, Dr., born in 1875 at Smyrna, he was educated at the local Greek school and studied from 1890 to 1895 at the Collège de la Sainte-Famille, Cairo. In 1898 he obtained the *diplôme de pharmacie* from the Faculté française de médecine, Beirut, and in 1901, the *licence ès sciences* from the Faculté des sciences, Bordeaux. Upon his return to Egypt in 1901 he became a member of the Administration sanitaire in Cairo, where he became *inspecteur en chef* in 1908. He was a member of the Institut égyptien since 1903, and contributed numerous articles concerning the water resources of Egypt and Arabia to its *bulletin*. He wrote *La Pharmacie en Égypte* (1906). He died in Cairo from typhoid fever on 25 July 1934. Bulletin de l'Institut égyptien 17 (1934/35), pp. xxi-xxv

Georgiades Arnakes, Georgios, 1912-1976 *see* Arnakis (Αρνάκης), George Georgiades

Georgiev, Vladimir Ivanov, born 3 February 1908 at Gabare, Rumania, he studied at Sofia, Wien, Paris, Berlin and Firenze; since 1931 he was a professor. His writings include *Die Träger der kretisch-mykenischen Kultur* (Sofia, 1936-38), *Le Déchiffrement des inscriptions minoennes* (Sofia, 1949), Словарь крито-микенсκих надписей (Sofia, 1955), and *Introduction to the history of Indo-European languages* (1981). He died 17 April 1986. Petia Asenova wrote Владимир Георгиевич (Sofia, 1990). EnBulg; IntWW, 1974/75-1990/91|; WhoSocC, 1978; WhoWor, 1974/75

Georgin, Pierre, born 20th cent., he received a doctorate in 1980 from the Université de Paris for his thesis, *Esquisse phonologique et détermination nominale du parler arabe d'Alger*. THESAM, 3

Gérard, Cécile *Jules* Basile, born in 1817 of humble parents at Pignans (Var), he early in life developed a passion for hunting. At age twenty-five he joined the Spahis and went to find his fortune in Algeria. By sheer coincident around a campfire of Muslim fellow spahis he learned of the lion of Archioua, one of several who were decimating local flocks. After more than a month of fruitless effort, he met the lion on a moonlit night and killed it with a lucky shot. With official sanction he subsequently killed twenty-five lions in the colony. He had an undeniable status among the Muslims and was one of the very few Frenchman who could mingle freely among the proud and sullen population and receive a genuine welcome wherever he went. He drowned in the Jong River, Sierra Leone, on the way to Kong country in 1864. His writings include *La chasse au lion* (1855), *Adventures of Gerard, the lion killer* (1856), *L'Afrique du nord* (1860), and *La caccia de leone* (1888). DBF; Hoefer; IndexBFr² (1); *Muslim world* 64 (1974), pp. 45-49; Vapereau

Gerard, James Gilbert, born 1795, he was since 1814 on the Bengal establishment as a surgeon. In 1831 he accompanied Sir Alexander Burnes in his expedition to Bukhara. The trip killed him, for he had several attacks of fever. On his return he was detained at Meshed and Herat for months, by fever, so that on his arrival at Subathoo he died on 31 March 1835. He had kept a painstaking travel journal from which a splendid map on a scale of 5 in. to the mile was produced. BritInd (1); Buckland; DNB; Riddick

Gérard de Nerval, 1808-1855 *see* Nerval, Gérard Labrunie de

Gérardin, P., fl. 1826, he was an *interprète de 1ère classe* with the Corps des interprètes de l'armée d'Afrique, and was sent to Tunis in April 1830 to find out the Bey's views towards possible French incursions into North Africa. On 6 July 1830 he was appointed to the *Commission de gouvernement d'Alger* by the order of General Bourmont. Féraud, p. 189; Peyronnet, p. 14

Gerasimov, Oleg Gerasimovich, born 20th cent., he wrote *В горах Южной Аравии* (1966), *10 000 километров по Месопотамии* (1968), *Иракская нефть* (1969), and *Саудовская Аравия* (1977), *Египет* (1980), *Ирак* (1984), *Миссия* (1988), and *Пятое время года* (1991). LC

Gerasimov, Todor Dimitrov, born 31 March 1903 at Sofia, he was an archaeologist, numismatist and epigrapher; he was affiliated with Sofia University and the National Archaeological Museum, Sofia. His writings include *Антични и средновековни монет в България* (1975), and *Antike Münzen in bulgarischen Gebieten geprägt* (1977). He died 8 March 1973. EnBulg; *Etudes balkaniques* 10 (1974), 246; LC

Gerasimova, Alevtina Sergeevna, born 13 August 1925 at Andijan, Eastern Uzbekistan, she graduated in 1949 from the Oriental Institute, Moscow, and received her first degree in 1968 for *Пути развития полевоенной афганской литературы*. Since 1956 she was affiliated with the Oriental Institute of the Soviet Academy of Science. Her writings include *Песни разлук и встреч* (1968), *Литература Афганистана на языке пушту* (1986), and she was joint author of *Литература Афганистана* (1963). Miliband; Miliband²

Geraty, Lawrence Thomas, born 21 April 1940 at St. Helena, Calif., he graduated in 1962 from Pacific Union College and received his Ph.D. in 1972 from Harvard for *Third century B.C. ostraca from Khirbet el-Kom*. In 1972 he was appointed a professor of archaeology and history of antiquities in Andrews University at Berrien Springs, Mich., a post which he still held in 1995. He was in 2003 a president, La Sierra University, Riverside, Cal. He was joint editor of *Archaeology of Jordan and other studies* (1986), and *Madaba Plains Project; the 1984 season* (1989). DrAS, 1974 H, 1978 P, 1982 P; Master (2); NatFacDr, 1995-2003

Gerber, Haim, born in 1945, he was in 1991 a senior lecturer in the Department of Islamic studies, Hebrew University, Jerusalem. His writings include *Ottoman rule in Jerusalem, 1890-1914* (1985), *Social origins of the modern Middle East* (1987), *Islam, guerilla war and revolution* (1988), and *State, society, and law in Islam* (1994). LC

Gerdts-Rupp, Elisabeth, 1888- *see* Rupp-Gerdts, Elisabeth

Ger'e (Guerrier), Vladimir Ivanovich, born in 1837, he was an historian and a professor at Moscow University. His writings include *Лейбниц и его век* (1868), and *Leibniz in seinen Beziehungen zu Russland und Peter dem Grossen* (1873). He died in 1919. GSE; EnSlovar; *Index Islamicus* (1); Wieczynski

Gerhardt, Dietrich Kurt, born 11 February 1911 at Breslau, Germany, he received a Dr.phil. in 1941 from the Universität Halle for *Gogol' and Dostojevskij in ihrem künstlerischen Verhältnis*. He was a professor of Slavic studies successively at Erlangen, Münster and Hamburg. HbDtWiss; Kürschner, 1950-2003; *Wer ist wer*, 1955-1971/73

Gerhardt, Mia Irene, born 28 December 1918 at Rotterdam, she received her doctorate in 1950 from the Rijksuniversiteit te Leiden for *Essai d'analyse littéraire de la pastorale dans les littératures italienne, espagnole et française*. She successively taught Romance languages at Leiden, Groningen and

Utrecht. Her writings include *Les Voyages de Sindbad le marin* (1957), *The Art of story-telling; a literary study of the Thousand and one nights* (1963), and *Zevenslapers en andere tijd-verliezers* (1968).   Wie is wie, 1984-1988

Gerholm, Tomas, born in 1942, he received a doctorate in 1977 from the Department of Social Anthropology, Stockholm, for *Market, mosque and mafraj; social inequality in a Yemeni town*. He was in 1993 a professor at his alma mater. He was joint editor of *The New Islamic presence in Western Europe* (1988).   EURAMES, 1993; LC

de **Gérin-Ricard**, Henry Marie Emmanuel Constance, born 8 November 1864 at Marseille, he joined the Compagnie des docks et entrepôts de Marseille in 1889. Early in life he began to pursue an interest in history and archaeology. A member of the Académie de Vaucluse of long standing, he was a sometime president of the Société de statstque de Marseille, Société archéologique de Provence, and vice-president of the Institut historique de Provence. From 1919 to 1932 he was curator at the Musée Borely. His many writings include *Actes concernant les vicomtes de Marseille et leurs descendants* (1926). He died in Marseille, 8 September 1944.   Curinier; DBF; *Revue archéologique* 27 (1947), pp. 77-80

Gerken, Egbert, born 20 March 1940 at Arnsberg, Germany, he received a Dr.rer.pol. in 1970 from the Freie Universität Berlin for *Die Industriestadt als Faktor sozialen Wandels*. Since 1978 he was affiliated with the Institut für Weltwirtschaft, Kiel, as well as the World Bank, Washington, D.C. In 1980 he gained a Dr.habil. His writings include *Land productivity and the employment problem of rural areas* (1973), and *Zur Theorie der dualistischen Entwicklung* (1973).   Kürschner, 1987-2003

Gerland, Ernst, born 19 May 1870 at Imshausen, near Fulda, he went to school in Halberstadt and studied at Jena, where he received a Dr.phil. in 1894 for *Die persischen Feldzüge des Kaisers Herakleios*. He served for nearly forty years as a high school teacher at Bad Homburg, being obliged to pursue his scholarly interest in Byzantine history in his spare time. It was only during the last years of his life that he had a chance to lecture in his chosen field at the Universität Frankfurt. His writings include *Geschichte des lateinischen Kaiserreiches von Konstantinopel* (1905). He died in Bad Homburg on 12 November 1934.   DtBE; *Echos d'Orient* 34, no. 179 (juillet/september 1935), pp. 368-374; Kürschner, 1925-1935

Gerland, Georg Carl Cornelius, born 29 January 1833 at Kassel, he received a Dr.phil. in 1859 from the Universität Marburg for *Der altgriechische Dativ*. He was a prolific scholar, a composer, linguist, ethnographer, geographer and geophysicist. He was instrumental in the establishment of the Station météorologique d'Alsace as well as the Station sismographique of the Jardin botanique at Straßburg. His writings include *Über das Aussterben der Naturvölker* (1868), and *Der Mythos der Sintflut* (1912). He died in Strasbourg, 26 February 1919.   Dickinson; DtBE; DtBIlnd (7); Hinrichsen; NDB; NDBA; *Wer ist's*, 1912

Germain, Adrien Adolphe Charles, born in 1837, he was a French marine engineer and a cartographer who, in 1867, conducted astronomical researches on the coasts of the Indian Ocean, particularly in Oman and Zanzibar. His writings include *Traité d'hydrographie* (1882). He died in 1895.   BN; Henze; NUC, pre-1956

Germain, Gabriel, born in 1903, he received a doctorate in 1954 at Paris for his two theses, *Essai sur les origines de certaines thèmes odysséens et sur la genèse de l'Odyssée*, and *La mystique des nombres dans l'épopée homérique*. His other writings include *La Genèse de l'Odyssée* (1954), and *Victor Segalen* (1982). He died in 1978.   LC; NUC, pre-1956

Germann, Raimund E., born 20th cent., he received a doctorate in 1968 from the Universität Freiburg, Switzerland, for *Verwaltung und Einheitspartei in Tunesien*. His writings include *Politische Innovation und Verfassungsreform* (1975), *Ausserparlamentarische Kommissionen* (Bern, 1981), and *Experts et commissions de la Confédération* (Lausanne, 1985).   Schwarz

Germanus, Abdul Kareem Gyula (Julius), born 6 November 1884 at Budapest, he studied at Constantinople, Budapest and Wien. He became a Muslim, and in 1934 made the pilgrimage to Mecca. From 1948 to 1965 he was a professor of Arabic and Islamic studies at Budapest as well as a visiting lecturer throughout the Muslim world. His writings include *Modern movements in the world of Islam* (1932), *Allah akbar* (Budapest, 1936), its translations, *Allah akbar* (Berlin, 1938), *Sulle erme di Maometto* (Milano, 1938). In 1974 he was honoured by *The Muslim East; studies in honour of Julius Germanus*. He died in Budapest in 1979.   IntWW, 1974/75-1979; Magyar; MEL, 1978-91; WhoSocC, 1978; WhoWor, 1974/75, 1976/77

Germanus (de Silesia), Dominicus, born in 1588, he studied Arabic under Tommaso Obicini. After the death of his teacher in 1633, he succeeded him in the lectureship in Oriental languages at the convent ad S. Petrum in Monte Aureo in Roma. His writings include *Fabrica overo Dittionario delle lingua volgare arabica* (1636), *Fabrica lingvæ arabicæ cum interpretatione, latina & italica, accomodata ad* *vsum lingvæ vulgaris, & scripturalis* (1639), he was *praeses* of *Antithesis fidei ventilabuntur in Conuentu* (1638), and he edited *Thesaurus Arabico Syro-Latinus*, of Thomas Obicinus (1636). He died in 1670. BN; Flück, pp. 77-78; NUC, pre-1956

Gern, Jean Pierre, born 17 August 1934 at Neuchâtel, he received a doctorate in economics at Neuchâtel as well as diplomas in law, economics and political science from the Université de Paris and L.S.E. He became affiliated with the World Bank and the Université de Neuchâtel. His writings include *L'Indexation des salaires* (1961), and he edited *Le Développement de l'Afrique confronté aux politiques d'ajustement structurel* (1987). WhoSwi, 1992/93-1996/97

Gerner-Adams, Deborah J., born 20th cent., she received a Ph.D. in 1982 in political science from Northwestern University, Evanston. She was in 1990 a professor in the University of Kansas at Lawrence, a post which she still held in 2003. Her writings include *One land, two peoples* (1991). *MESA Roster of members*, 1990; NatFacDr, 2003

Gernet, Jacques, born 22 December 1921 at Alger, he studied at Alger, the Sorbonne and Ecole nationale des langues orientales, Paris. He was from 1957 to 1974 a professor of Chinese studies at the Sorbonne; in 1975 he became a professor at the Collège de France. His writings include *La Vie quotidienne en Chine à la veille de l'invasion mongole, 1250-1276* (1959), and its translation, *Daily life in China* (1962). ConAu 163

Gernet, Louis, born in 1882, he was a graduate of the Ecole normale supérieure and gained his *agrégation* in 1907. He taught at La Flèche from 1911 to 1917, became a professor in the Université d'Alger from 1917 to 1947, and was from 1948 to 1962 a professor of sociology at the Ecole pratique des hautes études, Paris. He concurrently served as secretary general and editor-in-chief of *Année sociologique*, 1948-1962. His writings include *Le Genie grec dans la religion* (1932), its translation, *El genio grieco en la religión* (1937), and *Droit et société dans la Grèce ancienne* (1955). He died in 1962. *Revue archéologique* 1962 i, pp. 237-39; ThTwC, 1983, 1987

Gerő, Győző, born 16 May 1924 at Budapest, he was an archaeologist who was affiliated with the Museum of History, Budapest. His writings include *Pécs török müemlékei* (1960), *Török építészeti emlékek Magyarországon* (1976), its translation, *Türkische Baudenkmäler in Ungarn* (1976), and *Az oszmán-török építészet Magyarországon* (1980). LC; WhoSoCE, 1989

Gerrans, B., Rev., born 18th cent., he was a lecturer of St. Catherine, Coleman, and a teacher of Persian, Arabic, Hebrew, Syriac, Chaldaean, Greek, Latin, Italian, French and English. He was the author of two translations, *Travels of Rabbi Benjamin, son of Jonah, of Tudela* (1783), and *Tales of a parrot, from a Persian manuscript intiled Tooti Namêh* (1792). BritInd (1); Note

Gershevitch, Ilya, born 24 October 1914 at Zürich, he received a Ph.D. in 1954 from the University of London for *A grammar of Manichean Sogdian* as well as doctorates from the universities in Roma and Bern. His writings include *Philologia Iranica* (1985), and he edited and translated *The Avestan hymn to Mithra* (1959). He taught Iranian subjets at Cambridge from 1948 to 1965. He was a fellow of Jesus College, Cambridge, and also the British Academy. He died 11 April 2001. IntWW, 1989-2002; Who, 1974-2001

Gershoni, Israel, born 11 October 1946 in Palestine, he received a Ph.D. in 1978 from the Hebrew University, Jerusalem, and became affiliated with Tel Aviv University and the Center for Judiac Studies in the University of Pennsylvania. His writings include *The Emergence of Pan-Arabism in Egypt* (1981), and he was joint author of *Egypt, Islam, and the Arabs* (1987). ConAu 150; *MESA Roster of members*, 1990; Note

Gerson, Allan, born 19 June 1945 in Uzbekistan, he graduated in 1966 from the University of Buffalo, N.Y., and subsequently trained as a New York lawyer. He wrote *Israel, the West Bank, and international law* (1978), and he edited *Lawyer's ethics; contemporary dilemmas* (1980). WhoAmL, 1977/78

Gerson née **Kiwi**, Esther *Edith*, born 13 May 1908 at Berlin, she studied at the Konservatorium Berlin, Musikhochschule Leipzig and subsequently at the universities of Freiburg, Leipzig and Heidelberg, where she received a Dr.phil. in 1933 for *Studien zur Geschichte des italienischen Liedmadrigals im 16. Jahrhundert.* In 1947 she was a lecturer at the Palestine conservatory; since 1950 she held various appointments in her field throughout the world. Baker, 1992; BioHbDtE; IntWWM, 1975-1985|; Master (2); NewGrDM, 1980

von **Gerstenberg**, Carl, born 15 July 1846 at Weimar, he studied fine art and philosophy at Berlin and Jena, where he received a Dr.phil. He spent some years travelling in southern Russia, Italy and Switzerland, but also in the East. After his return home, he became an editor of the *Allgemeine*

Zeitung, Augsburg. From 1883 to his death he was the editor of his own journal, the *Allgemeine Rundschau auf dem Gebiete der Künste*. DtBilnd (1); Hinrichsen

Gerteiny, Alfred George(s), born 13 October 1930 at Heliopolis, Cairo, he studied at Cairo, Paris, den Haag and Columbia University, and received a Ph.D. in 1963 from Saint John's University, Jamaica, N.Y., for *The concept of positive neutralism in the United Arab Republic*. He was a foreign correspondent to French journals, affiliated with Unesco, and Grolier Encyclopedia, before embarking on an academic career as a professor of history first at his alma mater and then at the University of Bridgeport, Ct. He spent some time in Mauritania. His writngs include *Mauritania* (1967), and *Historical dictionary of Mauritania* (1981). ConAu 21-24; DrAS, 1969-1982 H; Master (1); Selim

Gerth van Wijk, D., born 19th cent., he wrote *Spraakleer der Maleische taal* (1890), and its translation, *Tata bahasa Melayn* (1985). His trace is lost after an article in 1893. LC

Gertsenberg, Leonard Georgevich, born 20th cent., he gained a doctorate in philosophy. His writings include *Хотано-сакский язык* (1965), *Морфологическая структура слова в древних тндоиранских языках* (1972), and *Вопросы реконструкции индоевропейской просодики* (1981). LC; Note

Gervais-Courtellemont, Jules, born 1 July 1863 at Avon (Seine-et-Marne), he studied classics and fine art at Alger, and was a pioneer of photographic journalism. He travelled widely throughout the Muslim world, and was a passenger on the first train into Medina. He photographed the inauguration of the Hejaz railway in 1908. In 1894 the governor of Algeria sent him on an official mission to Mecca, where he arrived in 1895, returning with probably the first photograph of the city. He lectured on Islam and the Orient and wrote *Jérusalem-Damas* (1893), *L'Algérie de nos jours* (1894), *Le Caire* (1894), *Mon voyage à La Mecque* (1896), and *La Civilisation* (1924-26). He died 31 October 1931. Bidwell; DBF; Henze

Gervers-Molnár, Veronika, born in 1939 at Hajdúnánás, Hungary, she received a doctorate in medieval history of art at Budapest, and became an associate curator at the Rákóczi Museum, Sárospatak, and later, a lecturer in the Institute of Historical Monuments, Budapest. She went to Canada in 1968 and joined the Textile Department of the Royal Ontario Museum. Her writings include *A középkori Magyarország rotundái* (1972), *The Hungarian szür* (1973), and *The Influence of Ottoman Turkish textiles in eastern Europe* (1982). She died in Toronto in 1979. BioIn 12; DrAS, 1978, 1982 H; MESA bulletin 13 (1979), p. 116

Gessain, Robert Henri Jean, born 11 April 1907 at Clermont-Ferrand, he was educated at the Lycée du Parc, Lyon, and received a medical doctorate at Paris. He was also a graduate of the Institut d'ethnologie. Since 1936 he was variously affiliated with the Musée de l'Homme, where he served from 1968 to his retirement in 1979 as its director. Since 1965 he was a professor without chair at the Muséum nationale d'histoire naturelle. His writings include *Les Esquimaux du Groenland à Alaska* (1947). He died in Paris, 8 April 1986. Hommes et destins vol. 9, pp. 197-98; Unesco; WhoFr, 1973/74-1985/86

Gessi, Romolo, born 30 April 1829 at Ravenna, or possibly Constantinople. After the completion of his study in Germany, he served with the British Army in the Crimean War under General G. Gordon. Since 1874 he was in the service of Gordon in the Sudan, where he explored the sources of the Nile. In 1880 he was sent on a punitive expedition against Sulayman Pasha, the slave merchant in Darfur, from which he returned gravely ill. His writings include *Sette anni nel Sudan egiziano* (1891), and its translation, *Seven years in the Sudan* (1892). He died in Suez, 19 January, or 30 April, 1881. Embacher; Henze; Hill; IndBl (7); VIA

Getchell, Dana King, born about 1870 at Glencoe, Minn., he attended Carleton College and went to Turkey in 1900 as a tutor in Anatolia College, Marsovan. He became a fully appointed missionary from his Board in 1903. He was in 1914 principal of the Preparatory Department in the College. Forced to leave Marsovan during the first World War, he stayed in Constantinople until able to return to Marsovan. In 1922 he was transferred to Thessaloniki, where he worked among Armenian and Greek refugees from Turkey. When Anatolia College removed to Thessaloniki in 1924 he rejoined it. He retired in 1937 and died on 2 November 1950. NYT, 4 November 1950, p. 17, col. 5

Geyer, Franz Xaver, born 3 December 1859 at Regen, Bavaria, he studied at Passau, München and Verona and was ordained in 1882. He was from 1883 to 1896 first in Khartoum and then in Egypt. He then entered the congregation of the Söhne des heiligsten Herzens Jesu in Verona, where he served as rector of its missionary seminary until 1903. In the same year he was consecrated in München titular bishop of Trocnade and vicar apostolic of Central Africa, a post which he held until 1922, when he returned to Germany and founded the Religiöse Gemeinschaft für die auslandsdeutsche Seelsorge. Since 1927 he was editor of the quarterly, *Deutsche Auslandsseelsorge*. His writings include *Durch*

Sand, Sumpf und Wald; Missionsreisen in Zentral-Afrika (1912), *Khartoum* (1912), and *50 Jahre auslandsdeutsche Missionsarbeit* (1936). He died in 1943. Hill; Kosch

Geyer, George Edwin, born 25 June 1938 at Milwaukee, Wisc., he graduated in 1961 from St. Francis Seminary and received a Ph.D. in 1967 from Marquette University, Milwaukee, for *The nature and content of first philosophy in the text of Ibn Rushd's great commentary on book twelve of Aristotle's Metaphysics*. Since 1965 he was a professor, and sometime chairman, St. Anselm's College, Manchester, N.H. DrAS, 1969 P

Geyer, Rudolf Eugen, born 28 June 1861 at Wien, he there first studied classics and Indian philology and then Semitic languages, mainly Arabic, and received a Dr.phil. in 1884 for *Das Buch über die Namen der wilden Tiere von al-Asma'ī*. He subsequently worked as an assistant at the k.k. Hofbibliothek until 1900, when he started teaching Arabic language and literature at the Universität. Since 1915 he was a director of Orientalisches Institut. His writings include *Gedichte und Fragmente des 'Aus Ibn Hagar* (1892), and *Zwei Gedichte von al-A'šā* (1906-1919). He died in Wien on 15 September 1929. DtBE; Fück, p. 257; Kürschner, 1925-1928/29; ÖBL; *Wer ist's*, 1928

Ghaffari-Farhangi, Setareh, born 13 July 1958 at Tehran, she studied at the Université de Paris, where she specialized in Islamic medias and the islamization of the medias. She was a member of several professional societies and a lecturer at the Université de Paris II. Private

Ghafurov, Olim, 1931- *see* Gafurov, Alimzhan Gafurovich

Ghaleb, Kamel Osman, 1882-1963 *see* Ghālib, Kāmil 'Uthmān

Ghali, Boutros Boutros, 1922- *see* Boutros Ghali, Boutros

Ghali, Mirrit Boutros, born 10 May 1908 at Cairo, he studied at the Sorbonne, where he received a law degree and a diploma in political science. He was a business executive, member of parliament, and cabinet minister. His writings include *Siyāsat al-ghad* (1938), and its translation, *The Policy of tomorrow* (1953). WhoWor, 1976/77

Ghali, Samir, born 17 June 1939 at Cairo, he received a Ph.D. in 1972 from the University of Nebraska for his thesis, *Deux écivains libanais d'expression français, Ferjallah Haïk et Georges Schehadé*. Selim

Ghālib (Ghaleb), Kāmil 'Uthmān, born in 1882 at Cairo, he was a trained engineer who spent his entire career with the Ministry of Public Works. When he retired in 1939 he held the post of under-secretary of state in the Ministry. He was a founding member of the Société d'archéologie copte. He died in 1963. *Bulletin de la Société d'archéologie copte*, 17 (1963/64), pp. 283-284; WhoEgypt, 1951, 1955 = AfrBioInd

Ghambashidze, David, born in 1884, he wrote *Mineral resources of Georgia and Caucasia* (London, 1919), *Der bolschewistische Osten* (Berlin, 1933), and *Comintern in Asia* (Berlin, 1939). LC; Master (1)

Ghānim, Shukrī, 1861-1929 *see* Ganem, Chékri

Gharatchehdaghi (Qarāchahdāghī), Cyrus, born 4 December 1928 at Tabriz, he studied agriculture from 1948 to 1951 at Tehran. After two years of military service he found employ with the Public Health Cooperative Organization and subsequently was involved in the governmental agrarian reform. From 1957 to 1960 he was a doctoral student at Landwirtschaftliche Hochschule Hohenheim, where he received a Dr.agr. for *Untersuchungen über die Frostresistenz und Möglichkeiten ihrer Erhöhung bei Tabaksetzlingen*. His writings include *Distribution of land in Varamin* (1967), and *Landverteilung in Waramin* (1967). Thesis

Ghassemlou (Qāsimlū), Abdul Rahman, born 22 December 1930 at Urmia, Persia, he received a doctorate in economics in Czechoslovakia. He was a Kurdish political activist in the anti-Shah movement of the 1970s. His writings include *Kurdistán a Kurdovia* (Bratislava, 1964), *Kurdistan and the Kurds* (Prague, 1965), and *Iranian Kurdistan* (1976). He was assassinated in Wien, 13 July 1989. Bidwell²

Ghate, Vinayak Sakharam, born 19th cent., his writings include *Lectures on Rigveda*, delivered at the University of Bombay (1915). He received a doctorate in 1918 from the Université de Paris for *Le Vedanta*, a work which was published in 1926 in an English version entitled *The Vedānta*. NUC, pre-1956

Ghattas, Emile, born 20th cent., he received a Ph.D. in 1964 from Columbia University for his thesis, *The functioning of the banking system in Lebanon*. Selim

Gheerbrandt, Jehan (Jean) Laurent, born 5 August 1882 at Sartène (Corsica), he studied law and practised his profession in Paris. Since 1907 he was a *stagiaire* in the Court de Cassation and at the Conseil d'Etat. Invalided in the Great War, he founded in 1920 the Institut colonial français and served

614

as its director until 1942. His writings include *Notre empire; un univers, un idéal* (1943), and *Pavia, le grand humain de l'Indochine* (1949). He died in Paris in 1965. DBF; Qui est-ce, 1934; WhoFr, 1953/4-1963/64

Gherardi, Pompeo, he wrote *La Reconquête de la Tripolitaine vue du camp des rebelles* (Paris, 1925). NUC, pre-1956

Ghermani, Dionisie, born 29 July 1922 at Govora, Rumania, he was caught studying in Germany at the end of the war and remained there to receive a Dr.phil. in 1967 from the Universität München for *Die kommunistische Unterdrückung der rumänischen Geschichte* (1967). He was successively a professor of political sciences at München and Bamberg. His other writings include *Rumänien* (1968). Kürschner, 1980-2003; WhoRom

Gherson, Randolph, born 20th cent. in Egypt, he served with the Middle East Supply Center and the British Embassy in Egypt, before studying at the Academy of International Law, den Haag, and L.S.E. Note

Gheusi, Pierre Barthélemy, born in 1865 at Toulouse, he was a lawyer, librettist, journalist, ministerial secretary, deputy director of the Paris Opéra and the Opéra comique. He was a prolific writer whose writings include *Galliéni, 1849-1916* (1922), and *Galliéni et Madagascar* (1931). He died in 1943. DBF

Gheyn, Joseph Marie Martin van den, 1854-1913 see Van den Gheyn, Joseph Marie Martin

Ghezelbash (Qizilbāsh), Abbas, born in 1930, he received a Ph.D. in 1954 from Ohio State University for *An econometric analysis of the greenhouse tomato market in Ohio*. In 1961 he was affiliated with the Iranian Plan Organization, Tehran. Note; NUC, 1956-67, 1968-72

Ghirelli, Angelo, he was in his later years affiliated with the C.S.I.C., Instituto de Estudios Africanos. His writings include *Monografia de la cabila de Beni Tuzin* (Madrid, 1923), *El norte de Marruecos* (Melilla, 1926), *El país berebere* (Madrid, 1942), *La renacimiento musulmán* (Barcelona, 1948), and *Pueblos árabes y pueblos arabizados* (Madrid, 1957). NUC, pre-1956-1967

Ghiron, Isaia, born in 17 December 1837 at Casale Monterrata, (Piedmont), he studied at Torino and became an archaeologist, Arabist and numismatist, serving successively as a librarian at Milano, Roma, and Brera. His writings include *Le iscrizioni arabe della Reale armeria di Torino* (1868), and *Bibliografia lombarda* (1884). He died in Milano in 1889, DizBI; IndBiltal (6); Wininger

Ghirshman, Roman, born 3 October 1895 at Kharkov, Ukraine, he was an officer who emigrated to Constantinople after the 1917 revolution. He made a living as a violinist at silent movies until he left for Palestine. In 1923 he went to Paris, where he worked in night clubs and during the day studied at the Sorbonne, where in due time he received a *doctorat ès lettres* as well as diplomas from the Ecole des Hautes études and Ecole du Louvre. He was director of the Délégation archéologique française in Iran from 1930 to 1972. His work also took him to Afghanistan and Iraq. His writings include *Bégram; recherches archéologiques* (1946), and *L'Iran des origines à l'islam* (1951), and its translation, *Iran from the earliest times to the Islamic conquest* (1954). He died in Budapest at a colloquium on 5 September 1979. BioB134; DBF; EncIran; IntWW, 1974/75-1983; Master (2); NDBC, 1968; Note: WhoWor, 1974/75-1978/79

Ghisalberti, Alessandro, born 5 October 1940 at Zogno, Lombardia, he was a professor of philosophy and affiliated with the Università cattolica di Milano. His writings include *Giovanni Buridano dalla metafisica alla fisica* (1976), *Introduzione a Ockham* (1976), and *Medioevo teologico* (1990). Lui, chi è, 1969

Ghobashy, Omar Zaki, born in 1924, he received a Ph.D. in 1955 from New York University for his thesis, *Egypt's attitude towards international law as expressed in the United Nations*. Selim

Ghorbal, Mohammed Shafik, 1894-1961 see Ghurbāl, Muhammad Shafīq

Ghrab, Saâd, born 20th cent., he received a doctorate in 1984 from the Université de Paris for his thesis, *Ibn Arafa et le malikisme en Ifriqiya au XIVe siècle*. THESAM, 2

Ghurbāl (Ghorbal), Muhammad Shafīq, born in 1894 at Alexxandria, Egypt, he was educated at the Higher Teachers' College, Cairo. During the first World War he studied modern history in England. After graduation from Liverpool University he took a M.A. at London. On his return to Egypt he began an academic career in history first at his alma mater and then at Cairo University, where he became the first Egyptian to hold the chair of history. Apart from a short appointment at the Ministry of Social Affairs, he remained with the Ministry of Education until his retirement in 1954. From 1956 until his death on 19 October 1961, he served as director of the Institute of Higher Arab Studies. Bulletin de la Société d'archéologique copte, 16 (1961/62), pp. 342-43; Goldschmidt; Index Islamicus (1); WhoEgypt, 1951, 1955 = AfrBioInd

al-**Ghusayn** (Ghusein), Fā'iz, born about 1870 in Hawrān, the son of a shaykh of al-Sulūt, he went to school in Constantinople, where he also studied law at the Darūlfünun. For practice work he was assigned to the staff of the Vali of Damascus for quite some time. He subsequently served for three years and a half as district chief (*kaymakam*) of Harput in the vilayet Elâzığ, before starting his own practice in Damascus. He represented Hawran at the provincial assembly in Damascus and later became a member of council. In 1914, at the outbreak of the war, he was designated *kaymakam* at Harput, but declined, preferring to keep on practising his profession. Accused of high treason, he was taken in chains to Âliye. Though acquitted in court, Ahmed Cemal Paşa had him sent to Erzurum under military escort. On account of the Russian threat to the city, the group were stalled at Diyarbakır. For no reason at all, he there had to spend three weeks in jail before being freed. He then spent another half a year at Diyarbakır. He became a witness to the Turkish treatment of the Armenians and, as a former *kaymakam* from the adjacent vilayet, he also had access to reliable sources in the military and civil service to what was happening. After some time, he escaped to Aleppo, whence he made his way to Basrah and on to Bombay. His writings include *Les Massacres en Arménie* (1917), *Martyred Armenia* (1917), *Gemarteld Armenië* (1917), *Armenisches Märtyrertum* (1922), *La Domination ottomane* (1917), and *Türkenherrschaft und Armeniens Schmerzensschrei* (1918). Note

Giaccardi, Alberto, fl. 1931, he wrote *L'Africa delle vicende politiche e diplomatiche dell'Europa dal Congresso di Vienna alla pace di Versaglia* (1938), *L'opera del fascimo in Africa* (1938-39), *La colonizzazione d'impero* (1939), and *La conquista di Tunisi* (1940). NUC, pre-1956

Giacobetti, A., born 19th cent., he belonged to the Pères blancs and was also an Arabist. His writings include *Receuil d'énigmes arabes populaires* (Alger, 1916), and *Les Tapis et tissages du Djebel Amour* (Paris, 1932). Note; NUC, pre-1956

di **Giacomo**, L., fl. 1954, he was an *inspecteur principal* with the Service de l'Instruction publique du Maroc. Note

Giacon, Carlo, born 28 December 1900 at Padova, he was a Jesuit and successively taught philosophy at Messina and Padova. His writings include *Il divenire in Aristotele* (1947), *L'oggettività in Antonio Rosmini* (1960), *Interiorità e metafisica* (1964), *Le grandi tesi del tomismo* (1967), and *Verità, esistenza, causa* (1973). He died in Gallarate in 1984. Chi è, 1957, 1961; IndBiltal (2); Vaccaro; Wholtaly, 1958

Giamberardini, Gabriele, O.F.M., born 14 January 1917 at Lucoli (Aquila), he was ordained in 1941 and received a doctorate in theology in 1944 from the Università di Roma. The taught theology and related subjects successively at Sulmona and Lanciano until 1950. He subsequently studied Coptic in Egypt. From 1956 to 1959 he was director of the journal, *La voce del Nilo*. In 1959 he became a founder of the Istituto di Missiologia at Cairo. His writings include *San Giuseppe nella tradizione Copta* (1966), and *Impegni del Concilio vaticano I per l'Oriente cristiano* (1975). IndBiltal (1)

Giani, Renato, born 28 January 1913 at Roma, he was a journalist and art critic. His writings include *Carbonia* (1940), *Filibustieri, corsari, pirati* (1962), and *Lo specchio del costume* (1965). IndBiltal (1): Lui, chi è, 1969; Vaccaro

Giannini, Amedeo, born 18 or 19 September 1886 at Napoli, he received a doctorate in law and subsequently entered Foreign Affairs. From 1924 to 1944 he was a professor of law at Roma. His writings include *Le costituzioni degli stati del vicino Oriente* (1931), and *L'ultima fase della questione orientale* (1933). He died in Roma, 18 December 1960. Chi è, 1928-1957; DizBl; IndBiltal (2); Wholtaly, 1958

Giannini, Torquato Carlo, born 31 July 1868 or 1869 at Fermo, Italy, he received a doctorate in law and successively was a professor of commercial law at Ferrara, Macerata and Roma. His writings include *Corso di diritto marittimo* (1937), and *Il passeggero marittimo istruito* (1939). Chi è, 1928-1961; IndBiltal (3); Wholtaly, 1958

Giannò, Salvatore, born 19th cent., he was a *dottore* whose writings include *La Cirenaica* (1902), and *Tripolitania* (1907). Firenze

Gianturco, Vito, fl. 1975, he wrote *Della responsabilità dello stato verso le vittime di errori giudiziari* (1956), *La prova indiziaria* (1958), and *I giudizi penali della Corte costituzionale* (1965). NUC, 1956-1967

Gianviti, François Paul Frédéric, born 2 August 1938 at Paris, he was a professor of law. Since 1970 he was affiliated with the International Monetary Fund, where he was since 1986 a director of legal affairs. IntWW, 1989-2002; WhoFr, 1990/91-2000|

Gibaudi, Ferdinando, called Dino, born 26 November 1902 at Torino, he received the classical education of his day and subsequently studied history and geography at the local university, completing his study in 1924 with a thesis entitled *Il Piemonte nella antichità classica*. His writings include *Profilo geografico del continente africano* (1959). He died in Torino on 5 January 1971. DizBI

Gibb, Elias John Wilkinson, born 3 June 1857 at Glasgow, he early in his youth started to pursue linguistic studies, mainly in Arabic, Persian and Turkish, which he completed at Glasgow. At the age of twenty-one, he attracted the attention of Sir James Redhouse, although Gibb had never been to Turkey. After his marriage in 1889, he resided almost entirely in London. His was the work of a student seated at his desk and drawing his knowledge from books and manuscripts. Unfortunately he died in 1901 before his great work, the *History of Ottoman poetry*, had left the press. It was left to his friend and colleague, E. G. Browne, to put it before the public. His other works include *Ottoman poems translated into English verse in the original form* (1882), *Ottoman literature* (1901) as well as translations from the Turkish. Asiatic review, n.s., 38 (1942), pp. 314-317; Athenaeum, 18 January 1902, pp. 81-82; DNB

Gibb, Sir Hamilton Alexander Rosskeen, born in 1895 at Alexandria, Egypt, he received an M.A. in 1922 from the University of London for *The Arabic conquest of Transoxania*. He was an editor of the *Encyclopaedia of Islam*, Laudian Professor of Arabic at Oxford, 1937-1955, and subsequently J. R. Jewitt Professor of Arabic at Harvard. He was a member of numerous learned socieites throughout the world. He suffered a massive stroke in the spring of 1964 and died in 1971 in the village of Cherington near Oxford. P. S. Rosenthal submitted a B.Phil. thesis in 1977 at Oxford entitled *Sir Hamilton Gibb; a critical historiography*. CentBritOr, pp.154-183; ConAu 1-4, 33-36, new rev. 6; DNB; *Index Islamicus* (6); Master (2); Sluglett; WhAm 5; WhE&EA; *Who was who* 7

Gibbon, Edward, born in 1737 at Putney, he was a historian and the author of the *History of the decline and fall of the Roman Empire* (1776), and its excerpts, *The Life of Mahomet* (1805), and *The Crusaders* (1869). He died in 1794. BritInd (24); DLB, 104 (1991), pp. 88-105; DNB; EncAm; EncBrit; EncicUni; EncItaliana; GDU; GSE; Magyar; Master (60)

Gibbons, Herbert Adams, born in 1880 at Annapolis, Md., he graduated from the University of Pennsylvania and was ordained in 1908; he received a Litt.D. in 1920 from his alma mater. From 1909 to 1913 he taught successively at St. Paul's College, Tarsus, and Robert College, Constantinople. A correspondent of the *New York herald tribune* and *Century magazine* from 1908 to 1918, he travelled extensively in Europe and Asia. He reported on the wars of Turkey with her subject peoples, Italy and the Balkan states. His writings include *The blackest page of modern history; events in Armenia in 1915* (1916), *The reconstruction of Poland and the Near East* (1917), and *The foundation of the Ottoman Empire* (1916). He died in 1934. DAB; NatCAB, vol. 49, pp. 231-232; Note; Shavit; WhAm 1

Gibbons, Richard, born about 1800, he was a sergeant with the British Military Mission in Persia. Under the command of captain B. Shee he and four other non-commissioned officers took part in a two-year campaign against the Turkomans and other turbulent elements in central and north-eastern Persia. They first marched from Tabriz to Yazd and Kirman and then continued by way of Isfahan and Kashan to Mashad. Finally, in December 1832, the group left Khorasan for their base at Tabriz, which they reached in March 1833. They covered little short of 4,000 miles on foot or mule, mostly across inhospitable deserts of the high Iranian Plateau, through towns and villages where civil war, plague and famine were rampant. They certainly earned the gold medals awarded them by the Crown Prince on their return, yet Gibbons, who wrote a paper for the Royal Geographical Society about the routes traversed on this long march, records nothing of the hardships. Henze; Wright, p. 55-56

Gibbons, Virginia Harris, born 12 August 1946 at Plymouth, Ind., she graduated in 1968 from Allegheny College and subsequently received an M.L.Sc. elsewhere. She was a librarian successively at Princeton and Northwestern University, Evanston, Illinois. WhoLibl, 1982

Gibbs, G. N., born 19th cent., he was a captain in the British Army. At the outbreak of the first World War he was an engineer on board the Tigris steamer *Khalifah*. Note

Gibbs, James, born in 1825, he was educated at Merchant Taylors' School, London, and the East India Company college of Haileybury. He entered the Bombay Civil Service in 1846, and was admitted to the bar from Inner Temple in 1864. From 1866 to 1879 he was a judge in the High Court, Bombay, and concurrently served for some years as vice-chancellor of the University of Bombay. He died in London in 1886. Boase; BritInd (1); Buckland; Riddick

Gibbs, Josiah Willard, born in 1790 at Salem, Mass., he graduated in 1809 from Yale College and subsequently studied Oriental languages at Andover. Since 1824 he taught Biblical studies at Yale University, New Haven, Conn. He was excessively modest and retiring. His writings include *Philological studies* (1857). He died in 1861. ANB; DAB; Magyar; Master (18); WhAm H & 1

Gibert Fenech, Soledad, born 20th cent., she received a doctorate in Semitic languages and was a sometime professor of Arabic at the Universidad Complutense de Madrid. She was affiliated with the

Instituto de Estudios Almerienses. She edited *El diwan de Ibn Jatima de Almería* (1975), and *Poetas árabes de Almería* (1987). Arabismo, 1992, 1994, 1997; LC

Gibson, John C. L., he was in 1955 affilliated with the University of Glasgow. His writings include *Textbook of Syrian Semitic inscriptions* (1971). Note; NUC, 1973-77

Gibson, Margaret Dunlop née Smith, born in 1843 at Irvine, Scotland, she was educated privately, learning Latin, French and German. When her father died, she inherited enough wealth to place her above her social class. She and her twin sister, Agnes Smith Lewis, thus travelled to the East and discovered the Mount Sinai Palimpsest. This discovery was the event that began their career as Biblical scholars. The sisters shared in this recognition and received honorary doctorates from St. Andrews, Heidelberg and Dublin. Their writings include *How the codex was found; a narrative of two visits to Sinai* (1893), *An Arabic version of the Acts of the Apostles* (1899), *Palestinian Syriac texts from palimpsest fragments* (1900), and *Apocrypha arabica* (1901). She died in 1920. Whigham A. Price wrote a biography, *The Ladies of Castlebrae* (1985). DLB 174; Master (2); Who was who 2

Gicquel, Roger Alphonse Raymond, born 22 February 1933 at Thiers-sur-Thère (Oise), he was a radio and television commentator. His writings include *Des virages et des hommes* (1981). BioIn 11, 12; WhoFr, 1975/76-2002/2003

Gide, Charles, born 29 June 1847 at Uzès (Gard), he was an economist whose writings include *Principes d'économie politique* (1884), a work which was translated into Dutch (1899), and Turkish (1909), and *Les Colonies communistes et coopératives* (1928), and its translation, *Communist and cooperative colonies* (1930). He died in 1932. Henri Desroche wrote a biography, *Charles Gide* (1982). DBF; Economic journal 42 (1932), pp. 333-38; Master (2); WhE&EA; WhoEc, 1981, 1986, 1999; Who was who 3

Gidel, Gilbert Charles, born 18 November 1880 at Paris, he went to school at the *lycées* Louis-le-Grand and Condorcet, Paris, and received degrees in 1898 and 1900, and his doctorate in law in 1904 for *Les Effets de l'annexion sur les concession.* He subsequently taught at the universities of Montpellier and Rennes, before teaching for twenty-eight years law of nations at the Faculté de droit de Paris. His writings include *De l'efficacité extraterritoriale des jugements répressifs* (1905), and *Travaux pratiques de droit public comparé* (1935). He died in Paris, 22 July 1958. DBFC, 1954/55; IndexBFr³ (3); Revue générale de droit international public 62 (1958), pp. 393-397; WhoFr, 1953/54-1957/58

Gidumal (Shahani), Dayaram, born in 1857 at Hyderabad, Sind, he was educated at Bombay and graduated in 1879 from Elphinston College. He became a district judge and retired as a judge at Bombay. Throughout his life he was engaged in humanitarian and social work. His writings include *The life and life-work of Behramji M. Malabari* (1888), its translation, *Un réformateur parsi dans l'histoire contemporaine de l'Inde, Behramji M. Malabari* (1898), and *The status of woman in India* (1889). He died in 1927. Eminent

Giebels, Lidwina (*Ludy*) Antonia Maria, born 20th cent., she was affiliated with the Library of the Universiteit van Amsterdam. Her writings include *De zionistische beweging in Nederland 1899-1941* (1975), *Inventaris van de archiven van Jacob Fränkel* (1986), and *Inventaris van het archief van Jacob Israël de Haan in de Bibliotheca Rosenthaliana* (1994). Brinkman's; LC

Gielgud, Adam Jerzy Konstanty, born 12 April 1834 at Krôlewiec (Königsberg), Poland, he was a journalist who emigrated to England, where he became a civil servant. He edited *Memoirs of Prince Adam Czartoryski and his correspondence with Alexander I* (1886). He died at Vevey, Switzerland, on 26 November 1920. PSB

Gielhammer, Lutz, born 24 April 1898 at Altötting, Bavaria, he trained as a banker and subsequently studied political science at Jena and Berlin. He received a Dr.jur. in 1929 from the Universität Bonn for *Die politischen Grundlagen der Strafrechtslehre Feuerbachs.* He was a banker in Germany and from 1929 to 1938 a director of the Bank-i Millī-i Irān. From 1940 to 1941 he served as a trade commissioner at Kabul. In 1955 he was a German ambassador to Iran. Wer ist wer, 1955, 1958|

Gies, Hermann, born 10 October 1851 at Hanau, Hesse, he studied at Marburg and Leipzig, where he received a Dr.phil. in 1879 for *Al-Funūn al-sab'atu; ein Beitrag zur Kenntnis sieben neuerer arabischer Versarten.* He was joint author of *Türkische Grammatik* (1889). Sezgin; Thesis

Giese, Friedrich Wilhelm Carl, born 11 December 1870 at Stargard, Prussia, he studied theology and Oriental languages at Greifswald, where he received a Dr.phil. in 1894 for *Untersuchungen über die Addād auf Grund von Stellen in den altarabischen Dichtern.* He subsequently studied at Straßburg under Theodor Nöldeke. Under the influence of Georg Jacob he became interested in Turkish studies. From 1899 to 1905 he became a teacher at Deutsche Realschule, Constantinople. He travelled extensively in central Anatolia. A professor at Seminar für Orientalische Sprachen, Berlin, he devoted his spare time to the study of early Ottoman history. From 1920 to 1936 he was a professor at Breslau. He published the text and translation of "Anonymus Giese," *die altosmanischen anonymen Chroniken* (1922-25), and also the text of 'Āšiqpašazāde in 1929 and *Die verschiedenen Textrezensionen des 'Āšiqpašazāde* (1936). His other writings include *Die Toleranz des Islam* (1915), and *Türkische Märchen* (1925). He died in Eichwalde near Berlin, 19 October 1944. DtBE; Kürschner, 1925-1940/41; NDB; *Wer ist's*, 1935; ZDMG 99 (1945-49), pp. 7-10

Giese, Wilhelm, born 20 February 1895 at Metz, he studied Romance languages and received a Dr.phil. in 1924 from the Universität Hamburg for *Waffen nach der spanischen Literatur des 12. und 13. Jahrhunderts*. He was a professor successively at Halle, Kiel, Posen, and Hamburg. His writings include *Anthologie der geistigen Kultur auf der Pyrenäenhalbinsel* (1927), and *Geschichte der spanischen und portugiesischen Literatur* (1949). In 1972 he was honoured by *Festschrift Wilhelm Giese*. Kürschner, 1931-1992|; *Wer ist wer*, 1955-1974/75

Giesecke, Heinz Helmut, born about 1915, he received a Dr.phil. in 1940 from the Universität Leipzig for *Das Werk des 'Azīz ibn Ardašīr Astārābādī; eine Quelle zur Geschichte des Spätmittelalters in Kleinasien*. His writings include *Richard Hartmann Bibliographie* (1951). Schwarz

Gießner, Klaus, born 28 February 1938 at Würzburg, he studied geography, chemistry and biology successively at the Universität Würzburg and Technische Hochschule Hannover, where he received a doctorate in 1964 for *Naturgeographische Landschaftsanalyse der tunesischen Dorsale*. In 1970 he was affiliated with Geographisches Institut, Hannover. His writings include *Klimageographie Nordafrika* (1985), and he was joint author of *Sudan - Sahel - Sahara* (1978). Thesis

Giesswein, Sándor (Alexandre), born 4 February 1856 at Tata, Hungary, he was a bishop, politician and a peace leader. His writings include *Die Hauptprobleme der Sprachwissenschaft in ihren Beziehungen zur Theologie, Philosophie und Anthropologie* (1892), and *A háború és a társadalomtudomány* (1915). He died in Budapest, 15 April 1923. BiDMoPL; Magyar; GeistigeUng

Gieysztor, Aleksandr, born 17 July 1916 at Moscow, he was a Polish medievalist at Uniwersytet Warszawski, who was granted numerous honorary degrees. His writings include *Ze studiów nad geneza wypraw krzyowych Encyklika Sergiusza IV* (1948), and he edited *Państwo, naród, stany w świadomości wieków średnich* (1990). He died 9 February 1999. IntWW, 1974/75-2000; NEP; WhoSocC, 1978; WhoSoCE, 1989; WhoWor, 1974/75-1978/79

Giffen, John Kelly, born in 1853, he graduated from Franklin College (Ohio) and the United Presbyterian Theological Seminary (Allegheny, Pa.) He was a missionary successively in Egypt and the Sudan from 1881 to 1932. His writings include *The Egyptian Sudan* (1905). He died in Khartoum in 1932. Hill; Master (1); Shavit; WhAm 1

Giffen, Lois Anita, born 28 July 1930 at Cambridge, Mass., she graduated in 1960 from Syracuse University and received a Ph.D. in 1970 from Columbia University for *The development of the Arabic literature on the theory of profane love; an historical study*. Since 1967 she taught her subject successively at New York University and the University of Utah. *MESA Roster of members*, 1977-1990; NatFacDr, 1995; Note; Selim

Giffen, Sir Robert, born in 1837 at Strathaven, Scotland, he was a journalist and sub-ediitor of the *Globe*, before he became a government official and statistician. His writings include *The progress of the working classes in the last half century* (1884), and *The growth of capital* (1889). He died in Strathaven in 1910. Bioln 14; Britlnd (5); DNB; Master (2); WhoEc, 1981, 1986, 1999; *Who was who* 1

Giggei(us), Antonius, born about 1600, most likely in Lombardia, he received a doctorate in theology and taught Hebrew, Arabic and Persian at the Collegio Ambrosiana of Milano. Pope Urban VIII called him in 1632 to Roma, but he died in Milano shortly before setting out for the Eternal City. His writings include *In proverbia Salomonis commentarij trium rabbinorum* (1620), and *Thesavrvs lingvae arabicae* (Milano, 1632), a work which is based on the *Qāmūs* of Firuzabadi and was printed at the expense of Cardinal Federigo Borromei, who thought highly of him. Casati; Encltaliana; Fück, p. 79; IndBiltal (1)

Gigineishvili, Otar Isidorovich, born in 1916 at Kutaisi, Georgia, he graduated in 1940 at Tiflis and received his first degree in 1954 for *Из истории экспансионистской политики младотурок*. Since 1960 he was affiliated with the Oriental Institute, Georgian Soviet Academy of Science first as a lecturer and since 1973 as a director. He received a doctorate in 1986. His writings include *Туркизм и внешняя политика Турции* (1963). He died 11 February 1990. Miliband; Miliband²

Giglio, Carlo, born 27 November 1911 at Apechio, Pesaro, he was affiliated with the Istituto italiano per l'Africa and also was a sometime professor of colonial history in the Università di Pavia. His writings include *La confraternita senussita dalle sue origine ad oggi* (1932), *Politica estera italiana*

(1936), *La colonizzazione demografica dell'Imperio* (1939), *Colonizzazione e decolonizzazione* (1964), and he was general editor of *Inventario delle fonti manoscritte relative alla storia dell'Africa del nord esistenti in Italia* (1971). Chi è, 1940-1961; Unesco

Giglioli, Enrico Hillyer, born 23 January 1845 at London to Anglo-Italian parents, he was educated in England and Italy, where he received a degree in 1863 from the Università di Pisa. He established strong relations with the English scientific community, which he maintained throughout his life. After participating in a three-year anthropological circumnavigation, he became an ethno-anthropologist at Italian museums. He died in Firenze, 16 December 1909. DizBI; IntDicAn

Gignoux, Philippe, born 1931, he was a scholar of pre-Islamic Persia, and in 1973 he was affiliated with the Ecole pratique des hautes études, Paris. He received a *doctorat d'état* in 1987 from the Université de Paris for *L'Anthroponymie de l'Iran sassanide à partir des sources épigraphiques*. He was joint author of *Sceaux sassanides de diverses collections* (1983), *Bulles et sceaux sassanides de diverses collections* (1985), and joint editor of *Études irano-aryennes offertes à Gilbert Lazard* (1989). AnEIFr, 1997; EURAMES, 1993; *Livres disponibles*, 2003, 2004; THESAM, 4

Gil, Isidor, born in 1843, he wrote *El castillo de Loarre y Alcázar de Segovia* (Burgos, 1905), and *Memórias históricas de Burgos y su provincia* (Burgos, 1913). He died in 1917. NUC, pre-1956

Gil, Moshe, born 8 February 1921 at Bialystok, Poland, he graduated in 1966 from Tel Aviv University and received a Ph.D. in 1970 from the University of Pennsylvania for *The institution of charitable foundations in the light of the Cairo Geniza*. His writings include *A history of Palestine, 634-1099* (1992), and he edited *Documents of the Jewish pious foundations from the Cairo Geniza* (1976). Selim

Gil, Pablo, born about 1850, he was in 1872-73 a lecturer in the Universidad de Zaragoza. His writings include *Colección de textos aljamiados* (Zaragoza, 1888). His trace is lost after a publication in 1904. Note about the author

Gil Benumeya, Rodolfo, 1901-1975 *see* Gil Torres Benumeya, Rodolfo

Gil Farrés, Octavio, born 22 November 1922 at Madrid, he graduated from the Universidad de Valencia and became an archivist, librarian and archaeologist, who was affiliated with the Museo Arqueológico Nacional. His writings include *Historia de la moneda española* (1959), *Moneda hispánica en la edad antigua* (1966), and *Historia universal de la moneda* (1974). RuizC

Gil Grimau, Rodolfo, born 1 August 1941 at Madrid, he studied at Madrid, where he received a doctorate in 1982. He was sussesively a director of the Centro Cultural Español, Tetuán, Instituto Cervantes, Lisboa, and Instituto Cervantes, Madrid. He conducted field work in North Africa and was awarded *Comendador del Mérito Civil*. He wrote *Aproximación a una bibliografía española sobre el norte de Africa, 1850-1980* (1988), and he was joint author of *Que por la rosa roja corrio mi sangre* (1977), and *Corpus aproximativo de una bibliografía española sobre al-Andalus* (1993). Arabismo, 1992-1997; Private

Gil-Torres Benumeya , Rodolfo, born in 1901 at Andújar (Jaén), he received an arts degree from the Universidad de Madrid. He was a lecturer in Spanish at Cairo and Alger, and a professor of Moroccan art and history at the Centro de Estudios Marroquíes de Tetuán. Throughout the 1940s he was a regular contributor to the daily, *Madrid*. He was a member of the Instituto de Estudios Políticos as well as the editorial board of the *Revista de política internacional*. His writings include *Cartilla del español en Marruecos* (1925), *Historia de la política árabe* (1951), *Hispanidad y arabidad* (1952), *Andalucismo africano* (1953), *España y al mondo árabe* (1955), and *España dentro de lo árabe* (1964). He died on 31 March 1975. DBEC; IndiceE³ (1); *Revista de política internacional* 138 (1975), pp. 5-7

Gil'adi, Avner, born 28 July 1947, he was a sometime lecturer in Islamic history, University of Haifa. His writings include *Children of Islam; concepts of childhood in medieval Muslim society* (1992). LC

Gilbar, Gad G., born 18 February 1944 at Haifa, he graduated in 1969 from the Hebrew University, Jerusalem, and received a Ph.D. in 1974 from SOAS. Since 1979 he served in the University of Haifa successively as a professor of economic history, chairman of department, and rector. He edited *Ottoman Palestine, 1800-1914* (1990). Note; WhoIsrael, 2001

Gilbert, Joan Elizabeth, born 20th cent., she received a Ph.D. in 1977 from the University of California at Berkeley for *The ulama of medieval Damascus and the international world of Islamic scholars.* Selim³

Gilbert, Pierre Jean Jacques, born 19 September 1904 at Uccle, Bruxelles, he completed his classics in 1929 with a doctorate and became a professor of Egyptology as well as director of museum. His writings include *Méditerranée antique et humanisme dans l'est* (1967). He died in Bruxelles in 1986. Egyptology; NBN, vol, 6, pp. 211-214; WhoBelgium, 1957/58; *Who's who in Belgium and Luxembourg*, 1962

Gilbert, Richard Vincent, born in 1902, he received a Ph.D. in 1930 from Harvard for *Theory of international payments*. He was in 1964 a supervisor, Harvard University Advisory Project, Planning Commission, Karachi. Note about the author

Gilbertson, George Waters, born in 1860 in Caithness, Scotland, he was educated at the University of Edinburgh and subsequently served in the Indian Army with the rank of major. His writings include *First Pakhtoo book* (1901), *The Baluchi language* (1923), and *The Pakkhto idiom* (1932). WhE&EA

Gilchrist, John Borthwick, born in 1759 at Edinburgh, he trained as a doctor at the local George Heriot's Hospital and then joined the East India Company's civil service as an assistant surgeon and proceeded to India in 1782. Being a hospital doctor he soon encountered the difficulty of conversing with the natives. He started to learn Hindustani and launched a campaign that British officers should do the same. He also acquired a good knowledge of other Indian languages before writing *A grammar of the Hindustani language* (1796), *The Oriental fabulist* (1803), *Hindoostanee philology* (1810), and *Oordoo risaluh* (1831). He was from 1818 to 1826 a professor of Hindustani at the Oriental Institution, London. He died in Paris, 9 January 1841. AsianBilnd (6); Bioln 5; BritInd (9); Buckland; DNB; *Libri* 28 (1978), pp. 196-204; Master (2); Riddick

Gildemeister, Johannes Gustav, born in 1812 at Klein Siemen, Mecklenburg, he had taken Hebrew at school before he studied theology and Oriental languages at Göttingen. He received a Dr.phil. in 1838 from the Universität Bonn for *De rebus Indiae quo modo in Arabum notitiam venerint*. He subsequently went to Leiden and Paris to study manuscripts. He returned to Bonn he there taught Indian philology, Oriental languages and Biblical subjects. He died 11 March 1890. ADtB, vol. 49, pp. 354-59; Bonner, vol. 8, pp. 305-9; Buckland; DtBE; DtBilnd (1); Fück; IndianBilnd (2); Stache-Rosen, pp. 40-41

Gil'ferding, Aleksandr Fedorovich, born 2 August 1831 at Warszawa, he was a Slavic scholar whose work on behalf of Slavic culture was such that the Philanthropic Committee established an award in his honour in 1887. His writings include *Geschichte der Serben und Bulgaren* (1856-64), *Die sprachlichen Denkmäler der Drevjaner und Glinjaner Elbslaven* (1957), *Bosnia, Hercegovina e Croazia-turca* (1962), and *Онежія былины* (1873). He died in Kargopol, Olonets Gouv., in 1872. EnSlovar; Wieczynski

Gill, Joseph, born 8 November 1901 at Killamarsh, England, he was a Jesuit since 1918, received a doctorate in 1926 from the Pontificia Università Gregoriana, Roma, and was ordained in 1932. With the exception of wartime service as a chaplain with the Royal Air Force, 1940-46, he was affiliated with the Pontifical Oriental Institute, Roma, from 1938 to 1968. He was a writer on medieval ecclesiastical history. His writings include *The Council of Florence* (1959), its translations, *Le Council de Florence* (1964), *Concilio di Firenze* (1967), *Eugenius IV, Pope of Christian union* (1961), its translation, *Eugenio IV, Papa de la unión de los cristianos* (1967), and *Personalities of the Council of Florence* (1964). Au&Wr, 1971; ConAu 9-12, new rev. 3; IntAu&W, 1976-1982; WhoWor, 1974/75, 1976/77; WrDr, 1982/84-1990/92|

Gill, William John, born 10 September 1843 at Bangladore, he was educated at Brighton College and the Royal Military Academy, Woolwich, and served from 1869 to 1871 as a captain with the Royal Engineers in India. In 1873 he travelled in north-eastern Persia. On 8 August 1880 he started from Suez for the desert but was murdered by Bedouins at Wadi Sudr three days later on the eleventh. He is best remembered for his travels in China and Tibet, 1876-78, for which he was awarded a gold medal from the Royal Geographical Society. Boase; DNB; Henze; Master (1); Riddick

Gillan, Sir James *Agnus*, born in 1885 at Aberdeen, he was educated at Magdalen College, Oxford, and in 1909 entered the Sudan Political Service. In 1928 he was governor of Kordofan Province. He died in 1981. WhE&EA; Who, 1946-1981; *Who was who 8*

Gille, Floriant (Florent), he wrote *Musée de Tzarskoe-Selo; ou, Collection d'armes de S.M. l'Empereur de toutes les Russies* (1835-53), *Antiquités du Bosphore cimmérien conservées au Musée de l'armure impérial de l'Ermitage* (1854), *Lettres sur le Caucase et la Crimée* (1859), and *Musée de l'Ermitage impérial; notice sur la formation de ce musée et descriptions des diverses collections* (1860). BN; NUC

Gillet, Lev, born in 1893 at S.-Marcellin (Isère). After the study of philosophy and natural sciences at Grenoble, Paris and Genève, he became attracted to monastic life and entered Farnborough Abbey, England. He visited Roma in 1922 and became interested in the oecomenical movement of the Eastern Catholic Church, but after the promulgation of the encyclical *Mortalium animos* in 1928, he turned Orthodox. In 1938 he became an Orthodox chaplain to the Fellowship of St. Alban and St. Sergius in Ladbroke Grove, England. He frequently visited Jerusalem and the Lebanon. His writings in French and English include *Communion in the Messiah* (1942), and *Jérusalem, symbole de convergences spirituelles* (1964). Most of his French works have been translated into the major Western European languages. He died in London, 29 March 1980. DBF; ConAu 97-100

Gillett, Sir Michael Cavenagh, born in 1907, he entered the British Consular Service in 1929. From 1957 to 1963 he was ambassador to Afghanistan. He died in 1971. Who, 1955-1971; *Who was who* 7

Gilliat-Smith, Bernard Joseph Leo, born in 1883, he was educated privately and at Caius College, Cambridge. He was a member of the Levant Consular Service. He died in 1973. BritInd (2); Who, 1943-1971; *Who was who* 7

Gilliot, Claude, born 20th cent., he received a doctorate in 1987 from the Université de Paris for *Aspects de l'imaginaire islamique commun dans le commentaire de Tabari.* He was a Dominican priest who was a sometime professor of Arabic and Islamic studies in the Université de Provence. His writings include *Exégèse, langue et théologie en islam; l'éxegèse coranique de Tabari* (1990). Note; THESAM, 3

Gilmozzi, Marcello, born 7 May 1925 at Imer (Trento), he was a journalist and a deputy director of *il Popolu.* He was at one time affiliated with the Istituto di sociologia internazionale di Gorizia. His writings include *Dieci anni di vita internazionale* (1971), and *La Cina tra passato futuro* (1972). IntBiItal (2)

Gilsenan, Michael Dermot Cole, born 6 February 1940, he studied Arabic at Oxford for his B.A. and then social anthropology for his D.Phil., based on fieldwork in Cairo (1964-66), entitled *The Sufi brotherhoods of Egypt* (1977). He conducted further fieldwork in northern Lebanon, 1971-72. He taught anthropology at UCLA and University College, London. In 1984 he became the first holder of the Khalid bin Abdullah al-Sa'ud Chair for the Study of the Contemporary Arab World at Oxford. His writings include *Saint and Sufi in modern Egypt* (1973), *Recognizing Islam* (1982), *Lebanon, the fractured country* (1987), and *Lords of the Lebanese marches* (1996). Note; Sluglett; Who, 1985-2002

Gilson, Étienne Henry, born 13 June 1884 at Paris, he was educated at the local Lycée Henri-IV, and the Faculté des Lettres. From 1932 to 1951 he was a professor at the Collège de France, and since 1946 a member of the Académie française. His writings include *The Mystical theology of Saint Bernard* (1940), *Le Thomisme* (1942), and *The Spirit of Thomism* (1964). He is the subject of *Étienne Gilson et nous; la philosophie et son histoire,* edited by Monique Couratier (1980). He died on 19 September 1978. *Who's who in France,* 1977-1978

Gimadi, Khairutdin Gimadeevich, born in 1912, he was from 1933 to 1943 a teacher at Kazan institutions of higher learning and subsequently became affiliated with the Institute of Philology, Literature and History, Soviet Academy of Science, Kazan Section. He wrote *Татария и дни первой русском революции* (1955), and *Советская Татария - детище словарь* (1957). He died in 1961. TatarES

Gimaret, Daniel, born 11 June 1933 at Saint-Didier-sur-Chalaronne (Ain), he studied at École Normale Supérieure, 1955-59, and received a *doctorat d'état ès lettres* in 1979. Since 1973 he was a *directeur d'études* at the École pratique des hautes études, Section des sciences religieuses, Sorbonne. A member of the Société asiatique, he served as editor-director of the *Journal asiatique* from 1973 to 1992; since 1984 he was also responsible for the *Bulletin critique des Annales islamologiques.* His writings include *Théories de l'acte humain en théologie musulmane* (1980), *Les Noms divins en islam* (1988), *La Doctrine d'al-Ash'ari* (1990), *Une Lecture mu'taziliste du Coran; le Tafsir d'Abu 'Ali al-Djubba'ï* (1994), *Dieu à l'image de l'homme* (1997), he edited *Kitāb Bilawhar wa-Būdhāsaf* (1972), and he translated *Le Livre de Bilawhar et Budasaf* (1971). AnEIFr, 1997; EURAMES, 1993; *Livres disponibles,* 2003; Private

Ginestous, G., born 19th cent., he received a doctorate in 1906 from the Faculté des science de Paris for *Etudes sur le climat de la Tunisie.* He was a sometime lecturer at the École coloniale d'agriculture de Tunis and affiliated with the Service météorologique, Tunis. His writings include *Esquisse géologiques de la Tunisie* (1911), *Resumé de la climatologie tunisienne* (1922), *Étude climatologique du golfe de Tunis* (1925), and *Le Régime des pluies en Tunisie* (1927). BN; NUC, pre-1956

Gini, Corrado, born 23 May 1884 at Motta di Livenza (Trevisa), he qualified for law at the Università di Bologna and after related post-graduate study he became a professor of statistics, political economy, constitutional law and demography successively at Cagliari, Padova and Roma. His writings include *Problemi sociologici della guerra* (1921), *Population* (Chicago, 1930), and *Teoria della popolazione* (1945). He died in Roma, 13 March 1965. Chi è, 1928-1961; DizBI; Vaccaro; Wholtaly, 1958

Giniewski, Paul, born 18 February 1926 at Wien, he studied at Paris and became an editor and Zionist leader. His writings include *Quand Israël combat* (1957), *Israël devant l'Afrique et Asie* (1958), *Bantustans* (1961), *Le Sionisme d'Abraham à Dayan* (1969), and *De Massada à Beyrouth* (1983). WhoWorJ, 1965, 1972, 1978

Gink, Károly, 1924-1987 *see* Gombos, Károly

van **Ginneken**, Wouter, born 28 June 1944, he was affiliated with the International Labour Office, Genève. His writings include *Rural and urban inequalities in Indonesia, Mexico, Pakistan, Tanzania and Tunisia* (1976), *Government and its employees* (1991), he was joint author of *De weg naar volledige werkgelegenheid* (1985), he edited *Finding the balance* (1996), and he was joint editor of *Generating internationally compatible income distribution estimates* (1984). LC

Ginoux, Irénée, fl. 1867-1894, he was an author of a number of biographical notes, all of which were published by the Académie du Gard, Nîmes. BN; Note

Gins (Guins), Georgii (George) Konstantinovich (Constantine), born in 1887 at Novogeorgievsk, Russia, he studied at St. Petersburg, Heidelberg and Paris. He received a law degree and then became a lecturer in Russia until 1919. Since 1920 he resided in the U.S.A. where he was affiliated with a variety of universities and the U.S. Information Agency. His writings include *Переселение и колонизация* (1913), *Право и сила* (1929), *Quo vadis Europa* (1941), *Soviet law and Soviet society* (1954), and *Communism on the decline* (1957). He died in 1971. Au&Wr, 1971

Gintl, Heinrich Eduard, born 13 July 1832 at Ungarisch Hradisch (Uherské Hradiště), Moravia, he received a Dr.phil. in 1872 from the Universität Rostock for *Der Nationalismus*. He subsequently trained as a railway engineer and found employ in Austrian Galicia. He wrote *Die Concurrenzfähigkeit des galizischen Petroleums* (Wien, 1885). He died in Abbazia (Opatija), 30 June 1892. Hinrichsen; ÖBL

Gintsburg (Гинцбург), David G., Baron von, 1857-1910 *see* Günzburg, David Goratsievich

Gintsburg, Iona Iosifovich, born in 1871, he studied Arabic, particularly Judeo-Arabic philology, under P. K. Kokovtsov. He was from 1934 to his death affiliated with the Oriental Institute, Soviet Academy of Science, Leningrad. During the siege of Leningrad he continued to prepare a comprehensive catalogue of Hebrew manuscripts in the Institute of Oriental Studies. He died 24 April 1942. Krachkovskii, pp. 141-42; Miliband; Miliband²

Ginzburg, Vul'f Veniaminovich, born in 1904, he was an anthropologist who received a doctorate in 1945. His writings include *Горные таджики* (1937), and he was joint author of *Палеоантропология Средней Азии* (1972). He died in 1969. KazakSE; KyrgyzSE

Ginzel, Friedrich Carl, born 26 February 1850 at Reichenberg, Bohemia, he trained from 1877 to 1886 in Wien as an astronomer at the private observatory of Th. von Oppolzer. He subsequently joined the Astronomisches Rechen-Institut, Berlin, where he remained until his retirement in 1920. He died in Berlin on 29 June 1926. DtBE; DtBiInd (3); Jaksch; Kosch; NDB

Giordani, Paolo, born 19th cent., he wrote *Sui campi d'Africa a Tripoli e Bengasi* (1912), *L'impero coloniale tedesco come nacque e come finisce* (1915), and its translation, *The German colonial empire* (1916). NUC, pre-1956

Giorgi, Luigi de, fl. 1965 *see* De Giorgi, Luigi

Giovannozzi, Ugo, born in 1876, he wrote *Nozioni elementari di fisica, chimica e mineralogia, ad uso della terze classe tecnica* (Firenze, 1909), *Studio sulla distribuzione delle masse montuose nell'Appennino centrale* (Firenze, 1914), and *Ugo Giovannozzi* (Milano, 193-). Firenze; NUC, pre-1956

Giraldo, Zaida Irene, born 30 April 1938 at N.Y.C., she received a Ph.D. in 1975 from New York University. She was a sometime research associate in family policy in the Institute of Policy Sciences, Duke University, Durham, N.C. Her writings include *Tax policy and the dual-income family* (1978), and *Public policy and the family* (1980). DrAS, 1978 H

Girard, Alain, born 13 March 1914 at Paris, he studied at the Sorbonne and received a *doctorat ès lettres*. He was a high school teacher, 1938-41, a curator at the Bibliothèque nationale, 1941-46, and a professor at the Sorbonne, 1964-82. His writings include *L'Homme et les nombre des hommes* (1984), and he edited *Les Immigrés du Maghreb* (1977). He died 11 January 1996. WhoFr, 1967/68-1995/96

Girard, André, born about 1900, he received a doctorate in law in 1933 from the Sorbonne for *Les Minorités nationales ethniques en Bulgarie*. NUC, pre-1956

Girard, Henri, born 18 January 1879 at Paris, he graduated in 1904 from the military college, Saint-Cyr and served for seven years with the Zouaves at Tunis. He subsequently passed through the Ecole supérieure de la guerre. In 1919 he served with the general staff of the Allied Forces at Constantinople. Upon the request of *maréchal* Lyautey, he was nominated in 1922 *chef d'État-major* of the Subdivision of Marrakesh, later serving in Rabat and Taza. After participating in the Riff campaign, during which he was seriously wounded, he spent two years of teaching at the École supérieure de

Guerre. He then returned to North Africa for final colonial duty until 1936. He died in Dijon on 10 March 1949. *Hommes et destins*, vol. 7, pp. 207-210

Girard, Jules, born in 1831 at Paris, he wrote *Nouvelle-Guinée* (1883), *L'évolution comparée des sables* (1903), and *Le modelé des sables littoraux* (1905). He died in 1902.

Girard, Pierre Marie *Benjamin*, born in 1830 at Loix (Île de Ré), he entered the offices of the Navy and at the same time worked as a copy clerk at a Rochefort lawyer. He served with the navy administration in French Guiana, Senegal and Japan. In 1869 he was named commissioner of the navy division in Egypt, and in 1881 he served in the same capacity with the navy division of the Levant on the battleship *La Galissonnière*. He participated in the entire campaign in Tunisia. After his retirement he served as a vice-consul of Greece for the departments of Charente-maritime and Vendée. His writings include *L'Égypte en 1882* (1883), *Souvenirs maritimes, 1881-1883* (1896), and *La Normandie maritime* (1899). He died in Finistère, 23 February 1905. DBF; IndexBFr² (1)

Girard de Rialle, Julien, born in 1841, he completed his education in 1861 and subsequently travelled in the Balkans. Under the pseudonym Dmitri Stephanowitch he published two brochures on the ethnic and linguistic affinity of the Yugoslavs, *Slaves et Grecs devant la Turquie* (1861), and *Belgrade* (1862). In 1866 the French government sent him on a scientific mission to Syria. Having learnt Sanscrit and Zend, he gave a course on the ancient Aryan civilizations of Asia at the Sorbonne in 1869/70. His writings include *Mémoire sur l'Asie centrale* (1875), *La mythologie comparée* (1878), and *Les peuples de l'Asie et de l'Europe* (1881). He died in Santiago de Chile on 23 November 1904 and was buried at Père Lachaise, Paris, 17 February 1905. DBF; Vapereau

Girardin, François Auguste *Marc*, 1801-1873 *see* Saint-Marc Girardin, *Marc*

Giraud, Ernest, born 19th cent., he was a president of the Chambre de commerce française, Constantinople, a counsellor on foreign trade and an officer of the Légion d'honneur. His writings include *La France à Constantinople*; réunion des articles parus sous ce titre dans la *Revue commercial du Levant* (1907). *Qui êtes-vous*, 1924

Giraud, Henri, born 18 January 1879 at Paris, he graduated in 1900 from the military college, Saint-Cyr, and subsequently served for seven years with the Zouaves in Tunisia. After the first World War he served for two years with the General Staff of the Allied Forces in Constantinople. Between 1922 and 1935 he was engaged for most of the time with the pacification of French North Africa. He retired with the rank of general. He died in Dijon, 10 March 1949. *Hommes et destins*, vol. 7, pp. 207-210

Giraud, Hubert Marie Julien, born 7 September 1865 at Nevers (Nièvre), the son of a bank director, he was educated at Marseille and started life as a representative of the Compagnie Paquet at Mogador, Morocco. In 1892 he started his affiliation with the Société générale des transports maritimes à vapeur, successively becoming director and *président du conseil d'administration*. In 1905 he joined the Chambre de commerce de Marseille, becoming secretary in 1913 and president from 1920 to 1923. From 1919 to 1924 he was *député* for Bouches-du-Rhône. He was a founder (1910) and president of the Comité marseillais du Maroc and a vice-president of the Société de géographie de Marseille. In its *Bulletin* he published several articles on Morocco and Islam. His writings include the off-print, *Itinéraire de Mogador à Marrakech, 1890-92* (1899). He died in Marseille in 5 August 1934. DBF

Giraud, René, born 29 August 1906 at Ménerville, Algeria, he studied classics and literature at the Université d'Alger and subsequently thought at secondary educational institutions until 1944, when the French Government sent him on a cultural mission to Ankara. He remained there for eighteen years as a teacher of French first at the Hukuk Fakültesi and then at the Siyasal Bilgiler Enstitüsü. In 1958 he received his doctorate for his two theses, *L'Empire des Turcs célestes* and *L'Inscription de Baïn Tsokto*, published in 1960 and 1961 respectively. Upon his return to France in 1962, he was invited to found the Département d'Études turques at Strasbourg, and in 1964 he was appointed to the chair of Turkish. He died in May of 1968. *Hommes et destins*, vol. 7, pp. 210-211; *Turcica* 1 (1969), pp. 242-46

Giraudo, Gianfranco, born in 1941, he wrote *Drakula; contributo alla storia delle idee politiche nel'Europa orientale alla avolta del XV secolo* (Venezia, 1972). LC

Girbal, Enrique Claudio, born 13 November 1839 at Gerona, he studied classics and local history and became a curator at the Museo de antigüedades, Gerona. He was a prominent member of Gerona learned associations and societies, and a founding director of four local periodicals, whose writings include *Los Judios en Gerona* (1870), *Album monumental de Gerona* (1876), *El castillo de Brunyola* (1885), and *Estudio histórico-artistico acerca de los llamados baños árabes de Gerona* (1888). He died in 1896. IndiceE³ (2)

Girgas (Guirgas), Vladimir Fedorovich, born in 1835, he went to school in St. Petersburg, where he also studied Oriental languages, particularly Arabic, but also Turkish, graduating in 1858. He subsequently spent two years and a half at Paris as a private teacher and concurrently studied Arabic at the Sorbonne. He then went on to the Levant for three years, before returning to St. Petersburg. He there received his master's degree in 1865 for *Права хримтиан на Востоке по тусуль-мананским законам* and began teaching Arabic. He received a doctorate in 1873 with a thesis on Arabic grammar. He was joint author of *Арабская хрестоматія* (1876), and he edited *Akhbār al-tiwāl*, of Abū Hanīfah al-Dīnawarī (1888). He died in 1887. Fück; Index Islamicus (1); Krachkovskii, pp. 131-133

Giron, Noël Joseph Antoine Justin, born 22 August 1884, he graduated from the École des langues orientales vivantes, Paris. He was a student interpreter in Damascus, 1907, and in Aleppo, 1910; an acting vice-consul in Mersin and Tarsus, 1910, and in Constantinople, 1912. He subsequently served as a dragoman in Jerusalem, Damascus, Tehran and Cairo. He was awarded *chevalier* of the Légion d'honneur, 7 March 1925. His writings include *Légendes coptes; fragments inédits* (Paris, 1907). IndexBFr² (1)

Giron Irueste, Fernando, born in 1945, he received a medical doctorate and became a professor of history of medicine at the Facultad de Medicina de Granada, specializing in medieval Arabic medicine. His writings include *El Maristán de Granada; un hospital islámico* (1989), and *Mujtasar fī 'l-tibb = compedio de medicina*, of 'Abd al-Malik Ibn Habīb (1992). Arabismo, 1992; EURAMES, 1993; LC

de **Gironcourt**, Georges, born in 1878 to a Lorraine family, he trained as an agronomist and specialized in Tropical agriculture. In the service of the ministries of Colonies and Instruction publique, he went on two missions to French West Africa in 1908-1909 and 1911-1912. His writings include *Missions de Gironcourt en Afrique occidentale* (1920), and *La géographie musicale* (1955). His apartment in Nancy, where he was still living in 1958, was full of rare African objects. DBF

Giroud, Auguste, he wrote *L'Union douanière France-Tunisie* (Paris, 1939). NUC, pre-1956

Girs, Georgii Fedorovich, born 11 November 1928 at Moscow, he graduated in 1952 from the Moscow Oriental Institute and received his first degree in 1955 for *Становление и развитие современной художественной прозы на пушту в Афганистане*. He was since 1955 affiliated with the Oriental Institute, Soviet Academy of Sciences. His writings include *Современная художественная проза на пушту в Афганистане* (1958), *Литература непокоренного народа* (1966), he translated *Стихи поэтов Афганистана* (1962), and he edited *Исторические песни пуштунов* (1984). He died on 9 June 1994. Miliband; Miliband²; Восток, 1995, no. 2, pp. 192-193

Giscard, Robert, born in 1900, he wrote *Les Praries permanentes au Maroc* (Salé, 1952). NUC, pre-1956

Giskra (Jiskra), Carl, born 29 January 1820 at Mährisch-Trübau, Moravia, he studied at Wien and received a Dr.phil. in 1840 and a Dr.jur. in 1843. He was an Austrian representative at the Parliament of Frankfurt, 1848. Later, as an Austrian minister, he was one of the most popular Liberals. He died in Baden near Wien, 1 Juni 1879. DtBE; DtBiInd (1); Kosch; ÖBL; Wurzbach

Gitelson, Susan Aurelia, born about 1942 at N.Y.C. she graduated in 1963 from Barnard College, New York, and received a Ph.D. in 1970 from Columbia University for *Multilateral aid for natural development and self-reliance*. She was a human rights and peace activist who was joint editor of *Israel in the Third World* (1976). WhoAmW, 1985/86, 1987/88; WhoE, 1989/90; WhoWor, 1987-1993/94

Gittée, August, born 5 January 1858 at Gent, he taught at the Atheneum, Charleroi. He was since 1888 an editor of *Volkskunde* (Gent). His writings include *Vraagboek tot het zamelen van vlaamsche folklore of volkskunde* (Gent, 1888), and *Curiosités de la vie enfantine* (Paris, 1899). BiBenelux (1)

Gittinger, James Price, born 13 October 1928 at Berkeley, Calif., he graduated in 1949 from the University of California at Davis, and received his Ph.D. in 1955 from Iowa State College for *Economic development through agrarian reform*. He at one time gave the Agricultural Projects Course at the Economic Development Institute of the World Bank, Washington, D.C. His writings include *Planning for agricultural development; the Iranian experiment* (1965), *Economic analysis of agricultural projects* (1972), and he edited *Agricultural projects case studies and work exercises* (1973). AmM&WSc, 1973 S; ConAu 41-44; WhoUN, 1975

Giunashvili, Dzhamshid Shalavovich, born 1 May 1931 at Tehran, he graduated in 1953 from the Oriental Faculty, Central Asian State University, and received his first degree for «Глагольный компонент детерминативных именных образованний персидского литературного языка.» Since 1958 he was affiliated with his alma mater. He received a doctorate in 1966 for *Филологическая структура литературного персидского языка*. He was appointed a professor in 1970. His writings include *Грузинско-персидский и персидского-грузинский карманный словарь* (1971),

Тбилисская рукопис Тарих-е Систан (1971), and *Филологические заметки* (1978). Miliband; Milibandl

Giunashvili, Liudmila Semenovna, born 15 July 1937 at Dushanbe, she graduated in 1959 from the Central Asian State University and received her first degree in 1963 at Tiflis for *Художественная проза Сфида Нафиси, 1916-1953*, and her doctorate in 1987 at Leningrad for *Крестьянский тема в современной персидской прозе*. Her writings include *Поэзия Саида Нафиса* (1971), and *Творческий путь Саида Нафиси* (1976), and *Проблесы становления и развития реализма в современной персидской прозе* (1985). Miliband; Miliband[2]

Giurescu, Constantin C., born 26 October 1901 at Focşani, Rumania, he received all his education at Bucureşti, including his doctorate in history in 1925 for *Contribuţiuni la studiol marilor dregătorii în secolele XIV şi XV*. Since 1930 he held the chair of history at Bucureşti University and served from 1931 to 1948 as a director of the Institutului de Istorie Naţională. As an individualist who shunned academic collectives, he was imprisoned from 1948 to 1953 for non-conformity, but re-instated after the death of Stalin. His writings include *Istoria Românilor* (1939), *Studii de istorie socială* (1943), and *Chronological history of Romania* (1972). He died in Bucureşti, 13 November 1977. DcEnc; MicDcEnc; Südost-Forschungen 37 (1978), pp. 201-202; WhoRom; WhoSocC, 1978; WhoWor, 1974/75

Giustolisi, Eugenio, born 20th cent., in Varese, Italy, he was a consultant in hospital technology. In this capacity he spent much time in the Muslim countries of Africa and the Middle East. Interested in Islamic culture, he later also took a degree in history in order to deepen his appreciation of Islam. He edited *Il vangelo di Barnaba; un vangelo per il musulmani?* (1991). Note

Giuzal'ian, Leon Tigranovich, born in 1901 at Tiflis, he graduated in 1929 from the Faculty of History and Material Culture, Leningrad, and received his first degree in 1948 for *Персидские поэтические отрывки на средневековых глиняных изделиях и их историко-литературная ценность*. Since 1935 he was affiliated with the Oriental Faculty, Leningrad. He was joint author of *Рукописи Шахнамэ и ленинградских собраниях* (1934), and *Миниатюры рукописи поэмы "Шахнаме" 1933 года* (1985). He died 11 October 1994. Miliband; Miliband[2]

Giuzelev, Vasil Todoro, born 19 October 1936 at Dmitrograd, he obtained a degree in history and archaeology in 1959 from "Св. Кл. Охридски," Sofia. He was from 1984 to 1989 a director of the Bulgarian research institute in Wien. His writings include *Славяни и прабългари в нашата история* (1966), *Княз Борис Първи* (1969), *Medieval Bulgaria* (1988), and he edited *Българските земи и българите и сбирките на Военния архив, Виенна, 1664-1878* (1986). Koi; 1998; LC

Gladden, Edgar Norman, born 4 August 1897 at Reading, he received a Ph.D. in 1936 from the University of London. He was from 1913 to 1958 with the British Civil Service. His writings include *The Civil Service* (1945), *The Essentials of public administration* (1953), its translation, *Principi essenziali della pubblica amministrazione* (1961), *Ypres 1917; a personal account* (1967). Under the pseudonym Norman Mansfield he wrote *The Failure of the left, 1919-1947* (1947). ConAu 21-24; Unesco

Glade, Dieter, born about 1935, he received a Dr.phil. in 1965 from the Universität Kiel for *Bremen und der Ferne Osten*. GV; NUC, 1968-72

Gladstone (Γκλάντστον), William Ewart, born in 1809 at Liverpool, he was educated at Eton and Christ Church College, Oxford. He was a politician and statesman. His writings include *The Turco-Servian war* (1876), and *The Hellenic factor in the Eastern problem* (1877). He died in 1898. AnaBrit; Boase; Britlnd; (26); DLB, 57, p. 184; DNB; EEE; EncAm; EncBrit; EncicUni; Encltaliana; GdeEnc; Master(48); Meyers; Pallas; Who was who i

Gladwin, Francis, born in 1789, he was an Orientalist in the Honorable East India Company and was in 1785 a founding member of the Asiatic Society of Bengal. He was appointed in 1801 a professor of Persian at the College of Fort William, and in 1802 a Collector of Customs. He initiated a series of translations and writings associated with Oriental literature and history, including *The Ayin Akbary; or, The Institutes of the Emperor Akbar* (1777), *The Memoirs of Khojeh Abdulkureem* (1788), *The Persian moonshee* (1801), *A Dictionary, Persian, Hindoostanee and English* (1809) and *The Gulistan; or, Rose garden* (1865). He died in Patna in 1812. Britlnd (3); Buckland; DNB; Riddick

Glagow, Rainer Karl-Heinz, born 17 December 1941 at Frankurt an der Oder, he studied Islamic subjects, history, and comparative religion and received a Dr.phil. in 1956 from the Universität Bonn for *Das Kalifat des al-Mu'tadid Billah*. From 1968 to 1971 he was affiliated with 'Ayn Shams University, Cairo, and subsequently served for seven years as a deputy director, Deutsches Orient-Institut, Hamburg. He was in 2003 a free-lance journalist and a director of a foundation in Berlin. Junge Freiheit (Berlin), 16 Mai 2003, p. 3; Note; Thesis

Glascott, A. G., fl. 1841, he was a British naval officer who accompanied the British vice-consul James Brant on his travels from Erzurum to Bayezit in 1838 and produced the first reliable map of Lake Van. Henze

von **Glasenapp**, Otto Max *Helmuth*, born 8 September 1891 at Berlin, he pursued Indian and religious studies and subsequently taught at Berlin, Königsberg and Tübingen, where he died 25 June 1963. His writings include *Die Philosophie der Inder* (1952). DtBE; IndianBilnd (1); KDtLK, Nekrolog, 1936-1970; Kürschner, 1950-1961; NDB; Stache-Rosen; Wer ist's, 1928, 1935; Wer ist wer, 1950-1963

Glaser, Eduard, born 15 March 1855 at Deutsch-Rust, Bohemia, he studied mathematics and geodesy at Prag, and astronomy and Oriental languages at Wien. From 1873 to 1875 he made several foot-marches to Paris, covering up to fifty-five miles a day. D. H. Müller roused his interest in southern Arabia and also introduced him to Sabaean. In 1878 he obtained employment at the Vienna observatory. In 1880 he went as a private tutor to Tunis, learning Arabic at the same time. In the service of the Vienna observatory he travelled to Suhaj in Upper Egypt to observe a total eclipse of the sun in May of 1882. In October of the same year he undertook the first of his four travels to southern Arabia, during which he collected numerous South Arabian inscriptions, which he donated to the libraries of Berlin, London, and Wien. Although the Universität Greifswald conferred on him an honorary doctorate in 1890, he was largely ignored and left without support by his contemporaries. His writings include *Skizze der Geschichte Arabiens von den aeltesten Zeiten bis zum Propheten Muhammad* (1889), *Altjemenische Nachrichten* (1908), and *Eduard Glasers Reise nach Mârib* (1913). He died in München on 7 May 1908. Walter Dostal wrote a biography, *Eduard Glaser; Forschungen im Yemen* (1990). Asien 11 (1889), p. 87; DtBE; EncJud; Filipisky; Fück, p. 256; GdeEnc; Henze; JüdLex; NDB; Pallas; RNL; Wininger

Glaser, Gisbert, born about 1935, he received a Dr.phil. in 1967 from the Universität Heidelberg for *Der Sonderkulturanbau zu beiden Seiten des nördlichen Rheins zwischen Karsruhe und Worms*. GV

Glasgow, George, born in 1891 in Bolton, he was educated at Bolton Grammar School and the University of Manchester. He was a journalist whose writings, partly under the pseudonym Logistes, include *The Janina murders and the occupation of Corfu* (1923), *MacDonald as a diplomatist* (1924), *From Dawes to Locarno* (1925), and *Diplomacy and God* (1941). His trace is lost after an article in 1956. Master (1); WhE&EA

Glasman, Pierre Wladimir, born 17 October 1942 at Rabat, he studied at Aix-en-Provence. He was from 1984 to 1988 an academic librarian at the Institut français d'Etudes arabes, Damascus, from 1988 to 1991 a press attaché at the Ambassade de France, Alger, and since 1992 a press attaché at Amman. He was a member of the Association française des Arabisants. Private

Glasneck, Johannes, born 22 February 1928 at Hirschberg, Germany, he received a Dr.phil. in 1972 from the Universität Hallle for *Die imperialistischen Großmächte und die Türkei am Vorabend und während des zweiten Weltkrieges*. He was a professor of modern history at his alma mater from 1970 to his retirement. His writings include *Methoden der deutsch-faschistischen Propagandatätigkeit in der Türkei* (1966), *Kemal Atatürk und die moderne Türkei* (1966), and he was joint author of *Türkei und Afghanistan, Brennpunkte der Orientpolitik im zweiten Weltkrieg* (1968), and *Die Rolle der Persönlichkeit Kemal Atatürks im nationalen Befreiungskampf der Völker des Nahen Ostens* (1983). Kürschner, 1992-2003; Schwarz

Glass, Charles, born 23 January 1951, he was a special Middle East correspondent for American television companies. He left his post as ABC's chief Middle East correspondent to write a book when he was kidnapped by Hizbullah guerrillas. He came into the headlines in 1987 when he escaped from Beirut after sixty-two days of captivity. He wrote *Tribes with flags; a dangerous passage through the chaos in the Middle East* (1990). ConAu 139; Note

Glassburner, John Bruce, born 4 December 1920 at Beatrice, Nebr., he graduated in 1943 from Iowa State University and received a Ph.D. in 1953 from the University of California at Berkeley. Since 1955 he was a professor of economics, temporarily also chairman of department, in the University of California at Davis. His writings include *Indonesia's new economic policy* (1974), and he was joint author of *An evaluation of Pakistan's third five-year plan* (1965), and *Macroeconomic policies, crises, and long-term growth in Indonesia, 1965-1990* (1994). AmM&WS, 1973, 1978 S; ConAu 33-36; Master (1); WhoWest, 1974/75

Glasse, Robert Marshall, born 3 April 1929 at Brooklyn, N.Y., he graduated in 1951 from the City College of New York and received a Ph.D. in 1968 from the Australian National University for *Huli of Papua*. He was since 1972 a professor of anthropology at Queens College, Flushing, N.Y. He was joint editor of *Pigs, pearlshells, and woman; marriage in New Guinea highlands* (1969). American men and women of science, 1973 F; ConAu 29-32, 140; WhoE, 1977/78

Glassen, Erika née Wendt, born about 1940, she received a Dr.phil. in 1968 from the Universität Freiburg im Breisgau for *Die frühen Safawiden nach Qāzī Qumī* and also a Dr.habil. in 1981 for *Der mittlere Weg; Studien zur Religionspolitik und Religiosität der späteren Abbasiden-Zeit*. She was a sometime lecturer at Freiburg. Kürschner, 1983-1996|; Sezgin

Glasser, Arthur Frederick, born 10 September 1914 at Paterson, N.J., he graduated from Cornell University, Ithaca, N.Y., and Princeton Theological Seminary. He served with the China Inland Mission and in 1970 became a dean, School of World Mission, Pasadena, Cal. His writings include *And some believed; a chaplain's experiences with the Marines in the South Pacific* (1946), and he edited *Crucial dimensions in world evangelization* (1976). WhoRel, 1975, 1977

Glassl, Horst, born 1 January 1934 at Silberbach, Germany, he received a Dr.phil. in 1965 and a Dr.habil. in 1973. Since 1980 he was a professor of political science and Balkan history at München. His writings include *Der mährische Ausgleich* (1967), *Die slovakische Geschichtswissenschaft nach 1945* (1971), and he was joint editor of *Das österreichische Einrichtungswerk in Galizien, 1772-1790* (1975). Kürschner, 1976-2003

Glassner, Martin Ira, born 7 July 1932 at Plainfield, N.J., he graduated in 1953 from Syracuse University and received a Ph.D. in 1968. After fellowships in Morocco, Tunisia and Egypt, he was for five years a U.S. Foreign Service officer. Since 1968 he was a professor of geography at Southern Connecticut State College, New Haven. His writings include *Access to the sea for developing land-locked states* (1970). AmM&WS, 1973 S, 1978 S; ConAu 41-44, new rev. 15, 34, 90; IntAu&W, 1977

Glatzer, Bernt, born in 1942, he received a Dr.phil. in 1975 from the Universität Heidelberg for *Nomaden von Charjistan; Aspekte der wirtschaftlichen, sozialen und politischen Organisation nomadischer Durrānī Paschtunen*. In 2001 he was an aid worker in the Third World and affiliated with Deutsche Stiftung für Internationale Entwicklung, Bad Honnef. LC; Note

Glaubitt, Klaus, born in 1944, he received a Dr.rer.oec. and subsequently carried on field-work in the Third World. After two years of research and teaching at Kabul, he joined the Institut für Entwicklungsforschung und Entwicklungspolitik in Ruhr-Universität, Bochum. His writings include *Effekte staatlicher Aktivität in Entwicklungsländern* (1979), and he was joint author of *Das System der Staatseinnahmen und seine Bedeutung für die Wirtschaftsentwicklung Afghanistans* (1975). Note

Glauert, Günter, born 29 August 1905 at Bonn, he received a Dr.phil. in 1936 from the Universität Graz and a Dr.habil. in 1942 from the Universität München. He taught geography from 1944 to 1945 at Graz and subsequently at München. His writings include *Siedlungsgeographie von Oberkrain* (1943), and *Die Alpen* (1975). He died in München, 18 March 1982. Kürschner, 1950-1983

Glavanis, Mrs. Kathy R. G., born 20th cent., she was affiliated with the Department of Sociology and Social Policy in the University of Durham. She was joint author of *The Sociology of agrarian relations in the Middle East* (1983), and *The Rural Middle East; peasant lives and modes of production* (1990). DrBSMES, 1993

Glavanis, Pandeli M., born 20th cent., he obtained a docorate and was affiliated with the Department of Sociology and Social Policy, University of Durham, until 1993. In the following year he became a lecturer in sociology in the University of Manchester and a director of its Development Studies Stream in the Graduate School. He served as a tresurer of BRISMES. He was joint author of *The Sociology of agrarian relations in the Middle East; the persistence of household production* (1983), and *The rural Middle East; peasant lives and modes of production* (1990). DrBSMES, 1993; Note

Glazer, Mark, born 22 January 1938 at Istanbul, he received a Ph.D. in 1971 from Northwestern University, Evanston, Illinois, for *Psychological intimacy among the Jews of north metropolitan Chicago and the Sephardic Jews of Istanbul, Turkey*. He was since 1974 a professor of anthropology in Purdue University, West Lafayette, Ind. AmM&WS P, 13th ed. (1976) [not sighted]

Glazer, Sidney S., born in 1911, he received a Ph.D. in 1937 from Yale University for *Abu Hayyan's commentary to the Alfiyya of Ibn Malik; studies in the grammatical literature of the Arabs*. Since 1947 he was an editor of *Bibliography of periodical literature on the Near and Middle East*. In 1956 he was a consultant in Near Eastern bibliography to the Library of Congress, Washington, D.C. His writings include the *Commentary to the Alfiyya of Ibn Malik; Kitāb Manhaj as-sālik* (1947). Master (1); Selim

Glazik, Josef, born 1 February 1913 at Hagen-Hapse, Germany, he received a Dr.theol. in 1953 from the Universität Münster for *Die russisch-orthodoxe Heidenmission seit Peter dem Großen* (1954), and also a Dr.habil. in 1958 for *Die Islammission der russisch-orthodoxen Kirche*. He was successively a professor of missionary sciences at the universities of Würzburg and Münster. His writings include *Warum Mission?* (1984). Kürschner, 1961-2001|; Schwarz

Gledhill, Alan, born 26 October 1895 at Leeds, he spent over twenty years in the Indian Civil Service, before becoming in 1955 a professor of Oriental laws at SOAS. In 1958 he received a LL.D. from the University of London. His writings include *The Republic of India* (1951), *Fundamental rights in India* (1955), *Pakistan; the development of its laws and constitution* (1957), and *The penal law of North Nigeria* (1968). He died 16 July 1983. ConAu P-1, 110; IndianBiInd (2); IntAu&W, 1976, 1977; Unesco; Who, 1959-1983; Who was who 8; WrDr, 1976/78-1984/86

Gleditsch, Nils Petter, born in 1942, he was since 1971 affiliated with the International Peace Research Institute, Oslo, and the Norwegian University of Science and Technology, Trondheim. His writings include *Krigsstaten Norge* (1970), *Rank theory, field theory, and attribute theory* (1970), *De utro tjenere* (1974), *The wages of peace* (1994), he was joint author of *Mardøla - aksjon* (1971), he edited *Peace divided* (1996), and he was joint editor of *Arms races* (1990). LC

Gleichen, Lord Albert *Edward* Wilfred, born in 1863 at London, he graduated from the Royal Military College, Sandhurst, and joined the Grenadier Guards. He served in various capacities with the Army, Intelligence, and the Foreign Service, retiring in 1919. His writings include *With the Camel Corps up the Nile* (1888), *With the Mission to Menelik, 1897* (1898), *Alphabets of foreign languages* (1921), and *A Guardsman's memories* (1932). AfrBioInd (1); Hill; WhE&EA; Who, 1903-1936; Who was who 3

Gleizes, Abbé Raymond, born 19th cent., he wrote *Jean Le Vacher, vicaire apostolique et consul de France à Tunis et à Alger* (Paris, 1914). His trace is lost after a publication in 1928. BN; NUC, pre-1956

Glennie, John Forbes, born 20 May 1912 at Singapore, he was educated at King's School, Canterbury, and the University of Bristol, where he received an M.Sc. in 1963 for *Studies of river control and regulation accompanied by a report on the Equatorial Nile Project and its effects in the Anglo-Egyptian Sudan.* He was in 1952 a divisional engineer (Upper Nile), and in 1955, chief hydrologist, with the Sudan Irrigation Department. Sluglett; *Who's who in Egypt and the Near East*, 1952, 1955

Glenny, Edward, born 19th cent., he was an honorary secretary, North African Mission, Barking, and joint author, with John Rutherfurd, of *The Gospel in North Africa* (London, 1900). His trace is lost after a publication in 1911. BLC; Note

Glick, Thomas Frederick, born 28 January 1939 at Cleveland, Ohio, he graduated in 1960 from Harvard, where he also received his Ph.D. in 1968 for *Irrigation and society in medieval Valencia.* He was since 1972 a professor of history and geography in the Department of History, Boston University. His writings include *Islamic and Christian Spain in the early middle ages* (1979). ConAu 29-32, new rev. 15; DrAS, 1969 H, 1974 H, 1978 H, 1982 H; WhoE, 1981/82

Glidden, Harold Walter, born 29 September 1910 at Rochester, N.Y., he graduated in 1932 from the University of Rochester, N.Y., and received a Ph.D. in 1937 from Princeton for *A comparative study of the Kay Kāwūs, Nimrod and Alexander ascensions in Oriental literature.* He served as a senior specialist in Arab affairs with the Bureau of Intelligence Research as well as other U.S. agencies. He was joint author of *Egyptian (National) Library* (1947). DrAS, 1969 F, 1974 F; MESA Roster of members, 1977-82

Glob, Peter Vilhelm, born 20 February 1911 at Kalundborg, Denmark, he studied at Københavns Universitet, where he also received a Dr.phil. in 1945 for *Studier over den Jyske Enkeltgravskultur.* He was a curator at the Nationalmuseet from 1937 to 1949, and a professor of archaeology in Århus Universitet from 1949 to 1960. He made repeated expeditions to the Persian Gulf and convinced the authorities of the value of archaeological research. It was partly thanks to his persuasive presence that the National Museum of Bahrain was established. His writings include *Danske oldtidsminder* (1942), and *Al-Bahrain; de Danske ekspeditioner til oldtidens Dilmun* (1968). He died in Ebeltoft, 20 July 1985. AnObit, 1985, pp. 346-47; ConAu 97-100, 117; DanskBL; IntDcAn; IntWW, 1974/75-1985/86; Kraks, 1985; WhoWor, 1974/75-1978/79

Glubb (Γκλαμπ), Sir John Bagot, born 16 April 1897 at Preston, England, he graduated from the Royal Military Academy, Woolwich, and entered the Royal Engineers. He served in Iraq from 1920 to 1926, when he resigned his commission and became an administrative inspector in the tribal districts in the Iraq Government. In 1930 he transferred to Transjordan, where he served from 1938 to 1956 as chief of the Arab Legion. He died in 1986. Biographies were published by a number of Arab academics in 1963 entitled غلوب باشا, also by James Lunt in 1982, and by Trevor Royle in 1992. ConAu 9-12, 118, new rev. 5; CurBio, 1951, 1986; DNB; EEE; IntWW, 1959-1985/86; Master (16); MidE, 1978-1982/83; Who, 1943-1985; Who was who 8; WhoWor, 1974/75, 1976/77; WrDr, 1980/82-1986/88; ZKO

Glück, Heinrich, born 11 July 1889 at Wien, he studied fine art at the Universität and travelled in the Near East before taking his doctorates in 1914 and 1923. He was a historian of Christian and Islamic art. Since 1928 he was a curator at Österreichisches Museum für Kunst und Industrie. His writings include *Der Breit- und Langhausbau in Syrien* (1916), *Die indischen Miniaturen des Hamzae-Romanes*

(1925), and he was joint author of *Die Kunst des Islam* (1925), and its translation, *Arte del Islam* (1932). He died in Wien, 24 June 1930. DtBE; Kürschner, 1925-1928/29; ÖBL; Schwarz

Glueck, Nelson, born in 1900 at Cincinnati, Ohio, he graduated from Hebrew Union College and studied at Cincinnati, Berlin, Heidelberg, and Jena. He was a professor of Biblical archaeology at Cincinnati. His writings include *The Other side of the Jordan* (1940), *The River Jordan* (1946), and *Rivers in the desert* (1949). He died in 1971. ANB; CnDiAmJBi; ConAu 17-18; CurBio, 1948, 1969, 1971; DrAS, 1969 H; Master (16); NatCAB, 56, pp. 170-171; NYT, 14 February 1971, p. 75, cols. 1-2; Shavit; WhAm, 5; WhoWorJ, 1965

Glukhoded, Vladimir Sergeevich, born 24 May 1930, he graduated in 1953 from the Moscow Oriental Institute and received his first degree in 1969 for a monograph. He was from 1963 to 1970 affiliated with the State Committee for Economic Relations (Afghanistan) and subsequently with the Ministry of Foreign Relations. His writings include *Проблемы экономического развития Ирана, 20-е - 30.е гг.* (1968). Miliband²

Glünz, Michael Thomas, born 21 June 1954 at Dauchingen, Germany, he studied at the universities of Basel and Bern, where he received a Dr.phil. in 1986 for *Die panegyrische Qasida bei Kamal ud-Din Isma'ili aus Isfahan*, a work which was published in 1993. He was successively a fellow, Schweizerischer Nationalfonds and an academic staff member, Institut für Islamwissenschaft, Bern. His other writings include *Intoxination, earthly and heavenly; seven studies on the poet Hafiz* (1991). He was a member of Schweizerische Asiengesellschaft. EURAMES, 1993; Private

Gluskina, Gita Mendelevna, born 6 July 1922 at Parichi, Belorussia, she graduated in 1949 from the Oriental Faculty, Leningrad, where she also received her first degree in 1968 for *Неизвестные рукописи сочинения Алхаризи «Тахкемони» в Государственной Публичной библиотеке имени М. Е. Салтыкова-Щедрина в Ленинграде*. She was affiliated with the Oriental Insitute in the Soviet Academy of Science since 1951 and in 1972 appointed a lecturer. Miliband; Miliband²

Glykatzi-Ahrweiler, Hélène, 1926- see Ahrweiler, Héléne

Gmelin, Julius Hermann Gotthelf, born 28 April 1859 at Ludwigsburg, he was since 1888 a pastor in Württemberg. He received a Dr.phil. in 1890. His writings include *Evangelische Freiheit* (1892), *Schuld oder Unschuld des Templerordens* (1893), and *Hällische Geschichte* (1896). He died in 1919. DtBiInd (1); Wer ist's, 1909-1912

Gnevusheva, Elizaveta Ivanovna, born in 1916 in Ukraine, she graduated in 1941 from the Faculty of History, Moscow State Pedagogical Institute, and received her first degree in 1948 for *Возникновение Всеиндийского национального конгресса*. Since 1956 she was affiliated with the Institute of Oriental Languages, Moscow State University. Her writings include *Забытый путешественник; жизнь и путешествие Петра Ивановича Пашино* (1958), and *В стране трех тысяч островов; русские ученые в Индонезии* (1962). She died 10 May 1994. Miliband; Miliband²

Gnoli, Gherardo, born 6 December 1937 at Roma, he was a professor of Iranian philology and successively affiliated with the Istituto universitario orientale di Napoli, and Istituto italiano per l'Africa e l'Oriente. His writings include *Le iscrizioni guideo-persiane del Ġūr, Afghanistan* (1964), *Richerche storiche su Sīstān antico* (1967), *The idea of Iran; essay on its origin* (1989), and he edited *Iranian studies* (1983). Wholtaly, 1998-2002

Goadby, Frédéric Maurice, born in 1875, he was in 1916 a professor at l'École sultaniyeh de droit, Cairo, and a member of the Société sultanieh d'économie politique, de statistique et de législation. His writings include *International and inter-religious private law in Palestine* (1916), and *The Land law of Palestine* (1935). Note; NUC, pre-1956

Gobeaux-Thonet, Jeanne, fl. 1932, she was from 1948 to 1953 associated with the Bibliothèque de l'Université de Liége. Note about the author

Göbel, Karl-Heinrich, born about 1950, his writings include *Moderne schiitische Politik und Staatsidee nach Taufīq al-Fukaikī, Muhammad Ġawād Muġnīya, Rūhullāh Humainī* (1984), a work which was originally presented in 1981 as his thesis at the Universität Hamburg. Note about the author; Sezgin

Gobert, Ernest Gustave, born 29 November 1879 at Charly near Château-Thierry (Aisne), he gained a medical doctorate in 1906 at Paris, and in the same year began his career at the Hôpital musulman de Tunis. After the first World War, he became *médecin de colonisation* at Mateur and Nabeul, Tunisia. From 1920 to his retirement in 1935, he was a director of Hygiène et de la Santé publique. He retired to Aix-en-Provence, where he pursued an interest in anthropology and archaeology. In 1962 he was elected a member of the Académie d'Aix-en-Provence. His writings include *Usages et rites alimen-*

taires des Tunisiens (1940), and *Le Capsien de l'abri 402* (1950). He died in Aix-en-Provence on 1 August 1973. Hommes et destins, vol. 7, pp. 211-215; Index Islamicus (1)

Gobillot, Geneviève Marie, born 3 January 1950, she received a *doctorat d'état* in Arabic and Islamic studies and was appointed a professor of Arabic and Islamic studies at Lyon in 1993. Private

de **Gobineau**, Joseph Arthur, born 14 July 1816 at Ville d'Avray, he served with the French diplomatic corps in various capitals, including Tehran (1855-58), and Athens (1864-68). He was a prolific writer of prose and poetry. His writings include *Les Religions et les philosophies dans l'Asie centrale* (1865); but he is best remembered for his *Essai sur l'inégalité des races humaines* (1853), and its translation, *The Moral and intellectual diversity of races* (1856). He died in Torino, 13 October 1882. DBF; DLB 123 (1992), pp. 101-117; EncAm; EncItaliana; IndexBFr² (4); Magyar; Master (16); MEW; Meyers; Pallas

Göbl, Robert, born in 1919 at Wien, he received a Dr.phil. in 1950 from the Universität Wien for *Die römische Reichsprägung als Quelle zur Geschichte der Kaiser Valerianus und Gallienus*. Influenced by Franz Altheim, he pursued an interest in classical numismatics, becoming in 1955 a professor in this field at his alma mater. In 1962 he went to Kabul as a Unesco expert to assist in the establishment of the coin collection in the National Museum. His writings include *Dokumente zur Geschichte der iranischen Hunnen* (1967), *Sasanische Numismatik* (1968), its translation, *Sasanian numismatics* (1971), and *A catalogue of coins from Butkara I, Swāt, Pakistan* (1976). He died in December, 1997. EncIran; Note; WhoAustria, 1964-1996

Goblet, Yann Morvan, born in 1881, he gained a *doctorat ès lettres*, and became well known for his work on political and economic geography, culminating in the chair of the geography of transport at the Conservatoire des Arts-et-Métiers, Paris. He was a great traveller and observer, keenly interested in the politics, economics and culture of the countries he visited, and with his wide and accurate knowledge he was well equipped as a correspondent of numerous journals, including *le Temps* and *le Monde*. He was in 1953 elected to the Académie des Sciences Coloniales. At the time of his death in July 1955, he was vice-president of the Société de Géographie Commerciale and of the Société d'Economie Politique, and an officer of the Légion d'Honneur. He was joint author of *La Vie politique orientale en 1909* (1910). Geographical journal 122 (1956), p. 140; NUC, pre-1956

Goblot, Henri Antoine, born early 20th cent., he received a *doctorat de 3ème cycle* in 1973 from the Université de Paris for *Histoire d'une des techniques de l'eau; les qanats*. He was an *ingénieur-conseil* whose writings include *Les qanats; une technique d'acquisition d'eau* (1979). Note; THESAM, 3

Gobronidze, Manana Georgievna, born 25 November 1949 in the Georgian Soviet Republic, she graduated in 1974 from the Oriental Faculty, Tiflis State University, and received her first degree in 1984. She was since 1977 affiliated with the Oriental Institute, Georgian Academy of Science. Her writings include *Shua saukuneebis arabuli phonetikuri theriis dzirithadi sakithebi, VIII-XIII ss.* (Tiflis, 1980), with the Russian added title Основные вопросы фонетической теории средневековых арабских яхыковедов (1980). Miliband²; OSK

Goby, Jean Édouard, fl. 1940, his writings include *Problèmes techniques de la conservation et de l'amélioration du canal de Suez* (Alexandrie, 1956), *Lexique biographique des membres de la Commission des sciences et arts et ceux du premier Institut d'Égypte, 1798-1801* (Alexandrie, 1967), and *Premier Institut d'Égypte* (1987). ZKO

Gochenour, Theodore S., born in 1933, he received a B.A. He was from 1963 to 1965 an executive director of the Fulbright Program in Afghanistan, and concurrently studied at Kabul University. In 1966 he started doctoral studies at Harvard University. Master (1); Note about the author

Godard, André, born in 1881, he was originally an architect, but subsequently became an award-winning student at l'École des Beaux-Arts de Paris. He specialized in history of art, particularly Middle Eastern art. He travelled widely in Syria and Iraq, and spent 1923 in Afghanistan as a member of the délégation française. Since the 1923/24 season he was actively engaged in Iranian archaeology and the preservation and restauration of the country's historical monuments. All in all he spent nearly thirty years in the Services archéologiques de l'Iran. His writings include *L'Art de l'Iran* (1962), and its translation, *The Art of Iran* (1965). He died in 1965. DBF; Journal asiatique 253 (1965), pp. 415-17

Godard, Jean, born 11 December 1921 at Fontainebleau (Seine-et-Marne), he graduated in 1947 from École Nationale d'Administration, and also gained a doctorate in law. In 1962 he was a *conseiller référendaire* in the Cour des Comptes. His writings include *L'Oasis moderne; essai d'urbanisme saharien* (1954), and he was joint author of *Sahara; organisation politique et administrative, droit pétrolier, régime des investissements* (1959-61). WhoFr., 1959/60-1961/62|

Godard, Léon Nicolas, l'abbé, born in 1825, his writings include *Cours d'archéologie sacrée* (Paris, 1851-54), *Soirées algériennes; corsairs, esclaves et martyrs de Barbarie* (Tours, 1857), *Le Maroc; notes d'un voyageur* (1859), *Description et histoire du Maroc* (1860), and *Espagne; mœurs et paysages, histoire et monuments* (Tours, 1862). He died in 1863. BN; NUC, pre-1956

Godard, Yedda, fl. 1972, she was a joint author of *Bronzes du Luristan, avec 33 reproductions: Collection E. Graeffe* (La Haye, 1954). NUC, 1968-1972

Godart, François Pierre Marie *Justin*, born 26 November 1871 at Lyon, he there studied and received in 1901 his doctorate in law for *L'ouvrier en soi*. He became a barrister in the Cour d'appel and concurrently taught both at the École de La Marinière and the Faculté de droit. He subsequently entered municipal and national politics, with a strong commitment to social welfare and health. His many travels abroad included visits to the French colonies. His many writings include *L'Albanie en 1921* (1922). He died in Paris on 13 December 1956. DBF; IndexBFr² (7); WhoFr, 1953/54, 1955/56

Godchot, Simon Maurice, born 14 April 1858 at Gondrecourt (Meuse), he was a graduate of the military college, Saint-Cyr, and also gained a degree in law, before entering an infantry unit, serving mainly in Algeria. He retired in 1918 with the rank of colonel. His writings include *Le 1er régiment de Zouaves, 1852-1895* (1898), and *Pages de guerre, Maroc-France, 1908-1918* (1918). He died after 1938. DBF

Godden, Gertrude M., born 20th cent., she was a contributor to the *Fortnightly*, and also wrote *Mussolini; the birth of a new democracy* (New York, 1923), *Conflict in Spain, 1920-1937* (London, 1937), and *Murder of a nation* (London, 1943). LC

Gödeke, Karl Ludwig Friedrich, 1814-1887 *see* Goedeke, Karl Ludwig Friedrich

Godel, Roger, his writings include *Cités et univers de Platon* (Le Caire, 1940), *Recherche d'une fois* (Paris, 1940), and *Terre de Socrate* (Le Caire, 1955). NUC, pre-1956

Gödel-Lannoy, E., fl. 1881, he contributed articles on Ottoman law to *Österreichische Monatsschrift für den Orient*, and also wrote *Notizen zur Orientirung in den durch den Sües-Kanal erschlossenen westasiatischen und ostafrikanischen Handelsgebieten* (Triest, 1879). GV

Godfrey, Sir Walter, born in 1907, he was a graduate of Jesus College, Cambridge, and subsequently entered the Department of Overseas Trade. He served as a UK Trade Commisioner in India, Pakistan, and Egypt. He died in 1976. Who, 1952-1976; Who was who, 7

von **Godin**, Marie *Amélie* Julie Anna, born 7 March 1882 at München, she was a novelist and translator. She visited Albania on several occasions and supported the Albanian struggle for independence. Her writings include *Aus dem neuen Albanien; politische und kulturhistorische Skizzen* (Wien, 1914), *Wörterbuch der albanischen und deutschen Sprache* (1930), as well as historical novels with Albanian themes. She died in München on 22 February 1956. DtBE; DiBiInd (1); KDtLK, Nekrolog, 1936-70

Goedeke (Gödeke), Carl Ludwig Friedrich, born in 1814 at Celle, Germany, he studied philology and history at Göttingen without taking a degree. He became a journalist who also wrote short stories as well as political poetry. In 1873 he was appointed a professor of history of literature at Göttingen. His writings include *Deutsche Dichtung im Mittelalter* (1854). He died in Göttingen on 27 October 1887. ADtB, vol. 49, pp. 422-430; DtBE; DtBiInd (4); NDB

Goehrke, Carsten, born 19 May 1937 at Hamburg, Germany, he received a Dr.phil. in 1968 from the Universität Münster for *Die Wüstungen in der Moskauer Rus'*. He was a professor of East European history at Zürich from 1971 to his retirement. His other writings include *Die Theorien über Entstehung und Entwicklung des "Mir"* (1964), and he edited *Rußland* (Frankfurt am Main, 1972), and its translation, *Russia* (Milano, 1973). Kürschner, 1976-2003

de **Goeje**, Michaël Jan, born 13 August 1836 at Dronrijp, Friesland, he studied theology and Oriental languages under Reinhart P. Dozy at Leiden, where he received a doctorate in 1860 for an edition and translation of al-Ya'qūbī's *K. al-Buldān*, entitled *Specimen e literis orientalibus*. He was a lifelong curator of Oriental manuscripts at Leiden, and the editor of a long list of Arabic works on geography and history. He is best remembered as the driving force behind the fifteen-volume Leiden edition of al-Tabari's *Annales* (1879-1901). He died 17 May 1909. BiBenelux² (5); EncIran; Fück, p. 211-216; GSE; *Index Islamicus* (4); NieuwNBW, vol. 1, cols. 946-947; Pallas

Goergens (Görgens), Ernst Peter, born 19th cent., his writings include *Mohammed, ein Charakterbild* (1878), *Islam und die moderne Kultur; ein Beitrag zur Lösung der orientalischen Frage* (1879); he and Reinhold Röhricht edited and translated from the Arabic of Abū Shāmah al-Maqdisī *Arabische Quellenbeiträge zur Geschichte der Kreuzzüge: (1) Zur Geschichte Salâh ad-dîn's* (1879).

Goerke, Franz, born 16 November 1856 at Königsberg, East Prussia, he was photographer, historian of art, a member of numerous learned societies, and a writer of illustrated German travel books. In 1918 he was a director of the Urania-Institut für Volkstümliche Naturkunde, Berlin. He died in 1931. Wer ist's, 1922, 1928

Goeseke, Gudrun, born about 1930, she was a student of Carl Brockelmann, and became affiliated with the German Oriental Society, Halle. Private

Goeseke, Horst, born 8 July 1922 at Halle/Saale, he received the education of his day and was then called to arms at the age of nineteen. He was released from a POW camp in October 1945. Since 1947 he studied Oriental languages at the Universität Halle, becoming an assistant in 1952. He received his Dr.phil. in 1954 from his alma mater for *Die Stellung des Ugaritischen innerhalb der semitischen Sprachen*. His trace is lost after a publication in 1969. He died young. Private; Schwarz; Thesis

Goetz, Hermann, born 17 July 1898 at Karlsruhe, he studied Oriental languages and fine art at München, where he received a Dr.phil. in 1923 for *Die Hoftrachten des Großmoghul-Reiches*. He subsequently worked at the Völkerkunde-Museum, Berlin, until 1931, when he accepted an invitation from the Instituut Kern at Leiden. From 1936 to 1961 he was intermittently in India, where he had been interned during the war. In 1961 he became a honorary professor in the Südasien-Institut at Heidelberg. His writings include *Indien; fünf Jahrtausende indischer Kunst* (1959), its translation, *The Art of India* (1959), and *Geschichte Indiens* (1962). He died in Heidelberg on 3 or 8 July 1976. BioIn 11; Kürschner, 1961-1976; Note; Stache-Rosen, pp. 229-230

Goetze, Albrecht Ernst Rudolf, born 11 January 1897 at Leipzig, he pursued ancient Near Eastern studies at München, Leipzig, Berlin, and Heidelberg, where he received a Dr.phil. in 1921 for *Zur relativen Chronologie von Lauterscheinungen insbesondere im Italienischen und Griechischen*, and also his Dr.habil. in 1923. He subsequently taught there until 1930, when he obtained a professorship at Marburg. Dismissed in 1933, he went in 1936 to America, where he served as a professor in his field at Yale University until his retirement in 1965. His writings include *Schatzhöhle; Überlieferung und Quellen* (1922), and *Kleinasien* (1957). He died in New Haven, Conn., on 15 August 1971. Au&Wr, 1971; BioHbDtE; BioIn 9 (3); ConAu, 33-36; DrAS, 1969; DtBE; GV; Kürschner, 1928/29-1935; NYT, 18 August 1971, p. 40, cols. 4-5; Sezgin; Shavit; WhAm, 5

Gogacz, Mieczysław, born 20th cent., he was in the 1970s affiliated with the Catholic University of Lublin. His writings include *Filozofia bytu w "Beniamin Major" Ryszarda ze Świętego Wiktora* (Lublin, 1957), *Problem istnienia Boga u Anzelma z Canterbury* (1961), and he translated into Polish Avicenna's *Dānishnāmah* entitled *Metafizyka; ze zbioru pt. Księga wiedzy* (1973). NUC

Goglia, Luigi, born in 1943 at Vico Equence, Italy, his writings include *Questione palestinese e nazionalismo arabo* (1980), *Storia fotografica dell'imperio fascista* (1985), and he was joint author of *Il colonialismo italiano da Adua all'imperio* (c1981, 1993) as well as *Mussolini, il mito* (1983). LC

Goguyer, Antonin, fl. 1890, his writings include the translation from the Arabic entitled *Pluie de rosée, étanchement de la soif, traité de flexion et syntaxe* (1887). BN; Note

Goharghi, Alfred, born 19th cent., he was in 1916 a lawyer resident in Mansurah, Egypt, and for over twelve years a member of the Société sultanieh d'économie politique, de statistique et de législation. Note about the author

Gohier, Urbain Degoulet, born 17 December 1862 at Versailles, he is well known to have been the natural son of Gustave Hervé and was adopted by one Gohier. A brilliant student at the Collège Stanislas, Paris, from 1874 to 1881, he took degrees in law and letters in 1884. Concurrently to taking courses at the Faculté, he served as a lecturer at Saint-Cyr. He was an editor and editorial writer to a variety of journals, and made the acquaintance of Zola, Clemenceau, Mirabeau, and all the celebrities of his day. He passionately fought for the re-opening of the Dreyfus case, denouncing the corruption of the République, criticizing both the Army and the Church. He delivered hundreds of lectures, and held public meetings at open universities. He travelled widely and was even a war correspondent in 1908 in Turkey, and in 1912 in the Balkans. He fought a dozen poliical court battles, some of which sensational. Twice he was aquitted in the Cour d'assises, but condemned several times to reformatory for antimilitary propaganda, serving one year at La Santé Prison, Paris. His writings include *Les Massacres d'Arménie* (1896), *La Terreure juive; le socialisme juif* (1906), and *Protocoles des sages d'Israël* (1924). He died in Saint-Satur (Cher) on 29 June 1951. Curinier, 5 (1906), pp. 245-47; DBF; DcBMOuvF, 12 (1974), p. 298; IndexBFr² (3)

Gohlman, Susan Ashley, born 22 December 1938 at Detroit, Mich. she graduated in 1961 from Western Michigan University and received a Ph.D. in 1973. She was successively a professor of

633

comparative literature at Eastern Michigan University, and Virginia Commonwealth University, Richmond. DrAS, 1978 E, 1982 E

Gohlman, William E., born 20th cent., he received a Ph.D. from the University of Michigan for *The Life of Ibn Sina; a critical edition and annotated translation*, a work which was published in 1974. LC

Goibov, Golib, born 10 September 1944 in Tajikistan, he graduated in 1967 from Tajik State University and received his first degree in 1980 for Ранние походы арабов в Среднюю Азию, 644-704 гг., a work which was published in 1989. He was since 1969 a research fellow in the Oriental Institute, Tajik Academy of Science. His writings include Мухаммад ибн Муса ал-Хорезми (1980), Мухаммад ибн Муса ал-Хорезми: Жизнь и творчество (1983), and he translated from the Arabic of Ahmad ibn Yahyá al-Balādhurī, Завоевание Хорасана (1987). Miliband²; OSK

Goichon, Amélie Marie, born in 1894 at Poitiers, she was an academic librarian first at Bordeaux and then from 1923 until her retirement at Paris. In 1938 she received doctorates from the Sorbonne for her theses, *La distinction de l'essence et de l'existence d'après Ibn Sina*, and *Lexique de la langue philosophique d'Ibn Sina*. Since 1959 she was a lecturer in contemporary history and civilization of the Arab countries at the Sorbonne. Her writings include *La vie féminine au Mzab* (1927), *La philosophie d'Avicenne et son influence en Europe médiévale* (1944), *L'eau, problème vital de la région du Jourdain* (1964), and she translated from the Arabic of Jamāl al-Dīn al-Afghānī, *Réfutation des matérialistes* (1942), and Avicenna's *Livre des directives et remarques* (1951). She died in Paris in 1977. DBF

Goicoecheva, Antonio, fl. 1966, his writings include *Alfonso XIII; epílogo de José de Yanguas Messía* (Madrid, 1965). NUC, 1973-1977

Goitein, Solomon (Shelomo) Dov Fritz, born 3 April 1900 at Burgkunstadt, Bavaria, he received the classical education of the time and gained his Dr.phil. in 1923 at Frankfurt for *Das Gebet im Koran*. Immediately thereafter he emigrated to Palestine, becoming a school-teacher at Haifa. He subsequently pursued an interest in the cultural history of the region and became a scholar of Arabic and Hebrew literature at the Hebrew University of Jerusalem. His writings include *Juifs et Arabes* (1957), *Jews and Arabs through the ages* (1964), and he edited the fifth volume of al-Balādhurī's *K. Ansāb al-ashraf*, as well as works in Hebrew. He died in Princeton, N.J., on 6 February 1985. AnObit, 1985, pp. 68-70; Bioln 15; CnDiAmJBi; ConAu, 61-64, 115, new rev., 8; DrAS, 1969 H, 1974 H, 1978 H, 1982 H; *Index Islamicus* (5); *MESA Roster of members*, 1977-1982; NYT, 10 February 1985, p. 40, cols. 4-6; WhoWorJ, 1965, 1972, 1978

Golan, Galia, born 20th cent., she was in the late 1980s a director of the Soviet and East European Research Centre at the Hebrew University of Jerusalem. Her writings include The *Soviet Union and the PLO* (1976), *Yom Kippur and after; the Soviet Union and the Middle East crisis* (1977), *Soviet policies in the Middle East* (1990), and *Moscow and the Middle East* (1992). Note; ZKO

Golan, Yona, born in 1909, she was in 1972 head of the Department of International Affairs at the Israeli Mapam. She was a joint compiler of *ha-Ishah ba-hevrah ha-modernit* (Tel-Aviv, 1966). Note

Golant, Veniamin IAkovlevich, fl. 1958, he was a geographer whose writings include Народ мудрец (1959), Планету открывали сообща (1971), and he was a joint author of Здесь, в самом сердце Африки (1965). NUC, 1956-1972

Golb, Norman, born 15 January 1928 at Chicago, he graduated in 1948 from Roosevelt College and received a Ph.D. in 1954 from Johns Hopkins University, Baltimore, Md. After teaching posts at a variety of American universities he became a professor of Hebrew and Judeo-Arabic studies at the University of Chicago. He was a joint author of *Khazarian Hebrew documents of the tenth century* (1982). CnDiAmJBi; DrAS, 1969 H, 1972 H, 1974 H, 1982 H

Golbert, Albert Sidney, born 26 November 1932 at Denver, Colo., he graduated in 1954 from the University of Southern California, and subsequently gained law degrees at the universities of Denver, Michigan, and Genève. He was an international attorney and a sometime member of the U.S. Supreme Court. Master (3); WhoAm, 1978/79-1988/89; WhoWor, 1980/81, 1982/83

Golczewski, Frank, born 8 October 1948 at Katowice, Poland, he received a Dr.phil. in 1973 and a Dr.habil. in 1979. He was successively a professor of East European history at Osnabrück and Hamburg. His writings include *Das Deutschlandbild der Polen, 1918-1939* (1974), a work which was originally presented as a thesis. Kürschner, 1983-2003; WhoWor, 1987/88, 1991/92

Gold, Martin, born in 1928, he was a longtime activist in Jewish and political affairs. Although not trained as an academic, his fascination for books and his passionate commitment to politics and history led him to research and write extensively on the Middle East. He died 27 March 1997. *MESA bulletin* 32 (1998), pp. 137-138

Goldberg, Arnold Maria, born 28 February 1928 at Berlin, he received a Dr.phil. in 1957 from the Universität Freiburg im Breisgau for *Die ägyptischen Elemente in der Sprache des Alten Testaments*, and also a Dr.habil. in 1965 for *Untersuchungen über die Vorstellung von der Schekhinah in der frühen rabbinischen Literatur*. He was in 1970 appointed a professor of Old Testament studies at the Universität Frankfurt am Main. His writings include *Das Buch Numeri* (1970). He died on 19 April 1991. Kürschner, 1980-1992

Goldberg, Arthur Joseph, born in 1908 at Chicago, he was a member of the Supreme Court of the United States, a U.S. representative to the U.N., and a professor of law. His writings include *AFL-CIO; labor united* (1956), *The Defenses of freedom* (1966), and *Equal justice* (1971). He died in Washington, D.C., on 19 January 1990. AnObit, 1990, pp. 29-31; CnDiAmJBi; Master (90); WhoAm, 1986/87-1988/90; *Who was who*, 8; WhoWorJ, 1965

Goldberg, Ellis Jay, born about 1950, he received a Ph.D. in 1983 from the University of California, Berkeley, for *Tinker, tailor, and textile worker; class and politics in Egypt, 1930-1954*, a work which was published in 1986. He was since 1990 a professor of political science in the University of Washington at Seattle, a post which he still held in 2003. In 1996 he edited *The Social history of labor in the Middle East*. MESA *Roster of members*, 1990; NatFacDr, 1995-2003; Note; Selim²

Goldberg, Harvey Ellis, born 16 May 1939 at Brooklyn, N.Y., he graduated in 1961 from Columbia University, and received his Ph.D. in 1967 from Harvard for *Acculturation, continuity and youth in an Israeli immigrant village*. He was a professor of anthropology at the University of Iowa, before he became a professor of sociology at the Hebrew University, Jerusalem. His writings include *Cave dwellers and citrus growers; a Jewish community in Libya and Israel* (1972). AmM&WS, 1973 S; ConAu, 45-48, new rev., 25; MESA *Roster of members*, 1977-1990; NUC, 1968-1972

Golden, Peter Benjamin, born 17 July 1941 at N.Y.C., he graduated in 1963 from Queen's College, and received his Ph.D. in 1970 from Columbia University for *The Q'azars; their history and languages as reflected in Islamic, Byzantine, Caucasian, Hebrew and Old Russian sources*. He was since 1974 a professor of history at Rutgers University, Newark, N.J. He was a member of the Turkish Studies Association. DrAS, 1974 H, 1978 H, 1982 H; NatFacDr, 1995; Schoeberlein; Selim

Gol'denberg, Abram Markovich *see* Argo, Abram M., pseud.

Goldenberg, Gideon, born 20th cent., he received a Ph.D. in 1966 from the Hebrew University, Jerusalem, for *Maa'rekhet ha-zemanim ha-amharit*, with the added title, *The Amharic tense-system*. NUC

Gol'denberg, Leonid Arkad'evich, his writings include *Russian maps and atlases as historical sources* (1971), *Михаил Федорович Соймонов, 1730-1804* (1973), *Каторжанин - сибирский губернатор; жизнь и труды Ф. И. Соймонова* (1979), and he edited *Первые русские научные исследования Устюрта* (1963). OSK

Goldfeld, Isiah, born 20th cent., he received a Ph.D. in 1969 from Cambridge University for *The tribal policy of the Prophet Muhammad*. Private; Sluglett

Goldfine, Yitzhak, born 13 September 1936 in Haifa, Palestine, he studied law at the Hebrew University, Jerusalem, and received a Dr.phil. in 1967 from the Universität Frankfurt am Main for *Herkunft und Quellen des gegenwärtigen israelischen Rechts*. His other writings include *Jüdisches und israelisches Eherecht* (1975). Thesis

Goldie, Sir George Dashwood Taubman, born in 1846 on the Isle of Man, he was educated at the Royal Military Academy, Woolwich. He became a British colonial administrator, and an expert on Niger questions. He died in 1925. John Ed. Flint wrote *Sir George Goldie and the making of Nigeria* (1960), and D. J. M. Muffet wrote *Empire builder extraordinary, Sir George Goldie* (1978). AfrBioInd (2); DNB; Master (1); Who, 1903-1924; *Who was who*, 2

Goldie, Henry Mountford, born in the last quarter of the nineteenth century. Before the first World War, he worked in a bank in Egypt. He fought in France until 1917 when he was sent to the Hejaz. He reported on tribal matters for the *Arab bulletin*. R.L. Bidwell, *Arab bulletin* 1 (1986 reprint), p. xxvi

Goldman, Bernard Marvin, born 30 May 1922 at Toronto, Ont., he received a Ph.D. in 1958 from the University of Michigan for *Oriental influences on Etruscan bronzes*. He was since 1966 a professor of ancient Near Eastern art at Wayne State University, where he became the director of their University Press in 1974. DrAS, 1969 H; WhoAm, 1976/77,1988/89

Goldman, Bosworth, fl. 1933, his writings include *Red road through Asia; a journey to Central Asia and Armenia* (London, 1934). NUC, pre-1956

Goldman, S., born 20th cent., he was in 1934 affiliated with the Glasgow Oriental Society, and received a D.Phil. in 1936 from Oxford University for *The development of historical writing among the Moslems in Spain*. Sluglett

Goldmann, Nahum, born 10 July 1894 at Visznevo (Wisnowo), he studied at Marburg, Berlin, and Heidelberg. He was a Zionist leader and from 1953 to 1977 a president of the World Jewish Congress. His writings include *Erez-Israel; Reisebriefe aus Palästina* (1914), *Der Geist des Militarismus* (1915), *The Reminiscences* (1975), and *Mein Leben als deutscher Jude* (1980). He died in Bad Reichenhall on 29 August 1982. AnObit, 1982, pp. 414-16; CnDiAmJB; DtBE; EncJud; Master (52); MidE, 1982/83; *Who was who*, 8; WhoWorJ, 1965, 1972, 1978

Goldobin, Aleksei Mikhailovich, born 26 June 1924 at Psikov (Pihkav), he graduated in 1950 from the Oriental Faculty, Leningrad, and received his first degree in 1953 for *Английские колонизаторы в Египте и мартовское восстание 1919 года*. He became a lecturer in 1961 and was from 1963 to 1972 affiliated with the Oriental Faculty, Leningrad. His writings include *Египетская революция 1919 года* (1958), *Социально-экономическое развитие арабских стран* (1966), *Национально-освободительная борьба народа Египта, 1918-1936 гг.* (1989), and he edited *История стран зарубежной Азии в средние века* (1970). Miliband²; OSK

Goldsack, William, Rev., born 19th cent., he was affiliated with the Christian Literature Society for India. His writings include *Christ in Islám* (London, 1905), *The Qur'án in Islám* (London, 1906), *The Origins of the Qur'án* (London, 1907), *God in Islám* (London, 1908), *Muhammad in Islám* (Madras,1916), *The Traditions in Islám* (Madras, 1919), and *A Mussulmani Bengali-English dictionary* (Calcutta, 1923). Note; NUC, pre-1956

Goldschmidt, Arthur Edward, born 17 March 1938 at Washington, D.C., he obtained a Ph.D. in 1968 from Harvard for his thesis, *The Egyptian Nationalist Party*. From the early 1970s until his retirement in 2000 he was a professor of Middle East history at Pennsylvania State University. Apart from his research on Egypt, Israel, and Turkey - his *Concise history of the Middle East* was a best-selling textbook in the field - he was equally concerned about biographical dictionaries of the area. His writings include *Modern Egypt* (1988), *The memoirs and diaries of Muhammad Farid* (1992), and *Historical dictionary of Egypt* (1994). His *Historical dictionary of modern Egypt* (2000) stands as a biographical pharos by which the work of others will be measured for a long time to come. DrAS, 1974 H, 1978 H, 1982 H; Private; Selim

Goldschmidt, Lazarus, born 17 December 1871, he studied Oriental languages at Berlin, particularly Ethiopic. He emigrated to the UK in the 1930s. His writings include *Bibliotheca æthiopica* (1893), *Die abessinischen Handsschriften der Stadtbibliothek zu Frankfurt am Main* (1897), and he was the translator of a German Koran in 1916. He died 18 April 1950. GV; *Isis*, 42 (1951), p. 146; NYT, 19 April 1950, p. 29, col. 4; Wininger

Goldsmid, Sir Frederick John, born in 1818 at Milano, he was educated privately, but also at King's College, London. Originally commissioned in the East India Company's Madras Native Infantry but after service in China transferred to the civilian establishment. He served many years in Sind. From 1861 to 1870, he was almost continously employed on Indo-European Telegraph work, and from 1871 to 1872 he served as Makran and Sistan Boundary Commissioner. He was a brilliant linguist whose writings include *Central Asia and its question* (1873), *Eastern Persia; an account of the journeys of the Persian Boundary Commission, 1870-72* (1887), and *James Outram; a biography* (1880). He died in 1908. Buckland; DNB; Henze; Riddick; *Who was who*, 1; Wright

Goldstein, Bernard Raphael, born 24 January 1938 at N.Y.C., he received a Ph.D. in 1963 from Brown University for his thesis, *The commentary of Ibn al-Muthanna to the astronomical tables of al-Khwarizmi*. He taught history of science and medicine at Yale University until 1973, when he was appointed a professor of Jewish studies at the University of Pittsburgh. His writings include *On the principles of astronomy; an edition of the Arabic and Hebrew versions, with translation from al-Bitrūjī* (1971), *The Astronomical tables of Levi ben Gerson* (1974), he was joint author of *Levi Ben Gershon's prognostication for the conjunction of 1345* (1990). ConAu, 57-60; NatFacDr, 1995-1999; Selim

Goldstücker, Theodor, born 18 January 1821 at Königsberg, he studied Oriental languages at Königsberg, Bonn, and again Königsberg, where he gained a doctorate. He studied Sanskrits manuscripts in Paris before going in 1850 to London. From 1851 to his death on 6 March 1872 he was a professor of Sanskrit at University College. Stache-Rosen, pp. 56-57

Goldziher, Ignaz (Isaak Jehudah), born 22 June 1860 at Stuhlweissenburg (Szekesfehervar), Hungary. "He was the greatest Hungarian Islamicist of his day, and one of the profoundest and most original scholars in Europe in an age that produced veritable giants in this field." However, he did not

636

attain a full stipendiary chair in his homeland until he was fifty-five years of age. His *Tagebuch*, which was published in 1977, "was hardly intended for undoctored publication, and it might well have been better had it in fact never been exposed to general view" (G. M. Wickens). Suffice it to mention the English translations of his books: *A Short history of Classical Arabic* literature (1966), *Muslim studies* (1967-1971); and *The Zahiris* (1971). At the time of writing an English translation of his *Richtungen der islamischen Koranauslegung* was been prepared by W. H. Behn. He died in Budapest on 14 November 1921. Róbert Simon wrote *Ignaz Goldziher, his life and scholarship as reflected in his works and correspondence* (1986). EncJud.; Fück, pp. 226-231; GeistigeUng; *Index Islamicus* (15); Magyar; MagyarZL; Pallas; RNL; TatarES; UjLex; Wininger

Golenishchev, Vladimir Semenovich, born in 1856 at St. Petersburg. He was an Egyptologist who left Russia in 1915 to work in Egypt, where he was sometime professor of Egyptology at Cairo University. He died in 1947. Egyptology; GSE

Goliger (Golinger), Moses, born about 1900, he received a Dr.phil. in 1922 from the Universität Wien for *Der Nachdruck in der nordsemitischen Syntax*. Both Schwarz and GV also know of a Moses Golinger who received a Dr.phil. in the same year from the same university, entitled *Die T-Nomina oder die ursemitische Wortbildung*. *Index Islamicus*, 1906-1955; Sezgin

Golino, Frank Ralph, born 26 October 1936 at Erie, Pa., he graduated in 1957 from Gannon College, and received an M.A. in 1960 from Fordham University, New York. He was a sometime foreign service officer with the Bureau of Inter-African Affairs. Master (2); *MESA Roster of members*, 1977-1990; Note; WhoAm, 1984/85, 1986/87; WhoE, 1979/80-1985/86

Golitsyn (Galitzin), Emmanuil Mikhailovich, born a Russian prince, 4 January 1804 at Paris. After completing his education in Paris, he went to St. Petersburg to become an officer in the Russian army. Severely wounded at Varna during the Turco-Russian war, he had to retire from the military soon after his return to St. Petersburg on account of his injuries. He devoted the rest of his life to the arts, travel and writing. He returned to Paris, where he became a member of the Société de géographie almost since its foundation. He translated Russian works into French, and wrote articles, notably for *Nouvelles annales de voyages* and *Annales forestières*. He was in the course of preparing the publication of *Aperçu de l'état social et politique de la Russie, de l'Espagne et de la France au milieu du XVIIe siècle* when he caught a cold while researching in the Bibliothèque Mazarine which, at that time, was still unheated, and died within a few days on 1 February 1853 at Quai Malaquais n° 1, where, by curious coincident, he had been born. His writings include *La conteur russe* (1846), *La Finlande* (1852), *La Russie du XVII siècle* (1855), and the translation *Sept ans en Chine*, by Peter Dobell (1842). *Bulletin de la Société de géographie*, 4e série, 6 (1853), pp. 373-378

Golius (Gool), Jacobus, born in 1596 at den Haag, he studied medicine, mathematics and astronomy at Leiden. His interest in the scientific legacy of the ancient Greeks, led him to the study of Oriental languages, particularly Arabic. In 1622 he had the chance to accompany an ambassador to Morocco in the service of the Staten Generaal. He returned to Leiden in 1624. When later in the year his teacher, Th. Erpenius, died, he succeeed him in the chair of Arabic. Only a year later his authorities granted him another leave of absence to travel in the East and acquire manuscripts. He spent a year and a half in Aleppo, visited Antioch (Antakya) as well as other cities of Syria, accompanied Turkish troops on their march against the Persians in Mesopotamia, and returned in 1629 to Leiden by way of Asia Minor and Constantinople. He brought back 250 manuscripts for the Leiden library. Apart from his Arabic teaching he held a cross appointment for mathematics, posts which he held unil his death in 1667. Apart from Arabic readers and a grammar, he is best remembered for his *Lexicon Arabico-Latinum* (1653). EncIran; Fück, pp. 79-84; Juynboll; NieuwNBW, vol. 10 (1937), cols. 287-89

Gollancz, Sir Hermann, born 30 November 1852 at Bremen, Germany, he studied at Jews College, London, and subsequently served at several English synagoges as a rabbi. After obtaining a doctorate in 1900 at London, he was appointed in 1902 a professor of Hebrew at University College. His writings include *Chronicle of events between the years 1623 and 1733 relating to the settlement of the Order of Carmelites in Mesopotamia* (1927). He died in 1930. DNB; JewEnc; JüdLex; *Who was who*, 3

Göllner, Carl/Carlos/Carol, born 5 October 1911 at Mediaş, Transylvania, he studied at Cluj (Kolozsvár) and received a Dr.phil. in 1934 from the Universität Wien for *Das Revolutionsjahr 1848 in den rumänischen Fürstentümern im Spiegel der siebenbürgisch-sächsichen Zeitungen*. In 1967 he received a second doctorate in Romania. He was a secondary school-teacher before he was appointed in 1970 a professor of history at the University of Sibiu. His writings include *Turcica; die europäischen Türckendrucke des XVI. Jahrhunderts* (Bucureşti, 1941-1958), *Michael der Tapfere im Lichte des Abendlandes* (Hermannstadt, 1943), and *Turcica, 3; die Türkenfrage in der öffentlichen Meinung Europas im 16. Jahrhundert* (Bucureşti, 1978). GV; WhoRom; WhoWor, 1974/75, 1976/77

Golobutskiĭ, Vladimir Alekseevich *see* Holobuts'kyĭ Volodymyr Oleksiĭovych

Golombek, Lisa Beth, born 27 November 1939, she was a graduate of Barnard College, and received a Ph.D. in 1968 from the University of Michigan. Thereafter she was a curator of the West Asian Collection at the Royal Ontario Museum, Toronto, and concurrently a professor in the University of Toronto. Her writings include *The Timurid shrine at Gazur Gah* (1969), and, with Donald N. Wilber, *The Timurid architecture of Central Asia and Iran* (1987); she was joint editor of *Timurid art and culture; Iran and Central Asia in the fifteenth century* (1992). DrASCan, 1983; *MESA Roster of members*; 1977-1990; Schoeberlein

Golovin, IUliĭ Mikhailovich, born 28 April 1927 at Vladimir, Russia, he received his first degree in 1961 for *Развитие внешнеэкономических связей Афганистана после второй мировой войны*. He was since 1953 affiliated with В.Н.И.К.И. His writings include *Афганистан; экономика и внешняя торговля* (1962), *Советский Союз и Афганистан; опыт экономического сотрудничества* (1962), *Марокко* (1964), and *Развтие обрабатыважщей промышленности в странах Ближнего и Среднего Востока,1946-1965 гг.* (1966). Miliband²

Gölpınarlı, Abdülbaki, born in 1900 at Constantinople, he was particularly noted for his study of Turkish Sufi orders, many of which he joined without remaining in any of them for long. His writings include *Yunus Emre* (1936). Between 1942 and 1946 he edited Mevlâna Rumî's *Mesnevi*. He died in Istanbul in 1982. AnaBrit; EncIran; Meydan; Necatigil

Goltz, Bogumil, born 20 March 1801 at Warszawa,he tried his hand at farming before embarking on a career as a writer. After his first literary success, *Buch der Kindheit* (1847), he travelled in Europe and Egypt, supporting himself by lectures and travel accounts. His other writings include *Ein Kleinstädter in Ägypten; eine Reise* (1853). He died in Toruń (Thorn) on 12 November 1870. ADtB, vol. 9, pp. 353-55; DtBE; DtBIlnd (2); Master (2)

von der Goltz, Wilhelm Leopold *Colmar*, born 12 August 1843 at Bielkenfeld, East Prussia. When he received his first commission, he was a lieutenant of modest means who supplemented his pay as a writer of short stories under the pseudonym W. von Dünheim. After serving in the Franco-Prussian war of 1870-71, he successively became a lecturer in the historical department of the general staff, and the war college. In 1883 he was appointed head of military training at Constantinople, a post which he held for thirteen years. After returning home, he was promoted through general officer grades, becoming lieutenant general in 1908, at which time he returned to Turkey for a two-year tour of duty. As general field marshall he was appointed military governor of the occupied portion of Belgium in 1914. In the autumn of 1914 he returned to Turkey as aide-de-camp-general to the Sultan, whom he advised on the defence of the Dardanelles. In 1915 he became commander of the 1st Turkish Army, which besieged General Charles Townshend at Kut al-Amarah, but died of typhoid fever in Baghdad, 19 April 1916, before the surrender. He was a man of exceptional physical and psychological resistance. His writings include *Das Volk in Waffen* (1883), its translations into French (1884), English (1887), Spanish, and Chinese (1926), *Ein Ausflug nach Macedonien* (1894), *Anatolische Ausflüge* (1896), *Der thessalonische Krieg und die türkische Armee* (1898), its translations into Greek (1899), and Turkish (1910), *Der jungen Türkei Niederlage und die Möglichkeit ihrer Wiedererhebung* (1913), and its translation *La défait de la jeune Turquie et la possibilité de son relèvement* (1913). *Deutsche Rundschau* 156 (1913), pp. 301-305; DtBE; DtBIlnd (13); EEE; EncAm; GSE; *Index Islamicus* (3); Master (1); Meydan; Meyers; *Wer ist's*, 1909-1912; WhoMilH

Golubeva, Ninel' Petrovna, born 31 December 1933 at Moscow, she graduated in 1956 from the Faculty of Philology, Moscow, and received her first degree in 1974 for *Синтагматические связи переходного турецкого глагола*. From 1958 to her death on 23 November 1979 she was affiliated with the Oriental Institute of the Soviet Academy of Sciences. Her writings include *Турецко-русскии словарь* (1977). Miliband²

Golubeva, Ol'ga Dmitrievna, fl. 1955, her writings include *Горький - издатель* (1968), *В. Д. Бонч-Бруевич - издатель* (1972), *На полках Публичной Библиотеки* (1978), and she edited *Рукописные фонды Ленинградских хранилищ* (1970). LC; OSK

Golubovich, Girolamo, born in 1865 at Constantinople to a Dalmatian family. He was a Franciscan missionary and a sometime lecturer in Greek at Limasol and Aleppo. His writings include *Serie cronologica dei reverendissimi superiori di Terra Santa* (1898), and *I frati minori nel possesso de' luoghi santi di posseduti dai Greco-Elleni* (1922). He died in Firenze in 1941. Chi è, 1928-1940; IndBIltal (3); DizBI

Golubovskaia, Elena Karlovna, born 12 January 1927 at Moscow, she graduated in 1952 from the Faculty of History, Moscow State University and received her first degree in 1967 from the Institute of the Peoples of Asia, Soviet Academy of Sciences for *Социально-экономические и политические предпосылки революции 1962 г. в Йемене*. Since 1956 she was affiliated with the Oriental Institute of the Soviet Academy of Sciences. Her writings include Йемен (1965), Револжция 1962 г. и Йемене (1971), and Политическое развитие Йеменской Арабской Республики, 1962-1985 гг. (1989). Miliband; Miliband²

Golvin, Jacques, born 20th cent., he was joint author of *Thulâ; architecture et urbanisme* (1984). ZKO

Golvin, Lucien, born 20th cent., his writings include *Aspects de l'artisanat en Afrique du Nord* (1957), *Le Magrib central à l'époque des Zirides* (1957), *La Mosquée; ses origines* (1960), *Essai sur l'architecture religieuse musulmane* (1974), *La Madrasa médiévale* (1995), and he was joint author of *Islamic architecture in North Africa; a photographic survey* (1976), and *Thulâ; architecture et urbanisme* (1984). Livres disponibles, 2003; ZKO

Gomane, Jean Pierre, born 20th cent., he was a director of the Centre des hautes études sur l'Afrique et de l'Asie moderne, and a founding member of the Institut du Pacifique. His writings include *Les Marins et l'outre-mer* (1988), and *L'Exploration du Mékong* (1994). Livres disponibles, 2003

Gombár, Eduard, born 14 October 1952 at Hranice, Moravia, he studied history, philosophy, and Arabic at Universita Karlova, Praha, where he also received a Ph.Dr. in 1981. His writings include *Moderní dějiny islámských zemí* (1999). Filipsky

Gombar, William, born 20th cent., he was with the U.S. Department of Health, Education and Welfare as a program officer for the Middle East, before he joined Lackawanna Junior College in Scranton, Pa., as a dean. Note about the author

Gombocz, Zoltán, born 18 June 1877 at Ödenburg (Sopron), Austria-Hungary, he studied at Budapest, where he received a doctorate in 1900 and subsequently joined Budapest University as a lecturer in phonetics and philology. His writings include *Az altáji nyelvek hangtörténetéhez* (1905), *Die bulgarisch-türkischen Lehnwörter in der ungarischen Sprache* (1912), and *Magyar etymologiai szótár* (1914-30). He died in Budapest on 1 May 1935. GeistigeUng; Index Islamicus (1), Magyar; Ungarische Jahrbücher 15 (1936), pp. 367-75, reprinted in PorLing, v. 2, pp.437-447

Gomboev, Galsan, born in 1822, he was a professor at a Siberian university. He died in 1863. In Ulan-Ude, Buryat Republic, Eastern Siberia, there is now the Arkhiv zasak-lamy Galsana Gomboeva, which is the subject of a Russian monograph by Georgiĭ Nikitich Rumiantsev (1959). EnSlovar

Gombos, Károlyi, born 2 January 1924 at Debrecen, Hungary, he was a trained teacher and became a director of museums. His writings, partly under the name Károlyi Gink, include *Régi Kaukazusi Azerbajdzsán szönyegek = Old Caucasian Azerbaijan rugs* (1977) *Régi anatóliai szönyegek* (1982), and *Aszkéták, dervisek, imaszönyegek* (1985). He died in Budapest on 9 January 1987. MEL, 1978-1991; WhoSoCE, 1989

Gomel, Charles, born in 1843 at Paris, he was a civil servant and a business executive who contributed to several periodicals. His writings include *Les causes financières de la Révolution française* (1892-93), and *Histoire financière de l'Assemblée constituante* (1896-97). He died in Paris on 15 January 1922. DBF

Gomez Aparicio, Pedro, born 1 August 1903 at Madrid, he studied liberal arts at the Universidad Central, Madrid, and became a journalist and editor. His writings include *Hacia una nueva guerra* (1948),*Una terceca guerra universel?* (1951), *España y el mondo árabe* (1952), *El Oriente Medio, en crucijada del mundo* (1956), and *Historia del periodismo español* (1957). Figuras, 1950; IndiceE³ (8); WhoSpain, 1963

Gómez Camarero, Marla del Carmen, born 20th cent., she received a diploma in Semitic philology, with particular reference to modern and contemporary Arabic literature. She was in 1992 affiliated with the Universidad de Granada. Her writings include *Estudios árabes contemporáneos* (1990). Arabismo, 1992

Gómez-Moreno y Martínez, Manuel, born 21 February 1870 at Granada, he received a doctorate from the Universidad Central, Madrid, and became a professor of history and fine art at the Centro de Estudios Históricos, and the Universidad Central. He was also an archaeologist, and art critic. His writings include *De arqueología mozárabe* (1913), *Alhambra* (1914), *Iglesias mozárabes* (1919), *Renaissance sculpture in Spain* (1931), and *Breve historia de la escultura español* (1935). He died in Madrid, 7 June 1970. BioIn, 9; Figuras, 1950; Index Islamicus (2); IndiceE³ (6); OxSpan; WhAm, 5; WhoSpain, 1963

Gómez Nogales, Salvador, born in 1913, he was a Jesuit who received a doctorate in philosophy from the Pontificia Università Gregoriana, Roma. He was a professor of metaphysics (ontology) at the Facultad de Filosofia de Alcalá de Henares, Madrid. His writings include *Horizonte de la metafisica aristotelica* (1955), and *La politica como unica ciencia religiosa en al-Farabi* (1980). He died in 1987. Index Islamicus (1); Note about the author

Gómez Renau, María de Mar, born 20th cent., she received a doctorate in Semitic philology, and was throughout the 1990s a professor at the Universidad de Valladolid. Her writings include *Los Moriscos* (1987). Arabismo, 1992, 1994, 1997

Gommans, Jozef Johannes Leon, born 1 April 1963 at Venlo, the Netherlands, he received a doctorate from the Rijksuniversiteit te Leiden on the Afghan state formation and the India trade in the eighteenth century. His writings include *The Rise of the Indo-Afghan empire, 1710-1780* (1995). He was since 1992 a research fellow at the Instituut Kern, Leiden. Brinkman's; Private

Gompert, A. V., M.C., B.E., born about 1880, he passed through the Royal Military Academy at Woolwich and was gazetted as a second lieutenant in the Royal Engineers in 1908. After a further two years of instruction at the School of Military Engineering at Chatham, he sailed for India and was posted to Quetta. With the rank of major he spent years on the Indian frontier. In 1918 he was awarded the prize essay of the United Service Institution of India. Asia, February 1931; NUC, pre-1956

Gonçalves, Aniceto dos Reis, 1840-1914 *see* Gonçalves Vianna, Aniceto dos Reis

Gonçalves, José Julio, born 19 January 1929 at Pampilhosa da Serra, Portugal, he became a professor of missions and social policy at the Instituto Superior de Estudos Ultramarinos, Lisboa. His writings include *O mundo árabo-islâmico e o ultramar português* (1958), *O islamismo na Guiné portuguesa* (1961), *Síntese religiosa de Africa* (1961), and *A informação na Guiné* (1966). Unesco

Gonçalves Vianna, Aniceto dos Reis, born in 1840, he was a philologist whose writings include *Vocabulário ortográfico e ortoépico da lingua portuguesa* (1909). At the 1892 Lisbon International Congress of Orientalist he read the paper "Simplification possible de la composition en caractères arabes." He died in 1914. NUC, pre-1956

Gonda, Jan, born 14 April 1905 at Gouda, the Netherlands, he studied philology at Utrecht, where he also received a doctorate in 1929 for *Δείκνυμι; semantische studie over den indo-germaanschen wortel deik*. He was a professor of Indo-Iranian philology at Utrecht, to which Indonesian was added later. His writings include *Austrisch en Arisch* (1932), *De indische letterkunde en haar betekenis voor uns* (1937), *Kurze Elementar-Grammatik der Sanskrit-Sprache* (1941), *Het Boeddhisme* (1943), and *De indische godsdiensten* (1955). In 1972 he was honoured by *India maior; congratulatory volume presented to J. Gonda*. BioB134; WhoNL, 1962/63; Wie is dat, 1948, 1956; Wie is wie, 1984/88

Gonsalès (Gonzales), Antoine, born 17th cent., at Malines (Mechelen), Belgium, he was a Franciscan priest who travelled in Egypt and Syria from 1665 to 1668. His writings include *Hiervsalemsche reyse van den Eerw. Pater P. Anthonius Gonsales* (Antwerpen, 1673), and its translation, *Voyage en Egypte*, traduit du néerlandais et annoté par Charles Libois (1977). BioNBelg, vol. 8 (1884-85), cols. 107-8; Benelux (3)

Gonţa, Alexandru I., born in 1918 at Glodeni (Gãseni), Bessarabia, he studied theology and law and became a professor at Iaşi University. He died in 1977. DcEnc; WhoRom

de Gonzague, Louis, born in 1820, he was a Franciscan priest who wrote *Les écrivains de l'Ordre de Prémontré* (1884), and *Esquisse de l'histoire littéraire de l'Ordre de Prémontré* (1888). He died in 1892. NUC, pre-1956

Gonzales, Antoine, 17th cent. *see* Gonsalès, Antoine

González Echegaray, Carlos, born 20th cent., his writings include *Morfología y sintaxis de la lengua bujeba* (Madrid, 1960), and *Historia del Africa negra* (Madrid, 1974). NUC, 1973-77

González Garbín, Antonio, born 19th cent., he received a doctorate and successively became a professor of Greek and Latin at the universities of Granada and Madrid. In 1886, at the opening of the academic year at Granada, he delivered an address on Aryan philology. EncicUni; IndiceE³ (3); NUC

González Palencia, Cándido *Angel*, born in 1889, he was a professor at the Universidad de Madrid, and a scholar of Arabic and Spanish literature as well as folklore. He edited *K. Taqwīm al-dhihn*, of Abū al-Salt Umayyah ibn 'Abd al-'Azīz (1915); his other writings include *Historia de la España musulmana* (1925), *Historia de la literatura arábigo-española* (1928), *El Islam y Occidente* (1931), and *España del siglo de oro* (1940). He died in 1949 in a traffic accident. DcSpL; *Index Islamicus* (1); IndiceE³ (5); *Isis*, 41 (1950), p. 56

Gonzalo Maeso, David, born 8 July 1902 at Hontoria de la Cantera (Burgos), he became a professor of Hebrew at the Universidad de Granada. He also was a sometime civil controller (*interventor civil adjunto*) of the Protectorate of Spain in Morocco, and a joint founder of the periodical, *Miscelánea de estudios árabes y hebraicos*. His writings include *Grandeza del pueblo hebreo* (1952), *Introducción a la filosofía* (1960), *Granāta al-Yahūd; Granada en la historia del judaismo español* (1963), *El tema del* *amor en los poetas hebraicoespañoles medievales* (1971), *El legato del judaismo español* (1972), and *La piel en las lenguas y las literaturas iberopeninsulares del medievo* (1975). IndiceE³ (2); WhoSpain, 1963

Gonzalvo, Luis, born 19th cent., his writings include the booklet, *La mujer musulmana en España* (Madrid, 1906). NUC, pre-1956

von **Gonzenbach**, Carl, born 19th cent., he wrote *Nilfahrt*; mit 203 Illustrationen im Text von Rafaello Mainella (Stuttgart, 1890), its translation, *Viaje por el Nilo* (1890), and *Pilgerritt; Bilder aus Palästina und Syrien*, mit Illustrationen von Rafaello Mainella (Berlin, 1896). Sezgin

Gooch, Brison Dowling, born 1 March 1925 at Bar Harbor, Me., he graduated in 1949 from Miami University and received a Ph.D. in 1955. He became a professor of modern European history. Since 1973 he taught a Texas A. & M. University. His writings include *Napoleon III, man of destiny* (1963), *Interpreting Western civilization* (1969), *The Origins of the Crimean War* (1969), and *Europe in the nineteenth century* (1970). DrAS, 1974 H, 1978 H, 1982 H; WrDr, 1976/78-1996/98|

Gooch, George Peabody, O.M., C.H., F.B.A., D.Litt., born in 1873, he studied successively at King's College, London, and Trinity College, Cambridge, and in German and French universities. He did not choose a university appointment. Financially secure, he rejoiced in that fact but saw that it meant he must make the greater contribution to society than otherwise he might. For forty-nine years he held the editorship of the *Contemporary review*. From 1906 to 1910, he sat in the House of Commons as a Liberal. He was blessed with a prodigious memory and wrote biographical articles adorned by perfect English. He died on 31 August 1968. DNB; GrBr; Master (20); Who, 1948-1969; *Who was who*, 8

Good, Mary-Jo DelVecchio, born 20th cent., she received a Ph.D. in sociology and Middle Eastern studies from Harvard. She spent two years with the Peace Corps, did sociological research in an Iranian town, and was a consultant on rural health care projects in Iran with the World Health Organization. In 1978, she taught medical sociology in the Department of Psychiatry, the University of California at Davis, a post which she still held in 1990. *MESA Roster of* members, 1982-1990; Note

Goodacre, Hugh J., born about 1945, he was since the 1970s a librarian for Arabic at the British Museum. In 1995 he was head of its Arabic Section. He was joint author of the *Guide to the Department of Oriental Printed Books and Manuscripts* (1977), and *Arabic language collection in the British Library* (1984). Private

Goodall, Norman, born in 1896 at Birmingham, he received a Ph.D. and became a clergy, but he is best remembered for his service to the ecumenical movement. He was a secretary of the Joint Committee of the International Missionary Council and the World Council of Churches. In 1956, he attended the Conference on Arab Refugees in Beirut, and paid and extensive visit to the Near East. His writings include *A History of the London Missionary Society* (1954), and *Christian missions and social ferment* (1964). He died in 1985. BioIn, 14, 16; ConAu, 115; DNB; Note; Who, 1980-85; *Who was who*, 8

Goodchild, Richard George, he was a British archaeologist whose writings include *Roman roads and milestones of Tripolitania* (1948), *Cyrene and Apollonia; an historical guide* (1959), and *Libyan studies*, edited by Joyce Reynolds (1976). NUC

Goodell, Grace E., born 20th cent., her writings include *The Elementary structures of political life; rural development in Pahlavi Iran* (1986), and she was joint author of *Traditionelle und moderne Formen der Landwirtschaft in Iran* (1975), *Conservative perspectives on economic development* (1983), and *The Peasant betrayed* (1986). NUC

Goodell, William, born in 1792 at Templeton, Mass., he was an ordained minister and became a missionary under the American Board of Commissioners for Foreign Missions. He served in the Middle East from 1823 to 1865, with only a two year interruption. He translated the Bible into Turkish. His writings include *The Old and the new; or, The changes of thirty years in the East* (1853), and *Forty years in the Turkish Empire* (1876). He died in Philadelphia, Pa., in 1867. ACAB; AmIndex (4); ANB; DAB; Master (7); NatCAB, vol. 5, pp. 198-199; Shavit; WhAm H

Goodenough, Edmund, born in 1785 at Ealing, Middlesex, he was educated at Westminster School, and graduated from Christ Church College, Oxford, including a D.D. in 1820. He served as a tutor and censor, curate, proctor, select preacher, vicar, and almoner to the king. He died suddenly at Wells in 1845. Sotheby published the sales *Catalogue of the valuable library of the late Rev. Edmund Goodenough, Dean of Wells* (1846). DNB

Goodfield, Gwyneth *June*, born 1 June 1927 at Stratford-on-Avon, she was educated at the universities of London and Leeds. She became a lecturer, professor, and visiting professor of history and philosophy of science at a variety of universities. Since 1990 she was a professor emerita at George

Mason University, Fairfax, Va. Her writings include *The Growth of scientific physiology* (1960), and *Playing God; genetic engineering and the manipulation of life* (1977). IntAu&W, 1991/92-2001/2; Master (1); WrDr, 1988/90-2003

Goodison, Ronald Alan Cameron, born in 1921, he received a Ph.D. in 1951 from Cornell University, Ithaca, N.Y., for *The Phonology of Czech*. He edited *Russian; an active introduction* (Washington, D.C., Foreign Service Institute, 1973). Master (1); NUC

Goodman, Cyril, born in 1870 at St. Ives, Hampshire, he was educated at St. John's College, Cambridge, and became a barrister. He was a sometime director-general of the Public Health Department in Egypt. He died in 1938. BritInd (1); Who, 1932; Who was who, 3

Goodman, George Jerome Waldo, born 10 August 1930 at St. Louis, Mo., he was a graduate of Harvard and a Rhodes scholar at Oxford who became a journalist, writer, and editor. Under the pseudonym Adam Smith he wrote such notable best sellers as *The Money game* (1968), its translation, *El juego de dinero* (1969), *Supermoney* (1972), and *Powers of the mind* (1975). ConAu 21-24, new rev. 31; Master (6); WhoAm, 1974/75-2003

Goodman, Lenn Evan, born 21 March 1944 at Detroit, Mich., he received a D.Phil. in 1969 from Oxford University for *The philosophical achievement of al-Ghazzali*. In the same year, he became a professor of philosophy at the University of Hawai, Manoa; in 2003 he was a professor at Vanderbilt University, Nashville, Tenn. His writings include *Ibn Tufayl's Hayy ibn Yaqzān* (1972), *The Case of the animals versus man before the king of the jinn*, translated from the Arabic of the Pure Brethren (1978), and *Jewish and Islamic philosophy* (1999). MESA Roster of members, 1977; ConAu 53-56; DrAS, 1974 P, 1978 P, 1982 P; Note; Sluglett; NatFacDr, 1995-2003; WhoWest, 1992/93, 1994/95

Goodman, Neville Marriott, born in 1898, he was educated at the Royal Military College, Sandhurst, and Pembrook College, Cambridge. A trained physician, he retired with the rank of captain and subsequently practised from 1925 to 1932. He later served as a health official with the League of Nations and the U.N.O. His writings include *International health organizations and their work* (1952), and *Alternatives in hospital care* (1963). He died in 1980. Who, 1959-1980; Who was who, 7

Goodman, Paul, born in 1875 at Dorpat (Tartu), Estonia, he was a Jewish historian and Zionist official who lived in the UK. His writings include *A History of the Jews* (1911), its translation, *Historia do povo Israel* (1927), *Zionism* (1916), and *The Jewish national home* (1943). He died in a London hospital on 13 August 1949. EncJud; JüdLex; NYT, 15 August 1949, p. 17, col. 4, Erratum, 25 September 1949, p. 17, col. 1; WhE&EA; Who was who, 4

Goodrich, Chauncey Shafter, born 18 March 1920 at San Francisco, he graduate in 1942 from Yale University, and received a Ph.D. in 1957 from the University of California at Berkeley for *The Nine bestowals during the Han-Wei period*. Since 1964 he was a professor of Chinese language and literature in the University of California at Santa Barbara. DrAS 1969 F, 1974 F, 1978 F, 1982 F

Goodrich-Freer, Ada (Adela), born in 1857 in England, she was married in 1905 to the Rev. Hans H. Spoer, a sometime district commander under Allied High Commissioner in Armenia. Mystery surrounds much of her life and parentage, and she appears to have been responsible for deliberate mystification on many details. She contributed to *Folk-lore* and other journals. Her writings include *In a Syrian saddle* (1905), *Things seen in Palestine* (1913), *A Visitors' guide to Constantinople* (1919), *Arabs in tent and town* (1924), and *Things seen in Constantinople* (1925). She died in 1931. BLC; EncO&P; Master (2); Who was who, 3

Goodsell, Fred Field, born 21 September 1880 at Montevideo, Minn., and a graduate of University of California and the Pacific School of Religion; he also studied at Marburg and Berlin; he was ordained in 1905. He served the mission of the Church for over four decades in a variety of capacities: he was missionary in Turkey as well as principal and president of schools of language and religion in Turkey, and executive vice-president of the American Board of Commissioners for Foreign Missions; he served the American Board in the capacity of historian. During the course of his retirement, he continued to teach at a number of schools and universities, including Hartford Theological Seminary in 1960. His writings include *Inductive Turkish lessons* (1927). He died quietly in his sleep in Auburndale, Mass., on 13 August 1976. Master (4); Muslim world 66 (1976), 313-314; Shavit; WhAm, 6

Goodwin, Godfrey, born 20th cent., his writings include *A History of Ottoman architecture* (1971), and *Ottoman Turkey* (1977). ZKO

Goody, Jack R., born about 1920. After passing part of his war-time military service in Africa, he returned to Cambridge in 1946 to read anthropology. He received a B.Litt. in 1951 at Oxford for *The Social organisation of the Lobi of the Gold Coast*, and his Ph.D. in 1954 at Cambridge for *A Study of the ritual institutions of the Wiililo and Dagabalo of the Gold Coast*. Since 1954 he taught social anthropology in Cambridge, where he later became a director of the African Studies Centre. He was a fellow of the Institute for Advanced Studies at Palo Alto, Calif., and a visiting professor in the Institute of African Studies at Legon, Ghana. His writings include *The Social organisation of the LoWiili* (1956). Note about the author; *Theses on Africa*, eds. Barry C. and Valerie Bloomfield, James D. Pearson, London, 1964

Gool, Jacob, 1596-1667 *see* Golius, Jacobus

Gooßens, Eduard, born 16 April 1887 at Straelen, Prussia, he received a Dr.theol. in 1914 from the Universität Münster for *Die Frage nach makkabäischen Psalmen*, and also a Dr.phil. in 1923 for *Ursprung und Bedeutung der koranischen Siglen*. He was in 1914 a rector of St. Josephs-Stift in Sendenhorst, Westphalia. GV

Goossens, Roger, born in 1894, he was a classicist whose writings include *L'Œuvre de Rome* (1944), and he was joint author of *Asklêpios, Apollon Smintheus et Rudra* (Bruxelles, 1949). He was honoured by *Mélanges Roger Goossens* (Bruxelles, 1954). He died in 1954. NUC, pre-1956

Gopčević, Spiridion, born 9 July 1855 at Triest, he was educated at schools in Melk and Wien. Since 1875 he fought with Montenegrin insurgents against the Turks as a battalion commander, but in 1879 he fell out with Duke Nicola of Montenegro. Since 1880 he was a war correspondent to the *Wiener Allgemeine Zeitung* and *Berliner Tageblatt* for Albania, Bosnia, and Bulgaria. He served as Serbian attaché in Berlin, 1886/87, and in Wien, 1887/88. Since 1890 he pursued an interest in astronomy, founded the Manora observatory in Lussin Piccolo, and from 1899 to 1907 edited the journal *Astronomische Rundschau*. His writings, partly under the pseudonyms Leon Brenner and Silvan Galena, include *Die Türken und ihre Freunde und die Ursachen der serbisch-bulgarischen Erhebung* (Wien, 1873), *Montenegro und Montenegriner* (Leipzig, 1877), *Der turco-montenegrische Krieg, 1876-1878* (1879), *Makedonien und Alt-Serbien* (Wien, 1889), its translation, *Стара Србија и Македонија* (1890), *Geschichte von Montenegro und Albanien* (Gotha, 1914), and *Rußland und Serbien von 1804-1915* (München, 1916) as well as works on atsronomy. He died in Wien in 1909. DtBE; DtBilnd (1); Master (1); NUC, pre-1956; ÖBL; *Wer ist's*, 1905-1909

Gorbatkina, Galina Arkad'evna, born 20th cent., her writings include *Пьесы-легенды Назыма Хикмета* (1967). OSK

Gorbold, Roland, born 19th cent., he was in 1921 a captain of the Mesopotamian Expeditionary Force and lived for more than two years in Baghdad. His trace is lost after an article in 1934. Note

Gorbunova, Natal'ia Maksovna, born 24 March 1944 at Moscow, she received her first degree in 1973 for *Ливанская коммунистическая партия в борьбе за создание единого национального фронта прогрессивних*. Since 1974 she was a research fellow in the Oriental Institute, Soviet Academy of Sciences. Her writings include *Фронт прогрессивних сил в Ливане, 1958-1982.* (1987) Miliband²

Gorce, Paul Marie de la, 1928- *see* La Gorce, Paul Marie de

Gorceix, Septime, born end of the 19th cent., his writings include *Le Miroir de la France* (Paris, 1923), *Evadé; des hauts de Meuse en Moldavie* (Paris, 1930), and *Bonneval pacha, pacha à trois queus* (Paris, 1953)., and he jointly edited and translated, with Nicolae Iorga, *Anthologie de la littérature roumaine des origines au XXe siècle* (Paris, 1920). BN; NUC, pre-1956

Gordillo Osuna, Manuel, born 20th cent., he was affiliated with the Instituto de Estudios Africanos, C.S.I.C. His writings include *Modelos procesales defectuosos* (1951), *Gravitación política de Ceuta* (1968), and *Geografía urbana de Ceuta* (1972). NUC, 1967-1977; ZKO

Gordimer, Nadine, born in 1923 in South Africa, she was a novelist who was awarded the Nobel prize for literature in 1991. Her writings include *The World of strangers* (1958), *The Late bourgeois world* (1966), and *African literature* (1972). IntWW, 1974/75-2002; Master (20); Who, 1973-2003; WhoAm, 1994-2003; WhoAmW, 1970/71, 1972/73; WhoWor, 1974-2003; WrDr, 1976/78-2003

Gordlevskii, Vladimir Aleksandrovich, born in 1876 at Sveaborg, Finland, he studied philology, particularly Turkish and Arabic, as well as history at Moscow, where he graduated in 1899 from Lazarev Institute. He later taught in his field at the Soviet Academy of Science. A professor since 1925, he received a doctorate in 1934. His writings include *Образцы османскаго народнаго творчества* (1916), *Государство сельджукидов Малой Азии* (1941), *Библиография Турции, 1713-1917*, and *Библиография Турции, 1917-1958*, in 1961 and 1959 respectively. He died in Moscow on 10 September 1956. BiobibSOT; GSE; *Index Islamicus* (6); Krachkovskiĭ; Miliband; Miliband²; TatarES

Gordon, Benjamin Lee, born in 1875 at Neustadt, Lithuania, he went to America as a boy and became a physician on the East Coast. His writings include *New Judea; Jewish life in modern Palestine and Egypt* (1919), *Medicine throughout antiquity* (1949), and *Between two worlds; the memoirs of a*

physician (1952). He died in Atlantic City, N.J., on 30 March 1965. CnDiAmJBi; NYT, 31 March 1965, p. 39, col. 1; WhoWorJ, 1965

Gordon, Charles George, born in 1833 at Woolwich, he was educated at the Royal Military Academy, Woolwich, and received his commission in the Royal Engineers. He served in the Crimean War, in boundary missions in the Balkans, Armenia and Turkestan. After crushing the Taiping rebellion, he became known as Chinese Gordon. Since 1873 he was in the service of the Khedive of Egypt, mainly in the Anglo-Egyptian Sudan, where he was killed in besieged Khartoum on 26 January 1885. His writings include *The Journals of Major-General C. G. Gordon at Khartoum* (1885). Hugh E. Wortham wrote *Gordon; an intimate portrait* (1933). DNB; Embacher; EncAm; EncBrit; Henze; Hill; Master (30)

Gordon, Cyrus Herzl, born 29 June 1908 at Philadelphia, Pa., he graduated and received his Ph.D. from the University of Pennsylvania. He was a professor of ancient Near Eastern studies, Assyriology, and Egyptology at Dropsie College, and Brandeis University, before he was appointed a professor of Hebrew at New York University. From 1931 to 1934 he was in the Near East in the service of the American Schools of Oriental Research. As an epigraphist he was connected with excavations in Iraq, Palestine, and Transjordan. His writings include *Ugaritic grammar* (1940), *The Living past* (1941), *The Loves and wars of Baal and Anat, and other poems from Ugarit* (1943), *Lands of the cross and crescent* (1948), and *Ugariti literature* (1949). He died 30 March 2001. CnDiAmJBi; DrAS, 1969 H, 1974 F, 1978 F, 1982 F; Master (15); Note; Who, 1969-2001; WhoAm, 1974/75-1996; WhoWorJ, 1965; WrDr, 1980/82-1996/98

Gordon, David C., born about 1925, he received a Ph.D. in 1957 from Princeton for *A "philosophe" views the French revolution, the Abbé Morellet*. He was in 1966 an associate professor of European history at AUB, and in 1990, a professor of history at Wright State University, Dayton, Ohio. His writings include *North Africa's French legacy* (1962), *The Passing of French Algeria* (1966), *Women of Algeria* (1968), *Self-determination and history in the Third World* (1971), and *Lebanon, the fragmented nation* (1979). MESA Roster of members, 1990; Note

Gordon, Ezékiel, born in 1904, he was a sometime professor at the Collège des sciences sociales de Paris, and the Faculté de droit du Caire. His writings include *La Réforme monétaire dans la Russie des soviets* (1924), *Les Nouvelles constitutions europénnes et le rôle du chef de l'état* (Paris, 1932), a work which won him the Prix Brossi for 1931 from the Faculté de droit de Paris, and he was joint author of *Eléments de droit public* (1937). He died on 15 February 1962. BN; Note; NYT, 16 February 1962, p. 29, cols. 1-2

Gordon, Leland James, born 28 September 1897 at Janesville, Minn., he received his Ph.D. in 1932 from the University of Pennsylvania for *American relations with Turkey, 1830-1930*, and subsequently served as a professor of economics at a variety of American universities. He was also a Fulbright lecturer. His other writings include *Economics for consumers* (1939), *Consumers in wartime* (1943), and *Elementary economics* (1950). He died in 1982. ConAu 41-44, 133; WhE&EA

Gordon, Leonid Abramovich, born 7 May 1930 at Moscow, he graduated in 1953 from Moscow State University where he also received his first degree in 1960 for *Из истории рабочего класса Индии*, and a Ph.D. in 1969 from Harvard University for *Bengal and the Indian national movement*. He was from 1956 to 1960 a bibliographer in the Oriental Section of the Fundamental Library of Social Sciences in the Soviet Academy of Science, from 1961 to 1965, a research fellow in the Institute of Asian Peoples in the Soviet Academy, and in 1966 he joined the Institut of the International Working Class Movement in the Soviet Academy. His writings include *Рабочий класс независимой Индии* (1968), and he was joint author of *Человек после работы* (1972), its translation, *Man after work* (1975), and *Социальное развитие рабочего класса СССР* (1974). Miliband; Miliband²; NUC, 1968-72

Gordon, Sir Thomas Edward, born in 1832, he was educated at the Scottish Naval and Military Academy. He was second in command of the mission to the Amir of Kashgar, an experience described in his *The Roof of the world; being a narrative of a journey over the high plateau of Tibet to the Russian frontier and the Oxus sources on Pamir* (1876). A good Persian linguist, he served from 1889 to 1893 at the British legation in Tehran. His other writings include *Persia; report on a journey from Tehran to Karun and Mohamrah* (1891), *Persia revisited, 1895* (1896), and *A varied life; a record of military and civil service, of sport and travels in India, Central Asia and Persia, 1849-1902* (1906). He died in 1914. BritInd (2); Buckland; DNB; Riddick; Who, 1903-1909; Who was who, 1

Gordon-Cumming, Constance Frederica, born 26 May 1837 at Altyre, Scotland, into a noble and wealthy Scottish family, the twelfth child of fifteen brothers and sisters, and fifty cousins scattered around the world. She was the perfect candidate for a life of leisurely travel. Having lost her parents in her youth, and not being married, she had few responsibilities, and she had the freedom to travel. Once she began travelling - and writing - it became difficult to stop. She died at home in Scotland on 4 September 1924. Her writings include *From the Hebrides to the Himalayas; a sketch of eighteen* *months' wanderings* (1876), *Via Cornwall to Egypt* (1885), *Wanderings in China* (1886), and *In the Himalayas and on the Indian plains* (1901). BritInd (4); Master (4); Robinson, pp. 93-95; *Who was who*, 2

Gordon-Polonskaia, Liudmila Rafailovna, 1922- *see* Polonskaia, Liudmila Rafailovna

Gorelik, Mikhail Viktorovich, born 2 October 1946 at Narva (Narova), Estonia, he graduated in 1969 from the Faculty of History, Moscow, and received his first degree in 1972 for *Месопотамские школы миниатюры II половины XII - I половины XIII в.* He was in 1979 a research fellow in the Oriental Institute, Department of Ancient Near Eastern Studies, Soviet Academy of Science. His writings include *Оружие Древнего Востока: IV тысячелетие - IV в. до н.э.* (1993). Miliband²; Note

Gorelikov, Semen Gerasimov, born in 1901 in Mogilev Oblast, he graduated in 1939 at Moscow and received his first degree in 1951 for *Полезные ископаемые Ирана*. He was from 1940 to 1947 in Iran and since 1952 he was affiliated with the Soviet Academy of Science as a geographer. His writings include *География технияеских культур Ирана* (1957), and *Иран; экономическо-географическая характеристика* (1961). Miliband; Miliband²

Görgens, Ernst Peter *see* Goergens, Ernst Peter

Gorguos, A., fl. 1849-62, he published all of his articles in the *Revue africaine*, with only one exeption. He also wrote *Cours d'arabe vulgaire* (Paris, 1849-50), a work which went through three editions until 1872.

Gorianov, Boris Timofeevich, he received a degree in 1956 for *Поздневизантийский феодализм; очерки внутренней истории Византии XVI-XV вв.* His writings include *Поздневизантийский феодализм* (1962). OSK

Gorini, Giovanni, born 20th cent., his writings include *Monete antiche a Padova* (Padova, 1972), *La monetazione incusa della Magna Grecia* (Milano, 1975), and he edited *Monete romane repubblicane del Museo Bottacin di Padova* (Venezia, 1974). NUC

Görlitz, Walter, born 24 February 1913 at Frauendorf near Stettin, Prussia, he studied medicine from 1931 to 1936, without taking a degree, and subsequently travelled throughout Europe and North Africa. He was a free lance writer until 1941, when he headed for two years the press and information bureau of the city of Rostock. After the war, he became a writer of historical biographies. Since 1954 he was also a weekly columnist of the Hamburg *die Welt*. In 1952 he published one of the first biographies of Hitler. His other writings, partly under the pseudonym Otto Julius Frauendorf, include *Hannibal, der Feldherr, der Staatsmann, der Mensch* (1935), *Hüter des Lebens; ärztliches Wirken in antiker Kultur* (1935), and *Wächter der Gläubigen; der arabische Lebenskreis und seine Ärzte* (1936). He died in Hamburg on 4 October 1991. DtBE; KDtLK, Nekrolog, 1971-1998; *Wer ist wer*, 1955-1990/91

de **Gorloff** (Gorlov), Valentin, born 19th cent., his writings include *La Question d'Orient au XXe siècle* (Nice, 1899), and *Origine et bases de l'alliance franco-russe* (Paris, 1913). BN; NUC, pre-1956

Gorodetskaia, A. A., born 20th cent., a translator from the Arabic, whose writings include *Современная арабская литература* (1960), *Современная арабская поэзии* (1961), and as joint translator *Поэты Ливана; Илия Абу Мады, Саид Акль, Шафик Маалюф* (1967). NUC, 1956-77; OSK

Gorodetskiĭ, V. D., born 19th cent., his writings include *Биобiографiя Туркестана* (Tashkent, 1913). His trace is lost after an article in 1927. OSK

Gorovei, Şefan S., born in 1948, he was a Romanian historian whose writings include *Dragoş şi Bogdan întemeietorii Moldovei* (Bucureşti, 1973), *Muşatinii* (1976), *Dragomirna* (1978), and *Petru Rareş* (1982). DcEnc; OSK

Gorra, Pierre, born about 1900, he received a doctorate in 1939 from the Université de Paris for *Méthode pour l'étude quantitative des répercussions économiques*. In 1952 he was a member of the Société Fouad Ier d'économie politique, de statistique et de législation, and in 1967 he was affiliated with the Faculté de droit de Beyrouth. Note; NUC, pre-1956

Gorrée, Georges, born 3 February 1908 at Lyon, he was educated by the Lazarists and at the Séminaire Saint-Sulpice. He was ordained in 1931 and subsequently spent some time in French North Africa. During the war he served as a chaplain, and since 1946 he was affiliated with les Invalides, Paris. In 1950 he organized the Exposition Foucauld l'Africain, and in 1952 he was elected a non-resident member of the Académie des sciences coloniales. His writings include *Le Transsaharien* (1941), *La Vérité sur l'assassinat du Père de Foucauld* (1941), *Sur les traces de Charles de Foucauld* (1947), *Soyez tous missionaires* (1955), *Laperrine, la plus belle amitié du Père de Foucauld* (1948),

Pasteur de peuples (1959), and *Amour sans frontière, Mère Teresa de Calcutte* (1972). He died in Paris on 16 January 1977. DBF

Görres, Franz Joseph, born 22 July 1844 at Wittlich, Prussia, he received a Dr.phil. in 1868 from the Universität Bonn for *De primis Aureliani principates temporibus.* His other writings include *Kritische Untersuchungen über die licinianische Christenverfolgung* (1875). His trace is lost after an article published in 1915. Sezgin; Thesis

Gorst, Sir John Eldon, born in 1835 at Preston, he was a barrister and parliamentarian who served 1893/94 as Lord Rector of Glasgow University. His writings include *The Children of the nation* (1897). He died in 1916. Peter Mellini wrote *Sir Eldon Gorst, the over-shadowed pro-consul* (1977). AusBioInd (4); BritInd (12); DNB; Hill; IndianBilnd (1); Master (2); Who was who, 2

Görtemaker, Manfred, born 28 April 1951 at Großoldendorf, Ostfriesland, Germany, he studied political science at the Universität Münster and Freie Universität Berlin, where he received a Dr.phil. in 1977 for *Entspannungspolitik und europäische Sicherheit.* He became a professor in Historisches Institut, Universität Potsdam. His writings include *Die unheilige Allianz* (1979), *Deutschland im 19. Jahrhundert* (1983), and *Geschichte Europas* (2002). Kürschner, 1996-2003; Thesis

Gorton, T. J., born 20th cent., he received a D.Phil. in 1976 at Oxford for *The Diwan of Ibn Quzman of Cordoba.* Sluglett

Gorvine, Albert, born 30 March 1922 at Boston, Mass., he graduated in 1944 from Harvard, and received a Ph.D. in 1950 from New York University for *The governor and administration, State of Nevada.* He spent his entire career teaching political science at C.U.N.Y. In 1970 he became chairman of the Department of Political Science. His other writings include *An Outline of Turkish provincial and local government* (1956), and he was joint author of *Organization and function of Turkish ministries* (1957), and *Dacca urban division* (1963). AmM&WS, 1973 S, 1978 S; Master (1); WhoAm, 1974/75, 1976/77

Goryński, Jan, of Ojrzanow, Poland, born about 1535, he studied in 1556 at Wittenberg and Frankfurt, and in 1560 he visited Palestine as a pilgrim. Dziekan; NEP; Polski (3); *Wielka encyklopedia PWN* (2002)

Gosche, Hermann *Richard* Adolf, born 4 June 1824 at Neuendorf, Lower Lusatia, he studied theology, classical and Oriental philology at Leipzig and Berlin, where he received a Dr.phil. in 1847 for *De Ariana linguae gentisque Armeniacae indole.* He subsequently became a librarian at the Royal Library, Berlin. After his Dr.habil. in 1853, he taught history of literature at the Prussian war college. Since 1862 he was a professor of Semitic languages at Halle. He was in 1865 the founding editor of *Jahrbuch für Literaturgeschichte,* and concurrently from 1870 to 1887 also an editor of *Archiv für Literaturgeschichte.* He died in Halle on 29 October 1889. ADtB, vol. 49, pp. 469-74; DtBE; DtBilnd (2); GV

Goshen-Gottstein, Moshe Henri, born 6 September 1925 at Berlin, he was since 1950 a professor of Biblical and Semitic philology at the Hebrew University, Jerusalem. His writings include *Hebrew and Semitic languages; an outline introduction* (1965), *A Syriac-English glossary* (1970), *A Modern dictionary, Arabic-Hebrew* (1976), as well as editions of medieval Hebrew works relating to the Islamic period. He died in 1991. BioHbDtE; IntAu&W, 1977; NYT, 25 October 1991, p. B-5, col. 2; WhoWor, 1974/75, 1976/77, 1991/92; WhoWor, 1972, 1978

Gosman, Khatib *see* Usmanov, Khatib Usmanovich

Gosnell, Harold Foote, born 24 December 1896 at Lockport, N.Y., he graduated in 1918 from the University of Rochester, N.Y., and received a Ph.D. in 1924 from the University of Chicago for *Boss Platt and his New York machine.* He spent twice twenty years each teaching political science at the American University, and Howard University. He was in 1958 an observer of the Sudan elections. His writings include *Getting out the vote* (1927), *Negro politicians* (1935), and *Grass roots politics* (1942). AmM&WS, 1973 S, 1978 S; ConAu 41-44; WhAm 10; WhE&EA; WrDr, 1982/84-1984/86

Goss, Charles Frederic, born in 1852 at Meridian, N.Y., he was a graduate of Hamilton College and Auburn (N.Y.) Theological Seminary. Ordained a Presbyterian minister in 1876, he served as a pastor throughout America, lastly at Cincinnati, Ohio. He died in 1930. Master (3); WhAm 10

Gosset, Alphonse, born 9 May 1835 at Reims (Marne), he studied from 1856 to 1861 at l'Ecole nationale des beaux-arts, Paris, and became an architect at Reims. He was a member and president of the Académie nationale de Reims. His writings include *Traité de la construction des théâtres* (1885), *Les Anciennes églises et mosquées de Constantinople* (1888), and *Les Coupoles d'Orient et d'Occident* (1894). He died in 1914. IndexBFr² (3)

Got'e, IUriĭ Vladimirovich, born in 1873, he was a Russian historian and archaeologist whose writings include Замосковный край в XVII веке (1906), Исторія областного управленія в Россіи от

Петра I до Екатерины II (1913-41), and he edited *Крымская война, 1853-1856 гг.* (1940). He died in 1943. Bioln 16; GSE; NUC, pre-1956; OSK

Gotsch, Carl H., born in 1933, he was in the late 1960s and early 1970s successively an assistant professor of economics, and a development adviser, at Harvard. He wrote a number of working papers on quantitative research in economic development of the Third World, and he was a joint author of the *World Bank staff working paper* entitled *Prices, taxes, and subsidies in Pakistan agriculture, 1960-1976* (Washington, D.C., 1980). Master (1)

Gotsiridze, Irana Sladoevna, born 8 January 1935 in Soviet Georgia, she graduated in 1958 from Tiflis State University, where she also received her first degree in 1965 for *Остовные мотивы творчества Мехмеда Эмина*. She was since 1961 affiliated with her alma mater. From 1969 to 1982 she served as deputy dean. She spent 1968 and 1973 in Turkey. Miliband²

Gott, Richard Willoughby, born 28 October 1938 at Aston Tirrold, Berkshire, he was from 1962 to 1972 successively a research assistant in the Royal Institute of International Affairs, London, the Universidad de Chile, Santiago, and a foreign editor with the *Standard*, Dar es Salaam, before becoming a free-lance writer. He wrote *Mobuto's Congo* (1968), *Rural guerillas in Latin America* (1973), and *Close your frontiers* (1983). ConAu 81-84; WrDr, 1980/82-2003

von **Gottberg**, Eduard, fl. 1845-1855, he was a German engineer in the service of the Egyptian government. In 1853 he was the first to survey accurately the caravan route from Keneh (Qina) on the Nile to Qusayr on the Red Sea. In 1857 he was sent on reconnaissance to the Nile cataracts with a view to improving river navigation. Henze; Hill

von **Gottberg**, Erika, born 23 June 1916 at Neustadt/Holstein, Germany, she was a writer of poetry and prose, whose writings include *Du bist wie Brot für mich; Gedichte* (1975). KDtLK, 1978-1988; Sezgin

Gottheil, Fred Monroe, born 1 December 1931 at Montreal, P.Q., he graduated in 1954 from the local McGill University, and received a Ph.D. in 1959. He was a professor in the Department of Economics, University of Illinois, Urbana-Champaign, as well as a visiting professor in the U.S.A. and Israel. His writings include two brief faculty working papers entitled *Arab immigration into pre-state Israel, 1922-1931*, and *An economic assessment of the military burden in the Middle East, 1960-1980*, both of which were published in 1971 by the College of Commerce and Business Administration, University of Illinois, Urbana-Champaign. Master (1); NatFacDr, 1995-1999; WhoAm, 1982/3; WhoAmJ, 1980

Gottheil, Richard James Horatio, born in 1862 at Manchester, he graduated in 1881 from Columbia University, N.Y., and subsequently studied at Berlin, Tübingen and Leipzig, where he received a Dr.phil. in 1896 for *A Treatise on Syriac grammar*. He was a professor of Semitic languages at Columbia, a head of the Oriental Department, N.Y.P.L., and an editor of the *Jewish encyclopedia*. In 1902 he edited *Persian literature*. He died in 1936. ANB; Bioln 11; CnDiAmJBi; EncJud; WhAm 1; *Index Islamicus* (1); NatCAB, vol. 14, pp. 276-277; Wininger

Gottlieb, Francis, fl. 19th cent., his surname is given in corrupt forms - captain François Akden (?) a son of Gobinet; Faraçu ou Fransu, fils de Gûst (Auguste) ou de Gûstîn (Augustin) - by A. Sprenger and Garcin de Tassy, but there seems to be little doubt that he is Farāsū Gōtlīb, i.e. Francis Gottlieb, a German born in Poland and educated in India, who wrote for Major Abraham Lockett in Persian a history of the Jāt Rājahs of Bharatpūr. Under the name Farāsū he wrote the *Fath-nāmah-i Angrēz*. Storey, *History of Persian literature*, vol. 1, pp. 647 & 690

Gottlieb, Gidon Alai Guy, born 9 December 1932 at Paris, he graduated from L.S.E., received a diploma at Cambridge, and a S.J.D. from Harvard Law School for *The logic of choice; an inquiry into the logic of judicial argument*. He was a human rights' activist, a practising lawyer, and a university lecturer, whose writings include *Of Suez, withdrawal, and Jarring; the search for a compromise* (1971). Master (2); NatFacDr, 1995-1999; NUC; WhoAm, 1982/83-2003

Gottmann, Jean, born 10 October 1915 at Kharkov, he was educated at Paris *lycées*. From 1940 to 1948 he held teaching posts in the United States, and subsequently taught geography at the Sorbonne, first at its Institut d'études politiques, and later at the Ecole des hautes études. His writings include *A Geography of Europe* (1950), and *La Politique des états et leur géographie* (1952). He died on 28 February 1994. Who, 1969-1994; WhoWorJ, 1965

Gottschalk, Hans Ludwig, born 24 March 1904 at Freiburg im Breisgau, Germany, he studied Semitic languages and ancient history at Freiburg, Berlin, Tübingen and München, where he received a Dr.phil. in 1928 for *Die Māḏarā'ijjūn; ein Beitrag zur Geschichte Ägyptens unter dem Islam*. He was an assistant in the Seminar für Geschichte und Kultur des Vorderen Orients, Universität Hamburg, from 1930 to 1933, when he was dismissed. He subsequently served as a keeper at Mingana Collection of

Oriental Manuscripts, Selly Oak Colleges Library, Birmingham. Since 1948 he was a professor of Arabic at Wien. His writings include *Al-Malik al-Kāmil von Egypten und seine Zeit* (1958), and he was a joint author of the fourth volume, the Islamic Arabic MSS., of the *Catalogue of the Mingana Collection of manuscripts* (1948-63). DtBE; *Index Islamicus* (2); Kürschner, 1950-1980; Note; Teichl; WhoAustria, 1954-1980; WhoWor, 1974/75, 1976/77; WZKM, 74 (1982), pp. 7-9

Gottschalk, Rudolph, born 6 October 1901 at Bernburg, Anhalt, he received a Dr.jur. in 1925 from the Universität Leipzig for *Zur Lehre von der ungerechtfertigten Bereicherung bei Leistungen an Dritte*, and he was called to the bar from Gray's Inn in 1936. Since 1934 he was resident in Palestine. His other writings include *Die Vollmacht zum Grundstücksverkauf* (1932), and *Impossibility of performance in contract* (London, 1938). GV; WhoWorJ, 1972, 1978

Gottschalk, Walter, born 29 January 1891 at Aachen, Germany, he received a Dr.phil. in 1919 at Berlin for *Das Gelübde nach älterer arabischer Auffassung*. He was a librarian at the Staatsbibliothek, Berlin, until 1933, when he had to emigrate to Turkey; he there set up a library system. He retired in 1954 to Frankfurt am Main. His writings include *Katalog der Handbibliothek der Orientalischen Abteilung* (1929). He died in Frankfurt am Main on 1 October 1974. BioHbDtE; JahrDtB, 1931-1934; Kürschner, 1950-1970; Sezgin

Gottschling, Caspar, born 28 February 1679 at Lobenau, Silesia, he studied the classical subjects of his day at Wittenberg, Halle, and Leipzig. He successively served as a teacher at the Universität Halle, and as a teacher, rector, and librarian at the Ritter-Schule, Brandenburg, where he died in 1739. His writings include *Staat von dem Königreiche Algier in Africa* (1712), *Staat von dem Königreiche Thunis* (1712), and *Staat von Egypten* (1712). DtBilnd (5); Sezgin

Gottwaldt, Josephus M. E., 1813-1897 *see* Gotva'ld, Iosif Fedorovich

Gotva'ld (Gottwaldt), Iosif Fedorovich, born in 1813 at Ratibor, Prussia, he studied Oriental languages, particularly Arabic, under C. M. Habicht. In 1849 he was appointed a professor of Arabic at Kazan. He edited and translated *Annalium libri X*, of Hamzah ibn al-Hasan al-Isfahānī (1844-48), and he edited *K. Khulāsat al-khālisah*, of Mahmūd ibn Ahmad al-Fārābī (1851). He died in 1897. Krachkovskiĭ, pp. 170-73; NUC, pre-1956; Slovar; TatarES

Götz, Manfred, born 7 January 1932 at Dresden, Germany, he received a Dr.phil. in 1956 from the Universität München for *Der Charakter der Prosabelege bei Sibawaih*, and a Dr.habil. in 1971 from the Universität Köln for *Die Funktionen der Tempora im Türkeitürkischen*. He was since 1980 a professor of Islamic studies at Köln. His other writings include *Türkische Handschriften* [in Germany] (1979). Kürschner, 1987-2003; Schwarz

Goubert, Paul, fl. 20th cent., his writings include *Byzance avant l'islam* (Paris, 1951). NUC, pre-1956

Goudard-Pacha, Jules M., 1828-1888 *see* Gaudard, Jules Maurice

Goudy, Henry, born in 1848, he studied at the universities of Glasgow, Edinburgh, and Königsberg, East Prussia. He was for over twenty years Regius Professor of Civil Law at Oxford. His writings include *Trichotomy in Roman law* (1910). He died in 1921. BritInd (3); OxCLaw; *Who was who, 2*

Gouffé, Claude, fl. 20th cent., he was in 1969 associated with l'Ecole nationale des langues orientales vivantes, Paris. Note

Gough, Sir Hugh Henri, born in 1833 at Calcutta, he was a soldier who fought in the Mutiny and in Afghanistan. In 1897 he retired with the rank of general. In 1898 he was appointed keeper of the crown jewels at the London Tower. He died in London in 1909. Buckland; DNB; Riddick; *Who was who 1*

Gouilly, Alphonse, born in 1910, his writings include *L'Islam devant le monde moderne* (Paris, 1945), and *L'Islam dans l'Afrique occidentale française* (Paris, 1952). His trace is lost after an article in 1965.

Goulven, Joseph Georges Arsène, born in 1886, he passed through the École coloniale in 1906 and was posted to Dakar with the Ministry of the Colonies. His 1911 thesis, *Étude sur l'évolution administrative, judiciaire et financière de l'Afrique équatoriale française*, won him a prize from the Faculté du droit de Paris. In 1913 he became *chef du cabinet* of Réunion. Apart from two hundred articles, his writings include *Le Cercle des Doukkala au point de vue économique* (1917), *La Place de Mazagan sous la domination portugaise, 1502-1769* (1917), *Le Maroc* (1920), *Les Mellahs de Rabat-Salé* (1927), and *Safi au vieux temps des Portugais* (1938). He died in Aix-en-Provence on 26 April 1972. *Hommes et destins*, vol. 7, p. 612; NUC

Gounaris, Demetrios P., born in 1867 at Patras, Greece, he took a doctorate in law and became a lawyer and politician. After the political deaster of 1922, he was condemned to death and executed in the same year in Athens. EEE; Megali, vol. 8 (1929), pp. 652-55; EncicUni; *Larousse du XXe siècle*

648

Gounot, André, born in 1878 at Palermo, he was admitted in 1898 to the École d'agriculture de Tunis. In 1902 he established one of the first estates on the Soukh el Khémis Plain, and in 1904 became the founding vice-president of the *commune*, a post which he held until his death. In 1905 he entered the *conférence consultative* and remained there when it became the *Grand Conseil*. After the war he returned to Tunisia, becoming honorary president of the Chambre d'agriculture, president of the Union des Travailleurs français, and director of the journal, *Le Colon français*. Since 1926 he was a corresponding member of the Académie des sciences d'Outre-Mer. He died in Tunis, 23 November 1936. *Hommes et destins*, vol. 7, p. 221

Gouraud, Henri Joseph Etienne, born in 1867 at Paris, he graduated from the Collège Stanislas, Paris, and the military college, Saint-Cyr. He was serving with the *chasseurs à pied* at Montbéliard when the defeat of the *Colonne* Bonnier at Timbuctu became known in 1894. He immediately volunteered for service in French Equatorial Africa, where he remained with short interruptions until 1906, when he served in the western Sahara and Morocco. His victory over the Germans under Ludendorff on 15 July 1918 projected him among the great heroes of the first World War. His writings include *La Pacification de la Mauritanie* (1911), *Au Soudan* (1939), *Zinder - Tchad; souvenirs d'un Africain* (1944), *Mauritanie, Adrar; souvenirs d'un Africain* (1945), and *Au Maroc, 1911-1914* (1949). He died in Paris on 16 September 1946. DBF; *Hommes et destins*, vol. 8, p. 162-165; IndexBFr² (5); *Revue indigène*, 7 (1912), pp. 424-426; *Who was who*, (1)

Gourdon, Jean, born in 1824 at Lyon, he was a professor at the École vétérinaire de Toulouse and from 1865 to 1870 he concurrently edited the *Revue agricole du Midi*. His writings include *Des réformes à apporter dans l'alimentation des animaux domestiques* (1860), and *Du cheval oriental et de son emploi dans l'amélioration des races françaises* (1864). He died in Toulouse in 1876. DBF

Goussault, Yves, born 20th cent., he was a writer on Third World affairs. His writings include *Interventions éducatives et animation dans les développements agraires* (1970), and *Sciences sociales et développement* (1993). *Livres disponibles*, 2003; Master (1)

de Gouvea (Gouveia), Antonio, born in 1575 at Beja, Portugal, he was an Augustinian missionary and Portuguese envoy who in 1602 was sent on a mission to Persia. Until 1613 he again made two more visits to the country. His writings include *Relaçem em que se tratam as guerras e grandes victorias que alcançou o grāde rey da Persia Xá Abbas do grāo Turco Mahometto* (Lisboa, 1611), and its translation, *Relation des grandes gverres et victoires obtenves par le roy de Perse, Cha Abbas* (Rouven, 1646). He died in Manzanares, Spain, in 1628. *Cambridge history of Iran*, vol. 6, pp. 389, 391-92; EncIran; GdeEnc; IndiceE³ (1)

Gover, Charles E., born 19th cent., he was "a principal and secretary of the Madras Military Orphan Asylum at Egmore since 1864, and a member of the Royal Asiatic Society, Society of Arts, and a fellow of the Anthropological Society." (Buckland) His writings include *Indian weights and measures* (1865), *An Uniform metrology in India* (1867), and *Folk-songs of Southern India* (1872). He died in 1872 in Madras. Buckland; DNB; IndianBilnd (2); Riddick

Govi, Mario, born 14 February or March 1880 at Carpi (Modena), he earned degrees in law and philosophy and became a lecturer at the Università di Pisa. His writings include *Il socialismo internazionalista e la guerra italo-balcanico-turca* (1912), and *Le basi psico-sociologiche del rinnovamento spirituale e sociale; lezioni di sociologia* (Pisa, 1945). *Chi è*, 1928-1957|

Gow, James John, born 24 July 1918 at Aberdeen, he was called to the Bar of British Columbia in 1968, and from 1987 to 1993, served as a judge in the Supreme Court of British Columbia. His writings include *The Law of hire-purchase in Scotland* (Edinburgh, 1961), and *The Mercantile and industrial law of Scotland* (Edinburgh, 1964). BLC; Canadian, 1989-1998

Gowing, Peter Gordon, born 9 May 1930 at Norwood, Mass., he was educated in New England, and ordained in 1954. From 1960 until his death on 10 July 1983 in the Philippines, he was professor of Christian history and world religions at a variety institutions of higher learning in Southeast Asia. His writings include *Mosque and Moro* (1964), *Mandate in Moroland* (1977) - a work which was originally presented as a thesis at Syracuse University - *Moros and Indians* (1977), *Muslim Filipinos* (1979); and he is edited *Understanding Islam and Muslims in the Philippines* (1988). Master (2); Shavit - Asia

Goyau, Georges Pierre Louis Théophile, born 31 May 1869 at Orléans, he was educated at the Lycée Louis-le-Grand, Paris, and in 1888 entered the École normale supérieure at the top of his class. From 1891 to 1894 he was a fellow at the École française de Rome, where he divided his time between the study of ancient history, and political activity for social Catholicism. In 1894 he joined the staff of the *Revue des deux mondes*, a post which occasioned travels throughout Europe and simultaneously confronted him with contemporary political problems, resulting in his book, *L'Allemagne religieuse; le* *protestantisme* (1898). In the ensuing struggle between Church and State he worked for avoidance of rupture. During years from 1910 to 1922 he produced the four volumes of *Kulturkampf* (1911-13) as well as the *Histoire religieuse de la France* (1922), works which were well received by Protestants and Catholics alike. A member of the Académie française since 1923, he became their permanent secretary in 1936. His writings also include *Orientations catholiques* (1925), *Missions et missionaires*, and its translation, *Missions and missionaries* (1932). He died in Bernay on 25 October 1939.   DBF; IndexBFr² (5); *Qui êtes-vous*, 1924

Gozalbes Busto, Guillermo, born in 1916, he received doctorates in history and law as well as a diploma in Semitic philology. His writings include *Marruecos poético* (1963), *Estudios sobre Marruecos en la edad media* (1989), and *Al-Mandari; el granadino de Tetuán* (1993). He died in 1999. Arabismo, 1992, 1994, 1997; *Index Islamicus* (1)

Gozalbes Cravioto, Carlos, born 20th cent., he received a degree in history, with special reference to medieval archaeology. His writings include *Las vias romanas de Málaga* (1986). Arabismo, 1992, 1994, 1997

Gozdović Paşa, Rifat, born 19th cent., he was an Austrian soldier whose writings include *Zwanzig Jahre in der bosnischen Fremdenlegion* (Prag, 1912), *Im blutigen Karst; Erinnerungen eines österreichischen Offiziers* (Stuttgart, 1915), and *Am Col di Lama; Erinnerungen aus dem Kriegsjahr 1915* (1916). OSK

de **Graaf**, Hermanus Johannes, born 2 December 1899 at Rotterdam, he began to study at Leiden. About 1925 he became posted to the Dutch East Indies, where he was from 1926 to 1935 first a teacher at Surabaya, later an employee at the library of the Museum in Batavia, and finally an inspector of secondary education. During his three years at Jakarta he learned Javanese. In the early 1930s he resigned his public functions and became a teacher in a private school run by Protestant missionaries. In 1935 he returned to Leiden to complete his study with a doctorate on the assassination of Captain François Tack in 1686 in Kartasura. In the late 1930s he again went to Java as a teacher in a Christian school in Surakarta, remaining there until 1950, when he decided to return to the Netherlands, partly for fear for the family's safety, a decision which might be interpreted as sign of his great deception. At home he was unable to fit into Dutch academia and was obliged to make a living as a simple school teacher until his retirement in 1967. On account of his impressive publications he must be considered the veritable founder of historical studies on Java during its Islamic period. His writings include *Chinese geschiedenis* (1941), *Geschiedenis van Indonesië* (1949), *De regering van Sultan Agung, Vorst van Mataram, 1613-45* (1958), *Indonesia* (1969), and *Islamic states in Java, 1500-1700* (1976). He died in 1984. Archipel, 31 (1986), pp. 3-6

Grabar, André, born 26 July 1896 at Kiev, he was successively a professor of fine art at the Faculté des lettres, Strasbourg (1928-37), and École pratique des hautes études, Paris (1937-66). His writings include *La Décoration byzantine* (1928), *La Peinture byzantine* (1953), *Early medieval painting* (1957), *L'Art de la fin de l'antiquité et du moyen âge* (1968), and a collection of his articles, *L'Art du moyen âge en Occident* (1980). He died 5 October 1990. ConAu 111; BioIn 17 (3); IntWW, 1974/75-1990/91; NYT, 9 October 1990, p. B-8, col. 3; WhoFr, 1969/70-1990/91; WhoWor, 1974/75-1978/79

Grabar, Oleg, born 11 March 1929 at Strasbourg, he was educated at the universities of Paris and Harvard, and obtained a Ph.D. from Princeton in 1955 for *Ceremonial and art at the Umayyad court*. In 1954 he became professor of history of art at the University of Michigan, and from 1969 until his retirement in 1990 he was professor at Harvard. Since 1990 he was with the Institute for Advanced Study at Princeton. He travelled and excavated in many of the principal centres of Islamic culture in the Middle East and Spain. He was honorary curator of Near Eastern art at the Freer Gallery, Washington, D.C., founding secretary of the American Research Institute in Turkey, and a sometime director of the American School of Oriental Research, Jerusalem. As one of the most productive scholars in Islamic studies in the second half of the twentieth century, he did more than any other person to establish Islamic art and architecture in the curriculum of American universities. In recognition of his scholarship he was awarded the Levi della Vida prize for 1996. His writings include *The Formation of Islamic art* (1973), *The Alhambra* (1978), *The Great Mosque of Isfahan* (1990), *The Shape of the holy: Islamic Jerusalem* (1996). ConAu 124, new rev. 51; DrAS, 1969-1982 H; Master (3); Shavit; WhoAm, 1974/75-1986/87, 2003

Graber, Doris Appel, born 11 November 1923 at St. Louis, Mo., she graduated in 1940 from the local Washington University, and received a Ph.D. in 1947 from Columbia University, N.Y.C. She was a newspaper writer and editor who also taught political science at a variety of colleges and universities. Her writings include *The Development of the law of belligerent occupation, 1863-1914; a historical survey* (1949), *Crisis diplomacy; a history of U.S. intervention policies and practices* (1959), and *Verbal behavior and politics* (1976). ConAu 33-36; NUC

Gråberg til Hemsö, Jacob, born 5 May 1776 at Gannarve on the Island of Gotland, Sweden, he was a prolific scholar, and also served as Swedish consul in Tanger, 1815-1822, and Tripoli, 1823-1828. His writings include *La Scandinavie vengée de l'accusation d'avoir produit les peuples barbares qui détruisirent l'empire de Rome* (1822), and *Specchio geografico e statistico dell'impero di Marocco* (1834). He died in Firenze, 29 November 1847. Henze; SMK

Grabham, George Walter, born in Madeira in 1882, he was educated at St. John's College, Cambridge, and subsequently served on the Geological Survey in Scotland from 1903 to 1906, when he became Government geologist to the Anglo-Egyptian Sudan. He retired automatically in 1934, but remained as geological adviser until 1939. He contributed to the reconstruction of the Sudan from the early years of the twentieth century by his development of water supplies and his advisory work on the siting of major irrigation installations. He was one of the pioneers of the use of motor transport in the Sudan and travelled extensively there and in Africa throughout his career. He and R. F. Black carried out the Lake Tana Mission in 1920-21. His writings include *Hints on collecting geological information and specimens* (1913), and *Report on the Mission to Lake Tana, 1920-21* (1925). He died in Khartoum on 29 January 1955. Bioln 3; *Geographical journal*, 121 (June 1955), p. 252; *Who was who*, 5

Grabill, Joseph Leon, born 21 July 1931 at Bluffton, Ohio, he graduated in 1954 from Fort Wayne Bible College, and received a Ph.D. in 1964 from the University of Indiana for *Missionaries amid conflict; their influence upon American relations with the Near East, 1914-1927.* He was associated with Malone College, Canton, Ohio, before he began a teaching career in the Department of History, Illinois State University at Normal. His writings include *Protestant diplomacy and the Near East* (1971). ConAu 29-32; NatFacDr, 1995; Selim

Grabmann, Martin, born in 1875, he studied philosophy and theology at Eichstätt, Franconia. After doctorates at Roma, he was from 1918 to 1939 a profesor of Christian philosophy at the Universität Wien. He was a historian of scholasticism, whose writings include *Der lateinische Averroismus des 13. Jahrhunderts und seine Stellung zur christlichen Weltanschauung* (1931). He died in 1946. Catholic authors, (1948-1952), vol. 2, pp. 213-25; DcCathB; DtBE; DtInd (5); Kosch; Kürschner, 1925-35; NDB; *Wer ist's*, 1922-35

Grabois, Aryeh, born 9 April 1930 at Odessa, he settled in 1948 in Israel and studied at the Hebrew University, Jerusalem, École des chartes, École pratique des hautes études, Paris, and the Université de Dijon, where he completed his Ph.D. thesis on the Capetian monarchy and the Church in the twelfth century. Upon returning to Israel, he took up a teaching position at the University of Haifa. Over the years he served as head of the Department of History (1968-70), dean of the Faculty of Humanities (1976-79), and dean of the Graduate School (1986-91). In 1995, he was honoured by *Cross cultural convergences in the crusader period; essays presented on his sixty-fifth birthday.* ConAu 105; WhoWorJ, 1972, 1978, 1987; WhoIsrael, 1978-2001

Grabowski, Adam, born in 1875 at Warszawa, he studied at München, Roma, and Paris. He was a painter, who visited greater Syria. He died in 1941. Dziekan; Polski (2)

Grabowsky, Adolf, born 31 August 1880 at Berlin, he received a Dr.jur. in 1907 from the Universität Würzburg for *Der sogenannte Verlust der Staatsangehörigkeit durch Fristablauf.* He was from 1912 to 1923 an editor of *Zeitschrift für Politik*, and from 1921 until his dismissal in 1933 he lectured in political science at Hochschule für Politik, Berlin. In 1934 he emigrated to Basel. From 1952 to 1965 he was a professor at Marburg and Gießen. His writings include *Grundlagen des Völkerbundes* (1919). He died on 23 August 1969 in Switzerland. BioHbDtE; KDtLK, Nekrolog, 1936-70; Kürschner, 1926-35, 1950-66; RHbDtG; Sezgin; Wininger

Gracey, George Frederick Handel, born in 1878 or 9 at Belfast, he was a missionary at Urfa (Edessa), Turkey, from 1904 to 1914. He was a member of the American Relief Expedition to the Caucasus to assist a quarter of a million Armenian refugees who fled from Turkey to Russia in 1915. He piloted the evacuation of 25,000 Armenians from Van to Igdir single-handed in 1916. He later served as an Intelligence Staff Officer to the British Mission in Tiflis. He died in 1958. WhE&EA; *Who was who* 5

Grach, Aleksandr Danielovich, fl. 20th cent., he was a historian whose writings include Археологические раскопки в Ленинграде (1957), Древнетюркские изваяния Тувы (1961), and Древние кочевники в центре Азии (1979). OSK

Gracia Guillén, Diego M., born 20th cent., he gained a doctorate in medicine, specializing in history of medicine, and later lectured in his field at Madrid. His writings include *Voluntad de verdad; para leer a Zubiri* (1986), *Fundamentos de bioética* (1989), he was joint author of *Historia del medicamento* (1984), and he was joint editor of *The Ethics of diagnosis* (1992). Arabismo, 1992

Grad, Marie Antoine *Charles*, born 8 December 1842 at Turckheim, Alsace, he completed his secondary education at the Collège libre de Colmar and then joined a textile firm in nearby Logelbach.

With increasing proficiency through evening study, he advanced rapidly, eventually rising to associate of the firm. Parallel to his business duties he pursued an interest in popular traditions, geology, hydrology, and climatology, subjects which he studied on his many business journeys throughout Alsace, the rest of Europe, the Near East, and North Africa. He became a contributor to many learned periodicals. After the German annexation in 1870, he represented Alsace at the Reichstag in Berlin. His writings include *Heimathskunde, Schilderungen aus Elsaß* (1878), and *L'Alsace, le pays et ses habitants* (1889), a work which won him the Prix Monthyon from the Académie française. He died a bachelor in Wintzenheim-Logelbach on 3 July 1890. DBF; NDBA; Vapereau

Gradis, Gaston, born 7 May 1889 at Paris, he was a graduate of the École polytechnique and became a business executive. In 1923 he was the first person to travel overland by car from Algeria to Dahomy by way of the French Sudan and Niger. His writings include *Les Ballons dirigeables* (1923), and *À la recherche du grand-axe; contribution aux études transsahariennes* (1924). He died 15 January 1968. Qui est-ce, 1924; WhoFr, 1957/58-1967/68

Gradmann, Robert Julius Wilhelm, born 18 July 1865 at Lauffen on Neckar, Württemberg, he studied theology at Tübingen, and in 1891 became a pastor in Forchtenberg. Concurrently he pursued an interest in geography and botany, culminating in his *Pflanzenleben der Schwäbischen Alb* (1898), a work which gained him a doctorate without formally having studied his subject. He subsequently became first a librarian at the university library, Tübingen, and later successively a professor of geography at Tübingen and Erlangen. His writings include *Die Steppen des Morgenlandes in ihrer Bedeutung für die Geschichte der menschlichen Gesittung* (1934), and his autobiography, *Lebenserinnerungen* (1965). He died in Sindelfingen on 16 September 1950. DtBE; DtBilnd (2); Geographers, 6 (1982), pp. 47-54) ; Kürschner, 1925-50; NDB; Wer ist's, 1950

Grady, Henry Francis, born 12 February 1882 at San Francisco, he was a graduate of St. Mary's University, Baltimore, and received a Ph.D. in 1927 from Columbia University for *British war finances, 1914-1919*. He entered the U.S. foreign and diplomatic service. In 1952 he was an ambassador to Iran. His writings include *A Survey of India's industrial production for war purposes* (1942). He died in 1957. ANB; DAB S6; WhAm, 3

von **Graefe**, Axel, born 27 May 1900 at Goldebee, Mecklenburg, he received a Dr.jur. in 1925 from the Universität Halle for *Mehrfach Beteiligung bei der eingetragenen Genossenschaft m.b.H.* He was a judge in Berlin, whose writings include *Männer unterm Spaten* (1936), its translation, *Shoulder spates* (1936), and *Iran, das neue Persien* (1937). DtBilnd (1)

Graefe, Erich, born 12 April 1886 at Halle, he studied classical and Oriental philology at the universities of Lausanne, Tübingen, Halle, and Leipzig, where he received a Dr.phil. in 1911 for an edition and translation entitled *Das Pyramidenkapitel in Al-Makrīzī's "Ḫiṭaṭ" nach 2 Berliner Drucken und 2 Münchener Handschriften herausgegeben und übersetzt.* He died on 25 September 1914 in a French hospital in St. Nazaire from wounds received near Septmonts (Aisne). der Islam, 6 (1915/16), pp. 88-90; ZDMG, 69 (1915), pp. 567-69

Graefe, John Edward, born in 1889, he was affiliated with the Theological Department of the Andhra Christian College, Guntur, India. His writings include *The Church in Corinth* (1936), *What is this Christianity in India?* (1937), and *Christ and the Hindu heart* (1938). Note; NUC, pre-1956

Graeff Wassink, Maria, born 20th cent., she received a doctorate and was in 1993 a technical adviser with the F.M.V.J. Her writings include *Rapport sur la population ouvrière marocaine en France* (1973), and *Enquête socio-économique sur échantillouage de bidonvilles marocaines* (1983). EURAMES, 1993

von **Graevenitz**, George, born 28 May 1858 at Danzig, Prussia, he studied at Berlin and Heidelberg, and was a retired Prussian army captain when he received his Dr.phil. in 1906 from the Universität Heidelberg for *Gattamelata (Erasmo da Narni) und seine Verherrlichung durch die Kunst.* His writings include *Geschichte des italienisch-türkischen Krieges* (1912), *Die militärische Vorbereitung der Jugend in Gegenwart und Zukunft* (1916), and *Musik in Freiburg* (1938). He died in 1939. KDtLK, 1913-1917; NUC, pre-1956; Thesis

von **Graevenitz**, Kurt Fritz Hermann Alfred Richard, born 21 August 1898 at Kreuth, Bavaria, he studied law at Tübingen and Leipzig and received a Dr.jur. in 1925 for *Die Tanger-Frage; eine öffentliche Studie* (1925). In the foreign service from 1922 to 1945 and posted throughout Europe and the Middle East, he was since 1951 in the foreign office and responsible for cultural affairs. From 1952 to 1955 he was in charge of the college of diplomatists, Speyer. He died in München on 20 November 1987. DtBE; Wer ist wer, 1955-63

Graf, András (Andreas), born 23 September 1909 at Budapest, he studied classical philology and received a doctorate in 1933. He was affiliated with the Érem- és Régisségtani Intézete (Institute of

Numismatics and Archaeology), Budapest University. His writings include *Jedrjiosz Zavírasz Budapesti könyvtárának katalógusa* (1935), and *Übersicht der antiken Geographie von Pannonien* (1936). He died in 1944. MEL, 1967-69

Graf, Arturo, born in 1848 at Athens of German parentage, he spent his youth in Romania, studied law at Napoli, and became a tutor at the Università di Roma. Since 1874 he was a professor at Torino. Apart from being a teacher of history of literature, he was a writer of poetry and prose in his own right. His writings include *La leggenda del paradiso terreste* (1878), *Miti, leggende e supertizioni del medio evo* (1892-93), and *L'anglomania e l'influsso inglese in Italia nel secolo XVIII* (1911). He died in 1913. BbD; CasWL; DizBI; EncicUni; IndBiltal (16); Magyar; Master (3); Megali, 8 (1928), p. 518; MEW; Meyers

Graf, Charles Henri (Karl Heinrich), born 28 February 1815 at Mulhouse (Haut-Rhin), he studied theology and Oriental languages at Strasbourg and Genève. In 1838 he went to Paris as a private tutor, concurrently completing his study in 1842 with a diploma in theology entitled *Essai sur la vie et les écrits de Jacques LeFèvre d'Étaples*. Since 1844 he was a teacher at Knabeninstitut, Kleinzschocher near Leipzig, Saxony, and since 1847 he taught French and Hebrew at Meißen, Saxony, where he became a titular professor in 1852. Throughout his life he pursued an interest in Persian literature. His writings include *Le Boustan de Sa'dî, texte persan avec un commentaire persan* (Wien, 1858), and *Die geschichtlichen Bücher des Alten Testaments* (1866). He died in Meißen on 16 July 1869. DBF; DtBE; EncJud; GV; IndexBFr² (3); NDB

Gräf, Erwin, born 16 February 1914 at Hückeswaden, Prussia, he studied Oriental languages and comparative religion at Bonn, where he received a Dr.phil. in 1948 for *Das Gerichtswesen der heutigen Beduinen*, a work which was published in 1952, and a Dr.habil. in 1959 from the Universität Köln for *Jagdbeute und Schlachttier im islamischen Recht*. He was a professor of Semitic studies at the Universität Bonn, and a chairman of its Oriental Seminary. His other writings include *Die Geschichte eines Chan's in Smyrna* (1952). He died in Tübingen on 2 February 1976. Index Islamicus (2); Kürschner, 1961-1976; Note

Graf, Georg, born 15 March 1875 at Munzingen im Ries, Bavaria, he received a Dr.phil. in 1905 from the Universität München for *Die christlich-arabische Literatur bis zur fränkischen Zeit*, and a Dr.theol. in 1918 at Freiburg im Breisgau. He was since 1930 a professor in the Theologische Fakultät, München. His writings include *Catalogue de manuscrits arabes chrétiens conservés au Caire* (1934), and *Geschichte der christlichen arabischen Literatur* (1944-50). He died in Dillingen on 18 September 1955. DtBE; DtBilnd (2); Kosch; Kürschner, 1931-1955; NDB; *Studia orientalia*, 1 (1956), pp. 305-307

Graf, Heinz Joachim, born 20th cent., he received a Dr.phil. in 1939 from the Universität Bonn for *Untersuchungen zur Gebärde in der Islendingasaga*. His writings include *Orientalische Berichte des Mittelalters über die Germanen* (1971). GV; Sezgin

Graf, Karl Heinrich, 1815-1869 see Graf, Charles Henri

Grafenauer, Bogo, born 16 March 1916 at Laibach (Ljubljana), Austria-Hungary, he received the classical education of his day and then studied history at the University where he received a doctorate in 1944. His writings include *Kmečki upori na Slovenskem* (1962), *Die ethnische Gliederung und geschichtliche Rolle der westlichen Südslawen im Mittelalter* (1966), and *Boj za staro pravdo v. 15. in 16. stoletju na Slovenskem* (1974). JugoslSa, 1970; Ko je ko, 1957; *Enciklopedija Slovenije* (1989)

Graff, Violette, born 20th cent., her writings include *Les Partis communistes indiens* (Paris, Foundation nationale des sciences politiques, 1974).

Graffam, Mary Louis, born in 1871 at Monson, Me., she graduated from Oberlin College, Ohio. She went in 1901 to Sivas in central Anatolia, where she served for twenty years as principal of the American girls' high school. She had a good deal of talent in languages and acquired a speaking knowledge of French. Her best foreign language was Armenian, but while in military hospital work she acquired a speaking knowledge of Turkish. She was thanked by the British and French governments for her service to their people, decorated by the Turkish government for her service to soldiers and civilians. She was awarded an honorary degree by her alma mater for humanitarian service during the Great War. After the armistice she refused to return home for a long overdue vacation, but she was loathe to leave her charges. She said that she had seen all the agony, and wanted to stay on and see things build up again. She tried to stick it out, but finally died in Sivas from an overworked heart, following an operation for cancer in 1922. Armenian affairs 1 (1949/50), pp. 62-65; Missionary herald, 117 (1921), p. 345; Shavit

Gragger, Robert, born 7 November 1887 at Aranyosmarót, Hungary, he became a professor, and director, Ungarisches Institut, Universität Berlin. He was the founding editor of *Ural-Altaische Jahrbücher* from 1921 to his death in Berlin on 10 November 1926. His writings include *Deutsche Hand-*

schriften in ungarischen Bibliotheken (1921), *Magyar népballadák* (1927), and he was joint author of *Literaturdenkmäler aus Ungarns Türkenzeit* (1927). Geistigeung; Kürschner, 1925, 1926; Magyar; *Wer ist's*, 1922

Graham, A. M. S., he received a Ph.D. in 1962 from the London School of Economics for *Rural water supplies and settlement in Gedara district, Sudan.* Sluglett

Graham, Sir Cyril Clerke, born in 1834, he was a private secretary to the Earl of Carnarvon, and a Secretary of State for Colonies. In 1857 he explored the eastern Hawran region in Syria, a totally *terra incognita* at the time. He died of paralysis at Cannes, 9 May 1895. Boase; Henze

Graham, Gail née Minault *see* Minault, Gail

Graham, Robert, M.A., born in 1942, he was from 1975 to 1977 a correspondent for the *Financial times* in Madrid and Tehran. His writings include *Iran; the illusion of power* (1979), and its translation, *Iran; die Illusion der Macht* (1979). Note

Graham, Stephen, born in 1884 at Edinburgh, he was a novellist and essayist who for years travelled in Russia. He later became associated with the Slavonic Service of the BBC, London. His writings include *Vagabond in the Caucasus* (1911), *Russia and the world* (1915), *Through Russian Central Asia* (1916), and *The Gentle art of tramping* (1926). He died in 1975. Britlnd (1); ConAu 93-96; DLB 195 (1998), pp. 137-154; IntAu&W, 1971, 1976; WhE&EA; *Who was who, 7*

Graham, William Albert, born 16 August 1943 at Raleigh, N.C., he studied at Göttingen before he graduated B.A. *summa cum laude* in 1966 from the University of North Carolina at Chapel Hill, and received his Ph.D. in 1973 from Harvard for *Divine word and prophetic word; the early Muslim understanding of revelation, with special reference to the divine saying, or so-called Hadīth qudsī*, a work which was published in 1977. He conducted field work in Cairo, Damascus as well as in northern India. He won a book prize of the American Council of Learned Societies for 1978, and was a Guggenheim Fellow (1981), and Alexander von Humboldt Fellow (1982). A professor of the history of religion and Islamic studies at Harvard, he became in 1990 a director of Harvard's Center for Middle Eastern Studies. In 1991 he became a master, Currier House, Harvard College. NatFacDr, 1995-2003; Private; Selim³; WhoAm, 1998-2003

Graham-Brown, Sarah, born in 1946, she was a free-lance writer on Middle Eastern affairs, and from 1991 to 1994 a coordinator of the Gulf Information Project of the British Refugee Council, London. Her writings include *Palestinian workers and trade unions* (1980), *Palestinians and their society, 1880-1946* (1980), *Education, repression & liberation, Palestinians* (1984), *Images of women; the portrayal of women in photography of the Middle East, 1860-1950* (1988), and *The Palestinian situation* (1989). LC

Grahame, Kenneth, born in 1859 at Edinburgh, he was a writer, particularly of books for young people. He died in 1932. ConAu 108, new rev. 80; DLB, vol. 34 (1985), pp. 181-89, vol. 141 (1994), pp. 87-102, vol. 178 (1997), pp. 98-102; DNB; Master (70); *Who was who, 3*

Graindorge, P., born 20th cent., he was in 1972 an International Labour Organization expert on co-operative development in Lebanon. Note about the author

Grame, Theodore C., born 28 January 1930 at N.Y.C., he graduated in 1953 from the Manhattan School of Music and subsequently taught musicology successively at Yale University and the Unversity of Pittsburgh. His writings include *America's ethnic music* (1976). DrAS, 1974 H, 1978 H

Gramenitskiĭ, Sergeĭ Mikhailovish, born in 1859, his writings include *Очерк развития народнаго образования Туркестанском крае* (Tashkent, 1916), and *Положение инородческаго образования в Сыр-Ларьинской област* (Tashkent, 1916). He died 5 February 1919. OSK; UzbekSE

Gramlich, Richard Alois, born about 1940, he received a Dr.phil. in 1969 from the Universität Basel for *Die schiitischen Derwischeorden Persiens.* He was an Arabist and a professor of history of religion at his alma mater until 1996, and subsequently until his retirement at the Universität Freiburg im Breisgau. His other writings include *Der reine Gottesglaube* (1983), *Die Wunder der Freunde Gottes* (1987), and he edited *Islamwissenschaftliche Abhandlungen Fritz Meier zum 60. Geburtstag* (1974). Kürschner, 1996-2003

de **Grammont**, Henri Delmas, born 5 August 1830 at Versailles to an old French family of army officers, he started to study law, but at the age of twenty he joined the Zouaves. After two years with an expeditionary force in Kabylia, his colonel was instrumental in having him enter the military school of Saint-Cyr in 1852. After graduation he participated in the Crimean War, returning in 1859 to North Africa, where he remained until 1864. In obedience with his father's wishes he then resigned in order to join the administration at Montbéliard. He participated in the Franco-Prussian War and then retired to Mustapha, Algeria, where he pursued his interest in writing. His writings include *Relations entre la*

France et la Régence d'Alger au XVIIe siècle (1879-85), and *Histoire d'Alger sous la domination turque* (1887). He died in Saint-Eugène on 12 September 1891 or 92. Revue africaine, 36 (1892), pp. 289-311

Gran, Peter, born 14 December 1941 at Jersey City, N.J., he received his Ph.D. in 1974 from the University of Chicago for *A Study in the indigenous origins and early development of modern culture in Egypt; the life and writings of Shaykh Hasan al-'Attār, 1766-1835*. He was a lecturer, or visiting lecturer, at many universities before and after his permanent appointment in 1979 as a professor of history at Temple University, Philadelphia, Pa., a post which he still held in 2003. His writings include *Islamic roots of capitalism; Egypt, 1760-1840* (1979), and *Beyond Eurocentrism* (1996). ConAu 156; DrAS, 1974 H, 1978 H; *MESA Roster of members*, 1977-1990; NatFacDr, 1995-2003; Selim³

Granberg, Beatrice, born in 1916, her writings include *Förteckning över kufiska myntfynd i Finland* (Helsinki, 1966). NUC

Grancsay, Stephen Vincent, born in 1897, he was affiliated with the Metropolitan Museum of Art, New York. His writings include *The Bashford Dean collection of arms and armor in the Metropolitan Museum of Art* (1933), *Historical arms and armor* (1938), as well as exhibition catalogues. He died in 1980. Note about the author; the only other reference found turned out to be wrong

de **Grancy**, Roger Senarclens, born in 1938, he was joint editor of *Großer Pamir; österreichisches Forschungsunternehmen 1975* (Graz, 1978). Note about the author

Grandchamp, Pierre Aubin Thomas Garrigou, born 16 June 1875 at Vitrac-Vincent (Charente), his writings include *La France en Tunisie de 1582 à 1705* (1920-23), *La Mission de Pléville-Le-Pelley à Tunis, 1793-1794* (1921), *Les Différends de 1832-1833 entre la Régence de Tunis et les Royaumes de Sardaigne et des Deux-Siciles* (1931), *Le Royaume de Sardaigne* (1933), and *Documents relatifs à la révolution de 1864 en Tunisie* (1935). He died in 1965 in Tunis. DBF; *Hommes et destins*, vol. 2, pp. 350-52; Index Islamicus (1)

Grande, Bentsion Meerovich, born in 1891 in Siberia, he was from 1929 to 1944 associated with the Institute of the Peoples of the East, Central Executive Committee SSSR. In 1946 he was appointed a professor. His writings include *Грамматические таблицы арабского литературного языка* (1950), *Курс арабской грамматики в сравнительно-историческом освещении* (1963), and *Введение в сравнительное изучение семитских языков* (1972). He died 8 July 1974. Miliband; Miliband²

Grandelehnus, Johannes, fl. 17th cent., he wrote *Türkische, Tartarische, Persianische und Venetianische Chronika oder ... Beschreibung ... von dessen Stifter Mahomet* (Frankfurt am Main, 1665), a work which was also published in the same year entitled *Hungarisch-Siebenbürgisch-Moldau-Wallach-Türk-Tartar-Persian-Venetzianische Chronika oder ... Beschreibung von deß Türkischen Reiches Auffnehemen*, a copy of which is located in Göttingen. From a communication from Prof. F. Sezgin to the writer

Grandgent, Charles Hall, born in 1862 at Dorchester, Mass., he was a graduate of Harvard and became a Romance philologist and a Dante scholar. From 1896 to his retirement in 1932 he served as a professor of Romance languages at his alma mater. He died in 1939. BioIn 3, 5; DAB S2; NatCAB, vol. 13, pp. 539-540; WhAm 4

Grandguillaume, Gilbert, born 20th cent., he received a *doctorat d'état* in 1981 from the Université de Paris for *Relations entre mutations linguistiques et dynamique sociale dans le Maghreb contemporain*. He was affiliated with the École des hautes études en sciences sociales, Paris. His writings include *Nédroma; l'évolution d'une médina* (1976), and *L'Arabisation et politique linguistique au Maghreb* (1983), and he was joint author of *Sanaa hors les murs; une ville arabe contemporaine* (1995). LC; Livres disponibles, 2003; Note; THESAM, 1

Grandguillot, Georges, born 19th cent., he received a law degree, and was in 1924 an *attaché commercial* of France in Egypt. His writings include *Étude sur la crise égytienne* (Alexandrie, 1909). NUC, pre-1956; WhoEgypt, 1952, 1955|

Grand'henry, Jacques, born 20th cent., his writings include *Le parler arabe de Cherchell, Algérie* (Louvain, 1972), and *Les parlers arabes de la région du Mzāb* (Leiden, 1976).

Grandi, Bruno, born 20th cent., his writings include *I conflitti di Cipro* (Milano, 1978), *Cipro e le Nazioni Unite* (Milano, 1978), and *Profili internazionali della questione di Cipro* (Milano, 1983).

Grandin, François *Léonce* Victor, born 1 November 1829 at Besançon (Doubs), he graduated from the military colleges of La Flèche and Saint-Cyr. With the rank of captain he went with his regiment in 1864 to southern Algeria, where he fought the Ouled Sidi Cheikh for four years, returning to metropolitan France in 1868. His writings include *Le Maréchal de Mac-Mahon* (1894), *Le Dahomey* (1895), and *Le Duc d'Aumale* (1897). Lamathière

Grandin-Blanc, Nicole, born 20th cent., she received a *doctorat de 3ème cycle* in 1975 from the Université de Paris for *Le Soudan nilotique et son administration coloniale britannique, 1898-1956; éléments d'interprétation socio-historique d'une expérience coloniale*, a work which was published in 1982. She was joint author of *Madrasa; la transmission du savoir dans le monde musulman* (1997). LC; *Livres disponibles*, 2003; THESAM, 3

de **Grandpré**, Louis Marie Joseph Ohier, born 7 May 1761 at St.-Malo (Ille-et-Vilaine), he became an *enseigne de vaisseau* in 1778, and then served in the East Indies. After his return to France in the 1780s, he resigned from the royal navy and prepared at La Rochelle three vessels for the trade of goods and slaves. When he arrived at Mauritius in 1789, he was suspected of having brought the small-pox to the island. To avoid all complications, he left for Pondichéry, and later, Bengal, before emigrating to England by way of Saint Helena. He returned to France at the time of the *consulat*. His writings include *Voyage à la côte occidentale d'Afrique fait dans les années 1786 et 1787* (1801), *Voyage dans l'Inde et au Bengal faits dans les années 1789 et 1790* (1801), and its translations, *Reise nach Indien und Arabien in den Jahren 1789 und 1790* (1802), and *A voyage to the Indian Ocean and to Bengal undertaken in the year 1790, containing an account of the Seychelles Islands and Trincomale ... to which is added a voyage in the Red Sea, including a description of Mocha, and of the trade of the Arabs of Yemen* (1803). He died in Paris on 7 January 1846. DBF; Hoefer; IndexBFr² (3); Master (1)

Grandval, Yves *Gilbert* Edmond, born 12 February 1904 at Paris, he was an executive in the chemical industry before his mobilization in 1940. Later that year he entered the movement "Ceux de la Résistance." After the war he was a military governor of the Sarre, and a resident-general of France in Morocco. He subsequently became a politician. His writings include *Ma mission au Maroc* (1956). He died in 1981. BioIn, 4, 7, 17; DBF; DBFC; IndexBFr² (2); IntWW, 1974/75-1981/82; NDNC, 1968; WhoFr, 1957/58-1981/82; WhoWor, 1974/75-1978/79

Grangeret de la Grange, Jean Baptiste André, born in 1790 at Paris, he was a student of Silvestre de Sacy in Arabic and Persian. A member of the Société asiatique since 1822, he was named a deputy librarian at the library of the Arsenal. He subsequently joined the Imprimérie royale as an Oriental editor. His writings include *Les Arabes en Espagne; extrait des historiens orientaux* (1824), and *Anthologie arabe ou choix de poésies arabes inédites* (1826). He edited and translated pieces of poetry from al-Mutanabbī and al-Safadī, which he published in the *Journal asiatique*, *Journal étrangère*, and in Hammer-Purgstall's *Fundgruben des Orients*. He died in Paris in 1859. DBF

de la **Granja Santamaría**, Fernando, born in 1928, he received a doctorate in Arabic literature in 1960 from the Universidad de Madrid for *Seleccion de la Fadalat al-jiwan*, of al-Tuyubi, and became a professor of Arabic and Islamic studies at the Universidad Complutense de Madrid. He was a member of the Real Academia de la Historia. His writings include *La Cocina arabigoandaluza segun un manu-scrito inedito* (1960), and *Maqāmas y risālas andaluzas* (1976). He died in Madrid, 24 February 1999. *Aljamía* 11 (1999), pp. 29-35; Arabismo, 1992; EURAMES, 1993; NUC

Grannes, Alf, born 31 July 1936 at Stavanger, Norway, he received a diploma in 1963 from the École nationale des langues orientales vivantes, Paris, and a dr.philos. in 1972 from the Universitetet i Bergen for Фонетические и морфологические элементы просторечного и диалектного харак-тера в языке русской комедии и комической оперы второй половины XVIII века. He was a professor of Russian at Bergen from 1971 to 1988, when he was appointed a professor of Slavic philology at Tampereen Yliopiston, Finland. His writings include *Études sur les turcismes en bulgare* (1970), and the published edition of his thesis, Просторечныеи диалектные элементы в языке русской комедии XVIII века (1972). Hvem er hvem, 1994

Granqvist, Hilma Natalia, born 17 July 1890 at Helsinki, she came to anthropology from Biblical studies. After graduating from Helsinki University in 1921 in pedagogy, history and philosophy, she took courses in Old Testament studies at Berlin with the intention of writing a book on women in the Old Testament. Realizing that the literature provided insufficient evidence on the subject, she resolved to go to Palestine to study contemporary village life. In 1925 she was granted financial support and left for Jerusalem in the summer of that year. There she attended a two-month course in Palestinian archaeology. Contacts with an Alsacian missionary family at Artas made her decide to chose this region as a centre of research. Three years of field work between 1925 and 1931 were the basis for most of her books. In 1931 the first volume of *Marriage conditions in a Palestinian village* was published, for which she was awarded her doctorate by the Åbo Academy, the Swedish University in Finland. Throughout the 1930s she tried to get financial support for a return visit to Palestine without success. It was not until 1959 that she returned for four months. Her other writings include *Arabskt Familjeliv* (1939), *Birth and death among the Arabs; studies in a Muhammadan village in Palestine* (c1947, 1975), and *Muslim death and burial; Arab customs and traditions studied in a village in Jordan*

(1965). She died in Helsinki on 25 February 1972. *Index Islamicus (2); Palestine exploration quarterly,* 104 (1972), pp. 169-70; *Vem och vad,* 1936-1970

Granstrem, Evgeniia Éduardovna, his writings on Byzantine and Slavic manuscripts include *Описание русских и славянских пергаменных рукописей* (Leningrad, 1953), and *О подготовке сводного каталога славянских рукописей* (Leningrad, 1958). OSK

Grant, Arnold Harrison, born 20th cent., he received a Ph.D. in 1973 from UCLA for his thesis, *The Tunisian ulema, 1873-1915; social structure and response to ideological currents.* Selim

Grant, Asahel, born in 1807 at Marshall, N.Y., he studied medicine and in 1835 went to Urmia, Persia, as a medical missionary. He travelled widely in Kurdistan, experiences which he described in his *The Nestorians* (1841), a work which was translated into French (1843) and Dutch (1844). He died in Mosul on 24 April 1844. ACAB; DAB; *Encyclopedia of missions* (1904); Henze; NatCAB, vol. 4, p. 457; Shavit; WhAm H

Grant, Sir Charles, born in 1836, he was educated at Harrow and Trinity College, Cambridge, as well as Haileybury. He went to India in 1858 and served in the North West Province and the Central Provinces. From 1881 to his retirement in 1885 he was a foreign secretary to the Government of India. His writings include *The Gazetteer of the Central Provinces of India* (1870). He died on 12 April 1903. Buckland; DNB; IndianBiInd (2); Riddick; *Who was who,* 1

Grant, Christina née Phelps, 1902-1972 *see* Harris, Christina née Phelps

Grant, Ethel Watts Mumford, born in 1878 at N.Y.C., she studied art at Julian Academy, Paris, and with Merle Guise in New York. She began writing in connection with illustration and travel. She was a playwright, poet, and novelist. She was a charter member of the Colony Club and a member of the American Oriental Society. She edited *The hundred love songs of Kamal ad-Din of Isfahan* (1903). She died in 1940. CurBio, 1940; NYT, 3 May 1940, p. 21, col. 6; WhAm 1; WhoAm, 1932/33-1936/37

Grant, Gillian M., born 13 May 1953 at Blackburn, Lancashire. In the 1980s she was for many years an archivist at the Middle East Centre, St Antony's College, Oxford, where she catalogued the Centre's collection of photographs. Concurrently she was an active member of the Middle East Libraries Committee. In the 1990s she became a free-lance archivist specializing in the care of photographic collections. Her writings include *Images of Istanbul, 1829-1988; an exhibition* (1988), and *Middle Eastern photographic collections in the United Kingdom* (1989). She was joint author of *The Emirates by the first photographers* (1996), *Saudi Arabia by the first photographers* (1996), and *Kuwait by the first photographers* (1998). Private

Grant, Sir John Peter, born in 1774, he studied law at Edinburgh and was called to the bar from Lincoln's Inn in 1802. He was a member of Parliament before he went in 1827 to India, where he served as a judge, first at Bombay and later at Calcutta. He wrote on legal subjects. He died on 17 May 1848 on his voyage homewards. Buckland; DNB; IndianBiInd (1); Riddick

Grant, Nathaniel Philip, born 18 November 1774 at New York, he entered the East India Company as a military officer. As a captain in the 15th Regiment of Bengal Sepoys, he was sent in 1809 by John Malcolm to explore the Makran coast to ascertain whether a European army could penetrate into India by the south coast of India. In early 1810 he was sent to explore Luristan where soon after arrival he was slain by a bandit near Khurramābād in April. There is a cenotaph in his memory on the river side at Barrackpore. EncIran; IndianBiInd (1); Wright, pp. 150-51

Grant, Sir Patrick, born in 1804 in Scotland, he spent forty years with the Bengal Army in India and retired with the rank of field-marshal. He died in London in 1895. Boase; BritInd (2); Buckland; DNB; IndianBiInd (1); Riddick

Grant-Duff, Sir Evelyn Mountstuart, born in 1863, he was a British diplomat who served in Persia from 1892-1894 and 1905-1906. He was in attendance on Muzaffar al-Din Shah during his state visit to London in 1902. He died in 1926 in Bath.. BritInd (1); EncIran; Who, 1916-1925; *Who was who* 2

Grant Duff, Sir Mountstuart Elphinstone, born in 1829 in Scotland, he was educated at Balliol College, Oxford, and became a barrister and member of Parliament. He served as colonial administrator in India. His writings include *Studies in European politics* (1866), *A Political survey* (1868), and *A History of the Mahrattas* (1918). He died in 1906 in London. Buckland; DNB; IndianBiInd (1); MembriiAR; Riddick; *Who was who,* 1

Grantovskiĭ, Édvin Ardivovich, born 16 February 1932 at Moscow, he was an Iranian scholar of Latvian descent who reeived his first degree in 1954 from the Moscow Faculty of History for *Ираноязычные письмена Передней Азии в IX-VIII вв. до н.э.* He subsequently spent his entire career with the Institute of Oriental Studies in the Soviet Academy of Science. His writings include

657

Ранняя история иранских племен Передней Азии (1970), and he was a joint author of *Om Скифии до Индии* (1974). He died 28 June 1995. EncIran; Miliband; Miliband²; OSK

Grasset, Jean *Daniel*, born 8 March 1819, he gained a diploma in letters and subsequently taught at lycées in Bordeaux, Paris, Rodez, Tournon, Avignon, Chaumont, Nîmes, Tarbes, and finally Alger, where he died in 1879. He was a *chevallier de la Légion d'honneur*. IndexBFr² (1)

Grasshoff, Richard, born in 1873, he received a Dr.phil. in 1895 from the Universität Königsberg for *Die allgemeinen Lehren des Obligationsrechts (Verpflichtungsfähigkeit, Strellvertretung, Bürgschaft, Konkurs und Vergleich) sowie die Lehre vom Kauf-, Vollmachts-, Gesellschaftsvertrage und von den Realkontrakten nach der Rechtsschule des Imam Esch-Schāfi'ī; ein Abschnitt aus dem Kitāb el-bujū' des Abū Ishāk Esch-Schīrāzī, übersetzt und kommentiert*, and also his Dr.jur. in 1899 for *Die Suftaġa und Hawâla der Araber; ein Beitrag zur Geschichte des Wechsels*. His other writings include *Droit de changes des Arabes* (1911), *Belgiens Schuld* (1915), and its translation, *La Belgique coupable* (1915). GV; Sezgin

Grassmann, Joachim, born 23 June 1886 at Köpenick near Berlin, he studied law and political economy at Berlin and Heidelberg, where he received a Dr.phil. in 1909 for *Deutsche Konsular-Berichterstattung*. His writings include *Die Schiffahrt in Mesopotamien* (1916). Thesis

Grassmuck, George Ludwig, born 17 September 1919 at Nebraska City, Nebr., he graduated in 1941 from U.C.L.A. and received his Ph.D. in 1949 from Johns Hopkins University, Baltimore, Md. He was a professor in his field at a variety of American universities, including A.U.B. His writings include *Sectional biases in Congress on foreign policy* (1951), he was joint author of *A Manual of Lebanese administration* (1955), and he edited *Afghanistan; some new approaches* (1969). AmM&WSc, 1973 S; 1978 S; Master (1); MESA Roster of members, 1977-1990; WhoAm, 1974/75-2000|

Gratzl, Emil, born 30 December 1877 at München, he studied classical and Oriental philology at Marburg and München, where he received a Dr.phil. in 1906 for *Die altarabischen Frauennamen, mit einer Einleitung über die Geschichte des arabischen Personennamens bis zum Ende der Ğâhilijja*. He became a chief librarian of Bayerische Staatsbibliothek, München. His writings include *Islamische Bucheinbände des 14. bis 19. Jahrhunderts* (1924). In 1953 he was honoured by *Festgabe der Bayerischen Staatsbibliothek Emil Gratzl zum 75. Geburtstag*. He died in München on 9 January 1957. DtBE; JahrDtB, 1955; Kosch; Kürschner, 1954; NDB; RHbDtG; Thesis

Gratzl, Karl, born in 1934, he edited *Hindukusch; Österreichische Forschungexpedition in den Wakhan, 1970* (Graz, 1972). Note; ZKO

Grau, Román Perpiñá, 1902- see Perpiñá y Grau, Román

Grau i Montserrat, Manuel, born 20th cent., he received a doctorate in Semitic philology, specializing in the history of Islam, particularly Muslim Spain. He taught history and geography at Barcelona. Arabismo, 1992

Graul, Carl Friedrich Leberecht, born 6 February 1821 at Wörlitz, Anhalt, the son of a simple, Christian weaver, he was initially educated by a friend of the family, before graduating in 1834 from the Gymnasium at Zerbst. He then matriculated in the Faculty of Theology at Leipzig, where he soon won a prize for the dating of the Epistles of Paul the Apostle. After the completion of his study he became for two years a private teacher with an English family in Italy. Having acquired also a knowldege of English and French, he returned to Dessau, where he taught at a private institute until 1843, when he accepted the directorship of the Dresden missionary society. This was the beginning of his theological career, during which he established Protestant missionary science as part of the theological university curriculum. From 1849 to 1853 he gathered practical experience during study travel in the East, a journey which he described in *Reise nach Ostindien über Palästina und Egypten* (1854-56). His other writings include *Die christlichen Missionsplätze der ganzen Erde* (1847). He died on 10 November 1864, less than five months after his inauguration lecture at the Faculty of Theology, Universität Erlangen. ADtB, vol. 9, pp. 604-605; DtBE; DtBilnd (3); Henze; Master (1); NDB; Stache-Rosen, pp. 46-47

Graul, Heidemarie, born 20th cent., her writings include *Künstlerische Urteile im Rahmen der staatlichen Förderungstätigkeit* (Berlin, 1970). Sezgin

Graul, Richard Ernst, born 24 June 1862 at Leipzig, he received a Dr.phil. in 1889 at Zürich for *Beiträge zur Geschichte der dekorativen Skulptur in den Niederlanden*. He was a sometime editor of *Zeitschrift für bildende Kunst* and a director of Kunstgewerbe-Museum, Leipzig. His writings include *Ostasiatische Kunst und ihr Einfluß auf Europa* (1906). DtBilnd (2); RHbDtG; Wer ist's, 1922-1935

Graulle, A., born 19th cent., he translated *La "Daouhat an-nâchir"* (1913), from the Arabic of Muhammad b. 'Alī ibn 'Askar, *Nachr al-mathânî* (1913) from M. b. al-Tayyib b. Abī M. Sîdî 'Abd al-

658

Salam al-Charif al-Qâdirî, and *Les Idrisis* (1925), from the *K. el-Istiqça li akhbar doual el-Maghrib el-Aqşa*, of Ahmed b. Khaled en-Naciri es-Slaoui. BN; GAL

Graulle, Eugène Vincent, born 19th cent., he was a *commandant* in the French army, stationed in Algeria, who retired from active service in 1892. He published numerous articles in the periodical press of Oranie. His *L'Insurrection de Bou Amama* (1905), profits from his intrinsic acquaintance with native affairs. Peyronnet, p. 899

Graven, Jean, born 27 April 1899 at Sion (Valai), he studied law at the Université de Genève and became a judge and university administrator. His writings include *Le code pénal de l'Empire d'Ethiopie de 23 juillet 1957* (1959), *L'Argot et la tatouage des criminels* (1962), *Penser agir, vivre selon le droit* (1962), and *Le Difficile progrès du règne de la justice et de la paix internationales par le droit, des origines à la Société des nations* (1970). In 1969 he was honoured by *Études en l'honneur de Jean Graven*. He was also awarded several honorary doctorates. WhoSwi, 1950/51-1992/93

Graven, Mortimer, born about 1900, he was since 1927 an administrative secretary of the American Council of Learned Societies, where he had particular charge of all developments in fields of scholarship not sufficiently worked by American scholars. His writings include *The Library of Congress' PL-480 foreign acquisition program* (1969). Note

Graves, Charles Iverson, born 26 July 1838 at Longwood, Ga., he was a graduate of Annapolis Naval Academy, 1857, and served in the Confederate Navy during the Civil War. In 1875 he joined the Khedivial service and was port officer at Massawa during the Egyptian-Abyssinian war, 1875-1876. Afterwards he was sent on scientific missions to the Somali coast. He published his report in the *Bulletin de la Société khédiviale de géographie*. He resigned from Egyptian service in 1878 and became a civil engineer in Rome, Ga., where he died on 5 November 1896. Hill; Shavit

Graves, Philip Perceval, born in 1876, he was educated at Haileybury and Oxford, and became a correspondent for the London *Times* in the Middle East for several years. He contributed to the exposure of the *Protocols of the Elders of Zion*. His writings include *Palestine, the land of three faiths* (1923), *The Question of the Straits* (1931), and *Briton and Turk* (1941). He died in 1953. BioIn, 2; BritInd (2); NYT, 4 June 1953, p. 24, col. 5; WhE&EA; Who, 1936-1953; Who was who, 5

Graves, Theodore Dumaine, born 2 June 1932 at Concord, Mass., he graduated in 1954 from Earlham College, and received a Ph.D. in 1962 from the University of Pennsylvania for *Time perspective and the deferred gratification pattern in a tri-ethnic community*. He was an anthropologist and social psychologist who taught at a variety of American universities. His writings include *A Bibliography of culture change* (1966). AmM&WS, 1973 S; AmM&WS, 1976 P; WhoWest, 1984/85

Gravier, Gabriel, born 17 February 1827 at Sancoins (Cher). With only elementary education, he joined the army at the age of eighteen and served until 1852, when he settled in Rouen and joined the Administration des Eaux-et-forêts. From 1856 to his retirement in 1895 he enjoyed a modest career with the French railway company. Although his large family prevented him from travelling, this did not stop him from pursuing an interest in geography. He was instrumental in the creation of the Société normande de géographie and served first as their president and later as secretary-general. He wrote a great many biographies of geographers and explorers. He died in Rouen on 18 November 1904. DBF

Gravier, Gaston, born in 1886 at Liffol-le-Grand (Vosges), he studied at the Université de Lille, where he took Russian. He taught at Kharkov and Beograd. He received a doctorate for a thesis on the natural regions of Serbia. In 1912, during the Balkan war, he visited various fronts of the Serbian army. He turned down a teaching position at one of the Austrian universities. His writings include *Les Frontières historiques de la Serbie* (1919), as well as articles in a variety of periodicals, including *Correspondance d'Orient*. He died in the war in Souchez (Pas-de-Calais), 10 June 1915. DBF

Gravier, Gustave, he was in 1956 a directeur général of Energie électrique du Maroc. Note

Gravina, Manfredi, born of Germano-Italian parentage on 14 June 1885 at Palermo, he was a militant nationalist who entered the Reale Accademia navale, Livorno, in 1900. In 1905 he accompanied an Italian naval detachment to East Asian waters. After his return home, he made use of his family connections to study new technologies in Germany. His participation in the conquest of Tripolitania resulted in the promotion to *tenente di vascello*. In 1920 he entered the Italian foreign service. Since 1924 a member of the Italian delegation to the League of Nations, he was appointed High Commissioner for Danzig in 1929. He died in Danzig on 19 September 1932. His writings include *Attualità politiche* (1926), and *Problemi italiani d'oltr'Alpe et d'oltre mare* (1930). DizBI; Sezgin

Gray, Albert Lewis, born 30 November 1917 at Philadelphia, Pa., he graduated in 1939 from Drexel University, and received a Ph.D. in 1958 from the University of Pennsylvania for *Secular movements*

and cycles in financial contributions to ten selected Protestant denominations, 1900 to 1954. He was a recipient of several post-doctoral fellowships, and for many years served as a professor of economics at Baldwin-Wallace College, Berea, Ohio, as well as visiting professor at Ahmadu Bello University, Laria, Nigeria. AM&WS, 1973 S, 1978 S; Note

Gray, Basil, born 21 June 1904, and educated a New College, Oxford, he was for over thirty years a keeper of Oriental antiquities at the British Museum, London. His writings include *Persian painting* (1930), and he was joint author of *Studies in Chinese and Islamic art* (1985). He died in 1989. BioIn, 14, 16, 17; ConAu, 9-10, 128; DNB; EncIran; *Index Islamicus* (3); Master (1); Who, 1959-1989; WhoWor, 1982/83-1989/90; *Who was who* 8

Gray, Ezio Maria, born 9 October 1885 at Novara (Piedmont), he was a journalist for provincial periodicals, and in 1911 became a correspondent of the Agenzia Stefani for the war in Tripolitania. From 1926 to 1934 he was an editor of *Economia nazionale.* He was arrested on 24 May 1945 for his political role during the Mussolini era and tried in the High Court of Justice. Condemned to twenty years in prison, he came free under a 1946 amnesty. In 1948 he founded the weekly, *Il Nazionale,* and in the 1950s he re-entered politics. His writings, partly under the pseudonym Caesar Niuska, include *Guerra senza sangue* (1916), its translation, *The Bloodless war* (1916), *Un Ulisside in terra d'Africa* (1935), *Noi e Tunisi* (1939), its translations, *Italien und die Frage von Tunis* (1939), and *Italy and the question of Tunis* (1939). He died in Roma on 8 February 1969. *Chi è,* 1928-1961; DizBI; IndBiItal (2); WhoItaly, 1958

Gray, John Alfred, born in 1858 at London, he was educated in London, where he later joined the St. Mary's Infirmary. He was a sometime surgeon to the Amir of Afghanistan, 'Abd al-Raḥmān Khān. His writings include *At the court of the Amir* (1895). *Medical who's who,* 1914

Gray, Sir John Milner, born in 1889 at Cambridge, he was educated at the local King's College, and called to the bar from Gray's Inn in 1932. He was a colonial judge who served as Judge of the Supreme Court, Gambia, 1934-1942, and Chief Justice, Zanzibar, 1943-1952. He wrote *A History of Gambia* (1940), *Early Portuguese missionaries in East Africa* (1958), *History of Zanzibar* (1962), as well as histories of Cambridge. He died in 1970. BritInd (1); ConAu, 29-32; Who, 1946-1970; *Who was who,* 6

Gray, John *Richard,* born 7 July 1929 at Weymouth, Dorset, he was educated at Downing College, Cambridge, and received a Ph.D. in 1957 from SOAS for *The Southern Sudan, 1839-1889.* He was since 1972 a professor of African history in the University of London. His writings include *The Two nations* (1960), *A History of the Southern Sudan* (1961), *Pre-colonial African trade* (1970), and he was joint author of *Materials for West African history in Italian archives* (1965). ConAu, 1-4, new rev. 5; Sluglett; Unesco; Who, 1973-2003; WhoWor, 1976/77

Gray, John Walton David, born 1 October 1936 at Burry Port, Carmarthenshire, he was educated at Cambridge and the foreign language school in Shemlan, Lebanon. He was a British diplomat who was predominantly posted to the Middle East. Who, 1982-2003; WhoWor, 1991/92

Gray, Louis Herbert, born 10 April 1875 at Newark, N.J., he received a Ph.D. in 1902 from Columbia University, New York, for *Indo-Iranian phonology, with special reference to the middle and new Indo-Iranian languages.* He was an editor for a variety of encyclopaedias before the first World War. From 1919 to 1920 he served with the American Peace Commission in Paris, before becoming a professor of philology successively at the University of Nebraska, and Columbia University. His writings include *The Foundations of the Iranian religions* (1925), and he translated from the Persian *The hundred love songs of Kamal ad-Din of Isfahan* (1903). He died 18 August 1955. EncIran; NatCAB, vol. 15, p. 194; NYT, 20 August 1955, p. 17, col. 6; WhAm 3

Grayson, Benson Lee, born 1 December 1932 at N.Y.C., he graduated in 1953 from New York University, and received graduate degrees from Harvard and Columbia universities. From 1957 to 1964 he was a foreign service officer with the U.S. Department of State. His writings include *United States-Iranian relations* (1980), and *Saudi-American relations* (1982). ConAu, 93-96

Graz, Liesl, born about 1950, she was a Swiss journalist specializing in Middle Eastern affairs. She wrote for the *Economist* as well as other periodicals. Her writings include *L'Irak au présent* (1979), *Les Omanis, nouveaux gardiens du Golfe* (1981), and *The Turbulent Gulf* (1990). Note

Grazhdankina, N. S., fl. 1963, she was joint author of *Архитектурная керамика Узбекистана; очерк исторического развития и опут реставрации* (Tashkent, 1968). NUC, 1968-1972

Graziani, Joseph Salvatore, born in 1938, he received a Ph.D. in 1972 from U.C.L.A. for *Arabic medicine in the eleventh century as represented in the works of Ibn Jazlah,* a work which was published in 1980. In the following year he was an instructor in Middle East history and foreign languages at U.N.L.V. LC; ZKO

Graziani, Rodolfo, born 11 August 1882 at Filettino (Frosinone), he was a colonial army officer who rose to the rank of general. He served first in Eritrea from 1908 to 1913 and later became a deputy governor of Cyrenaica. In 1950 he was condemned to death for collaboration with the Germans, but was freed four months later, falling under an amnesty. His writings include *Verso il Fezzan* (1930), and *Libia redenta; storia di trent'anni di passione italiana in Africa* (1948). He died in Roma, 11 January 1955. Chi è, 1931-1948; DizBI; EncItaliana; IndBiltal (3)

Gréard, Valéry Clément Octave, born 18 April 1828 at Paris, he graduated from the Collège de Versailles and in 1849 entered the École normale supérieure together with other celebrities of the century. After graduation he served successively at lycées in Metz, Versailles, and Paris until an illness affecting his vocal cordes put an end to his teaching career. Since 1864 he was an inspector of education in Paris and its surroundings. In 1879 he was nominated *vice-recteur* of the Académie de Paris, a post which he held for twenty-three years. More important than his professional career is the effect of his writings on French education, which include *L'Éducation des femmes par les femmes* (1886), and *Éducation et instruction* (1887). He was an elected member of the Académie des sciences morales et politiques, and the Académie française. A *grand officier* of the Légion d'honneur, he died in Paris on 25 April 1904. DBF; *Cyclopedia of education* (c1911, 1968) [not sighted]

Greaves, Rosa (Rose) Louise, born 12 February 1925 at Kansas City, Kan., she graduated in 1946 from the University of Kansas, and received her Ph.D. in 1952 from the University of London, for a work which was published in 1959 entitled *Persia and the defence of India, 1884-1892; a study in the foreign policy of the third Marquis of Salisbury*. She taught history at a variety of universities in America, England, Canada, and lastly the University of Kansas at Lawrence. DrAS, 1974 H, 1978 H, 1982 H

Greaves, John, born in 1602, he educated at Balliol College, Oxford. After a short spell of teaching geometry in Gresham College, London, he set off in 1637 with his friend, the Oxford professor of Arabic, Edward Pococke, for Constantinople. Greaves is an example of the amateur Arabist of the period. He was primarily interested in astronomy. After spending some months with Pococke in Constantinople, he went on to Egypt, where he collected a considerable number of Arabic, Persian, and Greek manuscripts, and made a more accurate survey of the pyramids than any traveller who had preceded him. In 1643 he was appointed to the Savilian professorship of astronomy at Oxford, but he was deprived of his Gresham professorshipfor having neglected his duties. In 1645 he attempted a reformation of the calendar, but his plan was not adopted. He died in London in 1652. BritInd (15); Dawson; DNB; Egyptology; EncBrit

Greaves, Thomas, born in 1612, he was educated at Charterhouse School, and Corpus Christi College, Oxford. He acted as Edward Pococke's deputy at Oxford, while the latter was making his second journey in the East, from 1637 to 1641. On 19 July 1637 he delivered his inaugural lecture entitled *De linguae arabicae utilitate et praestantia*, a work which was published in 1639. BritInd (6); DNB

Grech, Prosper(o), born 24 December 1925, he studied at St. Joseph and St. Catherine schools, and subsequently at the universities of Malta and London. In 1943 he entered the Augustinian Order and studied philosophy at the Order's College in Rabat, and theology at St. Monica's International College in Roma. Ordained in 1950, he was awarded in 1957 a British Council scholarship to study Oriental languages at Oxford. In the following year he was a rsearch assistant to Arthur J. Arberry at Cambridge, where he also gained a M.A. from Pembroke College. His writings include *The Atonement and God; the main theories in modern English theology* (1955), *Educating Christians* (1960), and *Acts of the Apostles explained* (1966). Mifsud, p. 165

Grech-Mifsud, John, born 19th cent., he was a lawyer and, in 1916, a member of the Société sultanieh d'économie politique, de statistique et de législation. His trace is lost after an article in 1917. Note about the author

Grecu, Vasile, born 31 July 1885 at Mitocu Dragomirnei, Romania, he studied at Wien and Cernăuţi. He was from 1920 to 1938 a professor of history at Cernăuţi, and from 1938 to 1947 at Bucureşti. His writings include *Darstellung altheidnischer Denker und Schriftsteller der Kirchenmalerei des Morgenlandes* (1924), he edited *Istoria turco-bizantină, 1341-1462* (1958), and he edited and translated *Din domnia lui Mahomed al II-lea, anii 1451-1467* (1963). He died in Bucureşti on 27 May 1972. DcEnc; Dicţionar; MembriiAR

Greely, John Nesmith, born 6 June 1885 at Washington, D.C., he was a brigadier general in the U.S. Army, whose writings include *War breaks down doors* (1929). He died in Washington, D.C., 13 June 1965. Shavit; WhAm, 4

Green, Arnold Harrison, born 2 July 1940 at Los Angeles, he received a Ph.D. in 1973 from U.C.L.A. for *The Tunisian ulama, 1873-1915; social structure and response to ideological currents*, a work which was published in 1978. He was a professor of history at American universities as well as A.U.C. He was joint author of *A Survey of Arab history* (1985). Selim; WhoWor, 1987/88

Green, James Wyche, born 5 August 1915 at Alton, Va., he was a sociologist and anthropologist who received a Ph.D. in 1953 from the University of New York. He was from 1954 to 1959 assigned to the U.S. Operations Mission to Pakistan, serving first as associate chief and then as chief community development advisor to the Government of Pakistan. He subsequently served as a university lecturer, or consultant, in rural and urban development affairs. Note; Master (1); WhoAm, 1974/75-1999|; WhoWor, 1980/81-1989/90

Green, Lawrence Winter, born 16 September 1940 at Bell, Calif., he graduated in 1962 from the University of California at Berkeley, where he also received a Ph.D. in 1968 for *Status inconsistency, reference group theory, and preventive health behavior.* He subsequently taught public health and community development at a variety of international universities. He was joint author of *Seven years of clinic experience under the 'traditional planned parenthood approach' in Karachi* (1965), and *Demographic implications of the first six years of family planning in Karachi, 1958-1964* (1966). AmM&WS, 1976-1992 P; ConAu 69-72, new rev., 12, 42; Master (2); WhoWest, 1992/93, 1994/95

Green, Leslie Claude, born 6 November 1920 at London, he took all his degrees at London. He was from 1965 to his retirement in 1991 a professor of law at the University of Alberta, Edmonton, and served also as a visiting professor throughout the world. His writings include *International law through the cases* (1951), and *The Position of the individual in international law* (1960). AmM&WS, 1973 S, 1978 S; Canadian, 1985-2003; ConAu, 13-16; DrAS, 1974 P, 1978 P, 1982 P; WhoAm, 1980-1995|; WhoWest, 1976-1994/95; WhoWorJ, 1965

Greenberg, Joseph Harold, born 28 May 1915 at Brooklyn, N.Y., he received a Ph.D. in 1941 from Northwestern University, Evanston, Illinois, for *The religion of a Sudanese culture as influenced by Islam*, a work which was carried out as a field fellow of the Social Science Research Council. He was from 1962 to 1985 a professor of anthropology and linguistics at Stanford University. His writings include *The Languages of Africa* (1963). He died in Palo Alto on 7 May 2001. AmM&WS, 1973 S; AmM&WS, 1976 P; ConAu 102, 196; DrAS,, 1978 F, 1982 F; IntWW, 1974/75-2001; Selim; Unesco

Greene, Brook A., born 20th cent., he received a Ph.D. in 1971 from Cornell University, Ithaca, N.Y., for *Rate of adoption of new farm practices in the Central Plains of Thailand*, a work which was published in 1973. He was in 1974 a member of the Faculty of Agricultural Sciences, A.U.B. He was joint author of *The Feed-livestock economy of Lebanon, with projection 1976 and 1981* (1973), and *Selected socio-economic characteristics of Kohistan and Panjsher Districts, Kapisa Province, Afghanistan* (1974). NUC, 1973-1977

Greene, Frederick Davis, born 19th cent., his writings include *The Armenian crisis in Turkey* (New York, 1895), *Armenian massacres* (London, 1896), and *The Rule of the Turk* (New York, 1896). NUC, pre-1956

Greene, Joseph Kingsbury, born 10 April 1834 at Auburn, Me., he graduated in 1855 from Bowdoin College, and in 1857 from Union Theological Seminary. In 1857 he married Elizabeth A. Davis, a graduate from Mount Holyoke Seminary. They sailed for Smyrna, 17 January 1859, arriving after a voyage of thirty-five days. He served three years at İzmit (Nicomedia) until he was transferred in 1862 to Bursa. Ill health obliged him to take a three-year holiday in America. Except two more furloughs, he remained in Turkey until 1909, editing the *Avedaper*, publishing mission periodicals, lesson books, and preparing the tenth edition of the Armenian hym and tune book. His own writings include *Kingdom of God* (1909), and *Leavening the Levant* (1916). He retired to Oberlin, Ohio, where he died on 10 February 1917. Missionary herald, 113 (1917), pp. 169-170

Greene, Ruth Altman (Mrs. Phillips F. Greene), born in 1896, and educated at Wellesley College, she spent the years 1921 to 1923 in Turkey, where her medical missionary husband was professor of anatomy at the Constantinople College. Because of the drastic law of the Turkish Government against American doctors, they left Turkey in 1923, to return first to the United States, and in the autumn of the same year, went to China. She wrote *Hsiang-Ya journal* (1977). Shavit - Asia

Greenfield, James, born in 1874 at Tabriz, Persia, he studied at Leipzig, Berlin, and Tübingen, where he received a Dr.jur. He was in 1935 a member of Deutsche Armenische Gesellschaft. His writings include *Die Verfassung des persischen Staates* (1904), and *Das Handelsrecht einschließlich des Obligationen- und Pfandrechts, das Urkundenrecht, Konkursrecht und das Fremdenrecht von Persien* (1908). Wer ist's, 1922-1935

Greenfield, Jonas Carl, born 30 October 1926 at New York, he graduated in 1949 from the City College of New York and subsequently studied also Arabic at the New School of New York. He received a Ph.D. in ancient Semitic languages in 1956 from Yale University, New Haven, Conn. He became an authority in Aramaic and in 1971 was appointed a professor in his field at the Hebrew University, Jerusalem. He edited *New directions of Biblical archaeology* (1969). He died in Jerusalem, 13 March 1995. ConAu 110; DrAS, 1969 F, 1974 F, 1978 F, 1982 F; REJ 156 (1997), pp. 495-497

Greenfield, William, born in 1799 at London, he was a prodigous linguist who began teaching at the age of sixteen. Since 1824 he devoted himself to languages and Biblical criticism. In 1830 he was engaged by the British and Foriegn Bible Society as superintendent of the editorial department. His writings include *The Syriac New Testament according to the Peshita version* (1895). He died in 1831. BritInd (3); DNB; Master (2)

Greenhow, Henry Martineau, born 6 September 1829 at Newcastle-on-Tyne, he was educated at Newcastle and University College, London, where he obtained the diploma of the College of Surgeons. He was appointed an assistant surgeon to the Bengal Army, sailing for India in 1854. On the annexation of Oudh in 1856, he was nominated by the governor-general to the charge of the 1st Cavalry Regiment of the Oudh Irregular Force. He participated in the Indian Mutiny. He was also a novelist. His writings include *Observations on goitre as seen in Oudh* (1859), *The Bow fate* (1893), and *Leila's lover* (1902). He died in Esher, Surrey, on 26 November 1912. BritInd (1); IndianBiInd (1)

Greenidge, Charles Wilton Wood, born in 1889 on Barbados, B.W.I., he was educated in Barbados and Cambridge, England. He served as a judge at Barbados, and as magistrate at Port-of-Spain, Trinidad. His writings include *Forced labour* (1943), *Slavery in the twentieth century* (1952), *Memorandum on Slavery* (1953), *Slavery at the United Nations* (1954), and *Slavery* (1958). He died in 1972. Au&Wr, 1971; Who was who, 7

Greenip, William E., born 20th cent., he was in 1962 a director, American Friends of the Middle East, Jordan. Note about the author

Greenslade, W. G., he certainly served from 1926 to 1937 in Beirut as a missionary of the Presbyterian Church (U.S.A). Note about the author

Greenstone, Julius Hillel, born in 1873 at Mariampol, Lithuania, he went to America in 1894, where he attended the City College of New York, received a rabbinical degree from the Jewish Theological Seminary of America, and a Ph.D. in 1905 from the University of Pennsylvania for his thesis, *The Turkoman defeat at Cairo, by Solomon ben Joseph Ha-Kohen*. In the same year, he joined the faculty of Gratz College, Philadelphia, Pa., where he taught for two generations, becoming a principal emeritus on his retirement. His writings include *The Religion of Israel* (1902), and *The Messiah idea in Jewish history* (1906). He died in Philadelphia on 7 March 1955. BioIn 3, 16; CnDiAmJBi; Master (1); NYT, 8 March 1955, p. 27, cols. 3-4; WhE&EA; Selim; WhAm, 3

Greenwald, Isidor, born 7 July 1887 at N.Y.C., he received a Ph.D. in 1911 from Columbia University for a thesis on physiological chemistry, and subsequently served from 1929 to 1952 as a professor of biochemistry, School of Medicine, New York University. He died in 1976. AmW&WS, 1976 P; CnDiAmJBi; WhoWorJ, 1972

Greenwell, Dora (Dorothy), born in 1821 at Greenwell Ford near Durham, the family home for centuries. She became a poet and essayist. Her writings include *Liber humanitatis; a series of essays on various aspects of spiritual and social life* (1875). She died in 1882. BioIn 16 (2); DLB, vol. 35 (1985), pp. 78-82, vol. 199 (1999), pp. 140-48; DNB; Master (10)

Grégoire, Henri, born 21 March 1881 at Huy, Belgium, he was a professor of classical philology at the Université libre de Bruxelles, and a joint author of *Les Persécutions dans l'Empire romain* (1950). He died in Rosières (Brabant) on 26 September 1964. BioNBelg, vol. 44 (1985-86), pp. 554-575; IntAu&Wr, 1977; IntWW, 1974/75-1993/94

Grégoire, Roger, born 29 August 1913 at Paris, he received a diploma in *études supérieures de droit public et d'économie politique* as well as the diploma of the École libre des sciences politiques. Named an auditor at the Conseil d'État in 1938, he served from 1944 to 1945 as a liaison officer for allied forces. He headed the Direction de la fonction publique from 1945 to 1954, when he was posted for seven years to the Organisation for European Economic Co-operation. In 1961 he resumed his functions as a *conseiller d'État*. His writings include *Fonction publique* (1954), *Administrations nationales et organisations internationales* (1955), its translation, *National administration and international organizations* (1956), *Les Sciences sociales dans l'enseignement supérieur* (1964), its translation, *The University teaching of social sciences* (1966), and *Education professionnelle* (1967). He died on 25 March 1990. NDNC, 1968; WhoFr, 1965/66-1989/90

Gregor, Werner, born 4 December 1896 at Görlitz, Prussia, he studied law at Berlin and Rostock, where he received a Dr.jur. in 1925 for *Das ökonomische Prinzip; ein Versuch zur Begründung einer*

ökonomischen Logik. He spent his entire career with the foreign service first in Berlin and later in Bonn. The Universidad de La Paz granted him an honorary doctorate in 1955. Wer ist wer, 1958-1968

Gregorian, Vartan, born in 1934 or 35 at Tabriz, Persia, he was a 1958 graduate of Stanford University, Palo Alto, Calif., where he also received a Ph.D. in 1964 for *The emergence of modern Afghanistan; politics of modernization, 1880-1930.* He was successively a professor of history, with special reference to the Middle East, at the Universities of California and Pennsylvania. He was the recipient of numerous honours and awards. His writings also include *The Emergence of modern Afghanistan; politics of reform and modernization, 1880-1946* (1969). ConAu 29-32; CurBio, 1985; DrAS, 1974 H, 1978 H, 1982 H; WhoAm, 1976/77-1994; WhoE, 1975-1993/94; WhoLibl, 1982; WhoWor, 1978/79-1993

Gregorio (*i.e.*, De Gregorio), Giacomo, marchese, born 1 June 1856 at Palermo, he was a professor of linguistics at the Università di Palermo. His writings include *Cenni di glottologia* (Torino, 1882), *Glottologia* (Milano, 1896), *Manual da sciencia da linguagem* (Lisboa, 1903), and *Contributi al lessico etimologico romanzo* (Torino, 1920). He died in 1936. Chi è, 1928, 1931, 1936; IndBiltal (5)

Gregorovius, Ferdinand Adolf, born in 1821 at Neidenburg, East Prussia, he studied at the Universität Königsberg. After spending some years teaching he took up residence in Italy in 1852, remaining there for over twenty years. He became a citizen of Roma. He is best remembered for his monumental *Geschichte der Stadt Rom im Mittelalter* (1859-1872) and its translation, *History of the city of Rome in the middle ages* (1894-1902). Having completed a similar history of Athens at an advanced age, he started with the preliminaries on a history of Jerusalem in the middle ages, a work which did not get beyond the two articles, "From Cairo to Jerusalem," and "A ride to the Dead Sea." Many of his works have been translated into other languages. He died in München on 1 May 1891. ADtB, vol. 49, pp. 524-532 BbD; CasWL; DizBI; DtBE; DtBilnd (8); EncAm; EncBrit; GdeEnc; OxCGer, 1986

Gregory, Lady Isabella *Augusta Persse*, born in 1852, she was a playwright, folklorist, and translator. Her writings include *Seventy years, being the autobiography of Lady Gregory* (1974). She died in 1932. ConAu 104, 184; DLB, vol. 10, part 1 (1982), pp. 208-212; DNB; Master (33); Who was who, 3

Gregory, John Walter, born in 1864, he was an assistant in the Geological Department of the British Museum, London, before he became a professor of geology at the University of Glasgow. In 1892-93 he made a five-month study tour of East Africa. His writings include *The Foundation of British East Africa* (1901), and *Africa; a geography reader* (1928). He died in 1932. BritInd (4); DNB; Henze; Master (2); Who was who, 3

Gregory, Sir William Henry, born in 1817 at Dublin, he was a sometime governor of Ceylon, who also took an interest in Egyptian affairs. His writings include *Egypt in 1855 and 1856* (1859), and *Sir William Gregory, K.C.M.G.; an autobiography*, edited by Lady Gregory (1974). He died in London in 1892. Brian Jenkins wrote *Sir William Gregory of Coole; the biography of an Anglo-Irishman* (1986). BioIn 11; DclrB, 1978 & 1988; DNB S 1

Gregson, Ronald Edgar, born in 1934, he received a Ph.D. in 1969 from Columbia University, N.Y.C., for *Work exchanges and leadership; the mobilization of agricultural labor among the Tumbuka of Hanga Valley.* NUC, 1973-1977

Greif, Franz, born about 1935, he was an Austrian geographer who received a Dr.phil. in 1966 from the Universität Wien for *Der Erwerbsgartenbau von Wien.* His writings include *Raumstruktur-Inventar für das österreichische Bundesgebiet* (1980), *Die Bevölkerung in Österreichs Höhengemeinden* (1989), and he was joint author of *Die Sozialbrache im Hochgebirge am Beispiel des Aussenferns* (1979).

Greig, Peter Edmond, born in 1944 at Hudson, Québec, he was a graduate of Queen's University, Kingston, Ontario, and took post-graduate degrees at the University of Toronto, and Leeds University. He was librarian at Massey Col-lege, Toronto, 1969-1970; indexer at the National Library of Canada, Ottawa, 1971-1979; and from 1980 to his retirement in 2002 an under-appreciated librarian at the Department of National Defense in Ottawa, where, during the last years of a not so useful career he was obliged to dispose of something in the range of sixty per-cent of the collections due to institutional stringency. He was a founding member of several library societes in Ottawa, and a sometime chairman of the Index Committee of the Bibliographical Society of Canada. Private

Grek, Tat'iana Vladimirovna, borm 4 December 1920 at Petrograd, she graduated in 1947 from the Leningrad Oriental Faculty, where she also received her first degree in 1966 for *Могольская портретная живопись первой половины XVII в.* She was from 1952 until her death on 7 January 1985 affiliated with the Ėrmitazh Museum, Leningrad. She was joint author of *Миниатюры кашмирских рукописей* (1976) and a joint editor of *Индийские миниатюры XVI-XVIII вв.* (1971). Miliband; Miliband²; OSK

Grempe, P. Max, born 23 December 1875 at Brandenburg/Havel, Germany, he was since 1928 resident in Berlin as an engineer and lecturer on technical and commercial matters. Wer ist's, 1935

Grenard, Joseph *Fernand*, born 4 July 1866 at Paris, he received a diploma from the École des sciences politiques. Together with J. L. Dutreuil de Rhins, he explored Turkestan, Tibet, Mongolia and China from 1891 to 1895. He later served as a vice-consul at Sivas and Erzurum. In 1916 he was a commercial attaché in the Levant. His writings include *La Haute Asie* (1929), *Baber, foundateur de l'empire des Indes*, its translation, *Baber, the first of the Moguls* (1930), *Gengis-Khan* (1935), and *Grandeur et décadence de l'Asie* (1939). Henze; Qui êtes-vous, 1924

Grenier de Fajal, Z., born 19th cent., he received a doctorate in 1865 from the Université de Strasbourg for *Tableau historique et critique du polythéisme chez les anciens Hébreux*. His trace is lost after a publication in 1877. BN; NUC, pre-1956

Gretton, George, Dr., fl. 1969, he was a writer and broadcaster, and a sometime head of the East European Services of the B.B.C., London. Note about the author

Gretton, John, born 20th cent., he was a free-lance journalist writing on current affairs. His writings include *Students and workers; an analytical account of dissent in France, May-June 1968* (Paris, 1969), *Western Sahara - the fight for self-determination* (London, 1976), and *William Tyndale; collapse of a school - or a system?* (London, 1976).

Greusing, Kurt, born 25 May 1946 at Lauterbach, Austria, he studied at the Wirtschaftsuniversität, Wien, and the Freie Universität Berlin, where he received a doctorate in 1983 for his thesis, *Vom "guten König" zum Imam*. Afterwards he was a free-lance writer for the Austrian radio and television network. In the middle 1990s, he was involved in development programs in Mozambique, from where he returned to Wien in December 1997. Private

Grevemeyer, Jan-Heeren, born 6 February 1940 at Norden, Germany. After the completion of his secondary education, he was a casual worker and globetrotter between Sweden and Nepal for over ten years before he started studying political science at the Freie Universität Berlin, where he obtained a doctorate in 1982 with his thesis, *Herrschaft, Raub und Gegenseitigkeit; die politische Geschichte Badakhshans, 1500-1883*. He was a man of roving disposition and too restless for patient research; he cared little about the acceptance of his writing. Throughout his life, he preferred casual research projects - or unemployment benefits - to regular work. Since the 1970s he was married to an Afghan refugee. In the 1990s he was a second-hand book peddler, operating from Spain. His writings include *Afghanistan; sozialer Wandel und Staat im 20. Jahrhundert* (1987). Private

Grévisse, F., fl. 1934-1967, he was in 1936 affiliated with the Association des étudiants de l'Université coloniale de Belgique, Anvers (Antwerpen). His writings include *Notes sur le droit coutumier des Balebi* (Élisabethville, 1934), *La Grande pitié des juridictions indigènes* (Bruxelles, 1949), and *Le Centre extra-coutumier d'Élisabethville* (Bruxelles, 1951). Note about the author

Grey, Charles, born about 1900, he was a writer on Indian history, whose writings include *European adventurers of northern India, 1785 to 1849* (Lahore, 1929), *The Merchant venturers of London* (London, 1932), and *Pirates of the eastern seas* (London, 1933). His trace is lost after a publication in 1934.

Grey, Henry George, born in 1802, he was the 3rd Earl Grey, and was educated at Trinity College, Cambridge. He entered the House of Commons as a Whig member. After his father's death, he took his seat in the House of Lords. In 1846 he was appointed Secretary for the Colonies. He died in 1894. John Manning Ward wrote *Earl Grey and the Australian colonies* (1958). BioInd 5, 6; BritInd (14); DNB; EncAm; Master (3)

Grey, Wliiam George, born in 1866 at Wellington, New Zealand, he joined the British Army in 1886 and transferred to the Indian Army in 1889. In 1902 he transferred to the Political Service and became vice-consul at Bandar Abbas, followed by Political Agent in Masqat (Muscat), 1904 to 1908, and served in the same capacity from 1914 to 1916 in Kuwait. He subsequently served until his retirement as a consul-general for Khorasan. His writings include *Hindustani manual* (1933). He died in 1953. IndianBiInd (2); Who was who 5

Griadunov, IUriĭ Stepanovich, he was a 20th century writer on Sudan, whose writings include *Новые горизонты Судана; внутриполитической развитие в годы независимости, 1956-1967* (1969), and *Демократическая Республика Судан* (1970). OSK

Griaznevich, Petr Afanas'evich, born 19 October 1929 at Pavlovka Sibirskogo kraia, he graduated in 1953 from Leningrad State University and received his first degree for a monograph. Since 1956 he was affiliated with the Leningrad Branch of the Oriental Institute, Soviet Academy of Sciences. His writings include *В поисках затерянных городов; йеменские репортажи* (1978), *Im Reich der Königin Saba* (1985); he edited *Арабской аноним XI века* (1960), *История халифов* (1967), *Ислам; религи, общество, государство* (1984); and he edited and translated from the Arabic of Muhammad ibn 'Alī al-Hamawī, *Am-ma'pux ал-Мансури* (1960-67). Miliband; Miliband²

Griaznov, Mikhail Petrovich, born about 1900, he was an archaeologist whose writings include *История древних племен Верхней Оби по раскопкам близ с. Большая Речка* (1956), *Древнее искусство Алтая* (1958), *The Ancient civilization of southern Siberia* (1969), *Sibérie du sud* (1969), *South Siberia* (1969), *Südsibirien* (1970), *Комплекс археологических памятников у горы Тепсей на Енисее* (1979), *Аржан; царский курган раннескифского времени* (1980), and he edited *История Киргизии* (1963). OSK

Gribaudi, Ferdinando, called Dino, the son of Pietro Gribaudi, born 26 November 1902 at Torino. His whole carrer was passed at the Università di Torino, where he was first assitant and lecturer in geology, becoming reader in geography in 1929 and professor of geography in 1935. In 1949 he succeeded his father in the chair of economic geography. His writings include *Profilo geografico del continente africano* (1959). He died in Torino on 5 January 1971. Chi è, 1957, 1961; DizBI; *Geographical journal*, 137 (1971), p. 273; Wholtaly 1958

Gribaudi, Pietro (Piero), born 27 June 1874 to a family of modest substance at Cambiano near Torino. Supported by a bursary, he studied local history at the Università di Torino and graduated in 1898. He subsequently studied geography at the Scuola di perfezionamento di Firenze. He started his teaching career in 1900 at the normal school of Nuoro. Since 1906, he successively taught at Istituto tecnico di Parma, Scuola superiore di commercio di Bari, and the Scuola superiore di commercio di Torino, which later attained faculty status. His writings include *La Più grande Italia* (1920), *Il mondo e l'Italia* (1923), and *Storia delle scoperte e delle esplorazioni geografiche* (1945). He died in Torino on 24 March 1950. Chi è, 1928-1948; DizBI; IndBiltal (1)

Gribbon, Walter Harold, born 19th cent., he was educated at Rugby School as well as a variety of military colleges. During the first World War he served in Mesopotamia and Constantinople. From 1931 to 1932 he was a commander of the Suez Canal Brigade. He retired with the rank of colonel and died in 1944. Who was who, 4

Griboedov, Aleksandr Sergeevich, born in 1795 or 95 at Moscow, he studied science in Moscow, and joined the army. He subsequently entered the ministry of foreign affairs. Early in 1819 he was sent to Persia to establish a Russian mission in Tehran. He was killed in Tehran on 11 February 1829. Cambridge history of Iran, vol. 7, pp. 328-29, 382; GSE; EncIran; EnSlovar; vol. 18, pp. 689-96; Magyar; Wieczynski

Griera y Gaja, Antoni, born in 1887 at San Bartomeu del Grau (Osona), he studied at Halle, Germany, Zürich, and Berlin, and received a Dr.phil. in 1914 from the Universität Zürich for *La frontera catalano-aragonesa; estudi geográfico lingüístico*. He was ordained in 1914 and became a professor of Spanish and Romance languages at the Universidad de Barcelona. His writings include *Dialectologia catalana* (1949). He died before 1978. Dicc bio; IndiceE³ (2); IntAu&W, 1977; IntWW, 1974/75-1978/79, necrology; WhoSpain, 1963

Grierson, Sir George Abraham, born in 1851 at Glenageary near Dublin, he entered the Indian Civil Service in 1873 and held a variety of posts in India for the next thirty-three years. He became the first director of the Linguistic Survey of India in 1899. He submitted his report in 1927 in eleven volumes. The work was the source of practically all the major research in the field of Indian and general linguistics of his day. His writings also include *Bihar peasant life* (1885), *A Manual of the Kashmiri language* (1911), *A Dictionary of the Kashmiri language* (1916-32), and *Gypsy languages* (1922). He was awarded a Dr.h.c. in 1894 from the Universität Halle, and a D.Lit. in 1902 from Trinity College, Dublin. He died in Camberley, Surrey, in 1941. AnaBrit; Buckland; DNB; EncAm; IndianBilnd (4); Magyar; Riddick; Who was who, 4

Grierson, Philip, born 15 November 1910 at Dublin, he was a professor of numismatics at Cambridge University, and a honorary keeper of coins, Fitzwilliam Museum, Cambridge. His writings include *Coins and medals; a select bibliography* (1954), and two selections from his periodical publications, *Dark age numismatics* (1979), and *Later medieval numismatics* (1979). ConAu 129, new rev., 71; IntAu&W, 1977, 1982; IntWW, 1989-2004; WhE&EA; Who, 1974-2003; WrDr, 1986/88-2004

Griesbach, Carl (Charles) Ludolf, born 11 December 1848 at Wien, he studied geology at the Universität, and did his practice work from 1869 to 1870 at Geologische Reichs-Anstalt. He subsequently became a member of a German geological expedition to Natal and Portuguese East Africa. In 1871 he joined the Museum of Natural History, London. In 1874 he entered the Royal Fusiliers. A member of the Geological Survey of India, Calcutta, since 1878, he was its director from

1884 to 1903. While on special service during the Afghan War, he was present at Maiwand, the siege and battle of Kandahar in 1880. From 1884 to 86 he served with the Afghan Boundary Commission. Folllowing the request of the Amir of Afghanistan, he did prospecting in the country, but the scientific aspect of the mission was secondary to its political purpose. He was awarded Companion of the Indian Empire. His writings include *Geology of the Ramkola and Tatapani coal-fields* (1880), and *Report on the geology of the section between the Bolan Pass in Baluchistan and Girishk in southern Afghanistan* (1881). He died in Graz on 13 April 1907. Buckland; DtBE; DtBiInd (5); Henze; IndianBiInd (1); ÖBL; Riddick; *Who was who*, 1

Grießbauer, Ludwig, born 19th cent., he was associated with the Deutsch-Asiatische Gesellschaft. His writings include *Die internationalen Verkehrs- und Machtfragen an den Küsten Arabiens* (Berlin, 1907), *Gegen sechsfache Übermacht* (Frankfurt am Main, 1917), *Die Lüge vom Eroberungskrieg* (Frankfurt am Main, 1918), and *Siegreich gegen zehnfache Übermacht* (Frankfurt am Main, 1918). GV

Griffen, David Alexander, born 25 January 1919 at Buffalo, N.Y., he graduated in 1947 from the University of Chicago, where he also received his Ph.D. in 1956 for *Elementos mozárabes del diccionario latino-arábigo atribuigo a Ramón Martí*. He subsequently taught at a variety of American universities before being appointed in 1961 a professor of Romance languages at Ohio State University. DrAS, 1969 F, 1974 F, 1978 F, 1982 F

Griffin, Keith Broadwell, born 6 November 1938 in Panama, he graduated in 1960 from Williams College and received a Ph.D. in 1965 from Oxford University. He became an advisor on agricultural planning to the Government of Algeria, 1963-64, and later became associated with the United Nations Research Institute for Social Development as well as the International Labour Office. His writings include *The Green revolution* (1972), *The Political economy of agrarian change* (1974), *Land concentration and rural poverty* (1976), and he was joint author of *The Economic development of Baghdad within a socialist framework* (1974). AmM&WS, 1973 S, 1978 S; ConAu 57-60, new rev., 7

Griffin, Sir Lepel Henry, born in 1840 at Watford, Hertfordshire, he entered the Civil Service in the Panjab in 1860. He was a chief secretary to the Panjab since 1870, and during the occupation of Afghanistan he held the special appointment of chief political officer in the northern and western districts. In 1881 he was joint founder of the *Asiatic quarterly review*. His writings include *The Panjab chiefs* (1865), *The Law of inheritance to chiefships* (1869), *The Rajas of the Punjab* (1870), and *Ranjit Singh* (1892). He died in 1908. BritInd (1); Buckland; DNB; IndianBiInd (4); Riddick; *Who was who*, 1

Griffini, Eugenio, born 26 December 1878 at Milano, he received the diploma in Arabic in 1898 from the R. Istituto orientale di Napoli. At that time, he made the acquaintance of the Magenta merchant G. Caprotti who concurrently with his commercial interests in Yemen collected Arabic manuscripts. Having received a law degree in 1902 at Genova for his thesis, *L'istituto giuridico dei beni di manomorta, o wakūf, nel diritto musulmano e nei rapporti col diritto internazionale privato*, Griffini went on an acquisition trip of Arabic manuscripts on behalf of Caprotti, the results of which are embodied in his *Catalogo dei manoscritti arabi di nuovo fondo della Biblioteca Ambrosiana di Milano* (1908-1910). During the 1911-1912 Italian campaign in Libya he was attached to the Ufficio politico militare as an Arabist. Since 1915 he successively taught Arabic at Roma, Milano, and Firenze, first as a lecturer and later as a professor. From 1920 to his death on 3 May 1925 he was a librarian at Cairo. His writings include *L'arabo parlato della Libia* (1913), *I manoscritti sudarabici di Milano* (1908-10), and he edited *Corpus iuris; la più antica racolta di legislazione e di giurisprudenza musulmana finora ritrovata*, of Zayd ibn 'Alī Zayn al-'Ābidīn (1919). DizBI; IndBiItal (1)

Griffith, Alfred Hume, born 10 January 1875 at Worcester, he received medical degrees from the universities of Edinburgh and Cambridge as well as a Turkish diploma enabling him to practise in the Ottoman Empire. In 1903 he received an M.D. from Edinburgh University for *Dysentry, with special reference to the disease as studied in Persia*. He went to Isfahan as a medical missionary under the Christian Missionary Society, London, in 1900. The following year he founded a medical mission in Kerman. In 1902 he was in charge of the mission hospital in Yazd; in 1903 he went to Nablus, Palestine, and in 1904 to Mosul. He was invalided to England in 1908, where he became in 1910 a superintendent and medical officer, Epileptic Homes, Lingfield. He contributed to his wife's *Behind the veil in Persia* (1909). Sluglett; *Medical who's who*, 1914

Griffith, Mrs. George (Lucinda) Darby, born 19th cent., she was a joint author of *A Journey across the desert, from Ceylon to Marseilles, comprising sketches of Aden, the Red Sea, Lower Egypt, Malta, Sicily, and Italy*, by Major George Darby and [Lucinda Darby] Griffith (1845). Robinson, p. 282

Griffith, Mrs. M. E. Hume, born 19th cent., she was the wife of the medical missionary Alfred Hume Griffith. She wrote *Behind the veil in Persia and Turkish Arabia; an account of an English woman's eight years' residence amongst the women of the East* (London, 1909).

Griffith, William Edgar, born 19 February 1920 at Remsen, N.Y., he graduated in 1940 from Hamilton College, and received a Ph.D. in 1950 from Harvard. After war-time service in France and Germany, he became head of the de-nazification of the U.S. occupation forces in Baveria. He received a Ph.D. in 1950 and subsequently served as a political adviser to Radio Free Europe, München. In 1958 he joined M.I.T. as a professor of political science, later becoming a project director at its Center for International Studies. His writings include *Albania and the Sino-Soviet rift* (1963), *The fourth Middle Eastern war* (1973), and he was joint editor of *The World and the great-power triangles* (1975). He died of a stroke on 29 September 1998. ConAu 61-64, 170; WhoAm, 1974/75-1988/89; WrDr, 1982/84-1998/2000

Griffiths, Arthur George Frederick, born in 1838 at Poona, India, and educated at William's College, Isle of Man, he entered the Army in 1855 and served in the Crimean War. After performing the duties of brigade-major at Gibraltar from 1864 to 1870, he resigned and obtained an appointment in the Prison Service. His writings include *Oriental prisons* (1900). He died in 1908. DNB; *Men and women of the time*, 1899

Griffiths, John, born 29 November 1837 at Llanfair Caereinion, he trained in fine arts in London and subsequently joined the South Kensington Museum. He was a painter in his own right and since 1865 also a professor of art at the Bombay School of Arts. It was under his superintendence that much of the decoration of the new public buildings of Bombay was designed. He was also a fellow of Bombay University. His writings include *The Paintings in the Buddhist cave-temples of Ajuntâ, Khandesh, India* (1896). He died in Norton, Sherborne, on 1 December 1918. BritInd (1); DcBrWA²; *Dictionary of Welsh biography down to 1940*; Master (2); Riddick

Griffiths, John Gwyn, born 7 December 1911 at Porth, Wales, he was educated at Cardiff, Liverpool, and Oxford. He graduated in 1932 from the University of Wales, and became successively a professor of classics and Egyptology in the University of Wales, Swansea, and Oxford. In 1965/66 he was a visiting professor at Cairo University. ConAu 106; Au&Wr, 1971; IntAu&W, 1977, 1982; Master (1); WhE&EA; WrDr, 1976/78-2004

Griffiths, Sir Percival Joseph, born in 1899, he graduated from Cambridge and London, and in 1922 entered the Indian Civil Service, from which he retired in 1937 to become an adviser to the Government of India. He later became a London businessman who was long connected with affairs in the Indo-Pakistan sub-continent. His writngs include *Better towns; a study of urban reconstruction in India* (1945); *The British impact on India* (1952), *Report on a visit to Nigeria and the Gold Coast* (1955), *Modern India* (1957), *The Road to freedom* (1965), and *A History of the Inchcape Group* (1977). He died on 14 July 1992. ConAu 103; Riddick; WhE&EA; Who, 1948-1992; WhoWor, 1974/75

Grignaschi, Mario, born 20 January 1917 at Triest, he studied Arabic, Turkish, and Persian at the former Konsular-Akademie, Wien, and subsequently Turkish at the Faculty of Letters, Istanbul, concentrating on the institutions of the Turkish feudalism, and the political ideas of the Oriental middle ages. His writings include *Une Polémique du moyen âge sur la primauté de Pierre* (1962), and he edited *Deux ourages inédits sur la rhétorique d'al-Farabi* (1971). He was honoured by *Studi eurasiatici in onore di Mario Grignaschi* (1988). BioB134

Grigoraş, N., born 20th cent., he wrote *Biserica Trei Ierarhi* (1965), *L'Église des Trois Hiérarques* (Bucureşti, 1965), *Instituţii feudale din Moldova* (Bucureşti, 1971),*Ţara Românească a Moldovei de la întemeierea statului pînă la Ştefan cel Mare, 1359-1457* (Iaşi, 1978), and he was joint author of *Biserici şi mănăstiri vechi din Moldova, pînă la mijlocul secolului al XV-lea* (Bucureşti, 1968), and *Nicolae Jorga; omul şi opera* (Iaşi, 1971). OSK

Grigor'ev, Arkadii Pavlovich, born 15 July 1931 in Russia, he graduated in 1955 from the Oriental Faculty, Leningrad, where he later became a member of the staff. His writings include *Монгольская дипломатика XIII-XV вв.* (1978). Miliband²

Grigor'ev, Vasiliĭ Vasilevich, born 15 August 1816 in St. Petersburg, he was a sometime civil governor of the Orenburg Kirghizes. From 1863 to 1878 he held the newly established chair of history of the East at St. Petersburg, and concurrently served from 1873 to 1878 also as dean of the faculty. Beginning with his term of office, scientific study began to prevail over practical language teaching. His writings include *Die Nomaden als Nachbarn und Eroberer zivilisierter Staaten* (1875). BiobibSOT; KazakSE; Kazakhskaia, vol. 3, p. 172; Krachkovskiĭ; EnSlovar; TatarES; Wieczynski

Grigorian (Grigoryan), Vardan/Vladimir Rubenovich (Rhowbeni), born 26 January 1929 at Dilizhan, Armenia, he graduated in 1952 from Erevan State University, where he also received his first degree for his monograph, *Ереваиское ханство в конце XVIII столетия, 1780-1800* (1958). His writings include *История армянской колоний Украины и Польски* (1980). Miliband; Miliband²

Grigorian (Grigoryan), Zaven Tigranovich, his writings include *Вековая борьба армянского народа за свою независимость и свободу* (Moscow, 1946), and *Присоединение Восточной Армений к России в начале 19 века* (Moscow, 1959). OSK

Grigortsevich, Stanislav Siliverstovich, fl. 20th cent., he wrote *Американская и японская интервенция на советском Дальнем Вомтоке* (Moscow, 1957), and *Дальневомточная политика империалических держав в 1906-1917 гг.* (Tomsk, 1965). OSK

Grigoryan, Vladimir Rhowbeni, 1929- see Grigorian, Vardan

Grigoryan, Z. T. see Grigorian, Zaven Tigranovich

Grigsby, William Ebenezer, born 3 April 1847, he studied at Glasgow and Balliol College, Oxford. He was the first professor of international law at Jeddo University from 1874 to 1878. Called to the bar from Inner Temple in 1881, he was a municipal politician from 1889 to 1892. From 1893 to his death in September, 1899, he was a puisne judge of Cyprus. He translated *The Medjellè, or, Ottoman civil law* (1895). Boase; BritInd (1)

Griguer, Jules, born 19th cent., he was in 1910 an *interprète auxiliaire* at Tiaret, Algeria, and in 1912 an interpreter with the Direction de la Dette marocaine at Tanger. His writings include *Des différents régimes de succession au Maroc* (1935), and *Traité théorique et pratique de législation et jurisprudence marocaines en matière domaniale* (Casablanca, 1939). Note about the author

Grigull, Theodor Fr., born 19th cent., he wrote *Der Koran, aus dem Arabischen mit Vorbemerkung und Index nebst Facsimile einer Koran-Handschrift* (Halle, 1901), and *Auf Römerpfaden in Tunis* (Werden an der Ruhr, 1912). GV

Gril, Denis, born 20th cent., he received a *doctorat de 3ème cycle* in 1983 from the Université d'Aix-Marseille for *La Risala de Safi al-Din Ibn Abi l-Mansour Ibn Zafir*. He was joint author of *Linteaux à épigraphes de l'oasis de Dakhla* (1981). In 1987 he was affiliated with the Université de Provence. He translated from the Arabic of Ibn al-'Arabī, *Le Dévoilement des effets du voyage* (1998). Livres disponibles, 2003; Note about the author; THESAM, 3

Grill, Heinz, born in 1909, his writings, partly under the pseudonym Hans Steinburg, include *Der Wüstenreiter, eine abenteuerliche Erzählung* (1950), and *Maximilian I. und seine Zeit* (1977).

von **Grill**, Julius, born 10 July 1840 at Graildorf, Württemberg, he studied theology and Oriental languages at Tübingen and Heidelberg, and received a Dr.phil. in 1873 from the Universität Tübingen. He successively taught at Maulbronn and Tübingen. His writings include *Die Erzväter der Menschheit* (1875), and *Die persische Mysterienreligion im Römischen Reich* (1903). He died in August 1930. DtBiInd (1); Kürschner, 1925-1928/29; Wer ist's, 1909-1928

Grillières, Georges, born 28 June 1868 at Mende (Lozère), he entered the army in 1893 as a regular soldier and in 1895 had advanced to the rank of lieutenant. In 1895 he was posted to the 4e Régiment de Zouaves in Tunisia; his brilliant qualities enabled him there to create an admirable morale. For lack of connections, he did not succeed in a projected expedition to central Africa. With youthful ethusiasm, but extremely modest means, he set out on a geographic-touristic journey to Russia and northern Persia. At the gates of Afghanistan he was turned away and had to return to Marseille by way of Tiflis and Baku. Partly supported by the Société de Géograhie, he embarked in 1903 on an exploration of southern China, a journey from which he did not return. He was a member of the Section tunisienne de la Société de Géographie Commerciale de Paris. He died from fever on 15 July 1905 in China. DBF; Hommes et destins, vol. 6, pp. 162-63

Grillon, Pierre, born 20th cent., he edited *Un chargé d'affaires français au Maroc; la correspondance du consul Louis Chénier, 1767-1782* (1970), and *Les Papiers de Richelieu* (1975-1980).

Grimaud, Nicole, born 20th cent., she received a *doctorat d'état* in 1982 from the Université de Paris for *La politique extérieure de l'Algérie, 1962-1978*. In 1977 she was affiliated with the Centre d'études et de recherches internationales, Fondation nationales des Sciences politiques. Her writings include *La politique extérieure de l'Algérie* (1984), and *La Tunisie à la recherche de la sécurité* (1995). Livres disponibles, 2003; THESAM, 2; ZKO

Grimley, William Henry, born about 1840, he was educated at King Edward's School, Birmingham, and Trinity College, Cambridge. In 1862 he entered the Indian Civil Service, arriving in 1863. He served as an assistant magistrate and collector as well as in other capacities until his retirement in December of 1890. His writings include *An Income tax manual* (1886), and *Report on the administration of the Indian Famine Charitable Relief Fund in Bengal* (1898). The India list and India Office list for 1900 [not sighted]

Grimm', Érvin Davidovich, born in 1870, his writings include *Изследовагія по исторіи развитія римской императорской власти* (St. Petersburg, 1900), *L'Époque de la Sainte-alliance* (Sofia, 1922), and he was joint editor of *Konstantinopel und die Meerenge* (Dresden, 1930-32). LC

Grimm, Gerhard, born 14 October 1929 at Karlsruhe, Germany, he received a Dr.phil. in 1964 from the Universität München for *Johann Georg von Hahn; Leben und Werk*. He was successively a lecturer and professor of East European history at the Universität München. GV; Kürschner, 1976-2003

Grimme, Hubert, born 24 January 1864 at Paderborn, Germany, he studied Oriental languages under E. Sachau at the Universität Berlin, where he received a Dr.phil. in 1886 for *Palmyrae sive Tadmur ubis fata quaeduerint tempore muslimico*. He taught since 1889 at the newly founded Universität Freiburg im Ochtland, Switzerland, where he remained until invited to the Universität Münster in 1910. He was an original and versatile scholar, and particularly lucky in his epigraphic researches. His writings include *Mohammed* (1892-95), *Die weltgeschichtliche Bedeutung Arabiens* (1904), *Plattdeutsche Mundarten* (1910), *Islam und der Weltkrieg* (1914), *Ein böswilliger Sprachstümper über "deutsche Kriegsgreuel;"* Entgegnung auf "Les crimes allemands, par Josef Bédier" (1915), *Der Koran; ausgewählt angeordnet und im Metrum des Originals übertragen* (1923), *Texte und Untersuchungen zur safatenisch-arabischen Religion* (1929), and *Altsinaitische Forschungen, Epigraphisches und Historisches* (1937). He died in Münster on 5 September 1942. DtBE; DtBilnd (1); Encyclopaedia Judaica (Berlin, 1931); Fück, p. 317; Kosch; Kürschner, 1925-1940/41; Wer ist's, 1909-1935

Grimwood-Jones, Diana, born in 1944 at Abingdon, Oxfordshire, she studied Arabic, Persian, and Turkish at Edinburgh. She was an assistant Middle Eastern librarian, Durham University Library, 1967-1974, a librarian and private papers assistant, Middle East Centre, St. Antony's College, Oxford, 1974-1979, and in the 1990s, she was a senior consultant with the Association for Information Management. From 1981 to 1984 she served as a bibliographic review editor, *BRISMES bulletin*. Her writings include *Sources for the history of the British in the Middle East, 1800-1878* (1979), and she was joint editor of *Middle East and Islam; a bibliographical introduction* (1972). Private

Grindal, Bruce Theodore, born at Geneva, Illinois, he graduated in 1963 from Northwestern University, Evanston, and received a Ph.D. in 1969 from Indiana University, Bloomington, for *Education and culture change among the Sisala of Northern Ghana*. In 1972 he was appointed a professor in the Department of Anthropology, Florida State University at Tallahassee, a post which he still held in 1999. His writings include *Growing up in two worlds; education and transition among the Sisala of Northern Ghana* (1972). AmM&WS, 1973 S; AmM&WS, 1976 P; ConAu 41-44; NatFacDr, 1995-1999

Grinkova, Nadzha Pavlovna, born in 1895, she was a linguist whose writings include *Изучение языка писателя* (1957), *Вопросы исторической лексикологий русского языка* (1962); she was joint author of *Практические занятия по диалектологии* (1962); and she was joint editor of *Кафедра русского языка* (1948). She died in 1961. NUC; OSK

Griscom, Mary W., born 19th cent., she had been a practising physician for twenty years in Philadelphia, Pa., when she decided about 1913 to go to the Orient. She was teaching and practising medicine in China when after the first World War she was asked by the American-Persian Relief Commission to serve in Persia, foregoing work in India. Her trace is lost after an article in 1921. Note

Griselle, Eugène, born 23 May 1861 at Mouchy-le-Châtel (Oise), he received a religious schooling at Beauvais and in 1844 entered the noviciate of the Jesuits at their exile in Gemert (Holland). There, and in Lille, he studied until 1888, when he received his *licence ès lettres*. He subsequently taught at Catholic faculties until 1904. Ordained priest in 1895, and with a doctorate from Caen, he was in 1904 appointed director of the Collège ecclésiastique du S.-Esprit at Beauvais, a post which he held until 1911, when he decided to leave the Compagnie de Jésus. In 1915 he became general secretary of the Comité catholique de propagande française. His writings include *Louis XIII et Richelieu* (1911), *Écurie, vénerie, fauconnerie et louveterie du rois Louis XIII* (1912), *Le Martyre du clergé français* (1915), and *Le Bon combat* (1918). He died in Sèvres on 2 August 1923. DBF

Grislis, Egil, born 19 February 1928 at Mitau, Latvia, he graduated in 1950 from Gettysburg College, and received a Ph.D. in 1957 from Yale University for *Luther's understanding of the wrath of God*. He was since 1958 a pastor and a professor at a variety of theological faculties. He was joint author of *Richard Hooker; a selected bibliography* (1971), and he was joint editor of *The Heritage of Christian thought* (1965). DrAS, 1969 P, 1974 P; WhoRel, 1985

Griswold, Hervey De Witt, born 24 May 1860 at Dryden, New York, he was a graduate of Union College Schenectady, N.Y., and Union Theological Seminary, who studied also at Oxford and Berlin. He was a missionary, professor, and Church official in India from 1890 to 1926. His writings include

Mirza Ghulam Ahmad, the Mehdi messiah of Qadian (1902). He died in Stratford, Conn., 15 May 1945. Shavit - Asia; WhAm, 3

Griswold, William James, born 31 December 1926 at Bellingham, Wash., he graduated in 1950 from Occidental College, Los Angeles, and received a Ph.D. in 1966 from U.C.L.A. for *Political unrest and rebellion in Anatolia, 1605-1609.* He was awarded fellowships from Fulbright, National Defense Education, and American Research Institute in Turkey. He was a high school teacher in America and Turkey. From 1966 to 1967 he served as an assistant program director, Peace Corps Training Program in Turkey as well as in Afghanistan. He subsequently was appointed a professor of history at Colorado State University, Fort Collins. He was from 1990 to 1992 a president of the Turkish Studies Association. His writings include *The Image of the Middle East in secondary school textbooks* (1975). DrAS, 1974 H, 1978 H, 1982 H; Private

Gritly (Gritley/Jirītlī), Aly Ahmad Ibrahim, born 16 April 1913 at Alexandria, Egypt, he studied at Cairo and London, where he received a Ph.D. in 1947 from LSE for *The structure of modern industry in Egypt.* He was successively a professor of economics at Alexandria University, a banking executive, and a minister of finance. His other writings include *al-Ta'rīkh al-iqtisādī li-al-thawrah, 1952-1966* (1974). Sluglett; Unesco

Griunberg-TSvetinovich, Aleksandr Leonovich, born 1 March 1930 at Leningrad, he graduated in 1952 from the Oriental Faculty, Leningrad, and received his first degree in 1963 for Язык сервероазербайджанских татов. He was since 1957 a research fellow in the Leningrad Branch of the Institute of Linguistics, Soviet Academy of Sciences. He spent from 1963 to 1968 in Afghanistan. His writings include Языки Восточного Гиндукуша: Мунджанский язык (1972), Язык Кати (1980), Очерк грамматики афганского языка (1987), *La Langue wakhi* (1988), and he was joint author of Языки Восточного Гиндукуша: Ваханский язык (1976). Miliband; Miliband²; OSK

Griveau, Robert, born 29 August 1881 at Paris. he graduated in 1903 from the École des chartes, Paris. He was an Arabist who specialized in Christian Arab subjects in al-Bīrūnī, and al-Maqrīzī. He also produced a handlist of recently acquired Christian Arabic manuscripts in the Bibliothèque nationale, Paris. He died 6 June 1929. DBF

Grivel, Louis Antoine *Richild*, born 20 January 1827 at Brest, he entered the École navale in 1846 and served in the Far East and the West Coast of Africa He participated in the Crimean campaign of 1854 as well as naval engagements in the western and eastern Mediterranean. He died on active duty in Dakar, Senegal, on 24 January 1883. His writings include *Attaques et bombardements maritimes avant et pendant la Guerre d'Orient* (1857), and *De la guerre maritime* (1869). DBF; IndexBFr² (1); Vapereau

Grobba, Fritz Conrad Ferdinand, born 18 July 1886 at Gartz, Prussia, he studied at the Universität Greifswald, where he received a Dr.jur. in 1913 for *Der Schadenersatzanspruch wegen positiver Vertragsverletzung beim Werkvertrag.* He entered the foreign service in 1913 and was posted as a student dragoman to the Jerusalem consulate. He was appointed in 1923 chargé d'affaires in Kabul, and in 1932 consul in Baghdad. In 1941 he returned briefly to Baghdad as a German representative during Rashid 'Alī al-Gaylanī's rebellion. His writings include *Die Getreidewirtschaft Syriens und Palästinas seit Beginn des Weltkrieges* (1923), and *Männer und Mächte im Orient; fünfundzwanzig Jahre diplomatischer Tätigkeit im Orient* (1967). DtBilnd (2); *Middle Eastern studies*, 23 (1987), pp. 376-78; Wer ist's, 1935

Grobba, Udo, born 18 January 1931 at Berlin, he grew up from 1932 to 1939 in Baghdad, where his father, Fritz Grobba, was German consul. In 1949 he began to study at Berlin, where he received a diploma in political science in 1956. After three years in private industry, he became affiliated with the Press and Information Bureau of the German Federal Government. In 1970 he joined the federal employment agency. Note about the author

Grodekov, Nikolaĭ Ivanovich, born in 1843 at Elizavetgrad (Kirovograd), he was an army colonel who is remembered mainly for his 1878 expedition from Tashkent to Pakhta-Gisar, where he crossed the Amu-Darya, and onwards to Herat. His detailed observations constituted an important contribution to cartography. His writings include *Colonel Grodekoff's ride from Samarkand to Herat, through Balkh and the Uzbek states of Afghan Turkestan* (1880), Война в Туркменіи (1883-84), Хивинскій походъ 1873 года (1888), Киргизы и каракиргихы Сыръ-Дарьинской области (1889). He died in 1913. Henze; OSK; Slovar

Groenveld, Douwe, born 20th cent., he received a doctorate in 1961 from the Landbouwhogeschool Wageningen, the Netherlands, for his thesis *Investment for food.* Brinkman's, 1961-65

Groff, William N., born in 1857 in Ohio, U.S.A., he studied Egyptology at Paris and throughout the 1890s he lived in Cairo. He died in 1901. His teacher, Gaston Maspero, edited his collected works, with a biographical note by his sister, *Œuvres égyptologiques de William N. Groff* (1908). Dawson; Egyptology; Shavit

Grohmann, Adolf, born 1 March 1887 at Graz, Austria, he studied Oriental languages, history, art and archaeology at the Universität Wien, and received his Dr.phil. in 1911, and Dr.habil. in 1916. Until 1918 he was a lecturer in Arabic at K.u.K. Öffentliche Lehranstalt für Orientalische Sprachen, Wien. After a five-year service as head of the Oriental division, Papyrussammlung in the Nationalbibliothek, Wien, he served successively since 1923 as a professor of Oriental antiquities at Deutsche Universität Prag, and, after the war, the Universität Innsbruck, where he died on 21 September 1977. His writings include *Südarabien als Wirtschaftsgebiet* (1922-33), *Denkmäler islamischer Buchkunst* (1929), *Studien zur historischen Geographie und Verwaltung des frühmittelalterlichen Ägypten* (1959), and *Arabien* (1963). DtBE; Filipsky; Jacksch; Kürschner, 1926-1976; Note about the author; Teichl; *Wer ist's*, 1935

Groisard, Louis, born 2 December 1899 in Vendée, he graduated in 1923 from the École normale, and served from 1923 to 1931 in Le Kef region, Tunisia, as an *instituteur*, and from 1931 to 1937 as a professor of letters, giving the *cours complémentaire* at Maxula-Radès, Tunisia. His promotion to *inspecteur de l'enseignement du 1er degré* necessitated his return to France. He returned to North Africa during the war and was responsible for Muslim education of the Département de Constantine (1941-42), and subsequently from 1942 to 1945 at Bizerte. He is best remembered for his literary and cultural activities during his Tunisian residence, during which he served from 1930 to 1934 as secretary-general of the Société des écrivains de l'Afrique du nord. He edited *Matins d'Afrique; le troisième livre de l'écolier africain* (1965). He died in 1986. *IBLA*, 49 ii (1986), pp. 389-90

Gromyko, Andreï Andreevich, born in 1909, he was a Soviet ambassador and representative on the United Nations' Security Council. He died 2 July 1989. AnaBrit; ConAu, 134; IntWW, 1974/75-1990/91; Master (65); Who, 1953-1989; *Who was who*, 8

Gromyko, Marina Mikhaïlovna, born 20th cent., her writings include *Западная Сибирь в XVIII в.; русское население и земледельческое освоение* (1965), *Трудовые традиции русских крестьян Сибири* (1975), and she edited *Из истории семьи и быта сибирского крестьянства в XVIII - начале XX в.* (1975). NUC, 1973-77; OSK

Grønbech, Kaare (Kåre), born 28 September 1901 at Frbg., Denmark, he studied philology at Københavns Universitet, visited Istanbul in 1928, and received his doctorate in 1936 at København for *Der türkische Sprachbau*, and its translation, *The Structure of the Turkish languages* (1979). In 1948 he founded the Central Asian Institute, København. His writings include *Komanisches Wörterbuch* (1942). He died in København on 21 January 1957. AnaBrit; DanskBL; *Index Islamicus* (3); Kraks, 1956

Grønbech, Vilhelm Peter, born 14 June 1873 at Allinge, Denmark, he studied at København, where he received a doctorate in 1902 for *Forstudier til turkisk lydhistorie*. He was a scholar of social history and comparative theology and since 1911 taught his field at his alma mater. His writings include *Vor Folkeæt i Oldtiden* (1909-1912). He died in Helsingførs on 21 April 1948. DanskBL; DanskBL²; DcScandL

Grønhaug, Reidar, born 2 December 1938 at Stavanger, Norway, he was since 1969 successively a lecturer and professor of social anthropolgy at the Universitetet i Bergen. His writings include *Micro-macro relations; social organization in Antalya, southern Turkey* (1974). Hvem er hvem, 1979, 1984, 1994

Gronke, Monika, born 28 March 1952 at Hannover, she studied at the Universität Göttingen, where she received her Dr.phil. in 1982 for *Arabische und persische Privaturkunden des 12. und 13. Jahrhunderts aus Ardabil*. She pursued post-doctoral research at Paris and Freiburg im Breisgau, specializing in Islamic history of the middle ages. In 1991 she was appointed a professor at the Universität Köln. AnEIFr, 1997; Kürschner, 1992-2003; Private

Groom, Arthur John Richard, born 20th cent., he received a doctorate and became a lecturer in law in the University of London. His writings include *Peacekeeping* (1973), *British thinking about nuclear weapons* (1974); and he was joint editor of *The Commonwealth in the 1980s* (1984), *International relations; a handbook in current theory* (1985), and *Frameworks for international co-operation* (1990). BLC; LC; Note about the author

Groom, Nigel, born 26 April 1924 at Wisbech, Cambs., he was educated at Haileybury College, and Magdalen College, Cambridge. He entered the British Colonial Service and was for ten years a political officer at Aden. His writings include *Frankincense and myrrh; a study of the Arabian incense trade* (1980), and *A Dictionary of Arabic topography and place names* (1983). ConAu, 117; Private; ZKO

Groome, Francis Hindes, born in 1851, he studied at Oxford, but without taking a degree. Since his student days he was interested in Gypsy folklore and life. In the early 1870s, he lived much with Gypsies, at home and abroad, but nothing is more remarkable than that he should have passed so swiftly from a veritable Bohemian of romance into the systematic bondage of labour in literary work at Edinburgh. His writings include *In Gypsy tents* (1880), *The Gypsies* (1881), *Gypsy folktales* (1899), and *Edward Fitzgeral; an aftermath* (1902). He died in 1902. Bioln 7; CasWL; DNB; *Who was who*, 1

de **Groot**, Alexander Hendrik, born in 1943, he received a doctorate for *The Ottoman Empire and the Dutch Republic*, a work which was published in 1978. His other writings include *Nederland en Turkije* (1986); he was joint author of *A Bibliography of Dutch publications on the Middle East, 1945-1981* (1981); and he edited *Het Midden-Oosten en Nederland in historisch perspectief* (1989). Brinkman's, 1986-1990

de **Groot**, Gerard René, born in 1951, he was affiliated with the Faculteit der Rechtsgeleerdheit, Rijksunversiteit Limburg. His writings include *Doeleinden en techniek der rechtsvergelijking* (1984), *Nationaliteitsrecht* (1986), and *Rechtsvergelijking* (1986). Brinkman's, 1996-2000

Groot, Joanna de, 1947- see De Groot, Joanna

Gropp, Gerd, born in 1935, he received a Dr.phil. in 1965 from the Universität Hamburg for *Wiederholungsformen im Jung-Awesta*. He was joint author of *Altiranische Funde und Forschungen* (1969). Thesis

Gros, Henri René Louis Augustin Eugène, born in 1861, he received a medical doctorate in 1883 from the Université de Lille. His writings include *Les Médecins de colonisation et l'assistance médicale aux indigènes en Algérie* (Paris, 1909). BN; NUC, pre-1956

Gros, Jules, born in 1829 at Montluel (Ain), he was a traveller and a sometime secretary of the Société de géographie, whose numerous travel accounts were published in large editions, assuring him publicity. His exploits in South America were the subject of mystification of the time. His writings include *Voyages, aventures et captivités de J. Bonnat chez les Achantis* (1884), *Les Français en Guyane* (1887), *Nos explorateurs en Afrique* (1888), and *Paul Soleillet en Afrique* (1888). He died in Vanves (Hauts-de-Seine) in 1891. DBF

Grose, John Henry, born before 1750, he was a writer in the East India Company's service and went to Bombay in 1750, an experience which he described in *A Voyage to the East Indies, containing authentic accounts of the Mogul government in general* (1772). He died after 1783. Britlnd (1); Buckland; DNB

Grose, Peter Bolton, born 27 October 1934 at Evanston, Illinois, he was a foreign correspondent for the *New York Times*, and a research associate with American organizations, including senior fellow and director of Middle Eastern studies, Council of Foreign Relations, New York. His writings include *The United States, NATO, and Israeli-Abrab peace* (1981), and *Israel in the mind of America* (1983). ConAu, 114, 119, new rev., 99; WhoFl, 1989/90, 1992/93; WhoAm, 1974/75-1976/77; WrDr, 1986/88-2004

Grose-Hodge, Humfrey, born in 1891 he was a classicist who entered the Indian Civil Service in 1914. During the first World War he served in India as well as in the Arab world. His writings include *Roman panorama* (1944). He died in 1962. Britlnd (1); Indianbilnd (1); Who, 1929-1962; *Who was who*, 6

Groseclose, Elgin Earl, born 25 November 1899 at Waukomis, Okla., he graduated in 1920 from the University of Oklahoma and received his Ph.D. in 1928. After the Great War he sailed for Persia, primarily in search of adventure. He taught one year at the Presbyterian mission school in Tabriz, before working from 1921 to 1922 for the Near East Relief with refugees and living among the villagers. He made one trip into Russia. From 1923 to 1926 he was a special agent with the U.S. Department of Commerce. He became an economist in government and business as well as an investment consultant. In 1943 he was appointed treasurer-general by the Iranian Government. His writings include *Currency systems of the Orient* (1927), *The Persian journey of the Reverend Ashley Wishard and his servant Fathi* (1937), *Ararat* (1939), *Near Eastern postwar monetary standards* (1943), and *Introduction to Iran* (1947). He died from a stroke in Washington, D.C., on 4 April 1983. AmM&WS, 1973 S, 1978 S; BlueB, 1973/74, 1975, 1976; ConAu 21-22, new rev. 76; IntWW, 1976/77-1982; Master (1); Note about the author; Shavit; WhAm 9; WhoAm, 1974/75-1984; WhoWor; 1974/75-1982; WrDr, 1976/78-1984/86

Groshev, Viktor Andreevich, born 10 September 1940 at Balkhash, Kazakhstan, he studied at Kazakhstan University, where he received his first degree in 1971. He was an archaeologist. Schoeberlein

Gross, Ernest Arnold, born 23 September 1906 at N.Y.C., he studied at Harvard and Oxford, and gained a law degree. He served from 1948 to 1953 as a U.S. deputy delegate to the United Nations.

His writings include *The United Nations; structure for peace* (1962), and *The new United Nations* (1957). He was a subject of the Oral History Research Office of Columbia University. He died in New York, 2 May 1999. Bioln 2, 7; ConAu 5-8, 179; NYT, 4 May 1999, B-14, cols. 5-6; *Washington Post*, 10 May 1999, p. B-5, col. 2; WhoAm, 1974/75-1994; WhoWor, 1974/75

Gross, Georges, born 19th cent., he studied medicine at the Université de Nancy, where he also received a medical doctorate. Later he there served as a professor in the Faculté de médicine. Note

Gross, Jo-Ann, born about 1950, she received a Ph.D. in 1982 from New York University for *Khoja Ahrar; a study of the perceptions of religious power and prestige in the late Timurid period.* In 1995, she was a professor in the Department of History, Trenton State College, Trenton, N.J., and in 1999 she served as a professor of history at the College of New Jersey, Ewing. She edited *Muslims in Central Asia; expressions of identity and change* (1992). LC; *MESA Roster of members*, 1982-1990

Gross, Leo, born 6 April 1903 at Krosno, Austrian Galicia, he emigrated to America, where he was from 1948 to 1980 a professor of international law and administration at Fletcher School of Law and Diplomacy, Tufts University, Medford, Mass. He also served as a visiting professor in the U.S. and abroad. His writings include *Pazifismus und Imperialismus* (1931), and *International law in the twentieth century* (1969). He died in 1990. AmM&WS, 1973 S, 1978 S; BioHbDtE; DrAS, 1974 P, 1978 P, 1982 P; Master (1); WhoE, 1991/92

Gross, Max L., born 20th cent., he received a Ph.D. in 1979 from Georgetown University for *Ottoman rule in the province of Damascus, 1860-1909.* He was in 1990 a professor of Middle Eastern studies at the Defense Intelligence College in Washington, D.C. He was a specialist in the modern history of Syria and Lebanon, about which he wrote numerous articles. *MESA Roster of members*, 1982-1990; Selim[3]

Große-Rüschkamp, Alois, born 20th cent., he received a Dr.phil. in 1979 from the Universität Bonn for *Optimale Planung der Mischfutterindustrie in Ägypten.* ZKO

Grossen, Jacques Michel, born 8 February 1931 at Neuchâtel, Switzerland, he was educated at L.S.E. and the Academy of International Law, den Haag. He received his Dr.jur. in 1954 from the Université de Neuchâtel for *Les présomptions en droit international public.* He was a professor of law at his alma mater, where he delivered his inaugural address in 1957 entitled *L'Égalité du mari et de la femme au regard du droit de la famille.* He was granted an honorary doctorate by the Université de Genève. WhoSwi, 1964/65-1992/93

Grosset(-Grange), Henri, born 20th cent., his writings include *Glossaire nautique arabe ancien et moderne de l'Océan indien; 1975* (Paris, 1993). *Livres disponibles*, 2003; Note

Grossman, Leonid Petrovich, born in 1888 at Odessa, he was a writer and literary historian who in a work published in 1941 recognized the popularization of Orientalism among the educated Rusians of the middle of the nineteenth century. He died in 1965. CasWL; Krachkovskiĭ, p. 268

Grossmann, Peter, born 20th cent., he was an archaeologist whose writings include *Kirche und spätantike Hausanlagen im Chnumtempelhof* (1980), and *Mittelalterliche Langhaus-Kuppelkirchen und verwandte Typen in Oberägypten.* (1982). ZKO

Grosso, Mario, born in 1887, his writings include *Cronologia delle colonie italiane* (1934), and its translation into Arabic *al-Tasalsul al-zamanī li-ahdāth al-musta'marāt al-Itālīyah* (1989). ZKO

Grothe, Albert Louis Hugo, also known as Grothe-Harkányi, born 15 August 1869 at Magdeburg, Prussia, he studied geography, Oriental languages and law at the universities of Leipzig, Berlin, München and Wien, and received a Dr.phil. in 1902 from the Universität Würzburg for *Die Bagdadbahn und das schwäbische Bauernelement in Transkaukasien und Palästina.* He was a foreign correspondent of the *Kölnische Zeitung* and travelled extensively in the Levant, North Africa, and the Balkans. In 1900 he founded the Orientalische Gesellschaft in München. A founding editor of *Orientalisches Archiv für Völkerkunde und Kunstgeschichte* in 1912 in Leipzig, he there established the Deutsche Kuturpolitische Gesellschaft as well as the Institut für Auslandskunde. His writings include *Tripolitanien; Landschaftsbilder und Völkertypen* (1898), *Zur Landeskunde von Rumänien* (1907), *Geographische Charakterbilder aus der asiatischen Türkei und dem südlichen mesopotamisch-iranischen Randgebirge* (1909), *Auf türkischer Erde; Reisebilder und Studien* [aus Libyen] (1913), *Durch Albanien und Montenegro* (1913), *Türkisch Asien und seine Wirtschaftswerte* (1916), and *Libyen und die italienischen Kraftfelder in Nordafrika* (1941). He died in Starnberg on 28 December 1954. DtBE; KDtLK, Nekrolog, 1936-70; Kürschner, 1925-1950; NDB; Schwarz; *Wer ist's*, 1909-1935

Grothusen, Klaus-Detlev, born 29 October 1928 near Bad Nauheim, Hessen, Germany, he received a Dr.habil. in 1967 from the Universität Gießen for *Entstehung und Geschichte Zagrebs bis zum Ausgang des 14. Jahrhunderts.* He was from 1969 to1992 a professor of East European history at the

Universität Hamburg. For many years he served as a vice-president of the Südosteuropa-Gesellschaft in München. He is best remembered as the editor of the eight-volume *Südosteuropahandbuch*. His other writings include *Die Entwicklung der wissenschaftlichen Bibliotheken Jugoslawiens seit 1945* (1958), *Die historische Rechtsschule Rußlands* (1962), and he edited *Die Türkei in Europa* (1979), and *Türkei = Turkey* (1985). He died in Hamburg on 16 July 1994. DtBE; *Südosteuropa Mitteilungen*, 34 (1994), pp. 250-52; WhoWor, 1991/92

Grotkopp, Wilhelm, born in 1900, he received a Dr.phil. in 1924 from the Universität Kiel for *Universalökonomische Gedanken bei den mittelalterlich-christlichen Socialphilosophen*. His other writings include *Der schwedische Zündholztrust* (1928), *Amerikas Schutzzollpolitik und Europa* (1929), *Frei vom Golde* (1934), its translation, *Monnaie sans or* (1943), and *Die große Krise* (1954). NUC, pre-1956

Grottannelli, Vinigi Lorenzo, born 13 August 1912 at Avigliana, near Torino, he studied at the Università de Torino, where he received a degree in economics in 1933, and one in law in 1945. In 1940 he participated in the Italian mission to the Mao in Welega (Wollega), which determined his future ethnological researches. He subsequently joined the Museo preistorico e etnografico «Luigi Pigorini». Since 1946 he successively served in various capacities in the Istituto orientale di Napoli, Università «La Sapienza» di Roma, and Università Urbaniana del Vaticano. His writings include *I Mao* (1940), *Ethnologia* (1965), *Pescatori dell'Oceano Indiano* (1965), and *Gerarchie etniche e conflitto culturale; saggi di etnologia nordest africana* (1976). Africa (Roma), 48 (1993), pp. 424-26; DizBI; IndBiItal (2); Unesco

Grötzbach, Erwin, born 11 April 1933 at Markt Wekelsdorf, Germany, he studied geography and history at München, where he received a Dr.phil. in 1963 for *Geographische Untersuchung über die Kleinstadt der Gegenwart in Süd-Deutschland*; he received his Dr.habil. in 1970 from the Universität Saarbrücken for *Kultur-geographischer Wandel in Nordost-Afghanistan seit dem 19. Jahrhundert*. He taught successively at Erlangen and Hannover, before he was appointed to the chair of cultural geography at the Katholische Universität Eichstädt, Bavaria, in 1980. His writings include *Städte und Bazare in Afghanistan* (1979), *Afghanistan; eine geographische Landeskunde* (1990), and he edited *Aktuelle Probleme der Regionalentwicklung und Stadtgeographie Afghanistans* (1979). Kürschner, 1976-2001|; ZKO

Grotzfeld, Heinz, born 12 December 1933 at Quierschied, Saargebiet, he received a Dr.phil. in 1961 from the Universität Münster for *Laut- und Formenlehre des Damaszenisch-Arabischen*, and the *venia legendi* in 1968 for *Das Bad im arabisch-islamischen Mittelalter* (1970). He was from 1968 to 1975 a professor of Arabic at Stockholms Universitet, and from 1975 to his retirement he taught his subject at Münster. His writings include *Syrisch-arabische Grammatik* (1965). Kürschner, 1976-2003; Private

Grotzfeld, Sopia née Schwab, born 8 June 1934 at Nürnberg, married to Heinz Grotzfeld, she received a Dr.phil. in 1962 from the Universität Münster for *Drei altarabische Erzählungen aus dem Beduinenleben*. She was a research assistant at the library of the Deutsche Morgenländische Gesellschaft, Beirut, 1963/64. After some years as a free-lance orientalist she followed her husband to Stockholm, where she taught Arabic at Stockholms Universitet, 1968-1971. From 1973 to 1975 she was a research assistant at Kungliga Myntkabinettet, Stockholm. She collaborated in the production of *Corpus Nummorum saeculorum IX-XI qui in Suecia reperti sunt*. Her studies since the 1980s focus on Arabic folk literature. She was a joint author of *Die Erzählungen aus "Tausendundeiner Nacht* (1984). Private; Schwarz

Grousset, René, born 5 September 1885 at Aubais (Gard), he was a brilliant student in Montpellier. In 1912 he joined the Administration des Beaux arts, Paris, as a *rédacteur* at the Bureau des bâtiments civils. It was during this time before the Great War that he made plans for a history of Asia. Mobilized in 1914, he fought at Tahure (Marne) and Verdun. Demobilized in 1918, he continued with his *Histoire de l'Asie*, which was published in 1922, and which seemed to some, particularly certain specialists, to be an unequalled work of popularization. This was followed by his earth-shaking *Réveil de l'Asie* (1924). Since 1925 he was a deputy keeper at the Musée Guimet, Paris. He subsequently pursued a triple career: professor of history and geography at the École des langues orientales, lecturer at the École des Sciences politiques, keeper at the Musée Cernuschi, keeper-in-chief at the Musée Guimet, and member of council of the Musées nationaux. His other writings include *L'Épopée des croisades* (1939), its translations, *La epopeya de las cruzades* (1944), *Das Heldenlied der Kreuzzüge* (1951), *L'Empire des steppes* (1939), *L'Empire du Levant* (1946), and *L'Homme et son histoire* (1954), its translation, *Orient und Okzident im geistigen Austausch* (1955). He died on 12 September 1952 in the Musée Cernuschi which so much bears his stamp. DBF; EncIran; *Hommes et destins*, vol. 2, pp. 355-56; IndexBFr² (4); *Isis*, 43 (1952), p. 367; Magyar; WhoFr, 1953/54; *Who was who*, 5

Grout, Lewis, born 28 January 1815 at Newfane, Vt., he was a 1842 graduate of Yale University, and a 1846 graduate of Andower Theological Seminary. Immediately after being ordained, he sailed for South Africa as missionary to the Zulus. He returned to the United States in 1862 to become pastor in

New England. His writings include *The Isizulu, a grammar of the Zulu language* (1859), *Zululand* (1864), and translations of parts of the Bible into Zulu. His *Autobiography of the Rev. Lewis Grout* was published posthumously in 1905. He died in Battleboro, Vt., 12 March 1905. Shavit - Africa; WhAm, 1

Grove, Alfred Thomas, born 8 April 1924 at Evesham, Worcestershire, he was educated at Cambridge University, where he served since 1949 as a lecturer in geography. His writings include *Land use and soil conservation in parts of Onitsha and Owerri provinces* (1951), *Land use and soil conservation on the Jos Plateau* (1952), *The Benue Valley* (1957), *Africa south of the Sahara* (1967), and *Africa*, 3rd ed. (1978). Au&Wr, 1971; LC

Grove, Noel, born 20th, he was a journalist affiliated with the National Geographic Society (U.S.A.). His writings include *Wild lands for wildlife; America's national refuges* (1984). Note about the author

Grover, B. L., born 21 January 1927, he studied at the Panjab University, where he received his M.A. in 1948 and his Ph.D. in 1959. He was in 1983 a senior lecturer in history at Hans Raj College, Delhi. His writings include *The Beginnings of modern postal system in India* (1957), *A Documentary study of British policy towards Indian nationalism, 1835-1909* (1967), and he was a joint author of *Studies in modern Indian history from 1707 to the present day* (1963). BLC; IndianBilnd (1)

Groves, Walter Alexander, born 10 March 1898 at Germantown, Pa., he graduated in 1919 from Lafayette College, and received a Ph.D. in 1925 from Princeton University for *An Analysis of obvious outcomes in a study of the life of Christ essential for character education in the denominational colleges.* He was a professor in Iran from 1925 to 1940. In 1936 he was affiliated with Alborz College, Tehran, and in 1962, he was a vice-chancellor, Pahlavi University, Shiraz. DrAS, 4th ed. (1963/64); Note

Growse, Frederick Salmon, born in 1836 or 37 in Suffolk, he was educated at Oriel College, and Queen's College, Oxford, and subsequently entered the Indian Civil Service and went to India, where he served in the North West Province in 1860 and later in Mathura and Bulandshahr. He built a Catholic church at Mathura. He ardently defended the purity of the vernacular Hindi, as opposed to the official Hindustani. He retired from the Service in 1890. His writings include *Mathurá; a district memoir* (1873-74), and *Materials for a history of the parish of Bildeston in the county of Suffolk* (1892). He died on 19 May 1893. Boase, vol. 5; Buckland, Riddick

Grozdanić, Sulejman, born 20th cent., his writings include *Stara arapska poezija* (Sarajevo, 1971), and *Na horizontima arapske književnosti* (Sarajevo, 1975). His trace is lost after an article in 1995.

Grozdanova, Elena, born 20th cent., she was affiliated with the Oriental division of the National Library, Sofia. Her writings include *Българската селска община през XV-XVIII век* (1979), *Българската народност през XVII век; демографско изследване* (1989),and she was joint author of *Солярството Българското Черноморие през XV-XVIII век* (1982), and *Българите през XVI век; по документи отнаши и чужи архиви* (1986). Note; OSK

Grube, Ernst J., born in 1932, he received a Dr.phil. in 1955 from the Freie Universität Berlin for *Untersuchungen über den Quellenwert bildkünstlerischer Darstellung für die Erforschung des mittelalterlichen Theaters.* He taught at the universities of Padova and Napoli and was associated with the Istituto Italiano per il Medio ed Estremo Oriente (Roma) in Isfahan. His writings include *The World of Islam* (1967), its translation, *De wereld van de Islam* (1967), *The Classical style in Islamic painting* (1968), *Islamic pottery of the eighth to the fifteenth century in the Keir Collection* (1976), and he was a joint author of *Islamic paintings from the 11th to the 18th century in the Collection of Hans P. Kraus* (1972), and he was a joint editor of the colloquium papers, *Between China and Iran; paintings from four Istanbul albums* (1985). LC; Master (1); *MESA Roster of members*, 1990; Note

Grudziecki (Gurdziecki), Bogdam (Bohdan), born early 17th cent. of Georgian-Armenian descent, he served the Polish crown since the early 1650s. He was the first permanent Polish resident in Persia. He left Persia in 1699 and died in 1700 in Moscow. EncIran; Polski = PSB

Grueber, Herbert Appold, born in 1846 at Hambridge, Somerset, he entered the British Museum in 1866 and served from 1906 to 1912 as keeper of Coins and Medals. His writings include *English personal medals from 1760* (1892), and *Coins of the Roman republic in the British Museum* (1910). He died in 1927. BritInd (2); Dawson; Egyptology; Who was who, 2

Gruen, George Emanuel, born 20th cent., he received a Ph.D. in 1970 from Columbia University, New York, for *Turkey, Israel and the Palestinian question, 1948-1960; a study in the diplomacy of ambivalence.* He was associated with the American Jewish Committee, New York. His writings include *The troubled Middle East; a survey of current issues.* Selim

Grühl, Max, born 26 March 1884 at Pinneberg, Germany, he was a private scholar and a traveller. From 1922 to 1924 he edited the journal *Stimme des Orients*. His writings include *Faltboot-Safari in Afrika; Fahrten durch blaue Meere am Rand der Wüste* (1931), *The Citadel of Ethiopia* (1932), *Abessinien, die Zitadelle Afrikas* (1935), *Abyssinia at bay* (1935), *L'Impero del negus neghesti* (1935), *Ägyptischer Sommer* (1942), and *Zum Kaisergott von Kaffa; als Forscher auf eigene Faust im dunkelsten Afrika* (1938). KDtLK, 1937/38-1943

Grulich, Rudolf, he gained a Dr. theol. habil. and became a professor at the Universität Gießen. His writings include *Der Islam in Jugoslawien* (1979), and he was a joint editor of *Nationale Minderheiten in Europa* (1975). Kürschner, 1992-2003

Grum-Grzhimaïlo, Grigoriĭ Efimovich, born in 1860, he was a geographer who explored Central Asia, Tuva, Mongolia, Sinkiang, and Tien Shan, visiting Bukhara, Kuldja and Urumji. His writings include *Описаніе Амурской области* (1894), *Западная Монголія и Урянхайскій край* (1914-30), and he was a joint author of *Описаніе путешествія въ Западный Китай* (1896-1907). He died in 1936. EnSlovar; Henze; GSE; UzbekSE; Wieczynski

Grumach, Ernst, born 7 November 1902 at Tilsit, East Prussia, he received a Dr.phil. in 1929 from the Universität Königsberg for *Physis und Agathon in der alten Stoa*. He was from 1937 to 1942 a lecturer at Lehranstalt für die Wissenschaft des Judentums, Berlin, and from 1949 to 1957 he served as a professor at Humboldt-Universität, Berlin. Concurrently he collaborated since 1952 with Deutsche Akademie der Wissenschaften zu Berlin in the publication of *Goethes Werke*. His other writings include *Goethe und die Antike* (1949), *Beiträge zur Goetheforschung* (1959), and *Bibliographie zur kretisch-mykeninschen Epigraphik* (1963). He died in London on 5 October 1967. DtBE; Kürschner, 1954; Wer ist wer, 1963 [Grumbach]

Grumel, Venance, fl. 1945, his writings include *La Chronologie* (1958), and he edited *Les Regestes des Actes du Patriarcat de Constantinople* (1932).

Freiherr von **Grünau**, Kurt O. W., born 10 February 1871 at Schloß Kreuz-Wertheim, Unterfranken, he entered the German diplomatic service in 1896. During his career he was also posted to Cairo. He travelled widely throughout the world and contributed articles to geographical journals. Wer ist's, 1922-1935

Freiherr von **Grünau**, Werner, Dr.jur., born 9 October 1874 at Karlsruhe, Germany, he studied at Berlin, München, Leipzig and Heidelberg, and in 1904 entered the German foreign service. He served from 1906 to 1908 as vice-consul in Alexandria, Egypt, and in 1925 he was consul-general in Kattowitz. His writings include *Die staats- und völkerrechtliche Stellung Ägyptens* (1903). RHbDtG; Wer ist's, 1928

Grünbaum, Max (Maier), born 12 August 1817 at Seligenstadt, Hessen, he received a classical Jewish education and subsequently studied philology and philosophy at the universities of Gießen and Bonn, without taking a degree. From 1840 to 1857 he worked as a private tutor in Budapest, Amsterdam, London, Triest, and Wien. In 1858 he became an inspector of a Jewish orphanage in New York, a post which he held until 1870, when he returned to München, where he died on 11 December 1898. His writings include *Neue Beiträge zur semitischen Sagenkunde* (1893), *Jüdisch-spanische Chrestomathie* (1896), and *Gesammelte Aufsätze zur Sprach- und Sagenkunde* (1901). ADtB, vol. 49, pp. 589-94; DtBE; Encyclopedia Judaica (Berlin, 1931); Wininger

Grundfest, IAkov Berkovich, born 4 April 1929 at Moscow, he graduated in 1951 from the Oriental Faculty, Leningrad, and received his first degree in 1966 for *Глагол в южноарабском языке*. Miliband

von **Grünebaum** (Von Grunebaum), Gustav Edmund, born 1 September 1909 at Wien, he received a Dr.phil. in 1931 from the Universität Wien for *Über die Jahre 78-117 H. in Ibn Kaṯīrs Weltgeschichte al-Bidāja wa'n-nihāja*. In 1941 he emigrated to America, where he became first a professor at the University of Chicago and later a professor of history and director of the Near Eastern Center, U.C.L.A. His writings include *Muhammadan festivals* (1958), *Modern Islam* (1962), and a collection of his articles, *Islam and medieval Hellenism* (1976). He died in 1972 in Los Angeles. BioHbDtE; CnDiAmJBi; ConAu 1-4, new rev. 3; Index Islamicus (14); IntWW, 1958-1971/72; WhAm, 5

Gruner, Christian Gottfried, born 8 November 1744 at Sagan, Silesia, he studied at Leipzig and Halle/Saale, received a Dr.med. in 1747 and subsequently practised his profession at Breslau. In 1773 he accepted an invitation to teach medicine and botany at the Universität Jena. He was one of the most important medical historians of the eighteenth century. His writings include *Bibliothek der alten Aerzte und Uebersetzungen und Auszügen* (1780-82), and *Kritische Nachrichten von kleinen medizinischen Schriften inn- und ausländischer Akademien vom Jahre 1780 und 1781* (1783-84). He died in Jena on 5 December 1815. ADtB, vol. 10, pp. 38-40; DtBE; DtBilnd (7); NDB

Gruner, Dorothee, born 20th cent., she received a Dr.phil. in 1972 from the Universität Frankfurt am Main for *Die Berber-Keramik am Beispiel der Orte Afir, Merkalla, Taher, Tiberguent und Roknia*, a work which was published in 1973. Her other writings include *Die Lehm-Moschee am Niger* (1990). Note

Gruner, Oskar Cameron, born 15 August 1877 at Altrincham, Cheshire, he studied at Manchester and London, received a medical doctorate, and became a member of the Royal College of Surgeons. Since 1910 he was successively a pathologist at the Royal Victoria Hospital, Montreal, P.Q., and a professor of pathology at McGill University, Montreal. He was a joint editor of *Descriptive catalogue of the Medical Museum of McGill University* (1915), and he translated *A Treatise on the Canon of medicine of Avicenna* (1930). Biographical encyclopedia of the world, 3rd ed. (1946) [not sighted]; WhE&EA

Grünert, Max Theodor, born 13 October 1849 at Brüx, Bohemia, he studied classical and Oriental philology at Wien and Leipzig, where he was a student of H. L. Fleischer in Arabic, and received a Dr.phil. in 1876 for *Über die Imâla*. He subsequently taught Semitic languages at Karl's Universität, Prag. His writings include *Neu-persische Chrestomathie* (1881), *Der Löwe in der Literatur der Araber* (1899), *Das Gebet im Islam* (1900), and he edited *Ibn Kutaiba's Adab al-kâtib* (1900), as well as other texts. He died in Praha on 10 February 1929. DtBilnd (2); Filipsky; ÖBL; Wer ist's, 1909

Grunin, Timofei Ivanovich, born in 1898, he graduated in 1927 from the Faculty of Near Eastern studies, Moscow, and received his first degree in 1944 for Половецкие документы Киевского Центрального архива древних актов. In the 1930s he was associated with the Committee for the new alphabets for the central Asian languages, a body which operated within the All-Russian Scientific Oriental Association. He was a lecturer since 1951. His writings include Турецкий язык; элементарная грамматика и новый алфавит (1930), and he was a joint author of Учебное пособие по турецкому языку (1949). He died 19 August 1970. Miliband; Miliband²

Grunina, Él'vira Aleksandrovna, born 26 November 1826 at Moscow, she graduated in 1949 from the Faculty of Philology, Moscow, where she also received her first degree in 1952 for Сложноподчиненное предложение и современном узбекском языке. She was since 1956 associated with the Institute for Oriental Languages, Moscow. Her writings include Учебное пособие по османско-турецие языку (1988). Miliband; Miliband²

Gruntzel (Grunzel), Josef, born 20 October 1866 at Alt-Paka, Bohemia, he studied Oriental languages and political science successively at Wien, Paris (Collège de France and École des langues orientales vivantes), and Berlin. After taking a Dr.phil. and Dr.jur., he was since 1890 a librarian and editor of *Consularberichte* at the k.u.k. Handelsmuseum, Wien. He frequently visited the Near East. Since 1908 he was a professor of political economy at the Exportakademie des Österreichischen Handelsmuseum (later, Hochschule für Welthandel). His writings include *Entwurf einer ver-gleichenden Grammatik der altaischen Sprachen* (1895), *Die wirtschaftlichen Verhältnisse Kleinasiens* (1897), and *Bericht über die wirtschaftlichen Verhältnisse Ägyptens* (1905). He died in Wien on 21 November 1934. DtBE; DtBilnd (2); Kosch; Kürschner, 1925-1931; NDB; ÖBL; Wer ist's, 1922-1928

Grunwald, Kurt, born 18 September 1901 at Hamburg, he received a Dr.rer.pol., and became an economist and a banker in Israel. His writings include *Das Recht der nationalen Minderheiten und der Völkerbund* (1926), *The government finances of the Mandate territories in the Near East* (1926), its translation, *Le finance statali dei territori sotto Mandato net Vicino Oriente* (1933), *Türkenhirsch; a study of Baron Maurice de Hirsch* (1966), and he was a joint author of *Industrialization in the Middle East* (1960). Wholsrael, 1958-1968|

Grünwedel, Albert, born 31 July 1856 at München, he studied archaeology, classical and Oriental philology at the Universität München, where he received a Dr.phil. in 1883 for *Das sechste Kapitel der Rûpasiddhi nach drei singhalesischen Pâli-Handschriften*. A Tibetan scholar and a leading authority in the history of Indian and Buddhist art, he joined in 1882 the royal museums in Berlin, becoming in 1904 a director of the Asiatic section of the Berlin Ethnographical Museum. He led two German Turfan expeditions in Chinese Turkistan. His writings include *Mythologie des Buddhismus in Tibet und der Mongolei* (1900), its translation, *Mythologie du Buddhisme au Tibet et en Mongolie* (1900), *Alt-buddhistische Kultstätten in Chinesisch-Turkistan* (1912), and *Die Teufel des Avesta und ihre Beziehungen zur Ikonographie des Buddhismus Zentral-Asiens* (1924). He died in Lenggries, Bavaria, in 1935. Buckland; DtBE; DtBilnd (3); EncIran; GV; Kürschner, 1926-1935; NDB; Stache-Rosen, pp. 131-132

Grunzel, Josef, 1866-1934 see Gruntzel, Josef

Grunzweig, Armand, born 16 July 1897 at Paris, he took his B.A. and M.A. at Columbia University, New York, and his doctorate at the Université libre de Bruxelles. He was a keeper at the Archives générales du Royaume, Bruxelles. He edited *Correspondance de la filiale de Bruges des Medici*

(1931), and *Les Livres des comptes des Gallerani* (1961-62). WhoBelgium, 1957/58; *Who's who in Belgium and Grand Duchy of Luxemburg*, 1962

Grütter, Irene, born 20th cent., she received a Dr.phil. in 1952 from the Universität Erlangen for *Arabische Bestattungsgebräuche in frühislamischer Zeit (nach Ibn Sa'd, Buḫārī und Abū Dā'ūd)*. Schwarz

Grützmacher, Richard Heinrich, born 3 December 1876 at Berlin, he gained a doctorate and became a professor of Protestant theology at the universities of Greifswald, Rostock, and Erlangen. His writings include *Konfuzius, Buddha, Zarathustra, Muhammed* (1921), *Religionsgeschichtliche Charakterkunde* (1937-38), and *Die Religionen in der Anschauung Goethes* (1950). He died in 1959. Kürschner; *Wer ist's*, 1909-1935

Grye, B. de la, 1827-1909 *see* Bouquet de la Grye, Jean Jacques *Anatole*

Grzegorzewski, Jan (Johann), born about 1849 in Volyn (Wołyń), Ukraine, he was an ethnographer and Orientalist who had studied at Odessa and Moscow. His writings include *Ein türk-tatarischer Dialekt in Galizien* (1903), *Z sidżyllatów rumelijskich epoki wyprawy wiedeńskiej* (1912), *Albania i Albanczycy* (1914), and *Język Łach-Laraitów* (1917). He died in 1922. Polski (5); PSB

Grzeskowiak, Martin, born 10 October 1939 at Dessau, he studied Arabic and Islamic subjects at the University Halle-Wittenberg where he also received a Dr.phil. in 1969 for *Die Darstellung des arabischen Propheten Muhammad bei Muhammad Husain Haikal, Taufīq al-Hakīm und 'Abbās Mahmud al-'Aqqād*. He was since 1963 a research assistent in the Institut für Orientforschung, Deutsche Akademie der Wissenschaften zu Berlin. Thesis

Grzybowski, Kazimierz, born 19 June 1911 at Czortków, Poland, he took law degrees at Lvov and Harvard. He taught law in Poland until 1939. After the war he spent ten years with the Library of Congress, European Law Division, Washington, D.C.. From 1967 until his retirement he was a professor of law and political science at Duke University, Durham, N.C. His writings include *Soviet private international law* (1965), *Freedom of expression and dissident in the Soviet Union* (1972), and he was the compiler of *East-West trade* (1974). AmM&WS, 1973 S, 1978 S; DrAS, 1974 P, 1978 P, 1982 P; WhoAm, 1974/75-1992; WhoWor, 1982-1993/94

Gschwind, Alexander, born about 1950, he received a Dr.phil. in 1977 from the Universität Basel for *Die Entwicklung von Partei und Staat im unabhängigen Algerien, 1962-1977*. Schwarz

Gsell, Stéphane Charles Émile, born 7 February 1864 at Paris, he originated from a Protestant Alsatian family who generations back had settled in St. Gallen, Switzerland. He grew up in Paris, where graduated from the Lycée Louis-le-Grand and the École normale supérieure, gaining the first place in the *agrégation* in history. He subsequently spent four years at l'École française de Rome. In the spring of 1889, he excavated at the Etruscan site of Vulci; in the following year, he was nominated a lecturer in archaeology at l'École des lettres d'Alger; and in 1894, he was appointed to the chair of African antiquities, which at that time was essentially a research appointment. Concurrently he was since 1900 inspector of Algerian antiquities, and since 1902 also director of the Musée des antiquités algériennes et d'art musulman. After the sudden and early death of his wife in 1910, he accepted an invitation from the Collège de France and left Algeria in the spring of 1912. His writings include *Recherches archéologiques en Algérie* (1893), *Guide archéologique des environs d'Alger* (1896), and *Monuments antiques de l'Algérie* (1901). He died in Paris on 1 January 1932. DBF; IndexBFr² (2); *Qui êtes-vous*, 1924; *Revue africaine*, vol. 72 (1931), pp. 361-64, vol. 73 (1932), pp. 20-36

Gstrein, Heinz, born 16 December 1941 at Innsbruck, he received a Dr.phil. in 1968 from the Universität Wien for *Unedierte Texte zur Geschichte der byzantinischen Osterpredigt*. He was a foreign correspondent for major periodicals in Austria and Germany. His writings include *Volk ohne Anwalt; die Kurdenfrage im Mittleren Osten* (1974), *Islamische Sufi-Meditation für Christen* (1977), *Unter Menschenhändlern im Sudan* (1978), and *Marx oder Mohammed; arabischer Sozialismus und islamische Erneuerung* (1979). IntAu&W, 1976, 1977, 1982; WhoWor, 1978-1980/81

Guadagni, Francesco, born in 1769 at Roma, he received the classical education of his day and subsequently began to study theology and philosophy at the Università Gregoriana, Roma, later changing to literature under the influence of G. Marotti. In 1804 became a barrister of the *congregazione dei Riti*, and in due course a public prosecutor. His writings include *Opuscoli postumi italiani e latini* (1838), a work which contains his partial Latin translation of Sa'di's *Gulistān*. He died in Roma on 9 July 1837. DizBl; IndBiltal (1)

Guadagni, Marco, born 20th cent., his writings include *Ethiopian labour law handbook* (1972), and *Islamic land law and colonial domains* (1978). BLC; NUC

Guadagnoli, Filippo, born in 1596 at Magliano (Abruzzo), he studied Oriental languages, including Hebrew and Persian, but particularly Arabic, which he later taught for quite some time at the Collegio Sapienta at Roma. On behalf of the Collegio de propaganda Fide, he translated the Bible into Arabic, a work which was published in 1671 at Roma. His writings include *Apologia pro christiana religione* (1631), a work which was published as a reply to the objections brought by Ahmad ibn Zayn al-'Ābidīn against an exposition of the truth of the Christian religion which was composed in Persian by Jerónimo Javier and entitled *Ayīnah-i haqqnumā*. His other writings include *Breves arabicae linguae institutiones* (1642), and *Considerationes ad Mahomettanos, cum responsione* (1649). He left the manuscript of an Arabic dictionary which remained at the cloister of St. Laurentii in Lucina. He died on 27 March 1656. Fück, 78; IndBiltal (15); Christian G. Jöcher, *Allgemeines Gelehrten-Lexikon*, vol. 2 (1750)

Guarmani, Carlo Claudio Camillo, born 11 November 1828 at Livorno, he lived in the Levant since 1850 as the agent of a French trading company in Jerusalem. Whenever possible he wandered with the nomadic tribes of greater Syria and became a specialist on horses. He obtained a commission to buy stallions for the royal studs of Paris and Turino. His journey took him to Taymā', and Hā'il in Inner Arabia. He returned with many compass-bearings and precise intervals in Jabal Shammar that he can claim the distinction not only of being the first to render scientific cartography of Central Arabia possible, but of having done more for the mapmakers than any successor except Charles Huber. His writings include *Il Neged settentrionale* (1866), its translations, *Guarmani's Reise nach dem Negd* (1865), *Northern Najd, a journey from Jerusalem to Anaiza in Qasim* (1938), and *Gl'Italiani in Terra Santa; reminiscenze* (1872). He died in 1884 in Genova. Bidwell; BioIn 11, 15; Freeth; Henze; IndBiltal (2)

Guasco, Alexandre, born 19th cent., he received a doctorate in 1878 from the Université de Bordeaux for *De la condition des étrangers en droit romain et en droit français*. He contributed to *Annales de la propagation de la foi*, and *Revue générale de droit international public*. BN; NUC, pre-1956

Guastavino Gallent, Guillermo, born 24 October 1904 at Valencia, he received a degree in liberal arts from the Universidad de Madrid, and a diploma in documentation. He was from 1932 to 1935 a director of the Museo Arqueólogos, Tarragona, from 1935 to 1939, a director of the Archivo de Hacienda, Salamanca, from 1939 to 1957, director of the Archivos y Bibliotecas del Protectorado de España en Marruecos, and from 1957 to 1967, head of the Servicio de Despósito Legal. In 1967, he was nominated director of the Biblioteca Nacional de Madrid. His writings include *Breve historia de Marruecos* (1944), *Pensamientos arabes* (1944), *Los bombardeos de Argel en 1783-1784 y su repercusión literaria* (1950), and *La acción española en los archivos y bibliotecas de la zona norte de Marruecos* (1958). In 1974, he was honoured by *Homenaje a Guillermo Guastavino; miscelánea de estudios*. DBEC; IntWW, 1971/72-1975/76; WhoWor, 1974/75

Gubaïdullin (Gubaidulin), Gaziz Salikhovich, born in 1887, he studied history and received a doctorate in 1927. In the same year he was appointed a professor. His writings include *Из прошлого татар* (s.d.), and *Развитие исторической литературы у тюрко-татарских народов* (Baku, 1926). He died in 1938. NYPL; TatarES

Guboglu, Mihail, born in 1911 at Ceadir-Lunga, Bessarabia, he was a historian and Orientalist as well as a sometime director of the National Archives, Bucureşti. He also served as a professor at Bucureşti, Paris, and Ankara. His writings include *Paleografia şi diplomatica turco-osmana* (1958), *Catalogul documentelor turceşti* (1960-65), and he was a joint author of *Cronici turceşti privind tarile române* (1966). He died in 1990. DcEnc; WhoRom

Guboglu, Mikhaïl Nikolaevich, born 20th cent., he became associated with the Institute of Ethnology and Anthropology, Soviet (and later, Russian) Academy of Science. His writings include *Развитие двуязычия в Молдавской ССР* (Kishinev, 1979), *Современные этноязыковые процессы в СССР* (Moscow, 1984), *Крымскотатарское национальное двизение* (1992), *Sprachengesetzgebung und Sprachenpolitik in der UdSSR und in den Nachfolgestaaten der UdSSR seit 1989* (Köln, 1994), *Мобильность и мобилизация* (2002), he was a joint author of *Баскортостан и Татарстан* (1994), and he edited *Язык и национализм в ростсоветских республиках* (1994). LC; OSK

Gubser, Peter Anton, born 9 May 1941 at Tulsa, Okla., he graduated in 1964 from Yale University, received his M.A. in 1966 from A.U.B., and his D.Phil. in 1969 from Oxford University for *Politics and power in a small Arab town; a study of al-Karak*. He was from 1972 to 1974 associated with the American Institutes for Research, Washington, D.C., and from 1974 to 1977 with the Ford Foundation, Beirut. Since 1977, he was a president of the American Near East Refugee Aid, a post which he still held in 1990. His writings include *Jordan; crossroads of Middle Eastern events* (1983), and *Historical dictionary of the Hashimite Kingdom of Jordan* (1990). MESA *Roster of members*, 1977-1990; Note; Sluglett; WhoAm, 1994-2003; WhoE, 1993/94, 2003

Gudkova, A. V., born 20th cent., she was aasociated with the Karakapak Branch of the Uzbek Academy of Science. Her writings include *Ток-кала* (Tashkent, 1964). OSK

Gudme, Peter de Hemmer, born 28 September 1897 at København. In accordance with a family tradition he studied theology at Marselisborg. As a twenty year old he volunteered for service in the Finnish war of independence. He completed his theology in the early 1920s and subsequently pursued an interest in Oriental subjects at Paris, Leipzig, and Uppsala. In the late 1920s he began a career as a journalist. In the 1940s he became caught in the wider implications of the Finno-German dilemma. Arrested by the German secret police, he committed suicide in prison on 30 November 1944. His writings include *Fra Nebukadnesar til Hitler* (1934). *Finland, Nordens Østvold* (1939) *Finlands Folk i Kamp* (1940), *Främre Orienten och Stormakterna* (1941), and *Nær-Orienten of Stormagtskampen* (1941), and he translated into Danish T. E. Lawrence's *Revolt in the Desert* entitled *Oprøret i Ørkenen*. Kraks; DanskBL

Guebhard, Paul, born 19th cent., his writings include *Au Fouta Dialon; cent-vingt ans histoire; état social et politique autrefois et de nos jours* (Paris, 1909). BN

Guedalla, Hayyim, born in 1915 at Jerusalem, he was a philanthropist and supporter of Jewish settlement in Palestine. His writings include *The Roumanian government and the Jews* (1872), and *Mitigating and extenuating circumstances in the recent Turkish default* (1876). He died in Jerusalem on 2 October 1904. EncJud; Wininger

Gueluy, Albert, born 23 April 1849 at Anvaing, he studied at the Collège d'Enghien, and there served from 1871 to 1876 as a professor. From 1877 to 1881 he was a missionary in China and Mongolia. After his return to Belgium, he was attached to the seat of his mission at Scheut. From 1888 to 1889, he served as a missionary in the Congo, and from 1890 to 1900, he was a rector of the Séminaire africain at Louvain. His writings include *Bouddhisme et sinilogie* (Louvain, 1896), and *Le Mouvement chrétien de Si-Ngan-Fou* (Bruxelles, 1897). He died in 1924. BiBenelux (1)

Guémard, Gabriel Alphonse Alfred, born 18 November 1878 at Farges-en-Septaine (Cher), he was a graduate of the Lycée Louis-le-Grand, Paris, and the Faculté de droit de Dijon, and received a doctorate in law. He practised his profession at Cairo. His writings include *Le Régime hypothécaire égyptien; étude critique de législation économique* (1914), *La Condition juridique des gens mariés en droit musulman (notammement dans le rite hanafite), comparé au droit français* (1915), *Aventuriers mameluks d'Égypte* (1928), and *Bibliographie critique de la Commission des sciences et arts et de l'Institut égyptien* (1936). He died in Cairo on 22 March 1937. DBF; *Hommes et destins* 4, pp. 353-4

Guénon, René Jean Marie Joseph, born 15 November 1886 at Blois, he was educated privately and subsequently attended first l'École Notre-Dame des Aydes and then the Collège Augustin Thierry, where he became exposed to pre-Socratic philosophy. In 1906 he abandoned the idea of preparing for the *grandes écoles* and made contact with occult circles. *Évêque gnostique* in 1909, he collaborated with Matgioi and the painter G. Agueli in the publication of the journal *La Gnose*. He was professionally introduced to Sufism by a shaykh, and also instructed by a Hindu master. Since 1907 he was involved with Masonic orders, but at the same time he worked for *La France antimaçonnique* of Clarin de La Rive. After the death of his first wife in 1927 he sought spiritual refuge in the Shādhilite brotherhood in Cairo, and in 1934 he married the daughter of Shaykh Muhammad Ibrahim. His writings include *Le Thésophisme; histoire d'une pseudo-religion* (1921), *Orient et Occident* (1924), *La Crise du monde moderne* (1927), its translation, *The Crisis of the modern world* (1962), and *L'Ésotérisme de Dante* (1925). He died in Cairo on 7 January 1951. Robin Waterfield wrote *René Guénon and the future of the West* (1987). BioIn 2 (1); DBF; IndexBFr² (1)

Guenther, Harry Palmer, born in 1933, he received a doctorate in business administration in 1959 from Indiana University for *Commercial bank lending and investment behavior during a period of restrictive Federal Reserve monetary policy*. He was successively a faculty member and chairman of the Department of Business Administration, A.U.B., a dean of the Beirut Management College, a lecturer in finance at the University of Minnesota, and a professor in the Department of Accounting and Finance, Northern Michigan University at Marquette, a post which he still held in 1999. NatFacDr, 1995-1999; Note about the author

Guéraud, Armand Laurent, born 31 August 1824 at Vieillevigne (Loire-Inférieure), he was a printer and bookseller at Nantes, but also a scholar, writer, and corresponding member of the Ministère de l'Instruction publique. He was the founding editor and director of the *Revue des provinces de l'Ouest*. He died in Nantes on 21 July 1861. IndexBFr² (1)

Guérin, Victor Honoré, born 15 September 1821 at Paris, he entered the École normale supérieure in 1840 and left it two years later as a *professeur* of rhetorique, a subject which he taught successively at

Agen, Bastia, Mâcon, Angers, and Alger. He obtained his *agrégation* in letters in 1850, and spent the year 1852 with the École française d'Athènes. In 1856 he received a doctorate from the Université de Paris for his theses, *De ora Palaestinae a promontorio Carmelo usque ad urbem Joppen pertinenti*, and *Étude sur l'île de Rhodes*. He went on many archaeological missions in the Aegaen Sea, the Near East as well as in Tunisia. His other writings include *La France catholique en Tunisie, à Malte et en Tripolitaine* (1886), *France catholique en Égypte* (1888), and *Jérusalem; son histoire, sa description, ses établissements religieux* (1889). He died in Paris 21 September 1891. Dawson; DBF; Egyptology; EncJud; Henze; Hill

Guérinot, Armant Albert, born in 1872 at Messon (Aube), he received a doctorate in letters in 1900 from the Université de Lyon for *De rhetorica vedica*, and also a medical doctorate. He was a proof-reader for Orientalia at the Imprimerie nationale. His writings include *Répertoire d'épigraphie jaina* (1908), *Recherches sur l'origine de l'idée de Dieu d'après le Rig-Veda* (1900), and *La Religion Djaïna* (1926). IndexBFr² (1)

Gueritz, John Elton Fortescue, born about 1900, he was a subaltern in the Royal Garhwal Rifles, then stationed in the United Provinces, and later in Baroda and other Indian States. He lived for several years in Baghdad and about 1950 in Tehran. He was a member of the Royal Central Asian Society since 1936. He was a joint author of *The Penguin handbook of first aid and home nursing* (1961). BLC; Note about the author

Guérnier, Eugène Joseph Léonard Marie, born 14 December 1882 at Saint-Malo (Ille-et-Vilaine), he went to school at Rennes and studied law at Paris, where he received his degree. From 1913 to 1922 he was an industrial executive in Morocco and concurrently served as president of the Chambre de Commerce de Casablanca, and since 1918 also as a member of the Conseil du gouvernement du Protectorat. From 1923 to 1927 he was a professor of political science in the Institut des hautes études marocianes. He returned to France in 1939 to teach until 1958 at the Institut d'études politiques de Paris. His writings include *L'Afrique, champ d'expansion de l'Europe* (1933), *Algérie et Sahara* (1946), *L'Afrique méditerranéenne* (1947), *Maroc* (1948), *La Berbérie, l'islam et la France* (1950), and *L'Apport de l'Afrique à la pensée humaine* (1952). He died in Paris on 29 March 1973. Hommes et destins, vol. 7, pp. 222-24; NDNC, 1968; Note about the author

Guerrero Lovillo, José, fl. 1955, his writings include *Las Cántigas; estudio arqueológico de sus miniaturas* (1949), *Sevilla* (1952), and *Miniatura gótica castellana* (1956).

Guerrier, V. I., 1837-1919 see Ger'e, Vladimir Ivanovich

Guerrier de Dumast, August *Prosper* François, baron, born 26 February 1796 at Nancy, where he was educated before studying law at Paris. With the Intendance militaire, he took part in the French campaign in Spain, 1823. In 1828 he took his leave from the military. Thereafter he worked without renumeration in civic and charitative positions. He was a member of the Académie de Stanislas, Nancy, and other learned societies. He died in Nancy, 26 January 1883. DBF; GdeEnc; Meyers; l'Orient, l'Algérie et les colonies françaises 1 (1866/67), pp. 95-96, 110-112

Guerrieri-Crocetti, Camillo, born 24 July 1892 at Teramo, Italy, he was successively a professor of literature at the universities of Genova and Pisa. His writings include *Antica poesia abruzzese* (1914), *La lirica del Camões* (1938), and *La Chanson de Roland* (1946). In 1971 he was honoured with *Omaggio a Camillo Guerrieri-Crocetti*. Chi è? 1957, 1961

de **Guerville**, Amédée Baillot, born in 1869 at Paris, his writings include *La nouvelle Égypte* (1905), and its translations, *New Egypt* (1905), *Das moderne Ägypten* (1906). BN; IndexBFr² (1); NUC, pre-1956

Guest, Arthur Rhuvon, born in 1869, his writings include and *Life and works of Ibn er Rumi* (1944), and he edited al-Kindī's *The Governors of Egypt* (1912). His trace is lost after an article in 1936. ZKO

Guest, Grace Dunham, born about 1900, she was in 1943 an assistant director at the Freer Gallery of Art, Washington, D.C. Her writings include *Annotated outlines of the history of ancient arts* (1943), and *Shiraz painting in the sixteenth century* (1949). Her trace is lost after a publication in 1961. Note about the author

Guest, John Spencer-Churchill, born, 14 May 1913 in England, he was educated at Trinity College, Cambridge, and Harvard Business School. From 1941 to 1946 he served with the British Army in Iraq, Iran, Egypt as well as in Europe. From 1946 to 1989, he was a merchant banker in New York. His writings include *Broken images* (1949), *The Euphrates Expedition* (1992), and *Survival among the Kurds; a history of the Yezidis* (1993), a work which was first published in 1987 entitled *The Yezidis*. Note about the author; ZKO

Guevara Bazán, Rafael A., born 20th cent., his writings include *Historia de la revolución islámica de Irán* (Lima, 1990).

Gueymard, L., his writings include *Almanach commercial de la province d'Alger* (1852). BN

Guglia, Eugen, born 24 August 1857 at Wien, he studied history and philology at the Universität Wien and gained a Dr.phil. in 1882. He subsequently became a school teacher at Wien and Prag. From 1893 to 1901 he was a professor of history and German literature at Theresianum, Wien. Since 1910 he taught history at the military college, and since 1919 at the Universität Graz. He died there on 8 July 1919. His writings include *Geschichte der Stadt Wien* (1892), and *Maria Theresia, ihr Leben und ihre Regierung* (1917). DtBilnd (4); KDtLK, 1907-1917; Kosch; ÖBL; Wer ist's, 1909-1912

Guibal, Michel, born 20th cent., he obtained his *agrégation* and was a lecturer in the Faculté des sciences juridiques, économiques et sociales, Rabat, and throughout the 1970s at the Université de Montpellier. His writings include *Memento des marchés publics*, 3rd ed. (2001), and he was a joint author of *Contrats des collectivités locales* (1989), and *L'avant-contrat* (2001). Livres disponibles, 2003

Guiberteau, Philippe, born 20th cent., his writings include *Les Hommes et les rites; le christianisme, achèvement de l'homme* (1953), *L'Enigme de Dante* (1973), and he edited Dante Alghieri's *Le Banquet, il Convivio* (1968), and *Dante et la suite de son itinéraire spirituel selon le Canzoniere* (1985). Livres disponibles, 2003

Guibon, Alice née Poulleau see Poulleau, Alice, Madame Guibon

Guichard, Beatrice Catherine née Baskerville, born in 1878 at Chatham, Kent, she was privately educated and became a newspaper correspondent. Her writings include *The Polish Jew* (1906), *The Playground of Satan* (1918), and *What next, o Duce?* (1937). She died 23 June 1955. Who was who, 5

Guichard, Frantz, born 1870, he received a doctorate in 1894 from the Université de Lyon for *Étude sur l'artérie fémorale des bourreliers*. He was in 1906 a *médecin-major de 2e classe*. Note

Guichard, Jules, born 11 December 1827 at Jouancy (Yonne), he was in charge of the agricultural exploitation of the paternal estate. His competence earned him in 1861 the invitation of the Suez Canal Company to develop the lands along the water-way, a task which he accomplished with the help of numerous Bedouins. Later he also organized the transit service and the navigation. After his return to France in 1872, he became successively an industrial executive and politician. In 1891 he succeeded to Fr. de Lesseps as president of the Compagnie universelle du canal de Suez. He was also president of the Société nationale d'encouragement à l'agriculture and vice-president of the Conseil supérieure de l'agriculture. He died in Forges on 17 July 1896. DBF; Hommes et destins, 7, pp. 224-27; IndexBFr² (1)

Guichard, Pierre, born in 1939, he received a *doctorat d'état* in 1972 from the Université de Lyon for *Les tribus arabes et berbères en Al-Andalus*. His writings include *Al-Andalus; estructura antropológica de una sociedad islámica en Occidente* (1973), and *Structures sociales "orientales" et "occidentales" dans l'Espagne musulmane* (1977), *Les Musulmans de Valence et la reconquête* (1990-91), *Al-Andalus* (2000), and he was a joint author of *Les Châteaux ruraux d'al-Andalus; histoire et archéologie des husûn du sud-est de l'Espagne* (1988), *Islam et chrétienté latine* (2000), and *Pays d'islam et le monde latine* (2000), Livres disponibles, 2003; THESAM, 4

Guida, Francesco, born 20th cent., his writings include *L'Italie e il Risorgimento balcanico* (1984), *La Bulgaria dalla guerra di liberazione sino al trattato di Neuilly* (1984), and he was a joint author of *Nascita di uno stato balcanico; la Bulgaria di Alessandro di Battenberg nella corrispondenza diplomatica italiana* (1988). LC

Guidi, Ignazio, born 31 July 1844 at Roma, he taught from 1876 until his retirement in 1919 Hebrew and comparative Semitic languages in the Università di Roma, where he had been nominated professor extraordinary in 1878 and ordinary in 1885 when his duties were extended to the teaching of the languages and history of Abyssinia. In 1914 he became a senator. The reputation which he acquired in his early years won him the respect of the leading European Semitists who in 1876 secured his cooperation in the monumental Leiden edition of *Annales quos scripsit at-Tabari* (1879-1901). His output to the end of his life continued to be immense, being chiefly divided between the literature of Islam, of the Christian Orient, and of Abyssinia. Besides editions of texts, and monographs on an extraordinary variety of themes, he found time to organize the *Tables alphabétiques du Kitab al-Agani* (1900), the *Khizanat al-adab*, and the *Vocabulario amarico-italiano* (1901). He died in Roma on 18 April 1935. Al-Andalus, 3 (1935), pp. 201-204; Baldinetti, pp. 81-84; DizBI; Fück; Index Islamicus (7); JRAS, 1935, p. 785; Levante, 20 (1973), pp. 17-19; Wininger

Guidi, Michelangelo, born 19 March 1886 at Roma, he was successively a professor of Arabic and Islamic institutions and history in the Istituto orientale di Napoli and the Università di Roma. From 1926 to 1929 he taught at Cairo in Arabic. His writings include *Gli scrittori zayditi e l'esegesi coranica mu'tazilita* (1925), *Storia della religione dell'islam* (1935), *Aspetti e problemi del mondo islamico* (1937), and *Storia e cultura degli Arabi fino alla morte di Maometto* (1951). He died 15 June 1946. *Al-Andalus* 11 (1946), pp. 489-490; *Chi è*, 1931-1940

Guidoni, Enrico, born in 1939, his writings include *Michelangelo-Mosé* (1970), *Architettura primitiva* (1975), its translation, *Primitive architecture* (1977), *Arte e urbanistica in Toscana* (1989), *L'Arte di progettarele città; Italia e Mediterraneo dal Medioevo al settecento* (1992). *Storia dell'urbanistica* (1998). *Catalogo dei libri in commercio*, 2002

de **Guignes**, Joseph, born 19 October 1721 at Pontoise (Val d'Oise), he studied Oriental languages under Étienne Fourmont. In 1741 he was a royal interpreter for Chinese, and in 1745 he succeeded to the post of secretary-interpreter for Oriental languages at the Bibliothèque royale. He soon became interested in the Turks and Huns and in 1748 he published a memorandum on the origin of the Huns and Turks, a work which won him in 1752 entry to the Royal Society, London, as well as the Académie des Inscriptions in 1753. In the same year, he became associated with the *Journal des savants* and was appointed royal censor. Since 1757 he held the chair of Syriac at the Collège de France, and in 1769 he was nominated a keeper of antiquities at the Louvre. Pensioned off by the Académie in 1772, he lost all his privileges at the time of the French revolution. His writings include *Histoire générale des Huns, des Turcs, des Mongols, et des autres Tartares occidentaux* (1750-58), and its translation, *Allgemeine Geschichte der Hunnen und Türken, der Mongolen und anderer occidentalischen Tartarn, vor und nach Christi Geburt* (1768-71). He died in Paris in 1800. Casanova; DBF; Egyptology; EncBrit; Hoefer: IndexBFr² (7); Master (1)

Guiho, Pierre Louis, born 19 February 1922 at Alençon (Orne), he was educated at Vire (Calvados) and studied law and letters at Caen, where he took a doctorate in law and a degree in letters. He taught law from 1950 to 1955 at the Faculté de droit d'Alger, and from 1955 to 1959 at the Faculté de droit at Rabat. He subsequently served until his retirement in 1988 as a professor of law at the Université de Lyon. His writings include *Les Recours contre l'auteur d'un dommage cuvrant droit à une indemnité d'assurance* (1951), and *La nationalité marocaine* (1961). WhoFr, 1973/74-2002/2003

Guilcher, André Julien, born 19 May 1913 at Brest (Finistère), he was educated at the Lycée de Brest, Lycée Louis-le-Grand, Paris. He took his doctorate in 1930 for *L'Habitat rural à Plouvien (Finistère)*, as well as his *agrégation* in history and geography at Paris. He subsequently taught his subjects at *lycées* in Brest and Nancy, before he became a professor successively at the universities of Nancy, Paris, and Bretagne occidentale. Since 1981 he was a professor emeritus. His writings include *Recherches sur la morphologie de la côte du Maroc* (1954). He died 4 December 1993. Unesco; WhoFr, 1973/74-1993/94

Guillain, Charles, born 18 May 1808 at Lorient (Morbihan), he was educated at the Collège de la marine, Angoulême. A navy lieutenant since 1835, he sailed the Indian Ocean from 1836 to 1839. As a commander of the *Dordogne* in 1840, he campaigned in the Red Sea and and eastern Africa, and later he explored the eastern coast of Africa as well as India, experiences which he described in his *Documents sur l'histoire, la géographie et le commerce de l'Afrique orientale* (1856-57). With the rank of governor and commander of the naval station in New Caledonia, he established the local penal colony. He met repeated penal revolts with excessive force and was pensioned off in 1870. His other writings include *Voyage à la côte d'Afrique* (1857). He died in Lorient on 17 February 1875. Dantès 1; DBF; Henze; Vapereau

Guillain, Robert, born in 1908, he was a journalist for *le Monde*, Paris, specializing in East Asian affairs. His writings include *600 millions de Chinois sous le drapeau rouge* (1956), and its translation, *600 million Chinese* (1957).

Guilland, Rodolphe Joseph, born 5 March 1888 at Lons-le-Saunier (Jura), he was educated at his home town and Lyon, and studied at Besançon and Paris. He was a *professeur* successively at *lycées* in Constantine, Grenoble, Lyon and Paris. Since 1937 he held the chair of history and Byzantine civilization at the Sorbonne. His writings include *L'Empire byzantin entre 1081-1453* (1947-49), *L'Empire byzantin de 717 à 867* (1952), *La Politique sociale des empereurs byzantins de 867 à 1081* (1954-55), and he edited and translated *Correspondance de Nicéphore Grégoras* (1927). He died in S.-Vérand (Isère) on 5 October 1981. DBF; DBFC, 1954/55

Guillaume, Albert, fl. 1946-1951 in Rabat, his writings include *L'Évolution économique de la société rurale marocaine* (1955), and *La Propriété collective au Maroc* (1960).

Guillaume, Alfred, born 8 November 1888, he studied at Oxford, where received a B.D. and D.D. in 1934 for *The scholasticism of Christianity and of Islam so far as they are represesented by the "Summa contra gentiles" of St Thomas Aquinas and the "Nihayat al-Iqdam fi-'Ilm al-Kalam" of al-Shahrastani.* In the first World War, he served in France and then in the Arab Bureau in Cairo. He was ordained to the ministry in the Church of England when he returned to England. He had a distinguished career teaching Hebrew and Arabic. During the second World War, the British Council invited him to accept a visiting professorship at A.U.B. where he greatly enlarged his circle of Muslim friends. The Arab Academy of Damascus and the Royal Academy of Baghdad elected him a member, and İstanbul Üniversitesi chose him as their first foreign lecturer on Christian and Islamic theology. His writings include *Traditions of Islam* (1924), *Islam* (1954), *Prophecy and divination among the Hebrew and other Semites* (1938), its translation, *Prophétie et divination chez les Sémites* (1950), and he edited and translated *The Life of Muhammad; a translation of Ishāq's Sirat rasūl Allāh* (1955). He died 30 November 1965. BritInd (1); ConAu 15-16; Note; Sluglett; WhE&EA; Who, 1929-1966; Who was who 6

Guillaume, Augustin Léon, born 30 July 1895 at Guillestre (Hautes-Alpes), he was a graduate of the military college, Saint-Cyr, and l'École supérieure de guerre. With the rank of captain he served in 1919 with the Armée d'Orient. Later he was posted to native affairs in Morocco, where he specialized in Berber affairs. From 1926 to 1928 he passed through the École supérieure de guerre, and subsequently spent the next five years in Morocco in the pacification of the country. During the second World War, he served with the rank of general first in North Africa and later in southern Europe. He returned to Morocco in 1951 to succeed Maréchal Juin as *résident général* of France in Morocco, a post which he held until 1956, when he resigned in protest against military politics. His writings include *Les Berbères marocains et la pacification de l'Atlas central* (1946), and his memoirs, *Homme de guerre* (1977). He died in his home town on 9 March 1983. DBF; DBFC, 1954/55; Master (1); WhoFr, 1953/54-1983/84

Guillaume de Vaudoncourt, Frédéric François, born in 1772, he was in 1791 a lieutenant with the 1st *bataillon de volontaires de la Moselle* and joined the *compagnie franche*, which his father had raised. Assigned to the Armée d'Italie in 1796, he organized the artillery of the République cisalpine, was taken prisoner in May 1799 and, after his release, served in a variety of functions in both units from 1800 to 1809. He became in April 1809 chief of the general staff of the Division Fontanelli of the Armée d'Italie. Promoted *général de brigade* on 30 May 1809, he was in the same year created a baron of the Kingdom of Italy. He served in 1812 in Russia where he became a prisoner of war. After returning to France in 1814, he was reintegrated in the forces with the rank of *maréchal de camp*, commanded the *gardes nationales actives* of the Département de la Moselle during the Hundred Days, was charged by the second *Restauration* of the attempted seizure of the Palace de Metz, but was able to escape abroad. Condemned to death in 1816 for insubordination, he had to wait nine years until pardoned. He was editor-in-chief of the *Journal des sciences militaires* from 1825 to 1829. He took an active part in the events of July 1830 as the commander of the Garde nationale of the Roule and Tuileries *quartiers*. In August of the same year he was recalled to active service where he remained until his retirement in 1834. His writings include *Relation impartiale du passage de la Bérézina en 1812* (1814), and *Mémoire pour servir à l'histoire de la guerre entre la France et la Russie en 1812* (1815). He died in 1845. Dantès I; DBF; Dezobry; Hoefer; IndexBFr² (1)

Guillemin, Marcelle, born in 1907 at Liège, she was a scholar of ancient Near Eastern musicology. She died in 1997 in Liège. EncIran

Guillemard, Robert, *pseud.*, 1792-1867 see Barbaroux, Charles Ogé

Guillen, Pierre, born 20th cent., his writings include *L'Allemagne et le Maroc de 1870 à 1905* (1967), *L'Empire allemand, 1871-1918* (1970), *L'Allemagne de 1848 à nos jours* (1970), and *Les Emprunts marocains, 1902-1904* (1971).

Guillén Robles, Francisco, born 8 October 1846 at Málaga, he received degrees in philosophy, letters, and law. He was an archivist and official Málaga chronicler. He later became head of the manuscript division of the Biblioteca Nacional. His writings include *Málaga musulmana* (1880), *Leyendas moriscas, sacadas de varios manuscritos* (1885-86), and *Catalogo de los manuscritos árabes existentes en la Biblioteca Nacional de Madrid* (1889). He died 17 November 1920. EncicUni; IndiceE³ (5); Manzanares

Guillet, Jacques, born 3 April 1910 at Lyon, he entered the Society of Jesus in 1927, and from 1935 to 1938 studied Oriental languages at Beirut. During the war he escaped from a German prisoner of war camp. In 1945 he was ordained. He was from 1951 to 1966 a professor of *théologie fondamentale et d'Écriture sainte* at Lyon. His writings include *Thèmes bibliques* (1950), and its translation, *Themes of the Bible* (1960). ConAu 102; IndexBFr² (1)

Guillot, Eugène, born in 1854, he received his *agrégation* in history and became a professor at the Lycée Charlemagne in Lille. He was a founding member of the Société de géographie de Lille, and a sometime secretary-general of the Société. His writings include *La Question d'Orient au XIXe siècle* (1886), *La Mer Rouge et l'Abyssinie, les Italiens à Massaouah* (1890), and *Précis de la guerre de 1914* (1917). Note about the author

Guillot, Gaëtan, born 19th cent., his writings include *Les Moines précurseurs de Gutenberg* (1906). His trace is lost after an article in 1914. BN; NUC, pre-1956

Guillou, André, born 18 December 1923 at Nantes, he studied at the Faculté des lettres de Paris, and l'École des chartes. He received a degree from l'École pratique des hautes études as well as a doctorate. He became an archivist and palaeographer. He was from 1952 to 1955 a member of the École française d'archéologie et d'histoire de Rome, and from 1955 to 1958 a member of the École française d'Athènes. Since 1968 a *directeur d'études* at l'École des hautes études en sciences sociales, he was from 1968 to 1971 a visiting fellow at Dumbarton Oaks, Harvard University. His writings include *Les Monnayages pehlevi-arabes; catalogue* (1953), *Essai bibliographique sur les dynastie musulmanes de l'Iran* (1957), *La Civilisation byzantine* (1974), and a collection of his articels, *Studies on Byzantine Italy* (1970). WhoFr, 1973/74-2002/2003

Guilmain, Jacques, born in 1926, he received a Ph.D. in 1960 from Columbia University, New York, for *An analysis of some major forms of ornament in Mozarabic illumination.* NUC, pre-1956

Guimet, Émile Étienne, born 22 July 1836 at Lyon, he was the son of an industrialist. Determined to study religions at their source, he went in 1865 to Egypt. In 1876 the Ministère de l'Instruction publique sent him on a mission to the Far East. From this time dates his wish to establish the museum at Lyon which carries his name. His writings include *Arabes et Kabyles, pasteurs et agriculteurs* (1873). He died at the family's estate in Fleurieu-sur-Saône on 12 October 1918. Curinier, vol. 4 (1903), pp. 309-11; Dawson; DBF; Egyptology; IndexBFr² (4); Vapereau

Guin, Louis Elie, born 25 November 1838 at Marseille, he was an interpreter in Algeria and rose from the rank of *interprète auxiliaire 2e classe* (1 March 1858) to *interprète titulaire de 1re classe* (11 June 1872). He was a member of the Société historique algérienne. His writings include *Conte arabe: le cure-dent du prophète* (1886). Féraud, pp. 340-341

Guiney, Alain, born 20th cent., he was in 1961 an Israeli correspondent of *France soir*, and a political commentator for the Israeli *Yedi'ot aharonot.* Note about the author

Guins, George Constantine, 1887-1971 see Gins, Georgii Konstantinovich

Guiral, Pierre, born 3 July 1909 at Marseille, where he attended the *lycées* Périer and Thiers as well as the *khâgne* at the Lycée Henri IV. After brilliant studies at the faculties of letters in Aix-en-Provence and Lyon, he received his *agrégation* in history and geography in 1931. He subsequently taught at secondary schools in Pau and Avignon, before returning to Marseille. In 1947 he went to the Université d'Aix-en-Provence, where he was appointed to the chair of history in 1955. His writings include the *thèse complémentaire, Marseille et l'Algérie, 1830-1841* (1957), and *La Vie quotidienne en France à l'âge d'or du capitalisme, 1852-1879* (1976). He died in Marseille on 1 January 1996. REJ 155 (1996), pp. 485-491

Guirgas, Vladimir Fedorovich, 1835-1887 see Girgas, Vladimir Fedorovich

Guise, Samuel, born 18th cent., he completed his medical training in 1775. From 1785 to 1795 he was a surgeon to the General Hospital at Surat. He resigned in 1796 while on furlough. He contributed to *Oriental collections*, a periodical which was published in London from 1795 to 1797. His writings also include *Catalogue and detailed account of the very valuable and curious collection of manuscripts collected in Hindostan* (London,1800). He died in 1811. BiDLA; BLC; IndianBilnd (1); Note

Guisinger, Stephen Edward, born 14 January 1941 at Kansas City, he graduated in 1963 from Yale University, and received his Ph.D. in 1970 from Harvard for *Effective protection, resource allocation and the characteristics of protected industries; a study case of Pakistan.* He was successively a professor of economics at Southern Mehtodist University and the Department of Busines, University of Texas at Dallas. In 1974 he served as an adviser at the Pakistan Institute of Development Economics, Karachi. His writings include *Investment incentives and performance requirements; patterns of international trade* (1985), and he edited *Private enterprise and the new global economic challenge* (1979). AmM&WS, 1973 S, 1978 S; ConAu 103

Guitard, Odette, fl. 20th cent., she wrote *Bandoeng et le reveil des anciens coloniés* (1961), *Les Rhodésies et le Nyassaland; Rhodésie, Zambie et Malawi* (1964), and she was a joint author of *L'Afrique au XXe siècle* (1966). BN

Guiton, Raymond Jan, born 20th cent. he was a free-lance journalist and in 1964 residening in Köln. His writings include *Französische Zustände* (1953), *Paris-Moskau; die Sowjetuinion in der auswärtigen Politik Frankreichs seit dem zweiten Weltkrieg* (1956), *Afrika im Widerspruch* (1967), and *Die Verfassung der Demokratischen Republik Kongo; Wortlaut und Kommentar* (1970). GV

Guitonneau, Raymond Edouard, born 13 August 1921 at Villeparisis (Seine-et-Marne), he was educated at the Lycée Louis-le-Grand and the Faculté des sciences de Paris, later graduating from the École polytechnique. He served as an engineer of Ponts et Chaussée, head of the Arrondissement hydraulique, first from 1948 to 1949 in Casablanca and then from 1949 to 1953 in Marrakesh. He was a contributor to technical periodicals. NDNC, vol. 2 (1963); WhoFr, 1973/74-1995/96|

Guitton, Louis, born 19th cent., he was a sometime resident of Le Havre. His writings include *Les Influences française et allemande en Russie* (Paris, 1894). BN; NUC, pre-1956

Gukasian (Gukasian-Ganzaketsi), Levon Gurgenovich, born 6 January 1928 at Giandzha (Kirovabad), Azerbaijan, he received his first degree in 1956 for Экспансия монополистического капитала США во французской промишленности после второй мировой войнй, 1946-1954 гг., and his doctorate in 1968 for Французский неоколониализм и развивающиеся страны Африки, 1956-1965. Since 1956 he was associated with Oriental Institute of the Soviet Academy of Sciences. His writings include Французский империализм и Африка (1962). Miliband; Miliband²

Gulak, Nikolai Ivanovich, born in 1822 at present day Zolotonosh Raion, Cherkassy Oblast, Ukraine, he graduated from Dorpat university and became affiliated with the Society of Cyril and Methodius. He was also a Turkish scholar. He died in Giandzha (Kirovabad), 25 or 26 May 1899. AzarbSE, vol. 3, p. 263; BiobibSOT, pp. 152-154; GSE

Gulbenkian, Roberto, Dr., born 20th cent., his writings include *L'Ambassade en Perse de Luis Pereira de Lacerda et des pères portugais de l'Ordre de Saint-Augustin, Belchior dos Anjos et Guilherme de Santo Agostinho, 1604-1605* (Lisbonne, 1972), and *The Translation of the Four Gospels into Persian* (Immensee, 1981).

Gul'dzhanov, Mamadzhan Usmondzhon Obidov, born 20th cent., his writings include Краткий техниго-экономический терминологический дари-русский словарь (Dushanbe, 1979). OSK

Guliamov (Гуломов), IAkh'ia Guliamovich, fl. 20th cent., his writings include История орошения Хорезма (1957), Узбекском ССР тарихи (Toshkent, 1958), Ҳозирги узбек адабий тили (1965), Грамматика ташкентского говора (Tashkent, 1968); he was a joint author of Первобытная культура и возникновение орошаемого земледелия в низовьях Зафаршана (1966); he edited Древности Ташкента (Tashkent, 1976); he was a joint editor of Бобир-нома (Toshkent, 1948), and Языкознание (1964). OSK

Gulick, John, born 18 April 1924 at Newton, Mass., he received a Ph.D. in 1953 from Harvard with a thesis entitled *Patterns of acculturation in a Lebanese village*. He was an anthropologist who in 1974 taught his subject at the University of North Carolina, Chapel Hill. He also served as a professor at A.U.B. and the universities of Isfahan, and Shiraz. His writings include *The Arab Levant* (1963), *Tripoli, a modern Arab city* (1967), and *The Middle East; an anthropological perspective* (1976). AmM&WS, 1976 P; *MESA Roster of members*, 1977-1990; Selim; Shavit; WhoAm, 1974/75-1999|

Gulick, Margaret E., born about 1925, she received an M.A. in sociology in the 1970s from the University of North Carolina, and continued to be associated with the University for a number of years. She was a joint compiler of *An annotated bibliography of sources concerned with women in the modern Muslim Middle East* (1974). Note about the author

Gulick, Robert Lee, born 6 October 1912 at Paradise, Calif., he graduated in 1933 from California State University, and received a Ph.D. in 1948 from the University of California for *Evaluation of pamphleteering techniques*. He was an examiner's aid with the U.S. Customs Servie, 1937-1943, an economist with the Carnegie Endowment for International Peace, New York, 1943-1947, and a senior lecturer, University of California until 1952. From 1958 to 1964 he served with the Libyan Government as a teacher of English as a secondary language. In 1964 he became dean of admissions and professor of international studies in the American Graduate School of International Management. His writings include *Imports, the gain from trade* (1946), *American higher education - uncertain trumpet*

(Cairo, 1960), and *Muhammad the educator* (1961). He died in Glendale, Ariz., on 3 May 1987. AmM&WS, 1973 S, 1978 S; ConAu, 122; IWWAS, 1976/76; *MESA Roster of members*, 1977-1982

Guliev, Abbasali Mukhtar-ogly, 1935- see Guliiev, Abbasali Mukhtar-ogly

Guliiev (Гулијев), Abbasali Mukhtar-ogly, born 23 February 1935 in Azerbaijan, he graduated in 1958 from the Oriental Faculty, Azerbaijan State University and received his first degree in 1965 at Baku for *Поэма «Юсуф и Зулуйха» Абдурахмана Джами*. He was since 1958 associated with the Institute of the Peoples of the Near and Middle East in the Azerbaijan Academy of Sciences. His writings include *Әбдуррәһман Чами; һәјам вә јарадычылыг јолу* (Baku, 1964), and *Әбдуррәһман Чаминин "Јусиф вә Зулејха" поемасы* (Baku, 1969). Miliband; Miliband²

Gulizade (Гулузадә), Mirzaaga IUzbashi ogly, born in 1907 in Azerbaijan, he graduated in 1936 from the Azerbaijan State Pedagogical Institute and received his first degree in 1953 for *Творчество Насими*, and his doctorate in 1966 for *Лирика Физули*. He was associated with the Azerbajan State Pedagogical Institute, 1937-1941, Azerbaijan State University, 1947-1956, and the Azerbaijan Pedagogical Institute for Languages since 1966. In 1968 he was appointed a professor. His writings include *Низами Кәнчәви; һәјат вә ярадычылығы* (Baku, 1953), and *Бејүк идеаллар шаири* (1973), and he was joint editor of the collective work, *Совет әдәбијјат-шунаслығынын актуал проблемләри; мәгаләләр мәчмуәси* (Baku, 1974). He died 9 December 1979. Miliband; Miliband²

Gulkowitsch, Lazar, born in 1898 or 1899 at Zirkin, he studied at the Universität Königsberg, Germany, where he received a Dr.phil. in 1923, and a Dr.med. in 1925. He subsequently pursued Semitic and Talmudic studies and qualified in the subject in 1927. He served as the Seminary for Jewish studies of the Old Testament, Leipzig, as a professor and director until 1934, when he emigrated to Estonia to serve in the same capacities at Universitas Dorpatensis/Tartu. He was a sometime visiting professor at Harvard and Columbia universities. His writings include *Das Wesen der maimonideischen Lehre* (Tartu, 1935), and *Zur Grundlegung einer begriffsgeschichtlichen Methode in der Sprachwissenschaft* (Tartu, 1937). He was shot by the Germans in Tartu in 1941. BioHBDtE; DtBE; RHbDtG

Gully, Adrian, born 20th cent., he received a Ph.D. and became a lecturer in contemporary Arabic in the Department of Arabic and Islamic Studies, Exeter University. His writings include *Grammar and semantics in medieval Arabic* (1995). EURAMES, 1993

Gulomov (Ғуломов), A. G. see Guliamov, IAkh'ia Guliamovich

Gulphe, Pierre, born 16 March 1925 at Constantine, Algeria, he studied at Alger, and Paris where he received a doctorate in law in 1944 for *L'immobilisation par destination*. He was a barrister, magistrate, and professor. His writings include *Les Ententes industrielles* (1961). He died 19 August 1990. WhoFr, 1977/78-1990/91

Gülübov (Гълъбов/Гължбовъ/Gälǎbov), Gülüb D., born 25 February 1892 at Adrianople (Edirne), he was a Turkologist and writer on Bulgarian history whose writings include *Мюсюлманско право* (Sofia, 1924), *Османо-турски извори за българската истории* (Sofia, 1938-60), and he was a joint editor of *Die Protokollbücher des Kadiamtes Sofia* (1960). He died 13 December 1972. *Народы Азии и Африки*, 1974, no. 1, pp. 247-248

Gumilёv, Lev Nikolaevich, born in 1912 at TSarskom Sele near St. Petersburg, he received his first degree in 1948 at Leningrad for *Подробная политическая история первого тюркского каганата*, and his doctorate in 1962 for *Древние тюрки; история Срединной Азии на грани древности и средневековья*. Since 1962 he was associated with the Faculty of Geography, Leningrad State University. His writings include *Хунны* (1960), *Открытие Хазарии* (1966), and *Хунны и Китае* (1974). He died on 15 June 1992. *Biographical dictionary of the Soviet Union, 1917-1988*, by Jeanne Vronskaya, with Vladimir Chugue (London, 1989); *Index Islamicus* (1); Miliband; Miliband²; TatarES

Gumpel, Werner, born 21 October 1930 at Buchholz, Germany, he studied economics at the universities of Nürnberg, and Hamburg, where he received a Dr.rer.pol. in 1962 for *Die Seehafen- und Schiffahrtspolitik des COMECOM*. After his Dr.habil. in 1970, he was appointed a professor of East European studies in the Institut für Wirtschaft und Gesellschaft Ost- und Südosteuropas in the Universität München. His writings include *Das Verkehrswesen Osteuropas* (1967), and he edited *Die Türken auf dem Weg in die EG* (1979). Hacettepe Üniversitesi, Ankara, granted him an honorary doctorate. Kürschner, 1976-2003; Note about the author

Gumprecht, Thaddäus Eudard, born 18 November 1801 at Posen, Prussia, he gained a Dr.phil. and served from 1843 to 1853 as a lecturer in geography and geology in the Universität Berlin. His writings include *Die Mineralquellen auf dem Festlande von Afrika* (1852), *Barth und Overwegs Untersuchungs-*

Reise nach dem Tchad-See und in das innere Afrika (1852), and he was a joint author of *Handbuch der Geographie und Statistik von Afrika und Australien* (1853). He died in Berlin on 7 December 1856. DtBilnd (1); GV

Gunda, Béla, born 25 December 1911 at Temesfüzes, Transylvania, he was an ethnographer and historian at Debrecen University. His writings include *Néprajzi gyüjtönton* (1956), *Ethnographica Carpatho-Balcanica* (1979), and he edited *Viehwirtschaft und Hirtenkultur* (1969). In 1971 he was honoured by *Studia ethnographica et folkloristica in honorem Béla Gunda*. He died in Debrecen on 30 July 1994. Magyar; MagyarNKK, 1990, 1992; WhoSoC, 1978; WhoSoCE, 1989

Gündisch, Gustav, born 19th cent., he was in 1937 resident in Hermannstadt, Transylvania. He received a Dr.phil. in 1932 from the Universität Wien for *Geschichte der Münzstätte Nagybanyn in habsburgischer Zeit von 1530 bis 1928*. His writings include *Urkundenbuch zur Geschichte der Deutschen in Siebenbürgen* (1892), and *Deutsches Volkswerden in Siebenbürgen* (1944). GV, 1911-1965

Gune, Vithal Trimbak, born about 1900, his writings include *The Judicial system of the Marathas; a detailed study of the judicial institutions in Maharashta from 1600-1818 A.D.* (1953), *Ancient shrines of Goa* (1965), and *A Guide to the collections of records from the Goa Archives, Panaji* (1973).

Gunkel, Johann Friedrich *Hermann*, born 23 May 1862 at Springe near Hannover, he was a Protestant theologian who had studied at Göttingen, Gießen, and Leipzig. In 1907 he was appointed a professor of Old Testament studies at Gießen, a post which he held until 1920, when he moved for the rest of his life to Halle. He died on 11 March 1932. DtBE; DtBilnd; Kürschner, 1925-1931; LuthC, 75

Gunning, Jan Willem, Rev., born 15 June 1862 at Utrecht, he studied theology at Amsterdam. He was a Protestant missionary who served from 1897 to 1923 as a director of Nederlandsch Zendeling-Genootschap, Rotterdam, and since 1905 also as a director of the Utrechtse Zendingsvereniging. In 1914 the Rijksuniversiteit te Groningen granted him a Dr. theol. h.c. His writings include *Heden-daagsche zending in onze Oost* (1914), and *Afscheidswoord* (1919). He died in Leiden on 25 November 1923. BiBenelux (1)

Gunsaulaus, Helen Cowen, born 6 April 1886 at Baltimore, Md., she graduated in 1908 from the University of Chicago. She was a curator at Field Museum, Chicago, before she joined in 1926 the Chicago Art Institute. She later succeeded Fr. W. Gookin as keeper of the Clarence Buckingham Collection. She retired in 1943 from active work, becoming honorary curator. Her writings include *Gods and heroes of Japan* (1924), and *Handbook of the Department of Oriental Art, the Art Institute of Chicago* (1933). She died in Yarmouth, Mass., on 1 August 1954. American women, 1935/36; Chicago Art Institute quarterly, 49 (Feb., 1955), p. 8; NYT, 2 August 1954, p. 17, col. 4

Gunter, John Wadsworth, born 17 February 1914 at Sanford, N.C., he graduated in 1935 from the University of North Carolina, and received a Ph.D. in 1942. He was from 1953 to 1977 associated with the Middle Eastern Department, International Monetary Fund, Washington, D.C. His writings include the booklet, *The Proposed international trade organization* (Austin, Tex., 1949). BlueB, 1973/74, 1975, 1976; IntYB, 1978-1998; Master (1); WhoFI, 1989/90; WhoUN, 1975; Shavit

Gunter, Michael Martin, born 26 March 1943 at Gastonia, N.C., he received a Ph.D. in 1972 from Kent (Ohio) State University for *Ministates and the United Nations system*. He subsequently became a professor of political science at Tennessee Technological University, Cookeville, a post which he still held in 2003. His writings include *The Kurds in Turkey; a political dilemma* (1990), *Transnational Armenian activism* (1990), *The Kurds of Iraq; tragedy and hope* (1992), *The Changing Kurdish problem in Turkey* (1994), and *The Kurdish predicament in Iraq; a political analysis* (1999). NatFacDr, 1995-2003; Note; WhoS&SW, 1991/92, 1993/94

Gunther, Robert William Theodore, born in 1869 in Surrey, he was educated at University College School, London, and Oriel College, Oxford. He was successively a lecturer, tutor, and reader in natural science and history of science at his alma mater. A fellow of the Linnean Society since 1920, he was granted in 1925 an honorary LL.D. by the University of St. Andrews. He was instrumental in the establishment of the Museum of the History of Science in 1935 in Oxford. His writings include *Early science in Oxford* (1923-45). He died in 1940. BritInd (3); DNB; Master (3); Who was who, 3

Gunthorpe, Edward James, born 19th cent., he was a colonel who wrote *Notes on criminal tribes residing in or frequenting the Bombay Presidency, Berar and the Central Provinces* (Bombay, 1882). Note about the author

von **Günzburg** (Гинцбург), David Goratsievich, baron, born 5 July 1857 at Kamenetz-Podolsk, Ukraine, he was educated privately and studied Hebrew and Arabic at St. Petersburg. From 1879 to 1880 he studied Arabic under T. W. Ahlwardt at Greifswald, Germany. He was a patron of Jewish art and had an important private library. He wrote on early Arabic poetry and was a joint author of

Collections scientifiques de l'Institut des langues orientales du Ministère des affaires étrangères (1891). But he is best remembered for the publication and translation of the unique St. Petersburg manuscript, *Der Diwan des Ibn Quzman* (Berlin, 1896). His other writings include *O русском стихо с ложетии* (1915). He died in St. Petersburg, in 1910 or 1911. EncJud; Fück, p. 267; JewEnc; JüdLex; Krachkovskii, p. 141; Wininger

Gurdziecki, Bohdan, d. 1700 *see* Grudziecki, Bogdam

Gurevich, Aleksandr Mikhaĭlovich, fl. 1948, his writings include *Афганистан* (Moscow, 1929). OSK

Gurevich, Boris Pavlovich, born 20 September 1919 at Khar'kov, he graduated in 1942 at Moscow and received his first degree in 1956 for «*Борьба народов Китая за мирное освобождение Тибета, 1946-1951 годы*», and his doctorate in 1971. He was an East Asian scholar and was from 1947 to 1957 asscociated with the journal *Новое время*. Since 1961 he was affiliated with the Oriental Institute, Soviet Academy of Science. Miliband; Miliband²; Schoeberlein

Gurevich, Naum Manuilovich, born 5 August 1922 at Ekaterinoslav, he graduated in 1947 from the Oriental Institute, Moscow, and received his first degree in 1956 for «*Внешняя торговля Афганистана до 2-й мировой войны и формирование национального торгового капитала*», and his doctorate in 1967 for *Экономическое развитие Афганистана*. He was associated with the Ministry of Foreign Trade from 1948-1956, and from 1956 to 1983 with the Oriental Institute of the Soviet Academy of Science. His other writings include *Государственный сектор в экономике Афганистана* (1962), *Очерк истории торгового капитала в Афганистане* (1967), *Афганистан* (1983) and *Внешняя торговля Афганистана в новейшее время* (1983). He died on 28 March 1983. Miliband; Miliband²

Gurevitz, Baruch, born in 1945, he received a Ph.D. in 1973 from the University of Rochester, N.Y., for *National communism in the Soviet Union*. His writings include *The Bolshevik revolution and the foundation of the Jewish Communist movement in Russia* (1976). NUC; OSK

Guriel, Boris, born 20th cent., he was in 1970 a director of the Weizmann Archives, Rehovot, Israel. Note about the author

Gurko-Kriazhin, Vladimir Aleksandrovich, born in 1887 at Tiflis, he graduated in 1912 from the Faculty of History and Philology, Moscow University. He was successively from 1918 to 1922 an editor of the journals *Вестник жизни* and *Новый Восток*. His writings include *Национадьно-освободительное лвиженте на Ближнем Востоке* (1923), *Послевоенные мировые конфликты* (1924), *Краткая история Персии* (1925), *Абхазия* (1926), and *Арабский Восток и империализм* (1926). He died 17 October 1931. Miliband; Miliband²

Gurlekian, Hagop, born about 1900, he was a student of Loofty Levonian, and in 1925 one of the first graduates of the School of Religion, Istanbul and Athens. Afterwards he served as a teacher and preacher in Syria and Lebanon for thirty-two years, after which he went to Chicago in 1958. His writings include *Hayown hrashali goyatewowte ew harhajdimowt'iwne* (1970). MW 53 (1963), p. 76

Gurlitt, Cornelius Gustav, born 1 January 1850 at Nischwitz, Saxony, he was a trained carpenter who subsequently studied at Stuttgart Polytechnikum. A practising architect until 1875, he was since 1879 an assistant at the Kunstgewerbe-Museum, Dresden. His *Geschichte des Barockstils* in three volumes gained him a doctorate. From 1890 to his retirement in 1920 he was a professor of architecture at the Technische Hochschule, Dresden. His writings include *Konstantinopel* (1908), and *Die Baukunst Konstantinopels* (1912). He died in Dresden on 25 March 1938. DtBE; Hinrichsen; NDB; Wer ist's, 1909-1935

Gurner, Sir Cyril *Walter*, born in 1880, he was educated at Merchant Taylors' School, London, Oriel College, Oxford, and University College, London. He joined the Indian Civil Service and arrived in India on 4 December 1911. He served as a magistrate and controller. In 1933 he was appointed chairman of Calcutta Improvement Trust. He died in 1960. Britlnd (1); IndianBilnd (2); Riddick; Who was who, 5

Gurney, John D., born about 1940, he received a D.Phil. in 1969 from Oxford University for *The Debts of the Nawab of Arcot, 1763-76*. He was in 1993 a lecturer in Persian in the Oriental Institute, Oxford. DrBSMES, 1993; EURAMES, 1993; Private; Sluglett

Gurvich, Il'ia Samoĭlovich, born 20th cent., his writings include *Этническая история северо-вомтока Сибири* (1966), *Таинственный чучуна* (1975), *Культура севеных якутов-оленеводов; к вопросу о поздних этапах формирования якутского народа* (1977), and he edited *Социальная организация и культура народов Севера* (1974). NUC; OSK

Gusarov, Vladilen Ivanovich, born 28 February 1934 at Irkutsk, he graduated in 1957 in economics at Moscow, and received his first degree in 1966 for *Эконом. связи араб. стран с мировой социалистия системой*. He was from 1957 to 1967 affiliated with the State Committee for Economic Relations; 1963-64 he spent in the Yemen. Since 1970 he was associated with the African Institute in the Soviet Academy of Science. His writings include *Страны срциализма - верные прузья арабских народов* (1971), *Экономика Йетенской Арабской Республики* (1972), *Тунис* (1974), *Арабская нефть* (1975), *Социально-экономическое развития Судана; актуальные проблемы* (1983), *Африка; испытания и надезы* (1988), and he was a joint author of *Легенды и были Арабского Востока* (1972), and *Экономика Народной Демократической Республики Йемен* (1976). Miliband[2]

Guse, Felix, born 19th cent., he served during the first World War with the rank of lieutenant colonel as chief of the general staff of the Turkish third Army. In 1923 he received a Dr.jur. from the Universität Freiburg im Breisgau for *Gründung einer Aktiengesellschaft*. His other writings include *Die Kaukasusfront im Weltkrieg* (1940), and *Die Türkei* (1944). GV

von **Guseck**, Bernd, 1803-1871, pseud. *see* Berneck, Karl Gustav von

Guseïnaev, Abachara Guseïnaevich born 20th cent., his writings include *Очерки лакской советской литературы* (1964), *Бадрижет; повесть и пассказы* (1975), *Остовы дагестанского стихсложения* (1979), and he edited *Лакрал агьалинал балайрду; «дагъусттаннал халкьуннал балайрды» тиисса сериялува = Лакские народные песни* (Makhachkala, Dagestan, 1970). OSK

Guseïnov, Abdulla Anbievich, born 25 October 1925 in Azerbaijan, he graduated in 1956 from Turkmen State University and received his first degree in 1972 for *Профсоюзное движение в Турции в 1960-1970 гг*. He spent two years each in Turkey and Iran. His writings include *Профсоюзы движение в Турции, 1960-1970* (1975), *Турецкое кино* (1978), *Средства массовой ниформации в общественно-политической жизни Турции* (1981), *Йылмаз ГюнейБ жизнь - подвиг.* (1987), *Землепашец на троне* (1990), and *Мухсин Эртугул в театре и кино* (1990). Miliband[2]

Guseïnov, Beiukata Murtazaevich (Бәјүкаға Муртуза оғлу һүсејнов), born 7 March 1926 at Baku, he graduated in 1949 from the Oriental Institute, Moscow, where he also received his first degree in 1962 for *Советская тема в прогрессивной персидской поэзии*. He received his doctorate in 1973 for *Традиции и новаторство в поэзии Ирана XX века*. He was from 1962 to 1983 associated with the Institute of the People of the Near and Middle East. His writings include *Поэты Ирана о Советском Союзе* (1965), and *XX әср фарс ше'риндә ән'әнә вә новаторлуг* (1975). He died on 31 May 1983. AzarbSE, vol. 10, p. 284; Miliband; Miliband[2]

Guseïnov, Gasan Bakharchi ogly, born 20th cent., he was associated with the Institute of Philosophy and Law, Azerbaijan Academy of Science. His writings include *Критика современной буржуазной социологии Ирана* (Baku, 1973), and *Место и роль Ислама в социально-политической жизни современного Ирана* (Baku, 1986). OSK

Guseïnov, Geïdar, fl. 20th cent., his writings include *Философские взгляды М. Ф. Ахундова* (Baku, 1942), *Об историческом содружестве и азербайджанского народов* (Baku, 1946), and *Из истории общественной и филосософкой мысли в Азербайджане* (1958). NUC

Guseïnov, Rauf Alishirovich, born 25 April 1929 at Baku, he graduated in 1951 from the Faculty of History, Azerbaijan State University, and received his first degree in 1955 for *«Хроника» Михаила Сирийца, как источник по истории тюрок XI-XII вв. в Передней Азии*, and his doctorate in 1969 for *Сельджуки и Закавказе*. Since 1955 he was associated with Institute of History, Azerbaijan Academy of Science. His writings include *Сирийские источники XII-XIII вв. об Азербайджане* (1960). Miliband; Miliband[2]

Guseïnov (Гусейнов/һүсејнов), Sadyg Mekhti-ogly, born 26 April 1923 at Baku, he graduated in 1948 from the Oriental Faculty, Azerbaijan State University, and received his doctorate in 1969 for *Творческий путь Сеил Азима Ширвани*. From 1951 to 1957 he was associated with the Institute of Azeri Language and Literature, Azerbaijan Academy of Science. His writings include *„Экинчи" гәзетинин изаьлы библиографијасы* (1963), and *Сејид Әзим Ширванинин јарадычылыг јолу* (1977). Miliband; Miliband[2]

Guseïnzade, Ali *see* Huseïnzadă (һүсејнзадә), Äli

Gusev, Aleksandr Nikolaevich, born in 1810, he was a student of the Arabist Osip I. Senkovski at St. Petersburg and the first Russian scholar to consider translating *Alf laylah wa-lailah* from the Arabic. He died from the plague in Cairo shortly before the end of his three-year study grant in 1835. Krachkovskii, p. 106

Gusmani, Roberto, born 18 October 1935 at Novara, Italy, he was successively associated with the universities of Messina and Udine as a professor of linguistics, particularly Indo-European langages. His writings include *Lydisches Wörterbuch mit grammatischer Skizze und Inschriftensammlung* (Heidelberg, 1964), *Introduzione allo studio comparativo delle lingue anatoliche* (Napoli, 1968), *Elementi di fonetica storica delle lingue indoeuropee* (Messina, 1971), *Aspetti del prestito linguistico* (Napoli, 1973), and *Neue epichoriche Schriftzeugnisse aus Sardis, 1958-1971* (Cambridge, Mass., 1975). IndBiltal³ (2)

Güßfeld, Richard *Paul* Wilhelm, born 14 October 1840 at Berlin, he studied natural sciences and mathematics at the universities of Heidelberg, Berlin, Gießen, and Bonn, gaining doctorates in 1865 and 1868. In 1873 he set out on his first exploration of Equatorial Africa in the service of a German Africa society. Three years later he travelled in Egypt and the Arabian Desert. Supported by the Prussian Akademie der Wissenschaften he subsequently explored South America. From 1892 to 1914 he was a professor and responsible for the natural sciences' subjects at the Berlin Institut für Orientalische Sprachen. He was a good mountaineer. He died in Berlin on 17 January 1920. DtBE; DtBilnd (4); Embacher; Henze; KDtLK, 1907-1917; NDB; Wer ist's, 1909-1912

Gustafson, William Eric, born 18 November 1933 at Pittsfield, Mass., he received a Ph.D. in 1959 in economics from Harvard for his thesis, *A locational study of the printing and publishing industry*. Since 1972 he was a professor of economics at the University of California., specializing in economic history, especially of South Asia. He edited *Sources on Punjab history* (1975), and *Pakistan and Bangladesh; bibliographical essays in social science* (1976). ConAu 57; AmM&WS, 1973-1978

Gustinčič, Jurij, born 3 August 1921 at Trieste, he was a journalist, who had studied at Moscow, and became a specialist in political affairs. His writings include *Češkoslovaška 1968* (Ljubljana, 1960), and *Britanija izmedu Atlantika b Evrope* (Beograd, 1962). Hrvatska enciklopedija (Zagreb, 2002); JugoslSa, 1970; Ko je ko, 1957

Gutbrot, Rolf, born 13 September 1910 at Stutgart, Germany, he studied architecture at Berlin and Stuttgart. He became a professor in his subject at Stuttgart, and in 1957, 1958, and 1959 served as a visiting professor at İstanbul Üniversitesi. Since 1961 he was a free-lance architect. He died about 1998. DtBilnd (3); Master (2); WhoWor, 1977/78; Wer ist wer, 1962-1998/99

Gutenschwager, Gerald A., born in 1932, he received a Ph.D. in 1967 from the University of North Carolina for *Awareness, culture and change; a study of modernization in Greece*. His writings include *Planning and social change; a selected bibliography* (1971). NUC, 1968-1972

Güterbock, Hans Gustav, born Jewish on 27 May 1908 at Berlin, he became a Protestant in the mid-1920s. After gaining a doctorate in ancient Near Eastern studies in 1934 at the Universität Leipzig, he joined in 1933 the Near Eastern Section of the Staatliche Museen in Berlin. He emigrated in 1935 and went to the University of Chicago by way of Ankara (1935-1948) and Uppsala (1949). He died in Chicago, 26 March 2000. BioHbDtE; Kürschner, 1961-1996; Master (2); Schwarz; Widmann, pp. 149, 264

Guthe, Hermann, born 10 May 1849 at Westerlinde, Braunschweig, he studied theology at the universities of Göttingen and Erlangen. He received a Dr.habil. in 1877 at Leipzig. In 1881 he excavated in Palestine, and in 1884 he was appointed a professor of theology at Leipzig. His writings include *Geschichte des Volkes Israel* (1899), *Palästina* (1908), and *Die Hedschasbahn von Damaskus nach Medina, ihr Bau und ihre Bedeutung* (1917). He died in 1936. DtBilnd (1)

Guthrie, A., born 20th cent., he was from Wishaw, Scotland, and received a Ph.D. in 1953 from Glagow University for *A Translation of the biography of Muhammad by Ibn Hisham*. Note; Sluglett

Gutkowski, Jerzy, born about 1916, he served for more than twenty years as an Arabic subject specialist at the Library of the Institute of Islamic Studies in McGill University, Montreal, and retired in 1981. His writings include *Guide to Arabic sources at the Library of the Institute of Islamic Studies* (1973). Private

Gutsche, Willibald, born 14 August 1926, he was a school teacher before he began to study history, gaining a Dr.phil. in 1959 at the Universität Jena for *Die Novemberrevolution in Erfurt*. After his Dr.habil. in 1967 he became head of local history at the Akademie der Wissenschaften, Berlin, a post which he held until his retirement in 1992. His writings include *Zur Imperialismus-Apologie in der BRD* (1974), *1. August 1914* (1976), and he was a joint author of *Von Sarajevo nach Versailles* (1974). Kürschner, 1992|; WhoSoCE, 1989

von **Gutschmidt**, Hermann *Alfred*, born in 1831 at Loschwitz near Dresden, he was a classicist and historian, who became a professor successively at ath universities of Kiel, Königsberg, Jena, and Tübingen. He pursued a special interest in the ancient Near East. Independent of Renan, he came to the conclusion that the writings of Ibn Wahshīyah contain forgeries. His writings include *Beiträge zur Geschichte des alten Orients* (1858). He died in Tübingen on 1 March 1887. ADtB, vol. 49, pp. 646-52; DtBilnd (6); Fück; EncIran; NDB

Guttmann, Egon, born 27 January 1927 at Neuruppin, Germany, he took his law degrees in 1950 and 1952 at London, and subsequently taught at a variety of American universities, before he became a professor of law at Washington College of Law, American University, Washington, D.C. DrAS, 1982 P; WhoAm, 1986-2003; WhoAmL, 1983-2003/2004; WhoE, 1989/90, 1991/92

Guttmann, Herbert M., born 19th cent., he was in 1908 a director of the Deutsche Orientbank. Note

Guttmann, Jacob, born 22 April 1845 at Beuthen, Prussia, he was educated at Jüdisch-Theologisches Seminar, and the Universität, Breslau, where he received a Dr.phil. in 1868 for his prize winning work, *De Cartesii et Spinoza doctrinis et ratione inter eas intercedente*. Ordained rabbi in 1870, he served as at Hildesheim from 1874 to 1892 and subsequently at Breslau, where he died on 29 September 1919. DtBE; DtBilnd (3); EncJud; JüfLex; Wininger

Guttmann, Julius, born 15 April 1880 at Hildesheim, Prussia, he studied at Jüdisch-Theologisches Seminar, and the Universität, Breslau, where he received a Dr.phil. in 1903 for *Der Gottesbegriff Kants*. After his *venia legendi* in 1910, he taught philosophy at Breslau. He served in the first Word War, and subsequently became the first full-time lecturer in Jewish philosophy of religion at the Hoch-schule für die Wissenschaft des Judentums, Berlin. Shortly after the publication of his main work, *Die Philosophie des Judentums* (1933), he went to Jerusalem, where he died on 19 May 1950. His other writings include *Die Scholastik des dreizehnten Jahrhunderts in ihren Beziehungen zum Judenthum und zur jüdischen Literatur* (1902), and he edited *The Guide of the perplexed*, with the translation from the Arabic by Chaim Rabin (1952). BioIn 6 (1); BioHBDtE; DtBE; EncJud (Guttman); Kürschner, 1926; Wininger

Guy, Anselme, born about 1800, he was in 1831 a *commandant* in the French Engineers. His writings include *Notice historique et littéraire sur M. le comte Anatole de Montesquiou Fezensac* (Paris, 1847). BN

Guy, Arthur, fl. 1928, his writings include *Les Robaï d'Omer Kheyyam* (Paris, 1935). NUC, pre-1956

Guy, Camille Lucien Xavier, born 18 May 1860 at Saint-Vit (Doubs), he was educated at Besançon and taught at a number of lycées, before studying history and geography at the Sorbonne. He subsequently taught at a variety of collèges. In 1895 he entered the Ministère des Colonies as head of the Service géographique et des Missions. In 1902 he became secretary general of the Gouvernement de l'Afrique Occidentale Française, serving successively as a governor of Senegal, la Réunion, Guinea, and Martinique. After his return to France he taught at the École coloniale and similar institutions. His writings include *La Prise en valeur de notre domaine coloniale* (1900). He died in Paris on 20 May 1929. DBF; *Hommes et destins*, 5, pp. 238-39; IndexBFr² (1) = Curinier

Guy, Claude, born about 1840, he was in 1876 a controller of customs, who contributed to the *Bulletin* of the Société impériale d'agriculture d'Alger. His writings include *L'Algérie, agriculture, industrie, commerce* (Alger, 1876), *La Révision des traités de commerce à la Société d'agriculture d'Alger* (Alger, 1887), and *Statistique du vignoble algérien* (Alger, 1895). BN; Note

Guy, Paul, he was in 1955 a public prosecutor at Diégo-Suarez, Madagascar. His writings include *Traité de droit musulman comorien* (Alger, 1954-55). He died about 1984. *Études Océan indien*, 6 (1985), pp. 3-4 [not sighted]; Note; NUC, pre-1956

Guyard, Stanislas, born in 27 September 1846 at Frotey-lès-Vésoul (Haute-Saône), he grew up in Russia until he came in 1861 to Paris, where he studied Oriental languages. In 1868 he became a tutor at the École des hautes études. He became successively deputy secretary of the Société asiatique, their librarian, and a member of the Commission des orientalistes. In February 1884 he succeeded to Ch. Fr. Defrémery in the chair of Arabic languague and literature at the Collège de France. His writings include *Manuel de la langue persane vulgaire* (1880), *Le Divan de Beha ed-Din Zoheir* (1883), *La Géographie d'Aboulféda*, traduit en français (1883), and *La Civilisation musulmane* (1884). He committed suicide in a bout of cerebral fever on 7 September 1884. Casanova; DBF; Fück, p. 249; IndexBFr² (2); Krachkovskiĭ, p. 163

Guyau, Augustin Antoine André, born 13 December 1883 at Menton (Alpes-Maritimes), he took degrees in mathematics, physics, and law, gaining a doctorate in 1913. In April 1914 he went on a journey of exploration to Morocco, returning the end of July. Although exempted from military service, he enlisted in the army and was killed on 1 July 1917 on the Meuse River. His writings include *Œuvres posthumes; voyages, feuilles* (1919). DBF

Guyer, Heinrich Johannes *Samuel*, born the son of a clergy on 31 May 1879 at Marseille, he grew up in the south of France and studied theology at Basel, Berlin, and Zürich. After a brief period in pastoral work, he pursued an interest in fine art, gaining a Dr.phil. in 1906 from the Universität Zürich for *Die christlichen Denkmäler des ersten Jahrtausends in der Schweiz*. His researches were mainly in the field of early Christian architecture of Asia Minor and northern Mesopotamia, two regions which he frequently visited. After the first World War, he lived in Firenze, München, and Basel, where he died on 26 August 1950. His writings include *Meine Tigrisfahrt auf dem Floß nach den Ruinenstätten Mesopotamiens* (1923), its translation, *My Journey on the Tigris* (1925), *Venedig, Bauten und Bilderwerke* (1927), and *Grundlagen mittelalterlicher abendländischer Baukunst* (1950. DtBE; GV; NDB

Guyot, Yves Prosper, born 6 September 1843 at Dinan (Côtes-du-Nord), he studied at Rennes and in 1864 went to Paris. He became to be reckoned almost more as an English economist than a French one. It was not, however, only in the field of commercial policy that he remained all his life an intransigent Liberal; he was just the same in all the different fields of social, economic and political life. He was one of the most ardent protagonists in the celebrated Dreyfus affair, 1897-1900, and one of the founders of the Ligue des droits des hommes at about the same time. He fought against every form of state intervention. The arguments which interventionists are wont to advance did not move him in the least, even when they were in support of morals. He was a member of the Royal Statistical Society, London, the Cobden Club, as well as numerous French societies. He died in Paris on 22 February 1928. BN; Curinier, 4 (1903), pp. 223-25; DBF; *Economic journal*, 38 (1928), pp. 332-335; IndexBFr² (7); *Who was who*, 2

Guys, Charles Édouard, born about 1800, his writings include *Les Philistins, colonie grecque de la Palestine* (Marseille, 1856), and *Le Guide de la Macédoine* (Paris, 1857), *Notice sur les îles de Bomba et Plate, le golfe de Bomba et ses environs* (Marseille, 1863). BN; NUC, pre-1956

Guys, Pierre Alphonse, born 27 August 1755 at Marseille, he was educated at the Collège du Plessis, Paris. In 1775 he became attached to the French ambassador at Constantinople. From 1777 to 1792 he held a variety of posts at French embassies. In 1793 he was appointed consul general and chargé d'affaires at Tripoli de Barberie. Upon his request in 1797 he was granted a transfer as consul general to Syria and Palestine, but captured in March 1798 by a British frigate on his outward voyage, he was taken back to Tripoli. The pasha set him free and put him on a Swedish vessel which took him to Malte. After his return to Paris he was appointed in June 1802 to the consulate at Tripoli in Syria, but it was not until the following spring that he could take office. He died there on 13 September 1812. His writings include *Lettres sur les Turcs* (Constantinople, 1776). DBF

Guys, Pierre Marie François *Henri*, born 12 October 1781 at Marseille, he travelled a great deal with his father, Pierre Alphonse Guys, on his many ambassadorial assignments, learning to speak fluently Greek, Italian, Arabic, and Turkish. He followed his father's career and became first an Arabic secretary at Tripoli and then successively consul at Latakia, Alger, Oran, Chios, and finally, from 1824 to 1828, at Beirut. Highly esteemed by Ibrahim Pasha, the governor of Syria, he became entrusted with the sanitation of Beirut. He was a member of the Académie de Marseille. His writings include *Relation d'un séjour de plusieurs années à Beyrouth et dans le Liban* (1847), *Voyage en Syrie* (1855), *La Nation druse* (1863), and *Étude sur les mœurs des Arabes et sur les moyens d'amener ceux d'Algérie à la civilisation* (1866). He died in Marseille in 1878. BN; DBF; IndexBFr² (1)

Guzeev, ZHamal Magomedovich, born 20th cent., he was associated with the Kabardino-Balkarian Institute of History, Philology and Economics, Ministry of the Kardino-Balkarian Autonomous Soviet Socialist Republic. He received a degree in 1972 at Frunze for *Сопоставительная фонетика русского и карачаево-балкарского языков*. His other writings include *Основы карачаево-балкарской орфографии* (1980); he was a joint author of *Къарачай-малъар тилни орфография сёзлюую*; and he edited *Вопросы лексики и семантики карачаево-балкарского языка* (1984), and *Проблемы исторической лексики карачаево-балкарского и ногайского языков* (1993). Note; OSK

Guzev, Viktor Grigor'evich, born 3 February 1939 at Voronezh, he graduated in 1962 from the Oriental Faculty, Leningrad, studied at Sofia, 1959-60, and received his first degree in 1967 for *Фонетика староанатолийского-тюркского языка*. From 1965 to 1973 he was a research fellow in the Leningrad Branch of the Oriental Institute in the Soviet Academy of Science. He subsequently became associated with the Oriental Faculty of the Leningrad State University. In 1978 he was appointed a lecturer. His writings include *Староосмансий язык* (1979), and *Очерки по теории тюркского словоизменения* (1987). Miliband; Miliband²

Guzman, Gregory George, born 25 December 1939 at Stevens Point, Wisc., he graduated in 1963 from Wisconsin State University, and received his Ph.D. in 1968 from the University of Cincinnati for *Simon of Saint-Quentin and the Dominican mission to the Mongols, 1245-1248*. From 1967 to his

694

retirement he taught in the Department of History, Bradley University, Peoria, Illinois. DrAS, 1969, 1974 H, 1978 H, 1982 H; NatFacDr, 1995-1999; Private

de **Guzmán y Gallo**, Juan Pérez, 1841-1928 *see* Pérez de Guzmán y Gallo, Juan

Guzzetti, Cherubino *Mario*, born middle of the 20th cent., he was educated at the Sorbonne, Paris, and received degrees from the University of London and the Università Cattolica di Milano. He spent thirty years in the Near and Middle East. His writings include *Il messaggio di Allàh* (1979), *Cristo e Allàh* (1984), *Bibbia e Corano* (1995), and his translation of the Koran, *Il Corano* (1989). Catalogo dei libri in commercio, 1990-2002; Note about the author

Gvakhariia, Aleksandr Akakievich, born 30 July 1930 at Tiflis, he graduated in 1952 at Tiflis and received his first degree in 1958, and his doctorate in 1970 for *Грузинские версии персидских народних дастанов*. Since 1959 he was associated with the Tiflis State University as a teacher of Persian. Appointed a lecturer in 1965, he became a professor in 1973. His writings include *Грусинские версии персидских народных дастанов Бахтяр-наме* (1968), *Из истории персидской народной прозы* (1973), *Персидские версии «Балавариани»* (1985), and he edited *Вис ва Рамин*, of Fakhr al-Dīn Gurgānī (1970). Miliband; Miliband²

von **Gwinner**, Arthur Philipp Friedrich Wilhelm, born 6 April 1856 at Frankfurt/Main, he trained as a banker and subsequently spent four years in London, and six years in Madrid as a bank manager and honorary consul. He was particularly interested in railway development and related industrial and agricultural matters in the Ottoman Empire, from the Balkans to Mesopotamia. He was a prominent banker of his day. His writings include *Die Handelspolitik Spaniens in den letzten Jahrzehnten* (1892). He died in Berlin on 29 December 1931. DtBE; DtBilnd (2); NDB; RHbDtG; Wer ist's, 1909-1928

Gwyer, G. D., born 20th cent., he was affiliated with the Institute of Development Studies, University of Nairobi. His writings include *Perennial crop supply response; the case of Tanzanian sisal* (1971), *East Africa and three international commodity agreements* (1972), and *Trends in Kenya agriculture in relation to employment* (1972). Note about the author

Gwynne, Michael Douglas, born 23 November 1932 at West Wickham, UK, he was educated at the universities of Edinburgh and Oxford. Since 1985 he was associated with the United Nations Environmental Programme as an environmentalist. His writings include *Current rangeland research projects in East Africa* (Nairobi, 1968), and he was joint author of *A Checklist of birds of the Muguga area* (1967). WhoUN, 1992

Gyalókay, Jenö, born 28 April 1874 at Nagyvárad, Hungary, his writings include *A mohácsi csata* (1926), *Az elsö mehszállás és Erdély felszabadítása* (1931), and *Az erdélyi hadjárat 1849 nyarán* (1938). He died in Budapest on 10 March 1945. MEL, 1967

Gyānī, Ranachhodalālā G., he was a writer on Indian architecture; his writings include *Guide to the Gallery of Miscellaneous Antiquities*, Prince of Wales Museum of Western India (Bombay, 1931). BLC

Gyford, Criss Barrington, fl. 1936-1945, he wrote *N'Gaga, king of the gorillas* (1937), *The Skipper ashore* (1938), and *British Empire in pictures* (1945). BLC

Györffy, György (George), born 20th cent., his writings include *Krónikáink és a magyar östörténet* (Budapest, 1948). OSK

Györffy, István, born 10 February 1884 at Karcag, Hungary, he studied geography and history. Since 1934 he was the first full professor of ethnography in Budapest University, where he established its Department of Ethnography. He died in Budapest on 3 October 1939. IntDcAn; Ki=kicsoda, 1937; Magyar

György, Aladár, born 11 April 1874 at Huszt, Hungary, he studied at home and abroad, and in 1871 joined the editorial staff of the daily, *A Hon*. In 1882 he was appointed to Statistics Hungary. His writings include *Az egyetemes müvelödéstörténelem vázlata* (1875), *Magyarország köz- és magánkönyvtárai* (1886-87), *Afrika, földrajzi és népismei leírása* (1904), *Azia, földrajzi és népismei leírása* (1906), and he edited *Magyarország* (1905). He died in Budapest on 16 January 1906. GeistigeUng; Magyar

Gyselen, Rika Marie Nellie, born 25 October 1942 at Veurne, Belgium, she studied at the universities of Gent and Louvain, and received a *doctorat de 3ème cycle* in 1979 from the Sorbonne nouvelle, Paris III, for *Trésors monétaires d'époque sassanide tardive; problème d'identification des ateliers monétaires*, as well as a doctorate in 1988 at Louvain. She was the recipient of the Prix Edm. Drouin (1982) and Prix R. & T. Ghirshman (1991). A director of the series *Res orientales*, and *Cahiers de studia Iranica*, her writings include *La géographie administrative de l'Empire sassanide* (1989), *Nouveaux matériaux pour la géographie historique de l'Empire sassanide* (2002), and she was a joint author of *Sceaux sassanides de diverses collections* (1983), *Une collection de monnaies de cuivre arabo-sassanides* (1984), *Bulles et sceaux sassanides des diverses collections* (1985), *Deux trésors monétaires de premiers temps de l'islam* (1983), and *Une Collection de monnaies de cuivre arabo-sasanides* (1984). AnEIFr, 1997; Livres disponibles, 2003, 2004; Private; THESAM, 4

Gysling, Erich, born in 1936, he was in 1992 a head of the foreign politics section at the Swiss television, D.R.S., Zürich, and made regular visits to the Middle East. As a speaker of Arabic he had direct access to the political leaders of the area. His writings include *Magnetfeld der Ungleichen: Amerika - Europa* (1974), *Arabiens Uhren gehen anders; Eigendynamik und Weltpolitik in Nahost* (1982), and *Zerreißprobe in Nahost; Menschen, Schicksale, Traditionen* (1986). EURAMES, 1993; Note

von **Gyurikovits**, Georg (György), born 12 July 1783 at Ivanocz near Trencsén (Trentschin), Hungary, he was educated at Protestant schools in Trentschin, and Preßburg, where he also trained with a renowned lawyer. Since 1818 he was a senator at Preßburg and held a position in the court of appeal. Privately he pursued an interest in Hungarian history and ethnography, subjects on which he published widely in periodicals. His writings include *De situ et ambitu Slavoniae et Croatiae, quem critice illustravit et de eo in usum Croatarum Latine* (Pesth, 1844). He died 25 January 1848. GeistigeUng; Wurzbach

DEBBIE MACOMBER

COUNTRY BRIDES

MIRA®

ISBN 1-55166-626-X

COUNTRY BRIDES
Copyright © 1998 by MIRA Books.

A LITTLE BIT COUNTRY
Copyright © 1990 by Debbie Macomber.

COUNTRY BRIDE
Copyright © 1990 by Debbie Macomber.

Visit us at www.mirabooks.com

Printed in U.S.A.

CONTENTS

A LITTLE BIT COUNTRY

arrangements to get the car repaired and then call the hotel to ask if they'd hold her room. Depending on how close she was to the nearest town, Rorie figured it would take at least an hour for a tow truck to get to her and then another for it to get her car to a garage. Once there, the repairs shouldn't require too much time. Just how much trouble could fixing a water pump be?

"How far is it to the phone?"

The youth grinned and pointed towards his horse. "Just over that ridge..."

Rorie relaxed. At least that part wasn't going to be much of a problem.

"...about ten miles," the teenager finished.

"Ten miles?" Rorie leaned her weight against the side of the car and let the frustration work its way through her weary bones. She swore this was the last time she'd ever take the scenic route and the last time she'd ever let Dan talk her into borrowing his car!

"Don't worry, you won't have to walk. Venture can handle both of us. You don't appear to weigh much."

"Venture?" Rorie was beginning to feel like an echo.

"My horse."

Rorie's gaze zoomed to the stallion, who had lowered his head to sample the tall sweet hillside grass. Now that she had a chance to study him, she realised what an extraordinarily large animal he was. Rorie hadn't been on the back of a horse since she was a child. Somehow, the experience of riding a pony in a slow circle with a bunch of other six-year-olds all those years ago didn't lend her much confidence now.

"You...you want me to ride double with you?" She was wearing a summer dress and mounting a horse might prove rather... interesting. She eyed the stallion, wondering how she could manage to climb into the saddle and still maintain her dignity.

"You wearing a dress and all could make that difficult." The boy rubbed the side of his jaw, looking doubtful.

"I could wait here until someone else comes along," she offered.

The teenager used his index finger to set his snap-brim hat further back on his head. "You might do that," he drawled lazily, "but it could be another day or so—if you're lucky."

"Oh, dear!"

"I suppose I could head back to the house and grab the pickup," he suggested.

It sounded like a stroke of genius to Rorie. "Would you? Listen, I'd be more than happy to pay you for your time."

He gave her an odd look. "Why would you want to do that? I'm only doing the neighbourly thing."

Rorie gave him a soft smile. She'd lived in San Francisco most of her life. She loved everything about the City by the Bay, but she couldn't have named the couple in the apartment next door had her life depended on it. People in the city kept to themselves.

"By the way," he said, wiping his hands with the bright blue handkerchief, "the name's Skip. Skip Franklin."

Rorie eagerly gave him her hand, overwhelmingly grateful he'd happened along when he did. "Rorie Campbell."

"Pleased to meet you, ma'am."

"Me too, Skip."

The teenager grinned. "Now you stay right here and I'll be back before you know it." He paused, apparently considering something else. "You'll be all right here by yourself, won't you?"

"Oh, sure, don't worry about me." She braced her feet wide apart and held up her hands in the classic karate position. "I can take care of myself. I've had three self-defence lessons."

Skip chuckled, ambled towards Venture and swung up into the saddle. Within minutes he disappeared over the ridge.

Rorie watched him until he was out of sight, then she walked over to the grassy hillside and plopped herself down. The cow she'd been conversing with earlier glanced in her direction and Rorie felt obliged to explain. "He's gone for help," she called out. "Said it was the neighbourly thing to do."

The heifer mooed loudly.

Rorie smiled. "I thought so, too."

An hour passed, and it seemed the longest in Rorie's life. With the sun out in full force now, she felt as if she was wilting more by the minute. Just when she began to suspect that Skip Franklin had been a figment of her overwrought imagination, she heard a loud chugging sound. She leaped to her feet and, shading her eyes with her hand, looked down the road. It was Skip, sitting atop a huge piece of farm equipment, heading in her direction.

Rorie gulped. Her gallant rescuer had come to get her on a tractor!

Skip removed his hat and waved. Even from this distance, she could see his eager grin.

Rorie feebly returned the gesture, but the smile on her lips felt brittle. Of the two modes of transportation, she would have preferred the stallion. Good grief, there was only one seat on the tractor. Where exactly did Skip plan for her to sit? On the engine?

Once the teenager reached the car, he steered the tractor in a wide circle until he faced the opposite direction from which he'd come. "Clay said we should tow the car to our place instead of leaving it on the road. You don't mind, do you?"

"Whatever he thinks is best."

"He'll be along any minute," Skip explained, jumping down from his perch. He reached for a hook and chain and began to connect the sports car to the tractor. "Clay had a couple of things he needed to do first."

Rorie nodded, grateful her options weren't so limited after all.

A couple of minutes later, the sound of another vehicle reached Rorie's ears. This time it was a late-model truck in critical need of a paint job. Rust showed through on the left front fender, which had been badly dented.

"That's Clay now," Skip announced, glancing towards the winding road.

Rorie busied herself brushing bits of grass from the skirt of her dress. When she'd finished, she looked up to see a tall muscular man sliding from the driver's side of the pickup. He was dressed in jeans and a denim shirt, and his hat was pulled low over his forehead, shading his eyes. Rorie's breath jammed in her throat as she watched the man's grace of movement—a thoroughly masculine grace. Something about Clay Franklin grabbed hold of her imagination. He embodied everything she'd ever linked with the idea of an outdoors man, a man's man. She could imagine him taming a wilderness or forging an empire. In his prominently defined features she sensed a strength that seemed to come from the land itself. The spellbinding quality of his steel-grey eyes drew her own and held them for a long moment. His nose was a bony protrusion with a slight curve, as though it had been broken once. He smiled, and a tingling sensation Rorie couldn't explain skittered down her spine.

His eyes still looked straight into hers and his hands rested lightly on his lean hips. "Looks as if you've got yourself into something of a predicament here." His voice was low, husky—and slightly amused.

His words seemed to wrap themselves around Rorie's throat,

choking off an intelligent reply. Her lips parted, but to her embarrassment no sound escaped.

Clay smiled and the fine lines that fanned out from the corners of his eyes crinkled appealingly.

"Skip thinks it might be the water pump," she said, pointing towards the MGB. The words came out weak and rusty and Rorie felt all the more foolish. She'd never had a man affect her this way. He wasn't really even handsome. Not like Dan Rogers. No, Clay wasn't the least bit like Dan, who was urbane and polished—and very proud of his neat little MGB.

"From the sounds of it, Skip's probably right." Clay walked over to the car, which his brother was connecting to the tractor. He twisted the same black hose Skip had earlier and frowned. Next he checked to see that the bumper of Dan's car was securely fastened to the chain. He nodded, lightly slapping the youth's back in approval. "Nice work."

Skip beamed under his brother's praise.

"I imagine you're interested in finding a phone. There's one at the house you're welcome to use," Clay said, looking directly at Rorie.

"Thank you." Her heart pounded in her ears and her stomach felt queasy. This reaction was so unusual for her. Normally she was a calm, levelheaded twenty-four-year-old, not a flighty teenager who didn't know how to act when an attractive male happened to glance in her direction.

Clay walked around to the passenger side of the pickup and held open the door. He waited for Rorie, then gave her his hand to help her climb inside. The simple action touched her heart. It had been a long time since anyone had shown her such unself-conscious courtesy.

Then Clay walked to the driver's side and hoisted himself in. He started the engine, which roared to life immediately, then shifted gears.

"I apologise for any inconvenience I've caused you," Rorie said stiffly, after several moments of silence.

"It's no problem," Clay murmured, concentrating on his driving, doing just the speed limit and not a fraction more.

They'd been driving for about ten minutes when Clay turned off the road and through a huge log archway with ELK RUN lettered across the top. Lush green pastures flanked the private road, and several horses were grazing calmly in one of them. Rorie knew next to nothing about horse breeds, but whatever type these were revealed a grace and beauty that was apparent even to her untrained eye.

The next thing Rorie noticed was the large two-storey house with a wide wraparound veranda on which a white wicker swing swayed gently in the breeze. Budding rosebushes lined the meandering brick walkway.

"It's beautiful," she said softly. Rorie would have expected something like this in the bluegrass hills of Kentucky, but never on the back roads of Oregon.

Clay made no comment.

He drove past the house and around the back towards the largest stable Rorie had ever seen. The sprawling wood structure must have had room enough for thirty or more horses.

"You raise horses?" she said.

A smile moved through his eyes like a distant light. "That's one way of putting it. Elk Run is a stud farm."

"Arabians?"

"No. American Saddlebreds."

"I don't think I've ever heard of that breed before."

"Probably not," Clay said, not unkindly.

He parked the truck, helped Rorie down and then led her towards the back of the house.

"Mary," he called, holding open the screen door for Rorie to precede him into the large country kitchen. She was met with the smell of cinnamon and apples. The delectable aroma came from a freshly baked pie, cooling on the counter. A black Labrador retriever slept on a braided rug. He raised his head and thumped his tail gently when Clay stepped over to him. Absently Clay bent down to scratch the dog's ears. "This is Blue."

"Hi, Blue," Rorie said, realising that the dog had probably been a childhood pet. He looked well advanced in years.

"Mary doesn't seem to be around."

"Mary's your wife?"

"Housekeeper," Clay informed her. "I'm not married."

That small piece of information gladdened Rorie's heart and she instantly felt foolish. Okay, so she was attracted to this man with eyes as grey as a San Francisco sky, but that didn't change anything. If her plans went according to schedule, she'd be in and out of his life within hours.

"Mary's probably upstairs," Clay explained when the housekeeper didn't immediately answer his call. "There's a phone against the wall." He pointed towards the other side of the kitchen.

While Rorie retrieved her AT&T card from her eelskin wallet, Clay crossed to the refrigerator and took out a brightly coloured ceramic jug.

"Iced tea?" he asked.

Rorie nodded. "Please." Her throat felt parched. She had to swallow several times before she could make her call.

As she spoke on the phone, Clay took two tall glasses down from a cupboard and half filled them with ice cubes. He poured in the tea, then added thin slices of lemon.

Rorie finished her conversation and walked over to the table. Sitting opposite Clay, she reached for the drink he'd prepared. "That was my hotel in Seattle. They won't be able to hold the room past six."

"I'm sure there'll be space in another," he said confidently.

Rorie nodded, although she thought that was unlikely. She was on her way to a writers' conference, one for which she'd paid a hefty fee, and she hated to miss one minute of it. Every hotel within a one-mile radius of the city was said to be filled.

"I'll call the garage in Nightingale for you," Clay offered.

"Is that close by?"

"About five miles down the road."

Rorie was relieved. She'd never heard of Nightingale and was grateful to hear it had a garage. After all, the place was barely large enough to rate a mention on the road map.

"Old Joe's been working on cars most of his life. He'll do a good job for you."

Once more Rorie nodded, not knowing how else to respond.

Clay quickly strode to the phone, punched out the number and talked for a few minutes. He was frowning when he replaced the receiver. Rorie wanted to question him, but before she could, he reached for an impossibly thin phone book and dialled a second number. His frown was deeper by the time he'd completed the call.

"I've got more bad news for you."

"Oh?" Rorie's heart had planted itself somewhere between her chest and her throat. She didn't like the way Clay was frowning, or the regret she heard in his voice. "What's wrong now?"

"Old Joe's gone fishing and isn't expected back this month. The mechanic in Riversdale, which is about sixty miles south of here, claims that if it is your water pump it'll take at least four days to ship a replacement.''

Two

"Four days!" Rorie cried. She felt the colour drain from her face. "But that's impossible! I can't possibly wait that long."

"Seems to me," Clay said in his smooth drawl, "you don't have much choice. George tells me he could have the water pump within a day if you weren't driving a foreign job."

"Surely there's someone else I could call."

Clay seemed to mull that over; then he shrugged. "Go ahead and give it a try if you like, but it isn't going to do you any good. If the shop in Riversdale can't get the part until Saturday, what makes you think someone else can do it any faster?"

Clay's calm acceptance of the situation infuriated Rorie. If she stayed four days here, in the middle of nowhere, she'd completely miss the writers' conference, which she'd been planning to attend for months. She'd scheduled her entire vacation around it. She'd made arrangements to travel to Victoria on British Columbia's Vancouver Island after the conference and on the way home take a leisurely trip down the Oregon coastline.

Clay handed her the telephone book, and feeling defeated Rorie thumbed through the brief yellow pages until she came to the section headed Automobile Repair. Only a handful were listed and none of them promised quick service, she noted.

"Yes, well," she muttered, expelling her breath, "there doesn't seem to be any help for it." Discouraged, she set the directory back on the counter. "You and your brother have been most helpful and I want you to know how much I appreciate everything you've done. Now if you could recommend a hotel in...what did you say was the name of the town again?"

"Nightingale."

"Right," she said, and offered him a wobbly smile, which was the best she could do at the moment. "Actually, any place that's clean will do."

Clay rubbed the side of his jaw. "I'm afraid that's going to present another problem."

"Now what? Has the manager gone fishing with Old Joe?" Rorie did her best to keep the sarcasm out of her voice, but it was difficult. Obviously the people in the community of...Nightingale, didn't take their responsibilities too seriously. If they were on the job when someone happened to need them, it was probably by pure coincidence.

"Old Joe's fishing trip isn't the problem this time," Clay explained, looking thoughtful. "Nightingale doesn't have a hotel."

"What?" Rorie exploded, slapping her hands against her legs in angry frustration. "No hotel...but there must be."

"We don't get much traffic through here. People usually stick to the freeway."

If he was implying that *she* should have done so, Rorie couldn't have agreed with him more. She might have seen some lovely scenery, but look where this little side trip had taken her! Her entire vacation was about to be ruined. Once more she slowly released her breath, trying hard to maintain her composure, which was cracking more with every passing minute.

"What about Riversdale? Surely they have a hotel?"

Clay nodded. "They do. It's a real nice one, but I suspect it's full."

"Full? I thought you just told me people don't often take this route."

"Tourists don't."

"Then how could the hotel possibly be full?"

"The Jerome family."

"I beg your pardon?"

"The Jerome family is having a big reunion. People are coming from all over the country. Jed was telling me just the other day that a cousin of his is driving out from Boston. The overflow will more than likely fill up Riversdale's only hotel."

One phone call confirmed Clay's suspicion.

"Terrific," Rorie murmured, her hand still on the telephone receiver. Her tension filled the kitchen. The way things were beginning to look, she'd end up sleeping on a park bench—if Nightingale even had a park.

The back door opened and Skip wandered in, looking pleased about something. He poured himself a glass of iced tea and leaned against the counter, glancing from Rorie to Clay and then back again.

"What's happening?" he asked, when no one volunteered any information.

"Nothing much," Rorie answered. "Getting the water pump for my car is going to take four days and it seems the only hotel within a sixty-mile radius is booked full for the next two weeks and—"

"Gee, that's no problem. You can stay here," Skip inserted quickly, his blue eyes flashing with eagerness. "We'd love to have you, wouldn't we, Clay?"

Rorie spoke before the elder Franklin had an opportunity to answer. "No, really, I appreciate the offer, but I can't inconvenience you any more than I already have."

"She wouldn't be an inconvenience, would she?" Once more Skip directed his attention to his older brother. "Tell her she wouldn't be, Clay."

"It's out of the question," Rorie returned, without giving Clay the chance to echo his brother's invitation. She didn't know these people. And, more important, they didn't know her and Rorie refused to impose on them further.

Clay looked into her eyes and a slow smile turned up the sensuous edges of his mouth. "It's up to you, Rorie. You're welcome on Elk Run if you want to stay."

"But you've already done so much. I really couldn't—"

"There's plenty of room," Skip announced ardently.

Those baby-blue eyes of his would melt the strongest resolve, Rorie mused.

"There's three bedrooms upstairs that are sitting empty. And you wouldn't need to worry about staying with two bachelors, because Mary's here."

It seemed inconceivable to Rorie that this family would take her in just like that. But, given her options, her arguments for refusing their offer grew weaker by the minute. "You don't even know me."

"We know all we need to, don't we, Clay?" Once more Skip glanced towards his older brother, seeking his support.

"You're welcome to stay here, if you like," Clay repeated, his gaze continuing to hold Rorie's.

Again she was gripped by the compelling quality of this man. He had a jutting, stubborn jaw and she doubted there were many confrontations where he walked away a loser. She'd always prided herself on her ability to read people. And her instincts told her firmly that Clay Franklin could be trusted. She sensed he was scrupulously honest, utterly dependable—and she already knew he was generous to a fault.

"I'd be most grateful," she said, swallowing an unexpected surge of tears at the Franklins' uncomplicated kindness to a complete stranger. "But, please, let me do something to make up for all the trouble I've caused you."

"It's no trouble," Skip said, looking as though he wanted to jump up and click his heels.

Clay frowned as he watched his younger brother.

"Really," Rorie stressed. "If there's anything I can do, I'd be more than happy to lend a hand."

"I don't suppose you know anything about computers?"

"A little," she admitted hesitantly. "We've been using them at the library for several years now."

"You're a librarian?"

Rorie nodded and brushed a stray dark curl from her forehead. "I specialise in children's literature." Someday she hoped to have her own work published. That had been the reason for attending this conference in Seattle. Three of the top children's authors in the country were scheduled to speak and Rorie had so wanted to meet them. "If you have a computer system, I'd be happy to do whatever I can...if I can figure out how to work it."

"Clay bought one last winter," Skip informed her proudly. "He claims it's the wave of the future, the way it records horse breeding and pedigrees up to the fourth and fifth generation."

A heavyset woman Rorie assumed was the housekeeper entered the kitchen, hauling a mop and bucket. She paused to inspect Rorie with a quick measuring glance and seemed to find her lacking. She grumbled something about city girls as she sidled past Skip.

"Didn't know you'd decided to hold a convention right in the middle of my kitchen."

"Mary," Clay said, "this is Rorie Campbell, from San Francisco. Her car broke down, so she'll be staying with us for the next few days. Could you see that a bed is made up for her?"

The older woman's wide face broke into a network of frown lines.

"Oh, please, I can do that myself," Rorie said quickly. "Don't trouble yourself, Mary."

Mary nodded. "Sheets are in the closet at the top of the stairs."

"Rorie is our guest." Clay didn't raise his voice, but his displeasure was evident in every syllable.

Mary shrugged, muttering, "I got my own things to do. If the girl claims she can make a bed, then let her."

Rorie couldn't contain her smile.

"You want to invite some city slicker to stay, then fine, but I got more important matters to attend to before I make up a bed for her." With that, Mary marched out of the kitchen.

"Mary's like family," Skip explained. "It's just her nature to be sassy. She doesn't mean anything by it."

"I'm sure she doesn't," Rorie said, smiling so Clay and Skip would know she wasn't offended. She gathered that the Franklins' housekeeper didn't hold a high opinion of anyone from the city and briefly wondered why.

"I'll get your suitcase from your car," Skip offered, already heading for the door.

Clay finished off the last of his drink and set the glass on the counter. "I've got to get back to work," he said, and pausing for a moment before he added, "You won't be bored by yourself, will you?"

"Not at all. Don't worry about me."

Clay nodded. "Dinner's at six."

"I'll be ready."

Rorie picked up the empty glasses and put them by the sink. While she waited for Skip to carry in her luggage, she phoned Dan. Unfortunately he was in a meeting and couldn't be reached, so she left a message, explaining that she'd been delayed and would call again. She felt strangely reluctant to give him the Franklins' phone number, but she decided there was no reason not to do so. She also decided not to examine that feeling too closely.

Skip had returned by the time she'd hung up. "Clay says you can have Mom and Dad's old room," the teenager announced on his way through the door. He hauled her large suitcase in one hand and her flight bag was slung over his shoulder. "Their room is at the other end of the house. They were killed in an accident several years back."

"But—"

"Their room's got the best view."

"Skip, really, any bedroom will do... I don't want your parents' room."

"But that's the one Clay wants for you." He bounded up the curving stairway with an energy reserved for the young.

Rorie followed him slowly. She slid her hand along the polished banister and glanced into the living room. A large natural-rock fireplace dominated one wall. The furniture was built of solid oak, made comfortable with thick chintz-covered cushions. Several braided rugs were strategically placed here and there on the polished wood floor. A piano with well-worn ivory keys stood to one side. The collection of family photographs displayed on top of it immediately caught her eye. She recognised a much younger Clay in what had to be his high-school graduation photo. The largest picture in an ornate brass frame was of a middle-aged couple, obviously Clay's and Skip's parents.

Skip paused at the top of the stairway and glanced over his shoulder. "My grandfather built this house over fifty years ago."

"It's magnificent."

"We think so," he admitted, eyes shining with pride.

The master bedroom, which was at the end of the hallway, opened onto a balcony that presented an unobstructed panorama of the entire valley. Rolling green pastures stretched as far as the eye could see. Rorie felt instantly drawn to this unfamiliar rural beauty. She drew a deep breath, and the thought flashed through her mind that it must be comforting to wake up to this serene landscape day after day.

"Everyone loves it here," Skip said from behind her.

"I can understand why."

"Well, I suppose I should get back to work," he said regretfully, setting her suitcases on the double bed. A colourful quilt lay folded at its foot.

Rorie slowly turned towards him, smiling. "Thank you, Skip. I hate to think what would have happened to me if you hadn't come along when you did."

He blushed and started backing out of the room, taking small steps as though he was loath to leave her. "I'll see you at dinner, okay?"

Rorie smiled again. "I'll look forward to it."

"Bye for now." He raised his right hand in a farewell gesture, then whirled around and dashed down the hallway. She could hear his feet pounding on the stairs.

It took Rorie only a few minutes to hang her things in the bare wardrobe. When she'd finished, she went back to the kitchen where Mary was busy peeling potatoes at the stainless steel sink.

"I'd like to help, if I could."

"Fine," the housekeeper answered gruffly, as she took another potato peeler out of a nearby drawer, slapping it down on the counter. "I suppose that's your fancy sports car there in the yard."

"The water pump has to be replaced...I think," Rorie answered, not bothering to mention that the MGB wasn't actually hers.

"Hmph," was Mary's only response.

Rorie sighed and reached for a fat potato. "The mechanic in Riversdale said it would take until Saturday to get a replacement part."

For the second time, Mary answered her with a gruff-sounding hmph. "If then! Saturday or next Thursday or a month from now, it's all the same to George. Fact is, you could end up staying here all summer."

Three

Mary's words echoed in Rorie's head as she joined Clay and Skip at the dinner table that evening. She stood just inside the dining room, dressed in a summer skirt and a cotton-knit cream-coloured sweater, and announced, "I can't stay any longer than four days."

Clay regarded her blankly. "I have no intention of holding you prisoner, Rorie."

"I know, but Mary told me that if I'm counting on George what's-his-name to fix the MG, I could end up spending the summer here. I've got to get back to San Francisco—I have a job there." She realised how nonsensical her little speech sounded, as if that last bit about having a job explained everything.

"If you want, I'll keep after George to be sure he doesn't forget about it."

"Please." Rorie felt a little better for having spoken her mind.

"And the Greyhound bus comes through on Mondays," Skip said reassuringly. "If worse comes to worst, you could take that back to California and return later for your friend's car."

"The bus," Rorie echoed, considering the option. "I *could* take the bus." As it was, the first half of her vacation was ruined, but it'd be nice to salvage what she could of the rest.

Both men were seated, but as Rorie approached the table Skip rose noisily to his feet, rushed around to the opposite side and pulled out a chair for her.

"Thank you," she said, smiling up at the youth. His dark hair was wet and slicked down close to his head. He'd changed out of his work clothes and into what appeared to be his Sunday best—a dress shirt, tie and pearl-grey slacks. With a good deal of ceremony, he pushed in her chair. As he leaned towards her, it was all Rorie could do to keep from grimacing at the overpowering scent of his spicy after-shave. He must have drenched himself in the stuff.

Clay's gaze tugged at hers and when Rorie glanced in his direction, she saw that he was doing his utmost to hold back a laugh.

He clearly found his brother's antics amusing, though he took pains not to hurt Skip's feelings, but Rorie wasn't sure how she should react. Skip was only in his teens, and she didn't want to encourage any romantic fantasies he might have.

"I hope you're hungry," Skip said, once he'd reclaimed his chair. "Mary puts on a good feed."

"I'm starved," Rorie admitted, eyeing the numerous serving dishes spread out on the table.

Clay handed her a large platter of fried chicken. That was followed by mashed potatoes, gravy, rolls, fresh green beans, a mixed green salad, milk and a variety of preserves. By the time they'd finished passing around the food, there wasn't any space left on Rorie's oversize plate.

"Don't forget to leave room for dessert," Clay commented, again with that slow, easy drawl of his. Here Skip was practically doing cartwheels to attract her attention and all Clay needed to do was look at her and smile and she became light-headed. Rorie couldn't understand it. From the moment Clay Franklin had stepped down from his pickup, she hadn't been the same.

"After dinner I thought I'd take you up to the stable and introduce you to King Genius," Skip said, waving a chicken leg as if conducting an orchestra.

"I'd be happy to meet him."

"Once you do, you'll feel the same way about Elk Run as you did when you stood on the balcony in the big bedroom and looked at the valley."

Obviously this King fellow wasn't a foreman, as Rorie had first assumed. More than likely, he was one of the horses she'd seen earlier grazing on the pasture in the front of the house.

"I don't think it would be a good idea to take Rorie around Hercules," Clay warned his younger brother, frowning slightly.

"Of course not." But it looked for a moment as if Skip wanted to argue.

"Who's Hercules?"

"Clay's stallion," Skip explained. "He has a tendency to act up if Clay isn't around."

Rorie could only guess what "act up" meant, but even if Skip didn't intend to heed Clay's advice, she gladly would. Other than the pony ride when she was six, Rorie hadn't been near a horse. One thing was certain, she planned to steer a wide path around the creature no matter how much Skip encouraged her. The largest pet she'd ever owned had been a guinea pig.

"When Hercules first came to Elk Run, the man who brought him claimed he was mean-spirited and untrainable. He wanted him destroyed, but Clay insisted on working with the stallion first."

"Now he's your own personal horse?" Rorie asked, directing the question to Clay.

He nodded. "We've got an understanding."

"But it's only between them," Skip added. "Hercules doesn't like anyone else getting close to him."

"He doesn't have anything to worry about as far as I'm concerned," Rorie was quick to assure both brothers. "I'll give him as much space as he needs."

Clay grinned, and once again she felt her heart turn over. This strange affinity with Clay was affirmed in the look he gave her. Unexpected thoughts of Dan Rogers sprang to mind. Dan was a divorced stockbroker she'd been seeing steadily for the past few months. Rorie enjoyed Dan's company and had recently come to believe she was falling in love with him. Now she knew differently. She couldn't be this powerfully drawn to Clay Franklin if Dan was anything more than a good friend to her. One of the reasons Rorie had decided on this vacation was to test her feelings for Dan. Two days out of San Francisco, and she had her answer.

Deliberately Rorie pulled her gaze from Clay, wanting to attribute everything she was experiencing to the clean scent of the country air.

Skip's deep blue eyes sparkled with pride as he started to tell Rorie about Elk Run's other champion horses. "But you'll love the King best. He was the five-gaited world champion four years running. Clay put him out to stud four years ago. We've been doing some cross-breeding with Arabians for the past couple of years. National Show Horses are commanding top dollar and we've produced three of the best. King's the sire, naturally."

"Do all the horses I saw in the pasture belong to you?"

"We board several," Skip answered. "Some of the others are brought here from around the country for Clay to break and train."

"You break horses?" She couldn't conceal her sudden alarm. The image of Clay sitting on a wild bronco that bucked and heaved in a furious effort to unseat him did funny things to Rorie's stomach.

"Breaking horses isn't exactly the way Hollywood pictures show it," Clay explained.

Rorie was about to ask him more when Skip planted his elbows on the table and leaned forward. Once more Rorie was assaulted by the overpowering scent of his after-shave. She did her best to smile, but if he remained in that position much longer, her eyes were sure to start watering. Already she could feel a sneeze tickling her nose.

"How old are you, Rorie?"

The question came so far out of the blue that she was too surprised to answer immediately. Then she said, "Twenty-four."

Clay shot his brother a exasperated look. "Are you interviewing Rorie for the *Independent*?"

"No. I was just curious."

"She's too old for you, little brother."

"I don't know about that," Skip returned fervently. "I've always liked my women more mature. Besides, Rorie's kind of cute."

"Kind of?"

Skip shrugged. "You know what I mean. She hardly acts like a city girl."

Rorie's eyes flew from one brother to the next. They were talking as if she weren't even in the room, and that annoyed her—especially since she was the main topic of conversation.

Unaware of her reaction, Skip helped himself to another roll. "Actually, I thought she might be closer to twenty. With some women it's hard to tell."

"I'll take that as a compliment," Rorie muttered to no one in particular.

"I beg your pardon, Rorie," Clay said contritely. "We were being rude."

She took time buttering her roll. "No offence taken."

"How old do you think I am?" Skip asked her, his eyes wide and hopeful.

It was Rorie's nature to be kind, and besides, Skip had saved her from an unknown fate. "Twenty," she answered with barely a pause.

The younger Franklin straightened and sent his brother a satisfied smirk. "I was seventeen last week."

"That surprises me," Rorie continued, setting aside her butter knife and swallowing a smile. "I could have sworn you were much older."

Looking all the more pleased with himself, Skip cleared his throat. "Lots of girls think that."

"Don't I remember you saying something about helping Luke Rivers tonight?" Clay reminded his brother.

Skip's face fell. "I guess I did at that."

"If Rorie doesn't mind, I'll introduce her to King."

Clay's offer appeared to surprise Skip, and Rorie studied the boy, a little worried now about causing problems between the two brothers. Nor did she want to disappoint Skip, who had offered first.

"But I thought..." Skip began, then swallowed. "You want to take Rorie?"

Clay's eyes narrowed, and when he spoke, his voice was cool. "That's what I just said. Is there a problem with that?"

"No...of course not." Skip stuffed half a roll in his mouth and shook his head vigorously. After a moment of chewing, he announced, "Clay will show you around the stable." Each word was measured and even, but his gaze continued to hold his brother's.

"I heard," Rorie said gently. She could only speculate on what was going on between them, but obviously something was amiss. There had been more than a hint of surprise in Skip's eyes at Clay's offer. She noticed that the younger Franklin seemed angry. Because his vanity was bruised? Rorie supposed so. "I could wait until tomorrow if you want, Skip," she suggested.

"No, that's all right," he answered and lowered his gaze. "Clay can do it, since that's what he seems to want."

When they finished the meal, Rorie cleared the table, but Mary refused to let her help with cleaning up the kitchen.

"You'd just be in the way," she grumbled, though her eyes weren't unfriendly. "Besides, I heard something about the boys showing you the barn."

"Tomorrow night I'll do the dishes. I insist."

Mary muttered a response, then asked brusquely, "How was the apple pie?"

"Absolutely delicious."

A satisfied smile touched the edges of the housekeeper's mouth. "Good. I did things a little differently this time, and I was just wondering."

Clay led Rorie out the back door and across the yard towards the barn. The minute Rorie walked through the enormous double doors she felt she'd entered another world. The wonderful smells of leather and liniments and saddle soap mingled with the fragrance of fresh hay and the pungent odour of the horses themselves. Rorie found it surprisingly pleasant. Flashes of bright colour from halters and blankets captured her attention, as did the gleam of steel bits against the far wall.

"King's over here," Clay said, guiding her with a firm hand beneath her elbow.

When Clay opened the top of the stall door, the most magnificent creature Rorie had ever seen turned to face them. He was a deep chestnut colour, so sleek and powerful it took her breath away. This splendid creature seemed to know he was royalty. He regarded Rorie with a keen eye, as though he expected her to show the proper respect and curtsy. For a wild moment, Rorie was tempted to do exactly that.

"I brought a young lady for you to impress," Clay told the stallion.

King took a couple of steps back and pawed the ground.

"He really is something," Rorie whispered, once she'd found her voice. "Did you raise him from a colt?"

Clay nodded.

Rorie was about to ask him more when they heard frantic whinnying from the other side of the aisle.

Clay looked almost apologetic when he explained. "If you haven't already guessed, that's Hercules. He doesn't like being ignored." He walked to the stall opposite King's and opened the upper half of the door. Instantly the black stallion stuck his head out and complained about the lack of attention in a loud snort, which brought an involuntary smile to Rorie's mouth. "I was bringing Rorie over to meet you, too, so don't get your neck all out of joint," Clay chastised.

"Hi," Rorie said, and raised her right hand in a stiff greeting. It amused her that Clay talked to his animals as if he honestly expected them to understand his remarks and join in the conversation. But then who was she to criticise? Only a few hours earlier, she'd been conversing with a cow.

"You don't need to be frightened of him," Clay told her when she stood, unmoving, a good distance from the stall. Taking into consideration what Skip had mentioned earlier about the moody stallion, Rorie decided to stay where she was.

Clay ran his hand down the side of Hercules's neck, a gesture that seemed to appease the stallion's obviously delicate ego.

Looking around her, Rorie was surprised by the size of the barn. "How many stalls are there all together?"

"Thirty-six regular and four foaling. But this is only a small part of Elk Run." He led her outside to a large arena and nodded at a building on the opposite side. "My office is over there, if you'd like to see it."

Rorie nodded, and they crossed to the office. Clay opened the door for her. Inside, the first thing that captured her attention was the collection of championship ribbons and photographs displayed on the walls. A large trophy case was filled with a variety of awards. When he noticed her interest in the computer, Clay explained the system he'd had installed and how it would aid him in the future.

"This is the same word-processing program we use at the library," Rorie told him.

"I've been meaning to hire a high-school kid to enter the data for me so I can get started, but I haven't got around to it yet."

Rorie sorted through the files. There were only a few hours of work and her typing skills were good. "There's no need to pay anyone. If I'm going to be imposing on your hospitality, the least I can do is type this into the system for you."

"Rorie, that isn't necessary. I don't want you to spend your time here stuck in the office doing all that tedious typing."

"It'll give me something productive to do instead of fretting over how long it's taking to get the MG repaired."

He glanced at her, his expression concerned. "All right, if you insist, but it really isn't necessary, you know."

"I do insist." Rorie clasped her hands behind her back, and decided to change the subject. "What's that?" she asked, nodding towards a large room off the office. Floor-to-ceiling windows looked out over the arena.

"The observation room."

"So you can have your own private shows?"

"In a manner of speaking. Would you like to go down there?"

"Oh, yes!"

Inside the arena, Rorie realised that it was much bigger than it had looked from above. They'd walked around for several minutes, then Clay checked his watch and frowned. "I hate to cut this short, but I've got a meeting. Normally I wouldn't leave company."

"Oh, please," she said hurriedly, "don't apologise. It's not as though I was expected or anything. I hardly consider myself company.''

Still Clay looked regretful. ''I'll walk you back to the house.''

He left in the pickup a couple of minutes later. The house was quiet. Mary had apparently finished her duties in the kitchen and had retired to her room. Skip, who had returned from helping his friend, was busy talking on the phone. He smiled when he saw Rorie, without interrupting his conversation.

Rorie moved into the living room and idly picked up a magazine, leafing through it. Restless and bored after a few minutes, she went so far as to read a heated article on the pros and cons of a new medication used for equine worming.

When Skip was finished on the phone, he suggested they play cribbage. Not until after ten did Rorie realise she was unconsciously waiting for Clay's return. But she wasn't quite sure why.

Skip yawned rather pointedly and Rorie took the hint.

''I suppose I should think about heading up to bed,'' she said, putting down the deck of playing cards.

''Yeah, it seems to be that time,'' he answered, yawning again.

''I didn't mean to keep you up so late.''

''Oh, that's no problem. It's just that we get started early around here. But you sleep in. We don't expect you to get up before the sun just because we do.''

By Rorie's rough calculation, getting up before the sun meant Clay and Skip started their workday between four-thirty and five in the morning.

Skip must have read the look in her eyes, because he chuckled and said, ''You get used to it.''

Rorie followed him up the stairs, and they said their good-nights. But later, even after a warm bath, she couldn't sleep. Wearing her flower-sprigged cotton pyjamas, she sat on the bed with the light still on and thought how everything was so different from what she'd planned. According to her schedule, she was supposed to be in Seattle now, at a cocktail party arranged for the first night of the conference; she'd hoped to talk to several of the authors there. But she'd missed that, and the likelihood of attending even one workshop was dim. Instead she'd made an unscheduled detour into a stud farm and stumbled upon a handsome rancher.

She grinned. Things could be worse. Much worse.

An hour later, Rorie heard a sound outside, behind the house. Clay must be home. She smiled, oddly pleased that he'd returned.

Yawning, she reached for the lamp on the bedside table and turned it off.

The discordant noise came again.

Rorie frowned. This time, whatever was making the racket didn't sound the least bit like a pickup truck parking, or anything else she could readily identify.

Grabbing her robe from the foot of the bed and tucking her feet into fuzzy slippers, Rorie went downstairs to investigate.

Once she reached the kitchen she realised the clamour was coming from the barn. Trouble with the horses?

Not knowing what else to do, she raced up the stairs, taking them two at a time, and hurried from room to room until she found Skip's bedroom. She had no idea where Mary slept.

The teenager was sprawled across his bed, snoring softly.

"Skip," she cried, "something's wrong with the horses!"

He continued to snore.

"Skip," she cried, louder this time. "Wake up!"

He remained deep in sleep.

"Skip, please, oh, please, wake up!" Rorie pleaded, shaking him so hard he was sure to have bruises in the morning. "I'm from the city. Remember? I don't know what to do."

The thumps and bangs coming from the barn were growing fiercer by the minute. Perhaps there was a fire. Oh, dear Lord, she prayed, not that. Rorie raced halfway down the stairs, paused, and then reversed her direction.

"Skip," she yelled. "Mary! Anyone!" Rorie heard the panic in her own voice. "Someone's got to do something!"

No one else seemed to think so.

Nearly frantic now, Rorie dashed back down the stairs and across the yard. Trembling, she entered the barn. A lone electric light shone from the ceiling, dimly illuminating the area.

Several of the Dutch stall doors were open and Rorie could sense the horses becoming increasingly restless. Walking on tiptoe, she slowly moved towards the source of the noise, somewhere in the middle of the stable. The horses were curious and their combined cries brought Rorie's heart straight to her throat.

"Nice horsey, nice horsey," she repeated soothingly over and over again until she reached the stall those unearthly sounds were coming from.

The upper half of the door was open and Rorie flattened herself against it before daring to peek inside. She saw a speckled grey mare, head thrown back and teeth bared, neighing loudly, ceaselessly. Rorie quickly jerked away and resumed her position against the outside of the door. She didn't know much about horses, but she knew this one was in dire trouble.

Racing out of the stable, Rorie picked up the hem of her robe and sprinted towards the house. She'd find a way to wake Skip or die trying.

She was breathless by the time she reached the yard. It was then she saw Clay's battered blue truck.

"Clay," she screamed, halting in the middle of the moonlit yard. "Oh, Clay."

He was at her side instantly, his hands roughly gripping her shoulders. "Rorie, what is it?"

She was so glad to see him, she hugged his middle and only just resisted bursting into tears. Her shoulders were heaving and her voice shook uncontrollably. "There's trouble in the barn...bad trouble."

Four

Clay raced towards the barn with Rorie right behind him. He paused to flip a switch, flooding the interior with bright light.

The grey mare in the centre stall continued to neigh and thrash around. Rorie found it astonishing that the walls had remained intact. The noise of the animal's pain echoed through the stable, reflected by the rising anxiety of the other horses.

Clay took one look at the mare and released a low groan, then he muttered something under his breath.

"What's wrong?" Rorie cried.

"It seems Star Bright is about to become a mother."

"But why isn't she in one of the foaling stalls?"

"Because two different vets palpated her and said she wasn't in foal."

"But..."

"She's already had six foals and her stomach's so stretched she looks pregnant even when she isn't." Clay opened the stall door and entered the cubicle. Rorie's hand flew to her heart. Good grief, he could get killed in there.

"What do you want me to do?" she said.

Clay shook his head. "This is no place for you. Get back to the house and stay there." His brow furrowed, every line a testament to his hard, outdoor life.

"But shouldn't I be phoning a vet or something?"

"It's too late for that."

"Boiling water—I could get that for you." She wanted to help; she just didn't know how.

"Boiling water?" he repeated. "What the hell would I need that for?"

"I don't know," she confessed lamely, "but they always seem to need it in the movies."

Clay gave an exasperated sigh. "Rorie, please, just go back to the house."

She made it all the way to the barn door, then abruptly turned back. If anyone were to ask her why she felt it so necessary to remain with Clay, she wouldn't have been able to answer. But something kept her there, something far stronger than the threat of Clay's temper.

She marched back to the centre stall her head and shoulders held stiff and straight. She stood with her feet braced apart, prepared for an argument.

"Clay," she announced, "I'm not leaving."

"Listen, Rorie, you're a city girl. This isn't going to be pretty."

"I'm a woman, too. The sight of a little blood isn't enough to make me faint."

Clay was doing his best to calm the frightened mare, but without much success. The tension in the air crackled like static electricity.

"I haven't got time to argue with you," he said through clenched teeth.

"Good."

Star Bright heaved her neck backward and gave a deep groan that seemed to bounce against the sides of the stall like the boom of a cannon.

"Poor little mother," Rorie whispered in a calm soothing voice. Led by instinct, she carefully unlatched the stall door and slipped inside.

Clay sent her a look hot enough to peel paint off the wall. "Get out of here before you get hurt." His voice was low and urgent.

Star Bright reacted to his tension immediately, jerking about, her body twitching convulsively. One of her hooves caught Clay in the forearm and, almost immediately, blood seeped through his sleeve. Rorie bit her lip to suppress a cry of alarm, but if Clay felt any pain he didn't show it.

"Hold her head," Clay said sharply.

Somehow Rorie found the courage to do as he asked. Star Bright groaned once more and her pleading eyes looked directly into Rorie's, seeming to beg for help. The mare's lips pulled back from her teeth as she flailed her head to and fro, shaking Rorie in the process.

"Whoa, girl," Rorie said softly, gaining control. "It's painful, isn't it, but soon you'll have a beautiful baby to show off to the world."

"Foal," Clay corrected from behind the mare.

"A beautiful foal," Rorie repeated. She ran her hand down the sweat-dampened neck in a caressing motion, doing what she could to reassure the frightened horse.

"Keep talking," Clay whispered.

Rorie kept up a running dialogue for several tense moments, but there was only so much she could find to say on such short acquaintance. When she ran out of ideas, she started to sing in a soft, lilting voice. She began with lullabies her mother had once sung to her, then she followed those with a few childhood ditties. Her singing lasted only minutes, but Rorie's lungs felt close to collapse.

Suddenly the mare's waters broke. Although Clay wasn't saying much, Rorie knew there were problems. She saw his frown, and the way he began to work furiously, though she couldn't see what he was doing. Star Bright tossed her neck in the final throes of birth and Rorie watched, fascinated, as two hooves and front legs emerged, followed by a white nose.

The mare lifted her head, eager to see. Clay tugged gently, and within seconds, the foal was free. Rorie's heart pounded like a locomotive struggling up a steep hill as Clay's strong hands completed the task.

"A filly," he announced, a smile lighting his face. He reached for a rag and wiped his hands and arms.

Star Bright turned her head to view her offspring. "See?" Rorie told the mare, her eyes moist with relief. "Didn't I tell you it would all be worth it in a little while?"

The mare nickered and her long tongue began the task of cleaning and caressing her newborn filly who was grey, like her mother, and finely marked with white streaks on her nose, mane and tail. Rorie watched, touched to her very soul by the sight. Tears blurred her vision and ran down her flushed cheeks. She wiped them aside so that Clay couldn't see them and silently chided herself for being such a sentimental fool.

It was almost another hour before they left Star Bright's stall. The mare stood guard over her long-legged baby, looking content and utterly pleased with herself. As they prepared to leave, Rorie whispered in the mare's ear.

"What was that all about?" Clay wanted to know, latching the stall door.

"I just told her she'd done a good job."

"That she did," Clay whispered. A moment later, he added, "And so did you, Rorie. I was grateful for your help."

Once more tears misted her eyes. She responded with a nod,

unable to trust her voice. Her heart was racing with exhilaration. She couldn't remember a time she'd felt more excited. It was well past midnight by then, but she'd never felt less sleepy.

"Rorie?" He was watching her, his eyes bright with concern.

She owed him an explanation, although she wasn't sure she could fully explain this sudden burst of emotion. "It was so...beautiful." She brushed the dark brown hair from her face and smiled up at him, hoping he wouldn't think she was just a foolish city girl. She wasn't sure why it mattered, but she doubted that any man had seen her looking worse, although Rorie was well aware she didn't possess a classic beauty. She was usually referred to as cute, with her turned-up nose and dark brown eyes.

"I understand." He walked to the sink against the barn's opposite wall and busily washed his hands, then splashed water on his face. When he'd finished, Rorie handed him a towel hanging on a nearby hook.

"Thanks."

"I don't know how to describe it," she said, after a fruitless effort to find the words to explain all the feeling that had surged up inside her.

"It's the same for me every time I witness a birth," Clay told her. He looked at her then and gently touched her face, letting his finger glide along her jaw. All the world went still as his eyes caressed hers. There was a primitive wonder in the experience of birth, a wonder that struck deep within the soul. For the first time Rorie understood this. And sharing it with Clay seemed to intensify the attraction she already felt for him. During those few short minutes in the stall, just before Star Bright delivered her foal, Rorie felt closer to Clay than she ever had to any other man. It was as though her heart had taken flight and joined his in a moment of sheer challenge and joy. That was a silly romantic thought, she realised. But it seemed so incredible to her that she could feel anything this strong for a man she'd known for such a short time.

"I've got a name for her," Clay said, hanging up the towel. "What do you think of Nightsong?"

"Nightsong," Rorie repeated in a soft whisper. "I like it."

"In honour of the woman who sang to her mother."

Rorie nodded as emotion clogged her throat. "Does this mean I did all right for a city slicker?"

"You did more than all right."

"Thanks for not sending me away... I probably would have gone if you'd insisted."

They left the barn, and Clay draped his arm across her shoulders as though he'd been doing it for years. Rorie was grateful for his touch, because it somehow helped to ground the unfamiliar feelings and sensations.

As they strolled across the yard, she noticed that the sky was filled with a thousand glittering stars, brighter than any she could remember seeing in the city. She paused midstep to gaze up at them.

Clay's quiet voice didn't dispel the serenity. "It's a lovely night, isn't it?"

Rorie wanted to hold on to each exquisite minute and make it last a lifetime. A nod was all she could manage as she realised that this time with Clay was about to end. They would walk into the house and Clay would probably thank her for her help. Then she'd climb the stairs to her room and that would be all there was.

"How about some coffee?" he asked once they'd entered the kitchen. Blue left his rug and wandered over to Clay. "The way I feel now, it would be a waste of time to go to bed."

"For me, too." Rorie leapt at the suggestion, pleased that he wanted to delay their parting, too. And when she did return to her room, she knew the adrenalin surging through her system would make sleep impossible, anyway.

Clay was reaching up for the canister of coffee, when Rorie suddenly noticed the bloodstain on his sleeve and remembered Star Bright's kick.

"Clay, you need to take care of that cut."

From the surprised way he looked at his arm, she guessed that he, too, had forgotten about the injury. "Yes, I suppose I should." Then he calmly returned to his task.

"Let me clean it for you," Rorie offered, joining him at the kitchen counter.

"If you like." He led her into the bathroom down the hall and took a variety of medical supplies from the cabinet above the sink. "Do you want to do it here or in the kitchen?"

"Here is fine."

Clay sat on the edge of the bath and unfastened the cuff, then rolled back the sleeve.

"Oh, Clay," Rorie whispered when she saw the angry torn flesh just above his elbow. Gently her fingers tested the edges, wondering if he was going to need stitches. He winced slightly at her probing fingers.

"Sorry."

"Just put some antiseptic on it and it'll be all right."

"But this is really deep—you should probably have a doctor look at it."

"Rorie, I'm as tough as old saddle leather. This kind of thing happens all the time. I'll recover."

"I don't doubt that," she said primly.

"Then just put on a bandage and be done with it."

"But—"

"I've been injured often enough to know when a cut needs a doctor's attention."

She hesitated, then conceded that he was probably right. She filled the sink with warm tap water and took care to clean the wound thoroughly. All the while, Rorie was conscious of Clay's eyes moving over her face, solemnly perusing the chin-length, dark brown hair and the big dark eyes that still displayed a hint of vulnerability. She was tall, almost five-eight, her figure willowy. But if Clay found anything attractive about her, he didn't mention it. Her throat muscles squeezed shut, and, although she was grateful for the silence between them, it confused her.

"You missed your vocation," he told her as she rinsed the bloody cloth. "You should have been a nurse."

"I toyed with the idea when I was ten, but decided I liked books better."

His shoulders were tense, Rorie noted, and she tried to be as gentle as possible. A muscle leapt in his jaw.

"I'm...hurting you?"

"No," he answered sharply.

After that, he was an excellent patient. He didn't complain when she dabbed on the antiseptic, although she was sure it must have stung like crazy. He co-oper-ated when she wrapped the gauze around his arm, lifting and lowering it when she asked him to. The silence continued as she secured the bandage with adhesive tape. But Rorie had the feeling that he wanted to escape the close confines of the bathroom as quickly as possible.

"I hope that stays."

He stood up and flexed his elbow a couple of times. "It's fine. You do good work."

"I'm glad you think so."

"The coffee's probably ready by now." He spoke quickly, as if eager to be gone.

She sighed. "I could use a cup."

She put the medical supplies neatly back inside the cabinet, while Clay returned to the kitchen. Rorie could smell the freshly perked coffee even before she entered the room.

He was leaning against the counter, already sipping a cup of the fragrant coffee, waiting for her.

"It's been quite a night, hasn't it?" she murmured, adding cream and sugar to the mug he'd poured for her.

A certain tension hung in the air, and Rorie couldn't explain or understand it. Only minutes before, they'd walked across the yard, spellbound by the stars, and Clay had laid his arm across her shoulders. He'd smiled down on her so tenderly. Now he looked as if he couldn't wait to get away from her.

"Have I done something wrong?" she asked outright.

"Rorie, no." He set his mug aside and gripped her shoulders with both hands. "There's something so intimate and...earthy in what we shared." His eyes were tense, strangely darker. "Wanting you this way isn't right."

Rorie felt a tremor work through him as he lifted his hands to cup her face. His callused thumbs lightly caressed her cheeks.

"I feel as if I've known you all my life," he whispered hoarsely, his expression uncertain.

"It's...been the same for me, from the moment you stepped out of the truck."

Clay smiled, and Rorie thought her knees would melt. She set her coffee aside and as soon as she did Clay eased her into his arms, his hands on her shoulders and back. Her heart stopped, then jolted back to frenzied life.

"I'm going to kiss you..."

He made the statement almost a question. "I know," she whispered in return, letting him know she'd welcome his touch. Her stomach fluttered as he slowly lowered his mouth to hers.

Rorie had never wanted a man's kiss more. His moist lips glided over hers in a series of gentle explorations. He drew her closer until their bodies were pressed full length against one another.

"Oh, Rorie," he breathed, dragging his mouth from hers. "You taste like heaven...I was afraid you would." His mouth found the pulse in her throat and lingered there.

"This afternoon I wanted to cry when the car broke down and now...now I'm glad...so glad," she said.

He kissed her again, nibbling on her lower lip, gently drawing it between his teeth. Rorie could hardly breathe, her heart was pounding so hard and fast. She slumped against him, delighting in the rise and fall of his broad chest. His hands moved down her back in slow restraint, but paused when he reached the rounded curve of her hips.

He tensed. "I think we should say goodnight."

A protest sprang to her lips, but, before she could voice it, Clay said, "Now."

She looked at him, dazed and uncertain. The last thing she wanted to do was leave him. "What about my coffee?"

"That was just an excuse and we both knew it."

Rorie said nothing.

The silence between them seemed to throb for endless minutes.

"Good night, Clay," she finally whispered. She broke away, but his hand caught her fingers, and with a groan he pulled her back into his arms.

"What the hell," he muttered fiercely, "sending you upstairs isn't going to help. Nothing's going to change."

His words brought confusion, but Rorie didn't question him, didn't want to. What she longed for was the warmth and security she found in his arms.

"Come on," he whispered, after his mouth had sampled hers once more. He led her through the living room and outside to the porch where the swing moved gently in the night breeze.

Rorie sat beside him and he wrapped his arm around her. She nestled her head against his shoulder, savouring these precious moments.

"I'll never forget this night."

"Neither will I," Clay promised, kissing her again.

Rorie awoke when the sun settled on her face and refused to leave her alone. Keeping her eyes closed, she smiled contentedly, basking in the memory of her night with Clay. They'd sat on the swing and talked for hours. Talked and kissed and laughed and touched as if they'd known each other all their lives.

Sitting up, Rorie raised her hands high above her head and stretched, arching her spine. She looked at her watch on the bedside table and was shocked to realise it was after eleven. By the time she'd climbed the stairs for bed the sky had already been dappled with faint shreds of light. She suspected Clay hadn't even bothered to sleep.

Tossing aside the blankets, Rorie slid to the floor, anxious to shower and dress. Anxious to see him again. Fifteen minutes later, she was on her way down the stairs.

Mary was dusting in the living room and glanced up when she saw Rorie. The housekeeper grinned, then resumed her task, but not before she muttered something about how city folks were prone to sleeping their lives away.

"Good morning, Mary," Rorie greeted cheerfully.

"'Mornin'."

"Where is everyone?"

"Where they ought to be this time of the day. Working."

"Yes, I know, but where?"

"Outside."

Rorie had trouble hiding her grin.

"I heard about you helping last night," Mary added gruffly. "Seems like you did all right for a city girl."

"Thank you, Mary, you don't do half bad for a country girl, either."

The housekeeper seemed uncomfortable with the praise, despite the lightness of Rorie's tone. "I suppose you want me to cook you some fancy breakfast."

"Good heavens, no, you're busy. I'll just help myself to toast."

"That's hardly enough to fill a growing girl," Mary complained.

"It'll suit me just fine."

Once her toast was ready, Rorie carried it outside with her. If she couldn't find Clay, then she wanted to check on Nightsong.

"Rorie."

She turned to discover Skip walking towards her, in animated conversation with a blonde. His girlfriend, she guessed. He waved and Rorie returned the gesture, smiling. The sun was glorious and the day held marvellous promise.

"I didn't think you were ever going to wake up," Skip said.

"I'm sorry—I don't usually sleep this late."

"Clay told me how you helped him deliver Star Bright's filly. You could have knocked me over with a feather when I heard she was ready to foal."

Rorie nodded, her heart warming with the memory. "Well, I

tried to get you up, fellow. It would have been easier to wake a dead man than to get you out of bed last night.''

Skip looked slightly embarrassed. ''Sorry about that, but I generally don't wake up too easily.'' As he spoke, he slipped his arm around the blonde girl's shoulders. ''Rorie, I want you to meet Kate Logan.''

''Hello, Kate.'' Rorie held out a hand and Kate shook it politely, smiling warmly up at her.

''Hello, Rorie,'' she said softly. ''Clay and Skip told me about your troubles. I hope everything turns out all right for you.''

''I'm sure it will. Do you live around here?'' Rorie already knew she was going to like her. At a closer glance, she saw that Kate was older than she'd first assumed. Maybe even close to her own age, which gave credence to Skip's comment about liking older, more mature women.

''I live pretty close,'' Kate explained. ''The Circle L is just down the road, only a few miles from here.''

''She's going to be living *with* us in the near future,'' Skip put in, looking fondly at Kate.

The young woman's cheeks reddened and she smiled shyly.

''Oh?'' Skip couldn't possibly mean he meant to marry her, Rorie thought. Good heavens, he was still in high school.

He must have read Rorie's look, and hurried to explain. ''Not me,'' he said with a short laugh. ''Kate is Clay's fiancée.''

Five

"**Y**ou and Clay are engaged," Rorie murmured as shock waves coursed through her blood. They stopped with a thud at her heart and spread out in ripples of dismay. She felt as if she'd been hit by a bombshell.

Somehow Rorie managed a smile, her outward composure unbroken. She was even able to offer her congratulations. To all appearances, nothing was wrong. No one would have known that those few simple words had destroyed a night she'd planned to treasure all her life.

"I hope you and Clay will be very happy," Rorie said—and she meant it. She'd just been introduced to Kate Logan, but already Rorie knew that this sweet friendly woman was exactly the kind of wife a man like Clay would need. They were perfect for each other.

"Skip's rushing things a little," Kate pointed out, but the glint of love in her eyes contradicted her words. "Clay hasn't even given me an engagement ring yet."

"But you and Clay have been talking about getting married, haven't you?" Skip pressed. "And you're crazy about him."

Kate blushed prettily. "I've loved Clay from the time I was ten years old. I wrote his name all over my books when I was in the fifth grade. Of course, Clay wouldn't have anything to do with me, not when he was a big important high-schooler. I was just the pesky little girl next door. It took a while for him to notice me—like ten years." She gave a small laugh. "We've been dating steadily for the past two years."

"But you and Clay *are* going to get married, right?" Skip continued, clearly wanting to prove his point.

"Eventually, but we haven't set a date, although I'm sure it'll be soon," Kate answered, casting a sharp look at Rorie.

The tightness that had gripped Rorie's throat eased and she managed to keep her smile intact. It was nearly impossible not to like Kate, but that didn't lessen the ache in Rorie's heart.

"The wedding's inevitable," Skip said offhandedly, "so I wasn't exaggerating when I said you were Clay's fiancée, now was I?"

Kate smiled. "I suppose not. We love each other, and have for years. We're just waiting for the right time." Her eyes continued to hold Rorie's, assessing her, but she didn't seem worried about competition.

Rorie supposed she should be pleased about that, at least.

"I was just taking Kate over to see Nightsong," Skip explained to Rorie.

"I actually came over to Elk Run to meet you," the other woman inserted. "Clay stopped by last night and told me about your car. I felt terrible for you. Your whole vacation's been ruined. You must be awfully upset."

"These things happen," Rorie said with a shrug. "Being upset isn't going to ship that part any faster. The only thing I can do is accept the facts."

Kate nodded, looking sympathetic. "Skip was about to show me the filly. You'll come with us, won't you?"

Rorie nodded, unable to excuse herself without sounding rude. If there'd been a way, she would have retreated, wanting only to lick her wounds in private. Instead, hoping she sounded more enthusiastic than she felt, she mumbled, "I was headed in that direction myself."

Skip led the way to the barn, which was alive with activity. Clay had explained that Elk Run employed five men full-time. Two men mucking out stalls paused when Skip and the women entered the building. Skip introduced Rorie and they touched the tips of their hats in greeting.

"I just don't understand Clay," Skip said as they approached the mare's stall. "When we bought Star Bright a few years back, all Clay could do was complain about that silly name. He even toyed with the idea of getting her registration changed."

"Star Bright's a perfectly good name, I think," Kate insisted, her sunny blue eyes intent on the newborn foal.

Nightsong was standing now on knobby, skinny legs that threatened to buckle, greedily feasting from her mother.

"Oh, she really is lovely, isn't she?" Kate whispered.

Rorie hadn't been able to stop looking at the filly from the moment they'd approached the stall. Finished with her breakfast, Nightsong gazed around, fascinated by everything she surveyed.

The young filly returned Rorie's look, not vacantly, but as though she recognised the woman who'd been there at her birth.

Rorie couldn't even identify all the emotions that wove their way around her heart. Some of these feelings were so new she couldn't put a name to them, but they gripped her heart and squeezed tight.

"What I can't understand," Skip muttered, "is why Clay would go and name her Nightsong. It doesn't sound the least bit like anything he'd ever come up with on his own, yet he insists he did."

"I know," Kate agreed, "but I'm glad, because the name suits her." She sighed. "Clay's always been so practical when it comes to names for his horses, but Nightsong has such a sweet romantic flavour, don't you think?"

Skip chuckled. "You know what Clay thinks about romance, and that makes it all the more confusing. But Nightsong she is, and she's bound to bring us a pretty penny in a year or two. Her father was a Polish Arabian, and with Star Bright's bloodlines Nightsong will command big bucks as a National Show Horse."

"Skip." Clay's curt voice interrupted them. He strode from the arena leading a bay mare. The horse's coat gleamed with sweat, turning its colour the shade of an oak leaf in autumn. The stableman approached to take the reins. Then Clay removed his hat, wiping his brow with his forearm, and Rorie noticed the now-grimy bandage she'd applied last night. No, this morning.

She gazed hungrily at his sun-bronzed face, a face that revealed more than a hint of impatience. The carved lines around his mouth were etched deep with poorly disguised regrets. Rorie recognised them, even if the others didn't.

Clay stopped short when he saw Kate, his eyes narrowing.

"Morning, Kate."

"Hello, Clay."

Then his gaze moved, slowly and reluctantly, to Rorie. The remorse she'd already sensed in him seemed to shout at her now.

"I hope you slept well," was all he said to her.

"Fine." She detected a tautness along his jaw line and decided he was probably concerned that she would do or say something to embarrass him in front of his fiancée. Rorie wouldn't, but not because she was worried about him. Her sense of fair play wouldn't allow her to hurt Kate, who so obviously adored this man.

"We're just admiring Nightsong," Kate explained, her expression tender as she gazed up at him.

"We were just talking about her, and I can't understand why you'd name her something like that," Skip said, his mouth twitching with barely suppressed laughter. "You like names like Brutus and Firepower, but Nightsong? Really, Clay, I think you may be going soft on us." Thinking himself particularly funny, Skip chuckled and added, "I suppose that's what love does to a man."

Kate's lashes brushed against the high arch of her cheek and she smiled, her pleasure so keen it was like a physical touch.

"Didn't I ask you to water the horses several hours ago?" Clay asked in a tone that could have chipped rock.

"Yes, but—"

"Then kindly see to it. The farrier will be here any minute."

The humour drained out of Skip's eyes; he was clearly upset by Clay's anger. His eyes moved from his brother to the two women and then back to Clay again. Hot colour rose from his neck and invaded his face. "All right," he muttered. "Excuse me for living." Then he stormed out of the barn, slapping his hat against his thigh in an outburst of anger.

Kate waited until Skip was out of the barn. "Clay, what's wrong?"

"He should have done what I told him long before now. Those horses in the pasture are thirsty because of his incompetence."

"I'm the one you should be angry with, not Skip." Kate's voice was contrite. "I should never have stopped in this way without calling first, but I...wanted to meet Rorie."

"You've only been here a few minutes," Clay insisted, his anger in check now. "Skip had plenty of time to complete his chores before you arrived."

Rorie tossed invisible daggers at Clay, angered at him for taking his irritation out on his younger brother. Skip had introduced her to Clay's fiancée. That was what really troubled him if he'd been willing to admit it—which he obviously wasn't.

"We came here to see Nightsong," Kate continued. "I'm glad you named her that, no matter what Skip thinks." She wrapped her arm around his waist, and rested her head against his broad chest. "He was just teasing you and you know how he loves to do that."

Clay gave her an absent smile, but his gaze settled with disturbing ease on Rorie. She met his eyes boldly, denying the emotions churning furiously in her stomach. The plea for patience and understanding he sent her was so clear, so obvious, that Rorie wondered how anyone seeing it wouldn't know what was happening.

As though she'd suddenly remembered something, Kate dropped her arm and hurriedly glanced at her watch. She hesitated and then groaned. "I promised Dad I'd meet him at lunch today. He's getting together with the other Town Council members in one of those horribly boring meetings. He needs me for an excuse to get away." She stopped abruptly, a chagrined expression on her face. "I guess that explains how informal everything is in Nightingale, doesn't it, Rorie?"

"The town seems to be doing very well." She didn't know if that was true or not, but it sounded good.

"He just hates these things, but he likes the prestige of being a Council member—something I tease him about."

"I'll walk you to your car," Clay offered.

"Oh, there's no need. You're busy. Besides I wanted to talk to Rorie and arrange to meet her tomorrow and show her around town. I certainly hope you remembered to invite her to the Grange dance tomorrow night. I'm sure Luke would be willing to escort her."

"Oh, I couldn't possibly intrude," Rorie blurted.

"Nonsense, you'd be more than welcome. And don't fret about having the right kind of clothes for a square dance, either, because I've got more outfits than I know what to do with. We're about the same size," Kate said, eyeing her. "Perhaps you're a little taller, but not so much that you couldn't wear my skirts."

Rorie smiled blandly, realising it wouldn't do any good to decline the invitation. But good heavens, square dancing? Her?

"Knowing you and Skip," Kate chastised Clay, "poor Rorie will be stuck on Elk Run for the next four days bored out of her mind. The least I can do is see she's entertained."

"That's thoughtful of you," said Rorie, thinking that the sooner she got back on the road, the safer her heart would be, and if Kate Logan offered to help her kill time, then all the better.

"I thought I'd give you a tour of our little town in the morning," Kate went on. "It's small, but the people are friendly."

"I'd love to see Nightingale."

"Clay." The brusque voice of a farmhand interrupted them. "Could you come here a minute?"

Clay glanced at the man and nodded. "I'd better find out what Don needs," he said quietly. As he met Rorie's eyes, a speculative look flashed into his own.

She nearly flinched, wondering what emotion her face had betrayed. From the minute Clay had walked into the barn, she'd been careful to school her expression, not wanting him to read anything into her words or actions. She'd tried to look cool and unconcerned, as if the night they'd shared had never happened.

"You two will have to excuse me." Weary amusement turned up the corners of his mouth and Rorie realised he'd readily seen through her guise.

"Of course," Kate said. "I'll see you later, sweetheart."

Clay nodded abruptly and departed with firm purposeful strides.

Kate started walking towards the yard. Rorie followed, eager to escape the barn and all the memories associated with it.

"Clay told us you're a librarian," Kate said when she reached the Ford parked in the curving driveway. "If you want, I can take you to our library. We built a new one last year and we're rather proud of it. I know it's small compared to where you probably work, but I think you'll like what we've done."

"I'd love to see it." Libraries were often the heart of a community, and if the good citizens of Nightingale had seen fit to pay tax dollars to upgrade theirs, then it was apparent they shared Rorie's love of literature.

"I'll pick you up around ten tomorrow, if that's convenient?"

"That'd be fine."

"Plan on spending the afternoon with me and we'll meet Clay and Skip at the dance later."

Rorie agreed, although her enthusiasm was decidedly low. How Dan would tease her if he ever discovered she'd spent part of her vacation square dancing with the folks at the Grange.

"'Bye for now," Kate said.

"'Bye," Rorie murmured, waving. She stood in the yard until Kate's car was out of sight. Not knowing what else to do, she wandered back into the house, where Mary was busy with preparations for lunch.

"Can I help?" she asked.

In response, Mary scurried to a drawer and once again handed her a peeler. Rorie started carefully whittling away at a firm red apple she'd scooped from a large bowlful of them.

"I don't suppose you know anything about cooking?" Mary demanded, pointing her own peeler at Rorie.

"I've managed to keep from starving the last several years," she retorted idly.

The merest hint of amusement flashed into the older woman's

weathered face. "If I was judging your talents in the kitchen on looks alone, I think you'd starve a man to death within a week."

Despite her glum spirits, Rorie laughed. "If you're telling me you think I'm thin, watch out, Mary, because I'm likely to throw my arms around your neck and kiss you."

The other woman chanced a grin at that. A few peaceful minutes passed while they pared apple after apple.

"I got a call from my sister," Mary said hesitantly, her eyes darting to Rorie, then back to her task. "She's coming as far as Riversdale and wants to know if I can drive over and see her. She's only going to be in Oregon one day."

This was the most Mary had said to Rorie since her arrival. The realisation pleased her. The older woman was lowering her guard and extending a friendly hand.

"I'd like to visit with my sister."

"I certainly think you should." It took Rorie another minute to figure out where Mary was directing this meandering conversation. Then suddenly she understood. "Oh, you're looking for someone to do the cooking while you're away."

Mary shrugged as if it didn't concern her one way or the other. "Just for one meal, two nights from now. I could manage lunch for the hands before I leave. It's the evening meal I'm worried about. There's only Clay and Skip who need to be fed—the other men go home in the evenings."

"Well, relax, because I'm sure I can manage one dinner without killing off the menfolk."

"You're sure?"

Mary was so completely serious that Rorie laughed outright. "Since my abilities do seem to worry you, how would you feel if I invited Kate Logan over to help?"

Mary nodded and sighed. "I'd rest easier."

Rorie stayed in the kitchen until the lunch dishes had been washed and put away. Mary thanked her for the help, then went into her bedroom to watch her daily soap operas.

Feeling a little lost, Rorie wandered outside and into the stable. Since Clay had already shown her the computer, she decided to spend the afternoon working in his office.

The area was deserted, which went some distance towards re-assuring her—but then, she'd assumed it would be. From what she'd observed, a stud farm was a busy place and Clay was bound to be occupied elsewhere. That suited Rorie just fine. She hoped to avoid him as much as possible. In three days she'd be out of his life, leaving hardly a trace, and that was the way she wanted it.

Rorie sat typing in data for about an hour before her neck and shoulders began to develop a cramp. She paused, flexing her muscles, then rotated her head to relieve the building tightness.

"How long have you been in here?"

The rough male voice behind her startled Rorie. Her hand flew to her heart and she expelled a shaky breath. "Clay! Good heavens, you frightened me."

"How long?" he repeated.

"An hour or so." She glanced at her watch and nodded.

Clay advanced a step toward her, his mouth a thin line of impatience. "I suppose you're looking for an apology."

Rorie didn't answer. She'd learned not to expect anything from him.

"I'm here to tell you right now that you're not going to get one," he finished gruffly.

Six

"You don't owe me anything, Clay," Rorie said, struggling to make her voice light. Clay looked driven to the limits of exhaustion. Dark shadows had formed beneath his eyes and fatigue lines fanned out from their corners. His shoulders sagged slightly, as if the weight he carried was more than he could bear. He studied her wearily, then turned away from her, stalking to the other side of the office. His shoulders heaved as he drew in a shuddering breath.

"I know I should feel some regrets, but God help me, Rorie, I don't."

"Clay, listen…"

He turned to face her then, and drove his fingers into his hair with such force Rorie winced. "I'd like to explain about Kate and me."

"No." The last thing Rorie wanted was to be forced to listen to his explanations or excuses. She didn't have a lot of room to be judgemental. She herself had, after all, been dating a man steadily for the past few months. "Don't. Please don't say anything. It isn't necessary."

He ignored her request. "Kate and I have known each other all our lives."

"Clay, stop." She pushed out the chair and stood up, wanting only to escape, and knowing she couldn't.

"For the last two years, it's been understood by everyone around us that Kate and I would eventually get married. I didn't even question the right or wrong of it, just calmly accepted the fact. A man needs someone to share his life."

"Kate will make you a wonderful wife," she said forcefully, feeling both disillusioned and indignant, but she refused to let him know how much his small indiscretion had hurt her. "If you owe anyone an apology, it's Kate, not me."

His responding frown was brooding and dark. "I know." He drew his fingers across his eyes, and she could feel his exhaustion from the other side of the room. "The last thing in the world I want is to hurt Kate."

"Then don't."

He stared at her, and Rorie forced herself to send him a smile, although she feared it was more flippant than reassuring. "There's no reason for Kate to know. What good would it do? She'd only end up feeling betrayed. Last night was a tiny impropriety and best forgotten, don't you agree?" Walking seemed to help, and Rorie paced the office, her fingers brushing the stack of books and papers on his cluttered desk.

"I don't know what's best any more," Clay admitted quietly.

"I do," Rorie said with unwavering confidence, still struggling to make light of the incident. "Think about it, Clay. We were alone together for hours—we shared something beautiful with Star Bright and...her foal. And we shared a few stolen kisses under the stars. If anything's to blame, I think it should be the moonlight. We're strangers, Clay. You don't know me and I don't know you." Afraid to look him directly in the eye, Rorie lowered her gaze and waited, breathless, for his next words.

"So it was the moonlight?" His voice was hoarse and painfully raw.

"Of course," she lied. "What else could it have been?"

"Yes, what else could it have been?" he echoed, then turned and walked out of the office.

It suddenly seemed as though the room's light had dimmed. Rorie felt so weak, she sank into the chair, shocked by how deeply the encounter had disturbed her.

Typing proved to be a distraction and Rorie left the office a couple of hours later with a feeling of accomplishment. She'd been able to enter several time-consuming pages of data into the computer system. The routine mechanical work was a relief because it didn't give her time to think. Sorting through her thoughts could be dangerous.

The kitchen smelled of roasting beef and simmering apple crisp when Rorie let herself in the back door. It was an oddly pleasant combination of scents. Mary was nowhere to be seen.

While she remembered, Rorie reached for the telephone book and dialled the number listed for the garage in Riversdale.

"Hello," she said abruptly when a gruff male voice answered. "This is Rorie Campbell...the woman with the broken water pump. The one in Nightingale."

"Yeah, Miss Campbell, what can I do for you?"

"I just wanted to be sure there wasn't any problem in ordering the part. I don't know if Clay...Mr Franklin told you, but I'm more or less stuck here until the car's repaired. I'd like to get back on the road as soon as possible—I'm sure you understand."

"Lady, I can't make that water pump come any faster than what it already is."

"I know, but I just wanted to check and be sure you'd been able to order one."

"It's on its way, at least that's what the guy in Los Angeles told me. They're shipping it by overnight freight to Portland. I've arranged for a man to pick it up the following day, but it's going to take him some time to get it to me."

"But that's only three days."

"You called too late yesterday for me to phone the order in. Lady, there's only so much I can do."

"I know, I'm sorry if I sound impatient."

"The whole world's impatient. Listen, I'll let you know the minute it arrives."

She sighed. "Thanks, I'd appreciate it."

"Clay got your car here without a hitch, so you don't need to worry about that—he saved you a bundle on towing charges. Shipping costs and long-distance phone bills are going to be plenty high, though."

Rorie hadn't even noticed that Dan's shiny sports car wasn't in the yard where Skip had originally left it. "So you'll be calling me within the next day or two?" she asked, trying to hide the anxiety in her voice. And trying not to think about the state of her finances, already depleted by this disastrous vacation.

"Right. I'll call as soon as it comes in."

"Thank you. I appreciate it more than I can say."

"No problem," the mechanic muttered, obviously eager to end their conversation.

When the call was finished, Rorie toyed with the idea of phoning Dan next. She'd been half expecting to hear from him, since she'd left the Franklins' number with his secretary the day before. He hadn't phoned her back. But there wasn't anything new to tell him, so she decided not to call a second time.

Hesitantly Rorie replaced the telephone receiver, pleased that everything was under control—everything except her heart.

* * *

Dinner that evening was a strained affair. If it hadn't been for Skip, who seemed oblivious to the tension between her and Clay, Rorie didn't think she could have endured it. Clay hardly said a word throughout the meal. But Skip seemed more than eager to carry the conversation and Rorie did her best to lighten the mood, wondering all the time whether Clay saw through her façade.

"While you're here, Rorie," Skip said with a sudden burst of enthusiasm, "you should think about learning to ride."

"No, thank you," she said pointedly, holding up her hand, as though fending off the suggestion. A mere introduction to King and Hercules was as far as she was willing to go.

"Rain Magic would suit you nicely."

"Rain Magic?"

"That's a silly name Kate thought up, and Clay went along with it," Skip explained. "He's gentle, but smart—the gelding I mean, not Clay." The younger Franklin needled his older brother, then laughed heartily at his own attempt at humour.

Clay smiled, but Rorie wasn't fooled; he hadn't been amused by the joke, nor, she suspected, was he pleased by the reference to Kate.

"No thanks, Skip," she said, before the subject could get out of control. "I'm really not interested." There, that said it plain enough.

"Are you afraid?"

"A little," she admitted truthfully. "I prefer all my horses on a merry-go-around, thank you. I'm a city girl, remember?"

"But even girls from San Francisco have been known to climb on the back of a horse. It'll be good for you, Rorie. Trust me—it's time to broaden your horizons."

"Thanks, but no thanks," she told him, emphasising her point by biting down on a crisp carrot stick. The loud crunch added an exclamation point to her words.

"Rorie, I insist. You aren't going to get hurt—I wouldn't let that happen, and Rain Magic is as gentle as they come. In fact—" he wiggled his eyebrows up and down several times "—if you want, we can ride double until you feel more secure."

Rorie laughed. "Skip, honestly."

"All right, you can ride alone, and I'll lead you around in a circle. For as long as you want."

Rorie shook her head and, amused at the mental picture that scenario presented, laughed again.

"Leave it," Clay said with sudden sharpness. "If Rorie doesn't want to ride, that should be the end of it."

Skip's shocked gaze flew from Rorie to his brother. "I was just having a little fun, Clay."

His older brother gripped his water goblet so hard that Rorie feared the glass would shatter. "Enough is enough. She said she wasn't interested in learning to ride and that should be the end of it."

The astounded look left Skip's features, but his eyes narrowed and he stiffened his shoulders in a display of righteous indignation. "What's with you, Clay?" he shouted. "You've been acting like a wounded bear all day, barking and biting at everyone. Who declared you king of the universe all of a sudden?"

"If you'll excuse me, I'll bring in the apple crisp," Rorie said, and hurriedly rose to her feet, not wanting to be caught in the crossfire between the two brothers. Whatever they had to say wasn't meant for her ears.

The exchange that followed ended quickly, Rorie noted gratefully from inside the kitchen. Their voices were raised and then there was a sudden hush followed by laughter. Rorie relaxed and picked up the dessert, carrying it into the dining room along with a carton of vanilla ice cream.

"I apologise, Rorie," Clay said soberly when she reentered the room. "Skip's right, I've been cross and unreasonable all day. I hope my sour mood hasn't ruined your dinner."

"Of course not," she murmured, offering him a smile.

Clay stood up to serve the dessert dishes, spooning generous helpings of apple crisp and ice cream in each bowl.

Skip chattered aimlessly, commenting on one subject and then bouncing to another without any logical connection, his thoughts darting this way and that.

"What time are you going over to Kate's tonight?" he asked Clay casually.

"I won't be. She's got some meeting with the women's group from the Grange. They're doing decorations for the dance tomorrow night."

"Now that you mention it, I seem to remember Kate saying something about being busy tonight, too." Without any pause he turned to Rorie. "You'll be coming, I hope. The Grange is putting on a square dance—the biggest one of the year and they usually do it up good."

"Kate already invited me. I'll be going with her," Rorie explained, although she hadn't the slightest idea how to square dance. Generally she enjoyed dancing although she hadn't done any for several months because Dan wasn't keen on it.

"You could drive there with us if you wanted," Skip offered. "I'd kinda like to walk in there with you on my arm. I know you'd cause quite a stir with the men, especially with Luke Rivers—he's the foreman at the Logan place. Most girls go all goo-goo-eyed over him."

Clay's spoon clanged loudly against the side of his glass dish and he murmured an apology.

"I'm sorry, Skip," Rorie said gently, "I already told Kate I'd drive over with her."

"Darn," Skip muttered.

The rest of the meal was completed in silence. Once, when Rorie happened to glance up, her gaze collided with Clay's. Her heart felt as though it might hammer its way out of her chest. She was oppressively aware of the chemistry between them. It simmered in Rorie's veins and she could tell that Clay felt everything she did. Throughout dinner, she'd been all too conscious of the swift stolen glances Clay had sent in her direction. She sent a few of her own, though she'd tried hard not to. But it was impossible to be in the same room with this man and not react to him.

A thousand times in the next couple of hours, Rorie told herself everything would be fine as soon as she could leave. Life would return to normal then.

After the dishes were finished, Skip challenged her to a game of cribbage, and grateful for the escape Rorie accepted. Skip sat with his back to his brother, and every time Rorie played her hand, she found her gaze wandering across the room to where Clay sat reading. To all outward appearances, he was relaxed and comfortable, but she knew he felt as tense as she did. She knew he was equally aware of the electricity that sparked between them.

Rorie's fingers shook as she counted out her cards.

"Fifteen eight," Skip corrected. "You forgot two points."

Her eyes fell to the extra ten, and she blinked. "I guess I did."

Skip heaved a sigh. "I don't think your mind's on the game tonight."

"I guess not," she admitted wryly. "If you don't mind, I think I'll head up to bed." She offered him an apologetic smile and reached for her coffee cup. Skip was right. Her mind hadn't been on the game at all. Her thoughts had been centred on a man who owed his loyalties to another woman—a woman whose roots were intricately bound with his. A woman Rorie had liked and respected from the moment they met.

Feeling depressed, she bade the two men good night and carried her cup into the kitchen. Dutifully, she rinsed it out and set it beside the sink, but when she turned around Clay was standing in the doorway, blocking her exit.

"Where's Skip?" she asked a little breathlessly. Heat seemed to throb between them and she retreated a step in a futile effort to escape.

"He went upstairs."

She blinked and faked a yawn. "I was headed in that direction myself."

Clay buried one hand in his jeans pocket. "Do you know what happened tonight at dinner?"

Not finding her voice, Rorie shook her head.

"I was jealous," he said between clenched teeth. "You were laughing and joking with Skip and I wanted it to be me your eyes were shining for. Me. No one else." He stopped abruptly and shook his head. "Jealous of a seventeen-year-old boy...I can't believe it myself."

Seven

Not knowing what to expect, Rorie decided to wear a dress for her outing with Kate Logan. Although she rose early, both Skip and Clay had eaten breakfast and left the house by the time she came downstairs. Which was just as well, Rorie thought.

Mary stood at the stove, frying chunks of beef for a luncheon stew. "I spoke to Clay about your cooking dinner later this week. He says that'll be fine if you're still around, but the way he sees it, you'll be headed north within a day or two."

Rorie poured herself a cup of coffee. "I'll be happy to do it if I'm here. Otherwise, I'm sure Kate Logan would be more than pleased."

Mary turned to face her, mouth open as if to comment. Instead her eyes widened in appreciation. "My, my, you look pretty enough to hog-tie a man's heart."

"Thank you, Mary," Rorie answered, grinning.

"I suppose you got yourself a sweetheart back there in San Francisco?" she asked, watching her closely. "A pretty girl like you is bound to attract plenty of men."

Rorie paused to consider her answer. She thought briefly about mentioning Dan, but quickly decided against it. She'd planned this separation to gain a perspective on their relationship. And within hours of arriving at Elk Run, Rorie had found her answer. Dan would always be a special friend—but nothing more.

"The question shouldn't require a week's thought," Mary grumbled, stirring the large pot of simmering beef.

"Sorry...I was just mulling something over."

"Then there is someone special?"

She shook her head lightly. "No."

The answer didn't seem to please Mary, because she frowned. "When did you say that fancy car of yours was going to be fixed?"

The abrupt question caught Rorie by surprise. Mary was openly concerned about the attraction between her and Clay. The housekeeper, who probably knew Clay better than anyone, clearly wasn't blind to what had been happening—and just as clearly didn't like it.

"The mechanic in Riversdale said it should be finished the day after tomorrow if all goes well."

"Good!" Mary proclaimed with a fierce nod, then turned back to her stew.

Rorie couldn't help grinning at the older woman's astuteness. Mary was telling her that the sooner she was off Elk Run the better for everyone concerned. In truth, Rorie couldn't agree with her more.

Kate Logan arrived promptly at ten. She wore tight-fitting jeans, red checked western shirt and a white silk scarf knotted at her throat. Her long honey-coloured hair was woven into thick braids that fell over her shoulders. At first glance, Kate looked closer to sixteen than the twenty-four Rorie knew her to be.

Kate greeted her with a warm smile. "Rorie, there wasn't any need to wear something so nice. I should have told you to dress casually."

Rorie's shoulders slumped. "I brought along more dresses than jeans. Am I really overdressed? I could change," she said hesitantly.

"Oh, no, you look fine...more than fine." But for the first time, Kate sounded worried. The doubt that played across her features would have been amusing if Rorie hadn't already been suffering from such a potent bout of guilt. It was all too clear that Kate viewed Rorie as a threat.

If Clay Franklin had chosen that moment to walk into the kitchen, Rorie would have turned on him, calling him every foul name she could think of. She was furious with him for doing this to her—and to Kate.

"I wear a lot of dresses because of my job at the library," Rorie rushed to explain. "I also date quite a bit. I've been seeing someone—Dan Rogers—for months now. In fact, it's his car I was driving."

"You're dating someone special?" Kate asked, looking relieved.

"Yes, Dan and I've been going together for several months."

Mary coughed noisily and threw Rorie an accusing glare; Rorie ignored her. "Shouldn't we be leaving?"

"Oh, sure, any time you're ready." When they were outside, Kate turned to face Rorie. Looking uncomfortable, she slipped her hands into the back pockets of her jeans. "I've embarrassed you and I apologise. I didn't mean to imply that I didn't trust you and Clay."

"There's no need for an apology, really. I'm sure I wouldn't feel any differently if Clay were my fiancé."

Kate shook her head. "But I feel as if I *should* apologise. I'm not going to be the kind of wife Clay wants if I can't trust him around a pretty girl once in a while."

Had the earth cracked open just then, Rorie would gladly have fallen in. That had to be better than looking at Kate and feeling the things she did about Clay Franklin.

"Don't have any worries about me," she said lightly, dismissing the issue as nonchalantly as she could. "I'll be out of everyone's hair in a day or two."

"Oh, Rorie, please, I don't mean for you to rush off because I had a silly attack of jealousy. Now I feel terrible."

"Don't, please. I have to leave...I want to leave. My vacation's on hold until I can get my car repaired and there's so much I'd planned to see and do." She dug in her bag for a brochure she'd been carrying with her. "Have you ever been up to Victoria on Vancouver Island?"

"Once, but I was only five, much too young to remember much of anything," Kate told her, scanning the pamphlet. "This does sound like a fun trip. It sounds like just the place Clay and I should honeymoon."

"It'd be perfect for that," Rorie murmured. Her heart constricted on a sudden flash of pain, but she ruthlessly forced down her emotions, praying Kate hadn't noticed. "I'm looking forward to visiting Canada. By the way, Mary's driving to Riversdale to visit her sister later in the week. She's asked me to take charge of cooking dinner if I'm still here. Would you like to help? We could have a good time and get to know each other better."

"Oh, that sounds great." Kate slipped her arm around Rorie's trim waist and gave her an enthusiastic squeeze. "Thank you, Rorie. I know you're trying to reassure me, and I appreciate it."

That had been exactly Rorie's intent.

"It probably sounds selfish," Kate continued, "but I'm glad your car broke down when it did. Without any difficulty at all, I can see us becoming the best of friends."

Rorie could, too, but it only added to her growing sense of uneasiness.

* * *

Nightingale was a sleepy kind of town. Businesses lined both sides of Main Street, with a beauty shop, an insurance agency, Nellie's Café and a service station on one side, a grocery store, pharmacy and five-and-dime on the other. Rorie had the impression that things happened in their own good time in Nightingale. Few places could have been more unlike San Francisco, where people always seemed to be rushing, always scurrying from one spot to another. Here, no one seemed to feel any need to bustle. It was as though this town, with its population of fifteen hundred, existed in a time warp. Rorie found the relaxed pace unexpectedly pleasant.

"The library is across from the high school on Maple Street," Kate explained as she parked her Ford on Main. "That way, students have easy access to the building."

Rorie climbed out of the car, automatically pressing down the door lock.

"You don't need to do that here. There hasn't been a vehicle stolen in...oh, at least twenty years."

Rorie's eyes must have revealed her surprise, because Kate added, "Actually, we had trouble passing our last bond issue for a new patrol car. People couldn't see the need since there hasn't been a felony committed here in over two years. About the worst thing that goes on is when Harry Ackerman gets drunk. That happens once or twice a year and he's arrested for disturbing the peace." She paused and grinned sheepishly. "He sings old love songs to Nellie at the top of his lungs in front of the café. They were apparently sweet on each other a long time back. Nellie married someone else and Harry never got over the loss of his one true love."

Looping the strap of her bag over her shoulder, Rorie looked around the quiet streets.

"The fire and police station are in the same building," Kate pointed out next. "And the one really nice restaurant is on Oak. If you want, we could have lunch there."

"Only if you let me treat."

"I wouldn't hear of it," Kate insisted with a shake of her head that sent her braids flying. "You're my guest."

Rorie decided not to argue, asking another question instead. "Where do the ranchers get their supplies?" It seemed to her that type of store would do a thriving business, yet she hadn't seen one.

"At Garner's Feed and Supply. It's on the outskirts of town— I'll take you past on the way out. In fact, we should take a driving tour so you can see a little more of the town. Main Street is only a small part of Nightingale.''

By the time Kate and Rorie walked over to Maple and the library, Rorie's head was swimming with the names of all the people Kate had insisted on introducing. It seemed that everyone had heard about her car problems and was eager to talk to her. Several mentioned the Grange dance that night and said they'd be looking for her there.

''You're really going to be impressed with the library,'' Kate promised as they walked the two streets over to Maple. ''Dad and the others worked hard to get the levy passed so we could build it. People here tend to be tightfisted. Dad says they squeeze a nickel so hard, the buffalo belches.''

Rorie laughed outright at that.

The library was the largest building in town, a sprawling one-storey structure with lots of windows. The hours were posted on the double glass doors, and Rorie noted that the library wouldn't open until the middle of the afternoon, still several hours away.

''It doesn't look open,'' she said, disappointed.

''Oh, don't worry, I've got a key. All the volunteers do.'' Kate rummaged in her bag and took out a large key ring. She opened the door, pushing it wide for Rorie to enter first.

''Mrs Halldorfson retired last year, a month after the building was finished,'' Kate told her, flipping on the lights, ''and the town's budget wouldn't stretch to hire a new full-time librarian. So several parents and teachers are taking turns volunteering. We've got a workable schedule, unless someone goes on vacation, which, I hate to admit, has been happening all summer.''

''You don't have a full-time librarian?'' Rorie couldn't disguise her astonishment. ''Why go to all the trouble and expense of building a modern facility if you can't afford a librarian?''

''You'll have to ask Town Council that,'' Kate returned, shrugging. ''It doesn't make much sense, does it? But you see, Mrs. Halldorfson was only part-time and the Council seems to think that's what her replacement should be.''

''That doesn't make sense, either.''

''Especially when you consider that the new library is twice the size of the old one.''

Rorie had to bite her tongue to keep from saying more. But she was appalled at the waste, the missed opportunities.

''We've been advertising for months for a part-time librarian, but so far we haven't found anyone interested. Not that I blame them—one look at the size of the job and no one wants to tackle it alone.''

''A library is more than a place to check books in and out,'' Rorie insisted, gesturing dramatically. Her voice rose despite herself. This was an issue close to her heart, and polite silence was practically impossible. ''A library can be the heart of a community. It can be a place for classes, community services, all kinds of things. Don't non-profit organisations use it for meetings?''

''I'm afraid not,'' Kate answered. ''Everyone gets together at Nellie's when there's any kind of meeting. Nellie serves great pies,'' she added, as though that explained everything.

Realising that she'd climbed on to her soapbox, Rorie dropped her hands and shrugged. ''It's a very nice building, Kate, and you have every reason to be proud. I didn't mean to sound so righteous.''

''But you're absolutely correct,'' Kate said thoughtfully. ''We're not using the library to its full potential, are we? Volunteers can only do so much. As it is, the library's only open three afternoons a week.'' She sighed expressively. ''To be honest, I think Dad and the other members of the Town Council are expecting Mrs. Halldorfson to come back in the fall, but that's unfair to her. She's served the community for over twenty years. She deserves to retire in peace without being blackmailed into coming back because we can't find a replacement.''

''Well, I hope you find someone soon.''

''I hope so, too,'' Kate murmured.

They ate a leisurely lunch, and as she'd promised, Kate gave Rorie a brief tour of the town. After pointing out several churches, the elementary school where she taught second grade and some of the nicer homes on the hill, Kate ended the tour on the outskirts of town near Garner's Feed and Supply.

''Luke's here,'' Kate explained, easing into the parking place next to a dusty pickup truck.

''Luke?''

''Our foreman. I don't know what Dad would do without him. He runs the ranch and has for years—ever since I was in high school. Dad's retirement age now, and he's more than willing to let Luke take charge of things.''

Kate got out of the car and leaned against the front fender, crossing her arms over her chest. Not knowing what else to do, Rorie joined her there.

"He'll be out in a minute," Kate explained.

True to her word a tall, deeply tanned man appeared with a sack of grain slung over his shoulder. His eyes were so dark they gleamed like onyx, taking in everything around him, but revealing little of his own thoughts. His strong square chin was balanced by a high intelligent brow. He was lean and muscular and strikingly handsome.

"Need any help, stranger?" Kate asked with a light laugh.

"You offering?"

"Nope."

Luke chuckled. "I thought not. You wouldn't want to ruin those pretty nails of yours now, would you?"

"I didn't stop by to be insulted by you," Kate chastised, clearly enjoying the exchange. "I wanted you to meet Rorie Campbell— she's the one Clay was telling us about the other night, whose car broke down."

"I remember." For the first time the foreman's gaze drifted from Kate. He tossed the sack of grain into the back of the truck and used his teeth to tug his glove free from his right hand. Then he presented his long calloused fingers to Rorie. "Pleased to meet you, ma'am."

"The pleasure's mine." Rorie remembered where she'd heard the name. Skip had mentioned Luke Rivers when he'd told her about the Grange square dance. He'd said something about all the girls being attracted to the Logan foreman. Rorie could understand why.

They exchanged a brief handshake before Luke's attention slid back to Kate. His eyes softened perceptibly.

"Luke's like a brother to me," Kate said fondly.

He frowned at that, but didn't comment.

"We're going to let you escort us to the dance tonight," she informed him.

"What about Clay?"

"Oh, he'll be by. I thought the four of us could go over together."

Rorie wasn't fooled. Kate was setting her up with Luke, who didn't look any too pleased at having his evening arranged for him.

"Kate, listen," she began, "I'd really rather skip the dance tonight. I've never done square dancing in my life—"

"That doesn't matter," Kate interrupted. "Luke will be glad to show you. Won't you, Luke?"

"Sure," he mumbled, with the enthusiasm of a man offered the choice between hanging and a firing squad.

"Honestly, Luke!" Kate gave an embarrassed laugh.

"Listen," Rorie said quickly. "It's obvious Luke has his own plans for tonight. I don't want to intrude—"

He surprised her by turning towards her, his eyes searching hers. "I'd be happy to escort you, Rorie."

"I'm likely to step all over your toes...I really think I'd do best to sit the whole thing out."

"Nonsense," Kate cried. "Luke won't let you do that and neither will I!"

"We'll have a good time," the foreman insisted. "Leave everything to me."

Rorie nodded, although she felt little enthusiasm.

A moment of awkward silence fell over the trio. "Well, I suppose I should get Rorie back to Circle L and see about finding her a dress," Kate said, smiling. She playfully tossed her car keys into the air and caught them deftly.

Luke tipped his hat when they both returned to the car. Rorie didn't mention his name until they were back on the road.

"He really is attractive, isn't he?" she asked, closely watching Kate.

The other woman nodded eagerly. "It surprises me that he hasn't married. There are plenty of girls around Nightingale who would be more than willing, believe me. At every Grange dance, the ladies flirt with him like crazy. I love to tease him about it—he really hates that. But I wish Luke *would* get married—I don't like the idea of him living his life alone. It's time he thought about settling down and starting a family. He was thirty last month, but the last time I mentioned it to him, he nearly bit my head off."

Rorie nibbled on her lower lip. She inhaled a deep breath and released it slowly. Her guess was that Luke had his heart set on someone special, and that someone was engaged to another man. God help him, Rorie thought. She knew exactly how he felt.

The music was already playing by the time Luke, Kate and Rorie arrived at the Grange Hall in Luke's ten-year-old four-door sedan. Rorie tried to force some enthusiasm for this outing, but had little success. She hadn't exchanged more than a few words with the

Logan foreman during the entire drive. He, apparently, didn't like this arranged-date business any better than she did. But they were stuck with each other, and Rorie at least was determined to make the best of it.

They entered the hall and were greeted with the cheery sounds of the male caller:

Rope the cow, brand the calf
Swing your sweetheart, once and a half...

Rorie hadn't known what to expect, but she was surprised by the smooth-stepping, smartly dressed dancers who twirled around the floor following the caller's directions. She felt more daunted than ever by the evening ahead of her. And to worsen matters, Kate had insisted Rorie borrow one of her outfits. Although Rorie liked the bright blue colours of the western skirt and matching blouse, she felt awkward and self-conscious in the billowing skirts.

The Grange itself was bigger than Rorie had anticipated. On the stage stood the caller and several fiddlers. Refreshment tables lined one wall and the polished dance floor was so crowded Rorie found it a wonder that anyone could move without bumping into others. The entire meeting hall was alive with energy and music, and despite herself, she felt her mood lift. Her toes started tapping out rhythms almost of their own accord. Given time, she knew she'd be out there, too, joining the vibrant, laughing dancers. It was unavoidable, anyway. She knew Kate, Clay and Skip weren't going to allow her to sit sedately in the background and watch.

"Oh, my feet are moving already," Kate cried, squirming with eagerness. Clay smiled indulgently, tucked his arm around her waist and the two of them stepped onto the dance floor. He glanced back once at Rorie, before a circle of eight opened up to admit them.

"Shall we?" Luke asked, eyeing the dance floor.

He didn't sound too enthusiastic and Rorie didn't blame him. "Would it be all right if we sat out the first couple of dances?" she asked. "I'd like to get more into the swing of things."

"No problem."

Luke looked almost grateful for the respite, which didn't lend Rorie much confidence. No doubt he assumed this city slicker was going to make a fool of herself and him—and she probably would. When he escorted her to the row of chairs, Rorie made the mistake of sitting down. Instantly her skirts leapt up into her face. Embarrassed, she pushed them down, then tucked the material under her thighs in an effort to tame the layers of stiff petticoats.

"Hello, Luke." A pretty blonde with sparkling blue eyes sauntered over. "I didn't know if you'd show tonight or not. Glad you did."

"Betty Hammond, this is Rorie Campbell."

Rorie nodded. "It's nice to meet you, Betty."

"Oh, I heard about you at the drugstore yesterday. You're the gal with the broken-down sports car, aren't you?"

"That's me." By now it shouldn't have surprised Rorie that everyone knew about her troubles.

"I hope everything turns out all right for you."

"Thanks." Although Betty was speaking to Rorie, her eyes didn't leave Luke. It was more than obvious that she expected an invitation to dance.

"Luke, why don't you dance with Betty?" Rorie suggested. "That way I'll gather a few pointers from watching the two of you."

"What a good idea," Betty chirped eagerly. "We'll stay on the outskirts of the crowd so you can see how it's done. Be sure and listen to Charlie—he's the caller. That way you'll see what each step is."

Rorie nodded, agreeably.

Luke gave Rorie a long sober look. "You're sure?"

"Positive."

All join hands, circle right around
Stop in place at your hometown...

Studying the dancers, Rorie quickly picked up the terms *do se do*, *allemande left* and *allemande right* and a number of others, which she struggled to keep track of. By the end of the dance, her mind was buzzing. Her foot tapped out the lively beat of the fiddlers' music and a smile formed as she listened to the perfectly rhyming words.

"Rorie," Skip cried, suddenly standing in front of her. "May I have the pleasure of this dance?"

"I...I don't think I'm ready yet."

"Nonsense." Without listening to her protest, reached for her hand and hauled her to her feet.

"Skip, I'll embarrass you," she protested in a low whisper. "I've never done this before."

"You've got to start some time." He tucked his arm around her waist and led her close to the stage.

"We got a newcomer, Charlie," Skip called out, "so make this one simple."

Charlie gave Skip a thumbs-up sign and reached for the microphone. "We'll go a bit slower this time," Charlie announced to his happy audience. "Miss Rorie Campbell from San Francisco has joined us and it's her first time on the floor."

Rorie wanted to curl up and die as a hundred faces turned to stare at her. But the dancers were shouting and cheering their welcome and Rorie shyly raised her hand, smiling into the crowd.

Getting through that first series of steps was the most difficult, but soon Rorie was in the middle, stepping and twirling—and laughing. Something she'd always assumed to be a silly, outdated activity turned out to be great fun.

By the time Skip led her back to her chair, she was breathless. "Want some punch?" he asked. Rorie nodded eagerly. Her throat felt parched.

When Skip left her, Luke Rivers appeared at her side. "You did just great," he said enthusiastically.

"For a city girl, you mean," she teased.

"As good as anyone," he insisted.

"Thanks."

"I suspect I owe you an apology, Rorie."

"Because you didn't want to make a fool of yourself with me on the dance floor?" she asked with a light laugh. "I don't blame you. Kate and Clay practically threw me in your lap. I'm sure you had other plans for tonight, and I'm sorry for your sake, that we got stuck with each other."

Luke grinned. "Trust me, I've had plenty of envious stares from around the room tonight. Any of a dozen different men would be more than happy to be 'stuck' with you."

That went a long way towards boosting her ego. She would have commented, but Skip returned just then with a paper cup filled with bright pink punch. A teenage girl was beside him, clutching his free arm and smiling dreamily up at him.

"I'm going to dance with Caroline now, okay?" he said to Rorie.

"That's fine," she answered, smiling, "and thank you for braving the dance floor with me that first time.'' Skip blushed as he slipped an arm around Caroline's waist and hurried her off.

''You game?'' Luke nodded towards the dancing couples.

Rorie didn't hesitate. She swallowed the punch in three giant gulps, and gave him her hand. Together they moved onto the crowded floor.

By the end of the third set of dances, Rorie had twirled around with so many different partners, she lost track of them. She'd caught sight of Clay only once, and when he saw her he waved. Returning the gesture, she promptly missed her footing and nearly fell into her partner's waiting arms. The tall sheriff's deputy was all too pleased to have her throw herself at him and told her as much, to Rorie's embarrassment.

Although it was only ten o'clock, Rorie was exhausted and so warm the perspiration ran in rivulets down her face and neck. She had to escape. Several times, she'd tried to sit out a dance, but no one would listen to her excuses.

In an effort to catch her breath and cool down, Rorie took advantage of a break between sets to wander outside. The night air was light and refreshing. Quite a few other people had apparently had the same idea, as the field that served as a car park was crowded with groups and strolling couples.

As she made her way through the dimly lit field, a handful of men were passing around a flask of whisky and entertaining each other with off-colour jokes. She steered a wide circle around them and headed towards Luke's parked car, deciding it was far enough away to discourage anyone from following her. In her eagerness to escape, she nearly stumbled over a couple locked in a passionate embrace against the side of a pickup.

Rorie mumbled an apology when the pair glanced up at her, irritation written all over their young faces. Good grief, she'd only wanted a few minutes alone in order to get a breath of fresh air— she hadn't expected to walk through an obstacle course!

When she finally arrived at Luke Rivers' car, she leaned on the fender and slowly inhaled the clean country air. All her assumptions about this evening had been wrong. She'd been so sure she'd feel lonely and bored and out of place. And she'd felt none of those things. If she were to tell Dan about the Grange dance, he'd laugh at the idea of having such a grand time with a bunch of what he'd refer to as ''country bumpkins''. The thought irritated her briefly. These were good, friendly, fun-loving people. They'd taken her under their wing, expressed their welcome without reserve, and now they were showing her an uncomplicated life-style that had more appeal than Rorie would have thought possible.

''I thought I'd find you out here.''

Rorie's whole body tensed as she recognised the voice of the man who had joined her.

''Hello, Clay.''

Eight

Rorie forced a cheerful note into her voice. She turned around, half expecting Kate to be with him. The two had been inseparable from the minute Clay had arrived at the Logan house. It was just as well that Kate was around, since her presence prevented Clay and Rorie from giving in to any temptation.

Clay's hands settled on her shoulders and Rorie flinched involuntarily at his touch. With obvious regret and reluctance, Clay dropped his hands.

"Are you having a good time?" he asked.

She nodded enthusiastically. "I didn't think I would, which tells you how prejudiced I've been about country life, but I've been pleasantly surprised."

"I'm glad." His hands clenched briefly at his sides, then he flexed his fingers a couple of times. "I would have danced with you myself, but—"

She stopped him abruptly. "Clay, no. Don't explain…it isn't necessary. I understand."

His eyes held hers with such tenderness that she had to look away. The magical quality was back in the air—Rorie could feel it as forcefully as if the stars had spelled it out across the heavens.

"I don't think you do understand, Rorie," Clay said, "but it doesn't matter. You'll be gone in a couple of days and both our lives will go back to the way they were meant to be."

Rorie agreed with a quick nod of her head. It was too tempting, standing in the moonlight with Clay. Much too tempting. The memory of another night in which they'd stood and gazed at the stars returned with powerful intensity. Rorie realised that even talking to each other, alone like this, was dangerous.

"Won't Kate be looking for you?" she asked carefully.

"No. Luke Rivers is dancing with her."

For a moment she closed her eyes, not daring to look up at Clay.

"I guess I'll be going inside now. I only came out to catch my breath and cool down a little."

"Dance with me first—here in the moonlight."

A protest surged within her, but the instant Clay slid his arms around her waist, Rorie felt herself give in. Kate would have him the rest of her life, but Rorie only had these few hours. Almost against her will, her hands found his shoulders, slipping around his neck with an ease that brought a sigh of pleasure to her lips. Being held by Clay shouldn't feel this good.

"Oh, Rorie," he moaned as she settled into his embrace.

They fitted together as if they'd been created for one another. His chin touched the top of her head and he gently caressed her hair with his jaw.

"This is a mistake," Rorie murmured, closing her eyes, savouring the warm, secure feel of his arms.

"I know…"

But neither seemed willing to release the other.

His mouth found her temple and he kissed her there softly. "God help me, Rorie, what am I going to do? I haven't been able to stop thinking about you. I don't sleep, I hardly eat…" His voice was raw, almost savage.

"Oh, please," she said with a soft cry. "We can't…we mustn't even talk like this." His grey eyes smouldered above hers, and their breaths merged as his mouth hovered so close to her own.

"I vowed I wouldn't touch you again."

Rorie looked away. She'd made the same promise to herself. But it wasn't in her to deny him now, although her mind frantically searched for the words to convince him how wrong they were to risk hurting Kate—and each other.

His hands drifted up from her shoulders, his fingertips grazing the sides of her neck, trailing over her cheeks and through the softness of her hair. He placed his index finger over her lips, gently stroking them apart.

Rorie moaned. She moistened her lips with the tip of her tongue. Clay's left hand dug into her shoulders as her tongue caressed the length of his finger, drawing it into her mouth and sucking it gently. She needed him so much in that moment, she could have wept.

"Just this once…for these few minutes," he pleaded, "let me pretend you're mine." His hands cupped her face and slowly brought her mouth to his, smothering her whimper of part welcome, part protest.

A long series of kisses followed. Deep, relentless, searching kisses that sent her heart soaring. Kisses that only made the coming loneliness more painful. A sob swelled within her and tears burned her eyes as she twisted away and tore her mouth from his.

"No," she cried, covering her face with her hands and turning her back to him. "Please, Clay. We shouldn't be doing this."

He was silent for so long that Rorie suspected he'd left her. She inhaled a deep, calming breath and dropped her hands limply to her sides.

"It would be so easy to love you, Rorie."

"No," she whispered, shaking her head vigorously as she faced him again. "I'm not the right person for you—it's too late for that. You've got Kate." She couldn't keep the pain out of her voice. Anything between them was hopeless, futile. Within a day or two her car would be repaired and she'd vanish from his life as suddenly as she'd appeared.

Clay fell silent, his shoulders stiff and resolute as he stood silhouetted against the light of the Grange Hall. His face was masked by the shadows and Rorie couldn't read his thoughts. He drew in a harsh breath.

"You're right, Rorie. We can't allow this...attraction between us get out of hand. I promise you, by all I hold dear, that I won't kiss you again."

"I'll...do my part, too," she assured him, feeling better now that they'd made this agreement.

His hand reached for hers and clasped it warmly. "Come on, I'll walk you back to the hall. We're going to be all right. We'll do what we have to do."

Clay's tone told her he sincerely meant it. Relieved, Rorie silently made the same promise to herself.

Rorie slept late the following morning, later than she would have thought possible. Mary was busy with lunch preparations by the time she wandered down the stairs.

"Did you enjoy yourself last night?" Mary immediately asked.

In response, Rorie curtsyed and danced a few steps with an imaginary partner, clapping her hands.

Mary tried to hide a smile at Rorie's antics. "Oh, get away with you now. All I was looking for was a yes or a no."

"I had a great time."

"It was nothing like those city hotspots, I'll wager."

ight about that,'' Rorie told her, pouring herself a cup

u seeing Kate today?''

Jrie shook her head and popped a piece of bread in the toaster. She's got a doctor's appointment this morning and a teachers' meeting this afternoon. She's going to try to stop by later if she has a chance, but if not I'll be seeing her for sure tomorrow.'' Rorie intended to spend as much time as she could with Clay's fiancée. She genuinely enjoyed her company, and being with her served two useful purposes. It helped keep Rorie occupied, and it prevented her from being alone with Clay.

"What are you going to do today, then?'' Mary asked, frowning.

Rorie laughed. "Don't worry. Whatever it is, I promise to stay out of your way.''

The housekeeper gave a snort of amusement—or was it relief?

"Actually, I thought I'd type the data Clay needs for his pedi-gree-research program into the computer. There isn't much left and I should be able to finish by this afternoon.''

"So if someone comes looking for you, that's where you'll be?''

"That's where I'll be,'' Rorie echoed. She didn't know who would "come looking for her'', as Mary put it. The housekeeper made it sound as though a posse was due to arrive any minute demanding to know where the Franklin men were hiding Rorie Campbell.

Taking her coffee cup with her, Rorie walked across the yard and into the barn. Once more, she was impressed with all the activity that went on there. She'd come to know several of the men by their first names and returned their greetings with a smile and a wave.

As before, she found the office empty. She set down her cup while she turned on the computer and collected Clay's data. She'd just started to type it in when she heard someone enter the room. Pausing, she twisted her head around.

"Rorie.''

"Clay.''

They were awkward with one another now. Afraid, almost.

"I didn't realise you were here.''

She stood abruptly. "I'll leave...''

"No. I came up to get something. I'll be gone in just a minute.''

She nodded and sat back down. "Okay.''

He walked briskly to his desk and sifted through the untidy

stacks of papers. His gaze didn't waver from the task, but his jaw was tight, his teeth clenched. Impatience marked his every move. "Kate told me you're involved with a man in San Francisco. I...didn't know."

"I'm not exactly involved with him—at least not in the way you're implying. His name is Dan Rogers, and we've been seeing each other for about six months. He's divorced. The MG is his."

Clay's mouth thinned, but he still didn't look at her. "Are you in love with him?"

"No."

Lowering his head, Clay rubbed his hand over his eyes. "I had no right to ask you that. None. Forgive me, Rorie." Then, clutching his papers, he stalked out of the office without a backward glance.

Rorie was so shaken by the encounter that when she went back to her typing, she made three mistakes in a row and had to stop to regain her composure.

When the phone rang, she ignored it, knowing Mary or one of the men would answer it. Soon afterwards, she heard running footsteps behind her and swivelled around in the chair.

A breathless Skip bolted into the room. Shoulders heaving, he pointed in the direction of the telephone. "It's for you," he panted.

"Me?" It could only be Dan.

He nodded several times, his hand braced theatrically against his heart.

"Hello," she said, her fingers closing tightly around the receiver. "This is Rorie Campbell."

"Miss Campbell," came the unmistakable voice of George, the mechanic in Riversdale, "let me put it to you like this. I've got good news and bad news."

"Now what?" she cried, pushing her hair off her forehead with an impatient hand. She had to get out of Elk Run and the sooner the better.

"My man picked up the water pump for your car in Portland just the way we planned."

"Good."

George sighed heavily. "There's a minor problem, though."

"Minor?" She repeated hopefully.

"Well, not that minor actually."

"Oh, great... Listen, George, I'd prefer not to play guessing games with you. Just tell me what happened and how long it's going to be before I can get out of here.''

"I'm sorry, Miss Campbell, but they shipped the wrong part. It'll be two, possibly three days more.''

Nine

"What's wrong?" Skip asked when Rorie indignantly replaced the telephone receiver.

She crossed her arms over her chest and breathed deeply, battling down the angry frustration that boiled inside her. The problem wasn't George's fault, or Skip's, or Kate's, or anyone else's.

"Rorie?" Skip asked again.

"They shipped the wrong part for the car," she returned flatly. "I'm going to be stuck here another two or possibly three days."

Skip didn't look the least bit perturbed at this bit of information. "Gee, Rorie, that's not so terrible. We like having you around—and you like it here, don't you?"

"Yes, but..." How could she explain that her reservations had nothing to do with their company, the stud farm or even with country life? She couldn't very well blurt out that she was falling in love with his brother, that she had to escape before she ruined their lives.

"But what?" Skip asked.

"My vacation."

"I know you had other plans, but you can relax and enjoy yourself here just as well, can't you?"

She didn't attempt to answer him, but closed her eyes and nodded, faintly.

"Well, listen, I've got to get back to work. Do you need me for anything?"

She shook her head. When the office door closed, Rorie sat back down in front of the computer again and poised her fingers over the keyboard. She sat like that, unmoving, for several minutes as her thoughts churned. What was she going to do? Every time she came near Clay the attraction was so strong that trying to ignore it was like swimming upstream. Rorie had planned on leaving Elk Run the following day. Now she was trapped here for God only knew how much longer.

She got up suddenly and started pacing the office floor. Dan hadn't called her, either. She might have vanished from the face of the earth as far as he was concerned. The stupid car was his, after all, and the least he could do was make some effort to find out what had happened. Rorie knew she wasn't being entirely reasonable, but she was caught up in the momentum of her anger and frustration.

Impulsively she snatched the telephone receiver, had the operator charge the call to her San Francisco number and dialled Dan's office.

"Rorie, thank God you phoned," Dan said.

The worry in his voice appeased her a little. "The least you could have done was call me back," she fumed.

"I tried. My secretary apparently wrote down the wrong number. I've been waiting all this time for you to call back. Why didn't you? What on earth happened?"

She told him in detail, from the stalled car to her recent conversation with the mechanic. She didn't tell him about Clay Franklin and the way he made her feel.

"Rorie, baby, I'm so sorry."

She nodded mutely, close to tears. If she weren't so dangerously close to falling in love with Clay, none of this would seem such a disaster.

The silence lengthened while Dan apparently mulled things over. "Shall I come and get you?" he finally asked.

"With what?" she asked with surprising calm. "My car? You were the one who convinced me it would never make this trip. Besides, how would you get the MG back?"

"I'd find a way. Listen, baby, I can't let you sit around in some backwoods farm town. I'll borrow a car or rent one." He hesitated, then expelled his breath in a short burst of impatience. "Damn, forget that. I can't come."

"You can't?"

"I've got a meeting tomorrow afternoon. It's important—I can't miss it. I'm sorry, Rorie, I really am, but there's nothing I can do."

"Don't worry about it," she said, defeat causing her voice to dip slightly. "I understand." In a crazy kind of way she did. As a rising stockbroker, Dan's career moves were critical to him, more important than rescuing Rorie, the woman he claimed to love… Somehow Rorie couldn't picture Clay making the same decision.

In her heart she knew Clay would come for her the second she asked.

They spoke for a few minutes longer before Rorie ended the conversation. She felt trapped, as though the walls were closing in around her. So far she and Clay had managed to disguise their feelings, but they wouldn't be able to keep it up much longer before someone guessed. Kate wasn't blind, and neither was Mary.

"Rorie?" Clay called her name as he burst into the office. "What happened? Skip just told me you were all upset—something about the car? What's going on?"

"George phoned." She whirled around and pointed towards the telephone. "The water pump arrived just the way it was supposed to—but it's the wrong one."

Clay dropped his gaze, then removed his hat and wiped his forehead. "I'm sorry, Rorie."

"I am, too, but that doesn't do a bit of good, does it?" The conversation with Dan hadn't helped matters, and taking her frustration out on Clay wasn't going to change anything, either. "I'm stuck here, and this is the last place on earth I want to be."

"Do you think I like it any better?" he challenged.

Rorie blinked wildly at the tears that burned for release.

"I wish to God your car had broken down a hundred miles away from Elk Run," he said. "Before you bombarded your way into my home, my life was set. I knew what I wanted, where I was headed. In the course of a few days you've managed to uproot my whole world."

Emotion clogged Rorie's throat at the unfairness of his accusations. She hadn't asked for the MGB to break down where it had. The minute she could, she planned to get out of his life and back to her own.

No, she decided, they couldn't wait that long—it was much too painful for them both. She had to leave now. "I'll pack my things and be gone before evening."

"Just where do you plan to go?"

Rorie didn't know. "Somewhere…anywhere." She had to leave for his sake, as well as her own.

"Go back inside the house, Rorie, before I say or do something else I'll regret. You're right—we can't be in the same room together. At least not alone."

She started to walk past him, her eyes downcast, her heart heavy with misery. Unexpectedly his hand shot out and caught her fingers, stopping her.

"I didn't mean what I said." His voice rasped warm and hoarse. "None of it. Forgive me, Rorie."

Her heart raced when his hand touched hers. It took all the restraint Rorie could muster, which at the moment wasn't much, to resist wrapping herself in his arms and holding on for the rest of her life.

"Forgive me, too," she whispered.

"Forgive you?" he asked, incredulous. "No, Rorie. I'll thank God every day of my life for having met you." With that, he released her fingers, slowly, reluctantly. "Go now, before I make an even bigger fool of myself."

Rorie ran from the office as though a raging fire were licking at her heels, threatening to consume her.

And in a way, it was.

For two days, Rorie managed to stay completely out of Clay's way. They saw each other only briefly and always in the company of others. Rorie was sure they gave Academy Award performances every time they were together. They laughed and teased and joked and the only one who seemed to suspect things weren't quite right was Mary.

Rorie was grateful the housekeeper didn't question her, but the looks she gave Rorie were frowningly thoughtful.

Three days after the Grange dance, Mary's sister arrived in Riversdale. Revealing more excitement than Rorie had seen in their brief acquaintance, Mary fussed with her hair and dress, and as soon as she finished the lunch dishes she was off.

Putting on Mary's well-worn apron, Rorie looped the long strands around her narrow waist twice and set to work. Kate joined her in mid-afternoon, carrying in a large bag of ingredients for the dessert she was planning to prepare.

"I've been cooking from the moment Mary left," Rorie told Kate, pushing the damp hair from her forehead, as she stirred wine into a simmering sauce. Rorie intended to razzle-dazzle Clay and Skip with her one speciality—seafood fettuccine. She hadn't admitted to Mary how limited her repertoire of dishes was, although the housekeeper had repeatedly quizzed her about what she planned to make for dinner. Rorie had insisted it was a surprise. She'd decided that this rich and tasty dish stood a good chance of impressing the Franklin men.

"And I'm making Clay his favourite dessert—homemade lemon meringue pie." Kate reached for the grocery bag on the kitchen counter and six bright yellow lemons rolled onto the counter.

Rorie was impressed. The one and only time she'd tried to bake a lemon pie, she'd used a pudding mix. Apparently, Kate took the homemade part seriously.

"Whatever you're cooking smells wonderful," Kate said, stepping over to the stove. Fresh cracked crab, large succulent shrimp and small bite-sized pieces of sole were waiting in the refrigerator, to be added to the sauce just before the dish was served.

Kate was busy whipping up a pie crust when the phone rang several minutes later. She glanced anxiously at the wall, her fingers sticky with flour and lard.

Rorie looked over at her. "Do you suppose I should answer that?"

"You'd better. Clay usually relies on Mary to catch the phone for him."

Rorie lifted the receiver before the next peal. "Elk Run."

"That Miss Campbell?"

Rorie immediately recognised the voice of the mechanic from Riversdale. "Yes, this is Rorie Campbell."

"Remember I promised I'd call you when the part arrived? Well, it's here, all safe and sound, so you can stop fretting. It just came in a few minutes ago—haven't even had a chance to take it out of the box. Just thought you'd want to know."

"It's the right one this time?"

"Here, I'll just check it now... Yup, this is it."

Rorie wasn't sure what she felt. Relief, yes, but regrets, too. "Thank you. Thank you very much."

"It's a little late for me to be starting the job this afternoon. My son's playing a little-league game and I told him I'd be there. I'll get to it first thing in the morning, and should be finished before noon. Just give me a call before you head out and I'll make sure everything's running the way it should be."

"Yes, I'll do that. Thanks again." Slowly Rorie replaced the telephone receiver. She leaned against the wall sighing deeply. At Kate's questioning gaze, she smiled weakly and explained, "That was the mechanic. The water pump for my car arrived and he's going to be working on it first thing in the morning."

"Rorie, that's great."

"I think so, too." She did—and she didn't. Part of her longed to flee Elk Run, and another part of her realised that no matter how far she travelled, no matter how many years passed, these days with Clay Franklin would always be special to her.

"Then tonight's going to be your last evening here," Kate murmured thoughtfully, looking disappointed. "Oh, dear, Rorie, as selfish as it sounds, I really hate the thought of you leaving."

"We can keep in touch."

"Oh, yes, I'd like that. I promise to send you a wedding invitation."

That reminder was the last thing Rorie needed. But once she was on the road again, she could start forgetting, she told herself grimly.

"Since this is going to be your last night, I think we should make it special," Kate announced brightly. "We're going to use the best china and set out the crystal wineglasses."

Rorie laughed, imagining Mary's face when she heard about it.

Even as she spoke, Kate was walking towards the dining-room china cabinet. In a matter of minutes, she'd set the table, cooked the sauce for the pie and poured it into the cooling pie shell that sat on the counter. The woman was a marvel!

Rorie was busy adding the final touches to the fettuccine when Clay and Skip came in through the back door.

"When's dinner?" Skip wanted to know. "I'm starved."

"In a few minutes." Rorie tested the boiling noodles to be sure they'd cooked all the way through but weren't overdone.

"Upstairs with the both of you," Kate said, shooing them out of the kitchen. "I want you to change into something nice."

"You want us to dress up for dinner?" Skip complained. He'd obviously recovered from any need to impress her with his sartorial elegance, Rorie noted, remembering that he'd worn his Sunday best that first night. "We already washed—what more do you want?"

"For you to change your clothes. We're having a celebration tonight."

"We are?" The boy's gaze slid from Kate to Rorie and then back again.

"That's right," Kate continued, undaunted by his lack of enthusiasm. "And when we're through with dinner, there's going to be a farewell party for Rorie. We're going to send her off country-style."

"Rorie's leaving?" Skip sounded as though that was the last thing he'd expected to hear. "But she just got here."

"The repair shop called from Riversdale. Her car will be finished tomorrow and she'll be on her way."

Clay's eyes burned into Rorie's. She tried to avoid looking at him, but when she did chance to meet his gaze, she could feel his distress. His jaw went rigid, and his mouth tightened as though he was bracing himself against Kate's words.

"Now hurry up, you two. Dinner's nearly ready," Kate said with a laugh. "Rorie's been cooking her heart out all afternoon."

Both men disappeared and Rorie set out the fresh green salad she'd made earlier, along with the seven-grain dinner rolls she'd warmed in the oven.

Once everyone was seated at the table and waiting, Rorie ceremonially carried in the platter of fettuccine, thick with seafood. She'd spent a good ten minutes arranging it to look as attractive as possible.

"Whatever it is smells good," Skip called out as she entered the dining room. "I'm so hungry I could eat a horse."

"Funny, Skip, very funny," Kate said.

Rorie set the serving dish in the middle of the table and stepped back, anticipating their praise.

Skip raised himself halfway out of his seat as he glared at her masterpiece. "That's it?" His young voice was filled with disappointment.

Rorie blinked, uncertain how she should respond.

"You've been cooking all afternoon and you mean to tell me that's everything?"

"It's seafood fettuccine," she explained.

"It just looks like a bunch of noodles to me."

Ten

"I'll have another piece of lemon pie," Skip said, eagerly extending his plate.

"If you're still hungry, Skip," Clay remarked casually, "there are a few dinner rolls left."

Skip's gaze darted to the small wicker basket and he wrinkled his nose. "No, thanks, there're too many seeds in those things. I got one caught in my tooth earlier and spent five minutes trying to suck it out."

Rorie did her best to smile.

Skip must have noticed how miserable she was because he added, "The salad was real good though. What kind of dressing was that?"

"Vinaigrette."

"Really? It tasted fruity."

"It was raspberry flavoured."

Skip's eyes widened. "I don't think I've ever heard of that kind of fancy vinegar. Did you buy it here in Nightingale?"

"Not exactly. I got the ingredients while Kate and I were out the other day and mixed it up last night."

"*That* tasted real good." Which was Skip's less-than-subtle method of telling her nothing else had. He'd barely touched the main course. Clay had made a show of asking for seconds, but Rorie was all too aware that his display of enthusiasm had been an effort to salve her injured ego.

Rorie wasn't fooled—no one had enjoyed her special dinner. Even old Blue had turned his nose up at it when she'd offered him a taste of the leftovers. The Labrador had covered his nose with a paw.

Clay and Skip did hard physical work; they didn't sit in an office all day like Dan and the other men she knew. She should have realised that Clay and his brother required a more substantial meal than noodles swimming in a creamy sauce. Rorie wished she'd discussed her menu with either Mary or Kate. A tiny voice inside her suggested that Kate might have said something to warn her...

"Anyone else for more pie?" Kate was asking.

Clay nodded and cast a guilty glance in Rorie's direction. "I could go for a second piece myself."

"The pie was delicious," Rorie told Kate, meaning it. She was willing to admit Kate's dessert had been the highlight of the meal.

"Kate's one of the best cooks in the entire country," Skip announced, licking the back of his fork. "Her lemon pie won a blue ribbon at the county fair last year." He leaned forward, planting his elbows on the table. "She's got a barbecue sauce so tangy and good that when she cooks up spareribs I just can't stop eating 'em." His face fell as though he was thinking about those ribs now and would have gladly traded all of Rorie's fancy city food for a plateful.

"I'd like the recipe to the fettuccine if you'd give it to me," Kate told Rorie, obviously doing her best to change the subject and spare Rorie's feelings. Perhaps she felt a little guilty, too, for not giving her any helpful suggestions.

Skip stared at Kate as if she'd volunteered to muck out the stalls.

"I'll write it down before I leave."

"Since Rorie and Kate put so much time and effort into the meal, I think Skip and I could be convinced to do our part and wash the dishes."

"We could?" Skip protested.

"It's the least we can do," Clay returned flatly, glaring at his younger brother.

Rorie was all too aware of Clay's ploy. He wanted to get into the kitchen so they could find something else to eat without being obvious about it.

"Listen, you guys," Rorie said brightly. "I'm sorry about dinner. I can see everyone's still hungry. You're all going out of your way to reassure me, but it just isn't necessary."

"I don't know what you're talking about, Rorie. Dinner was excellent," Clay said, patting his stomach.

Rorie nearly laughed out loud. "You're starving and you know it. Why don't we call out for a pizza?" she said, pleased with her solution. "I bungled dinner, so that's the least I can do to make it up to you."

Three faces stared at her blankly.

"Rorie," Clay said gently. "The closest pizza parlour is thirty miles from here."

"Oh."

Undeterred, Skip leapt to his feet. "No problem... You phone in the order and I'll go get it."

Empty pizza boxes littered the living-room floor along with several abandoned soft-drink cans.

Skip lay on his back staring up at the ceiling. "Anyone for a little music?" he asked lazily.

"Sure." Kate got to her feet and sat down at the piano. As her nimble fingers ran over the keyboard, the rich sounds echoed against the walls. "Anyone for a little Lee Greenwood?"

"All *right*," Skip called out with a yell, punching his fist into the air. He thrust two fingers in his mouth and gave a shrill whistle.

"Who?" Rorie asked once the commotion had died down.

"He's a country singer," Clay explained. Blue ambled to his side, settling down at his feet. Clay gently stroked his back.

"I guess I haven't heard of him," Rorie murmured.

Once more she discovered three pairs of curious eyes studying her.

"What about Johnny Cash?" Kate suggested next. "You probably know who he is."

"Oh, sure." Rorie looped her arms over her bent knees and lowered her voice to a gravelly pitch. "I hear that train a comin'."

Skip let loose with another whistle and Rorie laughed at his boisterous antics. Clay left the room and returned a moment later with a guitar, then seated himself on the floor again, beside Blue. Skip crawled across the braided rug in the centre of the room and retrieved a harmonica from the mantel. Soon Kate and the two men were making their own brand of music—country songs, from the traditional to the more recent. Rorie didn't know a single one, but she clapped her hands and tapped her foot to the lively beat.

"Sing for Rorie," Skip shouted to Clay and Kate. "Let's show her what she's been missing."

Clay's rich baritone joined Kate's lilting soprano, and Rorie's hands and feet stopped moving. Her eyes darted from one to the other in open-mouthed wonder at the beautiful harmony of their two voices, male and female. It was as though they'd been singing together all their lives. She realised maybe they had.

When they finished, Rorie blinked back tears, too dumbfounded for a moment to speak. ''That was wonderful,'' she told them and her voice caught with emotion.

''Kate and Clay sing duets at church all the time,'' Skip explained. ''They're good, aren't they?''

Rorie nodded, gazing at the two of them. She felt her heart might burst with the emotion that had welled up in her. Clay and Kate were right for each other—they belonged together, and once she was gone they would blend their lives as beautifully as they had their voices. Rorie happened to catch Kate's eye. The other woman slipped her arms around Clay's waist and rested her head against his shoulder, laying claim to this man and silently letting Rorie know it. Rorie couldn't blame Kate. In like circumstances she would have done the same.

''Do you sing, Rorie?'' Kate asked, leaving Clay and sliding onto the piano seat.

''A little, along with some piano.'' Actually her own singing voice wasn't half bad. She'd participated in several singing groups while she was in high school and had taken five years of piano lessons.

''Please sing something for us.'' Rorie recognised a hint of challenge in the words.

''Okay.'' She replaced Kate at the piano seat and started out with a little satirical ditty she remembered from her college days. Skip hooted as she knew he would at the clever words, and all three rewarded her with a round of applause when she'd finished.

''Go ahead and play some more,'' Kate encouraged. ''It's nice to have someone else do the playing for once.'' She sat next to Clay on the floor, resting her head against his shoulder. If it hadn't been for the guitar in his hands, Rorie knew he would have placed his arm over her shoulders and drawn her even closer. It would have been the natural thing to do.

''I don't think I know how to play the songs you usually sing, though.'' Rorie was more than a little reluctant now. She'd never heard of this Greenwood person they seemed to like so well.

''Play what you know,'' Kate said, ''and we'll join in.''

After a few seconds' thought, Rorie nodded. ''This is a song by Billy Ocean. You might have heard of him—his songs are more rock than country, but I think you'll recognise the music.'' Rorie wasn't more than a few measures into the ballad before she realised that Kate, Clay and Skip had never heard of Billy Ocean.

She stopped playing. ''What about Whitney Houston?''

Skip repeated the name a couple of times before his eyes lit up with recognition. "Hasn't she done Coke commercials?"

"Right," Rorie said, laughing. "She's had several big hits."

Kate slowly shook her head, looking discouraged. "Sorry, Rorie, I don't think I can remember the words to her songs."

"Barbra Streisand?"

"I thought she was an actress," Skip said with a puzzled frown. "You mean she sings, too?"

Reluctantly Rorie rose from the piano seat. "I'm sorry, Kate, you'll have to take over. It seems you three are a whole lot country and I'm a little bit rock and roll."

"We'll make you into a country girl yet!" Skip insisted, sliding the harmonica across his mouth with an ease Rorie envied.

Clay glanced at his watch. "We aren't going to be able to convert Rorie within the next twelve hours."

A gloom settled over them as Kate replaced Rorie at the piano.

"Are you sure we can't talk you into staying a few more days?" Skip asked. "We're just starting to know each other."

Rorie shook her head, more determined than ever to leave as soon as she could.

"It would be a shame for you to miss the county fair next weekend—maybe you could stop here on your way back through Oregon, after your trip to Canada," Kate added. "Clay and I are singing, and we're scheduled for the square-dance competition, too."

"Yeah," Skip cried. "And we've got pig races planned again this year."

"Pig races?" Rorie echoed faintly.

"I know it sounds silly, but it's really fun. We take the ten fastest pigs in the area and let them race towards a bowl of Oreos. No joke—cookies! Everyone bets on who'll win and we all have a really good time." Skip's eyes shone with eagerness. "Please think about it, anyway, Rorie."

"Mary's entering her apple pie again," Clay put in. "She's been after that blue ribbon for six years."

A hundred reasons for Rorie to fade out of their lives flew across her mind like particles of dust in the wind. And yet the offer was tempting. She tried, unsuccessfully, to read Clay's eyes, her own filled with a silent appeal. This was a decision she needed help making. But Clay wasn't helping. The thought of never seeing him again was like pouring salt onto an open wound; still, it was a reality she'd have to face sooner or later.

So Rorie offered the only excuse she could come up with at the moment. "I don't have the time. I'm sorry, but I'd be cutting it too close to get back to San Francisco for work Monday morning."

"Not if you cancelled part of your trip to Canada and came back on Friday," Skip pointed out, having given the matter some thought. "You didn't think you'd have a good time at the square dance, either, but you did, remember?"

It wasn't a matter of having a good time. So much more was involved...though the pig races actually sounded like fun. The very idea of such an activity would have astounded her only a week before, Rorie reflected. She could just imagine what Dan would say about it.

"Rorie?" Skip pressed. "What do you think?"

"I...I don't know."

"The county fair is about as good as it gets around Nightingale."

"I don't want to impose on your hospitality again." Clay still wasn't giving her any help with this decision.

"But having you stay with us isn't any problem," Skip insisted. "As long as you promise to stay out of the kitchen, you're welcome to stick around all summer. Isn't that right, Clay?"

His hesitation was so slight that Rorie doubted anyone else had noticed it. "Naturally Rorie's welcome to visit us any time she wants."

"If staying with these two drives you crazy," Kate inserted, "you could stay at my house. In fact, I'd love it if you did."

Rorie dropped her gaze, fearing what she might read in Clay's eyes. She sensed his indecision as she struggled with her own. She had to leave. Yet she wanted to stay...

"I think I should make what I can out of the rest of my vacation in Victoria," she finally told them.

"I know you're worried about getting back in time for work, but Skip's right. If you left Victoria one day early, then you could be here for the fair," Kate suggested again, but her offer didn't sound nearly as sincere as it had earlier.

"Rorie said she doesn't have the time," Clay said after an awkward silence. "I think we should all respect her decision."

"You sound as if you don't want her to come back," Skip accused.

"No," Clay murmured, his gaze finding hers. "I want her here, but I think Rorie should try to salvage some of the vacation she planned. She has to do what she thinks best.''

Rorie could feel his eyes moving over her hair and her face in loving appraisal. She tensed and prayed that Kate and Skip hadn't noticed.

During the next hour, Skip tried repeatedly to convince Rorie to visit on her way back or even to stay on until the fair. As far as Skip could see, there wasn't much reason to go to Canada now, anyway. But Rorie resisted. Walking away from Clay once was going to be painful enough. Rorie didn't know if she could do it twice.

Skip was yawning by the time they decided to call an end to the evening. With little more than a mumbled good night, he hurried up the stairs, abandoning the others.

Rorie and Kate took a few extra minutes to straighten the living room, while Clay drove the pickup around to the front of the house. ''I think I'd better burn the evidence before Mary sees these pizza boxes,'' Rorie joked. ''She'll have my hide once she hears about dinner.''

Kate laughed good-naturedly as she collected her belongings. When they heard Clay's truck, she put down her bags and ran to Rorie. ''You'll call me before you leave tomorrow?''

Rorie nodded and hugged her back.

''If something happens and you change your mind about the fair, please know that you're welcome to stay with me and Dad—we'd enjoy the company.''

''Thank you, Kate.''

The house felt empty and silent once Kate had left with Clay. Rorie knew it would be useless to go upstairs and try to sleep. Instead she wandered onto the front porch where she'd sat in the swing with Clay that first night. She sank down on the porch steps, one arm wrapped around a post, and gazed upward. The skies were alive with the glittering light of countless stars—stars that shone with a clarity and brightness one couldn't see in the city.

Clay belonged to this land, this farm, this small town. Rorie was a city girl to the marrow of her bones. This evening had proved the hopelessness of any dream that she and Clay might have of finding happiness together. There was his commitment to Kate. And there was the fact that he and Rorie were too different, their tastes too dissimilar. She certainly couldn't picture him making a life away from Elk Run.

Clay had accepted the hopelessness of it, too. That was the reason he'd insisted she travel to Canada. This evening Rorie had sensed a desperation in him that rivalled her own. It was a night filled with insights. Sitting under the heavens, she was beginning to understand some important things about life. For perhaps the first time, she'd fallen in love. The past six days she'd tried to deny what she was feeling, but on the eve of her departure it seemed silly to lie to herself any longer. Rorie couldn't believe something like this had actually happened to her. Meeting someone and falling in love with him in the space of a few days was an experience reserved for novels and movies. This wasn't like her normal sane, sensible self at all. Rorie had always thought she was too levelheaded to fall so easily in love.

Until she met Clay Franklin.

On the wings of one soul-searching realisation came another. Love wasn't what she'd anticipated. She'd assumed it meant a strong sensual passion that overwhelmed the lovers and left them powerless before it. But in the past few days, she'd learned that love marked the soul as well as the body.

Clay would forever be a part of her. Since that first night when Nightsong was born her heart had never felt more alive. Yet within a few hours she would walk away from the man she loved and consider herself blessed to have shared these days with him.

A tear rolled down the side of her face, surprising her. This wasn't a time for sadness, but joy. She'd discovered a deep inner strength she hadn't known she possessed. She wiped the moisture away and rested her head against the post, her gaze fixed on the heavens.

The footsteps behind Rorie didn't startle her. She'd known Clay would come to her this one last time.

Eleven

Clay draped his arm over Rorie's shoulders and joined her in gazing up at the sky. Neither spoke for several moments, as though they feared words would destroy the tranquil mood. Rorie stared, transfixed by the glittering display. Like her love for this man, the stars would remain forever distant, unattainable, but certain and unchanging.

A ragged sigh escaped her lips. "All my life I've believed that everything that befalls us has a purpose."

"I've always thought that, too," Clay whispered.

"Everything in life is deliberate."

"Our final hours together you're going to become philosophical?" He rested his chin on the crown of her head, gently ruffling her hair. "Are you sad, Rorie?"

"Oh, no," she denied quickly. "I can't be... I feel strange, but I don't know if I can find the words to explain it. I'm leaving tomorrow and I realise we'll probably never see each other again. I have no regrets—not a single one—and yet I think my heart is breaking."

His hand tightened on her shoulder in silent protest as if he found the thought of relinquishing her more than he could bear.

"We can't deny reality," she told him. "Nothing's going to change in the next few hours. The water pump on the car will be replaced, and I'll go back to my life. The way you'll go back to yours."

"I have this gut feeling there's going to be a hole the size of Grand Canyon in mine the minute you drive away." He dropped his arm and reluctantly moved away from her. His eyes held a weary sadness, but Rorie found an acceptance there, too.

"I'm an uncomplicated man," he stated evenly. "I'm probably nothing like the sophisticated man you're dating in San Francisco."

Her thoughts flew to Dan, so cosmopolitan and...superficial, and she recognised the truth in Clay's words. The two men were poles apart. Dan's interests revolved around his career and his car, but he was genuinely kind, and it was that quality that had attracted Rorie to him.

"Elk Run's given me a good deal of satisfaction over the years. My life's work is here and, God willing, some day my son will carry on the breeding programmes I've started. Everything I've ever dreamed of has always been within my hand's grasp." He paused, holding in a long sigh, then releasing it slowly. "And then you came," he whispered, and a brief smile crossed his lips, "and, within a matter of days, I'm reeling from the effects. Suddenly I'm left doubting what really is important in my life."

Rorie lowered her eyes. "Who would have believed a silly water pump would be responsible for all this wretched soul-searching?"

"I've always been the type of man who's known what he wants, but you make me feel like a schoolboy no older than Skip. I don't know what to do any more, Rorie. Within a few hours, you'll be leaving and part of me says if you do, I'll regret it the rest of my life."

"I can't stay." Their little dinner party had shown her how different their worlds actually were. She wouldn't fit into his life and he'd be an alien in hers. But Kate...Kate belonged to his world.

Clay rubbed his hands across his eyes and harshly drew in a breath. "I know you feel you should leave, but that doesn't mean I have to like it."

"The pull to stay is there for me, too," she whispered.

"And it's tearing both of us apart."

Rorie shook her head. "Don't you see? So much good has come out of meeting you, Clay." Her voice was strong. She had to make him realise that she'd always be grateful for the things he'd taught her. "In some ways I became a woman tonight. I feel I'm doing what's right for both of us, though it's more painful than anything I've ever known."

He looked at her with such undisguised love that she ached all the way to the core of her being.

"Let me hold you once more," he said softly. "Give me that, at least."

Rorie sadly shook her head. "I can't... I'm so sorry, Clay, but this is how it has to be with us. I'm so weak where you're concerned. I couldn't bear to let you touch me now and then leave tomorrow."

His eyes drifted shut as he yielded to her wisdom. "I don't know that I could, either."

They were no more than a few feet apart, but it seemed vast worlds stood between them.

"More than anything I want you to remember me fondly, without any bitterness," Rorie told him, discovering as she spoke the words how much she meant them.

Clay nodded. "Be happy, Rorie, for my sake."

Rorie realised that contentment would be a long time coming without this man in her life, but she would find it eventually. She prayed that he'd marry Kate someday, the way he'd planned. The other woman was the perfect wife for him—unlike herself. A thread of agony twisted around Rorie's heart.

She turned to leave him, fearing she'd dissolve into tears if she remained much longer. "Goodbye, Clay."

"Goodbye, Rorie."

She rushed past him and hurried up the stairs.

The following morning, both Clay and Skip had left the house by the time Rorie entered the kitchen.

"Good morning, Mary," she said, forcing a note of cheerfulness in her voice. "How did the visit with your sister go?"

"Fine."

Rorie stepped around the housekeeper to reach the coffeepot and poured herself a cup. A plume of steam rose enticingly to her nostrils and she took a tentative sip, not wanting to burn her lips.

"I found those pizza boxes you were trying so hard to hide from me," Mary grumbled as she wiped her hands on her apron. "You fed these good men restaurant pizza?"

Unable to stop herself, Rorie chuckled at the housekeeper's indignation. "Guilty as charged. Mary, you should have known better than to leave their fate in my evil hands."

"Near as I can figure, the closest pizza parlour is a half-hour or more away. Did you drive over and get it yourself or did you send Skip?"

"Actually he volunteered," she admitted reluctantly. "Dinner didn't exactly turn out the way I'd hoped."

The housekeeper snickered. "I should have known as much. You city slickers don't know nothing about serving up a decent meal to your menfolk."

Rorie gave a hefty sigh of agreement. "The only thing for me to do is stay on another month or two and have you teach me.'' As she expected, the housekeeper opened her mouth to protest. ''Unfortunately,'' Rorie continued, cutting Mary off before she could launch into her arguments, ''I'm hoping to be gone by afternoon.''

Mary's response was a surprise. The older woman turned to face Rorie, and her eyes narrowed, intense and troubled.

''I suspected you'd be going soon enough,'' she said in a tight voice, pulling out a chair. She sat down heavily and her hand brushed wisps of grey hair from her forehead. Her weathered face grew more and more thoughtful. ''It's for the best, you know.''

''I knew you'd be glad to be rid of me.''

Mary shrugged. ''It's other reasons that make your leaving right. You know what I'm talking about, even if you don't want to admit it to me. As a person you tend to grow on folks. Like I said before, for a city girl, you ain't half bad.''

Rorie reached for a banana from the fruit bowl in the centre of the table. She waved it like a baton, trying to lighten the mood, which had taken an unexpected turn towards the serious. ''For a stud farm, stuck out here in the middle of nowhere, this place isn't half bad, either. The people are friendly and the apple pie's been exceptional.''

Mary ignored the compliment on her pie. ''By people, I suppose you're referring to Clay. You're going to miss him, aren't you, girl?''

The banana found its way back into the bowl and, with it, the cheerful façade. ''Yes. I'll miss Clay.''

The older woman's frown deepened. ''From the things I've been noticing, he's going to be yearning for you, as well. But it's for the best,'' she said quietly. ''For the best.''

Rorie nodded and her voice wavered. ''Yes, I know...but it isn't easy.''

The housekeeper gave her a lopsided smile as she gently patted Rorie's hand. ''I know that, too, but you're doing the right thing. You'll forget him soon enough.''

A strong protest rose in her breast, closing off her throat. She wouldn't forget Clay. Ever. How could she forget the man who had so unselfishly taught her such valuable lessons about life and love? Lessons about herself.

''Kate Logan's the right woman for Clay,'' Mary said abruptly. Those few words cut Rorie to the quick. It was something she already knew, but hearing another person voice it made the truth almost unbearably painful.

"I...hope they're very happy."

"Kate loves him. She has from the time she was knee-high to a June bug. And there's something you don't know. Several years back, when Clay was in college, he fell in love with a girl from Seattle. She'd been born and raised in the city. Clay loved her, wanted to marry her, even brought her to Elk Run to meet the family. She stayed a couple of days, and the whole time, she was as restless as water on a hot skillet. Apparently she had words with Clay because the next thing I knew, she'd packed her bags and headed home. Clay never said much about her after that, but she hurt him bad. It wasn't until Kate was home from college that Clay thought seriously about marriage again."

Mary's story explained a good deal about Clay.

"Now, I know I'm just an old woman who likes her soaps and Saturday-night bingo. Most folks don't think I've got a lick of sense, and that's all right. What others choose to assume don't bother me much." She paused, and shook her head. "But Kate Logan's about the kindest, dearest person this town has ever seen. People like her—can't help themselves. She's always got a kind word and there's no one in this world she's too good for. She cares about the people in this community. Those kids she teaches over at the grade school love her like nothing you've ever seen. And she loves them. When it came to building that fancy library, it was Kate who worked so hard convincing folks they'd be doing what was best for Nightingale by voting for that bond issue."

Rorie kept her face averted. She didn't need Mary to tell her Kate was a good person; she'd seen the evidence of it herself.

"What most folks don't know is that Kate has seen plenty of pain in her own life. She watched her mother die a slow death from cancer. Took care of her most of the time herself, nursing Nora when she should have been off at college having fun like other nineteen-year-olds. Her family needed her and she was there. Kate gave old man Logan a reason to go on living when Nora passed away. She lives with him still, and it's long past time for her to be a carefree adult on her own. Kate's a good person clean through." Mary hesitated, then drew in a solemn breath. "Now, you may think I'm nothing but a meddling old fool, and I suspect you're right. But I'm saying it's a good thing you're leaving Elk Run before you break that girl's heart. She's got a chance now for some happiness, and God knows she deserves it. If she loses Clay, I know for certain it'd break her heart. She's too good to have that happen to her over some fancy city girl who's only passing through."

Rorie winced at the way Mary described her.

"I'm a plain talker," Mary said on the end of an abrupt laugh. "Always have been, always will be. Knowing Clay—and I do, as well as his mother did, God rest her soul—he'll pine for you awhile, but eventually everything will fall back into place. The way it was before you arrived."

Tears stung Rorie's eyes. She felt miserable as it was, and Mary wasn't helping. She'd already assured the housekeeper she was leaving, but Mary apparently wanted to be damn certain she didn't change her mind and return. The woman didn't understand...but then again, maybe she did.

"Have you ever been in love, Mary?"

"Once," came the curt reply. "Hurt so much the first time I never chanced it again."

"Are you sorry you lived your life alone now?" That was what Rorie saw for herself. Oh, she knew she was being melodramatic and over-emotional, but she couldn't imagine loving any man as much as she did Clay.

Mary lifted one shoulder in a shrug. "Some days I have plenty of regrets, but then on others it ain't so bad. I'd like to have had a child, but God saw to it that I was around when Clay and Skip needed someone... Knowing that made up for what I missed."

"They consider you family."

"Yeah, I suppose they do." Mary pushed out her chair and stood up. "Well, I better get back to work. Those men expect a good lunch. I imagine they're near starved after the dinner you fed them last night."

Despite her heartache, Rorie smiled and drained the last of her coffee. "And I'd better get upstairs and pack the rest of my things. The mechanic said my car would be ready around noon."

On her way to the bedroom Rorie paused at the framed photograph of Clay's parents that sat on the piano. She'd passed it several times and had given it little more than a fleeting glance. Now it suddenly demanded her attention, and she stopped in front of it.

A tremor went through her hand as she lightly ran her finger along the brass frame. Clay's mother smiled serenely into the camera, her grey eyes so like her son's that Rorie felt a knot twist in her stomach. Those same eyes seemed to reach across eternity and call out to Rorie, plead with her. Rorie's own eyes narrowed, certain her imagination was playing havoc with her troubled mind. She focused her attention on the woman's hair. That, too, was the same dark shade as Clay's, brushed away from her face in a carefully styled chignon. Clay had never mentioned his parents to her, not once, but just looking at the photograph Rorie knew intuitively that he'd shared a close relationship with his mother. Blue wandered out from the kitchen and stood at Rorie's side as though offering consolation. Grateful, she reached down to pet him.

Looking back at the photograph, Rorie noted that Skip resembled his father, with the same dancing blue eyes that revealed more than a hint of devilry.

Rorie continued to study both parents, but it was Clay's mother who captured her attention over and over again.

The phone ringing in the distance startled her, and her wrist was shaking when she set the picture back on the piano.

"Phone's for you," Mary shouted from the kitchen.

Rorie already knew it was George at the repair shop in Riversdale; she'd been waiting all morning to hear from him.

"Hello," she said, her fingers closing tightly around the receiver. Her biggest fear was that something had happened to delay her departure a second time.

"Miss Campbell," said the mechanic, "everything's fine. I got that part in and working for you without a hitch."

"Thank God," she murmured. Her hold on the telephone receiver relaxed, a little.

"I've got a man I could spare if you'd like to have your car delivered to Elk Run. But you've got to understand fifty miles is a fair distance and I'm afraid I'll have to charge you extra for it."

"That's fine," Rorie said eagerly, not even bothering to ask the amount. "How soon can he be here?"

Twelve

"So you're really going," Skip said as he picked up Rorie's bags. "Somehow I thought I might have talked you into staying on for the county fair."

"You seem intent on bringing me to ruin, Skip Franklin. I'm afraid I'd bet all my hard-earned cash on those pig races you were telling me about," Rorie teased. Standing in the middle of the master bedroom, she surveyed it one last time to be certain she hadn't forgotten anything.

A pang of wistfulness settled over her as she slowly looked around. Not for the first time, Rorie felt the love and warmth emanating from these brightly papered walls. Lazily, almost lovingly, she ran her fingertips along the top of the dresser, letting her hand linger there a moment, unwilling to pull herself away. This bedroom represented so much of what she was leaving behind. It was difficult to walk away.

Skip stood in the doorway impatiently waiting for her. "Kate phoned and said she's on her way over. She wants to say goodbye."

"I'll be happy to see her one last time." Rorie wished Skip would leave so she could delay her parting with this room a little longer. Until now, Rorie hadn't realised how much sleeping in Clay's parents' room had meant to her. Her appreciation had come too late.

"Mary's packing a lunch for you to take," Skip announced with a wry chuckle, "and, knowing Mary, it'll be enough to last you a week."

Rorie smiled and reluctantly followed him down the stairs. As Skip had claimed, the housekeeper had prepared two large bags, which sat waiting on the kitchen table.

"Might as well take those with you, too," Mary muttered gruffly. "I hate the thought of you eating restaurant food. This, at least, will stick to your ribs."

"Goodbye, Mary," Rorie said softly, touched by the housekeeper's thoughtfulness. On impulse she gently hugged the older woman. "Thank you for everything—including our talk this morning." The impromptu embrace surprised Rorie as much as it obviously did Mary.

"You drive careful now, you hear?" the housekeeper answered, squeezing Rorie tightly and patting her back several times.

"I will, I promise."

"A letter now and again wouldn't go amiss."

"All right," Rorie agreed, and rubbed the moisture from the corners of her eyes. These people had touched her in so many ways. Leaving them was far more difficult than she'd imagined.

The housekeeper rubbed the heel of her hand over her right eye. "It's time for you to get on the road. What are you doing standing in the kitchen chitchatting with me?" she asked brusquely.

"I'm going, I'm going." Mary's gruff voice didn't fool Rorie. The housekeeper's exterior might be a little crusty, and her tongue a bit surly, but she didn't succeed in disguising a generous, loving heart.

"I don't know where Clay is," Skip complained after he'd loaded the luggage into the MG's trunk. "I thought for sure he'd want to see you before you left. I wonder where he got off to."

"I'm...sure he's got better things to do than say goodbye to me."

"Nothing is more important than this," Skip countered, frowning. "I'm going to see if I can find him."

Rorie's first reaction was to stop Skip, then she quickly decided against it. If she made too much of a fuss, Skip might suspect something. She understood what had prompted Clay to stay away from the house all morning, and in truth she was grateful. Leaving Elk Run was hard enough without prolonging the agony in lengthy farewells to Clay.

Skip hesitated, kicking at the dirt with the pointed toe of his cowboy boot. "You two didn't happen to have a fight or anything, did you?"

"No. What makes you ask?"

Skip shrugged. "I don't know... It's just that every time I walked into a room with the two of you, I could feel something. If it weren't for Kate, I'd think my big brother was sweet on you."

"I'm sure you're imagining things."

"I suppose so," Skip said with a curt nod, quickly dismissing the notion. "Ever since you arrived, though, Clay's been acting weird."

"How do you mean?"

"Sort of cranky."

"My unexpected arrival added to his troubles, don't you think?" In so many ways it was the truth, and she felt guilty about that. The responsibilities for the farm and for raising Skip were sobering enough; he didn't need her there to wreak havoc with his personal life.

"You weren't any problem," Skip answered sharply. "In fact, having you around was a lot of fun. The only trouble is you didn't stay near long enough."

"Thank you, Skip," she managed. Once again she felt her throat clog with tears. She was touched by his sweet, simple hospitality and reminded of how much she would miss him.

"I still kinda wish you were going to stay for the fair," he mumbled. "You'd have a good time, I guarantee it. We may not have all the fancy entertainment you do in San Francisco, but when we do something like a country fair, we do it big."

"I'm sure it'll be great fun."

Skip braced his foot against the bumper of the faded blue pickup, apparently forgetting his earlier decision to seek out Clay, which was just as well.

"You don't like the country much, do you, Rorie?"

"Oh, but I do," she countered. "It's a different way of life, though. I feel like a duck in a pond full of swans here on Elk Run."

Skip laughed. "I suppose folks there in the big city don't think much of the country."

"No one has time to think," Rorie said with a small laugh.

"That doesn't make any sense. Everyone's got thoughts."

Rorie nodded, not knowing how to explain something so complex. When Skip had spent some time in the city, he'd figure out what she meant.

"The one thing I've noticed more than anything is how quiet it is here," she said pensively, looking around, burning into her memory each detail of the farmhouse and the yard.

"I like the quiet. Some places, the noise is so bad I worry about ear damage," Skip said.

"I imagine if I were to live here, I'd grow accustomed to the silence, too. I hadn't ever thought about how much I enjoy the sounds of the city. There's something invigorating about the clang of the trolley cars or the foghorn on the Bay early in the morning.''

Skip frowned and shook his head. "You honestly like all that racket?"

Rorie nodded. "It's more than that. There's something sensual about the city, exciting. I hadn't even realised how much living there meant to me before coming to Elk Run." Rorie didn't know how to describe the aroma of freshly baked sourdough bread, or the perfumed scent of budding rosebushes in the Golden Gate Park, to someone who had never experienced them. Country life had its appeal, she couldn't deny that, but she belonged to the city. At least, that was what she told herself over and over again.

"Ah," Skip said, and his foot dropped from the bumper with a thud, "here's Clay now."

Rorie tensed, gripping her hands together in front of her. Clay's lengthy strides quickly diminished the distance between the barn and the yard. Each stride was filled with purpose, as though he longed to get this polite farewell over with.

Rorie straightened and walked towards him. "I'll be leaving in a couple of minutes," she explained softly.

"Kate's coming over to say goodbye," Skip added.

Rorie noted how Clay's eyes didn't quite meet her own. He seemed to focus instead on the car behind her. They'd already said everything there was to say and this final parting only compounded the pain.

"Saying thank you seems so inadequate," Rorie told him in a voice that wasn't entirely steady. "I've appreciated your hospitality more than you'll ever know." Hesitantly she held out her hand to him.

Clay's hard fingers curled around her own, his touch light and impersonal. Rorie swallowed hard, unable to hold back the emotion churning so violently inside her.

His expression was completely impassive, she noted, but she sensed that he held on to his self-control with the thinnest of threads. In that moment, Rorie felt the desperate longing in him and knew that he recognised it in her, too.

"Oh, Clay…" she whispered, her eyes brimming with tears. The impulse to move into his arms was like a huge wave, threatening to sweep over her, and she didn't know how much longer she'd have the strength to resist.

"Don't look at me like that," Clay muttered grimly.

"I...can't help it." But he belonged to Kate and nothing was likely to change that.

He took a step towards her and stopped himself, suddenly remembering they weren't alone.

"Skip, go hold Thunder for Don. Don's trying to paste-worm him, and he's getting dragged all over the stall." Clay's words were low-pitched, sharp, full of demand.

"But, Clay, Rorie's about to—"

"Do it."

Mumbling something unintelligible under his breath, Skip trudged off to the barn.

The minute his brother was out of sight, Clay caught Rorie's shoulders, his fingers felt rough and urgent through the thin cotton of her blouse. The next instant, she was locked against him. The kiss was inevitable, Rorie knew, but when his mouth settled over hers she wanted to weep for the joy she found in his arms. He kissed her temple, her cheek, her mouth, until she clung to him with hungry abandonment. They were standing in the middle of the yard in full view of farmhands, but Clay didn't seem to care and Rorie wasn't about object.

"I told myself I wouldn't do this," he whispered huskily.

Rorie's heart constricted.

At the sound of a car in the distance, Clay abruptly dropped his arms, freeing her. His fingers tangled in her hair as if he had to touch her one last time.

"I was a fool to think I could politely shake your hand and let you drive away from me. We're more than casual friends and I can't pretend otherwise—to hell with the consequences."

Tears flooded Rorie's eyes as she stared up at Clay. Then from behind him, she saw the cloud of dust that announced Kate's arrival. She inhaled a deep breath in an effort to compose herself and, wiping her damp cheeks with the back of one hand, forced a smile.

Clay released a ragged sigh as he trailed a calloused hand down the side of her face. "Goodbye, Rorie," he whispered. With that, he turned and walked away.

A thick layer of fog swirled around Rorie as she paused to catch her breath on the path in Golden Gate Park. She bent forward and planted her hands on her knees, driving the oxygen into her heaving lungs. Not once in the two weeks she'd been on vacation had she followed her jogging routine, and now she was paying the penalty.

The muscles in her calves and thighs protested the strenuous exercise and her heart seemed about to explode. Her biggest problem was trying to keep up with Dan, who'd run ahead, unwilling to slow his pace to match hers.

"Rorie?"

"Over here." Her voice was barely more than a choked whisper. She meant to raise her hand and signal to him, but even that required more effort than she could manage. Seeing a bench in the distance, she stumbled over and collapsed into it. Leaning back, she stretched her legs in front of her.

"You *are* out of shape," Dan teased, handing her a small towel.

Rorie wiped the perspiration from her face and smiled her appreciation. "I can't believe two weeks would make such a difference." She'd been back in San Francisco only a couple of days. Other than dropping off the MG at Dan's place, this was the first time they'd had a chance to get together.

Dan stood next to her, hardly out of breath. Even after a three-mile workout, he didn't have a hair out of place.

"Two weeks *is* a long time," he said with the hint of a smile. "I suppose you didn't keep up with your vitamin programme, either," he chastised gently. "Well, Rorie, it's obvious how much you need me."

She chose to ignore that comment. "I used to consider myself in top physical condition. I ranked right up there with Jane Fonda and the rest of them. Not anymore. Good grief, I thought my heart was going to give out two miles back."

Dan, blond and debonair, was appealingly handsome in a clean-cut boyish way. He draped the towel around his neck and grasped the ends. Rorie's eyes were drawn to his hands, with their finely manicured nails and long tapered fingers. Stockbroker fingers. Nice hands. Friendly hands.

Still, Rorie couldn't help comparing them with another pair of male hands, darkly tanned from hours in the sun and roughly calloused. Gentle hands. Working hands.

"I meant what I said about you needing me," Dan murmured, watching her closely. "It's time we got serious, Rorie. Time we made some important decisions about our future."

When she least expected it, he dropped onto the bench beside her. With his so smooth fingers, he cupped her face, his thumbs stroking her flushed cheeks. "I had time to do a lot of thinking while you were away."

She covered his fingers with her own, praying for an easier way to say what she must. They'd been seeing each other for months and she hated to hurt him, but it would be even crueller to lead him on. When they'd first started dating, Dan had been looking for a casual relationship. He'd recently been divorced and wasn't ready for a new emotional commitment.

"Oh, Dan, I think I know what you're going to say. Please don't."

He paused, searching her face intently. "What do you mean?"

"I had time to think while I was away, too, and I realised that although I'll always treasure your friendship, we can't ever be more than friends."

His dark eyes ignited with resistance. "What happened to you on this vacation, Rorie? You left, and two weeks later you returned a completely different woman."

"I'm sure you're exaggerating," Rorie objected weakly. She knew she *was* different, from the inside out.

"You've hardly said a word to me about your trip," Dan complained, in a tone that suggested he felt hurt by her reticence. "All you've said is that the car broke down in the Oregon outback and you were stuck there for days until a part could be delivered. You don't blame me for that, do you? I had no idea there was anything wrong with the water pump."

She laughed at his apt description of Nightingale as the outback.

"You completely missed the writers' conference, didn't you?"

"That couldn't be helped, but I enjoyed the rest of my vacation. Victoria was like stepping into a small piece of England," she said, in an effort to divert his attention from the time she'd spent on the Franklin farm. Victoria had been lovely, but unfortunately she hadn't been in the proper mood to appreciate its special brand of beauty.

"You didn't so much as mail me a postcard."

"I know," she said with a twinge of guilt.

"I was lonesome without you," Dan said slowly, running his hand over her hair. "Nothing felt right with you gone."

Rorie realised it had taken a good deal for him to admit that, and it made what she had to tell him all the more difficult.

"Dan, please," she said, breaking away from him and standing. "I...I don't love you."

"But we're friends."

"Of course."

He seemed both pleased and relieved by that. "Good friends?" he coaxed.

Rorie nodded, wondering where this discussion was leading.

"Then there's really no problem, is there?" he asked, his voice gaining enthusiasm. "You went away, and I realised how much I love you, and you came back deciding you value my friendship—that, at least, is a beginning."

"Dan, honestly!"

"Well, isn't it?"

"Our relationship isn't going anywhere," she told him, desperate to clarify the issue. Dan was a good person and he deserved someone who was crazy in love with him. The way she was with Clay. Only Clay.

To Rorie's surprise, Dan drew her forward and soundly kissed her. Startled, she stood placidly in his arms, feeling his warm mouth move over hers. She experienced no feeling, no excitement, nothing. Kissing Dan held all the appeal of drinking flat soda.

Frustrated, he tried to deepen the kiss.

Rorie braced her hands against his chest and twisted her mouth free from him. He released her immediately, then stepped back, frowning. "Okay, okay, we've got our work cut out for us. But the electricity will come, in time."

Somehow Rorie doubted that.

Dan dropped her off in front of her apartment. "Can I see you soon?" he asked, his hands clenching the steering wheel. He didn't look at her but stared straight ahead as though he feared her answer.

Rorie hesitated. "I'm not going to fall in love with you, Dan, and I don't want to take advantage of your feelings. I think it'd be best if you started seeing someone else."

He appeared to mull that over for several awkward moments. "But the decision should be my own, don't you think?"

"Yes, but—"

"Then leave everything to me, and stop worrying. If I choose to waste my time on you, that's my problem, not yours. Personally I think you're going to change your mind. You see, Rorie, I love you enough for both of us."

"Oh, Dan." Her shoulders sagged with defeat. He hadn't believed a single word she'd said.

"Now stop looking so depressed. How about a movie Sunday? It's been a while since we've done that."

Exhausted, she shook her head. "Dan, no."

"I insist, so stop arguing."

She didn't have the energy to argue. Soon enough he'd learn she meant what she'd said. "All right."

"Good. I'll pick you up at six."

Rorie climbed out of the sedan and closed the door, turning to give Dan a limp wave. She paused in the foyer of her apartment building to unlock her mailbox.

There was a handful of envelopes. Absently, she shuffled through a leaflet from a prominent department store, an envelope with a Kentucky postmark and an electric bill. It wasn't until she was inside her apartment that Rorie noticed the letter postmarked Nightingale, Oregon.

Thirteen

Rorie set the letter on her kitchen counter and stared at it for several breathless moments. Her chest felt as if a dead weight were pressing against it. Her heart was pounding and her stomach churned. The post-office box number for the return address didn't tell her much. The letter could as easily be from Kate as Clay. It could even be from Mary.

Taking a deep, calming breath, Rorie reached for the envelope from Kentucky first. The return address left her blank—she didn't know anyone who lived in that state.

That single slip of paper inside confused her, too. She read it several times, not understanding. It appeared to be registration papers for Nightsong, from the National Show Horse Association. Rorie Campbell was listed as owner, with Clay's name given as breeder. The date of Nightsong's birth was also recorded. Rorie slumped into a kitchen chair and battled an attack of memories and tears.

Clay was giving her Nightsong.

It was Nightsong who had brought them together and it was by Nightsong that they would remain linked. Life would go on; the loss of one woman's love wouldn't alter the course of history. But now there was something—a single piece of paper—that would connect her to Clay, something that gave testimony to their sacrifice.

Rorie had needed that and Clay had apparently known it.

They'd made the right decision, Rorie told herself for the hundredth time. Clay's action confirmed it.

Clay was wide-open spaces and sleek, well-trained horses, while she thrived in the crowded city.

His strength came from his devotion to the land; hers came from the love of children and literature and the desire to create her own stories.

They were dissimilar in every way—and alike. In the most important matters, the most telling, they were actually very much alike. Neither of them was willing to claim happiness at the expense of someone else.

Tears spilled down her cheeks, and sniffling, Rorie wiped them aside. The drops dampened her fingertips as she reached for the second envelope, blurring the return address. But even before she opened it, Rorie realised the letter was from Kate. Clay wouldn't write her, and everything Mary had wanted to say she'd already said the morning Rorie left Elk Run.

Three handwritten sheets slipped easily from the envelope, with Kate's evenly slanted signature at the bottom of the last.

The letter was filled with chatty news about Nightingale and some of the people Rorie had met. There were so many, and connecting names with the faces taxed her memory. Kate wrote about the county fair, telling Rorie that she'd missed a very exciting pig race. The biggest news of all was that after years of trying, Mary had finally won a blue ribbon for her apple pie—an honour long overdue in Kate's eyes.

Toward the end of the letter, Clay's fiancée casually mentioned that Clay would be in San Francisco the first week of September for a horse show. The American Saddlebreds from Elk Run were well-known throughout the Pacific coast for their fire and elegance. Clay had high hopes of repeating last year's wins in the Five Gaited and Fine Harness Championships.

Rorie's pulse shifted into overdrive and her fingers tightened on the letter. Clay was coming to San Francisco. He hadn't mentioned the show to Rorie—not once, although he must have known about it long before she'd left Nightingale.

Kate went on to say that she'd asked Clay if he planned to look up Rorie while he was in town, but he'd claimed there wouldn't be time. Kate was sure Rorie would understand and not take offence. She closed by mentioning that her father might also be attending the horse show and, if he did, Kate would try to talk him into letting her tag along. Kate promised she'd phone Rorie the minute she arrived in town, if she could swing it with her father.

Not until Rorie folded the letter to return it to the envelope did she notice the postscript on the back of the last page. She turned over the sheet of pink stationery. The words seemed to jump off the page: Kate was planning an October wedding and would send Rorie an invitation. She ended with, "Write soon."

Rorie's breath caught in her lungs. An October wedding... In only a few weeks; Kate would belong to Clay. Rorie closed her eyes as her heart squeezed into a knot of pain. It wasn't that she hadn't realised this was coming. Kate's and Clay's wedding was inevitable, but Rorie hadn't thought Clay would go through with it quite so soon. With trembling hands, she set the letter aside.

"Rorie, love, I can't honestly believe you want to go to a horse show," Dan complained, scanning the entertainment section of the Friday-evening paper. They sat in the minuscule living room in her apartment and sipped their coffee while they tossed around ideas for something to do.

Rorie smiled blandly, praying Dan couldn't read her thoughts. He'd offered several suggestions for the night's amusement, but Rorie had rejected each one, until she pretended to hit upon the idea of attending the horse show.

"A horse show?" he repeated. "You never told me you were interested in horses."

"It would be fun, don't you think?"

"Not particularly."

"But, Dan, it's time to broaden our horizons—we might even learn something."

"Does this mean you're going to insist we attend a demolition derby next weekend?"

"Of course not. I read an article about this horse show and I just thought we'd enjoy the gaited classes and harness competitions. Apparently, lots of Saddlebreds and National Show Horses are going to be performing. Doesn't that interest you?"

"No."

Rorie shrugged, slowly releasing a sigh of regret. "Then a movie's fine," she said, not even trying to hide her disappointment. They'd seen each other only a handful of times since Rorie's return. Rorie wouldn't be going out with him tonight if he hadn't persisted. She hoped he'd soon get the message and start dating other women, but that didn't seem to be happening.

"I can't imagine why you'd want to see a horse show," Dan said once more.

For the past few days the newspapers had been filled with information regarding the country-wide show in which Kate had said several of Elk Run's horses would be participating. In all the years she'd lived in San Francisco, Rorie couldn't remember ever reading about a single equine exhibition, but then she hadn't exactly been looking for one, either.

If Dan refused to go with her, Rorie was determined to attend the event on her own. She didn't have any intention of seeking out Clay, but the opportunity to see him, even from a distance, was too tempting to let pass. It would probably be the last time she'd ever see him.

"I don't know what's got into you lately, Rorie," he complained, not for the first time. "Just when I think our lives are starting to even out, you throw me for a loop."

"I said a movie was fine." Her tone was testier than she meant it to be, but Dan had been harping on the same subject for weeks and she was tired of it.

If he didn't want her company, he should start dating someone else. She wasn't going to realise suddenly she was madly in love with him, as he seemed to expect. Again and again, Dan phoned to tell her that he loved her, that his love was enough for them both. She always stopped him there, unable to imagine spending the rest of her life with him. If she couldn't have Clay—and she couldn't—then she wasn't willing to settle for anyone else.

"I'm talking about a lot more than seeing a silly movie." He laid the newspaper aside and seemed to carefully consider his next words.

"Really, Dan, you're making a mountain out of a molehill," Rorie said. "Just because I wanted to do something a little out of the ordinary..."

"Eating at an Armenian restaurant is a little out of the ordinary," he muttered, frowning, "but horse shows... I can't even begin to imagine why on God's green earth you'd want to watch a bunch of animals running around in circles."

"Well, you keep insisting I've changed," she said flippantly. If she'd known Dan was going to react so strongly to her suggestion, she'd never have made it. "I guess this only goes to prove you're right."

"How much writing have you done in the past month?"

The question was completely unexpected. She answered him with a shrug, hoping he'd drop the subject, knowing he wouldn't.

"None, right? I've seen you sitting at your computer, staring into space with that sad look on your face. I remember how you used to talk about your stories. Your eyes would light up and spar-kle. Enthusiasm would just spill out of you." His hand reached for hers, tightly squeezing her fingers. "What happened to you, Rorie? Where's the joy? Where's the energy?"

"You're imagining things," she said, nearly leaping to her feet in an effort to sidestep the issues he was raising. She reached for her bag and a light sweater, eager to escape the apartment, which suddenly felt too small. "Are you going to take me to that movie, or are you going to sit here and ask questions I have no intention of answering?"

Dan stood, smiling faintly. "I don't know what happened while you were on vacation, and it's not important that I do know, but whatever it was hurt you badly."

Rorie tried to deny it, but couldn't force the lie past her tongue. She swallowed and turned her head away, her eyes burning.

"You won't be able to keep pretending forever, Rorie. I know you too well. Put whatever it is behind you. If you want to talk about it, I've got a sympathetic ear and a sturdy shoulder. I'm your friend, you know."

"Dan, please..."

"I know you're not in love with me," he said gently. "I suspect you met someone else while you were away, but that doesn't matter to me. Whatever happened during those two weeks is over."

"Dan..."

He reached for her hand, pulling her back onto the sofa, then sitting down beside her. She couldn't look at him.

"Given time, you'll learn to love me," he cajoled, holding her hand, his voice filled with kindness. "We're already good friends, and that's a lot more than some people have when they marry." He raised her fingers to his mouth and kissed them lightly. "I'm not looking for passion. I had that with my first wife. I learned the hard way that desire is a poor foundation for a solid marriage."

"We've talked about this before," Rorie protested. "I can't marry you, Dan, not when I feel the way I do about...someone else." Her mouth trembled with the effort to suppress tears. Dan was right. As much as she hadn't wanted to face the truth, she'd been heartbroken from the moment she'd left Nightingale.

She'd tried to forget Clay, believing that was the best thing for them both, yet she cherished the memories, knowing those few brief days were all she would ever have of this man she loved.

"You don't have to decide right now," Dan assured her.

"There isn't anything to decide," she persisted.

His fingers continued to caress hers, and when he spoke his voice was thick. "At least you've admitted there is someone else."

"Was," she corrected.

"I take it there isn't any chance the two of you—"

"None," she blurted, unwilling to discuss anything that had to do with Clay.

"I know it's painful for you right now, but all I ask is that you seriously consider my proposal. My only wish is to take care of you and make you smile again. Help you forget."

His mouth sought hers, and though his kiss wasn't unpleasant, it generated no more excitement than before, no rush of adrenalin, no urgency. She hadn't minded Dan's kisses in the past, but until she met Clay she hadn't known the warmth and magic a man's touch could create.

Dan must have read her thoughts, because he added in a soothing voice, "The passion will come in time—you shouldn't even look for it now, but it'll be there. Maybe not this month or the next, but you'll feel it eventually, I promise."

Rorie brushed the hair from her face, confused and uncertain. Clay was marrying Kate in just a few weeks. Her own life stretched before her, lonely and barren—surely she deserved some happiness, too. Beyond a doubt, Rorie knew Clay would want her to build a good life for herself. But if she married Dan, it would be an act of selfishness, and she feared she'd only end up hurting him.

"Think about it," Dan urged. "That's all I ask."

"Dan..."

"Just consider it. I know the score and I'm willing to take the risk, so you don't have to worry about me. I'm a big boy." He rubbed his thumb against the inside of her wrist. "Now, promise me you'll honestly think about us getting married."

Rorie nodded, although she already knew what her answer would have to be.

Dan heaved a sigh. "Now, are you really interested in that horse show, or are we going to see a movie?"

Rorie didn't need to think twice. "The movie." There was no use in tormenting herself with thoughts of Clay. He belonged to Kate in the same way that he belonged to the country. Rorie had no claim to either.

The film Dan chose was surprisingly good, a comedy, which was just what Rorie needed to lift her spirits. Afterward, they dined on linguini and drank wine and discussed politics. Dan went out of his way to be a pleasant companion, making no demands on her, and Rorie was grateful.

It was still relatively early when he drove her back to her apartment, and he eagerly accepted her invitation for coffee. As he eased the MG into the narrow space in front of her building, he suddenly paused, frowning.

"Do you have new neighbours?"

"Not that I know of. Why?"

Dan nodded towards the battered blue pickup across the street. "Whoever drives that piece of junk is about to bring down the neighbourhood property values."

Fourteen

"Clay." His name escaped Rorie's lips on a rush of excitement. She jerked open the car door and stepped onto the pavement, legs trembling. Her pulse was thundering so hard it echoed in her ears like sonic booms.

"Rorie?" Dan called, agitated. "Who is this man?"

She hardly heard him. A door slammed in the distance and Rorie whirled around and saw that Clay had been sitting inside his truck, apparently waiting for her return. He'd been parked in the shadows, and she hadn't noticed him there.

Dan joined her on the pavement and placed his hand possessively on her shoulder. His grip was the only thing that rooted her in reality, his hand the restraining force that prevented her from flying into Clay's arms.

"Who is this guy?" Dan asked a second time.

Rorie opened her mouth to explain and realised she couldn't, not in just a few words. "A...friend," she whispered, but that seemed so inadequate.

"He's a cowboy!" Dan hissed, making it sound as though Clay's close-fitting jeans and jacket were the garb of a man just released from jail.

Clay crossed the street and his long strides made short work of the distance separating him from Rorie.

"Hello, Rorie."

She heard the faint catch in his voice. "Clay."

A muscle moved in his cheek as he looked past her to Dan, who squared the shoulders of his Brooks Brothers suit. No one spoke for a long moment, until Rorie realised Clay was waiting for an introduction.

"Clay Franklin, this is Dan Rogers. Dan is the stockbroker I...I mentioned before. It was his sports car I was driving."

Clay nodded. "I remember now." His gaze slid away from Rorie to the man at her side.

Dan stepped around Rorie and accepted Clay's hand. She noticed that when Dan dropped his arm to his side, he flexed his fingers a couple of times, as though to restore the circulation. Rorie smiled to herself. Clay's handshake was the solid one of a man accustomed to working with his hands. When Dan shook hands, it was little more than a polite business greeting, an archaic but necessary exchange.

"Clay and his brother, Skip, were the family who helped me when the MG broke down," Rorie explained to Dan.

"Ah, yes, I remember your saying something about that now."

"I was just about to put on a pot of coffee," Rorie went on, unable to take her eyes off Clay. She drank in the sight of him, painfully noting the crow's feet that fanned out from the corners of his eyes. She couldn't remember their being quite so pronounced before.

"Yes, by all means join us." Dan's invitation lacked any real welcome.

Clay said nothing. He just stood there looking at her. Almost no emotion showed in his face, but she could feel the battle that raged inside him. He loved her still, and everything about him told her that.

"Please join us," she whispered.

Any lingering hope that Dan would take the hint and make his excuses faded as he slipped his arm protectively around Rorie's shoulders. "I picked up some Swiss mocha coffee beans earlier," he said, "and Rorie was going to brew a pot of that."

"Swiss mocha coffee?" Clay repeated, blinking quizzically.

"Decaffeinated, naturally," Dan hurried to add.

Clay arched his brow expressively, as if to say that made all the difference in the world.

With Dan glued to her side, Rorie reluctantly led the way into her building. "Have you been here long?" she asked Clay while they stood waiting for the lift.

"About an hour."

"Oh, Clay…" Rorie felt terrible, although it wasn't her fault; she hadn't known he intended to stop by. Perhaps he hadn't known himself and had been lured to her apartment the same way she'd been contemplating the horse show.

"You should have phoned." Dan's comment was casual, but it contained a hint of accusation. "But then, I suppose, you folks tend to drop in on each other all the time. Things are more casual in the country, aren't they?''

Rorie sent Dan a furious glare. He returned her look blankly, as if to say he had no idea what could have angered her. Rorie was grateful that the lift arrived just then.

Clay didn't comment on Dan's observation and the three stepped inside, facing the doors as they slowly closed.

''When you weren't home, I asked the neighbours if they knew where you'd gone,'' Clay mentioned.

''The neighbours?'' Dan echoed, making no effort to disguise his astonishment.

''What did they tell you?'' Rorie asked.

Clay smiled briefly, then sobered when he glanced at Dan. ''They claimed they didn't know *who* lived next door, never mind where you'd gone.''

''Frankly, I'm surprised they answered the door,'' Dan said conversationally. ''There's a big difference between what goes on in small towns and big cities.''

Dan spoke like a teacher to a grade-school pupil. Rorie wanted to kick him, but reacting in anger would only increase the embarrassment. She marvelled at Clay's tolerance.

''Things are done differently here,'' Dan continued. ''Few people have anything to do with their neighbours. People prefer to mind their own business. Getting involved can only lead to problems.''

Clay rubbed the side of his face. ''It seems to me *not* getting involved would lead to even bigger problems.''

''I'm grateful Clay and Skip were there when *your* car broke down,'' Rorie said to Dan, hoping to put an end to this tiresome discussion. ''Otherwise I don't know what would have happened. I could still be on that road waiting for someone to stop and help me,'' she said, forcing the joke.

''Yes,'' Dan admitted, clearing his throat. ''I suppose I should thank you for assisting Rorie.''

''I suppose I should accept your thanks,'' Clay returned.

''How's Mary?'' Rorie asked, quickly changing the subject, as the lift slid to a stop at her floor.

Humour sparked in Clay's grey eyes. ''Mary's strutting around proud as a peacock ever since she won a blue ribbon at the county fair.''

''She had reason to be proud.'' Rorie could just picture the housekeeper. Knowing Mary, she was probably wearing the ribbon pinned to her apron. "What about Skip?" Rorie asked next, hungry for news about each one. She took the keys from her bag and systematically began unlocking the three bolts on her apartment door.

"Fine. He started school last week—he's a senior this year."

Rorie already knew that, but she nodded.

"Kate wanted you to know she sends her best," Clay said next, his voice carefully nonchalant.

"Tell her I said hello, too."

"She hasn't heard from you. No one has."

"I know. I'm sorry. She wrote soon after I returned from Canada, but I hadn't had a chance to answer." On several occasions, Rorie had tried to force herself to sit down and write Kate a letter. But she couldn't. At the end of her second week back home, she'd decided it was better for everyone involved if she didn't keep in touch with Kate. When the wedding invitation came, Rorie planned to post an appropriate gift, and that would be the end of it.

Once they were inside the apartment, Rorie hung up her sweater and bag and motioned for both men to sit down. "It'll only take a minute to put on the coffee."

"Do you need me to grind the beans?" Dan asked, obviously eager to assist her.

"No, I don't need any help." His offer was an excuse to question her about Clay, and Rorie wanted to avoid that if she could. At least for now.

Her apartment had never felt more cramped than it did when she joined the two men in her tiny living room. Clay rose to his feet as she entered, and the simple courtly gesture made her want to weep. He was telling her that he respected her and cared for her, that...she was his lady...would always be his lady.

The area was just large enough for one sofa and a coffee table. Her desk and computer stood against the other wall. Rorie pulled the chair away from the desk, turned it to face her guests and perched on the edge. Only then did Clay sit back down.

"So," Dan said with a heavy sigh. "Rorie never did tell me what it is you do in...in..."

"Nightingale," Rorie and Clay said together.

"Oh, yes, Nightingale," Dan murmured, clearing his throat. "I take it you're some kind of farmer? Do you grow soy beans or wheat?"

"Clay owns a stud farm for American Saddlebreds," Rorie explained.

Dan looked as if she'd punched him in the stomach. He'd obviously made the connection between Clay and her earlier interest in attending the horse show.

"I see," he breathed, and his voice shook a little. "Horses. So you're involved with horses."

Clay looked at him curiously.

"How's Nightsong?" Rorie asked, before Dan could say anything else. Just thinking about the foal with her wide curious eyes and her long wobbly legs produced a feeling of tenderness in Rorie.

"She's a rare beauty," Clay told her softly, "showing more promise every day."

Rorie longed to tell Clay how much it had meant to her that he'd registered Nightsong in her name, how she cherished that gesture more than anything in her life. She also knew that Clay would never sell the foal, but would keep and love her all her life.

An awkward silence followed, and in an effort to smooth matters over she explained to Dan, "Clay was gone one night when Star Bright—one of the brood mares—went into labour...if that's what they call it in horses?" she asked Clay.

He nodded.

"Anyway, I couldn't wake up Skip, and I didn't know where Mary was sleeping and something had to be done—quick."

Dan leaned forward, his eyes revealing his surprise and shock. "You don't mean to tell me *you* delivered the foal?"

"Not exactly." Rorie wished now that she hadn't said anything to Dan about that night. No one could possibly understand what she and Clay had shared in those few hours. Trying to convey the experience to someone else only diminished its significance.

"I'll get the coffee," Rorie offered, standing. "I'm sure it's ready."

From her kitchen, she could hear Dan and Clay talking, although she couldn't make out their words. She filled three cups and placed them on a tray, then carried it into the living room.

Once more Clay stood. He took the tray out of her hands and set it on the coffee table. Rorie handed Dan the first cup and saucer and Clay the second. He looked uncomfortable as he accepted it.

"I'm sorry, Clay, you prefer a mug, don't you?" The cup seemed frail and tiny, impractical, cradled in his strong hand.

"It doesn't matter. If I'm going to be drinking Swiss mocha

coffee, I might as well do it from a china cup.'' He smiled into her eyes, and Rorie couldn't help reciprocating.

"Eaten any seafood fettuccine lately?'' she teased.

"Can't say that I have.''

"It's my favourite dinner,'' Dan inserted, apparently feeling left out of the conversation. "We had linguini tonight, but Rorie's favourite is sushi.''

Her eye caught Clay's and she noted how the corner of his mouth quirked with barely restrained humour. She could just imagine what the good people of Nightingale would think of a sushi bar. Skip would probably turn up his nose, insisting that the small pieces of raw fish looked like bait.

The coffee seemed to command everyone's attention for the next minute or so.

"I'm still reeling from the news of your adventures on this stud farm,'' Dan commented, laughing lightly. "You could have bowled me over with a feather when you announced that you'd helped deliver a foal. I would never have believed it of you, Rorie.''

"I brought along a picture of Nightsong,'' Clay said, cautiously putting down his coffee cup. He unsnapped the pocket of his wide-yoked shirt and withdrew two colour photographs, which he handed to Rorie. "I meant to show those to you earlier...but I got sidetracked.''

"Oh, Clay,'' she breathed, studying the filly with her gleaming chestnut coat. "She's grown so much in just this last month,'' she said, her voice full of wonder.

"I thought you'd be impressed.''

Reluctantly Rorie shared the pictures with Dan, who barely glanced at them before handing them back to Clay.

"Most men carry around pictures of their wife and kids,'' Dan stated, his eyes darting to Clay and then Rorie.

Rorie supposed this comment was Dan's less-than-subtle attempt to find out if Clay was married. Taking a deep breath, she explained. "Clay's engaged to a neighbour—Kate Logan.''

"I see.'' Apparently he did, because he set aside his coffee cup, and got up to stand behind Rorie. Hands resting on her shoulders, he leaned forward and lightly brushed his mouth over her cheek. "Rorie and I have been talking about getting married ourselves, haven't we, darling?''

Fifteen

No emotion revealed itself on Clay's face, but Rorie could sense the tight rein he held on himself. Dan's words had dismayed him.

"Is that true, Rorie?" he said after a moment.

Dan's fingers tightened almost painfully on her shoulders. "Just tonight we were talking about getting married. Tell him, darling."

Her eyes refused to leave Clay's. She *had* been talking to Dan about marriage, although she had no intention of accepting his offer. Dan knew where he stood, knew she was in love with another man. But nothing would be accomplished by telling Clay that she'd always love him, especially since he was marrying Kate within a few weeks. "Yes, Dan has proposed."

"I'm crazy about Rorie and have been for months," Dan announced, squarely facing his competition. He spoke for a few minutes more, outlining his goals. Within another ten years, he planned to be financially secure and hoped to retire.

"Dan's got a bright future," Rorie echoed.

"I see." Clay replaced his coffee cup on the tray, then glanced at his watch and rose to his feet. "I suppose I should head back to the Cow Palace."

"How...how are you doing in the show?" Rorie asked, distraught, not wanting him to leave. Kate would have him the rest of their lives; surely a few more minutes with him wouldn't matter. "Kate wrote that you were going after several championships."

"I'm doing exactly as I expected I would." The words were clipped, as though he was impatient to get away.

Rorie knew she couldn't keep him any longer. Clay's face was stern with purpose, drawn and resigned. "I'll see you out," she told him.

"I'll help you," Dan said.

She whirled around and glared at him. "No, you won't."

"Good to see you again, Rorie," Clay said, standing just inside her apartment, his hand on the door. His mouth was hard and flat and he held himself rigid, eyes avoiding hers. He stepped forward and shook Dan's hand.

"It was a pleasure," Dan said in a tone that conveyed exactly the opposite.

"Me, too." Clay dropped his hand.

"I'm glad you stopped by," Rorie told him quietly. "It was... nice seeing you." The words sounded inane, meaningless.

He nodded brusquely, opened the door and walked into the hallway.

"Clay," she said, following him out, her heart hammering so loudly it seemed to echo off the walls.

He stopped, and slowly turned around.

Now that she had his attention, Rorie didn't know what to say. "Listen, I'm sorry about the way Dan was acting."

He shook off her apology. "Don't worry about it."

Her fingers tightened on the doorknob, and she wondered if this was really to be the end. "Will I see you again?" she asked despite herself.

"I don't think so," he answered hoarsely. He looked past her as though he could see through the apartment door and into her living room where Dan was waiting. "Do you honestly love this guy?"

"He's...he's been a good friend."

Clay took two steps towards her, then stopped. As if it was against his better judgement, he raised his hand and lightly drew his finger down the side of her face. Rorie closed her eyes to the wealth of sensation the simple action provoked.

"Be happy, Rorie. That's all I want for you."

The rain hit during the last week of September, and the dreary dark afternoons suited Rorie's mood. Normally autumn was a productive time for her, but she remained tormented with what she felt sure was a terminal case of writer's block. She sat at her desk, her computer humming merrily as she read over the accumulation of an entire weekend's work.

One measly sentence.

There'd been a time when she could write four or five pages a night after coming home from the library. Perhaps the problem was the story she'd chosen. She wanted to write about a young filly named Nightsong, but every time she started her memories of the real Nightsong invaded her thoughts, crippling the creative flow.

Here it was Monday night and she sat staring at the screen, convinced nothing she wrote had any merit. The only reason she even kept on trying was that Dan had pressured her into it. He seemed to believe her world would right itself once Rorie was back to originating her warm, lighthearted children's stories.

The phone rang and, grateful for a reprieve, Rorie hurried into the kitchen to answer it.

The unmistakable hum of a long-distance call echoed in her ear. "Is this Miss Rorie Campbell of San Francisco, California?"

"Yes, it is." Her heart tripped with anxiety. In a matter of two seconds, every horrible scenario of what could have happened to her parents or her brother darted through Rorie's mind.

"This is Devin Logan calling."

He paused, as though expecting her to recognise the name. Rorie didn't. "Yes?"

"Devin Logan," he repeated, "from the Nightingale, Oregon, Town Council." He paused. "I believe you're acquainted with my daughter, Kate."

"Yes, I remember Kate." If her heart continued at this pace Rorie thought she'd keel over in a dead faint. Just as her pulse had started to slow, it shot up again. "Has anything happened?"

"The council meeting adjourned about ten minutes ago. Are you referring to that?"

"No...no, I mean has anything happened to Kate?"

"Not that I'm aware of. Do you know something I don't?"

"I don't think so." This entire conversation was quickly driving her crazy.

Devin Logan cleared his throat, and when he spoke his voice dropped to a deeper pitch. "I'm phoning on an official capacity," he said. "We voted at the Town Council meeting tonight to employ a full-time librarian."

He paused again, and, not knowing what else to say, Rorie murmured, "Congratulations. Kate mentioned the library was currently being run by part-time volunteers."

"It was decided to offer *you* the position."

Rorie nearly dropped the receiver. "I beg your pardon?"

"My daughter managed to convince the council that we need a full-time librarian for our new building. She also persuaded us that you're the woman for the job."

"But..." Hardly able to believe what she was hearing, Rorie slumped against the kitchen wall, glad of its support. Logan's next remark was even more surprising.

"We'll match whatever the San Francisco library is paying you and throw in a house in town—rent-free."

"I…" Rorie's mind was buzzing. Kate obviously thought she was doing her a favour, when in fact being so close to Clay would be utter torment.

"Miss Campbell?"

"I'm honoured," she said quickly, still reeling with astonishment, "truly honoured, but I'm going to have to refuse."

A moment of silence followed. "All right…I'm authorised to enhance the offer by ten percent over the amount you're currently earning, but that's our final bid. You'd be making as much money as the fire chief, and he's not about to let the Council pay a librarian more than he's bringing home."

"Mr Logan, please, the salary isn't the reason I'm turning down your generous offer. I…I want you to know how much I appreciate your offering me the job. Thank you, and thank Kate on my behalf, but I can't accept."

Another, longer silence vibrated across the line, as though he couldn't believe what she was telling him.

"You're positive you want to refuse? Miss Campbell, we're being more than reasonable…more than generous."

"I realise that. In fact, I'm quite amazed and flattered by your proposal, but I can't possibly accept this position."

"Kate had the feeling you'd leap at the job."

"She was mistaken."

"I see. Well, then, it was good talking to you. I'm sorry we didn't get a chance to meet while you were in Nightingale. Perhaps next time."

"Perhaps." Only there wouldn't be a next time.

Rorie kept her hand on the telephone receiver long after she'd hung up. Her back was pressed against the kitchen wall, her eyes closed.

She'd regained a little of her composure when the doorbell chimed. A glance at the wall clock told her it was Dan, who'd promised to drop by that evening. She straightened, forcing a smile, and slowly walked to the door.

Dan entered with a flourish, handing her a small white bag.

"What's this?" she asked.

"Frozen yoghurt. Just the thing for a girl with a hot keyboard. How's the writing going?" He leaned forward to kiss her on the cheek.

Rorie walked back into the kitchen and set the container in the freezer compartment of her refrigerator. "It's not. If you don't mind, I'll eat this later."

"Rorie." Dan caught her by her shoulders and studied her face. "You're as pale as chalk. What's wrong?"

"I...I just got off the phone. I was offered another job as head librarian..."

"But, darling, that's wonderful."

"...in Nightingale, Oregon."

The change in Dan's expression was almost comical. "And? What did you tell them?"

"I refused."

He gave a great sigh of relief. His eyes glowed and he hugged her impulsively. "Does this mean what I think it does? Are you finally over that cowpoke, Rorie? Will you finally consent to be my wife?"

Rorie lowered her gaze. "Oh, Dan, don't you understand? I'll never get over Clay. Not next week, not next month, not next year." Her voice was filled with pain, and with conviction. Everyone seemed to assume that, given time, she'd forget all about Clay Franklin, but she wouldn't.

Dan's smile faded quickly, and he dropped his arms to his sides. "I see." He leaned against the counter, and after a long moment he sighed pensively and said, "I'd do just about anything in this world for you, Rorie, but I think it's time we both faced a few truths."

Rorie had wanted to confront them long before now.

"You're never going to love me the way you do that horseman. We can't go on like this. It isn't doing either of us any good to pretend your feelings are going to change."

He looked so grim and so discouraged that she didn't point out that *he'd* been the one who'd been pretending.

"I'm so sorry to hurt you—it's the last thing I ever wanted to do," she told him sincerely.

"It isn't as if I didn't know," he admitted. "You've been honest with me from the start. I can't be less with you. That country boy loves you. I knew it the minute he walked across the street without even noticing the traffic. The whole world would know," he admitted ruefully. "All he had to do is look at you and everything about him shouts his feelings. He may be engaged to another woman, but it's you he loves."

"I wouldn't fit into his world."

"But, Rorie, love, you're lost and confused in your own now."

She bit her lower lip and nodded. Until Dan said it, she hadn't realised how true that was. But it didn't change the fact that Clay belonged to Kate. And she was marrying him within the month.

"I'm sorry, Rorie," Dan said, completely serious, "but the wedding's off."

She nearly laughed out loud at Dan's announcement. No wedding had ever been planned. He'd asked her to marry him at least ten times since she'd returned from her vacation, and each time she'd refused. Instead of wearing her down as he'd hoped, Dan had finally come to accept her decision. Rorie felt relieved, but she was sorry to lose her friend.

"I didn't mean to lead you on," she offered, genuinely contrite.

He shrugged. "The pain will only last a little while. I'm 'a keeper' as the girls in the office like to tell me. I guess it's time I let out the word that I'm available." He wiggled his eyebrows up and down, striving for some humour.

"You've been such a good friend."

He cupped her face and gently kissed her. "Yes, I know. Now don't let that yoghurt go to waste—you're too thin as it is."

She smiled and nodded. When she let him out of the apartment, Rorie bolted the door then leaned against it, feeling drained, but curiously calm.

Dan had been gone only a short while when Rorie's phone rang again. She hurried into the kitchen to answer it.

The long-distance hum greeted her a second time. "Rorie? This is Kate Logan."

"Kate! How are you?"

"Rotten, but I didn't call to talk about me. I want to know exactly why you're refusing to be Nightingale's librarian—after everything I went through. I can't believe you, Rorie. How can you do this to Clay? Don't you love him?"

Sixteen

"Kate," Rorie demanded. "What are you talking about?"

"You and Clay," she returned sharply, sounding quite unlike her normally gentle self. "Now, do you love him or not? I've got to know."

This day had been sliding steadily downhill from the moment Rorie had climbed out of bed that morning. To admit her feelings for Clay would only hurt Kate, and Rorie had tried so hard to avoid offending the other woman.

"Well?" Kate demanded, then gave a sob. "The least you can do is answer me."

"Oh, Kate," Rorie said, her heart in her throat, "why are you asking me if I love Clay? He belongs to you. It shouldn't matter one little bit if I love him or not. I'm out of your lives and I intend to stay out."

"But he loves you."

The tears in Kate's voice tore at Rorie's already battered heart. She would have given anything to spare her friend this pain. "I know," she whispered.

"Doesn't that mean anything to you?"

Only the world and everything in it. "Yes," she murmured, her voice growing stronger.

"Then how could you do this to him?"

"Do what?" Rorie didn't understand.

"Hurt him this way!"

"Kate," Rorie pleaded. "I don't know what you're talking about—I'd never intentionally hurt Clay. If you insist on knowing, I do love him, with all my heart, but he's your fiancé. You loved him long before I even knew him."

Kate's short laugh was riddled with sarcasm. "What is this? A game of first come, first served?"

"Of course not—"

"For your information, Clay isn't my fiancé any longer," Kate blurted, her voice trembling. "He hasn't been in weeks...since before he went to San Francisco for the horse show."

Rorie's head came up so fast she wondered whether she'd dislocated her neck. "He isn't?"

"That's...that's what I just told you."

"But I thought...I assumed..."

"I know what you assumed—that much is obvious—but it isn't that way now and it hasn't been in a long time."

"But you love Clay," Rorie insisted, feeling almost lightheaded.

"I've loved him from the time I was in pigtails. I love him enough to want to see him happy. Why...why do you think I talked my fool head off to a bunch of hard-nosed council members? Why do you think I ranted and raved about what a fantastic librarian you are? I as good as told them you're the only person who could possibly assume full responsibility for the new library. Do you honestly think I did all that for the fun of it? The challenge?"

"No, but, Kate, surely you understand why I have to refuse. I just couldn't bear to be—"

Kate wouldn't allow her to finish, and when she spoke, her voice was high and almost hysterical. "Well, if you think that, Rorie Campbell, then you've got a lot to learn about me...and even more to learn about Clay Franklin."

"Kate, I'm sorry. Now, please stop and listen to me. There's so much I don't understand. We've got to talk, because I can't make head or tail out of what you're telling me and I've got to know—"

"If you have anything to say to me, Rorie Campbell, then you can do it to my face. Now, I'm telling Dad and everyone else on the council that you've accepted the position we so generously offered you. The job starts in two weeks and you had damn well better be here. Understand?"

Rorie's car left a dusty trail on the long, curving driveway that led to the Circle L Ranch. It had been a week since her telephone conversation with Kate, and Rorie's mind still had trouble assimilating what the other woman had told her. Their conversation repeated itself over and over in her mind, until nothing made sense. But one thing stood out: Kate was no longer engaged to Clay.

Rorie was going to him, running as fast as she could, but first she had to settle matters with his former fiancée.

The sun had started to descend in an autumn sky when Rorie

parked her car at the Logan ranch and climbed out. Rotating her neck and shoulders to relieve some of the tension coiled there, Rorie looked around, wondering if anyone was home. She'd been on the road most of the day, so she was exhausted. And exhilarated.

Luke Rivers strolled out of the barn, and stopped when he saw Rorie. His smile deepened. It could have been Rorie's imagination, but she sensed the hard edge was missing from his look, as though life had unexpectedly tossed him a good turn.

"So you're back," he said by way of greeting.

Rorie nodded, then reached inside the car for her bag. "Is Kate around?"

"She'll be here any minute. Kate's usually home from the school around four. Come inside and I'll get you a cup of coffee."

"Thanks." At the moment, coffee sounded like nectar from the gods.

Luke opened the kitchen door for her. "I understand you're going to be Nightingale's new librarian?" he said, following her into the house.

"Yes." But that wasn't the reason she'd come back, and they both knew it.

"Good." Luke brought down two mugs from the cupboard and filled them from a coffeepot that sat on the stove. He placed Rorie's cup on the table, then pulled out a chair for her.

"Thank you, Luke."

The sound of an approaching vehicle drew his attention. He parted the lace curtain at the kitchen window and glanced out.

"That's Kate now," he said, his gaze lingering on the driveway, softening perceptibly. "Listen, if I don't get a chance to talk to you later, I want you to know I'm glad you're here. I've got a few things to thank you for myself. If it hadn't been for you, I might have turned into a crotchety old saddle bum."

Before Rorie could ask him what he meant, he was gone.

Kate burst into the kitchen a minute later and hugged Rorie as though they were long-lost sisters. "I don't know when I've been more pleased to see anyone!"

Rorie's face must have revealed her surprise because Kate hurried to add, "I suppose you think I'm a crazy woman after the way I talked to you on the phone last week. I don't blame you, but...well, I was upset, to put it mildly, and my thinking was a little confused." She tossed her bag on the counter and reached inside the cupboard for a mug. She poured the coffee very slowly, as if she needed the time to gather her thoughts.

Rorie's mind was buzzing with questions she couldn't wait for Kate to answer. "Did I understand you correctly the other night? Did you tell me you and Clay are no longer engaged?"

Kate wasn't able to disguise the flash of pain that leaped into her deep blue eyes. She dropped her gaze and nodded. "We haven't been in weeks."

"But..."

Kate sat down across the table from Rorie and folded her hands around the mug. "The thing is, Rorie, I knew how you two felt about each other since the night of the Grange dance. A blind man would have known you and Clay had fallen in love, but it was so much easier for me to pretend otherwise." Her finger traced the rim of the mug. "I thought once you returned to San Francisco, everything would go back the way it was before you arrived."

"I was hoping for the same thing. Kate, you've got to believe me when I tell you I'd have done anything in the world to spare you this. When I learned you and Clay were engaged I wanted to—"

"Die," Kate finished for her. "I know exactly how you must have felt, because that's the way I felt later. The night of the Grange dance, Clay kept looking at you. Every time you danced with a new partner, his frown grew darker. He might have had me at his side, but his eyes followed you all over the hall."

"He loves you, too," Rorie told her. "That's what made this all so difficult."

"No, he doesn't," Kate answered flatly, without a hint of doubt. "I accepted that a long time before you ever arrived. Oh, he respects and likes me, and to Clay's way of thinking that was enough." She hesitated, frowning. "To my way of thinking, it was enough, too. We probably would have married and found contentment over the years. But everything changed when Clay met you. You hit him square between the eyes, Rorie—a direct hit."

"I'm sure he feels more for you than admiration..."

"No," Kate said, reaching into her bag for a tissue. "He told me as much himself, but as I said it wasn't something I didn't already know. You see, I was so crazy about Clay, I was willing to take whatever he offered me, even if it was only second-best." She swabbed at the tears that sprang so readily to her eyes and paused in an effort to gather her composure. "I'm sorry, Rorie. It's still so painful. But you see, through all this, I've learned a great deal about what it means to love someone.''

Rorie's own eyes welled with involuntary tears, which she hurriedly wiped aside. Then, Kate's fingers clasped hers and squeezed tight in a gesture of reassurance.

''I learned that loving people means placing their happiness before your own. That's the way you love Clay, and the same way he loves you.'' Kate squared her shoulders and inhaled a quavery breath.

''Kate, please, this isn't necessary.''

''Yes, it is, because what I've got to say next is the hardest part. I need to ask your forgiveness for that terrible letter I wrote you soon after you left Nightingale. I don't have any excuse except that I was crazy with jealousy.''

''Letter? You wrote me a terrible letter?'' The only one Rorie had received was the chatty note that had told her about Mary's prize-winning ribbon and made mention of the upcoming wedding.

''I used a subtle form of viciousness,'' Kate replied, her voice filled with self-contempt.

Rorie discounted the fact Kate could ever be malicious. ''The only letter I received from you wasn't the least bit terrible.''

Kate lowered her eyes to her hands, neatly folded on the table. Her grip tightened until Rorie was sure her friend's long nails would cut her palms.

''I lied in that letter,'' Kate continued. ''When I told you that Clay wouldn't have time for you while he was at the horse show, I was trying to tell you that you didn't mean anything to him any more. I wanted you to think you'd easily slipped from his mind when nothing could have been further from the truth.''

''Don't feel so bad about it. I'm not sure I wouldn't have done the same thing.''

''No, Rorie, you wouldn't have. That letter was an underhand attempt to hold on to Clay... I was losing him more and more each day and I thought...I hoped that if you believed we were going to be married in October, then... Oh, I don't know, my thinking was so warped and desperate.''

''Your emotions were running high at the time.'' Rorie's had been, too—she understood Kate's pain because she'd been in so much pain herself.

''But I was pretending to be your friend when in reality I think I almost hated you.'' Kate paused, her shoulders shaking with emotion. "That was the crazy part. I couldn't help liking you and wanting to be your friend, and at the same time I was being eaten alive with selfish resentment."

"It's not in you to hate anyone, Kate Logan."

"I...I didn't think it was, either, but I was wrong. I can be a terrible person, Rorie. Facing up to that hasn't been easy.

"Then...a few days after I mailed that letter to you, Clay came over to the house wanting to talk. Almost immediately I realised I'd lost him. Nothing I could say or do would change the way he felt about you. I said some awful things to Clay that night... He's forgiven me now, but I need your forgiveness, too."

"Oh, Kate, of course, but it isn't necessary. I understand. I honestly do."

"Thank you," she murmured, blotting her eyes with the crumpled tissue. "Now I've got that off my chest, I feel a whole lot better."

"But if Clay had broken your engagement when he came to San Francisco, why didn't he say anything to me?"

Kate shrugged. "I don't know what happened while he was gone, but he hasn't been himself since. He never has been a talkative person, but he seemed to draw even further into himself when he came back from seeing you. He's working himself into an early grave, everyone says. Mary's concerned about him—we all are. Mary said if you didn't come soon, she was going after you herself."

"Mary said that?" The housekeeper had been the very person who'd convinced Rorie she was doing the right thing by getting out of Clay's life.

"Well, are you going to him? Or are you determined to stick around here and listen to me blubber all day? If you give me any more time," she said, forcing a laugh, "I'll manage to make an even bigger fool of myself than I already have." Kate stood abruptly, pushing back the kitchen chair. Her arms were folded around her waist, her eyes bright with tears.

"Kate," Rorie murmured, "you are a dear, dear friend. I owe you more than it's possible to repay."

"The only thing you owe me is one godchild—and about fifty years of happiness with Clay Franklin. Now get out of here before I start weeping in earnest."

Kate opened the kitchen door for her and Rorie gave her an impulsive hug before hurrying out.

Luke Rivers was standing in the yard, apparently waiting for her. When she came out of the house he sauntered over to her car and held open the driver's door. ''Did everything go all right with Kate?''

Rorie nodded.

''Well,'' he said soberly, ''there may be more rough water ahead for her. She doesn't know it yet, but I'm buying out the Circle L.'' Then he smiled, his eyes crinkling. ''She's going to be fine, though. I'll make sure of that personally.'' He extended his hand, gripping hers in a firm handshake. ''Let me be the first to welcome you to our community.''

''Thank you.''

He touched the rim of his hat in farewell, then glanced towards the house. ''I think I'll go inside and see how Kate's doing.''

Rorie's gaze skipped from the foreman to the house and then back again. ''You do that.'' If Luke Rivers had anything to say about it, Kate wouldn't be suffering from a broken heart for long. Rorie had suspected Luke was in love with Kate. But, like her, he was caught in a trap, unable to reveal his feelings. Perhaps now Kate's eyes would be opened—Rorie fervently hoped so.

The drive from the Logans' place to the Franklins' took no more than a few minutes. Rorie parked her car behind the house, her heart pounding like a piston in a hot engine. When she climbed out, the only one there to greet her was Mary.

''It's about time you got here,'' the housekeeper complained, marching down the porch steps with a vengeance.

''Could this be the apple-pie blue-ribbon holder of Nightingale, Oregon?''

Mary actually blushed, and Rorie laughed. ''I thought you'd never want to see the likes of me again,'' she teased.

''Fiddlesticks.'' The weathered face broke into a smile.

''I'm still a city girl,'' Rorie warned.

''That's fine 'cause you got the heart of one from the country.'' Wiping her hands dry on her apron, Mary reached for Rorie and hugged her.

After one brief, bone-crushing squeeze, she set her free. ''I'm a meddling old woman and I suspect the good Lord intends to teach me more than one lesson in the next year or two. I'd best tell you that I never should have said those things I did about Kate being the right woman for Clay.''

''Mary, you spoke out of concern. I know that.''

"Clay doesn't love Kate," she continued undaunted, "but my heavens, he does love you. That boy's been pining his heart out for want of you. He hasn't been the same from the minute you drove out of here all those weeks ago."

Rorie had suffered, too, but she didn't mention that to Mary. Instead, she slipped her arm around the housekeeper's broad waist and together they strolled towards the house.

"Clay's gone for the day, but he'll be back within the hour."

"An hour," Rorie repeated. She'd waited all this time; another sixty minutes shouldn't matter.

"It'll be dinnertime then, and it's not like Clay or Skip to miss a meal. Dinner's been the same time every night since I've been cooking for this family, and that's a good many years now." Mary's mouth formed a lopsided grin. "Now what we'll do is this. You be in the dining room waiting for him and I'll tell him he's got company."

"But won't he notice my car?" Rorie twisted around, gesturing at her old white Toyota—her own car this time—parked within plain sight.

Mary shook her head. "I doubt it. He's never seen your car, so far as I know, only that fancy sports car. Anyway, that boy's been working himself so hard, he'll be too tired to notice much of anything."

Mary opened the back door and Rorie stepped inside the kitchen. As she did, the house seemed to fold its arms around her in welcome. She paused, breathing in the scent of roast beef and homemade rolls. It might not be sourdough and Golden Gate Park rose blossoms, but it felt right. More than right.

"Do you need me to do anything?" Rorie asked.

Mary frowned then nodded. "There's only one thing I want you to do—make Clay happy."

"Oh, Mary, I intend to start doing that the minute he walks through that door."

An hour later, almost to the minute, Rorie heard Skip and Clay come into the kitchen.

"What's for dinner?" Skip asked immediately.

"It's on the table. Now wash your hands."

Rorie heard the teenager grumble as he headed down the hallway to the bathroom.

"How'd the trip go?" Mary asked Clay next.

He mumbled something Rorie couldn't hear.

"The new librarian stopped by to say hello. Old man Logan and Kate sent her over—thought you might like to meet her."

"I don't. I hope you got rid of her. I'm in no mood for company."

"Nope," Mary said flatly. "Fact is, I invited her to stay for dinner. The least you can do is wipe that frown off your face and go introduce yourself."

Rorie stood just inside the dining room, her heart ready to explode. By the time Clay stepped into the room, tears had blurred her vision and she could hardly make out the tall, familiar figure that blocked the doorway.

She heard his swift intake of breath, and the next thing she knew she was crushed in Clay's loving arms.

Seventeen

Rorie was locked so securely in Clay's arms that for a moment she couldn't draw a breath. But that didn't matter. What mattered was that she was being hugged by the man she loved and he was holding on to her as though he didn't plan to ever let her go.

Clay kissed her again and again, the way a starving man took his first bites of food, hesitant at first, then eager. The palms of Rorie's hands were pressed against his chest and she felt the quick surge of his heart. His own hand was gentle on her hair, caressing it, running his fingers through it.

"Rorie...Rorie, I don't believe you're here."

Rorie felt the power of his emotions, and they were strong enough to rock her, body and soul. This man really did love her. He was honest and hardworking, she knew all that, but even more, Clay Franklin was *good*, with an unselfishness and a loyalty that had touched her deeply. In an age of ambitious, hardhearted, vain men, she had inadvertently stumbled on this rare man of character. Her life would never be the same again.

Clay exhaled a deep sigh, and his hands framed her face as he dragged his head back to gaze into her eyes. The lines that marked his face seemed more deeply incised now, and she felt another pang of sorrow for the pain he'd endured.

"Mary wasn't teasing me, was she? You are the new librarian?"

Rorie nodded, smiling up at him, her happiness shining from her eyes. "There's no going back for me. I've moved out of my apartment, packed everything I own and quit my job with little more than a few days' notice."

Rorie had fallen in love with Clay, caught in the magic of one special night when a foal had been born. But her feelings stretched far beyond the events of a single evening and the few short days they'd spent together. Her love for Clay had become an essential part of her. Rorie adored him and would feel that way for as long as her heart continued to beat.

Clay's frown deepened and his features tightened briefly. "What about Dan? I thought you were going to marry him."

"I couldn't," she said, then smiled tenderly, tracing his face with her hands, loving the feel of him beneath her fingertips.

"But—"

"Clay," she interrupted, "why didn't you tell me that night in San Francisco you'd broken your engagement to Kate?" Her eyes clouded with anguish at the memory, at the anxiety they'd caused each other. It had been such senseless heartache, and they'd wasted precious time. "Couldn't you see how miserable I was?"

A grimace of pain moved across his features. "All I noticed was how right you and that stockbroker looked together. You both kept telling me what a bright future he had. I couldn't begin to offer you the things he could. And if that weren't enough, it was all too apparent that Dan was in love with you." Gently Clay smoothed her hair away from her temple. "I could understand what it meant to love you, and, between the two of us, he seemed the better man."

Rorie lowered her face, pressing her forehead against the hollow of his shoulder. She groaned in frustration. "How can you even think such a thing, when I love you so much?"

Clay moved her face so that he could gaze into her eyes. "But, Rorie..." He stopped and a muscle jerked in his jaw. "Dan can give you far more than I'll ever be able to. He's got connections, background, education. A few years down the road, he's going to be very wealthy—success is written all over him. He may have his faults, but basically he's a fine man."

"He *is* a good person and he's probably going to make some woman a good husband. But it won't be me."

"He could give you the kinds of things I may never be able to afford...."

"Clay Franklin, do you love me or not?"

Clay exhaled slowly, watching her. "You know the answer to that."

"Then stop arguing with me. I don't love Dan Rogers. I love you."

Still his frown persisted. "You belong in the city."

"I belong with you," she countered.

He said nothing for a long moment. "I can't argue with that," he whispered, his voice husky with emotion. "You do belong here, because God help me, I haven't got the strength to let you walk away a second time."

Clay kissed her again, his mouth sliding over hers as though he still couldn't believe she was in his arms. She held on to him with all her strength, soaking up his love. She was at home in his arms. It was where she belonged and where she planned to stay.

The sound of someone entering the room filtered through to Rorie's consciousness, but she couldn't bring herself to move out of Clay's arms.

"Rorie," Skip cried, his voice high and excited, "what are you doing here?"

Rorie finally released Clay and turned towards the teenager who had come to her rescue that August afternoon.

"Hello, Skip," she said softly. Clay slipped his arm around her waist and she smiled up at him, needing his touch to anchor her in the reality of their love.

"Are you back for good?" Skip wanted to know.

She nodded, but before she could answer Clay said, "Meet Nightingale's new librarian." His arm tightened around her.

The smile that lit up the teenager's eyes was telling. "So you're going to stick around this time." He blew out a gusty sigh. "It's a damn good thing, because my brother's been as hard to live with as a rattlesnake since you left."

"I'd say that was a bit of an exaggeration," Clay muttered, clearly not approving of his brother's choice of descriptions.

"You shouldn't have gone," Skip said, sighing again. "Especially before the county fair."

Rorie laughed. "You're never going to forgive me for missing that, are you?"

"You should have been here, Rorie. It was great."

"I'll be here next summer," she promised.

"The fact is, Rorie's going to be around a lifetime of summers," Clay informed his brother. "We're going to be married as soon as it can be arranged." His eyes held hers but they were filled with questions, as if he half expected her, even now, to refuse him.

Rorie swallowed the emotion that bobbed so readily to the surface and nodded wildly, telling him with one look that she'd marry him any time he wanted.

Skip folded his arms over his chest, and he gave them a smug look. "I knew something was going on between the two of you. Every time I was around you guys it was like getting zapped with one of those stun guns."

"We were that conspicuous?" It still troubled Rorie that Kate had known, especially since both she and Clay had tried so hard to hide their feelings.

Skip's shrug was carefree. "I don't think so, but I'm not much into love and all that nonsense."

"Give it time, little brother," Clay murmured, "because when it hits, it'll knock you for a loop."

Mary stepped into the room, carrying a platter of meat. "So the two of you are getting hitched?"

Their laughter signalled a welcome release from all the tensions of the past weeks. Clay pulled out Rorie's chair, then sat down beside her. His hand reached for hers, lacing their fingers together. "Yes," he said, still smiling, "we'll be married as soon as we can get the licence and talk to the pastor."

Mary pushed the basket of rolls closer to Skip. "Well, you don't need to fret—I'll stick around for a couple more years until I can teach this child the proper way to feed a man. She may be pretty to look at, but she don't know beans about whipping up a decent meal."

"I'd appreciate that, Mary," Rorie said. "I could do with a few cooking lessons."

The housekeeper's smile broadened. "Now, go ahead and eat before the potatoes get cold and the gravy gets lumpy."

Skip didn't need any further inducement. He reached for the rolls, piling three on the edge of his plate.

Mary reached down and playfully slapped his hand. "I've got apple pie for dessert, so don't go filling yourselves up on my buttermilk biscuits." Her good humour was evident as she surveyed the table, glancing at every one's plate, then bustled back to the kitchen.

Rorie did her best to sample a little of everything. Although the meal was delicious, she was too excited to do anything as mundane as eat.

After dinner, Skip made himself scarce. Mary delivered a tray with two coffee cups to the living room, where Clay and Rorie sat close together on the couch. "You two have lots to talk about, so you might as well drink this while you're doing it."

"Thank you, Mary," Clay said, sharing a smile with Rorie.

The older woman set the tray down, then patted the fine grey hair at the sides of her head. "I want you to know how pleased I am for you both. Have you set the date yet?"

"We're talking about that now," Clay answered. "We're going

to call Rorie's family in Arizona this evening and discuss it with them.''

Mary nodded. ''She's not the woman I would have chosen for you, her being a city girl and all, but she'll make you happy.''

Clay's hand reached for Rorie's. ''I know.''

''She's got a generous soul.'' The housekeeper looked at Rorie and her gaze softened. ''Fill this house with children—and with love. It's been quiet far too long.''

The phone rang in the kitchen and, with a regretful glance over her shoulder, the housekeeper hurried to answer it. A moment later, she stuck her head around the kitchen door.

''It's for you, Clay. Long distance.''

Clay's grimace was apologetic. ''I'd better answer it.''

''You don't need to worry that I'll leave,'' Rorie teased. ''You're stuck with me for a lot of years, Clay Franklin.''

He kissed her before he stood up, then headed towards the kitchen. Rorie sighed and leaned back, cradling her mug in both hands. By chance, her gaze fell on the photograph of Clay's parents, which rested on top of the piano. Once more, Rorie felt the pull of his mother's eyes. She smiled now, understanding so many things. The day she'd planned to leave Elk Run, this same photograph had captured her attention. The moment she'd walked into this house, Rorie had belonged to Clay, and somehow, looking at his mother's picture, she'd sensed that, from the furthest corners of her heart. She belonged to this home and this family.

Clay returned a few minutes later, with old Blue following him. ''Just a call from the owner of one of the horses I board. Just checking on his prize,'' he said, as he sat down beside Rorie and placed his arm around her shoulder. His eyes followed hers to the photo. ''Mom would have liked you.''

Rorie sipped her coffee and smiled. ''I know I would have loved her.'' Setting her cup aside, she reached up and threw both arms around Clay's neck. Gazing into his eyes, she brought his mouth down to hers.

Perhaps it was her imagination, or an optical illusion—in fact, Rorie was sure of it. But she could have sworn the elegant woman in the photograph smiled.

COUNTRY BRIDE

One

"I now pronounce you husband and wife."

A burst of organ music crescendoed through the largest church in Nightingale, Oregon, as a murmur of shared happiness rose from the excited congregation.

Standing at the altar, Clay Franklin claimed his right to kiss Rorie Campbell Franklin, his bride.

Kate Logan did her best to look delighted for her friends, even though she felt as if a giant fist had been slammed into her stomach. Tears gathered in her eyes and she lowered her gaze, unable to watch as the man she'd loved most of her life wrapped his arm around his new bride's waist.

Clay should be marrying me, Kate cried silently. *I should be the one he's looking at so tenderly. Me!* During the past few weeks, Kate had repeatedly reassured herself that she'd done the right thing in stepping aside to bring Clay and Rorie together. But that fact didn't lessen her pain now. Kate loved Clay, and that wasn't ever going to change. He was her best friend and confidant, her compass, her North Star. And now Clay was married to another woman— someone he loved far more than he could ever care for Kate.

A clean white handkerchief was thrust into her hand by Luke Rivers, her father's foreman. Kate knew he'd been waiting for this moment, convinced she'd dissolve into a puddle of tears.

She declined the use of his kerchief by gently shaking her head.

"I'm here," he whispered in her ear.

"So is half of Nightingale," she returned wryly. Luke seemed determined to rescue her from this pain—as if that were possible. All she wanted was to survive this day with her dignity intact, and his open sympathy threatened the outward composure she'd painfully mustered.

"You're doing fine."

"Luke," she muttered, "stop making a fuss over me. Please." She'd managed to get through the ceremony without breaking down. The last thing she needed now was to have Luke calling attention to her.

The ironic thing was that Kate had been the one responsible for bringing Clay and Rorie together. She should be feeling noble and jubilant and honorable. But the only emotion she felt was a deep, abiding sense of loss.

Rorie and Clay walked down the centre aisle, and from somewhere deep inside her, Kate found the strength to raise her head and smile blindly in their direction. Luke's hands gripped her shoulders as though to lend her strength. His concern should have been a comfort, but it wasn't.

"I'll walk you to the reception hall," Luke said, slipping his arm through hers.

"I'm perfectly capable of making it there on my own," she snapped, not wanting his pity. She would have argued more, but since they were sitting near the front of the church, they were among the first to be ushered out. Holding her head high, Kate walked past her friends and neighbours, doing her best to appear cheerful and serene.

At least she *looked* her best; Kate had made certain of that. She'd curled her thick blonde hair until it lightly brushed her shoulders. The style emphasised her blue eyes and sculptured cheekbones. She'd shopped long and hard for the perfect dress for this wedding and had found one that enhanced her tiny waist and outlined her trim figure. The minute she'd tried on the soft blue silk and viewed herself in the mirror, Kate had known the dress was perfect. Although the lines were simple, the look was both classic and sophisticated, a look she'd never bothered to cultivate before. Too often in the past, she'd been mistaken for a teenager, mostly, she supposed, because she dressed the part. Now, she was a woman though, and she had the broken heart to prove it.

Kate paused in the church vestibule, waiting for her father. Devin was sitting with Dorothea Murphy, his widow friend. Her father's interest in the older woman was something of a mystery to Kate. Tall and plump and outspoken, she was completely unlike Kate's late mother, who'd been delicate and reserved. Kate sometimes wondered what it was about Dorothea that so strongly attracted her father. The two had been seeing a lot of each other in recent weeks, but the possibility of their contemplating marriage filled Kate with a sudden, overwhelming sense of alarm. Kate pushed the thought from her mind. Losing Clay was all she could deal with right now.

"Are you all right, Princess?" Devin asked when he joined her.

"I wish everyone would stop worrying about me. I'm fine." It wasn't the truth, but Kate was well aware that she had to put on a breezy, unconcerned front. At least for the next few hours.

Her father patted her hand gently. "I know how hard this is for you. Do you want to go to the reception or would you prefer to head home?" His eyes were warm and sympathetic, and Kate felt a rush of love for him. A part of her longed to slip away unnoticed, but she couldn't and she knew it.

"Kate's already agreed to accompany me," Luke inserted, daring her to contradict him.

Indignation rose inside her. Instead of helping, Luke was making everything worse. The pain of watching Clay pledge his life to another woman was difficult enough, without Luke's unsought demands.

"I'm pleased to hear that," Devin Logan said, looking relieved. He smiled as he slipped his arm around Dorothea's thick waist. "Mrs Murphy invited me to sit with her and, frankly, I was looking forward to doing so." He released Kate's hand, kissed her on the cheek, then strolled nonchalantly away.

"Shall we?" Grinning, Luke reached for Kate's limp hand and tucked it into the crook of his arm. As if they'd been a couple for years, he casually led the way out of the church.

The early evening air was crisp and clear. Autumn had crested on an October tide of bronze and gold leaves, huge pumpkins and early twilights. Normally, this time of year invigorated Kate. If she hadn't been fortifying herself against Clay's wedding, she could have appreciated the season more.

The walk across the car park to the reception hall was a short one. Kate didn't say another word to Luke, mentally preparing herself for the coming encounter with Clay and his bride. With each step her heart grew heavier. Rorie had asked her to be a bridesmaid, and although Kate was honoured by the request, she'd declined. Rorie understood and hadn't pressured her. Despite the fact that they both loved the same man, Rorie and Kate had become close. Their friendship made everything more difficult for Kate, yet somehow easier, too.

By the time they reached the old brick building, Kate's pulse was so loud it echoed like a drum in her ear. Just outside the double doors leading into the hall, she stopped abruptly.

"I can't go in there," she told Luke. Panic had worked its way into her voice, which was low and trembling. ''I can't face them and pretend... I just can't do it.''

''You can—I'll help you.''

''How can you possibly know what I can and can't do?'' she demanded, wanting to bury her face in her hands and weep. These past few hours had taken their toll and she couldn't keep up the charade much longer. Luke gazed down on her and for the briefest of moments his eyes registered sympathy and regret.

''You can go in there and you will,'' he repeated.

Kate saw determination in his serious dark eyes and swallowed an angry retort, knowing he was right.

At six feet, Luke towered over her, and the hard set of his mouth did more than hint at determination and a will of iron. ''If you don't attend the reception, everyone in Nightingale will talk. Is that what you want?''

''Yes,'' she cried, then lowered her head, battling down wave after wave of depression and self-pity that threatened to swamp her. ''No,'' she said reluctantly, loath to agree with him.

''I'm here for you, Kate. Lean on me for once in your life, and let me help you through the next few hours.''

''I'm doing fine. I—''

He wouldn't allow her to finish. ''Quit fighting me. I'm your friend, remember?''

His words, hushed and tender, brought a burning to her eyes. Her fingers tightened around his arm and she nodded, calling upon a reserve of strength she didn't know she possessed. ''Just don't be so bossy with me. Please. I can bear almost anything but that.'' She'd made it through the wedding ceremony on her own reserves of strength. Now she needed someone at her side to help her appear strong and steady when she felt as though the entire universe was pitching and heaving.

''Anything you say, Princess.''

Although she'd objected earlier, she felt comforted by his strong arm pressing against her. She heard his voice, as if from a distance, too preoccupied with her own pain to respond to his gentle concern. But his presence restored her determination to acquit herself well during the long evening ahead.

''Only Daddy calls me Princess,'' she said distractedly.

''You mind?''

''I don't know... I suppose it's all right.''

"Good." His fingers intertwined with hers as he led her into the brightly decorated reception hall.

The next half-hour was a blur. Drawing upon Luke's silent strength, Kate managed to make it through the reception line without a problem. Still, her knees felt shaky by the time she reached Clay, who kissed her cheek and thanked her for being so wonderful. Kate certainly didn't *feel* wonderful—even particularly admirable—but she smiled. And she was sincere when she offered Clay and Rorie her very best wishes.

Somehow Luke must have known how frail she felt because he took her hand and led her to one of the round lace-covered tables. His fingers were cool and calloused, while Kate's were damp with her stubborn determination to hide her pain.

Wordlessly, she sat beside Luke until the cake had been cut and the first piece ceremonially fed to the bride and groom. The scene before her flickered like an old silent movie. Kate held herself still, trying not to feel anything, but not succeeding.

"Would you like me to get you something to eat?" Luke asked, when a line formed to gather refreshments.

She stared at him, hardly able to comprehend his words. Then she blinked and her eyes travelled across the hall to the three-tiered heart-shaped wedding cake. "No," she said automatically.

"When was the last time you ate?"

Kate didn't remember. She shrugged. "Breakfast, I guess." As she spoke she realised that wasn't true. Dinner the night before was the last time she'd eaten. No wonder she felt so shaky and light-headed.

"I'm getting you some wedding cake," Luke announced grimly.

"Don't. I'm—I'm not hungry."

He was doing it again! Taking over, making decisions on her behalf because he felt sorry for her. She would have argued with him, but he was already walking away, blithely unaware of her frustration.

Kate watched him, suddenly seeing him with fresh eyes. Luke Rivers had lived and worked on the Circle L for a decade, but Kate knew next to nothing of his past. His official title was foreman, but he was much more than that. He'd initiated several successful cattle-breeding programmes and had been involved in a profit-sharing venture with her father almost from the first. Devin had often remarked that Luke was more than capable of maintaining his own spread. But year after year, he continued to stay at the Circle L.

This realisation—that she knew so little of his past and even less about his thoughts and plans—shocked Kate. He'd always been just plain Luke. And he'd always been around, or so it seemed. She considered him a good friend, yet she hardly knew him. Not really. Especially considering the length of time he'd been at the Circle L.

She had to admit that Luke puzzled her. He was handsome enough, but he rarely dated any woman for long, although plenty of Nightingale's finest had made their interest obvious. He was a "catch" who refused to play ball. He could be as tough as leather and mean as a saddle sore when the mood struck him, but it seldom did. Tall, lean and rugged adequately described him on the surface. It was what lay below that piqued her interest now.

Kate's musings about Luke were disrupted by the man himself as he pulled out the chair beside her and sat down. He pushed a delicate china plate filled with cheese and mixed nuts in her direction.

"I thought you were bringing me cake." His own plate was loaded with a huge piece, in addition to a few nuts and pastel mints.

"I brought you some protein instead. Sugar's the last thing you need on an empty stomach."

"I don't believe you," she muttered, her sarcasm fuelled by his arrogance. "First you insist on bringing me cake, and then just when I'm looking forward to sampling it, you decide I shouldn't be eating sweets."

Luke ignored her, slicing into a thick piece of cake with the side of his fork. "Just a minute ago, you claimed it would be a waste of time for me to bring you anything. Fact is, you downright refused to eat."

"That...was before."

He smiled, and that knowing cocky smile of his infuriated her.

"You'll feel sick if you eat sugar," he announced in an authoritative voice.

So much for helping her through this evening! All he seemed to want to do was quarrel. "Apparently you know how my stomach is going to react to certain food groups. You amaze me, Luke Rivers. You honestly amaze me. I had no idea you knew so much about my body's metabolism."

"You'd be shocked if I told you all the things I know about you and your body, Princess."

Kate stood abruptly. "I don't think it's a good idea for you to call me that. I'm not your 'Princess'. I'm a woman, not a little girl.''

"Honey, you don't need to tell me that. I already know. Now sit down." His tone was brusque, and his smile humourless.

"I'll stand if I choose."

"Fine then. Look like a fool, if that's what you want."

No sooner had the words left his lips than she limply lowered herself back into the chair. The fight had gone out of her as quickly as it had come. Absently she scooped up a handful of nuts and chewed them vigorously, taking her frustration out on them.

Luke pushed his plate aside and reached for her hand, squeezing it gently. "I'm your friend. I've always been your friend and I'll continue to be your friend as long as I live. Don't ever doubt that."

Kate's eyes misted and her throat tightened painfully. "I know. It's just that this is so much more...exhausting than I thought it would be."

Voices drew Kate's eyes to the front of the room, where Clay and Rorie were toasting each other with tall, thin glasses of sparkling champagne. Soon flutes were being delivered around the room. Kate took one, holding the long stem with both hands as if the champagne would lend her strength.

When the newlyweds were toasted, she took a sip. It bubbled and fizzed inside her mouth, then slid easily down her throat.

The soft strains of a violin drifted around the hall, and, mesmerised, Kate watched as Clay claimed his bride and led her on to the dance floor. Just watching the couple, so much in love, with eyes only for each other, heaped an extra burden of pain on Kate's thin shoulders. She looked away and, when she did, her gaze met Luke's. She tried to smile, to convince him she wasn't feeling a thing, but the effort was a poor one. Ready tears brimmed at the corners of her eyes and she lowered her head, not wanting anyone to notice them, least of all Luke. He'd been wonderful; he'd been terrible. Kate couldn't decide which.

Soon others joined Clay and Rorie. First the matron of honour and then the bridesmaids and groomsmen, each couple swirling around the polished floor with practised ease.

Luke got to his feet, walked to Kate's side, and offered her his hand. His eyes held hers, silently demanding that she dance with him. Kate longed to tell him no, but she didn't have the energy to argue. It was simpler to comply than try to explain why she couldn't.

Together they approached the outskirts of the dance floor and Luke skilfully turned her into his arms.

"Everything's going to be all right," he whispered as his hand slipped around her waist.

Kate managed a nod, grateful for his concern. She needed Luke this evening more than she'd realised. One thing was certain—she'd never make it through the remainder of the night without him.

During the past several years, Luke had danced with Kate any number of times. She'd never given it a second thought. Now they danced one number and then another, but when she slipped into his embrace a third time, and his fingers spread across the small of her back, a shiver of unexpected awareness skidded up her spine. Kate paused, confused. Her steps faltered and in what seemed like an effort to help her, Luke pulled her closer. Soon their bodies were so close together Kate could hear the steady beat of Luke's heart against her own. The quickening rate of his pulse told her he was experiencing the same rush of excitement she was.

Kate felt so light-headed she was almost giddy. Luke's arms were warm and secure, a solid foundation to hold on to when her world had been abruptly kicked off its axis. It might have been selfish, but Kate needed that warmth, that security. Smiling up at him, she closed her eyes and surrendered to the warm sensations carried on the soft, lilting music.

"Kate, there's something I need to tell you about the Circle L—"

She pressed her fingers against his lips, afraid that words would ruin this feeling. Arms twined around his neck, she grazed his jaw with the side of her face, revelling in the feel of him. Male and strong. Lean and hard.

"All right," he whispered, "we'll talk about it later."

They continued dancing and Luke rubbed his face against her hair, mussing it slightly, but Kate didn't mind.

Like a contented cat, she purred softly, the low sound coming from deep in her throat. The music ended all too quickly and with heavy reluctance, she dropped her arms and backed up one small step. Silently they stood more than an inch apart until the music resumed, giving them the necessary excuse to reach for each other once again.

But this time Kate made an effort to work out what was happening between them. Knowing how much she loved Clay, Luke was determined to help her through the evening. Yes, that had to be it. And doing a fine job, too. She felt...marvellous. It didn't make sense to her that she should experience this strong, unexpectedly sensual attraction to Luke, but at the moment she didn't care. He was concerned and gentle and she needed him.

They remained as they were, not speaking, savouring these warm sensations, until Kate lost count of the number of dances they'd shared.

When the band took a ten-minute break, Luke released her with an unwillingness that made her heart soar. As though he couldn't bear to be separated from her, he reached for her hand, lacing her soft fingers with his strong ones.

He was leading her back to their table when they were interrupted by Betty Hammond, a pert blonde, who'd hurried toward them. "Hello, Luke," she said, ignoring Kate.

"Betty." He dipped his head politely, but it was clear he didn't appreciate the intrusion.

The other woman placed a proprietorial hand on his arm. "You promised me a dance, remember?"

Kate's eyes swivelled from Betty, who was pouting prettily, to Luke who looked testy and impatient.

"If you'll excuse me a minute, I'm going to get something to drink," Kate said. Her throat was parched and she didn't want to be left standing alone when the music started and Betty walked off with Luke.

The fruit punch was cold and refreshing, but she still felt warm. Kate decided to walk outside and let the cool night air clear her mind. She didn't really understand what was happening between her and Luke, but she thought it probably had to do with the confused state of her emotions.

The stars glittered like frost diamonds against a velvety black sky. Kate stood in the crisp evening air with her arms wrapped around her waist, gazing up at the heavens. She didn't hear Luke until he stepped behind her and lightly rested his hands on her shoulders. "I couldn't find you," he said in a voice that was softly accusing.

Kate didn't want to discuss Betty Hammond. For as long as she could remember, the other woman had been going out of her way to attract him.

"It's beautiful out tonight, isn't it?" she asked instead. Instinctively she nestled closer to Luke, reclining against the lean strength of his body, seeking his warmth.

"Beautiful," he repeated, running his hands down the length of her arms.

How content she felt with Luke, how comfortable—the way she imagined people felt when they'd been married twenty years. But along with this familiar sense of ease, she experienced a prickle of anticipation. Her feelings contradicted themselves, she realised wryly. Secure and steady, and at the same time this growing sense of giddy excitement. It must be that glass of champagne, she decided.

The band started playing again and the sweet sounds of the music wafted outside. Gently Luke turned her to face him, slipping his hands around her as if to dance. Her arms reached for his neck, resuming their earlier position.

"We should talk," he whispered close to her ear.

"No," she murmured with a sigh. Finding her way back into Luke's arms was like arriving home after an extended vacation. It seemed the most natural thing in the world to stand on the tips of her toes and brush her moist lips over his. Then she realised what she'd done. Her eyes rounded and she abruptly stepped back, her heart hammering inside her chest.

Neither spoke. In the light that spilled from the hall windows, they stared at each other, searching. Kate didn't know what her eyes told Luke, but his own were clouded with uncertainty. Kate half expected him to chastise her, or to tease her for behaving like such a flirt. Instead he reached for her once more, his eyes challenging her to stop him.

She couldn't.

The warmth of his mouth on hers produced a small sigh of welcome as her eyes slid languidly shut; she felt transported into a dreamworld, one she had never visited before. This couldn't actually be happening, she told herself, and yet it felt so very real. And so right.

Luke's kiss was surprisingly tender, unlike anything she'd expected. He held her as though she were made of the most delicate bone china and might shatter at the slightest pressure.

"My darling Kate," he breathed against her hair, "I've dreamed of this so often."

"You have?" To her own ears, her voice sounded as though it came from far, far away. Her head was swimming. If this was a dream, then she didn't want it to end. Sighing, she smiled beguilingly up at him.

"You little tease," he said, and laughed softly. He rained light kisses on her forehead, the corners of her eyes and her cheek, until she interrupted his meandering lips, seeking his mouth with her own.

He seemed to want the kiss as much as she did. But apparently saw no need to rush the experience, as if he feared hurrying would spoil it. Kate's mouth parted softly, inviting a deeper union. His willing compliance was so effective it buckled her knees.

"Kate?" Still holding her, he drew back, tilting his head to study her. Boldly she met his look, her eyes dancing with mischief. If he'd been kissing her out of pity, she was past caring.

A long moment passed before a slow, thoughtful smile played across his lips. "I think I'd better get you inside."

"No," she said, surprised at how vehement she felt about returning to the reception hall and the newlyweds. "I don't want to go back there."

"But—"

"Stay with me here. Dance with me. Hold me." He'd said he wanted to take care of her. Well, she was giving him the opportunity. She leaned her body into his and sighed, savouring his strength and support. This was Luke. Luke Rivers. Her trusted friend. Surely he understood; surely he would help her through this most difficult night of her life. "I want you with me." She couldn't explain what was happening between them any more than she could deny it.

"You don't know what you're asking me." He stared down at her, searching her features for a long, breathless moment. Then the cool tips of his fingers brushed her face, moving along her cheekbones, stroking her ivory skin as if he expected her to vanish.

Kate caught his hand with her own and recklessly gazed into his dark eyes. They glittered like freshly polished onyx, full of light and a deep inner fire.

"I want you to kiss me. You taste so good." She moistened her lips and leaned closer to him, so close that she could feel the imprint of his buttons against her body. So close that the beat of his heart merged with her own. Excitement shivered through her in tremors so intense they frightened her. But not enough to make her pull away.

Her words spurred Luke into action, and when he kissed her their lips met with hungry insistence. Sensation erupted between them until Kate was weak and dizzy, forced to cling to him for support, her fingers bunching the material of his jacket. When he lifted his head, ending the kiss, Kate felt nearly faint from the rush of blood to her pounding temples.

There was a look of shock on Luke's face. His eyes questioned her, but Kate's thoughts were as scattered as autumn leaves tossed by a brisk wind.

"How much champagne have you had?" he demanded softly.

"One glass," she answered with a sigh, resting her forehead against his heaving chest. Luke hadn't said taking care of her would be this wonderful. Had she known, she wouldn't have resented it quite so much earlier.

Luke expelled a harsh breath. "You've had more than one glass. I doubt you even know who I am."

"Of course I do!" she flared. "You're Luke. Now don't be ridiculous. Only..."

"Only what?"

"Only you never kissed me before. At least not like that. Why in heaven's name didn't you tell me you were so good at this?" Finding herself exceptionally witty, she began to laugh.

"I'm taking you home," Luke said firmly, grabbing her elbow with such force that she was half-lifted from the walkway.

"Luke," she cried, "I don't want to go back yet."

His grip relaxed immediately. "Kate Logan, I think you're drunk! Only you don't have the sense to know it."

"I most certainly am not!" She waved her index finger at him like a schoolmarm. "I'll have you know that it takes a lot more than one glass of champagne to do me in."

Luke obviously wasn't willing to argue the point. His hand cradling her elbow, he led her towards the car park.

"I want to stay," she protested.

He didn't answer. Then it dawned on her that perhaps she'd misread Luke. Maybe he wanted to be rid of her so he could return to Betty.

"Luke?"

"Kate, please, don't argue with me."

"Are you in love with Betty?"

"No." His answer was clipped and impatient.

"Thank heaven." Her hand fluttered over her heart. "I don't think I could bear it if you were."

Luke stopped abruptly and Kate realised they were standing in front of his truck. He opened the passenger door for her, but she had no intention of climbing in. At least not yet. She wanted to spend more time with Luke, their arms wrapped around each other the way they'd been before. The pain that had battered her heart for weeks had vanished the instant she stepped into his arms.

"I want you to kiss me again, okay?"

"Kate, no."

"Please?"

"Kate, you're drunk."

"And I tell you I'm not." The one glass of champagne had been just enough to make her a little...reckless. It felt so good to surrender to these new emotions—to lean on Luke. From the moment they'd arrived at the wedding, he'd been telling her how much she needed him. Maybe he was right. There'd been so much upheaval in her life, and Luke was here, warm and kind and solid.

"I'm going to drive you home," he insisted. From the sound of his voice, Kate could tell he was growing frustrated.

The house would be dark and cold. How Kate feared being alone, and with Clay out of her life, there was only her father. And Luke. If Devin did decide to marry Mrs Murphy, he might sell the ranch and then Luke would be gone, too. Alarmed at the thought, she placed her hands on his shoulders, her gaze holding his.

"Kate?" Luke coaxed softly.

"All right, I'll go back to the house, but on one condition."

"Kate, come on, be reasonable."

"I want you to do something for me. You keep telling me you're my friend and how much you want to help...."

"Just get inside the truck, would you, before someone comes along and finds us arguing?"

"I need your promise first."

Luke ignored her. "You've got a reputation to uphold. You can't let people in Nightingale see you tipsy. The school board will hear about this and that'll be the end of your career."

Kate smiled, shaking her head, then impulsively leaned forward and kissed him again. Being with Luke took the hurt away, and she didn't want to suffer that kind of pain ever again. "Will you kindly do what I want?"

"All right," he cried, clearly exasperated. "What is it?"

"Oh, good," she murmured, and sighed expressively. This was going to shock him, but no more than it had already shocked her.

She didn't know where the idea had come from, but it seemed suddenly, unarguably right.

Kate smiled at him, her heart shining through her eyes. "It's simple really. All I want you to do is marry me."

Two

Early the following day, Devin Logan walked hesitantly into the kitchen where Kate sat drinking her first cup of coffee. She smiled a greeting. "Morning, Dad."

"Morning, Princess." He circled the table twice before he sat down.

Kate watched him curiously, then rose to pour him a cup of coffee and deliver it to the table. It was a habit she'd begun after her mother's death several years earlier.

"Did you and Mrs Murphy have a good time last night?" Kate asked, before her father could comment on the rumours that were sure to be circulating about her and Luke Rivers. She hadn't seen Luke yet, but she would soon enough, and she was mentally bracing herself for the confrontation. What a fool she'd made of herself. She cringed at the thought of her marriage proposal and didn't doubt for a second that Luke was going to take a good deal of delight in tormenting her about it. She suspected it would be a good long while before he let her live this one down.

"Looks like rain," Devin mumbled.

Kate grinned good-naturedly, wondering at her father's strange mood. "I asked you about last night, not about the weather."

Devin's eyes flared briefly with some unnamed emotion, which he quickly disguised. His gaze fell to the steaming mug cupped in his hands.

"Dad? Did you and Mrs Murphy enjoy yourselves?"

"Why, sure, we had a grand time," he said with forced enthusiasm.

Knowing her father well, Kate waited for him to elaborate. Instead he reached for the sugar bowl and resolutely added three heaping teaspoons to his coffee. He stirred it so briskly the coffee threatened to slosh over the edge of his mug. All the while, he stared blankly into space.

Kate didn't know what to make of Devin's unusual behaviour.

"Dad," she said, trying once more, "is there something on your mind?"

His eyes darted about the room, reluctantly settling on Kate. "What makes you ask that?"

"You just added sugar to your coffee. You've been drinking it sugarless for forty years."

He glared down at the mug, surprise written on his tanned face. "I did?"

"I saw you myself."

"I did," he repeated firmly, as if that was what he'd intended all along. "I, ah, seem to have developed a sweet tooth lately."

It was becoming apparent to Kate that her father's experience at Clay's and Rorie's wedding reception must have rivalled her own. "Instead of beating around the bush all morning, why don't you just tell me what's on your mind?"

Once more, her father lowered his eyes, then nodded and swallowed tightly. "Dorothea and I had...a long talk last night," he began haltingly. "It all started out innocently enough. Then again, I'm sure the wedding and all the good feelings floating around Clay and Rorie probably had a good deal to do with it." He hesitated long enough to take a sip of his coffee. Grimacing at its sweetness. "The best I can figure, we started talking seriously after Nellie Jackson came by and told Dorothea and me that we made a handsome couple. At least that's how I think the conversation got started."

"It's true," Kate said kindly. Personally she would have preferred her father to see someone who resembled her mother a bit more, but Mrs Murphy was a pleasant, gentle woman and Kate was fond of her.

Her father smiled fleetingly. "Then the champagne was passed around and Dorothea and I helped ourselves." He paused, glancing at Kate as if that explained everything.

"Yes," Kate said, hiding a smile, "go on."

Slowly Devin straightened, and eyes, forthright and unwavering, held hers. "You know I loved your mother. When Nora died, there was a time I wondered if I could go on living without her, but I have, and so have you."

"Of course you have, Dad." Suddenly it dawned on Kate exactly where this conversation was leading. It shouldn't have surprised her, and yet... Kate's heart was beginning to hammer uncomfortably. Her father didn't need to say another word; she knew what was coming as surely as if he'd already spoken the words aloud. He was going to marry Dorothea Murphy.

"Your mother's been gone nearly five years now and, well, a man gets lonely," her father continued. "I've been thinking about doing some travelling and, frankly, I don't want to do it alone."

"You should have said something earlier, Dad," Kate interjected. "I'd have loved travelling with you. Still would. That's one of the nice things about being a schoolteacher," she rambled on. "My summers are free. And with Luke watching the ranch, you wouldn't have any worries about what's happening at home and—"

"Princess." His spoon made an irritating clicking sound against the sides of the ceramic mug, but he didn't seem to notice. "I asked Dorothea to marry me last night and she's graciously consented."

After only a moment's hesitation, Kate found the strength to smile and murmur, "Why, Dad, that's fantastic."

"I know it's going to be hard on you, Princess—so soon after Clay's wedding and all. I want you to know that I have no intention of abandoning you—you'll always be my little girl."

"Of course you aren't abandoning me." Tears edged their way into the corners of Kate's eyes and a cold numbness moved out from her heart and spread through her body. "I'm happy for you. Really happy." She meant it, too, but she couldn't help feeling a sense of impending loss. All the emotional certainties seemed to be disappearing from her life.

Her father gently squeezed her hand. "There are going to be some other changes, as well, I'm afraid. I'm selling the ranch."

Kate gasped before she could stop herself. He'd just confirmed all her fears. She'd lost Clay to another woman; now she was about to lose her father, and her home, too. Then another thought crystallised in her mind, although that had been half formed the night before. If the ranch was sold, Luke would be gone, too.

Clay. Her father. The Circle L. Luke. Everyone and everything she loved, gone in a matter of hours. It was almost more than she could absorb at one time. Pressing her hand over her mouth, she blinked back the blinding tears.

"Now I don't want you to concern yourself," her father hurried to add. "You'll always have a home with me. Dorothea and I talked it over and we both want you to feel free to live with us in town as long as you like. You'll always be my Princess, and Dorothea understands that."

"Dad," Kate muttered, laughing and crying at the same time,

unable to decide which was most appropriate. "That's ridiculous. I'm twenty-four years old and perfectly capable of living on my own."

"Of course you are, but—"

She stopped him by raising her hand. "There's no need to discuss it further. You and Dorothea Murphy are going to be married, and...I couldn't be happier for you. Now, don't you worry about me. I'll find a place of my own in town and make arrangements to move as soon as I can."

Her father sighed, clearly relieved by her easy acceptance of his plans, "Well, Princess," he said, shaking his head, his smile so bright it rivalled a July sun, "I can't tell you how pleased I am. Frankly, I was worried you'd be upset."

"Oh, Dad..."

Still grinning broadly, Devin stroked the side of his jaw. "Dorothea isn't a bit like your mother—I don't know if you noticed that or not. Fact is, the only reason I asked her out that first time was so she'd invite me over for some of her peach cobbler. Then before I knew it, I was making excuses to get into town and it wasn't because of her cobbler, either."

Kate made an appropriate reply although a minute later she wasn't sure what she'd said. Soon afterwards, her father kissed her cheek and then left the house, telling her he'd be back later that afternoon.

After her father left, Kate poured herself a second cup of coffee and leaned her hip against the kitchen counter, trying to digest everything that was happening to her well-organised life. She felt as though her whole world had been uprooted and tossed about—as though the winds of a hurricane had landed in Nightingale and swept away all that was good in her life.

Wandering aimlessly from room to room, she paused in front of the bookcase, where a photograph of her mother rested. Tears blurred her eyes as she picked it up and clutched it to her chest. Wave upon wave of emotion swept through her, followed by a flood of hot tears.

She relived the overwhelming grief she'd felt at her mother's death, and she was furious with her father for letting another woman take Nora's place in his life. At the same time, she couldn't find it in her heart to begrudge him his new happiness.

Mrs Murphy wasn't the type of woman Kate would have chosen for her father, but then she wasn't doing the choosing. Suddenly resolute, Kate dragged in a deep breath, exhaling the fear and uncertainty and inhaling the acceptance of this sudden change in both their lives.

The back door opened and instinctively Kate closed her eyes, mentally composing herself. It could only be Luke, and he was the last person she wanted to see right now.

"Kate?"

With trembling hands, she replaced the faded photograph and wiped the tears from her face. "Good morning, Luke," she said softly, as she entered the kitchen.

Luke had walked over to the cupboard and taken down a mug. "Your father just told me the news about him and Mrs Murphy," he said carefully. "Are you going to be all right?"

"Of course. It's wonderful for Dad, isn't it?"

"For your father yes, but it must be something of a shock to you so soon..."

"After Clay and Rorie," she finished for him. Reaching for the coffeepot, she poured his cup and refilled her own. "I'm going to be just fine," she repeated, but Kate didn't know whether she was telling him this for his benefit or her own. "Naturally, the fact that Dad's marrying Dorothea means a few changes in all our lives, but I'll adjust."

"I haven't seen your father this happy in years."

Kate did her best to smile through the pain. "Yes, I know." To her horror tears formed again, and she lowered her gaze and blinked wildly in an effort to hide them.

"Kate?"

She whirled around and set her coffee aside while she started wiping invisible crumbs from the perfectly clean kitchen counter.

Luke's hands settled on her shoulders, and before she knew what was happening, Kate had turned and buried her face against his clean-smelling denim shirt. A single sob shook her shoulders and she heaved out a quivering sigh, embarrassed to be breaking down in front of him like this.

"Go on, baby," he whispered gently, his hands rubbing her back, "let it out."

She felt like such a weakling to be needing Luke so much, but he was so strong and steady, and Kate felt as helpless as a rowing boat tossed about an angry sea. Even if she lasted through the storm, she didn't know if she could survive.

"Did...did you know Dad might sell the ranch?" she asked Luke.

"Yes." His voice was tight. "When did he tell you?"

"This morning, after he said he was marrying Mrs Murphy."

"You don't need to worry about it."

"But I do," she said, and sobbed softly. She felt Luke's chin caress the crown of her head and she snuggled closer into his warm, safe embrace. Luke was her most trusted friend. He'd seen her through the most difficult day of her life.

The thought of Clay and Rorie's wedding flashed into her mind, and with it came the burning memory of her marriage proposal to Luke. She stiffened in his arms, mortified at the blatant way she'd used him, the way she'd practically begged him to take care of her—to marry her. Breaking free of his arms, she straightened and offered him a watery smile.

"What would I do without you, Luke Rivers?"

"You won't ever need to find that out." He looped his arms around her waist and gently kissed the tip of her nose. His smile was tender. "There must have been something in the air last night. First us, and now your father and Mrs Murphy."

"About us," she began carefully. She drew in a steadying breath, but her eyes avoided Luke's. "I hope you realise that when I asked you to marry me I...didn't actually mean it."

He went very still and for a long moment he said nothing. "I took you seriously, Kate."

Kate freed herself from his arms and reached for her coffee, gripping the mug tightly. "I'd had too much champagne."

"According to you, it was only one glass."

"Yes, but I drank it on an empty stomach, and with the difficult emotions the wedding brought out and everything, I simply wasn't myself."

Luke frowned. "Oh?"

"No, I wasn't," she said, feigning a light laugh. "The way we were dancing and the way I clung to you, and...and kissed you. That's nothing like me. I'm not going to hold you to that promise, Luke."

As if he found it difficult to remain standing, Luke twisted around the rail-back chair and straddled it with familiar ease. Kate claimed the chair opposite him, grateful to sit down. Her nerves were stretched to the breaking point. For several minutes Luke said nothing. He draped his forearms over the back of the chair, cupping the hot mug with both hands, and studied Kate with an intensity that made her blush.

"Listen," Kate said hesitantly, "you were the perfect gentleman and I want you to know how much I appreciate everything you did to help me. But...I'm afraid I didn't mean half of what I said."

The sun-marked crow's feet at the corners of his eyes fanned out as Luke smiled slowly, confidently. "Now that raises some interesting questions."

"I don't think I understand." Surely Luke knew what she was talking about, yet he seemed to enjoy watching her make an even bigger fool of herself by forcing her to explain.

"Well," he said in an easy drawl, "if you only meant half of what you said, then it leads me to wonder what you did mean and what you didn't."

"I can't remember *everything* I said," she murmured, her cheeks hot enough to pop a batch of corn. "But I do know I'd greatly appreciate it if you'd forget the part about marrying me."

"I don't want to forget it."

"Luke, please," she cried, squeezing her eyes shut. "This is embarrassing me. Couldn't you kindly drop it?"

Luke rubbed his jaw thoughtfully. "I don't think I can."

So Luke was going to demand his pound of flesh. Kate supposed she shouldn't be so surprised. She had, after all, brought this on herself. "You were so good to me at the reception... After the wedding ceremony you kept saying that you wanted to help me and, Luke, you did, you honestly did. I don't think I could have made it through Clay's wedding without you, but..."

"You want to forget the kissing, too?"

"Yes, please." She nodded emphatically.

He frowned. "That's not what you said last night. In fact, you were downright surprised at how pleasant it was. As I recall you told me—and I quote—'Why in heaven's name didn't you tell me you were so good at this?'"

"Dear Lord, I said that?" Kate muttered, already knowing it was true.

"I'm afraid so."

She covered her face with both hands as the hot colour mounted in her cheeks.

"And you practically forced me to promise I'd marry you."

She bit down hard on her lower lip. "Anyone else in the world would have mercifully forgotten I suggested that."

With a certain amount of ceremony, Luke set his hat farther back on his head and folded his arms. His face was a study in concentration. "I have no intention of forgetting it. I'm a man of my word and I never break my promises."

Kate groaned. In light of her father's news this morning, she'd hoped Luke might be a little more understanding. "It's obvious you're deriving a good deal of pleasure from all this," she muttered angrily, and then pressed her lips together to keep from saying more.

"No, not exactly. When would you like to have the wedding? And while we're at it, you might as well find out now that—"

"You can't be serious!" she interrupted, incredulous that he'd suggest they set a date. If this was a joke, he was carrying it too far.

"I'm dead serious. You asked me to marry you, I agreed, and anything less would be a breach of good faith."

"Then I...I absolve you from your promise." She waved her hands as if she was granting some kind of formal dispensation.

He stroked the side of his face, his forehead creased in a contemplative frown. "My word is my word and I stand firm on it."

"I didn't know what I was saying—well, I did. Sort of. But you know as well as I do that the...heat of the moment was doing most of the talking."

Luke's frown deepened. "I suppose everybody in town will assume you're marrying me on the rebound. Either that, or I'll be the one they'll gossip about. That doesn't trouble me much, but I don't like the thought of folks saying anything about you."

"Will you kindly stop?" she cried. "I have no intention of marrying anyone! Ever!" She was finished with love, finished with romance. Thirty years from now she'd be living alone with a few companion cats and her knitting needles.

"That wasn't what you said last night."

"Would you quit saying that? I wasn't myself, for heaven's sake!"

"Well, our getting married sounded like a hell of a good idea to me. Now, I realise you've gone through a hard time, but our marriage will end all that."

Kate brushed a shaking hand across her eyes, hoping this scene was just part of a nightmare and she'd soon wake up. Unfortunately when she lowered her hand, Luke was still sitting there, as arrogant as could be. "I can't believe we're even having this discussion. It's totally unreasonable, and if you're trying to improve my mood, you've failed."

"I'm serious, Kate. I already explained that."

Keeping her head down, she spoke quickly, urgently. "It's really wonderful of you to even consider going through with the marriage, but it isn't necessary, Luke. More than anyone, you should understand that I can't marry you. Not when I love Clay Franklin the way I do."

"Hogwash."

Kate's head jerked up. "I beg your pardon?"

"You're in love with me. You just don't know it yet."

It took Kate only half a second to respond. "Of all the egotistical, vain, high-handed..." She paused to suck in a breath. If Luke's intent was to shock her, he'd succeeded. "I can't believe you!" She bolted to her feet and flailed the air with both hands. Unable to stand still, she started pacing the kitchen. "I don't understand you. I've tried, honestly I've tried. One moment you're the Rock of Gibraltar, steady and secure and everything I need, my best friend, and the next moment you're saying the most ridiculous things to me. It never used to be this way between us! What happened? Why have you changed?"

"Is it really that bad?" he cajoled softly, ignoring her questions.

"I don't know what happened to you—to us—at the wedding reception, but obviously something must have been in the air. Let's attribute it to the champagne and drop it before one of us ends up getting hurt."

"You know, if you gave the idea of our getting married some serious thought, it might grow on you," he suggested next.

Then he got to his feet and moved purposefully towards her. His mouth twisted into a cocky grin. "Maybe this will help you decide what's best."

"I—"

He laid a finger across her mouth to stop her. "It seems to me you've forgotten it's not ladylike to be quite so stubborn." With that, he slipped his arm around her waist and gently pulled her against him.

Knowing what he intended, Kate opened her mouth to protest, but he fastened his lips over hers, sealing off the words, and to her chagrin, soon erasing them altogether. Her fingers gripped the collar of his blue button-snap shirt and against every dictate of her will her mouth parted willingly, welcoming his touch.

When he released her, it was a minor miracle that she didn't collapse on the floor. He paused and a wide grin split his face.

"Yup," he said, looking more than pleased, "you love me all right."

Three

Kate had never felt more grateful for a Monday morning than she did the following day. At least when she was at school, she had the perfect excuse to avoid another confrontation with Luke. He seemed to believe he was somehow responsible for her and to take that responsibility quite seriously. She had no intention of holding him to his promise and couldn't understand why he was being so stubborn. To suggest she was in love with him simply because she'd proposed marriage and responded ardently to his kisses revealed how truly irrational Luke Rivers had become.

Kate paused and let that thought run through her mind once more, then laughed aloud. No wonder Luke insisted on marrying her. Kate had to admit she could see why he might have the wrong impression. Still, she wished she could think of some way to set him straight.

Luke was right about a few things, though. She *did* love him— but not the way he implied. She felt for him as a sister did towards a special older brother. As a woman did towards a confidant and companion of many years' standing. The feelings she'd experienced when he kissed her were something of a mystery, but could easily be attributed to the heightened emotions following Clay's wedding. So much had been going on in Kate's life the past few months that she barely understood herself any more.

She could never love Luke the way she had Clay. For as long as Kate could remember, she'd pictured herself as Clay's wife. Linking her life with any other man's seemed not only wrong but completely foreign.

"Good morning, Miss Logan," seven-year-old Taylor Morgenroth said as he casually strolled into the classroom. "I saw you at Mr Franklin's wedding on Saturday."

"You did?" It shouldn't surprise her, since nearly every family in town had been represented at the wedding. Probably more than one of her students had seen her.

"You were with Mr Rivers, weren't you? My mom kept asking my dad who you were dancing with. That was Mr Rivers, wasn't it?"

"Yes." Kate had to bite her tongue to keep from explaining that she hadn't actually been "with" Luke. He wasn't her official date, although they'd attended the wedding together. But explaining something like that to a second-grader would only confuse the child.

"My dad made me dance with my older sister. It was yucky."

Kate managed to mumble something about how much of a gentleman Taylor had been, but she doubted that he wanted to hear it.

Before long, the students of Nightingale Elementary were eagerly filing into the classroom and rushing towards their desks. From that point on, Kate didn't have time to think about Luke or Saturday night or anything else except her lesson plans for the day.

At noon she took her packed lunch to the staff room. Several of the other teachers were already seated at the circular tables.

"Kate!" Sally Daley, the sixth-grade teacher, waved her hand to gain Kate's attention. She smiled, patting the empty chair beside her.

Reluctantly Kate joined the older woman, sending an apologetic look to her friend Linda Hutton, the third-grade teacher, whom she usually joined for lunch. Sally had the reputation of being a busybody, but Kate couldn't think of a way to avoid her without being rude.

"We were just talking about you," Sally said warmly, "and we thought it would be nice if you'd sit with us today."

"I'll be happy to," Kate said, feeling a twinge of guilt at the lie. She opened her brown bag, taking out a container of peach-flavoured yogurt and two rye crisps.

"Clay's wedding was really lovely, wasn't it?" Sally asked without any preamble. "And now I understand your father and Dorothea Murphy are going to be tying the knot?" Her questioning tone indicated she wasn't certain of her facts.

"That's right," Kate said cheerfully.

"Kind of a surprise, wasn't it?"

"Kind of," was all Kate would admit, although now she realised she should have known her father was falling in love with Mrs Murphy. They'd been spending more and more time together since early summer. If Kate hadn't been so blinded by what was happening between her and Clay, she would have noticed how serious her father had become about Dorothea long before now.

"It's going to be difficult for you, isn't it, dear?" Sally asked sympathetically. "Everyone knows how close you and your father have been since Nora died."

"I'm very pleased my father's going to remarry." And Kate was. The initial shock had worn off; she felt genuinely and completely happy that her father had found someone to love. He'd never complained, but Kate knew he'd been lonely during the past few years.

"Still, it must be something of a blow," Sally pressed, "especially following on the heels of Clay and Rorie getting married? It seems your whole life has been turned upside down of late, doesn't it?"

Kate nodded, keeping her eyes focused on her sparse meal.

"Speaking of Clay and Rorie, their wedding was exceptionally lovely."

"I thought so, too," Kate said, smiling through the pain. "Rorie will make him a perfect wife." The words nearly stuck in her throat, although she was fully aware of their truth. Rorie was an ideal complement to Clay. From the moment she'd stepped into their lives, she'd obviously belonged with Clay.

"The new Mrs Franklin is certainly an ambitious soul. Why, the library hasn't been the same since she took over. There are education programmes going on there every other week. Displays. Lectures. I tell you, nothing but good has happened since she moved to Nightingale."

"I couldn't agree with you more."

Sally looked pleased. "I think you've taken this... disappointment over Clay rather well," she murmured with cloying sympathy. "And now your father remarrying so soon afterwards..." She gently patted Kate's hand. "If there's anything I can do for you, Kate, anything at all, during this difficult time, I don't want you to hesitate to call me. I know I speak for each and every staff member when I say that. Your father must see you've been a wonderful daughter, and I'm sorry all of this is being heaped on your shoulders just now. But if it's ever more than you can bear, your friends at Nightingale Elementary will be honoured to stand at your side. All you have to do is call."

If Sally was expecting a lengthy response, Kate couldn't manage it. "Thank you. That's...really wonderful to know," she said in a faltering voice. To hear Sally tell it, Kate was close to a nervous breakdown.

"We're prepared to stand at your side as you pick up the shattered pieces of your life. And furthermore, I think Luke Rivers is a fine man."

"Luke Rivers?" Kate repeated, nearly choking on her bite of rye crisp. A huge knot formed in her throat at Sally's implication.

"Why, yes." Sally paused and smiled serenely. "Everyone in Nightingale saw how the two of you were gazing into each other's eyes at the dance. It was the most romantic thing I've seen in years."

"Dance?"

"At the wedding-reception dance," Sally elaborated. "From what I understand, Betty Hammond's been so depressed she hasn't left her house since that night."

"Whatever for?"

Sally laughed lightly. "Surely there's no reason to be so reticent—you're among friends. Everyone knows how Betty's had her eye on Luke for years. From what I understand they dated a couple of times a year or so ago, but Luke's kept her dangling ever since."

"I don't have a clue what you mean," Kate said faintly, her heart beating hard enough to pound its way out of her chest. She'd hoped that with her father's engagement, the rumours about her and Luke would naturally fade away. So much for wishful thinking.

Sally exchanged a meaningful look with her friends. "Well, I thought that, you know...that you and Luke Rivers had a thing going."

"Luke and me?" Kate gave a short, almost hysterical laugh. "Nothing could be further from the truth. Luke's a dear friend, and we've known each other for years, but we're not romantically involved. There's nothing between us. Absolutely nothing." She spoke more vehemently than necessary, feeling pleased that for once Sally couldn't manage a single word.

After a moment, she made a show of looking at her watch. "Excuse me, ladies, but I've got to get back to my classroom."

As she left the staff room, she heard the whispers start. Groaning inwardly, Kate marched down the hall and into her own room. Sitting at her desk, she snapped the cracker in half and examined it closely before tossing it into the garbage.

"Don't you know it's wrong to waste food?" Linda Hutton said, leaning against the doorjamb, arms folded.

"I wished I'd never talked to that woman," Kate muttered, feeling foolish for allowing herself to be manipulated into conversation with a known busybody.

"Well, then," Linda said, with a knowing grin, "why did you?"

"If I knew the answer to that, I'd be enjoying my lunch instead of worrying about the tales Sally's going to spread all over town about me...and Luke Rivers."

Linda walked nonchalantly into the room.

"The least you could have done was rescue me," Kate complained.

"Hey, I leave that kind of work to the fire department." Linda leaned forward and planted her hands on the edge of Kate's desk. "Besides, I was curious myself."

"You're curious about what? Luke and me? Honestly, all we did was dance a couple of times. I...was feeling warm and went outside for a little bit. Luke met me there and after a few minutes, he... drove me home. What's the big deal, anyway?"

"A couple of dances...I see," Linda said, her words slow and thoughtful.

"I'd be interested in knowing exactly what you see. Everyone keeps making an issue of the dancing. Taylor came into class this morning and the first thing he mentioned was that he'd seen me at the wedding. He didn't talk about running into me at the grocery store earlier that same day."

"Did you have your arms wrapped around a man there, too?"

"Don't be silly!"

"I wasn't. Honestly, Kate, nearly everyone in Nightingale saw the way you and Luke were dancing. You acted as though there wasn't anyone else at the reception. Needless to say, rumours were floating in every direction. Everyone was watching the two of you, and neither you or Luke even noticed. Or cared. I heard the pastor mumble something about the possibility of performing another wedding soon, and he wasn't referring to your father and Dorothea Murphy—which is something else entirely." Linda paused to suck in a deep breath. "Are you sure you're going to be able to handle this on top of—"

"Clay and Rorie? Yes," Kate answered her own question emphatically. "Oh, I had a few bad moments when Dad first told me, but I got over it." The comfort she'd found in Luke's arms had helped her more than she cared to admit. He seemed to be making a habit of helping her through difficult moments.

Linda eyed her sceptically. "There's been so much upheaval in your life these past few weeks. You know sometimes people go into shock for weeks after a major change in their lives."

"Linda," Kate cried, "everyone keeps looking at me as though they expect me to have a nervous breakdown or something. What is it with you people?"

"It isn't us, Katie girl, it's you."

Kate pushed her hair off her forehead and kept her hand pressed there. "What do I have to do to convince you that I'm fine? I'm happy for Clay and Rorie. I like to think of myself as resilient and emotionally strong, but it makes me wonder why you and Sally and the others don't."

"I don't think anyone's waiting for you to fall apart," Linda countered. "We all have your best interests at heart. In fact with one obvious exception, everyone's really pleased you have Luke."

"But I don't *have* him. Luke isn't a possession, he's a man. We're friends. You know that." She expected Linda, of all her friends and colleagues, to recognise the truth when she heard it. Instead she'd made it sound as though Kate's dancing with Luke and then letting him take her home early meant instant wedding bells.

Linda took a moment to consider her answer. "To be honest, Kate, you're doing a whole lot of denying and I don't understand why. It seems to me that the person you're most trying to convince is yourself."

By the time Kate arrived home that evening, she was in a fine temper. Her father had already left for a meeting at the Eagles Lodge. He'd taped a note to the refrigerator door telling her not to worry about fixing him any dinner because he planned to stop off at Dorothea's for a bite to eat later.

Kate read his scrawled note, pulled it off the fridge and crumpled it with both hands. She was angry and impatient for no reason she could identify.

Heating herself a bowl of soup, Kate stood in front of the stove stirring it briskly when Luke let himself in the back door. After her encounter with Sally and Linda, Luke was the last person she wanted to see that evening. Nevertheless, her eyes flew anxiously to his.

"Evening, Kate."

"Hi."

He hung his hat on the peg next to the door, then walked to the kitchen counter and examined the empty soup can. "I hope you're going to eat more than this."

"Luke," she said, slowly expelling her breath. "I had a terrible day and I'm rotten company."

"What happened?"

Kate didn't want to talk about it. Dredging up her lunch-hour conversation with Sally Daley would only refuel her unhappiness.

"Kate?" Luke coaxed.

She shrugged. "The other teachers heard about Dad and Dorothea and seemed to think the shock would do me in, if you know what I mean."

"I think I do." As he was speaking, he took two bowls out of the cupboard and set them on the table.

Kate stirred the soup energetically, not looking at him, almost afraid of his reaction. "In addition, people are talking about us."

When she glanced in his direction, Luke nodded, his eyes twinkling. "I thought they might be."

"I don't like it!" she burst out. The least Luke could do was show the proper amount of concern. "Sally Daley told me how pleased she was with the way I'd rebounded from a broken heart." She paused, waiting for his response. When he didn't give her one, she added, "Sally seems to think you and I are perfect together."

Luke grinned. "And that upset you?"

"Yes!" she cried.

"Sally didn't mean anything. She's got a big heart."

"Her mouth is even bigger," Kate retorted. "We're in trouble here, Luke Rivers, and I want to know exactly how we're going to get out of it."

"The answer to that is simple. We should get married and put an end to speculation."

Kate's shoulders sagged in defeat. "Luke, please, I'm just not in the mood for your teasing tonight. The time has come for us to get serious about..."

Her voice dwindled as Luke, standing behind her, placed his hands on her shoulders and nuzzled her neck. "I'm willing."

His touch had a curious effect on Kate's senses, which seemed to leap to life. It took every ounce of fortitude she possessed to resist melting into his arms and accepting his gentle comfort. But that was how they'd got into this mess in the first place.

"The gossips are having a field day and I hate it."

Luke drew her away from the stove and turned her towards him.

He searched her face, but his own revealed not a hint of annoyance or distress. "I don't mind if folks talk. It's only natural, don't you think?"

"How can you say that?" This whole situation with Luke had completely unnerved her, while he seemed to take it in his stride.

"Kate, you're making this out to be some kind of disaster."

"But don't you see? It is! There are people out there who honestly believe we're falling in love."

"You do love me. I told you that earlier. Remember?"

"Oh, Luke," she cried, so disheartened she wanted to weep. "I understand what you're trying to do and I appreciate it with all my heart, but it isn't necessary. It really isn't."

Luke looked baffled. "I don't think I understand."

"You've been such a dear." She laid her hand against his clean-shaven cheek. "Any other man would have laughed in my face when I made him promise to marry me, but you agreed and now, out of consideration for *my* pride, *my* feelings, you claim you're going to go through with it."

"Kate," he said, guiding her to the table and gently pressing her into a chair. "Sit down. I have something important to tell you—something I've been trying to tell you since the night of the wedding."

"What is it?" she asked, once she was seated.

Luke paced the floor directly in front of her chair, frowning deeply. "I should have told you much sooner, but with everything else that's going on in your life, finding the right time has been difficult." He paused in his pacing and looked at her as though he was having trouble finding the words.

"Yes?" she coaxed.

"I'm buying the Circle L."

The kitchen started to sway. Kate reached out and gripped the edge of the table. She'd hoped it would be several months before a buyer could be found. And it had never occurred to her that Luke might be that buyer. "I see," she said, smiling through her shock. "I...I'd have thought Dad would've said something himself."

"I asked him not to."

Her troubled gaze clashed with Luke's. Despite her shock she felt curious. How could Luke afford to buy a ranch, especially one as large as this? She knew he'd been raised by an uncle, who had died years before. Had there been an inheritance? "Luke," she ventured shyly, "I know it's none of my business, but..."

"How did I come by the money?" he finished for her. "You have every right to ask, Princess. I inherited it from my Uncle Dan—I've told you about him. He owned a couple of businesses in Wyoming, where I grew up. There was a small sum left to me by my grandfather. I invested everything, together with most of what Devin's paid me over the years, and I've got enough now to buy the ranch outright—which'll leave your dad and Dorothea in good financial shape for their retirement. I'll be able to expand the operation, too."

Kate nodded absently. She hadn't known much about Luke's background, apart from the fact that he had very little family, that he'd lost his parents at an early age. She supposed those losses were the reason he'd been so sympathetic, such a comfort to her and Devin, at the time of Nora's death.

It still seemed too much to take in. Her home—it was going to belong to Luke. He'd move his things from the small foreman's house, though she knew he hadn't accumulated many possessions. But it meant that soon she would be sorting through and packing up the memories of a lifetime.... She frowned and bit her lip.

He knelt in front of her, gripping her fingers with his warm, hard hands. "I realise you've been through a lot of emotional upheaval lately, but this should help."

"Help!" she wailed. "How could it possibly—?"

"There isn't any reason for you to be uprooted now."

For a stunned second she didn't react. "I don't have the slightest idea what you're talking about."

"Once we're married, we'll live right here."

"Married!" she almost shouted. "I'm beginning to hate the sound of that word."

"You'd best get used to it, because the way I figure it we're going to be husband and wife before Christmas. We'll let Devin and Dorothea take their vows first—I don't want to steal their thunder—and then we'll wait a couple of weeks and have the Reverend Wilkins marry us."

"Luke, this is all very sweet of you, but *it isn't necessary.*" Although he hadn't said as much, Kate was convinced that this sudden desire to make her his wife was founded in sympathy. He felt sorry for her, because of all the unexpected jolts that had hit her recently. Including this latest one.

"I can't understand why you're arguing with me."

Her hand caressed his jaw. How square and strong it was, and

the eyes that gazed at her had never seemed darker or more magnetic. She smiled sadly. "Don't you think it's a little...odd to be
discussing marriage when you've never once said you loved me?"

"I love you."

Despite the seriousness of the moment, Kate laughed. "Oh, honestly, Luke, that was terrible."

"I'm serious. I love you and you love me."

"Of course we love each other, but what we feel is what *friends*
feel. The kind of love brothers and sisters share."

Fire leapt into his eyes, unlike anything she'd seen in him before.
With any other man, she would have been frightened—but this was
Luke....

"Instead of looking at me as if you're tempted to toss me over
your knee, you should be grateful I'm not holding you to your
word."

"Kate," he said forcefully. "we're getting married." He spoke
as though he were daring her to argue with him.

Gently she lowered her head and brushed his lips with her own.
"No, we're not. I'll always be grateful to have had a friend as good
as you, Luke Rivers. Every woman deserves someone just as kind
and thoughtful, but we'd be making the biggest mistake of our lives
if we went through with this marriage."

"I don't think that's true."

"I'm sane and rational and I'm not going to disintegrate under
the emotional stress of Clay's wedding or my father's remarriage,
or the selling of the ranch. Life goes on—I learned that after my
mother died. It sounds so clichéd, but it's true. I learned to deal
with losing her and I'll do the same with everything else that's
been happening."

"Kate, you don't understand. I *want* to marry you."

"Oh, Luke, it's so sweet of you. But you don't love me. Not the
way you should. Some day, you'll make some lucky woman a
fantastic husband." Kate had grown accustomed to his comfortable
presence. But while she felt at ease with him, she experienced none
of the thrill, the urgent excitement, that being in love entailed.

With Clay, the intensity of emotion had wrapped itself around
her so securely that she'd been certain it would last a lifetime. Kate
hadn't fooled herself into believing Clay felt as strongly for her.
He'd been fond of her, and Kate had been willing to settle for that.
But it hadn't been enough for him. She wasn't going to allow Luke
to settle for second best in his life.

"People are going to talk, so we both have to do our best to put an end to the rumours."

"I don't intend to do any such thing," Luke said, his jaw rigid. His eyes narrowed. "Kate, darling, a marriage between us is inevitable. The sooner you accept that, the better it will be for everyone involved."

Four

"The way I figure it," Kate said, munching hard on a carrot stick, "the only way to convince Luke I don't plan to marry him is to start dating someone else."

Linda looked as if she were about to swallow her apple whole. The two were seated in the school lunchroom late Friday afternoon, reviewing plans for the Thanksgiving play their two classes would present the following month.

"Start dating someone else?" Linda echoed, still wearing a stunned expression. "Not more than two days ago you announced that you were finished with love and completely opposed to the idea of men and marriage."

"I'm not looking to fall in love again," Kate explained impatiently. "That would be ridiculous."

"You talk about being ridiculous?" Linda asked, absently setting down her half-eaten apple. "We were discussing Pilgrim costume designs and suddenly you decide you want to start dating. I take it you're not referring to Miles Standish?"

"Of course not."

"That's what I thought."

Kate supposed she wasn't making a lot of sense to her friend. Luke and the issue of marriage had been on her mind all week, but she'd carefully avoided any mention of the subject. Until now. The rumours regarding her and Luke continued to burn like a forest fire through Nightingale, aided, Kate was sure, by the silly grin Luke wore about town, and the fact that he was buying her father's ranch. True, he hadn't pressured her into setting a wedding date again, but the thought was there, waiting to envelop her every time they were in the same room. She used to be able to laugh and joke with Luke, but lately, the minute they were together, Kate found herself raising her protective force field. She was beginning to feel like a character out of *Star Wars*.

"All right, you've piqued my curiosity," Linda said, her eyes flashing with humour. "Tell me about this sudden interest in the opposite sex."

"I want to stop the rumours naturally." And, she thought, convince Luke that her marriage proposal had been rooted in self-pity. He'd been so strong and she'd felt so fragile.

Linda pushed aside the pages of the Thanksgiving project notes. "Have you picked out anyone in particular?"

"No," Kate murmured, frowning. "I've been out of circulation for so long, I don't know who's available."

"No one," Linda told her in a despondent voice. "And I should know. If you want the truth, I think Nightingale would make an excellent locale for a convent. Have you ever considered the religious life?"

Kate ignored that. "Didn't I hear Sally Daley mention something about a new guy who recently moved to town? I'm sure I did and she seemed to think he was single."

"Eric Wilson. Attorney, mid-thirties, divorced, with a small mole on his left shoulder."

Kate was astonished. "Good heavens, how did Sally know all that?"

Linda shook her head slowly. "I don't even want to guess."

"Eric Wilson." Kate repeated the name slowly, letting each syllable roll off her tongue. She decided the name had a friendly feel, though it didn't really tell her anything about the man himself.

"Have you met him?" Kate asked her friend.

Linda shook her head. "No, but you're welcome to him, if you want. The only reason Sally mentioned him to me was that she assumed you and Luke would be married before the holidays were over."

A sense of panic momentarily swamped Kate. Luke had mentioned getting married around Christmas, too. "There's always Andy Barrett," Kate pointed out. Andy worked at the pharmacy, and was single. True, he wasn't exactly a heartthrob, but he was a decent-enough sort.

Linda immediately rejected that possibility. "No one in town would believe you'd choose Andy over Luke." A smile played across her mouth, as if she found the idea of Kate and Andy together somehow comical. "Andy's sweet, don't get me wrong," Linda amended, "but Luke's a real man."

"I'll think of someone," Kate murmured, her determination fierce.

Linda started to gather her Thanksgiving notes. "If you're serious about this, then you may have no choice but to import a man from Portland."

"You're kidding, I hope," Kate groaned.

"I'm dead serious," Linda said, shoving everything into her briefcase.

Her friend's words echoed depressingly through Kate's mind as she pushed her cart to the frozen-food section of the grocery store later that afternoon. She peered at the TV dinners, trying to choose something for dinner. Her father had dined with Dorothea every night since they'd become engaged, and the wedding was planned for early December.

"The beef burgundy is good," a resonant male voice said from behind her.

Kate turned to face a tall, friendly-looking man with flashing blue eyes and a lazy smile.

"Eric Wilson," he introduced himself, holding out his hand.

"Kate Logan," she said, her heart racing as they exchanged handshakes. It was all Kate could do not to mention that she'd been talking about him only minutes before and that she'd learned he was possibly the only decent single man in town—other than Luke, of course. How bizarre that they should run into each other almost immediately afterward. Perhaps not! Perhaps it was fate.

"The Salisbury steak isn't half-bad, either." As if to prove his point, he deposited both the beef burgundy and the Salisbury-steak frozen dinners in his cart.

"You sound as though you know."

"I've discovered frozen entrées are less trouble than a wife."

He frowned as he spoke, so she guessed that his divorce had been unpleasant. Sally would know, and Kate made a mental note to ask her later. She'd do so blatantly, of course, since Sally was sure to spread Kate's interest in the transplanted lawyer all over the county.

"You're new in town, aren't you? An attorney?"

Eric nodded. "At your service."

Kate was thinking fast. It had been a long time since she'd last flirted with a man. "Does that mean I can sue you if the beef burgundy isn't to my liking?"

He grinned at that, and although her comment hadn't been especially witty, she felt encouraged by his smile.

"You might have trouble getting the judge to listen to your suit, though," he told her.

"Judge Webster is my uncle," she said, laughing.

"And I suppose you're his favourite niece."

"Naturally."

"In that case, might I suggest we avoid the possibility of a lawsuit and I buy you dinner?"

That was so easy Kate couldn't believe it. She'd been out of the dating game for a long time, and she'd been sure it would take weeks to get the hang of it again. "I'd be honoured."

It wasn't until Kate was home, high on her success, that she realised Eric, as a new man in town, was probably starved for companionship. That made her pride sag just a little, but she wasn't about to complain. Within hours of declaring that she wanted to start dating, she'd met a man. An attractive, pleasant man, too. It didn't matter that he'd asked her out because he was lonely or that he was obviously still licking the wounds from his divorce. A date was a date.

Kate showered and changed into a mid-calf burgundy wool skirt and a rose-coloured silk blouse. She was putting the last coat of polish on her nails when her father strolled into the kitchen. Even from her position at the far side of the room, Kate caught a strong whiff of his spicy after-shave. She smiled a little.

"You look nice."

"Thanks," he said, tugging on the lapels of his tweed jacket, then brushing the sleeves.

"Do you want me to wait up for you?"

A light pink flush worked its way up Devin's neck. "Of course not."

Kate loved teasing him, and as their eyes met, they both started to laugh.

"You're looking awfully pretty yourself," Devin commented. "Are you and Luke going out?"

"Eric Wilson is taking me to dinner."

Devin regarded her quizzically. "Who? You're jesting, aren't you?"

"No." She gave him a warning frown. "Eric's new here. We met in the frozen-food section at the Safeway store this afternoon and he asked me to dinner."

"And you accepted?" His eyes were wide with astonishment.

"Of course. It beats sitting around here and watching reruns on television."

"But...but what about Luke?"

"What about him?"

"I thought...I'd hoped after Clay's wedding that the two of you might—"

"Dad, Luke's a dear friend, but we're not in love with each other."

For a moment Devin looked as if he wanted to argue, but apparently decided against it. "He's a good man, Princess."

"Trust me, I know that. If it weren't for Luke, I don't know how I would have survived the last couple of months."

"Folks in town got the impression you two might be falling in love, and I can't say I blame them after watching you at the wedding."

Kate focused her attention on polishing her nails, knowing that an identical shade of red had crept into her cheeks.

"Luke and I are friends, Dad, nothing more," she repeated.

"I don't mind letting you know, Kate, I think very highly of Luke. If I were to handpick a husband for you, it would be him."

"I...think Luke's wonderful, too," she said, her words faltering.

"Now that he's buying the ranch, well, it seems natural that the two of you—"

"Dad, please," she whispered. "I'm not in love with Luke, and he doesn't love me."

"That's a real pity," came Devin's softly drawled response. He reached for his hat, then paused by the door. "I don't suppose Luke knows you're going out tonight, does he?"

"There isn't any reason to tell him." She struggled to sound nonchalant. But the last thing she needed or wanted was another showdown with Luke. Pleadingly, she raised her eyes to her father. "You aren't going to tell him, are you?"

"I won't lie to him."

"Oh, no, I wouldn't expect you to do that," Kate murmured. She blew at the red polish on her nails, trying to dry them quickly. With luck Eric would arrive soon and she could make her escape before she encountered Luke.

Kate should have known that was asking too much. She was standing at the kitchen window beside the oak table, waiting for Eric's headlights to come down the long driveway, when Luke walked into the house.

Kate groaned inwardly, but said nothing. Her fingers tightened on the curtain as she changed her silent entreaty. Now she prayed that Eric would be late.

"You've got your coat on," Luke observed, as he helped himself to coffee.

"I'll be leaving in a couple of minutes," she said, hoping she didn't sound as tense as she felt. Then, a little guiltily, she added, "I baked some oatmeal cookies this afternoon. The cookie jar's full, so help yourself."

He did exactly that, then sat down at the table. "If I didn't know better, I'd think you were waiting for someone."

"I am."

"Who?"

"A...friend." Her back was to him, but Kate could feel the tension mounting in the air between them.

"Are you upset about something?"

"No. Should I be?" she asked in an offhand manner.

"You've been avoiding me all week," Luke murmured.

He was sitting almost directly behind her and Kate felt his presence acutely. Her knees were shaking, her breath coming in short, uneven gulps. She felt almost light-headed. It had to be nerves. If Luke discovered she was going to dinner with Eric there could be trouble. Yes, that explained the strange, physical reaction she was experiencing, she told herself.

"Kate, love—"

"Please," she implored, "don't call me that." She let go of the curtain and turned to face him. "I made a mistake, and considering the circumstances, it was understandable. Please, Luke, can't you drop this whole marriage business? Please?"

His look of shocked surprise didn't do anything to settle her nerves. A strained moment passed before Luke relaxed, chuckling. "I've broken stallions who've given me less trouble than you."

"I'm no stallion."

Luke chuckled again, and before she could move, his arms reached out and circled her waist to pull her on to his lap.

Kate was so astonished that for a crazy moment she didn't react at all. "Let me go," she said stiffly, holding her chin at a regal angle.

He ignored her demand and instead lightly ran the tips of his fingers along the side of her jaw and stroked downward to cup her chin. "I've missed you this week, Princess."

A trail of warmth followed his cool fingers, and a foreign sensation nibbled at her stomach. Kate didn't know what was wrong with her—and she didn't *want* to know.

"I've decided to give you a chance to think matters through before we contact Pastor Wilkins—"

"Before we what?" she flared.

"Before we're married," he explained patiently, his voice much too low and seductive to suit her. "But every time we're together, you run away like a frightened kitten."

"Did you stop to think there might be a perfectly logical reason for that?" She'd told him repeatedly that she wasn't going to marry him, but it didn't seem to do any good. "I'm sorry, I truly am, but I just don't think of you in that way."

"Oh?"

He raised his hand and threaded his fingers through her hair. She tried to pull away, to thwart him, with no effect.

"That's not the feeling I get when I kiss you."

She braced her hands against his shoulder, her fingers curling into the powerful muscles there. "I apologise if I've given you the wrong impression," she said, her voice feeble.

He cocked his brows at her statement, and his lips quivered with the effort to suppress a smile. That infuriated Kate, but she held on to her temper, knowing an argument would be pointless.

"It seems to me," he continued softly, "that we need some time alone to explore what's happening between us."

Alarm rose in Kate's throat, as she struggled to hide her response to him. The last thing she wanted was "time alone" with Luke.

"I'm afraid that's impossible tonight," she said hastily.

"Why's that?"

He was so close that his breath fanned her flushed face. It was all Kate could do to keep from closing her eyes and surrendering to the sensations that encircled her like lazy curls of smoke from a camp fire.

His mouth found her neck and he rained a long series of kisses there, each one a small dart of pleasure that robbed her of clear thought. For a wild moment, she couldn't catch her breath. His hands were in her hair, and his mouth was working its magic on her.

"No," she breathed, her voice low and trembling. Any resistance she'd managed to muster had vanished.

"Yes, my darling Kate."

He captured her mouth then, and excitement erupted inside her. She clung to him, her arms wrapped around his neck as his lips returned again and again to taste and tantalise her.

When he buried his face in the hollow of her throat, Kate moaned softly. She felt nearly faint from the rush of pleasure.

"Call Linda and cancel whatever plans you've made," he whispered.

Kate froze. "I can't."

"Yes, you can. I'll talk to her, if you want."

"I'm not going out with Linda." How weak she sounded.

"Then call whoever you're going out with and cancel."

"No..."

A flash of headlights through the kitchen window announced Eric's arrival. With a burst of desperate energy, Kate leapt off Luke's lap. She felt disoriented and bewildered for a moment. She rubbed her hands over her face, realising she'd probably smudged her make-up, but that didn't concern her as much as the unreserved way she'd submitted to Luke's touch. He'd kissed her before and it had been wonderful—more than wonderful. But in those brief moments when he'd held her, at the wedding and then again the next day, she hadn't experience this burning need. It terrified her.

"Kate?"

She looked at Luke without really seeing him. "I've got to go," she insisted.

"There's a man here."

Kate opened the door for Eric. "Hi," she greeted, doing her best to appear bright and cheerful, but knowing she looked and sounded as though she was coming down with a bad case of flu. "I see you found the place without a problem."

"I had one hell of a time," he said, glancing at his watch. "Didn't you notice I'm fifteen minutes late?"

Well, no, she hadn't. Not really.

"Kate, who is this man?" Luke demanded in a steely voice.

"Eric Wilson, this is Luke Rivers. Luke is buying the Circle L," she said, hoping she didn't sound as breathless as she felt.

The two men exchanged the briefest of handshakes.

Kate didn't dare look in Luke's direction. She didn't need to, she could feel the resentment and annoyance that emanated from him like waves of heat. "Well, I suppose we should be on our way," Kate said quickly to Eric, throwing him a tight, nervous smile.

"Yes, I suppose we should." Eric's gaze travelled from Kate to Luke, then back again. He looked equally eager to make an escape.

"I'll say goodnight, Luke," she said pointedly, her hand on the back door.

He didn't respond, which was just as well.

Once they were outside, Eric opened his car door for her. "You said Luke is buying the ranch?"

"Yes," she answered brightly.

"And nothing else?" he pressed, frowning. "The look he was giving me seemed to say you came with the property."

"That's not the least bit true." Even if Luke chose to believe otherwise. After tonight, she couldn't deny that they shared a strong physical attraction, but that was nothing on which to base a life together. She didn't *love* Luke; how could she, when she was still in love with Clay? She'd been crazy about Clay Franklin most of her life, and feelings that intense wouldn't change overnight simply because he'd married another woman.

When Clay and Rorie had announced their engagement, Kate had known with desolate certainty that she'd never love again. If she couldn't have Clay, then she would live the remainder of her life alone, treasuring the time they'd had together.

"You're sure Rivers has no claim on you?"

"None," Kate assured him.

"That's funny," Eric said with a humourless chuckle. "From the way he glared at me, I feel lucky to have walked away with my head still attached."

Kate forced a light laugh. "I'm sure you're mistaken."

Eric didn't comment further, but it was obvious he didn't believe her.

After their shaky beginning, dinner turned out to be an almost pleasant affair. Eric took Kate to the Red Bull, the one fancy restaurant in Nightingale, a steak house that specialised in thick T-bones and fat baked potatoes. A country-and-western band played local favourites in the lounge, which was a popular Friday-night attraction. The music drifted into the dining-room, creating a festive atmosphere.

Eric studied the menu, then requested a bottle of wine with their meal.

When the waitress had taken their order, he planted his elbows on the table and smiled at Kate. "Your eyes are lovely," he said, his voice a little too enthusiastic.

Despite herself, Kate blushed. "Thank you."

"They're the same colour as my ex-wife's." He announced this in bitter tones, as if he wished Kate's were any other colour but blue. "I'm sorry," he added, looking chagrined. "I've got to stop thinking about Lonni. It's over. Finished. Kaput."

"I take it you didn't want the divorce."

"Do you mind if we don't talk about it?"

Kate felt foolish for bringing up the subject, especially since it was obviously so painful for him. "I'm sorry, that was thoughtless. Of course, you want to let go of the past."

The bottle of wine arrived and when Eric had sampled and approved it the waitress filled their glasses.

"Actually you remind me a good deal of Lonni," he said, after taking a sip of the chardonnay. "We met when we were both in college."

Kate lowered her gaze to her wineglass, twirling the delicate stem between her fingers. Eric was so clearly in love with his ex-wife that she wondered what had torn them apart.

"You were asking about the divorce?" He replenished his wine with a lavish hand.

"If it's painful, you don't need to talk about it."

"I don't think either Lonni or I ever intended to let matters go so far," he said, and Kate was sure he hadn't even heard her. "I certainly didn't, but before I knew what was happening the whole thing blew up in my face. There wasn't another man—I would have staked my life on that."

Their dinner salads arrived and, reaching for her fork, Kate asked, "What brought you to Nightingale?"

Eric drank his wine as though he were gulping cool water on a summer afternoon. "Lonni, of course."

"I beg your pardon?"

"Lonni. I decided I needed to make a clean break. Get a fresh start and all that."

"I see."

"You have to understand that when Lonni first suggested we might be better off separated, I thought it was the right thing to do. We hadn't been getting along and, frankly, if she wanted out of the relationship, I wasn't going to stand in her way. It's best to discover these things before children arrive, don't you agree?"

"Oh, yes." Kate nibbled at her salad, wondering what she could say that would help or comfort Eric.

An hour and another bottle of wine later, Kate realised he'd drunk the better part of both bottles and was in no condition to drive home. Now she had to tactfully make her date realise that.

"Do you dance?" she asked, as he paid the dinner bill.

He frowned slightly. "This country-and-western stuff doesn't usually appeal to me, but I'm willing to give it a whirl, if you are."

Kate supposed the wine he'd been drinking had quelled his reservations.

As she'd expected, the lounge was filled to capacity. Smoke and good humour filled the air, and when the band played a lively melody, Eric led Kate to the dance floor.

Kate was breathless by the time the song ended. To her relief, the next number was a much slower one. She realised her mistake the minute Eric locked her in his embrace. His hands fastened at the small of her back, forcing her close. She tried to put some space between them, but Eric didn't seem to notice her efforts. His eyes were shut as he swayed to the leisurely beat. Kate wasn't fooled; her newfound friend was pretending he had Lonni in his arms. It was a good thing her ego wasn't riding on this date.

"I need a little more room," she whispered.

He loosened his grip for a moment, but as the song continued his hold gradually tightened again. Kate edged her forearms up and braced them on his chest, easing herself back an inch or two.

"Excuse me, please." A harsh male voice that was all too familiar came from behind Eric. Kate wanted to crawl into a hole and die the instant she heard it.

"I'm cutting in," Luke informed the other man, who turned his head and looked at the intruder incredulously.

Without a word of protest Eric dropped his arms and took a step in retreat. Neither man bothered to ask Kate what *she* wanted. She was about to complain when Luke reached for her hand and with a natural flair swept her into his arms. The immediate sense of welcome she experienced made her want to weep with frustration.

"Why did you cut in like that?" she demanded. She felt disheartened and irritable. Everything she'd worked for this evening was about to be undone.

"Did you honestly mean for that city slicker to hold you so close?"

"How Eric holds me isn't any of your business."

"I'm making it my business."

His face was contorted with anger. His arms were so tight around her that Kate couldn't have escaped him if she'd tried. Judging by the looks they were receiving from the couples around them, Kate realised they were quickly becoming the main attraction.

The instant the music ended, Kate abruptly left Luke's arms and returned to Eric. Her date stood at the corner of the room, nursing a shot glass filled with amber liquid. Kate groaned and hid her displeasure. Eric had already had enough wine to drink without adding hard liquor.

"I thought you said there was nothing between you and Luke Rivers," he accused, when she joined him.

"There isn't. We're just good friends."

"That's not the impression I'm getting."

Kate didn't know how to respond. "I apologise for the interruption. Do you want to dance?"

"Not if it's going to cost me my neck."

"It isn't," she promised.

Another lively song erupted from the band. Eric reached for Kate's hand and she smiled encouragingly up at him. As they headed for the dance floor, Kate tried to ignore Luke's chilly glare.

Midway through the song, Eric stopped dancing. "I'm not into this fancy footwork," he declared. With that, he pulled her into his arms, tucking her securely against him.

"This is much better," he whispered, his mouth close to her ear. Once more his hold tightened.

"Eric, please. I'm having trouble breathing," Kate told him in a strangled voice.

"Oh, sorry." Immediately he relaxed his grip. "Lonni and I used to dance like this all the time."

Kate had already guessed as much. It was on the tip of her tongue to remind him that she wasn't his ex-wife, but she doubted it would make any difference. Eric had spent much of the evening pretending she was.

At the moment, however, her date and his ex-wife were the least of Kate's problems. Tiny pinpricks moved up and down her spine, telling her that Luke was still glaring at her from the other side of the room. She did her best to act as though he wasn't there.

She smiled up at Eric; she laughed, she talked, but with each breath she drew she could feel Luke's eyes on her, scrutinising every move she made.

When the music ended, Eric returned to their table and his drink, swallowing the remainder of it in one gulp. The music started again and he pulled Kate towards him.

"I think I'll sit this one out." She hoped that would appease Luke, who looked as if he were about to rip Eric in two. She'd never seen anyone look more furious. With the least bit of encouragement, his eyes told her, he'd cross the room and paddle her behind.

Her gaze dropped to her lap and she folded her hands, concentrating on not letting him know how much a single glance from him affected her.

"How much have you had to drink, Wilson?"

While her eyes were lowered, Luke had come over to their table. His voice was filled with angry demand.

"I can't say that it's any of your concern, Rivers." For his part, Eric seemed unnerved. He leaned back in his chair, balancing on two legs, and raised his empty shot glass.

"I don't agree," Luke countered, moving closer. "From what I can see, you've had plenty. I'm taking Kate home with me."

"Luke," she protested, "please don't do this."

"Your date's in no condition to drive."

It was all Kate could do not to stand up and defend Eric. Unfortunately Luke was right. She'd known it even before they'd finished dinner, but she wanted to handle things her own way.

"I can hold my liquor as well as the next man," Eric said, daring to wave his glass under Luke's nose. It was apparent to everyone that his courage had been fortified by whisky. Few men would have dared to taunt Luke in his present mood.

Luke turned to Kate. "You've got better sense than this, Kate."

Kate did have. But she had no intention of telling him so. "I think Eric knows his own limit," she returned.

"Then you plan to ride home with him?"

"I'm not sure yet." She wouldn't, but she wasn't about to hand Luke an armful of ammunition to use against her.

Luke scowled at her with such fury that it was difficult for Kate to swallow normally.

Slowly he turned to Eric. "If you value your teeth, I suggest you stay exactly where you are. Bob," Luke shouted to the sheriff's deputy across the room, "would you see this newcomer gets home without a problem?"

"Sure thing, Luke."

"Kate," he said, addressing her next, "you're coming with me."

"I most certainly am not."

Luke didn't leave her any option. He leaned forward and pulled her upright, as if she weighed no more than a bag of popcorn.

She struggled briefly, but she knew it was useless. "Luke, don't do this. Please, don't do this," she pleaded through clenched teeth, humiliated to the very roots of her hair.

"Either you come with me willingly or I carry you out of here." Luke's composure didn't falter. When she resisted, he swept his arms behind her legs and lifted her from the floor.

"Luke," Kate cried, "put me down this instant. I *demand* that you put me down."

He completely ignored her threat as he strode toward the door, his gaze focused impassively ahead of them. The waitress who had served her dinner came running up to hand Kate her coat and bag. Her eyes were flashing with humour.

"Stick by your man, honey," she advised. "That city slicker can't hold a candle to Luke Rivers."

"Luke's the man for you," someone else shouted.

"When you two gonna tie the knot?"

Two men were holding open the lounge door for them. The last thing Kate heard as Luke carried her out into the cold night air was a robust round of applause from inside the lounge.

Five

"I have never been so embarrassed in my life," Kate stormed as Luke parked his pickup outside the house. "How could you do that to me? How could you?"

During the entire ride home, Luke hadn't spoken a word, nor had he even glanced at her. He'd held himself stiff, staring straight ahead. For all his concern about her riding with Eric, he drove as if the very devil were on their tail. Only when they entered the long, winding driveway that led to the house had he reduced his speed.

"I'll never live this down," she told him, reaching for the door handle and vaulting out of the truck. She couldn't escape him fast enough. Every tongue in Nightingale would be wagging by morning, telling how Luke Rivers had hauled Kate Logan out of the Red Bull.

To her dismay Luke followed her into the house.

"I couldn't care less if you forgive me or not," he said darkly.

"The women were laughing and the men snickering.... I won't be able to show my face in this town again."

"As far as I'm concerned, that problem is one of your own making."

"That's not true!" She'd had no way of knowing that Eric was going to start downing wine like soda . The last thing she needed from Luke was a lecture. All she wanted him to do was leave, so she could lick her wounds in private and figure out how long it would be before she dared go out in public again.

Luke started pacing the kitchen floor. Each step was measured and precise. Clipped, like his voice.

"Please go," she beseeched wearily.

"I'm not leaving until I get some answers from you."

Gathering what remained of her dignity, which at this point wasn't much, Kate sank on to a chair. She wouldn't argue with Luke. Every time she tried, she came out the loser. Better to get this over with now rather than wait for tomorrow morning. She sighed deeply.

"Who the hell is Eric Wilson and why were you having dinner with him?" Luke demanded. His heavy boots clicked against the kitchen floor as he paced.

Instead of answering, Kate asked, "What's happened to us?" She gazed sorrowfully up at Luke. "Do you remember how much fun we used to have together? Tonight wasn't fun, Luke. Just a few weeks ago I could laugh with you and cry with you. You were my friend and I was yours. Suddenly nothing's the same, and I don't understand what's happened." Her voice wavered slightly. She fought an overwhelming desire to hide her face in her hands and weep.

She didn't win. Tears of pride and anguish spilled on to her cheeks. She brought her hands up, trying to hide her distress.

Luke knelt in front of her and pried her hands away. His fingers lightly and tenderly caressed her face. "Everything has changed, hasn't it, Princess?"

She sucked in a quavery breath and nodded.

"You're still confused, aren't you?" His hands cradled her face and he eased forward to press his warm mouth over hers. Even as she kissed him back, her confusion grew. He'd been so angry with her, more furious than she could ever remember. Yet, when he kissed her, he was achingly gentle.

Luke seemed to believe that her ready response to his kiss would answer the questions that haunted her. Instead it raised more reservations, more qualms.

"Do you understand now?" he asked, his voice a husky murmur, his eyes closed.

How Kate wished she did. She shook her head and lowered her gaze, bewildered and more uncertain than ever.

Luke stroked her lips with his index finger. His most innocent touches brought her nerves to life with a prickling, wary excitement. Not understanding her own impulse, she held his hand to her mouth and brushed her lips across his calloused fingertips.

"Oh, love," he moaned, and bent forward, caressing her mouth with his once more. "We've got to put an end to this madness before I go insane."

"How?" she gasped, as she braced her hands against his broad chest. He felt so good, hard muscle and warm flesh, and so strong, as if nothing could stand in his way once he determined a course. Not heaven. Not hell. And nothing in between.

"How?" He repeated her question, then chuckled, the sound rumbling from deep from within his chest. "We're going to have to do as you suggested."

"What I suggested?"

His mouth continued to tease hers with a series of small, nibbling kisses that seemed almost to pluck at her soul. "There's only one way to cure what's between us, Kate, my love."

"One way," she echoed weakly.

"You'll have to marry me. There's no help for it and, frankly, the way I feel right now, the sooner the better."

Kate felt as if he'd dumped a bucket of ice water over her head. "Marry you," she cried, pushing him away with such force that he nearly toppled backward. "Your answer to all this confusion is for us to marry?"

"Kate, don't be unreasonable. We're perfect for each other. You need me now more than at any time in your life and I'm here for you."

"Luke, please—"

"No." He stopped her with one look. "You're about to lose everything in life that you thought was secure—your father and your home. I don't have any intention of taking over Devin's role, but the way I figure it, I'd make you a decent husband."

"What about love?" Kate cried.

Luke sighed in frustration. "We've gone over that ten times. You already love me—"

"Like a brother."

"Princess, sisters don't kiss their brothers the way you do me."

He apparently believed that was argument enough. Not knowing how else to respond, she shook her head. "I love Clay! You keep ignoring that or insisting I don't—but I do. I have for as long as I can remember. I can't marry you. I won't."

"For heaven's sake, forget Clay."

"It's not so easy!" she shouted.

"It would be if you'd try a little harder," Luke muttered, obviously losing patience. "I'm asking you to marry me, Kate Logan, and a smart woman like you should know a good offer when she hears one."

So much for love. So much for romance. Luke wasn't even listening to her, and Kate doubted he'd understood a single thing she'd said. "I don't think this conversation is getting us any-where."

"Kate—"

"I think you should leave."

"Kate," he said, firmly gripping her shoulders, "how long is it going to take for you to realise that I love you and you love me?"

"Love you? How can you say that? Until a few weeks ago I was engaged to marry Clay Franklin!" Angrily she pushed away his hands and sprang to her feet.

"Yes. And all that time you were going to marry the wrong man."

Luke didn't seem to find that statement the least bit odd, as if women regularly chose to marry one man when they were really in love with another. Kate pushed her hair off her forehead and released a harsh breath.

"It's the truth," he said calmly.

She glared at him. Reasoning with Luke was a waste of time. He repeated the same nonsensical statements over and over, like a broken record, as if his few words were explanation enough.

"I'm going to bed," she said, turning abruptly away from him. "You can do as you like."

A moment of stunned silence followed her words before he chuckled softly, seductively. "I'm sure you don't mean that the way it sounds."

As Kate expected, the small community buzzed with the news of her fiasco with Eric Wilson. Neighbour delighted in telling neighbour how Luke Rivers had swooped her into his arms and how the entire Friday-night crowd at the Red Bull had cheered as he'd carried her off the dance floor.

It took every ounce of courage Kate possessed just to walk down Main Street. Her smile felt stiff and false, like the painted smile on a china doll, and she was convinced she had the beginnings of an ulcer.

To worsen matters, all the townsfolk seemed to believe it was their place to offer her free advice.

"You stick with Luke Rivers. He's a far better man than that city slicker," the butcher told her Saturday afternoon.

Blushing heatedly, she ordered a pork roast and left as soon as she'd paid.

"I understand you and Luke Rivers caused quite a ruckus the

other night at the steak house,'' the church secretary said Sunday morning after the service. ''I heard about the romantic way Luke carried you outside.''

Kate hadn't found being carried off the least bit romantic but she smiled kindly, made no comment and returned home without a word.

''What's this I hear about you and Luke Rivers?'' The moment Kate entered her classroom Monday morning, Sally Daley appeared.

''Whatever you heard, I'm sure it was vastly exaggerated,'' Kate said hurriedly.

''That could be,'' Sally admitted with a delicate laugh. ''You certainly know how to keep this town buzzing. First Clay's wedding reception, and now this. By the way, Clay and Rorie are back from Hawaii, and I heard both of them have marvellous tans.''

''That often happens in Hawaii,'' Kate said, sarcastically, swallowing the pain and holding on to her composure by the thinnest of threads.

No sooner had Sally left when Linda showed up. ''Is it true?'' she demanded, her eyes as round as quarters.

Kate shrugged. ''Probably.''

''Oh, good grief, the whole thing about squelching the rumours backfired, didn't it?''

Miserably Kate nodded. She feared she would dissolve into a puddle of tears the next time someone mentioned Luke's name. ''After what happened to me Friday night, well...I just don't think it's possible to feel any more humiliated.''

''I thought you said you hadn't met Eric,'' Linda said, clearly puzzled.

''I hadn't when you and I talked. Eric and I ran into each other at the grocery not ten minutes after you mentioned his name.''

Linda slumped against the side of Kate's desk. ''I try for months to meet a new man and nothing happens. It doesn't make sense. A few minutes after you decide you're looking, one pops up in front of you like a bird in a turkey shoot!''

''Beginner's luck.'' Except that Friday night could in no way be classified as lucky.

''Oh, Kate, you've really done it now.''

''I know,'' she whispered in a tone of defeat.

Kate's day ended much as it had begun, which meant that by four o'clock she had a headache to rival all headaches. After school, she stopped at the pharmacy and bought a bottle of double-strength aspirin and some antacid tablets.

When she left the pharmacy, she headed for the library, wondering if Rorie would be back at work so soon following her honeymoon. Her friend's smiling face greeted Kate the instant she walked through the glass doors.

"Kate, it's so good to see you."

"Hi, Rorie." Kate still felt a little awkward with Clay's bride. She suffered no regrets about bringing them together, though it had been the most painful decision of her life.

"Sally Daley's right," Kate said with a light laugh, as she kissed Rorie's cheek. "You're so tanned. You look wonderful."

Rorie accept the praise with a lively smile that shone from her dark brown eyes. "To be honest, I never thought I'd get Clay to laze away seven whole days on the beach, but he did. Oh, Kate, we had the most wonderful time."

"I'm glad." And she was. Rorie and Clay belonged together—she'd known that almost from the beginning. Because of her sacrifice, their love had been given a chance. Rorie radiated happiness, and the glow of it warmed Kate's numb heart.

"I was just about to go on my coffee break. Have you got time to join me?" Rorie invited, glancing at her wristwatch.

"I'd love to." Kate crossed her fingers. With luck, Rorie wouldn't have heard any of the gossip—no doubt colourfully embroidered by now—about what had happened Friday night. At the moment, Kate needed a friend, a good friend, someone she could trust to be objective.

While Rorie arranged to leave the library in the hands of a volunteer assistant, Kate walked over to Nellie's Café, across the street from the pharmacy. She'd already ordered their coffee when Rorie slipped into the red upholstered booth across from her.

"Now what's this I've been hearing all day about you and Luke? Honestly, Kate, you know how to live dangerously, don't you? And now Luke's buying the Circle L and your father's marrying Mrs Murphy. We were only gone seven days, but I swear it felt like a year with all Mary had to tell us once we got home."

Kate trained her expression to remain perfectly stoic, although the acid in her stomach seemed to be burning a hole straight through her. There were no secrets in this town.

"To tell you the truth, Luke and I haven't been getting along very well lately,'' she admitted, keeping her eyes lowered so as not to meet her friend's questioning gaze.

Rorie took a tentative sip of her coffee. ''Do you want to talk about it?''

Kate nodded. She felt ridiculously close to tears and paid close attention to the silverware, repositioning the fork and the spoon several times as if their placement on the paper napkin were of dire importance.

''Luke was so gentle and good to me after you and Clay became engaged. He couldn't have been a better friend. Then...after the wedding I was feeling so lost and alone. Luke had been dancing with me and I felt so...secure in his arms, and I'm afraid I suggested something foolish... And now Luke keeps reminding me of it.''

''That doesn't sound like Luke.'' Rorie frowned in puzzlement. ''Nor does suggesting 'something foolish' sound like you.''

''I had a glass of champagne on an empty stomach,'' Kate offered as an excuse.

''What about Luke?''

''I don't know, but I swear, he's become so unreasonable about everything, and he keeps insisting the most ridiculous things.''

''Give me an example,'' Rorie said softly.

Kate shrugged. ''He claims I love him.''

Her remark was followed by a short silence. ''What *do* you feel for Luke?'' Rorie asked.

''I care about him, but certainly not in the way he assumes.'' Her finger idly circled the rim of the coffee cup while she composed her thoughts. ''What irritates me most is that Luke discounts everything I felt for Clay, as if my love for him was nothing more than wasted emotion.'' Kate felt uncomfortable explaining this to her ex-fiancé's wife, but Rorie was the one person who would understand.

''And now that Clay's married to me,'' Rorie said, ''Luke seems to think some giant light bulb has snapped on inside your brain.''

''Exactly.''

''He thinks you should have no qualms about throwing yourself into his loving arms?''

''Yes!'' Rorie explained it far better than Kate had. ''He keeps insisting I need him and that if I thought about it I'd realise I do love him. If it was only Luke I think I could deal with it, but everyone else in town, including my own father, thinks I should marry him.''

''That's when you agreed to have dinner with that new attorney. What's his name again?''

''Eric Wilson. Yes, that was exactly the reason I went out with him. Rorie, I tell you I was desperate. Every time I turned around, Luke was there wearing this smug, knowing look and casually announcing that we'd be married before Christmas. He makes the whole thing sound like it's a foregone conclusion and if I resist him I'd be going against nature or something.'' She paused and dramatically waved her hand. ''To hear Luke tell it, if I don't marry him by the end of the year, every herd in Nightingale is destined to deliver two-headed calves next spring.''

Rorie laughed. ''Is he really doing that?''

Kate nodded grimly. ''Actually there's more.'' Although the truth was she had to tell Rorie everything. ''To be fair you should know that I have no one to blame but myself. Luke may be doing all this talking about us getting married. But I was the one who...suggested it.''

''How? When? Oh. The 'something foolish' you mentioned.''

Shredding the paper napkin into tiny strips, Kate nodded again, swallowing painfully at the memory. ''Honestly, Rorie, I didn't mean it. We were standing in the moonlight at your wedding dance and everything was so serene and beautiful. The words just slipped out of my mouth before I stopped to think what I was saying.''

''The incident with the attorney didn't help.''

Kate sighed. ''And now that Dad's marrying Mrs Murphy and Luke's bought the ranch everything's just getting worse.''

''Luke can be a bit overpowering at times, can't he?''

Kate rolled her eyes in agreement.

''But you know, what bothers me even more than Luke's cavalier attitude is the way everyone else seems to be siding with him.''

''What do you mean?''

''Look at my dad—he's the perfect example. As far as he's concerned, marrying Luke is only a matter of time. And everyone in town seems to think that since Clay married you, it's the only thing left for me to do. If I'm foolish enough to let another good man slip through my fingers, then I'll be sure to end up thirty and a spinster.''

''That's ridiculous.''

Coming from San Francisco, Rorie couldn't understand how differently people in this small Oregon community viewed life, Kate mused. A woman already thirty years old and unmarried was more than likely to stay that way—at least in Nightingale. "You haven't lived here long enough to understand how folks around here think."

"Kate, you're over twenty-one. No one can force you into marrying Luke. Remember that."

Kate rested her elbows on the table and cradled her coffee cup in both hands. "I feel caught in a current that's flowing much too fast for me. I don't dare stand up for fear I'll lose my footing but I can't just allow it to carry me where it will, either."

"No, you can't," Rorie said and her mouth tightened.

"Luke—and just about everyone else—apparently sees me as a poor, spineless soul who can't possibly decide what's best for her own life."

"That's not the least bit true," Rorie declared. "And don't let anyone tell you you're weak! If that were the case, you would have married Clay yourself instead of working so hard to make sure we found each other."

Kate discounted that with a hard shake of her head. "I did the only thing I could."

"But not everyone would have been so unselfish. Clay and I owe our happiness to you." She paused and gripped Kate's hands with her own. "I wish I knew how to help you. All I can tell you is to listen to your own heart."

"Oh, Rorie, I feel so much better talking to you." Kate released a long, slow sigh, knowing her friend was right. She'd faltered for a step or two, but considering all that had happened to her in the past little while, that was understandable. Luke might believe she needed him, but she didn't, not really. In the weeks to come, she'd have the opportunity to prove it.

"Before I forget," Rorie said, her voice eager, "Clay and I want to invite you over for dinner one night soon. As I said, we feel deeply indebted to you and want to thank you for what you did for us."

"Dinner," Kate repeated, suddenly dismayed. She'd need time to fortify herself before facing Clay again. Here she was reassuring herself with one breath and then doubting herself in the next.

"Would next Tuesday be all right?" Rorie pressed.

"But you've barely had time to settle in with Clay," Kate said, turning her attention back to her friend. "How about giving it another week or two?"

"Are you worried that I'm going to serve my special seafood fettuccine?" Rorie asked with a light laugh. When she'd first found herself stranded in Nightingale, Rorie had cooked it for Clay and his younger brother, Skip, one night. But, unfortunately, because both men were involved in strenuous physical activity, they were far more interested in a hearty meat-and-potatoes meal at the end of the day. Neither of them had considered seafood swimming in a cream sauce and fancy noodles a very satisfactory repast, though Clay had politely tried to hide his disappointment. Skip hadn't.

Kate smiled at the memory of that night and slowly shook her head. "You serve whatever you want. I'm much easier to please than Skip."

"Actually Mary will probably do the cooking. She's been the Franklins' housekeeper for so many years that I don't dare invade her kitchen just yet. After the fettuccine disaster, she doesn't trust me around her stove any more than Skip does."

They both laughed, and to Kate, it felt good to forget her troubles, even for a few minutes.

"I should get back to library," Rorie announced reluctantly.

"I need to head home myself." Kate left some change on the table and slid out of the booth. Impulsively she hugged Rorie, grateful for the time they'd spent together and for the other woman's support. "I'm glad you're my friend," she whispered, feeling a little self-conscious.

"I am, too," Rorie said, and hugged her back.

By the time Kate pulled into the Circle L driveway, she was filled with bold resolution. She hurried inside just long enough to set a roast in the oven and change her clothes. Then, she went into the yard, intent on confronting Luke. The sooner she talked to him, the better she'd feel.

As luck would have it, Luke wasn't in any of the places where she normally found him. Bill Schmidt, a longtime ranch hand, was working in the barn by himself.

"Bill, have you seen Luke around?" she asked.

Bill straightened slowly and set his hat farther back on his head. "Can't say I have. At least, not in the past couple of hours. The last thing he said was he was going out to look for strays. I imagine he'll be back pretty soon now."

"I see." Kate gnawed her lower lip, wondering what she should do. Without pausing to question the wisdom of her decision, she reached for a bridle.

"Bill, would you get Nonstop for me?" Nonstop was the fastest horse in their stable. Kate was in the mood for some exercise; if she didn't find Luke, that was fine, too. She could use a good hard ride to vent some of the frustration that had been binding her all week.

"Sure, Mizz Logan." Bill left his task and headed for the corral, returning a few minutes later with Nonstop. "Luke seemed to be in the mood to do some riding himself this afternoon," he commented as he helped her cinch the saddle. "Must be something in the air."

"Must be," Kate agreed.

Minutes later Nonstop was cantering out of the yard. Kate hadn't ridden in several weeks and she was surprised to realise just how long it had been. When she was engaged to Clay, she'd spent many a summer afternoon in the saddle, many a Saturday or Sunday riding by his side. That had ended about the same time as their wedding plans. She felt a stinging sense of loss but managed to dispel it with the memory of her talk with Rorie earlier.

Bill pointed out the general direction Luke had taken, and Kate followed that course, at a gallop. She found it wonderfully invigorating to be in the saddle again.

The afternoon remained mild, but the breeze carried the distinctive scent of autumn. These past few days had been Indian summer, with rare clement temperatures. Within the hour, the sun would set, bathing the rolling green hills in a golden haze.

"Kate." Her name floated on a whisper of wind.

Pulling back on the reins, Kate halted the mare and twisted around to discover Luke trotting towards her. She raised her hand and waved. Much of her irritation had dissipated, replaced by a newly awakened sense of well-being. No longer did Kate feel her life was roaring out of control; she was in charge, and it exhilarated her.

Luke leapt out of the saddle as soon as he reached her. "Is everything all right?"

"Of course," she said, laughing a little. "I hope I didn't frighten you?"

"No. I rode into the yard not more than fifteen minutes after you left, according to Bill. I was afraid I wasn't going to catch you. You were riding like a demon."

"I...had some thinking to do."

"Bill said you were looking for me."

"Yes," she agreed. "I wanted to talk to you." There was no better time than the present. And no better place. They were at the top of a grassy knoll that looked out over the lush green valley below. Several head of cattle dotted the pasture spread out below them, lazily grazing in the last of the afternoon sun.

Luke lifted his hand to her waist, helping her out of the saddle. His eyes held hers as he slowly lowered her to the ground. Once again, she was aware that his touch had a curious effect on her, but she stringently ignored it.

Still, Kate's knees felt a little shaky and she was more breathless than she should have been after her ride. She watched Luke loop the reins over the horses heads to dangle on the ground. Both Nonstop and Silver Shadow, Luke's gelding, were content to graze leisurely.

"It's lovely out this afternoon, isn't it?" she said, then sank down on the grass and drew up her legs, resting on her knees.

Luke sat down beside her, looking out over the valley. "It's a rare day. I don't expect many more like it."

"Rorie and Clay are back from Hawaii."

Luke had removed his leather work gloves to brush a stray curl from her temple, then stopped abruptly and withdrew his hand. "I take it you saw Rorie?"

She nodded, adding, "We had coffee at Nellie's."

"You're not upset?"

"Not at all."

"I thought you looked more at peace with yourself." He leaned back and rested his weight on the palms of his hands. His long legs were stretched out in front of him, crossed at the ankles. "Did you finally recognise that you never did love Clay? That you're in love with me?"

"No," she said vehemently, amazed he could anger her so quickly.

Luke turned away. "I thought...I'd hoped you were willing to discuss a wedding date," he said stiffly.

"Oh, Luke," she whispered and closed her eyes. He was so worried for her, so concerned, and it really wasn't necessary. And she didn't know how to reassure him.

"Luke," she said softly, "we've been having the same discussion all week, and it's got to come to an end." Luke faced her and their eyes met with an impact that shocked her. "Luke, I think you're a wonderful man—I have for years and years," she continued quickly. "But I don't love you, at least not the way you deserve to be loved."

Luke's eyebrows soared, then his brow furrowed. He seemed about to argue, but Kate stopped him before he had the chance.

"I refuse to be coerced into a wedding simply because *you* feel it's the best thing for me—because you feel I need looking after. Frankly, I don't believe marriage is a good idea for us—at least not to each other."

"Kate, love—"

Lowering her lashes in an effort to disguise her frustration, Kate reminded him for what seemed the thousandth time, "I am not your 'love'."

His eyes became sharp, more intent. "Then explain," he said slowly, "why it feels so right when I hold you? How do you answer that?"

She avoided his gaze, her eyes focusing a fraction below his own, resting instead on the slight cleft in his chin. "I can't explain it any more than I can deny it." She'd willingly give him that much. "I do enjoy it when you kiss me, though I don't know why, especially since I'm still in love with Clay. My guess is that we've lived all these years in close proximity and we're such good friends that it was a natural, comforting, thing to do. But I don't think it should continue."

His nostrils flared briefly, and from the impatient look he gave her she could tell he was angered by her words.

"I'm asking you, Luke, pleading with you, if you—"

"Kate, would you listen to me for once?"

"No," she said firmly, holding her ground. "I want only one thing from you, and that's for you to drop this incessant pressure that we marry."

"But—"

"I want your word, Luke."

His entire countenance changed, and just looking at him told Kate how difficult he was finding this. "All right," he said heavily. "You have my word. I won't mention it again."

Kate sighed shakily and all her muscles seemed to go limp. "Thank you," she whispered. "That's all I want."

Luke lunged to his feet and reached for Silver Shadow's reins.

He eased himself back into the saddle, then paused to gaze down at her, his face dark and brooding. ''What about what I want, Kate? Did you stop to consider that?''

Six

Kate felt good. The lethargy and depression she'd been feeling since Clay's wedding had started to dissipate. She'd completely adjusted to the idea of her father's impending marriage. And even the sale of the Circle L—to Luke of all people—no longer seemed so devastating. Clearing the air between them had helped, too.

"Evening, Nellie," Kate called as she entered the small, homey café. She'd arrived home from school to discover a message from her father suggesting she meet him for dinner at Nellie's at six sharp.

"Howdy, Kate," Nellie called from behind the counter.

Kate assumed her father would be bringing Dorothea so they could discuss last-minute plans for their wedding, which was scheduled for Friday evening at the parsonage. Minnie Wilkins, Pastor Wilkins's wife, and Dorothea were close friends. Kate was to stand up for Dorothea and Luke for her father in the small, private ceremony.

Carrying the water glass in one hand, a coffeepot in the other and a menu tucked under her arm, Nellie followed Kate to the booth. "I'm expecting my dad and Dorothea Murphy to join me," Kate explained.

"Sure thing," Nellie said. "The special tonight is Yankee pot roast, and when your daddy gets here, you tell him I pulled a rhubarb pie out of the oven no more than fifteen minutes ago."

"I'll tell him."

"Nellie, I could use a refill on my coffee," Fred Garner called from the table closest to the window. He nodded politely in Kate's direction. "Good to see you again, Kate."

"You, too, Fred." She smiled at the owner of Garner Feed and Supply and noted that a couple of ranchers were dining with him. Glancing at her watch, Kate realised her father was a few minutes late, which wasn't like him.

To pass the time she began reading the menu; she was halfway through when the door opened. Smiling automatically, she glanced up and discovered Luke striding towards her. He slid into her booth, opposite her.

"Where's your dad?"

"I don't know. He asked me to meet him here for dinner."

"I got the same message."

"I think it's got something to do with the wedding."

"No," Luke muttered, frowning. "I've got some bank forms he needs to sign."

Nellie brought another glass of water, then poured coffee for both of them.

"Evening, Nellie."

"Luke Rivers, I declare I don't see near enough of you," the older woman said coyly, giving him a bold wink as she sauntered away with a swish of her hips.

Astonished that Nellie would flirt so openly with Luke, Kate took a sip of her coffee and nearly scalded her tongue. Why, Nellie had a good fifteen years on Luke!

"Does she do that often?" Kate asked, in a disapproving whisper.

"You jealous?"

"Of course not. It's just that I've never known Nellie to flirt quite so blatantly."

"She's allowed." Luke gazed down at his menu and to all appearances, was soon deep in concentration.

Kate managed to squelch the argument before it reached her lips. There wasn't a single, solitary reason for her to care if a thousand women wanted to throw themselves at Luke Rivers. She had no claim on him, and wanted none.

The restaurant telephone pealed, but with four plates balanced on her arms, Nellie let it ring until someone in the kitchen answered it.

No more than a minute later, she approached their table. "That was Devin on the phone. He says he's going to be late and you two should go ahead and order." She pulled a notepad from the pocket of her pink uniform. "Eat hearty since it's on his tab," she said, chuckling amiably.

"The roast-beef sandwich sounds good to me," Kate said. "With a small salad."

"I'll have chicken-fried steak, just so I can taste those biscuits of yours,'' Luke told the café owner, handing her the menu. ''I'll start with a salad, though.''

''I got rhubarb pie hot from the oven.''

''Give me a piece of that, too,'' Luke said, grinning up at Nellie. ''Kate?''

''Sure,'' she said, forcing a smile. ''Why not?''

Once Nellie had left, an awkwardness fell between Kate and Luke. To Kate if felt as though they'd become strangers with each other, standing on uncertain ground.

Luke ventured into conversation first. ''So how's school?''

''Good. Really good.''

''That's nice.''

She laughed nervously. ''I've started washing down cupboards at the house, clearing out things. I've got two piles. What Dad's going to take with him and what I'll need when I move.''

Instead of pleasing Luke, her announcement had the opposite effect. ''You're welcome to live on the ranch as long as you want,'' he said, his dark eyes narrowing. ''There's no need to move away.''

''I know that, but the Circle L belongs to you—or it will soon.''

''It's your home.''

''It won't be much longer,'' she felt obliged to remind him. ''I'm hoping to find a place in town. In fact, I'm looking forward to the move. You know what the roads are like in the winter. I should have done this long ago.''

''You wouldn't have to move if you weren't so damn stubborn,'' Luke muttered between clenched teeth, clearly struggling with his patience. ''I swear, Kate, you exasperate me. The last thing I want to do is take your home away from you.''

''I know that.'' She hadn't considered relocating to town earlier for a number of reasons, foremost being that her father had needed her. But he didn't anymore, and it was time for her to exhibit a little independence.

Nellie delivered their tossed green dinner salads, lingering at the table to flirt with Luke again. He waited until she'd left before he leaned forward, speaking to Kate in a low, urgent voice. His mouth was tight and his eyes were filled with regret. ''Kate, please stay on at the ranch. Let me at least do this much for you.''

She thanked him for his concern with a warm smile, but couldn't resist adding, ''People will talk.'' After all Luke had pointed that very fact out to her when she'd made her foolish proposal. The night of Clay's wedding…

"Let them talk."

"I'm a schoolteacher, remember?" she whispered. She felt genuinely grateful for his friendship and wanted to assure him that all this worry on her behalf wasn't necessary, that she was fully capable of living on her own.

Their dinner arrived before they'd even finished the salads. Another silence fell over them as they ate. Several possible subjects of conversation fluttered in and out of Kate's mind as the meal progressed. Her fear was that Luke would divert the discussion back to the ranch no matter what she said, so she remained silent.

A sudden commotion came from the pavement outside the café.

"It's Harry Ackerman again," Fred Garner shouted to Nellie, who was busy in the kitchen. "You want me to call the sheriff?"

"No, let him sing," Nellie shouted back. "He isn't hurting anyone."

Harry Ackerman was the town drunk. Back in his and Nellie's high-school days, they'd dated seriously, but then Harry went into the military and returned to Nightingale more interested in the bottle than a wife and family. Within six months, Nellie had married a mechanic who'd drifted into town. Problem was, when he left, he didn't take Nellie or their two children with him. But Nellie hadn't seemed to miss him much, and had supported her family by opening the café, which did a healthy business right from the first.

Fifteen years had passed, and Harry was still courting Nellie. Every time he came into town, he took it upon himself to sing love songs from the pavement outside the café. He seemed to believe that would be enough of an inducement for her to forget the past and finally marry him.

"Actually his singing voice isn't so bad," Kate murmured to Luke.

Luke chuckled. "I've heard better."

Fred Garner stood up and strolled towards the cash register. He glanced in Luke's direction and touched the rim of his hat in greeting. "I've been hearing things about the two of you," Fred said, grinning broadly.

Kate centred her concentration on the sandwich, refusing to look up from her plate.

Luke made a reply that had to do with the ranch and not Kate, and she was grateful.

"Be seeing you," Fred said as he headed towards the door. As he opened it, Harry's latest love ballad, sung badly off-key, could be heard with ear-piercing clarity.

Fred left and soon Harry Ackerman strolled inside. He glanced longingly at Nellie, placed his hand over his heart and started singing again at the top of his lungs.

"You get out of my restaurant," Nellie cried, reaching for the broom. "I don't want you in here disrupting my customers." She wielded the broom like a shotgun, and before she could say another word Harry stumbled outside. He pressed his forlorn face to the glass, content to wait until his one true love returned to his waiting arms.

"Sorry, folks," Nellie muttered, replacing the broom.

"No problem," Luke answered, and she tossed him a grateful smile, then hurried over to refill their coffee cups.

The disturbance died down when Harry wandered down the street to find a more appreciative audience. Luke sighed as he stirred his coffee slowly and carefully. "I don't think your father has any intention of showing up tonight," he began. "In fact—"

"Why, that's ridiculous," Kate said, cutting him off. "Dad wouldn't do that."

"He's trying to tell you something," Luke insisted.

"I can't imagine what." She could, but decided to pretend otherwise.

For a long moment, Luke said nothing. "You're smart enough to figure it out, Kate." He finished off the last bite of his pie and pushed the plate aside. "I've got some things to attend to, so I'd best be leaving." The crow's feet at the corners of his eyes crinkled with amusement as he glanced out the café window. "Who knows, you might be singing me love songs in a couple of years if you don't come to your senses soon."

Kate ignored the comment. "My father will be here any minute."

"No, Princess," Luke said, and the smile drained from his dark eyes. He leaned across the table to brush his hand gently against her cheek. "But his message is coming across loud and clear."

Kate stayed at the café another half-hour after Luke had left and it took her that long to admit he was right. Her father *had* been giving her a message, this one no more subtle than the rest. Expelling her breath in disgust, Kate dredged up a smile and said goodbye to Nellie.

* * *

Kate didn't see Luke again until Friday evening, when they met at the Wilkins' home for her father's wedding. Kate arrived with Devin, and Luke followed a few minutes later. Kate was busy arranging freshly baked cookies on a tray for the small reception to be held after the ceremony, when Luke walked into the dining room. Dorothea was with Minnie Wilkins in the back bedroom, and her father and Pastor Wilkins were talking in the living-room.

"Hello, Kate," Luke said from behind her.

"Hi," she responded, turning to give him a polite smile. Her breath stopped in her throat at the elegant yet virile sight he made. He was dressed in a dark, three-piece suit that did nothing to disguise his strong, well formed body, and his light blue silk tie enhanced the richness of his tan. Kate suspected that Luke was basking in the wonder she was unable to conceal, and yet still she couldn't stop looking at him.

Her heart skipped a beat, then leapt wildly as his penetrating brown eyes looked straight into hers. She felt the tears well up, knowing that only Luke truly understood how difficult this evening was for her.

Many of her emotions tonight were identical to the ones she'd experienced at Clay's and Rorie's wedding. All day, she'd worried her stomach into a knot of apprehension. The acceptance and strength of purpose she'd so recently been feeling had fled. Tonight, she was reminded again that everything she loved, everything familiar, had been taken from her life. First the man she'd planned to marry, now her father, and soon, so very soon, her childhood home. It was too much change, too quickly.

Just as she had at Clay's wedding, Kate forced herself to show pleasure, to behave appropriately. She *was* happy for her father and Dorothea—just as she'd been for Clay and Rorie. But why did everyone else's happiness need to cost Kate so much?

Luke must have read the apprehension in her eyes, because he hurried to her side. "Everything's going to be all right," he told her quietly.

"Of course it is," she said, braving a smile. She turned back to the flowers, although her fingers were trembling. "I couldn't have chosen a better wife for Dad myself. Dorothea's wonderful."

Luke's hands settled on her shoulders and began to caress them gently. "So are you, Princess."

It demanded every ounce of fortitude Kate possessed not to whirl around and bury her face in Luke's chest, to absorb his strength.

But this was exactly how she'd lost control before; she had to remember that.

A sound came from behind them, and Luke released her with a reluctance that echoed her own. She needed Luke now, just as she'd needed him a few weeks before. But this time, she was determined to be stronger.

The ceremony itself was brief. Kate felt almost wooden as she stood next to the woman her father had chosen to replace her mother. Memories of the lovely, soft-spoken Nora, and of their happy, close-knit family, almost overwhelmed Kate. Twice she felt tears threaten, but managed to hold them in. Both times she found Luke's eyes on her, his gaze warm with empathy.

When Pastor Wilkins closed his Bible and announced that Devin and Dorothea were now husband and wife, Devin took his bride in his arms and gently kissed her. Minnie Wilkins dabbed at her eyes with a lace hankie.

"You look so lovely," the woman murmured, hugging her friend.

Soon they were all hugging each other. When Kate's arms slipped around Luke it felt like a homecoming. It felt far too comfortable, too familiar, and that frightened her. She stiffened and let her arms drop. Luke would have none of that, however. Locking his hands on her upper arms, he drew her back to him.

"What I wouldn't give for a full moon and some champagne," he whispered in her ear.

Kate could have done without his teasing, but she refused to satisfy him with a reply.

The small reception began immediately afterwards, and Kate was busy for the next hour, dishing up pieces of wedding cake, passing trays of sugar cookies and pouring coffee.

Her father found her in the kitchen, his eyes bright with happiness. "You're going to be just fine, aren't you, Princess?"

"You know I am," she said, flashing him a brilliant smile.

"Dorothea and I will be leaving soon." He placed his arm around her shoulder and hugged her. "Don't forget I love you. You'll always be my little girl."

"You'll always be my hero."

Devin chuckled. "I think Luke would like to fill that position and I'd be more than pleased if he did. He's a good man, sweetheart. You could do a lot worse."

"Dad," she groaned, closing her eyes. "Luke is wonderful, and

I understand your concern. You'd like all the loose ends neatly tied up before you leave for your honeymoon, but I'm just not ready to make a commitment. At least not yet.''

"You'd make a lovely country bride, Princess. I just want you to be happy."

"I will be," she said, standing on the tips of her toes to kiss his cheek.

By the time Devin and Dorothea were ready to leave, more than twenty close friends had gathered at the parsonage. They crowded on to the porch to send the newlyweds off with a flourish of kisses and enthusiastic waves. Almost everyone returned to the warmth of the house but Kate lingered, not wanting to go back inside when tears were blurring her eyes.

Luke joined her, standing silently at her side until she'd composed herself.

"Your father asked me to see you home."

Kate nodded and swallowed a near-hysterical laugh. Despite their conversation Devin was still attempting to throw her together with Luke.

"You mean you aren't going to argue with me?" Luke asked with exaggerated surprise.

"Would it do any good?"

"No," he said and chuckled lightly. Then, suddenly, his strong arms encircled her stiff body. "It's been a long time since you let me kiss you," he said, his warm breath closer and closer to her mouth.

Kate stared at his chest, refusing to raise her eyes to his. Gathering her resolve, she snapped her head up to demand he release her. But Luke smothered her words with his mouth. Her hands closed into tight fists as soon as the initial shock had subsided and she fully intended to push him away. But once his mouth had settled over hers, he gentled the kiss, and her resolve all but disappeared.

Again and again his mouth sought hers. Luke's sweet, soft kisses seemed to erase all the pain from her heart. Only a moment before, she'd been intent on escaping. Now she clung to him, tilting her face towards him, seeking more. He deepened his kiss, sending jolts of excitement through her.

His hands were in her hair, holding her prisoner as he devoured her. When he stopped abruptly, Kate moaned her dissatisfaction.

"Kate..." he warned.

"Hmm...Luke, don't stop."

"I'm afraid we've attracted an audience," he returned mildly.

Sucking in her breath, Kate dropped her arms and whirled around so fast she would have stumbled if Luke's arms hadn't caught her. Her eyes felt as wide as the Columbia River as she stared into the faces of the twenty or more guests who'd stepped outside, preparing to leave.

"I thought Taylor Morgenroth should play the part of the Indian chief," Kate was saying to Linda when Sally Daley walked into the faculty lounge Monday afternoon. The two were discussing the final plans for their Thanksgiving play.

"Taylor's the perfect choice," Linda agreed.

"I see you girls are busy," Sally commented. "This play is such an ambitious project. You two are to be commended."

"Thanks." Linda answered for them both, trying to ignore the other woman as much as possible.

"Wasn't that Rorie Franklin I saw you with the other day, Kate, dear?"

"Yes. We had coffee together at Nellie's." She resumed her discussion with Linda, not wanting to be rude to Sally, but at the same time, hoping to dissuade her from further conversation.

But Sally refused to be thwarted. She settled in the chair opposite Kate, and said in confidential tones, "You're completely recovered from Clay Franklin now, aren't you, dear?"

Kate shared an exasperated look with Linda and nearly laughed out loud when the third-grade teacher playfully rolled her eyes towards the ceiling. To hear Sally talk, anybody would think Kate had recently recovered from a bad case of the flu.

"Sally, honestly!" Kate exclaimed when she realised how avidly the other woman was waiting for her reply. "How am I supposed to answer that?" She dramatically covered her heart with one hand and offered a look meant to portray misery and anguish. "Do you want me to tell you that my female pride's been shattered and that I'll never love again?"

Sally shook her head. "I wouldn't believe it, anyway."

"Then why ask?" Linda prompted.

"Well, because we all love Kate. She's such a dear, and she's been through so much lately."

"Thank you," Kate said graciously, then returned her attention to the Thanksgiving project.

"Most of the fuss about you and Eric Wilson and Luke Rivers has died down now," Sally assured her, as if this should lessen the keen embarrassment of that Friday night.

"I take it you haven't talked to Eric lately?" Linda asked, surprising Kate with her sudden interest. There'd been plenty of opportunity to enquire about the lawyer, but Linda hadn't done so until now.

"Talked to him?" Kate echoed with a short, derisive laugh. "I don't even shop at the Safeway store for fear I'll run into him again."

"I don't think you need to worry," Sally said blandly. "From what I understand, he's avoiding you, too."

Linda snickered softly. "No doubt. I'm sure Luke Rivers put quite a scare into him."

"How do you mean?" Kate demanded, already angry with Luke.

"You don't know?" Sally asked, her eyes sparkling with excitement.

"Know what?" Kate swung her gaze first to Linda, then to Sally. "Did Luke threaten him?" If he had, he was going to hear about it from her.

"I haven't got the foggiest idea what Sally's talking about," Linda said quickly.

"I didn't hear anything specific," Sally confirmed sheepishly. "I thought maybe you had…" The older teacher's expression suggested that she hoped Kate would fill in the succulent details herself. "My dear, surely you understand that everyone in town is speculating about you and Luke," she continued.

"Rumours have been floating around since the day of Clay's wedding," Linda added.

"But Sally just finished telling me those were dying down," Kate snapped, irritated with the entire discussion.

"They're not about you and that Wilson fellow," Sally rushed to explain. "As far as your one date with him is concerned, it's history. He's too smart to cross Luke."

"I'm sure he is," Kate said, anxious to quell the woman's gossip. "Aren't we about finished here, Linda?" she asked pointedly.

"Ah…yes."

"Now folks are talking about seeing you and Luke together at Nellie's last week just before your father's wedding, and there've been a few rumours flying around about seeing the two of you at Pastor Wilkins's, too."

As fast as her hands would co-operate, Kate started gathering up their materials. Sally seemed to accept that she was about to lose her audience. If she'd come to pump Kate for information she'd just have to realise Kate wasn't talking. Standing, Sally gave a deep sigh, clearly disappointed. She reached for her purse and headed out of the door, pausing to look back. ''Frankly, I think Fred Garner is carrying this thing between you and Luke just a little too far. I consider what he's doing in poor taste.'' With that, she left the room.

''Fred Garner?'' Linda echoed after a stunned second. ''What's that old coot doing now?''

''Fred Garner owns the feed store,'' Kate said, wondering what Sally could possibly mean.

''Yes, but what's he got to do with anything?''

''Beats me.'' Still, Kate couldn't help wondering. Fred had seen them at the restaurant, and he'd been at the reception for her father and Dorothea. Although she hadn't seen him on the porch when a number of guests had found her in Luke's arms, she had very little doubt that he was there.

When Kate drove home an hour later, Luke was working in the yard. She climbed out of the car, took two steps towards him and halted abruptly. The lump in her throat was so large she could hardly swallow, let alone speak.

The trembling had started the minute she left Garner Feed and Supply. She'd dropped in at the store following Sally's puzzling remark, and from then on everything had grown progressively worse. The way she felt right now, she could slam her bag over Luke's head, or something equally violent, and feel completely justified.

''Kate?'' he asked gently, looking concerned. ''What's wrong?''

She knew her feelings were written on her face. Her heart felt like a piston from a fired-up jalopy. She'd never been more scandalised in her life, which was saying a great deal considering the fiasco with Eric Wilson.

In fact, the blow her dignity had been dealt by Luke Rivers during that incident paled by comparison with this latest outrage. Dear Lord, there was only one thing for her to do. She'd have to move away from Nightingale.

''This is all your doing, isn't it?'' she demanded in a shaking voice. She held her head high, although it was a struggle to preserve her composure. Her pride was all she had left, and that was crumbling at her feet.

Luke advanced several steps toward her. "What are you talking about?"

She ground her fist into her hip. "I just got back from the feed store. Does that tell you anything?"

"No."

"I'll just bet."

He frowned. "Kate, I swear to you, I don't know what you're talking about."

She made a doubting noise that came out sounding and feeling like a painful sob. Yet he appeared so bewildered. She didn't know how any man could cause her such life-shattering embarrassment and maintain that look of faithful integrity.

The tears wouldn't be restrained any longer, and they slipped from her eyes, running down the sides of her face. They felt cool against her flushed cheeks.

"Kate? What's wrong?"

Kate turned and rapidly walked away from him rather than allow him to witness her loss of control. She hurried into the house and slumped in a chair, hiding her face in her hands as she battled the terrible urge to weep hysterically. The painful sensation in the pit of her stomach grew more intense every time she drew a breath.

The door opened and she said, "Go away."

"Kate?"

"Haven't...you...done...enough?" Each word rolled from her tongue on the end of a hiccuping sob.

He knelt in front of her and wrapped his arms around her, holding her close, but she pushed him away, refusing the comfort he offered.

Kate's shoulders still heaved. With an exasperated sigh, Luke stood back on his boot heels and buried his hands in his pockets. "All right, tell me about it."

"Pastor ... Wilkins ... bet ... twenty ... dollars ... on ... December," she told him between sobs. Her fingers curled into fists. "Even...Clay...put in a...wager."

Seeing his name on that huge blackboard had hurt more than anything.

"Kate, I swear to you by everything I hold dear that I don't know what you're talking about."

Furiously she wiped the tears from her face and tried to marshal her composure enough to speak clearly. "The...feed store," she managed.

"What about the feed store?"

"They're taking bets—it's a regular lottery," she cried, all the more furious with him because he was making her spell out this latest humiliation.

"Bets on what?" Luke's frown was growing darker by the second, and Kate could tell that he was dangerously close to losing his patience.

"On us!" she cried, as if that much, at least, should be obvious.

"For what?"

"When we're going to be married!" she shouted. "What else? Half the town's got money riding on the date of our wedding."

"Dear Lord," Luke moaned, briefly closing his eyes, as if he couldn't quite believe what she was telling him.

"You honestly didn't know?"

"Of course not." He was beginning to look perturbed as only Luke could. His dark eyes took on a cold glare that was enough to intimidate the strongest of men. "How'd you find out?"

"Sally Daley said something about it after school, and then in the school car park one of the mothers told me March is a lovely time of year for a wedding. March sixteenth, she said. Then...then I made the mistake of stopping in at the feed store on my way home to check out what was going on."

Luke nodded, but Kate had the impression he was only half listening to her.

"As far as I'm concerned, there's only one thing for me to do," she said, gaining strength from her decision. "I'll offer my resignation to the school board tomorrow morning and leave the district this weekend."

Luke flashed her a quick, angry look. "That won't be necessary. I'll take care of this my own way."

Seven

At one time Kate spent as many hours at Elk Run, the Franklin stud farm, as she did at the Circle L. But when she arrived Tuesday night for dinner, Elk Run no longer felt familiar. It seemed like years instead of weeks since her last visit. Kate's enthusiasm for this dinner with Clay and Rorie had never been high, but now she felt decidedly uncomfortable.

"Kate, welcome." Rorie flew out the door the minute Kate pulled into the driveway. She stepped from the car into Rorie's hug.

Clay Franklin followed his wife and briefly held Kate close, smiling down on her the same way he always had from the time she was thirteen. Back then, she'd worshipped him from afar, and she'd worshipped him more with each passing year. Kate paused, waiting for the surge of regret and pain she'd been expecting; to her astonishment, it didn't come.

"We're so pleased you could make it," Rorie said as she opened the door for her.

Recognising Kate, Clay's old dog, Blue, ambled over for his usual pat. Kate was more than happy to comply and bent down to playfully scratch his ears.

Mary, the Franklins' housekeeper, bustled about the kitchen, dressed in her bib apron, hair twisted into thick braids and piled on top of her head. Kate could scarcely remember a time she hadn't seen Mary in an apron. The scent of freshly baked pie permeated the room, mingling with the hearty aroma of roast beef and simmering vegetables.

"I hope that's one of your award-winning pies I'm smelling, Mary," Kate coaxed. "I've had my heart set on a thick slice all day."

"Oh, get away with you," Mary returned gruffly, but the happy light that sparked from her eyes told Kate how gratified the housekeeper was by her request.

"When are you going to give me your recipe?" Kate asked, although she didn't know whom she'd be baking pies for now that her father had remarried. "No one can bake an apple pie the way you do."

"Mary won't even share her secret with me," Rorie said, giving a soft laugh. "I don't think she's willing to trust a city slicker just yet."

"I never wrote down any recipe," Mary grumbled, casting Rorie a stern look. "I just make my pies the same way everybody else does."

"I wish I could bake like Mary does," Rorie said, slipping her arm around her husband's waist. They exchanged a meaningful glance. The way Clay smiled at his wife showed he couldn't care less whether or not she could bake a pie.

Once more Kate braced herself for the pain of seeing them together, gentle and loving, but to her surprise she didn't feel so much as a pinprick of distress. She relaxed, wondering at what was happening, or rather wasn't, and why.

"Where's Skip?" she asked suddenly. She missed Clay's younger brother almost as much as she did Clay. The two had been friends for years.

"Football practice," Clay explained. "He's quarterback this year and proud as a peacock about it. He'll be home later."

"About the time Mary serves her pie," Rorie whispered to Kate. Skip's appetite for sweets was legendary.

The small party headed into the homey living-room. The piano rested against one wall, and Kate noted the music on the stand. It had always been Kate who'd played that piano, but Rorie played for Clay now. There had been a time when Kate and Clay had sung together, their voices blending in a melodious harmony. But Clay sang with Rorie now.

Kate expected the knowledge to claw at her insides, and she did feel a small twinge of regret—but that was all.

"Skip's hoping to catch you later," Rorie explained.

"As I recall, you played quarterback your senior year of high school," Kate reminded Clay as she claimed the overstuffed chair. "That was the first year the Nightingale team made it to the state finals."

Rorie beamed a look of surprise at her husband. "You never told me that."

"There wasn't much to tell," Clay said with a short laugh. "We were eliminated in the first round.'' He sat beside Rorie and draped his arm around her shoulders as if he had to keep touching her to believe she was here at his side.

Mary carried in a tray of wineglasses and an unopened bottle of a locally produced sparkling white. ''I take it Devin and Dorothea arrived safely in California?'' she asked as she uncorked the wine.

''Yes, Dad phoned when they arrived at Dorothea's daughter's house.''

''We didn't get a chance to say more than a few words at the reception,'' Rorie apologised. ''You were so busy pouring coffee, there wasn't much opportunity to chat.''

''I know. It was good of you and Clay to come.''

''We wouldn't have missed it for the world,'' Clay said.

''I wanted to tell you how nice your father and Dorothea looked together. And for that matter, you and Luke, too,'' Rorie added.

''Thank you,'' Kate said simply, wondering if her friends had heard about the incident on the Wilkins' front porch. It still embarrassed Kate to think of all her father's friends seeing her and Luke together...like that. ''So much has happened in the last month,'' she said, trying to change the subject before either of them mentioned her father's wedding again. ''Who'd ever have believed Luke would end up buying the ranch?''

''I know it must have come as a shock to you,'' Clay said evenly, ''but I've been after him for years to get his own spread.''

''What are your plans now that the Circle L's been sold?'' Rorie wanted to know.

''I'm looking for a place in town,'' she explained, and sipped her wine.

''From what Luke told me, he'd rather you continued living on the ranch,'' Clay said, studying her as though he knew something she didn't.

''I know,'' Kate admitted. ''It's really very generous of him, but I'd prefer to get an apartment of my own.''

''Good luck finding one,'' Clay murmured.

They were both aware that a decent apartment might be difficult to locate. Nightingale was a place of family dwellings, not singles' apartments.

They chatted easily as they waited for Mary to announce dinner. Every now and again Kate saw Clay glance over at Rorie. His look was tender and warm and filled with the deep joy that came from loving completely and knowing that love was returned.

When Rorie Campbell had arrived in their midst, Kate had realised almost immediately that Clay was attracted to her. That was understandable, after all, since Rorie was a beautiful woman. In the beginning, Kate had done everything she could to combat her jealousy. Rorie had been due to leave Elk Run in a few days and once she was gone, Kate had told herself, their lives and feelings would return to normal.

Eventually Rorie did return to San Francisco, but Clay wasn't able to forget her. Kate had done her best to pretend; she'd even talked Clay into setting a wedding date, pressuring him in a not-so-subtle way to marry her quickly. They'd been talking about it for years, and Kate wanted the deed done before Rorie realised what she'd given up when she'd left Clay. Their getting married seemed the perfect solution. Then, if Rorie did decide to return to Nightingale, it would be too late.

Kate's strategy had been a desperate one, planned by a desperate woman. And as often happened in such cases, her scheme backfired.

Kate didn't think she'd ever forget the day Clay told her he wanted to break their engagement. The words had scarred her soul like lye on tender skin. He'd come to the ranch, and from the minute he'd asked to talk to her, Kate had known something was terribly wrong. She'd tried to fill the tension with talk of bridesmaids' dresses and floral arrangements, but Clay had stopped her.

He'd sat with his hands folded, his eyes regarding her sadly. ''I wouldn't hurt you for the world,'' he'd said, and his words rang with truth and regret.

''Clay, you could never hurt me.'' Which was a lie, because he was already inflicting pain.

He'd told her then, simply and directly, that it would be wrong for them to marry. Not once did he mention Rorie's name. He didn't need to. Kate had known for weeks that Clay was in love with the other woman. But she'd chosen instead to involve her heart in a painful game of pretend.

Instead of accepting the truth when Clay had come to her with his decision, she'd insisted he was wrong, that they *were* right for each other and had been all their lives. The memory humbled her now. She'd tried to convince him that all they needed was a little more time. By the next week, or maybe the next month, Clay would realise he'd made a mistake and would want to go through with the wedding. She could afford to be patient because she loved him so much. Kindly, and as gently as possible, Clay had told her time wouldn't alter the way he felt. Then he'd left, although she'd pleaded with him to stay.

In the week that followed, Kate had felt as though she were walking around in a thick fog. She laughed, she smiled, she slept, she ate. The school year hadn't started yet, so there was little else to occupy her mind. The days bled into each other, one indistinguishable from the next.

As Kate had known, Clay, soon after he'd broken their engagement, headed for San Francisco, purportedly to attend a horse show. In her heart, she'd expected Clay left to return with Rorie at his side. As hard as it had been, she'd tried to accept the fact Clay loved Rorie and nothing was ever going to change that.

To everyone's surprise, Clay returned home alone, and there was no mention of Rorie. Kate didn't know what had happened between them. Hope stirred in her chest, and she'd briefly entertained thoughts of Clay resuming their engagement, the two of them marrying and settling down together, the way she'd always dreamed.

Instead she stood helplessly by as Clay threw himself into his work, making unreasonable demands on himself and his men. At first she believed the situation would change. She began stopping off at Elk Run, trying to be the friend she knew Clay needed. But Clay didn't want her. He didn't want anyone.

Except Rorie.

Only then did Kate understand that it was in her power to help this man she loved. She talked over her idea with Luke, even before she approached her father. Luke, and Luke alone, had seemed to understand and appreciate her sacrifice. When she couldn't hold back the tears any longer, it had been Luke who'd held her in his arms and who'd beamed with pride over the unselfishness of her deed.

As she sat, listening to the pre-dinner conversation, even contributing now and then, she realised that Luke had been the one who'd helped her survive that most difficult time.

Luke.

Losing Clay had threatened to destroy her mentally and physically. But Luke hadn't allowed that to happen. It was then he'd started bullying her, she realised. She'd thought of him as a tyrant, with his unreasonable demands and his gentle harassments. At the time, Kate had been so furious with him for assuming command of her life that she'd overlooked the obvious. Only now could she understand and appreciate his strategy. Gradually, the fire had returned to her eyes and her life, although it had been fuelled by indignation. Nevertheless it was there, and Luke had been the person responsible.

She'd been furious with him when she should have been grateful. Luke had never stopped being her friend—the best friend she'd ever had. She'd leaned heavily on him in the days and weeks before Clay married Rorie, though she had never understood how much he'd done for her, how much he cared.

The wineglasses were replenished and Kate proposed a toast. "To your happiness," she said sincerely. It pained Kate to realise Clay and Rorie had nearly lost each other. Because of her...

Nightingale had needed a librarian, and with her father's help, Kate had convinced the town council to offer the job to Rorie Campbell. When she'd turned them down, Kate herself had called Rorie, and together they'd wept over the phone and later in each other's arms.

So Rorie had returned to Nightingale, and she and Clay had been married. In October. The same month Kate had planned for her own wedding to Clay.

Kate's thoughts were pulled back to the present when Clay said, "Rorie has a piece of good news." He cast a proud look at his wife.

"What's that?" Kate asked.

Rorie blushed becomingly. "Clay shouldn't have said anything. It's not for certain yet."

"Rorie," Kate said, studying her carefully, "you're not pregnant so soon, are you? Why, that's wonderful!"

"No, no." Rorie rushed to correct the impression. "Good grief, we've been married less than a month."

"It's about Rorie's book," Clay explained.

Vaguely Kate remembered that Rorie wrote children's books. In fact, she'd been on her way to a writers' conference when the car she was driving broke down on the road not far from Elk Run.

"Has one of your stories been accepted for publication?" Kate asked eagerly.

"Not exactly," Rorie said.

"An editor from New York phoned and asked for a few revisions, but she sounded enthusiastic about the book and there was some talk of a contract once the revisions are done," Clay said. His fingers were twined with his wife's and he looked as excited as if he'd created the story himself.

"Oh, Rorie, that's wonderful." Kate felt pleased and proud for her friend. "What's the book about?"

"Well, the story involves Star Bright and the night we delivered Nightsong, and it's told from the foal's point of view," Rorie said.

"I know I'm her husband," Clay broke in, "but I read it, and I don't mind telling you, the book's gripping. Any editor worth her salt would snap it up in a minute."

"Oh, Clay, honestly!"

"When will you know if it's sold?" Kate wanted to know. "I don't think Nightingale's ever had an author living here before. Dad could convince the town council to commission a sign so folks would know. You might even become a tourist attraction. Who knows what this could turn into?"

They all laughed, but Rorie cautioned, "It could be months yet before I hear a word, so don't go having your father commission any signs."

"You should have seen her after the call arrived," Clay said, his eyes twinkling with merriment. "I didn't know what to think. Rorie came running out of the house and started shrieking and jumping up and down."

"So I was a little excited."

Playfully Clay rolled his eyes. "A little! That's got to be the understatement of the year."

"I'd behave the same way," Kate defended. "And you seem pretty thrilled about all this yourself, Clay Franklin."

Clay admitted it, and then the discussion turned to the awards Clay had accumulated in several national horse shows this past year.

A few minutes later, Mary announced that dinner was ready and they moved into the dining-room. The meal was lively, and conversation flowed easily around the table.

Kate had been dreading this dinner almost from the moment Rorie had issued the invitation. Now she was pleasantly surprised by how enjoyable the evening had become. She'd been convinced that seeing Clay and Rorie's happiness would deepen her own pain. It hadn't happened. She'd expected to spend this evening nursing her wounds behind a brave front. Instead she felt almost giddy with a sense of release.

She *had* loved Clay, she realised, loved him with a youthful innocence. But she didn't feel the same way towards him now. Clay belonged to Rorie and Rorie to him. The tender relationship Kate had once shared with him was part of the past. He would always be a special person in her life, but those old feelings, that adulation she'd felt for him, were relegated to her adolescent fantasies.

Kate Logan was a woman now.

She wasn't sure exactly when the transformation had taken place, but it had. She'd struggled with it, fought the metamorphosis, because change, as always, was both painful and difficult. Kate realised for the first time that all the pain, all the uncertainty, had not been for nothing.

"Kate?" Luke called, as he let himself into the house. "You around?"

"In here." She was at the back of the house, packing away the library of books her father kept in his den. Every night she did a little more to get the main house ready for Luke to move in and her to move out.

She straightened up and tucked in a few wisps of hair that had escaped the red bandana. She wore blue jeans and an old grey sweatshirt and no doubt looked terrible. Despite that, she was pleased to see Luke, eager to talk to him. She was wiping her dusty palms on her jeans when he walked in.

"What are you doing?" He stood just inside the door, a dark frown creasing his forehead.

"What does it look like?" she said. "I'm packing."

He hesitated, then said, "I told you, I want you to live here, at least to the end of the school year. I thought you understood that."

"I do, Luke. It's just that this place is yours now—or will be soon, and there's no reason for me to stay on." For one despairing moment, she was swept away on a crashing wave of disbelief and misery at all she'd lost in so short a time. She could barely walk through her home and not feel an aching throb at the thought of leaving it behind. But the sale of the ranch was part of the new reality she was learning to face.

"Of course there's a reason for you to stay here," Luke insisted, his voice sharp with impatience. "It's where you belong—where I want you. Isn't that reason enough?"

Kate forced a light laugh. "Honestly, Luke, there's no excuse for me to continue living here. You don't need a housekeeper, or a cook or anything else. As I recall, you're completely self-sufficient. And I could do without all the gossip my living here would start in town." She paused a moment, then added gently, "I really *can* manage on my own, you know. I'm a big girl, Luke, and I don't need anyone to take care of me.''

He wanted to argue with her; Kate could sense it with every breath he drew. But when he spoke next, his remarks had nothing to do with her moving.

''I suppose I should tell you about the feed store,'' he said. His voice was controlled, though Kate heard a hint of steel in his words. He'd been just as angry as she was over the incident. Once she'd come to grips with her own outrage, she'd recognised how furious Luke was.

''No...well, yes, I guess I am curious to know how you handled that. Would you like some coffee?''

''Please.''

Kate led the way into the kitchen and filled two ceramic mugs. After handing Luke his, she moved into the living-room and sat on the sofa. Relaxing, she slipped off her shoes and tucked her feet underneath her. It felt good to sit here with Luke—almost like old times. So often over the years, they'd sat and talked like this. Friends. Confidants. Companions. She cradled the mug in both hands, letting the warmth seep up her arms.

''I had dinner with Clay and Rorie last night,'' she said, wanting to share with Luke what she'd discovered.

''Yes, I heard. Listen, I want you to know you can close the door on the situation with Fred Garner. You don't need to worry about it anymore.''

Kate lowered her gaze. ''Thanks,'' she murmured. There was so much she wanted to tell Luke. ''I had a great time at Elk Run last night, though I honestly didn't expect to.''

''I can personally guarantee the matter with Garner is over. If it isn't a dead issue, it soon will be.''

Kate didn't want to talk about the wedding lottery. The subject had become an embarrassing memory—a very embarrassing one— but as Luke said, it was finished. There were other, far more important issues to discuss.

Since her evening with Clay and Rorie, Kate had been doing a lot of serious thinking. For weeks, she'd been abrupt and impatient with Luke and only in the past twenty-four hours had she realised how grateful she should be to him. He'd helped her through the most difficult weeks of her life in ways she was only beginning to understand.

''All day I'd worried about that dinner,'' she said, starting over.

"I wondered how I'd ever be able to sit at a table with Clay, knowing he was married to Rorie. But I did. Oh, Luke, I can't tell you how happy they are. Deep down, I knew they would be, and I had to brace myself for that, expecting to find it unbearably painful. But something incredible happened, something wonderful. During the evening, I learned a valuable lesson about—"

"Good." Luke's response was clipped, detached.

Kate hesitated. From the moment he'd walked into her father's office, she'd felt something was wrong, but she hadn't been able to put her finger on it. "Luke, what is it?"

"Nothing. I'd prefer not talking about Clay and Rorie, all right?"

"I...suppose so," she said, feeling hurt. After an awkward moment, she attempted conversation once more. "You'll never guess who I got a letter from today." If Luke didn't want to talk about Clay and Rorie, then she'd try another topic that was sure to pique his interest. "Eric Wilson. Remember him?"

A slight smile touched Luke's mouth. "I'm not likely to forget him. What'd he have to say?"

"He's moved back to Portland and is talking to his ex-wife. Apparently she's been just as miserable as he has since their divorce. It looks as if they might get back together."

"That's good news."

"He asked me to give you his regards, and sends his thanks." Kate paused. "But he didn't say what I was to thank you for?" She made the statement a question, hoping Luke would supply an answer.

"We talked once."

"Oh," Kate returned, disappointed.

"I told him he was wasting his time on you because you're in love with me."

Kate was outraged. "Luke, you didn't! Please tell me you're joking."

He smiled briefly, then his eyes took on the distant look he'd been wearing a moment earlier. Kate couldn't ignore it any longer. "Luke, please, tell me what's bothering you."

"What makes you think anything is?"

"You don't seem yourself tonight." Something in his voice puzzled her. A reserved quality. It was as if he was distancing himself from her and that was baffling. After Clay's wedding, Luke had actually insisted they marry and now he was treating her like some casual acquaintance. She didn't know what to think.

Kate took another sip of coffee while she collected her thoughts. Luke was sitting as far away from her as he could and still be in the same room. His shoulders were straight and stiff and his dark eyes a shade more intense than she could remember. Gone was the laughing devilry she adored.

"I'll be out of town for a few days next week," he said stiffly. "I'm hoping to pick up a few pieces of new equipment from a wholesaler in New Mexico."

"When will the bank close the deal on the ranch?"

Luke paused and his eyes pinned hers. "Your father and I signed all the necessary papers the day before he married Dorothea Murphy."

Kate felt like bolting from the chair, the shock was so great. "Why didn't you say something?" she demanded, her heart racing. "Why didn't my father? I shouldn't even be here now. This is your home. Yours. Bought and paid for and—"

"Kate." He set his mug aside and wearily rubbed the back of his neck. "You're welcome to stay as long as you need. If you insist on leaving, that's fine, too, but there's no rush."

She brought her hands to her cheeks, which were feverishly hot one minute, numb and cold the next. "I'll be out as...as soon as I can find some place to move."

"Kate, for the love of heaven, why do you persist in being so stubborn?"

She shook her head, hardly understanding it herself. All she knew was that this place, which had been a part of her from the time she was born, no longer belonged to her family. Despite everything Luke said, she couldn't stay on at the Circle L, and she had no other place to go.

Eight

Kate had just finished correcting a pile of math papers when her friend, Linda Hutton, strolled into her classroom. Linda's third-grade class had been on a field trip and the two friends had missed talking at lunchtime.

"Hi," Kate said, smiling up at her. "How'd the tour of the jail and fire station go?"

Linda pulled up a child-size chair and sank heavily down on it, then started massaging her temples with her fingertips. "Don't ask. By noon I was ready to lock up the entire third-grade class and lose the key."

"It certainly was quiet around school."

Linda gave a soft snicker. "Listen, I didn't come in here to learn what a peaceful day *you* had. The only reason I'm not home in bed curled up with aspirin and a hot-water bottle is so I can tell you I was at Garner Feed and Supply yesterday afternoon."

"Oh?"

"Yes, and you aren't going to like what happened. While I was there, Mr. Garner asked me if I wanted to place a wager on the Rivers-Logan wedding."

Kate's heart stopped cold. "He didn't!"

"I'm afraid so."

"But Luke told me he'd taken care of the problem. He said it was a dead issue and that I shouldn't worry about it any longer." It wasn't like Luke to make careless promises.

"I wish I didn't have to tell you this," Linda said, with a sympathetic sigh.

"But Luke told me he'd personally talked to Fred Garner."

"He did. Mr Garner made a point of telling me that, too," Linda confirmed. "He claimed Luke was hotter than a Mexican chili pepper. Said Luke came into his place, ranted and raved and threatened him within an inch of his life. But, Kate, I'm telling you the whole time old Garner was talking to me he wore a grin so wide I could have driven a Jeep through it.''

Kate sagged against the back of her chair.

''Then Mr Garner started telling me that the harder a man fights marriage, the faster he falls. From what he said, he's taking bets from as far away as Riversdale and southward.''

Kate pressed a hand over her eyes. ''What am I going to do now?''

Linda shook her head. ''I don't know. At least Garner's taken it off the blackboard, but when I said something about that, he told me he had to, since half the county wants in on the action. Apparently the betting outgrew his blackboard space.''

''If nothing else it all proves how desperate this community is for entertainment,'' Kate returned stiffly. ''If the good people of Nightingale have nothing better to do than waste their time and money betting on something as silly as a wedding date, then it's a sad commentary on our lives here.''

Kate's friend cleared her throat, and looked suspiciously guilty.

Kate hesitated, studying Linda. No, she mused, her gaze narrowing. Not Linda. Her closest childhood friend wouldn't place a wager. Her expression confirmed that she would.

''You chose a date yourself, didn't you?'' Kate demanded.

Linda's gaze bounced all over the room, avoiding Kate's completely.

''You did, didn't you?'' Kate exclaimed, hardly able to believe Linda would do such a thing.

Linda's fingers were curling and uncurling in her lap. ''You're my oldest, dearest friend. How could I ever do anything like that?'' she wailed.

''I don't know, Linda. You tell me.''

''All right, all right,'' Linda confessed. ''I did put a wager on June. The first part of summer is such a lovely time of year for a wedding and you'd make a beautiful bride.''

''I can't believe I'm hearing this.'' Kate had the sinking suspicion that her father had probably gotten in on the action, too, before he left for his honeymoon.

''I had no intention of betting,'' Linda hurried to explain. ''In fact I never would have, but the odds were so good for June. For a five-dollar bet, I could collect as much as five hundred in return if you were to marry around the middle of the month—say the sixteenth. It's a Saturday. Weekends are always best for weddings, don't you think?''

Kate wasn't about to answer that. ''You know, I think this whole thing is illegal. Each and every one of you should thank your lucky stars I don't call the sheriff.''

''He's betting himself—on March. Said his own wedding anniversary is March tenth and he thinks Luke will be able to persuade you early in the spring. According to Fred, the sheriff thinks once Luke gets you to agree, he won't wait around for a big wedding. He'll want to marry you before you can change your mind.''

Kate gave her a furious look. ''If you're telling me all this to amuse me, you've failed miserably.''

''I'm sorry, Kate, I really am. The only reason I went into the feed store was so I could assure you the whole thing was over, only I can't and—''

''Instead you placed a wager of your own.''

''I feel guilty enough about that,'' Linda admitted, her voice subdued.

''Why don't we both forget the whole thing and concentrate on the Thanksgiving play?'' Instead of upsetting herself with more talk of this wedding lottery, Kate preferred to do something constructive with her time.

''I think I may be able to make it up to you, though,'' Linda murmured, fussing with the cuffs of her long-sleeved blouse.

''Whatever it is will have to be good.''

''It is.'' Linda brightened and pulled a slip of paper from her purse. ''I got this information from a friend of a friend, so I don't know how accurate it is, but I think it's pretty much for sure.''

''What's for sure?'' she asked when Linda handed her the paper. A local phone number was carefully printed on it.

Linda's sheepish look departed. ''It's Mrs Jackson's number—she's the manager of the apartment complex on Spruce Street. They may have a vacancy coming up early next week. If you're the first one to apply, you might have a decent chance of getting it.''

''Oh, Linda, that's great.''

''Am I forgiven?''

Kate laughed. ''This makes up for a multitude of sins.''

''I was counting on that.''

Kate called five times before she was able to get through. Mrs Jackson seemed surprised to be hearing from her.

"I thought you were marrying that Rivers chap," the elderly woman said. "Can't understand why you'd want to rent an apartment when you're engaged to that man. The whole town says it's just a matter of time."

"Mrs Jackson," Kate said loudly, because everyone knew the older woman was hard of hearing, "could I look at the apartment soon?"

"Won't be cleaned up for another day or two. I'll let you know once it's ready to be shown, but I can't help feeling it's a waste of time. Don't know what's wrong with you young women these days. In my time, we'd snap up a good man like Luke Rivers so fast it'd make your head spin."

"I'd still like to see the apartment," Kate pressed.

"Saturday, I guess. Yes, Saturday. Why don't you plan to come over then? I'll need a deposit if you decide to take the place."

"Will a cheque be all right?"

"Good as gold when it's got your name on it," the older woman said, chuckling. "Don't suppose you have any season or month that you're particularly partial to for weddings, would you?"

"No, I can't say that I do."

"Well, me and Ethel Martin think you and that Rivers fellow will tie the knot in April. April seems a mighty nice month for a country wedding."

"I'm sure it is," Kate said, clenching her teeth.

"Good. Now listen, soon as the word gets out, someone else will be wanting that apartment, so if you aren't here by noon Saturday, I'm afraid I'm going to have to give it to whoever else shows up. You understand?"

"I'll be there before noon."

"I'll look forward to seeing you then."

"Goodbye, Mrs Jackson."

"You keep thinking about April, you hear?"

"Yes, I will," Kate murmured, rolling her eyes as she replaced the receiver.

That night, Luke stopped in shortly after Kate had finished dinner, which consisted of a sandwich eaten while she emptied the living-room bookcases. She filled box after box with books, her own and her father's, as well as complete sets of Dickens, Thackeray, and George Eliot that had belonged to her mother. The physical activity gave her time to think. She'd realised the night she had dinner at the Franklins' that she wasn't in love with Clay. That same evening, Kate had also realised how much Luke had done for her in the weeks following her broken engagement. It troubled her to acknowledge how unappreciative she'd been of his support.

At Clay's wedding, she'd only added to the problem by asking Luke to marry her. He'd been willing to comply, willing to continue taking care of her through these difficult emotional times. In his own way, he did love her; Kate didn't doubt that. But he seemed far more concerned about protecting her from the harsh realities of life.

All the talk about weddings had brought the subject to the fore-front of Kate's mind. She tried to picture what her life would be like if she were to marry Luke. From the night of Clay's wedding, Luke had been telling her she was in love with him. It came as a shock to her to realise how right he was. She did love him, a thousand times more than she'd ever dreamed.

Luke claimed he loved her, too. If that was true, then why was she fighting him so hard? For one thing, Luke had delivered any declaration of love in such a matter-of-fact, unromantic way, it was hard to believe he really meant it. He seemed to prefer forcing her into admitting she loved him. If she could be sure that his feelings were rooted in something more than sympathy and a strong physical attraction, she would feel more confident. But Luke kept trying to shield her, as though she were a child. Now that she was moving into a place of her own, she'd be able to analyse her changing feelings more objectively. She'd be completely on her own, away from the environment they'd always shared. Once they were apart, once it was clear that she could manage on her own, Luke would be free to pursue a relationship with her as an equal, an adult woman—not a little girl who needed looking after.

''I see you're at it again,'' he said, standing in the doorway between the kitchen and the living-room.

''Luke—'' she slapped her hand over her heart ''—you startled me!'' Her thoughts had been full of him and then suddenly he was there.

As he did more and more often of late, Luke was frowning, but Kate wasn't going to let that destroy her mood. She was thrilled with the prospect of moving into her own apartment and settling into a different kind of life.

''I have good news. I'm going to look at an apartment Saturday morning.'' She dragged a heavy box of books across the carpet.

"So," she said, huffing, "I'll probably be out of here sooner than we thought."

Luke interrupted her, effortlessly picking up the cardboard box and depositing it on the growing stack at the far side of the room.

"Thanks," she murmured, grateful for his help.

"You shouldn't be doing this heavy work on your own."

"It's no problem," she countered, rubbing the dust from her hands. "The only trouble I'm having is with these books. I didn't realise we had so many."

"Kate, dammit, I wish you'd listen to reason."

"I'm being reasonable," she said, fixing a reassuring smile on her face. "The only thing I'm doing is giving you what's rightfully yours."

Luke's frown grew darker, and he dragged a hand through his hair. "Listen, I think we may have more of a problem with Fred Garner than I first realised."

"Yes, I know," Kate said, already filling the next box. "Linda told me after school that he's doing a thriving business."

Luke knelt on the floor beside her. "You're not upset?"

"Would it do any good? I mean, you obviously did your best and that only seemed to encourage the betting. As far as I can see, the only thing that will settle this issue is time." She kept her gaze averted and added, "When six months pass and we're still not married, most everyone will accept that nothing's going on between us."

"Nothing?" Luke asked bitterly.

Hope stirred briefly within her. "I like to think we'll always be friends." An absent smile touched her lips. "Now that I've decided to distance my emotions from this silly lottery business, I find it all rather comical. I think you should do the same."

"This whole thing amuses you?"

"The good citizens of Nightingale are amused, I suppose. Everyone seems to assume that because Clay and Dad both got married and the ranch has been sold, I should swoon into your arms."

"Personally, I don't think that's such a bad idea."

"Oh?" She chuckled and tucked a few more books in the box. Her heart was racing. If Luke was ever really going to declare his love, it would be now. "That wasn't the message I got the other night. I tried to have a serious talk with you about my evening with Clay and Rorie, and all you could do was glower at me." She glanced up at him and gently shook her head. "As you're doing now."

Luke walked away from her. He stood staring out the window, although Kate suspected the view was of little interest to him. "I just wish you'd be sensible for once in your life," he snapped.

"I didn't know I had a habit of not being sensible," she said conversationally, disheartened by his attitude. She rose and walked over to the larger bookcase, but even standing on the tips of her toes, she couldn't quite reach the trophies stored on the top shelf. Not to be defeated, she rolled the ottoman in front of the empty bookcase and climbed on to the thick cushioned seat. She stretched up and her fingers were just about to grasp the first trophy when she heard Luke's swift intake of breath.

"Kate, good Lord..."

Just as he spoke the ottoman started to roll out from under her feet. She flailed her arms in a desperate effort to maintain her balance.

Kate had never seen Luke move faster. His hands closed around her waist in an iron grip. Her cry of alarm caught in her throat as she was forcefully slammed against his solid chest.

"Of all the stupid, idiotic things I've ever seen—"

"I would have been perfectly fine if you hadn't called my name." Her heart was pounding so hard she could barely breathe.

Luke's hold relaxed. "You're all right?"

"Fine."

He closed his eyes, exhaling a ragged sigh. When he opened them, he assessed her carefully; he apparently concluded that she was unhurt because he gave her an impatient little shake. "Whatever possessed you to climb up on that ottoman in the first place?" he demanded.

"I couldn't reach the trophies."

"Couldn't you have asked me to get them for you? Why do you have such a difficult time accepting help from me?"

"I don't know," she admitted softly.

Still he held her and still Kate let him, trying to resist the comfort she felt in his arms. Her hands were braced against his powerful shoulders, but then she relaxed, unconsciously linking her fingers behind his neck.

Neither moved for a long moment.

Slowly Luke ran a provocative finger down the length of her cheek, and Kate's eyes drifted shut. She felt herself drawn inexorably towards him. Her lips parted and trembled, awaiting his kiss. When she realised what she was doing, her eyes snapped open and she broke away from him with such force that she would have stumbled had his hands not righted her.

Embarrassed now, she stepped back. Luke brought down the trophies and handed them to her, but she noted that his eyes had become distant and unreadable.

"I think that's enough packing for tonight," she murmured, her voice breathless even while she struggled to sound cheerful and bright.

He nodded slightly, then without another word stalked from the room. Kate didn't know what possessed her to follow him, certainly the last thing she should have done.

"Luke?"

He stopped halfway through the kitchen and turned towards her. His eyes were steely and intense, and just seeing that harsh edge in them drove her to take a step backward in retreat.

"You wanted something?" he asked when she didn't immediately explain.

"Just to say…" She could barely talk coherently. It occurred to her to ask if he loved her the way a man loves his wife, but she lacked the courage. "I thought maybe, I mean, I wanted to know if there was anything I could do for you before I left the house. Paint the living-room…or something?"

"No."

Briefly she toyed with the idea of following him outside. For all his words about wanting her to stay, he couldn't seem to get away from her fast enough. The thought of not having Luke for her friend anymore felt almost crippling. Her pride was the problem. Luke had told her repeatedly that she needed him, and she knew now that she did. But not in the way he meant. Not just as a friend who was willing to offer her the protection and peace of marriage, a friend who felt obliged to take care of her.

"I don't want you to move from the ranch," he said.

Her heart was begging him to give her a reason to stay—the reason she longed to hear. "Luke, please accept that I'm only doing what I think is best in my life."

"I realise that, but dammit, Kate, you're being so stubborn it's all I can do to remain sane. Why do you resist me when all I want to do is make things easier for you? We could be married, and you could settle down in the house, and nothing need change. Yet you insist on causing all this turmoil in your life.''

There wasn't anything Kate could say.

''You can't tell me we aren't physically attracted to each other. The electricity between us is powerful enough to light up Main Street.''

''I...know.''

''Say it, Kate. Admit that it felt good to have me hold you just now.''

''I...''

When Luke reached for her, Kate felt as if she'd lost some strategic battle. When his mouth found hers, her stomach tightened and fluttered wildly. Against her will, her lips parted, and before she realised what was happening she slid her arms tightly around his hard, narrow waist, wanting to hold on to him forever.

Luke moaned, then suddenly tore his lips away from hers. She felt a tremor go through him before he raised his head and gazed tenderly into her face, his eyes dark and gentle.

''Is it so difficult to say?'' he asked.

Nine

"This is the second bedroom," Mrs. Jackson was saying as she led Kate through the vacant apartment. From the moment she'd walked in the door, Kate had known that this place would suit her needs perfectly.

"I can't understand why you'd be wanting a two-bedroom place, but that's none of my business," Mrs. Jackson went on. Her hair was tightly curled in pink plastic rollers. To the best of her ability, Kate couldn't remember ever seeing the woman's hair *without* rollers.

"What did that Rivers fellow say when you told him you were moving into town?" She didn't wait for a response, but cackled delightedly, contemplating the thought. "Frankly, I wasn't sure you'd show this morning. My friend Ethel and me talked about it, and we thought Rivers would tie a rope around you and hightail it to Nevada and marry you quick. Offhand, I can't remember who's got money on November."

"I was determined to be here before noon," she said, ignoring the other comments.

"So I see. If Luke didn't stop you, I expected that snowstorm the weatherman's been talking about for the past two days would."

"Do you really think it's going to snow?" Kate asked anxiously. The sky had been dark all morning, and the temperature seemed to be dropping steadily. Normally Kate wouldn't have chanced driving into town by herself with weather conditions this uncertain, but if she hadn't come, she might have missed getting the apartment.

"If I was you, I'd stick around town for a while," Mrs Jackson advised. "I'd hate the thought of you getting trapped on the road in a bad storm."

"I'm sure I'll be all right." She'd driven her father's four-wheel-drive truck, and even if the storm did hit, she shouldn't have much trouble getting home. The Circle L was only twenty minutes away, and how much snow could settle in that time? Not much, she decided.

''Would you like me to write you a cheque now?'' Kate asked, eager to be on her way.

''That would be fine. There's still some cleaning to be done, but I'll make sure it's finished before the first of the month. Fact is, you can start moving your things in here next week if you want.''

''Thanks, I appreciate that.''

Mrs Jackson bundled her coat around her thin shoulders as they stepped outside. She glanced at the sky and shook her pink-curlered head. ''If you're going home, I'd suggest you do it quick. I don't like the look of them clouds. They seem downright angry to me.''

''If that's the case, I'd better write that cheque and hurry home.''

No more than five minutes later, Kate was sitting inside her father's truck. The sky was an oyster-grey and darkening by the minute. Shivering from the cold, she zipped her jacket all the way up to her neck and drew on a pair of fur-lined leather gloves.

Kate started the engine and shifted the gears. The radio was set on her dad's favourite country station and the music played softly, giving her a sense of peace. When she left the outskirts of town, she hit a couple of rough patches in the road and bounced so high her head nearly hit the roof of the cab. After that she kept her speed down. She drove at a steady pace, her gaze focused on the road ahead, scanning the horizon for any sign of snow.

When she was about ten miles from the ranch, the storm hit. Light, fluffy flakes whirled around the windshield. The morning sky darkened until it resembled dusk and Kate was forced to turn on the headlights.

A love song came on the radio, one the band at the Red Bull had played that fateful Friday night. The night Luke had lifted her in his arms and carried her off the dance floor. Embarrassed by the memory, she reached for the radio dial, intending to change to station.

She didn't see the rock that had rolled on to the roadway, not until she was on top of it, and then it was too late. Her instincts took control. She gripped the wheel with both hands, then swerved and slammed into the embankment. The truck stopped with a sudden jerk, and the engine went dead.

For a stunned moment, Kate couldn't so much as breathe. Her heart was in her throat and her hands clenched the steering wheel so tightly her fingers felt numb.

Finally, when she was able to move, Kate released a long, slow breath, grateful the accident hadn't been worse. She took a moment to compose herself and tried to restart the engine, but nothing happened. Twice more she tried to get the engine to kick over, but it wouldn't even cough or sputter.

Frustrated, she smacked the cushioned seat with her gloved hand and closed her eyes. The snow was coming down thick and fast now.

"Don't worry," she muttered, opening the door and climbing out. "Stay calm." Although everything Kate knew about the internal workings of engines would fit in a thimble, she decided to take a look to see if she could find the problem.

The snow and wind slapped at her viciously, as though to punish her for not listening to Mrs Jackson and staying in town.

After considerable difficulty finding the latch, Kate lifted the bonnet. With a prayer on her lips, she looked everything over, then touched two or three different parts as if that would repair whatever was broken. Certain that she was destined to sit out the storm huddled in the cab, she returned and tried the key once more.

The engine gave one sick cough and promptly died.

"Damn!"

Nothing remained but to sit and wait for someone to drive past. Leaving the truck and attempting to find her way to the house would be nearly as insane as driving around in a snowstorm in the first place.

Kate could almost hear Luke's lecture now. It would be hot enough to blister her ears. All she could do was hope her father never found out about this—or she'd have a lecture from him, too.

Half-hour passed and, hoping against hope, Kate tried the engine again. Nothing. But it was snowing so hard now that even if the truck had started, she probably wouldn't have been able to drive in these conditions. She tried to warm herself by rubbing her hands together and hugging her arms close to her body. Lord, it was cold, the coldest weather she could remember.

With little to take her mind off the freezing temperatures, she laid her head back and closed her eyes, forcing herself to relax. There was nothing to do but sit patiently and wait....

She must have dozed off because the next thing she knew, the truck door was jerked open and her arm gripped in a sudden, painful grasp.

"Have you lost your mind?" The fury in Luke's voice was like a slap in the face.

"Luke...Luke." She was so grateful to see him that she didn't question where he'd come from or how he'd found her. It all felt like a dream. Moving was difficult, but she slid her arms around his neck and hugged him, laughing and crying at the same time. "How did you ever find me?"

"Good Lord, don't you realise I was about to have heart failure worrying about you?"

"You're sick?" Her mind was so muddled. Of course he'd be worried, and how had he known where she was? And he seemed so angry now, but then, for the past several days he'd been continually upset with her.

Her arms tightened around his neck and she breathed in the fresh, warm scent of him. When she sat up and looked around, she was shocked by how dark it had become; if it weren't for the blowing, swirling snow, the stars would be twinkling. The storm had abated somewhat, but not by much.

"I can't believe you'd do anything so stupid." His voice was low and angry, his face blanched with concern. "Don't you realise you could have frozen to death out here? If you don't want to consider your own life or what you might have suffered as a result of your impulsiveness, then what about Devin away on his honeymoon? If anything happened to you, he'd never forgive himself."

Kate bore up well under Luke's tirade, refusing to cry even though she was trembling with shock and cold and the truth of his words. As for the part about being frozen, she was already halfway there, but he didn't seem to notice that.

"Kate, I don't know what I would have done if you'd left the truck and tried to make it back to the house on foot."

"I knew enough to stay here at least." She'd been a fool not to have taken the danger more seriously. "I'm sorry," she whispered.

He pulled her to him and held her so tight she couldn't move. His face was buried in her hair, one ungloved hand gently stroking her forehead, her cheek, her chin, as if he had to touch her to know he'd found her safe. When he lifted his head, he roughly brushed the hair from her face and gazed into her eyes, his own dark and filled with unspoken torment. "Are you all right?"

She nodded and tried to talk, but her teeth started to chatter. Luke shrugged out of his coat and draped it over her shoulders.

"Tell me what happened."

"I swerved to miss a rock and hit...something. It had already started to snow and I...the song...I changed stations and that's when it happened...I don't know what I did, but after I turned so sharply, the truck wouldn't start."

"I've got to get you back to the house." He half carried her to his truck and placed her in the passenger seat. He climbed into the driver's side and leaned over to wrap a warm blanket around her, then he reached for her hand and began to rub some warmth back into her fingers.

"What about Dad's truck?" Kate asked, shocked by how tired and weak she felt.

"We'll worry about that later. I'll send someone to fix it when the storm's over."

The blast from the heater felt like a tropical wind and Kate finally started to relax. She was terribly cold but dared not let Luke know.

All the way back to the ranch he didn't say a word. Driving was difficult at best, and she didn't want to disturb his concentration. So she sat beside him, her hands and feet numb despite the almost oppressive warmth, and her eyes heavy with weariness.

Several of the ranch hands ran towards the front porch when Luke pulled into the yard. Kate found the flurry of activity all centred on her disconcerting, but she tried to thank everyone and apologised profusely for the concern she'd caused.

If Luke had been impatient and demanding when he rescued her, it couldn't compare to the way he rapped out orders once she was inside the house.

"A bath," he said, pointing toward the bathroom as if she'd never been there before. "Warm water, not hot."

Bill Schmidt, Luke's newly appointed foreman, followed them to the doorway of the tiny room, looking pale and anxious. Kate felt so weak that she simply stood, leaning against the sink, while Luke ran the bathwater, testing it several times to check the temperature.

"It's stopped snowing. Do you think I should contact one of her female friends? Maybe Mizz Franklin?" Bill asked, shifting awkwardly from foot to foot. When Luke nodded, Bill charged out of the house, slamming the door behind him.

Luke turned off the bathwater and straightened. He shook his head, arms limp and at his sides, mouth stern and tight. "Dear Lord, Kate, what could have possessed you to drive in from town during the worst storm of the year? Can you imagine what went through my mind when I was looking for you?''

It took all her strength just to manage a few words. ''How'd...you know...where I was?''

''You told me you were going to town to look at an apartment on Saturday. Remember? When you weren't back after the blizzard hit, I started calling around town until I learned you were renting one of the apartments on Spruce Street. Mrs Jackson told me she'd warned you herself and that you'd left several hours earlier. Also that she was fond of April because of all the flowers, whatever the hell that means.''

''I'm...sorry I worried you.''

His hands gripped her shoulders and the anguish he'd endured the past few hours was written plainly on his face. The anger and pain in his eyes told her about the panic he'd felt. A rush of emotion crossed his expression and he pulled her close, wrapping his arms around her.

Luke didn't speak for a long moment. Instead, quietly, gently, his hand stroked her hair as he dragged in several deep breaths.

Kate's heart pounded wildly in her chest. She longed to look at him, to gaze into his eyes again. She was puzzled by the intensity she'd seen there. Fear, yes, doubt and anger, too, but there was something more, something deeper she couldn't recognise.

She longed to tell him she loved him, just the way he claimed she did, but the thought didn't make it to her lips. Love was a strange, unpredictable emotion, she'd learned, so painful and difficult. Her eyes held his and she tried to smile, but her mouth wouldn't co-operate.

Her fingertips mapped out the lines of his face, as she strove to reassure him with her touch, when her words couldn't. He captured her wrist and brought her palm to his lips.

She'd just opened her mouth to speak, when Bill Schmidt came crashing into the room. ''Rorie Franklin will be over as soon as she can.''

''Thanks, Bill,'' Luke said without looking away from Kate.

''Uh, I'll be leaving, now, if you don't need me.''

''Fine. Thanks again for your help.''

''No problem. Certainly glad you're all right, Kate.'' He touched his hat and then was gone.

''Someone should help you out of those clothes,'' Luke said, half smiling, ''and I don't think I should be the one to do it.''

"I'm fine. I can undress myself."

Luke didn't seem inclined to challenge her statement. She floated towards the bathroom door and ushered him out, then shut it softly.

Once she started undressing, she discovered that Luke hadn't been too far wrong when he'd suggested she needed help. By the time she sank into the warm water, she was shivering, exhausted and intensely cold again. The water felt wonderful although it stung her tender skin. When the prickling sensation left her, she was almost overwhelmed by the sensation of comfort. She sighed deeply, closed her eyes and lay back in the tepid water.

"Kate," Luke called from the other side of the door, "are you okay in there?"

"I'm fine."

"Do you need anything?"

"No," she assured him.

A sudden thought made her bolt upright, gasping. *Luke could have died searching for me.* She squeezed her eyes closed and whispered a prayer of thanks that the events of this traumatic afternoon had turned out as they had.

She must have sobbed because Luke cried out, "What's wrong? It sounds like you're crying."

"You...could have died trying to find me."

"I didn't."

"I know," she said hoarsely, biting into her lower lip. "I'm glad. I wouldn't want you to die."

"That's encouraging," he answered with a soft laugh.

Dressed in her flannel pyjamas and long robe, her hair hanging wetly against her shoulders, Kate let herself out of the bathroom. She looked like something the cat had proudly dragged on to the porch, but at least she felt better. A thousand times better.

Luke was sitting in the kitchen, nursing a shot glass of whisky. Kate had very rarely seen Luke drink straight liquor.

"I blame myself," he muttered. "I knew about the storm and didn't warn you."

"Warn me? It wouldn't have done any good. I would have gone into town, anyway. I had to be there before noon if I was going to get the apartment. You couldn't have stopped me, Luke. You know that."

Luke shook his head grimly. "What I can't understand is why moving away from here is so all-fired important that you'd risk your fool neck to do it."

"Mrs Jackson said she'd have to give the apartment to someone else if I wasn't there."

"She wouldn't have understood if you'd phoned? You had to go look at it in a blizzard?" He urged her into a chair and poured a cup of hot coffee, adding a liberal dose of whisky before handing her the cup.

"I already told you I couldn't wait," Kate said patiently. "Please don't be angry, Luke." She reached for his hand, needing to touch him.

He gripped her fingers with his own. "Kate, if anything should convince you we ought to get married, this is it. You need me, Princess, can't you see that?" He released her hand to brush the damp curls from her face, then framed her cheek with his index fingers. "How many times do I have to tell you that before you'll believe it?"

"Oh, Luke," she moaned, feeling close to tears.

"I want to take care of you, Kate. What nearly happened today, plus the fiasco with Eric Wilson, should tell you something."

She stared at him, feeling a little lost and disoriented. "There are women in this community, women my age, who already have children." Even as she spoke, she realised she wasn't really making sense.

Luke blinked in confusion. "You want children? Great, so do I. In fact, I'm hoping we'll have several."

"That's not what I meant," Kate said, exasperated. She tried again. "These women don't live with a guardian." Was that clearer? she wondered.

"Of course they don't—they're married," Luke countered sharply.

Kate closed her eyes. "Don't you understand? I'm old enough to be on my own. I don't need someone to protect me."

"We're not discussing your age," Luke snapped.

"You don't love me," she blurted. "You feel sorry for me, that's all. You think because Clay's married to Rorie and…and Dad married Dorothea that I don't have anyone. But I do! There's Linda and lots of other friends. I've got a good life. I don't need to get married."

Luke bolted from the chair and walked to the sink, pressing both hands against the edge, hunching his shoulders, his back towards her. He said nothing for several moments and when he finally spoke, his voice was cool, detached. "All I can say is that you must feel a lot more strongly about this than I realised. Apparently you're willing to risk your life to get away from me.''

"I didn't go to town knowing I was in any danger," she objected.

"Then leave, Kate. I won't try to keep you any longer, despite the fact that I love you and want to marry you. If you want your independence so badly, then take it.''

"Luke, please, you don't love me—not the way you should.''

"Oh, and what do you know about that? Obviously nothing.''

"I know you keep saying you want to take care of me.''

"That's so wrong?''

"Yes. A woman needs more.''

"My love and my life are all I've got to offer you, Kate. It's a take-it-or-leave-it proposition.''

"That's not fair," she said. "You make it sound as though I'm destined to live my life alone if I don't marry you within the next ten minutes.''

Slowly he turned to face her. His eyes were piercing and as dark as she'd ever seen them. "Fine. You've made your choice. I'm not going to stand here arguing with you. It's over between us, Kate. This is the last time we'll talk about marriage.''

She tried to say something, but couldn't think coherently. Even if she'd been able to work out her thoughts and give them voice, she doubted Luke was in any mood to listen. He avoided looking at her as he walked out of the house.

A fire was blazing in the fireplace and Kate stretched out on the nearby sofa, intending to mull over Luke's words. But her eyes felt as heavy as her heart, and almost as soon as she laid her head on the pillow, she was asleep.

Someone working in the kitchen stirred Kate to wakefulness, and when she glanced at her watch she was shocked to realise she'd slept for almost two hours.

Her heart soared when she thought it must be Luke. He'd been so angry with her earlier, though she supposed his anxiety about finding her in the snowstorm explained his attitude. She hoped they could clear the air between them.

But it wasn't Luke. Instead, Rorie peered into the living-room, her eyes gentle and concerned.

"I hope you don't mind. Luke let me in.''

"You're always welcome here, Rorie, you know that.''

''Bill Schmidt called with an incredible story about your being lost in the storm. I could hardly believe it. Clay drove me over as soon as he could, but to be honest I didn't know who was worse off—you or Luke.''

At the mention of his name, Kate lowered her gaze to the multicoloured quilt spread across her lap. Idly she smoothed the wrinkles, trying not to think about Luke.

''How are you feeling?''

''I'm okay. I just have a little headache.''

''A monster of one from the look of you. I've never seen you this pale.''

Kate's hands twisted the fringed edge of the homemade quilt. ''Luke was furious with me for going into town—I found an apartment, Rorie. He said it was over between us.'' She began to cry. ''He said he'd be glad when I was gone and that he'd...never bother me again.'' By the time Kate had finished, her voice was reduced to a hoarse whisper.

''I see,'' Rorie murmured.

''I don't even know Luke any more. We used to be able to talk to each other and joke together, but lately we're barely able to discuss anything in a rational manner. I've tried, Rorie, I really have, but Luke makes everything so difficult.''

''Men have a habit of doing that sometimes.''

''I wanted to tell Luke about the night I had dinner with you and Clay and—'' She stopped abruptly when she realised what she'd almost said.

''What about it?'' Rorie coaxed.

''It's just that I'd dreaded the evening because I was afraid of being with Clay again. I'm sorry, Rorie, I don't want to upset you, but I loved Clay for a long time, and getting over him was much harder than I ever thought it would be. That is, until the night we were all together.'' The words came rushing from her. ''I saw Clay with you and I assumed I'd experience all this pain, but instead I felt completely free. You're both so happy, and I knew, then and there, that I never loved Clay the way you do. True I adored him for years, but it was more of an adolescent infatuation. Clay was a part of my youth. When I realised all these things about myself, all these changes, I felt such hope, such excitement.''

''Oh, Kate, I'm so pleased to hear that.'' A shy smile dented Rorie's cheeks.

''I wanted to explain all this to Luke, but I never got the chance, and now it's all so much worse. I don't know if we'll ever be able to talk to each other again.''

''Of course you will.''

''But he sounded so angry.''

''I'm sure that was because of his concern for your safety.''

''I can't talk to him,'' Kate repeated sadly. ''At least not yet, and maybe not for a long time.''

''It'll be sooner than you think,'' Rorie advised. ''You won't be able to break off all those years of friendship, and neither will he. He'll be around in a day or two, ready to apologise for being so harsh. Just you wait and see.''

Kate shook her head. ''You make it all sound so easy.''

''Trust me, I know it isn't. When I think back to the way things went between Clay and me, I empathise all the more with what you're going through now.''

Kate remembered the dark days following Clay's visit to California. Neither Rorie nor Clay had ever told her what happened. But no one needed to spell it out for her. Clay had gone to San Francisco, intending to bring Rorie back with him, and instead had returned alone.

''Maybe we just need to get away from each other for a while,'' Kate said. She chewed her lower lip as she considered her own words. ''If we aren't in such close proximity, maybe the fog will clear and we'll be able to sort out what we really feel for each other.''

''When are you moving to town?''

''Monday,'' Kate said, looking at the cardboard boxes stacked against the opposite wall.

''Do you need help? Skip, Clay and I could easily lend a hand.''

''That would be wonderful.''

The remainder of the weekend passed in a blur. Kate didn't see Luke once. So much for Rorie's assurances that he'd be by soon to talk everything out. Apparently he meant everything he'd said.

Monday morning, when she was ready to leave for school, Kate paused before she got into her car, deciding she should at least say goodbye to Luke before she moved out.

Luke wasn't in the barn, but Bill Schmidt was.

''Good morning, Bill.''

''Howdy, Kate,'' he said with a wide grin. ''Glad to see there's no ill effects from your accident.''

"None, thanks. Is Luke around?"

Bill settled his hands in the pockets of his bib overalls. "No, I thought you knew. He left yesterday afternoon for New Mexico. There's some new equipment there he wants to look at. He won't be back until Thursday."

Ten

Kate was carrying the last of the cardboard boxes to the dumpster outside the apartment building onThursday evening when she saw Luke's pickup turn on to Spruce Street. He came to a grinding halt at the kerb, vaulted out of the cab and stood there scowling at her apartment building. His features were contorted, but for the life of her Kate couldn't understand why he should be so irritated.

She was about to make her presence known, but before she could act, Luke brought his fist down on the bonnet. She heard the sound from where she stood. It must have smarted because he rubbed the knuckles for a couple of moments, gazing intently at the redbrick building. Then, tucking his hands in the back pockets of his jeans, he squared his shoulders and strode towards the building. He stopped abruptly, then retreated to his truck. Opening the door, he balanced one foot on the side rail, as if he was about to leap into the cab.

Kate leaned forward on the tips of her toes and stretched out her hand to stop him. It took everything in her not to rush forward, but she didn't trust herself not to burst into tears. Viewing Luke's behaviour had moved something deep within her.

If Luke had planned to drive away, he apparently changed his mind, because he slammed the door shut and resolutely faced the apartment building again.

Knowing that the time to make her move was now, Kate casually turned the corner.

''Kate.''

''Luke,'' she said, pretending surprise.

For a moment, Luke didn't say a word. ''I just got back to the ranch and discovered that the main house was empty. I thought you'd be there when I returned.''

''Mrs Jackson said I could have the apartment Monday, and since Rorie, Clay and Skip were able to help me move, I couldn't see any reason to delay.''

"You might have told me."

Kate lowered her gaze, feeling a little guilty, since they'd parted on such unfriendly terms. "I tried, but you'd already left for New Mexico."

"Bill did say something about you wanting to talk to me," he conceded.

"Would you like to come inside?" she asked, opening the door for him.

"All right." He sounded reluctant.

Once in the apartment they stood looking at each other, and Kate felt terribly awkward. Luke's eyes were dark and luminous and his face had never seemed so dear to her—familiar, yet in some new exciting way, not fully known. She would have liked nothing better than to walk into his arms. She wanted to tell him how sorry she was for the way they'd last parted, to tell him she was ready to accept his proposal on any terms. But her pride made that impossible.

"Nice place you've got here," he said when the silence became painful. He tucked his fingers in his back pockets again.

"Can I take your coat?"

"Please." He took it off and gave it to her.

She motioned towards the sofa. "Would you like to sit down?"

He nodded and sat on the edge of the cushion. Leaning forward, he balanced his hands between his knees and rotated his hat with his fingers. Luke had sat on this very same sofa a thousand times, but he'd never looked as uncomfortable as he did now.

"I came to apologise for the last time we spoke."

"Oh, Luke," she whispered, sitting in the overstuffed chair across from him, "I felt bad afterwards, too. Why do we argue like that? Some days I feel as if we're growing further and further apart, and I don't want that."

"I'd like to suggest that we put an end to this nonsense, but you've made your views plain enough."

"You still want to take care of me?"

"I don't think that's so wrong."

"I know." She sighed, tired of repeating the same arguments. "But I'm fully capable of doing that myself."

"Right," he said with deadly softness. "You took care of yourself pretty well during that snowstorm, didn't you?"

"Why don't you throw Eric Wilson in my face while you're at

it? I thought you came because you regretted our last argument, but it looks to me as if you're eager to start another one.''

"All right," he shouted, "I'll stop! You asked me not to bring up the distasteful subject of marriage and I agreed. It's just that—" He clamped his mouth shut. "We're better off dropping the subject entirely," he finished stiffly.

"I feel terrible when we argue," Kate whispered.

"So do I, Princess."

Although his tone was light, Kate heard the distress in his voice. It filled her with regret and she longed for something comforting to say, something that would ease this awkwardness between them, and return a sense of balance to their relationship.

"Do you need anything, Kate?"

"No. I'm fine," she rushed to assure him. She might occasionally date the wrong men and take foolish risks in snowstorms, but she could manage her own life!

Luke glanced around the room, then slowly nodded as if accepting the truth of her words.

"It was thoughtful of you to stop in... I mean, it's good to see you and I really am grateful you wanted to clear the air, too."

"Are you saying you missed me while I was away?"

She had, terribly, but until that moment, Kate hadn't been willing to admit it even to herself. Unconsciously she'd been waiting for Thursday, hoping to hear from Luke—but not really expecting to. For the past few days, she'd worked like a demon to unpack her things and make her apartment presentable. And all along it had been an effort to prove to Luke how efficient and capable she actually was. After falling on her face so many times, she wanted this transition from the ranch house to her first apartment to go off without a hitch. It was a matter of pride.

They were like polite strangers with each other and Kate still couldn't think of any clever remark or probing question to ease this tension between them.

"Have you eaten?" Luke asked brusquely. "I thought I'd take you to dinner. I realise I'm not giving you much notice and I read somewhere that women don't like a man to take things for granted, so if you don't want to go, I'll understand."

He sounded as though he expected her to reject his invitation. "I'd love to have dinner with you," she said, unable to hide a smile.

Luke seemed shocked by her easy acquiescence.

Kate stood up, stretching luxuriously. "If you'll give me a moment, I'll freshen up," she said, unable to keep the happiness out of her voice.

Luke rose then, and his presence seemed to fill every corner of her compact living-room. Only a few scant inches separated them. With one finger, he tilted her chin and looked deeply into her eyes. "You honestly missed me?" he whispered.

For some unexplained reason, her throat squeezed shut and Kate was forced to answer him without words. She cradled his face between both hands and gazed up at him, nodding fervently.

Luke's eyes darkened and she thought he meant to kiss her. Just when she was prepared to slip into his arms and raise her mouth to his, he pulled loose from her light grasp and stepped back. Kate was forced to swallow her disappointment.

"I was thinking about that pizza parlour in Riversdale," he said gruffly.

"Pizza sounds wonderful," Kate said.

"Then it's settled."

Kate didn't bother to change clothes, but ran a brush through her hair and refreshed her make-up. A few minutes later, she was ready to leave. Luke stood at the front door, and as she approached him, his appreciative look sent small flutters of awareness through her body.

Companionably they drove the thirty miles to Riversdale. By mutual and unspoken agreement they both avoided any subject that would cause them to disagree.

The restaurant, Pizza Mania, was known throughout the county for its excellent Italian cuisine. The room was dimly lit, and the wooden tables were covered with red-checked cloths. Since it was a weeknight, the place didn't seem especially busy.

Luke's hand guided her to a table in the middle of the homey room. Service was prompt and they quickly placed their order for a large sausage-and-black-olive pizza. Kate also ordered a raw vegetable platter with yogurt-herb dip, and she laughed at the disdainful expression on Luke's face. A few minutes later, she laughed again.

"What's so funny now?"

"I just remembered the last time I ate pizza from Pizza Mania. It was when Rorie had just arrived—remember?—and she and I were cooking dinner for Clay and Skip. I made a lemon meringue pie and Rorie had spent the entire afternoon cooking up this seafood sauce.''

''Where does the pizza come in?''

Kate told Luke about the disastrous dinner, and the smiled slightly, shaking his head. ''Rorie must have been devastated.''

''Actually she was a pretty good sport about the whole thing. We called Pizza Mania, ordered two large pizzas, and afterwards sat in the living-room around the piano for a while.''

As she thought back to that night all those months ago, Kate realised it was then she'd realised how hard Clay was fighting not to fall in love with Rorie. Kate hadsuspected it when she'd noticed how he tried not to gaze in Rorie's direction. Then, later in the evening, when he drove Kate home, he said barely a word and gently kissed her cheek after he walked her to the door. A peck on the cheek, the way he'd kiss a younger sister.

''What's wrong?'' Luke asked gently.

''Nothing,'' Kate hurried to say, forcing a smile. ''What makes you ask?'' She was relieved at the appearance of their vegetable appetiser, immediately reaching for a carrot stick.

''Your eyes looked kind of sad just now.''

Kate concentrated on munching her carrot, amazed at the way Luke always seemed to know what she was thinking. But then, sometimes he didn't.... ''That night was the first time I realised I was losing Clay to Rorie. My whole world was about to fall in on me and I felt powerless to do anything to stop it. It didn't mean I stopped trying, of course—it hurt too much to accept without putting up a fight.'' She paused and helped herself to a courgette strip. ''Enough about me. It seems I'm the only one we ever discuss. How was your trip to New Mexico?'' she asked brightly, determined to change the subject.

''Good.'' He didn't elaborate. His gaze held hers, the mood warm and comfortable. ''There are going to be a few changes around the Circle L in the coming months. I don't want you to be surprised when you find out I'm adding a couple of outbuildings and doing some remodelling on the house.''

Although he spoke in a conversational tone, Kate wasn't fooled. ''The Circle L belongs to you now. I expect there'll be plenty of changes, but don't worry about offending me or Dad.''

He nodded and his dark eyes brightened with his dreams for the future. ''I intend to turn it into one of the top cattle ranches on the West Coast within the next fifteen years.''

"I'm sure you'll do it, Luke." And she was.

He seemed pleased by her confidence in him. Kate couldn't help believing in Luke. In the ten years he'd worked for her father, he'd initiated several successful breeding programs. With each passing year, Devin had turned more and more of the ranch business over to Luke. Her father had become only a figurehead. More than once, Kate could remember hearing Devin say that he couldn't understand why Luke would continue working for him when it was obvious the foreman was more than capable of maintaining his own spread. At one time, Kate had thought money was the issue, but that obviously wasn't the case.

"Why'd you delay buying your own ranch for so long?" Kate asked, just as their pizza arrived. Their waitress remained standing at their table and studied them so blatantly that Luke turned to her.

"Is something wrong?" he asked sharply.

"No...not at all. Enjoy your dinner." She backed away from their table and returned to the counter, where two other employees were waiting. Almost immediately the three huddled together and started whispering.

Luke chose to ignore their waitress's strange behavior and lifted a steaming piece, thick with gooey melted cheese and spicy sausage, on to Kate's dinner plate. Then he served himself.

"Now, where were we?" Luke asked.

"I wanted to know why you didn't buy your own ranch long before now."

"You don't want to know the answer to that, Princess."

"Of course I do. I wouldn't have asked you otherwise," she insisted.

"All right," Luke said, settling back in his chair. He looked at her, eyes thoughtful. "I had a minor problem. I was in love with the boss's daughter and she was crazy about me, only she didn't know it. In fact, she'd gotten herself engaged to someone else. I was afraid that if I moved away she'd never realise how I felt—or how she did—and frankly, I didn't think I could ever love anyone the way I do her."

Kate focused her attention on her meal. The knot in her throat was almost choking her. "You're right about...me not loving Clay," she admitted softly. No matter how hard she tried, she couldn't raise her eyes high enough to meet his.

"What did you just say?"

"I... You were right about me and Clay. I could never feel for him the things a wife should feel for her husband. I'd adored him for years, but that love was only an adolescent fantasy.''

She was well aware of the seriousness of her admission, and the room seemed to go still with her words. The music from the juke box faded, the clatter from the kitchen dimmed, and the voices from those around them seemed to disappear altogether.

''I didn't ever think I'd hear you admit that,'' Luke said softly, and his face filled with tenderness.

''I tried to tell you the night after I had dinner with Clay and Rorie, but you were so angry with me...because I was moving.'' She laughed lightly, hoping to break the unexpected tension that had leapt between them.

''Does this mean you're also admitting you love me?''

''I've never had a problem with that—''

Kate was interrupted by an elderly man who strolled up to their table. With a good deal of ceremony, he lifted a violin to his chin and played a bittersweet love song.

''I didn't know they had strolling violinists here,'' Kate said when the man had finished. Everyone in the restaurant stopped to applaud.

''This next song is dedicated to the two of you,'' the man said proudly, ''that the love in your hearts will blossom for each other into a bouquet of *May* flowers.''

It wasn't until he'd finished the third song that Kate noticed he didn't stroll to any of the other tables. He seemed to be playing only for them. Some of the customers apparently realised this, too, and gathered behind Luke and Kate in order to get a better view of the musician.

''Thank you,'' Kate said as the last notes faded.

The man lowered his instrument to his side. ''You two have become quite a sensation in Nightingale and beyond. We at Pizza Mania are honoured that you've chosen our restaurant for a romantic evening. We want to do our part to bring the two of you together in wedded bliss.''

''And you're suggesting the month of May?'' Kate asked, referring to his comment about a bouquet of flowers.

''It would be an excellent choice,'' the violinist said, grinning broadly.

''I think it's time we left,'' Luke said, frowning. He reached for his wallet, but the violinist stopped him. ''Please, your pizza's on the house. It's an honour that you chose to dine in our humble establishment.''

From the tight set of Luke's mouth, Kate realized he wanted to argue, but more urgent in his mind was the need to escape. He took Kate by the hand and headed for the door.

''Your leftover pizza,'' their waitress called after them, handing Luke a large white box, as she cast Kate an envious glance.

Luke couldn't seem to get out of the car park fast enough. Kate waited until they were on the road before she spoke. ''I take it this is the first time that's happened to you?''

Luke laughed shortly. ''Not really, only I didn't pick up on it as easily as you. Several people have made odd comments about certain months, but until now, I didn't realise what they were actually saying.''

''It's kind of funny when you think about it. Half the county's got money riding on our wedding day, and Fred Garner's making a killing raising and lowering the odds.'' Suddenly the lottery was the most comical thing Kate had ever heard of, and she started to laugh. She slumped against the side of the cab, holding her sides. She was laughing so hard, her stomach hurt. Tears ran down her cheeks and she wiped them away in an effort to regain control. The wedding lottery and everyone's subtle interference wasn't really so terribly funny, but Luke's disgruntled reaction was. He didn't seem to find any of this the least bit amusing.

''Come on, Luke,'' she said, still chuckling. ''There's a good deal of humour in this situation.''

He gave a short snort.

''Don't be such a killjoy. I've been getting free advice from the butcher, Sally Daley, the paperboy and just about everyone else in town. It's only fair that you put up with a few of their comments, too.''

''One might think you'd take some of that free advice.''

''What?'' she cried. ''And ruin their fun?''

Luke was oddly quiet for the remainder of the trip into Nightingale. He stopped at her building, walked her to her door with barely another word, then turned and walked away. No goodnight kiss, no mention of seeing her again.

This was the last thing she'd expected. For the entire drive home, she'd been thinking about how good it would feel when Luke held her and kissed her. She'd decided to invite him in for coffee, hoping he'd accept. But this was even worse than Clay's peck on the cheek all those months ago.

"Luke..."

He stopped abruptly at the sound of her voice, then turned back. His eyes seemed to burn into hers as he came toward her, and she stumbled into his arms. His mouth, hot and hungry, sought hers in a kiss that scorched her senses.

His fingers plunged deep into her hair, releasing the French braid and ploughing through the twisted strands of blonde hair.

Instinctively Kate reached up and slid her arms tightly around his shoulders, feeling so much at home in his arms that it frightened her. She trembled with the knowledge, but she didn't have time to analyse her feelings. Not when her world was in chaos. She clung to him as though she were rocketing into a fathomless sky.

Luke broke away from her, his face a study of hope and confusion. "I never know where I stand with you, Kate." With that, he stroked her hair and quickly returned to his truck.

Kate was reeling from the effects of Luke's kiss. If she hadn't leaned against the front door, she might have slumped on to the walkway, so profound was her reaction.

"Luke," she called, shocked by how weak her voice sounded. "Would you like to come inside for coffee? We could talk about... things."

Slowly a smile eased its way across his handsome features. "I don't dare, Princess, because the way I feel right now, I might not leave until morning. If then."

Flustered by the truth of his words, Kate unlocked her door and let herself inside.

She gulped a deep breath and stood in the middle of the living-room with her hand planted over her rampaging heart. "You're in love with him, Kate Logan," she told herself. "Head over heels in love with a man and fighting him every step of the way."

Groaning, she buried her face in her hands. She didn't understand why she'd been fighting him so hard. She did realise that Luke wouldn't have spent years building up her father's ranch if he hadn't loved her. He could have left any time, gone anywhere, to buy his own ranch, but he'd stayed at the Circle L. He honestly loved her!

Now that she knew what she wanted, Kate still didn't know what to do about it.

She guessed Luke was planning to court her; if that was the case, one more dinner with him would be enough. They'd be officially engaged by the end of the evening. She'd bet on it!

To her disappointment, Kate didn't hear from Luke the following day. Fridays were generally busy around the ranch, so she decided the next move would have to come from her.

Early Saturday morning she compiled a grocery list, intent on inviting Luke over for a home-cooked meal. She was reviewing her cookbooks, searching for a special dessert recipe, when she was suddenly distracted by the memory of her kiss. Closing her eyes, she relived the way she'd felt that night. She smiled to herself, admitting how eager she was to feel that way again.

If only she'd listened to her heart all these weeks instead of her pride. Happiness bubbled up inside her like the fizz in champagne.

She tried phoning Luke, but there wasn't any answer, so she decided to do the shopping first. She reached for her coat, and walked the few blocks to the Safeway store.

It must had been her imagination, but it seemed that everyone stopped what they were doing and watched her as she pushed her cart down the aisles.

When she'd finished buying her groceries, she headed over to the pharmacy and bought a couple of scented candles. Once again, everyone seemed to stop and stare at her.

"Kate," Sally Daley said, walking toward her. The older woman was shaking her head, eyes brimming with sympathy. She reached for Kate's hand and patted it gently. "How are you doing, dear?"

"Fine," Kate said, puzzled.

Sally's mouth dropped. "You don't know then, do you?"

"Know what?"

"Luke Rivers took Betty Hammond to dinner, and the two of them danced all night at the Red Bull. Why, everyone in town's buzzing with it. People are saying he's lost patience with you and is going to marry Betty. Really, dear, every woman in town thinks you'd be crazy to let a man like Luke Rivers get away."

Kate was so shocked she could hardly breathe. "I see," she murmured, pretending it really didn't matter.

"You poor child," Sally said compassionately. "Don't let your pride get in the way."

"I won't," Kate promised, barely able to find her voice.

"I do worry about you, Kate, dear. I have this terrible feeling you're going to end up thirty and all alone."

Eleven

Thirty and all alone. The words echoed in Kate's mind as she walked the short distance to her apartment. Tears burned her eyes, but somehow she'd dredged up the courage to smile and assure Sally that Luke was free to date whomever he pleased. In fact, she'd even managed to laugh lightly and say that she hoped Luke's dating Betty would finally put an end to all this wedding-lottery nonsense.

Walking at a clipped pace, she kept her head lowered and headed directly back to her apartment, clutching her purchases to her chest. By the time she let herself in the front door, her face was streaked with tears, although she'd used every ounce of fortitude she possessed to keep them at bay.

No doubt Sally would have the story of her meeting with Kate all over town by evening. Not that it mattered. By now, the residents of Nightingale should be accustomed to hearing gossip about her and Luke.

Luke. The mere thought of him, and her heart constricted painfully. He'd given up on her and now she'd lost him, too. Only it hurt so much more than when Clay had broken their engagement. A hundred times more.

Wiping the tears from her eyes, she struggled to take in all that had happened to her in the past few weeks. It seemed every time she found her balance and secured her footing, something would happen to send her teetering again. Would it never end? Was her life destined to be an endless struggle of one emotional pain following on the heels of another?

She set her bags on the floor, and without bothering to remove her coat, slumped into the overstuffed chair.

"Okay," she said aloud. "Luke took Betty Hammond out to dinner and dancing. It doesn't have to mean anything."

But it did. In her heart Kate was sure Luke planned to do exactly as Sally suggested. He'd made it plain from the first that he wanted a wife, and like a fool Kate had repeatedly turned him down. He loved her, or so he claimed, and Kate had doubted him. Now she wondered if perhaps he didn't love her enough. But over and over again, Luke had insisted she needed him—and he'd been right.

Closing her eyes, she tried to picture her life without Luke. A chill ran down her spine as an intense wave of loneliness swept over her.

Someone pounded at the door, but before Kate could answer it, Luke strode into the apartment. Having to face him this way, when she was least prepared, put her at a clear disadvantage. Hurriedly she painted on a bright smile.

"Hello, Luke," she said, trying to sound breezy and amused. "What's this I hear about you and Betty?"

"You heard already?" He looked stunned.

"Good heavens, yes. You don't honestly expect something like that to stay quiet, do you?"

"When...who told you?"

"I went to the grocery store and ran into Sally Daley."

"That explains it," he said, pacing her carpet with abrupt, impatient steps. He stopped suddenly and turned to study her. "It doesn't bother you that I'm seeing Betty?"

"Good grief, no," she lied. "Should it? Would you like some coffee?"

"No."

Desperate for a chance to escape and compose herself, Kate almost ran into the kitchen and poured herself a cup, keeping her back to him all the while.

"You seem to be downright happy about this," he accused, following her into the small, windowless room.

"Of course I'm pleased. I think it's wonderful when two people fall in love, don't you?"

"I'm not in love with Betty," he said angrily.

"Actually I think dating Betty is a wonderful way to kill all the rumours that are floating around about us," she said, finally turning to face him. She held her coffee cup close, though, for protection.

Rubbing his neck, Luke continued his pacing in the kitchen. "I thought you might be...jealous."

"Me?" She couldn't very well admit she'd been dying inside from the moment Sally had told her. Her pride wouldn't allow that. "Now why would I feel like that?"

"I don't know," Luke barked. "Why would you?"

Before Kate could answer, he stormed out of the apartment, leaving her so frustrated she wanted to weep.

"You could have told him how you feel," she reprimanded herself aloud. "Why are you such a fool when it comes to Luke Rivers? Why? Why? Why?"

"I saw Luke yesterday," Rorie said, watching Kate closely as they sat across from each other in a booth at Nellie's.

"That's nice," she said, pretending indifference and doing a grand job of it.

"He was with Betty Hammond."

Kate's breath caught in her throat at the unexpected rush of pain. "I...see."

"Do you?" Rorie inquired softly. "I swear I could shake the pair of you. I don't know when I've ever met two more stubborn people in my life. You look like one of the walking wounded, and Luke's got a chip on his shoulder the size of a California redwood."

"I'm sure you're mistaken." Kate concentrated on stirring her coffee, and she avoided Rorie's eyes. Her heart felt like a ball of lead.

"When was the last time you two talked?"

"A couple of days ago."

"Honestly, Kate, I can't understand what's wrong with you. Clay and I thought...we hoped everything would fall into place after you moved to the apartment. Now it seems exactly the opposite has happened."

"Luke's free to date whomever he pleases, just the way I am."

"There's only one person you want and that's Luke Rivers and we both know it," Rorie said with an exasperated sigh. "I shouldn't have said that. It's just that I hate the thought of you two being so miserable when you're both so much in love with each other."

"Is love always this painful?" Kate asked, her question barely audible.

Rorie shrugged. "It was with Clay and me, and sometimes I feel it must be for everyone sooner or later. Think about it, Kate. If you honestly love Luke, why are you fighting the very thing you want most?"

"I don't know," she admitted reluctantly.

They parted a few minutes later. Kate felt a new sense of certainty and resolve. She *did* love Luke and if she didn't do something soon, she was going to lose him.

She drove to the Circle L, her heart in her throat the entire way. Luke's truck was parked behind the house, and she left her car beside it, hurrying through the cold to the back door. Luke didn't respond to her knock, which didn't surprise her, since it was unusual for him to be in at this time of day. But she couldn't find him outside, either, and even Bill didn't know where he was.

Making a rapid decision, she let herself into the house and started preparations for the evening meal. It gave her a way of passing the time. Dinner was in the oven and she was busy making a fresh green salad, when the back door opened and Luke walked into the kitchen.

Apparently he hadn't noticed her car because he stopped dead, shock written in every feature, when he saw her standing at the sink.

Kate held her breath for a moment, then dried her hands on the dish towel she'd tucked into her waistband. She struggled to give the impression that she was completely at ease, tried to act as though she made dinner for him every evening.

"Hello, Luke," she said to break the silence that had been growing heavier by the second.

He blinked. "I suppose you're looking for an explanation."

Kate wasn't sure she knew what he meant.

"Taking Betty out Friday night was a mistake."

"Then why'd you do it?"

"So you'd be jealous. The night you and I went out, I was furious at the way you started laughing, and talking as though you never planned to marry me. I wanted you to know you weren't the only fish in the sea. Only my idea backfired."

"It did?" Not so far as Kate was concerned—she'd been pretty darn worried.

"That wasn't all that went wrong. Betty saw I was in town on Saturday and started following me," he explained. "I swear I had no intention of seeing her again, but before I knew what was happening, her arm was linked with mine and we were strolling through the middle of town together."

"Betty's a nice girl."

He frowned. "Yes, I suppose she is. I'd forgotten it doesn't bother you who I date, does it? You've never been one to give in to fits of jealousy."

"I was so jealous I wanted to die."

"You were? You could have fooled me."

"Believe me, I tried to," Kate murmured.

"Exactly what are you doing here?"

"I fixed dinner," Kate said sheepishly. She'd admitted how she felt about Luke seeing Betty and she'd be an idiot to stop there. "I've got pork chops in the oven, along with scalloped potatoes and an acorn squash," she rattled off without pausing for breath, then gathering her resolve, casually added, "and if you're still asking, I'll marry you."

That stopped Luke cold. When he finally spoke he sounded strangely calm. "What did you just say?"

"There's pork chops and potatoes and—"

"Not that. The part about marrying me."

She struggled to hold on to what remained of her tattered pride. "If you're still asking me to marry you, then I'd be honoured to be your wife."

"I'm still asking."

Kate dropped her gaze and her throat squeezed tight. "You've been right about so many things lately. I do need you. I guess I was waiting all this time for you to admit you needed *me*, only you never did."

Luke rubbed a hand over his face. "Not need you?" he asked, his voice filled with shock and wonder. "I think my life would be an empty shell without you, Kate. I couldn't bear the thought of living one day to the next if you weren't at my side to share everything with me—all the good things that are in store for us. I've waited so long, Kate."

"You honestly do love me, don't you?" she whispered.

For a long, long moment Luke said nothing. "I tried not to. For years I stood by helpless and frustrated, watching you break out in hives with excitement every time Clay Franklin came close. I realised then it was a schoolgirl crush, but you never seemed to get over him. Instead of improving, things got worse. How could I let you know how I felt?"

"Couldn't you have said something? Anything?"

A flicker of pain crossed his face. "No. You were so infatuated with Clay I didn't dare. It wouldn't have done any good—although only God knows how you managed not to figure it out yourself. The first time Rorie met me, she guessed."

"Rorie knew all along?"

Luke shook his head in bewildered amusement. "We were a lovesick pair a few months back—Rorie in love with Clay and me crazy about you. All this time, I thought I'd kept my feelings secret, and then I discovered everyone in town knew."

"Betty Hammond didn't," Kate countered.

"No, but she should have. I've never wanted anyone but you, Kate Logan. I haven't for years. Somehow I always kept hoping you'd see the light."

"Oh, Luke." She took a step toward him, her eyes full of emotion. "Are you going to stand way over there on the other side of the room? I need you so much."

For every step Kate took, Luke managed three. When they reached each other, she put her arms around his waist, hugging him tight. She felt the surge of his heart and closed her eyes, succumbing to the wave of love that threatened to overwhelm her.

Luke's hand was gentle on her hair. "Do you love me, Kate?"

She discovered she couldn't speak, so she wildly nodded her head. Her hands framed his face and she spread light, eager kisses over his mouth and nose and eyes, letting her lips explain what was in her heart.

"I love you," he whispered. "If you marry me, I promise I'll do everything I can to make you happy." His eyes shone with delight and a kind of humility that touched Kate's very soul. Gone was the remoteness he'd displayed so often these past few weeks.

"Oh, Luke, I can hardly wait to be your wife," she said. "Didn't you once say something about a December wedding?"

"Kate, that's only a few weeks from now."

"Yes, I know. But Christmas is such a lovely time of year for a wedding. We'll decorate the church in holly, and all the brides-maids will have long red dresses...."

"Kate, dear Lord, you mean it, don't you?" His voice was low and husky.

"I've never meant anything more in my life. I love you. We're going to have such a good life together, Luke Rivers."

He kissed her then, with a hunger that spoke of his years of longing. Dragging his mouth from hers, he buried it in the gentle curve of her neck.

"I want children, Kate. I want to fill this home with so much love that the walls threaten to burst with it."

For a breathless moment, they did nothing more than gaze at each other as they shared the dream.

Kate smiled up at him, and as her hands mapped his face, loving each strong feature, she was amazed at how easily this happiness had come to her once she let go of her pride.

Luke's mouth settled on hers, his kiss gentle, almost reverent, as though he couldn't yet believe she was in his home and eager to be his wife.

As Kate wrapped her arms around his neck, her gaze fell on the calendar. December was a good month, and she seemed to remember that Pastor Wilkins had placed a sizeable wager on the fifteenth. That sounded good to Kate.

Very good indeed.

Epilogue

The sun shone clear and bright in the late July afternoon, two years after Rorie Campbell's car had broken down near Nightingale. Kate was making a fresh pitcher of iced tea when Rorie knocked on the back door.

"Let yourself in," Kate called. "The screen door's unlocked."

A moment later Rorie entered the kitchen, looking slightly frazzled. "How did your afternoon at the library go?" Kate asked, as she added ice cubes to the tall pitcher.

"Very well, thanks."

"Katherine's still sleeping," Kate told her.

Rorie's eyes softened as she gazed out at the newly constructed patio where her baby slept under the shade of the huge oak tree.

"It was such a lovely afternoon I kept her outside." Kate wiped her hands dry. She poured them each a tall glass of iced tea, and carried a tray of tea and cookies on to the patio.

The nine-month-old infant stirred when Rorie stood over the portable crib and protectively placed her hand on the sleeping baby's back. When she turned, her eyes fell on Kate's protruding abdomen. "How are *you* feeling?"

"Like a blimp." Kate's hands rested on her swollen stomach and she patted it gently. "The doctor told me it would probably be another two weeks."

"Two weeks!" Rorie said, looking sympathetic.

"I know, and I was hoping Junior would choose to arrive this week. I swear to you, Rorie, when you were pregnant with Katherine you positively glowed. You made everything look so easy, so natural."

Rorie laughed. "I did?"

"I feel miserable. My legs are swollen, my hands and feet look like they've been inflated. I swear, there isn't a single part of my body that's normal-sized any more."

Rorie laughed. "The last few weeks are always like that. I think the main difference is that Katherine was born in October, when the weather was much cooler.''

With some difficulty Kate crossed her legs. "I only hope our baby will be as good-natured as Katherine. She barely fussed the whole time she was here.''

"Her Uncle Skip thinks she's going to start walking soon.''

"I think he's right." Pressing a hand to her ribs, Kate shifted her position. She was finding it difficult to sit comfortably for longer than a few minutes at a time.

"Oh—" Rorie set her iced tea aside "—I almost forgot.'' She hurried back into the kitchen and returned a moment later with a hardbound children's book. "I received my first copies of *Nightsong's Adventures* in the mail yesterday. Kate, I can't even begin to tell you how thrilled I was when I held this book in my hands.''

Kate reverently laid the book in her lap and slowly turned the pages. "The illustrations are fantastic—almost as good as the story!''

"The reviews have been excellent. One critic said he expected it to become a children's classic, which I know is probably ridiculous, but I couldn't help feeling excited about it.''

"It isn't ridiculous, and I'm sure your publisher knows that, otherwise they wouldn't have been so eager to buy your second book.''

"You know, the second sale was every bit as exciting as the first,'' Rorie admitted with a soft smile.

"Just think, within a few years our children will be reading your stories and attending school together. They're bound to be the best of friends.''

"It's enough to boggle the mind, isn't it?''

Before Rorie could respond, the baby woke and they watched, delighted, as she sat up in the portable crib. When she saw her mother sitting next to Kate, she grinned, her dark eyes twinkling. She raised her chubby arms, reaching for Rorie.

Rorie stood and lifted Katherine out of the crib, kissing the little girl's pudgy cheeks. "I'd better get back home. Thanks so much for watching Katherine for me. I promised I'd pinch-hit for the new librarian if she ever needed me, and I didn't think I could refuse her even if it was at the last minute like this.''

"It wasn't any problem, so don't worry. And tell Mary she should visit her sister more often so I get the opportunity to watch Katherine every once in a while.''

"Call me later and let me know how you're feeling.''

Kate nodded, promising that she would.

Ten minutes after Rorie and Katherine left, Luke drove up and parked in the back of the house. Standing on the porch, Kate waved to her husband.

Luke joined her, placing an arm around what once had been a trim waist, and led the way into the kitchen. "You okay?" His gaze was tender and warm.

Kate wasn't exactly sure how to answer that. She was miserable. Excited. Frightened. Eager. So many emotions were coming at her, she didn't know which one to respond to first.

"Kate?"

"I feel fine." There was no need to list her complaints, but all of a sudden she felt *funny*. She didn't know of any other way to describe it. As Rorie had explained, there were a dozen different aches and pains the last few weeks of any pregnancy. Given time, Kate figured she'd grow accustomed to this feeling, too.

Luke kissed her then, his mouth gentle over hers. "Did you have a busy day with Katherine?"

"She slept almost the entire time, but I think Rorie knew she would." Leaning forward, Kate kissed her husband's jaw. "I made some iced tea. Want some?"

"Please."

When Kate reached inside the cupboard for a glass, a sharp pain split her side. She let out a soft cry.

"Kate?"

Clenching her swollen abdomen, Kate's startled gaze flew to Luke. "Oh, my goodness. I just felt a pain."

Luke paled. "You're in labour?"

Smiling, wide-eyed, she nodded slowly. "I must be. I didn't expect them to start off so strong."

Luke was across the kitchen beside her. "Now what?"

"I think I should call the doctor."

"No." Luke's arm flew out as if holding out his hand would halt the course of nature. "I'll call. Stay there. Don't move."

"But, Luke—"

"For heaven's sake, Kate, don't argue with me now. We're about to have a baby!"

He said this as if it were a recent discovery. She noted as he reached for the phone that he'd gone deathly pale. When he finished talking to the doctor, he gave her a panicked look, then announced that Doc Adams wanted them to go straight to the hospital. As soon as the words left his mouth, he shot to the bedroom and returned a moment later with her packed suitcase. He halted abruptly when he saw she was on the phone.

"Who are you calling?"

"Dad and Dorothea. I promised I would."

"Dear Lord, Kate, would you kindly let me do the telephoning?"

"All right." She gave him the receiver and started toward the bedroom to collect the rest of her things. If he thought that talking on the phone was too taxing for her, fine. She'd let him do it. The years had taught her that arguing with Luke was fruitless.

"Kate," he yelled. "Don't wander off."

"Luke, I just want to gather my things before we leave." A pain started to work its way around her back and she paused, flattening her hands across her abdomen. Slowly she raised her head and smiled up at her husband. "Oh, Luke, the baby..."

Luke dropped the telephone and rushed to her side. "Now?"

"No." She laughed gently and touched his loving face. "It'll be hours yet. Oh! I just felt another pain—a bad one."

He swallowed hard and gripped both her hands in his own. "I've been waiting for this moment for nine months and I swear to you, Kate, I've never been more frightened in my life."

"Don't look so worried." Her hands caressed his face and she kissed him gently, offering him what reassurance she could.

He exhaled noisily, then gave her a brisk little nod. Without warning, he lifted her into his arms, ignoring her protests, and carried her out the door to the truck. Once he'd settled her in the seat, he returned to the house for her bag.

"Luke," she called after him, "I really would like to talk to Dad and Dorothea."

"I'll phone them from the hospital. No more arguing, Kate. I'm in charge here."

Only another sharp pain—and her regard for Luke's feelings—kept her from breaking out in laughter.

Ten long hours later, Kate lay in the hospital bed, eyes closed in exhaustion. When she opened them, she discovered her father standing over her. Dorothea was next to him, looking as pleased and proud as Kate's father. Devin took his daughter's hand in his own and squeezed it gently. "How do you feel, little mother?"

"Wonderful. Did they let you see him? Oh, Dad, he's so beautiful!"

Her father nodded, looking as though he were unable to speak for a moment. "Luke's with Matthew now. He looks so big sitting in that rocking chair, holding his son."

"I don't think I've ever seen Luke wear an expression quite like that before," Dorothea murmured. "So tender and loving."

Devin concurred with a hard nod of his head. "When Luke came into the waiting-room to tell us Matthew Devin had been born, there were tears in his eyes. I'll tell you, Kate, that man loves you."

"I know, Dad, and I love him, too."

Devin patted her hand. "You go ahead and rest, Princess. Dorothea and I'll be back tomorrow."

When Kate opened her eyes a second time, Luke was there. She held out her hand to him and smiled dreamily. "I couldn't have done it without you. Thank you for staying with me."

"Staying with you," he echoed softly, his fingers brushing the tousled curls from her face. "Nothing on this earth could have kept me away. I swear, Kate, I would have done anything to spare you that pain. Anything." His voice was raw with the memory of those last hours.

Her smile was one of comfort. "It only lasted a little while and we have a beautiful son to show for it."

"All these months when we've talked about the baby," he said, his eyes glazed, "he seemed so unreal to me, and then you were in the delivery-room and in so much agony. I felt so helpless. I wanted so much to be able to help you and there was nothing I could do. Then Matthew was born and, Kate, I looked at him and I swear something happened to my heart. The overwhelming surge of love I felt for that baby, that tiny person, was so strong, so powerful, I could barely breathe. I thought I was going to break down and start weeping right there in front of everyone."

"Oh, Luke."

"There's no way I could ever thank you for all you've given me, Kate Rivers."

"Yes, there is," she said with a smile. "Just love me."

"I do," he whispered, his voice husky with emotion. "I always will."

MIRA Books
is proud to invite you to read this preview of
Debbie Macomber's

DAKOTA HOME

Dakota Home is the second novel in this
New York Times bestselling author's blockbuster
Dakota trilogy.

Enjoy all three of these heartwarming and memorable stories.

Look for Dakota Home in August 2000
wherever books are sold.

One

It was the screaming that woke him.

Jeb bolted upright in bed and forced himself to look around the darkened room, to recognize familiar details. Four years had passed since the accident. Four years in which his mind refused to release even one small detail of that fateful afternoon.

Leaning against his headboard, he dragged in deep gulps of air until the shaking subsided. Invariably with the dream came the pain, the pain in his leg. The remembered pain of that summer's day.

His mind refused to forget and so did his body. As he waited for his hammering pulse to return to normal, pain shot through his badly scarred thigh, cramping his calf muscle. Instinctively cringing, he stiffened until the discomfort passed.

Then he started to laugh. Sitting on the edge of his bed, Jeb reached for his prosthesis and strapped it onto the stump of his left leg. This was the joke: The pain Jeb experienced, the charley horse that knotted and twisted his muscles, was in a leg that had been amputated four years earlier.

He'd cheated death that day, but death had gained its own revenge. The doctors had a phrase for it. They called it phantom pain, and assured him that eventually it would pass. It was all part of his emotional adjustment to the loss of a limb. Or so they said, over and over, only Jeb had given up listening a long time ago.

After he'd dressed, he made his way into the kitchen, eager to get some caffeine into his system and dispel the lingering effects of the dream. Then he remembered he was out of coffee.

It didn't take a genius to realize that Sarah had purposely forgotten coffee when she'd delivered his supplies. This was his sister's less-than-subtle effort to make him go into town. It wouldn't work. He wasn't going to let her manipulate him—even if it meant roasting barley and brewing that.

Jeb slammed out the back door and headed for the barn, his limp more pronounced with his anger. His last trip into Buffalo Valley had been at Christmas, almost ten months earlier. Sarah knew how he felt about people staring at him, whispering behind his back as if he wasn't supposed to know what they were talking about. He'd lost his leg, not his hearing or intelligence. Their pity was as unwelcome as their curiosity.

Jeb hadn't been particularly sociable before the accident and was less so now. Sarah knew that, too. She was also aware that his least favorite person in Buffalo Valley was Marta Hansen, the grocer's wife. The old biddy treated him like a charity case, a poor, pathetic cripple—as if it was her duty, now that his mother was gone, to smother him with sympathy. Her condescending manner offended him and hurt his already wounded pride.

Jeb realized he made people uncomfortable. His loss reminded other farmers of their own vulnerability. With few exceptions, namely Dennis, the men he'd once considered friends felt awkward and uneasy around him. Even more now that he'd given up farming and taken up raising bison.

Cursing his sister and her obstinate ways, he wrote a grocery list—if he was going into town he'd make it worth his while—and hurried toward his pickup. The October wind felt almost hot in his face. A few minutes later, he drove out of the yard, sparing a glance for the bison grazing stolidly on either side.

To his surprise, he enjoyed the fifty-minute trip to Buffalo Valley, although he rarely ventured into town. Usually he preferred to drive with no real destination, enjoying the solitude and the changing seasons and the feel of the road.

When he pulled into town, he was immediately struck by the changes the past ten months had brought to Buffalo Valley. Knight's Pharmacy was and always had been the brightest spot in town. Hassie Knight had been around as long as he could remember and served the world's best old-fashioned ice-cream sodas. He'd loved that place as a kid and had considered it a special treat when his mother had taken him there on Saturday afternoons.

Like Marta Hansen, Hassie Knight had been a friend of his mother's; she was also the one woman he knew, other than Sarah, who didn't make him feel like a cripple.

The Pizza Parlor was new, but now that he thought about it, he remembered Sarah mentioning that Calla had started working there part-time. Good thing—the kid needed an outlet. She was fifteen and full of attitude. Jeb suspected that Dennis and his sister would have been married by now if it wasn't for Calla.

Sarah's quilting store came into view next and despite his irritation with her, he couldn't squelch his sense of pride. She displayed her quilts in the front window of what had once been a florist shop. The Spring Bouquet had been closed for at least fifteen years. Folks didn't buy a luxury like hothouse flowers when it was hard enough just getting food on the table. Nor had there been much to celebrate in Buffalo Valley for a long time.

Still, the town showed more life than it had in years. Even the outside of Hansen's Grocery had recently been painted. God knew it could use a face-lift. The sign was down and propped against the building; it was probably worn out, like so much else in town.

Not delaying the unpleasant task any longer, Jeb parked and headed toward the grocery, determined to be as cold and aloof as possible until Marta Hansen got the message. If experience was anything to go by, that could take a while.

"Hello."

He wasn't two steps into the grocery when a friendly voice called out to greet him. His reply was more a grunt than words. Without stopping, he reached for a cart and started down the first aisle.

"I don't believe we've met," the woman said, following him.

Jeb turned. He didn't want to be rude, but he did want to get his point across. *Leave me alone.* He wasn't interested in exchanging gossip, didn't require assistance or company. He'd come for coffee and a few other groceries and that was it.

Confronting the woman with the friendly voice, Jeb got the shock of his life. She was young and blond and beautiful. Really beautiful. He couldn't begin to imagine what had brought a beauty like this to a town like Buffalo Valley. The next thing he noticed was how tall she was—just a couple of inches shorter than his own six feet. Her blue eyes held kindness and her smile was warm.

"I'm Maddy Washburn," she said, holding out her hand.

Jeb stared at it a second before he extended his own. "Jeb Mc-

Kenna,'' he said gruffly, certain he was making an ass of himself by gawking at her. Hell, he couldn't seem to stop.

''So *you're* Jeb,'' she returned, sounding genuinely pleased to make his acquaintance. ''I wondered when I'd have a chance to meet you. Sarah and Calla talk about you all the time.''

He nodded and turned back to his cart. It was adding up now, why his sister had ''forgotten'' to include coffee in his monthly supplies....

His love freed her at last.

MARGOT DALTON

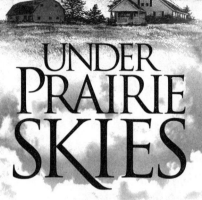

UNDER PRAIRIE SKIES

Allan Williamson might have been just a simple prairie farmer, but he went after what he wanted. And from the first day he met Mara Steen, his son's kindergarten teacher, he wanted her—as much as she wanted him.

Mara almost believed she and Allan could be happy. But she could never abandon the grandmother who'd raised her...though if she didn't, she'd never have a life of her own....

"Margot Dalton's a writer who always delivers: probing characterization, ingenious plotting, riveting pace and impeccable craft."
—Award-winning author Bethany Campbell

On sale mid-July 2000 wherever paperbacks are sold!